ENCYCLOPEDIA OF MARKS ON AMERICAN, ENGLISH, AND EUROPEAN EARTHENWARE, IRONSTONE, AND STONEWARE (1780-1980)

MAKERS, MARKS, AND PATTERNS IN BLUE AND WHITE, HISTORIC BLUE, FLOW BLUE, MULBERRY, ROMANTIC TRANSFERWARE, TEA LEAF, AND WHITE IRONSTONE

Arnold A. & Dorothy E. Kowalsky

Schiffer Publishing Ltd ®

4880 Lower Valley Road, Atglen, PA 19310 USA

DEDICATED TO:

Geoffrey A. Godden

"There are many unsolved problems in the ceramic world, some of which may be resolved in many volumes while others require no more than a modest article of a few hundred words. Every contribution to ceramic history is important and helps to complete the puzzle...Resolve to make a contribution."

This work is dedicated to one individual, Geoffrey A. Godden, whose scholarship and research has brought to life, as no author has done in this century, the history and romance of ceramics in the United Kingdom.

I am most grateful to Geoffrey for his erudition and strict approach in his dealing with me. As busy a gentleman as he is, Mr. Godden has never refused to help or guide me. He has continuously pushed me to further research in the quest for the correct answer. I am privileged to have him as a friend and mentor.

This Encyclopedia records just one part of the history of ceramics from 1780 - 1980. It is strongly advised that the reader and collector use this book in conjunction with Mr. Godden's two encyclopaedias: *Encyclopaedia of British Porcelain Manufacturers* and the *Encyclopaedia of British Pottery and Porcelain Marks*. The first includes substantial histories of potteries as well as notices of partnership dissolution. The second work, which I consider the "bible", cites hundreds of additional potters and marks that have not been incorporated into this author's work, due in part to a lack of information relative to the body of this book. Additional potters' marks, found in Mr. *Godden's Encyclopaedia of British Pottery and Porcelain Marks*, have not been included due to a lack of space.

Library of Congress Cataloging-in-Publication Data

Kowalsky, Arnold A.
Encyclopedia of Marks on American, English, and European Earthenware, Ironstone, and Stoneware, 1780-1980: makers, marks, and pattens in blue and white, historic blue, flow blue, mulberry, romantic transferware, tea leaf, and white ironstone / Arnold A. & Dorothy E. Kowalsky.
p. cm.
Includes bibliographical references and index.
ISBN 0-7643-0731-2 (hc.)
1. Pottery, American Encyclopedias. 2. Pottery--19th century--United States Encyclopedias. 3. Pottery--20th century--United States Encyclopedias. 4. Pottery, English Encyclopedias. 5. Pottery--19th century--England Encyclopedias. 6. Pottery--20th century--England Encyclopedias. 7. Pottery, European Encyclopedias. 8. Pottery--19th century--Europe Encyclopedias. 9. Pottery--20th century-- Europe Encyclopedias. I. Kowalsky, Dorothy E. II. Title.
NK4007.K69 1999
738'.09'034--dc21 99-26188
CIP

Book Design by Anne Davidsen
Type set in Dutch Roman

ISBN: 0-7643-0731-2
Printed in China

Published by Schiffer Publishing Ltd.
4880 Lower Valley Road
Atglen, PA 19310
Phone: (610) 593-1777; Fax: (610) 593-2002
E-mail: Schifferbk@aol.com
Please visit our web site catalog at
www.schifferbooks.com

This book may be purchased from the publisher.
Include $3.95 for shipping.
Please try your bookstore first.
We are interested in hearing from authors
with book ideas on related subjects.
You may write for a free catalog.

In Europe, Schiffer books are distributed by
Bushwood Books
6 Marksbury Rd.
Kew Gardens
Surrey TW9 4JF England
Phone: 44 (0)181 392-8585; Fax: 44 (0)181 392-9876
E-mail: Bushwd@aol.com

CONTENTS

FOREWORD

There is today a vast library of books on various aspects of European and North American ceramics. These have been written over a span of more than a hundred years. Llewellynn Jewitt's two-volume work *The Ceramic Art of Great Britain* was published in 1878. It still serves as almost a source book on British nineteenth century potters and their wares.

Since then a host of other authors have added to Jewitt's widely-spread foundation. In recent years, too, we have been treated to a series of welcome specialist books and a mass of articles or learned papers on different types, classes or makes of collectable ceramics. Many of these authors have carried out deep research in their chosen field. The end result may be rather uneven, due to personal taste, situation or pure chance but the benefit is undoubted.

Arnold Kowalsky, the American author of the present work has, I believe not been able to carry out first-hand research on European archives or source material but helpfully he stood back, enabling him to take a broad view of the whole field with a welcome fresh mind. He has painstakingly consulted the mass of published material, comparing the statements or views of dozens of authors. Importantly, he has questioned the many differences that came to light. He has sought the advice and help of numerous international authorities in an effort to resolve the differences and to fill in the many gaps that showed themselves.

This new enterprise, mainly concerned with the Anglo-American market and ceramics of the Ironstone-type, is the result of a very long painstaking work; of thousands of letters; of seemingly tens of thousands of long trans-Atlantic phone calls. Work in Europe has, at times, all but ceased as Arnold's questions have been answered!

In terms of time, the cost of reference books and of the combined years of experience of the authorities, this resulting work must be priceless! I, whilst at times almost despairing of Arnold's continued questions, have benefited greatly from his inquiring mind and on re-working a given problem have shown some of my original views or dates to be erroneous. We can, therefore, all learn from our new author's researches on this truly vast subject. No work on ceramics can be complete or faultless, but Arnold Kowalsky's new comparative study surely represents a useful step in that direction.

Geoffrey A. Godden,
Findon, U.K.
1996

ACKNOWLEDGMENTS

This Encyclopedia is first and foremost indebted to all researchers, past and present, without whose collective information and knowledge this work would not have been possible. My thanks go to the many authors, publishers, museums, manufacturers and other individuals too numerous to list, here in the United States, the United Kingdom and in Europe, who have put up with my incessant inquiries, in the continual search for the most current and accurate data possible. To the many clubs, societies and collectors, past present and future, thank you for sharing your research and information with me.

My thanks and appreciation go to the following authors, collectors and publishers in the United States: Dale Abrams, David Arman, Irene Beer, Dorothy & Elmer Caskey, Bea & Roy Coleman, Frank and Paul Davenport, Kimmey Decker, Bev & Ernie Dieringer, Gale Frederick, Mary Frank Gaston, William Gates, Sharon Glendenning, Shirley & James Hagerty, Annise Doring Heaivilin, Ellen R. Hill, Kyle Husfloen, William Kurau, James Kerr, Janice Kobach, Mary M. Lacombe, Lois Lehner, Louise & Charles Loehr, Dr. Warren L. Macy, Brinda & Ron Myers, James L. Murphy, Lou Nelson, Dana Ormerod, Daniel Overmyer, Robert & Joy Renshaw, Julie Rich, Connie Rogers, Jeffrey B. Snyder, Frank Stefano, Jr., Nancy J. Upchurch, William Van Buskirk, Eleanor Washburn, Marguerite Rose Weber, George Wells IV, Jean Wetherbee, Bill Wetherton, Petra Williams, The Antique Trader Books, Collectors Books, Fountain House East, Schiffer Publications Ltd., The Society for Historical Archaeology, Wallace-Homestead Book Co., the Flow Blue International Collectors Club, Tea Leaf Club International, and White Ironstone Collectors Association.

I also thank my English colleagues, without whose advice this work would not have been possible: John C. Baker, R.C. Bell, Michael Berthoud, John H.Y. Briggs, Robert E. Cluett, John Cockerill, Robert Copeland, A.W. Coysh, John P. Cushion, Kay Dickson, David Drakard and Paul Holdway, Diana Edwards, Neil Ewins, Geoffrey A. Godden, Reginald Haggar and Elizabeth Adams, Pat Halfpenny, Helen L. Hallesy, Rodney Hampson, Dr. Richard K. Henrywood, Joan Jones, Henry Kelly, Barry Lamb, Heather Lawrence, D.B. Leigh, Douglas Leishman, W.L. Little, Terence A. Lockett, Wolf Mankowitz, Julie McKeown, Steven Moore and Catherine Ross, Kathy Niblett, Tim H. Peake, John Potter, P.D. Pryce and S.H. Williams, Robert Pugh, Robin Reilly, Gabe Lake Roberts, Florence Sibson, Allan Smith, Mrs. Eileen Smith, Mrs. Anna Tomlinson, Sydney B. Williams, Anthony Wood, Antique Collectors Club, Barrie & Jenkins, B.T. Batsford Ltd., Blakeney Art Pottery, Burgess & Leigh Ltd., City Museum and Art Gallery - Stoke on Trent, The Churchill Group, David & Charles Ltd., Andre Deutsch Ltd., Doncaster Museum and Art Gallery, Faber & Faber, Longman Group Ltd., MacMillan Inc., Minton, Omega Books Ltd., T.H. Peake Publishers, Random House, Royal Doulton, Simon & Schuster, Studio Vista, Swan Hill Press, Tyne & Wear County Council Museum, Wedgwood, Arthur Wood & Son, The English Ceramics Circle, Friends of Blue, Northern Ceramics Society, and Scottish Ceramics Society.

My appreciation also goes to the many European authorities with whom I have corresponded: Nicole Balluloureiro, J. Bottema, Ludwig Danckert, Emile Decker, Claire Dumortier, Jacqueline DuPasquier, Clive Gilbert, K. Girard, Tord Gyllenhammar-Stockholms Stadmuseum, Heikki Hyvonen - National Board of Antiquities, Helsinki, Finland, J. Lefebvre - Service des Archives, La Louviere, Marie-Madeleine Masse, Dr. Waltraud Neuwirth, Joao Castel-Branco Pereira, J. Polling, Maria Queirozribeiro, Robert E. Rontgen, Barbara Scheffran, Ester Schneider, Tara Silverman - Finnish National Museum, Helsinki, Finland, Dr. Christa Svoboda, Antiek (Publishing), Ceramic Museum in Sacavem, Gulbenkian Museum, Robert Hale Ltd. (Publisher), Musee Dorsay, The Museum of Decorative Arts-Palais du Louvre, Museum of Decorative Arts-Bordeaux, National Museum of Azulego, Osterreichisches Museum, Prestel-Verlag (Publisher), The Royal Museum of Art & History, Brussels, Salzburger Museum, Sarreguemines Museum, Der Stadt Dortmund Museum, and Villeroy & Boch.

There were just so many people who assisted and encouraged me, that in my attempt to acknowledge everyone, I may have omitted some names. Thus, my thanks and apologies go to those inadvertently overlooked.

Special thanks and acknowledgment goes to: Geoffrey Godden for not only sharing his knowledge and expertise, but also for allowing me the use of selected marks in his *Encyclopedia of British Pottery and Porcelain Marks*; Deborah Joiner who graciously volunteered to computerize the appendices included in this book; Ellen Hill, Louise and Leonard Mason for their monumental proofreading efforts; and Barry Lamb of Reference Works and Steve Chun of the Art Book Services (Antique Collectors Club) for their friendship and help in building my research library.

My great appreciation goes to those who have shared their area of expertise with me and have taken the time to proofread, add to or correct the areas in which they specialize: Dale Abrams; David Arman; John Cockerill; Robert Copeland; Bev and Ernie Deiringer; Ellen Hill; Henry Kelly; Tim H. Peake; John Potter; Robert Pugh; Jean Wetherbee; and Norman Wolfe. Lest I forget, I would like to say thank you to Charles Washburne for his many hours in assisting to put this work onto computer. I would also like to thank Schiffer Publishing, Ltd. and Jeffrey Snyder for their encouragement and guidance in bringing this work to fruition.

Last, but not at all least, my thanks and love to my wife, Dorothy, and daughter, Francine, for their writing, typewriting and proofreading, and for generally putting up with me.

INTRODUCTION

The principal aim of this Encyclopedia on Earthenware, Ironstone and Stoneware is to bring together , in one volume, two hundred years of manufacture of Blue and White Transferware, Historic Blue, Romantic Transferware, Flow Blue, Mulberry Wares, White Ironstone and Tea Leaf/Copper Lustre. Since the 1950s a vast number of publications have appeared covering these categories. Every author writes from his or her own perspective, adding a valuable contribution to his or her specific topic. Through these works the foundation of information has been laid and expanded upon, adding to our understanding of the potters' art. One may refer to this book as an effort to pull together all materials known to this author in a logical and codified form, making them available to the reader, who does not have or is unable to obtain the untold corpus of works available on potters, marks and patterns as recorded to-date.

I believe that John Ramsay's *American Potters and Pottery* (1947, page vii), best sums up the methodology employed in writing this encyclopedia. This is not, however, to be taken as an apology but as an explanation; for each author writes from his own interest and viewpoint.

> "If this single volume were meant to be a study of the manufacture of pottery, it would be necessary to preface it with an apology. If it were intended as a history of the pottery industry of [sic], further apologies would be in order. Since I have written from the standpoint of a collector of pottery, both subjects have been considered, but topics of considerable historical and technical significance have been compressed into very small space, because their interest to the collector is slight, while other material, which does interest collectors, has been expanded to what may seem to others, unreasonable length. Thus "collectible" pottery — its types, manufacture and makers — is considered in detail, while other wares, as well as much early and recent ceramic history, are covered only sketchily."

The Industrial Revolution was the catalyst for expansion of the pottery industry. A middle class market evolved, and with bravura, the "Staffordshire" potter arose to meet the challenge of filling the needs of this new middle class. New ceramic body styles and techniques of manufacture, including the transfer printing process, were introduced. The ceramics industry was slowly transforming itself from one based on hand made work to one of mass production. The year 1780 seems to be the date that writers refer to as the beginning of the Blue and White period. The determination of this date was due, in part, to the introduction of new body styles, the transfer (printing) technique and the introduction of the now famous "Willow" pattern. (For an introduction to Creamware and Pearlware, refer to *Creamware & Pearlware, (May 18 - September 7, 1986)*. The Fifth Exhibition from the Northern Ceramics Society, Stoke-on-Trent, England, Pat Halfpenny and Terence A. Lockett, editors, as well as to Robert Copeland's *Brief History of Transfer-Printing on Blue and White Ceramics.* As the steam driven engine replaced water power in the nineteenth century, so too did ironstone type earthenware bodies replace Creamware/ Queensware and Pearlware. To capitalize on this expansion, body descriptions such as Ironstone, Stoneware, etc. were introduced. Strong, compact, durable and lasting wares became the "china" of the export and middle class market, whereas porcelain remained the china of choice of the upper classes.

This Encyclopedia deals with the three major categories: earthenware, stoneware and ironstone, defined as follows:

Earthenware is the most basic, made of potters' earth or clay and not vitrified. It is fired at the lowest temperatures, about 900-1000 degrees. When fired, earthenware is porous and opaque. It needs a glaze to make it impervious to liquids.

Ironstone/Stone China is by its definition Earthenware with the addition of ferrous elements (iron slag). It is fired at the highest temperatures, 1200 degrees and above, and is the strongest of the three categories.

Stoneware is also made of clay, but has additions such as fusible stone, calcium or flint. Without these additions stoneware is clay colored, but with the addition of calcium-like products the body becomes white. It is fired at higher temperatures than Earthenware, 1100-1200 degrees. Due to these high temperatures, Stoneware is vitrified, rendering it impervious to liquids, and can appear translucent when potted thinly.

It is not the purpose of this introduction to delve into potters' histories, techniques and decorative styles. If done, this would become a twenty-four volume work. Excellent works such as Drakard & Holdway's *Spode's Printed Ware* give the reader an insight into the printing technique of the period, as does the *Dictionary of Blue and White Printed Pottery, 1780-1880,* in two volumes, by A.W. Coysh and R.K. Henrywood. There are many other fine works that explore the industry and art of the potter which should not be ignored; e.g., Reilly's two-volume *Dictionary and History of Wedgwood*, and Geoffrey Godden's *Staffordshire Porcelain.*

I have asked various authorities in the field to write a section on their areas of expertise in order to give the reader an insight into the categories covered herein.

As astute businessmen, English potters found a way to exploit the American market by appealing to a new nation's patriotism through creating "Historic" Staffordshire wares, commonly referred to in America as "Historic American Blue." These wares had patriotic and American views (scenes) and found favor with and appeal to the young nation. These views, as sketched by English artists, were sometimes fanciful and even included European scenes. Historic Staffordshire subject matter is well documented and illustrated in works such as Ellouise Baker Larsen's *American Historical Views of Staffordshire China* and Jeffrey B. Snyder's *Historical Staffordshire, American Patriots and Views*.

White Ironstone-type wares continued to be manufactured during this period, both for home use and for the export market. The were produced in blue and white, as well as in a variety of colors such as pink, black, brown and green. The art of polychrome and lustre decoration was also employed by potters of the period. For in-depth reading, I would refer the reader to Geoffrey A. Godden and Michael Gibson's *Collecting Lustreware*, Godden's *Guide to Mason's China and the Ironstone*

Wares as well as Howard Davis' *Chinoiserie Polychrome Decoration on Staffordshire Porcelain, 1790-1850*.

Flow Blue and Mulberry Wares, the next categories, found favor with the American market and were produced by hundreds of potters. One must understand that potters did not "earn their keep" through the production of just one product. They stayed in business through producing a variety of wares; e.g., figurines, toy china, porcelain, parian ware, etc. Flown Blue was just one segment of the production line. Petra Williams' classic three volume work *Flow Blue China an Aid to Identification* is the standard reference work for collectors. Other works on Flow Blue, notably Mary Frank Gaston's *Collectors Guide to Patterns, History and Values*, and Ellen R. Hill's *Mulberry Ironstone, Flow Blue's Best Kept Little Secret* are major references for collectors.

Romantic Transferware was an outgrowth of the tastes of the early Victorian period. It was produced not only in blue but also in other shades and colors. In their three volumes, *Romantic Staffordshire*, Petra Williams and Marguerite Weber note that patterns and subject matter were executed in categories such as floral, classical, oriental, scenic, genre, juvenile and polychrome/chinoiserie. This "Romantic" period was an extremely prolific and productive one for English potters, as opportunity was never wasted.

White Ironstone bodies that were never decorated found a market just as they were, or embellished with various styles of simple leaf decorations with or without lustre and with or without colored bands (commonly referred to in America as Tea Leaf/Copper Lustre). It would appear that if potters could not sell their products in one form they sold it in another. I would call this "theme and variation based upon an ironstone-type earthenware body." Two significant works covering the categories of White Ironstone and Tea Leaf/Copper Lustre are Jean Wetherbee's *White Ironstone, A Collector's Guide* and Annise Heaivilin's *Grandma's Tea Leaf Ironstone, A History and Study of English and American Potteries*. Too late to make reference to, but very noteworthy as a source for American White Earthenwares, is William C. Ketchum, Jr's. *American Pottery and Porcelain, Identification and Price Guide*.

The European continent did not manufacture prolifically in the above categories. Potters on the Continent did, however, produce some Blue and White, Romantic Transferware and Flow Blue not only for home consumption but for the export market. There are two particularly good publications available on European ceramics: Ludwig Danckert's *Dictionary of European Porcelain* and Robert E. Rontgen's *Marks of German, Bohemian and Austrian Porcelain*.

The end of the Civil War and the philosophy of Manifest Destiny helped the U.S. to claim its share of the ceramics industry. Flow Blue, Tea Leaf/Copper Luster and White Ironstone were the most notable wares represented, even though these were a very small percent of the overall categories manufactured. However, the United States industry was depressed due, in part, to the large volume of inexpensive goods imported into the country from the United Kingdom. For further reading on U.S. ceramics refer to Edwin Atlee Barber's *The Pottery and Porcelain of the United States and Marks of American Potters*, William C. Gates & Dana E. Ormerod's *The East Liverpool Pottery District*, and Lois Lehner's *Lehner's Encyclopedia of U.S. Marks on Pottery & Porcelain China*.

Many potters of this period have been written about and well documented during the past fifty years. See this author's Bibliography section for information on the many excellent publications available. Additionally, clubs and societies have emerged at which ceramics collectors can share their interests and research. In the United Kingdom there is the Friends of Blue and the Northern Ceramics Society amongst others. Clubs in the United States are the Flow Blue International Collectors Club, Tea Leaf International Collectors Club and the White Ironstone Collectors Association.

As much as one would like to, the "whole world" cannot be included in a work such as this. Therefore, this Encyclopedia does not include porcelain, children's ware/toy china, brush stroke, gaudy wares and decorative wares. A few examples may be included for pattern reference, but they are not the main focus of this work.

It is my hope that readers, scholars, and collectors will avail themselves of the bibliography included in this work, and search out subjects, potters and technologies of production that prove to be of interest. A wonderful book available which touches upon the social fabric of the period is *Pottery and Porcelain, 1700-1914* by Bevis Hillier. There is so much more to the ceramics industry than just the production of the potter, with many forces coming into play in the evolution of the industry! Hillier's book delves into cause and effect as well as social and political influences on the arts, including the ceramics industry.

There is no better way to conclude this short introduction than by citing a section from Geoffrey A. Godden's *Staffordshire Porcelain*:

"Perhaps as the twentieth century draws to a close we can look back over the eighteenth and nineteenth century wares with more understanding and tolerance than past authorities, remembering as we do so that the commercial products of any age should rightly reflect the taste or requirements of that time."

This author has taken great care to include all known manufacturers of Staffordshire, ironstone and earthenware. However, I am sure that future research and studies will divulge new names, corrections, etc. I would be pleased to learn of such findings and to receive any corrections or additions.

Arnold A. Kowalsky
908 North Broadway
Yonkers, NY 10701

NOTES FROM SELECTED AUTHORS

In the past few years many fine and authoritative collectors and authors have emerged who specialize in the subject matter covered in this encyclopedia; Blue and White Transferware, Historic Staffordshire, Flow Blue, Mulberry Ironstone, White Ironstone and Tea Leaf/Copper Lustre. I have prevailed upon a number of these authorities to write short and concise commentaries on their areas of expertise. They graciously met this task as witnessed by the following selections.

A BRIEF HISTORY OF TRANSFER-PRINTING ON BLUE AND WHITE CERAMICS

Why is blue and white so popular? What are its origins? The Chinese realized that cobalt yielded the most attractive color which would withstand the high temperature of 1400c at which they fired their fine porcelain. The center of production was in the Province of Kiangsi at Ching-te-Chen and over the years a large export trade was developed. In the seventeenth century European traders reached China by sea; first, the Portuguese who imported Chinese porcelain wares into Lisbon, and later the Dutch, British and others. Teas, silks, lacquers, spices and porcelains were brought to Europe; soon the Chinese were exploiting this lucrative market by producing patterns which appealed to the Westerners. These included landscapes of a Chinese style which were skillfully hand painted in cobalt blue direct onto the dry, unfired clayware to which glaze was added before firing once at 1400c. Millions of pieces of tea, dinner and dessert wares were imported into Europe. However in Britain, due to the rise in popularity of the Georgian style of architecture with its Neo-classical ornamentation both outside and inside and the new forms of fine furniture made with fine-grained hardwoods like mahogany and walnut, Chinese tableware designs seemed out of place. The English East India Company also found that they were losing money on their 'chinaware'. These imports were sold at auction, mostly to dealers. Miles Mason, a china dealer in London, organized a dealers' auction 'ring' which cheated the Company of all competition, so not only were sales depressed by lower demand, it was losing money on the sales it did have. The East India Company reduced its imports of chinaware to nil in 1799, but the volume began to reduce quickly from 1783.

However, there were people who needed these wares; some because their families were growing in size or they had sustained losses through breakage. Even before this, some English potters had made earthenwares with naive pseudo-oriental designs painted in blue on creamware, but they had not learned the skills of the Chinese painters. It seems that the Worcester Porcelain Manufactory had introduced transfer-printing in blue underglaze direct onto the biscuit porcelain in 1761, but it was at Caughley, in Shropshire on the River Severn, that the earliest successful attempts were made to copy some of the Chinese landscapes, centers and border designs. Caughley did not produce the Willow Pattern, with the three socialists on the bridge (they go to the left) and the fence for them to sit on. But they did produce copies of about seven Chinese landscapes on their porcelain body. The porcelain biscuit had a fine, smooth surface which enabled the image from the engraved copper plate to be printed with a good degree of success. Attempts in Staffordshire to transfer prints onto the biscuit earthenware were not so successful because the surface of the biscuit was not so fine and smooth, being covered with thousands of minute holes which rendered the printed image incomplete. The credit for solving this difficulty is given to Josiah Spode I who, in 1784, found a method of ensuring the transfer of the complete image onto the surface of biscuit earthenware. I believe that the secret lay in the use of soft soap and water 'size' with which the tissue paper was wetted before it was applied to the copper engraving holding the color. This soft soap 'size' rendered the paper impervious to the oil with which the color was mixed, it rendered the tissue paper very flexible so that it could be easily moulded to the contours of the different items, it reduced the risk of the paper singeing on the hot copper engraving, and it made it easier to wash off the paper in water.

Initially, the blue color was very dark. This was due to the use of impure cobalt substances; in these days the two cobalt materials were 'zaffres' (cobalt ore roasted with a flux such as sand, or quartz) and 'smalts' (zaffres heated with potash to yield the double silicate of cobalt and potassium). However, this dark blue matched the Chinese ware quite well, so Spode began to engrave copper plates to match the Chinese pieces he was requested to reproduce. This willingness to assist his customers led him to copying some twenty or more Chinese patterns in order that customers might continue to enjoy the use of their blue and white services. Gradually, as chemists and producers of cobalt colors improved the purity of the product, the cobalt colors became paler; at the same time the skill of the engravers improved so that, instead of only fairly coarsely line-engraved designs being made, patterns having a range of tonal qualities emerged, partly due to the use of stipple-punchwork. Moreover, different shades of blue became available, such as cyanine, royal, ultramarine, and several more. (see *Spode's Willow Pattern and Other Designs After The Chinese*).

Blue and White became, and remains, very popular because it is a restful color and, most importantly, it enhances the appearance of the food which is served on it. It looks fresh and cheerful, and looks attractive on natural wood especially oak -

the predominant wood used for furniture in the days when Chinese blue and white wares were the principal fine tablewares. Incidentally, blue on creamware does not look as attractive as does blue on white.

The Spodes, having established themselves as the leaders in the field of blue and white earthenware moved into non-oriental patterns, and were followed closely by other manufacturers such as Rogers, Riley, Joshua Heath, Turner, Adams, Clews, Ridgway, etc. The quality of the engraving determined the final quality of the print; these potters achieved their fine results because the engravings were of the best standard. Other manufacturers, who appealed to the less well-off customers, could not afford to engrave their coppers to such a high standard with the consequence that their products were coarser in engraving and in the printing quality. It may be partly due to this lower standard that, in the 1840s, the emergence of flow blue took place. Coarsely engraved coppers, lower quality of cobalt color, and perhaps over thick glazing all led to the effect which was later made a special product by accentuating the flow by the addition of "flow powder".

Chinese porcelain was pale grey, rather than white, so, when in the late 1770s matching was needed for the Chinese services, cobalt stain was added to the prevailing earthenware body, cream colored or creamware, to counteract the yellow effect of the iron in the ball clay; the resultant pale grey tone was ideal for the purpose. This remained the principal body for blue and white, and today is called "pearlware". Then in the 1820s, improvements in body formulation led to true white biscuit ware which could be glazed with a transparent, colorless glaze; this became known as "whiteware" and superseded the pearlware after some years. In 1813, Mason's Ironstone was promoted; this began as a genuine stone ware, or vitreous earthenware which was very tough and hard-wearing, pale grey in color. Later, the quality deteriorated, and, although the name Ironstone was retained, the body was changed to white earthenware. By the middle of the nineteenth century many manufacturers were naming their medium (to poor) quality earthenwares, "Ironstone". "Stone China", however, made by Spode, Copeland, Davenport, Wedgwood, Hicks and Meigh, and a few others remained a pale grey, good quality, vitreous product. But the terms "Stone China", "Opaque China", "Semi-Porcelain", and similar euphemisms, have clouded the ceramic skies and misled many folk; they were all medium to low quality earthenware, very rarely vitreous, and certainly not china.

Dark cobalt blue does not have to flow. The "American Views on British Pottery" are printed in a very dark blue but generally it does not flow. Moreover, patterns printed in flow blue do not have to end up as large blobs of blue with matte black patches (due to there being more cobalt than can be absorbed by the glaze); Copeland's "Ruins" pattern shows a delicate diffusion of the blue around the clear printed image rather like a halo.

Whilst blue and white was the dominant color for underglaze earthenware decorations up until about the 1820s, other colors began to appear as chemists and color makers developed their knowledge of other metallic compounds, such as chromium, vanadium and tin. This increased the potters' opportunities to attract more business, and overseas markets were of huge importance to British potters. Many manufacturers developed the American market to the point where their patterns were never even offered in the United Kingdom and where treatments like Mulberry were seldom seen.

It is a pleasure to see the return of blue and white as a popular color for everyday tableware and dresser ware, as is evident in the mid-nineteen nineties.

Robert Copeland
June 1996

HISTORICAL STAFFORDSHIRE

Historical Staffordshire is but one small specialty in the field of collecting English Staffordshire pottery. Primarily, the collecting of Historical Staffordshire in the United States, means collecting various forms of transfer printed ceramics depicting American views. It would seem, though, that any dark blue transferware is called Historical Staffordshire by many.

Quite a few Staffordshire potters produced ceramics with American views. Early research, especially that by Ellouise Baker Larsen, has uncovered many of the source views used by the potters. These take the form of engravings and paintings by various artists, some of whom went to the United States and sketched items of interest. These sources are a great help in dating this ware, the bulk of which was produced in the 1820-1845 period. There are hundreds of views identified, and the research continues.

In the 1815-1820 period, ceramics were produced that depicted the War of 1812 naval battles and personages. It would seem that the enterprising potters put aside their national pride and showed American victories on their wares in the hopes that a profitable market could be produced. It must have proved successful, as shortly after many potteries were producing all sorts of dinnerware and utilitarian items with American views. There are many categories of collecting Historical Staffordshire that may be pursued by the collector. Some try to complete a series produced by a specific potter of choice. Others collect marine views, architecture, churches, colleges, historical events, regional views or the complete spectrum of American interest.

Most popular is the dark cobalt blue that found a ready market in the United States. Items produced with transfers for the home market [English] were generally printed in a lighter blue and were of a higher quality. The dark color would hide imperfections in the potting that would not suffice for home market use. In the mid 1830s and 1840s items were also printed in black, light blue, red, purple, brown, black and green.

Except for a few examples, potters employed border designs of their own that are useful in identifying the potter. Not all pieces were marked, so it is useful to learn the different borders. Historical Staffordshire has been collected and written about since the 1870s, and there are a number of fine reference books of which beginning collectors should avail themselves.

William Kurau
1995

TO FLOW OR NOT TO FLOW, THAT IS THE QUESTION?

An Occasional Paper Presented to the Flow Blue International Collectors Club Annual Convention, 1995

The development of blue designs was a matter of both technology and taste notes Robert Copeland.[1] "Flow[n] Blue ... a chemical technique achieved by introducing (Flow Poder), a chemical such as lime or ammonium chloride into the glost oven. The blue print (cobalt oxide) is allowed to run during fusion of the glaze, thus producing a blurred or halo effect." Copeland notes this process as "...putting flow powder - a mixture of sale (sodium chloride), with lead and calcium carbonate - into the saggars during firing."[2]

In a letter dated January 5, 1848, Herbert Minton relates "...as respect all FB (Flown Blue) patterns, we cannot, after taking all the pains in our power, guarantee that all the pieces of the service [Anemone] should be exactly of the same tint and color or degree of flow. The process is an uncertain one."[3]

Davenport's Flow Blue production during the approximate period of 1840-1860 was quite large and mass produced, as was that of his contemporary potters who were involved in the export market.[4]

> English potters shipped these "...calculated insult[s] to the engravers art with its deliberate effect of smudge and blur..."[5] These wares for export were "Poorly fired 'seconds' or 'thirds' ... at low price[s]...exclusively as export wares."[6]

English taste of the period lay in printed, clean, sharply defined wares.[7] Leonard Whiter writes on the subject that "Mercifully the full Flow Blue effect was never sought during the Spode period."[8]

In a series of articles in the "Art-Union" Magazine of June 1844, the editor notes, "...These abominations [as] 'floating blue' ..." [an] "...indulgence of bad taste...The only place where we can find anything like it is in the wash-house, where the laundress squeezes the blue-bag over wet flannel, and amuses herself by giving a rude configuration to the discharged contents."[9]

The formulae for these misguided wares, made for export, could fetch upwards of 100£ each.[10] William Evans' article "Art and History of the Potting Industry (1846)", reprinted in *The Journal of Ceramic History, No. 3*, 1970 states that "The flor for blue, although of recent introduction, has undergone several changes. That, now in use by W. Ridgway, esq., is considered to be the best. Instead of washing, or placing the flow in the saggars, it is introduced in the glaze; and a great savings of expense is thereby secured.[11] Various recipes for this "flowing" process are noted in detail in many publications including" *Copeland, Spode*, pp. 163-166; *Jones*, pp. 174-175; and *Whiter*, p. 347.

1. *Copeland, Spode*, p. 20.
   It is further noted that a rather compact and concise history of Staffordshire Blue can be found in *Little*.
2. *Copeland, Spode*, pp. 19-120
   P. Williams, Flow Blue, Vol. I, p. 5 notes that "this deep blurring covered printing faults and stilt marks and served to hide other defects such as glaze bubbles."
   Nance, p. 175 notes that between 1830-1840 "...The flow colors, although transferred in the ordinary way, differ from the usual printed colours in that when fired in the glost-kiln they run and produce a sort of blurring of the lines of the design, which was considered pleasant. ...The process seems to have been discovered by chance ... owing to some materials accidentally left in a saggar having given a result on firing that was afterwareds artificially retrograde." Nance further notes that "... Less care needed to be taken with the engraving ... and due to the flowing process faults in design were often disguised."
3. *Jones*, p. 48.
   Geoffrey Godden further notes in his *Minton Pottery and Porcelain of the First Period, 1792-1850*, that this process is described in W. White's book *The Complete Practical Potter*, 1847, that "The Flown Blue effect was mainly the result of firing the blue printed wares in an atmosphere containing volatile chlorides. This flown effect, in which the blue colour runs slightly into the glaze, giving a halo-like effect, was very popular in foreign markets during the 1840-1850 period."
   Further *P. Williams, Flow Blue*, p. 5 notes that "...some of the pieces so made are so flown that it is impossible to discern border detail or center pattern; and some are done so lightly that only a halo effect appears."
4. *Lockett & Godden*, pp. 1762-179.
5. *Whiter*, p. 144.
6. *Lockett & Godden*, p. 172.
7. Una des Fontaines (Contributor) *English Ceramic Circle Transactions*, Vol. II, Part 3, 1983. p. 219.
8. *Whiter*, p. 144.
9. *Lockett & Godden*, pp. 173-174.
   Further, *Williams-Wood, English Transfer*, pp. 35-36 and 235-239, includes an extensive glossary of color terms covering all hues and shades met with in the study of ceramis. This is accomplished by using a parallel system of color codings and terms described by the Munsell system in American and the British Standards Institution.
10. *Reilly, Wedgwood*, pp. 347-350; *Copeland, Spode*, pp. 163-166; and *Godden, Davenport*, pp. 174-175.
    Furthermore, Audrey Dudson. *Dudson, A Family of Potters Since 1800*. Hanley, England. Dudson Publications, states that it would appear that potters were engaged not only in selling formulae for colors and glazes but sold body shapes themselves. (See the Dudson Order Book for 1842-1844, Appendix D)
11. *Lockett & Godden*, p. 174 and *Copeland, Spode*, pp. 19-20 notes "...An underglaze colour must have two components, the color strain (which must be stable and brilliant when glazed and fired) and the flux to fasten the colour to the biscuit body. The glaze has an important effect on brilliance and unfortunately a glaze that gives particularly high brilliance may often have solvent action, which impairs equally the fineness of the pattern. So it is very unusual to find underglaze patterns in cobolt silicate blues, especially in which the lines and dots of the pattern are not to some degree blurred, for the intensity of the cobalt silicate reveals the slightest diffusion of colour into the glaze."

N.B. The books referenced here, in abbreviated form, will be completely listed and included in the Bibliography of the above-reference Encyclopedia.

FLOW BLUE IRONSTONE

The export market of the nineteenth century proved itself to be a very fertile and profitable endeavor for many English potters. Because of its durability, earthenware/ironstone/ stoneware, designed with blue and white transfer and American [historic] depictions were highly successful commodities. Potters were always seeking new opportunities during this period of great change and experimentation.[1] From the late 1830s through the 1870s "Flow Blue" followed these earlier successes.

Themes and patterns employed during this time were predominantly oriental. It is important to note that not all Flow Blue flowed. Whether by intent or happenstance, there are early patterns by Davenport, Minton and other potters that do not flow as much as do the overwhelming majority of wares of the period.

Over the years Flow Blue has been interpreted to mean different things to different people. As such, I feel obligated to define what Flow Blue means in the context of this Encyclopedia.

The title of this book describes the subject matter at hand as an **earthenware/ironstone/stoneware** body which, when fired in a bisque state is white or pale gray. Flow Blue patterns are to be found on this type of body. The transfer pattern and glazing were applied to this bisque body prior to its second firing.

These glazed, decorated bisque wares were placed into saggars along with a bowl containing flow powder. During this high temperature second firing volatilization occurred, whereby color diffused into the glaze with a blurring or halo effect taking place. Furthermore, due to gaps between objects in the saggar color was sometimes transferred from the printed image, settling on a piece next to it. The deposition of "flow ghosts" on the reverse sides of plates and platters is frequently and erroneously attributed to the color having flown *through* the pottery. (Breaking a piece quickly disproves the theory – the pottery remains white.) The flow ghosts originate at the upper surface of the item immediately below the surface on which they appear. During firing, the glaze melts, and the fluxes within release the gas carbon dioxide. Tiny bubbles of the gas rise to the surface and burst, in the same way that a carbonated beverage effervesces. The bursting bubbles splash small amounts of glaze on the underside of the plate stacked above. In areas where the transfer is dark, a significant amount of cobalt is dissolved in the glaze, and when some of it "splashes" on the surface above, it leaves a "ghost" of the image below. The closer the two surfaces are to each other, the sharper the ghost image will be.This is most evident in plates and flatware. The result was a blurred coloration on the back of an adjacent piece, giving the appearance of bleeding through the back of the piece on which the pattern was applied. However, such is not the case.

The period between c.1840 and the 1870s is known for having heavier bodies than those manufactured from the 1870s onward. The composition of these earthenware/ironstone/ stoneware blanks are exactly the same for both periods, only with the bodies of the latter era being made thinner.

The 1870s ushered in a change in style and taste whereby clear, clean and defined lines were in order. The demand for the earlier "flowing" style gave way to this new "photographic-type image." To more fully understand this transition period, I would refer the reader to Maureen Batkin's book *Wedgwood Ceramics, 1846-1959*, Richard Dennis, London, England, 1982. However, the color **Flow Blue** remained. The difference now was that the underglazed transfer color was not made to flow. Are there exceptions? Yes, there will always be exceptions caused by impurities in the cobalt, unclean saggars, uncontrolled heat, etc.

This author firmly believes that, to a large extent, most of the seconds and thirds produced during the early Flow Blue period of 1840 to 1870 were passed off to an export market in which America was predominant. Seconds and thirds imported into the United States were defective pieces and were priced accordingly. (In point of fact, manufacturers tried to set prices on these defective pieces.) Defects included but were not limited to the following: ill fitting lids; chips that were glazed over; irregular fitting and placed patterns; pieces that had kiln bruises and irregular coloring; pieces that were on imperfect blanks; and pieces that had irregular glazing.

As businessmen, fine potters of the early Victorian period (such as Samuel Alcock & Co., Davenport, etc.) faced a dilemma as to how to rid themselves of second and third quality undecorated blanks that did not meet their standards. A solution was found in the production of Flow Blue, whereby the copper plates were heavily and deeply etched which allowed for distortion of the printed scene when transferred onto a ceramic body.[2] With the addition of salts and acids to the saggar during the second firing, a blurring or flowing of the pattern was effected. The glazes were also tinted with the "blue poder" [powder] to produce not only a halo or "blue sheen" but to further exaggerate the blurring process into the glaze. Consequently, through this flown process imperfections were easily hidden.

As the popularity of these Flown Blue ironstone wares in America far exceeded manufacturers expectations, imperfect blanks were not the only bodies used for sale to the export market. This "full blown" media now found potters using first quality blanks - as, after all, business was business.

During the late Victorian period onward taste and circumstances dictated a clear, clean look. To a large extent, floral and art nouveau patterns replaced the romantic and oriental look. The "Flow Blue" [color] took on an almost clear and clean transfer appearance reminiscent of late eighteenth and early nineteenth century blue and white transferware. The difference, however, lay in the rich blue coloring of the Flow Blue as opposed to the early soft blue of transferware, so well noted and illustrated by *Coysh*, *Copeland*, *Whiter* and others in their works.[3]

England was not the only country that produced Flow Blue. Other counties such as France, Germany, Holland and Portugal also manufactured Flow Blue, as did American manufactories after the Civil War. Flow Blue production continued into the twentieth century and included a grab bag of styles and wares manufactured to meet the demands of the market. However, with the end of World War I production was reduced to a handful of potteries who continued the Flow Blue tradition. Such firms as Adams and Wood & Son reissued earlier patterns during the period after the war. The Second World War saw a further decline in production, and today there is an even smaller group of potteries manufacturing Flow Blue.

Arnold A. Kowalsky
April 1998

1 Michael Berthoud notes the following in his book *H. & R. Daniel, 1822-1846.* Kent, England, Micawber Publications, pp. 53-55 and 65: John Daniel [a potter of Stoke-on-Trent] experimented in Flow Blue and other flown colors (as noted by his ledger, prior to August 1840). "By October 1842 John Daniel was conducting trials for "Flow Blue", but was probably not the first in the field since he records that these were to match Dimmock's 'Blue Flowing Earthenware'.

2 For more complete data on Cobalt in the manufacture of Flow Blue refer to *English Blue & White Porcelain of the Eighteenth Century* by Bernard Watney, New York, NY. Thomas Yoseloff. 1963-1964, pp. 6-9. These four pages are a very good introduction into the history of Cobalt which dates from 2000 BC to the present. In these pages Mr. Watney states that "...cobalt is the essential colouring material in the manufacture of all Blue and White China, not only for underglaze painting, but also for tinting bodies and glazes to imitate the appearance of imported Chinese wares as nearly as possible." Also see Robert Copeland's Comments on cobalt in his commentary *A Brief History of Blue & White Ceramics* in this encyclopedia.

3 Maureen Batkin provides interesting and relevant information on Flow Blue and Transferware in *Wedgwood Ceramics, 1846-1959*. London, England. Richard Dennis. 1982, Chapter 6, Victorian Tablewares, pp. 89-108.

Located in the Wedgwood Archives is Clement Francis's notebook compiled in the early 1860s which cites the following:

"For Blue printed there are 7 different blues of different strengths, No. 1 & 2 being the strongest are used for Flowed patterns because the Flow weakens them in diffusing them. No. 3, 4 & 5 are used for still patterns. No. 5, 6 & 7 are used for seconds printed patterns so as to spend no more blue than will cover the plate." Ms. Batkin goes on to state that (Wedgwood) Flow Blue fell into the Common category and included patterns such as, "Ferrara, Cairo, Chinese, Landscape, Trent, Trophy, Gothic, Filigree, Willow, Brosley, Old Chain, Bead and Botanical."

MULBERRY IRONSTONE

What is Mulberry Ironstone? My definition of Mulberry Ironstone is: "Ironstone china made primarily in England between 1840 and 1870; transfer printed or hand-painted in any of several colorations: dark grays, browns or purplish-blacks, the design can flow." To understand the definition you need some background information: why, when and where Mulberry Ironstone was made. Let's take a look at England toward the end of the 1700s — the transfer printing process had been developed, a rise in the tax on silver caused an increased demand for pottery teapots, and the imports of china-ware from the Orient decreased. To replace the imports, large amounts of porcelain and pottery were produced in England. Many of the designs used were of oriental origin, and most of the pottery produced was blue, because the cobalt-based coloring fired reliably in the kilns of the day.

Exports from North Staffordshire accelerated after the completion of the Grand Trunk Canal to Liverpool. There were no very large potteries in the United States at that time, so "huge volumes of blue-printed wares were produced and some manufacturers specialized in supplying North America with designs scarcely seen in Britain from 1830 onwards patterns printed in Flow Blue became increasingly popular and were offered in addition to designs printed in non-flowing blue and in many other colors such as green, pink, brown, and especially mulberry."[1]

The mulberry color was probably produced as a cheaper alternative to the expensive cobalt used in blue transfer and flow blue. The Victorians were fascinated with the purple-black-brown shades and the manganese carbonate used to produce the color was readily available and made attractive dishes. Some authors claim that the public was bored with blue and white dishes; they had become available and cheap and were even considered "common" because everyone had them! Mulberry must have caught the public's fancy; for several years it was produced side-by-side with flow blue, by many of the same potters, and even in some of the exact same patterns. There were over four hundred different patterns made in Mulberry Ironstone; Floral patterns are the most numerous, followed by Scenic (Western), Asian, Brush Stroke and Marble.

Mulberry has been vastly underrated until recently. **Mulberry Ironstone** was first manufactured in the 1830s. There was other pottery made earlier using the mulberry color, but this pottery was not ironstone, and will not be covered here. Most of the patterns date from 1835-1855, with a few later ones made up to the 1870s. The late patterns are usually borderline in color and generally do not flow.

Mulberry Ironstone was manufactured primarily in the Staffordshire district of England. Staffordshire was a major pottery center because of the availability of coal, needed in vast quantities to fire the kilns. Other potteries were located in Glasgow, Newcastle-upon-Tyne, and in South Wales. A few patterns were manufactured in France, Germany and Sweden. Most of the non-British Isles ware was made late in the time period, 1870 and afterwards.

The largest manufacturers of Mulberry Ironstone were: W. Adams, J. Alcock, J. & M.P. Bell, E. Challinor, J. Clementson, W. Davenport, T. Dimmock, J. Edwards, J. Furnival, T. Furnival, J. & R. Godwin, J. Heath, T.J. & J. Mayer, C. Meigh, Mellor Venables, F. Morley, Podmore Walker, T. Walker, Wedgwood, Wedgwood & Co., J. Wedg Wood and Wood & Brownfield. There were at least sixty more minor makers of Mulberry, with numerous manufacturers still unidentified.

Ellen R. Hill
1993

WHITE IRONSTONE CHINA

In Staffordshire England, Charles James Mason patented in 1813 an improved china harder than earthenware and stronger than porcelain and called it "Mason's Patent Ironstone China." His patent lasted only fourteen years and by 1827, it is possible that a number of other potters had already experimented with his formulas. This early white ironstone took its forms from Chinese export ware. It had round, oval and rectangular bodies, with realistically sculptured pieces of nature for its handles and finials. There are natural branch handles on the early Mason's jugs, and Boar's head handles and Fu Dog finials on some covered dishes. Some of this early paneled ironstone was six, eight, ten or more sided and was usually decorated with transfer designs in combination with over and under glaze hand painting in various additional colors. Pieces most commonly known are of blue transfer designs. Occasionally one finds an undecorated piece of this plain-paneled early ironstone from the first half of the nineteenth century, and that's the beginning of what we call white ironstone china. (Some people suspect that flawed pieces were left undecorated and found their way out of the factories. These pieces were frequently warped or had ill fitting lids and kiln bruises.) Early ironstone seems to also have taken its form from silver and pewter services, with pedestals, handles and finials of a similar form, sometimes requiring six separate molds to make one covered bowl.

Around 1840 potters started to intentionally manufacture those same designs without transfer and painted decoration. This strong bodied, plainer and cheaper china was intended only for export to American colonies because it survived travel well and suited the colonial tastes. Between this time and 1880 over one hundred potters were producing a gleaming white china with a bluish cast, similar to Mason's ironstone.

Competition and changing tastes required new patterns to be introduced to the market every couple of years, and the flat-sided paneled plates and tureens, whose decoration existed only in and around the finials and handles, became more decorative. In place of transfer pattern decoration and hand painting which was extremely time consuming and expensive, potters switched to embossed designs carved in shallow relief before casting in molds, thus making the manufacture of the body of the piece synonymous with its surface decoration. This explosion of design extended the Chinese influence of natural forms from only the handles and finials to the entire body surface. Every imaginable part of a plant, bark, stems and leaves, seed pods and flowers, fruits, nuts and vegetables were used. Also shells, animals, fish and birds found their way on to both the surface decoration, the handles and the finials. The ribs of melons and pumpkins replaced many of the panel designs. These organic forms were well suited for the agricultural economy of the American and Canadian markets. Little, if any, of this ironstone can now be found in England.

After 1870, ironstone china was made both by English and American potters. Some of the potters were immigrants from England and helped improve American quality. They produced a plainer form suitable for the Shaker aesthetic as seen in Shaker museums. These round, oval and rectangular bodies with utilitarian handles and plain finials without decoration were forerunners of all our early twentieth century mass-produced china found in our restaurants, railroads, hotels, ocean liners and hospitals.

Ironstone china came in sets and special-order pieces. There are dinner, tea and bath sets. (There are also child's toy sets which are exact copies of the dinner and tea sets.) A dinner set included a large four piece soup tureen, (a pedestaled bowl, covered with a lid, resting on a tray, accompanied by a matching serving ladle) a smaller chowder tureen and two much smaller sauce tureens, identical except for size to the large soup tureen, (all with ladles and undertrays), a stew tureen which has no pedestal or underplate, covered vegetable tureens in several sizes, platters in seven or more graduated sizes, table plates in seven sizes from 4" to 10 1/2", and soup-type bowls in the same range of sizes, used for everything from honey to berries, cereal, chowder and soup. Relish or pickle dishes in imaginative shell, boat and leaf shapes, some exceptionally embossed with flowers, were also included. Special order pieces for the dinner set could include a well and tree platter, a wine cooler, a carafe, a reticulated fruit basket, a cheese keep and a compote with matching serving dishes, punch or toddy bowl with matching cups (and anything else the Victorians could imagine using). A tea set could include a tea pot and a coffee pot, a large sugar bowl, a cream pitcher, a waste bowl for used tea leaves and cups and saucers. Earlier cups had no handles. Special order pieces could be a cookie plate, a cake plate and spoon warmer. The bath set comprised a ewer and basin, a covered chamber pot, covered soap dish with liner, covered tooth brush holder, a shaving mug and a small pitcher for hot water. Sometimes a master waste jar and a sponge bowl were included. Vase shaped toothbrush holders with undertrays were certainly special order items since they are extremely rare, as are foot baths.

White Ironstone is becoming more popular each year and is even being reproduced by museums and catalog companies. However, they have not been able to match the quality of the glaze, the color or the detail (copies are always creamier yellow-white, while real ironstone china is a cooler blue-white). One of the well known reproductions was made by Red Cliff, an American company no longer in business, but careful enough to mark every one of their pieces with their name. One way to determine if a piece is ironstone china and not porcelain, is to hold it up to a light source. If light can be seen through it, it is probably not opaque white ironstone.

Beverly & Ernie Dieringer
1996

COPPER LUSTRE DECORATIVE MOTIFS ON WHITE IRONSTONE CHINA

For nearly 200 years, English-produced White Ironstone China has had a significant place at the American table. It was not long after the turn of the 19th Century that English potters developed and introduced Ironstone China, primarily for export to North America. Although William and John Turner patented the first of the inexpensive and durable opaque earthenwares in 1800 their pottery went bankrupt in 1806. Other manufacturers introduced similar wares including Spode, Davenport and Hicks & Meigh, but it wasn't until 1813 when Charles Mason made public his "Patent Ironstone China" that White Ironstone became a household word. Mason became the most well known of the early ironstone potters and held an exclusive patent on the formula for fourteen years. By the time his patent expired many of the other Staffordshire potters had developed formulas of their own.

Early White Ironstone production was generally sold after being decorated with any of a number of motifs: copies of Oriental patterns, Historical Blue, Flow Blue, Mulberry, all-over Lustre applications, gaudy designs and numerous others. It was in the 1840s that plain undecorated White Ironstone began to be sold in quantity to the world market. White Ironstone was a huge success with the North American consumer and sold well for many of the dozens of potters whose output was marketed in the States and Canada.

Tastes were ever-changing and consumer taste for copper/lustreware coincided with the popularity of undecorated white ironstone. As this new trend took hold, some potters began to enhance their wares with various copper lustre effects and motifs. Beginning simply with the addition of copper-colored lustre bands to pieces, decorators eventually employed a variety of fanciful floral and geometric motifs, many of which are shown in the following chart. The copper lustre treatment was obtained by the addition of gold or copper oxide to the glazes the potter used in the decorating phase of the firing. Copper lustre decorated ware is generally characterized by thin banding around the top and base rims of pieces, lustre accents to handles and finials, and often one of the motifs shown added prominently to flat and hollowware pieces.

In the mid-1850s Anthony Shaw introduced a new design that was destined to take the consumer market by storm - Tea Leaf. For almost fifty years Tea Leaf-decorated Ironstone was a favorite of the American family. More than thirty English potters adopted the Tea Leaf motif and used it on over 100 ironstone body styles. Although Tea Leaf popularity waned in the late 1800s, American potters eagerly entered the Tea Leaf market and eventually over twenty-five American manufacturers employed the Tea Leaf (or close variant) motif. American production was, however, relatively short-lived and, with the exception of a brief resurgence in the 1960s, copper lustre decorated White Ironstone did not recapture the hearts of the American consumer as it had their great-great grandmothers one hundred years earlier.

Today collectors eagerly search out Tea Leaf and all of its variant motifs. Copper lustre decorated White Ironstone has once again become prized for its durability, beauty, simplicity, craft and style.

Dale Abrams
1996

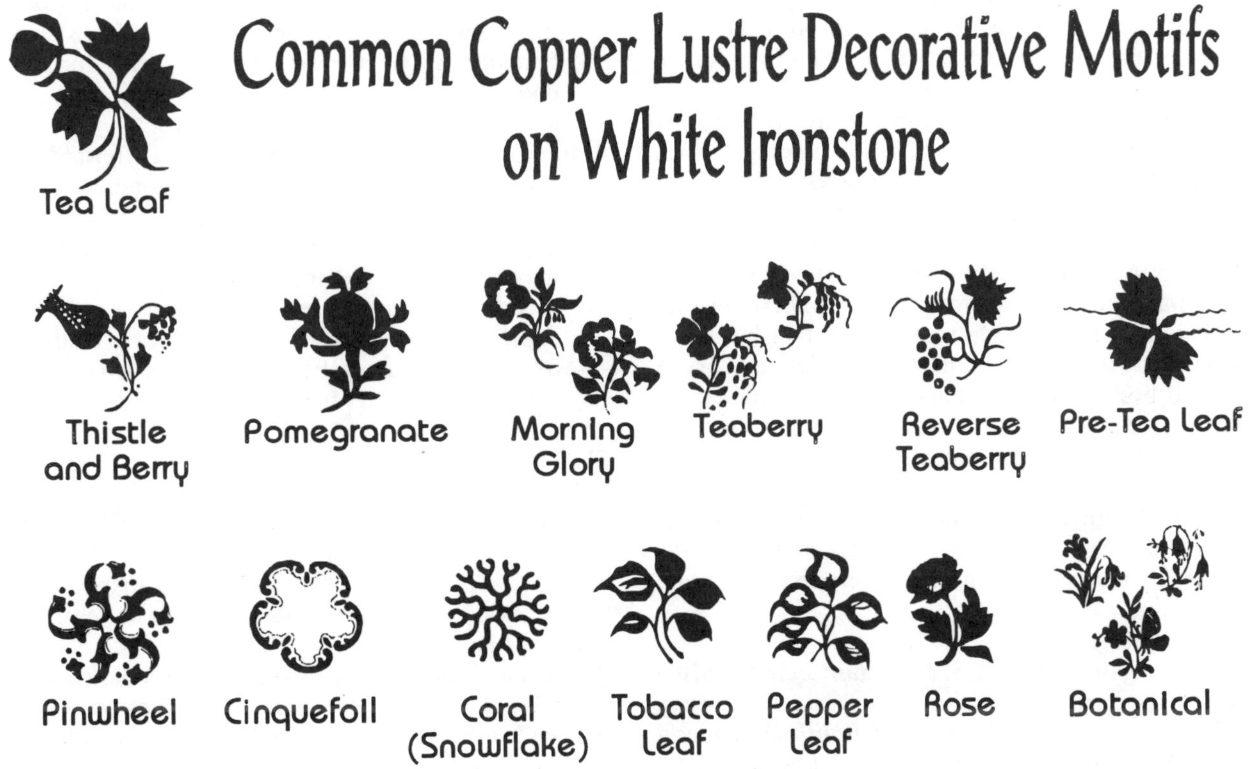

HOW TO USE THIS BOOK

English potters and potteries comprise the largest portion of this Encyclopedia. This English segment includes two main sections, Potters and Marks, and Patterns as well as ten appendices. The American portion is comprised of a section on Potters and Patterns in Flow Blue, White Ironstone and Tea Leaf/Copper Lustre, and four appendices. The European section includes Potters, Marks and Patterns, and two appendices.

A. **Potters and Marks**

Marks and dates noted in this Encyclopedia may differ, at times, from Mr. Godden's work, *Encyclopaedia of British Pottery and Porcelain Marks*, originally published in 1964 and revised in 1991. This is due to updated research that has come to light via my collating Mr. Godden's recent publications (see Bibliography), as well as through information from other publications and data supplied to me by Henry Kelly on the Scottish potteries. The Encyclopedia is set up alphabetically, giving name of potter, pottery location, and dates of manufacture. It also includes, when available, information on preceding and subsequent potters.

1. The use of **circa (c.)** indicates a three to five year leeway before and/or after the cited date, as the recording of dates by various authors can vary by a few years before or after the cited date. I would personally feel safer using **circa** with all dates, in that recorded data can be inconsistent and misleading; e.g., partnership entered into or land and building was purchased but production does not begin until a few years later. Likewise, dissolution of partnership notice may be after the fact, death of owner but pottery is continued by family for a number of years thereafter, bankruptcy proceedings have begun but production continues until company is liquidated. Unfortunately, exact dates may never be known.
2. An **asterisk (*)** noted next to the name of a potter in the heading indicates that the reader should refer to Appendix E3 for an Alphabetical Chronology of Selected Potters and Potteries; e.g.:

   *Benjamin Adams
   Greengates, Tunstall, Staffordshire, c. 1809-1820
3. The Marks Numbering System first established by Geoffrey A. Godden, in his *Encyclopaedia of British Pottery and Porcelain Marks* is continued. **(See comments under Part II, English Potters & Patterns for a brief explanation.)** Additional marks and/or potters have been included and a **dash (-)** means that no Godden number is indicated. A parallel reference system, devised by this author, is located to the left of Godden's number.

KAD NO.	GDN NO.	MARK	POTTERY INFORMATION
B 6	150	R.A.	Printed mark, c. 1860-1870.
B 7	-	(Mark)	Printed mark, c. 1860-1880.
B 8	151	R.A. & Co.	Printed Mark, "& CO." from 1870-1880

KEY TO LETTERS PRECEDING KAD NO.
A = American (Potters)
B = English (Potters)
C = European (Potters)

4. Additional source materials may be referenced at the end of each Potter/Mark section. Also see Bibliography.

B. **Patterns and Dating**

1. Recorded patterns are included from various sources. Classifications have been assigned to patterns where possible. Refer to listing of Pattern Categories and Abbreviations.
2. Impressed dates or printed patterns can prove problematic, as old blanks may have continued in use, registry designs may have been bought and sold or copied, and misspellings or misdating of significant potters' names may occur.
3. Registration dates are recorded via a Registry Mark or Number. If a Registration Year is given without the exact date, this is because only the registration year has been identified. See Appendices E7- E10.
4. Impressed Dates are included in the Pattern Section. The Impressed Date indicates a probable date of manufacture, not a registry mark. Blanks were often made with an impressed date prior to being decorated (and in some cases may have been decorated years later). The date may accompany a sign or device, as in the case of Davenport; e.g., Davenport mark with anchor does not indicate a date of registry, instead it indicates a possible date of manufacture. Refer to Appendices E7- E10.

C. **Abbreviations Used:**

1. **[ ]** indicates a secondary pattern name
2. **" "** around a pattern name indicates a contrived name made up by authors and collectors.
3. ( ) after a pattern indicates that multiple patterns have been recorded; e.g., (2) indicates that two patterns have been recorded.
4. **(att.)** cited after a pattern and/or pottery indicates that pattern has been attributed to being manufactured by pottery.
5. **(Ch)** Jean Wetherbee was kind enough to indicate children's pieces in White Ironstone. These are noted by the initials **(Ch)** after the pattern.

D. **Colors:** Blue and White Transfer is included as the category because it is the predominant color found in the Transferware category. Other colors such as brown, pink, purple, green, black, etc. have not been separated out, nor have varying colored back marks.

E. **Pattern Names for Blue & White Transferware:** Pattern names in the Blue & White Transferware category have not been reconciled. Various sources may have given a piece their own name. Thus multiple names for the same piece may exist. This applies to both contrived or actual names. A conflict of names would most likely exist where the category has not been indicated.

F. **Pattern Names for White Ironstone and Tea Leaf/Copper Lustre:** Pattern and shape names pose a problem solely in this category, in that these categories are frequently given descriptive rather than actual names. Furthermore, these descriptive shapes in both categories are often described by two different names. In order to be consistent with the quotes (" ") , I have employed a commonly used standard by which the exact name (with or without the addition of the word "shape") recognizes that between 1842 and 1883 potters either registered shapes or designs. This Encyclopedia was written for a global market and, as such, I have maintained these descriptive names by adding quote marks around a contrived name, while citing an actual name without quote marks. Further, when there is no true name even though there is a recorded registry date, I have added the word **shape** within the quote marks to alert the reader to the fact that a registry date exists even though no name was ascribed to the piece.

• An example would be **"Balanced Vine"** in both White Ironstone and Tea Leaf/Copper Lustre, where a true registry date of June 11, 1867 is recorded. I have, therefore, noted this as **"Balanced Vine" Shape.**

There can be two problems when a true name is cited:

• Examples of this problem would be the names Sevres Shape (by John Edwards) and Citron Shape. The first does not have a registry date but the true name is Sevres Shape (printed or impressed). The second, Citron Shape by Joseph Clementson, is a true registered shape for August 21, 1863. One would have to refer to the Pattern section of this Encyclopedia, under White Ironstone or Tea Leaf/Copper Lustre to see if there is a recorded registry date.

Alphabetical Listing of Patterns, Borders and Series as recorded by potter. Collectors are often confronted with only an accepted name. It is hoped that this listing will be an additional way to verify or attribute that name or particular pattern to a potter. I have taken the liberty of eliminating quote marks in this section, but have included both secondary and tertiary names. I would recommend that the reader refer to the original listing of Patterns by Potter for category of manufacture, as these have been eliminated in this section.

Of course there are inconsistencies in markings. Back marks may have been placed on wrong patterns, blanks of an earlier period may have been used, pieces in the same pattern may not have been marked, marks of two different potters (subcontractors) may be found on one piece, companies may have acquired other potters' copper plates, subsequent ownership of the pottery may have continued producing the line, etc. To further add to this conundrum, a shape may have been registered by another potter, sold to, shared by or acquired (due to a liquidation sale or purchase) by another potter. Thus, a proprietary shape may have gone through various ownerships and changes of name.

• The relationship between John Wedge Wood and Davenport was through marriage. Edmund T. Wood continued his brother's (John Wedge Wood) pottery and carried on the practice of using earlier shapes registered by his brother-in-law, Henry Davenport, and his uncle, William Davenport. What arrangements the Davenports had with John Wedge Wood and Edmund T. Wood for the use of their registered shapes can only be left to conjecture.

These are salient points to consider when studying marks and pattern names. See Appendix E7 for Dating Marks.

Always remember there are problems that will continue to exist as many of the potters' records have been destroyed, lost or were never accurately kept. Further adding to this problem, J.T. Shaw notes in *Sunderland Wear, The Potteries of Wearside*, (4th ed. revised) the issue of subcontracting and contracting for wares "...according to the firm's records [Southwick] and/or Scott's [Pottery] supplied earthenware to Moore's Wear Pottery and to the Bridge End Pottery presumably plain, for decoration. They also purchased wares from both Maling and Fell of Newcastle." How could the potters of yesterday have known that collectors of today would relish this information!

We live in an age of computers which, at times, have minds of their own - particularly in cases of sorting alphabetically. Alphabetical listings and names that include apostrophes may not always appear in sequence as one may wish them to. If in doubt, particularly when it pertains to plurals, (Maling's, Ridgway's, etc.) please refer to the Marks section of this book.

PATTERN CATEGORIES

Most transfer patterns fit into the **twelve** descriptive categories listed below. Frequently, books note the names of patterns but do not give an idea of the style of the pattern. Additionally, earlier transferware pieces often did not have a pattern name. In their two volumes on Romantic Staffordshire, Petra Williams and Marguerite Weber did an excellent job of separating patterns into categories. To assist all interested parties in communicating with each other clearly and identifying patterns, I have continued use of their categories. In reading this book you may come across a pattern that has not been categorized because no illustration was available, making classification impossible.

ABBREVIATIONS - PATTERN CATEGORIES

An abbreviated code listing for Pattern Categories is given throughout the Encyclopedia. These abbreviations are:

A = Art Nouveau
C = Classical
F = Floral
G = Genre
H = Historic
J = Juvenile
L = Literary
M = Miscellaneous
O = Oriental
P = Polychrome
S = Scenic
Z = Zoological

There are instances where multiple pattern descriptions are used. For example, a **Miscellaneous** designation was previously ascribed to a pattern, but in my determination another category, such as **Floral**, best suited the pattern. Therefore, the designation **F/M** is given to the pattern. Further, most **Polychrome** pieces fall into the **Oriental** category, so the designation **P/O** is given the pattern. However, this does not hold true for Mulberry Wares, as most **Polychrome** pieces are **Floral**. Thus the designation would be **P/F**.

The **Juvenile** designation, as included, is present only as a sampling. There are untold thousands of pieces comprising this subject - making it just too large a category to include at this time. In contrast, the **Literary** category is a very small one, with few examples.

The exhibition catalog *True Blue*, pp. 19-38, contains a section "Sources of Design" which is invaluable to the collector for its insight into origins and descriptive analysis.

PATTERN CATEGORIES

ART NOUVEAU:

The Art Nouveau period, which began in about 1885, represented a real shift in perspective on design. It presented a formal stylistic and linear approach, conveying the essence of a flower or design. Lines still swirled but the design was neither realistic nor romanticized. Floral depiction, which predominated, looked almost real, but upon close inspection were rather stylized.

CLASSICAL:

Three events occurred that determined and defined the Classical Period in Transferware: The installation of classical statuary in the British Museum; Josiah Wedgwood's enthusiasm over classical antiquities illustration; and Wedgwood's employment of an extraordinarily talented sculptor who was able to create designs of great beauty. Classical subjects were interpreted from statues, allegorical subjects, buildings and ruins, vases and urns.

FLORAL:

Floral patterns are taken mainly from gardens, estates and parks found in England as well as from botanical publications and prints. Florals can be natural and realistic or stylized, and can include urns, birds and exotic insects. Many potters produced floral patterns, but outstanding examples were made at the Wedgwood Etruria works.

GENRE:

Genre, as defined in art, is usually associated with common scenes and subjects of everyday life; i.e., farmers, innkeepers and their patrons, sportsmen, mothers and children, etc. Scenic depictions served merely as backdrops for human activities. Genre scenes, as designed, were more fanciful than just a representation of common people. Costumes were often elaborate and many of the designs, particularly the sporting scenes, showed the upper classes and aristocracy in action.

HISTORIC:

Historic patterns were made to commemorate notable events, people, battles, etc. Such designs could include the Coronation of George IV, Martha Washington, the Battle of Trafalgar, the opening of the first railway, Landing of Lafayette, the Hudson River, City Hall-Albany, etc.

JUVENILE:

Juvenile or children's patterns were designed to educate and amuse, while at the same time encourage proper dining habits. Pieces were made to scale and were to be used at meals or as toys. Dishes and juvenile other pieces were usually not backstamped.

LITERARY:

Literary patterns are depictions based on great novels, stories and plays of the period and are of imagined, idealized or contrived scenes, events or portraits.

MISCELLANEOUS:

This category includes all patterns that do not fit into any other category and includes subjects that are Allegorical and Moralistic, Gothic, Geometric, etc. Patterns which are a class unto themselves such as transportation patterns, "Arms of the States", etc. as well as Coats of Arms, Fraternal Orders, Advertising, Medical, etc. are also classified as Miscellaneous.

ORIENTAL:

Oriental patterns on blue transferware Flow Blue and Mulberry were derived from designs found on Chinese porcelain imported into Britain. Designs included ornate Chinese style borders, willow patterns, oriental flowers, fanciful birds, ornate urns and vases, pagodas, graceful and flowering trees and oriental garbed men and women. Oriental designs also included mid-Eastern, East-Indian and Arabic elements such as mosques, minarets, desert scenes, palm trees and camels. Except for scenes based on etchings in travel books, patterns designs were imaginary.

POLYCHROME (CHINOISERIE WITH LUSTRE):

Polychrome is defined as many colors. These patterns, which are predominantly Oriental or Floral in theme, are done in multi-colors of basically rose, celadon green, dark red, tan or buff, salmon or coral and dark green. Colors are fixed over a black transfer outline and all are decorated with lustre of gold, tan or bronze. Some patterns are toned down in color due to the pastel shades used, while some are brilliant and vividly colored. Most patterns are found on plain, unscalloped blanks.

SCENIC:

The introduction of underglaze transfer printing on earthenwares in c. 1750 enabled potters to print pictures on inexpensive dishes. Plates could now depict important commemorative and architectural scenes both American and British. Idyllic pastoral scenes were reproduced for the home market, and aside from including architectural and commemorative elements also included figures dressed in Medieval, Elizabethan or Empire costumes, and graceful hunting dogs. These all added elegance and sophistication to the designs.

ZOOLOGICAL:

Zoological patterns include those patterns and series that have identifiable birds and animals as the central theme or predominant figures in the piece.

FREQUENTLY REFERENCED WORKS

Often used books are referred to by author's name only and, where indicated, by volume number. In the case of multiple authorship, a brief phrase describing the book will be included after the author's name. Newsletters and Journals are referred to by the initials of the issuing organization.

BOOK REFERENCES

Book references appearing frequently are noted by giving the name of the author or the proper abbreviation. When cited, the number of page or reference is also given.

Arman	David & Linda Arman. *Historical Staffordshire, (with First Supplement)*
Arman, Anglo-American	Arman, David & Linda. *Anglo-American Series*, Part I.
Arman	David & Linda Arman. *The China and Glass Quarterly*
Baker	John C. Baker, *Sunderland Pottery*
Barber	Edwin Atlee Barber. *Anglo-American Pottery, Old English China With American Views*
Barber's Marks	Edwin Atlee Barber. *Marks of American Potters*
Batkin	Maureen Batkin. *Gifts for Good Children, Vol. II*
Bell	R.C. Bell, *Tyneside Pottery*
Blue Berry Notes (FBICC)	*Blue Berry Notes*, Newsletter of the Flow Blue International Collectors' Club, Inc.
Bunt, British Potters	Cyril G.E. Bunt, *British Potters & Pottery Today*
Camehl	Ada Walker Camehl. *The Blue-China Book, Early American Scenes and History Pictured in the Pottery of Time*
Cameron	Elisabeth Cameron. *Encyclopedia of Pottery & Porcelain, The Nineteenth and Twentieth Centuries*
Chaffers	William Chaffers. *Marks and Monograms on European and Oriental Pottery and Porcelain (14th rev. ed.)*
Cluett	Robert Cluett. *George Jones Ceramics, 1861-1951*
Collard, Potters View	Elizabeth Collard. *The Potter's View of Canada*
Collard, Pottery & Porcelain	Elizabeth Collard. *Nineteenth-Century Pottery and Porcelain in Canada*
Copeland	Robert Copeland. *Spode and Copeland Marks*
Copeland, Spode	Robert Copeland. *Spode's Willow Pattern and Other Designs After the Chinese*
Coysh, Vol. I, Vol. II	A.W. Coysh & R.K. Henrywood. *The Dictionary of Blue and White Printed Pottery, Vol. I & Vol.II*
Coysh, Transferware	A.W. Coysh. *Blue and White Transferware*
Coysh, Earthenware	A.W. Coysh. *Blue Printed Earthenware*
Coysh & Stefano	A.W. Coysh & Frank Stefano, Jr. *Ceramic Landscapes*
Cushion	J.P. Cushion & W.B. Honey. *Handbook of Pottery and Porcelain Marks*
Cushion, Manuel de la Ceramique	J.P. Cushion. *Manuel de la Ceramique Europeenne*
Cushion, British Ceramic Marks	J.P. Cushion. *Pocket Book of British Ceramic Marks*
Danckert	Ludwig Danckert. *Directory of European Porcelain*
Debolt	Gerald Debolt. *Debolt's Dictionary of American Pottery Marks*
Edwards, Basalt	Dana Edwards. *Black Basalt, Wedgwood & Contemporary Manufacturers*
English Ceramic Circle Transactions	*English Ceramic Circle Transactions.* Publication of the English Ceramic Circle
Ewins	*Journal of Ceramic History*, Vol. 15 "Supplying the Wants of Our Yankee Cousins..."
F.B.I.C.C.	(See: Blue Berry Notes)
Finlayson	R.W. Finlayson. *Portneuf Pottery & Other Early Wares*
Fleming	J. Arnold Fleming. *Scottish Pottery*
F.O.B.	*Friends of Blue Journal*
Gaston, Vol. I, Vol. 2	Mary Frank Gaston. *A Collector's Encyclopedia of Flow Blue China, First and Second Series*
Gates	William C. Gates & Dana E. Ormerod. *The East Liverpool Pottery District*
Godden	Geoffrey A. Godden. *Encyclopaedia of British Pottery and Porcelain Marks*
Godden, British Porcelain	Geoffrey A. Godden. *Encyclopaedia of British Porcelain Manufacturers*
Godden, British Pottery	Geoffrey A. Godden. *British Pottery, An Illustrated Guide, 1990*
Godden, Collecting Lustreware	Geoffrey A. Godden & Michael Gibson. *Collecting Lustreware*
Godden, Concise Guide	Geoffrey A. Godden. *The Concise Guide to British Pottery and Porcelain*
Godden, European Porcelain	Geoffrey A. Godden. *Godden's Guide to European Porcelain*
Godden, Handbook	Geoffrey A. Godden. *The Handbook of British Pottery and Porcelain Marks*
Godden, Illustrated Encylopedia	Geoffrey A. Godden. *An Illustrated Encyclopedia of British Pottery and Porcelain, 2nd ed.*
Godden, Jewitt	Geoffrey A. Godden. *Jewitt's Ceramic Art of Great Britian 1800-1900*
Godden, Mason's	Geoffrey A. Godden. *Godden's Guide to Mason's China and the Ironstone Wares.*
Godden, Ridgways	Geoffrey A. Godden. *Ridgways Porcelains*
Godden, Staffordshire	Geoffrey A. Godden. *Staffordshire Porcelain*
Halfpenny, Penny Plain	Pat Halfpenny (ed.). *Penny Plain Two Pence Coloured*
Hallesy	Helen Hallesy. *The Glamorgan Pottery, Swansea 1814-1838*
Hampson, Churchill	Rodney Hampson. *Churchill China, Great British Potters Since 1795*
Hampson	Rodney Hampson. *Longton Potters 1700-1865*
Henrywood, Guide to British Jugs	R.K. Henrywood, *An Illustrated Guide to British Jugs*
Henrywood	R.H. Henrywood. *Bristol Potters 1775-1906*
Henrywood, Relief Moulded Jugs	R.K. Henrywood. *Relief Moulded Jugs 1820-1900*

Heaivilin	Annise Doring Heaivilin. *Grandma's Tea Leaf Ironstone, A History and Study of English and American Potteries*
Hill	Ellen R. Hill. *Mulberry Ironstone, Flow Blue's Best Kept Little Secret*
Hughes, Vol. I & II	Kathy Hughes, *A Collector's Guide to Nineteenth Century Jugs, Vol. I & II*
Jewitt	Llewellyn Jewitt. *The Ceramic Art of Great Britain*
Jones	Joan Jones. *Minton, The First Two Hundred Years of Design and Production*
Karmason	Karmason, Marilyn G. & Stacke, Joan B. *Majolica, A Complete History*
Kelly	Henry E. Kelly. *Scottish Sponge Printed Pottery*
Ketchum, Jr.	William C. Ketchum, Jr. *Potters and Potteries of New York State*
Laidacker	Sam Laidacker. *Anglo-American China & Historical American Views and Subjects, Part I and Part II*
Larsen	Ellouise Baker Larsen. *American Historical Views of Staffordshire China, 3rd ed.*
Lawrence	Heather Lawrence. *Yorkshire Pots and Potters*
Lehner	Lois Lehner. *Lehner's Encyclopedia of U.S. Marks on Pottery and Porcelain China*
Lewis, Pratt Ware	John & Griselda Lewis. *Pratt Ware, English & Scottish Relief Decorated & Underglaze Colored Earthenware*
Little	W.K. Little. *Staffordshire Blue*
Lockett	Terence A. Lockett. *Davenport Pottery and Porcelain 1794-1887*
Lockett & Godden	Terence A. Lockett & Geoffrey A. Godden. *Davenport China, Earthenware and Glass 1794-1887*
Mankowitz & Haggar	Wolf Mankowitz & Reginald A. Haggar. *The Concise Encyclopedia of English Pottery and Porcelain*
Marques de Fabrique	Edition, *Association des Amis du Musee de Sarreguemines*
McVeigh	Patrick McVeigh. *Scottish East Coast Potteries, 1750-1840*
Nance	E. Morton Nance. *The Pottery & Porcelain of Swansea & Nantgarw, Vol. 1 & 2*
NCSJ	*Northern Ceramics Society Journal*
NCS Newsletter	*Northern Ceramics Society Newsletter*
Niblett	Kathy Niblett. *Dynamic Design; The British Pottery Industry, 1940-1990*
Ormsbee	Thomas H. Ormsbee. *English China and Its Marks*
Peake	Tim H. Peake. *William Brownfield*
Polling	A. Polling. *Maastrichtse Ceramiek, Merken en Dateringen*
Pryce	P.D. Pryce and S.H. Williams. *Swansea Blue and White Pottery*
Pugh, Welsh Pottery	Robert Pugh. *Welsh Pottery, A Towy Guide*
Ramsay	John Ramsay. *American Potters and Pottery*
Reilly, Wedgwood	Robin Reilly. *Wedgwood* (2 volumes), 1989
Reilly, Wedgwood II	Robin Reilly. *Wedgwood, The New Illustrated Dictionary*. 1995
Reilly & Savage	Robin Reilly & George Savage. *The Dictionary of Wedgood.* 1980.
Rhead	G. Woolliscroft Rhead. *British Pottery Marks*
Riley, Noel	*Gifts for Good Children*
Röntgen	Robert E. Röntgen. *Marks of German, Bohemian & Austrian Porcelain*
Scottish Pottery Historical Review	*Scottish Pottery Historical Review*
Shelley Potteries	Harvey & Senft Watkins. *Shelley Potteries*
Snyder, Fascinating Flow Blue	Jeffrey B. Snyder. *Fascinating Flow Blue*
Snyder, Vol. I & 2	Jeffrey B. Snyder. *Historic Flow Blue and Flow Blue, A Collector's Guide to Patterns, History and Values*
Snyder, Romantic Staffordshire	Jeffrey B. Snyder. *Romantic Staffordshire Ceramics*
Snyder, Historic Staffordshire	Jeffrey B. Snyder. *Historic Staffordshire*
Snyder, Pocket Guide	Jeffrey B. Snyder. *A Pocket Guide to Flow Blue*
Stefano	Frank Stefano, Jr. *Check List of Wedgwood Old Blue Historical Plates and Other Views of the United States*
Stoltzfus/Snyder	Dawn Stoltzfus & Jeffrey Snyder. *White Ironstone, A Survey of its Many Forms: Undecorated, Flow Blue, Mulberry, Copper Lustre.*
Sussman	Lynne Sussman. *The Wheat Pattern, An Illustrated Survey*
TLCI 1 & 2	*Tea Leaf Club International, Parts 1 & 2, White Ironstone Body Styles, Copper & Gold Lustre Decorated 1840-1900*
Tea Leaf Readings	*Tea Leaf Readings*. Bulletin of the Tea Leaf Club International
Thorn	D. Jordan Thorn. *Handbook of Old Pottery and Porcelain Marks*
Tiny Times	*Tiny Times*. Newsletter of the Toy Dish Collectors Society
True Blue	*True Blue Transfer Printed Earthenware*, edited by Gaye Blake Roberts
Wetherbee	Jean Wetherbee. *A Look at White Ironstone, and A Second Look at White Ironstone, rev. 1993*
Wetherbee, White Ironstone	Jean Wetherbee. *White Ironstone, A Collector's Guide*
White Ironstone Notes	*White Ironstone Notes*. Newsletter of the White Ironstone Association, Inc.
Whiter	Leonard Whiter. *Spode, A History of the Family, Factory & Wares from 1733-1833*
P. Williams, Flow Blue	Petra Williams. *Flow Blue China, An Aid to Identification, Vol. I, II, III*
P. Williams, Staffordshire	Petra Williams & Marguerite Weber. *Staffordshire Romantic Transfer Patterns, Vol. I and II*
Williams-Wood, English Transfer	Cyril Williams-Wood. *English Transfer-Printed Pottery and Porcelain*
Williams-Wood, Pot Lids	Cyril Williams-Wood. *Staffordshire Pot Lids and Their Potters*
Wood, No. I, No. VI	Heather Serry Wood. *English Staffordshire China, Classics*. Heather Serry Wood. *English Staffordshire China, Classics*.
Woolliscroft-Rhead	G. Woolliscroft-Rhead. *British Pottery Marks*
Yorkshire Pots	*A Celebration of Yorkshire Pots*, The Eighth Exhibition From the Northern Ceramic Society, June 29 - September 21, 1997

[1] Robert Copeland - *Blue and White Transfer-Printed Pottery*

Part I. AMERICAN POTTERS, PATTERNS & MARKS

Coverage of American potters and potteries is confined to three categories in this Encyclopedia: Flow Blue, Tea Leaf/Copper Lustre and White Ironstone. It is important to remember that the three groups do not represent the bulk of American ceramics production. Rather, they represent only a small segment in part due to stiff competition from abroad in these categories.

It is interesting to note how little has been written or researched on these categories. The major writers most commonly referred to for information are Edwin Barber, C. Gerald Debolt, William Gates and Dana Ormerod, Annise Doring Heaivilin, Sam Laidacker, Lois Lehner, George Savage, John Spargo and Jean Wetherbee. This area of American ceramics is ripe for further research.

- I would particularly like to thank Julie Rich, Editor Emeritus of the Tea Leaf Club International for allowing me to reproduce her motif drawing of American Tea Leaf. As Mr. Godden did not catalog American potters, there is no Godden number referenced in this section. The letter "A" will precede all KAD numbers, e.g.:

KAD NO.	MARK	DATING
A1	BENNETT & BROTHERS LIVERPOOL, OHIO	1841-1844
A2	E. & W. BENNETT	1848-1856
A3	E. B.	1856-1890
A4	E. BENNETT	1856-1890
A5	E. B. P. CO.	1890-1936

KEY TO LETTERS PRECEDING "KAD NO."

A = AMERICAN (POTTERS)
B = ENGLISH (POTTERS)
C = EUROPEAN (POTTERS)

Additionally, potters are listed in alphabetical order, so inclusions start with the letter "A" and continue on with "A Bros.", "A B", "A & B", etc.

AMERICAN

KAD NO. | **MARK**

American Beleek Co.
Fredericksburg, Ohio, USA, 1937
In operation for (6 months). See Fredericksburg
Art Pottery, and for further reading refer to *Lehner*, p. 154.

American China Co.
Toronto, Ohio, USA, c.1894-1910

A1 — **A.C. CO.** — Printed mark, c.1894-1910. "MADE IN USA" from c.1905-1910.
Typical Marks Include:

A2
A3

1897-1904 **1905-1910**

- American China Co. is not to be confused with The American Chinaware Corp. or the American Crockery Co. For further reading, refer to *Debolt*, p. 199 and *Lehner, p. 20.*

American Crockery Co.
Trenton, New Jersey, USA, c.1876-c.1900
Printed marks, c.1876-c.1900.

A4 — **A.C. CO.**
A5
A6

c.1876 **c.1890** **Tea Leaf Motif**

For further reading, refer to *Tea Leaf Readings*, Jan./Feb. 1991, p. 1 and 11; *Barber*, p. 175; and *Barber's Marks*, pp. 59-60.

AMERICAN

KAD NO.	MARK	

AMERICAN POTTERY CO.
See: JERSEY CITY POTTERY CO.

ANCHOR

Anchor Pottery Co.
Trenton, New Jersey, USA, 1893-1928
Subsequently owned by the Grand Union Tea Co. (c.1918-1926) and the Fulper Pottery Co. (1926-1930+)

KAD NO.	MARK	
A8	**A.P.**	Printed initial mark, 1893-1910.
A9	**J.E.N.**	Printed initial mark, 1893-1912(18).

Typical Marks Include:

A10
A11
A12
A13

c.1894

c.1898

c.1900

c.1904-c.1912

For further reading, refer to *Debolt*, pp. 18-19; and *Lehner*, pp. 24-25.

BAHL

Bahl Potteries Inc.
Carrolton, Ohio, USA, 1940-1941

A14 **AMERICAN BELLEEK BAHL CHINA**

Printed mark, 1940-1941. Company manufactured "Gold Tea Leaf".

- ***Tea Leaf Club International,*** Pamphlet No. 2, "Copper & Gold Lustre Decorated 1840-1900", p. 4, notes a possible relationship with the American Beleek Co. However, I believe this is incorrect. There is a three year span between both potteries (1937-1940). Further, the American Beleek Co. spells the name "Beleek" and Bahl spells it "Belleek". Lastly, the two potteries are located 70-80 miles apart. I believe the mark "AMERICAN BELLEEK' was merely a marketing tool used by Bahl.

BAUM

J.H. Baum
Schoolhouse Pottery,
Wellsville, Ohio, USA, c. 1888-1896

A15

Printed mark noted by *Wetherbee, White Ironstone*, p. 180, c.1888-1896.

For further reading, refer to *Gates*, p. 14; and *Lehner*, p. 39.

BEERBOWER

KAD NO. | **MARK**

Beerbower & Griffen
Phoenixville Pottery,
Phoenixville, Pennsylvania, USA, 1877-1879
Subsequently, L.B. Beerbower & Co.,
Elizabeth, New Jersey (1879-c.1904)

A16 **B. & G.**
Printed initial mark, 1877-1879.
- Printed mark "SEMI-GRANITE" noted.

A17

Printed "Coat of Arms" mark of the State of Pennsylvania,, 1877-1879.
- *Barber's Marks*, p. 28 notes that the style was continued by Griffen, Smith & Hill when Beerbower moved to Elizabeth, NJ.

Also refer to Phoenixville Pottery for chronology.

BEERBOWER

L.B. Beerbower & Co.
Elizabeth, New Jersey, USA, 1879-c.1904
Formerly, Beerbower & Griffen
(See: Phoenixville Pottery Co. 1877-1879)

A18 **L.B.B. & CO.**
A19 **L.B. BEERBOWER & CO.**
Printed marks, 1879-c.1904.

Typical Marks Include:

A20
A21
A22

For further reading, refer to *Debolt*, pp. 12, 113; and *Lehner*, p. 345 for "Phoenixville Pottery, Kaolin and Fire Brick Co."

BENNETT

Edwin Bennett Pottery/E. Bennett Pottery Co.

Baltimore, Maryland, USA,	**1846-1936**
Formerly, James Bennett	**(1839-1841)**
History:	
Bennett Brothers (E. Liverpool, Ohio)	1841-1844
E. Bennett Chinaware Factory	1846-1848
E. & W. Bennett	1848-1856
Edwin Bennett Pottery	1856-1890
Edwin Bennett Pottery Co.	1890-1936

A23 **BENNETT & BROTHERS LIVERPOOL, OHIO**
Impressed mark, "EAST LIVERPOOL, OHIO" noted on yellow-ware, 1841-1844.

A24 **E. & W. BENNETT**
Printed marks, 1848-1856.

A25 **E. B.**
A26 **E. BENNETT**
Printed marks, 1856-1890.

A27 **E. B. P. CO.**
A28 **EDWIN BENNETT/ POTTERY CO.**
Printed marks, 1890-1936.

KAD NO. **MARK**

Typical Marks Include:

A29
A30
A31
A32
A33

c.1870-c.1875

c.1873-c.1880

c.1884-c.1890

c.1886

c.1886

- Bevis Hillier's *Pottery & Porcelain, 1700-1914.* New York. Meredith Press, 1968, Plate 132 illustrates a Blue & White Platter "Scenes From the American Civil Ware", c. 1901.

- Additionally, Sam Laidacker notes this Blue & White American Historic pattern as "Pickett's Charge, Gettysburg". See *Anglo-American China, Part I*, Scranton, PA. 1938, p. 5

For further reading, refer to *Debolt,* pp. 21-23; *Lehner*, pp. 44-45; *Barber*, p. 180; and *Barber's Marks*, pp. 143-146 wherein he gives an extensive history of this potter.

BROCKMANN

Brockmann Pottery Co.
Cincinnati, Ohio, USA, 1887(8)-1912
History:

Tempest, Brockmann & Co.	1862-1881
Tempest, Brockmann & Sampson Pottery Co.	1881-1887(8)

A34 **B. P. CO.** Printed marks, c.1888-1912.

Typical Marks Include:

A35
A36
A37

Tea Leaf Motif

For further reading, refer to *Barber's Marks*, p. 118; *Debolt*, p. 24; and *Lehner*, p. 57;

BRUNT

William Brunt Co. (& Associates)
Phoenix Pottery(1859-1911)
Riverside Knob Works (1850-1910)
East Liverpool, Ohio, USA 1847-1911
Subsequently, Hall China Co. (1911-1926)
There is no listing or known marks for the following:

G.F. Brunt Porcelain Co.	1847-1851
& Co. (Henry)	—
H. Brunt Son & Co.	1856-1859
Wm. Brunt, Jr. (son of Henry)	1862-1866
Wm. (Brunt), Jr. & Mr. Hill (Great Western Pottery Works)	1867-1874

KAD NO.	MARK	
A38	**B. B. M. & CO.**	Printed mark, WM. BRUNT (JR.), BLOOR, MARTIN, 1875-1882.
A39	**W. B. JR. & CO.**	Printed mark, W.B. JR. & CO., 1877-1878.
A40	**W. B. S. & CO.**	Printed mark, WM. BRUNT SON & CO., 1878-1892.
A41	**W. B. P. CO.**	Printed mark, WM. BRUNT POTTERY CO., 1892-1911.
		- Company was incorporated in 1894.

Typical Marks Include:

A42
A43
A44
A45

1875-1882*

1877-1878

Tea Leaf Motif

1892-1911

*The marking "DRESDEN/WHITE GRANITE" was continued by the Potters Co-Operative (& Co.). Refer to *Gates*, p. 217, Mark "B".
Also refer to the Dresden Pottery (Works) Co.

-William Brunt is an example of a potter who manufactured in England and continued as a potter in the United States. The name William Brunt appears, as a potter in England, in partnership with William Allerton (1830-1833). Brunt died in 1859. The reader may be interested in doing further research on potters who manufactured in both England and the US. Refer to *NCSJ*, No. 11, 1994, p. 59 for an article by Ronald B. Brown titled "Potteries of Derbyshire; and p. 145 for an article titled "Rawdon Pottery, Woodville". Also refer to *Hamspon*, p. 2, no. 5 and p. 40, no 60.

For further reading, refer to *Debolt*, pp. 25-26; *Gates*, pp. 17-23; *Lehner,* pp. 60-61; and *Stoltzfus/Snyder*, p. 133.

BRUNT

BRUNT, BLOOR, MARTIN & CO.
See: WM. BRUNT & CO.

BUFFALO

Buffalo Pottery Co.
- & Various other potteries
Buffalo, New York, USA, 1901-1916
(in 1916 pottery changed over to the manufacture of China), 1916-present

A16 **VASSAR** Printed mark, 1901-1916

A47
A48

Tea Leaf Motif

For further reading, refer to *Heaivilin, pp. 154-156;* TLCI, pp. 6-7.
Note, however, that the marks are switched (in error) between Brockmann Pottery and Buffalo Pottery. Also refer to *Ketchum, Jr.*, pp. 427-429.

BURFORD

KAD NO.	MARK	
		Burford Bros. Pottery Co. **East Liverpool, Ohio, USA, c.1879(81)-1904** **Subsequently, Standard Pottery Co. (c.1904-c.1908)**
A49	**B. B.***	Printed marks, 1879(81)-1904.
A50	**B. B. P. CO.**	
A51	**BURFORD BROS.**	
A52	**BURFORDS**	
A53	**BURFORD BROS. E. L. O.**	

Typical Marks Include:

A54
A55
A56
A57

c.1881-1904*

c.1882

c.1900-1904

Tea Leaf Motif c.1900-1904

c.1881-1904* **c.1882** **c.1900-1904**

*Gates, p. 25 notes an additional marking with "B.B.".
For further reading, refer to *Gates*, pp. 24-30; and *White Ironstone Notes*, Vol. 4, No. 1, Summer 1997, p. 12 for pattern "Devotion".

BURROUGHS

KAD NO.	MARK	
		Burroughs & Mountford (& Co.) **Trenton, New Jersey, USA, 1879-c.1895** **Formerly, The Eagle Pottery (1876-1879)**
A58	**B-M**	Printed mark, 1879-1895. "& CO.", c.1890.
A59	**B. & M.**	- Additional marking "ROYAL CHINA" noted.
A60	**B. M. & CO.**	
A61	**B. & M. CO.**	

Various Printed marks, c.1879-1895, include:

A62
A63
A64
A65

Printed Marks found on Flow Blue c.1879-1895

White Granite c.1890-1895

White Granite c.1890-1895

- *Barber*, p. 105, notes that the Harker Pottery Co. of East Liverpool, Ohio decorated white granite wares for many companies including the Burroughs & Mountford Co.

For dating system refer to *Debolt*, p. 169, and for further reading, refer to *Barber's Marks*, p. 60.

CARROLLTON

Carrollton Pottery Co.
Carrollton, Ohio, USA, 1903-1929*
- In 1929 joined with other potteries to form the American Chinaware Corp. (1929-1931)

KAD NO.	MARK	
A66	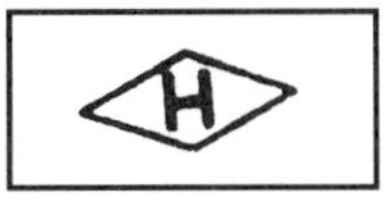	Printed initial mark, 1903-1929(36).
A67	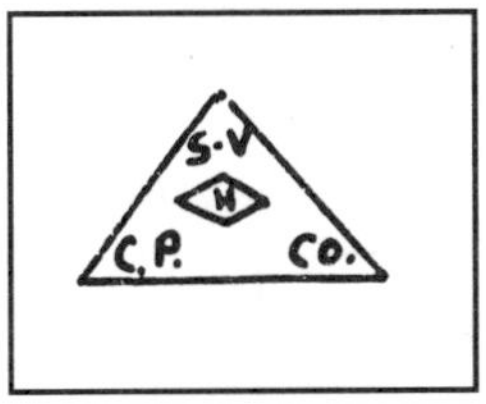	Printed initial mark with the addition of "C.P. CO." 1903-1929(36).

Printed Name Marks, 1907-1929(36), include:

A68
A69
A70

For further reading, refer to *Gates*, pp. 12-13.
**Lehner*, p. 83 notes that the pottery continued after the demise of the merger from 1931-1936.

CARTWRIGHT

Cartwright Bros. (Pottery Co.)
East Liverpool, Ohio, USA, 1864-1927
Formerly, Webster Stoneware Pottery
History:

Manley & Cartwright purchased company	1864
Holland & Manley	1864-1872
Manley, Cartwright & Co.	1872-1880
Cartwright Bros. Pottery Co.	1880-1896
Cartwright Bros. Co.	1896-1927

KAD NO.	MARK	
A71	**C. B. P. CO.**	Printed mark of crown on garter with elaborate monogram initials and "IRON STONE CHINA", 1880-1896.
A72	**CARTWRIGHT & BROS. LIVERPOOL**	Printed mark, 1887-1896.
A73	**CARTWRIGHT BROS. CO.**	Printed mark, 1896-1927.

Typical Marks Include:

A74
A75
A76

1887-1896

Tea Leaf

1887-1900

For further reading, refer to *Gates*, pp. 30-34; *Heaivilin*, pp. 157-160; and *TLCI*, p. 12.

KAD NO.	MARK	

CHELSEA

Chelsea China Co.
New Cumberland, West Virginia, USA, 1888-1896

A77 **CHELSEA** Printed name mark, 1888-1896.

Typical Marks Include:

A78
A79

c.1888

1890s

CHESAPEAKE

Chesapeake Pottery (Co.)
(& Various Partnerships)
Baltimore, Maryland, USA, 1887-1914
Subsequently, Sugar Refining Co. (1914-?)
History:

Henry & Isaac Brougham & John Tunstall	1880-1892
D.F. Haynes and Company	1882-1887
Chesapeake Pottery Co.	1887-1890
Haynes Bennett and Company	1890-1895
D.F. Haynes & Son	1896-1914

A80

Printed mark with the addition of "& CO.", 1882-1887.
Additional printed marks noted with the inclusion of "AVALON FAIENCE" OR "AVALON CHINA", 1882-1887.

KAD NO.	MARK	
A81	**ARUNDEL**	Printed mark, 1887-1890+
A82	**C. C. P.**	Printed mark, 1887-1890+
A83	**H. B. H.**	Printed mark, 1890-1895.
A84	**HAYNES BALT.º**	Printed mark, 1900+

- *Abbie's Encyclopedia of Flow Blue, Floral & Art Nouveau* by Thomas E. Nix, Sentinel Publication, July 1992, p. 28, illustrates a floral pattern "Pansy" with the above mark.

For further reading, refer to *Barber's Marks*, pp. 147-148; *Debolt*, pp. 32-22; *Karmason*, pp. 166-167; and *Lehner*, pp. 88-89.

CITY

City Pottery Co.
(& Various Ownerships),
Trenton, New Jersey, USA, 1859-c.1880
Formerly, The Hattersley Pottery

A85

Printed mark, c.1859-1880 ("& CO." from 1875).

KAD NO.	MARK	
A86	**R. & Y.**	Printed initial mark for Rhodes & Yates, 1859-c.1864.
A87	**Y. & T.**	Printed initial mark for Yates & Titus, 1865-1871.
A88	**Y. B. A.**	Printed initial mark for Yates, Bennett, Allan, 1871-c.1880.

KAD NO. | **MARK**

- The business was conducted under three different partnership names:
- Kenyon City Pottery
- Trenton City Pottery
- City Pottery Co.
- Further research indicates that in 1886 the City Pottery Co. was acquired by Thomas Maddock & Son, who were located directly across the street.

For further reading, refer to *Barber*, p. 46

COLONIAL

(The) Colonial Company (Colonial Pottery)
East Liverpool, Ohio, USA, 1903-1929
Formerly, East Liverpool Potteries (1901-1903)

A89

Printed mark, 1903-1929.

A90 **COLONIAL STERLING CHINA PATENTED**

Printed mark attributed to the Colonial Company, c.1919.

- *Gates*, pp. 305-306 notes the name "Colonial Pottery" was introduced by Wallace & Chetwynd (1881-1900). In 1901 they merged with the East Liverpool Potteries Co. and subsequently, in 1903, formed The Colonial Company.

For further reading, refer to *Debolt*, p. 171 for "Colonial Sterling" marks; *Gates*, pp. 35-36; and *Lehner*, pp. 100-101.

COOK

Cook (& Mellor) Pottery Co.
Trenton, New Jersey, USA, 1894-1920s
Formerly, Ott & Brewer Co., Etruria Pottery (1863-1893)
Subsequently, Cook Ceramics Mfg. Co. (c.1930-c.1959)

A91 **C. P. CO.**
Printed monogram within shield, c1894-1910.
- Also see Mellor & Co., mark no. A92.

A92 **MELLOR & CO.**
Printed "Trademark", 1894-c.1910.

A93 **COOK POTTERY CO. TRENTON, N.J.**
Printed mark, c.1910-1920's.

Typical Marks Include:

A94
A95
A96

1894-c.1900

1900-c.1910

c.1905

For further reading, refer to *Barber's Marks*, p. 54; *Debolt*, pp. 108-110 and (A22) p. 170; and *Lehner*, pp. 107 and 140 for "Etruria Pottery".

CRESCENT

KAD NO. | **MARK**

Crescent Pottery Co.
Trenton, New Jersey, USA, 1881-1907 & 1910-1924
- In 1892 joined the Trenton Potteries (former marks continued) (1892-1907)

A97 **COOK & HANCOCK** Printed marks, c.1886-c.1895.

A98

Printed mark of the Coat of Arms of the State of New Jersey, c.1885.

A99

Printed mark, c.1890-1895. "COOK & HANCOCK" does not appear after 1895.

Typical Marks Include:

A100
A101
A102

c.1890-1995

Tea Leaf Motif

A103

Printed mark, 1896-1898.

A104

Printed mark, 1899-1903. Monogram mark "CPO" and title "UTOPIA" dates from 1900-1902.

For further reading, refer to *Barber's Marks*, pp. 62-63; *Debolt*, pp. 37 & 150; *Lehner*, p. 473; and *White Ironstone Notes*, Vol. 2, No. 3, Winter 1995, p. 7, for a "Plain American Mug".

CROWN

Crown Pottery (& Potteries) Co.
Evansville, Indiana, USA, 1891-1901
Acquired the Peoria Pottery Co. in 1902, and both companies assumed the name "Crown Potteries Co." (c.1902-1955)
Formerly, Bennighof, Uhl & Co. (1884-1891)

A105 **C. P. CO.** Printed Royal Coat of Arms with initial monogram, c.1891-1904.
A106 **C. P. Coy** Printed initial marking, 1902-1905.

KAD NO. | **MARK**

A107
A108
A109
A110

Typical Marks Include:

c.1891-1904

c.1902-1905

c.1946

Tea Leaf Motif

For further reading, refer to *Barber's Marks*, pp. 163-164; *Debolt*, p. 40; and *Lehner,* pp. 117-118.

CUMBOW

Cumbow China Co.
Abingdon, Virginia, USA, 1932-1980

A111 **CUMBOW CHINA DECORATING CO. ABINGDON, VA**

Printed mark, 1932-1980.
- Cumbow was primarily a decorating firm that purchased blanks from various manufacturers. Refer to Homer Laughlin, Johnson Bros. and "Greenfield Village Pottery".

Typical Marks Include:

A112
A113

Design Patent dated May 24, 1960

Tea Leaf Motif

- Design Patent obtained from Advertising Pricing List Supplement and U.S. Patent Office information, c.1961.

For further reading, refer to *Heaivilin*, pp. 160-161; Richard Foil. *Cumbow China of Abingdon, Virginia,* Abingdon, Virginia, Richard Foil Publisher; and *Tea Leaf Readings*, Vol. 6, No. 5, Nov. 1986, pp. 4-5.

DRESDEN

Dresden Pottery (Works) Co. (Dresden Pottery Works)
East Liverpool, Ohio, USA, c.1876-1927
History:

Brunt, Bloor, Martin & Co.	c.1875-1882
Potters Co-Operative Co.*	c.1882-1925
Dresden Pottery (Works) Co.	c.1925-1927

A38 **B. B. M. & CO.** Printed mark, 1875-1882.

A115 **T. P. C. CO.** Printed mark, c.1882-1925.

A116 **POTTERS CO-OPERATIVE CO.** Printed mark, c.1915-1925.
A117 **DRESDEN POTTERY WORKS** Printed mark, c.1925-1927.

KAD NO. | **MARK**

Typical Marks Include:

A118
A119
A120
A121
A122

1880s

c.1890

1890s

c.1895+

*Mark "DRESDEN/WHITE GRANITE" was continued from The Potters Co-Operative (& Co.).
See KAD Mark No. A330. Also see *Gates,* p. 217, Mark "B".

For further reading on the Brunt family associations, refer to *Barber,* pp. 179-180; *Barber's Marks*, pp. 177-180; *Gates*, pp. 17, 19, 211-219 and 341; and *Lehner*, pp. 60-61 for "Brunt, Bloor, Martin & Co."

EAGLE

Eagle Pottery Co.
Trenton, New Jersey, USA, c.1876-c.1879
Subsequently, The Burroughs & Mountford Co. (1879-c.1895)
Little is known about this pottery. For further reading, however, refer to *Barber's Marks*, pp. 48 & 60; as well as *Gates*, p. 52 where he notes that John Goodwin established this pottery (1844-1853) which was subsequently operated by Samuel & William Baggott (1854-?).

EAST END

East End Pottery (China) Co.
North Side of Railroad Street,
East Liverpool, Ohio, USA, 1894-1909
Subsequently, Trenley (Blake) China Co. (1909-1966)
History:

East End Pottery Co.	c.1894-1901
East Liverpool Potteries Co.	c.1901-1903
East End Pottery Co.	c.1903-1907
East End China Co.*	c.1908-1909

A123 **E. E. P. CO.** Printed mark, 1894-1901/1903-1907.
A124 **E. E. C. CO.** Printed mark, 1908-1909.
*See Trenle (Blake) China Co. KAD 384 & 385.
Typical Marks Include:

A125
A126
A127

1894-1901/1903-1907

Tea Leaf Motif

For further reading, refer to *Gates*, pp. 40-41; *Heaivilin*, pp. 161-162; and *Stoltzfus/Snyder*, p. 140.

EAST LIVERPOOL

KAD NO. | MARK

East Liverpool Potteries Companies*
East Liverpool, Ohio, USA, c1901-1907
The United States Pottery Co. (Wellsville, Ohio) continued the name (c.1907-c.1932)
The six members were:*
East End Pottery, East Liverpool Pottery, Globe Pottery, George C. Murphy Pottery, United States Pottery Co., and Wallace & Chetwynd

A128 

Printed mark for the Capitol, the United States Pottery Co., c.1901-1907.
- The marking "E.L.P.CO." (see KAD Mark No. A402) was used only on semi-vitreous dinnerware. *The mark belongs to the East Liverpool Pottery Co.* (1907-1925+). "MADE IN USA/CHINA" added by the United States Pottery Co., Wellsville, Ohio (c.1925-1932).

*See individual potteries for additional markings.

For further reading, refer to *Debolt*, pp. 40-45 & 199 (A149); and *Gates*, pp. 44-45 & 299.

EAST LIVERPOOL

East Liverpool Pottery Co.
East Liverpool, Ohio, USA, 1894-1901
Subsequently, East Liverpool Potteries Company (1901-1907)

A129 **E. L. P. CO.** Printed initial mark, 1894-1896.

A130 

Printed mark, 1894-1896. Additional marking "WARRANTED" noted.

For further reading, refer to *Gates*, pp. 41-43.

EAST TRENTON

East Trenton Pottery Co.
Trenton, New Jersey, USA, c.1885-c.1905

A131 **E. T. P. CO.** Printed initial mark, c.1885-c.1905.
A132 **OPAQUE CHINA E. T. P. CO.** Impressed mark, after 1890.

Typical Marks Include:

A133
A134
A135

c.1880s

c.1890s

c.1890s

- *Debolt*, p. 174, notes an additional mark of an impressed initial "E" within an embossed border, also including the additional marking "OPAQUE/CHINA".

For further reading, refer to *Barber's Marks*, p. 47.

EMPIRE

KAD NO. **MARK**

Empire Pottery*
- and Various Ownerships*
Trenton, New Jersey, USA, c.1863-1892
Subsequently, Trenton Potteries Co., (1892-c.1950s)
- The name Empire Pottery was conceived by Alpaugh & Magowan
***Not to be confused with The Empire Pottery (New York State) which subsequently became The Syracuse China Co.**
History:

Coxon & Co.	c.1863-1880
Wood & Barlow	c.1880-1884
Alpaugh & Magowan	c.1884-1892

A136

Printed Royal Coat of Arms marked "COXON & CO.", c.1863-c.1870.
- Note script initial "C. & Co." within shield.

A137

Printed mark, c.1870s-1880s. For a variation of this mark, refer to *Lehner*, p. 112.
- The company is listed as "COXON & THOMPSON", with the "& CO." being J.F. Thompson.

A138

Impressed mark,c.1880-1884.

A139

Printed mark, c.1885-1890.

A140

Printed monogram initial mark "T.P. CO." may have been a transitional marking. Note the word "EMPIRE" above, c.1892.
- Also see Trenton Potteries Co.

For further reading, refer to *Barber*, p. 175; *Barber's Marks*, pp. 63-64; *Debolt*, pp. 47-48 & 172; *Ketchum, Jr.*, p. 296; and *Lehner*, pp. 139 & 474.

ETRURIA

KAD NO. | **MARK**

Etruria Pottery (& Co.)
Trenton, New Jersey, USA, 1863-1893
Subsequently, The Cook Pottery Co. (1894-1920s)
History:

Bloor, Ott & Booth	1863-1865
Ott, Brewer & Bloor	1865-1870
Etruria Pottery & Co. (of Ott & Brewer Co.)	1870-1893

A141 

Printed monogram initial "E. P. & CO." within English Coat of Arms, 1870-1893.

A142 

Printed mark, 1870s. Note "ETRURIA" above mark.

A143 **OTT & BREWER CO. TRENTON, N.J.**
Printed name mark, 1880s.

For further reading, refer to *Barber's Marks*, pp. 52-54; *Debolt*, pp. 108-110; and *Lehner*, p. 140 for "Etruria Pottery".

FELL

Fell & Thropp & Co.
Trenton, New Jersey, USA, c.1879-c.1901
Previously, Isaac Davis (c.1872-1879)
Subsequently, Thropp & Brewer (c.1901-1902)

A144 **F. & T. & CO.**
A145 **F. & T. CO.**
Printed initial marks, c.1879-1901.

Typical Marks Include:

A146
A147
A148
A149

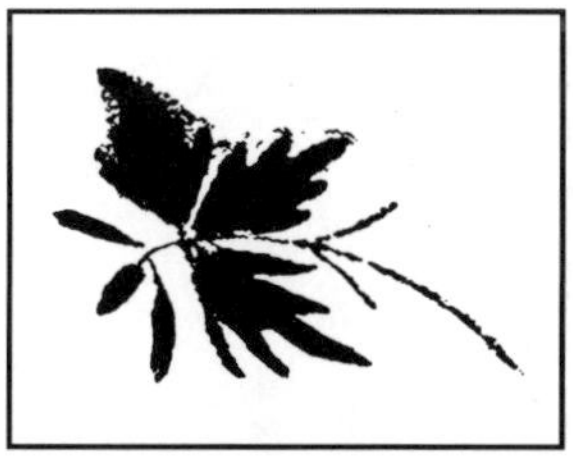

c.1879-1890 (1901)

Coat of Arms of State of New Jersey

Tea Leaf Motif

- Also refer to Trenton Pottery (Co.) (Works).

For further reading, refer to *Debolt,* pp. 48-49 & 148-149; and *Lehner*, p. 474.

FORD

KAD NO. | **MARK**

Ford China Co.
Ford City, Pennsylvania, USA, 1898-c.1904
Subsequently, Cook & Co. (c.1904-1912)

A150 **F. CO. CO.**

Printed mark with monogram. Pattern name often included, 1898-c.1904.

A151
A152

Tea Leaf Motif

For further reading, refer to *Barber's Marks*, p. 36 for additional body style marks; and *Tea Leaf Readings*, Sept. 1988, p. 8.

FRENCH

The French China Co. ("Klondike Pottery")
East Liverpool, Ohio, USA (1898-1908) and Sebring, Ohio, USA (1898-1929), 1898-1929
Subsequently, The Sebring Manufacturing Co. (c.1916-1929) which was a holding corporation for various Sebring potteries (c.1898-1929)
Subsequently, The American Chinaware Corporation (c.1929-1931)

A153 **F. C. CO.**
A154 **FRENCH CHINA CO.**

Printed marks of differing design. Pattern name or "body style" often included, c.1900-1916. (Initials "F.C. CO." from 1916-1929).

A155
A156
A157

c.1898-1916

1916-1929

1916-1929

- The above three marks are also noted on Flow Blue. This backstamp may be printed in colors other than blue.
- See Saxon China Co. for additional comments as well as Sebring Pottery Co. for chronology of holdings.

For further reading, refer to *Gates*, pp. 47-49; *Lehner*, pp. 155-156; and *Snyder*, Vol. 2, pp. 68-69.

FRENCH-SAXON

French-Saxon China Co.
Sebring, Ohio, USA, 1935-1964
Formerly, The American Chinaware Corp. (1929-1931)
Subsequently, The Royal China Co. (1964-1969+)

A158 **FRENCH SAXON**

Printed mark, 1935+.

- For marking "SAXON CHINA" see The Saxon China Co., (KAD No. A343) 1911-1929.

For further reading, refer to *Debolt*, p. 128 and *Gates*, pp. 229-230.

GLASGOW

KAD NO. | **MARK**

Glasgow Pottery Co.
Trenton, New Jersey, USA, c.1863-c.1900*
Subsequently, Thomas Maddock's Sons' Co. (c.1900) and hence, John Moses & Sons (c.1900-1905)

A159

Printed American Eagle and Shield mark noted with or without "IRONSTONE CHINA", c.1878.

A160

Printed initial mark, "G. P." c.1882.

A161

Printed initial mark "J.M." (John Moses) noted on Tea Leaf, c.1884.

A162
A163

Tea Leaf Motif
c.1884

Tea Leaf Motif
c.1895-1905

A164

Printed Royal Coat of Arms Mark. Shield includes monogrammed initial abbreviation "G.P. CO." for Glasgow Pottery Co., c.1890-1900.

A165 **J. M. & S. CO.**

Printed initial mark for "JOHN MOSES & SONS CO.", c.1900-1905.

A166 **TRILBY**

Trilby is a pattern name, and is also noted on Flow Blue by the English pottery Wood & Son(s)(Ltd.) of Burslem.

*Dating information seems to be contradictory. Lehner notes that the Glasgow pottery was purchased by Thomas Maddock Sons & Co. in 1900, but also notes that from 1900-1905 the company was called John Moses & Sons Co.

For further reading, refer to *Barber's Marks*, pp. 50-52 for additional marks; *Debolt*, pp. 54-56; *Karmason*, pp. 167-170; ,*Lehner*, pp. 172-173; *Stoltzfus/Snyder*, p. 151; and *TLCI*, 1992, pp. 22-23.

GLOBE

KAD NO.	MARK	

Globe Pottery Co.
East Liverpool, Ohio, USA, 1888-1900 & 1907-1912
Formerly, Frederick, Schenkle, Allen & Co. (1881-1888)
History:

Globe Pottery Co.	1888-1900
East Liverpool Potteries Companies	1901-1907
Globe Pottery Co.	1907-1917

KAD NO.	MARK	
A167	**G. P. CO.**	Printed initial mark, 1888-1901/1907-1912.
A168	**G. P. CO. ELO**	Printed initial mark, 1888-1901/1907-1912.

Typical Marks Include:

A169
A170
A171

1888-1901& 1907-1912

c.1898

1888-1901& 1907-1912

For further reading, refer to *Gates*, pp. 50-51.

GOODWIN

Goodwin (Bros.) Pottery Co.
Broadway Pottery Works, Liverpool, Ohio, USA, 1872-1912
Formerly, "The Broadway Pottery Works" (1868-1872)*
History:

John Goodwin	1872-1875
Goodwin Bros.	1876-1893
Goodwin Pottery Co.	1893-1912

- Also refer to "Eagle Pottery" and "Novelty Pottery Works" for an earlier history of Goodwin.

KAD NO.	MARK	
A172	**GOODWIN BROS.**	Printed mark, 1876-1893.
A173	**GOODWIN'S**	Printed mark, 1893-1906.
A174	**GOODWIN**	Printed mark, 1906-1912.

Typical Marks Include:

A175
A176
A177
A178
A179

Tea Leaf Motif c.1885-1897

c.1885-1897

c.1885-1898

c.1888-1893

c.1893-1906

*See Trenton Pottery Co. (1870-1872).
- In her books, *Potters View* and *Pottery & Porcelain*, Elizabeth Collard notes the presence of "Goodwin Bros." in Canada, c.1856. The reference is to George and Joseph, sons of John Goodwin of Longton, Staffordshire. Also see *Hampson*, pp. 77-78, No. 116.

For further reading, refer to *Gates,* pp. 52-55; and *Heaivilin*, pp. 163-176.

GREENFIELD

KAD NO. | **MARK**

Greenfield Village Pottery
Greenfield Village, Dearborn, Michigan, USA, (1933-present)

A180 — **GREENFIELD VILLAGE THE HENRY FORD MUSEUM**

Printed mark, 1933+.

A181

- Blanks were purchased from Simpsons, Ltd. and decorated by Cumbow in Tea Leaf/Copper Lustre for the Greenfield Village Pottery. See Cumbow China Co. (1932-1980) for printed mark. Simpson, a major retail chain, is still in existence in England. They also fill retail orders, worldwide, with reproduction of older patterns.

-*Heaivilin* gives a rather detailed history of the Cumbow China Decorating Co. see pp. 160-161, Mark CU3 "The Henry Ford Museum".

For further reading, refer to *Godden*, Mark no's. 3560-62; and *Snyder*, Vol. 1, p. 122 where he notes that Flow Blue pieces produced for Simpson's are well known.

GREENWOOD

Greenwood Pottery Co.
Trenton, New Jersey, USA, c.1868-c.1933
Formerly, Stephen Tams & Co. (1861-c.1868)

A182 — **G. P. CO.**

Printed or impressed mark, c.1868-1875.

A183

Printed mark with Coat of Arms of New Jersey, marked "G. P. CO." c.1868-1875.

- See Stephen Tams & Co.

A184 — **GREENWOOD CHINA**

Impressed mark, c.1886.

A185

Printed mark noted in *Wetherbee's White Ironstone*, p. 181, c.1886-1897.

For further reading, refer to *Debolt*, pp. 58-59; and *Lehner*, p. 180.

HALL

KAD NO. | **MARK**

Hall China Co.
East Liverpool, Ohio, USA, 1903-present
(Also see Red Cliff Co., 1955-1977)

A186 **HALL** Printed name mark, 1903-present.

- From the 1950s until 1960 Red Cliff subcontracted out for the production of blanks to both the Hall China Co. and the Walker China Co. The former manufactured hollow ware and the latter plates.

For further reading, refer to *Heaivilin*, pp. 175-181 & 205.

HARKER

Harker Potteries Etruria Pottery (1846-1931)
& Wedgwood Pottery (1877-1881)
East Liverpool, Ohio, USA, 1843-1972
Subsequently, The Jeanette Glass Corp.
History:

George S. Harker & Sons	1843-1846
Harker, Taylor & Co. (Etruria Pottery)	1846-1851
Harker, Thompson & Co.	1851-1853
George S. Harker (Sr. & Jr.) & Co.	1854-1877
Benjamin Harker joins firm (from 1877-1881, Ben. Harker & Son, and in 1881 Wedgwood Pottery was sold to Wallace & Chetwynd)	1877-1890
Harker Pottery Co. (Inc.)/or George S. Harker & Co.	1890-1910

A187 **GEO. S. HARKER & CO.** Printed mark, 1879-1890.
A188 **H. P. CO.** Printed initial mark, 1890-c.1910.

Typical Marks Include:

A189
A190
A191

c.1879-1890

c.1890-1900

- *Barber*, p. 105 notes that the Harker Pottery Co. decorated white granite wares for many companies. Also refer to Burroughs & Mountford Co.
For further reading, refer to *Gates*, pp. 79-94.

ILLINOIS

The Illinois China Co.
Lincoln, Illinois, USA, c.1919-1946
Subsequently, Stetson China Co. (1946-1966)

A192 

Printed mark found on Tea Leaf/Copper Lustre, c.1919-1946.

A193 **LINCOLN, ILL** Printed mark, as above, marked "LINCOLN, ILL" c.1919-1946.
For further reading, refer to *Lehner,* p. 218.

INTERNATIONAL

KAD NO. | **MARK**

International (Lincoln) Pottery Co.
Trenton, New Jersey, USA, 1860-1936
History:

International Pottery Co., Henry Speeler	1860-1868
International Pottery Co., Henry Speeler & Son	1868-1879
Lincoln Pottery Co., James Carr, Edward Clark & John & James Moses	1878-1879
International Pottery Co., Burgess & Campbell	1879-1903
International Pottery Co., Burgess & Co.	1903-1936

A194

Printed marks of differing design with pattern name often included, 1878-1879.*

A195

Printed marks of differing design with pattern name often included, 1879-1903.**

A196

Printed marks of differing design with pattern name often included, 1879-1903.
- See page 133 for additional comments.

A197 **B. & C.**
A198 **B-C**

Printed marks of differing design with pattern name often included, c.1891-1898.

Selected Marks Noted On Flow Blue, 1879-1903:

A199
A200
A201

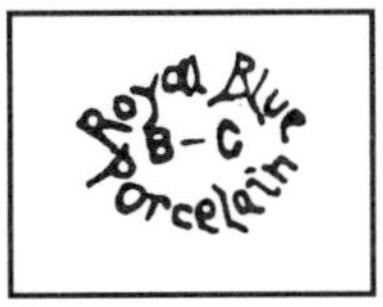

A202
A203

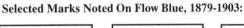

Printed mark noted on Flow Blue, c.1895-c.1902.

A204

Printed Maltese Cross mark with initials, c.1897. The addition of "INTERNATIONAL" is noted on Flow Blue, c.1910.

*Clarke returned to England, and from 1880-1887 he continued the use of the double shield mark at his Church Yard Works in Burslem.
- A research paper presented by Mary Bertram in *Tea Leaf Readings*, Nov. 1986, pp. 6-7, traces the history of Clarke in England and the United States.
**Evidently this double shield mark was very popular, as the Mercer Pottery Co. also used it for a few years from c.1879-1885 (see *Debolt*, p. 96); as did the New York City Pottery. To complicate this issue even further, John Wyllie used the same double shield marking between 1880 and 1883 (see *Debolt*, p. 164).
For a full discussion on the use of this mark, see *Gates,* pp. 200-201.

KAD NO. **MARK**

For further reading, refer to *Gaston*, Vol. 1, Mark Nos. 158-160. Also refer to *Godden's Collecting Lustreware*, pp. 115-116 for an extended history of Burgess; *Lehner*, p. 221; and *Snyder,* Vol. 2, pp. 67-68.

JERSEY CITY

Jersey City (American) Pottery Co.
- & Various Ownerships,
Jersey City, New Jersey, USA, c.1827-1892
History:

Jersey City Porcelain & Earthenware Co.	1825-1827
Jersey City Pottery	1827-1829
Pottery Closed	1829-1833
American Pottery Co.	1840-1892
Various owners, most important being 'Rouse & Turner'	1855-1892

A205

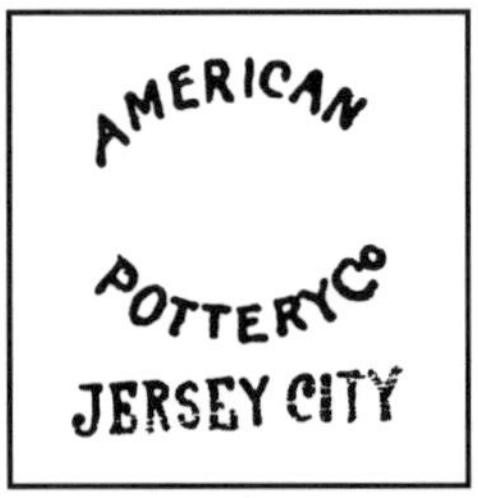

Printed marks of differing design, 1840-1845.
- *Barber*, pp. 118-125 & 438-440 gives a rather detailed history of this pottery.

A206

Barber, p. 545 illustrates a Creamware plate, in light blue transfer, marked "CANOVA" after a design by John Ridgway, Hanley, England, 1840-1845.
- CANOVA is recorded as "the first transfer printed decorated earthenware produced in America." So notes the exhibit catalog of 1947, The Pottery & Porcelain of New Jersey, 1688-1900. April 8-May 11, 1947, pp. 10 and 100 and plate 49.

A207 **R. & T.** Printed Royal Coat of Arms mark with initials of Rouse & Turner, c.1850s.

For further reading, refer to *Barber*, pp. 174-175; *Barber's Marks*, pp. 41-44; *Debolt*, p. 66; and *Lehner*, pp. 222-229.

KNOWLES

Edwin M. Knowles China Co.,
East Liverpool, Ohio, USA, 1900-1963
- Pottery located in Chester & Newell, West Virginia
- Offices located in East Liverpool, Ohio

A208 **E. M. K.**
C. CO. Printed initial mark, 1900-1905.

A209

Printed mark, 1900-1948.

For further reading, refer to *Debolt*, pp. 67-70, wherein he gives a rather extensive "dating system"; and *Gates*, pp. 99-114.

KNOWLES

KAD NO.	MARK

Knowles, Taylor, Knowles Co.
East Liverpool Pottery Works (c.1870-1929)
Buckeye Pottery Works (c.1881-1929)
East Liverpool, Ohio, USA, c.1854-1929
Subsequently, American Chinaware Corp. (c.1929-1931)
History:

Isaac Knowles & Isaac Harvey	c.1854-1856
Isaac Knowles	c.1856-1870
Knowles, Taylor, Knowles Co.	c.1870-1891
Knowles, Taylor, Knowles Inc.	c.1891
Knowles, Taylor, Knowles Ltd.	c.1891-1929

A210 **K. T. & K.**

Printed marks of various design. Pattern name often included, 1870-1891. May also be noted with Royal Coat of Arms, c.1872-1878. Initials "K.T. & K." used by John Wyllie & Son (1874-1893)and William Young & Sons, Trenton, New Jersey (c.1872-1893).

A211

Printed Royal Coat of Arms marked "K. T. K." Also noted marked "GRANITEWARE", "PATENTED" and "WARRANTED", c.1872-1878.

A212

Printed mark, c.1878-1885.
- *Gates*, pp. 115-116 notes that in 1881 the "Buckeye" Pottery was purchased for the production of White Ironstone. Also refer to *White Ironstone Notes*, Vol. 3, No. 3, Winter 1997 (Dec. 1996), p. 12.

Marks noted on Tea Leaf/Copper Lustre:

A213
A214
A215

c.1881-1920

Motif
Child's Set
Tea Leaf

Motif
Oak Leaf
Tea Leaf

A216
A217

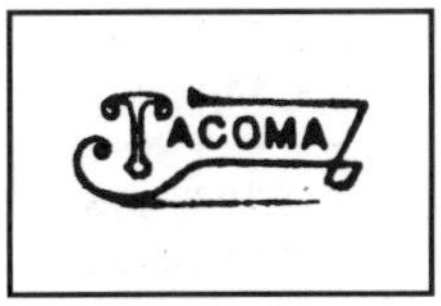

c.1905-1920*

Tacoma Motif
Tea Leaf

**Gates*, pp. 122-123 notes other shapes and pattern names for Semi-vitreous hotel and dinnerware of this period.

KAD NO.	MARK	

Typical Marks Include:

A218
A219
A220
A221

c.1879

c.1880-1890

c.1881

1890-1920

For further reading, refer to *Gates*, pp. 115-127; *Heaivilin*, pp. 182-190; *Lehner*, pp. 238-239; *Stoltzfus/Snyder*, pp. 140, 171; and *Tea Leaf Readings*, Vol. 14, No. 12, Apr. 1994

LAUGHLIN

Homer Laughlin (China & Co.)
Ohio Valley Pottery, East Liverpool, Ohio, USA
-& various other locations, 1877-present
History:

Homer Laughlin & Nathaniel Simms	1869-1872
(Homer) Laughlin & Bros.	1873-1877
Homer Laughlin	1877-1897
Homer Laughlin China Co.	1897-present

A222 **LAUGHLIN BROS.** Printed mark, c.1873-1877.

A223 

Printed mark found on Flow Blue, 1877-1900.

A224 **LAUGHLIN** Printed mark found on Flow Blue, 1877-1900.
A225 **HOMER LAUGHLIN** Printed mark, 1877-c.1900.
A226 **COLONIAL** Printed mark, 1877-c.1900.
A227 **LAUGHLIN CHINA** Impressed mark, c.1886.
A228 **H. L. & CO.** Printed mark, c.1897-present.

A229
A230

c.1940-1955
Cup/Saucer
Gold

Tea Leaf Motif

A231 

Printed mark “KITCHEN KRAFT” noted on Tea Leaf/ Copper Lustre, 1935-1950.

- Cumbow China Co. decorated white wares supplied and manufactured by Homer Laughlin China Co. in Tea Leaf/Copper Lustre. (See Cumbow).

KAD NO. **MARK**

For a full discussion on the use of this mark see *Gates*, pp. 200-201 and *Godden*, Mark No. 895, c.1880-1887.
For further reading, *Gates*, pp. 128-169; *Heaivilin*, pp. 190-197; *Stoltzfus/Snyder*, pp. 130-131; *TLCI*, p. 49, wherein Tea Leaf by Laughlin is noted. Also cited, on p. 51, is the marking "KITCHEN KRAFT" by Laughlin, c.1935-1950, which were Tea Leaf wares produced at the Newell , WV Pottery - titled "Fleur-de-lis". Also refer to *Tea Leaf Readings*, Vol. 14, No. 4, Sept. 1994, p. 25.

LIMOGES

Limoges China Co.,
Sebring, Ohio, USA, 1902-1949
Formerly, Sterling China Co. (1900-1902)
and briefly, Sebring China Co.
Subsequently, The American Limoges China Co. (1949-1955)

A232 Printed mark, c.1900-c.1902.

A233 These two marks present problems, as noted by *Debolt, Gates and Lehner*.
The use of the term "STERLING" to identify the pottery is, in the least, confusing. I believe these marks, which are from *Gates*, accurately reflect the 1900-1902 period. Also refer to The Sterling China Co. and Sebring Pottery Company - Chronology of Holdings.

A234 **LIMOGES** Printed mark, c.1902-1935.
A235 **L. C. CO.** Printed mark, c.1910-1930.

- The name "Sebring China Co." and "E. H. Sebring China Co.' was used during the transition period of c.1900-1902, until the name "LIMOGES CHINA CO." was finally settled upon. The mark "STERLING" was used by both the Colonial Pottery Co. (1903-1929) and J. & G. Meakin, Hanley, England.

Confusion exists when you look at *P. Williams, Flow Blue*, Vol. III, p. 50, "Calendar Plate #2" and p. 56 "Panama Canal". Petra notes President pictures up to the year 1913. Thus, one is led to believe that Limoges continued the Sterling marks to at least 1913.

To further complicate the issue of name marks, *Gates* cites the practice of using familiar British symbols, such as the Lion and Unicorn, in combination with a coat of arms, a heraldic escutcheon, or a shield. This practice was prevalent through the late 1880s. Occasionally, the diamond shape registry mark or the familiar garter-shaped mark also appeared on American pottery. Refer to *Gates*, pp. 9-10.

Also note that there is a company by the same name, Sterling China Co., 1917-present, located in Wellsville, Ohio. Refer to *Gates*, p. 250.

For further reading, refer to *Debolt*, pp. 135, & 188; *Gates*, p. 100; and *Lehner*, pp. 100, & 443-444 for additional comments and marks.

LINCOLN

LINCOLN POTTERY
See: INTERNATIONAL (LINCOLN) POTTERY CO.

MADDOCK

Thomas Maddock (& Sons)(& Co.)
- & Various Potteries.
Trenton, New Jersey, c.1882-1929
(Lamberton Works continued by Schammell China Co., c.1924-1954)*
History:

Astbury & Maddock	c.1875-1882
Thomas Maddock	c.1882
Thomas Maddock & Sons	c.1882-1902
Incorporated as Maddock Pottery Co.	1892
Lamberton Works*	c.1892-1922
(John) Maddock Pottery Co.	c.1895-1929
Thomas Maddock's Sons & Co.	c.1902-1915

KAD NO.	MARK	
A236	**T. M. & S.**	Printed mark, c.1882-1902.
A237		- Flow Blue marking noted "THOS. MADDOCK'S SONS CO., TRENTON, NJ" See *Gates*, pp. 182-183.
A238	**LAMBERTON***	Printed mark, c.1892-1922.
A239 A240	 	Printed marks, c.1893-1900 and c.1900-1915.
A241		Printed mark, c.1902-1915.

- Research indicates that in 1886 Thomas Maddock acquired the City Pottery Co. which was directly across the street.

Debolt, p. 86, notes a period between c.1900-c.1912, whereby decorative work for other potteries was taken on. Further, on p. 181, he notes a shield marking with or without wreath (c.1902) which was continued throughout various ownerships. Also refer to *Lehner*, p. 275.

Gates, p. 10 notes that subcontracting or even the copying of marks and patterns, including the English Diamond Registration, was not an unknown practice on both sides of the ocean. In fact, John Maddock & Sons of Burslem, England notes, as late as 1894, in a company price list that "this stamp is being imitated ... It is easier to imitate the stamp than the goods."

MARYLAND

Maryland Pottery Co.
Baltimore, Maryland, USA, c.1888-1910(14)
History:

Maryland Queensware Co.	c.1879-1880
Hamill, Brown & Co.	c.1880-1888
Maryland Pottery Co.	c.1888-1910(14)

After 1895 pottery produced only sanitary wares.

KAD NO.	MARK	
A242	**D. F. H. & CO. BALT°**	Printed marks belonging to Maryland Queensware Co. and
A243	**D. F. HAYNES & CO.**	their selling agent, c.1879-c.1881.
A244	**MARYLAND POTTERY WARRANTED**	Printed mark, c.1881-1883.

Typical Marks Include:

A245
A246
A247
A248
A249

c.1879-1881

c.1879-1881

c.1880-1892

c.1881-1883

c.1883-1891 Arms of Maryland

For further reading, refer to *Barber's* Marks, pp. 147-148; *Debolt,* p. 89; and *Lehner*, pp. 281-282.

MAYER

(J. & E.) Mayer Potteries Co., Ltd.
Beaver Falls, Pennsylvania, USA, 1881-1964
Subsequently, Shenango China Co.,
New Castle, Pennsylvania (1964-1968)
- In 1916 company moved to the production of hotel chinaware.

A250	**J. & E. MAYER**	Printed mark, c.1881-c.1888.
A251	**J. & E. M.**	Printed marks, c.1890-c.1910

A252

Printed marks of various designs. Pattern name often included. Pennsylvania Royal Coat of Arms may also be marked "SEMI VITREOUS CHINA", c.1890s-c.1910.
- Refer to *Gaston*, Vol. 1, Mark 164 - Flow Blue China.

A253

Printed mark and pattern name "TRIUMPH" noted by *Debolt*, p. 183, c.1890s-c.1905.

KAD NO. | **MARK**

Typical Marks Include:

A254
A255

c.1881- 91

c.1890's- 1910

A256
A257

c.1881-c.1888
Tea Leaf Motif

c.1890-1910
Oak Leaf Motif

For further marks and reading, refer to *Barber's Marks*, pp. 33-34; *Debolt*, pp. 89-92; *Heaivilin*, p. 196; *Lehner*, pp. 283-286, Marks 1, 3, 5, 9, and 10-13; *Snyder*, Vol. 2, pp. 69-70; and *Stoltzfus/Snyder*, p. 134.

McNICOL

McNicol, Burton & Co.,
Novelty Pottery Works
- and various ownerships,
East Liverpool, Ohio, USA, c.1870-1892
History:

John Goodwin	c.1863-1865
Manly & Riley	c.1865-1869
A. H. Marks	c.1869-1870
McNicol & Burton & Co.	c.1870-1892
D. E. McNicol Pottery Co.	c.1892-1928
D. McNicol Pottery Co.	c.1928-1954

- This last period concentrated on Vitrified China

A258 **McNICOL BURTON & CO.** Printed name mark, c.1870-1892
A259 **McN. B. & CO.** Printed mark with or without flower in center, c.1885-1892.

A260

- An additional marking has been noted for McNicol, Burton & Co. This marking is a shield, of which two variations exist. One is with initials and the other with the full name. Refer to *Gates*, pp. 184-185, figure 162c.

A261 - As above, but without flower, c. 1885-1892.

KAD NO.	MARK	
A262 A263		**Typical Tea Leaf/Copper Lustre Marks Include:**

Mark
c.1870-1892

Tea Leaf Motif

For further reading, refer to *Gates*, pp. 184-185; and *Lehner*, p. 325 for the "Novelty Pottery Co."

McNICOL

D.E. McNicol Pottery Co. (Novelty Pottery Works),
East Liverpool, Ohio, USA (1892-1928)
Wellsville, Ohio. (c.1899-1907)
Clarksburg, West Virginia (c.1914-1954),
c.1892-1954

KAD NO.	MARK	
A264	**D. E. McN. P. CO.**	Printed mark, c.1892-1910.
A265	**D. E. McN. P. CO.** **LIVERPOOL**	Printed initial mark, c.1892-1910.
A266	**D. E. McN. P. CO.** **WARRANTED**	Printed initial mark including "WARRANTED", c.1900.

- *Heaivilin*, p. 149 & 152 notes a marking "T. A. McNICOL, EAST LIVERPOOL, OHIO" from (1913-1929). This mark has not been located or identified. Also refer to *Gates*, p. 196.

Tea Leaf/Copper Lustre Markings Include:

A267
A268

c.1892-c.1910

Tea Leaf Motif

For further reading, refer to *Gates*, pp. 185-194.

McNICOL

McNicol-Smith Company
School House Pottery, Wellsville, Ohio, USA, 1889-1901
Formerly, Baum Pottery
Subsequently, McNicol-Corns China Co. (c.1907-1928)

A269 Printed mark, 1889-1901.

For further reading and additional marks, refer to *Gates*, pp. 196-197.

MERCER

KAD NO.	MARK	
		Mercer Pottery Co. **Trenton, New Jersey, USA, 1868-1930s(37)**
A270 A271	**M. C.** **M. C. CO.**	Printed marks, 1868-c.1930s.
		Typical Marks Include:
A272 A273 A274 A275 A276		

1879-c.1885*

c.1880-c.1885

1890s

1890s

c.1897

A277	**MERCER POTTERY** **TRENTON, N. J.**	Impressed mark, c.1880s.
A278		Impressed mark, c.1880s.
A279 A280	 	Printed marks found on "Flow Blue", 1890s.

- See the International Pottery Co. for comments on the Double Shield mark, as well as New York City Pottery and John Wyllie & Son.
*Waness & Campbell, a printed name mark noted in lieu of Mercer Pottery Co. is illustrated in *White Ironstone Notes*, Vol. 4, No. 2, Fall 1997, p. 11.

For further reading, refer to *Barber*, p. 181; *Barber's Marks*, p. 57; *Debolt*, pp. 96-97; *Lehner*, p. 293; and *Snyder*, Vol. 2, p. 70.

MILLINGTON

		Millington & Astbury (& Paulson) Pottery **Carrol Street Pottery, Trenton, New Jersey, USA, 1853-1859** **Subsequently, Millington, Astbury & Paulson (1859-1862), 1853-1862**
A281	**M. A.**	Printed mark, 1853-1859.
A282	**M. A. P** **TRENTON**	Printed or impressed mark, 1859-1862.
A283	**M.A.P.** **N.J.**	As above but with the addition of "N.J.", 1859-1862.

- Marks KAD No. 282 & 283 are noted for Millington, Astbury & Paulson (1859-1862).

For further reading, refer to *Barber's Marks*, pp. 47-48; *Debolt*, p. 97; and *Lehner*, p. 300.

MORLEY

KAD NO.	MARK	

Morley (& Son) or (& Sons) & Co.,
- Various locations and partnerships
Wellsville, Ohio, USA, 1879-1891

History:

PIONEER POTTERY WORKS

1879-1884	*Morley & Co.*	Clarke, Michaels & Morley	Pioneer Pottery Works
1884-1891	Pioneer Pottery Co.	Clarke & Michaels	Pioneer Pottery Works
1892-1895	-Co. in receivership	-	-
1896-1900	Wellsville Pottery Co.	B. Clarke	[Pioneer Pottery]
1902-1959	Wellsville China Co.	-	[Pioneer Pottery]
1959-1969	Sterling China Co.	-	[Pioneer Pottery]

LINCOLN POTTERY (WORKS)

1865	Thompson, Jobling, Taylor & Hardwick		[Lincoln Pottery]
1867-1883	West, Hardwick & Co.		Lincoln Pottery Works
1884-1891	*George Morley & Son* (acquire)		Lincoln Pottery Works
		-	Bankrupt in 1891

EAST LIVERPOOL OR SALAMANDER POTTERY

1849-1850	(R.) Harrison & (R.) Henderson		[East Liverpool Pottery]
1852-1853	Richard Harrison & Co.		[East Liverpool Pottery]
1855-1857	*Morley,* Godwin & Flentke		[East Liverpool Pottery]
1857-1878	*Morley,* Godwin & Flentke	(name changed to)	Salamander Pottery
1878-1882	Godwin & Flentke		Salamander Pottery
1882-1886	William Flentke		Salamander Pottery
1886-1927	Standard Pottery Co.	-	Moves to West Virginia

A284 **MORLEY & CO.** Printed name mark, c.1879-1884.

A285 

Printed initial mark, c. 1879-1884.

A286 **G. M. & SON** Printed marks, ("PIONEER POTTERY WORKS") c.1884-1891. Mark may also include "IRONSTONE CHINA".

A287 **G. M. C. SON**

-For various other partnerships see Pioneer Pottery Works.

For further reading, refer to *Gates*, pp. 46, 198-200; and *Karmason, pp. 165-166.*

NEW ENGLAND

New England Pottery Co.
East Boston, Massachusetts, USA, 1875-1914
Formerly, Frederick Meagher (1854-1875)

A288 **N. E. P. CO.** Printed mark, 1875-1914.
A289 **G. C.** Printed initial mark is for Gray & Clark Pottery, owners (1875-1914).

KAD NO.	MARK	

Typical Marks Include:

A290
A291
A292
A293

1878-1893 **1883-1886** **1886-1902** **1887-1904**

For further reading, refer to *Barber's Marks*, pp. 96-97; *Debolt*, p. 102; *Ketchum, Jr.*, p. 308; and *Lehner*, p. 315.

NEW YORK CITY

New York City Pottery
New York, New York, USA, 1852-1888
History:

James Carr, Swanhill Pottery	(South Amboy, NJ)	1852-1854
Carr & Smith	(NYC)	1855-1856
Morrison, Carr & Smith	(NYC)	1856-1857
Morris & Carr	(NYC)	1858-1871
-Morrison departs		
Carr, James	(NYC)	1871-1888

A294 **MORRISON & CARR** Impressed mark, c.1858-1871.

A295 Printed mark with monogram initials "J.C.", 1871-1888.
- *Wetherbee, White Ironstone* notes two additional markings:

A296 - STONE/PORCELAIN/J.C.
A297 - N. Y. C. P.

A298 **J. C.** Printed mark, 1871-1888.
A299 **JAMES CARR**

A300 Printed "Trade Mark", 1879.*

- In an article written in 1901, James Carr recalls his arrival in the United States in 1844, his work in Jersey City, his early pottery efforts in South Amboy (NJ), through to his involvement in the New York City Pottery. For reference to this article, see Lelyn Branin, *The Early Makers of Handcrafted Earthenware and Stoneware in Central and Southern New Jersey.* Cranbury, NJ. Associated University Presses. 1988, pp. 198-201. Also refer to Godden Mark No. 895.
*See the International Pottery Co., Mercer Pottery Co., and John Wyllie & Son for comments on the double shield mark.

For further reading, refer to *Barber*, p. 175; *Barber's Marks*, pp. 57, 77-79; Karmason, pp. 162-165; and *Ketchum, Jr.*, p. 66.

NORTON

KAD NO. **MARK**

Norton Pottery
Bennington, Vermont, USA, 1793-1894
History:

L. Norton & Co.	1800-1827
L. Norton	1828-1833
L. Norton and Son	1833-1840
Julius Norton and/or J. Norton	1841-1844
Norton and Fenton	1845-1847
Julius Norton	1847-1850
J. & E. Norton	1850-1859
J. & E. Norton & Co.	1859-1861
E. & L. P. Norton	1861-1881
E. Norton	1881-1883
Edward Norton & Co.	1883-1884

Printed marks bear printed names of the various partnerships, with the appropriate additions of "BENNINGTON, VT.", "EAST BENNINGTON, VT.", and "BENNINGTON".

For a full and extensive listing, refer to Richard Carter Barret. *Bennington Pottery and Porcelain*. New York, Bonanza Books, 1958; *Lehner,* pp. 322-323, 481; and *Wetherbee*, p. 156.

- Also see the U.S. Pottery Company, Bennington, Vermont.

OHIO

Ohio China Co.
East Palestine, Ohio, USA, c.1902-c.1912
Formerly, Ohio China Works (1896-1902)

A301 **O. C. CO. IMPERIAL CHINA** — Printed mark, c.1902-c.1912.

A302 

Printed mark, c.1902-c.1912.
- *Debolt*, p. 180 notes that this mark is found on "Flow Blue".

OLIVER

Oliver China Co.
Sebring, Ohio, USA, c.1899-c.1908
(Manufacturers of Porcelain or Semi-porcelain)

A303 **VERUS PORCELAIN** — Printed marks, c.1899-c.1908.

A304 **THE OLIVER CHINA CO. SEBRING, OHIO**

- Also refer to E. H. Sebring China Co.

For further reading, refer to *Gates*, p. 209; and *Lehner*, p. 330.

ONONDAGA

KAD NO. **MARK**

Onondaga Pottery Co.
Syracuse, New York, USA, 1871-1966
Formerly, Empire Pottery, Fayette Street (1868-1871)
Subsequently, Syracuse China Co. (1966-1970+)

A305 

Printed mark of the "Arms of the State of New York", c.1874-1893.

- The marking "C. P. CO." was also used by the Chittenango Pottery Co., 1897-early 1900s (Madison County, NY) on White Ironstone china wares.

A306 

Printed mark, c.1893-1895.

For further reading, refer to *Barber's Marks*, p. 81; *Ketchum, Jr.* p. 219; and *Lehner*, pp. 454-458.

OPERATIVE

Operative Pottery

A307 

- Neither Operative Pottery nor mark identified. William Gates states this pottery was definitely not located in East Liverpool, Ohio. It possibly may have been located in Trenton, New Jersey.

- J.L. Murphy observed that the Operative mark bears a close similarity to Standard Pottery Co. of East Liverpool, Ohio, which also began as a cooperative. If the above marking is for Standard Pottery then it is an earlier mark than that for the Operative Pottery.

PADEN

Paden City Pottery Co.
Paden City Pottery, Paden City, West Virginia, USA, c.1910-1963

A308 **P. C. P. CO.**

Printed mark, c.1910-1963.

Debolt notes that the manufacture of whiteware dates from the 1920s.

PEORIA

Peoria Pottery Co.
Peoria, Illinois, USA, 1873-1902(04)
Formerly, American Pottery Co. (1859-1973)
Subsequently, The Crown Potteries Co. (1902-1904)

A309 **P. P. CO.**
A310 **PEORIA POTTERY**

Printed marks, 1873-1904.

KAD NO. | **MARK**

Typical Marks Include:

A311
A312
A313

1880-1890 **1890-1904**

For further reading, refer to *Barber's Marks*, pp. 161-162; *Debolt*, p. 112; and *Lehner*, pp. 340-341.

PHOENIXVILLE

Phoenixville Pottery Co.
- and Various Ownerships,
Phoenixville, Pennsylvania, USA, 1867-1872
Subsequently, Schrieber & Betz (1872-1877)
History:

Phoenixville Pottery, Kaolin & Firebrick Co.	1867-1872
Schreiber & Betz	1872-1877
L. B. Beerbower & Henry B. Griffen	1877(79)
Griffen, Smith & Co.	1878
Griffen, Smith & Hill	1879-1882
Griffen, Smith & Co.	1888-1889
Griffen, Love & Co.	1890
Griffen China Co.	1891
Works Closed	1892
Chester Pottery	1894-1897
Penn China Co.	1899-1902
Tuxedo Pottery Co.	1902

A314 **PHOENIX POTTERY** Printed mark, 1867-1902.

- An elaborate printed or impressed coded system was devised to identify the Phoenix Pottery. See *Gates*, p. 114 and *Lehner*, p. 346.

A315 **B. & G.*** Impressed initial mark found on Majolica, 1877-(79)
A316 **G. S. H.** Printed initial mark, c.1879-1882.

*The initials "B. & G." were also used by Beerbower & Griffen at their Phoenixville Pottery (1877-1879).

For further reading, refer to *Barber's Marks,* pp. 28-31; and *Karmason,* pp. 141-142, 145-161.

PIONEER

Pioneer Pottery (Works) Co.
Wellsville, Ohio, USA, 1884-1891
History:

Morley & Co.* (Morley, Clark & Michaels)	1879-1884
- Morley (& Son) moves on to acquire Lincoln	
Pioneer Pottery Works (Clark & Michaels)	1884-1891
- Co. in receivership	1891-1895
Pioneer Pottery	1896-1900
- Barber notes name as Wellsville Pioneer Pottery Co. See *Barber's Marks*, p. 128	
Wellsville China Co. acquires pottery	1902-1959(+)

KAD NO.	MARK	
A317	**P. P. CO.**	Printed mark of various designs, 1884-c.1891. - The mark "P. P. CO.", as noted by *Barber*, p. 128, may have continued through to 1904.
A318	**PIONEER POTTERY WORKS**	The full name "PIONEER POTTERY WORKS" may occur with "IRONSTONE CHINA" printed above mark, 1884-1891.

Typical Marks, 1884-1891, Include:

A319
A320
A321

A322 **W. P. P. CO.** Printed mark of various designs, 1896-c.1900.

A323

(Noted on Tea Leaf)

- For various Morley partnerships refer to Morley (& Son) or (& Sons) & Co.

For further reading, refer to *Gates*, pp. 198-202; and *Tea Leaf Readings*, Vol. 12, No. 5, Dec. 1992, p. 11.

POTTERS

The Potters Co-Operative (& Co.)
Dresden Pottery Works, East Liverpool, Ohio, USA, 1882-1925
Formerly, The Dresden Pottery Works of Brunt, Bloor, Martin & Co. (1875-1882)
Subsequently, The Dresden Pottery Co. (1925-1927)

KAD NO.	MARK	
A324	**P. C.**	Printed English Royal Coat of Arms with monogram initials, c.1882-1895.
A115	**T. P. C. CO.**	- See Dresden Pottery.

Typical Marks, c.1882-1895, Include:

A326
A327
A328

A329 Printed mark as above (c.1882-1895). Additional markings "CHINA", "SEMI PORCELAIN" and "WHITE GRANITE" noted, see *Gates*, p. 217.

A42

Printed mark "DRESDEN WHITE-GRANITE" continued on from Brunt, Bloor, Martin & Co., c.1882-1895.

KAD NO.	MARK	
A330	**T. P. C. CO.** **E. L. O.**	Printed initial mark, c.1882-1895.

Tea Leaf Markings, c.1882-1895, Include:

A331
A332

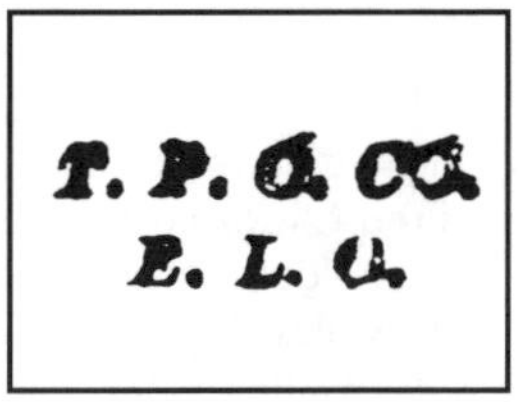

Tea Leaf

A328
A333

Tea Plum

For further reading, refer to *Gates*, pp. 18-19, 211-219.

PROSPECT

Prospect Hill Pottery
Trenton, New Jersey, USA, 1879-1894
Formerly, I. Davis (1872-1879)
Subsequently, Cook Pottery Co. (1894-1959)

KAD NO.	MARK	
A334	**I. DAVIS**	Printed mark, 1872-1879. (Referred to as the Isaac Davis Period/Trenton Pottery Works)
A335	**D - D**	Printed marks, 1879-1894.
A336	**D & D CHINA**	(Referred to as the Dale & Davis Period/Prospect Hill Pottery), 1879-1894.

Typical Marks Include:

A337
A338
A339

1872-1879

1872-1879

1879-1894

For further reading, refer to *Barber's Marks*, p. 61.

RED CLIFF

KAD NO. | **MARK**

Red Cliff Co. (Decorators)
Chicago, Illinois, USA, c.1957-1977
- Refer to Hall China Co. and Walker China Co.

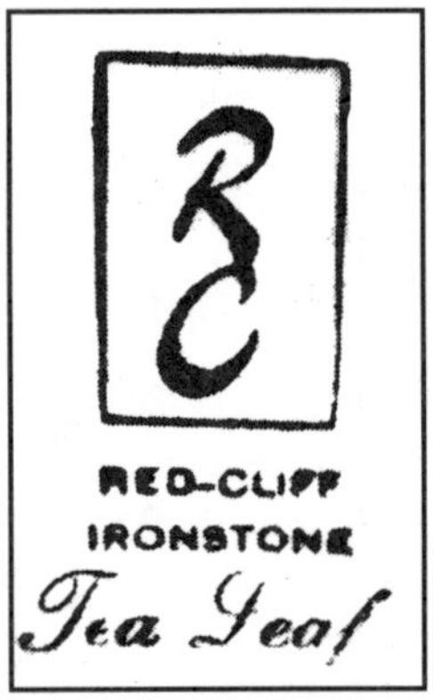

A340
A341

Printed marks noting "TEA LEAF", c.1950s-1960s.
-Fred Clifford of the Red Cliff Co. had decorated "Tea Leaf" reproductions made from older molds at Hall China Co. from the 1950s until 1960. English patterns of Shaw and Wedgwood, et.al. were reproduced and marked "RED-CLIFF" or "R. C." - Walker China Co. reproduced blank, flatware "plates" for the Red Cliff Co., while Hall reproduced the holloware blanks.

A342 **RC RED-CLIFF IRONSTONE**

Printed mark, see KAD No. A340 without "Tea Leaf" marking noted on White Ironstone, c.1950s-1960.

For further reading, refer to *Heaivilin*, pp. 175-181, 205; *Stoltzfus/Snyder*, pp. 74, 112-113;*Tea Leaf Readings*, Vol. 14, No. 4, Sept. 1994, pp. 25-26; and *White Ironstone Notes*, Vol. 2, No. 3, Winter 1995, p. 3 and Vol. 3, No. 3, Winter 1997 (Dec. 1996), p. 9 for an article titled "Red-Cliff Reproduction Ironstone.

SAXON

Saxon China Co.
Sebring, Ohio, USA, c.1911-1916
Acquired by O. H. Sebring, Sebring, Ohio (1916-1929)

A343 **SAXON CHINA**

Printed mark, c.1925-1929.

A344 **S. C. CO.**

Printed initial mark, c.1925-1929.

- *Debolt*, p. 127, remarks about the close relationship between the Saxon China Co. and The French China Co.
- *Gates*, p. 12 and 229 notes that from 1916-1929, the Saxon China Co. operated under the Sebring Manufacturing Co., a holding company. (Also see Sebring Pottery (Works) Co.). In 1929 it joined the American China Corp. (1929-1931) and was subsequently purchased by W. V. Oliver in 1935 and renamed the French Saxon China Co. (1935-1964).

For further reading, refer to *Gates*, p. 229 and *Lehner*, p. 407.

SAYERS

Don & Ruth Sayers
Morton, Illinois, USA, 1982 -
(Retailers)

A345 **R. S.**

Printed mark, 1982 -

- Retailers of a line of Tea Leaf, with backstamp reading "Copper Luster".
The color of the backstamp varies from year to year for purposes of identification.

For further reading, refer to *Tea Leaf Readings*, Vol. 14, No. 4, Sept. 1994, pp. 26-27.

SCOTT

KAD NO.	MARK	
		George Scott (& Sons) Pottery **Front Street, Cincinnati, Ohio, USA, 1853(54)-1900** **Subsequently, Sarah A. White (1901-1902)**
A346	**G. S.**	Printed initial mark, 1853(54)-1889.
A347	**GEORGE SCOTT**	"& SONS" added, 1889-1900
A348	**SCOTT**	
A349	**SCOTT & SONS**	

Tea Leaf Markings Include:

A350
A351

Tea Leaf Motif

- In *English Staffordshire China*. China Classics. Vol. VI. Century House. 1959, p. 70, Serry Wood includes an interesting history on Scott.

SEBRING

SEBRING POTTERY CO. — CHRONOLOGY OF HOLDINGS

DATE	POTTERY	LOCATION
1887-1902	American Pottery Co. (Sebring Pottery Works)	E. Liverpool, Ohio
	- Former Agner & Gaston Pottery Acquired	
	- Partners bought out	
	- 1902-1940 Moves to American Pottery Co.	
	- 1887-1940 Sebring Pottery Co.	Various Locations
	- 1902-1940 American Pottery Co. moved to	Sebring, Ohio
	- 1940-1948 Absorbed by Limoges China Co.	
1893-1912	East Palestine Pottery (Leased)	E. Palestine, Ohio
1896-1912	Ohio China Co. (Acquired)	E. Palestine, Ohio
1898-1900	French China Co.	E. Liverpool, Ohio
	- 1900-1929 Pottery moved to	Sebring, Ohio
	- 1916-1929 Sebring Manufacturing Corp. (a holding co.) is formed to include The Strong Manufacturing Co. and Saxon China Co.	
	- 1929-1931 Holding co. joins American Chinaware Corp.	
1899-1908	Oliver China Co. (Porcelain manufacturing co.)	Sebring, Ohio
	- 1908-1929 E. H. Sebring acquires pottery	
	- 1934 Subsequently acquired by the Royal China Co.	
1900-1949	(Sterling China Co.)/The Limoges China Co.	Sebring, Ohio
	- 1900 Sterling name gives way to Limoges	
	- 1940-1948 Sebring absorbed by Limoges	
	- 1949-1955 Subsequently, The American Limoges China Co.	
1900-1929	Saxon China Co.	Sebring, Ohio
	- 1929-1931 Subsequently, The American Chinaware Corp.	
	- 1935-1964 Finally, The French Saxon China Co.	
1908-1929	(E. H.) Sebring China Co.	Sebring, Ohio
	- 1899-1908 Formerly, Oliver China Co.	
	- 1929-1931 American Chinaware Corp.	
	- 1943 The Royal China Co.	
	ALSO SEE:	
1920-1927	Crescent China Co.	Alliance, Ohio
1927-1932	Leigh Potters Inc.	Alliance, Ohio

For further reading, refer to *Debolt*, pp. 37, 172-173.

SEBRING

KAD NO. | **MARK**

Sebring Pottery Co. (American Pottery Works)
- East Liverpool (c.1887-1902)
- Sebring, (c.1902-1940)
Ohio, USA, 1887-1940
Subsequently, Limoges China Co. (c.1940-1948)

A352

Printed English Royal Coat of Arms, marked "Sebring Bros. & Co.", c.1887-1902.

A353

As above with marking "ROYAL IRONSTONE/CHINA", c.1887-1902.

A354

Printed mark, "KOKUS STONE CHINA/WARRANTED", c.1895-1902.

A355

Tea Leaf Motif

The above marks have been noted on Tea Leaf with Copper Lustre, c.1887-1902.

A356

Printed mark in script noted on Flow Blue, c.1895-1902.

For further reading, refer to *Debolt,* Mark Nos. 12 & 189: *Gates*, pp. 231-233; *Heaivilin*, pp. 200-201; *Lehner*, p. 23; and *T.L.C.I.*, 1992, "American Tea Leaf Manufacturers, Potters and Decorators", pp. 38-39.

SEBRING

E. H. Sebring China Co.
Sebring, Ohio, USA, 1908-1929
Formerly, Oliver China Co. (1899-1908)
Subsequently, American China

A357 **E. H. S. C. CO.**
WINONA

Printed initial mark with pattern name often included, 1908-1929.

For further reading, refer to *Gates*, p. 240.

SHENANGO

KAD NO. **MARK**

Shenango China (Pottery) Co.
New Castle, Pennsylvania, USA, 1901(05)-1979
Formerly, New Castle Pottery Co. (1901-c.1905)
Subsequently, The Anchor Hocking Corp. (1979-)

A358 **SHENANGO** Printed marks, "CHINA CO.", 1901-C.1905, "POTTERY & CO." c.1905+, "SHENANGO", c. 1919.

Typical Marks Include:

A359
A360
A361

c.1901-1905

c.1905+

c.1915-c.1940

For further reading, refer to *Lehner*, p. 422.

STEPHENS

Stephens, Tams & Co.
Trenton, New Jersey, USA, 1861(62)-1868
Subsequently, The Greenwood Pottery Co., (c.1868-1930s)

A362 **G. P. CO.** Little is known about Stephens, Tams & Co. However, *Lehner*, p. 180, notes a New Jersey State of Arms Seal marked with the initial "G. P. CO."
- Also see Greenwood Pottery Co. and also see Tams et. al. KAD B2267-2272.

STERLING

STERLING CHINA CO.,
See: LIMOGES CHINA CO.

STEUBENVILLE

Steubenville Pottery Co.
Steubenville, Ohio, USA, 1879-1959
Acquired by Canonsburg Pottery Co. in 1959 who continued name until 1970s.

A363 

Printed mark, c.1885-c.1890s.

A364 

Printed mark, c.1885-1895.

- Company also issued advertising pieces for various clients. One example, in Flow Blue, includes the following text: "When You Eat Think Of Us When You Buy Come To Us" The company is H. S. Mill General Merchandise, Springtown, PA

KAD NO.	MARK	
A365 A366	  Pomegranate (Copper)	Printed Royal Coat of Arms noted on Tea Leaf pattern with initial mark "S. P. CO.", 1885-1895.
A367	**S. C.**	Printed initial mark "S. C.", 1890s+.
A368 A369	  Tea Leaf (Gold 2-Leaf)	Printed Royal Coat of Arms noted on Tea Leaf pattern with initial mark "S. C.", 1890s+.

For further reading, refer to *Barber's Marks*, pp. 129-130; *Debolt*, pp. 136-138; and *Lehner*, pp. 446-447.

TAYLOR

Taylor, Smith & Taylor Co. (Inc.)
Chester, West Virginia, USA, c.1901-1972
Formerly, Taylor & Smith (c.1899-1901)
Subsequently, Anchor Hocking Glass Corp. (c.1972-1981)

KAD NO.	MARK	
A370	**T. S. T.**	Printed marks, c.1901-1972. "INC" added from 1907.
A371	**TAYLOR/SMITH & TAYLOR**	Printed mark, c.1901-1972.

Typical Marks Include:

A372
A373
A374

c.1901-c.1915

c.1908-c.1915+

- Various shapes, pattern names and coding systems for dating are noted by *Debolt*, pp. 140-144. Examples of marked noted with coding date from c.1915+.

For further reading, refer to *Gates*, pp. 267-286.

TEMPEST

Tempest, Brockmann & Co.
Cincinnati, Ohio, USA, 1862-1881
Subsequent History:
Tempest, Brockmann Pottery Co.* 1881-1887(88)
Brockmann Pottery Co. 1887(88)-1912

KAD NO.	MARK	
A375	**T. B. & CO.**	Printed mark, 1862-1881.
A376		Printed mark, 1862-1881, noted in *Tea Leaf Readings*, Vol. 16, Issue No. 4, Sept. 1996, p.12 **Barber's Marks*, p. 118, notes the name of the company as Tempest, Brockmann & Sampson Pottery Co."

THOMPSON

C. C. Thompson & Co. (Pottery Co.)
East Liverpool, Ohio, USA, c.1868-1938
History:

Thompson & Herbert	c.1868-1870
C. C. Thompson & Company	c.1870-1889
C. C. Thompson Pottery Company	c.1889-1938

KAD NO.	MARK	
A377		Printed mark, c.1870-1889. -Although this mark is illustrated in *Ramsay*, it is questioned by Lehner. The mark appears to be a Phoenix as opposed to a Griffen. Refer to *Lehner*, pp. 470-471. - Also refer to Vodrey & Brothers (Pottery)(Co.) for a similar mark. See KAD No. A414.
A378		Printed initial mark, c.1889-1910.
A379	**<u>MELROSE</u>** **T**	Printed mark on Ironstone tableware, c.1894, with the addition of "SEMI-VITREOUS", c.1920.
A380		Printed Royal Coat of Arms mark, with or without "ELO". Also may be marked "EUREKA", c.1915. For further reading, refer to Debolt, pp. 145-147; *Gates*, pp. 288-294; and *Heaivilin*, pp. 201-203.

TRENLE

Trenle (Blake) China Co.
- East Liverpool, Ohio (1909-1937)
- Ravenswood, West Virginia, USA (1937-1966)
1909-1966
From 1942-1966 the name changed to Trenle, Blake China Co.
Formerly, East End China Co.* (1908-1909)

KAD NO.	MARK	
A381	**TRENLE**	Printed name mark, 1909-1942.
A382	**E. E. C. CO.***	Printed "East End" name mark, 1909-1966.
A383	**TRENLE/BLAKE**	Former printed mark of East End (Pottery) China Co., continued by Trenle, Blake China Co., 1942-1966.

Typical Marks Include:

A384
A385
A386
A387

1908-1909
***Marks of East End Pottery continued - see East End Pottery (China) Co.**

1909-1917
Trenle Mark

Mark noted on Flow Blue

TRENTON

Trenton China Co.
Trenton, New Jersey, USA, 1892-1950s

A388 **TRENTON CHINA CO. TRENTON, N.J.** — Impressed mark, 1859-1891.

For further reading, refer to *Debolt,* p. 148; and *Lehner*, p. 473.

TRENTON

Trenton Potteries Co.
Trenton, New Jersey, USA, 1892-c.1950
A partnership formed between six pottery companies in 1892: The Crescent, Delaware, Empire, Enterprise, Equitable and the Ideal (who joined in 1897). Later, in 1922, they were joined by the Mutual Pottery. The Crescent and Ideal Potteries continued their own marks.

A389	**THE TRENTON POTTERIES CO.**	Printed mark, 1892-c.1950s.
A390	**T. P. CO. CHINA**	Printed mark (Crescent Pottery), 1892-c.1920s. - Also see Trenton Potteries Co.
A391	**T/IDEAL P. CO.**	Printed mark (Ideal Pottery), 1897-c.1904.

A392 Printed mark, c.1915-1940s.

For further reading, refer to *Barber's Marks*, p. 64-65; *Gates*, p. 191; and *Lehner*, pp. 473-474 for a detailed history.

TRENTON

KAD NO. **MARK**

Trenton Pottery (1852-1865) (Co.)(Works)
Trenton, New Jersey, USA
- "& Co." (1865-1870),
- Pottery Works (1870-1894(1903), 1852-1894(1903)

History:

	MARKING	POTTERY	COMPANY	DATE
	-	Trenton Pottery	Taylor & Speeler	1852-1856
	-	Trenton Pottery	Taylor, Speeler & Bloor	1856-1859
	-	Trenton Pottery	Speeler & Taylor	1859-1865
A393	T. P. CO.	Trenton Pottery Co.	Taylor & Co.	1865-1870
A394	T. P. W.	Trenton Pottery Works	Taylor, Goodwin & Co.	1870-1872
A334	I. DAVIS*	Trenton Pottery Works	Isaac Davis	1872-1879

*Also see listing for Prospect Hill Pottery

The periods from 1879-c.1902 for this manufactory is confusing in that Lehner and Debolt show differing dates and ownership. I have listed the dates and ownerships from both these writers. (Refer to *Lehner*, p. 474 and *Debolt*, pp. 148-150.)

LEHNER

A144	**F. & T. CO.***	**Trenton Pottery Works**	**Fell & Thropp & Co.** *Also see listing for Fell & Thropp & Co.	**1879-c.1901**
	-	Trenton Pottery Works	Thropp & Brewer	1901-(02)
	-	Trenton Pottery Works	Hart Brewer Pottery Co.	1902(03)?

DEBOLT

A144	**F. & T. CO.***	**Trenton Pottery Works**	**Fell & Thropp & Co.** *Also see listing for Fell & Thropp & Co.	**1879-1890**
	-	Trenton Pottery Works	Fell & Brewer	1890-1893
	-	Trenton Pottery Works	Robert Gruessner	1894 (?)

Typical Marks, 1865-c.1900, Include:

A393A
A394A
A334A
A145A

c.1865-1870

c.1870-1872

c.1872-1879*

c.1879-1901**

*See Prospect Hill Pottery
**See Fell & Thropp, Co.
For further reading, refer to *Barber*, p. 175; and *Barber's Marks*, p. 66.

UNION

Union Pottery Co.
Trenton, New Jersey, USA, 1869-1883
Joined with the New Jersey Pottery Co. from 1883-1889.

A395 **U. P. CO.**

Printed Royal Coat of Arms mark with monogrammed initials "U. P. CO."*, 1870s. Attributed to the Union Pottery Co., Trenton, New Jersey. Additional marking "WARRANTED" and "IRONSTONE CHINA" noted.

KAD NO. | **MARK**

A396

Impressed mark, c.1880.

*The Royal Coat of Arms mark in question, as noted, is pictured in *Debolt*, p. 297, and attributed to the Union Potteries of East Liverpool, Ohio and Pittsburgh, Ohio, (c.1894-1905).

For further reading, refer to *Debolt*, pp. 152-153, 192; and *Gates*, pp. 297-298.

UNITED STATES

United States Pottery
Bennington, Vermont, USA, c.1847-1858

A397

Impressed mark noted on porcelain or semi-porcelain, c.1847-1858.
- Also refer to Norton Pottery Co., Bennington, Vermont.

For further reading, refer to *Art & Antiques Weekly*, Dec. 12, 1997, pp. 82-83, Newton, CT; Richard Carter Barret. *Bennington Pottery & Porcelain*. New York: Bonanza Books, 1958; *Ketchum, Jr.*, p. 219; and *Lehner,* pp. 322-323 for an early history of the pottery as well as p. 481.

UNITED STATES

(The) United States Pottery Co.
Wellsville, Ohio, USA, 1898-1932
History:

United States Pottery Co.	1898-1900
(joins) East Liverpool Potteries Co.*	1901-c.1907
United States Pottery Co.	c.1907-1932

A398

Printed shield marked "WELLSVILLE. O./U.S.A.", c.1899-1901 and 1907-c.1920.

A399

Tea Leaf Motif found with mark "WELLSVILLE, O./U.S.A.", 1899-1901.

A400 — **EAST LIVERPOOL O** — Printed mark with "EAST LIVERPOOL O", 1901-1907.

A401 — **EAST LIVERPOOL POTTERIES CO.** — Printed mark (without shield), c.1907-c.1920.

A402 — **E. L. P. CO.** — Printed initial mark noted on semi-vitreous ware, 1907-1932.
- The added marking "MADE IN U.S.A./CHINA" dates from 1925-1932.
* Also see comments under East Liverpool Potteries Companies.

For further reading, refer to *Gates*, p. 299.

VANCE

KAD NO.	MARK	
		Vance Faience (Pottery) Co. Tittonsville, Ohio, USA, 1902-1903 Subsequently, Wheeling Potteries Co. (1903-1909)
A403	**F. M. & CO.**	"F. M. & CO." may be noted in printed form, in script, or as
A404		
A405	VANCE/ F./CO.	"VANCE/F./CO.", 1902-1903. For further reading, refer to *Barber's Marks*, p. 152; *Debolt*, p. 162, and *Lehner*, p. 32 for "Avon Faience Pottery Co."

VODREY

Vodrey & Brothers (Pottery)(Co.)
Palissey Works and other Potteries,
East Liverpool, Ohio, USA, c.1858-1928

History:

Jabez Vodrey & William Woodward	—	c.1847-1848
Woodward, Blakeley & Co.	Phoenix Pottery	c.1849-1857
Vodrey & Bros. Pottery Co.	Phoenix Pottery	c.1858-1896
Vodrey Pottery Co.	Phoenix Pottery	c.1896-1928

A406
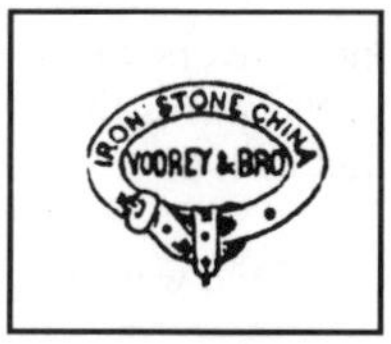

Printed mark, c.1876-1896.

A407
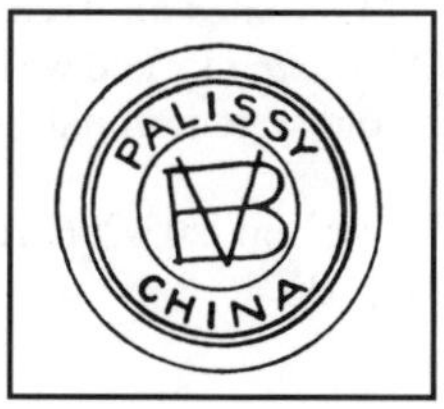

Printed or stamped mark of various styles. Pattern name may be included, c.1876-1896.

A408 **V. & B.** Printed mark with Royal Coat of Arms and monogrammed initials "V. & B.", c.1876-1896.

Typical White Ironstone & Tea Leaf Marks Include:

A409
A410
A411
A412

c.1876-1896

KAD NO.	MARK	
A413	**VODREY POTTERY CO.**	Printed name mark with "& Co.", 1896-1928.
A414		Printed mark noted by Wetherbee in *White Ironstone A Collector's Guide*, p. 181, c.1896-1928. - See C. C. Thompson & Co., KAD No. A377, for a similar Phoenix mark.

For further reading, refer to *Debolt*, pp. 155-156; *Gates*, pp. 300-304; *Heaivilin*, pp. 203-204; and *Lehner*, p. 493.

WALKER

Walker China Co. (a Division of Alcoa Corp.)
Bedford, Ohio, USA, 1943-c.1976(80)
Formerly, Bailey-Walker China Co., (c.1923-1943)
Subsequently, The Jeannete Corp (1976-c.1980)

KAD NO.	MARK	
A415		Printed name mark, c.1943.
A416	**WALKER CHINA PATENTED BEDFORD OHIO 181**	Printed mark noted on Tea Leaf, c. 1970s.

Heaivilin notes, via correspondence and phone conversations, that Tea Leaf was manufactured (by order) in the 1970s. Further, flat wares that were manufactured in the Red Cliff Line, c.1950s, were discontinued in 1960.

- In *Tea Leaf Readings*, Julia Rich remarks thatTea Leaf was also produced from the late 1920s to c.1980.
- The dating system provided by *Gates*, p. 224, creates an irreconcilable problem when applied to the back mark on p. 205 of *Heaivilin* marked with the numbers 181 and 22). The question posed is, when did the old system of dating end?

For further reading, refer to *Gates*, pp. 157, 224; , pp. 205-206; *Lehner*, p. 476; and *Tea Leaf Readings*, Vol. 14, No. 4, Sept. 1994, p. 26.

WALLACE

Wallace & Chetwynd
"Colonial" Pottery,
River Road, East Liverpool, Ohio, 1882-1901

History:

Harker Pottery Co. "Wedgwood Pottery"	1877-1881
Wallace & Chetwynd (renamed)"Colonial Pottery"	1882-1901
(Six *Autonomous* Potteries merge to form)	
East Liverpool Potteries Co.	1901-1903
(The) Colonial Co. "Colonial" Pottery	1903-1929

KAD NO.	MARK	
A417	**WALLACE & CHETWYND**	Printed name mark, 1882-1901.
A418		Printed initial mark "W. & C." noted on White Ironstone, 1882-1901.
A419	**W. & C. P. CO.**	Printed initial mark, c.1882-1901.

- "La Belle" Toilet Ware [mark] noted and illustrated by *Gates*, p. 306.
Also refer to Wheeling Potteries Co., (1893-1903) "La Belle China".

- See Harker Potteries, (The) East Liverpool Potteries Co. and (The) Colonial Co.

For further reading, refer to *Gates*, pp. 35, 44, 79-94, and 306-310 for additional pottery history; and *White Ironstone Notes*, Vol. 3, No. 2, Fall 1996, p. 9.

WARWICK

Warwick China (Co.)
Wheeling, West Virginia, USA, 1884-1951

KAD NO.	MARK	
A420	**WARWICK CHINA CO.**	Printed mark of varying designs, 1884-1951. "& CO." from 1887. Flow Blue noted with this marking dates from c.1900.
A421	**WARWICK CHINA**	Printed mark, c.1898-c.1910. - See *Snyder*, Vol. 2, pp. 70-71.

Typical Marks Include:

A422
A423
A424

c.1892-1900

1900-c.1915 (Flow Blue)

1920s

KAD NO.	MARK	
A425	**"TRADE MARK"**	Printed mark (Helmet) with "TRADE MARK" added below, c.1890s.
A426	**WARWICK WHEELING**	Printed name mark, c.1918.
A427	**W. C. CO.**	Typical Helmet mark with the initials "W. C. CO." noted in John Ramsay's *American Potters & Potteries*, New York, Tudor Publishing Co., 1947, p. 283.

For further reading, refer to *Antique Week*, March 9, 1998. pp. 1, 30 for an article on Warwick China by Susan & Jim Harran.

WELLSVILLE

KAD NO. | **MARK**

Wellsville China Company
Wellsville, Ohio, c.1902-1959(69)
Formerly, Pioneer Pottery Co. (c.1884-1900)
Subsequently owned by Sterling China Co. (c.1959-1969)

A428

Printed mark, "SEMI PORCELAIN", 1902-1930.
- See *Tea Leaf Readings*, Vol. 15, No. 1, Jan. 1995, p. 3.

For further reading, refer to *Gates*, pp. 309-315; and *Lehner*, p. 510.

WHEELING

Wheeling Pottery Co.
Wheeling, West Virginia, USA 1879-1903(10)

History:

Wheeling Pottery Co.	Wheeling, WV	1879-1903
LaBelle Pottery Co.	Wheeling, WV	1887-1893
Vance Faience Co. (Avon Works)	Tiltonsville, Ohio	1903-1908(10)
Riverside Pottery	Tiltonsville, Ohio	1903-1908(10)
Wheeling Sanitary Manufacturing Co.	Wheeling, WV	1910-1930s
Wheeling Potteries Co.	Wheeling, WV	1903-1908(10)
Wheeling Tile Co.	Wheeling, WV	1913-1933(34)

A429 **W. P. C. (CO.)**
Printed initial mark, 1880-1886.

A430 **WHEELING STONE CHINA POTTERY CO.**
Printed mark which may be found on White Ironstone, 1880-1886.

A431
A432

Printed Royal Coat of Arms mark, 1886-1896 found on Tea Leaf/Copper Lustre Ware. Circular marking "WHITE GRANITE" and "MADE IN AMERICA" date from 1896-c.1903.

A433 **ADAMANTINE CHINA**
Printed mark from "LaBelle" Works, 1887-1893.

A434

Printed mark "LA BELLE CHINA" appears after pottery's expansion program, 1893-c.1903.

A435
A436

- The term "LA BELLE" was used by the American potters Wallace & Chetwynd but the initials "WP" and the word "CHINA" was omitted. (See *Gates*, p. 306). Further, there are variations noted in the mark, whereby the initial "S" may appear to the left of the device, 1893-1903. Marks may have continued on to c.1904-1910.

A437 **AVON W. PTS. CO.**
Printed marks continued after the purchase by Wheeling Potteries Co., c.1904-1910.

KAD NO.	MARK	
A438	**THE WHEELING POTTERY CO.**	Printed mark, c.1904-1910.
A439	**XX CENTURY SEMI PORCELAIN**	Printed mark, c.1904-1910. Mark may be transitional, possibly appearing earlier.
A440	**ROYAL LA BELLE WHEELING POTTERIES CO.**	Printed mark, c.1904-1910.
A441		Printed mark, c. 1903(04), when name of the company changed. Probably used until company closed, 1909-1910. *Debolt*, p. 161, notes that "BONITA" may refer to the name of a shape."*

Typical Marks for Wheeling Pottery, 1879-1910, Include:

A442
A443
A444
A445

c.1880-1886

c.1880-1886

c.1893-1903

c.1893-1910

- LaBelle Pottery Co. marks have been noted by Donna V. Freter in nine different colors, with each color signifying the type of piece. Ms. Freter also cites a few pieces that include backmarks and artists' names; one reads Cecelia, Nov. 27, 192 and another reads Laura Beisuyeinger, March 16, 1898. She further notes that it was not unusual for designers to go back and forth between LaBelle and Warwick, as is evidenced by identical pieces.

For further reading, refer to *Barber*, p. 180; *Heaivilin*, pp. 206-208; and *Snyder*, Vol. 2, pp. 71-72.
*In an article for the *Antique Trader*, Sept. 24, 1997, pp. 78-80, titled "A Look at LaBelle and Wheeling Potteries", Dick Southern notes additional name shapes.
**In the same article, Dick Southern states that "Wheeling Potteries ... design[d] a collection of large vases and name[d] each one after a major city. Such were those named for New York, Buffalo, Cleveland and Chicago."

- Refer to the occasional paper written by Dick Southern titled *Victorian Flow Blue - A Look at LaBelle by Wheeling Potteries, Wheeling, West Virginia"* presented on July 22, 1995, at the Flow Blue International Collectors Club Convention in Kansas City, KS (40 plates, 10 color pages).
Also refer to the September 1906 Sales Catalog *"LaBelle/The Best Made in America"*, The Wheeling Potteries Co., Wheeling, West Virginia (60 pages).

FLOW BLUE

CAT.	PATTERN
-	"Bonita" Shape* ("Blue Diamond")
M	Chicago "Vases"**
M	"Dewey Jardiniere"
M	"Dolphin" Shape ("Blue Diamond")
M	Fish
G	"La Belle Lovely Ladies"
F	"Maroon Rose"
F	"Oriental"
F	"Rainbow"
F	"Surprise"
F	"Surprise & Evergreen"
F	"Surprise & Rainbow"
M	"Wild Turkeys": "The Governor's Set"
M	"Wild Turkeys": "His Majesty's Set"

WHEELOCK

KAD NO. **MARK**

C. E. Wheelock and Co. (Importers)
South Bend, Indiana & Peoria, Illinois, USA, 1888-1971
"Commemorative Wares" imported from English Manufacturers such as Adams & Beardmore.

These wares are considered Blue and White "Commemorative Wares" and not "Flow Blue". (For like wares also refer to Rowland & Marsellus.)

For further reading, refer to Arene Burgess' two books, *Souvenir Plates, A Collectors Guide*. Bethalto, IL, Private Publication, 1978; and *A Collector's Guide to Souvenir Plates.* Atglen, PA. Schiffer Publishing, Ltd., 1996.

WICK

Wick China Co. (The)
Wicksboro (Kittanning), Pennsylvania, USA, 1889-c.1905
Formerly, The Wick Chinaware Co., (c.1889)
Subsequently, The Pennsylvania China (Pottery) Co. (c.1905-1913)

A446 

Printed initial mark, "T. W. C. CO." Pattern name often included, 1889-1905.

A447 

Printed mark of the Royal Coat of Arms of Pennsylvania, c. 1900.

Typical Tea Leaf Marks Include:

A448
A449

c.1889-1905

c.1900

For further reading, refer to *Heaivilin*, pp. 208-209.

WILLETS

Willets Manufacturing Co.
Trenton, New Jersey, USA, 1879-c.1909
Formerly, William Young & Sons, "Excelsior Pottery Works", (1857-1879)

A450 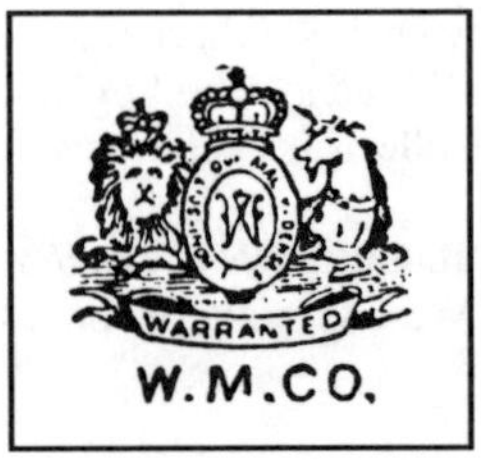

Printed Royal Coat of Arms mark with monogram "W", 1879-c.1884.

KAD NO. **MARK**

A451

Printed mark with pattern name often included, 1880s-1909.

A452

Printed or impressed mark with elaborate monogrammed initials, "W. M. & CO." 1884-c.1880.

A453

Printed snake mark with or without "BELLEEK" and/or "WILLETS", 1890s.

For further reading, refer to *Barber's Marks*, p. 45; *Debolt*, p. 163; and *Lehner*, p. 522.

WYLLIE

John Wyllie & Son,
Great Western Pottery Works
East Liverpool, Ohio, USA, 1874-c.1893
Formerly, The Great Western Pottery (1867-1874)
Subsequently, The Union Co-Operative Pottery Company (1894-1904)

A454

Printed English Royal Coat of Arms mark, c.1875-c.1883.

A455

Printed "American Eagle" mark, c.1875-c.1883.

A456

Printed American and English Coat of Arms mark (Double Shield), c.1880-1883.*
*See International Pottery Co., Mercer Pottery Co. and New York City Pottery for comments on the double shield mark.

A457 **G. W. P. CO.**

Same as above but with initials "G. W. P. CO." above trademark. (Mark appears after the death of John Wyllie, Sr. In 1882), c.1883-1888(93).

For further reading, refer to *Debolt*, p. 164; *Gates*, pp. 318-319; and *Lehner*, p. 479.

WYLLIE

KAD NO.	MARK	
		H. R. Wyllie China Co. **Huntington, West Virginia, USA, c.1910-c.1929**
A458	**H. R. WYLLIE CHINA**	Printed mark, c.1910-c.1929. - Mark is noted on Flow Blue. See *Debolt,* p. 165
A459		Printed name mark, c.1915-c.1920.

POTTERS & PATTERNS IN FLOW BLUE-IDENTIFIED

POTTERY	LOCATION	CATEGORY	PATTERN
American China Co.	Toronto, OH	M/F	"Grape Vine"
Burroughs & Mountford (& Co.)	Trenton, NJ	F	Grape Vine
Burroughs & Mountford (& Co.)		A	Honiton
Burroughs & Mountford (& Co.)		F	Wild Rose
Chesapeake Pottery (Co.)	Baltimore, MD	F	Pansy
Colonial (Sterling) Company (The)	East Liverpool, OH	M/A	"Sterling"
Colonial (Sterling) Company (The)		O	Togo
Cook (& Mellor) Pottery Co.	Trenton, NJ	M	Vernon
Crescent Pottery Co.	Trenton, NJ	A	Utopia
French China Co. (The)	Sebring, OH	M	Game Birds
French China Co. (The)		M	"La Francaise"
French China Co. (The)		H	"Pilgrims Landing"
French China Co. (The)		H	"Pilgrims Waving From Shore"
French China Co. (The)		H	U.S.S. Brooklyn
French China Co. (The)		H	U.S.S. Maine
French China Co. (The)		H	U.S.S. New York
French China Co. (The)		M	Winona
International (Lincoln) Pottery Co.	Trenton, NJ	M	"Balmoral"
International (Lincoln) Pottery Co.		M	"Cracked Ice"
International (Lincoln) Pottery Co.	(Burgess & Campbell)	M	Royal Blue
Knowles, Taylor, Knowles Co.	East Liverpool, OH	M	"Fernery"
Knowles, Taylor, Knowles Co.		M	"Snow Flake"
Knowles, Taylor, Knowles Co.		M	"Tiger"
Laughlin, Homer (China & Co.)	East Liverpool, OH	F	Angelus
Laughlin, Homer (China & Co.)		F	Colonial
Mayer (J&E) Potteries Co. Ltd.	Beaver Falls, PA	A	Argyle
Mayer (J&E) Potteries Co. Ltd.		S	Marine
Mayer (J&E) Potteries Co. Ltd.		-	Triumph
Mercer Pottery Co.	Trenton, NJ	F	"Carnations"
Mercer Pottery Co.		M/F	Hawthorne
Mercer Pottery Co.		F	Luzerne
Mercer Pottery Co.		M/F	Paisley
Pioneer (Wellsville) Pottery Co.	Wellsville, OH	M	"Red Raspberries"
Saxon China Co.	Sebring, OH	M	"Springtime"
Sebring, E. H. China Co.	Sebring, OH	F	"Floral Swag"
Sterling China Co. (Limoges China Co.)	Sebring, OH	M	"Calander II"
Sterling China Co. (Limoges China Co.)		M/F	"Panama Canal"
Taylor, Smith & Taylor Co. (Inc.)	Chester, WV	F	"Grapes"
Warwick China (Co.)	Wheeling, WV	F	Marble
Warwick China (Co.)		F	"Warwick"
Warwick China (Co.)		F	"Warwick Dogwood"
Warwick China (Co.)		F	"Warwick Pansy"
Wheeling Pottery Co.	Wheeling, WV	-	"Bonita" Shape (Blue Diamond)
Wheeling Pottery Co.		M	"Fish"
Wheeling Pottery Co.		F	"His Majesty"
Wheeling Pottery Co.		G	"LaBelle Lovely Ladies"
Wheeling Pottery Co.		F	"Maroon Rose"
Wheeling Pottery Co.		F	"Oriental"
Wheeling Pottery Co.		F	"Rainbow"
Wheeling Pottery Co.		F	"Surprise"
Wheeling Pottery Co.		F	"Surprise & Evergreen"
Wheeling Pottery Co.		F	"Surprise & Rainbow"
Wheeling Pottery Co.		M	"Wild Turkeys"

Many of the above patterns have been noted and illustrated in Gaston's two books,
Petra Williams' three volumes and Snyder's three volumes.
Also refer to *Debolt*, p. 240 "American Makers of Flow Blue Ware."

POTTERS of FLOW BLUE: NON- RECORDED PATTERNS

POTTERY	LOCATION
Buffalo Pottery Co.	Buffalo, NY
Carrollton Pottery Co.	Carrollton, OH
Chesapeake Pottery (Co.)	Baltimore, MD
Dresden Pottery (Works) Co.	East Liverpool, OH
Empire Pottery	Trenton, NJ
French-Saxon China Co.	Sebring, OH
Limoges China Co.	Sebring OH
Maddock (Thos.)(& Sons)(& Co.)	Trenton, NJ
McNicol Smith Company	Wellsville, OH
New England Pottery Co.	East Boston, MA
Ohio China Co.	East Palestine, OH
Oliver China Co.	Sebring, OH
Paden City Pottery Co.	Paden City, WV
Potters Cooperative (& Co.)(The)	East Liverpool, OH
Sebring, E.H. China Co.	Sebring OH
Steubenville Pottery Co.	Steubenville, OH
Trenle (Blake) China Co.	East Liverpool, OH
Wyllie, H.R. China Co.	Huntington, WV

POTTERS & PATTERNS IN TEA LEAF/COPPER LUSTRE

POTTERY	LOCATION	PATTERN
American Crockery Co.	Trenton, NJ	
Bahl Potteries Inc.	Carrollton, OH	
Brockmann Pottery Co.	Cincinnati, OH	"Vassar"
Brunt, William Jr. & Co.	East Liverpool, OH	
Brunt, William Son & Co.	East Liverpool, OH	
Buffalo Pottery Co.	Buffalo, NY	
Burford Bros. Pottery Co.	East Liverpool, OH	"Ideal"
Cartwright Bros. (Pottery Co.)	East Liverpool, OH	
Crescent Pottery Co.	Trenton, NJ	
Crown Pottery (& Potteries) Co.	Evansville, IN	
Cumbow China Decorating Co.	Abingdon, VA	
East End Pottery (China) Co.	East Liverpool, OH	
Fell & Thropp Co.	Trenton, NJ	
Ford China Co.	Ford City, PA	"Turin"
Glasgow Pottery Co.	Trenton, NJ	"Trilby"
Goodwin (Bros.) Pottery Co.	East Liverpool, OH	
Goodwin (Bros.) Pottery Co.	East Liverpool, OH	
Greenfield Village Pottery (Museum)	Dearborn, MI	
Hall China Co.	East Liverpool, OH	
Harker Potteries (Etruria Pottery)	East Liverpool, OH	
Illinois China Co. (The)	Lincoln, IL	
Knowles, Taylor, Knowles Co.	East Liverpool, OH	"Tacoma"
Laughlin, Homer China (& Co.)	East Liverpool, OH	
Mayer, (J. & E.) Potteries Co. (Ltd.)	Beaver Falls, PA	
McNicol, Burton & Co.	East Liverpool, OH	
McNicol, D. E. Pottery Co.	East Liverpool, OH	
Onandonga Pottery Co.	Syracuse, NY	
Potters Cooperative (&Co.) (The)	East Liverpool, OH	"Tea Plum"
Red Cliff Co. (Decorators)	Chicago, IL	"Gothic 1: Classic"
Red Cliff Co. (Decorators)	—	"Shaws Chinese Shape"
Red Cliff Co. (Decorators)	—	"Square Ridged IV"
Red Cliff Co. (Decorators)	—	"Wedgwood's Ribbed"
Sayers, Don & Ruth (Retailers)	Morton, IL	
Scott, George (& Sons) Pottery	Cincinnati, OH	
Sebring, E.H., China Co.	East Liverpool, OH	
Shenango China (Pottery) Co.	New Castle, PA	
Steubenville Pottery Co.	Steubenville, OH	
Tempest, Brockmann & Co.	Cincinnati, OH	
Thompson, C. C. & Co. (Pottery Co.)	East Liverpool, OH	
Trenton Potteries (Co.)(Works)	Trenton, NJ	
United States Pottery Co. (The)	Wellsville, OH	
Vodrey & Brothers (Pottery)(Co.)	East Liverpool, OH	
Walker China Co.	Bedford, OH	
Wellsville China Company	Wellsville, OH	
Wheeling Pottery Co.	Wheeling, WV	
Wick China Co. (The)	(Wickboro) Kittanning, PA	

For further reading, refer to *Debolt*, p. 241 "American Makers of Tea Leaf Lustre Ware."

POTTERS & PATTERNS IN WHITE IRONSTONE

POTTERY	LOCATION	PATTERN
American China Co.	Toronto, OH	
American Crockery Co.	Trenton, NJ	"Cable & Ring"
American Pottery Co.	Jersey City, NJ	
Anchor Pottery Co.	Trenton, NJ	
Beerbower & Griffin	Phoenixville, PA	
Beerbower, L. B. & Co.	Elizabeth, NJ	
Bennett, Edwin Pottery (Co.)	Baltimore, MD	
Brunt, William Co.	East Liverpool, OH	"Round Grape Leaf"
Burford Bros.	East Liverpool, OH	"Devotion"
Burroughs & Mountford (& Co.)	Trenton, NJ	
Cartwright Bros. (Pottery Co.)	East Liverpool, OH	
Chelsea China Co.	New Cumberland, WV	
Chesapeake Pottery (Co.)	Baltimore, MD	
City Pottery Co.	Trenton, NJ	
Cook (& Mellor) Pottery Co.	Trenton, NJ	
Crescent Pottery Co.	Trenton, NJ	"Cable & Ring"
Crown Pottery (& Potteries) Co.	Evansville, IN	
Eagle Pottery Co.	Trenton, NJ	
East Liverpool Potteries Companies	East Liverpool, OH	
East Liverpool Potteries Companies	East Liverpool, OH	
East Trenton Pottery Co.	Trenton, NJ	
Empire Pottery	Trenton, NJ	
Etruria Pottery (Co.)	Trenton, NJ	
Fell & Thropp Co.	Trenton, NJ	
Glasgow Pottery Co.	Trenton, NJ	"Rectangle"
Globe Pottery Co.	East Liverpool, OH	
Goodwin (Bros.) Pottery Co.	East Liverpool, OH	
Greenwood Pottery Co.	Trenton, NJ	"Cable & Ring"
Hall China Co.	East Liverpool, OH	
Harker Potteries	East Liverpool, OH	
International (Lincoln) Pottery Co.	Trenton, NJ	"Winterberry"
Jersey City Pottery	Jersey City, NJ	
Knowles, Edwin M. China Co.	Newell, WV	
Knowles, Taylor, Knowles Co.	East Liverpool, OH	
Maddock, Thomas (& Sons)(& Co.)		"Plain Round"
Maddock, Thomas (& Sons)(& Co.)		"Simple Rectangle"
Maddock, Thomas (& Sons)(& Co.)		"Simplicity"
Maddock, Thomas (& Sons)(& Co.)		"Stylized Berry"
Maddock, Thomas (& Sons)(& Co.)	Trenton, NJ	"Bar & Chain"
Maryland Pottery Co.	Baltimore, MD	
Mayer, (J. & E.) Potteries Co. (Ltd.)	Beaver Falls, PA	
McNicol, D. E. Pottery Co.	East Liverpool, OH	
Mercer Pottery Co.	Trenton, NJ	
Millington & Astbury (& Paulson) Pottery	Trenton, NJ	
Morley (& Son) or (& Sons) & Co.	Wellsville, OH	
New England Pottery Co.	East Boston, MA	
New York City Pottery	New York, NY	
Norton Pottery (& Co.)	Bennington, VT	
Onondonga Pottery Co.	Syracuse, NY	"Cameo Square"
Peoria Pottery Co.	Peoria, IL	
Phoenixville (Phoenix) Pottery Co.	Phoenixville, PA	
Potters Cooperative (& Co.) (The)	East Liverpool, OH	
Prospect Hill Pottery	Trenton, NJ	"Shaws Chinese Shape"
Steubenville Pottery Co.	Steubenville, OH	
Tams, Steven & Co.	Trenton, NJ	
Trenton China Co.	Trenton, NJ	
Trenton Pottery (Co.)(Works)	Trenton, NJ	
Union Pottery Co.	Trenton, NJ	
United States Pottery	Bennington, VT	
Vance Faience (Pottery) Co.	Tiltonsville, OH	
Vodrey & Brothers (Pottery) (Co.)	East Liverpool, OH	
Wallace & Chetwynd	East Liverpool, OH	
Warwick China Co.	Wheeling, WV	
Wheeling Pottery Co.	Wheeling, WV	"Leaf"
Willets Manufacturing Co.	Trenton, NJ	
Wyllie, John & Son	East Liverpool, OH	"Leaf & Grape Cluster"
Wyllie, John & Son	East Liverpool, OH	"Round Grape Leaf"

AMERICAN APPENDICES

Four appendices are included in this portion of the Encyclopedia which will prove helpful in sorting out the potters included. **Appendices A1-A3** will assist the reader in sorting out potters by their initials and/or backmarks which may be peculiar to them. The Cross Reference of Potters and Potteries by Name will be of further help, in that when initials and/or other markings are missing or indecipherable and/or the pottery or trade name is the only thing noted, it is often difficult to locate the name of the pottery. For example, "ADAMANTINE CHINA" is a marking used by the Wheeling Pottery Company. LaBelle China Co., similarly, would be noted under the Wheeling Pottery Company. Thus, in the Cross Reference Appendix the reader will be referred to Wheeling Pottery for information on LaBelle or "ADAMANTINE CHINA". Likewise, Burgess & Campbell, often noted on backstamps, is to be referenced via the International Pottery Company/Lincoln Pottery Company.

Appendix A4 is a listing of Flow Blue, Tea Leaf/Copper Lustre and White Ironstone as recorded by individual potteries.

APPENDIX A1: ALPHABETIC LISTING: POTTERS & POTTERIES BY INITIAL

INITIALS	POTTERY	LOCATION
A. & M.	EMPIRE POTTERY (CO.)	NEW JERSEY
A. C. CO.	AMERICAN CHINA CO.	OHIO
A. C. CO.	AMERICAN CROCKERY CO.	NEW JERSEY
A. P.	ANCHOR POTTERY CO.	NEW JERSEY
B & C (B. & C.)	INTERNATIONAL (LINCOLN) POTTERY CO.	NEW JERSEY
B. & G.	BEERBOWER & GRIFFIN	PENNSYLVANIA
B. & G.	PHOENIXVILLE (PHOENIX) POTTERY CO.	PENNSYLVANIA
B. & M.OR (B-M)	BURROUGHS & MOUNTFORD (& CO.)	NEW JERSEY
B. B.	BURFORD BROS. POTTERY CO.	OHIO
B. B. M. CO.	BRUNT, WILLIAM POTTERY CO.	OHIO
B. B. M. CO.	DRESDEN POTTERY (WORKS) CO.	OHIO
B. B. P. CO.	BURFORD BROS. POTTERY CO.	OHIO
B. O. B.	ETRURIA POTTERY CO.	NEW JERSEY
B. P. CO.	BROCKMANN POTTERY CO.	OHIO
B.-M. OR (B&M)	BURROUGHS & MOUNTFORD (& CO.)	NEW JERSEY
C. & CO.	EMPIRE POTTERY (CO.)	NEW JERSEY
C. B. P. CO.	CARTWRIGHT BROS. (POTTERY CO.)	OHIO
C. C. P.	CHESAPEAKE POTTERY (& CO.)	MARYLAND
C. C. T. (P. CO.)	THOMPSON, C. C. CO. (POTTERY CO.)	OHIO
C. P. CO.	CARROLLTON, H. POTTERY CO.	OHIO
C. P. CO.	CITY POTTERY CO.	NEW JERSEY
C. P. CO.	COOK (& MELLOR) POTTERY CO.	NEW JERSEY
C. P. CO.	CROWN POTTERY (POTTERIES) CO.	INDIANA
C. P. O.	CRESCENT POTTERY CO.	NEW JERSEY
C.P. COY	CROWN POTTERY (POTTERIES) CO.	INDIANA
D-D OR (D&D)	PROSPECT HILL POTTERY	NEW JERSEY
D. & D. OR (D-D)	PROSPECT HILL POTTERY	NEW JERSEY
D. E. MCN. P. CO.	MCNICOL, D. E. POTTERY CO.	OHIO
D. F. H. & CO., BALT-	MARYLAND POTTERY CO.	MARYLAND
D. F. H. & S. (CO.)	CHESAPEAKE POTTERY (& CO.)	MARYLAND
D. F. HAYNES & CO.	MARYLAND POTTERY CO.	MARYLAND
E. & L. P.	NORTON POTTERY (& CO.)	VERMONT
E. B.	BENNETT, EDWIN POTTERY (CO.)	MARYLAND
E. B. P. CO.	BENNETT, EDWIN POTTERY CO.	MARYLAND
E. E. C. CO.	EAST END POTTERY (CHINA) CO.	OHIO
E. E. C. CO.	TRENLE (BLAKE) CHINA CO.	OHIO
E. E. P. CO.	EAST END POTTERY (CHINA) CO.	OHIO
E. H. S. C. CO.	SEBRING, E. H. CHINA CO.	OHIO
E. L. O.	BURFORD BROS. POTTERY CO.	OHIO
E. L. O.	THOMPSON, C. C. CO. (POTTERY CO.)	OHIO
E. L. P. CO.	EAST LIVERPOOL POTTERY CO.	OHIO
E. L. P. CO.	UNITED STATES POTTERY (THE)	VERMONT
E. L. P. CO.	UNITED STATES POTTERY CO. (THE)	OHIO
E. M. K. C. CO.	KNOWLES, EDWIN M. CHINA CO.	WEST VIRGINIA
E. P. & CO.	ETRURIA POTTERY CO.	NEW JERSEY
E. T. P. CO.	EAST TRENTON POTTERY CO.	NEW JERSEY
F. & T. CO.	FELL & THROPP CO.(TRENTON POTTERY WORKS)	NEW JERSEY
F. C. CO.	FORD CHINA CO.	PENNSYLVANIA
F. C. CO.	FRENCH CHINA CO. (THE)	OHIO
F. M. & CO.	VANCE FAIENCE (POTTERY) CO.	OHIO
F. T. & CO.	TRENTON POTTERY WORKS (FELL & THROPP CO.)	NEW JERSEY
G. C.	NEW ENGLAND POTTERY CO.	MASSACHUSETTS
G. M. & SON	MORLEY & (SONS(S) & CO.	OHIO
G. M. C. SON	MORLEY & (SONS(S) & CO.	OHIO
G. P. CO.	GLASGOW POTTERY CO.	NEW JERSEY
G. P. CO.	GLOBE POTTERY CO.	OHIO
G. P. CO.	GREENWOOD POTTERY CO.	NEW JERSEY
G. P. CO.	TAMS, STEPHENS & CO.	NEW JERSEY
G. P. CO/E. L. O.	GLOBE POTTERY CO.	OHIO
G. S.	SCOTT, GEORGE (& SONS) POTTERY	OHIO
G. S. H.	PHOENIXVILLE (PHOENIX) POTTERY CO.	PENNSYLVANIA
G. W. P. CO.	WYLLIE, JOHN & SON	OHIO
H. B. H.	CHESAPEAKE POTTERY (& CO.)	MARYLAND
H. L. & CO.	LAUGHLIN, HOMER (CHINA& CO.)	OHIO
H. P. CO.	HARKER POTTERY CO.	OHIO
I. P. CO.	INTERNATIONAL (LINCOLN)POTTERY CO.	NEW JERSEY
I. V. W.	AMERICAN POTTERY CO./ JERSEY CITY POTTERY	NEW JERSEY
J. C.	NEW YORK CITY POTTERY	NEW YORK
J. & E. M.	MAYER, (J. & E.) POTTERY CO. (LTD.)	PENNSYLVANIA
J. E. N.	ANCHOR POTTERY CO.	NEW JERSEY
J. M.	JOHN MOSES & SONS	NEW JERSEY
J. M. & CO.	GLASGOW POTTERY CO.	NEW JERSEY
J. M. & S. CO.	GLASGOW POTTERY CO.	NEW JERSEY
J. W. & SON	WYLLIE, JOHN & SON	OHIO
K. T. & K.	KNOWLES, TAYLOR, KNOWLES & CO.	OHIO
K.T.K.	KNOWLES, TAYLOR, KNOWLES & CO.	OHIO
L. B. B. & CO.	BEERBOWER, L. B. & CO.	NEW JERSEY
L. C. CO.	LIMOGES CHINA CO.	OHIO
M. & CO.	MORLEY & (SONS(S) & CO.	OHIO
M. & S.	MC NICOL-SMITH COMPANY	OHIO
M. A.	MILLINGTON, ASTBURY (& PAULSON) POTTERY	NEW JERSEY
M. A. P./TRENTON	MILLINGTON & ASTBURY (& PAULSON) POTTERY	NEW JERSEY
M. C. (CO.)	MERCER POTTERY CO.	NEW JERSEY
MCN. B. & CO.	MCNICOL, BURTON & CO.	OHIO
N. E. P. CO.	NEW ENGLAND POTTERY CO.	MASSACHUSETTS
N.Y.C.P.	NEW YORK CITY POTTERY	NEW YORK
O. C. CO.	OHIO CHINA CO.	OHIO
O. P. CO.	ONONDONGA POTTERY CO.	NEW YORK
P. C.	POTTERS COOPERATIVE CO. (THE)	OHIO
P. C. P. CO.	PADEN CITY POTTERY CO.	WEST VIRGINIA
P. P. CO.	PEORIA POTTERY CO.	ILLINOIS
P. P. CO.	PIONEER (WELLSVILLE)POTTERY CO.	OHIO
P. P. WORKS	PIONEER (WELLSVILLE)POTTERY CO.	OHIO
R. & T.	AMERICAN POTTERY CO./ JERSEY CITY POTTERY	NEW JERSEY
R. & Y.	CITY POTTERY CO.	NEW JERSEY
R. C.	RED CLIFF CO. (DECORATORS)	ILLINOIS
R. S.	SAYERS, DON & RUTH (RETAILERS)	ILLINOIS
S. C.	STEUBENVILLE POTTERY CO.	OHIO
S. C. CO.	SAXON CHINA CO.	OHIO
S. C. CO.	STERLING CHINA CO.	OHIO
S. P. CO.	STEUBENVILLE POTTERY CO.	OHIO
T.	THOMPSON, C. C.& CO.(POTTERY CO.)	OHIO
T. IDEAL P. CO.	TRENTON POTTERIES CO.	NEW JERSEY
T. M. & S.	MADDOCK, THOMAS (& SONS)(& CO.)	NEW JERSEY
T. P. C. CO.	DRESDEN POTTERY (WORKS) CO.	OHIO
T. P. CO.	EMPIRE POTTERY (CO.)	NEW JERSEY
T. P. CO.	POTTERS COOPERATIVE (& CO.)(THE)	OHIO
T. P. CO.	TRENTON POTTERIES CO.	NEW JERSEY
T. P. CO. (ELO)	POTTERS COOPERATIVE CO. (THE)	OHIO
T. P. W.	TRENTON POTTERY (CO.)(WORKS)	NEW JERSEY
T. S. T.	TAYLOR, SMITH, TAYLOR CO. (INC.)	WEST VIRGINIA
T. W. C. CO.	WICK CHINA CO. (THE)	PENNSYLVANIA
T.B. (&) CO.	TEMPEST, BROCKMANN & CO.	OHIO
U. P. CO.	UNION POTTERY CO.	NEW JERSEY
V. & BROS.	VODREY & BROTHERS (& CO.)	OHIO
W. & B.	EMPIRE POTTERY (CO.)	NEW JERSEY
W. & C.	WALLACE & CHETWYND	OHIO
W. & C. P. CO.	WALLACE & CHETWYND	OHIO
W. B. JR. & CO.	BRUNT, WILLIAM JR. & CO.	OHIO
W. B. P. CO.	BRUNT, WILLIAM POTTERY CO.	OHIO
W. B. S. & CO.	BRUNT, WILLIAM SON & CO.	OHIO
W. C. CO.	WARWICK CHINA CO. (INC.)	WEST VIRGINIA
W. C. CO.	WELLSVILLE CHINA CO.	OHIO
W. M. CO.	WILLETS MANUFACTURING CO.	NEW JERSEY
W. P. C. (CO.)	WHEELING POTTERY CO.	WEST VIRGINIA

INITIALS	POTTERY	LOCATION
W. P. P. CO.	PIONEER (WELLSVILLE)POTTERY CO.	OHIO
W. PTS. CO.	WHEELING POTTERIES CO.	WEST VIRGINIA
XX CENTURY	WHEELING POTTERIES CO.	WEST VIRGINIA
Y. & T.	CITY POTTERY CO.	NEW JERSEY
Y. B. A.	CITY POTTERY CO.	NEW JERSEY

APPENDIX A2: ALPHABETIC LISTING: POTTERS & POTTERIES BY NAME

POTTERY	INITIALS	LOCATION
AMERICAN CHINA CO.	A. C. CO.	OHIO
AMERICAN CROCKERY CO.	A. C. CO.	NEW JERSEY
AMERICAN POTTERY CO./ JERSEY CITY POTTERY	I. V. W.	NEW JERSEY
AMERICAN POTTERY CO./ JERSEY CITY POTTERY	R. & T.	NEW JERSEY
ANCHOR POTTERY CO.	A. P.	NEW JERSEY
ANCHOR POTTERY CO.	J. E. N.	NEW JERSEY
BEERBOWER & GRIFFIN	B. & G.	PENNSYLVANIA
BEERBOWER, L. B. & CO.	L. B. B. & CO.	NEW JERSEY
BENNETT, EDWIN POTTERY (CO.)	E. B.	MARYLAND
BENNETT, EDWIN POTTERY CO.	E. B. P. CO.	MARYLAND
BROCKMANN POTTERY CO.	B. P. CO.	OHIO
BRUNT, WILLIAM JR. & CO.	W.B. JR. & CO.	OHIO
BRUNT, WILLIAM POTTERY CO.	B. B. M. CO.	OHIO
BRUNT, WILLIAM POTTERY CO.	W. B. P. CO.	OHIO
BRUNT, WILLIAM SON & CO.	W. B. S. & CO.	OHIO
BURFORD BROS. POTTERY CO.	B. B.	OHIO
BURFORD BROS. POTTERY CO.	B. B. P. CO.	OHIO
BURFORD BROS. POTTERY CO.	E. L. O.	OHIO
BURROUGHS & MOUNTFORD (& CO.)	B. & M.OR(B-M)	NEW JERSEY
BURROUGHS & MOUNTFORD (& CO.)	B.-M. OR(B&M)	NEW JERSEY
CARROLLTON, H. POTTERY CO.	C. P. CO.	OHIO
CARTWRIGHT BROS. (POTTERY CO.)	C. B. P. CO.	OHIO
CHESAPEAKE POTTERY (& CO.)	C. C. P.	MARYLAND
CHESAPEAKE POTTERY (& CO.)	D. F. H. & S. (CO.)	MARYLAND
CHESAPEAKE POTTERY (& CO.)	H. B. H.	MARYLAND
CITY POTTERY CO.	C. P. CO.	NEW JERSEY
CITY POTTERY CO.	R. & Y.	NEW JERSEY
CITY POTTERY CO.	Y. & T.	NEW JERSEY
CITY POTTERY CO.	Y. B. A.	NEW JERSEY
COOK (& MELLOR) POTTERY CO.	C. P. CO.	NEW JERSEY
CRESCENT POTTERY CO.	C. P. O.	NEW JERSEY
CROWN POTTERY (POTTERIES) CO.	C. P. CO.	INDIANA
CROWN POTTERY (POTTERIES) CO.	C.P. COY	INDIANA
DRESDEN POTTERY (WORKS) CO.	B. B. M. CO.	OHIO
DRESDEN POTTERY (WORKS) CO.	T. P. C. CO.	OHIO
EAST END POTTERY (CHINA) CO.	E. E. C. CO.	OHIO
EAST END POTTERY (CHINA) CO.	E. E. P. CO.	OHIO
EAST LIVERPOOL POTTERY CO.	E. L. P. CO.	OHIO
EAST TRENTON POTTERY CO.	E. T. P. CO.	NEW JERSEY
EMPIRE POTTERY (CO.)	A. & M.	NEW JERSEY
EMPIRE POTTERY (CO.)	C. & CO.	NEW JERSEY
EMPIRE POTTERY (CO.)	T. P. CO.	NEW JERSEY
EMPIRE POTTERY (CO.)	W. & B.	NEW JERSEY
ETRURIA POTTERY CO.	B. O. B.	NEW JERSEY
ETRURIA POTTERY CO.	E. P. & CO.	NEW JERSEY
FELL & THROPP CO. (TRENTON POTTERY WORKS)	F. & T. CO.	NEW JERSEY
FORD CHINA CO.	F. C. CO.	PENNSYLVANIA
FRENCH CHINA CO. (THE)	F. C. CO.	OHIO
GLASGOW POTTERY CO.	G. P. CO.	NEW JERSEY
GLASGOW POTTERY CO.	J. M. & CO.	NEW JERSEY
GLASGOW POTTERY CO.	J. M. & S. CO.	NEW JERSEY
GLOBE POTTERY CO.	G. P. CO.	OHIO
GLOBE POTTERY CO.	G. P. CO/ E. L. O.	OHIO
GREENWOOD POTTERY CO.	G. P. CO.	NEW JERSEY
HARKER POTTERY CO.	H. P. CO.	OHIO
INTERNATIONAL (LINCOLN) POTTERY CO.	B & C (B. & C.)	NEW JERSEY
INTERNATIONAL (LINCOLN) POTTERY CO.	I. P. CO.	NEW JERSEY
JOHN MOSES & SONS	J. M.	NEW JERSEY
KNOWLES, EDWIN M. CHINA CO.	E. M. K. C. CO.	WEST VIRGINIA
KNOWLES, TAYLOR, KNOWLES & CO.	K. T. & K.	OHIO
KNOWLES, TAYLOR, KNOWLES & CO.	K.T. K.	OHIO
LAUGHLIN, HOMER (CHINA& CO.)	H. L. & CO.	OHIO
LIMOGES CHINA CO.	L. C. CO.	OHIO
MADDOCK, THOMAS (& SONS)(& CO.)	T. M. & S.	NEW JERSEY
MARYLAND POTTERY CO.	D. F. H. & CO., BALT-	MARYLAND
MARYLAND POTTERY CO.	D. F. HAYNES & CO.	MARYLAND
MAYER, (J. & E.) POTTERY CO. (LTD.)	J. & E. M.	PENNSYLVANIA
MC NICOL-SMITH COMPANY	M. & S.	OHIO
MCNICOL, BURTON & CO.	MCN. B. & CO.	OHIO
MCNICOL, D. E. POTTERY CO.	D. E. MCN. P. CO.	OHIO
MERCER POTTERY CO.	M. C. (CO.)	NEW JERSEY
MILLINGTON & ASTBURY (& PAULSON) POTTERY	M. A. P./ TRENTON	NEW JERSEY
MILLINGTON, ASTBURY (& PAULSON) POTTERY	M. A.	NEW JERSEY
MORLEY & (SONS(S) & CO.	G. M. & SON	OHIO
MORLEY & (SONS(S) & CO.	G. M. C. SON	OHIO
MORLEY & (SONS(S) & CO.	M. & CO.	OHIO
NEW ENGLAND POTTERY CO.	G. C.	MASSACHUSETTS
NEW ENGLAND POTTERY CO.	N. E. P. CO.	MASSACHUSETTS
NEW YORK CITY POTTERY	J. C.	NEW YORK
NEW YORK CITY POTTERY	N.Y.C.P.	NEW YORK
NORTON POTTERY (& CO.)	E. & L. P.	VERMONT
OHIO CHINA CO.	O. C. CO.	OHIO
ONONDONGA POTTERY CO.	O. P. CO.	NEW YORK
PADEN CITY POTTERY CO.	P. C. P. CO.	WEST VIRGINIA
PEORIA POTTERY CO.	P. P. CO.	ILLINOIS
PHOENIXVILLE (PHOENIX) POTTERY CO.	B. & G.	PENNSYLVANIA
PHOENIXVILLE (PHOENIX) POTTERY CO.	G. S. H.	PENNSYLVANIA
PIONEER (WELLSVILLE) POTTERY CO.	P. P. CO.	OHIO
PIONEER (WELLSVILLE) POTTERY CO.	P. P. WORKS	OHIO
PIONEER (WELLSVILLE) POTTERY CO.	W. P. P. CO.	OHIO
POTTERS COOPERATIVE (& CO.)(THE)	T. P. CO.	OHIO
POTTERS COOPERATIVE CO. (THE)	P. C.	OHIO
POTTERS COOPERATIVE CO. (THE)	T. P. CO. (ELO)	OHIO
PROSPECT HILL POTTERY	D-D OR (D&D)	NEW JERSEY
PROSPECT HILL POTTERY	D. & D. OR (D-D)	NEW JERSEY
RED CLIFF CO. (DECORATORS)	R. C.	ILLINOIS
SAXON CHINA CO.	S. C. CO.	OHIO
SAYERS, DON & RUTH (RETAILERS)	R. S.	ILLINOIS
SCOTT, GEORGE (& SONS) POTTERY	G. S.	OHIO
SEBRING, E. H. CHINA CO.	E. H. S. C. CO.	OHIO
STERLING CHINA CO.	S. C. CO.	OHIO
STEUBENVILLE POTTERY CO.	S. C.	OHIO
STEUBENVILLE POTTERY CO.	S. P. CO.	OHIO
TAMS, STEPHENS & CO.	G. P. CO.	NEW JERSEY
TAYLOR, SMITH, TAYLOR CO. (INC.)	T. S. T.	WEST VIRGINIA
TEMPEST, BROCKMANN & CO.	T.B. (&) CO.	OHIO
THOMPSON, C. C. CO. (POTTERY CO.)	C. C. T. (P. CO.)	OHIO
THOMPSON, C. C. CO. (POTTERY CO.)	E. L. O.	OHIO
THOMPSON, C. C.& CO. (POTTERY CO.)	T.	OHIO
TRENLE (BLAKE) CHINA CO.	E. E. C. CO.	OHIO
TRENTON POTTERIES CO.	T. IDEAL P. CO.	NEW JERSEY
TRENTON POTTERIES CO.	T. P. CO.	NEW JERSEY
TRENTON POTTERY (CO.)(WORKS)	T. P. W.	NEW JERSEY
TRENTON POTTERY WORKS (FELL & THROPP CO.)	F. T. & CO.	NEW JERSEY
UNION POTTERY CO.	U. P. CO.	NEW JERSEY
UNITED STATES POTTERY (THE)	E. L. P. CO.	VERMONT
UNITED STATES POTTERY CO. (THE)	E. L. P. CO.	OHIO
VANCE FAIENCE (POTTERY) CO.	F. M. & CO.	OHIO
VODREY & BROTHERS (& CO.)	V. & BROS.	OHIO
WALLACE & CHETWYND	W. & C.	OHIO
WALLACE & CHETWYND	W. & C. P. CO.	OHIO
WARWICK CHINA CO. (INC.)	W. C. CO.	WEST VIRGINIA
WELLSVILLE CHINA CO.	W. C. CO.	OHIO
WHEELING POTTERIES CO.	W. PTS. CO.	WEST VIRGINIA
WHEELING POTTERIES CO.	XX CENTURY	WEST VIRGINIA
WHEELING POTTERY CO.	W. P. C. (CO.)	WEST VIRGINIA
WICK CHINA CO. (THE)	T. W. C. CO.	PENNSYLVANIA
WILLETS MANUFACTURING CO.	W. M. CO.	NEW JERSEY
WYLLIE, JOHN & SON	G. W. P. CO.	OHIO
WYLLIE, JOHN & SON	J. W. & SON	OHIO

APPENDIX A3: CROSS REFERENCE: POTTERS & POTTERIES BY NAME

POTTERY	REFER TO POTTERY
ALPAUGH & MAGOWAN	EMPIRE POTTERY (CO.)/TRENTON POTTERIES CO.
AMERICAN POTTERY CO.	JERSEY CITY AMERICAN POTTERY (CO.)
AMERICAN POTTERY CO.	JERSEY CITY POTTERY
AMERICAN POTTERY MANUFACTURING CO.	JERSEY CITY POTTERY/AMERICAN POTTERY (CO.)
AMERICAN POTTERY WORKS	SEBRING POTTERY CO.
AVON WORKS	VANCE FAIENCE (POTTERY) CO.
BEERBOWER, L.B. & GRIFFIN,HENRY, B.	PHOENIXVILLE POTTERY CO.
BENNINGTON, VT	UNITED STATES POTTERY (THE)
BLOOR, OTT & BOOTH	ETRURIA POTTERY (CO.)
BREWER, HART POTTERY CO.	TRENTON POTTERY WORKS
BRUNT, BLOOR, MARTIN & CO.	DRESDEN POTTERY (WORKS) CO.
BRUNT, WILLIAM CO. (& ASSOC.)	DRESDEN POTTERY (CO.)
BUCKEYE POTTERY	KNOWLES, TAYLOR, KNOWLES & CO.
BURGESS & CAMPBELL	INTERNATIONAL (LINCOLN) POTTERY CO.
BURGESSS & CO.	INTERNATIONAL (LINCOLN) POTTERY CO.
CARR, ET. AL.	NEW YORK CITY POTTERY
CARR, JAMES & CLARK, EDWARD & MOSES, JOHN & JAMES	LINCOLN POTTERY CO.

POTTERY	**REFER TO POTTERY**
CHESTER POTTERY	PHOENIXVILLE POTTERY CO.
CITY POTTERY CO.	MADDOCK, THOMAS (& SONS) (& CO.)
CLARK & MICHAEL	PIONEER POTTERY CO.
CLARK, B.	WELLSVILLE PIONEER POTTERY CO.
COLONIAL POTTERY	WALLACE & CHETWYND
COLONIAL STERLING	COLONIAL COMPANY (THE)
COOK & HANCOCK	CRESCENT POTTERY CO.
COXON & CO.	EMPIRE POTTERY (CO.)/TRENTON POTTERIES CO.
CRESCENT POTTERY CO.	TRENTON POTTERIES CO. (EMPIRE POTTERY)
CROWN POTTERIES CO.	CROWN POTTERY
DALE & DAVIS	PROSPECT HILL POTTERY
DAVIS, ISAAC	PROSPECT HILL POTTERY
DAVIS, ISAAC	TRENTON POTTERY WORKS
DELAWARE POTTERY CO.	TRENTON POTTERIES CO. (EMPIRE POTTERY)
DRESDEN POTTERY (WORKS) CO.	POTTERS COOPERATIVE (& CO.) (THE)
EAGLE POTTERY	BURROUGHS & MOUNTFORD (& CO.)
EAGLE POTTERY	GOODWIN (BROS.) POTTERY CO.
EAST END (POTTERY) CHINA CO.	TRENLE (BLAKE) CHINA CO.
EAST LIVERPOOL POTTERIES COMPANIES	UNITED STATES POTTERY CO. (THE)
EMPIRE POTTERY (CO.)	TRENTON POTTERY (CO.) (WORKS)
ENTERPRISE POTTERY CO.	TRENTON POTTERIES CO. (EMPIRE POTTERY)
EQUITABLE POTTERY CO.	TRENTON POTTERIES CO. (EMPIRE POTTERY)
ETRURIA CO.	COOK (& MELLOR) POTTERY CO.
ETRURIA POTTERY	HARKER POTTERIES
FELL & THROPP & CO.	TRENTON POTTERY WORKS
FLENTKE, ET.AL.	SALAMANDER POTTERY (SEE: MORLEY & CO.)
FORREST, J.M. & CO.	EAGLE POTTERY CO.
FREDERICKSBURG	AMERICAN BELEEK
GOODWIN, JOHN	MCNICOL, BURTON & CO.
GRAY & CLARK	NEW ENGLAND POTTERY CO.
GREAT WESTERN POTTERY	WYLLIE, JOHN & SON
GREAT WESTERN POTTERY WORKS	BRUNT, WILLIAM, JR.
GRIFFIN, ET, AL.	PHOENIXVILLE POTTERY CO.
GRUESSNER, ROBERT	TRENTON POTTERY WORKS
HAMMILL, BROWN & CO.	MARYLAND POTTERY CO.
HARKER, ET.AL.	HARKER POTTERIES
HARRISON & R. HENDERSON	EAST LIVERPOOL POTTERY CO.
HARRISON, RICHARD & CO.	EAST LIVERPOOL POTTERY CO.
HAYNES, D.F. & CO. OR (& SON)	CHESAPEAKE POTTERY (CO.)
HOLLAND & MANLEY	CARTWRIGHT BROS. (POTTERY CO.)
IDEAL POTTERY	TRENTON POTTERIES CO. (CRESCENT POTTERY)
INTERNATIONAL POTERY CO.	BURGESS & CAMPBELL
KENYON CITY POTTERY	CITY POTTERY CO.
LABELLE CHINA CO.	WHEELING POTTERY CO.
LAMBERTON (WORKS)	MADDOCK POTTERY CO.
LAMBERTON (WORKS)	MADDOCK, THOMAS (& SONS) (& CO.)
LAUGHLIN BROS.	LAUGHLIN, HOMER (CHINA CO.)
LINCOLN POTTERY CO.	INTERNATIONAL LINCOLN POTTERY CO.
MANLEY & CARTWRIGHT	CARTWRIGHT BROS. (POTTERY CO.)
MANLEY & RILEY	MC NICOL, BURTON & CO.
MARKS, A. H.	MC NICOL, BURTON & CO.
MARYLAND QUEENSWARE CO.	MARYLAND POTTERY CO.
MELLOR & CO.	COOK (& MELLOR) POTTERY CO.
MOSES, JOHN & SONS CO.	GLASGOW POTTERY
NOVELTY POTTERY CO.	MCNICOL BURTON POTTERY CO.
NOVELTY POTTERY WORKS	GOODWIN (BROS.) POTTERY CO.
NOVELTY POTTERY WORKS	MC NICOL, BURTON & CO.
NOVELTY POTTERY WORKS	MC NICOL, D. E. POTTERY CO.
OTT, BREWER & BLOOR	ETRURIA POTTERY (CO.)
PENN CHINA CO.	PHOENIXVILLE POTTERY CO.
PHOENIX POTTERY	BRUNT, WILLIAM CO. (& ASSOCIATES)
PHOENIX POTTERY	PHOENIXVILLE POTTERY CO.
PHOENIX POTTERY	VODREY & BROS. (POTTERY) (CO.)
PHOENIXVILLE POTTERY	BEERBOWER & GRIFFEN
RED CLIFF	HALL CHINA CO.
RED CLIFF	WALKER CHINA CO.
RHODES & YATES	CITY POTTERY CO.
RIVERSIDE KNOB WORKS	BRUNT, WILLIAM CO. (& ASSOCIATES)
RIVERSIDE POTTERY	WHEELING POTTERY CO.
ROUSE & TURNER	AMERICAN POTTERY CO./JERSEY CITY POTTERY
SCHREIBER & BETZ	PHOENIXVILLE POTTERY CO.
SEBRING CHINA CO.	LIMOGES CHINA CO.
SPEELER & TAYLOR	TRENTON POTTERY
SPEELER, HENRY (& SON)	INTERNATIONAL POTTERY CO.
STERLING CHINA CO.	LIMOGES CHINA CO.
SYRACUSE POTTERY (CHINA) CO.	ONONDAGA POTTERY CO.
TAYLOR & CO. (& VARIOUS PARNERSHIPS)	TRENTON POTTERIES (CO.) (WORKS)
THROPP & BREWER	TRENTON POTTERY WORKS
TRENTON CITY POTTERY	CITY POTTERY CO.
TRENTON POTTERY (CO.)	FELL & THROPP CO.
TRENTON POTTERY (CO.)	PROSPECT HILL POTTERY
TUXEDO POTTERY CO.	PHOENIXVILLE POTTERY CO.
UNITED STATES POTTERY	BENNINGTON, VT.
UNITED STATES POTTERY (THE)	EAST LIVERPOOL POTTERIES COMPANIES
VANCE FAIENCE CO. (AVON WORKS)	WHEELING POTTERY CO.
WELLSVILLE CHINA CO.	PIONEER POTTERY CO. (SEE: GATES, P. 309, LEHNER, P. 510)
WOOD & BARLOW	EMPIRE POTTERY (CO.)/TRENTON POTTERIES CO.
WOODWARD, BLAKELEY & CO.	PHOENIX POTTERY/PHOENIXVILLE POTTERY CO.
YATES & TITUS	CITY POTTERY CO.
YATES, BENNETT (& ALLAN)	CITY POTTERY CO.

APPENDIX A4: CROSS REFERENCE: POTTERS & POTTERIES BY POTTERY

REFER TO POTTERY	POTTERY
AMERICAN BELEEK	FREDERICKSBURG
AMERICAN POTTERY CO./ JERSEY CITY POTTERY	ROUSE & TURNER
BEERBOWER & GRIFFEN	PHOENIXVILLE POTTERY
BENNINGTON, VT.	UNITED STATES POTTERY
BRUNT, WILLIAM CO. (& ASSOC.)	PHOENIX POTTERY
BRUNT, WILLIAM CO. (& ASSOC.)	RIVERSIDE KNOB WORKS
BRUNT, WILLIAM, JR.	GREAT WESTERN POTTERY WORKS
BURGESS & CAMPBELL	INTERNATIONAL POTERY CO.
BURROUGHS & MOUNTFORD (& CO.)	EAGLE POTTERY
CARTWRIGHT BROS. (POTTERY CO.)	HOLLAND & MANLEY
CARTWRIGHT BROS. (POTTERY CO.)	MANLEY & CARTWRIGHT
CHESAPEAKE POTTERY (CO.)	HAYNES, D.F. & CO. OR (& SON)
CITY POTTERY CO.	KENYON CITY POTTERY
CITY POTTERY CO.	RHODES & YATES
CITY POTTERY CO.	TRENTON CITY POTTERY
CITY POTTERY CO.	YATES & TITUS
CITY POTTERY CO.	YATES, BENNETT (& ALLAN)
COLONIAL COMPANY (THE)	COLONIAL STERLING
COOK (& MELLOR) POTTERY CO.	ETRURIA CO.
COOK (& MELLOR) POTTERY CO.	MELLOR & CO.
CRESCENT POTTERY CO.	COOK & HANCOCK
CROWN POTTERY	CROWN POTTERIES CO.
DRESDEN POTTERY (CO.)	BRUNT, WILLIAM CO. (& ASSOCIATES)
DRESDEN POTTERY (WORKS) CO.	BRUNT, BLOOR, MARTIN & CO.
EAGLE POTTERY CO.	FORREST, J.M. & CO.
EAST LIVERPOOL POTTERIES COMPANIES	UNITED STATES POTTERY (THE)
EAST LIVERPOOL POTTERY CO.	HARRISON & R. HENDERSON
EAST LIVERPOOL POTTERY CO.	HARRISON, RICHARD & CO.
EMPIRE POTTERY (CO.)/TRENTON POTTERIES CO.	ALPAUGH & MAGOWAN
EMPIRE POTTERY (CO.)/TRENTON POTTERIES CO.	COXON & CO.
EMPIRE POTTERY (CO.)/TRENTON POTTERIES CO.	WOOD & BARLOW
ETRURIA POTTERY (CO.)	BLOOR, OTT & BOOTH
ETRURIA POTTERY (CO.)	OTT, BREWER & BLOOR
FELL & THROPP CO.	TRENTON POTTERY (CO.)
GLASGOW POTTERY	MOSES, JOHN & SONS CO.
GOODWIN (BROS.) POTTERY CO.	EAGLE POTTERY
GOODWIN (BROS.) POTTERY CO.	NOVELTY POTTERY WORKS
HALL CHINA CO.	RED CLIFF
HARKER POTTERIES	ETRURIA POTTERY
HARKER POTTERIES	HARKER, ET.AL.
INTERNATIONAL (LINCOLN) POTTERY CO.	BURGESS & CAMPBELL
INTERNATIONAL (LINCOLN) POTTERY CO.	BURGESSS & CO.
INTERNATIONAL LINCOLN POTTERY CO.	LINCOLN POTTERY CO.
INTERNATIONAL POTTERY CO.	SPEELER, HENRY (& SON)
JERSEY CITY AMERICAN POTTERY (CO.)	AMERICAN POTTERY CO.
JERSEY CITY POTTERY	AMERICAN POTTERY CO.
JERSEY CITY POTTERY/ AMERICAN POTTERY (CO.)	AMERICAN POTTERY MANUFACTURING CO.
KNOWLES, TAYLOR, KNOWLES & CO.	BUCKEYE POTTERY
LAUGHLIN, HOMER (CHINA CO.)	LAUGHLIN BROS.
LIMOGES CHINA CO.	SEBRING CHINA CO.
LIMOGES CHINA CO.	STERLING CHINA CO.
LINCOLN POTTERY CO.	CARR, JAMES & CLARK, EDWARD & MOSES, JOHN & JAMES
MADDOCK POTTERY CO.	LAMBERTON (WORKS)
MADDOCK, THOMAS (& SONS) (& CO.)	CITY POTTERY CO.
MADDOCK, THOMAS (& SONS) (& CO.)	LAMBERTON (WORKS)
MARYLAND POTTERY CO.	HAMMILL, BROWN & CO.
MARYLAND POTTERY CO.	MARYLAND QUEENSWARE CO.
MC NICOL, BURTON & CO.	MANLEY & RILEY
MC NICOL, BURTON & CO.	MARKS, A. H.
MC NICOL, BURTON & CO.	NOVELTY POTTERY WORKS
MC NICOL, D. E. POTTERY CO.	NOVELTY POTTERY WORKS
MCNICOL BURTON POTTERY CO.	NOVELTY POTTERY CO.
MCNICOL, BURTON & CO.	GOODWIN, JOHN
NEW ENGLAND POTTERY CO.	GRAY & CLARK
NEW YORK CITY POTTERY	CARR, ET. AL.
ONONDAGA POTTERY CO.	SYRACUSE POTTERY (CHINA) CO.
PHOENIX POTTERY/PHOENIXVILLE POTTERY CO.	WOODWARD, BLAKELEY & CO.
PHOENIXVILLE POTTERY CO.	BEERBOWER, L.B. & GRIFFIN, HENRY, B.
PHOENIXVILLE POTTERY CO.	CHESTER POTTERY
PHOENIXVILLE POTTERY CO.	GRIFFIN, ET, AL.
PHOENIXVILLE POTTERY CO.	PENN CHINA CO.
PHOENIXVILLE POTTERY CO.	PHOENIX POTTERY

REFER TO POTTERY	POTTERY
PHOENIXVILLE POTTERY CO.	SCHREIBER & BETZ
PHOENIXVILLE POTTERY CO.	TUXEDO POTTERY CO.
PIONEER POTTERY CO.	CLARK & MICHAEL
PIONEER POTTERY CO. (SEE: GATES, P. 309, LEHNER, P. 510)	WELLSVILLE CHINA CO.
POTTERS COOPERATIVE (& CO.) (THE)	DRESDEN POTTERY (WORKS) CO.
PROSPECT HILL POTTERY	DALE & DAVIS
PROSPECT HILL POTTERY	DAVIS, ISAAC
PROSPECT HILL POTTERY	TRENTON POTTERY (CO.)
SALAMANDER POTTERY (SEE: MORLEY & CO.)	FLENTKE, ET.AL.
SEBRING POTTERY CO.	AMERICAN POTTERY WORKS
TRENLE (BLAKE) CHINA CO.	EAST END (POTTERY) CHINA CO.
TRENTON POTTERIES (CO.) (WORKS)	TAYLOR & CO. (& VARIOUS PARNERSHIPS)
TRENTON POTTERIES CO. (CRESCENT POTTERY)	IDEAL POTTERY
TRENTON POTTERIES CO. (EMPIRE POTTERY)	CRESCENT POTTERY CO.
TRENTON POTTERIES CO. (EMPIRE POTTERY)	DELAWARE POTTERY CO.
TRENTON POTTERIES CO. (EMPIRE POTTERY)	ENTERPRISE POTTERY CO.
TRENTON POTTERIES CO. (EMPIRE POTTERY)	EQUITABLE POTTERY CO.
TRENTON POTTERY	SPEELER & TAYLOR
TRENTON POTTERY (CO.) (WORKS)	EMPIRE POTTERY (CO.)
TRENTON POTTERY WORKS	BREWER, HART POTTERY CO.
TRENTON POTTERY WORKS	DAVIS, ISAAC
TRENTON POTTERY WORKS	FELL & THROPP & CO.
TRENTON POTTERY WORKS	GRUESSNER, ROBERT
TRENTON POTTERY WORKS	THROPP & BREWER
UNITED STATES POTTERY (THE)	BENNINGTON, VT
UNITED STATES POTTERY CO. (THE)	EAST LIVERPOOL POTTERIES COMPANIES
VANCE FAIENCE (POTTERY) CO.	AVON WORKS
VODREY & BROS. (POTTERY) (CO.)	PHOENIX POTTERY
WALKER CHINA CO.	RED CLIFF
WALLACE & CHETWYND	COLONIAL POTTERY
WELLSVILLE PIONEER POTTERY CO.	CLARK, B.
WHEELING POTTERY CO.	LABELLE CHINA CO.
WHEELING POTTERY CO.	RIVERSIDE POTTERY
WHEELING POTTERY CO.	VANCE FAIENCE CO. (AVON WORKS)
WYLLIE, JOHN & SON	GREAT WESTERN POTTERY

APPENDIX A5: CROSS REFERENCE: BACK MARKINGS BY POTTERY

MARK	POTTERY
ADAMANTINE CHINA	WHEELING POTTERY CO.
AMERICAN BELLEEK	BAHL POTTERIES, INC.
AMERICAN CHINA	AMERICAN CROCKERY CO. (JERSEY CITY POTTERY)
ARUNDEL	CHESAPEAKE POTTERY (CO.)
AURORA CHINA	WICK CHINA CO. (THE)
AVALON CHINA	CHESAPEAKE POTTERY (CO.)
AVALON FAIENCE	CHESAPEAKE POTTERY (CO.)
AVON	WHEELING POTTERIES CO.
BALTIMORE	MARYLAND POTTERY CO.
BEAVER FALLS, PA	MAYER, (J. & E.) POTTERIES CO. LTD.
BELEEK	WILLETS MANUFACTURING CO.
BENNINGTON (VT)	NORTON POTTERY
BENNINGTON, VT.	UNITED STATES POTTERY CO. (THE)
BEST CHINA	CHESAPEAKE POTTERY (CO.)
BONITA	WHEELING POTTERIES CO.
BONITA SEMI PORCELAIN	WHEELING POTTERIES CO.
CHINA	CARROLLTON POTTERY CO.
CHINA	CHELSEA CHINA CO.
CHINA	EAST LIVERPOOL POTTERY CO.
CHINA	EMPIRE POTTERY (CO.) (TRENTON POTTERY CO.)
CHINA	GLOBE POTTERY CO.
CHINA	GREENWOOD POTTERY CO.
CHINA	LIMOGES CHINA CO. (STERLING CHINA CO.)
CHINA	MADDOCK, THOMAS (& SONS) (& CO.)
CHINA	MERCER POTTERY CO.
CHINA	ONONDAGA POTTERY CO.
CHINA	POTTERS COOPERATIVE (& CO.) (THE)
CHINA	PROSPECT HILL POTTERY
CHINA	SAXON CHINA CO.
CHINA	SHENANGO CHINA (POTTERY) CO.
CHINA	TAYLOR, SMITH & TAYLOR CO. (INC.)
CHINA	TRENTON POTTERIES CO. (EMPIRE POTTERY)
CHINA	UNION POTTERY CO.
CHINA	VODREY & BROTHERS (POTTERY) (CO.)
CHINA	WARWICK CHINA (CO.)
CHINA	WHEELING POTTERY CO.
COLONIAL	LAUGHLIN, HOMER (CHINA & CO.)
CROWN POTTERY	PIONEER POTTERY CO.
DRESDEN	BRUNT, WILLIAM CO.

MARK	POTTERY
DRESDEN STONE CHINA	DRESDEN POTTERY (WORKS) CO.
DRESDEN WHITE GRANITE	BRUNT, BLOOR, MARTIN & CO.
DRESDEN WHITE GRANITE	DRESDEN POTTERY (WORKS) CO.
DRESDEN WHITE GRANITE	POTTERS CO-OPERATIVE (& CO.) (THE)
E. LIVERPOOL	HARKER POTTERIES (ETRURIA POTTERY)
E. LIVERPOOL O.	EAST END POTTERY (CHINA) CO.
EAST LIVERPOOL O.	UNITED STATES POTTERY CO. (THE)
EAST LIVERPOOL OHIO	BENNETT, EDWIN POTTERY (CO.)
ETRURIA	COOK (& MELLOR) POTTERY CO.
ETRUSCAN	PHOENIXVILLE (PHOENIX) POTTERY CO.
EUREKA	THOMPSON, C. C. & CO. (POTTERY CO.)
EXTRA QUALITY	AMERICAN CHINA CO.
EXTRA QUALITY	BURROUGHS & MOUNTFORD (& CO.)
EXTRA QUALITY	DRESDEN POTTERY (WORKS) CO.
EXTRA QUALITY IRONSTONE CHINA	AMERICAN CHINA CO.
FORD CITY, PA	FORD CHINA CO. (THE)
FRENCH-SAXON	FRENCH-SAXON CHINA CO.
GRANIT	MC NICOL, BURTON & CO.
GRANITE WARE	KNOWLES, TAYLOR, KNOWLES CO.
HALL	GREENFIELD VILLAGE POTTERY (Museum)
HAYNES BALT	CHESAPEAKE POTTERY (CO.)
IDEAL CHINA	TRENTON POTTERIES CO. (EMPIRE POTTERY)
IMPERIAL CHINA	EMPIRE POTTERY (CO.) (TRENTON POTTERY CO.)
IMPERIAL CHINA	OHIO CHINA CO.
IMPERIAL CHINA	PIONEER POTTERY CO.
INTERNATIONAL (LINCOLN) POTTERY CO.	KNOWLES, TAYLOR, KNOWLES CO.
IOGA	WARWICK CHINA (CO.)
IRONSTONE	WALLACE & CHETWYND
IRONSTONE CHINA	AMERICAN CHINA CO.
IRONSTONE CHINA	AMERICAN CROCKERY CO.(JERSEY CITY POTTERY)
IRONSTONE CHINA	ANCHOR POTTERY CO.
IRONSTONE CHINA	BEERBOWER & GRIFFEN
IRONSTONE CHINA	BEERBOWER, L. B. & CO.
IRONSTONE CHINA	BRUNT, WILLIAM (JR.) & CO.
IRONSTONE CHINA	BRUNT, WILLIAM POTTERY CO.
IRONSTONE CHINA	BURFORD BROS. POTTERY CO.
IRONSTONE CHINA	CARTWRIGHT BROS. (POTTERY CO.)
IRONSTONE CHINA	COOK (& MELLOR) POTTERY CO.
IRONSTONE CHINA	CRESCENT POTTERY CO.
IRONSTONE CHINA	CROWN POTTERY (& POTTERIES) CO.
IRONSTONE CHINA	DRESDEN POTTERY (WORKS) CO.
IRONSTONE CHINA	EAST LIVERPOOL POTTERY CO.
IRONSTONE CHINA	EAST TRENTON POTTERY CO.
IRONSTONE CHINA	EMPIRE POTTERY (CO.) (TRENTON POTTERY CO.)
IRONSTONE CHINA	FELL & THROPP CO. (TRENTON POTTERY WORKS)
IRONSTONE CHINA	GLASGOW POTTERY CO.
IRONSTONE CHINA	GOODWIN (BROS.) POTTERY CO.
IRONSTONE CHINA	GREENWOOD POTTERY CO.
IRONSTONE CHINA	HARKER POTTERIES (ETRURIA POTTERY)
IRONSTONE CHINA	INTERNATIONAL (LINCOLN) POTTERY CO.
IRONSTONE CHINA	KNOWLES, TAYLOR, KNOWLES CO.
IRONSTONE CHINA	MARYLAND POTTERY CO.
IRONSTONE CHINA	MAYER, (J. & E.) POTTERIES CO. LTD.
IRONSTONE CHINA	MC NICOL, SMITH CO.
IRONSTONE CHINA	MERCER POTTERY CO.
IRONSTONE CHINA	MORLEY (& SON) or (& SONS) & CO.
IRONSTONE CHINA	NEW ENGLAND POTTERY CO.
IRONSTONE CHINA	ONONDAGA POTTERY CO.
IRONSTONE CHINA	PEORIA POTTERY CO.
IRONSTONE CHINA	PIONEER POTTERY CO.
IRONSTONE CHINA	POTTERS COOPERATIVE (& CO.) (THE)
IRONSTONE CHINA	PROSPECT HILL POTTERY
IRONSTONE CHINA	RED CLIFF CO. (Decorators)
IRONSTONE CHINA	STEUBENVILLE POTTERY CO.
IRONSTONE CHINA	TRENTON POTTERY (CO.) (WORKS)
IRONSTONE CHINA	UNION POTTERY CO.
IRONSTONE CHINA	VODREY & BROTHERS (POTTERY) (CO.)
IRONSTONE CHINA	WALLACE & CHETWYND
IRONSTONE CHINA	WYLLIE, JOHN & SON
KITCHEN KRAFT	CUMBOW CHINA CO. (Decorators)
KITCHEN KRAFT	LAUGHLIN, HOMER (CHINA & CO.)
KOKUS (STONE) CHINA	SEBRING POTTERY (WORKS) CO. or (SEBRING BROS. & CO.)
LA BELLE CHINA	WHEELING POTTERY CO.
LA FRANCAISE PORCELAIN	FRENCH CHINA CO. (THE)
LA FRANCAISE SEMI VITREOUS	FRENCH CHINA CO. (THE)
LAMBERTON (CHINA)	MADDOCK, THOMAS (& SONS) (& CO.)
LIMOGES	LIMOGES CHINA CO. (STERLING CHINA CO.)
LINCOLN ILLINOIS	ILLINOIS CHINA CO. (THE)
LIVERPOOL	CARTWRIGHT BROS. (POTTERY CO.)
LIVERPOOL	MC NICOL, D. E. POTTERY CO.
LIVERPOOL, OHIO	BENNETT, EDWIN POTTERY (CO.)
MADE IN AMERICA	WHEELING POTTERY CO.
MADE IN U. S. A.	AMERICAN CHINA CO.
MADE IN U. S. A.	TAYLOR, SMITH & TAYLOR CO. (INC.)
MADE IN U. S. A./ CHINA	UNITED STATES POTTERY (THE)
MELROSE	THOMPSON, C. C. & CO. (POTTERY CO.)
N. Y. C. P.	BAUM, J. H.

MARK	POTTERY
NEW CASTLE PA	SHENANGO CHINA (POTTERY) CO.
OPAQUE CHINA	EAST TRENTON POTTERY CO.
OPAQUE PORCELAIN	WILLETS MANUFACTURING CO.
PALISSY CHINA	VODREY & BROTHERS (POTTERY) (CO.)
PARIS WHITE	CRESCENT POTTERY CO.
PATENTED	COLONIAL POTTERY CO. (THE)
PATENTED	GREENWOOD POTTERY CO.
PATENTED	KNOWLES, TAYLOR, KNOWLES CO.
PATENTED	WALKER CHINA CO.
PEARL WHITE	FRENCH CHINA CO. (THE)
PEARL WHITE	GOODWIN (BROS.) POTTERY CO.
PORCELAIN	BURFORD BROS. POTTERY CO.
PORCELAIN	INTERNATIONAL (LINCOLN) POTTERY CO.
PORCELAIN	SEBRING POTTERY (WORKS) CO. or (SEBRING BROS. & CO.)
PORCELAIN	TRENLE (BLAKE) CHINA CO.
PORCELAIN OPAQUE	TRENLE (BLAKE) CHINA CO.
PORCELAINE OPAQUE	PROSPECT HILL POTTERY
PORCELAINE OPAQUE	TRENTON POTTERY (CO.) (WORKS)
ROYAL BLUE	INTERNATIONAL (LINCOLN) POTTERY CO.
ROYAL BLUE CHINA	INTERNATIONAL (LINCOLN) POTTERY CO.
ROYAL BLUE PORCELAIN	INTERNATIONAL (LINCOLN) POTTERY CO.
ROYAL CHINA	BURROUGHS & MOUNTFORD (& CO.)
ROYAL IRONSTONE	WHEELING POTTERY CO.
ROYAL IRONSTONE CHINA	EAST END POTTERY (CHINA) CO.
ROYAL IRONSTONE CHINA	SEBRING POTTERY (WORKS) CO. or (SEBRING BROS. & CO.)
ROYAL IRONSTONE CHINA	STEUBENVILLE POTTERY CO.
ROYAL LA BELLE	WHEELING POTTERIES CO.
ROYAL PORCELAIN	MADDOCK, THOMAS (& SONS) (& CO.)
SAXON CHINA	SAXON CHINA CO.
SEMI GRANITE	BAUM, J. H.
SEMI GRANITE	BEERBOWER & GRIFFEN
SEMI GRANITE	BEERBOWER, L. B. & CO.
SEMI GRANITE	CARTWRIGHT BROS. (POTTERY CO.)
SEMI GRANITE	CRESCENT POTTERY CO.
SEMI GRANITE	MC NICOL, BURTON & CO.
SEMI GRANITE	MC NICOL, D. E. POTTERY CO.
SEMI GRANITE	THOMPSON, C. C. & CO. (POTTERY CO.)
SEMI PORCELAIN	ANCHOR POTTERY CO.
SEMI PORCELAIN	CROWN POTTERY (& POTTERIES) CO.
SEMI PORCELAIN	PIONEER POTTERY CO.
SEMI PORCELAIN	POTTERS COOPERATIVE (& CO.) (THE)
SEMI PORCELAIN	VODREY & BROTHERS (POTTERY) (CO.)
SEMI PORCELAIN	WARWICK CHINA (CO.)
SEMI PORCELAIN	WELLSVILLE CHINA COMPANY
SEMI PORCELAIN	WHEELING POTTERIES CO.
SEMI VITREOUS	FRENCH CHINA CO. (THE)
SEMI VITREOUS	INTERNATIONAL (LINCOLN) POTTERY CO.
SEMI VITREOUS	KNOWLES, EDWIN, M. CHINA CO.
SEMI VITREOUS	MERCER POTTERY CO.
SEMI VITREOUS CHINA	MAYER, (J. & E.) POTTERIES CO. LTD.
SEMI VITREOUS PORCELAIN	EAST LIVERPOOL POTTERIES COMPANIES
SEMI VITREOUS PORCELAIN	MAYER, (J. & E.) POTTERIES CO. LTD.
SEMI VITREOUS PORCELAIN	UNITED STATES POTTERY CO. (THE)
SEMI WARRANTY	MC NICOL, BURTON & CO.
STERLING CHINA	COLONIAL POTTERY CO. (THE)
STERLING CHINA	LIMOGES CHINA CO. (STERLING CHINA CO.)
STERLING CHINA	POTTERS COOPERATIVE (& CO.) (THE)
STONE CHINA	BEERBOWER, L. B. & CO.
STONE CHINA	BENNETT, EDWIN POTTERY (CO.)
STONE CHINA	DRESDEN POTTERY (WORKS) CO.
STONE CHINA	EMPIRE POTTERY (CO.) (TRENTON POTTERY CO.)
STONE CHINA	ETRURIA POTTERY (CO.)
STONE CHINA	HARKER POTTERIES (ETRURIA POTTERY)
STONE CHINA	MAYER, (J. & E.) POTTERIES CO. LTD.
STONE CHINA	MERCER POTTERY CO.
STONE CHINA	NEW ENGLAND POTTERY CO.
STONE CHINA	NEW YORK CITY POTTERY
STONE CHINA	PIONEER POTTERY CO.
STONE CHINA	POTTERS COOPERATIVE (& CO.) (THE)
STONE CHINA	SCOTT, GEO. (& SONS) POTTERY
STONE CHINA	SEBRING POTTERY (WORKS) CO. or (SEBRING BROS. & CO.)
STONE CHINA	WHEELING POTTERY CO.
STONE CHINA	WYLLIE, JOHN & SON
STONE PORCELAIN	NEW YORK CITY POTTERY
THE POTTERS WHEEL	BURROUGHS & MOUNTFORD
TORONTO OHIO	AMERICAN CHINA CO.
TRADE MARK	BRUNT, WILLIAM (JR.) & CO.
TRADE MARK	FORD CHINA CO. (THE)
TRADE MARK	HARKER POTTERIES (ETRURIA POTTERY)
TRADE MARK	MERCER POTTERY CO.
TRADE MARK	NEW YORK CITY POTTERY
TRADE MARK	TAYLOR, SMITH & TAYLOR CO. (INC.)
TRADE MARK	THOMPSON, C. C. & CO. (POTTERY CO.)
TRADE MARK	WARWICK CHINA (CO.)
TRADE MARK	WYLLIE, JOHN & SON

MARK	POTTERY
TRENLE ROYAL	TRENLE (BLAKE) CHINA CO.
TRENTON N. J.	COOK (& MELLOR) POTTERY CO.
TRENTON N. J.	EMPIRE POTTERY (CO.) (TRENTON POTTERY CO.)
TRENTON N. J.	MADDOCK, THOMAS (& SONS) (& CO.)
TRENTON N. J.	MERCER POTTERY CO.
TRENTON N. J.	TRENTON CHINA CO.
TRENTON N. J.	TRENTON POTTERIES CO. (EMPIRE POTTERY)
TRENTON N. J.	MILLINGTON & ASTBURY (& PAULSON) POTTERY
U. S. (THE)	EAST LIVERPOOL POTTERIES COMPANIES
UNDERGLAZE BLUE	TRENLE (BLAKE) CHINA CO.
VASSAR	BUFFALO POTTERY CO.
VERUS	OLIVER CHINA CO.
VIRGINIA	EAST END CHINA CO. (THE) (SEE:TRENLE BLAKE CHINA CO.)
VITREOUS	TAYLOR, SMITH & TAYLOR CO. (INC.)
WARRANTED	AMERICAN CHINA CO.
WARRANTED	ANCHOR POTTERY CO.
WARRANTED	BEERBOWER, L. B. & CO.
WARRANTED	BENNETT, EDWIN POTTERY (CO.)
WARRANTED	BRUNT, WILLIAM POTTERY CO.
WARRANTED	BURFORD BROS. POTTERY CO.
WARRANTED	CARTWRIGHT BROS. (POTTERY CO.)
WARRANTED	CRESCENT POTTERY CO.
WARRANTED	CROWN POTTERY (& POTTERIES) CO.
WARRANTED	EAST END POTTERY (CHINA) CO.
WARRANTED	EAST LIVERPOOL POTTERY CO.
WARRANTED	EMPIRE POTTERY (CO.) (TRENTON POTTERY CO.)
WARRANTED	ETRURIA POTTERY (CO.)
WARRANTED	GLASGOW POTTERY CO.
WARRANTED	GOODWIN (BROS.) POTTERY CO.
WARRANTED	KNOWLES, TAYLOR, KNOWLES CO.
WARRANTED	MARYLAND POTTERY CO.
WARRANTED	MAYER, (J. & E.) POTTERIES CO. LTD.
WARRANTED	MC NICOL, D. E. POTTERY CO.
WARRANTED	OPERATIVE POTTERY
WARRANTED	PEORIA POTTERY CO.
WARRANTED	SEBRING POTTERY (WORKS) CO. or (SEBRING BROS. & CO.)
WARRANTED	STEUBENVILLE POTTERY CO.
WARRANTED	THOMPSON, C. C. & CO. (POTTERY CO.)
WARRANTED	TRENTON POTTERY (CO.) (WORKS)
WARRANTED	UNION POTTERY CO.
WARRANTED	VODREY & BROTHERS (POTTERY) (CO.)
WARRANTED	WHEELING POTTERY CO.
WARRANTED	WILLETS MANUFACTURING CO.
WARRANTED BEST IRONSTONE CHINA	BROCKMAN POTTERY CO.
WARRANTED BEST IRONSTONE CHINA	PEORIA POTTERY CO.
WARRANTED BEST IRONSTONE CHINA	TEMPEST, BROCKMANN & CO.
WARRANTED CHINA	MERCER POTTERY CO.
WARRANTED CHINA	UNION POTTERY CO.
WARRANTED IRONSTONE CHINA	KNOWLES, TAYLOR, KNOWLES & CO.
WARRANTED SUPERIOR	MERCER POTTERY CO.
WARRANTED SUPERIOR IRONSTONE CHINA	INTERNATIONAL (LINCOLN) POTTERY CO.
WHEELING	WARWICK CHINA (CO.)
WHITE GRANITE	BRUNT, WILLIAM CO.
WHITE GRANITE	CHELSEA CHINA CO.
WHITE GRANITE	MARYLAND POTTERY CO.
WHITE GRANITE	POTTERS COOPERATIVE (& CO.) (THE)
WHITE GRANITE	WHEELING POTTERY CO.
WINOMA	SEBRING, E. H. CHINA CO.
XX CENTURY SEMI PORCELAIN	WHEELING POTTERIES CO.

APPENDIX A6: CROSS REFERENCE: POTTERIES & BACK MARKINGS

POTTERY	MARK
AMERICAN CHINA CO.	EXTRA QUALITY
AMERICAN CHINA CO.	EXTRA QUALITY IRONSTONE CHINA
AMERICAN CHINA CO.	IRONSTONE CHINA
AMERICAN CHINA CO.	MADE IN U. S. A.
AMERICAN CHINA CO.	TORONTO OHIO
AMERICAN CHINA CO.	WARRANTED
AMERICAN CROCKERY CO. (JERSEY CITY POTTERY)	AMERICAN CHINA
AMERICAN CROCKERY CO. (JERSEY CITY POTTERY)	IRONSTONE CHINA
ANCHOR POTTERY CO.	IRONSTONE CHINA
ANCHOR POTTERY CO.	SEMI PORCELAIN
ANCHOR POTTERY CO.	WARRANTED
BAHL POTTERIES, INC.	AMERICAN BELLEEK
BAUM, J. H.	N. Y. C. P.
BAUM, J. H.	SEMI GRANITE
BEERBOWER & GRIFFEN	IRONSTONE CHINA
BEERBOWER & GRIFFEN	SEMI GRANITE

POTTERY	MARK
BEERBOWER, L. B. & CO.	IRONSTONE CHINA
BEERBOWER, L. B. & CO.	SEMI GRANITE
BEERBOWER, L. B. & CO.	STONE CHINA
BEERBOWER, L. B. & CO.	WARRANTED
BENNETT, EDWIN POTTERY (CO.)	EAST LIVERPOOL OHIO
BENNETT, EDWIN POTTERY (CO.)	LIVERPOOL, OHIO
BENNETT, EDWIN POTTERY (CO.)	STONE CHINA
BENNETT, EDWIN POTTERY (CO.)	WARRANTED
BROCKMAN POTTERY CO.	WARRANTED BEST IRONSTONE CHINA
BRUNT, BLOOR, MARTIN & CO.	DRESDEN WHITE GRANITE
BRUNT, WILLIAM (JR.) & CO.	IRONSTONE CHINA
BRUNT, WILLIAM (JR.) & CO.	TRADE MARK
BRUNT, WILLIAM CO.	DRESDEN
BRUNT, WILLIAM CO.	WHITE GRANITE
BRUNT, WILLIAM POTTERY CO.	IRONSTONE CHINA
BRUNT, WILLIAM POTTERY CO.	WARRANTED
BUFFALO POTTERY CO.	VASSAR
BURFORD BROS. POTTERY CO.	IRONSTONE CHINA
BURFORD BROS. POTTERY CO.	PORCELAIN
BURFORD BROS. POTTERY CO.	WARRANTED
BURROUGHS & MOUNTFORD	THE POTTERS WHEEL
BURROUGHS & MOUNTFORD (& CO.)	EXTRA QUALITY
BURROUGHS & MOUNTFORD (& CO.)	ROYAL CHINA
CARROLLTON POTTERY CO.	CHINA
CARTWRIGHT BROS. (POTTERY CO.)	IRONSTONE CHINA
CARTWRIGHT BROS. (POTTERY CO.)	LIVERPOOL
CARTWRIGHT BROS. (POTTERY CO.)	SEMI GRANITE
CARTWRIGHT BROS. (POTTERY CO.)	WARRANTED
CHELSEA CHINA CO.	CHINA
CHELSEA CHINA CO.	WHITE GRANITE
CHESAPEAKE POTTERY (CO.)	ARUNDEL
CHESAPEAKE POTTERY (CO.)	AVALON CHINA
CHESAPEAKE POTTERY (CO.)	AVALON FAIENCE
CHESAPEAKE POTTERY (CO.)	BEST CHINA
CHESAPEAKE POTTERY (CO.)	HAYNES BALT
COLONIAL POTTERY CO. (THE)	PATENTED
COLONIAL POTTERY CO. (THE)	STERLING CHINA
COOK (& MELLOR) POTTERY CO.	ETRURIA
COOK (& MELLOR) POTTERY CO.	IRONSTONE CHINA
COOK (& MELLOR) POTTERY CO.	TRENTON N. J.
CRESCENT POTTERY CO.	IRONSTONE CHINA
CRESCENT POTTERY CO.	PARIS WHITE
CRESCENT POTTERY CO.	SEMI GRANITE
CRESCENT POTTERY CO.	WARRANTED
CROWN POTTERY (& POTTERIES) CO.	IRONSTONE CHINA
CROWN POTTERY (& POTTERIES) CO.	SEMI PORCELAIN
CROWN POTTERY (& POTTERIES) CO.	WARRANTED
CUMBOW CHINA CO. (Decorators)	KITCHEN KRAFT
DRESDEN POTTERY (WORKS) CO.	DRESDEN STONE CHINA
DRESDEN POTTERY (WORKS) CO.	DRESDEN WHITE GRANITE
DRESDEN POTTERY (WORKS) CO.	EXTRA QUALITY
DRESDEN POTTERY (WORKS) CO.	IRONSTONE CHINA
DRESDEN POTTERY (WORKS) CO.	STONE CHINA
EAST END CHINA CO. (THE) (SEE: TRENLE BLAKE CHINA CO.)	VIRGINIA
EAST END POTTERY (CHINA) CO.	E. LIVERPOOL O.
EAST END POTTERY (CHINA) CO.	ROYAL IRONSTONE CHINA
EAST END POTTERY (CHINA) CO.	WARRANTED
EAST LIVERPOOL POTTERIES COMPANIES	SEMI VITREOUS PORCELAIN
EAST LIVERPOOL POTTERIES COMPANIES	U. S. (THE)
EAST LIVERPOOL POTTERY CO.	CHINA
EAST LIVERPOOL POTTERY CO.	IRONSTONE CHINA
EAST LIVERPOOL POTTERY CO.	WARRANTED
EAST TRENTON POTTERY CO.	IRONSTONE CHINA
EAST TRENTON POTTERY CO.	OPAQUE CHINA
EMPIRE POTTERY (CO.) (TRENTON POTTERY CO.)	CHINA
EMPIRE POTTERY (CO.) (TRENTON POTTERY CO.)	IMPERIAL CHINA
EMPIRE POTTERY (CO.) (TRENTON POTTERY CO.)	IRONSTONE CHINA
EMPIRE POTTERY (CO.) (TRENTON POTTERY CO.)	STONE CHINA
EMPIRE POTTERY (CO.) (TRENTON POTTERY CO.)	TRENTON N. J.
EMPIRE POTTERY (CO.) (TRENTON POTTERY CO.)	WARRANTED
ETRURIA POTTERY (CO.)	STONE CHINA
ETRURIA POTTERY (CO.)	WARRANTED
FELL & THROPP CO. (TRENTON POTTERY WORKS)	IRONSTONE CHINA
FORD CHINA CO. (THE)	FORD CITY, PA
FORD CHINA CO. (THE)	TRADE MARK
FRENCH CHINA CO. (THE)	LA FRANCAISE PORCELAIN
FRENCH CHINA CO. (THE)	LA FRANCAISE SEMI VITREOUS
FRENCH CHINA CO. (THE)	PEARL WHITE
FRENCH CHINA CO. (THE)	SEMI VITREOUS
FRENCH-SAXON CHINA CO.	FRENCH-SAXON

POTTERY	MARK
GLASGOW POTTERY CO.	IRONSTONE CHINA
GLASGOW POTTERY CO.	WARRANTED
GLOBE POTTERY CO.	CHINA
GOODWIN (BROS.) POTTERY CO.	IRONSTONE CHINA
GOODWIN (BROS.) POTTERY CO.	PEARL WHITE
GOODWIN (BROS.) POTTERY CO.	WARRANTED
GREENFIELD VILLAGE POTTERY (Museum)	HALL
GREENWOOD POTTERY CO.	CHINA
GREENWOOD POTTERY CO.	IRONSTONE CHINA
GREENWOOD POTTERY CO.	PATENTED
HARKER POTTERIES (ETRURIA POTTERY)	E. LIVERPOOL
HARKER POTTERIES (ETRURIA POTTERY)	IRONSTONE CHINA
HARKER POTTERIES (ETRURIA POTTERY)	STONE CHINA
HARKER POTTERIES (ETRURIA POTTERY)	TRADE MARK
ILLINOIS CHINA CO. (THE)	LINCOLN ILLINOIS
INTERNATIONAL (LINCOLN) POTTERY CO.	IRONSTONE CHINA
INTERNATIONAL (LINCOLN) POTTERY CO.	PORCELAIN
INTERNATIONAL (LINCOLN) POTTERY CO.	ROYAL BLUE
INTERNATIONAL (LINCOLN) POTTERY CO.	ROYAL BLUE CHINA
INTERNATIONAL (LINCOLN) POTTERY CO.	ROYAL BLUE PORCELAIN
INTERNATIONAL (LINCOLN) POTTERY CO.	SEMI VITREOUS
INTERNATIONAL (LINCOLN) POTTERY CO.	WARRANTED SUPERIOR IRONSTONE CHINA
KNOWLES, EDWIN, M. CHINA CO.	SEMI VITREOUS
KNOWLES, TAYLOR, KNOWLES CO.	GRANITE WARE
KNOWLES, TAYLOR, KNOWLES CO.	INTERNATIONAL (LINCOLN)POTTERY CO.
KNOWLES, TAYLOR, KNOWLES CO.	IRONSTONE CHINA
KNOWLES, TAYLOR, KNOWLES CO.	PATENTED
KNOWLES, TAYLOR, KNOWLES CO.	WARRANTED
KNOWLES, TAYLOR, KNOWLES CO.	WARRANTED IRONSTONE CHINA
LAUGHLIN, HOMER (CHINA & CO.)	COLONIAL
LAUGHLIN, HOMER (CHINA & CO.)	KITCHEN KRAFT
LIMOGES CHINA CO. (STERLING CHINA CO.)	CHINA
LIMOGES CHINA CO. (STERLING CHINA CO.)	LIMOGES
LIMOGES CHINA CO. (STERLING CHINA CO.)	STERLING CHINA
MADDOCK, THOMAS (& SONS) (& CO.)	CHINA
MADDOCK, THOMAS (& SONS) (& CO.)	LAMBERTON (CHINA)
MADDOCK, THOMAS (& SONS) (& CO.)	ROYAL PORCELAIN
MADDOCK, THOMAS (& SONS) (& CO.)	TRENTON N. J.
MARYLAND POTTERY CO.	BALTIMORE
MARYLAND POTTERY CO.	IRONSTONE CHINA
MARYLAND POTTERY CO.	WARRANTED
MARYLAND POTTERY CO.	WHITE GRANITE
MAYER, (J. & E.) POTTERIES CO. LTD.	BEAVER FALLS, PA
MAYER, (J. & E.) POTTERIES CO. LTD.	IRONSTONE CHINA
MAYER, (J. & E.) POTTERIES CO. LTD.	SEMI VITREOUS CHINA
MAYER, (J. & E.) POTTERIES CO. LTD.	SEMI VITREOUS PORCELAIN
MAYER, (J. & E.) POTTERIES CO. LTD.	STONE CHINA
MAYER, (J. & E.) POTTERIES CO. LTD.	WARRANTED
MC NICOL, BURTON & CO.	GRANIT
MC NICOL, BURTON & CO.	SEMI GRANITE
MC NICOL, BURTON & CO.	SEMI WARRANTY
MC NICOL, D. E. POTTERY CO.	LIVERPOOL
MC NICOL, D. E. POTTERY CO.	SEMI GRANITE
MC NICOL, D. E. POTTERY CO.	WARRANTED
MC NICOL, SMITH CO.	IRONSTONE CHINA
MERCER POTTERY CO.	CHINA
MERCER POTTERY CO.	IRONSTONE CHINA
MERCER POTTERY CO.	SEMI VITREOUS
MERCER POTTERY CO.	STONE CHINA
MERCER POTTERY CO.	TRADE MARK
MERCER POTTERY CO.	TRENTON N. J.
MERCER POTTERY CO.	WARRANTED CHINA
MERCER POTTERY CO.	WARRANTED SUPERIOR
MILLINGTON & ASTBURY (& PAULSON) POTTERY	TRENTON N.J.
MORLEY (& SON) or (& SONS) & CO.	IRONSTONE CHINA
NEW ENGLAND POTTERY CO.	IRONSTONE CHINA
NEW ENGLAND POTTERY CO.	STONE CHINA
NEW YORK CITY POTTERY	STONE CHINA
NEW YORK CITY POTTERY	STONE PORCELAIN
NEW YORK CITY POTTERY	TRADE MARK
NORTON POTTERY	BENNINGTON (VT)
OHIO CHINA CO.	IMPERIAL CHINA
OLIVER CHINA CO.	VERUS
ONONDAGA POTTERY CO.	CHINA
ONONDAGA POTTERY CO.	IRONSTONE CHINA
OPERATIVE POTTERY	WARRANTED
PEORIA POTTERY CO.	IRONSTONE CHINA
PEORIA POTTERY CO.	WARRANTED
PEORIA POTTERY CO.	WARRANTED BEST IRONSTONE CHINA

POTTERY	MARK
PHOENIXVILLE (PHOENIX) POTTERY CO.	ETRUSCAN
PIONEER POTTERY CO.	CROWN POTTERY
PIONEER POTTERY CO.	IMPERIAL CHINA
PIONEER POTTERY CO.	IRONSTONE CHINA
PIONEER POTTERY CO.	SEMI PORCELAIN
PIONEER POTTERY CO.	STONE CHINA
POTTERS CO-OPERATIVE (& CO.)(THE)	DRESDEN WHITE GRANITE
POTTERS COOPERATIVE (& CO.) (THE)	CHINA
POTTERS COOPERATIVE (& CO.) (THE)	IRONSTONE CHINA
POTTERS COOPERATIVE (& CO.) (THE)	SEMI PORCELAIN
POTTERS COOPERATIVE (& CO.) (THE)	STERLING CHINA
POTTERS COOPERATIVE (& CO.) (THE)	STONE CHINA
POTTERS COOPERATIVE (& CO.) (THE)	WHITE GRANITE
PROSPECT HILL POTTERY	CHINA
PROSPECT HILL POTTERY	IRONSTONE CHINA
PROSPECT HILL POTTERY	PORCELAINE OPAQUE
RED CLIFF CO. (Decorators)	IRONSTONE CHINA
SAXON CHINA CO.	CHINA
SAXON CHINA CO.	SAXON CHINA
SCOTT, GEO. (& SONS) POTTERY	STONE CHINA
SEBRING POTTERY (WORKS) CO. or (SEBRING BROS. & CO.)	KOKUS (STONE) CHINA
SEBRING POTTERY (WORKS) CO. or (SEBRING BROS. & CO.)	PORCELAIN
SEBRING POTTERY (WORKS) CO. or (SEBRING BROS. & CO.)	ROYAL IRONSTONE CHINA
SEBRING POTTERY (WORKS) CO. or (SEBRING BROS. & CO.)	STONE CHINA
SEBRING POTTERY (WORKS) CO. or (SEBRING BROS. & CO.)	WARRANTED
SEBRING, E. H. CHINA CO.	WINOMA
SHENANGO CHINA (POTTERY) CO.	CHINA
SHENANGO CHINA (POTTERY) CO.	NEW CASTLE PA
STEUBENVILLE POTTERY CO.	IRONSTONE CHINA
STEUBENVILLE POTTERY CO.	ROYAL IRONSTONE CHINA
STEUBENVILLE POTTERY CO.	WARRANTED
TAYLOR, SMITH & TAYLOR CO. (INC.)	CHINA
TAYLOR, SMITH & TAYLOR CO. (INC.)	MADE IN U. S. A.
TAYLOR, SMITH & TAYLOR CO. (INC.)	TRADE MARK
TAYLOR, SMITH & TAYLOR CO. (INC.)	VITREOUS
TEMPEST, BROCKMANN & CO.	WARRANTED BEST IRONSTONE CHINA
THOMPSON, C. C. & CO. (POTTERY CO.)	EUREKA
THOMPSON, C. C. & CO. (POTTERY CO.)	MELROSE
THOMPSON, C. C. & CO. (POTTERY CO.)	SEMI GRANITE
THOMPSON, C. C. & CO. (POTTERY CO.)	TRADE MARK
THOMPSON, C. C. & CO. (POTTERY CO.)	WARRANTED
TRENLE (BLAKE) CHINA CO.	PORCELAIN
TRENLE (BLAKE) CHINA CO.	PORCELAIN OPAQUE
TRENLE (BLAKE) CHINA CO.	TRENLE ROYAL
TRENLE (BLAKE) CHINA CO.	UNDERGLAZE BLUE
TRENTON CHINA CO.	TRENTON N. J.
TRENTON POTTERIES CO. (EMPIRE POTTERY)	CHINA
TRENTON POTTERIES CO. (EMPIRE POTTERY)	IDEAL CHINA
TRENTON POTTERIES CO. (EMPIRE POTTERY)	TRENTON N. J.
TRENTON POTTERY (CO.) (WORKS)	IRONSTONE CHINA
TRENTON POTTERY (CO.) (WORKS)	PORCELAINE OPAQUE
TRENTON POTTERY (CO.) (WORKS)	WARRANTED
UNION POTTERY CO.	CHINA
UNION POTTERY CO.	IRONSTONE CHINA
UNION POTTERY CO.	WARRANTED
UNION POTTERY CO.	WARRANTED CHINA
UNITED STATES POTTERY (THE)	MADE IN U. S. A./ CHINA
UNITED STATES POTTERY CO. (THE)	BENNINGTON, VT.
UNITED STATES POTTERY CO. (THE)	EAST LIVERPOOL O.
UNITED STATES POTTERY CO. (THE)	SEMI VITREOUS PORCELAIN
VODREY & BROTHERS (POTTERY) (CO.)	CHINA
VODREY & BROTHERS (POTTERY) (CO.)	IRONSTONE CHINA
VODREY & BROTHERS (POTTERY) (CO.)	PALISSY CHINA
VODREY & BROTHERS (POTTERY) (CO.)	SEMI PORCELAIN
VODREY & BROTHERS (POTTERY) (CO.)	WARRANTED
WALKER CHINA CO.	PATENTED
WALLACE & CHETWYND	IRONSTONE
WALLACE & CHETWYND	IRONSTONE CHINA
WARWICK CHINA (CO.)	CHINA
WARWICK CHINA (CO.)	IOGA
WARWICK CHINA (CO.)	SEMI PORCELAIN
WARWICK CHINA (CO.)	TRADE MARK
WARWICK CHINA (CO.)	WHEELING
WELLSVILLE CHINA COMPANY	SEMI PORCELAIN
WHEELING POTTERIES CO.	AVON
WHEELING POTTERIES CO.	BONITA
WHEELING POTTERIES CO.	BONITA SEMI PORCELAIN
WHEELING POTTERIES CO.	ROYAL LA BELLE
WHEELING POTTERIES CO.	SEMI PORCELAIN
WHEELING POTTERIES CO.	XX CENTURY SEMI PORCELAIN
WHEELING POTTERY CO.	ADAMANTINE CHINA
WHEELING POTTERY CO.	CHINA
WHEELING POTTERY CO.	LA BELLE CHINA
WHEELING POTTERY CO.	MADE IN AMERICA
WHEELING POTTERY CO.	ROYAL IRONSTONE
WHEELING POTTERY CO.	STONE CHINA
WHEELING POTTERY CO.	WARRANTED
WHEELING POTTERY CO.	WHITE GRANITE
WICK CHINA CO. (THE)	AURORA CHINA
WILLETS MANUFACTURING CO.	BELEEK
WILLETS MANUFACTURING CO.	OPAQUE PORCELAIN
WILLETS MANUFACTURING CO.	WARRANTED
WYLLIE, JOHN & SON	IRONSTONE CHINA
WYLLIE, JOHN & SON	STONE CHINA
WYLLIE, JOHN & SON	TRADE MARK

APPENDIX A7: CHECKLIST: PRODUCTION BY POTTERY IN FLOW BLUE, TEA LEAF, WHITE IRONSTONE

POTTERY	LOCATION	FB	TL	WH
AMERICAN CHINA CO.	TORONTO, OH	X		X
AMERICAN CROCKERY CO.	TRENTON, NJ		X	X
AMERICAN POTTERY CO.	JERSEY CITY, NJ			X
ANCHOR POTTERY CO. (JERSEY CITY POTTERY)	TRENTON, NJ			X
BAHL POTTERIES INC.	CARROLTON, OH		X	
BAUM, J. H.	WELLSVILLE, OH			X
BEERBOWER & GRIFFEN	PHOENIXVILLE, PA			X
BEERBOWER, L. B. & CO.	ELIZABETH, NJ			X
BENNETT, EDWIN POTTERY (CO.)	BALTIMORE, MD			X
BROCKMANN POTTERY CO.	CINCINNATI, OH		X	
BRUNT, WILLIAM JR. & CO.	EAST LIVERPOOL, OH		X	
BRUNT, WILLIAM POTTERY CO.	EAST LIVERPOOL, OH			X
BRUNT, WILLIAM SON & CO.	EAST LIVERPOOL, OH		X	
BUFFALO POTTERY CO.	BUFFALO, NY	X	X	
BURFORD BROS. POTTERY CO.	EAST LIVERPOOL, OH		X	X
BURROUGHS & MOUNTFORD (& CO.)	TRENTON, NJ		X	
CARROLTON POTTERY CO.	CARROLLTON, OH	X		
CARTWRIGHT BROTHERS (POTTERY CO.)	EAST LIVERPOOL, OH		X	X
CHELSEA CHINA CO.	NEW CUMBERLAND, WV			X
CHESAPEAKE POTTERY (CO.)	BALTIMORE, MD	X		X
CITY POTTERY CO.	TRENTON, NJ			X
COLONIAL POTTERY COMPANY (THE)	EAST LIVERPOOL, OH	X		
COOK (& MELLOR) POTTERY CO.	TRENTON, NJ	X		X
CRESCENT POTTERY CO.	TRENTON, NJ	X	X	X
CROWN POTTERY (& POTTERIES) CO.	EVANSVILLE, IN		X	X
CUMBOW CHINA CO.* (Decorators)	ABINGDON, VA		X	
DRESDEN POTTERY (WORKS) CO.	EAST LIVERPOOL, OH			X
EAGLE POTTERY CO.	TRENTON, NJ			X
EAST END POTTERY (CHINA) CO.	EAST LIVERPOOL, OH	X	X	
EAST LIVERPOOL POTTERIES CO.	EAST LIVERPOOL, OH			X
EAST LIVERPOOL POTTERY CO.	EAST LIVERPOOL, OH			X
EAST TRENTON POTTERY CO.	TRENTON, NJ			X
EMPIRE POTTERY	TRENTON, NJ	X		X
ETRURIA POTTERY (CO.)	TRENTON, NJ			X
FELL & THROPP CO.	TRENTON, NJ		X	X
FORD CHINA CO.	FORD CITY, PA		X	
FRENCH CHINA CO. (THE)	SEBRING, OH	X		
FRENCH-SAXON CHINA CO.	SEBRING, OH	X		
GLASGOW POTTERY CO.	TRENTON, NJ		X	X
GLOBE POTTERY CO.	EAST LIVERPOOL, OH		X	X
GOODWIN (BROS.) POTTERY CO.	EAST LIVERPOOL, OH		X	X
GREENFIELD VILLAGE POTTERY* (Museum)	DEARBORN, MI		X	
GREENWOOD POTTERY CO.	TRENTON, NJ			X
HALL CHINA CO.*	EAST LIVERPOOL, OH		X	X
HARKER POTTERIES	EAST LIVERPOOL, OH		X	X
ILLINOIS CHINA CO. (THE)	LINCOLN, IL		X	
INT'L (LINCOLN) POTTERY CO.- BURGESS & CAMPBELL	TRENTON, NJ	X		X
JERSEY CITY POTTERY (AMERICAN POTTERY CO.)	JERSEY CITY, NJ			X
KNOWLES, EDWIN, M. CHINA CO.	NEWELL, WV			X
KNOWLES, TAYLOR & KNOWLES & CO.	EAST LIVERPOOL, OH	X	X	X
LAUGHLIN, HOMER (CHINA CO.)*	EAST LIVERPOOL, OH	X	X	X
LIMOGES CHINA CO.	SEBRING, OH	X		X
MADDOCK, THOMAS & (SONS)(& CO.)	TRENTON, NJ	X		X
MARYLAND POTTERY CO.	BALTIMORE, MD			X
MAYER, (J&E) POTTERIES CO. (LTD.)	BEAVER FALLS, PA	X	X	X
MC NICOL, BURTON CO.	EAST LIVERPOOL, OH		X	
MC NICOL, D. E. POTTERY CO.	EAST LIVERPOOL, OH		X	X
MC NICOL, SMITH COMPANY	WELLSVILLE, OH	X		
MERCER POTTERY CO.	TRENTON, NJ	X		X

POTTERY	LOCATION	FB	TL	WH
MILLINGTON, ASTBURY (& PAULSON) POTTERY	TRENTON, NJ			X
MORELY & (SON(S)) & CO.	WELLSVILLE, OH			X
NEW ENGLAND POTTERY CO.	EAST BOSTON, MA	X		X
NEW YORK CITY POTTERY	NEW YORK, NY			X
NORTON POTTERY (& CO.)	BENNINGTON, VT			X
NORTON POTTERY (E. & L..P.)	BENNINGTON, VT			X
OHIO CHINA CO.	EAST PALESTINE, OH	X		
OLIVER CHINA CO.	SEBRING, OH	X		
ONONDANGA POTTERY CO.	SYRACUSE, NY		X	X
PADEN CITY POTTERY CO.	PADEN CITY, WV	X		
PEORIA POTTERY CO.	PEORIA, IL			X
PHOENIXVILLE (PHOENIX) POTTERY CO.	PHOENIXVILLE, PA			X
PIONEER (WELLSVILE) POTTERY CO.	WELLSVILLE, OH	X		
POTTERS COOPERATIVE CO. (THE)	EAST LIVERPOOL, OH	X	X	X
PROSPECT HILL POTTERY	TRENTON, NJ			X
RED CLIFF CO.* (Decorators)	CHICAGO, IL		X	
SAXON CHINA CO.	SEBRING, OH	X		
SAYERS, DON & RUTH * (Retailers)	MORTON, IL		X	
SCOTT, GEORGE (& SONS) POTTERY	CINCINNATI, OH		X	
SEBRING POTTERY CO. (SEBRING BROS. & CO.)	EAST LIVERPOOL, OH	X	X	
SEBRING, E. H. CHINA CO.	SEBRING, OH	X		
SHENANGO CHINA (POTTERY) CO.	NEWCASTLE, PA		X	
STERLING CHINA CO. (LIMOGES CHINA CO.)	SEBRING, OH	X		
STEUBENVILLE POTTERY CO.	STEUBINVILLE, OH	X	X	X
TAMS, STEPHEN & CO.	TRENTON, NJ			X
TAYLOR, SMITH & TAYLOR CO. (INC.)	CHESTER, WV	X		
TEMPEST, BROCKMANN & CO.	CINCINNATI, OH		X	
THOMPSON, C. C. & CO. (POTTERY CO.)	EAST LIVERPOOL, OH		X	
TRENLE (BLAKE) CHINA CO.	EAST LIVERPOOL, OH	X		
TRENTON CHINA CO.	TRENTON, NJ			X
TRENTON POTTERIES CO.	TRENTON, NJ	X		
TRENTON POTTERY (CO.)(WORKS)	TRENTON, NJ			X
UNION POTTERY CO.	TRENTON, NJ			X
UNITED STATES POTTERY CO.	BENNINGTON, VT			X
UNITED STATES POTTERY CO. (THE)	WELLSVILLE, OH		X	
VANCE FAIENCE (POTTERY) CO.	TITONSILLVE, OH			X
VANCE FAIENCE (POTTERY) CO.	TITONSILLVE, OH			X
VODREY & BROTHERS (POTTERY) (CO.)	EAST LIVERPOOL, OH		X	X
WALKER CHINA CO. *	BEDFORD, OH		X	
WALLACE & CHETWYND	EAST LIVERPOOL, OH			X
WARWICK CHINA CO.	WHEELING, WV	X		X
WELLSVILLE CHINA CO.	WELLSVILLE, OH		X	
WHEELING POTTERY CO.	WHEELING, WV	X	X	X
WICK CHINA CO. (THE)	(WICKSBORO) KITTERING, PA			X
WILLETS MANUFACTURING CO.	TRENTON, NJ			X
WYLLIE, H. R. CHINA CO.	HUNTINGTON, WV	X		
WYLLIE, JOHN & SON	EAST LIVERPOOL, OH			X

Abbreviations Used:
FB = Flow Blue
TL = Tea Leaf/Copper Lustre Band
WH = White Ironstone
* Denotes companies that had manufacturing/decorating relationships

N.B.: White Ironstone and Tea Leaf/Copper Lustre production has been very well documented by respective authors. Flow Blue, however, has not yet been totally explored. The foregoing information relies, to a large extent, upon the works of Debolt. After going through Leslie Bockol's *Willow Ware* and Connie Rogers *Willow Ware, Made in the U.S.A.*, Mary Frank Gaston's *Blue Willow*, as well as coming across examples noted by Debolt, I have listed all of the manufacturers cited by Mr. Debolt. It would appear that even without verification, Debolt's listing is accurate. However, a sufficient number of potters differ between what Debolt has cataloged as Flow Blue and/or as Willow Ware.Although slightly afield of the intent of this Encyclopedia, I felt it necessary to include a listing of American potters who manufactured **"Willow Ware"**, of which the predominant color was blue (see Appendix A4A). This color factor may have confused writers, who unintentionally mixed "Willow Ware" with Flow Blue.

APPENDIX A4A: AMERICAN MANUFACTURERS OF WILLOW WARE 19TH - 20TH CENTURY

POTTERY	MARK	LOCATION	DATES
American Chinaware Corp	American Chinaware Corp.	Cleveland, Ohio	1929-1933
Bailey-Walker China Co.	Bailey-Walker	Bedford, Ohio	1923-1941(43)
Bennett, Edwin Pottery (Co.)	Bennett S-V Willow Ware	Baltimore, MD	(1846)90-1936
Buffalo Pottery Co.	Buffalo Pottery or China	Buffalo, NY	1901/present
Canonsburg Pottery Co.	SIMPLICITY/NASCO	Canonsburg, PA	1901-1978
Carr China Co.	CARR CHINA/ GRAFTON CHOP	Grafton, WV	1916-1952
Cleveland China Co. or Geo. H. Bowman Co.**	CLEVELAND CHINA	Cleveland, Ohio Cleveland, Ohio & N.Y.C.	1890-1930s
Colonial Pottery Co.	THE COLONIAL CO.	E.Liverpool, Ohio	1903-1929
Cooks Pottery (or) China Co.	YE OLD BLUE WILLOW	Trenton, NJ	1894/c1959
Cronin China Co.	CRONIN CASUALS	Minerva, Ohio	1934-1956
Crooksville China Co.	QUADRO	Crooksville, Ohio	1902-1959
Flintridge China Co.	FLINTRIDGE	Pasadena, CA	1945-1970
George W.S., Pottery Co.	ASTER; DERWOOD; RADISSON	E. Palestine, Ohio	1898-1960
Greenwood China (or) Pottery	GREENWOOD	Trenton, NJ	1862(68)-1933
Hall China Co.	HALL	E. Liverpool, Ohio	1903/present
Hopewell China Co.	ENGLISH BRAMBLE BERRY; OSTROW CHINA	Hopewell, VA	1920-1938
Illinois China Co.	ILLINOIS CHINA CO./ LINCOLN HALL	Lincoln, IL	c.1919-1946
Jackson (Royal) China Co.	JACKSON	Falls Creek, PA	1920-1980s
Knowles, Edwin, M. China Co.	EDWIN M. KNOWLES CHINA CO.	Chester & Newell, WV	1901-1963
Laughlin, Homer (China & Co.)	BEST CHINA; KITCHEN KRAFT; WILLOW	E. Liverpool, Ohio & Newell, WV	(1873)77-present
Limoges (American) China Co.	BLUE WILLOW; LIMOGES	Sebring, Ohio	1902-1949 (55)
Mayer (J. & E.) Pottery Co. Ltd.	MAYER CHINA; WILLOW PATTERN	Beaver Falls, Ohio	1881-1916 (64)
McCoy, Nelson Pottery	MC COY	Roseville, Ohio	(1910)33-1990
McNicol, D.E., Pottery Co.	MC NICOL CHINA	E. Liverpool, Ohio & Clarksburg, WV	1892-1928 &1914-1954
Mercer Pottery Co.	MERCER	Trenton, NJ	1868-1930s
National China Co.	NATIONAL CHINA	E. Liverpool, Ohio & Salineville, Ohio	1899-1911 1911-1929 (31)
Paden City Pottery Co.	THE PADEN CITY POTTERY CO.	Paden City, WV	1914-1963
Pickard China	-PICKARD	Antioch, IL	(1894)& 38 - present
River, James Potteries	KING QUALITY	Hopewell, VA	1939-1945
Royal China Co. (The)	R.C.; BLUE WILLOW	Sebring, Ohio	1933-1987
Salem China Co. (The)	SALEM CHINA	Salem, Ohio	1898-1967 present
Scammell China Co.	SCAMMELL	Trenton, NJ	1924-1939 (54)
Scio Pottery Co.	—	Scio, Ohio	1887-1940 (48)
Sebring, E.H. China Co.	E.H.S./S.V./CHINA; IVORY PORCELAIN	Sebring, Ohio	1897-1940 (48)
Shenango China (Pottery) Co.	SHENANGO CHINA U.S.A.	Newcastle, PA	1901-1979-present
Southern Potteries Inc.	BLUE RIDGE, S.P.I	Erwin, TN	1917-1957
Sterling China Co.	STERLING (VITIRIFIED) CHINA CO.	Wellsville, Ohio	1917/present
Sterling China Co.	CARIBE	Vega Baja,Puerto Rico	1951-1977
Stetson China Co.	—	Lincoln, IL	1919-1966
Syracuse China Co.	O..P. CO.; OLD IVORY; CAREFREE	Syracuse, NY	1871/present
Taylor, Smith & Taylor Co. (The)	BELVA CHINA; IONA; T.S.T.	Chester, WV	1901-1973 (82)
Thompson, C.C. & Co. (Pottery Co.)	THOM/PSON/ MADISON	E. Liverpool, Ohio	(1868)1916-1938
Van Pottery	YE OLD BLUE CHINA	Trenton, NJ	1920-1932
Walker China Co.	WALKER CHINA	Bedford, Ohio	c.1941-1976 (80)
Warwick China Co.	WARWICK (CHINA)	Wheeling, WV	1884-1951
Wellsville China Company	WELLSVILLE/CHINA/ "WILLOW"	Wellsville, Ohio	1902-1959 (69)

*A sample selection of back markings
** George H. Bowman (Cleveland China Co.) was a major importer, wholesaler and retailer with retail outlets in both Cleveland, Ohio, and New York City (refer to Section IV). Willow ware was amongst the wares imported (e.g. Burgess Bros.).

In correspondence to me, Connie Rogers noted the following importers of willow ware: and further notes "Willow pattern china was produced from 1905 on."

IMPORTER	LOCATION	POTTER REPRESENTED &/OR MARK
BAMBERGER & CO.	NEWARK, [NJ]	—
BURLEY & CO.	CHICAGO [IL]	JOHN MADDOCK & SON
BRUCE FISHER & CO.	PHILADELPHIA [PA]	WM. ADAMS & SON
AUGUST HASHAGEN	NEW YORK [N.Y.C.]	"WILLOW PATTERN"
ALBERT PICK BARTH & CO.	CHICAGO [IL] & NEW YORK [NY]	WOOD & SONS
PITKIN & BROOKS	CHICAGO [IL]	HAMMERSLEY & CO.
RICH & FISHER	457 FIFTH AVE., NEW YORK [NY]	H. AYNSLEY & CO.

PART II. INTRODUCTION TO ENGLISH POTTERS AND PATTERNS

Over the last thirty years vast amounts of printed material, particularly relative to English ceramics, has been published. I have attempted to bring together, in one volume, this diverse material to aid and facilitate the collector and reader's pursuit of information. Where feasible, I have supplied an annotated listing of these publications to which the reader may refer.

Substantial amounts of English ceramics of ironstone-type earthenware were exported to the United States. As such, these marks and patterns were not available to the English researcher. Many of these marks and patterns are to be found in this section.

The Marks Numbering System, first established by Geoffrey A. Godden, in his *Encyclopaedia of British Pottery and Porcelain Marks* is continued. Additional marks and/or potters have been included and a **dash (-)** means that no Godden number is indicated. A parallel reference system, devised by this author, is located to the left of Godden's numbers, and called a **KAD** number.

KAD NO.	**GDN NO.**	**MARK**	**DATING**
B6	150	R.A.	Printed mark, 1860-1870.
B7		(Mark)	Printed mark, c. 1860-1880.
B8	151	R.A. & Co.	Printed mark, "& CO." from 1870-1880

KEY TO LETTERS PRECEDING "KAD NO."

A = American (Potters)
B = English (Potters)
C = European (Potters)

Additionally, potters are listed in alphabetical order; thus inclusions start with the letter "A" and continue on with "A Bros.", "AB", "A & B", etc.

It must be remembered that this is not a definitive work - as no work can be. This effort represents the vast majority of potters of ironstone-type earthenwares, their marks, patterns and brief histories.

As we approach the twenty-first century, the time may be ripe for English authors and researchers to provide us with published information on late nineteenth and twentieth century ceramics, an area of information that is sorely lacking for today's collector.

ADAMS

KAD NO.	**GODDEN NO.**	**MARK**	
			***Benjamin Adams** **Greengates,** **Tunstall, Staffordshire, c.1805-1820**
B1	10	**B. ADAMS**	Impressed name mark found on earthenware, c.1805-1820.

ADAMS

Harvey Adams & Co.
High Street & Sutherland Road,
Longton, Staffordshire, 1869-1887
Formerly, Adams, Scrivner & Co. (1862-1869)
Subsequently, Hammersley & Co. (1887-1932)

B2	14	**H. A. & CO.**	Printed initial mark over crown, c.1869-1887.

For further reading, refer to *Coysh*, Vol. 2, p. 12; and *Godden, British Porcelain*, pp. 71-72, 393.

ADAMS

KAD NO. | GODDEN NO. | MARK

***William Adams & Son(s), c.1772-1820**
- & Son, 1819+
- Stoke, 1818-1822
- & Sons, c.1829-1863
William Adams (Co. & Ltd.), c.1829-1865
Greenfield & Greengates Potteries, Tunstall, Staffordshire
- From 1784 - Under William II
- From 1787-1805 - William Adams & Son

B3 | 17 | **ADAMS & CO.** | Impressed name mark, c.1769-1800.

B4 | 18 | **ADAMS** | Impressed name mark, c.1800-1863.

B5 | 19

Printed or impressed mark on Blue Earthenware, c.1804-1840.
- Second marking of printed mark, but noted with impressed eagle, c.1804-1840.

Printed marks of various designs noted on Historic American/Canadian Views, which often include printed series and title names, c.1804-1840.

Typical Examples Include:

B6 | -
B7 | -

B8 | -

Importer's mark frequently noted on Historic American subjects, c.1804-1840.

B9 | 20

Impressed mark on earthenware, c.1810-1825.

- This impressed mark may also accompany a printed mark. See *P. Williams, Staffordshire*, Vol. 2, p. 658 for an example.

For further reading, refer to *Coysh & Stefano, Ceramic Landscapes*; *Godden, British Porcelain*, pp. 69-70; *Godden, Collecting Lustreware*, pp. 75-76; *Godden, Staffordshire*, pp. 369-374; and *Snyder, Historic Staffordshire,* pp. 39-41.

B10 | 22 | **W. ADAMS & SONS** | Printed marks of differing design. Pattern name often included, c.1829-1863.
B11 | 23 | **W. A. & S.**

Typical Examples Include:*

B12 | -
B13 | -
B14 | -
B15 | -

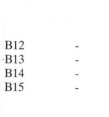

KAD NO.	GODDEN NO.	MARK	
B16	-		Printed marks of differing design. Pattern name often included, c.1829-1863. - For a continuation of the Chronology, refer to William & Thomas Adams.
B17	26	W. ADAMS	Printed marks of differing design. Pattern name often included, mid-19th century. Note the term "IMPERIAL/FRENCH PORCELAIN". **Typical Examples Include:**
B18	-		
B19	-		
B20	-		
B21	27		Printed marks of differing design. Pattern name often included, c.1893-1917. -Robert Nicholl's *Ten Generations of a Potting Family*, includes many overseas markets for Adams, and lists the export lines as "Flown Blue", "Ironstone", and "Painted Wares". - The Greenfield Pottery was sold in 1853 by William Adams IV and Edward to Thomas Adams. For further reading, refer to William Turner's *William Adams, An Old English Potter*, London, Chapman & Hall, 1904.
B22	27	W. A. & CO.	Printed marks of differing design. Pattern name often included, c.1893-1917. - Various printed marks used from c.1879 into the 20th century, with variations occurring: e.g.; a crown in place of an eagle, etc. for Godden Nos. 28 and 29. "ENGLAND" included after 1891. **Typical Examples Include:**
B23	28		
B24	29		
B25	30		
B26	31		
B27	32		

- For additional backstamps, refer to *Gaston*, Vol. 1, No. 1-10.
- In *F.O.B. Bulletin*, No. 89, Autumn 1995, p. 3, David Furniss' article "Adams-'Lasso' of Amazon Pattern and Petrus Regout 'Indian Traffic' Pattern", it is noted that George

KAD NO.	GODDEN NO.	MARK	
			Jones acquired the "Lasso" pattern and other patterns at the Stoke sale of April 10, 1861. He further notes that "...Adams 'Lasso' was in the sales literature until after 1917. A copper which survived at Tunstall until 1979 had the engraved title 'Amazon'. [Thus noting] in the Adams 1861 sale list there is a 'Lasso' but no 'Amazon'...'Amazon' may be a twentieth century title change.
B28	34		Printed mark introduced in 1879. "ENGLAND" added from 1891 on.
B29	-	**W. ADAMS TUNSTALL ENGLAND**	Printed marks of differing design. Pattern name often included, c.1890 1914. "TUNSTALL" appears, c.1896.

Typical Examples Include:

KAD NO.	GODDEN NO.	MARK	
B30	35		
B31	-		
B32	-		- *P. Williams' Flow Blue*, Vol. I, p. 54, notes the reissue of the pattern "Tonquin" as "Shanghai", c.1870s.
B33	38	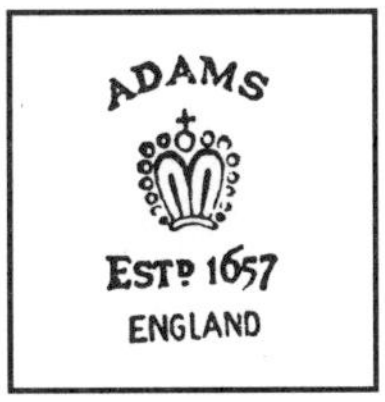	Printed name mark from 1914-1947.

Typical Examples of Printed Marks from 1950+ Include:

1950+

1950+

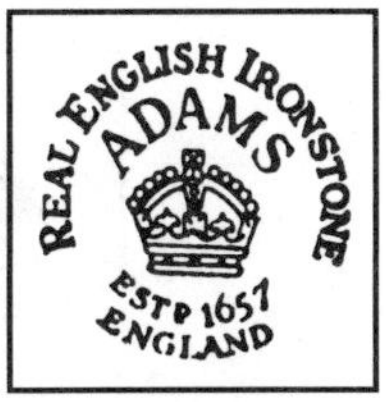

1962+

KAD NO.	GODDEN NO.	MARK	
B34	40		
B35	41		
B36	42		
B37	42A	**MICRATEX**	Trade name introduced commercially in 1963 for a new, extra strong body type.

- Production of Tea Leaf ceased in 1972.

KAD NO.	GODDEN NO.	MARK

Marks Noted on Tea Leaf, 1963-1972 Include:

B38 -
B39 -

- The company was acquired by Josiah Wedgwood & Sons, Ltd. in 1966.
For further reading, refer to *Tea Leaf Readings*, Vol. 12, No. 5, Dec. 1995, p. 8; *TLCI Educational Insert*, Vol. 10, No. 5, Dec. 1990; *Sussman*, pp. 73-74, "Wheat & Daisy" for further information of White Ironstone; and *Stoltzfus/Snyder*, pp. 16, 52; and *Cluett*, pp. 72-73 for comments relative to George Jones acquiring copper plates at the 1861 auction.

ADAMS

***William & Thomas Adams**
Greenfield,
Tunstall, Staffordshire, c.1866-1892
- In 1893 the name changed to William Adams & Co., c.1893-1917
(See KAD No's B22 - B27)

B40 43

Printed marks of differing design. Pattern name often included, c.1866-1892.

- Emblems other than Royal Arms are used with full name.
"ENGLAND" was added in 1891.

For further reading, refer to *Sussman*, pp. 16-17, wherein she notes a "Wheat" pattern with a registration date of Jan. 21, 1881. This pattern mark is noted as Eagle and Laurel. It was reissued under William Adams & Co. (See KAD Nos. B23-B24.)

ADDERLEY

***William Alsager Adderley (& Co.)**
Daisy Bank Works,
Longton, Staffordshire, c.1875-1905
Formerly, Hulsey & Adderley (1869-1874)

B41 47 **W. A. A.** Printed marks of differing design. Pattern name often included, c.1875-1885.

B42 -

B43 48 **W. A. A. & CO.** "& CO." added to mark KAD No. B41 from 1886-1905.

KAD NO.	GODDEN NO.	MARK	
B44	49		Printed Trade-mark, 1875-1905, with initials "W. A. A." (1875-1885) and the additional of "& CO." from (1886-1905). Trade-mark continued by Adderley's Ltd. (c.1905-1926). - See p. 243 for additional comments.

ADDERLEY

***Adderleys Ltd.**
Daisy Bank Works (Renamed Gainsborough Works)
Longton, Staffordshire, c.1905-1947+
Formerly, William Alsager Adderley (& Co.) (c.1875-1905)
Subsequently, Ridgway Potteries, Ltd. (1947+)

B45	50		Printed Trade-mark continued from predecessor, c.1905-1926. (See KAD No. B44.)

Typical Marks Include:

B46 51
B47 52
B48 53

1912-26 1926+

For additional (later) marks and comments, refer to *Godden, British Porcelain*, pp. 74-75.

ALCOCK

***Henry Alcock & Co. (Ltd.)**
Elder Pottery,
Cobridge, Staffordshire, c.1861-1910
Formerly, John Alcock (c.1850-1861)
Subsequently, Henry Alcock Pottery (c.1910-1935)

B49	64	**H. A. & CO.**	Printed or impressed marks of differing design. Pattern name often included, c.1861-1910. Various marks noted with "IMPERIAL IRONSTONE CHINA" and "IRONSTONE CHINA" in addition to those cited.
B50	-	**HENRY ALCOCK & CO. COBRIDGE**	
B51	-	**ALCOCK'S LTD. SEMI CHINA**	- The word "ENGLAND" added from c.1891 and "LTD" added from 1901.

Typical Marks Include:

B52 -
B53 65
B54 -
B55 -
B56 -

KAD NO.	GODDEN NO.	MARK	
B57	-	**ROYAL WARRANTED BEST IRONSTONE CHINA HENRY ALCOCK & CO. ENGLAND**	Printed mark noted on Tea Leaf/Copper Lustre, c.1891-1910.

For further reading, refer to *Stoltzfus/Snyder*, pp. 16, 52.

ALCOCK

***Henry Alcock Pottery**
Clarence Works,
Stoke, Staffordshire, c.1910-1935
Formerly, Henry Alcock & Co. (Ltd.) (c.1861-1910)

B58	66		Printed mark, c.1910-1935. - KAD No. B53 continued with the addition of "HENRY ALCOCK POTTERY", 1910-1935.

ALCOCK

***John Alcock**
Cobridge, Staffordshire, c.1850-1861

B59	67	**JOHN ALCOCK COBRIDGE**	Printed marks of differing design. Pattern name often included, c.1850-1861. - The "Scinde" pattern was continued from John & Samuel Alcock (Jr.) (1848-1850) Refer to mark KAD B 73 and B 75.
B60	69	**ORIENTAL STONE**	Printed or impressed marking, pattern and potter name often included, c. 1850-1861.

Typical Marks on Mulberry & White Ironstone Include:

B61 -
B62 -
B63 -
B64 -

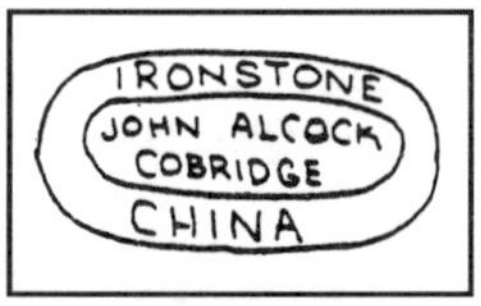

- For additional marks on Mulberry wares refer to Hill, No. 292.

For further reading, refer to *Stoltzfus/Snyder*, pp. 16, 45.

ALCOCK

***John & George Alcock**
Cobridge, Staffordshire, c.1839-1848

B65	68	**J. & G. ALCOCK COBRIDGE**	Impressed name mark, c.1839-1848.

KAD NO.	GODDEN NO.	MARK	
B66	69	**ORIENTAL STONE J. & G. ALCOCK**	Printed or impressed marks. Pattern & potter name often included, 1839-1848. - Terms "IRONSTONE","IRONSTONE CHINA", "PORCELAIN OPAQUE", "IMPERIAL STONE","WHITE GRANITE" or "ORIENTAL STONE" noted.
B67	69A	**J. & G. A.**	
B68	-	**J. & G. A. COBRIDGE**	
B69	70	**ALCOCK'S INDIAN STONE**	Impressed mark "...believed to relate to this firm", but has now been confirmed as being a mark for Samuel Alcock & Co.

Typical Marks Include:

B70 -
B71 -
B72* -
B73 -

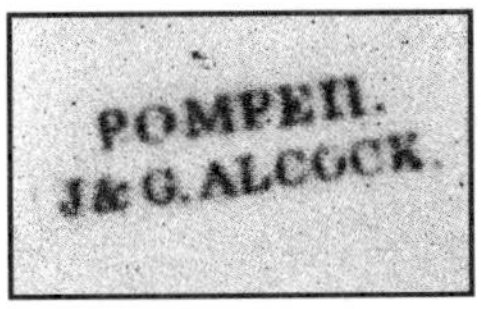

*Note the marking "IMPERIAL GRANITE CHINA". Predecessor John & Samuel Alcock KAD No. B76, who used the mark with wording "IMPERIAL FRENCH PORCELAIN."

- Various importers' marks noted:
1. Wright & Pike/Importers/North 3rd Street/Philadelphia
2. Thompson & Parish/79 Pearl Street/New York
3. Thompson & Parish/10 Pearl Street/New York
4. Hector Sears/226 Greenwich Street/New York
5. N. G. Bassett/:Importer/Newburyport [Massachusetts]

Also refer to Importers' section for additional information, p. 657.

ALCOCK

***John & Samuel Alcock (Jr.)**
Cobridge, Staffordshire, c.1848-1850

KAD NO.	GODDEN NO.	MARK	
B74	71	**J. & S. ALCOCK, JR.**	Printed or impressed marks of differing design. Pattern name often included, c.1848-1850.
B75	-	**JOHN ALCOCK COBRIDGE**	Printed name mark noted on "Scinde" pattern, with Registration Diamond dated March 27, 1848, for above partnership of J. & S. Alcock, Jr. - Other markings have been noted with or without "COBRIDGE" or "OPAQUE".
B76	-		Printed mark may be accompanied by an impressed marking of "J. & S. ALCOCK, JR.", 1848-1850. - Additional impressed marking "PORCELAIN OPAQUE" has been noted.
B60	69	**ORIENTAL STONE**	*Snyder, Fascinating Flow Blue*, p. 126, illustrates another impressed marking "ORIENTAL STONE".

ALCOCK

KAD NO. | GODDEN NO. | MARK

***Richard Alcock,**
Central Pottery, Market Place,
Burslem, Hanley, Staffordshire, 1870-1881
Subsequently, Wilkinson & Hulme (1881-1885)
and Arthur J. Wilkinson (1885-1970+)

B77 | - | **RICHARD ALCOCK BURSLEM STAFFORDSHIRE**

Printed and impressed marks of differing design. Pattern name often included, c.1870-1881.

B78 | - | **ROYAL PATENT IRONSTONE RICHARD ALCOCK BURSLEM, ENGLAND***

Printed Royal Arms mark, c.1870-1881.
Printed Royal Coat of Arms Mark (small) surrounded by impressed name mark, 1870-1881.
*Note the word "ENGLAND" appears considerably ahead of its time (c.1891).

B79 | -

For further reading, refer to *Godden, Mason's*, p. 230.

ALCOCK

***Samuel Alcock & Co.**
Cobridge China Works, Cobridge (1826-1853(+))
Hill Pottery, Burslem (1833-1859)
Staffordshire, 1826-1859
Formerly, Ralph Stevenson, Samuel Alcock &
Augustus Williams (1820-1826)*
Subsequently, J. Duke & Nephews (1860-1863)

B80 | 73 | **SAM^L ALCOCK & CO. COBRIDGE**

Printed or impressed name mark with address and Cobridge noted, 1826-1853(+).

B81 | 74 | **SAM^L ALCOCK & CO. BURSLEM**

Printed or impressed mark with address and "BURSLEM" noted, 1833-1859.

B82 | -

Printed or impressed mark. "HILL POTTERY" noted with or without "BURSLEM" designation, 1833-1859.

B83 | -

Printed mark with "HILL POTTERY" noted on Tea Leaf/Copper Lustre, 1850s.

B84 | - | **ALCOCK & CO. HILL POTTERY BURSLEM**

Printed name mark, 1833-1859.

KAD NO.	GODDEN NO.	MARK	
B85	-	**S. A.**	Printed or impressed marks of differing design. Pattern name often included, 1826-1859.
B86	75	**S. A. & CO.**	
B87	-	**ALCOCK**	- Godden notes that "ROYAL ARMS" or "BEE-HIVE" device marks and various names and/or initial combinations appear. Potter's marks may include "FRENCH PORCELAIN", "PEARLWARE" and "FLORENTINE CHINA", 1826-1859.
B88	-	**S. ALCOCK**	
B89	76	**S. ALCOCK & CO.**	
B90	77	**SAM^L ALCOCK & CO.**	
B91	-	**SM. A & Co.**	- At times a combination of a printed and impressed mark may appear.

Typical Examples Include:

B92 -
B93 -
B94 -
B95 -

- *P. Williams' Staffordshire*, Vol. 2, p. 29, shows an impressed Beehive mark, 1826-1859, as above. For additional marks refer to *Gaston*, Vol. 1 & 2; *Hill*; *Snyder*, Vol. 1 & 2; and *P. Williams' Staffordshire*, Vol. 1 & 2.

B96 78
B97

Royal Arms mark with or without initials. "PATENT" or "IMPERIAL IRONSTONE CHINA" included, 1826-1859.

KAD NO.	GODDEN NO.	MARK	
B98A	-	**S. ALCOCK & CO. PATENT IRONSTONE CHINA**	Impressed mark noted on White Ironstone with impressed name mark "ATLANTIC SHAPE", 1840s-1859. - See *White Ironstone Notes, Vol. 4, No. 3, Winter 1998, p. 12.*
B69	70	**ALCOCK'S INDIAN STONE**	Impressed mark, c.1840s. - See *Godden, Mason's*, p. 230 and *Staffordshire Porcelain*, p. 311.

This author has seen a Flow Blue plate by Samuel Alcock & Co. with a singularly unusual marking. The back of the plate has four marks, two printed and two impressed. The printed marks are the Beehive with the pattern name "ROSE" and a mark reading "By Order of S. Fenderich & Co., Odessa [Russia]". The impressed marks are a Beehive mark with "S. A. & CO." and to the side impressed initials "F. M.".
- Did Francis Morley order this to his specifications [and provide the blanks] for Alcock to manufacture for him, or did he obtain the copper plates and capitalize on the Alcock name? For further reading, refer to *Godden, British Porcelain*, pp. 76-85, 416; *Godden, Staffordshire Porcelain*, pp. 307-325; Pat Halfpenny's article in *NCSJ*, Vol. 2, 1975-1976, pp. 83-90; *Snyder*, Vol. 2; and *Henrywood*.
*Ralph Stevenson continued on with Samuel Alcock & Co. until his retirement in May 1831. See *Godden,* comments in his *British Porcelain*, pp. 711-712 as well as in his *Collecting Lustreware*, pp. 158-159.

ALLASON

KAD NO.	GODDEN NO.	MARK	
			John Allason **Seaham Harbour Pottery,** **Sunderland, Durham, c.1838-1841**
B98	82	**JOHN ALLASON SEAHAM POTTERY**	Printed name mark, c.1838-1841. For further reading, refer to *Sunderland Pottery*, as revised by John C. Baker. Thomas Reed Industrial Press, Ltd. & Tyne & Wear County Council Museums, 1984.

ALLERTON

Allerton, Brough & Green
Park Works, High Street, Lane End,
Longton, Staffordshire, c.1832-1859
Succeeded by Charles Allerton & Sons (Ltd.) (c.1860-1942)

KAD NO.	GODDEN NO.	MARK	
B99	-	**A. B. & G.**	Printed marks of differing design, c.1832-1859. - Godden notes the importance of this potter - as he owned five separate works (sic. and yet so few pieces are recorded.) For further reading, refer to *Godden, Collecting Lustreware*, p. 77; and *Hampson*, pp. 2-3, No. 5.

ALLERTON

Charles Allerton & Sons (Ltd.)
Park Works, High Street, Lane End,
Longton, Staffordshire, c.1860-1942
Formerly, Allerton, Brough & Green (c.1833-1859)
- In 1912 the company was taken over by Cauldon, Ltd.
under the name of Allerton's Ltd., c.1912-1942.
"LTD" was added from 1912.

KAD NO.	GODDEN NO.	MARK	
B100	85	**C. A. & SONS**	Printed or impressed marks of differing design. Pattern name often included, c.1860-1911.
B101	84	**CHAS. ALLERTON & SONS ENGLAND**	As above but with the addition of "ENGLAND", c.1890-1942.
B102	-		Printed name mark noted. See *Gaston*, Vol. 1, p. 21, Mark 15. This mark is also seen on Brushstroke patterns, c.1890-1942. - "MADE IN ENGLAND" added c.1920.

Selected Printed Marks, 1890-1915+, Include:

B103 86
B104 87
B105 88

c.1890+

c.1890+

c.1903-1911

KAD NO.	GODDEN NO.	MARK	
B106	89		
B107	90		
B108	91		

c.1912+

c.1915+

c.1915+

For further reading, refer to *Godden, Collecting Lustreware*, pp. 77-78.

ALLMAN

Allman, Broughton & Co.
Overhouse Works,
Burslem, Staffordshire, c.1861-1868
Formerly, Morgan, Wood & Co. (1858-1860)
Subsequently, Robinson, Kirkham & Co. (1868-1869)

KAD NO.	GODDEN NO.	MARK	
B109	94	**A. B. & CO.**	Printed or impressed marks of differing design. Pattern name often included, c.1861-1868.
B110	95	**A. B. & CO. WEDGWOOD PLACE BURSLEM**	
B111	-		- Mark may be that of Alexander Balfour & Co. See *Coysh*, Vol. I, p. 41. See KAD B160. For further reading, refer to *Godden, Jewitt*, p. 19, for "The Overhouse Works".

ASHWORTH

G. L. Ashworth & Bros. (Ltd.)
Broad Street, Hanley, Staffordshire, c.1862-1968
Formerly, Morley & Ashworth (c.1859-1862)
Subsequently, Mason's Ironstone China Ltd. (1968-1973)

History:

George L. Ashworth & Bros.	1862-1884
Company acquired by John Shaw Goddard	1883
A Limited "LTD" Company from	1884-1968
Company becomes Mason's Ironstone China, Ltd.	1968-1973
Company acquired by the Wedgwood Group	1973

KAD NO.	GODDEN NO.	MARK	
B112	137	**ASHWORTH**	Impressed mark "Ashworth" is normally noted accompanying printed marks, c.1862-1883. - Additional impressed marking "REAL IRONSTONE CHINA" noted.
B113	138	**A. BROS.**	Printed marks of differing design. Pattern name often included, c.1862-1883.
B114	-	**ASHWORTH BROS.**	
B115	-	**G. L. ASHWORTH BROS.**	
B116	-	**G. L. A. BROS(S)**	
B117	139	**G. L. A. & BROTHERS**	

- *Coysh*, Vol. 1, notes exports for Russia marked "FOR STIFFEL BROS./ODESSA"

KAD NO.	GODDEN NO.	MARK

Typical Examples Include:

B118 140
B119 141
B120 142
B121 -

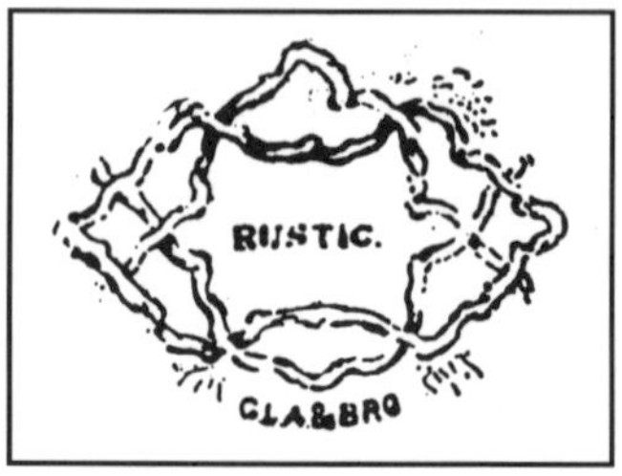

B122 -

Impressed mark of Crown and name "Ashworth", c.1862-1883.

- See *Gaston*, Vol. 2, Mark No. 17.

Printed marks noted to include "IRONSTONE", "REAL IRONSTONE CHINA" with the additional of the original Mason's "PATENT IRONSTONE CHINA" marking "ROYAL IRONSTONE", c.1862-1883.

Typical Examples Include:

B123 -
B124 -

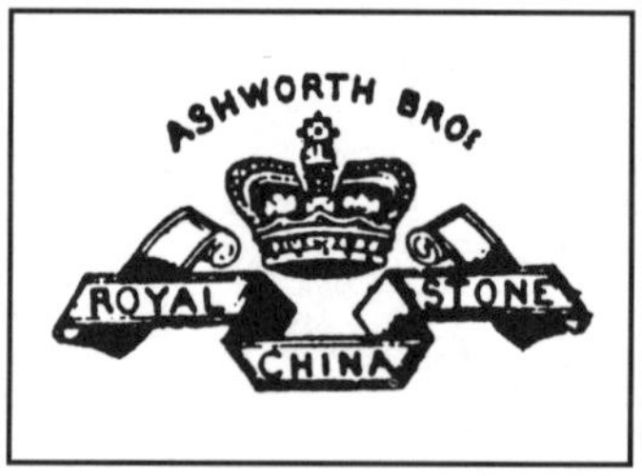

Printed marks adopted from original Mason's "Patent Ironstone". Additional marking "REAL IRONSTONE CHINA" noted, c.1862-1968.

B125 143
B126 144
B127 145

Former Mason mark continued

Name Ashworth added 1862+

"England" added below standard mark 1891+ (c.1968)

B128 146

Printed "Royal Arms" mark with pattern name included. The impressed name "Ashworth" is normally present. Note the term "IRONSTONE CHINA", c.1862-1968.

B129 147

Printed mark with slight variations in wording: "A. BROS." or "ASHWORTH", c.1880+.

KAD NO.	GODDEN NO.	MARK	
B130	148		Printed mark "ENGLAND" or "MADE IN ENGLAND", c.1891+.
B131	-		Printed mark noted on an American Historic View, with title, c.1862. Marks noted are: "G. L. A. & BROS." or "G. L. A. & T." - *Larsen*, p. 196 notes that Ashworth continued Morley's series but with a different name, and used the impressed mark "ASHWORTH".
B132	-		For further reading, refer to *Godden, Mason's*, pp. 131-132, 225, 231-235; Gaye Lake Roberts, *Mason's The First Two Hundred Years*. London, England, Merrell Holberton Publishers Ltd., 1996, pp. 124-126 for additional marks; and *Snyder, Historic Staffordshire*, pp. 70-71.

BADDELEY

John & Edward Baddeley
Albion Street,
Shelton, Staffordshire, c.1784-(1803) or 1807-(1811)

KAD NO.	GODDEN NO.	MARK	
B133	196	**B**	Impressed initial marks, c.1784-1811.
B134	197	**I. E. B.**	
B135	198	**I. E. B.** **W.**	

Godden stresses that one should take care in attributing "B" initial, as likely manufacturers include:

George Baggerley	c.1822
James Barlow	c.1822-1839
George Bettany	c.1822-1830
Charles Birks	c.1822-1835
William Bradshaw	c.1819-1823
John Breeze	c.1828-1830
Sampson Bridgwood	c.1822-1852

For further reading, refer to *Godden, British Porcelain*, pp. 102-107; and *Edward's Basalt*, pp. 112-118.

BADDELEY

Ralph & John Baddeley,
Broad Street Works, Shelton, Staffordshire, c.1750-1795

KAD NO.	GODDEN NO.	MARK	
B136	199	**BADDELEY**	Impressed name or initial mark, c.1775-1795.
B137	200	**R. & J.** **BADDELEY**	

For further reading, refer to *Coysh*, Vol. 1, p. 31; *Godden, British Porcelain*, p. 102; *Godden, Staffordshire*, p. 35; and *Little*, p. 47.

BAGGERLEY

KAD NO.	GODDEN NO.	MARK

Baggerley & Ball
High Street, Lane End, Longton,
Staffordshire, c.1822-1836
Formerly, George Baggerley & Co. (c.1820)

B138	207	

Printed mark, c.1822-1836.
- Also noted marked "WARRANTED IRONSTONE CHINA", "OPAQUE CHINA", or "B. & B., L."
- The name Baggerley can also be spelled "Baggeley".

For further reading, refer to *Coysh*, Vol. 1, p. 31; and *Hampson*, No. 13, p. 9.

BAGSHAW

Bagshaw & Meir (or Maier)
Burslem, Staffordshire, c.1802-1808
Formerly, Bagsahw, Taylor & Maier (1798-1802)

B139	208	**B. & M.**

Printed or impressed initial mark, c.1802-1808.

- Initials could also refer to Brougham & Mayer, c.1853-1855.

BAGSTER

JOHN DENTON BAGSTER
SEE: BAXTER

BAILEY

Bailey & Ball
Stafford Street, Longton, Staffordshire, c.1843-1850
Subsequently, John Bailey (c.1849-1858)

B140	-	**B. & B.**

Printed mark, c.1843-1850.

- *Godden, Collecting Lustreware*, p. 80 notes sixteen (+) firms with the name Bailey. As such, when researching or reading about initials "B. & B." please be aware that these can stand for Baggerley & Ball, Bailey & Batkin, Bates & Bennett, or Blackhurst & Bourne as well as Bailey & Ball.

For further reading, refer to *Godden, British Porcelain*, p. 113; and *Hampson*, No. 14, pp. 9-10, 183-184 wherein he notes change of street names for Longton potters from 1828-1969.

BAILEY

W. & D. Bailey
Flint Street Works, Land End, Longton, 1826-1830
Formerly, Bailey & Batkin (1814-1826)
Subsequently, Bailey's & Harvey's (1832-1835)

B141	-	**BAILEY**

Printed name mark, 1826-1830.

For further reading, refer to *Godden, British Porcelain*, p. 113; and *Hampson*, No. 17, p. 12.

BAKER

KAD NO.	GODDEN NO.	MARK	
			Baker & Chetwynd & Co. Nile Street, Burslem, Staffordshire, c.1869-1875 Subsequently, Charles G. Baker (c.1875-1876), and Holmes, Plant & Whitehurst (c.1876)
B142	-		Printed mark noted on Tea Leaf/Copper Lustre and White Ironstone, c.1869-1875. For further reading, refer to *Heaivilin*, pp. 46-47.

BAKER

(W.) Baker & Co. (Ltd.)
High Street (1839-1886)
Fenton Potteries (1886-1932)
Fenton, Stafordshire, 1839-1932
Formerly, William Baker (1836-1838)

KAD NO.	GODDEN NO.	MARK	
B143	-	**W. B. & CO.**	Printed or impressed initial mark. Additional marking "PEARL CHINA", "OPAQUE GRANITE CHINA" noted, c.1839-1893. - *White Ironstone Notes*, Vol. 4, No. 1, Summer 1997, p. 8, illustrates a child's tea set "Belted Octagon" with the impressed initial "W. B. & CO."
B144 B145	230 231	**W. BAKER & CO.** **BAKER & CO.**	Printed or impressed marks of differing design. Pattern name often included, c.1839-1932. - "LTD." from 1893

Typical Marks Include:

B146 -
B147 232
B148 -
B149 233

c.1860-1893

c.1893-1928

c.1893-1928

c.1928-1930

KAD NO.	GODDEN NO.	MARK	
B150	-	**BAKER & CO. FENTON STAFFORDSHIRE, ENGLAND IMPERIAL IRONSTONE CHINA**	Printed Royal Coat of Arms mark, c.1891+.

White Ironstone Marks, c.1860-1896, include:

B151 -
B152 -
B153 -
B154 -

KAD NO.	GODDEN NO.	MARK	
			- *Sussman*, pp. 63-64 notes that the pattern "Hyacinth" does not include the word "ENGLAND". Therefore, it [may] predates 1891. It is further noted by *Jewitt* that in 1878 the factory was producing "PEARL-WHITE GRANITE". This marking is noted as being elaborately scrolled in a circular mark with "W. B. & CO." and an eagle above the words "PEARL CHINA, FENTON". Additionally, a second impressed marking is noted as "P. W./IRONSTONE/CHINA/W. B. & CO." "P. W." evidently indicates Pearl Ware.

For further reading, refer to *Little*, p. 52; and *NCS Newsletter* No. 77, March 1990, pp. 43-45.

BAKER

***Baker, Bevans & Irwin**
Glamorgan Pottery, Swansea, Wales, c.1813-1838
(See Appendix B6: for Chronology of Glamorgan Pottery)

KAD NO.	GODDEN NO.	MARK	
B155	226		Printed or impressed (initial) marks of differing design. Pattern name often included. "Prince of Wales" mark (three plumes) as well as marking "OPAQUE CHINA" noted, c.1813-1838.
B156	227	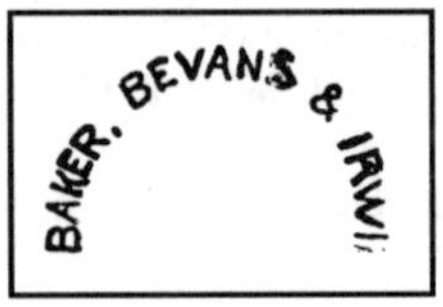	Printed or impressed name mark in a horseshoe, c.1819-1838.
B157	228	**B. B. & CO.**	Printed marks of differing design. Rare pattern name mark noted on the pattern "Campania", 1819-1838.
B158	229	**G. P. CO./S.**	- Printed initial mark "G. P. CO./S." found on the front of Glamorgan ship plates, (Glamorgan Pottery Co., Swansea), 1819-1838. - Dillwyn acquired the Cambrian Pottery in 1839 for the purpose of closing it; thus acquiring the moulds and copper plates.

For further reading, refer to *Hallesy; Nance*, pp. 203-227 as well as marks on Plate XCII; and *Pugh, Welsh Pottery*, pp. 34-40. Additional patterns have been noted in both Hallesy and Pugh.

BALFOUR

Alexander Balfour & Co.
(North-British Pottery)
Debbies Loan, Glasgow, c.1874-1904

KAD NO.	GODDEN NO.	MARK	
B159	-	**A. B. & CO.**	Printed initial mark, c.1874-1904.
B160	-		- See *Coysh*, Vol. 1, p. 41 for the initial marking "A. B. & CO." This mark was also used by Allman, Broughton & Co., Burslem (c.1861-1868).

For further reading, refer to *Fleming*, p. 139.

BARKER

KAD NO.	GODDEN NO.	MARK	
			***Barker & Son** **Hill Works, Burslem, Staffordshire, c.1850-1860** **Formerly, Samuel Alcock's Famous Hill Pottery** **Subsequently, Morgan Wood (& Co.) (c.1860-1870)**
B161	256		Printed initial marks B & S of differing design. Pattern name often included, c.1850-1860.
B162	256A	**BARKER & SON**	Printed or impressed name mark, c.1850-1860. - The name "E. Barker" relates to the Sunderland engraver. See *Godden*, p. 710.

For further reading, refer to *Godden, British Porcelain*, p. 121; and *Hampson*, No. 273, pp. 176-177.

BARKER

***Barker & Till**
Sytch Pottery, Burslem, Staffordshire, c.1846-1850
Preceded by Barker, Sutton & Till (1834-1846)

B163	-	**B. & T.**	Printed marks of differing design. Pattern name often included, c.1846-1850. - *Godden*, Appendix B notes that initial may fit other firms. The initial "B. & T." may also signify such potters as: Bettany & Tomlinson, Lane End, 1834-1844 and Barrow & Taylor, Hanley, 1859. - Pieces have been noted with the impressed marking "STONE CHINA".

For further reading, refer to *Henrywood*, p. 208.

BARKER

***Barker Bros. (Ltd.)**
Gold Street (c.1876-1882)
Meir Works, Barker Street, Longton, Staffordshire (1882+)
Acquired by Alfred Clough in 1959
Sold to John Tams Ltd. in 1982 and works demolished

B164	247	**B. B.**	Impressed initial mark, c.1876-1900.
B165	-	**B. B. LTD.**	- Barker Bros. became a "LTD." company in 1882. - *Godden* notes that most "LTD" markings date from 1901.
B166	248		Printed name mark, c.1880+.
B167	249		Printed name mark, c.1912-1930.

For further reading and additional marks, refer to *Godden*, p. 54; and *Godden, British Porcelain*, p. 121.

BARKER

***Samuel Barker & Son**
Don Pottery, Swinton, Nr Rotherham,
Yorkshire, c.1834(39)-1893
Also see "Don Pottery"

KAD NO.	GODDEN NO.	MARK	
B168	260	**BARKER DON POTTERY**	Impressed mark, c.1839.
B169	261		Printed or impressed mark "BARKER" or "B" may be interchangeable above crest, c.1834(39)+.
B170	262		Rare printed mark, c.1850.
B171	-	**S. B. & S.**	Printed marks of differing design. Pattern name often included. "& SONS" or & "S" occur from 1851+.
B172 B173 B174	263 - -		**Typical Marks Include:**

For further reading, refer to *Lawrence*, as well as the *"Don Pottery Exhibit Catalogue"* of the Doncaster Museum & Art Gallery.

BARKER

***Barker, Sutton & Till**
Sytch Pottery, Burslem, Staffordshire, 1834-1846
Formerly, J. Hall & Sons (c.1814-1832)
Subsequently, Barker & Till (c.1846-1850)

KAD NO.	GODDEN NO.	MARK	
B175	258	**B. S. & T.**	Printed or impressed marks of differing design. Pattern name often included. - "STONE CHINA" or "STONEWARE" markings noted, 1834-1836.
B176	259	**B. S. & T. BURSLEM**	

For further reading, refer to *Coysh*, Vol. 1, p. 33; and *Godden, Jewitt*, p. 25.

BARKER

***Barkers & Kent (Ltd.)**
Foley Pottery,
Fenton, Staffordshire, c.1889-1941
Formerly, John Hawley & Co. (1832-1893)

KAD NO.	GODDEN NO.	MARK	
B177	264	**B. & K.**	Printed marks of differing design. Pattern name often included, c.1889-1941.
B178	265	**B. & K. L.**	- "LTD." or "L" added from c.1898.
B179	-	**B. & K. LTD.**	
B180	266		- *Coysh*, Vol. 1, p. 48 notes that the pattern "Bosphorus" may, in fact, be from copper plates first produced by John Hawley & Co., c.1832-1893.

BARLOW

Thomas Barlow
Cyples Old Pottery, Market Street,
Longton, Staffordshire, 1849-1853(82)
Formerly, Cyples & Barker (1846-1847)
Subsequently, T. W. Barlow & Son Ltd. (1882-c.1940)

KAD NO.	GODDEN NO.	MARK	
B181	267	**B**	Printed initial mark. Pattern name often included, 1849-1853(82).
B182	-	**BARLOW**	Impressed name mark, 1849-1853(82). - The firm continued on after Thomas Barlow's death in 1853, notes *Hampson*, No. 88, pp. 56-58.

For further reading, refer to *Godden, Collecting Lustreware*, pp. 85-86.

BARROW

Barrow & Co.
Market Street, Longton, Staffordshire
(and/or Park Works, Fenton), c.1853-1856
- Godden notes that this firm is also listed as Barrow & Taylor

KAD NO.	GODDEN NO.	MARK	
B183	-		Printed or impressed mark. Pattern name often included, c.1853-1856. - *P. Williams' Staffordshire*, Vol. 2, p. 170 notes an impressed Royal Arms marking with "IRONSTONE/CHINA/BARROW & CO." below.
B184	-	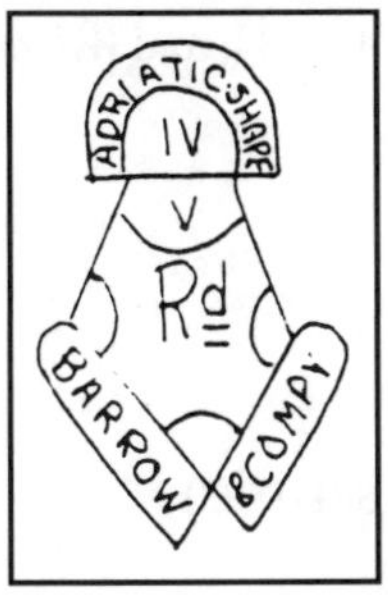	- See *Wetherbee*, p. 59 for "Adriatic Shape".

For further reading, refer to *Godden, British Porcelain*, p. 126; *Godden, Staffordshire*, pp. 383-384; *Stoltzfus/Snyder*, pp. 138; and *White Ironstone Notes*, Vol. 3, No. 3, Winter 1997 (Dec. 1996), p. 12 for an example of an impressed Royal Coat of Arms mark.

KAD NO.	GODDEN NO.	MARK	

BATES

***Bates, Brown-Westhead & Moore**
Cauldon Place,
Shelton, Hanley, Staffordshire, 1859-1861
Formerly, J. Ridgway, Bates & Co. (1855-1858)
Subsequently, Brown-Westhead, Moore & Co. (1862-1904)

B185 288 **B.. B. W. & M.**

Printed or impressed marks of differing design. Pattern name often included, 1859-1861. - *Godden, Collecting Lustreware*, p. 217 notes five registration dates for designs, two of which were for table services dated December 3, 1860 and October 28, 1861.

For further reading, refer to *Godden, Ridgways*, pp. 170-175.

BATES

***Bates & Bennett**
Lincoln Pottery,
Cobridge, Staffordshire, c.1868-1895
Formerly, John & Robert Godwin (1834-1867)

B186 287 **B. & B.**

Printed marks of differing design. Pattern name often included, c.1868-1895.

B187 -

- When researching or reading about the initials "B. & B.", be aware that these can stand for Baggerly & Ball, Bailey & Batkin, Bailey & Ball, or Blackhurst & Bourne, as well as Bates & Bennett.

For further reading, refer to *Godden, Jewitt*, p. 35; and *Godden, Collecting Lustreware* where he notes sixteen (+) firms with possible "B & B" markings.

BATES

***Bates, Elliott & Co.**
Dale Hall Works,
Burslem, Staffordshire, c.1870-1875
Subsequently, Bates Walker & Co. (c.1875-1878)

B188 289 **B. E. & CO.**

Printed marks of differing design. Pattern name often included, c.1870-1875.

B189 290

Printed Staple Trade-mark found incorporated in many marks, and continued by successors, c.1870-1875.

For further reading, refer to *Coysh*, Vol. 1, p. 34; and *Williams-Wood*, pp. 83-88.

BATES

***Bates, Gildea & Walker**
Dale Hall Works,
Burslem, Staffordshire, c.1878-1881
Subsequently, Gildea, Walker & Co. (c.1881-1885)

B190 292 **B. G. & W.**

Printed marks of differing design. Pattern name often included, c.1878-1881.
- Also see KAD Mark No. B189.

BATES

KAD NO.	GODDEN NO.	MARK	
			***Bates, Walker & Co. Dale Hall Works, Burslem, Staffordshire, c.1875-1878 Formerly, Bates, Elliott & Co. (c.1870-1875) Subsequently, Bates, Gildea & Walker (c.1878-1881)**
B191	293	**B. W. & CO.**	Printed marks of differing design. Pattern name often included, c.1875-1878.
B192	293A	**BATES WALKER & CO.**	

- A recently reported postcard notes the following, as addressed to Mr. Briggs, Boston (importer), dated Oct. 20, 1879: Bates, Gildea & Walker over the crossed out name of Bates, Bates & Co. It is possible that a transition partnership consisting of Bates, Bates & Co. existed between that of Bates, Walker & Co. (dissolution of partnership, Aug. 12, 1878) and Bates, Gildea & Walker, c.1878-1881.

BATHWELL

Bathwell & Goodfellow
Upper House Works, Burslem,
(and at Tunstall, 1820-1822), Staffordshire, c.1818-1823
Formerly, T. & C. Bathwell

KAD NO.	GODDEN NO.	MARK	
B193	294	**BATHWELL & GOODFELLOW**	Impressed (oval) name-mark, with printed pattern name often included, c.1818-1823.
B194	-		- Godden notes a spelling error: B*O*THWELL & GOODFELLOW.

For further reading, refer to *Coysh*, Vol. 1, p. 35; *Coysh, Blue Printed Earthenware*, p. 12; *NCSJ*, Vol. 13, 1996, p. 45 for "Anthony Keeling, China and Earthenware Manufacturer at Tunstall" for pottery dates relating to Bathwell & Goodfellow; *NCS* Newsletter No. 87, September 1992, p. 14, and No. 104, December 1996, pp. 15-17 for an article by Catriona & David Maisels, titled "Basket by Bathwell & Goodfellow and Others."

BATKIN

Batkin, Walker & Broadhurst
Church Street,
Lane End, Longton, Staffordshire, c.1840-1845
Subsequently, Thomas R. Walker (1846-1848)

KAD NO.	GODDEN NO.	MARK	
B195	-	**B. W. B.**	Printed marks of differing design. Pattern name often included, c.1840-1845.
B196	295	**B. W. & B.**	- Additional marking noted, "STAFFORDSHIRE/WARRANTED/STONE CHINA"
B197	-		

For further reading, refer to *Hampson*, No. 25, p. 18.

BAXTER

KAD NO.	GODDEN NO.	MARK

John Denton Baxter or (Bagster)
Church Works,
High Street, Hanley, Staffordshire, c.1823-1827
Formerly, Phillips & Bagster (1819-1823)
Subsequently, Joseph Mayer, son of Elijah Mayer (1828-1831)

B198 300 — Printed or impressed initial mark with Staffordshire Knot. The letter "I" was frequently used in place of "J" in the early part of the nineteenth century, c.1823-1827.

B199 301 **J. D. B.**

B200 301A — Printed mark comprising the Prince of Wales Feather Crest with the initials "J. D. B. " together with the Staffordshire Knot containing the words "CELTIC CHINA", c.1823-1827.

For further reading refer to *Coysh*, Vol. 1, p. 31 and Vol. 2, p. 24; *Godden*, pp. 62, 723; *Godden, British Pottery*, pp. 61-62 for comments on the spelling "Bagster"; and *Godden, British Porcelain*, pp. 108-109.

BEARDMORE

Beardmore & Edwards
Union Square,
Longton, Staffordshire, c.1858
Formerly, Colclough, Beardmore & Cartwright (c.1856-1857)
Subsequently, Cartwright & Newbon (1858)

B201 306 **B. & E.** — Printed marks of differing design, c.1858.

For further reading, refer to *Hampson*, No. 26, p. 19

BEARDMORE

Frank Beardmore & Co.
Sutherland Pottery, High Street,
Fenton, Staffordshire, c.1903-1914
Formerly, Christie & Beardmore (c.1902-1903)

B202 307 **F. B. & CO.**
F. — Printed or impressed initial marks of differing design, with or without "F" (Fenton) below. Pattern name often included, c.1903-1914.

B203 307A — Printed name mark, c.1903-1914.

- Frank Beardmore & Co. is not to be confused with "Beardmore & Co.", Longton, 1850-1854.

The ABC of English Ceramic Art by J.F. Blacker, London, Stanley Paul & Co., c.1911, pp. 187-187, notes that this enterprising firm was engaged in reproducing patterns and shapes of its predecessors and others such as Brownfield & Sons "…in a style and quality that are equal to anything then sent out, and in a variety of colors - flown neutral, flown green, flow blue, Berlin blue…"

BECK

KAD NO.	GODDEN NO.	MARK	

Beck, Blair & Co.
Beaconsfield Pottery,
Anchor Road, Longton, c.1879
Formerly, Beck, Wild & Co. (c.1878-1879)
Subsequently, Blair & Co. (1879-1911)
No further information available other than a registration date for March 29, 1879/ No. 333813, Parcel 4.
For further reading, refer to *Godden, British Porcelain*, p. 133.

BEECH

Beech & Hancock
Church Bank Works (c.1860-1862)
Swan Bank Pottery, High Street (c.1862-1876)
(Formerly Podmore Walker & Co.),
Tunstall, Staffordshire (c.1862-1876), c.1860-1876
Subsequently, James Beech (c.1878-1889)

KAD NO.	GODDEN NO.	MARK	
B204	312	**BEECH & HANCOCK**	Printed marks of differing design. Pattern name often included, c.1860-1876.
B205	-		- Godden notes, "A firm with a similar title was working at Burslem, c.1851-1855, but "& CO." should occur after their title or initials…"
B206	313	**B. & H.**	Printed initial mark, c.1860-1876.

For further reading, refer to *Coysh*, Vol. 2, p. 26; *Godden, Collecting Lustreware*, p. 89; and *Henrywood*, pp. 179-182;

BEECH

Beech & Lowndes
Lion Works,
Sandyford, Tunstall, c.1821-1834
Subsequently, James Beech (1834-1845)

KAD NO.	GODDEN NO.	MARK	
B207	-	**L. B.**	Printed initial mark, pattern name included, c.1821-1834. - *Coysh*, Vol. 1, p. 231 notes the title of the firm as Lowndes & Beech, while *Little*, p. 49, notes the name of the firm as above.

BEECH

Beech, Hancock & Co.
Swan Bank Pottery, High Street
Burslem, Staffordshire, c.1851-1855
Formerly, Thomas Pinder (c.1849-1851)

KAD NO.	GODDEN NO.	MARK	
B208	311	**B. H. & CO.**	Printed marks of differing design. Pattern name often included, c.1851-1855.

For further reading, refer to *Godden, Collecting Lustreware*, p. 89; and *Henrywood*, p. 179.

KAD NO. | **GODDEN NO.** | **MARK**

BEECH

James Beech
Swan Bank Pottery, High Street
Tunstall & Burslem, c.1878-1889
Formerly, Beech & Hancock (c.1860-1876)
Subsequently, Boulton, Machin & Tennant (1889-1899)

B209 314

Printed trade-mark of a Swan with initials J.B. below swan. Pattern name often included, c.1878-1889.

- The initials "J.B." may also refer to other potters. See *Godden*, p. 351 and comments on p. 723 of Appendix. *P. Williams', Staffordshire*, Vol. 1, p. 658 notes a problem with the initials "J.B." and the pattern "Pompadour". Further, the initials "J.B." are mentioned by *Larsen*, pp. 190-191 in conjunction with A. Shaw and "Texian Campaigne". I cite this point to the collector, as Godden stresses that one must be very careful with initials. *Little,* p. 49, mentioned "Texian Campaigne" as being made by "J.B." (James Beech). Also refer to *Godden, Porcelain Encyclopaedia*, p. 133 - James Beech (& Son), *Longton*, 1850-1858, (& Son) c.1860-1898.
- For further comments on "Texian Campaigne" refer to Anthony Shaw.
- For a lengthy listing for the initials "J. B." refer to Appendix B6: Chronology of Selected Potteries & Partnerships, see p. 548.

For further reading, refer to *Hamspon*, No. 29, p. 22; and *Henrywood*, p. 179.

BELFIELD

Belfield & Co.
Prestonpans Pottery,
Prestonpan, Scotland, c.1836-1941

B210 316 **BELFIELD & CO. PRESTOPANS**

Printed or impressed name marks, most dating from post 1870.

For further reading, refer to *Fleming,* pp. 151-155; *Godden, Jewitt*, p. 219; and *McVeigh*, pp. 104-109.

BELL

Bell, Cook & Co.
Phoenix Pottery,
Ouseburn, Newcastle-upon-Tyne, c.1859-1860

B211 - **BELL, COOK & CO.**

Printed or impressed name marks, c.1859-1860.

B212 -

For further reading, refer to *Bell*.

BELL

Isaac & Thomas Bell
Albion Pottery,
Newcastle, Tyneside, c.1860-1863
Formerly, Maling's (Robert) Ouseborn Bridge Pottery (1815(17)-1859)
Subsequently, Bell, Isaacs, Galloway & Atkinson (c.1863-1864)

KAD NO.	GODDEN NO.	MARK	
B213	-	**ALBION** **I. & T. BELL**	Printed marks of differing design, which may include the Albion Pottery mark, c.1860-1863.*
B214	-		Impressed mark found in conjunction with printed name mark, and noted on Willow patterns, c.1860-1863.

Noel Riley, p. 22, No. 16, cites four potteries using this London/Anchor marking:

John Carr (& Co.)(& Son(s), North Shields	1845-1900, see p. 140
Thomas Fell (& Co.)(Ltd.), Newcastle	1817-1890, see p. 192
Malkin, Walker & Hulse, Longton	1858-1864, see p. 264
Middlesborough Pottery Co., Yorkshire	1831-1844, see p. 286

**Noel Riley*, p. 134, No. 470 cites the pottery Galloway & Atkinson, Albion Pottery, Newcastle-upon-Tyne, 1865-1872 as using the mark "ALBION POTTERY". Care must be taken when attributing by this marking.
For further reading, refer to *Bell*, pp. 46 and 138.

BELL

J. & M. P. Bell (& Co.)(Ltd.)
"& Co." [Robert Clough], (1842-1844)
Glasgow Pottery,
Dobbies Loan, Glasgow, Scotland, c.1842-1910(23)

KAD NO.	GODDEN NO.	MARK	
B215	317	**J. B.**	Printed or impressed marks of differing design. Pattern name often included. Impressed mark "IMPERIAL" noted, c.1842-1860.
B216 B217	- 318	**J. & M. P. B. & CO.** **J. & M. P. BELL & CO.**	Printed or impressed marks of differing design. Pattern name often included, c.1850-1870. "GRANITE IMPERIAL" and "ROYAL" tend to date from the 1870s (and denote improvement in body style).
B218	-		- Refer to *P. Williams' Staffordshire*, Vol. 2, p. 531, pattern "Japan" for an example of the marking.
B219	-		Printed Royal Coat of Arms mark, c.1842-1910.
B220 B221	319 -		Impressed "BELL" trade-mark noted with or without printed or impressed initials "J. B." or "B", c.1842-1881.
B222	-	**B** (INITIAL)	Impressed B dates c. 1842-1881.

KAD NO.	GODDEN NO.	MARK	
			Typical Marks Include:
B223	-		
B223	-		
B225	-		

KAD NO.	GODDEN NO.	MARK	
B226	-		
B227	-		

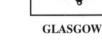

KAD NO.	GODDEN NO.	MARK	
B228	-	**J. & M. P. BELL & CO. LIMITED**	Printed marks. "LIMITED" may be noted as "LD" or "L", with the term "LTD" rarely being used, c.1881.
B229	320	 **GLASGOW**	Printed mark(s) with the additional of "GLASGOW", c.1881-1910.

- Henry Kelly has brought new research to light, indicating that the company ceased operation in 1910 and total liquidation was accomplished in 1923.

For additional patterns refer to *Blue Berry Notes*, Vol. 10, No. 1, Jan.-Feb. 1996, pp. 16-21 for an article by Henry Kelly titled "Mulberry Transfer Patterns in Scottish Pottery."

For further reading, refer to, *Scottish Industrial History*, Vol. 16, Business Archives Council of Scotland, 1993, pp. 9-19 for an article by Henry Kelly titled "The Glasgow Pottery of John and Matthew Perston Bell.; *Godden, Collecting Lustreware*, pp. 270-271; *Coysh & Stefano; Henrywood*, pp. 181-182; and various articles and publications by Henry Kelly: "Bell" in the *Scottish Pottery 16th Historical Review*, pp. 49-57; *The Glasgow Pottery of John and Matthew Perston Bell, China and Earthenware Manufacturers*. Glasgow, Scotland. The Lomondside Press Publishers, (1998/1999).

BELLE VUE

Belle Vue Pottery
Hull, Yorkshire, c.1802-1841
- There were various owners from c.1802

KAD NO.	GODDEN NO.	MARK	
B230	321		Printed marks of differing design. Pattern name often included, c.1829-1841.

KAD NO.	GODDEN NO.	MARK	
			Variation in Marks as Follows:
B231 B232	- -		 
B233	322	**BELLE VUE***	Printed name without Bell device, c.1829-1841.
B234	323	**TWO BELLS' DEVICE**	Impressed marks (as KAD No. B230) noted without title above "Belle Vue Pottery", c.1829-1841. *The mark "BELLE VUE" may be a series title. - "Allegheny Scenery" has been identified as an American Historic piece and is recorded in pink in Sam Laidacker's *Anglo-American China, Part I*. Bristol, PA, 1954, p. 6. Also refer to *Staffordshire, an Illustrated Checklist*, First Supplement by David & Linda Arman. Danville, VA, Arman Enterprises, 1977. p. 101; and *NCSJ*, Vol. 12, 1995 for an article by Elsie Blatch titled "Hull Potteries", pp. 215-269, in which she lists additional patterns and notes that the mark "BELLE VUE" may be a series title. Marks on this page reproduced by kind permission of the publishers, David & Charles, from Heather Lawrence, "Yorkshire Pots & Potteries", 1974.

BENNETT

J. Bennett & Co.
Hanley, Staffordshire, c.1896-1900
Subsequently, Bennett & Shenton (1900-1903)

B235	336	**J. B. & CO.**	Printed or impressed marks of differing design. Pattern name often included, c.1896-1900.

BEVINGTON

***(T. & J.) Bevington & Co.**
Cambrian Pottery,
Swansea, Wales, c.1811-1824
See Appendix B6 for Chronology of Swansea & Cambrian Potteries, p. 553.

B236	3767	**BEVINGTON & CO.**	Printed or impressed marks of differing design. "& CO."1811-1817. "& CO." omitted from 1817-1824.
B237	351	**BEVINGTON & CO. SWANSEA**	Dillwyn mark "SWANSEA"continued from 1817-1824. - "Potters trade-mark "OPAQUE CHINA" noted.
B238 B239	- -		 

In *Pugh, Welsh Pottery*, pp. 4-5, Mr. Pugh notes that Timothy Bevington and Dillwyn formed a partnership in 1811. Upon Lewis Weston Dillwyn's retirement in 1817 the Bevingtons formed a partnership with Haynes & Roby & Co. In 1821, upon the retirement of Haynes, the firm traded as T. & J. Bevington. In 1824 the leased pottery reverted back to the Dillwyn family (1824-1850).

For further reading, refer to *Coysh,* Vol. 1, p. 41; *Godden, Collecting Lustreware*, pp. 242-254; *Hallesy*; and *Nance*, pp. 108-138.

BIRKS

KAD NO.	GODDEN NO.	MARK	
			Birks Brothers & Seddon **Globe Pottery,** **Cobridge Works, Cobridge, Staffordshire, 1878-1886** **Formerly, Cockson & Seddon (1876-1878)**
B240	374		Printed Royal Arms mark. Full title and pattern name included, c.1878-1886.
B241	-	**B. B. & S.**	Printed initial mark, c.1878-1886. - One must be very careful not to confuse Thomas Birks & Co. of High Street, Longton with Birks Brothers & Seddon of Cobridge. Refer to *Godden, Collecting Lustreware*, p. 91, as well as to *Godden, British Porcelain*, p. 148.

BISHOP

			Bishop & Stonier (Ltd.) **Waterloo Works, Nelson Place** **Stafford Street Works, Miles Bank** **Church Street Works, High Street** **Hanley, Staffordshire, c.1891-1939** **Formerly, Powell, Bishop & Stonier (c.1878-1891)**
B242	384	**B. & S.**	Printed or impressed marks of differing design. Pattern name often included, c.1891-1910.
B243 B244	385-6	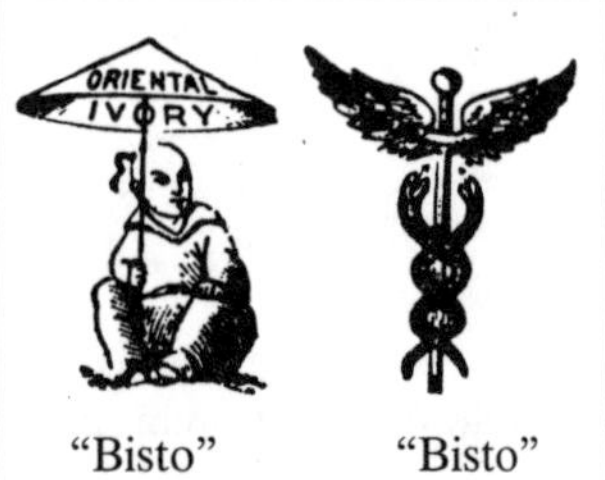"Bisto" "Bisto"	Printed marks of predecessors (KAD Nos. B1938 and 1935) continued with or without "BISTO" below, c.1891-1936. - "BISTO" an anagram for [Bi]shop and [Sto]nier.
B245 B246	387-8		Printed marks, c.1899-1936. Note continuation of mark KAD No. B244 but with the addition of "ENGLAND", c.1891. (For additional marks for the years 1936-1939 refer to *Godden*, p. 77.) - See Powell & Bishop as well as Powell, Bishop & Stonier for continuation and usage of earlier marks. - It would appear that Bishop & Stonier, Ltd. and their predecessors Powell, Bishop & Stonier were heavily involved in the manufacture of children's and toy wares, notes *Batkin*, pp. 43-44. For further reading, refer to *Godden, British Porcelain*, p. 149; *Jewitt*, pp. 497-499; and *Sussman*, pp. 73-74.

BLACKHURST

Blackhurst & Tunnicliffe
Hadderidge Pottery,
Burslem, Staffordshire, c.1879
Formerly, Heath & Blackhurst (c.1859-1877)
Subsequently, Blackhurst & Bourne (c.1880-1892)

KAD NO.	GODDEN NO.	MARK	
B247	401	**B. & T.**	Printed marks of differing design. Pattern name often included, c.1879.

BLACKWELL

John & Andrew Blackwell
Cobridge, Staffordshire, c.1802-1818
Subsequently, J. & R. Blackwell (c.1818)
No recorded marks have been noted by this author.
For further reading, refer to *Little*, p. 50.

BLAKENEY

Blakeney Pottery Ltd.
Stoke-on-Trent, Staffordshire, August 1968-Present

Blakeney Pottery Ltd. started production in August 1968 with the manufacture of Tea Leaf, which was followed by Flow Blue in 1970. Flow Blue is still a major production line.

Tea Leaf was produced and sold to "C.W. Allison & Sons" of Preston, England, who, it is understood, had a partnership with "Fred & Dottie's Antiques" in Birdsboro, PA. I would say that approximately from the 1960s to the mid-1970s backstamps are noted as follows:

KAD NO.	GODDEN NO.	MARK	
B248	-		Printed Royal Coat of Arms mark, with pattern name "Victoria" included, 1970-late 1970s.
B249	-		Printed Royal Arms mark, with pattern name "Victoria" included, 1970-late 1970s.
B250	-		Printed Royal Coat of Arms mark, with pattern name "Romantic" included, 1970-late 1970s.
B251	-		Printed Royal Coat of Arms mark, with initials "M. J. B." (Michael J. Bailey) included. This is the only mark to be printed in brown, 1970-late 1970s.

KAD NO.	GODDEN NO.	MARK	
B252	-		Printed mark with pattern name "Romantic" and "FLO BLUE/T.M. STAFFORDSHIRE/ENGLAND" included, 1970-late 1970s. - Pattern names used: "Victoria" and "Romantic". These pieces and patterns are not to be considered as reproductions, but as late potted Flow Blue wares. - Marks are to be found in *Cushion*, p. 157. For further reading, refer to *Tea Leaf Readings*, Vol. 12, Dec. 1993 and Vol. 13, September 1994; and *Antique Week, Central Edition*, Vol. 30, No. 51, Mar. 16, 1996, pp. 2 & 47 for an article by Connie Rogers titled "Is it Old or New? Know Before You Buy Willow Pattern China".

BODLEY

***Bodley & Co.**
Scotia Pottery,
Burslem, Staffordshire and other locations, c.1865-1865
Formerly, Bodley & Harrold (1863-1865)

KAD NO.	GODDEN NO.	MARK	
B253	419		Printed "Staffordshire Knot" mark. Pattern name often included, c.1865-1865. See mark KAD no. B264 for like mark but note "& Son."

BODLEY

***Bodley & Harrold**
Scotia Pottery,
Burslem, Staffordshire, c.1863-1865
Subsequently, Bodley & Co. (1865-1875)

KAD NO.	GODDEN NO.	MARK	
B254	431	**B. & H.**	Printed marks of differing design. Pattern name often included, c.1863-1865.
B255	432	**BODLEY & HARROLD**	

- Care should be taken in assigning initials, as these initials can also be attributed to:

Beech & Hancock	c.1860-1876, see KAD B206
Bednall & Heath	c.1879-1899, see *Godden, British Pottery*, p. 64.
Blackhurst & Hulme	c.1890-1932, see *Godden, British Pottery,* p. 79.

BODLEY

***Edward F. Bodley & Co.**
Scotia Pottery,
Burslem, 1865-1875

KAD NO.	GODDEN NO.	MARK	
B256	420	**E. F. B. & CO.**	Printed marks of differing design. Pattern name often included, 1865-1875.
B257	421	**E. F. B.**	
B258	-		Printed mark "E. F. BODLEY & CO., BURSLEM" with Staffordshire Knot included, 1865-1875.

KAD NO.	GODDEN NO.	MARK	
B259	422	**SCOTIA POTTERY**	Printed Staffordshire Knot with "SCOTIA POTTERY" within, 1865-1875.
B260	423	**BODLEY**	Impressed mark, c.1870-1875. Mark may relate to other firms of like name. - See *Collard*, Pottery & Porcelain, pp. 236-237; and *Godden, British Porcelain*, pp. 154-155 for clarification of Edward J. D. Bodley and Edward Fisher Bodley (& Co./& Son).

BODLEY

***Edward F. Bodley & Son**
Scotia Pottery (1875-1882)
New Bridge Pottery (1882-1898),
and other locations,
Burslem, Staffordshire, 1875-1898.

KAD NO.	GODDEN NO.	MARK	
B261 B262	424 425	**E. F. B. & SON** **E. F. B. & S.**	Printed or impressed marks of differing design. Pattern name often included, 1875-1898
B263	426		Printed trade-mark, Staffordshire Knot, c.1882-1898.
B264	427		- The marking "B. & S." should not be confused with E. F. Bodley & Son. It is only for Bodley & Son, 1874-1875. *See Godden*, p. 83.

BOLTON

James & Fletcher Bolton
Warrington, Lancashire, c.1797-1812
Blue and White printed wares are recorded, but very few appear to have been marked, c.1797-1812.
For further reading, refer to *Coysh*, Vol. 1, p. 47; *Godden, Collecting Lustreware*, pp. 280-281; and *Little*, p. 120.

BOOM

Joseph Boom
Shelton and Hanley, Staffordshire, 1784-1814

Blue and White printed wares are recorded, but very few appear to have been marked, c.1784-1814.
For further reading, refer to *Coysh*, Vol. 1, p. 47; *Godden*, p. 711; *Little*, p. 50; and *Mankowitz & Haggar*, p. 27.

BOOTE

T. & R. Boote Ltd. ("& Son" from 1872-1876)
Central Pottery (1842-(?)
Kilncroft Works (1842-1864)
Market Place Works (1849-1850)
Waterloo Pottery, Holehouse (1850-1963(66)),
Burslem, Staffordshire, 1842-1906(63)
- "Ltd." from 1894
In 1906 the Waterloo Pottery closed and the firm continued tile manufacture until 1963.

KAD NO.	GODDEN NO.	MARK	
B265	436	**T. & R. B.**	Printed marks of differing design. Pattern name often included, c. 1842-1871. Royal Arms mark noted on Victorian wares. "GRANITE", "GRANITE EARTHENWARE", "OPAQUE CHINA" AND "ROYAL IRONSTONE CHINA" also noted, c.1842+.
B266	-	**T. & R. BOOTE & CO.**	
B267	437	**T. & R. BOOTE**	
B268	-	**T. & R. BOOTE/ WARRANTED**	
B269	438	**T. B. & S.**	Printed initial mark "& SON", 1872-1876. **Typical Marks Include:**

B270 439
B271 -
B272 -
B273 440
B274 441

- G. Bernard Hughes notes in his *Victorian Pottery and Porcelain*. Spring Books, London, 1967, p. 57 the following as it relates to KAD No. B273 "ROYAL PATENT IRONSTONE": "...That the Royal Arms and reference to a patent have no association with Ironstone, but concern a method of making inlaid mosaic ware for which the firm were granted a patent in 1857."

Typical Marks on White Ironstone Include:

B275 -
B276 -
B277 -
B278 -
B279 -

- *White Ironstone Notes*, Vol. 1, No. 2, Winter 1994, shows an extensive collection of T. & R. Boote, featuring Sydenham and Octagon shapes, pp. 4-9.
Also refer to *Sussman*, p. 19, wherein she notes that the "firm confined itself to the production of ordinary White Graniteware from c.1865 to c.1906."

For further reading, refer to *Godden, British Porcelain*, p. 156; *Henrywood*, pp. 183-188; *Stoltzfus/Snyder*; and *White Ironstone Notes*, Vol. 3, No. 4, Spring 1997, p. 11.
- *Wetherbee, White Ironstone A Collector's Guide*, p. 51, shows an importer's mark for this potter:
"IMPORTED BY T. SWEENEY & SON, DEALERS IN QUEEN'S WARE & MANUFACTURERS OF FLINT GLASS, 63 MAIN ST., WHEELING, VA. WHEELING & LOUISVILLE UNION LINE."

B280 -

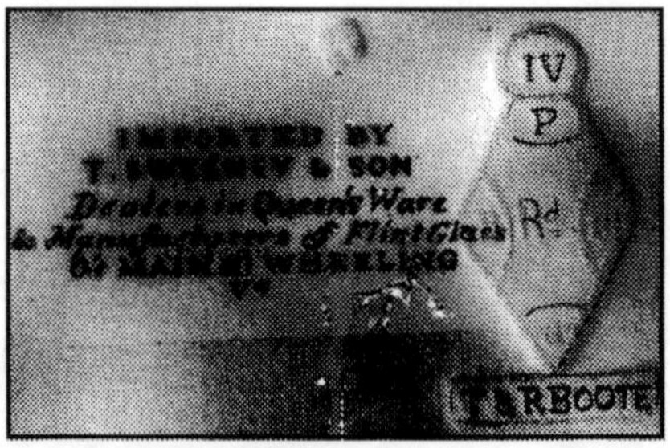

BOOTH

KAD NO.	GODDEN NO.	MARK	
			***Booth & Meigh** **Church Street, Lane End,** **Longton, Staffordshire, c.1837-1838**
B281	-	**B. & M.**	
B282	-	**BOOTH & MEIGH** **LANE END**	Printed and impressed mark noted. Pattern name often included. "IRONSTONE" mark also noted, c.1837-1838. - *Hampson*, No. 38, p. 28 cited the following dates: Richard Booth, Church Street, Longton c.1822-1838 Pye & Booth c.1822-1823 Richard Booth & Sons c.1824-1834 Abel Booth & Co. c.1837 Booth & Meigh c.1837-1838 Also refer to *P. Williams' Staffordshire*, Vol. 1, p. 386, and Vol. 2, p. 622 for the pattern "Rhine".

BOOTH

***Thomas Booth & Co.**
Knowles Street Works, Burslem (c.1868) and
Church Bank Works (from 1870),
Tunstall, Staffordshire, c.1868-1872
Formerly, Evans & Booth
Subsequently, Thomas Booth & Son

B283	-	**BOOTH**	Impressed name mark, 1868-1872.
B283A	447	**T. B. & CO.**	Printed marks of differing design. Pattern name often included, c.1868-1872. For further reading, refer to *Henrywood*, pp. 188-191.

BOOTH

***Thomas Booth & Son**
Waterloo Works (1872-1873)
Church Bank Works (1872-1876)
New Hall Pottery (1872-1876)
Tunstall & Hanley, Staffordshire, c.1872-1876

B284	448	**T. B. & S.**	Printed marks of differing design. Pattern name often included, c.1872-1876. - See comments under Thomas G. Booth

BOOTH

***Thomas G. Booth**
Church Bank Works,
Tunstall, Staffordshire, c.1876-1883
Formerly, T. Booth & Son
Subsequently, T. G. & F. Booth

B285	-	**T. G. B.**	Printed initial marks with pattern name often included, c.1876-1883.

KAD NO.	GODDEN NO.	MARK	
B286	449		
B287	-		

Typical Marks Include:

*The pattern "MADRAS" is noted in *P. Williams' Staffordshire*, Vol. 2, pp. 367-368 (photo plates are reversed) as registered first by Thomas Booth & Son, October 14, 1871, and evidently reissued by Thomas G. Booth. I believe the attribution of Madras and the registry thereof to be incorrect.
(See Appendix B6: Chronology of Selected Potteries & Partnerships):

Thomas G. Booth & Co.	1868-1872
Thomas Booth & Son	1872-1876
Thomas G. Booth	1876-1883

The original Blue & White Madras pattern was registered by Thos. Booth & Co. on Oct. 14, 1871/No. 256687, not by Thomas Booth & Son, and subsequently reissued by Thomas G. Booth (note initials "T. G. B.").

BOOTH

***T. G. & F. Booth**
Church Bank Works,
Tunstall, Staffordshire, c.1883-1891
Formerly, T. G. Booth
Subsequently, Booths (Ltd.)

B288	450	**T. G. & F. B.**	Printed marks of differing design. Pattern name often included, c.1883-1891.
B289	-		Printed mark with name of body style "PARISIAN GRANITE" noted. Also marked "ENGLAND" which was to comply with the American Tariff Act of 1891. (Example of marking noted is for polychrome, and is not for categories referenced in this work.)

BOOTH

***Booths (Ltd.)**
Church Bank Works (from 1891)
Swan Bank Pottery, High Street
and Soho Potteries (c.1912),
Tunstall, Staffordshire, c.1891-1948
Formerly, T. G. & F. Booth.
Subsequently, Booths & Colclough Ltd.
Merged with Ridgways in 1955

B290	-	**BOOTHS**	Impressed name mark, 1891-1912.

KAD NO.	GODDEN NO.	MARK	

B290A — 451

Printed marks of differing design. Pattern name often included, c.1891-1948.

B291 — 453

Printed mark, c.1906+. May also include "LTD", which dates from 1898.

B292 — 454

Printed mark, c.1912+. Terms "MADE IN ENGLAND" or word "ENGLAND" can be included. "1750" may also be included, but divided by mark; e.g. 17Mark50.

For further reading, refer to J.F. Blacker, *A .B .C. of XIX Century English Ceramic* Art. London, Stanley Paul & Co. Ltd., c. 1911, pp. 236-243; *Godden, British Porcelain*, pp. 158-161; and *NCSJ*, No. 68, Dec. 1987, pp. 16-22 for an article by David Richardson titled "The Bowers Family".

BOULTON

Boulton, Machin & Tennant
Swan Bank Pottery,
Tunstall, Staffordshire, c.1889-1899
Formerly, James Beech (1878-1889)

B293 — 469

Printed or impressed mark. Pattern name often included, c.1889-1899.
- "ENGLAND" included after 1891.

For further reading, refer to *Godden, Jewitt*, p. 141; and *Rhead*, p. 45.

BOURNE

***Bourne & Leigh (Ltd.)**
Albion & Leighton Potteries,
Burslem, Staffordshire, c.1892-1941
Formerly, Blackhurst & Bourne (1880-1892)
Subsequently, The Leighton Pottery, Ltd. 1940-1954

KAD NO.	GODDEN NO.	MARK	
B294	482	**B. & L.**	Printed marks of differing design. Pattern name often included, c.1892-1941. - The firm's name may also occur printed in full.
B295	483	**E. B. & J. E. L.**	
B296	484	**E. B. J. E. L.**	- *P. Williams' Flow Blue,* Vol. 2, p. 122, notes a floral pattern, "Azalea" only with a marking "J. E. L.". Also see KAD B298.
B297	485	**E. B. & J. E. L.** **B.**	

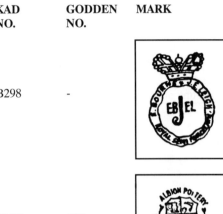

KAD NO.	GODDEN NO.	MARK	
B298	-		Printed mark c. 1892 - c. 1941.
B299	486		Printed mark, c.1912+. Note the inclusion of trade-mark "ALBION POTTERY".

BOURNE

***Bourne, Baker & Bourne**
Fenton Potteries,
Staffordshire, c.1796-1833
Subsequently, Bourne, Baker & Baker (1833-1835)
- Also listed as Bourne & Baker or Bourne, Baker & Co.

B300	-	**B. B. & B.***	Printed initial mark. Pattern name often included, c.1830s. -Additional marking "OPAQUE CHINA" noted.
B301	-		*Could this be the rare "B. B. & B." mark found on the "American Villa" pattern; see *Larsen*, 3rd ed. p. 234, No. 633.

For further reading, refer to *Godden, British Porcelain*, p. 163; *Little*, p. 52; and *NCS Newsletter*, No. 77, March 1990, pp. 43-45.

BOURNE

***Charles Bourne**
Grosvenor Works,
Foley, Fenton, Staffordshire, c.1817-1830
(Firm manufactured porcelain)

B302	-	**C. B.**	Coysh notes that while no blue-printed earthenwares have yet been recorded, a listing of copper plates for sale from the Bourne works (July 9, 1831) offers the possibility that earthenware may exist. Refer to *Coysh*, Vol. 1, p. 32; and *Godden, Staffordshire*, p. 239. - An extensive commentary on Charles Bourne, Foley Potteries, c.1817-1830 can be found in *Godden, Staffordshire Porcelain*, Ch. 16, pp. 238-247.

For further reading, refer to *Godden, British Porcelain*, pp. 238-247; and *Little,* pp. 51-52.

BOURNE

***Edward Bourne**
Longport, 1781-1815

B303	472	**E. BOURNE**	Impressed name mark, 1781-1815.

For further reading, refer to *Godden, Collecting Lustreware*, p.; 380; and *NCSJ*, Vol. 8, 1991, pp. 91-124 for an article by Ann Eatwell and Alex Werner titled "A London Staffordshire Warehouse - 1794-1825".

BOURNE

KAD NO.	GODDEN NO.	MARK	

***Joseph Bourne (& Son)(Ltd.)**
Bourne's Pottery,
Denby, Derbyshire, c.1809-1860+
History:

Mr. Jager	c. 1809-1812
Joseph Bourne	1812-1841
Joseph Bourne "& Son"	1841-1860
Joseph Harvey Bourne	1860-1869
J. Bourne (Joseph Harvey) & Son	1869-1898
"Ltd." from	1916
Acquired by Coloroll	1987
Acquired by Management	1990
Renamed The Denby Pottery Co.	1990

KAD NO.	GODDEN NO.	MARK	
B304	473	**BOURNES WARRANTED**	Various 19th century impressed marks, with the addition of "Codnor Park", related to the period of c.1833-1860. - Codnor Park Pottery was acquired in 1833.
B305	-		Printed mark noted on untitled White Ironstone as illustrated by *Wetherbee* on p. 48, as well as in *White Ironstone, A Collector's Guide*, p. 48, c.1840s+. - For later markings refer to *Godden*, pp. 89-90.

For further reading, refer to *NCSJ, Vol. 11,1994, Potteries of Derbyshire No. 29*, pp. 119-120, and *No. 31* pp. 121-123, for an article by Ronald B. Brown titled "Denby"; and Irene & Gordon Hopwood. *Denby Pottery 1809-1977.* Richard Dennis, London. 1997.

BOURNE

***Bourne, Nixon & Co.**
Tunstall, Staffordshire, c.1828-1830

KAD NO.	GODDEN NO.	MARK	
B306	489	**BOURNE NIXON & CO.**	Printed and impressed marks of differing design. Pattern name often included, c.1828-1830.
B307	489A	**B. N. & CO.**	Printed mark found on American/Canadian Historic Views, c.1828-1830. - Only one pattern has been cited by Larsen.

BOURNE

***William Bourne (Fenton)**
Fenton, Staffordshire, c.1843-1850

KAD NO.	GODDEN NO.	MARK	
B308	-	**W. BOURNE**	Printed marks of differing design. Pattern name often included, c.1843-1850.

For further reading, refer to *Hill*, Nos. 136 and 257.

BOURNE

***William Bourne (Longton)**
High Street, Alma Place,
Longton, Staffordshire, c.1857-1861

KAD NO.	GODDEN NO.	MARK	
B309	-		Printed mark noted with initial "B" on pattern "Lasso", attributed to William Bourne, Longton. 1857-1861.

KAD NO.	GODDEN NO.	MARK	
B310	-		Printed marks of differing design. Pattern name often included, c.1857-1861. For further reading, refer to *Hampson*, No. 42, p. 30; *Hill*, No. 257; and *P. Williams' Staffordshire*, Vol. 1, p. 720 and Vol. 2, p. 684. Also note the "Lasso" pattern by Petrus Regout & Co.

BOURNE

***William Bourne & Co.**
Bell Works,
Burslem, Staffordshire, c.1804-1818
Subsequently, Bourne & Cormie (1818-1829)

B311	-	**W. B. & C. STAFFORDSHIRE**	Printed initial mark, c.1812-1818. For further reading, refer to *Godden*, p. 735; and *Little*, p. 51. Also see William Adams and further comments by David Furniss on "Adams-Lasso..."

BOVEY

Bovey Pottery Co., Ltd.
Bovey Tracey,
Devon, c.1894-1957
Formerly, Bovey Tracey Pottery Co. (c.1842-1894)

B312		**B. P. CO. LTD.***	Printed initial mark, c.1894-1910. - *Mark used by Britannia Pottery Co. See KAD B362.
B312A	493		Printed or impressed mark, c.1894-1949.
B313	493A	**MADE BY BOVEY**	Printed or impressed mark, c.1937-1939. - For additional marks see *Godden*, p. 92.

BOVEY

Bovey Tracey Pottery Company
Bovey Tracey,
Devon, c.1842-1894
Subsequently, Bovey Pottery Co. Ltd. (c.1894-1957)
Previously known as The Foley Pottery
- see *Jewitt*, p. 154

B314	498	**B. T. P. CO.**	Printed or impressed marks of differing design. Pattern name often included, c.1842-1894. - Also see Indeo Pottery, p. 243. For further reading, refer to the *English Ceramics Circle Transactions*, Vol. 8, Park 2; and the *NCS Newsletter*, No. 76, Dec. 1989, pp. 39-45.

BOWERS

George Frederick Bowers (& Co.)
Brownhills Works,
Tunstall, Staffordshire, c.1841-1868
Company acquired by Brownhills Pottery Co. (1872-1896)
History:

"& Co." Edward Challinor	1841-1849
Bowers, Challinor & Woolliscroft	1850-1854
George Frederick Bowers*	1854-1868
Frederick Thomas Bowers	1868-1871

KAD NO.	GODDEN NO.	MARK	
B315	509	**G. F. B.**	Printed or impressed marks of differing design. Pattern name often included, c.1841-1868.
B316	510	**G. F. B. B. T.**	
B317	511		Printed Staffordshire Knot mark, c.1841-1868.
B318	512	**G. F. BOWERS**	Printed or impressed marks, c.1841-1868.
B319	512A	**G. F. BOWERS & CO.**	
B320	513	**IRONSTONE CHINA G. F. BOWERS**	
B321	514	**G. F. BOWERS TUNSTALL POTTERS (IES)**	

*The continuation of a pottery by family members without a change in title is not an uncommon practice.
For further reading, refer to *Godden, British Porcelain*, pp. 168-170; *Godden, Staffordshire*, pp. 391-393; and *NCSJ,* Vol. VI, 1987, pp. 167-192, for an article by David & Doreen Richardson and Bill Brown titled "The Start of A Dynasty, George Frederick Bowers."

BOYLE

Samuel Boyle (& Sons)
Church Street, Stoke-on-Trent (1845-1848)
High Street, Fenton (1849-1852),
Staffordshire, 1845-1852

KAD NO.	GODDEN NO.	MARK	
B322	-	**S. J. & J. B.**	Printed or impressed marks of differing design. Pattern name often included, 1845-1852.
B322A	-	**BOYLE & SONS**	

- See *True Blue*, p. 146 No. B5.
- (& Sons) dates from 1850-1852. Godden notes firm name given as "S. & J. Boyle". See *Godden, British Porcelain*, p. 171, as well as comments in his *Staffordshire Porcelain*, p. 393. Additionally, *P. Williams' Staffordshire*, Vol. 2, p. 154, notes the pattern "CIRCASSIA" as possibly being made by Samuel & James Boyle. However, the initials "S. J. & J. B." could stand for Samuel, James & John Boyle. Attribution is questionable.

BOYLE

Zacharia Boyle (& Co.) (& Son(s))
Keeling Lane, Hanley (c.1823-1830)
Bridge Works, Church Street,* (c.1828-1845),
Stoke-on-Trent*, c.1823-1845(47)
(& Son, 1828-1836) (& Sons, c. 1840-1845)

KAD NO.	GODDEN NO.	MARK	
B323	-	**BOYLE**	Impressed name mark with printed pattern name often included, c.1828-1844.
B324	522	**Z. B.**	Elaborately printed marks of differing design. Pattern name often included, c.1823-1844. "& S." from (1828-1836).
B325	523	**Z. B. & S.**	
B326	-		*Pottery formerly Church Street China Works of William Adams.
B327	-	**BOYLE & SON STOKE MANUFACTURERS**	Printed name mark, c.1828-1836(45).

- The former partnership was not officially dissolved until October 1847, although Zacharia Boyle died in December 1841 and Joseph retired in 1845.

For further reading, refer to *Godden, British Porcelain*, p. 172; *Little*, p. 52; and *NCSJ*, Vol. 14, Autumn 1997, pp. 105-129 for an article by Trevor Markin titled "Thomas Wolfe of Stoke-on-Trent and Liverpool."

BRADLEY

Bradley & Co.
Coalport, Shropshire, c.1796-1800

B328	530	**BRADLEY & CO. COALPORT**	Rare impressed mark, c.1800.

For further reading, refer to *Coysh*, Vol. 1, p. 207, *FOB* Bulletin No. 34; and *NCS Newsletter*, No. 62, pp. 31-35, for an article by Roger Edmundson titled "Walter Bradley & Co., Coalport, 1796-1800."

BRAMELD

Brameld & CO. (Rockingham Works)
Swinton, Old Pottery,
near Rotherham, Yorkshire, c.1806-1841(42)
Formerly operated by the Leeds firm of Hartley, Greens & Co. (c.1787-1806)

B329	3351	**BRAMELD**	Printed or impressed marks of differing design. Pattern name often included. c. 1806-1841(42)
B330	3355	**BRAMELD & Co.**	Various crosses, stars and numbers (1-16) were added after the name "Brameld", c.1806-1842. Many pieces were produced unmarked.

- Brameld may be noted as one of the first to use the term "GRANITE CHINA".
- Note mark of initial "B" in KAD B332.

Typical Examples, c.1820-1842, include:

B331 -
B332 3357
B333 -
B334 -

KAD NO.	GODDEN NO.	MARK	
B335	-		
B336	-		
B337	3356		
B338	-		

B339	3352	**ROYAL ROCKINGHAM WORKS BRAMELD**	Printed marks from c1826-1842. Impressed markings "ROCKINGHAM WORKS BRAMELD" or "ROCKINGHAM BRAMELD" noted. See Godden Nos. 3353-3354.

B340 3358 — Printed "Griffin" mark taken from the Crest of the Earl of Fitzwilliam, Marquis of Rockingham , c.1826-1842. "ROYAL" and "MANUFACTURED TO THE KING", c.1830-1842 noted.

B341 3359 — - For additional marks refer to *Rockingham Pottery & Porcelain, 1745-1842* by Alwyn & Angela Cox, London, Faber & Faber, 1983, pp. 219-228.

For further reading, refer to *Lawrence, Godden, Illustrated Encyclopedia*, p. 545 for "Rockingham"; *Godden, British Porcelain*, pp. 110-11, 176 and 660-663; *Edward's Basalt*, pp. 241-242; *Williams-Wood, English Transferware*, pp. 200-204 for "Swinton Pottery"; *NCSJ*, Vol. 12, 1995, pp. 93-150 for an article by Alwyn & Angela Cox titled "The Closure of the Rockingham Works, Part I; and *NCSJ*, Vol. 13, 1996, pp. 1-34 for Part II of "The Closure of the Rockingham Works". Also refer to *The Rockingham Pottery*, new rev. edition by Arthur A. Ealestone & T. A. Lockett, England, David & Charles, 1973; *NCS Newsletter*, No. 109, March 1998, pp. 4-16 for an article by Renard Broughton titled "Yorkshire Pottery: Identifying Early Blue Painted Patterns of the circa. 1785-1810."

BRANNAM

C. H. Brannam & Co. (Ltd.)
Litchdon Pottery,
Barnstaple, Devon, c.1879-

B342	-	**CHB. CO.**	*P. Williams' Flow Blue*, Vol. II, p. 142, notes a printed mark "CHB. CO." with the pattern name "Limoges". Godden (see *Godden*, p. 98) in a letter to me dated 9/12/94, states "This plate is nothing like Brannam and is probably not English."

For further reading, refer to *Cameron*, p. 59; *A Collectors' History of English Pottery*, by Griselda Lewis, "The Brannam Pottery, Barnstaple", England. Antique Collectors Club, 1992; pp. 276- 278 and John A. Bartlett. *British Ceramic Art 1870-1940.* Atglen, PA, Schiffer Publishing Ltd. 1993, pp. 32-37.

BRIDGETT

***Bridgett & Bates**
King Street,
Longton, Staffordshire, c.1882-1915
Formerly, Bridgett, Bates & Beech (c.1875-1882)
Subsequently, Beswick & Son(s) (c.1916-1930)

B343	587	**B. & B.**	Printed marks of differing design and impressed initials. Both may be found in combination with each other, c.1882-1915.

KAD NO.	GODDEN NO.	MARK	
B344	588		Printed mark, c.1912+. Continued by successors, Beswick & Son, c.1916-1930. - Firm was acquired by J. W. Beswick in 1908, who continued with production.

BRIDGWOOD

***Bridgwood & Clarke**
Church Yard, Burslem & Phoenix Works,
Tunstall, Staffordshire, c.1859-1864
Formerly, Thomas Goodfellow (1828-1859)
Subsequently, Edward Clarke & Co. (1865-1977+)

B345	589	**BRIDGWOOD & CLARKE**	Printed or impressed marks of differing design. Pattern name often included. "PORCELAIN OPAQUE " noted, c.1859-1864.
B346	590	**B. & C.**	
B347	590A	**B. & C. BURSLEM**	
B348	-		Printed Royal Coat of Arms mark. Additional markings "OPAQUE CHINE" and "PORCELAIN OPAQUE " noted, c.1859-1864. For further reading and marks refer to *Wetherbee*, p. 93.

BRIDGWOOD

***Sampson Bridgwood (& Son) (Ltd.)**
Lane End (1800-1817)
Market Street (1818-1853)
Stafford Street (1822-1854)
High Street (1832-1835)
Anchor Works (1854-1890+),
Longton, Staffordshire, 1854-1890+
Subsequently, Sampson Bridgwood & Son, Anchor Works (1854-1890+)
Acquired by James Broadhurst & Sons Ltd. in 1963

B349	-		Printed Royal Coat of Arms mark with initial "S. B.", c.1830.
B350	-	**BRIDGWOOD**	Impressed name mark, mid 19th century.
B351	591	**BRIDGWOOD & SON**	Printed marks of differing design. Pattern name often included, "& SON" dates from 1854. "BRIDGWOODS CHINA" variation of crest mark KAD B353 dates from c.1884. - "ENGLAND" added from 1891+. - "LTD" added from 1932.
B352	592	**S. BRIDGWOOD & SON**	
B353	**593**		

KAD NO.	GODDEN NO.	MARK
B354	594	
B355	595	
B356	596	
B357	597	
B358	598	

Typical Marks Include:

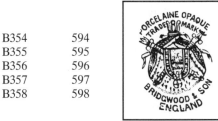

1885+

1885

"PARISIAN GRANITE" wares. 1870+

(with or without "Anchor China")

1912+

KAD NO.	GODDEN NO.	MARK
B359	-	
B360	-	

Selected Examples of White Ironstone Include:

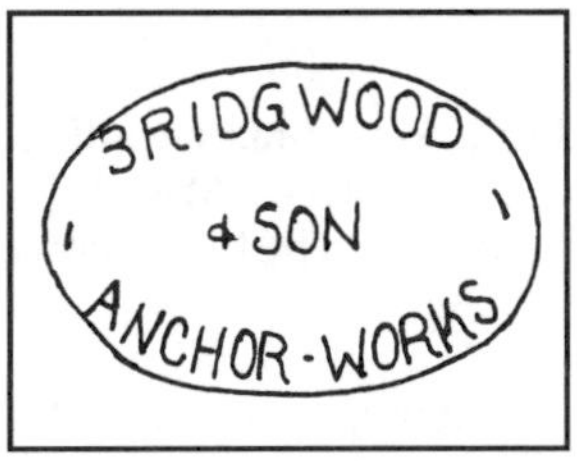

- As of 1879 no Bridgwood family member was involved with the company.

For further reading, refer to *Hampson*, No. 50, pp. 34-35; *Hamspon, Churchill, pp. 51-78; Godden, Masons*, p. 239; *Wetherbee*, p. 93' *NCS Newsletter*, No. 106, June 1997, pp. 28-31 for an article by Dr. G. A. Godden titled "Impressed Anchor Mark -Adams or Bridgwood".

BRINDLEY

John Brindley & CO.
Broad Street,
Shelton, Hanley, Staffordshire, c.1828

KAD NO.	GODDEN NO.	MARK	
B361	-	**BRINDLEY & CO. WARRANTED STAFFORDSHIRE**	Rare impressed mark, c.1828.

- The name John Brindley & Co. is not to be confused with the earlier firm John Brinley (& Co. is not included), 1773-1793.

For further reading, refer to *Godden, Jewitt*, p. 37 and *Jewitt*, pp. 397, 467-468.

BRISTOL

Bristol Pottery
See: Poutney, p. 98

BRITANNIA

***Britannia Pott. Co. Ltd.**
St. Rollox,
Glasgow, Scotland, c.1920-1935
Formerly, Cochran & Fleming (1896-1920)
- See R. Cochran & Co., pp. 155-156.

KAD NO.	GODDEN NO.	MARK	

History:

Britannia Pottery, St. Rollox, Glasgow, Scotland c.1855(57)-1935
R. Cochran & Co. c.1855(57)-1896
- Robert Cochran (Sr.),
Alexander Cochran & James Fleming,
- Robert, Sr. dies in 1869
Cochran & Fleming c.1896-1920
- Alexander Cochran & James Fleming
Britannia Pott. Co. Ltd. c.1920-1935
Britannia Pottery Co. Ltd. 1935-1939

- The company was sold to a group of Glasgow businessmen, named Woolfson, who continued the pottery until 1939 when it was closed.

B362 - **B. P. CO. LTD.*** Printed initial marks, 1920-1939.

B363 620

Printed trade-mark continued on "Quebec Views Series". Marking noted as "B. P CO. LTD., MADE IN SCOTLAND", 1920-1939.
* Mark used by Bovey Pottery Co., Ltd. See KAD B312.

B364 - **MADE IN ENGLAND** - As above, but marked "MADE IN ENGLAND", 1920-1939.
- The company name is not to be confused with the Britannia China Co. (1894-1906).

For further reading, refer to *Collard, Potters View*, pp. 74-80; and *Finlayson*.

BRITISH ANCHOR

British Anchor Pottery Co. Ltd.
Anchor Road, Longton, c.1884-1982
Formerly, John Thomas Hudden (1874-1883)

B365 - **B. P. CO. LTD.** Printed or impressed marks. Pattern name often included, c.1884.
- "ENGLAND" added from 1891.

Typical Examples Include:

B366 622
B367 623
B368 624

c.1884-1913

1910+

1913-1940(+)

- The pottery works closed during World War II, but under a concentration scheme production continued at the facilities of J. & G. Meakin Ltd. See *NCSJ*, No. 12, 1995, pp. 175-213 for an article by Kathy Niblett titled "Ten Plain Years, The British Pottery Industry, 1942-1952." Further, in 1970 the company was renamed Hostess Tableware Ltd. In 1973 the company merged with the Alfred Clough Group and the works were closed in 1982.

BROADHURST

KAD NO.	GODDEN NO.	MARK	
			***Broadhurst & Green** **Anchor Works,** **Longton, Staffordshire, c.1846-1852** **Formerly, Broadhurst & Green, New Street (c.1846)** **Subsequently, William Green (c.1853-1858)**
B369	-	**BROADHURST & GREEN**	Printed name mark, c.1846-1852. For further reading, refer to *Godden, Collecting Lustreware*, p. 95; and *Hampson*, No. 54, pp. 37-38.

BROADHURST

			***James Broadhurst (& Sons) (Ltd.)** **Crown Pottery, Stafford Street,** **Longton, Staffordshire, c.1854-1863** **Formerly, Bradbury, Mason & Broadhurst (1853-1854)** **Subsequently, James Broadhurst (c.1863-1870)**
B370	-	**WARRANTED** **BROADHURST & SONS** **CROWN POTTERY, LONGTON**	Printed mark, c.1870-1922. - Mark noted on "Willow" pattern. Refer to *Blue Willow*, 2nd ed. by Mary Frank Gaston, Paducah, KY, Collectors Books, 1996, pp. 19, 59.
B371	640	**J. B.**	*JAMES BROADHURST (Longton):* Printed initial marking, 1863-1870.
B372	639	**J. B. & S**	*JAMES BROADHURST & SONS (Fenton):* - Portland Pottery, Frederick Street Printed initial marking, 1870-1922
B373	641	**J. B. & S. LTD.**	*JAMES BROADHURST & SONS LTD (Fenton):* - Portland Pottery, Frederick Street Printed initial marking. "LTD" from 1922-1983. For further reading, refer to *Godden*, p. 107; *Godden, Collecting Lustreware*, p. 95; and *Hampson*, No. 53, p. 37.

BROUGHAM

			Brougham & Mayer **Lion Works,** **Sandyford, Tunstall, Staffordshire, c.1856-1862** **Formerly, Thomas Walker (c.1845-1856)**
B374	-	**B. & M.**	Printed marks of differing design. Pattern name often included, c.1856-1862.
B375	649	**BROUGHAM & MAYER**	- May include the wording "IRONSTONE". - Care must be taken with the initials "B. & M." when attributing potters. For further information, refer to *Hill*, No. 283 for the pattern "Tavoy".

BROWN

Brown & Steventon, Ltd.
Royal Pottery,
Burslem, Staffordshire, 1900-1923
Subsequently, J. Steventon & Son, Ltd. (1923-1936+)

KAD NO.	GODDEN NO.	MARK	
B375A	653	B. & S.	Printed marks of differing design, with initial "B. & S." Pattern name often included, 1900-1923.

B375B 654 Printed mark with full name. A variation of this mark is noted with "LTD./BURSLEM/ MADE IN ENGLAND", 1920-1923
- Registration marks for 1903/No. 414460 with the pattern name "Pansy" have been noted.
- This pattern is unattributed by *Gaston*. See Book II, p. 111, pl. 241. However, it is attributed to Johnson Bros. by *P. Williams*. See *Flow Blue*, Vol. II, p. 150.

BROWN

Brown-Westhead, Moore & Co.
Cauldon Place & Royal Victoria Works,
Shelton, Hanley, Staffordshire, c.1862-1904
Formerly, Bates, Brown, Westhead & Moore (1859-1861)
Subsequently, Cauldon, Ltd. (1905-1920)

KAD NO.	GODDEN NO.	MARK	
B376	675	B. W. M.	Printed or impressed marks of differing design. Pattern name often included, c.1862-1904.
B377	676	B. W. M. & CO.	
B378	677	T. C. BROWN-WESTHEAD MOORE & CO.	Impressed name marks, c.1862+.

Typical Marks Include:

B379 679
B380 682
B381 684
B382 684A

1862+

Word Variation noted

c.1895-1904

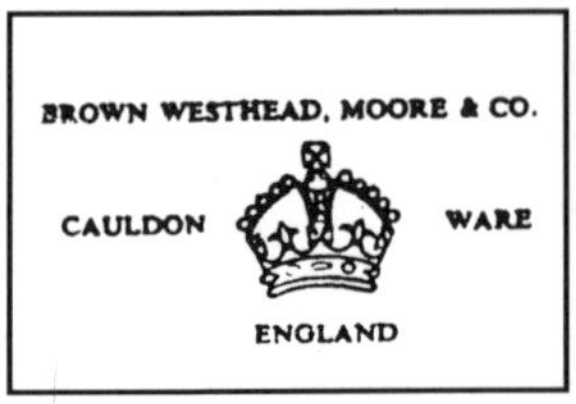

c.1894-1904

B383 680

Printed or impressed mark, c.1884+.

B384 683

"CAULDON" printed marking, c.1895-1904.

B385 681

Printed or impressed mark.
- "ENGLAND" included after 1891+.
-Patterns and marks may have been continued by Cauldon Potters Ltd. (1920-1962)

KAD NO.	GODDEN NO.	MARK	

Godden, Ridgway, notes a listing of registry shapes and design from 1862-1883. Refer to pp.217-218 and to pp. 173-175 for a more complete history of the pottery.

BROWNFIELD

***William Brownfield (& Son(s)),**
Cobridge Works, Cobridge, Staffordshire, 1850-1892
Formerly, Wood & Brownfield (1837-1850)
Subsequently, Brownfield's Guild Pottery Society Co. Ltd. (1892-1897)

Family Name History:

Robinson, Wood & Brownfield	c.1837
Wood & Brownfield	1837-1850
William Brownfield	1850-1871
William Brownfield & Son	1871-1876
William Brownfield & Sons	1876-1892
Brownfield Guild Pottery Society Co. Ltd.	1892-1897
Brownfield Guild Pottery Ltd.	1897-1900

KAD NO.	GODDEN NO.	MARK	
B386	660	**W. B.**	Printed or impressed initial marks of differing design. Pattern name often included, c.1850-1871.
B387	661		
B388	-		Printed Garter Mark with pattern name "THRACE" as well as retailer's marking "HIGGINBOTHAM & SON, 102 GRAFTON STREET, DUBLIN" noted by Peake, c.1856. See *Peake,* p. 111, Mark No. 39.
B389	662	**BROWNFIELD**	Impressed marks, 1860 onwards. The printed name also occurs with a crown above, 1850-1892.
B390	663	**BROWNFIELDS**	
B391	664	**W. B. & S.**	Printed initial marks "& S" or "& SON" appears after 1871.
B392	665	**W. B. & SON**	
B393	665A	**& SONS**	Printed "& SONS" appears after 1876.
B394	666		Printed mark, 1871-1892.
B395	-		Printed mark "TRADE MARK", 1871-1892. - *Hughes* Vol. 1, p. 105, notes a jug titled "Westminster" and impressed initials "W.B." but with the registration date Oct. 21, 1868 in the name of W. P. & G. Phillips.

KAD NO. | **GODDEN NO.** | **MARK**

For further reading, refer to *Woolliscroft-Rhead*, pp. 308-309; *Hampson, Churchill*; *Godden, British Porcelain*, pp. 199-200; *Shelley Potteries*, pp. 27-28; *Peake, William Brownfield*, pp. 17-80, 93-199 for additional marks for plate designs, pp. 119-129 for information on "& SONS" and pp. 170-172, Appendix 3, for a complete index of plate designs. Also refer to *NCSJ*, Vol. 4, 1980-1981, pp. 177-218 for an article by Rodney & Eileen Hampson titled "Brownfield, Victorian Potters."

BROWNFIELDS

***Brownfields Guild Pottery Society Ltd. (1892-1897)**
Subsequently, Brownfields Pottery Ltd. (1897-1900),
Cobridge Works, Cobridge, Staffordshire, 1892-1900
Formerly, William Brownfield & Sons (1850-1891)

B396 | 667 | **B. G. P. CO.** | Printed marks of differing design. Pattern name often included. Printed marks continued by Brownfields Pottery Ltd., 1892-1900.

Typical Marks Include:

B397 | 668
B398 | 669
B399 | 670

1892-1897 **1892-1900**

B400 | - |

Mark similar to KAD B397 but with additional wording "WORKMEN'S PRODCTIVE SOCIETY", 1892-1897. Note that the letter "U" has been omitted.
- See *Peake, William Brownfield*, pp. 76-80, where Mr. Peake notes that between December 1897 and early 1898 liquidation of the pottery was carried out on a voluntary basis. The Pottery was put up for sale in 1898. During this wind down period a new company was formed called Brownfield Pottery Ltd. In 1900 Wood & Brownfield, agents, came into being and by September 26, 1900, the Brownfield Pottery Co. was auctioned off, ending sixty-three years of production. For plate design index refer to Appendix 3, p. 172.

For further reading, refer to *Woolliscroft-Rhead*, pp. 297, 308-309; *Jewitt*, pp. 472, 476; *Hampson, Churchill*; *Shelley Potteries*, pp. 27-28; *Godden, British Porcelain*, p. 200; *Henrywood*, pp. 132-145; and *NCSJ*, Vol. 4, 1980-1981, pp. 177-218 for an article by Rodney & Eileen Hampson titled "Brownfields, Victorian Potters." Also refer to Flora E. Haines. *A Keramic Study, A Chapter in the History of Half a Dozen Dinner Plates*. Bangor, ME. (Published by the Author). 1895. pp. 104-110.

BROWNHILLS

Brownhills Pottery Co.
Brownhills China Works,
Tunstall, Staffordshire, c.1872-1896
Formerly, T.F. Bowers (1869-1871)
Subsequently, Salt Bros. (1897-1904)

B401 | 671 | **B. P. CO.** | Printed marks of differing design. Pattern name often included, c.1872-1896.

KAD NO.	GODDEN NO.	MARK	
B402	672		Typical printed initial mark, c.1872-1896. "ENGLAND" added from 1891.
B403 B404	673 674		Printed marks, c.1880-1896. - The initials "B. P. CO." are not to be confused with those of Cochran & Fleming, "BP CO. LTD." Also see KAD B194. For further reading, refer to *Henrywood*, p. 191.

BULLOCK

A. Bullock & Co.
Waterloo Pottery (1895-1902)
Kensington Pottery (1903-1915)
Hanley, Staffordshire, 1895-1915

B404A	704	**A. B. & CO./H.**	Printed or impressed initial marks of differing design. Pattern name often included, 1895-1915.
B404B	704A	**A. B. & CO.***	

* Allman, Broughton & Co. (1861-1868) used like initials. Care must be taken when attributing by initials. Refer to KAD B109.

BURGESS

***Burgess & Goddard, Importers (USA)**
Lane End,
Longton, Staffordshire, c.1840s-1890s
History:

Goddard & Co. (manufacturers)	Commerce Street, Lane End, Longton	c.1840-1848
Goddard, Dale & Burgess (exporters)	32 Church Street, or Stafford Street, Longton	c.1848(51)-1858
Goddard & Burgess (exporters)	32 Church Street or Stafford Street, Longton	c.1858-1890

- This company traded under the name of Burgess & Goddard in the US and under the name of Goddard & Burgess in Longton, Staffordshire.

It was the Burgess side of the partnership that managed the USA side of the business. In 1879 William Burgess and John Campbell purchased the International Pottery Company in Trenton, New Jersey. Burgess & Goddard traded as importers of earthenwares and represented such firms as John Edwards, Wedgwood & Co., S. Bridgwood & Son in the US. See KAD marks A195 and 196, p. 41.

B405	-	**BURGESS & GODDARD**	Printed name mark, c.1870s-1885. - This name mark should not mislead the reader in thinking Burgess & Goddard were potters. For further reading, refer to *Hampson*, No. 115, p. 76; *Hamspon, Churchill*, p. 58; *Godden, Collecting Lustreware*, pp. 115-166; *Ewins*, Ch. 7, pp. 105-127 "The Role of the Specialist Merchant and the Non-autonomous Manufacturer in the mid-Nineteenth Century."

BURGESS

Burgess & Leigh (Ltd.)
Central Pottery,
Stafford Street (Market Street) (1862-1870)
Hill (Top) Pottery, High Street (c.1862-1889)
Middleport Pottery (c.1889+)
Burslem, Staffordshire, c.1862+

KAD NO.	GODDEN NO.	MARK	
B406	712	**B. & L.**	Printed or impressed marks of differing design. Pattern name often included. Burslem may be added to initials, 1862-1889.
B407	715		Printed mark, c.1862+. Variations are noted. - *Godden* notes that the "Beehive mark was used by other earlier manufacturers (e.g. S. Alcock & Co.)*" See marks KAD B93 and 94. - *P. Williams, Flow Blue*, Vol. 1, p. 72 notes the pattern "Old Castle" marked W (for W. & E. Corn) as well as an impressed initial mark "B.&L." (for Burgess & Leigh). In Vol. 2, p.112 she notes a further printed marking "GERMANY" and impressed "B.&L." It is interesting to note that there were frequent occasions when potters "jobbed" work out to other potters for decorating and for distribution.
B408	-	**MIDDLEPORT POTTERY B & L**	Printed name mark in semi-circle over ornate initials "B. & L.", 1889-1912.
B409	716		Printed mark, "MIDDLEPORT", c.1889-1912.
B410	717		Printed name mark, c.1906-1912.
B411	718		Printed name mark, c.1912+. "LTD" added to style in 1919. -Willow ware was produced with a special backstamp after 1921.

*Burgess & Leigh acquired the moulds and copper plates of Samuel Alcock & Co., (See Appendix B6: Chronology for Alcock, pp. 539-540) some of which were continued until the mid 1950s.

For further reading, refer to *Blue Berry Notes*, Vol. 9, No. 1, Jan./Feb. 1995, p. 1 for a "Tongue Dish" located in the Margaret Strong Museum in Rochester, New York. Also refer to *Gaston*, Mark Nos. 24-28.

BURGESS

Henry Burgess
Kilncroft Works, Sylvester Square,
Burslem, Staffordshire, c.1864-1892
(Former pottery owner, T. & R. Boote, 1842-1864)

KAD NO.	GODDEN NO.	MARK	
B412	710		Printed or impressed Royal Coat of Arms mark with initials below. Pattern name often included, 1864-1892.
B413	-		Printed Royal Coat of Arms mark with name below, found on Tea Leaf with Copper Lustre, 1864-1892.
B414	-	**STONE CHINA H. BURGESS BURSLEM**	Printed Royal Coat of Arms mark, as above, but with name below, 1864-1892.
B415	711	**H. BURGESS**	Printed or impressed name mark, 1864-1892.

Selected Marks on Tea Leaf/Copper Lustre & White Ironstone Include:

B416 -
B417 -
B418 -

Reg'd. Nov. 5, 1878

Registration Diamond 1843-1883

Post 1883
Reg. No. 54421
& name H. BURGESS

Noted above are examples of pre and post 1883 registration markings. The early example illustrates the Registration Diamond for Nov. 5, 1878 and the later the printed Registration number Rd. 54421 (not shown) with the name H. BURGESS for the year 1886.

- See *Godden's* comments, pl. 8, on raised applied marks; and *Henrywood, Relief Moulded Jugs* for an excellent insight into the application of relief marks.

For further reading, refer to *Tea Leaf Readings, Educational Supplement*, May 1994; *Heaivilin*, pp. 48-51; *Wetherbee*, p. 112; *White Ironstone Notes*, Vol. 3, No. 4, Spring 1997, p. 8, for the pattern "Hyacinth Shape"; and *Stoltzfus/Snyder*.

BURN

Joseph Burn & Co.
Stepney Bank Pottery, Ouseburn,
Newcastle-upon-Tyne, c.1852-1860
Formerly, Thomas Bell & Co. (1847-1852)
Subsequently, John Charlton (1861-1875)

KAD NO.	GODDEN NO.	MARK	
B419	-		Printed Royal Coat of Arms mark with initials "B. & CO.", also marked "STONE WARE", c.1852-1860.
B420	-	**BURN & CO.**	Printed name mark, c.1852-1860.
B421	-	**J. BURN & CO.**	Impressed name mark, c.1852-1860.

For further reading, refer to *Bell*.

BURTON

Samuel & John Burton
New Street Pottery,
Hanley, Staffordshire, c.1832-1845
Formerly, James Keeling (1790-1832)

B422	734	**S. & I. B.**	Printed marks of differing design. Pattern name often included. "PEARL CHINA" marking noted, c.1832-1845. - *Coysh*, Vol. 1, p. 63, notes a shield marking containing the wording "IRONSTONE CHINA" and initials "S. & I. B." *Godden*, Mark No. 734 notes an impressed, raised pad on a moulded jug which is impressed "S. & J. B." Additional marking "IMPROVED STONE CHINA" in a hexagonal frame is also noted. - The letters "I" and "J" were used interchangeably during the mid 19th century.

BUTTERFIELD

William & James Butterfield
Globe Pottery,
Tunstall, Staffordshire, c.1854-1861
Formerly, W. & C. Butterfield (1854)

B423	736	**W. & J. B.**	Printed marks of differing design. Pattern name often included, c.1854-1861.
B424	-		For further reading, refer to Snyder, *Romantic Staffordshire*, p. 42.

CALEDONIAN

Caledonian Pottery
Glasgow, Scotland, c.1801-1850+
Pottery also known as Glasgow Pottery (1800-1807). Garngad Hill Pottery acquired in 1811 by Delftfield and merged into one pottery, Caledonian Pottery.

KAD NO.	GODDEN NO.	MARK	
			History:
B425	-	-	Reid, Patterson & Co. 1801
B426	-	-	Reid & Patterson 1801
B427	-	-	Archd. Patterson & Co.* 1802-1807
B428	-	**J. C.**	J. Aitchieson & Co.* 1807-1811 - Printed initial mark is questionable.
B429	-	-	Delftfield/Caledonia 1811-1820
B430	-	**KEMP & CO.**	John Kemp & Co. 1820-1825 - Impressed name mark is questionable.
B431	-	-	Murray & Co. 1826-1840
B432	-	**M. & C./G.**	Murray & Couper 1840-1850
B433	-	**M. & F.**	Murray & Fullerton 1850-1864
B434	-	-	Murray & Grosvenor 1864-1868
B435	-	**M. & CO.**	Murray & Co. 1868-1895
B436	-	-	W. F. Murray & Co. Ltd. 1895-1898
B437	-	-	W. P. Hartley 1898-1928 *From 1802-1811 Josiah Rowley was the pottery's manager. As a retailer he had his name put on wares. One such [printed] marking is noted.
B438	-	**ROWLEY, WILSON STREET GLASGOW-STONE CHINA**	- Godden questions the "STONE CHINA" mark being as early as 1802-1811.

For further reading, refer to *Fleming*, pp. 77-78; *Scottish Pottery History Review*, 15th Historical Review, 1992-1993, for an article by Irene McDonald; *The Story of the Caledonia Pottery, Glasgow*" by John S. Neil, and *Old Glasgow Club Transactions,* No. 5, Vol. II, Paper No. 3, pp. 318-325, 1912-1913. Also refer to Godden, *Collecting Lustreware*, pp. 268-269; and *Cameron*, pp. 68-69.

CALLAND

John F. Calland & Co.
Landore Pottery,
Swansea, Wales, c.1852-1856

KAD NO.	GODDEN NO.	MARK	
B439	746	**CALLAND SWANSEA**	Printed and impressed marks of differing design, c.1852-1856.
B440	747	**CALLAND & CO. LANDORE, SWANSEA**	- Godden notes, from a copper plate in his collection, the marking "C. & CO.", as well as the mark "IMPROVED WILLOW". He further notes "…its attribution to this firm is only tentative." See *Godden*, p. 123.
B441	748	**C. & CO.**	
B442	749	**J. F. CALLAND & CO. LANDORE POTTERY**	

For further reading, refer to *Godden, Jewitt,* pp. 230-231; *Coysh*, Vol. 1, p. 67; *Nance*, p. 202; and Pugh, *Welsh Pottery*, p. 54.

CAMBRIAN

***Cambrian Pottery**
Swansea, Wales, c.1786-1810
(Founded, c.1764 and referred to as Cambrian Pottery)
Also see Appendix B6: Chronology for Swansea Pottery & Bevington & Co.

KAD NO.	GODDEN NO.	MARK	
B443	3757	**SWANSEA**	Impressed pottery mark, c.1783-1810.
B444	3759	**CAMBRIAN**	Hand painted mark, c.1783-1810.

KAD NO.	GODDEN NO.	MARK	
B445 B446 B447	3761 3762 3763	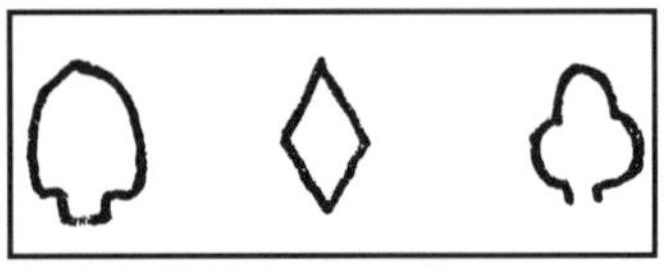	Impressed workmen's marks found on Swansea plates, etc. c.1800-1810. - The spade-like mark was used elsewhere such as at Leeds Pottery. - The impressed mark "SWANSEA" (KAD No. B443) may appear throughout the period, c.1783-1810, and was used as the factory mark. - For additional marks of Cambrian potters refer to *Nance,* pp. 444-452. For further reading, refer to *Godden, Collecting Lustreware*, pp. 242-254; *Little*, pp. 111-112; *Coysh*, Vol. 1, p. 354; *Cameron*, p. 70; Pugh, *Welsh Pottery*; and *Hallesy*. Additional patterns are noted in both *Pugh* and *Hallesy*.

CAMPBELLFIELD

Campbellfield Pottery Co. (Ltd.)
Springburn, Glasgow, Scotland, c.1850-1899

B448	757	**CAMPBELLFIELD**	Printed or impressed marks of differing design. Pattern name often included, c.1850-1881.
B449	758	**C. P. CO.***	*The marking "C. P. CO." has not been verified, and may be an error in marking, where "LTD" has been omitted.
B450	759		
B451	760	**C. P. CO. LTD.**	Printed mark, "LTD." included from 1881-1899.
B452	761		Printed initial mark, 1881-1899.

CAREY

Thomas & John Carey (John Carey & Sons)
Lane Delph, Fenton (1818-1842)
Anchor Works, Longton, (1828-1842)
Staffordshire, c.1818-1842
Formerly, John Carey (c.1813-1825) (& Sons, c.1818-1827)

B453	772	**CAREYS**	J. Carey c.1813-1825
B454	-	**CAREY & SON**	& Sons c.1818-1827
B455	-	**CAREYS** **J**	T. & J. Carey c.1828-1841(42)
B456	-		Printed marks of differing design. Pattern name often included. Note markings "FELSPAR" and "SAXON STONE", c.1828-1842. - A printed marking by Carey is noted in Peake, *William Brownfield*, p. 89 as a Royal Coat of Arms below 'IMPROVED/IRONSTONE CHINA".

KAD NO.	GODDEN NO.	MARK	
			Typical Examples Include:
B457	-		 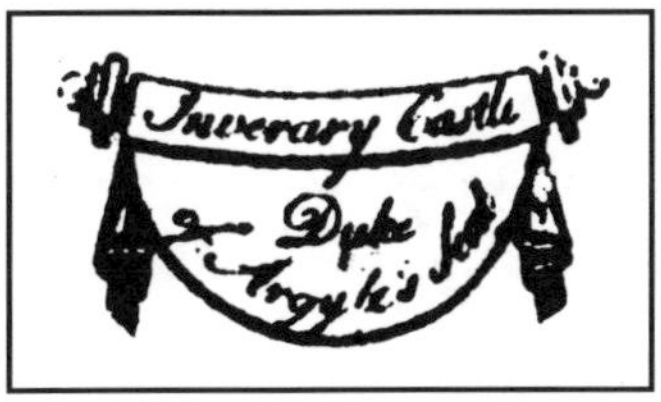 
B458	-		
B459	-		
B460	-		

- The impressed Anchor mark (KAD No. B457) may accompany other marks.

For further reading, refer to *Coysh, Transferware*, pp. 21-22; *Coysh*, Vol. 1, p. 70; *Hampson*, No. 65, pp. 64-65; *Godden, British Porcelain*, p. 211; *Godden, Staffordshire Porcelain*, p. 401; *Little*, p. 54; and *Coysh & Stefano*.

Carlton Ware, Ltd.
Carlton Works,
Stoke-on-Trent, Staffordshire, 1958-1966
Formerly, Wiltshaw & Robinson (1890-1957)
Subsequently, A. Wood & Son (Longport) Ltd. (1966-1987+)

B461 774 

Former printed marks on Staffordshire by Wiltshaw & Robinson continued by Carlton Ware, 1958-1966.
- See Wiltshaw & Robinson KAD Nos. B2466-68.
- In 1987 the company was renamed Carlton & Kent. The trade name, pattern books and some moulds were acquired by Grosvenor Ceramic Hardware, Ltd., Stoke, Staffordshire. Carlton was re-launched in 1990 and closed in 1992.

For further reading, refer to John A. Bartlett. *British Ceramic Art 1870-1940*. Atglen, PA. Schiffer Publishing Ltd. 1993, pp. 50-51.

CARR

Carr & Patton
Phoenix Pottery,
Ouseburn, Newcastle-Upon-Tyne
Northumberland, c.1847-1848
Bell notes "…It would appear there were two partnership periods at two different potteries." There was a one year partnership with John Carr continuing on at the Low Lights Pottery, Northshields, and with John Patton at the above Phoenix Works. Refer to *Bell*, p. 49; and *Coysh*, Vol. 1, p. 72. Further, *Godden, Jewitt*, p. 213 notes "…In about 1844, it passed (Phoenix Pottery) into the hands of Isaac Bell & Co., as was afterwards carried on successively by Carr & Patton (who at the same time operated the North Shields Pottery)…"

CARR

John Carr (& Co.) (& Son(s))
Low Lights Pottery,
North Shields, Northumberland, c.1845-1900
(& Co. 1850-1854) (& Son 1854-1861) (& Sons 1861-1900)

KAD NO.	GODDEN NO.	MARK	
B462	-	**CARR**	Printed marks of differing design. Pattern name often included, c.1845-1850.
B463	-	**J. CARR**	

KAD NO.	GODDEN NO.	MARK	
B464	-	**J. C. & C.**	Printed initial mark, c. 1850-1854. - Refer to *Bell*, p. 51.
B465	-		Impressed marking of Anchor with "LONDON" marking which may accompany printed initial marking. - See comments re "LONDON/ANCHOR" impressed mark under Isaac & Thomas Bell, see p. 109.
B466	-	**J. C. & CO. WARRANTED STAFFORDSHIRE**	Printed marks of differing design. Pattern name often included, c.1850-1854.
B467	778	**J. CARR & CO.**	Printed marks of differing design. Pattern name often included, c.1850-1854.
B468	-	**J. C. & SON WARRANTED STAFFORDSHIRE**	Printed marks of differing design. Pattern name often included, c.1854-1861.
B469	-	**J. CARR & SON PORCELAINE OPAQUE**	Impressed name mark, c.1854-1861.
B470	-	**J. C. & S.**	Printed initial mark noted on a floral designed pattern marked "Asiatic Pheasant", c.1861-1900. - Refer to *Bell*, p. 51.
B471	-	**J. CARR & SONS NORTH SHIELDS**	Impressed name mark, c.1861-1900.
B472	779		Impressed Stag's Head mark, c.1861-1900. - Refer to *Godden*, p. 128. - It was not uncommon in the history of the Carr's (or other potters) to use marks of a predecessor. Thus, two marks may appear on one piece, one impressed and one printed.

Typical Marks Include:

B473	-	
B474	-	
B475	-	

- Authors may reference this pottery as:
Low Lights Pottery
North Shields
Northumberland

For further reading, refer to *Bell*; *Coysh*, Vol. 1, pp. 72; *Godden, Collecting Lustreware*, p. 237; *Cameron*, p. 247; and *Cushion, British Ceramic Marks*.

CARTWRIGHT

KAD NO.	GODDEN NO.	MARK	
			Cartwright & Edwards (Ltd.) **Weston Place, Longton c.1858-1955** **Borough Pottery, Longton (1869+)** **Victoria Works, Longton [Porcelain from 1912 +]** **Heron Cross Pottery, Fenton, Staffordshire (1916-1988)** **Acquired by Alfred Clough Ltd. in (1955-1988)**
B476	-	**CARTWRIGHT & EDWARDS**	Printed marks of differing design. Pattern name often included, c.1858+.
B476A	796	**C. & E.**	- Cork & Edge also used the initial "C. & E." (1846-1860) - Initials, as in mark KAD B476A, noted from c.1880 onwards.
B477	797	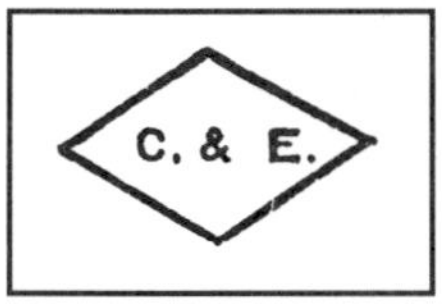	Printed or impressed initial in Diamond, from 1900+.
B478	798		Printed mark on porcelain from the Victoria Works, c.1912+. - "LTD." noted from 1926. - Blakeney Art Pottery also used the printed name mark "VICTORIA" (See KAD No. B248).

For further reading, refer to *Hampson,* No. 66, pp. 43-44; and *Godden, British Porcelain,* p.212; and *P. Williams*, *Staffordshire*, Vol. III, p. 258

CAULDON

KAD NO.	GODDEN NO.	MARK	
			Cauldon Ltd. **Cauldon Place,** **Shelton, Hanley, Staffordshire, c.1905-1962** **Formerly, Brown-Westhead, Moore & Co. (1862-1904)** **Subsequently, Cauldon (Potteries) Ltd. (1920-1962)***
B479	821	**CAULDON ENGLAND**	Printed marks of differing design. Pattern name often included. "CAULDON" marking may include the terms "LTD." or "LIMITED", c.1905-1920.
B480	822		Former Ridgway and Brown-Westhead, Moore & Co. marks used again with the addition of "CAULDON LTD." and "ENGLAND", c.1905-1920.

Typical Marks Include:

KAD NO.	GODDEN NO.
B481	823
B482	-
B483	682
B484	684

Former Brown-Westhead, Moore & Co. Marks
See KAD Nos. B380 - 381

KAD NO.	GODDEN NO.	MARK	

*For an extensive history, until the factory's closing in 1977, refer to *Batkin*, pp. 57-59. For further reading, refer to *Godden*, pp. 111-112; and Godden, *Ridgway*, pp. 51, 53, and 57; and *P. Williams, Staffordshire*, Vol. III, p. 112.

CERAMIC

Ceramic Art Co. Ltd.
Stoke Road,
Hanley, Staffordshire, c.1892-1903

B485	828	**THE CERAMIC ART CO. LTD. HANLEY STAFFORDSHIRE ENGLAND**	Printed mark. Pattern name often included, c.1892-1903. - Godden notes that KAD mark nos. B485 and B487 are differentiated by the marking "HANLEY" from a company with the exact same name title as above, but located in Stoke-on-Trent.

CERAMIC

Ceramic Art Co. (1905) Ltd.
Crown Pottery,
Stoke, Staffordshire, c.1905-1919

B486	829		Printed or impressed marks of differing design. Pattern name often included, c.1905-1919.
B487	830	**CERAMIC ART CO. LTD. CROWN POTTERY STOKE-ON-TRENT MANUF. OF FAIENCE**	Printed mark, c.1905-1919. - This marking is noted without the term "HANLEY". See comments under KAD B485.

CHALLINOR

Challinor & Mayer,
Fenton, Staffordshire, c.1887

- This was a short lived partnership about which little information is recorded.

B488	-		Printed mark, with a "Teaberry" Motif noted in June 1988 edition of *Tea Leaf Readings*, p. 7, c.1887.

CHALLINOR

***E. & C. Challinor**
Fenton Stone Works,
High Street, Lane Delph, Fenton, c.1862-1891
Subsequently, C. Challinor & Co. (1892-1896)

B489	837	**E. & C. C.**	Printed marks of differing design. Pattern name often included, c.1862-1891.
B490	-	**E. & C. CHALLINOR FENTON**	- The marking "IRONSTONE CHINA" is noted. Staffordshire knot, with name or initials, appears c.1862-1891.

KAD NO.	GODDEN NO.	MARK

B491 - 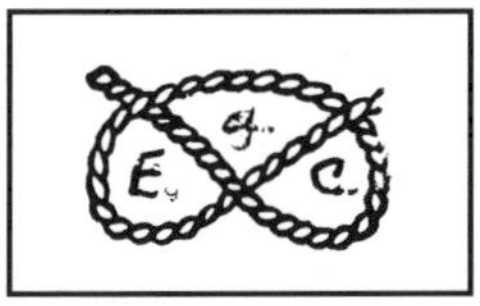

Printed Staffordshire Knot, 1862-1891.

Typical Examples Include:

B492 -
B493 -

Printed Royal Arms mark, with variations, noted on White Ironstone and Tea Leaf/Copper Lustre, 1862-1891.

- The mark "ENGLAND" normally appears after 1891. The collector must realize, however, that potters anticipated this change and may have started using this marking a few years earlier.
- An excellent accounting of additional patterns and marks is provided in *Jewitt*, p. 554.

For further reading, refer to *Sussman*, p. 19 for the patterns "Ceres", "Wheat", "Garland" and "Vine Leaf". Also refer to *Stoltzfus/Snyder,* p. 53; *Wetherbee*, p. 11; and *Woolliscroft-Rhead*, p. 69; and *Antique Week, Central Edition*, Vol. 30, No. 51, Mar. 16, 1996, pp. 2 & 47 for an article by Connie Rogers titled "Is it Old or New? Know Before You Buy Willow Pattern China."

CHALLINOR

***E. Challinor & Co.**
Fenton Stone Works, High Street,
Lane Delph, Fenton, c.1853-1862
Subsequently, E. & C. Challinor (1862-1891)

KAD NO.	GODDEN NO.	MARK
B494	-	**E. C. & CO.**
B495	-	**E. C. & C. CO.**
B496	-	**CHALLINOR & CO.**
B497	836	**E. CHALLINOR & CO.***

Printed marks of differing design. Pattern name often included, c.1853-1862.
- Markings "IRONSTONE" or "IRONSTONE CHINA" noted.

Typical Examples Include

:

B498 -
B499 -
B500 -

B501 -
B502

*Godden notes the firm name E. Challinor & Co. as being recorded at Tunstall in 1851 and 1853-1854.

CHALLINOR

KAD NO.	GODDEN NO.	MARK	
			***Edward Challinor** **Pinnock Works (1842-1847)** **Fenton Stone Works, High Street,** **Lane Delph, Fenton (1853-1862)** **Unicorn Pottery (1862-1867),** **Tunstall, Staffordshire, 1842-1867**
B503	835	**E. C.**	Printed marks of differing design. Pattern name often included, 1842-1867.
B504	835A	**E. CHALLINOR**	- "IRONSTONE" marking noted.
B505	-		Printed marks of differing design. Pattern name often included, 1862-1867. - "TUNSTALL" marking noted.
B506	-	**G. R.**	Printed initial mark "G. R." noted by *Coysh* for Oriental Sports "Series".
B507	-		- See *Coysh*, Vol. 1, pp. 267-268 "Groom Leading Out" and Vol. 2, pp. 148-149 "Battle With a Buffalo and a Tiger".
B508 B509 B509A	- - -		**Typical Printed Marks Include:** 
B510 B511	- -		**Typical Impressed Marks Include:** 

For additional markings refer to *P. Williams Staffordshire*, Vol. I & II; and *Hill.*

CHAPPELL

KAD NO.	GODDEN NO.	MARK	

S. & J. Chappell
(S. Chappell & Co.)
Leeds Pottery,
Yorkshire, c.1842-1847(9)
Formerly, The Leeds Pottery Co. (1832(34)-1842)
Subsequently, Warburton & Britton (1849(50)-1863)

No further information is available.
For further reading, refer to *Lawrence*, pp. 25, 55; *Little*, pp. 115-116; *Towner*, pp. 13, 21; and *NCSJ*, Vol. 6, 1987, pp. 23-48 for an article by Ron Morley titled "The Enigma of the Leeds Pottery's Co. Partnership Shares."

CHESWORTH

***Chesworth & Robinson**
Lane End,
Longton, Staffordshire, c.1825-1840
Formerly, Chesworth & Wood (1824-1825)

B512 | 874 | **C. & R.** | Printed marks of differing design. Pattern name often included, c.1825-1840.

B513 | - | - Printed initial mark noted by Coysh as either Chesworth & Robinson or Chetham & Robinson (1822-1834).
- Both Coysh and Godden note that care must be taken in attributing the initial "C. & R." See *Coysh*, Vol. 1, p. 80.
For further reading, refer to *Hampson*, No. 73, pp. 46-48 "Chetham & Robinson".

CHETHAM

***Chetham (& Son)**
Commerce Street,
Longton, c.1814-1821
Formerly, Mrs. Ann Chetham (1809-1811)
Subsequently, Chetham & Robinson (1822-1834)

B514 | 875 | **CHETHAM** | Impressed name mark, c.1809-1811 (Mrs. Ann Chetham).

B515 | 876 | **CHETHAM & SON** | Impressed name mark, c.1814-1821.
For further reading, refer to *Hampson,* No. 73, pp. 46-48.

CHETHAM

***Chetham & Robinson (& Son)**
Commerce Street,
Longton, c.1822-1840
- "& Son" from 1834
Subsequently, Jonathan Lowe Chetham (1841-1861)

B516 | - | **CHETHAM & ROBINSON** | Printed name mark, c.1822-1834.

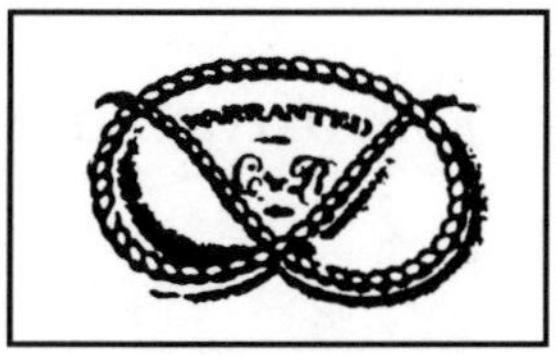

B517 | 879 | Printed Staffordshire Knot, with initials "C. & R.", c.1822-1834.
- This mark may also be that of Chesworth & Robinson.
- Note marking "WARRANTED".

KAD NO.	GODDEN NO.	MARK	
B518	-	**C. R. S.**	Printed initial mark, 'CHETHAM, ROBINSON & SON", c.1834-1840. For further reading, refer to *Edwards*, *Basalt*, pp. 137-140; *Godden, British Porcelain*, p. 233; *Godden, Collecting Lustreware*, pp. 96-97; and *Hampson*, No. 73, pp. 46-48.

CHETHAM

Chetham & Woolley
Commerce Street, Lane End,
Longton, Staffordshire, c.1796-1807
Subsequently, (Mrs.) Chetham & Woolley (c.1807-1809)

B519	-	**CHETHAM & WOOLLEY**	Impressed name mark, c.1796-1807. For further reading, refer to *Hampson*, No. 46, pp. 46-48; *Penny Plain*, p. 95, No. 184; and *Edward's, Basalt*, pp. 137-140.

CHETHAM

Jonathan Lowe Chetham
Commerce Street, Longton, 1841-1861
Formerly, Chetham & Robinson & Son (1834-1840)
Subsequently, J. R. & F. Chetham (1862)

B520	877	**J. L. C.**	Printed initial mark, 1841-1861. For further reading, refer to *Hampson*, No. 73, pp. 46-48.

CHILD

Child & Clive
Newfield,
Tunstall, Staffordshire, c.1811-1818(28)
Formerly, John Henry Clive (c.1802-1811)
Subsequently, Joseph Heath & Co. (c.1828-1841(42)

B521	883A	**CHILD**	Impressed name mark, c.1811-1818(28) - Additional printed mark "MORTLOCK'S OXFORD STREET" noted. - Coysh notes that the pattern "Quails" with painted mark may, in fact, be attributed to Child & Clive and not Smith Child, as printed marks did not appear until the 1820s. See *Coysh*, Vol. 1, p. 293. - The pattern and name "Quails" was later copied by Furnivals, Ltd. and dated 1913. - Also refer to Smith Child For further reading, refer to *Little*, p. 55, 57; and *Mankowitz & Haggar*, p. 53.

CHILD

Smith Child
Newfield,
Tunstall, Staffordshire, c.1763-1790
Subsequently, John Henry Clive (c.1802-1811)

B522	883	**CHILD**	Impressed name mark, c.1780-1790. - Additional printed mark "MORTLOCK'S OXFORD STREET" noted. - Also refer to Child & Clive

KAD NO.	GODDEN NO.	MARK	
			For further reading, refer to *Coysh*, Vol. 1, p. 293, wherein he states that the mark was possibly issued later under the name of Child & Clive. Also refer to *Little*, p. 57; *Mankowitz & Haggar*, p. 53; and *Woolliscroft-Rhead*, p. 73.

CLARKE

Edward Clarke (& Co.), 1865-1887
Phoenix Works, Tunstall (c.1865-1877)
New Bridge Works, Longport (c.1876-1880)
Churchyard Works, Burslem (c.1880-1887)
Formerly, Bridgwood & Clarke (c.1857-1864)
Subsequently, A. J. Wilkinson

KAD NO.	GODDEN NO.	MARK	
B523	893	**EDWARD CLARKE (TOWN)**	Printed marks of differing design. Pattern name often included. Address of firm added (helpful in dating), c.1865-1887.
B524	894	**EDWARD CLARKE & CO. (TOWN)**	- Tunstall Address c.1865-1877 - Longport Address c.1876-1880 - Burslem Address c.1880-1887
B525	895		Addresses are often indicated on a mark by the town and respective date.
B526	896	**ROYAL SEMI-PORCELAIN**	Printed or impressed term added from 1877+.

- Also refer to the American partnership of Edward Clarke and James Carr, the New York City Pottery, see p. 52, and the International (Lincoln)Pottery Co, Trenton, New Jersey, see p. 41. The same marks as KAD B525 was used at these potteries. Refer to *Debolt*, pp. 200-201.

For further reading on Clarke and Carr, refer to M. Lelyn Branin, *The Early Makers of Handcrafted Earthenware and Stoneware in Central and Southern New Jersey*. Cranbury, NJ, Associated University Press, 1988

CLEMENTSON

***Clementson & Young**
Broad Street,
Shelton, Hanley, Staffordshire, c.1845-1847
Formerly, Clementson, Young & Jameson (1844)

KAD NO.	GODDEN NO.	MARK	
B527	977	**CLEMENTSON & YOUNG**	Printed marks of differing design. Pattern name often included, c.1845-1847.
B528	-	**CLEMENTSON & YOUNG**	Impressed name mark, in cartouche, c.1845-1847. - An impressed Registration mark, No. 30701 has been noted with a Registration Diamond, surrounded by a double circle which reads: "REGISTERED BY CLEMENTSON & YOUNG, OCTOBER 22, 1845."
B529	-		Printed mark with the pattern name "COLUMBIA" is also noted, 1845-1847. - See *P. Williams, Flow Blue*, Vol. I, p. 62.

CLEMENTSON

KAD NO.	GODDEN NO.	MARK	

***Clementson Bros. (Ltd.)**
Phoenix Works and Bell Works,
Hanley, Staffordshire, c.1865-1916
"LTD" added from 1910

B530 905

Printed marks of differing design. Pattern name often included, c.1867-1880.
- Additional marking "STONE CHINA" noted.

B531 -

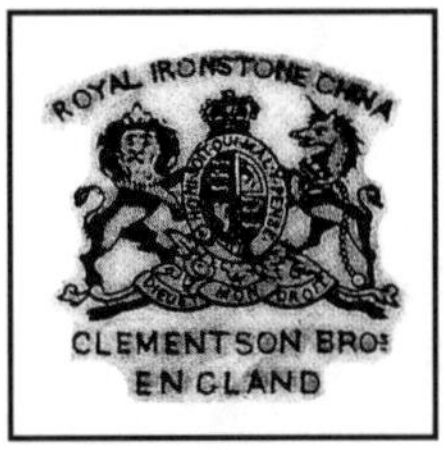

Printed marks of differing design. Pattern name often included, c.1870-1916.
- "ENGLAND" added after 1891.
- Many prior Joseph Clementson registration shapes were reissued by his sons. Refer to pattern section.

Typical Examples Include:

B532 -
B533 906
B534 907
B535 908
B536 909

1870+

1870+

1910+

1901-1913

1913-1916

- KAD B536 may be noted with the additions "SEMI PORCELAIN".

For further reading on Tea Leaf/Copper Lustre shapes, refer to *TLCI Educational Supplement*, April 1992, pp. 40-41, 49-50, 67-69, for an article by Sussman titled "Pouring Vessels"; *White Ironstone Notes*, Vol. 3, No. 4, Spring 1997, p. 11; *Snyder, Romantic Staffordshire*, p. 55; and *Stoltzfus/Snyder.*

CLEMENTSON

***Joseph Clementson**
Phoenix and Bell Works (1855),
Shelton, Hanley, Staffordshire, c.1839-1864
Formerly, Read & Co. (1837-1838)
Subsequently, Clementson Bros. (1865-1916)

KAD NO.	GODDEN NO.	MARK	
B537	910	**J. C.**	Printed marks of differing design. Pattern name often included, c.1839-1864.
B538	910A	**J. CLEMENTSON**	
B539	-	**J. CLEMENTSON SHELTON**	Impressed mark with or without registration mark and term "IRONSTONE" noted on White Ironstone, c.1848-1864.

KAD NO. **GODDEN NO.** **MARK**

B540 -

B540A -

Printed Phoenix Bird is the most commonly noted mark, c.1840s-1864.
- Godden notes an additional mark of "WARRANTED/STONE CHINA".

B541 -

Printed mark "RUSTIC SCENERY" registered Dec. 2, 1842. See *P. Williams, Staffordshire*, Vol. II, pp. 238-239.
- Additional marks for Blue & White Transferware are to be found in *P. Williams, Staffordshire*, Vol. I, II & III. Additional marks for Flow Blue will be found in both *Gaston* and *Snyder's* two volumes.

B542 - **J. CLEMENTSON HANLEY**

Printed or impressed mark, with or without registration marking, noted on White Ironstone and Tea Leaf/Copper Lustre. Pattern shape often included, c.1848-1864.

B543 -

Mark noted on "Classical Antiquities Series", registered March 13, 1849/No. 58874, 1848-1864.

For further reading, refer to *Snyder, Romantic Staffordshire*, pp. 44-45.

Joseph Clementson was a major exporter to the American and Canadian markets. Two examples of marks noted below date from the late 1850s, and may be found on either Tea Leaf/Copper Lustre or White Ironstone.

B544 -

B545 -

Selected Importers Marks Include:

B546 -

B547 -

B548 -

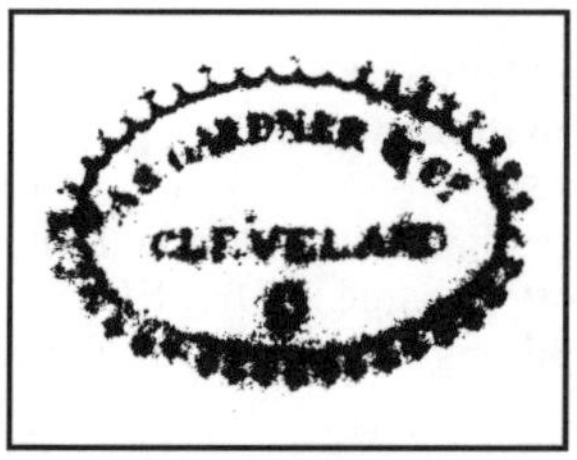

KAD NO.	GODDEN NO.	MARK	
			For further information on American/Canadian Importers refer to Appendix at the back of this encyclopedia titled "Importer, Retailer, Wholesaler and Auctioneers of Earthenware and Souvenir Wares, United States and Canada." See pp. 657-673.
B549	-		Printed Garter marked "CHICAGO SHAPE" normally associated with the "NEW YORK SHAPE" registered Dec. 8, 1858 noted in *White Ironstone Notes*, Vol. 3, No. 4, Spring 1997, p.11.
B550	-		- At an auction held by Gene Harris Antiques, Marshalltown, Iowa (Feb. 25, 1995),in the United States a transfer plate marked "MANUFACTURED FOR DAVENPORT, J. CLEMENTSON, SHELTON" was noted as Lot 168A - It would appear that between the years 1842 and 1890(92) J. Clementson had an agent in the United States (particularly in New York). Clementson has pieces marked specifically for this agent. The following marking is noted on the Claremont pattern registered June 30, 1856: For further reading on the Clementson family and potteries, refer to *NCSJ,* Vol. 5, 1984, pp. 177-205 for an article by Pat Halfpenny titled "Joseph Clementson: A Potter Remarkable for Energy of Character". For additional information on US importers' backstamps refer to *Blue Berry Notes*, Vol. 8, No. 7, Nov.-Dec. 1994, pp. 1-2. Also refer to *Sussman*, p. 49 and *Collard, Pottery & Porcelain*.

CLEMENTSON

***Joseph Clementson & Sons (J. C. & SONS),**
Phoenix Works and Bell Works
Shelton, Hanley, Staffordshire, c.1848+(?)

KAD NO.	GODDEN NO.	MARK	
B551	-	**J. C. & SONS**	Printed name mark. Pattern name often included, c.1848+(?). - During Joseph Clementson's tenure (1839-1864), I would suspect [sometime] after c.1848, that he took his sons into the company. Francis was in earlier partnerships from 1844-1847. Further complicating the issue is that James Colclough & Son (c.1837-1838) and John Carey & Sons (c.1825-1835) may also have used the initials "J. C. & SONS".

CLEMENTSON

***Clementson, Young & Jameson**
Broad Street,
Shelton, Hanley, Staffordshire, c.1844-1845
Subsequently, Clementson & Young (1845-1847)

KAD NO.	GODDEN NO.	MARK	
B552	912	**C. Y. & J.**	Printed initial mark and registry for Oct. 17, 1844, recorded in the name of the above firm.

CLEVELAND

Cleveland Pottery Co.
No information available

KAD NO.	GODDEN NO.	MARK	
B553	-	**PORCELAINE ROYAL CLEVELAND POTTERY/ COMPANY ENGLAND**	Printed mark, c.1891+. Marked with name in horseshoe style around crown, and above pottery name "PORCELAINE ROYAL", noted on a Flow Blue butter pat in this author's collection [Art Nouveau in design].

CLEWS

KAD NO. | **GODDEN NO.** | **MARK**

James & Ralph Clews
Bleak Hill Works, Elder Road (1813-1827)
Cobridge, Works,
Cobridge, Staffordshire, (c.1817-1834)
Globe Pottery, Cobridge Road (1817-1834)
Cobridge, Staffordshire, 1813-1834
- Cobridge Pottery works rented from William Adams on Sept. 29, 1817

B554 - **CLEWS**

Impressed name mark, c.1817-1834.

B554A 918

Impressed mark. Sometimes initials "G.R." may appear on either side of crown, c.1817-1834.
- Note that term "WARRANTED STAFFORDSHIRE" can appear either in one or two curved lines.

B554B - **CLEWS WARRANTED**

Impressed name mark within a double circle with crown in center, c.1817-1843.

B555 919

Impressed or printed marks noted with various and often elaborately designed marks. Name of individual pattern often included. Additional marking "CHINA WARRANTED" noted, c.1817-1834.

Typical Marks Include:

B556 -
B557 -
B558 -
B559 -

B559A -

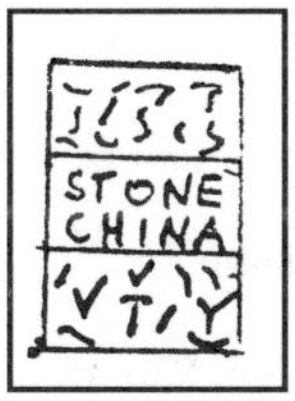

Printed variation of mark KAD B559, with addition of impressed mark KAD B554, c.1817-1834.
- See *Arman Quarterly*, Vol. 3, No. 3, July/August 1997, p. 7, for "Pointer and Rabbit".
- *P. Williams, Staffordshire*, Vol. II, p. 365 notes the pattern "Hunting Dog" showing an impressed mark KAD B555 and a rectangular printed mark "STONE/CHINA" KAD B559A.

B559B -

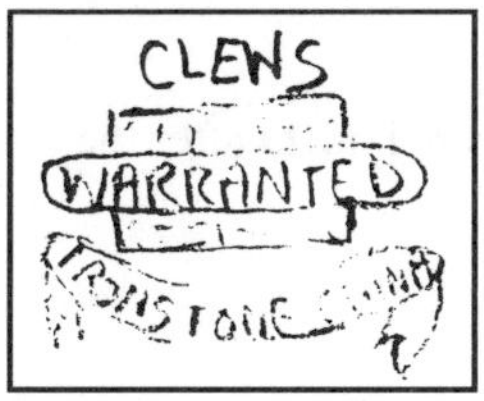

Printed mark noted on a pitcher with "Basket & Vase" pattern, c.1817-1834.
- See *Arman Quarterly*, Vol. 1, No. 3, p. 8.
Printed marks of various designs noted on Historic American/Canadian views which often include printed series and title names, c.1817-1834.

KAD NO.	GODDEN NO.	MARK	
			Typical Marks Include:
B560 B561 B562 B563	- - - -		

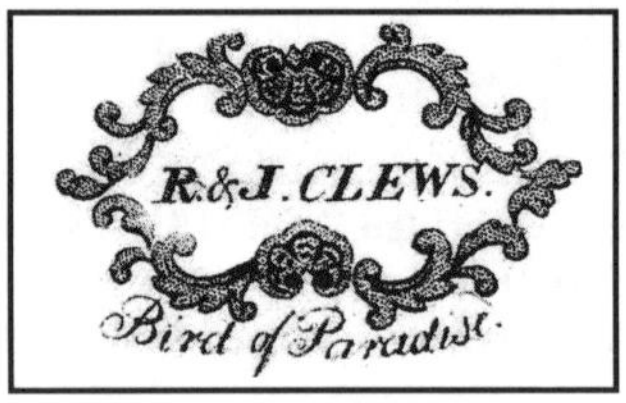

B564 -

This impressed Propeller (Potters Mark) was used by many potters and should not be misconstrued as being used only by Clews.
- See *Godden's* comments on reproductions, p. 152.

In correspondence to me dated Dec. 19, 1994, Frank Stefano notes an impressed importer mark for "GREENFIELD/PEARL STREET/NEW YORK". Further, an importer mark "WRIGHT TYNDAL & VAN RODEN/PHILADELPHIA" is noted.

For further reading, refer to *Edwards, Basalt*, pp. 140-141, *Coysh & Stefano*; *Snyder, Historic Staffordshire; Godden, British Porcelain*, pp. 238-239; *Little*, pp. 56-57, 146-147; *Hampson, Churchill*, pp. 124-125; and *Penny Plain*, p. 100, No. 25.
Also refer to *Cameron*, p. 82 for a short but interesting history of James Clews as a manufacturer in the United States (1836-1842); *Collard, Potters View*, pp. 81-85; and *Barber*, pp. 157-161 for a tract titled "James Clews in the United States at the Pottery at Troy, Indiana."

CLIVE

John Henry Clive
Newfield,
Tunstall, Staffordshire, c.1801-1811
Previously, Smith Child (1763-1790)
Subsequently, Child & Clive (c.1811-1818(28)

B565	920	**CLIVE**	Impressed name mark, c.1802-1811.

For further reading, refer to *Little*, p. 57; and *Mankowitz & Haggar*, p. 53.

CLOSE

Close & Co.
Church Street & Brook Street Potteries,
Stoke-upon-Trent, Staffordshire, c.1855-1863
Subsequently, J. T. Close (& Co.) (c.1864-1869)

B566	928	**CLOSE & CO. LATE W. ADAMS & SONS STOKE UPON TRENT**	Printed or impressed marks of differing design. Pattern name often included, c.1855-1863.

- Ormsbee notes three potteries were bought after the death of William Adams, IV plus one in Cliff Bank.

CLOSE

J. T. Close (& Co.)
Brook & High Street Potteries (1864-1865)
Church Street Pottery (1864-1869)
Stoke-upon-Trent, Staffordshire, 1864-1869
Formerly, Close & Co. (c.1855-1863)

KAD NO.	GODDEN NO.	MARK	
B567	-	**J. T. CLOSE**	Printed or impressed name mark, 1864-1869.
B568	-	**J. T. CLOSE & CO.**	- An example in White Ironstone was registered Jan. 3, 1866/No. 194194. See *Cushion*, p.181.
B569	-		- The name J. T. Close may also be noted as "I. T." Close, c.1864-1869.
B570	-	**J. T. CLOSE STONEWARE STAFFORDSHIRE**	Printed mark noted by *P. Williams, Flow Blue*, Vol. III, p. 10, pattern "SICILIAN", c.1864-1869. For further reading, refer to *Godden, Collecting Lustreware*, pp. 97-98.

CLOUGH

Cloughs Royal Art Pottery Ltd.
Barford Street,
Longton, 1961-1969
Formerly, Alfred Clough Ltd. (Royal Art Pottery) (1956-1961)

B571	929		Printed mark continued on from predecessor, Alfred Clough Ltd. (1956-1961) (Royal Art Pottery), 1961-1969. - See *Godden's* comments on Alfred Clough (Ltd.), p. 153.

CLYDE

Clyde Pottery Co. (Ltd.)
Greenock, Scotland, 1857-1903
"Ltd." noted from (1857-1861(62)

History:

		MARK	**PARTNERSHIP**	**DATE**
-	-	-	James Stevenson, James Muir & Alan Ker, Jr.	c.1815-1836
B572	-	**A. M.**	Andrew Muir & Co.	c.1836-1840(01)
B573	-	**S. & M.**	Thomas Shirley & Co.	c.1841-1857
B574-5		-	**T. S. & CO. (or) COY**	
B576	935	**C. P. CO.**	**(Clyde Pottery Co. (Ltd.)**	c.1857-1861(02)
B577	-	**CLYDE P. CO.**	Donald McLachlan & Brownie	c.1861(02)-1872
B578	-	**CLYDE POTTERY**	McLachlan & Brown	c.1872-1903
B579	932	**CLYDE**	Printed or impressed marks of differing design. Most early wares are unmarked.	
B580	933	**GREENOCK**	- Godden notes "Marked pieces probably date from c.1850s-1903."	
B581	934	**G. C. P. CO.**		
B576	935	**C. P. & CO.**	Marking "& CO." may relate to one of Charles Purvis' other ventures; i.e., Govan Pottery (c.1883-1887).	
B582	936	**G. P. CO. G.**	- Also see Elgin Pottery, p. 186.	
			New Research Notes the Following:	
B576	-	**C. P. CO.**	Printed or impressed marks of differing design, c.1857+.	
B578	-	**CLYDE POTTERY**	Printed or impressed marks of differing design after 1880+.	
B583	-	**CLYDE POTTERY GREENOCK**		
B577	-	**CLYDE P. CO.**		

KAD NO. | **GODDEN NO.** | **MARK**

For further reading, refer to *Little*, pp. 125-126; *Godden, Collecting Lustreware,* pp. 269-170; *The Scottish Pottery Review*, No. 15, 1993, pp. 57-75 for an article by Henry Kelly titled "The Muir & Clyde Pottery"; *Fleming*, pp. 209-210; and G. Bernard Hughes. *English and Scottish Earthenware*. London. Abbey Fine Arts. p. 213. Also refer to *Scottish Industrial History*, No. 17, 1994 for another article by Henry Kelly titled "The Beginning of the Pottery Industry in Greenock."

CO-OPERATIVE

Co-Operative Wholesale Society Ltd.
Crown Clarence Pottery,
Longton, Staffordshire, 1946-early 1970s
-Wholesalers/Retailers

B584 | - | **C. W. S.**

Printed initial mark noted on wares manufactured for their retail outlets.
- For additional marks refer to *Godden*, p. 169.
- "Shirley", a floral pattern, illustrated in *Blue Berry Notes*, Vol. 10, No. 2, March/April 1996, p. 25 is marked "F. & S." (Ford & Son) who may have reissued this pattern with the additional marking "C. W. S." for the above wholesaler.
- Further *Batkin* notes a Co-Operative Wholesale Society, Ltd., located at Windsor Pottery, Longton, Staffordshire from 1922-1989.

COCHRAN

***Cochran & Fleming**
Britannia Pottery, St. Rollox,
Glasgow, Scotland, c.1896-1920
Formerly, R. Cochran & Co. (1846-1917)
Subsequently, Britannia Pott. Co. Ltd. (c.1920-1935)

B585 | 968 | **C. & F. G**

Printed or impressed marks of differing design. Pattern name often included. "ROYAL IRONSTONE CHINA" marking noted, c.1896-1917.
- "G" may also be written out in full for "GLASGOW". "ENGLAND" appears after c.1891.

B586 | 969

B587 | - | **COCHRAN GLASGOW**

Printed mark with or without "TRADE MARK", c.1855-1890.

B588 | 970
B589 | -

Printed mark (Trade Mark). Seated Britannia appears with the style "COCHRAN & FLEMING", c.1896-1917.

B590 | 971

Printed Royal Arms mark, c.1900-1920.

KAD NO.	GODDEN NO.	MARK	
B591	972	**FLEMING**	Impressed mark "FLEMING" and "FLEMING GLASGOW", as well as other printed marks, based on the above wording and with or without crown, c.1900-1917.
B592	-	**FLEMING GLASGOW**	
B593	-	**PORCELAIN OPAQUE GLASGOW, BRITAIN FLEMING**	
B594	-	**BP CO. LTD. MADE IN SCOTLAND**	Printed mark with seated Britannia (Trade Mark) within a circle (see KAD No. B588). Also noted with marking "MADE IN GREAT BRITAIN", c. 1920-1939. - See Britannia Pott. Co. Ltd. for Chronology, pp. 127-128.

For further reading, refer to *Fleming*; as well as to "*Scottish Pottery 16th Historical Review*, pp.49-57 for an article by Henry Kelly.

COCHRAN

***R. Cochran & Co.**
Verreville Pottery, c.1846-1917
Britannia Pottery, c.1855-1896
Glasgow, Scotland
(China production ceased c.1856)
- Also refer to R. A. Kidston & Co., p. 252.

KAD NO.	GODDEN NO.	MARK	
B595	965	**R. C. & CO.**	Printed or impressed marks of differing design. Pattern name often included. Impressed marking "STONE CHINA" noted, c.1846.
B596	-	**R. & C. ST. ROLLOX GLASGOW**	Printed mark with crown, c. 1846-1896. - Britannia Pottery marking.
B597	-	**R. C. & CO. V. P.**	Printed mark with "V. P." added, c.1869-1917. - Verreville Pottery marking.
B598	-	**R. COCHRAN & CO. ST. ROLLOX GLASGOW**	Printed mark with or without initial "R" and with or without crown, c.1856-1896. - Britannia Pottery marking.

Selected Trade Marks Include:

B599 -
B600 -
B601 -

Typical Marks Include:

B602 966
B603 -
B604 -
B605 -

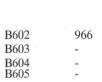

KAD NO.	GODDEN NO.	MARK	
B606	967	**COCHRAN GLASGOW**	Printed marks of various designs noted on Historic American/Canadian views; often including printed series and title names. Mark registered Sept. 21, 1875. - Britannia Pottery marking, c.1856-1890.
B607	-	**COCHRAN-S.ROLLOX GLASGOW**	

For further reading, refer to *Collard, Potter's View*, pp. 74-80 and *Pottery & Porcelain*, for "Robert Anderson" (Canada), pp. 86-88; *Godden, Collecting Lustreware*, p. 268, 272-273; *Tea Leaf Readings,* Vol. 17, Issue 3, July 1977, pp. 10-11 for an article by Henry E. Kelly titled "Robert Cochran's Potteries, White Ironstone and Tea Leaf Ware;" *Scottish Pottery 18th Historical Review*, 1996, for two articles" "The Anderston and Verreville Potteries and Glass Works, 1842" by Douglas A. Leishman, pp. 9-14, and "The North Woodside and Garrioch Mills on the Kelvin and their Connection with the Pottery Trade", by Henry E. Kelly, pp. 49-56.

COCKSON

***Cockson & Chetwynd (or Cockson Chetwynd & Co.)**
Globe Works,
Cobridge, Staffordshire, c.1867-1875
Subsequently, Cockson & Seddon (c.1876-1878)

B608	975	**COCKSON & CHETWYND**	Printed marks of differing design. Pattern name often included, c.1867-1875. - Impressed mark "PEARL" noted.
B609	976	**C. C. & CO.**	Printed initial marks, c.1867-1875.
B610	-	**IMPERIAL IRONSTONE CHINA**	Printed Royal Coat of Arms marked "IMPERIAL IRONSTONE CHINA" c.1867-1875.

For further reading, refer to *Godden, Jewitt*, p. 36; and *Godden, British Porcelain, p. 245.*

COCKSON

***Cockson & Harding**
New Hall Works,
Shelton, Hanley, Staffordshire, c.1856-1863
Formerly, T. Hackwood (1850-1855)
Subsequently, Charles Cockson
[who continued the Cobridge Porcelain Works] (1863-1866)

B611	977	**C. & H.**	Printed or impressed marks of differing design. Pattern name often included, c. 1856-1863.
B612	978	**C. & H. LATE HACKWOOD**	
B613	979		- *Coysh*, Vol. II, p. 122, notes that the "Institutions" pattern originated with Hackwood, but was found with the impressed marks of their successors.

- Winfield Harding died in 1856 and the partnership was continued as Cockson & Harding.
- Also refer to the Harding & Cockson partnership at the Globe Pottery, Cobridge, 1834-1863 as well as to W. & J. Harding, New Hall Works, Shelton, Hanley, 1863-1872. However, Please note that this firm should not be confused with this Harding & Cockson partnership, 1834-1863. See p. 224.

For further reading, refer to *Godden, British Porcelain*, pp. 245 & 400.

COCKSON

KAD NO. | GODDEN NO. | MARK

***Cockson & Seddon**
Globe Works,
Cobridge, Staffordshire, 1876-1878
Formerly, Cockson & Chetwynd (1867-1875)
Subsequently, Birks Bros. & Seddon (1878-1886)

B614 980 

Printed Royal Coat of Arms mark, 1876-1878.

- *Wetherbee, White Ironstone, A Collector's Guide*, p. 139, notes a single White Ironstone pattern, "Clover".

COLCLOUGH

Colclough & Co.
Stanley Pottery (and other addresses),
Longton, Staffordshire, 1887-1928
Subsequently, Stanley Pottery Ltd. (1928-1931)

B615 - C. & CO.

Printed marks of differing design. Pattern name often included, 1887-1928. "ENGLAND" added after 1891.

B616 983
B617 984

1903-1919

1919-1928

- Printed marks, formerly used by Colclough & Co. were continued by Stanley Pottery Ltd., Edensor Road, Longton, 1928-1931. See pp. 341-342.
- In correspondence to me dated June 15, 1995, Godden notes "The SR mark (KAD No. B617) occurs in the *Pottery Gazette* under Colclough & Co. before Stanley Pottery Ltd. came into being. But from the 1929 issue (prepared in 1928) the marks were transferred to appear under Stanley Pottery Ltd."
- See *P. Williams, Flow Blue*, Vol. I, p. 132 for comments regarding the Alcock and Stanley "Touraine" pattern.
- Charles Amison (& Co. Ltd.) worked the Stanley China Works, Wedgwood Street, Longton from 1878-1906, and from 1906-1930 marked their pieces "STANLEY CHINA". "& CO." was added in 1916.

For further reading, refer to *Snyder*, Vol. 1, pp. 138-140; and *Gaston*, Vol. 1, pp. 118-119.

COLLEY

Alfred Colley & Co., Ltd.
Gordon Pottery,
Tunstall, Staffordshire, c.1909-1914
Subsequently, A.G. Richardson & CO. Ltd. (c.1915(16)-1974)

B618 999 

Printed or impressed mark. Pattern name often included, c.1909-1914.

For further reading, refer to *Jewitt*, p. 142; *Godden, Jewitt*, p. 183 for the Well Street Pottery and The Old Works.

COLLINSON

KAD NO.	GODDEN NO.	MARK	
			Charles Collinson & Co. **Fountain Place,** **Burslem, Staffordshire, 1851-1873**
B619	1013	**C. COLLINSON & CO.**	Printed marks of differing design. Pattern name often included, 1851-1873.
B620	-		- Petra Williams notes a brushstroke pattern, "Peach Blossom" with the impressed marking "PEARL" dated July [26] 1851. See *P. Williams, Flow Blue*, Vol. II, p. 223, KAD No. B619. - For additional marks, refer to *Godden*, Mark No. 1014 and *Gaston*, Vol. 2, p. 62, plate 69 for the marking "IMPERIAL/IRONSTONE CHINA/C. COLLINSON & CO./BURSLEM" below a Royal Coat of Arms.

COPELAND

***Copeland & Garrett,**
Spode Works,
Stoke-on-Trent, Staffordshire, March 1833-1847
Formerly, Spode (c.1770-1833)
Subsequently, W. T. Copeland (1847-1867)
(Refer to Spode found in Chronology of Potters & Potteries)

- Numbers in ( ) denote reference to Robert Copeland's numbering system. For additional marks refer to Copeland, *Spode & Copeland Marks*, Studio Vista, London, 1993

KAD NO.	GODDEN NO.	MARK	
B621	1088	**C. & G.** **(130)**	Printed, rare initial mark which is rarely painted with pattern numbers,c.1833-1847.
B622	1089	**N. S.** **(8)**	Impressed initial mark continued on from Spode, (Godden No. 3653), c.1822-1840. - N. S. denotes "NEW STONE"
B623	-	**COPELAND** **& GARRETT** **(100)**	Impressed name mark, 1833-1847. Note variation with ampersand on either first or second line.
B624	1090	**COPELAND &** **GARRETT** **(101A)**	
B625	1091	 **(143)**	Printed mark in underglaze green or blue-green noted on Flow Blue, c.1838-1847. - The introduction of pattern names with this mark commenced 1844-1845.

KAD NO.	GODDEN NO.	MARK

B626 -

(151)

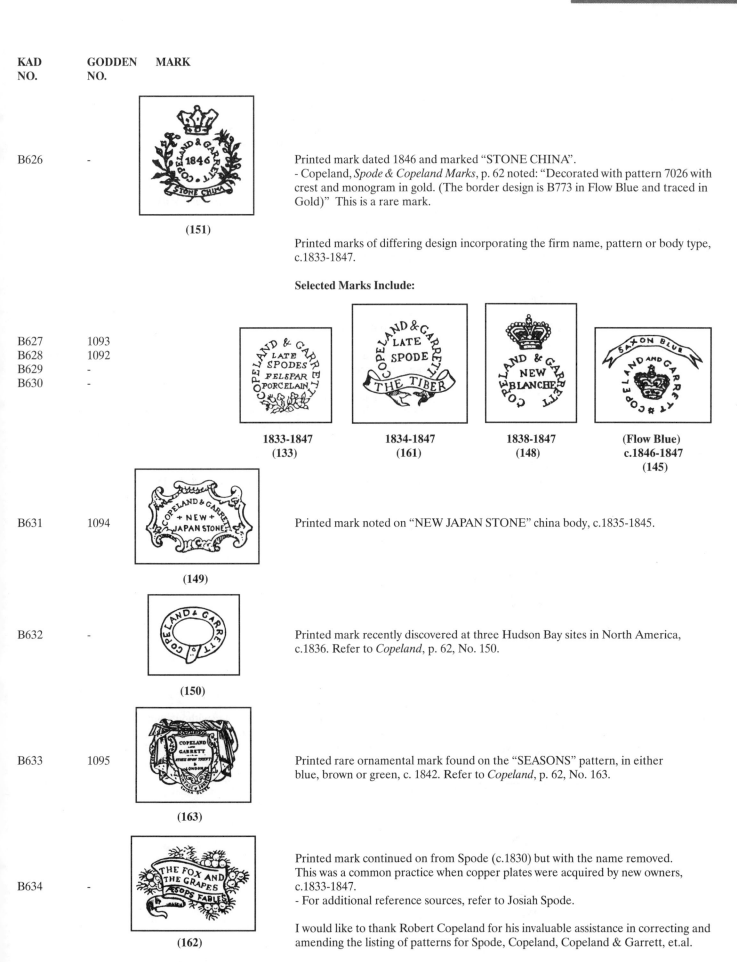

Printed mark dated 1846 and marked "STONE CHINA".
- Copeland, *Spode & Copeland Marks*, p. 62 noted: "Decorated with pattern 7026 with crest and monogram in gold. (The border design is B773 in Flow Blue and traced in Gold)" This is a rare mark.

Printed marks of differing design incorporating the firm name, pattern or body type, c.1833-1847.

Selected Marks Include:

B627 1093
B628 1092
B629 -
B630 -

1833-1847
(133)

1834-1847
(161)

1838-1847
(148)

(Flow Blue)
c.1846-1847
(145)

B631 1094

(149)

Printed mark noted on "NEW JAPAN STONE" china body, c.1835-1845.

B632 -

(150)

Printed mark recently discovered at three Hudson Bay sites in North America, c.1836. Refer to *Copeland*, p. 62, No. 150.

B633 1095

(163)

Printed rare ornamental mark found on the "SEASONS" pattern, in either blue, brown or green, c. 1842. Refer to *Copeland*, p. 62, No. 163.

B634 -

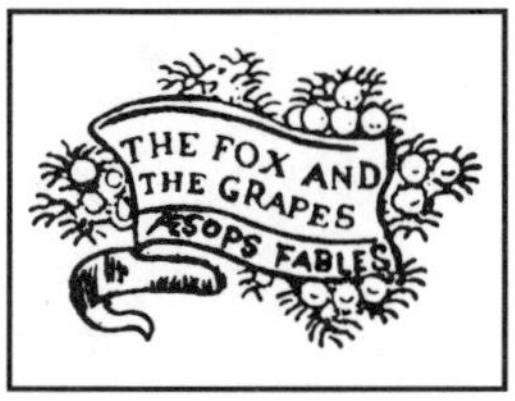

(162)

Printed mark continued on from Spode (c.1830) but with the name removed. This was a common practice when copper plates were acquired by new owners, c.1833-1847.
- For additional reference sources, refer to Josiah Spode.

I would like to thank Robert Copeland for his invaluable assistance in correcting and amending the listing of patterns for Spode, Copeland, Copeland & Garrett, et.al.

COPELAND

KAD NO.	GODDEN NO.	MARK	
			***W.T. Copeland (& Sons Ltd.),** **Spode Works,** **Stoke-on-Trent, Staffordshire, 1847-1867** **- "& Sons" from (1867-1932) "Ltd." from (1932-1970+)** - See Spode for Chronology of Pottery, pp. 552-553. - Numbers in ( ) denote reference to Robert Copeland's numbering system. For additional marks see Copeland's *Spode & Copeland Marks*, Studio Vista, London, 1993
B635	1068	**COPELAND, LATE SPODE (234 A&B)**	Printed name mark "LATE SPODE", 1847-1890. - Printed two or three line variations of "LATE SPODE" noted. - *Copeland* notes text in both upper and lower case.
B636	1069	**COPELAND (209)**	Printed name mark, c.1847-c.1855.
B637	-	**COPELAND (209)**	Impressed name mark, c.1847-1958. - Name appears in either straight line or curved. Size of mark may vary and may be noted with other devices. "ENGLAND" appears after 1891.
B638	-	**Y 88**	Impressed letter and date marking, c.1859-c.1900. This marking may accompany above impressed name mark. Letters "B", "I" and "Y" and numerals note the month and year. In this example the date is July 1888. This dating system continued into the twentieth century. - See *Copeland,* pp. 65, 92-93.
B639	-	 **(201)**	Impressed crown mark found on Flow Blue, c.1847-c.1855.
B640	-	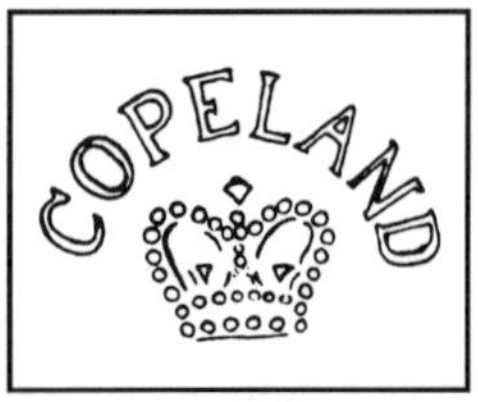 **(207)**	Impressed crown mark, c.1860-1969.
B641	1072	 **(237)**	Printed or impressed mark. Variations noted without name below wreath in either straight or curved line, 1847-1890. - "ENGLAND" added after 1891.
B642	1071	 **(236)**	Printed mark, 1847-1856.

KAD NO. | **GODDEN NO.** | **MARK**

B643 1073

(234)

Printed mark, as above, 1850-1890.
- The name "COPELAND" may be absent from mark.

B644 -

COPELAND'S
(407)

Printed name mark, with various devices, on earthenware and china, 1851-1920.

B645 1075

Printed mark on earthenware, 1867-1890.
- Variations marked "IRONSTONE" noted.

B646 1074

(252A)

Printed mark, 1883-1890.
- "ENGLAND" added after 1891.

B647
B648 1076

(265)

ENGLAND
(266)

Printed "FRANKS BOAT" mark, 1887-1894. Variation without "TRADE MARK" and with the addition of the Registration No. 180288 and
- "ENGLAND" date from 1894-1910.

B649 -

(419)

Printed mark, 1902-1970.

Selected "GRID IRON" printed marks, 19th to 20th century. "ENGLAND" added after 1891.
- See *Copeland*, p. 70 for additional variations and dating system.
- See Spode for a more complete bibliography.
For listing of series, Blue & White Transferware, Plain Printed Patterns, Flow Blue & Mulberry, refer to listing under Spode, pp. 452-455.

B650 -
B651 -
B652 1079
B653 1080
B654 1087

1890
(256)

1906
(257A)

1920-1957
(259)

1920-1960
(258)

1960-1969
(260)

CORK

KAD NO.	GODDEN NO.	MARK

***Cork & Edge**
Newport Pottery, Queen Street,
Burslem, Staffordshire, c.1846-1860
Formerly, Cork & Condliffe (1834-1843+)
Subsequently, Cork, Edge & Malkin (1860-1871)

KAD NO.	GODDEN NO.	MARK	
B655	1097	**C. & E.**	Printed marks of differing design. Pattern name often included, c.1846-1860.
B656	-	**CORK & EDGE**	- Note additional marks "STAFFORDSHIRE STONE WARE" and "PEARL WHITE IRONSTONE".

Typical Marks Include:

KAD NO.	GODDEN NO.
B657	1098
B658	1099
B659	1100

R. K. Henrywood *An Illustrated Guide to British Jugs, From Medieval Times to the Twentieth Century*. Swan Hill Press, Shrewsbury, England, 1997, pp. 236-238, cites the following: "Relief-moulding was one of the most important methods for decorating utilitarian jugs from 1840 onwards and literally hundreds of designs appears. …The phrase 'Patent Mosaic' dates from 1843 when Richard Boote invented various techniques for decorating pots with surface designs in contrasting colours. Whether he had any involvement with the rouletting process is unclear, but another of his techniques was adopted for use on relief-moulded jugs by Alcock and by Bradbury, Anderson & Bettany (see Chapter 8). A further process involving sprigged designs inlaid within the surface appears to have been used only by T. & R. Boote. Two distinctive and very typical jugs are shown, one in green with white figures (Plate 665), the other in white with drab figures (Plate 666). These are again marked 'Patent Mosaic', so the phrase covers at least three different techniques. It was also used for no apparent reason on ordinary sprigged and relief-moulded wares by Cork & Edge."
- Godden notes KAD No. B658 (Godden No. 1099) on a moulded pattern jug "Babes In The Woods". See *Godden, British Pottery*, pl. 93. *Wetherbee, White Ironstone A Collector's Guide*, pp. 198-199 notes two moulded jugs in White Ironstone, "Trunks With Ivy" and "Babes In The Woods".
- *Coysh*, Vol. 2, p. 67 notes the pattern "Dahlia" marked "C. & E."

For further reading, refer to *Edwards, Basalt*, p. 146 *Godden, Collecting Lustreware*, p. 100; *Henrywood*, pp. 193-198; *Hughes*, Vol. I & II; and *Stoltzfus/Snyder*, p. 150.

CORK

***Cork, Edge & Malkin**
Newport Pottery, Queen Street,
Burslem, Staffordshire, c.1860-1871
Formerly, Cork & Edge (1846-1860)
Subsequently, Edge, Malkin & Co. (Ltd.) (1871-1899)

Printed marks of differing design. Pattern name often included, c.1860-1871.
- Marks are noted with "IRONSTONE", "STONE CHINA" and "WHITE GRANITE".

KAD NO.	GODDEN NO.	MARK
B660	1101	**C. E. & M.**
B661	-	**CORK & EDGE BURSLEM**

KAD NO.	GODDEN NO.	MARK
B662	-	
B663	-	
B664	-	

Typical Marks Include:

- *Coysh*, Vol. I, p. 187 notes: "Indian Series … introduced by Thomas & Benjamin Godwin and later copied by Cork, Edge & Malkin and their successors Edge, Malkin & Co."
- Backstamp marks were copied as well. Note the similarity of "Versailles" by Thomas Godwin and Cork, Edge & Malkin. This practice was not uncommon.

KAD NO.	GODDEN NO.	MARK
B665	-	
B1064	-	

Cork, Edge & Malkin

Thomas Godwin

For further reading, refer to *Godden, Collecting Lustreware*, p. 101; and *Henrywood*, pp. 193-198.

CORMIE

John or James Cormie
Nile Street Works,
Burslem, Staffordshire, c.1820-1841
Formerly, Bourne & Cormie (1818-1820)

KAD NO.	GODDEN NO.	MARK
B667	-	**CORMIE**
B668	-	**J. C.**

Printed name and/or initial mark, c.1820-1841.

- Additional printed mark "IRONSTONE CHINA" noted. However, most pieces are unmarked. Further, Godden notes that the impressed initial "J. C." may possibly belong to J. Cormie.
For further reading, refer to *Godden, Jewitt*, pp. 10-12; *Godden, Handbook*; *Little*, pp. 51, 58; and *Mankowitz & Haggar*, p. 60.

CORN

Edward Corn
Navigation Road,
Burslem, Staffordshire, c.1853-c.1863
Subsequently, W. & E. Corn (1864-1904)

KAD NO.	GODDEN NO.	MARK
B669	-	

Printed or impressed mark noted on White Ironstone, c.1853-c.1863.
- Refer to *Wetherbee*, p. 58.

CORN

W. & E. Corn

Navigation Road, Burslem	**(c.1864-1891)**
Top Bridge Works, Longport	**(1891-1904)**
Burslem and Longport, Staffordshire,	**1864-1904**
Formerly, Edward Corn	**(c.1853-1863)**

KAD NO.	GODDEN NO.	MARK	
B670	-		Printed diamond mark with "W" is noted by Petra Williams in all three Flow Blue volumes. Sometimes found with mark KAD B679. - It is my opinion that this marking was used to identify items for export, as pieces marked "GERMANY" have also been noted, c.1900-1904.
B671	1109	**W. & E. C.**	Printed marks of differing design. Pattern name often included. Most pre-1900 wares are unmarked, c.1864-1904.
B672	1110	**W. E. C.**	

Typical White Ironstone and Tea Leaf/Copper Lustre Marks Include*:

B673 -
B674 -
B675 -
B676 -

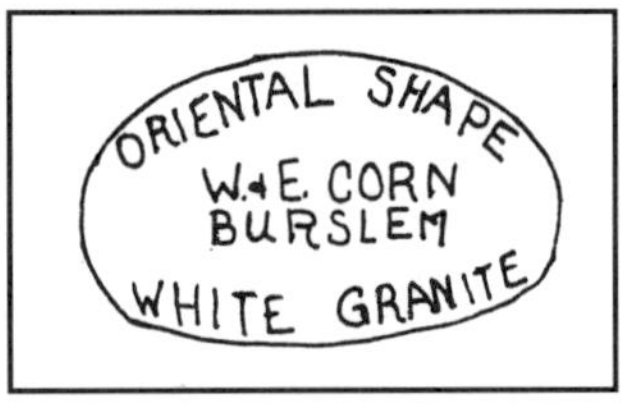

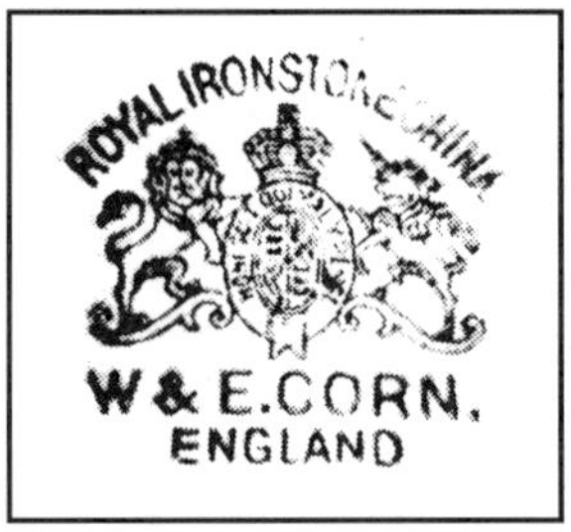

Other Printed Marks, c.1900 Include:

B677 1111
B678 1112
B679 1113

**Collard, Pottery & Porcelain*, p. 314 notes that "…Canadian decorators added a gold rim … at Crystal Hall, and then painted with a bird in flight and a spray of clover…"
- In addition to the mark "W. & E. CORN" on the back of the plate (underglaze printed) there is an ornate overglaze mark (in red) of "J. & W. REID" who were importers and decorators in London.
- Also refer to Burgess & Leigh for comments relative to decorating for other potters.

For further reading, refer to *Tea Leaf Readings Educational Supplement*, May 1994; and *White Ironstone Notes*, Vol. 3, No. 4, Spring 1997, p. 9.

CORNFOOT

Cornfoot, Colville & Co.
Low Lights Pottery,
North Shields, Northumberland, c.1829-1847
Formerly, Bird & Co. (c.1821-1823)
Subsequently, Carr & Patton (c.1847-1848)
History:

Cornfoot, Colville & Co.	c.1829-1832
Cornfoot, Patton & Co.	c.1832-1834
Cornfoot, Carr & Patton	c.1834-1847

KAD NO.	GODDEN NO.	MARK	
B680	-	**CORNFOOT COLVILLE & CO.**	Impressed circular mark, c.1829-1832.

For further reading, refer to *Bell*; *Coysh, Transferware*, p. 126; and *Godden, Collecting Lustreware*, p. 237.

COTTON

Cotton & Barlow
Coronation Works, Commerce Street,
Longton, Staffordshire, c.1850-1857
Subsequently, Thomas Waterhouse Barlow (c.1857-1865)

KAD NO.	GODDEN NO.	MARK
B681	1116	**C. & B.**
B682	-	**COTTON & BARLOW**

Printed or impressed marks. Pattern name often included, c.1850-1857.

For further reading, refer to Hampson, No. 22, p. 16.

CUMBERLIDGE

Cumberlidge & Humphreys
Gordon Pottery,
Tunstall, Staffordshire, 1886-1889 and 1893-1895
Formerly, Well Street Pottery (1880-1885)

-The interim period between 1889-1893 was a partnership of Cumberlidge, Humphreys & Hele.*

KAD NO.	GODDEN NO.	MARK
B683	1158	**C. & H.**
B684	1158A	**C. & H. TUNSTALL**

Printed or impressed marks of differing design. Patter name often included, 1886-1889 and 1893-1895.

* *Godden*, p. 183 notes the period between 1889 and 1893 as Cumberlidge, Humphreys & Hele. The initial style may have C. H. & H. as a marking - similar to the markings above.

DALTON

Dalton & Burn
Stepney Bank Pottery,
Newcastle-upon-Tyne, c.1833-1843(44)
Formerly, Davies, Cookson & Wilson (c.1822-1833)
Subsequently, John Harrison (c.1844)
- Company also known as Dalton, Burn & Co.

KAD NO.	GODDEN NO.	MARK
B685	-	**D. & B.**

Printed initial mark, possibly attributed to the above firm.
- Coysh notes a Blue & White pattern "Villa Scenery" with the initials "D. & B.", c.1833-1843(44).
- Initials may also be those of Deakin & Bailey or Deaville & Badderley.

For further reading, refer to *Bell*, p. 54; and *Little*, p. 124, wherein he notes a former partnership of Davies, Coxon & Wilson and the successor, G. R. Turnbull (1863-1875). However, *Cameron*, pp. 317-318 notes Thomas Bell & Co., (1840s) as the subsequent owner.

DANIEL

H. & R. Daniel
London Road, (Subsequently, H. Minton & Co.)
Stoke-on-Trent (and Bedford Row Pottery, Shelton, 1826-1835),
Staffordshire, 1822-1846

KAD NO.	GODDEN NO.	MARK
B686	-	**D.**
B687	-	**H. & R. D.**

Printed initial marks. Pattern name often included, 1826-1846.

- Markings "STONE CHINA", "STONE WARE" and "IRONSTONE CHINA" are noted.

KAD NO.	GODDEN NO.	MARK	
B688	-	**DANIELS REAL IRONSTONE**	Impressed name mark. Pattern name often included, 1826-1846. - *Godden*, p. 188 notes three additional markings on porcelain. See Godden mark nos. 1170-1172. - The name Daniel with one "L" is not to be confused with the London retailers Daniells, spelled with two "LL's". For further reading, refer to *Godden, British Porcelain*, pp. 279-283; *Godden, Staffordshire Porcelain*, Ch. 19, pp. 274-305; Michael Berthoud, *H. & R. Daniel, 1822- 1846.* Micawber Publications, England, 1980; and *NCS Newsletter*, No. 101, March 1996, p. 41.

DANIEL

Walter Daniel
Newport Pottery,
Burslem, Staffordshire, c.1786-1810
Subsequently, John Davenport

B689	-	**W. DANIEL**	Impressed name mark, c.1786-1810. - The name Walter Daniel is not to be confused with H. & R. Daniel of Stoke, c.1822-1846. For further reading, refer to *Coysh, Earthenware*, p. 22; and *Godden, Staffordshire Porcelain*, Ch. 19, pp. 274-296.

DAVENPORT

Davenport, Banks & Co.
Castlefield Pottery,
Hanley, Staffordshire, 1860-1873
Subsequently, Davenport, Beck & Co. (1873-1880)

B690	1196	**D. B. & CO.**	Printed marks of differing design. Pattern name often included, 1860-1873.
B691	1196A	**DAVENPORT BANKS & CO. ETRURIA**	Printed or impressed full name mark, 1860-1873. - Godden notes that the initials "D. B. & CO." were also used by the Davenport, Beck & Co. (see next entry)

DAVENPORT

Davenport, Beck & Co.
Castlefield Pottery,
Hanley, Staffordshire, 1873-1880
Formerly, Davenport, Banks & Co. (1860-1873)

B692	1197	**D. B. & CO.**	Printed mark noted as "comprising a castle, with the initials D. B. & CO. and 'Etruria' within an oval circle. 1873-1880.

DAVENPORT

KAD NO.	GODDEN NO.	MARK

DAVENPORT,
Longport, Staffordshire, c.1794-1887
History:

John Davenport		1794-1835
Henry & William Davenport	-	1835-1869
William Davenport	(& Co.)	1869-1881
Henry (Son of William)	(Ltd.)	1881-1887
Acquired by Thomas Hughes	-	1888-1957
Subsequently, Arthur Wood & Sons	-	1957

Locations:

John Davenport	Unicorn Pottery	1794-1835
	Top Bridge Pottery	1794-1835
	Newport Pottery	1806-1835
Henry & William Davenport	Newport Pottery	1835-1846
	Lower Bridge Works	1835-1869
	Top Bridge Pottery	1835-1869
	Unicorn Pottery	1835-1869
	New Bridge Pottery	1849-1869
William Davenport (& Co.)	New Bridge Pottery	1869-1876
	Top Bridge Pottery	1869-1881
	Lower Bridge Pottery	1869-1876
	Unicorn Pottery	1869-1881
Henry Davenport (Ltd.)	Unicorn Pottery	1881-1887

Impressed Anchor marks, with or without "DAVENPORT" in upper or lower case. Impressed and dated "LONGPORT" may appear in place of "DAVENPORT", c.1795-1820.

B693 1179
B694 1179A
B695 1180A
B696 1181

B697 1181A

Impressed Anchor mark with "DAVENPORT" in upper case and last two numbers of potted date on either side of Anchor, c.1830-1860+.
- A variation of impressed mark KAD B697 appears with "OPAQUE CHINA" below anchor, c.1850-1880s.

B697A -

- Printed variation found on White Ironstone, c.1850-1880s.

B698 - **DAVENPORT**

Printed mark "DAVENPORT" in upper case, c.1835-1887.

Selection of Printed Marks:

B699 1180
B700 1183
B701 1182

c.1805-1835

c.1815-1870s

c.1820-1870s

KAD NO.	GODDEN NO.	MARK

Typical Marks Include:

B702 -

Printed marks of differing design. Pattern name and name "DAVENPORT" often included, c.1820-1860s.

B703 1185
B704 1186
B705 1187

- KAD B704 is an exact mark used by Wood & Challinor (1828-1845). Also see KAD B2496.
- Arene Burgess notes a printed American importer's backstamp for Scott's Illustrations, "Legend of Montrose" with the impressed name "DAVENPORT" and printed mark reading: "HENDERSON & GAINES/IMPORTERS/45 CANAL ST./NEW ORLEANS".
- Additional US importers are cited in *Lockett;* and *Godden*, pp. 37-40.
- For further information refer to Importer section in this encyclopedia.

Typical Examples Also Include:

B706 -
B707 -
B708 -

B709 -
B710 -
B711 -

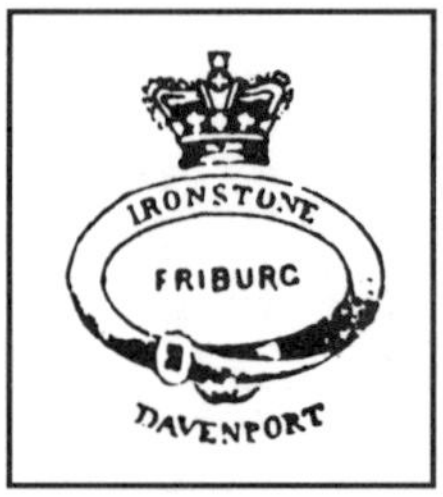

*See Grimwades Ltd. mark no. KAD B1119A for exact pattern reissued c.1915+.

B712 -

Printed Oriental mark with "DAVENPORT" in upper case noted on Mulberry Wares, c.1835-1860s.

B713 1192

Printed mark on wares of registered form or pattern, c.1842-1883. Impressed

For further reading, refer to *Wetherbee*, pp. 78-79; and *Sussman*, p. 56.
- Also refer to John Wedge Wood and Edmund T. Wood for the use of Cambridge, Erie and Union Shapes in White Ironstone. (See Pattern Section.)

KAD NO.	GODDEN NO.	MARK	
B714	-		Impressed mark on Stone China with date numbers impressed below mark. Term "IRONSTONE CHINA" noted, c.1850. - Mark noted on Tea Leaf/Copper Lustre in *Stoltzfus/Snyder*, pp. 17, 160.
B715	-	**STONEWARE**	Printed mark with Crown pattern and "STONEWARE" noted, c.1850+.
B716	-		Printed Royal Arms mark with "DAVENPORT/LONGPORT/STAFFORDSHIRE/ REAL IRONSTONE CHINA" noted alone or together with impressed mark (Godden No. 1189): **DAVENPORT** **LONGPORT** **9 80**
B717	1194		Printed mark noted on Flow Blue, c.1870-1886.
B718	-	**WM. DAVENPORT & CO.** **LONGPORT** **8 82** **L**	Impressed name and date mark for August 1882. Mark noted in conjunction with a printed double circle mark reading: Outer Circle: "DAVENPORT/ LONGPORT/STAFFORD". Inner Circle: "DOCALNING PLACE/LIVERPOOL/ QUEEN PLACE/CHARTER HOUSE/LONDON". The piece is in Flow Blue and shows and anchor within a wreath with the word "MARINE" above. The border is comprised of floral swags.
B719	1195	**DAVENPORTS LTD.**	Printed marks on earthenware. Note the use of "LTD" or "LIMITED", c.1881-1887.
B720	1195A	**DAVENPORTS** **LIMITED**	

-A transfer plate marked "MANUFACTURED FOR DAVENPORT, J. CLEMENTSON, SHELTON" was noted as lot 168A of the GeneHarris Auction, Marshalltown, Iowa, Feb. 25, 1995. For additional comments see Joseph Clementson. See p. 150.

For further reading, refer to *Edwards,* Basalt, pp. 149-152; *Godden, Collecting Lustreware*, pp.105-108; *Lockett, Davenport Pottery & Porcelain*; *Lockett & Godden*; and *Penny Plain*, p. 99, No. 237.

DAVIES

(Richard) Davies & Co.
Salt Meadows, South Shore,
Gateshead, Northumberland (Tyne Main Pottery), c.1833-1844
Subsequently, Robert Christopher Wilson (c.1844-1852)

KAD NO.	GODDEN NO.	MARK	
B721	1201	**DAVIES & CO.**	Impressed name mark, c.1833-1844.

For further reading, refer to *Bell*, p. 54; *Godden*, p. 512; and *Godden, Collecting Lustreware*, pp. 240-241.

DAVIS

Davis, Cookson & Wilson
Stepney Bank Pottery,
Newcastle-upon-Tyne, c.1822-1833
Formerly, John Dryden & Co. (c.1821-1822)
Subsequently, Dalton, Burn & Co. (c.1833-1843(44)

KAD NO.	GODDEN NO.	MARK	
B722	-	**D. C. & W.**	Printed initial mark, c.1822-1833.
B722A	-	**DAVIS, COCKSON & SON**	Impressed name mark, c.1822-1833. - See *True Blue*, p. 147, No. D9.

For further reading, refer to *Bell.*

DAVIS

J. H. & J. Davis
Trent Pottery,
Eastwood, Hanley, 1871-1875
Formerly, Livesley & Davis (1867-1871)
Subsequently, J. H. Davis (1875-1891)

KAD NO.	GODDEN NO.	MARK	
B723	-	**J. H. & J. DAVIS**	Printed mark and Royal Coat of Arms noted on White Ironstone and Tea Leaf/Copper Lustre. - Marked "ROYAL STONE CHINA/HANLEY", 1871-1875.

For further reading, refer to *Godden, Jewitt*, p. 73; and *Tea Leaf Readings*, Nov. 1988, p. 8 as well as Vol. 16, No. 5, Nov. 1996, p. 3.

DAVIS

John Heath Davis
Trent Pottery,
Eastwood, Hanley, Staffordshire, 1875-1891
Formerly, J. H. & J. Davis (1871-1875)

KAD NO.	GODDEN NO.	MARK	
B724	1204	**J. H. DAVIS** **HANLEY**	Printed name mark with pattern name often included, 1875-1891.
B725	1204A		Printed shield mark, 1875-1891. - *Wetherbee, White Ironstone,* fig. 18-9 illustrates a spittoon by this potter.

DAWSON

Dawson (John Dawson & Co., etc.)
South Hylton and Low Ford Potteries,
Sunderland, Durham, c.1799-1864
Formerly, Sanders & Co. (c.1794-1797)
History:
John Dawson & Co. c.1799-1848
Thomas Dawson & Co. c.1848-1864

KAD NO.	GODDEN NO.	MARK	
B726	1207	**DAWSON**	Printed or impressed marks of differing design. Pattern name may be included, c.1799-1864.
B727	1207A	**I. DAWSON**	
B728	1208	**DAWSON & CO.**	
B729	1209	**DAWSON & CO. LOW FORD**	Various printed marks including pottery name, "Low Ford" Pottery, c.1800-1850s.
B730	1210	**J. DAWSON & CO. LOW FORD**	
B731	1211	**FORD POTTERY**	
B732	1212	**J. DAWSON SOUTH HYLTON**	

For further reading, refer to *Cushion*, p. 105; *Godden, Collecting Lustreware*, p. 228; and *Sunderland Pottery*, Sunderland Libraries Publications, 1984, pp. 37-42.

DAWSON

Thomas Dawson & Co., c.1848-1864

(See previous entry: John Dawson & Co., Low Ford Pottery, South Hylton, Sunderland)
Marks presumably continued on from John Dawson & Co., c.1848-1864.
For further reading, refer to *Baker*, pp. 37-42; *Coysh,* Vol. I, p. 103; *Godden*, pp. 193- 194; and *Godden, Collecting Lustreware*, pp. 215, 228.

DEAKIN

Deakin & Bailey,
Waterloo Works,
Lane End, Longton, c.1828-1832
Formerly, Batkin, Dale & Deakin (1819-1827)
Subsequently, Deakin & Son (1832-1863)

KAD NO.	GODDEN NO.	MARK	
B733	4420	**D. & B.**	Printed marks of differing design. Pattern name often included, c.1828-1832.
B734	-	**DEAKIN & BAILEY**	
B735	-		
B736	-		

- Godden notes the potteries Dalton & Burn and Deaville & Badderley with similar initial markings "D. & B."

KAD NO.	GODDEN NO.	MARK

DEAKIN

***Deakin & Son(s) (& Co.)**
Waterloo Works,
Lane End (c.1832-1841)
Longton, Staffordshire, c.1832-1841
Formerly, Deakin & Bailey (1828-1832)

KAD NO.	GODDEN NO.	MARK	
B737	-	**D. & S.**	Printed or impressed marks of differing design. Pattern name often included, c.1832-1841. - See *P. Williams, Staffordshire*, Vol. II, p. 27.
B738	1218		
B739	-		
B740	-		

- This company traded as James Deakin & Son(s), 1832-1841 or as James Deakin & Co., c.1846-1851. There is an extensive account of Deakin in *Godden, Collecting Lustreware*, pp. 108-110.

For further reading, refer to *P. Williams, Staffordshire*, Vol. III, pp. 95-96 "Pickmany's Sevilla".
- Dates listed in Appendix B6, Chronology, are those noted in *Hampson*, No. 91, pp. 59-60.

DEAKIN

Edwin Deakin
Waterloo Place, Lane End,
Longton, Staffordshire, 1851-1854

KAD NO.	GODDEN NO.	MARK	
B741	-	**DEAKIN**	Impressed name marks, 1851-1854.
B742	-	**DEAKIN PEARL**	

-*Hampson*, No. 91, pp.59-60 notes a rather complex family history for the name Deakin.

For further reading, refer to *P. Williams, Flow Blue*, Vol. I, p. 175 for the pattern "Deakin Pearl" now residing in this author's collection.

DEAN

S. W. Dean
Newport Pottery,
Burslem, Staffordshire, c.1904-1910
Formerly, Edge, Malkin & Co. (1871-1903)
Subsequently, Deans (1910) Ltd. (1910-1919)

KAD NO.	GODDEN NO.	MARK	
B743	1219		Printed name mark, c.1904-1910.

- Other marks have been noted with the firm's title in full.

DEAN

KAD NO.	GODDEN NO	MARK	
			Dean's (1910) Ltd. **Newport Pottery,** **Burslem, Staffordshire, 1910-1919** **Formerly, S. W. Dean (1904-1910)** **Subsequently, Newport Pottery Co., Ltd. (1920-1962(87))**
B744	-	**ROYAL IRONSTONE CHINA DEANS (1910) LTD. BURSLEM ENGLAND**	Printed Royal Coat of Arms marks noted by *Sussman*, (p. 24), with illustrated saucer in White Ironstone in the "Wheat" Pattern, 1910-1919.
B745	1222	**DEANS (1910) LTD. BURSLEM ENGLAND**	Printed title mark, 1910-1919.

DIAMOND

Diamond Pottery Co. (Ltd.)
See Pearl Pottery Co. (Ltd.), p. 300

DILLON

Francis Dillon
Cobridge, Staffordshire, c.1830-1843
Formerly, Francis & Nicholas Dillon (c.1815-1830)

B746 1288 **DILLON** Impressed name mark, c.1830-1843.

B747 1288A
B748 -

Printed marks of differing design. Pattern name and initials "F. D." noted, c.1830-1843.
- The copper plates for "Asiatic Views" may have been acquired in 1843-1844 by Podmore Walker & Co., as the pattern and back mark noted by Petra Williams are quite similar.

For further reading, refer to *P. Williams, Staffordshire*, Vol. I, pp. 95-96, and Vol. II, pp. 383, 521; and *Mankowitz & Haggar*, pp. 25-26.

DILLWYN

***Dillwyn & Co.**
Cambrian Pottery,
Swansea, Wales, (c.1802)1811-1850
(Also refer to Swansea Pottery)

B749 3757 **SWANSEA** Impressed name mark in small capital letters, c.1783-1810.

B750 3764 **DILLWYN & CO.** Printed or impressed marks in various forms, c.1811-1817.
- "& CO." is Timothy and John Bevington

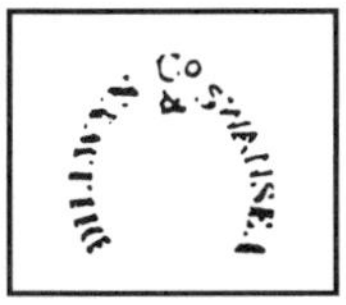

B751 3765 Impressed Horseshoe mark, c.1811-1817 and 1824-1850.
- Pottery was leased to T. & J. Bevington for the period 1817-1824.

B752 3768 Impressed name mark in a crescent shape, c.1824-1850.

KAD NO.	GODDEN NO.	MARK	
B753	3769	**DILLWYN SWANSEA**	Impressed name or initial mark, 1824-1850.
B754	3770	**D.**	
B755	3766	**D. & CO.**	Printed initial mark "D. & CO." and transfer pattern marks, c.1836-1850.
B756	-		Printed transferware marks of various designs. Pattern name often included, c.1836-1850. - "IMPROVED STONEWARE" noted on Flow Blue, c.1840-1850. **Typical Marks Include:**
B757 B758 B759	- - -		   **Additional printed transferware marks noted by *Pryce & Williams*, c.1836-1850.**
B760 B761	- -		 
B763	3771		Raised (molded) special body mark, 1847-1850.
B764	3772		Printed, ornate frame mark, 1847-1850, used only on green type wares and made of local red clay. - Additional patterns are noted in both *Pugh & Hallesy*.

Marks from Pryce & Williams *Swansea Blue and White Pottery* are reproduced with the kind permission of the publishers, Antique Collectors' Club Ltd.
For further reading, refer to *Nance; Edwards, Basalt*, pp. 131-134; *Godden, Collecting Lustreware*, pp. 242-254; *P. Williams, Flow Blue*, Vol. I, p. 170; *Snyder*, Vol. 2 (for photos/shapes of "Blue Bell" pattern); *Godden*, p. 605; *Pugh, Welsh Pottery*, pp. 5-33; and *Hallesy, Glamorgan Pottery*.

KAD NO.	GODDEN NO.	MARK	

DIMMOCK

Dimmock & Smith,
Tontine Street,
Hanley, Staffordshire, c.1826-1833 or c.1842-1859

B765 1302 **D. & S.**

Printed marks of differing design. Pattern name often included. Godden notes that this "Style" dictates the later (second) period, c.1842-1859.
- "Style" refers to the general design, marks and other characteristics leading one to determine an earlier or later period of production.

B766 -

Coysh, Vol. I, p. 107 notes "Plates bearing the same patterns as John Hall's "Quadrupeds" Series are known with the added initials "D & S" on the printed cartouche mark." Further *Edwards, Basalt*, p. 162 notes an earlier partnership with William Hackwood.

DIMMOCK

John Dimmock & Co.*
Albion Works,
Hanley, Staffordshire, c.1862-1904
Formerly, Thomas Dimmock & Co. (c.1828-1859)

B767 1289 **J. D. & CO.**

Printed marks of differing design with distinguishing initials or monogram noted, often accompanied by individual pattern name, c.1862-1878.

B768 1290

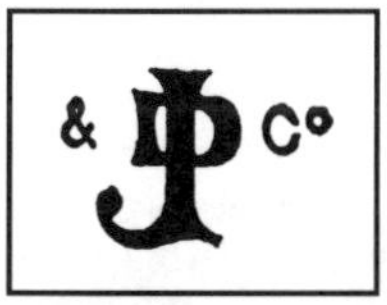

B769 1293

Printed marks from c.1878 under the proprietorship of W. D. Cliff, whose name often occurs on marked pieces, c.1878-1890.

Typical Printed Marks, 1878-1904, Include:

B770 -
B771 -
B772 -

B773 1291 **CLIFF ALBION CHINA**

Impressed mark, c.1879-1890.

*The name J. (John) Dimmock & Co. should not be confused with the like initial name J.(James) Dimmock & Co. of Hanley, 1840-1850.

For further reading, refer to *Little*, p. 60; and the extensive comments on partnerships by *Henrywood*, pp. 206-207; and *Cluett*, p. 14 for comments on George Jones acquiring moulds and shapes at an auction in 1904.

DIMMOCK

KAD NO.	GODDEN NO.	MARK	
			Thomas Dimmock (Jr.) & Co., Albion Street (c.1828-1859) Tontine Street (c.1830-1850) Hanley, Staffordshire, c.1828-1859 Formerly, Hackwood, Dimmock & Co. (c.1807-1827) Subsequently, Dimmock & Wood (c.1859-1878)
B774	1297	**D**	Printed marks of differing design. Pattern name often included, c.1828-1859.
B775	-	**T. D. KAOLIN**	- KAD No. B774 "D" may also occur impressed in conjunction with printed marks. Note trade-mark "KAOLIN WARE".
B776	-	**THOMAS DIMMOCK IMPROVED STONEWARE**	- Note trade-mark "KAOLIN WARE", c. 1828-1859.

B777 1298
B778 -

Printed marks with "D" noted by Godden may fit other firms of this period.
- However, KAD B778 is, in fact, a registered Dimmock pattern for 1844.

Typical Marks Include:

B779 -
B780 -
B781 -
B782 -

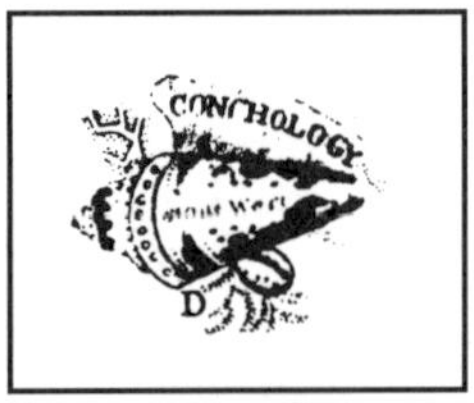

B783 1299

Many such printed marks occur, and may be dated from c.1828-1859.

B784 1300

Printed or impressed monogram marking may occur concurrent with printed mark, c.1828-1859.

B785 1301

- Godden notes that care must be taken, as many potters named Dimmock were working in Staffordshire during the nineteenth century.
- It is important to note that Thomas Dimmock & Co. produced many beautiful shapes and polychrome pieces.

For further reading, refer to *Snyder*, Vol. 2; and *Snyder, Romantic Staffordshire,* p. 55.

DON

KAD NO.	GODDEN NO.	MARK	

***Don Pottery**
Swinton, South Yorkshire, c.(1790s)1801-1834
(and various partnerships)
History:

Greens, Clark & Co.	1801-1810
John & William Green (& Co.)	1810-1823
Green & Co.	1823-1834
Pottery acquired by Samuel Barker	1834-1851
Continued by his son until closure	1851-1893

KAD NO.	GODDEN NO.	MARK	
B786	1309	**DON POTTERY**	Printed or impressed marks of differing design, c.1801-1834.
B787	1310	**DON POTTERY GREEN**	Printed or impressed marks of differing design, c.1801-1834.
B788	1311	**GREEN DON POTTERY**	
B789	1313		Relief Pad Mark may occur with the one word "DON", c.1801-1834.
B790 B791	1314 -	 	Printed or impressed Crest Mark. Variation noted with wording "GREEN DON POTTERY", c.1810-1834.

For further reading, refer to *Edwards Basalt*, pp. 152-153; *Godden, Collecting Lustreware*, p. 262; the *Don Pottery 1983 Exhibition Catalogue*. Doncaster Museum and Art Gallery; *Lawrence*, pp. 96-97, 248-251; *Towner*, pp. 156-157; *Little*, p. 117; and *NCS Newsletter*, No. 109, Mar. 1998, pp. 4-16 for an article by Renard Broughton titled "Yorkshire Pottery: Identifying Early Blue Printed Patterns of the Circa. 1785-1810."

DOULTON

Doulton & Co. (Ltd.)
Nile Street,
Burslem, Staffordshire, c.1882-1955
Formerly, Pinder Bourne & Co. (1862-1882)*
Retitled Doulton Fine China Ltd. from October 1955

*From 1878 until c.1882 Pinder Bourne & Co. marks were continued in use. Sometimes both Doulton & Pinder Bourne & Co. marks appear together. Doulton continued successful patterns with or without modification by using the new trade-mark.
- Numbers appearing in ( ) indicate reference to Desmond Eyles' numbering system. For additional marks refer to Desmond Eyles, *The Doulton Burslem Wares*. Barrie & Jenkins/Royal Doulton, London. 1980

KAD NO.	GODDEN NO.	MARK	
B792	1327	**DOULTON**	Impressed name mark, 1882+.
B793	-	**DOULTONS**	Printed name mark, 1882-1886.
B794	-	**ENGLAND**	Early printed or impressed marks, c.1891-1902. - "ENGLAND" added after 1891.

Selected Marks Include:

B795 -
B796 1329
B797 1332
B798 -

1882-1891
(B3)

1891-1902
(B3)

1886-1891
(B4)

1891-1902
(B4)

B799 -
B800 -

Printed "FLAT IRON MARK" usually associated with series ware, 1891-1901.*
- Noted on the backstamp for the pattern "Jeddo". See *Gaston*, Vol. 2, Mark 34A.
*Refer to *Royal Doulton Series Ware* (in four volumes) by Louise Irvine. Richard Dennis, London, 1980, 1984, 1986, 1988.

B801 -

Printed mark, 1895-1930s.

B802 -

Printed mark after 1902.
- Note the marking "ROYAL DOULTON/BURSLEM, ENGLAND".

B803 1333
B804 1531

(B7)

Printed or impressed marks from 1901-1922 and continued on from 1927-1936.
- US Patent dates from the 1880s.

B805 1337
B806 1355

(B8)

Printed marks without "crown", 1923-1927.
- Note variations.

KAD NO.	GODDEN NO.	MARK	
B807	1334	 (B9)	Printed mark "MADE IN ENGLAND" dates from 1923 onwards. - Desmond Eyles, p. 179, notes that many examples exist with the marking "MADE IN ENGLAND" dating from 1923-1927, but less frequently from 1928-1931. For additional marks and further reading, refer to *Godden*, pp. 213-219; *Desmond Eyles*, pp. 177-180; and additional comments under Pinder Bourne & Co.

DUDSON

James Dudson
Hope & Hanover Streets,
Hanley, Staffordshire, 1845-1888
Formerly, James & Charles Dudson (1835-1845)
Subsequently, Company continued by son after James Dudson's death (1882-1888)*
- J. T. Dudson, Hope Street, Hanley, Staffordshire, 1888-1898
- Subsequently, Dudson Bros., 1898-1918
-"LTD." from 1918-present

B808	1409	**DUDSON**	Impressed name mark (noted on jugs), c.1840s-1888.
B809	1410	**J. DUDSON**	Impressed name marks, 1888-1898
B810	1411	**J. DUDSON ENGLAND**	

For further reading, refer to Audrey M. Dudson. *Dudson, A Family of Potters Since 1800*. Dudson Publications. Hanley, England, 1985 wherein additional marks may be found on pp. 222-224. Many of the pieces by Dudson are unmarked. He was, however, one of the major manufacturers of Flow Blue and Copper Lustre Relief Moulded Jugs in the tulip motif. See Plate 3D, p. 21 and pp. 80-90.

Also refer to *Godden, British Porcelain, pp. 316-317;Collecting Lustreware*, pp. 110, 356 & 360; *Henrywood*, pp. 146-156; *Hughes*, Vol. I & II; and Jill Rumsey. *Relief Moulded Jugs and Exhibition Catalog*. Dec. 2-23, 1987. Richard Dennis, London,

DUDSON

Dudson, Wilcox & Till, Ltd.
Britannic Works, High Street
Hanley Staffordshire, c.1902-1926

B811	1412		Printed or impressed marks of differing design. Pattern name often included, c.1902-1926.
B812	1413		Mark, as above, but without double circle, c.1902-1926.

For further reading, refer to Audrey M. Dudson. *Dudson, A Family of Potters Since 1800*. Dudson Publications. Hanley, England, 1985, pp. 135 and 224.

DUNDERDALE

David Dunderdale & Co.
Castleford Pottery,
Castleford, West Yorkshire, c.1790-1821
Formerly William Taylor & Co.
Subsequently, Asquity & Co./George Bateson

KAD NO.	GODDEN NO.	MARK	
B813	1416	**D. D. & CO.**	Impressed initial marks, c.1790-1821.
B814	1417	**D. D. & CO. CASTLEFORD**	- "& CO." c. 1803
B815	1418	**D. D. & CO. CASTLEFORD POTTERY**	- Pieces are seldom marked.

For further reading, refer to, *Edwards, Basalt*, p. 154; *Godden, British Porcelain*, pp. 319-321; *Godden, Collecting Lustreware*, p. 261; and *Lawrence.*

DUNN

Dunn, Bennett & Co. (Ltd.)
Boothen Works,
Hanley (1875-1887)
Royal Victoria Works, Burslem (1887-1937)
Staffordshire, 1875-1937
Subsequently, Wade, Heath & Co. (1937-1968)
Acquired by Royal Doulton (1968)

KAD NO.	GODDEN NO.	MARK	
B816	-	**D. B. & C.**	Printed marks of differing design. Pattern name often included, c.1875- 1906.
B817	1421	**D. B. & CO.**	- "LTD." from 1907 onwards.
B818	-	**DUNN BENNETT & CO.**	
B819	1422		Printed Beehive mark noted from c.1875-1907. - For additional marks refer to *Godden,* p. 225.

For further reading, refer to *Godden, Jewitt*, p. 22 "Hill Works" Burslem, and p. 79 "Boothen Works", Hanley and Victoria, County History of Staffordshire, p. 135.

EDGE

***Edge, Barker & Barker**
Market Street,
Fenton, Staffordshire, 1836-1840
Formerly, Edge, Barker & Co. (1835-1836)

KAD NO.	GODDEN NO.	MARK	
B820	1437	**E. B. & B.**	Printed marks of differing design. Pattern name often included, 1836-1840.

EDGE

***Edge, Barker & Co.**
Market Street, Fenton & Lane End,
Staffordshire, c.1835-1836

KAD NO.	GODDEN NO.	MARK	
B821	1438	**E. B. & CO.**	Printed marks of differing design. Pattern name often included, c.1835-1836.

KAD NO.	GODDEN NO.	MARK	
B822	-		Typical mark, c.1835-1836. For further reading, refer to *Little*, p. 61.

EDGE

Edge, Malkin & Co. (Ltd.)
Newport & Middleport Potteries,
Burslem, Staffordshire, c.1870-1903
Formerly, Cork, Edge & Malkin (c.1860-1870)
Subsequently, S.W. Dean (1904-1910)

B823 — 1440 — **EDGE MALKIN & CO.** — Printed or impressed name mark, c.1870-1903.

B824 — - — 

Printed Royal Coat of Arms Mark noted on Tea Leaf with Copper Lustre, c.1891-1903.
- Refer to Stoltzfus/Snyder.

B825 — 1441 — **E. M. & CO.** — Printed marks of differing design. Pattern name often included, c.1870-1903.
- "LTD." added from 1899.

B826 — 1442 — **E. M. & CO. B**

B827 — 1443 — 

Printed mark (typical), c.1870-1880.

B828 — 1444 — **D. & K. R.** — Printed mark noted below Royal Arms, c.1873.
- Godden notes "The initial probably relate to the firm for whom the pattern was made."

B829 — 1445 — 

Printed "Trade Mark" registered in 1873. (Slight variations exist.) Pattern name may occur in place of "Trade Mark", c.1873-1903.
- Laidacker, *American Antique Collector*. Vol. 2, June-Aug. 1940, No. 1, p. 6, notes the pattern "Utica", a view from the American Historic Series, as having two marks: a printed mark "T. GODWIN, WHARF" and an impressed mark "EDGE, MALKIN & CO."
- Also refer to Thomas & Benjamin Godwin, p. 208.

For further reading, refer to *TLCI Educational Supplement*, April 1994; and *Godden, Collecting Lustreware*, pp. 110-111. Further, *Tiny Times*, Summer 1996, Vol. 4, Issue 4, p. 76, notes a "Missouri-like" pattern on a child's set with a Canadian importer's mark "ROYAL LONDON IRONSTONE, J. McD & S. IMPORTERS".

EDGE

KAD NO.	GODDEN NO.	MARK	
			***William & Samuel Edge** **Market Street, Lane Delph,** **Fenton, Staffordshire, c.1841-1848**
B830	1436	**W. & S. E.**	Printed marks of differing design. Pattern name often included, c.1841-1848.
B831	-		

EDWARDS

KAD NO.	GODDEN NO.	MARK	
			***James Edwards** **Dale Hall, Burslem,** **Staffordshire, 1842-1854** **Formerly, John Rogers & Son (c.1815-1841)** **"& Son" (1854-1876) "& Sons" (1877-1882)**
B832 B833	1449 -	**J. E.*** **J. E. EDWARDS**	Printed or impressed marks noted with various and often elaborately designed marks, c.1842-1854. - Individual pattern noted. - "WARRANTED" marking also noted.
B834	-	**JAS. EDWARDS** **REAL IRONSTONE**	- Additional impressed marking "PORCELAINE A LA PERLE" noted on "Boston Mails".**
B835	-	**JAMES EDWARDS**	Impressed name mark may accompany printed mark, 1842-1854.
B835A	-	**JAMES EDWARDS** **BURSLEM**	Impressed name mark with locale, 1842-1854. *Care in attributing by initials alone must be taken, as "J. E." was also used by John Edwards.
B836	-	**JAMES EDWARDS** **SAXON BLUE**	Impressed name mark with "SAXTON BLUE", 1842-1854.
B837	-		Printed Royal Arms mark with variation "IRONSTONE/JAMES EDWARDS" noted, c.1842-1854.

Typical Marks Include:

B838 -
B839 -
B840 -

-*White Ironstone Notes*, Vol. 4, No. 1, Summer 1997, p. 7, illustrates a child's tea set "Pedestaled Gothic" registered in 1847, with the impressed mark (KAD B840) "FELSPAR OPAQUE CHINA, DALE HALL".

- The Flow Blue pattern "COBURG" has been definitely attributed to James Edwards and *not* John Edwards. The piece has an impressed Registry Mark No. 9678 which dates the registry as August 30, 1843 by James Edwards.

KAD NO.	GODDEN NO.	MARK
B841	-	
B842	-	
B843	-	

Selected Registry Marks Include:

Oct. 26, 1846

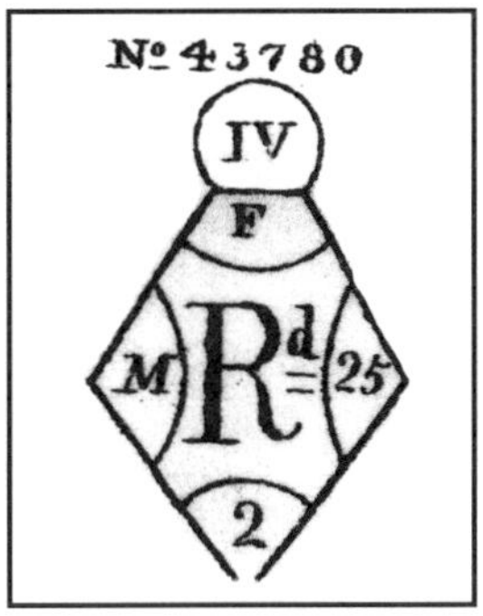

June 25, 1847

July 16, 1847

- Evidently the "COBURG" pattern was extremely popular and necessitated additional registries.
- For additional backstamp markings, refer to *P. Williams, Staffordshire*, Vol. I, p. 24 and Vol. II, pp. 568-569; *Tea Leaf Educational Supplement*, May 1994; and *Hampson*, No. 83, p. 53.
- See *White Ironstone Notes*, Vol. 5, No. 1, Summer 1998, pp. 10-11 for an article by Jean Wetherbee titled "Verifying a New Shape". The registry date of May 30, 1842 is printed with the text "TO PREVENT THIS SHAPE FROM BEING COPIED IT WAS ENTERED AT THE REGISTRY OFFICE OF DESIGNS, MAY 30, 1842 BY JAMES EDWARDS." Also noted is registry no. 1267. Jean Wetherbee catalogs this shape as "Fluted Double Swirl."

** *Collard, Potters View*, pp. 35-38 notes that "Boston Mails" may have been continued by James Edwards.

- Also see comments under James & Thomas Edwards.

For further reading, refer to *Jewitt,* pp., 456-457; and *Snyder's Fascinating Flow Blue*, pp. 55, 58 .

EDWARDS

***James Edwards & Son(s)**
Dale Hall,
Burslem, Staffordshire, 1854-1876
"& Sons" (1877-1882)

KAD NO.	GODDEN NO.	MARK	
B844	1446	**J. E. & S. STONE CHINA**	Printed and impressed marks of differing design. Pattern name often included, c.1854-1882.
B845	-	**J. E. & SON**	
B846	1447	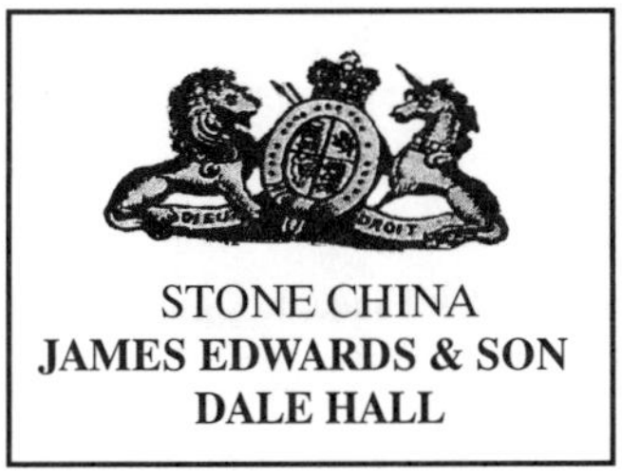	Printed mark noted on White Ironstone, c.1854-1882. - Full name of firm or initials may be noted along with the description "IRONSTONE CHINA", REAL IRONSTONE" or "STONE CHINA" added c.1854-1882. - "& SONS" from 1877-1882.
B847	1448	**EDWARDS D. H.**	- "DALE HALL" or "D. H." is noted from c.1854-1882.

- The initials "J. E." could be attributed to James Edwards, James & Thomas Edwards or John Edwards as well as others. Care must be taken with attribution.

KAD NO.	GODDEN NO.	MARK	
			For further reading, refer to *Godden, British Porcelain*, p. 324; *Cameron*, p. 119; and *Henrywood,* p. 198. - Also refer to Appendix B6: Chronology for comments about Edwards.

EDWARDS

***James & Thomas Edwards**
Kilncroft Works, Sylvester Square (c.1839-1842)
Burslem, Staffordshire c.1839-1842
Subsequently, James Edwards, Dale Hall (1842-1854)

KAD NO.	GODDEN NO.	MARK	
B848	1454	**J. & T. E.**	Printed or impressed marks of differing design. Pattern name often included, c.1839-1842.
B849	1455	**J. & T. EDWARDS** **B**	- "PORCELAIN OPAQUE" and "SEVRES" marks noted.
B850	1456	**EDWARDS**	Printed or impressed name mark, c.1839-1842.
B851	-		Printed mark with impressed name "EDWARDS" and term "IRONSTONE", c.1839-1842.
B852	-		Printed marks of various designs found on Historic American/Canadian views. -*Larsen* notes that "Boston Mails" was marked below "Entered at the Registry Office of Design, Sept. 2nd 1841.: -*Collard, Potters View*, pp. 35-38 illustrates different importer markings; e.g., "PORCELAINE/A LA PERLE/J. E." *Collard* further notes that "Boston Mails" may have been continued by James Edwards, as evidenced by the initials "J. E." For further reading, refer to *Collard, Pottery & Porcelain*, and *Potters View,* pp. 35-38; *Snyder, Historic Staffordshire*, p. 57; and *Godden, Illustrated Encyclopedia*, p. 159 for "Boston Mails" print registered Sept. 1841 which is illustrated from a pull of the original copper plate.

EDWARDS

***John Edwards (& Co.)**
King Street,
Fenton, Staffordshire (c.1853-1900)
- John Edwards began potting at Market Place, Longton (c.1847) and moved to King Street, Fenton in (1853), 1847-1900

KAD NO.	GODDEN NO.	MARK	
B853	1449	**J. E.***	Printed or impressed marks of differing design. Pattern name often included, c.1847-1900.
B854	1450	**J. E. & CO.**	- "& CO." from 1873-1879.
B855	-	**J. EDWARDS**	*Initials also used by James Edwards, 1842-1854.
B856	-	**JOHN EDWARDS**	

KAD NO.	GODDEN NO.	MARK

Typical Marks Include:

KAD NO.	GODDEN NO.
B857	1451
B858	1452
B859	-
B860	-
B861	-
B862	-
B863	-

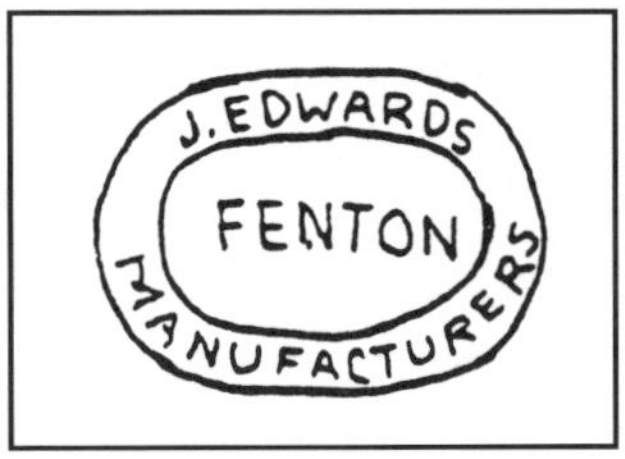

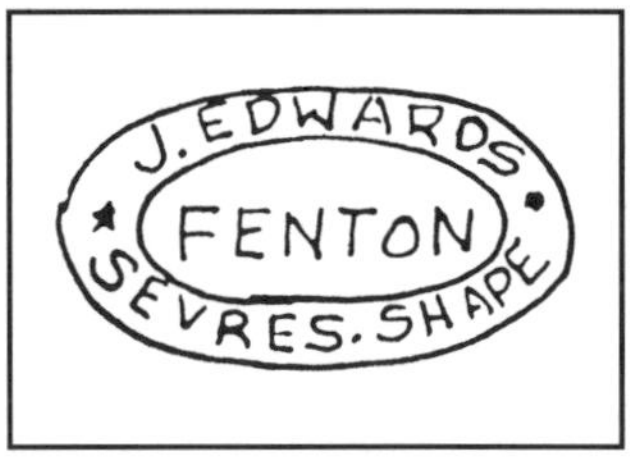

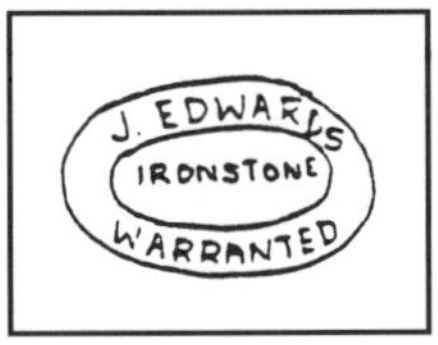

-An inconsistency in locations and dates is noted for John Edwards (& Co.) in that in 1853 he is recorded as being in Fenton, while Registry records indicate him as being in Longton.

Longton Registry Dates as noted by Cushion:

July 18, 1853	May 5, 1858
January 30, 1855	September 8, 1858
January 5, 1856	

- In response to my letter regarding this inconsistency, Geoffrey Godden notes: "…it could be he continued this Longton Pottery after 1853, or merely wrote-in on old-headed paper…"

For further information on the various partnerships and dates for Edwards, refer to the Appendix B6: Chronology for additional comments, see p. 545.

For further reading, refer to *Godden, British Porcelain*, pp. 324-325; and *Hampson*, No. 96, p. 62.

EDWARDS

***Thomas Edwards**
Waterloo Pottery, Holehouse,
Swan Bank Pottery, High Street
Burslem, Staffordshire, c.1841-(47)*

KAD NO.	GODDEN NO.	MARK	
B864	-	**T. E.**	Printed or impressed marks of differing design. Pattern name often included, c.1841-(47).
B865	-	**T. EDWARDS**	- Impressed marking "PORCELAIN OPAQUE" noted along with printed mark and pattern name "TEMPLE". See *P. Williams, Staffordshire,* Vol. II, p. 252.
B866	-	**THOMAS EDWARDS**	

Typical Marks Include:

KAD NO.	GODDEN NO.
B867	-
B868	-
B869	-
B870	-

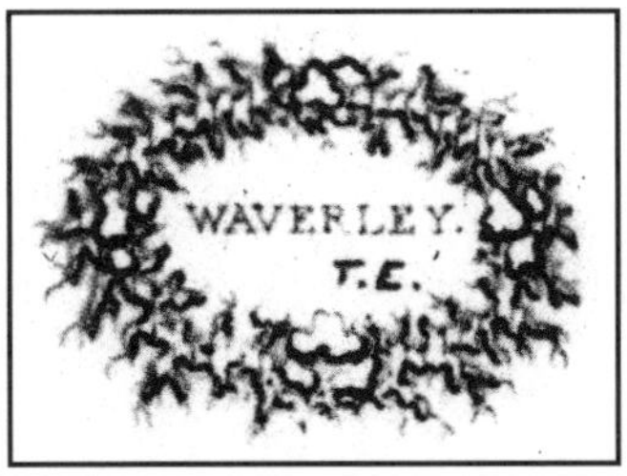

KAD NO.	GODDEN NO.	MARK	
B871	-	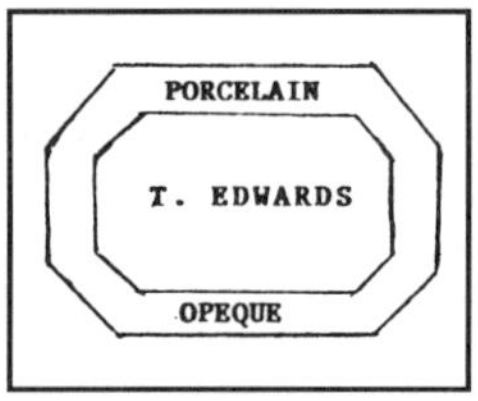	Impressed or printed cartouche marked "PORCELAIN/T. EDWARDS/OPEQUE" c.1841-(47). - Printed pattern name "ABBEY" noted by *P. Williams, Staffordshire*, Vol. I, p. 172 and Vol. II, p. 539. *Also refer to Appendix B6: Chronology for Thomas Edwards, Burslem, see p. 545.

ELGIN

Elgin Pottery
Davidson Street,
Glasgow, Scotland, c.1855-1870
History:

James Johnston, Wm. Reid, Joseph Vaughan & James Sellars, blacksmith	c.1855-1859
Pottery moves to larger premises	c.1859
Pottery is sequestrated	c.1860
Reid & Charles Purvis	c.1860-1861
Thomas Purvis (Pottery is sequestrated)	c.1867-1870

B872 - **ELGIN POTTERY C. P.** Printed initial and name marks, c.1855-1870.
- "SEMI CHINA" marking noted.

B873 - **C. P.**

- The name Purvis has caused a lot of confusion for purposes of attribution. Following are two other potteries with the name Purvis:

MILE END POTTERY*	**(P. D. & CO.)**
Charles Purvis & John Denny	c.1867-1868
Charles Purvis	c.1868-1870

- See Clyde Pottery Co., p. 153.

GOVAN POTTERY*	**(C. P. & CO.)**
Charles Purvis & James Watson Purvis	c.1883-1886
Charles Purvis	c.1886-1887

*They may have been cousins.

For further reading, refer to *Coysh*, Vol. I, p. 127; and *Fleming*, p. 129.

ELKIN

***Elkin & Newbon**
Stafford Street, Longton, 1845-1856

B874 1467 **E. & N.** Printed marks of differing design, 1845-1856.
- A date correction is noted in *Hamspon*, No. 98, pp. 63-64.

For further reading, refer to *Coysh*, Vol. I, pp. 48, 127, 402.

ELKIN

***Elkin, Knight & Bridgwood**
Foley Potteries, King Street,
Fenton, Staffordshire, c.1827-1840

B875 1464 **E. K. B.** Printed marks of differing design. Pattern name often included, c.1827-1840.
- Note marking "OPAQUE CHINA", see KAD B879.

KAD NO.	GODDEN NO.	MARK
B867	-	E. K. & B.
B877	-	K. E. & B.*

Typical Marks Include:

KAD NO.	GODDEN NO.
B878	-
B879	-
B880	-
B881	-

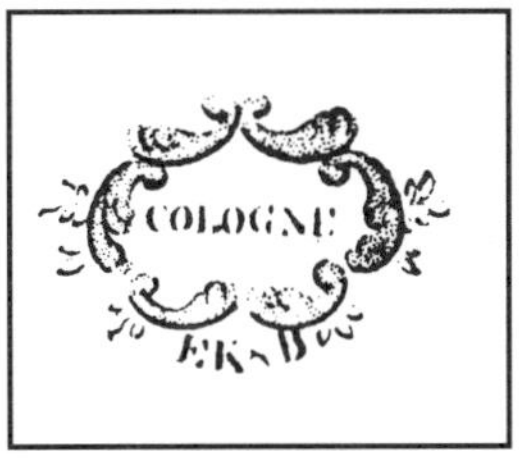

**Godden, British Porcelain*, p. 65 notes the name given on Trade Cards as Knight, Elkin & Bridgwood.

For further reading, refer to *Little,* p. 62.

ELKIN

***Elkin, Knight & Co.**
Foley Potteries, King Street,
Fenton, Staffordshire, c.1820(22)-1825
Subsequently, Elkin, Knight & Bridgwood
- Also see Knight, Elkin & Co.

KAD NO.	GODDEN NO.	MARK	
B882	1465	E. K. & CO.	Printed or impressed marks noted with various and often elaborately designed designed marks. Name of individual pattern often included, c.1820(22)-1825.
B883	1466	ELKIN KNIGHT & CO.	- Note marking "OPAQUE CHINA"
B884	-		Printed mark with impressed name "ELKIN/KNIGHT & CO." beneath a crown, c.1820(22)-1825 noted in *Coysh,* Vol. I, p. 146.

- It is important to note that marks appear to have been interchangeable between the various partnerships.

For further reading, refer to *P. Williams, Staffordshire*, Vol. II, pp. 283-285; and *Little*, p. 62.

ELKIN

***Elkins & Co.**
Church Street Pottery,
Fenton, Staffordshire, c.1822-1825
- "& Co." was partnership of Elkin, Knight & Elkin

KAD NO.	GODDEN NO.	MARK	
B885	-	E. & CO.	Printed marks of differing design. Pattern name often included, c.1822-1825.
B886	1468A	ELKINS & CO.	

KAD NO.	GODDEN NO.	MARK	
B887	-		Printed Royal Coat of Arms mark, c.1822-1825. - See *Coysh*, Vol. I, p. 393 for the mark "IRISH SCENERY" and retailer's mark "WARREN". For further reading, refer to *Godden*, p. 242; *Godden, British Porcelain*, p. 521 for "John Mayer"; and *Hamspon*, No. 99, p. 64.

ELSMORE

Elsmore & Forster
Clayhills Pottery,
Tunstall, Staffordshire, c.1853-1871
Formerly, John Holland (c.18852-1853)
Subsequently, Elsmore & Son (c.1872-1887)

KAD NO.	GODDEN NO.	MARK	
B888	-		Printed or impressed marks of differing design. Pattern name often included, c.1853-1871.
B889	-	**E. F. & CO.**	
B890	1476	**ELSMORE & FORSTER**	- Registry marks may appear on raised pads. Spelling errors noted in the name; i.e. "FOSTER", c.1853-1871.
B891	-	**ELSMORE, FORSTER & CO.**	- See comments in *White Ironstone Notes*, Vol. 3, No. 3, Winter 1997, (Dec. 1996), p. 14
B892	-	**ELSMORE & FORSTER & CO. TUNSTALL OPAQUE CHINA**	
B893	1477		Printed Royal Coat of Arms mark, c.1853-1871. -Godden notes additional variations. See KAD B893 with marking "WARRANTED IRONSTONE CHINA".
B894	-		Printed Royal Coat of Arms mark with script name-mark "E. FOR.", 1853-1871.

KAD NO. **GODDEN NO.** **MARK**

Typical Marks Noted on White Ironstone:

B895 -
B896 -
B897 -
B898 -

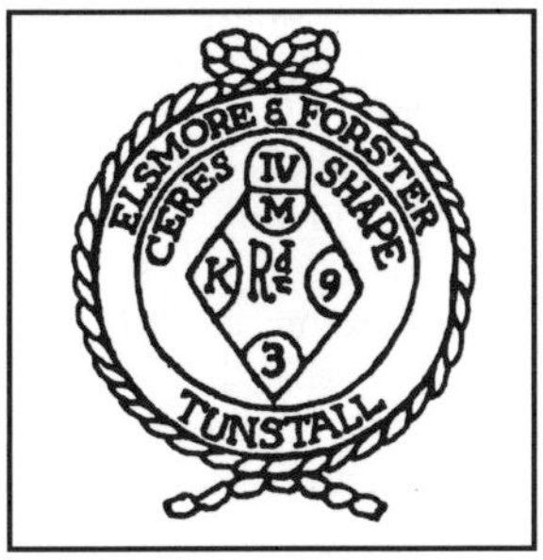

- A mark similar to KAD B900 was used by Elsmore & Son as well as KAD B1816 by The Old Hall (Earthenware) Pottery Co., Ltd., see p. 297.
- Arene Burgess notes, from pieces in her collection, that Thomas Walker also used many of the same patterns.
- Pattern [coppers] by Thomas Walker may have come into the possession of Elsmore & Forster.
- *Laidacker*, Part I, notes a tea and toilet set with a black transfer view of the Bust of Washington by Stuart, called "Laurel Wreath", registered Nov. 2, 1859/No. 123738-40.

For further reading, refer to *Heaivilin*, pp. 71-72; *Wetherbee; Sussman*, pp. 14-16; *Tea Leaf Readings*, Vol. 12, No. 1, Feb. 1992; *White Ironstone Notes* "Pattern Profile" by Bev. & Ernie Dieringer, Vol. 1, No. 3, Spring 1995, pp. 1-7, and "Variations on the Theme" by Arene Burgess, Vol. 2, No. 1, Summer 1995, pp. 10-11, and Vol. 2, No. 4, Spring 1996.

ELSMORE

Elsmore (Thomas) & Son
Clayhills Pottery,
Tunstall, Staffordshire, c.1872-1887

B899 1478 **ELSMORE & SON ENGLAND**

Printed and impressed marks of differing design. Pattern name seldom included, c.1872-1887.
- "PARISIAN GRANITE" (referring to body shape) is noted on White Ironstone.

B900 -

- This ornate, printed type or style mark was used by Elsmore & Forster (KAD B895) as well as by The Old Hall (Earthenware) Pottery Co., Ltd. (KAD B1826), see p. 297.
- Note the usage of "ENGLAND" prior to 1891. *Blue Berry Notes*, Vol. 10, No. 3, p. 12 illustrates an oriental design plate with a printed registry mark dating from May 14, 1878. Evidently this piece was registered on this date but not issued until a later date, as witnessed by the marking "ENGLAND" in anticipation of the McKinley Act of 1891. It was not uncommon to issue pieces at a later date or even to reregister pieces. The date of issue is possibly from 1885-1887.

- In correspondence to me dated April 1997, Geoffrey Godden states "…as to England…this is seemingly quite possible - nothing to stop anyone adding "England" in 1750, 1800 or 1850!" See *Godden's* entry No. 1478, p. 236.

EMBERTON

KAD NO.	GODDEN NO.	MARK	
			William Emberton (& Co.) **High Gate Pottery,** **Brownhills, Tunstall, Staffordshire, c.1846-1869** **Formerly, George Hood (1831-1846)** **Subsequently, T. I. & J. Emberton (c.1869-1882)**
B901	1485	**W. E.**	Printed marks of differing design. Pattern name often included, c.1851-1869.
B902	-	**W. E. & CO.**	- "& CO."* from c.1846-1851. - Several Garter shaped marks were used from 1851-1869.

**Abbie's Encyclopedia of Flow Blue, Oriental & Scenic*, Apopka, FL, (privately published), Vol. 1, p. 2, illustrates the pattern "Amoy" with the "& CO." marking.

For further reading, refer to *Godden, Collecting Lustreware*, p. 111; and *Edwards, Basalt*, p.181.

EMERY

KAD NO.	GODDEN NO.	MARK	
			Francis Joseph Emery **Church Yard Works (1878-1878)** **Crown Works (1878-1893)** **Bleak Hill Works (1880-1893)** **Burslem, Staffordshire, c.1878-1893** **- and other locations** **Formerly, W. E. Withinshaw (1873-1878)**
B903	-	**F. J. E.**	Printed marks of differing design. Pattern name often included, c.1878-1893.
B904	1485A	**F. J. EMERY**	

For further reading, refer to *Godden, Jewitt*, pp. 10, 25, 34, 38.

EMPIRE

KAD NO.	GODDEN NO.	MARK	
			Empire Porcelain Co. (Ltd.) **Empire Works, Stoke Road,** **Stoke-on-Trent, Staffordshire, c.1896-1967** **"Ltd." dates from (1963)**
B905	-	**E. P. CO.**	Printed marks of differing design. Pattern name often included, c.1896-1939.
B906	1488		
B907	1489		

Printed Mark c.1896-1912

Printed Mark c.1912-1928

- Elaborately printed monogram "E. P. CO." may appear in mark KAD B906.

- Printed marks from 1928-1939. Note month, potting year and potting numbers.

For additional marks, refer to *Godden, pp. 238-239.*

EVANS

***Evans & Glasson**
Cambrian Pottery,
Swansea, Wales, c.1850-1861
- Also see: Swansea Pottery

KAD NO.	GODDEN NO.	MARK	
B908	-	**E. & G.**	Printed initial mark, c. 1850-1861.
B908A	1519	**EVANS & GLASSON**	Printed marks of differing design. Pattern name often included, c.1850-1861.
B909	1519A	**EVANS & GLASSON SWANSEA**	- Note marking "BEST GOODS".
B910	-		
B911	-		

For further reading, refer to *Nance*, pp. 192-202.

EVANS

***D. J. Evans & Co.**
Cambrian Pottery,
Swansea, Wales, c.1861(62)-1870
Formerly, Evans & Glasson
Also see: Swansea, Cambrian Pottery

KAD NO.	GODDEN NO.	MARK	
B912	1514	**D. J. EVANS & CO. SWANSEA**	Printed marks of differing design. Pattern name often included, c. 1861(62)-1870. - Note Prince of Wales Feather mark (KAD B916).
B913	1515	**EVANS & CO.**	
B914	1516	**D. I. EVANS & CO.**	The marking "D, I. EVANS & CO." may also occur, c.1861(62)-1870. - The letters "I" and "J" were often interchangeable in mid-nineteenth century spelling; e.g., John/Iohn or James/Iames.

Typical Marks Include:

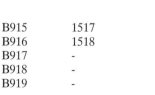

KAD NO.	GODDEN NO.
B915	1517
B916	1518
B917	-
B918	-
B919	-

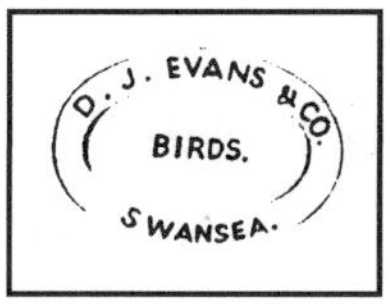

Marks from Pryce & William *Swansea Blue and White Pottery* reproduced with the kind permission of the publishers, Antique Collectors' Club Ltd.

For further reading, refer to *Pugh, Welsh Pottery*, pp. 28-33.

FARRALL

John Farrall
See: Pearson, Farrall & Meakin

FELL

Thomas Fell (& Co.) (Ltd.)
St. Peter's Pottery,
Newcastle-upon-Tyne, Northumberland, c.1817-1890
"& Co." (1830-1869), "Ltd." (1869-1890)

KAD NO.	GODDEN NO.	MARK	
B920	1530	**FELL**	Various impressed name marks, c.1817-1830.
B921	-	**FELL NEWCASTLE**	Printed or impressed marks of differing design. Pattern name often included, c.1817-1830.
B922 B923	1531 1532	 	Various impressed marks noted with anchor marking, c.1817-1830. - "& CO." from 1830-1869(90). - See comments re "LONDON/ANCHOR" impressed mark under Isaac & Thomas Bell, see p. 109.
B924	-	**FELL & CO.**	Printed marks of differing design. Pattern name often included, c.1830-1869(90).
B925	1533	**F. & CO.**	-Impressed mark "PORCELAIN/OPAQUE/FELL & CO." noted as well as printed Royal Coat of Arms mark, 1830-1869(90).
B926	1534	**T. F. & CO.**	
B927	1535	**T. FELL & CO.**	- Initial marks must be attributed with care in the case of "T. F. & Co." as this marking was also used by Thomas Furnival & Co., c.1844-1845.

Typical Marks (1830-1890) Include:

B928 -
B929 -
B930 -

B931 -
B932 -

For further reading, refer to *Bell*; *Lewis, Prattware*, p. 102; *Godden, Collecting Lustreware*, p.240; and *Snyder, Romantic Staffordshire*, pp. 59-60.

FENTON

KAD NO.	GODDEN NO.	MARK	
			Alfred Fenton & Sons **Brook Street,** **Hanley, Staffordshire, c.1887-1901** **Subsequently, Pearson Pottery Co.**
B933	1536	**A. F. & S.**	Printed or impressed initial marks. Pattern name often included, 1887-1901.
B934	1537		For further reading, refer to *Godden, British Porcelain*, pp. 106 and 334; and David Battle & Michael Turner. *The Price Guide to 19th and 20th Century British Pottery*, Antique Collectors Club Ltd., London, England, 1990.

FERRYBRIDGE

Ferrybridge Pottery (called Knottingley Pottery, c.1792-1804)
Various Partnerships, near Pontefract, Yorkshire, c.1792 to the present day

VARIOUS PRINTED AND IMPRESSED MARKS:

		PARTNERSHIP		**DATE**
B935	-	TOMLINSON FOSTER & CO.	Tomlinson, Foster & Co.	1793
B936	1538	TOMLINSON & CO.	—	—
B937	-	W. T. & CO.	Tomlinson, Foster, Wedgwood & Co.	1798
B938	1539	WEDGWOOD & CO.*	—	1798-1801
B936A	1538	TOMLINSON & CO.	Wm. Tomlinson & Co.	1801
B936B	1538	TOMLINSON & CO.	Tomlinson, Plowes & Co.	1804
B939	1540	FERRYBRIDGE	—	1804+
B936C	1538	TOMLINSON & CO.	Wm. Tomlinson	1828
B936D	1538	TOMLINSON & CO.	Edward Tomlinson	1830
B1966	3217	R. T. (& CO.)	Reed & Taylor (& Co.-1841-1848)	1832-1848
B940	-	B. T. & S.	Benjamin Taylor & Son	1848
B2558	4468	L. W.	Lewis Woolf	1851(56)
B2559	4468A	L. W. S. (or SONS)	Lewis Woolf & Sons	1870
B1912	3104	P. B.	Poulson Brothers	1884
B1913	3105	P. BROS.	—	—
B941	3482	S. & B.	Sefton & Brown	1897
B942	3483	S. & B./F. B.	—	—
B375A	655	T. B. & S./F. B.	T. Brown & Sons Ltd.	1919 -

*The patterns "Elephants" and "Greek Patterns" ("Classical Figure Patterns") were potted during Ralph Wedgwood's association, 1798-1801, and may have been carried over by Tomlinson & Co., 1804. *Coysh, Earthenware*, pp. 32-33 notes both these patterns. These two patterns have impressed markings "FERRYBRIDGE" or "WEDGWOOD & CO."

For further reading, refer to *Coysh,* Vol. I, p. 127, 136, 162 and Vol. II, p. 59; *Lawrence*, pp. 148-182 and marks pp. 252-257; *English Ceramic Circle Transactions*, pp. 255-264 and Plates 154-168 for an article by Dr. Minnie Holdaway titled "The Wares of Ralph Wedgwood"; *NCS Newsletter*, No. 109, March 1998, pp. 4-16 for an article by Renard Broughton titled "Yorkshire Pottery: Identifying Early Blue Printed Patterns of the Circa. 1785-1810 Period"; and *Williams-Wood, English Transfer*, pp. 196-200.

FIFE

KAD NO.	GODDEN NO.	MARK	

Fife Pottery
See: Robert Heron & Son

FLACKETT

Flackett & Toft
Church Street,
Longton, Staffordshire, c.1857
Formerly, Flackett, Chetham & Toft (c.1853-1856)
Subsequently, Flackett, Toft & Robinson (c.1858)

B943	-	**F. & T.**	Printed marks of differing design. Pattern name often included, c.1857.

For further reading, refer to *Hamspon*, No. 105, p. 67.

FLACKETT

Flackett, Toft & Robinson
Church Street,
Longton, Staffordshire, c.1858
Formerly, Flackett & Toft (c.1857)
Subsequently, William Toft (c.1859-1861)

B944	-	**F. T. R.**	Printed marks of differing design. Pattern name often included, c.1858
B945	1569	**F. T. & R.**	

For further reading, refer to Hampson, No. 105, p. 67.

FOLCH

Stephen Folch (& Sons)
Stoke Works, Church Street,
Stoke, Staffordshire, c.1819-1828

B946	1581	**FOLCH'S GENUINE STONE CHINA**	Impressed name mark, c.1819-1828.
B947	-	**IRONSTONE CHINA STOKE WORKS**	Impressed mark, c.1819-1828.
B948	-	**IMPROVED IRONSTONE CHINA STOKE WORKS**	Impressed mark, c.1819-1828.
B949	-	**FOLCH & SONS**	Printed (pre-1837) Royal Coat of Arms mark, with maker's name and/or with title "FOLCH & SONS" c.1819-1828. - See *True Blue*, p. 147, No. F3. For further reading, refer to *Little*, p. 63; *Edwards, Basalt*, p. 268; *Godden, Masons*, pp. 250-251; *Godden, British Porcelain*, pp. 343-344; and *Godden, Staffordshire,* p. 420.

FORD

KAD NO.	GODDEN NO.	MARK	
			***Ford & Challinor (or Ford & Challinor & Co.) Lion Works, Sandyford, Tunstall, Staffordshire, c.1865-1880**
B950	-	**F. & C.**	Printed marks of differing design. Pattern name often included, c.1865-1880.
B951	-	**F. C. & Co.**	
B952	1595		
B953	1595A		

For further reading, refer to *Sussman,* p. 59.

FORD

KAD NO.	GODDEN NO.	MARK	
			***Ford & Riley Newcastle Street, Burslem, Staffordshire, c.1882-1893**
B954	1601	**F. & R.**	Printed marks of differing design. Pattern name often included, c.1882-1893.
B955	1602		
B956	1603		

FORD

KAD NO.	GODDEN NO.	MARK	
			***Ford & Sons (Ltd.) Newcastle Street, Burslem, Staffordshire, c.1893-1938 Formerly, Ford & Riley (c.1882-1893) Subsequently, Ford & Sons (Crownford) Ltd. (c.1938-1986)**
B957	1582	**F. & S.**	Printed marks of differing design. Pattern name often included, c.1893-1938.
B958	1583	**F. & S. B**	
B959	1584	**F. & SONS LTD.**	Printed mark "LTD." c.1908+
			Typical Marks Include:
B960	1585		
B961	1586		

For additional marks, refer to *Godden*, pp. 283-284.

FORD

***John Ford & Co.**
39 Princes Street,
Edinburgh, Scotland, c.1891-1926
(Retailers)

KAD NO.	GODDEN NO.	MARK	
B962	1596	**JOHN FORD & CO. EDINBURGH**	Printed marks of differing design. Pattern name often included, c.1891-1926. For further reading, refer to *P. Williams, Staffordshire* Vol. II, p. 644.

FORD

***Samuel Ford & Co.**
Lincoln Pottery & Crown Pottery (from c.1913)
Burslem, Staffordshire, c.1898-1939
Formerly, Smith & Ford (1894-1898)

KAD NO.	GODDEN NO.	MARK	
B963	-	**S. F. & Co.**	Printed initial mark, c.1898-1939. - See *Gaston*, Mark 50A.
B964	1604		Printed mark (KAD B2147, previously used by Smith & Ford). Pattern name often included, c.1898-1939. - Smith & Ford (1895-1898) previously used the identical mark. See KAD B2147.
B965	-	**F. & CO.**	- The initials "F. & CO." may occur in place of "S. & F.".
B966	-	**SAMUEL FORD & CO. BURSLEM ENGLAND LIMITED**	Printed name mark, c.1898-1939.
B967	-	**LINCOLN POTTERY/ ENGLAND**	Printed name mark, c.1898-1913. - The above marking "LINCOLN POTTERY/ENGLAND" is illustrated in *Gaston*, Mark. No. 112.

FORD

***Thomas Ford (& Co.)**
Cannon Street,
Hanley, Staffordshire, c.1871-1874
Formerly, T. & C. Ford (c.1854-1871)
It must be noted that C. & T. Ford separated in 1871, and Charles continued alone at his new works at Eastwood, c.1871-1925.

KAD NO.	GODDEN NO.	MARK	
B968	1606	**T. F.**	Printed or impressed marks of differing design. Pattern name often included, c.1871- 1874. - *Godden*, pp. 255-256, Marks 1607 and 1608, notes examples of registration marks with the initials "T. F." Both *Larsen* and *Camehl* cite this pottery as "T. F. & Co." I however, have not been able to verify such a back mark.
B969	-	**T. F. & CO.**	*Godden, British Porcelain*, pp. 345-346 notes a partnership between Thomas and Charles dating from c.1854-1871. In addition to this partnership, Thomas Ford potted independently from 1865-1875. The "T. F. & CO." may then relate to their earlier partnership, or it may also stand for Thomas Forester & Co.

FORDY

KAD NO.	GODDEN NO.	MARK	
			Fordy, Patterson (& Co.) **Sheriff Hill (or Tyne) Pottery,** **Newcastle-upon-Tyne, Northumberland, c.1827-1829** **- See: Patterson & Co.**
B970	-		Impressed name mark, c.1827-1829. - See Jackson & Patterson for Sheriff Hill chronology, p. 244. For further reading, refer to *Godden, Collecting Lustreware*, p. 239; *Bell*; *Little*, p. 124; and *Cushion, British Ceramic Marks*, pp. 152-153.

FORDY

J. Fordy & Co.
Sheriff Hill (or Tyne) Pottery,
Newcastle-upon-Tyne, Northumberland, c.1824-1827
Subsequently, Fordy, Patterson (& Co.) (c.1827-1829)
No recorded marks, c.1824-1827.
For further reading, refer to *Bell*, pp. 28, 64; *Little*, p. 124; and *Godden, Collecting Lustreware*, p. 239.

FORESTER

***Thomas Forester Son & Co.**
Sutherland Pottery,
Fenton, Staffordshire, c.1884-1887
Subsequently, Forester & Hulme (c.1887-1892)

KAD NO.	GODDEN NO.	MARK	
B971	1613		Printed mark, c.1884-1887. - Note "ENGLAND" mark prior to 1891. For further reading, refer to *Godden, Staffordshire*, pp. 260-261.

FORESTER

***Thomas Forester & Son(s) (Ltd.)**
Phoenix Works, High Street,
Longton, Staffordshire, c.1884-1959
Formerly, Thomas Forester, Church Street Works, (1877-1883)

KAD NO.	GODDEN NO.	MARK	
B972	1614	T. F. & S.	Printed marks of differing design. Pattern name often included, c.1884-1891.
B973	1615		Printed mark, c.1891-1912. - Marks may include "LD" or "LTD."
B974	1616		Printed mark, c.1912-1959.

KAD NO.	GODDEN NO.	MARK	
B975	1617	**PHOENIX CHINA**	Printed names on various marks of differing design, c.1910-1959.
B976	1617A	**PHOENIX WARE**	

- Godden notes "A separate firm of similar name - Thomas Forester Son & Co. worked the Sutherland Pottery at Fenton in the 1880s." See *Godden, British Porcelain*, p. 347 as well as above listing.

For further reading, refer to *Karmason*, pp. 112-114.

FORRESTER

George Forrester
(Lower) Market Place, Lane End,
Longton, Staffordshire, c.1799-1830
Subsequently, Thomas E. Chesswas (1831-1835)

B977 - **G. F.** Impressed initial mark, c.1799-1830.

For further reading, refer to, *Coysh*, Vol. I, p. 145; and *Hampson*, No. 70, P. 45 and No. 108, p. 69.

FOWLER

Fowler Thompson & Co.
(Known as Watson's Pottery or Prestonpans)
Prestonpans, Scotland, c.1819-1838
- See, Watson & Co., p. 363.

B978 1625 **FOWLER THOMPSON & CO.** Printed or impressed name mark, c.1819-1838.
- Additional marking "SEMI CHINA" noted.
McVeigh notes the following Chronology:

Caldwell & Co.	1801
Anderson & Co.	1801-1809
David Thompson & Co.	1809-1819
Watson & Co. (Fowler Thompson & Co.)	1819-1838
Company in Liquidation	1839-1840

- *Fleming*, pp. 159-160 notes that the pottery was often referred to as "Thompson's", "Cadell's" or "Watson's" Pottery.
- *McVeigh*, p. 34 notes that Fowler Thompson and nephew had the controlling interest in the firm of David Thompson & Co.

For further reading, refer to *Coysh*, Vol. I, p. 147; and *Little*, p. 127.

FREAKLEY

Freakley & Farrall
Cannon Street, Shelton, Hanley, Staffordshire, c.1854-1855
Formerly, L. H. Meakin or Meakin & Farrall, (1850-1854)

B979 -

Printed Royal Coat of Arms marked "IRONSTONE CHINA, FREAKLEY & FARRALL" c.1854-1855.

- *Ewins*, p. 99 notes that the Staffordshire Advertiser of Aug. 1, 1855 publicized that the firm of L. H. Meakin & Co./Meakin & Farrall went bankrupt. He further cites an announcement of an impending auction on Sept. 12, 1855 by F. W. Bennett & Co. of 28

KAD NO.	GODDEN NO.	MARK	

& 30 Charles Street, Baltimore, MD of seventy-five crates of goods belonging to L. H. Meakin & Co. which were imported by Samuel B. Pierce & Co. of Boston.
- Refer to Pearson, Farrall & Meakin for additional comments, see p. 301.
- *Wetherbee, White Ironstone,* p. 104, fig. 11-34 illustrates a "Grape Octagon" ewer by this potter.

FURNIVAL

Jacob Furnival & Co.
Elder Road Pottery,
Cobridge, Staffordshire, c.1845-1870

KAD NO.	GODDEN NO.	MARK	
B980	-	**J. F.**	Printed marks of differing design. Pattern name often included, c.1845-1870.
B981	-	**J. F. & C.**	- Printed name of importers noted: "Huntington & Brooks/235 Main Street/ Cincinnati", and "J. C. Huntington & Co./162 Main St./Cincinnati".
B982	1643	**J. F. & CO.**	
B983	-	**J. FURNIVAL & CO.**	
B984	-	**JACOB FURNIVAL & CO.**	

Typical Marks Include:

B985 -
B986 -
B987 -
B988 -
B989 -

- *White Ironstone Notes*, Vol. 4, No. 1, Summer 1997, p. 13 notes a new pattern "Aquatic" Shape, registered in 1868, with an importer's mark.

For further reading, refer to *TLCI Educational Supplement*, Apr. 1994; *TLCI*, Vol. 15, No. 4, Aug. 1995, pp. 14-15; *Tea Leaf Readings*, Vol. 17, Issue No. 3, pp. 6-7 for an article by Nancy Upchurch about Jacob Furnival, as well as pp. 12-13 for an article by Anne Miller titled "Loop and Line or Grand Loop." For additional marks refer to *Stoltzfus/Snyder*, p. 18.

FURNIVAL

Jacob & Thomas Furnival
Stafford Street Works, Miles Bank
Shelton, Hanley, Staffordshire, c.1843
Subsequently, Thomas Furnival & Co. (c.1844-1845)

KAD NO.	GODDEN NO.	MARK	
B990		**J. & T. F.**	Printed marks of differing design. Pattern name often included, c.1843.
B991	1644		- It was not uncommon for successors to continue popular patterns. See Thomas Furnival & Co. as well as Cauldon (Potteries) Ltd. for the pattern "Indian Jar".

FURNIVAL

Thomas Furnival & Co.
Stafford Street Works, Miles Bank
Shelton, Hanley, Staffordshire, c.1844-1845
Formerly, Jacob & Thomas Furnival (c.1843)
Subsequently, Furnival & Clark (1845-1847)*

KAD NO.	GODDEN NO.	MARK	
B992	-	**T. F.**	Printed marks of differing design. Pattern name often included, c.1844-1845.
B993	-	**T. F. & C.**	- Additional markings noted with inclusion of "REAL IRONSTONE".
B994	1645	**T. F. & CO.**	
B995	-	**T. FURNIVAL & CO.**	

Typical Marks Include:

B996 -
B997 -

- Care must be taken with initials, particularly "T. F. & Co." as these were also used by Thomas Fell & Co. (c.1830-1890). Refer to KAD B926.
- It would also appear that patterns were continued from earlier partnerships. The pattern "Indian Jar" appears with the printed importer mark "Peter Wright/ Philadelphia" (USA). Further, Cauldon (Potteries) Ltd. (c.1905-1962) reissued this popular pattern in the twentieth century.

* *Hughes,* Vol. I, p. 50 illustrates a jug titled "Falstaff" registered on Dec. 30, 1845 in the name of Furnival & Clark, with the marking "T. F. & CO."

FURNIVAL

Thomas Furnival & Sons
Elder Road,
Cobridge, Staffordshire, c.1871-1890
Subsequently, Furnivals (Ltd.) (c.1890-1968)
- "& SONS" dates from c.1875

KAD NO.	GODDEN NO.	MARK	
B998	1648B	**FURNIVAL**	Impressed name mark, c.1871-1890. - *Snyder*, Vol. I, p. 61 shows a pattern titled "Ceylon". - Collard's two books illustrates a pattern called "Maple" which was commissioned for the Northwest Mounted Police [motto reads] "Maintiens Le Droit", c.1884, which is impressed "FURNIVAL" and also has a printed marking "T. FURNIVAL & SONS."
B999	-	**T. F. & SONS**	Printed marks of differing design. Pattern name often included, c.1875-1890.
B1000	-		- "ENGLAND" added after 1891. - Importers marks noted: "J. R. GIBNEY" [New York] and "PETER WRIGHT & SONS/IMPORTERS/PHILADELPHIA".
B1001	-	**T. FURNIVAL & SONS**	Printed name mark, c. 1875-1890.

KAD NO.	GODDEN NO.	MARK

Typical Monogrammed Marks, c.1875-1890, include:

B1002 1646
B1003 1647
B1004 1648
B1005 1648A

B1006 -

- *Wood*, No. I, p. 60 notes a White Ironstone platter in the "Roped Wheat" pattern with a printed mark "THE LORNE". This, in fact, may be the same as "Roped Wheat" noted below.
- "Roped Wheat" reg'd 1884/No. 5458 continued into the 1890s, as evidenced by the marking "ENGLAND", and was possibly continued by successors "Furnivals".
- The pattern "Florentine", reg'd Jan. 30, 1868, is a further example of the continuation of prior shapes and patterns (see Jacob Furnival & Co.), p. 199.

B1007 1649

B1008 -

Printed Royal Arms mark and variation, 1875-1890.

- The term "ENGLAND" was evidently printed prior to its requirement for the export market.

B1009 1650

Printed or impressed "Crest" mark registered 1878.
- Refer to *Collard, Potters View* pp. 65-67 and "Special Orders for Canada".

FURNIVAL

Furnivals (Ltd.)
Elder Road,
Cobridge, Staffordshire, 1890-1968
- "LTD" added from c.1895
Company name purchased by Enoch Wedgwood (Tunstall) Ltd. in 1969*
Printed marks of differing design. Pattern name often included, 1890-1968

B1010 1651 **FURNIVALS ENGLAND**

Printed name mark noted from 1890-1905.

B1011 1652

Printed or impressed anchor and dagger trade-mark found in several forms, 1890-1910.
- May accompany printed name mark.

Typical Marks Include:

B1012 1653
B1013 1654
B1014 1655

c.1905-1913

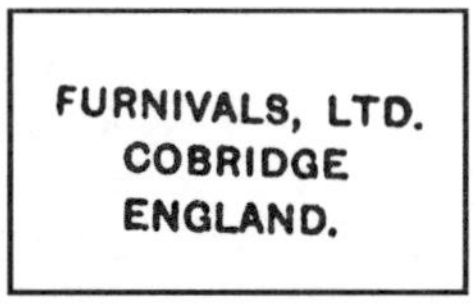

c.1895-1913

c.1910-1913

KAD NO.	GODDEN NO.	MARK	
B1014A	-	**FURNIVALS LTD.**	Printed marks of differing design. Pattern name often included, c.1895-1913 - Mark may also include an impressed anchor mark.

Typical (1913) Marks Include:

B1015 1656
B1016 1657
B1017 1658
B1018 1658A

Godden notes a style change in 1913 to "FURNIVALS" (1913) and "LTD". Further, *Coysh* gives an interesting insight into the reissuing of older patterns. Refer to the pattern "Quail" in Vol. I, p. 293 and "Bombay" in Vol. II, p. 57.

*The company was acquired by Barratts of Staffordshire, Ltd. in 1967 and was closed in December 1968. Furnivals Ltd. was subsequently purchased by Enoch Wedgwood, Tunstall, Ltd. in 1969.

GALLATOWN

Gallatown Potters
See: Robert Heron (& Son)

GARNER

Robert Garner (III)
Church Street,
Longton, Staffordshire, c.1789-1821
Formerly, Robert Garner, II (c.1777-1789)
Subsequently, Elkin, Knight & Elkin (Elkin & Co.) (c.1822-1825)

KAD NO.	GODDEN NO.	MARK	
B1019	-	**GARNER**	Impressed name mark, c.1777-1789.
B1020	1669	**R. G.**	Impressed initial mark, c.1789-1821

For further reading, refer to *F.O.B.*, No. 75, Spring 1992, p. 8; and *Hampson*, No. 99, p. 64 and No. 112, pp. 72-73.

GARRISON

Garrison Pottery
See: Sunderland Pottery

GATER

Gater, Hall & Co.
Furlong Lane Pottery, Burslem (1895-1899)
New Gordon Pottery, Tunstall (c.1899-1907)
Royal Overhouse Pottery (1907-1943)
Burslem, Staffordshire, 1895-1943
Formerly, Thomas Gater & Co. (c.1885-1894)
Subsequently, Barratt's of Staffordshire Ltd. (1943-1987)

KAD NO.	GODDEN NO.	MARK	
B1021	1671	**G. H. & CO.**	Printed initial marks of differing styles, 1895+.

KAD NO.	GODDEN NO.	MARK	
B1022 B1023	1672 -	 	Printed marks, 1914+. - The "CORONA" mark has been noted in Flow Blue (Art Nouveau style) with pattern being named "CORONA". - This mark was continued by Barratt's of Staffordshire Ltd. Refer to *Godden*, p. 58.
B1024	-	**OVERHOUSE**	Printed mark noted on Willow Ware, 1907-1943.

GEDDES

***John Geddes (& Son)**
Verreville Works,
Glasgow, Scotland, c.1806-1813
-Also see: R. Cochran & Co., p. 155

B1025	1674	**JOHN GEDDES VERREVILLE GLASGOW**	Impressed name mark, c.1806-1813.
B1026	-	**JOHN GEDDES VERREVILLE POTTERY GLASGOW**	Printed name mark, c.1806-1813. - This marking has been noted on a piece titled "New York Park Theatre" in a private collection, and is part of the American Historic Series. Refer to *Barber*, p. 83. - Sam Laidacker notes a second pattern in the "Oak & Acorn" Series as "Aqueduct Bridge at Rochester". Refer to the *Standard Catalog of Anglo-American China*. Scranton, PA, 1938, p.58, No. 358. - For additional comments refer to Robert Cochran, et.al. in Appendix B6: Chronology in this Encyclopedia, p. 543.

GELSON

Gelson Bros.
Cobden Works, High Street,
Hanley, Staffordshire, c.1867-1876
Subsequently, Thomas Gelson & Co. (c.1876-1878)

B1027	-	**GELSON BROS.**	Printed marks of differing design, c.1867-1876.
B1028	1675	**GELSON BROS. HANLEY**	
B1029	-		Printed Royal Coat of Arms mark noted on White Ironstone with an additional printed and impressed marking, in a circle, reading "Patented 9 November 1869". - Refer to *Stoltzfus/Snyder*, p. 51.

KAD NO.	GODDEN NO.	MARK	
B1030	1727	**G. BROS**	*Godden,* p. 278, notes that this printed mark may possibly belong to Gelson Bros. and not to John & Robert Godwin. See KAD B 1054.

GIBSON

Gibson & Sons (Ltd.)
Albany Pottery & Harvey Potteries,
Burslem, Staffordshire c.1884-1965+
Formerly, Gibson, Sudlow (& Co.) (c.1880-1884)
Subsequently, Manufactory transferred to the Howard Pottery Co. Ltd. (1965-1986)

KAD NO.	GODDEN NO.	MARK	
B1031	1679		Printed name mark, "HARVEY POTTERY", c.1904-1909.
B1032	1679A	**G. & S. LTD. B.**	Printed marks of differing design. Pattern name often included, 1884-1904. - "LTD." included from 1905.
B1033	1679B	**G. & S. LTD.**	
B1034	-	**GIBSON & SONS LTD.**	Printed name mark from c.1905.

Typical Marks Include:

B1035 1680
B1036 1681
B1037 1682
B1038 1683

c.1909+

c.1912+

c.1930+

c.1930+

For further reading, refer to *Edwards, Basalt*, p. 157; *Godden*, p. 271; *Godden, Jewitt*, pp. 74-75; *Godden, Collecting Lustreware,* p. 115; *Cushion, British Ceramic Marks*, p. 115; and *Niblett*, p. 51.

GILDEA

***James Gildea**
Dale Hall Works,
Burslem, Staffordshire, c.1885-1887
Formerly, Gildea, Walker & Co. (c.1881-1885)
Subsequently, Keeling & Co. (Ltd.) (1887-1936)

KAD NO.	GODDEN NO.	MARK	
B1039	1696		Printed initial mark, c.1885-1888. - Pattern name "Leaf" noted above "Staple Trade-mark". See KAD B189.

For further reading, refer to *Henrywood*, p. 172.

GILDEA

KAD NO.	GODDEN NO.	MARK	
			***Gildean, Walker (& Co.)** **Dale Hall Works,** **Burslem, Staffordshire, c.1881-1885** **Formerly, Bates, Gildea & Walker (c.1878-1881)** **Subsequently, James Gildea (c.1885-1887)**
B1040	1697	**G. & W.**	Printed marks of differing design, c.1881-1885.
B1041	1697A	**G. W. & CO.**	
B1042	1698		"Staple Trade-mark" incorporated into various marks, c.1881-1885. See KAD B189.
B1043	1699	**GILDEA & WALKER** **<u>2</u>** **84**	Impressed name mark with month and year numbers, c.1881-1885.

For further reading, refer to *Godden, Jewitt*, "Dale Hall", pp. 14-16; *Edwards, Basalt*, p. 172; and *Godden, British Porcelain*, p. 128.

GIMSON

Wallis Gimson & Co.
Lane Delph Pottery,
Fenton, Staffordshire, c.1883-1890
Formerly, Pratt & Simpson (c.1878-1883)

KAD NO.	GODDEN NO.	MARK	
B1044	1701	**WALLIS GIMSON & CO.**	Printed name mark. Title and Beehive below with name of firm noted, c.1883-1890. - Beehive mark style continued from predecessor Pratt & Simpson. See KAD B1940. - Printed marks noted on American/Canadian views often include printed series and title names. Examples noted have been marked, "Manufactured for Primavesi & Sons, Swansea." -*Coysh*, Vol. I, p. 290; *Godden*, Mark nos. 3167 and 3168, and *FOB*, Spring 1991, No. 71/5 by Ken Williams notes a marking of "F. PRIMAVESI & SONS, SWANSEA, NEWPORT & LONDON." This is an unrecorded combination. Variation, without "**LONDON**" but with [**MON**] noted.

For further reading, refer to *Collard, Potters View*, pp. 84-86.

GINDER

Samuel Ginder & Co.
Victoria Works, Lane Delph,
Fenton, Staffordshire, c.1811-1843

KAD NO.	GODDEN NO.	MARK	
B1045	1702		Printed marks of differing design. Pattern name often included, c.1811-1843.

For further reading, refer to *P. Williams, Staffordshire*, Vol. 2, p. 29.

GLAMORGAN

Glamorgan Pottery
See: Baker, Bevans & Irwin as well as Appendix B6: Chronology

GLOBE

KAD NO.	GODDEN NO.	MARK
B1046	1710	
B1047	1711	
B1048	1713	
B1049	1715	

Globe Pottery Co. Ltd.
Waterloo Road, Cobridge, Staffordshire
and at Shelton (from 1932), c.1914-1932+
Acquired by Ridgways and operated from The (Bedford Works), Shelton, Hanley (1932+)

History *(Cushion, British Ceramic Marks,* p. 162, notes the following chronology):

Purchased Ridgways and moved to Shelton	1932
Globe & Ridgways owned by Lawleys Ltd.	1948
Lawley Group taken over by S. Pearson & Son	1952
Renamed Allied English Potteries	1964
Allied English Potteries acquire Doulton	1971
Renamed Royal Doulton Tableware Ltd.	1973
Renamed Royal Doulton Ltd.	1984

Typical Printed Marks, c.1914-1954, Include:

1914+

1917+

c.1930-1932

1947-1954

Mark Dates:

Cobridge marking	c.1914-1934
Cobridge marking + LTD	c.1917+
Shelton marking	c.1932+
"CO. LTD." marking	c.1954+

- Globe made chinaware for Woolworth's (USA) and pieces were so marked.

For further reading, refer to *Gaston*, Vol. 2, Mark No. 126 "FIBRE", c.1917; and *Godden*, p.276 for additional marks.

GODDARD

***Goddard & Burgess, *Importers,* USA**
c.1870s-c.1885
Also see: Burgess & Goddard

B1050 - **GODDARD & BURGESS**

Printed name mark, c.1870s-c.1885.

For further reading, refer to *Ewins*, pp. 107-127.

GODWIN

***Benjamin E. Godwin**
Cobridge, Staffordshire, c.1834-1841
Formerly, T. & B. Godwin, c.1809-1834

B1051 1722 **B. G.**

Printed marks of differing design. Pattern name often included, c.1834-1841.
- Many child's toy services bear the mark "B. G."

B1052 1723

For further reading, refer to *Little*, pp. 65-66; and *Godden*, wherein he notes that another Benjamin Godwin was potting at Cobridge, c.1795-1811.

GODWIN

KAD NO.	GODDEN NO.	MARK

***John & Robert Godwin**
Lincoln Pottery (Sneyd Green),
Cobridge, Staffordshire, c.1834-1867
Subsequently, Bates & Bennett (1868-1895)

KAD NO.	GODDEN NO.	MARK	
B1053	1726	**J. & R. G.**	Printed marks of differing design. Pattern name often included, c.1834-1867.
B1054	1727	**G. BROS.**	

Typical Marks Include:

B1055 -
B1056 -
B1057 -

- KAD B1054 "G. BROS." may have been used by Gelson Bros. (See KAD B1030)

For further reading, refer to *Godden, Collecting Lustreware*, p. 116.

GODWIN

***Godwin, Rowley & Co.**
Market Place,
Burslem, Staffordshire, c.1828-1831

KAD NO.	GODDEN NO.	MARK	
B1058	1728	**G. R. & CO.**	Printed marks of differing design. Pattern name often included, c.1828-1831. - Marking may include "STAFFORDSHIRE STONE CHINA". - The "& CO." notes *Edwards, Basalt*, p.182, was a John Johnson. *Godden* notes that initials "G. R. & CO." may have been used by Godwin, Rathbone & Co. of the Market Place address, c.1822.

GODWIN

***Thomas Godwin**
Canal Works, Navigation Road,
Burslem, Staffordshire, c.1834-1854
Formerly, T. & R. Godwin (c.1809-1834)

KAD NO.	GODDEN NO.	MARK	
B1059	1729	**T. G.**	Printed marks of differing design. Pattern name often included, c.1834-1854.
B1060	-	**T. GODWIN**	- The initials "T. G." may also refer to Thomas Green. See KAD B1107.

Typical Marks Include:

B1061 1731
B1062 -
B1063 -
B1064 -

KAD NO.	GODDEN NO.	MARK	
B1065	1730	**THOS GODWIN BURSLEM STONE CHINA**	Printed or impressed marks employing full name, c.1834-1854.
B1066	1730A	**THOS GODWIN NEW WHARF**	
B1067	1730B	**OPAQUE CHINA T. GODWIN WHARF**	Printed marks of various designs noted on Historic/Canadian views, often including series and title name, c.1834-1854.

Typical Marks Include:

B1068 -
B1069 -

- Also see Thomas Green regarding mark KAD B1070, as well as Cork, Edge & Malkin for a continuation of "Indian Series" mark, see p. 163.
- It is worthy to note that another potter with the exact name was at Cobridge, c.1794-1814.

For further reading, refer to *Snyder, Historic Staffordshire*, p. 58; *Snyder, Romantic Staffordshire,* pp. 61-63; and the magazine *Antiques*, Vol. XVIII, No. 3, 1993 (New York City), pp. 91-94 for an article by Ellouise Baker Larsen titled "Thomas Godwin, Staffordshire Potter."

GODWIN

***Thomas & Benjamin Godwin**
New Wharf and New Basin Potteries,
Burslem, Staffordshire, c.1809-1834

KAD NO.	GODDEN NO.	MARK	
B1070	1732	**T. & B. G.**	Printed marks of differing design. Pattern name often included, c.1809-1834.
B1071	1733	**T. B. G.**	- Printed marks with full name may occur. - Note marking "STONE CHINA" and "SEMI CHINA".

Typical Marks Include:

B1072 -
B1073 -
B1074 -

KAD NO.	GODDEN NO.	MARK	
B1075	1734	**T. & B. GODWIN NEW WHARF**	Impressed name mark, c.1809-1834. - See *True Blue*, p. 147, No. G4
B1076	-	**T. & B. GODWIN NEW WHARFE**	Impressed name mark, c.1820s noted by *Coysh*, Vol. I, p. 381, "View of London".

- Godwin's copper plates evidently came into the possession of Cork & Edge, c.1846-1860 and their predecessors, Cork, Edge & Malkin, c.1860-1871 (see: "Indian Scenery" series). Also refer to p. 181 for added comments.

KAD NO.	GODDEN NO.	MARK

- *Laidacker, American Antique Collector*, Vol. 2, June - Aug. 1940, No. 1, p. 6, notes the scene "Utica" from the "American Historic" series with the printed mark "T. GODWIN, WHARF" as well as the impressed mark "EDGE, MALKIN & CO."

For further reading, refer to *Little*, pp. 65-66.

GOODFELLOW

Thomas Goodfellow
Phoenix Works, High Street,
Tunstall, Staffordshire, 1828-1859(60)
Formerly, Goodfellow & Bathwell (1822-1828)
Subsequently, Bridgwood & Clarke (1859-1864)

B1077 - **T. G.** Printed marks of differing design. Pattern name often included, c.1828-1859.

B1078 1738 **T. GOODFELLOW**

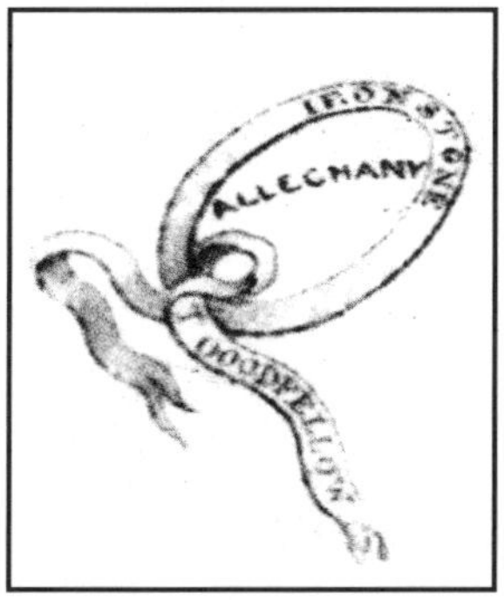

B1079 - - Importer's mark on Flow Blue pattern "Singan" noted: "Imported By/Babcock Brothers/Evansville/Indiana."

B1080 - Printed or impressed Anchor mark noted on White Ironstone, c.1850s.

B1081 - - Impressed marking, as above, which may accompany printed mark. Refer to *White Ironstone Notes*, Vol. 4, No. 1, Summer 1997, p. 7, for "Primary Shape".
- Details of the sale at Thomas Goodfellow's manufactory following his death in c.1860 are reported by *Hampson*, No. 65, pp. 35-36.

For further reading, refer to *Wetherbee*, p. 56; *FOB*, Bulletin No. 55, April 1987, p. 5 for an article by Harold Blakey titled "Thomas Goodfellow"; *NCS Newsletter* No. 65, March 1987, pp. 33-35 for an article by Rodney Hampson titled "Thomas Goodfellow, Tunstall". Both journals note many blue patterns.

GOODWIN

B1082 -

***John Goodwin (Longton)**
Crown Pottery,
Longton, Staffordshire, c.1841-1851 and
Seacombe Pottery, Liverpool, c.1852-1864

Printed marks of differing design. Pattern name often included, c.1841-1851.
- Printed mark "LONGTON" may appear with the potter's name.
- *Snyder, Romantic Staffordshire*, p. 64, notes a Blue & White classic scene titled

KAD NO.	GODDEN NO.	MARK	
B1083	-	J. G.	Printed name or initial mark "J. G." , 1841-1851 noted by *Godden*, p. 724.
B1084	-	G. C.	Impressed initial mark "G. C." or printed name "GOODWIN & CO." has been noted by Coysh, Hampson and others. However, the period of usage is speculative, c.1841-1864.
B1085	-		Printed marks of differing design, pattern name often included, c. 1841-1851. - See comments under mark, KAD B1098 and B1105. "Versailles" possibly by John Goodwin, illustrating a backmark "J. G.", c.1841-1851.
B1086	-		For further reading, refer to *Hampson,* No. 116, pp. 77-78; *Hampson, Churchill*, p. 119; and *Snyder, Fascinating Flow Blue,* p. 2.

GOODWIN

***John Goodwin (Seacombe)**
Seacombe Pottery, "Wallasey", Liverpool, c.1852-1864
History:

John Goodwin	c.1852-1857
Thomas Orton Goodwin (& Bros.)	c.1857-1860
Thomas Orton Goodwin	c.1861-1864

KAD NO.	GODDEN NO.	MARK	
B1087	-	J. GOODWIN	Printed mark with bird above, marked "SEACOMBE POTTERY, LIVERPOOL". Registry date, June 30, 1846 which was used in Longton and continued by Seacombe Pottery, c.1852-1864. - Also recorded in Flow Blue and Mulberry.
B1088	-	JOHN GOODWIN	
B1089	-	GOODWIN & CO.	
B1090	-		Printed mark has been noted by *Coysh*, Vol. I, p. 384, as found in "Views of London Series" with the pattern reported as "Royal Exchange", c.1852-1864.
B1091	-		Printed mark, c. 1852-1864. - *White Ironstone Notes*, Vol. 3, No. 3, Winter 1997 (Dec. 1996), p. 12 shows a Royal Coat of Arms with the additional marking "The Queens Royal Ironstone" and the printed name J. Goodwin. Also refer to *White Ironstone Notes,* Vol. 3, No. 4, Spring 1997, p. 11. For further reading, refer to *Hampson*, No. 116, pp. 77-78

GOODWIN

Goodwins & Bullock
Dresden Works,
Longton, c.1857-1859
- at High Street, (c.1858)
Subsequently, Mason, Holt & Co. (1857-1884)

KAD NO.	GODDEN NO.	MARK	
B1092	1740		Printed Staffordshire Knot mark, c.1857-1859.

For further reading, refer to *Hampson*, No. 117, p. 79.

GOODWINS

Goodwins & Ellis
Flint Street, Lane End,
Longton, c.1840

KAD NO.	GODDEN NO.	MARK	
B1093	1740A	**G. & E.***	Printed marks of differing design. Pattern name often included, c.1840.
B1094	-	**GOODWINS & ELLIS**	
B1905	-		*Printed initials "G. & E." have been noted on "Metropolitan Scenery" Series, c.1840.

GOODWINS

***Goodwins & Harris**
Crown Works, Lane End,
Longton, c.1832-1837

KAD NO.	GODDEN NO.	MARK	
B1096	-	**G. & H.**	Printed or impressed marks of differing design. Pattern name often included, c.1832-1837.
B1097	-	**G. H. & G.**	
B1098	1743	**GOODWINS & HARRIS**	Coysh notes markings other than Goodwins & Harris found on "Metropolitan Scenery" Series. The impressed mark "G. C." (Goodwin & Co.) (see KAD B1084) as well as an impressed Staffordshire Knot has been noted.

For further reading, refer to *Coysh*, Vol. I, p. 246 and Vol. II, p. 24, 135; *Coysh & Stefano, Ceramic Landscapes*; *Hampson*, No. 116, pp. 77-78; and *Penny Plain*, p. 99, No. 248.

GOODWINS

***Goodwins, Bridgwood & Co.**
High Street, Lane End,
Longton, c.1827-1829

KAD NO.	GODDEN NO.	MARK	
B1099	-	**GOODWINS, BRIDGWOOD & CO.**	*Hampson*, No. 116, p. 78 notes the existence of the pattern "Chinese Scenery" with a printed mark "GOODWINS, BRIDGWOOD & CO." However, no dates are noted, c. 1827-1829.

KAD NO.	GODDEN NO.	MARK

GOODWINS

***Goodwins, Bridgwood & Harris**
Crown Works, Lane End,
Longton, c.1829-1832

B1100 | 1739 | **G. B. H.** — Printed marks of differing design. Pattern name often included, c.1829-1832.

B1101 | - |

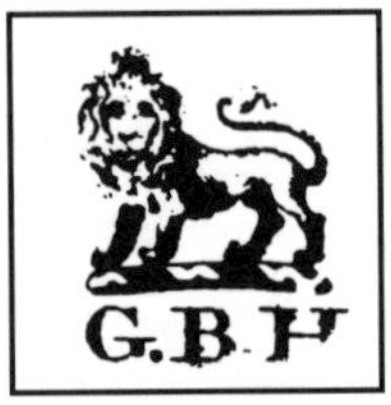

Printed mark noted on a rare jug commemorating the "Death of George IV", c.1829-1832.
- Godden notes that when two additional partners are noted, the "S" is used with the Goodwin surname. Refer to *Godden, Collecting Lustreware*, p. 117.

GOODWINS

***Goodwins, Bridgwood & Orton**
Ford Works, High Street,
Land End, Longton, c.1827-1829

B1102 | 1739A | **G. B. O.** — Printed marks of differing design. Pattern name often included, c.1827-1829

B1103 | 1739B | **G. B. & O.**

GORDON

George Gordon
Bankfoot Pottery, Prestonpans, Gordons Pottery (c.1795-1812)
Hyndford (Hilcote) Pottery at Morisons Haven (1812-1833)
Scotland, 1795-1833

B1104 | 1745 | **GORDON** — Impressed name mark, 1795-1833.

B1105 | 1746 | **G. G.** — Printed initial mark incorporating pattern name, early nineteenth century.
- Marked pieces as noted above are rare. *Coysh*, Vol. I, p. 139, notes an additional marking of "OPAQUE CHINA" appearing on a floral cartouche showing a dove holding an olive branch.
- See comments under Goodwins & Harris and John Goodwin (Longton), p. 211 & 209.

For further reading, refer to *McVeigh,* pp. 79-93.

GREEN

Green & Clay
Stafford Street,
Longton, Staffordshire, c.1888-1891
Formerly, Green, Clark & Clay (c.1882-1887)

B1106 | 1783 |

Printed or impressed mark noted on Tea Leaf/Copper Lustre, c.1888-1891.
- This Compass Point mark occurs on tiles made by The Campbell Tile Co. (Ltd.) from c.1882.

For further reading, refer to *Tea Leaf Readings*, Nov. 1986, p. 6.

GREEN

John & William Green (& Co.)
See: Don Pottery

GREEN

Thomas Green
Minerva Works,
Fenton, Staffordshire, c.1848-1858(59)
Formerly, Green & Richards (c.1833-1848)
Subsequently, M. Green & Co. (c.1859-1876)

KAD NO.	GODDEN NO.	MARK	
B1107	-	**T. G.***	Printed marks of differing design. Pattern name often included, c.1848-1859.
B1108	1794	**T. GREEN FENTON POTTERIES**	**Coysh* notes that the initial "T. G." may also refer to Thomas Godwin. (See KAD B1061).
B1109	1795		Printed crowned Staffordshire Knot, c.1848-1859.
B1061	-		Printed mark noted on Historic American/Canadian views, often including printed series and title names, c.1848-1859. For further reading, refer to *Godden, Collecting Lustreware*, p. 118; *Mankowitz & Haggar*, p.100 for the "Green Family"; and *Snyder, Historic Staffordshire*, pp. 58-59.

GREEN

T. A. & S. Green (Porcelain Manufacturer)
Minerva Works,
Fenton, Staffordshire, c.1876-1889
Formerly, M. Green & Co. (1859-1876)
Subsequently, Crown Staffordshire Porcelain Co. (1890-1943)

KAD NO.	GODDEN NO.	MARK	
B1110	1796		Printed Staffordshire Knot and Crown mark, c.1876-1889. - Other markings occur with initials "T. A. & S. G." For further reading, refer to, *Godden, Illustrated Encyclopedia,* p. 381.

GREEN

T. G. Green & Co. (Ltd.)
Church Gresley,
Near Burton-on-Trent, Derbyshire, c.1864-1967(+)
- Company acquired by P. H. Freeman in 1968
- Acquired by Clover Leaf Group in 1987
Formerly, Henry Wileman (1856-1864)

KAD NO.	GODDEN NO.	MARK	
B1111	-	**T. GREEN & CO.**	
B1112	-	**GRESLEY**	
B1113	-	**T. G. G. & CO. LTD.**	
B1114	-	**GREEN & CO. LTD.**	Printed mark with pattern name often included, c.1864+. - Church mark first registered in 1888. - Marked "ENGLAND" c.1892+. - "LTD" dates from the mid 1880s.
B1115	-	**T. GREEN & CO. LTD.**	

KAD NO.	GODDEN NO.	MARK	

Typical Marks Include:

B1116 1797
B1117 1798

c.1888-late 1930s **c.1892-c.1940**

For further reading, refer to *NCSJ*, Vol. 11, 1994, pp. 95-153 for an article by Ronald Brown titled "Potteries of Derbyshire"; *Godden*, p. 290 for additional marks; Paul Atterbury; *Cornish Ware, Kitchen and Domestic Pottery by T. G. Green of Church Gresley, Derbyshire*. England, Richard Dennis, 1996.

GRIFFITHS

***Griffiths, Beardmore & Birks**
Flint Street,
Lane End, Longton, c.1829-1831
Formerly, Beardmore & Griffiths (c.1823-1828)
Subsequently, Beardmore & Birks (c.1832-1842)

KAD NO.	GODDEN NO.	MARK	
B1118	1821	**G. B. & B.**	Printed mark of pre-Victorian Coat of Arms with the wording "STAFFORDSHIRE IRONSTONE CHINA". Pattern name often included, c.1829-1831.

For further reading, refer to *Hampson*, No. 119, pp. 79-80.

GRIMWADE

Grimwade Bros.
Winton Pottery, Hanley,
and Elgins Pottery, Stoke, Staffordshire, c.1886-1900
Subsequently, Grimwade's Ltd. (c.1900-1978)

B1119 1823

Printed name mark. Pattern name often included, c.1886-1900.

GRIMWADE

Grimwades Ltd.
Winton Pottery,
Hanley, Crown Potteries, Upper Hanley,
Elgins Pottery, Stoke, Staffordshire, c.1900-1978
Subsequently, part of The Howard Group (1978-1979+)

KAD NO.	GODDEN NO.	MARK	
B1119A	-	**GRIMWADES DAVENPORT MADE IN ENGLAND**	Printed mark with pattern name, c.1915+. - Grimwade Bros. acquired some Davenport copper in 1887 with the closing of the pottery. See KAD B707 for exact mark as reissued by Grimwades Ltd., c.1915+.

KAD NO.	GODDEN NO.	MARK
B1120	1824	
B1121	1825	
B1122	1826	
B1123	1827	
B1124	1828	
B1125	1832	

Typical Marks Include:

c.1900+

c.1906+

c.1906+

c.1906+

c.1911+

c.1930+

- See *Gaston*, Vol. II, Mark 58, where the term "SEMI PORCELAIN" is noted.
- In 1900 Grimwades Ltd. acquired the pottery of J. Plant & Co., and for a short time used a common backstamp. See KAD B1120.
- In 1913 Grimwades acquired the Rubian Art Pottery Co. (1906-1933).
- Also see the Rubian Art Pottery Ltd. (1906-1933).
- Grimwade also traded under the name "Atlas Bone China" from 1930-1936.

For additional marks and reading, refer to *Godden*, p. 293; *Batkin*, pp. 78-82, 88; and *Niblett*, p. 51.

GRINDLEY

W. H. Grindley & Co. (Ltd.)
Newfield Pottery (c.1880-1891)
Woodland Pottery (1891+)
Tunstall, Staffordshire, c.1880-1960
Acquired by Alfred Clough Ltd. (1960+) and in 1988 company reverted to trading under the name of Grindley

B1126 1842

Printed name mark, 1880-1914.
- "TUNSTALL" pre 1891.
- "ENGLAND" after 1891.
- "LTD" added in 1925.

B1127 1842A

"TRADE MARK" added, 1880-1914. See KAD B1126.

B1128 1842B **SEMI PORCELAIN**

As above, but marked "SEMI PORCELAIN" in place of pattern name, 1880-1914.

B1129 -

Printed Royal Coat of Arms noted on Tea Leaf/Copper Lustre and White Ironstone, c.1891-1925.

KAD NO. | **GODDEN NO.** | **MARK**

B1130 | - |

Printed mark in brown, c.1898+.
- Registration No. 326058, Nov. 8, 1898 noted on the pattern "Festoon" (in slate blue).

B1131 | 1843 |

Printed name mark, 1914-1925.

B1132 | - | **TRADE MARK**

As above, but with term "TRADE MARK" added, 1914-1925.
- Initial marking "F. B." noted, which may designated pattern as Flow Blue.

B1133 | 1850 |

Printed marks of differing design. Pattern name often included, c.1936-1954.

B1134 | - | **GRINDLEY MADE IN ENGLAND**

This author's collection has a Flow Blue piece in the Melbourne pattern with a green backstamp marked "GRINDLEY/MADE IN/ENGLAND" similar to mark KAD B1133, c. 1920+.

For additional marks and reading, refer to *Godden*, p. 294; *Hampson, Churchill*, p. 40; and William Van Buskirk's two research papers: *William Harry Grindley and His Flow Blue Dishes.* August 1996, and *William H. Grindley, Part II*. June 1997 both published by the Flow Blue International Collectors Club, Inc.

GROSE

Grose & Co.
Church Street,
Stoke-upon-Trent, Staffordshire, late 1860s

B1135 | - |

Printed Royal Coat of Arms mark recorded on a White Ironstone jug, late 1860s.

GROVE

Grove & Stark
Palissy Works,
Longton, Staffordshire, c.1875-1885
Formerly, Grove, Stark & Co. (1870-1875)
Subsequently, F. W. Grove (c.1885-1889)

B1136 | 1855 | **G. & S.**

Printed marks of differing design. Pattern name often included, c.1875-1885.

B1137 | 1855A | **GROVE & STARK LONGTON**

Printed or impressed name mark, written in full, c.1875-1885.

KAD NO.	GODDEN NO.	MARK	
B1138	1856		Impressed monogram initials "G. S." within an oval, noted on plates registered in the early 1880s.

For further reading, refer to *Godden, Jewitt*, p. 106; and *Godden, Collecting Lustreware*, p. 118.

HACKWOOD

***Hackwood & Co.**
Eastwood,
Hanley, Staffordshire, c.1807-1827
Subsequently, William Hackwood (c.1827-1843)

B1139	1863	**HACKWOOD & CO.**	Impressed name mark, c.1807-1827.
B1140	1864	**H. & CO.**	Impressed initial mark, c.1807-1827. There is the possibility that Hackwood & Co. and Hackwood, Dimmock & Co. were one and the same company, c.1807-1827.

For further reading, refer to *Coysh*, Vol. I, p. 169; *Edwards, Basalt,* p. 162; *Godden, British Porcelain, p. 385; Godden, Collecting Lustreware*, p. 119; and *Little*, p. 67.

HACKWOOD

***Hackwood & Keeling**
Market Street,
Hanley, Staffordshire, c.1835-1836

B1141	1865		Printed initials "H. & K." often noted on marks of differing design. Pattern name often included, c.1835-1836.

For further reading, refer to Audrey M. Dudson. *Dudson, A Family of Potters Since 1800*. Dudson Publications. England, 1985. p. 7; and *Edwards, Basalt*, p. 162.

HACKWOOD
Hackwood, Dimmock & Co.
See: Hackwood & Co.

HACKWOOD

***William Hackwood**
Eastwood,
Hanley, Staffordshire, c.1827-1843

-Godden notes several potters working in Shelton and/or Hanley by this name. The difficulty in attributing the name "Hackwood" or the initial "H" with any certainty is quite evident.

B1142 B1143	1860 1861	**HACKWOOD** **H**	Printed marks of differing design. Pattern name often included, c.1827-1843 and continued on to 1855. - The name Hackwood and the initial "H" was continued by various family potteries. See *Godden*, p. 299.
B1144	1862		Printed mark noted with impressed name "Hackwood", c.1830-1840. - Note additional marking "IRONSTONE CHINA".

KAD NO.	GODDEN NO.	MARK	
B1145	1866	**W. H. HACKWOOD**	"Distinguishing initials "W. H." found on several printed marks of differing design, c. 1827-1843.
B1146	1867	**HACKWOOD**	- A cup and saucer in the Godden collection has this form of printed initial mark as well as the impressed name "HACKWOOD", c.1827-1843.
B1147	-		Printed mark noted with printed initial marking "W. H." and title, noting the possible existence of a series titled "ARABIAN SKETCHES", c.1827-1843.
B1148	3199	**R** **HACKWOOD**	Printed mark noted on White and Printed wares, c.1827-1843. -*Little*, p. 90 notes the appearance of this mark on White and Printed wares as either printed or impressed - found on a Willow pattern under William Ratcliffe. Refer to Cockson & Harding (c.1856-1863).
B612	978	**C. & H. LATE HACKWOOD**	For further reading, photos and marks, refer to *Snyder,* Vol. II, p. 74 for pattern "Acadia"; *Coysh*, Vol. I, p. 168; *Godden*, pp. 299-300; *Godden, British Porcelain*, p. 386; *Godden, Collecting Lustreware*, pp. 118-199; *Little*, p. 90; and *Edwards, Basalt*, p. 162.

HACKWOOD

***William Hackwood & Son**
New Hall Pottery,
Shelton, Staffordshire, c.1843-1855

B1150	1868		Printed marks of differing design. Pattern name often included, c.1843-1855. - William Hackwood died in 1849 and his son Thomas continued until 1855. For further reading, refer to *Godden, Collecting Lustreware*, p. 118.

HALES

Hales, Hancock & Co. Ltd.
London, 1918-1921, *Retailers*
-See Hales, Hancock & Goodwin Ltd.

B1151	-	**H. H. & CO.**	Printed mark noted by *P. Williams, Flow Blue*, Vol. I, p. 80, with the addition of the Doulton Mark No. 1328 as noted by *Godden*, p. 213. - Evidently, as retailers, the firm of Hales, Hancock & Co. Ltd. ordered a set of "Watteau" through Doulton with the company's initials "H. H. & CO." printed on the back. This was a practice not uncommon with retail agents both in the domestic and export market. Not only did this firm act as retailers, but they were agents and wholesalers as well.

HALES

Hales, Hancock & Goodwin Ltd.
London (Agents, Retailers, Wholesalers, etc.), c.1922-1960
Formerly, Hales, Hancock & Co. Ltd. (c.1918-1921)
Subsequently, Hale Brothers (c.1960s)

B1152	1879	**H. H. & G. LTD.**	Printed mark of differing design, c.1922-1960. - See *Godden, British Porcelain*, p. 388.

HALL

KAD NO.	GODDEN NO.	MARK	
			***John & Ralph Hall** **Sytch Pottery, Burslem, Staffordshire (c.1802-1814),** **Swann Pottery, Tunstall, Staffordshire (c.1811-1822), c.1802-1822** **Subsequently, Ralph Hall (Son/& Co.) (c.1822-1849)**
B1153	1886	**HALL**	Printed or impressed marks of differing design. The mark "I. HALL" may have overlapped the partnership period, c.1802-1822.

For further reading, refer to *Edwards, Basalt*, p. 162; and *Godden*, p. 302.

HALL

***John Hall (& Sons)**
Sytch Pottery,
Burslem, Staffordshire, c.1814-1832
Formerly, John & Ralph Hall, Sytch Pottery (c.1802-1814)
Subsequently, Barker, Sutton & Till (c.1834-1846)

KAD NO.	GODDEN NO.	MARK	
B1154	1885	**I. HALL**	Printed or impressed marks of differing design, c.1814-1822.
B1155	1887	**I. (J.) HALL & SONS**	- "& SONS" c.1822-1832 - Additional mark "I. HALL" found on "Oriental Series" pattern "Mohamedan Mosque and Tomb".

Typical Marks Include:

B1156 -
B1157 -
B1158 -

For further reading, refer to *Snyder, Romantic Staffordshire*, pp. 65-67.

HALL

***Ralph Hall (& Son or & Co.)**
Swann Pottery,
Tunstall, Staffordshire, c.1822-1849
("& Son" 1836-1841) ("& Co." c.1841-1849)
Formerly, John & Ralph Hall (c.1811-1822)
Subsequently, Podmore, Walker & Co.

KAD NO.	GODDEN NO.	MARK	
B1159	1888	**R. HALL**	Printed marks of differing design. Pattern name often included, c.1822-1836.
B1160	-	**R. HALL'S**	

Typical Marks Include:

B1161 -
B1162 -
B1163 -
B1164 -

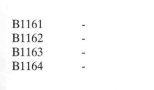

KAD NO.	GODDEN NO.	MARK	
B1165	1889	**R. HALL & SON**	Printed marks of differing design. Pattern name often included. American/Canadian views may also include series title, c.1836-1841.

Typical Marks Include:

B1166 -
B1167 -

B1168	1890	**R. HALL & CO.**	Printed marks of differing design. Pattern name often included, c.1841-1849.
B1169	1890A	**R. H. & CO.**	

Typical Marks Include:

B1170 -
B1171 -
B1172 -

-*Godden, British Porcelain*, pp. 388-389 notes the marking "R. HALL/LONGPORT"

For further reading, refer to *Coysh & Stefano*; *Snyder, Historic Staffordshire*, pp. 59-60; and *Snyder, Romantic Staffordshire*, pp. 67-69.

HALLAM

Hallam & Johnson (or Hallam, Johnson Co.)
Mt. Pleasant Works,
High Street, Longton, Staffordshire, c.1878-1880
Formerly, Hallam, Johnson & Taylor (c.1878)
Subsequently, Hallam & Day (c.1880-1883)

B1173	-	**H. & J.**	Printed initial marks, c.1878-1880.
B1174	-	**H. J. CO.**	

For further reading, refer to, *Godden, British Porcelain*, p. 390; and *P. Williams, Flow Blue*, Vol. I, p. 138.

HAMILTON

Robert Hamilton
"Big Works",
Stoke, Staffordshire, c.1810-1825
Formerly, Thomas Wolfe & Hamilton (c.1800-1810)

B1175	1901	**HAMILTON STOKE**	Printed or impressed name mark. Pattern name often included, c.1810-1825.

KAD NO.	GODDEN NO.	MARK	
B1176	-	**CALAIS**	

For further reading, refer to, *NCSJ*, Vol. 7, 1989, pp. 1-14 for an article by Trevor Markin; *NCS Newsletter*, No. 95, Sept. 1994, pp. 9-13; *NCS Newsletter*, No. 96, Dec. 1994 for information about blue and white wares made on the Continent in imitation of English wares; *NCS Newsletter*, No. 97, Mar. 1995, p. 3, for an article by Trevor Markin titled "Involvement with the Delftfield Co."; *Godden, British Porcelain*, pp. 390-391; and *FOB Bulletin*, No. 97, Autumn 1997, p. 10 for another article by Trevor Markin titled "Robert Hamilton Saucer."

HAMMERSLEY

Hammersley & Asbury
Prince of Wales Pottery, Sutherland Road (Now known as Sydney Works), Longton, Staffordshire, c.1870-1875
Formerly, Hammersley & Freeman, c.1864-1870
Subsequently, Edward Asbury Co. (c.1875-1925)

KAD NO.	GODDEN NO.	MARK	
B1177	1909	**H. & A.**	Printed marks of differing design. Pattern name often included, c.1870-1875.
B1178	1910		- Pieces marked without the Prince of Wales Crest may well have been used by other potters; i.e., Hulse & Adderley (c.1869-1875), see pp. 242-243. - Prince of Wales Crest in a Garter marked "H. & A." noted.
B1179	-	**ASBURY LONGTON**	Printed name mark and locale, 1870-1875.

For further reading, refer to *Godden, British Porcelain*, pp. 96-97; and *Hampson*, No. 234, p.148.

HAMMERSLEY

Ralph Hammersley (& Son(s))
Church Bank Pottery, Tunstall (c.1860-1883)
Overhouse Pottery, Burslem, (c.1884-1905)
Black Works, Tunstall (c.1885-1888), Staffordshire c.1860-1905

KAD NO.	GODDEN NO.	MARK	
B1180	1912	**R. H.**	Printed marks of differing design. Pattern name often included, c.1860-1883. - Garter mark noted on a registered pattern in 1868.
B1181	1913		
B1182	1914	**R. H. & S.**	Printed marks of differing design. Pattern name often included, c.1884-1905.
B1183	1915	**R. H. & S. LTD.***	- Godden notes that records do not confirm this or whether a "LTD" company was ever formed. It is noted, however, that "& SON" is from c.1884-1905.
B1184	-	**R. H. & SONS**	
B1185	-		Printed mark with Registry diamond noted on American Historic View with title "Gem", registered in 1868. - *Hill*, No. 289 notes the pattern "Venture" with a backstamp "RB". Possibly this is an engraver's error, as the same pattern is noted in *P. Williams, Staffordshire* and *Flow Blue*, Vol. III, p. 190 marked "R. H.".

KAD NO.	GODDEN NO.	MARK	

Godden, p. 730, Mark No. 4486 notes a marking "R. H. & S./LTD." for which he notes "I have been unable to fit these initials to a limited company."

For further reading, refer to, *Godden, British Porcelain*, pp. 393-395; and *Snyder, Historic Staffordshire*, p. 60.

HAMPSON

Hampson & Broadhurst
Green Dock Works,
Longton, Staffordshire, c.1849-1854
Formerly, Hampson, Broadhurst & Broadhurst (c.1847-1848)
Subsequently, Hamspon Bros. (c.1854-1870)

B1186 1919 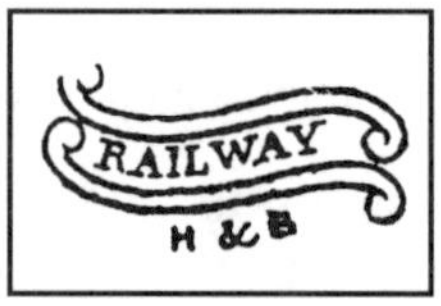

Printed initial marks of differing design. Pattern name often included, c.1849-1854.

For further reading, refer to *Hampson*, No. 128, pp. 83-84; *Godden, Collecting Lustreware,* p. 120; and *Hampson, Churchill*, pp. 17-19.

HANCOCK

Hancock & Wittingham
Bridge Works,
Stoke, Staffordshire, c.1873-1879
Formerly, Hancock, Wittingham & Co. (c.1863-1872)
Subsequently, B. & S. Hancock (c.1879-1882)

B1187	1937	**H. & W.**	Printed marks of differing design. Pattern name often included, c.1873-1879.

B1188 

- KAD B1188 is an illustration of this mark.

HANCOCK

Sampson Hancock (& Sons) (Ltd.)
Tunstall, (1858-1870), Bridge Street Works,
Stoke-on-Trent, (1871-1891),
Gordon Works,
Stoke-on-Trent (1892-1920),
Corona Pottery,
Hanley (1920-1935)
Staffordshire, c.1858-1937
- &"& Sons" dates from 1892-1935
- From 1935-1937 name of firm changes to
S. Hancock & Sons (Potters) Ltd., Corona Pottery, Hanley

B1189	1927	**S. H.**	Printed marks of differing design. Pattern name often included, c.1858-1891.
B1190	1928	**S. HANCOCK**	Printed marks with name in full, 1858+.
B1191	1929	**S. H. & S.**	Printed marks of differing design. Pattern name often included, c.1892-1935.
B1192	1929A	**S. H. & SONS**	

KAD NO.	GODDEN NO.	MARK	
B1193	1930		
B1194	1931		
B1195	1932		
B1196	1933		

Typical Marks Include:

c.1900-1906 **c.1906-1912**

B1197 1934 **THE "DUCHESS" CHINA**

Printed circular mark registered in 1911.

B1198 1935

Printed mark noted from 1912-1937.
- "Doris" pattern, in Flow Blue, is noted with this marking. Sampson Hancock (& Sons) (Ltd.), Stoke is not to be confused with the porcelain manufacturer, Sampson Hancock of King Street, Derby, 1866-1935+. Refer to John Twitchett & Betty Bailey, *Royal Crown Derby*, Clarkson N. Pottery, Inc. New York, NY, 1976. pp. 13-19.

For further reading, refer to *Godden, British Porcelain*, p. 396; and *Godden, Jewitt*, p. 133.

HANCOCK

Hancock & Wittingham & Co.
Swanbank Pottery,
Burslem, Staffordshire, c.1863-1872
Subsequently, Hancock & Wittingham (c.1873-1879)

B1199 1936 **H. W. & CO.**

Printed (initial) marks of differing design. Pattern name often included, c.1863-1872.

HANDLEY

James & William Handley
Kilncroft Works, Chapel Street, Burslem (1822-1824) and
High Street, Hanley, (1819-1828), Staffordshire, c.1819-1828
Subsequently, Marsh & Co. (c.1828-1829)

B1200 - **J. & W. HANDLEY**

Impressed name mark. Printed pattern names often included, c.1819-1828.
- Additional marking "STONE CHINA" noted.

For further reading, refer to *Godden, British Porcelain*, pp. 397-398; *Coysh*, Vol. 1, p. 170; *Godden, Collecting Lustreware*, p. 380; and *NCSJ*, Vol. 11, 1994, pp. 47-77 for an article by Molly Hosking titled "James & William Handley, Staffordshire Potters, 1819-1828."

HANLEY

Hanley Porcelain Co.
Burton Place,
Hanley, Staffordshire, c.1892-1898
Formerly, Thomas Bevington (c.1872-1891)
Subsequently, Hanley China Co. (c.1899-1901)

B1201 1940

Printed Staffordshire Rope Knot mark with initials "H. P. CO.", c.1892-1898.
- "ENGLAND" added after 1891.

For further reading, refer to *Godden, British Porcelain*, pp. 398-399.

HARDING

Harding & Cockson
Globe Pottery,
Cobridge, Staffordshire, c.1834-1863
Subsequently, Charles Cockson (c.1863-1866)
- These are china manufacturers.

KAD NO.	GODDEN NO.	MARK	
B1202	-	**HARDING & COCKSON**	Impressed mark noted only on a *bone china body plate* of heavy quality, c.1834-1863.
B1203	1946	**COBRIDGE H&C**	Printed marks of differing design. Pattern name often included, c.1834-1863. - The town name of Cobridge occurs on most marks.
B1204	1947		Harding died in 1856 and his sons continued the partnership with Cockson until January 1863. - Also refer to Cockson & Harding, p. 156. - The firm is listed here even though only china wares were produced. The firm Harding & Cockson, Cobridge, is not to be confused with a like name of Cockson & Harding, Hanley, who were china manufacturers from c.1856-1863. Refer to *Godden, British Porcelain*, pp. 245, 400.

HARDING

Joseph Harding
Furlong Works, Navigation Road,
Burslem, Staffordshire, c.1850-1851
Formerly, Bowers & Lloyd (c.1846-1850)
Subsequently, William & George Harding (c.1851-1854)

B1205	1949	**J. HARDING**	Printed marks of differing design. Pattern name often included, c.1850-1851.

HARDING

W. & G. Harding
Hadderidge Pottery & Furlong Works, Navigation Road,
Burslem, Staffordshire, c.1851-1854
Formerly, Thomas Phillips & Son (c.1845-1846)
Subsequently, Heath & Blackhurst (c.1859-1877)

B1206	-	**W. & G. HARDING**	Printed marks of differing design. Pattern name often included, c.1851-1854.
B1207	-		For further reading, refer to *P. Williams, Staffordshire*, Vol. I, p. 405.

HARDING

W. & J. Harding
New Hall Works,
Shelton, Hanley, Staffordshire, c.1863-1872
Formerly, Cockson & Harding (c.1856-1863)

B1208	1950	**W. & J. H.**	Printed (initial) marks of differing design. Pattern name often included, c.1863-1872.

HARLEY

KAD NO.	GODDEN NO.	MARK	
			Thomas Harley **High Street, Lane End** **and Longton, Staffordshire, c.1805-1808** **Formerly in partnership with J. G. & W. Weston (1799-1801)** **Subsequently, Harley & Seckerson (c.1808-1825)**
B1209	1951	**HARLEY**	Impressed name marks, c.1805-1808.
B1210	1952	**T. HARLEY***	
B1211	-	**TOM HARLEY**	Printed or written marks, in script letters, c.1805-1808.
B1212	1952A	**T. HARLEY** **LANE END**	
B1213	1952B	**MANUFACTURED BY** **T. HARLEY** **LANE END**	

*Printed wares may also bear the name "T. HARLEY". See *Godden*, p. 311 for comments; and *Hampson*, No. 130, pp. 84-85.

HARRIS

John Harris
(No information available. Refer to *P. Williams, Staffordshire*, Vol. II, p. 243)

B1214	-	**I. HARRIS**	Impressed name mark.

HARRISON

George Harrison (& Co.)
Lane Delph,
Fenton, Staffordshire, c.1790-1804

B1215	1958	**G. HARRISON**	Impressed name mark , c.1790-1795. - "& CO." from c.1795-1804.

For further reading, refer to *Little*, p. 68; *Coysh*, Vol. I, p. 171; *Godden*, p. 313; *Hampson*, No. 57, p. 57 and No. 131, p. 86 for comments on Thomas Brough and John Harrison, respectively. Also refer to *NCS Newsletter*, No. 107, Sept. 1997, pp. 28-30 for an article by Roger Pomfret titled "George Harrison of Lane Delph: A Manufacturer in Search of a Collector."

HARTLEY

Hartley, Greens & Co.
See: Leeds Pottery

HARVEY

KAD NO.	GODDEN NO.	MARK	

C. & W. K. Harvey (also Charles Harvey & Sons)

History:

Charles Harvey	Church Street Works (Works No. 119), Lane End	1799-1802
Charles Harvey	Stafford Street Works, Charles Street Lane End	1799-1805
Charles Harvey & Sons	Stafford Street Works, Charles Street Lane End	1805-1818
Charles & John Harvey	Stafford Street Works, Charles Street Lane End	1820-1827
C. & W. K. Harvey	Flint Street Works	1835-1843
C. & W. K. Harvey	Stafford Street Works, Charles Street Lane End	1842-1852

B1216 | 1967 | **HARVEY** | Impressed name mark, c.1835-1852.

B1217 | - | Impressed mark "HARVEY" and "OPAQUE CHINA" with printed pattern name and initial "H", c.1835-1852.

- See *P. Williams, Staffordshire*, Vol. I, p. 250 and Vol. 2, pp. 195-196.

B1218 | 1968 | **C. & W. K. H.** | Printed marks of differing design. Pattern name often included, , c.1835-1852.

B1219 | 1969 | Printed Royal Coat of Arms mark with initials and name, c.1835-1852.
- Note marking "REAL CHINA IRONSTONE".

B1220 | -

B1221 | -

B1222 | - | Printed mark found on "Cities and Town" Series, c.1835-1852.
-see *Coysh*, Vol. I, p. 85.
- A rather full history of the Harvey family of potters, merchants, bankers, etc. is documented in *Hampson*, pp. 86-89.
- *Hampson*, No. 134, p. 89 further notes that from c.1827-1831 John Hulme & Sons occupied the Charles Street Pottery. *Godden, Collecting Lustreware*, p. 121 notes a partnership of Harvey & Bailey or Harvey, Bailey & Co. from c.1832-1835.

For further reading, refer to *Godden, British Porcelain, pp. 401-402; NCSJ*, Vol. 4, 1980-1981, pp. 157-173, for an article by Allison Quinn titled "The Harvey Family of Potters at Lane End;" and *Snyder, Romantic Staffordshire*, pp. 70-71.

HAWLEY

KAD NO.	GODDEN NO.	MARK	
			Hawley Bros. (Ltd.) **Northfield Pottery,** **Rotherham, Yorkshire, c.1868-1903** **Formerly, W. & G. Hawley or Hawley Bros. (c.1855-1868)** **Subsequently, Northfield Hawley Pottery Co. Ltd. (1903-1916(19)**
B1223	1978	**H. B.**	Printed mark comprising the initials "H. B." (intertwined) within a shield, noted below the date 1790, c.1868-1898.
B1224	1978A	**HAWLEY BROS.**	Printed full name may also occur. - "LTD." dates from 1897.
B1225	1979		Printed "Trade-mark" registered in 1898. Mark was continued by the Northfield Hawley Pottery Co. Ltd. to c.1919. - This partnership name should not be confused with the Hawley Bros., a Bristol potter, c.1899-1901, as noted by *Henrywood*, p. 35.

For further reading, refer to *Lawrence*, and *Cameron*, p. 159.

HAWLEY

John Hawley (& Co.)
Longton (1827-1841); Fenton (1843-1893)
Staffordshire, c.1827-1893

History:

John Hulme & Sons	Stafford Street Works, Charles Street, Lane End	1827-1831
John Hawley	Stafford Street Works, Charles Street, Lane End	1832-1841
John Hawley & Co.	King Street (Foley), Fenton	1843-1893

KAD NO.	GODDEN NO.	MARK	
B1226	1980	**HAWLEY**	Impressed name mark, c.1832-1893.
B1227	-		Printed name mark, "J. HAWLEY" containing distinguishing details from printed marks of differing design. Pattern name often included, c.1832-1862. - Note marking "OPAQUE PEARL".
B1228	1981	**HAWLEY & CO.**	Printed name mark, c.1862-1893. - "& CO." added to style.

For further reading, refer to, *Snyder, Romantic Staffordshire*, p. 72; *Godden*, p. 720; *Godden, British Porcelain,* p. 403, for date corrections; and *Hampson*, No. 134, p. 89.

HAWTHORN

KAD NO.	GODDEN NO.	MARK	

John Hawthorn
Cobridge, Staffordshire, c.1879-1880

B1229 - 

Printed Royal Coat of Arms mark, c.1879-1880.

B1230 - **JOHN HAWTHORN COBRIDGE**

Printed name mark, 1879-1880.
- *Wetherbee, White Ironstone*, p. 148, fig. 15-22, notes "Hawthorn's Fern" Shape, registered March 19, 1879 at Cobridge.*
- *Godden, British Porcelain*, pp. 403, 775 notes other locations and dates for a **John Hawthorn:**

John Hawthorn (& John Nast),	Regent St. Works, Burslem	c.1851
John Hawthorn,	Regent St. Works, Burslem	c.1851-1854
John Hawthorn	Albert St. Works, Burslem	c.1860-1867
John Hawthorn & Son	Albert St. Works, Burslem	c.1868-1882
John Hawthorn	Burslem	c.1880-1882
John Hawthorn	Burslem	c.1882-1887

*Godden notes a similar potter, John Hawthorn<u>e</u>, with the last initial (E) working in Burslem from 1854-1869. See *Godden, British Porcelain*, p. 793, under William Wood & Co.

HEATH

Heath, Blackhurst & Co. (or Heath & Blackhurst)
Hadderidge Pottery,
Burslem, Staffordshire, 1859-1877
Formerly, W. & G. Harding
Subsequently, Blackhurst & Tunnicliffe (1879-1879)

B1230A 1997 **H. & B.**

Printed initial marks. Pattern name often included, 1859-1877.

B1230B 1998 **H. B. & CO.**

B1230C 1999 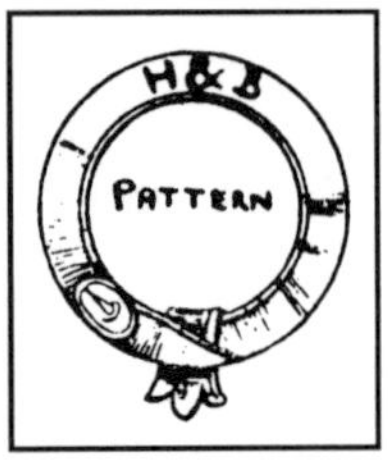

- *Godden* notes an earlier potter, Harvey, Bailey & Co., Lane End, (1832-1835) with the initials "H. B. & CO.", p. 313.

For further reading, refer to *Godden, Collecting Lustreware*, p. 121, *Hampson*, No. 17, p. 12; and *P. Williams, Staffordshire*, Vol. III, p. 66.

HEATH

***John Heath**
Sytch Pottery,
Burslem, Staffordshire, c.1810-1822

B1231 1989 **HEATH**

Impressed name mark, c.1810-1822.

HEATH

KAD NO.	GODDEN NO.	MARK	
			***J. (Joshua) Heath** **Albion Street Works, c.1796** **Hanley, Staffordshire, c.1770-1800**
B1232	1991	**I. H.**	Impressed mark either with initials "I. H." or name "HEATH" noted, c.1770-1800.
B1233	1992	**HEATH**	- Marks were previously attributed to John Heath of Derby.

HEATH

***Joseph Heath**
High Street,
Tunstall, Staffordshire, c.1845-1853

B1234	-	**J. H.**	Printed or impressed marks of differing design. Pattern name often included, c.1845-1853.
B1235	1993	**J. HEATH**	Printed or impressed name mark, 1845-1853.
B1235A	-		Printed Royal Coat of Arms mark may be accompanied by impressed name mark, 1845-1853. - *P. Williams, Staffordshire*, Vol. I, p. 353 and Vol. II, p. 612 notes an additional back stamp marking for "Ontario Lake Scenery" marked "B. & D.", as does Serry Wood, *English Staffordshire China Classics*, Vol. 1, Century House, Watkins Glenn, NY, 1959, p. 41 and *Little*, pp. 70-71.

Typical Marks Include:

B1237 -
B1238 -
B1239 -
B1240 -

- "Heath's Flower", a brush stroke pattern in both Flow Blue and Mulberry, is noted in this author's collection with the impressed marking "J. HEATH."
- Godden notes that "other J (John or Joseph) Heath's were working in Staffordshire in the first half of the nineteenth century."
- Coysh notes the pattern "Geneva" with the printed marking "J. HEATH" along with an impressed marking "HEATH" (See example: KAD B1237).
- See *Arman Quarterly*, Vol. 1, April-May 1997, No. 2, p. 12, for the importer's mark "H. P. Merrill, Sandusky, Ohio."

HEATH

***Joseph Heath & Co.**
Newfield Pottery,
Tunstall, Staffordshire, c.1828-1841(42)
Formerly, Child & Clive (c.1811-1818(28)

B1241	1994	**J. HEATH & CO.**	Printed marks of differing design. Pattern name often included, 1828-1841(42).

KAD NO.	GODDEN NO.	MARK	
B1242	1994A	**J. H. & CO.**	- Note that the initial "J" may also appear as an "I".
B1243	1994B	**I. H. & CO.**	

Typical Marks Include:
Printed marks of differing design found on Historic American/Canadian views, with pattern name often included, c.1828-1841(42).

B1244 -
B1245 -
B1246 -
B1247 -

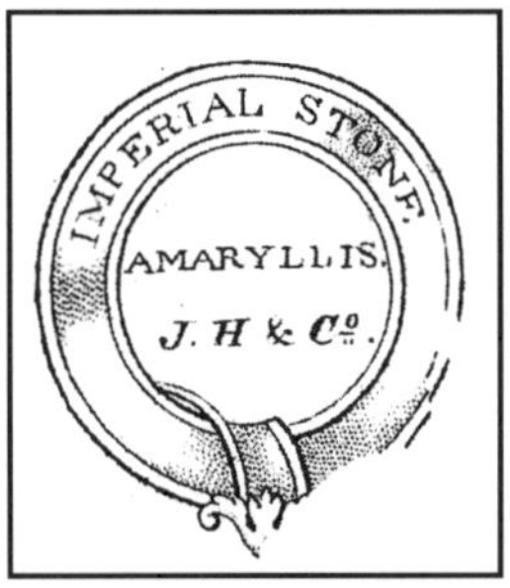

B1248 -

-The Impressed Potters' Wheel (three propellers) found on many pieces is often attributed to Joseph Heath & Co. when no initials or other markings are present, c.1828-1841(42).

For further reading, refer to *FOB*, No. 90, Winter 1995/1996, p. 8; and *P. Williams, Staffordshire*, Vol. III, p. 3.

HEATH

***Thomas Heath**
Hadderidge, Burslem and High Street, Tunstall,
Staffordshire, c.1812-1835

B1249	1995	**T. HEATH**	Printed or impressed marks of differing design. Pattern name often included, c.1812-1835.
B1250	1996	**T. HEATH BURSLEM**	- *Coysh* Vol. 1, p. 344, notes a pattern title "SPORTING SUBJECTS" with a printed mark "T. HEATH" which also has an impressed marking "DAVENPORT".

B1251 -

- *Godden, British Porcelain*, p. 404 notes the existence of a Thomas Heath, Lane End, Longton, c.1835.

For further reading, refer to, *Hampson*, No. 136, p. 90; *Little*, p. 70; and *Snyder, Romantic Staffordshire*, pp. 72-78.

HEATHCOTE

KAD NO.	GODDEN NO.	MARK	
			Charles Heathcote & Co. **Near Market Street Lane End,** **Longton, Staffordshire, 1819-1823**
B1252	2002	**C. HEATHCOTE & CO.**	Printed or impressed marks of differing design. Pattern name often included, 1819-1823. - The "C" in Charles may or may not appear in name markings.
B1253	-		- The "Prince of Wales" Three Feather Crest mark occurs on several pieces. - *Hampson*, No. 137, pp. 90-91, notes other printed or impressed markings; e.g., "HEATHCOTE" and "HEATHCOTE & CO." - See *True Blue* (9), p. 148.

HENSHALL

Henshall & Co.
Longport, Burslem, Staffordshire, c.1792-1800
"This firm consisted of several different partnerships. The style was Henshall & Clowes in the last decade of the eighteenth century [c.1790-1795]. But Clowes appears to have left soon after 1800 and the firm became **Henshall, Williamson(s) & Co. [c.1800-1830]** for a period. However, since the only recorded mark is Henshall & Co., which in any case is rare, it is virtually impossible to attribute pieces to a particular partnership." *Coysh*, Vol. I, p. 173 and Vol. II, 'Saxon Hall', p. 178 (fractional dating July 1824), and refer to *Little*, pp. 71-72.

KAD NO.	GODDEN NO.	MARK	
B1254	2005	**HENSHALL & CO.**	Impressed name mark, c.1792-1800.
B1255	-		Printed marks of differing design. Pattern name often included, c.1792-1800.
B1256	-		
B1257	-		Printed mark illustrated in *Snyder, Romantic Staffordshire*, p. 78, for the pattern "Gothic Scenery". Note the marking "HENSHALL & WILLIAMSON", c.1820s. - Printed marks would date from c.1810-1830. However, many authors date these marks from the 1820s. For further reading, refer to *Coysh*, Vol. I, p. 149; and *Snyder, Romantic Staffordshire*, pp. 61-62; *Mankowitz & Haggar*, p. 56.

HERCULANEUM

KAD NO.	GODDEN NO.	MARK

Herculaneum Pottery
In Toxteth on the banks of the Merses,
Liverpool, Lancashire, c.1793-1841
History:

Richard Abbey & Graham	c.1793-1796
Worthington, Humble & Holland or S. Worthington & Co.	c.1796-1806
Worthington, Humble & Holland & Partners - Pottery referred to as Herculaneum China & Earthenware Manufactory	c.1806-1833
Case, Mort & Co.	c.1833-1836
Mort & Simpson	c.1836-1841

Typical Impressed or Printed Marks, c.1796-1833:

B1258 2007 **HERCULANEUM**

B1259 2008
B1260 2009
B1261 2010

B1262 2997A **HERCULENEUM POTTERY** Impressed name mark, c.1822; subsequent to those above.

Other Selected Marks Include:

B1263 -
B1264 -
B1265 -

B1266 2011
B1267 2012

Printed or impressed "Liver Bird" marks. Pattern name often included, c.1833-1836.

For further reading, refer to, A. Smith, *The Illustrated Guide to Liverpool Herculaneum Pottery*. Barrie & Jenkins. London, 1970; *Made In Liverpool, Exhibit Catalog 1993* by the Walker Art Gallery, Liverpool. Also refer to *Godden, Collecting Lustreware*, pp. 276-179; *Godden, British Porcelain*, pp. 407-410; *Edwards, Basalt,*, pp. 175-176; *Williams-Wood, English Transfer*, pp. 192-196 "Herculaneum Pottery"; and *Penny Plain,* pp. 99, 103, Nos. 246 and 249 respectively.

HERON

Robert Heron (& Son)
Fife or Gallatown Pottery,
Sinclairtown, Kirkcaldy, Scotland, c.1837-1929
Formerly, J. Methven (Fife Pottery) (1830-1837)

B1268 2014 **R. H. & S.** Printed initial mark. Pattern name often included, c.1837-1929.

KAD NO. | **GODDEN NO.** | **MARK**

B1269 - **R. H. & S. (CO.)**

B1270 2015

Printed name mark, 1920-1929. Other marks include the firm name.

- In 1930 Bovey Tracy Pottery Co. purchased the rights to Wemyss Ware Designs.

- Due to recent research, a revised chronology for Robert Heron, et. al. has evolved:

Pottery built by Andrew & Archibald Gray	1730
Fife Pottery built	1817
Pottery bankrupt. Estate bought by John Methven	1826
Fife Pottery goes to Mary & Robert Heron (John's daughter and son-in-law)	1837
Their son was Robert Methven Heron	
Robert Methven goes to Europe, brings back Karol Nekola, who becomes principal painter of Wemyss Ware	1880
Robert Methven Heron dies	1906
Pottery closes	1930

For further history, marks and chronology refer to Peter Davis & Robert Rankine, *Wemyss Ware*, Scottish Academic Press, Edinburgh & London, 1986, pp. 38-41; and *Cameron*, p. 126 "Fife Pottery".

HICKS

Hicks & Meigh
Hill Street, (c.1803-1822)
Broad Street, (c.1812-1822)
Shelton, Staffordshire (c.1803-1822)
Subsequently, Hicks, Meigh & Johnson (1822-1835)*

B1271 2019 **HICKS & MEIGH** Printed or impressed marks with name in full, c.1803-1822.

B1272 - **HICKS, MEIGH & CO.**

B1273 - **HICKS & CO.**

B1274 2020

Printed Royal Coat of Arms mark, c.1803-1822.
- Note marking "STONE CHINA".
- Refer to *Godden, Mason's*, pp. 313-321 as well as *Godden, Staffordshire*, pp. 250-260 for an understanding of this firm's high grade production of Ironstone or Stone China in the style of Mason's Ironstone. Also refer to the article by Philip Miller "Hicks, Meigh and their Contemporaries", pp. 263-273 in the *English Ceramic Circle Transactions*, Vol. 14, Part 3, 1992.
*Hicks, Meigh & Johnson (1822-1835) was acquired by Ridgway, Morley, Wear & Co. and their successors. *Godden, British Porcelain*, pp. 411-413, notes an earlier partnership of Hicks & Boon at Shelton (c.1803-1804).

HICKS

Hicks, Meigh & Johnson
Broad Street & Hill Street Works,
Shelton, Staffordshire, c.1822-1835
Formerly, Hicks & Meigh (c.1803-1822)
Subsequently, Ridgway, Morley, Wear & Co. (1835-1842)

KAD NO.	GODDEN NO.	MARK	
			- *Godden, Staffordshire*, p. 350 notes that in 1835 Ridgway, Morley, Wear & Co. acquired, at auction, the above factory and its valuable assets; i.e. molds, copper plates, etc. (Also see Ridgway & Morley and other partnerships).
B1275	2021	**H. M. J.**	Printed marks of differing design. Pattern name often included, c.1822-1835.
B1276	2021A	**H. M. & J.**	- Note that the initial "J" may also appear as an "I".

B1277 -

- Godden notes that the firm's title for the years 1822-1827 was "Hicks, Meigh & Co." or "Hicks & Son." See *Godden, Staffordshire*, p. 250 and *Godden, British Porcelain*, pp. 412-413.

B1278 2022

Printed Royal Arms mark, c.1822-1835.
- Variations are noted with the pattern name or numbers below. Refer to KAD B1274 for a variation.

B1279 2023

Printed mark, c.1822-1835. This mark may have been used earlier by Hicks & Meigh.

B1280 2024

"Printed mark, c.1822-1830. This device occurs on the name and dated mark following, KAD B1281.

B1281 2025

"This mark may not have been used. The copper plate from which this was taken was found by the late Alfred Meigh on the premises. It is interesting as it includes the Crown and Laurel Wreath device which occurs on wares without any wording", mark KAD B1280.

"Messrs. Hicks, Meigh & Johnson produced a fine range of 'Stone China' (Ironstone) in the Mason's tradition. This is normally unattributed as the marks have not previously been published."

For further reading, refer to *Godden, Illustrated Encyclopedia,* pp. 323-324.

HILDITCH

KAD NO. | GODDEN NO. | MARK

Hilditch & Son(s) (& Co.) (or Hilditch Sons & Co.)
Church Street Works, Lane End,
Longton, Staffordshire, 1822-1836
Formerly, Hilditch & Martin (c.1815-1822)
Subsequently, Hilditch & Hopwood (c.1832-1859)*

B1282 2027

Printed initial marks, c.1822-1832(36).

B1283 2028

- Although "& CO." was added to the firm name in 1832, the initials "H. & S." did not change and continued until 1836.
*In c.1832, "Hopwood" entered into a partnership with Hilditch in a "second" pottery site on Church Street. A new marking "H. & H." appears.

B1284 2029

- For further reading, refer to *Godden, Staffordshire*, Ch. 18, pp. 260-272; *Hampson*, No. 139, pp. 92-95; and *Little*, p. 73. Further, *Godden, Collecting Lustreware*, p. 122 notes an earlier date of 1819. Mr. Godden also notes a listing of various names under which the pottery traded.

HOBSON

Charles Hobson (& Son),
Albert Street Pottery,
Burslem, Staffordshire, c.1865-1883
Formerly, Dix & Tundley (1862-1864)
Subsequently, G. & J. Hobson (c.1883-1901)

B1285 2039 **C. H.** Printed or impressed marks of differing design. Pattern name often included, c.1865-1883.

B1286 2040 **C. H. & S.** - "& S." added c.1873-1875.

B1287 2041

Printed name, in full, on a garter shaped design. Design registered in the name of G. & J. Hobson on April 6, 1883/No. 396576.

For further reading, refer to *Godden, Jewitt*, p. 26.

HOLDCROFT

Holdcroft, Hill & Mellor
High Street Pottery (c.1860-1865)
Queen Street (c.1866-1870),
Burslem, Staffordshire, c.1860-1870

B1288 2049 **H. H. & M.** Printed marks of differing design. Pattern name often included, c.1860-1870.

B1289 2049A

HOLDCROFT

Peter Holdcroft & Co.
Lower Works, Fountain Place,
Burslem, Staffordshire, c.1846-1852

KAD NO.	GODDEN NO.	MARK	
B1290	2048	**P. H. & CO.**	Printed marks of differing design. Pattern name often included, c.1846-1852.
B1291	-	**HOLDCROFT & CO.**	- Impressed mark "PEARL" noted.
B1292	-		
B1293	-		

Typical Marks Include:

HOLLAND

Holland & Green
Stafford Street Works, Charles Street, Lane End
Longton, Staffordshire, c.1853-1882
Formerly, C. & W. K. Harvey (c.1835-1853)
Subsequently, Green, Clarke & Clay (c.1882-1887)

KAD NO.	GODDEN NO.	MARK	
B1294	-	**H. & G.**	Printed or impressed marks of differing design. Pattern name often included, c. 1853-1882.
B1295	2064	**H. & G. LATE HARVEY**	Royal Arms mark noted on pieces as well as impressed name mark, c.1853-1882.
B1296	2065	**HOLLAND & GREEN**	

For further reading, refer to *Hampson*, No. 143, pp. 96-97; and *Stoltzfus/Snyder*, p. 67.

HOLLAND

John Holland
Clayhills Pottery,
Tunstall, Staffordshire, c.1852-1853
Subsequently, Elsmore & Forster (c.1853-1871).

KAD NO.	GODDEN NO.	MARK	
B1297	2060	**J. HOLLAND**	Registration and printed mark dated November 4, 1852.
B1298	-		- The only pattern recorded to-date in Blue & White is "Carrara". See *P. Williams, Staffordshire*, Vol. II, p. 59.

For further reading, refer to *Godden*, p. 330.

HOLLINS

T. & J. Hollins
Keeling Lane, Far Green,
Shelton, (Upper) Hanley, Staffordshire, c.1789-1809
Subsequently, T. J. & R. Hollins (c.1809-1820)

KAD NO.	GODDEN NO.	MARK	
B1299	2068	**T. & J. HOLLINS**	Impressed name marks, c.1789-1809.
B1300	-	**T. & I. HOLLINS**	

For further reading, refer to, *Godden, Collecting Lustreware*, p. 123; *Little*, p. 73; and *Edwards, Basalt*, pp. 180-181.

HOLLINS

Thomas, John & Richard Hollins
Keeling Lane, Far Green,
Shelton, (Upper) Hanley, Staffordshire, c.1809-1820
Formerly, T. & J. Hollins (c.1789-1809)
Subsequently, John & Richard Hollins (1821-1822)

KAD NO.	GODDEN NO.	MARK	
B1301	2069	**T. J. & R. HOLLINS**	Impressed name mark, 1809-1820. - *Godden* notes that dates are open to some slight doubt; and *Little* notes the date continuing to c.1829. - Also see comments in Diana Edwards & Rodney Hampson.*English Dry-Bodied Stoneware*, England. Antique Collectors Club, 1998. pp. 144-146. - T. & J. Hollins and T. J. & R. Hollins are not to be confused with Hollins of Vale Pleasant, 1773-1814

For further reading, refer to *Little*, p. 73, *Coysh*, Vol. I, p. 178; *Edwards, Basalt*, pp. 180-181; and *Godden, Collecting Lustreware*, p. 123.

HOLLINSHEAD

Hollinshead & Kirkham (Ltd.)
Burslem & Tunstall, 1870-1956
-New Wharf Pottery, Burslem (1870-1876)
-Woodlands Pottery off High Street, Tunstall (1876-1890)
-Unicorn Pottery, Amicable Street, Tunstall (1890-1956)
Acquired by Johnson Bros. (Hanley) Ltd. (1956-)

KAD NO.	GODDEN NO.	MARK	
B1302	2071	**H. & K.**	Printed or impressed marks of differing design. Pattern name often included, 1870-1900.
B1303	2072	**H. & K. TUNSTALL**	"TUNSTALL" marking from 1876-1900.
B1304	-	**H. & K. WOODLAND**	"WOODLAND" printed marking, c.1876-1890.
B1305	-	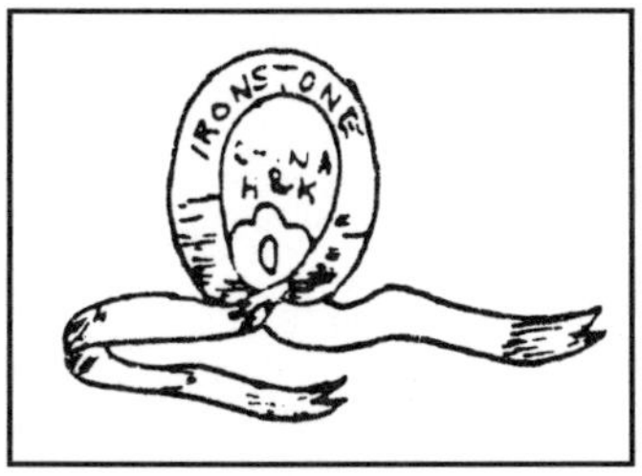	Printed initial mark, c.1890, when Wedgwood & Co.'s. Unicorn Pottery was acquired.
B1306	2072A	**H. & K. LATE WEDGWOOD**	Impressed mark, c. 1890, when Wedgwood & Co.'s. Unicorn Pottery was acquired.

KAD NO.	GODDEN NO.	MARK
B1307	2073	
B1308	2074	
B1309	2075	
B1310	2076	

Various Printed Marks, c.1900-1956, Include:

1900-1924

1924-1956

1933-1942

1954-1956

- *Sussman*, pp. 26-27 notes the purchase of the Unicorn Pottery from Wedgwood & Co. in 1890, and illustrates a White Ironstone pattern "Wheat". She further notes the purchase of the Woodland Pottery from Edmund T. Wood in 1876.

For further reading, refer to *Wetherbee*, p. 79; and *Sussman*, pp. 56-57; and *Jewitt*, p. 142.

HOLMES

Holmes, Stonier & Hollinshead
High Street, Upper Hanley Works,
Hanley, Staffordshire, 1875-1882
Fomerly, Hollinshead & Stonier
Subsequently, Stonier, Hollinshead & Oliver (1882-1891)

B1310A - **H. S. & H.**

Printed initial mark. Pattern name often included, 1875-1882.
- Two registration dates are recorded for this pottery:
August 1, 1877/ No. 312434 and January 15, 1881/No. 360806-7

For further reading, refer to *Jewitt*, p. 80.

HOPE

Hope & Carter
Fountain Place,
Burslem, Staffordshire, c.1862-1880
Formerly, Pinder, Bourne & Hope (c.1851-1860)
Subsequently, G. L. Ashworth & Bros. (c.1880-1968)

B1311 2088 **H. & C.**

Printed marks of differing design. Pattern name often included, 1862-1880.

B1312 -

- Printed Garter marks noted on registered patterns in the firm's name, c.1862-1880.

B1313 -

Printed Royal Coat of Arms marked "STONE CHINA" noted on White Ironstone, c.1862-1880.

For further reading, refer to *Wetherbee*, "Western Shape", p. 109.

HOPKIN

KAD NO.	GODDEN NO.	MARK	
			Hopkin & Vernon **Central Pottery,** **Burslem, Staffordshire, c.1836-1839** **Formerly, Peter Hopkin (or Peter Hopkin & Co.),** **Market Place, Burslem (c.1834-1835)** **Subsequently, Peter Hopkins & Co.** **Market Place, Burslem (c.1839-1943)**
B1314	-	**H. & V.**	Printed marks of differing design. Pattern name often included, c.1836-1839.
B1315	-	**HOPKINS & VERNON BURSLEM**	Impressed (partnership) name mark, c.1836-1839.

For further reading, refer to *Coysh*, Vol. I, p. 180 and *Godden, Jewitt*, p. 27.

HUDDEN

John Thomas Hudden
Stafford Street, (1861-1873)
British Anchor Works (c.1874-1883),
Longton Staffordshire, 1861-1883
Formerly, Wathen & Hudden (1859-1860)
Subsequently, British Anchor Pottery Co. Ltd. (1884-1982)

KAD NO.	GODDEN NO.	MARK	
B1316	2104	**J. T. H.**	Printed marks of differing design. Pattern name often included, c.1861-1883.
B1317	2105	**J. T. HUDDEN**	

- Patterns registered in the 1860s may have a garter shape mark.
-*Hampson*, No. 144, p. 97 notes registration markings for 1865 as a crown above a circle marked "LONGTON".

For further reading, refer to *Hampson*, *Churchill*, pp. 75-76.

HUGHES

***E. Hughes & Co. (China Manufacturer)**
Opal China Works,
Fenton, Staffordshire, 1889-1941*
Retitled, Hughes (Fenton) Ltd. (1940-1953)**
- Acquired by Lawley's Ltd. (1948-1953)
- This company is not to be confused with E. Hughes & Co. of Longton

KAD NO.	GODDEN NO.	MARK	
B1318	2114	**H**	Impressed initial mark, c.1889-1941.
B1319	2115		Impressed or printed initial mark, c.1889-1905. - "ENGLAND" used from 1914. - Company is not to be confused with Elijah Hughes & Co. of Cobridge. (See next entry)

Typical Marks Include:

B1320 2116
B1321 2117
B1322 2118
B1323 2119

1905-1912

1908-1912

1912-1941

1914-1941

KAD NO.	GODDEN NO.	MARK	
			**Godden, British Porcelain*, p. 448, notes the date as 1889. **Niblett*, p. 62, notes an earlier date of 1882 for E. Hughes & Co. **Kathy Niblett's article "The British Pottery Industry, 1942-1952" in *NCSJ*, Vol. 12, 1995, pp. 175-213, notes this period as the Ten Plain Years. Further, *Godden,* p. 295 notes the firm's closure during World Ware II (1941-1945).

HUGHES

***Elijah Hughes & Co.**
Bleak Hill Works,
Cobridge, Staffordshire, c.1853-1867

KAD NO.	GODDEN NO.	MARK	
B1324	-	**E. H.**	Printed initial mark, c.1853-1867.
B1325	2113	**E. HUGHES & CO.**	Impressed name mark, c.1853-1867. - The initial "E. H." may also be attributed to, but not limited to the following: E. Hallen, Burslem, c.1851-1854 Elijah Hodgkinson, Hanley, c.1864-1871

HUGHES

Stephen Hughes & Co. (or Stephen & Elijah Hughes*)
Bleak Hill Works,
Cobridge, Staffordshire, (c.1835-1853)
Subsequently, Elijah Hughes (1853-1867)

KAD NO.	GODDEN NO.	MARK	
B1326	-	**S. HUGHES & CO.**	Impressed name mark, c.1835-1853. **Godden, Collecting Lustreware*, p. 124 notes an alternative trade name, as Stephen & Elijah Hughes (c. 1846-1852). The partnership terminated January 1, 1853.

HUGHES

***Thomas Hughes**
Waterloo Road Works, Burslem (c.1856-1881)
Top Bridge Works, Longport (c.1872-1894)
Burslem & Longport, Staffordshire, c.1855-1894
Subsequently, Thomas Hughes & Son (Ltd.) (c.1895-1957)
- Thomas Hughes acquired Davenports Ltd. in 1887(88)

KAD NO.	GODDEN NO.	MARK	
B1327	2121	**THOMAS HUGHES IRONSTONE CHINA**	Printed or impressed name mark, c.1855-1894. - See *Tea Leaf Readings*, Vol. 18, No. 4, July 1998, p. 23 for an example of this mark in printed version. - "GRANITE CHINA" marking noted in *Godden, Mason's*, p. 261, and used in place of Ironstone on Blue Transferware.
B1327A	-	**THOMAS HUGHES BURSLEM**	
B1328	-		Printed mark noted on Tea Leaf/Copper Lustre, c.1855-1894. - "IMPERIAL/FRENCH CHINA" marking noted. - Refer to *TLCI,* Vol. 15, No. 4, Aug. 1995, p. 15 for notes on the pattern "Grape Octagon" possibly registered in 1851. (This registration date may be in error.)

KAD NO. | **GODDEN NO.** | **MARK**

B1329 - **HUGHES LONGPORT ENGLAND**

Impressed name mark, 1872-1894.
- "ENGLAND" added after 1891.

B1330 -

Impressed, registered shape mark found on White Ironstone, 1855-1879.
- Registered April 17, 1855, No. 99876 in the name of Stephen Hughes & Son.
-*Little*, p. 74 notes that the period 1855/1856 is a possible transition period between Stephen Hughes & Co. (1835-1855) and Thomas Hughes & Co. (1855-1876).
- Further, *Coysh* notes two registration dates for Thomas Hughes, February 24, 1877 and December 19, 1878 - both for Burslem.

For further reading, refer to, *Wetherbee, White Ironstone*, p. 60 as well as *A Second Look at White Ironstone*, p. 70; *Heaivilin*, pp. 80-81; and *Henrywood*, p. 200.

HUGHES

***Thomas Hughes & Son (Ltd.)**
Unicorn Pottery,
Longport, Staffordshire, 1895-1957
Formerly, Thomas Hughes (1855-1894)
Subsequently, A. Wood & Son (Longport) Ltd.
- Unicorn Pottery acquired in 1888 by Thomas Hughes from Davenport Ltd.

B1331 2122 **THOS. HUGHES & SON ENGLAND**

Printed or impressed marks of differing design. Pattern name often included, c.1895+.
"LTD" added after 1910.

B1332 -
B1333 -

Printed Royal Coat of Arms mark noted on White Ironstone, c.1895-1910.

- "ENGLAND" added after 1891.
- Refer to *Heaivilin*, pp. 80-81.

B1334 2123

Printed name mark, 1910-1930.
- Earlier versions exist without "LTD" and "MADE IN ENGLAND".

Typical Marks Include:

B1335 -
B1336 2124
B1337 2125

c.1910-1930*

1930-1935

1935-1957

*This pattern and mark is recorded in Flow Blue by Thomas Hughes & Sons' predecessors (c.1855-1894) and evidently was continued.

KAD NO.	GODDEN NO.	MARK	

HULME

***Hulme & Booth**
Central Pottery, Market Place,
Burslem, Staffordshire, c.1851-1854

B1338	-	**HULME & BOOTH**	Printed name mark, c.1851-1854.

- *Hill* notes a pattern marked "Flora" by Hulme & Booth with a registration diamond mark for Nov. 14, 1851. This date was registered by G. B. Sander of 319 High, Holborn, London, a *retailer* who was very active in the 1840s and 1850s. Godden states the following in a letter to me dated 9/1/94: "He registered patterns or shapes in his own name and used his own name and address marks."
- Also refer to *Wetherbee*, p. 116 for "Grape Octagon".

HULME

***(John) Hulme & Sons**
St. Charles Street, (Harvey Works), Lane End,
Longton, Staffordshire, c.1827-1831
Subsequently, John Hawley (c.1832-1841)

B1339 2128

Printed marks of differing design. Pattern name often included, c.1827-1831.

For further reading, refer to *Hampson*, No. 134, p. 89.

HULME

***Henry Hulme & Sons**
Garfield Pottery,
Burslem, Staffordshire, c.1906-1932
Formerly, Wood & Hulme (c.1882-1905)

B1340	2129	**W. & H. B**	Printed or impressed initials of Wood & Hulme, continued from previous partnership, c.1906-1932.

- Also see Wood & Hulme (KAD B2506).

HULME

***Thomas Hulme**
Central Pottery, Market Place,
Burslem, Staffordshire, c.1860-1861

B1341 -

Impressed name mark, c.1860-1861.
- Mark is illustrated in *Wetherbee*, p. 55.

HULSE

Hulse & Adderley
Daisy Bank Works,
Longton, Staffordshire, c.1869-1874
Subsequently, William A. Adderley (c.1875-1886)

B1342	-	**H. & A.**	Printed initial mark, c.1869-1874.

- One must be careful in attributing through initials alone, as "H. & A." may also be attributed to Hammersley & Asbury (c.1870-1875), see p. 221.

KAD NO.	GODDEN NO.	MARK	
B1343	2132		Trade Mark continued by William (Alsagar) Adderley (& Co.), c.1875-1905 and Adderleys Ltd. c.1906-1926, see pp. 88-89. For further reading, refer to *Hampson*, No. 148, pp. 99-100; and *Godden, British Porcelain,* p.429.

HULSE

Hulse, Nixon & Adderley
Daisy Bank Works,
Longton, Staffordshire, c.1853-1869
Formerly, C. J. Mason (1851-1853)
Subsequently, Hulse & Adderley (c.1869-1874)

KAD NO.	GODDEN NO.	MARK	
B1344	2133	**H. N. & A.**	Printed marks of differing design. Pattern name often included, c.1853-1869. - Patterns were continued by William Alsagar Adderley (& Co.) and marked "W. A. A." SeeKAD B41.
B1345	-		- *P. Williams, Staffordshire*, Vol. II, pp. 516-517, notes additional initials of "H. N. & A." for Hulse, Nixon & Adderley. For further reading, refer to *Hampson*, No. 148, pp. 99-100; and *Godden, British Porcelain,* p.429.

HUMPHREYS

Humphreys Bros.
Park Pottery
Tunstall, Staffordshire, c.1893-1903
Subsequently, J. P. Humphreys (1904-1908)

KAD NO.	GODDEN NO.	MARK	
B1346	-	**H. BROS. TUNSTALL**	Printed name mark, c.1893-1903. - Refer to *Gaston*, Mark no. 62.

INDEO

Indeo Pottery
Bovey Tracey,
Devon, c.1766-1836
- Also see Bovey Tracey Pottery Co.

KAD NO.	GODDEN NO.	MARK	
B1347	2138	**INDEO**	Rare, impressed name mark, c.1766-1836. - Most pieces are unmarked. - The "I" in Indeo may appear or look like a "J". For further reading, refer to *FOB* Journal No. 80, Summer, 1993, pp. 10-11, for an article on the Indeo Pottery by Brian Adams and Howard Mumford; *"English Ceramics Circle Transactions"*, Vol. 8, Part 2, 1972; *Godden, British Porcelain*, pp. 164-167; and *Prattware, English & Scottish Relief Decorated and Underglaze Coloured Earthenware*. by J. & G. Lewis. Dyfed, UK, Shire Publications, 1993, pp. 106-107.

INGLEBY

KAD NO.	GODDEN NO.	MARK	
			Thomas Ingleby & Co. **High Street,** **Tunstall, Staffordshire, c.1834-1835**
B1348	2140	**T. I. & Co.**	Printed marks of differing design. Pattern name often included, c.1834-1835.
B1349	-		

JACKSON

Jackson & Patterson
Sheriff Hill Pottery,
Newcastle-upon-Tyne, Northumberland, 1833-1838
History:
-Bell, pp. 29 and 67 notes the following dates for the Sheriff Hill Pottery:

J. Fordy & Co.	1824-1827
Fordy & Patterson*	1827-1833
Jackson & Patterson	1833-1838
John Ferry	1837
Patterson & Co.	
(George Patterson)*	1837-1844
Patterson & Codling	1844-1847
Thomas Patterson	1844-1851

*Also see Fordy & Patterson and Patterson & Co. See p. 197 & pp. 299-300.

- The names Sheriff Hill and Gateshead Fell were used interchangeably.

B1350	2169	**J. & P.**	Printed initial marks of differing design. Pattern name often included, c.1833-1838.

For further reading, refer to *Godden, Collecting Lustreware*, p. 239.

JACKSON

J. Jackson & Co.
Holmes Pottery,
Rotherham, Yorkshire, c.1870-1887
Formerly, Jackson, Dickinson, Greaves & Shaw (c.1855-1870)
Subsequently, George Shaw & Sons (c.1887-1948)

B1351	2153	**J. J. & CO.**	Printed marks of differing design. Pattern name often included, c.1870-1887.
B1352	2154	**J. & CO.**	- The initials "J. & CO." may refer to this pottery.

For further reading, refer to the *Annual Report of the Yorkshire Philosophical Society*. England, Coultas & Volans, Ltd., 1916, pp. 92-93.

JACKSON

Job & John Jackson
Church Yard Works,
Burslem Potteries, c.1831-1835

KAD NO.	GODDEN NO.	MARK	
B1353	2155	**J. & J. JACKSON**	Printed or impressed marks of differing design. Pattern name often included, c.1831-1835.
B1354	2156	**JACKSKON'S WARRANTED**	
B1355	-	**JACKSON**	

Typical Marks Include:

KAD NO.	GODDEN NO.
B1356	-
B1357	-
B1358	-

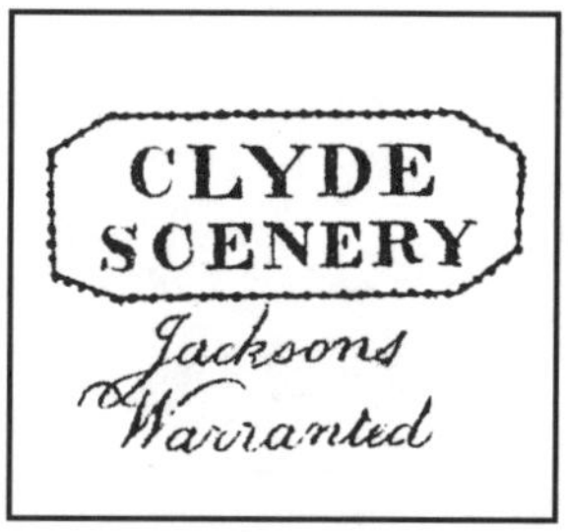

B1359 -

Printed marks with pattern names often included noted on "American/Canadian Historic Staffordshire, c.1831-1835.

For further reading, refer to *Coysh*, Vol. I, p. 197; *Little*, p. 74; *Snyder, Historic Staffordshire*, pp. 62-65; and *Snyder, Romantic Staffordshire*, pp. 81-85.

JAMIESON

James Jamieson & Co.
Bo'ness (Borrowstounness) Pottery,
Scotland, c.1826-1854
Formerly, Shaw & Sons
Subsequently, Redding Coal Co. (c.1854) and sold in 1854 to John Marshall (c.1854-1866)
- Also see John Marshall (& Co.) (Ltd.), see p. 266.

KAD NO.	GODDEN NO.	MARK	
B1360	-	**J. J.**	Printed or impressed marks of differing design. Pattern name often included, c.1826-1854.
B1361	-	**J. J. & CO.**	
B1362	-	**J. J. & CO. B**	- Impressed mark "PORCELAINE OPAQUE' noted a well as potter's impressed (eight petal) propeller mark.
B1363	-	**JAMIESON WARRANTED**	
B1364	-	**I. JAMIESON & CO.**	- An additional marking "B. P. & CO." may relate to the above pottery name in abbreviated form.
B1365	-	**J. JAMIESON BO'NESS**	

- It is interesting to note that *Coysh*, Vol. I, p. 250 cites the pattern "Modern Athens" with three back marks on one piece: an impressed oval mark, a printed mark, and a potter's impressed (eight petal) propeller mark.

For further reading and pattern listings, refer to *Scottish Pottery 14th Historical Review*, 1990-1992, pp. 39-48; *Fleming;* and *McVeigh*, p. 158.

KAD NO.	GODDEN NO.	MARK

JOHN

John King Knight
See: Knight, John King

JOHNSON

Johnson Bros. (Hanley) Ltd.
Hanley Pottery (& other Hanley potteries),
and at Tunstall, (c.1889-1939)
Staffordshire, c.1883-1968
Formerly, J. W. Pankhurst & Co. (c.1850-1882)
Subsequently, acquired by the Wedgwood Group (1968)
History:

Charles Street Works, Hanley	1883-1888
Hanley Pottery, Eastwood Road, Hanley	1888-
Imperial Pottery, Eastwood Road, Hanley	1891-
Alexander Pottery, Tunstall	1889-1939
Trent Sanitary Works, Hanley	1895-
Eastwood Pottery, Hanley	1958-
Company acquired by Wedgwood Group	1968

B1366 2176

Printed or impressed mark "JOHNSON BROS." noted with varying designs. Pattern name often included, c.1883-1913.
- "ENGLAND" added after 1891.
- "LTD." dates from 1896

Typical Marks Include:

B1367 2177
B1368 2178
B1369 2179

c.1900+

c.1913+

c.1913+

-*Mankowitz & Haggar*, pp. 118-119 note the four brothers as Henry, Robert, Alfred and Fred Johnson.

For further reading, refer to *Tea Leaf Readings Educational Supplement*, May 1994; and *Sussman*, p. 75 for "Wheat & Daisy" pattern; and *The Johnson Bros., A Dynasty in Clay* by William Van Buskirk, (paper presented at the Flow Blue International Collector's Club National Convention, Nashville, TN, 1998).

JOHNSON

Samuel Johnson, Ltd.
Hill Pottery,
Burslem, Staffordshire, c.1887-1931

KAD NO.	GODDEN NO.	MARK	
B1370	2186	**S. J.**	Printed marks of differing design. Pattern name often included, c.1887-1931.
B1371	2187	**S. J. B.**	- "LTD." dates from 1912.
B1372	2188	**S. J. LTD.**	

KAD NO.	GODDEN NO.	MARK	
B1373	2189		Printed mark "BRITANNIA POTTERY" from c.1916-1931. - An additional mark is noted in *Gaston*, Book 1, Plate 347, Mark no. 74.

JONES

Jones & Son
Hall Lane,
Hanley, Staffordshire, c.1826-1828(+)

B1374	-	**JONES***	Printed or impressed marks of differing design. Pattern name often included, c.1826-1828(+). * "JONES" mark was also used to identify Elijah Jones (1831-1839). See KAD B1381.
B1375	2223A	**JONES & SON**	
B1376	-		Printed "type" mark on "British History Series", c.1826-1828 noted by *Coysh*, Vol. I, p 169. -*Coysh*, Vol. I, p. 58 shows an impressed mark which possibly indicates a later date, c.1826-1828(+). - The name Jones may also be attributed to other potters of the period; i.e., Elijah Jones.

JONES

Jones & Walley
Villa Pottery,
Cobridge, 1841-1845
Subsequently, Edward Walley (1845-1858)

B1377	2224A	**J. & W.**	Printed initial mark of differing design. Pattern name often included, 1841-1845. - "Marble" type candlesticks with the initials "J. & W." are noted in *Snyder, Fascinating Flow Blue*, p. 18.
B1377A	-	**NEW PORCELAIN JONES & WALLEY**	Impressed name mark, c. 1841-1845. With printed mark, see KAD B2384.

JONES

Albert E. Jones (Longton) Ltd. (from c.1930)
Palissy Pottery (Formerly, Garfield Pottery),
Longton, Staffordshire, c.1905-1946
Formerly, A. E. Jones & A. E. Jones & Co., 1905-1929
Subsequently, Palissy Pottery Ltd. (1946-1989)

B1378	-	**A. JONES**	Printed marks of differing design. Pattern name often included, c.1905-1915.
B1379	2203		Printed or impressed name mark, c.1908-1936. - "Palissy Pottery Ltd." from c.1930.
B1380	2205	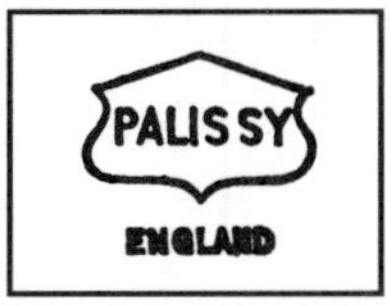	Printed name mark, c.1937-1946. - Also see the Palissy Pottery, Ltd. for a continuation of marks. - Acquired by Royal Worcester (1946-1982) and then Hammersley China until 1988. Pottery was demolished in 1989.

For further reading, refer to *Hampson*, *Churchill*, pp. 35-36.

JONES

KAD NO.	GODDEN NO.	MARK	

Elijah Jones,
Villa Pottery,
Cobridge, Staffordshire, c.1831-1839
Subsequently, Jones & Walley (c.1841-1845) and
eventually, Edward Walley (c.1845-1863)
Other Possible Potters:

Elijah Jones	Hall Lane, Hanley	c.1828-1831
Elijah Jones	Phoenix Works, Shelton	c.1831-1832
Elijah Jones	Mill Street, Shelton	c.1847-1848

- The coincidence that the initials "E. J." belong to the 'Villa Pottery' is that it is the most likely to be the pottery having produced Blue & White wares. It is important to be aware that the name Jones could present a problem in attribution.

KAD NO.	GODDEN NO.	MARK	
B1381	-	**JONES**	Printed or impressed marks of differing design. Pattern name often included, c.1831-1839. *-Jones was also used to identify Jones & Son, Hanley, 1826-1828(+), see KAD B1374.
B1382	2214	**E. J.**	
B1383	-		
B1384	-		*Coysh*, Vol. II, p. 69 "Denors Egypt", notes a "Sphinx" mark similar to C. T. Maling's "Sphinx in Front of Pyramids". For further reading, refer to *Henrywood,* pp. 96-105.

JONES

Frederick Jones (& Co.)
Stafford Street (c.1865-1873),
Chadwick Street (c.1879-1886),
Longton, Staffordshire, 1865-1886
- This firm is also listed as Frederick Jones & Co.
Formerly, Jones & Ellis (c.1863-1864) and Jones & Thompson (c.1879)

KAD NO.	GODDEN NO.	MARK	
B1385	2215	**F. JONES LONGTON**	Printed marks of differing design. Pattern name often included, c.1865-1886.

Typical Printed and Impressed Marks Noted on White Ironstone:

B1386 -
B1387 -
B1388 -

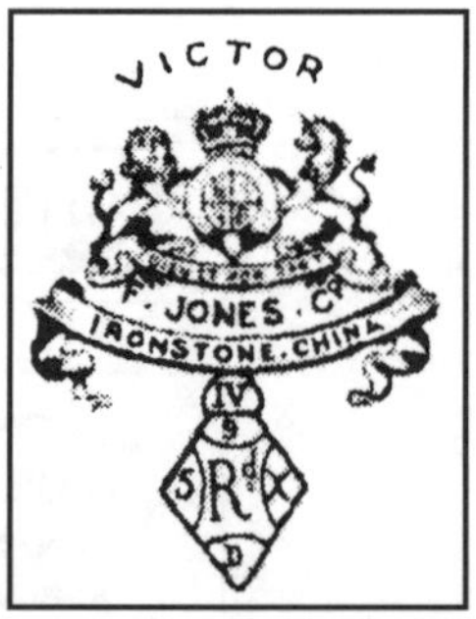

For further reading, refer to *Hampson*, No. 162, p. 104; *Wetherbee*, pp. 81, 126; *Godden, British Porcelain*, pp. 438, 440; *White Ironstone Notes*, Vol. 2, No. 4, Spring 1996.

JONES

George Jones (& Sons, Ltd.)
Bridge Works (1861-1865)
Trent Pottery (c.1865-1907),
Renamed Crescent Pottery (c.1907-1957), Stoke,
- From 1936-1950 company traded as Crescent Pottery
Staffordshire, 1861-1957
Acquired by E. Brain (1958-1967+)

KAD NO.	GODDEN NO.	MARK	
B1389	2217		Printed or impressed relief monogram mark (G. J.) 1861-1873. - Some marks may incorporate "STONE CHINA" and "STOKE ON TRENT".
B1390	2218		Printed marks of differing design. Pattern name often included, 1873-1929. - "& SONS" dates from 1873. - "LTD" dates from 1894 - "CRESCENT CHINA" may occur under mark name from c.1893.

Typical Marks Include:

KAD NO.	GODDEN NO.	MARK	
B1391	-		
B1392	-		
B1392A	-		- From 1862-1865 George Jones manufactured White Granite Ware for J. & G. Meakin as well as for himself. See *Cluett's* comments, pp. 10-11, 24, and 261.
B1393	-	**IRONSTONE G. F. JONES & SONS STOKE ON TRENT**	Impressed name mark noted on White Ironstone, c.1873+. - *Gaston*, Vol. I, p. 39, shows a "Shredded Wheat" dish in the "Abbey" pattern which was used as a redemption for a cereal purchase. Petrus Regout & Co. identically copied this popular pattern. Also see *Cluett* pp. 72-94, for a history of the Abbey pattern; which was acquired from the 1861 William Adams auction.
B1394	2219		Printed or impressed mark, c.1924-1951.

For further reading, refer to *Godden, British Porcelain*, p. 439; and *FOB Bulletin*, No. 89, August 1995, p. 3, for an article by David Furniss titled, "Adams 'Lasso' or 'Amazon' Pattern and Petrus Regout 'Indian Traffic' Pattern;" and *Cluett*, pp. 10, 14, 24, 72-73. Also see comments under William Adams & Sons.

KEELING

***Keeling & Co. (Ltd.)**
Swan Bank Pottery, High Street (1886-1888)
Dale Hall Works (from 1888),
Burslem, Staffordshire, c.1886-1936
Formerly, J. Gildea (c.1885-1887)

KAD NO.	GODDEN NO.	MARK	
B1395	2241	**K. & CO.**	Printed marks of differing design. Pattern name often included, c.1886-1936. "ENGLAND" added after 1891.
B1396	2242	**K. & CO. B.**	
B1397	2242A	**& K. CO.**	
B1398	-	**KEELING & CO.**	
B1399	2243		Printed "Trade-mark", 1886-1936. - "LTD." added after 1909. - Potter's trade-mark used by James Gildea & Gildea & Walker, see pp. 204-205.
B1400	2244	**LASOL**	Printed "Trade-name" c.1912+.
B1401	2245		Printed "Lasol Ware" mark, c.1912-1936.

KEELING

*** Charles Keeling**
Broad Street,
Shelton, Staffordshire, 1822-1826

B1402	2240	**C. K.**	Printed initial marks of differing design. Pattern name often included, 1822-1826.

KEELING

***James Keeling**
New Street,
Hanley, Staffordshire, c.1790-1832
Subsequently, S. & J. Burton (1832-1845)

-Godden gives an in depth accounting of the name Keeling from 1738 into the mid 1850s. A complexity of partnerships is quite evident. The methodology of historical research is one in which collectors only see the surface. Godden gives us an insight into this complexity in his *Encyclopedia of British Porcelain Manufacturers*, pp. 441-456. This truly is must reading in order for the collector to understand that research into potteries, locations and partnerships is, at times, very complex and time consuming.

B1403	-		No known name marks, c.1790-1832. - "Views in Mesopotamia" has been attributed to James Keeling. See *Coysh*, Vol. II, p. 206. For further reading, refer to *Dudson, A Family of Potters Since 1800* by A. M. Dudson, Hanley, England. Dudson Publications, 1985; and *Penny Plain*, pp. 99, 102, Nos. 238 and 285 respectively.

KEELING

KAD NO.	GODDEN NO.	MARK	
			***Samuel Keeling & Co.** **Market Street Works,** **Hanley, Staffordshire, c.1838-1849** **Formerly, Hackwood & Keeling (c.1834-1836)** **Subsequently, J. & G. Meakin (c.1851-1970)** **- In 1970 became part of the Wedgwood Group**
B1404	2247	**S. K. & CO.**	Printed marks of differing design. Pattern name often included, c.1838-1849.
B1405	2248	**S. KEELING & CO.**	
B1406	-	**S. K. & CO. HANLEY NEW STONE**	Impressed, octagonal marked recorded, 1838-1849. - See *FOB*, No. 71, Spring 1991, p. 4.
B1407 B1408	2249 -	 	Printed marks, (typical), c.1840-1850.

KENT

KAD NO.	GODDEN NO.	MARK	
			James Kent (Ltd.) **Old Foley Pottery, King Street,** **Longton (or Fenton), Staffordshire, c.1897-1989** **Renamed James Kent (1989) Ltd. and sold in April 1989 to Hadida Fine Bone China**
B1409	2263		Printed marks of differing design. Pattern name often included, c.1897-1989. *-P. Williams, Staffordshire*, Vol. II, p. 235 notes a marking, in script, "G. KENT, SOLE MANUFACTURER, 199 HIGH HALBORN. F. HAHN DANCHELL'S PATENT."
B1410 B1411 B1412 B1413	2264 2265 2266 2267		

Typical Marks Include:

c.1897-1901

c.1901+

c.1910+

c.1913+

- "LTD" added to title from 1913+.
- "Pieces marked "OLD FOLEY" date from c.1955+.
- The location of the pottery may be noted as Foley Pottery, Fenton and/or Foley or Old Foley Pottery, Fenton or Longton.

- It is important to note that several firms potted at various Foley potteries or Foley China Works.
- "Foley is the farthest portion of the three-fold division we make of the Fentons, and is situated wholly in Fenton Culvert" notes Geoffrey Godden in his letter dated July 11, 1995.
- *Hampson*, *Churchill*, p. 35 notes that James Kent succeeded Moore & Co. [Moore, Leason & Co.] at the Old Foley Pottery Co., Longton.

For further reading, refer to *Godden, Collecting Lustreware*, p. 126.

KIDSTON

KAD NO.	GODDEN NO.	MARK	
			***R. A. Kidston & Co.** **Verreville Works,** **Glasgow, Scotland, c.1834-1841** **- Also see R. A. Cochran & Co.**
B1414	-	**R. A. K. & CO.**	Printed marks of differing design. Pattern name often included, c.1834-1841.

For further reading, refer to *Scottish Pottery 15th Historical Review*, 1993, pp. 65-70; and *Scottish Pottery 18th Historical Review*, 1996, pp. 49-55, for an article by Henry E. Kelly titled "The North Woodside and Garrioch Mills on the Kelvin and their Connection with the Pottery Trade."

KILNHURST

Kilnhurst Old Pottery
South Yorkshire
History:

William Malpass	1746
Thomas Hawley	1783-1790s
Turner & Co.	1790s
Turner & Thomas Hawley	1798-1808
Turner & Philip Hawley	1808-1814
Philip Hawley & Cook	1814-1816
Philip Hawley & Co.	1816-1817
Turner & Philip Hawley	1818-1823
Under Management of Philip Hawley (1808-1830)	1823-1830
George Green	1830-1832
Bramelds & Co. (sublet)	1832-1839
Benjamin & John Twigg (The Twigg Brothers)	1839-1853
John Twigg	1853-1877
Daniel Twigg	1877-1884
Simpson Hepworth & Bowman Heald	1884-1888
Simpson Hepworth	1888-1928
William Heald Hepworth	1928-1929
Closed	1929

For further reading, refer to *Lawrence*; and *The Annual Report of the Council of the Yorkshire Philosophical Society*, York, England, 1916.

KNIGHT

***Knight Elkin & Bridgwood**
Foley Potteries, King Street,
Fenton, Staffordshire, c.1827-1840
-Also see Elkin Knight & Bridgwood (and *Godden*, p. 376)

KAD NO.	GODDEN NO.	MARK	
B1415	2304	**K. E. & B.**	Printed marks noted on Blue Printed Earthenware, c.1827-1840.
B1416	2304a	**K. E. B.**	

KNIGHT

***Knight Elkin & Co. (also listed a Elkin & Knight)**
Foley Potteries, King Street,
Fenton, Staffordshire, c.1822-1825
Subsequently, Elkin Knight & Bridgwood (c.1827-1840)

KAD NO.	GODDEN NO.	MARK	
B1417	2301	**K. E. & CO.**	Printed marks of differing design. Pattern name often included, c.1822-1825.

KAD NO.	GODDEN NO.	MARK	
B1418	2302	**KNIGHT ELKIN & CO.**	- Interchangeable marks of various partnerships noted. - Further markings noted are of an impressed eagle perched on a branch and an impressed marking "OPAQUE FELSPAR CHINA".
B1419	2303	**K. & E.**	
B1420	2301A		Printed mark and pattern name noted on Historic American/Canadian wares, c.1822-1825. - Only one pattern has been located, that being "PENNSYLVANIA". For further reading, refer to *Larsen*, p. 247, No. 696; *Coysh & Stefano;* and *Snyder, Romantic Staffordshire*, pp. 87-88.

KNIGHT

***Knight Elkin & Knight (also listed as Knight, Elkin & Co.)**
Foley Potteries, King Street,
Fenton, Staffordshire, c.1841-1844

B1421	2305	**K. E. & K.**	Printed marks of differing design. Pattern name often included, c.1841-1844.

KNIGHT

***John King Knight**
Foley Potteries, King Street,
Fenton, Staffordshire, c.1846-1853
Formerly, Knight, Elkin & Co.
Subsequently, Knight & Wileman (1853-1856)*

B1422	2306	**J. K. KNIGHT**	Printed marks of differing design. Pattern name often included, c.1846-1853.
B1423	2307	**I. K. KNIGHT**	- The name "FOLEY" may occur with these marks.
B1424	-	**KNIGHT FOLEY**	Printed name mark, c.1846-1853.
B1425	-		Printed or impressed Royal Coat of Arms mark with shield and printed initials "J. K. K.", c.1846-1853.**
B1426	-	**PUBLISHED BY JOHN KING KNIGHT THE FOLEY POTTERIES OCTOBER 1, 1846**	Mark noted on a jug "English Ale", c.1846-1853. -See *Flow Blue China*. by Norma Jean Hoener, Rockford, IL. Flow Blue International Collector's Club, 1996. p. 97.

**Godden, British Porcelain*, p. 465 notes the dates as 1853-1856.
- Subsequent research notes that in 1853 John Knight, surviving partner of Elkin, Knight took Henry Wileman as a partner. Upon his retirement in 1856, the company's name was changed to Wileman & Co.

***Coysh*, Vol. II, p. 89 notes the printed title "Geneva" marked "J. K. K.", as well as one impressed example "OPAQUE GRANITE CHINA" with distinct initials marks "W. R. & Co." Knight may have over printed these white wares; a practice which was not uncommon in the potteries.
For further reading, refer to *Godden, Collecting Lustreware*, p. 126; and *Snyder, Romantic Staffordshire*, p. 87.

KNOTTINGLY

KAD NO.	GODDEN NO.	MARK

Knottingley Pottery
See: Ferrybridge Pottery

LADYBURN

Ladyburn Pottery

Partnership Data	**Date**
James Stevenson, Jr. & David Ker	1819 — 1829/1830
James Stevenson, Sr. acquires full ownership of pottery	1831/1832
Company assets sold	1841
Thomas Crawford acquires pottery	1846
(W.) Clough, (H. & M.) Geddes & Co. acquire pottery	1849
Company goes bankrupt	1850
William Shirley takes over as Trustee for "Thomas Shirley & Co."	1850
Pottery Sold	1856

No recorded marks noted.

Also refer to Clyde Pottery, Muir, and Thomas Shirley, pp. 153-154.

For further reading, refer to *Fleming*, pp. 111-112 and *Kelly*, pp. 57-75.

LAKIN

***Thomas Lakin (& various partnerships)**
Burslem (1791-1812)
and Stoke-on-Trent (1810-1818)
Staffordshire, c.1791-1818

History:

Parternship	**Pottery**	**Date**
Lakin & Poole	Hadderidge, Burslem	1791-1795
Poole, Shrigley & Lakin	Burslem	1796
Thomas Lakin	Bournes Bank Pottery, Burslem	1797-1799
Thomas Lakin	Employed by John Davenport, Longport	1790s-1810
Lakin & Son or Lakin & Co.	Thomas Wolfe (& Co's.) Pottery, Stoke	1810-1812
Thomas Lakin	Thomas Wolfe (& Co's.) Pottery, Stoke	1812-1817
Thomas Lakin	(2nd) Pottery Leased from Josiah Spode, Stoke	1815-1817
Thomas Lakin	Manager at Leeds Pottery, Yorkshire	1818-1821

KAD NO.	GODDEN NO.	MARK	
B1427	-	**LAKIN & POOLE**	Impressed name mark, 1791-1975. - See *True Blue*, p. 148, No. L1
B1427A	2311	**LAKIN**	Impressed name mark, 1812-1817.

For further reading, refer to *Godden, Collecting Lustreware*, pp. 126-128; *NCSJ*, No. 5, 1984, pp. 79-114 for an article by Harold Blakey, titled "Thomas Lakin"; and *Edwards, Basalt*, pp.187-188.

LAWLEYS

Lawleys Limited
Ash Hall,
Stoke-on-Trent, Staffordshire 1921-1964+
- Retailers and Manufacturers

KAD NO.	GODDEN NO.	MARK	

History:

Established in Birmingham	1908
Renamed Lawleys (1921) Ltd.	1921
Renamed Lawleys Ltd.	1929
Manufacturing begins	1936
Acquired North Staffordshire Pottery Co.	1940
Acquires over ten companies as Lawley Group Ltd. (by)	1948
Acquired by Pearson & Son Ltd.	1952
Renamed Allied English Potteries Ltd.	1964
Merges with Royal Doulton	1972

KAD NO.	GODDEN NO.	MARK	
B1428	2340	**LAWLEYS**	Printed marks employed on wares manufactured on special order, 1925-1940.
B1429	2341	**LAWLEYS LTD.**	- Marks subsequent to 1940 may well include potters marks, 1921-1964.
B1430	-	**LAWLEYS NORFOLK POTTERY STONE**	- *Snyder*, Vol. I, p. 122 illustrates a Minton jardiniere for Lawleys with KAD mark B1756 for Minton, 1921-1964.

LEAR

Samuel Lear
Mayer Street (1877-1886)
High Street (1882-1886)
Hanley, Staffordshire, 1877-1886

KAD NO.	GODDEN NO.	MARK	
B1431	2360	**LEAR**	Impressed name mark noted on Jasper-type wares and earthenware, 1877-1886. - A White Ironstone Cheesekeep "Lily of the Valley with Ferns" is illustrated in *White Ironstone Notes*, Vol. 4, No. 1, Summer 1997, p. 13, and is unmarked. - Audrey M. Dudson illustrates an identical piece in Majolica which is impressed "LEAR" in her book *"Cheese Dishes" A Guide to Cheese Dishes From 1750-1940*. Dudson Publications, Ltd. England, 1993. p. 59, Plate 37. This is possibly an undecorated copy!

For further reading, refer to *Karmason*, pp. 112-114.

LEEDS

Leeds Pottery (c.1758-1850)
Jack Lane, Hunslet,
Leeds, Yorkshire, c.1758-1820
- See *Godden*, p. 386 for listings of various potters or firms who worked the Leeds Pottery, c,1820-1878.*

KAD NO.	GODDEN NO.	MARK	
B1432	-	**LEEDS**	Impressed name mark, c. 1820.
B1433	2362	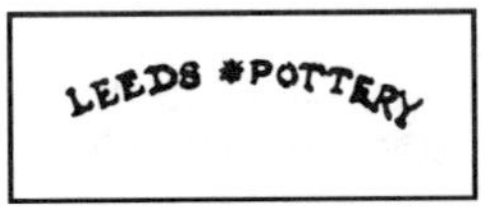	Impressed name mark, (concave arc), c.1775-1800+.
B1434	-		

Impressed (crisscross) markings, c.1791-1820:

B1435 -
B1436 -

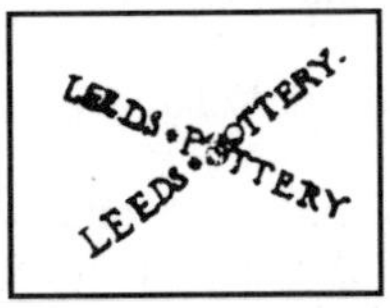

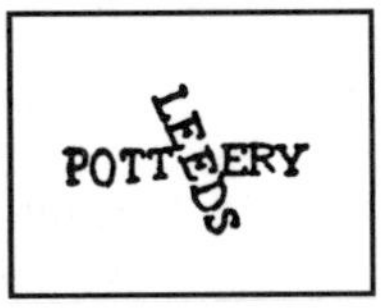

KAD NO.	GODDEN NO.	MARK	
B1437	2363	**LEEDS POTTERY**	Printed name mark on transfer painted Creamware, c.1790+.
B1438	2364	**L. P.**	Printed or impressed initial mark (rare), 1780+.
B1439	2365	**HARTLEY GREENS & CO.**	Printed or impressed name mark, c.1781-1820.
B1440	-		
B1441	-		
B1442	1963		

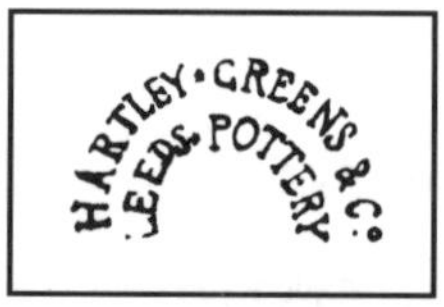

**Godden*, p. 386 notes the succession of firms after the 1820 bankruptcy.

For further reading, refer to *Lawrence*; *The Annual Report of the Yorkshire Philosophical Society*, February 1916; *The Leeds Pottery*, by Donald Towners, 1963; *Edwards, Basalt*, pp. 165-174; *Godden*, p. 313, Mark 1963; *Williams-Wood, English Transfer*, pp. 176-186; *Creamware and Other English Pottery at Temple Newsam House, Leeds*. by Peter Walton, Manningham Press, England, 1976; *NCSJ*, Vol. 8, 1991, pp. 1-13 for an article by Ron Morley titled "Mr. Hartley of Hartley, Greens & Co."; and *NCS Newsletter*, No. 109, March 1998, pp. 4-16, for an article by Renard Broughton titled "Yorkshire Pottery: Identifying Early Blue Printed Patterns of the Circa 1785-1810 Period."

For a complete and most up-to-date bibliography for the Yorkshire potteries, refer to *A Celebration of Yorkshire Pots*, The 8th Exposition for the Northern Ceramics Society, June 29 - September 21, 1997, Coordinated by John D. Griffin. Clifton Park Museum, Rotherham, England. pp. 178-184

LIDDLE

Liddle, Elliot & Son
Dale Hall Pottery,
Longport, Staffordshire, c.1860-1870
- Firm may also be listed as Elliot, Liddle & Son
Formerly, Mayer & Elliot (c.1858-1860)
Subsequently, Bates, Elliot & Co. (c.1870-1875)

KAD NO.	GODDEN NO.	MARK	
B1443	1472	**L. E. & S.**	Printed or impressed marks of differing design. Pattern name often included, c.1860-1870.
B1444	-	**L. E. & S.** (in elaborate script monogram)	- *Godden, British Porcelain*, p. 326 notes "within a short period, Liddle Elliot took his son into the business and by 1862 the company's trade style had been changed to Liddle Elliot & Son."
B1445	-		Printed English Royal Arms mark noted on White Ironstone, marked "BERLIN IRONSTONE/LIDDLE ELLIOT & SON", c.1860-1870.

Mayer Bros. & Elliot or Mayer & Elliot	1855-1860
Elliot Bros. or Liddle, Elliot & Co.*	1860-1862
Liddle Elliot & Son	1862-1870

For further reading, refer to *Wetherbee*, p. 38; *Godden, Jewitt*, p. 14; *Godden, Staffordshire*, p.442; and *Godden, British Porcelain*, p. 523.

- *Henrywood*, p. 172 notes the following partnership dates:

*Both *Bell*, pp. 28, 58, and *Riley*, p. 202, No. 779 notes a Tyneside potter, "Elliot, H. & Co.", c. 1821-1823, with the impressed mark "ELLIOT & CO." and a printed marking "SEMI-CHINA". Care in like name attribution is advised.

LIVESLEY

Livesley & Davis
Trent Pottery,
Eastwood, Hanley, c.1867-1871
Subsequently, J. H. & J. Davis (c.1871-1875)

KAD NO.	GODDEN NO.	MARK	
B1446	-	**LIVESLEY & DAVIS**	Printed name mark, 1867-1871.

LIVESLEY

Livesley, Powell & Co.
Old Hall Lane (1851-1860)
Stafford Street Works, Miles Bank
Hanley, Staffordshire, c.1851-1865*
Subsequently, Powell & Bishop (1866-1878)

KAD NO.	GODDEN NO.	MARK	
B1447	2385	**LIVESLEY POWELL & CO.**	Printed or impressed marks of varying design. Pattern name often included, c.1851-1865. "IRONSTONE" and "IRONSDIE CHINA" markings noted.
B1448	2386	**L. P. & CO.**	
B1449	2387	**BEST L. P. & CO.**	
B1450	-		
B1451	-		
B1452	-		

Typical Marks Include:

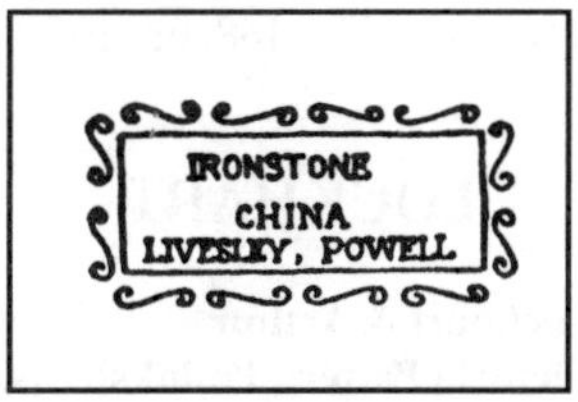

**Godden, Collecting Lustreware*, p. 128, notes that William Livesley potted at various addresses from about 1844 (three locations are noted in *Godden, British Porcelain*, pp. 608-609) "…and he [William] seemingly continued (with his son W. H. Livesley) after the dissolution of the Livesley, Powell & Co. partnership, until at least September 1870."

For further reading on Tea Leaf shapes refer to *TLCI Educational Supplement*, Apr. 1992 for an article called "Pouring Vessels"; *TLCI Educational Supplement*, April 1994 for an article by Dale Abrams titled "Climbing the Tea Leaf Family Tree"; *White Ironstone Notes*, Vol. 4, No. 2, Fall 1997, pp. 8-9 for an article by Kathy Banks titled "Excavations of White Ironstone China".

LLANELLY

Llanelly Pottery
See: South Wales Pottery

LOCKETT

***Lockett & Hulme**
King Street, Lane End,
Longton, Staffordshire, c.1818-1826

KAD NO.	GODDEN NO.	MARK	
B1453	-	**L. & H.**	Printed initial mark, 1818-1826.

KAD NO.	GODDEN NO.	MARK	
B1454	2396		Printed marks of differing design, c.1818-1826.
B1455	-	**LOCKETT & HULME**	Impressed name mark, c.1818-1826.

For further reading, refer to *Godden, British Porcelain*, pp. 485-488; *Hampson*, pp. 106-112; and *Little*, p. 78.

LOCKETT

***John & Thomas Lockett**
King Street, (c.1835-1855)
Market Street (c.1841-1855)
Longton, Staffordshire, c.1835-1855
Formerly, John Lockett & Son (c.1827-1835)
Subsequently, John Lockett (c.1855-1878)

B1456	-	**J. & T. L.**	Printed initial mark, c.1835-1855.

For further reading, refer to *Godden*, pp. 393-394; *Godden, Staffordshire*, pp. 445-445; *Godden, Collecting Lustreware*, pp. 129-130; *Little*, p. 78; *Edwards, Basalt*, p. 190; and *Hampson*, No. 168, pp. 106-112.

LOCKHART

Lockhart & Arthur
Victoria Pottery, Pollokshaws,
Glasgow, Scotland, c.1855-1864

B1457	2401	**L. & A.**	Printed or impressed marks of differing design. Pattern name often included, c.1855-1864.
B1458	2402	**LOCKHART & ARTHUR**	

LOCKHART

David Lockhart (& Co.)
Victoria Pottery, Pollokshaws,
Glasgow, Scotland, c.1865-1898

B1459	-	**L. & CO.**	Printed marks of differing design. Pattern name often included, c.1865-1876.
B1460	-	**L. & COY.**	
B1461	-	**LOCKHART & COY.**	
B1462	2403	**D. L. & CO.**	Initial Marking, c. 1876-1898. - Refer to *Hill,* p. 307 for printed "Garter" mark.

LOCKHART

David Lockhart & Sons (Ltd.)
Victoria Pottery, Pollokshaws,
Glasgow, Scotland, c.1898-1953

KAD NO. | **GODDEN NO.** | **MARK**

B1463 2404

Printed or impressed marks of differing design. Pattern name often included, c.1898-1953.
- Initials "D. L. & S." and/or "& SONS" included.

B1464 2405 **D. L. & SONS**

For further reading, refer to *Scottish Pottery 14th Historical Review, 1990-1992* pp. 16-38 for an article by Henry E. Kelly; and *Fleming*, pp. 141-142.

LOCKITT

William H. Lockitt
Wellington Pottery,
Hanley, Staffordshire 1901-1919
Formerly, Wellington Pottery Co. (1899-1901)

B1464A 2406 **W. H. L.**
H.

Printed initial mark. Pattern name often included, 1901-1919.

B1464B 2407

Printed name mark, 1913-1919.

LONGTON

Longton Pottery Co. Ltd.
Blue Bell Works,
Longton, Staffordshire, 1946-1955

B1465 2418 **L. P. CO. LTD.**

Printed initial mark. Pattern name often included, 1946-1955.
- See *Snyder*, Vol. II, p. 155 for additional marks.

B1466 2419

This company is not to be confused with the Longton (New) Art Pottery Co., Ltd. established in 1932.

LOWNDES

Lowndes & Beech
See: Beech & Lowndes

MACHIN

Machin & Potts
Waterloo Pottery, Nile Street,
Burslem, Staffordshire, 1833-1838
Formerly, Machin & Co. (c.1818-1832)

KAD NO.	GODDEN NO.	MARK	
B1467	-	**M. & P.**	Printed marks of differing design. Pattern name often included, 1833-1838.
B1468	2456	**MACHIN & POTTS**	
B1469	2456A	**MACHIN & POTTS PATENT**	

- Machin & Co. was the first to introduce a patent (1831) for a rotary press to print transfer (by steam presses) in a single color.

Typical Marks Include:

KAD NO.	GODDEN NO.
B1470	-
B1471	-
B1472	-

For additional marks and further reading, refer to *Godden, British Porcelain*, p. 500; *Godden, Staffordshire*, Ch. 13, pp. 201-208; *Godden, Collecting Lustreware*, pp. 130-131; *P. Williams, Staffordshire*, Vol. II, pp. 159-160; *Williams-Wood, English Transfer*, pp. 208-211; and *Henrywood*, pp. 56-58.

MAC INTYRE

James MacIntyre (& Co.) (Ltd.)
Washington Works,
Burslem, Staffordshire, c.1860-1867
Formerly, Kennedy & MacIntyre (c.1854-1860)
Subsequently, James MacIntyre & Co. (Ltd.) (c.1868-1928+)
- "LTD." added to title c.1894-1928+.

KAD NO.	GODDEN NO.	MARK	
B1473	2818	**MACINTYRE**	Printed marks of differing design. Pattern name often included, c.1860-1867.
B1474	2819	**J. MACINTYRE**	- Without "& CO." c.1860-1867.
B1475	2820	**J. M. & CO.**	- With "& CO." c.1868-1894.
B1476	2821	**J. MACINTYRE & CO.**	- Additional marking "IRONSTONE CHINA" noted.

Typical Marks Include:

KAD NO.	GODDEN NO.
B1477	2822
B1478	2823
B1479	2824
B1480	2825

- Only electrical wares were manufactured from c.1928+.

For further reading, refer to *Rhead*; *FOB*, 1989, Spring & Summer issues Nos. 63 and 64 for the pattern "Vinaigrette"; and *Godden, British Porcelain*, p. 501.

MADDOCK

KAD NO.	GODDEN NO.	MARK	

***Maddock & Gater**
Burslem, Staffordshire, c.1875

B1481 - Printed Royal Coat of Arms mark, c.1875.
- A registration date for June 12, 1875 is noted by *Cushion*.
- *Wetherbee*, notes a pattern with this date as "Plain Uplift".

For further reading, refer to *Wetherbee*, p. 36; and *Wetherbee, White Ironstone*, pp. 142 and 149.

MADDOCK

***Maddock & Seddon**
Newcastle Street,
Burslem, Staffordshire, c.1839-1842
Formerly, Maddock & Edwards (c.1837-1839)
Subsequently, John Maddock (1842-1855)

B1482 2476 **M. & S.** Printed marks of differing design. Pattern name often included, 1839-1842.
- The initials "M. & S." may also be attributed to Meir & Son (1837-1897).

B1485 - Printed initial mark, c.1839-1842.
- Also see comments under John Maddock, mark no. KAD B1485.

For further reading, refer to *Little*, p. 79.

MADDOCK

***John Maddock**
Newcastle Street,
Burslem, Staffordshire, 1842-1855
Formerly, Maddock & Seddon (1839-1842)
Subsequently, Maddock & Son(s) (Ltd.) (1855-1987)

B1483 - **I. M.** Printed initial mark. Pattern name often included, 1842-1855.
- Noted together with impressed mark, KAD B1487.

B1484 - **JOHN MADDOCK** Printed initial or name mark. Pattern name often included, 1842-1855.

B1485 2460 Printed mark with initial "M" at left side. Pattern name included, 1842-1855.
- Also see Maddock & Seddon.
- Minton's letter M is noted in cursive, , (c.1822-1836).

B1486 2460A **MADDOCK** Printed or impressed name mark. Pattern name often included, 1842-1855.

KAD NO.	GODDEN NO.	MARK	
B1487	2461		Printed or impressed mark. Pattern name often included, 1842-1855. - Impressed mark KAD B1487 is often noted along with a printed pattern name (in Flow Blue). -*P. Williams, Flow Blue*, Vol. I, p. 17, notes a pattern "Chen-si" as being made by John Meir. Evidently the initials "I. M." without the impressed mark KAD B1487 could be attributed to either John Meir or John Maddock. As previously stated, during the mid 19th century the name John could have been spelled either with an "I" or a "J". There are numerous pieces in this author's collection with the initials "I. M." and pattern name, along with the impressed mark KAD B1486. It would, therefore, hold that this pattern noted by Petra Williams as being by John Meir may be in error. In conclusion, as a rule only large pieces (e.g., hollowware, platters, etc.) show the impressed mark as well as a printed initial and pattern mark of Maddock. Therefore, confusion may have arisen by not having these large marked pieces at hand for attribution purposes.

MADDOCK

***John Maddock & Son(s) (Ltd.)**
Newcastle Street (1855-1987)
Dale Hall (until 1930)
Burslem, Staffordshire, 1855-1987
Formerly, John Maddock (1842-1855)
- "& Son" from 1855

B1488	-	**MADDOCK & SON**	Printed marks of differing design, c.1855+.
B1489	-	**JOHN MADDOCK & SONS**	Printed name mark, 1880-1896.
B1490 B1491	2462 2463	 	Printed marks of differing design. Pattern name often included, 1880-1896.
B1492	-	**MADDOCK & SONS LTD.**	As above, but with the addition of "LTD." after 1896.

Selected Marks, 1896-1930, include:

B1493 2464
B1494 2465
B1495 2466
B1496 2467

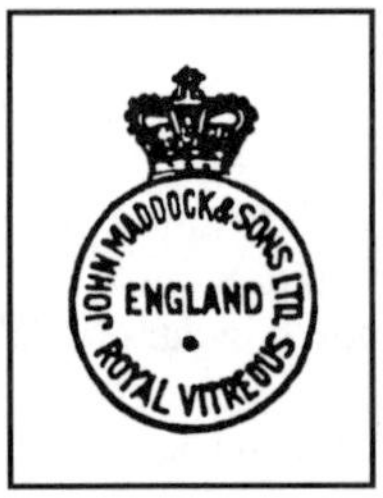

c.1896+ **c.1906+**

- For additional marks, after 1906, see *Godden*, pp. 406-407.

For further reading, refer to *Cushion, British Ceramic Marks*, pp. 234-235.

MALING

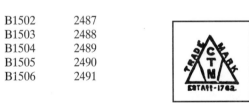

KAD NO.	GODDEN NO.	MARK	
			***C. T. Maling** **A & B Ford Potteries,** **Newcastle-upon-Tyne, Northumberland, 1859-1890** **Subsequently, C. T. Maling & Sons (1890-1947)**
B1497	2486	**MALING**	Impressed name mark, c.1859-1890. - "MALING" marking was in use prior to 1815 and continued through Maling's (Robert) to C. T. Maling, c.1815-1890.
B1498	2486A	**C. T. MALING**	Impressed name mark, c.1859+.
B1499	2486B	**C. T. M.**	Printed initial marks, 1859-1890. - May also include the name "Ford Pottery".
B1500	2487		Impressed or printed initial mark, 1875. - Continued by C. T. Maling & Sons until c.1908.

For further reading, refer to *Coysh*, Vol. II, p. 69 for his comments on "Denons Egypt" and the potter Elijah Jones (1831-1839); *Cameron*, p. 212; and *Penny Plain*, p. 100, No. 256. See KAD B1384.

MALING

***C. T. Maling & Sons (Ltd.)**
A & B Ford Potteries*,
Newcastle-upon-Tyne, Northumberland, 1890-1947
- "Ltd." from (1947-1963)
Formerly, C. T. Maling (1859-1890)

KAD NO.	GODDEN NO.	MARK	
B1501	-	**C. T. M. & SONS**	Printed marks of differing design. Pattern name often included, 1890-1947.

Typical Marks (1890-1963) Include:

B1502 2487
B1503 2488
B1504 2489
B1505 2490
B1506 2491

C. T. MALING mark continued 1890-1908

1890+

c.1908+

c.1924+

c.1949-1963

*The "B" Pottery closed in 1936.
- For additional backstamps refer to *Bell*, pp. 141-144; *Baker*, p. 45; *Maling, The Trade Mark of Excellence* by S. Moore & C. Ross. (rev. ed.) Tyne & Wear Museums. Newcastle, England, 1992; and *Godden, Collecting Lustreware*, pp. 237-239.

MALING

***Maling's (Robert)**
Ouseburn Bridge Pottery,
Newcastle, Tyneside, 1815(17)-1859
Subsequently, C. T. Maling (1859-1890)
- Pottery reopened in 1860 under Bell Bros. as "Albion Pottery", see pp. 108-109.

KAD NO.	GODDEN NO.	MARK	
B1507	2484	**MALING**	Impressed name mark, c.1815-1859.
B1508	2485	**M**	Impressed initial mark, c.1815-1830.
B1509	-	**R. M.**	Printed initial mark within banner and bell below, 1815-1859. - All appear within a laurel wreath separated by a crown at the top. - Impressed mark "C. T. MALING" can also be found. - *Bell*, notes that C. T. Maling took over the firm from his father in c.1853.

For further reading, refer to *Cameron*, p. 252 "Ouseburn Bridge Pottery".

MALKIN

Ralph Malkin
Park Works, Market Street,
Fenton, Staffordshire, c.1864-1881
Formerly, Malkin, Walker & Hulse (1858-1864)
Subsequently, R. Malkin & Sons (1882-1894)

B1510 2493

Printed marks of differing design. Pattern name often included, c.1864-1881.

For further reading, refer to *Godden, Collecting Lustreware*, p. 131.

MALKIN

Malkin, Walker & Hulse
British Anchor Pottery,
Anchor Road, Longton, 1858-1864
Subsequently, Walker, Bateman & Co. (1864-1866)

KAD NO.	GODDEN NO.	MARK	
B1511	-	**M. W. & H.**	Printed marks of differing design. Pattern name often included, 1858-1864.

B1512 2496

B1513 2497

Impressed mark dated January 1864.
- Malkin, Walker & Hulse also used the lesser known title of Malkin, Walker & Co.
- See *Godden's* comments, p. 411.
- Also see comments relative to "LONDON/ ANCHOR" impressed mark under Isaac & Thomas Bell, p. 109.

For further reading, refer to *Godden, Collecting Lustreware*, p. 131; and *Hampson*, No. 174, p. 118.

MANN

KAD NO.	GODDEN NO.	MARK	
			Mann & Co. **Cannon Street,** **Hanley, Staffordshire, c.1858-1860** **Subsequently, Mann, Evans & Co.**
B1514	2498	**MANN & CO. HANLEY**	Printed or impressed marks of differing design. Pattern name often included, c.1858-1860.

MARE

John Mare
Shelton, Hanley, Staffordshire, c.1802-1825

B1515	2504	**MARE**	Impressed name mark, c.1802-1825. - A printed mark "British Cobalt Blue" is noted on a version of the "Italian" pattern. See *Dreweatt-Neate Auction Catalog*, March 1997, "The Gibb Collection of Blue Printed and Other Pottery, p. 24, Lot No. 164. - An illustration is shown in *Godden, Illustrated Encyclopedia,* p. 212.

For further reading, refer to *Godden*, p. 413, 726; *Coysh*, Vol. I, p. 237; and *Little*, p. 80.

MARPLE

Marple, Turner & Co.
Upper Hanley Pottery,
Hanley, Staffordshire, c.1851-1858

B1516	-	**M. T. & CO.**	Printed marks of differing design. Pattern name often included, c.1851-1858.
B1517	-		

For further reading, refer to *Snyder, Romantic Staffordshire*, p. 116.

MARSH

Marsh & Willett
Kilncroft Works, Silvester Square,
Burslem, Staffordshire, c.1829-1834
Formerly, Samuel Marsh & Co. (1828-1829)
Subsequently, Samuel Marsh (1834-1836)

History of Kilncroft Works:
- After abstracting various sources, Geoffrey Godden was kind enough to straighten out the following dates, via his letter dated July 11, 1995.

James & William Handley	1819-1828
Samuel Marsh & Co. (Dissolution of Partnership 10/22/1829)	1828-1829
Marsh & Willett	1829-1834
Samuel Marsh	1834-1836
James & Thomas Edwards	1839-1842
T. & R. Boote	1842-1864
Henry Burgess	1864-1892

B1518	-	**M. & W.**	Printed initial mark, pattern name included, c.1829-1834.

For further reading, refer to *Coysh*, Vol. I, p. 239; and *Edwards, Basalt*, p. 193.

MARSH

KAD NO.	GODDEN NO.	MARK	
			Jacob Marsh **Church Street, Lane End,** **Longton, Staffordshire, 1819-1832** **Subsequently, John Riley Marsh (1832-1836)**
B1519	-	**MARSH**	Impressed name mark, c.1819-1832.
B1520	-	**OPAQUE CHINA WARRANTED**	Printed Royal Arms mark with text below, accompanied by impressed name mark, c.1819-1832.

For further reading, refer to *Hampson*, No. 176, p. 120; and *Coysh*, Vol. I, p. 239.

MARSHALL

John Marshall (& Co.) (Ltd.)
Bo'ness Pottery,
Bo'ness Scotland, c.1854-1899
Formerly, James Jamieson (1826-1854)/Redding Coal Co. (1854)

History:

John Marshall	c.1854-1866
"& Co." added (Partner, William McNay)	c.1867-1895
"Ltd." added	c.1895-1899
- Marshall dies in	1870
- McNay dies in	1881
- Charles McNay becomes Senior partner	c.1881-1886

KAD NO.	GODDEN NO.	MARK	
B1521	-	**J. M. & CO.**	Printed and impressed marks. Pattern name often included, c.1867-1895.
B1522	2509	**J. MARSHALL & CO.**	- See *True Blue*, p. 148, No. M2
B1523	-	**JOHN MARSHALL & CO. LTD. BO'NESS GREAT BRITAIN**	Printed oval mark, c.1895-1899. - Note wording "GREAT BRITAIN". - Additional marking "B. P. CO." may relate to the above pottery name in abbreviated form, c.1850s. - The "Canadian Sports" Series is noted with the marking "J. M. & CO."

For further reading, refer to *Collard, Pottery & Porcelain*, pp. 70-72; the *Scottish Pottery Historic Review*, Vol. 16, 1994, *Godden, Collecting Lustreware*, p. 268; *Finlayson*; and Henry Kelly's comments in *Blue Berry Notes*, Vol. 10, No. 1, Jan. - Feb. 1996, pp. 16-21.

MASON

MASON'S - SELECTED MARK CHRONOLOGY, 1800-1968

B1524 -
B1525 -
B1526 -

IMPRESSED ROYAL ARMS 1800-1813(25)

IMPRESSED ROYAL ARMS
WITH THE
NAME
MILES MASON
IMPRESSED

1813-1830+

POST 1813

KAD NO.	GODDEN NO.	MARK

ROUND SIDED CROWN MARKS, 1813+

B1527	2530	
B1528	-	
B1529	2530A	
B1530	2526	

BASIC MARK
1813-1830+

NO NAME
OVER CROWN
1813-1830

C.1820+

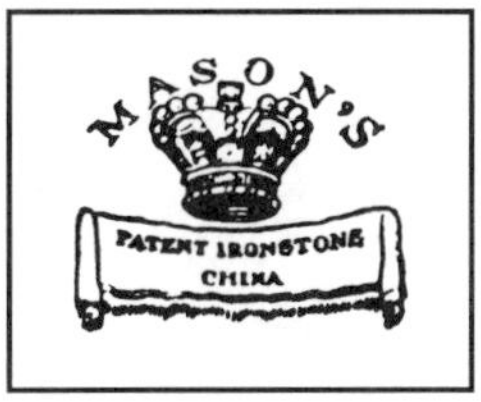

1845+

CUT SIDE (ANGULAR) CROWN MARKS, 1840+

B1531	2534	
B1532	2527	
B1533	2528	
B1534	2528A	

c.1835+

1835-1840(48)

1845+

1849-1854*

B1535	2530	
B1536	144	
B1537	-	
B1538	145	

MORLEY &
PARTNERSHIPS
1848-1862

1862+

BASIC MARK
WITH WORDING
"REAL IRONSTONE
CHINA" & NAME
ASHWORTH

1862+

1891+

*Mark for registration date of C. J. Mason, Longton, April 16, 1849.

Godden, Mason's, p. 225, notes "It must be understood that very many slight variations of the basic crowned Mason's Patent Ironstone mark occur, for most Mason's standard designs were based on a printed outline and the mark formed part of each engraved copper plate. In effect we have one mark to each printed design." For further reading, refer to *Godden, Mason's*, pp. 126-132; and *Mankowitz & Haggar*.

MASON

***Charles James Mason**
Mill Street, Lane Delph,
Fenton (1849-1851)
Daisy Bank Works, Lane End, Longton, (1850-1853)
Staffordshire, c.1849-1853

B1539	-	**C. J. M.**	Printed basic marks (and variations). Pattern name often included, c.1849-1853.

B1530	2526	
B1532	2527	
B1533	2528	

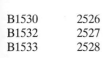

KAD NO.	GODDEN NO.	MARK	
B1540	2528A		Printed marks continued from predecessor, C. J. Mason & Co. - Registered April 16, 1849 [Lane Delph] Longton Mark Style Differences: - Early/Crown with Rounded Sides, c.1813-1849. - Later/Crown with Cut Sides (angular), c.1835+.
B1535 B1541	2530 2529		  **1813-1830+** **1835-1840**

See *Godden, Mason's*, pp. 128-132, relative to the Bankruptcy sale of April 3-8, 1848, and the purchase by Francis Morley of the Mason moulds and engraved copper plates.

For further reading, refer to *Godden, British Porcelain*; *Hampson*, No. 179, p. 122; and *Penny Plain*, p. 101, No. 264.

MASON

***Charles James Mason & Co.**
Fenton Stone Works,
High Street, Lane Delph,
Fenton, Staffordshire, c.1826-1840(48)

B1542	-	**C. J. M. & CO.**	Printed marks of differing design. Pattern name often included, c.1826-1840(48). - Marking "C. J. MASON & CO." rarely noted.
			Additional markings noted:
B1543	-		"BRITISH NANKEEN CHINA"
B1544	-		"GRANITE CHINA"
B1545	-		"SEMI CHINA/WARRANTED"
B1546	-		"NEW STONE CHINA"
B1547 B1548 B1549 B1550	2531 2532 2533 -		   

- For additional marks, refer to *Mankowitz & Haggar*, pp. 143-144.

B1551 B1552	2530 2534	 	Printed basic marks (and variations) continued, c.1826-1840(48). - "IMPROVED" added c. 1840-1848.

KAD NO.	GODDEN NO.	MARK	
B1553	2535	**MASONS CAMBRIAN ARGIL**	Printed mark noted on special bodies, c.1840s-1850.
B1554	2536	**MASON'S BANDANA WARE**	See *Godden*, pp. 188, 224-226.

MASON

***G. M. & C. J. Mason**
Fenton Stone Works,
High Street, Lane Delph,
Fenton, Staffordshire, 1813(15)-1826
Subsequently, C. J. Mason & Co. (1826-1840(48)

- Godden notes that the company was also listed as G. & C. Mason.

B1555	2537	**G. M. & C. J. MASON**	Marks incorporating the initials of George Miles and Charles James Mason occur before 1830.
B1556	2538	**G. & C. J. M.**	
B1557	2539	**MASONS PATENT IRONSTONE CHINA**	Impressed mark "MASONS IRONSTONE CHINA" (Patented in July 1813), c.1813-1826.
B1558	2540	**PATENT IRONSTONE CHINA***	Godden notes "These early marks … occur in different forms … and may be placed in unexpected places." - Impressed in one line - Impressed in two or more lines - In circular form
B1559	(2530B)		Printed basic mark occurs from 1813 onwards. See mark KAD B1541 for later version. Early versions occur without the word "MASONS" over crown. Impressed name marks KAD B1563 and B1564 may also occur with the above printed basic mark.
B1560	2541		Printed mark, c.1825+. "No. 306" refers to the pattern book number.
B1561	-	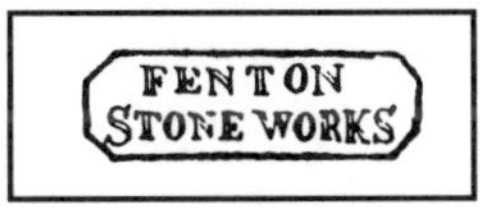	Printed variation of the above mark.
B1562	-	**SEMI-CHINA WARRANTED**	Printed mark, 'SEMI-CHINA/WARRANTED", c.1820-1835.

*Miles Mason was the inventor of Ironstone China for which his son Charles James Mason, as the Patentee in July 1813 reaped all the credit (for a period of 14 years).
- Subsequently, c.1813-1814, Josiah Spode introduced "STONE CHINA", later (1821) to be called "NEW STONE".
- Lest we forget, it was John Turner who patented a durable, compact earthenware body (No. 2367, January 1800) for the manufacture of porcelain and earthenware.

For further reading, refer to *Godden, Mason's*, pp. 283, 276-280 as well as Ch. 4, pp. 116-136; *Mason Porcelain and Ironstone 1796-1853* by Reginald Haggar & Elizabeth Adams, Faber & Faber, London, England, 1977.

MASON

KAD NO.	GODDEN NO.	MARK	
			***Miles Mason** **Islington Pottery,** **Liverpool (1796-1800)** **The Victoria Pottery (c.1800-1806),** **and Minerva Works, (1806-1813),** **Lane Delph, Fenton** **Liverpool & Fenton, 1796-1813**
B1563	2543	**M. MASON**	Impressed name marks found on *porcelain*, but not on all pieces, c.1802-1813.
B1564	2544	**MILES MASON**	Impressed name mark "MILES MASON" noted with impressed Royal Arms, c.1800-1813(25). - When accompanied by the impressed word "PATENT" mark dated from c.1813.
B1565 B1566	2545 -	 	Printed "mock" Chinese seal mark on Willow (and other Chinese type) patterns. - The name "MILES MASON" may occur with this type marking, c.1800(07)-1813. - Mark KAD B1565 dated c.1802-1810. - Mark B1566 (unnumbered) dates c.1807-1813. -*Coysh, Transferware*, p. 46, notes a printed marking attributed to Miles Mason, "BRITISH NANKEEN CHINA" which was continued by his sons. - As new research comes to light, it would appear that many dates may shift. Exact pinpointing of dates is difficult due to the absence of hard data. This is true not only for Mason's, but with many other potters as well. For further reading, refer to, *Godden, Mason's*, p. 22; *Chaffers*, p. 734; *Miles Mason Porcelain, A Guide To Patterns & Shapes*. by D. Skinner & V. Young. City Museum & Art Gallery, Stoke-on-Trent, 1991; *Mason's The First Two Hundred Years*. by Gaye Lake Roberts, Merrell Holberton Publishers, London, England, 1996, pp. 124-126; and *The Raven Mason Collection: The Catalogue of the Collection at Keele University* by Gaye Lake Roberts & John Twitchett. Keele University Press, 1997.

MASON

***William Mason (Miles Mason & Son)**
Lane Delph,
Fenton, Staffordshire, c.1811-1824
Formerly, Sampson Bagnall

B1567	2546	**W. MASON**	Printed name mark (rare), c.1811-1824.

For further reading, refer to *Godden, Mason's*, pp. 121-122 and 125.

MAUDESLEY

J. Maudesley & Co.
Well Street & Cross Street,
Tunstall, Staffordshire, 1862-1864
Subsequently, Cooper & Keeling

B1568	2557	**STONE WARE** **J. M. & CO.**	Printed marks noted by *Godden*, pp. 724-725, "... is believed to relate to this firm..." He notes that these initials were also used by other firms, c. 1862-1864.

MAY

Robert May
Charles Street Works,
Hanley, Staffordshire, c.1829-1830
Formerly, Toft & May (c.1825-1829)
- This is one of five potteries acquired by Ridgway in 1830

KAD NO.	GODDEN NO.	MARK	
B1569	-	**MAY**	Impressed name mark, c.1829-1830. - *P. Williams, Staffordshire*, Vol. II, p. 181, does not note a back mark for the "Fountain" pattern.

For further reading, refer to *Coysh*, Vol. I, p. 145; and *Little*, p. 77.

MAYER

***Mayer & Elliott**
Fountain Place and Dale Hall,
Longport, Staffordshire, c.1858-1860
Formerly, Mayer Bros. & Elliott (c.1855-1858)
Subsequently, Liddle, Elliott & Son (c.1860-1870)

B1570 2563

Printed, distinguishing initials "M & E" noted with differing designs. Pattern name often included, 1858-1860.
- Godden notes the occurrence of impressed month and year number 11/60 for November 1860.

B1571 2563A

Printed initial mark, 1858-1860.

B1572 - **MAYER & ELLIOTT**

Printed Royal Coat of Arms mark. Pattern name often included, c.1858-1860.
- "IRONSTONE" marking noted.

B1573 -

Wetherbee, p. 38 notes that the pattern "Berlin" was continued from predecessors, Mayer Bros. & Elliott and subsequently Liddle, Elliott & Son, c.1860-1870.

For further reading, refer to *Henrywood*, , p. 172; and *Godden, British Porcelain*, p. 523.

Henrywood, p. 172 notes the following partnership dates:

*1855-1860	Mayer Bros. & Elliott or Mayer & Elliott
1860-1862	Elliott Bros. or Liddle, Elliott & Co.
1862-1870	Liddle, Elliott & Son

**Godden, British Porcelain*, p. 523 notes a separate partnership of Mayer Bros. & Elliott dating from c.1855-1858.

MAYER

***Mayer & Newbold**
Lower Market Place (1817-1832)
Caroline Street (1818-1832)
Green Dock (1825-1832)
Lane End, Longton, Staffordshire, c.1817-1832
Formerly, Johnson & Blackwell (c.1815-1817)
Subsequently, Richard Newbold (c.1833-1837)

KAD NO.	GODDEN NO.	MARK	
B1574	2574	**M. & N.**	Printed marks of differing design. Pattern name often included, c.1817-1832. - "OPAQUE CHINA" marking noted.
B1575	2575	**May^{R} & New B^{D}**	
B1576	2576	**MAYER & NEWBOLD**	

KAD NO.	GODDEN NO.	MARK	
B1577	2577		- *Hampson*, No. 182, pp. 124-125 notes three pot works in operation.

For further reading, refer to *Godden, British Porcelain*, pp. 523-524; and *Godden, Collecting Lustreware*, p. 138.

MAYER

***Mayer Brothers & Elliott**
Dale Hall Pottery,
Longport, Staffordshire, c.1855-1858
Formerly, T. J. & J. Mayer (c.1842-1855)
Subsequently, Mayer & Elliott (c.1858-1860)

B1578 - **MAYER BROS. & ELLIOTT**

Printed name mark, c.1855-1858.
- Three (untitled) earthenware examples are noted, one bearing the registration mark of October 17, 1857. Refer to *Penny Plain*, pp. 103-104, Nos. 301, 302, 308.
- A White Ironstone pattern called "Berlin Swirl" was registered by Mayer Bros. & Elliott on Dec. 18, 1856.
- Also refer to Mayer & Elliott for a continuation of this pattern, see p. 271.
- An additional back mark for an American importer reads:

MANUFACTURED FOR AND IMPORTED
BY
CHAUNCEY J. FILLEY
ST. LOUIS
M. O.

Henrywood, p. 172 notes the following partnership dates:

1843-1855	T. J. & J. Mayer
1855-1860	Mayer Bros. & Elliott or Mayer & Elliott
1860-1862	Elliott Bros. or Liddle, Elliott & Co.

For further reading, refer to *Godden, British Porcelain*, p. 523 wherein he notes a separate partnership of Mayer & Elliott from c.1858-1860.

MAYER

***Thomas Mayer**
Cliff Bank Works, Stoke-on-Trent (c.1826-1835)
Brook Street (c.1836-1838)
Longport, Staffordshire, c.1826-1838

B1579	-	**MAYER**	Printed or impressed marks of differing design. Pattern name often included, c.1826-1838.
B1580	2568	**T. MAYER**	
B1581	2569	**T. MAYER, STOKE***	*Stoke predates c.1836.
B1582	-	**T. MAYER STOKE UPON TRENT**	

KAD NO.	GODDEN NO.	MARK	
			Typical Marks Include:
B1583	-		
B1584	-		
B1585	-		

c.1826-1835 c.1836-1838 *

*Printed "importer's mark" with Coat of Arms of New York State noted with the impressed name mark "T. MAYER", 1826-1835.

KAD NO.	GODDEN NO.	MARK	
B1586	-		Circular impressed mark, c.1826-1835.
B1587	-		Printed marks with pattern names often included on American/Historic Staffordshire, c.1826-1835.

- *Larsen,* p. 118 notes an impressed eagle facing right with the words "T. MAYER, STOKE, STAFFORDSHIRE". Other markings noted above printed "T. MAYER" and a Blue Printed Eagle marked "E. PLURIBUS UNUM".

- The name Thomas Mayer poses a problem, as indicated by comments in *Godden, British Porcelain*, pp. 520-524. Mr. Godden notes various potters by the name of Thomas Mayer, but only one at Brook Street, c.1841-1854 (a figure maker) and Hope Street, Shelton, c.1841-1854.

For further reading and marks, refer to *Snyder, Staffordshire*, pp. 65-68; and *Snyder, Romantic Staffordshire*, p. 128.

MAYER

***Thomas & John Mayer**
Dale Hall Pottery,
Longport, Staffordshire, c.1838-1842

KAD NO.	GODDEN NO.	MARK	
B1588	-	**T. & J. MAYER**	Printed name mark, c.1838-1842.
B1589	-		- *P. Williams, Staffordshire*, Vol. I, p. 350 and Vol. II, pp. 610-611 notes a "Non Pareil" pattern with the printed marking "T. & J. MAYER, LONGPORT". Dates for this pottery may be noted as c.1838-1842. The Brook Street Pottery may have been worked jointly prior to the Thomas, John & Joseph Mayer family pottery, c.1842-1855. - See next entry, Thomas, John & Joseph Mayer.

KAD NO.	GODDEN NO.	MARK

A most interesting marked piece is illustrated in the *NCS Newsletter*, No. 101, March 1996, p. 42 is a photograph of a color printed earthenware table made by Mayer with four distinct and different marks:
1. Impressed "J. MAYER LONGPORT 1840"
2. Brown printed mark "T. MAYER LONGPORT"
3. Brown printed mark "NON PAREIL" "T. & J. MAYER LONGPORT"
4. Impressed mark "T. MAYER STOKE" and "10"

B1590 -

To further add to this confusion, note the printed mark "T. MAYER, LONGPORT" on the pattern "Abbey Ruins". Refer to *Snyder, Romantic Staffordshire*, pp. 118-128. c. 1838-1842.

For further reading on the various Mayer partnerships, refer to *Coysh*, Vol. I, p. 242; and *Henrywood*, pp. 172-174.

MAYER

***Thomas, John & Joseph Mayer**
Furlong Works, Burslem and Dale Hall Pottery, Longport,
Longport, Burslem, Staffordshire, c.1842-1855
- Middle Works, Burslem was purchased in 1852 from the Enoch Wood Estate and sold in the same year.
Subsequently, Mayer Bros. & Elliott (1855-1858)

B1591 2570 **T. J. & J. MAYER**

Printed marks noted with various, and often elaborately designed cartouches. Pattern name often included, c.1842-1855.

B1592 -

B1593 2571 **MAYER BROS.**

- T. J. & J. Mayer exhibited at the 1851, 1853 and 1855 exhibitions, at which they received various awards.
- Printed marks "STONE WARE", "IMPROVED IRONSTONE" and "CHINESE PORCELAIN" may be found, as well as the printed title "MAYER BROS."

B1594 -

Printed mark noted on White Ironstone, registered Jan. 21, 1845.

Typical Marks Include:

B1595 -
B1596 -
B1597 -
B1598 -

KAD NO.	GODDEN NO.	MARK	
B1599	-		- Note mark "BARONIAL HALLS" with the wording "LONGPORT" For further reading, refer to *Godden, Collecting Lustreware*, pp. 133-134; *Henrywood*, p. 172; *Wetherbee*, pp. 34, 38, 44-48; *Williams-Wood, Pot Lids*, pp. 73-74; *Penny Plain*, p. 103, No. 304 & 307, and p. 104, No. 316 for additional patterns; *White Ironstone Notes*, Vol. 3, No. 2, Fall 1996, pp. 1-8 for an article titled "T. J. & J. Mayer"; *Wetherbee, White Ironstone*, pp. 45, 48; and *Snyder, Romantic Staffordshire,* pp. 118-128.

MEAKIN

***Meakin & Co. also known as Meakin Bros. & Co.**
Elder Road Works,
Cobridge, Staffordshire, c.1865-1882
Formerly, James Meakin, New Town Pottery, High Street, Longton (1845-1850)
Subsequently, The Crystal Porcelain Pottery Co. Ltd. (c.1882-1886)

KAD NO.	GODDEN NO.	MARK	
B1600	-	**MEAKIN BROS. COBRIDGE**	Printed Royal Coat of Arms mark noted on White Ironstone, c.1865-1882. - May also be marked "IRONSTONE CHINA".
B1601	-	**MEAKIN & CO.**	

For further reading, refer to *Godden, Jewitt*, p. 36, *Godden, Mason's*, p. 263; and *Wetherbee*, pp. 132, 145, and 148.

MEAKIN

***J. & G. Meakin (Ltd.), 1851-1970+**
Cannon Street Pottery (1851)
Market Street (1852-1859)
Eagle Factory (1859-1970+)
Eastwood Pottery (1889-1958)
Hanley, Staffordshire, 1851-1970+
"Ltd." dates from 1890
Formerly James Meakin, Newtown Pottery, High Street, Longton, 1845-1850.

KAD NO.	GODDEN NO.	MARK	
B1602	2598	**J. & G. MEAKIN**	Printed or impressed marks of differing design. Pattern name often included, 1851-1970+.
B1603	-	**J. & G. MEAKIN HANLEY**	- "ENGLAND" added after 1891 for the American export market.
B1604	-	**J. & G. MEAKIN REAL CHINA**	- *Noel Riley*, p. 230, No. 916, notes an additional impressed mark "K" on children's ware.
B1605	-	**J. & G. MEAKIN IRONSTONE**	
B1606	2599		
B1607	2600		
B1608	2601		
B1609	2602		
B1610	-		

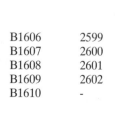

Typical Marks Include:

c.1890+

c.1890+

c.1890+

c.1907+

WITH THE
ADDITION OF
SEMI-PORCELAIN

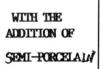

c.1907+

KAD NO.	GODDEN NO.	MARK
B1611	2603	
B1612	2604	
B1613	2605	
B1614	2606	

c.1912+

c.1912+

c.1912+

c.1939+

- *Godden*, p. 427. notes additional marks.

Selected Printed Marks on "White Ironstone"

KAD NO.	GODDEN NO.
B1615	-
B1616	-
B1617	-

Selected Impressed Marks on "White Ironstone"

KAD NO.	GODDEN NO.
B1618	-
B1619	-

- Variations in wording, with or without Royal Arms, may occur.
- The Eastwood Pottery was sold in 1958.
- The company may also be known as Meakin Bros. for the period 1851-1859.
- The company merged with W.R.M. Midwinter (Ltd.) in 1968.

For further reading, refer to *Sussman*, pp. 43-45; *Cameron*, p. 219; *Bunt, British Potters*, pp. 36-37; *Niblett,* p. 83; and Bernard Hollowood. *The Story of J. & G. Meakin*. London, England. Bimrose Publicity Co. Ltd., 1951; and *Cluett*, pp. 10, 24.

MEAKIN

***Alfred Meakin (Ltd.)**
Royal Albert, Victoria and Highgate Potteries,
Tunstall, Staffordshire, 1875-1913
Formerly, Pearson & Hancock
- The pottery was retitled Alfred Meakin (Tunstall) Ltd. in c.1913.
- The Newfield Pottery was acquired in c.1930+.
- In 1974 the Meakin holdings were acquired by Myott & Son, Co. Ltd. and restructured in 1982 as Myott-Meakin Ltd. Finally, in 1991 the company was acquired by the Churchill Group.

KAD NO.	GODDEN NO.	MARK	
B1620	2581	**ALFRED MEAKIN**	Printed or impressed marks of differing design. Pattern name often included, 1875-1930. - Marking "REAL IRONSTONE" noted.
B1621	2582	**ALFRED MEAKIN LTD.**	- Additional impressed marking "PARIS, WHITE/IRONSTONE" noted. See *Stoltzfus/Snyder*, p. 20. - "LTD." dates from 1897-1930.

KAD NO.	GODDEN NO.	MARK	
B1622	-		Printed mark c.1891-1897 (+) - "ENGLAND" added after 1891. - The term "LTD." does not appear on marks post-1930. Refer to *Godden*, p. 426.
B1623	-	**ALFRED MEAKIN ENGLAND**	Printed mark of Unicorn within Wreath, c.1891-1896.

Typical Marks Include:

B1624 2583
B1625 2584
B1626 2585

c.1875-1897

c.1897+

c.1897+

B1627 2586
B1628 2587
B1629 2589

c.1897+

c.1907+

c.1914+

For further reading, refer to *Hampson, Churchill*, pp. 123-128; *Sussman*, pp. 42 and 77-78; and Govin Starey, *Pottery, The Story of Alfred Meakin (Tunstall) Ltd.* London, Ruthien Publications Press, 1949.

MEAKIN

***Charles Meakin**
Trent Pottery, Burslem (1876-1882), and
Eastwood Pottery, Hanley (c.1883-1889)*
Staffordshire, 1876-1889

KAD NO.	GODDEN NO.	MARK	
B1630	-		Printed Royal Coat of Arms mark, c.1876-1882.
B1631	-		Mark, as above, with additional marking "HANLEY", c.1883-1889. - *Cushion, British Ceramic Marks* records a registry in the name of J. F. Meakin of 84 Baker Street, London, for the date Dec. 2, 1878, No. 329902. This was a designer who registered a pierced handled form. No further information is available. *Pottery acquired by J. & G. Meakin (Ltd.) in 1889.

MEAKIN

KAD NO.	GODDEN NO.	MARK	

***Henry Meakin**
Abbey Pottery, Cobridge,
Staffordshire, c.1873-1876
Formerly, Edward Pearson & Son (1868-1873)
Subsequently, Wood & Hawthorne (1879-1887)

B1632 2597

Printed Royal Coat of Arms mark, c.1873-1876.
-*Wetherbee, White Ironstone*, p. 99, notes the pattern "Wheat" in White Ironstone.
-*Godden*, p. 426 cites other H. Meakins as potting during this period.

MEAKIN

***Lewis Meakin**
Cannon Street,
Shelton, Staffordshire, c.1853-1855
No marks have been located for this potter.
For further reading, refer to *Godden, Mason's*, p. 264.

MEIGH

***Charles Meigh**
Old Hall Works
Hanley, Staffordshire, c.1832-1850

KAD NO.	GODDEN NO.	MARK	
B1633	2164A	**C. M.**	Printed and impressed marks of differing design. Pattern name often included, c.1832-1850.
B1634	-	**C. MEIGH**	
B1635	2614	**CHARLES MEIGH**	- Most marks incorporate the initials "C. M." with the name of the pattern and body type. - Printed importer's name "A. REEVES & CO., LOUISVILLE, KY" noted.

Typical Marks Include:

B1636 -
B1637 -
B1638 -
B1639 -

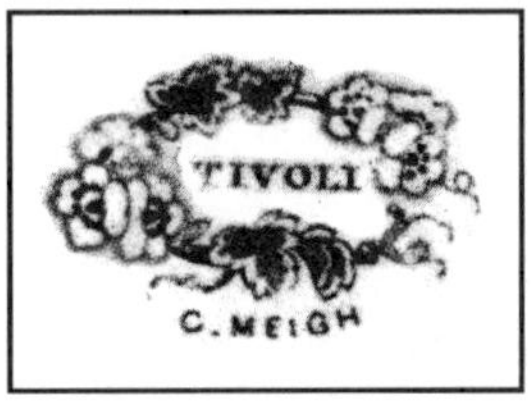

- Printed or impressed body types are noted quite frequently. Terms such as "FRENCH CHINA", "PORCELAIN OPAQUE", "ENAMEL PORCELAIN" or "IRONSTONE CHINA" are noted. These markings were continued by Charles Meigh & Son.

Typical Examples Include:

B1640 2617
B1641 2619

KAD NO. **GODDEN NO.** **MARK**

B1642 2618

In *FOB*, No. 71, Spring 1991, p. 4, C. Howard Mumford notes that the name "MEIGH" appears in Greek letter (X. MEIVN/HAVTEY) and is transcribed into English for convenience. With reference to the Minton mark, KAD B1735, Mumford notes "the symbols in the border appear to be meaningless." This same would apply to a marking with the term "INDIAN STONE CHINA".

B1643 - **INDIAN STONE CHINA**

B1644 -

Printed marks of various designs noted on Historic American/Canadian views, often including printed series and title names, c.1832-1850.
- Impressed mark KAD B1642 often accompanies the above.
- Margaret Ironside's article in *NCS Newsletter* No. 89, March 1993, and No. 95, Sept. 1994, notes fifty differing pseudo-Chinese marks.

For further reading, refer to *Snyder, Romantic Staffordshire*, pp. 68-69; *Henrywood*, pp. 106-119; *Woolliscroft-Rhead*, pp. 1993-194; and *Echoes and Reflections*. Occasional Paper No. 2 of The Northern Ceramic Society. Wells, England. 1990, pp. 14-20 for an article by Ronald Brown titled "The Meighs of Hanley, Staffordshire. Also see Job Meigh for additional comments.

MEIGH

***Charles Meigh & Son**
Old Hall Pottery
Hanley, Staffordshire, c.1850-1861
Subsequently, Old Hall Earthenware Co., Ltd. (1862-1867)

B1645 2620 **C. M. & S.** Printed marks of differing design. Pattern name often included, c.1850-1861.

B1646 2620A **M. & S.**

B1647 2621 **C. MEIGH & SON**

Typical Marks Include:

B1648 -
B1649 -
B1650 -

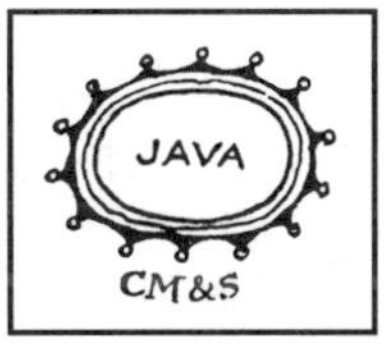

B1651 2622

Printed marks, including Royal Arms, occur with the name "MEIGH", "MEIGH'S" or "C. MEIGH & SON", c.1850-1861.

B1652 -

Printed or impressed mark "OPAQUE PORCELAIN" noted alone or in conjunction with other marks, c.1850-1861.

KAD NO.	GODDEN NO.	MARK	
B1653	-		Printed mark noted on White Ironstone, c.1850-1861. - KAD Nos. B1640, B1641 and B1642 continued to be used, c.1850-1861.
B1654	-	**IMPROVED FELSPAR C. MEIGH & SON**	Impressed mark, as above, noted on White Ironstone, c.1850-1861. - Refer to *Stoltzfus/Snyder*, p. 20.

For further reading, refer to *Henrywood*, pp. 106-119; and *Godden, Collecting Lustreware*, pp. 134-135.

MEIGH

***Charles Meigh, Son & Pankhurst**
Old Hall Pottery
Hanley, Staffordshire, c.1850

KAD NO.	GODDEN NO.	MARK	
B1655	2624	**C. M. S. & P.**	Printed marks of differing design. Pattern name often included, c.1850
B1656	-		

MEIGH

***Job Meigh (& Son)**
Old Hall Pottery,
Hanley, Staffordshire, c.1805-1811
- "& Son" dates from 1812-1832
Job Meigh died in 1817, but the name continued on as Job Meigh & Son (c.1812-1832)

KAD NO.	GODDEN NO.	MARK	
B1657	2625	**MEIGH**	Impressed name mark, c.1805-1832.
B1658	2626	**OLD HALL**	Printed or impressed mark, c.1805+.
B1659	2627	**J. M. & S.**	Printed initial mark, c.1812-1832.
B1660	2628		Printed marks on good quality printed plate found in the Godden collection, c.1815-1832.
B1661	-		

- *Coysh*, Vol. II, p. 110 and KAD No. B1642 notes the wording "MEIGH" above and "HANLEY" below, found on "Zoological Sketches" series. This is a mark frequently found on earthenwares of Charles Meigh, c.1832-1850. See p. 278.

- *Godden* indicates a further complication, stating that depending upon the period, the initials "J. M. & S." usually relate to J. Meir & Son (1837-1860).

For further reading, refer to *Godden, Collecting Lustreware*, pp. 134-136; and *Godden, British Porcelain*, p. 526.

MEIKLE

KAD NO.	GODDEN NO.	MARK	

Meikle Bros. [Canadian?]
(Potter nor Pottery located. Possibly an Importer's mark.)

B1662 - MEIKLE BROS

Printed marks noted on White Ironstone.
- See *Wetherbee*, p. 58.

Typical Marks Include:

B1663 -
B1664 -

- *Sussman,* pp. 67-69, notes that the "Canada" pattern was first introduced by Clementson Bros. in 1877.

For further reading, refer to *Collard, Pottery & Porcelain*, p. 133.

MEIR

John Meir
Greengates Pottery,
Tunstall, Staffordshire, c.1812-1836
- Greengates Pottery was acquired in 1822. Other pottery remains unidentified.
Subsequently, J. Meir & Son (c.1837-1897)

B1665 - **MEIR**

Printed or impressed marks of differing design. Pattern name often included, c.1812-1836.
- See comments under John Maddock, pp. 261-262.

B1666 2632 **I. M.**
B1667 - **I. MEIR**
B1668 2631 **J. M.**

B1669 - **G/R & CROWN**

B1670 - **WARRANTED STAFFORDSHIRE**

B1671 -

- "Chen-si" may be one of the earliest Flow Blue patterns dating from the mid-1830s period. I suspect, however, that this pattern was issued by J. Meir & Son (1837- 1860) in the late 1830s-1840s using the initials of John Meir, as is evident by the Flow Blue manufactured by "& SON". "Chen-si" is the only Flow Blue pattern recorded to-date.
-Additional marking "STONE CHINA" noted, see *Penny Plain*, p. 96, No. 205.
- The hypotheses given above, while rational, still leads this author to believe that Maddock was the manufacturer of the "Chen-si" pattern, especially after having seen at least a dozen platters with the exact pattern and printed mark. (See KAD No. B 1487 for John Maddock.)
- These marks and patterns were continued by J. Meir & Son (c.1837-1897). Refer to *Coysh*, Vol. I and II; *FOB* Occasional Papers, No. 1, Spring 1990, pp. 1-10 for an article by Doreen Otto.

KAD NO.	GODDEN NO.	MARK

- *Edwards, Basalt*, **pp. 192-193 notes the following history for the name Meir:**

John & Richard Meir	Market Square, Shelton, Hanley	1770-1785
Richard Meir	Hanley	1785-1794
John Meir	Market Square, Shelton, Hanley	1785-1808
John & Matthew Meir	Market Square, Shelton, Hanley	1808-1814
Matthew Meir & Co.	Shelton	1814
John Meir	John Street, Shelton	1814-1826

MEIR

John Meir & Son
Greengates Pottery,
Tunstall, Staffordshire, c.1837-1897*
Formerly, John Meir (c.1812-1836)
Subsequently acquired by Wm. Adams & Sons (Potters) Ltd. (c.1896)

B1672 2633 **J. M. & S.** Printed or impressed marks of differing design. Pattern name often included, c.1837-1897.

B1673 2634 **I. M. & S.***

B1674 2635
B1675 -

- Pattern names and marks were continued from John Meir (c.1812-1836). (See "Crown Acorn Series).

- Additional marking "J. MEIR & CO." noted. This mark, however, may not relate to "& SON".

B1675A - **JOHN MEIR & SON IVY WREATH** Impressed circular name mark with Registry Diamond and pattern name, 1844-1897.

*Care with the initials "J. M. & S." must be taken, as these initials may also relate to Job Meigh & Son (c.1812-1832).

B1676 - Printed Royal Coat of Arms mark noted on White Ironstone, c.1837-1897.
- Refer to *Stoltzfus/Snyder*.

B1677 - **JOHN MEIR & SON TUNSTALL** Printed name mark, c.1837-1897.
- "WARRANTED" added, c.1860-1897.

B1678 2637 **MEIR & SON** Printed name mark, c.1837-1897.
- "ENGLAND" added after 1891.

Typical Marks Include:

B1679 -
B1680 2639
B1681 2640
B1682 2641

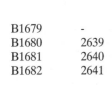

KAD NO.	GODDEN NO.	MARK	

- John Meir & Son purchased registered designs from both D. Chetwynd and G. W. Reade. *Wetherbee, White Ironstone*, p. 213, notes that the registered Baltic Shape (October 25, 1885, No. 102325) was purchased from G. W. Reade. It was not an uncommon practice to sell one's registry to another potter at this time, nor was it uncommon to have a shape or design registered by a retailer, or designer, etc.

- Also refer to Robert H. Penman & Co. for "Columbia Shape", p. 302.

*In a letter dated April 15, 1996, Geoffrey Godden notes "...John Meir & Son dates. The available records do not seem complete. John is recorded to 1836 then there is a gap until John Meir & Son occurs in 1841. The change over was somewhere between these dates!"

MELLOR

Mellor, Taylor & Co.
Top Bridge Works (c.1880-1883)
The Cleveland Works (c.1884-1904)
Burslem, Staffordshire, c.1880-1904

KAD NO.	GODDEN NO.	MARK	
B1683	-	**MELLOR TAYLOR & CO.**	Printed or impressed name marks, c.1880-1904. - Note trade terms such as "ROYAL IRONSTONE", "SEMI PORCELAIN" and "WARRANTED STONE CHINA".

Typical Marks Include:

KAD NO.	GODDEN NO.
B1684	2647
B1685	2648
B1686	-
B1687	-

For further reading, refer to *Tea Leaf Readings*, Educational Supplement, May 1994; *Heaivilin*, pp. 99-103; and *Stoltzfus/Snyder*, p. 171.

MELLOR

Mellor, Venables & Co.
Hole House, Nile Street,
Burslem, Staffordshire, c.1834-1851
- "& Co." - Thomas Pindar who left in 1847

KAD NO.	GODDEN NO.	MARK	
B1688	2645	**M. V. & CO.**	Printed or impressed marks with various designs. Name of individual pattern often included, c.1834-1851.
B1689	2646	**MELLOR VENABLES & CO.**	- Impressed marking "IRONSTONE" may be noted accompanying registration marks, which may be printed or impressed, c. 1834-1851.
B1690	-		Impressed Royal Coat of Arms mark noted on a "Whampoa" Flow Blue soup, c.1850. - "ROYAL PATENT" notes a prior processing patent issued.

KAD NO.	GODDEN NO.	MARK	
B1691	-		Printed or impressed mark noted on Historic American/Canadian Views, often including printed series and title names, c.1834-1851. - For additional marks and registration marks refer to *P. Williams, Staffordshire*, Vol. I, p. 333 and Vol. II, pp. 603-604 wherein reference is made to "Medici" pattern registered in July 1847. Also refer to *Hill*, p. 299 for "Windsor" pattern registered August 27, 1849. For further reading, refer to *Snyder, Historic Staffordshire*, pp. 69-70; and *Snyder, Romantic Staffordshire*, pp. 130-131; and *Cluett*, pp. 72-73.

METHVEN

David Methven & Sons
Kirkcaldy Pottery, Kirkcaldy, Scotland, 1847-1928
Formerly, George Methven (1837-1847)
Subsequently, Andrew R. Young (who joined as partner in 1870)
- Firm's marks and name continue until 1928.

History:

Wm. Robertson (Robertson's son-in-law) & Wm. Adams (the architect father of Robert and James) start a brick and tile works.	1714
Wm. Adams dies and his son John takes over.	1748
David Methven becomes manager.	1773
David Methven buys works for 400£ (no pottery is made at this time).	1776
John Methven starts to make brownware.	1805
Builds a second pottery.	1809
Pottery is inherited by John, with brick works by George Methven.	1827
John dies and pottery is left to daughter Mary (Methven) and her husband Robert Heron; but is sold to George Methven.	1837
George dies and pottery goes to nephew, David Methven.	1847
A. R. Young becomes a partner with James Methven (David's son).	1870
Partners in pottery are A. R. Young and his sons, William, Andrew and James.	1887
Brick works is closed and a new pottery is built.	1897
A. R. Young dies.	1944
Pottery closes.	1928

KAD NO.	GODDEN NO.	MARK	
B1692	2651	**D. M. & S.**	Printed marks of differing design. Pattern name often included, c.1870-1928.
B1693	-	**D. M. & SS**	
B1694	-	**D. M. & SONS**	- Earlier wares, c.1847-1870, were generally unmarked.
B1695	-	**IMPERIAL** **D. M. & SONS**	-Impressed marking including term "IMPERIAL" noted, c.1870s. - Refer to *Finlayson*, pp. 55-63.
B1696	2652	**METHVEN**	Printed Royal Coat of Arms mark noted on White Ironstone "Wheat" pattern, c.1870-1890.
B1697	2653	**D. METHVEN & SONS**	- Refer to *Sussman*, p. 34.
B1698	-		- A variation in spelling of "SONS" as "SO" is further noted, possibly due to a flawed mark impression, c. 1870-1928. - "ENGLAND" after 1891.

KAD NO.	GODDEN NO.	MARK	
B1699	-		Printed marks, in Flow Blue, with sponge printed border noted. c.1870s.
B1700	-		- Note Registered Trade Mark "Methven"

For further reading, refer to *Kelly*, p. 18; Graeme Cruickshank's article "Scottish Spongeware" in the *Scottish Pottery Studies*, Edinburgh, Scotland, Scottish Pottery Society, 1982; Peter Davis and Robert Rankine. *Wemyss Ware*, Edinburgh and London, Scottish Academic Press. 1986, for a further family history and chronology. Also refer to *McVeigh*, pp. 129-143; and *Finlayson.*

MIDDLESBROUGH

Middlesbrough Earthenware Co.
Middlesbrough-on-Tees, Yorkshire, c.1844-1852
Formerly, Middlesbrough Pottery Co. (c.1831-1844)
Subsequently, Isaac Wilson & Co. (c.1852-1887)

B1701 2654 **M. E. CO.** Printed or impressed marks of differing design. Pattern name often included, c.1844-1852.

B1702 - 

Impressed Middlesbrough mark is normally attributed to the c.1831-1844 period, but was definitely carried on by this company until 1852. (Refer to Mark KAD B1712)

For further reading, refer to *Lawrence*; and *Godden, Collecting Lustreware*, p. 263.

MIDDLESBROUGH

Middlesbrough Pottery Co.
Middlesbrough-on-Tees, Yorkshire, c.1831-1844
Subsequently, Middlesbrough Earthenware Co. (1844-1852)

KAD NO.	GODDEN NO.	MARK	
B1703	2655	**M. P. CO.**	Printed or impressed marks of differing design. Pattern name often included, c.1831-1844.
B1704	2656	**MIDDLESBRO' POTTERY CO.**	
B1705	2656A	**MIDDLESBRO' POTTERY**	

Typical Marks Include:

B1706
B1707 -
B1708 -
B1709 -
B1710 -

B1711 - **MIDDLESBRO POTTERY** Printed Anchor mark, c.1831-1852.
- Several variations exist, all marked around the anchor.
- Marks were continued by Middlesbrough Earthenware Co., c.1844-1852.

KAD NO.	GODDEN NO.	MARK
B1712	2657	
B1713	2657A	
B1714	-	

B1715 2658

Printed or impressed mark, c.1831-1844.
- Numbers may appear above mark.
- *Godden* notes this mark as of a later period.
- A similar mark (KAD B1513) was issued by Malkin, Walker & Hulse (c.1858-1864).
- See comments relative to the "LONDON/ANCHOR" impressed mark under Isaac & Thomas Bell, p. 109.
- *Noel Riley,* p. 40, No. 111 notes an additional marking/signature by the engraver "T. ROBSON", 1834-1852.
- Also refer to Middlesbrough Earthenware Co., p. 285.

For further reading, refer to *Lawrence*, pp. 209-210; *Godden, Collecting Lustreware*, p. 263; and *Penny Plain*, p. 102, No. 280.

MIDWINTER

W. R. Midwinter (Ltd.)
Bourne's Bank Pottery, Burslem (1910-1916)
Albion Pottery, (1916-1932)
Hadderidge Potteries (1932-1968)
Burslem, Staffordshire, 1910-1968
- In 1964 Midwinter acquired A. J. Wilkinson, Ltd. and the Newport Pottery. In 1968 they merged with J. & G. Meakin, Ltd. and then in 1980 merged with the Wedgwood Group.

B1716 - **W. R. MIDWINTER**

Printed name marks, c.1932-1941.
- Early wares were generally unmarked.

KAD NO.	GODDEN NO.
B1717	2664
B1718	2665

c.1932-1941

- For additional marks from 1941 to the post-ware period see *Godden*, p. 436, as well as his comment on p. 295 relative to "Group Letters" which were introduced because of war time controls.
- Additionally, *NCSJ*, Vol. 12, 1995, pp. 175-213 includes an article by Kathy Niblett titled "The British Pottery Industry 1942-1952", wherein Ms. Niblett documents this period as Ten Plain Years.

For further reading, refer to *Bunt, British Potters*, pp. 37-38; *Niblett*, p. 83; *Batkin*, pp. 106-111; and *Midwinter Pottery, A Revolution in British Tableware.* Steven Jenkins (ed. by Paul Atterbury), England, Richard Dennis. 1997

MILLER

KAD NO.	GODDEN NO.	MARK	
			James Miller & Co., Ltd. **Port-Dundas Pottery, Bishop Street,** **Glasgow, Scotland, c.1869-1904** **- Miller was a Stoneware pottery** **- Also see North British Pottery, p. 296.**
1719	-	**PORT DUNDAS POTTERY CO. GLASGOW**	Printed oval mark noted on stoneware pottery, c.1869-1904.

For further reading, refer to *Godden*, p. 504 for comments on the Port-Dundas Pottery Co., Ltd.; *Cameron*, p. 224 for an extensive history; and *Fleming*, pp. 226-227.

MINTON

***Minton (& Various Partnerships)**
Stoke-on-Trent, Staffordshire, 1793-Present

- Early wares were either unmarked or noted with a pattern number.
Printed marks of differing design. Pattern name often included.
- Many patterns were reissued at later dates.

Minton, 1824-1836

B1720 -  Printed letter M in script, c. 1824-1836.

B1721 2688 **MINTON**
B1722 -
B1723 -
B1724 -

Minton & Boyle, 1836-1841

B1725 2693 **M. & B.**
B1726 2693A
B1727 -
B1728 -

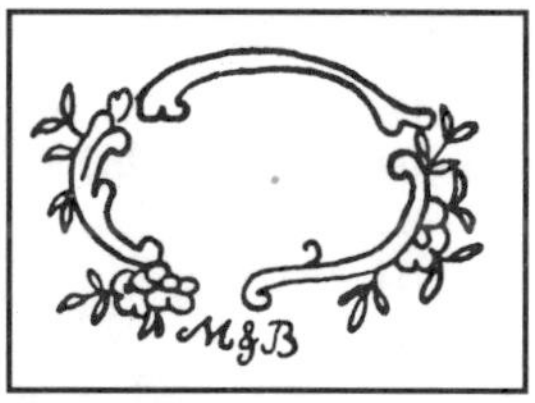

Minton & Co., 1841-1873

B1729 2694 **M. & CO.**
B1730 2696
B1731 -

KAD NO.	GODDEN NO.	MARK

Minton & Hollins, 1845-1868

B1732	2697	M. & H.
B1733	2698	
B1734	-	

Note: "ENGLAND"

- In 1868 Michael Hollins opened his own pottery, Minton Hollins (& Co.) (Ltd.). Care must be taken when attributing the initials "M. H. & Co." This new company was in the business of manufacturing tile.

B1735 -

Printed or impressed trade-markings in various combinations, with or without name or pattern markings, 1820s-1871.

- F. Howard Mumford notes in *FOB*, No. 71, Spring 1991, p. 4 the confusion that arises in attributing the "IMPROVED/STONE CHINA" mark of C. H. Meigh, Hanley and Minton. The characteristic differences between both markings is in the text. Meigh's is written in Greek while Minton's "...symbols in the border appear to be meaningless." Also see KAD B1642.

B1736	-	FLORENTINE CHINA
B1737	-	NEW STONE
B1738	-	OPAQUE CHINA
B1739	-	SEMI-CHINA
B1740	-	SEMI-NANKIN CHINA
B1741	-	STONE CHINA

Printed Marks of 1850-1870:

B1742	2695
B1743	2702
B1744	2704
B1745	2705

Selected Marks Noted on Various Wares, 1824-1875:

B1746	2685
B1747	2690
B1748	2701
B1749	-
B1750	2708

1824-1836 FELSPAR

1830-1860 RELIEF PAD

1846-1856 RELIEF MARK PARIAN FIGURE

c.1870 COLEMAN'S NATURALIST MOTIFS

1871-1875 DECORATED MARK

For further reading about Minton's involvement with the Willow Pattern during the eighteenth century, when he worked as an engraver, see *Willow*, David Richard Quinter, Ontario, Canada. General Store Publishing House, 1997

KEY TO MONTH LETTERS

J	January
F	February
M	March
A	April
E	May
I	June
H	July
Y	August
S	September
O	October
N	November
D	December

YEAR CIPHERS

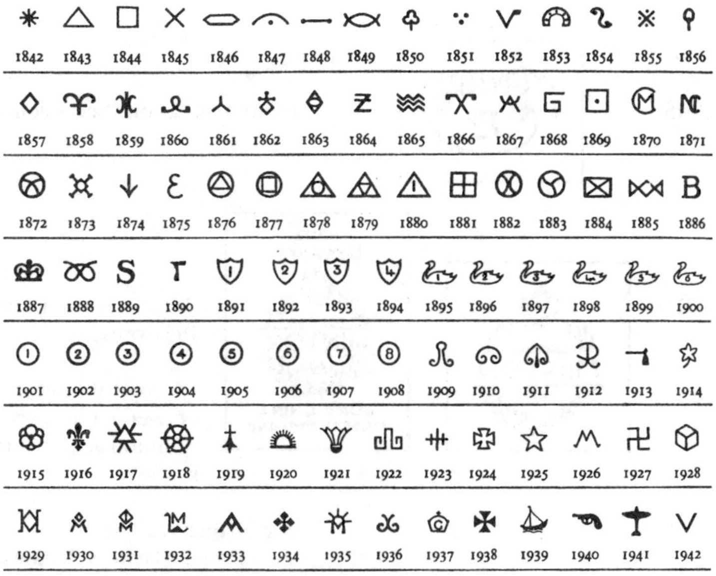

Impressed Year Cyphers from 1842-1942. Such marks occur in sets of three: month letter, potter's mark and the year cypher. From 1920-1968 the last two figures of the year were impressed.
- Cypher Chart reproduced by permission of Minton Museum, Royal Doulton PLC.

B1751 2705 **B. B.** Impressed initials "B. B." found on some earthenware. The initials stand for "BEST BODY", c.1830-1850.

B1752 2706 **MINTON** Impressed name mark, c.1862-1872.
- This mark usually occurs along with impressed year cyphers.

B1753 2711 **MINTONS** As above, but note the addition of "S" to the name "MINTON*S*", 1873-1951.
Printed Standard Globe Trade-mark, c.1863+

B1754 2707
B1755 -
B1756 2713
B1757 -
B1758 -

1863-1872

1873-1891

1875-1891

1891-c.1920

c.1920-1951

- The crown was deleted on some earthenware from c.1901 Printed marks commemorating special events or incorporating a retailer name. Such marks usually include date.

Typical Examples of Special Event Marks Include:

B1759 2712
B1760 -
B1761 -

B1762 2714 **MINTONS ENGLAND** Impressed or molded mark, c.1891-1910.

KAD NO.	GODDEN NO.	MARK	
B1763	2715		Printed marks on "Secessionist" earthenware, 1902-1914.
B1764	2717		Printed, revised, current marking. May include pattern name and number, 1951-present.
B1765	-		

- A copy of Minton's sales ledger from January-July 1882, including a listing of twenty-four importers, is illustrated by *Ewins*, p. 72, Table 12.
- Minton acquired the copper plates of Bathwell & Goodfellow from a sale in 1861.

For further reading, refer to Geoffrey A. Godden. *Minton Pottery & Porcelain of the First Period*. Barrie & Jenkins. London. 1968; *Godden, Collecting Lustreware*, pp. 136-147; P. Atterbury & M. Batkin. *The Dictionary of Minton*. Antique Collectors Club. England, 1990; *Jones*; *Henrywood, Relief Moulded Jugs*, Ch. 7, pp. 81-94; and *NCSJ*, Vol. 7, 1998, pp. 27-43 for an article by Geoffrey Priestman titled "In Search of Early Minton Blue & White."

MOORE

Moore & Co.
Old Foley Pottery,
Fenton, Staffordshire, 1872-1892
Subsequently, Moore, Leason & Co. (1892-1896)

B1766	2748	**M. & CO.**	Printed or impressed marks of differing design. Pattern name often included, 1872-1892.

- The initials "M. & CO." were used by Minton & Co. as well as (M) Moore & Co. Care must be taking in attributing initials for all potters.
- *Godden, British Porcelain*, p. 546 notes "…at an unknown date between 1889-1892, the style was changed to Moore, Leason & Co."

For further reading, refer to *Godden*, p. 448, "Moore, Leason & Co.;" *Hampson, Churchill*, pp. 35, 69.

MOORE

(Samuel) Moore & Co.
Wear Pottery,
Southwick, Sunderland, Durham, 1803-1874
Formerly, John Brunton (1789-1805)
Subsequently, Glaholm, Lisle & Robinson (1875-1882)
- R. T. Wilkinson, using old style from (1866-1875)
History:

Samuel Moore & Co.	
(Co. - Peter Austin)	1803-1831
Charles Moore	1831-1847
Charles & George S. Moore	1847-1856
George S. Moore	1856-1861
Ralph Seddon (Manager)	1861-1874

KAD NO.	GODDEN NO.	MARK	
B1767	2743	**MOORE & CO. SUNDERLAND**	Printed or impressed marks of differing design. Pattern name often included, 1803-1874. - Various forms of initials or names are noted.
B1768	2744	**MOORE & CO.**	
B1769	2745	**S. MOORE & CO.**	
B1770	2746	**S. M. & CO.**	
B1771	2747	**SAMUEL MOORE & CO.**	

For further reading, refer to the various illustrations found in *Godden, Illustrated Encyclopaedia*; *Baker*, pp. 56-59; *Williams-Wood, English Transfer*, pp. 206-207; *NCS Newsletter* No 104, Dec. 1996, pp. 24-29 for an article by John Cockerill titled "A Potters' Flint Mill at Beamish Co., Durham;" and *Woolliscroft-Rhead*, p. 183 for "Moore & Co. (Southwick)."

MORLEY

Morley & Ashworth
Broad Street,
Shelton, Hanley Staffordshire, 1859-1862
Formerly, F. Morley (1845-1858)
Subsequently, G. L. Ashworth & Bros., (1862-1968)

KAD NO.	GODDEN NO.	MARK	
B1772	2754	**M. & A.**	Printed marks of differing design. Pattern name often included, 1859-1862
B1773	2755	**MORLEY & ASHWORTH HANLEY**	

Typical Marks Include:

KAD NO.	GODDEN NO.
B1774	2756
B1775	2757
B1776	2758
B1777	-

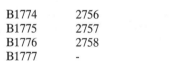

Godden notes this partnership as a vital link in the preservation of the original Mason designs, plates, molds, etc.
For further reading, refer to *Godden, Mason*.

MORLEY

Francis Morley (& Co.)
Broad Street,
Shelton, Hanley, Staffordshire, c.1845-1859
Formerly, Ridgway & Morley (c.1842-1845)
Subsequently, Morley & Ashworth (c.1859-1862)
- "& CO." from 1850-1859

KAD NO.	GODDEN NO.	MARK	
B1778	2759	**F. M.**	Printed or impressed marks noted with various and often elaborately designed marks. Name of individual pattern is often included, c.1845-1859.
B1779	2760	**F. M. & CO.**	
B1780	2761	**F. MORLEY & CO.**	

KAD NO.	GODDEN NO.	MARK
B1781	-	

Note marking and usage of "IRONSTONE", "REAL IRONSTONE", "REAL STONE CHINA", "ROYAL STONE CHINA" and "OPAQUE CHINA", c. 1850-1859.

- Importer's mark noted" "BEST QUALITY/TYNDALE/& MITCHELL/ NO. 219 CHESTNUT STREET/PHILADELPHIA/F. M. & CO."

Typical Marks Include:

KAD NO.	GODDEN NO.
B1782	2462
B1783	2463
B1784	-
B1785	2464

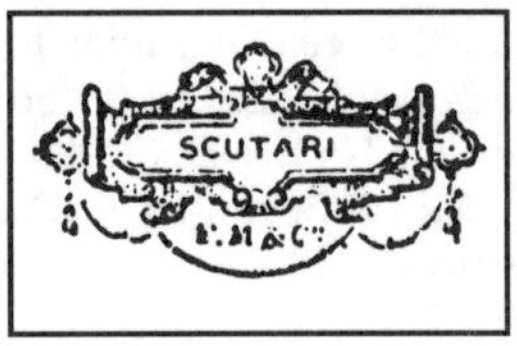

KAD NO.	GODDEN NO.
B1786	-
B1787	-
B1788	-
B1789	-

KAD NO.	GODDEN NO.
B1790	-

- The use of copper engraving plates (for patterns and marks) from one partnership into another, or the purchasing of copper plates from manufactories that went out of business seems to have been a fairly common occurrence among potters of the nineteenth century. Note the reissued printed stamp of Masons' marked "Morley's", c.1848(+) and continued by G. L. Ashworth up to 1968.

KAD NO.	GODDEN NO.
B1791	-

Printed marks of various design, as well as a rare, impressed Registration Mark dated May 31, 1845/No. 2;7800 (for Lake Series) noted on Historic America/Canadian Views, which often included printed series and title names, c.1845-1849.

KAD NO.	GODDEN NO.	MARK
B1792	-	**F. M. (& CO)**

- Elizabeth Collard extensively mentions Morley's Bartlett Views (Lake Series) in Chapter 8 of *Collard, Potter's View*. I have abstracted her listing of this series as it differs from those of *Arman* and *Larsen*, see p. 439. This series was registered by Morley on May 31, 1845 and had the design number 278000. The same series was continued by Morley & Ashworth and then registered by Ashworth [alone] in February 1884.

For further reading, refer to *Godden, Mason's*, pp. 131, 267; *Godden, British Porcelain*, pp.650-651; *Godden, Ridgway*, pp. 166-169; and *Snyder, Historic Staffordshire*, pp. 70-71.

MOSELEY

John Moseley
(John & William Moseley)
Church Yard Works, Cobridge, 1801-1822
and Black Works, Burslem, c.1809-1822
Formerly, Moseley & Dale (1801-1809)*

KAD NO.	GODDEN NO.	MARK	
B1793	2791	**MOSELEY**	Impressed name mark, 1801-1822. **Edwards, Basalt*, pp. 205-207 notes a partnership of John & William Moseley, "... in the manufacture of earthenware in Burslem...sometime after 1801 and prior to 1809..." Their partnership dissolved on November 11, 1809.

For further reading, refer to *Godden, Collecting Lustreware*, p. 380; *Little*, p. 86; and *NCSJ*, Vol. 8, 1991, pp. 91-124 for an article by Ann Eatwell & Alex Werner titled "A London Staffordshire Warehouse, 1794-1825."

MOUNTFORD

George Thomas Mountford
Alexander Pottery, Wolfe Street,
Stoke-on-Trent, Staffordshire, c.1888-1898
Subsequently, Myott, Son & Co. (Ltd.)(1898-1902)

KAD NO.	GODDEN NO.	MARK	
B1794	2796		Printed mark, pattern name often included, c.1888-1898.

MUIR

Andrew Muir (& Co.)
Clyde Pottery,
Greenock, Scotland, c.1816-1840(41)
- "& Co." c.1836-1840(41)
Subsequently, Thomas Shirley & Co. (c.1840(41)-1857)
Also see: Clyde Pottery, pp. 153-154

KAD NO.	GODDEN NO.	MARK	
B572	-	**A. M.**	Printed mark, c.1816-1840(41). - Initial "A. M." dates from 1836-1841 period. - Partners were Andrew Muir, Andrew Muir, Jr. and James Youngerson.

Henry E. Kelly's article in the *Scottish Pottery 15th Historical Review, 1993*. pp. 19-23, titled "The Muir Brothers and The Clyde Pottery" notes that "...The Andrew Muir's played no part in the Clyde Pottery before the death of James in December 1834." He further notes that in "...The Register of Seisins for the County of Renfrew, (dated Sept. 15th) there is an entry describing James Stevenson, James Muir, and Alan Ker, Jr. ...co-partners in the Clyde Pottery Company as taking possession of the land on the North side..."

MYOTT

Myott, Son & Co. (Ltd.) c.1898-1977
Alexander Pottery,
Wolfe Street, Stoke-on-Trent (c.1898-1902) and (1927-1969)
Cobridge Works, Cobridge (c.1902-1947(69)
Hanley (c.1947-1986)
Formerly, G. Mountford (1888-1898)
- Retitled, Myott-Meakin Ltd. from 1977

KAD NO.	GODDEN NO.	MARK	
B1795	-	**M. S. & Co.**	Printed marks of differing design. Pattern name often included, 1898-1977.

Typical Marks Include:

KAD NO.	GODDEN NO.
B1796	2809
B1797	2810
B1798	2811

c.1898-1902

c.1900+

c.1907+

For further reading, refer to *Hampson*, *Churchill*. Also refer to Appendix B6, Chronology for Churchill, p. 543.

NAUTILUS

Nautilus Porcelain Co.
Denmark Pottery, Possil Park,
Glasgow, Scotland, c.1896-1911
Formerly, Possil Pottery Co. (c.1895-1896)
- Also see Possil Pottery for a chronology

KAD NO.	GODDEN NO.
B1799	2838
B1800	2839

The Nautilus Porcelain Company renamed itself as the Possil Pottery from c.1896-1911, see p. 308.
- Printed Nautilus Porcelain Trade-mark was registered in 1892 under the name Nautilus Porcelain Co., Reg. No. 189577.

For further reading, refer to J. F. Blacker. *The ABC of [XIX Century] English Ceramic Art*. London, England. Stanley Paul & Co. Ltd. c. 1911. p. 505; and *Godden, British Porcelain*, pp.553-554.

NEALE

(James) Neale & Co.
Church Works,
Hanley, Staffordshire, c.1778-1782
and Neale & Wilson [Partnership], 1783-1792
Formerly, Humphrey Palmer (1750s-1778)
Subsequently, Robert Wilson (1792-1801)

KAD NO.	GODDEN NO.	MARK	
B1801	2841	**N**	Impressed initial or name marks, c.1778-1782.
B1802	2842	**NEALE**	- Additional marking "NEALE HANLEY" noted.
B1803	2843	**I. NEALE**	
B1804	2844	**I. NEALE & CO.**	Impressed name mark in circular form, c.1778-1782.
B1805	2845	**NEALE & CO.**	Impressed name mark, "& CO." added, c.1778-1782.

KAD NO.	GODDEN NO.	MARK	
B1806	2846		The Crown and "C" (or "G") is sometimes found in conjunction with earlier name or initial markings. - *Godden* notes the "G" and crown mark on wares of the 1820 period.
B1807	2850	**NEALE & WILSON**	Impressed [partnership] marks, c.1783-1792.

For further reading, on Neale & Co. refer to *Edwards, Basalt;* and *Godden, Staffordshire*, Ch. 4, pp. 46-56. For information on Neale & Wilson refer to Diana Edwards, *Neale Pottery and Porcelain, 1763-1820.* London. Barrie & Jenkins, 1987. Also refer to *Williams-Wood, English Transfer*, pp. 171-172; *Godden*, p. 463; *Godden, Collecting Lustreware*, pp. 176-177; and Pat Halfpenny, *English Earthenware Figures, 1740-1840*, England. Antique Collectors Club. 1991, pp. 140-151.

NEW WHARF

New Wharf Pottery Co.
New Street, Burslem, Staffordshire, c.1878-1894
Subsequently, Wood & Son(s) (Ltd.) (1894-1982)

KAD NO.	GODDEN NO.	MARK	
B1808	2882	**N. W. P. CO.**	Printed marks of differing design. Pattern name often included, 1878-1894.
B1809	2884	**N. W. P. CO. B.**	- Wood & Son(s) (Ltd.) reissued the "CONWAY" and many prior patterns.
B1810	2885	**N. W. P. CO. BURSLEM**	

Typical Marks (1890-1894) Include:

B1811 2886
B1812 -
B1813 -
B1814 -

B1815 -

Printed Beehive mark with urn to the left c.1878-1894. This is similar to Samuel Alcock markings, see KAD B93 & B94.

For additional marks refer to *Gaston*, Vol. II, Mark. 100A, p. 33.

NEWPORT

Newport Pottery Co. Ltd.
Newport Lane, Burslem, Staffordshire, 1920-1964
Formerly, Deans (1910) Ltd. (1910-1919)
Subsequently, acquired by W. R. Midwinter in 1964
- Merged with J. & G. Meakin in 1968, then acquired by the Wedgwood Group in 1870
-Newport Works closed in 1987

KAD NO.	GODDEN NO.	MARK	
B1816	2876		Printed marks of differing design, c.1920-1964.
B1817	-	 **c.1920+**	Printed mark with "Greyhound" standing on base (similar to Edge Malkin & Co., KAD No. B829), c.1920-1964. - Marked above "NEWPORT POTTERY CO. LTD." - For exact mark refer to *Gaston*, Vol. II, pp. 33, Mark 97A. - Shorter & Son acquired the Newport Pottery in 1920. In turn, it was acquired by Crown Devon (S. Fielding & Co., Ltd.) in 1964 and closed in 1982.

For further reading, refer to *Niblett,* p. 83.

NICHOLSON

Thomas Nicholson & Co.
Castleford Pottery,
Castleford, Yorkshire, c.1854-1871
Formerly, Wood & Nicholson (1837-1854)
Subsequently, Clokie & Masterman (1871-1885)

B1818	2887	**T. N. & CO.**	Printed marks of differing design. Pattern name often included, c.1854-1871.
B1819	2888		For further reading, refer to *Lawrence* and *True Blue*, p. 49, No. 1, for pattern "WILD ROSE".

NORTH BRITISH

North British Pottery
Dobbies Loan,
Glasgow, Scotland, c.1867-1874
-Also see: James Miller & Co., Ltd., Robert H. Penman & Co., and Alexander Balfour & Co.

B1820	2896	**J. M. & CO.**	Printed marks of differing design. Pattern name often included, c.1867-1874. - To separate this pottery from the Marshall Pottery of Bo'ness, who used the same initials, the term **"GLASGOW"** is usually included in the markings of the North British Pottery.
B1821	297	**I. M. & CO.**	- Initials "I" and "J" were used interchangeably during the early nineteenth century.
B1822	2898	**J. M. & CO.**	

For further reading, refer to *Godden*, p. 469; *Coysh*, Vol. I, p. 313 for the "Rural" pattern; and the *Scottish Society Archive News*, No. 4, 1979, pp. 53-54 for an article by Gerald Quail titled "The North British Pottery of A. & J. Winkles, Leith."

OLD HALL

Old Hall (Earthenware) Pottery Co. Ltd.*
Old Hall Pottery,
Hanley Staffordshire, 1862-1886
Formerly, Charles Meigh & Son (1850-1861)
Subsequently, Old Hall Porcelain Works, Ltd. (1886-1902)

KAD NO.	GODDEN NO.	MARK	
B1823	2917	**O. H. E. C.**	Printed marks of differing design. Pattern name often included, 1862-1886.
B1824	2918	**O. H. E. C. (L).**	
B1825	2919		Printed or impressed initial mark, 1862-1886.
B1826	2920		One of several ornate printed marks with the full title of the pottery, c.1862-1886. - See *White Ironstone Notes*, Vol. 4, No. 2, Fall 1997, p. 11. - Note the similarity to Elsmore & Forster, KAD B895, as well as to Elsmore & Son, KAD B 900.
B1827	2921	**INDIAN/STONE/CHINA**	Impressed marks continued in conjunction with printed marks from Charles Meigh & Son, c. 1862+.
B1828	2623	**OPAQUE/PORCELAIN**	- The words **"INDIAN STONE CHINA"** and **"OPAQUE PORCELAIN"** are slightly curved. See *Godden*, pp. 428 and 474.
B1829	2922		Printed trade-mark, registered in 1884 and continued by Old Hall Porcelain Works, Ltd. (1886-1902). Refer to *Godden*, p. 475.

For further reading, refer to *Godden, British Porcelain*, p. 572; *Henrywood*, p. 106; and *Cluett*, pp. 14, 73, where he notes that Jones acquired two lots of Old Hall's engravings in 1907.
*Both *Godden* and *Henrywood* note this firm as The First Liability (Ltd.) Co. in the Staffordshire Potteries.

OULSNAM

W. E. Oulsnam (& Sons)
Tunstall (1867-1871) and Burslem (1872-1892),
Staffordshire, 1867-1892
- "& Sons" from 1872

KAD NO.	GODDEN NO.	MARK	
B1830	-	**W. E. OULSNAM**	Printed name mark, c.1867-1871.
B1831	-	**W. E. OULSNAM & SONS**	Printed name mark, c.1872-1892.

Wetherbee, White Ironstone, p. 101, records and illustrates a design in White Ironstone for "Wheat & Hops".

PALISSY

KAD NO.	GODDEN NO.	MARK	
			Palissy Pottery Ltd. **Chancery Lane,** **Longton, Staffordshire, 1946-1989** **Formerly, A. E. Jones (Longton) Ltd. (1905-1946)** **Subsequently owned by Royal Worcester (1958-1989) and demolished August 1989**
B1832 B1833	 2943A	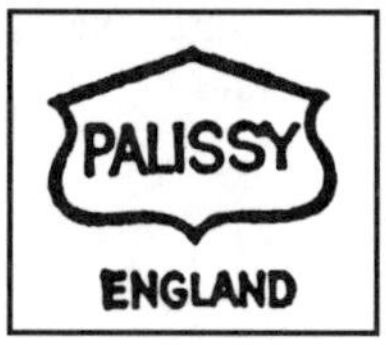 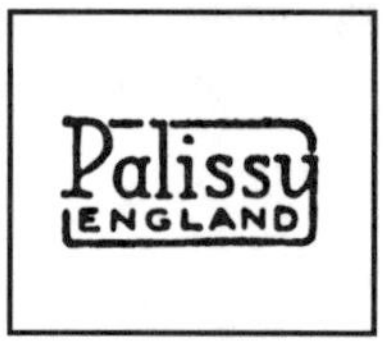	Printed mark formerly of A. E. Jones (Longton) continued, 1946+.
			For additional marks refer to *Godden*, p. 480.
B1833A		**ROYAL WORCESTER** **1st SUBSIDIARY** **1790** **AVON SCENES** **PALISSY** **STAFFORDSHIRE** **ENGLAND**	- In 1958 Palissy was acquired by Royal Worcester which continued the pottery until 1989. During this period Palissy acquired earlier copper plates from an unspecified pottery. A scenic pattern has appeared marked "AVON SCENES". - Mark is noted as a printed cartouche, c.1958-1989. - Additional marking notes "HAND ENGRAVED". - This practice of reissuing acquired copper plates was not an uncommon practice.

PANKHURST

Pankhurst & Dimmock*
Charles Street & Old Hall Street Works,
Hanley, Staffordshire, 1852-1858
- Also refer to J. W. Pankhurst

***From 1852-1882, John Pankhurst & John Dimmock conducted business as J. W. Pankhurst & Co. (Refer to next entry, J. W. Pankhurst (& Co.).**

Wetherbee, White Ironstone, p. 135, fig. 14-13 illustrates a creamer in the "Reeded Grape" pattern with an impressed diamond marking for January 19, 1855 (Rd. No. 99086). *Cluett*, pp. 260-261notes the following **Chronology:**

Charles Meigh, Son & Pankhurst		1849-1850
- J. W. Pankhurst		1850-1852
- J. W. Pankhurst & Co.	(& Co. - John Dimmock)*	1852-1858
J. W. Pankhurst & Co.	(& Co. - Meakin)	1858-1883
Co. sold to Johnson	(Johnson & Co.)	1883

PANKHURST

J. W. Pankhurst (& Co.)
Charles Street & Old Hall Street,
Hanley, Staffordshire, c.1850-1882
Formerly, William Ridgway (Charles Street Works, 1835-1849)
- From 1858-1882 John Pankhurst and John Dimmock conducted business as J. W. Pankhurst & Co. (Refer to previous entry, Pankhurst & Dimmock)

KAD NO.	GODDEN NO.	MARK	
B1834	2952	**J. W. P.**	Printed marks of differing design. Pattern name often included, c.1850-1882.
B1835	2953	**J. W. PANKNURST**	- "& CO." added from 1852.

KAD NO.	GODDEN NO.	MARK	
B1836	-		Printed Royal Coat of Arms mark found on White Ironstone with wording "STONE CHINA" from. c.1850-1852. - See *Wetherbee, White Ironstone*, p. 121 for the above marking.
B1837	-	**IRONSTONE CHINA PANKHURST & CO.**	Impressed name mark in elaborate scroll, c.1852-1882.
B1838	2954	**J. W. P. & CO.**	Printed marks of differing design. Pattern name often included, c.1852-1882.
B1839	2955	**J. W. PANKHURST & CO.**	
B1840	2956	**J. W. PANKHURST & CO.**	
B1841	-		

Henrywood, p. 206 notes that "The history of the firm is particularly confusing since there are six different trading styles recorded in the Patent Office Design Registry between 1852 and 1863:

J. Pankhurst & Co.	1852
J. Pankhurst & J. Dimmock	1852-1853
J. W. Pankhurst & Co.	1853
Pankhurst & Dimmock	1853-1855
James Pankhurst & Co.	1856
J. W. Pankhurst	1863

- It is probable that these all relate to the same company, the proprietors being James Pankhurst and J. Dimmock (the "& Co."). It is tempting to suggest that the former partner was the Pankhurst part of Charles Meigh Son & Pankhurst, the short-lived partnership which operated only between 1850 and 1851, in which case he may have developed a taste for moulded jugs from the famous Meigh products. J. Dimmock could be the John Dimmock who succeeded Thomas Dimmock & Co. in 1862 at the Albion Works, Hanley. At this stage Dimmock may have terminated his partnership with Pankhurst, and this could explain the lack of "& Co." in the entry for 1863 given above.
- See previous entry, Pankhurst & Dimmock for Cluett's chronology.

For further reading, refer to *White Ironstone Notes*, Vol. 4, No. 2, Fall 1997, pp. 8-9 for an article by Kathy Banks titled "Excavations of White Ironstone China".

PATTERSON

Patterson & Co. (George Patterson)
Sheriff Hill Pottery*,
Newcastle-upon-Tyne, Northumberland, c.1837-1844

KAD NO.	GODDEN NO.	MARK	
B1842	-	**G. P.**	Printed initial marks of differing design, c.1837-1844. - "& Co." was a Mr. Fordy, with date undetermined.
B1843	2976	**G. PATTERSON & CO.**	Printed or impressed marks of differing design. Pattern name often included, c.1837-1844.
B1844	-		
B1845	-		

KAD NO.	GODDEN NO.	MARK	
B1846	2977	**PATTERSON & CO. TYNE POTTERY**	Other firms or potteries named Patterson worked nearby at the Carr Hill Pottery as well as at the St. Carr's Hill Pottery.

*Sheriff Hill or Gateshead Fell were interchangeable names. See Jackson & Patterson for "Sheriff Hill" chronology, p. 244.
For further reading, refer to *Godden*, p. 485; *Bell*, p. 98; and *Godden, Collecting Lustreware*, p.239.

PATTON

John Patton
Phoenix Pottery,
Ouseburn, Newcastle-Upon-Tyne
Northumberland, c.1848-1856
Formerly, Carr & Patton (c.1847-1848)
Subsequently, Bell Cook & Co. (c.1859-1860)
No recorded marks, c.1848-1856
For further reading, refer to *Bell*, pp. 30, 98.

PEARL

Pearl Pottery Co. (Ltd.)*
Brook Street Potteries,
Hanley, Staffordshire, 1894-1936
Subsequently, New Pearl Pottery Co. Ltd. (1936-1941)

B1847 2982

Printed or impressed mark. Pattern name often included, 1894-1912.

B1848 2983

Printed initial mark, 1912+.

B1849 2984

Printed initial mark, c.1914-1936.

*Pottery also known as Diamond Pottery Co. (Ltd.) (1908-1936)

-*Godden* notes "...From 1930-1942 a similarly named firm Pearl Pottery (Burslem) Ltd. was working the Sytch Pottery, Burslem."
For further reading, refer to *Godden, Jewitt*, p. 75.

PEARSON

Pearson & Co.
Whittington Moor Potteries,
Chesterfield, Derbyshire, est. c.1805-1924
In 1925 company was renamed "Pearson & Co. (Chesterfield) Ltd."

KAD NO.	GODDEN NO.	MARK	
B1850	2985	**P. & CO.**	Early impressed marks, prior to 1880+.
B1851	2986	**PEARSON & CO. WHITTINGTON MOOR**	

KAD NO.	GODDEN NO.	MARK	
B1852	2987		Printed or impressed marks. Pattern name often included, c.1880+.

For further reading, refer to *Cameron*, p. 257.

PEARSON

Edward (Meakin) Pearson (& Son)
Liverpool Road, Burslem (1850-1853)
Sneyd Street, Cobridge from (1853-1868)
Staffordshire, c.1850-1873
Subsequently, Henry Meakin (1873-1876)
- "& Son" from c.1868-1873

B1853	-	**E. PEARSON**	Printed or impressed mark noted on White Ironstone, c.1850-1873.
B1853A	-	**EDWARD PEARSON**	
B1854	-		
B1855	-		
B1856	-		

Printed **Impressed**

- Marks included above do not reflect a registration date. The only registration date noted is that of May 11, 1863. This raises the question as to the registration dates noted for both "Tulip Shape" and "Mississippi Shape" noted by Wetherbee as *1845* and *1855* respectively. *Wetherbee*, pp. 54-55 and 92 illustrates a design for Registration No. 95587 dated April 11, 1854, registered by Pearson, Farrall and Meakin (Shelton/ Hanley). This, evidently, was a short lived partnership. (Refer to next entry.)

For further reading, refer to *Cushion,* p. 179; *Godden, British Porcelain*, p. 586; *Sussman,* p. 35; *Cameron*, p. 257; *Barber*, pp. 300-311 wherein he notes that Edward Meakin Pearson left England in 1873 for the United States (see Wheeling Potteries), pp. 70-71; *Little*, p. 87; and *White Ironstone Notes*, Vol. 5, No. 1, Summer 1998, p. 6.

PEARSON

Pearson, Farrall & Meakin
Shelton/Hanley,
Staffordshire, c.1854

B1857	-	**JOHN FARRALL**	Printed name marks, c.1854
B1858	-		
B1859	-		

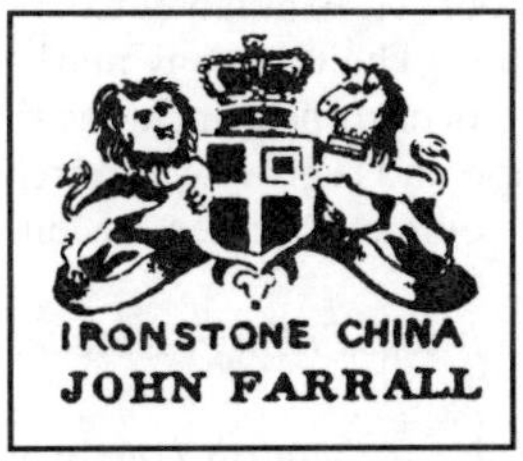

- I have included John Farrall under this listing for no other reason than the complex chronology recorded below.
Available records elude further data, as Godden notes in correspondence dated August 11, 1995. "I have not traced a dissolution of partnership notice for them, the firm must have been of very short duration."

KAD NO.	GODDEN NO.	MARK	

- Further records note the following potters working during this time frame as:

Meakin (Thomas) & Procter (John)	Stoke	1845-1845
Meakin (Thomas) & Procter (John)	Longton	1845-1847
Meakin (L. H.) & Farrall (John)	Shelton/Hanley	1850-1854
- or titled L. H. Meakin & Co.		
John Farrall*	Shelton/Hanley	1854-1854
- Formerly, Wm. Freakley & Co.	Shelton/Hanley	1853
Freakley (Wm.) & Farrall (John)	Shelton/Hanley	1854-1855
Pearson, Farrall & Meakin	Shelton/Hanley	1854-1854
James Meakin	Longton	1845-1850
- Subsequently, J. & G. Meakin		
Edward (Meakin) Pearson	Burslem	1850-1853
Edward (Meakin) Pearson	Cobridge	1853-1868
Edward (Meakin) Pearson & Son	Cobridge	1868-1873
- Subsequently, Henry Meakin	Cobridge	1873-1876

- Refer to Freakley & Farrall, p. 198-199 and Edward (Meakin) Pearson, p. 301, for additional comments.

* *Cushion* notes a double registration entry of April 11, 1854, No. 95587 and 95588 for this firm.

For further reading, refer to *Tea Leaf Readings*, Vol. 15, No. 4, august 1995, pp. 14-15, for an article by Nancy Upchurch; *Cameron*, p. 257; *Godden, British Porcelain*, p. 525; and Dennis Stuart. *People of the Potteries, A Dictionary of Local Biography*, Vol. 1, Keele, England. Department of Adult Education, University of Keele, p. 170.

PENMAN

Robert H. Penman & Co.
Armitage Pottery, Dobbies Loan,
Glasgow, Scotland, c.1860-1867*
- Also see North British Pottery, p. 296
History:

Robert H. Penman & Co.	Armitage Pottery	1860-1867
Penman, Brown & Co. (Trade Style)		
(Partners: Robert Hedderwick Penman, Joseph Brown, & John W. Oslear)		1860-1864
Robert Hedderwick Penman	Armitage Pottery	1865-1867
James Miller & Co. (Ltd.)	renamed: North British Pottery	1868-1874
Alexander Balfour & Co.	North British Pottery	1874-1904

KAD NO.	GODDEN NO.	MARK	
B1860	-	**ARMITAGE****	Printed marks, c.1860-1867.
B1861	-	**R. H. P. & CO.****	Printed mark, c. 1865-1867.
B1862	-	**PENMAN, BROWN & CO.**	Printed and/or impressed name mark, 1860-1864.

- Robert H. Penman & Co. purchased a registry design "Columbia Shape" from G. W. Reade. The company marks note "Robert H. Penman & Co." impressed, and for a rare occurrence, includes the designer's name, G. W. Reade, in printed form. This shape and registry was purchased earlier by J. Meir & Son.

See comments under J. Meir & Son, pp. 282-283.

*Refer to *Edinburgh Gazette*, 1864 and 1865.

**Refer to *Scottish Pottery Society Newsletter* (with amendments), No. 7, Sept. 1976. Glasgow, Scotland, pp. 10-13.

For further reading, refer to *Wetherbee, White Ironstone*, p. 58.

PETTY

KAD NO.	GODDEN NO.	MARK	
			Petty & Co. **Hunslet Hall Pottery,** **Holbeck Leeds, Yorkshire, c.1814-1824** **Formerly, Rainforth & Co. (c.1809-1814)** **Subsequently, Samuel Petty & Son (c.1825-1845)**
B1863	-	**PETTYS & CO. LEEDS**	Impressed name mark, c.1814-1824.

For further reading, refer to *Coysh, Transferware*, No. 66; *Coysh*, Vol. II, p. 214, "Wiseton Hall, Nottinghampshire"; *Lawrence*, pp. 47-49; *FOB Bulletin* No. 89, Autumn 1995, p. 2, for a new titled noted as "Castle Scenery"; *Cameron*, p. 167 for a short history of "Hunslet Hall Pottery or Petty's and Victoria Pottery."

PHILLIPS

Edward & George Phillips
New Bridge Works
Longport, Staffordshire, c.1822-1834
Subsequently, George Phillips (1834-1848)
Subsequently, Davenport (1849-1876)

B1864	3008	**PHILLIPS, LONGPORT**	Printed marks of differing design. Elaborately designed marks and name of individual pattern often included, c.1822-1834.
B1865	3008A	**E. & G. P.**	
B1866	3009		

Typical Marks Include:

B1867 -
B1868 -
B1869 -

Larsen, p. 155 "Franklins Tomb" notes a rare marked example on Historic American/ Canadian views, but does not indicate the marking. Also refer to *Arman*, No. 512.

For further reading and additional back stamps, refer to *P. Williams, Staffordshire*, Vol. II, pp. 92, 133, 330 (patterns: "Ancona", "Africana", "Chinese Views"); *Snyder, Historic Staffordshire*, p. 71; and *Little*, p. 87.

PHILLIPS

George Phillips
New Bridge Works
Longport, Staffordshire, c.1834-1848
Subsequently, Davenport (1849-1876)

B1870	-	**G. P.**	Printed or impressed marks of differing design. Pattern name often included, c.1834-1848.
B1871	3010	**PHILLIPS**	- The name Phillips or G. Phillips is often noted with the pattern name. - A body name "OPAQUE CHINA" or "IRONSTONE" occurs, as will a registry mark.
B1872	-	**G. PHILLIPS LONGPORT**	

KAD NO.	GODDEN NO.	MARK	
			Typical Marks Include:
B1873	3012		
B1874	-		
B1875	-		
B1876	-		

B1877 3011

Printed and/or impressed Staffordshire Knot device noted marked Phillips and Longport, 1834-1848.

B1878 -

Coysh, Vol. I, p. 282, notes a backwards "Staffordshire Knot" with the letter "N" in reverse.

- *P. Williams, Staffordshire*, Vol. II, pp. 601 and 616, shows two back stamps, "Marino" and "Parisian".

For further reading, refer to *Coysh & Stefano* and *Snyder, Romantic Staffordshire*, pp. 136-137.

PHILLIPS

Thomas Phillips & Son
Furlong Pottery, Navigation Road,
Burslem, Staffordshire, c.1845-1846

B1879 3016A **T. PHILLIPS & SON BURSLEM**

Printed and impressed marks, c.1845-1846.

For further reading, refer to *Coysh*, Vol. I, p. 283.

PHOENIX

Phoenix Pottery Co.
Phoenix Pottery,
Ouseburn, Northumberland, c. 1856-1858
Formerly, John Patton (c.1848-1856)
Subsequently, Bell Cook * Co. (c.1858-1859)

B1880 - **PHOENIX POTTERY CO.**

Printed name mark, c.1856-1858.

-*Bell*, p, 102, illustrates a "Willow" pattern with the marking "PHOENIX/N'CASTLE" shown on p. 145, No. 104.

PINDER

Pinder, Bourne & Co.
Nile Street Works,
Burslem, Staffordshire, c.1862-1882
Formerly, Pinder, Bourne & Hope (c.1860-1862)
Subsequently, Doulton & Co., Ltd. (1882-1955*)
-Retitled "Doulton Fine China Ltd. (1955-)

KAD NO.	GODDEN NO.	MARK	
B1881	3038	**P. B. & CO.**	Printed or impressed marks of differing design. Pattern name often included, c.1862-1882.
B1882	3039	**PINDER BOURNE & CO.**	- Marking "IMPERIAL WHITE GRANITE" noted.
B1883	3040		
B1884	3041		
B1885	3042		

Typical Marks Include:

- Doulton acquired this firm in 1878 and retained the title Pinder, Bourne & Co. until 1882. Marks were also continued in use. Sometimes both Doulton and Pinder, Bourne & Co. appear together. Doulton continued successful patterns with or without modification by using the new trade mark.
- Impressed dates have been noted; e.g. 9-81 for September 1881.
- For a history of Pinder, Bourne & Co. and its acquisition by Doulton, refer to Desmond Eyles, *The Doulton Burslem Wares*, London, Barrie & Jenkins Ltd., 1980, pp. 11-15.

PINDER

Pinder, Bourne & Hope
Fountain Place (c.1851-1860)
Nile Street Works (c.1860-1862)
Burslem, Staffordshire, c.1851-1862
Formerly, Thomas Pinder at
Swan Bank Pottery, High Street (c.1849-1851)
Subsequently, Pinder, Bourne & Co. (c.1862-1882)

KAD NO.	GODDEN NO.	MARK	
B1886	3043	**P. B. & H.**	Printed marks of differing design. Pattern name often included, c.1851-1862.
B1887	3044	**PINDER BOURNE & HOPE**	
B1888	3045		For further reading, refer to *Cameron*, p. 261.

PITCAIRNS

Pitcairns Ltd.
Pinnox Pottery,
Tunstall, 1895-1901

KAD NO.	GODDEN NO.	MARK	
B1889	3052		Printed mark. Pattern name often included, 1895-1901.

PLANT

KAD NO. | **GODDEN NO.** | **MARK**

***Enoch Plant**
Crown Pottery,
Burslem, Staffordshire, 1898-1905
Formerly, A. Heath & Co. (1892-1897)

B1890 3055

Printed or impressed Crown mark. Pattern name often included, 1898-1905.

- Care must be taken in attribution solely by the Crown mark, as other manufacturers also used this mark. See *Godden*, pp. 757-758; and *Godden, Jewitt*, p. 22.

PLANT

***J. Plant & Co.**
Stoke Pottery,
Stoke-on-Trent, Staffordshire, 1893-1900
Formerly, J. & R. Plant (1889-1893)
Subsequently, Grimwade Bros. (c.1900)

B1891 3056

Printed mark, pattern name often included, 1893-1900.

- Mark may have been continued from predecessor, J. & R. Plant (1889-1893) and continued through to Grimwades Bros. Ltd. (1900+).

PLANT

***R. H. & S. L. Plant (Ltd.)**
Tuscan Works, Forester Street,
Longton, Staffordshire, 1898-1915
Formerly, R. H. Plant & Co., Carlisle Works, High Street (1891-1898) and
Plant Bros., Stanley Works, Bagnell Street (1889-1898)
- "Ltd." after 1915-1966*

B1892 - **R. H. & S. L. P.**

Printed marks of differing design, incorporating the initials "R. H." and "S. L. P." or the trade-name "TUSCAN", 1898-1915.

Typical Marks Include:

B1893 3059
B1894 3060
B1895 3061

c.1898+

c.1902+

c.1907+

*In 1966 pottery became part of the Wedgwood Group.

For a further history refer to *Batkin*, pp. 114-115.

For further reading, refer to *Godden, British Porcelain*, p. 597; *Cameron*, p. 262; and *Woolliscroft-Rhead*, p. 202.

PLYMOUTH

Plymouth Pottery Co. Ltd.
Coxside, Plymouth, Devon, c.1856-1863

B1896 3072

Printed mark. Pattern name may be included, c.1856-1863.

- The initials "P. P. COY. L." may be attributed to other firms. Care must be taken in attribution. Refer to *Godden*, p. 500.

PODMORE

Podmore, Walker (& Co.)
(Podmore, Walker & Wedgwood, c.1856-1859)
Newfield Pottery (c.1856-1859)
Well Street (c.1834-1853)
Amicable Street (c.1850-1859)
Swan Bank (c.1853-1859)
Tunstall, Staffordshire, c.1834-1859
Subsequently, Wedgwood & Co. (Ltd.) (1860-1965)

KAD NO.	GODDEN NO.	MARK	
B1897	3075	**P. W. & CO.**	Printed marks of differing designs. Name of individual pattern often included, c.1834-1859.
B1898	-	**PODMORE WALKER**	
B1899	-	**(& CO.)**	The "& CO." was Enoch Wedgwood.
B1900	3077	**P. W. & W.**	Printed and/or impressed trade marks noted to include: "IRONSTONE", "PEARL STONEWARE", and "STONEWARE", c. 1856-1859. - An impressed potters marks is frequently noted on Flow Blue wares, c.1856-1859. - Importer's mark "EVANS & HILL, CONCORD, N. H." noted on "Corean" pattern.

Typical Marks Include:

B1901 3076
B1902 -
B1903 -
B1904 -

KAD NO.	GODDEN NO.	MARK	
B1905	3078	**WEDGWOOD**	Printed Registration mark with "WEDGWOOD" or "WEDGWOOD & CO." noted.
B1906	3079	**WEDGWOOD & CO.**	- *Godden, Mason's*, cites an earlier example registered in 1849, thus establishing an earlier date for the name "Wedgwood". - In 1860 the firm was retitled "Wedgwood & Co."

B1907 3080

- Wedgwood reissued the patterns of his predecessor and partner, Podmore, Walker.

These pieces may be stamped with the Wedgwood & Co. markings, c.1860+.

B1908 -

Printed Royal Arms mark noted with initials P. W. & Co. on Historic American/Canadian views. Title names and series names often included, c.1834-1859.

B1909 -

- Impressed trade mark "PEARL STONE WARE" often noted, c. 1834-1859, as is impressed name mark "P. W. & CO./IMPERIAL GRANITE".

KAD NO.	GODDEN NO.	MARK	
B1910	-		Printed marks with pattern name noted on White Ironstone, including date of registry, c.1834-1859. For further reading, refer to *Snyder, Historic Staffordshire*, p. 72; and *Wetherbee*, p. 129.

POSSIL

Possil Pottery
Denmark Pottery, Possil Park,
Glasgow, Scotland, c.1896-1911
Formerly, Possil Pottery Co. (c.1895-1896)
- Also see Nautilus Pottery, p. 294

History:

Pottery Name	Initial Marks	Impressed Marks	Date
Bayley, Murray & Bramer	B. M. & B.	Saracen Pottery	c.1875-1878
Murray, Grieve & Co.	M. G. & Co.	Saracen Pottery	c.1878-1879
Grieve, Ellis & Co.	G. E. & Co.	Saracen Pottery	c.1879-1880
Saracen Pottery Co.	—	Saracen Pottery Co.	c.1881-1895
Possil Pottery Co.	—	Possil Pottery Co.	c.1895-1896
		PRINTED MARKS	
MacDougall & Sons formcompany	—	Nautilus Porcelain Co.	c.1894-1918
MacDougall & Son (acquire)	—	Possil Pottery	c.1896-1911

B1911 3101
B1800 2839

Printed trade marks, c.1896-1911.

- Possil Pottery connotes Earthenware.

- Nautilus Porcelain Co. connotes fine Porcelain, see p. 294.

- Henry E. Kelly notes a void between 1911 and 1918, when the pottery was taken over by tenants who produced lager and other beers.

- See picture of unidentified pattern in *Blue Berry Notes*, Vol. 9, No. 1, Jan.- Feb. 1995, p. 15.

POULSON

Poulson Bros. (Ltd.)
West Riding Pottery,
Ferrybridge, Yorkshire, c.1884-1927
- Also refer to Ferrybridge Pottery, p. 193

KAD NO.	GODDEN NO.	MARK	
B1912	3104	**P. B.**	Printed marks of differing design. Pattern name often included, c.1884-1927.
B1913	3105	**P. BROS.**	- T. & E. L. Poulson worked the "Ferrybridge Pottery" prior to [1897], and are not to be confused with their dates at "West Riding Pottery".
B1914	-	**POULSON BRO'S**	

For further reading, refer to *Lawrence*, pp. 161 and 257.

POUNTNEY

***Pountney & Allies**
Bristol Pottery, Temple Backs,
Bristol, Gloucestershire, c.1816-1835
Formerly, Carter & Pountney (c.1813-1815)
Subsequently, John D. Pountney (c.1836)

KAD NO.	GODDEN NO.	MARK	
B1915	3120	**P**	Printed or impressed marks of differing design. Pattern name often included, c.1816-1835.
B1916	3121	**P. & A.**	
B1917	3122	**P. S.** **B. P.**	- Additional markings noted: Impressed "IMPROVED STONE CHINA" and in a circular medallion mark "P/FANCY VASE/A".
B1918	3123	**P. A.** **BRISTOL POTTERY**	- Refer to *Coysh, Earthenware*, No. 70.
B1919	3124		Printed or impressed "horse-shoe" style mark, c.1816-1835. - This style was continued by Pountney & Goldney.
B1920	3125	**HAMILTON**	Printed written name decorated in the classical style, c.1820-1830. - Many of the patterns were continued by successors Pountney & Goldney. For further reading, refer to *Penny Plain*, p. 99, No. 240.

POUNTNEY

***Pountney & Co. (Ltd.)**
Bristol Pottery (1859-1962)
Victoria Pottery (1873-1906)
Crown Pottery (1891-1906)
Temple Backs, Bristol, Gloucestershire (1859-1962)
- A new pottery built at Causeway, Fish Ponds (1906-1969)
Formerly, Pountney, Edwards & Co. (c.1858)
- From 1962 known as Cauldon Bristol Potteries, Ltd.
- From 1985 known as Cauldon Potteries Ltd.
Early wares were generally unmarked.

KAD NO.	GODDEN NO.	MARK	
B1921	3106	**P. & Co.**	Printed or impressed marks of differing design. Pattern name often included, 1859-1889.
B1922	3107	**POUNTNEY & CO.**	- "GRANITE CHINA" marking noted. - Marks KAD B1921 and B1922 are frequently noted.
B1923	3109	**P. & CO. LTD.**	Printed marks of differing design. Pattern name often included. - "LTD." from 1889-1962.
B1924	3110	**POUNTNEY & CO. LTD.**	

KAD NO.	GODDEN NO.	MARK	
B1925	3111		
B1926	3112		
B1927	3113		

Typical Marks Include:

c.1889+

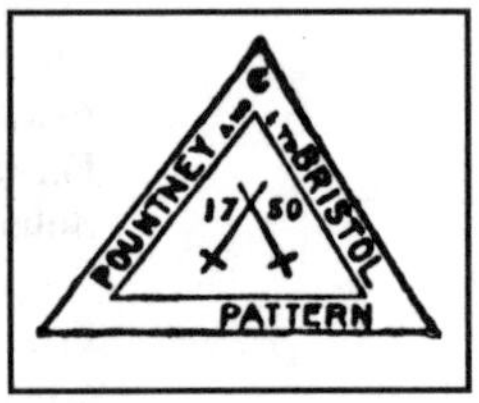

c.1900+

c.1900+

- For additional marks refer to *Godden*, p. 507.

For further reading and additional late marks, refer to *Godden, British Porcelain*, pp. 506-507; *Godden, Jewitt*, pp. 157-158; *Cameron*, p. 61; *Bunt, British Potters*, pp. 46-47; and *Henrywood*, pp. 52-56.

POUNTNEY

***Pountney & Goldney**
Bristol Pottery,
Temple Backs, Bristol, Gloucestershire, c.1837-1850
Formerly, John D. Pountney (c.1836)
Subsequently, John D. Pountney (c.1851-1853)

B1928 3126 **BRISTOL POTTERY** Impressed pottery name mark, c.1837-1850.

B1929 3127 

Printed or impressed "horse shoe" type mark continued from Pountney & Allies. Pattern name often included, c. 1837-1850.

- Marking "MANDARIN OPAQUE CHINA" noted.

B1930 - **P. & G.** Printed initial mark, 1837-1850.
- Many patterns were continued from the previous partnership of Pountney & Allies, c.1816-1835.

For further reading and additional marks, refer to *Ormsbee*, p. 98, *Henrywood*, pp. 52-56; and *Godden, Collecting Lustreware*, pp. 285-286.

POWELL

Powell & Bishop
Church Street Works, High Street (1866-1878)
Stafford Street Works, Miles Bank (1866-1878)
Waterloo Works, Nelson Place (1875-1878)
Hanley, Staffordshire, 1866-1878
Formerly, Livesley, Powell & Co. (c.1851-1865)
Subsequently, Powell, Bishop & Stonier (1878-1891)

B1931 3132 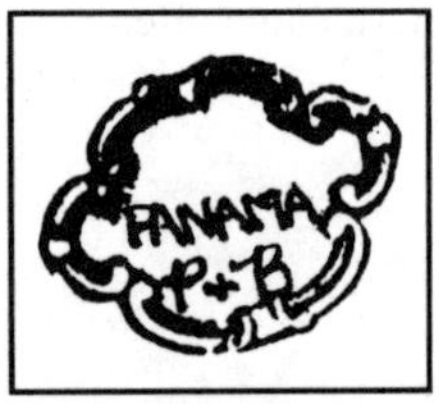

Printed or impressed marks of differing design. Pattern name often included, c.1866-1878.

B1932 3132A **BEST P. & B.** Printed initial mark, may also be noted as "P.B.", 1866+

B1933 3133 **POWELL & BISHOP**

KAD NO.	GODDEN NO.	MARK	
B1934	-		Printed Royal Coat of Arms mark noted on Tea Leaf with Copper Lustre, 1866-1878. - Refer to *Stoltzfus/Snyder*, p. 21.
B1935	3135		Printed or impressed "Caduceus" trade-mark, registered 1876. - Mark may occur with "P. & B." or with initials "P.B." or names of succeeding partnership, 1878-1891+.
B1936	3136		Examples of printed mark (KAD B1936) continued by succeeding partnerships. - "ENGLAND" appears after 1891. - See Powell, Bishop & Stonier as well as Bishop & Stonier for further dating. - *Sussman* p. 65, notes a "Wheat In The Meadow" pattern registered on Oct. 29, 1869, which may have been continued by successors. For further reading, refer to *Jewitt*, and *Godden, British Porcelain*, pp. 608-609.

POWELL

Powell, Bishop & Stonier
Waterloo Works, Nelson Place
Stafford Street Works, Miles Bank
Church Street Works, High Street
Hanley, Staffordshire, c.1878-1891
Formerly, Powell & Bishop (1866-1878)
Subsequently, Bishop & Stonier (1891-1939)

KAD NO.	GODDEN NO.	MARK	
B1937		**P. B. & S.**	Printed or impressed marks of differing design. Pattern name often included, c.1878-1891.
B1938	3138		Printed trade-mark registered in c.1880+ and continued by Bishop & Stonier (Ltd.) (c.1891-1939).
B1938A	-	**P. S. & S.**	-Mark KAD B1935 "Caduceus" similarly continued, but with the initials "P. S. & S.", c.1878-1891. For further reading, refer to *Heaivilin*, pp. 104-106; and *Godden, British Porcelain*. p. 149.

PRATT

KAD NO.	GODDEN NO.	MARK	

Pratt & Simpson
Lane Delph Pottery, High Street, Lane Delph
Fenton, Staffordshire, 1878-1883
Formerly, John Pratt & Co., Ltd. (1847-1878)
Subsequently, Wallis Gimson & Co. (1883-1890)

B1939 3156 **P. & S.** Printed, simple circular mark with pattern names and initials, 1878-1883.

B1940 - * Printed "Bee Hive" mark with full name, noted on White Ironstone, 1878-1883*.

- Mark style continued by Wallis Gimson & Co. See KAD B1044.

*See *White Ironstone Notes*, Vol. 4, No. 1, Summer 1997, p. 14 for "Eagle Soup Tureen".

PRATT

F. & R. Pratt & Co. (Ltd.)
Fenton Potteries, Lane Delph,
Fenton, Staffordshire, c.1840-1916
Formerly, Felix Pratt (c.1780-1815)
Subsequently, Cauldon Ltd. (1916-1962)

B1941 3143 **F. & R. P.** Printed marks of differing design. Pattern name often included, c.1840-1862.

B1942 3144 **F. & R. P. CO.** - *Snyder, Fascinating Flow Blue,* Vol. I, pp. 59-60 notes a marking "KAOLIN WARE NO. 9", c. 1840+.
- "& CO." dates from 1840 and "ENGLAND" from 1891.

B1943 3145 **PRATT** Printed name marks, c.1870-1880s.

B1944 -

Typical Marks Include:

B1945 3146
B1946 3147
B1947 3148
B1948 3152
B1949 3153

pre-1840

post-1840

c.1847-1860

1925-1945

post-war, 1945-1962

- Marks continued and marked "MADE BY CAULDON", c. 1916+.

For further reading, refer to *Lewis, Pratt Ware*, *Godden, Illustrated Encyclopedia*; *Penny Plain*, p. 104, Ns 309, 312, 313, 317, and p. 103, No. 305 for additional patterns.

PRATT

KAD NO.	GODDEN NO.	MARK	
			John Pratt & Co. (Ltd.) Lane Delph Pottery, High Street, Lane Delph Fenton, Staffordshire, 1847-1878 Formerly, John (Jr.) & William Pratt (1847) Subsequently, Pratt & Simpson (1878-1883)
B1950	-	**J. P. & CO.**	Printed marks of differing design. Pattern name often included, 1847-1878.
B1951	-	**J. P. & CO. (L)**	Printed marks of differing design. Pattern name often included, 1847-1878.
B1952	3154	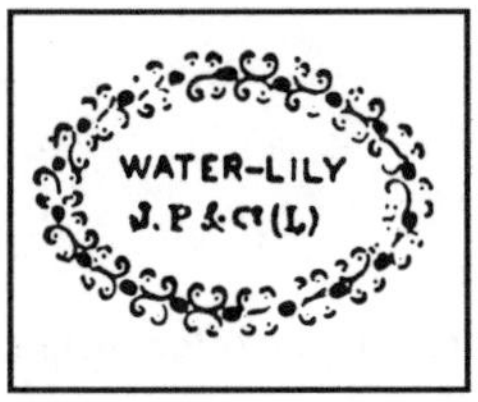	- "LTD." dates from 1870-1878. - Marks "J. P. & Co." without the "(L)" could also relate to J. Pratt & Co. (1847-1878) or Joseph Peake & Co. (c.1835), or James Pope & Co. (c.1849-1850). For further reading, refer to *Godden, British Porcelain*, p. 610; and J. F. Blacker. *The A. B. C. of English Ceramic Art*. London, Stanley Paul & Co., c.1911, pp. 166-168; and *Lewis, Pratt Ware*, p. 21.

PRESTOPANS

Prestopans
See: Fowler Thompson & Co.

PURVIS

Charles Purvis
See: Elgin Pottery

RAINFORTH

			Rainforth & Co. Hunslet Hall Potteries, Holbeck, Leeds, Yorkshire, c.1809-1814 Subsequently, Petty & Hewitt or Petty & Co. (c.1814-1824)
B1953	3195	**RAINFORTH & CO.**	Impressed name mark, c.1809-1814
B1954	3195A	**RAINFORTH & C.**	
B1955	3196	**H. M.**	- *Godden*, p. 520 notes that impressed initial mark KAD B1955 "H. M. ... may relate to this pottery at Holbeck Moor or to the Leeds Pottery period, after c.1775." For further reading, refer to *Coysh*, Vol. I, p. 296, *Little*, p. 118; *Lawrence*, pp. 47-51; *Cameron*, p. 167 "Hunslet Hall Pottery"; and Donald Towner. *The Leeds Pottery*. Cory, Adams & MacKay, London, 1963, p. 150.

RATCLIFFE

			William Ratcliffe, New Hall Works, Shelton, Hanley, Staffordshire, c.1831-1841(43) Formerly, Thomas Taylor (1819-1830) Subsequently, William & Thomas Hackwood (c.1843-1850)
1956	3199	**R** **HACKWOOD**	Printed or impressed name mark, c.1831-1843.

KAD NO.	GODDEN NO.	MARK	
B1957	3200		Printed mark in Underglaze Blue, c.1831-1843.

- *Godden, British Porcelain*, p. 619, notes that this mark (KAD B1957) is confirmed as that of Samuel and John Rathbone, c.1812-1818 and c.1823-1835. It is *not* that of William Ratcliffe.

For further reading, refer to *Little*, p. 90. Also refer to Hackwood for further information.

RATHBONE

T. Rathbone & Co.
Newfield Pottery,
Tunstall, Staffordshire, 1898-1923

KAD NO.	GODDEN NO.	MARK	
B1958	3207	**T. R. & CO.***	Printed marks of differing design. Pattern name often included, 1898-1923.
B1959	-	**RATHBONE & CO.**	

Typical Marks Include:

B1960 3204
B1961 3205
B1962 3206

c.1898+

c.1912+

c.1919-1923

*The initials "T. R. & CO." were also used by Thomas Rathbone & Co., an earlier potter, at the Portobello Pottery, c.1810-1845.

For further reading, refer to *Scottish Pottery Society Archive News*, No. 4, 1979, pp. 30-31 for an article by Robin Armstrong Hill titled "Thomas Rathbone of Portobello and a Spode Design."

READ

***Read & Clementson**
High Street,
Shelton, Hanley, Staffordshire, c.1833-1835

KAD NO.	GODDEN NO.	MARK	
B1963	3212	**R. & C.**	Printed marks of differing design. Pattern name often included, c.1833-1835.

- Refer to Appendix B6: Chronology for Clementson.

- The mark "R. & C." was also used by Read & Co. as well as later in the century by other potters.

B1964	3212A		Printed typical mark, c. 1833-1835.

READ

KAD NO.	GODDEN NO.	MARK	
			***Read, Clementson & Anderson** **High Street,** **Shelton, Hanley, Staffordshire, c.1836** **Formerly, Read & Clementson (1833-1835)** **Subsequently, Read & Co. (c.1837-1838)**
B1965	3213	**R. C. & A.**	Printed marks of differing design. Pattern name often included, c.1836. - Refer to Appendix B6: Chronology for Clementson, p. 543.

REED

***Reed & Taylor**
Rock Pottery (c.1820-1839)
Swillington Bridge Pottery (c.1832-1838)
Ferrybridge Pottery (c.1841-1848)
Yorkshire, c.1830-1848

KAD NO.	GODDEN NO.	MARK	
B1966	3217	**R. & T.**	Printed initial marks. Pattern name often included, c.1820-1848.
B1967	-	**R. T. & CO.**	- "& CO." from 1820-1839. - "OPAQUE CHINA" and "STONE CHINA" markings noted. - Also refer to Ferrybridge Pottery, p. 193, and Swillington Bridge Pottery, p. 347. - Initials "R. & T." could also refer to the potter Ray & Tideswell, Lane End, Staffordshire (c.1830-1837).

For further reading, refer to *FOB* No. 70, 1990, p. 10; and *Lawrence*, pp. 73-77, 117, and 150-151.

REED

James Reed
Rock Pottery,
Mexborough, Yorkshire, c.1839-1849
Subsequently, John Reed (c.1849-1873)

History:

Reed & Taylor*	Rock Pottery	1820-1838
Reed, Taylor & Co.	Rock Pottery	1838-1839
James Reed	Rock Pottery	1839-1849
John Reed	Rock Pottery (renamed Mexborough Pottery)	1849-1873
Sydney Woolf & Co.*	Rock Pottery	1873-1883

KAD NO.	GODDEN NO.	MARK	
B1968	3216	**REED**	Printed or impressed name marks. Pattern name often included, c.1839-1873. *See Ferrybridge Pottery, p. 193 and Swillington Bridge Pottery, p. 347.
B1969	-	**J. REED**	- Rockingham copper plates were acquired in 1843, after the Rockingham Works financial failure. See pp. 124-125.

For further reading, refer to *Lawrence*, as well as the *Annual Report of the Yorkshire Philosophical Society*, Yorkshire, 1916, pp. 77-78.

REEVES

KAD NO.	GODDEN NO.	MARK	
			James Reeves **Victoria Works, Market Street,** **Fenton, Staffordshire, 1870-1948**
B1970	3218	**J. R.**	Printed marks of differing design. Pattern name often included, 1870-1948.
B1971	3218A	**J. R.** **F**	- "ENGLAND" or "MADE IN ENGLAND" included, c. 20th century. - Godden, British Porcelain, p. 628, notes that James Reeves & Co. may possibly be a retailer or wholesaler and should not be confused with James Reeves (without the "& CO." marking).
B1972	3219	**J. REEVES**	
B1973	3221		

REID

William Reid (& Son) or (& Sons)
Newbigging Pottery,
Musselburgh, East Lothian, (West Pans), Scotland, c.1800-1855
History:

Wm. Reid (& Sons)	(1797) 1800-1835
Wm. Reid & Son	1835-1855
A. J. Winkles	1857-1859
James Forster	1862-1885
Jonathan Forster	1886-1893
W. A. Gray & Sons (Ltd.)	1894-1928
James Turner	1867-1868
Pottery Subdivided in	1868
W. A. Gray & Sons (Ltd.)	1869-1928

KAD NO.	GODDEN NO.	MARK	
B1974	-	**W. REID**	Printed name marks, c.1820-1855.
B1975	-	**WM. REID**	
B1976	-	**MUSSELBURGH POTTERY JT.**	Printed pottery mark noted on transfer printed ware, with printed back marks and pattern name "CHING", c.1840s-1855.
B1977	-	**"MUSSELBURGH COAT OF ARMS"**	Printed shield of three anchors and three mussel shells in two files of alternating figures, c.1840-1855.

For a detailed history and additional marks, refer to *Scottish Pottery 18th Historical Review*, 1996, pp. 15-37 for an article by George Haggarty titled "Newbigging Pottery Musselburgh, East Lothian"; and *McVeigh*, pp. 94-97.

RIDGWAY

Ridgway Chronology - Shelton/Hanley

The Ridgway family history is very complex. This chronology is an introduction into the Ridgway family and its holdings. It provides the reader with some background prior to reading about the various Ridgway potteries included below. For further information, I would suggest the reader refer to *Godden, Ridgway and Godden, British Porcelain, pp. 641-651*

DATE	POTTERY	PROPRIETOR
1792-1797	Bell Works (Bell Bank)	Job & George Ridgway
1797-1798	Bell Works (Bell Bank)	Ridgway, Smith & Ridgway
1798-1801	Bell Works (Bell Bank)	Job & George Ridgway
1802-1804	*Belle Vue Pottery, Hull, Yorkshire*	*Smith, Ridgway & Co.*
1802-1808	Cauldon Place Works	Job Ridgway
1802-1814	Bell Works (Bell Bank)	George Ridgway (& Son)
1808-1813	Cauldon Place Works	Job Ridgway & Sons
1813-1830	Bell Works & Cauldon Place Works	John (& William) Ridgway & Co.
1830-1855	Cauldon Place Works - & Co. from 1841-1855	John Ridgway (& Co.)
1830-1854*	Bell Works (1) - Church Street Works, High Street 1831 (2) - Cobden Street Works, High Street, 1832 (3) - Charles Street Pottery, Old Hall Street, 1834 (4) - Thomas Taylor's Works, High Street, 1835	William Ridgway (& Co.)
1835-1860	Church Street Works, High Street	Ridgway & Abington
1836-1842	Broad Street Works - & Co. (Abington) - Pottery formerly, Hicks, Meigh & Johnson	Ridgway, Morley, Wear & Co.
1837-1840	-	Ridgway & Robey
1838-1845	Church Street Works, High Street Cobden Street Works, High Street from 1841-1845	William Ridgway Son & Co.
1842-1845	Broad Street Works - Subsequently, Francis Morley	Ridgway & Morley
1856-1858	Cauldon Place Works - Subsequently, Bates-Brown-Westhead-Moore - Also see Chronology for Bates	Ridgway, Bates & Co.
1860-1872	- Bedford Works, Vale Road -& Church Street Works High Street, until 1866 - & Son from 1870-1872	E. J. Ridgway Son
1872-1878	Bedford Works, Vale Road	Ridgway, Sparks & Ridgway
1878-1920	Bedford Works, Vale Road	Ridgways
1920-1952	Bedford Works, Vale Road	Ridgways (Bedford Works) Ltd.
1952-1955	Bedford Works, Ash Hall, Stoke	Ridgways & Adderley, Ltd.
1955-1955	-	Ridgway, Adderley, Booths & Colcloughs Ltd.
1955-1964	-	Ridgway Potteries, Ltd.
1964-1972	-	Allied English Potteries, Ltd.
1973-Present	-	Royal Doulton Tableware, Ltd.

***See** *Godden, Ridgway*

(1) Subsequently, Joseph Clementson
(2) Formerly, Elijah Mayer & Son, acquired by Joseph Mayer in 1828 and rented to Ridgway in 1831
(3) Formerly, Elijah Mayer & Son
(4) Formerly, Toft & May

KAD NO.	GODDEN NO.	MARK	
			***Ridgway & Abington** **Church Works,** **Hanley, Staffordshire, c.1835-1860**
B1978	-		Printed Royal Arms mark. Pattern name often included, c.1835-1860. - *Godden*, p. 533 cites that the name Abington may occur with either one or two "b's". For further reading, refer to *Godden, Ridgway;* W. P. Jervis & Serry Wood, *Jervis (China Classics II & III)*, p. 108, Pl. 3, Mark 8, Century House, Watkins Glen, NY, 1953; and *P. Williams, Flow Blue*, Vol. I, p. 200.

RIDGWAY

Ridgway & Morley
Broad Street,
Shelton, Hanley, Staffordshire, c.1842-1845

KAD NO.	GODDEN NO.	MARK	
B1979	3276	**R. & M.**	Printed and impressed marks with various and often elaborately designed
B1980	-	**RIDGWAY & MORLEY**	cartouches. Name of pattern often included, c.1842-1845. - Various markings include: "IMPROVED GRANITE CHINA", "OPAQUE CHINA", "PATENT IRONSTONE", "STONEWARE" AND "REAL IRONSTONE CHINA".
B1980A	-	**RIDGWAY & MORLEY PATENT IRONSTONE CHINA SHELTON**	Printed circular mark with crown above noted on White Ironstone, 1842-1845.

Typical Marks Include:

B1981 -
B1982 3278
B1983 3279
B1984 3280

B1985 3281
B1986 3282
B1987 3283
B1988 -

B1989 3278A

Marking found on a printed mark for pattern "Cashmere", one of the most popular Flow Blue patterns. Note term "PATENT" above Royal Arms mark, c.1842-1845.

For further reading, refer to *Godden, Ridgway*.

RIDGWAY

KAD NO.	GODDEN NO.	MARK	
			Job Ridgway **Cauldon Place,** **Shelton, Hanley, Staffordshire, c.1802-1808** **Subsequently, Job Ridgway & Sons (1808-1813)**
B1990	3250		Printed mark. Chinese type square seal marked "R" has been noted, c.1802-1808.
B1991	3251	**J. R.**	Printed mark, which in most cases is related to John Ridgway 1830-1855. - Job Ridgway wares were usually unmarked.

For further reading, refer to *Godden, Ridgway.*

RIDGWAY

Job Ridgway & Sons
Cauldon Place,
Shelton, Hanley, Staffordshire, c.1808-1813
Formerly, Job Ridgway (1802-1808)
Subsequently, J. & W. Ridgway (1813-1830)

KAD NO.	GODDEN NO.	MARK	
B1992	3552	**RIDGWAY & SONS**	Printed or impressed marks with "RIDGWAY & SONS" incorporated into marking, 1808-1813.

- E. J. Ridgway & Sons (c.1860-1872) may have used the above marking "RIDGWAY & SONS".

For further reading, refer to *Godden, Ridgway*.

RIDGWAY

John Ridgway (& Co.)
Cauldon Place,
Shelton, Hanley, Staffordshire, c.1830-1855
- "& Co." from 1841-1855
Formerly, J. & W. Ridgway (1818-1830)

KAD NO.	GODDEN NO.	MARK	
B1993	3253	**J. R.**	Printed or impressed marks noted with various and often elaborately designed marks. Name of individual pattern is often included, c.1830-1855.
B1994	3254	**JOHN RIDGWAY**	
B1995	3255	**JHN RIDGWAY**	- Registered and unmarked pieces have been noted. Refer to *Godden, Ridgway*, pp. 215-219.
B1996	3256	**I. RIDGWAY**	

Typical Marks Include:

KAD NO.	GODDEN NO.
B1997	-
B1998	3257
B1999	-

KAD NO.	GODDEN NO.
B2000	-
B2001	-
B2002	-

KAD NO.	GODDEN NO.	MARK	
B2003	3258		Printed or impressed Royal Arms mark, c.1830-1855. - Refer to *Godden, Ridgway*, Plate 179. - Many variations of this mark occur; some without initials "J. R." or "J. R. & CO." under arms. - Printed marks "STONE CHINA" may also be included. Printed marks of various design noted on Historic American/Canadian views, often including printed series and title names, c.1830+. **Typical Marks Include:**
B2004 B2005	- -		 
B2006	3259	**J. R. & CO.**	Printed marks of differing design. Pattern name often included, c.1841-1855.
B2007	3259A	**J. RIDGWAY & CO.**	
B2008	3259B	**JOHN RIDGWAY & CO.**	
			Typical Marks Include:
B2009 B2010 B2011	- - -		  
B2012	-		Printed or impressed mark on Tea Leaf/Copper Lustre, marked "J. R. & CO.", "PORCELAINE A LA FRANCIASE" and "& CO.", c.1841-1855. - Patterns and marks may have been continued by Brown-Westhead, Moore & Co. as well as by Cauldon Ltd. For further reading, refer to *Godden, Ridgway*, pp. 140-147; *Snyder, Historic Staffordshire*, pp.72-80; and *Penny Plain*, pp. 101, 102, Nos. 267 and 268, respectively.

RIDGWAY

KAD NO.	GODDEN NO.	MARK	
			John & William Ridgway **Cauldon Place and Bell Works,** **Shelton, Hanley, Staffordshire, c.1813-1830** **Formerly, Job Ridgway & Sons (c.1808-1813)**
B2013	3260	**J. W. R.**	Printed or impressed marks with various, and often elaborately designed cartouches. Pattern names often included, c.1813-1830.
B2014	3261	**J. & W. R.**	
B2015	3262	**J. & W. RIDGWAY**	- "OPAQUE CHINA/STONE CHINA" also noted.

Typical Marks Include:

KAD NO.	GODDEN NO.	MARK	
B2016	3263		
B2017	3264		
B2018	3265		
B2019	-		

KAD NO.	GODDEN NO.	MARK	
B2020	3266		Printed, impressed or relief "Vase & Anchor" mark, c.1813+. - See William Ridgway who also used this mark (c.1830-1854), KAD B2046, as did William Ridgway Son & Co., KAD B2051. -*Henrywood*, p. 61, notes that mark usage was probably discontinued c.1838.
B2021	-	**J. & W.** or	Printed or impressed marks of various designs. The American/Canadian Historic wares often include printed series and title names, c.1813-1830.
B2022		**I. & W.**	

Typical Marks Include:

KAD NO.	GODDEN NO.
B2023	-
B2024	-
B2025	-

Impressed **Printed**

For further reading, refer to *Snyder, Historic Staffordshire*, pp. 72-80; and for additional marks refer to *NCS Newsletter*, No. 107, Sept. 1997, pp. 14-19, for an article by K. Church titled "Anonymous Marks."

RIDGWAY

John Ridgway Bates & Co.
Cauldon Place,
Shelton, Hanley, Staffordshire, c.1856-1858

KAD NO.	GODDEN NO.	MARK	
B2026	-	**J. R./B**	Printed initial mark, c.1856-1858.
B2027	3268	**J. R. B. & CO.**	Printed marks incorporating initials and pattern name, c.1856-1858.
B2028	3269		Typical mark, c.1856-1858. - Also see mark KAD B 2005. For further reading, refer to *Godden, Ridgway*.

RIDGWAY

KAD NO.	GODDEN NO.	MARK	
			Ridgway, Morley, Wear & Co. **Broad Street,** **Shelton, Hanley, Staffordshire, c.1836-1842**
B2029	3271	**R. M. W. & CO.**	Printed mark noted with various and often elaborately designed cartouches, c. 1836-1842.
B2030	3272	**RIDGWAY, MORLEY WEAR & CO.**	Pattern name often included, c.1836-1842. - Note use of printed or impressed term "IMPROVED/GRANITE CHINA". - *Collard* notes that the pattern "Agricultural Vase" was also used by Ridgway & Morley and Francis Morley & Co. **Typical Marks Include:**

B2031 3273
B2032 3274
B2033 3275
B2034 -

- See *Coysh*, Vol. I, p. 108 for an illustrated example of a special backstamp for the Sheffield Mounting Company.

For further reading, refer to *Godden, Ridgway*; and *Snyder, Romantic Staffordshire*, pp. 152-153, and *NCSJ*, Vol. 4, 1980-1981, pp. 219-236 for an article by Leonard G. King titled "Ridgway, Wear & Morley at the Broad Street Works".

RIDGWAY

Ridgway, Sparks & Ridgway
Bedford Works,
Shelton, Hanley, Staffordshire, c.1872-1878

B2035 3299 **R. S. R.** Printed or impressed initials noted along with various marks of differing design. Pattern name often included, c.1872-1878.

B2036 3299A

Impressed Staffordshire Knot Rope is a typical marking noted on White Ironstone, c.1872-1878.

B2037 -

"Quiver and Bow" trademark. This early version does not include marking "STOKE ON TRENT", c.1872-1878.
- See KAD B2056 for additional comments.

RIDGWAY

William Ridgway (& Co.)
Bell Works & Church Works,
Shelton, Hanley, Staffordshire, c.1830-1854
Formerly, J. & W. Ridgway (c.1813-1830)

KAD NO.	GODDEN NO.	MARK	
B2038	3300	**W. RIDGWAY**	Printed or impressed marks noted with various and often elaborately designed cartouches. Pattern name often included, c.1830-1854.
B2039	3301	**W. R.**	- Note markings "IMPROVED CHINA" "OPAQUE CHINA" and "GRANITE CHINA".

Typical Marks Include:

B2040 -
B2041 -
B2042 -

B2043 -

Printed mark noted on Historic American/Canadian views, including title name, c.1830-1854.

- See American Scenery Series, p. 446.

- William Kurau notes examples of American Scenery Series with a impressed Lion and Unicorn (KAD B2042) marked "W. R. & CO."

- Marking "OPAQUE GRANITE CHINA" has also been noted. See *Snyder, Historic Staffordshire*, pp. 72-80.

B2044	3302	**W. RIDGWAY & CO.**	Printed or impressed marks. Pattern name often included, c.1830-1834.
B2045	3303	**W. R. & CO.**	- "& CO." dates from 1834-1854.

Typical Marks Include:

B2046* 3033A
B2047 -
B2048** -

- Multi-markings have also been noted with an impressed Lion & Unicorn mark along with a second mark of a vase and anchor, c. 1834-1854.

*See a similar mark used by John & William Ridgway, KAD B2020 and B2051.
- Patterns and marks overlapped from William Ridgway to William Ridgway & Co.
**See a similar marked used by Swillington Bridge Pottery, KAD B2263.

For further reading, refer to *Godden, Ridgway*; *Penny Plain*, p. 96, No. 192; and *Snyder, Romantic Staffordshire*, pp. 147-150.

RIDGWAY

KAD NO.	GODDEN NO.	MARK	
			William Ridgway Son & Co. **Church Works (1838-1845)** **Cobden Works (1841-1845)** **Hanley, Staffordshire, 1838-1845**
B2049	3306	**PUBLISHED BY W. RIDGWAY, SON & CO. HANLEY OCTOBER 5, 1841**	Printed marks, dated, in form noted. "PUBLISHED BY" and pattern name often included, c.1838+.
B2050	3307	**W. R. S. & CO.**	Printed or impressed mark noted with differing designs, often including pattern name, c.1838-1845. - Style mark KAD B2048 noted with the initials "W. R. S. & CO."

Typical Marks Include:

B2051* 3308
B2052* 3309
B2053 -

B2054 -

Printed mark noted with differing designs found on American/Canadian
*Marks continued by various Ridgways.
Historic Staffordshire. Pattern name often included, c.1838-1845.

B2055 4416

- *Little*, p. 92, notes that the initials "C. C." were registered December 16, 1844. See "Catskill Moss Series", p. 446.
- Also refer to the European Pottery Section for Clairmont & Chainaye, who also used the initials "C. & C.", p. 646.

For further reading, refer to *Godden, Ridgway*; *Godden*, p. 713; *Snyder, Historic Staffordshire*, p. 78; and *Snyder, Romantic Staffordshire*, pp. 151-152.

RIDGWAY

Ridgways
Bedford Works,
Shelton, Hanley, Staffordshire, c.1878-1920
Formerly, Ridgway, Sparks & Ridgway (1872-1878)
Subsequently, Ridgways (Bedford Works), Ltd. (1920-1952)

B2056 3310

"Quiver & Bow" Trademark registered c.1880.
- 'Early versions' are not marked "STOKE ON TRENT", "BEDFORD WORKS" which are trade names for Ridgways.
- Note change of (Bedford Works) Ltd. and inclusion of "BEDFORD", "BEDFORD WARE" or "BEDFORD WORKS", c.1920+.

KAD NO.	GODDEN NO.	MARK

Typical Marks Include:

KAD NO.	GODDEN NO.
B2057	3311
B2058	3312
B2059	3313
B2060	3314

c.1905+

c.1905+

c.1912+

c.1912+

The following marks were reissued with the word "ENGLAND", and were introduced after 1891.

KAD NO.	GODDEN NO.
B2052*	3309
B2061**	3315
B2062***	3316

*Text as follows: note earlier marks, KAD B2018, B 2052.
**Text as follows: note earlier mark, KAD B2051.
***Text as follows: note earlier mark, KAD B2042.
For further reading, refer to *Godden, Ridgway*.

RIDGWAY

Ridgways (Bedford Works) Ltd.
Bedford Works, Shelton,
Hanley, Staffordshire, 1920-1952+
Formerly, Ridgways (1878-1920)
Subsequently retitled Ridgway & Adderley Ltd. (1952-1955)
Former Marks of Ridgways Continued:

KAD NO.	GODDEN NO.
B2063	3318
B2064	3321
B2065	3323
B2066	-

c.1927+

c.1930+

c.1930+

c.1934+

For further reading, refer to *Godden, Ridgway*; *Godden*. p. 530; and *Godden, Collecting Lustreware*, pp. 146-148.

RILEY

KAD NO.	GODDEN NO.	MARK

John & Richard Riley
Hole House Works, Nile Street (1796-1817)
Hill Works (c.1811-1828)
Burslem, Staffordshire, c.1796-1828

KAD NO.	GODDEN NO.	MARK	
B2067	3328		Several different, painted, printed or impressed marks. Pattern name often included, c.1796-1828.
B2068	3330	**RILEY 1823**	
B2069	-	**RILEY**	- "Gaudy Deutsch" or "Gaudy Dutch" was heavily exported to the state of Pennsylvania, USA, where there was a large German immigrant population.

Typical Marks Include:

KAD NO.	GODDEN NO.
B2070	3329
B2071	-
B2072	-

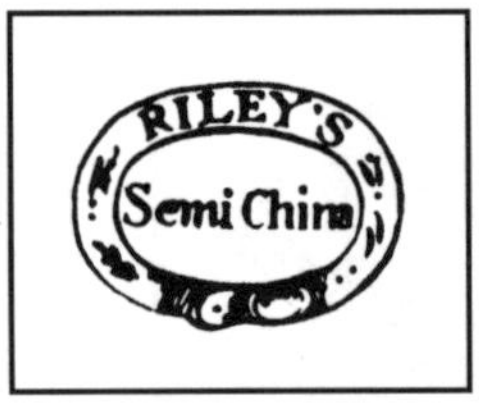

KAD NO.	GODDEN NO.
B2073	-
B2074	-
B2075	-

For further reading, refer to *Journal of Ceramic History*, Vol. 13, 1998, Stoke-on-Trent, City Museum & Art Gallery for an article by Roger Pomfret titled "John & Richard Riley, China & Earthenware Manufacturers;" *Godden, British Porcelain*, p. 653; *Godden, Collecting Lustreware*, p. 148; *Penny Plain*, p. 95, No. 189; *Edwards, Basalt*, pp. 223-226; and *True Blue*, p.66, No. 9 & p. 149, No. R12A.

ROBINSON

***Robinson & Wood**
Broad Street,
Shelton, Hanley, Staffordshire, c.1832-1836
Subsequently, Robinson, Wood & Brownfield (1837-1841)

KAD NO.	GODDEN NO.	MARK	
B2076	3344	**R. & W.**	Printed marks of differing design. Pattern name often included, c.1832-1836.
B2077	-		- "STONE CHINA" marking noted.

For further reading, refer to *Henrywood*, p. 132.

ROBINSON

John Robinson (& Sons)
Hill Works,
Burslem, Staffordshire, c.1786-1818
- "& Sons"* (1812-1822)
Subsequently, John Robertson (Jr.) (c.1822-1827)

KAD NO.	GODDEN NO.	MARK	
B2078	-	**ROBINSON**	Impressed name mark, c.1786-1818. *The initials "J. R. & S." may refer to John Robinson & Son, Castleford, Yorkshire, 1902-1933, and should not be attributed to the above potter. *Godden, British Porcelain*, p. 656 notes another potter, (John) Robinson & Son, Longton, 1863-1870 and 1881-1903. - See *Coysh*, Vol. 2, p. 168 for the pattern "Temple Parkland."

ROBINSON

Joseph Robinson
Knowle Works,
Burslem, Staffordshire, 1876-1898

KAD NO.	GODDEN NO.	MARK	
B2079*	3337		Printed or impressed marks of differing design. Pattern name often included, 1876-1898. - The initials "J. R./B." denote the potter and town Burslem.
B2080	3337A	**J. ROBINSON**	- This type of marking, "J. R./B." can be confusing. It has been noted, evidently in error, as John Ridgway, Bates & Co. See *Snyder, Pocket Guide*, p. 69 for an illustration and mark for the pattern "Cyprus."

ROBINSON

***Robinson, Wood & Brownfield**
Brownfields Works,
Cobridge, Staffordshire, c.1837-1841
Formerly, Robinson & Wood (c.1832-1836)

KAD NO.	GODDEN NO.	MARK	
B2081	3345	**R. W. & B.**	Printed marks of differing design. Pattern name often included, c.1837.
B2483	4242	**W. & B.***	Printed or impressed initials oftern with pattern name c.1838-40
B2082	-		- "STONE/WARE" and "OPAQUE STONE CHINA" markings noted. Refer to *Peake, William Brownfield*, pp. 87-88.

* *Peake, William Brownfield*, notes that the initials "R. W. & B." were used until Noah Robinson's death in September 1837. Thereafter only the initials "W. & B." were used, with one noted exception - a rare registration in July 1839. See pp. 1-2 and p. 87, marks 27 and 29. See Wood & Brownfield, pp. 376-377.

For further reading, refer to *Hampson, Churchill*, as well as to Appendix B6, Chronology for the Churchill Group. For a complete index of plate designs refer to *Peake, William Brownfield*, Appendix 3, p. 170; and *Henrywood*, "William Brownfield", pp. 132-145.

ROCKINGHAM

Rockingham Works
See: Brameld (& Co.), see pp. 124-125

ROGERS

John & George Rogers
Dale Hall,
Longport, Staffordshire, c.1784-1815
Subsequently, J. Rogers & Son (c.1815-1841)

KAD NO.	GODDEN NO.	MARK	
B2084	3367	**ROGERS**	Impressed marks, c.1784-1815+. - Mark noted as having been used by John Rogers & Son, c.1815-1841.
B2085	3368	**J. R. L.**	*Chaffers* notes this initial mark as belonging to John & George Rogers. *Godden* notes this marking as "unlikely" to relate to either firm. (See John Rogers & Son) - John Rogers died in 1815 and George Rogers in 1816. However, the firm continued on as John Rogers & Son (the son was Spencer Rogers).

For further reading, refer to *Godden, Collecting Lustreware*, pp. 148-149; and *Henrywood*, p.172.

ROGERS

John Rogers & Son (Spencer Rogers)
Dale Hall Pottery, Fountain Place
Longport, Staffordshire, c.1815-1841
Subsequently, James Edwards (1842-1854)

KAD NO.	GODDEN NO.	MARK	
B2086	3369	**ROGERS**	Impressed name mark, c.1815-1841.
B2087	-		- This is a continuation of the John & George Rogers' mark (c.1874-1815). - Occasionally the "IRON OF MARS" device may appear with or without accompanying name.
B2088	-		Printed marks of varying designs. Pattern names often included in later wares, c.1815-1841. - Note the Prince of Wales Feather mark and the use of "SEMI CHINA".

Typical Marks Include:

B2089 -
B2090 -
B2091 -

KAD NO. | **GODDEN NO.** | **MARK**

B2092 | - |

Printed and impressed marks of varying designs noted on American/Canadian Views, which often include printed series and title names, c.1815-1841.
- Name "ROGERS" noted. See KAD B2086.

B2093 | 3370 | **J. R.**

Mark noted by *Godden* as being "unlikely" to relate to either the firm of J. & G. Rogers or J. Rogers & Son.

B2094 | 3371 | **J. R. S. L.**

Impressed marks noted by *Ormsbee*, p. 109, c. 1815-1841.

B2095 | 3372 | **ROGERS & SON**

For further reading, refer to *FOB* Occasional Papers, Summer, 1992, No. 2, pp. 1-22, for an article by Minnie Holdaway titled "Rogers Blue-Printed Earthenwares; *Coysh & Stefano*; *Penny Plain*, p. 96, Nos. 197, 238; *Godden, Collecting Lustreware*, pp. 148-149; *Snyder, Historic Staffordshire*, pp. 80-82; and *Snyder, Romantic Staffordshire*, pp. 155-156.

ROWLAND

Rowland & Marsellus Importers
New York (City) USA, c.1893-1933
- I have included this series on Rowland & Marsellus in order to give the collector an idea of the complexity and magnitude involved in researching commemorative/souvenir plates. *In my opinion souvenir and commemorative ware is a category unto its own, and are neither truly historic nor flow blue.*

B2096 | - |

Printed initial and name marks, c.1893-1933.

B2097 | - |

- Arene Burgess' book *Souvenir Plates, A Collector's Guide*. Bethalto, IL, 1978, pp. 84-96, finally clears up the confusion about Rowland & Marsellus. Until the research and publication of Burgess' book, everyone was under the misapprehension that this company was a manufacturer due to the appearance of their marks and to the fact that a manufacturer's mark is seldom found on their wares. However, Rowland & Marsellus were New York importers. From 1893-1910 the wares they imported were manufactured by Hancock, and after 1910 by Royal Fenton and other companies. It is important to note that the two features most commonly associated with Rowland & Marsellus are the Fruit and Flower Border and the Rolled Edge Border.

For further reading, refer to *Arman*, pp. 224-226; Frank Stefano, Jr. *Pictorial and Commemoratives of North America*, New York, NY. E. P. Dutton & Co., 1976; Ian T. Henderson. *Pictorial Souvenirs of Britain*. London,. David & Charles, 1974; A. W. Coysh & Frank Stefano, Jr. *Collecting Ceramic Landscapes*. London. Lund Humphries, 1981.

B2098 | - |

ST. ANTHONY' S

St. Anthony's Pottery
See: Sewell(s) Pottery, p. 331

ST. JOHNS

St. Johns Stone Chinaware Co.
St. Johns (Province of Quebec) *Canada*, c.1873-1899
Manufacturers of White Ironstone
History:

c.1873-1877	Founded by George Whitfield Farrar
c.1877-1896	Subsequently, Duncan & Edward MacDonald
c.1896-1899	Purchased by a French group.

KAD NO.	GODDEN NO.	MARK	
B2099	-	**ST. JOHNS P. Q.**	Printed marks (in brown or black), c.1873-1899. - Also noted with Royal Arms marking which may include "ST. JOHNS, P. Q." and/or "Q. U. E."
B2100	-	**IMPERIAL IRONSTONE CHINA**	
B2101	-	**Q. U. E.**	
B2102	-	**IRONSTONE CHINA ST. JOHNS**	

- According to *Collard, Pottery & Porcelain*, pp. 281-290, the company produced mainly White Ironstone c.1873-1899.

For further reading, refer to *Sussman*, pp. 36-37 for the "Wheat Pattern" as well as p. 46; and *Antiques*, October 1976 for an article by Elizabeth Collard titled "The St. Johns Stone Chinaware Company."

SCOTT

Scott Brothers
Portobello,
near Edinburgh, Scotland, 1786-1796
Subsequently, Cookson & Jardine (1796-1808),
Thomas Yoole (1808-1810), and
Thomas Rathbone & Co. (1810-1845)

KAD NO.	GODDEN NO.	MARK	
B2103	3473	**SCOTT BROS.***	Impressed name marks, c.1786-1796.
B2104	3473	**SCOTT BROTHERS**	- Marks noted here should not be confused with "Scott Bros." of the Southwick Pottery, Sunderland, Durham.
B2105	3475	**SCOTT P. B.**	

* Refer to Southwick Pottery for like name-mark "SCOTT", p. 339.

For further reading, refer to *Fleming,* pp. 170-171; *McVeigh*, pp. 122-128; *Godden*, pp. 587-588; and *Godden, Collecting Lustreware*, pp. 229-230.

SEWELL

KAD NO.	GODDEN NO.	MARK	
			Sewell(s) & Co. **St. Anthony's Pottery at Newcastle-upon-Tyne, Northumberland, c.1804-1878** **Formerly, Foster & Cutter (c.1800-1804)** **Subsequently, W. Lloyd (1882-1884)** **History:** Joseph Sewell 1804-1819 Sewell(s) & Donkin 1819-1852 Sewell(s) & Co. 1852-1878
B2106	3664A	**SEWELL**	Impressed name marks of differing design. Printed pattern name often included, 1804-1878.
B2107	3665	**SEWELL & DONKIN**	- For additional comments refer to *Godden*, "St. Anthony's Pottery" pp. 591-592.
B2108	3666	**SEWELLS & DONKIN**	
B2109	3667	**SEWELL & CO.**	
B2110	-	**SEWELLS & CO.**	

For further reading, refer to *Bell*; *FOB*, No. 56, Summer 19897, p. 11 and No. 63, 1989, p. 10; and *Godden, Collecting Lustreware*, pp. 239-240;and *NCS Newsletter*, No. 98, June 1995, pp. 4-6 for an article by Alwyn & Angela Cox titled "Sewell or Dawson".

SHARPE

Sharpe Brothers & Co. (Ltd.)
Swadlincote Potteries,
Burton-on-Trent, Derbyshire, c.1838-1895
Formerly, Thomas Sharpe (c.1821-1838)

KAD NO.	GODDEN NO.	MARK	
B2111	3494	**S. B. & CO.**	Printed initial mark, c.1838-1895. - "LTD." dates from 1895. - *Godden*, p. 570, notes that the firm produced mainly toilet wares.

For further reading, refer to *Collard, Pottery & Porcelain*, pp. 142-143; and *NCSJ* Vol. 11, 1994 for an article by Ronald B. Brown titled "Potteries of Derbyshire", No. 50, pp. 138-141.

SHARPE

Thomas Sharpe
Swadlincote Potteries,
Burton-on-Trent, Derbyshire, c.1821-1838
Subsequently, Sharpe Brothers & Co. (1838-1895)

KAD NO.	GODDEN NO.	MARK	
B2112	3490	**SHARPE MANUFACTURER SWADLINCOTE**	Impressed name marks, c.1821-1838. - Care must be taken in not confusing this firm with (William) Sharpe & Co., (c.1803-1807).
B2113	3491	**T. SHARPE**	
B2114	3492	**THOMAS SHARPE**	

For further reading, refer to *Little*, p. 115; *Coysh*, Vol. I, p. 330; *Cameron*, pp. 304-305; *NCSJ*, No. 11, 1994 (No. 50), pp. 138-141, for an article on Swadlincote Potteries by Ronald B. Brown titled "Potteries of Derbyshire".

SHAW

Anthony Shaw (& Son(s) (& Co.)
Child Works, Tunstall (c.1851-1858)
Mersey Works, Burslem (c.1858-1900)
Staffordshire, c.1851-1900
Subsequently, A. J. Wilkinson Ltd. (1900+)

KAD NO.	GODDEN NO.	MARK	
B2115	3496	**ANTHONY SHAW**	Printed or impressed marks noted with various, and often elaborately designed marks. Pattern name is often included, c.1851-1900.
B2116	3497	**A. SHAW**	
B2117	3498	**A. SHAW BURSLEM**	Printed or impressed marks of varying design marked "BURSLEM", 1851-1858.
B2118	3499	**SHAWS**	
B2119	3500	**SHAW BURSLEM**	
B2120	-	**ANTHONY SHAW BURSLEM**	
B2121	-	**ANTHONY SHAW TUNSTALL**	Printed marks of varying design marked "TUNSTALL", 1858-1898.

Typical Marks Include:

B2122 -
B2123 -
B2124 -
B2125 -

B2126 -
B2127 -
B2128 -
B2129 -

B2130 -
B2131 -

Printed marking "& SON" added from 1882-1898.

B2132 -

Printed marking "& SONS", "& CO." added from 1898-1900.

KAD NO. | **GODDEN NO.** | **MARK**

B2133 - 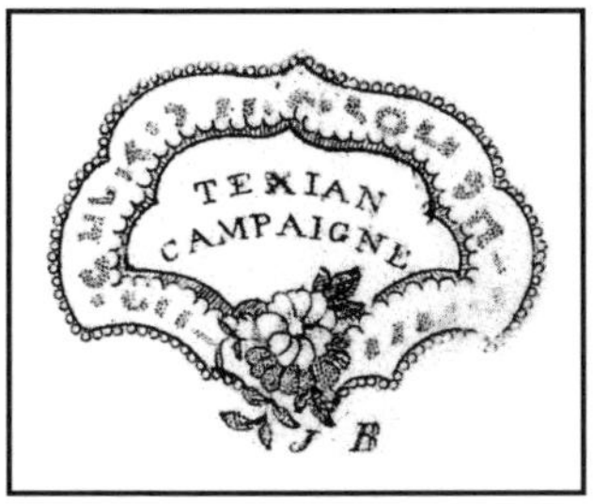

Printed marks of various designs noted on Historic American/Canadian views, often including printed series and title names, c.1851-c.1860.
- Importer's mark "J. L. ALTENBAUGH/TIFFEN, OHIO" noted. *P. Williams, Staffordshire*, Vol. II, p. 650 notes the existence of "TEXAS CAMPAIGN" in Mulberry.
- It is thought that the initials "J. B." may be those of the designer and not the potter. Nevertheless, care must be taken when attributing these initials, as they may belong to many other potters as well. I would refer the reader back to James Beech and to the initials "J. B." under Appendix B6: Chronology, p. 548.
- *Arman, Quarterly*, Vol. 1, April/May 1997, No. 2, pp. 22-23 includes a report on the March 1997 sales by Northeast Auctions of "Texian Campaigne".

For further reading, refer to *Heaivilin*, pp. 106-107 "Tea Leaf Shapes"; *TLCI*, Vol. 7, No. 2, Aug. 1987; *Tea Leaf Readings Educational Supplement*, April 1992, "Pouring Vessels"; *White Ironstone Notes*, Vol. 3, No. 4, Spring 1997, p. 7, "Lily of the Valley by Anthony Shaw"; *Stoltzfus/Snyder*; *Godden, Mason's*, p. 276; *Snyder, Romantic Staffordshire*, pp. 156-157; and Dennis Stuart. *People of the Potteries*. Keele, England. Dept. of Adult Education, Univ. of Keele, 1985.

SHAW

C. & J. Shaw (Junior)
Green Dock Works,
Longton, Staffordshire, 1832-1837
Formerly, Thomas Brough (1816-1822)
Subsequently, Deakins & Procter (1836-1838)

B2134 - **C. & J. SHAW** Printed garter mark with Latin inscription "Vincit Veritas"/Truth Conquers, c.1832-1837, noted in *Snyder, Romantic Staffordshire*, p. 157.

- See *P. Williams, Staffordshire*, Vol. III, p. 120 for an illustration.

B2135 - 

B2136 4495 **C. & J. SHAW JUNIOR** Printed name mark noted by *Godden*, Appendix p. 731.

- It is my opinion that C. & J. Shaw and Shaw Junior may have been one and the same. See information provided by *Hampson*, No. 224, p. 142. However, research is needed to verify this, and the reader is advised to treat this cautiously.

SHIRLEY

Thomas Shirley & Co.
Clyde Pottery,
Greenock, Scotland, c.1840(41)-1857
Formerly, Andrew Muir & Co. (c.1836-1840(41)
Subsequently, Clyde Pottery Co. (c.1857-1862)

B2137 3522 **T. S. & C.** Impressed initial marks, c.1840(41)-1857.

B574 - **T. S. & CO.** - Printed trade-mark "SAXON" and "WARRANTED" noted.

B575 3521 **T. S. & COY** - For further information on Thomas Shirley, refer to the Clyde Pottery and Andrew Muir & Co., pp. 153-154 and p. 293 respectively.

For further reading, refer to *Scottish Pottery 16th Historical Review*, pp. 44-48 for an article by Heather Jack titled "The Thomas Shirley Document."

SHORE

Shore, Coggins & Holt
Edensor Works,
Longton, Staffordshire, 1905-1910
Formerly, J. Shore & Co. (1887-1905)
Subsequently, Shore & Coggins (1911-1966)

KAD NO.	GODDEN NO.	MARK	
B2137A	3531		Printed initial mark. Pattern name often included, 1905-1910.

SHORTHOUSE

Shorthouse & Heath (or & Co.)
Tontine & High Street Potteries,
Shelton, Hanley, Staffordshire, c.1794-1823

History:

Shorthouse & Heath	Hanley	1794-1815
John Shorthouse	Hanley	1815-1823
Shorthouse & Co.	Shelton	1817-1818

KAD NO.	GODDEN NO.	MARK	
B2138	3537	**SHORTHOUSE & HEATH**	Impressed name mark, c.1794-1815.
B2139	3539	**SHORTHOUSE**	Printed, impressed or written name marks. Pattern name included, c.1815-1823.
B2140	-	**I. SHORTHOUSE**	
B2141	3536	**SHORTHOUSE & CO.**	Impressed, printed or written name mark, c.1817-1818. - See *True Blue*, p. 150, Nos. S1 & S2. - *Godden*, p. 576 notes that "John Shorthouse was probably connected with [all] these firms."

For further reading, refer to *Godden, Collecting Lustreware*, p. 151; *Coysh*, Vol. I, pp. 397-398; *Edwards, Basalt*, pp. 231-232; and *Little*, pp. 95-96.

SKINNER

***Skinner & Walker**
Stafford Pottery,
Stockton-on-Tees, Yorkshire, 1875-1877**
Formerly, George Skinner & Co. (c.1855-1870)
Subsequently, Ambrose Walker & Co. (1880-1893)
- Pottery closed in 1905
- See Stafford Pottery for Chronology, p. 553

KAD NO.	GODDEN NO.	MARK	
B2142	3569	**S. & W. QUEENSWARE STOCKTON**	Printed or impressed marks of differing design, c.1875-1877.
B2143	3569A	**S. & W.^{S} PEARLWARE**	
B2144	3570	**QUEENSWARE STOCKTON**	

- The foregoing information was obtain from *Lawrence*, pp. 212-213

**Godden, Collecting Lustreware*, p. 264, notes the dates for Skinner & Walker as 1870-1880.

SKINNER

KAD NO.	GODDEN NO.	MARK	

***George Skinner & Co.**
Stafford Pottery,
Stockton-on-Tees, Yorkshire, c. 1855-1870
Formerly, William Smith & Co. (c.1825-1855)
- See Stafford Pottery for Chronology, p. 553

B2145	3568	**G. S. & CO.**	Printed marks of differing design. Pattern name often included, c.1855-1870.

- *Godden*, p. 580 notes "Some wares bearing "G. S. & CO." printed mark may also have the impressed mark of William Smith & Co..." Wares were potted by one firm and decorated by another (G. Skinner & Co.).

For further reading, refer to *Lawrence*, pp. 212-213; *Cameron*, p. 316; and *Williams-Wood, Pot Lids*, p. 98.

SMITH

Smith & Binall
Soho Pottery,
Tunstall, Staffordshire, c.1897-1900
Formerly, Rathbone, Smith & Co. (c.1883-1897)
Subsequently, Soho Pottery Ltd. (1901-1944)

B2146 | 3577

Printed Staffordshire Knot mark, c.1897-1900.

For further reading, refer to *Cushion,* pp. 165-166; and *Bunt, British Potters*, pp. 52-53.

SMITH

Smith & Ford
Lincoln Pottery,
Burslem, Staffordshire, 1894-1898
Formerly, Smith, Ford & Jones (c.1889-1894)
Subsequently, Samuel Ford & Co. (1898-1939)

B2147 | 3578

Printed marks of differing design. Pattern name often included, 1895-1898.

- Mark KAD B2147 was continued by Samuel Ford & Co. See KAD B964.

B2148 | -

For further reading, refer to *Blue Berry Notes*, Vol. 11, No. 3, May-June 1997, pp. 14-15.

SMITH

Smith, Ford & Jones
Lincoln Pottery,
Burslem, Staffordshire, c.1889-1894
Subsequently, Smith & Ford (1894-1898)

B2149	-	**S. F. & J.**	Printed marks of differing design. Pattern name often included, c.1889-1894.
B2150	-	**LINCOLN POTTERY PARISIAN WHITE ENGLAND**	Initial mark absent. Marking "LINCOLN POTTERY" noted, 1889-1894.

KAD NO.	GODDEN NO.	MARK	
			- The pattern "Regalia", in semi-porcelain, is noted in *The Handbook of Tea Leaf Body Styles*, 1995, published by Tea Leaf Collector's International, as possibly being made by the above firm.

SMITH

***George F. Smith (& Co.)**
North Shore Pottery,
Stockton-on-Tees, Durham, c.1851-1857
Formerly, W. Smith Jr. & Co. (1845-1848)
- See North Shore Pottery for chronology, p. 551

B2151	3579	**G. F. S.**	Printed or impressed marks of differing design. Pattern name often included, 1851-1857.
B2152	3580	**G. F. S. & CO.**	- "& CO." from 1851-1857.

For further reading, refer to *Godden, Jewitt*, p. 223; and *The Catalog of the Boynton Collection of Yorkshire Pottery*, by A. Hurst. The Yorkshire Philosophical Society, 1922, pp. 22-23.

SMITH

Theophilus Smith
Smithfield Works,
Tunstall, Staffordshire, c.1790-1797
- John Breeze (& Son) renamed the pottery "Greenfield" (in 1801)

B2153	-	**T. SMITH**	Impressed name mark, c.1790-1797.

For further reading, refer to *Little*, pp. 53, 135; *Godden, British Porcelain*, p. 184; and *Penny Plain*, pp. 65-66 and p. 98 No. 229.

SMITH

***William Smith (& Co.)**
Stafford Pottery,
Thornaby/Stockton-on-Tees, Yorkshire, c.1825-1855
- See Appendix B6: Chronology for Stafford Pottery

B2154	3596		Printed marks of differing design. Pattern name often included, c.1825-1855.
B2155	3597	**W. S. & CO. STAFFORD/POTTERY**	
B2156	3598	**W. S. & CO'S WEDGEWOOD [POTTERY]**	The name "WEDGWOOD" or "WEDGEWOOD", impressed or otherwise marked, ceased in 1848 due to a successful injunction granted to Wedgwood.
B2157	3599	**W. S. & CO'S QUEEN'S WARE STOCKTON**	The firm of William Smith (& Co.) greatly benefited from this deceptive practice so cleverly conceived that no other deceptions were devised. The marking "QUEEN'S WARE" was probably adopted and used for several decades.

KAD NO.	GODDEN NO.	MARK	
B2158	3600	**W. S. & CO. WEDGWOOD WARE**	- Additional marking "JOHN WILKINSON, WEDGWOOD POTTERY, STAFFORD, AUGUST 10TH 1836" noted by *Noel Riley*, p. 256, No. 1030.
B2159	3601	**W. SMITH & CO.**	
B2160	-	**WILLIAM SMITH & CO.**	
B2161	-	**STAFFORD POTTERY SOUTH STOCKTON**	
B2162	-	**VEDGWOOD**	"VEDGWOOD" is noted by Godden as a marking used by William Smith & Co. Doubts do exist as to whether the marking was used by William Smith. However, it was used by Carr & Patton.
B2163	-		Printed mark of William Smith, agent and partner in Brussels, Belgium (1847-1857).

- Refer to European potter "J.B. Cappellemans/William Smith & Sie", p. 635.

- *Blue Berry Notes*, Vol. 9, No. 3, May-June 1995, p. 15 illustrates a New York importer's mark "L. WEAFELAER & CO., NEW YORK" for the pattern "Geranium". Also refer to *Gaston*, Vol. II, p. 75, for the pattern "Down the Street She Passed" which is impressed "WEDGEWOOD" and has an additional printed marking "MADE FOR THE LINTON & SINCLAIR CO."

For further reading, refer to *Coysh*, Vol. I, pp. 220, 340 and Vol. 2, p. 47; *Little*, Pl. 106; *Hill*, No. 117 "Fruit Basket"; *The Catalog of the Boynton Collection of Yorkshire Pottery*, by A. Hurst. The Yorkshire Philosophical Society, 1922, pp. 22-23; *NCS Newsletter*, No. 98, June 1995, pp. 14-16 for an article by John Cockerill titled "The Wedgewood Pottery"; *NCS Newsletter*, No. 100, Dec. 1995, pp. 39-46 for a further article by John Cockerill titled "English Earthenware Made in Belgium"; *NCS Newsletter,* No. 105, March 1997, pp. 12-187 for an article by John Cockerill titled "Multi-Colour Printing by W. Smith & Co. at the Stafford/Wedgewood Pottery, South Stockton in the 1840s"

SNEYD

Sneyd & Hill
Miles Bank,
Shelton, Hanley, c.1845
Subsequently, Thomas Sneyd (1846-1847)

- *Snyder, Fascinating Flow Blue* illustrates two patterns "Claremont Groups" and "Windsor Scrolls" with the initials "S. & H."* that may refer to this potter.

KAD NO.	GODDEN NO.	MARK	
B2164	-	**S. & H.***	Printed initial mark. Pattern name often included, c.1845.
B2165	3610	**SNEYD & HILL HANLEY STAFFORDSHIRE POTTERIES**	Printed name mark, c.1845.

*The following are potters with like initials:

Shorthouse & Heath	1794-1815
Sheridan & Hewitt	1805-1808
Sheridan & Hyatt	1807-1811
Shaw & Hallum	1827

These potters are, however, too early to be considered.

*The following potters are not recorded as earthenware manufacturers:

Shelley & Hartshorn	1858-1861
Stanway & Horne	1862-1864
Stevenson & Hancock	1862-1866
Spencer & Hines	1876-1882

KAD NO.	GODDEN NO.	MARK	

SNEYD

Thomas Sneyd
Miles Bank,
Shelton, Hanley, Staffordshire, c.1846-1847
Formerly, Sneyd & Hill (c.1845)

KAD NO.	GODDEN NO.	MARK	
B2166	3609	**T. SNEYD HANLEY**	Impressed name mark, c.1846-1847.

- Lorraine Punchard, *Playtime Pottery and Porcelain from the United Kingdom and the United States*. Atglen PA, Schiffer Publishing Ltd., 1966, p. 62 illustrates a child set in Flow Blue. Additionally, *Blue Berry Notes*, Vol. 6, No. 1, July/Aug. 1991, p. 4, records a child's pattern "Lily" in an article by Judy Peabody titled "Children's Play Dishes."

SOHO

Soho Pottery (Ltd.)
Soho Pottery, Tunstall (1901-1906)
Elder Works, Cobridge (1906-1944)
Staffordshire, 1901-1944
Formerly, Smith & Binall (1897-1900)
Subsequently, Simpsons (Potters) Ltd. (1944-)

KAD NO.	GODDEN NO.	MARK	
B2167	-	**SOHO POTTERY TUNSTALL**	Printed marks of differing design. Pattern name often included, 1901-1944.
B2168	-	**SOHO POTTERY COBRIDGE**	- "ENGLAND" appears after 1891. - "LTD" added from 1904

Typical Marks Include:

B2169 3612
B2170 3613
B2171 3614

1901-1906

1906-1922

1913-1930

- For additional marks refer to *Godden*, p. 585.

For further reading, refer to *Bunt, British Potters*, pp. 52-53 for Simpsons (Potters) Ltd.

SOUTH WALES

South Wales Potters,
Llanelly, Wales, c.1839-1922

History:

Chambers & Co.	1839-1855
Coombs & Holland	1855-1858
William (W. T.) Holland	1859-1868
Guest & Dewsberry	1877-1906
Guest & Family	1910-1922
Richard Guest, owner	1906-1922
"& Co." (& Ltd.) dates from	1910-1922

KAD NO.	GODDEN NO.	MARK	
B2172	3626	**CHAMBERS, LLANELLY**	Printed and impressed marks Nos. KAD B2172-B2175 of differing design. Pattern name often included, c.1839-1855.

KAD NO.	GODDEN NO.	MARK		
B2173	3627	**SOUTH WALES POTTERY W. CHAMBERS**	- *Noel Riley*, notes the following impressed markings: "SOUTH WALES POTTERY", p. 262 No. 1049 Four "blobs" which signify "S. W. P.", p. 280 No. 1125. - Additional impressed markings "IRONSTONE" or "IRONSTONE CHINA" may be noted in addition to proprietors' printed marks, c.1855-1868.	
B2174	3626A	**SOUTH WALES POTTERY**		
B2175	3628	**S. W. P.**		
B2176	-	**W. C. JR. L. P.**	William Chambers Jun.	1839-1855
B2177	-	**C. & H.***	Coombs & Holland	1855-1858
B2178	-	**W. T. H.**	*William Holland	1859-1868
B2179	-	**G. & D.**	Guest & Dewsberry	1877-1906

*Initials "C. & H." and patterns continued in use by William Holland.

For further reading, refer to *Nance*; Gareth Hughes & Robert Pugh. *Llanelly ottery*. Llanelli Wales, Llanelli Borough Council, 1990; *Godden, Collecting Lustreware*, pp. 254-255; *Pugh, Welsh Pottery*, pp. 41-53 "Llanelly Pottery" and pp. 52-54 for additional markings. Additional patterns are to be found in both *Pugh*, and *Hallesy*.

SOUTHWICK

Southwick Pottery
Sunderland, Durham, c.1800-1896
Formerly, Atkinson & Co. (1788-1800)
The following are printed or impressed marks of differing designs, with pattern name often included, c.1800-1896.

		MARK	COMPANY NAME	DATE
B2180	3629	**A. SCOTT & CO.**	Anthony Scott & Co.	1800-1829
B2181	3629A	**SCOTT, SOUTHWICK**		
B2182	3630	**ANTHONY SCOTT/& SONS**	Scott & Sons	1829-1841
B2183	3630A	**A. SCOTT & SONS**		
B2184	3631	**SCOTT & SONS**		
B2185	3632	**SCOTT & SONS/SOUTHWICK**		
B2186	3633	**S. & S.**		
B2187	3634	**SCOTT BROTHERS/& CO.**	Scott Bros. & Co.	1841-1854
B2188	3635	**SCOTT BROTHERS**		
B2189	3636	**SCOTT BROS.**		
B2199	3637	**S. B. & CO.**		
B2191	3638	**SCOTT**		
B2192	3639	**A. SCOTT**	Anthony Scott	1854-1872
B2193	3638	**SCOTT**		
B2194	3640	**A. SCOTT & SON**	Anthony Scott & Son	1872-1882
B2195	3641	**S. & S.**		
B2196	3638	**SCOTT**		
B2197	3639	**A. SCOTT**	Anthony Scott	1882-1896
B2198	3638	**SCOTT**		

- The above marks should not be confused with "Scott Bros." of Portobello Pottery (1786-1796).
*Mark "SCOTT" was used from c.1841-1896.

For further reading, refer to *Baker*; J. T. Shaw. *Sunderland Ware: The Potteries of Wearside*. (4th ed.) Sunderland, England, Sunderland Public Libraries, Museum & Art Gallery, 1973; *Riley,* Part I; and *Godden, Jewitt*, p. 211.

SPODE

KAD NO. | GODDEN NO. | MARK

***Josiah Spode**
Stoke-on-Trent,
Staffordshire, c.1770-1833
Subsequently, Copeland & Garrett (1833-1847)
- Number appearing in ( ) denote reference to Robert Copeland's numbering system. For additional marks refer to Copeland. *Spode & Copeland Marks*. London. Studio Vista, 1993.

B2199 | 3648 | **SPODE (21-24)** | Impressed or blue printed marks on earthenware, c.1784-1830.

Impressed Marks (selection) Include:

B2200 | -
B2201 | -
B2202 | -
B2203 | -

1785-1790 (10)

1790-1802 (2A)

1800-1820 (3A)

1815-1833 (4)

- Note No. (4), KAD B2203 with Serifs on letter "S"

B2204 | 3650 | **SPODE** | Printed marks, as above, 1800-1833.

Printed Marks (selection) Include:

B2205
B2206 | -
B2207 | -

1800-1820 (31)

1810-1833 (33)

1810-1833 (34)

B2208 | 3648B | **SPODE 967 SPODE 1106** | Written (pattern) marks with individual identifying pattern number found on earthenware and porcelain, c.1790-1820.

B2209 | 3651
B2210 | -

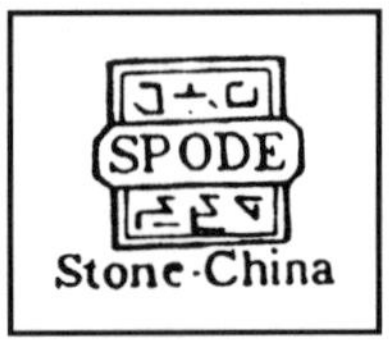

(47)

(48)

Printed marks, in black, on stone-china, c.1812-1833, and in blue, c.1815-1833.

B2211 | 3652

(7B)

Impressed marks on "NEW STONE" earthenware, 1822-1833.
- This seal was a popular marking among Spode's contemporaries. Refer to Miles Mason and J. Ridgway's marks noting special earthenware bodies, c.1805-1833.

B2212 | 3653 | **N. S. (8)** | - Abbreviations for "NEW STONE", 1822-1833.

Selected Marks on "NEW BODY STYLE" Include:

B2213 | 3654
B2214 | 3656
B2215 | 3655

1805-1815 (37)

1821-1833 (49)

1826-1833 (51A)

KAD NO. **GODDEN NO.** **MARK**

B2216 -

(63)

Printed marks in elaborate cartouche are few in number for Spode. This practice of marking, though late in Spode's life, was to become popular among nearly all potters or printed wares during the Victorian period, c.1830.

- Under Spode patterns, all listings are as noted and continued by subsequent partnerships and owners. Spode patterns are cited as being in Blue & White, while all others can be in any color.

- I would like to thank Robert Copeland for his invaluable assistance in correcting and amending the listing of patterns for Spode, Copeland & Garrett, et.al.

B2217 -

(64)

For further reading on Spode, Copeland and Copeland & Garrett, refer to:

- Sydney B. Williams. *Blue and White Spode*, Omega Books Ltd., London, 1987.
- Lynne Sussman. *Canadian Historic Sites, Spode/Copeland Transfer-Printed Patterns*. Minister responsible for Parks, Ottawa, Canada, 1979.
- Howard Davis. *Chinoiserie, Polychrome Decoration on Staffordshire Porcelain, 1780-1850*, Rubicom Press, London, 1991, pp. 73-75.
- Robert Copeland. *Copeland*, Shire Album 309. Shire Publications, Ltd. Aylesbury, Bucks, England, 1993.
- V. Wilkinson. *Copeland*. Shire Album 306. Shire Publications, Ltd. Aylesbury, Bucks, England, 1993.
-Leonard White. *Spode*, Barrie & Jenkins, London, 1978.
- Robert Copeland. *Spode & Copeland Marks*. Studio Vista, England. 1st & 2nd editions, 1993 and 1997.
- D. Drakard & P. Holdway. *Spode Printed Ware*. Longman Group Ltd., Essex, England, 1983.
- Robert Copeland. *Spode's Willow Pattern* and Other Designs After The Chinese. Studio Vista, London, 1980 and 1990.
- Geoffrey Godden. *Staffordshire Porcelain*, Chapter 8.

STANLEY

Stanley Pottery Co.
Newport Lane,
Middleport, Burslem, c.1909-1937

B2218 - **S. P. CO.** Printed name or initial marks, c.1909-1937.

B2219 - **STANLEY POTTERY CO. ENGLAND**

B2220 -

Printed crown mark, c.1909-1937.

STANLEY

Stanley Pottery Ltd.
Edensor Road,
Longton, Staffordshire, 1928-1931
Formerly, Colclough & Co. (1887-1928)
Printed marks used by Colclough & Co. (1887-1928) continued by the Stanley Pottery Ltd., 1928-1931.

KAD NO.	GODDEN NO.	MARK
B2221	983	
B617	984	

In correspondence to me dated 6/15/95, Geoffrey Godden notes:
"...The initial [C. & Co.] may not occur on newly engraved Stanley patterns." The initial "C. & CO." relates to the earlier company of Colclough & Co. (1887-1928). For further comments refer to Colclough & Co., p. 157.

STEVENSON

Stevenson & Godwin
Upper & Lower Manufactory,
Cobridge, Staffordshire, 1804-1810
Formerly, Stevenson, Godwin & Dale (1802-1804)
Subsequently, Benjamin Godwin & Sons (B. & S. Godwin)
Upper Manufactory (1810-1818), and
Ralph Stevenson, Lower Manufactory (1810-1833)

No Further Information Available.

For further reading, refer to *Edwards, Basalt*, pp. 160-161; *Godden, Collecting Lustreware*, pp. 158-159; and *NCSJ*, Vol. 8, 1991 for an article by Ann Eatwell & Alex Werner titled "A London Staffordshire Warehouse, 1794-1825."

STEVENSON

***Andrew Stevenson**
Cobridge, Staffordshire, c.1816-1836
Formerly, Stevenson & Bucknall (c.1811-1816)

KAD NO.	GODDEN NO.	MARK	
B2223	3699	**STEVENSON**	Impressed name marks, c.1816-1836.
B2224	3699A	**A. STEVENSON**	
B2225	3700		Impressed name mark, c.1816-1836.
B2226	3701		Impressed circular mark, c.1816-1836.
B2227	3702		Printed mark found predominantly on Blue Earthenware with variously designed cartouches, c.1816-1836.

KAD NO. | **GODDEN NO.** | **MARK**

B2228 -

In "AMERICAN VIEWS ON STAFFORDSHIRE CHINA", c. 1816-1836.
Larsen, pp. 43-44, notes signed pieces by the famed artist W. G. Wall of New York.*
Other printed markings are:
- "Eagle with Widespread Wings Faces Left" [and] Scroll.
- Urn With Scarf and Pattern Name.
- Boy With Scroll and Printed Pattern Name.

B2229 -

**Little*, p. 27, provides an interesting insight into the Irish artist W. G. Wall whosettled in the United States. Wall supplied Andrew Stevenson with the drawings for at least twelve designs.

B2230 -

Printed mark often accompanied by Impressed Mark KAD B2226, c.1816-1836.

For further reading, refer to *Godden, Collecting Lustreware*, pp. 158-159; *Little*, p. 98; *NCS Newsletter*, No. 97, March 1995, pp. 8-10 for an article by Anthony Bruce titled "Chinoiseries"; *Snyder, Historic Staffordshire*, , p. 29 and p. 83 wherein he illustrates additional backstamps which feature the W. G. Wall attribution; and *Hampson, Churchill*, pp. 123-124.

STEVENSON

***Ralph Stevenson (Stephenson) [at times noted with this spelling]**
Lower Manufactory,
Cobridge, Staffordshire, c.1810-1833
Formerly, Stevenson & Godwin (c.1805-1810)
- Godden notes that "Marks may have been used by either Andrew or Ralph Stevenson."

B2231 3703

Impressed name mark, c.1810-1833.

B2232 3704 **R. STEVENSON** Impressed name mark, c.1810-1833.

B2233 3705 **R. S.** Printed initial mark, c.1810-1833.
Printed marks of differing design. Pattern names often included in series, c.1810-1833.

Typical Marks Include:

B2234 -
B2235 -
B2236 -

Coysh, Vol. I, pp. 349-350 notes that "Stevenson's Acorn & Oak Leaf Border Series" and "British" or "American" Views are marked either "R. S." or "R. S. W."

For further reading, refer to *Little*, pp. 98-99; *Snyder, Historic Staffordshire*, pp. 86-99; and *Godden, Collecting Lustreware*, pp. 158-159.

STEVENSON

***Ralph Stevenson & Son**
Lower Manufactory,
Cobridge, Staffordshire, c.1833-1835+
Formerly, Ralph Stevenson (c.1810-1833)

KAD NO.	GODDEN NO.	MARK	
B2237	3706	**R. S. & S.**	Printed marks of differing design. Pattern name often included, c.1833-1835+.
B2238	3707	**R. STEVENSON & SON**	- "NEW STONE CHINA" and "IMPERIAL STONE" markings noted.

Typical Marks Include:

B2239 -
B2240 -

P. Williams, Staffordshire, Vol. I & II, pp. 205 and 553-555 respectively, notes a number of unidentified pieces in the "British Lake Series."

For further reading, refer to *Little*, pp. 98-99; *Snyder, Historic Staffordshire*, pp. 86-99; *Godden, Collecting Lustreware*; pp. 158-159; and *Snyder, Romantic Staffordshire*, pp. 160-164.

STEVENSON

***R. Stevenson & Williams**
Lower Manufactory,
Cobridge, Staffordshire, c.1825-1827

KAD NO.	GODDEN NO.	MARK	
B2241	3713	**R. S. W.**	Printed or impressed marks of differing design and initials. Pattern name often included the printed marking "ROYAL STONE CHINA" or "STONE CHINA", c.1825-1827.
B2242	-	**R. W. & W.**	
B2243	-	**R. S. & W.**	

Typical Marks Include:

B2244 3714
B2245 -
B2246 -

- There was a two year span involving two distinct partnerships; Stevenson, Alcock & Williams and Stevenson & Williams, (1822-1826) and (1825-1827) respectively.
- *Snyder, Historic Staffordshire*, pp. 86-99 notes that "British" or "American" Views are marked either "R. S." or "R. S. W."

For further reading, refer to R. T. Haines Halsey, *Pictures of Early New York on Dark Blue Staffordshire Pottery*, Dover Publications, New York, 1974. pp. 285-286; *Godden, Collecting Lustreware*, pp. 158-159; *Godden, British Porcelain*, pp. 77, 83-85, & 88; Leslie Bockol. *Willow Ware*. Schiffer Publishing, Ltd. Atglen, PA. 1995, p. 132; and *Snyder, Romantic Staffordshire*, p.160.

STEVENTON

KAD NO.	GODDEN NO.	MARK	
			John Steventon & Son, Ltd. Royal Pottery, Burslem, Staffordshire, c.1923-1936+
B2247	3715		Printed name mark, as noted, c.1923-1936. - After 1936 firm continued in the production of sanitary wares and tile.

STUBBS

Stubbs & Kent
Dale Hall,
Longport, Burslem,
Staffordshire, c.1828-1830

KAD NO.	GODDEN NO.	MARK	
B2248	3730		Impressed or printed mark in circular form, c.1828-1830.

STUBBS

Joseph Stubbs
Dale Hall,
Longport, Burslem,
Staffordshire, c.1822-1834
Formerly, Benjamin Stubbs (c.1818-1822)

KAD NO.	GODDEN NO.	MARK	
B2249	3728	**STUBBS**	Impressed name mark, c.1822-1834.
B2250	-		- Also noted with printed pattern marks of various designs on American/Canadian views, often including printed series and title names, c. 1822-1834.
B2251	3729		Impressed or printed name mark in circular form, c.1822-1834.

For further reading, refer to *Little*, pp. 99-100; *Godden, Collecting Lustreware*, p. 159; *Henrywood*, p. 172; and *Snyder, Historic Staffordshire*, pp. 99-106.

SUNDERLAND

Sunderland or "Garrison" Pottery,
Sunderland, Durham, c.1807-1865
History:

John Phillips	1807-1812
Phillips & Co. and/or Dixon & Co.	1813-1819
Dixon, Austin & Co.	1820-1826
Dixon, Austin, Phillips & Co.	1827-1834(39)
Dixon, Phillips & Co.	1834-1839(65)

KAD NO.	GODDEN NO.	MARK	
B2252	3740	**J. PHILLIPS**	Most Sunderland marks incorporate the various partnership names, c.1807-1812.

KAD NO.	GODDEN NO.	MARK	
B2253	3741	**J. PHILLIPS SUNDERLAND POTTERY**	- Impressed marks (names) are most frequently noted, c. 1807-1812.
B2254	3742	**PHILLIPS & CO.**	
B2255	3743	**DIXON & CO.***	*"DIXON & CO." is frequently found impressed along with the printed pattern name, often accompanying one of the other partnership names, c.1813-1819.
B2256	3744	**DIXON, AUSTIN & CO.**	Name mark, c.1820-1826.
B2257	3745	**DIXON, AUSTIN PHILLIPS & CO.**	- Care must be taken as names and marks may be of a later period, c.1827-1840.
B2258	3746	**DIXON, AUSTIN & CO.**	- "Garrison's" copper plates were acquired by Ball Bros. See *Godden, Collecting Lustreware*, pp. 342-343.
B2259	3747	**DIXON, PHILLIPS & CO.**	Name mark, c.1840-1865.
B2260	3748	**SUNDREX**	"SUNDERLAND POTTERY CO. (LTD.)" a later firm, c.1913-1927. - Also refer to the Maling partnership, c.1780-1815, and the later acquisition of the North Hylton Pottery, c.1815-1840, p. 549.

For further reading, refer to John Baker, *Sunderland Pottery*, Thomas Reed Industrial Press, Ltd. & Tyne & Wear County Council Museums, 1984. pp. 66-67; *Godden, Collecting Lustreware*, pp. 209-232 (which includes a chronology) & pp. 341-345; *Lewis, Prattware*, pp. 102-105.

SWANSEA

Swansea Pottery
See: Cambrian Pottery, pp.137-138

SWIFT

Swift & Elkin
Flint & Stafford Streets
Longton, 1840-1843

History:

Swift, Elkin & Nicholls	[Flint Street]	1839-1840
Swift & Elkin	Flint Street	1840-1843
	Stafford Street	1841-1843
Swift & Brindley	Stafford Street	1843-1844
John Swift	Stafford Street	1844 -1844
Elkin & Newbon	Stafford Street	1845-1856
Samuel Elkin	Stafford Street	1856-1867
	Mill Works	1860-1863
John Swift	St. Martins Lane	1860-1861

B2260B	3773	**S. & E.**	Printed marks of differing design. Pattern name often included, 1840-1843.

KAD NO.	GODDEN NO.	MARK
B2260B	-	
B2260C	-	

Typical Marks Include:

For further reading, refer to *Godden, Collecting Lustreware*, p. 159; and *Hampson*, No. 98, p.63 and No. 247, p. 154.

SWILLINGTON

Swillington Bridge Pottery,
West Bank of the River Aire and South of the Road at Swillington Bridge, Yorkshire, c.1791-1844
History:

Wm. Taylor		1791
Wm. Butterill & Richard Rhodes	Traded as Butterill & Co.	1795
James Clarkson & Co.		1807
John Hindale & Co.		1810
Hordhirst, Greasbath	Greatpatch & Co.	-
Wm. Wildblood*	Traded as Wildblood & Co.	1814
James Reed & Benjamin Taylor	Traded as Reed & Taylor	1832
Reed Taylor & Co.	(Reed & Taylor)**	1838
Benjamin Taylor (& Son)	Traded as Messrs. Taylor	1840
Thomas Wildblood, Jr.		1843-1844

This pottery has been included due to the significance of one mark, the Royal Coat of Arms with the marking "OPAQUE CHINA" which is the same marking used by William Ridgway & Co. (See Mark KAD B2048).
- Collectors should be careful not to attribute by mark alone, as noted by this example.
- The Crown mark is a marking also used by the Kilnhurst Old Pottery, with the only difference being the word "IRON" in the Swillington version, c. 1832-1838.

Selected Printed Marks Include:

KAD NO.	GODDEN NO.
B2261	-
B2262	-
B2263	

c.1820-1832(42)

c.1820-1842

c.1832-1838***

KAD NO.	GODDEN NO.
B2264	-
B2265	-
B2266	-

c.1832-1838

- All markings included above were noted in the Blue & White category on the "Willow" pattern, except for the mark denoting the pattern "Fibre".
*See John Wildblood & Co., p. 370.
**See Reed & Taylor, p. 315.
***Refer to William Ridgway (& Co.) for a like marking, KAD B2048.

For further reading, refer to *Godden, Mason's*, pp. 280-282; and *Lawrence*, pp. 73-76 and 243-245.

SWINNERTONS

Swinnertons Ltd.
(Various Addresses)
Hanley, Staffordshire, 1906-1970
- "Ltd." dates from 1911
- Acquired by the Lawley Group in 1959

KAD NO.	GODDEN NO.	MARK	
B2266A	3774		Printed marks of differing design. Pattern name often included, 1906-1917.
B2266B	3775		Printed marks of differing design. Pattern name often included, 1917-1930. - For additional marks refer to *Godden*, p. 606.

SWINTON

Swinton Old Pottery
See: Brameld & Co., pp. 124-125

TAMS

Tams (et.al.)
Longton (?) Staffordshire, c.1820-1840s
- There is very little recorded information on either dating or patterns available. Partnerships appear to have been subdivided into three groupings:
I. Tams
- Tams & Co.
- S. Tams & Co.
II. Tams & Anderson
III. Tams, Anderson & Tams

KAD NO.	GODDEN NO.	MARK	
B2267	-	**TAMS**	Printed name mark, c.1820-1840s.
B2268	-	**TAMS & CO.**	Printed name mark, c.1820-1840s.
B2269	-	**S. TAMS & CO.**	Printed name mark, c.1820-1840s.
B2270		**S. TAMS & CO. WARRANTED STAFFORDSHIRE**	Impressed circular name mark with eagle in center and marking "SEMI CHINA" above, c.1820-1840s.
B2271	-	**TAMS & ANDERSON**	Impressed name mark, c.1820-1840s.
B2272	-	**TAMS, ANDERSON & TAMS . . . POTTERY**	Circular impressed name mark with twelve point sun burst in center. c. 1820-1840s. - Printed pattern name may include marking "SEMI CHINA". - See *True Blue*, "Four Courts, Dublin", p. 71, No. 12 and p. 150, No. T1.
B2272A	-	**TAMS, ANDERSON & TAMS WARRANTED STAFFORDSHIRE**	Printed name mark, c.1820-1840s. - See *True Blue*, "Richmond Castle, Yorkshire", p. 84, No. 1 and p. 150, No. T2. In a current article in the *NSC Newsletter, No. 112, December 1998,* Titled "Tams, Anderson & Tams: - A Phantom Factory Revealed – as a Phantom: By Roger Pomfret, pp. 54-57, Mr. Pomfret concludes that "… the wares under discussion were

manufactured in Staffordshire on a subcontracted basis for the substantial American-based Tams importing concerns, who at most retained a local forwarding agent in the potteries. Any marks incorporating the word Tams were applied by the sub-contractor at the direction of the customer."

For further reading, refer to *Coysh*, Vol. I, p. 356; *Larsen*, p. 122, 184-185; *Little*, pp. 100-101; *Snyder, Historic Staffordshire*, pp. 106-107; *FOB* No. 90, Winter 1995-1996, pp. 5-6; and *Niblett,* p. 78.

TAMS

John Tams (& Son) (Ltd.)
Crown Pottery, Stafford Street,
Longton, Staffordshire, c.1875-1982

History:
John Tams & Son c.1903-1912
John Tams Ltd. c.1912+
-John Tams Ltd. acquired Barker Bros. in 1982

KAD NO.	GODDEN NO.	MARK	
B2273	3791	**J. T.**	Printed marks of differing design. Pattern name often included, c.1875-1903.
B2274	3792	**J. TAMS**	
B2275	-		
B2276	3793		Printed trade mark. Center monogram may be replaced by initials "J. T.", c.1875-1903.
B2277	3794	**J. T. & S.**	Printed marks of differing design. Pattern name often included, c.1903-1912.
B2278	3795		Printed trade mark. Center monogram may be replaced by initials "J. T. S.", c.1903-1912.
B2279	3801	**CHININE**	Various printed and impressed marks used by John Tams Ltd., incorporating the words "TAMS ENGLAND", c.1912+.
B2280	3798	**ELEPHANT BRAND**	
B2281	3796	**NANKIN-WARE**	
B2282	3800	**TAMS-REGENT**	

- *Godden, Collecting Lustreware*, p. 160 notes a prior partnership of Tams & Lowe, c.1865-1875 at St. Gregory's Works, High Street, Longton, Staffordshire. This firm may have preceded John Tams.

For further reading, refer to *Hampson*, pp. 154-155, No. 250; *Little*, pp. 100-101; and *Niblett,* p. 78.

TAYLOR

Taylor Bros.
Market Street Works,
Renamed in 1865 to Opaque Porcelain Manufactory
(Factory demolished in by 1875)
Hanley, Staffordshire, 1862-1871
Formerly, J. & G. Meakin (1851+)

KAD NO.	GODDEN NO.	MARK	
B2283	-	**IRONSTONE CHINA TAYLOR BROS. HANLEY**	Printed name mark noted on White Ironstone, 1862-1871. For further reading, refer to *Godden, Jewitt*, p. 58.

TAYLOR

George Taylor (Sr.)
High Street,
Hanley, Staffordshire, (1784-1809)
George Taylor (Jr.)
Broad Street, Hanley, (1807-1811)
- Taylor Dating: 1784-1811

KAD NO.	GODDEN NO.	MARK	
B2284	3805	**G. TAYLOR**	Impressed or incised name marks, 1784-1811.
B2285	3806	**GEO. TAYLOR**	For further reading, refer to *Edwards, Basalt*, p. 243; and *NCSJ* Vol. 8, 1991, pp. 91-124 for an article by Ann Eatwell & Alex Werner titled "A London Staffordshire Warehouse, 1794-1825."

TAYLOR

Taylor, Harrison & Co.
Mere Pottery,
Castleford, Yorkshire, c.1830s-1841
Subsequently, Taylor & Harrison (c.1841-1867)

KAD NO.	GODDEN NO.	MARK	
B2286	-	**T. H. & CO.**	Printed initial and name marks, 1830s-1841.
B2287	-	**TAYLOR & CO.**	For further reading, refer to *Little*, p. 119; *Lawrence*, p. 172; and *Godden, Collecting Lustreware*, p. 261.

TAYLOR

William Taylor
Pearl Pottery, Brook Street,
Hanley, Staffordshire, 1860-1881
Formerly, Booth, William & Willet (1843-1860)
Subsequently, Wood, Hines & Winkle (c.1881-1885)

KAD NO.	GODDEN NO.	MARK	
B2288	-	**W. TAYLOR**	Printed name marks noted on White Ironstone, c.1860-1881.
B2289	-	**W. TAYLOR HANLEY**	
B2290	-		Printed Royal Coat of Arms mark found on White Ironstone, 1860-1881. For further reading, refer to *Godden, Jewitt*, p. 75; and *Sussman*, pp. 38, 47, 59.

THOMSON

John Thomson (& Sons)*
Annfield Pottery,
Glasgow, Scotland, c.1826-1888(96)
- "& Sons" from 1870

KAD NO.	GODDEN NO.	MARK	
B2291	-	**THOMSON**	Printed or impressed marks of differing design. Pattern name often included, 1826-1888(96).
B2292	-	**JOHN THOMSON**	
B2293	3844	**J. T.**	- Impressed markings "GRANITE" and "STONE/WARE" noted.
B2294	3845	**J. T. ANNFIELD**	
B2295	-	**J. T. & S.**	Printed or impressed marks of differing design. Pattern name often included, c.1870-1888(96).
B2296	3846	**J. T. & SONS**	- Marking "GRANITE" noted.
B2297	3847	**J. T. & SONS GLASGOW**	Printed or impressed marks of differing design. Pattern name often included, c.1870-1888(96). - Marking "STONE WARE" noted.

Typical Marks Include:

B2293 -
B2296 -

KAD B2293

KAD B2296

- *Fleming*, pp. 147-148 states: "…Sometimes the name of the pattern appears in a circular ribbon over these initial [J. T. & S.]". Further, on pp. 159-160, he notes the partnership of Thomson & Fowler.
- *Cushion*, p. 353, notes additional marks and dates for Thomson. Also refer to the *Scottish Pottery Society Bulletin*, No. 19, Oct. 1994, pp. 7-12, wherein additional patterns and marks are noted.

**Finlayson*, pp. 94-95 notes an impressed anchor marking spelled "JOHN THOMSON". In Scotland the name Thomson may be spelled with or without the letter "P".

For further reading, refer to *FOB*, No. 72, Summer 1991, pp. 7-8 "The Coulters Memorial Service", A Tribute to the Memory of the late Mr. Samuel Coulters. Also refer to *Little*, p. 126; *Finlayson*; *Scottish Pottery 17th Historical Review*, 1995, pp. 7-13, for an article by Lynn Sussman titled "John Thomson's Wares Found at a Canadian Site."

TILL

Thomas Till & Son(s) (Ltd.)
Sytch Pottery,
Burslem, Staffordshire, 1850-1928
Formerly, Barker & Till (1846-1850)
Subsequently, The Pearl Pottery (Burslem) Ltd. (1930-1942)

KAD NO.	GODDEN NO.	MARK	
B2301	3853	**TILL**	Printed or impressed marks of differing design. Pattern name often included, 1850-1928.
B2302	-	**T. TILL**	
B2303	3854	**TILL & SON**	- "& SONS" appear from 1861.

KAD NO.	GODDEN NO.	MARK	
B2304	3855	**T. TILL & SON**	- “ENGLAND” appear after 1891.
B2305	-	**THOMAS TILL & SON**	- “LTD.” appear from 1922.

Typical Marks Include:

B2306 3856
B2307 3857
B2308 3585

c.1861+

Registration Mark for Mar. 3, 1869

c.1880+

B2309	-	**THOS. TILL & SONS SYTCH POTTERY N°**	Printed mark noted on Flow Blue, 1861-1921.

- For additional marks refer to *Godden*, p. 617.
- *Wetherbee, White Ironstone*, p. 49 notes that two shapes were available in “White Granite” or “Pearl White Granite” for the pattern shapes “Albany” and “Virginia”, but neither have been located to-date.

For further reading, refer to *Godden, Collecting Lustreware*, p. 160; and *Henrywood*, p. 208.

TITTENSOR

Charles Tittensor
(Various Locations)
Shelton,
Staffordshire, c.1815-1823
Formerly, Tittensor & Simpson (1807-1813)

B2310	3861	**TITTENSOR**	Printed (rare) mark, c.1815-1823.
B2311	-	**C. T.**	Impressed mark noted on figures.

For further reading, refer to *Godden, Illustrated Encyclopedia*; *Little*, p. 101; Reginald G. Haggar, *Staffordshire Chimney Ornaments*, Ch. VIII, pp. 82-88, titled “The Tittensor Family”, Pitman Publishing Corp., New York, 1955; *NCS Newsletter*, No. 103, Sept. 1996, pp. 26-27 for an article by Joyce & Derek Chitty titled “A Little More About the Tittensor Family”; and Pat Halfpenny. *English Earthenware Figures 1740-1840*. Antique Collectors Club, England 1991, pp. 113-115.

TOFT

Toft & May
Charles Street Works,
Hanley, Staffordshire, 1825-1829
History:

Keeling, Toft & Co.	1801-1824
Toft & May	1825-1829
Robert May	1829-1830
William Ridgway (& Co.)	1830-1834

B2312	-	**TOFT & MAY**	Impressed mark and printed pattern name, c.1825-1829.

KAD NO.	GODDEN NO.	MARK	

For further reading, refer to *Coysh*, Vol. II, p. 63; *Godden, British Porcelain*, pp. 453-454 for information on Keeling, Toft & Co. (1806-1824/27); *Edwards, Basalt*, pp. 124-126; *Penny Plain*, p. 99, No. 238; and *Little*, p. 77.

TOMPKINSON

Tompkinson Bros. & Co.
Columbia Works,
Hanley, Staffordshire, c.1867-1870*

B2313 -

Printed Royal Coat of Arms mark noted on White Ironstone, c.1867-1870.
- No further information has been noted except for a registration date noted by *Coysh* of August 4, 1869.
* *Ewins*, p. 92 records Tompkinson Bros. & Co. as shipping a consignment in 1868 to its company's outlet in Philadelphia who was "...recorded as chinaware importers briefly in 1862, and permanently in Philadelphia Trade Directories after the end of the Civil War. [Andrew S. Tompkinson] Tompkinson Bros. & Co. (Philadelphia) became Tompkinson & McElveney towards the end of the 60s; advertising themselves as 'agents for Staffordshire potteries.' "

For further reading, refer to *Wetherbee,* p. 100.

TOWNSEND

George Townsend
St. Gregory's Works,
High Street, Longton, 1850-1865
***Hampson* notes the following locations:**

Gower Street,	1850-1853
St. Gregory's Works, High Street,	1850-1865
Chadwick Street,	1854-1865
Formerly, Sampson, Beardmore,	1843-1848
Subsequently, Tams & Lowe	(1865-1875)

B2314 3879 **G. TOWNSEND** Printed marks of differing design. Pattern name often included, 1860-1865.

B2315 -

Printed Royal Coat of Arms marked "TOWNSEND/LONGTON".

For further reading, refer to *Hampson*, No. 27, p. 20, No. 254, p. 156; and *Edwards, Basalt*, p.244.

TROUTBECK

E. T. Troutbeck
Sandyford,
Tunstall, Staffordshire, c.1846

B2316 - **E. T. TROUTBECK** Printed or impressed marks of differing design. Pattern name often included, c.1846.

B2317 -

KAD NO.	GODDEN NO.	MARK	
B2318	-	**M. T. & T.**	Printed initial mark, c.1846.
B2319	-	**TROUTBECK**	Printed name mark, c.1846.
B2320	-	**TROUTBECK TUNSTALL**	*Coysh*, Vol. II, p. 199 notes an impressed marking "…Maker's name and the address ' Tunstall' within concentric circules surrounding an anchor," c. 1846.

For further reading, refer to *Snyder, Romantic Staffordshire*, p. 167.

TUNNICLIFF(E)

Michael Tunnicliff(e)
High Street,
Tunstall, Staffordshire, 1828-1841

B2321	3887	**TUNNICLIFF TUNSTALL**	Printed or impressed name mark on raised scroll, 1828-1841. - *Wetherbee*, p. 63, fig. 168-43, records a "Paneled Decagon Shape."

For further reading, refer to *Godden, British Porcelain*, p. 730.

TURNBULL

G. R. Turnbull
Stepeny Street Pottery,
Ouseburn, Newcastle-upon-Tyne,
Northumberland, c.1863-1875

B2322	-	**TURNBULL STEPNEY**	Impressed name marks, 1863-1875.
B2323	-	**TURNBULL STEPENY POTTERY**	

For further reading, refer to *FOB*, No. 46, Winter 1984/85, p. 5; and *Bell,* pp. 32, 109, 146.

TURNER

***Turner & Abbott**
Lower Works (Far Bank),
Market & Kingcross Streets, Lane End,
Longton, Staffordshire, 1781-1787
Formerly, John Turner (I) (1762-1781)
Subsequently, Turners, Abbott & Newbury (1788-1792)

B2324	3888	**TURNER & ABBOTT**	Impressed name mark, 1781-1787.

- *Hampson*, No. 255, p. 157 notes that John Turner, I, Andrew Abbott and Benjamin Newburn were in partnership, c.1781-1792, long after John Turner's death in 1787.

For further reading, refer to *Hampson*, No. 255, pp. 157-166; *NCSJ*, Vol. 13, 1996 for an article by Jack Howarth titled "Andrew Abbott and the Fleet Street Partnerships."

TURNER

***Turner & Tomkinson**
Victoria Works, High Street,
Tunstall, Staffordshire, c.1860-1872
Subsequently, G. W. Turner & Sons (c.1873-1895)

KAD NO.	GODDEN NO.	MARK	
B2325	3903	**TURNER & TOMKINSON**	Printed marks of differing design. Pattern name often included, c.1860-1872.
B2326	3904	**T. & T.**	Printed initial mark, c.1860-1872.
B2327	3905	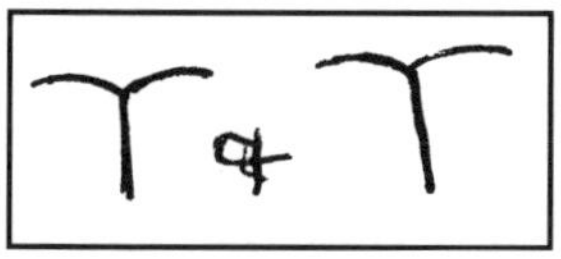	Printed initials, often noted in fancy form, c.1860-1872.

For further reading, refer to *Godden*, p. 626.

TURNER

***Turner, Goddard & Co.**
Royal Albert Pottery,
Tunstall, Staffordshire, 1867-1874

KAD NO.	GODDEN NO.	MARK	
B2328	3889	**TURNER, GODDARD & CO.**	Printed or impressed marks of differing design. Pattern name often included, c.1867-1874.

Typical Marks Include:

B2329 -
B2330 -

Impressed mark on White Ironstone

For further reading, refer to *Sussman*, pp. 27-28; and *Wetherbee*, pp. 92, 101.

TURNER

***G. W. Turner & Sons**
Victoria Works,
High Street, Tunstall, c.1873-1895
Formerly, Turner & Tomkinson (c.1860-1872)

KAD NO.	GODDEN NO.	MARK	
B2331	3890	**TURNERS**	Impressed name mark, c.1873-1895.
B2332	3891	**G. W. T. & SONS**	Printed marks of differing design. Pattern name often included, c.1873-1895.
B2333	2892	**G.W.T.S.**	
B2334	2893	**G. W. T. & S.**	
B2335	3894	**G. T. & S.**	

For further reading, refer to *Godden, Mason's*, p. 283; and Bevis Hillier. *Master Potters of the Industrial Revolution, The Turners of Lane End.* Cory, Adams & Mackay. London. 1965.

TURNER

KAD NO.	GODDEN NO.	MARK	
			***John Turner (I)** **Upper Works, (Nr. Bank),** **Market Street & Uttoxeter Rd., &** **Lower Works (Far Bank), Market & Kingcross Streets,** **Lane End, Longton, Staffordshire, 1762-1781** **Subsequently, Turner & Abbott or "& Co." (1781-1787)**
B2336	3896	**TURNER**	Impressed name mark, 1770+.
B2337	3897	**I. TURNER**	Impressed name mark (rare), c.1770-1787.
B2338	3898		Printed or Impressed "Prince of Wales" mark noted from 1784 visit and appointment thereof as potter to the Prince.
B2339	3899	**TURNER & CO.**	Impressed name mark. "& CO." probably used from 1781-1787 and 1803-1804 when company was referred to as Turners, Glover & Simpson.
B2340	3900	**TURNER'S-PATENT**	Painted mark (rare) noted on stone-ware type earthenwares, January 1800-1804. - Patent (body) rights were sold to Josiah Spode in 1805.

For further reading, refer to *Little*, pp. 102-103 on wares by Turner & Davenport marked "C. R. S."; *Hampson*, No. 255, pp. 157-166; *Godden, Illustrated Encyclopaedia; Coysh, Earthenware* and *Transferware*; and Bevis Hillier. *Master Potters of The Industrial Revolution, The Turners of Lane End*. Cory Adams & Mackay. London, 1965.

TURNER

***John & William Turner**
Lower Works, (Far Bank)
Market & Kingcross Street Lane End,
Longton, Staffordshire, 1792-1803
Formerly, Turners, Abbott & Newbury (1788-1792)
Subsequently, Turners, Glover & Simpson (c.1803-1804)

KAD NO.	GODDEN NO.	MARK	
B2341	3896	**TURNER**	Impressed name mark, c.1792-1803.
B2342	3900	**TURNERS-PATENT**	Printed mark "PATENTED STONE CHINA" dated January 19, 1800 (No. 2367). - Known as "The Tabberner's Mine Rock", "Little Mine Rock" and "New Rock", made from local stone ground and mixed with calcined flint.

For further reading, refer to Bevis Hillier. *Master Potters of The Industrial Revolution, The Turners of Lane End*. Cory Adams & Mackay. London, 1965, pp. 22, 62, 71-82; *Godden, Staffordshire*, pp. 96-99; *Godden, British Porcelain*, pp. 731-734; *Hampson*, No. 255, pp. 157-166; *Little*, pp. 101-103; and *Penny Plain*, p. 96, No. 196.

TURNER

KAD NO.	GODDEN NO.	MARK	

***William Turner**
Foley Works, (Jos. Myatt Works),
Foley, Fenton (c.1807-1812)
High Street Works, (Wm. Waller's Works),
Lane End, Longton (c.1824-1829)
Fenton & Longton, Staffordshire, c.1807-1829

KAD NO.	GODDEN NO.	MARK	
B2343	-	**TURNER**	Impressed name mark, c.1815-1829.

- John Turner died in 1787 and his sons William and John, II continued the business, in partnerships as noted:

(Wm. & John) Glover & Simpson	c.1803-1804
W. Turner, Glover & Simpson	c.1804-1806

- *Godden*, p. 626 notes a Turner mark dating from 1770+. Care must be taken in attributing by name mark only.

For further reading, refer to *Godden, British Porcelain*, p. 731; *Coysh*, Vol. I, p. 371; *Hampson*, No. 225, pp. 157-166; *Edwards, Basalt*, pp. 244-253; and *Henrywood*, pp. 123-124.

TURPIN

Turpin & Co.
Ouseburn Pottery,
Ouseburn, Newcastle-Upon-Tyne,
Northumberland, c.1841

KAD NO.	GODDEN NO.	MARK	
B2344	-	**TURPIN**	Impressed name mark, c.1841.

TWIGG

Joseph Twigg (& Brothers) (& Co.)
Newhill Pottery, c.1820-1881
Kilnhurst Pottery, nr. Swinton, Yorkshire (1839-1881)
- "& Co." from c.1841
- "& Bros." from c.1843-1881
Subsequently, Daniel & Puntil

- Refer to Kilnhurst Old Pottery for History, p. 252

KAD NO.	GODDEN NO.	MARK	
B2345	3908	**J. T.**	Printed or impressed mark. Pattern name included, c.1822-1866.
B2346	3909	**TWIGG**	Impressed mark which may be found within an impressed oval, c.1822+.
B2347	-		
B2348	3910	**TWIGG'S**	Impressed name mark, c.1822+.
B2349	3911	**TWIGG NEW HILL**	Impressed name mark for New Hill Pottery, c.1820-1881.
B2350	3912	**TWIG(G) K. P.**	Impressed name mark for Kilnhurst Pottery, c.1839-1881.
B2351	-	**T (FOR TWIGG) STONE CHINA K. P.**	Printed marks found on "Willow Pattern" of Kilnhurst Pottery. Marked with or without initials "K. P.", c.1839-1881.

Typical Marks Include:

KAD NO.	GODDEN NO.	MARK	
B2352	-		
B2353	-		
B2354	-		
B2355	-	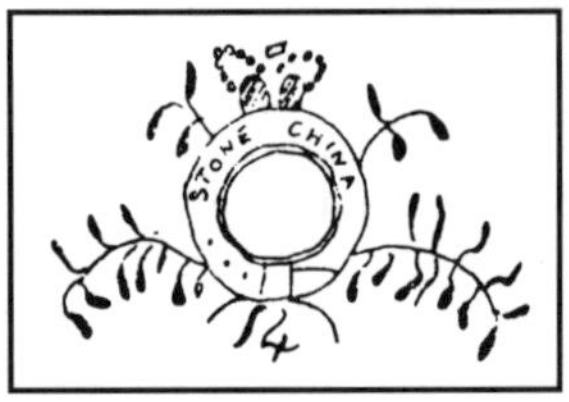	
B2356	3913	**J. TWIGG & CO.**	Rare printed mark, c.1841-1846. - *Godden* notes that marking "& CO." is very small and found below "J. TWIGG". - Marks KAD B2346 and B2352-2355 are taken from Heather Lawrence, *Yorkshire Pots and Potteries*, (David & Charles, 1974) by kind permission of the publishers. For further reading, refer to *Annual Report of the Yorkshire Philosophical Society*, February, 1916; Norman Dacre. *Kilnhurst Old Potter 1746-1929*. Kilnhurst, Rotherham. 1987; and *NCS Newsletter*, No. 106, June 1997, pp. 11-12 for an article by Alwyn & Angela Cox titled "Yorkshire Potteries: Some Personal Notes".

UPPER HANLEY

Upper Hanley Pottery Co. (Ltd.)
Hanley, Staffordshire (c.1895-1902)
Brownfield Works, Cobridge (c.1902-1910)
Hanley & Cobridge, Staffordshire, c.1895-1910

KAD NO.	GODDEN NO.	MARK	
B2357	3927	**U. H. P. CO. ENGLAND**	Printed or impressed marks of differing design. Pattern name often included. - "ENGLAND" included after 1895-1900.
B2358	3928		Printed name mark with "& CO." included, c.1895-1900.
B2359	3929	**U. H. P. CO. LTD. ENGLAND**	Printed initial mark with "LTD." included, c.1900-1910.
B2360	3930		- *Hampson, Churchill*, p. 127 notes that the firm continued, in name, until at least 1912, and from 1906 was acquired as part of the Grimwade syndicate.

VENABLES

KAD NO.	GODDEN NO.	MARK	
			Venables & Baines **Nile Street,** **Burslem, Staffordshire, c.1851-1853** **Subsequently, Venables, Mann & Co. (c.1853-1855)**
B2361	3930A	**VENABLES & BAINES**	Printed or impressed name mark, c.1851-1853. For further reading, refer to *Godden, Mason's*, p. 286; and *Godden, British Porcelain*, p. 529.

VENABLES

			John Venables & Co. **Nile Street,** **Burslem, Staffordshire, c.1853-1855** **- Also traded as Venables, Mann & Co.** **Formerly, Venables & Baines (c.1851-1853)**
B2362	3930B	**J. VENABLES & CO.**	Printed or impressed name mark on White Ironstone, c.1853-1855.
B2363	-		Impressed mark noted on White Ironstone, c.1853-1855. For further reading, refer to *Godden, British Porcelain*, p. 738.

VERNON

			James Vernon (& Son) **Waterloo Pottery,** **Burslem, Staffordshire, 1860-1880** **Formerly, James Vernon & Co. (1841-1860)** **Subsequently, J. & G. Vernon (1880-1889)**
B2364	3934	**J. V.**	Printed marks of differing design. Pattern name often included, 1860-1874.
B2365	3934A	**J. V. & S.**	- "& SON" or "JUNR." appears, 1875-1880.
B2366	3934B	**J. V. JUNR.**	

WALKER

			***Walker & Carter** **British Anchor Pottery,** **Anchor Road (c.1866-1872)** **Stoke (c.1872-1889)** **Longton, Staffordshire, c.1866-1889** **Formerly, Walker, Bateman & Co. (1864-1865)**
B2367	3981	**W. & C.**	Printed (initial) marks of differing design. Pattern name often included, c.1866-1889. For further reading, refer to *Godden, Collecting Lustreware*, p. 131.

WALKER

KAD NO.	GODDEN NO.	MARK	
			Thomas Walker **Lion Works, Sandyford,** **Tunstall, Staffordshire, 1845-1856** **Formerly, James Beech (1834-1845)** **Subsequently, Brougham & Mayer (1856-1862)**
B2368	-	**T. W.***	Printed or impressed marks of differing design. Pattern name often included, 1845-1856.
B2369	3982	**T. WALKER**	
B2370	3983	**THOS. WALKER**	
B2371	-		
B2372	-		
B2373	-		
B2374	-		

Typical Marks Include:

- Walker patterns present an interesting understanding into clever marketing (repackaging) of patterns:

- "Tavoy" and "Washington" are the same pattern.

- "Hong" and "Scinde" have the same center scene.

- Brougham & Mayer (c.1856-1862) and Elsmore & Forrester (1853-1871) may have acquired T. Walker's copper plates after his death, as "Tavoy" was reissued by Brougham & May as was "Simla" by Elsmore & Forrester.

* The initials "T. W." may relate to the following potters as well as T. Walker. Thus, care must always be taken when attributing by initials alone.

Thomas Wright	Hanley	1822-1835
Thomas Williams	Stoke	1827
Thomas White	Hanley	1840-1841
Thomas Worthington	Hanley	1842
Thomas Walker	Tunstall	1845-1851
Thomas Wynne	Longton	1847-1853

For further reading, refer to *Godden*, pp. 643, 734; and *Snyder, Romantic Staffordshire*, pp. 167-168.

WALKER

Thomas Henry Walker
Church Street,
Longton, Staffordshire, 1846-1848
Formerly, Batkin, Walker & Broadhurst (1840-1845)

KAD NO.	GODDEN NO.	MARK	
2375	-	**T. H. W.** **WARRANTED STONE CHINA**	Printed initial mark noted on "Willow" pattern, 1846-1848.

For further reading, refer to *Hampson*, No. 25, pp. 18-19; and "The Gibbs Collection" *Dreweatt Neate Auction Catalog*, p. 5, Lot. 32, March 26, 1997.

WALLACE

KAD NO.	GODDEN NO.	MARK	
			James Wallace & Co. Newcastle or Forth Bank Pottery, Newcastle-upon-Tyne, Northumberland, c.1838-1893
B2376	-	**J. W.**	Printed or impressed marks of differing design. Pattern name often included, c.1838-1893. - "SEMI-CHINA" marking noted.
B2377	-	**J. W. CO.**	
B2378	3984	**WALLACE & CO.**	- Refer to *Bell*, p. 109 for firm's chronology: T. Wallace & Son c.1838-1840 J. Wallace & Co. c.1840-1857 Wallace & Co. c.1858-1893 Other addresses are also noted. Wallace continued until 1904 as manufacturers of flower pots. For further reading, refer to *Coysh*, Vol. II, p. 197; and *Bell*, p. 146, No. 120-124 for additional marks.

WALLEY

KAD NO.	GODDEN NO.	MARK	
			***Edward Walley Villa Pottery, Cobridge, Staffordshire, c.1845-1858 Formerly, Jones & Walley (c.1841-1845) Subsequently, Edward Walley & Son (c.1858-1862)**
B2379	3988		Printed Royal Coat of Arms mark, c.1845-1858.
B2380	-	**E. WALLEY**	Printed or impressed name mark, c.1845-1858.
B2381	-		Printed Garter mark, c.1845-1858. - Marking "STAF." and "GARTER" noted on Tea Leaf/Copper Lustre.
B2382	3988	**IRONSTONE CHINA E. WALLEY**	Impressed name mark, c.1845-1858. - Additional markings "IRONSTONE/CHINA", "PEARL WHITE" and variation "COBRIDGE/CHINA" noted.
B2383	3990	**W**	Printed or impressed initial mark. Pattern name often noted with printed name mark, c.1845-1858. - Markings "INDIAN STONE"*, "IRONSTONE CHINA" and "STONE CHINA" also noted. *"INDIAN STONE", a body style term first introduced by Jones & Walley has been adopted as a pattern name by Flow Blue collectors. See KAD B1377A. - The marking "W" was also used by other potters, notably: Thomas Wolfe c.1781-1810 & c.1810-1818 Enoch Wood c.1784-1792 John Warburton c.1802-1823 Care must be taken when attributing potters by initials alone.
B2384	-		

Typical Marks Include:

B2385 -
B2386 -
B2387 -
B2388 -

Printed Mark

Printed Mark

Printed Mark on Tea Leaf

Impressed on White Ironstone & printed on Tea Leaf

- *Collard, Potter's View*, pp. 61-64 and *Pottery & Porcelain*, pp. 81, 223-224, notes a Canadian pattern "Ontario" ["Beavers & Maple Leaves"] registered Nov. 29, 1856, with the French National Slogan.
- *Jewitt*, p. 478 notes dates for Walley different from the above:

Jones & Walley	c.1835-1850, see p. 247
- Edward Walley	c.1850-1865
- Villa Pottery Vacant	c.1862-1869
Subsequently Wood, Son & Co.	c.1869-1879, see p. 385

For further reading, refer to *Godden, Collecting Lustreware*, pp. 161-162; *TLCI*, Educational Supplements, April 1992, April 1994; *TLCI*, Vol. 15, No. 4, Aug. 1995, p. 15; *TLCI*, Vol. 17, No. 1, Jan. 1997, for an article by Nancy Upchurch titled "Edward Walley, Lustre Magician"; *Henrywood*, pp. 96-105; and *White Ironstone Notes*, Vol. 4, No. 2, Fall 1997, p. 10, for an illustration of "Sidney's Patent Measure Jug" made by Edward Walley.

WALSH

William Walsh
Newcastle Street,
Burslem, Staffordshire, c.1815-1822

B2389 - **WALSH** Printed name mark, c.1815-1822.

For further reading, refer to *Coysh*, Vol. II, p. 209.

WARBURTON

John Warburton
Hot Lane,
Cobridge, Staffordshire, 1802-1823
Formerly, in partnership with his brother Jacob

B2390 - **W** Impressed initial or name mark, 1802-1823.

B2391 4004 **WARBURTON** - Care in attributing by initial alone is advisable. See comments under Edward Walley, mark KAD B2384.

For further reading, refer to *Godden, Staffordshire*, pp. 64-65, 569; *Godden, Collecting Lustreware*, pp. 162-163; *Williams-Wood, English Transfer*, p. 176; *NCS Newsletter*, No. 104, Dec. 1996, pp. 24-29 for an article by John Cockerill titled "A Potters' Flint Mill at Beamish Co., Durham"; and *Edwards, Basalt*, pp. 260-261.

WARDLE

KAD NO.	GODDEN NO.	MARK	

James Wardle & Co. (Hanley) (Ltd.)
Various Locations:
Hope Street, Shelton (1854-1859)
James Street, Shelton (1859-1863)
William Street, Hanley (1865-1881)
Washington Works, Victoria Road, Hanley (1881-1909)
Wolfe Street, Stoke (1910-1924)
Cauldon Place, Shelton (1924-1935)
Staffordshire, 1854-1909(+)

History:

J. W. Wardle*	1854-1871
Wardle & Co.	1871-1903
Wardle & Co. Ltd.	1903-1909
Wardle Art Pottery Co. Ltd.**	1910-1924(35)
- Company acquired by J. A. Robinson & Sons Ltd.	(1909)
- Company amalgamated with Cauldon Potteries Ltd.	(1924-1935)

KAD NO.	GODDEN NO.	MARK	
B2392	-	**J. W.**	Impressed initial mark, 1854-1871.
B2392	4013	**WARDLE ENGLAND**	Impressed name mark, 1871+. - "ENGLAND" appears after 1891.

Typical "Wardle & Co." Marks Include:

B2394 4014
B2395 4015

1885-1890

1890-1935

- It is important to note that the name or initials "J. W." may also belong to John Wardle (& Co.) of the Denaby Pottery, Yorkshire, c.1866-1868. Refer to *Lawrence*, p. 119.
* Wardle died in 1871 but firm continued on as Wardle & Co.
**The company was renamed Wardle Art Pottery Co. Ltd., 1910-1924. See *Godden*, p. 648 for additional comments.

For further reading, refer to *Godden, British Porcelain*, p. 752; John A. Bartlett. *British Ceramic Art 1870-1940*, Schiffer Publishing Ltd. Atglen, PA, 1993; and *Karmason*, pp. 125-126.

WATSON

Watson & Co.
Watsons Pottery,
Prestonpans, Scotland, c.1819-1838
Formerly, David Thompson & Co. (1809-1819)
- See Fowler Thompson & Co., p. 198

KAD NO.	GODDEN NO.	MARK	
B2396	4038	**WATSON**	Impressed name mark, late 18th-early 19th century.
B2397	4039	**WATSON & CO.**	Printed marks of differing design. Pattern name often included, 1819-1838.

For further reading, refer to *Fleming*, pp. 157-160; *Little*, p. 127; and *Coysh*, Vol. I, p. 395.

WEATHERBY

KAD NO. | **GODDEN NO.** | **MARK**

J. H. Weatherby & Sons (Ltd.)
Pinnox Works, Pinnox Street (1891-1892)
Falcon Pottery, High Street (1893-Present)
Tunstall & Hanley, Staffordshire 1891-Present
"LTD." from 1908

B2398 4043 **J. H. W. & SONS** — Printed marks of differing design. Pattern name often included, 1891-.

B2399 4043A

Printed mark, "TUNSTALL", with pattern name often included, 1891-1892.

B2400 4044

Printed mark, "HANLEY", with pattern name often included, 1893-1925.

B2401 4045 **FALCON WARE** — From 1925, with the introduction of this new trade name, the production of earthenware was discontinued.
- *Sussman*, pp. 27-30, notes that "Wheat" pattern production began in 1970 when Weatherby "acquired the blocks, cases and master moulds from A. J. Wilkinson (Ltd.)"

For further reading, refer to *Wetherbee, p. 90;* and Susan Jean Verbeek, *The Falcon Ware Story"*, Pottery Publications, London, 1996, pp. 5-93.

WEDGWOOD

Wedgwood & Co. (Ltd.)
Unicorn, Amicable Street* (1890-1956)
Pinnox Works, Woodland Street (1860-1965+)
Tunstall, Staffordshire, 1860-1965
Formerly, Podmore, Walker & Co. (1834-1859)
Subsequently, Wedgwood (Tunstall), Ltd. - present

B2402 4055 **WEDGWOOD & CO.** — Impressed name mark. Body style such as "IMPERIAL STONE CHINA" often included 1860+.
- Additional markings noted include: "STONE WARE", "IMPERIAL IRONSTONE CHINA" and "PATENT PARIS WHITE IRONSTONE".

B2403 -
B2404 -

Printed marks with pattern name and body styles often included, 1860-1890.
- "ENGLAND" noted after 1891.

KAD NO. | **GODDEN NO.** | **MARK**

Typical Marks Include:

B2405 -
B2406 -
B2407 -

B2408 4056
B2409 -

Printed **Unicorn** trade-mark subsequent to the Act of 1863.

- Style of mark changed in 1908. See KAD B2414.

- "ENGLAND" noted after 1891.

B2410 4057

Impressed name mark, 1890-1906.

B2411 4058 **WEDGWOOD & CO. LTD.**

Impressed name mark, 1900+.
"LTD." noted from this date on (1965+).

Typical Marks Include:

B2412 4059
B2413 4060
B2414 -
B2415 4061

c.1906+ Imperial Porcelain

c.1908+ Pattern name or Body Style added

1908+

1925+

**Jewitt* notes that the Unicorn Pottery "...were entire devoted to the production of plain White Graniteware for the American trade." See *Godden, Jewitt*, p. 142, wherein he cites that the pottery was sold to Hollinshead & Kirkham (1890), p. 237.

DIFFERENTIATING WEDGWOOD

Confusion abounds when it comes to the name Wedgwood. No less than six potters have used this name on their wares. Mis-cataloging has further added to the confusion, as well as the fact that copying and capitalizing on this famous name was not beyond other potters of the period. Refer to *Hampson*, No. 1, p. 1 re: Wedgewood & Ackerley and Wedgwood & Co. It is hoped that the simplified name listing below, with the addition of KAD reference numbers, will assist the reader. (As a further guide, I have underlined important data for clarification).

MARKINGS	TYPE OF MARK	KAD REFERENCE #	POTTERY & PARTNERSHIP	DATES
WEDGWOOD & CO.	Impressed	B938	Knottingly Pottery Partners-Tomlinson, (Ralph) Wedgwood, Foster & Co. (From 1804 pottery was named Ferrybridge Pottery)	*1798-1801(4)*
W.S. & CO'S WEDG*E*WOOD	Printed or Impressed	B2156	William Smith & Co. Injunction of 1848 prohibited usage of name.	1825-1855
J. WEDG*.*WOOD WEDG WOOD (note the space between G & W)	Printed	B2547	John Wedge Wood (Capitalized on the famous name)	1848-1857(75)
WEDG*E*WOOD & CO.	Impressed	—	Pottery continued by brother Edmund T. Wood (1857-1875)	1845-1857
WEDGWOOD	Printed	B1905	Podmore, Walker & Co. (or Podmore, Walker & Wedgwood)	1856-1859
WEDGWOOD & CO.	Printed	B1906	The "& CO." was Enoch Wedgwood Company retitled Wedgwood & Co. (Ltd.) (1860-1965+)	
WEDGWOOD & CO.	Printed or Impressed	B2402	Wedgwood & Co. Many marks and patterns continued	1860-1895
WEDGWOOD & CO.	Printed Trademark	B2408	from Podmore, Walker & Co.	
WEDGWOOD	Impressed	B2419-9	Josiah Wedgwood	*1759+*
WEDGWOOD*S*	Printed	B2421		1827-1861
WEDGWOOD	Impressed	B2423-4	Additional Marks: ETRURIA or PEARL	1840-1868

WEDGWOOD

KAD NO.	GODDEN NO.	MARK	
			***Josiah Wedgwood (& Sons, Ltd.)** **Burslem, c.1759+** **Etruria, c.1769+** **Barlaston, 1840+** **Staffordshire, c.1759-Present**
B2417 B2418	4073 4074		Impressed name mark, stamped individually and sometimes in a curve, c.1759-1769. - Very early wares were unmarked.
B2419	4075		Impressed mark, in varying sizes dating from 1769-1780. - From 1780 onward the name "WEDGWOOD" was carried forward unless otherwise noted.
B2420	4080	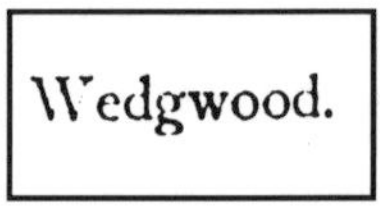	Impressed name mark, varying in size and used for all wares from 1780 to c.1795. - Known as the "Upper and Lower Case" mark.

KAD NO.	GODDEN NO.	MARK	
B2421	4084	**WEDGWOOD'S STONE CHINA**	Printed name mark on stone china, 1820-1861. - *Godden, Mason's*, pp. 288-289 notes early experimentation (in 1818) to compete compete with Spode's successful earthenware.
B2422	4085	**WEDGWOOD ETRTURIA**	Impressed name mark, in various sizes, c.1840-1845.
B2423	4086	**PEARL**	Impressed name denoting Pearl Body, 1840-1868.
B2424	4087	**P**	Impressed initial used after 1869.
B2425	-	**WEDGWOOD PEARL**	The impressed mark KAD B2419 "WEDGWOOD" is often noted along with the impressed mark KAD B2423 "PEARL" on late Blue & White and Flow Blue.

Typical Marks (for 1840-1868) Include:

B2426 -
B2427 -
B2428 -
B2429 -

For additional marks refer to *Godden*, pp. 657-661.

For further reading, refer to *Godden*, p. 657 for the "Wedgwood & Bentley" partnership; *Coysh*, Vol. I, pp. 396-397; Howard Davis. *Chinoiserie, Polychrome Decoration on Staffordshire Porcelain, 1790-1850*. Rubicom Press, London, 1991. pp. 62-73; *English Ceramic Circle Transactions*, Vol. 11, Part 3, pp. 212-221- and pl. 105-111 for an article by Una des Fontaines titled "Wedgwood Blue-Printed Wares, 1805-1843, and Vol. 14, Part 1, 1990 for an article by Barbara Horn; *Godden, Collecting Lustreware*; *Hill*; *Reilly, Wedgwood*, (in 2 volumes); Reilly & Savage; *Wetherbee*; Griselda Lewis. *A Collector's History of English Pottery*, Antique Collectors Club, England. 1992, Ch. 8, pp. 99-117 "Josiah Wedgwood 1730-1795"

WEDGWOOD
TABLES OF THREE LETTER IMPRESSED MARKS, 1860-1906

- First Letter Indicates Month
- Second Letter Indicate Potter
- Third Letter Indicates Year

(Note: Workman errors in numbers and letters are to be noted)
The Impressed Wedgwood Mark also occurs on all examples bearing the three letter code.

Month(1)	First Letter	Year	Code(1)	Year	Code	Year	Code	Year
January	J	-	O	1860	E	1876	U	1892
February	F	-	P	1861	F	1877	V	1893
March	M	1860-63	Q	1862	G	1878	W	1894
	R	1864-1907	R	1863	H	1879	X	1895
April	A	-	S	1864	I	1880	Y	1896
May	Y	1860-63	T	1865	J	1881	Z	1897
	M	1864-1907	U	1866	K	1882	A	1898**
June	T	-	V	1867	L	1883	B	1899
July	Y	1860-63	W	1868	M	1884	C	1900
	L	1864-1907	X	1869	N	1885	D	1901
August	W	-	Y	1870	O	1886	E	1902
September	S	-	Z	1871	P	1887	F	1903
October	O	-	A	1872	Q	1888	G	1904
November	N	-	B	1873	R	1889	H	1905
December	D	-	C	1874	S	1890	I	1906
			D	1875	T	1891*	-	-

*After 1891 note term "ENGLAND"
**After 1898 note term "MADE IN ENGLAND", but not in general use until 1908
(1) Due to letter duplication, months and dates may repeat, e.g. JBO - January 1860 or 1866.

DATING CHART FROM 1907- 1923

		1907-1923*						1924-1929**	1930***-1935		MONTHS		MONTHS
3	J	1907	3	S	1916	4	A	1924	1930	1	January	7	July
3	K	1908	3	T	1917	4	B	1925	1931	2	February	8	August
3	L	1909	3	U	1918	4	C	1926	1932	3	March	9	September
3	M	1910	3	V	1919	4	D	1927	1933	4	April	10	October
3	N	1911	3	W	1920	4	E	1928	1934	5	May	11	November
3	O	1912	3	X	1921	4	F	1929	1935	6	June	12	December
3	P	1913	3	Y	1922								
3	Q	1914	3	Z	1923								
3	R	1915											

*From 1907-1923 The Figure 3 was substituted for the month.
**From 1924-1929 The Figure 4 was substituted for the month.
***From 1930 the actual date (2 digits) were impressed. The months were numbered in sequence (1-12).
In later years only the 2 digit year code may appear; e.g., 3BK - 1908, 4AC - 1926, 1A33 - Jan. 1933

WHITEHAVEN

KAD NO. **GODDEN NO.** **MARK**

Whitehaven Pottery
West Cumberland, Cumbria, 1800-1910
History:

Woodnorth & Co.	W. & Co. or W. H. H. (Woodnorth, Harrison & Hall)	Printed Initials	1800-1824
John Wilkinson	I. W.	Printed Initials	1824-1863
Mary Wilkinson	M. W.	Printed Initials	1863-1877
Randle Wilkinson	R. W.	Printed Initials	1877-1910

KAD NO.	GODDEN NO.	MARK	
B2430	-	**W. H. H. WHITEHAVEN**	Printed initial mark, 1800-1824.
B2431	-	**WOODNORTHS WHITEHAVEN**	Printed name mark in small capital letters within a circle, 1800-1824.
B2432	4515	**WOODNORTH & CO.**	Impressed name mark, c.1815-1824.
B2433	-	**W. & CO.**	Printed initial mark within scroll, 1820-1824.
B2434	-	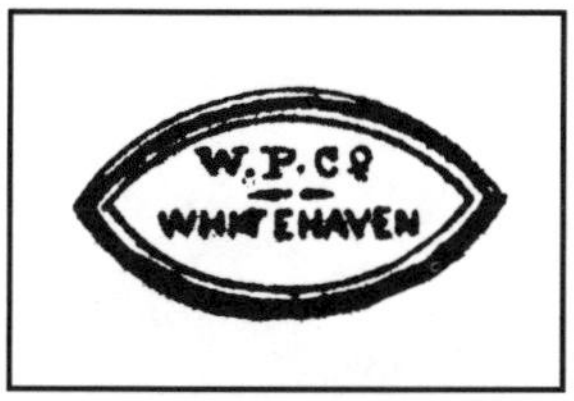	Printed initials and pottery name, 1824-1840.
B2435	-	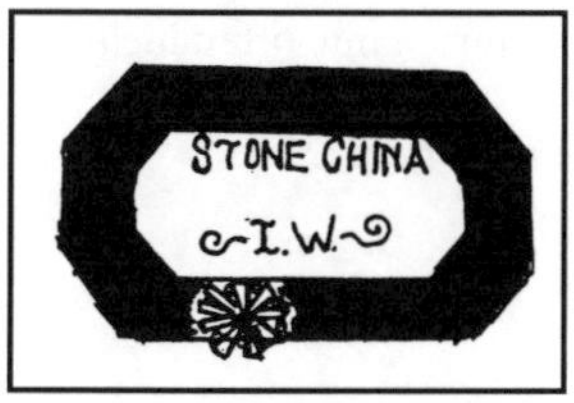	Printed marks of differing design. Pattern name often included, 1824-1840. - "STONE CHINA", "WARRANTED STONE CHINA" markings noted, as is the potter's wheel.
B2436	-		Printed marks of differing design. Pattern name often included, 1840-1863.
B2437	-	**WILKINSON POTTERY CO. WHITEHAVEN**	Printed name mark, 1863-1877. - Additional marking "W. P. C. WHITEHAVEN" noted.
B2438	-	**R. WILKINSON WHITEHAVEN**	Printed name mark, 1877-1910. For further reading, refer to Florence Sibson, *The History of the West Cumberland Potteries*. Cumbria, England (privately published) 1991; *Coysh*, Vol. I, p. 399; *FOB*, Spring 1991, No. 71, P. 5 and Autumn 1992, No. 77, p. 10 for an article by Florence Sibson titled "Potteries of West Cumbria"; *FOB Bulletin*, No. 86, Jan 1995, p. 12 wherein Florence Sibson records fourteen patterns; and *True Blue*, p. 88

WHITTAKER

Whittaker & Co.
Hallfield Pottery
Hanley, Staffordshire, c.1886-1892
Formerly, Whittaker, Edge & Co. (c.1882-1886)
Subsequently, Whittaker, Heath & Co. (1892-1898)

KAD NO.	GODDEN NO.	MARK	
B2439	4127		Printed mark, with pattern name occurring in central cross bar, c.1886-1892. - Lorraine Punchard's *Playtime Pottery and Porcelain From the United Kingdom and the United States*, Schiffer Publishing Ltd. Atglen, PA, 1996, p. 94, illustrates two transferware patterns "Nursery Rhymes" and "Alaska", the first in brown and the second in red.

WHITTAKER

Whittaker, Heath & Co.
Hallfield Pottery, Grafton Street,
Hanley, Staffordshire, 1892-1898
Formerly, Whittaker & Co. (1886-1891)

KAD NO.	GODDEN NO.	MARK	
B2439A	4128	**W. H. & CO.**	Printed initial mark. Pattern name often included, 1892-1898. - Additional marking "HANLEY" noted.

WHITTINGHAM

Whittingham, Ford & Co.
Union Banks or High Street
Burslem, Staffordshire, 1868-1873
Subsequently, Buckley, Wood & Co. (1873-1885)

KAD NO.	GODDEN NO.	MARK	
B2440	4130	**W. F. & CO.**	Printed marks of differing design. Pattern name often included, 1868-1873.

For further reading, refer to *Godden, Jewitt*, p. 23.

WHITTAKER

Whittingham, Ford & Riley
Newcastle Street,
Burslem, Staffordshire, 1876-1882
Subsequently, Ford & Riley (1882-1893)

KAD NO.	GODDEN NO.	MARK	
B2441	4131	**W. F. & R.**	Printed marks of differing design. Pattern name often included, 1876-1882.
B2442	-	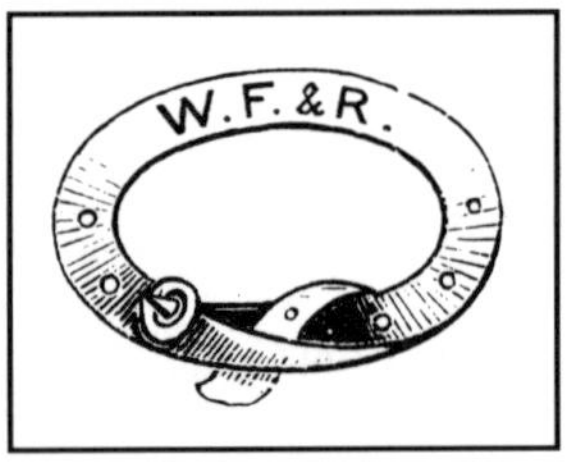	

WILDBLOOD

John Wildblood & Co.
Swillington Bridge Pottery,
Near Methley, Yorkshire, c.1814-1832

- See Swillington Bridge Pottery for history, p. 347.

Few printed or impressed marks exist, and those that do are inconclusive.
For further reading, refer to *Godden* pp. 670-671, Mark No. 4153; *Coysh*, Vol. I, p. 401; and *Lawrence*, pp.74-75.

WILEMAN

***Henry Wileman**
Foley China Works,
Fenton, Staffordshire, 1856-1864
Formerly, Knight & Wileman (1853-1856)
Subsequently, J. & C. Wileman (1864-1870)
No marked specimens recorded.

For further reading, refer to *Godden, British Porcelain*, p. 770; *Godden, Staffordshire*, p. 498; and *Shelley Pottery*, p. 171.

WILEMAN

James (F.) & Charles (F.) Wileman
Foley China Works*,
Fenton, Longton, Staffordshire, 1864-1870
Formerly, Henry Wileman (1856-1864)
Subsequently, James F. Wileman (1870-1892)

KAD NO.	GODDEN NO.	MARK	
B2443	4156	**J. & C. W.**	Printed marks of differing design. Pattern name often included, 1864-1870.
B2444	4157	**J. F. & C. W.**	- Additional markings "PEARL CHINA" and "WARRANTED" noted. - *Wetherbee's White Ironstone, A Collector's Guide*, p. 99,, notes a Royal Coat of Arms markings with "Poppy Shape".
B2445	4158	**C. J. W.**	Incorporated initials of Charles J. Wileman, c.1869. (rare)
B2446	4159	**J. W. & CO.**	Initials note the trade name for the above partnership as J. Wileman & Co., 1864-1870. *The Foley China Works was built in 1860, whereas the Foley *Potteries* were built about 1820. Refer to *Shelley Potteries*, pp. 18-20.

WILEMAN

***James F. Wileman**
Foley China Works,
Fenton Culvert, Fenton, Staffordshire, 1870-1892
Subsequently, Wileman & Co., Foley Potteries
& Foley China Works (1892-1925)

B2447	4160	**J. F. W.**	Printed marks of differing design. Pattern name often included, 1870-1892.
B2448	4161	**J. F. WILEMAN**	
B2449	4162		
B2450	-		

Typical Marks Include:

- Refer to *Wetherbee, White Ironstone*, p. 77, for the pattern "Richelieu Shape".

For further reading, refer to *Godden, Jewitt*, pp. 52-53; *Heaivilin*, p. 124; *Godden, Collecting Lustreware*, pp. 175-176; and *Shelley Potteries*, pp. 164-165 for additional marks.

WILKINSON

Wilkinson & Hulme
Central Pottery, Market Street,
Burslem, Staffordshire, 1881-1885
Formerly, Richard Alcock (1870-1881)
Subsequently, Arthur J. Wilkinson (1885-1896)

B2451	-	**WILKINSON & HULME BURSLEM, ENGLAND**	Printed mark noted on Tea Leaf/Copper Lustre, 1881-1885.

For further reading, refer to *Heaivilin*, p. 127; and *Godden, Jewitt*, p. 27.

WILKINSON

KAD NO. | **GODDEN NO.** | **MARK**

Arthur J. Wilkinson (Ltd.)
Central Pottery,
Stafford Street (Market Street) (1885-1898)
Church Yard Works (1887-)
Royal Staffordshire Pottery (1898-1965+)
Burslem, Staffordshire, 1885-1965
Formerly, Wilkinson & Hulme (1881-1885)
Subsequently, W. R. Midwinter, Ltd. (1965-1968)
- Merged with J. & G. Meakin in 1968 and acquired by the Wedgwood Group in 1970

B2452 -
B2453 -

Printed marks of differing design. Pattern name often included, 1885-1970.
- "LTD" from 1896.
- *Ormsbee*, p. 152 records a printed marking "LATE R. ALCOCK", 1885-1895.
- Richard Alcock (1870-1881) was acquired by Wilkinson & Hulme (1881-1885) who, in turn, became Arthur J. Wilkinson (Ltd.). Thus, the notation "LATE R. ALCOCK."

Typical Marks Include:

B2454 -
B2455 4168
B2456 4169
B2457 4170
B2458 4171

c.1891+

c.1891+

c.1896

c.1907

c.1910

- Shorter & Boulton acquired A. J. Wilkinson in 1894. The company was subsequently acquired by Crown Devon (S. Fielding & So. Ltd.) in 1964 and closed in 1982. For further information refer to, Gordon Hopwood. *The Shorter Connection*. Richard Dennis, England, 1992.

For further reading and additional marks, refer to *Godden*, p. 673; *Coysh*, Vol. I, p. 127; *Heaivilin*, pp. 125-130; *Gaston*, Vol. I & II; *Snyder*, Vol. I & II; *Sussman*, pp. 27-29; *Cameron*, pp. 355-356; *Niblett*, pp. 83-84; and *Batkin*, pp. 181-182.

WILLIAMS

William Williams
Ynysmeudwy Pottery,
Near Swansea, Wales, c.1856-1859
Formerly, Michael & William Williams (1845-1856)
Subsequently, G. Lewis & Morgan (c.1860-1870)

B2459 -

Printed name mark "WILLIAMS", c.1856-1859.

- Also refer to Ynysmeudwy Pottery.

For further reading, refer to *Godden, Mason's*, pp. 290-291; *Nance*, p. 197; *Pugh, Welsh Pottery*, pp. 55-56 for additional marks and patterns.

WILSON

KAD NO.	GODDEN NO.	MARK	

David Wilson (& Son(s))
Church Works,
Hanley Staffordshire, c.1801-1817
Formerly, Robert Wilson (1791-1801)
Subsequently, Phillips & Thompson (c.1817-1819)
and Phillips & Bagster (c.1818-1823)

B2460 | 4192 | **WILSON**

Impressed name mark, c.1801-1817.
"& SONS" from c.1809-1814.
"& SON" from c.1814-1817.
- Mark was also used by Robert Wilson (1791-1801)

B2461 | -

Impressed Crown and letter "G", 1801-1817.

- This device, as noted by Godden, may also have been used by Neale & Co. (c.1778-1792). Also refer to Diane Edwards, *Neale Pottery and Porcelain, 1763-1820*. Barrie & Jenkins. London, 1987.

For further reading, refer to *Godden, British Porcelain*, p. 773; *Godden, Collecting Lustreware*, pp. 176-177, 190-191; *Godden, Staffordshire*, p. 495; *Henrywood*, p. 53; *Coysh*, Vol. I, p. 403; and *Edwards, Basalt*, pp. 266-268.

WILSON

Isaac Wilson & Co.
Middlesbrough Pottery,
Middlesbrough, Yorkshire, 1852-1887
Formerly, Middlesbrough Earthenware Co. (1844-1852)

B2462 | 4193 | **I. W. & CO.**

Printed marks of differing design. Pattern name often included, 1852-1887.

B2463 | 4193A | **I. W. & CO. MIDDLESBROUGH**

B2464 | 4194

Impressed crown mark, printed "I. WILSON & CO.", 1852-1887.

- Godden notes mark 2658A with an impressed crown as most probably belonging to the Middlesbrough Earthenware Co. (1844-1852). Refer to KAD B1712 and *Godden*, p. 435.

For further reading, refer to the *Annual Report of the Yorkshire Philosophical Society*, pp. 79-81; *Lawrence*, pp. 209-210; *Little*, p. 118; and *Godden, Collecting Lustreware*, p. 263.

WILTSHAW

Wiltshaw & Robinson (Ltd.)
Carlton Works, Copeland Street
Stoke-upon-Trent, Staffordshire, 1890-1957
- Purchased by A. Wood & Son (Longport) Ltd. in 1966.
- In 1987 pottery was purchased by County Properties Plc
and renamed Carlton Ware, Ltd. (1958-1986+)

KAD NO.	GODDEN NO.	MARK	
B2465	-	W. & R.	Printed marks of differing design. Pattern name often included, 1890-1914(57).
B2466	4200		
B2467	4201		
B2468	4202		

c.1890+

c.1894 onward
variations occur

c.1906 onward

- KAD B2468 was continued by Carlton Ware, Ltd. 1958-1966.
- Refer to KAD B461 and p. 139.
- It is interesting to note that Harold Taylor Robinson (1877-1953) was quite an industrialist within the porcelain and pottery community. His history of acquisitions, in manufactories he either bought or controlled, is notable and most impressive. Those potteries Robinson bought or controlled include: (See *Cameron*, p. 282)

Henry Alcock & Co.	Hewitt Bros.
Allertons Ltd.	George Jones/Crescent Pottery
G. L. Ashworth & Bros. Ltd.	F. R. Pratt & Co. Ltd.
Bishop & Stonier	Ridgways (Bedford) Works Ltd.
Cauldon Pottery Co. Ltd.	Robinson & Leadbeater
Coalport China Co.	Royal Crown Derby
Charles Ford	The Wardle Art Pottery Co.
Ford & Pointon	Wedgwood & Co. (Tunstall)
W. H. Goss	Willow Potteries Ltd.
Grindley Hotel Ware Co.	Worcester Royal Porcelain

For further reading, refer to *Godden, Jewitt*, p. 137; *Godden, British Porcelain*, p. 775; *Cameron*, p. 282, 357; *Bunt, British Potters*, pp. 57-58; and *Niblett,* p. 40.

WINKLE

F. Winkle & CO. (Ltd.)
Colonial Pottery,
Stoke-on-Trent, Staffordshire, 1890-1931
Formerly, Winkle & Wood (1885-1890)
Subsequently, Ridgways (Bedford Works) Ltd. (1931-1955)

KAD NO.	GODDEN NO.	MARK	
B2469	4213	F. W. & CO. ENGLAND	Printed or impressed marks of differing design. Pattern name often included, 1890-1910.
B2470	4214	F. WINKLE & CO.	Several marks, incorporating full name, 1890-1910.
			- "LTD." appears from 1911.
B2471	4215		Printed initial mark, 1890-1925.

KAD NO.	GODDEN NO.	MARK	
B2472	4216		Printed or impressed mark, 1908-1925. - *Abbie's Encyclopedia of Flow Blue, Floral & Art Nouveau* by Thomas E. Nix, Sentinel Publications, July 1992, p. 11, notes the pattern "Kingston" with the printed marks KAD B2469 and KAD B2472.

WOLFE

Wolfe & Hamilton
Big Works, Church Street,
Stoke-on-Trent, Staffordshire, c.1800-1809
Formerly, Thomas Wolfe & Co. (c.1796-1800)
Subsequently, Wolfe, Hamilton & Arrowsmith (c.1809-1810)

B2473	4227	**WOLFE & HAMILTON**	Printed or impressed name marks, c.1800-1809.
B2474	4227A	**WOLFE & HAMILTON STOKE**	- *Godden*, p. 681, notes that these marks are taken from Creamware.
B2475	4230	**WOLFE & CO.**	This marking may relate to an earlier partnership (porcelain) with Miles Mason and John Luckcock at Islington, Liverpool (c.1796-1800) or to the above Wolfe & Hamilton partnership.

For further reading, refer to *Godden, British Porcelain*, pp. 785-786; *Little*, p. 106; *Godden, Collecting Lustreware*, pp. 49, 50, 141, 171-178; *Edwards, Basalt*, p. 268; *Godden, Staffordshire*, pp. 427-428, 496-497; *Coysh*, Vol. I, pp. 406-407; and *Godden, Guide to English Porcelain*, pp. 139-140.

WOLFE

Thomas Wolfe(s)
"Big Works", Church Street,
Stoke-on-Trent, Staffordshire, c.1781-1818
Subsequently, Rachael Wolfe

History:
I. Thomas Wolfe (in various partnerships) 1781-1810
II: Pottery subdivided and leased:

T. Wolfe's Half		***Sublet Half***	
T. Wolfe & Wm. Arrowsmith	**1810-1818***	**R. Hamilton**	**1810-1828***
- T. Wolfe died in	**1818**	**Z. & J. Boyle & Sons**	**1828-1844**
- Pottery void from	**1819-1823**	**S. & J. Boyle (& Sons)**	**1844-1852**
Wm. Adams	**1823-1862**	**Minton & Hollins**	**1852-1877**
		Walker & Carter	**1878-1889**

*Arrowsmith & Hamilton were T. Wolfe's sons-in-law.

For a detailed history of T. Wolfe, including his Liverpool period and his Old China Works, Stoke-on-Trent, see *NCSJ*, Vol. 14, Autumn 1997, pp. 105-129 for an article by Trevor Markin titled "Thomas Wolfe of Stoke-on-Trent and Liverpool."

B2476	4228	**WOLFE**	Impressed name mark, 1781-1818.
B2477	4229	**W**	Impressed letter "W" attributed to both Thomas Wolfe and/or his son, 1781-1810. - Mark was also used by Enoch Wood.

For further reading, refer to *Coysh*, Vol. I, pp. 406-407; *Little*, pp. 105-106; *Godden, British Porcelain*, pp.171-172, 782-786; *Godden, Staffordshire*, pp. 32-34; *Godden, Collecting Lustreware*, pp. 177-178; *FOB*, Spring 1992, No. 75, p. 8; and *Williams-Wood, English Transfer*, pp. 140, 174.

WOOD

KAD NO.	GODDEN NO.	MARK	

***Wood & Baggaley**
Hill Works,
Burslem, Staffordshire, c.1870-1880
Formerly, Morgan (& Co.) (1860-1870)
Subsequently, Jacob Baggaley (c.1880-1886)

B2478 - Printed marks of differing design. Pattern name often included, c.1870-1880.

B2479 4239 W. & B. Mark, as above, c.1870-1880.

- Note marking "W. & B.", not to be confused with Wood & Brownfield or Wood & Bretell.

WOOD

***Wood & Barker Ltd.**
Queen Street Pottery,
Burslem, Staffordshire, c.1897-1903
Formerly, Thomas Wood & Sons (1896-1897)

B2480 4240 Printed initial mark. Pattern name often included, c.1897-1903.

WOOD

***Wood & Brettel**
Brownhills Pottery,
Tunstall, Staffordshire, c.1818-1823

B2481 - **W. & B.** Impressed initial mark, c.1818-1823.
- Pattern pieces not as yet located.
- The initials "W. & B." an also be attributed to Wood & Baggaley, Wood & Bower or Wood & Brownfield.

WOOD

***Wood & Brownfield**
Cobridge Works,
Cobridge, Staffordshire, c.1837-1850

B2482 4242 **W. & B.** Printed or impressed initial mark, often elaborately designed and including printed pattern name, c.1837-1850.
- Marking "REAL IRONSTONE" noted.

B2483 -
B2484 -

Printed marks of elaborate design with pattern name included, c.1837-1850.
- *Peake,* notes that Wood & Brownfield continued patterns from predecessor, Robinson, Wood & Brownfield, a common practice during this time. See *Peake,* p. 3 for "Nankin" pattern as well as p. 106 for "Pekin" pattern. Also see p. 327.

KAD NO.	GODDEN NO.	MARK	
B2485	-		Printed Royal Coat of Arms marked with WARRANTED REAL IRONSTONE CHINA" and retailer's marking "HIGGINBOTHAM & SONS, 17 SACKVILLE STREET, DUBLIN", c.1842. See *Peake*, p. 89.
B2486	4243	**W. & B. PEARL WHITE COBRIDGE**	Impressed initial mark, within borders, c.1837-1850. - Godden notes that the initials "W. & B." may be attributed to Wood & Baggaley, Wood & Bowers or Wood & Brettel.

Typical Marks Include:

KAD NO.	GODDEN NO.	MARK
B2487 B2488 B2489 B2490	- - - -	

For further reading, refer to *Hampson, Churchill*; *Peake*, pp. 1-2, 88-93 for additional marks, and p. 170, Appendix 3 for a complete index of plate designs.

WOOD

***Wood & Caldwell**
Fountain Place Works,
Burslem, c.1793-1818
Formerly, Enoch Wood & Co. (1790-1792)
Subsequently, Enoch Wood & Sons (c.1818-1845)
- Sons: Joseph & Edward

KAD NO.	GODDEN NO.	MARK	
B2491	4256	**WOOD & CALDWELL**	Impressed name mark, c.1793-1818.
B2492	-	**HENSHAW & JARVES IMPORTERS OF EARTHENWARE AND CHINA WARE BOSTON FROM WOOD AND CALDWELL'S MANUFACTORY BURSLEM, STAFFORDSHIRE**	Printed name mark, with importer's mark, found on Historical Blue, c.1793-1818. - Refer to *Larsen*, p. 258. - Markings "IRONSTONE", OPAQUE CHINA" AND "STONE CHINA" noted.

For further reading, refer to *Coysh*, Vol. I, p. 408; *Godden*; and *Godden, Collecting Lustreware*, pp. 188-189.

WOOD

KAD NO.	GODDEN NO.	MARK	
			***Wood & Challinor** **Brownhill Pottery (1828-1834)** **Woodland Pottery (1834-1845)** **Tunstall, Staffordshire, 1828-1845** **- Also see John Wedg Wood, pp. 383-384**
B2493	-	**W. C.**	Printed marks of differing design. Pattern name often included, c.1828-1845.
B2494	4244	**W. & C.**	-
B2495	-	**WOOD & CHALLINOR**	

Typical Marks Include:

B2496* -
B2497 -
B2498 -

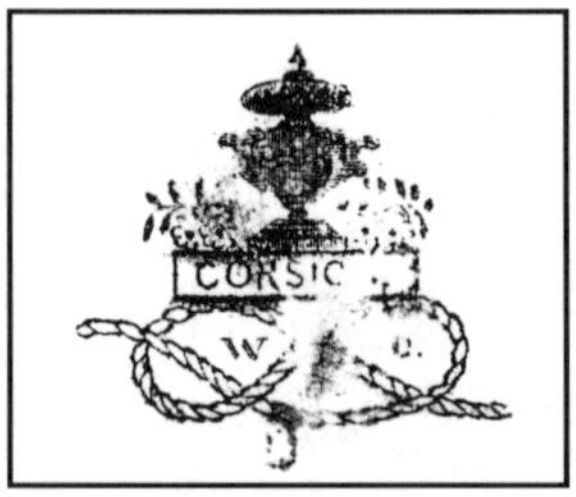

B2499 -
B2500 -
B2501 -

*KAD B2496 was used exactly as is by Davenport. See *P. Williams, Staffordshire*, Vol. III, p. 51 and KAD B703.

For further reading, refer to *Snyder, Romantic Staffordshire*, pp. 169-170.

WOOD

KAD NO.	GODDEN NO.	MARK	
			***Wood & Challinor & Co.** **Well Street Pottery,** **Tunstall, Staffordshire, c.1860-1864**
B2502	-	**W. & CO.**	Printed marks of differing design. Pattern name often included, c.1860-1864.
B2503	4245	**W. C. & CO.**	

WOOD

KAD NO. | **GODDEN NO.** | **MARK**

Wood & Hawthorne
Abbey Pottery,
Cobridge, Staffordshire, 1882-1887
Subsequently, Sant & Vodrey (1887-1893)

B2504 4272 

Printed Royal Coat of Arms mark. Pattern name often included, 1882-1887.
- Marking "IRONSTONE CHINA" noted.
- Note marking "ENGLAND" prior to the McKinley Act of 1891.

For further reading, refer to *White Ironstone Notes*, Vol. 3, No. 2, Fall 1996, p. 9.

WOOD

***Wood & Hulme**
Garfield Pottery,
Burslem, Staffordshire, c.1882-1905
Subsequently, H. Hulme & Sons (1906-1932)

B2505 - **W. H.** Printed or impressed initial mark. Pattern name often included, c.1882-1905.

B2506 4273 **W. & H. B.**

Godden, p. 341 notes that marks were continued by H. Hulme & Sons.
See Henry Hulme & Sons, mark no. KAD B1340.

WOOD

***Wood & Pigott**
Well Street Pottery,
Tunstall, Staffordshire, 1869-1871

B2506A 4277 **W. & P.** Printed initial mark. Pattern name often included, 1869-1871.
- The name Pigott many occur with one or two "G's".
- The exact pattern [Madras] was also made by Doulton.
- Refer to *Snyder, Historic Flow Blue*, p. 153, where this "Madras" pattern is illustrated, though wrongly attributed.

WOOD

KAD NO. | **GODDEN NO.** | **MARK**

***Wood & Son(s) (Ltd.)**
Trent & New Wharf Potteries (from 1894),
Burslem, Staffordshire, c.1865-
Subsequently, Wood & Sons (1982) Ltd.

B2507 4285 

B2508 - 

Printed name mark, c.1865-1907.
- "& Sons" dates from 1907.
- "LTD." dates from 1910-1981.
- **Advertising markings noted:**
"Compliments, Geo. T. Horan House Furnishers, Charleston, Mass."
"Clifford Black & Co., Malden, Mass."
"Geo. A. Folsom & Co., Teas & Coffees, Boston, Mass"
"W. B. Fuller Co., Mansfield, Mass."
- Wood & Sons reissued many patterns from the New Wharf Pottery which were acquired in 1894.

For further reading, refer to *Edwards, Basalt*, pp. 269-272; *P. Williams, Flow Blue*, Vol. II, p. 172 for the pattern "Waldorf"; *Godden*, pp. 689-690 for additional marks; and *Bunt, British Potters*, pp. 58-59.

KAD NO.	GODDEN NO.	MARK

WOOD

***Arthur Wood**
Bradwell Works,
Longport, Staffordshire, c.1904-1928
Formerly, Capper & Wood (1895-1904)

B2509 4233

Printed or impressed mark. Pattern name often included, c.1904-1928.

WOOD

***Arthur Wood & Son (Longport) Ltd.**
Bradwell Works,
Longport, Staffordshire, c.1928-

B2510 4234

Printed marks of differing design. Pattern name often included, c.1928-.
- In 1966 Arthur Wood & Son (Longport) Ltd. acquired Carlton Ware Ltd., which was formerly Wiltshaw & Robinson.
- For additional marks refer to *Godden*, p. 683.

WOOD

***Edmund T. Wood**
Woodland Pottery,
Tunstall, 1857-1875
Formerly, John Wedge Wood (1841-1857)
Subsequently, Hollinshead & Kirkham

- Also see Wood & Challinor and John Wedge Wood

It is probable that Edmund T. Wood continued the marks of his brother John, as there are no recorded marks in the name of Edmund T. Wood.

Evidently there was a continuing relationship between Edmund T. Wood and his brother-in-law, William Davenport, whereby a registry of William Davenport, "ERIE SHAPE" registered on April 12, 1861, was used by Edmund T. Wood and referred to as "SHARON ARCH" Shape by White Ironstone collectors.

A second example of this practice was a White Ironstone piece by Davenport, Banks & Co. "CORN ON THE COB" registered on Jan. 12, 1863. This shape was also used by Edmund T. Wood and registered by him on Oct. 31, 1863. White Ironstone collectors refer to this as "CORN & OATS". Refer to *Sussman*, pp. 55-56; and *Peake*, p. 182. - Also refer to John Wedge Wood for other registries of William Davenport which were used by John Wedge Wood on White Ironstone.

For further reading, refer to *Wetherbee*, *White Ironstone*, p. 106; *Godden, Davenport*, pp. 21, 63-64; and *Sussman*, p. 57.

WOOD

***Enoch Wood**
Fountain Place Works,
Burslem, Staffordshire, c.1784-1789
- "& SONS" (c.1818-1845)

KAD NO.	GODDEN NO.	MARK	
B2511	4247	**WOOD**	Impressed name or initial mark, c.1784-1789.
B2512	4248	**E. WOOD**	- Also noted with the initial "N" or with "#8" and impressed mark "WHITE ENAMEL CHINA", c. 1784-1789.

- The initials "W M B" can also be attributed to WOOD & BAGGALEY, WOOD & BOWER, or WOOD & BROWNFIELD.

KAD NO.	GODDEN NO.	MARK	
B2513	4249	**E. W.**	- Patterns noted may be of a later date and marked:
B2514	4250		"E. W. & Son" or impressed "WOOD".
B2515	-	**W** (impressed)	*P. Williams, Staffordshire*, Vol. I and II, notes patterns in Blue & White with the marks KAD B2511, B2512 and B2514. She also notes a possible later date of issue for Enoch Wood & Sons of c.1818-1845. Printed backstamp marks date from c.1800s. For further reading, refer to *Edwards, Basalt*, pp. 269-272; *Coysh*, Vol. I, p. 408; and *Penny Plain*, p. 101, No. 272.

WOOD

***Enoch Wood & Sons**
Fountain Place Works,
- and other potteries
Burslem, Staffordshire, c.1818-1845
Formerly, Wood & Caldwell (1793-1818)
- Fountain Place Works acquired by Pinder, Bourne & Hope in 1851

KAD NO.	GODDEN NO.	MARK	
B2516	4257		Impressed name marks, c.1818-1845. - Additional marking noted with inclusion of "STAFFORDSHIRE".
B2517	4258	**ENOCH WOOD & SONS BURSLEM STAFFORDSHIRE**	- Marks KAD B2511 and B2512 were continued on from Enoch Wood.
B2518 B2519	4259 -	 	Impressed name marks, c. 1818-1845. - Additional marking with double inner circle KAD B2519 noted, c.1818-1845.
B2520	4260	**E. W. & S(o)**	Printed initials noted with various and often elaborately designed marks. Name of pattern and/or series noted: - Initials "E. W. & S." used c.1818-1845 - Initials "E. & E. W." used c.1840 - Initials "E. & E." related to Enoch & Edward Wood
B2521	4261	**E. WOOD & SON(S)**	Printed name marks, c.1818-1845.
B2522	4262	**E. E. WOOD**	
B2523	4263	**E. E. WOOD BURSLEM**	

KAD NO.	GODDEN NO.	MARK	
B2524	4264	**E. & E. W.**	Printed initial mark, c.1840.

- Pieces may be marked "CELTIC CHINA", IMPERIAL CHINA" OR "SEMI CHINA". Marking "PEARL CHINA" is found impressed on "Damascus" pattern.
- "WOOD" or "E. WOOD" are marks associated with Enoch Wood.
- The impressed name mark "WOOD" or "E. WOOD" is noted by Ellen Hill on Mulberry wares of the relating to the latter years of E. Wood & Sons, c. 1840.

Typical Historic Marks Include:

B2525 -
B2526 -
B2527 -
B2528 -

B2529 -
B2530 -
B2531 -
B2532 -

Printed marks of various designs noted on Historic American/Canadian views, often including printed series and title names, c.1818-1845.
- The printed or impressed name "WOOD" are found on occasion.
- Impressed marks KAD B2516, B2518 and B2519 often accompany the printed marks noted above.

Typical Marks Include:

B2533 -
B2534 -
B2535 -

For further reading, refer to *Godden, British Porcelain*, pp. 787-788; and *Snyder, Romantic Staffordshire*, pp. 171-177; *Godden, Collecting Lustreware*, pp. 178-188; *Edwards, Basalt*, pp. 269-272; *Snyder, Historic Staffordshire*, pp. 115-150; *Coysh & Stefano*; and *Little*, pp. 106-108.

WOOD

***H. J. Wood (Ltd.)**
Alexandra Pottery,
Burslem, Staffordshire, c.1884-

B2536 4266

Printed Staffordshire Knot with the initials "H. J. W./B.", c.1884-.

For additional marks refer to *Godden*, p. 686; and *Gaston*, Vol. II, p. 68.

WOOD

KAD NO.	GODDEN NO.	MARK	
			***John Wood & Co. (Ltd.)** **New Stepney Pottery,** **Ouseburn, Newcastle-upon-Tyne, Northumberland, c.1877-1912** **- "Ltd." dates from 1892**
B2537	-	**J. WOOD** **NEWCASTLE**	Impressed mark noted with printed marking and pattern name, c.1877-1912.
B2538	-	**J. WOOD** **STEPENY POTTERY** **NEWCASTLE ON TYNE**	Printed marks of differing design. Pattern name often included, c.1877-1912. - TYNE" marking which refer to Tyneside noted. - *Bell,* p. 148 notes an impressed marking "SEWELL'S" and states, "…that when Sewell & Co. ceased production, part at least of their stock of biscuit-ware passed into the hands of John Wood." This was a common practice when acquiring bankrupt pottery inventory. - *Godden, Staffordshire*, p. 498 records a John Wood & Co. at Mt. Pleasant, Longton (1867-1871).

For further reading, refer to *Hampson*, No. 64, p. 42; *Lawrence*, p. 113; *Coysh*, Vol. I, p. 108; and *Bell*, pp. 113-114 and 146.

WOOD

John Wedge Wood
Brownhills & Hadderidge, Burslem (1841-1844(45))
Woodland Pottery, Tunstall (1845-1857(75/76))
Staffordshire, 1841-1875(76)
- John Wedge Wood died in 1857, whereupon his youngest brother, Edward Thomas Wood, continued pottery until 1875/76.
- See Edmund T. Wood and Wood & Challinor for the Woodland Pottery.

KAD NO.	GODDEN NO.	MARK	
B2539	4276	**W. W.**	Impressed mark with printed name mark, 1841-1857(75/76). - See *P. Williams, Staffordshire*, Vol. II, p. 380 for the "Sea Fan" pattern.
B2540	-	**J. WEDGWOOD**	Printed or impressed marks of differing design, 1841-1857(75/76).
B2540A	-	**J. W. W.**	

Typical Marks Include:

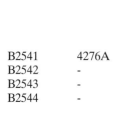

B2541 4276A
B2542 -
B2543 -
B2544 -

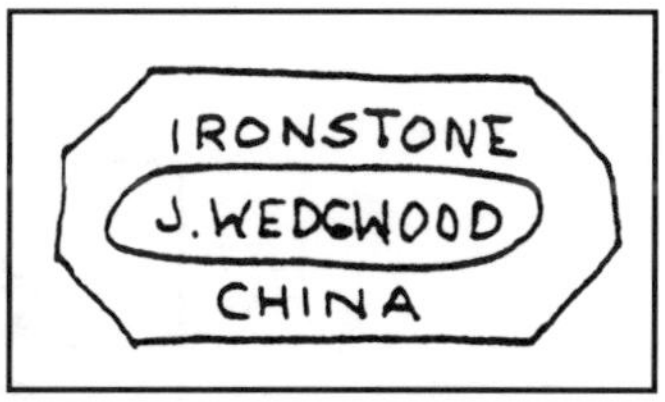

Printed **Impressed**

B2545 -

Impressed mark, c.1845-1857.

- See *White Ironstone Notes*, Vol. 3, No. 4, Spring 1997, p. 8; and *Godden, Jewitt*, pp. 222-223.

- The marking "WEDG*E*WOOD & CO." is not to be confused with the famous Wedgwood & Co. of the Unicorn Pottery, Tunstall, 1860-1965.

KAD NO.	GODDEN NO.	MARK	
B2546	4276B		Printed name mark, 1841-1857(75/76).

- Refer to *P. Williams, Staffordshire*, Vol. II, p. 200 for the "Hibernia" pattern.

- Una des Fontaine's article "Wedgwood or Wedg Wood" Filling a Gap in Ceramic History" in the *NCSJ*, Vol. 6, 1987, pp. 143-166, notes the "following tentative dates for the marks..." as follows:

B2547	-	**WEDG WOOD**	1837-1840/44
B2548	-	**WedgWooD**	1840-1850
B2549	-	**WEDG.WOOD**	1850-1859(?)

- The name "J. WEDGWOOD" is often mistaken for Josiah Wedgwood, who firm did not sign its wares with a "J".

For further reading, refer to *Sussman*, pp. 26-27 and 56-57; and *Wetherbee*, p. 79.

- A relationship existed between William Davenport and John Wedge Wood, who were brothers-in-law, as noted by two registered shapes of William Davenport that were used by John Wedge Wood:

William Davenport's Cambridge Shape, registered on Oct. 6, 1854, is noted as also being used by John Wedge Wood, but referred to as "Scalloped Decagon" by White Ironstone collectors and marked "John Wedg Wood."

Further, William Davenport's Union Shape, registered on Nov. 14, 1856, is found on White Ironstone. It is referred to as "Fig Shape" by White Ironstone collectors and marked "John Wedg Wood."

- Also refer to Edmund T. Wood for shapes registered by Davenport and employed by Edmund T. Wood.

- *Ewins*, pp. 60-74, records an extensive trade market established by John Wedge Wood and continued by Edmund T. Wood; recording a customer base of 188 establishments in the United States. This is a clear illustration of how the English proliferated the US market. Also refer to pp. 48 and 67, pl. 10 and 13 respectively for tear pulls of the "Union Shape."

WOOD

***Wood, Rathbon & Co.**
Cobridge, Staffordshire, c.1868

B2550	-		Printed American Eagle and Shield, c.1868.

Wetherbee, White Ironstone, p. 121 notes the pattern "Forget-Me-Not" in White Ironstone.

WOOD

KAD NO.	GODDEN NO.	MARK	

***Wood, Son & Co.**
Villa Pottery,
Cobridge, Staffordshire, 1868-1877
Formerly, Edward Walley & Son (1858-1862(65))
Subsequently, W. E. Cartlidge (1879-1892)

B2551 4298 

Printed Royal Coat of Arms mark, c.1868-1877.

-*Wetherbee, White Ironstone*, has noted the pattern "Hyacinth Shape."

B2552 - 

Printed mark noted on White Ironstone, 1868-1877.

- Note wording "COBRIDGE".

For further reading, refer to *White Ironstone Notes*, Vol. 3, No. 4, Spring 1997, p. 8, for "Hyacinth Shape".

WOOD

***Thomas Wood & Co.**
Wedgwood & Queen Street Potteries
Burslem, Staffordshire, c.1885-1896
Subsequently, Thomas Wood & Sons (c.1896-1897)

B2553 4283 **T. W. & CO.** Printed or impressed initial marks, c.1885-1896.

WOOD

***Thoms Wood & Sons**
Queen Street Pottery
Burslem, Staffordshire, c.1896-1897
Subsequently, Barker, Wood & Co. (c.1897-1903)

B2554 4284 

Printed marks of differing design. Pattern name often included, c.1896-1897.

WOOD

***William Wood & Co.**
Albert Street Works,
Burslem, Staffordshire, 1873-1932
Formerly, Wiltshaw, Wood & Co. (1870-1873)

B2555 4299 **W. W. & CO.*** Printed or impressed marks of differing design, 1873+.*

B2556 4300 

Printed Staffordshire Knot, 1880-1915.

B2557 4301 

Printed Staffordshire Knot with crown, 1915-1932.

* Godden notes that the initials "W. W. & CO." may be a carry over from the preceding firm, Wiltshaw, Wood & Co. Refer to *Godden, British Porcelain*. pp. 775 and 793.

WOODNORTH

Woodnorth & Co.
See: Whitehaven Pottery, pp. 368-369

WOOLF

Lewis Woolf (& Sons) (& Co.)*
Ferrybridge, Australian Pottery & Rock Pottery,
Mexborough, Yorkshire, 1851-1887
*** See Ferrybridge Pottery**

KAD NO.	GODDEN NO.	MARK	Printed Initial Marks & Proprietors		
B2558	4468	L. W.	Lewis Woolf	Ferrybridge Pottery	1851-1870
B2559	4468A	L. W. S.	Lewis Woolf & Sons	Ferrybridge Pottery	1870-1883
B2560	-	L. W. & SONS			
B2558	4468	L. W.	Lewis Woolf	Australian Pottery	1857-1877
B2561	-	S. W.	Sydney Woolf	Australian Pottery	1877-1887
B2562	-	[S. W. CO.]	Sydney Woolf & Co.	Rock Pottery, Mexborough	1873-1883

For further reading, refer to *Coysh*, Vol. II, p. 215; *Lawrence;* the *Annual Report of the Yorkshire Philosophical Society, 1916*; and *Godden, Jewitt*, p. 192.

WOOLISCROFT

George Wooliscroft (& Co.)
Well Street (c.1851)
High Street (c.1853)
Sandyford Potteries (c.1860-1864),
Tunstall, Staffordshire, 1851-1853 and 1860-1864

KAD NO.	GODDEN NO.	MARK	
B2563	4308	**G. WOOLISCROFT**	Printed or impressed marks of differing design. Pattern name often included, 1851-1853 and 1860-1864.
B2563A	-	**IRONSTONE CHINA G. WOOLISCROFT**	Impressed Royal Arms mark with name below, 1860-1864.

Typical Marks Include:

B2564 -
B2565 -
B2566 -

- Woolscroft is spelled with either one or two "l's".

For further reading, refer to *Wetherbee*, pp. 54-56, 71-72 and 144.

WOOLLEY

KAD NO.	GODDEN NO.	MARK	
			Richard Woolley **Late Turner's Works, Lane End,** **Longton, Staffordshire, c.1809-1811** **Formerly, Chetham & Woolley (c.1796-1809)** **Subsequently, Harley & Seckerson (c.1808)(c. 1812-1835)**
B2567	4309	**WOOLLEY**	Impressed name mark, c.1809-1811.

For further reading, refer to *Hampson*, No. 270, p. 174; and *Godden, British Porcelain*, pp.174-175.

WORTHINGTON

Worthington & Harrop
Dresden Works,
Hanley, Staffordshire, 1856-1873
Subsequently, William Harrop (1874-1894)

B2568	4365	**W. & H.**	Printed marks of differing design. Pattern name often included, 1856-1873.

For further reading, refer to *Godden, Jewitt*, p. 78.

YALE

Yale & Barker
Victoria Place Works,
Longton, Staffordshire, c.1841-1842
Formerly, Shaw & Yale (1838-1841)
Subsequently, Yale, Barker & Barker (1843-1846)

B2569	4381	**Y. & B.**	Printed marks of differing design. Pattern name often included, 1841-1842.
B2570	4382	**SEMI CHINA WARRANTED Y. & B.**	

For further reading, refer to *Hampson*, No. 273, pp. 176-177; and *Coysh*, Vol. I, p. 216.

YATES

Yates & May
Broad Street,
(Shelton) Hanley, Staffordshire, c.1835-1843
Formerly, John Yates and John & Williams Yates (1770-1835)

B2571	-	**Y. & M.**	Printed initial mark, 1835-1843.

For further reading, refer to *Little*, p. 109; *Godden, British Porcelain*, pp. 808-809; and *Godden, Staffordshire*, Ch. 20, pp. 298-305.

YATES

John Yates
Keeling Lane (c.1770-1808)
Broad Street (High Street), (c.1784-1835)
Shelton, Hanley, Staffordshire, c.1770-1835

***Edwards, Basalt*, notes the following chronology:**

John Yates (The Elder)	c.1770-1796
John Yates (The Younger) & Wm. Yates	c.1794-1814
John Yates (The Younger)	c1820-1835
Yates & May	c.1835-1843
John Yates	c.1844

KAD NO.	GODDEN NO.	MARK	
B2572	4383	**J. Y.**	Printed or impressed initial mark, c.1784-1835.
B2573	-	**WARRANTED STONE CHINA FENTON**	Printed mark, c.1784-1835. - Godden notes the period of c.1820-1835 as the period of high grade production.
B2574	-	**YATES**	Impressed name mark, c.1820-1835.

For further reading, refer to *Godden*, p. 704; *Godden, British Porcelain*, pp. 807-808; *Little*, p. 109; *Edwards, Basalt*, pp. 90, 137, 175 and 273-274; and *Coysh*, Vol. I, p. 411.

YNYSMEUDWY

Ynysmeudwy Pottery
(Various Ownerships)
Near Swansea, Wales, 1845-1875
History:

Michael & William Williams	1845-1856
William Williams*	1856-1859
Charles Williams	1859-1860
Griffith Lewis & John Morgan	1860-1870
W. T. Holland (owner of Llanelly Pottery)**	1870
W. T. Holland (Manufacturer of Bricks, Chimney Pots, Garden Ornaments, Pipes, etc.)	1871-1875

KAD NO.	GODDEN NO.	MARK	
B2575	4395	**Y. M. P.**	Impressed initial mark, c.1850+.
B2576	4396	**Y. P.**	Impressed initial mark, with initials below, c.1850.
B2577	4397	**L. & M.**	Printed initial mark, possibly 1860-1870.
B2578	-	**W. T. HOLLAND**	Printed name mark, 1871-1875.

* Refer to William Williams, p. 372
** Refer to South Wales Potters, pp. 338-339

For further reading, refer to *Nance*, p. 197; *Pugh, Welsh Pottery*, pp. 55-57, and 109-115.

PATTERNS BY POTTERS

BENJAMIN ADAMS

BLUE AND WHITE TRANSFERWARE
SERIES
1. MISCELLANEOUS
Ruins
"Scene After Claude Lorraine"
"Tendril Pattern"
"Willow" Pattern

WILLIAM ADAMS
BLUE AND WHITE TRANSFERWARE
SERIES
1. REGENT'S PARK SERIES
Bank of England, London
Church of England Missionary College, London
Clarence House
Clarence Terrace, Regent's Park, London
The Coliseum
Cornwall Terrace, Regent's Park, London
Hanover Terrace, Regent's Park, London
Highbury College, London
The Holme, Regent's Park
The London Institution
Part of Regent Street, London
The Regent's Quadrant, London
Royal Hospital, Regent's Park, London
St. George's Chapel, Regent Street, London
St. Paul's School, London
Sussex Place, Regent's Park
Villa in the Regent's Park, London (3)
York Gate, Regent's Park, London
2. "ROCKS AND FOLIAGE BORDER" SERIES
"Denton Park, Yorkshire"
"Normanton Park, Rutlandshire"
"Thatched Cottage By Bridge"
3. "SCOTTISH SCENES" SERIES
Caledonia
4. SEASONS (PATTERNS) SERIES*
February
Winter
Refer to Snyder, *Romantic Staffordshire*, pp. 27-28.

WILLIAM ADAMS & SON(S) (POTTERS) LTD.
BLUE AND WHITE TRANSFERWARE
SERIES:
1. "BLUEBELL BORDER SERIES"
Bamborough Castle, Northumberland
Beckenham Place, Kent
Bothwell Castle, Clydesdale
Branxholm Castle, Roxburghshire [is Melrose Abbey, Roxburghshire view]
Brecon Castle, Brecknockshire
Bywell Castle, Northumberland
Caister Castle, Norfolk
The Chantry, Suffolk
Dilston Tower, Northumberland
Hawthornden, Edinburghshire
Jedburgh Abbey, Roxburghshire
Ludlow Castle, Salop
Lyme Castle, Kent (sic)
Melrose Abbey, Roxburghshire [is Branxholm Castle, Roxburghshire view]
Morpeth Castle, Northumberland
Moorland Castle, Staffs
Northumberland Castle
St. Mary's Abbey, York
Scaleby Castle, Cumberland
Windsor Castle, Berkshire
Wolvesey Castle, Hampshire
2. "FLOWERS AND LEAVES BORDER SERIES"
Armidale, Invernesshire
Beckenham Place, Kent
Berkley Castle, Gloucestershire
Blaise Castle, Gloucestershire
Blenheim Castle, Oxfordshire
Bramham Park, Yorkshire
Carstairs, Lanarkshire
Denton Park, Yorkshire
Dews Hall, Essex
Fleurs, Roxburghshire
Fonthill Abbey
Glanbran, Carmarthenshire
Gracefield, Queen's County, Ireland
Kimberly Hall, Norfolk*
Murthly, Perthshire
Normanton Park, South View, Rutlandshire
Pishobury, Hertfordshire
Plasnewydd, Anglesey
Polesden, Surrey
Rode Hall, Cheshire
The Rookery, Surrey
Sunning Hill Park, Berkshire
Tixall, Staffordshire,
Warleigh House, Somersetshire
Wellcombe, Warwickshire
Wells Cathedral
Wilton House, Wiltshire
*See *True Blue*, p. 82, No. 6
3. FOLIAGE & SCROLL BORDER SERIES
Alnwick Castle, Northumberland
Gable's Farm
Kirkstall Abbey
St. Catherine's Hill, Near Guildford
4. CUPID SERIES
"Cupid Pattern"
"Cupid & Roses"
"Cupid & Virgin"

WILLIAM ADAMS & SON(S) (POTTERS) LTD.
BLUE AND WHITE TRANSFERWARE
SINGLE PATTERNS

CATEGORY	PATTERN	
-	Amazon	
G	Andalusia	
F	Asiatic Pheasants	
M/F	Athecus	
S	Athens	Reg'd. Jan 3, 1849/No. 56978
F	"Basket of Flowers"	
S	Bear Forest, Ireland*	
M/S	Beehive	
-	"Bird & Basket Chinoiserie"	
G	Black Eyed Susan	
M	"Blue Concentric"	
-	Blue Lawnton	
G	Bologna	
O	"Burmese Garden"	
G	Caledonia (possible series)	
S	Cassino (2) (possible series)	
-	Castle Scenery	
G	Chess Players	
P/O	Chinese Ching	
F	Chinese Flowers ["Windsor Flowers"]	
O	Chinoiserie After Pillemont	
F	"Chrysanthemum" ("Snowy Shrubs")	
S	Columbia (2)	
G	Columbus (see Series, Landing Of Columbus)	
-	"Cupid Pattern", "Cupid & Roses",. "Cupid & Virgin"	
S	Cyrene	
O	Damascus**	
S	Delphi	
G	DuBarry	
S	Florence	
G	"Forget-Me-Not"	
S	Fountain Scenery	
F	"Gables Farm"	
G	Garden Sports	
G	Gazelle	
S	Genoa	
S	Grecian Font (2)	
G	Habana	Reg'd. July 26, 1845/No. 29173
F	"Hibiscus in Pot"	
G	Huntsman	
S	Isola Belle (2)	
P/O	Kyber	
-	Lasso	
Z	"Lion Patterns"	
S	Lorraine	
S	Maddle, Jenny Lind	
S	"Manor House"	
O	Mazara	
S	Milan	
-	"Milking Time" [Thatched Cottage]	
M	"Miscellanea"	
-	"Native Pattern"	
S	Navarine	
S	New York	
-	Oriental	
M/Z	Ornithology ["Game Birds"]	
G	Palestine** (possible series)	
F	"Peony in Vase"	

S	Persia	
G	Pirates [The]***	
P/F	"Red & Green Roses"	
S	Ruins	
G	Sea [The]***	
G	Seasons (possible series)	

BLUE AND WHITE TRANSFERWARE
SINGLE PATTERNS

CATEGORY	PATTERN
P/O	Shanshai
G	"Sower" [The]
S	Spanish Convent (possible series)
-	Spanish Marriages, Madrid
-	"Three Cows"
S	United States View
-	"Urns, Scrolls & Flowers"
S	Venetian Temple
-	"Whitby Harbor" ["View of Whitby"]
S	Wild Rose
O	"Willow" Pattern
F	Windsor Rose

*See *Coysh*, Vol. 1, p. 36 and *P. Williams, Staffordshire*, Vol. III, p. 53
**Refer to *Snyder, Romantic Staffordshire*, pp. 23-25 for a possible series.
***Refer to *Snyder, Romantic Staffordshire*, pp. 26-27 for a possible series.

HISTORIC STAFFORDSHIRE SERIES
AMERICAN
1. HUDSON RIVER VIEWS SERIES
"Fairmont" (So Called)
Fort Edwards, Hudson River
View Near Sandy Hill, Hudson River
2. LANDING OF COLUMBUS SERIES
Columbus: Boat Scene
Columbus: Camp Scene
Columbus: Cavalry Scene
Columbus: Fleet Scene "Two Caravels, One Man in Each, et.al."
Columbus: Fleet Scene "One Companion, et.al."
Columbus: Fleet Scene "Two Companions, et.al."
Columbus: Greyhound Scene
Columbus: Hunting Scene
Columbus: Indian Scene "Indian Girl Kneeling, Two Indians Standing, et.al."
Columbus: Indian Scene "One Tent, Three Indians, et.al."
Columbus: Indian Scene "Squaw Seated, Indian Standing, et.al."
Columbus: Landing Scene "Several Indians, Columbus & Companions, et.al."
Columbus: Landing Scene "Three Indians & Procession of White Men, et.al."
Columbus: Pavilion Scene
Columbus: Spanish Scene
3. U.S. VIEWS SERIES
Catskill Mountain House, U.S.
The Falls of Niagara, U.S.
Harper's Ferry, U.S.
Headwaters of the Juniata, U.S.
Lake George, U.S.
Montevideo, Connecticut, U.S.
New York, U.S.
Shannondall Springs, Virginia, U.S.
Skenectady on the Mohawk River, U.S.
View Near Conway, N. Hampshire, U.S.
West Point, Military School, New York, U.S.
White Mountains, N. Hampshire, U.S.
4. MISCELLANEOUS
Log Cabin(Wm. Adams)
"Mitchell & Freeman's China & Glass Warehouse, Chatham Street, Boston" (Wm. Adams)
New York ["River and City"] (Wm. Adams & Sons)
Seal of the United States ["Eagle, Scroll in Beak"] (Wm. Adams)

FLOW BLUE

CATEGORY	PATTERN	
S	Abbey	-
O	Amoy	-
S	Athens	Reg'd. Jan. 3, 1849/No. 56978
F	"Berlin Group"	-
F	Doric	-
F	Fairy Villas (I)	-
F	"Fern"	-
O	Jeddo	Reg'd. Jan 3, 1849/No.56978
A	Ivy	-
O	Kyber	-
F	Lily	-
A	Medallion	-
G	Old English Rural Scenes	-
M	Ornithology	-
A	Poppy	-
F	Rhoda	-
F	Rose Sprays	-
O	Tonquin [Shanghai]	-
S	Wild Rose	-

MULBERRY WARES

CATEGORY	PATTERN	
S	Abbey	Reg'd. Jan. 3, 1849/No.56978
S	Athens	Reg'd. Jan. 3, 1849/No. 56978
F	Floral	Reg'd. Jan. 3, 1849/No. 56978
S	Caledonia	-
A/O	Jeddo	Reg'd. Jan. 3, 1849/No. 56978
S	Palestine	-

TEA LEAF/COPPER LUSTRE

"Empress Shape"*	-
Huron Shape	Reg'd. May 31, 1858/No. 113903
Vintage Shape ["Grape & Medallion"]	-

*This is a 20th century shape produced by Adams during the Tea Leaf revival of the 1950s and 1960s. Production ceased in 1972. The "Empress Shape" is a 20th century design and is not to be confused with 19th century shapes.

WHITE IRONSTONE

"Adams Scallop Shape"	Reg'd. Apr. 23, 1853/No. 90876
"Athenia Shape"*	-
"Cable and Ring"	-
Columbia Shape	-
Dover Shape	Reg'd. Mar. 13, 1862/No. 149939
Huron Shape	Reg'd. May 31, 1858/No. 113903
Vintage Shape	-
"Wheat"	-
"Wheat and Daisy"	-

*Subsequently registered by J.T. Close (& Co.), Jan. 3, 1866/No. 194194

WILLIAM ADAMS & CO. LTD.
BLUE AND WHITE TRANSFERWARE
SINGLE PATTERNS

CATEGORY	PATTERN
O	Asiatic Pheasants
O	Shanghai [Tonquin]

FLOW BLUE

CATEGORY	PATTERN
F	Asiatic Pheasants
O	Canton
F	Christmas Roses
F	Doric
O	Fairy Villas (I)
F	Fairy Villas (II)
O	Fairy Villas (III)
F	Festoon
S	"Game Birds"
F	Garland
O	Geisha
O	Jeddo
O	Kyber
F	Lilly
S	Mazara
S	Northern Scenery
G	"Pastoral"
A	Poppy
F	Queen Charlotte ["Queens Border"]
-	Regal
S	St. Petersburg
O	Shanghai [Tonquin]
S	Venetian Scenery
S	"Wild Rose"

MULBERRY WARES

CATEGORY	PATTERN
M	Marble

WHITE IRONSTONE
"Plain Wheat"*
*Wetherbee notes reproduced in mid and late 20th century in a light, creamy body.

WILLIAM & THOMAS ADAMS
BLUE AND WHITE TRANSFERWARE
SINGLE PATTERNS

CATEGORY	PATTERN
F	Asiatic Pheasants
O	Shanghai

FLOW BLUE

CATEGORY	PATTERN	
F	Queens Border	Reg'd. Jan. 21, 1881/No.360954

MULBERRY WARES

CATEGORY	PATTERN
M	Marble

WHITE IRONSTONE
"Wheat"

WILLIAM (ALSAGER) ADDERLEY (& CO.)
BLUE AND WHITE TRANSFERWARE
SINGLE PATTERNS

CATEGORY	PATTERN
F	"Cherry Blossom"
J	Berlin

CATEGORY	PATTERN	
C	Mycene (possible series)	
S	Rhone*	

See *P. Williams, Staffordshire*, Vol. III, pp. 99-100.

FLOW BLUE

CATEGORY	PATTERN	
-	Allexis	-
F	Alma	Reg'd. 1900/No. 365882
M/F	Constance	Reg'd. 1902/No. 397963
M/F	Imperial	Reg'd. 1900/No. 356790
F	Lily	-
-	Malta	-
F	Melbourne	-
A	Oxford	Reg'd. 1901/No. 368266
F	Pansy	-
-	Paris	-
F	Richmond	-
F	Sola	-
-	Spero	-

ADDERLEY'S LTD.

FLOW BLUE

CATEGORY	PATTERN	
D	Amoy	
F	"Budding Dogwood"	
F	Milan	Reg'd. 1893/No. 213153

HENRY ALCOCK & CO. (LTD.)

BLUE AND WHITE TRANSFERWARE

SINGLE PATTERNS

CATEGORY	PATTERN
G	Chase
A	Kenilworth
S	Priory

FLOW BLUE

CATEGORY	PATTERN	
A	Alma	
A	Beverly	
F	Bouquet	
A	Burmese	
A	Clarendon	
-	Clive	
A	Delamere	
F	Dresden Flowers	
M/A	Gem	
F	Grenada	
F	Herald	
F	Manhattan	
M	Minwood	
F	Mira	Reg'd. 1890/No. 149950
S	Old Castles	
O	Oriental Garden	
-	"Royal Premium"	
F	Sybil	
F	Touraine	Reg'd. 1898/No. 329815
F	Vine	

TEA LEAF/COPPER LUSTRE

"Blanket Stitch" ["Piecrust"]

"Jumbo"

WHITE IRONSTONE

Chinese Shape*	-
"Draped Leaf "	-
"Forget-Me-Not"	-
"Jumbo"	-
Oxford ["Floral Ray"]	-
Paris Shape*	-
"Pie Crust" ["Blanket Stitch"]	-
"Prunus Blossoms"	-
"Ribbed Berry"	-
"Square Ridged"	-
"Stylized Flower"	-
Trent Shape**	Reg'd. June 7, 1855/No. 100246-7
Wheat Pattern Shape	Reg'd. 1903/No. 414424

*Originally patented by John Alcock, March 20, 1857/No. 109427 and continued by Henry Alcock.

**Also registered by John Alcock. See *White Ironstone Notes*, Vol. 4, Spring 1998, pp. 4-6.

JOHN ALCOCK

BLUE AND WHITE TRANSFERWARE

SINGLE PATTERNS

CATEGORY	PATTERN
O	Celeste
O	Circassia
S	Cologne
S	Moselle
S	Priory (possible series)

FLOW BLUE

CATEGORY	PATTERN	
O	Celeste	-
S	Vincennes*	Reg'd. May 7, 1853/No. 91121-4

MULBERRY WARES

CATEGORY	PATTERN	
S	Cologne	-
S	Vincennes*	Reg'd. May 7, 1853/No. 91121-4

*Registered by J. & S. Alcock, Jr., March 27, 1848

WHITE IRONSTONE

"Bordered Gothic"	-
"Boxy Decagon"	-
Chinese Shape	Reg'd. Mar. 20, 1857/No. 109427
"Cora Shape" (att.)	-
"Divided Gothic"	-
Flora Shape ["Forget-Me-Not"]	Reg'd. Feb. 7, 1855/No. 99310
"Gothic Cameo"	-
Hebe Shape	Reg'd. May 7, 1853/No. 91121-4
"Little Pear"Shape	Reg'd. May 7, 1853/No. 91121-4
"Long Octagon"	-
Paris Shape	Reg'd. Mar. 20, 1857/No. 109427
"Pierced Scroll"*	-
"Ribbed Berry"	-
"Split Pod" (with concave & convex panels)	-
"Stafford Shape"**	Reg'd. Sept. 5, 1854/No. 96773
Trent Shape	Reg'd. June 7, 1855/No. 100246-7
"True Scallop"	-
"Wheat Harvest"	-

*See Wetherbee, *White Ironstone* p. 48, fig. 7-51

**Also registered by S. Alcock & Co., Sept. 5, 1854. See *White Ironstone Notes,* Vol. 4, No. 4, Spring 1998, pp. 4-6 for illustrations and discussion on the use of this shape by both John Alcock and Samuel Alcock.

JOHN & GEORGE ALCOCK

BLUE AND WHITE TRANSFERWARE

SINGLE PATTERNS

CATEGORY	PATTERN
S	Blyantre
O	Circassia
S	Cologne
M/F	Fern
S	Moselle
O	Napier
M	Neptune
M/F	Paradise
C	Pompeii
F	"Rosetta Wreath"
S	Tyrol
S	Vintage

FLOW BLUE

CATEGORY	PATTERN
O	Circassia
F	"Flowers of Beads"
O	Napier
O	Scinde

MULBERRY WARES

CATEGORY	PATTERN
S	Cologne
S	Moselle
O	Scinde

WHITE IRONSTONE

"Classic Gothic"

"Pierced Scroll"

JOHN & SAMUEL ALCOCK (JR.)

FLOW BLUE

CATEGORY	PATTERN
O	Scinde

MULBERRY WARES

CATEGORY	PATTERN	
S	Vincennes	Reg'd. Mar. 27, 1848/ No. 51185-91

WHITE IRONSTONE

"Alcock's Long Octagon Shape"	Reg'd. Mar. 27, 1848/ No. 51185-91
"Bordered Gothic"	-
"Pierced Scroll"	-

N.B.: See Wetherbee's White Ironstone, p. 48, f. 7-51 and p. 81.

SAMUEL ALCOCK & CO.

BLUE AND WHITE TRANSFERWARE

SINGLE PATTERNS

CATEGORY	PATTERN	
O	Abbeville	
-	"Beehives & Country House"	
S	Blenheim	
M/Z	British Birds	Reg'd. June 11, 1855/ No. 100299 Impressed F.M.
F	Carlton	
M/F	Carroll	
S	Commerce (2)	
C	Etruscan Vase	
M/F	Fern (att.)	
S	Forest	
S	Fountain Scenery	

F	Hawthorne Blossom	
O	Indian Bridge	
M/F	Japanese*	
S	Manila	
S	Maryland	
M	Ontario	
S	Pearl	
M	Royal Star	
M	Sea Leaf	
S	Statue	
O	"The Sacred Tree of the Hindoos at Gyansohar"	
M	Toronto	
D	Van Dyke	
G	Victoria	
H	William III	

*See *Coysh*, p.20

FLOW BLUE

CATEGORY	PATTERN	
M/O	Bamboo	Reg'd. June 14, 1843/No. 7503-5
F	Basket (att.)	
F	"Bleeding Heart"* (Brush Stroke)	Reg'd. June 14, 1843/No. 7503-5
O	Bombay Japan	
O	Carlton	
-	Celtic	
O	Chinese Bells (att.)	
O	Coral Japan	
M	Eclipse	
O	Hyson	
O	Kremlin	Reg'd. June 14, 1843/No. 7503-5
O	Madras	
F	Malo	
O	Manila	
O	Oriental	
O	Oriental Fan	
O	Oriental Rose	Reg'd. June 14, 1843/No. 7503-5
O	Sobraon	
F	"Summer Flowers"	
S	Swan	
O	Tonquin	
F	Velarian	
F	Wild Flower	

*See *Snyder's Fascinating Flow Blue*, p. 63 for illustration.

SAMUEL ALCOCK & CO.

MULBERRY WARES

CATEGORY	PATTERN
F	Althea
F	Bouquet
F	Flora
P/F	Indian Bridge
S	Loretta
S	Percy
P/F	Summer Flowers
F	Velarian

WHITE IRONSTONE

Atlantic Shape*	-
"Classic Gothic Shape"	Reg'd. 1847
"Divided Gothic"	-
"Framed Leaf"	-
"Grape Octagon Shape"	Reg'd. April 1847
"Many Paneled Gothic"	-
Stafford Shape**	Reg'd. Sept. 5, 1854/No. 96773

*See *White Ironstone Notes*, Vol. 4, No. 3, Winter 1998, p. 12 and Vol. 5, No. 3, Winter 1998, p. 11

**Also registered by J. Alcock Sept. 5, 1854. See *White Ironstone Notes,* Vol. 4, No. 4, Spring 1998, pp. 4-6 for illustrations and discussion on the use of this shape by both John Alcock and Samuel Alcock.

JOHN ALLASON

BLUE AND WHITE TRANSFERWARE

SINGLE PATTERNS

CATEGORY	PATTERN
-	Forest
P/O	Sana
Z	Stag
O	"Willow" Pattern

CHARLES ALLERTON & SONS

BLUE AND WHITE TRANSFERWARE

SINGLE PATTERNS

CATEGORY	PATTERN
O	Toro*

See *Cluett*, p. 73

FLOW BLUE

CATEGORY	PATTERN	
-	Chinese	
F	"Dahlia" (Brush Stroke)	
M/F	Danube	
A	Don	Reg'd. 1904/No. 428270
F	France	
M/F	Mabel	
M	Onion	
M/F	Racine	
F	Roslin	
P/M	"Wheel" (Lustre Decorated)	

ALLERTON, BROUGH & GREEN

BLUE AND WHITE TRANSFERWARE

SINGLE PATTERNS

CATEGORY	PATTERN
O	Ching-Tien
O	"Willow" Pattern

ALLMAN, BROUGHTON & CO.

BLUE AND WHITE TRANSFERWARE

SINGLE PATTERNS

CATEGORY	PATTERN
G	Berties Hope
-	Fountain

G.L. ASHWORTH & BROS. (LTD.)

BLUE AND WHITE TRANSFERWARE

SINGLE PATTERNS

CATEGORY	PATTERN	
C	Acropolis	
M	"Artichoke"	
O	Blue Pheasant	
A	Bow Bells	
P/O	"China Flora"	
P/O	"Chinese Flowers"	
P/O	"Chinese Pattern"	
P/O	Corean	
-	Cross Leaf	
A	Empress	
P/O	"Exotic Bird"	
S	Florentine	
O	India Temple	
S	"Italian Village"	
-	"King's College Chapel, Cambridge" (see Masons)	
P/O	"Mandarin"	
P/O	Medallion	
P/A	"Medallions"	
-	Melrose	
P/O	"Mock-Willow"	
P/O	"Mogul"	
O	Nang Po	
S	Oak Vista	
F	"Old World Rose"	
C	Olympia	
P/Z	"Peacock"	
S	Rustic	
S	St. Petersburg (Russian Script)	Reg'd. 1866
P/O	"Tree of Life"	
S	Victoria	
S	Vista	
S	Watteau	
P/F	"Wild Floral"	
F	"Wild Roses"	
O	"Willow" Pattern	
P/O	Yin	

HISTORIC STAFFORDSHIRE SERIES

AMERICAN & CANADIAN

1. MISCELLANEOUS

American Marine*

Lake Series* (see Francis Morley)

*Series was carried on by Ashworth, successors to Francis Morley

FLOW BLUE

CATEGORY	PATTERN
S	Ancient Ruins
M/F	Bedford
F	Blossom
-	Blue Bell
F	Bouquet
O	Canton
O/A	"Chinese Basket"
O	"Chinese Dragon"
O	"Chinese Landscape"
O	Chusan
M/Z	Flamingo
O	Hizen
O	India Temple
O	Indian
F	Iris
-	Kiji

-	Koaa	
S	Lake	
M/F	Lincoln	
F	Morning Glory	
M/F	Nankin	
F	Nankin Jar	
F	Persiana	
S	Ruins	
O	"Table & Flower Pot"	
O	"Willow" Pattern	
O	Yeddo	
O	Yin	

MULBERRY WARES

CATEGORY	PATTERN
P/F	Chusan
O	Lake
O	Yin

WHITE IRONSTONE

Nile Shape	Reg'd. Apr. 14, 1866/No. 196552-4

JOHN & EDWARD BADDELEY
BLUE AND WHITE TRANSFERWARE
SINGLE PATTERNS

CATEGORY	PATTERN
F	"Peony"
-	"Stilted House"

BAILEY & BALL
BLUE AND WHITE TRANSFERWARE
SINGLE PATTERNS

CATEGORY	PATTERN	
M	The Rabbit	Reg'd. Nov. 15, 1845/No. 31128
J	Robinson Crusoe	

W. & D. BAILEY
BLUE AND WHITE TRANSFERWARE
SINGLE PATTERNS

CATEGORY	PATTERN
-	"Woodbine"

BAKER, BEVANS & IRWIN
BLUE AND WHITE TRANSFERWARE
SINGLE PATTERNS

CATEGORY	PATTERN
G	Archers
G	"The Cottage Girl"
-	"Cowherd"
S	Free Trade
G	The Haymaker
-	"Horse & Cart"
G	"The Ladies of Llangollen"
S	Newstead Abbey
G	Pulteney Bridge, Bath
H	"Ship Pattern"
F	Vine
O	"Willow" Pattern

(W.) BAKER & CO. (LTD.)
BLUE AND WHITE TRANSFERWARE
SINGLE PATTERNS

CATEGORY	PATTERN
O	Damascus
F	Persian Rose
M/F	Spiral
O	"Willow Pattern"
G	Woodland

FLOW BLUE

CATEGORY	PATTERN
F	Peony
O	Shanghai*

*Pattern is exactly the same as "Tonquin" by Adams & Co.

WHITE IRONSTONE

"Belted Octagon"*	-
"Bordered Hyacinth"**	-
"Dominion Shape"	Reg'd. June 13, 1877/No. 310909
"Draped Leaf C"	-
"Meadow Bouquet"	-
"Plain Round"	-
Potomac Shape ["Blackberry"]	Reg'd. Oct. 23, 1862/No. 156715-7
"Wheat"	-

*See *White Ironstone Notes*, Vol. 4, No. 1, Summer 1997, p. 9 for illustration of a child's set
**Same as Lily Shape by W. & E. Corn.

TEA LEAF/COPPER LUSTRE
"Draped Leaf"
"Plain Round: Bulbous"

BAKER & CHETWYND & CO.
WHITE IRONSTONE
"Round Acorn"
TEA LEAF/COPPER LUSTRE
"Plain Round: Bulbous"

ALEXANDER BALFOUR & CO.
BLUE AND WHITE TRANSFERWARE
SINGLE PATTERNS

CATEGORY	PATTERN
G	Berties Hope
-	Fountain
-	Windsor

BARKER BROS (LTD.)
FLOW BLUE

CATEGORY	PATTERN
F	Alton

BARKER & SON
BLUE AND WHITE TRANSFERWARE
SINGLE PATTERNS

CATEGORY	PATTERN	
O	Chinese Marine	
S	Claremont	
C	Corrella	
S	Missouri	Reg'd. June 5, 1850/No. 69685
-	Regal	
S	Royal Cottage	

FLOW BLUE

CATEGORY	PATTERN
S	Clematis
F	Corella

MULBERRY WARES

CATEGORY	PATTERN	
F	Corella	Reg'd. June 5, 1850/No. 69685
F	Festoon	-
S	Missouri	Reg'd. June 5, 1850/No. 69685
P/S	Scroll	Reg'd. June 5, 1850/No. 69685

BARKER & TILL
BLUE AND WHITE TRANSFERWARE
SINGLE PATTERNS

CATEGORY	PATTERN	
S	Laconia	Reg'd. Jan. 1, 1848/No. 48540-2
S	Royal Cottage	

FLOW BLUE

CATEGORY	PATTERN
O	Lahore

BARKER, SUTTON & TILL
BLUE AND WHITE TRANSFERWARE
SINGLE PATTERNS

CATEGORY	PATTERN
S	Royal Cottage

SAMUEL BARKER & SON
BLUE AND WHITE TRANSFERWARE
SINGLE PATTERNS

CATEGORY	PATTERN
F	Asiatic Pheasants
-	Delhi
-	Floral Scenery
S	Gem
-	Manila
-	Persian
-	Royal Exchange
-	Savoy
-	Syrian
S	Wild Rose
O	"Willow" Pattern
-	York

FLOW BLUE

CATEGORY	PATTERN
F	Clematis

BARKERS & KENT (LTD.)
BLUE AND WHITE TRANSFERWARE
SINGLE PATTERNS

CATEGORY	PATTERN
F	Asiatic Pheasants
-	Bosphorus

FLOW BLUE

CATEGORY	PATTERN
F	Bavaria
M/A	Cairo
F	Clematis

F Coburg
S Florence
F Foley
F Hoey

THOMAS BARLOW
BLUE AND WHITE TRANSFERWARE
SINGLE PATTERNS

CATEGORY	PATTERN
O	Chinese Juvenile Sports
M	Persians
S	Scroll

BARROW & CO.
BLUE AND WHITE TRANSFERWARE
SINGLE PATTERNS

CATEGORY	PATTERN
S	Doria

WHITE IRONSTONE
Adriatic Shape Aug. 27, 1855/No. 101229-31
"Cherub Jug"
"Double Leaf"
"Fruit Garden"

BATES & BENNETT
FLOW BLUE

CATEGORY	PATTERN
F	Anemone

BATES, GILDEA & WALKER
MULBERRY WARES

CATEGORY	PATTERN	
O	"Bird & Fan"	Reg'd. Aug. 27, 1879/No. 338872

BATES, WALKER & CO.
BLUE AND WHITE TRANSFERWARE
SINGLE PATTERNS

CATEGORY	PATTERN
P/O	"Tea House"

BATHWELL & GOODFELLOW
BLUE AND WHITE TRANSFERWARE
SERIES
1. RURAL SCENERY "SERIES"
"Clinging Girl"
"Conversations"
"Firewood Pattern"
"Laird"
"Milkmaid Pattern"
"Mule & Goat"
"Reaper Pattern"
"Resting Farm Girl"
"Shepherd Pattern" ["Shepherd & Maid"]
BLUE AND WHITE TRANSFERWARE
SINGLE PATTERNS

CATEGORY	PATTERN
F	"Basket & Flowers" ("Large Basket")
S	"Bridge of Lucano"
-	"Castle" (Spode pattern)
F	"Flower Arrangement & Birds"

BATKIN, WALKER & BROADHURST
BLUE AND WHITE TRANSFERWARE
SINGLE PATTERNS

CATEGORY	PATTERN
-	"Bridge & Statue"
S	Versailles

JOHN DENTON BAXTER (BAGSTER)
BLUE AND WHITE TRANSFERWARE
SERIES
1. VIGNETTE SERIES
"The Cows, et.al."
"Haymaking, et.al."
"Horses Trotting, et.al."
"The Meeting, et.al."
"Reaping Scene, et.al."
"Resing Family, et.al."
"Rural Beggars, et.al."
"Scottish Shepherd, et.al."
"Sheep at Hay Rack, et.al."
"The Topers, et.al." ["Peasants Repast"]
"Watering Place, et.al."
"Woman with Basket, et.al." ["Shopping"]
"Woodcutters Lunch, et.al."

2. METROPOLITAN SCENERY SERIES (?)
BLUE AND WHITE TRANSFERWARE
SINGLE PATTERNS

CATEGORY	PATTERN
-	Bee
-	Birds & Nest
-	Broseley
-	Empress
-	Filigree
-	Flower Basket
-	Gothic
-	Grape & Bird
-	Haymaker
-	Japan
-	Jar
-	Lucano
-	New Fruit
-	New Rose
-	Nun
-	Rustic Bridge
-	Toy Plate
-	Wine Press

BEARDMORE & EDWARDS
BLUE AND WHITE TRANSFERWARE
SINGLE PATTERNS

CATEGORY	PATTERN
S	Claremont
M	Railway "Express"

FRANK BEARDMORE & CO.
FLOW BLUE

CATEGORY	PATTERN	
A	Bristol	
F	Dunkfield	
M/F	Pomona	Reg'd. 1910/No. 567811
S	Scenes of Quebec	
S	Stag Island	

BECK, BLAIR & CO.
BLUE AND WHITE TRANSFERWARE
SINGLE PATTERNS

CATEGORY	PATTERN
-	"Birds on Grass"

BEECH, HANCOCK & CO.
BLUE AND WHITE TRANSFERWARE
SINGLE PATTERNS

CATEGORY	PATTERN
O	Aurora
-	Eva

MULBERRY WARES

CATEGORY	PATTERN
F	Flora

BEECH & HANCOCK
BLUE AND WHITE TRANSFERWARE
SINGLE PATTERNS

CATEGORY	PATTERN
A	Aurora
A	Unique

FLOW BLUE

CATEGORY	PATTERN
O	Siam

MULBERRY WARES

CATEGORY	PATTERN
F	Fuchsia
F	Gothic
F	Jeddo

BEECH & LOWNDES
BLUE AND WHITE TRANSFERWARE
SINGLE PATTERNS

CATEGORY	PATTERN
-	"Birds & Fruit"

JAMES BEECH
BLUE AND WHITE TRANSFERWARE
SINGLE PATTERNS

CATEGORY	PATTERN
M	Alton
O	Aurora
O	Pekin
O	Perak

FLOW BLUE

CATEGORY	PATTERN
M/A	Princess

ISAAC & THOMAS BELL
BLUE AND WHITE TRANSFERWARE
SINGLE PATTERNS

CATEGORY	PATTERN
O	"Willow" Pattern

J. & M.P. BELL (CO.) & (LTD.)
BLUE AND WHITE TRANSFERWARE
SINGLE PATTERNS

CATEGORY	PATTERN	
S	Abergeldie	
F	Aboyne	
C	Achilles	
S	Agra	
-	Alhambra	(possibly Annfield and not Bell)
-	Amboina	
O	Amoy	
O	Antoinette	
-	Arcadia	
F	Asiatic Pheasants	
C	Athens	(only recorded in brown)
F	Autumn	
-	Ayam Jantam	(Cockerel)*
F	Ballater	
S	Balmoral	
-	Banda*	
-	Bangkok*	
-	Batavia	
F	Bavaria	
G	Bohemia	
-	Borneo*	
-	Braemar	
F	Brazil	
O	"Broseley"	
-	Buah and Nanas*	
-	Buah Buah*	
-	Burmania*	
-	Burns	
-	Burong Kupu*	
-	Burong Metak*	
-	Burong Supam*	
M	Butterfly	
F	Cadzow	
S	California	
G	Callcott, Sir Augustus Wall	
S	Canova	
F	Castile	
-	Celebes*	
O	Chinese Sports	
O	Chinese Vase	
O	Chinese Villa	
-	Classical Dancers	
F	Clematis	
S/H	Crystal Palace	
-	Damascus	
M	"Deer Stalking"	
-	Delhi	
S	Domestic	(questionable)
F	Dumblane	
-	Durian and Nanas*	
-	Eviction	
H	Exhibition	
-	Gauda	
G	"German Stag Hunt"	
F	Glasgow Exhibition (1901)	
F	Glenartney	
G	Going to Market	
O	Haarlem	
G	Harvest	
G	"Harvest Scene"	
G	Hawking	
-	Hawking in Olden Time	
-	Hawthorn Blossom	(not recorded in blue)
-	Ikan China*	(Chinese Fish)
-	Indian Cress	
F	Invercauld	
-	Ionia	Reg'd. Feb. 13, 1850/No.67413
G	"Italian Lakes"	(possible series)
-	Ivy Wreath	
O	Japan	
O	Jeddo	
M	Jenny Lind	
-	Johore*	
-	Kalantan*	
-	Kapal Basar*	
-	Keelin Hong*	
-	Kembang Bintang*	
-	Kwantung*	
-	Linnet	
M	Louise	
-	Makassar*	
-	Malacca	
-	Marine	
-	Malaga	
G	May Morn	
-	Mayflower	
O	Mikado	
-	Morning & Even	
-	Mossgiel	
M	Neuilly	
-	Oban	
-	Ochil	
-	Old Dutch	
S	Oriental	
-	Orleans	
S	Palestine	
G	Paraguay	
-	Parisian Sprig	
-	Peacock & Lilies*	
-	Pekin	
-	Reindeer	
-	Royal Conservatory	
-	Royal Palace	
F	Sandhurst	
-	Sarawak*	
-	Sardinia	
A	Sexagon	
F	Seymour	
-	Siam*	
G	Sporting Subjects	
M	"Stray Leaves"	
-	Sumatra*	
-	Swiss Cantons	
G	Swiss Subjects	
S	Swiss Water Mill	
P/O	Tamerlaine	
-	Tarlalu Bagus*	
F	Tokio	
M	Trojan	
C	Triumphal Car	
F	Tullibardine	
M	Vases	
F	Victoria Regia	
S	Warwick Vase	Reg'd. June 4, 1850/No. 69679
-	Watteau	
C	Webster Vase	
S	Wild Rose	
O	"Willow" Pattern	

For a complete listing of Transfer patterns, see *Scottish Pottery Society*, No. 24 [Fall '96] for an article by Henry Kelly, "List of Names, Transfer Pattern From The Glasgow Pottery For the Period 1841-1880.", pp. 6-12
*These patterns were made specifically for the Far East market, in countries such as Java, Borneo, Indonesia, etc.

HISTORIC STAFFORDSHIRE SERIES
AMERICAN
1. MISCELLANEOUS
Allegheny Scenery*
*See *Arman Historic Staffordshire*, First Supplement, p. 87.

FLOW BLUE

CATEGORY	PATTERN	
M	Alhambra	
A	Aurora	
A	Clifton	
S	Coburg	
M	Derby	
S	Gondola	
F	Indian Sprig	
O	Japan	
F	Jeddo	
M	Kensington	Reg'd. 1862
F	Kew Gardens	
C	Marine	
F	"Leaf Border"	
F	"Morning Glory"	[Vine Border]
M	Mushrooms	
F	Persian Sprigs	
F	Victoria Scroll	Reg'd. Mar. 10, 1853/No. 90253
F	Vine Border	["Morning Glory"]

MULBERRY WARES

CATEGORY	PATTERN	
F	Aden	
A	Anemone	Reg'd. Feb. 3, 1855/No. 99231
A	Aurora	
S	California	
O	"Ching"	
M	Fungus	
F	Golden Flower	
S	Gondola	
F	Indian Sprig	
O	Japan	

M	Kensington	Reg'd. 1862
C	Marine	
O	Ningpo	
O	Pekin	
F	Royal Conservatory	
F	Victoria Scroll	Reg'd. Mar. 10, 1853/No. 90253
F	Vine Border	["Morning Glory"]
S	Warwick Vase	

WHITE IRONSTONE
"Long Octagon"
N.B.: Bell always shortened "Ltd" to "Ld ".

BELL, COOK & CO.
BLUE AND WHITE TRANSFERWARE
SINGLE PATTERNS

CATEGORY	PATTERN
S	Wild Rose

BELLE VUE POTTERIES
BLUE AND WHITE TRANSFERWARE
SERIES
1. "BELLE VUE VIEWS SERIES"
Abbotsford, Sir Walter Scott' s
Blytheswood on the Clyde
Cambusnetham on the Clyde
Carstairs on the Clyde
Durham Cathedral
Guys Cliff, Warwickshire
Hinchinbrooke, Huntington
Lee House on the Clyde
Newstead Abbey
BLUE AND WHITE TRANSFERWARE
SINGLE PATTERNS

CATEGORY	PATTERN	
O	"Chinese Marine"	(possible series)
-	"Fruit Basket"	
O	"Garden Scenery"	
F	"Hydrangea"	
M	"Lightening"	
G	"Milkmaid"	
M	"Peacock Eye"	
F	"Pedestal & Bouquet"	
G	"The Proposal"	
G	"Rustic Cottage"	
G	"The Shepherd"	
-	"Swan"	
-	"Vermicelli"	
O	"Willow" Pattern	

Many of the above pattern listings and marks have been taken from Heather Lawrence's *"Yorkshire Pots & Potteries",* (David & Charles, London, 1974), by kind permission of the publisher.
HISTORIC STAFFORDSHIRE
AMERICAN & CANADIAN - SERIES
1. MISCELLANEOUS
Allegheny Scenery

J. BENNETT & CO.
FLOW BLUE

CATEGORY	PATTERN
F	Florence

T. & J. BEVINGTON (& CO.)
BLUE AND WHITE TRANSFERWARE
SINGLE PATTERNS

CATEGORY	PATTERN
S	"Castle" ["Castled Gateway"]
S	"Cows Crossing Stream"
H	"Monopteros"
S	"Remains of an Ancient Building Near "Firoz Shah's Cotilla, Delhi"
H	"Ship"
M	"Vine"

BIRKS BROTHERS & SEDDON
FLOW BLUE

CATEGORY	PATTERN
F	Bouquet

BISHOP & STONIER (LTD.)
BLUE AND WHITE TRANSFERWARE
SINGLE PATTERNS

CATEGORY	PATTERN
-	Bull

FLOW BLUE

CATEGORY	PATTERN
F	Anemone
O	Ceylon
S	Chelsea
F	Dove
A	Esdale
F	"Floral"
F	Gresham
F	Greville
P/O	India
F	Khan
F	Lancaster
A	Lawrence
P/M	Lincoln
F	Meadow
F	Pembroke
A	Persia
A	Pomeroy
F	Poppy
F	Rathbone
F	Torbay
A	Trent
S	Venice
F	Yuletide

WHITE IRONSTONE
"Golden Scroll"*
"Simple Square"
"Square Ridged"
"Wheat & Flowers" ["Daisy"]
TEA LEAF/COPPER LUSTRE
"Golden Scroll"*
"Simple Square"
"Square Ridged: Iona"
*First introduced by Powell & Bishop

BLACKHURST & TUNNICLIFFE
FLOW BLUE

CATEGORY	PATTERN
O	Delhi
F	Lanconia
F	Lily

EDWARD F. BODLEY & CO. (& SON)
BLUE AND WHITE TRANSFERWARE
SINGLE PATTERNS

CATEGORY	PATTERN	
S	Bonaparte	Reg'd. Aug. 17, 1868/No. 220828
S	"Roman Vista"	-

HISTORIC STAFFORDSHIRE
AMERICAN - SERIES
1. MISCELLANEOUS
Alabama*
**Larsen*, p. 239, No. 649 notes a possible registry year for 1862. However, according to the Registry records no date for Bodley exists for this year; the first recorded date is 1860. See Appendix E10 for a listing of Registry dates.

BODLEY & HARROLD
BLUE AND WHITE TRANSFERWARE
SINGLE PATTERNS

CATEGORY	PATTERN	
F	Asiatic Pheasants	
S	The Princess Alexander	Reg'd. Mar. 23, 1863/No. 160792

T. & R. BOOTE (LTD.) (& SON)
BLUE AND WHITE TRANSFERWARE
SINGLE PATTERNS

CATEGORY	PATTERN
O	Lahore
A	Tournay
S	Yosemite

FLOW BLUE

CATEGORY	PATTERN
O	Shapoo

MULBERRY WARES

CATEGORY	PATTERN
O	Shapoo

WHITE IRONSTONE

Atlantic Shape (A)*	Reg'd. Oct. 17, 1857/No.111643-4
Atlantic Shape (B)*	Reg'd. Apr. 22, 1858/No.113565
Atlantic Shape (C)*	Reg'd. Dec. 8, 1858/No.117336-8
Atlantic Shape (D)*	Reg'd. Mar. 29, 1859/No.119137
"Boote's Gothic" -	
"Boote's 1851 Octagon Shape" (Ch)	Reg'd. July 21, 1851/No. 79750-3 & Oct. 10, 1851/No. 80913
Chinese Shape	Reg'd. Dec. 8, 1858/No. 117336-8
Classic Shape ["Gothic"]	Reg'd. Jan. 8, 1868/No. 215674
Floral Shape ["Prairie Flower Shape"]**	Reg'd. Aug. 30, 1862/No.154221 & Jan. 30, 1863/No.159573
Garibaldi Shape	Reg'd. Nov.23, 1860/No. 136032
Grenade Shape	-
Mocho Shape	Reg'd. Oct. 17, 1863/No. 167374
New Grenade Shape	Reg'd. Dec. 8, 1858/No.117336-8
"One Large & Two Little Ribs"	-

Prairie Flower Shape ["Floral Shape"]**	Reg'd.Aug. 30, 1861/ No. 154221 & Jan. 30, 1863/159573
Roman Shape	-
"Scallop Shape" ["1851 Relish Dish"]	Reg'd. Sept.19, 1851/No. 80629-30
Senate Shape	Reg'd. Nov. 26, 1870/ No. 248114-6
"Starred Leaf"	-
Sydenham Shape (Ch)	Reg'd. Sept. 3, 1853/ No. 92340
Sydenham Shape	Reg'd. June 21, 1854/ No. 96085-6
Sydenham Shape	Reg'd. July 18, 1854/ No. 96296
Union Shape	Reg'd. Aug. 22, 1856/ No. 105955-9
"Winding Vine Shape"	Reg'd. Mar. 22, 1862/ No. 150152

**Ewins*, pp. 107-127 gives an insight into Boote's marketing in the US. *Peake*, Appendix 7, p. 182 notes a teapot design for T. & R. Boote titled Atlantic for March 29, 1859/No. 119137.
**Same pattern, but evidently registered with two distinct names.
N.B.: Refer to *Wetherbee's White Ironstone*, pp. 50-56

BOOTH & MEIGH
BLUE & WHITE TRANSFERWARE
SINGLE PATTERNS

CATEGORY	PATTERN
S	Rhine

THOMAS BOOTH & CO.
BLUE AND WHITE TRANSFERWARE
SINGLE PATTERNS

CATEGORY	PATTERN	
O	Madras	Reg'd. Oct. 14, 1871/No.256687

FLOW BLUE

CATEGORY	PATTERN
-	Hoya
F	Victor

THOMAS BOOTH & SON
BLUE AND WHITE TRANSFERWARE
SINGLE PATTERNS

CATEGORY	PATTERN	
O	Madras	(Has not been confirmed)

THOMAS G. BOOTH
BLUE AND WHITE TRANSFERWARE
SINGLE PATTERNS

CATEGORY	PATTERN	
A	Fans	
M/Z	Madras	(Has not been confirmed)

T.G. & F. BOOTH
BLUE AND WHITE TRANSFERWARE
SINGLE PATTERNS

CATEGORY	PATTERN
F	Indian Ornament
F	May Blossom

FLOW BLUE

CATEGORY	PATTERN
M	"Strawberry"

BOOTHS (LTD.)
BLUE AND WHITE TRANSFERWARE
SINGLE PATTERNS

CATEGORY	PATTERN
S	British Scenery
F	Hawthorne
P/F	Pompadour, The
O	"Willow" Pattern

FLOW BLUE

CATEGORY	PATTERN	
S	Avon (att.)	
-	Canterbury	
-	Cedric	
A	Chippendale	
F	El Brau	
F	Flanders	
A	Indian Ornament	
F	Princess	Reg'd. 1891/No. 183183
F	Rosa	
-	Simplex	

BOULTON, MACHIN & TENNANT
FLOW BLUE

CATEGORY	PATTERN
M	Herbs
F	Mallow

BOURNE & LEIGH (LTD.)
FLOW BLUE

CATEGORY	PATTERN	
F	Aberdeen	
F	Azalea	Reg'd. 1897/No. 306084
O	Chinese	
M	Delph	
F	Deva	
M/F	Erie	
F	Florentine	
F	Garland	
F	Kew	
F	Kioto	
F	Loraine	
F	Marguerite	
A	Melrose	
F	Ophir	
M	Regal	
F	Rose	
-	Selwyn	

BOURNE, BAKER & BOURNE
BLUE AND WHITE TRANSFERWARE
SINGLE PATTERNS

CATEGORY	PATTERN
-	American Villa
G	British Castle
F	Jessamine
S	"River Bridge & Boat Scene, et.al."
S	Wild Rose

CHARLES BOURNE
BLUE AND WHITE TRANSFERWARE
SINGLE PATTERNS

CATEGORY	PATTERN
S	British Views (possible series)
S	Lucano Pattern
O	"Willow" Pattern (old)
Z	Zebra Pattern

N.B.: Refer to Coysh, Vol. 2, p. 32

EDWARD BOURNE
BLUE AND WHITE TRANSFERWARE
SINGLE PATTERNS

CATEGORY	PATTERN
-	Abbey
-	Ship
-	"Willow" Pattern

JOSEPH BOURNE (& SON)(LTD.)*
WHITE IRONSTONE
**Wetherbee, White Ironstone*, p. 48 notes a mark on White Ironstone for the above potter with the additional marking "IRONSTONE/CHINA".

BOURNE, NIXON & CO.
HISTORIC STAFFORDSHIRE SERIES
AMERICAN
1. MISCELLANEOUS
Primitive Methodist Preachers, 1830*
*See *Larsen*, p. 247, No. 698.

WILLIAM BOURNE
BLUE AND WHITE TRANSFERWARE (LONGTON)
SINGLE PATTERNS

CATEGORY	PATTERN
O	Lasso

MULBERRY WARES (FENTON)

CATEGORY	PATTERN
F	May-Flower
G	Lasso

WILLIAM BOURNE & CO.
BLUE AND WHITE TRANSFERWARE
SINGLE PATTERNS

CATEGORY	PATTERN
O	"Willow" Pattern

BOVEY POTTERY CO. LTD.
FLOW BLUE

CATEGORY	PATTERN	
M/A	Stella	Patented 1918

BOVEY TRACY POTTERY COMPANY
BLUE AND WHITE TRANSFERWARE
SINGLE PATTERNS

CATEGORY	PATTERN
M/F	Asiatic Pheasants
O	Chinese Pagoda
G	The Gem
S	Wild Rose

GEORGE FREDERICK BOWERS (& CO.)
BLUE AND WHITE TRANSFERWARE

SINGLE PATTERNS

CATEGORY	PATTERN
-	Cable
-	Clermont
F	"Gazunda"*
-	Pekin
-	Picciola
P/O	Poonah
-	Rubella
P/O	Scinde
-	Vintage

*See *FOB Bulletin* No. 95, Spring 1997, p. 11.

FLOW BLUE

CATEGORY	PATTERN
O	"Bird & Font"

WHITE IRONSTONE

Baltic Shape*

Mobile Shape** Reg'd. Apr. 18, 1856/No. 104393

*Originally registered by D. Chetwynd, Oct. 25, 1855/No. 102325. This same shape was used by J. Meir and G. Woolliscroft. Refer to *Wetherbee, White Ironstone,* p. 57, fig.8-21.

**Registered by Ralph Scragg

SAMUEL BOYLE (& SONS)

BLUE AND WHITE TRANSFERWARE

SINGLE PATTERNS

CATEGORY	PATTERN
S	Circassia

ZACHARIAH BOYLE (& CO.)(& SON(S)

BLUE AND WHITE TRANSFERWARE

SINGLE PATTERNS

CATEGORY	PATTERN
G	"Blue Italian"
O	"Canton Vase"
M	Clarence Star

BRADLEY & CO.

BLUE AND WHITE TRANSFERWARE

SINGLE PATTERNS

CATEGORY	PATTERN
-	"Carnations"
-	"Chinoiserie Bridges"
-	"Mandarin"
-	"Mythological Sea Scape"
-	"Pastoral"
-	"Pearl River House" ["Trench Mortar"]
-	"Two Figures"
-	"Two Temples"
O	"Violin"

BRAMELD & CO.

BLUE AND WHITE TRANSFERWARE

SERIES

1. DON QUIXOTE "SERIES"

"Don Quixote & Sancho Panza"

"Don Quixote & the Shepherdess"

"Peasant Girl Mistaken"

"Tilting at Windmills"

BLUE AND WHITE TRANSFERWARE

SINGLE PATTERNS

CATEGORY	PATTERN
-	"Bo Peep"
F	"Brameld Roses"
G	"Boys Fishing" ["Fishing Scene"]
L	Burns Cotter
S	"Castle of Rochefort, South France"
-	"Fisher Boys"
S	Floral Sketches
F	Flower Groups
H	Forfarshire
-	"Girl With a Bird"
O	India ["Twisted Tree"]
-	"Indian Flowers"
F	"Llandig's Blackberry"
J/M	"Lord's Prayer"
S	Masaniello
G	Packhorses (2)
-	Paris Stripe
F	Parroquet
G	"Picking Apples" ["Apple Gatherers"]
G	"The Returning Woodman" ["Pheasant"]
-	"Rocking Horse"
-	"Rose Jar"
-	"Shepherd Pattern"
F	"Sweet Peas"
O	"Willow" Pattern

BRIDGETT & BATES

FLOW BLUE

CATEGORY	PATTERN	
F	Martha	Reg'd. 1896/No. 288120

BRIDGWOOD & CLARKE

WHITE IRONSTONE

"Alternate Loops"

"Draped Leaf"

"Grape Wreath"

"Leaf Fan"

SAMPSON BRIDGWOOD (& SON)(LTD.)

BLUE AND WHITE TRANSFERWARE

SINGLE PATTERNS

CATEGORY	PATTERN
Z	"Bird Nest"
O	"Chinamen Hawking"
F	"Ivy"

FLOW BLUE

CATEGORY	PATTERN
S	Brig O' Doon
A	"Castle Shield"
M	Crawford "Ranges"
F	Double Poppy
A	"Fleur de Lis"
-	Luzerne
F	Portland
A	"Surreal"
-	Tycoon
F	Tyne

MULBERRY WARES

CATEGORY	PATTERN
F	Kew

WHITE IRONSTONE

"(The) Box"

"Full Ribbed"*

"Hexagon Strap"

Napier Shape

"Scroll Border"

TEA LEAF/COPPER LUSTRE

"Full Ribbed"*

*Not to be confused with "Full Ribbed" by J.W. Pankhurst.

JOHN BRINDLEY & CO.

BLUE AND WHITE TRANSFERWARE

SINGLE PATTERNS

CATEGORY	PATTERN
S	"Wild Rose"

BRITANNIA POTTERY CO. LTD.

BLUE AND WHITE TRANSFERWARE

SINGLE PATTERNS

CATEGORY	PATTERN
-	A Bit of Devon
F	Daisy
-	Dragon
-	Lomond
-	Moyen
O	Ming
F	Peony
F	Pheasant [Asiatic Pheasants]
F	Rosebud
S	Rural England
F	Wild Rose
O	"Willow" Pattern

BRITISH ANCHOR POTTERY CO., LTD.

BLUE AND WHITE TRANSFERWARE

SINGLE PATTERNS

CATEGORY	PATTERN
S	Castle
O	Japan

FLOW BLUE

CATEGORY	PATTERN
M	Chelsea
M	"Onion"
O	Temple
S	Watteau

BROADHURST & GREEN

FLOW BLUE

CATEGORY	PATTERN
O	Font

BROUGHAM & MAYER
BLUE AND WHITE TRANSFERWARE
SINGLE PATTERNS

CATEGORY	PATTERN
-	Archipelago
F	Hybla

FLOW BLUE

CATEGORY	PATTERN
F	Hybla

MULBERRY WARES

CATEGORY	PATTERN
S	Tavoy*

*Same pattern as Tavoy by Thomas Walker

WHITE IRONSTONE

Baltimore Shape	-
"Grape Octagon"	-
Virginia Shape	Reg'd. Jan. 15, 1855/No. 99051

BROWN & STEVENTON, LTD.
FLOW BLUE

CATEGORY	PATTERN	
F	Pansey	Reg'd. 1903/No. 414460

BROWN WESTHEAD, MOORE & CO.
BLUE AND WHITE TRANSFERWARE
SINGLE PATTERNS

CATEGORY	PATTERN
-	Laurelia
F	Pansy
-	Pro Deo, Rege Et Patria
-	Rhine
-	Teutonic
-	Tournay

FLOW BLUE

CATEGORY	PATTERN	
S	Breadalebane	-
O	Byzantium	-
M/A	Burlington*	Reg'd. Dec. 4, 1845/No. 31670-3
F	Chantrey	-
A	Crystal	Reg'd. 1894/No. 227133
-	Entwined Ribbon	-
M	Fable	-
M/Z	France	Reg'd. 1868
M	Indian Empress	-
O	Jeddo	-
-	Kew	-
O	Mandalay	-
-	Mauritas	-
O	Medallion	-
F	Messina	-
F	Mow Cop	Reg'd. 1887/No. 70235
M/A	Par	Reg'd. 1879
A	Plymouth	Reg'd 1899/No. 332002
M/F	Pomona	-
G	"Romeo"	-
F	Rose & Ivy	Reg'd. 1870
O	Satsuma	-
M/F	Springtime	Reg'd. 1891/No. 184291
S	Sylvan	-
-	Teutonic	-
F	Trentham	-
O	Tripod	-
M/F	Volante	Dated 1882
M/A	York	Reg'd. 1892/No. 199522

*Registered by John Ridgway

WILLIAM BROWNFIELD (& SON(S)
BLUE AND WHITE TRANSFERWARE
SINGLE PATTERNS

CATEGORY	PATTERN
A	Berne
S	Inkermann
O	Madras
S	Maltese
S	Ravenna
S	Wild Rose

FLOW BLUE

CATEGORY	PATTERN	
F	Anemone	-
M/F	Bouquet	Dated 1851
O	"Chinese Key & Basket"	-
M	Ciris	-
G	Field Sports	-
M	Ida	-
S	Medieval	-
Z	Sylvania	Reg'd. June 10, 1875/No. 292005
O	Suez	-
O	Tycoon	-
S	Watteau	Reg'd. 1900/No. 355592
O	Windsor Wreath	-
G	Woodland	-

MULBERRY WARES

CATEGORY	PATTERN	
M	Cyprus	-
F	"Flower Sprig"	Reg'd. Mar. 14, 1862/No. 149957-8

BROWNFIELDS GUILD POTTERY SOCIETY, LTD. and BROWNFIELDS POTTERY LTD.
FLOW BLUE

CATEGORY	PATTERN	
A	Delft	Reg'd. 1893/No. 210792
M	Devon	
F	Dunkfield	
S	"Grecian Statue"	
S	Watteau	

BROWNHILLS POTTERY CO.
BLUE AND WHITE TRANSFERWARE
SINGLE PATTERNS

CATEGORY	PATTERN
M	Irene
O	Kioto
F	Mercia

BULLOCK, A. & CO.
BLUE AND WHITE TRANSFERWARE
SINGLE PATTERNS

CATEGORY	PATTERN
P/O	Poonah

BURGESS & GODDARD
(or Goddard & Burgess)
WHITE IRONSTONE

"Bow & Tassel"	Dated 1878*	
"Plain"		-
"Plain Round"	-	
"Wheat"		-

*Manufactured with impressed or printed potting dates, that are not to be confused with registry dates.

BURGESS & LEIGH (LTD.)
BLUE AND WHITE TRANSFERWARE
SINGLE PATTERNS

CATEGORY	PATTERN	
S	Barbarini Vase	Reg'd. Jan. 17, 1866/No. 194537
F	"Blue Rose Border"	
F	Clematis	
M	Farmers Arms (The)	
O	"Japy Posies"	
S	Norman	

FLOW BLUE

CATEGORY	PATTERN	
-	Alexandra	-
F	Apsley Plant	-
F	Athol	Reg'd. 1898/No. 324171
F	Briar	Reg'd. 1886/No. 443008
A	Burleigh	Reg'd. 1903/No. 413995
P/O	Celeste	-
F	Cranesbill	-
F	Cranston	Reg'd. 1892/No. 191212
F	Daisy	Reg'd. 1896/No. 272768
F	Derby	-
A	Dresden	Reg'd. 1896/No. 272767
F	Dresden Flowers	-
-	Erie	-
-	Florentine	-
A	Florette	-
F	Florian	Reg'd 1909
F	Florida	-
F	Garland	-
A	Haarlem	Reg'd. 1905/No. 457960
-	Halford	-
-	Halia	-
F	Italia	Reg'd. 1905/No. 451959
F	Ivy	-
A	Leicester	Reg'd. 1900/No. 364190
A	Leighton	-
F	Lilac	-
F	Mabelle	Reg'd. 1896/No. 274526
A	Milford	Reg'd. 1910/No. 565728
O	Nankin	-
F	Napoli	Reg'd. 1907
A	Newlyn	Reg'd. 1914/No. 640182
P/O	Nizan (Tongue Dish)	-
S	Non Pareil	-
-	Premier	-

A	Raleigh	Reg'd. 1902/No. 393237
M/A	Richmond	Reg'd. 1904/No. 438212
-	Rosette	-
A	Selwyn	-
A/F	Stratford	-
F	Sweetbrier	-
F	Venice	-
F	Vermont	Reg'd. 1895/No. 250791
F	Windflower	Reg'd. 1895/No. 249191

HENRY BURGESS
WHITE IRONSTONE

"Barred Wreath"	-
"Cable & Ring"	-
"Chrysanthemum Shape"	Reg'd. 1886
"Grape Cluster with Chain"	-
"Hyacinth Shape"	-
"Lily Shape"* ("Calla Lily")	-
"Square Ridged"	-

*This is an 1860's shape. Also see Lily Shape by W. & E. Corn as illustrated in Wetherbee, *White Ironstone, A Collector's Guide*, pp. 123-124.

TEA LEAF/COPPER LUSTRE

"Cable Shape"	-
"Chrysanthemum Shape"	Reg'd. 1886
"Embroidered Chelsea Shape"	Reg'd. 1884
"Grenade Shape"	-
"Plain Round"	-
Senate Shape	-
"Simple Square: Pagoda"	-
"Square Ridged Shape: Beaded Handle Shape"	Reg'd. 1896

JOSEPH BURN & CO.
BLUE AND WHITE TRANSFERWARE
SINGLE PATTERNS

CATEGORY	PATTERN
S	Wild Rose
O	"Willow" Pattern

SAMUEL & JOHN BURTON
BLUE AND WHITE TRANSFERWARE
SINGLE PATTERNS

CATEGORY	PATTERN
S	Domestic Scenery
P/O	Palestine
O	"Willow" Pattern

WILLIAM & JAMES BUTTERFIELD
BLUE AND WHITE TRANSFERWARE
SINGLE PATTERNS

CATEGORY	PATTERN
S	Alma

CALEDONIAN POTTERY
BLUE AND WHITE TRANSFERWARE
SINGLE PATTERNS

CATEGORY	PATTERN
-	"Castle" Pattern (att.)
-	"Lugano" (att.)

CAMBRIAN POTTERY
BLUE AND WHITE TRANSFERWARE
SINGLE PATTERNS

CATEGORY	PATTERN
S	"Bridge at Lucano"
O	"Cambrian Border"
O	"Cambrian Palm" ["Chinoiserie Palm"]
Z	"Cheetah"
O	"Chinese Scene After Pillemont"
F	"Chrysanthemum"
-	"Cockle & Whelk"
G	"Cow Herd"
S	"Cows Crossing Stream Pattern"
O	"Dancing Fisherman"
O	"Elephant Pattern"
O	"Elephant & Howdah"
G	"The Ladies of Langollen"*
S	"Long Bridge"
O	"Precarious Chinaman"
S	"Pulteney Bridge at Bath"
M	"St. Michael's Mount"
S	Scene of Tintern (?) Abbey**

*See *P. Williams, Staffordshire*, Vol. III, pp. 149-151.
**See *FOB Bulletin*, No. 95, Spring 1997, p. 8.

FLOW BLUE

CATEGORY	PATTERN
F	"Bell" or "Bluebell"
M	Lazuli
F	"Shell & Flower"
O	Whampoa

For additional patterns refer to *Pugh's Welsh Pottery* and Hallesy's *Glamorgan Pottery*

CAMPBELLFIELD POTTERY CO. (LTD.)
FLOW BLUE

CATEGORY	PATTERN
F	Chrysanthemum

THOMAS & JOHN CAREY
(or John Carey & Sons)
BLUE AND WHITE TRANSFERWARE
SERIES
1. "CATHEDRAL SERIES"
Bath & Bristol Cathedrals
Chichester Cathedral
Christchurch, Oxford*
Litchfield Cathedral
St. Paul's Cathedral
York Cathedral
See *FOB*, No. 98, Winter 1997/98, p. 10
2. "DOMESTIC CATTLE SERIES"*
"Donkeys & Campfire"
"Donkeys & Tent"
"Five Sheet in Foreground"
"Goats & Lamb"
"Grazing Deer"
"Horses & Top Hat"
"Lying Bull"
"Man Filling Trough"
"Shepherd & Dog with Sheep"
"White Rabbits" (or Two Rabbits)
*Refer to *Coysh*, Vol. I, p. 111 and Vol. 2, p. 71; and *True Blue*, p. 86, No. 2.
3. "INDIAN TEMPLES SERIES"
Temple & Castle
Temple & Ox Cart
Temple & Sailboats
4. "IRISH VIEWS SERIES"
Black Rock Castle, Near Cork
Carrickfergus Castle, and Town
The Lower Lake of Killarney
The Upper Lake of Killarney
5. "TITLED SEATS SERIES"
Alton Abbey, Earl of Shrewsbury Seat
Belvoir Castle, Leicestershire, Duke of Rutland Seat
Castle Frede, Cork Ireland, Lord Carbery's Seat
Dunraven Castle, Honorable Wm. Wyndham Quinn's Seat
Eaton Hall, Cheshire, Earl Grosvenor's Seat
Hollywell Cottage, Ireland, Lord Tara's Seat
Inverary Castle, Duke of Argyle's Seat (sic.)
Kilruddery Hall, Wicklow, Earl of Meath's Seat
Luton Hoo, Bedfordshire, Marquis of Bute's Seat
Plas-Newydd, Wales, Marquess of Anglesey's Seat
Sandon Hall, Earl of Harrowby's Seat
Shugborough Hall, Staffordshire, Viscount Anson's Seat
Woburn Abbey, Duke of Bedford's Seat
6. UNIDENTIFIED SERIES
Large Country House on Hills (2 views)
BLUE AND WHITE TRANSFERWARE
SINGLE PATTERNS

CATEGORY	PATTERN
S	"Ancient Rome"
F	Asiatic Scenery
O	"Bridge and Pagoda"
-	"Cottar's Saturday Night"
C	Grecian Statue*
M	"Grazing Rabbits"
O	Indian Temples (possible series)
G	Lady of the Lake**

*Refer to *Peake, William Brownfield*, pp. 89 & 91, wherein he notes a Chinoiserie pattern titled Grecian Statue.
**See *P. Williams, Staffordshire*, Vol. III, pp. 152-153

CARLTON WARE LTD.
FLOW BLUE

CATEGORY	PATTERN
F	Arvista

CARR & PATTON
BLUE AND WHITE TRANSFERWARE
SINGLE PATTERNS

CATEGORY	PATTERN
O	"Willow" Pattern

JOHN CARR (& CO.) (& SON(S))
BLUE AND WHITE TRANSFERWARE
SINGLE PATTERNS

CATEGORY	PATTERN
F	Asiatic Pheasants
-	Dacca (2) (possible series)
S	Gem
-	London
S	Park Scenery
A	"Persian Lion"
O	Tonquin Ware
O	"Willow" Pattern

FLOW BLUE

CATEGORY	PATTERN
O	Tonquin

CARTWRIGHT & EDWARDS (LTD.)
BLUE AND WHITE TRANSFERWARE
SINGLE PATTERNS

CATEGORY	PATTERN
F	Asiatic Pheasants
J/Z	Tiger Hunt

FLOW BLUE

CATEGORY	PATTERN
S	Grange
F	Rosa

CAULDON, LTD.
BLUE AND WHITE TRANSFERWARE
SINGLE PATTERNS

CATEGORY	PATTERN
C	Arcadian Chariots (Reissue)
F	"Floral"
P/F	"Floral Paradise"
P/F	"Peony"
C	"Roman Chariot
S	Tiber

FLOW BLUE

CATEGORY	PATTERN	
F	Bentick	
M/A	Burlington* (Reissue)	Reg'd. Dec. 4, 1845/No. 31670-3
O	Byzantium	
F	Candia	
A	Crystal	
M/A	Corinthian Flute	
O	"Dragon"	
S	"Fish Plate II"	
F	Delftland**	
O	"Dragon"	
F	"Herb Garden"	
-	Hibiscus	
-	Indian	
F	Iris	
O	Japan	
F	Messina	
O	Nankin	
A	Pagoda	
-	Peking Star**	Reg'd. Dec. 4, 1845 (John Ridgway)
A	Plymouth	
F	Romeo	
F	Ruskin	
-	Siam	
-	Teutonic	
S/A	"Turkey" (Wild)	
F	York	Impressed Reg. No. 183243 or 8/1891 and Printed Reg. No. 199552/1892

*Registered by John Ridgway, and continued by Brown, Westhead, Moore & Co.
** Refer to *P. Williams, Flow Blue, Vol.* 2, p. 58

CERAMIC ART CO. LTD.
FLOW BLUE

CATEGORY	PATTERN	
F	Lynton	Reg'd. 1896/No. 276958

CERAMIC ART CO. (1905) LTD.
FLOW BLUE

CATEGORY	PATTERN	
A	Empire	Reg'd. 1906/No. 473633

EDWARD CHALLINOR
BLUE AND WHITE TRANSFERWARE
SERIES
1. "ORIENTAL SPORTS SERIES"
"Battle Between a Buffalo and a Tiger"
"Chase After a Wolf"
"The Dead Hog"
"Death of the Bear"
"Decoy Elephants Leaving the Male Fastened to a Tree"
"Dooreahs Leading Out Dogs" ("Dooreahs or Dog Keepers Leading Out Dogs")
"Driving a Bear Out of Sugar Canes"
"Groom Leading Out" ("Syces or Grooms Leading Out Horses")
"(The) Hog at Bay"
"The Hog Deer at Bay"
"Hog Hunters Meeting by Surprise a Tiger and Her Cubs"
"Hounds Chasing a Hare"
"Hunting a Buffalo" ("Hunting an Old Buffalo")
"Hunting a Civet Cat" ("Hunting a Kuttauss or Civet Cat")
"Hunting a Hog Deer"
"Shooting at the Edge of a Jungle"
"Shooting a Leopard in a Tree"
BLUE AND WHITE TRANSFERWARE
SINGLE PATTERNS

CATEGORY	PATTERN	
S	Ancona*	
S	Ardenne(s)	
F	Canella	
S	Corinthia	
S	Corsica	
M/O	Florilla	
G	Font	
S	Italian	
S	Lozere	
G	Maddle Jenny Lind	
O	Nanking (possible series)	
F	Neva	
S	Panama	
S	Parma**	
S	Pastoral	
M/F	Princess Feather	
S	Priory	
F	Rosetta	
S	Sciro	Reg'd. Dec. 29, 1846/No. 37903
S	Union	
M	Vase	
S	Verona	

See *P. Williams, Staffordshire*, Vol. III, pp. 48-49.
***P. Williams, Staffordshire* Vol. II, p. 617 notes pattern was reproduced by J. Ridgway & Co., but named Belvedere.

EDWARD CHALLINOR
FLOW BLUE

CATEGORY	PATTERN	
O	Cabul*	Reg'd. Aug. 26, 1847/No. 45367
O	Calcutta	
M/F	Dahlia	
S	Lozere	
O	Pelew	
O	Puck	
O	Rock	
M/F	Shell	

MULBERRY WARES

CATEGORY	PATTERN	
O	Cabul*	Reg'd. Aug. 26, 1847/No. 45367
O	Calcutta	-
F	Dresden	-
F	Neva	-
O	Pelew	-
F	Rose*	Reg'd. Aug. 26, 1847/No. 45367

*Note: There seems to be somewhat of a puzzle with this registration date. Godden notes, in a letter to me dated 9/19/94, that the Aug. 26th registration is in the name of J. Edwards. Neither of us can reconcile why Challinor has this registration date. A possibility is that he did the work but never registered (or pulled his registry forms). Further, Challinor is not recorded in Cushion for this date - only Edwards is. Additionally, Edwards is noted as being in Burslem when, in fact, he was in Tunstall.
WHITE IRONSTONE
"Little Pear"*
*This is a relish dish and is not to be confused with the "Little Pear" Shape registered May 7, 1853/No. 91121-4 by John Alcock.

E. CHALLINOR & CO.
BLUE AND WHITE TRANSFERWARE
SINGLE PATTERNS

CATEGORY	PATTERN	
F	Amula	
F	Anthos	
S	Dora	Reg'd. July 28, 1856/No. 105492
S	Egina	
S	Panama	
S	Priory	

FLOW BLUE

CATEGORY	PATTERN
O	Kin Shan

E. CHALLINOR & CO.
MULBERRY WARES

S	Coburg
S	Egina

O	Kin Shan
S	Lozere
S	Panama
F	"Rose"

WHITE IRONSTONE
"Grape Octagon"
"Panelled Octagon"

E. & C. CHALLINOR
BLUE AND WHITE TRANSFERWARE
SINGLE PATTERNS

CATEGORY	PATTERN
M	Gordon
S	Woldens

WHITE IRONSTONE
"Cable & Ring"
Columbia Shape
"Forget-Me-Not"
"Grape Octagon"
"Little Pear"
"Loop & Dot"
"Nosegay"
"Panelled Decagon"
"True Scallop"
Vintage Shape ["Grape & Medallion"]
"Wheat"
TEA LEAF/COPPER LUSTRE
"Cable Shape"
"Plain Round Bulbous"
"Victorian Beauty"

S. & J. CHAPPELL
BLUE AND WHITE TRANSFERWARE
SINGLE PATTERNS

CATEGORY	PATTERN
-	Eton College

CHESWORTH & ROBINSON
BLUE AND WHITE TRANSFERWARE
SERIES
1. "TERNI SERIES"
The Guitar
The Offering
A Romantic District of Italy
The Social Party
BLUE AND WHITE TRANSFERWARE
SINGLE PATTERNS

CATEGORY	PATTERN
C	"Grecian Figures"
S	"Parkland Scenery"
F	Parisian Basket

JONATHAN LOWE CHETHAM
BLUE AND WHITE TRANSFERWARE
SINGLE PATTERNS

CATEGORY	PATTERN
-	Festoon
F	Nosegay
-	Swiss

CHETHAM & (SON)
BLUE AND WHITE TRANSFERWARE
SINGLE PATTERNS

CATEGORY	PATTERN
F	Chetham

CHETHAM & ROBINSON
BLUE AND WHITE TRANSFERWARE
SINGLE PATTERNS

CATEGORY	PATTERN
-	"Horseman, Woman & Child"

CHETHAM & WOOLLEY
BLUE AND WHITE TRANSFERWARE
SINGLE PATTERNS

CATEGORY	PATTERN
-	"Fruit"
O	"Two Men on Bridge" ["Two Part Willow"]

SMITH CHILD
BLUE AND WHITE TRANSFERWARE
SINGLE PATTERNS

CATEGORY	PATTERN
F	Quails

CHILD & CLIVE
BLUE AND WHITE TRANSFERWARE
SINGLE PATTERNS

CATEGORY	PATTERN
F	Quails

EDWARD CLARKE (& CO.)
FLOW BLUE

CATEGORY	PATTERN
F	Lucania (att.)

WHITE IRONSTONE
"Winterberry"

JOSEPH CLEMENTSON
BLUE AND WHITE TRANSFERWARE
SERIES
1. CLASSICAL ANTIQUITIES SERIES*
Reg'd. Mar. 13, 1849/No. 58874
"Diomed Casting His Spear Against Mars"
"Homer Invoking the Muses"
"Juno's Command"
"Nestor's Sacrifice"
"Penelope Carrying the Bow to the Suitors"
"Phemius Singing to the Suitors"
"Ulysses at the Table of Circe"
"Ulysses Following the Car of Nausicaa"
"Ulysses Weeps at the Song of Demodocus"
BLUE AND WHITE TRANSFERWARE
SINGLE PATTERNS

CATEGORY	PATTERN	
C	Antique Vases	-
S	British Star	-
O	Chusan	-
C	Claremont*	Reg'd. June 30, 1856/No. 105258
-	Eastern Sketches	-
M	Forest	-
M	Hop Border	-
S	Leipsic	-
S	Loretto**	Reg'd. Jan. 7, 1846/No. 32698
S	Lucerne	Reg'd. Dec. 2, 1842/No. 2599-00
S	Palermo	-
O	Pekin Sketches	-
S	"Ruins"	-
C	Rustic Scenery	Reg'd. Dec. 2, 1842/No. 2599-00
O	Siam	Reg'd. Apr. 8, 1850/No. 68720
C	Sydenham	-
-	Taiwan	-
S	Tessino**	Reg'd. Jan. 7, 1846/No. 32698
F	"Trumpet Vine"	-
S	Udina	-
H	Viscount Clive Attaining His Majority, Nov. 1839	
S	Wild Rose	-

*Claremont reissued 1892, No. 19886
**Both patterns share the same center scene. Refer to *Snyder, Romantic Staffordshire*, p. 64.

FLOW BLUE

CATEGORY	PATTERN
M	"Aster & Grapeshot"
O	Chusan
O	Hyson
S	Leipsic
S	Palermo
F/O	Sylvia
-	Taiwan
O	Tillenberg

N.B: P. Williams, *Staffordshire* Vol. 1 & 2, notes three additional patterns, "Chili", "Holly" and "Persian Rose" with the marking "M.T. & Co." as possibly made by Joseph Clementson (also see pattern "Delhi" in Mulberry Wares).
MULBERRY WARES

CATEGORY	PATTERN	
F	Citron	
C	Classical Antiquities*	Reg'd. Mar. 13, 1849/No. 58874
O	Corea	
O	Delhi**	
M	Fossils	
F	Grape	
C	"Hector & Paris"*	
O	Hyson	
S	Leipsic	
P/F	Oak & Ivy	
P/F	Parisian Group	
C	"Phemius Singing to the Suitors"*	
O/F	Sylvia	
S	Sydenham	
O	Tillenberg	
P/F	Woodbine	

*These are all part of the "Classical Antiquities Series". Other patterns may exist. Refer to Blue & White Transferware series.
**Delhi pattern has been noted with the marking of importer "M.T. & CO."

WHITE IRONSTONE

Augusta Shape	-
"Chinese Shape"	-

Citron Shape	Reg'd. Aug. 21, 1863/No. 165317
"Classic Gothic"	-
Columbia Shape	-
Dallas Shape	-
"Grape Octagon"	-
Hill Shape	Reg'd. Oct. 19, 1860/No. 134555-7
Lafayette Shape	-
"Nautilus Shape" ["Dolphin Shape"]	-
New York Shape* (Ch)	Reg'd. Dec. 8, 1858/ No. 117339 (and 1861, 1862)
"Panelled Grape"	-
Prairie Shape	Reg'd. Nov. 15, 1861/ No. 146352-4 (and 1862)
"Sevres Shape"	-
Sydenham Shape	-

*Printed garter mark with name Chicago Shape noted on New York Shape is illustrated in *White Ironstone Notes*, Vol. 3, No. 4, Spring 1997, p. 11.

N.B.: Many shapes were continued on by Clementson Bros. (see Clementson Bros.)

TEA LEAF/COPPER LUSTRE

Augusta Shape	-
Chinese Shape	-
"Classic Gothic"	-
Columbia Shape	-
Dallas Shape	-
"Full Paneled Gothic"	-
"Grape Octagon"	-
Hill Shape ["Medallion Scroll"]	Reg'd. Oct. 19, 1860/ No. 134555-7
"Nautilus"	-
New York Shape (Ch)	Reg'd. Dec. 8, 1858/ No. 117339 (and 1861, 1862)
"Panelled Grape"	-
Prairie Shape (Ch)	Reg'd. Nov. 15, 1861/ No. 146352-4

CLEMENTSON BROS. (LTD.)

BLUE AND WHITE TRANSFERWARE

SINGLE PATTERNS

CATEGORY	PATTERN	
C	Claremont	Reissued 1892/No. 19856
-	Delft	-
S	Tillenberg	
S	Vienna	

FLOW BLUE

CATEGORY	PATTERN
F	Iris
F	Oriel
M	Saxon

WHITE IRONSTONE

"Balanced Vine Shape"(Ch)	Reg'd. June 11, 1867/ No. 208819
Canada Shape*	Reg'd. Mar. 20, 1877/ No. 308650-2
Citron Shape**	Reg'd. Aug. 21, 1863/ No. 165317
"Heavy Square Shape"	Reg'd. 1885
Hill Shape**	Reg'd. Oct. 19, 1860/ No. 134555-7
New York Shape (Ch)**	Reg'd. Dec. 8, 1858/ No. 117339 (and 1861, 1862)
"Plain Uplift"	-
Prairie Shape** (Ch)	Reg'd. Nov. 15, 1861/ No. 146352-4
"Wheat & Hops"	-

TEA LEAF/COPPER LUSTRE

"Balanced Vine Shape" (Ch)	Reg'd. Jun. 11, 1867/ No. 208819
"Beaded Band" ["Plain Round"]	-
"Elegance Shape"	Reg'd. 1884
"Gothic IV: Many Panelled"	-
"Grape Vine"	-
"Heavy Square Shape"	Reg'd. 1885
"Hill Shape"**	Reg'd. Oct. 19, 1860/ No. 134555-7
New York Shape**	Reg'd. Dec. 8, 1858/ No. 117339 (and 1861, 1862)
Prairie Shape**	Reg'd. Nov. 15, 1861/ No. 146352-4

*See Meikle Bros. (Canadian wholesalers) whose mark was found on Canada Shape.

**Previously registered by Joseph Clementson.

JOSEPH CLEMENTSON & SONS

BLUE AND WHITE TRANSFERWARE

SINGLE PATTERNS

CATEGORY	PATTERN
O	Alexandria
O	Equestrian Vase

CLEMENTSON & YOUNG

BLUE AND WHITE TRANSFERWARE

SINGLE PATTERNS

CATEGORY	PATTERN	
S	Ionic	
S	Washington	Reg'd. Oct. 22, 1845/No. 30701

FLOW BLUE

CATEGORY	PATTERN	
S	Columbia	Reg'd. Oct. 22, 1845/No. 30701
M	"Feather Edge"	-
O	Tonquin	-

MULBERRY WARES

CATEGORY	PATTERN
O	Tonquin

CLEMENTSON, YOUNG & JAMESON

BLUE AND WHITE TRANSFERWARE

SINGLE PATTERNS

CATEGORY	PATTERN	
S	Aleppo	Reg'd. Oct. 17, 1844/No. 22192

CLEVELAND POTTERY CO.

FLOW BLUE

CATEGORY	PATTERN
F	Coronation

JAMES & RALPH CLEWS

BLUE AND WHITE TRANSFERWARE

SERIES

1. BLUE BELL BORDER VIEWS
Dunfermline Abbey, Fifeshire
Dulwich Castle
Fonthill Abbey, Wiltshire (Distant View)
Fonthill Abbey, Wiltshire (Near View)
Gloucester Cathedral
Lumley Castle, Durham
Palace of Linlithgow, West Lothian
Remains of the Church, Thornton Abbey
Rothesay Castle, Buteshire
St. Mary's Abbey, York
Stratford-on-Avon, Warwickshire
Tintern Abbey, Monmouthshire
Warkworth Castle, Northumberland
Wells Cathedral

2. FOLIAGE AND SCROLL BORDER SERIES
N.B.: This series was also executed by William Adams
"Alnwick Castle, Northumberland"
Canterbury Cathedral
Greenwich
Melrose Abbey
Nottingham
Rochester Castle
St. Catherine's Hill, Near Guildford
Windsor Castle

3. HUNTING VIEWS SERIES
"Bird Shooting"
"Duck Hunting"
"Goose Hunting"*
"Rabbit Pie"
"Return From the Hunt"
"Snipe Hunting"
*See *FOB Bulletin*, No. 97, Autumn 1997, p. 4
N.B.: New series identified, FOB No. 96, Summer 1997, p. 10.

4. SELECT SCENERY SERIES
Aysgill Force in Wensleydale
Cheddar, Somersetshire
Donemark Mill
Fountains Abbey
Ivy Bridge, Devon
Kilcolman Castle
Killin, Head of Loch Tay
Norwich
Rippon, Yorkshire
Rivax Abbey
St. Catherine's Hill Near Guildford
View in Glencyle
Windsor

5. WILKIE SERIES
Christmas Eve
The Errand Boy
The Escape of the Mouse
The Letter of Introduction
Playing at Draughts
The Rabbit on the Wall
The Valentine

6. ZOOLOGICAL GARDENS SERIES
"Aviary"
Bear Cages
Bird Cages
Camel, Cow and Gnu
Deer
Foxes
Goats
Ostriches, Zebra and other Animals
Swans
Wolf

JAMES & RALPH CLEWS

BLUE AND WHITE TRANSFERWARE

SINGLE PATTERNS

CATEGORY	PATTERN
F	"Basket and Vase"
Z	"Birds of Paradise"

M	"Blue and White Sheet Pattern"
S	Canovian (3)
G	"Castle"
O	"Chinese Landscape" ["Riverside Temple"]
-	"Chrysanthemum & Bamboo"
G	"Church and Fisherman"
M/O	"Clews, Double Prints" ["Mirror Lakeside"]
O	"Clews Oriental" ["Crane & Peony"]
S	"Colossal Sarcophagus Near Castle Rosso"
-	"Corinthian Ornaments"
F	"Cornucopia of Flowers"*
F	Coronation
M	Crown Apple**
S	Genevese
M/Z	Haddington
-	"Half-built Bridge"
-	"Heron"
M/Z	"Hunting Dog"
S	Jessamine
P/M	"Man With Bird"
M	Moral Maxims (possible series)
M	Mosaic Tracery
M	"Neptune" ["Victory" or "Apotheosis of Nelson"]
M/Z	"Pointer and Rabbit"*** ["Hunting Dog"]
S	"River Scene with Fort, et.al."
G	"Romantic Ruins" ["Ruins and Mule"]
-	"Shell & Flowers"
S	Sicilian Beauties
S	Solar Ray
F	Summer Rose
-	"Temple & Child"
F	Tuscan Rose
O	Two Temples ["Clews Willow"]
S	"Village Church"
S	Virginia
G	Water Girl

*See *FOB Bulletin*, No. 97, Autumn 1997, p. 4
**See *Arman Quarterly*, Vol. 1, Oct.-Nov. 1997, No. 4, p. 23, photos 12 & 13
***See *FOB Bulletin*, No. 95, Spring 1997, p. 3

JAMES & RALPH CLEWS
HISTORIC STAFFORDSHIRE SERIES
AMERICAN
1. AMERICA AND INDEPENDENCE OF STATES SERIES
"Bear Forest, Ireland" ["Three Story Building With Curved Drive"]*
"Belton House, Lincolnshire" ["Mansion, Winding Drive"]**
"Bishton Hall, Staffordshire" ["Building, Fisherman With Net"]***
"Building in Distance, Woman in Foreground"
"Building, Sheep on Lawn"
"Building, Two Wings, Water in Foreground"
"Bushey Park, Middlesex" ["Building, Deer on Lawn"]***
"Castle with Flag, Boats in Foreground"
"Dock, With Large Building and Ships"
"Mansion, Circular Drive"
"Mansion, Foreground a Lake With Swans"
"Mansion, Small Boat With Flag in Foreground"
"Three Story Building, Two Wings and Center Section"
"Two Story Mansion, Small Extension onto Left"
*See *Arman Quarterly*, Vol. 1, 1997, p. 6
**See *Arman Quarterly*, Vol. 2, 1997, p. 5
*** See *Arman Quarterly, Vol. 1*, 1997, pp. 8-10
2. CITIES SERIES
(Cities Series has been attributed to Davenport)
Albany [New York, Albany]
Baltimore [Maryland, Baltimore]
Buenos Ayres [South America, Buenos Ayres (Aires)]
Chillicothe (with Cows) [Ohio]
Chillicothe (with Raft) [Ohio, Three Boatmen on the River]
Chillicothe (with Sailboat) [Ohio]*
Columbus [Ohio]
Detroit [Michigan, Detroit]
Harbor Scene (Unidentified)
Hobart Town
Louisville, Kentucky
Near Fishkill (New York)
Near Philadelphia [A View Near Philadelphia]
Philadelphia [Penn's Treaty Tree]
Quebec
Sandusky (Ohio)
Washington [District of Columbia, Washington]
Wright's Ferry on the Susquehanna
*See Arman *Quarterly*, Vol. 1, 1997, p. 8
3. DR. SYNTAX SERIES
N.B.: It would appear that American Collectors have adopted this series as a part of the American Historic Series.
The Advertisement For a Wife
The Bans Forbidden
Death of Punch
The Garden Trio
The Harvest Home
The Noble Hunting Party
Dr. Syntax Amused with Pat in the Pond
Dr. Syntax and the Bees
Dr. Syntax and the Gypsies
Dr. Syntax Bound to a Tree by Highwaymen
Dr. Syntax Copying the Wit of the Widow
Dr. Syntax Disputing His Bill With Landlady
Dr. Syntax Drawing After Nature

DR. SYNTAX SERIES
Dr. Syntax Entertained at College
Dr. Syntax Making a Discovery
Dr. Syntax Mistakes a Gentleman's House for an Inn
Dr. Syntax Painting a Portrait
Dr. Syntax Presenting a Floral Offering
Dr. Syntax Pursued by a Bull
Dr. Syntax Reading His Tour
Dr. Syntax Returning From His Tour
Dr. Syntax Sells Grizzle
Dr. Syntax Setting Out In Search of a Wife
Dr. Syntax Setting Out On His First Tour
Dr. Syntax Setting Out On His Second Tour
Dr. Syntax Sketching the Lake
Dr. Syntax Star Gazing
Dr. Syntax Stopt by Highwaymen
Dr. Syntax Taking Possession of His Living
Dr. Syntax Turned Nurse
Dr. Syntax With a Blue Stocking Beauty
Dr. Syntax With Dairy Maid
4. DON QUIXOTE SERIES
(Don Quixote Series has been attributed to Davenport)
Don Quixote
Don Quixote and the Princess
Don Quixote and the Shepherdess
Don Quixote and Sancho Panza [Don Quixote Entreated by Sancho Panza]
Don Quixote and Sancho Panza
Don Quixote's Attack Upon The Mills
Don Quixote's Library
The Enchanted Bark
The Knight of the Wood Conquered
Knighthood Conferred on Don Quixote
Mambrino's Helmet
The Meeting of Don Quixote and Sancho Panza
The Meeting with the Duchess
The Meeting of Sancho and Dapple
Peasant Girl Mistaken For the Lady Dulcinea
Repose in the Wood
Sancho Panza
Sancho Panza and the Duchess
Sancho Panza and the Messenger
Sancho and the Priest and the Barber
Sancho Panza at the Boar Hunt
Sancho Panza's Debate With Teresa
Sancho Panza Hoisted in the Blanket
Shepherd Boy Rescued
Teresa, Panza and the Messenger
Yanquesian Conflict
5. FLOWER AND FOLIAGE SERIES
City Hall, New York
Insane Asylum, New York
"Three Story Building with Columned Entrance on Front and Side"
"Three Story Building With Large Two Story Extension to the Left"
"[Prison] With Four Two-Story Towers Joined By One Story Walls"

6. PICTURESQUE VIEWS SERIES
Bakers Falls, Hudson River
"Fairmount" [Fairmont Water Works on the Schuylkill]
Fort Edward, Hudson River
Fort Montgomery, Hudson River [Near Hudson, Hudson River]
From Fishkill, Hudson River
Glenn's [Glenss] Falls
Hadley's Falls
Hudson, Hudson River
Jessup's Landing, Hudson River
Junction of the Sacandaga And Hudson River
Little Falls at Luzerne, Hudson River
Near Fishkill, Hudson River
Near Fort Miller, Hudson River
Near Hudson, Hudson River [Fort Montgomery] (2)
Near Sandy Hill, Hudson River (2)
Newburgh, Hudson River [Glenn's Falls]
New York, Hudson River [View From Governors' Island] (2)
Penitentiary in Allegheny, Near Pittsburgh, PA
Pittsburgh-Steamboat, Pennsylvania [Pennsylvania Steamboat]
Pittsburgh [Home, Lark, and Nile Steamboat]
Rapids Above Hadley's Falls [Junction of Sacandaga and Hudson Rivers

or Near Sandy Hill, Hudson River]
Troy From Mount Ida
West Point, Hudson River
7. WILKIE (BURNET) SERIES:*
(Scrolls and Large Flowers)
Christmas Eve
The Errand Boy
The Escape of the Mouse
The Letter of Introduction
Playing at Draughts
The Rabbit on the Wall
The Valentine
*See *Larsen*, pp. 78-80
8. MISCELLANEOUS
American Eagle on Urn
Lafayette (See Welcome Lafayette ...)
The Landing of General Lafayette at Castle Garden, New York, 16, August 1824
Mount Pleasant Classical Institution, Amherst, Mass.
New York Hospital
Peace and Plenty
Virginia (3)
Virginia [Monument]
Welcome Lafayette The Nation's Guest and Our Country's(3)
Glory (with or without inscription)
Winter View of Pittsfield, Mass
For further reading, refer to *Arman Quarterly*, Clews Part 1 and Part 2, Vol. 1, No. 2&3 for comments by Norman Wolfe.

CLOSE & CO.
BLUE AND WHITE TRANSFERWARE
SINGLE PATTERNS

CATEGORY	PATTERN
M	Maddle Jenny Lind

FLOW BLUE

CATEGORY	PATTERN
O	Tonquin

J.T. CLOSE (& CO.)
FLOW BLUE

CATEGORY	PATTERN
O	Sicilian

WHITE IRONSTONE
Athenia Shape* Reg'd. Jan. 3, 1866/No. 194194
*See William Adams & Son(s) for prior shape.

CLYDE POTTERY CO. (LTD.)
BLUE AND WHITE TRANSFERWARE
SINGLE PATTERNS

CATEGORY	PATTERN
F	Asiatic Pheasants
S	British Rivers
-	Caledonian
G	Gondola
-	Mario
S	Melrose
S	Tyrolese
G	Victoria
-	Washington
O	"Willow" Pattern

FLOW BLUE

CATEGORY	PATTERN
F	Chrysanthemum

MULBERRY WARES

CATEGORY	PATTERN
S	Gothic
F	Passion Flowers

R. COCHRAN & CO. - VERREVILLE POTTERY
BLUE AND WHITE TRANSFERWARE
SINGLE PATTERNS

CATEGORY	PATTERN
-	Australia
S	California*
O	"Chinese Tea Garden"
-	Colombo
-	Damascus
F	Dresden Sprigs
-	Duchess
-	Empress
S	Exhibition (Crystal Palace)
M/G	Fairy
S	Genoa
H	Greek
S	Grotto
-	Holly
-	Loch Winnock
-	Lorne
-	Mogul
S	Oriental
M	Osborne
G	Pastoral
M	"Prince of Wales"
-	Sebastopol
S	Syria
H	Wellington
S	"Wild Rose"
O	"Willow" Pattern

*See *P. Williams, Staffordshire*, Vol. III, p. 64.
N.B.: For an additional listing of patterns refer to the *Scottish Pottery Society Bulletin* No. 21, September 1995, pp. 2-7
HISTORIC STAFFORDSHIRE SERIES (Britannia Pottery)
CANADIAN
1. QUEBEC VIEWS SERIES
"Abraham Hill" (no French Title)
Basilica & Seminary: Basilique & Seminaire
Breakneck Steps: Escalier Champlain
Cape Diamond: Cap Diamant
Chaudiere Falls: Chute De La Chaudiere
Dufferin Terrace & Citadel: Place Dufferin & Citadelle
"Indian Chief": Chef Sauvage
"Lorette Falls" Chutes De Lorette
"Lorette Squaw": "Sauvagesse De Lorette"
Montmorency Falls: Chute De Montmorency
Montmorency Falls Winter View (no French Title)
Natural Steps, Montmorency River: Marches Naturelle, Riviere Montmorency
Quebec Harbor & Levis: Havre De Quebec & Levis
Quebec From Point Levis: Quebec, Vue De Point Levis
N.B.: See Elizabeth Collard's *Potter's View*, pp. 74-80

R. COCHRAN & CO. - VERREVILLE POTTERY
FLOW BLUE

CATEGORY	PATTERN	
F	Dresden Sprigs	
F	Lotus	Dated 1846
S	Syria	

MULBERRY WARES

CATEGORY	PATTERN
G	Castile
F	Dresden Sprigs
F	Lotus
S	Syria
S	Triumphal Car

WHITE IRONSTONE
"Arched Wheat"
"Cochran's Ring" ["Cochran's Hyacinth"]
"Four Square Wheat", "Wheat & Hops" ["Wheat & Blackberry"]
TEA LEAF/COPPER LUSTRE
"Hyacinth"*
*Same as "Cochran's Ring" in White Ironstone.

COCHRAN & FLEMING - BRITANNIA POTTERY
BLUE AND WHITE TRANSFERWARE
SINGLE PATTERNS

CATEGORY	PATTERN
F	Asiatic Pheasants
F	"Bee & Rose"
M	"Duchess"
Z	"Stag"
H	"Wide Awake"

FLOW BLUE

CATEGORY	PATTERN
-	"China"
-	"Rowena"

COCKSON & CHETWYND
(or Cockson, Chetwynd & Co.)
BLUE AND WHITE TRANSFERWARE
SINGLE PATTERNS

CATEGORY	PATTERN
M	Musk Deer*

*See *P. Williams, Staffordshire*, Vol. III, p. 186.
FLOW BLUE

CATEGORY	PATTERN
F	Flora

WHITE IRONSTONE
"Cable & Ring"
"Garland"
Gothic*
"Plain Uplift Shape" Reg'd. Jan. 7, 1868/215642
*Found with impressed year 78 (1878).

COCKSON & HARDING
BLUE AND WHITE TRANSFERWARE
SINGLE PATTERNS

CATEGORY	PATTERN
-	"Institutions"
O	"Willow" Pattern

FLOW BLUE

CATEGORY	PATTERN
F	Flora
O	Hindoostan
F	Lotus

COCKSON & SEDDON
WHITE IRONSTONE
"Clover Shape"
"Plain Round"

COLCLOUGH & CO.
FLOW BLUE

CATEGORY	PATTERN	
F	Tine	Reg'd. 1898/329815
F	Torbex	-
F	Touraine	Reg'd. 1898/329815

ALFRED COLLEY & CO. LTD.
FLOW BLUE

CATEGORY	PATTERN
A	Lusitania
A	Paris
F	Roslyn

CHARLES COLLINSON & CO.
BLUE AND WHITE TRANSFERWARE
SINGLE PATTERNS

CATEGORY	PATTERN
F	"Water Lily"

FLOW BLUE

CATEGORY	PATTERN
S	Chusan
F	"Peach Blossom" (Brush Stroke)

COPELAND & GARRETT/W.T. COPELAND/W.T. COPELAND & SON
BLUE AND WHITE TRANSFERWARE
SERIES
1. ARABESQUE SERIES
Dover
Eton
Folkestone
Greenwich
Greenwich Hospital
Hastings
Margate
Plymouth
Pope's Villa
Portsmouth
Richmond Bridge
Richmond Hill
Tower of Lucano
West Cowes
2. BYRON VIEWS SERIES
"Bay of Naples"
"Bellagio, Lago di Como"
"Bologna"
"Cintra" (2)
"Franciscan Convent, Athens"
"The Hague"
"Interlachen" (sic)
"Lachin y Gair"
"Lausanne"
"Mount Etna"
Mount Olympus
"Patrass" (sic)
"Rhodes"
"Salamis"
"Sicily"
"The Simplon"
"Soracte"
"Spoleto"
"Thun"
"The Tiber"
"Tivoli"
"Tomb of Cecilia Metella"
"Venice"
"Yanina"
3. SEASONS SERIES
January - Untitled
February - The Alps
March - Untitled
April - Untitled [Italian Garden]
May - Untitled
June - Italian Garden
July - Untitled
August - Italian Garden
September - Windsor Castle
October - Untitled
November - Untitled
(December)
Spring - Richmond Hill
Summer - -
Autumn - Vintage of Sorrento
Winter —
N.B.: For Seasons Series, refer to *Sussman*, pp. 194-203, No. 206-215
BLUE AND WHITE TRANSFERWARE
SINGLE PATTERNS - W. & T. COPELAND
CATEGORY PATTERN
Alba
Albert Richard Smith (sepia center)
Animum Rege
Garden Flowers
Gothic Ruins
Inspe Crescentis
Koran
"Louis Quatorze Border"
Severn
"Skinner's Arms"
Tower
Union Club
"Upside Down Bird"
Varina*
Virtus Vera Nobilitas
Wild Rose & Bluebell
*See *P. Williams, Staffordshire*, Vol. III, p. 117.

COPELAND & GARRETT/W.T. COPELAND/W.T. COPELAND & SON
COPELAND & GARRETT PATTERNS RECORDED AS "FLOW BLUE"

B772	Printed in Dresden Blue
B773	Printed in Dresden Blue
B776	Aquatic printed in Dresden Blue
B777	RAD SPRIGS printed in Dresden Blue
B779	DRESDEN BORDER printed in Royal Saxon Blue
B782	ARABESQUE with floral centre printed in Mazarine
B798	FLOWER VASE printed in Royal Saxon Blue
B800	Un-named printed in Mazarine Blue
B801	RAFAELESQUE printed in Royal Saxon Blue
B803	WEEPING WILLOW (Bamboo & Rock) printed in Royal Saxon Blue
B805	Arabesque border and small floral spray in center, printed in Royal Saxon Blue
B806	INDIAN TREE printed in Royal Saxon Blue
B810	MAY printed in Royal Saxon Blue
B811	(Sheet Pattern) printed in Royal Saxon Blue
B812	Kendal Sheet printed in Royal Saxon Blue
B813	Un-named sheet printed in Royal Saxon Blue
B828	"Starlike" Sprays printed in Royal Saxon Blue
B918	"Sprays and Bead" printed in Royal Saxon Blue
B919	Sprays printed in Royal Saxon Blue
B942	Scrolls printed in Royal dark Saxon Blue
B943	BANG UP printed in Royal Saxon Blue

N.B.: Dresden Blue & Royal Saxon Blue are the names of the Flow Blue colors as recorded in the Pattern Book.
COPELAND FLOW BLUE PATTERNS WITH EXTRA COLORING

D1	Blue Rose
D4	Chinese Plants Sprays
D5	British Flowers
D6	Flower Vase
D7	Sprays
D8	Sprays printed in Royal Gray
D13	Border of Enoch Wood's DETROIT
D14	Border of Enoch Wood's DETROIT
D239	DRESDEN SPRAYS (Like English Sprays but reversed with a different bead at edge).
D262	as B772

N.B.: The B numbers are pattern numbers for underglaze decorations, the D numbers are also pattern numbers; both series embrace all body styles. Refer to Robert Copeland. *Spode & Copeland Marks and Other Relevant Intelligence.* London, Studio Vista, 1993, pp. 119-121.

SPODE/COPELAND & GARRETT/W.T. COPELAND & SUCCESSORS

FLOW BLUE

PATTERN	CATEGORY	SPODE	COPELAND & GARRETT	W.T. COPELAND	W.T. COPELAND & SON	W.T. COPELAND LTD.	SPODE	ROYAL WORCESTER	COMMENTS
Asiatic Pheasant	F	-	-	-	-	X	-	-	
Chinese Bouquet	O	-	-	-	X	-	-	-	Dated 1884
Copeland's "Turkey"	M	-	-	-	X	-	-	-	Reg'd. 1891/No. 180288
Fleur de Lis	M	-	-	X	X	-	-	-	Mar. 16, 1852 & Impressed 1894
Floral Arrangements	F	-	X	-	-	-	-	-	
Game Birds	M	-	-	-	X	-	-	-	Dated 1904
Garland	F	-	-	X	-	-	-	-	
Landscape	O	X(1)	-	X	X	X	-	-	
Louis Quatorze	S	-	X	-	-	-	-	-	Reg'd. Dec. 2, 1844
"Marble"	M	-	-	X	-	-	-	-	
Oriental Landscape)	O	X(1)	-	-	-	-	-	-	Imp. N.S. (may be not seen
Ruins	S	-	-	X	-	-	-	-	Jan. 15, 1848
Sevres [Rose & Sprig]	F	-	X	-	-	-	-	-	
Spode's Tower	S	X(1)	X	X	X	X	X	-	
Sunflower	F	-	X	-	-	-	-	-	Mkd."Late Spode"
Water Lily	F	-	-	X	-	-	-	-	Dated 1850

(1) Introduced earlier but not produced in Flow Blue until Copeland & Garrett

Note: *Hoener*, p. 12, illustrates a scenic Flow Blue pattern Louis Quatorze, Reg'd. Dec. 2, 1844

Also see patterns and comments under Spode.

SPODE/COPELAND & GARRETT/W.T. COPELAND & SUCCESSORS

MULBERRY

PATTERNS RECORDED AS BEING PRINTED IN MULBERRY

B934 (Sprays) printed in Mulberry

B935 (Sprays) printed in Mulberry

B936 (Sprays) printed in Mulberry

N.B: *Hill* notes a scenic view "Continental Views" Reg'd. Oct. 21, 1845/No. 30699 in Mulberry.

CORK, EDGE & MALKIN

BLUE AND WHITE TRANSFERWARE

SERIES

1. "INDIAN SCENERY SERIES"

Delhi, Hindoostan

Surseya Ghaut, Khanpore

Tomb of Jeswuntnagurth

Tomb of Shere Shah

Tombs Near Etaya on the Jumna River

BLUE AND WHITE TRANSFERWARE

SINGLE PATTERNS

CATEGORY	PATTERN	
-	Cashmere	
J/G	Fishers	
F	Marina	(possible series)
S	Marino	
F	Mesieres	
S	Missouri	
S	Royal Cottage	
S	Theatre	Reg'd. 1868
S	Verona	

FLOW BLUE

CATEGORY	PATTERN
O	Singa*

*Pattern continued by Edge, Malkin & Co. (Ltd.)

MULBERRY WARES

CATEGORY	PATTERN	
O	Hong	Reg'd. March 12, 1864/No. 172559
S	Versaille*	

*Same pattern as Versaille by Thomas Godwin

CORK & EDGE

BLUE AND WHITE TRANSFERWARE

SINGLE PATTERNS

CATEGORY	PATTERN
F	Asiatic Pheasants
-	Dahlia
S	Royal Cottage

WHITE IRONSTONE

"Babes In The Woods" (Heavy Relief)

"Tree Trunk With Ivy" (Heavy Relief)

JOHN CORMIE

BLUE AND WHITE TRANSFERWARE

SINGLE PATTERNS

CATEGORY	PATTERN
O	"Two Exotic Birds on a Flowering Tree"

EDWARD CORN

WHITE IRONSTONE

"Grape Octagon"

Maltese Shape*

Persia Shape

*See *Wetherbee, White Ironstone A Second Look*, p. 60 where she notes that Edward Pearson named this shape Mississippi and I Meir and George Woolliscroft named theirs Baltic Shape.

W. & E. CORN

FLOW BLUE

CATEGORY	PATTERN
M	Albion
O	Amoy
F	Ayr
O	Burmese
O	Celeste
O	Delhi
F	Dorothy
M/A	Elsa
F	Flannel Daisy
F	Garland
F	Iris
S	Italia
-	Jewel
O	Lahore
F	Lancaster
A	Lucania
F	Mikado
-	Old Castle
A	Ormonde
O	Shanghai
F	York

MULBERRY WARES

CATEGORY	PATTERN
F	Elsa
O	Shanghai

WHITE IRONSTONE

Centennial Shape	Reg'd. Nov. 3, 1874/No. 286720-2
"Double Sydenham"	["Wrapped Sydenham"]
"Bordered Hyacinth"*	
"Flowering Vine"	
Oriental Shape	
"Plain Round"	
"Ribbed Grape"	
"Ribboned Oak"	
"Seashore"	
"Square Ridged"	
"Western Shape"	
"Wheat"	
"Wrapped Sydenham"	["Double Sydenham"]

*Called Lily Shape by Henry Burgess.

TEA LEAF/COPPER LUSTRE

"Bellflower"

"Corn's Cloverleaf with Gold Luster"

"Coronet"

"Square Ridged: Square Pear"

"Woodland"

CORNFOOT, COLVILLE & CO.

BLUE AND WHITE TRANSFERWARE

SINGLE PATTERNS

CATEGORY	PATTERN
S	"Country Church"

COTTON & BARLOW

BLUE AND WHITE TRANSFERWARE

SINGLE PATTERNS

CATEGORY	PATTERN
S	Medina

FLOW BLUE

CATEGORY	PATTERN
O	Maltese

CUMBERLIDGE & HUMPHREYS
FLOW BLUE

CATEGORY	PATTERN
F	Petunia

DALTON & BURN
BLUE AND WHITE TRANSFERWARE
SINGLE PATTERNS

CATEGORY	PATTERN
S	"Villa Scenery" (att.)

H. & R. DANIEL
BLUE AND WHITE TRANSFERWARE
SINGLE PATTERNS

CATEGORY	PATTERN
S	Canovian Statues
O	Chinese Scenery
-	"Fancy Birds"
S	"Goats & Swiss Chalets"
F	"Japan Group"
S	Neapolitan
F	Oriental Vases/Ne Plus Ultra
M	Peacock
O	"Raised Dragons"
F	"Shell"

For additional patterns see Michael Berthoud's, *H. & R. Daniel, 1822-1846*, Micawber Publications, England, 1980, Nos. 96-102; and *The Daniel Tableware Patterns*, Micawber Publications, England, 1982 .

WALTER DANIEL
BLUE AND WHITE TRANSFERWARE
SINGLE PATTERNS

CATEGORY	PATTERN
O	"Parasol Willow Pattern"

WILLIAM DAVENPORT
BLUE AND WHITE TRANSFERWARE
SERIES
1. "CHINESE VIEWS" SERIES
"Fenced Pagoda"
"Island Temple"
"Pagodas & Fishermen"
"Vase on the Bridge"
2. CITIES SERIES
(Cities Series has been attributed to Davenport and is also listed under American Historic.)
Albany [New York, Albany]
Baltimore [Maryland, Baltimore]
Buenos Ayres [South America, Buenos Ayres (Aires)]
Chillicothe (with Cows) [Ohio]
Chillicothe (with Raft) [Ohio, Three Boatmen on the River]
Chillicothe (with Sailboat) [Ohio]
Columbus [Ohio]
Detroit [Michigan, Detroit]
Harbor Scene (Unidentified)
Hobart Town
Indianapolis, Indiana
Louisville, Kentucky
Near Fishkill (New York)
Near Philadelphia [A View Near Philadelphia]
Philadelphia [Penn's Treaty Tree]
Quebec
Richmond, Virginia
Sandusky (Ohio)
Washington [District of Columbia, Washington]
Wright's Ferry on the Susquehanna
3. CORNUCOPIA FLOWER BORDER SERIES
Laidacker, Part II, p. 38 notes a possible series.
4. DON QUIXOTE SERIES
(Don Quixote Series has been attributed to Davenport)
Don Quixote
Don Quixote and the Princess
Don Quixote and the Shepherdess
Don Quixote and Sancho Panza [Don Quixote Entreated by Sancho Panza]
Don Quixote and Sancho Panza
Don Quixote's Attack Upon The Mills
Don Quixote's Library
The Enchanted Bark
The Knight of the Wood Conquered
Knighthood Conferred on Don Quixote
Mambrino's Helmet
The Meeting of Don Quixote and Sancho Panza
The Meeting of Sancho and Dapple
The Meeting With the Duchess
Peasant Girl Mistaken For the Lady Dulcinea
Repose in the Wood
Sancho Panza
Sancho Panza and the Duchess
Sancho Panza and the Messenger
Sancho and the Priest and the Barber
Sancho Panza at the Boar Hunt
Sancho Panza's Debate With Teresa
Sancho Panza Hoisted in the Blanket
Shepherd Boy Rescued
Teresa, Panza and the Messenger
Yanquesian Conflict
5. "THE FISHERMAN" SERIES [GOTHIC RUINS SERIES]
"By The River" (Dated 1856)
"The Catch"
"Cows Under Trees"
"Fisherman & Fence"
"Fisherman and Friend"
"Fisherman and Woman With Basket"
"Fisherman's Advise"
"Fisherman, Old Man With Stick and Fence"
"Fisherman's Tale"
"Fisherman With Boat"
"Fishing Talk"
"Norman Tower"
"Peaceful Fisherman"
"Resting Fisherman and Friend"
"Seated Fisherman, Man With Stick, Boat on River"
"Solitary Fisherman"
6. "MARE AND FOAL" SERIES
"Cows Under Trees Resting by a Tree"
"Fisherman on an Island, background country house, et.al."
"Fisherman with rod in hand on an Island, country house, et.al."
"Five cows on the near bank of a river, et.al."
"Large cottage, one mounted rider talking to a standing figure, et.al." ["Two Cows"]
"Mare and foal at riverside, et.al."
"Timber-framed house, cattle and two seated figures, et.al." ["Tudor Cottage"]
"Traveler with bundle of sticks, dog, cottage and two standing figures, et.al." ["Traveler & Woman"]
"Two fishermen, two large spreading trees, bridge with ornamental wall, et.al." ["Fishermen & Bucket"]
"Two men on horseback talking to a woman, et.al."
"Two seated and two standing cows and seated man, et.al." ["Cattlemen & Spire"]
7. MULETEER SERIES
"The Muleteer mounted, preceded by dog, two women standing by shore, et.al."
"The Muleteer stands with the two women and child, et.al."
"The Mounted Muleteer has left the woman and proceeds towards the village, et.al." (P. Williams, Staffordshire, Vol. 1, p. 347)
"The Muleteer and two women walk with mules alongside a wall, et.al." (dated 1836)
8. "RHINE" SERIES ["Close-lined Border"]
(A series of six view are recorded.)
WILLIAM DAVENPORT
9. "RURAL SCENERY" SERIES
"Boy seated with a collie-type dog, two cottages in background, et.al."
"Humped back bridge, boat and two seated figures, floral foliage, et.al."
"Three youthful figures seated by the water, bridge and sail boat, et.al."
10. "RUSTIC SCENES" SERIES
"Camp Fire"
"Castle gateway, two gentlemen walk with their dog, et.al."
"Cottage and bridge, horse and rider followed by dog, et.al."
"The Drover, man drives a cow and calf in front of a gnarled tree, et.al."
"Farm and cattle shed, thatched cottage with very tall chimneys, et.al."
"Gothic Ruins, large tree on left, tall ruined Gothic tower on right, et.al." ["Two-arch Ruins"]
"Man on Cart-horse, talking to another man seated beneath tree, et.al."
"Milking Time, Thatched cottage with two cows, one being milked, et.al."
"Resting time, Two men, one seated, the other standing, dog lies nearby, two cows in front of cottage, et.al."
"Returning home, man with stick, bundle on his shoulder and holding young girl by the hand"
"Senior Citizens"
"Spreading Tree & Bridge"
"Thatched cottage, cottage with a central corner window, two cows and their calves, et.al."
"Thatched farm, extensive thatched farm buildings, moored boat and a group of figures, et.al."
"Thatched farm shed"
"Trewkers & Dogs"
"Two Riders"
"Watermill, scene #1, two men talking by a horse and cart, left - watermill, et.al."
"Watermill, scene #2, large watermill on left, two fishermen in the foreground, church on right, et.al."
"Watermill, scene #3, as above, but tree different and village replaced by windmill"
11. SCOTT'S ILLUSTRATIONS SERIES
The Bride of Lammermoor I
The Bride of Lammermoor II
Guy Mannering
Heart of Midlothian
Legend of Montrose
Old Mortality
Rob Roy
Waverly

BLUE AND WHITE TRANSFERWARE
SINGLE PATTERNS

CATEGORY	PATTERN	
G	Agriculture	-
J/G	Archery	-
F	"Bamboo & Peony"	-

G	"Bisham Abbey Berkshire" ["Tudor Mansion"]	-
F	Botanical Beauties	-
O	"Bridge and Temple"	-
O	"Bullfight"	-
S	Canton	Reg'd. Oct. 23, 1852/No. 87219
O	Chian	Dated 1844
O	Chinese Banana Tree ["Chinese Beekeepers"]	-
M/Z	Chinese Birds	-
O	"Chinese Fishermen" ["Fishing Family"]	-
O	"Chinese Flag Bearers"	-
O	"Chinese Garden Scene" ["Chinese Scenery"?]	-
O	"Chinese Marine"	-
O	"Chinese Pastime" (possible series)	-
O	"Chinoisere Bridgeless"	-
O	"Chinoisere High Bridge"	-
O	"Chinoisere Ruins" [Chinese Ruins]	-
S	"Classical Buildings and City"	-
M/F	Cornice	-
G	"Cornucopia Flower Border" (3) (possible series)	-
O	"Cows Crossing Stream" ["View Near Colnebrook"]	-
O	"Cranes & Peony Tree"	-
O	Cyprus*	-
O	"Donovan Fisherman" ["Dragons No. 2"]	-
F	Eastern Birds	Reg'd. Oct. 23, 1852/No. 87219
F	Eaton	-
O	Erica	Dated 1844
A	Fan	-
G	Floral	Reg'd. Oct. 23, 1852/No. 87219
G	"Fisherman and Ferns"	-
M/S	Florentine Fountain	-
F	French Groups	-
S	Friburg	Dated 1844
M/F	"Fruit & Wild Rose Border"	-
S	"Fur Trapper"	-
S	Gazebo	-
	(2) ["Chinese In Gazebo" ?]	-
G	Genoa	Dated 1848
S	Gondola (a)	-
S	Gothic	Dated 1844
F	Hawthorne	-
-	"Henry Marriott"	-
O	"High Bridge"	
F	"Hop"	-
F	Hydrographic	-
O	Iolanthe	-
S	Isola Bella	-
Z	"Java"	Dated 1842
F	Madras	Dated 1844
-	Marine	-
-	Mersey	-
G	"Milkmaid"	-
S	Montilla	-
O	"Mosque and Fisherman"	-
G	"Mt. Chalet and Two Walking Gentlemen"	-
F	Orissa	-
M	Pepper Pot I & II**	
*M/Z	Persian Bird	-
G	"Rhenish Views" ["Rhine"]	Dated 1836
	"Swiss Lake & Village", ["Swiss Scenery"]***	-
O	"River Scene" ["View of the Imperial Park at Gehol"]	-
S	Rocaille	-
G	"Romantic Castles" (4) (possible series)	-
O	"Rose"	-

BLUE AND WHITE TRANSFERWARE
SINGLE PATTERNS

CATEGORY	PATTERN	
F	Rose	-
F	Rose and Lily	-
S	"Rural Cottage"	-
S	"Rural Lake & Village"	Dated 1836
S	"Rural Scene"	Dated 1836
S	"Snow Scenes" (2)	-
F	Spanish Rose	Dated 1848
S	"Swiss"	Dated 1836
G	Swiss Pastime	Dated 1848
S	"Swiss Chalet"	-
O	Temple	-
G	"Tudor Mansion"**** ["Bisham Abbey"]	-
S	"Turkish Archer"	-
S	Tyrol Hunters	-
F	"Vase of Flowers" ["Flowers on a Tree"]	-
F	"Vase on a Wall" (possible series)	Dated 1836 and 1844
G	View in Geneva	-
S	"View on the Thames" (2)	-
G	"The Villagers"	-
S	Villaris	-
S	Wild Rose	-
O	"Willow" Pattern	-

*See *P. Williams, Staffordshire,* Vol. III, p. 26
**See *P. Williams, Staffordshire*, Vol. III, pp. 188-189
***See *P. Williams, Staffordshire* Vol.II, pp. 249, 622.
*****FOB* No. 96, Summer 1997, pp. 6-7.

BLUE AND WHITE TRANSFERWARE
SINGLE PATTERNS - As Recorded and Supplied by Friends of Blue (UK)*

CATEGORY	PATTERN
-	Alpine
-	Amusements
-	Arabesque
-	Auspicio Reges et Senatus Anglia
-	Bird & Berry
-	Bird & Star
-	Boat & Castle
-	Bramble
-	Ceres
-	Citron
-	Cross & Statue
-	Crosslet
-	Danish
-	Delaware
-	Eskimo on Snowshoes ["Snow Scenes" ?]
-	Festoon & Bird
-	Fisherman & Cross
-	Floral Trellis
-	French Fan
-	Garland
-	Grapes
-	Italian Honeysuckle
-	Italian Verandah
-	Junks & Rowboats
-	King's Head
-	Marbles
-	Nectarine
-	Old Florida
-	Ribbon
-	Scots
-	Squirrel
-	Statuary
-	Sunflower
-	Swans & Horses
-	Syrian
-	Tendril
-	Tree, Mansion & Cows
-	Venetian Meeting
-	Versailles
-	Woodland

*Some of these names may be alternative and/or fabricated.

HISTORIC STAFFORDSHIRE SERIES
AMERICAN
1. "CITY SERIES" (att.)
Albany, New York
Baltimore, Maryland
Buenos Ayres, South America [Aires]
Chillicothe [Ohio] (variation with cows)*
Chillicothe [Ohio] (variation with three men on rafts)*
Chillicothe [Ohio] (variation with sailboat)*
Columbus [Ohio]
Detroit, Michigan
Fishkill, Near [N.Y.]
Hobart Town
Harbor Scene (Unidentified)
Indianapolis, Indiana
Louisville, Kentucky

Philadelphia, A View Near
Philadelphia [Penn's Treaty Tree]
Quebec
Richmond, Virginia
Sandusky [Ohio]
Washington, District of Columbia
Wright's Ferry On The Susquehanna
* See Arman *Quarterly*, Vol. 1, 1997, pp. 8-10.
2. "FRANKLIN'S MORALS" SERIES
The Eye of the Master Will Do More Work Than Both His Hands
Man a Little Makes a Mickle
No Gains Without Pains
If You Would Know The Value of Money Try to Borrow Some
3. MISCELLANEOUS
Franklin "Flying a Kite"
Jones* ["Captain Jones of the Macedonian"]
Montreal (City of) ["British American"]
Perry (Oliver Hazard)
Perry, Hero of the Lake Pike
*See *Larsen*, p. 229, No. 614

FLOW BLUE

CATEGORY	PATTERN	
O	Amoy	Dated 1844
S	British Scenery	Reg'd. 1856
O	Chantilly	-
O	Ching	Dated 1840
F	Clematis	Dated 1848
F	Cornice	Dated 1844
M/F	Cuba	-
O	Cyprus	Reg'd. Jan. 3, 1850/ No. 65884
F	Damask Rose	Dated 1860
F	Flora	Dated Jan. 3, 1850
O	Gothic	Dated 1844 & 1847
M	Griffin	-
-	Ideal	-
S	Isola Bella	-
F	Ivy	Dated 1844
O	"Japan Pattern"	-
F	"Lady Bug"	-
S	Las Palmas Canaria	-
M	Lazuli	-
F	Lily	Dated 1866
O	Macao	-
F	Madras	-
S	Montilla	Dated 1844
F	Nankin	Reg'd. Jan. 3, 1850/ No. 65884
-	Nile	-
P/O	Orissa	Dated 1856
S	Pastoral	-
O	Pekin	Dated 1847
O	Persian Bird	-
F	Rose & Lily	-
-	Seaweed	-
-	Spanish Rose	Dated. 1862
-	Suez*	Reg'd. March 13, 1879/ No. 333241-4
M/F	Vine ["Vine Border"]	Dated 1883
S	Watteau	Dated 1844
P/O	Whampoa	-

*See *FOB*, No. 97, Autumn 1997, p. 12
N.B.: For ease of reading I have taken the liberty of filling in the complete date when impressed marking notes only last two digits;
e.g. '44.

MULBERRY WARES

CATEGORY	PATTERN	
S	Bisham Abbey	-
F	"Blackberry"	Dated 1850
F	Clematis	-
O	Cyprus	Reg'd. Oct. 23, 1852/No. 87219
F	Floresque	Reg'd Jan. 3, 1850/No. 65884
S	Genoa	Reg'd. Oct. 23, 1852/No. 87219
S	Gondola	-
F	Hawthorn	-
F	Ivy	Dated 1866
F	Lilium	-
F	Lily	-
M	Marble	-
F	Nankin	-
F	Oriental Flower	Dated 1848
F	Seine	-
F	Spanish Rose	-

WHITE IRONSTONE

"Bordered Gothic Shape"	-
Cambridge Shape ["Scalloped Decagon Shape"]	Reg'd. Oct. 6, 1854/No. 97141
"Classic Gothic Shape"	Reg'd. 1856
"Corn & Oats"*	-
"Daily Bread Platter"	-
"Davenport's Gothic"	Reg'd. Oct. 23, 1852/No. 87219
"Eagle Head"	-
"Early Cameo Shape" ["Gothic Cameo"]	Dated 1848
Erie Shape ["Sharon Arch Shape"](Ch)	Reg'd. Apr. 12, 1861/No. 139714-5
"Fig Cousin Shape" [Niagara Shape]** (Ch)	Reg'd. Jan. 14, 1853/No. 88987
"Grape Vine Motif Shape" ["Grape Cluster"]	Reg'd. May 27, 1869/No. 229642-4
Niagara Shape ["Fig Cousin Shape"]** (Ch)	Reg'd. Jan. 14, 1853/No. 88987
Plain French ["Squat Oval Teapot"]	Reg'd. Jan. 18, 1853/No. 89050
"Relish Dish"	-
Union Shape ["Fig"]*** (Ch)	Reg'd. 1856[1]
"Vineyard Shape"	Reg'd. 1856

[1] A dinner set was registered on Nov. 14, and a tea ware and table ware set was registered on Nov. 27.
*Confusion with this name and/or the name Corn-on-the-Cob exists. The full name Corn-on-the-Cob is a shape that was originally registered by Davenport, Banks & Co., Jan. 12, 1863 and used by (registered by) Edmund T. Wood on Oct. 31, 1863.
**In order to differentiate the true name Niagara Shape of Niagara Shape between Davenport and Walley, the White Ironstone collectors refer to this as "Fig Cousin".
***In order to differentiate Union Shape by T. & R. Boote, White Ironstone collectors have nicknamed William Davenport's Union Shape "Fig".

TEA LEAF/COPPER LUSTRE

"Early Cameo"	Dated 1848
Niagara Shape ["Fig Cousin Shape"] (Ch)	Reg'd. Jan. 14, 1853/No. 88987
"Rondeau" ["Plain Round"]	-

The following registered (named) shapes are noted by Lockett & Godden's *Davenport*, pp. 294-295.

Davenports & Co.	Jan. 18, 1853	Plain French Shape
Wm. Davenport & Co	Mar. 13, 1879	Berlin Shape, Empress Shape, Regina Shape, Cyprus Shape
	Aug. 14, 1880	Regent Shape
Davenports Ltd.	Sept. 30, 1881	Grecian Shape
	Jan. 9, 1883	Clifton Shape
	July 19, 1883	Antique Shape
	Nov. 1, 1883	Hanley Shape

For further information on marks, paterns and importers refer to Lockett & Godden's *Davenport,* and particularly p. 294 for an update of pattern and registry dates, as follows:

Davenports & Co.	Jan. 14, 1853	Niagara
	Jan.18, 1853	Plain French
	Oct.6, 1854	Cambridge
	Nov.14, 1856	Union
	Apr. 12, 1861	Erie
	Oct. 9, 1868	Parisian
Wm. Davenport & Co.	Mar. 13, 1879	Berlin
	Mar. 13, 1879	Empress
	Mar. 13, 1879	Regina
	Mar. 13, 1879	Cyprus
	Aug. 14, 1880	Regent
Davenports Ltd.	Sept. 30, 1881	Grecian
	Jan. 9, 1883	Clifton
	Feb. 20, 1883	Delaware
	July 19, 1883	Antique
	Nov. 1, 1883	Hanley

Peake, p. 187, Appendix 7, "Teapot Designs" notes "Niagara" as the title for a shape registered on Jan. 14, 1853 by William Davenport.

DAVENPORT, BANKS & CO.
WHITE IRONSTONE
Corn-on-the-Cob Shape ["Corn & Oats Shape"]* Reg'd. Jan. 12, 1863/No. 159083
*This shape was also used by Edmund T. Wood and registered on Oct. 31, 1863, and referred to as "Corn & Oats Shape" by White Ironstone collectors.

RICHARD DAVIES & CO.
BLUE AND WHITE TRANSFERWARE
SINGLE PATTERNS

CATEGORY	PATTERN
M	"Eel Plate"
-	Milanese Villas
-	"Poet & Child"
O	"Willow" Pattern

DAVIS, COOKSON & WILSON
BLUE AND WHITE TRANSFERWARE
SINGLE PATTERNS

CATEGORY	PATTERN
O	"Brosley" ["Two Temples"]*
S	"Country Church"

*See *True Blue*, p. 68, No. 4.

J. H. & J. DAVIS
BLUE AND WHITE TRANSFERWARE
SINGLE PATTERNS

CATEGORY	PATTERN
F	Chatsworth
S	Lucerne
M	Victor

FLOW BLUE

CATEGORY	PATTERN
M	Victor (?)

WHITE IRONSTONE
"Spittoon Gargoyle"
"Wheat" Pattern
TEA LEAF/COPPER LUSTRE
"Plain Round"

DAWSON (JOHN DAWSON & CO., ETC.)
BLUE AND WHITE TRANSFERWARE
SINGLE PATTERNS

CATEGORY	PATTERN
G	"Birds Nest"
G	"Classical Ruins" (possible series)
-	Docility
-	"Girl, Dog & Bucket"
-	"Goatherd"
S	"Romantic" ["Romantic Landscape"]
S	"Squire & Lackey"

FLOW BLUE

CATEGORY	PATTERN
O	Arabia
O	Temple

DEAKIN & BAILEY
BLUE AND WHITE TRANSFERWARE
SINGLE PATTERNS

CATEGORY	PATTERN
G	Crusaders
S	Villa Scenery

DEAKIN & SON(S) (& CO.)
BLUE AND WHITE TRANSFERWARE
SINGLE PATTERNS

CATEGORY	PATTERN
F	Geranium
O	Ortolan
S	Seville
S	Spanish Beauties

FLOW BLUE

CATEGORY	PATTERN
F	"Grape Vine"
M	Japanese Scroll (att.)

EDWIN DEAKIN
FLOW BLUE

CATEGORY	PATTERN
P/M	"Deakin Pearl"

S.W. DEAN
FLOW BLUE

CATEGORY	PATTERN	
F	Blossom	
-	Fernwood	
F	Florentine	Reg'd. 1898/No. 330453
-	Japan	
A	Seraph	
F	"Shamrock"	

DEANS (1910) LTD.
WHITE IRONSTONE
"Wheat"

FRANCIS DILLON
BLUE AND WHITE TRANSFERWARE
SINGLE PATTERNS

CATEGORY	PATTERN
G	Arabian
S	Asiatic Views ["Bridge & Pagoda"?]
-	British Scenery
G	Gardening

DILLWYN & CO.
BLUE AND WHITE TRANSFERWARE
SINGLE PATTERNS

CATEGORY	PATTERN
O	Amoy
S	"Bridge of Lucano"
O	"Chinese Harbor Scene"
O	"Chinese Rose"
O	"Chinese Views"
M	"Cockle Plater" ["Cockle & Whelk"?]
G	"Cow Herd"
S	"Cows Crossing Stream"
S	Cuba
G	"Drover" ["Herdsman"]
O	"Elephant Pattern" ["Elephant & Howdah"] (Haynes, Dillwyn & Co.)
-	"Hawthorn"
M	Lazuli
S	Mignonette
G	Ne Plus Ultra (No Farther)
O	Oriental Basket
G	Ottoman
O	"Peony and Willow"
S	Pulteney Bridge, Bath
S	Rhine
M	Seaweed (Sea Leaf)
H	"Ship" Pattern
S	Swiss Villa
S	Tintern Abbey
M	Unity
-	"Villager"
O	Whampoa
O	"Willow" Pattern
S	"Women With Basket"

FLOW BLUE

CATEGORY	PATTERN
M/F	"Blue Bell"
M	Lazuli
O	Whampoa

N.B.: In their book *Swansea Blue & White Pottery*, p. 16, Pryce and Williams note a series of named views in Black & White Transferware, which include the following:

Barnstable & Bude, Cornwall	Ryde, Isle of Wright
Church of St. Austell, Cornwall	St. Mary's Church, Truro
Church of the Holy Trinity	St. Mary Magdalen, Taunton
Clifton Rocks	St. Michael's Mt., Cornwall
Guernsey College	Swansea Harbor & Town
Mt. Orguel, Jersey	Wilton Church, Wilts
Osborne, Isle of Wright	Winchester Cathedral

J. DIMMOCK & CO.
BLUE AND WHITE TRANSFERWARE
SINGLE PATTERNS

CATEGORY	PATTERN
S	Madras*

*See *P. Williams, Staffordshire*, Vol. III, p. 183.
FLOW BLUE

CATEGORY	PATTERN	
P/F	Bird & Font	
F	Lucerne	Reg'd. 1893/No. 221056
S	McNette	
A	Senator*	
S	Vignette	

*Pattern used by Burgess & Campbell for "Royal Blue" and "Balmoral", as well as by Hughes for "Floral". Refer to section on American potters.

DIMMOCK & SMITH
BLUE AND WHITE TRANSFERWARE
SINGLE PATTERNS

CATEGORY	PATTERN
H	Victoria

FLOW BLUE

CATEGORY	PATTERN
J/O	Amherst Japan
O	Chino
F	Delhi
O	Shantong
O	Scinde

THOMAS DIMMOCK (JR.) & CO.
BLUE AND WHITE TRANSFERWARE
SERIES
1. "CHEVY CHASE" SERIES
"Hunter returning home"
"Hunters and urn"
"Hunters resting"
"Stag and urn"
"White horse and hunting horn"
2. "SELECT SKETCHES SERIES"
Antwerp
Cowes
Menai Bridge
New York
Rhodes
Tivoli
BLUE AND WHITE TRANSFERWARE
SINGLE PATTERNS

CATEGORY	PATTERN
-	"Birds"
O	"Chinese"
O	"Chinese Tree"
-	"Clarendon"
N	Conchology
M/F	"Coral Border"
F	"Filigree"
S	Gothic
M	"Grecian Border"
-	"Indian"
-	"Ruined Temple & Tower"

P/O	Japanese	
F	Lily	Reg'd. June 29, 1844/No. 19182
-	Morea (att.)	
O	Nankin	
S	Neopolitan	
-	Oriental Vase	
O	Pekin	
S	Vignette	
S	"Village Church"*	
O	"Willow" Pattern	

See *P. Williams Staffordshire,* Vol. III, pp. 118-119.
HISTORIC STAFFORDSHIRE SERIES
AMERICAN
1. MISCELLANEOUS
"Burning of Coenties Slip" (2)
"Exchange, New York"* (3)
"Ruined Merchants Exchange"**
*See *Larsen*, 3rd edition, No. 687, 690 & 691
**See Snyder, *Historic Staffordshire*, p. 112.
N.B.: This pottery is controversial. Two other views may exist.
FLOW BLUE

CATEGORY	PATTERN	
A/F	Argyll	-
O	Bamboo	-
F	Bohemia	Reg'd. Nov. 22, 1844/No. 22834
F	"Bouquet"	Reg'd. Nov. 28, 1843/No. 11690
O	Chinese	-
O	Chinese Garden	-
P/O	Chinese Key	-
F	Coburg	-
O	Dagger Border	-
O	Dragon	-
F	Florentine	-
O	Indian Plant	-
P/F	Ivy	-
F	Lily	Reg'd. June 29, 1844/No. 19182
F	Lotus	-
O	Mandarin	Reg'd. 1844
M	Marble	-
O	Oriental	-
F	Orleans	-
M	Oxonian	-
O	Pekin	-
O	Rhine	Reg'd. May 7, 1844/No. 18207
M/F	Royal Rose (att.)	-
M	Shells	-
S	Shrine	-
M/A	Windsor Scroll	-

MULBERRY WARES

CATEGORY	PATTERN	
F	Argyll	-
F	Balmoral	-
P/F	Bohemia	Reg'd. Nov. 22, 1844/No. 22834
F	Chaplet Wreath	Reg'd. 1844
O	Chinese	-
F	Chintz	-
P/F	Florentine	-
F	Lily	Reg'd. June 29, 1844/No. 19182
O	Mandarin	Reg'd. 1844
F	Tripod	-
F	Vienna	-
F	Wild Flowers	

***DON POTTERY**
BLUE AND WHITE TRANSFERWARE
SERIES
1."NAMED" ITALIAN VIEWS SERIES
Aetna from the Augustines
Ancient Cistern Near Catania
Black Swan
The Bridge of Staves
Brundisium
Cascade at Isola
The Church of Resina at the Foot of Vesuvius
The Drying Green
Etna from the Adorines
Grotto of St. Rosalie Near Palermo
Isola
Monastery at Tre Castagne
Obelisk at Catania
On the Heights of Corigliano
Port of Ansetta
Port of Turenium
Residence of Solimenes near Vesuvius (2)
Ruins Near Agrigenti
Ruins of the Castle of Canna
Temple of Serapis at Pouzzuoli
Terrace of the Naval Amphitheatre at Taorminum
Tomb of Theron at Agrigentum
View in Palma
View in the Valley of Oretho Near Palermo
View Near Taormina
View of Alicata
View of Camping and Carting
View of Canada
View of Corigliano
View of Part of Mont Peloet in Sicily
View of Stromboli from the part facing to the Northeast
View of Temple on the Hill
View of the Cave of the Goats on Etna
View of the Countryside at Agrigento
View of the Rocks or Cape of Scaretia
View of the Ruins of the Temple of Juno at Agrigento
View of the Tower Pulicoro on the Gulf of Tarento
Coysh, p. 256, of his Dictionary, mentions that there are two other views which are doubtful; On the Po and Port of Alicata.
N.B.: Views, above, marked with a "T" are also known by Twigg (Twigg/Newhill)
2. "LANDSCAPE SERIES"
"Castello St. Angelo"
"Italian Fountains"
"Reading Woman"
3. "VERMICELLI BORDER" SERIES
Abbey Cloister
Bridge and Gatehouse
Cottages
Packhorse and Cottages
Round Tower
Sailing Boat by Cliffs
BLUE AND WHITE TRANSFERWARE
SINGLE PATTERNS

CATEGORY	PATTERN
S	"Bridge of Lucano"
O	Broseley
O	"Chinoiserie Bridgeless" (2)
S	Eyaopia
G	"Milkmaid"
O	Oriental
O	"Reindeer Pattern"
S	"Sun and Fountain"
O	"Two Temples"
S	"Wild Horse"

DOULTON & CO. (LTD.)
BLUE AND WHITE TRANSFERWARE
SINGLE PATTERNS

CATEGORY	PATTERN
F	Asiatic Pheasants
A	Belmont
A	Borrento
A	Elaine
S	Glendale, The
O	Mandarin
A	Oxford
F	Pomeroy
O	"Willow" Pattern

FLOW BLUE

CATEGORY	PATTERN	
F/A	Adelaide	-
F	Adderley	-
O	Amoy	-
F	Arundel	-
A	Aubrey	Dated 1903
G	Babes In The Woods	-
F	Beverly	-
A	Briar Rose	Reg'd. 1905/No. 453404
F	Buttercup	-
S	Chase (The)	-
-	Clifton	-
F	Daffodil	-
A	Edgerton	-
H	Eglinton Tournament	-
M/S	Empire	Reg'd. 1899/No. 344750
F	Festoon	-
F	Flora	-
F	Fruit & Flowers	Dated May 1904
S	Geneva	-
O	Genevesa	-
S	Gibson Widow*	-
F	Gladiolus	-
F	Gloire de Dijon	Reg'd. 1897/No. 307815
F	Gloire de Gulian	-
A	Howard	Reg'd. 1901/No. 374874
F	Iris	-
H	Isthmian Games	-
M	Jacobean	Reg'd. 1901/02 (continued to1935)
O	Jedo	-
F	Jessica	-
A	Kensington	-

A	Kent	-
F	Klemscot	Reg'd. 1901/No. 374820/74
O	Madras**	-
F	Matsumai	-
M	Melbourne	-
F	Melrose	Reg'd. 1898/No. 316420
G	Morrisan	-
S	Nankin	-
F	Nanking	-
F	Norbury	-
S	Norfolk	-
F	Oxford	-
O	Oyama	-
A	Paisley	-
M	Persian Spray***	-
F	Poppy	-
-	Provence	-
S	Rabbits	-
A	Sandhurst****	Reg'd. 1885/No. 35324
A	Simplicitas	-
F	Sutherland	-
S	Switzerland	-
L	The Tempest	-
-	Turkey	-
F	Vernon	-
A	Veronica	-
F	Virginia	-
S	"Volga-Villa"	-
S	Watteau	-
O	"Willow" Pattern	-
A	Willow & Aster	-

*For a complete listing of the Gibson (Rack Plates) refer to Louise Irvine, *Royal Doulton Series Ware, Vol. I*. London, Richard Dennis, 1980. pp. 70-75.
**Pattern appears to be the same as Wood & Baggaley
***Registered in the US in 1906, Patent No. 25792, title "Cheer Up".
****Sandhurst reregistered 1901, No. 370821

DUDSON BROS.
(James Dudson/J(ames) T. Dudson)
BLUE AND WHITE TRANSFERWARE
SINGLE PATTERNS

CATEGORY	PATTERN
-	Galloping Horses
-	Irish Hero
-	Wanderer (att.)

DUDSON, WILCOX & TILL, LTD.
FLOW BLUE

CATEGORY	PATTERN
F	Albert
-	Daisy

DAVID DUNDERDALE & CO.
BLUE AND WHITE TRANSFERWARE
SINGLE PATTERNS

CATEGORY	PATTERN
O	"Buffalo and Ruins"
O	"Long Bridge"
S	"Village Church"
-	"Violin"

DUNN BENNETT & CO. (LTD.)
BLUE AND WHITE TRANSFERWARE
SINGLE PATTERNS

CATEGORY	PATTERN
A	Marlborough
A	Ravenscliffe

FLOW BLUE

CATEGORY	PATTERN
-	Delft
F	Duchess
F	Florence
F	Hawthorne
F	Lilac
F	Recherche
F	Roserie
F	Rutland

WILLIAM & SAMUEL EDGE
BLUE AND WHITE TRANSFERWARE
SINGLE PATTERNS

CATEGORY	PATTERN
G	Humulus
O	"Willow" Pattern

EDGE, BARKER & CO.
BLUE AND WHITE TRANSFERWARE
SINGLE PATTERNS

CATEGORY	PATTERN
G	Humulus

EDGE, MALKIN & CO. (LTD.)
BLUE AND WHITE TRANSFERWARE
SERIES
1. "INDIAN SCENERY SERIES"
Delhi, Hindoostan
Surseya Ghaut, Khanpore
Tomb of Shere Shah
Tombs Near Etaya on the Jumna River
BLUE AND WHITE TRANSFERWARE
SINGLE PATTERNS

CATEGORY	PATTERN
F	Avon
J	Bower (The)
M	Cashmere
P/O	Chang
C	Corella
S	Genevese
S	Italy
S	Lisbon
S	Marino
S	Missouri
J	Peat Goat
S	Verona
J/O	"Willow" Pattern

FLOW BLUE

CATEGORY	PATTERN	
-	Argyle	
F	Empress	
S	Genevese	
F	Iris	
-	Paris	
O	Sciao	
O	Singa*	
F	Summertime	
A	Watteau	Reg'd. 1899/No. 3421681

*The Singa pattern was continued on from Cork, Edge & Malkin. Refer to *Godden* mark No. 1445.
TEA LEAF/COPPER LUSTRE BAND
"Polonaise"

JAMES EDWARDS
BLUE AND WHITE TRANSFERWARE
SINGLE PATTERNS

CATEGORY	PATTERN	
M/Z	American Bird	-
S	Coburg*	Reg'd. Aug. 30, 1843/No. 9678-80
S	Corinth	-
S	Domestic	-
O	Erford	-
M	Flensburg	-
M	The Roby Day & Sunday School	-
S	Shield	-

HISTORIC STAFFORDSHIRE SERIES
AMERICAN
1. BOSTON MAILS "SERIES"*
Boston Mails "Gentlemen's Cabin" (With Three-Five Passengers and Steward) (3)
Boston Mails "Ladies Cabin" (Three Passengers)
Boston Mail "Saloon", et.al. (Eleven Men and Woman besides Steward)
* Originally registered by James & Thomas Edwards Sept. 2, 1841/ No. 808.
\- See comments under Marks section.
FLOW BLUE

CATEGORY	PATTERN	
O	Cabul	Reg'd. Aug. 26, 1847/No. 45367
O	Canton	-
S	Coburg*	Reg'd. Aug. 30, 1843/No. 9678-80
M	Flensburg	-
M	Lazuli	-
S	Salem	-

*Registered on Oct. 26, 1846/No. 37864 June 25, 1847/No. 43780 and July 16, 1847/No.44036.
MULBERRY WARES

CATEGORY	PATTERN	
O	Bochara	Reg'd. Aug. 1847
S	Coburg*	Reg'd. June 25, 1847/No. 43780
S	Foliage	-

WHITE IRONSTONE

"Ball & Stick"	-
"Classic Gothic"	-
"Crabstock Dozen"	-
"Curved Gothic Shape"	Reg'd. Aug. 30, 1843/No. 9678-80
"Double Leaf"	-

"Edward's Leaf"	-
"Edward's Lily of the Valley"	
"Fluted Double Swirl"*	Reg'd. May 30, 1842/No. 1267
"Fluted Gothic"	-
"Fluted Panels"	-
"Framed Classic"	-
"Full Panelled Gothic"["Hexagonal" or "Octagonal"]	-
"Gothic Cameo"	-
"Husk"	-
"Line Trim"	-
"Open Roses"	-
"Pedestaled Gothic Shape" (Ch)	Reg'd. July 16, 1847/No. 44036-9
"Pinch Neck Gothic Shape"	-
"Pond Lily Pad"	-
"Rolling Star"	-
"Split Pod"	-
"Square Acorn"	-
"Square Open Flower Shape"	Reg'd. Dec. 16, 1848/No. 56631-3
"Square Rose Bud Shape"	Reg'd. Dec. 16, 1848/No. 56631-3
"Square Tumbling Petals Shape"	Reg'd. Dec. 16, 1848/No. 56631-3
"Triple Border Shape"	Reg'd. Sept. 21, 1853/No. 92631-2
"True Scallop"	-
"Twin Leaves Shape" ["Hexagon Shape"]	Reg'd. Sept. 29, 1851/No. 80815-16 (possibly registered Sept. 30, 1851)
"Wild Rose Twig"	-

*See *White Ironstone Notes*, Vol. 5, No. 1, Summer 1998, pp. 10-11 for an article by Jean Wetherbee titled "Verifying a New Shape".

JAMES EDWARDS & SON
BLUE AND WHITE TRANSFERWARE
SINGLE PATTERNS

CATEGORY	PATTERN	
F	Arabic	Reg'd. Mar. 24, 1852/No. 84406
M	Vintage	

FLOW BLUE

CATEGORY	PATTERN	
F	Arabic	Reg'd. Mar. 24, 1852/No. 84406
O	Windsor Royal	-

WHITE IRONSTONE

"Alternate Octagon Shape"	Reg'd. Mar. 22, 1854/No. 95397
"Draped Leaf Shape"	Reg'd. Sept. 1, 1859/No. 121833
"Fluted Panels" (12 panels)	-
"Edward's Lily of the Valley Shape"*	Reg'd. Sept. 1, 1859/No. 121833 & Feb. 27, 1861/No.138535
"Gourd"	-
"Hanging Arch Shape"	Reg'd. Sept. 6, 1858/No. 115197
"Husk"	-
"Line Trim"	-
"True Scallop"	-
"Twisted Ribbon"	-

*Lily of the Valley shapes vary according to potter.

JOHN EDWARDS (& CO.)
BLUE AND WHITE TRANSFERWARE
SINGLE PATTERNS

CATEGORY	PATTERN
S	Chateau
M/F	Eastern Plants
A	Eola
A	Fleur de Lis
S	Salem

FLOW BLUE

CATEGORY	PATTERN
F	Morning Glory

WHITE IRONSTONE

"Bamboo Shape"	-
"Bellflower"	-
Harve Shape	Reg'd. June 12, 1866/ No. 198135-7
Peerless "Shape" ["Feather"]	Reg'd. 1887/No. 53184
President Shape	Reg'd. Jan. 30, 1855/No. 99188 & Jan. 5, 1856/No. 103103
Royal "Shape" ["Lion's Head" "Sheep's Head"]	Reg'd. 1877
St. Louis Shape	-
Seine	-
Sevres Shape	-
Tuscan Shape	Reg'd. July 18, 1853/No. 91737
Victory "Shape" ["Dolphin"]	Reg'd. 1884/No. 10959, and 1888

TEA LEAF/COPPER LUSTRE BAND

"Bamboo Shape"	Reg'd. 1887
Peerless "Shape" ["Feather"]	Reg'd. 1887/No.58184
Royal "Shape" ["Lion's Head"]	Reg'd. 1877
Victory "Shape" ["Dolphin"]	Reg'd. 1884/No. 10959 and 1888

THOMAS EDWARDS
BLUE AND WHITE TRANSFERWARE
SINGLE PATTERNS

CATEGORY	PATTERN
S	Abbey
S	Hudson
S	Sirius
S	Temple
S	Waverly

WHITE IRONSTONE

"Fluted Pearl Shape"	Reg'd. Apr. 3, 1844/No. 17566-72
"Fluted Panels Shape"	Reg'd. Apr. 3, 1844/No. 17566-72

JAMES & THOMAS EDWARDS
BLUE AND WHITE TRANSFERWARE
SINGLE PATTERNS

CATEGORY	PATTERN
S	Mansion
O	Sirius

HISTORIC STAFFORDSHIRE SERIES
AMERICAN
1. BOSTON MAILS "SERIES"*
Boston Mails "Gentlemen's Cabin" (With Three-Five Passengers and Steward) (3)
Boston Mails "Ladies Cabin" (Three Passengers)
Boston Mail "Saloon", et.al. (Eleven Men and Woman besides Steward)
*Designs were Reg'd. Sept. 2, 1841/No. 808.
-See comments under James Edwards in Marks Section
FLOW BLUE
SINGLE PATTERNS

CATEGORY	PATTERNS
H	Acadia
H	Britannia
H	Caldonia
H	Columbia

MULBERRY WARES

CATEGORY	PATTERN
M	Boston Mails "Ladies Cabin"* (Three Passengers)

*Designs were Reg'd. Sept. 2, 1841/No. 808.

ELGIN POTTERY
BLUE AND WHITE TRANSFERWARE
SINGLE PATTERNS

CATEGORY	PATTERN
-	Elgin
-	Mile End
-	Windsor

ELKIN, KNIGHT & BRIDGWOOD
BLUE AND WHITE TRANSFERWARE
SERIES
1. "CANTON VIEWS" SERIES
"Chinese River Scene"
"Three Men in Boat"
"Two Men on Rocks"
2. "ETRUSCAN" SERIES
"Britannia"
"Greek Maiden with Lamb"
"Greek Musicians"
"Rams Head Tripod"
"Urn on Column"
BLUE AND WHITE TRANSFERWARE
SINGLE PATTERNS

CATEGORY	PATTERN
G	"Archery"
O	Canton Views
O	Chinese Fountains
O	Chinese Pagoda
S	Cologne
C	Etruscan ["Classical Figure"]
O	Indian Temple

FLOW BLUE

CATEGORY	PATTERN
-	Rome

ELKIN, KNIGHT & CO.
BLUE AND WHITE TRANSFERWARE
SERIES
1. "ROCK CARTOUCHE MARK SERIES"
By Land, Abbey, Yorkshire
Craig Castle ["Castle Richard in Waterford"]
Fountains Abbey, Yorkshire
Guy's Cliffe
Jedburgh Abbey
Lancaster
Mill at Ambleside
Nant Mill
Near Newark
Near Patterdale
Sweetheart Abbey
BLUE AND WHITE TRANSFERWARE
SINGLE PATTERNS

CATEGORY	PATTERN
O	Canton

MULBERRY WARES
P. Williams, Staffordshire, Vol. 2, p. 201, records an Irish Scenery pattern in Mulberry of a castle high on a bluff.

ELKIN & NEWBON
BLUE AND WHITE TRANSFERWARE
SERIES
1. "BOTANICAL BEAUTIES" SERIES
"Giant Lily"
"Passion Flower"
BLUE AND WHITE TRANSFERWARE
SINGLE PATTERNS

CATEGORY	PATTERN
F	Botanical Beauties
S	Warwick Vase
O	"Willow" Pattern

ELKIN & CO.
BLUE AND WHITE TRANSFERWARE
SERIES
1. IRISH SCENERY "SERIES"
Castle Richard in Waterford ["Craig Castle]*
Fonthill Abbey, Wiltshire
The Haining, Selkirkshire
Stackpole Court, Pembrokeshire
Warren
Warwick Castle
**Coysh* notes this as Castle Richard [Craig Castle] Waterford, Refer to Vol. 2, p. 49
BLUE AND WHITE TRANSFERWARE
SINGLE PATTERNS

CATEGORY	PATTERN
-	"Floral Sheet"
-	"Pastoral"
M	"The Pet Goat"
S	Warwick Vase

ELSMORE & FORSTER
BLUE AND WHITE TRANSFERWARE
SINGLE PATTERNS

CATEGORY	PATTERN
A	Osborne
P/Z	"Pheasant"
G	Vaquero*
-	"Wheat"

* Only recorded in purple
FLOW BLUE

CATEGORY	PATTERN
M	"Lustre Band"
O	Simla
M	"Strawberry Lustre"*

*Named "Tulip & Sprig" in Brush Stroke
MULBERRY WARES

CATEGORY	PATTERN
F	"Bittersweet"
-	"Gaudy" (Brush Stroke)
P/F	"Grandmother's Flowers"*
P/F	"Lily & Vase"
O	Simla
F	"Trumpet Flower"*
P/F	"Trumpet Flower Variant"

*Made in purple, not in Mulberry.
WHITE IRONSTONE

"Arched Forget-Me-Not Shape"	Reg'd. Nov. 10, 1864/ No. 181214-5
"Arched Panel"	-
"Big & Little Ribs" ["1 Big & 2 Little Ribs"]	-
Ceres Shape* (Ch) ["Wheat"]	Reg'd. Nov. 2, 1859/ No. 123738-40
"Ceres With Cable"	-
"Ceres Without Cable"	-
"Classic Gothic"	-
Columbia Shape (Ch)	Reg'd. Mar. 5, 1855/ No. 99579
"Double Sydenham" ["Wrapped Sydenham"]	-
"Fanfare"	-
"Fuchsia" (or "Lily & Vase")	-
"Gothic Shape"	-
"Grape Octagon"	-
"Green Band"	-
Laurel Wreath Shape/Victory Shape**	Reg'd. Apr. 4, 1867/ No. 207201
Morning Glory Shape [Halleck Shape]	Reg'd. Apr. 4, 1867/ No. 207201
Olympic Shape ["Greek Key"]	Reg'd. Nov. 10, 1864/ No. 181214-5
"One Large & Two Little Ribs"	-
Pacific Shape	Reg'd. Feb. 20, 1871/ No. 250478-9
"Paneled Decagon"	-
"Paneled Grape"	-
"Plain Scallop" (Ch) ["Crystal"]	-
"Pod"	-
Portland Shape (Ch)	Reg'd. Apr. 4, 1867/ No. 207201
"Rose Banded"	-
"Sydenham"	-
Tulip "Shape" (Ch) ["Little Scroll"] (No. 2)	Reg'd. Mar. 5, 1855/ No. 99579
Victory Shape/Laurel Wreath Shape**	Reg'd. Apr. 4, 1867/ No. 207201

TEA LEAF/COPPER LUSTRE BAND

"Arched Forget-Me-Not Shape"	Reg'd. Nov. 10, 1864/ No. 181214-5
Ceres Shape* ["Wheat"]	Reg'd. Nov. 2, 1859/ No. 123738-40
Columbia Shape***	Reg'd. Mar. 5, 1855/ No. 99579
"Crystal Shape" ["Plain Scallop"]	-
"Fanfare"	-
"Gothic IV: Many Panelled"	-
"Grape Octagon"	-
Laurel Wreath Shape/Victory Shape**	Reg'd. Apr. 4, 1867/No. 207201
"Many Paneled Gothic"	-
Portland Shape	Reg'd. Apr. 4, 1867/No. 207201
Tulip Shape ["Little Scroll"](No. 2)	Reg'd. Mar. 5, 1855/No. 99579
Victory Shape/Laurel Wreath Shape**	Reg'd. Apr. 4, 1867/No. 207201

*Ceres Shape was manufactured as a tea, dinner and toilet set, each with a distinct registry number.
**See *White Ironstone Notes*, Vol. 2, No. 4, Spring 1996 for two shapes registered on the same date.
***Spelling error in name, reading Elsmore & *Foster* noted on some Copper Lustre pieces.
N.B.: Refer to *Appendix E5A*, Additional Potters Recorded in White Ironstone by Arene Burgess
Sam Laidacker notes a Laurel Wreath registered Nov. 2, 1859/No. 123738-40 in his *Anglo-American China, Part I*. Bristol, PA. 1954, p.15, as follows: "This is a tea and toilet set of heavy white ironstone with a black transfer of the Stuart bust of Washington inside a wreath in heavy relief. The title is over the Registry mark [Laurel Wreath] reading 1859. The same pattern is found without the transfer decoration..."

ELSMORE (THOMAS) & SON
WHITE IRONSTONE
Crystal "Shape"*
"Plain Round"
*See *White Ironstone Notes*, Vol. 4, No. 2, Fall 1997, p. 11 for impressed name mark Crystal.
TEA LEAF/COPPER LUSTRE BAND
"Plain Round"
Portland Shape

WILLIAM EMBERTON (& CO.)
BLUE AND WHITE TRANSFERWARE
SINGLE PATTERNS

CATEGORY	PATTERN
F	Asiatic Pheasant
A	Berber
S	Cottage Scenery

FLOW BLUE

CATEGORY	PATTERN
O	Amoy

FRANCIS J. EMERY
BLUE AND WHITE TRANSFERWARE
SINGLE PATTERNS

CATEGORY	PATTERN
S	Cyprus
O	Satsuma

FLOW BLUE

CATEGORY	PATTERN
O	Burmese

EMPIRE PORCELAIN CO. (LTD.)
BLUE AND WHITE TRANSFERWARE
SINGLE PATTERNS

CATEGORY	PATTERN
A	"Star Center"

FLOW BLUE

CATEGORY	PATTERN
-	Arabic
A	Astoria
O	Oriental
F	Pansies
F	"Pomegranate"
F	Savoy
O	"Willow" Pattern

D.J. EVANS & CO.
BLUE AND WHITE TRANSFERWARE
SINGLE PATTERNS

CATEGORY	PATTERN
M	Birds
F	Floral
O	Verandah
O	"Willow" Pattern

EVANS & GLASSON
BLUE AND WHITE TRANSFERWARE
SINGLE PATTERNS

CATEGORY	PATTERN
S	"Cows Crossing Stream Pattern"
S	Cuba
S	"Swiss Scenery"
O	Whampoa
O	"Willow" Pattern

THOMAS FELL (& CO.) (LTD.)
BLUE AND WHITE TRANSFERWARE
SINGLE PATTERNS

CATEGORY	PATTERN	
S	Antiquarian	
F	Asiatic Pheasants	
S	Bosphorus (The)	
G	"Boy & Man"*	
S	"Cattle Scenery"	
-	"Charlotte"	
O	"Chinese Marine"	
G	Chinese Sports	
S	Corinth	Dated 1845
-	"Ferns & Flowers"	
-	Fountain	
-	"Four Deer"	
S	Italia	
-	"La Mancha"	
-	"Lady on the Lake"	
S	Lasso	
S	Ne Plus	
L	Pickwick	
S	Rhine	
-	"Swans & Vase"**	
G	"Tea Party"	
G	"Tomb Pattern"	
S	Wild Rose	
S	Woodland	
G	"Woodman"	
O	"Willow" Pattern	

*See *True Blue*, p. 83, No. 6.
**See *True Blue*, p. 92, No. 15.

FLOW BLUE

CATEGORY	PATTERN
S	Excelsior
O	Japan
M	Northumberland

MULBERRY WARES

CATEGORY	PATTERN	
O	Chusan*	
F	Fuschia	
P/O	Japan	
O	Segapore	
S	Trafik	Dated 1846

*See *P. Williams*, *Flow Blue, Vol. 3,* p. 149, Chusan by T. Fell

FERRYBRIDGE POTTERY
BLUE AND WHITE TRANSFERWARE
SERIES
1. "GREEK PATTERN" SERIES
(Classical Figure Patterns)
"Bull Rider"
"Chariot with Rearing Horses"
"Classical Grecian"
"Greek Altar"
"Seated & Kneeling Ladies"
"Trotting Chariot"

BLUE AND WHITE TRANSFERWARE
SINGLE PATTERNS

CATEGORY	PATTERN
-	"Bridge & Church"
-	"Elephant & Castle"
O	"Elephant & Howdah" (2)
O	"Elephants"
O	"Gardener & Butterfly"
O	"Gazebo" (att.)
-	"Indiana"
-	"Pearl River House" ["Trench Mortar"]
O	Polka
P/F	Schizanthus
O	"Three Chinamen"
O	"Willow Nanking" ["Mandarin"]
O	"Willow Pattern"

FLACKETT & TOFT
BLUE AND WHITE TRANSFERWARE
SINGLE PATTERNS

CATEGORY	PATTERN
O	Chian

FLACKETT, TOFT & ROBINSON
FLOW BLUE

CATEGORY	PATTERN
O	Bimrah

STEPHEN FOLCH
BLUE AND WHITE TRANSFERWARE
SINGLE PATTERNS

CATEGORY	PATTERN
O	"Peonies & Birds"
O	"Temple Landscape II"

FORD & SONS (LTD.)
FLOW BLUE

CATEGORY	PATTERN
M/A	Argyle
F	Arley
F	Avon
S	Bay
A	Belmont
M/A	Berkley
-	Boston
A	Brampton
A	Brentford
-	Brentwood
M/F	Bristol
M/A	Bute
M/A	Carlton
F	Chatsworth
F	Clifton
M	Corona
A	Devon
A	Douglas
A	Dover
A	Dudley
F	Florida
M/F	Floris
P/O	Geisha
M/A	Grecian
A	Halford
M/F	Ilford
M/F	Jewell
F	Lily
F	Mareshal
F	Melbourne
M	Milan
A	Norman
-	Osborne
A	Oxford
O	Pekin
F	Primrose
F	Queen
M/F	Richmond
M/A	Richmond
-	Rio
S	Ruskin
F	Salisbury
-	Sandon
F	Shirley
-	Tokio
M/F	Trent (I&II)
M/A	Trellis
S	Verona
F	Verona
F	Walton
A	Watford
M/F	Weir
M/F	Windsor

FORD & CHALLINOR
(or Ford & Challinor & Co.)
BLUE AND WHITE TRANSFERWARE
SINGLE PATTERNS

CATEGORY	PATTERN	
S	Monument (Russian Script)	Reg'd. Oct. 24, 1867/No. 212765
S	Russian Views	Reg'd. Nov. 18, 1867/No. 214000

FLOW BLUE

CATEGORY	PATTERN
F	Groop (The)
-	Pansy

WHITE IRONSTONE
"Wheat & Clover" (with concave ribs)

JOHN FORD & CO.
BLUE AND WHITE TRANSFERWARE
SINGLE PATTERNS

CATEGORY	PATTERN
G	Humphreys Clock

SAMUEL FORD & CO.
FLOW BLUE

CATEGORY	PATTERN
F	Arbor
O	Cypress
F	Lonsdale
F	Martel
F	Milan
F	McKinley
M/A	Penang
-	Savoy
M	Tokio

THOMAS FORD (& CO.)
HISTORIC STAFFORDSHIRE SERIES
AMERICAN
1. MISCELLANEOUS
America
FLOW BLUE

CATEGORY	PATTERN
O	Ming

FORD & PATTERSON (& CO.)
BLUE AND WHITE TRANSFERWARE
SINGLE PATTERNS

CATEGORY	PATTERN
O	"Willow" Pattern

THOMAS FORESTER SON & CO.
FLOW BLUE

CATEGORY	PATTERN
F	"Forester's Flowers" (att.)
F	Ponseters

THOMAS FORESTER & SONS (LTD.)
FLOW BLUE

CATEGORY	PATTERN
F	"Forester's Flowers" (att.)
F	Windsor

GEORGE FORRESTER
BLUE AND WHITE TRANSFERWARE
SINGLE PATTERNS

CATEGORY	PATTERN
O	"Chinoiserie Design" ["Bridgeless Temple/Four Pavilions"]

FOWLER THOMPSON & CO.
BLUE AND WHITE TRANSFERWARE
SINGLE PATTERNS

CATEGORY	PATTERN
-	"Bird & Fly"
-	"Willow" Pattern

FREAKLEY & FARRELL
WHITE IRONSTONE
Grape Octagon"

JACOB FURNIVAL & CO.
BLUE AND WHITE TRANSFERWARE
SINGLE PATTERNS

CATEGORY	PATTERN	
S	Castle Scenery	
M	Coral	
S	Gothic (att.)	
M/F	Grape	
F	Lily	
O	Mecca	
S	Medina	
S	Palmyra	Reg'd. Apr. 30, 1845/No. 27383
F	Phantasia	

FLOW BLUE

CATEGORY	PATTERN
O	Chinese Sports
A	Delaware
S	Gothic
S	Medina
F	Moss Rose III
S	Rhine
O	Shanghae
M	"Strawberry" (Brush Stroke)

MULBERRY WARES

CATEGORY	PATTERN
S	Castle Scenery
P/F	Coral
P/F	Cotton Plant #100
S	Gothic
F	Lily
S	Medina
F	Moss Rose
P/F	Phantasia
O	Shanghae #36
M	"Strawberry" (Brush Stroke)

WHITE IRONSTONE
"Aquatic Shape"* Reg'd. Jan 30, 1868/No. 216333
"Berry Cluster"
"Classic Cameo"
"Classic Gothic"
"Floral Gothic"
"Flower Blanket"
"Fluted Hills"
"Fruit Garden"
"Gooseberry"
"Gothic Grape"
"Grand Loop"
"Grape Octagon"
"Hidden Motif"
"J.F.'s Wheat"
"Lily of the Valley with Thumb Prints"
"Loop & Line"
"Panelled Grape" (Ch)
"Panelled Lily"
"Pomegranate"
"Quartered Rose"
"Ring O'Hearts"
"Short Octagon"
"Texas Furnival"
"Two Fish"
"Walled Octagon"
"Wheat & Hops" ["Wheat & Blackberry"]
*See *White Ironstone Notes,* Vol. 4, No. 1, Summer 1997, p. 13
TEA LEAF/COPPER LUSTRE BAND
"Berry Cluster"
"Cockscomb Handle" (att.)
"Floral Gothic"
"Full Paneled Gothic"
"Grand Loop"
"Grape Octagon"
"Panelled Grape"
"Quartered Rose"
"Ring O'Hearts"
"Walled Octagon"
"Wheat"*
*Same as J.F.'s Wheat in White Ironstone.

JACOB & THOMAS FURNIVAL
BLUE AND WHITE TRANSFERWARE
SINGLE PATTERNS

CATEGORY	PATTERN
O	Indian Jar
S	Medina

FLOW BLUE

CATEGORY	PATTERN
O	Indian Jar

THOMAS FURNIVAL & CO.
BLUE AND WHITE TRANSFERWARE
SINGLE PATTERNS

CATEGORY	PATTERN	
M/H	America*	Reg'd. Nov. 21, 1846/No. 38291-2
O	Chinese Sports	
-	Eagle on Globe	Reg'd. Nov. 21, 1846/No. 38291-1
S	Italy	
S	Palmyra	
F	Rose (The)	

FLOW BLUE

CATEGORY	PATTERN	
S	Castle Scenery	
O	Chinese (att.)	
S	Florentine	Reg'd. Jan. 30, 1868/No. 216333
O	Formosa	
O	Indian Jar	
O	Japan	
F	Orchard Blossom	
O	Oriental Flowers	
S	Rhone	
S	Tivoli	

MULBERRY WARES

CATEGORY	PATTERN
S	Rhone
F	Wreath*

*Often found with only importer's mark of Peter Wright, Philadelphia

THOMAS FURNIVAL & SONS
BLUE AND WHITE TRANSFERWARE
SINGLE PATTERNS

CATEGORY	PATTERN
F	Spray

HISTORIC STAFFORDSHIRE SERIES
CANADIAN
SINGLE PATTERNS

CATEGORY	PATTERN	
F	Maple	Reg'd. Sept. 20, 1884

FLOW BLUE

CATEGORY	PATTERN	
O	Bombay	
O	Ceylon	
M	Florentine	
O	Mikado	Reg'd. July 2, 1881/No. 366643
F	Meissen	
F	Versailles	

WHITE IRONSTONE

"Cable & Ring"*	-
"Fox & Grapes"	-
"Gentle Square Shape" ["Rooster"]	Reg'd. Apr. 21, 1876 and Nov. 24, 1876
"Hanging Basket"**	-
"Plain Round Shape"	Reg'd. 1885/No. 30039
The Lorne "Shape" ["Roped Wheat"]	Reg'd. Apr. 20, 1878/No. 320606 and 1884/No. 5458
"Wheat"	-

*Copper Tea Leaf collectors refer to this as "Cable".
**Refer to *White Ironstone Notes*, Vol. 4, No. 2, Fall 1997, p. 10 for an illustration

TEA LEAF/COPPER LUSTRE BAND

"Cable Shape"	-
"Gentle Square Shape" ["Rooster"]	Reg'd. Apr. 21, 1876 and Nov. 24, 1876
"Little Cable"	-

FURNIVALS (LTD.)
BLUE AND WHITE TRANSFERWARE
SINGLE PATTERNS

CATEGORY	PATTERN
M	Fabric
F	Quails

FLOW BLUE

CATEGORY	PATTERN	
M/F	Acorn	-
S	Adelphi	-
-	Bombay	-
F	Bouquet	-
F	Capri	Reg'd. 1895/No. 26891
F	Carnation	-
M/F	Cluny	Reg'd. 1902/No.394104
M	Denmark	-
M	Derby	Reg'd. 1902/No. 388682
F	English Rose	-
M	Roman	-
F	Rosedale	Reg'd. 1899/No. 339344
F	Shanghae	-

WHITE IRONSTONE
"Gentle Square"

ROBERT GARNER (III)
BLUE AND WHITE TRANSFERWARE
SINGLE PATTERNS

CATEGORY	PATTERN
O	"Buddleia"
O	"Temple Landscape First"

GATER, HALL & CO.
FLOW BLUE

CATEGORY	PATTERN
A	Corona

JOHN GEDDES - VERREVILLE POTTERY
BLUE AND WHITE TRANSFERWARE
SERIES
1. MISCELLANEOUS
"Danesford House" (The Home of Warren Hastings)
"Taymouth Castle, Perthshire"
"York Minster"
HISTORIC STAFFORDSHIRE SERIES
AMERICAN
1. MISCELLANEOUS
New York Park Theatre
GELSON BROS.
BLUE AND WHITE TRANSFERWARE
SINGLE PATTERNS

CATEGORY	PATTERN
S	Bickley

WHITE IRONSTONE

"Eagle Shape" ["Dove", "Diamond with Thumb Print"]	Reg'd. Sept. 21, 1869/No. 233411

GIBSON & SONS (LTD.)
FLOW BLUE

CATEGORY	PATTERN
F	Begonia
F	Locarno
F	"Tulip"

JAMES GILDEA
FLOW BLUE

CATEGORY	PATTERN
P/O	Chaing ("The Chinese Pattern")

GILDEA & WALKER (& CO.)
BLUE AND WHITE TRANSFERWARE
SINGLE PATTERNS

CATEGORY	PATTERN
P/O	"Tea House"

MULBERRY WARES

CATEGORY	PATTERN
F	"Ivy & Flowers"

WALLIS GIMSON & CO.
BLUE AND WHITE TRANSFERWARE
SERIES
1. THE WORLD
(CANADIAN SCENES) SERIES Reg'd. May 27, 1884, Design#7624
"The Bank Stand"
"The Federal Parliament Buildings, Ottawa"
"The Governor General's Residence (Rideau Hall), Ottawa"
"Grand Battery at Quebec"
"Lieutenant-Governor's Residence"
"Niagara Falls" (2) Two Scenes "Summer" and "Winter"
"The Normal School, Toronto"
"Notre Dame Church in Montreal"
"The University of Toronto"
"Wolf's Monument, Quebec"
For further information on this series refer to Collard's *Potters View*, pp. 84-86
BLUE AND WHITE TRANSFERWARE
SINGLE PATTERNS

CATEGORY	PATTERN
S	Castillo
A	Garfield
P/A	Venice

SAMUEL GINDER & CO.
BLUE AND WHITE TRANSFERWARE
SINGLE PATTERNS

CATEGORY	PATTERN
G	Bavarian
G	Mandoline

GLOBE POTTERY CO. LTD.
FLOW BLUE

CATEGORY	PATTERN
M	Delph
M	Fibre*

*Made for Woolworths, see Godden No. 1711

GODDARD & BURGESS
(or Burgess & Goddard)
WHITE IRONSTONE
"Bow & Tassel"*
"Plain Round"*
"Wheat"*
*All the above are noted as marked Burgess & Goddard.

BENJAMIN E. GODWIN
BLUE AND WHITE TRANSFERWARE
SINGLE PATTERNS

CATEGORY	PATTERN
-	"Bamboo & Sprigs"
-	"Bridge"
-	"Broseley"
-	"Canton"
S	Cottage
-	"Cow"
-	"Cow & Waterfall"
-	"Fox Chase"
-	"Geranium"
S	Gothic
-	"Ivy"
Z	Peacock
-	"Primrose"
-	"Rose"
-	"Ruins"
-	"Shepherd"
-	"Shepherd Boy"
-	"Stream & Cow"
-	"Temple"
-	"Waterfall"
-	"Wellington"
-	"Wild Rose"
-	"Woodman"

JOHN & ROBERT GODWIN
BLUE AND WHITE TRANSFERWARE
SINGLE PATTERNS

CATEGORY	PATTERN
S	Albany
G	Goat
-	"Pavilion"
S	Venice
G	Waverly

FLOW BLUE

CATEGORY	PATTERN
S	Cottage
G	Goat
F	"Lilies"
F	#22
S	#104 ["Ancient Ruins"]

MULBERRY WARES

CATEGORY	PATTERN
S	Albany
O	Albany #110
F	Talli
S	Venice #125
P/F	"Vine"
S	#104
F	#112

THOMAS GODWIN
BLUE AND WHITE TRANSFERWARE
SERIES
1. ARCTIC SCENERY SERIES (att.)
"A Man With A Gun, Two Eskimos and Two Dogs, et.al."
"A Scene With Dogs and a Sledge, A Group of Huntsmen, et.al."
"An Eskimo Family Group in Front of Igloos...With Two Small Sailing Boats, et.al."
"An Eskimo Family Seated With Their God...With Two Ships, Hella & Griper, et.al."
"Eskimos Building Igloos"
"Esquimaux Building a Snow Hut"*
"Large Naval Litter and Several Small Boats on a Lake, et.al."
"Sledge Bearing Eskimos, et.al."
"Two Men By a Sledge With Covered Long Boats, et.al."
"Two Men, One Aiming His Rifle and Two Dogs, et.al." ["Winter Camp"]
*See *True Blue*, p. 75, No. 1.
2. WILLIAM PENN'S TREATY SERIES
"Cloaked Figure"
"Kneeling Brave"
"Kneeling Squaw I & II"
"Squaw Lying Down"
"Three Seated Indians"
*Refer to *Snyder*, *Romantic Staffordshire*, pp. 62-63.

BLUE AND WHITE TRANSFERWARE
SINGLE PATTERNS

CATEGORY	PATTERN
S	Crystal Palace
S	Marino
O	Medina*
F	Mezieres
J	Pet Paris
M	Polish Star
S	Seasons
G	Tams O' Shanter
S	Versailles
O	"Willow" Pattern

*See *P. Williams*, *Staffordshire*, Vol. III, p. 35 where a second border is recorded.
HISTORIC STAFFORDSHIRE SERIES
AMERICAN
1. AMERICAN VIEWS SERIES
Baltimore [City of Baltimore]
Boston and Bunker Hill (Godden Mark No.1730B)
Brooklyn Ferry
Caldwell, Lake George
The Capitol, Washington
Columbia Bridge (On the Susquehanna)
East Port and Passamaquoddy Bay
The Narrows From Fort Hamilton
Outlet of Lake Memphremacog
The President's House
Schuylkill Water Works
Utica, N.Y. (also mark impressed Edge, Malkin & Co.)
Village of Cedars, St. Lawrence
Yale College [New Haven, Conn]
N.B.: Some of the American Views Series were reissued by Edge, Malkin & Co., 1871-1903 (Godden Mark No. 1445)

FLOW BLUE

CATEGORY	PATTERN
O	Linton
O	Macao
O	Singa
F	Versatility

MULBERRY WARES

CATEGORY	PATTERN
O	Lintin
S	Versaille*

*Same pattern as Versaille by Cork, Edge & Malkin

THOMAS & BENJAMIN GODWIN
BLUE AND WHITE TRANSFERWARE
SERIES
1. "INDIAN SCENERY SERIES"
Beejapore (sic.)
Delhi, Hindoostan
Lucknow
"Mosque of Mustopha Khan"
Pagoda Below Patna Azimabad
Part of the City of Moorhedabad
Sicre Gully Pass, Bengal
Surseya Ghaut, Khanpore
The Taj Mahal, Tomb of the Emperor
Tomb of Jeswuntnagurh
Tomb of Shere Shah
Tombs Near Etaya on the Jumna River
Village and Pagoda on the Ganges
BLUE AND WHITE TRANSFERWARE
SINGLE PATTERNS

CATEGORY	PATTERN
-	"Acorn"
-	"Ass"
-	"Cat"
S	Genevese
-	"Hawks"
L	"The Heart of Midlothian"
-	"Pyramid"
-	"Ship"
-	"Ship Willow"
-	"Stag"
S	View of London
O	"Willow" Pattern
S	Windmill, The

THOMAS GOODFELLOW
BLUE AND WHITE TRANSFERWARE
SINGLE PATTERNS

CATEGORY	PATTERN
S	Alleghany
-	"Arcade"
-	"Basket"
O	Broseley
-	"Chaplet"
-	Cologne
C	"Colonna"*
-	"Formosa"
-	"Grecian Temple"
-	"Indian"
-	"Lucerne"
-	"Marine"
-	"Moselle"
-	"Polish Star"
-	"Rhone"
-	"Royal Persian"
-	"Rural Scenery"
-	"Tyrian"
S	Wild Rose
O	"Willow" Pattern

*See *P. Williams*, *Staffordshire*, Vol. III, p. 13.
FLOW BLUE

CATEGORY	PATTERN
-	Colonial
O	Singan

MULBERRY WARES

CATEGORY	PATTERN
S	Alleghany
O	Singan

WHITE IRONSTONE
"Classic Gothic" (Ch)
"Double Sydenham" ["Wrapped Sydenham"]
"Grape Octagon"
"Primary Shape"

JOHN GOODWIN/LONGTON
BLUE AND WHITE TRANSFERWARE
SINGLE PATTERNS

CATEGORY	PATTERN	
O	Chiang	
G	Lasso*	-
S	Morea**	Reg'd. June 30, 1846/No. 35795
S	Rousillon** (2)	Reg'd. Dec. 16, 1846/No. 39519
C	Versailles	-
S	Views of London	-

FLOW BLUE

CATEGORY	PATTERN	
O	Japan Flowers	
G	Lasso*	-
S	Morea**	Reg'd. Dec. 16, 1846/No. 39519
M	Tiger Hunt***	

***Pattern continued by Thomas Goodwin

MULBERRY WARES

CATEGORY	PATTERN	
-	Montezuma	
S	Morea**	Reg'd. June 30, 1846/No. 35795

*See *Collard's Pottery & Porcelain in Canada*, pl. No. 13.
**Patterns were reissued at Seacombe (1852-1864). See next entry.

WHITE IRONSTONE
"Paneled Grape" -

JOHN GOODWIN, THOMAS ORTON GOODWIN (& BROS)., THOMAS ORTON GOODWIN SEACOMBE POTTERY

BLUE AND WHITE TRANSFERWARE
SERIES
1. VIEW OF LONDON "SERIES"
The Bank
Buckingham Palace
Colosseum
The Royal Exchange
Westminster Palace
Windsor Castle

BLUE AND WHITE TRANSFERWARE
SINGLE PATTERNS

CATEGORY	PATTERN	
S	Alhambra	-
G	Lasso	-
S	Montezuma	-
S	Morea*	Reg'd. June 30, 1846/No. 35895
-	"Riverside Steps"	-
S	Rousillon**	Reg'd. Dec. 16, 1846/No. 39519

**P. William, Flow Blue*, Vol. 2, p. 97, notes a platter titled "Morea" in Flow Blue which was registered c. 1878 [Longton]. It is marked J. Goodwin and impressed "IRONSTONE". The "Morea" pattern also appeared in Mulberry. See *Godden's Masons,* p. 276 for backstamp marking, which is probably dated June 30, 1846. Also refer to *Cushion's Handbook*, p. 174. See John Goodwin/Longton as well.
**First registered at Longton and reissued.

FLOW BLUE

CATEGORY	PATTERN
M	Tiger Hunt*

*Originally manufactured by John Goodwin.

GOODWINS, BRIDGWOOD & ORTON

BLUE AND WHITE TRANSFERWARE
SINGLE PATTERNS

CATEGORY	PATTERN
F	Daisy
F	Oriental Flower Garden (2)

GOODWIN & ELLIS

BLUE AND WHITE TRANSFERWARE
SERIES
1. MISCELLANEOUS
"Grecian Vases"
"Oriental Flower Garden"
"Peruvian Hunters" (possible series)

GOODWINS & HARRIS

BLUE AND WHITE TRANSFERWARE
SERIES
1. METROPOLITAN SCENERY SERIES
Bow Bridge
Hampton House
Kingston on Thames
Near Highgate Road
North End, Hampstead ["Grand Cricket & Match"]
Osterley Park
St. Albans Abbey
View From Blackheath
View Near Colnebrook (sic)
View of Eton Chapel
View of Greenwich
View of Richmond
View Near Twickenham
Waltham Cross
Windsor Castle
Woolwich
2. BYRON GALLERY SERIES
Bride of Abydos
Don Juan
The Dream
Hebrew Melodies
Mazeppa

BLUE AND WHITE TRANSFERWARE
SINGLE PATTERNS

CATEGORY	PATTERN
F	"Coral Border" ["Stylised Flowers"]
S	"Cows Crossing Stream"
S	Genevese
O	"Willow" Pattern

GEORGE GORDON [GORDON'S POTTERY]

BLUE AND WHITE TRANSFERWARE
SINGLE PATTERNS

CATEGORY	PATTERN
F	Florentine
-	"Lord Owen's Daughter"
F	"Watering Can"
O	"Willow" Pattern

JOHN & WILLIAM GREEN

BLUE AND WHITE TRANSFERWARE
SINGLE PATTERNS

CATEGORY	PATTERN
-	"Broseley"
-	"Garden

THOMAS GREEN

HISTORIC STAFFORDSHIRE SERIES
AMERICAN & CANADIAN
1. MISCELLANEOUS
William Penn's Treaty

FLOW BLUE

CATEGORY	PATTERN
O	Chinese Jar
A	Royal

THOMAS G. GREEN & CO. (LTD.)

BLUE AND WHITE TRANSFERWARE
SINGLE PATTERNS

CATEGORY	PATTERN
O	Ming
F	Regal
F	"Sweet Pea"

GRIFFITHS, BEARDMORE & BIRKS

BLUE AND WHITE TRANSFERWARE
SERIES
1. "LIGHT BLUE ROSE BORDER SERIES"
Castle Richard
Denton Park
Gunton Hall
Kirkstall Abbey
The Rookery
Tedesley Hall
Wolseley Hall

BLUE AND WHITE TRANSFERWARE
SINGLE PATTERNS

CATEGORY	PATTERN
O	"Willow" Pattern

GRIMWADE BROS.

BLUE AND WHITE TRANSFERWARE
SINGLE PATTERNS

CATEGORY	PATTERN
F	Gypsy
M/F	Indian Tree
-	Venice
S	Winton

FLOW BLUE

CATEGORY	PATTERN
S	Crete

GRIMWADES LTD.

BLUE AND WHITE TRANSFERWARE
SINGLE PATTERNS

CATEGORY	PATTERN
P/S	Carro
S	Genoa

FLOW BLUE

CATEGORY	PATTERN	
A	Athens	Reg'd. 1903/No. 414421
S	Genoa	-
M	Linnea	Reg'd. 1903/No. 407851
A	Nancy	Reg'd. 1900/No. 359029
M	Nelson	-
F	Poppea	-
F	Roseate	-

W.H. GRINDLEY & CO. (LTD.)
BLUE AND WHITE TRANSFERWARE
SINGLE PATTERNS

CATEGORY	PATTERN	
F	Brussels	
F	Burmah	
F	Daffodil	
A	Dresden	
A	Elysian	
A	Haddon	
S	Hay Wain, The	
S	Lambeth	
F	Mersey	Reg'd. 1889/No.135130

FLOW BLUE

CATEGORY	PATTERN	
-	Agra	-
M/A	Alaska	-
F	Albany*	-
M/F	Aldine	Reg'd. 1898/No. 325874
-	Allen	-
A	Alton	-
-	Arabic	Reg'd. 1889/No. 134743
M/A	Argyle/Stratford	Reg'd. 1896/No. 289457
F	Ashburton	-
A	Astoria	-
A	Astral	Reg'd. 1904/No. 426592
M	Athena	Reg'd. 1897/No. 303231
M	Atlanta	-
F	Atlas	-
A	Baltic	Reg'd. 1904/No. 433097
A	Beaufort	Reg'd. 1903/No. 408448
F	Beauty Roses	Reg'd. 1922/No. 690339
F	Belgrave	-
A	Belmont*	-
A	Bisley	-
F	Blue Rose	-
M	Blytheswood/Regal (The)	-
F	Boston	Reg'd. 1893/No. 219411
F	Brazil	-
F	Brussels	Reg'd. 1897/No. 303723
M	Burton	-
F	Campion	Reg'd.1894/No. 245688
F	Catherine**	Reg'd.1894/No. 233436
F	Catherine Merrett**	-
A	Celtic	Reg'd. 1897/No. 310588
F	Charleston	-
F	Chatsworth	Reg'd. 1896/No. 274727
O	Chinese	-
F	Clarence	-
F	Clematis	Reg'd. 1897/No. 303250
A	Clifton	-
M/A	Clover	-
-	Clytie	-
M/A	Countess (Polychrome)	-
A	Crescent	Reg'd. 1904/No. 433102
M/F	Delmar	-
M	Denmark	-
F	Denton	-
F	Derby (Polychrome)	-
A	Derwent/Dutchess (The)	-
F	Doreen	-
A	Doris/Ochis	-
M	Dorothy	Reg'd. 1897/No. 305973
M/F	Dover	-
P/F	Dutchess	Reg'd. 1891/No. 184834
A	Dutchess (The)/ Derwent	-
F	Eileen	-
M/F	England	-
F	Eton	-
M/A	Festoon*	Reg'd. Nov. 8, 1989/No. 326058
F	Flora	-
F	Florida	-
F	Gironde	Reg'd. 1897/No. 293169
A	Girton	Reg'd. 1905/No. 457960
F	Glenmore/Glentine	-
F	Glentine/Glenmore	-
F	Gordon	-
F	Grace	Reg'd. 1905/No. 303495
A	Haddon	-
A	Hampton	-
F	Hampton Spray	-
F	Harley	-
A	Hartington	-
M/A	Hofburg (The)	-
F	Ideal	Reg'd. 1893/No. 213154
A	Idris	-
F	Imperial (The)/ Somerset	-
F	Janette	Reg'd. 1897/No. 292398
M/A	Keele	-
M/A	Kent	-
F	LaBelle	Reg'd. 1893/No. 213120
-	Lawrence	-
F	Le Pavot	Reg'd. 1896/No. 277089
A	Lorne	-
A	Lotus	-
F	Louise	Reg'd. 1896/No. 269029
A	Lyndhurst	-
A	Lynton	-
M	Lyric	-
M/F	Malta	Reg'd. 1887/No. 69160
M	Manila	-
F	Marachal Neil	Reg'd. 1896/No. 269030
F	Margot	Reg'd. 1896/No. 269028
F	Marguerite	-
A	Marie	Reg'd. 1895/No. 250387
M/A	Marlborough	-
M	Marquis (The)	Reg'd. 1906/No. 473313
M/A	Marquis II (The)	-
F	May	Reg'd. 1895/No. 256165
F	Melbourne	-
F	Merion	Reg'd. 1897/No. 292307
M/F	Milan	Reg'd. 1893/No. 213153
A	Missouri	Reg'd. 1890/No. 150034
A	Ochis/Doris	-
F	Olympia*	Reg'd. 1899/No. 233436
M	Olympic (The)/Shangrila	-
F	Osborne	-
-	Penshurst	-
F	Perth	-
F	Poppy	-
A	Portman	-
F	Primula	Reg'd. 1893/No. 218411
F	Progress	Reg'd. 1894/No. 233435
M	Regal (The)/Blytheswood	-
F	Richmond	-
F	Rose	Reg'd. 1893/No. 213117
F	Rustic	-
F	Seine	-
S	Shanghai	-
F	Shangrila/Olympic (The)	-
F	Somerset/Imperial (The)	-
F	Spring	Reg'd. 1886/No. 51058
M/A	Stratford/Argyle	-
M/A	Syrian	Reg'd. 1897/No. 303260
F	Teresa	Reg'd. 1898/No. 326059
M	Trellis	-
F	Triumph	Reg'd. 1893/No. 219411
M/A	Troy	Reg'd. 1886/No. 64490
F	Unique	-
A	Victoria	-
A	Victory	-
A	Waverly	-
M	Wentworth	-
F	Widflower	-
F	Woodbine	-
-	Woodville	-

*William VanBuskirk notes there are two distinct patterns with the same name.
- Also noted as patented October 19, 1897.
**Catherine, Catherine Merrett & Olympia are the same pattern.
Various dish and wash set body styles were registered with the U.S. Patent Office by William H. Grindley:
Dish body styles were registered on: February 2, 1897
October 19, 1897
November 8, 1898
October 31, 1899
May 9, 1906
Wash set body styles were registered on: September 21, 1897
For additional information on patterns and body styles for William H. Grindley, refer to the research paper, *William H. Grindley, Part I & II.* by William Van Buskirk, published by the Flow Blue International Collectors Club, June 1996 and 1997
N.B.: William VanBuskirk notes that the following patterns may, in fact, be body style names and not pattern names. They are: The Duchess, The Imperial, The Marquis, The Olympic The Regal,

WHITE IRONSTONE

"Bamboo"	-
"Favorite Shape"	Reg'd. 1885/No. 51059
"Flower Garden Border"	-

TEA LEAF/COPPER LUSTRE

"Bamboo"	-
"Favorite Shape"	Reg'd. 1885/No. 51059

For further reading, refer to *Heaivilin*, pp. 77-80

GROVE & STARK
FLOW BLUE

CATEGORY	PATTERN	
M	Dora*	Reg'd. Jan 30, 1882/No. 376529
M/S	Rosebud*	Reg'd. Sept. 25, 1883/No. 404328
F	Swallow*	Reg'd. Jan. 20, 1877/No. 307028

*All three patterns were registered in the name of F.W. Grove and J. Stark.

WILLIAM HACKWOOD
BLUE AND WHITE TRANSFERWARE
SINGLE PATTERNS

CATEGORY	PATTERN
O	Arabian Sketches/The March
M	Exotic Birds
-	"Girl, Bird-catcher"
S	"Falls of Killarney"
S	"Institutions" or "Monastery Hill"
O	Rhoda Gardens
M	"Sheet Pattern"
O	"Willow" Pattern

FLOW BLUE

CATEGORY	PATTERN
H	Acadia*
O	Rhoda Gardens
O	Sobreon (att.)

*Refer to *Snyder*, Vol. 2, p. 74 for photos and marks. However, attribution of the initial "H" to William Hackwood, as illustrated by *Snyder* is open to debate.

HACKWOOD & KEELING
BLUE AND WHITE TRANSFERWARE
SINGLE PATTERNS

CATEGORY	PATTERN
-	"Pomona"

WILLIAM HACKWOOD & SON
BLUE AND WHITE TRANSFERWARE
SINGLE PATTERNS

CATEGORY	PATTERN
S	"Hackwood's Garland"
O	Hindoostan
F	Wild Rose

HALES, HANCOCK & CO. LTD.
FLOW BLUE

CATEGORY	PATTERN
S	Watteau

JOHN HALL
BLUE AND WHITE TRANSFERWARE
SERIES
1. QUADRUPEDS "SERIES"
"Antelope"
"Beaver"
"Brown Bear"
"Camel and other animals"
"Deer"
"Dog"
"Dog and Rabbit"
"Elk"
"Fox"
"Gazelle"
"Genet and Civet Cat"
"Goats"
"Hedgehog"
"Horse and Colt"
"Hyena"
"Lion"
"Mole"
"Moose and Hunters"
"Nylghau"
"Otter"
"Polar Bear"
"Rabbit and Hunters"
"Raccoon"
"Rhinoceros"
"Seal"
"Tibetan Musk"
"Wolverine"
"Zebra"

JOHN HALL (& SONS)
BLUE AND WHITE TRANSFERWARE - SERIES
1. ORIENTAL SCENERY "SERIES"
City of Benares
Elephants & Tomb
Fakeer's Rock
Ghaut of Cutwa
Hindoo Ghaut
Hindoo Pagoda
Hindoo Temple
Hindoo Village
Lucknow
Mahomeda Mosque and Tomb (sic)
Palace of the King of Delhi
Sicre Gully Pass
Surseya Ghaut, Khanpore
Tomb of the Emperor Shah Jehan
Tomb at Jeswunthnagure
Tombs of Etaya
BLUE AND WHITE TRANSFERWARE
SINGLE PATTERNS

CATEGORY	PATTERN
S	Antiquities (possible series)
S	Castle Toward

RALPH HALL (& CO.) or (& SONS)
BLUE AND WHITE TRANSFERWARE
SERIES
1. PICTURESQUE SCENERY "SERIES"
Alton Abbey, Staffordshire, England
Broadlands, Hampshire
Cashiobury, Hertfordshire
Croe House
Crome Court, Worcester
Culford Hall, Suffolk
Dreghorn House, Scotland
Dunsany Castle, Ireland
Fulham Church, Middlesex
Klostenburg, Germany
Llanarth Court, Monmouthshire
Norwich Cathedral, Norfolk
Palace of St. Cloud, France
Palace of St. Germain, France
Panshanger, Hertfordshire
St. Woolston's, Kildare, Ireland
Terwin Water, Hertfordshire
Trematon Castle
Worcester Cathedral
2. SELECT VIEWS "SERIES"
Biddulph Castle, Staffordshire
Boughton House, Northamptonshire
Bramber Church, Sussex
Castle Prison, St. Albans, Hertfordshire
Church of St. Charles and Polytechnic School, Vienna, Germany
Conway Castle, Caernarvonshire, Wales
Eashing Park, Surrey
Gyrn, Flintshire, Wales
The Hospital Near Poissy, France
Knole, Kent
Laxton Hall, Northamptonshire
Luscombe, Devonshire
Oatlands, Surrey
Pains Hill, Surrey
A Scene in the Campania of Rome, Italy
Thoresby Park, Nottinghamshire
Valley Crusis Abbey, Wales
Warleigh House, Somersetshire
Wilderness, Kent

RALPH HALL
BLUE AND WHITE TRANSFERWARE
SINGLE PATTERNS

CATEGORY	PATTERN
F	Asiatic Pheasants
S	Carolina
S	Italian Buildings
G	Parisian Chateau (possible series)
G	Sheltered Peasants
M	Variety
S	Wells Cathedral, Somersetshire (att.)

HISTORIC STAFFORDSHIRE SERIES
AMERICAN
1. MISCELLANEOUS
Carolina (2)

RALPH HALL & SON
BLUE AND WHITE TRANSFERWARE
SINGLE PATTERNS

CATEGORY	PATTERN
O	Japanese

HISTORIC STAFFORDSHIRE SERIES
AMERICAN
1. MISCELLANEOUS
"Eagle" ["Eagle Riding on a Shell"]
Fayette, The Nation's Guest/Washington, His Country's Father* (Dated 1824)
"Franklin, Lafayette, Washington"
*See *Snyder, Historic Staffordshire*, p. 59, and *Larsen*, p. 264, No. 740.
RALPH HALL & CO.
BLUE AND WHITE TRANSFERWARE
SINGLE PATTERNS

CATEGORY	PATTERN
S	Bosphorus (The)
O	Chapoo

F Favorite (The)
M Feather
S Moselle
S Sardinia
S Singanese*
S Veranda
*Same pattern used by John Wedgwood, but called Tippecanoe. Refer to Snyder, *Romantic Staffordshire*, p. 60.
FLOW BLUE
CATEGORY PATTERN
O Nanking
O Ning Po
MULBERRY WARES
CATEGORY PATTERN
O Ning Po

HALLAM & JOHNSON (CO.)
FLOW BLUE
CATEGORY PATTERN
F Flora

ROBERT HAMILTON
BLUE AND WHITE TRANSFERWARE
SINGLE PATTERNS
CATEGORY PATTERN
- "Chinese Market Stall"
- "Colossal Sarcophagus at Cacamo" (att.)
S "Country Scene With Ram and Sheep"
- "Cowmen"
S "Fishermen With Nets"
S "Gothic Ruins"
S "Hut on the Canton River"
- "Milkmaid"
S "Ruined Castle"
- "Strawberry Border"
O "Willow" Pattern

HAMMERSLEY & ASBURY
BLUE AND WHITE TRANSFERWARE
SINGLE PATTERNS
CATEGORY PATTERN
- God is Our Strength* (This is an example of Armorial Wares)
Found on Asiatic Pheasants pattern.

RALPH HAMMERSLEY (& SON(S))
BLUE AND WHITE TRANSFERWARE
SINGLE PATTERNS
CATEGORY PATTERN
Z Heron
P/O Manila
O Stanley
S Venture
HISTORIC STAFFORDSHIRE SINGLE PATTERNS
AMERICAN
M/H Gem*["Arms of the United States"] Reg'd. April 23, 1868/No. 218386
FLOW BLUE
CATEGORY PATTERN
M/H Gem*["Arms of the United States"] Reg'd. April 23, 1868/No. 218386
F Hatfield
*See *Larsen*, pp. 240, 258, Nos. 658 and 724 (2) and *Arman*, pp. 208-209, No. 575.
MULBERRY WARES
CATEGORY PATTERN
F Agra
S Venture*
*An example in Ellen Hill's collection is found with the marking "R.B."

HAMPSON & BROADHURST
BLUE AND WHITE TRANSFERWARE
SINGLE PATTERNS
CATEGORY PATTERN
F Asiatic Pheasant
- Railway
FLOW BLUE
CATEGORY PATTERN
F Chints

SAMPSON HANCOCK (& SONS)
BLUE AND WHITE TRANSFERWARE
SINGLE PATTERNS
CATEGORY PATTERN
S Albion
F Palmyra
FLOW BLUE
CATEGORY PATTERN
M/A Acme
M/A Alexandra
- Baronet
A Blenheim Reg'd. 1902/No. 391504
F Blossoms
F Bridal Veil Reg'd. 1894/No. 246962
F Chadsworth
F Claremont Group
- Corinth
F Coronet
A Doris
M Dresden
F Glen
F Harvest
A Hawksey Reg'd. 1903/No. 411972
M/H Hudson*
F Larch
A Leicester
F Margot Reg'd. 1896/No. 269028
- Mattean
F Melton
F Millais
- Nitre (& Sons)
F Rosetta
M/H Saratoga*
F Summer
S Valencia
A Walbeck
A Waldorf (& Sons)
- Warwick (& Sons) Reg'd. 1898/No. 319525
M/A Westbourne
*Commemorative Ware

HANCOCK & WITTINGHAM & CO.
BLUE AND WHITE TRANSFERWARE
SINGLE PATTERNS
CATEGORY PATTERN
C Etruscan
MULBERRY WARES
CATEGORY PATTERN
P/F Roses

JAMES & WILLIAM HANDLEY
BLUE AND WHITE TRANSFERWARE
SINGLE PATTERNS
CATEGORY PATTERN
- "Blue Landscape"
O "Broseley"
- "Jar"
- "Ponte Molle"
O "Printed Chinese"
F "Village Fisherman" (att.)
S "Wild Rose"
O "Willow" Pattern
N.B.: Additional patterns in Blue & White are noted by Molly Hosking. See *NCSJVol. 11*, 1994, p. 70

HANLEY PORCELAIN CO.
FLOW BLUE
CATEGORY PATTERN
F Argyle

JOSEPH HARDING
BLUE AND WHITE TRANSFERWARE
SINGLE PATTERNS
CATEGORY PATTERN
O Asiatic Scenery
M "Sheet Pattern"
O "Willow" Pattern

W. & J. HARDING
BLUE AND WHITE TRANSFERWARE
SINGLE PATTERNS
CATEGORY PATTERN
S Rustic

THOMAS HARLEY
BLUE AND WHITE TRANSFERWARE
SINGLE PATTERNS
CATEGORY PATTERN
- "Tendril"
- "Thatched Cottage With Outside Stairs"
M "Violin"

JOHN HARRIS
BLUE AND WHITE TRANSFERWARE
SINGLE PATTERNS
CATEGORY PATTERN
S Sevres

GEORGE HARRISON (& CO.)
BLUE AND WHITE TRANSFERWARE
SINGLE PATTERNS

CATEGORY PATTERN
O "Bridgeless Willow*
O "Fitzhugh" Pattern (known as "Trophies-Dagger")
*See *True Blue*, p. 56, No. 25
N.B.: See *Penny Plain*, p. 98, No. 230

C. & W.K. HARVEY
BLUE AND WHITE TRANSFERWARE - SERIES
1. "CITIES AND TOWNS SERIES"
Cambridge
Canterbury
Dublin
Edinburgh
Gloucester
Greenwich
Oxford
Richmond
Worcester
York
BLUE AND WHITE TRANSFERWARE
SINGLE PATTERNS
CATEGORY PATTERN
S Atlantis
M "Birds and Flowers" ["Exotic Birds and Flowers"]
S Delaware
G "Girl at the Well"
S Gothic Temple
FLOW BLUE
CATEGORY PATTERN
F "Cherry Blossom"*
WHITE IRONSTONE
"Classic Gothic"
Florentine Shape Reg'd. July 16, 1850/No. 70364
**Gaston, Vol. 2*, p. 170, pl. 462, notes an unidentified pattern that has now been recorded with the impressed name "Harvey" in Flow Blue with Copper Lustre. The name given to this pattern is "Cherry Blossom".

HAWLEY BROS (LTD.)
BLUE AND WHITE TRANSFERWARE
SINGLE PATTERNS
CATEGORY PATTERN
F Asiatic Pheasants

JOHN HAWLEY & CO.
BLUE AND WHITE TRANSFERWARE
SINGLE PATTERNS
CATEGORY PATTERN
S Valetta

JOHN HAWTHORN
WHITE IRONSTONE
"Hawthorn's Fern Shape" Reg'd. Mar. 19, 1879/No. 333485

HEATH, BLACKHURST & CO.
BLUE AND WHITE TRANSFERWARE
SINGLE PATTERNS
CATEGORY PATTERN
S Canovian Statues

JOHN HEATH
BLUE AND WHITE TRANSFERWARE
SINGLE PATTERNS
CATEGORY PATTERN
G "Girl At The Well"
O Rhoda Gardens

JOSEPH HEATH
BLUE AND WHITE TRANSFERWARE
SINGLE PATTERNS
CATEGORY PATTERN
S Albano
S Belvoir
S Cintra
S Geneva
- Gotha
S Monterey
S Ontario Lake Scenery
F Phantasia*
O Rhoda Gardens
O Tonquin
*See *P. Williams, Staffordshire*, Vol. II & II, pp. 658 and 262 respectively.
FLOW BLUE
CATEGORY PATTERN
F Garden Flowers (att.)
S Gotha
F "Heath's Flower"* (brush stroke)
S Monterey
- Ontario
O Tonquin
MULBERRY WARES
CATEGORY PATTERN
F "Heath's Flower"* (brush stroke)
S Monterey
O Rhoda Gardens
O Tonquin
*"Heath's Flower," a brush stroke floral found in both Flow Blue and Mulberry, are noted by various authors as manufactured by Thomas Heath. The two pieces in this author's collection are, however, impressed "J. Heath". Also refer to Thomas Heath.

JOSEPH HEATH & CO.
BLUE AND WHITE TRANSFERWARE
SINGLE PATTERNS
CATEGORY PATTERN
F Amaryllis
S Asia Displayed
S Cathedral (att.)
S Egyptian
G Indian Chief
S Italian Villas (possible series)
S Lombardy
S Milanese Pavilions
G Military Sketches*
S Persian
S Rural Scenery
G Woodman (The)
**Snyder' s Romantic Staffordshire*, pp. 70 (pattern Albion) and 75 shows two potters' initial marks with "S.H. & CO." The potter has not been identified. It would appear that when looking at the mark for Military Sketches, the first initial "J" has been re-engraved as an "S". *P. Williams Staffordshire*, Vol. 1, p. 292 illustrates the exact same back mark for Military Sketches as Snyder. The question remains, which potter obtained and re-engraved these as well as the other copper plates of Joseph Heath & Co. (whose manufactory closed in 1853).
HISTORIC STAFFORDSHIRE SERIES
AMERICAN & CANADIAN
1. MISCELLANEOUS
Monterey
Ontario, Lake Scenery
The Residence of the Late Richard Jordan, New Jersey
MULBERRY WARES
CATEGORY PATTERN
S Milanese Pavilions

J (JOSHUA) HEATH
BLUE AND WHITE TRANSFERWARE
SINGLE PATTERNS
CATEGORY PATTERN
1. CHINOISERIE (style)
O "Buffalo"
O "Chantilly Sprigs"*
O "Chinese Design With Trophies"
O "Chinese Design Wheel" ["Violin"]
O Conversation Pattern"*
O Full Nankin" (att.)*
O Lady With Parasol I"* (att.)
O Lady With Parasol II"* (att.)
O Modified Lady With Parasol"* (att.)
O "Palladian Pagoda"
O "Reindeer Pattern"
O "Two Figures"
O "Violin" ["Chinese Design Wheel"]
O "Willow" Pattern
*For further reference, refer to *NCS Newsletter No. 102*, April 1996, pp. 35-37 Observations On The "Lady With Parasol" pattern by Christopher Tyzack.
2. MISCELLANEOUS
CATEGORY PATTERN
M Long Live The King

THOMAS HEATH
BLUE AND WHITE TRANSFERWARE
SINGLE PATTERNS
CATEGORY PATTERN
M "Feather Edge"
G "Sporting Subject"
FLOW BLUE
CATEGORY PATTERN
F "Heath's Flower" (Brush Stroke)
MULBERRY WARES
CATEGORY PATTERN
F "Heath's Flower" (Brush Stroke)
N.B.: "Heath's Flower", a brush stroke floral found in both Flow Blue and Mulberry, is noted by various authors as manufactured by Thomas Heath. The two pieces in this author's collection are, however, impressed "J. Heath".

CHARLES HEATHCOTE & CO.
BLUE AND WHITE TRANSFERWARE
SINGLE PATTERNS
CATEGORY PATTERN
- Cambria
S "Cattle and River Pattern"

G "The Villager"*
*See *True Blue*, p. 148, No. H9

HENSHALL & CO.
BLUE AND WHITE TRANSFERWARE
SERIES
1. "FRUIT AND FLOWER BORDER SERIES"
Beaumont Lodge
Bellinzona
Blenheim, Oxfordshire
Bradfield
The Bridge of Martoviele
British Views (various examples)
Cashiobury*
Castle of Furstenfeld
Compton, Verney
Halstead, Essex
Hanover Place
The Harbor of Messina
Hollywood Cottage
Kimberley Hall
Langley Park
Milford Green
Old Castle of Martigny
Ostend Gates at Bruges
St. Clous
Saxham Hall
Scene in Campania, Rome
Spring Hall
The Temple of Friendship
Tweekenham, Surrey
Vae House
*See *True Blue*, p. 82, No. 7.
BLUE AND WHITE TRANSFERWARE
SINGLE PATTERNS

CATEGORY	PATTERN
S	"Castle and Bridge" ["St. Albins"]*
F	"Flowers and Leaves"
S	Gothic Scenery**

*See *P. Williams, Staffordshire*, Vol. III, p. 262 where an additional scene is illustrated.
**Refer to *Snyder*, *Romantic Staffordshire*, p. 78.

HENSHALL & CO.
HISTORIC STAFFORDSHIRE SERIES
AMERICAN
1. FRUIT AND FLOWER BORDER SERIES [AMERICAN OR BRITISH VIEWS]
"Building" ("Two Story Structure with Two Apparently Central Chimney Stacks")
Court House, Baltimore
The Dam and Water Works, Philadelphia (Side-Wheel Steamboat)*
The Dam and Water Works, Philadelphia (Stern-Wheel Steamboat)
Exchange, Baltimore
Holliday Street Theatre, Baltimore
Vevay, Indiana (?)
York Minster
* See *Arman Quarterly*, Vol. 1, 1997, p. 35 for picture.

HERCULANEUM POTTERY
BLUE AND WHITE TRANSFERWARE
SERIES
1. "CHERUB MEDALLION BORDER SERIES"
Caernarvon Castle
Cambridge
Canterbury
Chester
Cluny Castle
Conway Castle
Edinburgh
Darsie Castle
Dumfries
Greenwich
Kilkenny
Knaresborough
Lancaster (2)
Oxford
Scarborough
Shrewsbury
Worcester
York
2. "FIELD SPORTS SERIES"
"Duck Hunters With Boat"
"Field Sports"
"Fox Head and Horn"
"Hunting Scene, Two Hunters With Dog"
"Two Hunters and Two Pointers Flushing Birds"
"Two Men Fishing Below Falls, Mill in Background"
3. "INDIA SERIES"
"The Charlees Satoon in the Ford of Allahabad on the River Jumna"
"Gate of a Mosque Built by Hafizramut, Pillibeat"
"Mausoleum of Nawaub Assoph Khan, Rajemahel"
"Mausoleum of Sultan Purveiz, Near Allahabad"*
"View in the Fort Madura"
*Now attributed to William Walsh, Burslem.
4. "LIVERPOOL VIEWS SERIES"
"Castle Street and St. George's, Crescent, Liverpool"
"Duke of Bridgewater's House, Liverpool"
"The Duke's Warehouse, Liverpool"
"Exchange Buildings and Nelson's Monument, Liverpool"
"Ferry Over the River Mersey at Birkenhead"
"Fort and Lighthouse, Liverpool"
"The House of Correction, Kirkdale, Liverpool"
"Liverpool From the Mersey"
"Liverpool From the Seacombe Slip"
"Lord Street, Liverpool"
"Royal Institution, Liverpool"
"St. Paul's Church"
"Wellington Rooms, Liverpool"
BLUE AND WHITE TRANSFERWARE
SINGLE PATTERNS

CATEGORY	PATTERN	
G	"Archery" [Casal]	(Also in Mulberry)
S	"Bell Tower"	
-	"Cattle Resting"	
-	"Country Cottage"	
-	"Curling Bridge and Temple"	
M	Etruscan Pattern" (possible series)	
F	"Flowers and Leaves"	
S	"French Scenery"	
L	"Holy Bible Series"* (att.)	
S	"Italian Fountain"	
-	"Laughing Dog"	
-	"Liverpool Arms"	
-	"Louvre"	
-	"Mr. Miller" ["Honest Lawyer"]	
G	"Mushroom Picker"	
M	"Net Pattern"	
G	"Pekin Palm"	
C	"Roman Garden"	
F	"Rose Chintz"	
-	"Thatched Cottage With Outside Staircase"	
S	"Two Men, Two Arches" ["Flying Pennant"]	
-	"Vatican"	
O	"Willow" Pattern	

*For further reading, refer to *Coysh,* Vol. 2, p. 107

ROBERT HERON (& SON)
BLUE AND WHITE TRANSFERWARE
SINGLE PATTERNS

CATEGORY	PATTERN
O	Canton
S	Florence
G	"Hawking"
S	"Taymouth Castle, Perthshire"
-	Temple
O	"Willow" Pattern

FLOW BLUE

CATEGORY	PATTERN
F	Bath
F	Primrose

HICKS & MEIGH
BLUE AND WHITE TRANSFERWARE
SINGLE PATTERNS

CATEGORY	PATTERN
M	"Exotic Birds"

HICKS, MEIGH & JOHNSON
BLUE AND WHITE TRANSFERWARE
SINGLE PATTERNS

CATEGORY	PATTERN
P/O	"Bridgeless Willow"
O	"Chinese Fishing Scene"
O	"Chinese Landscape"
P/S	Edelaide's Bower
M	"Exotic Birds"
P/F	"Floral"
M/F	Fruit & Flowers
M	"Oriental Shells" (possible series)
-	"Priory"
-	Sal Sapit Omnia*

*Refer to *Coysh*, Vol. 1, pp. 117-118
FLOW BLUE

CATEGORY	PATTERN
O	Mandarin

HILDITCH & HOPWOOD
FLOW BLUE

CATEGORY	PATTERN	
F	Chian Sprigs*	Reg'd. April 11, 1844/No. 17714

*See *Snyder's Fascinating Flow Blue*, p. 64 for illustration.

HILDITCH & SONS (& CO.)
BLUE AND WHITE TRANSFERWARE
SINGLE PATTERNS

CATEGORY	PATTERN
P/O	"Garden Scene"

CHARLES HOBSON (& SON)
BLUE AND WHITE TRANSFERWARE
SINGLE PATTERNS

CATEGORY	PATTERN
P/O	Ning Po

PETER HOLDCROFT & CO.
BLUE AND WHITE TRANSFERWARE
SINGLE PATTERNS

CATEGORY	PATTERN
S	Peru

FLOW BLUE

CATEGORY	PATTERN
O	Chusan

MULBERRY WARES

CATEGORY	PATTERN
O	Chusan
S	Peru

HOLDCROFT, HILL & MELLOR
BLUE AND WHITE TRANSFERWARE
SINGLE PATTERNS

CATEGORY	PATTERN
F	Asiatic Pheasants
-	Flaxman

JOHN HOLLAND
BLUE AND WHITE TRANSFERWARE
SINGLE PATTERNS

CATEGORY	PATTERN	
C	Carrara	Reg'd. Nov. 4, 1852/No. 87541

HOLLAND & GREEN
BLUE AND WHITE TRANSFERWARE
SINGLE PATTERNS

CATEGORY	PATTERN
Z	Borneo
A	Bracelet
P/O	Pekin

WHITE IRONSTONE

"Arched Panel"	-
"Bell Tracery"	-
"Double Sydenham" ["Wrapped Sydenham"]	-
Gothic "Shape"	Reg'd. Mar. 31, 1854/No. 95469
Haveloch Shape	-
"White Oak & Acorn Shape"*	Reg'd. Oct. 19, 1860/No. 134558-9

*Full name has not been deciphered off of registry mark, therefore contrived name noted.

T. & J. HOLLINS
BLUE AND WHITE TRANSFERWARE
SINGLE PATTERNS

CATEGORY	PATTERN
-	"Abbey"
-	"India"
-	"Star"
-	"Temple"
O	"Willow" Pattern

HOLLINSHEAD & KIRKHAM (LTD.)
BLUE AND WHITE TRANSFERWARE
SINGLE PATTERNS

CATEGORY	PATTERN
M	"Buttons & Bows"
O	Lahore

FLOW BLUE

CATEGORY	PATTERN	
F	Alexandria	Reg'd. 1893/No. 218832
F	Anemone	
A	Cambridge	
F	Davenport	
A	Natal	
F	Persian	
A	Togo	
F	Tyrian	

WHITE IRONSTONE
"Corn & Oats"
"Wheat"

HOLMES, STONIER & HOLLINSHEAD
BLUE AND WHITE TRANSFERWARE
SINGLE PATTERNS

CATEGORY	PATTERN
M	Anna

HOPE & CARTER
BLUE AND WHITE TRANSFERWARE
SINGLE PATTERNS

CATEGORY	PATTERN	
S	Acropolis	
-	Ballet	Reg'd. July 25, 1867/No. 209726
P/F	Bramble	
P/O	"Chinese Pattern"	
G	Horsehunt	
P/O	Indian Tree	
S	Mexico	Reg'd. 1868
S	Odessa	

FLOW BLUE

CATEGORY	PATTERN
F	Hindoostan (att.)

MULBERRY WARES

CATEGORY	PATTERN
O	Bamboo

WHITE IRONSTONE

"Bluet Shape"*	Reg'd.
"Twin Leaves" (Ch)	
Western Shape	Reg'd. Sept. 17, 1862/No. 154812 or Sept. 26, 1862/No. 155220-2

*Registry date has not been deciphered, but was late 1860s+.

HOPKIN & VERNON
BLUE AND WHITE TRANSFERWARE
SINGLE PATTERNS

CATEGORY	PATTERN
S	British Lakes
S	Ruins

JOHN THOMAS HUDDEN
BLUE AND WHITE TRANSFERWARE
SINGLE PATTERNS

CATEGORY	PATTERN
F	Asiatic Pheasants
S	Bosphorus
F	"Flora"
S	Grecian Statue
J/G	Lasso
S	Rhine
O	"Willow" Pattern

Hampson, p. 97, No. 144 notes the following registrations:

"Toulon" Pattern	May 15, 1865/No. 186841		
"Prelew" Pattern	June 6, 1865/No. 187358	"Orleans" Pattern	June 6, 1865/No. 187359
"Choice" Pattern	June 15, 1865/No. 187576		

ELIJAH HUGHES & CO.
FLOW BLUE

CATEGORY	PATTERN
A	Paladin China
S	Walmer

MULBERRY WARES

CATEGORY	PATTERN
S	Walmer

THOMAS HUGHES
FLOW BLUE

CATEGORY	PATTERN
F	Regalia
F	Roseville
O	Shapoo

WHITE IRONSTONE

DeSoto Shape*	Reg'd. Apr. 17, 1855/No. 99876
"Plain Round"	
"Primary Shape"	

*Registry marking notes T. Hughes, but registry date is recorded as Stephen Hughes & Son. See *Cushion.*

TEA LEAF/COPPER LUSTRE
"Plain Round: Bulbous"

THOMAS HUGHES & SON (LTD.)
BLUE AND WHITE TRANSFERWARE
SINGLE PATTERNS

CATEGORY	PATTERN
S	Avon Cottage

FLOW BLUE

CATEGORY	PATTERN
M/F	Asiatic Pheasants
M/F	Floral
F	Morning Glory
F	Regalia
F	Roseville
O	Shapoo

WHITE IRONSTONE

DeSoto Shape	Reg'd. Apr. 17, 1855/No. 99876
"Plain Acanthus"	-
"Plain Round"	-

TEA LEAF/COPPER LUSTRE
"Plain Round"

THOMAS HULME
WHITE IRONSTONE
Baltic Shape

HULME & BOOTH
MULBERRY WARES

CATEGORY	PATTERN	
F	Flora	Reg'd. Nov. 14, 1851*

*Registered to Geo.B. Sander, London, No. 81558
WHITE IRONSTONE
"Grape Octagon"

(JOHN) HULME & SONS
BLUE AND WHITE TRANSFERWARE
SINGLE PATTERNS

CATEGORY	PATTERN
-	Alva
S	Montes Pyrenees
M	Vas Floreat

HULSE & ADDERLEY
BLUE AND WHITE TRANSFERWARE
SINGLE PATTERNS

CATEGORY	PATTERN
M	God Is Our Strength

HULSE, NIXON & ADDERLEY
BLUE AND WHITE TRANSFERWARE
SINGLE PATTERNS

CATEGORY	PATTERN
C	Mycene

HUMPHREYS BROS.
FLOW BLUE

CATEGORY	PATTERN
F	Dresden
F	Marguerite
F	Petunia

INDEO POTTERY
BLUE AND WHITE TRANSFERWARE
SINGLE PATTERNS

CATEGORY	PATTERN
-	"Buffalo and Fisherman"
M	"Huntsman and Greyhound"
M	"Indeo Chinoiserie"
M	"Italian"
M	"Oriental Birds"
M	"Ornate Pagoda"
-	"Pagoda and Water Birds"
M	"Riding a Buffalo"
M	"Spotted Deer"
-	"Two Kilns"
M	"Two Temples"
M	"Willow" Pattern

THOMAS INGLEBY & CO.
BLUE AND WHITE TRANSFERWARE
SINGLE PATTERNS

CATEGORY	PATTERN
S	Gothic Beauties

J. JACKSON & CO.
BLUE AND WHITE TRANSFERWARE
SINGLE PATTERNS

CATEGORY	PATTERN
S	Wild Rose
O	"Willow" Pattern

JOB & JOHN JACKSON
BLUE AND WHITE TRANSFERWARE
SERIES
1. Holy Bible Series
2. Holy Bible
3. Tadmore in the Desert
BLUE AND WHITE TRANSFERWARE
SINGLE PATTERNS

CATEGORY	PATTERN
M/G	Antelope
G	Archery
O	Asiatic Scenery (2)
M/F	Bird Pattern
S	Clyde Scenery*
S	Florentine Villas
S/C	Grecian Gardens
-	Grecian Scenery
G	Harvest Scenery
G	Haymaker, The
O	India Pagoda
-	Marine
G	Swiss Boy
F	Tuscan Rose
S	Valencia

*Possibly a series. Refer to *Snyder, Romantic Staffordshire*, pp. 82-84.
HISTORIC STAFFORDSHIRE SERIES
AMERICAN
1. AMERICAN SCENERY SERIES
Albany, New York
American Scenery ("...View of Newburgh, et.al.")
At Richmond, Virginia
Battery & C. New York
Battle Monument, Baltimore
Bunker Hill Monument
Castle Garden, New York
City Hall, New York
"Conway, New Hampshire" (Mkd. American Scenery) ["N. Hampshire, US, View Near Conway, et.al."]
Court House, Richmond (VA.)
Deaf & Dumb Asylum, Philadelphia
Fort Conanicut, Rhode Island
Fort Ticonderoga, New York* (2)
Girard's Bank, Philadelphia
Hancock House, Boston
Hartford, Connecticut
Harvard Hall, Massachusetts
Iron Works at Saugerties (N.Y.)
Lake George* [Fort Ticonderoga, New York]
Montevideo [Wadsworth Tower] Hartford
New Haven, Connecticut
Newport, Rhode Island
The President's House, Washington
The Race Bridge, Philadelphia
Shannondale Springs, Virginia
Skenectady* [Schenectady] On the Mohawk River [Fort Ticonderoga, New York]
State House, Boston
University Hall, Harvard (Massachusetts)
Upper Ferry Bridge Over the River Schuylkill
View of the Canal, Little Falls, Mohawk River
View of the Catskill Mountain House, N.Y.
View of Newburgh [Junction of the Sacandage & Hudson River or Fort Ticonderoga, New York, or Upper Ferry
Bridge over the River Schuylkill]
The Water Works, Philadelphia
Yale College and State House, New Haven
*Fort Ticonderoga is noted on two other scenes, Lake George and Schenectady.
2. MISCELLANEOUS
"American Scenery" ["Jackson Warranted"]
New York [From Weehawk]
Skenectady On the Mohawk River
White Sulphur Springs, Town of Delaware, Ohio, 22 Miles from City of Columbus

JAMES JAMIESON & CO.
BLUE AND WHITE TRANSFERWARE
SERIES
1. MODERN ATHENS "SERIES"
"Burns Monument"
"Dean Bridge"
"Dean Bridge From Water of Leith"
"Donaldson's Hospital"
"Dugald Stewart's Monument"
"Princes Street from Calton Hill"
"George Heriot's Hospital"
"Holy Trinity Episcopal Church"
"Royal High School"
"Royal Scottish Academy"
"St. John's Church"
"Scott Monument"
BLUE AND WHITE TRANSFERWARE
SINGLE PATTERNS

CATEGORY	PATTERN
-	Australia
O	Bosphorus
S	California
-	Falconry
-	Florentine Villas
-	Forth
-	Goat
-	Gothic
-	Grecian Scenery
-	Hawthorn Blossom
-	Loch Winnock
H	"Queen Victoria"
G	Rajah
F	Rose
-	Royal Vase
-	Rural
S	Swiss Scenery
C	Triumphal Car
O	"Willow" Pattern

MULBERRY WARES

CATEGORY	PATTERN
F	Coral

JOHN KING KNIGHT

BLUE AND WHITE TRANSFERWARE

SINGLE PATTERNS

CATEGORY	PATTERN
S	Geneva
F	Lily
O	"Willow" Pattern

JOHNSON BROS. (HANLEY), LTD.

BLUE & WHITE TRANSFERWARE

SERIES

1. OLD BRITISH CASTLES SERIES

BLUE AND WHITE TRANSFERWARE

SINGLE PATTERNS

CATEGORY	PATTERN
F	Begonia
S	Blarney Castle
F	Bouquet
A	English Chippendale
A	Glenwood
A	Lace
A	Regis
A	Rolland
A	Sylvan

FLOW BLUE

CATEGORY	PATTERN	
A	Albany	Reg'd. 1896/No. 285152
A	Andora	
A	Argyle	Reg'd. 1908/No. 526896
F	Astoria	
-	Aubrey	
F	Begonia	
F	Blackberry/Kenworth	
A	Blue Danube (The)	
A	Brittany	
A	Brooklyn	
F	Claremont	
F	Clarissa	Reg'd. 1894/No. 235459
F	Clayton	Reg'd. 1900/No. 355159
F	Clayton	Reg'd. 1902/No. 396702
F	Clematis	
M	Columbia	
F	Constance	
M/F	Coral	
F	Delmonte	
M/F	Dorothy	
F	Dresden	
M/A	Eclipse	
F	English Gardens (?)	
F/M	Exeter	
A	Florida	
F	Fortuna	Reg'd. 1894
A	Fulton	
A	Georgia	Reg'd. 1903/No. 417778
M/A	Glenwood	Reg'd. Oct. 24, 1902
M/F	Hague	
M/F	Holland ["Blue Meissen"]	Reg'd. 1906/No. 483405
F	Japan	
A	Jewel	
M/F	Kenworth /"Blackberry"	
F	Lily	
F	Manhattan	
F	Mentone	
M/Z	Mongolia	
F	Montana	
F	Neapolitan	Reg'd. 1895/No. 260049
M/F	Normandy	Reg'd. 1905/No. 457...
M	"Onion Pattern"	
A	Oregon	
O	Oriental	
A	Oxford	
F	Pansy*	
F	Paris	
F	Peach/ Peach Blossom	Reg'd. 1893/No. 208597
F	Peach Blossom/ Peach	Reg'd. 1893/No. 208597
F	Pekin	Reg'd. Oct. 24, 1902[1]
A	Persian	
F	Poppy	
A	Princeton	Reg'd. 1899/No. 347009
F	Raleigh	
A	Regent	
F	Richmond	
A	Royston	
F	St. Louis	
A	Savoy	
M/A	Stanley**	
A	Sterling	Reg'd. 1906/No. 483400
A	Tokio	
A	Trieste (The)	
F	Tulip	Reg'd. 1893/No. 208691
F	Turin	
F	Venice***	Reg'd. 1893/No. 208595
F	Vienna	
F	Warwick	
F	Waverly	

(1)Johnson patented body styles in the United States: June 27, 1893, Nov. 11, 1898, Oct. 21, 1900, Oct. 21, 1902, Oct. 24, 1902.

*See comments under Brown & Steventon, Ltd.

**Patent date, Nov. 7, 99 (1899)

***Registered in 1895, No. 250791

MULBERRY WARES

CATEGORY	PATTERN
F	Savannah
F	Vienna

WHITE IRONSTONE

"Acanthus"

"Chelsea"

"Double Swirl"

"Plain Square"

"Square Ridged"

"Tracery"

"Wheat & Daisy"

TEA LEAF/COPPER LUSTRE

"Acanthus"

"Chelsea

JONES & SON

BLUE AND WHITE TRANSFERWARE

SERIES

1. BRITISH HISTORY "SERIES"

Alfred as a "Minstrel"

Battle of Waterloo

Canute Reproving His Courtiers

Caractacus Before Claudius

Charles I Ordering the Speaker to Give Up the Five Members

Coronation of George IV

Cromwell Dismissing the Long Parliament

Death of General Wolfe

Death of Lord Nelson

Elizabeth Addressing the Troops

Hamden Mortally Wounded

Interview of Wallace and Bruce

Landing of William of Orange

The Seven Bishops Conveyed to the Tower

Signing the Magna Carta

N.B.: Refer to Penny Plain, p. 100, No. 251

BLUE AND WHITE TRANSFERWARE

SINGLE PATTERNS

CATEGORY	PATTERN
M	"Neptune" Pattern ["The Apotheosis of Nelson"]
S	Picturesque Asiatic Beauties (possible series)

JONES & WALLEY

FLOW BLUE

CATEGORY	PATTERN
M	"Marble"
O	Indian Stone

ALBERT E. JONES (LONGTON), LTD.

FLOW BLUE

CATEGORY	PATTERN	
O	Pekin	Reg'd. 1909/No. 538202

ELIJAH JONES

BLUE AND WHITE TRANSFERWARE

SINGLE PATTERNS

CATEGORY	PATTERN
O	Asiatic Scenic Beauties
M/F	Cabinet
S	Cambrian Bridges
M	Country Sports
S	Denon's Egypt (possible series)
G	The Hop
O	Oriental Beauties
O	Palestine (Sheckem)
O	Palestine (Sidom)
M	Pomona
G	"The Villager"

FREDERICK JONES (& CO.)
FLOW BLUE

CATEGORY	PATTERN	
O	Formosa	

WHITE IRONSTONE

Scotia Shape*	-
Victor Shape	Reg'd. Sept. 9, 1868/No. 221312

**Wetherbee, White Ironstone A Second Look*, p. 99, notes a similar body style used by J.&C. Wileman and marked Poppy

GEORGE JONES (& SONS LTD.)
BLUE AND WHITE TRANSFERWARE
SINGLE PATTERNS

CATEGORY	PATTERN	
-	Abbey	
P/A	Alpine	
F	Briar	
S	Casino	
A	Chatsworth	
F	Chinese Flowers	
-	Christs Hospital	
F	Congo	
S	Cyrene	
O	Dragon	
S	Farm	
G	Indian Traffic	
M	Kent	Reg'd. Mar. 3, 1874/No. 280907
G	Lasso	
S	Medici	
S	Pastoral	
F	Shandon	
O	Sing An	
F	Sistovia	
S	Spanish Festivity	
F	Sunbury	
G	Toro	
O	"Willow" Pattern	
S	Woodland	

See *Cluett*, pp. 72-75.
FLOW BLUE

CATEGORY	PATTERN	
S	Abbey	-
S	Abbey "Shredded Wheat Dish"	-
F	Azalea	-
A	Bristol	-
F	Chatsworth	Reg'd. 1885/No. 22781
G	Farm*	-
G	Indian Traffic*	-
O	Jeddo	-
M	Lasso*	-
S	Paisley	-
F	Peachblow	Reg'd. 1886/No.56152
M/A	Rebecca	Reg'd. 1886/No. 57681
G	Spanish Festivities	-
M	"Spinach" (Brush Stroke)	-
G	Toro*	-
F	Wild Rose	-
O	Willow*	-
G	Woodland*	-

*See *Cluett*, pp. 94-96
N.B.: *Blue Berry Notes*, Vol. 11, No. 3, May-June 1997, p. 12 illustrates a "Gaudy Pitcher and Bowl" registered Nov. 8, 1876/No.305080.
WHITE IRONSTONE

"Fuchsia Shape"	Reg'd. July 12, 1867/No. 209530
"Nautilus"	-
"Plain Round"	-
"Summer Garden"	-

KEELING & CO. (LTD.)
FLOW BLUE

CATEGORY	PATTERN	
-	Alton	
M	Andes	
F	Avon	
M/F	Cavendish	
F	Chatsworth	
O	Chusan	
P/F	Chusan	
F	Colesberg	
A	Croxon	Reg'd. 1910/No. 571753
F	Flora	
F	Ilford	
O	Indian Tree	
A/F	Kensington	
-	Kingston	
A/P	Napier	
-	Ormonde	
M	Parisian	
M	Pekin	
A	Pompadour	
F	Rose	
F	Sevres	
F	Tokio	
O	Whampoa	
O	"Willow" Pattern ("Two Temples II")	

JAMES KEELING
BLUE AND WHITE TRANSFERWARE
SERIES
1. VIEWS OF MESOPOTAMIA "SERIES" (att.)
The Fountain Near Aleppo
"Oriental Converazione and ..."
"Return From a Desert Excursion..."
"Tomb of Zobeida ..."
"Turkish Coffee-House..."
"View of Birs Nimroud"
BLUE AND WHITE TRANSFERWARE
SINGLE PATTERNS

CATEGORY	PATTERN
S	"Grazing Rabbits" (att.)
G	"Lakeside Meeting" (att.)
G	"Master and Servant" (att.)
G	"Tea Party" (att.)
-	"View of Clare College, Cambridge"
O	"Willow" Pattern

SAMUEL KEELING & CO.
BLUE AND WHITE TRANSFERWARE
SERIES
1. BARONIAL VIEWS "SERIES" (Country Houses)
Clumber
Statfield Saye
BLUE AND WHITE TRANSFERWARE
SINGLE PATTERNS

CATEGORY	PATTERN
S	Abbey

FLOW BLUE

CATEGORY	PATTERN
F	Cowes
M/F	Pekin
M	Parisian

JAMES KENT (LTD.)
FLOW BLUE

CATEGORY	PATTERN
M/A	Arabesque
M	Brugge
F	Delph
F	Dora
-	Empress
-	Fenton
S	Oriental
F	Osaka

R.S. KIDSTON & CO. - VERREVILLE
BLUE AND WHITE TRANSFERWARE
SERIES
1. UNITED KINGDOM "SERIES"
Dublin From Phoenix Park
Dunkel
Edinburgh (2)
BLUE AND WHITE TRANSFERWARE
SINGLE PATTERNS

CATEGORY	PATTERN
S	Abbey
M	"Peruvian Hunters"
O	"Syrian"
O	"Willow" Pattern

KNIGHT, ELKIN & CO.
BLUE AND WHITE TRANSFERWARE
SERIES
1. BARONIAL HALLS "SERIES" Reg'd. Aug. 15, 1844/No. 20779
Chip Chase
Cobham Hall
Stow Hall
BLUE AND WHITE TRANSFERWARE
SINGLE PATTERNS

CATEGORY	PATTERN
O	Bouquet
C	De Fete
C	Etruscan ["Classical Figure"]
S	"Garden Scene"
G	Hannibal Passing the Alps (3)
-	Milan
O	Oriental Vase
S	Pennsylvania

HISTORIC STAFFORDSHIRE SERIES
AMERICAN
1. MISCELLANEOUS
Pennsylvania*
*See *Larsen*, p. 247, No. 696.

KNIGHT, ELKIN & BRIDGWOOD
BLUE AND WHITE TRANSFERWARE
SINGLE PATTERNS

CATEGORY	PATTERN
G	Guitary No. 24
F	Moss-Rose No. 35
M	Sun of Righteousness (The)

THOMAS LAKIN
BLUE AND WHITE TRANSFERWARE
SINGLE PATTERNS

CATEGORY	PATTERN
-	"Chinamen"
-	"Classical Ruins"
-	"Eight Storey Pagoda"
-	"Prince of Wales Feathers"
S	"Rome" ["Tiber"]
-	"Thistle & Rose"
-	"Twin Obelisks"

SAMUEL LEAR
WHITE IRONSTONE
"Lily of the Valley with Ferns"

LEEDS POTTERY
BLUE AND WHITE TRANSFERWARE
SINGLE PATTERNS
CATEGORY PATTERN
1. CHINOISERIE PATTERNS
"Buffalo Pattern" ["Boy on a Buffalo"]
"Conservation"
"Jar and Fisherman"
"Junk Pattern" ["Chinese Junk"]
"The Great Wall of China"
"Long Bridge Pattern"
"Two Figure Pattern" ["Invented V Shape Bridge"] ["Willow"]
"Two Men on a Bridge, et.al." (2)
"Zebra"
2. MISCELLANEOUS PATTERNS

M	"An All-over Shell Design"
M	"Basket"
-	"Camel"
-	"Castellated Manor House"
-	"Church With Flagstaff"
S	"Cottage and Vase"
S	"Cow Standing in a Distant Landscape, et.al."
F	"Floral Spray"
F	"Flowers and Butterflies"
-	"Griffon"
S	Italian (After Claud Lorraine) ["Ponte Del Palazzo Near Florence"]
G	Italian Scenery ["Winding Road"]
-	"Jar and Fisherman"
-	"Near Currah, on the River Ganges"*
Z	"Parrot and Fruit"
S	"Scene after Claude Lorraine"**
S	"Swans on a Pond, et.al."
S	"Two Cows in a Ruined Abbey, et.al."
G	"The Wanderer"

*See *FOB Bulletin* No. 95, Spring 1997, p. 10.
**See *P. Williams Staffordshire,* Vol. III, p. 104.
HISTORIC STAFFORDSHIRE SERIES
AMERICAN
1. MISCELLANEOUS
James Gant/General Mercer & Captain Morres, 1801*
*Refer to *Yorkshire Pots*, p. 48, No. 57

LIDDLE, ELLIOT & SON
FLOW BLUE

CATEGORY	PATTERN	
S	Florentine	-

MULBERRY WARES

CATEGORY	PATTERN	
F	Fern	Reg'd. Nov. 15, 1869/ No. 236203-7
-	Mooresque*	
F	Panel	Reg'd. Nov. 15, 1869/ No. 236203-7
F	"Scrolled Leaf"	-

*Ellen Hill notes this as a geometric pattern.
WHITE IRONSTONE

"Berlin Swirl" *	Dated 1864
"Hanging Pear"	-
"Plain Berlin"	Dated 1864,
"Trumpet Vine Shape"	Reg'd. Sept. 18, 1865/No.189782 2/68 indicates a reissued date for February 1868 of this earlier registered design.

*Originally registered by T.J. & J. Mayer, 1845 and continued by his successors Mayer & Elliot and Liddle Elliot & Son.

LIVESLEY, POWELL & CO.
BLUE AND WHITE TRANSFERWARE
SINGLE PATTERNS

CATEGORY	PATTERN
S	Abbey
G	For-get-me-not
F	Hawthorne
M/F	Indian
-	Panama
M/F	Paradise
J	Rose Chintz

FLOW BLUE

CATEGORY	PATTERN
M/F	Indian

MULBERRY WARES

CATEGORY	PATTERN
S	Abbey
F	"Rose & Bell"*
F	Water Lily

*Made in purple, not in Mulberry
WHITE IRONSTONE

"Classic Gothic"	-
Columbia Shape	-
"Double Sydenham" ["Wrapped Sydenham"]	-
"Fern & Floral" (Ch)	-
"Full Paneled Gothic"	-
"Fruit Garden"	-
"Grape Octagon"	-
"Leaf & Crossed Ribbon"	-
"Paneled Columbia" (Ch)	-
"Prairie Flowers"	-
"Ring O' Hearts Shape" A&B (Ch)	Reg'd. Oct. 12, 1853/No. 92868-9
"Wheat in the Meadow"	-

TEA LEAF/COPPER LUSTRE

Columbia Shape	-
"Classic Gothic"	-
"Full Panelled Gothic"	-
"Grape Octagon"	-
"Ring O'Hearts" (Ch)	Reg'd. Oct. 12, 1853/No. 92868-9
"Wrapped Sydenham" ["Double Sydenham"]	-

JOHN & THOMAS LOCKETT
BLUE AND WHITE TRANSFERWARE
SINGLE PATTERNS

CATEGORY	PATTERN
S	Melton

LOCKETT & HULME
BLUE AND WHITE TRANSFERWARE
SINGLE PATTERNS

CATEGORY	PATTERN
H	Ponte Rotto

LOCKHART & ARTHUR
BLUE AND WHITE TRANSFERWARE
SINGLE PATTERNS

CATEGORY	PATTERN
F	Anemone
S	Athens
M	"Clan Mackenzie"
S	Country Scenery
F	Lily and Rose
S	Palermo
S	Pastoral
S	"Sevres"
C	Verona
-	Virginia
S	Wild Rose

DAVID LOCKHART (and LOCKHART & CO.)
BLUE AND WHITE TRANSFERWARE
SINGLE PATTERNS

CATEGORY	PATTERN
G	"Arab"
-	Athens
Z	Antelope
F	Batavia
M	Brussels
J	"Charlie"
A	Cuba

CATEGORY	PATTERN
C	Etruscan
J	"Greyhound"
J	"Innocence"
M	"Life Buoy"
F	Palermo
A	Persia
-	Peru
S	Rhine
-	Scotia

MULBERRY WARES

CATEGORY	PATTERN
C	Etruscan
S	Rothsay

DAVID LOCKHART & SONS (LTD.)
BLUE AND WHITE TRANSFERWARE

CATEGORY	PATTERN
M	Auld Lang Syne
M	Britannia
M	King & Queen
M	Scotland Forever
M	Thistle
A	Verona

MULBERRY WARES

CATEGORY	PATTERN
G	Fidelity
-	Lochee

WILLIAM H. LOCKITT
BLUE AND WHITE TRANSFERWARE
SINGLE PATTERNS

CATEGORY	PATTERN
S	Marne

LONGTON POTTERY CO. LTD.
FLOW BLUE

CATEGORY	PATTERN
-	Benton

LOWNDES & BEECH
(see: BEECH & LOWNDES)

MACHIN & POTTS
BLUE AND WHITE TRANSFERWARE
SERIES
1. CONTINENTAL VIEWS (SERIES)
Mt. Olympus
Socrates ["Beehive and Poet"]
BLUE AND WHITE TRANSFERWARE
SINGLE PATTERNS

CATEGORY	PATTERN
M	Cavendish

JAMES MAC INTYRE & CO. (LTD.)
BLUE AND WHITE TRANSFERWARE
SINGLE PATTERNS

CATEGORY	PATTERN
F	Devon
O	Vinagrette
O	"Willow" Pattern

MacIntrye & Co. registered a pedestal salt on December 3, 1878, No. 329992. See *Sussman*, p. 48.

JOHN MADDOCK
BLUE AND WHITE TRANSFERWARE
SINGLE PATTERNS

CATEGORY	PATTERN
S	Campanile
O	Fairy Villas
S	Korea
A	Tudor (att.)
O	"Willow" Pattern

FLOW BLUE

CATEGORY	PATTERN
O	Canton
O	Chen-si
O	Cimerian
O	Fairy Villas
O	Mandarin

WHITE IRONSTONE
"Double Sydenham" ["Wrapped Sydenham"]
"Great Ivy & Berries"
"Holly"
"Lined Glory"
"Maddock's Pear"
"Primary Shape"
"Squash & Vine"

JOHN MADDOCK & SONS (LTD.)
BLUE AND WHITE TRANSFERWARE
SINGLE PATTERNS

CATEGORY	PATTERN
O	Bombay
S	Campania
O	Fairy Villas
O	Indian Tree
S	Korea
F	"Pansy Border"
A	Tudor (att.)
S	Verano
O	"Willow" Pattern

FLOW BLUE

CATEGORY	PATTERN	
F	Abbot	
F	Beatrice	
F	Belfort	
F	Brooklyn	
A/F	Dainty	
F	Duchess	
F	Gem	Reg'd. 1897/No. 308970
F	Grapevine	
F	Hamilton	
O	Hindustan	
M/A	Heuman	
F	Iris	
M	Jewel	
F	Linda	
F	Louise	
F	Marlborough	
M	Meissen	
F	Oakland	
F	Orchard	
F	Rialto	
A	Rococo	
A	Roseville	
F	"Rose & Ribbons"	
A	Triumph*	Reg'd. 1903/No. 405093
-	Victor	
M/F	Virginia	
F	Waverly	

*In addition to registry date and number, shape number 405538 is recorded.
WHITE IRONSTONE
"Bar & Chain"
"Cable & Ring"
"Holly"
"Hyacinth"
"Lined Glory"
"Simple Square"
"Simplicity"
"Squash & Vine"
"Stylized Berry"
"Trailing Ivy"
TEA LEAF/COPPER LUSTRE
"Square Ridged"

MADDOCK & GATER
WHITE IRONSTONE
"Plain Uplift"

MADDOCK & SEDDON
BLUE AND WHITE TRANSFERWARE
SINGLE PATTERNS

CATEGORY	PATTERN
G	"Children's Pets" (att.)
O	Fairy Villas

C.T. MALING
BLUE AND WHITE TRANSFERWARE
SINGLE PATTERNS

CATEGORY	PATTERN
M	Denon's Egypt
O	"Willow" Pattern

FLOW BLUE

CATEGORY	PATTERN	
O	Chang	-
O	Ning Po	-
F	Windsor	Reg'd. 1887/No. 71430
O	"Willow" Pattern	-

C.T. MALING & SONS (LTD.)
FLOW BLUE

CATEGORY	PATTERN
S	Egypt
F	Vine
O	"Willow" Pattern

MALING'S (ROBERT)
BLUE AND WHITE TRANSFERWARE
SINGLE PATTERNS

CATEGORY	PATTERN	
S	Albion	
M	"Bee Catcher" (att.)	
M	"Pillar With Urn"	

RALPH MALKIN
BLUE AND WHITE TRANSFERWARE
SINGLE PATTERNS

CATEGORY	PATTERN	
G	Dancers	
S	"Rumanian Inscription"	Reg'd. Aug. 21, 1868/No. 220906

MALKIN, WALKER & HULSE
BLUE AND WHITE TRANSFERWARE
SINGLE PATTERNS

CATEGORY	PATTERN
O	Pekin

MANN & CO.
FLOW BLUE

CATEGORY	PATTERN
F	Balmoral

N.B.: *Blue Berry Notes*, Vol. 11, No. 4, July/August 1997, p. 19, illustrates a 19.5" Charger (no name) in Flow Blue.

JOHN MARE
BLUE AND WHITE TRANSFERWARE
SINGLE PATTERNS

CATEGORY	PATTERN
S	"Italian Pattern"
O	"Willow" Pattern

MARPLE, TURNER & CO.
BLUE AND WHITE TRANSFERWARE
SINGLE PATTERNS

CATEGORY	PATTERN	
C	Athena	Reg'd. Oct. 30, 1852/No. 87464
S	Holly	

JACOB MARSH
BLUE AND WHITE TRANSFERWARE
SINGLE PATTERNS

CATEGORY	PATTERN
G	"The Village"

MARSH & WILLETT
BLUE AND WHITE TRANSFERWARE
SINGLE PATTERNS

CATEGORY	PATTERN
M	Top Piper

JOHN MARSHALL (& CO.)(LTD.)
BLUE AND WHITE TRANSFERWARE
SERIES
1. CANADIAN SPORTS "SERIES"
"Child With Snow Shovel"
"Girl Feeding a Goose"
"LaCrosse Player" (2)
"Male Skaters"
"Male Snowshoer Striding Along"
"Male Snowshoer Trips Over Fence"
"The Skating Girl"
"Snowshoes Being Tied"
"Toboganners"
"Two Children on Sled"
BLUE AND WHITE TRANSFERWARE
SINGLE PATTERNS

CATEGORY	PATTERN
S	Bosphorus

FLOW BLUE

CATEGORY	PATTERN
S	Bosphorus
S	Rural

CHARLES JAMES MASON
BLUE AND WHITE TRANSFERWARE
SINGLE PATTERNS

CATEGORY	PATTERN
O	"Chinese Landscape" (Reissued by G.L. Ashworth Bros. in Flow Blue)
O	"Oriental Pheasants"

N.B.: The question of whether these patterns emanated with G.M. and C.J. Mason and continued through various ownerships is a subject well documented and illustrated in *Godden Masons*, see pp. 21, 97, 144, pl. 154 and pp. 140 and 149.

CHARLES JAMES MASON & CO.
BLUE AND WHITE TRANSFERWARE
SERIES
1. "BRITISH LAKES SERIES"
Buttermere*
Derwentwater
Elterwater
Loweswater
Thirlmere
Ullswater
Windermere
*See *P. Williams, Staffordshire*, Vol. III, p. 59.
2. "COLLEGE VIEWS" SERIES
"King's College Chapel, Cambridge"
"King's College Provost Lodge"
"Main Entrance to Queens College, Cambridge"
"Walnut Tree Court"
3. "NAPOLEON SERIES"
Napoleon (3)
"Napoleon at the Battle of" Austerlitz
"Napoleon at the Battle of" Marengo
"Napoleon Battles" - Return from Elba
"Napoleon Battles" - Revolt of Cairo
N.B.: Title names appear in script. For further reading, refer to *Laidacker*, Pt. II, p. 57.
BLUE AND WHITE TRANSFERWARE
SINGLE PATTERNS

CATEGORY	PATTERN
M/A	Basket
S	"Classical Landscape"
S	Damascus
S	Loadicea
O	Mogul
O	"Opium Smokers"
P/O	"Pekin Japan"
F	"Roses" (att.)
S	"Trentham Hall" ["Hercules Fountain"]

FLOW BLUE

CATEGORY	PATTERN
O	"Yellow River"*

*See Snyder's Fascinating Flow Blue, p. 137 for pattern.
WHITE IRONSTONE
Fenton Shape*
"Foo Dog"
Hydra Shape*
"Scalloped Edge"
*Wetherbee notes that Fenton Shape and Hydra Shape were shapes used as blanks for transfer patterns.
For additional patterns and further reading, refer to *Godden's Masons*; *Coysh, Vol. 1 & 2*

G.M. & C.J. MASON
BLUE AND WHITE TRANSFERWARE
SINGLE PATTERNS

CATEGORY	PATTERN
O	"Blue Pheasants"
M/F	"Butterfly Japan"
F	"Roses"
F	"Sharpus" et.al.*
O	"Table & Flower Pot"
O	"Two-Man Chinoiserie"

*Refer to Coysh, Vol. 2, p. 181

MILES MASON
BLUE AND WHITE TRANSFERWARE
SINGLE PATTERNS

CATEGORY	PATTERN
O	"Willow" Pattern

WILLIAM MASON
BLUE AND WHITE TRANSFERWARE
SINGLE PATTERNS

CATEGORY	PATTERN
S	"Furness Abbey, Lancashire"
S	"Netley Abbey"
O	"Two Temples"

ROBERT MAY
BLUE AND WHITE TRANSFERWARE
SINGLE PATTERNS

CATEGORY	PATTERN
S	Fountain ["Bird Fountain"]

MAYER & ELLIOTT
(or Mayer Bros. & Elliott)
BLUE AND WHITE TRANSFERWARE
SINGLE PATTERNS

CATEGORY	PATTERN
-	"Blue Acorn"
-	"Gothic"

-	"Temple"
-	"Tower"
O	"Willow" Pattern

MULBERRY WARES

CATEGORY	PATTERN
F	Berry
S/C	Etruscan Vases
F	Flora

WHITE IRONSTONE

Berlin "Swirl Shape"*	Reg'd. Dec. 18, 1856/No. 108052
"Cabbage Shape"	Reg'd. Jan. 23, 1860/No. 125863

*Marking notes "BERLIN IRONSTONE CHINA" first made by T.J. & J. Mayer. See *Wetherbee, White Ironstone,* p. 45.

THOMAS MAYER

BLUE AND WHITE TRANSFERWARE
SERIES
1. ILLUSTRATIONS OF THE BIBLE SERIES
Flight into Egypt
Foot of Mount Sinai
Fords of the Jordan
Fountain of Elisha at Jericho
Nazareth
Tomb of Absalom, Village of Siloan
The Brook, Kedron
2. OLYMPIC GAMES SERIES
Animal Prize Fight
Archery, Oly Game
Charioteers,The
Darting
Discus, The
Running
Spanish Bullfight
Victors Crowned
BLUE AND WHITE TRANSFERWARE
SINGLE PATTERNS

CATEGORY	PATTERN
S	Abbey Ruins*
S	Canova**
S	Cattle Scenery (3)
G	"Gaignault"***
S	Gothic
O	Mogul Scenery**** (also produced in Mulberry)
S	Non Pareil

*Possibly a series. Refer to *Snyder, Romantic Staffordshire,* pp. 121-123.
**Possibly a series. Refer to *Snyder, Romantic Staffordshire*, pp. 123-125.
***See *P. Williams, Staffordshire*, Vol. III, pp. 142-143.
****Possibly a series. Refer to *Snyder, Romantic Staffordshire*, pp. 127.
HISTORIC STAFFORDSHIRE SERIES
AMERICAN
1. ARMS OF THE AMERICAN STATES
Connecticut, Arms of
Delaware, Arms of
Georgia, Arms of
Maryland, Arms of
Massachusetts, Arms of
New Hampshire, Arms of*
New Jersey, Arms of
New York, Arms of
North Carolina, Arms of
Pennsylvania, Arms of
Rhode Island, Arms of
South Carolina, Arms of
Virginia, Arms of
*To-date this has not been located.
2. MISCELLANEOUS
Franklin's [Tomb] ["Lafayette at the Tomb of Franklin"]
Washington(s) [Tomb] ["Lafayette at the Tomb of Washington"]

THOMAS, JOHN & JOSEPH MAYER

BLUE AND WHITE TRANSFERWARE
SINGLE PATTERNS

CATEGORY	PATTERN
F	Ava (Prize Medal 1851)
S	Baronial Halls (possible series)
S	Bosphorus (The)
S	E.B. & S. Wards Steamers*
S/C	Etruscan Vase
S	1851 Exposition Building
S	Florentine
S	Garden Scenery (possible series)
S	Gem (The)
H	Grape & Vine
S	Grecian Scroll
S	Rhone Scenery
S	Rural Scenery (Prize Medal 1851)

* See Arman *Quarterly*, Vol. 1, 1997, p. 34

FLOW BLUE

CATEGORY	PATTERN	
S	Arabesque	
O	Formosa	
S	Grecian Scroll	
O	Oregon	Reg'd. Oct. 9, 1854/No. 97160
S	Rhone Scenery	

MULBERRY WARES

CATEGORY	PATTERN	
F	Ava	Reg'd. Oct. 22, 1853/No. 93008-9
S/C	Etruscan Vases	
S	Florentine	
P/F	Flower Vase (Prize Medal 1851)	
F	Heraldic Swirls	
F	"Ivy & Flowers"	
F	Lily	
F	"Lily & Bluebell"	
O	Oriental Scenery	
S	Rhone Scenery	
F	"Scrolls"	

WHITE IRONSTONE

"Berlin Inverted Diamond"	-
"Berlin Swirl" Shape*	Reg'd. Jan 21, 1845/No. 25199
"Classic Gothic Octagon Shape"**	Reg'd. July 27, 1847/No. 44398
"Curved Gothic"	-
"Inverted Diamond"	-
"Long Octagon Shape"	Reg'd. July 27, 1847/No. 44398
"Mayer's Classic Gothic Shape" ["Gothic Shape"]***	Reg'd. July 27, 1847/No. 44398
"Primary Shape"	-
"Pumpkin Primary Octagon Shape"****	-
"Prize Nodding Bud Shape" ["Narrow Waist Gothic"]	Reg'd. Dec. 2, 1851/No. 81815
"Prize Bloom Shape"	Reg'd. Oct. 22, 1853/No. 93008-9
"Prize Puritan Shape"	Reg'd. Sept. 2, 1851/No. 80365

*See *White Ironstone Notes*, Vol. 5, No. 3, Winter 1998, pp. 1-7
**Reg'd. by Mayer & Elliott in 1856 and Liddle & Elliott in 1864.
***Referred to by many as "Mayer's Classic Gothic Shape" with same registry date as for "Long Octagon Shape".
****See *Wetherbee*, p. 34, fig. 7-5, for "Hexagon Shape", which is actually "Octagon Shape".

MEAKIN & CO.
(Also Known as Meakin Bros. & Co.)

WHITE IRONSTONE

"Budded Vine"	-
"Moss Rose"	-
"Plain Round"	Impressed Date 1869
"Strawberry"	-

ALFRED MEAKIN (LTD.)

BLUE AND WHITE TRANSFERWARE
SINGLE PATTERNS

CATEGORY	PATTERN
F	Oban
F	Spray
A	Superior
-	Washington

FLOW BLUE

CATEGORY	PATTERN
F	Albermarle/Medway
-	Alhambra
F	Belmont
-	Bentick
F	Bramble
F	Brier
-	Burns
A	Cambridge
F	Carnations
A/N	Chesterfield
F	Claridge
F	Clifton
F	Daisy
F	Devon
-	Genoa
-	Hanley
F	Hanwell
F	Harvard
F	Harvest
M/A	Holland (The)
F	Kelvin
-	Kent
F	Kenwood
F	Leighton
A	Lenox
F	Lily
F	Luciville
F	Medway/Albemarle

F	Mentone
F	Messina
F	Normandy
F	Oakley
F	Oban
F	Ormonde
F	Ovando
F	Peony
F	Persian
A	Raleigh
A	Regent
F	Richmond
F	Ripon
F	Rosalina
-	Selwyn
F	Severn
F	Springfield
-	Tokiyo
F	Vane
A	Vernon
A	Verona
F	Wellington
F	West Meath

WHITE IRONSTONE
"Bamboo" (?)
"Basketweave With Band"
"Brocade"
"Chelsea"
"Fishhook"
"Plain Round"
"Plain Uplift Shape"
"Wheat & Hops" (LTD)*
"Wheat & Rose" (LTD)*
*Back marking "LTD" notes date after 1897.
TEA LEAF/COPPER LUSTRE
"Bamboo"
"Brocade"
"Chelsea"
"Crewel"
"Fishhook"
"Scroll"
"Senate Shape"
"Simple Pear"

CHARLES MEAKIN
WHITE IRONSTONE
"Curved Rectangle" (Burslem)
"Plain Round"

HENRY MEAKIN
WHITE IRONSTONE
"Wheat"

J. & G. MEAKIN
BLUE AND WHITE TRANSFERWARE
SINGLE PATTERNS

CATEGORY	PATTERN
S	Americana
A	Avondale
M/A	Chaplet
A	Chatham
A	Coniston
J	Farmer (The)
G	Millennium
S	Priory
J	Resurrection
F	Rosalie
S	Virginia

FLOW BLUE

CATEGORY	PATTERN	
F	Acantha	
A	Anglesea	
P/A	Balmoral	
-	Cairo	
M/A	Castro/Colonial	
M/A	Chaplet	
F	Claridge	
M/A	Colonial/Castro	
F	Columbia	
F	Delaware	
M/F	Diana	
F	Dunrobbin	
M/F	Fleur-de-Lis	
M/F	Fortuna	
M	Geisha	
F	Gem	
-	Genoa	
S	Hanley	
F	"Harebell"	
F	Harvest	
S	Homestead	
-	Hope Louise	
F	Hudson	
A/N	Jackson	
F	Japan	Reg'd. 1909/No. 545904
O	"Japan Pattern"	
F	Leon	
M/F	Louvre	
M/F	Madison	
S	"Mountain Stream"	
F	Non Pareil	
O	Pagoda	
-	Queen	
A	Regal	Reg'd. 1885 and Oct. 1899/No. 33283
F	Regina	
F	Rosalie	
F	Sevres	
F	Sol	Reg'd. 1902/No.391413
F	Stafford	
-	"Sweet Pea"	
A	Tenneriffe	
S	Virginia	
S	"Waterfall"	
F	Wellington	
M/F	Wentworth	
M/F	York	
M/A	Zuyder	

WHITE IRONSTONE
"Acorn"
"Block Optic"***
"Border of Leaves"
"Bow Knot"
"Budded Vine"*** Impressed Date 1869
"Cable & Ring"***
"Chain of Tulips"***
"Cherry Scroll"***
"Fern"
"Fern With Medallion"**
"Fruit of the Vine"***
"Fuchsia"
"Garden Sprig"***
"Miniature Scroll"
"Moss Rose"
"One Large & Two Little Ribs"***
"Panelled Leaves"
"Panelled Leaves With Berries"
"Pearl Sydenham"
"Piecrust" ["Blanket Stitch"]
"Plain Round"***
"Plain (Uplift)"***
"Plum Decagon"
"Ribbed Berry With Bloom"
"Safety Pin"
"Square Melon/Ribbed" ["Rope & Melon Ribs"]***
"Strawberry"* (Ch)
"Wheat & Hops" (Ch)
*See *White Ironstone Notes*, Vol. 4, No. 1, Summer 1997, p. 9 or illustration of a child's tea set
**See *Wetherbee*, *White Ironstone*, p. 140, fig. 15-3, marked "Medallion".
****Wetherbee*, *White Ironstone*, notes these as being manufactured in the last decade of the 1800s whereas those without asterisks are from the 1850s and 1860s.

CHARLES MEIGH
BLUE AND WHITE TRANSFERWARE
SERIES
1. MISCELLANEOUS
British Cathedral "Series"
St. Pauls
BLUE AND WHITE TRANSFERWARE
SINGLE PATTERNS

CATEGORY	PATTERN
M/F	Asiatic Birds (att.)
S	Athens
S	Boston
S	Ceylon
O	Chinese Bells
O	"Chinese Children's Games"
O	Dimity (att.)
S	Gothic
S	Gothic Ruins
-	Plover
F	"Rose Lattice"
S	Royal Persian
S	Scroll Frond Border
-	Sicilian
-	Susa
S	Tivoli
-	Valenciennes
S	Verona

S	Veronese
S	Village of Little Falls
S	Watteau

CHARLES MEIGH
HISTORIC STAFFORDSHIRE SERIES
AMERICAN
1. AMERICAN CITIES AND SCENERY SERIES
Albany
Ascent to the Capitol, Washington
Ballston Springs ["N.Y."]
Baltimore
Boston
Boston From Dorchester Heights
Caldwell, Lake George
Capitol at Washington
City Hall, New York
Gothic Church, New Haven
Hudson City ["N.Y."]
New York (From Weehawken)
Northampton, Mass.
Schuylkill Water Works (Philadelphia)
Utica ["N.Y."]
View From Mount Ida ["N.Y."]
Village of Little Falls ["N.Y."]
Washington (From the President's House)
Yale College, New Haven
FLOW BLUE

CATEGORY	PATTERN
M	Angelsea
S	Athens
F	Botanical
O	Chinese Bells
M/F	Corbeille (att.)
M/O	"Eastern Vines"
F	Eglantine
F	Gem
P/O	"Grasshopper & Flowers" (att.)
M/F	Heron
P/O	Hong Kong
F	Iris
O	Kyber
F	Lily
M	"Navy Marble" (att.)
F	Oriental Bouquet
P/M	"Pinwheel"
F	Poonah
M	"Sphinx"
M	Sprigs
F	Susa
S	Tivoli
S	Troy
S	Watteau
F	Wreath

MULBERRY WARES

CATEGORY	PATTERN
S	Athens
P/F	Ceylon
O	Chinese Bells
M/F	Eglantine
F	"Flower & Rose"
P/F	Hawthorne
P/F	Hopberry
F	Japan Flowers
F	Lauristinus
F	Lily
F	[# 1069]
P/O	Oleaster
F	Passion Flower
P/F	Plover
F	Poonah
S	Tivoli
S	Troy

CHARLES MEIGH & SON
BLUE AND WHITE TRANSFERWARE
SINGLE PATTERNS

CATEGORY	PATTERN
F	Grosvenor
M	Harebell
S	Italy
F	Java
S	Jenny Lind
P/F	Silistria
S	Sousa
S	Tivoli

FLOW BLUE

CATEGORY	PATTERN
P/F	Aberdeen
F	"Forget-Me-Not"
M/F	Gothic
F	Grosvenor
F	Impmoea
S	Jenny Lind
F	Poppy
F	Passiflora
M/F	Sutherland Border

MULBERRY WARES

CATEGORY	PATTERN
F	Concordia
F	Heath
F	Pansey
F	Passiflora
F	Sutherland Border

WHITE IRONSTONE

"Arcaded Trumpet Shape"	Reg'd. July 24, 1855/No. 100816
"Framed Panels Shape"*	Reg'd. Aug. 23, 1861/No. 142850
"Gothic Rose"	-
"Paneled Grape"	-
"Wild Rose Twig"	Dated 1860

*Registered by G.W. Reade

CHARLES MEIGH, SON & PANKHURST
BLUE AND WHITE TRANSFERWARE
SINGLE PATTERNS

CATEGORY	PATTERN
S	California
F	Java
S	Medina

MULBERRY WARES

CATEGORY	PATTERN
S	Susa

JOB MEIGH (& SON)
BLUE AND WHITE TRANSFERWARE
SERIES
1. ZOOLOGICAL SKETCHES "SERIES"
"Armadillo"
"Badger" [Skunk]
"Cheetah"
"Elks" (?)
"Foxes Raiding A Farmyard"
"Gazelle"
"Leopard"
"Otter, Elephant, Rhinoceros"
"Polecat"
"Racoon, Nylghau"
"Reindeer, Zebra, Camel"
"Ring-tailed Lemur"
"Tiger"
"Two Rabbits"
"Zebra"
N.B.: Additions to Coysh's listing is taken from the *Friends of Blue* publications, No. 61, 62, 71-73, 80

MEIKLE BROS.
(Canadian Importers)
WHITE IRONSTONE
Canada*
"Wheat & Hops"
Manufactured by Clementson Bros. but marked Meikle Bros.

JOHN MEIR
BLUE AND WHITE TRANSFERWARE
SERIES
1. "CROWN ACORN AND OAK LEAF BORDER" SERIES
Amport House, Hampshire
Barlborough Hall, Derbyshire
Bedfords, Essex
Cole Orton Hall, Leicestershire
Dalguise, Perthshire
Gorhambury, Hertfordshire
Hylands, Essex
Kincardine Castle, Perthshire
Lambton Hall, Durham
Lindertis, Forfarshire
Lowther Castle, Westmorland
Luscombe, Devon
Moxhull Hall, Warwickshire
Plas Nwydd, Anglesey
Spetchley, Worcestershire
Tewin Water, Hertfordshire
Wakefield Lodge, Warwickshire
Worstead House, Norfolk

2. "BYRON'S ILLUSTRATIONS" SERIES
Patas
Simplon
BLUE AND WHITE TRANSFERWARE
SINGLE PATTERNS

CATEGORY	PATTERN	
-	"Cottagers"	
-	"Cowper Gardening"	
F	"Flora" Pattern	
G	"Fortune Teller"	
-	Mazara	Reg'd. Dec. 24, 1844/ No. 23843
O	Mohamedan Mosque & Tomb ["Oriental Scenery"]	
H	Queen Caroline	
S	"River Fishing"	
O	"Three Man Willow"	

FLOW BLUE

CATEGORY	PATTERN
O	Chen-si (att.)

JOHN MEIR & SON
BLUE AND WHITE TRANSFERWARE
SERIES
1. "CROWN ACORN AND OAK LEAF BORDER" SERIES
(See John Meir)
2. NORTHERN SCENERY "SERIES"
Bothwell Castle
Dunolly Castle, Near Oban
Inverness
Kilchurn Castle, Loch Awe
Loch Achray
Loch Awe
Loch Creran with Bar Caldine Castle
Loch Katrine, Looking Towards Ellen's Isle
Loch Levan Looking Towards Ballachulish Ferry
Loch Linnhe Looking South
Loc Oich and Invergarry Castle
Pass of the Trossachs, Loch Katrine
BLUE AND WHITE TRANSFERWARE
SINGLE PATTERNS

CATEGORY	PATTERN	
F	Albert	
O	Bamboo	
-	Brighton	
F	British Flora (The)	
O	Chinese Bottle (att.)	
S	Chinese Temple	
A	Chios	
S	Como	
O	Cyprean	
S	Fairy Villas (possible series)	
M	Gem	
S	Italian Scenery (17 Views)	
S	Korea (Corea)	
S	Mazara	Reg'd. Dec. 24, 1844/No. 23843
M	Ornithology	
S	Rhine	
S	Roselle	Reg'd. Aug. 26, 1848/No. 54067
G	Vintage	
S/F	Wild Rose	
O	"Willow" Pattern	

FLOW BLUE

CATEGORY	PATTERN
M/F	"Antique Bottle"
M/F	Asiatic Pheasants
O	Chinese
M	Gem
O	Kirkee
O	Kyber
O	Tonquin

MULBERRY WARES

CATEGORY	PATTERN
O	Kirkee
O	Kyber
F	Lily of the Valley
S	Rhine
S	Roselle

WHITE IRONSTONE

Baltic Shape*	Reg'd. Oct. 25, 1855/No. 102325
"Classic Gothic"**	-
Columbia Shape***	Reg'd. Oct. 29, 1855/No. 102355
"Early Gothic" (10 sided)	-
Ivy Wreath "Shape"	Reg'd. May 2, 1860/No. 128476
Memnon Shape	Reg'd. Feb. 4, 1857/No. 108854-5
"Nut & Bud"	-
"Primary Shape"	-
Washington Shape (Ch)	Reg'd. Nov. 3, 1863/No. 168132

*Registered in the name of D. Chetwynd
**Compotes were usually ten or twelve sided.
***Registered in the name of G.W. Reade. Also see *White Ironstone Notes*, Vol. 4, No. 3, Winter 1998, p. 12

MELLOR, TAYLOR & CO.
BLUE AND WHITE TRANSFERWARE
SINGLE PATTERNS

CATEGORY	PATTERN
A	Niagara

FLOW BLUE

CATEGORY	PATTERN
F	Niagara

WHITE IRONSTONE

"Fleur-de-Lys Shape"	Reg'd. 1891
"Fuchsia With Band"	-
"Lion's Head"	-
"Plain Square"	-
"Square Ridged"	-
"Wheat"	-

TEA LEAF/COPPER LUSTRE

"Fleur-de-Lys Shape"	Reg'd. 1891
"Lion's Head"	
"Plain Round" (Ch)	
Senate Shape	
"Square Ridged: Hearts"	

MELLOR, VENABLES & CO.
BLUE AND WHITE TRANSFERWARE
SINGLE PATTERNS

CATEGORY	PATTERN	
M/Z	British Tambourine	-
S	Burmese	-
S	Medici	Reg'd. July 5, 1847/No. 43916-7
O	Ning Po	-
M	Olive	-
G	Union*	-
S	Windsor	Reg'd. Aug. 27, 1849/No. 62316

*See Venables & Baines
HISTORIC STAFFORDSHIRE SERIES
AMERICAN
1. ARMS OF THE STATES (SCENIC) SERIES
Albany
Boston and Bunker Hill
Caldwell (Lake George)
The Narrows (From Fort Hamilton) [New York, Fort Hamilton]
The President's House from the River
The Tomb of Washington, Mount Vernon
View From Gowanus Heights, Brooklyn
View of Baltimore
View of Hudson City and the Catskill Mountains
View of New York From Weehawken
View of the Capitol at Washington
Village of Little Falls (Mohawk River)
Washington's House, Mount Vernon [View of Mount Vernon]
2. MISCELLANEOUS - ARMS OF THE STATES
"Arms of Delaware" (4)
"Arms of Maryland" (5)
"Arms of Massachusetts, New York, Massachusetts"
"Arms of North Carolina"
"Arms of Pennsylvania"
"Arms of Virginia"
FLOW BLUE

CATEGORY	PATTERN	
M	"Aster & Grapeshot"* (Brush Stroke)	
O	Beauties of China	
O	Bengal	
F	"Blackberry"	
M	"Daisy & Leaf" (Brush Stroke)	Reg'd. July 15, 1847/No. 44014-5
O	Eastern Flowers	
O	Nankin	
O	Niagara	
P/M	"Strawberry Luster"	
O	Whampoa	

*See Blue Berry Notes, Vol. 11, No. 3, May-June 1997, Supplement "Brush Stroke Gems", p. 4
MULBERRY WARES

CATEGORY	PATTERN	
M	"Aster & Grapeshot" (Brush Stroke)	-
O	Beauties of China	-
F	"Blackberry Luster"	Reg'd. 1849
P/F	Brunswick	Reg'd. 1849
P/F	Eastern Flowers	Reg'd. 1849
O	Whampoa	Reg'd. 1849
S	Windsor	Reg'd. Aug. 27, 1849/No. 62316

WHITE IRONSTONE

"Many Panelled Gothic Shape"	Reg'd. Sept. 21, 1850/No. 72057
"Primary Shape"	-
"Wheat & Hops"	-

DAVID METHVEN & SONS
BLUE AND WHITE TRANSFERWARE
SINGLE PATTERNS

CATEGORY	PATTERN
F	Blossom
S	Canova
-	"Chariots & Gazebo"
-	Chile
F	Daffodil
O	Damascus
S	Florence
S	Fountain
G	Garland
H	"Germanstag Hunt"
-	Imperial
S	Kent
-	Lorne
S	Palestine
H	Peace
-	Squirrel
-	Sultana
-	Tom Tit
S	Tudor (att.)
-	The Turk
S	Verona
O	"Willow" Pattern
S	Windsor

FLOW BLUE

CATEGORY	PATTERN
A	Garland
F	Wild Rose

MULBERRY WARES

CATEGORY	PATTERN
S	Gazebo (att.)

WHITE IRONSTONE
"Wheat"

MIDDLESBOROUGH EARTHENWARE CO.
MULBERRY WARES

CATEGORY	PATTERN
P/A	Chili

MIDDLESBOROUGH POTTERY CO.
BLUE AND WHITE TRANSFERWARE
SINGLE PATTERNS

CATEGORY	PATTERN
S	Arabian Nights
-	Caledonia
-	Caprera
-	Cyprian Bower
-	Devon
S	Dresden Views
S	Granada
-	Hop Pickers
G	Horse Guards
-	Orient
S	Rhine
S	Romania
F	Wild Rose
O	"Willow" Pattern

FLOW BLUE

CATEGORY	PATTERN
S	Rhine

MULBERRY WARES

CATEGORY	PATTERN
S	Rhine

W.R. MIDWINTER (LTD.)
BLUE AND WHITE TRANSFERWARE
SINGLE PATTERNS

CATEGORY	PATTERN
S	Bandstand
S	Landscape
S	Moyen
S	Rural England

FLOW BLUE

CATEGORY	PATTERN
A	Medallion

JAMES MILLER & CO. (LTD)
(North British Pottery)
BLUE AND WHITE TRANSFERWARE
SINGLE PATTERNS

CATEGORY	PATTERN
-	"Rural"

MINTON
EARLY MINTON PATTERNS (1824-1836)
BLUE AND WHITE TRANSFERWARE
SINGLE PATTERNS

CATEGORY	PATTERN
O	"Bamboo and Flowers"
O	"Basket" ["Basket of Flowers"]
-	"Berlin Chaplet"
-	"Berlin Roses"
O	"Bowl" - Chinoiserie
S	"Bridge" ["Italian Ruins"]
S	"Bridge Views"
S	"British Views" (possible series)
M	"Broseley"
O	"Chinese Marine" (possible series)
S	"Chinoiserie Landscape"
F	Claremont
-	Corinthia
-	Corinthian
F	"Dresden Flowers"
S	"English Scenery"
F	Epping Fruit
-	Eugenie/Pandah
M	"Fibre"
O	"Fig-Tree Chinoiserie"
O	"Fishermen"
F	"Floral Pattern"
C	Florentine
F	"Florette"
F	"Floweret"
-	"Foliage"
S	Genevese (possible series)
O	"Hermit" ["Senchenal" or "Bridgeless Chinoiserie"]
M	"Lace Border"
F	Lily
O	"Mandarin"
-	"Minton Filigree"
O	"Pagoda in the Montpelier Garden"
F	"Rose & Violet Wreath"
-	"Quintal Flower Horn"
-	"Porter Mug"
-	Royal Persian
-	Sicilian
-	"Shepherd" ["Chinese Pilgrim"]
S	Swiss Cottage
-	Verona
O	Willow
-	"Wreath"

For further reading and for a listing of hundreds of more patterns, as well as various combinations of services and shapes, refer to *Jones*, pp. 321-325.

FLOW BLUE

CATEGORY	PATTERN
F	Anemone
F	Eugenie/Pandah

MINTON
TOY/CHILD DINNERWARE & TEAWARE - DINNER/DESSERTWARE - TEAWARE
TOY OR CHILD'S TEAWARE
1810-1817
"Castle" Village
"Chinese Figures"
"Grotto"
"Maypole" (listed twice)
"Nanking"
"Pagoda"
(Refer to *Jones*, p. 34)
TOILETWARE
1810-1817
Village
1820s & 1830s

Chintz	c. 1830s
Dresden Flowers	c. 1830s
Fibre	c. 1830s
Lily	c. 1830s
Willow	c. 1830s

TOY/CHILD'S DINNERWARE - 19TH & 20TH CENTURY
Abbey Mill
Asgill House, Richmond
Brandenburg House
Bysham Monastery
Corf Castle (sic)
DeGaunt Castle
Donington Park
Embdon Castle
Entry to Blaize Castle
Kenelworth Priory (sic)
Lanercost Priory (c. 1874-1915)
Lechlade Bridge
St. Mary's Dover

Tewkesbury Church
Refer to Coysh, Vol. 1, p. 249
TEAWARE - 1810-1817 (Continued into 20th Century)
Apple Tree
Bamboo
Broseley
China Temple
Chinese Figure
Chinese Temple
Cottage
Dragon
Farmyard
Image
India
Jessamine
Key
Leaf
Lily
Nanking
Nelson
Pagoda
Peony
Pine
Red House
Floer
Shepherd
MINTON
TOY/CHILD DINNERWARE & TEAWARE - DINNER/DESSERTWARE - TEAWARE
TEAWARE - 1810-1817 (Continued into 20th Century)
Sprig
Steed
Trophy
Tulip
Turkish Figure
Willow
Refer to Jones, p. 34

MINTON
DINNER/DESSERTWARE
1810-1817
"Basket"
"Bird"
"Brick"
"China Pattern"
"Cottage"
"Dove"
"Hermit"
"Image"
"Landscape"
"Lily"
"Plant"
"Roman"
"Rose & Flower"
"Star"
"Trophy"
"Tulip"
"Willow"
"Windsor Castle"
Refer to *Jones*, p. 34
N.B.: *Jones* lists hundred of patterns as well as various combinations of services and shapes in her book, see Appendix A, pp. 321-325

MINTON & BOYLE
BLUE AND WHITE TRANSFERWARE
SINGLE PATTERNS

CATEGORY	PATTERN
S	Angoulie
O	Asian Bird
M	Chintz
S	Dacca (possible series)
S	Devon
S	The Gem
S	Genevese
O	Spot & Wreath

FLOW BLUE

CATEGORY	PATTERN
M	Dagger Border

MULBERRY WARES

CATEGORY	PATTERN
S	Dacca

MINTON & CO.
BLUE AND WHITE TRANSFERWARE
SINGLE PATTERNS

CATEGORY	PATTERN	
P/O	Amherst Japan	-
O	Bamboo Flowers	Dated 1866
C	Cameo	-
M	Delph	Reg'd. 1871
M	Delft	Dated 1872
O	Filigree	Impressed 1863
F	Flora	-
F	Fuchsia	-
S	Genevese	-
M	Grecian Border	-
P/F	Mona	-
P/O	"Oriental Japan"	-
M/F	Ribbon Wreath	Reg'd. Nov. 12, 1851/ No. 81510-12
P/O	Scinde	-
S	Swiss Cottage	-
G	"Travelers"	-
S	"Villa"	-
P/O	Woodseat	Dated 1866

FLOW BLUE

CATEGORY	PATTERN	
O	Amherst Japan	-
F	Anemone	-
F	Botanical	-
F	Carnation	Dated 1855
-	China Aster	-
O	D'Orsay Japan	Dated 1868
M	Delph	Reg'd. 1871
M	Delft	Dated 1872
F	Denmark	-
-	Eva	-
S	The Gem ("Eagle & Shield")	-
O	Japanese Crane	-
S	Marina	-
M/F	Meissen	-
O	Minton's Japan	Dated 1846
F	Passion Flower	Reg'd. Nov. 16, 1846/ No. 38113
F	Ribbon Wreath	Reg'd. Nov. 12, 1851/ No. 81510-12
O	Smith's Japan	Dated 1852
A	Truro	-
-	"Wreath Japan"	-

MULBERRY WARES

CATEGORY	PATTERN
P/F	"Water Lilies"

WHITE IRONSTONE
"Grape With Vine Shape" (High Relief) Reg'd. May 21, 1846/No. 35030-1
White Ironstone Notes, Vol. 5, No. 3, Winter 1998, p. 11 "New & Unusual" notes and illustrates an infant feeder patented February 25, 1879

MINTON & HOLLINS
BLUE AND WHITE TRANSFERWARE
SINGLE PATTERNS

CATEGORY	PATTERN	
S	The Gem	-
F	Sea Flowers	Reissued After 1891
G	Watteau Figures	-

FLOW BLUE

CATEGORY	PATTERN
S	Watteau Figures

MULBERRY WARES

CATEGORY	PATTERN
S	Watteau Figures

MINTONS
BLUE AND WHITE TRANSFERWARE
SINGLE PATTERNS

CATEGORY	PATTERN	
A	"Andirons"	-
F	Basket	-
S	Gem, The	Reg'd. 1896
O	Indian Tree	-
S	Lanercost Priory	-
G	"Mushroom Pickers"	-
P/O	Woodseat	-

FLOW BLUE

CATEGORY	PATTERN
A	"Andirons"
A	"Garland"
F	Passion Flower

MINTONS, LTD.
FLOW BLUE

CATEGORY	PATTERN	
	Alunwick	
	Arundel	
	Astor	Dated 1879
	Bamboo & Fan	
	Beaconsfield	
	Bombay	
	Border of Chinese Blossom	
	Boston Japan	
	Bow	
	Brunswick	
	Byzantine	
	Cameos	
	Canadian Leaves	

Carnation Spray
Chinese
Chinese Blossom
Chinese Dragon — Reg'd. March 19, 1853/No. 90372
Chinese Flowers
Chrysanthemum
Dacca
Delft
M/A Denmark
D'Orsay Japan
Epping
Faisan
Florentine Border
Fly & Blackberry
Gangees
Grasses & Flies
Halifax
Hexham
Hollins Japan
Inverary
Iris & Flies
Japanese Crane
Java
Keele
Kenmore
Kent
Kildare
Kings Ware
Lincoln
Lismore
Litchfield
Meissen
Merrion Japan
Milan
Norfolk
Oriental Japan
Portland
Putney
Ribbons & Roses
Roman
Roseberry Chrysanthemum
Rosette Border
Rossalyn
Rotterdam Castle
Rouen
Shah Japan
Sprigs & Flies
Stork & Fan
Strathearn
Thames
Thanet
Wheel Japan
Willow

N.B.: *P. Williams*, *Flow Blue*, Vol. 1&2, notes two additional patterns, "Amherst Japan" and "China Aster". I believe both to be reissues of earlier patterns.

The foregoing list reflects a research effort by Anna Tomlinson of the records available in the Minton Archives. I wish to thank her for her research and for compiling this list by locating "F.B.'s" and "F. Blues" through reading the old copper plate writings located in the Archives. This is a truly monumental undertaking, even though Mrs. Tomlinson was not able to categorize the various patterns. I am grateful for the assistance and spirit of cooperation tendered by the wonderful people at Minton, as well as for the assistance offered by so many other people both abroad and here in the U.S.

(SAMUEL) MOORE & CO.

BLUE AND WHITE TRANSFERWARE
SINGLE PATTERNS

CATEGORY	PATTERN
O	"Chinese Garden"
S	Excelsior
M	Gazelle
G	"Girl Holding a Parrot"
S	Oriental
-	"Ruined Castle"
S	Scotia
O	Takoo
G	Tournament
S	Villa D'Este
F	Wild Rose

MOORE & CO.

FLOW BLUE

CATEGORY	PATTERN
F	Hampton

MULBERRY WARES

CATEGORY	PATTERN
M	Birds of Paradise
O	Takoo

MORLEY & ASHWORTH

WHITE IRONSTONE
"Ropes & Anchor"*
*See *White Ironstone Notes*, Vol. 4, No. 1, Summer 1997, p. 13 for an illustrated pitcher marked "M.&A."

FRANCIS MORLEY (& CO.)

BLUE AND WHITE TRANSFERWARE
SINGLE PATTERNS

CATEGORY	PATTERN	
M	American Marine*	
M	Aurora	
O	Basket and Vase	
-	Bijou	
F	California	
O	Cashmere	
C	Cleopatra	Reg'd. May 31, 1845/No. 27800
-	"Harvesters Gossip"	
S	Lake	
F	Paxton	
-	Persiana	
S	Rhine	
S	Scroll	
-	Scutari	
S	Shannon	
F	Sydenham	
M	Watteau	
S	Vista	
M	Zamara	

*See Series which was continued on by G.L. Ashworth & Bros.
N.B.: *Copeland II*, p. 101, makes reference to the "Caledonian" pattern by Francis Morley & Co., registered July 21, 1846/No. 36278.

HISTORIC STAFFORDSHIRE SERIES -
AMERICAN & CANADIAN
1. AMERICAN MARINE SERIES
American Marine

2. *LAKE SERIES (LARSEN)	*LAKE SERIES (E. COLLARD)
The Chaudiere Bridge	Chaudiere Bridge
The Church at Point Levi	Church at Point-Levi
Georgeville	Georgeville
Hallowell ("Bay of Quinte")	Hallowell ("Bay of Quinte")
Rideau Canal, Bytown	Kingston
View on the St. Lawrence,	Outlet at Lake Memphremagog
("Indian Encampent, et.al.")	The Rideau Canal, Bytown
Village of Cedars, River St. Lawrence	St. Lawrence (Indian Scene)
Scene Among the Thousand Isles St. Lawrence	Village of Cedars

*Lake Series was registered May 31, 1845. Series continued by G. L. Ashworth & Bros.

FLOW BLUE

CATEGORY	PATTERN	
M/F	Aurora	
F	Blackberry	
F	California	
O	Cashmere	
C	Cleopatra	Reg'd. May 31, 1845/No. 27800
F	"Golden Ivy"	
F	Lily	
C	Lyra	
F	Paxton	
S	Percy	
M/F	Pheasant	
M	Scroll	
O	Sobraon	

MULBERRY WARES

CATEGORY	PATTERN	
F	Aurora	
F	"Basket & Vine"	
F	Blackberry	
F	Blossom	
F	California	
F	Casket Japan	
C	Cleopatra	Reg'd. May 31, 1845/No. 27800
F	"Flower Birds"	
F	Fruit Basket	
F	Lady Peel	
S	Lake	
P/F	Lily	
F	Paxton*	
S	Percy	
S	Shannon	
S	Vista	

*May also appear in polychrome.

WHITE IRONSTONE

"Classic Gothic"	-
"Early Swirl Shape"	Reg'd. May 31, 1845/No. 27800
"Fluted"	-
"Footed Primary"	-
"Many Faceted" (16 Facets)	-
"Rittenhouse, Cambridge 1850"	-

JOHN MOSELEY
BLUE AND WHITE TRANSFERWARE
SINGLE PATTERNS

CATEGORY	PATTERN
-	"Indian Villa"
-	"Milkmaid"
-	"Piper"
O	"Willow" Pattern

GEORGE THOMAS MOUNTFORD
BLUE AND WHITE TRANSFERWARE
SINGLE PATTERNS

CATEGORY	PATTERN
S	Seville

FLOW BLUE

CATEGORY	PATTERN
-	Clyde
-	Indiana
A	Regent
F	Windsor

ANDREW MUIR (& CO.)
BLUE AND WHITE TRANSFERWARE
SINGLE PATTERNS

CATEGORY	PATTERN
S	British Rivers
G	Caledonia
-	Grecian*
O	"Willow" Pattern*
S	Windsor*

*The attribution of these three patterns to Andrew Muir & Co. is questionable.

MYOTT, SON & CO. (LTD.)
BLUE AND WHITE TRANSFERWARE
SINGLE PATTERNS

CATEGORY	PATTERN
A	Kendal
A	Sevres

FLOW BLUE

CATEGORY	PATTERN
F	Acton
F	Argyle
F	Brooklyn
-	Bermuda
F	Chatsworth
F	Chrysanthemum
A	Crumlin
F	Doris
F	Dudley
A	Flora
M	"Grapes"
F	Grosvenor
A	Iris
M/F	Ivy
-	Krumlin
M/F	Monarch
F	Oban
F	Oriel
F	Rose
-	Sanito
-	Sefton

NEALE (JAMES) & CO.
(or Neale & Wilson)
BLUE AND WHITE TRANSFERWARE
SINGLE PATTERNS

CATEGORY	PATTERN
M	"Feather Edge"
S	"Trial Plate"

NEW WHARF POTTERY CO.
BLUE AND WHITE TRANSFERWARE
SINGLE PATTERNS

CATEGORY	PATTERN
F	Clyde
F	Harwood
M/F	Lois

FLOW BLUE

CATEGORY	PATTERN	
F	Astoria	
F	Berwick	
F	Brunswick	
F	Cambridge	
F	Clyde	
F	Colwyn	
M/A	Conway	
F	Dunbarton	
F	Eastwood	
F	Edgar	
F	Elsie	
F	Geneva	
A	Gladys	
F	Harwood	
-	Ilan	
F	Killarney	
F	Kiswick	
A	Knox	
F	Lancaster	
M/F	Lois	
F	Louise	
M/F	Lucerne	
A	Madras	
M/A	Maple Leaf	
F	Melrose	
M	Monarch	
F	Milan	
F	Monmouth	
F	Nelson	
O	Oriental	
A	Paris	
F	Plymouth	
A	Poppy	
A	Portsmouth	
A	Seville	
F	Sevres	Reg'd. 1902/No. 412412
F	Sterling	
F	Sydney	
F	Touraine	
A	Trent	
M/F	Verona	
F	Waldorf	
S	Watteau	
A	Woodbine	

MULBERRY WARES

CATEGORY	PATTERN
F	Harwood

N.B.: Many patterns were reissued by Wood & Sons upon the acquisition of New Wharf Pottery Co. in 1894.

NEWPORT POTTERY CO. LTD.
BLUE AND WHITE TRANSFERWARE
SINGLE PATTERNS

CATEGORY	PATTERN
O	Tonquin

FLOW BLUE

CATEGORY	PATTERN
M	"Burslem Berrie"

THOMAS NICHOLSON & CO.
BLUE AND WHITE TRANSFERWARE
SINGLE PATTERNS

CATEGORY	PATTERN
-	"Eton College"
F	Wild Rose*

*See *True Blue*, p. 149, No. N1

OLD HALL (EARTHENWARE) POTTERY CO. LTD.
BLUE AND WHITE TRANSFERWARE
SINGLE PATTERNS

CATEGORY	PATTERN
F	"Asiatic Pheasants"
S	"Farm"
A	Hampden
F	Tasnoda

FLOW BLUE

CATEGORY	PATTERN
F	Tasnoda

WHITE IRONSTONE*
*Children's pieces recorded by this pottery.

PALISSY POTTERY LTD.
FLOW BLUE

CATEGORY	PATTERN
S	Avon Scenes

W.E. OULSNAM (& SONS)
WHITE IRONSTONE
"Wheat & Hops"

J.W. PANKHURST (& CO.)
BLUE AND WHITE TRANSFERWARE
SINGLE PATTERNS

CATEGORY	PATTERN
S	Lucerne
M	Spray

WHITE IRONSTONE

"Elaborated Six Panelled Trumpet"	-
"Fleur-de-Lis With Leaves"	-
"Fluted Hops Shape"*	Reg'd. Feb. 4, 1853/No. 89469

"Framed Leaf"* (Ch) (J.W. Pankhurst & Co.) -
"Full Ribbed"(Ch) -
"Gothic Octagon" -
"Greek Key Shape"* (J.W. Pankhurst & Co.) Reg'd. Dec. 2, 1863/No. 169774
"Lily Pad" -
"Panelled Lily" -
"Ribbed Bud"* (J.W. Pankhurst & Co.) -
"Ribbed Chain" -
"Scalloped Compote" -
"Scrolled Bubble" -
"Six Panelled Trumpet" (Ch) -
"Star Flower" -
"Tiny Oak & Acorn" -
*Registered in the name of J. Pankhurst and J. Dimmock.
See Pankhurst & Dimmock.

PANKHURST & DIMMOCK
WHITE IRONSTONE
"Fluted Hops Shape" Reg'd. Feb. 4, 1853/No. 89469
"Reeded Grape Shape" Reg'd. Jan. 19, 1855/No. 99086

PATTERSON & CO.
(or George Patterson)
BLUE AND WHITE TRANSFERWARE
SINGLE PATTERNS

CATEGORY	PATTERN
S	Albion
-	"Bacchanalian Cherubs"
O	Bosphorus
-	Grecian
O	"Willow" Pattern

PEARL POTTERY CO. (LTD.)
BLUE AND WHITE TRANSFERWARE
SINGLE PATTERNS

CATEGORY	PATTERN
F	"Cluster of Peaches & Leaves"

FLOW BLUE

CATEGORY	PATTERN
F	Iris

EDWARD PEARSON (& SON)
WHITE IRONSTONE
Ceres Shape ["Wheat & Hops"] -
"Dangling Tulip Shape"* Reg'd. Apr. 11, 1854/No. 95587-8
Mississippi Shape** -
No. 5 Shape -
No. 6 Shape -
"Panelled Grape" -
"Peas & Pod Shape"*** Reg'd. May 11, 1863/No. 162261-2
*Registered under the names of Pearson, Farrall & Meakin.
***Wetherbee, White Ironstone, A Second Look*, p. 60 notes that two other potters used the exact shape, but with different names: Edward Corn marked his Maltese Shape and G. Woolliscroft marked his Baltic Shape.
***See *White Ironstone Notes*, Vol. 4, No. 3, Winter 1998, p. 12

PEARSON, FARRALL & MEAKIN
TEA LEAF/COPPER LUSTRE
"Grape Octagon"

PENMAN, BROWN & CO.
WHITE IRONSTONE
Columbia Shape* Reg'd. Oct. 25, 1855/No. 102325
*Also refer to John Meir & Son.

PETTY & CO.
BLUE AND WHITE TRANSFERWARE
SINGLE PATTERNS

CATEGORY	PATTERN
S	"Wiseton Hall, Nottinghampshire" ["Gazebo"]

EDWARD & GEORGE PHILLIPS
BLUE AND WHITE TRANSFERWARE
SERIES
1. POLISH VIEWS SERIES
The Enquiry
The Messenger
Patriot's Departure
Polish Prisoner
A Tear For Poland
Wearied Poles
BLUE AND WHITE TRANSFERWARE
SINGLE PATTERNS

CATEGORY	PATTERN
M/Z	Africana
S	Ancona
F	British Flowers (possible series)
O	"Chinese Views"
O	Commerce
G	"The Cottage Door"
S	Grecian Scenery
F	Guitar
G	"Pastoral Scene"
J/G	Pet Lamb
O	"Willow" Pattern
F	Windsor Groups

HISTORIC STAFFORDSHIRE SERIES
AMERICAN
1. MISCELLANEOUS
Franklin(s)["Tomb"]

GEORGE PHILLIPS
BLUE AND WHITE TRANSFERWARE
SINGLE PATTERNS

CATEGORY	PATTERN	
S	Cambrian	-
S	Canova	-
M/Z	Ceylonese	-
-	Columbian	-
S	Corinth	Reg'd. Jan. 11, 1845/No. 24846
G	Eaton College	-
S	Friburg	Reg'd. Nov 5, 1846/No. 37986
F	Lobelia	Reg'd. June 19, 1845/No 28150
-	Marine	-
S	Marino	-
S	Parisian	-
S	Park Scenery	-
O	Segapore	Reg'd. Sept. 3, 1846/No. 37170
S	Verona	-
S	Wild Rose	-

N.B.: *Copeland II*, p. 101, makes reference to "Lobelia" pattern by George Phillips, Longport, registered June 19, 1845/No. 28150.
FLOW BLUE

CATEGORY	PATTERN	
F	Lobelia	Reg'd. June 19, 1845/No 28150

MULBERRY WARES

CATEGORY	PATTERN
S	Cambrian
S	Park Scenery

WHITE IRONSTONE
"Primary Shape" (Ch)

THOMAS PHILLIPS & SON
BLUE AND WHITE TRANSFERWARE
SINGLE PATTERNS

CATEGORY	PATTERN
S	Marino
O	"Willow" Pattern

FLOW BLUE

CATEGORY	PATTERN
O	Lahore
O	Pagoda Bells

PHOENIX POTTERY CO.
BLUE AND WHITE TRANSFERWARE
SINGLE PATTERNS

CATEGORY	PATTERN
O	"Willow" Pattern

PINDER BOURNE & CO.
FLOW BLUE

CATEGORY	PATTERN	
M	"Nautilus Shell"*	
O	"Tea Ceremony"	Impressed Date (3/1879)
O	"Willow" Pattern	
F	Zinnia	Impressed Date (9-81)

* See *Snyder' s Historic Flow Blue*, p. 129, pieces may or may not be marked.
MULBERRY WARES

CATEGORY	PATTERN
A	Whampoa

PINDER BOURNE & HOPE
BLUE AND WHITE TRANSFERWARE
SINGLE PATTERNS

CATEGORY	PATTERN
P/S	Baltic

FLOW BLUE

CATEGORY	PATTERN
O	Honc
O	Mongolia
M/F	Venice

MULBERRY WARES

CATEGORY	PATTERN
F	Baltic
H	Crystal Palace

WHITE IRONSTONE
Columbia Shape

PITCAIRNS LTD.
BLUE AND WHITE TRANSFERWARE
SINGLE PATTERNS

CATEGORY	PATTERN
F	Asiatic Pheasants
M	Myra
F	Rosslyn

FLOW BLUE

CATEGORY	PATTERN
F	Aquilla
A	Astoria
A	Rivona
F	Vera

ENOCH PLANT
FLOW BLUE

CATEGORY	PATTERN
M/A	Arcadia

J. PLANT & CO.
FLOW BLUE

CATEGORY	PATTERN
F	Crete

PLYMOUTH POTTERY CO. LTD.
BLUE AND WHITE TRANSFERWARE
SINGLE PATTERNS

CATEGORY	PATTERN
O	"Elephant Pattern"
F	Wild Rose

PODMORE, WALKER (& CO.)
BLUE AND WHITE TRANSFERWARE
SINGLE PATTERNS

CATEGORY	PATTERN	
-	"Acropolis"	
F	Asiatic Pheasants	
S	Asiatic Scenery	
O	Asiatic Views	
-	"Blue Italian"	
S	California	Reg'd April 2, 1849/No. 59308
-	"Chusan"	
M/Z	Eagle	
S	Florentine	
S	Ivanhoe	
J	Juvenile	
M	Maude	
C	Minerva	
S	Olympia	
S	Spartan	
M/O	Swans	
O	Temple	
S	Venus	
S	Warwick	
C	Washington Vase	
S	Wild Rose [Blue Rose]	
O	"Willow" Pattern	

HISTORIC STAFFORDSHIRE SERIES
AMERICAN & CANADIAN
1. BRITISH AMERICA SERIES
(BRITISH AMERICA VIEWS SERIES)
Brockville
Chaudiere Bridge
Fort Chambly
Fredericton (2)
Halifax
Kingston, Lake Ontario (2)
Lake of Two Mountains
Lily Lake
Montreal
Navy Island (Niagara River)
Port Hope
Quebec
Saint John
St. Lawrence (Indian Scene)
Saint Regis (Indian Scene)
Toronto
Village of Cedars
Windsor
2. MISCELLANEOUS
British America ("Kingston, Lake Ontario, et.al.")
British America ("Montreal, et.al.")
British America ("Navy Island/Niagara River, et.al.")
British America ("Quebec, et.al.")
British America ("View on the St. Lawrence/Indian (scene) Encampment, et.al.")
FLOW BLUE

CATEGORY	PATTERN	
F	"Althea"	-
M/F	Amerillia	-
-	Bohemia	-
S	California	Reg'd. Apr. 2, 1849/No. 59308
O	Chusan	-
O	Corean	-
O	"Fisherman" (The)	-
F	Geranium	Reg'd. 1849
O	Juvenile (Child's Tea set)	-
O	Kaolin	-
O	Manilla	-
F	Pansy	-
O	Peking	-
M/F	"Shell & Flowers"	Reg'd. 1849
O	Temple (The)	Reg'd. 1849
S	Warwick	-
S	Washington Vase	-

MULBERRY WARES

CATEGORY	PATTERN	
F	Amerillia	-
S	California	Reg'd. Apr. 2, 1849/No. 59308
O	Corean	-
S	Eagle	-
F	Geranium	Reg'd. 1849
O	Manilla	-
F	"Shell & Flowers"	Reg'd. 1849
S	Spartan	-
O	Temple (The)	Reg'd. 1849
S	Venus	Reg'd. 1849
S	Washington Vase	-

WHITE IRONSTONE
Athens Shape ["Fleur-de-Lis"] Reg'd. Feb. 23, 1857/No. 109180

POULSON BROS. (LTD.)
BLUE AND WHITE TRANSFERWARE
SINGLE PATTERNS

CATEGORY	PATTERN
F	Asiatic Pheasants

POUNTNEY & CO. (LTD.)
BLUE AND WHITE TRANSFERWARE
SINGLE PATTERNS

CATEGORY	PATTERN
P/F	Ashton

FLOW BLUE

CATEGORY	PATTERN
A	Ashton
M/A	Florentine
A	Hilton
F	Lind
O	Mandarin
F	Milton
-	Utopia
F	Windsor Wreath

POUNTNEY & ALLIES
BLUE AND WHITE TRANSFERWARE
SERIES
1. BRISTOL VIEWS "SERIES"
(Also produced by Successor - Pountney & Goldney)
Bristol
Bristol Hot Wells
Chepstow Castle
Clifton
Clifton Rocks
Cook's Folly
Reach of the River Avon, Roman Encampment
St. Vincent's Rocks
View Near Bristol, River Avon
2. RIVER THAMES "SERIES"
(Also produced by Successor - Pountney & Goldney)
Oxford
Park Place, Henley (2)
Richmond Bridge
Temple House
BLUE AND WHITE TRANSFERWARE
SINGLE PATTERNS

CATEGORY	PATTERN
S	Abbey
-	"Arms of Bristol"
S	"Bridge at Lucano"
-	"Bristol Leaves"
S	"British Cobalt Blue" (att.)*
"	"Coral Border"
Z	Dromedary
-	Egyptian Scene
C	Fancy Vase
S	Gothic Ruins
G	Italian
M	"Sheet Pattern"
S	Sicilian
O	"Willow" Pattern

*See *Coysh*, Vol. 2, p. 34

POUNTNEY & GOLDNEY
BLUE AND WHITE TRANSFERWARE
SERIES
1. "ANTIQUE SUBJECTS" SERIES
Annunciation
Pursuit
2. BRISTOL VIEWS "SERIES"
(See Pountney & Allies)
3. RIVER THAMES "SERIES"
(See Pountney & Allies)
4. THE DRAMA SERIES
(Also refer to John Rogers & Son)
The Adopted Child
As You Like It, Act 2 Scene 2
As You Like It, Act 4 Scene 2
As You Like It, Act 4 Scene 3
The Deserter, Scene 1
Douglas, Act 5 Scene 1
Henry IV, Act 2 Scene 2
Henry IV, Act 5 Scene 4
Love in a Village, Act 1 Scene 4
The Maid at the Mill, Act 1 Scene 1
"Maypole"
Merchant of Venice, Act 4 Scene 1
Merchant of Venice, Act 5 Scene 4
Merry Wives of Windsor, Act 5 Scene 5
Midas, Act 1 Scene 3
Much Ado About Nothing
The Quaker, Act 2 Scene 2
The Revenge
The Taming of the Shrew, Act 4 Scene 1
The Taming of the Shrew, Act 4 Scene 3
The Tempest, Act 1 Scene 2
Two Gentlemen of Verona, Act 5 Scene 4
Winter's Tale, Act 4 Scene 3
BLUE AND WHITE TRANSFERWARE
SINGLE PATTERNS

CATEGORY	PATTERN
M	"Birds & Flowers"
S	Gothic Ruins
G	"Italian"
O	Lind
S	Sicilian
O	"Willow" Pattern

FLOW BLUE

CATEGORY	PATTERN
O	Portland

POWELL & BISHOP
BLUE AND WHITE TRANSFERWARE
SINGLE PATTERNS

CATEGORY	PATTERN
C	Abbey
S	Parma
O	"Willow" Pattern

WHITE IRONSTONE

"Britannia"	-
"Medallion Sprig"	-
"Square Ridged Shape"	Reg'd. 1876
"Tulip Border"	-
Washington Shape	Reg'd. 1869
"Wheat in the Meadow Shape"	Reg'd. Oct. 29, 1869/No. 235401-2

TEA LEAF/COPPER LUSTRE

"Chelsea"	-
"Golden Scroll"	-
"Prairie Flowers"	-
"Simple Square: Puffy"	-
"Simplicity"	-
"Square Ridged: Iona Shape"	Reg'd. 1876
Washington Shape	Reg'd. 1869
"Wheat in the Meadow"	Reg'd. Oct. 29, 1869/No. 235401-2

POWELL, BISHOP & STONIER
BLUE AND WHITE TRANSFERWARE
SINGLE PATTERNS

CATEGORY	PATTERN
F	Chelsea
F	Honfleur
P/F	Hong Kong

FLOW BLUE

CATEGORY	PATTERN	
-	Coburg	
S	London	Reg'd. 1882
O	Pagoda	
-	Song Birds	

WHITE IRONSTONE
Iona

PRATT & SIMPSON
WHITE IRONSTONE
"Eagle Soup Tureen"*
*See *White Ironstone Notes,* Vol. 4, No. 1, Summer 1997, p. 14

F. & R. PRATT & CO. (LTD.)
BLUE AND WHITE TRANSFERWARE
SINGLE PATTERNS

CATEGORY	PATTERN
F	Asiatic Marine
S	Lake Scenery
F	"Pratt's Botanical"
S	"Pratt's Italian"
S	"Pratt's Native Scenery"

FLOW BLUE

CATEGORY	PATTERN
F	Basket
-	Ching
O	"Chrysanthemum"
O	Indian*
O	Mandarin
O	Nankin
O	Shusan
S	Theban

*Indian pattern ascribed to the above potter may have been done by Charles Meigh. (See Godden Mark No. 2617), as the oriental cartouche is not characteristic of Pratt's back marks.
MULBERRY WARES

CATEGORY	PATTERN
-	"Marble - Pratt"*

*Picture illustrated in *Stoltzfus/Snyder*, p. 158.

JOHN PRATT & CO. LTD.
BLUE AND WHITE TRANSFERWARE
SINGLE PATTERNS

CATEGORY	PATTERN
S	Abbey
F	Water Lily

RAINFORTH (LEEDS)
BLUE AND WHITE TRANSFERWARE
SINGLE PATTERNS

CATEGORY	PATTERN
-	"Parasol & Birds"
-	"Rainforth's Willow"

T. RATHBONE & CO.
BLUE & WHITE TRANSFERWARE
SERIES
1. "NORTHERN VIEWS" SERIES
"Durham" ["Ruined Castle and Bridge"]
BLUE AND WHITE TRANSFERWARE
SINGLE PATTERNS

CATEGORY	PATTERN
G	"The Font" ["Girl at the Well"]
G	"Milkmaid"
-	"Sisters"
O	"Willow" Pattern

FLOW BLUE

CATEGORY	PATTERN	
A	Bell	
F	Belmont	
O	Burmese	
A	Clive	
F	Countess	
F	Hamden	
F	Harrow	
M/F	Japan	Reg'd. 1909/No. 545204
-	Jewel	
F	Norah	
A	Osborne	
-	Princess	
M/A	Queen	
F	Rose	
F	Sapho	
M/S	Shanghai	
-	Trentham	
F	Victor	

READ & CLEMENTSON
BLUE AND WHITE TRANSFERWARE
SINGLE PATTERNS

CATEGORY	PATTERN
-	"British Star"
O	Japan Beauty
S	Mantua
S	Terni
O	"Willow" Pattern

READ, CLEMENTSON & ANDERSON
BLUE AND WHITE TRANSFERWARE
SINGLE PATTERNS

CATEGORY	PATTERN
S	Chantillian
-	"Gazebo & Urn"
S	Priory
-	"Queen Victoria & the Duchess of Kent"
S	Stagg
S	Wild Rose

JAMES REED
BLUE AND WHITE TRANSFERWARE
SINGLE PATTERNS

CATEGORY	PATTERN
S	"Goatherd Piping"
M	India
M	"Tapestry" ["Twisted Tree"]
S	Wild Rose

REED & TAYLOR
BLUE AND WHITE TRANSFERWARE
SINGLE PATTERNS

CATEGORY	PATTERN
O	Chinese Figure
S	"Genevese"
-	Imperial Filigree
F	Indian Bird

JAMES REEVES
BLUE AND WHITE TRANSFERWARE
SINGLE PATTERNS

CATEGORY	PATTERN
F	Asiatic Pheasants

WILLIAM REID (& SON) or (SONS)
BLUE AND WHITE TRANSFERWARE
SINGLE PATTERNS

CATEGORY	PATTERN
S	"Bridge Of Lucano" (Variations of Spode)
O	Ching
G	"The Milkmaid"
O	"Two Temples"
O	"Willow" Pattern

RIDGWAY & ABINGTON
FLOW BLUE

CATEGORY	PATTERN
M/F	Smyrna

RIDGWAY & MORLEY
BLUE AND WHITE TRANSFERWARE
SINGLE PATTERNS

CATEGORY	PATTERN
F	Albion
C	Archipelago
O	Cashmere
S	Nice
C	Pantheon (possible series)
F	Sunflower

FLOW BLUE

CATEGORY	PATTERN
M	Arabian
O	Cashmere
O	Chusan
M/F	"Feather Flower"
F	Nankin Jar
F	Moss Rose
S	Pantheon
M/Z	Pheasant

MULBERRY WARES

CATEGORY	PATTERN
F	Nankin Jar
F	Pheasant
F	Sunflower

JOB RIDGWAY
BLUE AND WHITE TRANSFERWARE
SINGLE PATTERNS

CATEGORY	PATTERN
O	"Chinoiserie Ruins"
O	"Curling Palm"
O	"Net Pattern"

JOB RIDGWAY & SONS
BLUE AND WHITE TRANSFERWARE
SINGLE PATTERNS

CATEGORY	PATTERN
-	"Blind Boy"
-	"Chinoiserie Ruins"
-	"Curling Palm"
-	"Net"
-	"Parasol"
-	"Temple"

JOHN RIDGWAY (& CO.)
BLUE AND WHITE TRANSFERWARE
SERIES
1. POMERANIA "SERIES"*
"Artist and Chateau"
"Mill"
"Mill and Obelisk"
"Sailing Barge and Chateau"
**P. Williams Staffordshire*, 1, p. 378 depicts two scenes. *FOB Bulletin*, No. 95, Spring 1997, p. 10, illustrates an additional scene.
BLUE AND WHITE TRANSFERWARE
SINGLE PATTERNS

CATEGORY	PATTERN	
O	Aladdin	Reg'd. July 17, 1846/No. 36263
P/O	Amherst Japan	-
S	Archipelago (possible series)	-
S	Baronial Castles*	Reg'd. Mar. 13, 1852/No. 84329
G	Beauties I, II	-
S	Belvedere**	-
F	Bentick	-
C	Berlin Vase	
-	"Berlin Wreath"	
M/A	Burlington***	Reg'd. Dec. 4, 1845/No. 31670-3
S	Byzantium	Reg'd. Nov. 10, 1854/No. 97659
M	Camden	-
O	Canada	-
O	Celestial	-
M	Charmontel	-
O	Chinese	-
M	Chintz	-
M/F	Chusan	-
S	Clara	-
F	Clarendon	-
S	Columbia Star	Reg'd. Sept. 28, 1849/No. 62690-4
F	Coterie	-
M	Cottage	-
S	Delaware	-
S	Doria	Reg'd. July 20, 1844/No. 19977-9
M/Z	Giraffe	Published Aug. 30, 1836
-	"Girl & Lamb" (possible series)	-
M/F	Hampton Court	-
-	"Hare & Leverets"	-
O	India Temple	-
O	Japonica	-
O	Napier	-
S	Olympian	-
S	Palestine	-
F	Persian Sun Flower	-
S	Rhone (att.)	
M/Z	Ribonaire	-
F	Royal Flora	-
M	Seaweed	-
S	Scottish Minstrel	-
F	Shiraz	-
G	Souvenir	-
P/F	Tripoli	-
S	University (2)	-
-	Victoria	-
S	Villa	-
-	Vintage	Reg'd. Oct. 2, 1847/No. 26192-4
-	"Two Vases"	-
S	Warwick	Reg'd. 1847
M/F	Water Lily	-

*Date is recorded as registered by William Ridgway.
***P. Williams, Staffordshire II*, p. 617 notes pattern is the same as "Parma" by Edward Challinor.
***Reissued by Brown, Westhead, Moore & Co. Also see Cauldon, Ltd. for pattern Peking Star.
HISTORIC STAFFORDSHIRE SERIES
AMERICAN
1. COLUMBIAN STAR, OCT. 28TH, 1840 - SERIES
Log Cabin (End View with Two Men)
Log Cabin (Side View)
Log Cabin (Side View, Man Plowing with Two Horse Team)
2. MISCELLANEOUS
Capitol, Washington
Delaware
Yale
FLOW BLUE

CATEGORY	PATTERN	
F	Bentick	-
-	Bordeaux	-
A	Canada	-
O	Celestial	-

S	Columbian Star	Impressed 1840
F	Geranium	Reg'd. Jan. 9, 1847/No. 40104-5
S	Italian Urn	-
F	Morning Glory	-
F	Moss Rose	Reg'd. Oct. 2, 1847/No. 46192-4
S	Pantheon	-
O	Peking	Reg'd. Dec. 4, 1845/No. 31670-3

MULBERRY WARES

CATEGORY	PATTERN
S	Berlin Vase
S	Delaware
F	Seaweed
F	Tripoli

WHITE IRONSTONE

"Classic Gothic"	-
"Gothic Style"	-
"Montpelier Double Scallop Shape"	Reg'd. 1854
"Montpelier Gothic"	-
"Montpelier Grape"	-
"Montpelier Graybeard"	-
"Montpelier Hexagon Shape"	Reg'd. Sept. 30, 1848/No. 54662
"Primary Hexagon Shape"	Reg'd. Sept. 19, 1844/No. 21700-1
"Primary Shape"	-

JOHN & WILLIAM RIDGWAY
BLUE AND WHITE TRANSFERWARE
SERIES
1. "ANGUS SEATS" SERIES
"The Angus Drover"
"Comb Bank, Kent"
"Cusworth, Yorkshire"
"Gunnersbury House, Middlesex"
"Lacy House, Middlesex"
"Lanercost Priory, Cumberland"
"Lee, Kent"
"Lumley Castle, Durham"
"Melville Castle, Midlothian"
"Newham Court, Oxfordshire"
"Parish Church at Nettlecomb Court"
"Raby Castle, Durnham"
"Sheffield Place, Succes"
"Tong Castle, Shropshire"
2. BRITISH SCENERY SERIES (Att.)
"Cashiobury, Hertfordshire"
"Cottages and Castle, et.al."
"Curved Path, et.al."
"Family Group, et.al." ["Lechlade" ?]
"Herdsman, Bridge and Tower"
"Lakeside Castle, et.al."
"Leamington Baths, et.al."
"Palladian Mansion, et.al." [Wanstead House in Essex]
"Riverside Cottage, et.al."
"Thatched Barns, et.al."
"Tintern Abbey, et.al." [Old Octagon]
"Village Fishermen, et.al."
"The Water Mill, et.al."
"The Wind Mill, et.al."
3. OTTOMAN EMPIRE SERIES (Att.)
Caravansary at Kustchiuk Czenege
Cialka [Ciala] Kavak
Eski Estamboul
Kaskerat*
Monumental Arch in Latachia
Mosque in Latachia
Mosque of Sultan Achmet
Multi-arched Wall
Near Bucharest
Pera
Piccolo Bent
Pillar of Absalom
Port of Latachia
Tchiurluk
Tomb of Jeremiah
Views in Caramania
*See *FOB*, No. 98, Winter 1997/98, p. 7.
4. OXFORD AND CAMBRIDGE COLLEGE SERIES
Views in Cambridge:
Caius College, Cambridge
Christ's College, Cambridge
Clare Hall, Cambridge
Downing College, Cambridge
"The Fountain, Trinity College, Cambridge"
King's College, Cambridge
Library Of Trinity College, Cambridge
Pembroke Hall, Cambridge
St. Peter's College, Cambridge
Senate House, Cambridge
Sidney Sussex College, Cambridge
Trinity Hall, Cambridge
Views In Oxford:
All Souls College & St. Mary's Church, Oxford
Christ Church (Two Views), Oxford
Magdalen Tower and Bridge, Oxford
Merton College, Oxford
Observatory, Oxford
Radcliffe Library, Oxford
Theatre Printing House & C., Oxford
Trinity College, Oxford
Wadham College, Oxford
5. RURAL SCENERY SERIES
"A Drover With His Dog, et.al."
"Horse Drawn Covered Wagon, et.al."
"Horseman With Four Cows, et.al."
"Man With Horse Pulling a Harrow, et.al."
"Scything"
"Three Deer, et.al."
BLUE AND WHITE TRANSFERWARE
SINGLE PATTERNS

CATEGORY	PATTERN
O	Asiatic Temples
-	"Bamboo"
M/Z	Bandanna
G	The Blind Boy
-	"Broseley"
H	"Byzantium & Olympian"*
-	"Chinese Bird"
O	"Chinese Export Boat"
F	Columbia
O	Eastern Port
-	"Fruit"
O	India Temple
S	Italian Flower Garden
F	Japan Flowers
H	"Olympian & Byzantium"*
M/F	Oriental Birds
O	"Oriental Flower Tree"
G	"Osterley Park"
-	"Picnic"
-	"Portland Basket"
M	Sylvan
F	Tuscan Rose
-	"Union Medallions"
F	Windsor Festoon

*See *P. Williams, Staffordshire*, Vol. III, p. 238 for additional comments on four views.
HISTORIC STAFFORDSHIRE SERIES
AMERICAN
1. BEAUTIES OF AMERICA
Almshouse, Boston
Almshouse, New York
Athenaeum, Boston
Bank, Savannah
Cambridge College, Massachusetts
Capitol, Washington [at]
City Hall, New York
Court House, Boston
Custom House, Philadelphia
Deaf and Dumb Asylum, Hartford, Conn.
Exchange, Baltimore
Exchange, Charleston
Hospital, Boston
Insane Hospital, Boston
Library, Philadelphia
Masonic Hall, Philadelphia
Mount Vernon Near Washington
Octagon Church, Boston [New South Church]
Pennsylvania Hospital, Philadelphia
St. Paul's Church, Boston
Staughton's Church, Philadelphia
State House, Boston
II. MISCELLANEOUS
Virginia

JOHN RIDGWAY, BATES & CO.
BLUE AND WHITE TRANSFERWARE
SINGLE PATTERNS

CATEGORY	PATTERN
M	Leafall

FLOW BLUE

CATEGORY	PATTERN
Z	Antelope
M	Osborne

WHITE IRONSTONE

Girard Shape	Reg'd. July 30, 1857/No. 110780

RIDGWAY, MORLEY, WEAR & CO.

BLUE AND WHITE TRANSFERWARE

SINGLE PATTERNS

CATEGORY	PATTERN
C	Agricultural Vase
M	Albert Star
-	Arabian
C	Archipelago
M	Caledonia
M	Eglinton
-	"Floral"
F	Florence Rose
M	"Hot Water Plate"
O	Japan Flowers (2)
-	"Nice"
F	Non Pareil

FLOW BLUE

CATEGORY	PATTERN
M	Arabian
O	Cashmere
-	Pheasant
-	Syria

RIDGWAY, SPARKS & RIDGWAY

BLUE AND WHITE TRANSFERWARE

SINGLE PATTERNS

CATEGORY	PATTERN	
P/F	Corey Hill	-
Z	Indus	Reg'd. June 15, 1877/No. 310972
O	Tree Of Life	Reg'd. June 15, 1877/No. 310972
-	Yeddo	-

FLOW BLUE

CATEGORY	PATTERN
P/F	Corey Hill

WILLIAM RIDGWAY (& CO.)

BLUE AND WHITE TRANSFERWARE

SERIES

1. "HUMPHREY'S CLOCK" SERIES

"Little Girl and her Grandfather"

"Little Girl by the River"

"Little Girl in the Graveyard"

BLUE AND WHITE TRANSFERWARE

SINGLE PATTERNS

CATEGORY	PATTERN
-	"Acacia"
F	Albion
S	Alpine
O	Amoy
-	"Ancient Ruins"
F	Asiatic Plants
M	Beehive
M/F	"Berry"
F	"Bluebell"
-	"Bouquet"
F	British Flowers (possible series)
O	Byzantium
O	Canton
F	Etruscan Festoon
S	Euphrates
M	Fairy Queen
M	Flosculous
F	"Flower Pods"
G	For-Get-Me-Not
-	"Fruit Basket"
S	Gem
-	"Geometric Scrolls"
S	Grecian
M	"Heart With Arrow"
M	"Hot Water Plate"
S	Marcella
S	Marmora
O	Medina
S	Neva
O	Oriental
O	Pekin
O	Pekin Jar*
O	Persian (2)
S	Rome [Italian]
M/F	Russell
S	Shenandoah
S	Tyrolean
"S	"Tyrolean Scene"
M	Vermicelli
S	Villa
F	Vista De La Habana
M	Western Star

*See *P. Williams, Staffordshire*, Vol. III, p. 42.

HISTORIC STAFFORDSHIRE SERIES

AMERICAN

1. AMERICAN SCENERY SERIES

Albany

Caldwell, Lake George

Columbia Bridge on the Susquehanna

Crows Nest From Bull Hill (Hudson River)

Delaware Water Gap, Pa.

Harper's Ferry From the Potomac Side (W.Va.)

Meredith (N.H.)

Narrows From Fort Hamilton, (The) (N.Y.)

Narrows From Staten Island, (The) (N.Y.)

Peekskill Landing, Hudson river

Pennsylvania Hospital, Philadelphia

Undercliff Near Cold Spring (N.Y.)

The Valley of the Shenandoah From Jefferson Rock (Pa.)

View From Port [Fort] Putnam, Hudson River

View From Ruggle's House, Newburgh, Hudson River

View of The Capitol at Washington

Wilkes-Barre, Vale of Wyoming (Pa.)

FLOW BLUE

CATEGORY	PATTERN
F	Astoral
F	Berry
F	"Bluebell"
O	Euphrates*
F	"Forget-me-not"
O	Formosa/Penang
M/F	Hanging Basket
F	Mariteus
O	Pagoda
O	Penang/Formosa
F	Sloe Blossom
S	Tyrolean

**Although Petra Williams notes this as Flow Blue, it is in reality just a darker blue and belongs in the Blue and White Transferware category.

MULBERRY WARES

CATEGORY	PATTERN
F	Berry
S	Marmora

WILLIAM RIDGWAY, SON & CO.

BLUE AND WHITE TRANSFERWARE

SINGLE PATTERNS

CATEGORY	PATTERN
F	Apple Blossom
O	Asiatic Palaces
S	Field Sports
S	"Forget-Me-Not"
P/O	Hong Kong
G	Humphrey's Clock*
O	Oriental
P/F	"Poppies"
S	Rural Scenery
M	Vermicelli
G	Union
S	Villa

*See William Ridgway & Co. for series.

HISTORIC STAFFORDSHIRE SERIES

AMERICAN

1. CATSKILL MOSS SERIES*

Anthony's Nose

Baltimore

"Boston and Bunkers' Hill" ["Boston from Chelsea Heights"]

Caldwell, Lake George

Capitol, Washington ["View of the Capitol at Washington"]

Centre Harbour

Columbia Bridge on the Susquehanna

East Port

Fairmount

Fairmount Gardens ("Philadelphia")

Hudson, New York

Kosciusko's Tomb (N.Y.)

Little Falls, N.Y.

Meredith (N.H.)

The Narrows From Fort Hamilton

The Narrows, Lake George

Near Troy, N.Y.

Near Weehawken

New York Bay ("Brooklyn From Gowanus Heights")

President's House

Saw Mill at Centre Harbour (N.H.)

Undercliff Near Cold Spring

Utica

Valley of Wyoming

Village of Catskill (N.Y.)

Washington's Tomb

Wilkes-Barre, Vale of Wyoming

*Reg'd. Dec. 16, 1844/No. 23593

FLOW BLUE

CATEGORY	PATTERN	
F	Berry	
F	"Candlestick with Push Up"	Reg'd. July 16, 1846/No. 36167
F	Convolvolus	
O	Hong Kong	
S	Old Curiosity Shop* (see "Humphrey's Clock" Series by William Ridgway & Co.)	

*See P. Williams, *Flow Blue*, Vol. 2, p. 100.

WHITE IRONSTONE

"Candlestick Shape" Reg'd. July 16, 1846/No. 36167

RIDGWAYS (BEDFORD WORKS) LTD.

BLUE AND WHITE TRANSFERWARE

SINGLE PATTERNS

CATEGORY	PATTERN
A	Burlington
S	Canterbury
P/O	"Chinese Vase"
S	Eton
S	Grecian
F	Hawthorn
S	Humphrey's Clock
Z/O	Indus
S	Ludlow Castle
F	Lugano
S	Nell's Lonely Walk
O	"Oriental"
P/O	Simlay
S	Tyrolean

FLOW BLUE

CATEGORY	PATTERN	
F	Alberta	
-	Athol	
F	Bolingbroke (The)	
F	"Bridal Array"	
F	Brighton	
A	Burlington	
A	Burnham	
M/A	Cathlyn	
-	Celestial	
O	"Chinese Japan"	
F	Chiswick	Reg'd. 1897/No. 295284
F	Clevedon	
-	Coronation Moss	
M	"Cows"	
-	Dado	
F	Debora	
M/L	"Dickins" ["Pickwick"]	Reg'd. 1903/No. 419412
F	Dinan	
F	Dog Rose	
F	Dundee	
F	Ebor	
M/A	Gainsborough	
S	Grecian	
F	Hawthorn	
F	Jacqueminot	
F	Josephine	
F	Kendal	
F	Ladas	
A	Lichfield	Reg'd. 1888/No. 114297
M/F	Lonsdale	
F	Lorraine	
-	Lucania	
F	Lugano	
S	Medici	
M/F	Meissen	
P/F	Moyune	
F	"Narcissus"	
F	Nestor	
S	Old Curiosity Shop	
O	Oriental	
F	Osborne	
F	Paqueminot	
M	Penhurst	
F	Peony	
F	Pomona	
-	Rabbit	
M	"Ridgways Japan"	
F	Rose	
S	Saskia	
S	"Scenes"	Dated 1888
M	Sefton	
F	Stratford	
F	Suggton	
F	Suhrnglen	
F	Sutton	
S	"Turkey"	
S	Tyrolean	
M	Verona	

JOHN & RICHARD RILEY

BLUE AND WHITE TRANSFERWARE - SERIES

1. "LARGE SCROLL BORDER SERIES"

"Alton Abbey, Staffordshire"
"Balloch Castle, Dunbartonshire" (sic)
"Bickley, Kent"
"Bretton Hall, Yorkshire"
"Cannon Hall, Yorkshire"
"Denton Park, Yorkshire"
"Esholt Hall, Yorkshire"
"Ettington Hall, Warwickshire"
"Goggerddam, Cardiganshire"
"Gracefield, Queen's County"
"Hollywell Cottage," ["Cavan"]
"The Kings Cottage, Windsor Park"
"Kingsweston, Glouchestershire"
"Orielton, Pembrokeshire"
"Orwell Park, Suffolk"
"The Rookery, Surrey"
"Taymouth Castle, Perthshire"
"Wistow Hall, Leicestershire"

2. "UNION BORDER SERIES"

"Two Cows and a Donkey"
"Cattle and Sheep ..."
"Cattle and Herdsman"
"Cattle by Stream"
"Girl with Basket on Head"
"Goat, Sheep and Cow ..."
"Herdsman with White Cow"
"Horse, Goat, Sheep, Cows ..."
"Lowing Cow"

BLUE AND WHITE TRANSFERWARE

SINGLE PATTERNS

CATEGORY	PATTERN
S	Calcutta
Z	"Camel"
-	"Castle"
-	"Children Feeding Chickens"
Z	Dromedary
O	"Eastern Street Scene" ["The Blue Indian Villa"]
S	Europa
S	"Fishing Boat, House & Windmill"*
F	"Flower Arrangement" ["Flower Vase"]
G	"Girl Gardeners"**
G	"Girl Musician" ["Landscape With Musicians"]
-	"Goatherds"
F	"Midnight Flowers"
O	Nanking
O	"Oriental Garden"
-	"Peonies/Mosaic"
F	"Riley's Bowl of Flowers"
S	"The Sacred Tree of the Hindoos at Gyah, Bahar" [see "Eastern Street Scene"]
S	"Scene After Claude Lorraine" ["Waterfall"]
-	"Shipyards"
-	"Wild Fowl"
O	"Willow" Pattern

*See *True Blue*, p. 66, No. 11.

**An impressed hand mark is noted in *True Blue*, p. 66, No. 9 and p. 149, No. R12a.

JOHN ROBINSON (& SONS)

BLUE AND WHITE TRANSFERWARE

SINGLE PATTERNS

CATEGORY	PATTERN
S	Cypress
S	"Temple Parkland"

FLOW BLUE

CATEGORY	PATTERN
A	Oxford

JOSEPH ROBINSON

FLOW BLUE

CATEGORY	PATTERN
Z	Cypress

ROBINSON & WOOD

BLUE AND WHITE TRANSFERWARE

SINGLE PATTERNS

CATEGORY	PATTERN
O	Chinese Views
S	Venetian Scenery

ROBINSON, WOOD & BROWNFIELD

BLUE AND WHITE TRANSFERWARE - SERIES

1. ZOOLOGICAL "SERIES"

"Antelope"
"Camel"
"Lion"
"Pheasants"

"Tiger Cages"
"Unidentified Birds" ["Spoonbill & Heron"]
"Zebra Pen"

BLUE AND WHITE TRANSFERWARE
SINGLE PATTERNS

CATEGORY	PATTERN
O	Canton
-	"Ewer in Basin"
P/O	"Floral Urn"
M	Peace
M	Stripe
S	Versailles

JOHN ROGERS (& SON)
BLUE AND WHITE TRANSFERWARE - SERIES
1. "DRAMA SERIES"
(Copied by Poutney & Allies)
The Adopted Child
As You Like It, Act 2 Scene 2
As You Like It, Act 4 Scene 2
As You Like It, Act 4 Scene 3
The Deserter, Scene 1
Douglas, Act 5 Scene 1
Henry IV, Act 2 Scene 2
Henry IV, Act 5 Scene 4
Love in a Village, Act 1 Scene 4
Love's Labours Lost
The Maid at the Mill, Act 1 Scene 1
"Maypole"
Merchant of Venice, Act 4 Scene 1
Merchant of Venice, Act 5 Scene 4
Merry Wives of Windsor, Act 5 Scene 5
Midas, Act 1 Scene 3
Much Ado About Nothing
The Quaker, Act 2 Scene 2
The Revenge
The Taming of the Shrew, Act 4 Scene 1
The Taming of the Shrew, Act 4 Scene 3
The Tempest, Act 1 Scene 2
The Wheel of Fortune, Act 1 Scene 3
Two Gentlemen of Verona, Act 5 Scene 4
Winter"s Tale, Act 4 Scene 3
2. "ROGERS VIEW SERIES"
"Byland Abbey, Yorkshire"
"Cattle Foreground"
"Durham"
"Galleon at Anchor"
"Lakeside Scene"
"Lancaster"
"Ludlow Castle"
"Maidstone Jail"
"Osterley Park"
"Richmond Bridge"
"Rural Ferry"
"Teston Bridge" ["River Medway"]
"Two Castles"
"Yorkminster"

BLUE AND WHITE TRANSFERWARE
SINGLE PATTERNS

CATEGORY	PATTERN
-	"Abbey Ruins"
C	Athens (5) (series)
O	"Bamboo Flowers & Rocks"
-	"Bridge & Pensioner"
-	"Britannia"
O	"Broseley"
S	Bungalow
Z	"Camel Pattern"
-	"Chinese Garden" ["Swan & Parasol"]
O	Chinese Porcelain
O	"Chinoiserie Ruins"
Z	"Church Zebra" [Rogers]
F	Crescent
-	"Dragon & Flowers"
M/O	"Elephant"* [Rogers]
M/Z	Fallow Deer
O	"Figure Vase & Fence" ["Vase & Fence"]
G	"First Steps"
F	Flora
F	"Floral Pattern"
S	Florence
-	"Flowers With Butterflies"
F	"Fruit & Flowers" ["Van Huysun's"]
S	"Gothic Ruins"
C	"Greek Statue"
F	"Hexagonals & Dragons"
-	"India"
F	Indian Reed
M	"Leaf Sheet Pattern"
-	"Masque"
C	"Monopteros Pattern"
S	"More Bungalows"
G	"Musketeer"
F	"Net Trellis & Flowers"
-	"Pavilion"
M/F	"Pink Peonies"
C	Pompeii
M/F	Prunus Wreath
-	"Pyramid"
F	"Queen's Lily"
M/H	Shannon
-	"Shepherd With Lute"
J	Taking a Walk
-	"Tall Spire"
-	"Temple"
C	Tivoli
O	"Toy Chinamen Chinoiserie"
-	"Vase"
M/F	Vine
O	"Willow" Pattern
-	"Wood Nymph"
Z	Zebra

*Reproduced at the Elephina Hadderidge Pottery, Burslem, 1920s.

HISTORIC STAFFORDSHIRE SERIES
AMERICAN
1. "SHELLS AND SEAWEED SERIES"
"Approaching Port"
"Day Sea Battle"
"Fishing Dinghy"
"Fleet Scene I"*
"Fleet Scene II" (lower portion)*
"Frigate I" ["Shannon"] (2)
"Frigate II" ["Chesapeake"]
"Frigate III"
"Harbor Scene I"
"Harbor Scene II"
"Landing Scene"
"Night Sea Battle" ("Blanche", "LaPique")
"Sailing Galley"
"Shipwreck Scene"
*See *Arman*, No. 440A and B
N.B.: For a listing of the above see *Coysh*, Vol. 2, pp. 182-184.
2. MISCELLANEOUS
Boston Harbor
Boston State House (Cows With One or Two Trees/or no Cows) (3)

ROWLAND AND MARSELLUS
HISTORIC STAFFORDSHIRE SERIES
AMERICAN & CANADIAN
1. FRUIT AND FLOWER BORDER SERIES
Battle of Bunker Hill
Battle of Germantown, Attack on Judge Chew's House
Biltmore House, Ashville, N.C.
"Blockade" (so called) "Shows many sided buildings, et.al."
Boston Massacre
Bunker Hill Monument
Capitol at Washington, D.C.
Clara Barton Birthplace
Commodore Paul Jones' Capturing The Serapis
D.A.R., Fort Griswald
Death of Capt. Lawrence
Delaware Water Gap
DeSoto's Discovery of the Mississippi
Elm at Cambridge, Mass.
Faneuil Hall
Faneuil Hall, Boston From the Harbor
Federal Hall, Wall Street, New York
Forefather's Monument, Plymouth
Hermitage
Horseshoe Curve, Pa.
House of Oliver Ellsworth
Independence Hall
John Alden House, Duxbury, Conn.
"John and Priscilla Speak For Yourself, John"
Landing of the Pilgrims
Lexington, Battle of
Lowell Mass., City Hall
Massachusetts State House
Mayflower at Plymouth Harbor
Molly Pitcher at the Battle of Monmouth
Mount Vernon
Newport, R.I., Old Stone Mill
New Library at Boston
Niagara Falls
Oliver and Abigail Ellsworth
Old City Gate, St. Augustine, Fl.

Old South Church
Patrick Henry Addressing the Virginia Assembly
Perry's Victory at Lake Erie
Pilgrim Hall
Plymouth Rock
Retreat From Concord of the British
Ride of Paul Revere
Shaw Mansion, Conn.
Standish House
Surrender of Col. Ledyard
Valley Forge 1777-78, Washington's Headquarters
Waltham Watch Co.
Washington at Prayer, Valley Forge
Washington Crossing the Delaware
Whirlpool Rapids
White House
William Penn's Treaty With the Indians
Valley Forge 1777-78, Washington's Headquarters
2. ROLLED EDGE SERIES
Alaska-Yukon Centennial
Albany, N.Y. (Capitol)
Albany, N.Y.
Allentown, Pa.
Altoona, Pa.
Arlington, Va.
Asbury Park, N.J.
Atlantic City, N.J.
Baltimore, Indiana
Baltimore, Md.
Bangor, Maine
Battle Creek, Mich.
Bermuda
Bermuda (Somer's Island)
Bermuda 1609-1909
Boston, Mass.
Boston ... Historical
Bridgeport, Conn.
Brooklyn, N.Y.
Buffalo, N.Y.
Carlisle, Pa.
Charleston, W. Va.
Charlotte, N.C.
Chicago, Ill.
Cincinnati, Ohio
Cleveland, Ohio
Columbus, Ohio
Cornell College
Coven Hoven, Nova Scotia
Daytona, Fla.
Decatur, Il.
Denver, Colo.
Detroit, Mich.
Dickens, Charles
East Hampton, N.Y.
Fall River, Mass.
Fort Williams
Grand Rapids, Mich.
Hamilton, Canada
Harrisburg, Pa.
Hartford, Conn.
Haverhill, Mass.
Hawaii
Hendrick Hudson
Hudson River
Hot Springs, Va.
Indianapolis, Ind.
Jacksonville, Fl.
Kalamazoo, Mich.
Kansas City, Mo.
Keokuk, Iowa
Lake Champlain, N.Y.
Lake George, N.Y.
Lakewood, N.J.
Lenox, Mass.
Leavenworth, Kan.
Lewis and Clark Centennial
Lincoln, Neb.
Lima, Ohio
Longfellow's Early Home
Lookout Mtn., Tenn.
Los Angeles, Calif.
Memphis, Tenn.
Miami, Fl.
Miles Standish
Miles Standish Monument
Milwaukee, Wisc.
Minneapolis, Minn.
Mobile, Ala.
Montreal, Canada
Nantucket Island
Nashville, Tenn.
New Bedford (Statue)
New Bedford (Wharf)
New London, Conn.
New Orleans, La.
New York, N.Y. (Six Vignettes)
New York, N.Y. (Eight Vignettes)
Old Detroit
Omaha, Neb.
Onset, Mass.
Panama-Pacific International Expo
Peoria, Ill.
Philadelphia, Pa.
Philadelphia ...Independence Hall
Pittsburgh, Pa.
Plymouth Rock
Providence, R.I.
Put-In-Bay, Ohio
Quincy, Ill.
Richfield Springs, N.Y.
Richmond, Va... City Hall
Richmond, Va...Capitol
Robert Burns
Rochester, N.Y.
Sag Harbor, N.Y.
Salem, Mass.
Salt Lake City, Utah
San Francisco, Calif.
Saratoga, N.Y.
Scranton, Pa.
Seattle, Wash

2. ROLLED EDGE SERIES
Shakespeare
Sherbrooke, Quebec, Canada
Smith, Captayne John
Spirit of '76
Spokane, Washington
St. Augustine, Fl.
St. Joseph, Mo.
St. Louis, Mo.
St. Louis World's Fair
St. Louis Centennial
St. Patrick's Cathedral, Harrisburg
St Paul, Minn.
St. Paul's Church, Trexlertown, Pa.
St. Peter's Church, Rittersville, Pa.
Syracuse ... Fairgrounds
Syracuse ... Indian Chief
Tacoma, Wash.
Taft and Sherman
Tampa, Fl. (four vignettes)
Tampa, Fl. (six vignettes)
Teddy Roosevelt
Thomas Jefferson
Trexlertown, Pa.
Thousand Islands
Toledo, Ohio
Topeka, Kan.
Toronto, Canada
Trenton, N.J.
Troy, N.Y.
Valley Forge ... Summer
Valley Forge - Winter
Valley Forge
Vassar College
Washington, D.C.
Waterbury, Conn.
West Point, N.Y.
White House
White Mtns.
Williams College
Williamsport, Pa.
Winegar's Store ... Grand Rapids
Winnepeg, Manitoba, Canada
Worcester, Mass
Yale College
Yarmouth, Nova Scotia
Wilkes-Barre, Pa.
Zanesville, Ohio
Zion Union Church, Berks County, Pa.

2. MISCELLANEOUS VIEWS
American Musicians
American Poets
Ashville, N.C.

Bath, Maine, City of Ships
Chicago, Il.
Declaration of Independence
Denver, Colo.
Harrisburg, Pa.
Landing of Columbus
Landing of the Pilgrims
Mayflower
Miami, Fl.
Mohawk, Indiana
Niagara Falls
Old Chicago
Palm Beach, Fl.
Plymouth
Portland, Ore.
Mrs. Robinson by Sir Joshua Reynolds
San Antonio, Tex.
Souvenir of Detroit, Mich.
Souvenir of Plymouth, Mass.
Souvenir of Put-in-Bay, Ohio
Spots in California
University of Pennsylvania
Views of Atlantic City, M.J.
Whittier's Birthplace
Yale University

ST. JOHN'S STONE CHINAWARE CO. (CANADA)
WHITE IRONSTONE
"Daily Bread"
"Scallop"
"Wheat"
"Wheat and Hops" ["Wheat & Blackberry"]

SEWELL(S) & CO.
BLUE AND WHITE TRANSFERWARE
SINGLE PATTERNS

CATEGORY	PATTERN
F	"All Over Floral"
-	"Bernstroff"
-	"Iremitagen" ["Hermitage"]
G	Canovian
-	"Knippels Broe" ["Bridge"]
S	Tourist
S	Wild Rose
O	"Willow" Pattern

ANTHONY SHAW (& SON(S)) (& CO.)
BLUE AND WHITE TRANSFERWARE
SINGLE PATTERNS

CATEGORY	PATTERN	
S	Castanette Dancer	Reg'd. May 25, 1858/No. 113864
M/Z	Peruvian Horse Hunt	Reg'd. Aug. 8, 1853/No. 92001
C	Pomona	-
G/H	Texian Campaign	-

HISTORIC STAFFORDSHIRE SERIES
AMERICAN
1. TEXIAN [TEXAN] CAMPAIGN SERIES
Battle of Buena Vista
Battle of Chapultepec ("Gen'l Taylor in Mexico")
Battle of Monterey
Battle of Palo Alto
Battle of Resaca de la Palma
"General On Rearing Horse, ... Battle in the Distance,
"Officer on Foot, et.al."
"Officer and Men at Rest Around Fire, et.al."
"Two Officers on Horse, et.al."
FLOW BLUE

CATEGORY	PATTERN	
O	Hong	
M	Marble/Cracked Ice	
M/Z	Peruvian Horse Hunt	Reg'd. Aug. 8, 1853/No. 92001

MULBERRY WARES

CATEGORY	PATTERN
F	"Birds"
M	Marble/Cracked Ice
S/C	Pomona

WHITE IRONSTONE

"Basketweave"	-
"Bordered Fuchsia"	-
"Britannia Shape"	Reg'd. Dec. 7, 1878/No. 330097
"Bullet Shape"	-
"Cable & Ring"	-
Chinese Shape (Ch)	Reg'd. Apr. 7, 1856/No. 104313-16
"Chinese Sydenham"	-
"Classic Gothic"	-
"Daisy Shape"	-
DeSoto Shape	-
"Hanging Leaves" ["Shaw - Spray"]	-
"Hexagon Sunburst" ["Daisy"]	-
"(Shaw's) Lily-of-the-Valley" (Ch)	-
Niagara Shape* ["Niagara Fan Shape"]	Reg'd. Apr. 7, 1856/No. 104313-16
"Shaw's Pear"	-
"Shield"	-
"Twelve Paneled Gothic" (Ch)	-
"Vintage Beauty" ["The Gift"]	-
"Wrapped Sydenham Shape" ["Double Sydenham"]	Reg'd. 1885/No. 2965

*See comments under Davenport.

TEA LEAF/COPPER LUSTRE

"Basketweave Shape"	Reg'd. 1886/No. 4825
"Bordered Fuchsia"	-
"Bullet"	-
"Cable Shape"*	Reg'd. 1884
"Cattail"	-
Chinese Shape	Reg'd. April 7, 1856/ No. 104313-16
"Daisy Shape"	Reg'd. 1885/No. 2965
DeSoto Shape	-
"Hanging Leaves"	-
"Hexagon" ["Sunburst"]	-
"Lily-of-the-Valley" [Shaw's] (Ch)	-
"Many Paneled Gothic"	-
"Niagara Fan Shape"	Reg'd. April 7, 1856/ No. 104313-16
"Pear" [Shaw's] (Ch)	-
"Shield"	-
"Simplicity"	-
"Vintage Beauty"	-
"Wrapped Sydenham" ["Double Sydenham"]	Reg'd. 1885/No. 2965

*Same as Cable & Ring in White Ironstone.

THOMAS SHIRLEY & CO.
BLUE AND WHITE TRANSFERWARE
SINGLE PATTERNS

CATEGORY	PATTERN
-	"Abbotsford"
-	"Balustrade & Pillars"
O	"Broseley" Pattern
O	Cabul
S	Continental Cathedral
-	"Dragon"
-	"Dragon Fly"
F	Floral
S	Mansion
-	"The Reader"
-	Stag
-	"The Wheel"

MULBERRY WARES

CATEGORY	PATTERN
S	Rio

SHORE, COGGINS & HOLT
BLUE AND WHITE TRANSFERWARE
SINGLE PATTERNS

CATEGORY	PATTERN
P/O	"Yin Willow"

SHORTHOUSE & CO.
BLUE AND WHITE TRANSFERWARE
SINGLE PATTERNS

CATEGORY	PATTERN
G	"The Itinerant" ["Gypsy Fire"]*
-	"One Man/Insect Willow"
-	"Palladian Temple"
-	"Spinning Wheel Children"
-	"Two Swans"
H	"Wellington Hotel, Waterloo"

*See *True Blue*, p. 74, No. 17.

GEORGE SKINNER & CO.
BLUE AND WHITE TRANSFERWARE
SINGLE PATTERNS

CATEGORY	PATTERN
G	Napoleon's Victory

SKINNER & WALKER
FLOW BLUE

CATEGORY	PATTERN
S	Brooklyn (att.)
F	China-Aster (att.)

SMITH & BINNALL
FLOW BLUE

CATEGORY	PATTERN
-	Ashley
-	Richmond

SMITH & FORD
FLOW BLUE

CATEGORY	PATTERN
F	Anemone

SMITH, FORD & JONES

FLOW BLUE

CATEGORY	PATTERN	
F	Anemone	Reg'd. 1892/No. 198330
-	Lonsdale	

TEA LEAF/COPPER LUSTRE
"Regalia"

GEORGE F. SMITH (& CO.)

BLUE AND WHITE TRANSFERWARE
SINGLE PATTERNS

CATEGORY	PATTERN
-	"Castle Scene"
-	"Eton College"
S	Florentine
-	"Indian Jar"*

*Marked William Smith, Jr. & Co.

THEOPHILUS SMITH

BLUE AND WHITE TRANSFERWARE
SINGLE PATTERNS

CATEGORY	PATTERN
O	"Long Bridge"

WILLIAM SMITH (& CO.)

BLUE AND WHITE TRANSFERWARE
SERIES
1. BARONIAL HALLS "SERIES"
Baronial Halls
BLUE AND WHITE TRANSFERWARE
SINGLE PATTERNS

CATEGORY	PATTERN	
M	Armorial	
-	"Banner Floral"	
-	Bacchus*	(Pattern #80)
P/S	"Baronial Halls"	Dated 1838, 1839
O	"Bird On Branch"**	(Pattern #37)
O	"Broseley"**	(Pattern #13)
-	"Buy A Broom"*	(Pattern #99)
-	Canova	
-	"Chinese Temple"*	(Pattern #18)
-	"Coral Border"	
-	"Coral Border"*	(Pattern #30)
-	Cupid	
-	Fountain*	(Pattern #64)
P/M	Fruit Basket	Dated 1838, 1839, 1840, 1842
-	"Girls With Dog"	
-	Helvetia*	(Pattern #67)
Z	"Horse"	
M	"Lion Antique"	
-	"Musk Deer"	
P/H	Napoleon*	(Pattern #65) (possible series)
H	Napoleon's Victories	
-	Orphans*	(Pattern #2)
P/G	Pastimes* (Pattern # 101)	Impressed Dates 1844, 1845
-	"Pheasant"	
G	Reapers	
S	Selected Views (2) (series)	
-	"Syrian Flowers"	
G	"Tea Party"	
-	Tourist*	(Pattern #71)
-	Turkish Pavilion*	(Pattern #1)
M	"Two Exotic Crested Birds"	
-	Tyrian*	(Pattern #91)
P/G	Unnamed Pattern for German Market	
P/R	Unnamed Religious Pattern	
-	"Vase & Books"	
F	"Wild Rose"**	(Pattern #15)
O	"Willow"**	(Pattern #14)

FLOW BLUE

CATEGORY	PATTERN
-	Active
-	Genevese

MULBERRY WARES

CATEGORY	PATTERN
F	Fruit Basket***

* For further information, refer to *NCS Newsletter* No. 86, June 1992, pp. 37-39, for an article by John & Joyce Cockerill *"The Tees Pottery."*
**For further information, refer to *NCS Newsletter* No. 102, April 1996, pp. 19-21, for an article on William Smith by John Cockerill.
***Pattern has also been found marked "F. (Francis) Morely"

SNEYD & HILL

FLOW BLUE

CATEGORY	PATTERN
F	"Claremont Groups"
M	Windsor Scrolls

SOHO POTTERY (LTD.)

BLUE AND WHITE TRANSFERWARE
SINGLE PATTERNS

CATEGORY	PATTERN
O	"Poon-Tang"

FLOW BLUE

CATEGORY	PATTERN
A	Empire
-	Imperial
S	Pandora
M	Venice

SOUTH WALES POTTERS

BLUE AND WHITE TRANSFERWARE
SINGLE PATTERNS

CATEGORY	PATTERN
H	Albert
F	Alhambra
O	Amherst Japan
F	Anemone
F	Asiatic Pheasant
S	Athens
M	Avis
F	Bombay Japan
F	Botanical
M	Caledonia
O	Colandine
S	Damask Border
F	Eastern
H	Entente Cordiale
M	Etruria
F	Fern
M	"Fleur de Lys" (att.)
F	Flora
F	Floral Spray
M	Fest Florentine China
H	Garibaldi
M	Gower
C	Grecian
F	Ivy Wreath
S	Jersey Scenes (Marine)
O	Lahore (Amherst Lahore)
F	"Llanelly Bouquet"
S	Livinium
S	Milan
F	Moss Rose
M	Nautilus
G	Oriental
S	Panorama
S	Rural
S	Sirius
S	Swiss Sketches
-	Syria
O	"Willow" Pattern

N.B.: For additional patterns refer to *Pugh's Welsh Pottery* and Hallesy's *Glamorgan Pottery*.

FLOW BLUE

CATEGORY	PATTERN
F	"Bird in a Tree" (att.)
F	"Llanelly Bouquet"
O	"Oriental Birds"
F	"Persian Rose"
O	Whampoa

MULBERRY WARES

CATEGORY	PATTERN
S	Milan

SOUTHWICK POTTERY

BLUE AND WHITE TRANSFERWARE
SINGLE PATTERNS

CATEGORY	PATTERN
-	"Dutch United Provinces"
S	Laodicea
S	Statue
G	"Tea Party"
G	Vase

FLOW BLUE

CATEGORY	PATTERN
-	"Dot Flower"
O	Formosa

MULBERRY WARES

CATEGORY	PATTERN
S	Castle
S	Haddon

SPODE'S BLUE PRINTED WARES

1. CHINESE LANDSCAPES

PATTERN NAME	PAGES*	SUGGESTED DATES OF INTRODUCTION	COPPER-PLATE USED
BRIDGE I	92-96	C. 1808	-
BRIDGE II	92-96	C. 1816	-
NEW BRIDGE (QUEEN CHARLOTTE)	92-96	1884	1884
BROSELEY (TWO TEMPLES II)	53-66	C. 1817	-
BUDDLEIA (TEMPLE-LANDSCAPE, FIRST)	80-82	C. 1792	C. 1800
BUFFALO	100-116	C. 1786	C. 1795
BUNGALOW	80	C. 1818	-
FLYING PENNANT	91	C. 1805	C. 1805
FOREST LANDSCAPE I	83-84	C. 1795	-
FOREST LANDSCAPE II	83-84	C. 1805	-
LAKE	99	C. 1825	C. 1835
(DAGGER-LANDSCAPE, SECOND)	99	C. 1825	-
(LONG BRIDGE)	117-124	C. 1800	-
MANDARIN	45-48	C. 1788	C. 1814
(DAGGER-LANDSCAPE, THIRD)	45-48	C.1788	C. 1814
NET	91	C. 1800	-
PEARL RIVER HOUSE	72-77	C.1800	-
(TRENCH MORTAR)	72-77	C. 1800	-
ROCK	50-52	C. 1790	-
SPODE'S LANDSCAPE	125,128-129	-	-
TALL DOOR	89	C. 1818	C. 1818
TEMPLE (TWO TEMPLES I)**	53-66	C. 1815	-
TEMPLE-LANDSCAPE I	96-99	C. 1813	-
(TEMPLE-LANDSCAPE, SECOND)	96-99	C. 1813	-
TEMPLE -LANDSCAPE II	96-99	C. 1814	C. 1814
TEMPLE LANDSCAPE VAR. PARASOL	96-99	C. 1808	-
TEMPLE WITH PANEL	83-85	C. 1798	C. 1800
(DAGGER-LANDSCAPE, FIRST)	83-85	C. 1798	C. 1800
TWO FIGURES I	67-69	C. 1784	-
TWO FIGURES II	67-74	C. 1786	-
TWO TEMPLES I (TEMPLE)	53-66	C. 1817	C. 1820
TWO TEMPLES II (BROSELEY)	53-66	C. 1817	C. 1820
WILLOW I	33-44	C. 1790	-
WILLOW II	33-44	C. 1795	C. 1800
WILLOW III	33-44	C. 1810	-

SPODE'S WILLOW PATTERN AND OTHER DESIGNS AFTER THE CHINESE (c) R. COPELAND, DEC. 1993

**"TWO TEMPLES I": AN UNRECORDED SPODE VERSION, SEE *FOB BULLETIN* No. 93, AUTUMN 1996, P.11 BY RENARD BROUGHTON.

SPODE'S BLUE PRINTED WARES

II. NON-LANDSCAPE

PATTERN NAME	PAGES*	SUGGESTED DATES OF INTRODUCTION
ASTER (CHINESE PLANTS)	154	C. 1834
BAMBOO [BAMBOO & ROCK]	150	C. 1806
BLUE ITALIAN	154	1816
BOWPOT	136	C. 1812
BROSELEY DRAGON	14	-
BUDE	136	C. 1814
CHINESE FLOWERS	145	C. 1815
CHINESE PLANTS [ASTER]	154	C. 1834
CHINESE OF RANK	154	C. 1805
CRACKED ICE & PRUNUS (MARBLE)	136-141	C. 1821
DRAGONS I	145-146	C. 1815
DRAGONS II	145-146	C. 1828
ETRUSCAN	130	C. 1825
FENCE	136	1800-1805
FILIGREE	167	C. 1823
FITZHUGH (TROHIES - DAGGER)	92, 95-97	C. 1800
GLOUCESTER	96, 148	C. 1800
GRASSHOPPER	85, 125, 142	(1770) C. 1812
GROUP	136, 144	C. 1809
HOUSE & FENCE (PAINTED)	14	C. 1780
INDIA	144-145	C. 1815
JAPAN	148	C. 1815
JAR & SCROLL	150	C. 1825
LANGE LIJSEN [LONG ELIZA]	143	1815-1825
LATTICE SCROLL	136	C. 1810
LILY	148	C. 1803
LOVE CHASE	89	C. 1808
(BORDER 1119?) LYRE	150	1800-1805
MARBLE (MOSAIC)	136	1821
NEW JAPAN	148	-
OLD PEACOCK (ORIENTAL BIRDS)	154	1800-1805
PANEL JAPAN	148	C. 1819
PEONY	-	C. 1814
PEPLOW	148	C. 1819

SPODE'S WILLOW PATTERN AND OTHER DESIGNS AFTER THE CHINESE (c) R. COPELAND, DEC. 1993

ROME (TIBER)	167	1811
SHIP & STAR	150	C. 1823
SPODE'S PHOENIX (OLD PEACOCK)	154	C. 1820
SPOTTED DEER	136	-
TROPHIES - DAGGER (FITZHUGH)	92, 95-97	C. 1800
TROPHIES - ETRUSCAN	130	1823
TROPHIES - MARBLE	130	1823
TROPHIES - NANKIN	130	1800-1805
TUMBLEDOWN DICK	136	1823

SPODE'S WILLOW PATTERN AND OTHER DESIGNS AFTER THE CHINESE (c) R. COPELAND, DEC. 1993

SPODE'S BLUE PRINTED WARES OTHER DESIGNS

Pattern Name	Page/ LRW*	Pattern No.	Suggested Date of Introduction
AESOP'S FABLES	170-171	-	c. 1828-1830
BLUE ROSE	164-165	4162	1826
BOTANICAL	162-163	B146, 4565	1826
BRITISH FLOWERS	162-163	4749	1831
BYRON VIEWS/GROUPS	-	-	c. 1833
CAMILLA	162-163	B406, 5419	1834
CARAMANIAN	170-171	-	c. 1809
CASTLE	168-169	-	c. 1806
CHANTILLY SPRIG	158-159	-	c. 1801
CONTINENTAL VIEWS	-	-	1845
CONVOLVULUS & SUNFLOWER	168-169	1864, 1831	1813
COUNTRY SCENE	166-167	B87 BORDER	c. 1825
DAISY	156-157	-	c. 1800
DAISY & BEAD	-	-	c. 1820
DRESDEN BORDER	168-169	3499, 3663 GILDED	1822
DRESDEN SPRAYS (as English Sprays but reversed)	160-161	4615	C. 1830
ENGLISH SPRAYS	160-161	4697, 4760	C. 1829
FLORAL	160-161	4977	C. 1831
FLOWER CROSS (PERSIAN QUATREFOIL)	156-157	-	C. 1800
FRENCH BIRDS	-	-	C. 1831
FRUIT & FLOWERS "MAY"	160-161	B 139, B 184	C. 1826
GERANIUM	162-163	3037	C. 1821
GIRL AT THE WELL	164-165	3661	1823
GOTHIC CASTLE	166-167	1966	C. 1814
GREEK	170-171	1111	1806
HONEYSUCKLE & PARSLEY	-	3244	C. 1821
INDIAN SPORTING	170-171	-	C.1807 (Possibly c. 1815)
ITALIAN	168-169	2614	1816
JASMINE (JESSAMINE)	162-163	B118, 4540	1826
LEAF	156-157	-	C. 1800
LOVE CHASE	-	-	C. 1810
LUCANO [BRIDGE OF LUCANO]	168-169	-	C. 1819
MILK MAID	166-167	-	C. 1814

MUSICIANS (VILLAGE SCENE)	166-167	4207	1826
NETTLE	-	-	c. 1823
PORTLAND VASE	17000-171	5057	1832
ROME [TIBER]	168-169	-	1811
ROTUNDA	-	-	c. 1790
SEASONS	-	-	1837
SHEPHERDESS	-	-	c. 1815
THE TURK	-	-	c. 1809
TOWER	168-169	3166, BORDER	1814
TURKISH CASTLE	-	-	c. 1809
UNION WREATH I	164-165	4158	1826
UNION WREATH II (BLUE ROSE CENTER)	164-165	B145, 4169	1826
UNION WREATH III (GIRL AT WELL BORDER/UNION BOUQUET CENTER)	164-165	3813	1824
VANDYKE	-	-	c. 1822
WARWICK VASE/GROUPS	170-171	-	c. 1834
WATERLOO (ITALIAN CHURCH)**		166-167 3395 BORDER	c. 1822
WOODMAN	166-167	-	c. 1816

*REFER TO *SPODE* BY LEONARD WHITER
**SEE *FOB BULLETIN*, No. 95, SPRING 1997, P. 4-5

JOSIAH SPODE
BLUE AND WHITE TRANSFERWARE - SERIES
1. AESOPH'S FABLES
(SPODE/COPELAND & GARRETT/W.T. COPELAND/W.T. COPELAND & SONS)
"The Ass, the Lion and the Cock"
"The Crow and the Pitcher"
"The Dog in the Manger"
"The Dog and the Shadow"
"The Dog and the Sheep"
"The Dog and the Wolf"
"The Fox and the Goat"
"The Fox and the Grapes"
"The Fox and the Lion"
"The Fox and the Sick Lion"
"The Fox and the Tiger"
"The Fox, The Hare and The Tortoise"
"The Hare and the Tortoise"
"The Horse and the Loaded Ass"
"The Leopard and the Fox"
"The Lion, the Bear and the Fox"
"The Lion in Love"
"The Lioness and the Fox"
"The Mountains in Labour"
"The Oak and the Reed"
"The Peacock and the Crane"
"The Sow and the Wolf"
"The Stag Looking into the Water"
"The Wolf and the Crane"
"The Wolf and the Lamb"
"The Wolf, the Lamb and the Goat"
2. CARAMANIAN SERIES (c. 1808-1809) (Series continued into 20th Century)
Ancient Bath at Cacamo in Caramania
Ancient Granary at Cacamo
Antique Fragments at Limissio
Caramania
Caramania Castle
Caramania Vase
The Castle of Bourdon in the Gulf of Stancio
Citadel Near Corinth
City of Corinth
A Colossal Sarcophagus at Cacamo
Colossal Sarcophagus Near Castle Rosso
A Colossal Vase Near Limissio in Cyprus
Entrance to Ancient Granary
Necropolis or Cemetery of Cacamo
Part of the Harbor of Macri
Principal Entrance to the Harbor of Cacamo
Ruins of Ancient Temple Near Corinth
Sarcophagi at Cacamo
Sarcophagus and Sepulchres at the Head of the Harbor of Cacamo
"Sepulchre with Annexe"*
A Triumphal Arch at Tripoli in Barbary
The "Turk"*
*Refer to *Coysh*, Vol. 2, pp. 181, 200
BLUE AND WHITE TRANSFERWARE - SERIES
3. "SPODE GREEK PATTERN SERIES"*
"Acratus With Female Carrying Myrtle"
"Advice to the Young"
"Artemis Drawn by a Griffon and a Lynx"
"Artemis With Two Lynx"
"Beautiful Penelope"
"Bellerophon's Victory Over the chimaera"
"Centaurs Battling Theseus"
"Cynisca Winning the Chariot Race"
"Demeter With Priestesses"
"A Domestic Ceremony"
"Four Figures in Battle"
"Gift of a Dove"
"Hephaestus (Vulcan) Presenting Arms to Aphrodite (Venus)"
"Hercules Fighting Hippolya"
"Iphegenia Told of the Death of Agamemnon"
"The Nuptial Bath"
"Offering to Demeter"
"Presentation of the Missing Son"
"Refreshments for Philasian Horsemen"
"Row Boat Fishermen"
"Sacrifice to Dionysus"
"Two Satyrs"
"Winner Crown at Temple of Venus"
"A Wreath for the Victor"
*See *Coysh, Vol. 1, p. 95* [Both center and border were often interchangeable. Probably more patterns exist.]
4. INDIAN SPORTING SERIES (c. 1805-1806)
(Copied by James & Ralph Clews, Edward Challinor used the title
"Oriental Sports" for the Indian Sports Series)
"Battle Between a Buffalo and a Tiger"
"Chase After a Wolf"
"Common Wolf Trap"
"The Dead Hog"
"Death of the Bear"
"Dooreahs Leading Out Dogs" ["Dooreahs or Dog Keepers Leading Out Dogs"]
"Driving a Bear out of Sugar Canes"
"Groom Leading Out" ["Syces or Grooms Leading Out Horses"]
"The Hog at Bay"
"The Hog Deer at Bay"
"Hog Hunters Meeting by Surprise a Tigress and Her Cubs" ["Her Cubs" sometimes missing]
"Hounds Chasing a Hare"
"Hunting a Buffalo" ["Hunting an Old Buffalo"]
"Hunting a Civiet Cat" ["Hunting a Cuttauss or Civiet Cat"]
"Hunting a Hog Deer"
"Koomkies Leaving the Male"
"Shooting at the Edge of a Jungle"
"Shooting a Leopard in a Tree" [Words "in a tree" often missing]

SPODE/COPELAND MANUFACTORY PLAIN PRINTED PATTERNS, IN ANY COLOR

PATTERN	CATEGORY	SPODE Up To 1833	COPELAND & GARRETT 1833 To 1847	COPELAND 1847 To 1867	COPELAND & SONS 1867 To 1932	SPODE LTD. 1932 To 1970	SPODE 1970	COMMENTS & REGISTRY DATE
ADEN	M	-	-	-	X	-	-	
AESOP'S FABLES	L	X	X	X	-	-	-	
ALBION	M	-	-	-	X	-	-	
ALHAMBRA	M	-	X	X	-	-	-	JUNE 30, 1848
ANTIQUE VASE (MIMOSA)	C	-	X	X	X	-	-	
ANTOINETTE	F	-	X	X	-	-	-	
AQUATIC	F	-	X	X	-	-	-	
ARABESQUE	S	-	X	X	X	-	-	
ATHENIAN	C	-	X	X(?)	-	-	-	
BANG UP	O	X	X	X	-	-	-	
BEDFORD	F	-	X	-	-	-	-	
BEVERLY (GRECIAN)	M	-	X	X	X	X	-	
BLUE ROSE	F	X	X	-	-	-	-	
BOTANICAL	F	X	X	-	-	-	-	
BRAMBLE	F	-	-	X	-	-	-	
BRITISH FLOWERS	F	X	X	X	X	X	-	
BROSELEY	O	X	X	X	X	X	-	
B700	F	-	X	X	-	-	-	
B772	F	-	X	X	-	-	-	
B773	F	-	X	X	-	-	-	
BYRON GROUPS	F	-	X	X	-	-	-	
BYRON VIEWS	L	-	X	X	-	-	-	
BYRON	G	-	-	X	-	X	-	JUNE 19, 1851
CAIRO	S	-	-	-	X	-	-	

PATTERN	CATEGORY	SPODE Up To 1833	COPELAND & GARRETT 1833 TO 1847	COPELAND 1847 TO 1867	COPELAND & SONS 1867 TO 1932	LTD. 1932 TO 1970	SPODE 1970	COMMENTS & REGISTRY DATE
CAMILLA	F	-	X	X	X	X	X	
CASTLE	S	X	X	-	-	-	-	
CEYLON	F	-	X	X	X	-	-	
CHATSWORTH	F	-	X	X	X	-	-	
CHINA ROSE	F	-	X	X	-	-	-	
CHINA FLOWERS	F	X	X	X	-	-	-	
CHINESE GARDENS	O	-	X	X	-	-	-	
CHINESE PLANTS	F	-	X	X	-	X*	-	
CONGRESS	M	-	-	-	X	-	-	
CONNAUGHT	M	-	-	-	X	-	-	
CONTINENTAL VIEWS	S	-	X	X	-	-	-	OCT. 21, 1845
CONVOLVULUS	F	-	X	X	-	-	-	** AUG. 17, 1849/ No. 62003
CORAL	F	-	X	X	-	-	-	
CORINTHIAN	C	-	-	X	X	-	-	
CORN & POPPY	F	-	-	X	X	-	-	MAY 22, 1863/ No. 162618
CORONAL	M	-	-	X	X	-	-	MAY 22, 1863/ No. 162619
COVENTRY	M	-	-	X	X	-	-	JUNE 11, 1861/ No. 141326-7
CRACKED & PRUNUSO	X	X	X	X	-	-	**	
CRETE	M	-	-	-	X	-	-	APRIL 4, 1892
CYRIL	F	-	-	-	X	-	-	APRIL 4, 1892
DAISY GRASS	F	-	-	-	X	-	-	
DELHI	A	-	-	X	X	-	-	
DENMARK	A	-	-	X	X	-	-	JULY 24, 1863/ No. 164468-9
DUNCAN SCENES	S	-	-	X	X	-	-	SEPT. 19, 1850/ No. 71989
ELCHO	M	-	-	-	X	-	-	JULY 24, 1863/ No. 164468-9
ETNA	M	-	-	X	X	-	-	JAN. 10, 1860/ No. 125365
ETRUSCAN (TROPHIES-ETRUSCAN)	O	X	X	X	X	-	-	
FABLES	M	-	-	-	X	-	-	JAN. 28/No. 331597 & MAR. 12, 1879/ No. 333235-6
FERN	M	-	-	X	X	-	-	
FIELD SPORTS	S	-	X	X	X	-	-	SEPT. 14, 1846/ No. 37254
FILLIGREE	O	X	X	-	-	-	-	
FLEUR DE LYS	M	-	-	X	X	X	X	AUG. 4, 1852/ No. 86070-1
FLORAL	F	X	-	-	-	-	-	
FLOWER VASE	F	X	X	-	-	-	-	
FRENCH RADIATING SPRIGS	F	-	X	X	-	-	-	
FRUIT & FLOWERS (MAY)	F	X	X	X	X	-	-	
GAME BIRDS (VARIOUS BORDERS)	M	-	-	-	X	X	X	
GARLAND	F	-	X	X	X	-	-	AUG. 17, 1849/ No. 62003
GERANIUM	F	X	X	X	X	-	X	
GRANADA	M	-	-	X	X	-	-	
HARLEAN	M	-	-	X	-	-	-	
HAWTHORN	F	-	-	-	X	-	-	
HONEYCOMB	M	-	-	X	-	-	-	JAN. 3, 1853/ No. 88808-9
HONEYSUCKLE (ITALIC)	M	-	-	-	X	-	-	
HONEYSUCKLE EMPIRE	M	-	-	X	X	-	-	APR. 7, 1855/ No. 99814
ILIUM	M	-	-	-	X	-	-	
INDIAN TREE	F	-	-	-	X	X	-	
IONIAN	S	-	-	X	X	-	-	JUNE 11, 1851/ No. 79183
ITALIAN	S	X	X	X	X	X	X	
IVY	F	-	X	-	-	-	-	
JAPONICA	F	-	-	X	X	-	-	MAR. 9, 1850/ No. 67987
JASMINE	F	X	X	-	-	-	-	
KEW (CHINESE BOUQUET)	F	-	-	-	X	-	-	
LAKE	O	X	X	-	-	-	-	
LANDSCAPE	O	X	-	-	X	X	-	
LILY	F	-	X	X	X	-	-	
LILY & ROSE	F	-	-	X	-	-	-	SEPT. 16, 1847/ No. 45822
LOBELIA	F	-	-	X	-	-	-	JUNE 19, 1845/ No. 28150
LOTUS	F	-	-	X	-	-	-	DEC. 20, 1850/ No. 75148
LOUIS QUATORZE	S	-	X	X	-	-	-	DEC. 2, 1844/ No. 22919-20
MACAW	M	-	X	X	X	-	-	
MANDARIN	O	X	X	X	X	X	-	
MARBLE/SHEET PATTERN*	O	X	-	-	-	-	-	SHEET PATTERN
SELDOM SEEN								
MEANDER	F	-	-	-	X	-	-	
MILKMAID	S	X	X	X	-	-	-	
MOROCCO	A	-	-	-	X	-	-	
NINEVEH	M	-	-	-	X	-	-	
NYMPHEA	F	-	-	-	X	-	-	MAR. 13, 1862/ No. 149938
OLD SALEM	S	-	-	-	-	X	X	
ONYX (SPHINX)	M	-	-	-	X	-	-	
OPEN IVY	F	-	-	X	X	-	-	
OSBORNE	M	-	-	-	X	-	-	
PAGODA	O	-	X	X	X	-	-	
PARTHENON	C	-	-	X	X	-	-	MAR. 19, 1861/ No. 139053
PASSION FLOWER	F	-	-	-	X	-	-	
PEARLS	M	-	-	X	X	-	-	
"PERGOLA"	F	-	-	-	X	-	-	
PEKIN	O	-	-	X	X	-	-	SEPT. 6, 1864/ No. 178264
PERSIAN	M	-	-	X	X	-	-	OCT. 14, 1859/ No. 123116
PERSIAN BIRD	M	-	-	-	X	-	-	**
PERSIAN RABBITS	-	-	-	-	X	-	-	
PORTLAND VASE	M	-	X	X	X	-	-	
PRIMROSE	A	-	-	-	X	X	-	APR. 28, 1881/ No. 364488
RAFAELESQUE	F	-	X	X	-	-	-	APR. 25, 1845/ No. 27350
RHINE (SEVERN)	S	-	-	-	X	X	X	*
RIBBON	M	-	-	X	-	-	-	
RICHMOND	S	-	-	X	X	-	-	APR. 29, 1856/ No. (?)
ROMA	A	-	-	X	X	-	-	
ROMAN BEADS	M	-	-	X	-	-	-	
ROSE & SPRIGS	F	-	-	X	-	-	-	JAN. 9, 1847/ No. 40110
ROSE WREATH (PICCADILLY)	F	-	-	X	X	-	-	SEPT. 9, 1847/ No. 45730
RUINS (MELROSE)	S	-	-	X	X	-	-	SEPT. 15, 1848/ No. 54438

*Pattern with the addition of color, called Aster.
**Garland Border ***Often called "Marble"

*See *Copeland, 2nd ed.,* Appendix IV, p. 181, for further information.
**Ex Davenport

RURAL SCENES	S	-	-	X	X	X	-	SEPT. 19, 1850/ No. 71989
SARDINIA	M	-	-	X	X	X	-	DEC. 17, 1858/ No. 117443
SEASONS	S	-	X	X	X	-	-	
SEASONS STAR	M	-	X	X	-	-	-	
SEAWEED	M	-	X	X	-	-	-	
SEVRES	M	-	X	X	-	-	-	
SHAGREEN (BROTH)	M	-	X	-	-	X	-	
SHAMROCK	M	-	-	X	X	-	-	SEPT. 17, 1861/ No. 143702
SHIP BORDER	O	X	X	X	X	-	-	
SIAM	-	-	-	X	X	X	X	**
SILVESTER	M	-	-	-	X	-	-	
SOUVENIR	F	-	-	X	X	-	-	OCT. 18, 1861/ No. 145157
STAR	M	-	-	X	X	-	-	
STATICE	F	-	X	X	-	-	-	
STELLA	A	-	-	-	X	-	-	
STORK	M	-	-	-	X	-	-	
STRAWBERRY	F	-	-	X	X	-	-	OCT. 1, 1852/ No. 86931
SUEZ KEY	C	-	-	X	X	-	-	
SUNFLOWER & CONVOLVULUS	F	X	-	-	-	-	X	

*Ex Davenport
**Ex Enoch Wood

SYRINGA OR MOCK ORANGE	F	-	-	X	X	-	-	NOV. 22, 1849/ No. 64319
TEMPLE	O	X	X	-	X	-	-	
THISTLE	M	-	-	-	X	-	-	
TOWER	S	X	X	X	X	X	X	
TULIP	M	-	X	-	X	-	-	
TURCO	M	-	-	-	X	-	-	
TUSCAN	A	-	-	-	X	-	-	JUNE 14, 1852/ No. 85354
UNION	F	X	X	X	-	-	-	
"VASE & PEONY"	F	-	?	-	-	-	-	
VENETIA	A	-	-	-	X	-	-	
VIOLET	F	-	-	X	X	-	-	
WARWICK GROUPS	F	-	X	X	-	-	-	
WARWICK VASE	C	-	X	-	-	-	-	
WATERLOO	S	X	-	-	-	-	-	
WATTEAU	S	-	-	X	X	-	-	
WEEPING WILLOW	O	X	X	X	X	-	-	
WELLINGTON	O	X	X	X	X	-	-	
WILLOW	O	X	X	X	X	-	-	

Robert Copeland, in his revised edition of *Spode and Copeland Marks,* 1997, pp, 186-187, Appendix VII, includes tables of designs that bear several different names.

STANLEY POTTERY LTD.
BLUE AND WHITE TRANSFERWARE
SINGLE PATTERNS

CATEGORY	PATTERN
A	Ostend

FLOW BLUE

CATEGORY	PATTERN	
-	Paris	-
F	Tine	Reg'd. 1898/No. 329815
-	Torbex	-
F	Touraine	Reg'd. 1898/No. 329815

STEVENSON & GODWIN
BLUE AND WHITE TRANSFERWARE
SINGLE PATTERNS

CATEGORY	PATTERN
O	"Willow" Pattern

ANDREW STEVENSON
BLUE AND WHITE TRANSFERWARE
SERIES
1. ORNITHOLOGICAL SERIES
"Birds of Prey"
"Birds of Prey Attacking"
"Birds and Willow" ["Pied Flycatcher and Snipe"]
"Duck Shooting"*
"Dusky Grebe"
"Grouse"
"Herons"
"The Kingfisher"
"The Peacock and Turkey"
"Pheasant"
"Stone Curlew"
"Wild Duck"
*See *True Blue*, p. 84, No. 10.
2. ROSE BORDER SERIES
Ampton Hall, Suffolk
Audley End, Essex
Barrington Hall
Boreham House, Essex
The Chantry, Suffolk
Culford Hall, Suffolk
Dulwich College, Essex
Duston Hall
Enville Hall, Staffordshire
Faulkbourn Hall
Felix Hall
Halstead, Essex
Haughton Hall, Norfolk
Kidbrook, Sussex
Mereworth House
Niagara
Oatlands, Surrey
Remains of Covet Hall, Essex*
Summer Hall, Kent
Tunbridge Castle, Surrey
Walsingham Priory, Norfolk
Wanstead House, Essex
Wolvesey Castle
Writtle Lodge, Essex
*Correct title may be "Remains of Covenham Hall, Essex"
BLUE AND WHITE TRANSFERWARE
SINGLE PATTERNS

CATEGORY	PATTERN
O	"Chinese Traders"
O	"Chinoiserie Bridgeless"
O	"Chinoiserie Ruins"
F	Nankeen
S	Netley Abbey [Gothic Ruins]
O	New Canton
G	"Pastoral Courtship" ["Pastoral Scene"]
S	"Rural Scene" ["Country Park"]
M	Sheep*
M	"Sheet Pattern" ["Acorns and Oak Leaves"]
G	"Shepherdess"
O	"Stevenson's Willow"
-	"Vase Acanthus"

See *P. Williams, Staffordshire*, Vol. III, p. 194.
HISTORIC STAFFORDSHIRE SERIES
AMERICAN
1. FLORAL AND SCROLL BORDER SERIES
Almshouse, New York
Catholic Cathedral, New York
Church and Buildings Adjoining Murray Street, New York
City Hall, New York
Columbia College, New York
The Junction of the Sacandage and Hudson Rivers
New York From Heights Near Brooklyn
The Temple of Fame ... To The Memory of Commodore Perry
Troy From Mt. Ida
View Near Catskill on the Hudson River
"Unidentified View"* [Edinburgh Scotland] (mkd. W.G. Wall)
View of New York From Weehawken
*See *Arman*, p. 149, No. 405.
2. FLORAL BORDER SERIES
New York From Brooklyn Heights
View of Governor's Island
View On the Road to Lake George
3. "FOUR PORTRAIT MEDALLION SERIES"
(Rose Border)
Dulwich College, Essex*
- Erie Canal View/Aqueduct Bridge at Rochester
Faulkbourn Hall* (3)
- Erie Canal View/With Aqueduct Bridge at Little Falls
- Erie Canal View/With Aqueduct Bridge at Rochester
- Erie Canal View/With Entrance of the Erie Canal into the Hudson at Albany
Niagara (3)
- Erie Canal View/With Aqueduct Bridge at Little Falls
- Erie Canal View/With Aqueduct Bridge at Rochester
- Erie Canal View/With Entrance of the Erie Canal into the Hudson at Albany
Oatlands, Surrey*
- Erie Canal View/With Aqueduct Bridge at Little Falls
- Erie Canal View/With Aqueduct Bridge at Rochester
- Erie Canal View/With Entrance of the Erie Canal into the Hudson at Albany
Summer Hall, Kent*
- Erie Canal View/With Aqueduct Bridge at Little Falls
Writtle Lodge, Essex
- Erie Canal View/With Entrance of the Erie Canal into the Hudson at Albany
*These may be referred to as "Four Medallions with English Views"

4. "TWO PORTRAIT MEDALLION BORDER SERIES"
(Rose Border)
Halstead, Essex (No canal views)
5. URN-BORDER AND SCROLL BORDER SERIES
Washington & Lafayette ("Welcome Lafayette, The Nation's Guest, Aug. 6, 1824") (2)
6. MISCELLANEOUS
Charter Oak, Connecticut*
Dutch Church at Albany
"General Lafayette ...Welcome to the Land of Liberty ... Born 1757; Joined the ...Struggle in 1777, ...Returned ...[to] the Land Whose Liberty he in Part Gave Birth to."
Hartford State House
Niagara** (Sheep Shearing View)
Wadsworth Tower***
*See *Snyder, Historic Staffordshire*, p. 99.
**See *Larsen*, p. 51, No. 107
***See *Larsen*, p. 11, No. 10 and p. 52, No. 108

RALPH STEVENSON
BLUE AND WHITE TRANSFERWARE SERIES
1. "ACORN AND OAK LEAF SERIES/STEVENSON'S"
Belvoir Castle
Cave Castle, Yorkshire
Compton, Verney
Dorney Court
Endsleigh Cottage
Gorhambury, Hertfordshire
Harewood House
Holliwell Cottage
Kenmount House
Lowther Castle, Westmorland
Oxburgh Hall
Sufton Court
Windsor Castle
BLUE AND WHITE TRANSFERWARE SERIES
2. "LACE BORDER SERIES"*
British Palaces [Windsor Castle]**
Eaton Hall
Kenilworth
View on the Ganges
Virginia Water
Windsor Castle [British Views]
*See *Coysh*, Vol. 1, p. 206.
See *P. Williams, Staffordshire*, Vol. II, p. 206 for comments.
3. "PANORAMIC SCENERY SERIES"
Canterbury Cathedral
Chichester Cathedral
Fonthill Abbey
York Minster
4. "PASTORAL SERIES"
"Girl With Birdcage"
"Girl With Shepherd"
5. "SEMI-CHINA WARRANTED SERIES"
"Boys and Dogs"
"The Bull" ["The Young Bull"]
"Girl with Sheep and Goat"
"Horseman at the Ford" ["Riding into the Water"]
"Milkmaid and Goats" ["Man with Rake"]
"Piping Shepherd Boy"
"The Three Donkeys" ["Donkey Ride"]
BLUE AND WHITE TRANSFERWARE SINGLE PATTERNS

CATEGORY	PATTERN
O	"Chinoiserie Ruins"
-	College
S	Harp
-	India
-	"Johuguel"
S	Palestine
Z	Paroquet
G	Pastoral
G	"Springer Spaniel"
S	Swiss
-	Villa

HISTORIC STAFFORDSHIRE SERIES AMERICAN
1. ACORN & OAK LEAVES BORDER SERIES
Washington Capitol*
*For full listing see Ralph Stevenson & Williams
2. "LACE BORDER SERIES"*
"Erie Canal at Buffalo"
"New Orleans"
"Riceborough at Georgia"
"Shipping Port of the Ohio, Kentucky"
*See *Arman*, pp. 143-144.
3. "LACE BORDER WITH VASES AND FLOWERS SERIES"
City Hall, Albany
Thorps and Sprague, Albany

4. SINGLE MEDALLION BORDER SERIES
(Oak Leaf Border)
Columbia College, New York (7)
- Clinton
- Erie Canal View/With Aqueduct Bridge at Little Falls
- Jefferson
- Erie Canal View/With Aqueduct Bridge at Little Falls
- Erie Canal View/With Entrance of the Erie Canal into the Hudson at Albany
- Lafayette
- Erie Canal View/With Aqueduct Bridge at Little Falls
- Erie Canal View/With Aqueduct Bridge at Rochester
- Washington
- Erie Canal View/With Aqueduct Bridge at Rochester
- Erie Canal View/With Entrance of the Erie Canal into the Hudson at Albany
St. Paul's Chapel, New York (6)
- Clinton
- Erie Canal View/With Aqueduct Bridge at Little Falls
- Erie Canal View/With Aqueduct Bridge at Rochester
-Jefferson
- Erie Canal View/With Entrance of the Erie Canal into the Hudson at Albany
-Lafayette
- Erie Canal View/With Aqueduct Bridge at Rochester
- Erie Canal View/With Entrance of the Erie Canal into the Hudson at Albany
- Washington
- Erie Canal View/With Aqueduct Bridge at Little Falls
5. SINGLE MEDALLION BORDER SERIES
(Vine Border)
Battery, New York* (Flagstaff Pavillion)
-Erie Canal View/With Aqueduct Bridge at Rochester
*See Arman, Quarterly, Vol. 1, 1997, p. 41 for illustration.
6. TWO MEDALLION BORDER SERIES
(Oak Leaf Border)
City Hotel, New York (7)
- Jefferson - Clinton
- Erie Canal View/With Aqueduct Bridge at Little Falls
- Erie Canal View/With Aqueduct Bridge at Rochester
- Erie Canal View/With Entrance of the Erie Canal into the Hudson at Albany
- Washington - Clinton
- Erie Canal View/With Entrance of the Erie Canal into the Hudson at Albany
- Washington - Lafayette
- Erie Canal View/With Aqueduct Bridge at Little Falls
- Erie Canal View/With Aqueduct Bridge at Rochester
- Erie Canal View/With Entrance of the Erie Canal into the Hudson at Albany
Park Theatre, New York (5)
- Jefferson - Clinton
- Erie Canal View/With Aqueduct Bridge at Little Falls
- Erie Canal View/With Entrance of the Erie Canal into the Hudson at Albany
- Washington - Jefferson
- Erie Canal View/With Entrance of the Erie Canal into the Hudson at Albany
- Washington - Clinton
- Erie Canal View/With Aqueduct Bridge at Little Falls
- Erie Canal View/With Entrance of the Erie Canal into the Hudson at Albany
7. TWO MEDALLION BORDER SERIES
(Vine Border)
Capitol, Washington (5)
-Jefferson & Lafayette *with*
- Erie Canal View/With Aqueduct Bridge at Little Falls
- Erie Canal View/With Aqueduct Bridge at Rochester
- Washington & Lafayette *with*
- Erie Canal View/With Aqueduct Bridge at Little Falls
- Washington & Jefferson *with*
- Erie Canal View/With Entrance of the Erie Canal into the Hudson at Albany
- Washington & Clinton *with*
- Erie Canal View/With Entrance of the Erie Canal into the Hudson at Albany
- Hospital, Boston (5)
- Jefferson & Clinton *with*
- Erie Canal View/With Aqueduct Bridge at Rochester
- Erie Canal View/With Entrance of the Erie Canal into the Hudson at Albany
- Jefferson & Lafayette *with*
- Erie Canal View/With Aqueduct Bridge at Rochester
- Erie Canal View/With Entrance of the Erie Canal into the Hudson at Albany
- Washington & Clinton *with*
- Erie Canal View/With Entrance of the Erie Canal into the Hudson at Albany
8. VINE BORDER SERIES*
(Or referred to as "Leaves & Vines" or "Vine Leaf")
Almshouse, New York
American Museum
Battery, New York [Flagstaff Pavilion]
Battle of Bunker Hill
Brooklyn Ferry
Capitol, Washington
City Hall, New York
Columbia College, New York
Deaf and Dumb Asylum, Hartford, Conn.
Esplanade and Castle Garden, New York
Exchange, Charleston
Fort Ganesvoort, New York
Fulton Market, New York
Hospital, Boston (With or Without Sea Wall) (2)

Hospital, New York
Insane Asylum, New York
Lawrence Mansion, Boston [Boston Athenaeum] or [American Villa]
Masonic Hall, Philadelphia
Pennsylvania Hospital, Philadelphia [PA]
St. Patrick's Cathedral, Mott Street, [N.Y.]
Savannah Bank**
State House, Boston
*See *Arman Quarterly*, Vol. 1, Apr./May 1997, No. 2, pp. 13, 54, for illustrations and an article by Ted Gallagher titled "Vine Leaf Border Series."
**See *Larsen*, p. 137, No. 316.

RALPH STEVENSON & SON
BLUE AND WHITE TRANSFERWARE
SERIES
1. BRITISH LAKE "SERIES"
Derwentwater
Elterwater
Loweswater
Thirlmere
Ullswater
Windermere
BLUE AND WHITE TRANSFERWARE
SINGLE PATTERNS*

CATEGORY	PATTERN
F	Amaryllis
S	Cologne
O	Manhattan
M	Millennium

*A Series of Biblical Prophesy Scenes
FLOW BLUE

CATEGORY	PATTERN
S	Swiss

RALPH STEVENSON & WILLIAMS
BLUE AND WHITE TRANSFERWARE
SINGLE PATTERNS

CATEGORY	PATTERN
C	Ancient Greece
M	"Beehive and Vases"
F	"Butterfly with Rose"
O	"Chinese Bird Catchers"
-	"Eton Jacket Fishermen"
-	"Fishing Party"
G	Pastoral
O	"Temple Landscape I" [Nankin]

HISTORIC STAFFORDSHIRE SERIES
AMERICAN
1. "ACORN & OAK LEAVES BORDER SERIES"
Albany Theatre, 1824
Almshouse, Boston
Baltimore Exchange
City Hotel, New York
Columbia College, New York (2)
Court House, Boston
Dutch Church at Albany
Harvard College "End of University Hall, With Two People in Foreground, et.al."
Harvard College "Four Buildings, et.al."
Harvard College "University Hall with Horseman in Foreground, et.al."
Nahant Hotel Near Boston (With or Without Tree) (2)
Octagon Church, Boston [Staughton's Church, Philadelphia]
Park Theatre, New York
St. Paul's Chapel, New York [St. Paul's Church, New York]
Scudder's American Museum
State House, Boston (Scudder's Museum)
Staughton's Church, Philadelphia ["Octagon Church"]
Water Works, Philadelphia
2. FOUR MEDALLION BORDER SERIES
(Acorn & Oak Leaves)
"A View of the Late Protestant Church in the City of Albany ... Erected in 1715 ... Pulled Down in 1806"*
Albany Theatre, 1824*
Dorney Court
Harewood House, Yorkshire
- Erie Canal View/With Entrance of the Erie Canal into the Hudson at Albany
Park Theatre, New York (3)
- Erie Canal View/With Aqueduct Bridge at Little Falls
- Erie Canal View/With Aqueduct Bridge at Rochester
- Erie Canal View/With Entrance of the Erie Canal into the Hudson at Albany
- Windsor Castle
- Erie Canal View/With Aqueduct Bridge at Rochester
Only covered piece has medallion, the base does not.
3. FOUR MEDALLION BORDER SERIES
(Urn Border)
Portrait Medallion
4. ONE MEDALLION
President Washington*
*Found on a cup plate.

5. ONE MEDALLION BORDER SERIES
(Acorn & Oak Leaves)
Columbia College, New York (7)
- Clinton *with*
- Erie Canal View/With Aqueduct Bridge at Little Falls
-Jefferson *with*
- Erie Canal View/With Aqueduct Bridge at Little Falls
- Erie Canal View/With Entrance of the Erie Canal into the Hudson at Albany
- Lafayette *with*
- Erie Canal View/With Aqueduct Bridge at Little Falls
- Erie Canal View/With Aqueduct Bridge at Rochester
- Washington *with*
- Erie Canal View/With Aqueduct Bridge at Rochester
- Erie Canal View/With Entrance of the Erie Canal into the Hudson at Albany
St. Paul's Chapel, New York (6)
-Clinton *with*
- Erie Canal View/With Aqueduct Bridge at Little Falls
- Erie Canal View/With Aqueduct Bridge at Rochester
-Jefferson *with*
- Erie Canal View/With Entrance of the Erie Canal into the Hudson at Albany
- Lafayette *with*
- Erie Canal View/With Aqueduct Bridge at Rochester
- Erie Canal View/With Entrance of the Erie Canal into the Hudson at Albany
-Washington *with*
- Erie Canal View/With Aqueduct Bridge at Little Falls
6. SCROLLS, FLOWERS & URNS SERIES
Washington and Lafayette*
*See *Larsen*, p. 224, No. 586
7. TWO MEDALLION BORDER SERIES
(Acorn & Oak Leaves)
City Hotel, New York
- Erie Canal View/With Aqueduct Bridge at Little Falls
- Erie Canal View/With Aqueduct Bridge at Rochester
- Erie Canal View/With Entrance of the Erie Canal into the Hudson at Albany
Park Theatre, New York (5)
- Jefferson & Clinton *with*
- Erie Canal View/With Aqueduct Bridge at Little Falls
- Erie Canal View/With Entrance of the Erie Canal into the Hudson at Albany
- Washington & Clinton *with*
- Erie Canal View/With Aqueduct Bridge at Little Falls
- Erie Canal View/With Aqueduct Bridge at Rochester
- Washington & Jefferson *with*
- Erie Canal View/With Entrance of the Erie Canal into the Hudson at Albany
8. TWO MEDALLION BORDER SERIES
(Floral-Urn and Scroll)
Capitol, Albany*
-Clinton & Washington
*Noted on a water pitcher without Erie Canal View. See Arman, p. 155, No. 424.
9. FOUR MEDALLION BORDER SERIES
(Vine Border)
Hospital, Boston (5)
- Jefferson - Clinton
- Erie Canal Views/With Aqueduct Bridge at Rochester
- Erie Canal Views/With Entrance of the Erie Canal into the Hudson at Albany
- Jefferson - Lafayette
- Erie Canal Views/With Aqueduct Bridge at Little Falls
- Erie Canal Views/With Aqueduct Bridge at Rochester
- Washington - Clinton
- Erie Canal Views/With Entrance of the Erie Canal into the Hudson at Albany

JOHN STEVENTON & SONS, LTD.
BLUE AND WHITE TRANSFERWARE
SINGLE PATTERNS

CATEGORY	PATTERN
Z	"Elephant"

FLOW BLUE

CATEGORY	PATTERN
O	Kato

JOSEPH STUBBS
BLUE AND WHITE TRANSFERWARE
SINGLE PATTERNS

CATEGORY	PATTERN
G	"Italian" ["Blue Italian"]
S	Milanese Scenery*
S	Jedburgh Abbey/Roxburghshire
S	"Rome"
M	"Seashells"** (2)
S	Swiss Scenery

*See *P. Williams, Staffordshire*, Vol. III, p. 253.
**See *FOB Bulletin*, No. 95, Spring 1997, p. 6
HISTORIC STAFFORDSHIRE SERIES
AMERICAN
1. "SPREAD EAGLE BORDER SERIES"
Bank of the United States, Philadelphia
Church in the City of New York ("Dr. Mason's")
City Hall, New York
Fair Mount Near Philadelphia (with and without Sheep) (2)

Highlands, North River
Hoboken in New Jersey ("Steven's House")
Mendenhall Ferry
Nahant Hotel, Near Boston
New York Bay
Park Theatre, New York
State House, Boston
Upper Ferry Bridge Over the River Schuylkill
View at Hurl Gate, East River
Woodlands, Near Philadelphia
2. "ROSE BORDER SERIES"
Boston State House
City Hall, New York

STUBBS & KENT
BLUE AND WHITE TRANSFERWARE
SINGLE PATTERNS

CATEGORY	PATTERN
F	"Peach & Cherry Pattern"*

*Refer to *Snyder, Romantic Staffordshire*, pp. 165-166.

SUNDERLAND OR "GARRISON" POTTERY
BLUE AND WHITE TRANSFERWARE
SINGLE PATTERNS

CATEGORY	PATTERN
G	Accepted
-	"African Daisies"
M	Australian
F	"Camel"
-	"Dresden"
G	"Eel Plate"
S	Gothic
G	"Lady of the Lake"
G	"Man of the Lake"
-	Medina
-	"Mediterranean Group"
F	Non Pareil
S	Royal Cottage
O	Turkish Pavillion
O	"Willow" Pattern

BLUE AND WHITE TRANSFERWARE
SINGLE PATTERNS

CATEGORY	PATTERN
F	Non Pareil*

*Produced by Dixon & Co./Dixon & Phillips
MULBERRY WARES

CATEGORY	PATTERN
F	Non Parril*

*Produced by Dixon, Phillips

SWIFT & ELKIN
BLUE AND WHITE TRANSFERWARE
SINGLE PATTERNS

CATEGORY	PATTERN
S	Swiss Scenery

SWINNERTON (LTD.)
BLUE AND WHITE TRANSFERWARE
SINGLE PATTERNS

CATEGORY	PATTERN
S	Silverdale
O	"Willow Pattern"

TAMS (et.al.)
Partnerships Include:
Tams & Co.
S. Tams & Co.
Tams & Anderson
Tams, Anderson & Tams
BLUE AND WHITE TRANSFERWARE - SERIES
1. "FLORAL CITY SERIES"
"Ludlow Castle" (Tams, Anderson & Tams)
"Richmond Castle, Yorkshire"*
"Worcester Cathedral"
*See *True Blue*, p. 84, No. 1.
2. "TAMS FOLIAGE BORDER SERIES" (Recorded Partnerships: S. Tams & Co., Tams, Anderson & Tams)
Broke Hall, Suffolk
Bruce Castle, Tottenham*
Covent Garden Theatre, London
Custom House, London
Drury Lane Theatre, London
Eton College
Four Courts, Dublin
The Guild Hall, London**
Haymarket Theatre, London
New Post Office, London
Opera House, London
Post Office, Dublin
Residence of General Sir Herbert ...***
Royal Coburg Theatre
Royal Exchange, London
Somerset House, London
*See *True Blue*, p. 83, No. 9.
**See *True Blue*, p. 83, No. 10.
***See *True Blue*, p. 83, No. 12.
3. MISCELLANEOUS

CATEGORY	PATTERN
O	"Fishermen With Nets"
S	"Ruined Castle"
O	"Willow" Pattern

BLUE AND WHITE TRANSFERWARE
SINGLE PATTERNS

CATEGORY	PATTERN
-	"Tams Urn" (Tams, Anderson & Tams)
-	"Fruit & Scrolls" (S. Tams & Co.)

HISTORIC STAFFORDSHIRE SERIES
AMERICAN
1. MISCELLANEOUS
Capitol at Harrisburg, PA (S. Tams & Co.)
The Capitol, Washington (Tams, Anderson & Co.)(Tams, Anderson & Tams)
General W.H. Harrison ... Hero of the Thames 1813*
Henry Clay ... Star of the West
United States Hotel, Philadelphia (Tams, Anderson & Tams)**
*The marking for General W.H. Harrison ... is not by Tams. Rather, it was designed by John Tams and has a stencil mark "JAMES TAMS & CO., PHILADELPHIA". *Larsen*, pp. 122 and 184-185 and *Snyder's Historic Staffordshire*, pp. 106-107, cite two conflicting Tams partnerships for the same piece.
**See *Arman Quarterly*, Vol. 1, 1997, p. 35 for picture.
N.B.: When attribution to a particular partnership has been verified, this has been noted with the name of the partnership in parentheses.

JOHN TAMS (& SON)(LTD)
BLUE AND WHITE TRANSFERWARE
SINGLE PATTERNS

CATEGORY	PATTERN
G	Imperial Quart ["Imperial Measure"]
S	Seine

FLOW BLUE

CATEGORY	PATTERN
F	Aurora
S	Castle
F	Glenwood
M/A	Jewel
S	Stork

S. TAMS & CO.
BLUE AND WHITE TRANSFERWARE
SINGLE PATTERNS

CATEGORY	PATTERN
F	"Fruit & Scrolls"

TAMS, ANDERSON & TAMS
BLUE AND WHITE TRANSFERWARE
SINGLE PATTERNS

CATEGORY	PATTERN
M	"Tam's Urn"

WILLIAM TAYLOR
WHITE IRONSTONE
"Wheat & Blackberry" ["Wheat & Hops"]
"Wheat"

TAYLOR BROS.
WHITE IRONSTONE
"Forget-Me-Not"
"Leaf Focus"
"Wheat & Clover"

GEORGE TAYLOR
(T. & J. Taylor/Lindop & Taylor)
BLUE AND WHITE TRANSFERWARE
SINGLE PATTERNS

CATEGORY	PATTERN
-	"Cottage"
O	"Willow" Pattern

TAYLOR, HARRISON & CO.
BLUE AND WHITE TRANSFERWARE
SINGLE PATTERNS

CATEGORY	PATTERN
-	"Lion Hunter"
O	"Ornate Pagodas"

JOHN THOMSON (& SONS)
BLUE AND WHITE TRANSFERWARE
SINGLE PATTERNS

CATEGORY	PATTERN
S	Alhambra
S	Alma
-	Andalusia
-	Athenian
S	Castle ["Cowherd & Castle"]
-	Cavendish
-	"Chantilly"
-	Chariot
-	Grecian
-	"Ivanhoe"
M/Z	Peacock
-	Pekin
-	Triumphal
-	Watteau
-	"Willow" Pattern

FLOW BLUE

CATEGORY	PATTERN
S	Alhambra
M/C	Alma
O	Madras

MULBERRY WARES

CATEGORY	PATTERN
M/C	Alma
S	Cynthia
F	Royal Rose
S	Watteau

THOMAS TILL & SON
BLUE AND WHITE TRANSFERWARE
SINGLE PATTERNS

CATEGORY	PATTERN
-	"Clyde"
S	Marino
-	Royal Cottage
P	Shanghai
O	"Willow" Pattern
S	Woodbine

THOMAS TILL & SONS
FLOW BLUE

CATEGORY	PATTERN	
F	Blenheim	
F	Cecil	
M/A	Eton	
O	Manila	
F	Navy	
A	Osborne	
O	Pagoda	Reg'd. 1887
F	Poppy	
-	Prunus	
-	Rajah	
-	Rheims	
M/F	Syton	
-	Tulip	
M/A	Venus	

CHARLES TITTENSOR
BLUE AND WHITE TRANSFERWARE
SINGLE PATTERNS

CATEGORY	PATTERN
O	"Net Pattern" (att.)

TOFT & MAY
BLUE AND WHITE TRANSFERWARE
SINGLE PATTERNS

CATEGORY	PATTERN
-	"Coursing Scene"
O	"Elephant" Pattern
-	"Wild Rose"
Z	"Zebra"*

*Also used by John Rogers & Son

TOMPKINSON BROS. & CO.
WHITE IRONSTONE
"Wheat & Clover Shape" ["Pearl"] Reg'd. Aug. 4, 1869/No. 231613

GEORGE TOWNSEND
BLUE AND WHITE TRANSFERWARE
SINGLE PATTERNS

CATEGORY	PATTERN
O	"Chinese Marine"
S	Wild Rose ["Nuneham Courtney"]

E.T. TROUTBECK
BLUE AND WHITE TRANSFERWARE
SINGLE PATTERNS

CATEGORY	PATTERN
S	Epirus
O	Chinese Gem

MICHAEL TUNNICLIFF(E)
WHITE IRONSTONE
"Paneled Decagon"

G.R. TURNBULL
BLUE AND WHITE TRANSFERWARE
SINGLE PATTERNS

CATEGORY	PATTERN
O	Albion
-	"Lake & Bridge"

TURNER, GODDARD & CO.
WHITE IRONSTONE

Ceres Shape	Reg'd. Nov. 25, 1870/No. 248052
"Ceres Without Cable"	
"Wheat"	-

G.W. TURNER & SONS
BLUE AND WHITE TRANSFERWARE
SINGLE PATTERNS

CATEGORY	PATTERN
S	Brazil

FLOW BLUE

CATEGORY	PATTERN
M/Z	Heron

JOHN TURNER (TURNER & CO., etc.)
BLUE AND WHITE TRANSFERWARE
SINGLE PATTERNS

CATEGORY	PATTERN
-	"Archery Lesson"
-	"Bailiff's Report"
F	"Botanical Beauties" (possible series)
O	"Buffalo"
O	"Chinaman With Rocket"
F	"Daffodil Pattern"
Z	"Elephant" ["Day on an Elephant"]
-	"Flame Plant"
-	"Floral"
-	"Palm Tree & Bridge"
O	"Stag"
-	"Swooping Bird"
M	"Turner's Windmill"
O	"Two Men Willow"
-	"The Villager" ["Villager Pattern"]

JOHN & WILLIAM TURNER
BLUE AND WHITE TRANSFERWARE
SINGLE PATTERNS

CATEGORY	PATTERN
O	"Chinese-Style" Scene With Figure of a One Legged Duck* ["Traveler & Duck"]

*Refer to *Penny Plain*, p. 96, No. 196

TURNER & TOMKINSON
BLUE AND WHITE TRANSFERWARE
SINGLE PATTERNS

CATEGORY	PATTERN
-	Cattle
F	Pell*

*See *Christies South Kensington Auction*, April 23, 1998, Lot 96.

MULBERRY WARES

CATEGORY	PATTERN
F	Lily

WHITE IRONSTONE
"Wheat"
"Wheat & Clover" (Ch)

TURPIN & CO.
BLUE AND WHITE TRANSFERWARE
SINGLE PATTERNS

CATEGORY	PATTERN
O	"Willow" Pattern

JOSEPH TWIGG (& CO.)
or (& Bros).(& Co.)
BLUE AND WHITE TRANSFERWARE
SINGLE PATTERNS
CATEGORY PATTERN
1. "NAMED ITALIAN VIEWS SERIES"
Cascade at Isola
Grotto of St. Rosalie
Obelisk at Catania

Residence of Solimenes Near Vesuvius
Temple of Serapis at Pouzzuoli
BLUE AND WHITE TRANSFERWARE
SINGLE PATTERNS

CATEGORY	PATTERN
S	Andalusia
-	"Basket of Eggs"
G	Eton College
M	Independent Order of Oddfellows (2)
M	Ivanhoe
S	Wild Rose
O	"Willow" Pattern

HISTORIC STAFFORDSHIRE SERIES
AMERICAN
1. MISCELLANEOUS
"Temple at Nauvoo" (Illinois) ["Mormon Temple"]*
* See *Arman Quarterly*, Vol. 1, 1997, pp. 37-38 for picture and *Larsen*, p. 244, No. 680.

UPPER HANLEY POTTERY CO. (LTD.)
BLUE AND WHITE TRANSFERWARE
SINGLE PATTERNS

CATEGORY	PATTERN
O	Geisha
A	Victoria

FLOW BLUE

CATEGORY	PATTERN
F	Aster
M/F	Astoria
-	Bern
F	Ceicel
M	Crawford
F	Dahlia
M/F	Dorothy
A	Elgar
-	Florence
O	Geisha
-	"Grape Pod"
M	Madras
A	Martha
A	Muriel
F	Naida
-	Nelson
F	Pearl
M	Venice

MULBERRY WARES

CATEGORY	PATTERN
F	Bryonia

VENABLES, MANN & CO.
(or John Venables & Co.)
WHITE IRONSTONE
"Twelve Paneled Gothic Shape" Reg'd. Oct.5, 1853/No. 92768-70

VENABLES & BAINES
BLUE AND WHITE TRANSFERWARE
SINGLE PATTERNS

CATEGORY	PATTERN	
G	Union	Reg'd. Feb. 17, 1852/No. 83826

MULBERRY WARES

CATEGORY	PATTERN
-	"Marble"

JOHN VENABLES & CO.
(or Venables, Mann & Co.)
WHITE IRONSTONE

"Arcaded Panels"	-
Baltic Shape	Reg'd. Oct. 5, 1853/No. 92768-70
"Grape Octagon"	-
"Twelve Paneled Gothic Shape"	Reg'd. Oct. 5, 1853/No.92768-70
"Closed Bud Finial"	

JAMES VERNON (& SON)
BLUE AND WHITE TRANSFERWARE
SINGLE PATTERNS

CATEGORY	PATTERN
O	Kin Shan*
O	"Willow" Pattern

*See *P. Williams, Staffordshire I*, p. 136.

THOMAS WALKER
BLUE AND WHITE TRANSFERWARE
SINGLE PATTERNS

CATEGORY	PATTERN
O	Kan-Su
O	Simla
S	Tavoy
S	Washington

FLOW BLUE

CATEGORY	PATTERN
M/F	Flora
O	Nankin (att.)
O	Scinde
O	Simla
M	"Strawberry"* (Brush Stroke)
F	"Tulip & Sprig" (Brush Stroke)
S	Washington
M	"Wild Strawberry"* (Brush Stroke)

*Ellen Hill notes attribution may be in error; with potter being Jacob Furnival.
MULBERRY WARES

CATEGORY	PATTERN
M/F	Flora
S	Florentine
F	"Grape & Sprig" (Brush Stroke)
O	Hong
O	Kan-Su
F	Rose
O	Scinde
S	Tavoy*
S	Washington*

*Ellen Hill notes patterns are the same, but with different names, and Ms. Hill further notes the pattern Tavoy recorded with initials "B & M" (Brougham & Mayer).
WHITE IRONSTONE
"Bordered Gothic"
"Grape Octagon"
"Primary Shape"

THOMAS HENRY WALKER
BLUE AND WHITE TRANSFERWARE
SINGLE PATTERNS

CATEGORY	PATTERN
O	"Willow" Pattern

JAMES WALLACE & CO.
BLUE AND WHITE TRANSFERWARE
SERIES
1. RURAL SCENERY "SERIES"
"Abbey Ruins and Horses"
"Castle and Cattle"
"Herdsman and Gothic Cottage"
"Water Mill and Packhorse"
"Woman With Baby"
BLUE AND WHITE TRANSFERWARE
SINGLE PATTERNS

CATEGORY	PATTERN
S	Cambrian
S	"Kirkstall Abbey" ["Abbey Ruins & Sailing Boat"]
M	Shell
S	Wild Rose
O	"Willow" Pattern

EDWARD WALLEY
BLUE AND WHITE TRANSFERWARE
SINGLE PATTERNS

CATEGORY	PATTERN
S	Amaranthine Flower
P/F	"Grape Clusters"
O	Hindu
S	Wild Rose
O	"Willow" Pattern

FLOW BLUE

CATEGORY	PATTERN	
S	Cleopatra	-
O	Indian Stone	-
F	Niagara Shape* (Gaudy Ironstone)	Reg'd. Nov. 29, 1856/ No. 107783-5
P/F	Queen's Own	-
F	"Sleepy Eye"** ["Seeing Eye"] (Gaudy Ironstone")	Reg'd. Nov. 29, 1856/ No. 107783-5
O	Takoo	-

*Sam Laidacker's *Anglo-American China, Part II*. Bristol, PA. 1951, p. 131 notes the following: "There are a few instances where different potters use the same design and the same name but this name as used by this maker [is] in a class by itself...Illustrated is a typical piece of the ware called Gaudy Ironstone which bears this pattern name ["Niagara Shape"]...Large sets of plain White Ironstone have been made with this same pattern name. Also: plain white with an embossed wreath; with a luster and around the rim and with a luster leaf..."
**Also see *Anglo-American China, Part I*, p. 85, No. 936 "Seeing Eye".

MULBERRY WARES

CATEGORY	PATTERN	
S	Foliage*	
P/O	Hong	

*Hill notes this is exact pattern as James Edwards.

WHITE IRONSTONE

"Ceres"	-
"Double Sydenham" ["Wrapped Sydenham"]	-
"Full Panelled Gothic"	-
Niagara Shape*	Reg'd. Nov. 29, 1856/ No. 107783-5

TEA LEAF/COPPER LUSTRE

"Cameo Gothic"	-
"Classic Gothic"	-
"Full Paneled Gothic"	-
"Grape Octagon"	-
Niagara Shape*	Reg'd. Nov. 29, 1856/ No. 107783-5
"Wrapped Sydenham" ["Double Sydenham"]	-

*Niagara Shape is also a true registered name by William Davenort. In order to differentiate between both potters, the White Ironstone Collectors have given Davenport's Niagara Shape the nickname "Fig Cousin". This may be confusing, however, this only relates to White Ironstone, not to Flow Blue/Gaudy Ironstone.

WILLIAM WALSH

BLUE AND WHITE TRANSFERWARE

SINGLE PATTERNS

CATEGORY	PATTERN
-	"Camel"
O	"Mausoleum of Sultan Purveiz, Near Allahabad"*
O	"View in the Fort, Madura"
O	"Willow" Pattern

*See Herculaneum Pottery's "Indian Series" for previous attribution.

(JAMES) WARDLE & CO. (HANLEY) LTD.

FLOW BLUE

CATEGORY	PATTERN
S	Countryside

WATSON & CO.

(or Watson's Pottery)

BLUE AND WHITE TRANSFERWARE

SINGLE PATTERNS

CATEGORY	PATTERN
-	"Bird & Fly"
S	"Edinburgh from Port Hopetown"
S	"The Gentle Shepherd"
O	"Willow" Pattern
-	"The Witch Spinning"

J.H. WEATHERBY & SONS (LTD.)

BLUE AND WHITE TRANSFERWARE

SINGLE PATTERNS

CATEGORY	PATTERN
S	Medina
S	Trentham

FLOW BLUE

CATEGORY	PATTERN	
M/F	Belmont	
-	Sandon	
F	Welbeck	Reg'd. 1905/No. 461702

WHITE IRONSTONE

"Wheat"

WEDGWOOD & CO. (LTD.)

BLUE AND WHITE TRANSFERWARE

SINGLE PATTERNS

CATEGORY	PATTERN	
S	Alexander	Reg"d. Sept. 9, 1868/No. 221313
F	Beatrice	Reg'd. June 16, 1880/No. 350972
S	Corinthia	-
M	Eagle	-
F	Hague	-
F	Ladygrass	-
S	Lozere	-
P/M	Melton	-
A	Oceanic	-
S	Parma	-
A	Raleigh	-
S	Woronzoff (Patent Teapot)	Reg'd. Sept. 17, 1867/No. 211290

FLOW BLUE

CATEGORY	PATTERN
S	Atlanta
A	Beryl
F	Burlington
F	Camelia
O	Chinese
O	Chusan
S	Clytie
-	Corea
-	Corinthia
S	"Cows"
F	Dahlia
F	Daphne
M	Eagle
-	Evangeline
F	Fern
M	"Fish Plate"
-	Granada
F	Hague
F	Hastings
-	Hilda
F	Horticulture
M/F	Indiana
A	Irene
A	Lace
A	Montrose
F	Nancy
A	Navarre
F	Niobe
F	Peach Blossom
-	Phoebe
A	Poppy
F	Roma
F	Romeo
-	Shannon
-	Shell
F	Sibyl
-	Swallow
M	Tavarre
O	Temple*
-	Venus
M/F	Vine
F	Violet

*See Podmore Walker

MULBERRY WARES

CATEGORY	PATTERN
F	Camelia
P/O	Chusan #1
P/O	Chusan #2
S	Corinthia
S	Eagle
M	Garland

WHITE IRONSTONE

"Arbor Vine"
Athens Shape
"Bordered Gooseberry"*
"Flora"
"Hyacinth Shape"
"Late Tulip"
Laurel "Shape"
"Plain Round"
"Plain Square"
"Square Ridged"

*Once known as "Branch of Three Leaves"

TEA LEAF/COPPER LUSTRE

"Chelsea"
"Daisy & Tulip"
"Fleur-de-lis Chain" ["Daisy Chain"]
"Simple Square: Wedgwood Plain"
"Square Ridged"
"Wedgwood's Ribbed"

JOSIAH WEDGWOOD (& SONS LTD.)

BLUE AND WHITE TRANSFERWARE

SERIES

1. BLUE ROSE BORDER SERIES
(Landscape Patterns) c. 1824

"Blue Rose"
"A Country House & River"
"An Estuary"
"Greenwich Hospital"
"A Harbor Scene" ["Sicilian Pattern"]
"Landscape With Blue Rose Border"
"Many-storied Pagoda"
"A River Scene"
"A Scene With a River and Church"
"Tower of London"
"A View of Kirkstall Abbey"
"A View of the Rookery Surrey"

N.B.: *Coysh*, Vol. 1, p. 45, notes that "it is possible that some of the marked Wedgwood patterns with this [Blue Rose] border are made by Podmore Walker & Co."

2. BOTANICAL PATTERNS, c. 1807-1809
(90 Numbered Floral Prints)
BLUE AND WHITE TRANSFERWARE
SINGLE PATTERNS - EARLY
N.B.: No Categories are Noted

DATE	PATTERN
c.1834	"Arch Border" ["Medieval"]
c.1822-5	"Absalom's Tomb ["Absalom's Pillar"]
c.1820	"Basket of Flowers"
1805	Blue Bamboo ["Chinese Vase"]
1805	Blue Basket ["Fruit Basket"]
1829	Blue Birds and Nets (2) ["Blue Bird Cage"]
1809	Blue Botanical Flowers (series)
1811	Blue Bridge* ["Chinese Economy of Time"]
1817	Blue Broseley
1834	Blue Cairo
1822	Blue Claude
1822	Blue Convolvulus Border
1811	Blue Corinth
1832	Blue Ferrara
1830	Blue Garland
1842	Blue Goats
1819	Blue Group
1821	Blue Lotus
1812	Blue Pagoda
1815	Blue Palisade
1822	Blue Pavillion
1806	Blue Peony
1823	Blue Poppy
1824	Blue Rose
1811	Blue Water Lily
1841	Blue Zodiac

*Noted on Earthenware and China

c.1806-10	"Chinese Garden" ["Palisade"]
c.1827	"Cows and Herdsman"
c.1825-35	"Crane" Pattern
c.1812	"Dogs of Fo"*
c.1843	"Fruit Basket"
c,1830-40	"Golden Palm"
c.1825	"Gothic Ruins"
c.1806-7	"Hibiscus"
c.1843	"Landscape With Grapes and Chain"
1828	"New Chinese Temples"
c.1822	"Pavillion
c.1860+	"Pearl"
c.1807	"Peony"
c.1830-35	"Rococo Scrolls"
c.1830-40	"Roses and Butterflies"
c.1830-35	"Swan"
c.1860+	"Two Crested Exotic Birds"
c.1817	"Two Temples"
c.1808-11	"Water Lily" ["Lotus"]
c.1827	"Water Tower"
c. 1818-20	"Willow" Pattern ["Minton's Willow"]
1843	Windmill**

*Noted on Earthenware and China
**Reg'd. Mar. 21, 1843/No. 5266-70
The following patterns do not have a date or approximate date of issuance.
"Dragon"
"Fishspearing"
March (True pattern name)
"Mounted Procession on Bridge"
"Poterat"
BLUE AND WHITE TRANSFERWARE*
SINGLE PATTERNS - LATE

CATEGORY	PATTERN	
F	Bouquet	Reg'd. Aug. 3, 1846/No. 36441-8
O	"Chinese Baroque"	Impressed Wedgwood S.S.
M	Corinth	-
S	Edinburgh	-
S	Ferrara	-
Z	Grouse	-
S	"Harbor Scene"	-
S	Landscape	Dated 1878 & Reissued after 1891
	"ENGLAND"	
-	Marguerite	Reg'd. Feb. 19, 1869/No. 227345
M	Marigold	-
P/O	Pekin	-

*See *Reilly's Wedgwood* 1995, pp. 436-437 for Blue & White Underglazed blue printing.
FLOW BLUE

CATEGORY	PATTERN	
F	Bramble	-
-	Bull Finch**	-
O	Chinese	-
O	Chusan/Oriental	(Two names, same pattern)
F	Clover	Dated 1860
O	Crown Imperial	-
P/O	Eastern Flowers	-
S	Ferrara	-
S	Festoon	-
S	Festoon, The	-
F	Flowers**	-
F	Garland	-
-	Hinse	-
F	Hollyhock	-
L	Ivanhoe	c. 1901 (Commemorative Ware)
-	Key Border**	-
-	Nankin	-
O	Oriental/Chusan	(Two names/same pattern)
F	Raleigh	-
S	Raphael	-
F	Rose & Jessamine	-
M/F	Shannon	-
F	Swallow	Dated March 1900
M	Trophy	
-	Vermicelli**	-
M/F	Vine	Dated 1860
F	Water Nymph	-

**See *Reilly's Wedgwood* 1995, p. 185, for Woodbine information on "Flow (Flown) Blue"
MULBERRY WARES

CATEGORY	PATTERN	
F	Arabesque	-
F	Bouquet	Reg'd. 1846
S	Festoon, The	-
P/F	Hollyhock	-
F	Horticultural	-
F	Moresque	Reg'd. 1846
F	Napier	Reg'd. 1846
F	Nymphaea*	Reg'd. 1872
P/F	Ranunculus	-
F	Rose & Jessamine	Reg'd. 1846
F	"Woodland Glen"	-

*Same pattern as Water Nymph in Flow Blue

WHITEHAVEN POTTERY
PATTERNS IN BLUE & WHITE TRANSFERWARE

JOHN WILKINSON
(INITIALS I.W. (OR) J.W.)
-Antiques
-Amoy
-Bosphorus (or J.W.)
-Charity (or. J.W.)
-Marseillaise (or J.W.)
-"Mayfield"
-Minstrel
-"Peel Castle, Isle of Man"
-Pekin
-Terrace
-"Willow" Pattern

MARY WILKINSON
(INITIALS M.W.)
-Asiatic Pheasants
-Marble Ice

RANDLE WILKINSON
(INITIALS R.W.)
-Pagoda

WHITEHAVEN POTTERY
(INITIALS W.P. CO.)
-Marseillaise

WHITEHAVEN
(WOODNORTH, HARRISON & HALL)
-Country House on the River
N.B.: Additional comments on Whitehaven Pottery patterns are noted in *F.O.B.* No. 86, January 95, p. 12, in an article by Florence Sibson. Further, *Coysh*, Vol. 1 and Vol. 2 notes additional Blue & White Transferware patterns as follows:

CATEGORY	PATTERN
S	"Church & College of St. Bees"
M	"Free Trade" ["Masonic"]
S	"Hillis Bowl"
M	"Littledale" Mug
M	Loretta
G	Puzzle ["Marriage Puzzle"]
S	Rhine
G	The Ruined Family ["The Drunkard Doom"]
S	"Seaweed"

WHITTAKER, HEATH & CO.
BLUE AND WHITE TRANSFERWARE
SINGLE PATTERNS

CATEGORY	PATTERN
S	Fairy

WHITTAKER & CO.
BLUE AND WHITE TRANSFERWARE
SINGLE PATTERNS

CATEGORY	PATTERN	
-	Alaska	
O	Bombay	Reg'd. 1887/No. 71582
O	Oriental*	

*See *P. Williams Staffordshire*, Vol. III, p. 21 for illustration and registry date 1887.

WHITTINGHAM, FORD & CO.
FLOW BLUE

CATEGORY	PATTERN
O	Singanese
S	Temple

WHITTINGHAM, FORD & RILEY
BLUE AND WHITE TRANSFERWARE
SINGLE PATTERNS

CATEGORY	PATTERN
J/G	Rustic

JAMES F. WILEMAN
BLUE AND WHITE TRANSFERWARE
SINGLE PATTERNS

CATEGORY	PATTERN
-	Etruscan
F	Moss Rose
P/O	Nankin
S	Rhine
Z	"Swallow"
F	Victoria

FLOW BLUE

CATEGORY	PATTERN
F	Albert

WHITE IRONSTONE
Richelieu Shape
TEA LEAF/COPPER LUSTRE
Richelieu Shape
"Wheat"

J. & C. WILEMAN
WHITE IRONSTONE
"Poppy Shape"*
*Same as Scotia Shape by F. Jones & Co., both are concave.

ARTHUR J. WILKINSON (LTD.)
BLUE AND WHITE TRANSFERWARE
SINGLE PATTERNS

CATEGORY	PATTERN
F	Arcadia
S	Harvest
F	Iris
G	Jenny Lind
A	Marseilles
O	Tonquin
P/O	Yeddo

FLOW BLUE

CATEGORY	PATTERN
F	Arcadia
F	Carnation
-	Conway
F	Davenport
M/F	Festoon
F	Flora
S	Harvest
-	Ideal
F	Iowa
F	Iris
G	Jenny Lind
A	Lichfield
M	Mikado
P/O	Pekin
A	Renown
-	Worcester
O	Yeddo

WHITE IRONSTONE
"Bow Knot (Wilkinson's)"
"Cable & Ring"
"Daisy 'n Chain"
"Forget-Me-Not"
"Hawthorn"
"Maidenhair Fern"
"Plain Square"
"Ribbed Fern"
Senate Shape
"Sunburst"
"Wheat"
TEA LEAF/COPPER LUSTRE
"Bow Knot"
"Daisy 'n Chain"
"Hawthorn"
"Maidenhair Fern"
Senate Shape
"Sunburst"

WILLIAM WILLIAMS
FLOW BLUE

CATEGORY	PATTERN
O	Rio

MULBERRY WARES

CATEGORY	PATTERN
O	Rio

ISAAC WILSON & CO.
BLUE AND WHITE TRANSFERWARE
SINGLE PATTERNS

CATEGORY	PATTERN
S	Caledonia
O	"Willow" Pattern

MULBERRY WARES

CATEGORY	PATTERN
F	Rosa Centifolia

WILTSHAW & ROBINSON (LTD.)
FLOW BLUE

CATEGORY	PATTERN	
F	Arvista	-
O	Chusan	-
F	Florida	Reg'd. 1892/No. 201360
F	Petunia	Reg'd. 1895, 1896 & 1899/ No. 337779
F	Vine Flowers	-

F. WINKLE & CO. (LTD.)
BLUE AND WHITE TRANSFERWARE
SINGLE PATTERNS

CATEGORY	PATTERN
P/O	Old Chelsea
P/O	Pekin
P/Z	Pheasant
S	Togo

FLOW BLUE

CATEGORY	PATTERN	
S	Agra	
M	Byron	
-	Clifton	
-	Dart	
F	Huron	
A	Kelmscott	Reg'd. 1902/No. 396132
A	Kingston	
F	Lucerne	
A	Malverne	Reg'd. 1903/No. 406306
F	Matlock	
F	Ripon	
F	Royal	
A	Rudyard	
S	Togo	
F	Zeeland	

THOMAS WOLFE(S)
BLUE AND WHITE TRANSFERWARE
SINGLE PATTERNS

CATEGORY	PATTERN
M	"Basket" ["Twig Basket"]
O	"Buddleia"
-	"Buffalo"
O	Conversation*

*Refer to Penny Plain, p. 98, No. 228

WOOLFE, HAMILTON & CO.
BLUE AND WHITE TRANSFERWARE
SINGLE PATTERNS

CATEGORY	PATTERN
-	"Cupids"

ARTHUR WOOD & SON (LONGPORT) LTD.
FLOW BLUE

CATEGORY	PATTERN
S	"Country Pastures"

MULBERRY WARES

CATEGORY	PATTERN
D	Keswick

WOOD & BAGGALEY

FLOW BLUE

CATEGORY	PATTERN
-	Amerilla
O	Ciris
M	Doric
F	Eastern Plants
O	Hindoostan
O	Japanese No. __
O	Madras*
F	Viola

MULBERRY WARES

CATEGORY	PATTERN
O	Madras*

*Pattern appears identical to pattern by Doulton & Co.

WOOD & BARKER LTD.

FLOW BLUE

CATEGORY	PATTERN
F	Viola

WOOD & BRETTEL

BLUE AND WHITE TRANSFERWARE

SINGLE PATTERNS

CATEGORY	PATTERN
F	"Bird Feeding Its Young, et.al." ["Bird's Nest"]
O	Chinese Gardener
M	"Dairy Pail"

WOOD & BROWNFIELD

BLUE AND WHITE TRANSFERWARE

SINGLE PATTERNS

CATEGORY	PATTERN
-	Albion
-	"Bird's Nest"
S	Grecian Statue
O	Indian Tree
O	Japanese
G	Juvenile
S	Palmyra

FLOW BLUE

CATEGORY	PATTERN
F	Ambrosia
F	Arcadia
O	Birmah (att.)
F	Chantilly
O	Ciris
M	Doric
M/F	Etruscan
O	Field Sports
S	Grecian Stone
O	Hindoostan
O	Nankin
O	Pekin
S	Rhone
O	Temple
F	Windsor Wreath

MULBERRY WARES

CATEGORY	PATTERN	
F	Althea	
F	Botanical	
F	Chantilly ["Floral"]	Reg'd. Mar. 20, 1848/No. 50994
F	Chinese Tree	
F	Chiswick	
F	Claremont	
F	Corinthian	
F	Etruscan	
F	Floral Scroll, #3159	
F	Indian Tree	
O	Madras	
F	Moultan	
F	Oriental	
F	Pomona	
F	"Ribbon Flower"	Reg'd. Mar. 20, 1848/No. 50994
F	Sweaborg	Reg'd. Mar. 20, 1848/No. 50994
F	Windsor Wreath	

WOOD & CALDWELL

BLUE AND WHITE TRANSFERWARE

SINGLE PATTERNS

CATEGORY	PATTERN
-	"Fishing"
-	"Temple"

HISTORIC STAFFORDSHIRE SERIES

AMERICAN & CANADIAN

1. MISCELLANEOUS

Ames, Fisher

N.B.: See Arman, *Anglo-American*, Ch. 2 "The Enoch Wood & Sons Group".

WOOD & CHALLINOR

BLUE AND WHITE TRANSFERWARE

SERIES

1. "CONTINENTAL VIEWS" SERIES

Bachrach

Castle Mount Dragon

Lake Como

Rimini

Viege

BLUE AND WHITE TRANSFERWARE

SINGLE PATTERNS

CATEGORY	PATTERN
S	Blue Italian
S	Castle of Beaucaire
M	Centenary
O	Chinese Temples
S	Cologne
G	Corsica
M/F	Feather
S	Font (The) ["Girl at the Well"]
F	"Italian"
S	Klumn
M/F	Lily
S	Messina
O	Pagoda
S	Patras
Z	Pheasant
F	Tower of Mauconseil
F	"Wounded Leg"* (Pap Boat)

*See *True Blue*, p. 83, No. 5.

FLOW BLUE

CATEGORY	PATTERN
M/F	Shell

MULBERRY WARES

CATEGORY	PATTERN
S	Messina

WOOD & CHALLINOR & CO.

BLUE AND WHITE TRANSFERWARE

SINGLE PATTERNS

CATEGORY	PATTERN
S	Corsica
S	Messina

WOOD & HULME

FLOW BLUE

CATEGORY	PATTERN
F	Ripon

WOOD & PIGOTT

BLUE AND WHITE TRANSFERWARE

SINGLE PATTERNS

CATEGORY	PATTERN	
O	Madras	
S	Wien*	Reg'd. Apr. 1, 1869/No. 228290

*See *Victorian Pottery* by Hugh Wakefield, London, England, Herbert Jenkins, 1962. p. 186

FLOW BLUE

CATEGORY	PATTERN
O	Madras

EDMUND T. WOOD

WHITE IRONSTONE

"Coral"

Corn-on-the-Cob Shape ["Corn & Oats"]*

*Reg'd. Oct. 31, 1863/No. 167761-3.

ENOCH WOOD

BLUE AND WHITE TRANSFERWARE

SINGLE PATTERNS

CATEGORY	PATTERN
S	"British Countryside"
O	"Dagger Border Chinoiserie"
O	"Diamond Sunburst Border" (att.)
J	"Little Girls Playing Ball"
O	Pekin
-	"Sportsman"
S	"Swiss Farm"
-	"Thatched Cottage & Wicker Settee"
S	"Thames River Scene"
S	Virginia
O	"Willow" Pattern

FLOW BLUE CATEGORY	PATTERN
O	"Rock" (?)

ENOCH WOOD & SONS
BLUE AND WHITE TRANSFERWARE SERIES
1. CUPID PATTERN SERIES
The Bride
Cupid Imprisoned
Cupid's Escape
Girl Behind Grape Fence
The Young Philosopher
2. ENGLISH CITIES SERIES
Chester
Chichester
Coke, Denton
Coventry
Durham
Edinburgh
Ely
Exeter
Hereford
Leeds
Lincoln
Litchfield
Liverpool (2 views)
London
Norwich
Oxford (2 views)
Peterborough
Rochester
Salisbury
Wells
Worcester
York
3. GRAPEVINE BORDER SERIES
Armitage Park, Staffordshire
Barlborough Hall, Derbyshire
Bedfords, Essex
Belsay Castle, Northumberland
Belvoir Castle, Leichestershire
Bickley, Kent
Brancepeth Castle, Durham
Cashiobury, Hertfordshire
Castle Forbes, Aberdeenshire
Castle Huntley, Perthshire
Cathedral at York
Cave Castle, Yorkshire
City of Canterbury
Claremont, Surrey
Cokethorpe Park, Oxfordshire
Compton Verney, Warwickshire
Culzean Castle, Ayrshire
Dalguise, Perthshire
Dorney Court, Buckinghamshire
Dunraven, Glamorgan
Durham Cathedral
Esholt House, Yorkshire
Fonthill Abbey, Wiltshire (2 views, near and distant)
Gnoll Castle, Glamorganshire
Goodridge Castle, Kent
Gubbins, Hertfordshire
Gunton Hall, Norfolk
Guy's Cliff, Warwickshire
Hagley, Worcestershire
Hare Hall, Essex*
Harewood House, Yorkshire
Hollywell Cottage, Cavan
Holyrood House, Edinburgh
Hylands, Essex
Kenilworth Castle, Warwickshire
Kenmount, Dumfriesshire
Lambton Hall, Durham
Luscombe, Devon
Maxstoke Castle, Warwickshire
Moditonham House, Cornwall
Orielton, Pembrokeshire
Oxburgh Hall, Norfolk
Part of Goodridge Castle, Kent
Powderham Castle, Devonshire
Rochester Castle
The Rookery, Surrey
Ross Castle, Monmouthshire
Saltwood Castle
Sharon Castle
Sherbourn Castle**
Shirley House, Surrey ["Coombs House"]
Spring Vale, Staffordshire
Sproughton Chantry, Suffolk
Sufton Court, Herefordshire
Taymouth Castle, Perthshire
Thornton Castle, Staffordshire
Thrybergh, Yorkshire
View of Greenwich
View of Richmond
View of Worcester
Wardour Castle, Wiltshire (2 slight variants)
Warwick Castle
Wellcombe, Warwickshire
Windsor Castle
N.B.:See *Arman Quarterly*, Vol. 1, April/May 1997, No. 2, pp. 14-18 for new patterns finds for the Grapevine Border Series by Norman Wolf.
*See *Arman Quarterly*, Vol. 1, July/August 1997, No. 3, p. 38.
**See *FOB*, No. 99, Spring 1998, pp. 4-5.
4. ITALIAN SCENERY SERIES
The Arch of Janus
"Between Sarzano & Massa, et.al."
Bridge of Lucano
Castle of Lavenza
Castle of Nepi, Italy
Castle of St. Angelo, Rome
Chateau de Chillon
Coliseum
Fisherman's Island, Lago Maggiori
Florence
Genoa
La Riccia
Lake of Albano
Lake Avernus
Naples from Capo di Chino
Ponte del Palazzo
Ponte Rotto
St. Peter's, Rome
Sarento
Temple of Venus, Rome
Terni
Tivoli
Turin
Venice
Vesuvius
View Near Florence
Villa Borghese, Near Florence
Villa on the Coast of Posilepo
5. "LONDON VIEWS" SERIES
"Bank of England, London"
"Church of England Missionary College, London"
"Clarence House"
"Clarence Terrace, Regent's Park, London"
"The Coliseum"
"Cornwall Terrace, Regent's Park, London"
"Cumberland Terrace, Regent's Park, London"
"Doric Villa in Regent's Park, London"
"Eastgate, Regent's Park, London"
"Finsbury Chapel"
"Hanover Lodge, Regent's Park, London"
"Hanover Terrace, Regent's Park, London"
"Highbury College, London"
"The Holme, Regent's Park, London"
"The Lake, Regent's Park, London"
"Limehouse Dock, Regent's Canal, London"
"The London Institution"
"Macclesfield Bridge, Regent's Park, London"
"Part of Regent Street, London"
"The Regent's Quadrant, London" ["The Limehouse Dock & Regent's Canal"]
"Royal Hospital, Regent's Park, London"
"St. George's Chapel, Regent Street, London"
"St. Paul's School, London"
"St. Phillip's Chapel, Regent Street, London"
"Sussex Place, Regent's Park, London"
"Ulster Terrace, Regent's Park, London"
"Villa in the Regent's Park, London" (3 views)
"York Gate, Regent's Park, London"
6. SCRIPTURAL SERIES
Christ and the Woman of Samaria
The Coming of the Wise Men
Death of Abel
The Flight Into Egypt
Jacob and the Angel
The Nativity
Peter in the Garden
The Return
Revelation
7. SPORTING SERIES
Antelope
Beaver

Deer Hunting
Elephant
Hunter Shooting Ducks
Hunter Shooting Fox
Hyena [Spotted Hyena]
Leopard
Lion
Moose
Pointer and Quail
Polar Bear Hunting
Ram, Ewe and Lamb
Squirrel
Tibetan Musk
Tiger Hunt
Two Whippets
Wolf and Other Animals
Zebra
BLUE AND WHITE TRANSFERWARE
SINGLE PATTERNS

CATEGORY	PATTERN	
S	"Beehive & Cottage"	
O	Belzoni* (4)	
-	"Bird"	
O	Canton #107	
S	Cetara	
G	Chevy Chase	
S	"Country Manor"	
S	Damascus	
S	Eastern Scenery No. I & II** (possible series)	
C	Etruscan Vase	
S	European Scenery	
G	"Feeding the Swans"	
S	Festoon Border	
G	Fisherman	
S	Fountain	
G	"Girl Holding a Parrot"	
-	"Goat"	
-	"Gondola"	
S	Grecian Scenery	
J	"Hen and Chicks"	
S	Lake Scenery (2)	
S	Lucerne	Reg'd. July 5, 1845/No. 28672
-	"Newburg"	
P/O	No. 107	
P/S	Railway	
F	Regina	
G	"Sleigh Ride"***	
S	Suspension Bridge	
S	Swiss	
S	Valenciennes	
S	Venetian Scenery	
C	Warwick Vase	
C	Washington	
S	Wreath and Flowers	

*Possibly a series. Refer to *Snyder, Romantic Staffordshire,* pp. 171-172.
**Also recorded in Mulberry
***See *FOB Bulletin*, No. 95, Spring 1997, p. 3.
HISTORIC STAFFORDSHIRE SERIES
AMERICAN & CANADIAN
1. REGULAR SHELL BORDER SERIES
(Canadian Views)
Montmorenci Falls ["Fall of Montmorenci Near Quebec"]
Quebec (Heights of)
Table Rock At Niagara
2. REGULAR SHELL BORDER SERIES
(Hudson River Scenes)
Albany, City of, State of New York
Baltimore & Ohio Railroad (Level)
Baltimore & Ohio Railroad (Inclined Plane)
Belleville On The Passaic River
Capitol at Washington [Mount Vernon]
Castle Garden, Battery, New York [Niagara Falls or Lake George] (3)
Catskill, Hope Mill, State of New York
Catskill (Katskill) House, Hudson
Catskill Mountain, Pass, In The
Catskill Mountains, Hudson River (Palisades, River, and Steamboat)
Gilpin's Mills On the Brandywine Creek
Greensburg, Tappan Zee, (From)
Highlands, Hudson River [Lake George]
Highlands, At West Point, Hudson River
Highlands, Hudson River, Near Newburgh [Highlands at West Point, Hudson River]
Hudson River View
Lake George, State of New York
Marine Hospital, Louisville, KY (2)
Mount Vernon [Capitol at Washington]
New York Bay
Niagara Falls From the American Side
Passaic Falls, State of New Jersey [Belleville on the Passaic River]
Pine Orchard House, Catskills [Trenton Falls]
Pine Orchard House, Catskill Mountain (Distant View of Inn)
See: "Ships With American Flags Series"
Table Rock, Niagara
Trenton Falls, View of (Three People on Overhanging Rock)
Trenton Falls, View of [Catskill House] (One Man At Foot of Falls)
Washington* [White House, President's House Washington] (2)
West Point Military Academy
White House, Wash.*
*See Snyder, *Historic Staffordshire*, p. 127
3. CELTIC CHINA SERIES
Belleville on the Passaic River
Buffalo on Lake Erie
Castle Garden, Battery, New York
Columbus ["GA"]
Fairmount Water Works on the Schuylkill (Philadelphia)
Fishkill, Hudson River (Near)
Harvard College
Highlands, Hudson River
Lake George, State of New York
Natural Bridge, Virginia
New York From Staten Island
Niagara Falls
Pass In The Catskill Mountains
Riceborough, Georgia
Shipping Port On the Ohio, Kentucky
Transylvania University, Lexington, KY
Trenton Falls
West Point Military Academy
Wooding Station On The Mississippi
4. ERIE CANAL SERIES
Entrance of Erie Canal into the Hudson at Albany
View of the Aqueduct Bridge at Little Falls
Aqueduct Bridge at Rochester
5. FLORAL BORDER/IRREGULAR CENTER
Commodore MacDonnough's Victory
Entrance of the Erie Canal into the Hudson
Erie Canal, Aqueduct Bridge at Rochester
Erie Canal, View of the Aqueduct Bridge at Little Falls
6. FOUR MEDALLION/FLORAL BORDER SERIES
Castle Garden
Department of State, Washington
Dumb Asylum, Philadelphia
Harvard University
Monte Video
New Haven, State House
Northampton, Mass.
Pace Bridge, Philadelphia
President's House, Washington
Residence of S. Russell
7. FRANKLIN'S TOMB SERIES
Lafayette at Franklin's Tomb
Lafayette at Washington's Tomb
Washington Standing at his Tomb, Scroll in Hand
8. FRENCH VIEWS SERIES [FRENCH SERIES]
Cascade De Gresy Pres Chambery
Chapelle De Guillaume Tell
Chateau Coucey (Vue du)
Chateau Ermenonville (Vue du)
East View of La Grange (The Residence of The Marquis de Lafayette)
Environs De Chambery
"French View, Buildings at Left, et.al."
"French View, Building with Covered Terrace"
"French View, Horses in Foreground, et.al."
"French View, Long Stone Bridge With One Arched Section, Building on Left, et.al."
"French View, Stone Bridge With One Arched Section, et.al."
Hermitage En Dauphne
La Grange, The Residence of the Marquis Lafayette
Maison De Raphael
Moulin Pres De Royal, Dept. Du Puy De Dome
Moulin Sur La Marne A Charenton
Moulin Sur La Marne A Charenton (Varient)
Northwest View of La Grange (The Residence of Marquis Lafayette)
Southwest View of La Grange (The Residence of Marquis Lafayette)
Peter Morton Hartford (mkd)
Vue De La Porte Romaine Andernac
Vue Du Temple De La Philosophie, Ermenonville
Vue D'Une Ancienne Abbaye
Vue Prise Aux Environs De Francfort
Vue Prise En Savoie
N.B.: Also see Coysh, Vol. 1, French Series
9. "IRREGULAR SHELL BORDER SERIES"
(Ships With American Flags)
The Beach at Brighton
"Cadmus" (So Called) (2)
"Cadmus" ("At Anchor") ["Ship at Anchor"]
"Cadmus" ("Under Full Sail")
"Cadmus" ("Under Half Sail")
Cape Coast Castle On the Gold Coast, Africa
Chief Justice Marshall, Troy ["Troy Line, Steamboat"]
Chiswick On The Thames
Christianburg, Danish Settlement On The Gold Coast, Africa

Commodore MacDonnough's Victory (3)
Constitution And (The) Guerriera (So Called)
Cowes Harbor
Dartmouth
Dix Cove On the Gold Coast, Africa
East Cowes, Isle of Wight
The Eddistone Light ["Lighthouse"]
Erith on the Thames
The Kent,, East Indiaman
Marine Hospital, Louisville, Kentucky (2)
Near Calcutta
Ship Of The Line in the Downs
Southampton, Hampshire
"Ship, Two Sailboats, et.al."
"Ship, Two Sailboats & Rowboat, et.al."
"Ship Under Half Sail, et.al."
Union Line
View of Dublin
View of Liverpool
Wadsworth Tower (2)
Whitby
Yarmouth, Isle of Wight
For further information, refer to *Coysh*, Vol. 1, p. 333; *Laidacker*, Part II, pp. 103-104; and *Arman*, pp. 57-67
10. "TREFOIL" BORDER SERIES
Cadmus
Castle Garden, Battery, New York
Cottage in the Woods
11. MISCELLANEOUS
Boston State House
Brown* ["Major Gen. Brown, Niagara"]
"Chancellor Livingston" [Steamboat]
Eagle on Rock (Steamboat in Background)
General Jackson, Hero of New Orleans
Lafayette and Washington
Lafayette at Franklin's Tomb
Lafayette at Washington's Tomb
The Landing of the Fathers at Plymouth, Dec. 22, 1620
Lawrence (Captain James)
"Rural Homes"*
Wadsworth Tower**
Washington [Statue of Washington by Canova]
Washington Standing at His Tomb, Scroll In Hand
*Refer to *Laidacker*, Part 2, p. 107
***Larsen*, p. 52, No. 108 and p. 228, No. 607

H.J. WOOD (LTD.)
FLOW BLUE

CATEGORY	PATTERN
S	Countryside

JOHN WEDGE WOOD
BLUE AND WHITE TRANSFERWARE
SINGLE PATTERNS

CATEGORY	PATTERN	
S	Brussels	
F	Cashmere	
S	Columbia	Reg'd. Aug. 23, 1848/No. 54018
S	Festoon	
S	Geneva	Reg'd. 1847
S	Hibernia	
F	Japan Daisy	
M	Jessamine	
M	Marble	
S	Milesian	
S	Peruvian	Reg'd. May 24, 1849/No. 60081
M	Sea Fan	
S	Seine	
S	Singanese	
O	Tippecanoe	
-	Trafalgar	
S	Tyrol	

HISTORIC STAFFORDSHIRE SERIES
AMERICAN & CANADIAN
1. MISCELLANEOUS
Log Cabin/North Bend*
* See *Arman Quarterly*, Vol. 1, 1997, p. 36 pictured with Importer's marking "James Tams & Co."
FLOW BLUE

CATEGORY	PATTERN	
O	Chapoo	Teaset Reg'd. Sept. 25 (16 Paneled) 1847/ No. 45992
O	Chapoo	Dinner Set Reg'd. Oct. 8, 1847/ No.46265
F	Geranium	-
S	Peruvian	Reg'd. May 24, 1849/No. 60081

MULBERRY WARES

CATEGORY	PATTERN	
S	Peruvian	Reg'd. May 24, 1849/No. 60081

WHITE IRONSTONE

"Angled Leaf"	-
"Coral Shape"	Reg'd. Mar. 17, 1847/No. 42044
"Corn & Oats Shape" [Corn-on-the-Cob Shape]*	Reg'd. Oct. 31, 1863/No. 167762
"Eagle"	-
"Early Cameo"	-
"Fenton Jug"	-
"Fig Cousin"[Niagara Shape][1]	-
"Fig Shape" [Union Shape]**	-
"Fluted Band Shape"	Reg'd. Sept. 25, 1847/No. 45992
"Fluted Pearl Shape"	Reg'd. Oct. 8, 1847/No. 46265
"Gothic Cameo Shape"	Reg'd. Aug. 23, 1848/No. 54018
"Hyacinth"	-
"Primary"	-
"Relish Dish"***	-
"Scalloped Decagon Shape" [Cambridge Shape]****	-
"Sharon Arch Shape" [Erie Shape]*****	-

[1]See comments under William Davenport.
*Originally registered as Corn-on-the-Cob Shape by Davenport, Banks & Co. on Jan. 12, 1863 and referred to as "Corn & Oats Shape" by White Ironstone collectors.
**Originally registered by William Davenport on Nov. 14, 1856/No. 107038 as "Union Shape" and referred to as "Fig Shape" by White Ironstone collectors.
***Originally registered by William Davenport on Oct. 23, 1852/No. 87219
****Originally registered by William Davenport on Oct. 6, 1854 as "Cambridge Shape" and referred to as "Scalloped Decagon Shape" by White Ironstone collectors.
*****Originally registered by William Davenport as Erie Shape on April 12, 1861/No. 139714-5

JOHN WOOD & CO. (LTD.)
BLUE AND WHITE TRANSFERWARE
SINGLE PATTERNS

CATEGORY	PATTERN
F	Albion
S	Wild Rose
O	"Willow" Pattern

THOMAS WOOD & CO.
BLUE AND WHITE TRANSFERWARE
SINGLE PATTERNS

CATEGORY	PATTERN
O	"Willow" Pattern

THOMAS WOOD & SONS
BLUE AND WHITE TRANSFERWARE
SINGLE PATTERNS

CATEGORY	PATTERN
S	Balmoral

WOOD & SON(S) (LTD.)
BLUE AND WHITE TRANSFERWARE
SINGLE PATTERNS

CATEGORY	PATTERN
A	Aquatic
A	Aquila
F	Argyle
A	Cambridge
O	Canton
S	Cashiobury Hertfordshire (Reissue, c. 1931)
S	English Scenery
F	Forest Flowers
F	Hyde
H	"Martha Washington" ["Chain of States"]
H	Mountain House
O	"Nankow Willow"
O	"Old-Bow-Kakiyem"
A	Sea Forth
F	Sevres
P/S	Verona
O	"Willow" Pattern
S	Wortham Abbey (Reissue, c. 1931)
O	Yuan

FLOW BLUE

CATEGORY	PATTERN	
M/A	Adams	-
A	Alva	-
F	Argyle	-
A	Baronia	-
A	Berkley	-
F	Brunswick	-
S	Brunswick Evangeline	-
F	Byzantine	-
-	Carlton	-
F	Carmania	-
M/A	Conway	-
S	Country Scenes	-
A	Davenport	-
M	Delph	-
-	Denton	-
M	Duchess	-
-	Dudley	-
-	Eagle	-
A	Elise	-

-	Evangeline	-
F	Excelsior	-
M/A	Florence	Reg'd. 1891/No. 180288
F	Garland	-
A	Glenwood	-
F	Keswick	-
O	Khotan	-
A	Lakewood	Reg'd. 1899/No. 348700
F	Leicester	-
A	Lusitania	-
F	Madras	-
M	Manskillan	-
F	Marlborough	-
H	Martha Washington ["Chain of States"]	-
F	Milan	Reg'd. 1903/No. 412413
F	Milton	-
F	Monarch	-
S	Moselle	-
-	"Oriental Birds"	-
F	Paris Royal	-
O	Pekin	-
F	Prince	-
F	Princess	-
-	St. Regis	-
F	Seurer	-
A	Seville	-
F	Sevres	Reg'd. 1903/No. 412432
F	Sydney	-
M/C	Trent (I)	-
F	Trent (II)	Reg'd. 1891/No. 180288
F	Trilby	-
-	Venice	-
S	Verona	-
F	Victoria	-
F	Waldorf	-
O	Wincanton	
F	Wisteria	-
A	Woodbine	-
F	Woodland	Reg'd. 1899/No. 339529
O	Yuan	-

N.B.: Many patterns were reissued after the acquisition of the New Wharf Pottery Co. in 1894

MULBERRY WARES

CATEGORY	PATTERN
F	Seville
F	Sydney
F	Royal
S	Woodland

WOOD, RATHBONE & CO.
WHITE IRONSTONE
"Forget-Me-Not"

WOOD, SON & CO.
WHITE IRONSTONE
Hyacinth

LEWIS WOOLF (& SONS)(& CO.)
BLUE AND WHITE TRANSFERWARE
SINGLE PATTERNS

CATEGORY	PATTERN
(LEWIS WOOLF)	
F	Albion
O	Chinese Marine (possible series)
S	Marseillaise
S	Rhine*

*Refer to *Yorkshire Pots*, p. 76, No. 111

(SYDNEY WOOLF)	
S	"Eton College"

MULBERRY WARES

CATEGORY	PATTERN
O	Chinese Flora (att.)

GEORGE WOOLISCROFT (& CO.)
BLUE AND WHITE TRANSFERWARE
SINGLE PATTERNS

CATEGORY	PATTERN	
F	Amula	-
P/S	Eon (possible series)	Reg'd. June 24, 1853/No. 91487
F	Excelsior	Reg'd. Feb. 10, 1853/No. 89626
F	Rosetta	-

WHITE IRONSTONE

Asia Shape	-
Baltic Shape*	Reg'd. Oct. 25, 1855/No. 102325
Columbia Shape	-
"Gothic Shell" Shape**	Reg'd. Feb. 10, 1853/No. 89626
"Lily-of-the-Valley" (Molded)	-
"Line Trim"	-
"Peach"	-
"Primary Shape"	

*Wetherbee, *White Ironstone, A Second Look*, pp. 57, 60, notes two other potters using the exact shape but with different names; Edward Pearson named his Mississippi Shape and Edward Corn named his Maltese Shape. This shape was registered in the name of D. Chetwynd. Additionally, John Meir (& Son) used this exact registry.
**See *White Ironstone Notes*, Vol. 4, No. 3, Winter 1998, p. 8

RICHARD WOOLLEY
BLUE AND WHITE TRANSFERWARE
SINGLE PATTERNS

CATEGORY	PATTERN
O	"Ornate Pagodas"

WORTHINGTON & HARROP
BLUE AND WHITE TRANSFERWARE
SINGLE PATTERNS

CATEGORY	PATTERN
F	Asiatic Pheasants
S	Rhine

YALE & BARKER
BLUE AND WHITE TRANSFERWARE
SINGLE PATTERNS

CATEGORY	PATTERN
S	Lavinia

YATES & MAY
BLUE AND WHITE TRANSFERWARE
SINGLE PATTERNS

CATEGORY	PATTERN
F	"Snowdrop"*

*See *P. Williams, Staffordshire II*, p. 47.

YNYSMEDW POTTERY
FLOW BLUE

CATEGORY	PATTERN
F	Alhambra
-	"Floral Center"
O	Kyber* (Rio)
O	Nankin
O	Rio* (Kyber)

*N.B.: These two are the same pattern with different names.

ALPHABETIC INDEX OF RECORDED ENGLISH PATTERNS, SHAPES, BORDERS & SERIES

See Addendum for Additional Patterns

POTTER	PATTERN
BRITANNIA POTTERY CO. LTD.	A Bit of Devon
SPODE/COPELAND & GARRETT, et.al.	A Colossal Sarcophagus at Cacamo
SPODE/COPELAND & GARRETT, et.al.	A Colossal Vase Near Limissio in Cyprus
JOSIAH WEDGWOOD (& SONS LTD.)	A Country House & River
SPODE/COPELAND & GARRETT, et.al.	A Domestic Ceremony
JOHN & WILLIAM RIDGWAY	A Drover With His Dog, et.al.
JOSIAH WEDGWOOD (& SONS LTD.)	A Harbor Scene
THOMAS GODWIN	A Man With A Gun, Two Eskimos and Two Dogs, et.al.
JAMES & RALPH CLEWS	A Noble Hunting Party
JOSIAH WEDGWOOD (& SONS LTD.)	A River Scene
CHESWORTH & ROBINSON	A Romantic District of Italy
RALPH HALL (& CO.) or (& SONS)	A Scene in the Campania of Rome, Italy
JOSIAH WEDGWOOD (& SONS LTD.)	A Scene With a River and Church
THOMAS GODWIN	A Scene With Dogs and a Sledge, A Group of Huntsmen, et.al.
EDWARD & GEORGE PHILLIPS	A Tear For Poland
SPODE/COPELAND & GARRETT, et.al.	A Triumphal Arch at Tripoli in Barbary
JAMES & RALPH CLEWS	A View Near Philadelphia
WILLIAM DAVENPORT	A View Near Philadelphia
JOSIAH WEDGWOOD (& SONS LTD.)	A View of Kirkstall Abbey
RALPH STEVENSON & WILLIAMS	A View of the Late Protestant Church in the City of Albany ...et.al.
JOSIAH WEDGWOOD (& SONS LTD.)	A View of the Rookery Surrey
SPODE/COPELAND & GARRETT, et.al.	A Wreath for the Victor
SAMUEL ALCOCK & CO.	Abbeville
EDWARD BOURNE	Abbey
ENOCH WOOD & SONS	Abbey
GEORGE JONES (& SONS LTD.)	Abbey
JOHN PRATT & CO. LTD.	Abbey

LIVESLEY, POWELL & CO.	Abbey
POUNTNEY & ALLIES	Abbey
POWELL & BISHOP	Abbey
R.S. KIDSTON & CO. - VERREVILLE	Abbey
SAMUEL KEELING & CO.	Abbey
T. & J. HOLLINS	Abbey
THOMAS EDWARDS	Abbey
WILLIAM ADAMS & SON(S)(POTTERS) LTD.	Abbey
GEORGE JONES (& SONS LTD.)	Abbey / Shredded Wheat Dish
DON POTTERY	Abbey Cloister
MINTON	Abbey Mill
JOHN ROGERS (& SON)	Abbey Ruins
THOMAS MAYER	Abbey Ruins
JAMES WALLACE & CO.	Abbey Ruins & Sailing Boat
JAMES WALLACE & CO.	Abbey Ruins and Horses
JOHN MADDOCK & SONS (LTD.)	Abbot
THOMAS SHIRLEY & CO.	Abbotsford
BELLE VUE POTTERIES	Abbotsford, Sir Walter Scott' s
BOURNE & LEIGH (LTD.)	Aberdeen
CHARLES MEIGH & SON	Aberdeen
J. & M.P. BELL (CO.) & (LTD.)	Abergeldie
J. & M.P. BELL (CO.) & (LTD.)	Aboyne
R. COCHRAN & CO. - VERREVILLE POTTERY	Abraham Hill
JOSIAH WEDGWOOD (& SONS LTD.)	Absalom's Pillar
JOSIAH WEDGWOOD (& SONS LTD.)	Absalom's Tomb
WILLIAM RIDGWAY (& CO.)	Acacia
JAMES & THOMAS EDWARDS	Acadia
WILLIAM HACKWOOD	Acadia
J. & G. MEAKIN	Acantha
JOHNSON BROS. (HANLEY), LTD.	Acanthus
SUNDERLAND OR "GARRISON" POTTERY	Accepted
J. & M.P. BELL (CO.) & (LTD.)	Achilles
SAMPSON HANCOCK (& SONS)	Acme
FURNIVALS LTD.	Acorn
J. & G. MEAKIN	Acorn
THOMAS & BENJAMIN GODWIN	Acorn
RALPH STEVENSON & WILLIAMS	ACORN & OAK LEAVES
RALPH STEVENSON	ACORN & OAK LEAVES BORDER SERIES
RALPH STEVENSON & WILLIAMS	ACORN & OAK LEAVES BORDER SERIES
ANDREW STEVENSON	ACORN & OAK LEAVES SERIES
SPODE/COPELAND & GARRETT, et.al.	Acratus With Female Carrying Myrtle
G.L. ASHWORTH & BROS. (LTD.)	Acropolis
HOPE & CARTER	Acropolis
PODMORE, WALKER (& CO.)	Acropolis
WILLIAM SMITH (& CO.)	Active
MYOTT, SON & CO. (LTD.)	Acton
WOOD & SON(S) (LTD.)	Adams
WILLIAM ADAMS & SON(S) (POTTERS) LTD.	Adams Scallop Shape
DOULTON & CO. (LTD.)	Adderley
DOULTON & CO. (LTD.)	Adelaide
FURNIVALS LTD.	Adelphi
J. & M.P. BELL (CO.) & (LTD.)	Aden
SPODE/COPELAND & GARRETT, et.al.	Aden
BARROW & CO.	Adriatic Shape
SPODE/COPELAND & GARRETT, et.al.	Advice to the Young
SPODE/COPELAND & GARRETT, et.al.	Aesop's Fables
SPODE'S BLUE PRINTED WARES	Aesop's Fables
DON POTTERY	Aetna from the Augustines
SUNDERLAND OR "GARRISON" POTTERY	African Daisies
EDWARD & GEORGE PHILLIPS	Africana
F. WINKLE & CO. (LTD.)	Agra
J. & M.P. BELL (CO.) & (LTD.)	Agra
RALPH HAMMERSLEY (& SON(S)	Agra
W.H. GRINDLEY & CO. (LTD.)	Agra
RIDGWAY, MORLEY, WEAR & CO.	Agricultural Vase
WILLIAM DAVENPORT	Agriculture
EDWARD F. BODLEY & CO. (& SON)	Alabama
JOHN RIDGWAY (& CO.)	Aladdin
W.H. GRINDLEY & CO. (LTD.)	Alaska
WHITTAKER & CO.	Alaska
ROWLAND AND MARSELLUS	Alaska-Yukon Centennial
COPELAND & GARRETT, ET. AL.	Alba
JOSEPH HEATH	Albano
CHARLES MEIGH	Albany
JOHN & ROBERT GODWIN	Albany
JOHNSON BROS. (HANLEY), LTD.	Albany
MELLOR, VENABLES & CO.	Albany
W.H. GRINDLEY & CO. (LTD.)	Albany
WILLIAM DAVENPORT	Albany
WILLIAM RIDGWAY (& CO.)	Albany
RALPH STEVENSON & WILLIAMS	Albany Theatre, 1824
ENOCH WOOD & SONS	Albany, City of, State of New York
ROWLAND AND MARSELLUS	Albany, N.Y./ Capitol
JOB & JOHN JACKSON	Albany, New York
WILLIAM DAVENPORT	Albany, New York
JAMES & RALPH CLEWS	Albany/ New York, Albany
JOHN & ROBERT GODWIN	Albany/#110
ALFRED MEAKIN (LTD.)	Albermarle
DUDSON, WILCOX & TILL, LTD.	Albert
JAMES F. WILEMAN	Albert
JOHN MEIR & SON	Albert
SOUTH WALES POTTERS	Albert
COPELAND & GARRETT, ET. AL.	Albert Richard Smith
RIDGWAY, MORLEY, WEAR & CO.	Albert Star
RIDGWAYS (BEDFORD WORKS) LTD.	Alberta
G.R. TURNBULL	Albion
JOHN WOOD & CO. (LTD.)	Albion
LEWIS WOOLF (& SONS)(& CO.)	Albion
MALING'S (ROBERT)	Albion
PATTERSON & CO.	Albion
RIDGWAY & MORLEY	Albion
SAMPSON HANCOCK (& SONS)	Albion
SPODE/COPELAND & GARRETT, et.al.	Albion
W. & E. CORN	Albion
WILLIAM RIDGWAY (& CO.)	Albion
WOOD & BROWNFIELD	Albion
JOHN & SAMUEL ALCOCK (JR.)	Alcock's Long Octagon Shape
W.H. GRINDLEY & CO. (LTD.)	Aldine
CLEMENTSON, YOUNG & JAMESON	Aleppo
WEDGWOOD & CO. (LTD.)	Alexander
BURGESS & LEIGH (LTD.)	Alexandra
SAMPSON HANCOCK (& SONS)	Alexandra
HOLLINSHEAD & KIRKHAM (LTD.)	Alexandria
JOSEPH CLEMENTSON & SONS	Alexandria
JONES & SON	Alfred as a Minstrel
ALFRED MEAKIN (LTD.)	Alhambra
J. & M.P. BELL (CO.) & (LTD.)	Alhambra
JOHN GOODWIN/SEACOMBE POTTERY	Alhambra
JOHN THOMSON (& SONS)	Alhambra
SOUTH WALES POTTERS	Alhambra
SPODE/COPELAND & GARRETT, et.al.	Alhambra
YNYSMEDW POTTERY	Alhambra
SEWELL(S) & CO.	All Over Floral
JOHN & WILLIAM RIDGWAY	All Souls College & St. Mary's Church, Oxford
THOMAS GOODFELLOW	Alleghany
BELLE VUE POTTERIES	Allegheny Scenery
J. & M.P. BELL (CO.) & (LTD.)	Allegheny Scenery
W.H. GRINDLEY & CO. (LTD.)	Allen
ROWLAND AND MARSELLUS	Allentown, Pa.
WILLIAM (ALSAGER) ADDERLEY (& CO.)	Allexis
HENRY ALCOCK & CO. (LTD.)	Alma
JOHN THOMSON (& SONS)	Alma
WILLIAM & JAMES BUTTERFIELD	Alma
WILLIAM (ALSAGER) ADDERLEY (& CO.)	Alma
JOHN & WILLIAM RIDGWAY	Almshouse, Boston
RALPH STEVENSON & WILLIAMS	Almshouse, Boston
ANDREW STEVENSON	Almshouse, New York
JOHN & WILLIAM RIDGWAY	Almshouse, New York
RALPH STEVENSON	Almshouse, New York
JAMES & RALPH CLEWS	Alnwick Castle, Northumberland
WILLIAM ADAMS & SON(S) (POTTERS) LTD.	Alnwick Castle, Northumberland
GEORGE JONES (& SONS LTD.)	Alpine
WILLIAM DAVENPORT	Alpine
WILLIAM RIDGWAY (& CO.)	Alpine
BRIDGWOOD & CLARKE	Alternate Loops
JAMES EDWARDS & SON	Alternate Octagon Shape
PODMORE, WALKER (& CO.)	Althea
SAMUEL ALCOCK & CO.	Althea
WOOD & BROWNFIELD	Althea
BARKER BROS (LTD.)	Alton
JAMES BEECH	Alton
KEELING & CO. (LTD.)	Alton
W.H. GRINDLEY & CO. (LTD.)	Alton
THOMAS & JOHN CAREY/ JOHN CAREY & SONS	Alton Abbey, Earl of Shrewsbury Seat
JOHN & RICHARD RILEY	Alton Abbey, Staffordshire
RALPH HALL (& CO.) or (& SONS)	Alton Abbey, Staffordshire, England
ROWLAND AND MARSELLUS	Altoona, Pa.
MINTONS, LTD.	Alunwick
HULME, JOHN & SONS	Alva
WOOD & SON(S) (LTD.)	Alva
EDWARD WALLEY	Amaranthine Flower
JOSEPH HEATH & CO.	Amaryllis
RALPH STEVENSON & SON	Amaryllis
WILLIAM ADAMS & SON(S) (POTTERS) LTD.	Amazon
J. & M.P. BELL (CO.) & (LTD.)	Amboina
WOOD & BROWNFIELD	Ambrosia
THOMAS FORD & CO.	America
THOMAS FORD (& CO.)	America
THOMAS FURNIVAL & CO.	America
JAMES & RALPH CLEWS	AMERICA AND INDEPENDENCE OF STATES SERIES
JAMES EDWARDS	American Bird
CHARLES MEIGH	AMERICAN CITIES AND SCENERY SERIES
JAMES & RALPH CLEWS	American Eagle on Urn
FRANCIS MORLEY (& CO.)	American Marine
G.L. ASHWORTH & BROS. (LTD.)	American Marine
FRANCIS MORLEY (& CO.)	AMERICAN MARINE SERIES

RALPH STEVENSON	American Museum
ROWLAND AND MARSELLUS	American Musicians
ROWLAND AND MARSELLUS	American Poets
JOB & JOHN JACKSON	American Scenery
JOB & JOHN JACKSON	AMERICAN SCENERY SERIES
WILLIAM RIDGWAY (& CO.)	AMERICAN SCENERY SERIES
THOMAS GODWIN	AMERICAN VIEWS SERIES
BOURNE, BAKER & BOURNE	American Villa
RALPH STEVENSON	American Villa
J. & G. MEAKIN	Americana
WOOD & BAGGALEY	Amerilla
PODMORE, WALKER (& CO.)	Amerillia
WOOD & CALDWELL	Ames, Fisher
SOUTH WALES POTTERS	Amherst
DIMMOCK & SMITH	Amherst Japan
JOHN RIDGWAY (& CO.)	Amherst Japan
MINTON & CO.	Amherst Japan
SOUTH WALES POTTERS	Amherst Japan
ADDERLEY'S LTD.	Amoy
DILLWYN & CO.	Amoy
DOULTON & CO. (LTD.)	Amoy
J. & M.P. BELL (CO.) & (LTD.)	Amoy
W. & E. CORN	Amoy
WHITEHAVEN POTTERY	Amoy
WILLIAM ADAMS & SON(S) (POTTERS) LTD.	Amoy
WILLIAM DAVENPORT	Amoy
WILLIAM EMBERTON (& CO.)	Amoy
WILLIAM RIDGWAY (& CO.)	Amoy
JOHN MEIR	Amport House, Hampshire
ANDREW STEVENSON	Ampton Hall, Suffolk
E. CHALLINOR & CO.	Amula
GEORGE WOOLISCROFT (& CO.)	Amula
WILLIAM DAVENPORT	Amusements
LEEDS POTTERY	An All-over Shell Design
THOMAS GODWIN	An Eskimo Family Group in Front of Igloos...With Two Small Sailing Boats, et.al.
THOMAS GODWIN	An Eskimo Family Seated With Their God...With Two Ships, Hella & Griper, et.al.
JOSIAH WEDGWOOD (& SONS LTD.)	An Estuary
SPODE/COPELAND & GARRETT, et.al.	Ancient Bath at Cacamo in Caramania
DON POTTERY	Ancient Cistern Near Catania
SPODE/COPELAND & GARRETT, et.al.	Ancient Granary at Cacamo
RALPH STEVENSON & WILLIAMS	Ancient Greece
THOMAS & JOHN CAREY/ JOHN CAREY & SONS	Ancient Rome
G.L. ASHWORTH & BROS. (LTD.)	Ancient Ruins
JOHN & ROBERT GODWIN	Ancient Ruins
WILLIAM RIDGWAY (& CO.)	Ancient Ruins
JOHN & ROBERT GODWIN	Ancient Ruins [# 104]
EDWARD & GEORGE PHILLIPS	Ancona
EDWARD CHALLINOR	Ancona
JOHN THOMSON (& SONS)	Andalusia
JOSEPH TWIGG (& CO.)	Andalusia
WILLIAM ADAMS & SON(S) (POTTERS) LTD.	Andalusia
KEELING & CO. (LTD.)	Andes
MINTONS	Andirons
JOHNSON BROS. (HANLEY), LTD.	Andora
BATES & BENNETT	Anemone
BISHOP & STONIER (LTD.)	Anemone
HOLLINSHEAD & KIRKHAM (LTD.)	Anemone
J. & M.P. BELL (CO.) & (LTD.)	Anemone
LOCKHART & ARTHUR	Anemone
MINTON	Anemone
MINTON & CO.	Anemone
SMITH & FORD	Anemone
SMITH, FORD & JONES	Anemone
SOUTH WALES POTTERS	Anemone
WILLIAM BROWNFIELD (& SON(S)	Anemone
CHARLES MEIGH	Angelsea
JOHN WEDG WOOD	Angled Leaf
J. & G. MEAKIN	Anglesea
MINTON & BOYLE	Angoulie
JOHN & WILLIAM RIDGWAY	ANGUS SEATS SERIES
THOMAS MAYER	Animal Prize Fight
COPELAND & GARRETT, ET. AL.	Animum Rege
HOLMES, STONIER & HOLLINSHEAD	Anna
POUNTNEY & GOLDNEY	Annunciation
DAVID LOCKHART (and LOCKHART & CO.)	Antelope
ENOCH WOOD & SONS	Antelope
JOB & JOHN JACKSON	Antelope
JOHN HALL	Antelope
JOHN RIDGWAY, BATES & CO.	Antelope
ROBINSON, WOOD & BROWNFIELD	Antelope
WILLIAM RIDGWAY, SON & CO.	Anthony's Nose
E. CHALLINOR & CO.	Anthos
THOMAS FELL (& CO.) (LTD.)	Antiquarian
JOHN MEIR & SON	Antique Bottle
SPODE/COPELAND & GARRETT, et.al.	Antique Fragments at Limissio
DAVENPORT'S LTD.	Antique Shape
WILLIAM DAVENPORT	Antique Shape
POUNTNEY & GOLDNEY	ANTIQUE SUBJECTS SERIES
SPODE/COPELAND & GARRETT, et.al.	Antique Vase
JOSEPH CLEMENTSON	Antique Vases
WHITEHAVEN POTTERY	Antiques
JOHN HALL (& SONS)	Antiquities
J. & M.P. BELL (CO.) & (LTD.)	Antoinette
SPODE/COPELAND & GARRETT, et.al.	Antoinette
THOMAS DIMMOCK (JR.) & CO.	Antwerp
WILLIAM RIDGWAY, SON & CO.	Apple Blossom
BRAMELD & CO.	Apple Gatherers
MINTON	Apple Tree
JOHN ROGERS (& SON)	Approaching Port
COPELAND & GARRETT, ET. AL.	April - Untitled / Italian Garden
BURGESS & LEIGH (LTD.)	Apsley Plants
SPODE/COPELAND & GARRETT, et.al.	Aquatic
WOOD & SON(S) (LTD.)	Aquatic
JACOB FURNIVAL & CO.	Aquatic Shape
ENOCH WOOD & SONS	Aqueduct Bridge at Rochester
WOOD & SON(S) (LTD.)	Aquilia
PITCAIRNS LTD.	Aquilla
DAVID LOCKHART (and LOCKHART & CO.)	Arab
COPELAND & GARRETT, ET. AL.	Arabesque
JAMES KENT (LTD.)	Arabesque
JOSIAH WEDGWOOD (& SONS LTD.)	Arabesque
SPODE/COPELAND & GARRETT, et.al.	Arabesque
THOMAS, JOHN & JOSEPH MAYER	Arabesque
WILLIAM DAVENPORT	Arabesque
COPELAND & GARRETT, ET. AL.	ARABESQUE SERIES
DAWSON (JOHN DAWSON & CO., ETC.)	Arabia
FRANCIS DILLON	Arabian
RIDGWAY & MORLEY	Arabian
RIDGWAY, MORLEY, WEAR & CO.	Arabian
MIDDLESBOROUGH POTTERY CO.	Arabian Nights
WILLIAM HACKWOOD	Arabian Sketches
EMPIRE PORCELAIN CO. (LTD.)	Arabic
JAMES EDWARDS & SON	Arabic
W.H. GRINDLEY & CO. (LTD.)	Arabic
SAMUEL FORD & CO.	Arbor
WEDGWOOD & CO. (LTD.)	Arbor Vine
THOMAS GOODFELLOW	Arcade
JOHN VENABLES & CO.	Arcaded Panels
CHARLES MEIGH & SON	Arcaded Trumpet Shape
ARTHUR J. WILKINSON (LTD.)	Arcadia
ENOCH PLANT	Arcadia
J. & M.P. BELL (CO.) & (LTD.)	Arcadia
WOOD & BROWNFIELD	Arcadia
CAULDON, LTD.	Arcadian Chariots
JOSIAH WEDGWOOD (& SONS LTD.)	Arch Border
ELSMORE & FORSTER	Arched Forget-Me-Not Shape
ELSMORE & FORSTER	Arched Panel
HOLLAND & GREEN	Arched Panel
R. COCHRAN & CO. - VERREVILLE POTTERY	Arched Wheat
BAKER, BEVANS & IRWIN	Archers
ELKIN, KNIGHT & BRIDGWOOD	Archery
HERCULANEUM POTTERY	Archery
JOB & JOHN JACKSON	Archery
WILLIAM DAVENPORT	Archery
JOHN TURNER / TURNER & CO., etc.	Archery Lesson
THOMAS MAYER	Archery, Oly, Game
BROUGHAM & MAYER	Archipelago
JOHN RIDGWAY (& CO.)	Archipelago
RIDGWAY & MORLEY	Archipelago
RIDGWAY, MORLEY, WEAR & CO.	Archipelago
THOMAS GODWIN	ARCTIC SCENERY SERIES
EDWARD CHALLINOR	Ardenne(s)
EDGE, MALKIN & CO. (LTD.)	Argyle
FORD & SONS (LTD.)	Argyle
HANLEY PORCELAIN CO.	Argyle
JOHNSON BROS. (HANLEY), LTD.	Argyle
MYOTT, SON & CO. (LTD.)	Argyle
W.H. GRINDLEY & CO. (LTD.)	Argyle
WOOD & SON(S) (LTD.)	Argyle
THOMAS DIMMOCK (JR.) & CO.	Argyll I
THOMAS DIMMOCK (JR.) & CO.	Argyll II
FORD & SONS (LTD.)	Arley
ROWLAND AND MARSELLUS	Arlington, Va.
JOB MEIGH (& SON)	Armadillo
WILLIAM ADAMS & SON(S) (POTTERS) LTD.	Armidale, Invernesshire
ENOCH WOOD & SONS	Armitage Park, Staffordshire
WILLIAM SMITH (& CO.)	Armorial
POUNTNEY & ALLIES	Arms of Bristol
MELLOR, VENABLES & CO.	Arms of Delaware
MELLOR, VENABLES & CO.	Arms of Maryland
MELLOR, VENABLES & CO.	Arms of Massachusetts, New York, Massachusetts
MELLOR, VENABLES & CO.	Arms of North Carolina
MELLOR, VENABLES & CO.	Arms of Pennsylvania
THOMAS MAYER	ARMS OF THE AMERICAN STATES
MELLOR, VENABLES & CO.	ARMS OF THE STATES, SCENIC SERIES

RALPH HAMMERSLEY (& SON(S))	Arms of the United States
MELLOR, VENABLES & CO.	Arms of Virginia
SPODE/COPELAND & GARRETT, et.al.	Artemis Drawn by a Griffon and a Lynx
SPODE/COPELAND & GARRETT, et.al.	Artemis With Two Lynx
G.L. ASHWORTH & BROS. (LTD.)	Artichoke
JOHN RIDGWAY (& CO.)	Artist and Chateau
DOULTON & CO. (LTD.)	Arundel
MINTONS, LTD.	Arundel
CARLTON WARE LTD.	Arvista
WILTSHAW & ROBINSON (LTD.)	Arvista
JOHN ROGERS (& SON)	As You Like It, Act 2 Scene 2
POUNTNEY & GOLDNEY	As You Like It, Act 2 Scene 2
JOHN ROGERS (& SON)	As You Like It, Act 4 Scene 2
POUNTNEY & GOLDNEY	As You Like It, Act 4 Scene 2
JOHN ROGERS (& SON)	As You Like It, Act 4 Scene 3
POUNTNEY & GOLDNEY	As You Like It, Act 4 Scene 3
ROWLAND AND MARSELLUS	Asbury Park, N.J.
CHARLES MEIGH	Ascent to the Capitol, Washington
MINTON	Asgill House, Richmond
W.H. GRINDLEY & CO. (LTD.)	Ashburton
SMITH & BINNALL	Ashley
POUNTNEY & CO. (LTD.)	Ashton
ROWLAND AND MARSELLUS	Ashville, N.C.
JOSEPH HEATH & CO.	Asia Displayed
GEORGE WOOLISCROFT (& CO.)	Asia Shape
MINTON & BOYLE	Asian Bird
CHARLES MEIGH	Asiatic Birds
F. & R. PRATT & CO. (LTD.)	Asiatic Marine
WILLIAM RIDGWAY, SON & CO.	Asiatic Palaces
COPELAND & GARRETT, ET. AL.	Asiatic Pheasant
HAMPSON & BROADHURST	Asiatic Pheasant
SOUTH WALES POTTERS	Asiatic Pheasant
WILLIAM EMBERTON (& CO.)	Asiatic Pheasant
BARKERS & KENT (LTD.)	Asiatic Pheasants
BODLEY & HARROLD	Asiatic Pheasants
BOVEY TRACY POTTERY COMPANY	Asiatic Pheasants
BRITANNIA POTTERY CO. LTD.	Asiatic Pheasants
CARTWRIGHT & EDWARDS (LTD.)	Asiatic Pheasants
CLYDE POTTERY CO. (LTD.)	Asiatic Pheasants
COCHRAN & FLEMING - BRITANNIA POTTERY	Asiatic Pheasants
CORK & EDGE	Asiatic Pheasants
DOULTON & CO. (LTD.)	Asiatic Pheasants
HAWLEY BROS. (LTD.)	Asiatic Pheasants
HOLDCROFT, HILL & MELLOR	Asiatic Pheasants
J. & M.P. BELL (CO.) & (LTD.)	Asiatic Pheasants
JAMES REEVES	Asiatic Pheasants
JOHN CARR (& CO.) (& SON(S)	Asiatic Pheasants
JOHN MEIR & SON	Asiatic Pheasants
JOHN THOMAS HUDDEN	Asiatic Pheasants
MARY WILKINSON	Asiatic Pheasants
OLD HALL (EARTHENWARE) POTTERY CO. LTD.	Asiatic Pheasants
PITCAIRNS LTD.	Asiatic Pheasants
PODMORE, WALKER (& CO.)	Asiatic Pheasants
POULSON BROS. (LTD.)	Asiatic Pheasants
RALPH HALL	Asiatic Pheasants
SAMUEL BARKER & SON	Asiatic Pheasants
THOMAS FELL (& CO.) (LTD.)	Asiatic Pheasants
THOMAS HUGHES & SON (LTD.)	Asiatic Pheasants
WHITEHAVEN POTTERY	Asiatic Pheasants
WILLIAM & THOMAS ADAMS	Asiatic Pheasants
WILLIAM ADAMS & CO. LTD.	Asiatic Pheasants
WORTHINGTON & HARROP	Asiatic Pheasants
WILLIAM RIDGWAY (& CO.)	Asiatic Plants
JOB & JOHN JACKSON	Asiatic Scenery
JOSEPH HARDING	Asiatic Scenery
PODMORE, WALKER (& CO.)	Asiatic Scenery
THOMAS & JOHN CAREY/ JOHN CAREY & SONS	Asiatic Scenery
ELIJAH JONES	Asiatic Scenic Beauties
JOHN & WILLIAM RIDGWAY	Asiatic Temples
FRANCIS DILLON	Asiatic Views
PODMORE, WALKER (& CO.)	Asiatic Views
SPODE'S BLUE PRINTED WARES	Aspidistra
THOMAS & BENJAMIN GODWIN	Ass
SPODE/COPELAND & GARRETT, et.al.	Aster
SPODE'S BLUE PRINTED WARES	Aster
UPPER HANLEY POTTERY CO. (LTD.)	Aster
JOSEPH CLEMENTSON	Aster & Grapeshot
MELLOR, VENABLES & CO.	Aster & Grapeshot
MINTONS, LTD.	Astor
WILLIAM RIDGWAY (& CO.)	Astoral
EMPIRE PORCELAIN CO. (LTD.)	Astoria
JOHNSON BROS. (HANLEY), LTD.	Astoria
NEW WHARF POTTERY CO.	Astoria
PITCAIRNS LTD.	Astoria
UPPER HANLEY POTTERY CO. (LTD.)	Astoria
W.H. GRINDLEY & CO. (LTD.)	Astoria
W.H. GRINDLEY & CO. (LTD.)	Astral
JOB & JOHN JACKSON	At Richmond, Virginia
WILLIAM ADAMS & SON(S) (POTTERS) LTD.	Athecus
MARPLE, TURNER & CO.	Athena
W.H. GRINDLEY & CO. (LTD.)	Athena
JOHN & WILLIAM RIDGWAY	Athenaeum, Boston
J.T. CLOSE (& CO.)	Athenia Shape
WILLIAM ADAMS & SON(S) (POTTERS) LTD.	Athenia Shape
JOHN THOMSON (& SONS)	Athenian
SPODE/COPELAND & GARRETT, et.al.	Athenian
CHARLES MEIGH	Athens
DAVID LOCKHART (and LOCKHART & CO.)	Athens
GRIMWADES LTD.	Athens
J. & M.P. BELL (CO.) & (LTD.)	Athens
JOHN ROGERS (& SON)	Athens
LOCKHART & ARTHUR	Athens
SOUTH WALES POTTERS	Athens
WILLIAM ADAMS & SON(S) (POTTERS) LTD.	Athens
PODMORE, WALKER (& CO.)	Athens Shape
WEDGWOOD & CO. (LTD.)	Athens Shape
BURGESS & LEIGH (LTD.)	Athol
RIDGWAYS (BEDFORD WORKS) LTD.	Athol
W.H. GRINDLEY & CO. (LTD.)	Atlanta
WEDGWOOD & CO. (LTD.)	Atlanta
ROWLAND AND MARSELLUS	Atlantic City, N.J.
SAMUEL ALCOCK & CO.	Atlantic Shape
T. & R. BOOTE (LTD.) (& SON)	Atlantic Shape (A)
T. & R. BOOTE (LTD.) (& SON)	Atlantic Shape (B)
T. & R. BOOTE (LTD.) (& SON)	Atlantic Shape (C)
T. & R. BOOTE (LTD.) (& SON)	Atlantic Shape (D)
C. & W.K. HARVEY	Atlantis
W.H. GRINDLEY & CO. (LTD.)	Atlas
DOULTON & CO. (LTD.)	Aubrey
JOHNSON BROS. (HANLEY), LTD.	Aubrey
ANDREW STEVENSON	Audley End, Essex
COPELAND & GARRETT, ET. AL.	August - Italian Garden
JOSEPH CLEMENTSON	Augusta Shape
DAVID LOCKHART & SONS (LTD.)	Auld Lang Syne
BEECH & HANCOCK	Aurora
BEECH, HANCOCK & CO.	Aurora
FRANCIS MORLEY (& CO.)	Aurora
J. & M.P. BELL (CO.) & (LTD.)	Aurora
JAMES BEECH	Aurora
JOHN TAMS (& SON) (LTD)	Aurora
WILLIAM DAVENPORT	Auspicio Reges et Senatus Anglia
JAMES JAMIESON & CO.	Australia
R. COCHRAN & CO. - VERREVILLE POTTERY	Australia
SUNDERLAND OR "GARRISON" POTTERY	Australian
J. & M.P. BELL (CO.) & (LTD.)	Autumn
COPELAND & GARRETT, ET. AL.	Autumn - Vintage of Sorrento
THOMAS, JOHN & JOSEPH MAYER	Ava
JAMES & RALPH CLEWS	Aviary
SOUTH WALES POTTERS	Avis
BOOTHS (LTD.)	Avon
EDGE, MALKIN & CO. (LTD.)	Avon
FORD & SONS (LTD.)	Avon
KEELING & CO. (LTD.)	Avon
THOMAS HUGHES & SON (LTD.)	Avon Cottage
J. & G. MEAKIN	Avondale
PALISSY POTTERY LTD.	Avon Scenes
J. & M.P. BELL (CO.) & (LTD.)	Ayam Jantam
W. & E. CORN	Ayr
JAMES & RALPH CLEWS	Aysgill Force in Wensleydale
BOURNE & LEIGH (LTD.)	Azalea
GEORGE JONES (& SONS LTD.)	Azalea
SPODE/COPELAND & GARRETT, et.al.	B700
SPODE/COPELAND & GARRETT, et.al.	B772
SPODE/COPELAND & GARRETT, et.al.	B773
CORK & EDGE	Babes In The Woods
DOULTON & CO. (LTD.)	Babes In The Woods
PATTERSON & CO.	Bacchanalian Cherubs
WILLIAM SMITH (& CO.)	Bacchus
WOOD & CHALLINOR	Bachrach
JOB MEIGH (& SON)	Badger
JOHN TURNER / TURNER & CO., etc.	Bailiff's Report
JAMES & RALPH CLEWS	Bakers Falls, Hudson River
CLEMENTSON BROS. (LTD.)	Balanced Vine Shape
JAMES EDWARDS	Ball & Stick
J. & M.P. BELL (CO.) & (LTD.)	Ballater
HOPE & CARTER	Ballet
JOHN & RICHARD RILEY	Balloch Castle, Dunbartonshire... sic
CHARLES MEIGH	Ballston Springs, N.Y.
J. & G. MEAKIN	Balmoral
J. & M.P. BELL (CO.) & (LTD.)	Balmoral
MANN & CO.	Balmoral
THOMAS DIMMOCK (JR.) & CO.	Balmoral
THOMAS WOOD & SONS	Balmoral

PINDER BOURNE & HOPE	Baltic
W.H. GRINDLEY & CO. (LTD.)	Baltic
GEORGE FREDERICK BOWERS (& CO.)	Baltic Shape
GEORGE WOOLISCROFT (& CO.)	Baltic Shape
JOHN MEIR & SON	Baltic Shape
JOHN VENABLES & CO.	Baltic Shape
THOMAS HULME	Baltic Shape
CHARLES MEIGH	Baltimore
THOMAS GODWIN	Baltimore
WILLIAM DAVENPORT	Baltimore
WILLIAM RIDGWAY, SON & CO.	Baltimore
ENOCH WOOD & SONS	Baltimore & Ohio Railroad / Inclined Plane
ENOCH WOOD & SONS	Baltimore & Ohio Railroad / Level
RALPH STEVENSON & WILLIAMS	Baltimore Exchange
BROUGHAM & MAYER	Baltimore Shape
ROWLAND AND MARSELLUS	Baltimore, Indiana
WILLIAM DAVENPORT	Baltimore, Maryland
ROWLAND AND MARSELLUS	Baltimore, Md.
JAMES & RALPH CLEWS	Baltimore/ Maryland, Baltimore
THOMAS SHIRLEY & CO.	Balustrade & Pillars
ALFRED MEAKIN (LTD.)	Bamboo
HOPE & CARTER	Bamboo
JOHN & WILLIAM RIDGWAY	Bamboo
JOHN MEIR & SON	Bamboo
MINTON	Bamboo
SAMUEL ALCOCK & CO.	Bamboo
SPODE'S BLUE PRINTED WARES	Bamboo
THOMAS DIMMOCK (JR.) & CO.	Bamboo
W.H. GRINDLEY & CO. (LTD.)	Bamboo
MINTONS, LTD.	Bamboo & Fan
WILLIAM DAVENPORT	Bamboo & Peony
COPELAND & GARRETT, ET. AL.	Bamboo & Rock
SPODE'S BLUE PRINTED WARES	Bamboo & Rock
BENJAMIN E. GODWIN	Bamboo & Sprig
MINTON	Bamboo and Flowers
MINTON & CO.	Bamboo Flowers
JOHN ROGERS (& SON)	Bamboo Flowers & Rocks
JOHN EDWARDS (& CO.)	Bamboo Shape
WILLIAM ADAMS & SON(S) (POTTERS) LTD.	Bamborough Castle, Northumberland
J. & M.P. BELL (CO.) & (LTD.)	Banda-
JOHN & WILLIAM RIDGWAY	Bandanna
W.R. MIDWINTER (LTD.)	Bandstand
COPELAND & GARRETT, ET. AL.	Bang Up
SPODE/COPELAND & GARRETT, et.al.	Bang Up
J. & M.P. BELL (CO.) & (LTD.)	Bangkok
ROWLAND AND MARSELLUS	Bangor, Maine
ENOCH WOOD & SONS	Bank of England, London
WILLIAM ADAMS	Bank of England, London
JOSEPH STUBBS	Bank of the United States, Philadelphia
JOHN & WILLIAM RIDGWAY	Bank, Savannah
WILLIAM SMITH (& CO.)	Banner Floral
JOHN MADDOCK & SONS (LTD.)	Bar & Chain
BURGESS & LEIGH (LTD.)	Barbarini Vase
ENOCH WOOD & SONS	Barlborough Hall, Derbyshire
JOHN MEIR	Barlborough Hall, Derbyshire
DILLWYN & CO.	Barnstable & Bude, Cornwall
SAMPSON HANCOCK (& SONS)	Baronet
WOOD & SON(S) (LTD.)	Baronia
JOHN RIDGWAY (& CO.)	Baronial Castles
THOMAS, JOHN & JOSEPH MAYER	Baronial Halls
WILLIAM SMITH (& CO.)	Baronial Halls
KNIGHT, ELKIN & CO.	BARONIAL HALLS SERIES
WILLIAM SMITH (& CO.)	BARONIAL HALLS SERIES
SAMUEL KEELING & CO.	BARONIAL VIEWS SERIES
HENRY BURGESS	Barred Wreath
ANDREW STEVENSON	Barrington Hall
R. COCHRAN & CO. - VERREVILLE POTTERY	Basilica & Seminary: Basilique & Seminaire
CHARLES JAMES MASON & CO.	Basket
F. & R. PRATT & CO. (LTD.)	Basket
LEEDS POTTERY	Basket
MINTON	Basket
MINTONS	Basket
SAMUEL ALCOCK & CO.	Basket
THOMAS GOODFELLOW	Basket
THOMAS WOLFE(S)	Basket
BATHWELL & GOODFELLOW	Basket & Flowers
FRANCIS MORLEY (& CO.)	Basket & Vine
FRANCIS MORLEY (& CO.)	Basket and Vase
JAMES & RALPH CLEWS	Basket and Vase
JOSEPH TWIGG (& CO.)	Basket of Eggs
JOSIAH WEDGWOOD (& SONS LTD.)	Basket of Flowers
MINTON	Basket of Flowers
WILLIAM ADAMS & SON(S) (POTTERS) LTD.	Basket of Flowers
ANTHONY SHAW (& SON(S) (& CO.)	Basketweave
ANTHONY SHAW (& SON(S) (& CO.)	Basketweave Shape
ALFRED MEAKIN (LTD.)	Basketweave With Band
DAVID LOCKHART (and LOCKHART & CO.)	Batavia
ROBERT HERON (& SON)	Bath
THOMAS & JOHN CAREY/ JOHN CAREY & SONS	Bath & Bristol Cathedrals
ROWLAND AND MARSELLUS	Bath, Maine, City of Ships
JOB & JOHN JACKSON	Battery & C. New York
RALPH STEVENSON	Battery, New York
EDWARD CHALLINOR	Battle Between a Buffalo and a Tiger
SPODE/COPELAND & GARRETT, et.al.	Battle Between a Buffalo and a Tiger
ROWLAND AND MARSELLUS	Battle Creek, Mich.
JOB & JOHN JACKSON	Battle Monument, Baltimore
ANTHONY SHAW (& SON(S) (& CO.)	Battle of Buena Vista
RALPH STEVENSON	Battle of Bunker Hill
ROWLAND AND MARSELLUS	Battle of Bunker Hill
ANTHONY SHAW (& SON(S) (& CO.)	Battle of Chapultepec
ROWLAND AND MARSELLUS	Battle of Germantown, Attack on Judge Chew's House
ANTHONY SHAW (& SON(S) (& CO.)	Battle of Monterey
ANTHONY SHAW (& SON(S) (& CO.)	Battle of Palo Alto
ANTHONY SHAW (& SON(S) (& CO.)	Battle of Resaca de la Palma
JONES & SON	Battle of Waterloo
BARKERS & KENT (LTD.)	Bavaria
J. & M.P. BELL (CO.) & (LTD.)	Bavaria
SAMUEL GINDER & CO.	Bavarian
FORD & SONS (LTD.)	Bay
COPELAND & GARRETT, ET. AL.	Bay of Naples
FRANCIS MORLEY (& CO.)	Bay of Quinte
MINTONS, LTD.	Beaconsfield
CLEMENTSON BROS. (LTD.)	Beaded Band
JAMES & RALPH CLEWS	Bear Cages
JAMES & RALPH CLEWS	Bear Forest, Ireland
WILLIAM ADAMS & SON(S) (POTTERS) LTD.	Bear Forest, Ireland
JOHN MADDOCK & SONS (LTD.)	Beatrice
WEDGWOOD & CO. (LTD.)	Beatrice
W.H. GRINDLEY & CO. (LTD.)	Beaufort
HENSHALL & CO.	Beaumont Lodge
JOHN RIDGWAY (& CO.)	Beauties I,
JOHN RIDGWAY (& CO.)	Beauties II,
JOHN & WILLIAM RIDGWAY	BEAUTIES OF AMERICA
MELLOR, VENABLES & CO.	Beauties of China
SPODE/COPELAND & GARRETT, et.al.	Beautiful Penelope
W.H. GRINDLEY & CO. (LTD.)	Beauty Roses
ENOCH WOOD & SONS	Beaver
JOHN HALL	Beaver
WILLIAM ADAMS & SON(S) (POTTERS) LTD.	Beckenham Place, Kent
G.L. ASHWORTH & BROS. (LTD.)	Bedford
SPODE/COPELAND & GARRETT, et.al.	Bedford
ENOCH WOOD & SONS	Bedfords, Essex
JOHN MEIR	Bedfords, Essex
JOHN DENTON BAXTER (BAGSTER)	Bee
COCHRAN & FLEMING - BRITANNIA POTTERY	Bee & Rose
MALING'S (ROBERT)	Bee Catcher
WILLIAM ADAMS & SON(S) (POTTERS) LTD.	Beehive
WILLIAM RIDGWAY (& CO.)	Beehive
ENOCH WOOD & SONS	Beehive & Cottage
MACHIN & POTTS	Beehive and Poet
RALPH STEVENSON & WILLIAMS	Beehive and Vases
SAMUEL ALCOCK & CO.	Beehives & Country House
THOMAS & BENJAMIN GODWIN	Beejapore... sic.
GIBSON & SONS (LTD.)	Begonia
JOHNSON BROS. (HANLEY), LTD.	Begonia
JOHN MADDOCK & SONS (LTD.)	Belfort
W.H. GRINDLEY & CO. (LTD.)	Belgrave
T. RATHBONE & CO.	Bell
CAMBRIAN POTTERY	Bell or Bluebell
HERCULANEUM POTTERY	Bell Tower
HOLLAND & GREEN	Bell Tracery
COPELAND & GARRETT, ET. AL.	Bellagio, Lago di Como
BELLE VUE POTTERIES	BELLE VUE VIEWS SERIES
SPODE/COPELAND & GARRETT, et.al.	Bellerophon's Victory Over the chimaera
ENOCH WOOD & SONS	Belleville on the Passaic River
JOHN EDWARDS (& CO.)	Bellflower
W. & E. CORN	Bellflower
HENSHALL & CO.	Bellinzona
ALFRED MEAKIN (LTD.)	Belmont
DOULTON & CO. (LTD.)	Belmont
FORD & SONS (LTD.)	Belmont
J.H. WEATHERBY & SONS (LTD.)	Belmont
T. RATHBONE & CO.	Belmont
W.H. GRINDLEY & CO. (LTD.)	Belmont
ENOCH WOOD & SONS	Belsay Castle, Northumberland
W. BAKER & CO. (LTD.)	Belted Octagon
JAMES & RALPH CLEWS	Belton House, Lincolnshire
JOHN RIDGWAY (& CO.)	Belvedere
JOSEPH HEATH	Belvoir
RALPH STEVENSON	Belvoir Castle
THOMAS & JOHN CAREY/ JOHN CAREY & SONS	Belvoir Castle, Leicestershire, Duke of Rutland Seat
ENOCH WOOD & SONS	Belvoir Castle, Leichestershire
ENOCH WOOD & SONS	Belzoni
MELLOR, VENABLES & CO.	Bengal
ALFRED MEAKIN (LTD.)	Bentick

CAULDON, LTD.	Bentick
JOHN RIDGWAY (& CO.)	Bentick
LONGTON POTTERY CO. LTD.	Benton
WILLIAM EMBERTON (& CO.)	Berber
FORD & SONS (LTD.)	Berkley
WOOD & SON(S) (LTD.)	Berkley
WILLIAM ADAMS & SON(S) (POTTERS) LTD.	Berkley Castle, Gloucestershire
WILLIAM (ALSAGER) ADDERLEY (& CO.)	Berlin
MINTON	Berlin Chaplet
WILLIAM ADAMS & SON(S) (POTTERS) LTD.	Berlin Group
THOMAS, JOHN & JOSEPH MAYER	Berlin Inverted Diamond
MINTON	Berlin Roses
WM. DAVENPORT & CO.	Berlin Shape
WILLIAM DAVENPORT	Berlin Shape
LIDDLE, ELLIOT & SON	Berlin Swirl
MAYER(BROS.)& ELLIOT	Berlin Swirl Shape
THOMAS, JOHN & JOSEPH MAYER	Berlin Swirl Shape
JOHN RIDGWAY (& CO.)	Berlin Vase
JOHN RIDGWAY (& CO.)	Berlin Wreath
MYOTT, SON & CO. (LTD.)	Bermuda
ROWLAND AND MARSELLUS	Bermuda
ROWLAND AND MARSELLUS	Bermuda 1609-1909
UPPER HANLEY POTTERY CO. (LTD.)	Bern
WILLIAM BROWNFIELD (& SON(S)	Berne
SEWELL(S) & CO.	Bernstroff
MAYER(BROS.)& ELLIOT	Berry
WILLIAM RIDGWAY (& CO.)	Berry
WILLIAM RIDGWAY, SON & CO.	Berry
JACOB FURNIVAL & CO.	Berry Cluster
ALEXANDER BALFOUR & CO.	Berties Hope
ALLMAN, BROUGHTON & CO.	Berties Hope
NEW WHARF POTTERY CO.	Berwick
WEDGWOOD & CO. (LTD.)	Beryl
ENOCH WOOD & SONS	Between Sarzano & Massa, et.al.
DOULTON & CO. (LTD.)	Beverly
HENRY ALCOCK & CO. (LTD.)	Beverly
SPODE/COPELAND & GARRETT, et.al.	Beverly
GELSON BROS.	Bickley
ENOCH WOOD & SONS	Bickley, Kent
JOHN & RICHARD RILEY	Bickley, Kent
RALPH HALL (& CO.) or (& SONS)	Biddulph Castle, Staffordshire
ELSMORE & FORSTER	Big & Little Ribs
FRANCIS MORLEY (& CO.)	Bijou
ROWLAND AND MARSELLUS	Biltmore House, Ashville, N.C.
FLACKETT, TOFT & ROBINSON	Bimrah
ENOCH WOOD & SONS	Bird
MINTON	Bird
WILLIAM DAVENPORT	Bird & Berry
BATES, GILDEA & WALKER	Bird & Fan
FOWLER THOMPSON & CO.	Bird & Fly
WATSON & CO.	Bird & Fly
GEORGE FREDERICK BOWERS (& CO.)	Bird & Font
J. DIMMOCK & CO.	Bird & Font
WILLIAM DAVENPORT	Bird & Star
JAMES & RALPH CLEWS	Bird Cages
WOOD & BRETTEL	Bird Feeding Its Young, et.al.
ROBERT MAY	Bird Fountain
SOUTH WALES POTTERS	Bird in a Tree
SAMPSON BRIDGWOOD (& SON) (LTD.)	Bird Nest
JAMES & RALPH CLEWS	Bird of Paradise
WILLIAM SMITH (& CO.)	Bird On Branch
BECK, BLAIR & CO.	Bird on Grass
JOB & JOHN JACKSON	Bird Pattern
JAMES & RALPH CLEWS	Bird Shooting
WOOD & BRETTEL	Bird's Nest
WOOD & BROWNFIELD	Bird's Nest
ANTHONY SHAW (& SON(S) (& CO.)	Birds
D.J. EVANS & CO.	Birds
THOMAS DIMMOCK (JR.) & CO.	Birds
WILLIAM ADAMS & SON(S) (POTTERS) LTD.	Birds & Basket Chinoiserie
POUNTNEY & GOLDNEY	Birds & Flowers
BEECH & LOWNDES	Birds & Fruit
JOHN DENTON BAXTER (BAGSTER)	Birds & Nest
C. & W.K. HARVEY	Birds and Flowers
ANDREW STEVENSON	Birds and Willow
DAWSON (JOHN DAWSON & CO., ETC.)	Birds Nest
MOORE & CO.	Birds of Paradise
ANDREW STEVENSON	Birds of Prey
ANDREW STEVENSON	Birds of Prey Attacking
WOOD & BROWNFIELD	Birmah
WILLIAM DAVENPORT	Bisham Abbey
WILLIAM DAVENPORT	Bisham Abbey Berkshire
JAMES & RALPH CLEWS	Bishton Hall, Staffordshire
W.H. GRINDLEY & CO. (LTD.)	Bisley
ELSMORE & FORSTER	Bittersweet
THOMAS & JOHN CAREY/ JOHN CAREY & SONS	Black Rock Castle, Near Cork
DON POTTERY	Black Swan
FRANCIS MORLEY (& CO.)	Blackberry
JOHNSON BROS. (HANLEY), LTD.	Blackberry
MELLOR, VENABLES & CO.	Blackberry
W. BAKER & CO. (LTD.)	Blackberry
WILLIAM DAVENPORT	Blackberry
MELLOR, VENABLES & CO.	Blackberry Luster
WILLIAM ADAMS & SON(S) (POTTERS) LTD.	Black-Eyed Susan
WILLIAM ADAMS & SON(S) (POTTERS) LTD.	Blaise Castle, Gloucestershire
JOHN ROGERS (& SON)	Blanche
HENRY ALCOCK & CO. (LTD.)	Blanket Stitch
J. & G. MEAKIN	Blanket Stitch
JOHNSON BROS. (HANLEY), LTD.	Blarney Castle
SAMUEL ALCOCK & CO.	Bleeding Heart
SAMPSON HANCOCK (& SONS)	Blenheim
SAMUEL ALCOCK & CO.	Blenheim
THOMAS TILL & SONS	Blenheim
WILLIAM ADAMS & SON(S) (POTTERS) LTD.	Blenheim Castle, Oxfordshire
HENSHALL & CO.	Blenheim, Oxfordshire
JOB RIDGWAY & SONS	Blind Boy
J. & G. MEAKIN	Block Optic
ROWLAND AND MARSELLUS	Blockade Shows many sided buildings, et.al.
DAVID METHVEN & SONS	Blossom
FRANCIS MORLEY (& CO.)	Blossom
G.L. ASHWORTH & BROS. (LTD.)	Blossom
S.W. DEAN	Blossom
SPODE'S BLUE PRINTED WARES	Blossom
SAMPSON HANCOCK (& SONS)	Blossoms
MAYER(BROS.)& ELLIOT	Blue Acorn
JAMES & RALPH CLEWS	Blue and White Sheet Pattern
JOSIAH WEDGWOOD (& SONS LTD.)	Blue Bamboo
JOSIAH WEDGWOOD (& SONS LTD.)	Blue Basket
DILLWYN & CO.	Blue Bell
G.L. ASHWORTH & BROS. (LTD.)	Blue Bell
JAMES & RALPH CLEWS	BLUE BELL BORDER VIEWS SERIES
JOSIAH WEDGWOOD (& SONS LTD.)	Blue Bird Cage
JOSIAH WEDGWOOD (& SONS LTD.)	Blue Birds and Nets
JOSIAH WEDGWOOD (& SONS LTD.)	Blue Botanical Flowers
JOSIAH WEDGWOOD (& SONS LTD.)	Blue Bridge
JOSIAH WEDGWOOD (& SONS LTD.)	Blue Broseley
JOSIAH WEDGWOOD (& SONS LTD.)	Blue Cairo
JOSIAH WEDGWOOD (& SONS LTD.)	Blue Claude
WILLIAM ADAMS & SON(S) (POTTERS) LTD.	Blue Concentric
JOSIAH WEDGWOOD (& SONS LTD.)	Blue Convolvulus Border
JOSIAH WEDGWOOD (& SONS LTD.)	Blue Corinth
JOHNSON BROS. (HANLEY), LTD.	Blue Danube, The
JOSIAH WEDGWOOD (& SONS LTD.)	Blue Ferrara
JOSIAH WEDGWOOD (& SONS LTD.)	Blue Garland
JOSIAH WEDGWOOD (& SONS LTD.)	Blue Goats
JOSIAH WEDGWOOD (& SONS LTD.)	Blue Group
JOSEPH STUBBS	Blue Italian
PODMORE, WALKER (& CO.)	Blue Italian
SPODE'S BLUE PRINTED WARES	Blue Italian
WOOD & CHALLINOR	Blue Italian
ZACHARIAH BOYLE (& CO.)(& SON(S)	Blue Italian
JAMES & WILLIAM HANDLEY	Blue Landscape
WILLIAM ADAMS & SON(S) (POTTERS) LTD.	Blue Lawton
JOSIAH WEDGWOOD (& SONS LTD.)	Blue Lotus
JOHNSON BROS. (HANLEY), LTD.	Blue Meissen
JOSIAH WEDGWOOD (& SONS LTD.)	Blue Pagoda
JOSIAH WEDGWOOD (& SONS LTD.)	Blue Palisade
JOSIAH WEDGWOOD (& SONS LTD.)	Blue Pavillion
JOSIAH WEDGWOOD (& SONS LTD.)	Blue Peony
G.L. ASHWORTH & BROS. (LTD.)	Blue Pheasant
G.M. & C.J. MASON	Blue Pheasants
JOSIAH WEDGWOOD (& SONS LTD.)	Blue Poppy
COPELAND & GARRETT, ET. AL.	Blue Rose
JOSIAH WEDGWOOD (& SONS LTD.)	Blue Rose
PODMORE, WALKER (& CO.)	Blue Rose
SPODE/COPELAND & GARRETT, et.al.	Blue Rose
SPODE'S BLUE PRINTED WARES	Blue Rose
W.H. GRINDLEY & CO. (LTD.)	Blue Rose
BURGESS & LEIGH (LTD.)	Blue Rose Border
JOSIAH WEDGWOOD (& SONS LTD.)	BLUE ROSE BORDER SERIES
COPELAND & GARRETT, ET. AL.	Blue Saxon
JOSIAH WEDGWOOD (& SONS LTD.)	Blue Water Lily
JOSIAH WEDGWOOD (& SONS LTD.)	Blue Zodiac
WILLIAM RIDGWAY (& CO.)	Bluebell
WILLIAM ADAMS & SON(S) (POTTERS) LTD.	BLUEBELL BORDER SERIES
CAMBRIAN POTTERY	Bluebell or Bell
HOPE & CARTER	Bluet Shape
JOHN & GEORGE ALCOCK	Blyantre
W.H. GRINDLEY & CO. (LTD.)	Blytheswood
BELLE VUE POTTERIES	Blytheswood on the Clyde
BRAMELD & CO.	Bo Peep
WILLIAM DAVENPORT	Boat & Castle
JAMES EDWARDS	Bochara
J. & M.P. BELL (CO.) & (LTD.)	Bohemia
PODMORE, WALKER (& CO.)	Bohemia
THOMAS DIMMOCK (JR.) & CO.	Bohemia

RIDGWAYS (BEDFORD WORKS) LTD.	Bolingbroke, The
COPELAND & GARRETT, ET. AL.	Bologna
WILLIAM ADAMS & SON(S) (POTTERS) LTD.	Bologna
FURNIVALS LTD.	Bombay
JOHN MADDOCK & SONS (LTD.)	Bombay
MINTONS, LTD.	Bombay
THOMAS FURNIVAL & SONS	Bombay
WHITTAKER & CO.	Bombay
SAMUEL ALCOCK & CO.	Bombay Japan
SOUTH WALES POTTERS	Bombay Japan
EDWARD F. BODLEY & CO. (& SON)	Bonaparte
T. & R. BOOTE (LTD.) (& SON)	Boote's 1851 Octagon Shape
T. & R. BOOTE (LTD.) (& SON)	Boote's Gothic
JOHN RIDGWAY (& CO.)	Bordeaux
MINTONS, LTD.	Border of Chinese Blossom
J. & G. MEAKIN	Border of Leaves
ANTHONY SHAW (& SON(S) (& CO.)	Bordered Fuchsia
WEDGWOOD & CO. (LTD.)	Bordered Gooseberry
JOHN ALCOCK	Bordered Gothic
THOMAS WALKER	Bordered Gothic
JOHN & SAMUEL ALCOCK (JR.)	Bordered Gothic Shape
WILLIAM DAVENPORT	Bordered Gothic Shape
W. & E. CORN	Bordered Hyacinth
W. BAKER & CO. (LTD.)	Bordered Hyacinth
ANDREW STEVENSON	Boreham House, Essex
HOLLAND & GREEN	Borneo
J. & M.P. BELL (CO.) & (LTD.)	Borneo
DOULTON & CO. (LTD.)	Borrento
BARKERS & KENT (LTD.)	Bosphorus
JAMES JAMIESON & CO.	Bosphorus
JOHN MARSHALL (& CO.)(LTD.)	Bosphorus
JOHN THOMAS HUDDEN	Bosphorus
PATTERSON & CO.	Bosphorus
WHITEHAVEN POTTERY	Bosphorus
RALPH HALL & CO.	Bosphorus, The
THOMAS FELL (& CO.) (LTD.)	Bosphorus, The
THOMAS, JOHN & JOSEPH MAYER	Bosphorus, The
CHARLES MEIGH	Boston
FORD & SONS (LTD.)	Boston
W.H. GRINDLEY & CO. (LTD.)	Boston
ROWLAND AND MARSELLUS	Boston ... Historical
MELLOR, VENABLES & CO.	Boston and Bunker Hill
THOMAS GODWIN	Boston and Bunker Hill
WILLIAM RIDGWAY, SON & CO.	Boston and Bunkers' Hill
RALPH STEVENSON	Boston Athenaeum
WILLIAM RIDGWAY, SON & CO.	Boston from Chelsea Heights
CHARLES MEIGH	Boston From Dorchester Heights
JOHN ROGERS (& SON)	Boston Harbor
MINTONS, LTD.	Boston Japan
JAMES & THOMAS EDWARDS	Boston Mail / Saloon, et.al.
JAMES EDWARDS	Boston Mail / Saloon, et.al.
JAMES & THOMAS EDWARDS	Boston Mails / Gentlemen's Cabin
JAMES EDWARDS	Boston Mails / Gentlemen's Cabin
JAMES & THOMAS EDWARDS	Boston Mails / Ladies Cabin
JAMES EDWARDS	Boston Mails / Ladies Cabin-Three Passengers
JAMES & THOMAS EDWARDS	BOSTON MAILS SERIES
JAMES EDWARDS	BOSTON MAILS SERIES
ROWLAND AND MARSELLUS	Boston Massacre
ENOCH WOOD & SONS	Boston State House
JOHN ROGERS (& SON)	Boston State House
JOSEPH STUBBS	Boston State House
ROWLAND AND MARSELLUS	Boston, Mass.
CHARLES MEIGH	Botanical
MINTON & CO.	Botanical
SOUTH WALES POTTERS	Botanical
SPODE/COPELAND & GARRETT, et.al.	Botanical
SPODE'S BLUE PRINTED WARES	Botanical
WOOD & BROWNFIELD	Botanical
JOHN TURNER / TURNER & CO., etc.	Botanical Beauties
WILLIAM DAVENPORT	Botanical Beauties
ELKIN & NEWBON	BOTANICAL BEAUTIES SERIES
JOSIAH WEDGWOOD (& SONS LTD.)	BOTANICAL PATTERNS
JOHN MEIR & SON	Bothwell Castle
WILLIAM ADAMS & SON(S) (POTTERS) LTD.	Bothwell Castle, Clydesdale
RALPH HALL (& CO.) or (& SONS)	Boughton House, Northamptonshire
BIRKS BROTHERS & SEDDON	Bouquet
FURNIVALS LTD.	Bouquet
G.L. ASHWORTH & BROS. (LTD.)	Bouquet
HENRY ALCOCK & CO. (LTD.)	Bouquet
JOHNSON BROS. (HANLEY), LTD.	Bouquet
JOSIAH WEDGWOOD (& SONS LTD.)	Bouquet
KNIGHT, ELKIN & CO.	Bouquet
SAMUEL ALCOCK & CO.	Bouquet
THOMAS DIMMOCK (JR.) & CO.	Bouquet
WILLIAM BROWNFIELD (& SON(S)	Bouquet
WILLIAM RIDGWAY (& CO.)	Bouquet
MINTONS, LTD.	Bow
BURGESS & GODDARD	Bow & Tassel
GODDARD & BURGESS/ Burgess & Goddard	Bow & Tassel
G.L. ASHWORTH & BROS. (LTD.)	Bow Bells
GOODWINS & HARRIS	Bow Bridge
ARTHUR J. WILKINSON (LTD.)	Bow Knot
J. & G. MEAKIN	Bow Knot
EDGE, MALKIN & CO. (LTD.)	Bower, The
MINTON	Bowl - Chinoiserie
SPODE'S BLUE PRINTED WARES	Bowpot
SAMPSON BRIDGWOOD (& SON)(LTD.)	Box,The
JOHN ALCOCK	Boxy Decagon
THOMAS FELL (& CO.) (LTD.)	Boy & Man
LEEDS POTTERY	Boy on a Buffalo
WILLIAM DAVENPORT	Boy seated with a collie-type dog, two cottages in background, et.al.
RALPH STEVENSON	Boys and Dogs
BRAMELD & CO.	Boys Fishing
HOLLAND & GREEN	Bracelet
HENSHALL & CO.	Bradfield
J. & M.P. BELL (CO.) & (LTD.)	Braemar
RALPH HALL (& CO.) or (& SONS)	Bramber Church, Sussex
ALFRED MEAKIN (LTD.)	Bramble
HOPE & CARTER	Bramble
JOSIAH WEDGWOOD (& SONS LTD.)	Bramble
SPODE/COPELAND & GARRETT, et.al.	Bramble
WILLIAM DAVENPORT	Bramble
BRAMELD & CO.	Brameld Roses
WILLIAM ADAMS & SON(S) (POTTERS) LTD.	Bramham Park, Yorkshire
FORD & SONS (LTD.)	Brampton
ENOCH WOOD & SONS	Brancepeth Castle, Durham
WEDGWOOD & CO. (LTD.)	Branch of Three Leaves
MINTON	Brandenburg House
WILLIAM ADAMS & SON(S) (POTTERS) LTD.	Branxholm Castle, Roxburghshire
G.W. TURNER & SONS	Brazil
J. & M.P. BELL (CO.) & (LTD.)	Brazil
W.H. GRINDLEY & CO. (LTD.)	Brazil
BROWN WESTHEAD, MOORE & CO.	Breadalebane
R. COCHRAN & CO. - VERREVILLE POTTERY	Breakneck Steps: Escalier Champlain
WILLIAM ADAMS & SON(S) (POTTERS) LTD.	Brecon Castle, Brecknockshire
FORD & SONS (LTD.)	Brentford
FORD & SONS (LTD.)	Brentwood
JOHN & RICHARD RILEY	Bretton Hall, Yorkshire
BURGESS & LEIGH (LTD.)	Briar
GEORGE JONES (& SONS LTD.)	Briar
DOULTON & CO. (LTD.)	Briar Rose
MINTON	Brick
RIDGWAYS (BEDFORD WORKS) LTD.	Bridal Array
SAMPSON HANCOCK (& SONS)	Bridal Veil
GOODWINS & HARRIS	Bride of Abydos
BENJAMIN E. GODWIN	Bridge
MINTON	Bridge
SEWELL(S) & CO.	Bridge
FERRYBRIDGE POTTERY	Bridge & Church
FRANCIS DILLON	Bridge & Pagoda
JOHN ROGERS (& SON)	Bridge & Pensioner
BATKIN, WALKER & BROADHURST	Bridge & Statue
DON POTTERY	Bridge and gatehouse
THOMAS & JOHN CAREY/ JOHN CAREY & SONS	Bridge and Pagoda
WILLIAM DAVENPORT	Bridge and Temple
CAMBRIAN POTTERY	Bridge at Lucano
POUNTNEY & ALLIES	Bridge at Lucano
SPODE'S BLUE PRINTED WARES	Bridge I
SPODE'S BLUE PRINTED WARES	Bridge II
BATHWELL & GOODFELLOW	Bridge of Lucano
DILLWYN & CO.	Bridge of Lucano
DON POTTERY	Bridge of Lucano
ENOCH WOOD & SONS	Bridge of Lucano
WILLIAM REID (& SON) or (SONS)	Bridge Of Lucano
JOB & JOHN JACKSON	Bridge over the River Schuylkill
MINTON	Bridge Views
MINTON	Bridgeless Chinoiserie
GEORGE FORRESTER	Bridgeless Temple
GEORGE HARRISON (& CO.)	Bridgeless Willow
HICKS, MEIGH & JOHNSON	Bridgeless Willow
ROWLAND AND MARSELLUS	Bridgeport, Conn.
ALFRED MEAKIN (LTD.)	Brier
SAMPSON BRIDGWOOD (& SON)(LTD.)	Brig O' Doon
JOHN MEIR & SON	Brighton
RIDGWAYS (BEDFORD WORKS) LTD.	Brighton
FORD & SONS (LTD.)	Bristol
FRANK BEARDMORE & CO.	Bristol
GEORGE JONES (& SONS LTD.)	Bristol
POUNTNEY & ALLIES	Bristol
POUNTNEY & ALLIES	Bristol Hot Wells
POUNTNEY & ALLIES	Bristol Leaves
POUNTNEY & ALLIES	BRISTOL VIEW SERIES
POUNTNEY & GOLDNEY	BRISTOL VIEWS SERIES
DAVID LOCKHART & SONS (LTD.)	Britannia
ELKIN, KNIGHT & BRIDGWOOD	Britannia
JAMES & THOMAS EDWARDS	Britannia

JOHN ROGERS (& SON)	Britannia
POWELL & BISHOP	Britannia
ANTHONY SHAW (& SON(S) (& CO.)	Britannia Shape
JOHNSON BROS. (HANLEY), LTD.	Britanny
PODMORE, WALKER (& CO.)	British America
PODMORE, WALKER (& CO.)	BRITISH AMERICA SERIES
WILLIAM DAVENPORT	British American
SAMUEL ALCOCK & CO.	British Birds
BOURNE, BAKER & BOURNE	British Castle
CHARLES MEIGH	BRITISH CATHEDRAL SERIES
POUNTNEY & ALLIES	British Cobalt Blue
ENOCH WOOD	British Countryside
JOHN MEIR & SON	British Flora, The
COPELAND & GARRETT, ET. AL.	British Flowers
EDWARD & GEORGE PHILLIPS	British Flowers
SPODE/COPELAND & GARRETT, et.al.	British Flowers
SPODE'S BLUE PRINTED WARES	British Flowers
WILLIAM RIDGWAY (& CO.)	British Flowers
JONES & SON	BRITISH HISTORY SERIES
RALPH STEVENSON & SON	BRITISH LAKE SERIES
HOPKIN & VERNON	British Lakes
CHARLES JAMES MASON & CO.	BRITISH LAKES SERIES
RALPH STEVENSON	British Palaces
ANDREW MUIR (& CO.)	British Rivers
CLYDE POTTERY CO. (LTD.)	British Rivers
BOOTHS (LTD.)	British Scenery
FRANCIS DILLON	British Scenery
WILLIAM DAVENPORT	British Scenery
JOHN & WILLIAM RIDGWAY	BRITISH SCENERY SERIES
JOSEPH CLEMENTSON	British Star
READ & CLEMENTSON	British Star
MELLOR, VENABLES & CO.	British Tambourine
CHARLES BOURNE	British Views
HENSHALL & CO.	British Views
MINTON	British Views
RALPH STEVENSON	British Views
RALPH HALL (& CO.) or (& SONS)	Broadlands, Hampshire
ALFRED MEAKIN (LTD.)	Brocade
PODMORE, WALKER (& CO.)	Brockville
TAMS / et.al.	Broke Hall, Suffolk
JOHN MADDOCK & SONS (LTD.)	Brooklyn
JOHNSON BROS. (HANLEY), LTD.	Brooklyn
MYOTT, SON & CO. (LTD.)	Brooklyn
SKINNER & WALKER	Brooklyn
RALPH STEVENSON	Brooklyn Ferry
THOMAS GODWIN	Brooklyn Ferry
WILLIAM RIDGWAY, SON & CO.	Brooklyn From Gowanus Heights
ROWLAND AND MARSELLUS	Brooklyn, N.Y.
BENJAMIN E. GODWIN	Broseley
DAVIS, COOKSON & WILSON	Broseley
DON POTTERY	Broseley
J. & M.P. BELL (CO.) & (LTD.)	Broseley
JAMES & WILLIAM HANDLEY	Broseley
JOHN & WILLIAM GREEN	Broseley
JOHN & WILLIAM RIDGWAY	Broseley
JOHN DENTON BAXTER (BAGSTER)	Broseley
JOHN ROGERS (& SON)	Broseley
MINTON	Broseley
SPODE/COPELAND & GARRETT, et.al.	Broseley
SPODE'S BLUE PRINTED WARES	Broseley
THOMAS GOODFELLOW	Broseley
WILLIAM SMITH (& CO.)	Broseley
SPODE'S BLUE PRINTED WARES	Broseley Dragon
THOMAS SHIRLEY & CO.	Broseley Pattern
ENOCH WOOD & SONS	Brown
JOHN HALL	Brown Bear
TAMS / et.al.	Bruce Castle, Tottenham
JAMES KENT (LTD.)	Brugge
DON POTTERY	Brundisium
MELLOR, VENABLES & CO.	Brunswick
MINTONS, LTD.	Brunswick
NEW WHARF POTTERY CO.	Brunswick
WOOD & SON(S) (LTD.)	Brunswick
WOOD & SON(S) (LTD.)	Brunswick Evangeline
DAVID LOCKHART (and LOCKHART & CO.)	Brussels
JOHN WEDG WOOD	Brussels
W.H. GRINDLEY & CO. (LTD.)	Brussels
SPODE/COPELAND & GARRETT, et.al.	Bryon
SPODE/COPELAND & GARRETT, et.al.	Bryon Groups
UPPER HANLEY POTTERY CO. (LTD.)	Bryonia
J. & M.P. BELL (CO.) & (LTD.)	Buah and Nanas
J. & M.P. BELL (CO.) & (LTD.)	Buah Buah
JOHN GOODWIN/SEACOMBE POTTERY	Buckingham Palace
J. & G. MEAKIN	Budded Vine
MEAKIN (BROS) & CO.	Budded Vine
ADDERLEY'S LTD.	Budding Dogwood
ROBERT GARNER (III)	Buddleia
SPODE'S BLUE PRINTED WARES	Buddleia
THOMAS WOLFE(S)	Buddleia
SPODE'S BLUE PRINTED WARES	Bude
JAMES & RALPH CLEWS	Buenos Ayres
WILLIAM DAVENPORT	Buenos Ayres
WILLIAM DAVENPORT	Buenos Ayres, South America / Aires
J (JOSHUA) HEATH	Buffalo
JOHN TURNER / TURNER & CO., etc.	Buffalo
SPODE'S BLUE PRINTED WARES	Buffalo
THOMAS WOLFE(S)	Buffalo
INDEO POTTERY	Buffalo & Fishermen
DAVID DUNDERDALE & CO.	Buffalo and Ruins
ENOCH WOOD & SONS	Buffalo on Lake Erie
LEEDS POTTERY	Buffalo Pattern
ROWLAND AND MARSELLUS	Buffalo, N.Y.
HENSHALL & CO.	Building
JAMES & RALPH CLEWS	Building in Distance, Woman in Foreground
JAMES & RALPH CLEWS	Building, Deer on Lawn
JAMES & RALPH CLEWS	Building, Fisherman With Net
JAMES & RALPH CLEWS	Building, Sheep on Lawn
JAMES & RALPH CLEWS	Building, Two Wings, Water in Foreground
BISHOP & STONIER (LTD.)	Bull
JOSIAH WEDGWOOD (& SONS LTD.)	Bull Finch
FERRYBRIDGE POTTERY	Bull Rider
ANTHONY SHAW (& SON(S) (& CO.)	Bullet
ANTHONY SHAW (& SON(S) (& CO.)	Bullet Shape
WILLIAM DAVENPORT	Bullfight
JOHN ROGERS (& SON)	Bungalow
SPODE'S BLUE PRINTED WARES	Bungalow
JOB & JOHN JACKSON	Bunker Hill Monument
ROWLAND AND MARSELLUS	Bunker Hill Monument
BURGESS & LEIGH (LTD.)	Burleigh
BROWN WESTHEAD, MOORE & CO.	Burlington
CAULDON, LTD.	Burlington
JOHN RIDGWAY (& CO.)	Burlington
RIDGWAYS (BEDFORD WORKS) LTD.	Burlington
WEDGWOOD & CO. (LTD.)	Burlington
W.H. GRINDLEY & CO. (LTD.)	Burmah
J. & M.P. BELL (CO.) & (LTD.)	Burmania
FRANCIS J. EMERY	Burmese
HENRY ALCOCK & CO. (LTD.)	Burmese
MELLOR, VENABLES & CO.	Burmese
T. RATHBONE & CO.	Burmese
W. & E. CORN	Burmese
WILLIAM ADAMS & SON(S) (POTTERS) LTD.	Burmese Garden
RIDGWAYS (BEDFORD WORKS) LTD.	Burnham
THOMAS DIMMOCK (JR.) & CO.	Burning of Coenties Slip
ALFRED MEAKIN (LTD.)	Burns
J. & M.P. BELL (CO.) & (LTD.)	Burns
BRAMELD & CO.	Burns Cotter
JAMES JAMIESON & CO.	Burns Monument
J. & M.P. BELL (CO.) & (LTD.)	Burong Kupu
J. & M.P. BELL (CO.) & (LTD.)	Burong Metak
J. & M.P. BELL (CO.) & (LTD.)	Burong Supam
NEWPORT POTTERY CO. LTD.	Burslem Berrie
W.H. GRINDLEY & CO. (LTD.)	Burton
JAMES & RALPH CLEWS	Bushey Park, Middlesex
FORD & SONS (LTD.)	Bute
DOULTON & CO. (LTD.)	Buttercup
J. & M.P. BELL (CO.) & (LTD.)	Butterfly
G.M. & C.J. MASON	Butterfly Japan
RALPH STEVENSON & WILLIAMS	Butterfly Rose
CHARLES JAMES MASON & CO.	Buttermere
HOLLINSHEAD & KIRKHAM (LTD.)	Buttons & Bows
WILLIAM SMITH (& CO.)	Buy a Broom
ELKIN, KNIGHT & CO.	By Land, Abbey, Yorkshire
WILLIAM DAVENPORT	By The River
JOHN ROGERS (& SON)	Byland Abbey, Yorkshire
F. WINKLE & CO. (LTD.)	Byron
GOODWINS & HARRIS	BYRON GALLERY SERIES
SPODE/COPELAND & GARRETT, et.al.	Byron Views
COPELAND & GARRETT, ET. AL.	BYRON VIEWS SERIES
SPODE'S BLUE PRINTED WARES	Byron Views/Groups
JOHN MEIR	BYRON'S ILLUSTRATIONS SERIES
MINTON	Bysham Monastery
WILLIAM ADAMS & SON(S) (POTTERS) LTD.	Bywell Castle, Northumberland
MINTONS, LTD.	Byzantine
WOOD & SON(S) (LTD.)	Byzantine
BROWN WESTHEAD, MOORE & CO.	Byzantium
CAULDON, LTD.	Byzantium
JOHN RIDGWAY (& CO.)	Byzantium
WILLIAM RIDGWAY (& CO.)	Byzantium
JOHN & WILLIAM RIDGWAY	Byzantium & Olympian
MAYER(BROS.)& ELLIOT	Cabbage Shape
ELIJAH JONES	Cabinet
GEORGE FREDERICK BOWERS (& CO.)	Cable
ANTHONY SHAW (& SON(S) (& CO.)	Cable & Ring
ARTHUR J. WILKINSON (LTD.)	Cable & Ring
COCKSON & CHETWYND	Cable & Ring
E. & C. CHALLINOR	Cable & Ring
HENRY BURGESS	Cable & Ring

J. & G. MEAKIN	Cable & Ring
JOHN MADDOCK & SONS (LTD.)	Cable & Ring
THOMAS FURNIVAL & SONS	Cable & Ring
WILLIAM ADAMS & SON(S) (POTTERS) LTD.	Cable and Ring
ANTHONY SHAW (& SON(S) (& CO.)	Cable Shape
E. & C. CHALLINOR	Cable Shape
HENRY BURGESS	Cable Shape
THOMAS FURNIVAL & SONS	Cable Shape
EDWARD CHALLINOR	Cabul
JAMES EDWARDS	Cabul
THOMAS SHIRLEY & CO.	Cabul
ENOCH WOOD & SONS	Cadmus
ENOCH WOOD & SONS	Cadmus / At Anchor
ENOCH WOOD & SONS	Cadmus / So Called
ENOCH WOOD & SONS	Cadmus / Under Full Sail
ENOCH WOOD & SONS	Cadmus / Under Half Sail
J. & M.P. BELL (CO.) & (LTD.)	Cadzow
HERCULANEUM POTTERY	Caernarvon Castle
BARKERS & KENT (LTD.)	Cairo
J. & G. MEAKIN	Cairo
SPODE/COPELAND & GARRETT, et.al.	Cairo
WILLIAM ADAMS & SON(S) (POTTERS) LTD.	Caister Castle, Norfolk
JOHN & WILLIAM RIDGWAY	Caius College, Cambridge
EDWARD CHALLINOR	Calcutta
JOHN & RICHARD RILEY	Calcutta
JAMES & THOMAS EDWARDS	Caldonia
MELLOR, VENABLES & CO.	Caldwell
CHARLES MEIGH	Caldwell, Lake George
THOMAS GODWIN	Caldwell, Lake George
WILLIAM RIDGWAY (& CO.)	Caldwell, Lake George
WILLIAM RIDGWAY, SON & CO.	Caldwell, Lake George
ANDREW MUIR (& CO.)	Caledonia
ISAAC WILSON & CO.	Caledonia
MIDDLESBOROUGH POTTERY CO.	Caledonia
RIDGWAY, MORLEY, WEAR & CO.	Caledonia
SOUTH WALES POTTERS	Caledonia
WILLIAM ADAMS	Caledonia
WILLIAM ADAMS & SON(S) (POTTERS) LTD.	Caledonia
CLYDE POTTERY CO. (LTD.)	Caledonian
CHARLES MEIGH, SON & PANKHURST	California
FRANCIS MORLEY (& CO.)	California
J. & M.P. BELL (CO.) & (LTD.)	California
JAMES JAMIESON & CO.	California
PODMORE, WALKER (& CO.)	California
R. COCHRAN & CO. - VERREVILLE POTTERY	California
HENRY BURGESS	Calla Lily
J. & M.P. BELL (CO.) & (LTD.)	Callcott, Sir Augustus Wall
CHARLES HEATHCOTE & CO.	Cambria
GEORGE PHILLIPS	Cambrian
JAMES WALLACE & CO.	Cambrian
CAMBRIAN POTTERY	Cambrian Border
ELIJAH JONES	Cambrian Bridges
CAMBRIAN POTTERY	Cambrian Palm
ALFRED MEAKIN (LTD.)	Cambridge
C. & W.K. HARVEY	Cambridge
HERCULANEUM POTTERY	Cambridge
HOLLINSHEAD & KIRKHAM (LTD.)	Cambridge
NEW WHARF POTTERY CO.	Cambridge
WOOD & SON(S) (LTD.)	Cambridge
JOHN & WILLIAM RIDGWAY	Cambridge College, Massachusetts
DAVENPORT'S & CO.	Cambridge Shape
JOHN WEDG WOOD	Cambridge Shape
WILLIAM DAVENPORT	Cambridge Shape
BELLE VUE POTTERIES	Cambusnetham on the Clyde
JOHN RIDGWAY (& CO.)	Camden
JOHN & RICHARD RILEY	Camel
LEEDS POTTERY	Camel
ROBINSON, WOOD & BROWNFIELD	Camel
SUNDERLAND OR "GARRISON" POTTERY	Camel
WILLIAM WALSH	Camel
JOHN HALL	Camel and other animals
JOHN ROGERS (& SON)	Camel Pattern
JAMES & RALPH CLEWS	Camel, Cow and Gnu
WEDGWOOD & CO. (LTD.)	Camelia
MINTON & CO.	Cameo
EDWARD WALLEY	Cameo Gothic
MINTONS, LTD.	Cameos
SPODE/COPELAND & GARRETT, et.al.	Camilla
SPODE'S BLUE PRINTED WARES	Camilla
WILLIAM DAVENPORT	Camp fire
JOHN MADDOCK & SONS (LTD.)	Campania
JOHN MADDOCK	Campanile
W.H. GRINDLEY & CO. (LTD.)	Campion
JOHN RIDGWAY (& CO.)	Canada
MEIKLE BROS.	Canada
CLEMENTSON BROS. (LTD.)	Canada Shape
MINTONS, LTD.	Canadian Leaves
JOHN MARSHALL (& CO.)(LTD.)	CANADIAN SPORTS SERIES
ENOCH WOOD & SONS	CANADIAN VIEWS

CAULDON, LTD.	Candia
WILLIAM RIDGWAY, SON & CO.	Candlestick Shape
WILLIAM RIDGWAY, SON & CO.	Candlestick with Push Up
EDWARD CHALLINOR	Canella
JOHN & RICHARD RILEY	Cannon Hall, Yorkshire
DAVID METHVEN & SONS	Canova
GEORGE PHILLIPS	Canova
J. & M.P. BELL (CO.) & (LTD.)	Canova
THOMAS MAYER	Canova
WILLIAM SMITH (& CO.)	Canova
JAMES & RALPH CLEWS	Canovian
SEWELL(S) & CO.	Canovian
H. & R. DANIEL	Canovian Statues
HEATH, BLACKHURST & CO.	Canovian Statues
BOOTHS (LTD.)	Canterbury
C. & W.K. HARVEY	Canterbury
HERCULANEUM POTTERY	Canterbury
RIDGWAYS (BEDFORD WORKS) LTD.	Canterbury
JAMES & RALPH CLEWS	Canterbury Cathedral
RALPH STEVENSON	Canterbury Cathedral
BENJAMIN E. GODWIN	Canton
ELKIN, KNIGHT & CO.	Canton
G.L. ASHWORTH & BROS. (LTD.)	Canton
JAMES EDWARDS	Canton
JOHN MADDOCK	Canton
ROBERT HERON (& SON)	Canton
ROBINSON, WOOD & BROWNFIELD	Canton
WILLIAM ADAMS & CO. LTD.	Canton
WILLIAM DAVENPORT	Canton
WILLIAM RIDGWAY (& CO.)	Canton
WOOD & SON(S) (LTD.)	Canton
ENOCH WOOD & SONS	Canton #107
ZACHARIAH BOYLE (& CO.)(& SON(S)	Canton Vase
ELKIN, KNIGHT & BRIDGWOOD	Canton Views
ELKIN, KNIGHT & BRIDGWOOD	CANTON VIEWS SERIES
JONES & SON	Canute Reproving His Courtiers
ENOCH WOOD & SONS	Cape Coast Castle On the Gold Coast, Africa
R. COCHRAN & CO. - VERREVILLE POTTERY	Cape Diamond: Cap Diamant
TAMS / et.al.	Capitol at Harrisburg, PA
CHARLES MEIGH	Capitol at Washington
ENOCH WOOD & SONS	Capitol at Washington
ROWLAND AND MARSELLUS	Capitol at Washington, D.C.
RALPH STEVENSON & WILLIAMS	Capitol, Albany
JOHN RIDGWAY (& CO.)	Capitol, Washington
RALPH STEVENSON	Capitol, Washington
WILLIAM RIDGWAY, SON & CO.	Capitol, Washington
JOHN & WILLIAM RIDGWAY	Capitol, Washington,at
MIDDLESBOROUGH POTTERY CO.	Caprera
FURNIVALS LTD.	Capri
ENOCH WOOD & SONS	Captain James
WILLIAM DAVENPORT	Captain Jones of the Macedonian
JONES & SON	Caractacus Before Claudius
SPODE/COPELAND & GARRETT, et.al.	Caramania
SPODE/COPELAND & GARRETT, et.al.	Caramania Castle
SPODE/COPELAND & GARRETT, et.al.	Caramania Vase
SPODE'S BLUE PRINTED WARES	Caramanian
SPODE/COPELAND & GARRETT, et.al.	CARAMANIAN SERIES
JOHN & WILLIAM RIDGWAY	Caravansary at Kustchiuk Czenege
ROWLAND AND MARSELLUS	Carlisle, Pa.
FORD & SONS (LTD.)	Carlton
SAMUEL ALCOCK & CO.	Carlton
WOOD & SON(S) (LTD.)	Carlton
WOOD & SON(S) (LTD.)	Carmania
ARTHUR J. WILKINSON (LTD.)	Carnation
FURNIVALS LTD.	Carnation
MINTON & CO.	Carnation
MINTONS, LTD.	Carnation Spray
ALFRED MEAKIN (LTD.)	Carnations
BRADLEY & CO.	Carnations
RALPH HALL	Carolina
JOHN HOLLAND	Carrara
THOMAS & JOHN CAREY/ JOHN CAREY & SONS	Carrickfergus Castle, and Town
GRIMWADES LTD.	Carro
SAMUEL ALCOCK & CO.	Carroll
BELLE VUE POTTERIES	Carstairs on the Clyde
WILLIAM ADAMS & SON(S) (POTTERS) LTD.	Carstairs, Lanarkshire
HERCULANEUM POTTERY	Casal
DON POTTERY	Cascade at Isola
JOSEPH TWIGG (& CO.)	Cascade at Isola
ENOCH WOOD & SONS	Cascade De Gresy Pres Chambery
HENSHALL & CO.	Cashiobury
ENOCH WOOD & SONS	Cashiobury, Hertfordshire
JOHN & WILLIAM RIDGWAY	Cashiobury, Hertfordshire
RALPH HALL (& CO.) or (& SONS)	Cashiobury, Hertfordshire
WOOD & SON(S) (LTD.)	Cashiobury, Hertfordshire
CORK, EDGE & MALKIN	Cashmere
EDGE, MALKIN & CO. (LTD.)	Cashmere
FRANCIS MORLEY (& CO.)	Cashmere

JOHN WEDG WOOD	Cashmere
RIDGWAY & MORLEY	Cashmere
RIDGWAY, MORLEY, WEAR & CO.	Cashmere
GEORGE JONES (& SONS LTD.)	Casino
FRANCIS MORLEY (& CO.)	Casket Japan
WILLIAM ADAMS & SON(S) (POTTERS) LTD.	Cassino
ANTHONY SHAW (& SON(S) (& CO.)	Castanette Dancer
LEEDS POTTERY	Castellated Manor House
DON POTTERY	Castello St. Angelo
J. & M.P. BELL (CO.) & (LTD.)	Castile
R. COCHRAN & CO. - VERREVILLE POTTERY	Castile
WALLIS GIMSON & CO.	Castillo
BATHWELL & GOODFELLOW	Castle
BRITISH ANCHOR POTTERY CO., LTD.	Castle
JAMES & RALPH CLEWS	Castle
JOHN & RICHARD RILEY	Castle
JOHN TAMS (& SON) (LTD)	Castle
JOHN THOMSON (& SONS)	Castle
MINTON	Castle
SOUTHWICK POTTERY	Castle
SPODE/COPELAND & GARRETT, et.al.	Castle
SPODE'S BLUE PRINTED WARES	Castle
T. & J. BEVINGTON (& CO.)	Castle
HENSHALL & CO.	Castle and Bridge
JAMES WALLACE & CO.	Castle and Cattle
ENOCH WOOD & SONS	Castle Forbes, Aberdeenshire
THOMAS & JOHN CAREY/ JOHN CAREY & SONS	Castle Frede, Cork Ireland, Lord Carbery's Seat
ENOCH WOOD & SONS	Castle Garden
ENOCH WOOD & SONS	Castle Garden, Battery, New York
JOB & JOHN JACKSON	Castle Garden, New York
WILLIAM DAVENPORT	Castle gateway, two gentlemen walk with their dog, et.al.
ENOCH WOOD & SONS	Castle Huntley, Perthshire
WOOD & CHALLINOR	Castle Montdragon
WOOD & CHALLINOR	Castle of Beaucaire
HENSHALL & CO.	Castle of Furstenfeld
ENOCH WOOD & SONS	Castle of Lavenza
ENOCH WOOD & SONS	Castle of Nepi, Italy
BRAMELD & CO.	Castle of Rochefort, South France
ENOCH WOOD & SONS	Castle of St. Angelo, Rome
CALEDONIAN POTTERY	Castle Pattern
RALPH HALL (& CO.) or (& SONS)	Castle Prison, St. Albans, Hertfordshire
GRIFFITHS, BEARDMORE & BIRKS	Castle Richard
ELKIN & CO.	Castle Richard in Waterford
ELKIN, KNIGHT & CO.	Castle Richard in Waterford
GEORGE F. SMITH (& CO.)	Castle Scene
JACOB FURNIVAL & CO.	Castle Scenery
THOMAS FURNIVAL & CO.	Castle Scenery
SAMPSON BRIDGWOOD (& SON)(LTD.)	Castle Shield
HERCULANEUM POTTERY	Castle Street and St. George's, Crescent, Liverpool
JOHN HALL (& SONS)	Castle Toward
JAMES & RALPH CLEWS	Castle with Flag, Boats in Foreground
T. & J. BEVINGTON (& CO.)	Castled Gateway
J. & G. MEAKIN	Castro
THOMAS & BENJAMIN GODWIN	Cat
JOSEPH HEATH & CO.	Cathedral
ENOCH WOOD & SONS	Cathedral at York
THOMAS & JOHN CAREY/ JOHN CAREY & SONS	CATHEDRAL SERIES
W.H. GRINDLEY & CO. (LTD.)	Catherine
W.H. GRINDLEY & CO. (LTD.)	Catherine Merrett
RIDGWAYS (BEDFORD WORKS) LTD.	Cathlyn
ANDREW STEVENSON	Catholic Cathedral, New York
ENOCH WOOD & SONS	Catskill House, Hudson
WILLIAM RIDGWAY, SON & CO.	CATSKILL MOSS SERIES
WILLIAM ADAMS & SON(S) (POTTERS) LTD.	Catskill Mountain House, U.S.
ENOCH WOOD & SONS	Catskill Mountain, Pass, In The
ENOCH WOOD & SONS	Catskill Mountains, Hudson River
ENOCH WOOD & SONS	Catskill, Hope Mill, State of New York
ANTHONY SHAW (& SON(S) (& CO.)	Cattail
TURNER & TOMKINSON	Cattle
JOHN & RICHARD RILEY	Cattle and Herdsman
CHARLES HEATHCOTE & CO.	Cattle and River Pattern
JOHN & RICHARD RILEY	Cattle and Sheep ...
JOHN & RICHARD RILEY	Cattle by Stream
JOHN ROGERS (& SON)	Cattle Foreground
HERCULANEUM POTTERY	Cattle Resting
THOMAS FELL (& CO.) (LTD.)	Cattle Scenery
THOMAS MAYER	Cattle Scenery
WILLIAM ADAMS & SON(S) (POTTERS) LTD.	Cattle Scenery
WILLIAM DAVENPORT	Cattleman and Spire
ENOCH WOOD & SONS	Cave Castle, Yorkshire
RALPH STEVENSON	Cave Castle, Yorkshire
JOHN THOMSON (& SONS)	Cavendish
KEELING & CO. (LTD.)	Cavendish
THOMAS TILL & SONS	Cecil
BOOTHS (LTD.)	Cedric
UPPER HANLEY POTTERY CO. (LTD.)	Ceicel

J. & M.P. BELL (CO.) & (LTD.)	Celebes
BURGESS & LEIGH (LTD.)	Celeste
JOHN ALCOCK	Celeste
W. & E. CORN	Celeste
JOHN RIDGWAY (& CO.)	Celestial
RIDGWAYS (BEDFORD WORKS) LTD.	Celestial
SAMUEL ALCOCK & CO.	Celtic
W.H. GRINDLEY & CO. (LTD.)	Celtic
ENOCH WOOD & SONS	CELTIC CHINA SERIES
SPODE/COPELAND & GARRETT, et.al.	Centaurs Battling Theseus
WOOD & CHALLINOR	Centenary
W. & E. CORN	Centennial Shape
WILLIAM RIDGWAY, SON & CO.	Centre Harbour
EDWARD WALLEY	Ceres
WILLIAM DAVENPORT	Ceres
EDWARD PEARSON (& SON)	Ceres Shape
ELSMORE & FORSTER	Ceres Shape
TURNER, GODDARD & CO.	Ceres Shape
ELSMORE & FORSTER	Ceres With Cable
ELSMORE & FORSTER	Ceres Without Cable
TURNER & GODDARD	Ceres Without Cable
TURNER, GODDARD & CO.	Ceres Without Cable
ENOCH WOOD & SONS	Cetara
BISHOP & STONIER (LTD.)	Ceylon
CHARLES MEIGH	Ceylon
SPODE/COPELAND & GARRETT, et.al.	Ceylon
THOMAS FURNIVAL & SONS	Ceylon
GEORGE PHILLIPS	Ceylonese
SAMPSON HANCOCK (& SONS)	Chadsworth
WOOD & SON(S) (LTD.)	Chain of States
J. & G. MEAKIN	Chain of Tulips
JAMES GILDEA	Chaing
ENOCH WOOD & SONS	Chancellor Livingston
C.T. MALING	Chang
EDGE, MALKIN & CO. (LTD.)	Chang
READ, CLEMENTSON & ANDERSON	Chantillian
JOHN THOMSON (& SONS)	Chantilly
WILLIAM DAVENPORT	Chantilly
WOOD & BROWNFIELD	Chantilly
SPODE'S BLUE PRINTED WARES	Chantilly Sprig
J (JOSHUA) HEATH	Chantilly Sprigs
BROWN WESTHEAD, MOORE & CO.	Chantrey
ENOCH WOOD & SONS	Chapelle De Guillaume Tell
J. & G. MEAKIN	Chaplet
THOMAS GOODFELLOW	Chaplet
THOMAS DIMMOCK (JR.) & CO.	Chaplet Wreath
JOHN WEDG WOOD	Chapoo
RALPH HALL & CO.	Chapoo
JOHN THOMSON (& SONS)	Chariot
FERRYBRIDGE POTTERY	Chariot with Rearing Horses
THOMAS MAYER	Charioteers, The
DAVID METHVEN & SONS	Chariots and Gazebo
WHITEHAVEN POTTERY	Charity
JONES & SON	Charles I Ordering the Speaker to Give Up the Five Members
W.H. GRINDLEY & CO. (LTD.)	Charleston
ROWLAND AND MARSELLUS	Charleston, W. Va.
DAVID LOCKHART (and LOCKHART & CO.)	Charlie
THOMAS FELL (& CO.) (LTD.)	Charlotte
ROWLAND AND MARSELLUS	Charlotte, N.C.
JOHN RIDGWAY (& CO.)	Charmontel
ANDREW STEVENSON	Charter Oak, Connecticut
HENRY ALCOCK & CO. (LTD.)	Chase
EDWARD CHALLINOR	Chase After a Wolf
SPODE/COPELAND & GARRETT, et.al.	Chase After a Wolf
DOULTON & CO. (LTD.)	Chase, The
JOHN EDWARDS (& CO.)	Chateau
ENOCH WOOD & SONS	Chateau Coucey / Vue du
ENOCH WOOD & SONS	Chateau de Chillon
ENOCH WOOD & SONS	Chateau Ermenonville / Vue du
J. & G. MEAKIN	Chatham
FORD & SONS (LTD.)	Chatsworth
GEORGE JONES (& SONS LTD.)	Chatsworth
J. H. & J. DAVIS	Chatsworth
KEELING & CO. (LTD.)	Chatsworth
MYOTT, SON & CO. (LTD.)	Chatsworth
SPODE/COPELAND & GARRETT, et.al.	Chatsworth
W.H. GRINDLEY & CO. (LTD.)	Chatsworth
PODMORE, WALKER (& CO.)	Chaudiere Bridge
R. COCHRAN & CO. - VERREVILLE POTTERY	Chaudiere Falls: Chute De La Chaudiere
JAMES & RALPH CLEWS	Cheddar, Somersetshire
CAMBRIAN POTTERY	Cheetah
JOB MEIGH (& SON)	Cheetah
ALFRED MEAKIN (LTD.)	Chelsea
BISHOP & STONIER (LTD.)	Chelsea
BRITISH ANCHOR POTTERY CO., LTD.	Chelsea
JOHNSON BROS. (HANLEY), LTD.	Chelsea
POWELL & BISHOP	Chelsea
POWELL, BISHOP & STONIER	Chelsea

WEDGWOOD & CO. (LTD.)	Chelsea
JOHN MADDOCK	Chen-si
JOHN MEIR	Chen-si
POUNTNEY & ALLIES	Cheptow Castle
C. & W.K. HARVEY	Cherry Blossom
WILLIAM (ALSAGER) ADDERLEY (& CO.)	Cherry Blossom
J. & G. MEAKIN	Cherry Scroll
BARROW & CO.	Cherub Jug
HERCULANEUM POTTERY	CHERUB MEDALLION BORDER SERIES
JOHN ROGERS (& SON)	Chesapeake
WILLIAM ADAMS & SON(S) (POTTERS) LTD.	Chess Players
ENOCH WOOD & SONS	Chester
HERCULANEUM POTTERY	Chester
ALFRED MEAKIN (LTD.)	Chesterfield
CHETHAM & (SON)	Chetham
ENOCH WOOD & SONS	Chevy Chase
THOMAS DIMMOCK (JR.) & CO.	CHEVY CHASE SERIES
FLACKETT & TOFT	Chian
WILLIAM DAVENPORT	Chian
HILDITCH & HOPWOOD	Chian Sprigs
JOHN GOODWIN/LONGTON	Chiang
ROWLAND AND MARSELLUS	Chicago, Il.
ROWLAND AND MARSELLUS	Chicago, Ill.
ENOCH WOOD & SONS	Chichester
RALPH STEVENSON	Chichester Cathedral
THOMAS & JOHN CAREY/ JOHN CAREY & SONS	Chichester Cathedral
ENOCH WOOD & SONS	Chief Justice Marshall, Troy
JOHN MARSHALL (& CO.)(LTD.)	Child With Snow Shovel
JOHN & RICHARD RILEY	Children Feeding Chickens
MADDOCK & SEDDON	Children's Pets
DAVID METHVEN & SONS	Chile
MIDDLESBOROUGH EARTHENWARE CO.	Chili
WILLIAM DAVENPORT	Chillicothe / Ohio / variation with cows
WILLIAM DAVENPORT	Chillicothe / Ohio / variation with sailboat
WILLIAM DAVENPORT	Chillicothe / Ohio / variation with three men on rafts
WILLIAM DAVENPORT	Chillicothe, with Cows,Ohio
WILLIAM DAVENPORT	Chillicothe, with Sailboat,Ohio
JAMES & RALPH CLEWS	Chillicothe/ with Cows, Ohio
JAMES & RALPH CLEWS	Chillicothe/ with Raft
JAMES & RALPH CLEWS	Chillocothe with Sailboat
WILLIAM DAVENPORT	Chillothe with Raft
COCHRAN & FLEMING - BRITANNIA POTTERY	China
MINTON & CO.	China Aster
MINTON	China Pattern
SPODE/COPELAND & GARRETT, et.al.	China Rose
MINTON	China Temple
SKINNER & WALKER	China-Aster
G.L. ASHWORTH & BROS. (LTD.)	China-Flora
SAMPSON BRIDGWOOD (& SON)(LTD.)	Chinaman Hawking
JOHN TURNER / TURNER & CO., etc.	Chinaman With Rocket
THOMAS LAKIN	Chinamen
BOURNE & LEIGH (LTD.)	Chinese
CHARLES ALLERTON & SONS	Chinese
JOHN MEIR & SON	Chinese
JOHN RIDGWAY (& CO.)	Chinese
JOSIAH WEDGWOOD (& SONS LTD.)	Chinese
MINTONS, LTD.	Chinese
THOMAS DIMMOCK (JR.) & CO.	Chinese
THOMAS FURNIVAL & CO.	Chinese
W.H. GRINDLEY & CO. (LTD.)	Chinese
WEDGWOOD & CO. (LTD.)	Chinese
WILLIAM DAVENPORT	Chinese Banana Tree
JOSIAH WEDGWOOD (& SONS LTD.)	Chinese Baroque
G.L. ASHWORTH & BROS. (LTD.)	Chinese Basket
WILLIAM DAVENPORT	Chinese Beekeepers
CHARLES MEIGH	Chinese Bells
SAMUEL ALCOCK & CO.	Chinese Bells
JOHN & WILLIAM RIDGWAY	Chinese Bird
RALPH STEVENSON & WILLIAMS	Chinese Bird Catchers
WILLIAM DAVENPORT	Chinese Birds
MINTONS, LTD.	Chinese Blossom
JOHN MEIR & SON	Chinese Bottle
COPELAND & GARRETT, ET. AL.	Chinese Bouquet
SPODE/COPELAND & GARRETT, et.al.	Chinese Bouquet
CHARLES MEIGH	Chinese Children's Games
WILLIAM ADAMS & SON(S) (POTTERS) LTD.	Chinese Ching
J (JOSHUA) HEATH	Chinese Design Wheel
J (JOSHUA) HEATH	Chinese Design With Trophies
G.L. ASHWORTH & BROS. (LTD.)	Chinese Dragon
MINTONS, LTD.	Chinese Dragon
JOSIAH WEDGWOOD (& SONS LTD.)	Chinese Economy of Time
JOHN & WILLIAM RIDGWAY	Chinese Export Boat
MINTON	Chinese Figure
REED & TAYLOR	Chinese Figure
MINTON	Chinese Figures
J. & M.P. BELL (CO.) & (LTD.)	Chinese Fish
WILLIAM DAVENPORT	Chinese Fishermen
HICKS, MEIGH & JOHNSON	Chinese Fishing Scene
WILLIAM DAVENPORT	Chinese Flag Bearers
LEWIS WOOLF (& SONS)(& CO.)	Chinese Flora
GEORGE JONES (& SONS LTD.)	Chinese Flowers
MINTONS, LTD.	Chinese Flowers
SPODE/COPELAND & GARRETT, et.al.	Chinese Flowers
SPODE'S BLUE PRINTED WARES	Chinese Flowers
WILLIAM ADAMS & SON(S) (POTTERS) LTD.	Chinese Flowers
ELKIN, KNIGHT & BRIDGWOOD	Chinese Fountains
JOHN ROGERS (& SON)	Chinese Garden
JOSIAH WEDGWOOD (& SONS LTD.)	Chinese Garden
MOORE (SAMUEL) & CO.	Chinese Garden
THOMAS DIMMOCK (JR.) & CO.	Chinese Garden
WILLIAM DAVENPORT	Chinese Garden Scene
WOOD & BRETTEL	Chinese Gardener
SPODE/COPELAND & GARRETT, et.al.	Chinese Gardens
SPODE'S BLUE PRINTED WARES	Chinese Gardens
E.T. TROUTBECK	Chinese Gem
DILLWYN & CO.	Chinese Harbor Scene
WILLIAM DAVENPORT	Chinese in Gazebo
RIDGWAYS (BEDFORD WORKS) LTD.	Chinese Japan
THOMAS GREEN	Chinese Jar
LEEDS POTTERY	Chinese Junk
THOMAS BARLOW	Chinese Juvenile Sports
THOMAS DIMMOCK (JR.) & CO.	Chinese Key
WILLIAM BROWNFIELD (& SON(S)	Chinese Key & Basket
CHARLES JAMES MASON	Chinese Landscape
G.L. ASHWORTH & BROS. (LTD.)	Chinese Landscape
HICKS, MEIGH & JOHNSON	Chinese Landscape
JAMES & RALPH CLEWS	Chinese Landscape
SPODE'S BLUE PRINTED WARES	Chinese Landscapes
BARKER & SON	Chinese Marine
BELLE VUE POTTERIES	Chinese Marine
GEORGE TOWNSEND	Chinese Marine
LEWIS WOOLF (& SONS)(& CO.)	Chinese Marine
MINTON	Chinese Marine
THOMAS FELL (& CO.) (LTD.)	Chinese Marine
WILLIAM DAVENPORT	Chinese Marine
ROBERT HAMILTON	Chinese Market Stall
SPODE'S BLUE PRINTED WARES	Chinese of Rank
BOVEY TRACY POTTERY COMPANY	Chinese Pagoda
ELKIN, KNIGHT & BRIDGWOOD	Chinese Pagoda
WILLIAM DAVENPORT	Chinese Pastime
G.L. ASHWORTH & BROS. (LTD.)	Chinese Pattern
HOPE & CARTER	Chinese Pattern
MINTON	Chinese Pilgrim
SPODE/COPELAND & GARRETT, et.al.	Chinese Plants
SPODE'S BLUE PRINTED WARES	Chinese Plants
COPELAND & GARRETT, ET. AL.	Chinese Plants Sprays
JOHN ROGERS (& SON)	Chinese Porcelain
ELKIN, KNIGHT & BRIDGWOOD	Chinese River Scene
DILLWYN & CO.	Chinese Rose
WILLIAM DAVENPORT	Chinese Ruins
CAMBRIAN POTTERY	Chinese Scene After Pillemont
H. & R. DANIEL	Chinese Scenery
WILLIAM DAVENPORT	Chinese Scenery
ANTHONY SHAW (& SON(S) (& CO.)	Chinese Shape
HENRY ALCOCK & CO. (LTD.)	Chinese Shape
JOHN ALCOCK	Chinese Shape
JOSEPH CLEMENTSON	Chinese Shape
T. & R. BOOTE (LTD.) (& SON)	Chinese Shape
J. & M.P. BELL (CO.) & (LTD.)	Chinese Sports
JACOB FURNIVAL & CO.	Chinese Sports
THOMAS FELL (& CO.) (LTD.)	Chinese Sports
THOMAS FURNIVAL & CO.	Chinese Sports
ANTHONY SHAW (& SON(S) (& CO.)	Chinese Sydenham
R. COCHRAN & CO. - VERREVILLE POTTERY	Chinese Tea Garden
JOHN MEIR & SON	Chinese Temple
MINTON	Chinese Temple
WILLIAM SMITH (& CO.)	Chinese Temple
WOOD & CHALLINOR	Chinese Temples
ANDREW STEVENSON	Chinese Traders
THOMAS DIMMOCK (JR.) & CO.	Chinese Tree
WOOD & BROWNFIELD	Chinese Tree
J. & M.P. BELL (CO.) & (LTD.)	Chinese Vase
JOSIAH WEDGWOOD (& SONS LTD.)	Chinese Vase
RIDGWAYS (BEDFORD WORKS) LTD.	Chinese Vase
DILLWYN & CO.	Chinese Views
EDWARD & GEORGE PHILLIPS	Chinese Views
ROBINSON & WOOD	Chinese Views
WILLIAM DAVENPORT	CHINESE VIEWS SERIES
J. & M.P. BELL (CO.) & (LTD.)	Chinese Villa
G.L. ASHWORTH & BROS. (LTD.)	Chinese-Flowers
JOHN & WILLIAM TURNER	Chinese-Style Scene With Figure of a One Legged Duck
F. & R. PRATT & CO. (LTD.)	Ching
J. & M.P. BELL (CO.) & (LTD.)	Ching
WILLIAM DAVENPORT	Ching

WILLIAM REID (& SON) or (SONS)	Ching
ALLERTON, BROUGH & GREEN	Ching-Tien
DIMMOCK & SMITH	Chino
DIMMOCK & SMITH	Chino
WILLIAM DAVENPORT	Chinoisere Bridgeless
WILLIAM DAVENPORT	Chinoisere High Bridge
WILLIAM DAVENPORT	Chinoisere Ruins
WILLIAM ADAMS & SON(S) (POTTERS) LTD.	Chinoiserie After Pillemont
ANDREW STEVENSON	Chinoiserie Bridgeless
DON POTTERY	Chinoiserie Bridgeless
BRADLEY & CO.	Chinoiserie Bridges
GEORGE FORRESTER	Chinoiserie Design
MINTON	Chinoiserie Landscape
CAMBRIAN POTTERY	Chinoiserie Palm
ANDREW STEVENSON	Chinoiserie Ruins
JOB RIDGWAY	Chinoiserie Ruins
JOB RIDGWAY & SONS	Chinoiserie Ruins
JOHN ROGERS (& SON)	Chinoiserie Ruins
RALPH STEVENSON	Chinoiserie Ruins
RALPH HAMMERSLEY (& SON(S)	Chints
JOHN RIDGWAY (& CO.)	Chintz
MINTON	Chintz
MINTON & BOYLE	Chintz
THOMAS DIMMOCK (JR.) & CO.	Chintz
JOHN MEIR & SON	Chios
KNIGHT, ELKIN & CO.	Chip Chase
BOOTHS (LTD.)	Chippendale
RIDGWAYS (BEDFORD WORKS) LTD.	Chiswick
WOOD & BROWNFIELD	Chiswick
ENOCH WOOD & SONS	Chiswick On The Thames
JOHN THOMAS HUDDEN	Choice Pattern
ENOCH WOOD & SONS	Christ and the Woman of Samaria
JOHN & WILLIAM RIDGWAY	Christ Church, Oxford
JOHN & WILLIAM RIDGWAY	Christ's College, Cambridge
THOMAS & JOHN CAREY/ JOHN CAREY & SONS	Christchurch, Oxford
ENOCH WOOD & SONS	Christianburg, Danish Settlement On The Gold Coast, Africa
JAMES & RALPH CLEWS	Christmas Eve
WILLIAM ADAMS & CO. LTD.	Christmas Roses
GEORGE JONES (& SONS LTD.)	Christs Hospital
CAMBRIAN POTTERY	Chrysanthemum
CAMPBELLFIELD POTTERY CO. (LTD.)	Chrysanthemum
CLYDE POTTERY CO. (LTD.)	Chrysanthemum
F. & R. PRATT & CO. (LTD.)	Chrysanthemum
MINTONS, LTD.	Chrysanthemum
MYOTT, SON & CO. (LTD.)	Chrysanthemum
WILLIAM ADAMS & SON(S) (POTTERS) LTD.	Chrysanthemum
JAMES & RALPH CLEWS	Chrysanthemum & Bamboo
HENRY BURGESS	Chrysanthemum Shape
WHITEHAVEN POTTERY	Church & College of St. Bees
ANDREW STEVENSON	Church and Buildings Adjoining Murray Street, New York
JAMES & RALPH CLEWS	Church and Fisherman
JOSEPH STUBBS	Church in the City of New York / Dr. Mason's
ENOCH WOOD & SONS	Church of England Missionary College, London
WILLIAM ADAMS	Church of England Missionary College, London
DILLWYN & CO.	Church of St. Austell, Cornwall
RALPH HALL (& CO.) or (& SONS)	Church of St. Charles and Polytechnic School, Vienna, Germany
DILLWYN & CO.	Church of the Holy Trinity
LEEDS POTTERY	Church with Flagstaff
JOHN ROGERS (& SON)	Church Zebra
CHARLES COLLINSON & CO.	Chusan
G.L. ASHWORTH & BROS. (LTD.)	Chusan
JOHN RIDGWAY (& CO.)	Chusan
JOSEPH CLEMENTSON	Chusan
JOSIAH WEDGWOOD (& SONS LTD.)	Chusan
KEELING & CO. (LTD.)	Chusan
PETER HOLDCROFT & CO.	Chusan
PODMORE, WALKER (& CO.)	Chusan
RIDGWAY & MORLEY	Chusan
THOMAS FELL (& CO.) (LTD.)	Chusan
WEDGWOOD & CO. (LTD.)	Chusan
WILTSHAW & ROBINSON (LTD.)	Chusan
WEDGWOOD & CO. (LTD.)	Chusan #1
WEDGWOOD & CO. (LTD.)	Chusan #2
JOHN & WILLIAM RIDGWAY	Ciala Kavak
JOHN MADDOCK	Cimerian
ROWLAND AND MARSELLUS	Cincinnati, Ohio
COPELAND & GARRETT, ET. AL.	Cintra
JOSEPH HEATH	Cintra
JOHN & GEORGE ALCOCK	Circassia
JOHN ALCOCK	Circassia
SAMUEL BOYLE (& SONS)	Circassia
WILLIAM BROWNFIELD (& SON(S)	Ciris
WOOD & BAGGALEY	Ciris
WOOD & BROWNFIELD	Ciris
SPODE/COPELAND & GARRETT, et.al.	Citadel Near Corinth

C. & W.K. HARVEY	CITIES AND TOWNS SERIES
JAMES & RALPH CLEWS	CITIES SERIES
WILLIAM DAVENPORT	CITIES SERIES
JOSEPH CLEMENTSON	Citron
WILLIAM DAVENPORT	Citron
CLEMENTSON BROS. (LTD.)	Citron Shape
JOSEPH CLEMENTSON	Citron Shape
RALPH STEVENSON	City Hall, Albany
ANDREW STEVENSON	City Hall, New York
CHARLES MEIGH	City Hall, New York
JAMES & RALPH CLEWS	City Hall, New York
JOB & JOHN JACKSON	City Hall, New York
JOHN & WILLIAM RIDGWAY	City Hall, New York
JOSEPH STUBBS	City Hall, New York
RALPH STEVENSON	City Hotel New York
RALPH STEVENSON & WILLIAMS	City Hotel, New York
THOMAS GODWIN	City of Baltimore
JOHN HALL (& SONS)	City of Benares
ENOCH WOOD & SONS	City of Canterbury
SPODE/COPELAND & GARRETT, et.al.	City of Corinth
LOCKHART & ARTHUR	Clan Mackenzie
JOHN RIDGWAY (& CO.)	Clara
ROWLAND AND MARSELLUS	Clara Barton Birthplace
JOHN & WILLIAM RIDGWAY	Clare Hall, Cambridge
BARKER & SON	Claremont
BEARDMORE & EDWARDS	Claremont
CLEMENTSON BROS. (LTD.)	Claremont
JOHNSON BROS. (HANLEY), LTD.	Claremont
JOSEPH CLEMENTSON	Claremont
MINTON	Claremont
WOOD & BROWNFIELD	Claremont
SAMPSON HANCOCK (& SONS)	Claremont Group
SNEYD & HILL	Claremont Groups
ENOCH WOOD & SONS	Claremont, Surrey
W.H. GRINDLEY & CO. (LTD.)	Clarence
ENOCH WOOD & SONS	Clarence House
WILLIAM ADAMS	Clarence House
ZACHARIAH BOYLE (& CO.)(& SON(S)	Clarence Star
ENOCH WOOD & SONS	Clarence Terrace, Regent's Park, London
WILLIAM ADAMS	Clarence Terrace, Regent's Park, London
HENRY ALCOCK & CO. (LTD.)	Clarendon
JOHN RIDGWAY (& CO.)	Clarendon
THOMAS DIMMOCK (JR.) & CO.	Clarendon
ALFRED MEAKIN (LTD.)	Claridge
J. & G. MEAKIN	Claridge
JOHNSON BROS. (HANLEY), LTD.	Clarissa
JACOB FURNIVAL & CO.	Classic Cameo
ANTHONY SHAW (& SON(S) (& CO.)	Classic Gothic
C. & W.K. HARVEY	Classic Gothic
EDWARD WALLEY	Classic Gothic
ELSMORE & FORSTER	Classic Gothic
FRANCIS MORLEY (& CO.)	Classic Gothic
JACOB FURNIVAL & CO.	Classic Gothic
JAMES EDWARDS	Classic Gothic
JOHN & GEORGE ALCOCK	Classic Gothic
JOHN MEIR & SON	Classic Gothic
JOHN RIDGWAY (& CO.)	Classic Gothic
JOSEPH CLEMENTSON	Classic Gothic
LIVESLEY, POWELL & CO.	Classic Gothic
THOMAS GOODFELLOW	Classic Gothic
THOMAS, JOHN & JOSEPH MAYER	Classic Gothic Octagon Shape
SAMUEL ALCOCK & CO.	Classic Gothic Shape
WILLIAM DAVENPORT	Classic Gothic Shape
T. & R. BOOTE (LTD.) (& SON)	Classic Shape
JOSEPH CLEMENTSON	Classical Antiquities
JOSEPH CLEMENTSON	CLASSICAL ANTIQUITIES SERIES
WILLIAM DAVENPORT	Classical Buildings and City
J. & M.P. BELL (CO.) & (LTD.)	Classical Dancers
ELKIN, KNIGHT & BRIDGWOOD	Classical Figure
KNIGHT, ELKIN & CO.	Classical Figure
FERRYBRIDGE POTTERY	Classical Grecian
CHARLES JAMES MASON & CO.	Classical Landscape
DAWSON (JOHN DAWSON & CO., ETC.)	Classical Ruins
THOMAS LAKIN	Classical Ruins
JOHNSON BROS. (HANLEY), LTD.	Clayton
BARKER & SON	Clematis
BARKERS & KENT (LTD.)	Clematis
BURGESS & LEIGH (LTD.)	Clematis
J. & M.P. BELL (CO.) & (LTD.)	Clematis
JOHNSON BROS. (HANLEY), LTD.	Clematis
SAMUEL BARKER & SON	Clematis
W.H. GRINDLEY & CO. (LTD.)	Clematis
WILLIAM DAVENPORT	Clematis
EDWARD WALLEY	Cleopatra
FRANCIS MORLEY (& CO.)	Cleopatra
GEORGE FREDERICK BOWERS (& CO.)	Clermont
RIDGWAYS (BEDFORD WORKS) LTD.	Clevedon
ROWLAND AND MARSELLUS	Cleveland, Ohio
JAMES & RALPH CLEWS	Clews Oriental

JAMES & RALPH CLEWS	Clews, Double Prints
ALFRED MEAKIN (LTD.)	Clifton
DOULTON & CO. (LTD.)	Clifton
F. WINKLE & CO. (LTD.)	Clifton
FORD & SONS (LTD.)	Clifton
J. & M.P. BELL (CO.) & (LTD.)	Clifton
POUNTNEY & ALLIES	Clifton
W.H. GRINDLEY & CO. (LTD.)	Clifton
DILLWYN & CO.	Clifton Rocks
POUNTNEY & ALLIES	Clifton Rocks
DAVENPORT'S LTD.	Clifton Shape
WILLIAM DAVENPORT	Clifton Shape
BATHWELL & GOODFELLOW	Clinging Girl
RALPH STEVENSON	Clinton
RALPH STEVENSON & WILLIAMS	Clinton
RALPH STEVENSON & WILLIAMS	Clinton & Washington
HENRY ALCOCK & CO. (LTD.)	Clive
T. RATHBONE & CO.	Clive
THOMAS GODWIN	Cloaked Figure
JOHN VENABLES & CO.	Closed Bud Finial
WILLIAM DAVENPORT	CLOSE-LINED BORDER
JOSIAH WEDGWOOD (& SONS LTD.)	Clover
W.H. GRINDLEY & CO. (LTD.)	Clover
COCKSON & SEDDON	Clover Shape
SAMUEL KEELING & CO.	Clumber
FURNIVALS LTD.	Cluny
HERCULANEUM POTTERY	Cluny Castle
PEARL POTTERY CO. (LTD.)	Cluster of Peaches & Leaves
GEORGE THOMAS MOUNTFORD	Clyde
NEW WHARF POTTERY CO.	Clyde
THOMAS TILL & SON	Clyde
JOB & JOHN JACKSON	Clyde Scenery
W.H. GRINDLEY & CO. (LTD.)	Clytie
WEDGWOOD & CO. (LTD.)	Clytie
KNIGHT, ELKIN & CO.	Cobham Hall
BARKERS & KENT (LTD.)	Coburg
E. CHALLINOR & CO.	Coburg
J. & M.P. BELL (CO.) & (LTD.)	Coburg
JAMES EDWARDS	Coburg
POWELL, BISHOP & STONIER	Coburg
THOMAS DIMMOCK (JR.) & CO.	Coburg
R. COCHRAN & CO. - VERREVILLE POTTERY	Cochran's Hyacinth
R. COCHRAN & CO. - VERREVILLE POTTERY	Cochran's Ring
J. & M.P. BELL (CO.) & (LTD.)	Cockerel
CAMBRIAN POTTERY	Cockle
CAMBRIAN POTTERY	Cockle & Whelk
DILLWYN & CO.	Cockle & Whelk
DILLWYN & CO.	Cockle Plater
JACOB FURNIVAL & CO.	Cockscomb Handle
ENOCH WOOD & SONS	Coke, Denton
ENOCH WOOD & SONS	Cokethorpe Park, Oxfordshire
SOUTH WALES POTTERS	Colandine
JOHN MEIR	Cole Orton Hall, Leicestershire
KEELING & CO. (LTD.)	Colesberg
ENOCH WOOD & SONS	Coliseum
RALPH STEVENSON	College
CHARLES JAMES MASON & CO.	COLLEGE VIEWS SERIES
ELKIN, KNIGHT & BRIDGWOOD	Cologne
JOHN & GEORGE ALCOCK	Cologne
JOHN ALCOCK	Cologne
RALPH STEVENSON & SON	Cologne
THOMAS GOODFELLOW	Cologne
WOOD & CHALLINOR	Cologne
R. COCHRAN & CO. - VERREVILLE POTTERY	Colombo
J. & G. MEAKIN	Colonial
THOMAS GOODFELLOW	Colonial
THOMAS GOODFELLOW	Colonna
ROBERT HAMILTON	Colossal Sarcophagus at Cacamo
JAMES & RALPH CLEWS	Colossal Sarcophagus Near Castle Rosso
SPODE/COPELAND & GARRETT, et.al.	Colossal Sarcophagus Near Castle Rosso
JOHN GOODWIN/SEACOMBE POTTERY	Colosseum
CLEMENTSON & YOUNG	Columbia
J. & G. MEAKIN	Columbia
JAMES & THOMAS EDWARDS	Columbia
JOHN & WILLIAM RIDGWAY	Columbia
JOHN WEDG WOOD	Columbia
JOHNSON BROS. (HANLEY), LTD.	Columbia
WILLIAM ADAMS & SON(S) (POTTERS) LTD.	Columbia
THOMAS GODWIN	Columbia Bridge
WILLIAM RIDGWAY (& CO.)	Columbia Bridge on the Susquehanna
WILLIAM RIDGWAY, SON & CO.	Columbia Bridge on the Susquehanna
ANDREW STEVENSON	Columbia College, New York
RALPH STEVENSON	Columbia College, New York
RALPH STEVENSON & WILLIAMS	Columbia College, New York
E. & C. CHALLINOR	Columbia Shape
ELSMORE & FORSTER	Columbia Shape
GEORGE WOOLISCROFT (& CO.)	Columbia Shape
JOHN MEIR & SON	Columbia Shape
JOSEPH CLEMENTSON	Columbia Shape
LIVESLEY, POWELL & CO.	Columbia Shape
PENMAN, BROWN & CO.	Columbia Shape
PINDER BOURNE & HOPE	Columbia Shape
WILLIAM ADAMS & SON(S) (POTTERS) LTD.	Columbia Shape
JOHN RIDGWAY (& CO.)	Columbia Star
GEORGE PHILLIPS	Columbian
JOHN RIDGWAY (& CO.)	Columbian Star
JOHN RIDGWAY (& CO.)	COLUMBIAN STAR, OCT. 28TH, 1840 - SERIES
WILLIAM ADAMS & SON(S) (POTTERS) LTD.	Columbus
WILLIAM DAVENPORT	Columbus / Ohio
ENOCH WOOD & SONS	Columbus, GA
ROWLAND AND MARSELLUS	Columbus, Ohio
WILLIAM DAVENPORT	Columbus, Ohio
JAMES & RALPH CLEWS	Columbus/Ohio
WILLIAM ADAMS & SON(S) (POTTERS) LTD.	Columbus: Boat Scene
WILLIAM ADAMS & SON(S) (POTTERS) LTD.	Columbus: Camp Scene
WILLIAM ADAMS & SON(S) (POTTERS) LTD.	Columbus: Cavalry Scene
WILLIAM ADAMS & SON(S) (POTTERS) LTD.	Columbus: Fleet Scene, One Companion, et.al.
WILLIAM ADAMS & SON(S) (POTTERS) LTD.	Columbus: Fleet Scene, Two Caravels, One Man in Each, et.al.
WILLIAM ADAMS & SON(S) (POTTERS) LTD.	Columbus: Fleet Scene, Two Companions, et.al.
WILLIAM ADAMS & SON(S) (POTTERS) LTD.	Columbus: Greyhound Scene
WILLIAM ADAMS & SON(S) (POTTERS) LTD.	Columbus: Hunting Scene
WILLIAM ADAMS & SON(S) (POTTERS) LTD.	Columbus: Indian Scene, Indian Girl Kneeling, Two Indians Standing, et.al.
WILLIAM ADAMS & SON(S) (POTTERS) LTD.	Columbus: Indian Scene, One Tent, Three Indians, et.al.
WILLIAM ADAMS & SON(S) (POTTERS) LTD.	Columbus: Indian Scene, Squaw Seated, Indian Standing, et.al.
WILLIAM ADAMS & SON(S) (POTTERS) LTD.	Columbus: Landing Scene, Several Indians, Columbus & Companions, et.al.
WILLIAM ADAMS & SON(S) (POTTERS) LTD.	Columbus: Landing Scene, Three Indians & Procession of White Men, et.al.
WILLIAM ADAMS & SON(S) (POTTERS) LTD.	Columbus: Pavilion Scene
WILLIAM ADAMS & SON(S) (POTTERS) LTD.	Columbus: Spanish Scene
NEW WHARF POTTERY CO.	Colwyn
JOHN & WILLIAM RIDGWAY	Comb Bank, Kent
EDWARD & GEORGE PHILLIPS	Commerce
SAMUEL ALCOCK & CO.	Commerce
ENOCH WOOD & SONS	Commodore MacDonnough's Victory
ROWLAND AND MARSELLUS	Commodore Paul Jones' Capturing The Serapis
SPODE/COPELAND & GARRETT, et.al.	Common Wolf Trap
JOHN MEIR & SON	Como
ENOCH WOOD & SONS	Compton Verney, Warwickshire
HENSHALL & CO.	Compton, Verney
RALPH STEVENSON	Compton, Verney
THOMAS DIMMOCK (JR.) & CO.	Conchology
CHARLES MEIGH & SON	Concordia
GEORGE JONES (& SONS LTD.)	Congo
SPODE/COPELAND & GARRETT, et.al.	Congress
J. & G. MEAKIN	Coniston
SPODE/COPELAND & GARRETT, et.al.	Connaught
THOMAS MAYER	Connecticut, Arms of
LEEDS POTTERY	Conservation
JOHNSON BROS. (HANLEY), LTD.	Constance
WILLIAM (ALSAGER) ADDERLEY (& CO.)	Constance
ENOCH WOOD & SONS	Constitution And The Guerriera / So Called
THOMAS SHIRLEY & CO.	Continental Cathedral
SPODE/COPELAND & GARRETT, et.al.	Continental View
SPODE'S BLUE PRINTED WARES	Continental Views
WOOD & CHALLINOR	CONTINENTAL VIEWS SERIES
THOMAS WOLFE(S)	Conversation
J (JOSHUA) HEATH	Conversation Pattern
BATHWELL & GOODFELLOW	Conversations
WILLIAM RIDGWAY, SON & CO.	Convolvolus
SPODE/COPELAND & GARRETT, et.al.	Convolvulus
SPODE'S BLUE PRINTED WARES	Convolvulus & Sunflower
ARTHUR J. WILKINSON (LTD.)	Conway
NEW WHARF POTTERY CO.	Conway
WOOD & SON(S) (LTD.)	Conway
HERCULANEUM POTTERY	Conway Castle
RALPH HALL (& CO.) or (& SONS)	Conway Castle, Caernarvonshire, Wales
JOB & JOHN JACKSON	Conway, New Hampshire
POUNTNEY & ALLIES	Cook's Folly
ENOCH WOOD & SONS	Coombs House
COPELAND & GARRETT, ET. AL.	Copeland's / Turkey
JOHN ALCOCK	Cora Shape
EDMUND T. WOOD	Coral
JACOB FURNIVAL & CO.	Coral
JAMES JAMIESON & CO.	Coral
JOHNSON BROS. (HANLEY), LTD.	Coral
SPODE/COPELAND & GARRETT, et.al.	Coral
GOODWINS & HARRIS	Coral Border
POUNTNEY & ALLIES	Coral Border
THOMAS DIMMOCK (JR.) & CO.	Coral Border
WILLIAM SMITH (& CO.)	Coral Border
SAMUEL ALCOCK & CO.	Coral Japan
JOHN WEDG WOOD	Coral Shape
CHARLES MEIGH	Corbeille

JOHN MEIR & SON	Corea
JOSEPH CLEMENTSON	Corea
WEDGWOOD & CO. (LTD.)	Corea
G.L. ASHWORTH & BROS. (LTD.)	Corean
PODMORE, WALKER (& CO.)	Corean
BARKER & SON	Corella
EDGE, MALKIN & CO. (LTD.)	Corella
RIDGWAY, SPARKS & RIDGWAY	Corey Hill
MINTON	Corf Castle... sic
GEORGE PHILLIPS	Corinth
JAMES EDWARDS	Corinth
JOSIAH WEDGWOOD (& SONS LTD.)	Corinth
SAMPSON HANCOCK (& SONS)	Corinth
THOMAS FELL (& CO.) (LTD.)	Corinth
EDWARD CHALLINOR	Corinthia
MINTON	Corinthia
WEDGWOOD & CO. (LTD.)	Corinthia
MINTON	Corinthian
SPODE/COPELAND & GARRETT, et.al.	Corinthian
WOOD & BROWNFIELD	Corinthian
CAULDON, LTD.	Corinthian Flute
JAMES & RALPH CLEWS	Corinthian Ornaments
EDMUND T. WOOD	Corn & Oats
HOLLINSHEAD & KIRKHAM (LTD.)	Corn & Oats
WILLIAM DAVENPORT	Corn & Oats
DAVENPORT, BANKS & CO.	Corn & Oats Shape
JOHN WEDG WOOD	Corn & Oats Shape
SPODE/COPELAND & GARRETT, et.al.	Corn & Poppy
W. & E. CORN	Corn's Cloverleaf with Gold Luster
ROWLAND AND MARSELLUS	Cornell College
WILLIAM DAVENPORT	Cornice
DAVENPORT, BANKS & CO.	Corn-on-the-Cob Shape
EDMUND T. WOOD	Corn-on-the-Cob Shape
JOHN WEDG WOOD	Corn-on-the-Cob Shape
WILLIAM DAVENPORT	CORNUCOPIA BORDER SERIES
JAMES & RALPH CLEWS	Cornucopia of Flowers
ENOCH WOOD & SONS	Cornwall Terrace, Regent's Park, London
WILLIAM ADAMS	Cornwall Terrace, Regent's Park, London
FORD & SONS (LTD.)	Corona
GATER, HALL & CO.	Corona
SPODE/COPELAND & GARRETT, et.al.	Coronal
CLEVELAND POTTERY CO.	Coronation
JAMES & RALPH CLEWS	Coronation
RIDGWAYS (BEDFORD WORKS) LTD.	Coronation Moss
JONES & SON	Coronation of George IV
SAMPSON HANCOCK (& SONS)	Coronet
W. & E. CORN	Coronet
EDWARD CHALLINOR	Corsica
WOOD & CHALLINOR	Corsica
WOOD & CHALLINOR & CO.	Corsica
JOHN RIDGWAY (& CO.)	Coterie
BENJAMIN E. GODWIN	Cottage
GEORGE TAYLOR	Cottage
JOHN & ROBERT GODWIN	Cottage
JOHN RIDGWAY (& CO.)	Cottage
MINTON	Cottage
WILLIAM DAVENPORT	Cottage and bridge, horse and rider followed by dog, et.al.
LEEDS POTTERY	Cottage and Vase
ENOCH WOOD & SONS	Cottage in the Woods
WILLIAM EMBERTON (& CO.)	Cottage Scenery
DON POTTERY	Cottages
JOHN MEIR	Cottages
JOHN & WILLIAM RIDGWAY	Cottages and Castle, et.al.
THOMAS & JOHN CAREY/ JOHN CAREY & SONS	Cottar's Saturday Night
JACOB FURNIVAL & CO.	Cotton Plant #100
W.H. GRINDLEY & CO. (LTD.)	Countess
T. RATHBONE & CO.	Countess
CORNFOOT, COLVILLE & CO.	Country Church
DAVIS, COOKSON & WILSON	Country Church
HERCULANEUM POTTERY	Country Cottage
WHITEHAVEN POTTERY	Country House on the River
SAMUEL KEELING & CO.	COUNTRY HOUSES
ENOCH WOOD & SONS	Country Manor
ANDREW STEVENSON	Country Park
ARTHUR WOOD & SON (LONGPORT) LTD.	Country Pastures
SPODE'S BLUE PRINTED WARES	Country Scene
ROBERT HAMILTON	Country Scene With Ram and Sheep
LOCKHART & ARTHUR	Country Scenery
WOOD & SON(S) (LTD.)	Country Scenes
ELIJAH JONES	Country Sports
H.J. WOOD (LTD.)	Countryside
WARDLE (JAMES) & CO. (HANLEY) LTD.	Countryside
TOFT & MAY	Coursing Scene
HENSHALL & CO.	Court House, Baltimore
JOHN & WILLIAM RIDGWAY	Court House, Boston
RALPH STEVENSON & WILLIAMS	Court House, Boston
JOB & JOHN JACKSON	Court House, Richmond, VA.
ROWLAND AND MARSELLUS	Coven Hoven, Nova Scotia
TAMS / et.al.	Covent Garden Theatre, London
ENOCH WOOD & SONS	Coventry
SPODE/COPELAND & GARRETT, et.al.	Coventry
BENJAMIN E. GODWIN	Cow
BENJAMIN E. GODWIN	Cow & Waterfall
CAMBRIAN POTTERY	Cow Herd
DILLWYN & CO.	Cow Herd
LEEDS POTTERY	Cow Standing in a Distant Landscape, et.al.
SAMUEL KEELING & CO.	Cowes
THOMAS DIMMOCK (JR.) & CO.	Cowes
ENOCH WOOD & SONS	Cowes Harbor
BAKER, BEVANS & IRWIN	Cowherd
JOHN THOMSON (& SONS)	Cowherd & Castle
ROBERT HAMILTON	Cowmen
JOHN MEIR	Cowper Gardening
RIDGWAYS (BEDFORD WORKS) LTD.	Cows
WEDGWOOD & CO. (LTD.)	Cows
JOSIAH WEDGWOOD (& SONS LTD.)	Cows and Herdsman
DILLWYN & CO.	Cows Crossing Stream
EVANS & GLASSON	Cows Crossing Stream
GOODWINS & HARRIS	Cows Crossing Stream
T. & J. BEVINGTON (& CO.)	Cows Crossing Stream
WILLIAM DAVENPORT	Cows Crossing Stream
CAMBRIAN POTTERY	Cows Crossing Stream Pattern
WILLIAM DAVENPORT	Cows Under Trees
WILLIAM DAVENPORT	Cows under trees resting by a tree
JOHN ROGERS (& SON)	Cows With One or Two Trees/or no Cows
JAMES EDWARDS	Crabstock Dozen
SPODE/COPELAND & GARRETT, et.al.	Cracked & Prunus
ANTHONY SHAW (& SON(S) (& CO.)	Cracked Ice
SPODE'S BLUE PRINTED WARES	Cracked Ice & Prunes
ELKIN & CO.	Craig Castle
ELKIN, KNIGHT & CO.	Craig Castle
JAMES & RALPH CLEWS	Crane & Peony
JOSIAH WEDGWOOD (& SONS LTD.)	Crane Pattern
WILLIAM DAVENPORT	Cranes & Peony Tree
BURGESS & LEIGH (LTD.)	Cranesbill
BURGESS & LEIGH (LTD.)	Cranston
UPPER HANLEY POTTERY CO. (LTD.)	Crawford
SAMPSON BRIDGWOOD (& SON)(LTD.)	Crawford , Ranges
JOHN ROGERS (& SON)	Crescent
W.H. GRINDLEY & CO. (LTD.)	Crescent
GRIMWADE BROS.	Crete
J. PLANT & CO.	Crete
SPODE/COPELAND & GARRETT, et.al.	Crete
ALFRED MEAKIN (LTD.)	Crewel
RALPH HALL (& CO.) or (& SONS)	Croe House
RALPH HALL (& CO.) or (& SONS)	Crome Court, Worcester
JONES & SON	Cromwell Dismissing the Long Parliament
WILLIAM DAVENPORT	Cross & Statue
G.L. ASHWORTH & BROS. (LTD.)	Cross Leaf
WILLIAM DAVENPORT	Crosslet
JOHN MEIR	CROWN ACORN AND OAK LEAF BORDER SERIES
JOHN MEIR & SON	CROWN ACORN AND OAK LEAF BORDER SERIES
JAMES & RALPH CLEWS	Crown Apple
JOSIAH WEDGWOOD (& SONS LTD.)	Crown Imperial
WILLIAM RIDGWAY (& CO.)	Crows Nest From Bull Hill
KEELING & CO. (LTD.)	Croxon
MYOTT, SON & CO. (LTD.)	Crumlin
DEAKIN & BAILEY	Crusaders
BROWN WESTHEAD, MOORE & CO.	Crystal
CAULDON, LTD.	Crystal
ELSMORE & FORSTER	Crystal
J. & M.P. BELL (CO.) & (LTD.)	Crystal Palace
PINDER BOURNE & HOPE	Crystal Palace
R. COCHRAN & CO. - VERREVILLE POTTERY	Crystal Palace
THOMAS GODWIN	Crystal Palace
ELSMORE & FORSTER	Crystal Shape
ELSMORE (THOMAS) & SON	Crystal Shape
DAVID LOCKHART (and LOCKHART & CO.)	Cuba
DILLWYN & CO.	Cuba
EVANS & GLASSON	Cuba
WILLIAM DAVENPORT	Cuba
ANDREW STEVENSON	Culford Hall, Suffolk
RALPH HALL (& CO.) or (& SONS)	Culford Hall, Suffolk
ENOCH WOOD & SONS	Culzean Castle, Ayrshire
ENOCH WOOD & SONS	Cumberland Terrace, Regent's Park, London
WILLIAM SMITH (& CO.)	Cupid
WILLIAM ADAMS & SON(S) (POTTERS) LTD.	Cupid & Roses
WILLIAM ADAMS & SON(S) (POTTERS) LTD.	Cupid & Virgin
ENOCH WOOD & SONS	Cupid Imprisoned
WILLIAM ADAMS & SON(S) (POTTERS) LTD.	Cupid Pattern
ENOCH WOOD & SONS	CUPID PATTERN SERIES
WILLIAM ADAMS & SON(S) (POTTERS) LTD.	CUPID SERIES
ENOCH WOOD & SONS	Cupid's Escape
WOLFE, HAMILTON & CO.	Cupids

HERCULANEUM POTTERY	Curling Bridge & Temple
JOB RIDGWAY	Curling Palm
JOB RIDGWAY & SONS	Curling Palm
THOMAS, JOHN & JOSEPH MAYER	Curved Gothic
JAMES EDWARDS	Curved Gothic Shape
JOHN & WILLIAM RIDGWAY	Curved Path, et.al.
CHARLES MEAKIN	Curved Rectangle
TAMS / et.al.	Custom House, London
JOHN & WILLIAM RIDGWAY	Custom House, Philadelphia
JOHN & WILLIAM RIDGWAY	Cusworth, Yorkshire
SPODE/COPELAND & GARRETT, et.al.	Cynisca Winning the Chariot Race
JOHN THOMSON (& SONS)	Cynthia
JOHN MEIR & SON	Cyprean
JOHN ROBINSON (& SONS)	Cypress
JOSEPH ROBINSON	Cypress
SAMUEL FORD & CO.	Cypress
MIDDLESBOROUGH POTTERY CO.	Cyprian Bower
FRANCIS J. EMERY	Cyprus
WILLIAM BROWNFIELD (& SON(S)	Cyprus
WILLIAM DAVENPORT	Cyprus
WILLIAM DAVENPORT	Cyprus Shape
WM. DAVENPORT & CO.	Cyprus Shape
GEORGE JONES (& SONS LTD.)	Cyrene
WILLIAM ADAMS & SON(S) (POTTERS) LTD.	Cyrene
SPODE/COPELAND & GARRETT, et.al.	Cyril
ROWLAND AND MARSELLUS	D.A.R., Fort Griswald
MINTON & CO.	D'Orsay Japan
MINTONS, LTD.	D'Orsay Japan
JOHN CARR (& CO.) (& SON(S)	Dacca
MINTON & BOYLE	Dacca
MINTONS, LTD.	Dacca
RIDGWAYS (BEDFORD WORKS) LTD.	Dado
DAVID METHVEN & SONS	Daffodil
DOULTON & CO. (LTD.)	Daffodil
W.H. GRINDLEY & CO. (LTD.)	Daffodil
JOHN TURNER / TURNER & CO., etc.	Daffodil Pattern
SPODE'S BLUE PRINTED WARES	Dagger - Landscape, First
SPODE'S BLUE PRINTED WARES	Dagger - Landscape, Second
SPODE'S BLUE PRINTED WARES	Dagger - Landscape, Third
MINTON & BOYLE	Dagger Border
THOMAS DIMMOCK (JR.) & CO.	Dagger Border
ENOCH WOOD	Dagger Border Chinoiserie
CHARLES ALLERTON & SONS	Dahlia
CORK & EDGE	Dahlia
EDWARD CHALLINOR	Dahlia
UPPER HANLEY POTTERY CO. (LTD.)	Dahlia
WEDGWOOD & CO. (LTD.)	Dahlia
ST. JOHN'S STONE CHINAWARE CO. (CANADA)	Daily Bread
WILLIAM DAVENPORT	Daily Bread Platter
JOHN MADDOCK & SONS (LTD.)	Dainty
WOOD & BRETTEL	Dairy Pail
ALFRED MEAKIN (LTD.)	Daisy
ANTHONY SHAW (& SON(S) (& CO.)	Daisy
BISHOP & STONIER (LTD.)	Daisy
BRITANNIA POTTERY CO. LTD.	Daisy
BURGESS & LEIGH (LTD.)	Daisy
DUDSON, WILCOX & TILL, LTD.	Daisy
GOODWINS, BRIDGWOOD & ORTON	Daisy
SPODE'S BLUE PRINTED WARES	Daisy
SPODE'S BLUE PRINTED WARES	Daisy & Bead
MELLOR, VENABLES & CO.	Daisy & Leaf
WEDGWOOD & CO. (LTD.)	Daisy & Tulip
ARTHUR J. WILKINSON (LTD.)	Daisy 'n Chain
WEDGWOOD & CO. (LTD.)	Daisy Chain
SPODE/COPELAND & GARRETT, et.al.	Daisy Grass
ANTHONY SHAW (& SON(S) (& CO.)	Daisy Shape
ENOCH WOOD & SONS	Dalguise, Perthshire
JOHN MEIR	Dalguise, Perthshire
JOSEPH CLEMENTSON	Dallas Shape
CHARLES JAMES MASON & CO.	Damascus
DAVID METHVEN & SONS	Damascus
ENOCH WOOD & SONS	Damascus
J. & M.P. BELL (CO.) & (LTD.)	Damascus
R. COCHRAN & CO. - VERREVILLE POTTERY	Damascus
W. BAKER & CO. (LTD.)	Damascus
WILLIAM ADAMS & SON(S) (POTTERS) LTD.	Damascus
SOUTH WALES POTTERS	Damask Border
WILLIAM DAVENPORT	Damask Rose
RALPH MALKIN	Dancers
CAMBRIAN POTTERY	Dancing Fisherman
JOHN GEDDES - VERREVILLE POTTERY	Danesford House
EDWARD PEARSON (& SON)	Dangling Tulip Shape
WILLIAM DAVENPORT	Danish
CHARLES ALLERTON & SONS	Danube
WEDGWOOD & CO. (LTD.)	Daphne
HERCULANEUM POTTERY	Darsie Castle
F. WINKLE & CO. (LTD.)	Dart
THOMAS MAYER	Darting
ENOCH WOOD & SONS	Dartmouth
ARTHUR J. WILKINSON (LTD.)	Davenport
HOLLINSHEAD & KIRKHAM (LTD.)	Davenport
WOOD & SON(S) (LTD.)	Davenport
WILLIAM DAVENPORT & CO.	Davenport's Gothic
JOHN TURNER / TURNER & CO., etc.	Day on an Elephant
JOHN ROGERS (& SON)	Day Sea Battle
ROWLAND AND MARSELLUS	Daytona, Fla.
KNIGHT, ELKIN & CO.	De Fete
JOB & JOHN JACKSON	Deaf & Dumb Asylum, Philadelphia
JOHN & WILLIAM RIDGWAY	Deaf and Dumb Asylum, Hartford, Conn.
RALPH STEVENSON	Deaf and Dumb Asylum, Hartford, Conn.
EDWIN DEAKIN	Deakin Pearl
JAMES JAMIESON & CO.	Dean Bridge
JAMES JAMIESON & CO.	Dean Bridge From Water of Leith
ENOCH WOOD & SONS	Death of Abel
ROWLAND AND MARSELLUS	Death of Capt. Lawrence
JONES & SON	Death of General Wolfe
JONES & SON	Death of Lord Nelson
JAMES & RALPH CLEWS	Death of Punch
EDWARD CHALLINOR	Death of the Bear
SPODE/COPELAND & GARRETT, et.al.	Death of the Bear
RIDGWAYS (BEDFORD WORKS) LTD.	Debora
ROWLAND AND MARSELLUS	Decatur, Il.
COPELAND & GARRETT, ET. AL.	December
ROWLAND AND MARSELLUS	Declaration of Independence
EDWARD CHALLINOR	Decoy Elephants Leaving the Male Fastened to a Tree
JAMES & RALPH CLEWS	Deer
JOHN HALL	Deer
ENOCH WOOD & SONS	Deer Hunting
J. & M.P. BELL (CO.) & (LTD.)	Deer Stalking
MINTON	DeGaunt Castle
HENRY ALCOCK & CO. (LTD.)	Delamere
C. & W.K. HARVEY	Delaware
J. & G. MEAKIN	Delaware
JACOB FURNIVAL & CO.	Delaware
JOHN RIDGWAY (& CO.)	Delaware
WILLIAM DAVENPORT	Delaware
ROWLAND AND MARSELLUS	Delaware Water Gap
WILLIAM RIDGWAY (& CO.)	Delaware Water Gap, Pa.
THOMAS MAYER	Delaware, Arms of
BROWNFIELDS(GUILD) POTTERY SOCIETY LTD.	Delft
CLEMENTSON BROS. (LTD.)	Delft
DUNN BENNETT & CO. (LTD.)	Delft
MINTON & CO.	Delft
MINTONS, LTD.	Delft
CAULDON, LTD.	Delftland
BLACKHURST & TUNNICLIFFE	Delhi
DIMMOCK & SMITH	Delhi
J. & M.P. BELL (CO.) & (LTD.)	Delhi
JOSEPH CLEMENTSON	Delhi
SAMUEL BARKER & SON	Delhi
SPODE/COPELAND & GARRETT, et.al.	Delhi
T. & J. BEVINGTON (& CO.)	Delhi
W. & E. CORN	Delhi
CORK, EDGE & MALKIN	Delhi, Hindoostan
EDGE, MALKIN & CO. (LTD.)	Delhi, Hindoostan
THOMAS & BENJAMIN GODWIN	Delhi, Hindoostan
W.H. GRINDLEY & CO. (LTD.)	Delmar
JOHNSON BROS. (HANLEY), LTD.	Delmonte
BOURNE & LEIGH (LTD.)	Delph
GLOBE POTTERY CO. LTD.	Delph
JAMES KENT (LTD.)	Delph
MINTON & CO.	Delph
WOOD & SON(S) (LTD.)	Delph
WILLIAM ADAMS & SON(S) (POTTERS) LTD.	Delphi
SPODE/COPELAND & GARRETT, et.al.	Demeter With Priestesses
FURNIVALS LTD.	Denmark
MINTON & CO.	Denmark
MINTONS, LTD.	Denmark
SPODE/COPELAND & GARRETT, et.al.	Denmark
W.H. GRINDLEY & CO. (LTD.)	Denmark
C.T. MALING	Denon's Egypt
ELIJAH JONES	Denon's Egypt
W.H. GRINDLEY & CO. (LTD.)	Denton
WOOD & SON(S) (LTD.)	Denton
GRIFFITHS, BEARDMORE & BIRKS	Denton Park
JOHN & RICHARD RILEY	Denton Park, Yorkshire
WILLIAM ADAMS	Denton Park, Yorkshire
WILLIAM ADAMS & SON(S) (POTTERS) LTD.	Denton Park, Yorkshire
ROWLAND AND MARSELLUS	Denver, Colo.
ENOCH WOOD & SONS	Department of State, Washington
BURGESS & LEIGH (LTD.)	Derby
FURNIVALS LTD.	Derby
J. & M.P. BELL (CO.) & (LTD.)	Derby
W.H. GRINDLEY & CO. (LTD.)	Derby
W.H. GRINDLEY & CO. (LTD.)	Derwent

CHARLES JAMES MASON & CO.	Derwentwater
RALPH STEVENSON & SON	Derwentwater
ANTHONY SHAW (& SON(S) (& CO.)	DeSoto Shape
THOMAS HUGHES	DeSoto Shape
THOMAS HUGHES & SON (LTD.)	DeSoto Shape
ROWLAND AND MARSELLUS	DeSoto's Discovery of the Mississippi
WILLIAM DAVENPORT	Detroit
ROWLAND AND MARSELLUS	Detroit, Mich.
WILLIAM DAVENPORT	Detroit, Michigan
JAMES & RALPH CLEWS	Detroit/ Michigan, Detroit
BOURNE & LEIGH (LTD.)	Deva
ALFRED MEAKIN (LTD.)	Devon
BROWNFIELDS(GUILD) POTTERY SOCIETY LTD.	Devon
FORD & SONS (LTD.)	Devon
JAMES MAC INTYRE (& CO.) (LTD.)	Devon
MIDDLESBOROUGH POTTERY CO.	Devon
MINTON & BOYLE	Devon
WILLIAM ADAMS & SON(S) (POTTERS) LTD.	Dews Hall, Essex
ENOCH WOOD	Diamond Sunburst Border
GELSON BROS.	Diamond with Thumb Print
J. & G. MEAKIN	Diana
ROWLAND AND MARSELLUS	Dickens, Charles
RIDGWAYS (BEDFORD WORKS) LTD.	Dickins
WILLIAM ADAMS & SON(S) (POTTERS) LTD.	Dilston Tower, Northumberland
CHARLES MEIGH	Dimity
RIDGWAYS (BEDFORD WORKS) LTD.	Dinan
JOSEPH CLEMENTSON	Diomed Casting His Spear Against Mars
THOMAS MAYER	Discus, The
ENOCH WOOD & SONS	Distant View of Inn
JAMES & RALPH CLEWS	District of Columbia, Washington
WILLIAM DAVENPORT	District of Columbia, Washington
SAMUEL ALCOCK & CO.	Divided Gothic
JOHN ALCOCK	Divided Gothic Shape
ENOCH WOOD & SONS	Dix Cove On the Gold Coast, Africa
DAWSON (JOHN DAWSON & CO., ETC.)	Docility
JAMES & RALPH CLEWS	Dock, With Large Building and Ships
JOHN HALL	Dog
JAMES & RALPH CLEWS	Dog & Rabbit
JOHN HALL	Dog and Rabbit
RIDGWAYS (BEDFORD WORKS) LTD.	Dog Rose
JOSIAH WEDGWOOD (& SONS LTD.)	Dogs of Fo
JOHN EDWARDS (& CO.)	Dolphin
JOSEPH CLEMENTSON	Dolphin Shape
J. & M.P. BELL (CO.) & (LTD.)	Domestic
JAMES EDWARDS	Domestic
THOMAS & JOHN CAREY/ JOHN CAREY & SONS	DOMESTIC CATTLE SERIES
SAMUEL & JOHN BURTON	Domestic Scenery
W. BAKER & CO. (LTD.)	Dominion Shape
CHARLES ALLERTON & SONS	Don
GOODWINS & HARRIS	Don Juan
JAMES & RALPH CLEWS	Don Quixote
WILLIAM DAVENPORT	Don Quixote
BRAMELD & CO.	Don Quixote & Sancho Panza
BRAMELD & CO.	Don Quixote & the Shepherdess
JAMES & RALPH CLEWS	Don Quixote and Sancho Panza
WILLIAM DAVENPORT	Don Quixote and Sancho Panza
JAMES & RALPH CLEWS	Don Quixote and Sancho Panza /Don Quixote Entreated by Sancho Panza
JAMES & RALPH CLEWS	Don Quixote and the Princess
WILLIAM DAVENPORT	Don Quixote and the Princess
JAMES & RALPH CLEWS	Don Quixote and the Shepherdess
WILLIAM DAVENPORT	Don Quixote and the Shepherdess
WILLIAM DAVENPORT	Don Quixote Entreated by Sancho Panza
BRAMELD & CO.	DON QUIXOTE SERIES
JAMES & RALPH CLEWS	DON QUIXOTE SERIES
WILLIAM DAVENPORT	DON QUIXOTE SERIES
JAMES & RALPH CLEWS	Don Quixote's Attack Upon The Mills
WILLIAM DAVENPORT	Don Quixote's Attack Upon The Mills
JAMES & RALPH CLEWS	Don Quixote's Library
WILLIAM DAVENPORT	Don Quixote's Library
JAMES JAMIESON & CO.	Donaldson's Hospital
JAMES & RALPH CLEWS	Donemark Mill
MINTON	Donington Park
RALPH STEVENSON	Donkey Ride
THOMAS & JOHN CAREY/ JOHN CAREY & SONS	Donkeys & Campfire
THOMAS & JOHN CAREY/ JOHN CAREY & SONS	Donkeys & Tent
WILLIAM DAVENPORT	Donovan Fisherman
EDWARD CHALLINOR	Dooreahs Leading Out Dogs
SPODE/COPELAND & GARRETT, et.al.	Dooreahs Leading Out Dogs
EDWARD CHALLINOR	Dooreahs or Dog Keepers Leading Out Dogs
SPODE/COPELAND & GARRETT, et.al.	Dooreahs or Dog Keepers Leading Out Dogs
E. CHALLINOR & CO.	Dora
GROVE & STARK	Dora
JAMES KENT (LTD.)	Dora
W.H. GRINDLEY & CO. (LTD.)	Doreen
BARROW & CO.	Doria
JOHN RIDGWAY (& CO.)	Doria
WILLIAM ADAMS & CO. LTD.	Doric
WOOD & BAGGALEY	Doric
WOOD & BROWNFIELD	Doric
ENOCH WOOD & SONS	Doric Villa in Regent's Park
MYOTT, SON & CO. (LTD.)	Doris
SAMPSON HANCOCK (& SONS)	Doris
W.H. GRINDLEY & CO. (LTD.)	Doris
RALPH STEVENSON	Dorney Court
RALPH STEVENSON & WILLIAMS	Dorney Court
ENOCH WOOD & SONS	Dorney Court, Buckinghamshire
JOHNSON BROS. (HANLEY), LTD.	Dorothy
UPPER HANLEY POTTERY CO. (LTD.)	Dorothy
W. & E. CORN	Dorothy
W.H. GRINDLEY & CO. (LTD.)	Dorothy
SOUTHWICK POTTERY	Dot Flower
BARROW & CO.	Double Leaf
JAMES EDWARDS	Double Leaf
SAMPSON BRIDGWOOD (& SON)(LTD.)	Double Poppy
JOHNSON BROS. (HANLEY), LTD.	Double Swirl
ANTHONY SHAW (& SON(S) (& CO.)	Double Sydenham
EDWARD WALLEY	Double Sydenham
ELSMORE & FORSTER	Double Sydenham
HOLLAND & GREEN	Double Sydenham
JOHN MADDOCK	Double Sydenham
LIVESLEY, POWELL & CO.	Double Sydenham
THOMAS GOODFELLOW	Double Sydenham
W. & E. CORN	Double Sydenham
FORD & SONS (LTD.)	Douglas
JOHN ROGERS (& SON)	Douglas, Act 5 Scene 1
POUNTNEY & GOLDNEY	Douglas, Act 5 Scene 1
BISHOP & STONIER (LTD.)	Dove
GELSON BROS.	Dove
MINTON	Dove
COPELAND & GARRETT, ET. AL.	Dover
FORD & SONS (LTD.)	Dover
W.H. GRINDLEY & CO. (LTD.)	Dover
WILLIAM ADAMS & SON(S) (POTTERS) LTD.	Dover Shape
JOHN & WILLIAM RIDGWAY	Downing College, Cambridge
JAMES & RALPH CLEWS	Dr. Syntax Amused with Pat in the Pond
JAMES & RALPH CLEWS	Dr. Syntax and Dairy Maid
JAMES & RALPH CLEWS	Dr. Syntax and the Bees
JAMES & RALPH CLEWS	Dr. Syntax and the Gypsies
JAMES & RALPH CLEWS	Dr. Syntax Bound to a Tree by Highwaymen
JAMES & RALPH CLEWS	Dr. Syntax Copying the Wit of the Widow
JAMES & RALPH CLEWS	Dr. Syntax Disputing His Bill With Landlady
JAMES & RALPH CLEWS	Dr. Syntax Drawing From Nature
JAMES & RALPH CLEWS	Dr. Syntax Entertained at College
JAMES & RALPH CLEWS	Dr. Syntax Making a Discovery
JAMES & RALPH CLEWS	Dr. Syntax Mistakes a Gentleman's House for an Inn
JAMES & RALPH CLEWS	Dr. Syntax Painting a Portrait
JAMES & RALPH CLEWS	Dr. Syntax Presenting a Floral Offering
JAMES & RALPH CLEWS	Dr. Syntax Pursued by a Bull
JAMES & RALPH CLEWS	Dr. Syntax Reading His Tour
JAMES & RALPH CLEWS	Dr. Syntax Returning From His Tour
JAMES & RALPH CLEWS	Dr. Syntax Sells Grizzle
JAMES & RALPH CLEWS	DR. SYNTAX SERIES
JAMES & RALPH CLEWS	Dr. Syntax Setting Out In Search Of A Wife
JAMES & RALPH CLEWS	Dr. Syntax Setting Out On His First Tour
JAMES & RALPH CLEWS	Dr. Syntax Setting Out On His Second Tour
JAMES & RALPH CLEWS	Dr. Syntax Sketching the Lake
JAMES & RALPH CLEWS	Dr. Syntax Star Gazing
JAMES & RALPH CLEWS	Dr. Syntax Stopt by Highwaymen
JAMES & RALPH CLEWS	Dr. Syntax Taking Possession of His Living
JAMES & RALPH CLEWS	Dr. Syntax Turned Nurse
JAMES & RALPH CLEWS	Dr. Syntax With a Blue Stocking Beauty
BRITANNIA POTTERY CO. LTD.	Dragon
CAULDON, LTD.	Dragon
GEORGE JONES (& SONS LTD.)	Dragon
MINTON	Dragon
THOMAS DIMMOCK (JR.) & CO.	Dragon
THOMAS SHIRLEY & CO.	Dragon
THOMAS SHIRLEY & CO.	Dragon Fly
JOSIAH WEDGWOOD (& SONS LTD.)	Dragons
JOHN ROGERS (& SON)	Dragons & Flowers
SPODE'S BLUE PRINTED WARES	Dragons I
SPODE'S BLUE PRINTED WARES	Dragons II
WILLIAM DAVENPORT	Dragons No. 2
JOHN ROGERS (& SON)	DRAMA SERIES
BRIDGWOOD & CLARKE	Draped Leaf
HENRY ALCOCK & CO. (LTD.)	Draped Leaf
W. BAKER & CO. (LTD.)	Draped Leaf
W. BAKER & CO. (LTD.)	Draped Leaf C
JAMES EDWARDS & SON	Draped Leaf Shape
RALPH HALL (& CO.) or (& SONS)	Dreghorn House, Scotland
BURGESS & LEIGH (LTD.)	Dresden

EDWARD CHALLINOR	Dresden
HUMPHREYS BROS.	Dresden
JOHNSON BROS. (HANLEY), LTD.	Dresden
SAMPSON HANCOCK (& SONS)	Dresden
SUNDERLAND OR "GARRISON" POTTERY	Dresden
W.H. GRINDLEY & CO. (LTD.)	Dresden
COPELAND & GARRETT, ET. AL.	Dresden Border
SPODE'S BLUE PRINTED WARES	Dresden Border
BURGESS & LEIGH (LTD.)	Dresden Flowers
HENRY ALCOCK & CO. (LTD.)	Dresden Flowers
MINTON	Dresden Flowers
COPELAND & GARRETT, ET. AL.	Dresden Sprays
SPODE'S BLUE PRINTED WARES	Dresden Sprays
R. COCHRAN & CO. - VERREVILLE POTTERY	Dresden Sprigs
MIDDLESBOROUGH POTTERY CO.	Dresden Views
EDWARD CHALLINOR	Driving a Bear Out of Sugar Canes
SPODE/COPELAND & GARRETT, et.al.	Driving a Bear out of Sugar Canes
JOHN & RICHARD RILEY	Dromedary
POUNTNEY & ALLIES	Dromedary
DILLWYN & CO.	Drover
TAMS / et.al.	Drury Lane Theatre, London
WILLIAM ADAMS & SON(S) (POTTERS) LTD.	DuBarry
C. & W.K. HARVEY	Dublin
R.S. KIDSTON & CO. - VERREVILLE	Dublin From Phoenix Park
COCHRAN & FLEMING - BRITANNIA POTTERY	Duchess
DUNN BENNETT & CO. (LTD.)	Duchess
JOHN MADDOCK & SONS (LTD.)	Duchess
R. COCHRAN & CO. - VERREVILLE POTTERY	Duchess
W.H. GRINDLEY & CO. (LTD.)	Duchess
WOOD & SON(S) (LTD.)	Duchess
W.H. GRINDLEY & CO. (LTD.)	Duchess, The
HERCULANEUM POTTERY	Duck Hunters with Boat
JAMES & RALPH CLEWS	Duck Hunting
ANDREW STEVENSON	Duck Shooting
FORD & SONS (LTD.)	Dudley
MYOTT, SON & CO. (LTD.)	Dudley
WOOD & SON(S) (LTD.)	Dudley
R. COCHRAN & CO. - VERREVILLE POTTERY	Dufferin Terrace & Citadel: Place Dufferin & Citadelle
JAMES JAMIESON & CO.	Dugald Stewart's Monument
HERCULANEUM POTTERY	Duke of Bridgewater's House, Liverpool
JAMES & RALPH CLEWS	Dulwich Castle
ANDREW STEVENSON	Dulwich College, Essex
ENOCH WOOD & SONS	Dumb Asylum, Philadelphia
J. & M.P. BELL (CO.) & (LTD.)	Dumblane
HERCULANEUM POTTERY	Dumfries
NEW WHARF POTTERY CO.	Dunbarton
SPODE/COPELAND & GARRETT, et.al.	Duncan Series
RIDGWAYS (BEDFORD WORKS) LTD.	Dundee
JAMES & RALPH CLEWS	Dunfermline Abbey, Fifeshire
R.S. KIDSTON & CO. - VERREVILLE	Dunkeld
BROWNFIELDS(GUILD) POTTERY SOCIETY LTD.	Dunkfield
FRANK BEARDMORE & CO.	Dunkfield
JOHN MEIR & SON	Dunolly Castle, Near Oban
THOMAS & JOHN CAREY/ JOHN CAREY & SONS	Dunraven Castle, Honorable Wm. Wyndham Quinn's Seat
ENOCH WOOD & SONS	Dunraven, Glamorgan
J. & G. MEAKIN	Dunrobbin
RALPH HALL (& CO.) or (& SONS)	Dunsany Castle, Ireland
ENOCH WOOD & SONS	Durham
JOHN ROGERS (& SON)	Durham
T. RATHBONE & CO.	Durham
BELLE VUE POTTERIES	Durham Cathedral
ENOCH WOOD & SONS	Durham Cathedral
J. & M.P. BELL (CO.) & (LTD.)	Durian and Nanas
ANDREW STEVENSON	Dusky Grebe
ANDREW STEVENSON	Duston Hall
ANDREW STEVENSON	Dutch Church at Albany
RALPH STEVENSON & WILLIAMS	Dutch Church at Albany
SOUTHWICK POTTERY	Dutch United Provinces
THOMAS, JOHN & JOSEPH MAYER	E.B. & S. Wards Steamers
JOHN WEDG WOOD	Eagle
PODMORE, WALKER (& CO.)	Eagle
RALPH HALL & SON	Eagle
WEDGWOOD & CO. (LTD.)	Eagle
WOOD & SON(S) (LTD.)	Eagle
MINTON & CO.	Eagle & Shield
WILLIAM DAVENPORT	Eagle Head
THOMAS FURNIVAL & CO.	Eagle on Globe
ENOCH WOOD & SONS	Eagle on Rock
RALPH HALL & SON	Eagle Riding on a Shell
GELSON BROS.	Eagle Shape
PRATT & SIMPSON	Eagle Soup Tureen
WILLIAM ADAMS & SON(S) (POTTERS) LTD.	Eagle, Scroll in Beak
JOHN WEDG WOOD	Early Cameo
WILLIAM DAVENPORT	Early Cameo

WILLIAM DAVENPORT	Early Cameo Shape
JOHN MEIR & SON	Early Gothic
FRANCIS MORLEY (& CO.)	Early Swirl Shape
RALPH HALL (& CO.) or (& SONS)	Eashing Park, Surrey
ENOCH WOOD & SONS	East Cowes, Isle of Wight
ROWLAND AND MARSELLUS	East Hampton, N.Y.
WILLIAM RIDGWAY, SON & CO.	East Port
THOMAS GODWIN	East Port and Passamaquoddy Bay
ENOCH WOOD & SONS	East View of La Grange
SOUTH WALES POTTERS	Eastern
WILLIAM DAVENPORT	Eastern Birds
JOSIAH WEDGWOOD (& SONS LTD.)	Eastern Flowers
MELLOR, VENABLES & CO.	Eastern Flowers
THOMAS MAYER	Eastern Palace
JOHN EDWARDS (& CO.)	Eastern Plants
WOOD & BAGGALEY	Eastern Plants
JOHN & WILLIAM RIDGWAY	Eastern Port
ENOCH WOOD & SONS	Eastern Scenery No. I
ENOCH WOOD & SONS	Eastern Scenery No.II
JOSEPH CLEMENTSON	Eastern Sketches
JOHN & RICHARD RILEY	Eastern Street Scene
CHARLES MEIGH	Eastern Vines
ENOCH WOOD & SONS	Eastgate, Regent's Park, London
NEW WHARF POTTERY CO.	Eastwood
WILLIAM DAVENPORT	Eaton
GEORGE PHILLIPS	Eaton College
RALPH STEVENSON	Eaton Hall
THOMAS & JOHN CAREY/ JOHN CAREY & SONS	Eaton Hall, Cheshire, Earl Grosvenor's Seat
RIDGWAYS (BEDFORD WORKS) LTD.	Ebor
JOHNSON BROS. (HANLEY), LTD.	Eclipse
SAMUEL ALCOCK & CO.	Eclipse
HICKS, MEIGH & JOHNSON	Edelaides Bower
NEW WHARF POTTERY CO.	Edgar
DOULTON & CO. (LTD.)	Edgerton
C. & W.K. HARVEY	Edinburgh
ENOCH WOOD & SONS	Edinburgh
HERCULANEUM POTTERY	Edinburgh
JOSIAH WEDGWOOD (& SONS LTD.)	Edinburgh
R.S. KIDSTON & CO. - VERREVILLE	Edinburgh
WATSON & CO.	Edinburgh from Port Hopetown
ANDREW STEVENSON	Edinburgh Scotland
JAMES EDWARDS	Edward's Leaf
JAMES EDWARDS	Edward's Lily of the Valley
JAMES EDWARDS & SON	Edward's Lily of the Valley Shape
RICHARD DAVIES & CO.	Eel Plate
SUNDERLAND OR "GARRISON" POTTERY	Eel Plate
E. CHALLINOR & CO.	Egina
CHARLES MEIGH	Eglantine
RIDGWAY, MORLEY, WEAR & CO.	Eglinton
DOULTON & CO. (LTD.)	Eglinton Tournament
C.T. MALING & SONS (LTD.)	Egypt
JOSEPH HEATH & CO.	Egyptian
POUNTNEY & ALLIES	Egyptian Scene
THOMAS LAKIN	Eight Storeyed Pagoda
W.H. GRINDLEY & CO. (LTD.)	Eileen
BOOTHS (LTD.)	El Brau
J.W. PANKHURST (& CO.)	Elaborated Six Paneled Trumpet
DOULTON & CO. (LTD.)	Elaine
SPODE/COPELAND & GARRETT, et.al.	Elcho
CLEMENTSON BROS. (LTD.)	Elegance Shape
ENOCH WOOD & SONS	Elephant
JOHN ROGERS (& SON)	Elephant
JOHN STEVENTON & SONS, LTD.	Elephant
JOHN TURNER / TURNER & CO., etc.	Elephant
FERRYBRIDGE POTTERY	Elephant & Castle
CAMBRIAN POTTERY	Elephant & Howdah
DILLWYN & CO.	Elephant & Howdah
FERRYBRIDGE POTTERY	Elephant and Howdah
CAMBRIAN POTTERY	Elephant Pattern
DILLWYN & CO.	Elephant Pattern
PLYMOUTH POTTERY CO. LTD.	Elephant Pattern
TOFT & MAY	Elephant Pattern
FERRYBRIDGE POTTERY	Elephants
JOHN HALL (& SONS)	Elephants & Tomb
UPPER HANLEY POTTERY CO. (LTD.)	Elgar
ELGIN POTTERY	Elgin
WOOD & SON(S) (LTD.)	Elise
JONES & SON	Elizabeth Addressing the Troops
JOHN HALL	Elk
JOB MEIGH (& SON)	Elks
ROWLAND AND MARSELLUS	Elm at Cambridge, Mass.
W. & E. CORN	Elsa
NEW WHARF POTTERY CO.	Elsie
CHARLES JAMES MASON & CO.	Elterwater
RALPH STEVENSON & SON	Elterwater
ENOCH WOOD & SONS	Ely
W.H. GRINDLEY & CO. (LTD.)	Elysian
MINTON	Embdon Castle

HENRY BURGESS	Embroidered Chelsea Shape
CERAMIC ART CO. (1905) LTD.	Empire
DOULTON & CO. (LTD.)	Empire
SOHO POTTERY (LTD.)	Empire
EDGE, MALKIN & CO. (LTD.)	Empress
G.L. ASHWORTH & BROS. (LTD.)	Empress
JAMES KENT (LTD.)	Empress
JOHN DENTON BAXTER (BAGSTER)	Empress
R. COCHRAN & CO. - VERREVILLE POTTERY	Empress
WILLIAM ADAMS & SON(S) (POTTERS) LTD.	Empress Shape
WILLIAM DAVENPORT	Empress Shape
WM. DAVENPORT & CO.	Empress Shape
RALPH STEVENSON	Endsleigh Cottage
W.H. GRINDLEY & CO. (LTD.)	England
JOHNSON BROS. (HANLEY), LTD.	English Chippendale
ENOCH WOOD & SONS	ENGLISH CITIES SERIES
JOHNSON BROS. (HANLEY), LTD.	English Gardens
FURNIVALS LTD.	English Rose
MINTON	English Scenery
WOOD & SON(S) (LTD.)	English Scenery
SPODE'S BLUE PRINTED WARES	English Sprays
SOUTH WALES POTTERS	Entente Cordiale
ENOCH WOOD & SONS	Entrance of Erie Canal into the Hudson at Albany
ENOCH WOOD & SONS	Entrance of the Erie Canal into the Hudson
SPODE/COPELAND & GARRETT, et.al.	Entrance to Ancient Granary
MINTON	Entry to Blaize Castle
BROWN WESTHEAD, MOORE & CO.	Entwined Ribbon
ANDREW STEVENSON	Enville Hall, Staffordshire
ENOCH WOOD & SONS	Environs De Chambery
JOHN EDWARDS (& CO.)	Eola
GEORGE WOOLISCROFT (& CO.)	Eon
E.T. TROUTBECK	Epirus
MINTONS, LTD.	Epping
MINTON	Epping Fruit
JOSEPH CLEMENTSON & SONS	Equestrian Vase
JAMES EDWARDS	Erford
WILLIAM DAVENPORT	Erica
BOURNE & LEIGH (LTD.)	Erie
BURGESS & LEIGH (LTD.)	Erie
RALPH STEVENSON	Erie Canal at Buffalo
ENOCH WOOD & SONS	ERIE CANAL SERIES
ANDREW STEVENSON	Erie Canal View/With Aqueduct Bridge at Little Falls
RALPH STEVENSON	Erie Canal View/With Aqueduct Bridge at Little Falls
RALPH STEVENSON & WILLIAMS	Erie Canal View/With Aqueduct Bridge at Little Falls
ANDREW STEVENSON	Erie Canal View/With Aqueduct Bridge at Rochester
RALPH STEVENSON	Erie Canal View/With Aqueduct Bridge at Rochester
RALPH STEVENSON & WILLIAMS	Erie Canal View/With Aqueduct Bridge at Rochester
ANDREW STEVENSON	Erie Canal View/With Entrance of the Erie Canal into the Hudson at Albany
RALPH STEVENSON	Erie Canal View/With Entrance of the Erie Canal into the Hudson at Albany
RALPH STEVENSON & WILLIAMS	Erie Canal View/With Entrance of the Erie Canal into the Hudson at Albany
ENOCH WOOD & SONS	Erie Canal, Aqueduct Bridge at Rochester
ENOCH WOOD & SONS	Erie Canal, View of the Aqueduct Bridge at Little Falls
JOHN WEDG WOOD	Erie Shape
WILLIAM DAVENPORT	Erie Shape
ENOCH WOOD & SONS	Erith on the Thames
BISHOP & STONIER (LTD.)	Esdale
JOHN & RICHARD RILEY	Esholt Hall, Yorkshire
ENOCH WOOD & SONS	Esholt House, Yorkshire
JOHN & WILLIAM RIDGWAY	Eski Estamboul
WILLIAM DAVENPORT	Eskimo on Snowshoes
THOMAS GODWIN	Eskimos Building Igloos
RALPH STEVENSON	Esplanade and Castle Garden, New York
THOMAS GODWIN	Esquimaux Building a Snow Hut
SPODE/COPELAND & GARRETT, et.al.	Etna
DON POTTERY	Etna from the Adorines
COPELAND & GARRETT, ET. AL.	Eton
RIDGWAYS (BEDFORD WORKS) LTD.	Eton
THOMAS TILL & SONS	Eton
W.H. GRINDLEY & CO. (LTD.)	Eton
GEORGE F. SMITH (& CO.)	Eton College
JOSEPH TWIGG (& CO.)	Eton College
S. & J. CHAPPELL	Eton College
SIDNEY WOOLF	Eton College
TAMS / et.al.	Eton College
THOMAS NICHOLSON & CO.	Eton College
RALPH STEVENSON & WILLIAMS	Eton Jacket Fishermen
SOUTH WALES POTTERS	Etruria
DAVID LOCKHART (and LOCKHART & CO.)	Etruscan
ELKIN, KNIGHT & BRIDGWOOD	Etruscan
HANCOCK & WITTINGHAM & CO.	Etruscan
JAMES F. WILEMAN	Etruscan
KNIGHT, ELKIN & CO.	Etruscan
SPODE'S BLUE PRINTED WARES	Etruscan
WOOD & BROWNFIELD	Etruscan
WILLIAM RIDGWAY (& CO.)	Etruscan Festoon
HERCULANEUM POTTERY	Etruscan Pattern
ELKIN, KNIGHT & BRIDGWOOD	ETRUSCAN SERIES
ENOCH WOOD & SONS	Etruscan Vase
SAMUEL ALCOCK & CO.	Etruscan Vase
THOMAS, JOHN & JOSEPH MAYER	Etruscan Vase
MAYER(BROS.)& ELLIOT	Etruscan Vases
SPODE/COPELAND & GARRETT, et.al.	Etruscan/Trophies-Etruscan
JOHN & RICHARD RILEY	Ettington Hall, Warwickshire
MINTON	Eugenie
WILLIAM RIDGWAY (& CO.)	Euphrates
JOHN & RICHARD RILEY	Europa
ENOCH WOOD & SONS	European Scenery
BEECH, HANCOCK & CO.	Eva
MINTON & CO.	Eva
WEDGWOOD & CO. (LTD.)	Evangeline
WOOD & SON(S) (LTD.)	Evangeline
J. & M.P. BELL (CO.) & (LTD.)	Eviction
ROBINSON, WOOD & BROWNFIELD	Ewer & Basin
GEORGE WOOLISCROFT (& CO.)	Excelsior
MOORE (SAMUEL) & CO.	Excelsior
THOMAS FELL (& CO.) (LTD.)	Excelsior
WOOD & SON(S) (LTD.)	Excelsior
HERCULANEUM POTTERY	Exchange Buildings and Nelson's Monument, Liverpool
HENSHALL & CO.	Exchange, Baltimore
JOHN & WILLIAM RIDGWAY	Exchange, Baltimore
JOHN & WILLIAM RIDGWAY	Exchange, Charleston
RALPH STEVENSON	Exchange, Charleston
THOMAS DIMMOCK (JR.) & CO.	Exchange, New York
ENOCH WOOD & SONS	Exeter
JOHNSON BROS. (HANLEY), LTD.	Exeter
J. & M.P. BELL (CO.) & (LTD.)	Exhibition
R. COCHRAN & CO. - VERREVILLE POTTERY	Exhibition
G.L. ASHWORTH & BROS. (LTD.)	Exotic Bird
HICKS & MEIGH	Exotic Birds
HICKS, MEIGH & JOHNSON	Exotic Birds
WILLIAM HACKWOOD	Exotic Birds
C. & W.K. HARVEY	Exotic Birds and Flowers
THOMAS, JOHN & JOSEPH MAYER	Exposition Building, 1851
DON POTTERY	Eyaopia
BROWN WESTHEAD, MOORE & CO.	Fable
SPODE/COPELAND & GARRETT, et.al.	Fables
FURNIVALS LTD.	Fabric
JOSEPH STUBBS	Fair Mount Near Philadelphia with Sheep
JOSEPH STUBBS	Fair Mount Near Philadelphia without Sheep
WILLIAM ADAMS & SON(S) (POTTERS) LTD.	Fairmont, So Called
WILLIAM RIDGWAY, SON & CO.	Fairmount
JAMES & RALPH CLEWS	Fairmount / [Fairmont Water Works on the Schuylkill]
WILLIAM RIDGWAY, SON & CO.	Fairmount Gardens
ENOCH WOOD & SONS	Fairmount Water Works on the Schuylkill / Philadelphia
R. COCHRAN & CO. - VERREVILLE POTTERY	Fairy
WHITTAKER, HEATH & CO.	Fairy
WILLIAM RIDGWAY (& CO.)	Fairy Queen
JOHN MADDOCK	Fairy Villas
JOHN MADDOCK & SONS (LTD.)	Fairy Villas
JOHN MEIR & SON	Fairy Villas
MADDOCK & SEDDON	Fairy Villas
WILLIAM ADAMS & SON(S) (POTTERS) LTD.	Fairy Villas
WILLIAM ADAMS & CO. LTD.	Fairy Villas (I)
WILLIAM ADAMS & CO. LTD.	Fairy Villas (II)
WILLIAM ADAMS & CO. LTD.	Fairy Villas (III)
MINTONS, LTD.	Faisan
JOHN HALL (& SONS)	Fakeer's Rock
JAMES JAMIESON & CO.	Falconry
ENOCH WOOD & SONS	Fall of Montmorenci Near Quebec
ROWLAND AND MARSELLUS	Fall River, Mass.
JOHN ROGERS (& SON)	Fallow Deer
WILLIAM HACKWOOD	Falls of Killarney
JOHN & WILLIAM RIDGWAY	Family Group, et.al.
WILLIAM DAVENPORT	Fan
H. & R. DANIEL	Fancy Birds
POUNTNEY & ALLIES	Fancy Vase
ROWLAND AND MARSELLUS	Faneuil Hall
ROWLAND AND MARSELLUS	Faneuil Hall, Boston From the Harbor
ELSMORE & FORSTER	Fanfare
THOMAS G. BOOTH	Fans
GEORGE JONES (& SONS LTD.)	Farm
OLD HALL (EARTHENWARE) POTTERY CO. LTD.	Farm
WILLIAM DAVENPORT	Farm and cattle shed, thatched cottage with very tall chimneys, et.al.
J. & G. MEAKIN	Farmer, The
BURGESS & LEIGH (LTD.)	Farmers Arms,The
MINTON	Farmyard

ANDREW STEVENSON	Faulkbourn Hall
W.H. GRINDLEY & CO. (LTD.)	Favorite Shape
RALPH HALL & CO.	Favorite, The
RALPH HALL & SON	Fayette, The Nation's Guest/Washington, His Country's Father / Dated 1824
JOHN EDWARDS (& CO.)	Feather
RALPH HALL & CO.	Feather
WOOD & CHALLINOR	Feather
CLEMENTSON & YOUNG	Feather Edge
NEALE (JAMES) & CO.	Feather Edge
THOMAS HEATH	Feather Edge
RIDGWAY & MORLEY	Feather Flower
WILLIAM ADAMS	February
COPELAND & GARRETT, ET. AL.	February - The Alps
ROWLAND AND MARSELLUS	Federal Hall, Wall Street, New York
ENOCH WOOD & SONS	Feeding the Swans
ANDREW STEVENSON	Felix Hall
SPODE'S BLUE PRINTED WARES	Fence
WILLIAM DAVENPORT	Fenced Pagoda
JAMES KENT (LTD.)	Fenton
JOHN WEDG WOOD	Fenton Jug
CHARLES JAMES MASON & CO.	Fenton Shape
J. & G. MEAKIN	Fern
JOHN & GEORGE ALCOCK	Fern
LIDDLE, ELLIOT & SON	Fern
SAMUEL ALCOCK & CO.	Fern
SOUTH WALES POTTERS	Fern
SPODE/COPELAND & GARRETT, et.al.	Fern
WEDGWOOD & CO. (LTD.)	Fern
WILLIAM ADAMS & SON(S) (POTTERS) LTD.	Fern
LIVESLEY, POWELL & CO.	Fern & Floral
J. & G. MEAKIN	Fern With Medallion
THOMAS FELL (& CO.) (LTD.)	Ferns & Flowers
S.W. DEAN	Fernwood
JOSIAH WEDGWOOD (& SONS LTD.)	Ferrara
HERCULANEUM POTTERY	Ferry Over the River Mersey at Birkenhead
SOUTH WALES POTTERS	Fest Florentine China
ARTHUR J. WILKINSON (LTD.)	Festoon
BARKER & SON	Festoon
DOULTON & CO. (LTD.)	Festoon
JOHN WEDG WOOD	Festoon
JONATHAN LOWE CHETHAM	Festoon
JOSIAH WEDGWOOD (& SONS LTD.)	Festoon
W.H. GRINDLEY & CO. (LTD.)	Festoon
WILLIAM ADAMS & CO. LTD.	Festoon
WILLIAM DAVENPORT	Festoon & Bird
ENOCH WOOD & SONS	Festoon Border
JOSIAH WEDGWOOD (& SONS LTD.)	Festoon, The
GLOBE POTTERY CO. LTD.	Fibre
MINTON	Fibre
DAVID LOCKHART & SONS (LTD.)	Fidelity
HERCULANEUM POTTERY	Field Sports
SPODE/COPELAND & GARRETT, et.al.	Field Sports
WILLIAM BROWNFIELD (& SON(S))	Field Sports
WILLIAM RIDGWAY, SON & CO.	Field Sports
WOOD & BROWNFIELD	Field Sports
HERCULANEUM POTTERY	FIELD SPORTS SERIES
WILLIAM DAVENPORT	Fig
JOHN WEDG WOOD	Fig Cousin
WILLIAM DAVENPORT	Fig Cousin Shape
JOHN WEDG WOOD	Fig Shape
MINTON	Fig-Tree Chinoiserie
JOHN ROGERS (& SON)	Figure Vase & Fence
JOHN DENTON BAXTER (BAGSTER)	Filigree
MINTON & CO.	Filigree
SPODE/COPELAND & GARRETT, et.al.	Filigree
SPODE'S BLUE PRINTED WARES	Filigree
THOMAS DIMMOCK (JR.) & CO.	Filigree
ENOCH WOOD & SONS	Finsbury Chapel
BATHWELL & GOODFELLOW	Firewood Pattern
T. & J. BEVINGTON (& CO.)	Firoz Shah's Cotilla
JOHN ROGERS (& SON)	First Steps
WEDGWOOD & CO. (LTD.)	Fish Plate
CAULDON, LTD.	Fish Plate II
BRAMELD & CO.	Fisher Boys
ENOCH WOOD & SONS	Fisherman
MINTON	Fisherman
WILLIAM DAVENPORT	Fisherman & Cross
WILLIAM DAVENPORT	Fisherman & Fence
JOSIAH WEDGWOOD (& SONS LTD.)	Fisherman / Fish Spearing
WILLIAM DAVENPORT	Fisherman and Bucket
WILLIAM DAVENPORT	Fisherman and Ferns
WILLIAM DAVENPORT	Fisherman and Friend
WILLIAM DAVENPORT	Fisherman and Woman With Basket
ENOCH WOOD & SONS	Fisherman I & II
WILLIAM DAVENPORT	Fisherman on an Island, background country house, et.al.
WILLIAM DAVENPORT	Fisherman With Boat
WILLIAM DAVENPORT	Fisherman with rod in hand on an Island, country house, et.al.
WILLIAM DAVENPORT	Fisherman, Old Man With Stick and Fence
PODMORE, WALKER (& CO.)	Fisherman, The
WILLIAM DAVENPORT	Fisherman's Advise
ENOCH WOOD & SONS	Fisherman's Island, Lago Maggiori
WILLIAM DAVENPORT	Fisherman's Tale
ROBERT HAMILTON	Fishermen With Nets
TAMS / et.al.	Fishermen With Nets
CORK, EDGE & MALKIN	Fishers
ALFRED MEAKIN (LTD.)	Fishhook
WOOD & CALDWELL	Fishing
JOHN & RICHARD RILEY	Fishing Boat, House & Windmill
JOHN ROGERS (& SON)	Fishing Dinghy
WILLIAM DAVENPORT	Fishing Family
RALPH STEVENSON & WILLIAMS	Fishing Party
BRAMELD & CO.	Fishing Scene
WILLIAM DAVENPORT	Fishing Talk
ENOCH WOOD & SONS	Fishkill, Hudson River, Near
WILLIAM DAVENPORT	Fishkill, Near / N.Y.
SPODE'S BLUE PRINTED WARES	Fitzhugh
GEORGE HARRISON (& CO.)	Fitzhugh Pattern
WILLIAM DAVENPORT	Five cows on the near bank of a river, et.al.
THOMAS & JOHN CAREY/ JOHN CAREY & SONS	Five Sheep in Foreground
RALPH STEVENSON	Flagstaff Pavillion
JOHN TURNER / TURNER & CO., etc.	Flame Plant
G.L. ASHWORTH & BROS. (LTD.)	Flamingo
BOOTHS (LTD.)	Flanders
W. & E. CORN	Flannel Daisy
HOLDCROFT, HILL & MELLOR	Flaxman
JOHN ROGERS (& SON)	Fleet Scene I
JOHN ROGERS (& SON)	Fleet Scene II
JAMES EDWARDS	Flensburg
COPELAND & GARRETT, ET. AL.	Fleur de Lis
PODMORE, WALKER (& CO.)	Fleur de lis
SOUTH WALES POTTERS	Fleur de Lys
SPODE/COPELAND & GARRETT, et.al.	Fleur de Lys
J. & G. MEAKIN	Fleur-de-Lis
JOHN EDWARDS (& CO.)	Fleur-de-Lis
SAMPSON BRIDGWOOD (& SON)(LTD.)	Fleur-de-Lis
WEDGWOOD & CO. (LTD.)	Fleur-de-lis Chain
J.W. PANKHURST (& CO.)	Fleur-de-Lis With Leaves
MELLOR, TAYLOR & CO.	Fleur-de-Lys Shape
WILLIAM ADAMS & SON(S) (POTTERS) LTD.	Fleurs, Roxburghshire
THOMAS MAYER	Flight into Egypt
ARTHUR J. WILKINSON (LTD.)	Flora
BEECH, HANCOCK & CO.	Flora
COCKSON & CHETWYND	Flora
COCKSON & HARDING	Flora
DOULTON & CO. (LTD.)	Flcra
HALLAM & JOHNSON (CO.)	Flora
HULME & BOOTH	Flora
JOHN ROGERS (& SON)	Flora
JOHN THOMAS HUDDEN	Flora
KEELING & CO. (LTD.)	Flora
MAYER(BROS.)& ELLIOT	Flora
MINTON & CO.	Flora
MYOTT, SON & CO. (LTD.)	Flora
SAMUEL ALCOCK & CO.	Flora
SOUTH WALES POTTERS	Flora
THOMAS WALKER	Flora
W.H. GRINDLEY & CO. (LTD.)	Flora
WEDGWOOD & CO. (LTD.)	Flora
WILLIAM DAVENPORT	Flora
JOHN MEIR	Flora Pattern
JOHN ALCOCK	Flora Shape
BISHOP & STONIER (LTD.)	Floral
CAULDON, LTD.	Floral
D.J. EVANS & CO.	Floral
HICKS, MEIGH & JOHNSON	Floral
JOHN TURNER / TURNER & CO., etc.	Floral
RIDGWAY, MORLEY, WEAR & CO.	Floral
SPODE/COPELAND & GARRETT, et.al.	Floral
THOMAS HUGHES & SON (LTD.)	Floral
THOMAS SHIRLEY & CO.	Floral
WILLIAM ADAMS & SON(S) (POTTERS) LTD.	Floral
WILLIAM DAVENPORT	Floral
WOOD & BROWNFIELD	Floral
ANDREW STEVENSON	FLORAL AND SCROLL BORDER SERIES
COPELAND & GARRETT, ET. AL.	Floral Arrangements
ANDREW STEVENSON	FLORAL BORDER SERIES
ENOCH WOOD & SONS	FLORAL BORDER/IRREGULAR CENTER
YNYSMEDW POTTERY	Floral Centre
TAMS / et.al.	FLORAL CITY SERIES
JACOB FURNIVAL & CO.	Floral Gothic
JACOB FURNIVAL & CO.	Floral Gothic With Band
CAULDON, LTD.	Floral Paradise
JOHN ROGERS (& SON)	Floral Pattern
MINTON	Floral Pattern
HENRY ALCOCK & CO. (LTD.)	Floral Ray
SAMUEL BARKER & SON	Floral Scenery

JOHN HALL	Fox
THOMAS FURNIVAL & SONS	Fox & Grapes
BENJAMIN E. GODWIN	Fox Chase
HERCULANEUM POTTERY	Fox Head and Horn
JAMES & RALPH CLEWS	Foxes
JOB MEIGH (& SON)	Foxes Raiding A Farmyard
JAMES EDWARDS	Framed Classic
J.W. PANKHURST (& CO.)	Framed Leaf
SAMUEL ALCOCK & CO.	Framed Leaf
CHARLES MEIGH & SON	Framed Panels Shape
BROWN WESTHEAD, MOORE & CO.	France
CHARLES ALLERTON & SONS	France
COPELAND & GARRETT, ET. AL.	Franciscan Convent, Athens
WILLIAM DAVENPORT	Franklin / Flying a Kite
EDWARD & GEORGE PHILLIPS	Franklin(s)Tomb
RALPH HALL & SON	Franklin, Lafayette, Washington
WILLIAM DAVENPORT	FRANKLIN'S MORALS SERIES
ENOCH WOOD & SONS	FRANKLIN'S TOMB SERIES
THOMAS MAYER	Franklin's Tomb
PODMORE, WALKER (& CO.)	Fredericton
BAKER, BEVANS & IRWIN	Free Trade
WHITEHAVEN POTTERY	Free Trade
SPODE'S BLUE PRINTED WARES	French Birds
WILLIAM DAVENPORT	French Fan
WILLIAM DAVENPORT	French Groups
SPODE/COPELAND & GARRETT, et.al.	French Radiating Sprigs
HERCULANEUM POTTERY	French Scenery
ENOCH WOOD & SONS	French View, Building with Covered Terrace
ENOCH WOOD & SONS	French View, Buildings at Left, et.al.
ENOCH WOOD & SONS	French View, Horses in Foreground, et.al.
ENOCH WOOD & SONS	French View, Long Stone Bridge With One Arched Section, Building on Left, et.al.
ENOCH WOOD & SONS	French View, Stone Bridge With One Arched Section, et.al.
ENOCH WOOD & SONS	FRENCH VIEWS SERIES
GEORGE PHILLIPS	Friburg
WILLIAM DAVENPORT	Friburg
JOHN ROGERS (& SON)	Frigate I
JOHN ROGERS (& SON)	Frigate II
JOHN ROGERS (& SON)	Frigate III
JAMES & RALPH CLEWS	From Fishkill, Hudson River
MELLOR, VENABLES & CO.	From Fort Hamilton
CHARLES MEIGH	From The President's House
JOB & JOHN JACKSON	From Weehawk
CHETHAM & WOOLLEY	Fruit
JOHN & WILLIAM RIDGWAY	Fruit
DOULTON & CO. (LTD.)	Fruit & Flowers
HICKS, MEIGH & JOHNSON	Fruit & Flowers
JOHN ROGERS (& SON)	Fruit & Flowers
SPODE/COPELAND & GARRETT, et.al.	Fruit & Flowers - May
SPODE'S BLUE PRINTED WARES	Fruit & Flowers - May
S. TAMS & CO.	Fruit & Scroll
TAMS / et.al.	Fruit & Scrolls
WILLIAM DAVENPORT	Fruit & Wild Rose Border
HENSHALL & CO.	FRUIT AND FLOWER BORDER SERIES
ROWLAND AND MARSELLUS	FRUIT AND FLOWER BORDER SERIES
BELLE VUE POTTERIES	Fruit Basket
FRANCIS MORLEY (& CO.)	Fruit Basket
JOSIAH WEDGWOOD (& SONS LTD.)	Fruit Basket
WILLIAM RIDGWAY (& CO.)	Fruit Basket
WILLIAM SMITH (& CO.)	Fruit Basket
BARROW & CO.	Fruit Garden
JACOB FURNIVAL & CO.	Fruit Garden
LIVESLEY, POWELL & CO.	Fruit Garden
J. & G. MEAKIN	Fruit of the Vine
BEECH & HANCOCK	Fuchsia
ELSMORE & FORSTER	Fuchsia
J. & G. MEAKIN	Fuchsia
MINTON & CO.	Fuchsia
GEORGE JONES (& SONS LTD.)	Fuchsia Shape
MELLOR, TAYLOR & CO.	Fuchsia With Band
RALPH HALL (& CO.) or (& SONS)	Fulham Church, Middlesex
J (JOSHUA) HEATH	Full Nankin
EDWARD WALLEY	Full Paneled Gothic
JACOB FURNIVAL & CO.	Full Paneled Gothic
JOSEPH CLEMENTSON	Full Paneled Gothic
LIVESLEY, POWELL & CO.	Full Paneled Gothic
JAMES EDWARDS	Full Paneled Gothic, Hexagonal
JAMES EDWARDS	Full Paneled Gothic, Octagonal
J.W. PANKHURST (& CO.)	Full Ribbed
SAMPSON BRIDGWOOD (& SON)(LTD.)	Full Ribbed
JOHNSON BROS. (HANLEY), LTD.	Fulton
RALPH STEVENSON	Fulton Market, New York
J. & M.P. BELL (CO.) & (LTD.)	Fungus
WILLIAM DAVENPORT	Fur Trapper
WILLIAM MASON	Furness Abbey, Lancashire
THOMAS FELL (& CO.) (LTD.)	Fuschia
WILLIAM ADAMS & SON(S) (POTTERS) LTD.	Gable's Farm
THOMAS MAYER	Gaignault
RIDGWAYS (BEDFORD WORKS) LTD.	Gainsborough
JOHN ROGERS (& SON)	Galleon at Anchor
DOULTON & CO. (LTD.)	Galloping Horse
DUDSON BROS.	Galloping Horses
COPELAND & GARRETT, ET. AL.	Game Birds
SPODE/COPELAND & GARRETT, et.al.	Game Birds
WILLIAM ADAMS & SON(S) (POTTERS) LTD.	Game Birds
MINTONS, LTD.	Gangees
JOHN & WILLIAM GREEN	Garden
COPELAND & GARRETT, ET. AL.	Garden Flowers
JOSEPH HEATH	Garden Flowers
HILDITCH & SONS (& CO.)	Garden Scene
KNIGHT, ELKIN & CO.	Garden Scene
BELLE VUE POTTERIES	Garden Scenery
THOMAS, JOHN & JOSEPH MAYER	Garden Scenery
WILLIAM ADAMS & SON(S) (POTTERS) LTD.	Garden Sports
J. & G. MEAKIN	Garden Sprig
FERRYBRIDGE POTTERY	Gardener and Butterfly
FRANCIS DILLON	Gardening
WALLIS GIMSON & CO.	Garfield
SOUTH WALES POTTERS	Garibaldi
T. & R. BOOTE (LTD.) (& SON)	Garibaldi Shape
BOURNE & LEIGH (LTD.)	Garland
BURGESS & LEIGH (LTD.)	Garland
COCKSON & CHETWYND	Garland
COPELAND & GARRETT, ET. AL.	Garland
DAVID METHVEN & SONS	Garland
JOSIAH WEDGWOOD (& SONS LTD.)	Garland
MINTONS	Garland
SPODE/COPELAND & GARRETT, et.al.	Garland
W. & E. CORN	Garland
WEDGWOOD & CO. (LTD.)	Garland
WILLIAM ADAMS & SON(S) (POTTERS) LTD.	Garland
WILLIAM DAVENPORT	Garland
WOOD & SON(S) (LTD.)	Garland
SPODE/COPELAND & GARRETT, et.al.	Garland Border
HERCULANEUM POTTERY	Gate of a Mosque Built by Hafizramut, Pillibeat
J. & M.P. BELL (CO.) & (LTD.)	Gauda
ELSMORE & FORSTER	Gaudy
DAVID METHVEN & SONS	Gazebo
FERRYBRIDGE POTTERY	Gazebo
PETTY & CO.	Gazebo
WILLIAM DAVENPORT	Gazebo
READ, CLEMENTSON & ANDERSON	Gazebo & Urn
JOB MEIGH (& SON)	Gazelle
JOHN HALL	Gazelle
MOORE (SAMUEL) & CO.	Gazelle
WILLIAM ADAMS & SON(S) (POTTERS) LTD.	Gazelle
GEORGE FREDERICK BOWERS (& CO.)	Gazunda
FORD & SONS (LTD.)	Geisha
J. & G. MEAKIN	Geisha
UPPER HANLEY POTTERY CO. (LTD.)	Geisha
WILLIAM ADAMS & SON(S) (POTTERS) LTD.	Geisha
CHARLES MEIGH	Gem
HENRY ALCOCK & CO. (LTD.)	Gem
J. & G. MEAKIN	Gem
JOHN CARR (& CO.) (& SON(S)	Gem
JOHN MADDOCK & SONS (LTD.)	Gem
JOHN MEIR & SON	Gem
RALPH HAMMERSLEY (& SON(S)	Gem
SAMUEL BARKER & SON	Gem
WILLIAM RIDGWAY (& CO.)	Gem
THOMAS, JOHN & JOSEPH MAYER	Gem, The
ANTHONY SHAW (& SON(S) (& CO.)	Gen'l on Rearing Horse ... Battle in The Distance, et. al.
ANTHONY SHAW (& SON(S) (& CO.)	Gen'l Taylor in Mexico
ENOCH WOOD & SONS	General Jackson, Hero of New Orleans
ANDREW STEVENSON	General Lafayette ...Welcome to the Land of Liberty ...et. al.
TAMS / et.al.	General W.H. Harrison ... Hero of the Thames 1813
JOHN HALL	Genet and Civet Cat
DOULTON & CO. (LTD.)	Geneva
JOHN KING KNIGHT	Geneva
JOHN WEDG WOOD	Geneva
JOSEPH HEATH	Geneva
NEW WHARF POTTERY CO.	Geneva
DOULTON & CO. (LTD.)	Genevesa
EDGE, MALKIN & CO. (LTD.)	Genevese
GOODWINS & HARRIS	Genevese
JAMES & RALPH CLEWS	Genevese
MINTON	Genevese
MINTON & BOYLE	Genevese
MINTON & CO.	Genevese
REED & TAYLOR	Genevese
THOMAS & BENJAMIN GODWIN	Genevese
WILLIAM SMITH (& CO.)	Genevese
ALFRED MEAKIN (LTD.)	Genoa
ENOCH WOOD & SONS	Genoa
GRIMWADES LTD.	Genoa

J. & G. MEAKIN	Genoa
R. COCHRAN & CO. - VERREVILLE POTTERY	Genoa
WILLIAM ADAMS & SON(S) (POTTERS) LTD.	Genoa
WILLIAM DAVENPORT	Genoa
FURNIVALS LTD.	Gentle Square
THOMAS FURNIVAL & SONS	Gentle Square Shape
WILLIAM RIDGWAY (& CO.)	Geometric Scrolls
JAMES JAMIESON & CO.	George Heriot's Hospital
FRANCIS MORLEY (& CO.)	Georgeville
JOHNSON BROS. (HANLEY), LTD.	Georgia
THOMAS MAYER	Georgia, Arms of
BENJAMIN E. GODWIN	Geranium
DEAKIN & SON(S) (& CO.)	Geranium
JOHN RIDGWAY (& CO.)	Geranium
JOHN WEDG WOOD	Geranium
PODMORE, WALKER (& CO.)	Geranium
SPODE/COPELAND & GARRETT, et.al.	Geranium
SPODE'S BLUE PRINTED WARES	Geranium
J. & M.P. BELL (CO.) & (LTD.)	German Stag Hunt
DAVID METHVEN & SONS	Germanstag Hunt
JOHN HALL (& SONS)	Ghaut of Cutwa
ELKIN & NEWBON	Giant Lily
DOULTON & CO. (LTD.)	Gibson Widow
SPODE/COPELAND & GARRETT, et.al.	Gift of a Dove
ENOCH WOOD & SONS	Gilpin's Mills On the Brandywine Creek
JOHN RIDGWAY (& CO.)	Giraffe
JOHN RIDGWAY, BATES & CO.	Girard Shape
JOB & JOHN JACKSON	Girard's Bank, Philadelphia
JOHN RIDGWAY (& CO.)	Girl & Lamb
C. & W.K. HARVEY	Girl at the Well
JOHN HEATH	Girl at the Well
SPODE'S BLUE PRINTED WARES	Girl at the Well
T. RATHBONE & CO.	Girl at the Well
WOOD & CHALLINOR	Girl at the Well
ENOCH WOOD & SONS	Girl Behind Grape Fence
JOHN MARSHALL (& CO.)(LTD.)	Girl Feeding a Goose
JOHN & RICHARD RILEY	Girl Gardeners
RILEY, JOHN & RICHARD	Girl Gardeners
ENOCH WOOD & SONS	Girl Holding a Parrot
MOORE (SAMUEL) & CO.	Girl Holding a Parrot
JOHN & RICHARD RILEY	Girl Musician
BRAMELD & CO.	Girl With a Bird
JOHN & RICHARD RILEY	Girl With Basket on Head
RALPH STEVENSON	Girl With Birdcage
WILLIAM SMITH (& CO.)	Girl With Dog
RALPH STEVENSON	Girl with Sheep and Goat
RALPH STEVENSON	Girl With Shepherd
WILLIAM HACKWOOD	Girl, Bird-chatcher
DAWSON (JOHN DAWSON & CO., ETC.)	Girl, Dog & Bucket
W.H. GRINDLEY & CO. (LTD.)	Gironde
W.H. GRINDLEY & CO. (LTD.)	Girton
DOULTON & CO. (LTD.)	Gladiolus
NEW WHARF POTTERY CO.	Gladys
WILLIAM ADAMS & SON(S) (POTTERS) LTD.	Glanbran, Carmarthenshire
J. & M.P. BELL (CO.) & (LTD.)	Glasgow Exhibition,1901
SAMPSON HANCOCK (& SONS)	Glen
J. & M.P. BELL (CO.) & (LTD.)	Glenartney
DOULTON & CO. (LTD.)	Glendale, The
W.H. GRINDLEY & CO. (LTD.)	Glenmore
JAMES & RALPH CLEWS	Glenn's Falls
W.H. GRINDLEY & CO. (LTD.)	Glentine
JOHN TAMS (& SON) (LTD)	Glenwood
JOHNSON BROS. (HANLEY), LTD.	Glenwood
WOOD & SON(S) (LTD.)	Glenwood
DOULTON & CO. (LTD.)	Gloire de Dijon
DOULTON & CO. (LTD.)	Gloire de Gulian
C. & W.K. HARVEY	Gloucester
SPODE'S BLUE PRINTED WARES	Gloucester
JAMES & RALPH CLEWS	Gloucester Cathedral
ENOCH WOOD & SONS	Gnoll Castle, Glamorganshire
ENOCH WOOD & SONS	Goat
JAMES JAMIESON & CO.	Goat
JOHN & ROBERT GODWIN	Goat
JOHN & RICHARD RILEY	Goat, Sheep and Cow
DAWSON (JOHN DAWSON & CO., ETC.)	Goatherd
JAMES REED	Goatherd Piping
JOHN & RICHARD RILEY	Goatherds
JAMES & RALPH CLEWS	Goats
JOHN HALL	Goats
THOMAS & JOHN CAREY/ JOHN CAREY & SONS	Goats & Lamb
H. & R. DANIEL	Goats & Swiss Chalets
HAMMERSLEY & ASBURY	God is Our Strength
HULSE & ADDERLEY	God Is Our Strength
JOHN & RICHARD RILEY	Goggerddam, Cardiganshire
J. & M.P. BELL (CO.) & (LTD.)	Going to Market
J. & M.P. BELL (CO.) & (LTD.)	Golden Flower
FRANCIS MORLEY (& CO.)	Golden Ivy
JOSIAH WEDGWOOD (& SONS LTD.)	Golden Palm
BISHOP & STONIER (LTD.)	Golden Scroll
POWELL & BISHOP	Golden Scroll
CLYDE POTTERY CO. (LTD.)	Gondola
ENOCH WOOD & SONS	Gondola
J. & M.P. BELL (CO.) & (LTD.)	Gondola
WILLIAM DAVENPORT	Gondola
WILLIAM SMITH (& CO.)	Gondola
ENOCH WOOD & SONS	Goodridge Castle, Kent
JAMES & RALPH CLEWS	Goose Hunting
JACOB FURNIVAL & CO.	Gooseberry
E. & C. CHALLINOR	Gordon
W.H. GRINDLEY & CO. (LTD.)	Gordon
JOHN MEIR	Gorhambury, Hertfordshire
RALPH STEVENSON	Gorhambury, Hertfordshire
JOSEPH HEATH	Gotha
BEECH & HANCOCK	Gothic
BENJAMIN E. GODWIN	Gothic
CHARLES MEIGH	Gothic
CHARLES MEIGH & SON	Gothic
CLYDE POTTERY CO. (LTD.)	Gothic
COCKSON & CHETWYND	Gothic
JACOB FURNIVAL & CO.	Gothic
JAMES JAMIESON & CO.	Gothic
JOHN DENTON BAXTER (BAGSTER)	Gothic
MAYER(BROS.)& ELLIOT	Gothic
SUNDERLAND OR "GARRISON" POTTERY	Gothic
T. & R. BOOTE (LTD.) (& SON)	Gothic
THOMAS DIMMOCK (JR.) & CO.	Gothic
THOMAS MAYER	Gothic
WILLIAM DAVENPORT	Gothic
THOMAS INGLEBY & CO.	Gothic Beauties
JAMES EDWARDS	Gothic Cameo
JOHN ALCOCK	Gothic Cameo
WILLIAM DAVENPORT	Gothic Cameo
JOHN WEDG WOOD	Gothic Cameo Shape
SPODE'S BLUE PRINTED WARES	Gothic Castle
CHARLES MEIGH	Gothic Church, New Haven
JACOB FURNIVAL & CO.	Gothic Grape
CLEMENTSON BROS. (LTD.)	Gothic IV - Many Paneled
ELSMORE & FORSTER	Gothic IV: Many Panelled
J.W. PANKHURST (& CO.)	Gothic Octagon
CHARLES MEIGH & SON	Gothic Rose
ANDREW STEVENSON	Gothic Ruins
CHARLES MEIGH	Gothic Ruins
COPELAND & GARRETT, ET. AL.	Gothic Ruins
JOHN ROGERS (& SON)	Gothic Ruins
JOSIAH WEDGWOOD (& SONS LTD.)	Gothic Ruins
POUNTNEY & ALLIES	Gothic Ruins
POUNTNEY & GOLDNEY	Gothic Ruins
ROBERT HAMILTON	Gothic Ruins
WILLIAM DAVENPORT	GOTHIC RUINS SERIES
WILLIAM DAVENPORT	Gothic Ruins, large tree on left, tall ruined Gothic tower on right, et.al.
HENSHALL & CO.	Gothic Scenery
ELSMORE & FORSTER	Gothic Shape
HOLLAND & GREEN	Gothic Shape
THOMAS, JOHN & JOSEPH MAYER	Gothic Shape
GEORGE WOOLISCROFT (& CO.)	Gothic Shell Shape
JOHN RIDGWAY (& CO.)	Gothic Style
C. & W.K. HARVEY	Gothic Temple
JAMES EDWARDS & SON	Gourd
SOUTH WALES POTTERS	Gower
W.H. GRINDLEY & CO. (LTD.)	Grace
JOHN & RICHARD RILEY	Gracefield, Queen's County
WILLIAM ADAMS & SON(S) (POTTERS) LTD.	Gracefield, Queen's County, Ireland
MIDDLESBOROUGH POTTERY CO.	Granada
SPODE/COPELAND & GARRETT, et.al.	Granada
WEDGWOOD & CO. (LTD.)	Granada
WALLIS GIMSON & CO.	Grand Battery at Quebec
GOODWINS & HARRIS	Grand Cricket & Match
JACOB FURNIVAL & CO.	Grand Loop
ROWLAND AND MARSELLUS	Grand Rapids, Mich.
ELSMORE & FORSTER	Grandmother's Flowers
CARTWRIGHT & EDWARDS (LTD.)	Grange
JOSEPH CLEMENTSON	Grape
JOHN DENTON BAXTER (BAGSTER)	Grape & Bird
E. & C. CHALLINOR	Grape & Medallion
WILLIAM ADAMS & SON(S) (POTTERS) LTD.	Grape & Medallion
THOMAS WALKER	Grape & Sprig
THOMAS, JOHN & JOSEPH MAYER	Grape & Vine
WILLIAM DAVENPORT	Grape Cluster
HENRY BURGESS	Grape Cluster with Chain
EDWARD WALLEY	Grape Clusters
BROUGHAM & MAYER	Grape Octagon
E. & C. CHALLINOR	Grape Octagon
E. CHALLINOR & CO.	Grape Octagon
EDWARD CORN	Grape Octagon
EDWARD WALLEY	Grape Octagon

ELSMORE & FORSTER	Grape Octagon
FREAKLEY & FARRELL	Grape Octagon
HULME & BOOTH	Grape Octagon
JACOB FURNIVAL & CO.	Grape Octagon
JOHN VENABLES & CO.	Grape Octagon
JOSEPH CLEMENTSON	Grape Octagon
LIVESLEY, POWELL & CO.	Grape Octagon
PEARSON, FARRALL & MEAKIN	Grape Octagon
THOMAS GOODFELLOW	Grape Octagon
THOMAS WALKER	Grape Octagon
SAMUEL ALCOCK & CO.	Grape Octagon Shape
UPPER HANLEY POTTERY CO. (LTD.)	Grape Pod
CLEMENTSON BROS. (LTD.)	Grape Vine
DEAKIN & SON(S) (& CO.)	Grape Vine
WILLIAM DAVENPORT	Grape Vine Motif Shape
MINTON & CO.	Grape With Vine Shape
BRIDGWOOD & CLARKE	Grape Wreath
MYOTT, SON & CO. (LTD.)	Grapes
WILLIAM DAVENPORT	Grapes
JOHN MADDOCK & SONS (LTD.)	Grapevine
ENOCH WOOD & SONS	GRAPEVINE BORDER SERIES
MINTONS, LTD.	Grasses & Flies
SPODE'S BLUE PRINTED WARES	Grasshopper
CHARLES MEIGH	Grasshopper & Flowers
THOMAS & JOHN CAREY/ JOHN CAREY & SONS	Grazing Deer
JAMES KEELING	Grazing Rabbits
THOMAS & JOHN CAREY/ JOHN CAREY & SONS	Grazing Rabbits
JOHN MADDOCK	Great Ivy & Berries
ANDREW MUIR (& CO.)	Grecian
FORD & SONS (LTD.)	Grecian
JOHN THOMSON (& SONS)	Grecian
PATTERSON & CO.	Grecian
RIDGWAYS (BEDFORD WORKS) LTD.	Grecian
SOUTH WALES POTTERS	Grecian
SPODE/COPELAND & GARRETT, et.al.	Grecian
WILLIAM RIDGWAY (& CO.)	Grecian
MINTON & CO.	Grecian Border
THOMAS DIMMOCK (JR.) & CO.	Grecian Border
CHESWORTH & ROBINSON	Grecian Figures
WILLIAM ADAMS & SON(S) (POTTERS) LTD.	Grecian Font
JOB & JOHN JACKSON	Grecian Gardens
EDWARD & GEORGE PHILLIPS	Grecian Scenery
ENOCH WOOD & SONS	Grecian Scenery
JAMES JAMIESON & CO.	Grecian Scenery
JOB & JOHN JACKSON	Grecian Scenery
THOMAS, JOHN & JOSEPH MAYER	Grecian Scroll
DAVENPORT'S LTD.	Grecian Shape
WILLIAM DAVENPORT	Grecian Shape
BROWNFIELDS(GUILD) POTTERY SOCIETY LTD.	Grecian Statue
JOHN THOMAS HUDDEN	Grecian Statue
THOMAS & JOHN CAREY/ JOHN CAREY & SONS	Grecian Statue
WOOD & BROWNFIELD	Grecian Statue
WOOD & BROWNFIELD	Grecian Stone
THOMAS GOODFELLOW	Grecian Temple
GOODWIN & ELLIS	Grecian Vases
R. COCHRAN & CO. - VERREVILLE POTTERY	Greek
SPODE/COPELAND & GARRETT, et.al.	Greek
SPODE'S BLUE PRINTED WARES	Greek
FERRYBRIDGE POTTERY	Greek Altar
ELSMORE & FORSTER	Greek Key
J.W. PANKHURST (& CO.)	Greek Key Shape
ELKIN, KNIGHT & BRIDGWOOD	Greek Maiden with Lamb
ELKIN, KNIGHT & BRIDGWOOD	Greek Musicians
FERRYBRIDGE POTTERY	GREEK PATTERN SERIES
SPODE/COPELAND & GARRETT, et.al.	GREEK PATTERNS SERIES
JOHN ROGERS (& SON)	Greek Statue
ELSMORE & FORSTER	Green Band
ENOCH WOOD & SONS	Greensburg, Tappan Zee, From
C. & W.K. HARVEY	Greenwich
COPELAND & GARRETT, ET. AL.	Greenwich
HERCULANEUM POTTERY	Greenwich
JAMES & RALPH CLEWS	Greenwich
COPELAND & GARRETT, ET. AL.	Greenwich Hospital
JOSIAH WEDGWOOD (& SONS LTD.)	Greenwich Hospital
HENRY ALCOCK & CO. (LTD.)	Grenada
HENRY BURGESS	Grenade Shape
T. & R. BOOTE (LTD.) (& SON)	Grenade Shape
BISHOP & STONIER (LTD.)	Gresham
BISHOP & STONIER (LTD.)	Greville
DAVID LOCKHART (and LOCKHART & CO.)	Greyhound
WILLIAM DAVENPORT	Griffin
LEEDS POTTERY	Griffon
EDWARD CHALLINOR	Groom Leading Out
SPODE/COPELAND & GARRETT, et.al.	Groom Leading Out
FORD & CHALLINOR	Groop, The
CHARLES MEIGH & SON	Grosvenor
MYOTT, SON & CO. (LTD.)	Grosvenor
MINTON	Grotto
R. COCHRAN & CO. - VERREVILLE POTTERY	Grotto
JOSEPH TWIGG (& CO.)	Grotto of St. Rosalie
DON POTTERY	Grotto of St. Rosalie Near Palermo
SPODE'S BLUE PRINTED WARES	Group
ANDREW STEVENSON	Grouse
JOSIAH WEDGWOOD (& SONS LTD.)	Grouse
ENOCH WOOD & SONS	Gubbins, Hertfordshire
DILLWYN & CO.	Guernsey College
EDWARD & GEORGE PHILLIPS	Guitar
KNIGHT, ELKIN & BRIDGWOOD	Guitary No. 24
JOHN & WILLIAM RIDGWAY	Gunnersbury House, Middlesex
GRIFFITHS, BEARDMORE & BIRKS	Gunton Hall
ENOCH WOOD & SONS	Gunton Hall, Norfolk
WILLIAM DAVENPORT	Guy Mannering
ENOCH WOOD & SONS	Guy's Cliff, Warwickshire
ELKIN, KNIGHT & CO.	Guy's Cliffe
BELLE VUE POTTERIES	Guys Cliff, Warwickshire
GRIMWADE BROS.	Gypsy
SHORTHOUSE & CO.	Gypsy Fire
RALPH HALL (& CO.) or (& SONS)	Gyrn, Flintshire, Wales
BURGESS & LEIGH (LTD.)	Haarlem
J. & M.P. BELL (CO.) & (LTD.)	Haarlem
WILLIAM ADAMS & SON(S) (POTTERS) LTD.	Habana
WILLIAM HACKWOOD & SON	Hackwood's Garland
JAMES & RALPH CLEWS	Haddington
SOUTHWICK POTTERY	Haddon
W.H. GRINDLEY & CO. (LTD.)	Haddon
JAMES & RALPH CLEWS	Hadley's Falls
ENOCH WOOD & SONS	Hagley, Worcestershire
JOHNSON BROS. (HANLEY), LTD.	Hague
WEDGWOOD & CO. (LTD.)	Hague
JAMES & RALPH CLEWS	Half Built Bridge
BURGESS & LEIGH (LTD.)	Halford
FORD & SONS (LTD.)	Halford
BURGESS & LEIGH (LTD.)	Halia
MINTONS, LTD.	Halifax
PODMORE, WALKER (& CO.)	Halifax
ELSMORE & FORSTER	Halleck Shape
FRANCIS MORLEY (& CO.)	Hallowell
ANDREW STEVENSON	Halstead, Essex
HENSHALL & CO.	Halstead, Essex
T. RATHBONE & CO.	Hamden
JONES & SON	Hamden Mortally Wounded
JOHN MADDOCK & SONS (LTD.)	Hamilton
ROWLAND AND MARSELLUS	Hamilton, Canada
OLD HALL (EARTHENWARE) POTTERY CO. LTD.	Hampden
MOORE & CO.	Hampton
W.H. GRINDLEY & CO. (LTD.)	Hampton
JOHN RIDGWAY (& CO.)	Hampton Court
GOODWINS & HARRIS	Hampton House
W.H. GRINDLEY & CO. (LTD.)	Hampton Spray
JOB & JOHN JACKSON	Hancock House, Boston
JAMES EDWARDS & SON	Hanging Arch Shape
THOMAS FURNIVAL & SONS	Hanging Basket
WILLIAM RIDGWAY (& CO.)	Hanging Basket
ANTHONY SHAW (& SON(S) (& CO.)	Hanging Leaves
LIDDLE, ELLIOT & SON	Hanging Pear
ALFRED MEAKIN (LTD.)	Hanley
J. & G. MEAKIN	Hanley
DAVENPORT'S LTD.	Hanley Shape
WILLIAM DAVENPORT	Hanley Shape
KNIGHT, ELKIN & CO.	Hannibal Passing the Alps
ENOCH WOOD & SONS	Hanover Lodge, Regent's Park, London
HENSHALL & CO.	Hanover Place
ENOCH WOOD & SONS	Hanover Terrace, Regent's Park, London
WILLIAM ADAMS	Hanover Terrace, Regent's Park, London
ALFRED MEAKIN (LTD.)	Hanwell
SPODE/COPELAND & GARRETT, et.al.	Harbor of Cacamo
JAMES & RALPH CLEWS	Harbor Scene
JOSIAH WEDGWOOD (& SONS LTD.)	Harbor Scene
WILLIAM DAVENPORT	Harbor Scene
JOHN ROGERS (& SON)	Harbor Scene I
JOHN ROGERS (& SON)	Harbor Scene II
JOHN RIDGWAY (& CO.)	Hare & Leverets
ENOCH WOOD & SONS	Hare Hall, Essex
CHARLES MEIGH & SON	Harebell
J. & G. MEAKIN	Harebell
RALPH STEVENSON	Harewood House
ENOCH WOOD & SONS	Harewood House, Yorkshire
RALPH STEVENSON & WILLIAMS	Harewood House, Yorkshire
SPODE/COPELAND & GARRETT, et.al.	Harlean
W.H. GRINDLEY & CO. (LTD.)	Harley
RALPH STEVENSON	Harp
WILLIAM RIDGWAY (& CO.)	Harper's Ferry From the Potomac Side, W.Va.
WILLIAM ADAMS & SON(S) (POTTERS) LTD.	Harper's Ferry, U.S.

ROWLAND AND MARSELLUS	Harrisburg, Pa.
T. RATHBONE & CO.	Harrow
ANDREW STEVENSON	Hartford State House
ROWLAND AND MARSELLUS	Hartford, Conn.
JOB & JOHN JACKSON	Hartford, Connecticut
W.H. GRINDLEY & CO. (LTD.)	Hartington
ALFRED MEAKIN (LTD.)	Harvard
ENOCH WOOD & SONS	Harvard College
RALPH STEVENSON & WILLIAMS	Harvard College / End of University Hall, With Two People in Foreground, et.al.
RALPH STEVENSON & WILLIAMS	Harvard College / Four Buildings, et.al.
RALPH STEVENSON & WILLIAMS	Harvard College / University Hall with Horseman in Foreground, et.al.
JOB & JOHN JACKSON	Harvard Hall, Massachusetts
ENOCH WOOD & SONS	Harvard University
JOHN EDWARDS (& CO.)	Harve Shape
ALFRED MEAKIN (LTD.)	Harvest
ARTHUR J. WILKINSON (LTD.)	Harvest
J. & G. MEAKIN	Harvest
J. & M.P. BELL (CO.) & (LTD.)	Harvest
SAMPSON HANCOCK (& SONS)	Harvest
JAMES & RALPH CLEWS	Harvest Home
J. & M.P. BELL (CO.) & (LTD.)	Harvest Scene
JOB & JOHN JACKSON	Harvest Scenery
FRANCIS MORLEY (& CO.)	Harvester's Gossip
NEW WHARF POTTERY CO.	Harwood
COPELAND & GARRETT, ET. AL.	Hastings
WEDGWOOD & CO. (LTD.)	Hastings
RALPH HAMMERSLEY (& SON(S)	Hatfield
ANDREW STEVENSON	Haughton Hall, Norfolk
HOLLAND & GREEN	Haveloch Shape
ROWLAND AND MARSELLUS	Haverhill, Mass.
ROWLAND AND MARSELLUS	Hawaii
J. & M.P. BELL (CO.) & (LTD.)	Hawking
ROBERT HERON (& SON)	Hawking
J. & M.P. BELL (CO.) & (LTD.)	Hawking in Olden Time
THOMAS & BENJAMIN GODWIN	Hawks
SAMPSON HANCOCK (& SONS)	Hawksey
ARTHUR J. WILKINSON (LTD.)	Hawthorn
DILLWYN & CO.	Hawthorn
RIDGWAYS (BEDFORD WORKS) LTD.	Hawthorn
SPODE/COPELAND & GARRETT, et.al.	Hawthorn
WILLIAM DAVENPORT	Hawthorn
J. & M.P. BELL (CO.) & (LTD.)	Hawthorn Blossom
JAMES JAMIESON & CO.	Hawthorn Blossom
JOHN HAWTHORN	Hawthorn's Fern Shape
WILLIAM ADAMS & SON(S) (POTTERS) LTD.	Hawthornden, Edinburghshire
BOOTHS (LTD.)	Hawthorne
CHARLES MEIGH	Hawthorne
DUNN BENNETT & CO. (LTD.)	Hawthorne
LIVESLEY, POWELL & CO.	Hawthorne
WILLIAM DAVENPORT	Hawthorne
SAMUEL ALCOCK & CO.	Hawthorne Blossom
W.H. GRINDLEY & CO. (LTD.)	Hay Wain, The
JOHN DENTON BAXTER (BAGSTER)	Haymaker
JOB & JOHN JACKSON	Haymaker, The
JOHN DENTON BAXTER (BAGSTER)	Haymaking, et.al.
TAMS / et.al.	Haymarket Theatre, London
WILLIAM ADAMS & SON(S) (POTTERS) LTD.	Headwaters of the Juniata, U.S.
WILLIAM DAVENPORT	Heart of Midlothian
WILLIAM RIDGWAY (& CO.)	Heart With Arrow
CHARLES MEIGH & SON	Heath
JOSEPH HEATH	Heath's Flower
THOMAS HEATH	Heath's Flower
CLEMENTSON BROS. (LTD.)	Heavy Square Shape
JOHN ALCOCK	Hebe Shape
GOODWINS & HARRIS	Hebrew Melodies
JOSEPH CLEMENTSON	Hector & Paris
JOHN HALL	Hedgehog
WILLIAM SMITH (& CO.)	Helvetia
ENOCH WOOD & SONS	Hen and Chicks
ROWLAND AND MARSELLUS	Hendrick Hudson
TAMS / et.al.	Henry Clay ... Star of the West
JOHN ROGERS (& SON)	Henry IV, Act 2 Scene 2
POUNTNEY & GOLDNEY	Henry IV, Act 2 Scene 2
JOHN ROGERS (& SON)	Henry IV, Act 5 Scene 4
POUNTNEY & GOLDNEY	Henry IV, Act 5 Scene 4
WILLIAM DAVENPORT	Henry Marriott
SPODE/COPELAND & GARRETT, et.al.	Hephaestus Presenting Arms to Aphrodite
HENRY ALCOCK & CO. (LTD.)	Herald
THOMAS, JOHN & JOSEPH MAYER	Heraldic Swirls
CAULDON, LTD.	Herb Garden
BOULTON, MACHIN & TENNANT	Herbs
SPODE/COPELAND & GARRETT, et.al.	Hercules Fighting Hippolya
CHARLES JAMES MASON & CO.	Hercules Fountain
DILLWYN & CO.	Herdsman
JAMES WALLACE & CO.	Herdsman and Gothic Cottage
JOHN & RICHARD RILEY	Herdsman With White Cow
JOHN & WILLIAM RIDGWAY	Herdsman, Bridge and Tower
ENOCH WOOD & SONS	Hereford
MINTON	Hermit
ROWLAND AND MARSELLUS	Hermitage
SEWELL(S) & CO.	Hermitage
ENOCH WOOD & SONS	Hermitage En Dauphne
CHARLES MEIGH	Heron
G.W. TURNER & SONS	Heron
JAMES & RALPH CLEWS	Heron
RALPH HAMMERSLEY (& SON(S)	Heron
ANDREW STEVENSON	Herons
JOHN MADDOCK & SONS (LTD.)	Heuman
ANTHONY SHAW (& SON(S) (& CO.)	Hexagon
JAMES EDWARDS	Hexagon Shape
SAMPSON BRIDGWOOD (& SON)(LTD.)	Hexagon Strap
ANTHONY SHAW (& SON(S)) (& CO.)	Hexagon Sunburst
JOHN ROGERS (& SON)	Hexagonals & Dragons
MINTONS, LTD.	Hexham
JOHN WEDG WOOD	Hibernia
CAULDON, LTD.	Hibiscus
JOSIAH WEDGWOOD (& SONS LTD.)	Hibiscus
WILLIAM ADAMS & SON(S) (POTTERS) LTD.	Hibiscus in Pot
JACOB FURNIVAL & CO.	Hidden Motif
WILLIAM DAVENPORT	High Bridge
ENOCH WOOD & SONS	Highbury College, London
WILLIAM ADAMS	Highbury College, London
ENOCH WOOD & SONS	Highlands at West Point, Hudson River
ENOCH WOOD & SONS	Highlands, Hudson River
ENOCH WOOD & SONS	Highlands, Hudson River, Near Newburgh
JOSEPH STUBBS	Highlands, North River
WEDGWOOD & CO. (LTD.)	Hilda
CLEMENTSON BROS. (LTD.)	Hill Shape
JOSEPH CLEMENTSON	Hill Shape
WHITEHAVEN POTTERY	Hillis Bowl
POUNTNEY & CO. (LTD.)	Hilton
BELLE VUE POTTERIES	Hinchinbrooke, Huntington
JOHN HALL (& SONS)	Hindoo Ghaut
JOHN HALL (& SONS)	Hindoo Pagoda
JOHN HALL (& SONS)	Hindoo Temple
JOHN HALL (& SONS)	Hindoo Village
HOPE & CARTER	Hindoostan
WILLIAM HACKWOOD & SON	Hindoostan
WOOD & BAGGALEY	Hindoostan
WOOD & BROWNFIELD	Hindoostan
HOPE & CARTER	Hindostas
EDWARD WALLEY	Hindu
JOHN MADDOCK & SONS (LTD.)	Hindustan
JOSIAH WEDGWOOD (& SONS LTD.)	Hinse
G.L. ASHWORTH & BROS. (LTD.)	Hizen
JAMES & RALPH CLEWS	Hobart Town
WILLIAM DAVENPORT	Hobart Town
JOSEPH STUBBS	Hoboken in New Jersey
BARKERS & KENT (LTD.)	Hoey
W.H. GRINDLEY & CO. (LTD.)	Hofburg, The
EDWARD CHALLINOR	Hog at Bay,The
EDWARD CHALLINOR	Hog Hunters Meeting by Surprise a Tigress and Her Cubs
SPODE/COPELAND & GARRETT, et.al.	Hog Hunters Meeting by Surprise a Tigress and Her Cubs
JOHNSON BROS. (HANLEY), LTD.	Holland
ALFRED MEAKIN (LTD.)	Holland, The
HENSHALL & CO.	Holliday Street Theatre, Baltimore
MINTONS, LTD.	Hollins Japan
RALPH STEVENSON	Holliwell Cottage
JOHN MADDOCK	Holly
JOHN MADDOCK & SONS (LTD.)	Holly
MARPLE, TURNER & CO.	Holly
R. COCHRAN & CO. - VERREVILLE POTTERY	Holly
JOSIAH WEDGWOOD (& SONS LTD.)	Hollyhock
ENOCH WOOD & SONS	Hollywell Cottage, Cavan
JOHN & RICHARD RILEY	Hollywell Cottage, Cavan
THOMAS & JOHN CAREY/ JOHN CAREY & SONS	Hollywell Cottage, Ireland, Lord Tara's Seat
HENSHALL & CO.	Hollywood Cottage
JOB & JOHN JACKSON	Holy Bible
HERCULANEUM POTTERY	Holy Bible Series
JOB & JOHN JACKSON	HOLY BIBLE SERIES
JAMES JAMIESON & CO.	Holy Trinity Episcopal Church
ENOCH WOOD & SONS	Holyrood House, Edinburgh
JOSEPH CLEMENTSON	Homer Invoking the Muses
J. & G. MEAKIN	Homestead
PINDER BOURNE & HOPE	Honc
HERCULANEUM POTTERY	Honest Lawyer
SPODE/COPELAND & GARRETT, et.al.	Honeycomb
SPODE/COPELAND & GARRETT, et.al.	Honeysucke Empire
SPODE/COPELAND & GARRETT, et.al.	Honeysuckle
SPODE'S BLUE PRINTED WARES	Honeysuckle & Parsley
POWELL, BISHOP & STONIER	Honfleur
ANTHONY SHAW (& SON(S) (& CO.)	Hong

CORK, EDGE & MALKIN	Hong
EDWARD WALLEY	Hong
THOMAS WALKER	Hong
CHARLES MEIGH	Hong Kong
POWELL, BISHOP & STONIER	Hong Kong
WILLIAM RIDGWAY, SON & CO.	Hong Kong
WILLIAM DAVENPORT	Hop
JOSEPH CLEMENTSON	Hop Border
MIDDLESBOROUGH POTTERY CO.	Hop Pickers
CHARLES MEIGH	Hopberry
J. & G. MEAKIN	Hope Louise
WILLIAM SMITH (& CO.)	Horse
BAKER, BEVANS & IRWIN	Horse & Cart
THOMAS & JOHN CAREY/ JOHN CAREY & SONS	Horse & Top Hat
JOHN HALL	Horse and Colt
JOHN & WILLIAM RIDGWAY	Horse Drawn Covered Wagon, et.al.
MIDDLESBOROUGH POTTERY CO.	Horse Guards
JOHN & RICHARD RILEY	Horse, Goat, Sheep, Cows
HOPE & CARTER	Horsehunt
RALPH STEVENSON	Horseman at the Ford
JOHN & WILLIAM RIDGWAY	Horseman With Four Cows, et.al.
CHETHAM & ROBINSON	Horseman, Woman & Child
JOHN DENTON BAXTER (BAGSTER)	Horses Trotting, et.al.
ROWLAND AND MARSELLUS	Horseshoe Curve, Pa.
JOSIAH WEDGWOOD (& SONS LTD.)	Horticultural
WEDGWOOD & CO. (LTD.)	Horticulture
JOHN & WILLIAM RIDGWAY	Hospital, Boston
RALPH STEVENSON	Hospital, Boston
RALPH STEVENSON & WILLIAMS	Hospital, Boston
RALPH STEVENSON	Hospital, Boston With Sea Wall
RALPH STEVENSON	Hospital, Boston Without Sea Wall
RALPH STEVENSON	Hospital, New York
ROWLAND AND MARSELLUS	Hot Springs, Va.
RIDGWAY, MORLEY, WEAR & CO.	Hot Water Plate
WILLIAM RIDGWAY (& CO.)	Hot Water Plate
EDWARD CHALLINOR	Hounds Chasing a Hare
SPODE/COPELAND & GARRETT, et.al.	Hounds Chasing a Hare
SPODE'S BLUE PRINTED WARES	House & Fence
ROWLAND AND MARSELLUS	House of Oliver Ellsworth
DOULTON & CO. (LTD.)	Howard
THOMAS BOOTH & CO.	Hoya
J. & G. MEAKIN	Hudson
SAMPSON HANCOCK (& SONS)	Hudson
THOMAS EDWARDS	Hudson
CHARLES MEIGH	Hudson City, N.Y.
ROWLAND AND MARSELLUS	Hudson River
WILLIAM RIDGWAY (& CO.)	Hudson River
ENOCH WOOD & SONS	HUDSON RIVER SCENES
ENOCH WOOD & SONS	Hudson River View
WILLIAM ADAMS & SON(S) (POTTERS) LTD.	HUDSON RIVER VIEWS SERIES
JAMES & RALPH CLEWS	Hudson, Hudson River
WILLIAM RIDGWAY, SON & CO.	Hudson, New York
WILLIAM DAVENPORT	Humped back bridge, boat and two seated figures, floral foliage, et.al.
RIDGWAYS (BEDFORD WORKS) LTD.	Humphrey's Clock
WILLIAM RIDGWAY, SON & CO.	Humphrey's Clock
WILLIAM RIDGWAY (& CO.)	HUMPHREY'S CLOCK SERIES
JOHN FORD & CO.	Humphreys Clock
EDGE, BARKER & CO.	Humulus
WILLIAM & SAMUEL EDGE	Humulus
THOMAS DIMMOCK (JR.) & CO.	Hunter returning home
ENOCH WOOD & SONS	Hunter Shooting Ducks
ENOCH WOOD & SONS	Hunter Shooting Fox
THOMAS DIMMOCK (JR.) & CO.	Hunters and urn
THOMAS DIMMOCK (JR.) & CO.	Hunters resting
EDWARD CHALLINOR	Hunting a Buffalo
SPODE/COPELAND & GARRETT, et.al.	Hunting a Buffalo
EDWARD CHALLINOR	Hunting a Civet Cat
SPODE/COPELAND & GARRETT, et.al.	Hunting a Civiet Cat
SPODE/COPELAND & GARRETT, et.al.	Hunting a Cuttauss or Civiet Cat
EDWARD CHALLINOR	Hunting a Hog Deer
SPODE/COPELAND & GARRETT, et.al.	Hunting a Hog Deer
EDWARD CHALLINOR	Hunting a Kuttauss or Civet Cat
EDWARD CHALLINOR	Hunting an Old Buffalo
SPODE/COPELAND & GARRETT, et.al.	Hunting an Old Buffalo
JAMES & RALPH CLEWS	Hunting Dog
HERCULANEUM POTTERY	Hunting Scene, Two Hunters With Dog
JAMES & RALPH CLEWS	HUNTING VIEWS SERIES
WILLIAM ADAMS & SON(S) (POTTERS) LTD.	Huntsman
INDEO POTTERY	Huntsman and Greyhound
F. WINKLE & CO. (LTD.)	Huron
WILLIAM ADAMS & SON(S) (POTTERS) LTD.	Huron Shape
JAMES EDWARDS	Husk
JAMES EDWARDS & SON	Husk
ROBERT HAMILTON	Hut on the Canton River
JOHN MADDOCK & SONS (LTD.)	Hyacinth
JOHN WEDG WOOD	Hyacinth
R. COCHRAN & CO. - VERREVILLE POTTERY	Hyacinth

WOOD, SON & CO.	Hyacinth
WEDGWOOD & CO. (LTD.)	Hyacinth Shape
HENRY BURGESS	Hyacinth Shape
BROUGHAM & MAYER	Hybla
WOOD & SON(S) (LTD.)	Hyde
CHARLES JAMES MASON & CO.	Hydra Shape
BELLE VUE POTTERIES	Hydrangea
WILLIAM DAVENPORT	Hydrographic
ENOCH WOOD & SONS	Hyena
JOHN HALL	Hyena
ENOCH WOOD & SONS	Hylands, Essex
JOHN MEIR	Hylands, Essex
JOSEPH CLEMENTSON	Hyson
SAMUEL ALCOCK & CO.	Hyson
WILLIAM BROWNFIELD (& SON(S)	Ida
ARTHUR J. WILKINSON (LTD.)	Ideal
W.H. GRINDLEY & CO. (LTD.)	Ideal
WILLIAM DAVENPORT	Ideal
W.H. GRINDLEY & CO. (LTD.)	Idris
WILLIAM DAVENPORT	If You Would Know The Value of Money Try to Borrow Some
J. & M.P. BELL (CO.) & (LTD.)	Ikan China
NEW WHARF POTTERY CO.	Ilan
FORD & SONS (LTD.)	Ilford
KEELING & CO. (LTD.)	Ilford
SPODE/COPELAND & GARRETT, et.al.	Ilium
THOMAS MAYER	ILLUSTRATIONS OF THE BIBLE SERIES
MINTON	Image
DAVID METHVEN & SONS	Imperial
SOHO POTTERY (LTD.)	Imperial
WILLIAM (ALSAGER) ADDERLEY (& CO.)	Imperial
REED & TAYLOR	Imperial Filigree
JOHN TAMS (& SON) (LTD)	Imperial Measure
JOHN TAMS (& SON) (LTD)	Imperial Quart
W.H. GRINDLEY & CO. (LTD.)	Imperial, The
CHARLES MEIGH & SON	Impmoea
INDEO POTTERY	Indeo Chinoiserie
ROWLAND AND MARSELLUS	Independence Hall
JOSEPH TWIGG (& CO.)	Independent Order of Oddfellows
BISHOP & STONIER (LTD.)	India
BRAMELD & CO.	India
JAMES REED	India
JOHN ROGERS (& SON)	India
MINTON	India
RALPH STEVENSON	India
SPODE'S BLUE PRINTED WARES	India
T. & J. HOLLINS	India
JOB & JOHN JACKSON	India Pagoda
HERCULANEUM POTTERY	INDIA SERIES
G.L. ASHWORTH & BROS. (LTD.)	India Temple
JOHN & WILLIAM RIDGWAY	India Temple
JOHN RIDGWAY (& CO.)	India Temple
JOHN MADDOCK & SONS (LTD.)	India Tree
CAULDON, LTD.	Indian
F. & R. PRATT & CO. (LTD.)	Indian
G.L. ASHWORTH & BROS. (LTD.)	Indian
LIVESLEY, POWELL & CO.	Indian
THOMAS DIMMOCK (JR.) & CO.	Indian
THOMAS GOODFELLOW	Indian
REED & TAYLOR	Indian Bird
SAMUEL ALCOCK & CO.	Indian Bridge
JOSEPH HEATH & CO.	Indian Chief
R. COCHRAN & CO. - VERREVILLE POTTERY	Indian Chief/ Chef Sauvage
J. & M.P. BELL (CO.) & (LTD.)	Indian Cress
BROWN WESTHEAD, MOORE & CO.	Indian Empress
FRANCIS MORLEY (& CO.)	Indian Encampent, et.al.
BRAMELD & CO.	Indian Flowers
GEORGE F. SMITH (& CO.)	Indian Jar
JACOB & THOMAS FURNIVAL	Indian Jar
THOMAS FURNIVAL & CO.	Indian Jar
BOOTHS (LTD.)	Indian Ornament
T.G. & F. BOOTH	Indian Ornament
THOMAS DIMMOCK (JR.) & CO.	Indian Plant
JOHN ROGERS (& SON)	Indian Reed
FRANCIS MORLEY (& CO.)	Indian Scene
CORK, EDGE & MALKIN	INDIAN SCENERY SERIES
EDGE, MALKIN & CO. (LTD.)	INDIAN SCENERY SERIES
THOMAS & BENJAMIN GODWIN	INDIAN SCENERY SERIES
SPODE'S BLUE PRINTED WARES	Indian Sporting
SPODE/COPELAND & GARRETT, et.al.	INDIAN SPORTING SERIES
J. & M.P. BELL (CO.) & (LTD.)	Indian Sprig
EDWARD WALLEY	Indian Stone
JONES & WALLEY	Indian Stone
ELKIN, KNIGHT & BRIDGWOOD	Indian Temple
THOMAS & JOHN CAREY/ JOHN CAREY & SONS	Indian Temples
THOMAS & JOHN CAREY/ JOHN CAREY & SONS	INDIAN TEMPLES SERIES
GEORGE JONES (& SONS LTD.)	Indian Traffic

BARKER & TILL	Lahore
HOLLINSHEAD & KIRKHAM (LTD.)	Lahore
SOUTH WALES POTTERS	Lahore
SOUTH WALES POTTERS	Lahore
T. & R. BOOTE (LTD.) (& SON)	Lahore
THOMAS PHILLIPS & SON	Lahore
W. & E. CORN	Lahore
BATHWELL & GOODFELLOW	Laird
FRANCIS MORLEY (& CO.)	Lake
G.L. ASHWORTH & BROS. (LTD.)	Lake
SPODE/COPELAND & GARRETT, et.al.	Lake
SPODE'S BLUE PRINTED WARES	Lake
G.R. TURNBULL	Lake & Bridge
ENOCH WOOD & SONS	Lake Avernus
ROWLAND AND MARSELLUS	Lake Champlain, N.Y.
WOOD & CHALLINOR	Lake Como
ENOCH WOOD & SONS	Lake George
JOB & JOHN JACKSON	Lake George
MELLOR, VENABLES & CO.	Lake George
ROWLAND AND MARSELLUS	Lake George, N.Y.
ENOCH WOOD & SONS	Lake George, State of New York
WILLIAM ADAMS & SON(S) (POTTERS) LTD.	Lake George, U.S.
ENOCH WOOD & SONS	Lake of Albano
PODMORE, WALKER (& CO.)	Lake of Two Mountains
ENOCH WOOD & SONS	Lake Scenery
F. & R. PRATT & CO. (LTD.)	Lake Scenery
FRANCIS MORLEY (& CO.)	LAKE SERIES
G.L. ASHWORTH & BROS. (LTD.)	Lake Series
JOHN & WILLIAM RIDGWAY	Lakeside Castle, et.al.
JAMES KEELING	Lakeside Meeting
JOHN ROGERS (& SON)	Lakeside Scenes
WOOD & SON(S) (LTD.)	Lakewood
ROWLAND AND MARSELLUS	Lakewood, N.J.
W.H. GRINDLEY & CO. (LTD.)	Lambeth
ENOCH WOOD & SONS	Lambton Hall, Durham
JOHN MEIR	Lambton Hall, Durham
BISHOP & STONIER (LTD.)	Lancaster
ELKIN, KNIGHT & CO.	Lancaster
HERCULANEUM POTTERY	Lancaster
JOHN ROGERS (& SON)	Lancaster
NEW WHARF POTTERY CO.	Lancaster
W. & E. CORN	Lancaster
BLACKHURST & TUNNICLIFFE	Lanconia
ROWLAND AND MARSELLUS	Landing of Columbus
WILLIAM ADAMS & SON(S) (POTTERS) LTD.	LANDING OF COLUMBUS SERIES
ROWLAND AND MARSELLUS	Landing of the Pilgrims
JONES & SON	Landing of William of Orange
JOHN ROGERS (& SON)	Landing Scene
COPELAND & GARRETT, ET. AL.	Landscape
JOSIAH WEDGWOOD (& SONS LTD.)	Landscape
MINTON	Landscape
SPODE/COPELAND & GARRETT, et.al.	Landscape
W.R. MIDWINTER (LTD.)	Landscape
DON POTTERY	LANDSCAPE SERIES
JOSIAH WEDGWOOD (& SONS LTD.)	Landscape With Blue Rose Border
JOSIAH WEDGWOOD (& SONS LTD.)	Landscape with Grapes and Chain
JOHN & RICHARD RILEY	Landscape With Musicians
MINTON	Lanercost Priory
MINTONS	Lanercost Priory
JOHN & WILLIAM RIDGWAY	Lanercost Priory, Cumberland
SPODE'S BLUE PRINTED WARES	Lange Lijsen
HENSHALL & CO.	Langley Park
SOUTHWICK POTTERY	Laodicea
JOHN ROGERS (& SON)	Lapique
SAMPSON HANCOCK (& SONS)	Larch
BATHWELL & GOODFELLOW	Large Basket
WILLIAM DAVENPORT	Large cottage, one mounted rider talking to a standing figure, et.al.
THOMAS & JOHN CAREY/ JOHN CAREY & SONS	Large Country House on Hills, View 1
THOMAS & JOHN CAREY/ JOHN CAREY & SONS	Large Country House on Hills, View 2
THOMAS GODWIN	Large Naval Litter and Several Small Boats on a Lake, et.al.
JOHN & RICHARD RILEY	LARGE SCROLL BORDER SERIES
WILLIAM DAVENPORT	Las Palmas Canaria
GEORGE JONES (& SONS LTD.)	Lasso
JOHN GOODWIN/LONGTON	Lasso
JOHN GOODWIN/SEACOMBE POTTERY	Lasso
JOHN THOMAS HUDDEN	Lasso
THOMAS FELL (& CO.) (LTD.)	Lasso
WILLIAM ADAMS & SON(S) (POTTERS) LTD.	Lasso
WILLIAM BOURNE	Lasso
WEDGWOOD & CO. (LTD.)	Late Tulip
SPODE'S BLUE PRINTED WARES	Lattice Scroll
HERCULANEUM POTTERY	Laughing Dog
WEDGWOOD & CO. (LTD.)	Laurel Shape
ELSMORE & FORSTER	Laurel Wreath Shape
BROWN WESTHEAD, MOORE & CO.	Laurelia

CHARLES MEIGH	Lauristinus
COPELAND & GARRETT, ET. AL.	Lausanne
YALE & BARKER	Lavinia
BISHOP & STONIER (LTD.)	Lawrence
ENOCH WOOD & SONS	Lawrence
W.H. GRINDLEY & CO. (LTD.)	Lawrence
RALPH STEVENSON	Lawrence Mansion, Boston
RALPH HALL (& CO.) or (& SONS)	Laxton Hall, Northamptonshire
CAMBRIAN POTTERY	Lazuli
DILLWYN & CO.	Lazuli
JAMES EDWARDS	Lazuli
WILLIAM DAVENPORT	Lazuli
W.H. GRINDLEY & CO. (LTD.)	Le Pavot
MINTON	Leaf
SPODE'S BLUE PRINTED WARES	Leaf
LIVESLEY, POWELL & CO.	Leaf & Crossed Ribbon
J. & M.P. BELL (CO.) & (LTD.)	Leaf Border
BRIDGWOOD & CLARKE	Leaf Fan
TAYLOR BROS.	Leaf Focus
JOHN ROGERS (& SON)	Leaf Sheet Pattern
JOHN RIDGWAY, BATES & CO.	Leafall
JOHN & WILLIAM RIDGWAY	Leamington Baths, et.al.
ROWLAND AND MARSELLUS	Leavenworth, Kan.
RALPH STEVENSON	LEAVES & VINES
JOHN & WILLIAM RIDGWAY	Lechlade
MINTON	Lechlade Bridge
BELLE VUE POTTERIES	Lee House on the Clyde
JOHN & WILLIAM RIDGWAY	Lee, Kent
ENOCH WOOD & SONS	Leeds
WILLIAM DAVENPORT	Legend of Montrose
BURGESS & LEIGH (LTD.)	Leicester
SAMPSON HANCOCK (& SONS)	Leicester
WOOD & SON(S) (LTD.)	Leicester
ALFRED MEAKIN (LTD.)	Leighton
BURGESS & LEIGH (LTD.)	Leighton
JOSEPH CLEMENTSON	Leipsic
ALFRED MEAKIN (LTD.)	Lenox
ROWLAND AND MARSELLUS	Lenox, Mass.
J. & G. MEAKIN	Leon
ENOCH WOOD & SONS	Leopard
JOB MEIGH (& SON)	Leopard
ROWLAND AND MARSELLUS	Lewis and Clark Centennial
ROWLAND AND MARSELLUS	Lexington, Battle of
JOHN & WILLIAM RIDGWAY	Library Of Trinity College, Cambridge
JOHN & WILLIAM RIDGWAY	Library, Philadelphia
ARTHUR J. WILKINSON (LTD.)	Lichfield
RIDGWAYS (BEDFORD WORKS) LTD.	Lichfield
WALLIS GIMSON & CO.	Lieutenant-Governor's Residence
DAVID LOCKHART (and LOCKHART & CO.)	Life Buoy
GRIFFITHS, BEARDMORE & BIRKS	LIGHT BLUE ROSE BORDER SERIES
BELLE VUE POTTERIES	Lightening
ENOCH WOOD & SONS	Lighthouse
BURGESS & LEIGH (LTD.)	Lilac
DUNN BENNETT & CO. (LTD.)	Lilac
JOHN & ROBERT GODWIN	Lilies
WILLIAM DAVENPORT	Lilium
WILLIAM ADAMS & CO. LTD.	Lilly
ALFRED MEAKIN (LTD.)	Lily
BLACKHURST & TUNNICLIFFE	Lily
CHARLES MEIGH	Lily
FORD & SONS (LTD.)	Lily
FRANCIS MORLEY (& CO.)	Lily
JACOB FURNIVAL & CO.	Lily
JOHN KING KNIGHT	Lily
JOHNSON BROS. (HANLEY), LTD.	Lily
MINTON	Lily
SPODE/COPELAND & GARRETT, et.al.	Lily
SPODE'S BLUE PRINTED WARES	Lily
THOMAS DIMMOCK (JR.) & CO.	Lily
THOMAS, JOHN & JOSEPH MAYER	Lily
TURNER & TOMKINSON	Lily
WILLIAM (ALSAGER) ADDERLEY (& CO.)	Lily
WILLIAM ADAMS & SON(S) (POTTERS) LTD.	Lily
WILLIAM DAVENPORT	Lily
WOOD & CHALLINOR	Lily
THOMAS, JOHN & JOSEPH MAYER	Lily & Bluebell
COPELAND & GARRETT, ET. AL.	Lily & Rose
SPODE/COPELAND & GARRETT, et.al.	Lily & Rose
ELSMORE & FORSTER	Lily & Vase
LOCKHART & ARTHUR	Lily and Rose
PODMORE, WALKER (& CO.)	Lily Lake
JOHN MEIR & SON	Lily of the Valley
SAMUEL LEAR	Lily of the Valley with Ferns
JACOB FURNIVAL & CO.	Lily of the Valley with Thumb Prints
J.W. PANKHURST (& CO.)	Lily Pad
HENRY BURGESS	Lily Shape
GEORGE WOOLISCROFT (& CO.)	Lily-of-the-Valley
ROWLAND AND MARSELLUS	Lima, Ohio
ENOCH WOOD & SONS	Limehouse Dock, Regent's Canal, London

ENOCH WOOD & SONS	Limehouse Dock, The, Regent's Canal
BISHOP & STONIER (LTD.)	Lincoln
ENOCH WOOD & SONS	Lincoln
G.L. ASHWORTH & BROS. (LTD.)	Lincoln
MINTONS, LTD.	Lincoln
ROWLAND AND MARSELLUS	Lincoln, Neb.
POUNTNEY & CO. (LTD.)	Lind
POUNTNEY & GOLDNEY	Lind
JOHN MADDOCK & SONS (LTD.)	Linda
JOHN MEIR	Lindertis, Forfarshire
GEORGE WOOLISCROFT (& CO.)	Line Trim
JAMES EDWARDS	Line Trim
JAMES EDWARDS & SON	Line Trim
JOHN MADDOCK	Lined Glory
JOHN MADDOCK & SONS (LTD.)	Lined Glory
GRIMWADES LTD.	Linnea
J. & M.P. BELL (CO.) & (LTD.)	Linnet
THOMAS GODWIN	Lintin
THOMAS GODWIN	Linton
ENOCH WOOD & SONS	Lion
JOHN HALL	Lion
ROBINSON, WOOD & BROWNFIELD	Lion
WILLIAM SMITH (& CO.)	Lion Antique
TAYLOR, HARRISON & CO.	Lion Hunter
WILLIAM ADAMS & SON(S) (POTTERS) LTD.	Lion Patterns
MELLOR, TAYLOR & CO.	Lion's Head
JOHN EDWARDS (& CO.)	Lion's Head
EDGE, MALKIN & CO. (LTD.)	Lisbon
MINTONS, LTD.	Lismore
ENOCH WOOD & SONS	Litchfield
MINTONS, LTD.	Litchfield
THOMAS & JOHN CAREY/ JOHN CAREY & SONS	Litchfield Cathedral
THOMAS FURNIVAL & SONS	Little Cable
JAMES & RALPH CLEWS	Little Falls at Luzerne, Hudson River
WILLIAM RIDGWAY, SON & CO.	Little Falls, N.Y.
WILLIAM RIDGWAY (& CO.)	Little Girl & Her Grandfather
WILLIAM RIDGWAY (& CO.)	Little Girl By The River
WILLIAM RIDGWAY (& CO.)	Little Girls In The Graveyard
ENOCH WOOD	Little Girls Playing Ball
WILLIAM RIDGWAY (& CO.)	Little Nell and her Grandfather
WILLIAM RIDGWAY (& CO.)	Little Nell by the River
WILLIAM RIDGWAY (& CO.)	Little Nell in the Graveyard
E. & C. CHALLINOR	Little Pear
EDWARD CHALLINOR	Little Pear
JOHN ALCOCK	Little Pear Shape
ELSMORE & FORSTER	Little Scroll
WHITEHAVEN POTTERY	Littledale Mug
ENOCH WOOD & SONS	Liverpool
HERCULANEUM POTTERY	Liverpool Arms
HERCULANEUM POTTERY	Liverpool From the Mersey
HERCULANEUM POTTERY	Liverpool From the Seacombe Slip
HERCULANEUM POTTERY	LIVERPOOL VIEWS SERIES
SOUTH WALES POTTERS	Livinium
RALPH HALL (& CO.) or (& SONS)	Llanarth Court, Monmouthshire
BRAMELD & CO.	Llandig's Blackberry
SOUTH WALES POTTERS	Llanelly Bouquet
CHARLES JAMES MASON & CO.	Loadicea
GEORGE PHILLIPS	Lobelia
SPODE/COPELAND & GARRETT, et.al.	Lobelia
JOHN MEIR & SON	Loc Oich and Invergarry Castle
GIBSON & SONS (LTD.)	Locarno
JOHN MEIR & SON	Loch Achray
JOHN MEIR & SON	Loch Awe
JOHN MEIR & SON	Loch Creran with Bar Caldine Castle
JOHN MEIR & SON	Loch Katrine, Looking Towards Ellen's Isle
JOHN MEIR & SON	Loch Levan Looking Towards Ballachulish Ferry
JOHN MEIR & SON	Loch Linnhe Looking South
JAMES JAMIESON & CO.	Loch Winnock
R. COCHRAN & CO. - VERREVILLE POTTERY	Loch Winnock
DAVID LOCKHART & SONS (LTD.)	Lochee
WILLIAM ADAMS & SON(S) (POTTERS) LTD.	Log Cabin
JOHN RIDGWAY (& CO.)	Log Cabin, End View with Two Men
JOHN RIDGWAY (& CO.)	Log Cabin, Side View
JOHN RIDGWAY (& CO.)	Log Cabin, Side View, Man .. with Two Horse Team
JOHN WEDG WOOD	Log Cabin/North Bend
NEW WHARF POTTERY CO.	Lois
ENOCH WOOD & SONS	Loke Denton
JOSEPH HEATH & CO.	Lombardy
BRITANNIA POTTERY CO. LTD.	Lomond
ENOCH WOOD & SONS	London
JOHN CARR (& CO.) (& SON(S)	London
POWELL, BISHOP & STONIER	London
ENOCH WOOD & SONS	LONDON VIEWS SERIES
CAMBRIAN POTTERY	Long Bridge
DAVID DUNDERDALE & CO.	Long Bridge
SPODE'S BLUE PRINTED WARES	Long Bridge
THEOPHILUS SMITH	Long Bridge
LEEDS POTTERY	Long Bridge Pattern
SPODE'S BLUE PRINTED WARES	Long Eliza
J (JOSHUA) HEATH	Long Live The King
J. & M.P. BELL (CO.) & (LTD.)	Long Octagon
JOHN ALCOCK	Long Octagon
THOMAS, JOHN & JOSEPH MAYER	Long Octagon Shape
ROWLAND AND MARSELLUS	Longfellow's Early Home
RIDGWAYS (BEDFORD WORKS) LTD.	Lonsdale
SAMUEL FORD & CO.	Lonsdale
SMITH, FORD & JONES	Lonsdale
ROWLAND AND MARSELLUS	Lookout Mtn., Tenn.
E. & C. CHALLINOR	Loop & Dot
JACOB FURNIVAL & CO.	Loop & Line
BOURNE & LEIGH (LTD.)	Loraine
GEORGE GORDON [GORDON'S POTTERY]	Lord Owen's Daughter
HERCULANEUM POTTERY	Lord Street, Liverpool
BRAMELD & CO.	Lord's Prayer
SAMUEL ALCOCK & CO.	Loretta
WHITEHAVEN POTTERY	Loretta
R. COCHRAN & CO. - VERREVILLE POTTERY	Lorette Falls Chutes De Lorette
R. COCHRAN & CO. - VERREVILLE POTTERY	Lorette Squaw/ Sauvagesse De Lorette
JOSEPH CLEMENTSON	Loretto
DAVID METHVEN & SONS	Lorne
R. COCHRAN & CO. - VERREVILLE POTTERY	Lorne
W.H. GRINDLEY & CO. (LTD.)	Lorne
RIDGWAYS (BEDFORD WORKS) LTD.	Lorraine
WILLIAM ADAMS & SON(S) (POTTERS) LTD.	Lorraine
ROWLAND AND MARSELLUS	Los Angeles, Calif.
COCKSON & HARDING	Lotus
JOSIAH WEDGWOOD (& SONS LTD.)	Lotus
R. COCHRAN & CO. - VERREVILLE POTTERY	Lotus
SPODE/COPELAND & GARRETT, et.al.	Lotus
THOMAS DIMMOCK (JR.) & CO.	Lotus
W.H. GRINDLEY & CO. (LTD.)	Lotus
COPELAND & GARRETT, ET. AL.	Louis Quatorze
SPODE/COPELAND & GARRETT, et.al.	Louis Quatorze
J. & M.P. BELL (CO.) & (LTD.)	Louise
JOHN MADDOCK & SONS (LTD.)	Louise
NEW WHARF POTTERY CO.	Louise
W.H. GRINDLEY & CO. (LTD.)	Louise
JAMES & RALPH CLEWS	Louisville, Kentucky
WILLIAM DAVENPORT	Louisville, Kentucky
HERCULANEUM POTTERY	Louvre
J. & G. MEAKIN	Louvre
SPODE'S BLUE PRINTED WARES	Love Chase
JOHN ROGERS (& SON)	Love in a Village, Act 1 Scene 4
POUNTNEY & GOLDNEY	Love in a Village, Act 1 Scene 4
JOHN ROGERS (& SON)	Love's Labours Lost
ROWLAND AND MARSELLUS	Lowell Mass., City Hall
CHARLES JAMES MASON & CO.	Loweswater
RALPH STEVENSON & SON	Loweswater
JOHN & RICHARD RILEY	Lowing Cow
JOHN MEIR	Lowther Castle, Westmorland
RALPH STEVENSON	Lowther Castle, Westmorland
E. CHALLINOR & CO.	Lozere
EDWARD CHALLINOR	Lozere
WEDGWOOD & CO. (LTD.)	Lozere
EDWARD CLARKE (& CO.)	Lucania
RIDGWAYS (BEDFORD WORKS) LTD.	Lucania
W. & E. CORN	Lucania
JOHN DENTON BAXTER (BAGSTER)	Lucano
SPODE'S BLUE PRINTED WARES	Lucano
CHARLES BOURNE	Lucano Pattern
ENOCH WOOD & SONS	Lucerne
F. WINKLE & CO. (LTD.)	Lucerne
J. DIMMOCK & CO.	Lucerne
J. H. & J. DAVIS	Lucerne
J.W. PANKHURST (& CO.)	Lucerne
JOSEPH CLEMENTSON	Lucerne
NEW WHARF POTTERY CO.	Lucerne
THOMAS GOODFELLOW	Lucerne
ALFRED MEAKIN (LTD.)	Luciville
JOHN HALL (& SONS)	Lucknow
THOMAS & BENJAMIN GODWIN	Lucknow
JOHN ROGERS (& SON)	Ludlow Castle
RIDGWAYS (BEDFORD WORKS) LTD.	Ludlow Castle
TAMS / et.al.	Ludlow Castle
WILLIAM ADAMS & SON(S) (POTTERS) LTD.	Ludlow Castle, Salop
CALEDONIAN POTTERY	Lugano
RIDGWAYS (BEDFORD WORKS) LTD.	Lugano
JAMES & RALPH CLEWS	Lumley Castle, Durham
JOHN & WILLIAM RIDGWAY	Lumley Castle, Durham
ENOCH WOOD & SONS	Luscombe, Devon
JOHN MEIR	Luscombe, Devon
RALPH HALL (& CO.) or (& SONS)	Luscombe, Devonshire
ALFRED COLLEY & CO. LTD.	Lusitania
WOOD & SON(S) (LTD.)	Lusitania
ELSMORE & FORSTER	Lustre Band
THOMAS & JOHN CAREY/ JOHN CAREY & SONS	Luton Hoo, Bedfordshire, Marquis of Bute's Seat
SAMPSON BRIDGWOOD (& SON)(LTD.)	Luzerne

THOMAS & JOHN CAREY/ JOHN CAREY & SONS	Lying Bull
WILLIAM ADAMS & SON(S) (POTTERS) LTD.	Lyme Castle, Kent...sic
W.H. GRINDLEY & CO. (LTD.)	Lyndhurst
CERAMIC ART CO. LTD.	Lynton
W.H. GRINDLEY & CO. (LTD.)	Lynton
FRANCIS MORLEY (& CO.)	Lyra
SPODE'S BLUE PRINTED WARES	Lyre
W.H. GRINDLEY & CO. (LTD.)	Lyric
CHARLES ALLERTON & SONS	Mabel
BURGESS & LEIGH (LTD.)	Mabelle
THOMAS GODWIN	Macao
WILLIAM DAVENPORT	Macao
SPODE/COPELAND & GARRETT, et.al.	Macaw
ENOCH WOOD & SONS	Macclesfield Bridge, Regent's Park
CLOSE & CO.	Maddle Jenny Lind
EDWARD CHALLINOR	Maddle Jenny Lind
WILLIAM ADAMS & SON(S) (POTTERS) LTD.	Maddle, Jenny Lind
JOHN MADDOCK	Maddock's Pear
J. & G. MEAKIN	Madison
DOULTON & CO. (LTD.)	Madras
J. DIMMOCK & CO.	Madras
JOHN THOMSON (& SONS)	Madras
NEW WHARF POTTERY CO.	Madras
SAMUEL ALCOCK & CO.	Madras
THOMAS BOOTH & CO.	Madras
THOMAS BOOTH & SON	Madras
THOMAS G. BOOTH	Madras
UPPER HANLEY POTTERY CO. (LTD.)	Madras
WILLIAM BROWNFIELD (& SON(S)	Madras
WILLIAM DAVENPORT	Madras
WOOD & BAGGALEY	Madras
WOOD & BROWNFIELD	Madras
WOOD & PIGOTT	Madras
WOOD & SON(S) (LTD.)	Madras
JOHN & WILLIAM RIDGWAY	Magdalen Tower and Bridge, Oxford
JOHN HALL (& SONS)	Mahomeda Mosque and Tomb... sic
ARTHUR J. WILKINSON (LTD.)	Maidenhair Fern
JOHN ROGERS (& SON)	Maidstone Jail
CHARLES JAMES MASON & CO.	Main Entrance to Queens College, Cambridge
ENOCH WOOD & SONS	Maison De Raphael
ENOCH WOOD & SONS	Major Gen. Brown, Niagara
J. & M.P. BELL (CO.) & (LTD.)	Makassar
J. & M.P. BELL (CO.) & (LTD.)	Malacca
J. & M.P. BELL (CO.) & (LTD.)	Malaga
JOHN MARSHALL (& CO.)(LTD.)	Male Skaters
JOHN MARSHALL (& CO.)(LTD.)	Male Snowshoer Striding Along
JOHN MARSHALL (& CO.)(LTD.)	Male Snowshoer Trips Over Fence
BOULTON, MACHIN & TENNANT	Mallow
SAMUEL ALCOCK & CO.	Malo
W.H. GRINDLEY & CO. (LTD.)	Malta
WILLIAM (ALSAGER) ADDERLEY (& CO.)	Malta
COTTON & BARLOW	Maltese
WILLIAM BROWNFIELD (& SON(S))	Maltese
EDWARD CORN	Maltese Shape
F. WINKLE & CO. (LTD.)	Malverne
JAMES & RALPH CLEWS	Mambrino's Helmet
WILLIAM DAVENPORT	Mambrino's Helmet
WILLIAM DAVENPORT	Man a Little Makes a Mickle
THOMAS & JOHN CAREY/ JOHN CAREY & SONS	Man Filling Trough
SUNDERLAND OR "GARRISON" POTTERY	Man of the Lake
WILLIAM DAVENPORT	Man on Cart-horse, talking to another man seated beneath tree, et.al.
JAMES & RALPH CLEWS	Man With Bird
JOHN & WILLIAM RIDGWAY	Man With Horse Pulling a Harrow, et.al.
RALPH STEVENSON	Man with Rake
BROWN WESTHEAD, MOORE & CO.	Mandalay
BRADLEY & CO.	Mandarin
DOULTON & CO. (LTD.)	Mandarin
F. & R. PRATT & CO. (LTD.)	Mandarin
FERRYBRIDGE POTTERY	Mandarin
G.L. ASHWORTH & BROS. (LTD.)	Mandarin
HICKS, MEIGH & JOHNSON	Mandarin
JOHN MADDOCK	Mandarin
MINTON	Mandarin
POUNTNEY & CO. (LTD.)	Mandarin
SPODE/COPELAND & GARRETT, et.al.	Mandarin
SPODE'S BLUE PRINTED WARES	Mandarin
THOMAS DIMMOCK (JR.) & CO.	Mandarin
SAMUEL GINDER & CO.	Mandoline
HENRY ALCOCK & CO. (LTD.)	Manhattan
JOHNSON BROS. (HANLEY), LTD.	Manhattan
RALPH STEVENSON & SON	Manhattan
RALPH HAMMERSLEY (& SON(S)	Manila
SAMUEL ALCOCK & CO.	Manila
SAMUEL BARKER & SON	Manila
THOMAS TILL & SONS	Manila
W.H. GRINDLEY & CO. (LTD.)	Manila
PODMORE, WALKER (& CO.)	Manilla
WILLIAM ADAMS & SON(S) (POTTERS) LTD.	Manor House
JAMES & THOMAS EDWARDS	Mansion
THOMAS SHIRLEY & CO.	Mansion
JAMES & RALPH CLEWS	Mansion, Circular Drive
JAMES & RALPH CLEWS	Mansion, Foreground a Lake With Swans
JAMES & RALPH CLEWS	Mansion, Small Boat With Flag in Foreground
JAMES & RALPH CLEWS	Mansion, Winding Drive
WOOD & SON(S) (LTD.)	Manskillan
READ & CLEMENTSON	Mantua
FRANCIS MORLEY (& CO.)	Many Faceted
ANTHONY SHAW (& SON(S) (& CO.)	Many Paneled Gothic
ELSMORE & FORSTER	Many Paneled Gothic
SAMUEL ALCOCK & CO.	Many Paneled Gothic
MELLOR, VENABLES & CO.	Many Paneled Gothic Shape
JOSIAH WEDGWOOD (& SONS LTD.)	Many-storied Pagoda
THOMAS FURNIVAL & SONS	Maple
NEW WHARF POTTERY CO.	Maple Leaf
W.H. GRINDLEY & CO. (LTD.)	Marachal Neil
ANTHONY SHAW (& SON(S) (& CO.)	Marble
COPELAND & GARRETT, ET. AL.	Marble
F. & R. PRATT & CO. (LTD.)	Marble
JOHN WEDG WOOD	Marble
JONES & WALLEY	Marble
SPODE'S BLUE PRINTED WARES	Marble
THOMAS DIMMOCK (JR.) & CO.	Marble
VENABLES & BAINES	Marble
WILLIAM & THOMAS ADAMS	Marble
WILLIAM ADAMS & CO. LTD.	Marble
WILLIAM DAVENPORT	Marble
MARY WILKINSON	Marble Ice
SPODE/COPELAND & GARRETT, et.al.	Marble/Sheet Pattern
WILLIAM DAVENPORT	Marbles
WILLIAM RIDGWAY (& CO.)	Marcella
JOSIAH WEDGWOOD (& SONS LTD.)	March
COPELAND & GARRETT, ET. AL.	March - Untitled
WILLIAM HACKWOOD	March, The
WILLIAM DAVENPORT	Mare and foal at riverside, et.al.
WILLIAM DAVENPORT	MARE AND FOAL SERIES
FORD & SONS (LTD.)	Mareshal
COPELAND & GARRETT, ET. AL.	Margate
SAMPSON HANCOCK (& SONS)	Margot
W.H. GRINDLEY & CO. (LTD.)	Margot
BOURNE & LEIGH (LTD.)	Marguerite
HUMPHREYS BROS.	Marguerite
JOSIAH WEDGWOOD (& SONS LTD.)	Marguerite
W.H. GRINDLEY & CO. (LTD.)	Marguerite
W.H. GRINDLEY & CO. (LTD.)	Marie
JOSIAH WEDGWOOD (& SONS LTD.)	Marigold
CORK, EDGE & MALKIN	Marina
MINTON & CO.	Marina
GEORGE PHILLIPS	Marine
J. & M.P. BELL (CO.) & (LTD.)	Marine
JOB & JOHN JACKSON	Marine
SOUTH WALES POTTERS	Marine
THOMAS GOODFELLOW	Marine
WILLIAM DAVENPORT	Marine
ENOCH WOOD & SONS	Marine Hospital, Louisville, KY
CORK, EDGE & MALKIN	Marino
EDGE, MALKIN & CO. (LTD.)	Marino
GEORGE PHILLIPS	Marino
THOMAS GODWIN	Marino
THOMAS PHILLIPS & SON	Marino
THOMAS TILL & SON	Marino
CLYDE POTTERY CO. (LTD.)	Mario
WILLIAM RIDGWAY (& CO.)	Mariteus
DUNN BENNETT & CO. (LTD.)	Marlborough
JOHN MADDOCK & SONS (LTD.)	Marlborough
W.H. GRINDLEY & CO. (LTD.)	Marlborough
WOOD & SON(S) (LTD.)	Marlborough
WILLIAM RIDGWAY (& CO.)	Marmora
WILLIAM H. LOCKITT	Marne
W.H. GRINDLEY & CO. (LTD.)	Marquis II, The
W.H. GRINDLEY & CO. (LTD.)	Marquis, The
WHITEHAVEN POTTERY	Marriage Puzzle
LEWIS WOOLF (& SONS)(& CO.)	Marseillaise
WHITEHAVEN POTTERY	Marseillaise
ARTHUR J. WILKINSON (LTD.)	Marseilles
SAMUEL FORD & CO.	Martel
BRIDGETT & BATES	Martha
UPPER HANLEY POTTERY CO. (LTD.)	Martha
WOOD & SON(S) (LTD.)	Martha Washington
SAMUEL ALCOCK & CO.	Maryland
THOMAS MAYER	Maryland, Arms of
WILLIAM DAVENPORT	Maryland, Baltimore
BRAMELD & CO.	Masaniello
WHITEHAVEN POTTERY	Masonic
JOHN & WILLIAM RIDGWAY	Masonic Hall, Philadelphia
RALPH STEVENSON	Masonic Hall, Philadelphia
JOHN ROGERS (& SON)	Masque
ROWLAND AND MARSELLUS	Massachusetts State House

THOMAS MAYER	Massachusetts, Arms of
JAMES KEELING	Master and Servant
F. WINKLE & CO. (LTD.)	Matlock
DOULTON & CO. (LTD.)	Matsumai
SAMPSON HANCOCK (& SONS)	Mattean
PODMORE, WALKER (& CO.)	Maude
BROWN WESTHEAD, MOORE & CO.	Mauritas
HERCULANEUM POTTERY	Mausoleum of Nawaub Assoph Khan, Rajemahel
HERCULANEUM POTTERY	Mausoleum of Sultan Purveiz, Near Allahabad
WILLIAM WALSH	Mausoleum of Sultan Purveiz, Near Allahabad
ENOCH WOOD & SONS	Maxstoke Castle, Warwickshire
W.H. GRINDLEY & CO. (LTD.)	May
COPELAND & GARRETT, ET. AL.	May - Untitled
T.G. & F. BOOTH	May Blossom
J. & M.P. BELL (CO.) & (LTD.)	May Morn
THOMAS, JOHN & JOSEPH MAYER	Mayer's Classic Gothic Shape
WHITEHAVEN POTTERY	Mayfield
WILLIAM BOURNE	May-Flower
J. & M.P. BELL (CO.) & (LTD.)	Mayflower
ROWLAND AND MARSELLUS	Mayflower
ROWLAND AND MARSELLUS	Mayflower at Plymouth Harbor
JOHN ROGERS (& SON)	Maypole
MINTON	Maypole
POUNTNEY & GOLDNEY	Maypole
JOHN MEIR	Mazara
JOHN MEIR & SON	Mazara
WILLIAM ADAMS & CO. LTD.	Mazara
WILLIAM ADAMS & SON(S) (POTTERS) LTD.	Mazara
GOODWINS & HARRIS	Mazeppa
SAMUEL FORD & CO.	McKinley
J. DIMMOCK & CO.	McNette
BISHOP & STONIER (LTD.)	Meadow
W. BAKER & CO. (LTD.)	Meadow Bouquet
SPODE/COPELAND & GARRETT, et.al.	Meander
JACOB FURNIVAL & CO.	Mecca
BROWN WESTHEAD, MOORE & CO.	Medallion
G.L. ASHWORTH & BROS. (LTD.)	Medallion
W.R. MIDWINTER (LTD.)	Medallion
WILLIAM ADAMS & SON(S) (POTTERS) LTD.	Medallion
JOSEPH CLEMENTSON	Medallion Scroll
POWELL & BISHOP	Medallion Sprig
G.L. ASHWORTH & BROS. (LTD.)	Medallions
GEORGE JONES (& SONS LTD.)	Medici
MELLOR, VENABLES & CO.	Medici
RIDGWAYS (BEDFORD WORKS) LTD.	Medici
JOSIAH WEDGWOOD (& SONS LTD.)	Medieval
WILLIAM BROWNFIELD (& SON(S)	Medieval
CHARLES MEIGH, SON & PANKHURST	Medina
COTTON & BARLOW	Medina
J.H. WEATHERBY & SONS (LTD.)	Medina
JACOB & THOMAS FURNIVAL	Medina
JACOB FURNIVAL & CO.	Medina
SUNDERLAND OR "GARRISON" POTTERY	Medina
THOMAS GODWIN	Medina
WILLIAM RIDGWAY (& CO.)	Medina
SUNDERLAND OR "GARRISON" POTTERY	Mediterranean Group
ALFRED MEAKIN (LTD.)	Medway
JOHN MADDOCK & SONS (LTD.)	Meissen
MINTON & CO.	Meissen
MINTONS, LTD.	Meissen
RIDGWAYS (BEDFORD WORKS) LTD.	Meissen
THOMAS FURNIVAL & SONS	Meissen
FORD & SONS (LTD.)	Melbourn
DOULTON & CO. (LTD.)	Melbourne
W.H. GRINDLEY & CO. (LTD.)	Melbourne
WILLIAM (ALSAGER) ADDERLEY (& CO.)	Melbourne
BOURNE & LEIGH (LTD.)	Melrose
CLYDE POTTERY CO. (LTD.)	Melrose
DOULTON & CO. (LTD.)	Melrose
G.L. ASHWORTH & BROS. (LTD.)	Melrose
NEW WHARF POTTERY CO.	Melrose
SPODE/COPELAND & GARRETT, et.al.	Melrose
SPODE/COPELAND & GARRETT, et.al.	Melrose
JAMES & RALPH CLEWS	Melrose Abbey
WILLIAM ADAMS & SON(S) (POTTERS) LTD.	Melrose Abbey, Roxburghshire
JOHN & THOMAS LOCKETT	Melton
SAMPSON HANCOCK (& SONS)	Melton
WEDGWOOD & CO. (LTD.)	Melton
JOHN & WILLIAM RIDGWAY	Melville Castle, Midlothian
JOHN MEIR & SON	Memnon Shape
ROWLAND AND MARSELLUS	Memphis, Tenn.
THOMAS DIMMOCK (JR.) & CO.	Menai Bridge
JOSEPH STUBBS	Mendenhall Ferry
ALFRED MEAKIN (LTD.)	Mentone
JOHNSON BROS. (HANLEY), LTD.	Mentone
JOHN ROGERS (& SON)	Merchant of Venice, Act 4 Scene 1
POUNTNEY & GOLDNEY	Merchant of Venice, Act 4 Scene 1
JOHN ROGERS (& SON)	Merchant of Venice, Act 5 Scene 4
POUNTNEY & GOLDNEY	Merchant of Venice, Act 5 Scene 4
BROWNHILLS POTTERY CO. (LTD.)	Mercia
WILLIAM RIDGWAY (& CO.)	Meredith, N.H.
WILLIAM RIDGWAY, SON & CO.	Meredith, N.H.
ANDREW STEVENSON	Mereworth House
W.H. GRINDLEY & CO. (LTD.)	Merion
MINTONS, LTD.	Merrion Japan
JOHN ROGERS (& SON)	Merry Wives of Windsor, Act 5 Scene 5
POUNTNEY & GOLDNEY	Merry Wives of Windsor, Act 5 Scene 5
W.H. GRINDLEY & CO. (LTD.)	Mersey
WILLIAM DAVENPORT	Mersey
JOHN & WILLIAM RIDGWAY	Merton College, Oxford
CORK, EDGE & MALKIN	Mesieres
ALFRED MEAKIN (LTD.)	Messina
BROWN WESTHEAD, MOORE & CO.	Messina
CAULDON, LTD.	Messina
WOOD & CHALLINOR	Messina
WOOD & CHALLINOR & CO.	Messina
GOODWINS & HARRIS	METROPOLITAN SCENERY SERIES
JOHN DENTON BAXTER (BAGSTER)	METROPOLITAN SCENERY SERIES
HOPE & CARTER	Mexico
THOMAS GODWIN	Mezieres
ROWLAND AND MARSELLUS	Miami, Fl.
WILLIAM DAVENPORT	Michigan, Detroit
JOHN ROGERS (& SON)	Midas, Act 1 Scene 3
POUNTNEY & GOLDNEY	Midas, Act 1 Scene 3
JOHN & RICHARD RILEY	Midnight Flowers
DILLWYN & CO.	Mignonette
ARTHUR J. WILKINSON (LTD.)	Mikado
J. & M.P. BELL (CO.) & (LTD.)	Mikado
THOMAS FURNIVAL & SONS	Mikado
W. & E. CORN	Mikado
ADDERLEY'S LTD.	Milan
FORD & SONS (LTD.)	Milan
KNIGHT, ELKIN & CO.	Milan
MINTONS, LTD.	Milan
NEW WHARF POTTERY CO.	Milan
SAMUEL FORD & CO.	Milan
SOUTH WALES POTTERS	Milan
W.H. GRINDLEY & CO. (LTD.)	Milan
WILLIAM ADAMS & SON(S) (POTTERS) LTD.	Milan
WOOD & SON(S) (LTD.)	Milan
JOSEPH STUBBS	Milanaise Scenery
JOSEPH HEATH & CO.	Milanese Pavilions
RICHARD DAVIES & CO.	Milanese Villas
ELGIN POTTERY	Mile End
ROWLAND AND MARSELLUS	Miles Standish
ROWLAND AND MARSELLUS	Miles Standish Monument
JOHN WEDG WOOD	Milesian
BURGESS & LEIGH (LTD.)	Milford
HENSHALL & CO.	Milford Green
JOSEPH HEATH & CO.	Military Sketches
WILLIAM ADAMS & SON(S) (POTTERS) LTD.	Milking Time
WILLIAM DAVENPORT	Milking Time, Thatched cottage with two cows, one being milked, et.al.
BELLE VUE POTTERIES	Milkmaid
DON POTTERY	Milkmaid
JOHN MOSELEY	Milkmaid
ROBERT HAMILTON	Milkmaid
SPODE/COPELAND & GARRETT, et.al.	Milkmaid
SPODE'S BLUE PRINTED WARES	Milkmaid
T. RATHBONE & CO.	Milkmaid
WILLIAM DAVENPORT	Milkmaid
RALPH STEVENSON	Milkmaid and Goats
BATHWELL & GOODFELLOW	Milkmaid Pattern
JOHN RIDGWAY (& CO.)	Mill
JOHN RIDGWAY (& CO.)	Mill and Obelisk
ELKIN, KNIGHT & CO.	Mill at Ambleside
SAMPSON HANCOCK (& SONS)	Millais
J. & G. MEAKIN	Millennium
RALPH STEVENSON & SON	Millennium
POUNTNEY & CO. (LTD.)	Milton
WOOD & SON(S) (LTD.)	Milton
ROWLAND AND MARSELLUS	Milwaukee, Wisc.
SPODE/COPELAND & GARRETT, et.al.	Mimosa
PODMORE, WALKER (& CO.)	Minerva
BRITANNIA POTTERY CO. LTD.	Ming
THOMAS FORD & CO.	Ming
THOMAS FORD (& CO.)	Ming
THOMAS G. GREEN & CO. (LTD.)	Ming
J. & G. MEAKIN	Miniature Scroll
ROWLAND AND MARSELLUS	Minneapolis, Minn.
WHITEHAVEN POTTERY	Minstrel
MINTON	Minton Filigree
MINTON & CO.	Minton's Japan
JOSIAH WEDGWOOD (& SONS LTD.)	Minton's Willow
HENRY ALCOCK & CO. (LTD.)	Minwood
HENRY ALCOCK & CO. (LTD.)	Mira
JAMES & RALPH CLEWS	Mirror Lakeside
WILLIAM ADAMS & SON(S) (POTTERS) LTD.	Miscellania

KEELING & CO. (LTD.)	Napier
SAMPSON BRIDGWOOD (& SON)(LTD.)	Napier Shape
ENOCH WOOD & SONS	Naples from Capo di Chino
CHARLES JAMES MASON & CO.	Napoleon
WILLIAM SMITH (& CO.)	Napoleon
CHARLES JAMES MASON & CO.	Napoleon at the Battle of Austerlitz
CHARLES JAMES MASON & CO.	Napoleon at the Battle of Marengo
CHARLES JAMES MASON & CO.	Napoleon Battles - Return from Elba
CHARLES JAMES MASON & CO.	Napoleon Battles - Revolt of Cairo
CHARLES JAMES MASON & CO.	NAPOLEON SERIES
WILLIAM SMITH (& CO.)	Napoleon's Victories
GEORGE SKINNER & CO.	Napoleon's Victory
BURGESS & LEIGH (LTD.)	Napoli
RIDGWAYS (BEDFORD WORKS) LTD.	Narcissus
THOMAS, JOHN & JOSEPH MAYER	Narrow Waist Gothic
WILLIAM RIDGWAY (& CO.)	Narrows From Fort Hamilton, The, N.Y.
WILLIAM RIDGWAY (& CO.)	Narrows From Staten Island, The, N.Y.
ROWLAND AND MARSELLUS	Nashville, Tenn.
HOLLINSHEAD & KIRKHAM (LTD.)	Natal
WILLIAM ADAMS & SON(S) (POTTERS) LTD.	Native Pattern
ENOCH WOOD & SONS	Natural Bridge, Virginia
R. COCHRAN & CO. - VERREVILLE POTTERY	Natural Steps, Montmorency River: Marches
R. COCHRAN & CO. - VERREVILLE POTTERY	Naturelle, Riviere Montmorency
GEORGE JONES (& SONS LTD.)	Nautilus
JOSEPH CLEMENTSON	Nautilus
SOUTH WALES POTTERS	Nautilus
JOSEPH CLEMENTSON	Nautilus Shape
PINDER BOURNE & CO.	Nautilus Shell
WILLIAM ADAMS & SON(S) (POTTERS) LTD.	Navarine
WEDGWOOD & CO. (LTD.)	Navarre
THOMAS TILL & SONS	Navy
PODMORE, WALKER (& CO.)	Navy Island
CHARLES MEIGH	Navy Marble
THOMAS MAYER	Nazareth
THOMAS FELL (& CO.) (LTD.)	Ne Plus
DILLWYN & CO.	Ne Plus Ultra / No Farther
H. & R. DANIEL	Neapolitan
JOHNSON BROS. (HANLEY), LTD.	Neapolitan,
JOHN & WILLIAM RIDGWAY	Near Bucharest
ENOCH WOOD & SONS	Near Calcutta
LEEDS POTTERY	Near Curran on the River Ganges
WILLIAM DAVENPORT	Near Fishkill / New York
JAMES & RALPH CLEWS	Near Fishkill, Hudson River
JAMES & RALPH CLEWS	Near Fishkill/ New York
JAMES & RALPH CLEWS	Near Fort Miller, Hudson River
GOODWINS & HARRIS	Near Highgate Road
JAMES & RALPH CLEWS	Near Hudson, Hudson River/ Fort Montgomery
ELKIN, KNIGHT & CO.	Near Newark
ELKIN, KNIGHT & CO.	Near Patterdale
JAMES & RALPH CLEWS	Near Philadelphia
WILLIAM DAVENPORT	Near Philadelphia
JAMES & RALPH CLEWS	Near Sandy Hill, Hudson River
WILLIAM RIDGWAY, SON & CO.	Near Troy, N.Y.
WILLIAM RIDGWAY, SON & CO.	Near Weehawken
SPODE/COPELAND & GARRETT, et.al.	Necropolis or Cemetery of Cacamo
WILLIAM DAVENPORT	Nectarine
RIDGWAYS (BEDFORD WORKS) LTD.	Nell's Lonely Walk
GRIMWADES LTD.	Nelson
MINTON	Nelson
NEW WHARF POTTERY CO.	Nelson
UPPER HANLEY POTTERY CO. (LTD.)	Nelson
THOMAS DIMMOCK (JR.) & CO.	Neopolitan
JAMES & RALPH CLEWS	Neptune
JOHN & GEORGE ALCOCK	Neptune
JONES & SON	Neptune Pattern
RIDGWAYS (BEDFORD WORKS) LTD.	Nestor
JOSEPH CLEMENTSON	Nestor's Sacrifice
SPODE'S BLUE PRINTED WARES	Net
CHARLES TITTENSOR	Net Pattern
HERCULANEUM POTTERY	Net Pattern
JOB RIDGWAY	Net Pattern
JOB RIDGWAY & SONS	Net Pattern
JOHN ROGERS (& SON)	Net Trellis & Flowers
ANDREW STEVENSON	Netley Abbey
WILLIAM MASON	Netley Abbey
SPODE'S BLUE PRINTED WARES	Nettle
J. & M.P. BELL (CO.) & (LTD.)	Neuilly
EDWARD CHALLINOR	Neva
WILLIAM RIDGWAY (& CO.)	Neva
ROWLAND AND MARSELLUS	New Bedford Statue
ROWLAND AND MARSELLUS	New Bedford Wharf
SPODE'S BLUE PRINTED WARES	New Brdige Queen Charlotte
ANDREW STEVENSON	New Canton
JOSIAH WEDGWOOD (& SONS LTD.)	New Chinese Temples
JOHN DENTON BAXTER (BAGSTER)	New Fruit
T. & R. BOOTE (LTD.) (& SON)	New Grenade Shape
THOMAS MAYER	New Hampshire, Arms of
THOMAS GODWIN	New Haven, Conn
JOB & JOHN JACKSON	New Haven, Connecticut
ENOCH WOOD & SONS	New Haven, State House
SPODE'S BLUE PRINTED WARES	New Japan
THOMAS MAYER	New Jersey, Arms of
ROWLAND AND MARSELLUS	New Library at Boston
ROWLAND AND MARSELLUS	New London, Conn.
RALPH STEVENSON	New Orleans
ROWLAND AND MARSELLUS	New Orleans, La.
TAMS / et.al.	New Post Office, London
JOHN DENTON BAXTER (BAGSTER)	New Rose
JOHN & WILLIAM RIDGWAY	New South Church
JOB & JOHN JACKSON	New York
THOMAS DIMMOCK (JR.) & CO.	New York
WILLIAM ADAMS & SON(S) (POTTERS) LTD.	New York
ENOCH WOOD & SONS	New York Bay
JOSEPH STUBBS	New York Bay
WILLIAM RIDGWAY, SON & CO.	New York Bay
ANDREW STEVENSON	New York From Brooklyn Heights
ANDREW STEVENSON	New York From Heights Near Brooklyn
ENOCH WOOD & SONS	New York From Staten Island
JAMES & RALPH CLEWS	New York Hospital
JOHN GEDDES -VERREVILLE POTTERY	New York Park Theatre
CLEMENTSON BROS. (LTD.)	New York Shape
JOSEPH CLEMENTSON	New York Shape
THOMAS MAYER	New York, Arms of
MELLOR, VENABLES & CO.	New York, Fort Hamilton
CHARLES MEIGH	New York, From Weehawken
JAMES & RALPH CLEWS	New York, Hudson River
ROWLAND AND MARSELLUS	New York, N.Y.
WILLIAM ADAMS & SON(S) (POTTERS) LTD.	New York, U.S.
WILLIAM DAVENPORT	New York,Albany
ENOCH WOOD & SONS	Newburg
JAMES & RALPH CLEWS	Newburgh, Hudson River
JOHN & WILLIAM RIDGWAY	Newham Court, Oxfordshire
BURGESS & LEIGH (LTD.)	Newlyn
ROWLAND AND MARSELLUS	Newport, R.I., Old Stone Mill
JOB & JOHN JACKSON	Newport, Rhode Island
BAKER, BEVANS & IRWIN	Newstead Abbey
BELLE VUE POTTERIES	Newstead Abbey
ANDREW STEVENSON	Niagara
MELLOR, TAYLOR & CO.	Niagara
MELLOR, VENABLES & CO.	Niagara
WILLIAM DAVENPORT	Niagara
ENOCH WOOD & SONS	Niagara Falls
ROWLAND AND MARSELLUS	Niagara Falls
ENOCH WOOD & SONS	Niagara Falls / Lake George
ENOCH WOOD & SONS	Niagara Falls From the American Side
WALLIS GIMSON & CO.	Niagara Falls/ Summer
WALLIS GIMSON & CO.	Niagara Falls/Winter
ANTHONY SHAW (& SON(S) (& CO.)	Niagara Fan Shape
PODMORE, WALKER (& CO.)	Niagara River
ANTHONY SHAW (& SON(S) (& CO.)	Niagara Shape
DAVENPORT'S & CO.	Niagara Shape
EDWARD WALLEY	Niagara Shape
JOHN WEDG WOOD	Niagara Shape
WILLIAM DAVENPORT	Niagara Shape
RIDGWAY & MORLEY	Nice
RIDGWAY, MORLEY, WEAR & CO.	Nice
JOHN ROGERS (& SON)	Night Sea Battle
WILLIAM DAVENPORT	Nile
G.L. ASHWORTH & BROS. (LTD.)	Nile Shape
JAMES & RALPH CLEWS	Nile Steamboat
SPODE/COPELAND & GARRETT, et.al.	Nineveh
C.T. MALING	Ning Po
CHARLES HOBSON (& SON)	Ning Po
MELLOR, VENABLES & CO.	Ning Po
RALPH HALL & CO.	Ning Po
J. & M.P. BELL (CO.) & (LTD.)	Ning Po
WEDGWOOD & CO. (LTD.)	Niobe
SAMPSON HANCOCK (& SONS)	Nitre
BURGESS & LEIGH (LTD.)	Nizan
WILLIAM DAVENPORT	No Gains Without Pains
CHARLES MEIGH	No. 1069
ENOCH WOOD & SONS	No. 107
JOHN & ROBERT GODWIN	No. 22
EDWARD PEARSON (& SON)	No. 5 Shape
EDWARD PEARSON (& SON)	No. 6 Shape
JOHN & ROBERT GODWIN	No.104
JOHN & ROBERT GODWIN	No.112
BURGESS & LEIGH (LTD.)	Non Pareil
J. & G. MEAKIN	Non Pareil
RIDGWAY, MORLEY, WEAR & CO.	Non Pareil
SUNDERLAND OR "GARRISON"POTTERY	Non Pareil
THOMAS MAYER	Non Pareil
THOMAS, JOHN & JOSEPH MAYER	Non Pareil
T. RATHBONE & CO.	Norah
DOULTON & CO. (LTD.)	Norbury
DOULTON & CO. (LTD.)	Norfolk
MINTONS, LTD.	Norfolk
BURGESS & LEIGH (LTD.)	Norman

FORD & SONS (LTD.)	Norman
WILLIAM DAVENPORT	Norman Tower
ALFRED MEAKIN (LTD.)	Normandy
JOHNSON BROS. (HANLEY), LTD.	Normandy
WILLIAM ADAMS	Normanton Park, Rutlandshire
WILLIAM ADAMS & SON(S) (POTTERS) LTD.	Normanton Park, South View, Rutlandshire
THOMAS MAYER	North Carolina, Arms of
GOODWINS & HARRIS	North End, Hampstead
CHARLES MEIGH	Northampton, Mass.
ENOCH WOOD & SONS	Northampton, Mass.
WILLIAM ADAMS & CO. LTD.	Northern Scenery
JOHN MEIR & SON	NORTHERN SCENERY SERIES
T. RATHBONE & CO.	NORTHERN VIEWS SERIES
THOMAS FELL (& CO.) (LTD.)	Northumberland
WILLIAM ADAMS & SON(S) (POTTERS) LTD.	Northumberland Castle
ENOCH WOOD & SONS	Northwest View of La Grange / The Residence of Marquis Lafayette
ENOCH WOOD & SONS	Norwich
JAMES & RALPH CLEWS	Norwich
RALPH HALL (& CO.) or (& SONS)	Norwich Cathedral, Norfolk
FORD & SONS (LTD.)	Norwood
E. & C. CHALLINOR	Nosegay
JONATHAN LOWE CHETHAM	Nosegay
WALLIS GIMSON & CO.	Notre Dame Church in Montreal
JAMES & RALPH CLEWS	Nottingham
COPELAND & GARRETT, ET. AL.	November - Untitled
JOHN DENTON BAXTER (BAGSTER)	Nun
GEORGE TOWNSEND	Nuneham Courtney
JOHN MEIR & SON	Nut & Bud
JOHN HALL	Nylghau
JOSIAH WEDGWOOD (& SONS LTD.)	Nymphaea
SPODE/COPELAND & GARRETT, et.al.	Nymphea
JOSEPH CLEMENTSON	Oak & Ivy
RALPH STEVENSON	OAK LEAF BORDER
G.L. ASHWORTH & BROS. (LTD.)	Oak Vista
JOHN MADDOCK & SONS (LTD.)	Oakland
ALFRED MEAKIN (LTD.)	Oakley
ANDREW STEVENSON	Oatlands, Surrey
RALPH HALL (& CO.) or (& SONS)	Oatlands, Surrey
ALFRED MEAKIN (LTD.)	Oban
J. & M.P. BELL (CO.) & (LTD.)	Oban
MYOTT, SON & CO. (LTD.)	Oban
DON POTTERY	Obelisk at Catania
JOSEPH TWIGG (& CO.)	Obelisk at Catania
JOHN & WILLIAM RIDGWAY	Observatory, Oxford
WEDGWOOD & CO. (LTD.)	Oceanic
J. & M.P. BELL (CO.) & (LTD.)	Ochil
W.H. GRINDLEY & CO. (LTD.)	Ochis
RALPH STEVENSON & WILLIAMS	Octagon Church
JOHN & WILLIAM RIDGWAY	Octagon Church, Boston
RALPH STEVENSON & WILLIAMS	Octagon Church, Boston
COPELAND & GARRETT, ET. AL.	October - Untitled
HOPE & CARTER	Odessa
SPODE/COPELAND & GARRETT, et.al.	Offering to Demeter
ANTHONY SHAW (& SON(S) (& CO.)	Officer and Men at Rest Around Fire, et.al.
ANTHONY SHAW (& SON(S) (& CO.)	Officer on Foot
JAMES & RALPH CLEWS	Ohio, Three Boatmen on the River
WILLIAM DAVENPORT	Ohio, Three Boatmen on the River
JOHNSON BROS. (HANLEY), LTD.	OLD BRITISH CASTLES
W. & E. CORN	Old Castle
HENSHALL & CO.	Old Castle of Martigny
HENRY ALCOCK & CO. (LTD.)	Old Castles
F. WINKLE & CO. (LTD.)	Old Chelsea
ROWLAND AND MARSELLUS	Old Chicago
ROWLAND AND MARSELLUS	Old City Gate, St. Augustine, Fl.
RIDGWAYS (BEDFORD WORKS) LTD.	Old Curiosity Shop
WILLIAM RIDGWAY, SON & CO.	Old Curiosity Shop
ROWLAND AND MARSELLUS	Old Detroit
J. & M.P. BELL (CO.) & (LTD.)	Old Dutch
WILLIAM ADAMS & SON(S) (POTTERS) LTD.	Old English Rural Scenes
WILLIAM DAVENPORT	Old Florida
WILLIAM DAVENPORT	Old Mortality
JOHN & WILLIAM RIDGWAY	Old Octagon
SPODE'S BLUE PRINTED WARES	Old Peacock
SPODE/COPELAND & GARRETT, et.al.	Old Salem
ROWLAND AND MARSELLUS	Old South Church
G.L. ASHWORTH & BROS. (LTD.)	Old World Rose
WOOD & SON(S) (LTD.)	Old-Bow-Kakiyem
CHARLES MEIGH	Oleaster
MELLOR, VENABLES & CO.	Olive
ROWLAND AND MARSELLUS	Oliver and Abigail Ellsworth
WILLIAM DAVENPORT	Oliver Hazard
G.L. ASHWORTH & BROS. (LTD.)	Olympia
PODMORE, WALKER (& CO.)	Olympia
W.H. GRINDLEY & CO. (LTD.)	Olympia
JOHN RIDGWAY (& CO.)	Olympian
JOHN & WILLIAM RIDGWAY	Olympian & Byzantium
THOMAS MAYER	OLYMPIC GAMES SERIES
ELSMORE & FORSTER	Olympic Shape

W.H. GRINDLEY & CO. (LTD.)	Olympic, The
ROWLAND AND MARSELLUS	Omaha, Neb.
DON POTTERY	On the Heights of Corigliano
THOMAS GODWIN	On the Susquehanna
ELSMORE & FORSTER	One Large & Two Little Ribs
J. & G. MEAKIN	One Large & Two Little Ribs
T. & R. BOOTE (LTD.) (& SON)	One Large & Two Little Ribs
ENOCH WOOD & SONS	One Man At Foot of Falls
SHORTHOUSE & CO.	One Man/Insect Willow
RALPH STEVENSON & WILLIAMS	ONE MEDALLION
RALPH STEVENSON & WILLIAMS	ONE MEDALLION BORDER SERIES
BRITISH ANCHOR POTTERY CO., LTD.	Onion
CHARLES ALLERTON & SONS	Onion
JOHNSON BROS. (HANLEY), LTD.	Onion Pattern
ROWLAND AND MARSELLUS	Onset, Mass.
JOSEPH HEATH	Ontario
SAMUEL ALCOCK & CO.	Ontario
JOSEPH HEATH	Ontario Lake Scenery
SPODE/COPELAND & GARRETT, et.al.	Onyx
SPODE/COPELAND & GARRETT, et.al.	Open Ivy
JAMES EDWARDS	Open Roses
TAMS / et.al.	Opera House, London
BOURNE & LEIGH (LTD.)	Ophir
CHARLES JAMES MASON & CO.	Opium Smokers
JOHN MADDOCK & SONS (LTD.)	Orchard
THOMAS FURNIVAL & CO.	Orchard Blossom
JOHNSON BROS. (HANLEY), LTD.	Oregon
THOMAS, JOHN & JOSEPH MAYER	Oregon
CLEMENTSON BROS. (LTD.)	Oriel
MYOTT, SON & CO. (LTD.)	Oriel
ENOCH WOOD & SONS	Orielton, Pembrokeshire
JOHN & RICHARD RILEY	Orielton, Pembrokeshire
MIDDLESBOROUGH POTTERY CO.	Orient
COPELAND & GARRETT, ET. AL.	Oriental
DON POTTERY	Oriental
EMPIRE PORCELAIN CO. (LTD.)	Oriental
J. & M.P. BELL (CO.) & (LTD.)	Oriental
JAMES KENT (LTD.)	Oriental
JOHNSON BROS. (HANLEY), LTD.	Oriental
JOSIAH WEDGWOOD (& SONS LTD.)	Oriental
MOORE (SAMUEL) & CO.	Oriental
NEW WHARF POTTERY CO.	Oriental
R. COCHRAN & CO. - VERREVILLE POTTERY	Oriental
RIDGWAYS (BEDFORD WORKS) LTD.	Oriental
SAMUEL ALCOCK & CO.	Oriental
SOUTH WALES POTTERS	Oriental
THOMAS DIMMOCK (JR.) & CO.	Oriental
WHITTAKER & CO.	Oriental
WILLIAM ADAMS & SON(S) (POTTERS) LTD.	Oriental
WILLIAM RIDGWAY (& CO.)	Oriental
WILLIAM RIDGWAY, SON & CO.	Oriental
WOOD & BROWNFIELD	Oriental
DILLWYN & CO.	Oriental Basket
ELIJAH JONES	Oriental Beauties
INDEO POTTERY	Oriental Birds
JOHN & WILLIAM RIDGWAY	Oriental Birds
SOUTH WALES POTTERS	Oriental Birds
SPODE'S BLUE PRINTED WARES	Oriental Birds
WOOD & SON(S) (LTD.)	Oriental Birds
CHARLES MEIGH	Oriental Bouquet
JAMES KEELING	Oriental Converzazione and ...et, al.
SAMUEL ALCOCK & CO.	Oriental Fan
WILLIAM DAVENPORT	Oriental Flower
GOODWIN & ELLIS	Oriental Flower Garden
GOODWINS, BRIDGWOOD & ORTON	Oriental Flower Garden
JOHN & WILLIAM RIDGWAY	Oriental Flower Tree
THOMAS FURNIVAL & CO.	Oriental Flowers
HENRY ALCOCK & CO. (LTD.)	Oriental Garden
JOHN & RICHARD RILEY	Oriental Garden
MINTON & CO.	Oriental Japan
MINTONS, LTD.	Oriental Japan
CHARLES JAMES MASON	Oriental Pheasants
SAMUEL ALCOCK & CO.	Oriental Rose
JOHN MEIR	Oriental Scenery
THOMAS, JOHN & JOSEPH MAYER	Oriental Scenery
JOHN HALL (& SONS)	ORIENTAL SCENERY SERIES
W. & E. CORN	Oriental Shape
HICKS, MEIGH & JOHNSON	Oriental Shells
EDWARD CHALLINOR	ORIENTAL SPORTS SERIES
SPODE/COPELAND & GARRETT, et.al.	ORIENTAL SPORTS SERIES
KNIGHT, ELKIN & CO.	Oriental Vase
THOMAS DIMMOCK (JR.) & CO.	Oriental Vase
H. & R. DANIEL	Oriental Vases/Ne Plus Ultra
WILLIAM DAVENPORT	Orissa
J. & M.P. BELL (CO.) & (LTD.)	Orleans
THOMAS DIMMOCK (JR.) & CO.	Orleans
JOHN THOMAS HUDDEN	Orleans Pattern
ALFRED MEAKIN (LTD.)	Ormonde
KEELING & CO. (LTD.)	Ormonde

W. & E. CORN	Ormonde
INDEO POTTERY	Ornate Pagoda
TAYLOR, HARRISON & CO.	Ornate Pagoda
RICHARD WOOLLEY	Ornate Pagodas
ANDREW STEVENSON	ORNITHOLOGICAL SERIES
JOHN MEIR & SON	Ornithology
WILLIAM ADAMS & SON(S) (POTTERS) LTD.	Ornithology
WILLIAM SMITH (& CO.)	Orphans
DEAKIN & SON(S) (& CO.)	Ortolan
JOHN & RICHARD RILEY	Orwell Park, Suffolk
JAMES KENT (LTD.)	Osaka
ELSMORE & FORSTER	Osborne
FORD & SONS (LTD.)	Osborne
JOHN RIDGWAY, BATES & CO.	Osborne
R. COCHRAN & CO. - VERREVILLE POTTERY	Osborne
RIDGWAYS (BEDFORD WORKS) LTD.	Osborne
SPODE/COPELAND & GARRETT, et.al.	Osborne
T. RATHBONE & CO.	Osborne
THOMAS TILL & SONS	Osborne
W.H. GRINDLEY & CO. (LTD.)	Osborne
DILLWYN & CO.	Osborne, Isle of Wright
STANLEY POTTERY LTD.	Ostend
HENSHALL & CO.	Ostend Gates at Bruges
GOODWINS & HARRIS	Osterley Park
JOHN & WILLIAM RIDGWAY	Osterley Park
JOHN ROGERS (& SON)	Osterley Park
JAMES & RALPH CLEWS	Ostriches, Zebra and other Animals
JOHN HALL	Otter
JOB MEIGH (& SON)	Otter, Elephant, Rhinoceros
DILLWYN & CO.	Ottoman
JOHN & WILLIAM RIDGWAY	OTTOMAN EMPIRE SERIES
JOHN TURNER / TURNER & CO., etc.	Out on an Elephant
FRANCIS MORLEY (& CO.)	Outlet at Lake Memphremagog
THOMAS GODWIN	Outlet of Lake Memphremacog
ALFRED MEAKIN (LTD.)	Ovando
RALPH STEVENSON	Oxburgh Hall
ENOCH WOOD & SONS	Oxburgh Hall, Norfolk
C. & W.K. HARVEY	Oxford
DOULTON & CO. (LTD.)	Oxford
ENOCH WOOD & SONS	Oxford
FORD & SONS (LTD.)	Oxford
HENRY ALCOCK & CO. (LTD.)	Oxford
HERCULANEUM POTTERY	Oxford
JOHN ROBINSON (& SONS)	Oxford
JOHNSON BROS. (HANLEY), LTD.	Oxford
POUNTNEY & ALLIES	Oxford
WILLIAM (ALSAGER) ADDERLEY (& CO.)	Oxford
JOHN & WILLIAM RIDGWAY	OXFORD AND CAMBRIDGE COLLEGE SERIES
THOMAS DIMMOCK (JR.) & CO.	Oxonian
DOULTON & CO. (LTD.)	Oyama
ENOCH WOOD & SONS	Pace Bridge, Philadelphia
ELSMORE & FORSTER	Pacific Shape
DON POTTERY	Pack horse and cottages
BRAMELD & CO.	Packhorses
CAULDON, LTD.	Pagoda
J. & G. MEAKIN	Pagoda
MINTON	Pagoda
POWELL, BISHOP & STONIER	Pagoda
RANDLE WILKINSON	Pagoda
SPODE/COPELAND & GARRETT, et.al.	Pagoda
THOMAS TILL & SONS	Pagoda
WHITEHAVEN POTTERY	Pagoda
WILLIAM RIDGWAY (& CO.)	Pagoda
WOOD & CHALLINOR	Pagoda
INDEO POTTERY	Pagoda & Water Birds
THOMAS PHILLIPS & SON	Pagoda Bells
THOMAS & BENJAMIN GODWIN	Pagoda Below Patna Azimabad
MINTON	Pagoda in the Montpelier Garden
WILLIAM DAVENPORT	Pagodas & Fishermen
RALPH HALL (& CO.) or (& SONS)	Pains Hill, Surrey
DOULTON & CO. (LTD.)	Paisley
GEORGE JONES (& SONS LTD.)	Paisley
JAMES & RALPH CLEWS	Palace of Linlithgow, West Lothian
RALPH HALL (& CO.) or (& SONS)	Palace of St. Cloud, France
RALPH HALL (& CO.) or (& SONS)	Palace of St. Germain, France
JOHN HALL (& SONS)	Palace of the King of Delhi
ELIJAH HUGHES & CO.	Paladin China
DAVID LOCKHART (and LOCKHART & CO.)	Palermo
JOSEPH CLEMENTSON	Palermo
LOCKHART & ARTHUR	Palermo
DAVID METHVEN & SONS	Palestine
J. & M.P. BELL (CO.) & (LTD.)	Palestine
JOHN RIDGWAY (& CO.)	Palestine
RALPH STEVENSON	Palestine
SAMUEL & JOHN BURTON	Palestine
WILLIAM ADAMS & SON(S) (POTTERS) LTD.	Palestine
ELIJAH JONES	Palestine, Sheckem
ELIJAH JONES	Palestine, Sidom
JOSIAH WEDGWOOD (& SONS LTD.)	Palisade
ENOCH WOOD & SONS	Palisades, River, and Steamboat
JOHN & WILLIAM RIDGWAY	Palladian Mansion, et.al.
J (JOSHUA) HEATH	Palladian Pagoda
SHORTHOUSE & CO.	Palladian Temple
ROWLAND AND MARSELLUS	Palm Beach, Fl.
JOHN TURNER / TURNER & CO., etc.	Palm Tree & Bridge
JACOB FURNIVAL & CO.	Palmyra
SAMPSON HANCOCK (& SONS)	Palmyra
THOMAS FURNIVAL & CO.	Palmyra
WOOD & BROWNFIELD	Palmyra
E. CHALLINOR & CO.	Panama
EDWARD CHALLINOR	Panama
LIVESLEY, POWELL & CO.	Panama
ROWLAND AND MARSELLUS	Panama-Pacific International Expo
MINTON	Pandah
SOHO POTTERY (LTD.)	Pandora
LIDDLE, ELLIOT & SON	Panel
SPODE'S BLUE PRINTED WARES	Panel Japan
LIVESLEY, POWELL & CO.	Paneled Columbia
E. & C. CHALLINOR	Paneled Decagon
ELSMORE & FORSTER	Paneled Decagon
MICHAEL TUNNICLIFF(E)	Paneled Decagon
CHARLES MEIGH & SON	Paneled Grape
EDWARD PEARSON (& SON)	Paneled Grape
ELSMORE & FORSTER	Paneled Grape
JACOB FURNIVAL & CO.	Paneled Grape
JOHN GOODWIN/LONGTON	Paneled Grape
JOSEPH CLEMENTSON	Paneled Grape
J. & G. MEAKIN	Paneled Leaves
J. & G. MEAKIN	Paneled Leaves With Berries
J.W. PANKHURST (& CO.)	Paneled Lily
JACOB FURNIVAL & CO.	Paneled Lily
E. CHALLINOR & CO.	Paneled Octagon
SOUTH WALES POTTERS	Panorama
RALPH STEVENSON	PANORAMIC SCENERY SERIES
CHARLES MEIGH & SON	Pansey
RALPH HALL (& CO.) or (& SONS)	Panshanger, Hertfordshire
EMPIRE PORCELAIN CO. (LTD.)	Pansies
BROWN & STEVENTON, LTD.	Pansy
BROWN WESTHEAD, MOORE & CO.	Pansy
FORD & CHALLINOR	Pansy
JOHNSON BROS. (HANLEY), LTD.	Pansy
PODMORE, WALKER (& CO.)	Pansy
WILLIAM (ALSAGER) ADDERLEY (& CO.)	Pansy
JOHN MADDOCK & SONS (LTD.)	Pansy Border
JOHN RIDGWAY (& CO.)	Pantheon
RIDGWAY & MORLEY	Pantheon
RIDGWAYS (BEDFORD WORKS) LTD.	Paqueminot
BROWN WESTHEAD, MOORE & CO.	Par
JOHN & GEORGE ALCOCK	Paradise
LIVESLEY, POWELL & CO.	Paradise
J. & M.P. BELL (CO.) & (LTD.)	Paraguay
JOB RIDGWAY & SONS	Parasol
RAINFORTH (LEEDS)	Parasol & Birds
WALTER DANIEL	Parasol Willow Pattern
ALFRED COLLEY & CO. LTD.	Paris
EDGE, MALKIN & CO. (LTD.)	Paris
JOHNSON BROS. (HANLEY), LTD.	Paris
NEW WHARF POTTERY CO.	Paris
STANLEY POTTERY LTD.	Paris
WILLIAM (ALSAGER) ADDERLEY (& CO.)	Paris
WOOD & SON(S) (LTD.)	Paris Royal
HENRY ALCOCK & CO. (LTD.)	Paris Shape
JOHN ALCOCK	Paris Shape
BRAMELD & CO.	Paris Stripe
JOHN & WILLIAM RIDGWAY	Parish Church at Nettlecomb Court
GEORGE PHILLIPS	Parisian
KEELING & CO. (LTD.)	Parisian
SAMUEL KEELING & CO.	Parisian
CHESWORTH & ROBINSON	Parisian Basket
RALPH HALL	Parisian Chateau
JOSEPH CLEMENTSON	Parisian Group
DAVENPORT'S & CO.	Parisian Shape
J. & M.P. BELL (CO.) & (LTD.)	Parisian Sprig
POUNTNEY & ALLIES	Park Place, Henley
GEORGE PHILLIPS	Park Scenery
JOHN CARR (& CO.) (& SON(S)	Park Scenery
JOSEPH STUBBS	Park Theatre, New York
RALPH STEVENSON	Park Theatre, New York
RALPH STEVENSON & WILLIAMS	Park Theatre, New York
CHESWORTH & ROBINSON	Parkland Scenery
EDWARD CHALLINOR	Parma
POWELL & BISHOP	Parma
WEDGWOOD & CO. (LTD.)	Parma
RALPH STEVENSON	Paroquet
BRAMELD & CO.	Parroquet
LEEDS POTTERY	Parrot and Fruit
ENOCH WOOD & SONS	Part of Goodridge Castle, Kent
ENOCH WOOD & SONS	Part of Regent Street, London

WILLIAM ADAMS	Part of Regent Street, London
THOMAS & BENJAMIN GODWIN	Part of the City of Moorhedabad
SPODE/COPELAND & GARRETT, et.al.	Part of the Harbor of Macri
SPODE/COPELAND & GARRETT, et.al.	Parthenon
ENOCH WOOD & SONS	Pass In The Catskill Mountains
JOHN MEIR & SON	Pass of the Trossachs, Loch Katrine
ENOCH WOOD & SONS	Passaic Falls, State of New Jersey
CHARLES MEIGH & SON	Passiflora
CHARLES MEIGH	Passion Flower
ELKIN & NEWBON	Passion Flower
MINTON & CO.	Passion Flower
MINTONS	Passion Flower
SPODE/COPELAND & GARRETT, et.al.	Passion Flower
CLYDE POTTERY CO. (LTD.)	Passion Flowers
WILLIAM SMITH (& CO.)	Pastimes
BRADLEY & CO.	Pastoral
EDWARD CHALLINOR	Pastoral
ELKIN & CO.	Pastoral
GEORGE JONES (& SONS LTD.)	Pastoral
LOCKHART & ARTHUR	Pastoral
R. COCHRAN & CO. - VERREVILLE POTTERY	Pastoral
RALPH STEVENSON	Pastoral
RALPH STEVENSON & WILLIAMS	Pastoral
WILLIAM ADAMS & CO. LTD.	Pastoral
WILLIAM DAVENPORT	Pastoral
ANDREW STEVENSON	Pastoral Courtship
ANDREW STEVENSON	Pastoral Scene
EDWARD & GEORGE PHILLIPS	Pastoral Scene
RALPH STEVENSON	PASTORAL SERIES
JOHN MEIR	Patas
WOOD & CHALLINOR	Patras
COPELAND & GARRETT, ET. AL.	Patrass
ROWLAND AND MARSELLUS	Patrick Henry Addressing the Virginia Assembly
EDWARD & GEORGE PHILLIPS	Patriot's Departure
JOHN & ROBERT GODWIN	Pavilion
JOHN ROGERS (& SON)	Pavilion
JOSIAH WEDGWOOD (& SONS LTD.)	Pavillion
FRANCIS MORLEY (& CO.)	Paxton
DAVID METHVEN & SONS	Peace
ROBINSON, WOOD & BROWNFIELD	Peace
WILLIAM DAVENPORT	Peaceful Fisherman
GEORGE WOOLISCROFT (& CO.)	Peach
JOHNSON BROS. (HANLEY), LTD.	Peach
STUBBS & KENT	Peach & Cherry Pattern
CHARLES COLLINSON & CO.	Peach Blossom
JOHNSON BROS. (HANLEY), LTD.	Peach Blossom
WEDGWOOD & CO. (LTD.)	Peach Blossom
GEORGE JONES (& SONS LTD.)	Peachblow
BENJAMIN E. GODWIN	Peacock
G.L. ASHWORTH & BROS. (LTD.)	Peacock
H. & R. DANIEL	Peacock
JOHN THOMSON (& SONS)	Peacock
J. & M.P. BELL (CO.) & (LTD.)	Peacock & Lilies
BELLE VUE POTTERIES	Peacock Eye
JOSIAH WEDGWOOD (& SONS LTD.)	Pearl
SAMUEL ALCOCK & CO.	Pearl
TOMKINSON BROS. & CO.	Pearl
UPPER HANLEY POTTERY CO. (LTD.)	Pearl
BRADLEY & CO.	Pearl River House
FERRYBRIDGE POTTERY	Pearl River House
SPODE'S BLUE PRINTED WARES	Pearl River House
J. & G. MEAKIN	Pearl Sydenham
SPODE/COPELAND & GARRETT, et.al.	Pearls
EDWARD PEARSON (& SON)	Peas & Pod Shape
BRAMELD & CO.	Peasant Girl Mistaken
JAMES & RALPH CLEWS	Peasant Girl Mistaken For the Lady Dulcinea
WILLIAM DAVENPORT	Peasant Girl Mistaken For the Lady Dulcinea
JOHN DENTON BAXTER (BAGSTER)	Peasants' Repast
EDGE, MALKIN & CO. (LTD.)	Peat Goat
BELLE VUE POTTERIES	Pedestal & Bouquet
JAMES EDWARDS	Pedestaled Gothic Shape
WILLIAM RIDGWAY (& CO.)	Peekskill Landing, Hudson River
JOHN EDWARDS (& CO.)	Peerless Shape
JOHNSON BROS. (HANLEY), LTD.	Pekia
ALBERT E. JONES (LONGTON), LTD.	Pekin
ARTHUR J. WILKINSON (LTD.)	Pekin
ENOCH WOOD	Pekin
F. WINKLE & CO. (LTD.)	Pekin
FORD & SONS (LTD.)	Pekin
GEORGE FREDERICK BOWERS (& CO.)	Pekin
HOLLAND & GREEN	Pekin
J. & M.P. BELL (CO.) & (LTD.)	Pekin
JAMES BEECH	Pekin
JOHN THOMSON (& SONS)	Pekin
JOHNSON BROS. (HANLEY), LTD.	Pekin
JOSIAH WEDGWOOD (& SONS LTD.)	Pekin
KEELING & CO. (LTD.)	Pekin
MALKIN, WALKER & HULSE	Pekin
SAMUEL KEELING & CO.	Pekin
SPODE/COPELAND & GARRETT, et.al.	Pekin
THOMAS DIMMOCK (JR.) & CO.	Pekin
WHITEHAVEN POTTERY	Pekin
WILLIAM DAVENPORT	Pekin
WILLIAM RIDGWAY (& CO.)	Pekin
WOOD & BROWNFIELD	Pekin
WOOD & SON(S) (LTD.)	Pekin
CHARLES JAMES MASON & CO.	Pekin Japan
WILLIAM RIDGWAY (& CO.)	Pekin Jar
HERCULANEUM POTTERY	Pekin Palm
JOSEPH CLEMENTSON	Pekin Sketches
JOHN RIDGWAY (& CO.)	Peking
PODMORE, WALKER (& CO.)	Peking
CAULDON, LTD.	Peking Star
EDWARD CHALLINOR	Pelew
TURNER & TOMKINSON	Pell
WHITEHAVEN POTTERY	Pell Castle, Isle of Man
BISHOP & STONIER (LTD.)	Pembroke
JOHN & WILLIAM RIDGWAY	Pembroke Hall, Cambridge
SAMUEL FORD & CO.	Penang
WILLIAM RIDGWAY (& CO.)	Penang/Formosa
JOSEPH CLEMENTSON	Penelope Carrying the Bow to the Suitors
RIDGWAYS (BEDFORD WORKS) LTD.	Penhurst
JAMES & RALPH CLEWS	Penitentiary in Allegheny, Near Pittsburgh, PA
JAMES & RALPH CLEWS	Penn's Treaty Tree
WILLIAM DAVENPORT	Penn's Treaty Tree
KNIGHT, ELKIN & CO.	Pennsylvania
JOHN & WILLIAM RIDGWAY	Pennsylvania Hospital, Philadelphia
WILLIAM RIDGWAY (& CO.)	Pennsylvania Hospital, Philadelphia
RALPH STEVENSON	Pennsylvania Hospital, Philadelphia, PA.
JAMES & RALPH CLEWS	Pennsylvania Steamboat
THOMAS MAYER	Pennsylvania, Arms of
W.H. GRINDLEY & CO. (LTD.)	Penshurst
STEPHEN FOLCH	Peonies & Birds
JOHN & RICHARD RILEY	Peonies / Mosaic
ALFRED MEAKIN (LTD.)	Peony
BRITANNIA POTTERY CO. LTD.	Peony
CAULDON, LTD.	Peony
JOHN & EDWARD BADDELEY	Peony
JOSIAH WEDGWOOD (& SONS LTD.)	Peony
MINTON	Peony
RIDGWAYS (BEDFORD WORKS) LTD.	Peony
SPODE'S BLUE PRINTED WARES	Peony
W. BAKER & CO. (LTD.)	Peony
DILLWYN & CO.	Peony and Willow
WILLIAM ADAMS & SON(S) (POTTERS) LTD.	Peony in Vase
ROWLAND AND MARSELLUS	Peoria, Ill.
SPODE'S BLUE PRINTED WARES	Peplow
WILLIAM DAVENPORT	Pepper Pot I & II
JOHN & WILLIAM RIDGWAY	Pera
JAMES BEECH	Perak
FRANCIS MORLEY (& CO.)	Percy
SAMUEL ALCOCK & CO.	Percy
SPODE/COPELAND & GARRETT, et.al.	Pergola
WILLIAM DAVENPORT	Perry
WILLIAM DAVENPORT	Perry, Hero of Lake Pike
JAMES & RALPH CLEWS	Perry, The Temple of Fame
ROWLAND AND MARSELLUS	Perry's Victory at Lake Erie
BISHOP & STONIER (LTD.)	Persia
DAVID LOCKHART (and LOCKHART & CO.)	Persia
WILLIAM ADAMS & SON(S) (POTTERS) LTD.	Persia
EDWARD CORN	Persia Shape
ALFRED MEAKIN (LTD.)	Persian
HOLLINSHEAD & KIRKHAM (LTD.)	Persian
JOHNSON BROS. (HANLEY), LTD.	Persian
JOSEPH HEATH & CO.	Persian
SAMUEL BARKER & SON	Persian
SPODE/COPELAND & GARRETT, et.al.	Persian
WILLIAM RIDGWAY (& CO.)	Persian
SPODE/COPELAND & GARRETT, et.al.	Persian Bird
WILLIAM DAVENPORT	Persian Bird
JOHN CARR (& CO.) (& SON(S)	Persian Lion
SPODE'S BLUE PRINTED WARES	Persian Quatrefoil
SPODE/COPELAND & GARRETT, et.al.	Persian Rabbits
SOUTH WALES POTTERS	Persian Rose
W. BAKER & CO. (LTD.)	Persian Rose
DOULTON & CO. (LTD.)	Persian Spray
J. & M.P. BELL (CO.) & (LTD.)	Persian Sprigs
JOHN RIDGWAY (& CO.)	Persian Sun Flower
FRANCIS MORLEY (& CO.)	Persiana
G.L. ASHWORTH & BROS. (LTD.)	Persiana
THOMAS BARLOW	Persians
W.H. GRINDLEY & CO. (LTD.)	Perth
DAVID LOCKHART (and LOCKHART & CO.)	Peru
PETER HOLDCROFT & CO.	Peru
JOHN WEDG WOOD	Peruvian
ANTHONY SHAW (& SON(S) (& CO.)	Peruvian Horse Hunt
GOODWIN & ELLIS	Peruvian Hunters
R.S. KIDSTON & CO. - VERREVILLE	Peruvian Hunters

EDWARD & GEORGE PHILLIPS	Pet Lamb
THOMAS GODWIN	Pet Paris
ENOCH WOOD & SONS	Peter in the Garden
ENOCH WOOD & SONS	Peter Morton Hartford (mkd)
ENOCH WOOD & SONS	Peterborough
CUMBERLIDGE & HUMPHREYS	Petunia
HUMPHREYS BROS.	Petunia
WILTSHAW & ROBINSON (LTD.)	Petunia
JACOB FURNIVAL & CO.	Phantasia
JOSEPH HEATH	Phantasia
ANDREW STEVENSON	Pheasant
BRAMELD & CO.	Pheasant
BRITANNIA POTTERY CO. LTD.	Pheasant
ELSMORE & FORSTER	Pheasant
F. WINKLE & CO. (LTD.)	Pheasant
FRANCIS MORLEY (& CO.)	Pheasant
RIDGWAY & MORLEY	Pheasant
RIDGWAY, MORLEY, WEAR & CO.	Pheasant
WILLIAM SMITH (& CO.)	Pheasant
WOOD & CHALLINOR	Pheasant
ROBINSON, WOOD & BROWNFIELD	Pheasants
JOSEPH CLEMENTSON	Phemius Singing to the Suitors
JAMES & RALPH CLEWS	Philadelphia
WILLIAM DAVENPORT	Philadelphia
WILLIAM RIDGWAY, SON & CO.	Philadelphia
ROWLAND AND MARSELLUS	Philadelphia ...Independence Hall
WILLIAM DAVENPORT	Philadelphia, A View Near
ROWLAND AND MARSELLUS	Philadelphia, Pa.
WEDGWOOD & CO. (LTD.)	Phoebe
SPODE/COPELAND & GARRETT, et.al.	Piccadilly
GEORGE FREDERICK BOWERS (& CO.)	Picciola
JOHN & WILLIAM RIDGWAY	Piccolo Bent
BRAMELD & CO.	Picking Apples
RIDGWAYS (BEDFORD WORKS) LTD.	Pickwick
THOMAS FELL (& CO.) (LTD.)	Pickwick
JOHN & WILLIAM RIDGWAY	Picnic
JONES & SON	Picturesque Asiatic Beauties
RALPH HALL (& CO.) or (& SONS)	PICTURESQUE SCENERY SERIES
JAMES & RALPH CLEWS	PICTURESQUE VIEWS SERIES
HENRY ALCOCK & CO. (LTD.)	Pie Crust
J. & G. MEAKIN	Piecrust
ANDREW STEVENSON	Pied Flycatcher and Snipe
JOHN & GEORGE ALCOCK	Pierced Scroll
JOHN & SAMUEL ALCOCK (JR.)	Pierced Scroll
JOHN ALCOCK	Pierced Scroll
ROWLAND AND MARSELLUS	Pilgrim Hall
JOHN & WILLIAM RIDGWAY	Pillar of Absalom
MALING'S (ROBERT)	Pillar With Urn
JAMES EDWARDS	Pinch Neck Gothic Shape
MINTON	Pine
ENOCH WOOD & SONS	Pine Orchard House, Catskill Mountain
ENOCH WOOD & SONS	Pine Orchard House, Catskills
JOHN ROGERS (& SON)	Pink Peonies
CHARLES MEIGH	Pinwheel
JOHN MOSELEY	Piper
RALPH STEVENSON	Piping Shepherd Boy
WILLIAM ADAMS & SON(S) (POTTERS) LTD.	Pirates,The
WILLIAM ADAMS & SON(S) (POTTERS) LTD.	Pishobury, Hertfordshire
ROWLAND AND MARSELLUS	Pittsburgh, Pa.
JAMES & RALPH CLEWS	Pittsburgh/ Home/ Lark
JAMES & RALPH CLEWS	Pittsburgh-Steamboat, Pennsylvania
BURGESS & GODDARD	Plain
THOMAS HUGHES & SON (LTD.)	Plain Acanthus
LIDDLE, ELLIOT & SON	Plain Berlin
WILLIAM DAVENPORT	Plain French
DAVENPORT'S & CO.	Plain French Shape
WILLIAM DAVENPORT	Plain French Shape
ALFRED MEAKIN (LTD.)	Plain Round
BURGESS & GODDARD	Plain Round
CHARLES MEAKIN	Plain Round
CLEMENTSON BROS. (LTD.)	Plain Round
COCKSON & SEDDON	Plain Round
ELSMORE (THOMAS) & SON	Plain Round
GEORGE JONES (& SONS LTD.)	Plain Round
GODDARD & BURGESS/ Burgess & Goddard	Plain Round
HENRY BURGESS	Plain Round
J. & G. MEAKIN	Plain Round
J. H. & J. DAVIS	Plain Round
MEAKIN (BROS) & CO.	Plain Round
MELLOR, TAYLOR & CO.	Plain Round
THOMAS HUGHES	Plain Round
THOMAS HUGHES & SON (LTD.)	Plain Round
W. & E. CORN	Plain Round
W. BAKER & CO. (LTD.)	Plain Round
WEDGWOOD & CO. (LTD.)	Plain Round
THOMAS HUGHES	Plain Round - Bulbous
W. BAKER & CO. (LTD.)	Plain Round - Bulbous
BAKER & CHETWYND	Plain Round Bulbous
E. & C. CHALLINOR	Plain Round Bulbous

THOMAS FURNIVAL & SONS	Plain Round Shape
ELSMORE & FORSTER	Plain Scallop
ARTHUR J. WILKINSON (LTD.)	Plain Square
JOHNSON BROS. (HANLEY), LTD.	Plain Square
MELLOR, TAYLOR & CO.	Plain Square
WEDGWOOD & CO. (LTD.)	Plain Square
CLEMENTSON BROS. (LTD.)	Plain Uplift
J. & G. MEAKIN	Plain Uplift
MADDOCK & GATER	Plain Uplift
ALFRED MEAKIN (LTD.)	Plain Uplift Shape
COCKSON & CHETWYND	Plain Uplift Shape
WILLIAM ADAMS & CO. LTD.	Plain Wheat
MINTON	Plant
JOHN MEIR	Plas Newydd, Anglesey
WILLIAM ADAMS & SON(S) (POTTERS) LTD.	Plasnewydd, Anglesey
THOMAS & JOHN CAREY/ JOHN CAREY & SONS	Plas-Newydd, Wales, Marquess of Anglesey's Seat
JAMES & RALPH CLEWS	Playing at Draughts
CHARLES MEIGH	Plover
J. & G. MEAKIN	Plum Decagon
BROWN WESTHEAD, MOORE & CO.	Plymouth
CAULDON, LTD.	Plymouth
COPELAND & GARRETT, ET. AL.	Plymouth
NEW WHARF POTTERY CO.	Plymouth
ROWLAND AND MARSELLUS	Plymouth
ROWLAND AND MARSELLUS	Plymouth Rock
ELSMORE & FORSTER	Pod
RICHARD DAVIES & CO.	Poet & Child
ENOCH WOOD & SONS	Pointer and Quail
JAMES & RALPH CLEWS	Pointer and Rabbit
JOHN HALL	Polar Bear
ENOCH WOOD & SONS	Polar Bear Hunting
JOB MEIGH (& SON)	Polecat
WILLIAM ADAMS & SON(S) (POTTERS) LTD.	Polesden, Surrey
EDWARD & GEORGE PHILLIPS	Polish Prisoner
THOMAS GODWIN	Polish Star
THOMAS GOODFELLOW	Polish Star
EDWARD & GEORGE PHILLIPS	POLISH VIEWS SERIES
FERRYBRIDGE POTTERY	Polka
EDGE, MALKIN & CO. (LTD.)	Polonaise
EMPIRE PORCELAIN CO. (LTD.)	Pomegranate
JACOB FURNIVAL & CO.	Pomegranate
JOHN RIDGWAY (& CO.)	POMERANIA SERIES
BISHOP & STONIER (LTD.)	Pomeroy
DOULTON & CO. (LTD.)	Pomeroy
ANTHONY SHAW (& SON(S) (& CO.)	Pomona
BROWN WESTHEAD, MOORE & CO.	Pomona
ELIJAH JONES	Pomona
FRANK BEARDMORE & CO.	Pomona
HACKWOOD & KEELING	Pomona
RIDGWAYS (BEDFORD WORKS) LTD.	Pomona
WOOD & BROWNFIELD	Pomona
KEELING & CO. (LTD.)	Pompadour
BOOTHS (LTD.)	Pompadour, The
JOHN & GEORGE ALCOCK	Pompeii
JOHN ROGERS (& SON)	Pompeii
JAMES EDWARDS	Pond Lily Pad
THOMAS FORESTER SON & CO.	Ponseters
ENOCH WOOD & SONS	Ponte del Palazzo
LEEDS POTTERY	Ponte Del Palazzo Near Florence
JAMES & WILLIAM HANDLEY	Ponte Molle
ENOCH WOOD & SONS	Ponte Rotto
LOCKETT & HULME	Ponte Rotto
BULLOCK, A. & CO.	Poonah
CHARLES MEIGH	Poonah
GEORGE FREDERICK BOWERS (& CO.)	Poonah
SOHO POTTERY (LTD.)	Poon-Tang
COPELAND & GARRETT, ET. AL.	Pope's Villa
GRIMWADES LTD.	Poppea
WILLIAM RIDGWAY, SON & CO.	Poppies
BISHOP & STONIER (LTD.)	Poppy
CHARLES MEIGH & SON	Poppy
DOULTON & CO. (LTD.)	Poppy
JOHNSON BROS. (HANLEY), LTD.	Poppy
NEW WHARF POTTERY CO.	Poppy
THOMAS TILL & SONS	Poppy
W.H. GRINDLEY & CO. (LTD.)	Poppy
WEDGWOOD & CO. (LTD.)	Poppy
WILLIAM ADAMS & CO. LTD.	Poppy
J. & C. WILEMAN	Poppy Shape
PODMORE, WALKER (& CO.)	Port Hope
DON POTTERY	Port of Ansetta
JOHN & WILLIAM RIDGWAY	Port of Latachia
DON POTTERY	Port of Turenium
MINTON	Porter Mug
MINTONS, LTD.	Portland
POUNTNEY & GOLDNEY	Portland
SAMPSON BRIDGWOOD (& SON)(LTD.)	Portland
JOHN & WILLIAM RIDGWAY	Portland Basket

ELSMORE & FORSTER	Portland Shape
ELSMORE (THOMAS) & SON	Portland Shape
SPODE/COPELAND & GARRETT, et.al.	Portland Vase
SPODE'S BLUE PRINTED WARES	Portland Vase
ROWLAND AND MARSELLUS	Portland, Ore.
W.H. GRINDLEY & CO. (LTD.)	Portman
RALPH STEVENSON & WILLIAMS	Portrait Medallion
COPELAND & GARRETT, ET. AL.	Portsmouth
NEW WHARF POTTERY CO.	Portsmouth
TAMS / et.al.	Post Office, Dublin
JOSIAH WEDGWOOD (& SONS LTD.)	Poterat
W. BAKER & CO. (LTD.)	Potomac Shape
ENOCH WOOD & SONS	Powderham Castle, Devonshire
T. & R. BOOTE (LTD.) (& SON)	Prairie Flower Shape
LIVESLEY, POWELL & CO.	Prairie Flowers
POWELL & BISHOP	Prairie Flowers
CLEMENTSON BROS. (LTD.)	Prairie Shape
JOSEPH CLEMENTSON	Prairie Shape
F. & R. PRATT & CO. (LTD.)	Pratt's Botanical
F. & R. PRATT & CO. (LTD.)	Pratt's Italian
F. & R. PRATT & CO. (LTD.)	Pratt's Native Scenery
CAMBRIAN POTTERY	Precarious Chinaman
JOHN THOMAS HUDDEN	Prelew Pattern
BURGESS & LEIGH (LTD.)	Premier
SPODE/COPELAND & GARRETT, et.al.	Presentation of the Missing Son
JOHN EDWARDS (& CO.)	President Shape
RALPH STEVENSON & WILLIAMS	President Washington
WILLIAM RIDGWAY, SON & CO.	President's House
ENOCH WOOD & SONS	President's House, Washington
JOHN WEDG WOOD	Primary
JOHN RIDGWAY (& CO.)	Primary Hexagon Shape
GEORGE PHILLIPS	Primary Shape
GEORGE WOOLISCROFT (& CO.)	Primary Shape
JOHN MADDOCK	Primary Shape
JOHN MEIR & SON	Primary Shape
JOHN RIDGWAY (& CO.)	Primary Shape
MELLOR, VENABLES & CO.	Primary Shape
THOMAS GOODFELLOW	Primary Shape
THOMAS HUGHES	Primary Shape
THOMAS WALKER	Primary Shape
THOMAS, JOHN & JOSEPH MAYER	Primary Shape
BOURNE, NIXON & CO.	Primitive Methodist Preachers,1830
BENJAMIN E. GODWIN	Primrose
FORD & SONS (LTD.)	Primrose
ROBERT HERON (& SON)	Primrose
SPODE/COPELAND & GARRETT, et.al.	Primrose
W.H. GRINDLEY & CO. (LTD.)	Primula
WOOD & SON(S) (LTD.)	Prince
R. COCHRAN & CO. - VERREVILLE POTTERY	Prince of Wales
THOMAS LAKIN	Prince of Wales Feathers
JAMES JAMIESON & CO.	Princes Street from Calton Hill
BOOTHS (LTD.)	Princess
JAMES BEECH	Princess
T. RATHBONE & CO.	Princess
WOOD & SON(S) (LTD.)	Princess
EDWARD CHALLINOR	Princess Feather
JOHNSON BROS. (HANLEY), LTD.	Princeton
SPODE/COPELAND & GARRETT, et.al.	Principal Entrance to the Harbor of Cacamo
JAMES & WILLIAM HANDLEY	Printed Chinese
E. CHALLINOR & CO.	Priory
EDWARD CHALLINOR	Priory
HENRY ALCOCK & CO. (LTD.)	Priory
HICKS, MEIGH & JOHNSON	Priory
J. & G. MEAKIN	Priory
JOHN ALCOCK	Priory
READ, CLEMENTSON & ANDERSON	Priory
JAMES & RALPH CLEWS	Prison With Four Two-Story Towers Joined By One Story Walls
THOMAS, JOHN & JOSEPH MAYER	Prize Bloom Shape
THOMAS, JOHN & JOSEPH MAYER	Prize Nodding Bud Shape
THOMAS, JOHN & JOSEPH MAYER	Prize Puritan Shape
BROWN WESTHEAD, MOORE & CO.	Pro Deo, Rege et Patria
W.H. GRINDLEY & CO. (LTD.)	Progress
DOULTON & CO. (LTD.)	Provence
ROWLAND AND MARSELLUS	Providence, R.I.
THOMAS TILL & SONS	Prunus
HENRY ALCOCK & CO. (LTD.)	Prunus Blossoms
JOHN ROGERS (& SON)	Prunus Wreath
EDWARD CHALLINOR	Puck
BAKER, BEVANS & IRWIN	Pulteney Bridge, Bath
DILLWYN & CO.	Pulteney Bridge, Bath
CAMBRIAN POTTERY	Pultney Bridge at Bath
THOMAS, JOHN & JOSEPH MAYER	Pumpkin Primary Octagon Shape
POUNTNEY & GOLDNEY	Pursuit
ROWLAND AND MARSELLUS	Put-In-Bay, Ohio
MINTONS, LTD.	Putney
WHITEHAVEN POTTERY	Puzzle
JOHN ROGERS (& SON)	Pyramid
THOMAS & BENJAMIN GODWIN	Pyramid
JOHN HALL	QUADRUPEDS SERIES
CHILD & CLIVE	Quails
FURNIVALS LTD.	Quails
SMITH CHILD	Quails
JACOB FURNIVAL & CO.	Quartered Rose
JAMES & RALPH CLEWS	Quebec
PODMORE, WALKER (& CO.)	Quebec
WILLIAM DAVENPORT	Quebec
R. COCHRAN & CO. - VERREVILLE POTTERY	Quebec From Point Levis/ Quebec, Vue De Point Levis
R. COCHRAN & CO. - VERREVILLE POTTERY	Quebec Harbor & Levis/ Havre De Quebec & Levis
R. COCHRAN & CO. - VERREVILLE POTTERY	QUEBEC VIEWS SERIES
ENOCH WOOD & SONS	Quebec, Heights of
FORD & SONS (LTD.)	Queen
J. & G. MEAKIN	Queen
T. RATHBONE & CO.	Queen
JOHN MEIR	Queen Caroline
WILLIAM ADAMS & CO. LTD.	Queen Charlotte
JAMES JAMIESON & CO.	Queen Victoria
READ, CLEMENTSON & ANDERSON	Queen Victoria & the Duchess of Kent
JOHN ROGERS (& SON)	Queen's Lily
EDWARD WALLEY	Queen's Own
WILLIAM & THOMAS ADAMS	Queens Border
WILLIAM ADAMS & CO. LTD.	Queens Border
ROWLAND AND MARSELLUS	Quincy, Ill.
MINTON	Quintal Flower Horn
RIDGWAYS (BEDFORD WORKS) LTD.	Rabbit
JOHN HALL	Rabbit and Hunters
JAMES & RALPH CLEWS	Rabbit Pie
DOULTON & CO. (LTD.)	Rabbits
JOHN & WILLIAM RIDGWAY	Raby Castle, Durnham
JOHN HALL	Raccoon
CHARLES ALLERTON & SONS	Racine
JOB MEIGH (& SON)	Racoon, Nylghau
JOHN & WILLIAM RIDGWAY	Radcliffe Library, Oxford
SPODE/COPELAND & GARRETT, et.al.	Rafaelesque
COPELAND & GARRETT, ET. AL.	Rafaelesquer
ENOCH WOOD & SONS	Railway
HAMPSON & BROADHURST	Railway
BEARDMORE & EDWARDS	Railway Express
RAINFORTH (LEEDS)	Rainforth's Willow
H. & R. DANIEL	Raised Dragons
JAMES JAMIESON & CO.	Rajah
THOMAS TILL & SONS	Rajah
ALFRED MEAKIN (LTD.)	Raleigh
BURGESS & LEIGH (LTD.)	Raleigh
JOHNSON BROS. (HANLEY), LTD.	Raleigh
WEDGWOOD & CO. (LTD.)	Raleigh
ENOCH WOOD & SONS	Ram, Ewe and Lamb
ELKIN, KNIGHT & BRIDGWOOD	Rams Head Tripod
JOSIAH WEDGWOOD (& SONS LTD.)	Ranunculus
JOSIAH WEDGWOOD (& SONS LTD.)	Raphael
JAMES & RALPH CLEWS	Rapids Above Hadley's Falls
BISHOP & STONIER (LTD.)	Rathbone
WILLIAM BROWNFIELD (& SON(S)	Ravenna
DUNN BENNETT & CO. (LTD.)	Ravenscliffe
POUNTNEY & ALLIES	Reach of the River Avon, Roman Encampment
DON POTTERY	Reading Woman
BATHWELL & GOODFELLOW	Reaper Pattern
WILLIAM SMITH (& CO.)	Reapers
JOHN DENTON BAXTER (BAGSTER)	Reaping Scene, et.al.
GEORGE JONES (& SONS LTD.)	Rebecca
DUNN BENNETT & CO. (LTD.)	Recherche
WILLIAM ADAMS & SON(S) (POTTERS) LTD.	Red & Green Roses
MINTON	Red House
PANKHURST & DIMMOCK	Reeded Grape Shape
SPODE/COPELAND & GARRETT, et.al.	Refreshments for Philasian Horsemen
BARKER & SON	Regal
BOURNE & LEIGH (LTD.)	Regal
J. & G. MEAKIN	Regal
THOMAS G. GREEN & CO. (LTD.)	Regal
WILLIAM ADAMS & CO. LTD.	Regal
W.H. GRINDLEY & CO. (LTD.)	Regal, The
SMITH, FORD & JONES	Regalia
THOMAS HUGHES	Regalia
THOMAS HUGHES & SON (LTD.)	Regalia
ALFRED MEAKIN (LTD.)	Regent
GEORGE THOMAS MOUNTFORD	Regent
JOHNSON BROS. (HANLEY), LTD.	Regent
DAVENPORT'S LTD.	Regent Shape
WILLIAM DAVENPORT	Regent Shape
WM. DAVENPORT & CO.	Regent Shape
WILLIAM ADAMS	REGENT'S PARK SERIES
ENOCH WOOD & SONS	Regina
J. & G. MEAKIN	Regina
WILLIAM DAVENPORT	Regina Shape

WM. DAVENPORT & CO.	Regina Shape
JOHNSON BROS. (HANLEY), LTD.	Regis
ENOCH WOOD & SONS	REGULAR SHELL BORDER SERIES
J. & M.P. BELL (CO.) & (LTD.)	Reindeer
DON POTTERY	Reindeer Pattern
J (JOSHUA) HEATH	Reindeer Pattern
JOB MEIGH (& SON)	Reindeer, Zebra, Camel
JOHN WEDG WOOD	Relish Dish
WILLIAM DAVENPORT	Relish Dish
T. & R. BOOTE (LTD.) (& SON)	Relish Dish, 1851
T. & J. BEVINGTON (& CO.)	Remains of an Ancient Building Near Firoz Shah's, et.al.
ANDREW STEVENSON	Remains of Covenham Hall, Essex
ANDREW STEVENSON	Remains of Covet Hall, Essex
JAMES & RALPH CLEWS	Remains of the Church, Thornton Abbey
ARTHUR J. WILKINSON (LTD.)	Renown
JAMES & RALPH CLEWS	Repose in the Wood
WILLIAM DAVENPORT	Repose in the Wood
TAMS / et.al.	Residence of General Sir Herbert ...
ENOCH WOOD & SONS	Residence of S. Russell
DON POTTERY	Residence of Solimenes near Vesuvius
JOSEPH TWIGG (& CO.)	Residence of Solimenes Near Vesuvius
JOHN DENTON BAXTER (BAGSTER)	Resing Family, et.al.
BATHWELL & GOODFELLOW	Resting Farm Girl
WILLIAM DAVENPORT	Resting Fisherman and Friend
WILLIAM DAVENPORT	Resting time, Two men, one seated, the other standing, dog lies nearby,et.al.
J. & G. MEAKIN	Resurrection
ROWLAND AND MARSELLUS	Retreat From Concord of the British
JAMES KEELING	Return From a Desert Excursion...
JAMES & RALPH CLEWS	Return From the Hunt
WILLIAM DAVENPORT	Returning home, man with stick, bundle on his shoulder and holding young girl by the hand, et.al.
ENOCH WOOD & SONS	Revelation
THOMAS TILL & SONS	Rheims
WILLIAM DAVENPORT	Rhenish Views
BOOTH & MEIGH	Rhine
BROWN WESTHEAD, MOORE & CO.	Rhine
DAVID LOCKHART (and LOCKHART & CO.)	Rhine
DILLWYN & CO.	Rhine
FRANCIS MORLEY (& CO.)	Rhine
JACOB FURNIVAL & CO.	Rhine
JAMES F. WILEMAN	Rhine
JOHN MEIR & SON	Rhine
JOHN THOMAS HUDDEN	Rhine
LEWIS WOOLF (& SONS)(& CO.)	Rhine
MIDDLESBOROUGH POTTERY CO.	Rhine
SPODE/COPELAND & GARRETT, et.al.	Rhine
THOMAS DIMMOCK (JR.) & CO.	Rhine
THOMAS FELL (& CO.) (LTD.)	Rhine
WHITEHAVEN POTTERY	Rhine
WILLIAM DAVENPORT	Rhine
WORTHINGTON & HARROP	Rhine
WILLIAM DAVENPORT	RHINE SERIES
JOHN HALL	Rhinoceros
WILLIAM ADAMS & SON(S) (POTTERS) LTD.	Rhoda
JOHN HEATH	Rhoda Gardens
JOSEPH HEATH	Rhoda Gardens
WILLIAM HACKWOOD	Rhoda Gardens
THOMAS MAYER	Rhode Island, Arms of
COPELAND & GARRETT, ET. AL.	Rhodes
THOMAS DIMMOCK (JR.) & CO.	Rhodes
JOHN RIDGWAY (& CO.)	Rhone
THOMAS FURNIVAL & CO.	Rhone
THOMAS GOODFELLOW	Rhone
WILLIAM (ALSAGER) ADDERLEY (& CO.)	Rhone
WOOD & BROWNFIELD	Rhone
THOMAS, JOHN & JOSEPH MAYER	Rhone Scenery
JOHN MADDOCK & SONS (LTD.)	Rialto
HENRY ALCOCK & CO. (LTD.)	Ribbed Berry
JOHN ALCOCK	Ribbed Berry
J. & G. MEAKIN	Ribbed Berry With Bloom
J.W. PANKHURST (& CO.)	Ribbed Bud
J.W. PANKHURST (& CO.)	Ribbed Chain
ARTHUR J. WILKINSON (LTD.)	Ribbed Fern
W. & E. CORN	Ribbed Grape
SPODE/COPELAND & GARRETT, et.al.	Ribbon
WILLIAM DAVENPORT	Ribbon
WOOD & BROWNFIELD	Ribbon Flower
MINTON & CO.	Ribbon Wreath
W. & E. CORN	Ribboned Oak
MINTONS, LTD.	Ribbons & Roses
JOHN RIDGWAY (& CO.)	Ribonaire
RALPH STEVENSON	Riceborough at Georgia
ENOCH WOOD & SONS	Riceborough, Georgia
JAMES F. WILEMAN	Richelieu Shape
ROWLAND AND MARSELLUS	Richfield Springs, N.Y.
ALFRED MEAKIN (LTD.)	Richmond
BURGESS & LEIGH (LTD.)	Richmond

C. & W.K. HARVEY	Richmond
FORD & SONS (LTD.)	Richmond
JOHNSON BROS. (HANLEY), LTD.	Richmond
SMITH & BINNALL	Richmond
SPODE/COPELAND & GARRETT, et.al.	Richmond
W.H. GRINDLEY & CO. (LTD.)	Richmond
WILLIAM (ALSAGER) ADDERLEY (& CO.)	Richmond
COPELAND & GARRETT, ET. AL.	Richmond Bridge
JOHN ROGERS (& SON)	Richmond Bridge
POUNTNEY & ALLIES	Richmond Bridge
TAMS / et.al.	Richmond Castle, Yorkshire
COPELAND & GARRETT, ET. AL.	Richmond Hill
ROWLAND AND MARSELLUS	Richmond, Va... City Hall
ROWLAND AND MARSELLUS	Richmond, Va...Capitol
WILLIAM DAVENPORT	Richmond, Virginia
ROWLAND AND MARSELLUS	Ride of Paul Revere
FRANCIS MORLEY (& CO.)	Rideau Canal, Bytown
RIDGWAYS (BEDFORD WORKS) LTD.	Ridgways Japan
INDEO POTTERY	Riding a Buffalo
RALPH STEVENSON	Riding into the Water
JOHN & RICHARD RILEY	Riley's Bowl of Flowers
WOOD & CHALLINOR	Rimini
LIVESLEY, POWELL & CO.	Ring O' Hearts Shape A
LIVESLEY, POWELL & CO.	Ring O' Hearts Shape B
JACOB FURNIVAL & CO.	Ring O'Hearts
LIVESLEY, POWELL & CO.	Ring O'Hearts
JOB MEIGH (& SON)	Ring-tailed Lemur
FORD & SONS (LTD.)	Rio
THOMAS SHIRLEY & CO.	Rio
WILLIAM WILLIAMS	Rio
YNYSMEDW POTTERY	Rio
ALFRED MEAKIN (LTD.)	Ripon
F. WINKLE & CO. (LTD.)	Ripon
WOOD & HULME	Ripon
JAMES & RALPH CLEWS	Rippon, Yorkshire
FRANCIS MORLEY (& CO.)	Rittenhouse, Cambridge 1850
JAMES & RALPH CLEWS	Rivax Abbey
WILLIAM ADAMS & SON(S) (POTTERS) LTD.	River and City
BOURNE, BAKER & BOURNE	River Bridge & Boat Scene, et.al.
JOHN MEIR	River Fishing
JOHN ROGERS (& SON)	River Medway
WILLIAM DAVENPORT	River Scene
JAMES & RALPH CLEWS	River Scene with Fort, et.al.
POUNTNEY & ALLIES	RIVER THAMES SERIES
POUNTNEY & GOLDNEY	RIVER THAMES SERIES
JOHN & WILLIAM RIDGWAY	Riverside Cottage, et.al.
JOHN GOODWIN/SEACOMBE POTTERY	Riverside Steps
JAMES & RALPH CLEWS	Riverside Temple
PITCAIRNS LTD.	Rivona
WILLIAM DAVENPORT	Rob Roy
ROWLAND AND MARSELLUS	Robert Burns
BAILEY & BALL	Robinson Crusoe
WILLIAM DAVENPORT	Rocaille
ENOCH WOOD & SONS	Rochester
ENOCH WOOD & SONS	Rochester Castle
JAMES & RALPH CLEWS	Rochester Castle
ROWLAND AND MARSELLUS	Rochester, N.Y.
EDWARD CHALLINOR	Rock
ENOCH WOOD	Rock
SPODE'S BLUE PRINTED WARES	Rock
ELKIN, KNIGHT & CO.	ROCK CARTOUCHE MARK SERIES
BRAMELD & CO.	Rocking Horse
WILLIAM ADAMS	ROCKS AND FOLIAGE BORDER SERIES
JOHN MADDOCK & SONS (LTD.)	Rococo
JOSIAH WEDGWOOD (& SONS LTD.)	Rococo Scrolls
WILLIAM ADAMS & SON(S) (POTTERS) LTD.	Rode Hall, Cheshire
JOHN ROGERS (& SON)	ROGERS VIEW SERIES
JOHNSON BROS. (HANLEY), LTD.	Rolland
ROWLAND AND MARSELLUS	ROLLED EDGE SERIES
JAMES EDWARDS	Rolling Star
SPODE/COPELAND & GARRETT, et.al.	Roma
WEDGWOOD & CO. (LTD.)	Roma
FURNIVALS LTD.	Roman
MINTON	Roman
MINTONS, LTD.	Roman
SPODE/COPELAND & GARRETT, et.al.	Roman Beads
CAULDON, LTD.	Roman Chariot
HERCULANEUM POTTERY	Roman Garden
T. & R. BOOTE (LTD.) (& SON)	Roman Shape
EDWARD F. BODLEY & CO. (& SON)	Roman Vista
MIDDLESBOROUGH POTTERY CO.	Romania
RALPH MALKIN	Romanian Inscriptions
DAWSON (JOHN DAWSON & CO., ETC.)	Romantic
WILLIAM DAVENPORT	Romantic Castles
DAWSON (JOHN DAWSON & CO., ETC.)	Romantic Landscape
JAMES & RALPH CLEWS	Romantic Ruins
ELKIN, KNIGHT & BRIDGWOOD	Rome
JOSEPH STUBBS	Rome
SPODE'S BLUE PRINTED WARES	Rome

THOMAS LAKIN	Rome
WILLIAM RIDGWAY (& CO.)	Rome, Italian
SPODE'S BLUE PRINTED WARES	Rome, Tiber
BROWN WESTHEAD, MOORE & CO.	Romeo
CAULDON, LTD.	Romeo
WEDGWOOD & CO. (LTD.)	Romeo
WILLIAM DAVENPORT	Rondeau
THOMAS FURNIVAL & SONS	Rooster
J. & G. MEAKIN	Rope & Mellon Ribs
THOMAS FURNIVAL & SONS	Roped Wheat
MORLEY & ASHWORTH	Ropes & Anchor
BOOTHS (LTD.)	Rosa
CARTWRIGHT & EDWARDS (LTD.)	Rosa
ISAAC WILSON & CO.	Rosa Centifolia
J. & G. MEAKIN	Rosalie
ALFRED MEAKIN (LTD.)	Rosalina
BENJAMIN E. GODWIN	Rose
BOURNE & LEIGH (LTD.)	Rose
E. CHALLINOR & CO.	Rose
EDWARD CHALLINOR	Rose
JAMES JAMIESON & CO.	Rose
KEELING & CO. (LTD.)	Rose
MYOTT, SON & CO. (LTD.)	Rose
RIDGWAYS (BEDFORD WORKS) LTD.	Rose
T. RATHBONE & CO.	Rose
THOMAS WALKER	Rose
W.H. GRINDLEY & CO. (LTD.)	Rose
WILLIAM DAVENPORT	Rose
LIVESLEY, POWELL & CO.	Rose & Bell
MINTON	Rose & Flower
BROWN WESTHEAD, MOORE & CO.	Rose & Ivy
JOSIAH WEDGWOOD (& SONS LTD.)	Rose & Jessamine
WILLIAM DAVENPORT	Rose & Lily
JOHN MADDOCK & SONS (LTD.)	Rose & Ribbons
COPELAND & GARRETT, ET. AL.	Rose & Sprig
SPODE/COPELAND & GARRETT, et.al.	Rose & Sprigs
MINTON	Rose & Violet Wreath
ANDREW STEVENSON	ROSE BORDER
ANDREW STEVENSON	ROSE BORDER SERIES
JOSEPH STUBBS	ROSE BORDER SERIES
HERCULANEUM POTTERY	Rose Chintz
LIVESLEY, POWELL & CO.	Rose Chintz
BRAMELD & CO.	Rose Jar
CHARLES MEIGH	Rose Lattice
WILLIAM ADAMS & SON(S) (POTTERS) LTD.	Rose Sprays
SPODE/COPELAND & GARRETT, et.al.	Rose Wreath
THOMAS FURNIVAL & CO.	Rose, The
GRIMWADES LTD.	Roseate
MINTONS, LTD.	Roseberry Chrysanthemum
BRITANNIA POTTERY CO. LTD.	Rosebud
GROVE & STARK	Rosebud
FURNIVALS LTD.	Rosedale
JOHN MEIR & SON	Roselle
DUNN BENNETT & CO. (LTD.)	Roserie
CHARLES JAMES MASON & CO.	Roses
G.M. & C.J. MASON	Roses
HANCOCK & WITTINGHAM & CO.	Roses
JOSIAH WEDGWOOD (& SONS LTD.)	Roses and Butterflies
EDWARD CHALLINOR	Rosetta
GEORGE WOOLISCROFT (& CO.)	Rosetta
SAMPSON HANCOCK (& SONS)	Rosetta
JOHN & GEORGE ALCOCK	Rosetta Wreath
BURGESS & LEIGH (LTD.)	Rosette
MINTONS, LTD.	Rosette Border
JOHN MADDOCK & SONS (LTD.)	Roseville
THOMAS HUGHES	Roseville
THOMAS HUGHES & SON (LTD.)	Roseville
CHARLES ALLERTON & SONS	Roslin
ALFRED COLLEY & CO. LTD.	Roslyn
ENOCH WOOD & SONS	Ross Castle, Monmouthshire
MINTONS, LTD.	Rossalyn
PITCAIRNS LTD.	Rosslyn
JAMES & RALPH CLEWS	Rothesay Castle, Buteshire
DAVID LOCKHART (and LOCKHART & CO.)	Rothsay
MINTONS, LTD.	Rotterdam Castle
SPODE'S BLUE PRINTED WARES	Rotunda
MINTONS, LTD.	Rouen
BAKER & CHETWYND	Round Acord
DON POTTERY	Round Tower
JOHN GOODWIN/LONGTON	Rousillon
JOHN GOODWIN/SEACOMBE POTTERY	Rousillon
SPODE/COPELAND & GARRETT, et.al.	Row Boat Fishermen
COCHRAN & FLEMING - BRITANNIA POTTERY	Rowena
F. WINKLE & CO. (LTD.)	Royal
THOMAS GREEN	Royal
WOOD & SON(S) (LTD.)	Royal
TAMS / et.al.	Royal Coburg Theatre
J. & M.P. BELL (CO.) & (LTD.)	Royal Conservatory
BARKER & SON	Royal Cottage
BARKER & TILL	Royal Cottage
BARKER, SUTTON & TILL	Royal Cottage
CORK & EDGE	Royal Cottage
CORK, EDGE & MALKIN	Royal Cottage
SUNDERLAND OR "GARRISON" POTTERY	Royal Cottage
THOMAS TILL & SON	Royal Cottage
SAMUEL BARKER & SON	Royal Exchange
TAMS / et.al.	Royal Exchange, London
JOHN RIDGWAY (& CO.)	Royal Flora
JAMES JAMIESON & CO.	Royal High School
ENOCH WOOD & SONS	Royal Hospital, Regent's Park, London
WILLIAM ADAMS	Royal Hospital, Regent's Park, London
HERCULANEUM POTTERY	Royal Institution, Liverpool
J. & M.P. BELL (CO.) & (LTD.)	Royal Palace
CHARLES MEIGH	Royal Persian
MINTON	Royal Persian
THOMAS GOODFELLOW	Royal Persian
HENRY ALCOCK & CO. (LTD.)	Royal Premium
JOHN THOMSON (& SONS)	Royal Rose
THOMAS DIMMOCK (JR.) & CO.	Royal Rose
JAMES JAMIESON & CO.	Royal Scottish Academy
JOHN EDWARDS (& CO.)	Royal Shape
SAMUEL ALCOCK & CO.	Royal Star
JAMES JAMIESON & CO.	Royal Vase
JOHNSON BROS. (HANLEY), LTD.	Royston
GEORGE FREDERICK BOWERS (& CO.)	Rubella
F. WINKLE & CO. (LTD.)	Rudyard
MOORE (SAMUEL) & CO.	Ruined Castle
ROBERT HAMILTON	Ruined Castle
TAMS / et.al.	Ruined Castle
T. RATHBONE & CO.	Ruined Castle and Bridge
THOMAS DIMMOCK (JR.) & CO.	Ruined Temple and Tower
BENJAMIN ADAMS	Ruins
BENJAMIN E. GODWIN	Ruins
COPELAND & GARRETT, ET. AL.	Ruins
G.L. ASHWORTH & BROS. (LTD.)	Ruins
HOPKIN & VERNON	Ruins
JOSEPH CLEMENTSON	Ruins
SPODE/COPELAND & GARRETT, et.al.	Ruins
WILLIAM ADAMS & SON(S) (POTTERS) LTD.	Ruins
JAMES & RALPH CLEWS	Ruins and Mule
THOMAS DIMMOCK (JR.) & CO.	Ruins Merchants Exchange
DON POTTERY	Ruins Near Agrigenti
SPODE/COPELAND & GARRETT, et.al.	Ruins of Ancient Temple Near Corinth
DON POTTERY	Ruins of the Castle of Canna
THOMAS MAYER	Running
JAMES JAMIESON & CO.	Rural
JAMES MILLER & CO. (LTD)	Rural
JOHN MARSHALL (& CO.)(LTD.)	Rural
SOUTH WALES POTTERS	Rural
JOHN DENTON BAXTER (BAGSTER)	Rural Beggars, et.al.
WILLIAM DAVENPORT	Rural Cottage
BRITANNIA POTTERY CO. LTD.	Rural England
W.R. MIDWINTER (LTD.)	Rural England
JOHN ROGERS (& SON)	Rural Ferry
ENOCH WOOD & SONS	Rural Homes
WILLIAM DAVENPORT	Rural Lake & Village
ANDREW STEVENSON	Rural Scene
WILLIAM DAVENPORT	Rural Scene
JOSEPH HEATH & CO.	Rural Scenery
THOMAS GOODFELLOW	Rural Scenery
THOMAS, JOHN & JOSEPH MAYER	Rural Scenery
WILLIAM RIDGWAY, SON & CO.	Rural Scenery
BATHWELL & GOODFELLOW	RURAL SCENERY SERIES
JAMES WALLACE & CO.	RURAL SCENERY SERIES
JOHN & WILLIAM RIDGWAY	RURAL SCENERY SERIES
WILLIAM DAVENPORT	RURAL SCENERY SERIES
SPODE/COPELAND & GARRETT, et.al.	Rural Scenes
CAULDON, LTD.	Ruskin
FORD & SONS (LTD.)	Ruskin
WILLIAM RIDGWAY (& CO.)	Russell
G.L. ASHWORTH & BROS. (LTD.)	Rustic
W. & J. HARDING	Rustic
W.H. GRINDLEY & CO. (LTD.)	Rustic
WHITTINGHAM, FORD & RILEY	Rustic
JOHN DENTON BAXTER (BAGSTER)	Rustic Bridge
BELLE VUE POTTERIES	Rustic Cottage
JOSEPH CLEMENTSON	Rustic Scenery
WILLIAM DAVENPORT	RUSTIC SCENES SERIES
DUNN BENNETT & CO. (LTD.)	Rutland
DILLWYN & CO.	Ryde, Isle of Wright
SPODE/COPELAND & GARRETT, et.al.	Sacrifice to Dionysus
J. & G. MEAKIN	Safety Pin
ROWLAND AND MARSELLUS	Sag Harbor, N.Y.
JOHN RIDGWAY (& CO.)	Sailing Barge and Chateau
DON POTTERY	Sailing boat by cliffs
JOHN ROGERS (& SON)	Sailing Galley
PODMORE, WALKER (& CO.)	Saint John

PODMORE, WALKER (& CO.)	Saint Regis
HICKS, MEIGH & JOHNSON	Sal Sapit Omnia
COPELAND & GARRETT, ET. AL.	Salamis
JAMES EDWARDS	Salem
JOHN EDWARDS (& CO.)	Salem
ROWLAND AND MARSELLUS	Salem, Mass.
ENOCH WOOD & SONS	Salisbury
FORD & SONS (LTD.)	Salisbury
ROWLAND AND MARSELLUS	Salt Lake City, Utah
ENOCH WOOD & SONS	Saltwood Castle
ROWLAND AND MARSELLUS	San Antonio, Tex.
ROWLAND AND MARSELLUS	San Francisco, Calif.
JOHN ALLASON	Sana
JAMES & RALPH CLEWS	Sancho and the Priest and the Barber
WILLIAM DAVENPORT	Sancho and the Priest and the Barber
JAMES & RALPH CLEWS	Sancho Panza
WILLIAM DAVENPORT	Sancho Panza
JAMES & RALPH CLEWS	Sancho Panza and the Duchess
WILLIAM DAVENPORT	Sancho Panza and the Duchess
JAMES & RALPH CLEWS	Sancho Panza and the Messenger
WILLIAM DAVENPORT	Sancho Panza and the Messenger
JAMES & RALPH CLEWS	Sancho Panza at the Boar Hunt
WILLIAM DAVENPORT	Sancho Panza at the Boar Hunt
JAMES & RALPH CLEWS	Sancho Panza Hoisted in the Blanket
WILLIAM DAVENPORT	Sancho Panza Hoisted in the Blanket
JAMES & RALPH CLEWS	Sancho Panza's Debate With Teresa
WILLIAM DAVENPORT	Sancho Panza's Debate With Teresa
DOULTON & CO. (LTD.)	Sandhurst
J. & M.P. BELL (CO.) & (LTD.)	Sandhurst
FORD & SONS (LTD.)	Sandon
J.H. WEATHERBY & SONS (LTD.)	Sandon
THOMAS & JOHN CAREY/ JOHN CAREY & SONS	Sandon Hall, Earl of Harrowby's Seat
WILLIAM DAVENPORT	Sandusky / Ohio
JAMES & RALPH CLEWS	Sandusky/ Ohio
MYOTT, SON & CO. (LTD.)	Sanito
T. RATHBONE & CO.	Sapho
SAMPSON HANCOCK (& SONS)	Saratoga
ROWLAND AND MARSELLUS	Saratoga, N.Y.
J. & M.P. BELL (CO.) & (LTD.)	Sarawak
SPODE/COPELAND & GARRETT, et.al.	Sarcophagi at Cacamo
SPODE/COPELAND & GARRETT, et.al.	Sarcophagus and Sepulchres at the Head of the Harbor of Cacamo
RALPH HALL & CO.	Sardinia
SPODE/COPELAND & GARRETT, et.al.	Sardinia
ENOCH WOOD & SONS	Sarento
RIDGWAYS (BEDFORD WORKS) LTD.	Saskia
BROWN WESTHEAD, MOORE & CO.	Satsuma
FRANCIS J. EMERY	Satsuma
JOHNSON BROS. (HANLEY), LTD.	Savannah
RALPH STEVENSON	Savannah Bank
EMPIRE PORCELAIN CO. (LTD.)	Savoy
JOHNSON BROS. (HANLEY), LTD.	Savoy
SAMUEL BARKER & SON	Savoy
SAMUEL FORD & CO.	Savoy
WILLIAM RIDGWAY, SON & CO.	Saw Mill at Centre Harbour, N.H.
HENSHALL & CO.	Saxham Hall
CLEMENTSON BROS. (LTD.)	Saxon
WILLIAM ADAMS & SON(S) (POTTERS) LTD.	Scaleby Castle, Cumberland
ST. JOHN'S STONE CHINAWARE CO. (CANADA)	Scallop
T. & R. BOOTE (LTD.) (& SON)	Scallop Shape
J.W. PANKHURST (& CO.)	Scalloped Compote
JOHN WEDG WOOD	Scalloped Decagon Shape
WILLIAM DAVENPORT	Scalloped Decagon Shape
CHARLES JAMES MASON & CO.	Scalloped Edge
HERCULANEUM POTTERY	Scarborough
BENJAMIN ADAMS	Scene After Claude Lorraine
JOHN & RICHARD RILEY	Scene After Claude Lorraine
LEEDS POTTERY	Scene After Claude Lorraine
FRANCIS MORLEY (& CO.)	Scene Among the Thousand Isles
HENSHALL & CO.	Scene in Campania, Rome
CAMBRIAN POTTERY	Scene of Tintern Abbey
RIDGWAYS (BEDFORD WORKS) LTD.	Scenes
FRANK BEARDMORE & CO.	Scenes of Quebec
FERRYBRIDGE POTTERY	Schizanthus
THOMAS GODWIN	Schuylkill Water Works
CHARLES MEIGH	Schuylkill Water Works, Philadelphia
EDGE, MALKIN & CO. (LTD.)	Sciao
DIMMOCK & SMITH	Scinde
GEORGE FREDERICK BOWERS (& CO.)	Scinde
JOHN ALCOCK	Scinde
JOHN & GEORGE ALCOCK	Scinde
JOHN & SAMUEL ALCOCK (JR.)	Scinde
MINTON & CO.	Scinde
THOMAS WALKER	Scinde
EDWARD CHALLINOR	Sciro
DAVID LOCKHART (and LOCKHART & CO.)	Scotia
MOORE (SAMUEL) & CO.	Scotia

FREDERICK JONES (& CO.)	Scotia Shape
DAVID LOCKHART & SONS (LTD.)	Scotland Forever
WILLIAM DAVENPORT	Scots
JAMES JAMIESON & CO.	Scott Monument
WILLIAM DAVENPORT	SCOTT'S ILLUSTRATIONS SERIES
JOHN RIDGWAY (& CO.)	Scottish Minstrel
WILLIAM ADAMS	SCOTTISH SCENES SERIES
JOHN DENTON BAXTER (BAGSTER)	Scottish Shepherd, et.al.
ROWLAND AND MARSELLUS	Scranton, Pa.
ENOCH WOOD & SONS	SCRIPTURAL SERIES
ALFRED MEAKIN (LTD.)	Scroll
BARKER & SON	Scroll
FRANCIS MORLEY (& CO.)	Scroll
THOMAS BARLOW	Scroll
SAMPSON BRIDGWOOD (& SON)(LTD.)	Scroll Border
CHARLES MEIGH	Scroll Frond Border
J.W. PANKHURST (& CO.)	Scrolled Bubble
LIDDLE, ELLIOT & SON	Scrolled Leaf
COPELAND & GARRETT, ET. AL.	Scrolls
THOMAS, JOHN & JOSEPH MAYER	Scrolls
JAMES & RALPH CLEWS	Scrolls and Large Flowers
RALPH STEVENSON & WILLIAMS	SCROLLS, FLOWERS & URNS SERIES
RALPH STEVENSON & WILLIAMS	Scudder's American Museum
RALPH STEVENSON & WILLIAMS	Scudder's Museum
FRANCIS MORLEY (& CO.)	Scutari
JOHN & WILLIAM RIDGWAY	Scything
JOHN WEDG WOOD	Sea Fan
MINTON & HOLLINS	Sea Flowers
WOOD & SON(S) (LTD.)	Sea Forth
DILLWYN & CO.	Sea Leaf
SAMUEL ALCOCK & CO.	Sea Leaf
WILLIAM ADAMS & SON(S) (POTTERS) LTD.	Sea,The
JOHN HALL	Seal
WILLIAM ADAMS & SON(S) (POTTERS) LTD.	Seal of the United States
JOSEPH STUBBS	Seashells
W. & E. CORN	Seashore
SPODE/COPELAND & GARRETT, et.al.	Seasons
SPODE'S BLUE PRINTED WARES	Seasons
THOMAS GODWIN	Seasons
WILLIAM ADAMS & SON(S) (POTTERS) LTD.	Seasons
WILLIAM ADAMS	SEASONS PATTERNS SERIES
COPELAND & GARRETT, ET. AL.	SEASONS SERIES
SPODE/COPELAND & GARRETT, et.al.	Seasons Star
FERRYBRIDGE POTTERY	Seated and Kneeling Ladies
WILLIAM DAVENPORT	Seated Fisherman, Man With Stick, Boat on River
ROWLAND AND MARSELLUS	Seattle, Wash
DILLWYN & CO.	Seaweed
JOHN RIDGWAY (& CO.)	Seaweed
SPODE/COPELAND & GARRETT, et.al.	Seaweed
WHITEHAVEN POTTERY	Seaweed
WILLIAM DAVENPORT	Seaweed
R. COCHRAN & CO. - VERREVILLE POTTERY	Sebastopol
EDWARD WALLEY	Seeing Eye
MYOTT, SON & CO. (LTD.)	Sefton
RIDGWAYS (BEDFORD WORKS) LTD.	Sefton
GEORGE PHILLIPS	Segapore
THOMAS FELL (& CO.) (LTD.)	Segapore
JOHN EDWARDS (& CO.)	Seine
JOHN TAMS (& SON) (LTD)	Seine
JOHN WEDG WOOD	Seine
W.H. GRINDLEY & CO. (LTD.)	Seine
WILLIAM DAVENPORT	Seine
JAMES & RALPH CLEWS	SELECT SCENERY SERIES
THOMAS DIMMOCK (JR.) & CO.	SELECT SKETCHES SERIES
RALPH HALL (& CO.) or (& SONS)	SELECT VIEWS SERIES
WILLIAM SMITH (& CO.)	Selected Views
ALFRED MEAKIN (LTD.)	Selwyn
BOURNE & LEIGH (LTD.)	Selwyn
BURGESS & LEIGH (LTD.)	Selwyn
RALPH STEVENSON	SEMI-CHINA WARRANTED SERIES
JOHN & WILLIAM RIDGWAY	Senate House, Cambridge
ALFRED MEAKIN (LTD.)	Senate Shape
ARTHUR J. WILKINSON (LTD.)	Senate Shape
HENRY BURGESS	Senate Shape
MELLOR, TAYLOR & CO.	Senate Shape
T. & R. BOOTE (LTD.) (& SON)	Senate Shape
J. DIMMOCK & CO.	Senator
MINTON	Senchenal
WILLIAM DAVENPORT	Senior Citizens
COPELAND & GARRETT, ET. AL.	September - Windsor Castle
SPODE/COPELAND & GARRETT, et.al.	Sepulchre with Annexe
S.W. DEAN	Seraph
WOOD & SON(S) (LTD.)	Seurer
ALFRED MEAKIN (LTD.)	Severn
COPELAND & GARRETT, ET. AL.	Severn
SPODE/COPELAND & GARRETT, et.al.	Severn
DEAKIN & SON(S) (& CO.)	Seville
GEORGE THOMAS MOUNTFORD	Seville

NEW WHARF POTTERY CO.	Seville
WOOD & SON(S) (LTD.)	Seville
COPELAND & GARRETT, ET. AL.	Sevres
J. & G. MEAKIN	Sevres
JOHN HARRIS	Sevres
KEELING & CO. (LTD.)	Sevres
LOCKHART & ARTHUR	Sevres
MYOTT, SON & CO. (LTD.)	Sevres
NEW WHARF POTTERY CO.	Sevres
SPODE/COPELAND & GARRETT, et.al.	Sevres
WOOD & SON(S) (LTD.)	Sevres
JOHN EDWARDS (& CO.)	Sevres Shape
JOSEPH CLEMENTSON	Sevres Shape
J. & M.P. BELL (CO.) & (LTD.)	Sexagon
J. & M.P. BELL (CO.) & (LTD.)	Seymour
SPODE/COPELAND & GARRETT, et.al.	Shagreen/Broth
MINTONS, LTD.	Shah Japan
ROWLAND AND MARSELLUS	Shakespeare
S.W. DEAN	Shamrock
SPODE/COPELAND & GARRETT, et.al.	Shamrock
GEORGE JONES (& SONS LTD.)	Shandon
FURNIVALS LTD.	Shanghae
JACOB FURNIVAL & CO.	Shanghae
JACOB FURNIVAL & CO.	Shanghae #36
T. RATHBONE & CO.	Shanghai
THOMAS TILL & SON	Shanghai
W. & E. CORN	Shanghai
W. BAKER & CO. (LTD.)	Shanghai
W.H. GRINDLEY & CO. (LTD.)	Shanghai
WILLIAM & THOMAS ADAMS	Shanghai
WILLIAM ADAMS & CO. LTD.	Shanghai
WILLIAM ADAMS & SON(S) (POTTERS) LTD.	Shanghai
W.H. GRINDLEY & CO. (LTD.)	Shangrila
FRANCIS MORLEY (& CO.)	Shannon
JOHN ROGERS (& SON)	Shannon
JOSIAH WEDGWOOD (& SONS LTD.)	Shannon
WEDGWOOD & CO. (LTD.)	Shannon
JOB & JOHN JACKSON	Shannondale Springs, Virginia
WILLIAM ADAMS & SON(S) (POTTERS) LTD.	Shannondall Springs, Virginia, U.S.
DIMMOCK & SMITH	Shantong
T. & R. BOOTE (LTD.) (& SON)	Shapoo
THOMAS HUGHES	Shapoo
THOMAS HUGHES & SON (LTD.)	Shapoo
JOHN WEDG WOOD	Sharon Arch Shape
WILLIAM DAVENPORT	Sharon Arch Shape
ENOCH WOOD & SONS	Sharon Castle
G.M. & C.J. MASON	Sharpus et.al.
ROWLAND AND MARSELLUS	Shaw Mansion, Conn.
ANTHONY SHAW (& SON(S) (& CO.)	Shaw's, Lily-of-the-Valley
ANTHONY SHAW (& SON(S) (& CO.)	Shaw's, Pear
ANTHONY SHAW (& SON(S) (& CO.)	Shaw's, Spray
ANDREW STEVENSON	Sheep / Shearing View
JOHN DENTON BAXTER (BAGSTER)	Sheep at Hay Rack, et.al.
JOHN EDWARDS (& CO.)	Sheep's Head
ANDREW STEVENSON	Sheet Pattern
COPELAND & GARRETT, ET. AL.	Sheet Pattern
JOSEPH HARDING	Sheet Pattern
POUNTNEY & ALLIES	Sheet Pattern
WILLIAM HACKWOOD	Sheet Pattern
JOHN & WILLIAM RIDGWAY	Sheffield Place, Succes
EDWARD CHALLINOR	Shell
H. & R. DANIEL	Shell
JAMES WALLACE & CO.	Shell
WEDGWOOD & CO. (LTD.)	Shell
WOOD & CHALLINOR	Shell
CAMBRIAN POTTERY	Shell & Flower
PODMORE, WALKER (& CO.)	Shell & Flowers
THOMAS DIMMOCK (JR.) & CO.	Shells
JAMES & RALPH CLEWS	Shells & Flower
JOHN ROGERS (& SON)	SHELLS AND SEAWEED SERIES
RALPH HALL	Sheltered Peasants
WILLIAM RIDGWAY (& CO.)	Shenandoah
BENJAMIN E. GODWIN	Shepherd
MINTON	Shepherd
THOMAS & JOHN CAREY/ JOHN CAREY & SONS	Shepherd & Dog With Sheep
BATHWELL & GOODFELLOW	Shepherd & Maid
BENJAMIN E. GODWIN	Shepherd Boy
JAMES & RALPH CLEWS	Shepherd Boy Rescued
WILLIAM DAVENPORT	Shepherd Boy Rescued
BATHWELL & GOODFELLOW	Shepherd Pattern
BRAMELD & CO.	Shepherd Pattern
JOHN ROGERS (& SON)	Shepherd With Lute
ANDREW STEVENSON	Shepherdess
SPODE'S BLUE PRINTED WARES	Shepherdess
ENOCH WOOD & SONS	Sherbourn Castle
ROWLAND AND MARSELLUS	Sherbrooke, Quebec, Canada
ANTHONY SHAW (& SON(S) (& CO.)	Shield
JAMES EDWARDS	Shield

SAMPSON BRIDGWOOD (& SON)(LTD.)	Shield Border
EDWARD BOURNE	Ship
T. & J. BEVINGTON (& CO.)	Ship
THOMAS & BENJAMIN GODWIN	Ship
SPODE'S BLUE PRINTED WARES	Ship & Star
ENOCH WOOD & SONS	Ship at Anchor
SPODE/COPELAND & GARRETT, et.al.	Ship Border
ENOCH WOOD & SONS	Ship Of The Line in the Downs
BAKER, BEVANS & IRWIN	Ship Pattern
DILLWYN & CO.	Ship Pattern
ENOCH WOOD & SONS	Ship Under Half Sail, et.al.
THOMAS & BENJAMIN GODWIN	Ship Willow
ENOCH WOOD & SONS	Ship, Two Sailboats & Rowboat, et.al.
ENOCH WOOD & SONS	Ship, Two Sailboats, et.al.
RALPH STEVENSON	Shipping Port of the Ohio, Kentucky
ENOCH WOOD & SONS	Shipping Port On the Ohio, Kentucky
ENOCH WOOD & SONS	SHIPS WITH AMERICAN FLAGS
JOHN ROGERS (& SON)	Shipwreck Scene
JOHN & RICHARD RILEY	Shipyards
JOHN RIDGWAY (& CO.)	Shiraz
FORD & SONS (LTD.)	Shirley
ENOCH WOOD & SONS	Shirley House, Surrey
EDWARD CHALLINOR	Shooting a Leopard in a Tree
SPODE/COPELAND & GARRETT, et.al.	Shooting a Leopard in a Tree
EDWARD CHALLINOR	Shooting at the Edge of a Jungle
SPODE/COPELAND & GARRETT, et.al.	Shooting at the Edge of a Jungle
JOHN DENTON BAXTER (BAGSTER)	Shopping
JACOB FURNIVAL & CO.	Short Octagon
HERCULANEUM POTTERY	Shrewsbury
THOMAS DIMMOCK (JR.) & CO.	Shrine
THOMAS & JOHN CAREY/ JOHN CAREY & SONS	Shugborough Hall, Staffordshire, Viscount Anson's Seat
F. & R. PRATT & CO. (LTD.)	Shusan
BEECH & HANCOCK	Siam
CAULDON, LTD.	Siam
J. & M.P. BELL (CO.) & (LTD.)	Siam
JOSEPH CLEMENTSON	Siam
SPODE/COPELAND & GARRETT, et.al.	Siam
WEDGWOOD & CO. (LTD.)	Sibyl
CHARLES MEIGH	Sicilian
J.T. CLOSE (& CO.)	Sicilian
MINTON	Sicilian
POUNTNEY & ALLIES	Sicilian
POUNTNEY & GOLDNEY	Sicilian
JAMES & RALPH CLEWS	Sicilian Beauties
COPELAND & GARRETT, ET. AL.	Sicily
JOHN HALL (& SONS)	Sicre Gully Pass
THOMAS & BENJAMIN GODWIN	Sicre Gully Pass, Bengal
HENSHALL & CO.	Side-Wheel Steamboat
JOHN & WILLIAM RIDGWAY	Sidney Sussex College, Cambridge
JONES & SON	Signing the Magna Carta
CHARLES MEIGH & SON	Silistria
SWINNERTON (LTD.)	Silverdale
SPODE/COPELAND & GARRETT, et.al.	Silvester
ELSMORE & FORSTER	Simla
THOMAS WALKER	Simla
RIDGWAYS (BEDFORD WORKS) LTD.	Simlay
ALFRED MEAKIN (LTD.)	Simple Pear
BISHOP & STONIER (LTD.)	Simple Square
JOHN MADDOCK & SONS (LTD.)	Simple Square
WEDGWOOD & CO. (LTD.)	Simple Square
HENRY BURGESS	Simple Square - Pagoda
POWELL & BISHOP	Simple Square: Puffy
BOOTHS (LTD.)	Simplex
DOULTON & CO. (LTD.)	Simplicitas
ANTHONY SHAW (& SON(S) (& CO.)	Simplicity
JOHN MADDOCK & SONS (LTD.)	Simplicity
POWELL & BISHOP	Simplicity
JOHN MEIR	Simplon
GEORGE JONES (& SONS LTD.)	Sing An
CORK, EDGE & MALKIN	Singa
EDGE, MALKIN & CO. (LTD.)	Singa
THOMAS GODWIN	Singa
THOMAS GOODFELLOW	Singan
JOHN WEDG WOOD	Singanese
RALPH HALL & CO.	Singanese
WHITTINGHAM, FORD & CO.	Singanese
RALPH STEVENSON	SINGLE MEDALLION BORDER SERIES
JAMES & THOMAS EDWARDS	Sirius
SOUTH WALES POTTERS	Sirius
THOMAS EDWARDS	Sirius
T. RATHBONE & CO.	Sisters
GEORGE JONES (& SONS LTD.)	Sistovia
J.W. PANKHURST (& CO.)	Six Paneled Trumpet
JOB & JOHN JACKSON	Skenectady / Schenectady, On the Mohawk River
JOB & JOHN JACKSON	Skenectady On the Mohawk River
WILLIAM ADAMS & SON(S) (POTTERS) LTD.	Skenectady on the Mohawk River, U.S.

COPELAND & GARRETT, ET. AL.	Skinner's Arms
JOB MEIGH (& SON)	Skunk
THOMAS GODWIN	Sledge Bearing Eskimos, et.al.
EDWARD WALLEY	Sleepy Eye
ENOCH WOOD & SONS	Sleigh Ride
WILLIAM RIDGWAY (& CO.)	Sloe Blossom
ROWLAND AND MARSELLUS	Smith, Captayne John
MINTON & CO.	Smith's Japan
RIDGWAY & ABINGTON	Smyrna
JAMES & RALPH CLEWS	Snipe Hunting
WILLIAM DAVENPORT	Snow Scenes
YATES & MAY	Snowdrop
JOHN MARSHALL (& CO.)(LTD.)	Snowshoes Being Tied
WILLIAM ADAMS & SON(S) (POTTERS) LTD.	Snowy Shrubs
FRANCIS MORLEY (& CO.)	Sobraon
SAMUEL ALCOCK & CO.	Sobraon
WILLIAM HACKWOOD	Sobreon
MACHIN & POTTS	Socrates
J. & G. MEAKIN	Sol
WILLIAM (ALSAGER) ADDERLEY (& CO.)	Sola
JAMES & RALPH CLEWS	Solar Ray
WILLIAM DAVENPORT	Solitary Fisherman
ROWLAND AND MARSELLUS	Somer's Island
W.H. GRINDLEY & CO. (LTD.)	Somerset
TAMS / et.al.	Somerset House, London
POWELL, BISHOP & STONIER	Song Birds
COPELAND & GARRETT, ET. AL.	Soracte
CHARLES MEIGH & SON	Sousa
JAMES & RALPH CLEWS	South America, Buenos Ayres/ Aires
THOMAS MAYER	South Carolina, Arms of
ENOCH WOOD & SONS	Southampton, Hampshire
ENOCH WOOD & SONS	Southwest View of La Grange / The Residence of Marquis Lafayette
JOHN RIDGWAY (& CO.)	Souvenir
SPODE/COPELAND & GARRETT, et.al.	Souvenir
ROWLAND AND MARSELLUS	Souvenir of Detroit, Mich.
ROWLAND AND MARSELLUS	Souvenir of Plymouth, Mass.
ROWLAND AND MARSELLUS	Souvenir of Put-in-Bay, Ohio
WILLIAM ADAMS & SON(S) (POTTERS) LTD.	Sower,The
DEAKIN & SON(S) (& CO.)	Spanish Beauties
THOMAS MAYER	Spanish Bullfight
WILLIAM ADAMS & SON(S) (POTTERS) LTD.	Spanish Convent
GEORGE JONES (& SONS LTD.)	Spanish Festivity
WILLIAM ADAMS & SON(S) (POTTERS) LTD.	Spanish Marriages, Madrid
WILLIAM DAVENPORT	Spanish Rose
PODMORE, WALKER (& CO.)	Spartan
WILLIAM (ALSAGER) ADDERLEY (& CO.)	Spero
JOHN MEIR	Spetchley, Worcestershire
CHARLES MEIGH	Sphinx
SPODE/COPELAND & GARRETT, et.al.	Sphinx
GEORGE JONES (& SONS LTD.)	Spinach
SHORTHOUSE & CO.	Spinning Wheel Children
W. BAKER & CO. (LTD.)	Spiral
ROWLAND AND MARSELLUS	Spirit of '76
J. H. & J. DAVIS	Spittoon Gargoyle
JAMES EDWARDS	Split Pod
JOHN ALCOCK	Split Pod
COPELAND & GARRETT, ET. AL.	Spode's Tower
SPODE'S BLUE PRINTED WARES	Spode's Landscape
SPODE'S BLUE PRINTED WARES	Spode's Phoenix
ROWLAND AND MARSELLUS	Spokane, Washington
COPELAND & GARRETT, ET. AL.	Spoleto
ROBINSON, WOOD & BROWNFIELD	Spoonbill and Heron
ENOCH WOOD & SONS	SPORTING SERIES
THOMAS HEATH	Sporting Subject
J. & M.P. BELL (CO.) & (LTD.)	Sporting Subjects
ENOCH WOOD	Sportsman
MINTON & BOYLE	Spot & Wreath
ROWLAND AND MARSELLUS	Spots in California
SPODE'S BLUE PRINTED WARES	Spotted Dear
INDEO POTTERY	Spotted Deer
ENOCH WOOD & SONS	Spotted Hyena
ALFRED MEAKIN (LTD.)	Spray
J.W. PANKHURST (& CO.)	Spray
COPELAND & GARRETT, ET. AL.	Sprays
COPELAND & GARRETT, ET. AL.	Sprays and Bead
COPELAND & GARRETT, ET. AL.	Sprays printed in Royal Gray
JOSEPH STUBBS	SPREAD EAGLE BORDER SERIES
WILLIAM DAVENPORT	Spreading tree and bridge
MINTON	Sprig
CHARLES MEIGH	Sprigs
MINTONS, LTD.	Sprigs & Flies
W.H. GRINDLEY & CO. (LTD.)	Spring
COPELAND & GARRETT, ET. AL.	Spring - Richmond Hill
HENSHALL & CO.	Spring Hall
ENOCH WOOD & SONS	Spring Vale, Staffordshire
RALPH STEVENSON	Springer Spaniel
ALFRED MEAKIN (LTD.)	Springfield
BROWN WESTHEAD, MOORE & CO.	Springtime
ENOCH WOOD & SONS	Sproughton Chantry, Suffolk
JAMES EDWARDS	Square Acorn
J. & G. MEAKIN	Square Melon/Ribbed
JAMES EDWARDS	Square Open Flower Shape
W. & E. CORN	Square Pear
BISHOP & STONIER (LTD.)	Square Ridged
HENRY ALCOCK & CO. (LTD.)	Square Ridged
HENRY BURGESS	Square Ridged
JOHN MADDOCK & SONS (LTD.)	Square Ridged
JOHNSON BROS. (HANLEY), LTD.	Square Ridged
MELLOR, TAYLOR & CO.	Square Ridged
W. & E. CORN	Square Ridged
WEDGWOOD & CO. (LTD.)	Square Ridged
POWELL & BISHOP	Square Ridged Shape
HENRY BURGESS	Square Ridged/Beaded Handle Shape
MELLOR, TAYLOR & CO.	Square Ridged/Hearts
BISHOP & STONIER (LTD.)	Square Ridged/Iona
POWELL & BISHOP	Square Ridged: Iona Shape
JAMES EDWARDS	Square Rose Bud Shape
JAMES EDWARDS	Square Tumbling Petals Shape
JOHN MADDOCK	Squash & Vine
JOHN MADDOCK & SONS (LTD.)	Squash & Vine
WILLIAM DAVENPORT	Squat Oval Teapot
THOMAS GODWIN	Squaw Lying Down
DAWSON (JOHN DAWSON & CO., ETC.)	Squire & Lackey
DAVID METHVEN & SONS	Squirrel
ENOCH WOOD & SONS	Squirrel
WILLIAM DAVENPORT	Squirrel
ROWLAND AND MARSELLUS	St Paul, Minn.
GOODWINS & HARRIS	St. Albans Abbey
HENSHALL & CO.	St. Albins
ROWLAND AND MARSELLUS	St. Augustine, Fl.
JAMES & RALPH CLEWS	St. Catherine's Hill, Near Guildford
WILLIAM ADAMS & SON(S) (POTTERS) LTD.	St. Catherine's Hill, Near Guildford
HENSHALL & CO.	St. Cloud
ENOCH WOOD & SONS	St. George's Chapel, Regent Street, London
WILLIAM ADAMS	St. George's Chapel, Regent Street, London
JAMES JAMIESON & CO.	St. John's Church
ROWLAND AND MARSELLUS	St. Joseph, Mo.
FRANCIS MORLEY (& CO.)	St. Lawrence
PODMORE, WALKER (& CO.)	St. Lawrence
JOHNSON BROS. (HANLEY), LTD.	St. Louis
ROWLAND AND MARSELLUS	St. Louis Centennial
JOHN EDWARDS (& CO.)	St. Louis Shape
ROWLAND AND MARSELLUS	St. Louis World's Fair
ROWLAND AND MARSELLUS	St. Louis, Mo.
DILLWYN & CO.	St. Mary Magdalen, Taunton
JAMES & RALPH CLEWS	St. Mary's Abbey, York
WILLIAM ADAMS & SON(S) (POTTERS) LTD.	St. Mary's Abbey, York
DILLWYN & CO.	St. Mary's Church, Truro
MINTON	St. Mary's Dover
CAMBRIAN POTTERY	St. Michael's Mount
DILLWYN & CO.	St. Michael's Mt., Cornwall
ROWLAND AND MARSELLUS	St. Patrick's Cathedral, Harrisburg
RALPH STEVENSON	St. Patrick's Cathedral, Mott Street, N.Y.
THOMAS & JOHN CAREY/ JOHN CAREY & SONS	St. Paul's Cathedral
RALPH STEVENSON	St. Paul's Chapel, New York
RALPH STEVENSON & WILLIAMS	St. Paul's Chapel, New York
HERCULANEUM POTTERY	St. Paul's Church
JOHN & WILLIAM RIDGWAY	St. Paul's Church, Boston
ROWLAND AND MARSELLUS	St. Paul's Church, Trexlertown, Pa.
ENOCH WOOD & SONS	St. Paul's School, London
WILLIAM ADAMS	St. Paul's School, London
CHARLES MEIGH	St. Pauls
ROWLAND AND MARSELLUS	St. Peter's Church, Rittersville, Pa.
JOHN & WILLIAM RIDGWAY	St. Peter's College, Cambridge
ENOCH WOOD & SONS	St. Peter's, Rome
G.L. ASHWORTH & BROS. (LTD.)	St. Petersburg
WILLIAM ADAMS & CO. LTD.	St. Petersburg
ENOCH WOOD & SONS	St. Phillip's Chapel, Regent Street
WOOD & SON(S) (LTD.)	St. Regis
POUNTNEY & ALLIES	St. Vincent's Rocks
RALPH HALL (& CO.) or (& SONS)	St. Woolston's, Kildare, Ireland
PODMORE, WALKER (& CO.)	St.Lawrence/Indian Encampment, et.al.
THOMAS & JOHN CAREY/ JOHN CAREY & SONS	Stackpole Court
ELKIN & CO.	Stackpole Court, Pembrokeshire
J. & G. MEAKIN	Stafford
JOHN ALCOCK	Stafford Shape
SAMUEL ALCOCK & CO.	Stafford Shape
COCHRAN & FLEMING - BRITANNIA POTTERY	Stag
JOHN ALLASON	Stag
JOHN TURNER / TURNER & CO., etc.	Stag
THOMAS & BENJAMIN GODWIN	Stag
THOMAS SHIRLEY & CO.	Stag
THOMAS DIMMOCK (JR.) & CO.	Stag and urn
FRANK BEARDMORE & CO.	Stag Island

READ, CLEMENTSON & ANDERSON	Stagg
ROWLAND AND MARSELLUS	Standish House
JOHNSON BROS. (HANLEY), LTD.	Stanley
RALPH HAMMERSLEY (& SON(S)	Stanley
MINTON	Star
SPODE/COPELAND & GARRETT, et.al.	Star
T. & J. HOLLINS	Star
EMPIRE PORCELAIN CO. (LTD.)	Star Center
J.W. PANKHURST (& CO.)	Star Flower
COPELAND & GARRETT, ET. AL.	Starlike Sprays
T. & R. BOOTE (LTD.) (& SON)	Starred Leaf
JOB & JOHN JACKSON	State House, Boston
JOHN & WILLIAM RIDGWAY	State House, Boston
JOSEPH STUBBS	State House, Boston
RALPH STEVENSON	State House, Boston
RALPH STEVENSON & WILLIAMS	State House, Boston
SAMUEL KEELING & CO.	Statfield Saye
SPODE/COPELAND & GARRETT, et.al.	Statice
WILLIAM DAVENPORT	Statuary
SAMUEL ALCOCK & CO.	Statue
SOUTHWICK POTTERY	Statue
ENOCH WOOD & SONS	Statue of Washington by Canova
JOHN & WILLIAM RIDGWAY	Staughton's Church, Philadelphia
RALPH STEVENSON & WILLIAMS	Staughton's Church, Philadelphia
ENOCH WOOD & SONS	Steamboat
ENOCH WOOD & SONS	Steamboat in Background
MINTON	Steed
BOVEY POTTERY CO. LTD.	Stella
SPODE/COPELAND & GARRETT, et.al.	Stella
JOHNSON BROS. (HANLEY), LTD.	Sterling
NEW WHARF POTTERY CO.	Sterling
HENSHALL & CO.	Stern-Wheel Steamboat
JOSEPH STUBBS	Steven's House
ANDREW STEVENSON	Stevenson's Willow
JOHN & EDWARD BADDELEY	Stilted House
ANDREW STEVENSON	Stone Curlew
JOHN TAMS (& SON) (LTD)	Stork
SPODE/COPELAND & GARRETT, et.al.	Stork
MINTONS, LTD.	Stork & Fan
KNIGHT, ELKIN & CO.	Stow Hall
BURGESS & LEIGH (LTD.)	Stratford
RIDGWAYS (BEDFORD WORKS) LTD.	Stratford
W.H. GRINDLEY & CO. (LTD.)	Stratford
JAMES & RALPH CLEWS	Stratford-on-Avon, Warwickshire
MINTONS, LTD.	Strathearn
J. & G. MEAKIN	Strawberry
JACOB FURNIVAL & CO.	Strawberry
MEAKIN (BROS) & CO.	Strawberry
SPODE/COPELAND & GARRETT, et.al.	Strawberry
T.G. & F. BOOTH	Strawberry
THOMAS WALKER	Strawberry
ROBERT HAMILTON	Strawberry Border
MELLOR, VENABLES & CO.	Strawberry Luster
ELSMORE & FORSTER	Strawberry Lustre
J. & M.P. BELL (CO.) & (LTD.)	Stray Leaves
BENJAMIN E. GODWIN	Stream & Cow
ROBINSON, WOOD & BROWNFIELD	Stripe
GOODWINS & HARRIS	Stylised Flowers
JOHN MADDOCK & SONS (LTD.)	Stylized Berry
HENRY ALCOCK & CO. (LTD.)	Stylized Flower
WILLIAM BROWNFIELD (& SON(S)	Suez
WILLIAM DAVENPORT	Suez
SPODE/COPELAND & GARRETT, et.al.	Suez Key
RALPH STEVENSON	Sufton Court
ENOCH WOOD & SONS	Sufton Court, Herefordshire
RIDGWAYS (BEDFORD WORKS) LTD.	Suggton
RIDGWAYS (BEDFORD WORKS) LTD.	Suhrnglen
DAVID METHVEN & SONS	Sultana
WILLIAM SMITH (& CO.)	Sultana
J. & M.P. BELL (CO.) & (LTD.)	Sumatra
COPELAND & GARRETT, ET. AL.	Summer
SAMPSON HANCOCK (& SONS)	Summer
SAMUEL ALCOCK & CO.	Summer Flowers
GEORGE JONES (& SONS LTD.)	Summer Garden
ANDREW STEVENSON	Summer Hall, Kent
JAMES & RALPH CLEWS	Summer Rose
EDGE, MALKIN & CO. (LTD.)	Summertime
DON POTTERY	Sun and Fountain
KNIGHT, ELKIN & BRIDGWOOD	Sun of Righteousness, The
ANTHONY SHAW (& SON(S) (& CO.)	Sunburst
ARTHUR J. WILKINSON (LTD.)	Sunburst
GEORGE JONES (& SONS LTD.)	Sunbury
COPELAND & GARRETT, ET. AL.	Sunflower
RIDGWAY & MORLEY	Sunflower
WILLIAM DAVENPORT	Sunflower
SPODE/COPELAND & GARRETT, et.al.	Sunflower & Convolvulus
WILLIAM ADAMS & SON(S) (POTTERS) LTD.	Sunning Hill Park, Berkshire
ALFRED MEAKIN (LTD.)	Superior
SAMPSON BRIDGWOOD (& SON)(LTD.)	Surreal

ROWLAND AND MARSELLUS	Surrender of Col. Ledyard
CORK, EDGE & MALKIN	Surseya Ghaut, Khanpore
EDGE, MALKIN & CO. (LTD.)	Surseya Ghaut, Khanpore
JOHN HALL (& SONS)	Surseya Ghaut, Khanpore
THOMAS & BENJAMIN GODWIN	Surseya Ghaut, Khanpore
CHARLES MEIGH	Susa
CHARLES MEIGH, SON & PANKHURST	Susa
ENOCH WOOD & SONS	Suspension Bridge
ENOCH WOOD & SONS	Sussex Place, Regent's Park
WILLIAM ADAMS	Sussex Place, Regent's Park
DOULTON & CO. (LTD.)	Sutherland
CHARLES MEIGH & SON	Sutherland Border
RIDGWAYS (BEDFORD WORKS) LTD.	Sutton
GROVE & STARK	Swallow
JAMES F. WILEMAN	Swallow
JOSIAH WEDGWOOD (& SONS LTD.)	Swallow
WEDGWOOD & CO. (LTD.)	Swallow
BELLE VUE POTTERIES	Swan
JOSIAH WEDGWOOD (& SONS LTD.)	Swan
SAMUEL ALCOCK & CO.	Swan
JOHN ROGERS (& SON)	Swan & Parasol
JAMES & RALPH CLEWS	Swans
PODMORE, WALKER (& CO.)	Swans
WILLIAM DAVENPORT	Swans & Horses
THOMAS FELL (& CO.) (LTD.)	Swans & Vase
LEEDS POTTERY	Swans on a Pond, et.al.
DILLWYN & CO.	Swansea Harbor & Town
WOOD & BROWNFIELD	Sweaborg
J. & G. MEAKIN	Sweet Pea
THOMAS G. GREEN & CO. (LTD.)	Sweet Pea
BRAMELD & CO.	Sweet Peas
BURGESS & LEIGH (LTD.)	Sweetbrier
ELKIN, KNIGHT & CO.	Sweetheart Abbey
ENOCH WOOD & SONS	Swiss
JONATHAN LOWE CHETHAM	Swiss
RALPH STEVENSON	Swiss
RALPH STEVENSON & SON	Swiss
WILLIAM DAVENPORT	Swiss
JOB & JOHN JACKSON	Swiss Boy
J. & M.P. BELL (CO.) & (LTD.)	Swiss Cantons
WILLIAM DAVENPORT	Swiss Chalet
MINTON	Swiss Cottage
MINTON & CO.	Swiss Cottage
ENOCH WOOD	Swiss Farm
WILLIAM DAVENPORT	Swiss Lake & Village
WILLIAM DAVENPORT	Swiss Pastime
EVANS & GLASSON	Swiss Scenery
JAMES JAMIESON & CO.	Swiss Scenery
JOSEPH STUBBS	Swiss Scenery
SWIFT & ELKIN	Swiss Scenery
WILLIAM DAVENPORT	Swiss Scenery
SOUTH WALES POTTERS	Swiss Sketches
J. & M.P. BELL (CO.) & (LTD.)	Swiss Subjects
DILLWYN & CO.	Swiss Villa
J. & M.P. BELL (CO.) & (LTD.)	Swiss Water Mill
DOULTON & CO. (LTD.)	Switzerland
JOHN TURNER / TURNER & CO., etc.	Swooping Bird
HENRY ALCOCK & CO. (LTD.)	Sybil
EDWARD CHALLINOR	Syces or Grooms Leading Out Horses
SPODE/COPELAND & GARRETT, et.al.	Syces or Grooms Leading Out Horses
ELSMORE & FORSTER	Sydenham
FRANCIS MORLEY (& CO.)	Sydenham
JOSEPH CLEMENTSON	Sydenham
JOSEPH CLEMENTSON	Sydenham Shape
T. & R. BOOTE (LTD.) (& SON)	Sydenham Shape
NEW WHARF POTTERY CO.	Sydney
WOOD & SON(S) (LTD.)	Sydney
BROWN WESTHEAD, MOORE & CO.	Sylvan
JOHN & WILLIAM RIDGWAY	Sylvan
JOHNSON BROS. (HANLEY), LTD.	Sylvan
WILLIAM BROWNFIELD (& SON(S)	Sylvania
JOSEPH CLEMENTSON	Sylvia
ROWLAND AND MARSELLUS	Syracuse ... Fairgrounds
ROWLAND AND MARSELLUS	Syracuse ... Indian Chief
R. COCHRAN & CO. - VERREVILLE POTTERY	Syria
RIDGWAY, MORLEY, WEAR & CO.	Syria
SOUTH WALES POTTERS	Syria
R.S. KIDSTON & CO. - VERREVILLE	Syrian
SAMUEL BARKER & SON	Syrian
W.H. GRINDLEY & CO. (LTD.)	Syrian
WILLIAM DAVENPORT	Syrian
WILLIAM SMITH (& CO.)	Syrian Flowers
SPODE/COPELAND & GARRETT, et.al.	Syringa
THOMAS TILL & SONS	Syton
G.L. ASHWORTH & BROS. (LTD.)	Table & Flower Pot
G.M. & C.J. MASON	Table & Flower Pot
ENOCH WOOD & SONS	Table Rock At Niagara
ENOCH WOOD & SONS	Table Rock, Niagara
ROWLAND AND MARSELLUS	Tacoma, Wash.

WALLIS GIMSON & CO.	The Federal Parliament Buildings, Ottawa
WILLIAM DAVENPORT	THE FISHERMAN SERIES
ENOCH WOOD & SONS	The Flight Into Egypt
T. RATHBONE & CO.	The Font
JAMES KEELING	The Fountain Near Aleppo
JOHN & WILLIAM RIDGWAY	The Fountain, Trinity College, Cambridge
SPODE/COPELAND & GARRETT, et.al.	The Fox
SPODE/COPELAND & GARRETT, et.al.	The Fox and the Goat
SPODE/COPELAND & GARRETT, et.al.	The Fox and the Grapes
SPODE/COPELAND & GARRETT, et.al.	The Fox and the Lion
SPODE/COPELAND & GARRETT, et.al.	The Fox and the Sick Lion
SPODE/COPELAND & GARRETT, et.al.	The Fox and the Tiger
JAMES & RALPH CLEWS	The Garden Trio
BOVEY TRACY POTTERY COMPANY	The Gem
MINTON & BOYLE	The Gem
MINTON & CO.	The Gem
MINTON & HOLLINS	The Gem
MINTONS	The Gem
WATSON & CO.	The Gentle Shepherd
ANTHONY SHAW (& SON(S) (& CO.)	The Gift
WALLIS GIMSON & CO.	The Governor General's Residence / Rideau Hall, Ottawa
LEEDS POTTERY	The Great Wall of China
TAMS / et.al.	The Guild Hall, London
CHESWORTH & ROBINSON	The Guitar
COPELAND & GARRETT, ET. AL.	The Hague
ELKIN & CO.	The Haining, Selkirkshire
HENSHALL & CO.	The Harbor of Messina
SPODE/COPELAND & GARRETT, et.al.	The Hare and the Tortoise
JAMES & RALPH CLEWS	The Harvest Home
BAKER, BEVANS & IRWIN	The Haymaker
THOMAS & BENJAMIN GODWIN	The Heart of Midlothian
SPODE/COPELAND & GARRETT, et.al.	The Hog at Bay
EDWARD CHALLINOR	The Hog Deer at Bay
SPODE/COPELAND & GARRETT, et.al.	The Hog Deer at Bay
ENOCH WOOD & SONS	The Holme, Regent's Park
WILLIAM ADAMS	The Holme, Regent's Park
JOHN GEDDES - VERREVILLE POTTERY	The home of Warren Hastings
ELIJAH JONES	The Hop
SPODE/COPELAND & GARRETT, et.al.	The Horse and the Loaded Ass
RALPH HALL (& CO.) or (& SONS)	The Hospital Near Poissy, France
HERCULANEUM POTTERY	The House of Correction, Kirkdale, Liverpool
SHORTHOUSE & CO.	The Itinerant
ANDREW STEVENSON	The Junction of the Sacandage and Hudson Rivers
ENOCH WOOD & SONS	The Kent,, East Indiaman
ANDREW STEVENSON	The Kingfisher
JOHN & RICHARD RILEY	The Kings Cottage, Windsor Park
JAMES & RALPH CLEWS	The Knight of the Wood Conquered
WILLIAM DAVENPORT	The Knight of the Wood Conquered
CAMBRIAN POTTERY	The Ladies of Langollen
BAKER, BEVANS & IRWIN	The Ladies of Llangollen
ENOCH WOOD & SONS	The Lake, Regent's Park
JAMES & RALPH CLEWS	The Landing of General Lafayette at Castle Garden, New York, 16, August 1824
ENOCH WOOD & SONS	The Landing of the Fathers at Plymouth, Dec. 22, 1620
SPODE/COPELAND & GARRETT, et.al.	The Leopard and the Fox
JAMES & RALPH CLEWS	The Letter of Introduction
SPODE/COPELAND & GARRETT, et.al.	The Lion in Love
SPODE/COPELAND & GARRETT, et.al.	The Lion, the Bear and the Fox
SPODE/COPELAND & GARRETT, et.al.	The Lioness and the Fox
ENOCH WOOD & SONS	The London Institution
WILLIAM ADAMS	The London Institution
THOMAS FURNIVAL & SONS	The Lorne Shape
THOMAS & JOHN CAREY/ JOHN CAREY & SONS	The Lower Lake of Killarney
JOHN ROGERS (& SON)	The Maid at the Mill, Act 1 Scene 1
POUNTNEY & GOLDNEY	The Maid at the Mill, Act 1 Scene 1
JAMES & RALPH CLEWS	The Meeting of Don Quixote and Sancho Panza
WILLIAM DAVENPORT	The Meeting of Don Quixote and Sancho Panza
JAMES & RALPH CLEWS	The Meeting of Sancho and Dapple
WILLIAM DAVENPORT	The Meeting of Sancho and Dapple
JAMES & RALPH CLEWS	The Meeting With the Duchess
WILLIAM DAVENPORT	The Meeting With the Duchess
JOHN DENTON BAXTER (BAGSTER)	The Meeting, et.al.
EDWARD & GEORGE PHILLIPS	The Messenger
WILLIAM REID (& SON) or (SONS)	The Milkmaid
SPODE/COPELAND & GARRETT, et.al.	The Mountains in Labour
WILLIAM DAVENPORT	The Mounted Muleteer has left the woman and proceeds towards the village
WILLIAM DAVENPORT	The Muleteer and two women walk with mules alongside a wall, et.al.
WILLIAM DAVENPORT	The Muleteer mounted, preceded by dog, two women standing by shore, et.al.
WILLIAM DAVENPORT	The Muleteer stands with the two women and child, et.al.
MELLOR, VENABLES & CO.	The Narrows
THOMAS GODWIN	The Narrows From Fort Hamilton
WILLIAM RIDGWAY, SON & CO.	The Narrows From Fort Hamilton
WILLIAM RIDGWAY, SON & CO.	The Narrows, Lake George
ENOCH WOOD & SONS	The Nativity
WALLIS GIMSON & CO.	The Normal School, Toronto
SPODE/COPELAND & GARRETT, et.al.	The Nuptial Bath
SPODE/COPELAND & GARRETT, et.al.	The Oak and the Reed
CHESWORTH & ROBINSON	The Offering
SPODE/COPELAND & GARRETT, et.al.	The Peacock and the Crane
ANDREW STEVENSON	The Peacock and Turkey
ELKIN & CO.	The Pet Goat
THOMAS GODWIN	The President's House
MELLOR, VENABLES & CO.	The President's House from the River
JOB & JOHN JACKSON	The President's House, Washington
BODLEY & HARROLD	The Princess Alexander
BELLE VUE POTTERIES	The Proposal
JOHN ROGERS (& SON)	The Quaker, Act 2 Scene 2
POUNTNEY & GOLDNEY	The Quaker, Act 2 Scene 2
BAILEY & BALL	The Rabbit
JAMES & RALPH CLEWS	The Rabbit on the Wall
JOB & JOHN JACKSON	The Race Bridge, Philadelphia
THOMAS SHIRLEY & CO.	The Reader
ENOCH WOOD & SONS	The Regent's Quadrant, London
WILLIAM ADAMS	The Regent's Quadrant, London
JOSEPH HEATH	The Residence of the Late Richard Jordan, New Jersey
ENOCH WOOD & SONS	The Residence of The Marquis de Lafayette
ENOCH WOOD & SONS	The Return
BRAMELD & CO.	The Returning Woodman
JOHN ROGERS (& SON)	The Revenge
POUNTNEY & GOLDNEY	The Revenge
JAMES EDWARDS	The Roby Day and Sunday School
GRIFFITHS, BEARDMORE & BIRKS	The Rookery
ENOCH WOOD & SONS	The Rookery, Surrey
JOHN & RICHARD RILEY	The Rookery, Surrey
WILLIAM ADAMS & SON(S) (POTTERS) LTD.	The Rookery, Surrey
JOHN GOODWIN/SEACOMBE POTTERY	The Royal Exchange
WHITEHAVEN POTTERY	The Ruined Family
JOHN & RICHARD RILEY	The Sacred Tree of the Hindoos at Gyah, Bahar
SAMUEL ALCOCK & CO.	The Sacred Tree of the Hindoos at Gyansohar
JONES & SON	The Seven Bishops Conveyed to the Tower
BELLE VUE POTTERIES	The Shepherd
COPELAND & GARRETT, ET. AL.	The Simplon
JOHN MARSHALL (& CO.)(LTD.)	The Skating Girl
CHESWORTH & ROBINSON	The Social Party
SPODE/COPELAND & GARRETT, et.al.	The Sow and the Wolf
SPODE/COPELAND & GARRETT, et.al.	The Stag Looking into the Water
THOMAS & BENJAMIN GODWIN	The Taj Mahal, Tomb of the Emperor
JOHN ROGERS (& SON)	The Taming of the Shrew, Act 4 Scene 1
POUNTNEY & GOLDNEY	The Taming of the Shrew, Act 4 Scene 1
JOHN ROGERS (& SON)	The Taming of the Shrew, Act 4 Scene 3
POUNTNEY & GOLDNEY	The Taming of the Shrew, Act 4 Scene 3
DOULTON & CO. (LTD.)	The Tempest
JOHN ROGERS (& SON)	The Tempest, Act 1 Scene 2
POUNTNEY & GOLDNEY	The Tempest, Act 1 Scene 2
ANDREW STEVENSON	The Temple of Fame ... To The Memory of Commodore Perry
HENSHALL & CO.	The Temple of Friendship
RALPH STEVENSON	The Three Donkeys
COPELAND & GARRETT, ET. AL.	The Tiber
MELLOR, VENABLES & CO.	The Tomb of Washington, Mount Vernon
JOHN DENTON BAXTER (BAGSTER)	The Topers, et.al.
DAVID METHVEN & SONS	The Turk
SPODE/COPELAND & GARRETT, et.al.	The Turk
SPODE'S BLUE PRINTED WARES	The Turk
WALLIS GIMSON & CO.	The University of Toronto
THOMAS & JOHN CAREY/ JOHN CAREY & SONS	The Upper Lake of Killarney
JAMES & RALPH CLEWS	The Valentine
WILLIAM RIDGWAY (& CO.)	The Valley of the Shenandoah From Jefferson Rock, Pa.
JACOB MARSH	The Village
CHARLES HEATHCOTE & CO.	The Villager
ELIJAH JONES	The Villager
JOHN TURNER / TURNER & CO., etc.	The Villager
WILLIAM DAVENPORT	The Villagers
LEEDS POTTERY	The Wanderer
JOHN & WILLIAM RIDGWAY	The Water Mill, et.al.
JOB & JOHN JACKSON	The Water Works, Philadelphia
JOHN ROGERS (& SON)	The Wheel of Fortune, Act 1 Scene 3
JOHN & WILLIAM RIDGWAY	The Wind Mill, et.al.
WATSON & CO.	The Witch Spinning
SPODE/COPELAND & GARRETT, et.al.	The Wolf and the Crane
SPODE/COPELAND & GARRETT, et.al.	The Wolf and the Lamb
SPODE/COPELAND & GARRETT, et.al.	The Wolf, the Lamb and the Goat
WALLIS GIMSON & CO.	THE WORLD / CANADIAN SCENES- SERIES
RALPH STEVENSON	The Young Bull
ENOCH WOOD & SONS	The Young Philosopher
CORK, EDGE & MALKIN	Theatre
JOHN & WILLIAM RIDGWAY	Theatre Printing House & C., Oxford
F. & R. PRATT & CO. (LTD.)	Theban

CHARLES JAMES MASON & CO.	Thirlmere
RALPH STEVENSON & SON	Thirlmere
DAVID LOCKHART & SONS (LTD.)	Thistle
SPODE/COPELAND & GARRETT, et.al.	Thistle
THOMAS LAKIN	Thistle & Rose
ROWLAND AND MARSELLUS	Thomas Jefferson
RALPH HALL (& CO.) or (& SONS)	Thoresby Park, Nottinghamshire
ENOCH WOOD & SONS	Thornton Castle, Staffordshire
RALPH STEVENSON	Thorps and Sprague, Albany
ROWLAND AND MARSELLUS	Thousand Islands
FERRYBRIDGE POTTERY	Three Chinamen
WILLIAM ADAMS & SON(S) (POTTERS) LTD.	Three Cows
JOHN & WILLIAM RIDGWAY	Three Deer, et.al.
JOHN MEIR	Three Man Willow
ELKIN, KNIGHT & BRIDGWOOD	Three Men in Boat
ENOCH WOOD & SONS	Three People on Overhanging Rock
THOMAS GODWIN	Three Seated Indians
JAMES & RALPH CLEWS	Three Story Building with Columned Entrance on Front and Side
JAMES & RALPH CLEWS	Three Story Building With Curved Drive
JAMES & RALPH CLEWS	Three Story Building With Large Two Story Extension to the Left
JAMES & RALPH CLEWS	Three Story Building, Two Wings and Center Section
WILLIAM DAVENPORT	Three youthful figures seated by the water, bridge and sail boat, et.al.
ENOCH WOOD & SONS	Thrybergh, Yorkshire
COPELAND & GARRETT, ET. AL.	Thun
CAULDON, LTD.	Tiber
THOMAS LAKIN	Tiber
ENOCH WOOD & SONS	Tibetan Musk
JOHN HALL	Tibetan Musk
JOB MEIGH (& SON)	Tiger
ROBINSON, WOOD & BROWNFIELD	Tiger Cages
CARTWRIGHT & EDWARDS (LTD.)	Tiger Hunt
ENOCH WOOD & SONS	Tiger Hunt
JOHN GOODWIN/LONGTON	Tiger Hunt
JOHN GOODWIN/SEACOMBE POTTERY	Tiger Hunt
CLEMENTSON BROS. (LTD.)	Tillenberg
JOSEPH CLEMENTSON	Tillenberg
BRAMELD & CO.	Tilting at Windmills
WILLIAM DAVENPORT	Timber-framed house, cattle and two seated figures, et.al.
COLCLOUGH & CO.	Tine
STANLEY POTTERY LTD.	Tine
DILLWYN & CO.	Tintern Abbey
JOHN & WILLIAM RIDGWAY	Tintern Abbey, et.al.
JAMES & RALPH CLEWS	Tintern Abbey, Monmouthshire
J.W. PANKHURST (& CO.)	Tiny Oak & Acorn
JOHN WEDG WOOD	Tippecanoe
THOMAS & JOHN CAREY/ JOHN CAREY & SONS	TITLED SEATS SERIES
CHARLES MEIGH	Tivoli
CHARLES MEIGH & SON	Tivoli
COPELAND & GARRETT, ET. AL.	Tivoli
DON POTTERY	Tivoli
ENOCH WOOD & SONS	Tivoli
JOHN ROGERS (& SON)	Tivoli
THOMAS FURNIVAL & CO.	Tivoli
WILLIAM ADAMS & SON(S)(POTTERS) LTD.	Tixall, Staffordshire,
JOHN MARSHALL (& CO.)(LTD.)	Toboganners
F. WINKLE & CO. (LTD.)	Togo
HOLLINSHEAD & KIRKHAM (LTD.)	Togo
FORD & SONS (LTD.)	Tokio
J. & M.P. BELL (CO.) & (LTD.)	Tokio
JOHNSON BROS. (HANLEY), LTD.	Tokio
KEELING & CO. (LTD.)	Tokio
SAMUEL FORD & CO.	Tokio
ALFRED MEAKIN (LTD.)	Tokiyo
ROWLAND AND MARSELLUS	Toledo, Ohio
DAVID METHVEN & SONS	Tom Tit
JOHN HALL (& SONS)	Tomb at Jeswunthnagure
THOMAS MAYER	Tomb of Absalom, Village of Siloan
COPELAND & GARRETT, ET. AL.	Tomb of Cecilia Metella
JOHN & WILLIAM RIDGWAY	Tomb of Jeremiah
THOMAS & BENJAMIN GODWIN	Tomb of Jeswuntnagurh
CORK, EDGE & MALKIN	Tomb of Jeswuntnagurth
CORK, EDGE & MALKIN	Tomb of Shere Shah
EDGE, MALKIN & CO. (LTD.)	Tomb of Shere Shah
THOMAS & BENJAMIN GODWIN	Tomb of Shere Shah
JOHN HALL (& SONS)	Tomb of the Emperor Shah Jehan
DON POTTERY	Tomb of Theron at Agrigentum
JAMES KEELING	Tomb of Zobeida ...et.al.
THOMAS FELL (& CO.) (LTD.)	Tomb Pattern
CORK, EDGE & MALKIN	Tombs Near Etaya on the Jumna River
EDGE, MALKIN & CO. (LTD.)	Tombs Near Etaya on the Jumna River
THOMAS & BENJAMIN GODWIN	Tombs Near Etaya on the Jumna River
JOHN HALL (& SONS)	Tombs of Etaya
JOHN & WILLIAM RIDGWAY	Tong Castle, Shropshire
ARTHUR J. WILKINSON (LTD.)	Tonquin
CLEMENTSON & YOUNG	Tonquin
CLOSE & CO.	Tonquin
JOHN CARR (& CO.) (& SON(S)	Tonquin
JOHN MEIR & SON	Tonquin
JOSEPH HEATH	Tonquin
NEWPORT POTTERY CO. LTD.	Tonquin
SAMUEL ALCOCK & CO.	Tonquin
WILLIAM ADAMS & CO. LTD.	Tonquin
MARSH & WILLETT	Top Piper
ROWLAND AND MARSELLUS	Topeka, Kan.
BISHOP & STONIER (LTD.)	Torbay
COLCLOUGH & CO.	Torbex
STANLEY POTTERY LTD.	Torbex
CHARLES ALLERTON & SONS	Toro
GEORGE JONES (& SONS LTD.)	Toro
PODMORE, WALKER (& CO.)	Toronto
SAMUEL ALCOCK & CO.	Toronto
ROWLAND AND MARSELLUS	Toronto, Canada
JOHN THOMAS HUDDEN	Toulon Pattern
COLCLOUGH & CO.	Touraine
HENRY ALCOCK & CO. (LTD.)	Touraine
NEW WHARF POTTERY CO.	Touraine
STANLEY POTTERY LTD.	Touraine
SEWELL(S) & CO.	Tourist
WILLIAM SMITH (& CO.)	Tourist
MOORE (SAMUEL) & CO.	Tournament
BROWN WESTHEAD, MOORE & CO.	Tournay
T. & R. BOOTE (LTD.) (& SON)	Tournay
COPELAND & GARRETT, ET. AL.	Tower
MAYER(BROS.)& ELLIOT	Tower
SPODE/COPELAND & GARRETT, et.al.	Tower
SPODE'S BLUE PRINTED WARES	Tower
JOSIAH WEDGWOOD (& SONS LTD.)	Tower of London
COPELAND & GARRETT, ET. AL.	Tower of Lucano
WOOD & CHALLINOR	Tower of Mauconseil
JOHN ROGERS (& SON)	Toy Chinamen Chinoiserie
JOHN DENTON BAXTER (BAGSTER)	Toy Plate
JOHNSON BROS. (HANLEY), LTD.	Tracery
JOHN WEDG WOOD	Trafalgar
THOMAS FELL (& CO.) (LTD.)	Trafik
JOHN MADDOCK & SONS (LTD.)	Trailing Ivy
ENOCH WOOD & SONS	Transylvania University, Lexington, KY
JOHN & WILLIAM TURNER	Traveler & Duck
WILLIAM DAVENPORT	Traveler and Woman
WILLIAM DAVENPORT	Traveler with bundle of sticks, dog, cottage and two standing figures, et.al.
MINTON & CO.	Travelers
G.L. ASHWORTH & BROS. (LTD.)	Tree of Life
RIDGWAY, SPARKS & RIDGWAY	Tree Of Life
CORK & EDGE	Tree Trunk With Ivy
WILLIAM DAVENPORT	Tree, Mansion & Cows
ENOCH WOOD & SONS	TREFOIL BORDER SERIES
FORD & SONS (LTD.)	Trellis
W.H. GRINDLEY & CO. (LTD.)	Trellis
RALPH HALL (& CO.) or (& SONS)	Trematon Castle
BRADLEY & CO.	Trench Mortar
FERRYBRIDGE POTTERY	Trench Mortar
SPODE'S BLUE PRINTED WARES	Trench Mortar
BISHOP & STONIER (LTD.)	Trent
NEW WHARF POTTERY CO.	Trent
HENRY ALCOCK & CO. (LTD.)	Trent Shape
JOHN ALCOCK	Trent Shape
FORD & SONS (LTD.)	Trent, I
WOOD & SON(S) (LTD.)	Trent, I
WOOD & SON(S) (LTD.)	Trent, II
FORD & SONS (LTD.)	Trent, II
BROWN WESTHEAD, MOORE & CO.	Trentham
J.H. WEATHERBY & SONS (LTD.)	Trentham
T. RATHBONE & CO.	Trentham
CHARLES JAMES MASON & CO.	Trentham Hall
ENOCH WOOD & SONS	Trenton Falls
ENOCH WOOD & SONS	Trenton Falls, View of
ENOCH WOOD & SONS	Trenton Falls, View of / Catskill House
ROWLAND AND MARSELLUS	Trenton, N.J.
WILLIAM DAVENPORT	Trewkers and dogs
ROWLAND AND MARSELLUS	Trexlertown, Pa.
NEALE (JAMES) & CO.	Trial Plate
JOHNSON BROS. (HANLEY), LTD.	Trieste, The
WOOD & SON(S) (LTD.)	Trilby
JOHN & WILLIAM RIDGWAY	Trinity College, Oxford
JOHN & WILLIAM RIDGWAY	Trinity Hall, Cambridge
JAMES EDWARDS	Triple Border Shape
BROWN WESTHEAD, MOORE & CO.	Tripod
THOMAS DIMMOCK (JR.) & CO.	Tripod
JOHN RIDGWAY (& CO.)	Tripoli
W.H. GRINDLEY & CO. (LTD.)	Triumph
JOHN MADDOCK & SONS (LTD.)	Triumph
JOHN THOMSON (& SONS)	Triumphal
J. & M.P. BELL (CO.) & (LTD.)	Triumphal Car

JAMES JAMIESON & CO.	Triumphal Car
R. COCHRAN & CO. - VERREVILLE POTTERY	Triumphal Car
J. & M.P. BELL (CO.) & (LTD.)	Trojan
SPODE'S BLUE PRINTED WARES	Trophies - Dagger
SPODE'S BLUE PRINTED WARES	Trophies - Etruscan
SPODE'S BLUE PRINTED WARES	Trophies - Marble
SPODE'S BLUE PRINTED WARES	Trophies - Nankin
GEORGE HARRISON (& CO.)	Trophies-Dagger
JOSIAH WEDGWOOD (& SONS LTD.)	Trophy
MINTON	Trophy
FERRYBRIDGE POTTERY	Trotting Chariot
CHARLES MEIGH	Troy
W.H. GRINDLEY & CO. (LTD.)	Troy
JAMES & RALPH CLEWS	Troy From Mount Ida
ANDREW STEVENSON	Troy From Mt. Ida
ENOCH WOOD & SONS	Troy Line, Steamboat
ROWLAND AND MARSELLUS	Troy, N.Y.
E. & C. CHALLINOR	True Scallop
JAMES EDWARDS	True Scallop
JAMES EDWARDS & SON	True Scallop
JOHN ALCOCK	True Scallop
ELSMORE & FORSTER	Trumpet Flower
ELSMORE & FORSTER	Trumpet Flower Variant
JOSEPH CLEMENTSON	Trumpet Vine
LIDDLE, ELLIOT & SON	Trumpet VineShape
MINTON & CO.	Truro
DAVID METHVEN & SONS	Tudor
JOHN MADDOCK	Tudor
JOHN MADDOCK & SONS (LTD.)	Tudor
WILLIAM DAVENPORT	Tudor Cottage
WILLIAM DAVENPORT	Tudor Mansion
GIBSON & SONS (LTD.)	Tulip
MINTON	Tulip
SPODE/COPELAND & GARRETT, et.al.	Tulip
THOMAS TILL & SONS	Tulip
ELSMORE & FORSTER	Tulip & Sprig
THOMAS WALKER	Tulip & Sprig
POWELL & BISHOP	Tulip Border
ELSMORE & FORSTER	Tulip Shape
JOHNSON BROS. (HANLEY), LTD.	Tulip,
J. & M.P. BELL (CO.) & (LTD.)	Tullibardine
SPODE/COPELAND & GARRETT, et.al.	Tumble Down Dick
SPODE'S BLUE PRINTED WARES	Tumbledown Dick
ANDREW STEVENSON	Tunbridge Castle, Surrey
SPODE/COPELAND & GARRETT, et.al.	Turco
ENOCH WOOD & SONS	Turin
JOHNSON BROS. (HANLEY), LTD.	Turin
DOULTON & CO. (LTD.)	Turkey
RIDGWAYS (BEDFORD WORKS) LTD.	Turkey
CAULDON, LTD.	Turkey, Wild
WILLIAM DAVENPORT	Turkish Archer
SPODE'S BLUE PRINTED WARES	Turkish Castle
JAMES KEELING	Turkish Coffee-House...et.al.
MINTON	Turkish Figure
WILLIAM SMITH (& CO.)	Turkish Pavilion
SUNDERLAND OR "GARRISON" POTTERY	Turkish Pavillion
JOHN TURNER / TURNER & CO., etc.	Turner's Windmill
SPODE/COPELAND & GARRETT, et.al.	Tuscan
JAMES & RALPH CLEWS	Tuscan Rose
JOB & JOHN JACKSON	Tuscan Rose
JOHN & WILLIAM RIDGWAY	Tuscan Rose
JOHN EDWARDS (& CO.)	Tuscan Shape
HENSHALL & CO.	Tweekenham, Surrey
ANTHONY SHAW (& SON(S) (& CO.)	Twelve Paneled Gothic
JOHN VENABLES & CO.	Twelve Paneled Gothic Shape
JOHN VENABLES & CO.	Twelve Paneled Gothic Shape
VENABLES, MANN & CO.	Twelve Paneled Gothic Shape
THOMAS WOLFE(S)	Twig Basket
HOPE & CARTER	Twin Leaves
JAMES EDWARDS	Twin Leaves Shape
THOMAS LAKIN	Twin Obelisks
JAMES EDWARDS & SON	Twisted Ribbon
BRAMELD & CO.	Twisted Tree
JAMES REED	Twisted Tree
JOHN ROGERS (& SON)	Two Castles
JOHN MARSHALL (& CO.)(LTD.)	Two Children on Sled
WILLIAM DAVENPORT	Two Cows
JOHN & RICHARD RILEY	Two Cows and a Donkey
LEEDS POTTERY	Two Cows in a Ruined Abbey, et.al.
JOSIAH WEDGWOOD (& SONS LTD.)	Two Crested Exotic Birds
JOHN CORMIE	Two Exotic Birds on a Flowering Tree
WILLIAM SMITH (& CO.)	Two Exotic Crested Birds
LEEDS POTTERY	Two Figure Pattern
BRADLEY & CO.	Two Figures
J (JOSHUA) HEATH	Two Figures
SPODE'S BLUE PRINTED WARES	Two Figures I
SPODE'S BLUE PRINTED WARES	Two Figures II
JACOB FURNIVAL & CO.	Two Fish
WILLIAM DAVENPORT	Two fishermen, two large spreading trees, bridge with ornamental wall, et.al.
JOHN ROGERS (& SON)	Two Gentlemen of Verona, Act 5 Scene 4
POUNTNEY & GOLDNEY	Two Gentlemen of Verona, Act 5 Scene 4
HERCULANEUM POTTERY	Two Hunters and Two Pointers Flushing Birds
INDEO POTTERY	Two Kilns
RALPH STEVENSON	TWO MEDALLION BORDER SERIES
RALPH STEVENSON & WILLIAMS	TWO MEDALLION BORDER SERIES
THOMAS GODWIN	Two Men By a Sledge With Covered Long Boats, et.al.
HERCULANEUM POTTERY	Two Men Fishing Below Falls, Mill in Background
LEEDS POTTERY	Two Men on a Bridge, et.al.
CHETHAM & WOOLLEY	Two Men on Bridge
WILLIAM DAVENPORT	Two men on horseback talking to a woman, et.al.
ELKIN, KNIGHT & BRIDGWOOD	Two Men on Rocks
JOHN TURNER / TURNER & CO., etc.	Two Men Willow
THOMAS GODWIN	Two Men, One Aiming His Rifle and Two Dogs, et.al.
HERCULANEUM POTTERY	Two Men, Two Arches
ANTHONY SHAW (& SON(S) (& CO.)	Two Officers on Horse, et.al.
CHETHAM & WOOLLEY	Two Part Willow
ANDREW STEVENSON	TWO PORTRAIT MEDALLION BORDER SERIES
JOB MEIGH (& SON)	Two Rabbits
WILLIAM DAVENPORT	Two riders
SPODE/COPELAND & GARRETT, et.al.	Two Satyrs
WILLIAM DAVENPORT	Two seated and two standing cows and seated man, et.al.
JAMES & RALPH CLEWS	Two Story Mansion, Small Extension onto Left
HENSHALL & CO.	Two Story Structure with two Apparently Central Chimney Stacks
SHORTHOUSE & CO.	Two Swans
BRADLEY & CO.	Two Temples
DAVIS, COOKSON & WILSON	Two Temples
DON POTTERY	Two Temples
INDEO POTTERY	Two Temples
JOSIAH WEDGWOOD (& SONS LTD.)	Two Temples
WILLIAM MASON	Two Temples
WILLIAM REID (& SON) or (SONS)	Two Temples
SPODE'S BLUE PRINTED WARES	Two Temples I
KEELING & CO. (LTD.)	Two Temples II
SPODE'S BLUE PRINTED WARES	Two Temples II
JAMES & RALPH CLEWS	Two Temples... Clews Willow
JOHN RIDGWAY (& CO.)	Two Vases
ENOCH WOOD & SONS	Two Whippets
G.M. & C.J. MASON	Two-Man Chinoiserie
SAMPSON BRIDGWOOD (& SON)(LTD.)	Tycoon
WILLIAM BROWNFIELD (& SON(S))	Tycoon
SAMPSON BRIDGWOOD (& SON)(LTD.)	Tyne
HOLLINSHEAD & KIRKHAM (LTD.)	Tyrian
THOMAS GOODFELLOW	Tyrian
WILLIAM SMITH (& CO.)	Tyrian
JOHN & GEORGE ALCOCK	Tyrol
JOHN WEDG WOOD	Tyrol
WILLIAM DAVENPORT	Tyrol Hunters
RIDGWAYS (BEDFORD WORKS) LTD.	Tyrolean
WILLIAM RIDGWAY (& CO.)	Tyrolean
WILLIAM RIDGWAY (& CO.)	Tyrolean Scene
CLYDE POTTERY CO. (LTD.)	Tyrolese
WILLIAM ADAMS & SON(S)(POTTERS) LTD.	U.S. VIEWS SERIES
JOSEPH CLEMENTSON	Udina
CHARLES JAMES MASON & CO.	Ullswater
RALPH STEVENSON & SON	Ullswater
ENOCH WOOD & SONS	Ulster Terrace, Regent's Park
JOSEPH CLEMENTSON	Ulysses at the Table of Circe
JOSEPH CLEMENTSON	Ulysses Following the Car of Nausicaa
JOSEPH CLEMENTSON	Ulysses Weeps at the Song of Demodocus
WILLIAM RIDGWAY, SON & CO.	Undercliff Near Cold Spring
WILLIAM RIDGWAY (& CO.)	Undercliff Near Cold Spring, N.Y.
ROBINSON, WOOD & BROWNFIELD	Unidentified Birds
ANDREW STEVENSON	Unidentified View
EDWARD CHALLINOR	Union
MELLOR, VENABLES & CO.	Union
SPODE/COPELAND & GARRETT, et.al.	Union
VENABLES & BAINES	Union
WILLIAM RIDGWAY, SON & CO.	Union
JOHN & RICHARD RILEY	UNION BORDER SERIES
COPELAND & GARRETT, ET. AL.	Union Club
ENOCH WOOD & SONS	Union Line
JOHN & WILLIAM RIDGWAY	Union Medallions
DAVENPORT'S & CO.	Union Shape
JOHN WEDG WOOD	Union Shape
T. & R. BOOTE (LTD.) (& SON)	Union Shape
WILLIAM DAVENPORT	Union Shape
SPODE'S BLUE PRINTED WARES	Union Wreath I
SPODE'S BLUE PRINTED WARES	Union Wreath II
SPODE'S BLUE PRINTED WARES	Union Wreath III
BEECH & HANCOCK	Unique
W.H. GRINDLEY & CO. (LTD.)	Unique
R.S. KIDSTON & CO. - VERREVILLE	UNITED KINGDOM SERIES
TAMS / et.al.	United States Hotel, Philadelphia
WILLIAM ADAMS & SON(S) (POTTERS) LTD.	United States View
DILLWYN & CO.	Unity
JOHN RIDGWAY (& CO.)	University

JOB & JOHN JACKSON	University Hall, Harvard, Massachusetts
ROWLAND AND MARSELLUS	University of Pennsylvania
WILLIAM SMITH (& CO.)	Unnamed Pattern for German Market
WILLIAM SMITH (& CO.)	Unnamed Religious Pattern
THOMAS & JOHN CAREY/ JOHN CAREY & SONS	UNNAMED SERIES
ENOCH WOOD & SONS	Unrecorded View
JOB & JOHN JACKSON	Upper Ferry Bridge Over the River Schuylkill
JOSEPH STUBBS	Upper Ferry Bridge Over the River Schuylkill
COPELAND & GARRETT, ET. AL.	Upside Down Bird
RALPH STEVENSON & WILLIAMS	URN BORDER
ELKIN, KNIGHT & BRIDGWOOD	Urn on Column
ANDREW STEVENSON	URN-BORDER AND SCROLL BORDER SERIES
WILLIAM ADAMS & SON(S)(POTTERS) LTD.	Urns, Scrolls & Flowers
WILLIAM RIDGWAY, SON & CO.	Utica
CHARLES MEIGH	Utica, N.Y.
THOMAS GODWIN	Utica, N.Y.
POUNTNEY & CO. (LTD.)	Utopia
HENSHALL & CO.	Vae House
JOB & JOHN JACKSON	Valencia
SAMPSON HANCOCK (& SONS)	Valencia
CHARLES MEIGH	Valenciennes
ENOCH WOOD & SONS	Valenciennes
JOHN HAWLEY & CO.	Valetta
RALPH HALL (& CO.) or (& SONS)	Valley Crusis Abbey, Wales
ROWLAND AND MARSELLUS	Valley Forge
ROWLAND AND MARSELLUS	Valley Forge ... Summer
ROWLAND AND MARSELLUS	Valley Forge 1777-78, Washington's Headquarters
ROWLAND AND MARSELLUS	Valley Forge... Winter
WILLIAM RIDGWAY, SON & CO.	Valley of Wyoming
SAMUEL ALCOCK & CO.	Van Dyke
JOHN ROGERS (& SON)	Van Huysun' s
SPODE'S BLUE PRINTED WARES	Vandyke
ALFRED MEAKIN (LTD.)	Vane
ELSMORE & FORSTER	Vaquero
RALPH HALL	Variety
COPELAND & GARRETT, ET. AL.	Varina
HULME, JOHN & SONS	Vas Floreat
EDWARD CHALLINOR	Vase
JOHN ROGERS (& SON)	Vase
SOUTHWICK POTTERY	Vase
JOHN ROGERS (& SON)	Vase & Fence
SPODE/COPELAND & GARRETT, et.al.	Vase & Peony
ANDREW STEVENSON	Vase Acanthus
WILLIAM SMITH (& CO.)	Vase and Books
WILLIAM DAVENPORT	Vase of Flowers
WILLIAM DAVENPORT	Vase on a Wall
WILLIAM DAVENPORT	Vase on the Bridge
J. & M.P. BELL (CO.) & (LTD.)	Vases
ROWLAND AND MARSELLUS	Vassar College
HERCULANEUM POTTERY	Vatican
SAMUEL ALCOCK & CO.	Velarian
SPODE/COPELAND & GARRETT, et.al.	Venetia
WILLIAM DAVENPORT	Venetian Meeting
ENOCH WOOD & SONS	Venetian Scenery
ROBINSON & WOOD	Venetian Scenery
WILLIAM ADAMS & CO. LTD.	Venetian Scenery
WILLIAM ADAMS & SON(S) (POTTERS) LTD.	Venetian Temple
BISHOP & STONIER (LTD.)	Venice
BURGESS & LEIGH (LTD.)	Venice
COPELAND & GARRETT, ET. AL.	Venice
ENOCH WOOD & SONS	Venice
GRIMWADE BROS.	Venice
JOHN & ROBERT GODWIN	Venice
JOHNSON BROS. (HANLEY), LTD.	Venice
PINDER BOURNE & HOPE	Venice
SOHO POTTERY (LTD.)	Venice
UPPER HANLEY POTTERY CO. (LTD.)	Venice
WALLIS GIMSON & CO.	Venice
WOOD & SON(S) (LTD.)	Venice
JOHN & ROBERT GODWIN	Venice #125
RALPH HAMMERSLEY (& SON(S)	Venture
PODMORE, WALKER (& CO.)	Venus
THOMAS TILL & SONS	Venus
WEDGWOOD & CO. (LTD.)	Venus
PITCAIRNS LTD.	Vera
RALPH HALL & CO.	Veranda
D.J. EVANS & CO.	Verandah
JOHN MADDOCK & SONS (LTD.)	Verano
BELLE VUE POTTERIES	Vermicelli
JOSIAH WEDGWOOD (& SONS LTD.)	Vermicelli
WILLIAM RIDGWAY (& CO.)	Vermicelli
WILLIAM RIDGWAY, SON & CO.	Vermicelli
DON POTTERY	VERMICELLI BORDER SERIES
BURGESS & LEIGH (LTD.)	Vermont
ALFRED MEAKIN (LTD.)	Vernon
DOULTON & CO. (LTD.)	Vernon
ALFRED MEAKIN (LTD.)	Verona
CHARLES MEIGH	Verona
CORK, EDGE & MALKIN	Verona
DAVID LOCKHART & SONS (LTD.)	Verona
DAVID METHVEN & SONS	Verona
EDGE, MALKIN & CO. (LTD.)	Verona
EDWARD CHALLINOR	Verona
FORD & SONS (LTD.)	Verona
GEORGE PHILLIPS	Verona
LOCKHART & ARTHUR	Verona
MINTON	Verona
NEW WHARF POTTERY CO.	Verona
RIDGWAYS (BEDFORD WORKS) LTD.	Verona
WOOD & SON(S) (LTD.)	Verona
CHARLES MEIGH	Veronese
DOULTON & CO. (LTD.)	Veronica
CORK, EDGE & MALKIN	Versaille
BATKIN, WALKER & BROADHURST	Versailles
JOHN GOODWIN/LONGTON	Versailles
ROBINSON, WOOD & BROWNFIELD	Versailles
THOMAS FURNIVAL & SONS	Versailles
THOMAS GODWIN	Versailles
WILLIAM DAVENPORT	Versailles
THOMAS GODWIN	Versatility
ENOCH WOOD & SONS	Vesuvius
HENSHALL & CO.	Vevay, Indiana
J. H. & J. DAVIS	Victor
JOHN MADDOCK & SONS (LTD.)	Victor
T. RATHBONE & CO.	Victor
THOMAS BOOTH & CO.	Victor
FREDERICK JONES (& CO.)	Victor Shape
CLYDE POTTERY CO. (LTD.)	Victoria
DIMMOCK & SMITH	Victoria
G.L. ASHWORTH & BROS. (LTD.)	Victoria
JAMES F. WILEMAN	Victoria
JOHN RIDGWAY (& CO.)	Victoria
SAMUEL ALCOCK & CO.	Victoria
UPPER HANLEY POTTERY CO. (LTD.)	Victoria
W.H. GRINDLEY & CO. (LTD.)	Victoria
WOOD & SON(S) (LTD.)	Victoria
J. & M.P. BELL (CO.) & (LTD.)	Victoria Regia
J. & M.P. BELL (CO.) & (LTD.)	Victoria Scroll
E. & C. CHALLINOR	Victorian Beauty
THOMAS MAYER	Victors Crowned
W.H. GRINDLEY & CO. (LTD.)	Victory
JAMES & RALPH CLEWS	Victory or Apotheosis of Nelson
ELSMORE & FORSTER	Victory Shape
JOHN EDWARDS (& CO.)	Victory Shape
WOOD & CHALLINOR	Viege
CLEMENTSON BROS. (LTD.)	Vienna
JOHNSON BROS. (HANLEY), LTD.	Vienna
THOMAS DIMMOCK (JR.) & CO.	Vienna
JOSEPH STUBBS	View at Hurl Gate, East River
GOODWINS & HARRIS	View From Blackheath
JAMES & RALPH CLEWS	View From Governors' Island
MELLOR, VENABLES & CO.	View From Gowanus Heights, Brooklyn
JAMES & RALPH CLEWS	View From Jessup's Landing, Hudson River
CHARLES MEIGH	View From Mount Ida, N.Y.
WILLIAM RIDGWAY (& CO.)	View From Port [Fort] Putnam, Hudson River
WILLIAM RIDGWAY (& CO.)	View From Ruggle's House, Newburgh, Hudson River
JAMES & RALPH CLEWS	View in Clencyle
WILLIAM DAVENPORT	View in Geneva
DON POTTERY	View in Palma
HERCULANEUM POTTERY	View in the Fort Madura
WILLIAM WALSH	View in the Fort, Madura
DON POTTERY	View in the Valley of Oretho Near Palermo
POUNTNEY & ALLIES	View Near Bristol, River Avon
ANDREW STEVENSON	View Near Catskill on the Hudson River
WILLIAM DAVENPORT	View Near Colnebrook
GOODWINS & HARRIS	View Near Colnebrook... sic
WILLIAM ADAMS & SON(S)(POTTERS) LTD.	View Near Conway, N. Hampshire, U.S.
ENOCH WOOD & SONS	View Near Florence
WILLIAM ADAMS & SON(S)(POTTERS) LTD.	View Near Sandy Hill, Hudson River
DON POTTERY	View Near Taormina
GOODWINS & HARRIS	View Near Twickenham
DON POTTERY	View of Alicata
MELLOR, VENABLES & CO.	View of Baltimore
JAMES KEELING	View of Birs Nimroud
DON POTTERY	View of Camping and Carting
DON POTTERY	View of Canada
JAMES KEELING	View of Clare College, Cambridge
DON POTTERY	View of Corigliano
ENOCH WOOD & SONS	View of Dublin
GOODWINS & HARRIS	View of Eton Chapel
ANDREW STEVENSON	View of Governor's Island
ENOCH WOOD & SONS	View of Greenwich
GOODWINS & HARRIS	View of Greenwich
MELLOR, VENABLES & CO.	View of Hudson City and the Catskill Mountains
ENOCH WOOD & SONS	View of Liverpool
JOHN GOODWIN/LONGTON	View of London
THOMAS & BENJAMIN GODWIN	View of London
JOHN GOODWIN/SEACOMBE POTTERY	VIEW OF LONDON SERIES
MELLOR, VENABLES & CO.	View of Mount Vernon

ANDREW STEVENSON	View of New York From Weehawken
MELLOR, VENABLES & CO.	View of New York From Weehawken
JOB & JOHN JACKSON	View of Newburgh
JOB & JOHN JACKSON	View of Newburgh, et.al.
DON POTTERY	View of Part of Mont Peloet in Sicily
ENOCH WOOD & SONS	View of Richmond
GOODWINS & HARRIS	View of Richmond
DON POTTERY	View of Stromboli from the part facing to the Northeast
DON POTTERY	View of Temple on the Hill
ENOCH WOOD & SONS	View of the Aqueduct Bridge at Little Falls
JOB & JOHN JACKSON	View of the Canal, Little Falls, Mohawk River
MELLOR, VENABLES & CO.	View of the Capitol at Washington
WILLIAM RIDGWAY (& CO.)	View of The Capitol at Washington
WILLIAM RIDGWAY, SON & CO.	View of the Capitol at Washington
JOB & JOHN JACKSON	View of the Catskill Mountain House, N.Y.
DON POTTERY	View of the Cave of the Goats on Etna
DON POTTERY	View of the Countryside at Agrigento
WILLIAM DAVENPORT	View of the Imperial Park at Gehol
DON POTTERY	View of the Rocks or Cape of Scarletia
DON POTTERY	View of the Ruins of the Temple of Juno at Agrigento
DON POTTERY	View of the Tower Pulicoro on the Gulf of Tarento
WILLIAM ADAMS & SON(S)(POTTERS) LTD.	View of Whitby
ENOCH WOOD & SONS	View of Worcester
RALPH STEVENSON	View on the Ganges
ANDREW STEVENSON	View On the Road to Lake George
FRANCIS MORLEY (& CO.)	View on the St. Lawrence,
WILLIAM DAVENPORT	View on the Thames
JOHN & WILLIAM RIDGWAY	Views in Cambridge
JOHN & WILLIAM RIDGWAY	Views in Caramania
JOHN & WILLIAM RIDGWAY	Views In Oxford:
ROWLAND AND MARSELLUS	Views of Atlantic City, N.J.
JAMES KEELING	VIEWS OF MESOPOTAMIA SERIES
J. DIMMOCK & CO.	Vignette
THOMAS DIMMOCK (JR.) & CO.	Vignette
JOHN DENTON BAXTER (BAGSTER)	VIGNETTE SERIES
JOHN RIDGWAY (& CO.)	Villa
MINTON & CO.	Villa
RALPH STEVENSON	Villa
WILLIAM RIDGWAY (& CO.)	Villa
WILLIAM RIDGWAY, SON & CO.	Villa
ENOCH WOOD & SONS	Villa Borghese, Near Florence
MOORE (SAMUEL) & CO.	Villa D'Este
ENOCH WOOD & SONS	Villa in the Regent's Park, London
WILLIAM ADAMS	Villa in the Regent's Park, London
ENOCH WOOD & SONS	Villa on the Coast of Posilepo
DALTON & BURN	Villa Scenery
DEAKIN & BAILEY	Villa Scenery
MINTON	Village
THOMAS & BENJAMIN GODWIN	Village and Pagoda on the Ganges
DAVID DUNDERDALE & CO.	Village Church
JAMES & RALPH CLEWS	Village Church
THOMAS DIMMOCK (JR.) & CO.	Village Church
JAMES & WILLIAM HANDLEY	Village Fisherman
JOHN & WILLIAM RIDGWAY	Village Fishermen, et.al.
WILLIAM RIDGWAY, SON & CO.	Village of Catskill, N.Y.
PODMORE, WALKER (& CO.)	Village of Cedars
FRANCIS MORLEY (& CO.)	Village of Cedars, River
THOMAS GODWIN	Village of Cedars, St. Lawrence
MELLOR, VENABLES & CO.	Village of Little Falls
CHARLES MEIGH	Village of Little Falls, N.Y.
SPODE'S BLUE PRINTED WARES	Village Scene
DILLWYN & CO.	Villager
JOHN TURNER / TURNER & CO., etc.	Villager Pattern
WILLIAM DAVENPORT	Villaris
JAMES MAC INTYRE (& CO.) (LTD.)	Vinagrette
JOHN & SAMUEL ALCOCK (JR.)	Vincennes
JOHN ALCOCK	Vincennes
BAKER, BEVANS & IRWIN	Vine
C.T. MALING & SONS (LTD.)	Vine
HENRY ALCOCK & CO. (LTD.)	Vine
JAMES EDWARDS	Vine
JOHN & ROBERT GODWIN	Vine
JOHN ROGERS (& SON)	Vine
JOSIAH WEDGWOOD (& SONS LTD.)	Vine
T. & J. BEVINGTON (& CO.)	Vine
WEDGWOOD & CO. (LTD.)	Vine
WILLIAM DAVENPORT	Vine
J. & M.P. BELL (CO.) & (LTD.)	Vine Border
RALPH STEVENSON	VINE BORDER
RALPH STEVENSON & WILLIAMS	VINE BORDER
WILLIAM DAVENPORT	Vine Border
RALPH STEVENSON	VINE BORDER SERIES
WILTSHAW & ROBINSON (LTD.)	Vine Flowers
RALPH STEVENSON	VINE LEAF
WILLIAM DAVENPORT	Vineyard Shape
GEORGE FREDERICK BOWERS (& CO.)	Vintage
JAMES EDWARDS & SON	Vintage
JOHN & GEORGE ALCOCK	Vintage
JOHN MEIR & SON	Vintage
JOHN RIDGWAY (& CO.)	Vintage
ANTHONY SHAW (& SON(S) (& CO.)	Vintage Beauty
E. & C. CHALLINOR	Vintage Shape
WILLIAM ADAMS & SON(S)(POTTERS) LTD.	Vintage Shape
WOOD & BAGGALEY	Viola
WOOD & BARKER LTD.	Viola
SPODE/COPELAND & GARRETT, et.al.	Violet
WEDGWOOD & CO. (LTD.)	Violet
BRADLEY & CO.	Violin
DAVID DUNDERDALE & CO.	Violin
J (JOSHUA) HEATH	Violin
THOMAS HARLEY	Violin
DOULTON & CO. (LTD.)	Virginia
ENOCH WOOD	Virginia
J. & G. MEAKIN	Virginia
JAMES & RALPH CLEWS	Virginia
JOHN & WILLIAM RIDGWAY	Virginia
JOHN MADDOCK & SONS (LTD.)	Virginia
LOCKHART & ARTHUR	Virginia
JAMES & RALPH CLEWS	Virginia Monument
BROUGHAM & MAYER	Virginia Shape
RALPH STEVENSON	Virginia Water
THOMAS MAYER	Virginia, Arms of
COPELAND & GARRETT, ET. AL.	Virtus Vera Nobilitas
JOSEPH CLEMENTSON	Viscount Clive Attaining His Majority, Nov. 1839
FRANCIS MORLEY (& CO.)	Vista
G.L. ASHWORTH & BROS. (LTD.)	Vista
WILLIAM RIDGWAY (& CO.)	Vista De La Habana
BROWN WESTHEAD, MOORE & CO.	Volante
DOULTON & CO. (LTD.)	Volga-Villa
ENOCH WOOD & SONS	Vue D'Une Ancienne Abbaye
ENOCH WOOD & SONS	Vue De La Porte Romaine Andernac
ENOCH WOOD & SONS	Vue Du Temple De La Philosophie, Ermenonville
ENOCH WOOD & SONS	Vue Prise Aux Environs De Francfort
ENOCH WOOD & SONS	Vue Prise En Savoie
JOHN & WILLIAM RIDGWAY	Wadham College, Oxford
ANDREW STEVENSON	Wadsworth Tower
ENOCH WOOD & SONS	Wadsworth Tower
JOB & JOHN JACKSON	Wadsworth Tower
JOHN MEIR	Wakefield Lodge, Warwickshire
SAMPSON HANCOCK (& SONS)	Walbeck
NEW WHARF POTTERY CO.	Waldorf
SAMPSON HANCOCK (& SONS)	Waldorf
WOOD & SON(S) (LTD.)	Waldorf
JACOB FURNIVAL & CO.	Walled Octagon
ELIJAH HUGHES & CO.	Walmer
CHARLES JAMES MASON & CO.	Walnut Tree Court
ANDREW STEVENSON	Walsingham Priory, Norfolk
GOODWINS & HARRIS	Waltham Cross
ROWLAND AND MARSELLUS	Waltham Watch Co.
FORD & SONS (LTD.)	Walton
DOULTON & CO. (LTD.)	Wanderer
DUDSON BROS.	Wanderer
JOHN & WILLIAM RIDGWAY	Wanstead House in Essex
ANDREW STEVENSON	Wanstead House, Essex
ENOCH WOOD & SONS	Wardour Castle, Wiltshire
JAMES & RALPH CLEWS	Warkworth Castle, Northumberland
RALPH HALL (& CO.) or (& SONS)	Warleigh House, Somersetshire
WILLIAM ADAMS & SON(S)(POTTERS) LTD.	Warleigh House, Somersetshire
ELKIN & CO.	Warren
JOHN RIDGWAY (& CO.)	Warwick
JOHNSON BROS. (HANLEY), LTD.	Warwick
PODMORE, WALKER (& CO.)	Warwick
SAMPSON HANCOCK (& SONS)	Warwick
ELKIN & CO.	Warwick Castle
ENOCH WOOD & SONS	Warwick Castle
SPODE/COPELAND & GARRETT, et.al.	Warwick Groups
ELKIN & CO.	Warwick Vase
ELKIN & NEWBON	Warwick Vase
ENOCH WOOD & SONS	Warwick Vase
J. & M.P. BELL (CO.) & (LTD.)	Warwick Vase
SPODE/COPELAND & GARRETT, et.al.	Warwick Vase
SPODE'S BLUE PRINTED WARES	Warwick Vase/Groups
ALFRED MEAKIN (LTD.)	Washington
CHARLES MEIGH	Washington
CLEMENTSON & YOUNG	Washington
CLYDE POTTERY CO. (LTD.)	Washington
ENOCH WOOD & SONS	Washington
JAMES & RALPH CLEWS	Washington
RALPH STEVENSON	Washington
RALPH STEVENSON & WILLIAMS	Washington
THOMAS WALKER	Washington
WILLIAM DAVENPORT	Washington
RALPH STEVENSON & WILLIAMS	Washington & Clinton
RALPH STEVENSON & WILLIAMS	Washington & Lafayette

RALPH STEVENSON	Washington & Clinton
RALPH STEVENSON	Washington & Jefferson
RALPH STEVENSON & WILLIAMS	Washington & Jefferson
ANDREW STEVENSON	Washington & Lafayette
RALPH STEVENSON	Washington & Lafayette
ROWLAND AND MARSELLUS	Washington at Prayer, Valley Forge
RALPH STEVENSON	Washington Capitol
ROWLAND AND MARSELLUS	Washington Crossing the Delaware
JOHN MEIR & SON	Washington Shape
POWELL & BISHOP	Washington Shape
ENOCH WOOD & SONS	Washington Standing at His Tomb, Scroll in Hand
PODMORE, WALKER (& CO.)	Washington Vase
THOMAS MAYER	Washington(s)Tomb
ROWLAND AND MARSELLUS	Washington, D.C.
WILLIAM DAVENPORT	Washington, District of Columbia
WILLIAM RIDGWAY, SON & CO.	Washington's Tomb
MELLOR, VENABLES & CO.	Washington's House, Mount Vernon
JAMES & RALPH CLEWS	Water Girl
MINTON & CO.	Water Lilies
CHARLES COLLINSON & CO.	Water Lily
COPELAND & GARRETT, ET. AL.	Water Lily
JOHN PRATT & CO. LTD.	Water Lily
JOHN RIDGWAY (& CO.)	Water Lily
JOSIAH WEDGWOOD (& SONS LTD.)	Water Lily
LIVESLEY, POWELL & CO.	Water Lily
JAMES WALLACE & CO.	Water Mill and Packhorse
JOSIAH WEDGWOOD (& SONS LTD.)	Water Nymph
JOSIAH WEDGWOOD (& SONS LTD.)	Water Tower
THOMAS SHIRLEY & CO.	Water Wheel
RALPH STEVENSON & WILLIAMS	Water Works, Philadelphia
ROWLAND AND MARSELLUS	Waterbury, Conn.
BENJAMIN E. GODWIN	Waterfall
J. & G. MEAKIN	Waterfall
JOHN & RICHARD RILEY	Waterfall
GEORGE GORDON [GORDON'S POTTERY]	Watering Can
JOHN DENTON BAXTER (BAGSTER)	Watering Place, et.al.
SPODE/COPELAND & GARRETT, et.al.	Waterloo
SPODE'S BLUE PRINTED WARES	Waterloo
WILLIAM DAVENPORT	Watermill, scene #1, two men talking by a horse and cart, left - watermill, et.al.
WILLIAM DAVENPORT	Watermill, scene #2, large watermill on left, two fishermen in the foreground, church on right, et.al.
WILLIAM DAVENPORT	Watermill, scene #3, as above, but tree different and village replaced by windmill
FORD & SONS (LTD.)	Watford
BRITISH ANCHOR POTTERY CO., LTD.	Watteau
BROWNFIELDS(GUILD) POTTERY SOCIETY LTD.	Watteau
CHARLES MEIGH	Watteau
DOULTON & CO. (LTD.)	Watteau
EDGE, MALKIN & CO. (LTD.)	Watteau
FRANCIS MORLEY (& CO.)	Watteau
G.L. ASHWORTH & BROS. (LTD.)	Watteau
HALES, HANCOCK & CO. LTD.	Watteau
J. & M.P. BELL (CO.) & (LTD.)	Watteau
JOHN THOMSON (& SONS)	Watteau
NEW WHARF POTTERY CO.	Watteau
SPODE/COPELAND & GARRETT, et.al.	Watteau
WILLIAM BROWNFIELD (& SON(S)	Watteau
WILLIAM DAVENPORT	Watteau
MINTON & HOLLINS	Watteau Figures
JOHN & ROBERT GODWIN	Waverly
JOHN MADDOCK & SONS (LTD.)	Waverly
JOHNSON BROS. (HANLEY), LTD.	Waverly
THOMAS EDWARDS	Waverly
W.H. GRINDLEY & CO. (LTD.)	Waverly
WILLIAM DAVENPORT	Waverly
EDWARD & GEORGE PHILLIPS	Wearied Poles
J. & M.P. BELL (CO.) & (LTD.)	Webster Vase
WEDGWOOD & CO. (LTD.)	Wedgwood Plain
WEDGWOOD & CO. (LTD.)	Wedgwood's Ribbed
COPELAND & GARRETT, ET. AL.	Weeping Willow
SPODE/COPELAND & GARRETT, et.al.	Weeping Willow
FORD & SONS (LTD.)	Weir
J.H. WEATHERBY & SONS (LTD.)	Welbeck
JAMES & RALPH CLEWS	Welcome Lafayette The Nation's Guest and Our Country's Glory
ANDREW STEVENSON	Welcome Lafayette, The Nation's Guest, Aug. 6, 1824
ENOCH WOOD & SONS	Wellcombe, Warwickshire
WILLIAM ADAMS & SON(S) (POTTERS) LTD.	Wellcombe, Warwickshire
ALFRED MEAKIN (LTD.)	Wellington
BENJAMIN E. GODWIN	Wellington
J. & G. MEAKIN	Wellington
R. COCHRAN & CO. -VERREVILLE POTTERY	Wellington
SPODE/COPELAND & GARRETT, et.al.	Wellington
SHORTHOUSE & CO.	Wellington Hotel, Waterloo
HERCULANEUM POTTERY	Wellington Rooms, Liverpool
ENOCH WOOD & SONS	Wells
JAMES & RALPH CLEWS	Wells Cathedral
WILLIAM ADAMS & SON(S)(POTTERS) LTD.	Wells Cathedral
RALPH HALL	Wells Cathedral, Somersetshire
J. & G. MEAKIN	Wentworth
W.H. GRINDLEY & CO. (LTD.)	Wentworth
COPELAND & GARRETT, ET. AL.	West Cowes
ALFRED MEAKIN (LTD.)	West Meath
ENOCH WOOD & SONS	West Point Military Academy
JAMES & RALPH CLEWS	West Point, Hudson river
WILLIAM ADAMS & SON(S)(POTTERS) LTD.	West Point, Military School, New York, U.S.
ROWLAND AND MARSELLUS	West Point, N.Y.
SAMPSON HANCOCK (& SONS)	Westbourne
HOPE & CARTER	Western Shape
W. & E. CORN	Western Shape
WILLIAM RIDGWAY (& CO.)	Western Star
JOHN GOODWIN/SEACOMBE POTTERY	Westminster Palace
CAMBRIAN POTTERY	Whampoa
DILLWYN & CO.	Whampoa
EVANS & GLASSON	Whampoa
KEELING & CO. (LTD.)	Whampoa
MELLOR, VENABLES & CO.	Whampoa
PINDER BOURNE & CO.	Whampoa
SOUTH WALES POTTERS	Whampoa
WILLIAM DAVENPORT	Whampoa
ARTHUR J. WILKINSON (LTD.)	Wheat
BURGESS & GODDARD	Wheat
DAVID METHVEN & SONS	Wheat
DEANS (1910) LTD.	Wheat
E. & C. CHALLINOR	Wheat
ELSMORE & FORSTER	Wheat
GODDARD & BURGESS/ Burgess & Goddard	Wheat
HENRY MEAKIN	Wheat
HOLLINSHEAD & KIRKHAM (LTD.)	Wheat
J.H. WEATHERBY & SONS (LTD.)	Wheat
JACOB FURNIVAL & CO.	Wheat
JAMES F. WILEMAN	Wheat
MELLOR, TAYLOR & CO.	Wheat
ST. JOHN'S STONE CHINAWARE CO. (CANADA)	Wheat
THOMAS FURNIVAL & SONS	Wheat
TURNER & TOMKINSON	Wheat
TURNER, GODDARD & CO.	Wheat
W. & E. CORN	Wheat
W. BAKER & CO. (LTD.)	Wheat
WILLIAM & THOMAS ADAMS	Wheat
WILLIAM ADAMS & SON(S) (POTTERS) LTD.	Wheat
WILLIAM TAYLOR	Wheat
JACOB FURNIVAL & CO.	Wheat & Blackberry
R. COCHRAN & CO. - VERREVILLE POTTERY	Wheat & Blackberry
ST. JOHN'S STONE CHINAWARE CO. (CANADA)	Wheat & Blackberry
WILLIAM TAYLOR	Wheat & Blackberry
FORD & CHALLINOR	Wheat & Clover
JOHN THOMSON (& SONS)	Wheat & Clover
TAYLOR BROS.	Wheat & Clover
TOMKINSON BROS. & CO.	Wheat & Clover
TURNER & TOMKINSON	Wheat & Clover
JOHNSON BROS. (HANLEY), LTD.	Wheat & Daisy
BISHOP & STONIER (LTD.)	Wheat & Flowers
ALFRED MEAKIN (LTD.)	Wheat & Hops
CLEMENTSON BROS. (LTD.)	Wheat & Hops
EDWARD PEARSON (& SON)	Wheat & Hops
J. & G. MEAKIN	Wheat & Hops
JACOB FURNIVAL & CO.	Wheat & Hops
MEIKLE BROS.	Wheat & Hops
MELLOR, VENABLES & CO.	Wheat & Hops
R. COCHRAN & CO. - VERREVILLE POTTERY	Wheat & Hops
W.E. OULSNAM (& SONS)	Wheat & Hops
WILLIAM TAYLOR	Wheat & Hops
ALFRED MEAKIN (LTD.)	Wheat & Rose
WILLIAM ADAMS & SON(S) (POTTERS) LTD.	Wheat and Daisy
ST. JOHN'S STONE CHINAWARE CO. (CANADA)	Wheat and Hops
JOHN ALCOCK	Wheat Harvest
LIVESLEY, POWELL & CO.	Wheat in the Meadow
POWELL & BISHOP	Wheat in the Meadow Shape
J. H. & J. DAVIS	Wheat Pattern
HENRY ALCOCK & CO. (LTD.)	Wheat Pattern Shape
CHARLES ALLERTON & SONS	Wheel
MINTONS, LTD.	Wheel Japan
ROWLAND AND MARSELLUS	Whirlpool Rapids
ENOCH WOOD & SONS	Whitby
WILLIAM ADAMS & SON(S)(POTTERS) LTD.	Whitby Harbor
THOMAS DIMMOCK (JR.) & CO.	White horse and hunting horn
ROWLAND AND MARSELLUS	White House
ENOCH WOOD & SONS	White House, President's House Washington
ENOCH WOOD & SONS	White House, Wash

THOMAS GODWIN	Willow Pattern
THOMAS GOODFELLOW	Willow Pattern
THOMAS HENRY WALKER	Willow Pattern
THOMAS PHILLIPS & SON	Willow Pattern
THOMAS TILL & SON	Willow Pattern
THOMAS WOOD & CO.	Willow Pattern
TURPIN & CO./ & BROS	Willow Pattern
W. BAKER & CO. (LTD.)	Willow Pattern
WATSON & CO.	Willow Pattern
WHITEHAVEN POTTERY	Willow Pattern
WILLIAM & SAMUEL EDGE	Willow Pattern
WILLIAM ADAMS & SON(S)(POTTERS) LTD.	Willow Pattern
WILLIAM BOURNE & CO.	Willow Pattern
WILLIAM DAVENPORT	Willow Pattern
WILLIAM HACKWOOD	Willow Pattern
WILLIAM REID (& SON) or (SONS)	Willow Pattern
WILLIAM SMITH (& CO.)	Willow Pattern
WILLIAM WALSH	Willow Pattern
WOOD & SON(S) (LTD.)	Willow Pattern
DILLWYN & CO.	Wilton Church, Wilts
WILLIAM ADAMS & SON(S)(POTTERS) LTD.	Wilton House, Wiltshire
WOOD & SON(S) (LTD.)	Wincanton
DILLWYN & CO.	Winchester Cathedral
CHARLES JAMES MASON & CO.	Windermere
RALPH STEVENSON & SON	Windermere
BURGESS & LEIGH (LTD.)	Windflower
LEEDS POTTERY	Winding Road
T. & R. BOOTE (LTD.) (& SON)	Winding Vine Shape
JOSIAH WEDGWOOD (& SONS LTD.)	Windmill
THOMAS & BENJAMIN GODWIN	Windmill, The
ALEXANDER BALFOUR & CO.	Windsor
ANDREW MUIR (& CO.)	Windsor
C.T. MALING	Windsor
DAVID METHVEN & SONS	Windsor
ELGIN POTTERY	Windsor
FORD & SONS (LTD.)	Windsor
GEORGE THOMAS MOUNTFORD	Windsor
JAMES & RALPH CLEWS	Windsor
MELLOR, VENABLES & CO.	Windsor
PODMORE, WALKER (& CO.)	Windsor
THOMAS FORESTER & SONS (LTD.)	Windsor
ENOCH WOOD & SONS	Windsor Castle
GOODWINS & HARRIS	Windsor Castle
JAMES & RALPH CLEWS	Windsor Castle
JOHN GOODWIN/SEACOMBE POTTERY	Windsor Castle
MINTON	Windsor Castle
RALPH STEVENSON	Windsor Castle
RALPH STEVENSON & WILLIAMS	Windsor Castle
RALPH STEVENSON	Windsor Castle / British Views
WILLIAM ADAMS & SON(S) (POTTERS) LTD.	Windsor Castle, Berkshire
JOHN & WILLIAM RIDGWAY	Windsor Festoon
WILLIAM ADAMS & SON(S) (POTTERS) LTD.	Windsor Flowers
EDWARD & GEORGE PHILLIPS	Windsor Groups
WILLIAM ADAMS & SON(S) (POTTERS) LTD.	Windsor Rose
JAMES EDWARDS & SON	Windsor Royal
THOMAS DIMMOCK (JR.) & CO.	Windsor Scroll
SNEYD & HILL	Windsor Scrolls
POUNTNEY & CO. (LTD.)	Windsor Wreath
WILLIAM BROWNFIELD (& SON(S))	Windsor Wreath
WOOD & BROWNFIELD	Windsor Wreath
JOHN DENTON BAXTER (BAGSTER)	Wine Press
ROWLAND AND MARSELLUS	Winegar's Store ... Grand Rapids
ROWLAND AND MARSELLUS	Winnepeg, Manitoba, Canada
SPODE/COPELAND & GARRETT, et.al.	Winner Crown at Temple of Venus
COPELAND & GARRETT, ET. AL.	Winter
WILLIAM ADAMS	Winter
JAMES & RALPH CLEWS	Winter View of Pittsfield, Mass
EDWARD CLARKE (& CO.)	Winterberry
JOHN ROGERS (& SON)	Winter's Tale, Act 4 Scene 3
POUNTNEY & GOLDNEY	Winter's Tale, Act 4 Scene 3
GRIMWADE BROS.	Winton
PETTY & CO.	Wiseton Hall, Nottinghampshire
WOOD & SON(S) (LTD.)	Wisteria
JOHN & RICHARD RILEY	Wistow Hall, Leicestershire
THOMAS & JOHN CAREY/ JOHN CAREY & SONS	Woburn Abbey, Duke of Bedford's Seat
E. & C. CHALLINOR	Woldens
JAMES & RALPH CLEWS	Wolf
ENOCH WOOD & SONS	Wolf and Other Animals
WALLIS GIMSON & CO.	Wolf's Monument, Quebec
GRIFFITHS, BEARDMORE & BIRKS	Wolseley Hall
JOHN HALL	Wolverine
ANDREW STEVENSON	Wolvesey Castle
WILLIAM ADAMS & SON(S) (POTTERS) LTD.	Wolvesey Castle, Hampshire
JAMES WALLACE & CO.	Woman With Baby
JOHN DENTON BAXTER (BAGSTER)	Woman with Basket, et.al.
DILLWYN & CO.	Women With Basket
JOHN ROGERS (& SON)	Wood Nymph
JOSEPH CLEMENTSON	Woodbine
NEW WHARF POTTERY CO.	Woodbine
THOMAS TILL & SON	Woodbine
W. & D. BAILEY	Woodbine
W.H. GRINDLEY & CO. (LTD.)	Woodbine
WOOD & SON(S) (LTD.)	Woodbine
JOHN DENTON BAXTER (BAGSTER)	Woodcutters Lunch, et.al.
ENOCH WOOD & SONS	Wooding Station On The Mississippi
GEORGE JONES (& SONS LTD.)	Woodland
THOMAS FELL (& CO.) (LTD.)	Woodland
W. & E. CORN	Woodland
W. BAKER & CO. (LTD.)	Woodland
WILLIAM BROWNFIELD (& SON(S))	Woodland
WILLIAM DAVENPORT	Woodland
WOOD & SON(S) (LTD.)	Woodland
JOSIAH WEDGWOOD (& SONS LTD.)	Woodland Glen
JOSEPH STUBBS	Woodlands, Near Philadelphia
BENJAMIN E. GODWIN	Woodman
SPODE'S BLUE PRINTED WARES	Woodman
THOMAS FELL (& CO.) (LTD.)	Woodman
JOSEPH HEATH & CO.	Woodman, The
MINTON & CO.	Woodseat
MINTONS	Woodseat
W.H. GRINDLEY & CO. (LTD.)	Woodville
GOODWINS & HARRIS	Woolwich
ARTHUR J. WILKINSON (LTD.)	Worcester
C. & W.K. HARVEY	Worcester
ENOCH WOOD & SONS	Worcester
HERCULANEUM POTTERY	Worcester
RALPH HALL (& CO.) or (& SONS)	Worcester Cathedral
TAMS / et.al.	Worcester Cathedral
ROWLAND AND MARSELLUS	Worcester, Mass
WEDGWOOD & CO. (LTD.)	Woronzoff
JOHN MEIR	Worstead House
WOOD & SON(S) (LTD.)	Wortham Abbey
WOOD & CHALLINOR	Wounded Leg
ANTHONY SHAW (& SON(S) (& CO.)	Wrapped Sydenham
EDWARD WALLEY	Wrapped Sydenham
ELSMORE & FORSTER	Wrapped Sydenham
HOLLAND & GREEN	Wrapped Sydenham
JOHN MADDOCK	Wrapped Sydenham
LIVESLEY, POWELL & CO.	Wrapped Sydenham
THOMAS GOODFELLOW	Wrapped Sydenham
W. & E. CORN	Wrapped Sydenham
ANTHONY SHAW (& SON(S) (& CO.)	Wrapped Sydenham Shape
CHARLES MEIGH	Wreath
MINTON	Wreath
THOMAS FURNIVAL & CO.	Wreath
ENOCH WOOD & SONS	Wreath and Flowers
MINTON & CO.	Wreath Japan
JAMES & RALPH CLEWS	Wright's Ferry on the Susquehanna
WILLIAM DAVENPORT	Wright's Ferry on the Susquehanna
ANDREW STEVENSON	Writtle Lodge, Essex
JOHN RIDGWAY (& CO.)	Yale
ROWLAND AND MARSELLUS	Yale College
THOMAS GODWIN	Yale College
JOB & JOHN JACKSON	Yale College and State House, New Haven
CHARLES MEIGH	Yale College, New Haven
ROWLAND AND MARSELLUS	Yale University
COPELAND & GARRETT, ET. AL.	Yanina
JAMES & RALPH CLEWS	Yanquesian Conflict
WILLIAM DAVENPORT	Yanquesian Conflict
ENOCH WOOD & SONS	Yarmouth, Isle of Wight
ROWLAND AND MARSELLUS	Yarmouth, Nova Scotia
ARTHUR J. WILKINSON (LTD.)	Yeddo
G.L. ASHWORTH & BROS. (LTD.)	Yeddo
RIDGWAY, SPARKS & RIDGWAY	Yeddo
CHARLES JAMES MASON & CO.	Yellow River
G.L. ASHWORTH & BROS. (LTD.)	Yin
SHORE, COGGINS & HOLT	Yin Willow
BROWN WESTHEAD, MOORE & CO.	York
C. & W.K. HARVEY	York
CAULDON, LTD.	York
ENOCH WOOD & SONS	York
HERCULANEUM POTTERY	York
J. & G. MEAKIN	York
SAMUEL BARKER & SON	York
W. & E. CORN	York
THOMAS & JOHN CAREY/ JOHN CAREY & SONS	York Cathedral
ENOCH WOOD & SONS	York Gate, Regent's Park, London
WILLIAM ADAMS	York Gate, Regent's Park, London
HENSHALL & CO.	York Minster
JOHN GEDDES - VERREVILLE POTTERY	York Minster
RALPH STEVENSON	York Minster
JOHN ROGERS (& SON)	Yorkminster
T. & R. BOOTE (LTD.) (& SON)	Yosemite
WOOD & SON(S) (LTD.)	Yuan
BISHOP & STONIER (LTD.)	Yuletide
FRANCIS MORLEY (& CO.)	Zamara

ROWLAND AND MARSELLUS	Zanesville, Ohio
ENOCH WOOD & SONS	Zebra
JOB MEIGH (& SON)	Zebra
JOHN HALL	Zebra
JOHN ROGERS (& SON)	Zebra
LEEDS POTTERY	Zebra
TOFT & MAY	Zebra
CHARLES BOURNE	Zebra Pattern
ROBINSON, WOOD & BROWNFIELD	Zebra Pen
F. WINKLE & CO. (LTD.)	Zeeland
PINDER BOURNE & CO.	Zinnia
ROWLAND AND MARSELLUS	Zion Union Church, Berks County, Pa.
JAMES & RALPH CLEWS	ZOOLOGICAL GARDENS SERIES
ROBINSON, WOOD & BROWNFIELD	ZOOLOGICAL SERIES
JOB MEIGH (& SON)	ZOOLOGICAL SKETCHES SERIES
J. & G. MEAKIN	Zuyder

ADDENDUM TO ALPHABETIC INDEX OF RECORDED PATTERNS, SHAPES, BORDERS & SERIES

The following data was compiled too late to include into the body of the Alphabetic Index of Recorded Patterns, Shapes, Borders and Series.

Patterns noted with an asterisk (*) indicate added registration and/or patent numbers and dating.

All other patterns in this Addendum have not been included in the English Pattern Section of this Encyclopedia.

POTTERY	PATTERN	CAT.	FB	B&W	REG. NO.
HIBBERT & BROUGHEY	ANEMONE	PF	X		135869/1889
J. & G. MEAKIN	FERN	F	X		-
F. WINKLE & CO. (LTD.)	FLOWERS	F		X	27608/1885
ENOCH WOOD	PAGODA	O		X	-
BURGESS & LEIGH (LTD.)	SHEAF/WHEAT	F	X		-
BURGESS & LEIGH (LTD.)	TULIP SWIRL	A	X		406612/1903
GIBSON & SONS (LTD.)	TULIP*	M	X		699663/1923
W. H. GRINDLEY & CO. (LTD.)	ALBANY*	F	X		PATENT 12 OCT.1931
"PINDER, BOURNE & HOPE"	ALMA	PF	X		-
"DUDSON, WILCOX & TILL, LTD."	ANEMONE	F	X		
SAMPSON BRIDGWOOD (& SON) (LTD.)	ANEMONE	F	X		-
W. H. GRINDLEY & CO. (LTD.)	ANTIQUE	F		X	250386/1895
DOULTON & CO. (LTD.)	APPLE BLOSSOM	A	X		6327/1886
WEDGWOOD & CO. (LTD.)	ARCADE	A	X		-
EVANS & GLASSON	ASIATIC PHEASANT	O	X		-
RIDGWAYS (BEDFORD WORKS) LTD.	ASIATIC PLACES	O	X		-
JAMES KENT (LTD.)	ATHENS	F		X	-
DOULTON & CO. (LTD.)	AUBREY*	A	X		403830/1902
DOULTON & CO. (LTD.)	AUBREY*	A	X		399945/1902
BOURNE & LEIGH (LTD.)	AVON	F	X		276166/1896
"HOLMES, STONIER & HOLLINGSHEAD"	AVONA	A		X	"360806-7/ JAN.15, 1881"
J. & G. MEAKIN	BEAUVAIS	F	X		-
JOHN MADDOX & SONS (LTD.)	BELFORT	F	X		-
TAMS & CO.	BLUE WILLOW	O		X	-
W. H. GRINDLEY & CO. (LTD.)	BOMBAY	F	X		-
WILLIAM HULME	BRAMBLE	F		X	-
S. FIELDING & CO. (LTD.)	BRAY	F		X	-
SAMUEL FORD & CO.	BRAY	F	X		-
"JOHNSON BROS. (HANLEY), (LTD.)"	BROOKLYN*	A	X		326410/1898
RIDGWAYS (BEDFORD WORKS) LTD.	BURLINGTON	F		X	72235/1887
FORD & SONS (LTD.)	BURMA	O	X		-
"EDGE, MALKIN & CO. (LTD.)"	CASTLE	F		X	-
J. & G. MEAKIN	CATHY	F		X	-
ENOCH WOOD	CELIA	PF		X	-
ALFRED MEAKIN (LTD.)	CHARLOTTE	F		X	-
"POWELL, BISHOP & STONIER"	CHELSEA*	F		X	2665/1884
EVANS & GLASSON	CHINESE TEMPLE	O	X		-
GEORGE JONES (& SONS LTD.)	CHRYSANTHEMUM	F	X		21391/1885
KEELING & CO. (LTD.)	CLAYTON	F	X		-
"JOHNSON BROS. (HANLEY), (LTD.)"	CLAYTON*	F	X		US PATENT 10/21/1909
HENRY ALCOCK & CO. (LTD.)	CLIFTON	F	X		216253/1893
RIDGWAYS (BEDFORD WORKS) LTD.	COMO	M	X		-
CLEVELAND POTTERY CO.	CORONATION	M	X		-
POUNTNEY & CO. (LTD.)	CUBA	F		X	-
DOULTON & CO. (LTD.)	DAFFODIL*	F	X		258549/1895
KEELING & CO. (LTD.)	DAISY	F	X		-
KEELING & CO. (LTD.)	DOROTHY	F	X		-
POSSIL POTTERY CO.	DORIC	F	X		-
COCKSON & HARDING	DRESDEN	F	X		-
BURGESS & LEIGH (LTD.)	EATON	M	X		389974/1902
WILLIAM (ALSAGER) ADDERLEY (& CO.)	EATON	F		X	-
T. RATHBONE & CO.	ETON	M	X		-
BURGESS & LEIGH (LTD.)	EVERSLEY	F	X		-
J. DIMMOCK & CO.	FERN	F	X		-
"JOHNSON BROS. (HANLEY), (LTD.)"	FLORA	F	X		-
W. H. GRINDLEY & CO. (LTD.)	FLORA*	F	X		152444/1890
"THOMAS, JOHN & JOSEPH MAYER "	FLORENTINE*	S		X	"93008-9/1888 OCT.22, 1853"
GRIMWADES LTD.	FRESCO	M	X		-
J. & G. MEAKIN	GEISHA	M	X		-
NEWPORT POTTERY CO. LTD.	GENEVESE	S	X		-
ALFRED MEAKIN (LTD.)	GLENMERE	F	X		-
"WHITTINGHAM, FORD & RILEY"	GOAT	G		X	-
BURGESS & LEIGH (LTD.)	HAARLEM	F	X		-
J. & G. MEAKIN	HAGUE	F	X		-
J. & G. MEAKIN	HAMBURCO	A		X	-
MINTON & CO.	HAMPTON	PF	X		-
KEELING & CO. (LTD.)	HAWKSTONE	PO	X		-
THOMAS DIMMOCK (JR.) & CO.	HEDERA	F	X		-
C. T. MALING & SONS (LTD.)	HOLLYHOCK	F	X		-
W. H. GRINDLEY & CO. (LTD.)	HOMELAND	S		X	-
G. L. ASHWORTH & BROS. (LTD.)	INDIA	O	X		-
WEDGWOOD & CO. (LTD.)	INDIAN STAR	M		X	"147823/1890 DEC.20, 1861"
NEW WHARF POTTERY CO.	INDIANA	PF	X		-
F. WINKLE & CO. (LTD.)	IRVING	F	X		-
F. WINKLE & CO. (LTD.)	IVY	F	X		-
MINTON & CO.	JEROME	A		X	-
DALEHALL POTTER CO.	JESSAMINE	F	X		-
DOULTON & CO. (LTD.)	KEW	F	X		116918/1889
"ARTHUR, J. WILKINSON (LTD.)"	KIMBERLEY	F	X		-
SAMPSON HANCOCK (& SONS)	LAUREL	F		X	661490/1917
BURGESS & LEIGH (LTD.)	LEIGHTON*	A	X		567168/1910
BOOTHS (LTD.)	LONDON	M	X		-
GRIMWADES LTD.	LOUVRE	F	X		-
ALFRED MEAKIN (LTD.)	LUTON	F	X		-
F. WINKLE & CO. (LTD.)	MADELEY	F	X		-
THOMAS FURNIVAL & SONS	MADRAS	O		X	-
WILLIAM BROWNFIELD (& SON(S))	MADRAS*	O		X	JAN. 1883
F. WINKLE & CO. (LTD.)	MALVERN*	F		X	406306/1903
HOLLINSHEAD & KIRKHAM (LTD.)	MAX	F	X		-
BURGESS & LEIGH (LTD.)	MAY	F	X		-
KEELING & CO. (LTD.)	MEADFORD	F	X		-
BISHOP & STONIER (LTD.)	MELVILLE	M	X		-
W. H. GRINDLEY & CO. (LTD.)	MERSEY	F	X		135130/1889
ALFRED MEAKIN (LTD.)	MILAN	F		X	-
WOOD & SON(S) (LTD.)	MILTON*	F	X		233066/1894
HENRY ALCOCK & CO. (LTD.)	MINWOOD	M	X		-
J. & G. MEAKIN	MODERNA	F	X		409774/1903
WILLIAM (ALSAGER) ADDERLEY (& CO.)	MONTROSE	A	X		-
RIDGWAYS (BEDFORD WORKS) LTD.	MR. PICKWICK BENEATH THE MISTLE-TOE	L	X		419438/1903
RIDGWAYS (BEDFORD WORKS) LTD.	NARCISSUS	F	X		-
J. & G. MEAKIN	NORDIC	F	X		-
DOULTON & CO. (LTD.)	NORFOLK*	S	X		597783/1912
DOULTON & CO. (LTD.)	NORFOLK*	S	X		251612/1895
WILLIAM DAVENPORT	ORIEL	PO		X	-
WILCOX & TILL	PATRICIA	M	X		-
"BEECH, HANCOCK & CO."	PEKIN	PO		X	-
"JOHNSON BROS. (HANLEY), (LTD.)"	PERSIAN ROYAL	F	X		-
T. & R. BOOTE (LTD.) (& SON)	PICTURESQUE	S		X	-
WOOD & SON(S) (LTD.)	PRIMROSE	A	X		-
DOULTON & CO. (LTD.)	PROVENCE	PH	X		-

LEIGHTON POTTERY LTD.	REGAL	M	X		-
DOULTON & CO. (LTD.)	ROSAMOND	M		X	-
WOOD & BROWNFIELD	ROSEA	PO	X		-
KEELING & CO. (LTD.)	SHANGHAI	F	X		-
"ARTHUR, J. WILKINSON (LTD.)"	SOPHIE	A		X	-
W. H. GRINDLEY & CO. (LTD.)	SPRING	F		X	51058/1886
GRIMWADES LTD.	STELLA	M	X		-
HULME & CHRISTE	STELLA	F		X	-
"JOHNSON BROS. (HANLEY), (LTD.)"	SULTANA	M		X	-
BISHOP & STONIER (LTD.)	SUSSEX	M	X		-
W. H. GRINDLEY & CO. (LTD.)	THE LAHAYA	S	X		-
J. & G. MEAKIN	THE SANDOWN	S		X	-
RALPH HAMMERSLEY (& SON(S))	TIVOLI	F		X	180051/1891
T. & R. BOOTE (LTD.) (& SON)	TOURNAY*	F		X	33645/1885
CARLTON WARE (LTD.)	TRENTHAM/ BABY PLATE	Z	F		-
JOSIAH WEDGWOOD (& SONS LTD.)	TROPHY	O	X		-
"BROWN WESTHEAD, MOORE & CO."	VARIETE	Z	F		80107/1887
NEW WHARF POTTERY CO.	VIENNA	M	X		-
RIDGWAYS (BEDFORD WORKS) LTD.	VIRGINIA	F	X		-
WOOD & SON(S) (LTD.)	WAGNER	A	X		-
KEELING & CO. (LTD.)	WATFORD	F	X		-
J. H. WEATHERBY & SONS (LTD.)	WELBECK*	M	X		161702/1890
W. BAKER & CO. (LTD.)	WEMBLEY	M		X	-
SAMPSON BRIDGWOOD (& SON) (LTD.)	WILDFLOWER	F	X		-

INTRODUCTION TO APPENDICES B1 THROUGH B15

Appendices B1 and B2:

These two appendices provide the reader with a listing of those potters included in the British Marks Section of this Encyclopedia, with initial marks and dates of production when recorded. Appendix B1 is an alphabetic listing by initials and respective potter. Appendix B2 is an alphabetic listing by potter and respective initials.

Appendices B3 and B4:

Appendices B3 and B4 are as above, but include potters and their respective recorded initial marks and dates that do not appear under the British Marks Section of this Encyclopedia.

Appendix B5:

This appendix contains a listing of initials and patterns that are unidentified, but have been attributed to the respective initials included herein.

Appendix B6:

This very complex appendix is a Chronology of Selected Potteries, Partnerships and given names. It provides the reader with a "pottery tree" by date, name of pottery, locale and partnership involvement, when available.

Appendicies B7 and B8:

These appendices record backmark terms as recorded by respective potters. At times the only marking that may appear on a piece of ceramics is a term employed by a potter. These terms are only an aid to help the reader identify a possible potter. Appendix B7 is an alphabetic listing of terms with corresponding potter. Appendix B8 is an alphabetic listing of potters with corresponding term.

Appendix B9:

This appendix contains a listing of potters and the categories of manufacture as included in this Encyclopedia. The categories are: Blue & White, Historic Blue, Flow Blue, Mulberry, White Ironstone, and Tea Leaf/Copper Lustre. Also included are corresponding Godden reference numbers.

Appendix B10:

Appendix B10 includes a listing of additional potters who produced White Ironstone, along with location and dates of production.

Appendix B11:

This appendix is a listing of White Ironstone produced by the firm of Elsmore & Forster, as recorded by Arene Burgess.

Appendix B12:

Appendix B12 contains a listing of significant dates, terms and backmarks that is meant as a time line and aid to identification for the reader.

Appendix B13:

Appendix B13 is to be used as a tool to aid the reader in Dating & Deciphering the Registration Diamond. Registry periods (1842-1883) are discussed, as is application of the Registry Diamond. Also included is a code chart for determining the date that appears on the diamond.

Appendix B14:

This appendix is a listing of registry dates in chronological sequence from 1842 - 1900. It includes the registry date, parcel number, registration number, pottery and location.

The Parcel Number was a numerical logging system for daily entries. Each day began with the number one (1).

Appendix B15:

Appendix B15 is a listing of registry numbering sequences in two parts. Part I includes dates and numbering sequences from 1839 - 1884 and Part II includes dates and registry numbering sequences from 1884 - 1996.

Appendix B 16, 17, 18, 19 & 20:

Introduction to Alphabetical and Chronological Listings of Registry Dates, 1842-1883.

For full details of these appendices refer to the Introduction of the aforementioned appendices.

APPENDIX B1: ALPHABETIC LISTING: PRIMARY POTTERS BY INITIAL & NAME

INITIALS	POTTERY	DATE
A. B. & CO.	ALLMAN, BROUGHTON & CO.	1861-1868
A. B. & CO.	BALFOUR, ALEXANDER & CO.	1874-1904
A. B. & CO.	BULLOCK, A. & CO.	1895-1915
A. B. & CO./H.	BULLOCK, A. & CO.	1895-1915
A. B. & G.	ALLERTON, BROUGH & GREEN	1832-1859
A. BROS.	ASHWORTH, G. L. & BROS.	1862-1883
A. F. & S.	FENTON, ALFRED & SONS	1887-1901
A. M.	MUIR, ANDREW (& CO.) (CLYDE POTTERY CO.)	1836-1841
A. W. / L.	WOOD, ARTHUR	1904-1928
B.	BADDELEY, GEORGE	c1822
B.	BADDELEY, JOHN & EDWARD	1784-1811
B.	BARKER, SAMUEL (& SON(S))	1834-1851
B.	BARLOW, JAMES	1822-1839
B.	BARLOW, THOMAS	1849-1853-(1882)
B.	BELL, J. & M. P. & CO. (LTD.)	1850-1870
B.	BETTANY, GEORGE	1822-1830
B.	BIRKS, CHARLES	1822-1835
B.	BOURNE, WILLIAM (LONGTON)	1857-1861
B.	BRADSHAW, WILLIAM	1819-1823
B.	BRAMELD & CO.	1806-1841(1842)
B.	BREEZE, JOHN	1828-1830
B.	BRIDGWOOD, SAMPSON	1822-1853
B. & B.	BAGGERLEY & BALL	1822-1836
B. & B.	BAILEY & BALL	1843-1850
B. & B.	BAILEY & BATKIN	1814-1826
B. & B.	BATES & BENNETT	1868-1895
B. & B.	BEARDMORE & BIRKS	1832-1843
B. & B.	BLACKHURST & BOURNE	1880-1892
B. & B.	BRIDGETT & BATES	1882-1915
B. & B.	BRIDGWOOD & BURGESS	1846-1847
B. & B. /L.	BAGGERLEY & BALL	1822-1836
B. & C.	BRIDGWOOD & CLARKE	1859-1864
B. & CO.	BODLEY & CO.	1865-1865
B. & CO.	BURN, JOSEPH & CO.	1852-1860
B. & E.	BEARDMORE & EDWARDS	c1858
B. & H.	BEDNALL & HEATH	1879-1899
B. & H.	BEECH & HANCOCK	1860-1876
B. & H.	BLACKHURST & HULME	1889-1932
B. & H.	BODLEY & HAROLD	1863-1865
B. & K. (L.)	BARKERS & KENT (LTD.)	1889-1941
B. & L.	BOURNE & LEIGH (LTD.)	1892-1941
B. & L.	BURGESS & LEIGH (LTD.)	1862-1889
B. & M.	BAGSHAW & MEIR	1802-1808
B. & M.	BOOTH & MEIGH	1837-1838
B. & M.	BROUGHAM & MAYER	1856-1862
B. & M.	BURTON & MORRIS	1882-1897
B. & S.	BARKER & SON	1850-1860
B. & S.	BISHOP & STONIER (LTD.)	1891-1910
B. & S.	BROWN & STEVENTON, LTD.	1900-1923
B. & T.	BARKER & TILL	1846-1850
B. & T.	BLACKHURST & TUNNICLIFFE	1879-1879
B. B.	MINTON	1830-1850
B. B. & B.	BOURNE, BAKER & BAKER	1833-1835
B. B. & B.	BOURNE, BAKER & BOURNE	1796-1833
B. B. & CO.	BAKER, BEVANS & IRWIN	1813-1838
B. B. & I.	BAKER, BEVANS & IRWIN	1813-1838
B. B. & S.	BIRKS, BROS. & SEDDON	1878-1886
B. B. (LTD.)	BARKER BROS. (LTD.)	1876-1900-(1959)
B. B. B.	BOOTHS (LTD.)	1891-1912
B. B. W. & M.	BATES, BROWN-WESTHEAD & MOORE	1859-1861
B. E. & CO.	BATES, ELLIOTT & CO.	1870-1875
B. G.	GODWIN, BENJAMIN, E.	1834-1841
B. G. & W.	BATES, GILDEA & WALKER	1878-1881
B. G. P. CO.	BROWNFIELDS GUILD POTTERY LTD.	1892-1897
B. H. & CO.	BEECH, HANCOCK & CO.	1851-1855
B. M. & T.	BOULTON, MACHIN & TENNANT	1889-1899
B. N. & CO.	BOURNE, NIXON & CO.	1828-1830
B. P. CO.	BROWNHILLS POTTERY CO.	1872-1896
B. P. CO. LTD.	BOVEY POTTERY CO. LTD.	1894-1947
B. P. CO. LTD.	BRITANNIA POTTERY CO. LTD.	1920-1935
B. P. CO. LTD.	BRITISH ANCHOR POTTERY CO. LTD.	1884-1982
B. P. CO. LTD.	COCHRAN & FLEMING	1920-1939
B. S. & T.	BARKER, SUTTON & TILL	1834-1846
B. T. & S.	TAYLOR, BENJAMIN & SON	c1848
B. T. P. CO.	BOVEY TRACEY POTTERY CO.	1842-1894
B. W. & CO.	BATES, WALKER & CO.	1875-1878
B. W. (&) B.	BATKIN, WALKER, & BROADHURST	1840-1845
B. W. M. (& CO.)	BROWN-WESTHEAD, MOORE & CO.	1862-1904
B.B.B.	BRIDGET, BATES & BEECH	1875-1882
C. & B.	COTTON & BARLOW	1850-1857
C. & CO.	CALLAND, JOHN F. & CO.	1852-1856
C. & CO.	COLCLOUGH & CO.	1887-1928
C. & CO.	STANLEY POTTERY LTD.	1928-1931
C. & E.	CORK & EDGE	1846-1860
C. & E. (LTD)	CARTWRIGHT & EDWARDS (LTD.)	1858-1926-(1988)
C. & F. /G.	COCHRAN & FLEMING	1896-1917
C. & G.	COPELAND & GARRETT	1833-1847
C. & H.	COCKSON & HARDING	1856-1863
C. & H.	COOMBS & HOLLAND	1855-1858
C. & H.	CUMBERLIDGE & HUMPHREYS	1886-1889 & 1893-1895
C. & R.	CHESWORTH & ROBINSON	1825-1840
C. & R.	CHETHAM & ROBINSON	1822-1834
C. & W. K. H.	HARVEY, C. & W. K.	1835-1852
C. A. & CO. LTD.	CERAMIC ART CO. (1905) LTD.	1905-1919
C. A. & SONS	ALLERTON, CHARLES & SONS (LTD.)	1860-1911
C. B.	BOURNE, CHARLES	1817-1830
C. C.	RIDGWAY, WILLIAM SON & CO.	1838-1845
C. C. & CO.	COCKSON & CHETWYND (& CO.)	1867-1875
C. E. & M.	CORK, EDGE & MALKIN	1860-1871
C. H. & H.	CUMBERLIDGE, HUMPHREYS & HELE	1889-1893
C. H. (& S.)	HOBSON, CHARLES (& SON)	1865-1883
C. J. M.	MASON, CHARLES JAMES	1849-1853
C. J. M. & CO.	MASON, CHARLES JAMES & CO.	1826-1840-(1848)
C. J. W.	WILEMAN, CHARLES J.	c1869
C. K.	KEELING, CHARLES	1822-1826
C. M.	MEIGH, CHARLES	1832-1850
C. M. & S.	MEIGH, CHARLES & SON	1850-1861
C. M. S. & P.	MEIGH, CHARLES, SON & PANKHURST	1850
C. or G.	NEAL & CO.	1820s
C. P.	ELGIN POTTERY	1855-1870
C. P.	PURVES, CHARLES	1855-1870
C. P. CO.	CLYDE POTTERY CO. (LTD.)	1857-1861
C. P. CO. (LTD.)	CAMPBELLFIELD POTTERY CO. (LTD.)	1850-1880-(1899)
C. R. S.	CHETHAM & ROBINSON & SON	1834-1840
C. T.	TITTENSOR, CHARLES	1815-1823
C. T. M.	MALING, C. T.	1859-1890
C. T. M. & SONS (LTD.)	MALING, C. T. & SONS (LTD.)	1890-1947
C. W. S.	CO-OPERATIVE WHOLESALE SOCIETY LTD.	1946-1970s
C. Y. & J.	CLEMENTSON, YOUNG & JAMESON	1844-1845
CC (NO DOTS)	COPELAND, W. T. (& SONS LTD.)	1846-1856
D.	DANIEL, H. & R.	1822-1846
D.	DILLWYN & CO.	1824-1850
D.	DIMMOCK, THOMAS (JR.) (& CO.)	1828-1859
D.	SWANSEA POTTERY	1824-1850
D. & B.	DALTON & BURN	1833-1843
D. & B.	DEAKIN & BAILEY or (BAILEY & DEAKIN)	1828-1832
D. & CO.	DILLWYN & CO.	1836-1850
D. & CO.	SWANSEA POTTERY	1836-1850
D. & K. R.	EDGE, MALKIN & CO.	1870-1880
D. & S.	DEAKIN & SON(S) (& CO.)	1832-1841
D. & S.	DIMMOCK & SMITH	1842-1859
D. B. & C. (CO.)	DUNN BENNETT & CO. (LTD.)	1875-1907
D. B. & CO.	DAVENPORT, BANKS & CO.	1860-1873
D. B. & CO.	DAVENPORT, BECK & CO.	1873-1880
D. C. & W.	DAVIS, COOKSON, & WILSON	1822-1833
D. D. & CO.	DUNDERDALE, DAVID & CO.	1803-1821
D. H. (DALE HALL)	EDWARDS, JAMES & SON(S)	1854-1882
D. L. & CO.	LOCKHART, DAVID & CO.	1876-1898
D. L. & S. (SONS)	LOCKHART, DAVID & SONS (LTD.)	1898-1953
D. M. & S. (SONS)	METHVEN, DAVID & SONS	1847-1928
E. & C. C.	CHALLINOR, E. & C.	1862-1891
E. & CO.	ELKINS & CO.	1822-1825
E. & E. W.	WOOD, ENOCH & SONS	1840s
E. & F. or E. FOR.	ELSMORE & FORSTER	1853-1871
E. & G.	EVANS & GLASSON	1850-1861
E. & G. P.	PHILLIPS, EDWARD & GEORGE	1822-1834
E. & N.	ELKIN & NEWBON	1845-1856
E. & W.	WALLEY, EDWARD & SON	1858-1862
E. B. & B.	EDGE, BARKER & BARKER	1836-1840
E. B. & CO.	EDGE, BARKER & CO.	1835-1836
E. B. (&) J. E. L. (B.)	BOURNE & LEIGH (LTD.)	1892-1941
E. C.	CHALLINOR, EDWARD	1842-1867
E. C. & C. CO.	CHALLINOR, E. & CO.	1853-1862
E. C. & CO.	CHALLINOR, E. & CO.	1853-1862
E. F. & CO.	ELSMORE & FORSTER	1853-1871
E. F. B. & S. or (& SON)	BODLEY, EDWARD F. & SON	1875-1898
E. F. B. (&CO.)	BODLEY, EDWARD F. & CO.	1862-1875
E. H.	HUGHES, ELIJAH & CO.	1853-1867
E. J.	JONES, ELIJAH	1831-1839
E. J. R. (& S.)	RIDGWAY, E. J. (& SON)	1860-1866-(1872)
E. K. & CO.	ELKIN, KNIGHT & CO.	1822-1825
E. K. B. (& B.)	ELKIN, KNIGHT & BRIDGWOOD	1827-1840
E. M. & CO. (/B.)	EDGE, MALKIN & CO. (LTD.)	1870-1899-(1903)
E. P. CO.	EMPIRE PORCELAIN CO. (LTD.)	1896-1939-(1963)
E. W.	WOOD, ENOCH	1784-1789
E. W. & S.	WOOD, ENOCH & SONS	1818-1845
F.	FELL, THOMAS	1817-1830

F. & C.	FORD & CHALLINOR & CO.	1865-1880
F. & CO.	FELL, THOMAS & CO. (LTD.)	1830-1869-(1890)
F. & CO.	FORD, SAMUEL & CO.	1898-1939
F. & H.	FORESTER & HULME	1887-1892
F. & R. (/B.)	FORD & RILEY	1882-1893
F. & R. P. (& CO.)	PRATT, F. & R. (& CO.) (LTD.)	1840-1862(+)
F. & S. (/B.) (& SONS LTD)	FORD & SONS (LTD.)	1893-1908-(1938)
F. (&) T.	FLACKETT & TOFT	c1857
F. B. & CO. /F.	BEARDMORE, FRANK & CO.	1903-1914
F. C. & CO.	FORD & CHALLINOR & CO.	1865-1880
F. C. & CO.	FORD, (&) CHALLINOR & CO.	1865-1880
F. D.	DILLON, FRANCIS	1830-1843
F. J. E.	EMERY, FRANCIS J.	1878-1893
F. M.	MORLEY, FRANCIS	1845-1850
F. M. & CO.	MORLEY, FRANCIS & CO.	1850-1859
F. T. R. or (& R.)	FLACKETT, TOFT & ROBINSON	c1858
F. W. & CO.	WINKLE, F. & CO. (LTD.)	1890-1925-(1931)
G.	WILSON, DAVID (& SON(S))	1801-1817
G. & B.	GOODWINS & BULLOCK	1857-1859
G. & B.	GOODWINS, BRIDGWOOD & CO.	1827-1829
G. & C. J. M.	MASON, G. M. & C. J.	PRIOR TO 1830
G. & D.	GUEST & DEWSBERRY	1877-1906
G. & E.	GOODWINS & ELLIS	1839-1840
G. & H.	GOODWINS & HARRIS	1832-1837
G. & S.	GROVE & STARK	1875-1885
G. & S. LTD. (/B.)	GIBSON & SONS LTD.	1884-1904
G. & W. (& CO.)	GILDEA & WALKER (& CO.)	1881-1885
G. B.	GRIMWADES LTD.	1900-1978
G. B. & B.	GRIFFITHS, BEARDMORE (& CO.) & BIRKS	1829-1831
G. B. H.	GOODWINS, BRIDGWOOD (&) HARRIS	1829-1832
G. B. O. or (& O.)	GOODWINS, BRIDGWOOD & ORTON	1827-1829
G. BROS.	GODWIN, JOHN & ROBERT	1834-1867
G. BROS.	GRIMWADES BROS.	1886-1900
G. C.	GOODWIN & CO. (LONGTON)	1841-1864
G. C.	GOODWIN, JOHN (LONGTON)	1841-1864
G. C. P. CO. (G.)	CLYDE POTTERY CO. (LTD.)	1850s
G. C. P. CO. LTD.	CLYDE POTTERY CO. LTD.	1857-1861
G. F.	FORRESTER, GEORGE	1799-1830
G. F. B. (B.T.)	BOWERS, GEORGE FREDERICK(&CO.)	1841-1868
G. F. S. (& CO.)	SMITH, GEORGE F. (& CO.)	1857-1867
G. G.	GORDON, GEORGE	1795-1833
G. H. & CO.	GATER, HALL & CO.	1895-1914
G. H. & G.	GOODWIN, HARRIS & GOODWIN	1832-1838
G. J.	JONES, GEORGE	1861-1873
G. J. & SONS	JONES, GEORGE & SONS	1873-1893
G. J. & SONS LTD.	JONES, GEORGE & SONS LTD.	1894-1957
G. L. A. & BROS.	ASHWORTH, G. L. & BROS. (LTD.)	1862-1883
G. L. A. & T.	ASHWORTH, G. L. & BROS. (LTD.)	1862-1883
G. M. & C. J. M.	MASON, G. M. & C. J.	PRIOR TO 1830
G. P.	PATTERSON, GEORGE (PATTERSON & CO.)	1837-1844
G. P.	PHILLIPS, GEORGE	1834-1848
G. P. & CO.	PURVES, CHARLES	1883-1887
G. P. CO.	GLAMORGAN POTTERY CO.	1819-1838
G. P. CO. (G.) (& CO.)	CLYDE POTTERY (GREENOCK)	1816-1903
G. P. CO. /S.	BAKER, BEVANS & CO.	1819-1838
G. R.	CHALLINOR, EDWARD	1842-1867
G. R.	CLEWS, JAMES & RALPH	1817-1834
G. R. & CO.	GODWIN, ROWLEY & CO.	1828-1831
G. R. (& crown)	MEIR, JOHN	1812-1836
G. S. & CO.	SKINNER, GEORGE & CO.	1855-1870
G. T. & S.	TURNER, G. W. & SONS	1873-1895
G. T. M.	MOUNTFORD, GEORGE THOMAS	1888-1898
G. W. & CO.	GILDEA & WALKER & CO.	1881-1885
G. W. T. & S. (SONS)	TURNER, G. W. & SONS	1873-1895
G. W. T. S. (& S.)	TURNER, G. W. & SONS	1873-1895
H.	HACKWOOD, WILLIAM	1827-1843
H.	HARVEY, C. & W. K.	1835-1852
H.	HUGHES, E. & CO. (CHINA MANUFACTURER)	1889-1941
H. & A.	HAMMERSLEY & ASBURY	1870-1875
H. & A.	HULSEY & ADDERLEY	1869-1874
H. & B.	HAMPSON & BROADHURST	1849-1854
H. & B.	HEATH & BLACKHURST	1859-1877
H. & C.	HARDING & COCKSON (& SON) (& CO.)	1834-1863
H. & C.	HOPE & CARTER	1862-1880
H. & C. (CO.)	HAMMERSLEY & CO.	1887-1932(+)
H. & CO.	HACKWOOD & CO.	1807-1827
H. & CO.	HACKWOOD, WILLIAM & CO.	1827-1843
H. & G.	HOLLAND & GREEN	1853-1882
H. & G.	HOLLAND & GUEST	1868-1875
H. & G./B	HEATH & GREATBATCH	1891-1893
H. & H.	HILDITCH & HOPWOOD	1832-1859
H. & J.	HALLAM & JOHNSON	1878-1880
H. & K.	HACKWOOD & KEELING	1835-1836
H. & K.	HOLLINSHEAD & KIRKHAM (LTD.)	1870-1956
H. & K. /T.	HOLLINSHEAD & KIRKHAM (LTD.)	1924-1956
H. & R. D.	DANIEL, H. & R.	1822-1846
H. & S.	HILDITCH & SON(S) (& CO.)	1822-1836
H. & V.	HOPKIN & VERNON	1836-1839
H. & W.	HANCOCK & WITTINGHAM	1873-1879
H. A. & CO.	ADAMS, HARVEY & CO.	1869-1887
H. A. & CO.	ALCOCK, HENRY & CO. (LTD.)	1861-1901-(1910)
H. B.	BURGESS, HENRY	1864-1892
H. B.	HAWLEY BROS.	1868-1898
H. B. & CO.	HEATH, BLACKHURST & CO.	1859-1877
H. BROS.	HUMPHREYS BROS.	1893-1903
H. F.	HUGHES, E. & CO. (CHINA MANUFACTURER)	1898-1905
H. H. & CO.	HALES, HANCOCK & CO. LTD. (RETAILERS)	1918-1921
H. H. & G. LTD.	HALES, HANCOCK & GODWIN LTD. (RETAILERS)	1922-1960
H. H. & M.	HOLDCROFT, HILL & MELLOR	1860-1870
H. H. (&) A.	HULSE, NIXON & ADDERLEY	1853-1869
H. J. CO.	HALLAM & JOHNSON	1878-1880
H. J. W. /B.	WOOD, H. J. (LTD.)	1884-PRESENT
H. M.	RAINFORTH & CO.	1809-1814
H. M. J. (& J.)	HICKS, MEIGH & JOHNSON	1822-1835
H. N. & A.	HULSE, NIXON & ADDERLEY	1853-1869
H. P. CO.	GIBSON & SONS (LTD)	1904-1909
H. P. CO.	HANLEY PORCELAIN CO.	1892-1898
H. S. & H.	HOLMES, STONIER & HOLLINSHEAD	1875-1882
H. W. & CO.	HANCOCK, WITTINGHAM & CO.	1863-1872
HHM (NO DOTS)	HOLDCROFT, HILL & MELLOR	1860-1870
I. & W.	RIDGWAY, JOHN & WILLIAM	1813-1830
I. D. B.	BAGSTER, JOHN DENTON (or BAXTER)	1823-1827
I. H.	HEATH, J. (JOSHUA)	1770-1800
I. H. & CO.	HEATH, JOSEPH & CO.	1828-1841 (1842)
I. M.	MADDOCK, JOHN	1842-1855
I. M.	MEIR, JOHN	1812-1836
I. M. & S.	MEIR, JOHN & SON	1837-1897
I. M. (&) CO.	NORTH BRITISH POTTERY	1867-1874
I. M. CO.	MILLER, JAMES & CO.	1840s-1920s
I. W.	WHITEHAVEN POTTERY	1824-1863
I. W. & CO.	WILSON, ISAAC & CO.	1852-1887
J. & C. W.	WILEMAN, JAMES & CHARLES	1864-1870
J. & CO.	JACKSON, J. & CO.	1870-1887
J. & G. A.	ALCOCK, JOHN & GEORGE	1839-1848
J. & M. P. B. & CO.	BELL, J. & M. P. & CO. LTD.	1850-1870
J. & P.	JACKSON & PATTERSON	1833-1838
J. & R. G.	GODWIN, JOHN & ROBERT	1834-1867
J. & T. E.	EDWARDS, JAMES & THOMAS	1839-1842
J. & T. F.	FURNIVAL, JACOB & THOMAS	c1843
J. & T. L	LOCKETT, JOHN & THOMAS	1835-1855
J. & W.	JONES & WALLEY	1841-1845
J. & W.	RIDGWAY, JOHN & WILLIAM	1813-1830
J. & W. R.	RIDGWAY, JOHN & WILLIAM	1813-1830
J. B.	BEECH, JAMES	1878-1889
J. B.	BELL, J. & M. P. & CO. LTD.	1842-1881
J. B.	BROADHURST, JAMES (LONGTON)	1863-1870
J. B. & CO.	BENNETT, J. & CO.	1896-1900
J. B. & S.	BROADHURST, JAMES & SONS (FENTON)	1870-1922
J. B. & S. LTD.	BROADHURST, JAMES & SONS LTD. (FENTON)	1922-1983
J. C.	CLEMENTSON, JOSEPH	1839-1864
J. C.	CORMIE, JOHN or JAMES	1820-1841
J. C. & C. (CO.)	CARR, JOHN & CO.	1850-1854
J. C. & S. or (& SONS)	CARR, JOHN & SON(S)	1861-1900
J. C. & SONS	CLEMENTSON, JOSEPH & SONS	c1848+
J. D. & CO.	DIMMOCK, JOHN & CO.	1862-1878
J. D. B.	BAGSTER, JOHN DENTON (or BAXTER)	1823-1827
J. E.	EDWARDS, JAMES	1842-1854
J. E.	EDWARDS, JOHN & CO.	1847-1873
J. E. & CO.	EDWARDS, JOHN & CO.	1873-1879
J. E. & S.	EDWARDS, JAMES & SON(S)	1854-1882
J. E. B. (W.)	BADDELEY, JOHN & EDWARD	1784-1811
J. F. & C. W.	WILEMAN, JAMES & CHARLES	1864-1870
J. F. (& C.) or (& CO.)	FURNIVAL, JACOB & CO.	1845-1870
J. F. W.	WILEMAN, JAMES, F.	1870-1892
J. G.	GILDEA, JAMES	1885-1888
J. G.	GOODWIN, JOHN (LONGTON)	1841-1851
J. H.	HEATH, JOSEPH	1845-1853
J. H. & CO.	HEATH, JOSEPH & CO.	1828-1841 (1842)
J. H. W. & SONS (LTD)	WEATHERBY, J. H. & SONS (LTD.)	1891-1908-(1925)
J. J. & CO.	JACKSON, J. & CO.	1870-1887
J. J. (& CO.)(/B)	JAMIESON, JAMES & CO.	1826-1854
J. K. (L.)	KENT, JAMES (LTD.)	1897-1913-(1989)
J. K. K.	KNIGHT, JOHN KING	1846-1853
J. L. C.	CHETHAM, JONATHAN LOWE	1841-1861
J. M.	MEIR, JOHN	1812-1836
J. M. & CO.	MACINTYRE, JAMES & CO. (LTD.)	1868-1894-(1928+)
J. M. & CO.	MAUDESLEY, J. & CO.	1862-1864
J. M. & CO.	MILLER, JAMES & CO.	1869-1904
J. M. & CO. (LTD)	MARSHALL, JOHN & CO. (LTD.)	1867-1895-(1899)
J. M. & S.	MEIGH, JOB & SON	1812-1832
J. M. & S.	MEIR, JOHN & SON	1837-1897
J. M. (&) CO.	NORTH BRITISH POTTERY	1867-1874
J. P. & CO. (L.)	PRATT, JOHN & CO. (LTD.)	1847-1878
J. R.	RIDGWAY, JOB	1802-1808
J. R.	RIDGWAY, JOHN	1830-1841
J. R.	ROGERS, JOHN & SON	1815-1841

J. R. & CO.	RIDGWAY, JOHN & CO.	1841-1855
J. R. /B.	RIDGWAY, JOHN BATES & CO.	1856-1858
J. R. /B.	ROBINSON, JOSEPH	1876-1898
J. R. /F.	REEVES, JAMES	1870-1948
J. R. /L. S.	ROGERS, JOHN & GEORGE	1815-1841
J. R. B. (& CO.)	RIDGWAY, JOHN, BATES & CO.	1856-1858
J. R. S. /L	ROGERS, JOHN & SON	1815-1841
J. T.	TAMS, JOHN	1875-1903
J. T.	TWIGG, JOSEPH	1822-1866
J. T. & S. or J. T. S.	TAMS, JOHN & SON (LTD.)	1903-1912-(1988)
J. T. (& S.)	TWIGG, JOSEPH (& CO.) (KILNHURST)	1839-1881
J. T. (& SONS)	THOMSON, JOHN (& SONS)	1826-1870-(1888) (1896)
J. T. H.	HUDDEN, JOHN THOMAS	1861-1883
J. V.	VERNON, JAMES	1860-1874
J. V. & S. or JUNR.	VERNON, JAMES & SON	1875-1880
J. W.	WARDLE, JAMES & CO. (HANLEY) (LTD.)	1854-1871
J. W. & CO.	WILEMAN, JAMES & CHARLES	1864-1870
J. W. (CO.)	WALLACE, (J.) & CO.	1838-1893
J. W. P. (& CO.)	PANKHURST, J. W. (& CO.)	1850-1852-(1882)
J. W. R.	RIDGWAY, JOHN & WILLIAM	1813-1830
J. W. W.	WOOD, JOHN WEDG	1841-1875
J. Y.	YATES, JOHN	1770-1835
K. & CO. (/B.) (/LTD.)	KEELING & CO. (LTD.)	1886-1909-(1936)
K. & E.	KNIGHT, ELKIN & CO.	1822-1825
K. E. & B.	ELKIN, KNIGHT & BRIDGWOOD	1827-1840
K. E. & K.	KNIGHT, ELKIN & KNIGHT	1841-1844
K. E. (& CO.)	KNIGHT, ELKIN & CO.	1822-1825
K. E. B. (& B.)	KNIGHT, ELKIN & BRIDGWOOD	1827-1840
K. P.	TWIGG, JOSEPH	1839-1881
L. & A.	LOCKHART & ARTHUR	1855-1864
L. & CO. (COY)	LOCKHART, DAVID	1865-1876
L. & D.	LIVESLEY & DAVIS	1867-1871
L. & H.(/ L. E.)	LOCKETT & HULME or LOCKETT(S)(& CO.)	1818-1826
L. & M.	YNYSMEUDWY POTTERY	1860-1870
L. (&) B.	BEECH & LOWNDES	1821-1834
L. (&) B.	LOWNDES & BEECH	1821-1834
L. E. & S.	LIDDLE, ELLIOT & SON	1860-1870
L. P.	LEEDS POTTERY	c1780
L. P.	PLANT, R. H. & S. L. LTD.	1898-1915-(1970)
L. P. & CO.	LIVESLEY, POWELL & CO.	1851-1865
L. P. CO. LTD.	LONGTON POTTERY CO. LTD.	1946-1955
L. W.	WOOLF, LEWIS	1851-1877
L. W. (S.) or (& SONS)	WOOLF, LEWIS (& SON(S)) (& CO.)	1857-1883
M.	MADDOCK, JOHN	1842-1855
M.	MAILING'S (ROBERT)	1815-1830
M.	MINTON	1824-1836
M. & A.	MORLEY & ASHWORTH	1859-1862
M. & B.	MINTON & BOYLE	1836-1841
M. & CO.	MINTON & CO.	1841-1873
M. & CO.	MOORE & CO. (LONGTON)	1872-1892
M. & CO.	MOORE, (S.) & CO. (FENTON)	1841-1873
M. & E.	MAYER & ELLIOTT	1858-1860
M. & H.	MINTON & HOLLINS	1845-1868
M. & N.	MAYER & NEWBOLD	1817-1832
M. & P.	MACHIN & POTTS	1833-1838
M. & S.	MADDOCK & SEDDON	1839-1842
M. & S.	MEIGH, CHARLES & SON	1850-1861
M. & W.	MARSH & WILLETT	1829-1834
M. B. & E.	MAYER, BROS. & ELLIOT	1855-1858
M. E. CO.	MIDDLESBROUGH EARTHENWARE CO.	1844-1852
M. J. B.	BLAKENEY POTTERY LTD.	1968+
M. P. CO.	MIDDLESBROUGH POTTERY CO.	1831-1844
M. S. & CO. (LTD.)	MYOTT SON & CO. (LTD.)	1898-1977
M. T. & CO.	MARPLE, TURNER & CO.	1851-1858
M. T. & T.	TROUTBECK, E. T.	c1846
M. V. & CO.	MELLOR , VENABLES & CO.	1834-1851
M. W.	WHITEHAVEN POTTERY	1863-1877
M. W. & H.	MALKIN, WALKER & HULSE	1858-1864
N.	NEAL & CO.	1778-1792
N. S.	COPELAND & GARRETT	1822-1840
N. S.	SPODE, JOSIAH	1822-1833
N. W. P. CO. (B.)	NEW WHARF POTTERY CO.	1878-1894
N. W. P. CO./ BURSLEM	NEW WHARF POTTERY CO.	1878-1894
O. H. E. C. (L.)	OLD HALL EARTHENWARE CO.LTD.	1862-1886
P.	POUNTNEY & ALLIES	1816-1835
P.	WEDGWOOD, JOSIAH (& SONS LTD.)	AFTER 1869
P. & A.	POUNTNEY & ALLIES	1816-1835
P. & B.	POWELL & BISHOP	1866-1878
P. & CO.	PEARSON & CO.	1880(+)
P. & CO.	POUNTNEY & CO.	1859-1889
P. & CO. LTD	POUNTNEY & CO. LTD.	1889-1962
P. & G.	POUNTNEY & GOLDNEY	1837-1850
P. & S.	PRATT & SIMPSON	1878-1883
P. A. / B. P.	POUNTNEY & ALLIES (BRISTOL POTTERY)	1816-1835
P. B.	POWELL & BISHOP	1866-1878
P. B. & CO.	BOURNE, PINDER & CO.	1862-1882
P. B. & CO.	PINDER, BOURNE & CO.	1862-1882
P. B. & H.	BOURNE, PINDER & HOPE	1851-1862
P. B. & H.	PINDER, BOURNE & HOPE	1851-1862
P. B. & S.	POWELL, BISHOP & STONIER	1878-1891
P. B. (BROS.)	POULSON BROS. (LTD.)	1884-1927
P. H. & CO.	HOLDCROFT, PETER & CO.	1846-1852
P. P. (CO. LTD.)	PEARL POTTERY CO. (LTD.)	1894-1912-(1936)
P. P. COY. L.	PLYMOUTH POTTERY CO. LTD.	1856-1863
P. S. & S.	POWELL, BISHOP & STONIER	1878-1891
P. S. / B. P.	POUNTNEY & ALLIES	1816-1835
P. W. & CO.	PODMORE, WALKER & CO.	1834-1859
P. W. & W.	PODMORE, WALKER & WEDGWOOD	1856-1859
Q. U. E.	ST. JOHNS STONE CHINAWARE CO. (CANADA)	1873-1899
R.	RATHBONE, SAMUEL & JOHN	1812-1818 & 1823-1835
R.	RIDGWAY, JOB	1802-1808
R. & C.	REED & CLEMENTSON	1833-1835
R. & C.	REED & CO.	1837-1838
R. & M.	RIDGWAY & MORLEY	1842-1845
R. & M. CO.	ROWLAND & MARSELLUS	1893-1933
R. & T.	REED & TAYLOR	1820-1848
R. & W.	ROBINSON & WOOD	1832-1836
R. A. K. & CO.	KIDSTON, R. A. & CO.	1834-1841
R. C. & A.	READ, CLEMENTSON & ANDERSON	c1836
R. C. & CO.	COCHRAN, ROBERT & CO.	1846-1896- (1917)
R. C. & CO. /V . P.	COCHRAN, ROBERT & CO.	1869-1917
R. G.	GARNER, ROBERT (III)	1789-1821
R. H.	HAMMERSLEY, RALPH	1860-1883
R. H. & CO.	HALL, RALPH (& SON or & CO.)	1841-1849
R. H. & S. L. P.	PLANT, R. H. & S. L. (LTD.)	1898-1915-(1970)
R. H. & S. LTD.	HAMMERSLEY, RALPH & SON(S) LTD.	1884-1905
R. H. (& S.) S. or (/CO.)	HERON, ROBERT (& SON)	1837-1929
R. H. P. & CO.	PENMAN, ROBERT H. & CO.	1865-1867
R. M.	MAILING'(S), ROBERT	1815-1859
R. M.	MALKIN, RALPH	1864-1881
R. M. W. & CO.	RIDGWAY, MORLEY, WEAR & CO.	1836-1842
R. S.	STEVENSON, RALPH	1810-1833
R. S. & S.	STEVENSON, RALPH & SON	1833-1835
R. S. & W.	STEVENSON, RALPH & WILLIAMS	1825-1827
R. S. (&) R.	RIDGWAY, SPARKS & RIDGWAY	1872-1878
R. S. W.	STEVENSON, RALPH & WILLIAMS	1825-1827
R. T. (& CO.)	REED & TAYLOR (& CO.)	1841-1848
R. W.	WHITEHAVEN POTTERY	1877-1910
R. W. & B.	ROBINSON, WOOD & BROWNFIELD	1837
R. W. & CO.	RIDGWAY, WILLIAM & CO.	1834-1854
R. W. & W.	STEVENSON, RALPH & WILLIAMS	1825-1827
R./HACKWOOD	RATCLIFFE, WILLIAM (ATT.)	1831-1843
S. & B. (F. B.)	SEFTON & BROWN	1897-1919
S. & B. /T.	SMITH & BINNALL	1897-1900
S. & E.	SWIFT & ELKIN	1840-1843
S. & F.	FORD, SAMUEL & CO.	1898-1939
S. & F.	SMITH & FORD	1895-1898
S. & H.	SNEYD & HILL	c. 1845
S. & J. B.	BURTON, SAMUEL & JOHN	1832-1845
S. & M.	SHIRLEY, T. & JOHN MILLIGAN (CLYDE)	1841-1857
S. & S. (SONS.)	SCOTT & SONS	1829-1841-(1882)
S. & W.	SKINNER & WALKER	1875-1877
S. (& SONS)	SOUTHWICK POTTERY	1829-1841
S. A. (& CO.)	ALCOCK, SAMUEL (& CO.)	1826-1859
S. B.	BRIDGWOOD, SAMPSON	1830
S. B. & CO.	SCOTT BROS. & CO.	1841-1854
S. B. & CO.	SHARPE BROS. & CO. (LTD.)	1838-1895(+)
S. B. & CO.	SOUTHWICK POTTERY	1841-1854
S. B. & S.	BARKER, SAMUEL & SON(S)	1851-1893
S. B. & S. or (& SON)	BRIDGWOOD, SAMPSON & SON, (LTD.)	1854-1962
S. C. H. /L.	SHORE, COGGINS & HOLT	1905-1910
S. F. & CO.	FORD, SAMUEL & CO.	1898-1939
S. F. & J.	SMITH, FORD & JONES	1889-1894
S. H.	HANCOCK, SAMPSON	1858-1891
S. H. (& S.) or (& SONS)	HANCOCK, SAMPSON (& SONS)	1892-1935
S. J. & J. B.	BOYLE, SAMUEL	1823-1844
S. J. (B.)	JOHNSON, SAMUEL (LTD.)	1887-1912
S. J. LTD.	JOHNSON, SAMUEL LTD.	1912-1931
S. K. & CO.	KEELING, SAMUEL & CO.	1838-1849
S. M. & CO.	MOORE, SAMUEL & CO.	1803-1874
S. P. CO.	STANLEY POTTERY CO.	1909-1937
S. R.	COLCLOUGH & CO.	1919-1928
S. W. (& CO.)	WOOLF, SYDNEY (& CO.)	1873-1887
S. W. P.	SOUTH WALES POTTERS	1839-1922
T.	TWIGG, JOSEPH	1839-1881
T. & B. G.	GODWIN, THOMAS & BENJAMIN	1809-1834
T. & R. B.	BOOTE, T. & R.	1842-1894-(1963)
T. & T.	TURNER & TOMKINSON	1860-1872
T. A. & S. G.	GREEN, T. A. & S.	1876-1889
T. B. & CO.	BOOTH, THOMAS & CO.	1868-1872
T. B. & S.	BOOTE, T. & R. & SON.	1872-1876
T. B. & S.	BOOTH, THOMAS & SON	1872-1876
T. B. & S./FB	BROWN, T. & SONS, LTD.	c1919
T. B. G.	GODWIN, THOMAS & BENJAMIN	1809-1834
T. E.	EDWARDS, THOMAS	1841-1847

T. F.	FORD, THOMAS	1871-1874
T. F. & CO.	FORD, THOMAS & CO.	1871-1874
T. F. & S.	FORESTER, THOMAS & SON(S) (LTD.)	1884-1891-(1959)
T. F. & SONS	FURNIVAL, THOMAS & SONS	1875-1890
T. F. (& C.) or (& CO.)	FURNIVAL, THOMAS & CO.	1844-1845
T. F. (& C.) (& CO.)	FELL, THOMAS & CO. (LTD.)	1830-1869-(1890)
T. G.	GODWIN, THOMAS	1834-1854
T. G.	GOODFELLOW, THOMAS	1828-1860
T. G.	GREEN, THOMAS	1848-1859
T. G. & F. B.	BOOTH, T. G. & F. B.	1883-1891
T. G. B.	BOOTH, THOMAS G.	1876-1883
T. G. G. & CO. (LTD.)	GREEN, T. G. & CO. (LTD.)	1880s-1967(+)
T. H. & CO.	TAYLOR, HARRISON & CO.	1830s-1841
T. H. W.	WALKER, THOMAS HENRY	1846-1848
T. I. & CO.	INGLEBY, THOMAS & CO.	1834-1835
T. M.	BLAKENEY POTTERY LTD.	1968+
T. N. & CO. /C.	NICHOLSON, THOMAS & CO.	1854-1871
T. R. & CO.	RATHBONE, THOMAS & CO.	1898-1923
T. S. or (& CO. or & COY.)	SHIRLEY, THOMAS & CO.	1840-1857
T. W.	WALKER, THOMAS	1845-1856
T. W. & CO.	WOOD, THOMAS & CO.	1885-1896
T. W. & S.	WOOD, THOMAS & SONS.	1896-1897
U. H. P. CO. (LTD.)	UPPER HANLEY CO. (LTD.)	1895-1900-(1910)
W.	CORN, W. & E.	1900-1904
W.	WALLEY, EDWARD	1845-1858
W.	WARBURTON, JOHN (COBRIDGE)	1802-1823
W.	WARDLE, JAMES & CO. (HANLEY) LTD.	1890-1935
W.	WOLFE, THOMAS (SR.)	1781-1810
W.	WOOD, ENOCH	1784-1789
W. & B.	ROBINSON (&) WOOD	1837-1841
W. & B.	WOOD & BAGGALEY	1870-1880
W. & B.	WOOD & BRETTEL	1818-1823
W. & B.	WOOD & BROWNFIELD	1837-1850
W. & B. LTD. /B.	WOOD & BARKER LTD.	1897-1903
W. & C.	WALKER & CARTER	1866-1889
W. & C.	WILEMAN & CO.	1892-1925
W. & C.	WOOD & CHALLINOR	1828-1845
W. & CO.	WHITTAKER & CO.	1886-1892
W. & CO.	WOOD & CHALLINOR & CO.	1860-1864
W. & CO.	WOODNORTH & CO.	1800-1824
W. & E. C.	CORN, W. & E.	1864-1904
W. & H.	WORTHINGTON & HARROP	1856-1873
W. & H. /B.	HULME, HENRY & SONS	1906-1932
W. & H. /B.	WOOD & HULME	1882-1905
W. & J. B.	BUTTERFIELD, WILLIAM & JAMES	1854-1861
W. & J. H.	HARDING, W. & J.	1863-1872
W. & P.	WOOD & PIGOTT	1869-1871
W. & R.	CARLTON WARE LTD.	1958-1986
W. & R.	WILTSHAW & ROBINSON (LTD.)	1890-1957-(1958+)
W. & S. E.	EDGE, WILLIAM & SAMUEL	1841-1848
W. & T. A.	ADAMS, WILLIAM & THOMAS	1866-1892
W. A. & CO.	ADAMS, WILLIAM & CO.	1893-1917
W. A. & S.	ADAMS, WILLIAM & SON(S)	1829-1863
W. A. A. (& CO.)	ADDERELY, WILLIAM ALSAGER (& CO.)	1875-1886-(1905)
W. B. & C.	BOURNE, W. & CO. (BURSLEM)	1804-1818
W. B. & CO.	BAKER, (W.) & CO. (LTD.)	1839-1893
W. B. (& S.) or (& SON(S))	BROWNFIELD, WILLIAM & SON(S)	1850-1870-(1892)
W. C.	WOOD & CHALLINOR	1828-1845
W. C. & CO.	WOOD & CHALLINOR & CO.	1860-1864
W. C. JR. L.P.	CHAMBERS, WILLIAM JR.	1839-1855
W. E.	EMBERTON, WILLIAM	1851-1869
W. E. & CO.	EMBERTON, WILLIAM & CO.	1846-1851
W. E. C.	CORN, W. & E.	1864-1904
W. F. & CO.	WHITTINGHAM, FORD & CO.	1868-1873
W. F. & R.	WHITTINGHAM, FORD & RILEY	1876-1882
W. H.	WOOD & HULME	1882-1905
W. H. & CO.	WHITTAKER, HEATH & CO.	1892-1898
W. H. (& S.)	HACKWOOD, WILLIAM (& SON)	1843-1855
W. H. (/H.)	HACKWOOD, WILLIAM	1827-1843
W. H. L./H.	LOCKITT, WILLIAM H.	1901-1919
W. P. & CO.	WHITEHAVEN POTTERY	1824-1840
W. P. C.	WILKINSON POTTERY CO.	1863-1877
W. R. (& CO.)	RIDGWAY, WILLIAM (& CO.)	1830-1834-(1854)
W. R. S. & CO.	RIDGWAY, WILLIAM SON & CO.	1838-1845
W. S. & CO.	SMITH, WILLIAM & CO.	1825-1855
W. S. & CO'S .	SMITH, WILLIAM & CO. (WEDG WOOD)	1825-1855
W. T. & CO.	TOMLINSON, FOSTER, WEDGWOOD & CO.	c1798
W. T. H.	HOLLAND, WILLIAM T.	1859-1868
W. W.	WILKINSON, ARTHUR, J. (LTD)	1885-1965
W. W.	WOOD, JOHN WEDG	1841-1857-(1875)
W. W. & CO.	WOOD, WILLIAM & CO.	1873-1932
Y. & B.	YALE & BARKER	1841-1842
Y. & M.	YATES & MAY	1835-1843
Y. M. P.	YNYSMEUDWY POTTERY	1850(+)
Y. P.	YNYSMEUDWY POTTERY	1850s
Z. B. (& S.)	BOYLE, ZACHARIAH (& SON(S))	1828-1836

APPENDIX B2: ALPHABETIC LISTING: PRIMARY POTTERS BY NAME & INITIAL

POTTERY	INITIALS	DATE
ADAMS, HARVEY & CO.	H. A. & CO.	1869-1887
ADAMS, WILLIAM & CO.	W. A. & CO.	1893-1917
ADAMS, WILLIAM & SON(S)	W. A. & S.	1829-1863
ADAMS, WILLIAM & THOMAS	W. & T. A.	1866-1892
ADDERELY, WILLIAM ALSAGER (& CO.)	W. A. A. (& CO.)	1875-1886-(1905)
ALCOCK, HENRY & CO. (LTD.)	H. A. & CO.	1861-1901-(1910)
ALCOCK, JOHN & GEORGE	J. & G. A.	1839-1848
ALCOCK, SAMUEL (& CO.)	S. A. (& CO.)	1826-1859
ALLERTON, BROUGH & GREEN	A. B. & G.	1832-1859
ALLERTON, CHARLES & SONS (LTD.)	C. A. & SONS	1860-1911
ALLMAN, BROUGHTON & CO.	A. B. & CO.	1861-1868
ASHWORTH, G. L. & BROS.	A. BROS.	1862-1883
ASHWORTH, G. L. & BROS. (LTD.)	G. L. A. & BROS.	1862-1883
ASHWORTH, G. L. & BROS. (LTD.)	G. L. A. & T.	1862-1883
BADDELEY, GEORGE	B.	c1822
BADDELEY, JOHN & EDWARD	B.	1784-1811
BADDELEY, JOHN & EDWARD	J. E. B. (W.)	1784-1811
BAGGERLEY & BALL	B. & B.	1822-1836
BAGGERLEY & BALL	B. & B. /L.	1822-1836
BAGSHAW & MEIR	B. & M.	1802-1808
BAGSTER, JOHN DENTON (or BAXTER)	I. D. B.	1823-1827
BAGSTER, JOHN DENTON (or BAXTER)	J. D. B.	1823-1827
BAILEY & BALL	B. & B.	1843-1850
BAILEY & BATKIN	B. & B.	1814-1826
BAKER, (W.) & CO. (LTD.)	W. B. & CO.	1839-1893
BAKER, BEVANS & CO.	G. P. CO. /S.	1819-1838
BAKER, BEVANS & IRWIN	B. B. & CO.	1813-1838
BAKER, BEVANS & IRWIN	B. B. & I.	1813-1838
BALFOUR, ALEXANDER & CO.	A. B. & CO.	1874-1904
BARKER & SON	B. & S.	1850-1860
BARKER & TILL	B. & T.	1846-1850
BARKER BROS. (LTD.)	B. B. (LTD.)	1876-1900-(1959)
BARKER, SAMUEL & SON(S)	S. B. & S.	1851-1893
BARKER, SAMUEL (& SON(S))	B.	1834-1851
BARKER, SUTTON & TILL	B. S. & T.	1834-1846
BARKERS & KENT (LTD.)	B. & K. (L.)	1889-1941
BARLOW, JAMES	B.	1822-1839
BARLOW, THOMAS	B.	1849-1853-(1882)
BATES & BENNETT	B. & B.	1868-1895
BATES, BROWN-WESTHEAD & MOORE	B. B. W. & M.	1859-1861
BATES, ELLIOTT & CO.	B. E. & CO.	1870-1875
BATES, GILDEA & WALKER	B. G. & W.	1878-1881
BATES, WALKER & CO.	B. W. & CO.	1875-1878
BATKIN, WALKER, & BROADHURST	B. W. (&) B.	1840-1845
BEARDMORE & BIRKS	B. & B.	1832-1843
BEARDMORE & EDWARDS	B. & E.	c1858
BEARDMORE, FRANK & CO.	F. B. & CO. /F.	1903-1914
BEDNALL & HEATH	B. & H.	1879-1899
BEECH & HANCOCK	B. & H.	1860-1876
BEECH & LOWNDES	L. (&) B.	1821-1834
BEECH, HANCOCK & CO.	B. H. & CO.	1851-1855
BEECH, JAMES	J. B.	1878-1889
BELL, J. & M. P. & CO. (LTD.)	B.	1850-1870
BELL, J. & M. P. & CO. LTD.	J. & M. P. B. & CO.	1850-1870
BELL, J. & M. P. & CO. LTD.	J. B.	1842-1881
BENNETT, J. & CO.	J. B. & CO.	1896-1900
BETTANY, GEORGE	B.	1822-1830
BIRKS, BROS. & SEDDON	B. B. & S.	1878-1886
BIRKS, CHARLES	B.	1822-1835
BISHOP & STONIER (LTD.)	B. & S.	1891-1910
BLACKHURST & BOURNE	B. & B.	1880-1892
BLACKHURST & HULME	B. & H.	1889-1932
BLACKHURST & TUNNICLIFFE	B. & T.	1879-1879
BLAKENEY POTTERY LTD.	M. J. B.	1968+
BLAKENEY POTTERY LTD.	T. M.	1968+
BODLEY & CO.	B. & CO.	1865-1865
BODLEY & HAROLD	B. & H.	1863-1865
BODLEY, EDWARD F. & CO.	E. F. B. (&CO.)	1862-1875
BODLEY, EDWARD F. & SON	E. F. B. & S. or (& SON)	1875-1898
BOOTE, T. & R.	T. & R. B.	1842-1894-(1963)
BOOTE, T. & R. & SON.	T. B. & S.	1872-1876
BOOTH & MEIGH	B. & M.	1837-1838
BOOTH, T. G. & F. B.	T. G. & F. B.	1883-1891
BOOTH, THOMAS G.	T. G. B.	1876-1883
BOOTH, THOMAS & CO.	T. B. & CO.	1868-1872
BOOTH, THOMAS & SON	T. B. & S.	1872-1876
BOOTHS (LTD.)	B. B. B.	1891-1912
BOULTON, MACHIN & TENNANT	B. M. & T.	1889-1899
BOURNE & LEIGH (LTD.)	B. & L.	1892-1941

BOURNE & LEIGH (LTD.)	E. B. (&) J. E. L. (B.)	1892-1941
BOURNE, BAKER & BAKER	B. B. & B.	1833-1835
BOURNE, BAKER & BOURNE	B. B. & B.	1796-1833
BOURNE, CHARLES	C. B.	1817-1830
BOURNE, NIXON & CO.	B. N. & CO.	1828-1830
BOURNE, PINDER & CO.	P. B. & CO.	1862-1882
BOURNE, PINDER & HOPE	P. B. & H.	1851-1862
BOURNE, W. & CO. (BURSLEM)	W. B. & C.	1804-1818
BOURNE, WILLIAM (LONGTON)	B.	1857-1861
BOVEY POTTERY CO. LTD.	B. P. CO. LTD.	1894-1947
BOVEY TRACEY POTTERY CO.	B. T. P. CO.	1842-1894
BOWERS, GEORGE FREDERICK(&CO.)	G. F. B. (B.T.)	1841-1868
BOYLE, SAMUEL	S. J. & J. B.	1823-1844
BOYLE, ZACHARIAH (& SON(S))	Z. B. (& S.)	1828-1836
BRADSHAW, WILLIAM	B.	1819-1823
BRAMELD & CO.	B.	1806-1841(1842)
BREEZE, JOHN	B.	1828-1830
BRIDGET, BATES & BEECH	B.B.B.	1875-1882
BRIDGETT & BATES	B. & B.	1882-1915
BRIDGWOOD & BURGESS	B. & B.	1846-1847
BRIDGWOOD & CLARKE	B. & C.	1859-1864
BRIDGWOOD, SAMPSON	B.	1822-1853
BRIDGWOOD, SAMPSON	S. B.	1830
BRIDGWOOD, SAMPSON & SON, (LTD.)	S. B. & S. or (& SON)	1854-1962
BRITANNIA POTTERY CO. LTD.	B. P. CO. LTD.	1920-1935
BRITISH ANCHOR POTTERY CO. LTD.	B. P. CO. LTD.	1884-1982
BROADHURST, JAMES & SONS (FENTON)	J. B. & S.	1870-1922
BROADHURST, JAMES & SONS LTD. (FENTON)	J. B. & S. LTD.	1922-1983
BROADHURST, JAMES (LONGTON)	J. B.	1863-1870
BROUGHAM & MAYER	B. & M.	1856-1862
BROWN & STEVENTON, LTD.	B. & S.	1900-1923
BROWN, T. & SONS, LTD.	T. B. & S./FB	c1919
BROWNFIELD, WILLIAM & SON(S)	W. B. (& S.) or (& SON(S))	1850-1870-(1892)
BROWNFIELDS GUILD POTTERY LTD.	B. G. P. CO.	1892-1897
BROWNHILLS POTTERY CO.	B. P. CO.	1872-1896
BROWN-WESTHEAD, MOORE & CO.	B. W. M. (& CO.)	1862-1904
BULLOCK, A. & CO.	A. B. & CO.	1895-1915
BULLOCK, A. & CO.	A. B. & CO./H.	1895-1915
BURGESS & LEIGH (LTD.)	B. & L.	1862-1889
BURGESS, HENRY	H. B.	1864-1892
BURN, JOSEPH & CO.	B. & CO.	1852-1860
BURTON & MORRIS	B. & M.	1882-1897
BURTON, SAMUEL & JOHN	S. & J. B.	1832-1845
BUTTERFIELD, WILLIAM & JAMES	W. & J. B.	1854-1861
CALLAND, JOHN F. & CO.	C. & CO.	1852-1856
CAMPBELLFIELD POTTERY CO. (LTD.)	C. P. CO. (LTD.)	1850-1880-(1899)
CARLTON WARE LTD.	W. & R.	1958-1986
CARR, JOHN & CO.	J. C. & C. (CO.)	1850-1854
CARR, JOHN & SON(S)	J. C. & S. or (& SONS)	1861-1900
CARTWRIGHT & EDWARDS (LTD.)	C. & E. (LTD)	1858-1926-(1988)
CERAMIC ART CO. (1905) LTD.	C. A. & CO. LTD.	1905-1919
CHALLINOR, E. & C.	E. & C. C.	1862-1891
CHALLINOR, E. & CO.	E. C. & C. CO.	1853-1862
CHALLINOR, E. & CO.	E. C. & CO.	1853-1862
CHALLINOR, EDWARD	E. C.	1842-1867
CHALLINOR, EDWARD	G. R.	1842-1867
CHAMBERS, WILLIAM JR.	W. C. JR. L.P.	1839-1855
CHESWORTH & ROBINSON	C. & R.	1825-1840
CHETHAM & ROBINSON	C. & R.	1822-1834
CHETHAM & ROBINSON & SON	C. R. S.	1834-1840
CHETHAM, JONATHAN LOWE	J. L. C.	1841-1861
CLEMENTSON, JOSEPH	J. C.	1839-1864
CLEMENTSON, JOSEPH & SONS	J. C. & SONS	c1848+
CLEMENTSON, YOUNG & JAMESON	C. Y. & J.	1844-1845
CLEWS, JAMES & RALPH	G. R.	1817-1834
CLYDE POTTERY (GREENOCK)	G. P. CO. (G.) (& CO.)	1816-1903
CLYDE POTTERY CO. (LTD.)	C. P. CO.	1857-1861
CLYDE POTTERY CO. (LTD.)	G. C. P. CO. (G.)	1850s
CLYDE POTTERY CO. LTD.	G. C. P. CO. LTD.	1857-1861
COCHRAN & FLEMING	B. P. CO. LTD.	1920-1939
COCHRAN & FLEMING	C. & F. /G.	1896-1917
COCHRAN, ROBERT & CO.	R. C. & CO.	1846-1896- (1917)
COCHRAN, ROBERT & CO.	R. C. & CO. /V . P.	1869-1917
COCKSON & CHETWYND (& CO.)	C. C. & CO.	1867-1875
COCKSON & HARDING	C. & H.	1856-1863
COLCLOUGH & CO.	C. & CO.	1887-1928
COLCLOUGH & CO.	S. R.	1919-1928
COOMBS & HOLLAND	C. & H.	1855-1858
CO-OPERATIVE WHOLESALE SOCIETY LTD.	C. W. S.	1946-1970s
COPELAND & GARRETT	C. & G.	1833-1847
COPELAND & GARRETT	N. S.	1822-1840
COPELAND, W. T. (& SONS LTD.)	CC (NO DOTS)	1846-1856
CORK & EDGE	C. & E.	1846-1860
CORK, EDGE & MALKIN	C. E. & M.	1860-1871
CORMIE, JOHN or JAMES	J. C.	1820-1841
CORN, W. & E.	W.	1900-1904
CORN, W. & E.	W. & E. C.	1864-1904
CORN, W. & E.	W. E. C.	1864-1904
COTTON & BARLOW	C. & B.	1850-1857
CUMBERLIDGE & HUMPHREYS	C. & H.	1886-1889 & 1893-1895
CUMBERLIDGE, HUMPHREYS & HELE	C. H. & H.	1889-1893
DALTON & BURN	D. & B.	1833-1843
DANIEL, H. & R.	D.	1822-1846
DANIEL, H. & R.	H. & R. D.	1822-1846
DAVENPORT, BANKS & CO.	D. B. & CO.	1860-1873
DAVENPORT, BECK & CO.	D. B. & CO.	1873-1880
DAVIS, COOKSON, & WILSON	D. C. & W.	1822-1833
DEAKIN & BAILEY or (BAILEY & DEAKIN)	D. & B.	1828-1832
DEAKIN & SON(S) (& CO.)	D. & S.	1832-1841
DILLON, FRANCIS	F. D.	1830-1843
DILLWYN & CO.	D.	1824-1850
DILLWYN & CO.	D. & CO.	1836-1850
DIMMOCK & SMITH	D. & S.	1842-1859
DIMMOCK, JOHN & CO.	J. D. & CO.	1862-1878
DIMMOCK, THOMAS (JR.) (& CO.)	D.	1828-1859
DUNDERDALE, DAVID & CO.	D. D. & CO.	1803-1821
DUNN BENNETT & CO. (LTD.)	D. B. & C. (CO.)	1875-1907
EDGE, BARKER & BARKER	E. B. & B.	1836-1840
EDGE, BARKER & CO.	E. B. & CO.	1835-1836
EDGE, MALKIN & CO.	D. & K. R.	1870-1880
EDGE, MALKIN & CO. (LTD.)	E. M. & CO. (/B.)	1870-1899-(1903)
EDGE, WILLIAM & SAMUEL	W. & S. E.	1841-1848
EDWARDS, JAMES	J. E.	1842-1854
EDWARDS, JAMES & SON(S)	D. H. (DALE HALL)	1854-1882
EDWARDS, JAMES & SON(S)	J. E. & S.	1854-1882
EDWARDS, JAMES & THOMAS	J. & T. E.	1839-1842
EDWARDS, JOHN & CO.	J. E.	1847-1873
EDWARDS, JOHN & CO.	J. E. & CO.	1873-1879
EDWARDS, THOMAS	T. E.	1841-1847
ELGIN POTTERY	C. P.	1855-1870
ELKIN & NEWBON	E. & N.	1845-1856
ELKIN, KNIGHT & BRIDGWOOD	E. K. B. (& B.)	1827-1840
ELKIN, KNIGHT & BRIDGWOOD	K. E. & B.	1827-1840
ELKIN, KNIGHT & CO.	E. K. & CO.	1822-1825
ELKINS & CO.	E. & CO.	1822-1825
ELSMORE & FORSTER	E. & F. or E. FOR.	1853-1871
ELSMORE & FORSTER	E. F. & CO.	1853-1871
EMBERTON, WILLIAM	W. E.	1851-1869
EMBERTON, WILLIAM & CO.	W. E. & CO.	1846-1851
EMERY, FRANCIS J.	F. J. E.	1878-1893
EMPIRE PORCELAIN CO. (LTD.)	E. P. CO.	1896-1939-(1963)
EVANS & GLASSON	E. & G.	1850-1861
FELL, THOMAS	F.	1817-1830
FELL, THOMAS & CO. (LTD.)	F. & CO.	1830-1869-(1890)
FELL, THOMAS & CO. (LTD.)	T. F. (& C.) (& CO.)	1830-1869-(1890)
FENTON, ALFRED & SONS	A. F. & S.	1887-1901
FLACKETT & TOFT	F. (&) T.	c1857
FLACKETT, TOFT & ROBINSON	F. T. R. or (& R.)	c1858
FORD & CHALLINOR & CO.	F. & C.	1865-1880
FORD & CHALLINOR & CO.	F. C. & CO.	1865-1880
FORD & RILEY	F. & R. (/B.)	1882-1893
FORD & SONS (LTD.)	F. & S. (/B.)(& SONS LTD)	1893-1908-(1938)
FORD, (&) CHALLINOR & CO.	F. C. & CO.	1865-1880
FORD, SAMUEL & CO.	F. & CO.	1898-1939
FORD, SAMUEL & CO.	S. & F.	1898-1939
FORD, SAMUEL & CO.	S. F. & CO.	1898-1939
FORD, THOMAS	T. F.	1871-1874
FORD, THOMAS & CO.	T. F. & CO.	1871-1874
FORESTER & HULME	F. & H.	1887-1892
FORESTER, THOMAS & SON(S) (LTD.)	T. F. & S.	1884-1891-(1959)
FORRESTER, GEORGE	G. F.	1799-1830
FURNIVAL, JACOB & CO.	J. F. (& C.) or (& CO.)	1845-1870
FURNIVAL, JACOB & THOMAS	J. & T. F.	c1843
FURNIVAL, THOMAS & CO.	T. F. (& C.) or (& CO.)	1844-1845
FURNIVAL, THOMAS & SONS	T. F. & SONS	1875-1890
GARNER, ROBERT (III)	R. G.	1789-1821
GATER, HALL & CO.	G. H. & CO.	1895-1914
GIBSON & SONS (LTD)	H. P. CO.	1904-1909
GIBSON & SONS LTD.	G. & S. LTD. (/B.)	1884-1904
GILDEA & WALKER & CO.	G. W. & CO.	1881-1885
GILDEA & WALKER (& CO.)	G. & W. (& CO.)	1881-1885
GILDEA, JAMES	J. G.	1885-1888
GLAMORGAN POTTERY CO.	G. P. CO.	1819-1838
GODWIN, BENJAMIN, E.	B. G.	1834-1841
GODWIN, JOHN & ROBERT	G. BROS.	1834-1867
GODWIN, JOHN & ROBERT	J. & R. G.	1834-1867
GODWIN, ROWLEY & CO.	G. R. & CO.	1828-1831
GODWIN, THOMAS	T. G.	1834-1854
GODWIN, THOMAS & BENJAMIN	T. & B. G.	1809-1834
GODWIN, THOMAS & BENJAMIN	T. B. G.	1809-1834
GOODFELLOW, THOMAS	T. G.	1828-1860
GOODWIN & CO. (LONGTON)	G. C.	1841-1864
GOODWIN, HARRIS & GOODWIN	G. H. & G.	1832-1838
GOODWIN, JOHN (LONGTON)	G. C.	1841-1864
GOODWIN, JOHN (LONGTON)	J. G.	1841-1851
GOODWINS & BULLOCK	G. & B.	1857-1859

GOODWINS & ELLIS	G. & E.	1839-1840
GOODWINS & HARRIS	G. & H.	1832-1837
GOODWINS, BRIDGWOOD & CO.	G. & B.	1827-1829
GOODWINS, BRIDGWOOD & ORTON	G. B. O. or (& O.)	1827-1829
GOODWINS, BRIDGWOOD (&) HARRIS	G. B. H.	1829-1832
GORDON, GEORGE	G. G.	1795-1833
GREEN, T. A. & S.	T. A. & S. G.	1876-1889
GREEN, T. G. & CO. (LTD.)	T. G. G. & CO. (LTD.)	1880s-1967(+)
GREEN, THOMAS	T. G.	1848-1859
GRIFFITHS, BEARDMORE (& CO.) & BIRKS	G. B. & B.	1829-1831
GRIMWADES BROS.	G. BROS.	1886-1900
GRIMWADES LTD.	G. B.	1900-1978
GROVE & STARK	G. & S.	1875-1885
GUEST & DEWSBERRY	G. & D.	1877-1906
HACKWOOD & CO.	H. & CO.	1807-1827
HACKWOOD & KEELING	H. & K.	1835-1836
HACKWOOD, WILLIAM	H.	1827-1843
HACKWOOD, WILLIAM	W. H. (/H.)	1827-1843
HACKWOOD, WILLIAM & CO.	H. & CO.	1827-1843
HACKWOOD, WILLIAM (& SON)	W. H. (& S.)	1843-1855
HALES, HANCOCK & CO. LTD. (RETAILERS)	H. H. & CO.	1918-1921
HALES, HANCOCK & GODWIN LTD. (RETAILERS)	H. H. & G. LTD.	1922-1960
HALL, RALPH (& SON or & CO.)	R. H. & CO.	1841-1849
HALLAM & JOHNSON	H. & J.	1878-1880
HALLAM & JOHNSON	H. J. CO.	1878-1880
HAMMERSLEY & ASBURY	H. & A.	1870-1875
HAMMERSLEY & CO.	H. & C. (CO.)	1887-1932(+)
HAMMERSLEY, RALPH	R. H.	1860-1883
HAMMERSLEY, RALPH & SON(S) LTD.	R. H. & S. LTD.	1884-1905
HAMPSON & BROADHURST	H. & B.	1849-1854
HANCOCK & WITTINGHAM	H. & W.	1873-1879
HANCOCK, SAMPSON	S. H.	1858-1891
HANCOCK, SAMPSON (& SONS)	S. H. (& S.) or (& SONS)	1892-1935
HANCOCK, WITTINGHAM & CO.	H. W. & CO.	1863-1872
HANLEY PORCELAIN CO.	H. P. CO.	1892-1898
HARDING & COCKSON (& SON) (& CO.)	H. & C.	1834-1863
HARDING, W. & J.	W. & J. H.	1863-1872
HARVEY, C. & W. K.	C. & W. K. H.	1835-1852
HARVEY, C. & W. K.	H.	1835-1852
HAWLEY BROS.	H. B.	1868-1898
HEATH & BLACKHURST	H. & B.	1859-1877
HEATH & GREATBATCH	H. & G./B	1891-1893
HEATH, BLACKHURST & CO.	H. B. & CO.	1859-1877
HEATH, J. (JOSHUA)	I. H.	1770-1800
HEATH, JOSEPH	J. H.	1845-1853
HEATH, JOSEPH & CO.	I. H. & CO.	1828-1841 (1842)
HEATH, JOSEPH & CO.	J. H. & CO.	1828-1841 (1842)
HERON, ROBERT (& SON)	R. H. (& S.) S. or (/CO.)	1837-1929
HICKS, MEIGH & JOHNSON	H. M. J. (& J.)	1822-1835
HILDITCH & HOPWOOD	H. & H.	1832-1859
HILDITCH & SON(S) (& CO.)	H. & S.	1822-1836
HOBSON, CHARLES (& SON)	C. H. (& S.)	1865-1883
HOLDCROFT, HILL & MELLOR	H. H. & M.	1860-1870
HOLDCROFT, HILL & MELLOR	HHM (NO DOTS)	1860-1870
HOLDCROFT, PETER & CO.	P. H. & CO.	1846-1852
HOLLAND & GREEN	H. & G.	1853-1882
HOLLAND & GUEST	H. & G.	1868-1875
HOLLAND, WILLIAM T.	W. T. H.	1859-1868
HOLLINSHEAD & KIRKHAM (LTD.)	H. & K.	1870-1956
HOLLINSHEAD & KIRKHAM (LTD.)	H. & K. /T.	1924-1956
HOLMES, STONIER & HOLLINSHEAD	H. S. & H.	1875-1882
HOPE & CARTER	H. & C.	1862-1880
HOPKIN & VERNON	H. & V.	1836-1839
HUDDEN, JOHN THOMAS	J. T. H.	1861-1883
HUGHES, E. & CO. (CHINA MANUFACTURER)	H.	1889-1941
HUGHES, E. & CO. (CHINA MANUFACTURER)	H. F.	1898-1905
HUGHES, ELIJAH & CO.	E. H.	1853-1867
HULME, HENRY & SONS	W. & H. /B.	1906-1932
HULSE, NIXON & ADDERLEY	H. H. (&) A.	1853-1869
HULSE, NIXON & ADDERLEY	H. N. & A.	1853-1869
HULSEY & ADDERLEY	H. & A.	1869-1874
HUMPHREYS BROS.	H. BROS.	1893-1903
INGLEBY, THOMAS & CO.	T. I. & CO.	1834-1835
JACKSON & PATTERSON	J. & P.	1833-1838
JACKSON, J. & CO.	J. & CO.	1870-1887
JACKSON, J. & CO.	J. J. & CO.	1870-1887
JAMIESON, JAMES & CO.	J. J. (& CO.)(/B)	1826-1854
JOHNSON, SAMUEL (LTD.)	S. J. (B.)	1887-1912
JOHNSON, SAMUEL LTD.	S. J. LTD.	1912-1931
JONES & WALLEY	J. & W.	1841-1845
JONES, ELIJAH	E. J.	1831-1839
JONES, GEORGE	G. J.	1861-1873
JONES, GEORGE & SONS	G. J. & SONS	1873-1893
JONES, GEORGE & SONS LTD.	G. J. & SONS LTD.	1894-1957
KEELING & CO. (LTD.)	K. & CO. (/B.) (/LTD.)	1886-1909-(1936)
KEELING, CHARLES	C. K.	1822-1826
KEELING, SAMUEL & CO.	S. K. & CO.	1838-1849
KENT, JAMES (LTD.)	J. K. (L.)	1897-1913-(1989)
KIDSTON, R. A. & CO.	R. A. K. & CO.	1834-1841
KNIGHT, JOHN KING	J. K. K.	1846-1853
KNIGHT, ELKIN & BRIDGWOOD	K. E. B. (& B.)	1827-1840
KNIGHT, ELKIN & CO.	K. & E.	1822-1825
KNIGHT, ELKIN & CO.	K. E. (& CO.)	1822-1825
KNIGHT, ELKIN & KNIGHT	K. E. & K.	1841-1844
LEEDS POTTERY	L. P.	c1780
LIDDLE, ELLIOT & SON	L. E. & S.	1860-1870
LIVESLEY & DAVIS	L. & D.	1867-1871
LIVESLEY, POWELL & CO.	L. P. & CO.	1851-1865
LOCKETT & HULME or LOCKETT(S)(& CO.)	L. & H.(/ L. E.)	1818-1826
LOCKETT, JOHN & THOMAS	J. & T. L	1835-1855
LOCKHART & ARTHUR	L. & A.	1855-1864
LOCKHART, DAVID	L. & CO. (COY)	1865-1876
LOCKHART, DAVID & CO.	D. L. & CO.	1876-1898
LOCKHART, DAVID & SONS (LTD.)	D. L. & S. (SONS)	1898-1953
LOCKITT, WILLIAM H.	W. H. L./H.	1901-1919
LONGTON POTTERY CO. LTD.	L. P. CO. LTD.	1946-1955
LOWNDES & BEECH	L. (&) B.	1821-1834
MACHIN & POTTS	M. & P.	1833-1838
MACINTYRE, JAMES & CO. (LTD.)	J. M. & CO.	1868-1894-(1928+)
MADDOCK & SEDDON	M. & S.	1839-1842
MADDOCK, JOHN	I. M.	1842-1855
MADDOCK, JOHN	M.	1842-1855
MAILING'(S), ROBERT	R. M.	1815-1859
MAILING'S (ROBERT)	M.	1815-1830
MALING, C. T.	C. T. M.	1859-1890
MALING, C. T. & SONS (LTD.)	C. T. M. & SONS (LTD.)	1890-1947
MALKIN, RALPH	R. M.	1864-1881
MALKIN, WALKER & HULSE	M. W. & H.	1858-1864
MARPLE, TURNER & CO.	M. T. & CO.	1851-1858
MARSH & WILLETT	M. & W.	1829-1834
MARSHALL, JOHN & CO. (LTD.)	J. M. & CO. (LTD)	1867-1895-(1899)
MASON, CHARLES JAMES	C. J. M.	1849-1853
MASON, CHARLES JAMES & CO.	C. J. M. & CO.	1826-1840-(1848)
MASON, G. M. & C. J.	G. & C. J. M.	PRIOR TO 1830
MASON, G. M. & C. J.	G. M. & C. J. M.	PRIOR TO 1830
MAUDESLEY, J. & CO.	J. M. & CO.	1862-1864
MAYER & ELLIOTT	M. & E.	1858-1860
MAYER & NEWBOLD	M. & N.	1817-1832
MAYER, BROS. & ELLIOT	M. B. & E.	1855-1858
MEIGH, CHARLES	C. M.	1832-1850
MEIGH, CHARLES & SON	C. M. & S.	1850-1861
MEIGH, CHARLES & SON	M. & S.	1850-1861
MEIGH, CHARLES, SON & PANKHURST	C. M. S. & P.	1850
MEIGH, JOB & SON	J. M. & S.	1812-1832
MEIR, JOHN	G. R. (& crown)	1812-1836
MEIR, JOHN	I. M.	1812-1836
MEIR, JOHN	J. M.	1812-1836
MEIR, JOHN & SON	I. M. & S.	1837-1897
MEIR, JOHN & SON	J. M. & S.	1837-1897
MELLOR , VENABLES & CO.	M. V. & CO.	1834-1851
METHVEN, DAVID & SONS	D. M. & S. (SONS)	1847-1928
MIDDLESBROUGH EARTHENWARE CO.	M. E. CO.	1844-1852
MIDDLESBROUGH POTTERY CO.	M. P. CO.	1831-1844
MILLER, JAMES & CO.	I. M. CO.	1840s-1920s
MILLER, JAMES & CO.	J. M. & CO.	1869-1904
MINTON	B. B.	1830-1850
MINTON	M.	1824-1836
MINTON & BOYLE	M. & B.	1836-1841
MINTON & CO.	M. & CO.	1841-1873
MINTON & HOLLINS	M. & H.	1845-1868
MOORE & CO. (LONGTON)	M. & CO.	1872-1892
MOORE, (S.) & CO. (FENTON)	M. & CO.	1841-1873
MOORE, SAMUEL & CO.	S. M. & CO.	1803-1874
MORLEY & ASHWORTH	M. & A.	1859-1862
MORLEY, FRANCIS	F. M.	1845-1850
MORLEY, FRANCIS & CO.	F. M. & CO.	1850-1859
MOUNTFORD, GEORGE THOMAS	G. T. M.	1888-1898
MUIR, ANDREW (& CO.) (CLYDE POTTERY CO.)	A. M.	1836-1841
MYOTT SON & CO. (LTD.)	M. S. & CO. (LTD.)	1898-1977
NEAL & CO.	C. or G.	1820s
NEAL & CO.	N.	1778-1792
NEW WHARF POTTERY CO.	N. W. P. CO. (B.)	1878-1894
NEW WHARF POTTERY CO.	N. W. P. CO./BURSLEM	1878-1894
NICHOLSON, THOMAS & CO.	T. N. & CO. /C.	1854-1871
NORTH BRITISH POTTERY	I. M. (&) CO.	1867-1874
NORTH BRITISH POTTERY	J. M. (&) CO.	1867-1874
OLD HALL EARTHENWARE CO.LTD.	O. H. E. C. (L.)	1862-1886
PANKHURST, J. W. (& CO.)	J. W. P. (& CO.)	1850-1852-(1882)
PATTERSON, GEORGE (PATTERSON & CO.)	G. P.	1837-1844
PEARL POTTERY CO. (LTD.)	P. P. (CO. LTD.)	1894-1912-(1936)
PEARSON & CO.	P. & CO.	1880(+)
PENMAN, ROBERT H. & CO.	R. H. P. & CO.	1865-1867
PHILLIPS, EDWARD & GEORGE	E. & G. P.	1822-1834
PHILLIPS, GEORGE	G. P.	1834-1848
PINDER, BOURNE & CO.	P. B. & CO.	1862-1882
PINDER, BOURNE & HOPE	P. B. & H.	1851-1862

PLANT, R. H. & S. L. (LTD.)	R. H. & S. L. P.	1898-1915-(1970)
PLANT, R. H. & S. L. LTD.	L. P.	1898-1915-(1970)
PLYMOUTH POTTERY CO. LTD.	P. P. COY. L.	1856-1863
PODMORE, WALKER & CO.	P. W. & CO.	1834-1859
PODMORE, WALKER & WEDGWOOD	P. W. & W.	1856-1859
POULSON BROS. (LTD.)	P. B. (BROS.)	1884-1927
POUNTNEY & ALLIES	P.	1816-1835
POUNTNEY & ALLIES	P. & A.	1816-1835
POUNTNEY & ALLIES	P. S. / B. P.	1816-1835
POUNTNEY & ALLIES (BRISTOL POTTERY)	P. A. / B. P.	1816-1835
POUNTNEY & CO.	P. & CO.	1859-1889
POUNTNEY & CO. LTD.	P. & CO. LTD	1889-1962
POUNTNEY & GOLDNEY	P. & G.	1837-1850
POWELL & BISHOP	P. & B.	1866-1878
POWELL & BISHOP	P. B.	1866-1878
POWELL, BISHOP & STONIER	P. B. & S.	1878-1891
POWELL, BISHOP & STONIER	P. S. & S.	1878-1891
PRATT & SIMPSON	P. & S.	1878-1883
PRATT, F. & R. (& CO.) (LTD.)	F. & R. P. (& CO.)	1840-1862(+)
PRATT, JOHN & CO. (LTD.)	J. P. & CO. (L.)	1847-1878
PURVES, CHARLES	C. P.	1855-1870
PURVES, CHARLES	G. P. & CO.	1883-1887
RAINFORTH & CO.	H. M.	1809-1814
RATCLIFFE, WILLIAM (ATT.)	R./HACKWOOD	1831-1843
RATHBONE, SAMUEL & JOHN	R.	1812-1818 & 1823-1835
RATHBONE, THOMAS & CO.	T. R. & CO.	1898-1923
READ, CLEMENTSON & ANDERSON	R. C. & A.	c1836
REED & CLEMENTSON	R. & C.	1833-1835
REED & CO.	R. & C.	1837-1838
REED & TAYLOR	R. & T.	1820-1848
REED & TAYLOR (& CO.)	R. T. (& CO.)	1841-1848
REEVES, JAMES	J. R. /F.	1870-1948
RIDGWAY & MORLEY	R. & M.	1842-1845
RIDGWAY, E. J. (& SON)	E. J. R. (& S.)	1860-1866-(1872)
RIDGWAY, JOB	J. R.	1802-1808
RIDGWAY, JOB	R.	1802-1808
RIDGWAY, JOHN	J. R.	1830-1841
RIDGWAY, JOHN & CO.	J. R. & CO.	1841-1855
RIDGWAY, JOHN & WILLIAM	I. & W.	1813-1830
RIDGWAY, JOHN & WILLIAM	J. & W.	1813-1830
RIDGWAY, JOHN & WILLIAM	J. & W. R.	1813-1830
RIDGWAY, JOHN & WILLIAM	J. W. R.	1813-1830
RIDGWAY, JOHN BATES & CO.	J. R. /B.	1856-1858
RIDGWAY, JOHN, BATES & CO.	J. R. B. (& CO.)	1856-1858
RIDGWAY, MORLEY, WEAR & CO.	R. M. W. & CO.	1836-1842
RIDGWAY, SPARKS & RIDGWAY	R. S. (&) R.	1872-1878
RIDGWAY, WILLIAM & CO.	R. W. & CO.	1834-1854
RIDGWAY, WILLIAM (& CO.)	W. R. (& CO.)	1830-1834-(1854)
RIDGWAY, WILLIAM SON & CO.	C. C.	1838-1845
RIDGWAY, WILLIAM SON & CO.	W. R. S. & CO.	1838-1845
ROBINSON & WOOD	R. & W.	1832-1836
ROBINSON (&) WOOD	W. & B.	1837-1841
ROBINSON, JOSEPH	J. R. /B.	1876-1898
ROBINSON, WOOD & BROWNFIELD	R. W. & B.	1837
ROGERS, JOHN & GEORGE	J. R. /L. S.	1815-1841
ROGERS, JOHN & SON	J. R.	1815-1841
ROGERS, JOHN & SON	J. R. S. /L	1815-1841
ROWLAND & MARSELLUS	R. & M. CO.	1893-1933
SCOTT & SONS	S. & S. (SONS.)	1829-1841-(1882)
SCOTT BROS. & CO.	S. B. & CO.	1841-1854
SEFTON & BROWN	S. & B. (F. B.)	1897-1919
SHARPE BROS. & CO. (LTD.)	S. B. & CO.	1838-1895(+)
SHIRLEY, T. & JOHN MILLIGAN (CLYDE)	S. & M.	1841-1857
SHIRLEY, THOMAS & CO.	T. S. or (& CO. or & COY.)	1840-1857
SHORE, COGGINS & HOLT	S. C. H. /L.	1905-1910
SKINNER & WALKER	S. & W.	1875-1877
SKINNER, GEORGE & CO.	G. S. & CO.	1855-1870
SMITH & BINNALL	S. & B. /T.	1897-1900
SMITH & FORD	S. & F.	1895-1898
SMITH, FORD & JONES	S. F. & J.	1889-1894
SMITH, GEORGE F. (& CO.)	G. F. S. (& CO.)	1857-1867
SMITH, WILLIAM & CO.	W. S. & CO.	1825-1855
SMITH, WILLIAM & CO. (WEDG WOOD)	W. S. & CO'S .	1825-1855
SNEYD & HILL	S. & H.	c. 1845
SOUTH WALES POTTERS	S. W. P.	1839-1922
SOUTHWICK POTTERY	S. (& SONS)	1829-1841
SOUTHWICK POTTERY	S. B. & CO.	1841-1854
SPODE, JOSIAH	N. S.	1822-1833
ST. JOHNS STONE CHINAWARE CO. (CANADA)	Q. U. E.	1873-1899
STANLEY POTTERY CO.	S. P. CO.	1909-1937
STANLEY POTTERY LTD.	C. & CO.	1928-1931
STEVENSON, RALPH	R. S.	1810-1833
STEVENSON, RALPH & SON	R. S. & S.	1833-1835
STEVENSON, RALPH & WILLIAMS	R. S. & W.	1825-1827
STEVENSON, RALPH & WILLIAMS	R. S. W.	1825-1827
STEVENSON, RALPH & WILLIAMS	R. W. & W.	1825-1827
SWANSEA POTTERY	D.	1824-1850
SWANSEA POTTERY	D. & CO.´	1836-1850
SWIFT & ELKIN	S. & E.	1840-1843
TAMS, JOHN	J. T.	1875-1903
TAMS, JOHN & SON (LTD.)	J. T. & S. or J. T. S.	1903-1912-(1988)
TAYLOR, BENJAMIN & SON	B. T. & S.	c1848
TAYLOR, HARRISON & CO.	T. H. & CO.	1830s-1841
THOMSON, JOHN (& SONS)	J. T. (& SONS)	1826-1870-(1888) (1896)
TITTENSOR, CHARLES	C. T.	1815-1823
TOMLINSON, FOSTER, WEDGWOOD & CO.	W. T. & CO.	c1798
TROUTBECK, E. T.	M. T. & T.	c1846
TURNER & TOMKINSON	T. & T.	1860-1872
TURNER, G. W. & SONS	G. T. & S.	1873-1895
TURNER, G. W. & SONS	G. W. T. & S. (SONS)	1873-1895
TURNER, G. W. & SONS	G. W. T. S. (& S.)	1873-1895
TWIGG, JOSEPH	J. T.	1822-1866
TWIGG, JOSEPH	K. P.	1839-1881
TWIGG, JOSEPH	T.	1839-1881
TWIGG, JOSEPH (& CO.) (KILNHURST)	J. T. (& S.)	1839-1881
UPPER HANLEY CO. (LTD.)	U. H. P. CO. (LTD.)	1895-1900-(1910)
VERNON, JAMES	J. V.	1860-1874
VERNON, JAMES & SON	J. V. & S. or JUNR.	1875-1880
WALKER & CARTER	W. & C.	1866-1889
WALKER, THOMAS	T. W.	1845-1856
WALKER, THOMAS HENRY	T. H. W.	1846-1848
WALLACE, (J.) & CO.	J. W. (CO.)	1838-1893
WALLEY, EDWARD	W.	1845-1858
WALLEY, EDWARD & SON	E. & W.	1858-1862
WARBURTON, JOHN (COBRIDGE)	W.	1802-1823
WARDLE, JAMES & CO. (HANLEY) (LTD.)	J. W.	1854-1871
WARDLE, JAMES & CO. (HANLEY) LTD.	W.	1890-1935
WEATHERBY, J. H. & SONS (LTD.)	J. H. W. & SONS (LTD)	1891-1908-(1925)
WEDGWOOD, JOSIAH (& SONS LTD.)	P.	AFTER 1869
WHITEHAVEN POTTERY	I. W.	1824-1863
WHITEHAVEN POTTERY	M. W.	1863-1877
WHITEHAVEN POTTERY	R. W.	1877-1910
WHITEHAVEN POTTERY	W. P. & CO.	1824-1840
WHITTAKER & CO.	W. & CO.	1886-1892
WHITTAKER, HEATH & CO.	W. H. & CO.	1892-1898
WHITTINGHAM, FORD & CO.	W. F. & CO.	1868-1873
WHITTINGHAM, FORD & RILEY	W. F. & R.	1876-1882
WILEMAN & CO.	W. & C.	1892-1925
WILEMAN, CHARLES J.	C. J. W.	c1869
WILEMAN, JAMES & CHARLES	J. & C. W.	1864-1870
WILEMAN, JAMES & CHARLES	J. F. & C. W.	1864-1870
WILEMAN, JAMES & CHARLES	J. W. & CO.	1864-1870
WILEMAN, JAMES, F.	J. F. W.	1870-1892
WILKINSON POTTERY CO.	W. P. C.	1863-1877
WILKINSON, ARTHUR, J. (LTD)	W. W.	1885-1965
WILSON, DAVID (& SON(S))	G.	1801-1817
WILSON, ISAAC & CO.	I. W. & CO.	1852-1887
WILTSHAW & ROBINSON (LTD.)	W. & R.	1890-1957-(1958+)
WINKLE, F. & CO. (LTD.)	F. W. & CO.	1890-1925-(1931)
WOLFE, THOMAS (SR.)	W.	1781-1810
WOOD & BAGGALEY	W. & B.	1870-1880
WOOD & BARKER LTD.	W. & B. LTD. /B.	1897-1903
WOOD & BRETTEL	W. & B.	1818-1823
WOOD & BROWNFIELD	W. & B.	1837-1850
WOOD & CHALLINOR	W. & C.	1828-1845
WOOD & CHALLINOR	W. C.	1828-1845
WOOD & CHALLINOR & CO.	W. & CO.	1860-1864
WOOD & CHALLINOR & CO.	W. C. & CO.	1860-1864
WOOD & HULME	W. & H. /B.	1882-1905
WOOD & HULME	W. H.	1882-1905
WOOD & PIGOTT	W. & P.	1869-1871
WOOD, ARTHUR	A. W. / L.	1904-1928
WOOD, ENOCH	E. W.	1784-1789
WOOD, ENOCH	W.	1784-1789
WOOD, ENOCH & SONS	E. & E. W.	1840s
WOOD, ENOCH & SONS	E. W. & S.	1818-1845
WOOD, H. J. (LTD.)	H. J. W. /B.	1884-PRESENT
WOOD, JOHN WEDG	J. W. W.	1841-1875
WOOD, JOHN WEDG	W. W.	1841-1857-(1875)
WOOD, THOMAS & CO.	T. W. & CO.	1885-1896
WOOD, THOMAS & SONS.	T. W. & S.	1896-1897
WOOD, WILLIAM & CO.	W. W. & CO.	1873-1932
WOODNORTH & CO.	W. & CO.	1800-1824
WOOLF, LEWIS	L. W.	1851-1877
WOOLF, LEWIS (& SON(S)) (& CO.)	L. W. (S.) or (& SONS)	1857-1883
WOOLF, SYDNEY (& CO.)	S. W. (& CO.)	1873-1887
WORTHINGTON & HARROP	W. & H.	1856-1873
YALE & BARKER	Y. & B.	1841-1842
YATES & MAY	Y. & M.	1835-1843
YATES, JOHN	J. Y.	1770-1835
YNYSMEUDWY POTTERY	L. & M.	1860-1870
YNYSMEUDWY POTTERY	Y. M. P.	1850(+)
YNYSMEUDWY POTTERY	Y. P.	1850s

APPENDIX B3: ALPHABETIC LISTING SECONDARY POTTERS BY INITIAL & NAME

INITIALS	POTTERY	DATE	LOCATION
A. & B.	ADAMS & BROMLEY	1873-1886	HANLEY
A. & C.	ADAMS & COOPER	1850-1877	LONGTON
A. & CO.	ARROWSMITH & CO.	1900-1905	LONGTON
A. & CO.	ASBURY, EDWARD & CO.	1875-1925	LONGTON
A. & CO.	ASHWELL & CO.	c1832	LONGTON
A. & E. K.	KEELING, ANTHONY & ENOCH	1802-1811	TUNSTALL
A. & R. G.	GALLIMORE, AMBROSE & ROBERT	1832-1837	LONGTON
A. & S.	ARKINSTALL & SONS, LTD.	1904-1925	STOKE
A. B.	BALL, ALFRED	1883-1886	LONGTON
A. B.	BRIDGWOOD, A.	1894-1897	FENTON
A. B. (& CO.)	BEVINGTON, AMBROSE (& CO.)	1880-1891	HANLEY
A. B. J. (& S.) (LTD.)	JONES, A. B. (& SONS) (LTD.)	1880-1900-(55)-(72)	LONGTON
A. G. H. J./H.J.	JONES, A.G. HARLEY	1907-1934	FENTON
A. J. H.	HULL, A. J.	1896-1901	LONGTON
A. J. M.	MOUNTFORD, ARTHUR J.	1897-1901	BURSLEM
A. K.	KEELING, ANTHONY	1781-1801	TUNSTALL
A. K. & S.	KEELING, ANTHONY (& SON(S))	1792-1795	TUNSTALL
A. L. B. (LTD.)	ALCOCK, LINDLEY & BLOORE (LTD.)	1919-1959	HANLEY
A. M. /L.	MACKEE, ANDREW	1892-1906	LONGTON
A. S. & CO.	SMITH, AMBROSE & CO.	1784-1786	BURSLEM
A. W. & CO.(LTD)	WALKER, AMBROSE & CO.	1880-1893	YORKSHIRE
B.	BARLOW, T. W. & SON, LTD.	1882-1940	LONGTON
B. & B.	BAILEY & BEVINGTON or BEVINGTON & CO.	1867-1868	HANLEY
B. & B.	BEVINGTON & BRADLEY	1868-1869	HANLEY
B. & B.	BEVINGTON & CO. or BAILEY & BEVINGTON	1867-1868	HANLEY
B. & B.	BIRKS & BLOOD	1854-1854	LONGTON
B. & CO.	BIRKS, L. A. & CO.	1896-1898	STOKE
B. & CO.	BOULTON & CO.	1892-1902	LONGTON
B. & F.	BADDELEY & FLETCHER	1759-1775	SHELTON
B. & G.	BROUGH & GREEN	1842-1842	LONGTON
B. & J. M. & CO.	MYOTT, B. & J. & CO.	1818-1825	LANE END (LONGTON)
B. & L.	BILL & LAWRENCE	c.1832	LANE END (LONGTON)
B. & L.	BOWERS & LLOYD	1846-1850	BURSLEM
B. & L.	BROWNING & LEWIS	1899-1900	HANLEY
B. & L.	BRYAN & LAWTON	c1854	LONGTON
B. & N.	BOLD & NASH	1850-1851	BURSLEM
B. & S.	BARLOW, T. W. & SON	1882-1940	LONGTON
B. & S.	BARTON & SWIFT	c1811	BURSLEM
B. & S.	BESWICK & SON	1916-1930	LONGTON
B. & S.	BOULTON & SON	-	-
B. & S.	BROADHURST, JAMES & SONS	1855-1863	LONGTON
B. & S. (SON)	BODLEY & SON	1874-1875	BURSLEM
B. & S. H.	HANCOCK, BENJAMIN & SAMPSON	1876-1881	STOKE
B. & T.	BARROW & TAYLOR	c1859	HANLEY
B. & T.	BETTANEY & TOMLINSON	1843-1844	LANE END (LONGTON)
B. & W.	BOUGHEY & WILTSHAW	1892-1894	LONGTON
B. A. & B.	BRADBURY, ANDERSON & BETTANNY	1844-1850	LONGTON
B. B.	BERESFORD BROS.	1900-1930	LONGTON
B. B.	BROOKFIELD BROS.	1892-1903	LONGTON
B. B. & B.	BEARDMORE, BIRKS & BLOOD	1850-1854	LONGTON
B. B. & B.	BOURNE, BAKER & BAKER	1833-1835	FENTON
B. C. G.	GODWIN, B. C.	1851-1851	BURSLEM
B. C. T. & CO.	BEACH, COOPER, TILL & CO.	1872-1873	LONGTON
B. F.	FLOYD, BENJAMIN	1843-1843	LANE END (LONGTON)
B. F. & S.	BAILEY, FLOYD & SHUBOTHAM	1836-1837	LANE END (LONGTON)
B. H. & CO.	BAILEY, HACKNEY & CO.	c1889	HANLEY
B. H. & CO.	BENNETT, HURD & CO.	1865-1866	BURSLEM
B. H. & CO.	BUCKLEY, HEATH & CO.	1885-1890	BURSLEM
B. K. & C.	BRADBURY, KELLETT & CO.	1882-1887	LONGTON
B. LTD.	BARLOWS (LONGTON) LTD.	1920-1952	LONGTON
B. M. & B.	BAYLEY, MURRAY & BRAMMER	1875-1878	GLASGOW, SCOTLAND
B. M. & B.	BRADBURY, MASON, & BRADBURY	1852-1853	LONGTON
B. M. & B.	BRADBURY, MASON, & BROADHURST	1853-1854	LONGTON
B. M. & CO.	MURRAY, BAYLEY & CO.	1875-1884	GLASGOW, SCOTLAND
B. M. & CO.	SARACEN POTTERY CO.	1875-1884	GLASGOW, SCOTLAND
B. R. & CO.	BIRKS, RAWLINS & CO. (LTD.)	1898-1932	STOKE
B. R. & T.	BAXTER, ROWLEY & TAMS	1882-1885	LONGTON
B. T. & S.	TAYLOR, BENJAMIN & SON	c.1840s	FERRYBRIDGE
B. W. & CO.	BUCKLEY, WOOD & CO.	1873-1885	BURSLEM

C. & B.	CYPLES & BARKER	1846-1847	LONGTON
C. & CO.	CLOKIE & CO.	1871-1875	YORKSHIRE
C. & CO.	COOPERS & CO.	1877-1882	LONGTON
C. & D.	COOPER & DETHICK	1876-1888	LONGTON
C. & G.	COLLINGWOOD & GREATBACH	1870-1887	LONGTON
C. & H.	COOMBS & HOLLAND	1855-1858	LLANELLY, WALES
C. & M.	CLOKIE & MASTERMAN	1871-1885	YORKSHIRE
C. & P.	COOMER & PRATT	1807-1809	FENTON
C. & R.	CYPLES & ROBEY	1845-1845	LONGTON
C. & W.	CAPPER & WOOD	1895-1904	LONGTON
C. /N. A.	CANDY & CO., LTD.	c1882	DEVON
C. A. /L.	AMISON, CHARLES (& CO.)(LTD.)	1889-1916-(30)-(62)	LONGTON
C. B. (/F.)	CHRISTIE & BEARDMORE	1902-1903	FENTON
C. C. & CO.	CORNFOOT, COLVILLE & CO.	1829-1832	NORTHUMBER-LAND
C. F.	FORD, CHARLES	1874-1904	HANLEY
C. H.	HARRISON, CHARLES	1887-1897	LONGTON
C. P. CO.	CENTURY POTTERY CO.	1903-1920s	BURSLEM
C. P. CO. (LTD.)	CAMPBELLFIELD POTTERY CO., (LTD.)	1850-1884	SCOTLAND
C. P. P. CO.	CRYSTAL PORCELAIN POTTERY CO. LTD.	1882-1886	COBRIDGE
C. S.	SALT, CHARLES	1837-1864	HANLEY
C. S. A.	CARTER, STABLER & ADAMS	c1921	DORSET
C. T. & CO.	COOPERS, TILL & CO.	1873-1877	LONGTON
D.	DUDSON BROTHERS (LTD.)	1898-present	TUNSTALL
D. & B.	DEAVILLE & BADDERLEY	c1854	HANLEY
D. & C. (/L)	DEWES & COPESTAKE	1894-1915	LONGTON
D. & H.	DOWNS & HULME	c1882	LONGTON
D. & S.	DEAN & STOKES	1867-1868	BURSLEM
D. B. (LTD.)	DUDSON BROTHERS (LTD.)	1898-present	HANLEY & TUNSTALL
D. C. & B	DAVIS, COXON & BASKET	1816-1822	NORTHUMBER-LAND
D. C. & D.	DEAN, CAPPER & DEAN	1882-1888	HANLEY & BURSLEM
D. C. & W.	DAVIS, COXON & WILSON	1822-1833	NORTHUMBER-LAND
D. E.	EDGE, DANIEL	1834-1842	BURSLEM
D. P. CO. (LTD.)	DIAMOND POTTERY CO. (LTD.)	1908-1935	HANLEY
D. T.	THOMSON, DAVID	1802-1818	SCOTLAND
E. & B.	EVANS & BOOTH	1856-1869	BURSLEM
E. & C.	EVANS & COYNE	1867-1868	HANLEY
E. & H.	EARDLEY & HAMMERSLEY	1862-1866	TUNSTALL
E. B.	BLOOD, EDWIN	1860-1862	LONGTON
E. B. & CO./F	BRAIN, E. & CO. LTD.	1903-1963	FENTON
E. B. (& S.)	BOOTH, EPHRAIM (& SONS)	1790-1808	STOKE & SHELTON
E. C. & T.	EVERAD, COLCLOUGH & TOWNSEND	1838-1845	LONGTON
E. G. & C.	EVERAD, GLOVER & COLCLOUGH	1847-1847	LONGTON
E. G. & T.	EVERAD, GLOVER & TOWNSEND	c1837	LONGTON
E. H.	HALLEM, E.	1851-1854	BURSLEM
E. H.	HODGKINSON, ELIJAH	1864-1871	HANLEY
E. J.	JONES, ELIJAH	1831-1839	HANLEY
E. J.	JONES, ELIJAH (MILL STREET)	1847-1848	SHELTON
E. J. D. B.	BODLEY, E. J. D.	1882-1892	BURLSEM
E. L. & CO.	LAWRENCE, E. & CO.	1880-1883	LONGTON
E. M.	MILLS, ELIZABETH (MRS.)	1852-1873	SHELTON (HANLEY)
E. M. (& S.)	MAYER, ELIJAH (& SON)	1784-1834	HANLEY
E. P.	PHILLIPS, EDWARD	1855-1862	SHELTON (HANLEY)
E. S.	STEEL, EDWARD	1875-1900	HANLEY
E. S. & CO.	EARDLEY, SPEAR & CO.	c1873	TUNSTALL
E. U. & M.	ELLIS, UNWIN & MOUNTFORD	1860-1861	HANLEY
E. W.	WOOD, ENOCH (JR.)	1822-1822	BURSLEM
F. & H.	FRANSHAWE & HUGHES	1882-1889	FENTON
F. & N. D.	DILLON, FRANCIS & NICHOLAS	1815-1830	COBRIDGE
F. & S.	FOLCH & SCOTT	1821-1822	STOKE
F. & T.	FLETCHER & TITTENSOR	c1794	SHELTON (HANLEY)
F. B.	BOOTH, FREDERICK	c1881	YORKSHIRE
F. B. (& S.)	BREWER, FRANCIS, H. (& SON) or (& CO.)	1862-1866	LONGTON
F. C. & T.	FLACKETT, CHETHAM & TOFT	1853-1856	FENTON
F. D. & C.	FENTON, DOWNS & CO.	1881-1882	LONGTON
F. H. H.	HAWLEY, FELIX H.	1851-1851	FENTON
F. J.	JONES, FREDERICK	1879-1886	LONGTON
F. P. C.	FENTON POTTERY CO.	c1851	FENTON
F. S. & L.	FLOYD, SHUBOTHAM & LEAKE	1834-1835	LANE END (LONGTON)
G. & A.	GALLOWAY & ATKINSON	1865-1872	NORTHUMBER-LAND
G. & B. B.	BURTON, GEORGE & BENJAMIN	1882-1900	HANLEY
G. & C.	GLOVER & COLCLOUGH	1848-1855	LONGTON
G. & CO. /L.	GALLIMORE & CO. LTD.	1906-1934	LONGTON
G. & D. /L.	GUEST & DEWSBURY	1877-1927	LLANELLY- WALES
G. & J.	GOODWIN & JARVIS	1805-1808	STOKE
G. & L.	GRIFFITHS & LOWNDS	c1845	SHELTON (HANLEY)
G. & S.	GALLIMORE & SHUBOTHAM	1840-1841	LONGTON
G. & S. T.	TAYLOR, GEORGE & SAMUEL	1837-1866	LEEDS/YORKSHIRE
G. & T. P.	POULSON, G. & T.	1801-1812	COBRIDGE & STOKE
G. B. & CO.	BENNETT, GEORGE & CO.	1894-1902	STOKE
G. B. & F.	GOODWIN, BARKER & FANSHAWE	1881-1882	FENTON

G. E. & CO.	GRIEVE, ELLIS & CO.	1879-1889	GLASGOW, SCOTLAND
G. H.	HAWLEY, GEORGE	1855-1868	YORKSHIRE
G. L. B. & CO. (LTD.)	BENTLEY, G. L. & CO. (LTD.)	1898-1904-(12)	LONGTON
G. M. C.	CREYKE, G. M. & SONS	1920-1948	HANLEY
G. P.	POULSON, GEORGE	1801-1812	COBRIDGE & STOKE
G. P. & CO. (L.)	PROCTER, GEORGE & CO. (LTD.)	1892-1940	LONGTON
G. P. CO.	GRANVILLE POTTERY CO.	1899-1900	HANLEY
G. R.	RIDGWAY, GEORGE (& SON)	1802-1814	SHELTON (HANLEY)
G. R. B. (& CO.)	BOOTH, G. R. (& CO.)	1829-1844	HANLEY
G. R. C.	CURTIS, G. R.	c1839	YORKSHIRE
G. S. & S.	SHAW, GEORGE & SONS (LTD.)	1887-1948	YORKSHIRE
G. W.	WESTON, GEORGE (& CO.)	1799-1829	LANE END (LONGTON)
G. W.	WOOD, GEORGE	1850-1853 & 1864	SHELTON (HANLEY)
G. W.	WOOLISCROFT, GEORGE	1851-1853 & 1860-1864	TUNSTALL
G. W.	WRIGLEY, GEORGE	c1860	BURSLEM
G. W. & CO.	WESTON, GEORGE & CO.	1799-1851	LANE END (LONGTON)
H.	HULME, WILLIAM (LTD)	1891-1925-(41)	BURSLEM
H. & B.	BURGESS, THOMAS	1903-1917	HANLEY
H. & B.	HARROP & BURGESS	1894-1903	HANLEY
H. & B.	HIBBERT & BOUGHEY	1889-1889	LONGTON
H. & B.	HULME & BOOTH	1851-1854	BURSLEM
H. & C. /B.	HEATH & GREATBACH	1891-1893	BURSLEM
H. & C. /F.	HULME & CHRISTIE	1893-1902	FENTON
H. & CO.	HAMPSON & CO.	1854-1870	LONGTON
H. & CO.	HETT & CO.	c1864	HANLEY
H. & CO.	HOBSON & CO.	1876-78& 1889-93	LONGTON
H. & CO.	HODSON (RICHARD) & CO.	1849-1885	LONGTON
H. & CO.	HOLDCROFT & CO.	1870-1871	BURSLEM
H. & CO.	HOPKINS & CO.	1841-1843	BURSLEM
H. & D.	HALLAM & DAY	1880-1883	LONGTON
H. & G.	HOLLINSHEAD & GRIFFITHS	1890-1909	BURSLEM
H. & H.	HALL & HOLLAND	1838-1843	TUNSTALL
H. & H.	HARRIS & HULME	1839-1840	LONGTON
H. & M.	HAMILTON & MOORE	1841-1858	LONGTON
H. & P.	HARRISON & PHILLIPS	1914-1915	BURSLEM
H. & R.	HALL & READ	1882-1888	HANLEY
H. & R.	HALL & READ	1882-1882	BURSLEM
H. & R.	HUGHES & ROBINSON	1888-1894	COBRIDGE
H. & SON	HOLMES & SON	1898-1903	LONGTON
H. & W.	HANCOCK & WRIGHT	1838-1840	TUNSTALL
H. & W. & CO.	HAWLEY, WEBBERLEY & CO.	1895-1902	LONGTON
H. A. & CO. (L.)	AYNSLEY, H. & CO. (LTD.)	1873-present	LONGTON
H. B.	BOOTH, HUGH	1781-1789	STOKE
H. B.	HAINES, BATCHELOR & CO. (RETAILERS)	1880-1890	LONDON
H. B.	HINES BROTHERS	1886-1907	FENTON
H. B. & CO.	BROWN, HENRY & CO.	1828-1830	LONGTON
H. B. & CO.	HARVEY, BAILEY & CO./BAILEYS & HARVEYS	1832-1843	LANE END (LONGTON)
H. D. & CO.	HACKWOOD, DIMMOCK & CO.	1807-1827	HANLEY
H. D. (& CO.)	DANIEL, HENRY (& CO.)	1826-1836	SHELTON
H. F. W. & CO. LTD.	WEDGWOOD, H.F. & CO., LTD.	1941-1954	LONGTON
H. J.	JONES, A. G. HARVEY	1907-1934	FENTON
H. J. C. /L.	COLCLOUGH, HERBERT JOSEPH	1897-1937	LONGTON
H. J. W. /B.	WOOD, H. J. (LTD.)	1884-present	BURSLEM
H. M. W. & CO.	WILLIAMSON, H. M. & CO.	1866-1866	LONGTON
H. P. & CO. (LTD.)	HILL POTTERY CO. (LTD.)	1861-1867	BURSLEM
H. P. & M.	HOLMES, PLANT & MAYDEW	1876-1885	BURSLEM
H. P. & S.	HASSALL, POOLE & STANWAY	1872-1873	STOKE
H. S. (& S.)	SIMKIN, HUGH (& SON)	1819-1841	LONGTON
H. W. & B.	HANCOCK, WRIGHT & BURGESS	1840-1840	TUNSTALL
H. W. & CO.	HAWLEY, WEBBERLEY & CO.	1895-1902	LONGTON
I. B. & G. A.	BELL, ISACC & GALLOWAY & ATKINSON	c. 1836	NORTHUMBER-LAND
J. & B.	JONES & BROMLEY	1882-1887	LONGTON
J. & C. D.	DUDSON, JAMES & CHARLES	1835-1845	SHELTON (HANLEY)
J. & G. (/L.)	JACKSON & GOSLING (LTD.)	1866-1961	FENTON & LONGTON
J. & L.	JARVIS & LOVE	1818-1818	LANE END (LONGTON)
J. & P.	JACKSON & PATTERSON	1833-1838	NORTH-UMBERSIDE
J. & R. H.	HAMMERSLEY, J. & R.	1877-1917	HANLEY
J. & T.	JONES & THOMPSON	1879-1879	LONGTON
J. & T. B.	BEVINGTON, JAMES & THOMAS	1865-1878	HANLEY
J. & W.	JONES & WALLEY	1841-1843	COBRIDGE
J. & W. H.	HANDLEY, JAMES & WILLIAM	1819-1828	BURSLEM
J. A. & CO.	BRINDLEY, JOHN & CO.	1824-1830	HANLEY
J. B.	BAGGALEY, JACOB	1880-1886	BURSLEM
J. B.	BAILEY, JOHN	1851-1858	LONGTON
J. B.	BARKER, JOSEPH	1860-1861	LONGTON
J. B.	BIRCH, JOSEPH	1847-1851	HANLEY
J. B.	BLACKWELL, JOHN	1784-1814	COBRIDGE
J. B.	BROADHURST, JAMES	1863-1870	LONGTON
J. B. & CO.	BARLOW, JAMES & CO.	1822-1839	HANLEY
J. B. & CO.	BRINDLEY, JOHN & CO.	1824-1830	SHELTON /HANLEY
J. B. & CO.	BUCKLEY, JOHN & CO.	1885-1890	BURSLEM
J. B. & CO. /H.	BEVINGTON, JOHN & CO.	1860-1892	HANLEY
J. B. & S.	BROADHURST, JAMES & SONS	1870-1894	FENTON
J. B. & S. (LTD.)	BROADHURST, JAMES & SONS (LTD.)	1922 -1939	FENTON
J. B. & S.(SON)	BEECH, JAMES & SON	1860-1898	LONGTON
J. B. E. & CO.	EVANS, J. B. & CO.	1861-1870	HANLEY
J. B. J.	BRIDGWOOD, JOHN JR.	1870-1870	HANLEY
J. B. W. (/F.)	WATHEN, JAMES B. (& CO.)	1864-1869	FENTON
J. C.	AITCHIESON, J. & CO.	1807-1811	SCOTLAND
J. D.	DAWSON, J.	1799-1848	SUNDERLAND
J. E. J.	JONES, JOSIAH ELLIS	1868-1872	LONGTON
J. F.	FLOYD, JAMES	1845-1847	LONGTON
J. F. A.	ADDERLEY, J. FELLOWS	1901-1905	LONGTON
J. F. E. & CO. (LTD.)	ELTON, J. F. & CO. (LTD.)	1901-1910	BURSLEM
J. G.	GERRARD, JOHN	1824-1836	HANLEY
J. G.	GERRARD, JOHN	1846-1853	HANLEY
J. G.	GIBSON, JOHN	1840-1846	TUNSTALL
J. G.	GODWIN, JAMES	1846-1850	COBRIDGE
J. G.	GODWIN, JOHN	1805-1808	STOKE
J. G.	GREEN, JOHN	1872-1877	LONGTON
J. G. (& CO.)	GIBSON, JAMES (& CO.)	c1891	LONGTON
J. G. S. & CO.	GOODWIN, J., STODDARD & CO.	1898-1940	FOLEY, LONGTON, COBRIDGE
J. H.	HEBB, JOHN	1856-1857	FENTON
J. H.	HOLLAND, JOHN	1852-1853	TUNSTALL
J. H.	HOLLISON, JAMES	1899-1907	LONGTON
J. H.	HOLLOWAY, JOHN	1862-1867	HANLEY
J. H.	HUGHES, JOHN	1864-1864	COBRIDGE
J. H. (& CO.)	HAWLEY, JOHN (& CO.)	1832-1892	FOLEY (FENTON)
J. K.	KNIGHT, JOSEPH	1859-1879 & 1882-1883	FENTON
J. K. (& S.)	KENT, JOHN (& SONS)	1858-1868-(1876)	LONGTON
J. L.	LLOYD, JOHN (REBECCA)	1834-1852	SHELTON (HANLEY)
J. L.	LOCKETT, JOHN	1855-1879	LANE END (LONGTON)
J. L. & S.	LOCKETT, JOHN & SON (KING ST.)	1827-1835	LONGTON
J. M.	MACHIN, JOSEPH	c1841	BURSLEM
J. M.	MACHIN, JOSEPH	1802-1818	BURSLEM
J. M. & CO.	MACHIN, JOSEPH & CO.	1818-1832	BURSLEM
J. M. & CO.	MAYER, JOSEPH & CO.	c1841	BURSLEM
J. M. & S.	MADDOCK, JOHN & SON	1855-1859	BURSLEM
J. M. (&) CO.	NORTH BRITISH POTTERY	1867-1874	SCOTLAND
J. M. (/F.)	MAYER, JOHN	1832-1841	FENTON
J. O. (& CO.)	OLDHAM, JAMES (& CO.)	1860-1877	HANLEY
J. P. & CO.	PLANT, J. & CO.	1882-1884	LONGTON
J. P. /L.	PROCTER, JOHN	1845-1847	LANE END (LONGTON)
J. P. LTD.	PEARSON, JAMES LTD.	1880-1937(+)	CHESTERFIELD
J. R.	RATHBONE, JANE	1832-1835	TUNSTALL
J. R. & F. C.	CHETHAM, J. R. & F.	1862-1869	LONGTON
J. S.	SMITH, JAMES	1898-1922	STOKE
J. S. & CO.	SHEPHERD, JONES & CO.	1867-1868	LONGTON
J. S. & S. (LTD.)	SHAW, JOHN & SONS, (LONGTON), LTD.	1931-1963	LONGTON
J. S. H.	HILL POTTERY CO. (LTD.)	1861-1867	BURSLEM
J. S. S. B.	SADLER, JAMES & SONS (LTD.)	1899-	BURSLEM
J. T.	TWEMLOW, JOHN	1795-1797	SHELTON
J. T. C. & CO.	COPE, J. T. & CO.	1885-1889	HANLEY
J. V. & M.	VENABLES, JOHN & MARTYN	c1861	BURSLEM
J. W.	WALLEY, JOHN	1845-1867	BURSLEM, (& OTHER LOCALES)
J. W.	WALTON, JAMES	1846-1860	SHELTON (HANLEY)
J. W.	WARREN, JAMES	1843-1852	LONGTON
J. W.	WHITEHEAD, JAMES & CO.	1790-1810	SHELTON (HANLEY)
J. W.	WOOD, JOHN	1822-1837	NORTHUMBER-LAND
J. W.	WOOD, JOHN	1781-1797	BURSLEM
J. W. & CO.	WOOD, JOHN & CO.	1865-1871	LONGTON
J. W. & S.	WILSON, JAMES & SONS	1900-1926	FENTON
J. W. B.	BESWICK, J. W.	1894-1920	LONGTON
J. W. T. & CO.	THOMAS, J. W. & CO.	1886-1887	LONGTON
K. & B.	KING & BARRATT (LTD.)	1898-1940	BURSLEM
K. & B.	KNAPPER & BLACKHURST	1867-71 (&1883-88)	TUNSTALL (& BURSLEM)
K. & B.	KNIGHT & BRIDGWOOD	1884-1886	LONGTON
K. & CO.	KIRKBY, WILLIAM & CO.	1879-1885	FENTON
K. & CO.	KIRKLAND & PIDDOCK	1897-1898	ETRURIA
K. & CO./E.	KIRKLAND & CO.	1892-1938	ETRURIA
K. & M.	KEYS & MOUNTFORD	1850-1857	STOKE
K. & O.	KEELING & OGILVY	1807-1809	TUNSTALL
K. & W.	KNIGHT & WILEMAN	1853-1856	FENTON
K. E. & B.	KING, EDGE & BARATT	1896-1897	BURSLEM
K. F. A. P. CO.	KENSINGTON FINE ART POTTERY CO.	1892-1899	HANLEY
K. P. H.	KENSINGTON POTTERY CO. (LTD.)	1922-1937	HANLEY & BURSLEM
K. T. & CO.	KEELING, TOFT & CO. or (TOFT & CO.)	1801-1824	HANLEY

K. W. & CO.	KEELING, WALKER & CO./KEELING & CO.	1864-	LONGTON
L. & C.	LOCKETT & COOPER	1861-1863	SHELTON (HANLEY)
L. & N.	LEWIS & NICKLIN	1893-1894	LONGTON
L. & S. LTD.	LANCASTER & SUNDLAND LTD.	1906-1944	HANLEY
L. & SONS LTD.	LANCASTER & SONS, LTD.	1944-1968	HANLEY
L. /F.C.	LEEDS FIRECLAY CO. LTD.	1904-1914(+)	YORKSHIRE
L. B. & C.	LOCKETT, BAGULEY & COOPER	1855-1861	SHELTON (HANLEY)
L. C.	CYPLES, LYDIA	1811-1832	LANE END (LONGTON)
L. E. (& S.)	ELLIOTT, LIDDLE (& SON)	1860-1870	LONGPORT/ BURSLEM
L. L. & CO.	LOVATT & LOVATT	1895-1931	NOTTINGHAM
L. R. & CO.	LOWE, RATCLIFFE & CO.	1882-1892	LONGTON
L. S.	LANCASTER & SONS	1900-1944	HANLEY
L. S. & B.	LEA, SMITH & BOULTON	1865-1869	BURSLEM
L. S. & G.	RUBIAN ART POTTERY CO.	1906-1933	FENTON
M. & B.	MACHIN & BAGGALEY	1809-1817	BURSLEM
M. & C. /L.	MATTHEWS & CLARK	1902-1906	LONGTON
M. & C. I.G.	MURRAY & CO.	1826-1840	SCOTLAND
M. & CO.	MC NEAL & CO. (LTD.)	1894-1906	LONGTON
M. & CO.	MURRAY & CO. (LTD.)	1870-1898	SCOTLAND
M. & F.	MURRAY & COUPER	1850-1864	SCOTLAND
M. & H.	MARSH & HAYWOOD	1817-1837	BROWNHILLS/ TUNSTALL
M. & H.	MOSS & HOBSON	1859-1862	LONGTON
M. & M.	MAYER & MAUDESLEY	1837-1838	TUNSTALL
M. & P.	MEAKIN & PROCTER	1842-1845	LANE END (LONGTON)
M. & P.	MINTON & POULSON (& POWNALL)	1796-1808	STOKE
M. & S.	MILLS & SWAN(N)	1862-1862	HANLEY
M. & S./L.	MAYER & SHERRATT (CHINA)	1906-1941	LONGTON
M. & T.	MACHIN & THOMAS	1831-1832	BURSLEM
M. B.	MANSFIELD BROS. (LTD.)	c1890	SCOTLAND
M. F. (& CO.)	MORLEY, FOX & CO. LTD.	1906-1944	FENTON
M. G. & CO.	MURRAY, GRIEVE & CO.	1878-1879	GLASGOW, SCOTLAND
M. H. & CO.	MASON, HOLT & CO.	1857-1884	LONGTON
M. H. (& CO.)	HOLLINS, MINTON (& CO.)(LTD.)	1868-1950s	STOKE
M. L. & CO.	MOORE, LEASON & CO.	1892-1896	FENTON
M. N. & CO./ LONGTON	MC NEAL & CO. LTD.	1894-1906	LONGTON
M. S. & C.	MARTIN, SHAW & COPE/MARTIN & SHAW	1815-1824	LANE END (LONGTON)
M. V. P. & CO.	MELLOR, VENABLES & PINDER & CO.	1831-1851(4)	BURSLEM
M. W. & CO.	WILDBLOOD, MASSEY & CO.	1887-1889	LONGTON
M. W. & CO.	WOOD, MORGAN & CO.	1860-1870	BURSLEM
N. B.	NOAH BENTLEY	1865-1867	HANLEY
N. C. & A.	NICHOLS, COPE & ADAMS	1843-1843	LONGTON
N. H. & CO.	NEALE, HARRISON & CO.	1875-1882 & 1885	HANLEY
P.	PROCTER, J. & H. (& CO.)	1856-1884	LONGTON
P. & B.	PHILLIPS & BAGSTER	1818-1828	HANLEY
P. & C.	PHYSICK & COOPER	1899-1900	HANLEY
P. & C.	PROCTER & COLLINGWOOD	1850	LONGTON
P. & CO. LTD.	POINTON & CO. LTD.	1883-1916	HANLEY
P. & F. W.	WARBURTON, PETER & FRANCIS	1795-1802	COBRIDGE
P. & S. /L.	PLANT, (R.) & SONS	1895-1901	LONGTON
P. & T.	PHILLIPS & THOMPSON	1817-1819	HANLEY
P. & U.	POOLE & UNWIN	1871-1876	LONGTON
P. B.	PRICE BROS. (BURSLEM) LTD.	1903-1961	BURSLEM
P. B. B.	POULSON BROS. LTD.	1884-1927	YORKSHIRE
P. H. (&) G.	PRATT, HASSALL & GERRARD	1821-1834	FENTON
P. J.	JOHNSON, PHOEBE (& SON)	1824-1836-(1839)	HANLEY
P. S. & W.	POOL, STANWAY & WOOD	1875-1878	STOKE
R. & B.	RAY & BALL	1849-1850	LONGTON
R. & C.	RIVERS & CLOWES	1816-1822	SHELTON (HANLEY)
R. & C.	ROBINSON & CHAPMAN	1875-1881	LONGTON
R. & CO.	RITCHIE & CO.	1901-1903	STOKE
R. & M.	ROPER & MEREDITH	1913-1924	LONGTON
R. & N.	ROWLEY & NEWTON (LTD.)	1896-1901	LONGTON
R. & P.	REID & PATTERSON	1801-1803	SCOTLAND
R. & P.	RHODES & PROCTOR	1883-1885	BURSLEM
R. & S.	RIGBY & STEVENSON	1894-1954	HANLEY
R. & T.	RAY & TIDESWELL	1830-1837	LONGTON
R. & W.	RAY & WYNNE	1846-1847	LONGTON
R. B. & S.	BRITTON, RICHARD & SON	1872-1878	YORKSHIRE
R. C. & CO.	ROBINSON, CHAPMAN & CO.	1872-1875	LONGTON
R. C. A. & CO.	STEVENSON, ALCOCK & WILLIAMS	1820-1826	COBRIDGE
R. D.	DUDSON, RICHARD	1838-1843	HANLEY
R. D. (& CO.)	DANIEL, RICHARD (& CO.)	1841-1854	BURSLEM & OTHER LOCATIONS
R. F. & S.	FLOYD, R. & SON	1907-1930	STOKE
R. G.	GALLIMORE, ROBERT	1840-1850	FENTON
R. G. S. & CO.	SCRIVENER, R. G. & CO.	1870-1880	HANLEY
R. H.	HALL, R.	1854-1854	LONGPORT
R. H. G.	GROVE, RICHARD HENRY	1859-1869	LONGTON
R. J.	JOHNSON, REUBEN	1817-1823	HANLEY
R. M. A.	ASTBURY, RICHARD MEIR	c1790	SHELTON
R. M. S.	MALKIN, RALPH & SONS	1882-1894	FENTON

R. P. & CO.	REID, PATTERSON & CO.	1800-1801	SCOTLAND
R. R. & B.	RAY, RAY & BENTLEY	1853-1854	LONGTON
R. R. & CO.	RAY, RICHARD & CO.	1850-1852	LONGTON
R. S.	SALT, RALPH	1820-1842	HANLEY
R. S.	SHAW, RALPH	1828-1858	LONGTON
R. S. & CO.	RATHBONE, SMITH & CO.	1883-1897	TUNSTALL
R. W.	WOOD, RALPH (II)	1789-1795	BURSLEM
R. W.	WOOD, RALPH (III)	1795-1802	BURSLEM
S.	SHORTHOUSE, JOHN	1815-1823	SHELTON /HANLEY
S. & B.	SADLER & BENNETT	1895-1895	TUNSTALL
S. & B.	STUBBS & BIRD	1850-1853	HANLEY
S. & C.	SHAW & COPESTAKE	1905-1957	LONGTON
S. & C. LTD.	SANDLANDS & COLLEY LTD.	1907-1910	HANLEY
S. & CO.	SHORTHOSE, JOHN & CO.	1817-1818	HANLEY
S. & H.	SHORTHOSE & HEATH	1794-1815	SHELTON (HANLEY)
S. & L.	STANLEY & LAMBERT	1850-1855	LONGTON
S. & R.	SIMKIN & RIDGE	1839-1840	LANE END (LONGTON)
S. & S.	SADLER & SON	1895-1901	TUNSTALL
S. & S.	SHORTER & SON LTD.	1905-present	STOKE
S. & S.	SPENCER & STANWAY	1883-1886	LONGTON
S. & S.	STANWAY & SON	1878-1879	STOKE
S. & S. /S.	SHAW & SONS	1892-1910	TUNSTALL
S. & V.	SANT & VODREY	1887-1893	COBRIDGE
S. BROS.	SHORTER BROS.	1906-1912	BURSLEM
S. C. (& CO.)	CLIVE, STEPHEN (& CO.)	1875-1880	TUNSTALL
S. E.	ELKIN, SAMUEL	1856-1865	LONGTON
S. F. & CO.	FIELDING, S. & CO. (LTD.)	1879-1917-(1982)	FENTON
S. H.	HALL, SAMUEL	1841-1856	HANLEY
S. H.	HALLEM, SAMUEL	1851-1854	BURSLEM
S. H.	HUGHES, STEPHEN	1853-1855	BURSLEM
S. H. & CO.	HAMILTON, SAMPSON & CO.	1840-1840	LANE END (LONGTON)
S. H. & CO.	HUGHES, STEPHEN & CO.	1835-1852	COBRIDGE
S. J. P.	PRESTON, S. J.	1899-1900	LONGTON
S. L.	LEAR, SAMUEL	1882-1886	HANLEY
S. L.	LONGBOTTOM, SAMUEL	late 19c-1899	YORKSHIRE
S. LTD.	SANDLANDS, LTD.	1904-1907	HANLEY
S. S.	SMITH, SAMPSON (LTD.)	1851-1916-(1963)	LONGTON
T. & B.	TOMKINSON & BILLINGTON (& SON)	1868-1870	LONGTON
T. & CO.	TIPPER & CO.	1847-1862	LONGTON
T. & E. H. & CO.	HOBSON, T. & E. & CO.	1863-1866	LONGTON
T. & L.	TAMS & LOWE	1865-1875	LONGTON
T. & M.	TRANTER & MACHIN	1886-1898	LONGTON
T. & W.	TURNER & WOOD	1878-1888	STOKE
T. B.	BEVINGTON, THOMAS	1878-1891	HANLEY
T. B. (& S.)	BIRKS, THOMAS	1854-1877	LONGTON
T. C.	COOPER, THOMAS	1859-1865	SHELTON /HANLEY
T. C.	COPE, THOMAS	1822-1827(8)	LANE END (LONGTON)
T. C. /L.	CONE, THOMAS, LTD.	1892-1912-(67)	LONGTON
T. F. & CO.	FORESTER, THOMAS & CO.	c1888	LONGTON
T. F. (& CO.)	FLETCHER, THOMAS (& CO.)	1794-1800	SHELTON (HANLEY)
T. G. & S.	TURNER (S), GLOVER & SIMPSON	1803-1806	LANE END (LONGTON)
T. H. & CO.	HANSON, THOMAS & CO.	c1841	HANLEY
T. H. & CO.	HOBSON, THOMAS & CO.	1863-1866	LONGTON
T. H. & P.	TURNER, HASSALL & PEAKE	1865-1871	STOKE
T. H. & P.	TURNER, HASSALL & POOLE	1871-1872	STOKE
T. I. & J. E.	EMBERTON, T.I. & J.	1869-1882	TUNSTALL
T. P. & S.	TURNER, POOLE & STANWAY	1873-1873	STOKE
T. P. L.	LEDGAR, THOMAS P.	1900-1905	LONGTON
T. R. & CO.	RATHBONE, THOMAS & CO.	1810-1845	SCOTLAND
T. R. & P.	TUNDLEY, RHODES & PROCTOR	1873-1883	BURSLEM
T. S. R.	REPTON, T. S.	1883-1888	LONGTON
T. T. (& CO.)	TAYLOR, TUNNICLIFFE (&CO.)(LTD.)	1868-present	HANLEY
T. T. /H.	TWYFORD, THOMAS	1860-1888	HANLEY
T. W.	WILLIAMS, THOMAS	c1827	STOKE
T. W.	WORTHINGTON, THOMAS	1842-1843	HANLEY
T. W.	WRIGHT, THOMAS	1822-25 & 1840-1841	HANLEY
T. W.	WYNNE, THOMAS	1847-1853	LONGTON
U. H. & W.	UNWIN, HOLMES & WORTHINGTON	1865-1868	HANLEY
U. M. & T.	UNWIN, MOUNTFORD & TAYLOR	1864-1864	HANLEY
U. T. & CO.	THOMAS, URIAH	1888-1905	HANLEY
V. F. A. P. CO.	VINCENT FINE ART POTTERY CO.	1900-1910	BURSLEM
V. M. & CO.	VENABLES, MANN & CO.	1853-1855	BURSLEM
V. P. CO.	VICTORIA POTTERY CO.	1895-1927	HANLEY
W. & A.	WARDLE & ASH	1859-1865	SHELTON (HANLEY)
W. & A.	WILD & ADAMS (LTD.)	1909-1923-(27)	LONGTON
W. & B.	WOOD & BOWERS	1839-1839	BURSLEM
W. & B.	WRIGHT & BURGESS	1840-1841	TUNSTALL
W. & B. (LONGTON)	WAGSTAFF & BRUNT	1879-1927	LONGTON
W. & C.	WARRILOW & COPE	1880-1887	LONGTON
W. & C.	WOOD & CLARKE	1871-1872	BURLSEM
W. & CO.	WARRINGTON & CO.	186-1863	HANLEY
W. & CO.	WILSON & CO.	1897-1899	FENTON

W. & CO.	WILSON, ROBERT CHRISTOPHER	1844-1852	NORTHUMBER-LAND
W. & CO. /B.	WADE & CO.	1887-1927	BURSLEM
W. & F.	WOOD & FORD	1853-1853	SHELTON (HANLEY)
W. & G.	WORTHINGTON & GREEN	1844-1864	HANLEY
W. & H.	WESTON & HULL	1796-1798	LANE END (LONGTON)
W. & H.	WILDBLOOD & HEATH (CHINA)	1888-1898	LONGTON
W. & J. B.	BAKER, WILLIAM & JOHN	1835-1836	FENTON
W. & J. R.	RATHBONE, WM. & JOHN	1810-1813	TUNSTALL
W. & J. T.	TURNER, WM. & JOHN	1773-1803	LANE END (LONGTON)
W. & L.	WATHEN & LICHFIELD	1862-1864	FENTON
W. & L.	WILDBLOOD & LEDGAR	1896-1898	LONGTON
W. & R. /L.	WAYTE & RIDGE	1864-1864	LONGTON
W. & T. B.	BARKER, WILLIAM & THOMAS	c1860	BURSLEM
W. & W.	WEBB & WALTERS	1860-1867	LONGTON
W. & W.	WILKINSON & WARDLE	1864-1866	YORKSHIRE
W. & W. /B.	WOOLDRIDGE & WALLEY	1898-1901	BURSLEM
W. (&) D. B. & CO.	BAILEY, W. & D. & CO.	1827-1830	LONGTON
W. A.	ARROWSMITH, WILLIAM	1810-1819	STOKE
W. B.	BAKER, WILLIAM	1836-1838	FENTON
W. B.	BETTANY, W. (BETTENEY)	1882-1902	HANLEY
W. B. & T. (CO.)	WRIGHT, BURGESS & TAYLOR (& Co.)	1841-1843	TUNSTALL
W. B. /H.	BENNETT, WILLIAM LTD.	1882-1937	HANLEY
W. C. JR. L. P.	CHAMBERS, WM. JR.	1839-1855	LLANELLY, WALES
W. C. JR./L.P.	COPESTAKE, WM. JUNIOR	1834-1861	LONGTON
W. E.	EVERSFIELD, WILLIAM	1894-1895	HANLEY
W. E. W.	WITHINSHAW, W. E.	1873-1878	BURSLEM
W. G. & S.	GILL, WILLIAM & SON(S)	1880-1932	YORKSHIRE
W. H.	HUDSON, WILLIAM	1889-1941	LONGTON
W. H. & A.	WOLFE, HAMILTON & ARROWSMITH	1809-1810	STOKE
W. H. & CO.	KIRKBY, WILLIAM & CO.	1879-1885	FENTON
W. H. & S.	WILDBLOOD & HEATH (CHINA)	1888-1898	LONGTON
W. H. & W.	WOOD, HINES & WINKLE	1881-1885	HANLEY
W. H. G.	GIBBONS, W. H.	1883-1886	HANLEY
W. H. G.	GOSS, WILLIAM HENRY (LTD.)	1858-1944	STOKE
W. H. M.	MILLWARD, W. H.	1901-1902	LONGTON
W. H. S.	SKELSON, W. H. JR.	1893-1896	LONGTON
W. J.	JARVIS, WILLIAM OR (JERVIS)	1818-1847	LANE END (LONGTON)
W. K. & CO.	KIRKBY, WILLIAM & CO.	1879-1885	FENTON
W. L. & S. (& CO.)	LARGE, WM. & SON (& CO.)	1853-1855	SHELTON (HANLEY)
W. L. (/L)	LOWE, WILLIAM	1875-1930	LONGTON
W. P. & CO.	PLANT, WM. & CO.	1853-1855	FENTON
W. P. CO.	WELLINGTON POTTERY	1899-1901	HANLEY
W. R. & CO.	RIVERS, WM. & CO.	1816-1822	SHELTON (HANLEY)
W. R. (& CO.)	ROBINSON, W. (& CO.)	1872-1888	FOLEY (FENTON)
W. R. (& S.)	REID, WM. (& SON(S))	1800-1855	SCOTLAND
W. S.	SANDLAND, WM.	1898-1904	HANLEY
W. S.	SMITH, WM.	1870-1874	DURHAM
W. S.	STUBBS, WM.	1847-1897	HANLEY
W. S. & CO.	SKINNER, WM. & CO.	1865-1866	LONGTON
W. S. & J. R.	RATHBONE, WM., SAMUEL & JOHN	1810-1823	TUNSTALL
W. S. (JR.) & CO.	SMITH, WM. (JR.) & CO.	1845-1855	DURHAM
W. S. K.	KENNEDY, WILLIAM SADDLER	1843-1853	BURSLEM
W. T. H.	HOLLAND, WILLIAM	1859-1868	LLANELLY, WALES
W. W.	WARRINGTON, WILLIAM	1863-1867	HANLEY
W. W. & CO.	WOOD, WILLIAM & CO.	1873-1932	BURSLEM
Y. B. & B.	YALE, BARKER & BARKER	1843-1846	LONGTON
Y. B. & S.	YALE, BARKER & SON	1841-1843	LONGTON

BAGGALEY, JACOB	J. B.	1880-1886	BURSLEM

APPENDIX B4: ALPHABETIC LISTING: SECONDARY POTTERS BY NAME & INITIAL

POTTERY	INITIALS	DATE	LOCATION
ADAMS & BROMLEY	A. & B.	1873-1886	HANLEY
ADAMS & COOPER	A. & C.	1850-1879	LONGTON
ADDERLEY, J. FELLOWS	J. F. A.	1901-1905	LONGTON
AITCHIESON, J. & CO.	J. C.	1807-1811	SCOTLAND
ALCOCK, LINDLEY & BLOORE (LTD.)	A. L. B. (LTD.)	1919-1930(+)	HANLEY
AMISON, CHARLES (& CO.) (LTD.)	C. A. /L.	1889-1916-(30)-(62)	LONGTON
ARKINSTALL & SONS, LTD.	A. & S.	1904-1925	STOKE
ARROWSMITH & CO.	A. & CO.	1900-1905	LONGTON
ARROWSMITH, WILLIAM	W. A.	1810-1819	STOKE
ASBURY, EDWARD & CO.	A. & CO.	1875-1925	LONGTON
ASHWELL & CO.	A. & CO.	c1832	LONGTON
ASTBURY, RICHARD MEIR	R. M. A.	c1790	SHELTON
AYNSLEY, H. & CO. (LTD.)	H. A. & CO. (L.)	1873-1932-(82)	LONGTON
BADDELEY & FLETCHER	B. & F.	1759-1775	SHELTON
BAILEY & BEVINGTON or BEVINGTON & CO.	B. & B.	1867-1868	HANLEY
BAILEY, FLOYD & SHUBOTHAM	B. F. & S.	1835-1837	LANE END (LONGTON)
BAILEY, HACKNEY & CO.	B. H. & CO.	c1889	HANLEY
BAILEY, JOHN	J. B.	1849-1858	LONGTON
BAILEY, W. & D. & CO.	W. (&) D. B. & CO.	1826-1830	LONGTON
BAKER, WILLIAM	W. B.	1836-1838	FENTON
BAKER, WILLIAM & JOHN	W. & J. B.	1835-1836	FENTON
BALL, ALFRED	A. B.	1883-1886	LONGTON
BARKER, JOSEPH	J. B.	1860-1861	LONGTON
BARKER, WILLIAM & THOMAS	W. & T. B.	c1860	BURSLEM
BARLOW, JAMES & CO.	J. B. & CO.	1822-1839	HANLEY
BARLOW, T. W. & SON	B. & S.	1882-1940	LONGTON
BARLOW, T. W. & SON, LTD.	B.	1882-1940	LONGTON
BARLOWS (LONGTON) LTD.	B. LTD.	1923-1952	LONGTON
BARROW & TAYLOR	B. & T.	c1859	HANLEY
BARTON & SWIFT	B. & S.	c1811	BURSLEM
BAXTER, ROWLEY & TAMS	B. R. & T.	1882-1885	LONGTON
BAYLEY, MURRAY & BRAMMER	B. M. & B.	1875-1878	GLASGOW, SCOTLAND
BEACH, COOPER, TILL & CO.	B. C. T. & CO.	1872-1873	LONGTON
BEARDMORE, BIRKS & BLOOD	B. B. & B.	1851-1854	LONGTON
BEECH, JAMES & SON	J. B. & S.(SON)	1853-1898	LONGTON
BELL, ISACC & GALLOWAY & ATKINSON	I. B. & G. A.	C. 1836	NORTHUM-BERLAND
BENNETT, GEORGE & CO.	G. B. & CO.	1894-1902	STOKE
BENNETT, HURD & CO.	B. H. & CO.	1865-1866	BURSLEM
BENNETT, WILLIAM LTD.	W. B. /H.	1882-1937	HANLEY
BENTLEY, G. L. & CO. (LTD.)	G. L. B. & CO.(LTD.)	1898-1904-(12)	LONGTON
BERESFORD BROS.	B. B.	1900-1930	LONGTON
BESWICK & SON	B. & S.	1916-1930	LONGTON
BESWICK, J. W.	J. W. B.	1894-1920	LONGTON
BETTANY & TOMLINSON	B. & T.	1843-1844	LANE END (LONGTON)
BETTANY, W. (BETTENEY)	W. B.	1882-1902	HANLEY
BEVINGTON & BRADLEY	B. & B.	1868-1869	HANLEY
BEVINGTON & CO. or BAILEY & BEVINGTON	B. & B.	1867-1868	HANLEY
BEVINGTON, AMBROSE (& CO.)	A. B. (& CO.)	1871-1891	HANLEY
BEVINGTON, JAMES & THOMAS	J. & T. B.	1865-1878	HANLEY
BEVINGTON, JOHN & CO.	J. B. & CO. /H.	1860-1892	HANLEY
BEVINGTON, THOMAS	T. B.	1878-1891	HANLEY
BILL & LAWRENCE	B. & L.	c1832	LANE END (LONGTON)
BIRCH, JOSEPH	J. B.	1847-1851	HANLEY
BIRKS & BLOOD	B. & B.	c1854	LONGTON
BIRKS, L. A. & CO.	B. & CO.	1896-1899	STOKE
BIRKS, RAWLINS & CO. (LTD.)	B. R. & CO.	1898-1932	STOKE
BIRKS, THOMAS	T. B.	1845-1880	LONGTON
BLACKWELL, JOHN	J. B.	1784-1814	COBRIDGE
BLOOD, EDWIN	E. B.	1856-1862	LONGTON
BODLEY & SON	B. & S. (SON)	1874-1875	BURSLEM
BODLEY, E. J. D.	E. J. D. B.	1875-1892	BURLSEM
BOLD & NASH	B. & N.	1850-1851	BURSLEM
BOOTH, EPHRAIM (& SONS)	E. B. (& S.)	1790-1808	STOKE & SHELTON
BOOTH, FREDERICK	F. B.	c1881	YORKSHIRE
BOOTH, G. R. (& CO.)	G. R. B. (& CO.)	1829-1838-(40)	HANLEY
BOOTH, HUGH	H. B.	1791-1799	STOKE
BOUGHEY & WILTSHAW	B. & W.	1892-1894	LONGTON
BOULTON & CO.	B. & CO.	1892-1902	LONGTON
BOULTON & SON	B. & S.	-	-
BOURNE, BAKER & BAKER	B. B. & B.	1833-1835	FENTON
BOWERS & LLOYD	B. & L.	c1846	BURSLEM
BRADBURY, ANDERSON & BETTANNY	B. A. & B.	1844-1850	LONGTON
BRADBURY, KELLETT & CO.	B. K. & C.	1882-1887	LONGTON
BRADBURY, MASON, & BRADBURY	B. M. & B.	1852-1854	LONGTON
BRADBURY, MASON, & BROADHURST	B. M. & B.	c1854	LONGTON
BRAIN, E. & CO. LTD.	E. B. & CO./F	1903-1963	FENTON
BREWER, FRANCIS, H. & CO.	F. B. & C.	1863-1865	LONGTON
BREWER, FRANCIS, H. (& SON)	F. B. (& S.)	1862-1863	LONGTON
BRIDGWOOD, A.	A. B.	1894-1897	FENTON
BRIDGWOOD, JOHN JR.	J. B. J.	c1870	HANLEY
BRINDLEY, JOHN & CO.	J. A. & CO.	1824-1830	HANLEY
BRINDLEY, JOHN & CO.	J. B. & CO.	1824-1830	HANLEY
BRITTON, RICHARD & SON	R. B. & S.	1872-1878	YORKSHIRE
BROADHURST & SONS	B. & S.	1853-1863	LONGTON
BROADHURST, JAMES	J. B.	1863-1870	LONGTON
BROADHURST, JAMES & SONS	J. B. & S.	1870-1922	FENTON
BROADHURST, JAMES & SONS (LTD.)	J. B. & S. (LTD.)	1922 - 1983	FENTON
BROOKFIELD BROS.	B. B.	1892-1903	LONGTON
BROUGH & GREEN	B. & G.	1842-1852	LONGTON
BROWN, HENRY & CO.	H. B. & CO.	1828-1830	LONGTON

BROWNING & LEWIS	B. & L.	1899-1900	HANLEY
BRYAN & LAWTON	B. & L.	c1854	LONGTON
BUCKLEY, HEATH & CO.	B. H. & CO.	1885-1890	BURSLEM
BUCKLEY, JOHN & CO.	J. B. & CO.	1885-1890	BURSLEM
BUCKLEY, WOOD & CO.	B. W. & CO.	1875-1885	BURSLEM
BURGESS, THOMAS	H. & B.	1903-1917	HANLEY
BURTON, GEORGE & BENJAMIN	G. & B. B.	1882-1900	HANLEY
CAMPBELLFIELD POTTERY CO., (LTD.)	C. P. CO. (LTD.)	1850-1884	SCOTLAND
CANDY & CO., LTD.	C. /N. A.	c1882	DEVON
CAPPER & WOOD	C. & W.	1895-1904	LONGTON
CARTER, STABLER & ADAMS	C. S. A.	c1921	DORSET
CENTURY POTTERY CO.	C. P. CO.	1903-1920s	BURSLEM
CHAMBERS, WM. JR.	W. C. JR. L. P.	1839-1855	LLANELLY, WALES
CHETHAM, J. R. & F.	J. R. & F. C.	1864-1869	LONGTON
CHRISTIE & BEARDMORE	C. B. (/F.)	1902-1903	FENTON
CLIVE, STEPHEN (& CO.)	S. C. (& CO.)	1875-1880	TUNSTALL
CLOKIE & CO.	C. & CO.	1881-1961	YORKSHIRE
CLOKIE & MASTERMAN	C. & M.	1888-1961	YORKSHIRE
COLCLOUGH, HERBERT JOSEPH	H. J. C. /L.	1897-1937	LONGTON
COLLINGWOOD & GREATBACH	C. & G.	1870-1887	LONGTON
CONE, THOMAS, LTD.	T. C. /L.	1892-1912-(67)	LONGTON
COOMBS & HOLLAND	C. & H.	1855-1858	LLANELLY, WALES
COOMER & PRATT	C. & P.	1807-1809	FENTON
COOPER & DETHICK	C. & D.	1876-1888	LONGTON
COOPER, THOMAS	T. C.	1863-1865	SHELTON
COOPERS & CO.	C. & CO.	1877-1878	LONGTON
COOPERS, TILL & CO.	C. T. & CO.	1873-1877	LONGTON
COOPESTAKE, WM. JUNIOR	W. C. JR./L.P.	1834-1860	LONGTON
COPE, J. T. & CO.	J. T. C. & CO.	1885-1889	HANLEY
COPE, THOMAS	T. C.	1822-1827(8)	LANE END (LONGTON)
CORNFOOT, COLVILLE & CO.	C. C. & CO.	C. 1829	NORTHUM-BERLAND
CREYKE, G. M. & SONS	G. M. C.	1920-1948	HANLEY
CRYSTAL PORCELAIN POTTERY CO. LTD.	C. P. P. CO.	1883-1886	COBRIDGE
CURTIS, G. R.	G. R. C.	c1839	YORKSHIRE
CYPLES & BARKER	C. & B.	1846-1848	LONGTON
CYPLES & ROBEY	C. & R.	1844-1846	LONGTON
CYPLES, LYDIA	L. C.	1811-1832	LANE END (LONGTON)
DANIEL, HENRY (& CO.)	H. D. (& CO.)	1826-1836	SHELTON
DANIEL, RICHARD (& CO.)	R. D. (& CO.)	1841-1854	BURSLEM & OTHER LOCATIONS
DAVIS, COXON & BASKET	D. C. & B	1816-1822	NORTHUM-BERLAND
DAVIS, COXON & WILSON	D. C. & W.	1822-1833	NORTHUM-BERLAND
DAWSON, J.	J. D.	1800-1848	SUNDERLAND
DEAN & STOKES	D. & S.	1867-1868	BURSLEM
DEAN, CAPPER & DEAN	D. C. & D.	1882-1888	HANLEY & BURSLEM
DEAVILLE & BADDERLEY	D. & B.	c1854	HANLEY
DEWES & COPESTAKE	D. & C. (/L)	1893-1915	LONGTON
DIAMOND POTTERY CO. (LTD.)	D. P. CO. (LTD.)	1908-1935	HANLEY
DILLON, FRANCIS & NICHOLAS	F. & N. D.	1815-1830	COBRIDGE
DOWNS & HULME	D. & H.	c1882	LONGTON
DUDSON BROTHERS (LTD.)	D.	1898-PRESENT	TUNSTALL
DUDSON BROTHERS (LTD.)	D. B. (LTD.)	1898-PRESENT	HANLEY & TUNSTALL
DUDSON, JAMES & CHARLES	J. & C. D.	1835-1845	SHELTON (HANLEY)
DUDSON, RICHARD	R. D.	1838-1843	HANLEY
EARDLEY & HAMMERSLEY	E. & H.	1862-1866	TUNSTALL
EARDLEY, SPEAR & CO.	E. S. & CO.	c1873	TUNSTALL
EDGE, DANIEL	D. E.	1834-1842	BURSLEM
ELKIN, SAMUEL	S. E.	1856-1864	LONGTON
ELLIOTT, LIDDLE (& SON)	L. E. (& S.)	1860-1869	LONGPORT
ELLIS, UNWIN & MOUNTFORD	E. U. & M.	1860-1861	HANLEY
ELTON, J. F. & CO. (LTD.)	J. F. E. & CO. (LTD.)	1901-1911	BURSLEM
ELTON, J. F. & CO. LTD.	J. F. E. CO. LTD.	1901-1910	BURSLEM
EMBERTON, T.I. & J.	T. I. & J. E.	1869-1882	TUNSTALL
EVANS & BOOTH	E. & B.	1856-1869	BURSLEM
EVANS & COYNE	E. & C.	1867-1868	HANLEY
EVANS, J. B. & CO.	J. B. E. & CO.	1877-1879	HANLEY
EVERAD, COLCLOUGH & TOWNSEND	E. C. & T.	1837-1845	LONGTON
EVERAD, GLOVER & COLCLOUGH	E. G. & C.	c1847	LONGTON
EVERAD, GLOVER & TOWNSEND	E. G. & T.	c1837	LONGTON
EVERSFIELD, WILLIAM	W. E.	1894-1895	HANLEY
FENTON POTTERY CO.	F. P. C.	c1851	FENTON
FENTON, DOWNS & CO.	F. D. & C.	1881-1882	LONGTON
FIELDING, S. & CO. (LTD.)	S. F. & CO.	1879-1917-(1982)	FENTON
FLACKETT, CHETHAM & TOFT	F. C. & T.	c1853	FENTON
FLETCHER & TITTENSOR	F. & T.	c1794	SHELTON (HANLEY)
FLETCHER, THOMAS (& CO.)	T. F. (& CO.)	1794-1800	SHELTON (HANLEY)
FLOYD, BENJAMIN	B. F.	c1843	LANE END (LONGTON)
FLOYD, JAMES	J. F.	1845-1847	LONGTON
FLOYD, R. & SON	R. F. & S.	1907-1930	STOKE
FLOYD, SHUBOTHAM & LEAKE	F. S. & L.	1834-1835	LANE END (LONGTON)
FOLCH & SCOTT	F. & S.	1821-1822	STOKE
FORD, CHARLES	C. F.	1871-1904(25)	HANLEY
FORESTER, THOMAS & CO.	T. F. & CO.	c1888	LONGTON
FRANSHAWE & HUGHES	F. & H.	1882-1889	FENTON
GALLIMORE & CO. LTD.	G. & CO. /L.	1906-1934	LONGTON
GALLIMORE & SHUBOTHAM	G. & S.	1840-1841	LONGTON
GALLIMORE, AMBROSE & ROBERT	A. & R. G.	1832-1837	LONGTON
GALLIMORE, ROBERT	R. G.	1840-1850	FENTON
GALLOWAY & ATKINSON	G. & A.	c. 1864	NORTHUM-BERLAND
GALLOWAY & ATKINSON	G. & A.	1865-1872	NEWCASTLE
GERRARD, JOHN	J. G.	1846-1853	HANLEY
GERRARD, JOHN	J. G.	1824-1836	HANLEY
GIBBONS, W. H.	W. H. G.	1883-1886	HANLEY
GIBSON, JAMES (& CO.)	J. G. (& CO.)	c1891	LONGTON
GIBSON, JOHN	J. G.	1841-1846	TUNSTALL
GILL, WILLIAM & SON(S)	W. G. & S.	1880-1932	YORKSHIRE
GLOVER & COLCLOUGH	G. & C.	1847-1854	LONGTON
GODWIN, B. C.	B. C. G.	c1851	BURSLEM
GODWIN, JAMES	J. G.	1846-1850	COBRIDGE
GODWIN, JOHN	J. G.	1805-1808	STOKE
GOODWIN & JARVIS	G. & J.	1805-1808	STOKE
GOODWIN, BARKER & FANSHAWE	G. B. & F.	1881-1882	FENTON
GOODWIN, J., STODDARD & CO.	J. G. S. & CO.	1898-1940	FOLEY, LONGTON, COBRIDGE
GOSS, WILLIAM HENRY (LTD.)	W. H. G.	1858-1931-(56)+	STOKE
GRANVILLE POTTERY CO.	G. P. CO.	1899-1900	HANLEY
GREEN, JOHN	J. G.	1872-1877	LONGTON
GRIEVE, ELLIS & CO.	G. E. & CO.	1879-1889	GLASGOW, SCOTLAND
GRIFFITHS & LOWNDS	G. & L.	c1845	SHELTON (HANLEY)
GROVE, RICHARD HENRY	R. H. G.	1859-1869	LONGTON
GUEST & DEWSBURY	G. & D. /L.	1877-1927	LLANELLY- WALES
HACKWOOD, DIMMOCK & CO.	H. D. & CO.	1807-1827	HANLEY
HAINES, BATCHELOR & CO. (RETAILERS)	H. B.	1880-1890	LONDON
HALL & HOLLAND	H. & H.	1838-1843	TUNSTALL
HALL & READ	H. & R.	c1882	BURSLEM
HALL & READ	H. & R.	1883-1888	HANLEY
HALL, R.	R. H.	c1854	LONGPORT
HALL, SAMUEL	S. H.	1834&1841-56	HANLEY
HALLAM & DAY	H. & D.	1880-1883	LONGTON
HALLEM, E.	E. H.	1851-1854	BURSLEM
HALLEM, SAMUEL	S. H.	1851-1854	BURSLEM
HAMILTON & MOORE	H. & M.	c. 1840-1858	LONGTON
HAMILTON, SAMUEL & CO.	S. H. & CO.	c1840	LANE END (LONGTON)
HAMMERSLEY, J. & R.	J. & R. H.	1877-1917	HANLEY
HAMPSON & CO.	H. & CO.	c1865	LONGTON
HANCOCK & WRIGHT	H. & W.	1838-1840	TUNSTALL
HANCOCK, BENJAMIN & SAMPSON	B. & S. H.	1876-1881	STOKE
HANCOCK, WRIGHT & BURGESS	H. W. & B.	c1840	TUNSTALL
HANDLEY, JAMES & WILLIAM	J. & W. H.	1822-1830	BURSLEM
HANSON, THOMAS & CO.	T. H. & CO.	c1841	HANLEY
HARRIS & HULME	H. & H.	1839-1840	LONGTON
HARRISON & PHILLIPS	H. & P.	1914-1915	BURSLEM
HARRISON, CHARLES	C. H.	1887-1897	LONGTON
HARROP & BURGESS	H. & B.	1894-1903	HANLEY
HARVEY, BAILEY & CO./ BAILEYS & HARVEYS	H. B. & CO.	1832-1835	LANE END (LONGTON)
HASSALL, POOLE & STANWAY	H. P. & S.	1872-1873	STOKE
HAWLEY, FELIX H.	F. H. H.	c1851	FENTON
HAWLEY, GEORGE	G. H.	1855-1868	YORKSHIRE
HAWLEY, JOHN (& CO.)	J. H. (& CO.)	1832-1893	FOLEY(FENTON)
HAWLEY, WEBBERLEY & CO.	H. & W. & CO.	1895-1902	LONGTON
HAWLEY, WEBBERLEY & CO.	H. W. & CO.	1895-1902	LONGTON
HEATH & GREATBACH	H. & C. /B.	1891-1893	BURSLEM
HEBB, JOHN	J. H.	1856-1857	FENTON
HETT & CO.	H. & CO.	c1864	HANLEY
HIBBERT & BOUGHEY	H. & B.	1889-1890	LONGTON
HILL POTTERY CO. (LTD.)	H. P. & CO. (LTD.)	1861-1867	BURSLEM
HILL POTTERY CO. (LTD.)	J. S. H.	1861-1867	BURSLEM
HINES BROTHERS	H. B.	1886-1907	FENTON
HOBSON & CO.	H. & CO.	1876-78&1889-93	LONGTON
HOBSON, T. & E. & CO.	T. & E. H. & CO.	1863-1866	LONGTON
HOBSON, THOMAS & CO.	T. H. & CO.	1863-1866	LONGTON
HODGKINSON, ELIJAH	E. H.	1864-1871	HANLEY
HODSON (RICHARD) & CO.	H. & CO.	1849-1885	LONGTON
HOLDCROFT & CO.	H. & CO.	1870-1871	BURSLEM
HOLLAND, JOHN	J. H.	1852-1854	TUNSTALL
HOLLAND, WILLIAM	W. T. H.	1859-1868	LLANELLY, WALES
HOLLINS, MINTON (& CO.) (LTD.)	M. H. (& CO.)	1868-1950s	STOKE
HOLLINSHEAD & GRIFFITHS	H. & G.	1890-1909	BURSLEM
HOLLISON, JAMES	J. H.	1899-1907	LONGTON

HOLLOWAY, JOHN	J. H.	1862-1867	HANLEY
HOLMES & SON	H. & S.	1898-1903	LONGTON
HOLMES, PLANT & MAYDEW	H. P. & M.	1876-1885	BURSLEM
HOPKINS & CO.	H. & CO.	1841-1843	BURSLEM
HUDSON, WILLIAM	W. H.	1889-1941	LONGTON
HUGHES & ROBINSON	H. & R.	1888-1894	COBRIDGE
HUGHES, JOHN	J. H.	c1864	COBRIDGE
HUGHES, STEPHEN	S. H.	1853-1855	BURSLEM
HUGHES, STEPHEN & CO.	S. H. & CO.	1835-1852	COBRIDGE
HULL, A. J.	A. J. H.	1896-1901	LONGTON
HULME & BOOTH	H. & B.	1851-1854	BURSLEM
HULME & CHRISTIE	H. & C. /F.	1893-1902	FENTON
HULME, WILLIAM (LTD)	H.	1891-1925-(41)	BURSLEM
JACKSON & GOSLING (LTD.)	J. & G. (/L.)	1866-1961	FENTON & LONGTON
JACKSON & PATTERSON	J. & P.	1833-1838	NORTHUM-BERSIDE
JARVIS & LOVE	J. & L.	c1818	LANE END (LONGTON)
JARVIS, WILLIAM OR (JERVIS)	W. J.	1818-1846	LANE END (LONGTON)
JOHNSON, PHOEBE (& SON)	P. J.	1824-1836-(1839)	HANLEY
JOHNSON, REUBEN	R. J.	1817-1823	HANLEY
JONES & BROMLEY	J. & B.	1882-1887	LONGTON
JONES & THOMPSON	J. & T.	c1879	LONGTON
JONES & WALLEY	J. & W.	1841-1843	COBRIDGE
JONES, A. B. (& SONS) (LTD.)	A. B. J. (& S.)(LTD.)	1880-1900-(55)-(72)	LONGTON
JONES, A. G. HARVEY	H. J.	1907-1934	FENTON
JONES, A.G. HARLEY	A. G. H. J./H.J.	1907-1934	FENTON
JONES, ELIJAH	E. J.	1828-1831	HANLEY
JONES, ELIJAH (MILL STREET)	E. J.	1847-1848	SHELTON
JONES, FREDERICK	F. J.	1865-72&1879/86	LONGTON
JONES, JOSIAH ELLIS	J. E. J.	1868-1872	LONGTON
KEELING & OGILVY	K. & O.	1807-1809	TUNSTALL
KEELING, ANTHONY	A. K.	1738-1815	TUNSTALL/ HANLEY
KEELING, ANTHONY & ENOCH	A. & EK.	1795-1814	TUNSTALL
KEELING, ANTHONY (& SON(S))	A. K. & S.	1792-1795	TUNSTALL
KEELING, TOFT & CO. or (TOFT & CO.)	K. T. & CO.	1801-1824	HANLEY
KEELING, WALKER & CO./ KEELING & CO.	K. W. & CO.	1856-1866	LONGTON
KENNEDY, WILLIAM SADDLER	W. S. K.	1843-1853	BURSLEM
KENSINGTON FINE ART POTTERY CO.	K. F. A. P. CO.	1892-1899	HANLEY
KENSINGTON POTTERY CO. (LTD.)	K. P. H.	1922-1961	HANLEY & BURSLEM
KENT, JOHN (& SONS)	J. K. (& S.)	1858-1868-(1876)	LONGTON
KEYS & MOUNTFORD	K. & M.	1850-1853	STOKE
KING & BARRATT (LTD.)	K. & B.	1898-1940	BURSLEM
KING, EDGE & BARATT	K. E. & B.	1896-1897	BURSLEM
KIRKBY, WILLIAM & CO.	K. & CO.	1879-1885	FENTON
KIRKBY, WILLIAM & CO.	W. H. & CO.	1879-1885	FENTON
KIRKBY, WILLIAM & CO.	W. K. & CO.	1879-1885	FENTON
KIRKLAND & CO.	K. & CO./E.	c1892	ETRURIA
KIRKLAND & PIDDOCK	K. & CO.	1897-1898	ETRURIA
KNAPPER & BLACKHURST	K. & B.	1867-71(&1883-88)	TUNSTALL (& Burslem)
KNIGHT & BRIDGWOOD	K. & B.	1884-1886	LONGTON
KNIGHT & WILEMAN	K. & W.	1853-1856	FENTON
KNIGHT, JOSEPH	J. K.	1859-1879	FENTON
LANCASTER & SONS	L. S.	1906-1944	HANLEY
LANCASTER & SONS, LTD.	L. & SONS LTD.	1944-	HANLEY
LANCASTER & SUNDERLAND LTD.	L. & S. LTD.	1906-1944	HANLEY
LARGE, WM. & SON (& CO.)	W. L. & S. (& CO.)	1853-1855	SHELTON (HANLEY)
LAWRENCE, E. & CO.	E. L. & CO.	1880-1883	LONGTON
LEA, SMITH & BOULTON	L. S. & B.	1865-1869	BURSLEM
LEAR, SAMUEL	S. L.	1877-1886	HANLEY
LEDGAR, THOMAS P.	T. P. L.	1898-1905	LONGTON
LEEDS FIRECLAY CO. LTD.	L. /F.C.	1904-1914(+)	YORKSHIRE
LEWIS & NICKLIN	L. & N.	1893-1894	LONGTON
LLOYD, JOHN (REBECCA)	J. L.	1834-1852	SHELTON (HANLEY)
LOCKETT & COOPER	L. & C.	1861-1863	SHELTON (HANLEY)
LOCKETT, BAGULEY & COOPER	L. B. & C.	1855-1861	SHELTON (HANLEY)
LOCKETT, JOHN	J. L.	1830-1850	LANE END (LONGTON)
LOCKETT, JOHN & SON (KING ST.)	J. L. & S.	1827-1835	LONGTON
LOCKETT, JOHN (KING & MARKET ST.)	J. L.	1859-1879	LONGTON
LONGBOTTOM, SAMUEL	S. L.	LATE 19c-1899	YORKSHIRE
LOVATT & LOVATT	L. L. & CO.	1895-1931	NOTTINGHAM
LOWE, RATCLIFFE & CO.	L. R. & CO.	1882-1892	LONGTON
LOWE, WILLIAM	W. L. (/L)	1874-1930	LONGTON
MACHIN & BAGGALEY	M. & B.	1828-1830	BURSLEM
MACHIN & THOMAS	M. & T.	1831-1832	BURSLEM
MACHIN, JOSEPH	J. M.	c1841	BURSLEM
MACHIN, JOSEPH	J. M.	1802-1818	BURSLEM
MACHIN, JOSEPH & CO.	J. M. & CO.	1818-1833	BURSLEM
MACKEE, ANDREW	A. M. /L.	1892-1906	LONGTON
MADDOCK, JOHN & SON	J. M. & S.	1855-1859	BURSLEM

MALKIN, RALPH & SONS	R. M. S.	1882-1894	FENTON
MANSFIELD BROS. (LTD.)	M. B.	c1890	SCOTLAND
MARSH & HAYWOOD	M. & H.	1817-1837	BROWNHILLS/ TUNSTALL
MARTIN, SHAW & COPE/ MARTIN & SHAW	M. S. & C.	1815-1824 (LONGTON)	LANE END
MASON, HOLT & CO.	M. H. & CO.	1857-1884	LONGTON
MATTHEWS & CLARK	M. & C. /L.	1902-1906	LONGTON
MAYER & MAUDESLEY	M. & M.	1837-1838	TUNSTALL
MAYER & SHERRATT (CHINA)	M. & S./L.	1906-1941	LONGTON
MAYER, ELIJAH (& SON)	E. M. (& S.)	1784-1805-(1821)	HANLEY
MAYER, JOHN	J. M. (/F.)	1832-1841	FENTON
MAYER, JOSEPH & CO.	J. M. & CO.	c1841	BURSLEM
MC NEAL & CO. (LTD.)	M. & CO.	1894-1906	LONGTON
MC NEAL & CO. LTD.	M. N. & CO./ LONGTON	1894-1906	LONGTON
MEAKIN & PROCTER	M. & P.	c1845	LANE END (LONGTON)
MELLOR, VENABLES & PINDER & CO.	M. V. P. & CO.	1831-1851(4)	BURSLEM
MILLS & SWAN(N)	M. & S.	c1862	HANLEY
MILLS, ELIZABETH (MRS.)	E. M.	1862-1873	SHELTON (HANLEY)
MILLWARD, W. H.	W. H. M.	1901-1902	LONGTON
MINTON & POULSON (& POWNALL)	M. & P.	1796-1808	STOKE
MOORE, LEASON & CO.	M. L. & CO.	1892-1896	FENTON
MORLEY, FOX & CO. LTD.	M. F. (& CO.)	1906-1944	FENTON
MOSS & HOBSON	M. & H.	1859-1862	LONGTON
MOUNTFORD, ARTHUR J.	A. J. M.	1897-1901	BURSLEM
MURRAY & CO.	M. & C. I.G.	1826-1840	SCOTLAND
MURRAY & CO.	M. & CO.	1868-1895	SCOTLAND
MURRAY & COUPER	M. & F.	1850-1864	SCOTLAND
MURRAY, BAYLEY & CO.	B. M. & CO.	1875-1884	GLASGOW, SCOTLAND
MURRAY, GRIEVE & CO.	M. G. & CO.	1878-1879	GLASGOW, SCOTLAND
MYOTT, B. & J. & CO.	B. & J. M. & CO.	1818-1825	LANE END (LONGTON)
NEALE, HARRISON & CO.	N. H. & CO.	1875-1882	HANLEY
NICHOLS, COPE & ADAMS	N. C. & A.	c1843	LONGTON
NOAH BENTLEY	N. B.	1865-1867	HANLEY
NORTH BRITISH POTTERY	J. M. (&) CO.	1869-1875	SCOTLAND
OLDHAM, JAMES (& CO.)	J. O. (& CO.)	1860-1877	HANLEY
PEARSON, JAMES LTD.	J. P. LTD.	1880-1937(+)	CHESTERFIELD
PHILLIPS & BAGSTER	P. & B.	1819-1823	HANLEY
PHILLIPS & THOMPSON	P. & T.	1816-1819	HANLEY
PHILLIPS, EDWARD	E. P.	1855-1862	SHELTON (HANLEY)
PHYSICK & COOPER	P. & C.	1899-1900	HANLEY
PLANT, (R.) & SONS	P. & S. /L.	1895-1901	LONGTON
PLANT, J. & CO.	J. P. & CO.	1882-1884	LONGTON
PLANT, WM. & CO.	W. P. & CO.	1853-1855	FENTON
POINTON & CO. LTD.	P. & CO. LTD.	1883-1916	HANLEY
POOL, STANLEY & WOOD	P. S. & W.	1875-1878	STOKE
POOLE & UNWIN	P. & U.	1871-1877	LONGTON
POULSON BROS. LTD.	P. B. B.	1884-1897	YORKSHIRE
POULSON, G. & T.	G. & T. P.	1801-1812	COBRIDGE & STOKE
POULSON, GEORGE	G. P.	1801-1812	COBRIDGE & STOKE
PRATT, HASSALL & GERRARD	P. H. (&) G.	1822-1834	FENTON
PRESTON, S. J.	S. J. P.	1899-1900	LONGTON
PRICE BROS. (BURSLEM) LTD.	P. B.	1903-1961	BURSLEM
PROCTER, COLLINGWOOD	P. & C.	c. 1850	STAFFORDSHIRE
PROCTER, GEORGE & CO. (LTD.)	G. P. & CO. (L.)	1892-1940	LONGTON
PROCTER, J. & H. (& CO.)	P.	1856-1884	LONGTON
PROCTER, JOHN	J. P. /L.	1846-1847	LANE END (LONGTON)
RATHBONE, JANE	J. R.	1832-1835	TUNSTALL
RATHBONE, SMITH & CO.	R. S. & CO.	1883-1887	TUNSTALL
RATHBONE, THOMAS & CO.	T. R. & CO.	1810-1845	SCOTLAND
RATHBONE, WM. & JOHN	W. & J. R.	1810-1813	TUNSTALL
RATHBONE, WM., SAMUEL & JOHN	W. S. & J. R.	1810-1823	TUNSTALL
RAY & BALL	R. & B.	1849-1850	LONGTON
RAY & TIDESWELL	R. & T.	1830-1837	LONGTON
RAY & WYNNE	R. & W.	1846-1847	LONGTON
RAY, RAY & BENTLEY	R. R. & B.	1853-1854	LONGTON
RAY, RICHARD & CO.	R. R. & CO.	1850-1852	LONGTON
REID & PATTERSON	R. & P.	1801-1803	SCOTLAND
REID, PATTERSON & CO.	R. P. & CO.	1800-1801	SCOTLAND
REID, WM. (& SON(S))	W. R. (& S.)	1820s-1830s	SCOTLAND
REPTON, T. S.	T. S. R.	1883-1888	LONGTON
RHODES & PROCTOR	R. & P.	1883-1885	BURSLEM
RIDGWAY, GEORGE	G. R.	1805-1815	SHELTON (HANLEY)
RIGBY & STEVENSON	R. & S.	1894-1954	HANLEY
RITCHIE & CO.	R. & CO.	1901-1903	STOKE
RIVERS & CLOWES	R. & C.	1816-1822	SHELTON (HANLEY)
RIVERS, WM. & CO.	W. R. & CO.	1816-1822	SHELTON (HANLEY)
ROBINSON & CHAPMAN	R. & C.	1875-1881	LONGTON
ROBINSON, CHAPMAN & CO.	R. C. & CO.	1872-1875	LONGTON
ROBINSON, W. (& CO.)	W. R. (& CO.)	1872-1888	FOLEY (FENTON)

ROPER & MEREDITH	R. & M.	1913-1924	LONGTON
ROWLEY & NEWTON (LTD.)	R. & N.	1895-1901	LONGTON
RUBIAN ART POTTERY CO.	L. S. & G.	1906-1933	FENTON
SADLER & BENNETT	S. & B.	c1895	TUNSTALL
SADLER & SON	S. & S.	1895-1901	TUNSTALL
SADLER, JAMES & SONS (LTD.)	J. S. S. B.	c1899	BURSLEM
SALT, CHARLES	C. S.	1837-1864	HANLEY
SALT, RALPH	R. S.	1818-1842	HANLEY
SANDLAND, WM.	W. S.	1898-1904	HANLEY
SANDLANDS & COLLEY LTD.	S. & C. LTD.	1907-1910	HANLEY
SANDLANDS, LTD.	S. LTD.	1904-1907	HANLEY
SANT & VODREY	S. & V.	1887-1893	COBRIDGE
SARACEN POTTERY CO.	B. M. & CO.	1875-1884	GLASGOW, SCOTLAND
SCRIVENER, R. G. & CO.	R. G. S. & CO.	1870-1883	HANLEY
SHAW & COPESTAKE	S. & C.	1901-1982 or 1894-1989	LONGTON
SHAW & SONS	S. & S. /S.	1892-1910	TUNSTALL
SHAW, GEORGE & SONS (LTD.)	G. S. & S.	1887-1948	YORKSHIRE
SHAW, JOHN & SONS, (LONGTON), LTD.	J. S. & S. (LTD.)	1931-1963	LONGTON
SHAW, RALPH	R. S.	1828-1858	LONGTON
SHEPHERD, JONES & CO.	J. S. & CO.	1867-1868	LONGTON
SHORTER & SON LTD.	S. & S.	1905-	STOKE
SHORTER BROS.	S. BROS.	1906-1912	BURSLEM
SHORTHOSE & HEATH	S. & H.	1794-1815	SHELTON (HANLEY)
SHORTHOSE, JOHN & CO.	S. & CO.	1815-1823	HANLEY
SHORTHOUSE, JOHN	S.	1807-1823	HANLEY
SIMKIN & RIDGE	S. & R.	c1840	LANE END (LONGTON)
SIMKIN, HUGH (& SONS)	H. S. (& S.)	1839-1840	LONGTON
SKELSON, W. H. JR.	W. H. S.	1893-1896	LONGTON
SKINNER, WM. & CO.	W. S. & CO.	1865-1866	LONGTON
SMITH, AMBROSE & CO.	A. S. & CO.	1784-1786	BURSLEM
SMITH, JAMES	J. S.	1898-1922	STOKE
SMITH, SAMPSON (LTD.)	S. S.	1851-1916-(1963)	LONGTON
SMITH, WM.	W. S.	1870-1874	DURHAM
SMITH, WM. (JR.) & CO.	W. S. (JR.) & CO.	1845-1855	DURHAM
SPENCER & STANWAY	S. & S.	1883-1886	LONGTON
STANLEY & LAMBERT	S. & L.	1850-1854	LONGTON
STANWAY & SON	S. & S.	1878-1879	STOKE
STEEL, EDWARD	E. S.	1875-1900	HANLEY
STEVENSON, RALPH, ALCOCK & WILLIAMS	R. C. A. & CO.	1820-1826	COBRIDGE
STUBBS & BIRD	S. & B.	1850-1853	HANLEY
STUBBS, WM.	W. S.	1847-1897	HANLEY
TAMS & LOWE	T. & L.	1865-1875	LONGTON
TAYLOR, BENJAMIN & SON	B. T. & S.	c.1840s	FERRYBRIDGE
TAYLOR, GEORGE & SAMUEL	G. & S. T.	1837-1866	LEEDS/YORKSHIRE
TAYLOR, TUNNICLIFFE (&CO.)(LTD.)	T. T. (& CO.)	1868+	HANLEY
THOMAS, J. W. & CO.	J. W. T. & CO.	1886-1887	LONGTON
THOMAS, URIAH	U. T. & CO.	1888-1905	HANLEY
THOMSON, DAVID	D. T.	1802-1818	SCOTLAND
TIPPER & CO.	T. & CO.	1847-1862	LONGTON
TOMKINSON & BILLINGTON	T. & B.	1868-1870	LONGTON
TRANTER & MACHIN	T. & M.	1886-1898	LONGTON
TUNDLEY, RHODES & PROCTOR	T. R. & P.	1873-1883	BURSLEM
TURNER & WOOD	T. & W.	1878-1888	STOKE
TURNER, GLOVER & SIMPSON	T. G. & S.	1803-1806	LANE END (LONGTON)
TURNER, HASSALL & PEAKE	T. H. & P.	1863-1871	STOKE
TURNER, HASSALL & POOLE	T. H. & P.	1871-1872	STOKE
TURNER, POOLE & STANWAY	T. P. & S.	c1873	STOKE
TURNER, WM. & JOHN	W. & J. T.	1787-1803	LANE END (LONGTON)
TWEMLOW, JOHN	J. T.	1795-1797	SHELTON
TWYFORD, THOMAS	T. T. /H.	1860-1898(+)	HANLEY
UNWIN, HOLMES & WORTHINGTON	U. H. & W.	1865-1868	HANLEY
UNWIN, MOUNTFORD & TAYLOR	U. M. & T.	c1864	HANLEY
VENABLES, JOHN & MARTYN	J. V. & M.	c1861	BURSLEM
VENABLES, MANN & CO.	V. M. & CO.	1853-1855	BURSLEM
VICTORIA POTTERY CO.	V. P. CO.	1895-1927	HANLEY
VINCENT FINE ART POTTERY CO.	V. F. A. P. CO.	1900-1910	BURSLEM
WADE & CO.	W. & CO. /B.	1887-1927	BURSLEM
WAGSTAFF & BRUNT	W. & B. (LONGTON)	1879-1927	LONGTON
WALKER, AMBROSE & CO.	A. W. & CO.(LTD)	1877-1890s	YORKSHIRE
WALLEY, JOHN	J. W.	1850-1867	BURSLEM
WALTON, JAMES	J. W.	1846-1860	SHELTON (HANLEY)
WARBURTON, PETER & FRANCIS	P. & F. W.	1795-1802	COBRIDGE
WARDLE & ASH	W. & A.	1859-1865	SHELTON (HANLEY)
WARREN, JAMES	J. W.	1843-1852	LONGTON
WARRILOW & COPE	W. & C.	1880-1887	LONGTON
WARRINGTON & CO.	W. & CO.	186-1863	HANLEY
WARRINGTON, WILLIAM	W. W.	1863-1867	HANLEY
WATHEN & LICHFIELD	W. & L.	1860-1864	FENTON
WATHEN, JAMES B. (& CO.)	J. B. W. (/F.)	1864-1869	FENTON
WAYTE & RIDGE	W. & R. /L.	1864-1865	LONGTON
WEBB & WALTERS	W. & W.	1862-1867	LONGTON
WEDGWOOD, H.F. & CO., LTD.	H. F. W. & CO. LTD.	1941-1959	LONGTON
WELLINGTON POTTERY	W. P. CO.	1899-1901	HANLEY
WESTON & HULL	W. & H.	1796-1798	LANE END (LONGTON)
WESTON, GEORGE	G. W.	1807-1829	LANE END (LONGTON)
WESTON, GEORGE & CO.	G. W. & CO.	1799-1829	LANE END (LONGTON)
WHITEHEAD, JAMES & CO.	J. W.	1790-1810	SHELTON (HANLEY)
WILD & ADAMS (LTD.)	W. & A.	1909-1923-(27)	LONGTON
WILDBLOOD & HEATH (CHINA)	W. & H.	1889-1899	LONGTON
WILDBLOOD & HEATH (CHINA)	W. H. & S.	1899-1927	LONGTON
WILDBLOOD & LEDGAR	W. & L.	1896-1900	LONGTON
WILDBLOOD, MASSEY & CO.	M. W. & CO.	1887-1889	LONGTON
WILKINSON & WARDLE	W. & W.	1864-1866	YORKSHIRE
WILLIAMS, THOMAS	T. W.	c1827	STOKE
WILLIAMSON, H. M. & CO.	H. M. W. & CO.	c1866	LONGTON
WILSON & CO.	W. & CO.	1897-1899	FENTON
WILSON, JAMES & SONS	J. W. & S.	1898-1926	FENTON
WILSON, ROBERT CHRISTOPHER NORTHUMBERLAND	W. & CO.	1844-1851	
WITHINSHAW, W. E.	W. E. W.	1873-1878	BURSLEM
WOLFE, HAMILTON & ARROWSMITH	W. H. & A.	1800-1810	STOKE
WOOD & BOWERS	W. & B.	c1839	BURSLEM
WOOD & CLARKE	W. & C.	1871-1872	BURLSEM
WOOD & FORD	W. & F.	c1853	SHELTON (HANLEY)
WOOD, ENOCH (JR.)	E. W.	c1822	BURSLEM
WOOD, GEORGE	G. W.	1850-54&1864	SHELTON (HANLEY)
WOOD, H. J. (LTD.)	H. J. W. /B.	c1884	BURSLEM
WOOD, HINES & WINKLE	W. H. & W.	1882-1885	HANLEY
WOOD, JOHN	J. W.	1781-1797	BURSLEM
WOOD, JOHN	J. W.	1822-1837	NORTHUMBERLAND
WOOD, JOHN & CO.	J. W. & CO.	1865-1871	LONGTON
WOOD, MORGAN & CO.	M. W. & CO.	1860-1870	BURSLEM
WOOD, RALPH (II)	R. W.	1789-1795	BURSLEM
WOOD, RALPH (III)	R. W.	1795-1801	BURSLEM
WOOD, WILLIAM & CO.	W. W. & CO.	1873-1932	BURSLEM
WOOLDRIDGE & WALLEY	W. & W. /B.	1898-1901	BURSLEM
WOOLISCROFT, GEORGE	G. W.	1851-54&1860-64	TUNSTALL
WORTHINGTON & GREEN	W. & G.	1844-1864	HANLEY
WORTHINGTON, THOMAS	T. W.	c1842	HANLEY
WRIGHT & BURGESS	W. & B.	1840-1841	TUNSTALL
WRIGHT, BURGESS & TAYLOR (& CO.)	W. B. & T. (CO.)	1841-1843	TUNSTALL
WRIGHT, THOMAS	T. W.	1822-25&1840-41	HANLEY
WRIGLEY, GEORGE	G. W.	c1860	BURSLEM
WYNNE, THOMAS	T. W.	1847-1853	LONGTON
YALE, BARKER & BARKER	Y. B. & B.	1846-1852	LONGTON
YALE, BARKER & SON	Y. B. & S.	1841-1843	LONGTON

APPENDIX B5: UNIDENTIFIED INITIALS AND PATTERNS

Initial	Pattern	Category	Ref. Bk.	Vol.	Page	Media
A & CO.	THOMSON'S SEASONS	S	COY	II	195	B&W
B	CHINESE JUVENILE SPORTS	O	PS	I, II	112/525	B&W
B	CHINESE JUVENILE SPORTS	O	COY	II	54	B&W
-	-	-	-	-	375	-
B	PERSIANS	M	PS	II	409	B&W/M
B	SCROLL	S	PS	I		B&W
B.F.	CHUSAN	O	HILL	-	#10	M
B. J. & CO.	POMONA	S	PS	I	379	B&W
B&B	POPPY	F	COY	II	160	B&W
B&D	ONTARIO LAKE SCENERY	S	PS	I	353	B&W
-	-	-	PS	11	612	-
B&G	ASIATIC PHEASANTS	S	COY	II	20	B&W
B&G	CHINESE MARINE	O	COY	II	55	B&W
B.J. & CO.	POMONA	S	PS	I	379	-
B.K.	BAVARIA	F	PET	II	123	FB
B.T.S.	LINTIN	O	PET	III	195	FB
C.B.	CLAREMONT, REG. #19886(?)	C	PS	II	513	B&W
C & CO.	STAG	S	HILL	-	#280	M
C&P	REGINA	G	COY	I	297	B&W
D&B	VILLA SCENERY (att. Doulton & Burn)	S	COY	II	207	B&W
D&B	VILLA SCENERY (att. Doulton & Burn)	S	PS	II	266	B&W
D.W.	SCOTT'S ILLUSTRATIONS (SERIES)	S	COY	I	324	B&W

E & CO.	THE PET GOAT	S	COY	II	156	B&W
E.M.G.	LAVINIA	C	PS	I	71	B&W
E.N. & N.	CHINESE VILLA	O	COY	II	56	B&W
F.R. & CO.	ETON COLLEGE	S	FOB		56,7,68	B&W
F&W	ARCADIA	S	PS	II, III	425/279	B&W
F&W	BOUQUET	F	PET	I	59	FB
F&W	QUAN TYNG	O	PET	II	59	FB
F. W.	ARCADIA	S	PS	III	51	B&W
G.	SINGAN	O	PS	I	162	B&W
G.H.	PERELINE	—	FOB	#60	4	B&W
G.H.	VENETIAN	S	PS	I	444	B&W
G&R	PICNIC	G	PS	I	518	B&W
H	INDIAN SCENERY	S	COY	II	111	B&W
H.R.S.L.	SYRIAN	O	PS	I	166	B&W
H.W.	NYMPH	F	PS	II	39	B&W
I.W.	THE MINSTREL (att. John Wilkinson)	—	COY	II	138	B&W
J. B.	POMPADOUR	M	PS	I	658	B&W
J.G.	VERSAILLES	C	PS	II	518	B&W
J.L.	MEXICAN	G	PS	II	291	B&W
J&V	KIN SHAN	O	PS	II	136	B&W
J.E.L.	AZALEA	F	PET	II	122	FB
J.J.J.	BOUQUET	M	PS	II	337	B&W
J. L.	MEXICAN	G	PS	II	291	B&W
J.S.	GRECIAN BOAT	S	PS	III	81	B&W
	SWISS SCENERY	S	-	-	-	-
K.E.P.	—	—	WH	I	169	WH. IRON
A.S. KNIGHT	CHINESE PLANT	O	PET	II	239	FB
L...	LYME CASTLE	S	COY	II	128	B&W
L. B.	—	O	PS	I	694	B&W
L.W.	CHINESE FLORA	O	HILL	-	93	M
M.W. & H.	SPORTSMAN	S	H	-	307.14	M
M. T.	PERSIAN ROSE	F	PS	II	40	B&W
N	ANCIENT RUINS	S	PS	I	184	B&W
N	ANCIENT RUINS	S	PS	II	542/3	B&W
P.D. WARDS	CORINTH	S	PS	II	569	B&W
P. V.	HONG	O	PET	I	28	FB
P. V.	RAILWAY	M	PS	I	662	B&W
R.B.	VENTURE	S	HILL	-	289	M
R. D.	PEKIN	O	COY	I	278	B&W
R.F.F.T.	COLADINE	O	PS	II	94	B&W
R.K. & CO.	PEKIN	P/O	PS	I	582	B&W
R.K. & CO.	ASIATIC PHEASANTS	S	COY	II	20	B&W
R&D	BOTANICAL BEAUTIES	F	COY	II	-	B&W
S	LAWRENCE	S	PS	I	216	B&W
S	LAWRENCE	S	HILL	-	#258	M
S & CO.	WILLOW PATTERN	O	COY	II	212	B&W
S. & H.	WINDSOR SCROLLS	—	FFB	-	41	FB
S. & H.	CLAREMONT GROUPS	P/F	FFB	-	136	FB
S.B. & CO.	-	—	FOB	67	P.9	B&W
S. H. & CO.	ALBION	S	PS	III	270	B&W
S. H. & CO.	MILITARY SKETCHES	S	COY	II	212	B&W
S. H. & CO.	MILITARY SKETCHES	S	SN	-	75	B&W
T.H.W.	ARABIAN SKETCHES	S	COY	II	16	B&W
T.H.W.	RIBBON	O	HILL	-	#33	M
W	-	—	COY	II	13	B&W
W	AMARANTHINE FLOWER	—	COY	II	13	B&W
W&B*	FLORAL SCROLL	F	COY	II	84	B&W
Y&M	SNOWDROP (att: Yates & May)	F	PS	II	47	B&W

LEGEND:

Category:
O - Oriental
S - Scenic
F - Floral
C - Classical

Media:
B&W - Blue & White Transfer
FB - Flown Blue
M - Mulberry
WH. IRON - White Ironstone
M - Miscellaneous
P - Polychrome
(P/O - Polychrome w/Oriental Pattern)

Reference Book:
COY - Coysh, *Encyclopedia*, Vol. 1 & II
FFB - Jeffrey Snyder, *Fascinating Flow Blue*
FOB - *Friends of Blue Bulletin*
HILL - Ellen Hill, *Mulberry Ironstone, Flow Blue's Best Kept Little Secret*
PS - P. Williams, *Staffordshire Romantic Transfer Patterns*, Vol. I, II & III
SN - Jeffrey Snyder, *Romantic Staffordshire Ceramics*
WH - Jean Wetherbee, *A Second Look at White Ironstone*

Please note that neither Jean Wetherbee's new publications, *White Ironstone, A Collector's Guide,* nor Nancy Upchurch's *Handbook of Tea Leaf Body Styles* have been referenced in cataloging these unidentified patterns, as they were received by this author after this listing was compiled.

*Ellen Hill's reference work on Mulberry notes and illustrates a pattern "Floral Scroll" with initials W&B, refer to #211.47.

APPENDIX B6: CHRONOLOGY OF *SELECTED* POTTERIES AND PARTNERSHIPS

An explanation of the Potteries and Partnerships found in this Chronology is in order. I have tried to use the most up-to-date, reliable sources possible. Nevertheless, confusion relative to names (and their spelling), potteries and locations, titles, dates, and misattribution of patterns abounds. I have tried to simplify matters by including the foregoing chronologies of potteries, partnerships, locations, and dates.

It is important to note that I have included those partnerships and potteries that produced earthenware, ironstone and stoneware, although a few examples of manufacturers of other media may be included. Indeed, often times, even the best sources conflict in their information. This is particularly true in relation to dates. In recording the data I have omitted the use of ***circa.*** I would, however, advise the reader to consider that dates may be a year or two before or after the fact; due, in part, to whether the particular author noted the actual date of manufacture, partnership date, or dissolution date as opposed to the actual date that manufacture ceased.

Furthermore, at times it would seem that conflicting addresses appear when providing a specific pottery locale, thus misleading the reader into thinking that there were multiple potters at one location. This, however, is definitely not the case. For instance, Broad Street, High Street, Lane End, etc. may have been a street or locale that continued on for a mile or more with no intersecting cross streets (or numbered addresses - as we know these streets today). There may have been numerous potters along such a one mile stretch, with none having an address other than the name of the street. Likewise, due to subdivisions of potteries, two or more potters may have been located at the same pottery or address.

Additionally, the names Lane End and Longton were interchangeable from 1848 when Lane End changed its name to Longton. Street locales also create ambiguities notes *Hampson*, No. 134, p. 89, "... Great Charles Street, Flint Street and Stafford Street ... all referring to the same location." Many potters, however, continued to use the name Lane End for their address. The same applies to Shelton, Hanley. In 1812 Shelton and Hanley were officially noted as Hanley, but people continued to call each town by its own name; e.g. Shelton or Hanley. I cite an example in my own geographic locale of New

York City, wherein Riverdale is a part of the borough of the Bronx, but people still refer to it and address their mail to Riverdale. Nevertheless, the postman would know exactly where and to whom to deliver a letter.

Please remember that this Chronology (of both names, dates and locations) is in no way definitive; e.g., there are countless more Woods to be found than are actually listed.

ADAMS CHRONOLOGY: POTTERIES & PARTNERSHIPS

MARK	POTTERY NAME	DATES	FAMILY NAME	RELATIONSHIP	BIRTH/ DEATH
ADAMS	*Brick House Works, Burslem	c.1767-1794(3)	William Adams (1)	Cousin of 2 & 3	1748-1831
ADAMS & CO.	Sneyd Green, Cobridge	c.1774-1813			
W. ADAMS & CO.	Cobridge Hall, Hanley	c.1775			
CONTINUED	Greengates Works, Tunstall	1779-1820	William Adams (2)	Cousin of 1 & 3	1745-1805
AS ABOVE	Alsosee Benjamin Adams	1779-1805			
	Newfield Pottery, Tunstall -				
	Hadderidge Pottery,				
	Burslem**	1793-1804			
CONTINUED	(Upper) Cliff Bank Works,				
	Stoke Church Street China				
	Works, Stoke	1804-1829	William Adams (3)	Cousin of 1 & 2	1772-1829
AS ABOVE		1818-1824		Father of (4)	
(& SON)	As above	1804-1829	William Adams (Son)	Son of 3	1798-1865
(1819-1820)		1818-1829	of (4)	- Brother of (4)	
ADAMS	(Upper) Cliff Bank Works, Stoke	1804-1829	William Adams	Son of 3 &	
			(Sons) (4)	Brother of (4)	1798-1865
W. ADAMS & CO.	Greengates Works, Tunstall	1828-1861	Edward	- Brother of (4)	1803-1872
(& SONS)	Greenfields Pottery, Tunstall	1834-	Lewis	- Brother of (4)	1805-1850
(1820s-1861)	Newfield Pottery, Tunstall				
	(***See comments below)	1857-	Thomas	- Brother of (4)	1807-1863
LTD	Greenfields Pottery,		Wm. &		
	Tunstall	1834-	Thomas Adams (5)	Sons of (4)	-
(1861-1893)	Newfield Pottery, Tunstall	1872-1879	William		1833-1905
	Greengates Works, Tunstall	1861-Present	Thomas		1838-1905
& CO.	Greenfields Pottery,		William		
	Tunstall	Till 1959	Adams & Co.	-	-
(1893-1917)	Greengates Works,				
	Tunstall (& Successors)	Present			

*Brick House Works was established in c.1657, In 1757 it was leased to Wedgwood. and again, in 1774/75 it was leased to William Bourne.
**Hadderige Pottery in partnership with Lewis Heath.
***By the early nineteenth century William Adams had six factories, five in Stoke and one in Greenfield. There were also two in Burslem, one of which was rented to John Wedgwood and the other to Enoch Wood & Sons.
The Adams family dates and marks may confuse anyone. I would refer the reader back to this Chronology for more accurate dating. Please note that one must be very careful when referring to or researching Adams, as there are so many "Adams" who were potters. Thus, the exact pottery and town are extremely important.
N.B. The style William Adams & Sons used over many years is still retained today. For further information on the Chronology of the Adams family refer to *William Adams, An Old English Potter,* ed, by William Turner, F.S.S., Shapman & Hall, Ltd. 1904; *NCS Newsletter*, No. 66, June 1987, Item No. 11, pp. 29-31; *Godden, Staffordshire*, pp. 369-374; *Little,* pp. 42-46; and *British Potters and Pottery Today*, by Cyril G. E. Brunt, F. Lewis Publishers, Ltd., Leigh-on-Sea, England, 1956, pp. 19, 20.

ADDERLEY CHRONOLOGY: POTTERIES & PARTNERSHIPS

DATE	POTTERY	PARTNERSHIP
1853-1869	Daisy Bank Works, Longton	Hulse, Nixon & Adderley
1869-1874	Daisy Bank Works, Longton	Hulse & Adderley
1875-1905	Daisy Bank Works, Longton	William (Alsagar) Adderley & Co.
1905-1947+	(Renamed) Gainsborough Works, Longton	Adderleys Ltd.
1880	Salisbury Works, Edensor Road, Longton	Adderley & Amison
1881-1892	Salisbury Works, Edensor Road, Longton	Adderley & Lawson
1902-1905	Jubilee Works, Chatfield Place, Longton	John Fellow Adderley

ALCOCK CHRONOLOGY: POTTERIES & PARTNERSHIPS

POTTERY		DATES
King Street, Burslem	May have been working with Ralph Stevenson	c.1822-1823
Cobridge China Works, Cobridge	Cobridge China Works continued until 1848	
Elder Road Pottery, Cobridge	Partnership with Ralph Stevenson & Augustus Lloyd Williams. Company traded as (under name) Ralph Stevenson until c. 1826. (Stevenson, Alcock & Williams)	c.1822-1826
	Alcock carried on business as Samuel Alcock & Co. (although company was still really Ralph Stevenson). In 1831 partnership with Stevenson dissolved	c.1826-1831
Hill Pottery, Burslem	Samuel Alcock in partnership with Charles Keeling	c.1828(30)-1848
	Samuel Alcock now focuses more attention on Hill Pottery,by taking on an expansion program	c.1838-1840
Elder Road Pottery, Cobridge	John & George Alcock become partners with Samuel in Cobridge in 1838 and end partnership Jan. 20, 1848	c.1838-1848
	John and Samuel Jr. in partnership	c.1848-1850
	John Alcock now owner of Elder Road Pottery	c.1853-1861
	Henry Alcock acquires Elder Road Pottery now known as Henry Alcock & Co. (Ltd.)	c.1861-1890
Hill Pottery, Burslem	Alcock in partnership with nephews Joseph & John under the title of Alcock & Co. (John of Burslem is a silent partner and banker for company)	c.1833(34)
	Samuel Alcock purchases Joseph's half share and now had two "silent financial" partners - Charles Keeling and Richard Edward Alcock (Charles and Richard had no shares in pottery). Partnership dissolved Oct. 27, 1848	
	(I would suspect that somewhere between 1839 and 1847 Richard Edward Alcock came in as a money partner.)	
	Samuel Alcock in financial difficulty	c.1848
	Samuel Alcock dies	1848
	Alcock's will settled and business is carried on by widow with sons Samuel, Jr. and James Empson as trustees. (Joseph Locker, a 3rd son, resides in London)	c.1851-1859
	Business goes bankrupt	1859
	Sir James Duke and nephews acquire pottery in Oct. 1859, and continue using molds, etc.	c.1860-1863
	Thomas Ford purchases business	c.1863(64)- 1865

Hill Pottery, Burslem Business sold to Earthenware & Porcelain Co., using the name Hill Pottery, Co. Ltd, Late S. Alcock & Co.	c.1866-1867
Thomas Ford reacquires pottery and sells it off in two parts.	
Porcelain works sold to Alcock and Diggory	c. 1867-1870
Earthenware works sold to Burgess & Leigh & Co.	c.1867-1889

For further reading, refer to *Godden, British Porcelain*, pp. 76-85, 309-325 and 416; Pat Halfpenny's monograph on Alcock in *NCSJ*, Vol. 2, 1975-1976, pp. 83-90.

N.B.: To-date there is no verifiable information available on the familial relationship between the foregoing Alcocks and one Richard Alcock, Market Place, Hanley (1870-1881).

ALCOCK CHRONOLOGY: POTTERIES & PARTNERSHIPS

DATE	POTTERY	PARTNERSHIP
1796-1799	High Street, Lane End (Longton)	Alcock (Thomas & Edward) & Ward
1802-1804	High Street, Lane End (Longton)	Ward & Alcock (Edward)
1820-1826	Cobridge China Works, Cobridge	Stevenson (Ralph), Alcock & Williams
1822-1823	King Street, Burslem	Samuel Alcock
1825-1827	Elder Road Pottery, Cobridge	Alcock & Williams
1825-1827	Elder Road Pottery, Cobridge	Alcock & Williams
1825-1830	High Street, Lane End (Longton)	Alcock, Mason & Co.
1828-1828	Elder Road Pottery, Cobridge	Alcock & Stevenson (Sm. Alcock & Co.)
1828-1828	Elder Road Pottery, Cobridge	Alcock & Stevenson (Sm. Alcock & Co.)
1826-1848	Elder Road Pottery, Cobridge	Samuel Alcock & Co.
1826-1848	Elder Road Pottery, Cobridge	Samuel Alcock & Co.
1828-1833	Hill Works, Liverpool Road, Burslem	Alcock & Keeling (Charles)
1833-1859	Hill Works, Liverpool Road & Hilltop Pottery, Burslem	Samuel Alcock & Co.
1839-1848	Elder Road Pottery, Cobridge	John & George Alcock
1848-1850	Elder Road Pottery, Cobridge	John & Samuel Alcock, Jr.
1853-1861	Elder Road Pottery, Cobridge	John Alcock
1860-1861	Market Street, Longton	William Alcock
1861-1910	Elder Road Pottery, Cobridge	Henry Alcock & Co. (Ltd.)
1864-1866	St. Martins Lane, Longton	Alcock & Williamson
1867-1870*	Hill (Top) Pottery, Burslem	Alcock, Diggory & Co.
1870-1881	Central Pottery, Burlsem	Richard Alcock
1910-1935	Clarence Works, Stoke	Henry Alcock Pottery, The
1919-1959	Vulcan Pottery, Hanley	Alcock, Lindley & Bloor (Ltd.)

*Refer to Bodley in this Chronology.

ALCOCK CHRONOLOGY: HILL WORKS, HILL TOP POTTERY & HILL (TOP) POTTERY

DATE	POTTERY	PARTNERSHIP
	HILL WORKS, LIVERPOOL ROAD, BURSLEM	
1715-1772		Ralph Wood, I*
1787-1790		Enoch & Ralph Wood*
1789-1795		Ralph Wood, II*
1795-1801		Ralph Wood, III*
1798-1808		John Taylor*
1811-1828		John & Richard Riley*
1828-1833		Alcock & Keeling*
1833-1859		Samuel Alcock & Co.
1859-1860		William Barker & Son or (& Co.)
1860-1869		Morgan Wood & Co.
1870-1880		Wood & Baggaley
1880-1886		Jacob Baggaley
1887-1905		Dunn, Bennett & Co. (Ltd.)
	HILL TOP POTTERY, BURSLEM	
1833-1859		Samuel Alcock & Co.
1859-1863		Sir James Duke & Nephews
1864-1864		Thomas Ford
1864-1867		Hill Pottery Co. Ltd.
1867-1867		Thomas Ford
1867-1889		Burgess & Leigh
	HILL (TOP) POTTERY, BURSLEM	
1867-1870		Alcock, Diggory & Co.
1870-1871		Bodley & Diggory
1871-1874		Edward Fisher Bodley
1874-1874		Bodley & Son
1875-1892		Edwin J. D. Bodley & Son
1895-1897		A. Heath & Co.

*These early potters and their pottery sites were acquired and reconfigured into one large pottery known as the Hill Works.

In 1859 the Hill Works was sold and broken up into two entities, one being the Hill Works and the other being the Hill Top Pottery.

Subsequently, in 1867 another realignment took place where by the pottery was again split between Burgess & Leigh and Alcock, Diggory & Co...

BAILEY CHRONOLOGY: POTTERIES & PARTNERSHIPS

DATE	POTTERY	PARTNERSHIP
1799-1799	—Lane End	Bailey & Freeman or Bailey & Co.
1807-1810	Flint Street Works, Stafford Street, Lane End, Longton	Bailey, William
1811-1814	Flint Street Works, Stafford Street, Lane End, Longton	Bailey, William & Co.
1814-1826	Flint Street Works, Stafford Street, Lane End, Longton	Bailey & Batkin
1823-1827	Flint Street Works, Stafford Street, Lane End, Longton	Bailey & Martin/Martin & Bailey
1826-1830	Flint Street Works, Stafford Street, Lane End, Longton	Bailey, William & David & Co.
1827	Flint Street Works, Stafford Street, Lane End, Longton	Bailey & Greatbatch
1827-1830	Flint Street Works, Stafford Street, Lane End, Longton	Bailey, William & David
1828-1832	Waterloo Pottery, Lane End, Longton	Bailey & Deakin/Deakin & Bailey
1832	Flint Street Works, Stafford Street, Lane End, Longton	Bailey, John
1832-1835	Flint Street Works, Stafford Street, Lane End, Longton	Bailey(s) & Harvey/Harvey, Bailey(s) & Co.
1835-1843	Flint Street Works, Longton	Bailey, C. & W. K.
1836	Flint Street Works, Stafford Street, Lane End, Longton	Bailey & Floyd
1836-1837	Flint Street Works, Stafford Street, Lane End, Longton	Bailey, Floyd & Co. or Bailey, Floyd & Shubotham
1840-1841	Park Works Site, High Street, Longton	Bailey, Goodwin & Robey/ Bailey, Robey & Goodwin
1841-1843	High Street, Longton	Bailey, Robey & Deakin/Bailey, Robey & Co.
1843-1849	Stafford Street & Flint Street, Longton	Bailey & Ball
1849-1858	Stafford Street, Longton	Bailey, John
1855-1908	Alloa Pottery, Alloa, Scotland	Bailey, W. & J.A.
1860-1862	Bryan Street Works, Hanley	Bailey, John
1864-1866	Kensington Works, Broad Street, Hanley	Bailey, John & Co.
1867-1868	Kensington Works, Broad Street, Hanley	Bailey & Bevington/Bevington & Co.
1868-1870	Brewery Street Works, Hanley	Bailey, John & Co.
1870-1870	Brewery Works, Hope Street, Hanley	Bailey, Beech & Cooke
1889-1889	—, Hanley	Bailey, Hackney & Co.
1912-1914	Gordon Pottery, Longton	Bailey, William & Sons

BARKER CHRONOLOGY: POTTERIES & PARTNERSHIPS

DATE	POTTERY	PARTNERSHIP
1784-1787	#126 Works, East Side of Flint St. Longton	John Barker
1784-1810	#126 Works, East Side of Flint St. Longton	Richard Barker (I)
1790s-1810	Low Pot, Rawmarsh, Yorkshire	Barker & Co. (Wainwright & Barker)
1809-1818	Flint Street, & Ship Lane, Oxford Lane End. Longton	Richard (II), John & James Barker
1809-1812	Mexborough Pottery, Yorkshire	Jess Barker
1809-1820s	Mexborough Pottery, Yorkshire	Jess & Peter Barker
1818-1818	#126 Works, East Side of Flint St. Longton	William Barker
1818-1819	High Street, Lane End, Longton	Barker (Joseph)
1818-1831	High Street, Lane End, Longton	William & Joseph (James Barker)
1820-1830	High Street, Lane End, Longton	Barker, John & Joseph
1820-1822 & 1832-1835	Flint Street, Lane End, Longton	Richard Barker II (John & James)
1820s-1840s	Mexborough Pottery, Yorkshire	Samuel Barker
1834-1841	Flint Street, Lane End, Longton	Thomas Barker
1834-1846	Sytch Pottery, Liverpool Rd., Burslem	Barker, Sutton & Till
1834-1893	Don Pottery, Swinton, Yorkshire	Samuel Barker & Son
1835-1836	Market Street, Lane Delph, Fenton	Edge, Barker & Co.
1836-1840	Lane End, Longton	Edge, Barker & Barker
1846-1848	Market Street, Lane End, Longton	Cyples & Barker
1846-1850	Sytch Pottery, Liverpool Rd., Burslem	Barker & Till
1846-1852	Viaduct Works, Anchor Lane, Longton	Yale, Barker & Hall

1850-1860	Hill Works, Liverpool Road, Burslem	William Barker & Son
1851-1882	Don Pottery, Swinton, Yorkshire	Samuel Barker & Sons (See Don Pottery)
1853-1857	Viaduct Works, Longton	Barker & Hall
1859-1859	—, Longton	Barker & Hilditch
1860-1861	Stafford Street, Longton	Joseph Barker
1868-1868	King & Stafford Street, Longton	Barker & Hill
1876-1882	Meir Works, Barker Street, Longton	Barker Bros. (Ltd.)
1881-1882	Canning Street Works, Fenton	Goodwin, Barker & Fanshawe
1882-1959 (81)	Meir Works, Barker Street, Longton	Barker Bros. Ltd. (A division of Grindley of Stoke)
1889-1941	Foley Pottery, Fenton	Barkers & Kent, Ltd.
1897-1903	Queen Street Pottery, Burslem	Wood & Barker, Ltd.

For further reading, refer to *Hampson*, No. 19, pp. 13-14; *Godden*; *Woolliscroft-Rhead*, pp. 24-26; *Godden, Jewitt*.

BATES CHRONOLOGY: POTTERIES & PARTNERSHIPS

DATE	POTTERY	PARTNERSHIP
1855-1858	Cauldon Place, Shelton, Hanley	(J.) Ridgway, Bates & Co.
1859-1861	Cauldon Place, Shelton, Hanley	Bates, Brown-Westhead & Moore
1868-1895	Lincoln Pottery, Sneyd Green, Cobridge	Bates & Bennett
1870-1875	Dale Hall Works, Burslem	Bates, Elliott & Co.
1875-1878	Dale Hall Works, Burslem	Bates, Walker & Co.
1875-1881	King Street China Works, Longton	Bridgett, Bates & Beech
1878-1881	Dale Hall Works, Burslem	Bates, Gildea & Walker
1882-1914	King Street China Works, Longton	Bridgett & Bates
1892-1896	Albert Works, Longton	Thomas Bates & Son
1900-1900	Mayer Street, Hanley	Bates, Dewbury & Co.

BEARDMORE CHRONOLOGY: POTTERIES & PARTNERSHIPS

DATE	POTTERY	PARTNERSHIP
1800-1826	Stafford Street, Longton	Booth & Beardmore
1809-1809	High Street, Longton	Stirrup & Beardmore
1810-1822	High Street, Longton	Beardmore & Carr
1819-1822	Stafford Street, Longton	Shaw, Griffiths & Beardmore
1823-1828	Flint Street, Longton	Beardmore & Griffiths
1829-1831	Flint Street, Longton	Griffiths, Beardmore & Birks
1832-1842	St. Gregory's Pottery, High Street, Longton	Beardmore & Birks
1842-1843	High Street, Longton	Beardmore, Cope & Adams
1843-1848	Gladstone Works, High Street, Longton	Henry Beardmore
1843-1847	St. Gregory's Pottery, High Street, Longton	Sampson Beardmore
1847-1848	High Street, Longton	Sampson Beardmore
1850-1854	St. Gregory's Pottery, High Street, Longton	Beardmore, Birks & Blood (or Beardmore & Co.)
1856-1857	Union Market Square, Longton	Colclough, Beardmore & Cartwright
1858-1858	Union Market Square, Longton	Beardmore & Edwards
1859-1863	Commerce Street, Longton	Newborn & Beardmore
1863-1863	Commerce Street, Longton	Beardmore & Dawson
1864-1865(67)	Coronation Works, Heathcote Road, Longton	Thomas Beardmore
1902-1903	Sutherland Pottery, High Street, Fenton	Christie & Beardmore
1903-1914	Sutherland Pottery, High Street, Fenton	Frank Beardmore & Co. (Ltd.)

For further reading, refer to *Hampson*, No's. 26, 38, 113, and 199.

BEECH CHRONOLOGY: POTTERIES & PARTNERSHIPS

DATE	POTTERY	PARTNERSHIP
1821-1834	Lion Works, Sandyford, Tunstall	Lowndes & Beech (Beech & Lowndes)
1834-1862	Bell Works, Queen Street, (formerly Wedgwood), Burslem	William Beech
1834-1845	Lion Works, Sandyford, Tunstall	James Beech
1836-1839	Bell Works, Queen Street, (formerly Wedgwood), Burslem	Beech & Jones
1840-1846	Bell Works, Queen Street, (formerly Wedgwood), Burslem	James Beech
1847-1853	High Street, Longton	Edgerton, Beech & Birks
1850-1858	High Street, Longton	James Beech
1851-1855	Swan Bank Pottery, High Street, Burslem	Beech , Hancock & Co.
1853-1855	Bell Works, Queen Street, (formerly Wedgwood), Burslem	Beech & Brock
1855-1865	Bell Works, Queen Street, (formerly Wedgwood), Burslem	James Beech, Jr.
1859-1859	Albert Street Works, Longton	James & Thomas Beech
1860-1862		
1862-1876	Church Bank Works, Tunstall Swan Bank Pottery, High Street, Tunstall	Beech & Hancock
1860-1898	Albert & Sunderland Works, Longton	James Beech & Son (& Co.)
1864-1873	Bell Works, Queen Street, (formerly Wedgwood), Burslem	Jane Beech
1870-1870	Brewery Works, Hope Street, Hanley	Bailey, Beech & Cooke
1872-1873	New Street, Longton	Beech, Cooper, Till & Co.
1873-1876	Bleak Hill Works, Cobridge	Beech & Podmore (Succeeded by Podmore)
18738-1876	Bell Works, Burslem	Beech & Podmore
1875-1881	King Street China Works, Longton	Bridget, Bates & Beech
1878-1889	Swan Bank Pottery, Tunstall	James Beech
1880-1882	Waterloo Works, Hanley	Beech & Morgan
1882-1885	Lincoln Pottery, Cobridge	(Frederick) Beech & Tellwright
1885-1890	Lincoln Pottery, Cobridge	Frederick Beech & Co. U.S.A.
1845-1857	Kensington, Philadelphia, PA	Ralph B. Beech

For further reading, refer to *Godden's Collecting Lustreware.*

BODLEY CHRONOLOGY: POTTERIES & PARTNERSHIPS

DATE	POTTERY	PARTNERSHIP
	SCOTIA POTTERY, ET.AL.	
1862-1875	Scotia Pottery, Burslem	Edward Fisher Bodley & Co.
1863-1865	Scotia Pottery, Burslem	Bodley & Harold
1865-1865	Scotia Pottery, Burslem	Bodley & Co.
1875-1881	Scotia Pottery, Burslem	Edwin Fisher Bodley & Son

HILL TOP POTTERY (OLD)

1859-1863	(Old) Hill Pottery, Burslem	Sir. James Duke & Nephews
1864-1867	(Old) Hill Pottery, Burslem	Hill Pottery Co. (Ltd.)
1867-1889	(Old) Hill Pottery, Burslem	Burgess & Leigh

HILL (TOP) CHINA WORKS

1867-1870	Hill (Top) Pottery, Burslem	Alcock & Diggory
1870-1871	Hill (Top) Pottery, Burslem	Bodley & Diggory
1871-1874	Hill (Top) Pottery, Burslem	Edward Fisher Bodley
1874-1874	Hill (Top) Pottery, Burslem	Bodley & Son
1875-1888	Hill (Top) Pottery, Burslem	Edwin James D. Bodley
1888-1892	Hill (Top) Pottery, Burslem	Edwin J. D. Bodley & Son
1895-1897	Hill (Top) Pottery, Burslem	A. Heath & Co.

NEW BRIDGE POTTERY

1882-1898	New Bridge Pottery, Longton	Edwin Fisher Bodley & Son

*Refer to Alcock in this Chronology.
For further reading, refer to *Godden's British Porcelain*, pp. 154-155.

BOOTH CHRONOLOGY: POTTERIES & PARTNERSHIPS

DATE	POTTERY	PARTNERSHIP
1781-1790	Cliff Bank, Stoke	Hugh Booth
1792-1802	Cliff Bank, Stoke	Ephraim Booth & Sons (Hugh & Joseph)
1793-1807	Shelton	Booth & Marsh
1800	Stafford Street, Longton	Booth & Beardmore
1800-1806	#127 Works, Longton	Booth & Bridgwood
1802-1807	Cliff Bank, Shelton	Hugh & Joseph Booth
1807-1830	Stafford Street, Longton	J. & T, Booth (Joseph & Thomas)
1811-1830	Green Dock Works, Longton	J. & T, Booth (Joseph & Thomas)
1812-1822	Cliff Bank, Shelton	Hugh & Joseph Booth
1815-1816	High Street, Hanley	Booth & Bentley
1822-1823	Church Street, Lane End, Longton	Pye & Booth
1824-1835	Church Street, Lane End, Longton	(R) Booth & Sons (Richard & Abel)
1825-?	New Market Works	Abel Booth
1829-1844	Waterloo Works, Canal Side, Hanley	G.R. Booth & Co. (George & Robbin)
1832-1835	Peaerl Pottery, Brook Street, Hanley	Richard Booth
1836-1836	Church Street, Lane End, Longton	Meigh, Goodwin & Booth (January - September)
1836-1837	Central Pottery, Burslem	Hopkins & Booth
1837-1837	Church Street, Lane End, Longton	Booth & Co. / Abel Booth & Co.
1837-1838	Church Street, Lane End, Longton	Booth & Meigh
1840-1845	Railway Works, Longton	Joseph Booth
1842-1842	Lane End, Longton	James Booth
1842-1963	Waterloo Pottery, Kilncroft Works, Central Pottery, & other addresses, Burslem	T. & R. Boote, Ltd.

1843-1860	Pearl Pottery, Brook Street, Hanley	Booth, William & Willett
1851-1854	Central Pottery, Stafford Street, Burslem	Hulme & Booth
1851-1873	Waterloo Works, Lower Charles Street, Hanley	Thomas Booth & Son
1864-1868	Knowles Works, Burslem	Evans & Booth
1868-1868	Knowles Works, Burslem	Thomas Booth & Co.
1868-1872	Church Bank Works, Tunstall	Thomas Booth & Co.
1872-1876	Church Bank Works, Tunstall	Thomas Booth & Son
1872-1879	New Hall Pottery, Hanley	Thomas Booth & Son
1876-1883	Church Bank Works, Tunstall	Thomas G. Booth
c. 1881	Broad Street, Bradford, Yorkshire	Frederick Booth
1883-1891	Church Bank Works, Tunstall	T.G.&F. Booth (& various partnerships)
1891-1898	Church Bank Works, Tunstall	Booths
1898-1948	Church Bank Pottery (& Swan and Soho Potteries) (from 1912), Tunstall	Booths Ltd.
1948-1953	Hanley, Staffordshire	Booths & Colclough Ltd.
1948-1953	Church Bank Works, Tunstall	Booths & Colclough Ltd.
1948-1953	Soho Pottery, Tunstall	Booths & Colclough Ltd.
1954	Hanley, Staffordshire	Ridgway, Adderley, Booth & Colclough, Ltd.
1955	Hanley, Staffordshire	Ridgway Potteries Ltd.

BOURNE CHRONOLOGY: POTTERIES & PARTNERSHIPS

DATE	POTTERY	PARTNERSHIP
1781-1811	Bottom Bridge Works, Longport	Edward Bourne
1786	Burslem	Bourne & Malkin
1786-1803	Burslem, Shelton, Hanley	Samuel & John Bourne (partnership)
1796-1833	Fenton Potteries, High Street, Fenton	Bourne, Baker & Bourne (& various parternships)
1802 (?)	Shelton	Bourne & Co.
1804-1818	Bell (Brickhouse) Works, Nile Street, Burslem	William Bourne & Co.
1807-1817	Foley, Lane Delph & other potteries, FentonFenton Culvert, Lane Delph (from 1810)	Charles Bourne (Pottery)
1809-1860	Bourne Pottery, Denby, Derbyshire	*Pottery History:* Mr. Jager, 1809-1812 William Bourne, 1812-1833 Joseph Bourne, 1833-1850 Joseph Bourne & Son Ltd., 1850-1860
1817-1830	Grosvenor Works & Foley Pottery, Fenton	Charles Bourne
1818-1820	Bell (Brickhouse) Works, Nile Street, Burslem	Bourne & Cormie
1827-1840	Foley Pottery, King Street, Fenton	Bourne & Clark
1828-1830	Tunstall	Bourne, Nixon & Co.
1833-1835	Fenton Potteries, High Street, Fenton	Bourne, Baker & Bourne
1843-1850	Fenton	William Bourne
1851-1860	Fountain Place, Burslem	Pinder, Bourne & Hope
1856-1857	Bow Street/High Street, Hanley	Bourne & Roe
1857-1861	Alma Place China Works, Foley, Longton	William Bourne
1859-1860	Foley, Longton	Till, Bourne & Brown
1860-1862	Alma Place China Works, Foley, Longton	Bourne & Brown
1860-1862	Nile Street, Burslem	Pinder, Bourne & Hope
1862-1882	Nile Street, Burslem	Pinder, Bourne & Co. (Firm acquired in 1878)
1870-1883	Norfolk Street Works, Hanley	R.C. Scrivener & Co. (& Co.-Thomas Bourne)
1874-1878	Queen Street Pottery, Burslem	Bourne, (Tinsley & Bourne)
1880-1892	Hadderidge Pottery, Burslem	Blackhurst & Bourne
1892-1941	Albion & Leighton Potteries, Burslem	Bourne & Leigh (Ltd.)

For further reading, refer to *Little*, pp. 51-52; *Hampson* No. 42, p. 30; the various books of Geoffrey A. Godden, including *British Porcelain Manufacturers*. For information on the Bourne Pottery, Denby, Derbyshire see *NCSJ*, Vol. 11, 1994 "Potteries of Derbyshire" by Ronald Brown, pp. 95-153. *Refer to Godden's *British Porcelain*, p. 163.

BRIDGWOOD FAMILY (1795-1876) & OTHER OWNERSHIPS CHRONOLOGY: POTTERIES & PARTNERSHIPS

DATE	POTTERY	PARTNERSHIP
1795-1799	at the junction of Market Street and Transportation Road, Longton	Samuel Bridgwood (I) & Richard Johnson
1799-1805	#120 Works, (St. John's Church),Longton	Samuel Bridgwood (I)
1806-1818	#130 Works, Longton	Kitty Bridgwood
1807-1809	JNO Plant Works, Longton	Samuel Bridgwood (II)
1810-1811	Market Street, Longton	Maria Bridgwood
1812-1825	JNO Plant Works, Longton	Platt, Bridgwood & Johnson
1814-1818	Johnson Works, Longton	Kitty Bridgwood
1818-1821	Market Street Works & Wood Street Works, Longton	Kitty Bridgwood & Son(Samuel III)
1822-1825	Market Street Works, Longton (Sublet)	Edward Royle
1825-1853	Market Street, High Street and Stafford Street (from 1832-1853), Longton	Sampson Bridgwood
1827-1832	Market Street & Wood St. Works, Longton	Sampson Bridgwood
1846-1847	Market Street, Longton	(Samuel) Bridgwood (II) & Burgess
1846(?)	Mossfield Colliery, Longton	(John) Bridgwood, Goodwin & Hawley
1853-1876	Stafford Street (until 1854) & Anchor Pottery, Longton	Sampson Bridgwood & Son
1856-1864	Market Street, Longton	John Aynsley & Co. (& Co-Samuel Bridgwood)
1876-1879	Anchor Pottery Works, Longton	Bridgwood & Sons (name continues under his daughters, Mrs. Napier & Mrs. Walker)
1879-1887	Anchor Pottery Works, Longton	Mrs. Walker continues on alone
1887-1890	Anchor Pottery Works, Longton	Company is insolvent
1890-1932	Anchor Pottery Works, Longton	Aynsley's Pottery
1932-1965	Anchor Pottery Works, Longton	Sampson Bridgwood Son, Ltd.
1965-1978(+)	Anchor Pottery Works, Longton	James Broadhurst & Son Ltd.

VARIOUS OTHER BRIDGWOOD AND/OR FAMILY PARTNERSHIPS - LAND END/LONGTON
(N.B.: The Name *Lane End* changed to *Longton* in 1848)

1800-1806	#127 Works, Longton	Booth & Bridgwood
1827-1829	Ford Works, High Street, Longton	Goodwins, Bridgwood & Orton
1827-1829	High Street, formerly, R. Baker Works, Longton	Goodwins, Bridgwood & Orton
1829-1831	Crown Works, Flint Street, Longton	Goodwins, Bridgwood & Harris/Goodwins & Harris
	(Bridgwood in above 3 associations is unidentified)	
1836-1837	High Street, Lane End, Longton	(Wm) Bridgwood & Ravenscroft
1839-1839	High Street, Lane End, Longton	(Wm) Bridgwood & Hallam
1851-1852	Church Street, Longton	Weston, Colclough & Bridgwood
1884-1886	Granville Works, Longton	Knight & Bridgwood
1886-1913	Granville Works, Longton	Richard Bridgwood

See Goodwin (John) of Longton and Seacombe in this Chronology.
For further reading, refer to *Hampson*, No. 116, pp. 77-78 where he notes a printed mark for Goodwin's, Bridgwood & Co. (1827-1829).

VARIOUS OTHER BRIDGWOOD AND/OR FAMILY PARTNERSHIPS - BURSLEM/FENTON/HANLEY/TUNSTALL

1827-1840	Foley Potteries, King Street, Fenton and Church Street, (from 1822-1825) Lane End, Longton	Knight, Elkin & Bridgwood/ Elkin, Knight & Bridgwood
1854-1957	Phoenix Works, Tunstall	Jess Bridgwood
1857-1864	Church Yard Works, Burslem	Bridgwood & Clarke
1859-1864	Phoenix Works, Tunstall	Bridgwood & Clarke
1870-1870	Hanley	Bridgwood & Stonier
1870-1870	Hanley	John Bridgwood, Jr.
1894-1897	Park Road Works, Fenton	A. Bridgwood

N.B.: Also refer to Elkin & Knight
For further reading, refer to *Godden's Encyclopaedia, British Porcelain* and *Collecting Lustreware*; *Hampson* and *Hampson, Churchill*; as well as *Woolliscroft-Rhead*

BROADHURST CHRONOLOGY: POTTERIES & PARTNERSHIPS

DATE	POTTERY	PARTNERSHIP
1835-1838	Flint Street, Lane End, Longton	Broadhurst, Hulme & Bridget
1840-1845	Church Street, Lane End, Longton	Batkin, Walker & Broadhurst
1846-1846	New Street, Longton	Broadhurst & Green
1847-1852	Anchor Works, Longton	Broadhurst & Green
1847-1853	Green Dock Works, Longton	James Broadhurst (I) & partnership*
1850-1851	Fenton	Perry & Broadhurst
1853-1854	Crown Works, Stafford Street, Longton	Bradbury, Mason & Broadhurst
1854-1863	Crown Works, Stafford Street, Longton	James Broadhurst (I) & Sons
1860-1860	Gold Street, Longton	James & Samuel Broadhurst
1861-1861	Commerce Street, Longton	James & Samuel Broadhurst
1862-1862	Gold Street, Longton	Samuel Broadhurst
1862-1862	Commerce Street, Longton	James Broadhurst
1863-1870	Crown Works, Stafford Street, Longton	James Broadhurst (II)
1870-1892	Crown Works, Stafford Street, Longton	James Broadhurst & Sons
1870-1894	Portland Pottery, Frederick Street, Fenton	James Broadhurst (II)
1894-1922	Portland Pottery, Frederick Street, Fenton	James Broadhurst (II) & Sons
1922-1939	Portland Pottery, Frederick Street, Fenton	James Broadhurst & Sons Ltd.

*See *Hampson*, No. 128, p. 83 where partnership is noted as Hamspon & Broadhurst.
For further reading, refer to *Hampson, Churchill,* pp. 139-141.

CHALLINOR CHRONOLOGY: POTTERIES & PARTNERSHIPS

DATE	POTTERY	PARTNERSHIP
1819-1825(?)	Unicorn Pottery, Tunstall	Edward Challinor
1819-1828	Overhouse Works, Burslem	Edward Challinor
1827-1834	Greenfield Pottery, Tunstall	Wood & (Edward) Challinor
1828-1834	Brownhills Pottery, Tunstall	Wood & (Edward) Challinor
1834-1845	Woodlands, Tunstall	Wood & (Edward) Challinor
1842-1861	Pinnocks Works, Tunstall	E. (Edward) Challinor & Co.
1848-1865	High Street, Tunstall	Charles Challinor
1850-1854	Brownhills Pottery, Tunstall	Bowers, (Edward) Challinor & Woolliscroft
1851-1852/ 1853-1854	Fenton Potteries, Tunstall & Tunstall Works, Tunstall	E. (Edward) Challinor & Co.
1853-1862	Fenton Stone Works, High Street, Lane Delph, Fenton	E. (Edward) Challinor & Co.
1860-1864	Well Street Pottery, Tunstall	Wood, (Edward) Challinor & Co.
1862-1867	Unicorn Pottery, Tunstall	E. (Edward) Challinor
1862-1891	Fenton Stone Works, High Street, Lane Delph, Fenton	E. (Edward) & C. (Charles) Challinor
1865-1880	Lion Works, Sandyford, Tunstall	Ford & Challinor or (Ford & Challinor & Co.)
1887-1887	Fenton	Challinor & Mayer
1892-1896	Fenton Stone Works, High Street, Fenton	C. (Charles) Challinor & Co.

CHESWORTH CHRONOLOGY: POTTERIES & PARTNERSHIPS

DATE	POTTERY	PARTNERSHIP
1807-1809	G. Wood's Work & G. Barnes Works, Longton	G. Chesworth & Co.
1824-1825	Lane End, Longton	Chesworth & Wood
1825-1840	Lane End, Longton	Chesworth & Robinson/ Chesworth & Wood
1843-1844	Miles Bank, Shelton (Hanley)	Lomax & (John) Chesworth

CHETHAM CHRONOLOGY: POTTERIES & PARTNERSHIPS

DATE	POTTERY	PARTNERSHIP
1780s-1818	Longton	Chethams, Turners & Cypley
1796-1807	Commerce Street, Longton	Chetham & Woolley
1807-1809	Commerce Street, Longton	(Mrs.) Chetham & Woolley
1809-1811	Commerce Street, Longton	Mrs. Ann Chetham
1814-1821	Commerce Street, Longton	Chetham (& Son)
1822-1834	Commerce Street, Longton	Chetham & Robinson
1834-1840	Commerce Street, Longton	Chetham, Robinson & Son
1841-1861	Commerce Street, Longton	Jonathan Lowe Chetham
1861-1871	Commerce Street/Chancery Lane, Longton	Frederick Chetham & Co.
1862-1865	Commerce Street, Longton	J. R. & F. Chetham
1865-1869	Chancery Lane, Longton	J. R. & F. Chetham

Although *Hampson* and *Godden's* dates differ, *Godden, Collecting Lustreware*, pp. 96-97 gives a fine insight into the Lustreware production of Chetham. Also refer to *Edwards, Basalt,* pp. 137-140.

CHURCHILL GROUP/ALEXANDER WORKS (FORMERLY - COBRIDGE WORKS)CHRONOLOGY: POTTERIES & PARTNERSHIPS & ASSOCIATIONS

DATE	POTTERY	PARTNERSHIP & ASSOCIATION
1794-1808	Owner of "Site", Cobridge	Ralph Bucknall
1808-1816	Cobridge Works, Cobridge	Robert Bucknall & Andrew Stevenson
1816-1836	Cobridge Works, Cobridge	Andrew Stevenson
1828-1834	Cobridge Works, Cobridge	Ralph & James Clews
1834-1837	Cobridge Works, Cobridge	Vacant
1837-1837	Cobridge Works, Longton	Robinson, Wood & Brownfield
1837-1850	Brownfield Works, Cobridge	Wood & Brownfield
1850-1871	Brownfield Works, Cobridge	William Brownfield
1871-1876	Brownfield Works, Cobridge	William Brownfield & Son
1876-1892	Brownfield Works, Cobridge	William Brownfield & Sons
1880s-1892	Brownfield Works, Cobridge	Arthur Brownfield
1892-1897	Brownfield Works, Cobridge	Brownfields Guild Pottery Society Ltd.
1898-1900	Brownfield Works, Cobridge	Brownfields Pottery Ltd.
(1900-1902)	WORKS RECONSTRUCTED INTO 2 POTTERIES	
1902-1912(27)	Brownfield Works, Cobridge	Upper Hanley Pottery Co. Ltd.
1902-1927	Alexander Works, Stoke	Myott, Son & Co.
	WORKS REUNITED	
1927-1969	Alexander Works, Stoke	Myott, Son & Co's, Ltd.
1969-1976	Alexander Works, Stoke	Interpace Corp.
1976-1991	Alexander Works, Stoke	Myott-Meakin, Ltd. (& Various Partnerships)
1991-	Alexander Works, Stoke	Churchill Group

CLEMENTSON CHRONOLOGY: POTTERIES & PARTNERSHIPS

DATE	POTTERY	PARTNERSHIP
1833-1835	Broad & High Street, Shelton, Hanley	Read & Clementson
1836-1836	Broad & High Street, Shelton, Hanley	Read, Clementson & Anderson
1837-1839	Broad & High Street, Shelton, Hanley	Read & Co. (& Co.-Clementson)
1839-1864	Phoenix Works High Street, Shelton, Hanley	Joseph Clementson
1844-1845	Broad & High Street, Shelton, Hanley	Clementson, Young & Anderson
1845-1847	Broad & High Street, Shelton, Hanley	Clementson & Young
1848-1848	Phoenix Works, High Street, Shelton, Hanley (J.C. & SONS)	Joseph Clementson & Sons
1855-1864	The Bell Works, Shelton, Hanley (acquired in 1855)	Joseph Clementson
1865-1916	Bell Works, Shelton, Hanley	Clementson Bros.
1916-1919	Phoenix Works & Bell Works, Shelton, Hanley	Clementson Bros. Ltd.

N.B.: For additional marks for the Clementson partnerships, refer to *P. Williams, Staffordshire*, Vol. II and Gaston, Vol. 1.
For further reading on Clementson, refer to Pat Halfpenny, "Joseph Clementson: A Pottery 'Remarkable For Energy of Character'." *NCSJ*, Vol. 5, 1984, pp. 177-205.

ROBERT COCHRAN & CO./COCHRAN & FLEMING VERREVILLE POTTERY/BRITANNIA POTTERY CHRONOLOGY: POTTERIES & PARTNERSHIPS

John Geddes acquired the Verreville Glass Works in 1806; however the pottery date is uncertain with a c. 1820-1830 marking noted as John Geddes or J.G. From 1830-1833 Robert Montgomerie acquired pottery and the marking "M" with "WARRANTED" appears on scroll. Subsequent ownerships and dates are noted below.

DATE	MARK	PARTNERSHIP
VERREVILLE POTTERY		
1834-1838	R.A.K. & CO. & C. & CO.	Robert Alexander Kidston & Hugh Price
1838-1841	As Above	
1841-1846	R. COCHRAN & CO.	Robert Cochran, Alexander Cochran
	K. & CO.	Robert Alexander Kidston and others
1846-1867	R.C. & CO.	Robert and Alexander Cochran
1867-1869	R.C. & CO.	Robert Cochran, Jr. and Alexander Balfour
1869-1873	R.C. & CO.	Robert Cochran, Jr. and Alexander Balfour (also possible marking "V.P." for Verreville Pottery)
1873-1917	R.C. & CO.	Robert Cochran, Jr. and (later) Robert Conrad Cochran. (also possible marking "V.P." for Verreville Pottery)
BRITANNIAPOTTERY		
1855-1867	R.C. & CO.	Robert Cochran
1867-1869	Marks as above	Robert Cochran, Alexander Cochran, Jr. & James Fleming
1869-1896	Marks as above, plus R. COCHRAN & CO.	Alexander Cochran, Jr. & James Fleming
1896-1899	Marks as above, plus COCHRAN & FLEMING	Alexander Cochran, Jr., James Fleming & James Arnold Fleming
1899-1906	Marks as above, plus FLEMING, GLASGOW	James Fleming and James Arnold Fleming
1906-1920	Marks as above	James Arnold Fleming
ADDITIONAL POTTERY/PARTNERSHIPS, C. 1813-1838		
1813-1820	Anderston/Lancefield	Geddes, Kidston & Co.
1820-1824	Anderston/Lancefield	Anderston Pottery built
1825-1834	Anderston/Lancefield	Geddes Kidston (Holding Co.)
1835-1838	Anderston/Lancefield	Company sold to Anderston Pottery Co.
1838	Anderston/Lancefield	R.A. Kidston moves works to Verreville

COCKSON/HARDING CHRONOLOGY: POTTERIES & PARTNERSHIPS

DATE	POTTERY	PARTNERSHIP
COCKSON		
1834-1856	Globe Pottery, Cobridge (Cobridge Works), Cobridge	Harding & Cockson
1856-1863	Globe Pottery, Cobridge	Harding, Cockson & Sons (& Co.)
1856-1863	New Hall Works, Shelton, Hanley	Cockson & Harding
1863-1866	Globe Pottery, Cobridge	Charles Cockson
1867-1875	Globe Pottery, Cobridge	Cockson & Chetwynd (Cockson,Chetwynd & Co.)
1876-1878	Globe Pottery, Cobridge	Cockson & Seddon
HARDING		
1850-1851	Furlong Works, Navigation Road, Burslem	Joseph Harding
1856-1861	Globe Pottery, Cobridge	Harding & Cockson & Sons & Co.
1856-1863	New Hall Works, Shelton, Hanley	Cockson & Harding
1863-1872	New Hall Works, Shelton, Hanley	W. & J. Harding

CORK, ET.AL. CHRONOLOGY: POTTERIES & PARTNERSHIPS

DATE	**POTTERY**	**PARTNERSHIP**
CORK		
1834-1843	Newport Pottery, Queen Street Burslem	Cork and Condliffe
1846-1860	Newport Pottery, Queen Street, Burslem	Cork & Edge
1860-1870	Newport Pottery, Queen Street, Burslem	Cork, Edge & Malkin
1867-1869	Navigation Road, Burslem	Daniel & Cork
EDGE		
1830	Tunstall	Edge & Grocott*
1834-1842	Waterloo Road, Burslem	Daniel Edge
1835-1836	Market Street, Lane Delph, Fenton	Edge, Barker & Co.
1836-1840	Market Street, Lane Delph, Fenton	Edge, Barker & Barker
1841-1848	Market Street, Lane Delph, Fenton	William & Samuel Edge
1850-1854	Waterloo Road, Burslem	Timothy Edge
1870-1899	Newport & Middleport Potteries, Burslem	Edge, Malkin & Co.
1871	High Street, Longton	Edge & Co. **& Co. - Hill & Enoch Palmer
(?)-1874	Queen Street Pottery, Burslem	J. Edge (See Jewitt, p.464 for further information)
1882-1886	Hallfield Pottery, Hanley	Whittaker, Edge & Co. Whittaker & Co.***
1896-1897	Bourne's Bank Pottery, Burslem	King, Edge & Barratt
1899 - 1903	Newport & Middleport Potteries, Burslem	Edge, Malkin & Co., Ltd.
MALKIN		
1712-1834	Knowle Street Works, Burslem	Samuel Malkin
1850-1860	Longton	Malkin, Walker & Co.
1858-1864	British Anchor Pottery, Longton	Malkin, Walker & Hulse
1864-1881	Park Works, Market Street, Fenton	Ralph Malkin
1882-1893(4)	Park Works, Market Street, Fenton	Ralph Malkin & Sons
1891-1905	Bell Works, Burslem	Frederick Malkin

* Refer to *Cushion's Handbook*, p. 164 & *Little*, p. 61
**Refer to *Cushion* for reg. Date of 10/31/1871
*** Refer to *Jewitt*, p. 507,
For further reading, refer to Annise Doring Heaivilin. *Grandma's Tea Leaf*, Wallace Homestead, Des Moines, IA, 1981, pp. 63-66.

DEAKIN CHRONOLOGY: POTTERIES & PARTNERSHIPS

DATE	POTTERY	PARTNERSHIP
1815-1818	Waterloo Works, Lane End, Longton	Batkin & Deakin or (Deakin & Batkin)
1819-1827	Waterloo Works, Lane End, Longton	Batkin, Dale & Deakin
1824-1827	Waterloo Works, Lane End, Longton	William & James Deakin
1828-1832	Waterloo Works, Lane End, Longton	Deakin & Bailey/ Bailey & Deakin
1831-1838	Charles Street Works, Lane End, Longton	Deakin(s) & Procter
1833-1841	Waterloo Works, Lane End, Longton	Deakin & Son(s)
1836-1838	Green Dock Works, Longton	Deakin(s) & Proctor
1836-1841	Green Dock Works, Longton	Deakin & Sons or (Deakin, Deakin & Deakin)
1841-1863	Pell Pottery, Stafford Street, Longton	Deakin & Son(s) (& Co.)
1841-1846	Pell Pottery, Stafford Street, Longton	James & John Deakin
1841-1846	Waterloo Works, Lane End, Longton	James & John Deakin
1846-1851	Pell Pottery, Stafford Street, Longton	James Deakin & Co.
1846-1851	Waterloo Works, Lane End, Longton	James Deakin & Co.
1849-1850	High Street, Longton	Cyples & Deakin
1851-1854	Waterloo Place, Lane End, Longton	Edward Deakin
1851-1863	Pell Pottery, Stafford Street, Longton	James Deakin & Sons

DEAKIN CHRONOLOGY: POTTERIES & PARTNERSHIPS

DATE	POTTERY	PARTNERSHIP
1815-1818	Waterloo Place, Lane End, Longton	Batkin & Deakin - Thomas Deakin I
1819-1827	Waterloo Place, Lane End, Longton	Batkin, Dale & Deakin - Thomas I
1824-1827	Waterloo Place, Lane End, Longton	William & James Deakin
1828-1832	Waterloo Place, Lane End, Longton	Deakin & Bailey/Bailey & Deakin - Thomas I
1831-1838	Charles Street Works, Lane End, Longton	Deakin(s) & Procter
1833-1836	Waterloo Place, Lane End, Longton	Deakin & Son - " & Son" – James
1836-1841	Waterloo Place, Lane End, Longton & Green Dock, Lane End, Longton	Deakin & Son(s) - "& Sons" – James & John - Thomas died in 1838
1836-1839	Green Dock, Lane End, Longton	Deakin(s) & Procter - James & John
1841-1846	Waterloo Place, Lane End, Longton and Peel Pottery, Stafford Street, Longton	James & John Deakin - John Died in 1846
1846-1851	Waterloo Place, Lane End, Longton and Peel Pottery, Stafford Street, Longton	James Deakin & Co. - James & John
1849-1850	High Street, Longton	Cyples & Deakin - Thomas Deakin
1851-1854	Waterloo Place, Lane End, Longton	Edwin Deakin - Son of James
1851-1863	Peel Pottery, Stafford Street, Longton	James Deakin & Son(s) - Thomas II, his son Edwin
1864-?	Waterloo Potters	acquired by Lowe & Abberley
1864-1867	Peel Pottery	acquired by Webb & Walters

For further reading, refer to *Godden, Collecting Lustreware*, pp. 108-110; and *Hampson*, No. 91, pp. 59-60

DON POTTERY, SWINTON CHRONOLOGY: POTTERIES & PARTNERSHIPS

DATE	COMPANY NAME	COMMENTS
1801-1803	Don Pottery	Partnership: John Green, Richard Clark & William Brameld
1803-1807	Green, Don Pottery Green's son, John, William	Additional partners: John Clark, John Miller & John Wade
1805-1816	Green, Don Pottery	John Green dies and his son, William Green,
1807-1817	Green, Clark & Co.	joins as partner
1816-1817	Greens, Clark & Co.	New partner added: Samuel Thompson Lunn
1817-1822	John & William Green & Co.	As original partners died, other family members stepped in as partners: or Greens & Co. Thomas & George Frederick, John Brameld, William & Richard Clark, Elizabeth, Sarah, John, Joseph & William Green, John Birk & Lunn
1822-1823	as above	Lunn sells his share
1823-1824	as above	Partnership changes include: John Greaves Clark, John Wager Brameld & Marianne Milner. Joseph & Charles Green acted on behalf of family interests
1824-1834	as above	Green family acquires total interest in pottery in 1824
1834	as above	John and William Green declare bankruptcy
1835	—	Don Pottery and its stock sold off
1835-1839	—	Pottery (let) rented to various potters
1839-1851	Barker, Don Pottery	Samuel Barker of Mexborough Old Pottery buys Don Pottery. Continues both potteries until 1848 when Mexborough production (earthenwares) is transferred to Don Works
1851-1882	Barker & Son(s)	
1856-1882	Samuel Barker & Son	Samuel dies and pottery is carried on by his three sons

1882-1893	Samuel Barker & Son	Works are let out (rented) to John Adamson, John Williamson, Edward Smith and Charles Scorah. The back marking is carried on
1893	—	Pottery is closed and stock sold off

For further reading, refer to *Don Pottery Catalogue,* 1983 Exhibition by the Doncaster Museum and Art Gallery, Swinton, S. Yorkshire, *Lawrence; Little*, p. 117 and *Annual Report of Yorkshire Philosophical Society*, Feb. 1916.
Marks reproduced herein from *Yorkshire Pots and Potteries* (David and Charles, 1974) is by the kind permission of the publishers.

EDGE CHRONOLOGY: POTTERIES & PARTNERSHIPS

DATE	POTTERY	PARTNERSHIP
1830	—, Tunstall	Edge & Grocott
1834-1842	Waterloo Road, Burslem	Daniel Edge
1835-1836	Market Street, Lane Delph, Fenton	Edge, Barker & Co.
1836-1840	Market Street, Lane Delph, Fenton	Edge, Barker & Barker
1841-1848	Market Street, Lane Delph, Fenton	William & Samuel Edge
1846-1860	Newport Pottery, Burslem	Cork & Edge
1850-1854	Waterloo Road, Burslem	Timothy Edge
1860-1870	Newport Pottery, Burslem	Cork, Edge & Malkin
1870-1899	Newport Pottery, Burslem	Edge & Malkin & Co.
1871*	High Street, Burslem	Edge & Co.
1882-1886	Hallfield Pottery, Hanley	Whitaker, Edge & Co.
1896-1897	Bourne's Bank Pottery, Burslem	King, Edge & Barratt
1899-1903 (Ltd.)	Newport & Middleport Potteries, Burslem	Edge & Malkin & Co. Ltd.

*See additional comments under Cork, et.al.

EDWARDS CHRONOLOGY: POTTERIES & PARTNERSHIPS

DATE	POTTERY	PARTNERSHIP
1737-1737	Lane End, Longton	Edwards, Bullock & Nixon
1784-1796	Lane End, Longton	William Edwards (I)
1823-1823	H. Boulton's Works, Longton	Bettaney & Edwards
1828-1833	Flint Street, High Street, & Lower Market Street, Longton	William Edwards (II)
1834-1835	Commerce Street, Longton	Riddle & Co. (Edwards was one of partners)
1837-1839	Dale Hall, Kilncroft & Newcastle Works, Burslem	(John) Maddock & Edwards
1839-1842	Kilncroft Works, Sylvester St, Burslem	James & Thomas Edwards
1841(47)*	Waterloo & Swan Bank Pottery, Burslem	Thomas Edwards
1842-1851 (54)***	Dale Hall, Burslem	James Edwards
1844-1858	Market Street, Longton	Cope & Edwards
1847-1853	Market Street, Longton	John Edwards (& Co.)
1849-1859	Chancery Lane, Longton	John Edwards
1853-1872	Market Place, Longton	John Edwards
1853-1900	King Street, Fenton	John Edwards & Co.
1854-1876	Market Street & Sutherland Road, Longton	James Edwards & Son
1855-1881*	Dale Hall, Burslem	James Edwards (& Son(s))
1858-1863	Meadow Works, Rawmarsh, Yorkshire	Edwards & Howard
1859-1862	Market Street, Longton	James Edwards
1859-1867	King Street, Fenton	James Edwards
1862-1864	Market Street, Longton	James & John Edwards
1863-1867**	Market Street, Longton	James Edwards & Son (George)
1865-1865	King Street, Fenton	John Edwards & Son
1867-1873	Cyples Lane, Longton (1867) & Sheridan Works, King Street, Longton (1868-1873)	George Edwards (& Co.)
1873-1879	Cyples Lane, Longton	John Edwards & Co.
1873-1900	Market Place, Longton	John Edwards & Co.
1873-1904	Sheridan Works, King Street, Longton	George Edwards
1879-1900	Cyples Lane, Longton	John Edwards
1882-1933	Victoria Works, High Street, Longton	Edwards & Brown
1885-1898	Gordon Pottery, Anchor Works, Longton	R.J. Edwards & Co.
1887-1900	Trent Works, Hanley	Edwards & Son
1895-1904	Hadderidge Pottery, Burslem	W. Edwards & Son
1901-1933	Victoria Works, High Street, Longton	Joseph Edwards

*There is a difference in dates noted between *Godden* , p. 230, and *Henrywood*. *Henrywood*, p. 198 notes that dates for James Edwards was until 1854 "when his son Richard was admitted to partnership." Style was continued beyond James Edwards' retirement in 1861.

**The names Jas. Edwards & Son or James Edwards & Son are interchangeable. Evidently there were many surnames of Edwards during this period. In order to distinguish one from the other, James Edwards & Son, Market Street, Longton is referred to as Jas. Edwards thus distinguishing the name from James Edwards & Son, Dale Hall, Burslem. Refer to *Journal of Ceramic History*, No. 9, Stoke on Trent, City Museum, 1977, "II A Trade Union Year: 1864 an Extract from the Transactions of the Executive Committee for the Hollow Ware Pressers Union" by Paul Anderton, p. 32, *fn* 69.
***The rate records for Thomas Edwards are incomplete. There are two registry dates for 1844, which are April 3, 1844/ No. 17566-72 and Dec. 7, 1844/No. 23207-10 . In that the registry protection was for three years, it would appear unlikely that for at least the period of 1845 would not have been in any financial or other difficulty. Further investigation is warranted.

ELKIN/KNIGHT (TRADING UNDER NUMEROUS TITLES AND AT VARIOUS LOCATIONS) CHRONOLOGY: POTTERIES & PARTNERSHIPS

DATE	POTTERY	PARTNERSHIP
1820-1825	Foley Potteries, Church Street, Fenton	Elkin & Co. (Co.-Elkin, Knight & Elkin) Elkin Knight & Co. (Co.-Bridgwood) Elkin & Knight
1822-1825	Church Street, Longton	Thomas Elkin
1826-1846	Foley Potteries, King Street, Fenton	Elkin & Knight or Knight, Elkin & Co.
1827-1840	Foley Potteries, King Street, Fenton & Church Street, Lane End, Longton	Elkin, Knight & Bridgwood Elkin, Knight & Elkin (formerly Elkin & Co.) Knight, Elkin & Bridgwood
1840-1843	Flint Street & Stafford Street Potteries, Longton	Swift & Elkin
1840-1846		Elkin & Knight
	Church Street, Lane End, Longton	Knight & Elkin
1841-1844	Foley Potteries, King Street, Fenton	Knight, Elkin, Knight (Knight Elkin & Co.)
1845-1856	Stafford Street, Longton	Elkin & Newbon (Subsequently, Samuel Elkin)
1846-1856	Foley Potteries, King Street, Fenton	John King Knight (Subsequently, Knight & Wileman)
1853-1856	Foley Potteries, King Street, Fenton	Knight & Wileman
1856-1865	Stafford Street & Mill Street, Longton	Samuel Elkin
1859-1879	Foley Potteries, King Street, Fenton	Joseph Knight
1873-1878	Market Street Works, Longton	Knight & Rowley
1878-1880	Market Street Works, Longton	Knight & Colclough
1882-1883	Stafford Street, Longton	Joseph Knight
1884-1886	Granville Works, Stafford Street, Longton	Knight & Bridgwood

For further reading on individual potters, Elkin & Knight, refer to *Hampson*, No's. 98 and 99, pp. 63-64; and *Godden, British Porcelain*, pp. 326, 464 and 465.

FERRYBRIDGE POTTERY CHRONOLOGY: POTTERIES & PARTNERSHIPS

DATE	POTTERY	PARTNERSHIP
1792-1796	(Known as) Knottingly Pottery until 1804	Wm. Tomlinson & Co.
1796-1801	Knottingly Pottery	Tomlinson, Foster, Wedgwood & Co.
1801-1834	Knottingly Pottery; Renamed Ferrybridge in 1804	Tomlinson & Co.
1834-1840	Ferrybridge Pottery	Tomlinson, Plowes & Co.
1840-1843	Ferrybridge Pottery	Reed, Taylor & Kelsall
1843-1856	Ferrybridge Pottery	Reed & Taylor
1856-1883	Ferrybridge Pottery and (c.1877) The Australian Pottery	Lewis Woolf & Sons
1884-1897	Ferrybridge Pottery	Poulson Bros. (Ltd.)
1897-1919	Ferrybridge Pottery	Sefton & Brown
1919-	Ferrybridge Pottery	T. Brown & Sons (Ltd.)

For further reading, refer to *Godden*, p. 246 for additional dates, partnerships and markings; *Lawrence*; *Little*, p. 119; the *Annual Report of the Yorkshire Philosophical Society, Yorkshire*, 1916, pp. 31-37; and *Cushion*, p. 146.

FORD CHRONOLOGY: POTTERIES & PARTNERSHIPS

DATE	POTTERY	PARTNERSHIP
1799-1864	South Hylton, Sunderland, Durham	Ford Pottery
1805-1809*	Lane End, Longton	Ford & Hulme
1811-1815*	—, Longton	Singleton, Barlow & Ford
1815-1828*	Bridge Street, Flint Street & Lane End, Longton	Barlow & Ford
1818	Green Dock, Lane End, Longton	Hugh Ford
1827-1845	Sheriff Hill Pottery, Newcastle Upon Tyne, Northumberland	Ford & Patterson
1841-1853	Mere Pottery, Castleford, Yorkshire	Asquith, Ford & Co.
1854-1871	Cannon Street, Hanley	T. & C. Ford (Thomas & Charles)
1862-1880	Lion Works, Sandyford, Tunstall	Ford, Challinor & Co. (Ford & Challinor & Co.)
1868-1873	Union Bank/High Street Potteries, Burslem	Whittingham, Ford & Co.
1871-1874	Cannon Street, Hanley	Thomas Ford (& Co.)
1871-1912	Eastwood, Hanley	Charles Ford
1876-1882	Newcastle Street, Burslem	Whittingham, Ford & Riley
1880-1890	Lion Works, Sandyford, Tunstall	T. Ford & Co.
1882-1893	Newcastle Street, Burslem	Ford & Riley
1887-1893	Victoria Pottery, Whitwood Mere, Yorkshire	Ford Bros.
1889-1894	Lincoln Pottery, Burslem	Smith, Ford & Jones
1891-1926	39 Prince Street, Edinburgh, Scotland (Retailers)	John Ford & Co.
1893-1908 (1938)	Newcastle Street, Burslem	Ford & Sons (Ltd.)
1895-1898	Lincoln Pottery, Burslem	Smith & Ford
1898-1913	Lincoln Pottery, Burslem	Samuel Ford & Co.
1912-1925	Alexander Works, Stoke	Charles Ford
1913-1939	Crown Pottery, Burslem	Samuel Ford & Co.
1917-1936	Norfolk Works, Hanley	Ford & Pointon Ltd. (Cauldon Group in 1921)
1938 -	Crownford, Burslem	Ford & Sons (Crownford) Ltd.

* Refer to *Hampson*, p. 15, No. 20 and p. 68, No. 107.

FORESTER, FORRESTER, FORRISTER, FORSTER CHRONOLOGY: POTTERIES & PARTNERSHIPS

DATE	POTTERY	PARTNERSHIP
FORESTER		
1802-1817	Lane Delph, Staffordshire	Thomas Forester
1818-1830	Market Place, Lane End, Longton	George Forester
1877-1879	Church Works, Longton	Thomas Forester
1879-1883	Phoenix Works, Church Street, Longton	Thomas Forester
1883-1886	Melbourne Works, Church Street, Longton	Meigh & Forester
1880-1959	Phoenix Works, Church Street, Longton	Thomas Forester & Sons (Ltd.)
1884-1887	Sutherland Pottery, High Street, Fenton	Thomas Forester Son & Co.
1887-1887	Alexander Works, Longton	Thomas Forester & Co.
1887-1892	Melbourne Works, Church Street, Longton	Thomas Forester or (Taylor & Forester)
1887-1892	Sutherland Pottery, High Street, Fenton	Forester (Joseph Booth) & Hulme
1888	Melbourne Works, Church Street, Longton	Thomas Forester & Co.
FORRESTER		
1776-1790	Church Street, Lane End, Longton	John Forrester, Shufflebotham & Smith
1784-1787	Lower Market Place, Longton	Forrester & Meredith
1790-1796	Church Street, Lane End, Longton	John Forrester II & Charles Harvey
1799-1830	Lower Market Place, Lane End, Longton	George Forrester
1802-1802	Church Street, Lane End, Longton	John Forrester II & Thomas Mayer
1802-1809	Church Street, Lane End, Longton	John Forrester II
1884-1888	Alma Works, Marsh Street, Hanley (Decorator)	T.W. Forrester
- 1895	Blyth Works, Longton	T. Forrester & Son
FORRISTER (OR FORESTER?)		
1815	Lane Delph, Staffordshire	Forrister & Co.
1848-1851	Foley (Fenton) Staffordshire	Forrister, Copestake & Forrister
1851-1852	King Street, Foley, Fenton	Martin & John Forrister
FORSTER		
1853-1871	Clay Hills Pottery, Tunstall	Elsmore & Forster
1862-1885	New Biggins Pottery, Scotland	James Forster
1886-1893	New Biggins Pottery, Scotland	Jonathan Forster

For further reading, refer to *Hampson*, No. 108, p. 69 and No. 109 pp. 69-70 109.

THE GLAMORGAN POTTERY - SWANSEA (WALES) CHRONOLOGY: POTTERIES & PARTNERSHIPS

DATE	COMPANY NAME	NAME OF PARTNERS, ETC.
1813-1819	Baker, Bevans & Irwin	Founded by William Baker in partnership with William Bevans and Thomas Irwin
1819-1838	Glamorgan Pottery	Pottery name continued after the death of William Baker
1837	Glamorgan Pottery	Dillwyn negotiates to purchase Glamorgan Pottery
1839	Glamorgan Pottery	Pottery purchase is finalized and all equipment, moulds, etc. are transferred to the Cambrian Pottery by Dillwyn (with a view to closing down the Glamorgan Works)

For further reading, refer to *Nance*; *Little*, pp. 112-113; Gareth Hughes & Robert Pugh. *Llanelly Pottery*. Llanelli Borough Council, Llanelli Wales, 1990; *Pugh, Welsh Pottery*, pp. 36-30; *Godden, Collecting Lustreware*, pp. 252-254; and *Hallesy*.

GODDARD & BURGESS/BURGESS & GODDARD

Importers of Earthenware, c. 1870-c.1885, U.S.A. & Longton, Staffordshire (See Appendices)

"Pottery and Glassware Reporter" p. 7 notes a full page advertisement, reading in part: "Burgess & Goddard" Season of 1884. 49 Barclay St., and 52 Park Place, New York, as well as other U.S. locations in Boston, Baltimore and Philadelphia. Representing in the U.S. such firms as John Edwards, Wedgwood & Co., Bridgwood & Son, Burgess & Goddard, G.W. Turner & Sons, Dunn Bennett & Co., J.F. Wileman and Blair & Co."

Godden notes that in the 1870s the following were partners: John Burgess, John Hackwood, Goddard (son of Thomas), William Burgess and John Wilson Burgess. The firm traded as Goddard & Burgess, Longton. [John Burgess retired in 1875 and Thomas Goddard, father of John H. died in 1872.]

Hampson, No. 115, p. 76, notes that by 1861 John Hackett Goddard, who was known as the "American Merchant" was described as being a "large exporter to the U.S.A." and was known as Goddard & Burgess.

BURGESS — GODDARD CHRONOLOGY: POTTERIES & PARTNERSHIPS

DATE	POTTERY	PARTNERSHIP
	BURGESS	
1840-1840	Amicable Street, Tunstall	Hancock, Wright & (Richard) Burgess
1841-1843	Amicable Street, Tunstall	Wright & (Richard) Burgess
1846-1847	Market Street, Longton	Bridgwood & (John) Burgess
1862-	Hill Pottery, High Street, Burslem, 1862-1889 & Middleport Pottery & Central Pottery, (1862-1870) Dale Hall, Burslem, 1889+	Burgess & Leigh (Ltd.)
1864-1892	Kilncroft Works, Sylvester Square, Burslem	Henry Burgess
1903-1917	Mt. Pleasant Works, Hanley	Thomas Burgess
1922-1939	Carlisle Works, Longton	Burgess Bros.
	GODDARD	
1827-1828	Richard Plants Works, Longton	Thomas Goddard
1840-1848	Commerce Street, Longton	(John Hackett) Goddard & Co.
1841-1843	Lane End, Longton	(John Hackett) Goddard & Salt

Very little has been written about Goddard. However, for further information, refer to *Mankowitz & Haggar*, p. 97; *Hampson*; and *Godden, Collecting Lustreware*, pp. 115-116. For extensive information on the firm's marketing history see *Ewins*, pp. 107-127.

GODWIN CHRONOLOGY: POTTERIES & PARTNERSHIPS

DATE	POTTERY	PARTNERSHIP
1786-1795	—, Cobridge	Thomas & Benjamin Godwin
1789-1811	—, Cobridge	Benjamin Godwin
1794-1814	—, Cobridge	Thomas Godwin
1802-1804	Upper & Lower Manufactory, Cobridge	Stevenson, Godwin & Dale
1804-1810	Upper & Lower Manufactory, Cobridge	Stevenson & Godwin
1805-1820	—, Cobridge	James & Benjamin Godwin
1809-1834	New Basin Pottery, Navigation Road & New Wharf Potteries, Burslem	Thomas & Benjamin Godwin
1810-1818	Upper Manufactory, Cobridge	Benjamin Godwin & Sons
1818	—, Cobridge	B. & S. Godwin
1822-1822	Market Place, Burslem	Godwin, Rathbone & Co.
1828-1831	Market Place, Burslem	Godwin, Rowley & Co.
1834-1841	New Wharf Potteries, Cobridge	Benjamin Endon Godwin
1834-1854	Canal Works, Navigation Road, Burslem	Thomas Godwin
1834-1864 (67)	Lincoln Pottery, Sneyd Green, Cobridge	John & Robert Godwin
1836-1836	—, Cobridge	B. C. Godwin
1839-1843	—, Cobridge	John & James Godwin
1846-1850	—, Cobridge	James Godwin
1851	Navigation Road, Burslem	B. C. Godwin

For further reading, refer to *Edwards, Basalt,* pp. 160-161; and *Godden, Collecting Lustreware*, pp. 116-117.

GOODWIN (JOHN) OF LONGTON & SEACOMBE CHRONOLOGY: POTTERIES & PARTNERSHIPS

DATE	POTTERY	PARTNERSHIP
1822-1823	High Street, Longton	Robinson, Ash, Ball & Goodwin
1822-1827	R. Barker's Works (Flint Street) Lane End, Longton	Goodwin & Orton
1825	R. Barker's Works (Flint Street) Lane End, Longton	Goodwin, Taylor & Co.
1825-1827	R. Barker's Works (Flint Street) Lane End, Longton	Goodwin & Taylor
1827-1829*	R. Barker's Works (Flint Street)	Goodwins, Bridgwood & Orton & Ford's Works, Lane End, Longton (Sons, James & Thomas)
1829-1832	Crown Works, Flint Street, Lane End, Longton	Goodwins, Bridgwood & Harris
1832-1837	Crown Works, Flint Street, Lane End, Longton	Goodwins & Harris/Harris & Goodwins
1836(Jan. - Sept.)	Church Street Works, Land End, Longton	Meigh, Goodwin & Booth
1837-1838	Crown Works, Flint Street Lane End, Longton	John & James Goodwin
1839-1840	Crown Works, Flint Street Lane End, Longton	Goodwin & Ellis
1841-1851	Crown Works, Flint Street Lane End, Longton	John Goodwin
	JOHN GOODWIN MOVES TO SEACOMBE	
1852-1857	On the Wirral Peninsula, Wallasey,Liverpool	John Goodwin
1857-1860	On the Wirral Peninsula, Wallasey, Liverpool	Thomas Orton Goodwin (and three brothers)
1861-1864	On the Wirral Peninsula, Wallasey, Liverpool	Thomas Orton Goodwin (alone)

**Hampson*, No. 116, pp. 77-78 notes a printed mark "Goodwin's, Bridgwood & Co." High Street, Lane End, Longton. This possibly dates from 1827-1829.
N.B.: Also see Bridgwood Family in this Chronology.
For further reading on the Goodwins, see the article by Helen Williams, pp. 15-26, in the *NCSJ*, Vol. 7, 1989; the *Journal of Ceramic History*, Vol. 14; as well as *Hampson;* and *Godden, Collecting Lustreware*, p. 117.

HACKWOOD CHRONOLOGY: POTTERIES & PARTNERSHIPS

DATE	POTTERY	PARTNERSHIP
1807-1827	Eastwood Pottery, Shelton, Hanley	Hackwood & Co. (or) Hackwood, Dimmock & Co.
1827-1843	Eastwood Pottery, Shelton, Hanley	William Hackwood
1834-1836	Market Street Works, Shelton, Hanley	Hackwood & Keeling
1842-1843	Upper High Street, Shelton, Hanley	Josiah Hackwood
1843-1846*[1]	New Hall Pottery, Shelton, Hanley	William & Thomas Hackwood
1843-1855	New Hall Pottery, Shelton, Hanley	William Hackwood & Son
1850-1855*	New Hall Pottery, Shelton, Hanley	Thomas Hackwood
1853-1854	Hope Street, Shelton, Hanley	William Hackwood
Subsequently:[1]		
1856-1863	New Hall Pottery, Shelton, Hanley	Cockson & Harding

*The New Hall Pottery of William Ratcliffe (1831-1842) was acquired by William & Thomas Hackwood.
For further reading, refer to *Godden, Collecting Lustreware*, pp. 118-119; *Edwards, Basalt*, p. 162; and *Little*, p. 90.

HALL CHRONOLOGY: POTTERIES & PARTNERSHIPS

DATE	POTTERY	PARTNERSHIP
1802-1814	Sytch Pottery, Liverpool Road, Burslem	John & Ralph Hall
1811-1822	Sytch Pottery, Liverpool Road, Burslem	John & Ralph Hall
1814-1822	Sytch Pottery, Liverpool Road, Burslem	John Hall
- 1829	Rawdon Pottery, Derbyshire	John Hall
1822-1832	Sytch Pottery, Liverpool Road, Burslem	John Hall & Sons
1822-1835	Swan Pottery, Tunstall	Ralph Hall
1836-1841	Swan Pottery, Tunstall	Ralph Hall & Son
1836-1849	Swan Pottery, Tunstall	Ralph Hall & Co. or (& Son)
1838-1843	—, Tunstall	Hall & Holland
1841-1856	Marsh Street, Shelton, Hanley	Samuel Hall
1846-1852	Viaduct Works, Anchor Road, Longton	Yale, Barker & Hall
1851-1854	Dale Hall, Longport, Burslem (Lustrer)	Reuben Hall
1853-1857	Dale Hall, Longton, Burslem	Barker & Hall
1882-1882	Wellington Works, Burslem	Hall & Read
1883-1883	Dresden Works, Hanley	Hall & Read
1883-1888	Victoria Square & George Street, Hanley	Hall & Read
1895-1899	Furlong Pottery, Burslem	Hall, Gater & Co. or (Gater, Hall & Co.)
1895-1899	New Gordon Pottery, Tunstall	Hall, Gater & Co. or (Gater, Hall & Co.)
1907-1943	Royal Overhouse Pottery, Tunstall	Hall, Gater & Co. or (Gater, Hall & Co.)
1947-1982	Radnor Works, Longton	Hall Bros. (Longton) Ltd.

N.B.: Also see Swan Bank Pottery, Tunstall and Sytch Pottery, Burslem in this Chronology.

HEATH CHRONOLOGY: POTTERIES & PARTNERSHIPS

DATE	POTTERY	PARTNERSHIP
1745-	—, Hanley	Joshua Heath
1770-1800	Hanley	J. (Joshua) Heath
1780-1812	Hadderidge Pottery, Burslem	Lewis Heath
1782-1787	New Hall, Hanley	Heath, Warburton & Co.
1786	Shelton	Heath & Bagnall
1794-1815	Tontine Pottery, High Street, Shelton, Hanley	(John) Shorthouse & (Thomas) Heath
1797-1800	Hill Works, near Newcastle Turnpike, Burslem	Heath & Son
1799-1804	Walter Daniel Works nr. Newcastle Turnpike, Burslem	Nathan Heath & Son
1802	Hanley	Heath & Shorthouse
1802-1810	Hill Works, near Newcastle Turnpike, Burslem	John & Nathan Heath
1810-1822	Sytch Pottery, Burslem	John Heath
1812-1835	Hadderidge Pottery , Burslem & High St., (1830-1835) Tunstall	Thomas Heath
1828-1841	Newfield Pottery, Tunstall	Joseph Heath & Co.
1830-1835	Lane End or High St., Longton	Thomas Heath
1831	Lane End, Longton	Samuel Heath & Co.
1841-1841	Watergate Street, Tunstall	Heath, Boulton, Greenbanks & Co.
1845-1853	High Street, Tunstall	Joseph Heath
1859-1877	Hadderidge Pottery, Burslem	Heath & Blackhurst (& Co.)
1860-1860	Lane End or High St., Longton	William Heath
1879-1899	Wellington Pottery, Hanley	Bednall & Heath
1885-1890	Union Pottery, Burslem	Buckley, Heath & Co.
1888-1898	Pell Works, Longton	Wildblood & Heath
1891-1893	Union Pottery, Burslem	Heath & Greatbatch
1892-1898	Hallfield Pottery, Hanley	Whittaker, Heath & Co.
1895-1897	Hill Pottery, Burslem	A. Heath & Co.
1899-1927	Pell Works, Longton	Wildblood, Heath & Sons (Ltd.)
1951-Present	Albert Potteries, Burslem	J. E. Heath Ltd.

HUGHES CHRONOLOGY: POTTERIES & PARTNERSHIPS

DATE	POTTERY	PARTNERSHIP
1786-1798	Daisy Bank Works, Longton	Samuel Hughes & Sons
1797-1802	Daisy Bank Works, Longton	Samuel Hughes
1799-1802	High Street, Longton	William Hughes
1799-1804	Daisy Bank Works, Longton	Mary Hughes
1804-1810	Daisy Bank Works, Longton	Peter & Thomas Hughes
1810-1810	Greendock Works, Longton	Thomas Hughes
1810-1811	Daisy Bank Works, Longton	Peter Hughes

1822-1828	—, Cobridge	Cowap & Hughes
1822-1834	Villa Pottery, Cobridge	Thomas Hughes (Sr.)
1835-1852	Bleak Hill Works, Cobridge	S. & E. Hughes or (Stephen Hughes & Co.)
1835-1856	Waterloo Road Works, Longport	Stephen Hughes (& Co.)
1845-1846	High Street, Longton	Cyples & Hughes
1853-1854	Burslem	Stephen Hughes
1853-1867	Bleak Hill Works, Cobridge	Elijah Hughes & Co.
1855-1856	Waterloo Road Works, Longport	Stephen Hughes & Son
1856-1881	Waterloo Road Works, Longport	Thomas Hughes (Jr.)
1864-1864	Cobridge	John Hughes
1881-1882	Top Bridge Works, Longport	Thomas Hughes (Jr.)
1882-1889	Canning Street Works, Fenton	Fanshawe & Hughes
1882-1883	Chancery Lane China Works, Longton	Maddock, Ridge & Hughes
1883-1886	Peel Pottery, Longton	Massey, Wildblood & Co.
—	—	"& Co."(Edward Hughes one of many partners)
1883-1884	Chancery Lane China Works, Longton	Ridge & Hughes
1887-1894	— Unicorn Pottery, Longport, Burslem	Thomas Hughes (Jr.) acquires Davenport Ltd.
1888-1894	Globe Pottery, Cobridge	Hughes & Robinson
1889-1941	Opal China Works, Fenton	E. Hughes & Co.
1895-1910	Unicorn Pottery, Longport, Burslem	Thomas Hughes & Son
1910-1957	Unicorn Pottery, Longport, Burslem	Thomas Hughes & Son, Ltd.
1940-1953	Opal China Works, Fenton	Hughes (Fenton) Ltd.

HULME CHRONOLOGY: POTTERIES & PARTNERSHIPS

DATE	POTTERY	PARTNERSHIP
1814-1815	Shelton, Hanley	Hulme & Hammersley
1816-1818	King Street, Lane End, Longton	Lockett, Robinson & Hulme
1819-1826	King Street, Lane End, Longton	Lockett & Hulme
1822-1826	Chancery Lane, Lane End, Longton	Lockett & Hulme
1825-1827	High Street Works (Wm. Glass's Small Works), Hanley	Barlow, Ellis & Hulme
1827-1831*	Charles Street Works, Stafford Street, Lane End, Longton	John Hulme & Sons
1832-1841*	Charles Street Works, Stafford Street, Lane End, Longton	[John Hawley, son-in-law of John Hulme]
1834-1834	Central Pottery, Stafford Street, Longton	(James) Hulme & Hawley
1835-1838	Flint Street, Lane End, Longton	Broadhurst (James) Hulme & Bridgett
1839-1840	Flint Street, Lane End, Longton	Harris & (James) Hulme or (Hulme & Harris)
1841-1842	Flint Street, Lane End, Longton	James Hulme
1843-1847	Victoria Place, Longton	James Hulme
1851-1854	Central Pottery, Market Place, Burslem	Hulme & Booth
1854-1861	Central Pottery, Market Place, Burslem	Thomas Hulme
1881-1885	Central Pottery, Market Place, Burslem	Wilkinson & Hulme
1882-1882	Chadwick Street Works, Longton	Downs & Hulme
1882-1905	Garfield Pottery, Burslem	Wood & Hulme
1883-1886	Pell Works, Longton	Hulme & Massey or Massey, Wildblood & Co.
1886-1886	Belgrave Works, High Street, Longton	Blackhurst, Hand & Hulme
1886-1886	Belgrave Works, High Street, Longton	Cartlidge, Hand & Hulme
1887-1888	Belgrave Works, High Street, Longton	Blackhurst, Hulme & Berkin
1887-1892	Sutherland Pottery, Fenton	Forester (J. Booth) & Hulme
1889-1932	Belgrave Works, High Street, Longton	Blackhurst & Hulme
1891-1925 (1941)	Wedgwood Works, Burslem	William Hulme (Ltd.)
1893-1902	Sutherland Pottery, Fenton	Hulme & Christie
1906-1932	Garfield Pottery, Burslem	Henry Hulme & Sons
1925-1941	Wedgwood Works, Burslem	William Hulme (Burslem) Ltd.
1948-1954	Argyle Works, Cobridge	William Hulme

**Hampson*, No. 134, p. 89 notes that street descriptions varied, but were not limited to Great Charles Street, Flint Street and Stafford Street - all referring to the same location.

"J.B."

Attribution by initials alone, as noted by the potter James Beech, has and will continue to cause concern for ceramic historians and collectors alike. *Little*, p. 49, notes James Beech (1834-1845) as the possible potter for the "Texian Campaigne" (American War of 1846-1848), while *Larsen*, pp. 190-193, notes Anthony Shaw (1851-1881) as the potter of record due, in part, to the discovery of a specimen marked "A. SHAW". Thus, *Larsen* reasons that the initials "J.B." were that of the designer. The question one may ask is, is one example sufficient evidence for conclusive attribution? Isn't it possible that the potter "J.B." could have purchased additional blanks from another potter (a common practice)?

To add to this uncertainty and confusion, I cite the following selected examples of potters whose names may have been noted in the initial form of "J.B." In conclusion, in reviewing the Texian Campaigne (American War of 1846-1848), one could make a case for any potter from 1846 onwards as the potter of record. After all is said and done, *Larsen* may well have been correct.

POTTERS WITH THE INITIALS OF "J.B."

Date	Potter Name	Location	Date	Potter Name	Location
1759-1761	John Baddeley	Shelton	1840-1845	Joseph Booth	Longton
1770-1796	James Broadhurst	Longton	1842	James Booth	Lane End/ Longton
1784-1814	Joseph Boon	Hanley	1842-1860	J.&M.P.Bell & Co.	Glasgow
1784-1814	John Blackwell	Cobridge	1847-1851	Joseph Birch	Hanley
1786	Joseph Bourne	Burslem	1847-1853	James Broadhurst, I	Longton
1786	James Brindley	Stoke Upon Trent	1849-1858	John Bailey	Longton
1789-1805	John Brunton	Sunderland	1850-1858	James Beech	Longton
1795-1801	John Breeze	Burslem	1850-1860	Joseph Bourne & Sons, Ltd.	Derbyshire
1805	Joseph Booth	Hanley	1850-1883	John Bamford	Hanley
1806	John Brammer	Longton	1855-1865	James Beech, Jr.	Burslem
1810-1822	John Breeze	Tunstall	1860	James Bradshaw	Longton
1812-1834	James Bennett	Derbyshire	1860-1861	Joseph Barker	Longton
1818	Joseph Bradshaw	Cobridge	1860-1892	John Bevington	Hanley
1818	Joseph Burrow(s)	Fenton	1863-1870	James Broadhurst, II	Longton
1820s	Joseph Baggerley	Longton	1868	John Bebbington	Hanley
1822-1828	Joseph Burrows (Jr.)	Longton	1869-1880	John Bell	Glasgow
1822-1839	James Barlow	Hanley	1870	John Bridgwood, Jr.	Hanley
1826-1836	John Boyle	Hanley	1870-1894	James Broadhurst, II	Fenton
1828-1830	John Breeze	Tunstall	1872-1883	Jabez Blackhurst	Tunstall
1830-1850s	Joseph Brunt	Derbyshire	1878-89	James Beech	Tunstall
1833-1850	Joseph Bourne	Derbyshire	1880-1886	Jacob Baggaley	Burslem
1833-1861	John Boden	Tunstall	1882-1895	Joseph Ball	Longton
1837-1854	John Bagshaw	Tynside	1880s-1914	James Brown	Glasgow
1838-1845	James Beech	Tunstall	20th cent.	John Beswick	Longton
1839-1840	James Bridgett	Longton			

KEELING CHRONOLOGY: POTTERIES & PARTNERSHIPS

DATE	POTTERY	PARTNERSHIP
1765-1810	Enoch Booth's Pottery, Tunstall	Anthony Keeling
1781-1782	Keeling China Works, Hanley	Keeling, Turner, Hollins, Warburton & Co.
1781-1799	Keeling China Works, Hanley	Edward Keeling
1784-1789	Keeling China Works, Hanley	Anthony Keeling
1790-1832	New Street Pottery, Shelton	James Keeling
1792-1792	Keeling China Works, Hanley	Anthony Keeling & Co. (Keeling, Perry & Co.)
1792-1795	Enoch Booth's Pottery, Tunstall	Anthony Keeling & Son(s)
1795-1814	Enoch Booth's Pottery, Tunstall	Anthony & Enoch Keeling
1795-1814	Phoenix Works, Tunstall	Anthony & Enoch Keeling
1801-1824	Charles Street Pottery, Hanley	Keeling, Toft & Co. (Toft & Co.)
1802-1808	Keeling China Works, Hanley	Joseph Keeling
1807-1809	Keeling Works, Tunstall	Keeling & Ogilvy
1807-1811	—Shelton, Hanley	John Keeling
1811-1817	—Shelton, Hanley	Elizabeth Keeling
1822-1826	Broad St, Shelton, Hanley	Charles Keeling
1824-1837	Enoch Booth's Pottery, Tunstall	Keeling & Co. or (Keeling, Toft & Co.)
1826	—Shelton, Hanley	James & Charles Keeling
1827-1829	Charles Street Works, Hanley	Keeling, Toft & May
1834-1836	Market Street, (John Glass's Small Works), Hanley	Hackwood & Keeling
1840-1850	Market Street Works, Hanley	Samuel Keeling & Co.
1856-1863*	High Street, Longton	Keeling, Walker & Cooper
1862-1866*	Hope Street, Longton	Keeling, Walker & Cooper
1864-1866*	High Street, Longton	Keeling, Walker & Co.
1866-1872*	High Street, Longton	Keeling & Walker
1886-1988	Swan Bank Pottery, High Street, Burslem	Keeling & Co.
1887-1909	Dale Hall, Burslem	Keeling & Co.
1909-1936	Dale Hall, Burslem	Keeling & Co., Ltd.

For further reading, refer to *Godden, British Porcelain*, pp. 441-457; *Hampson* No. 163, pp. 104-105; *Godden*, *Collecting Lustreware*, p. 125; *Godden*, *British Porcelain* pp. 367-368; and *Little*, pp. 76-77.

*Note conflicting names, titles, and dates. Refer to *Godden, Collecting Lustreware* and *Hampson*.

LAKIN CHRONOLOGY: POTTERIES & PARTNERSHIPS

DATE	POTTERY	PARTNERSHIP
1791-1795	Hadderidge, Burslem	Lakin & Poole
1795-1795	Hadderidge, Burslem	Lakin, Poole & Shrigley
1795-1796	Hadderidge, Burslem	Poole, Shrigley & Lakin
1797-1799	Bournes Bank, Burslem	T. Lakin
1799-1810	Longport	Employed by Davenport
1810-1817	Thomas Wolfe's (& Co's) Pottery, Stoke-on-Trent	Lakin & Son or (Thomas Lakin (& Co.))
1815-1818	Stoke-on-Trent (Pottery Leased from Josiah Spode)	T. Lakin
1817-1818	Stoke-on-Trent	T. Lakin (Enamelers)
1818-1821	Yorkshire	Moves to Leeds Pottery
1821	Yorkshire	T. Lakin dies
1821-1824	Yorkshire	Succeeded by son

LOCKETT CHRONOLOGY: POTTERIES & PARTERNSHIPS

DATE	POTTERY	PARTNERSHIP
1796-1804	King Street Works #133, Lane End, Longton	Lockett(s) & Shaw (George & John [I] Lockett & George Shaw)
1805-1816	King Street, Lane End, Longton - John (I) & George Lockett - John (I) died in 1816	George Lockett (I) & Co. or Locketts & Co.
1816-1818	King Street, Lane End, Longton	Lockett (II), Robinson & Hulme
1819-1826	King Street & Chancery Lane (Lane End 1822-1858), Longton	Lockett (II) & Hulme (John)
1827-1835	King Street & Chancery Lane - John (II) died in 1835	John Lockett (II) & Son ("& Son" John Lockett (III))
1836-1858	King Street & Chancery Lane - UnionMarket Street Works acquired in 1842 from H. Simpkin - Thomas died in 1854	John Lockett (III) & Thomas (They are brothers)
1859-1877	King Street & Chancery Lane - UnionMarket Street Works acquired in 1842 from H. Simpkin - Thomas died in 1854	John Lockett (III)
1878(9)-1956	King Street, Longton - Firm continued by "Hancock family"	John Lockett & Co.
1956-1960 (+)	King Street, Longton - Factory demolished in 1960	Burgess & Leigh, Ltd. Acquire trade name and "good will"
	JOHN LOCKETT	
1855-1858	Chancery Lane, Lane End	John Lockett
1880-Present	King Street, Longton	John Lockett (& Co.)
	OTHER LOCKETTS	
1740-1780+	St. Ann's Street, Nottingham	William Lockett
- 1800	Waterloo Pottery, Holehouse, Burslem	Timothy & John Lockett
1855-1861	Victoria Works, Shelton, Hanley	Lockett, Baguley & Cooper
1861-1863	Royal Victoria Works, Shelton, Hanley	Lockett & Cooper
1861-1863	Victoria Works, Shelton, Hanley	Lockett & Cooper
1901-1919	Wellington Pottery, Hanley	William H. Lockett

For further reading, refer to *Godden, British Porcelain*, pp. 485-488; *Godden, Collecting Lustreware*, pp. 128-130; *Hampson*, pp. 106-112; and *Edwards, Basalt*, p. 190

MADDOCK CHRONOLOGY: POTTERIES & PARTNERSHIPS

DATE	POTTERY	PARTNERSHIP
1837-1839	Kilncroft Works, Sylvester Square, Burslem	Maddock & Edwards
1837-1839	Dale Hall Works, Burslem	Maddock & Edwards
1837-1839	Newcastle Street Works, Burslem	Maddock & Edwards
1839-1842	Newcastle Street Works, Burslem	Maddock & Seddon
1842-1855	Newcastle Street Works, Burslem	John Maddock
1855-1896	Dale Hall Works, Burslem	Maddock & Son(s) (Ltd.)
1855-1896 (1930)	Kilncroft Works, Sylvester Square, Burslem	Maddock & Son(s) (Ltd.)
1875	—, Burslem	Maddock & Gater
1881-1882	Chancery Lane China Works, Longton	Maddock & Ridge
1882-1883	Chancery Lane China Works, Longton	Maddock, Ridge & Hughes
1896-1987	Kilncroft Works, Sylvester Square, Burslem	Maddock & Sons (Ltd.)

MALING CHRONOLOGY: POTTERIES & PARTNERSHIPS

DATE	POTTERY	PARTNERSHIP
1762-1765	North Hylton Pottery, Sunderland Durhato - William dies in 1765	William Maling
1765-1815	North Hylton Pottery, Sunderland Durhato - Christopher Thompson died in 1810 - Pottery acquired by John Phillips (1815-1850) (See Sunderland/Garrison Pottery)	Christopher Thompson & John Maling
1815 (17)-1853 (59)	Ouseburn Bridge Pottery is built, Newcastle Upon-Tyne,Northumberland - Subsequenlty, Christopher Thompson (son of Robert Maling)	John Maling
1840s-1864	Old Ouseburn Pottery, Newcastle-Upon-Tyne, Northumberland, acquired - Robert Maling dies in 1863	Robert Maling
1853-1859	Ouseburn Bridge Pottery, Newcastle-Upon-Tyne, Maling Northumberland, taken over - Pottery acquired by Bell Bros. & renamed Albion Pottery	Christopher Thompson
1859-1878	- Builds Ford "A" Pottery, Ford Street Maling - Christopher Thompson Maling dies in 1901	Christopher Thompson
1878-1889	Ford "B" Pottery built Maling	Christopher Thompson
1889-1947	Ford "A" & "B" Pottery, Newcastle-Upon-Tyne, Northumberland - John Ford, Christopher Thompson & Frederick Theodore	C.T. Maling & Sons
1947-1963	Ford "A" & "B" Pottery, Newcastle-Upon-Tyne, Northumberland	C.T. Maling & Sons, Ltd.

MASON'S CHRONOLOGY: POTTERIES & PARTNERSHIPS

DATE	PARTNERSHIP	POTTERY
	MILES MASON	
1796	Thomas Wolfe & Co. - "& CO." = Miles Mason & John Lucock	Islington China Works, Liverpool
1796-1800	Wolfe (Geo.) & Mason (Miles)	Victoria Works, Lane Delph, Fenton
1800-1806	Miles Mason - of "Mason & Co."	Victoria Works, Lane Delph, Fenton
1806-1813	Miles Mason (& Son) - William Joins Firm	Minerva Works, Lane Delph, Fenton
1811-1816	Miles & William Mason - Miles seemingly retires in 1813 - Miles Mason acquires Bagnall's Pottery from William (1817-1822)	Sampson Bagnall's Works Lane Delph, Fenton
1813-1816	George & Charles take over Minerva Works	Minerva Works, Lane Delph, Fenton
1822	Miles Mason Dies	—
1822-1825	Estate Passes to Executors	—
	WILLIAM MASON	
1811-1813	Miles & William Mason (or Miles Mason & Son) - Miles Retires in 1813 and C.J. Mason continues firm.	Sampson Bagnall's Works, Lane Delph, Fenton
1817-1822	Miles Mason acquires Bagnall's Pottery from William	Sampson Bagnall's Works, Lane Delph, Fenton
1822-1824	William Mason	Fenton Stone Works, High Street, Lane Delph, Fenton
	G.M. & C.J. MASON	
1815-1826	G. & C. Mason - William is inactive partner	Fenton Stone Works, High Street, Lane Delph, Fenton
1825-1826	G. & C. Mason - George Retires in 1826	Sampson Bagnall's Works, Lane Delph, Fenton
1826-1845	C.J. Mason & Co.	Fenton Stone Works, High Street Lane Delph, Fenton
1841-1843	Mason (C.J.) & Faraday - Faraday dies in 1844	Fenton Stone Works, High Street Lane Delph, Fenton
1846-1848	Richard Daniel leases works (1846-1847) - Subsequently Samuel Boyle (& Son) (1849)	Fenton Stone Works, High Street, Lane Delph, Fenton
1848*	C.J. Mason Declared Bankrupt	—
1849-1851	C. J. Mason	Mill Street (Lane End), Longton
1851-1853	C. J. Mason Daisy Bank Works, - Subsequently, Hulse, Nixon & Adderley	(Lane End) Longton

MASON CHRONOLOGY (CONT.) SUCCEEDING FIRMS

DATE	PARTNERSHIP	POTTERY
1845-1850*	Francis Morley	Broad Street, Shelton, Hanley
1850-1858	Francis Morley & Co.	Broad Street, Shelton, Hanley
1858-1862	Francis Morley & Ashworth	Broad Street, Shelton, Hanley
1862-1968	G.L. Ashworth & Bros. (Ltd.)	Broad Street, Shelton, Hanley
1968-1973	Mason's Ironstone China, Ltd.	Broad Street, Shelton, Hanley
1973 -	Acquired by Wedgwood Group	Broad Street, Shelton, Hanley

*Francis Morley acquired a majority of the moulds, engravings and equipment prior to the April 1848 Auction Sale, thus enabling succeeding firms to match and reproduce his (Morley's) most successful patterns.

For further reading, refer to *Godden, Mason's*, pp. 126-133; *Hampson*, pp. 122-123, No. 179; Michael Berthoud, *H. & R. Daniel*, England, Micawber Publishing, 1980, pp. 31, 56; Gaye Lake Roberts. *Mason's The First Two Hundred Years*. London, England, Merrell Holberton Publishers, Ltd., 1996; and *The Raven Mason Collection, The Catalogue of the Collection at Keele University*, edited by Gaye Lake Roberts & John Twitchett, Keele University Press. 1997, Ch. 7, pp. 42-43.

MAYER CHRONOLOGY: POTTERIES & PARTNERSHIPS

Beginning with the early nineteenth century the name Mayer appears frequently in the history of Staffordshire potteries. There were numerous manufactories operated by potters of this name, many of whom were probably related.

DATE	POTTERY	PARTNERSHIP
1787-1800	Cobden Works, Hanley	Elijah Mayer
1800-1831	Cobden Works, High Street and Upper High Street, Hanley (Elijah Mayer died in 1813 but marking "& SON" continued until 1821)	Elijah Mayer "& Son"
1802-1802	Church Street or Lower Market Place, Lane End, Longton	John Forrester, II & Thomas Mayer
1809-1815	Keeling Lane, Hanley	Mayer & Hollins
1817-1832	Market Place, Caroline Street, Lane End, & Green Dock Works (from 1825), Longton	Mayer & Newbold
1821-1831	Cobden Works, Hanley	Joseph Mayer & Co. or (E. Mayer & Co.)
1822-1827	Upper High Street, Hanley	Joseph Mayer
1823-1825	High Street Works (Wm. Glass's Small Works), Hanley	John Mayer or (Mare)
1826-1835	Cliff Bank Works, Stoke	Thomas Mayer
1828-1828	Old Hall Street Pottery, Hanley	Mayer & Venable
1828-1829	Old Hall Street Pottery, Hanley	(Samuel) Mayer & Morris
1828-1831	Church Works, High Street, Hanley	Joseph Mayer & Co. or (E. Mayer & Co.)
1830-1845	Old Hall Street Pottery, Hanley	Samuel Mayer
1831-1833	Church Works, Hanley	Joseph Mayer & Co.
1832-1841	Foley Potteries, Fenton	John Mayer
1834-1841	Green Dock Works, Longton	John Mayer
1835-1838	Hope Street, Longport/Burslem	Thomas Mayer
1836-1838	Brook Street, Longport/Burlsem	Thomas Mayer
1837-1838	Pell Works, Longton	Mayer & Maudesley
1841	Dale Hall, Fountain Place, Longport, Burslem	Thomas & John Mayer or (Joseph Mayer & Co.)
1842-1855	Furlong Works & Dale Hall Works, Longport, Burslem	Thomas, John & Joseph Mayer
1855-1858	Dale Hall, Fountain Place, & Furlong Works Longport, Burslem	Mayer Bros. & Elliott
1858-1860	Dale Hall, Fountain Place, Longport, Burslem	Mayer & Elliott
1860-1870	Dale Hall, Fountain Place, Longport, Burslem	Liddle, Elliott & Son (Successors to Mayer)
1887-1887	Fenton	Challinor & Mayer
1906-1941	Clifton Works, Longton	Mayer & Sherratt (Manufacturers of Bone China)
1956-	Elton Pottery, Stoke	Thomas Mayer (Elton Pottery Ltd.)

N.B.: Mayer is a very complicated name, as dates and various partnerships overlap. (There is a similar problem with Godwin and Goodwin)
Refer to next Chronology, as *Williams-Wood* has conflicting dates.
For further reading on the Mayer potteries, refer to *Godden, Staffordshire*, pp. 520-524; *Godden, Collecting Lustreware*, p. 133; *Coysh*, Vol. 1; *Little*; and *Edwards, Basalt*, pp. 195-204. Note conflicting dates in *Williams-Wood, Pot Lids*, pp. 73-74.

MAYER *(WILLIAMS-WOOD) CHRONOLOGY: POTTERS & PARTNERSHIPS

DATE	POTTERY	PARTNERSHIP
1784	Cobden Works, Hanley	Elijah Mayer
1804	Cobden Works, Hanley	Joseph Mayer (oldest son) joins firm
1826-1835	Cliff Street Works, Stoke-on-Trent	Thomas Mayer
1833	Foley near Fenton	John Mayer
1835	—	Elijah Mayer dies
1835	—	Joseph Mayer continues firm as: (?) E. Mayer & Son 1820-1831 Joseph Mayer & Co.,Church St., Hanley (?) Mayer & Co.
1835	Brook Street, Longport, Burslem	Thomas Mayer
1836-1837	Dale Hall, Longport, Burslem	Thomas & John Mayer
1837-1856	Dale Hall, Longport, Burslem	T.J. & J. Mayer (3 brothers)
1857	—	Joseph Mayer dies and Liddle Elliott joins firm
1858-1862	—	Thomas Mayer retires and firm becomes Mayer & Elliott
1862	—	John Mayer dies and firm becomes Elliott Brothers
1862-1870	Dale Hall, Longport, Burslem	Firm is now Liddle Elliott (& Son), Dale Hall, Longport
1870-1875	Dale Hall, Longport, Burslem	Firm is now Bates Elliott & Co., Dale Hall, Longport

*Refer to *Williams-Wood, English Transfer*, pp. 74-75 for complete Chronology, as listed above.

MEAKIN CHRONOLOGY: POTTERIES & PARTNERSHIPS

DATE	POTTERY	PARTNERSHIP
1845-1845	Stafford Street, Lane End, Longton	(T) Meakin & Procter (or Proctor)
1845-1850	New Town Pottery, High Street, Longton	James Meakin
1848-1852	Cannon Street Pottery, Shelton	James Meakin
1850-1855	Cannon Street Pottery, Shelton	Meakin & Farrall or (L. H. Meakin & Co.)
1851-1970 (+)	Cannon Street Pottery 1851-1851 Market Street Pottery 1852-1859 Eagle Factory* 1859-1870 Eastwood Pottery 1889-1958 *Acquired by Wedgwood 1970+	J. & G. Meakin (Ltd.) - or Meakin Bros. (1852-1859)
1853-1855	Cannon Street, Shelton, Hanley	Lewis Meakin
1865-1882	Elder Road Works, Cobridge	Meakin & Co. (Also known as Meakin Bros. & Co.)
1870-1870	Litchfield Street, Hanley	Harry Meakin
1873-1876	Abbey Pottery, Cobridge	Henry Meakin
1875-1913	Royal Albert, Victoria & Highgate Potteries, Tunstall, Staffordshire	Alfred Meakin (Ltd.) "LTD." From 1897
1876-1882	Trent Pottery, Hanley, Burslem	Charles Meakin
1882-1882	Grove Street Pottery, Cobridge	Henry Meakin
1883-1889*	Eastwood Pottery, Hanley	Charles Meakin
1913-1974	Royal Albert, Victoria & Highgate Potteries (and The Newfield Pottery, acquired in 1930-1958), Tunstall	Alfred Meakin (Tunstall) Ltd.
1974+	As above	Acquired by Myott & Son Co. Ltd.

*Pottery acquired by J. & G. Meakin, Ltd. in 1889.
For further reading, refer to *Cameron*, p. 219. Also refer to Chronology for the Churchill Group.

MEIGH CHRONOLOGY: POTTERIES & PARTNERSHIPS

DATE	POTTERY	PARTNERSHIP
1790-1802	Old Hall Pottery, Hill Street, Hanley	Job Meigh (& Peter Walthall)
1802-1811	Old Hall Pottery, Hill Street, Hanley	Job Meigh
1803-1822	Broad Street, Shelton, Hanley	Hicks & Meigh
1806-1822	Albion Street Works, Shelton, Hanley	Hicks & Meigh
1812-1832	Old Hall Pottery, Hill Street, Hanley	Job Meigh & Son
1817	—	Job Meigh dies
1822-1835	Broad Street (High Street), Shelton, Hanley	Hicks, Meigh & Johnson or known as Hicks Meigh & Co. or Hicks & Co.
1832-1850	Old Hall Pottery, Hill Street, Hanley	Charles Meigh
1836-1836	Church Street, Lane End, Longton (Jan.-Sept.)	Meigh, Goodwin & Booth
1837-1837	Church Street, Lane End, Longton	Meigh & Booth (Sept.-)

1837-1838	Church Street, Lane End, Longton	Booth & Meigh
1850-1850	Old Hall Pottery, Hill Street, Hanley	Charles Meigh, Son & Pankhurst
1850-1861	Old Hall Pottery, Hill Street, Hanley	Charles Meigh & Son
1862-1886	Old Hall Pottery, Hill Street, Hanley	Old Hall Earthenware Co. (Ltd.)
1865	—	Charles Meigh Sr. dies
1867-1883	Melbourne Works, Church St., Longton	Ridge, Meigh & Co.
1883-1886	Melbourne Works, Church St., Longton	Meigh & Forester
1886-1902	Old Hall Pottery, Hill Street, Hanley	Old Hall Porcelain Works Co. (Ltd.)
1894-1899	Bridge Works, Stoke-on-Trent	W. & R. Meigh
1900	—	Charles Meigh Jr. dies

For further reading, refer to *Godden*, *Collecting Lustreware*, pp. 134-136; *Godden*, *Mason's*, pp. 265-266; and *Edwards*, *Basalt*, pp. 176-177.

MINTON CHRONOLOGY: PRINCIPALS & PARTNERSHIPS POTTERY IS LOCATED IN STOKE-ON-TRENT, STAFFORDSHIRE

DATE	PRINCIPAL	PARTNERSHIP
Thomas Minton purchased land in 1793 to build the Minton Factory.		
1796-1808	Thomas Minton	William Pownall (died 1814) and Joseph Poulson
1808-1817	Thomas Minton	William Pownall until 1814
1817-1823	Thomas Minton & Sons	Thomas Webb & Herbert join firm
1823-1836	Thomas Minton	Thomas Webb leaves to enter Church
1836-1841	Minton & Boyle	William Boyle
1841-1873	(Herbert) Minton & Co.	Includes family partnerships and period of Minton & Hollins (Hollins is nephew by marriage)
1845-1868	Minton & Hollins	Michael Hollins joins firm. In 1868 Hollins leaves to form his own company, Minton Hollins (& Co.)
1849-1873	Minton & Co.	Colin Minton Campbell (nephew) joins firm. In 1868 Colin gains control and Hollins forms his own company.
1873-1883	Minton	Under Colin Minton Campbell until 1885.
1883-1951	Mintons Ltd.	Colin Minton Campbell dies in 1885.
1951-Present	Minton	Acquired by Royal Doulton group in 1968.

For further reading, refer to *Godden*; *Godden, Staffordshire*, ch. 9, pp. 130-147; *Godden, British Porcelain*, pp. 532-533; *Godden, Collecting Lustreware*, pp. 136-137; *Coysh*, Vol. I, pp. 248-249 and Vol. 2, p. 138; *Jones*; and Howard Davis,' *Chinoiserie, Polychrome Decoration of Staffordshire Porcelain, 1790-1850.* London, Rubicom Press, 1991, pp. 88-199.

MOORE CHRONOLOGY: POTTERIES & PARTNERSHIPS

DATE	POTTERY	PARTNERSHIP
1805-1874	Wear Pottery, Southwick, Durham, Sunderland	(Samuel) Moore & Co.
1830-1858	St. Marys Works, Longton	Hamilton & Moore
1859-1861	Cauldon Place, Shelton, Hanley	Bates, Brown-Westhead & Moore
1859-1862	Mt. Pleasant Works, High Street, Longton	Samuel Moore (& Son)
1862-1872	St. Marys Works, Longton	Samuel Moore (& Son)
1872-1872	Bleak Hill Works, Burslem	Moore Bros.
1872-1905	St. Marys Works, Longton	Moore (Bros.)
1872-1892	Old Foley Pottery, King Street, Fenton	Moore & Co.
1892-1896	Old Foley Pottery, King Street, Fenton	Moore, Leason & Co.
1898-1903	Victoria Works, Hanley	(M) Moore & Co.
1905-1915 (20s)	Wolf Street, Stoke-on-Trent	Bernard Moore

For further reading, refer to *Godden*, pp. 446-448; *Godden, British Porcelain*, pp. 544-546; and *Hampson*, No. 125, p. 81.

NORTH SHORE POTTERY STOCKTON-ON-TEES, DURHAM CHRONOLOGY: PARTNERSHIPS

DATE	PARTNERSHIP
1845	James Smith (Brother of William Smith, Stafford Pottery) built North Shore Pottery
1845-1848	William Smith Jr. & Co. (Son of William Smith and nephew of James) operates North Shore Pottery
1848-1851	James Smith (Pottery managed by Thomas or Robert Ainsworth)
1851-1857	G.F. Smith & Co. (George Fothergill Smith, son of James Smith)
1857-1867	G. & W. Smith (George F. and William, sons of James Smith)
1867-1880	William Smith (North Shore Pottery closed permanently in 1882 and William Smith transferred to West Hartleford Pottery in 1880)

N.B.: Also refer to Chronology of Stafford/Thornaby Pottery, Stockton-on-Tees, Yorkshire.

In correspondence to me dated March 27, 1997, John Cockerill notes the following in regards to the North Shore Pottery:

> "William Smith, Jr. Was declared bankrupt in 1848 and nothing is known of him after this date.
>
> James Smith tried unsuccessfully to sell the pottery in 1848 and then employed either Thomas or Robert Ainsworth to manage the pottery until 1851, when his eldest son George Fothergill Smith attained the age of 21 and took over.
>
> In c. 1851 Thomas Ainsworth began the Stockton Pottery located about 200 yards from the North Shore Pottery and operated there, at first on his own then after his death, through his sons W.H. and J.H. Ainsworth, until c. 1900."

PLANT CHRONOLOGY: POTTERIES & PARTNERSHIPS

DATE	POTTERY	PARTNERSHIP
1797	Market Street, Lane End, Longton	John Plant
1801-1814	Lane End, Longton	Benjamin Plant
1825-1850	Lane End, Longton	Thomas Plant
1841-1841	—, Longton	Ephraim Plant
1853-1853	—, Longton	Plant & Hallem
1853-1855	Foley, Fenton	William Plant & Co.
1860-1860	Sheaf & George Street, Shelton, Hanley	Plant & Wild
1864-c.1866	New Market Works, Chancery Lane, Longton	Stubbs & (William) Plant
1874-1877	Waterloo Works, Shelton, Hanley	Holmes & Plant
1876-1876	Nile Street, Burslem	Holmes, Plant & Whithurst
1876-1885	Sylvester Pottery, Burslem	Holmes, Plant & Maydew
1880-1885	Heathcote Road Works, Longton	Johnson & Plant
1881-1898*	Carlisle Works, High Street, Longton	R.H. Plant & Co.
1882-1884	Clayton Street, Longton	J. Plant & Co.
1889-1893	Stoke Pottery, Stoke-on-Trent	J.R. Plant
1889-1898*	Crown Pottery, Burslem	Plant Bros.
1889-1907*	Stanley Works, Bagnell Street, Longton	Plant Bros.
1892-1898	New Hall Works, Shelton, Hanley	Plant & Gilmore
1893-1900	Stoke Pottery, Stoke-on-Trent	J. Plant & Co.
- 1895	Warwick China Works, Longton	Plant & Baggaley
1895-1901	Warwick China Works, Longton	R. Plant & Sons
1898-1905*	Crown Pottery, Burslem	Enoch Plant
1898-1915*	Tuscan Works, Forrester Street, Longton	R.H. & S.L. Plant
1915-1970	Tuscan Works, Forrester Street, Longton	R.H. & S.L. Plant, Ltd.

*Merged with R.H. & S.L. Plant in 1898.

For further reading, refer to *Hampson*, No. 199-202, p. 132-133; and *Godden, Collecting Lustreware*, pp. 142-143.

POUNTNEY (BRISTOL POTTERY) CHRONOLOGY: POTTERIES & PARTNERSHIPS

DATE	**POTTERY**	**POTTER**
1784	Bristol Pottery	Joseph Ring
1797	Bristol Pottery	Henry Carter
1798-1805	Bristol Pottery	Ring & Carter or Joseph Ring & Co.
1805-1813	Bristol Pottery	Henry Carter & Co.
1813-1815	Bristol Pottery	Carter & Pountney
1816-1835	Bristol Pottery	Pountney & Allies
1836-1836	Bristol Pottery	John D. Pountney
1837-1850	Bristol Pottery	Pountney & Goldney
1851-1853	Bristol Pottery	John D. Pountney
1854-1857	Bristol Pottery	John D. Pountney & Co.

1858-1858	Bristol Pottery	Pountney, Edward & Co.
1859-1888	Bristol Pottery & Victoria Pottery	Pountney & Co.
1889-1962	Victoria Pottery	Pountney & Co. Ltd.
	ACQUISITIONS FROM 1958 - 1985	
1958	Purchased Cauldon Potteries, Ltd.	
1962	Name changes to Cauldon Bristol Potteries Ltd.	
1985	Acquired by Perks Ceramic Group, Yorkshire	
1985	Names changes to Cauldon Potteries, Ltd.	
	LOCATION OF POTTERIES	
1784-1885	Bristol Pottery, Water Lane, Temple Backs	
1873-1906	Victoria Pottery, Feeder Rd., St. Philips Marsh	
1891-1906	Crown Pottery, St. George	
1906-1969	New pottery was built at Causeway Fish Ponds	
1969-	Pottery moved to Redruth, Cornwall	

RIDGWAY CHRONOLOGY: POTTERIES & PARTNERSHIPS

DATE	POTTERY	PARTNERSHIP
1792-1797	Bell Works, Hanley	Job & George Ridgway
1797-1798	Bell Works, Hanley	Ridgway, Smith & Ridgway
1798-c.1801	Bell Works, Hanley	Job & George Ridgway
1802-1808	Cauldon Place, Shelton, Hanley	Job Ridgway
1802-1813	Bell Works, Hanley	George Ridgway (& Sons)
1808-1813	Cauldon Place, Shelton, Hanley	Job Ridgway & Sons
1813-1830	Bell Works, Hanley	John & William Ridgway
1813-1830	Cauldon Place, Shelton, Hanley	J. Ridgway & Co. or J. & W. Ridgway & Co.
1830-1849	Charles Street Works, Hanley	William Ridgway
1830-1854	Bell Works, Hanley	William Ridgway (& Co.) (& Co. from 1834)
1830-1855	Cauldon Place, Shelton, Hanley	John Ridgway (& Co. from 1841)
1835-1860	Church Works, Hanley	Ridgway & Abington
1836-1842	Broad Street, Shelton, Hanley	Ridgway, Morley, Wear & Co.
1837-1840	Hanley	Ridgway & Robey
1838-1845	Church Works, Hanley	William Ridgway Son & Co.
1838-1845	Cobden Works, Shelton, Hanley	William Ridgway Son & Co.
1842-1845	Broad Street, Shelton, Hanley	Ridgway & Morley
1855-1858	Cauldon Place, Shelton, Hanley	Ridgway, Bates & Co.
1858	—	(John Ridgway retires)
1860-1872	Church & Cobden Works, Hanley	E.J. Ridgway (& Son) (& Son from 1867-1872)
1872-1878	Bedford Works, Shelton, Hanley	Ridgway, Sparks & Ridgway
1878-1920	Bedford Works, Shelton Hanley	Ridgways
1920-1952	Bedford Works, Shelton, Hanley	Ridgways (Bedford Works) Ltd.
1947-1964	Daisy Bank Works, Stoke	Ridgway Potteries Ltd.
1954	Hanley, Staffordshire	Ridgway, Adderly, Booth & Colclough, Ltd.

It would appear that patterns were continued and/or reissued by the various potters, and may appear more than once, but with differing marks.
For additional partnerships, titles and reading refer to *Godden*, *Ridgways*, pp. 51-53; *Godden*; and *Godden*, *Collecting Lustreware*, pp. 146-148

ROBINSON CHRONOLOGY: POTTERIES & PARTNERSHIPS

DATE	POTTERY	PARTNERSHIP
1760-1763	Briggate Leeds, Yorkshire	Robinson & Rhodes
1784-1787	Kilnhurst Bridge Pottery, Yorkshire, Kilnhurst	Robinson, Newton, Malpass, Hawkes & Ledger
1786-1818(22)	Hill Works, Burslem	John Robinson (& Sons from 1818)
1787-1795	Kilnhurst Bridge Pottery, Yorkshire, Kilnhurst	Newton & Robinson
1815-1819	Waterloo Pottery, Longton	Robinson & Rowley
1816-1818	King Street, Longton	Lockett, Robinson & Hulme
1819-1820	High Street, Longton	John Robinson
1821-1824	High Street, Longton	Robinson, Ash & Ball or (Robinson, Ash & Co.)
1822-1823	High Street, Longton	Robinson, Ash, Ball & Goodwin
1822-1827	Hill Works, Burslem	John Robinson, Jr.
1822-1834	Commerce Street, Longton	Chetham & Robinson
1825-1840	Lane End, Longton	Chesworth & Robinson
1826-1827	High Street, Longton	Noah Robinson
1827-1838	Great Charles Street & George Street, Longton	Faulkner & Robinson
1832-1836	Broad Street, Shelton, Hanley	Robinson & Wood
1834-1840	Commerce Street, Longton	Chetham, Robinson & Son
1837-1837	Cobridge Works, Cobridge	Robinson, Wood & Brownfield
1837-1841	Cobridge Works, Cobridge	Wood & Brownfield
1840-1842	Robinsons or Jack Lane Pottery, Hunslet, Yorkshire	Cooper, Hardy & Robinson
1841-1843	New Street or City Road, Longton	Robinson & Dale
1842-1848	Robinsons or Jack Lane Pottery, Hunslet, Yorkshire	Hardy & Robinson
1848-1866	Robinsons or Jack Lane Pottery, Hunslet, Yorkshire	William Robinson
1853-1863	King Street, Foley China Works, Foley, Fenton	Robinson, Stubbs & Hudson or (Robinson, Stubbs & Co.)
1857-1861	Soil Hill Pottery, Ovenden, Halifax, Yorkshire	James Robinson
1858-1858	Church Street, Longton	Flackett, Toft & Robinson
1862-1863	Wellington Works, Longton	(G.L.) Robinson & Cooper
1862-1924	Globe Street & Wharf Street Works, (from 1870-1924)	Robinson & Leadbeater (Ltd.) Stoke-on-Trent
1863-1863	Stafford Street, Wellington Works, Longton	(G.L.) Robinson & Cooper
1863-1870	Stafford Street, Wellington Works, Longton	Robinson & Son
1864-1867	Foley China Works, King Street, Foley, Fenton	Robinson, Hudson & Co.
1866-1896	Robinsons or Jack Lane Pottery, Hunslet, Yorkshire	William Robinson & Sons
1868-1869	Overshouse Works, Burslem	Robinson, Kirkham & Co.
1868-1872	Foley China Works, King Street, Foley, Fenton	Robinson & Hudson
1870-1876	Stafford Street, Wellington Works, Longton	Robinson, Repton & Robinson
1872-1875	Royal Porcelain Works, Longton	Robinson Chapman & Co. (or Robinson & Co.)
1872-1888	Foley China Works, King Street, Foley, Fenton	W. Robinson & Co. (or Robinson & Co.)
1875-1881	Royal Porcelain Works, Longton	Robinson & Chapman
1876-1879	Stafford Street, Wellington Works, Longton	Robinson & Repton
1876-1898	Knowle Works, Burslem	Joseph Robinson
1879	Sutherland Road, Longton	G.A. Robinson
1881-1903	Foley China Works, Foley, Fenton & Wellington Works (1863-1879), Longton	Robinson & Son
1882-	Victoria Pottery, Stoke	Robinson, Leadbeater & Leason
1888-1894	Globe Pottery, Cobridge	Hughes & Robinson
1895-1903	Sheriff Hill Pottery, Gateshead, Tyneside	Robinson, Gray & Burns
1897-1902	Castleford & Allerton Potteries, Castleford, Yorkshire	Robinson Bros.
1901-1901	Albion Street, Baltimore Works, Longton	Robinson & Jones
1901-1904	Albion Street, Baltimore Works, Longton	W.H. Robinson
1901-1907	Albion Street, Baltimore Works, Longton	Robinson & Beresford
1902-1933	Castleford & Allerton Potteries, Castleford, Yorkshire	John Robinson & Son
1905-	Wharf Street, Stoke	Frederick Robinson
1905-1924	Globe & Wharf Street Works, Stoke-on-Trent	Robinson & Leadbeater, Ltd.
1910-1932	Alexander China Works, Stoke & Cannon Street, Hanley	J.A. Robinson & Sons, Ltd.

For further reading, refer to *Chaffers*; *Jewitt*; *Little*; *Hampson*; and *Bell*.

SPODE, COPELAND & GARRETT, COPELAND CHRONOLOGY: PARTNERSHIPS

DATE	COMPANY	POTTERY
1761	Josiah Spode I, self employed	Shelton
1767-1779	Josiah Spode I and Tomlinson	Stoke
1772-1779	Josiah Spode I and Mountford	Shelton
1774-1797	Josiah Spode I	Stoke
1797-1827	Josiah Spode II	Stoke
1827-1829	Josiah Spode III	Stoke
1829-1833	Under Trusteeship of Hugh Henshall Williamson & Thomas Fenton	Stoke
1833-1847	Copeland & Garrett	Stoke
1847-1867	William Taylor Copeland (W.T. Copeland)	Stoke
1867-1932	W.T. Copeland & Sons (Copelands)	Stoke
1932-1966(70)	W.T. Copeland & Sons Ltd.	Stoke
1966(70)-1976	Spode Ltd.	Stoke
1976-1983	Royal Worcester Spode Ltd.	Stoke
1983-1984	Crystalate PLC	Stoke
1984-1988	London Rubber Co.	Stoke
1988(+)	Derby International Co.	Stoke
1989	(named) The Porcelain & Fine China Companies Ltd.	Stoke
	London Retail Business Partnership Periods 1805-1833	
1805-1811	William Spode & Co. (& Co.-Wm. Copeland)	London
1812-1823	Spode & Copeland (Spode II & Wm. Taylor Copeland)	London
1824-1826	Spode, Copeland & Son (& Son - Wm. Taylor Copeland)	London
1826-1833	Spode & Copeland (Spode II & Wm. Taylor Copeland)	London

STAFFORD POTTERY, THORNABY/STOCKTON-ON-TEES, YORKSHIRE CHRONOLOGY: POTTERIES & PARTNERSHIPS

DATE	POTTERY	PARTNERSHIP
1825-1826	Stafford Pottery	William Smith
1826-1855	Stafford Pottery	William Smith & Co.
1855-1870	Stafford Pottery	George Skinner & Co.
1860-1875	Stafford Pottery	Skinner, Parrington & Walker
1870-1877	Stafford Pottery	Skinner, Walker & Co.
1877-1890	Stafford Pottery	Ambrose Walker & Co.
1891-1900	Stafford Pottery	Ambrose Walker & Co., Ltd.
1901-1909	Stafford Pottery	Thornaby Pottery Co. Ltd.

N.B.: Also refer to Chronology for North Shore Pottery. For further reading, refer to *Lawrence*, pp. 212-213; and *Godden, Collecting Lustreware*, p. 264 wherein Mr. Godden notes the dates for Skinner & Walker as 1870-1880.

In correspondence to me dated March 27, 1997, John Cockerill noted the following in regards to the Stafford Pottery:

> "In all probability, William Smith was in partnership with William Skinner, Jr. and George Skinner (Stockton bankers) from the outset but the formal partnership agreement is dated 1826.
>
> William Smith probably left the partnership about 1855 but the legal agreement setting out the terms of his leaving is dated 1860.
>
> George Skinner and William Skinner, Jr. became the dominant partners in 1843 following a major financial rearrangement, but W. Smith continued to be a partner.
>
> Parrington and Walker were mortgagees of the pottery but so far as I know were never owners or operators.
>
> George Skinner died in 1870. His daughters, as his executors, were in partnership with Ambrose Walker until 1877 when he bought them out.
>
> Ambrose Walker died in 1890 but the pottery continued to trade as Ambrose Walker Co. Ltd. with his son Thomas Speck Walker as managing director.
>
> By 1901 the company name had changed to the Thornaby Pottery Co. Ltd. and it continued to operate until 1909.
>
> In 1912 the premises were sold to the local council for use as a depot."

STEVENSON (ANDREW/JOSEPH/RALPH) OF COBRIDGE CHRONOLOGY: POTTERIES & PARTNERSHIPS

DATE	POTTERY	PARTNERSHIP
	ANDREW (c.1799-1836)	
1806-1811	Cobridge Works, Cobridge	J. & A. Stevenson
1811-1816	Cobridge Works, Cobridge	Stevenson & Bucknall
1816-1836	Cobridge Works, Cobridge	Andrew Stevenson
	RALPH STEVENSON (c.1799-1835+)	
1799-1800	Lower Manufactory, Cobridge	Ralph Stevenson & Co.
1800-1802	Upper & Lower Manufactory, Cobridge	Stevenson & Dale
1802-1804	Upper & Lower Manufactory, Cobridge	Stevenson, Godwin & Dale
1804-1810	Upper & Lower Manufactory, Cobridge	Stevenson & Godwin
1810-1833	Lower Manufactory, Cobridge	Ralph Stevenson
1820-1826	Elder Road Pottery, Cobridge	Ralph Stevenson & Samuel Alcock
1825-1827	Elder Road Pottery &Lower Manufactory, Cobridge	Stevenson & Williams
1828-1828	Elder Road Pottery, Cobridge	Alcock & Stevenson
1833-1835(+)	Lower Manufactory, Cobridge	Ralph Stevenson & Son

N.B. Andrew & Ralph Stevenson are not to be confused with James Stevenson of the Greenock-Clyde Pottery-Ladyburn Pottery. For further reading, refer to *Godden, British Porcelain*, pp. 710-712 and *Godden, Collecting Lustreware*, pp. 158-159.

SWAN BANK POTTERY - TUNSTALL CHRONOLOGY: POTTERIES & PARTNERSHIPS

DATE	POTTERY	PARTNERSHIP
1811-1822	Swan Bank Pottery, High Street, Tunstall	Ralph & John Hall
1822-1835	Swan Bank Pottery, High Street, Tunstall	Ralph Hall
1836-1841	Swan Bank Pottery, High Street, Tunstall	Ralph Hall & Son
1841-1849	Swan Bank Pottery, High Street, Tunstall	Ralph Hall & Co. (or Hall & Holland)
1853-1859	Swan Bank Pottery, High Street, Tunstall	Podmore Walker & Co.
1860-1862	— Church Bank Works, Tunstall	Beech & Hancock
1862-1876	Swan Bank Pottery, High Street, Tunstall	Beech & Hancock
1878-1889	Swan Bank Pottery, High Street, Tunstall	James Beech
1889-1899	Swan Bank Pottery, High Street, Tunstall	Boulton, Machin & Tennant
1912-1948	Swan Bank Pottery, High Street, Tunstall	Booths, Ltd.

N.B.: Also see Hall and Sytch Pottery, Burslem, in this Chronology.

SWANSEA CAMBRIAN POTTERY (WALES) c.1764-1870 CHRONOLOGY: POTTERIES & PARTNERSHIPS

DATE	COMPANY NAME	PARTNERSHIP
1764-1786	—	Stoneware Pottery founded
1786-1802	Cambrian Pottery	George Haynes, under various partnerships
1802-1810	Dillwyn & Co.	Haynes, Dillwyn & Co.
1810-1811	L.W. Dillwyn & Co.	Lewis Weston Dillwyn - sole proprietor
1811-1817	Dillwyn & Co.	L.W. Dillwyn & Bevington & Son (with others) form partnership
1817-1821	T.J. Bevington & Co.	Timothy & John (son) and others are partners in Cambrian Pottery (leased by Bevington(s) from Dillwyn)
1821-1825	T. & J. Bevington	(Other partners are out) Company dissolves and lease continued on own with Timothy & John Bevington
1825	—	T.&J. Bevington partnership dissolves
1825-1831	Dillwyn & Co.	Pottery reverted back to L.W. Dillwyn
1831-1836	Dillwyn & Co.	Dillwyn re-acquires firm and Lewis Llewellyn Dillwyn (younger son) joins firm
1836-1850	Dillwyn & Co.	Lewis Llewellyn acquires firm
1850-1852	Evans & Glasson	Evans & Glasson acquire pottery
1852	Evans & Glasson	Glasson dies
1852-1861	Evans & Glasson	D.J. Evans joins father's firm
1861(62)-1870	D.J. Evans & Co.	D.J. Evans acquires full control

For further reading, refer to the *Catalog of the Sir Leslie Joseph Collection Sale by Sotheby's*, May 1992; *Pryce*; *Little*, pp. 111-112; Gareth Hughes & Robert Pugh. *Llanelly Pottery*. Llanelli Borough Council. Llanelli, Wales, 1990; *Edwards, Basalt*, pp. 131-134; *Pugh, Welsh Pottery*, pp. 5-33 for history and marks; Kildare S. Meager, *Swansea and Nantgarw Potteries*. Swansea, Swansea Corp., 1949; *Hallesy; and Nance*, pp. 166-167, 171, 174-175 and plates LXXII and LXXVI for comments on Flow Blue.

SYTCH POTTERY - BURSLEM CHRONOLOGY: POTTERIES & PARTNERSHIPS

DATE	POTTERY	PARTNERSHIP
1802-1814	Sytch Pottery, Liverpool Road, Burslem	John & Ralph Hall
1810-1822	Sytch Pottery, Liverpool Road, Burslem	John Heath
1814-1822	Sytch Pottery, Liverpool Road, Burslem	John Hall
1822-1832	Sytch Pottery, Liverpool Road, Burslem	John Hall & Sons
1834-1846	Sytch Pottery, Liverpool Road, Burslem	Barker, Sutton & Till
1836-1841	Sytch Pottery, Liverpool Road, Burslem	R. Hall & Sons
1846-1850	Sytch Pottery, Liverpool Road, Burslem	Barker & Till
1850-1928	Sytch Pottery, Liverpool Road, Burslem	Thomas Till & Son(s) (Ltd.)

N.B.: Also see Hall and Swan Bank Pottery, Tunstall, in this Chronology.

TILL CHRONOLOGY: POTTERIES & PARTNERSHIPS

DATE	POTTERY	PARTNERSHIP
1822-1822	Thomas Shelley's Works, High Street, Longton	Hammersley & Till
1824-1827	Jacksons Works, High Street, Longton	Edgerton, Till & Co.
1834-1846	Sytch Pottery, Liverpool Road, Burslem	Barker, Sutton & Till
1846-1850	Sytch Pottery, Liverpool Road, Burslem	Barker & Till
1850-1928	Sytch Pottery, Liverpool Road, Burslem	Thomas Till & Son(s) (Ltd.)
1859-1860	Alma Place China Works, Foley, Longton	Till, Bourne & Brown
1868-1868	Stafford Street & King Street, Longton	Barker & Hill
1872-1873	New Street, Longton	Beech, Cooper, Till & Co.
1873-1877	New Street, Longton	Coopers, Till & Co.

1873-1873	Commonside Pottery, Church Gresley, Derbyshire	Masons, Grough & Till
1874-1883	Commonside Pottery, Church Gresley, Derbyshire	Till & Grough
1884-1895	Commonside Pottery, Church Gresley, Derbyshire	J. Till
1904-1933	Brownhill's China Works, Tunstall	Till & Sons (1904)

TURNER CHRONOLOGY: POTTERIES & PARTNERSHIPS

DATE	POTTERY	PARTNERSHIP
1756-1762	—, Stoke	Turner & Banks
1762-1781	Upper Works, Market & Uttoxeter Road, Lane End, Longton	John Turner (I)
1762-1781	Lower Works, Market & Kingcross Street, Lane End, Longton	John Turner (I)
1781-1787	Lower Works, Market & Kingcross Street, Lane End, Longton	Turner & Abbott (Also Turner & Co.)
1787-1801	Lower Works, Market & Kingcross Street, Lane End, Longton	Turners, Abbott & Newbury
1790s-1798	Kilnhurst Old Pottery, Yorkshire	Turner & Co.
1792-1803	Lower Works, Market & Kingcross Street, Lane End, Longton	John & William Turner
1796-1803	Works No's 136 & 138, Lane End, Longton	William & John Turner (II) (Also Turner & Co.)
1798-1808	Kilnhurst Old Pottery, Yorkshire	Turner & Hawley (Thomas)
1803-1804	Lower Works, Market & Kingcross Street, Lane End, Longton	Turner, Glover & Simpson
1804-1806	Lower Works, Market & Kingcross Street, Lane End, Longton	Turners, Glover & Simpson
1806-1813	Kilnhurst Old Pottery, Yorkshire	Turner & Hawley (Phillip)
1807-1812	Foley Works, Lane Delph, (Joseph Myatt Works) Lane Delph, Fenton	William Turner (& Co.)
1814-1814	Nr. Longton Town Hall, Lane End, Longton	John Turner (II)
1824-1829	High Street Works, (William Waller's Works) Lane End, Longton	William Turner
1830	Church Street (Widow Garners Works?) Longton	John Turner (IV)
1859-1862	Albert Works, Liverpool Road, Stoke-on-Trent	Turner, Hassall & Bromley or (Bromley, Turner & Co.)
1860-1872	Victoria Works, High Street, Tunstall	Turner & Tomkinson
1863-1871	Copeland Street Works, Stoke-on-Trent	Turner, Hassall & Peake (or Turner & Co.)
1867-1868	New Biggins Pottery, Scotland	James Turner
1867-1874	Royal Albert Pottery, Tunstall	Turner, Goddard & Co.
1869-1871	Copeland Street Works, Stoke-on-Trent	Turner, Hassall Peake & Poole
1871-1872	Copeland Street Works, Stoke-on-Trent	Turner, Hassall & Poole
1873-1873	Copeland Street Works, Stoke-on-Trent	Turner, Poole & Stanway
1873-1895	Victoria Works & Alexander Works, High Street, Tunstall	G.W. Turner & Sons
1878-1888	Copeland Street Works, Stoke-on-Trent	Turner & Wood
1879	Stepny Lane, Yorkshire	Turner & Rhodes

WALKER CHRONOLOGY: POTTERIES & PARTNERSHIPS

DATE	POTTERY	PARTNERSHIP
1757-1765	Lowestoft Porcelain Factory, Suffolk	Walker & Co.
1765-1799	Lowestoft Porcelain Factory, Suffolk	Walker & Brown(e)
1772	Rotherham, Yorkshire	Walker (& Son)
1807-1809	Keeling Works, Tunstall	Keelings & Ogilvy
1834-1856(59)	Well Street (1834-1853), Newfield Potters (1848-1853), Unicorn Pottery, Amicable Street (1850-1895), Swan Bank Pottery (1853-1859), Tunstall	Podmore, Walker & Co. (Podmore, Walker & Wedgwood)
1840-1845	Church Street, Lane End, Longton Walker & Broadhurst	Batkin (Thomas Henry)
1844-1851	Carr's Hill Pottery, Warburton's Place, Tynside	Kendall & Walker
1845-1856	Lion Works, Tunstall	Thomas Walker
1846-1848	Church Street, Longton	Thomas & H(Henry) Walker
1853-1858	Victoria Place, Longton	(Thomas) Walker & Finney
1856-1863*	High Street, Longton	Keeling, (John) Walker & Cooper
1858-1864	British Anchor Pottery, Longton	Malkin, (Thomas) Walker & Hulse
1860-1875	Stafford Pottery, Thornaby, Stockton-on-Tees, Yorkshire	Skinner, Parrington & Walker
1864-1865	British Anchor Pottery, Longton	Walker (Thomas) & Bateman & Co.
1866-1872*	High Street, Longton	Keeling, (John) Walker & Co.
1866-1872	British Anchor Pottery, Longton	Walker (Thomas) & Carter
1870-1880	Stafford Pottery, Thornaby, Stockton-on-Tees, Yorkshire	Skinner, Walker & Co.
1872-1880	High Street, Longton	John Walker
1872-1889	Anchor Works, Stoke-upon-Trent	Walker (Thomas) & Carter
1875-1878	Dale Hall Works, Burslem	Bates, Walker & Co.
1877-1880	Bleak Hill Works, Burslem	Podmore Walker
1878-1881	Dale Hall Works, Burslem	Bates, Gildea & Walker
1880-1900	Stafford Pottery, Thornaby, Stockton-on-Tees, Yorkshire	Ambrose Walker & Co. (Ltd.)
1881-1885	Dale Hall Works, Burslem	Gildea & Walker (& Co.)

*See Chronology for Keeling

For information on Platt & Walker, (Samuel) Walker (& Son), William Walker, and Walker & Nash refer to *Godden, Jewitt*; and for further reading on Skinner & Walker, Stafford Pottery, Stockton, refer to *Godden, Jewitt,* pp. 222-223; (also refer to this section under Stafford Pottery) and *Godden, British Porcelain*, pp. 714-715.

WALLEY CHRONOLOGY: POTTERIES & PARTNERSHIPS

DATE	POTTERY	PARTNERSHIP
1813-1813	—, Shelton, Hanley	John Walley
1815-1818	—, Tunstall, Staffordshire	Nixon & Walley (George)
1818-1822	—, Tunstall, Staffordshire	George Walley
1841	Flint Street, Longton	George Walley
1841-1842	Marsh Street, Shelton, Hanley	William Walley
1841-1845	Villa Pottery, Cobridge	Jones (Elijah) & Edward Walley
1845*	Burslem, Cobridge & Hanley	T.R. Boote, Walley (Edward) & Elijah Jones
1845**	Cobridge & Burslem	Walley (Edward) & T.R. Boote
1845-1856	Villa Pottery, Cobridge	John Walley
1845-1858	Villa Pottery, Cobridge	Edward Walley
1850-1867	High Street, Burslem	John Walley
1853-1864	Hope Street, Hanley	John Walley
1854-1854	Market Street, Tunstall	John Walley
1858-1862	Villa Pottery, Cobridge	Edward Walley & Son (William) or (E. W. Walley)
1898-1901	Knowles Works, Burslem	Woolridge & Walley

* Shared registry design, April 26, 1845

**Shared registry design, May 10, 1845

N.B.: See *Lawrence*, pp. 212-213 wherein a Staffordshire potter, John Walley, is mentioned in partnership with William Smith, c. 1825-1855 as "William Smith & Co.", Stafford Pottery, Thornaby, Stockton-on-Tees. Walley continued on renting until c. 1860. This Walley should not be confused with John Walley of Burslem.

DIFFERENTIATING WEDGWOOD

Confusion abounds when it comes to the name Wedgwood. No less than six potters have used this name on their wares. Mis-cataloging has further added to the confusion, as well as the fact that copying and capitalizing on this famous name was not beyond other potters of the period. Refer to Hampson, No. 1, p. 1 re: Wedgewood & Ackerley and Wedgwood & Co.

It is hoped that the simplified name listing below, with the addition of Godden's reference numbers, should assist the reader. (As a further guide, I have underlined important criteria for clarification.)

Markings	Type of Mark	Godden #	Pottery & Partnership	Dates
WEDGWOOD & CO.	Impressed	1539	Knottingly Pottery Partners-Tomlinson, (Ralph) Wedgwood, Foster & Co. (From 1804 pottery was named Ferrybridge Pottery)	1798-1801(4)
W.S. & CO' S WEDG*E*WOOD	Printed or Impressed	3598	William Smith & Co. Injunction of 1848 prohibited usage of name	1825-1855
J. WEDG*.*WOOD WEDG WOOD	Printed	4276B	John Wedge Wood (Capitalized on the famous name) (note the space between G & W) Pottery continued by brother, Edmund T. Wood	1841-1857(75)
WEDG*E*WOOD & CO.	Impressed		—	(1857-1875)
WEDGWOOD	Printed	3078	Podmore, Walker &Co. (or Podmore, Walker & Wedgwood)	1856-1859

WEDGWOOD & CO	Printed	3079	The "& CO. was Enoch Wedgwood. Company retitled Wedgwood & Co. (Ltd.)	(1860-1965).
WEDGWOOD & CO.	Printed	4055	Wedgwood & Co. Many marks and patterns continued	1860-1895
WEDGWOOD & CO.	Printed or Impressed Trademark	4056	from Podmore Walker & Co.	
WEDGWOOD	Impressed	4073-5	Josiah Wedgwood	*1759+*
WEDGWOOD*S*	Printed	4084		1827-1861
WEDGWOOD	Impressed	4086-7	Additional Marks: ETRURIA or PEARL,	1840-1868

PROPRIETORS OF WEDGWOOD

DATE	PROPRIETOR
1759	Josiah Wedgwood I
1766-1788	Josiah I and Thomas Wedgwood
1768-1780	Josiah I and Thomas Bentley
1790	Josiah I, his sons John, Josiah II and Thomas Wedgwood, and Thomas Byerley
1793	Josiah I, Josiah II and Thomas Byerley
1795	Josiah II and Thomas Byerley
1800	Josiah II, John Wedgwood and Thomas Byerley
1811	Josiah II
1823	Josiah II and Josiah III
1827	Josiah II with his sons Josiah III and Francis
1841	Josiah III and Francis
1841	Francis
1843	Francis and John Boyle
1845	Francis and Robert Brown
1859	Francis & son Godfrey
1863	Francis with his sons Godfrey and Clement Francis
1868	Francis with his sons Godfrey, Clement Francis and Lawrence
1870	Godfrey with his brothers Clement Francis and Lawrence
1891	Lawrence with his nephews Cecil and Francis Hamilton
1895	Incorporation as Josiah Wedgwood & Sons Ltd.
1919-1955	Overseas companies formed in America, Canada, Australia
1967	Registration as a public company
1986	Acquired by Waterford Glass; titled Waterford, Wedgwood, Plc.

For further reading, refer to *Reilly*, *Wedgwood*. 1995, pp. 352-353 and 501-502, as well as the 1980 edition, p. 290.

WEDGWOOD GROUP FORMED (AS PUBLIC COMPANY) 1966 COMPANIES ACQUIRED (1966-1979)

	DATE	NAME OF COMPANY
1.	—	Josiah Wedgwood & Sons Ltd.
2.	1966	William Adams
3.	1966	Royal Tuscan
4.	1967	Coalport
6.	1968	Johnson Brothers
7.	1969	King Lynn Glass
8.	1969	Merseyside Jewelers
9.	1970	J. & G. Meakin
10.	1970	Midwinter
11.	1973	Crown Staffordshire
12.	1973	Mason's Ironstone
13.	1973	Precision Studios
14.	1974	Galway Crystal

WILEMAN CHRONOLOGY: POTTERIES & PARTNERSHIPS

DATE	POTTERY	PARTNERSHIP
1846-1853	Foley Pottery, King Street, Fenton	John King Knight
1853-1856	Foley Pottery, King Street, Fenton	Knight & Wileman
1856-1864	Foley Pottery, King Street, Fenton	Henry Wileman
1860	Foley Pottery, King Street, Fenton	New Foley China Works built
1864-1870	Foley Pottery, King Street, Fenton	James F. and Charles J. Wileman
1870-1892	Foley Pottery, King Street, Fenton	James F. Wileman
1872-1896	Foley Pottery, King Street, Fenton	Joseph Shelley joins firm
1872-1925	Foley Pottery, King Street, Fenton	Name changed to Wileman & Co. or James Wileman & Co.
1881	Foley Pottery, King Street, Fenton	Percy Shelley joins firm
1884	Foley Pottery, King Street, Fenton	Wileman leaves firm and it becomes totally a Shelley family business
1884-1925	Foley Pottery, King Street, Fenton	Joseph Ball Shelley
1890-1910	Foley Pottery, King Street, Fenton	Trade Name of Foley Pottery adopted
1910-1916	Foley Pottery, King Street, Fenton	Trade Name of Late Foley Adopted
1926-1966	Name changed to Shelley	Foley Pottery
1966	Foley Pottery, King Street, Fenton	Acquired by Allied English Potteries

For further reading, refer to Chris Watkins, William Harvey & Robert Senft. *Shelley Potteries, The History and Production of a Staffordshire Family of Potters.* England. Barrie & Jenkins & Ebury Press. 1994, p. 171.

WOOD CHRONOLOGY: POTTERIES & PARTNERSHIPS

DATE	POTTERY	PARTNERSHIP
1710-1715	"Back of George", Burslem	Isiah Wood
1771-1773	—, Burslem	Ralph Wood II & John Wood
1775	Staffordshire Potteries	Thomas Wood
1778-1787	Rockingham Works, Swinton	Bingley, Wood & Co.
1782-1795	Fountain Place Works, (Hill House Works), Burslem	Ralph Wood
1782-1795	Fountain Place Works, (Hill House Works), Burslem	Ralph Wood I
1782-1797	Brown Hill, Tunstall & Burslem	John Wood
1783-1784	Fountain Place Works, (Hill House Works), Burslem	Enoch & Ralph Wood
1784-1789	Fountain Place Works, (Hill House Works), Burslem	Enoch Wood
1786-1796	Overhouse Works, Burslem	Enoch Wood
1790-1792	Fountain Place Works, (Hill House Works), Burslem	Enoch Wood & Co.
1793-1818	Fountain Place Works, (Hill House Works), Burslem	Wood & Caldwell
1795-1801	Hill (Top) Pottery, Liverpool Road, Burslem	Ralph Wood II
1797-1817	Brownhills Pottery, Tunstall & Burslem	John Wood
1801-1812	Grainger Works, Worcester	Grainger & Wood or (Grainger, Wood & Co.)
1802	—, Burslem	William Wood & Co.
1813-1818	Shelton, Hanley	George Wood
1814-1818	John Tomlinson's Pottery, Shelton, Hanley	Wood & Chetwin (or Chetwyn)
1818-1821	John Tomlinson's Pottery, Shelton, Hanley	Samuel Wood
1818-1829	Brownhills Pottery, Tunstall	Wood & Britell (or Brettel)
1818-1830	Hole House Works, Burslem (Lusterer)	Ephraim Wood
1818-1845	Fountain House (& other addresses) Burslem	Enoch Wood (& Sons)
1820-1837	Hepworth Shore, Gateshead, Tyneside	Joseph Wood
1821-1835	Knowl Street Works, Burslem	Enoch Wood & Sons
1822-1822	Bleak Hills, Burslem	Enoch Wood, Jr.
1824-1825	Elizabeth Wood's Works, Longton	Wood, Chesworth & Co. or (Chesworth & Wood)
1827-1830	St. Gregory's Pottery, High Street (north side), Longton	Wood & Blood
1827-1834	Greenfield Pottery, Tunstall	Wood & Challinor
1827-1838	Felling Shore, Gateshead, Tyneside	Joseph Wood
1828-1845	Brownhills (1828-1845) & Woodland (1834-45), Tunstall	Wood & Challinor
1832-1836	Broad Street, Shelton, Hanley	Robinson & Wood
1837-1837	Cobridge Works, Cobridge	Robinson, Wood & Brownfield
1837-1850	BrownfieldWorks, Cobridge	Wood & Brownfield
1837-1854	Castleford, Yorkshire	Wood & Nicholson
1839-1839	Waterloo Road, Burslem	Wood & Bowers
1841-1875	Burslem (1841-44), Tunstall (1845-75)	John Wedge Wood
1849-1849	—, Longton	Webberley & Wood
1850-1853	Hope Street Pottery, Shelton, Hanley	George Wood
1851-	Newport Street, Burslem	John Wood
1853-1853	Hope Street, Shelton, Hanley	Wood & Ford
1857-1875	Woodland Pottery, Tunstall	Edmund T. Wood
1858-1860	Overhouse Works, Wedgwood Place, Burslem	Morgan, Wood & Co.
1860-1864	Well Street Pottery, Tunstall	Wood & Challinor & Co.
1860-1870	Hill (Top) Pottery, Liverpool Road, Burslem	Morgan, Wood & Co.
1863-1865	Mt. Pleasant Works, High Street,Longton	Burton, Wood & Co.
1864-1864	William Street, Hanley	Wood & Frost
1864-1864	William Street, Hanley	Wood, George
1865-1954	Trent & New Wharf Potteries (from 1894), Burslem	Wood & Son(s)(Ltd) ("LTD" 1954-1982)
1865-1871	Mt. Pleasant Works & Bagnall Street Works, Longton	(John) Wood & Co.
1868-1868	—, Cobridge	Wood, Rathbone & Co.
1869-1871	Well Street Pottery, Tunstall	Wood & Pigott (or Piggott)

1869-1879	Villa Pottery, Cobridge	Wood, Son & Co.
1870-1880	Hill (Top) Pottery, Liverpool Road, Burslem	Wood & Baggarley
1870-1873	Albert Street Works, Burslem	Wiltshaw Wood & Co.
1871-1872	Church Works, Burslem	Wood & Clarke
1873-1885	High Street, Burslem	Buckley, Wood & Co.
1873-1932	Albert Street Works, Burslem	William Wood & Co.
1875-1878	Copeland Street Works, Stoke-on Trent	Poole, Stanway & Wood
1877-1879	Villa Pottery, Cobridge	Wood & Dunn
1877-1912	New Stepney Pottery, Ouseburn, Northumberland	John Wood & Co. (Ltd.)
1878-1888	Copeland Street Works, Stoke-on-Trent	Turner & Wood
1881-1882	Pearl Pottery, Brook Street, Hanley	Wood, Hines & Frost
1881-1885	Pearl Pottery, Brook Street, Hanley	Wood, Hines & Winkle
1882-1887	Abbey Pottery, Cobridge	Wood & Hawthorne
1882-1905	Garfield Pottery, Burslem	Wood & Hulme
1884-Present	Chapel Lane (1884-1888) &Alexandra Pottery, Burslem	H.J. Wood (Ltd.) (Wood & Sons Ltd.)
1885-1896	Wedgwood & Queen St. Pottery, Burslem	Thomas Wood & Co.
1885-1889	Pearl Pottery, Brook Street, Hanley	Winkle & Wood
1892-1892	Pearl Pottery, Brook Street, Hanley	Wood & Bennett
1895-1904	Bradwell Works, Longton	Capper & Wood
1896-1897	Queen Street Pottery, Burslem	Thomas Wood & Sons
1897-1926	Heathcote Works, Longton	J.B. Wood & Co.
1897-1903	Queen Street Pottery, Burslem	Wood & Barker, Ltd. or (Barker, Wood & Co.)
1904-1928	Bradwell Works, Longport	Arthur Wood
1928-Present	Bradwell Works, Longport	Arthur Wood & Son (Longport) Ltd.
1952-1981	New Wharf Pottery, Burslem	Wood & Sons (Holdings) Ltd.
1952-1982	Trent Pottery, Burslem	Wood & Sons (Holdings) Ltd.
1957-Present	Unicorn Pottery, Amicable Street, Longport	Arthur Wood & Sons
1982-Present	Trent & New Wharf Potteries, Burslem	Wood & Sons (1982) Ltd.

This listing is by no means complete. There are more "Woods." For further reading, refer to *Godden, Collecting Lustreware*, p. 178-190.

APPENDIX B7: CROSS REFERENCE OF BACK MARKINGS

BACK MARKING	POTTERY
ALBANY & HARVEY POTTERIES	GIBSON & SONS (LTD.)
ALBION	BELL, ISAAC & THOMAS
ALBION CHINA (OR WORKS)	DIMMOCK, J. & CO.
ALBION POTTERY	BOURNE & LEIGH (LTD.)
ALBION POTTERY	GALLOWAY & ATKINSON
ALBION WORKS	DIMMOCK, J. & CO.
ALDWYCH CHINA	BESWICK & SON (CHINA)
ALDWYCH CHINA	BRIDGETT & BATES
ANCHOR CHINA (OR WORKS)	BRIDGWOOD, SAMPSON & SON (LTD.)
ANCHOR WORKS	BRIDGWOOD, SAMPSON & SON (LTD.)
ANNENFIELD	THOMSON, JOHN (& SONS)
ARMITAGE	PENMAN, BROWN & CO.
ARMITAGE	PENMAN, ROBERT H. & CO.
ATLAS BONE CHINA	GRIMWADE BROS.
B.B. (BEST BODY)	MINTON (Mid 19th c.)
BANDANA WARE	MASON, CHARLES JAMES (& CO.)
BARNSTAPLE	BRANNAM, C. H. (LTD.)
BAXTER	BAGSTER, JOHN DENTON
BEDFORD WARE (OR WORKS)	RIDGWAYS (BEDFORD WORKS) LTD.
BEDFORD WORKS (OR WARE)	RIDGWAYS (BEDFORD WORKS) LTD.
BERLIN IRONSTONE	LIDDLE, ELLIOT & SON
BERLIN IRONSTONE	MAYER & ELLIOTT (See MAYER BROS. & ELLIOTT)
BEST	LIVESLEY, POWELL & CO.
BEST	POWELL & BISHOP
BEST GOODS	EVANS & GLASSON
BEST GOODS	MARSHALL, JOHN (& CO.)(LTD.)
BISTRO	BISHOP & STONIER (LTD.)
BLUE BELL WARE	LONGTON POTTERY CO. LTD.
BO'NESS	JAMIESON, JAMES & CO.
BO'NESS (POTTERY)	MARSHALL, JOHN & CO.
BRISTOL	POUNTNEY & CO. (LTD.)
BRISTOL ALKALON CHINA	POUNTNEY & CO. (LTD.)
BRISTOL PORCELAIN	POUNTNEY & CO. (LTD.)
BRISTOL POTTERY	POUNTNEY & CO. (LTD.)
BRISTOL POTTERY	POUNTNEY & GOLDNEY
BRISTOL SEMI PORCELAIN	POUNTNEY & CO. (LTD.)
BRITAIN	COCHRAN & FLEMING
BRITANNIA POTTERY	JOHNSON, SAMUEL LTD.
BRITISH COBALT BLUE	MARE, JOHN
BRITISH NANKIN CHINA	MASON, MILES
BRITISH NANKIN CHINA (OR POTTERY)	MASON, CHARLES JAMES (& CO.)
BROOK STREET, HANLEY	TAYLOR, WILLIAM
BULLOCH	METHVEN, DAVID & SONS
BURLEIGH WARE	BURGESS & LEIGH (LTD.)
BURLEIGH WARE	WILKINSON, ARTHUR J. (LTD.)
BURSLEM	HUGHES, THOMAS
BURSLEM	ALCOCK, RICHARD
BURSLEM	ALCOCK, SAMUEL & CO.
BURSLEM	ALLMAN, BROUGHTON & CO.
BURSLEM	BARKER, SUTTON & TILL
BURSLEM	BODLEY & CO.
BURSLEM	BRIDGWOOD & CLARKE
BURSLEM	BROWN & STEVENTON, LTD.
BURSLEM	BURGESS & LEIGH (LTD.)
BURSLEM	BURGESS, HENRY
BURSLEM	CHALLINOR, EDWARD
BURSLEM	CLARKE, EDWARD (& CO.)
BURSLEM	COLLINSON, CHARLES & CO.
BURSLEM	CORK, EDGE & MALKIN
BURSLEM	CORN, EDWARD
BURSLEM	CORN, W. E.
BURSLEM	DEAN, S. W.
BURSLEM	DEANS (1910) LTD.
BURSLEM	DOULTON (& CO.) (LTD.)
BURSLEM	EDWARDS, THOMAS
BURSLEM	FORD & SONS (LTD.)
BURSLEM	FORD, SAMUEL & CO.
BURSLEM	GIBSON & SONS (LTD.)
BURSLEM	GODWIN, THOMAS
BURSLEM	HEATH, THOMAS
BURSLEM	HOPE & CARTER
BURSLEM	HOPKIN & VERNON
BURSLEM	JOHNSON, SAMUEL, LTD.
BURSLEM	KEELING & CO. (LTD.)
BURSLEM	MACINTYRE, JAMES & CO. (LTD.)
BURSLEM	MADDOCK, JOHN & SONS (LTD.)
BURSLEM	MIDWINTER, W. R. (LTD.)
BURSLEM	NEW WHARF POTTERY CO.
BURSLEM	NEWPORT POTTERY CO., LTD.
BURSLEM	PHILLIPS, GEORGE
BURSLEM	PHILLIPS, THOMAS & SON
BURSLEM	ROBINSON, JOSEPH
BURSLEM	SHAW, ANTHONY (& CO.)(&SON(S))
BURSLEM	TILL, THOMAS & SON(S)(LTD.)
BURSLEM	VENABLES, JOHN & CO.
BURSLEM	VENABLES, MANN & CO.
BURSLEM	WILKINSON & HULME
BURSLEM	WILKINSON, ARTHUR J. (LTD.)
BURSLEM	WOOD, ENOCH & SON(S)
BURSLEM WARRANTED	WOOD, ENOCH & SON(S)
BURSLEM, STAFFORDSHIRE	PINDER, BOURNE & CO.
CALEDONIAN POTTERY	AITCHIESON, J. & CO.
CALEDONIAN POTTERY	GLASGOW POTTERY
CALEDONIAN POTTERY	KEMP & CO.
CALEDONIAN POTTERY	ROWLEY, JOSEPH
CALIS	HAMILTON, ROBERT
CALYXWARE	ADAMS, WM. (& SONS)(& CO.)
CAMBRIA	HEATHCOTE, CHARLES & CO.
CAMBRIAN ARGIL	MASON, CHARLES JAMES (& CO.)
CAMBRIAN POTTERY	SWANSEA POTTERY
CAMBRIAN POTTERY	WALLACE & CO.
CAREYS	CAREY, THOMAS & JOHN
CARLTON CHINA (OR WARE)	WILTSHAW & ROBINSON (LTD.)
CASTLEFORD (POTTERY)	DUNDERDALE, DAVID & CO.
CAULDON (WARE)	BROWN-WESTHEAD, MOORE & CO.
CAULDON LTD.	ALLERTON, CHARLES & SONS
CAULDON PLACE	CAULDON LTD.
CELTIC CHINA	BAGSTER, JOHN DENTON
CELTIC CHINA	WOOD, ENOCH & SON(S)
CETEM WARE	MAILING, C. T. & SONS (LTD.)
CHINA	BOWERS, GEO. FREDERICK (& CO.)
CHINA	MEIGH, CHARLES & SON
CHINA GLAZE	COPELAND & GARRETT
CHINESE PORCELAIN	ROGERS, JOHN (& SON)
CHINESE PORCELAINE	MAYER, T. J. & J.
CHININE	TAMS, JOHN (& SON)(LTD.)
CITY POTTERY GLASGOW	COUPER, JAMES & SONS
CLIFF	DIMMOCK, J. & CO.
CLYDE (OR) LADYBURN POTTERY	SHIRLEY, THOMAS & CO.
CLYDE POTTERY CO.	GREENOCK POTTERY
CLYDE POTTERY CO. (LTD.)	MCLACHLAN, DONALD & BROWN
CLYDE POTTERY CO. (LTD.)	MUIR, ANDREW & CO.
CLYDE POTTERY CO. (LTD.)	STEVENSON, JAMES & CO.
COALPORT	BRADLEY & CO.
COBRIDGE	ALCOCK, HENRY & CO. (LTD.)
COBRIDGE	ALCOCK, JOHN
COBRIDGE	ALCOCK, JOHN & GEORGE
COBRIDGE	ALCOCK, SAMUEL & CO.
COBRIDGE	BROWNFIELD, WM. (& SON(S))

COBRIDGE	COCKSON & CHETWYND (& CO.)
COBRIDGE	FURNIVAL, JACOB & CO.
COBRIDGE	FURNIVAL, THOMAS & SONS
COBRIDGE	FURNIVALS (LTD.)
COBRIDGE	GLOBE POTTERY CO. LTD.
COBRIDGE	HARDING & COCKSON
COBRIDGE	MEAKIN & CO.
COBRIDGE	PEARSON, EDWARD (& SON)
COBRIDGE	SOHO POTTERY LTD.
COBRIDGE	STEVENSON, RALPH & WILLIAMS
COBRIDGE	WALLEY, EDWARD
COBRIDGE	WOOD & BROWNFIELD
COBRIDGE	WOOD, SON & CO.
COLONIAL POTTERY	WINKLE, F. & CO. (LTD.)
CONDOR PARK	BOURNE, JOSEPH (& SON)(LTD.)
CORONA	BARRATT'S OF STAFFORDSHIRE LTD.
CORONA	GATER, HALL & CO.
CORONA WARE	GATER, HALL & CO.
CRESENT (POTTERY) CHINA	JONES, GEORGE (& SONS)(LTD.)
CROWN POTTERY	BROADHURST, JAMES & SONS (LTD.)
CROWN POTTERY	CERAMIC ART CO. (1905) LTD.
CROWN POTTERY	TAMS, JOHN (& SON)(LTD.)
CROWN POTTERY	TAMS, JOHN (& SONS)(LTD.)
CROWN SEMI PORCELAIN	ADAMS, WM. & CO.
CROWN SEMI PORCELAIN	DIMMOCK, J. & CO.
CYMBRO STONE CHINA	DILLWYN & CO.
CYMBRO STONE CHINA	SWANSEA POTTERY
DALE HALL	EDWARDS, JAMES & SON
DALE HALL POTTERY	MAYER, T. J. & J.
DEAKIN PEARL	DEAKIN & CO.
DENABY POTTERY(IES)	WILKINSON & WARDLE
DENBY	BOURNE, JOSEPH (& SON)(LTD.)
DERBYSHIRE	POTTS, WM. WAINWRIGHT
DON	DON POTTERY
DON POTTERY	BARKER, SAMUEL & SON
DON POTTERY	GREEN(S)
DRESDEN OPAQUE CHINA	CLEWS, JAMES & RALPH
DRESDEN OPAQUE CHINA	DIXON, AUSTIN & CO.
DRESDEN OPAQUE CHINA	RIDGWAY, JOHN & WILLIAM
DURABILITY	WEATHERBY, J. H. & SONS (LTD.)
DURA-WARE	LOCKITT, WILLIAM H.
DUTCHESS CHINA (THE)	HANCOCK, SAMPSON (& SONS)
EASTWOOD WORKS	MEAKIN, J. & G. (LTD.)
EDINBURGH	FORD, JOHN & CO.
EDINBURGH SCOTLAND	SCOTT BROS.
ELEPHANT BRAND	TAMS, JOHN (& SON)(LTD.)
ELGIN POTTERY	PURVES, CHARLES
ELLIOT BROS. (See)	LIDDLE, ELLIOT & SON
EMPIRE WORKS	EMPIRE PORCELAIN CO. (LTD.)
ENAMEL PORCELAIN	MEIGH, CHARLES
ENGLISH STONE CHINA	CHALLINOR & MAYER
ETRURIA	DAVENPORT, BANKS & CO.
ETRURIA	DAVENPORT, BECK & CO.
ETRURIA	WEDGWOOD, JOSIAH (& SONS, LTD.)
ETRUSCAN FESTOON	RIDGWAY, WM. (& CO.)
ETRUSCAN WARE	CAMBRIAN POTTERY
ETRUSCAN WARE	DILLWYN'S
FALCON WARE	WEATHERBY, J. H. & SONS (LTD.)
FELSPAR	CAREY, THOMAS & JOHN
FELSPAR	EDWARDS, JAMES
FELSPAR CHINA	MINTON
FELSPAR PORCELAIN	COPELAND & GARRETT
FELSPAR PORCELAIN	MINTON
FENTON	BAKER, (W.) & CO. (LTD.)
FENTON	BEARDMORE, FRANK & CO.
FENTON	CHALLINOR & MAYER
FENTON	CHALLINOR, E. & C.
FENTON	EDWARDS, JAMES
FENTON	EDWARDS, JOHN (& CO.)
FENTON	GREEN, THOMAS
FENTON	HUGHES, E. & CO.
FENTON	MASON, C. J. (& CO.)
FENTON	PRATT, F. & R. & CO. (LTD.)
FENTON	REEVES, JAMES
FENTON	YATES, JOHN
FENTON POTTERIES	GREEN, THOMAS
FENTON STONE WORKS	MASON, C. J. (& CO.)
FENTON STONE WORKS	MASON, G. M. & C. J.
FERRYBRIDGE	WOOLF, SYDNEY & CO.
FERRYBRIDGE POTTERY	KNOTTINGLEY POTTERY
FERRYBRIDGE POTTERY	POULSON BROTHERS
FERRYBRIDGE POTTERY	REED & TAYLOR (& CO.)
FERRYBRIDGE POTTERY	TOMLINSON & CO.
FERRYBRIDGE POTTERY	WEDGWOOD & CO.
FERRYBRIDGE POTTERY	WOOLF, LEWIS (& SONS)
FINE STONE	BRAMELD & CO.
FLEMING	COCHRAN & FLEMING
FLO-BLUE	BLAKENEY POTTERY CO.
FLORENTINE CHINA	ALCOCK, SAMUEL & CO.
FLORENTINE CHINA	MINTON
FLORENTINE CHINA	RIDGWAY, JOHN, BATES & CO.
FOLEY	KNIGHT, JOHN KING
FOLEY POTTERIES	WILEMAN, JAMES F.
FORESTERS	FORESTER, THOMAS SON & CO.
FOSTER	ELSMORE & FORSTER
FOWLER THOMSON & CO. (See)	WATSON, WILLIAM (& CO.)
FRENCH CHINA	HICKS & MEIGH
FRENCH CHINA	MEIGH, CHARLES
FRENCH PORCELAIN	ALCOCK, SAMUEL & CO.
GARRISON POTTERY	DIXON & CO.
GARRISON POTTERY	DIXON, AUSTIN & CO.
GARRISON POTTERY	DIXON, AUSTIN PHILLIPS & CO.
GARRISON POTTERY	DIXON, PHILLIPS (& CO.)
GARRISON POTTERY	PHILLIPS & CO.
GARRISON POTTERY	PHILLIPS, J.
GATESHEAD FELL	SHERIFF HILL POTTERY
GENUINE IRONSTONE CHINA	BODLEY, EDWARD F. & CO.
GENUINE STONE CHINA	FOLCH, STEPHEN (& SONS)
GERMANY	CORN, W. & E.
GLAMORGAN POTTERY	BAKER, BEVANS & IRWIN
GLASGOW	BELL, J. & M. P. & CO. (LD.)
GLASGOW	CAMPBELLFIELD POTTERY COMPANY LTD.
GLASGOW	COCHRAN & FLEMING
GLASGOW	COCHRAN, R. & CO.
GLASGOW	GEDDES, JOHN (&SON)
GLASGOW	MILLER, JAMES & CO. LTD.
GLASGOW	POSSIL POTTERY CO.
GLASGOW	ROWLEY, JOSIAH
GLASGOW	THOMSON, JOHN (& SONS)
GLASGOW POTTERY	CALEDONIAN POTTERY
GLASGOW STONE CHINE	CALEDONIAN POTTERY
GRAFTON CHINA	JONES, A.B. & SONS (LTD.)
GRANITE	ALCOCK, J. & S.
GRANITE	ALCOCK, RICHARD
GRANITE	BOOTE, T. & R. (& SON) LTD.
GRANITE	BRIDGWOOD & CLARKE
GRANITE	CORN, W. E.
GRANITE	RIDGWAY, MORLEY, WEAR & CO.
GRANITE	THOMSON, JOHN (& SONS)
GRANITE CHINA	BRAMELD & CO.
GRANITE CHINA	FERRYBRIDGE POTTERY
GRANITE CHINA	HUGHES, THOMAS
GRANITE CHINA	MASON, C. J. (& CO.)
GRANITE CHINA	POUNTNEY & CO. (LTD.)
GRANITE CHINA	RIDGWAY & MORLEY
GRANITE CHINA	RIDGWAY, MORLEY, WEAR & CO.
GRANITE CHINA	RIDGWAY, WM. (& CO.)
GRANITE CHINA	SWILLINGTON BRIDGE POTTERY
GRANITE EARTHENWARE	BOOTE, T. & R. (& SON) LTD.
GRANITE IMPERIAL	BELL, J. & M. P. & CO. (LD.)
GRANITE IRONSTONE CHINA	RIDGWAY & MORLEY
GRANITE OPAQUE PEARL	CLEMENTSON, JOSEPH & SONS
GRANITE WARE	ALCOCK, HENRY & CO. (LTD.)
GRANITE WARE	CLEMENTSON, JOSEPH & SONS
GREEN(S)	DON POTTERY (See)
GREENOCK (POTTERY)	CLYDE POTTERY CO. (LTD.)
GRESLEY	GREEN, T. G. & CO. (LTD.)
HACKWOOD	RATCLIFFE, WILLIAM
HAMILTON	POUNTNEY & ALLIES
HANLEY	ALCOCK, RICHARD
HANLEY	ASHWORTH, G. L. & BROS. (LTD.)
HANLEY	CERAMIC ART CO. LTD.
HANLEY	CLEMENTSON BROS. LTD.
HANLEY	CLEMENTSON, JOSEPH & SONS
HANLEY	DAVIS, J. H. & J.
HANLEY	DAVIS, JOHN HEATH
HANLEY	DUDSON, WILCOX & TILL LTD.
HANLEY	GELSON BROS.
HANLEY	JOHNSON, REUBEN
HANLEY	KEELING, SAMUEL & CO.
HANLEY	LOCKITT, WILLIAM H.
HANLEY	MANN & CO.
HANLEY	MEAKIN, CHARLES
HANLEY	MEAKIN, J. & G. (LTD.)
HANLEY	MEIGH, CHARLES & SON
HANLEY	MEIGH, JOB (& SON)
HANLEY	MORLEY & ASHWORTH
HANLEY	NEAL (JAMES) & CO.
HANLEY	PANKHURST, J. W. & CO.
HANLEY	RIDGWAY & ABINGTON
HANLEY	RIDGWAY & MORLEY
HANLEY	RIDGWAY, WM. SON & CO.
HANLEY	SNEYD & HILL
HANLEY	SNEYD, THOMAS
HANLEY	SWINNERTON (LTD.)
HANLEY	TAYLOR BROS.
HANLEY	TAYLOR, WILLIAM
HANLEY	WEATHERBY, J. H. & SONS (LTD.)

HANLEY	WHITTAKER & CO.
HARVEY	HARVEY, C. & W. K.
HARVEY POTTERY	GIBSON & SONS (LTD.)
HERCULANEUM	JACKSON, JOB & JOHN
HILL POTTERY	ALCOCK, SAMUEL & CO.
HILL POTTERY	BURGESS & LEIGH (LTD.)
HILL, I. (See)	CLEWS, RALPH & JAMES
HOLKIRKWARE	HOLLINSHEAD & KIRKHAM (LTD.)
HULL (See)	BELLE VUE POTTERY
HYLTON POT WORKS	MAILING, C. T. & SONS (LTD.)
HYLTON POT WORKS	PHILLIPS, JOHN
HYLTON POTTERY	PHILLIPS, JOHN
IMPERIAL	ADAMS, WM. (& SONS)(& CO.)
IMPERIAL	METHVEN, DAVID & SONS
IMPERIAL CHINA	WOOD, ENOCH & SON(S)
IMPERIAL FRENCH PORCELAIN	ADAMS, WM. (& SONS)(& CO.)
IMPERIAL FRENCH PORCELAIN	ALCOCK, J. & S.
IMPERIAL FRENCH PORCELAIN	HUGHES, THOMAS
IMPERIAL GRANITE	PODMORE, WALKER & (CO.)
IMPERIAL GRANITE CHINA	ALOCK, JOHN & GEORGE
IMPERIAL GRANITE CHINA	RIDGWAY, WM. (& CO.)
IMPERIAL IRONSTONE	MORLEY & ASHWORTH
IMPERIAL IRONSTONE CHINA	ALCOCK, HENRY & CO. (LTD.)
IMPERIAL IRONSTONE CHINA	ALCOCK, JOHN
IMPERIAL IRÖNSTONE CHINA	ALCOCK, SAMUEL & CO.
IMPERIAL IRONSTONE CHINA	BAKER & CHETWYND & CO.
IMPERIAL IRONSTONE CHINA	BAKER, (W.) & CO. (LTD.)
IMPERIAL IRONSTONE CHINA	BIRKS BROS. & SEDDON
IMPERIAL IRONSTONE CHINA	COCHRAN, R. & CO.
IMPERIAL IRONSTONE CHINA	COCKSON & CHETWYND (& CO.)
IMPERIAL IRONSTONE CHINA	COCKSON & HARDING
IMPERIAL IRONSTONE CHINA	COCKSON & SEDDON
IMPERIAL IRONSTONE CHINA	COLLINSON, CHARLES & CO.
IMPERIAL IRONSTONE CHINA	CORN, W. & E.
IMPERIAL IRONSTONE CHINA	HOLLINSHEAD & KIRKHAM (LTD.)
IMPERIAL IRONSTONE CHINA	PODMORE, WALKER & (CO.)
IMPERIAL IRONSTONE CHINA	SHAW, ANTHONY (& CO.)(&SON(S))
IMPERIAL IRONSTONE CHINA	ST. JOHN'S STONE CHINAWARE CO. (Canadian)
IMPERIAL IRONSTONE CHINA	WEDGWOOD & CO. (LTD.)
IMPERIAL PARISIAN GRANITE	OLD HALL (EARTHENWARE) CO. LTD.
IMPERIAL PORCELAIN	WEDGWOOD & CO. (LTD.)
IMPERIAL SEMI CHINA	ALLERTON, CHARLES & SONS
IMPERIAL SEMI PORCELAIN	MYOTT, SON & CO. (LTD.)
IMPERIAL STONE	ALCOCK, JOHN & GEORGE
IMPERIAL STONE	HEATH, J. & CO.
IMPERIAL STONE	RIDGWAY & ABINGTON
IMPERIAL STONE	RIDGWAY & MORLEY
IMPERIAL STONE	RIDGWAY, JOHN (& CO.)
IMPERIAL STONE	RIDGWAY, WM. SON & CO.
IMPERIAL STONE	STEVENSON, RALPH & SON
IMPERIAL STONE CHINA	MEIGH, CHARLES
IMPERIAL STONE CHINA	RIDGWAY, JOHN (& CO.)
IMPERIAL STONE CHINA	STEVENSON, RALPH & SON
IMPERIAL STONE CHINA	WEDGWOOD & CO. (LTD.)
IMPERIAL STONE WARE	ADAMS, WM. (& SONS)(& CO.)
IMPERIAL WHITE GRANITE	PINDER, BOURNE & CO.
IMPERIAL WREATH	COCKSON & HARDING
IMPROVED BERLIN IRONSTONE	MAYER, T. J. & J.
IMPROVED CHINA	MEIGH, JOB (& SON)
IMPROVED CHINA	RIDGWAY, WM. (& CO.)
IMPROVED FELSPAR	MEIGH, CHARLES & SON
IMPROVED GRANITE CHINA	RIDGWAY & MORLEY
IMPROVED GRANITE CHINA	RIDGWAY, MORLEY, WEAR & CO.
IMPROVED GRANITE CHINA	RIDGWAY, WM. (& CO.)
IMPROVED IRONSTONE	ADAMS, WM. (& SONS)(& CO.)
IMPROVED IRONSTONE	MAYER, T. J. & J.
IMPROVED IRONSTONE	MEIGH, CHARLES
IMPROVED IRONSTONE CHINA	BROWNFIELD, WM. (& SON(S))
IMPROVED IRONSTONE CHINA	CAREY, THOMAS & JOHN
IMPROVED IRONSTONE CHINA	FOLCH, STEPHEN (& SONS)
IMPROVED IRONSTONE CHINA	MASON, CHARLES JAMES (& CO.)
IMPROVED IRONSTONE CHINA	MAYER, T. J. & J.
IMPROVED IRONSTONE CHINA	MEIGH, CHARLES
IMPROVED IRONSTONE CHINA STOKE WORKS	FOLCH, STEPHEN (& SONS)
IMPROVED OPAQUE CHINA	ELSMORE, FORESTER & CO.
IMPROVED SAXON BLUE	DILLWYN & CO.
IMPROVED STONE	RIDGWAY, WM. (& CO.)
IMPROVED STONE CHINA	BURTON, SAMUEL & JOHN
IMPROVED STONE CHINA	COCHRAN, R. & CO.
IMPROVED STONE CHINA	DAVENPORT (various styles)
IMPROVED STONE CHINA	HICKS & MEIGH
IMPROVED STONE CHINA	MAYER, THOMAS
IMPROVED STONE CHINA	MEIGH, CHARLES
IMPROVED STONE CHINA	MEIGH, JOB (& SON)
IMPROVED STONE CHINA	MINTON
IMPROVED STONE CHINA	MINTON & BOYLE
IMPROVED STONE CHINA	POUNTNEY & ALLIES
IMPROVED STONEWARE	DILLWYN & CO.
IMPROVED STONEWARE	DIMMOCK , THOMAS (JR.) & CO.
IMPROVED STONEWARE	FELL, THOMAS (& CO.)(LTD.)
INDIAN IRONSTONE	ALCOCK, JOHN & GEORGE
INDIAN IRONSTONE	ALCOCK, SAMUEL & CO.
INDIAN STONE	ALCOCK, JOHN & GEORGE
INDIAN STONE	JONES & WALLEY
INDIAN STONE	WALLEY, EDWARD
INDIAN STONE CHINA	HICKS & MEIGH
INDIAN STONE CHINA	OLD HALL (EARTHENWARE) CO. LTD.
IRONSTONE	ADAMS, WM. (& SONS)(& CO.)
IRONSTONE	ALCOCK, HENRY & CO. (LTD.)
IRONSTONE	ASHWORTH, G. L. & BROS. (LTD.)
IRONSTONE	BAKER, (W.) & CO.
IRONSTONE	BISHOP & STONIER (LTD.)
IRONSTONE	BOOTE, T. & R. (& SON) LTD.
IRONSTONE	BOOTH & MEIGH
IRONSTONE	BOWERS, GEO. FREDERICK (& CO.)
IRONSTONE	BROUGHAM & MAYER
IRONSTONE	CHALLINOR, E. & CO.
IRONSTONE	CHALLINOR, EDWARD
IRONSTONE	CLEMENTSON, JOSEPH & SONS
IRONSTONE	CLEMENTSON, YOUNG & ANDERSON
IRONSTONE	COCKSON & CHETWYND (& CO.)
IRONSTONE	CORK, EDGE & MALKIN
IRONSTONE	DAVENPORT (various styles)
IRONSTONE	DAVENPORT, JOHN
IRONSTONE	EDGE, MALKIN & CO. (LTD.)
IRONSTONE	EDWARDS, JAMES
IRONSTONE	EDWARDS, JAMES & THOMAS
IRONSTONE	EDWARDS, JOHN (& CO.)
IRONSTONE	FURNIVAL, JACOB & CO.
IRONSTONE	FURNIVAL, THOMAS & CO.
IRONSTONE	FURNIVAL, THOMAS & SONS
IRONSTONE	GODWIN, THOMAS
IRONSTONE	GOODFELLOW, THOMAS
IRONSTONE	GOODWIN, JOHN
IRONSTONE	GOODWIN, JOHN & CO.
IRONSTONE	GOODWIN, JOSEPH
IRONSTONE	HARVEY, C. & W. K.
IRONSTONE	HOLLINSHEAD & KIRKHAM (LTD.)
IRONSTONE	JONES, G. F.
IRONSTONE	LIVESLEY, POWELL & CO.
IRONSTONE	MAYER & ELLIOTT (See MAYER BROS. & ELLIOTT)
IRONSTONE	MAYER, T. J. & J.
IRONSTONE	MEAKIN & CO.
IRONSTONE	MEAKIN, J. & G. (LTD.)
IRONSTONE	MEIGH, CHARLES
IRONSTONE	MEIR, JOHN & SON
IRONSTONE	MELLOR, VENABLES & CO.
IRONSTONE	MORLEY, FRANCIS (& CO.)
IRONSTONE	PHILLIPS, GEORGE & SON
IRONSTONE	PODMORE, WALKER & (CO.)
IRONSTONE	POWELL & BISHOP
IRONSTONE	SHAW, ANTHONY (& CO.)(&SON(S))
IRONSTONE	SOUTH WALES POTTERY
IRONSTONE	TILL, THOMAS & SON(S)(LTD.)
IRONSTONE	WALKER, THOMAS
IRONSTONE	WALLEY, EDWARD
IRONSTONE	WILLIAMS, WILLIAM
IRONSTONE	WOOD & CHALLINOR
IRONSTONE	WOOD, JOHN WEDGE
IRONSTONE	WOOLISCROFT, GEORGE (& CO.)
IRONSTONE	YNYSMEDW POTTERY
IRONSTONE CHINA	ADAMS, WM. (& SONS)(& CO.)
IRONSTONE CHINA	ALCOCK, JOHN
IRONSTONE CHINA	ASHWORTH'S (BROS.)
IRONSTONE CHINA	ASHWORTH, G. L. & BROS. (LTD.)
IRONSTONE CHINA	BAKER, (W.) & CO. (LTD.)
IRONSTONE CHINA	BARKER, SAMUEL & SON
IRONSTONE CHINA	BARROW & CO.
IRONSTONE CHINA	BISHOP & STONIER (LTD.)
IRONSTONE CHINA	BOURNE, JOSEPH (& SON)(LTD.)
IRONSTONE CHINA	BOWERS, GEO. FREDERICK (& CO.)
IRONSTONE CHINA	BURGESS, HENRY
IRONSTONE CHINA	BURTON, SAMUEL & JOHN
IRONSTONE CHINA	CHALLINOR, E. & C.
IRONSTONE CHINA	CHALLINOR, E. & CO.
IRONSTONE CHINA	CLEMENTSON BROS.
IRONSTONE CHINA	CLEWS, JAMES & RALPH
IRONSTONE CHINA	CORMIE, JOHN
IRONSTONE CHINA	CORN, W. & E.
IRONSTONE CHINA	DANIEL, H. & R.
IRONSTONE CHINA	DAVENPORT (various styles)
IRONSTONE CHINA	DILLON, FRANCIS
IRONSTONE CHINA	DUNN, BENNETT & CO. (LTD.)
IRONSTONE CHINA	EDWARDS, JAMES
IRONSTONE CHINA	EDWARDS, JAMES & SON
IRONSTONE CHINA	EDWARDS, JAMES & THOMAS
IRONSTONE CHINA	EDWARDS, JOHN

IRONSTONE CHINA	ELSMORE & FORSTER
IRONSTONE CHINA	FREAKLY & FARRALL
IRONSTONE CHINA	FURNIVAL, JACOB & CO.
IRONSTONE CHINA	GOODFELLOW, THOMAS
IRONSTONE CHINA	HACKWOOD & CO.
IRONSTONE CHINA	HUGHES, THOMAS
IRONSTONE CHINA	HUGHES, THOMAS & SON (LTD.)
IRONSTONE CHINA	JONES, GEORGE & SONS
IRONSTONE CHINA	KNIGHT, ELKIN & CO.
IRONSTONE CHINA	LIVESLEY, POWELL & CO.
IRONSTONE CHINA	MACINTYRE, JAMES & CO. (LTD.)
IRONSTONE CHINA	MADDOCK, JOHN
IRONSTONE CHINA	MADDOCK, JOHN & SONS (LTD.)
IRONSTONE CHINA	MARPLE, TURNER & CO.
IRONSTONE CHINA	MASON, G. M. & C. J.
IRONSTONE CHINA	MEAKIN & CO.
IRONSTONE CHINA	MEAKIN, HENRY
IRONSTONE CHINA	MEAKIN, J. & G. (LTD.)
IRONSTONE CHINA	MEIGH, CHARLES & SON
IRONSTONE CHINA	MEIR, JOHN & SON
IRONSTONE CHINA	PANKHURST, J. W. & CO.
IRONSTONE CHINA	PEARSON, EDWARD
IRONSTONE CHINA	PEARSON, FARRALL & MEAKIN
IRONSTONE CHINA	POWELL & BISHOP
IRONSTONE CHINA	RIDGWAY, JOHN & WILLIAM
IRONSTONE CHINA	RIDGWAYS (BEDFORD WORKS) LTD.
IRONSTONE CHINA	SOUTH WALES POTTERY
IRONSTONE CHINA	ST. JOHN'S STONE CHINAWARE CO. (Canadian)
IRONSTONE CHINA	SWILLINGTON BRIDGE POTTERY
IRONSTONE CHINA	TAYLOR BROS.
IRONSTONE CHINA	WALKER, THOMAS
IRONSTONE CHINA	WALLEY, EDWARD
IRONSTONE CHINA	WILEMAN, JAMES F.
IRONSTONE CHINA	WILKINSON, ARTHUR J. (LTD.)
IRONSTONE CHINA	WOOD & HAWTHORNE
IRONSTONE CHINA	WOOD & SON(S) (LTD.)
IRONSTONE CHINA	WOOD, JOHN WEDGE
IRONSTONE CHINA	WOOD, RATHBON & CO.
IRONSTONE CHINA	WOOD, SON & CO.
IRONSTONE CHINA	WOOLISCROFT, GEORGE (& CO.)
IRONSTONE CHINA STOKE WORKS	FELL, THOMAS (& CO.)(LTD.)
IRONSTONE CHINA WARRANTED	SHAW, ANTHONY (& CO.)(&SON(S))
IRONSTONE STAFFORDSHIRE	BLAKENEY POTTERY CO.
IRONSTONE WARE	HUGHES, THOMAS & SON (LTD.)
IRONSTONE WARE	RIDGWAYS (BEDFORD WORKS) LTD.
IVORY CHINA	RIDGWAYS (BEDFORD WORKS) LTD.
IVORY WARE	CLEMENTSON BROS. LTD.
JANROTH (American Importer)	RIDGWAYS (BEDFORD WORKS) LTD.
JAPAN OPAQUE CHINA	RIDGWAY, JOHN & WILLIAM
JOHN FARRALL (See)	PEARSON, FARRALL & MEAKIN
KAOLIN (WARE)	DIMMOCK , THOMAS (JR.) & CO.
KAOLIN (WARE)	PRATT, F. & R. & CO. (LTD.)
KILNHURST OLD POTTERY	BRAMELDS & CO.
KILNHURST OLD POTTERY	GREEN, GEO.
KILNHURST OLD POTTERY	GREEN, GEORGE
KILNHURST OLD POTTERY	HAWLEY, PHILIP & CO.
KILNHURST OLD POTTERY	HAWLEY, PHILIP & COOK
KILNHURST OLD POTTERY	HAWLEY, SIMPSON
KILNHURST OLD POTTERY	HAWLEY, THOMAS
KILNHURST OLD POTTERY	HEALD, WILLIAM
KILNHURST OLD POTTERY	SIMPSON-BOWMAN HEALD
KILNHURST OLD POTTERY	TURNER & CO.
KILNHURST OLD POTTERY	TURNER & PHILLIP HAWLEY
KILNHURST OLD POTTERY	TURNER & THOMAS HAWLEY
KILNHURST OLD POTTERY	TWIGG, BENJAMIN & JOHN
KILNHURST OLD POTTERY	TWIGG, DANIEL
KILNHURST OLD POTTERY	TWIGG, JOHN
KIRKCALDY POTTERY	METHVEN, DAVID & SONS
KIRKCALDY, SCOTLAND	HERON, ROBERT (& SON)
KNOTTINGLEY POTTERY	FERRYBRIDGE POTTERY
KNOTTINGLEY POTTERY	TOMLINSON & CO.
KNOTTINGLEY POTTERY	WEDGWOOD & CO.
LADYBURN POTTERY	SHIRLEY, THOMAS & CO.
LANDORE POTTERY	CALLAND, JOHN F. & CO.
LANE DELPH	MASON, C. J. (& CO.)
LANE END	BOOTH & MEIGH
LANE END	HARLEY, THOMAS
LANE END	WALLEY, THOMAS
LASOL (WARE)	KEELING & CO. (LTD.)
LATE ADAMS, (W.) & SONS	CLOSE & CO.
LATE ALCOCK, (R.)	WILKINSON, ARTHUR J. (LTD.)
LATE HACKWOOD	COCKSON & HARDING
LATE HARVEY	HOLLAND & GREEN
LATE MAYERS	GILDEA, WALKER (& CO.)
LATE MAYERS	KEELING & CO. (LTD.)
LATE SPODE	COPELAND & GARRETT
LATE SPODE	COPELAND, W. T. (& SONS LTD.)
LATE WEDGWOOD	HOLLINSHEAD & KIRKHAM (LTD.)
LAWLEYS LTD. (Retailers)	MINTON
LEEDS	PETTY & CO.
LEEDS POTTERY	HARTLEY GREENS & CO.
LIMITED	DAVENPORT (various styles)
LIMOGES/P. G.	BRIDGWOOD, SAMPSON & SON (LTD.)
LINCOLN POTTERY	FORD, SAMUEL & CO.
LINCOLN POTTERY	SMITH & FORD
LINCOLN POTTERY	SMITH, FORD & JONES
LIVERPOOL	GOODWIN, JOHN & CO.
LIVERPOOL	HERCULANEUM POTTERY
LIVERPOOL	MEIKLE BROS. (Canadian Importers)
LLANELLY	SOUTH WALES POTTERY
LONDON	BELL, ISAAC & THOMAS
LONDON	CARR, JOHN & CO.
LONDON	FELL, THOMAS (& CO.)(LTD.)
LONDON	MALKIN, WALKER & HULSE
LONDON (See)	MIDDLESBROUGH POTTERY
LONDON RETAILERS	SHARPUS
LONGPORT	CLARKE, EDWARD (& CO.)
LONGPORT	CORN, W. & E.
LONGPORT	HUGHES, THOMAS
LONGPORT	MAYER, T. & J.
LONGPORT	MAYER, T. J. & J.
LONGPORT	MAYER, THOMAS
LONGPORT	PHILLIPS, EDWARD & GEORGE
LONGPORT	PHILLIPS, GEORGE
LONGPORT	PHILLIPS, THOMAS & SON
LONGPORT	STUBBS & KENT
LONGPORT	STUBBS, JOSEPH
LONGPORT	WOOD, ARTHUR & SON (LONGPORT) LTD.
LONGTON	BAGGERLEY & BALL
LONGTON	BARKER BROS. (LTD.)
LONGTON	BOURNE, WILLIAM (LONGTON)
LONGTON	BROADHURST, JAMES & SONS (LTD.)
LONGTON	COLCLOUGH & CO.
LONGTON	DAVENPORT (various styles)
LONGTON	GOODWIN, JOHN
LONGTON	GROVE & STARK
LONGTON	HAMMERSLEY & ASBURY
LONGTON	HUDDEN, JOHN THOMAS
LONGTON	JONES, FREDERICK (& CO.)
LONGTON	KENT, JAMES (LTD.)
LONGTON	LONGTON POTTERY CO. LTD.
LONGTON	STANLEY POTTERY LTD.
LONGTON	TAMS, JOHN (& SON)(LTD.)
LONGTON	TOMKINSON BROS. & CO.
LOW FORD	DAWSON (JOHN DAWSON & CO.)
LOWLIGHTS POTTERY	CARR, JOHN (& CO.)(& SON(S))
LOWNDES & BEECH	BEECH & LOWNDES
LUSTROSA	ASHWORTH, G. L. & BROS. (LTD.)
M./STONE	MINTON
MADE IN GREAT BRITTAIN	COCHRAN & FLEMING
MADE IN SCOTLAND	BRITANNIA POTTERY CO. LTD.
MADE IN SCOTLAND	COCHRAN & FLEMING
MALPASS, WILLIAM	KILNHURST OLD POTTERY
MANDARIN OPAQUE CHINA	POUNTNEY & GOLDNEY
MANUFACTURED	SHAW, ANTHONY (& CO.)(&SON(S))
MANUFACTURED BY	MORLEY & ASHWORTH
MANUFACTURED TO THE KING	BRAMELD & CO.
MASON'S	ASHWORTH, G. L. & BROS. (LTD.)
MASON'S	MASON, CHARLES JAMES (& CO.)
MASON'S	MASON, G. M. & C. J.
MASON'S IRONSTONE	MORLEY, FRANCIS (& CO.)
MASON'S PATENT IRONSTONE CHINA	MASON, G. M. & C. J.
MEAKIN & CO. (See)	MEAKIN BROS. & CO.
MEIR WORKS/LONGTON	BARKER BROS. (LTD.)
MELLOR, VENABLES & CO.	MELLOR, VENABLE, PINDER & CO. (See)
MICRATEX	ADAMS, WM. (& SONS)(& CO.)
MIDDLEPORT POTTERY (POTTERS)	BURGESS & LEIGH (LTD.)
MIDDLESBROUGH (POTTERY)	WILSON, ISAAC & CO.
MUSE	REID, WILLIAM (Scotland)
MUSE	REID, WM. (& SON(S))
MUSSELBURGH	REID, WM. (& SON(S))
N'CASTLE	PHOENIX POTTERY CO.
NANKIN WARE	TAMS, JOHN (& SON)(LTD.)
NAUTILUS PORCELAIN	NAUTILUS PORCELAIN CO.
NAUTILUS PORCELAIN	POSSIL POTTERY CO.
NEW BIGGINS POTTERY	REID, WM. & FORSTER
NEW BIGGINS POTTERY	REID, WM. (& SON(S))
NEW CANTON	STEVENSON, ANDREW
NEW CASTLE	FELL, THOMAS (& CO.)(LTD.)
NEW CASTLE (ON TYNE)	MAILING, C. T. & SONS (LTD.)
NEW CASTLE (ON TYNE)	WOOD, JOHN & CO. (LTD.)
NEW FAYENCE	SPODE, JOSIAH
NEW HILL	TWIGG, JOSEPH (& CO.)
NEW JAPAN STONE	COPELAND & GARRETT
NEW OPAQUE	MAYER & NEWBOLD
NEW PORCELAIN	JONES & WALLEY
NEW STONE	COPELAND, W. T. (& SONS LTD.)
NEW STONE	KEELING, SAMUEL & CO.
NEW STONE	SPODE, JOSIAH

NEW STONE CHINA	MASON, C. J. (& CO.)
NEW STONE CHINA	STEVENSON, RALPH & SON
NEW WHARF	GODWIN, THOMAS
NEW WHARF(E)	GODWIN, THOMAS & BENJAMIN
NEWBRIDGE POTTERY	BODLEY, EDWARD F. & SON
NEWCASTLE UPON TYNE	BELL, COOK & CO.
NEWCASTLE-ON-TYNE	MAILING, C. T. & SONS (LTD.)
NILE ST., BURSLEM	PINDER, BOURNE & CO.
NORFOLK POTTERY STONE	LAWLEY'S LTD. (Retailers)
NORTH BRITISH POTTERY	BALFOUR, ALEXANDER & CO.
NORTH BRITISH POTTERY	MILLER, JAMES & CO. LTD.
NORTHSHIELDS	CARR, JOHN & SON
NORTHUMBERLAND	CARR, JOHN & SON
OLD ENGLISH BONE CHINA	ALLERTON, CHARLES & SONS
OLD HALL	MEIGH, JOB (& SON)
OLD HALL	OLD HALL (EARTHENWARE) CO. LTD.
OLD HALL	OLD HALL PORCELAIN WORKS LTD.
OPAQUE CHINA	BAGGERLEY & BALL
OPAQUE CHINA	BAKER, BEVANS & IRWIN
OPAQUE CHINA	BELLE VUE POTTERY
OPAQUE CHINA	BEVINGTON, T. J. (& CO.)
OPAQUE CHINA	BOOTE, T. & R. (& SON) LTD.
OPAQUE CHINA	BOURNE, BAKER & BOURNE
OPAQUE CHINA	BRIDGWOOD & CLARKE
OPAQUE CHINA	DAVENPORT (various styles)
OPAQUE CHINA	EDWARDS, JAMES
OPAQUE CHINA	ELKIN, KNIGHT & BRIDGWOOD
OPAQUE CHINA	ELKIN, KNIGHT & CO.
OPAQUE CHINA	ELSMORE & FORSTER
OPAQUE CHINA	GODWIN, THOMAS
OPAQUE CHINA	GOODWIN(S) & HARRIS
OPAQUE CHINA	GORDON, GEORGE
OPAQUE CHINA	HANCOCK, SAMPSON (& SONS)
OPAQUE CHINA	HARVEY, C. & W. K.
OPAQUE CHINA	LOCKETT & HULME
OPAQUE CHINA	MAYER & NEWBOLD
OPAQUE CHINA	MINTON
OPAQUE CHINA	MORLEY, FRANCIS (& CO.)
OPAQUE CHINA	PHILLIPS, EDWARD & GEORGE
OPAQUE CHINA	PHILLIPS, GEORGE
OPAQUE CHINA	REED & TAYLOR (& CO.)
OPAQUE CHINA	RIDGWAY & MORLEY
OPAQUE CHINA	RIDGWAY, JOHN & WILLIAM
OPAQUE CHINA	RIDGWAY, JOHN & WILLIAM
OPAQUE CHINA	RIDGWAY, JOHN (& CO.)
OPAQUE CHINA	RIDGWAY, MORLEY, WEAR & CO.
OPAQUE CHINA	RIDGWAY, WM. (& CO.)
OPAQUE CHINA	RIDGWAYS (LTD.)
OPAQUE CHINA	RILEY, JOHN & RICHARD
OPAQUE CHINA	SWIFT & ELKIN
OPAQUE CHINA	WOOD & CHALLINOR
OPAQUE CHINA WARRANTED	MARSH, JACOB
OPAQUE FELSPAR CHINA	ELKIN, KNIGHT/KNIGHT, ELKIN & CO.
OPAQUE FELSPAR CHINA	KNIGHT, ELKIN & CO.
OPAQUE GRANITE	RIDGWAY, WM. (& CO.)
OPAQUE GRANITE CHINA	AUSTRALIAN POTTERY
OPAQUE GRANITE CHINA	BAKER, (W.) & CO.
OPAQUE GRANITE CHINA	FERRYBRIDGE POTTERY
OPAQUE GRANITE CHINA	KNIGHT, JOHN KING
OPAQUE GRANITE CHINA	RIDGWAY, WM. (& CO.)
OPAQUE GRANITE CHINA	SWILLINGTON BRIDGE POTTERY
OPAQUE PEARL	CLEMENTSON, JOSEPH & SONS
OPAQUE PEARL	HARVEY, J. & CO.
OPAQUE PORCELAIN	BRIDGWOOD & CLARKE
OPAQUE PORCELAIN	HARVEY, C. & W. K.
OPAQUE PORCELAIN	MEIGH, CHARLES & SON
OPAQUE PORCELAIN	OLD HALL (EARTHENWARE) CO. LTD.
OPAQUE PORCELAINE	FURNIVAL, THOMAS (& CO.)
OPAQUE STONE	ALCOCK, JOHN & GEORGE
OPAQUE STONE	ALCOCK, JOHN & SAMUEL
OPAQUE STONE	ROBINSON, WOOD & BROWNFIELD
OPAQUE STONE CHINA	ROBINSON, WOOD & BROWNFIELD
OPAQUE STONE CHINA	SHAW, ANTHONY (& CO.)(&SON(S))
ORIENTAL IVORY	BISHOP & STONIER (LTD.)
ORIENTAL IVORY	POWELL, BISHOP & STONIER
ORIENTAL STONE	ALCOCK, JOHN
ORIENTAL STONE	ALCOCK, JOHN & GEORGE
ORIENTAL STONE	ALCOCK, JOHN & SAMUEL
ORTOLAN	DEAKIN & SON
OVERHOUSE	GATER, HALL & CO.
PALISSY	JONES, ALBERT E. (LONGTON) LTD.
PALISSY	PALISSY POTTERY LTD.
PANKHURST & DIMMOCK (see)	PANKHURST, J. W. & CO.
PARIS WHITE	WALLEY, EDWARD
PARIS WHITE IRONSTONE	MEAKIN, ALFRED (LTD.)
PARIS WHITE IRONSTONE	MEAKIN, J. & G.
PARISIAN GRANITE	BOOTH, T. G. & F.
PARISIAN GRANITE	ELSMORE (THOMAS) & SON
PARISIAN GRANITE	MEAKIN, ALFRED (LTD.)
PARISIAN PORCELAIN	ALCOCK, HENRY & CO. (LTD.)
PARISIAN PORCELAIN	ALCOCK, JOHN
PARISIAN WHITE	SMITH, FORD & JONES
PATENT	ALCOCK, SAMUEL & CO.
PATENT	FORD & CHALLINOR & CO.
PATENT	GOODFELLOW, THOMAS
PATENT	MACHIN & POTTS
PATENT	MAYER, T. J. & J.
PATENT	MORLEY, FRANCIS (& CO.)
PATENT	POTTS, WM. WAINWRIGHT
PATENT	RIDGWAY & MORLEY
PATENT	WOOD, ENOCH & SON(S)
PATENT IRONSTONE CHINA	ALCOCK, SAMUEL & CO.
PATENT IRONSTONE CHINA	ASHWORTH, G. L. & BROS. (LTD.)
PATENT IRONSTONE CHINA	DAVENPORT (various styles)
PATENT IRONSTONE CHINA	JONES, FREDERICK (& CO.)
PATENT IRONSTONE CHINA	MASON, C. J. (& CO.)
PATENT IRONSTONE CHINA	MASON, G. M. & C. J.
PATENT IRONSTONE CHINA	MASON, JAMES
PATENT IRONSTONE CHINA	MORLEY & ASHWORTH
PATENT IRONSTONE CHINA	MORLEY, FRANCIS (& CO.)
PATENT IRONSTONE CHINA	RIDGWAY & MORLEY
PATENT IRONSTONE CHINA	SPODE, JOSIAH
PATENT IRONSTONE CHINA	TURNER, (JOHN) & CO.
PATENT MOSAIC	BOOTE, T. & R. (& SON) LTD.
PATENT MOSAIC	CORK & EDGE
PATENT OPAQUE CHINA	MORLEY, FRANCIS (& CO.)
PATENT PARIS WHITE IRONSTONE	WEDGWOOD & CO. (LTD.)
PATENT STAFFORDSHIRE	CLEWS, JAMES & RALPH
PEARL	CHALLINOR, CHARLES & CO.
PEARL	COCKSON & CHETWYND (& CO.)
PEARL	COLLINSON, CHARLES & CO.
PEARL	DEAKIN & CO.
PEARL	HOLDCROFT, PETER & CO.
PEARL	PODMORE, WALKER & (CO.)
PEARL	TOMKINSON BROS. & CO.
PEARL	WEDGWOOD, JOSIAH (& SONS, LTD.)
PEARL CHINA	BAKER, (W.) & CO. (LTD.)
PEARL CHINA	BURTON, SAMUEL & JOHN
PEARL CHINA	MEAKIN, J. & G. (LTD.)
PEARL CHINA	WOOD, ENOCH & EDWARD
PEARL IRONSTONE	JONES, FREDERICK (& CO.)
PEARL IRONSTONE CHINA	FORD & CHALLINOR & CO.
PEARL IRONSTONE CHINA	JONES, FREDERICK (& CO.)
PEARL IRONSTONE CHINA	PHILLIPS, GEORGE
PEARL IRONSTONE CHINA	TURNER & TOMKINSON
PEARL STONE CHINA	PODMORE, WALKER & (CO.)
PEARL STONE WARE	PODMORE, WALKER & (CO.)
PEARL STONE WARE	WEDGWOOD & CO. (LTD.)
PEARL VITRIFIED IRONSTONE CHINA	FURNIVAL, JACOB & CO.
PEARL WARE	ALCOCK, SAMUEL & CO.
PEARL WARE	DIMMOCK , THOMAS (JR.) & CO.
PEARL WARE	SKINNER & WALKER
PEARL WHITE	BAKER, (W.) & CO. (LTD.)
PEARL WHITE	WALLEY, EDWARD
PEARL WHITE	WOOD & BROWNFIELD
PEARL WHITE GRANITE	BAKER, (W.) & CO. (LTD.)
PEARL WHITE IRONSTONE	CORK & EDGE
PEARL WHITE IRONSTONE	SOUTH WALES POTTERY
PENMAN, BROWN & CO. (See)	PENMAN, ROBERT, H. & CO.
PHOENIX CHINA	FORESTER, THOMAS & SON(S)(LTD.)
PHOENIX WARE	FORESTER, THOMAS & SON(S)(LTD.)
PORCELAIN	EDWARDS, JAMES
PORCELAIN A LA PERLE	EDWARDS, JAMES & THOMAS
PORCELAIN OPAQUE	ALCOCK, J. & S.
PORCELAIN OPAQUE	BOOTE, T. & R. (& SON) LTD.
PORCELAIN OPAQUE	BRIDGWOOD & CLARKE
PORCELAIN OPAQUE	BRIDGWOOD, SAMPSON & SON (LTD.)
PORCELAIN OPAQUE	CARR, JOHN & SON
PORCELAIN OPAQUE	COCHRAN & FLEMING
PORCELAIN OPAQUE	EDWARDS, JAMES & THOMAS
PORCELAIN OPAQUE	EDWARDS, THOMAS
PORCELAIN OPAQUE	FELL, THOMAS (& CO.)(LTD.)
PORCELAIN OPAQUE	JAMIESON, JAMES & CO.
PORCELAIN OPAQUE	MEIGH, CHARLES
PORCELAIN OPAQUE	METHVEN, DAVID & SONS
PORCELAIN OPAQUE	SHAW, ANTHONY (& CO.)(&SON(S))
PORCELAIN ROYAL	CLEVELAND POTTERY
PORCELAIN ROYALE	PITCAIRNS LTD.
PORCELAIN ROYALE (ART-WARE)	CORN, W. & E.
PORCELAINE A LA FRANCAISE	RIDGWAY, JOHN (& CO.)
PORCELAINE A LA PERLE	EDWARDS, JAMES
PORCELAINE DE TERRE	EDWARDS, JOHN
PORCELAINE OPAQUE	BOOTE, T. & R. (& SON) LTD.
PORCELON	MIDWINTER, W. R. (LTD.)
PORT DUNDAS POTTERY CO.	MILLER, JAMES & CO. LTD.
POTTERS TO HER MAJESTY	CAULDON LTD.
POTTERY	TURNBULL, G. R.

PRESTOPANS	BELFIELD & CO.
PRESTOPANS	FOWLER THOMPSON & CO.
PUBLISHED BY	RIDGWAY, WM. SON & CO.
QUARTZ CHINA	RIDGWAY, WM. (& CO.)
QUEENS-WARE/STOCKTON	SKINNER & WALKER
QUEENS-WARE/STOCKTON	SMITH, WILLIAM (& CO.)
REAL CHINA	MEAKIN, J. & G. (LTD.)
REAL ENGLISH IRONSTONE	ADAMS, WM. (& SONS)(& CO.)
REAL IRONSTONE	DANIEL, H. & R.
REAL IRONSTONE	EDWARDS, JAMES
REAL IRONSTONE	FELL, THOMAS (& CO.)(LTD.)
REAL IRONSTONE	FURNIVAL, THOMAS & CO.
REAL IRONSTONE	MORLEY, FRANCIS (& CO.)
REAL IRONSTONE	WOOD & BROWNFIELD
REAL IRONSTONE CHINA	ADAMS, WM. (& SONS)(& CO.)
REAL IRONSTONE CHINA	ASHWORTH, G. L. & BROS. (LTD.)
REAL IRONSTONE CHINA	DAVENPORT (various styles)
REAL IRONSTONE CHINA	DAVENPORT, JOHN
REAL IRONSTONE CHINA	EDWARDS, JAMES & SON
REAL IRONSTONE CHINA	FURNIVAL, JACOB & CO.
REAL IRONSTONE CHINA	HARVEY, C. & W. K.
REAL IRONSTONE CHINA	HOLLAND & GREEN
REAL IRONSTONE CHINA	MEAKIN, ALFRED (LTD.)
REAL IRONSTONE CHINA	MELLOR, TAYLOR & CO.
REAL IRONSTONE CHINA	MORLEY & ASHWORTH
REAL IRONSTONE CHINA	MORLEY, FRANCIS (& CO.)
REAL IRONSTONE CHINA	RIDGWAY & MORLEY
REAL IRONSTONE CHINA	RIDGWAY, JOHN & WILLIAM
REAL IRONSTONE CHINA	RIDGWAY, JOHN (& CO.)
REAL IRONSTONE CHINA	RIDGWAY, MORLEY, WEAR & CO.
REAL IRONSTONE CHINA	RIDGWAY, WM. (& CO.)
REAL IRONSTONE CHINA	WOOD & BROWNFIELD
REAL STONE CHINA	ASHWORTH'S (BROS.)
REAL STONE CHINA	DAVENPORT (various styles)
REAL STONE CHINA	HICKS, MEIGH & JOHNSON
REAL STONE CHINA	MORLEY, FRANCIS (& CO.)
REAL STONE CHINA	RIDGWAY, JOHN (& CO.)
REAL VITRIFIED IRONSTONE CHINA	FURNIVAL, J. & CO.
ROCK STONE	TAMS, JOHN (& SON)(LTD.)
ROCKINGHAM POTTERY (WORKS)	BRAMELD & CO.
ROCKINGHAM WORKS	BRAMELD & CO.
ROMANTIC	BLAKENEY POTTERY CO.
ROYAL ART POTTERY	CLOUGH'S ROYAL ART POTTERY
ROYAL ART POTTERY	CLOUGH, ALFRED (LTD.)
ROYAL CHINA	HUGHES, E. & CO.
ROYAL CORONATION WARE	HANCOCK, SAMPSON (& SONS)
ROYAL CROWNFORD IRONSTONE	WEATHERBY, J. H. & SONS (LTD.)
ROYAL DOULTON	DOULTON (& CO.) (LTD.)
ROYAL IRONSTONE	MEAKIN, CHARLES
ROYAL IRONSTONE CHINA	ALCOCK, HENRY & CO. (LTD.)
ROYAL IRONSTONE CHINA	BAKER, (W.) & CO. (LTD.)
ROYAL IRONSTONE CHINA	BOOTE, T. & R. (& SON) LTD.
ROYAL IRONSTONE CHINA	CALEDONIAN POTTERY
ROYAL IRONSTONE CHINA	CLEMENTSON BROS.
ROYAL IRONSTONE CHINA	COCHRAN & FLEMING
ROYAL IRONSTONE CHINA	CORN, W. & E.
ROYAL IRONSTONE CHINA	DEANS (1910) LTD.
ROYAL IRONSTONE CHINA	GRINDLEY, W. H. & CO. (LTD.)
ROYAL IRONSTONE CHINA	JOHNSON BROS. (HANLEY) LTD.
ROYAL IRONSTONE CHINA	MEAKIN, ALFRED (LTD.)
ROYAL IRONSTONE CHINA	MEAKIN, CHARLES
ROYAL IRONSTONE CHINA	MELLOR, TAYLOR & CO.
ROYAL IRONSTONE CHINA	WILKINSON, ARTHUR J. (LTD.)
ROYAL IRONSTONE CHINA	WOOD & SON(S) (LTD.)
ROYAL IRONSTONE WARE	JOHNSON BROS. (HANLEY) LTD.
ROYAL IVORY	MADDOCK, JOHN & SONS (LTD.)
ROYAL OPAQUE CHINA	MEIKLE BROS. (Canadian Importers)
ROYAL PATENT	BOOTE, T. & R. (& SON) LTD.
ROYAL PATENT	CLEMENTSON BROS. LTD.
ROYAL PATENT	MELLOR, VENABLES & CO.
ROYAL PATENT IRONSTONE	BOOTE, T. & R. (& SON) LTD.
ROYAL PATENT IRONSTONE	HUGHES, THOMAS & SON (LTD.)
ROYAL PATENT IRONSTONE	JONES, GEORGE
ROYAL PATENT IRONSTONE	TURNER, GODDARD & CO.
ROYAL PATENT IRONSTONE	WILKINSON, ARTHUR J. (LTD.)
ROYAL PATENT STONE WARE	CLEMENTSON BROS. LTD.
ROYAL PREMIUM IRONSTONE	BOOTE, T. & R. (& SON) LTD.
ROYAL PREMIUM SEMI PORCELAIN	BOOTE, T. & R. (& SON) LTD.
ROYAL ROCKINGHAM WORKS	BRAMELD & CO.
ROYAL SEMI CHINA	KENT, JAMES (LTD.)
ROYAL SEMI PORCELAIN	ADAMS, WM. & CO.
ROYAL SEMI PORCELAIN	BOOTE, T. & R. (& SON) LTD.
ROYAL SEMI PORCELAIN	BOOTH'S (LTD.)
ROYAL SEMI PORCELAIN	BOURNE & LEIGH (LTD.)
ROYAL SEMI PORCELAIN	BURGESS & LEIGH (LTD.)
ROYAL SEMI PORCELAIN	CLARKE, EDWARD (& CO.)
ROYAL SEMI PORCELAIN	CLEMENTSON BROS. LTD.
ROYAL SEMI PORCELAIN	COLLEY , ALFRED & CO., LTD.
ROYAL SEMI PORCELAIN	FURNIVALS (LTD.)
ROYAL SEMI PORCELAIN	JOHNSON BROS. (HANLEY) LTD.
ROYAL SEMI PORCELAIN	MADDOCK, JOHN & SONS (LTD.)
ROYAL SEMI PORCELAIN	MEAKIN, ALFRED (LTD.)
ROYAL SEMI PORCELAIN	RIDGWAYS (LTD.)
ROYAL SEMI PORCELAIN	WEDGWOOD & CO. (LTD.)
ROYAL SEMI PORCELAIN	WILKINSON, ARTHUR J. (LTD.)
ROYAL SEMI PORCELAIN	WOOD & SON
ROYAL STAFFORDSHIRE POTTERY	WILKINSON, ARTHUR J. (LTD.)
ROYAL STANLEY (WARE)	COLCLOUGH & CO.
ROYAL STANLEY (WARE)	STANLEY POTTERY LTD.
ROYAL STONE	MORLEY, FRANCIS (& CO.)
ROYAL STONE CHINA	ASHWORTH, G. & L. (BROS.)(LTD.)
ROYAL STONE CHINA	BELL, J. & M. P. & CO. (LD.)
ROYAL STONE CHINA	DAVIS, J. H. & J.
ROYAL STONE CHINA	MADDOCK, JOHN & SONS (LTD.)
ROYAL STONE CHINA	STEVENSON, RALPH & WILLIAMS
ROYAL STONE CHINA	WEDGWOOD & CO. (LTD.)
ROYAL VENTON WARE	STEVENTON, JOHN & SONS LTD.
ROYAL VITREOUS	MADDOCK, JOHN & SONS (LTD.)
ROYAL VITRESCENT ROCK CHINA	MACHIN & POTTS
ROYAL VITRIFIED	MADDOCK, JOHN & SONS (LTD.)
ROYAL VITRIFIED	RIDGWAYS (LTD.)
ROYAL WARRANTED BEST IRONSTONE CHINA	ALCOCK, HENRY & CO.
ROYAL WARRANTED BEST IRONSTONE CHINA	ALCOCK, JOHN
ROYAL WORCESTER	PALISSY POTTERY LTD.
SAXON	CLYDE POTTERY CO. (LTD.)
SAXON	SHIRLEY, THOMAS & CO.
SAXON BLUE	EDWARDS, JAMES
SAXON BLUE	DILLWYN & CO.
SAXON STONE CHINA	CAREY, THOMAS & JOHN
SCOTIA POTTERY	BODLEY & HAROLD
SCOTIA POTTERY	BODLEY, EDWARD F. & CO.
SCOTLAND	METHVEN, DAVID & SONS
SEACOMBE POTTERY	GOODWIN, JOHN
SEAHAM POTTERY	ALLASON, JOHN
SEMI CHINA	ALCOCK, HENRY & CO. (LTD.)
SEMI CHINA	CLEMENTSON BROS. LTD.
SEMI CHINA	ELGIN POTTERY
SEMI CHINA	FOWLER THOMPSON & CO.
SEMI CHINA	GODWIN, THOMAS & BENJAMIN
SEMI CHINA	MINTON
SEMI CHINA	RIDGWAYS (BEDFORD WORKS) LTD.
SEMI CHINA	RILEY, JOHN & RICHARD
SEMI CHINA	ROGERS, JOHN (& SON)
SEMI CHINA	STEVENSON, RALPH & WILLIAMS
SEMI CHINA	TAMS & CO.
SEMI CHINA	TAMS (ET. AL.)
SEMI CHINA	THOMPSON, FOWLER (& CO.)
SEMI CHINA	WALLACE, JAMES & CO.
SEMI CHINA	WOOD, ENOCH & SON(S)
SEMI CHINA	YALE & BARKER
SEMI CHINA WARRANTED	MASON, C. J. (& CO.)
SEMI CHINA WARRANTED	MASON, G. M. & C. J.
SEMI CHINA WARRANTED	RILEY, JOHN & RICHARD
SEMI CHINA WARRANTED	STEVENSON, RALPH
SEMI IMPERIAL PORCELAIN	BISHOP & STONIER (LTD.)
SEMI NANKIN CHINA	MINTON
SEMI NANKIN CHINA	STEVENSON, ANDREW
SEMI PORCELAIN	ALCOCK, HENRY POTTERY, THE
SEMI PORCELAIN	BOOTE, T. & R. (& SON) LTD.
SEMI PORCELAIN	BRIDGWOOD, SAMPSON & SON (LTD.)
SEMI PORCELAIN	BURGESS & LEIGH (LTD.)
SEMI PORCELAIN	CLEMENTSON BROS. LTD.
SEMI PORCELAIN	FORD, SAMUEL & CO.
SEMI PORCELAIN	GLOBE POTTERY CO. LTD.
SEMI PORCELAIN	GRIMWADES LTD.
SEMI PORCELAIN	GRINDLEY, W. H. & CO. (LTD.)
SEMI PORCELAIN	HUGHES, THOMAS & SON (LTD.)
SEMI PORCELAIN	MEAKIN, J. & G. (LTD.)
SEMI PORCELAIN	MELLOR, TAYLOR & CO.
SEMI PORCELAIN	MYOTT, SON & CO. (LTD.)
SEMI PORCELAIN	NEW WHARF POTTERY CO.
SEMI PORCELAIN	POUNTNEY & CO. (LTD.)
SEMI PORCELAIN	RIDGWAYS (BEDFORD WORKS) LTD.
SEMI PORCELAIN	SMITH & FORD
SEMI PORCELAIN	SWINNERTON (LTD.)
SEMI PORCELAIN	SOHO POTTERY LTD.
SEMI PORCELAIN	UPPER HANLEY POTTERY CO. (LTD.)
SEMI PORCELAIN	WEATHERBY, J. H. & SONS (LTD.)
SEMI PORCELAIN IMPERIAL	BISHOP & STONIER (LTD.)
SEMI PORCELAINE	PRATT & SIMPSON
SEMI ROYAL PORCELAIN	WEDGWOOD & CO. (LTD.)
SEMI ROYAL PORCELAIN	WEDGWOOD, JOSIAH (& SONS, LTD.)
SEVRES	EDWARDS, JAMES & THOMAS
SHELTON	CLEMENTSON, JOSEPH & SONS
SHELTON	GLOBE POTTERY CO. LTD.
SHELTON	MORLEY, FRANCIS (& CO.)

SHELTON	RIDGWAY, WM. (& CO.)
SHELTON	RIDGWAYS (BEDFORD WORKS) LTD.
SHERIFF HILL	PATTERSON (GEORGE) & CO.
SHERIFF HILL POTTERY	FORDY & PATTERSON (& CO.)
SILICON CHINA	BOOTH'S (LTD.)
SILICON CHINA	DILLWYN & CO.
SOL	MEAKIN, J. & G. (LTD.)
SOLIAN WARE	SOHO POTTERY LTD.
SOUTH HYLTON	DAWSON (JOHN DAWSON & CO.)
SOUTH WALES POTTERY	CHAMBERS, LLANELLY
SOUTH WALES POTTERY	CHAMBERS, WILLIAM
SOUTH WALES POTTERY	COOMBS & HOLLAND
SOUTH WALES POTTERY	GUEST & DEWSBERRY
SOUTH WALES POTTERY	HOLLAND & GUEST
SOUTH WALES POTTERY	HOLLAND, WILLIAM
SOUTHWICK	SOUTHWICK POTTERY
SOUTHWICK POTTERY	SCOTT (BROS.)(& CO.)(& SONS)
SPECIAL WHITE STONE WARE	CLEMENTSON BROS. LTD.
SPODES IMPERIAL	COPELAND & GARRETT
ST. ANTHONY'S POTTERY	SEWELL(S) & CO.
ST. ANTHONY'S POTTERY	SEWELL(S) POTTERY
ST. ROLLOX	COCHRAN, R. & CO.
STAFF	FURNIVAL, JACOB & CO.
STAFFORD POTTERY	SMITH, WILLIAM (& CO.)
STAFFORDSHIRE	BAGSTER, JOHN DENTON
STAFFORDSHIRE	BAKER, (W.) & CO. (LTD.)
STAFFORDSHIRE	BATKIN, WALKER & BROADHURST
STAFFORDSHIRE	BOOTH'S (LTD.)
STAFFORDSHIRE	BOURNE, WILLIAM & CO.
STAFFORDSHIRE	CERAMIC ART CO. LTD.
STAFFORDSHIRE	CHALLINOR, EDWARD
STAFFORDSHIRE	CLOSE, J. T. (& CO.)
STAFFORDSHIRE	CORK & EDGE
STAFFORDSHIRE	CORN, W. & E.
STAFFORDSHIRE	DAVENPORT (various styles)
STAFFORDSHIRE	EDWARDS, THOMAS
STAFFORDSHIRE	FURNIVAL, J. & CO.
STAFFORDSHIRE	GODWIN, ROWLEY & CO.
STAFFORDSHIRE	GRIMWADES LTD.
STAFFORDSHIRE	MAYER, THOMAS
STAFFORDSHIRE	MEIGH, CHARLES & SON
STAFFORDSHIRE	MEIR, JOHN & SON
STAFFORDSHIRE	MYOTT, SON & CO. (LTD.)
STAFFORDSHIRE	PALISSY POTTERY LTD.
STAFFORDSHIRE	REEVES, JAMES
STAFFORDSHIRE	STEVENSON, ANDREW
STAFFORDSHIRE	STEVENSON, RALPH
STAFFORDSHIRE	STEVENSON, RALPH & WILLIAMS
STAFFORDSHIRE	WALLEY, EDWARD
STAFFORDSHIRE	WOOD, ENOCH & SON(S)
STAFFORDSHIRE IRONSTONE CHINA	GRIFFITHS, BEARDMORE & BIRKS
STAFFORDSHIRE IRONSTONE CHINA	TOWNSEND, GEORGE
STAFFORDSHIRE POTTERIES	MADDOCK & GATER
STAFFORDSHIRE POTTERIES	MADDOCK, JOHN & SONS (LTD.)
STAFFORDSHIRE POTTERIES	MASON, C. J. (& CO.)
STAFFORDSHIRE POTTERIES	SNEYD & HILL
STAFFORDSHIRE STONE CHINA	GODWIN, ROWLEY & CO.
STAFFORDSHIRE STONE CHINA	SWIFT & ELKIN
STAFFORDSHIRE STONEWARE	CORK & EDGE
STAFFORDSHIRE WARRANTED	ADAMS, WM. (& SONS)(& CO.)
STAFFORDSHIRE WARRANTED	STEVENSON, ANDREW
STAFFS	BROWNFIELD, WM. (& SON(S))
STAFFS	FURNIVAL, THOMAS & SONS
STANLEY CHINA	AMISON, CHARLES (& CO. LTD.) (China)
STEPNEY (POTTERY)	TURNBULL, G. R.
STEPNEY (POTTERY)	WOOD, JOHN & CO. (LTD.)
STOCKTON	RIDGWAY, JOHN & WILLIAM
STOCKTON	SKINNER & WALKER
STOCKTON	SMITH, W. (JR.) & CO.
STOKE	HAMILTON, ROBERT
STOKE	MAYER, THOMAS
STOKE	MOUNTFORD, GEORGE THOMAS
STOKE	MYOTT, SON & CO. (LTD.)
STOKE	WINKLE, F. & CO. (LTD.)
STOKE	WOLFE & HAMILTON
STOKE MANUFACTURERS	BOYLE, ZACHARIA (& CO.) (&SON(S))
STOKE ON TRENT	CARLTON WARE LTD.
STOKE ON TRENT	CERAMIC ART CO. (1905) LTD.
STOKE ON TRENT	COLCLOUGH & CO.
STOKE ON TRENT	EMPIRE PORCELAIN CO. (LTD.)
STOKE ON TRENT	GRIMWADES LTD.
STOKE ON TRENT	HANCOCK, SAMPSON (& SONS)
STOKE ON TRENT	JONES, G. F.
STOKE ON TRENT	JONES, GEORGE (& SONS)(LTD.)
STOKE ON TRENT	RIDGWAYS (LTD.)
STOKE ON TRENT	STANLEY POTTERY LTD.
STOKE ON TRENT	WILTSHAW & ROBINSON (LTD.)
STOKE POTTERY	GRIMWADES LTD.
STOKE POTTERY	PLANT, J. & CO.
STOKE UPON TRENT	CLOSE & CO.
STOKE UPON TRENT	CLOSE, J. T. (& CO.)
STOKE UPON TRENT	GRIMWADE BROS.
STOKE UPON TRENT	GROSE & CO.
STOKE UPON TRENT	MAYER, THOMAS
STOKE UPON TRENT	MINTON
STOKE WORKS	FOLCH, STEPHEN (& SONS)
STONE	MEIGH, CHARLES
STONE	MINTON
STONE CHINA	ADAMS, WM. (& SONS)(& CO.)
STONE CHINA	BAKER, (W.) & CO. (LTD.)
STONE CHINA	BARKER & TILL
STONE CHINA	BARKER, (W.) & CO. (LTD.)
STONE CHINA	BARKER, SUTTON & TILL
STONE CHINA	BATKIN, WALKER & BROADHURST
STONE CHINA	BRAMELD & CO.
STONE CHINA	BURGESS, HENRY
STONE CHINA	CALEDONIAN POTTERY
STONE CHINA	CHALLINOR, E. & C.
STONE CHINA	CLARKE, EDWARD (& CO.)
STONE CHINA	CLEMENTSON BROS. LTD.
STONE CHINA	CLEMENTSON, JOSEPH & SONS
STONE CHINA	CLEWS, JAMES & RALPH
STONE CHINA	CLOSE, J. T. (& CO.)
STONE CHINA	COCHRAN, R. & CO.
STONE CHINA	CORK & EDGE
STONE CHINA	CORK, EDGE & MALKIN
STONE CHINA	DANIEL, H. & R.
STONE CHINA	DAVENPORT (various styles)
STONE CHINA	EDGE, MALKIN & CO.
STONE CHINA	EDGE, WILLIAM & SAMUEL
STONE CHINA	EDWARDS, JAMES & SON
STONE CHINA	FELL, THOMAS (& CO.)(LTD.)
STONE CHINA	FURNIVAL, JACOB & THOMAS
STONE CHINA	GODWIN, ROWLEY & CO.
STONE CHINA	GODWIN, THOMAS
STONE CHINA	GODWIN, THOMAS & BENJAMIN
STONE CHINA	GROSE & CO.
STONE CHINA	HALL, RALPH (& CO.) or (& SON)
STONE CHINA	HANDLEY, JAMES & WILLIAM
STONE CHINA	HICKS & MEIGH
STONE CHINA	HICKS, MEIGH & JOHNSON
STONE CHINA	HOPE & CARTER
STONE CHINA	JOHNSON, REUBEN
STONE CHINA	JONES, GEORGE (& SONS)(LTD.)
STONE CHINA	MADDOCK & SEDDON
STONE CHINA	MADDOCK, JOHN
STONE CHINA	MADDOCK, JOHN & SONS (LTD.)
STONE CHINA	MEIR, JOHN
STONE CHINA	MEIR, JOHN & SON
STONE CHINA	MINTON
STONE CHINA	MORLEY & ASHWORTH
STONE CHINA	PLYMOUTH POTTERY CO. LTD.
STONE CHINA	PRATT & SIMPSON
STONE CHINA	REED & TAYLOR (& CO.)
STONE CHINA	REED, JAMES
STONE CHINA	RIDGWAY, JOHN & WILLIAM
STONE CHINA	RIDGWAY, JOHN (& CO.)
STONE CHINA	ROBINSON & WOOD
STONE CHINA	ROBINSON, WOOD & BROWNFIELD
STONE CHINA	ROWLEY & CO.
STONE CHINA	SHAW, ANTHONY (& CO.)(&SON(S))
STONE CHINA	SHAW, C. & J.
STONE CHINA	SPODE, JOSIAH
STONE CHINA	STEVENSON, RALPH & WILLIAMS
STONE CHINA	TAYLOR, WILLIAM
STONE CHINA	TWIGG, JOSEPH (& CO.)
STONE CHINA	WALLEY, EDWARD
STONE CHINA	WEDGWOOD & CO. (LTD.)
STONE CHINA	WEDGWOOD'S (J.) WEDGWOOD & SONS (LTD.)
STONE CHINA	WEDGWOOD, JOSIAH (& SONS, LTD.)
STONE CHINA	WHITEHAVEN POTTERY
STONE CHINA	WOOD & BROWNFIELD
STONE CHINA	WOOD & CHALLINOR
STONE CHINA WARRANTED	SHAW, ANTHONY (& CO.)(&SON(S))
STONE CHINAWARE CO.	ST. JOHN'S STONE CHINAWARE CO. (Canadian)
STONE GRANITE	SMITH, WM. & CO.
STONE GRANITE	WEDGWOOD & CO. (LTD.)
STONE GRANITE	WOOD, EDMUND, T.
STONE GRANITE	WOOD, J. WEDGE
STONEWARE	ALCOCK, SAMUEL & CO.
STONEWARE	BARKER & TILL
STONEWARE	BARKER, (W.) & SON, LTD.
STONEWARE	BARKER, SUTTON & TILL
STONEWARE	BATES & BENNETT
STONEWARE	BURN, JOSEPH & CO.
STONEWARE	CLEMENTSON BROS. LTD.
STONEWARE	CLEMENTSON, JOSEPH & SONS
STONEWARE	CLOSE, J. T. (& CO.)

STONEWARE	CORK & EDGE
STONEWARE	DANIEL, H. & R.
STONEWARE	DAVENPORT (various styles)
STONEWARE	DILLWYN & CO.
STONEWARE	DIMMOCK , THOMAS (JR.) & CO.
STONEWARE	MAUDESLEY, J. & CO.
STONEWARE	MAYER, T. J. & J.
STONEWARE	MORLEY, FRANCIS (& CO.)
STONEWARE	PODMORE, WALKER & (CO.)
STONEWARE	READ & CLEMENTSON
STONEWARE	READ & CO.
STONEWARE	REED, JAMES
STONEWARE	RIDGWAY & MORLEY
STONEWARE	RIDGWAY, JOHN (& CO.)
STONEWARE	ROBINSON, WOOD & BROWNFIELD
STONEWARE	THOMSON, JOHN (& SONS)
STONEWARE	TILL, THOMAS & SON(S)(LTD.)
STONEWARE	WEDGWOOD & CO. (LTD.)
STONEWARE	WOOD & BROWNFIELD
SUNDERLAND	MOORE, (SAMUEL) & CO.
SUNDERLAND POTTERY	DIXON & CO.
SUNDERLAND POTTERY	DIXON, AUSTIN & CO.
SUNDERLAND POTTERY	PHILLIPS & CO.
SUNDERLAND POTTERY	PHILLIPS, J.
SUNDERLAND POTTERY	PHILLIPS, JOHN
SUNDREX	SUNDERLAND POTTERY CO. (LTD.)
SUPERIOR STAFFORDSHIRE WARE	JONES & SON
SUPERIOR STONE CHINA	RIDGWAY, JOHN (& CO.)
SUTHERLAND ARTWARE	BEARDMORE, FRANK & CO.
SWADLINCOTE	SHARPE, THOMAS
SWANSEA	BEVINGTON, T. J. (& CO.)
SWANSEA	CALLAND, JOHN F. & CO.
SWANSEA	CAMBRIAN POTTERY
SWANSEA	DILLWYN & CO.
SWANSEA	EVANS & GLASSON
SWANSEA	EVANS, D. J. & CO.
SWANSEA POTTERY	DILLWYN & CO.
SWANSEA POTTERY	EVANS & GLASSON
SWANSEA POTTERY	EVANS, D. J. & CO.
SYTCH POTTERY	TILL, THOMAS & SON(S)(LTD.)
TAMS (ET. AL.)	TAMS & ANDERSON
TAMS (ET. AL.)	TAMS & CO.
TAMS (ET. AL.)	TAMS, ANDERSON & TAMS
TAMS (ET. AL.)	TAMS, S. & CO.
TAMS REGENT	TAMS, JOHN (& SON)(LTD.)
THE QUEEN'S ROYAL IRONSTONE	GOODWIN, JOHN
TRADE MARK	ADAMS, WM. & CO.
TRADE MARK	ADDERLEY'S LTD.
TRADE MARK	ADDERLEY, WILLIAM ALSAGER (& CO.)
TRADE MARK	ALCOCK, HENRY & CO.
TRADE MARK	BARKER BROS. (LTD.)
TRADE MARK	BARKERS & KENT, LTD.
TRADE MARK	BEECH, JAMES
TRADE MARK	BELL, J. & M. P. & CO. (LD.)
TRADE MARK	BODLEY, EDWARD F. & SON
TRADE MARK	BRIDGWOOD, SAMPSON & SON (LTD.)
TRADE MARK	BRITANNIA POTTERY CO. LTD.
TRADE MARK	BROWNFIELD, WM. (& SON(S))
TRADE MARK	CHALLINOR & MAYER
TRADE MARK	CLARKE, EDWARD (& CO.)
TRADE MARK	COPELAND, W. T. (& SONS LTD.)
TRADE MARK	EDGE, MALKIN & CO. (LTD.)
TRADE MARK	EDWARDS, JOHN
TRADE MARK	FORD & RILEY
TRADE MARK	FURNIVAL, THOMAS & SONS
TRADE MARK	FURNIVALS (LTD.)
TRADE MARK	GILDEA, WALKER (& CO.)
TRADE MARK	GREEN & CLAY
TRADE MARK	GRIMWADE BROS.
TRADE MARK	GRINDLEY, W. H. & CO. (LTD.)
TRADE MARK	HOLLINSHEAD & KIRKHAM (LTD.)
TRADE MARK	HUGHES, THOMAS & SON (LTD.)
TRADE MARK	HULSEY & ADDERLEY
TRADE MARK	MADDOCK & GATER
TRADE MARK	MADDOCK, JOHN & SONS (LTD.)
TRADE MARK	MAILING, C. T. & SONS (LTD.)
TRADE MARK	PEARSON & CO.
TRADE MARK	PLANT, R. H. & S. L. (LTD.)
TRADE MARK	POSSIL POTTERY CO.
TRADE MARK	RATHBONE, T. & CO.
TRADE MARK	SHAW, ANTHONY (& CO.)(&SON(S))
TRADE MARK	TILL, THOMAS & SON(S)(LTD.)
TRADE MARK	WEDGWOOD & CO. (LTD.)
TUNSTALL	ADAMS, WILLIAM & THOMAS
TUNSTALL	BOOTH, T. G. & F.
TUNSTALL	BOWERS, GEO. FREDERICK (& CO.)
TUNSTALL	CHALLINOR, EDWARD
TUNSTALL	CLARKE, EDWARD (& CO.)
TUNSTALL	COLLEY , ALFRED & CO., LTD.
TUNSTALL	CUMBERLIDGE & HUMPHREY'S
TUNSTALL	ELSMORE & FORSTER
TUNSTALL	EMBERTON, WILLIAM
TUNSTALL	GOODWIN, JOSEPH
TUNSTALL	GRINDLEY, W. H. & CO. (LTD.)
TUNSTALL	HOLLINSHEAD & KIRKHAM (LTD.)
TUNSTALL	HUMPHREY'S BROS.
TUNSTALL	MEAKIN, ALFRED (LTD.)
TUNSTALL	MEIR, JOHN & SON
TUNSTALL	PITCAIRNS LTD.
TUNSTALL	RATHBONE, T. & CO.
TUNSTALL	SHAW, ANTHONY (& CO.)(&SON(S))
TUNSTALL	SOHO POTTERY LTD.
TUNSTALL	TROUTBECK, E. T.
TUNSTALL	TUNNICLIFF(E), MICHAEL
TUNSTALL	TURNER, G. W. & SONS
TUNSTALL	WALKER, THOMAS
TUNSTALL	WEATHERBY, J. H. & SONS (LTD.)
TUNSTALL POTTERIES	BOWERS, GEO. FREDERICK (& CO.)
TURNER'S PATENT	TURNER, (JOHN) & CO.
TURNERS	TURNER, G. W. & SONS
TUSCAN CHINA	PLANT, R. H. & S. L. (LTD.)
TYNE POTTERY	PATTERSON (GEORGE) & CO.
TYNSIDE	BELL, COOK & CO.
UPPER HANLEY POTTERY	GRIMWADES LTD.
UPPER HANLEY POTTERY CO. (LTD.)	GRIMWADES LTD.
VEDGWOOD	CARR & PATTON
VEDGWOOD	SMITH, WILLIAM (& CO.)
VENABLES, MANN & CO. (See)	VENABLES, JOHN & CO.
VERREVILLE GLASGOW	GEDDES, JOHN (&SON)
VICTORIA	BLAKENEY POTTERY CO.
VICTORIA	CARTWRIGHT & EDWARDS LTD.
VICTORIA CHINA	REEVES, JAMES
VINCIT VERITAS	SHAW, C. & J.
VINE	BELL, J. & M. P. & CO. (LD.)
VITREOUS IRONSTONE	DUNN, BENNETT & CO. (LTD.)
VITRIFIED	GLOBE POTTERY CO. LTD.
VITRIFIED	MADDOCK, JOHN & SONS (LTD.)
VITRIFIED	RIDGWAYS (BEDFORD WORKS) LTD.
WALL, W. G. (See)	STEVENSON, A.
WARRANTED	ADAMS, WM. & CO.
WARRANTED	BATKIN, WALKER & BROADHURST
WARRANTED	BOOTE, T. & R. (& SON) LTD.
WARRANTED	BOURNE, JOSEPH (& SON)(LTD.)
WARRANTED	BRINDLEY, JOHN & CO.
WARRANTED	BROADHURST, JAMES & SONS (LTD.)
WARRANTED	CHALLINOR & MAYER
WARRANTED	CHALLINOR, EDWARD
WARRANTED	CHESWORTH & ROBINSON
WARRANTED	CHETHAM & ROBINSON
WARRANTED	CLEMENTSON, JOSEPH & SONS
WARRANTED	CLEWS, JAMES & RALPH
WARRANTED	CLYDE POTTERY CO. (LTD.)
WARRANTED	DEAKIN & BAILEY
WARRANTED	EDGE, WILLIAM & SAMUEL
WARRANTED	EDWARDS, JAMES
WARRANTED	EDWARDS, JOHN (& CO.)
WARRANTED	JACKSON, JOB & JOHN
WARRANTED	MASON, CHARLES JAMES (& CO.)
WARRANTED	MEIR, JOHN & SON
WARRANTED	PRATT & SIMPSON
WARRANTED	RILEY, JOHN & RICHARD
WARRANTED	SHAW, ANTHONY (& CO.)(&SON(S))
WARRANTED	SHIRLEY, THOMAS & CO.
WARRANTED	STEVENON, RALPH & WILLIAMS
WARRANTED	STEVENSON, ANDREW
WARRANTED	STEVENSON, RALPH
WARRANTED	WOOD & BROWNFIELD
WARRANTED	WOOD, ENOCH & SON(S)
WARRANTED	YALE & BARKER
WARRANTED ENGLISH STONE CHINA	CHALLINOR & MAYER
WARRANTED IRONSTONE CHINA	BAGGERLEY & BALL
WARRANTED IRONSTONE CHINA	BATKIN, WALKER & BROADHURST
WARRANTED IRONSTONE CHINA	CLEWS, JAMES & RALPH
WARRANTED IRONSTONE CHINA	EDWARDS, JOHN (& CO.)
WARRANTED IRONSTONE CHINA	ELSMORE & FORSTER
WARRANTED REAL IRONSTONE CHINA	WOOD & BROWNFIELD
WARRANTED STAFFORDSHIRE	ADAMS, WM. & SONS
WARRANTED STAFFORDSHIRE	BRINDLEY, JOHN & CO.
WARRANTED STAFFORDSHIRE	CARR, JOHN & SON
WARRANTED STAFFORDSHIRE	CLEWS, JAMES & RALPH
WARRANTED STAFFORDSHIRE	MEIR, JOHN
WARRANTED STAFFORDSHIRE	MEIR, JOHN & SON
WARRANTED STAFFORDSHIRE	TAMS, S. & CO.
WARRANTED STONE CHINA	CLEMENTSON, JOSEPH & SONS
WARRANTED STONE CHINA	CLEWS, JAMES & RALPH
WARRANTED STONE CHINA	MELLOR, TAYLOR & CO.
WARRANTED STONE CHINA	WALKER, THOMAS HENRY
WARRANTED STONE CHINA	WHITEHAVEN POTTERY

WARRANTED/STONE CHINA/FENTON	YATES, JOHN
WATERLOO POTTERIES	BOOTE, T. & R. (& SON) LTD.
WATSON'S POTTERY (See)	FOWLER THOMPSON & CO.
WATSON, WM. & CO. (See)	FOWLER, THOMPSON (& CO.)
WEDGEWOOD & CO.	WOOD, JOHN WEDGE
WEDGWOOD	PODMORE, WALKER & (CO.)
WEDGWOOD	WEDGWOOD, JOSIAH (& SONS, LTD.)
WEDGWOOD	WEDGWOOD, RALPH & CO.
WEDGWOOD & CO.	PODMORE, WALKER & (CO.)
WEDGWOOD & CO.	WEDGWOOD & CO. (LTD.)
WEDGWOOD & CO.	WEDGWOOD, RALPH & CO.
WEDGWOOD PLACE, BURSLEM	ALLMAN, BROUGHTON & CO.
WEDGWOOD WARE	SMITH, WILLIAM (& CO.)
WHARF	GODWIN, THOMAS
WHITE ENAMEL CHINA	WOOD, ENOCH
WHITE GRANITE	ALCOCK, JOHN & GEORGE
WHITE GRANITE	CORK & EDGE
WHITE GRANITE	CORK, EDGE & MALKIN
WHITE GRANITE	CORN, W. & E.
WHITE GRANITE	FURNIVAL, JACOB & CO.
WHITE GRANITE	SHAW, ANTHONY (& CO.)(&SON(S))
WHITE GRANITE IRONSTONE	BISHOP & STONIER (LTD.)
WHITE GRANITE WARE	ALCOCK, JOHN
WHITE STONEWARE	ASHWORTH, G. L. & BROS. (LTD.)
WHITEHAVEN	WHITEHAVEN POTTERY
WHITEHAVEN POTTERY	WILKINSON (JOHN) POTTERY
WHITEHAVEN POTTERY	WOODNORTH & CO.
WHITTINGTON MOOR	PEARSON & CO.
WIELDON WARE	WINKLE, F. & CO. (LTD.)
WOOD	WOOD, ENOCH
WOOD, EDMUND T. (See)	WOOD, JOHN WEDGE
WOODLAND	HOLLINSHEAD & KIRKHAM (LTD.)
WOODLAND (POTTERY)	HOLLINSHEAD & KIRKHAM (LTD.)
WOODS	WOOD & SON(S) (LTD.)
YE OLD FOLEY WARE	KENT, JAMES (LTD.)
YNYSMEDW POTTERY	WILLIAMS, WILLIAM
YNYSMEDW POTTERY	HOLLAND, W. T.

APPENDIX B8: ALPHABETIC CROSS REFERENCE: BACK MARKINGS BY POTTER

POTTER	BACK MARKING
ADAMS, WILLIAM & THOMAS	TUNSTALL
ADAMS, WM. & CO.	CROWN SEMI PORCELAIN
ADAMS, WM. & CO.	ROYAL SEMI PORCELAIN
ADAMS, WM. & CO.	TRADE MARK
ADAMS, WM. & CO.	WARRANTED
ADAMS, WM. & SONS	WARRANTED STAFFORDSHIRE
ADAMS, WM. (& SONS)(& CO.)	CALYXWARE
ADAMS, WM. (& SONS)(& CO.)	IMPERIAL
ADAMS, WM. (& SONS)(& CO.)	IMPERIAL FRENCH PORCELAIN
ADAMS, WM. (& SONS)(& CO.)	IMPERIAL STONE WARE
ADAMS, WM. (& SONS)(& CO.)	IMPROVED IRONSTONE
ADAMS, WM. (& SONS)(& CO.)	IRONSTONE
ADAMS, WM. (& SONS)(& CO.)	IRONSTONE CHINA
ADAMS, WM. (& SONS)(& CO.)	MICRATEX
ADAMS, WM. (& SONS)(& CO.)	REAL ENGLISH IRONSTONE
ADAMS, WM. (& SONS)(& CO.)	REAL IRONSTONE CHINA
ADAMS, WM. (& SONS)(& CO.)	STAFFORDSHIRE WARRANTED
ADAMS, WM. (& SONS)(& CO.)	STONE CHINA
ADDERLEY, WILLIAM ALSAGER (& CO.)	TRADE MARK
ADDERLEY'S LTD.	TRADE MARK
AITCHIESON, J. & CO.	CALEDONIAN POTTERY
ALCOCK, HENRY & CO.	ROYAL WARRANTED BEST IRONSTONE CHINA
ALCOCK, HENRY & CO.	TRADE MARK
ALCOCK, HENRY & CO. (LTD.)	COBRIDGE
ALCOCK, HENRY & CO. (LTD.)	GRANITE WARE
ALCOCK, HENRY & CO. (LTD.)	IMPERIAL IRONSTONE CHINA
ALCOCK, HENRY & CO. (LTD.)	IRONSTONE
ALCOCK, HENRY & CO. (LTD.)	PARISIAN PORCELAIN
ALCOCK, HENRY & CO. (LTD.)	ROYAL IRONSTONE CHINA
ALCOCK, HENRY & CO. (LTD.)	SEMI CHINA
ALCOCK, HENRY POTTERY, THE	SEMI PORCELAIN
ALCOCK, J. & S.	GRANITE
ALCOCK, J. & S.	IMPERIAL FRENCH PORCELAIN
ALCOCK, J. & S.	PORCELAIN OPAQUE
ALCOCK, JOHN	COBRIDGE
ALCOCK, JOHN	IMPERIAL IRONSTONE CHINA
ALCOCK, JOHN	IRONSTONE CHINA
ALCOCK, JOHN	ORIENTAL STONE
ALCOCK, JOHN	PARISIAN PORCELAIN
ALCOCK, JOHN	ROYAL WARRANTED BEST IRONSTONE CHINA
ALCOCK, JOHN	WHITE GRANITE WARE
ALCOCK, JOHN & GEORGE	COBRIDGE
ALCOCK, JOHN & GEORGE	IMPERIAL GRANITE CHINA
ALCOCK, JOHN & GEORGE	IMPERIAL STONE
ALCOCK, JOHN & GEORGE	INDIAN IRONSTONE
ALCOCK, JOHN & GEORGE	INDIAN STONE
ALCOCK, JOHN & GEORGE	OPAQUE STONE
ALCOCK, JOHN & GEORGE	ORIENTAL STONE
ALCOCK, JOHN & GEORGE	WHITE GRANITE
ALCOCK, JOHN & SAMUEL	OPAQUE STONE
ALCOCK, JOHN & SAMUEL	ORIENTAL STONE
ALCOCK, RICHARD	BURSLEM
ALCOCK, RICHARD	GRANITE
ALCOCK, RICHARD	HANLEY
ALCOCK, SAMUEL & CO.	BURSLEM
ALCOCK, SAMUEL & CO.	COBRIDGE
ALCOCK, SAMUEL & CO.	FLORENTINE CHINA
ALCOCK, SAMUEL & CO.	FRENCH PORCELAIN
ALCOCK, SAMUEL & CO.	HILL POTTERY
ALCOCK, SAMUEL & CO.	IMPERIAL IRONSTONE CHINA
ALCOCK, SAMUEL & CO.	INDIAN IRONSTONE
ALCOCK, SAMUEL & CO.	PATENT
ALCOCK, SAMUEL & CO.	PATENT IRONSTONE CHINA
ALCOCK, SAMUEL & CO.	PEARL WARE
ALCOCK, SAMUEL & CO.	STONEWARE
ALLASON, JOHN	SEAHAM POTTERY
ALLERTON, CHARLES & SONS	CAULDON LTD.
ALLERTON, CHARLES & SONS	IMPERIAL SEMI CHINA
ALLERTON, CHARLES & SONS	OLD ENGLISH BONE CHINA
ALLMAN, BROUGHTON & CO.	BURSLEM
ALLMAN, BROUGHTON & CO.	WEDGWOOD PLACE, BURSLEM
AMISON, CHARLES (& CO. LTD.) (China)	STANLEY CHINA
ASHWORTH'S (BROS.)	IRONSTONE CHINA
ASHWORTH'S (BROS.)	REAL STONE CHINA
ASHWORTH, G. & L. (BROS.)(LTD.)	ROYAL STONE CHINA
ASHWORTH, G. L. & BROS. (LTD.)	HANLEY
ASHWORTH, G. L. & BROS. (LTD.)	IRONSTONE
ASHWORTH, G. L. & BROS. (LTD.)	IRONSTONE CHINA
ASHWORTH, G. L. & BROS. (LTD.)	LUSTROSA
ASHWORTH, G. L. & BROS. (LTD.)	MASON'S
ASHWORTH, G. L. & BROS. (LTD.)	PATENT IRONSTONE CHINA
ASHWORTH, G. L. & BROS. (LTD.)	REAL IRONSTONE CHINA
ASHWORTH, G. L. & BROS. (LTD.)	WHITE STONEWARE
AUSTRALIAN POTTERY	OPAQUE GRANITE CHINA
BAGGERLEY & BALL	LONGTON
BAGGERLEY & BALL	OPAQUE CHINA
BAGGERLEY & BALL	WARRANTED IRONSTONE CHINA
BAGSTER, JOHN DENTON	BAXTER
BAGSTER, JOHN DENTON	CELTIC CHINA
BAGSTER, JOHN DENTON	STAFFORDSHIRE
BAKER & CHETWYND & CO.	IMPERIAL IRONSTONE CHINA
BAKER, (W.) & CO.	IRONSTONE
BAKER, (W.) & CO.	OPAQUE GRANITE CHINA
BAKER, (W.) & CO. (LTD.)	FENTON
BAKER, (W.) & CO. (LTD.)	IMPERIAL IRONSTONE CHINA
BAKER, (W.) & CO. (LTD.)	IRONSTONE CHINA
BAKER, (W.) & CO. (LTD.)	PEARL CHINA
BAKER, (W.) & CO. (LTD.)	PEARL WHITE
BAKER, (W.) & CO. (LTD.)	PEARL WHITE GRANITE
BAKER, (W.) & CO. (LTD.)	ROYAL IRONSTONE CHINA
BAKER, (W.) & CO. (LTD.)	STAFFORDSHIRE
BAKER, (W.) & CO. (LTD.)	STONE CHINA
BAKER, BEVANS & IRWIN	GLAMORGAN POTTERY
BAKER, BEVANS & IRWIN	OPAQUE CHINA
BALFOUR, ALEXANDER & CO.	NORTH BRITISH POTTERY
BARKER & TILL	STONE CHINA
BARKER & TILL	STONEWARE
BARKER BROS. (LTD.)	LONGTON
BARKER BROS. (LTD.)	MEIR WORKS/LONGTON
BARKER BROS. (LTD.)	TRADE MARK
BARKER, (W.) & CO. (LTD.)	STONE CHINA
BARKER, (W.) & SON, LTD.	STONEWARE
BARKER, SAMUEL & SON	DON POTTERY
BARKER, SAMUEL & SON	IRONSTONE CHINA
BARKER, SUTTON & TILL	BURSLEM
BARKER, SUTTON & TILL	STONE CHINA
BARKER, SUTTON & TILL	STONEWARE
BARKERS & KENT, LTD.	TRADE MARK
BARRATT'S OF STAFFORDSHIRE LTD.	CORONA
BARROW & CO.	IRONSTONE CHINA
BATES & BENNETT	STONEWARE
BATKIN, WALKER & BROADHURST	STAFFORDSHIRE
BATKIN, WALKER & BROADHURST	STONE CHINA
BATKIN, WALKER & BROADHURST	WARRANTED
BATKIN, WALKER & BROADHURST	WARRANTED IRONSTONE CHINA
BEARDMORE, FRANK & CO.	FENTON
BEARDMORE, FRANK & CO.	SUTHERLAND ARTWARE
BEECH & LOWNDES	LOWNDES & BEECH
BEECH, JAMES	TRADE MARK

BELFIELD & CO.	PRESTOPANS
BELL, COOK & CO.	NEWCASTLE UPON TYNE
BELL, COOK & CO.	TYNSIDE
BELL, ISAAC & THOMAS	ALBION
BELL, ISAAC & THOMAS	LONDON
BELL, J. & M. P. & CO. (LD.)	GLASGOW
BELL, J. & M. P. & CO. (LD.)	GRANITE IMPERIAL
BELL, J. & M. P. & CO. (LD.)	ROYAL STONE CHINA
BELL, J. & M. P. & CO. (LD.)	TRADE MARK
BELL, J. & M. P. & CO. (LD.)	VINE
BELLE VUE POTTERY	HULL (See)
BELLE VUE POTTERY	OPAQUE CHINA
BESWICK & SON (CHINA)	ALDWYCH CHINA
BEVINGTON, T. J. (& CO.)	OPAQUE CHINA
BEVINGTON, T. J. (& CO.)	SWANSEA
BIRKS BROS. & SEDDON	IMPERIAL IRONSTONE CHINA
BISHOP & STONIER (LTD.)	BISTRO
BISHOP & STONIER (LTD.)	IRONSTONE
BISHOP & STONIER (LTD.)	IRONSTONE CHINA
BISHOP & STONIER (LTD.)	ORIENTAL IVORY
BISHOP & STONIER (LTD.)	SEMI IMPERIAL PORCELAIN
BISHOP & STONIER (LTD.)	SEMI PORCELAIN IMPERIAL
BISHOP & STONIER (LTD.)	WHITE GRANITE IRONSTONE
BLAKENEY POTTERY CO.	FLO-BLUE
BLAKENEY POTTERY CO.	IRONSTONE STAFFORDSHIRE
BLAKENEY POTTERY CO.	ROMANTIC
BLAKENEY POTTERY CO.	VICTORIA
BODLEY & CO.	BURSLEM
BODLEY & HAROLD	SCOTIA POTTERY
BODLEY, EDWARD F. & CO.	GENUINE IRONSTONE CHINA
BODLEY, EDWARD F. & CO.	SCOTIA POTTERY
BODLEY, EDWARD F. & SON	NEWBRIDGE POTTERY
BODLEY, EDWARD F. & SON	TRADE MARK
BOOTE, T. & R. (& SON) LTD.	GRANITE
BOOTE, T. & R. (& SON) LTD.	GRANITE EARTHENWARE
BOOTE, T. & R. (& SON) LTD.	IRONSTONE
BOOTE, T. & R. (& SON) LTD.	OPAQUE CHINA
BOOTE, T. & R. (& SON) LTD.	PATENT MOSAIC
BOOTE, T. & R. (& SON) LTD.	PORCELAIN OPAQUE
BOOTE, T. & R. (& SON) LTD.	PORCELAINE OPAQUE
BOOTE, T. & R. (& SON) LTD.	ROYAL IRONSTONE CHINA
BOOTE, T. & R. (& SON) LTD.	ROYAL PATENT
BOOTE, T. & R. (& SON) LTD.	ROYAL PATENT IRONSTONE
BOOTE, T. & R. (& SON) LTD.	ROYAL PREMIUM IRONSTONE
BOOTE, T. & R. (& SON) LTD.	ROYAL PREMIUM SEMI PORCELAIN
BOOTE, T. & R. (& SON) LTD.	ROYAL SEMI PORCELAIN
BOOTE, T. & R. (& SON) LTD.	SEMI PORCELAIN
BOOTE, T. & R. (& SON) LTD.	WARRANTED
BOOTE, T. & R. (& SON) LTD.	WATERLOO POTTERIES
BOOTH & MEIGH	IRONSTONE
BOOTH & MEIGH	LANE END
BOOTH'S (LTD.)	ROYAL SEMI PORCELAIN
BOOTH'S (LTD.)	SILICON CHINA
BOOTH'S (LTD.)	STAFFORDSHIRE
BOOTH, T. G. & F.	PARISIAN GRANITE
BOOTH, T. G. & F.	TUNSTALL
BOURNE & LEIGH (LTD.)	ALBION POTTERY
BOURNE & LEIGH (LTD.)	ROYAL SEMI PORCELAIN
BOURNE, BAKER & BOURNE	OPAQUE CHINA
BOURNE, JOSEPH (& SON)(LTD.)	CONDOR PARK
BOURNE, JOSEPH (& SON)(LTD.)	DENBY
BOURNE, JOSEPH (& SON)(LTD.)	IRONSTONE CHINA
BOURNE, JOSEPH (& SON)(LTD.)	WARRANTED
BOURNE, WILLIAM & CO.	STAFFORDSHIRE
BOURNE, WILLIAM (LONGTON)	LONGTON
BOWERS, GEO. FREDERICK (& CO.)	CHINA
BOWERS, GEO. FREDERICK (& CO.)	IRONSTONE
BOWERS, GEO. FREDERICK (& CO.)	IRONSTONE CHINA
BOWERS, GEO. FREDERICK (& CO.)	TUNSTALL
BOWERS, GEO. FREDERICK (& CO.)	TUNSTALL POTTERIES
BOYLE, ZACHARIA (& CO.) (&SON(S))	STOKE MANUFACTURERS
BRADLEY & CO.	COALPORT
BRAMELD & CO.	FINE STONE
BRAMELD & CO.	GRANITE CHINA
BRAMELD & CO.	MANUFACTURED TO THE KING
BRAMELD & CO.	ROCKINGHAM POTTERY (WORKS)
BRAMELD & CO.	ROCKINGHAM WORKS
BRAMELD & CO.	ROYAL ROCKINGHAM WORKS
BRAMELD & CO.	STONE CHINA
BRAMELDS & CO.	KILNHURST OLD POTTERY
BRANNAM, C. H. (LTD.)	BARNSTAPLE
BRIDGETT & BATES	ALDWYCH CHINA
BRIDGWOOD & CLARKE	BURSLEM
BRIDGWOOD & CLARKE	GRANITE
BRIDGWOOD & CLARKE	OPAQUE CHINA
BRIDGWOOD & CLARKE	OPAQUE PORCELAIN
BRIDGWOOD & CLARKE	PORCELAIN OPAQUE
BRIDGWOOD, SAMPSON & SON (LTD.)	ANCHOR CHINA (OR WORKS)
BRIDGWOOD, SAMPSON & SON (LTD.)	ANCHOR WORKS
BRIDGWOOD, SAMPSON & SON (LTD.)	LIMOGES/P. G.
BRIDGWOOD, SAMPSON & SON (LTD.)	PORCELAIN OPAQUE
BRIDGWOOD, SAMPSON & SON (LTD.)	SEMI PORCELAIN
BRIDGWOOD, SAMPSON & SON (LTD.)	TRADE MARK
BRINDLEY, JOHN & CO.	WARRANTED
BRINDLEY, JOHN & CO.	WARRANTED STAFFORDSHIRE
BRITANNIA POTTERY CO. LTD.	MADE IN SCOTLAND
BRITANNIA POTTERY CO. LTD.	TRADE MARK
BROADHURST, JAMES & SONS (LTD.)	CROWN POTTERY
BROADHURST, JAMES & SONS (LTD.)	LONGTON
BROADHURST, JAMES & SONS (LTD.)	WARRANTED
BROUGHAM & MAYER	IRONSTONE
BROWN & STEVENTON, LTD.	BURSLEM
BROWN-WESTHEAD, MOORE & CO.	CAULDON (WARE)
BROWNFIELD, WM. (& SON(S))	COBRIDGE
BROWNFIELD, WM. (& SON(S))	IMPROVED IRONSTONE CHINA
BROWNFIELD, WM. (& SON(S))	STAFFS
BROWNFIELD, WM. (& SON(S))	TRADE MARK
BURGESS & LEIGH (LTD.)	BURLEIGH WARE
BURGESS & LEIGH (LTD.)	BURSLEM
BURGESS & LEIGH (LTD.)	HILL POTTERY
BURGESS & LEIGH (LTD.)	MIDDLEPORT POTTERY (POTTERS)
BURGESS & LEIGH (LTD.)	ROYAL SEMI PORCELAIN
BURGESS & LEIGH (LTD.)	SEMI PORCELAIN
BURGESS, HENRY	BURSLEM
BURGESS, HENRY	IRONSTONE CHINA
BURGESS, HENRY	STONE CHINA
BURN, JOSEPH & CO.	STONEWARE
BURTON, SAMUEL & JOHN	IMPROVED STONE CHINA
BURTON, SAMUEL & JOHN	IRONSTONE CHINA
BURTON, SAMUEL & JOHN	PEARL CHINA
CALEDONIAN POTTERY	GLASGOW POTTERY
CALEDONIAN POTTERY	GLASGOW STONE CHINE
CALEDONIAN POTTERY	ROYAL IRONSTONE CHINA
CALEDONIAN POTTERY	STONE CHINA
CALLAND, JOHN F. & CO.	LANDORE POTTERY
CALLAND, JOHN F. & CO.	SWANSEA
CAMBRIAN POTTERY	ETRUSCAN WARE
CAMBRIAN POTTERY	SWANSEA
CAMPBELLFIELD POTTERY COMPANY LTD.	GLASGOW
CAREY, THOMAS & JOHN	CAREYS
CAREY, THOMAS & JOHN	FELSPAR
CAREY, THOMAS & JOHN	IMPROVED IRONSTONE CHINA
CAREY, THOMAS & JOHN	SAXON STONE CHINA
CARLTON WARE LTD.	STOKE ON TRENT
CARR & PATTON	VEDGWOOD
CARR, JOHN & CO.	LONDON
CARR, JOHN & SON	NORTHSHIELDS
CARR, JOHN & SON	NORTHUMBERLAND
CARR, JOHN & SON	PORCELAIN OPAQUE
CARR, JOHN & SON	WARRANTED STAFFORDSHIRE
CARR, JOHN (& CO.)(& SON(S))	LOWLIGHTS POTTERY
CARTWRIGHT & EDWARDS LTD.	VICTORIA
CAULDON LTD.	CAULDON PLACE
CAULDON LTD.	POTTERS TO HER MAJESTY
CERAMIC ART CO. (1905) LTD.	CROWN POTTERY
CERAMIC ART CO. (1905) LTD.	STOKE ON TRENT
CERAMIC ART CO. LTD.	HANLEY
CERAMIC ART CO. LTD.	STAFFORDSHIRE
CHALLINOR & MAYER	ENGLISH STONE CHINA
CHALLINOR & MAYER	FENTON
CHALLINOR & MAYER	TRADE MARK
CHALLINOR & MAYER	WARRANTED
CHALLINOR & MAYER	WARRANTED ENGLISH STONE CHINA
CHALLINOR, CHARLES & CO.	PEARL
CHALLINOR, E. & C.	FENTON
CHALLINOR, E. & C.	IRONSTONE CHINA
CHALLINOR, E. & C.	STONE CHINA
CHALLINOR, E. & CO.	IRONSTONE
CHALLINOR, E. & CO.	IRONSTONE CHINA
CHALLINOR, EDWARD	BURSLEM
CHALLINOR, EDWARD	IRONSTONE
CHALLINOR, EDWARD	STAFFORDSHIRE
CHALLINOR, EDWARD	TUNSTALL
CHALLINOR, EDWARD	WARRANTED
CHAMBERS, LLANELLY	SOUTH WALES POTTERY
CHAMBERS, WILLIAM	SOUTH WALES POTTERY
CHESWORTH & ROBINSON	WARRANTED
CHETHAM & ROBINSON	WARRANTED
CLARKE, EDWARD (& CO.)	BURSLEM
CLARKE, EDWARD (& CO.)	LONGPORT
CLARKE, EDWARD (& CO.)	ROYAL SEMI PORCELAIN
CLARKE, EDWARD (& CO.)	STONE CHINA
CLARKE, EDWARD (& CO.)	TRADE MARK
CLARKE, EDWARD (& CO.)	TUNSTALL
CLEMENTSON BROS.	IRONSTONE CHINA
CLEMENTSON BROS.	ROYAL IRONSTONE CHINA
CLEMENTSON BROS. LTD.	HANLEY
CLEMENTSON BROS. LTD.	IVORY WARE

CLEMENTSON BROS. LTD.	ROYAL PATENT
CLEMENTSON BROS. LTD.	ROYAL PATENT STONE WARE
CLEMENTSON BROS. LTD.	ROYAL SEMI PORCELAIN
CLEMENTSON BROS. LTD.	SEMI CHINA
CLEMENTSON BROS. LTD.	SEMI PORCELAIN
CLEMENTSON BROS. LTD.	SPECIAL WHITE STONE WARE
CLEMENTSON BROS. LTD.	STONE CHINA
CLEMENTSON BROS. LTD.	STONEWARE
CLEMENTSON, JOSEPH & SONS	GRANITE OPAQUE PEARL
CLEMENTSON, JOSEPH & SONS	GRANITE WARE
CLEMENTSON, JOSEPH & SONS	HANLEY
CLEMENTSON, JOSEPH & SONS	IRONSTONE
CLEMENTSON, JOSEPH & SONS	OPAQUE PEARL
CLEMENTSON, JOSEPH & SONS	SHELTON
CLEMENTSON, JOSEPH & SONS	STONE CHINA
CLEMENTSON, JOSEPH & SONS	STONEWARE
CLEMENTSON, JOSEPH & SONS	WARRANTED
CLEMENTSON, JOSEPH & SONS	WARRANTED STONE CHINA
CLEMENTSON, YOUNG & ANDERSON	IRONSTONE
CLEVELAND POTTERY	PORCELAIN ROYAL
CLEWS, JAMES & RALPH	DRESDEN OPAQUE CHINA
CLEWS, JAMES & RALPH	IRONSTONE CHINA
CLEWS, JAMES & RALPH	PATENT STAFFORDSHIRE
CLEWS, JAMES & RALPH	STONE CHINA
CLEWS, JAMES & RALPH	WARRANTED
CLEWS, JAMES & RALPH	WARRANTED IRONSTONE CHINA
CLEWS, JAMES & RALPH	WARRANTED STAFFORDSHIRE
CLEWS, JAMES & RALPH	WARRANTED STONE CHINA
CLEWS, RALPH & JAMES	HILL, I. (See)
CLOSE & CO.	LATE ADAMS, (W.) & SONS
CLOSE & CO.	STOKE UPON TRENT
CLOSE, J. T. (& CO.)	STAFFORDSHIRE
CLOSE, J. T. (& CO.)	STOKE UPON TRENT
CLOSE, J. T. (& CO.)	STONE CHINA
CLOSE, J. T. (& CO.)	STONEWARE
CLOUGH'S ROYAL ART POTTERY	ROYAL ART POTTERY
CLOUGH, ALFRED (LTD.)	ROYAL ART POTTERY
CLYDE POTTERY CO. (LTD.)	GREENOCK (POTTERY)
CLYDE POTTERY CO. (LTD.)	SAXON
CLYDE POTTERY CO. (LTD.)	WARRANTED
COCHRAN & FLEMING	BRITAIN
COCHRAN & FLEMING	FLEMING
COCHRAN & FLEMING	GLASGOW
COCHRAN & FLEMING	MADE IN GREAT BRITTAIN
COCHRAN & FLEMING	MADE IN SCOTLAND
COCHRAN & FLEMING	PORCELAIN OPAQUE
COCHRAN & FLEMING	ROYAL IRONSTONE CHINA
COCHRAN, R. & CO.	GLASGOW
COCHRAN, R. & CO.	IMPERIAL IRONSTONE CHINA
COCHRAN, R. & CO.	IMPROVED STONE CHINA
COCHRAN, R. & CO.	ST. ROLLOX
COCHRAN, R. & CO.	STONE CHINA
COCKSON & CHETWYND (& CO.)	COBRIDGE
COCKSON & CHETWYND (& CO.)	IMPERIAL IRONSTONE CHINA
COCKSON & CHETWYND (& CO.)	IRONSTONE
COCKSON & CHETWYND (& CO.)	PEARL
COCKSON & HARDING	IMPERIAL IRONSTONE CHINA
COCKSON & HARDING	IMPERIAL WREATH
COCKSON & HARDING	LATE HACKWOOD
COCKSON & SEDDON	IMPERIAL IRONSTONE CHINA
COLCLOUGH & CO.	LONGTON
COLCLOUGH & CO.	ROYAL STANLEY (WARE)
COLCLOUGH & CO.	STOKE ON TRENT
COLLEY , ALFRED & CO., LTD.	ROYAL SEMI PORCELAIN
COLLEY , ALFRED & CO., LTD.	TUNSTALL
COLLINSON, CHARLES & CO.	BURSLEM
COLLINSON, CHARLES & CO.	IMPERIAL IRONSTONE CHINA
COLLINSON, CHARLES & CO.	PEARL
COOMBS & HOLLAND	SOUTH WALES POTTERY
COPELAND & GARRETT	CHINA GLAZE
COPELAND & GARRETT	FELSPAR PORCELAIN
COPELAND & GARRETT	LATE SPODE
COPELAND & GARRETT	NEW JAPAN STONE
COPELAND & GARRETT	SPODES IMPERIAL
COPELAND, W. T. (& SONS LTD.)	LATE SPODE
COPELAND, W. T. (& SONS LTD.)	NEW STONE
COPELAND, W. T. (& SONS LTD.)	TRADE MARK
CORK & EDGE	PATENT MOSAIC
CORK & EDGE	PEARL WHITE IRONSTONE
CORK & EDGE	STAFFORDSHIRE
CORK & EDGE	STAFFORDSHIRE STONEWARE
CORK & EDGE	STONE CHINA
CORK & EDGE	STONEWARE
CORK & EDGE	WHITE GRANITE
CORK, EDGE & MALKIN	BURSLEM
CORK, EDGE & MALKIN	IRONSTONE
CORK, EDGE & MALKIN	STONE CHINA
CORK, EDGE & MALKIN	WHITE GRANITE
CORMIE, JOHN	IRONSTONE CHINA
CORN, EDWARD	BURSLEM
CORN, W. & E.	GERMANY
CORN, W. & E.	IMPERIAL IRONSTONE CHINA
CORN, W. & E.	IRONSTONE CHINA
CORN, W. & E.	LONGPORT
CORN, W. & E.	PORCELAIN ROYALE (ART-WARE)
CORN, W. & E.	ROYAL IRONSTONE CHINA
CORN, W. & E.	STAFFORDSHIRE
CORN, W. & E.	WHITE GRANITE
CORN, W. E.	BURSLEM
CORN, W. E.	GRANITE
COUPER, JAMES & SONS	CITY POTTERY GLASGOW
CUMBERLIDGE & HUMPHREY'S	TUNSTALL
DANIEL, H. & R.	IRONSTONE CHINA
DANIEL, H. & R.	REAL IRONSTONE
DANIEL, H. & R.	STONE CHINA
DANIEL, H. & R.	STONEWARE
DAVENPORT (various styles)	IMPROVED STONE CHINA
DAVENPORT (various styles)	IRONSTONE
DAVENPORT (various styles)	IRONSTONE CHINA
DAVENPORT (various styles)	LIMITED
DAVENPORT (various styles)	LONGTON
DAVENPORT (various styles)	OPAQUE CHINA
DAVENPORT (various styles)	PATENT IRONSTONE CHINA
DAVENPORT (various styles)	REAL IRONSTONE CHINA
DAVENPORT (various styles)	REAL STONE CHINA
DAVENPORT (various styles)	STAFFORDSHIRE
DAVENPORT (various styles)	STONE CHINA
DAVENPORT (various styles)	STONEWARE
DAVENPORT, BANKS & CO.	ETRURIA
DAVENPORT, BECK & CO.	ETRURIA
DAVENPORT, JOHN	IRONSTONE
DAVENPORT, JOHN	REAL IRONSTONE CHINA
DAVIS, J. H. & J.	HANLEY
DAVIS, J. H. & J.	ROYAL STONE CHINA
DAVIS, JOHN HEATH	HANLEY
DAWSON (JOHN DAWSON & CO.)	LOW FORD
DAWSON (JOHN DAWSON & CO.)	SOUTH HYLTON
DEAKIN & BAILEY	WARRANTED
DEAKIN & CO.	DEAKIN PEARL
DEAKIN & CO.	PEARL
DEAKIN & SON	ORTOLAN
DEAN, S. W.	BURSLEM
DEANS (1910) LTD.	BURSLEM
DEANS (1910) LTD.	ROYAL IRONSTONE CHINA
DILLON, FRANCIS	IRONSTONE CHINA
DILLWYN & CO.	CYMBRO STONE CHINA
DILLWYN & CO.	IMPROVED SAXON BLUE
DILLWYN & CO.	IMPROVED STONEWARE
DILLWYN & CO.	SAXON BLUE
DILLWYN & CO.	SILICON CHINA
DILLWYN & CO.	STONEWARE
DILLWYN & CO.	SWANSEA
DILLWYN & CO.	SWANSEA POTTERY
DILLWYN'S	ETRUSCAN WARE
DIMMOCK , THOMAS (JR.) & CO.	IMPROVED STONEWARE
DIMMOCK , THOMAS (JR.) & CO.	KAOLIN (WARE)
DIMMOCK , THOMAS (JR.) & CO.	PEARL WARE
DIMMOCK , THOMAS (JR.) & CO.	STONEWARE
DIMMOCK, J. & CO.	ALBION CHINA (OR WORKS)
DIMMOCK, J. & CO.	ALBION WORKS
DIMMOCK, J. & CO.	CLIFF
DIMMOCK, J. & CO.	CROWN SEMI PORCELAIN
DIXON & CO.	GARRISON POTTERY
DIXON & CO.	SUNDERLAND POTTERY
DIXON, AUSTIN & CO.	DRESDEN OPAQUE CHINA
DIXON, AUSTIN & CO.	GARRISON POTTERY
DIXON, AUSTIN & CO.	SUNDERLAND POTTERY
DIXON, AUSTIN PHILLIPS & CO.	GARRISON POTTERY
DIXON, PHILLIPS (& CO.)	GARRISON POTTERY
DON POTTERY	DON
DON POTTERY (See)	GREEN(S)
DOULTON (& CO.) (LTD.)	BURSLEM
DOULTON (& CO.) (LTD.)	ROYAL DOULTON
DUDSON, WILCOX & TILL LTD.	HANLEY
DUNDERDALE, DAVID & CO.	CASTLEFORD (POTTERY)
DUNN, BENNETT & CO. (LTD.)	IRONSTONE CHINA
DUNN, BENNETT & CO. (LTD.)	VITREOUS IRONSTONE
EDGE, MALKIN & CO.	STONE CHINA
EDGE, MALKIN & CO. (LTD.)	IRONSTONE
EDGE, MALKIN & CO. (LTD.)	TRADE MARK
EDGE, WILLIAM & SAMUEL	STONE CHINA
EDGE, WILLIAM & SAMUEL	WARRANTED
EDWARDS, JAMES	FELSPAR
EDWARDS, JAMES	FENTON
EDWARDS, JAMES	IRONSTONE
EDWARDS, JAMES	IRONSTONE CHINA
EDWARDS, JAMES	OPAQUE CHINA
EDWARDS, JAMES	PORCELAIN

EDWARDS, JAMES	PORCELAINE A LA PERLE
EDWARDS, JAMES	REAL IRONSTONE
EDWARDS, JAMES	SAXON BLUE
EDWARDS, JAMES	WARRANTED
EDWARDS, JAMES & SON	DALE HALL
EDWARDS, JAMES & SON	IRONSTONE CHINA
EDWARDS, JAMES & SON	REAL IRONSTONE CHINA
EDWARDS, JAMES & SON	STONE CHINA
EDWARDS, JAMES & THOMAS	IRONSTONE
EDWARDS, JAMES & THOMAS	IRONSTONE CHINA
EDWARDS, JAMES & THOMAS	PORCELAIN A LA PERLE
EDWARDS, JAMES & THOMAS	PORCELAIN OPAQUE
EDWARDS, JAMES & THOMAS	SEVRES
EDWARDS, JOHN	IRONSTONE CHINA
EDWARDS, JOHN	PORCELAINE DE TERRE
EDWARDS, JOHN	TRADE MARK
EDWARDS, JOHN (& CO.)	FENTON
EDWARDS, JOHN (& CO.)	IRONSTONE
EDWARDS, JOHN (& CO.)	WARRANTED
EDWARDS, JOHN (& CO.)	WARRANTED IRONSTONE CHINA
EDWARDS, THOMAS	BURSLEM
EDWARDS, THOMAS	PORCELAIN OPAQUE
EDWARDS, THOMAS	STAFFORDSHIRE
ELGIN POTTERY	SEMI CHINA
ELKIN, KNIGHT & BRIDGWOOD	OPAQUE CHINA
ELKIN, KNIGHT & CO.	OPAQUE CHINA
ELKIN, KNIGHT/KNIGHT, ELKIN & CO.	OPAQUE FELSPAR CHINA
ELSMORE & FORSTER	FOSTER
ELSMORE & FORSTER	IRONSTONE CHINA
ELSMORE & FORSTER	OPAQUE CHINA
ELSMORE & FORSTER	TUNSTALL
ELSMORE & FORSTER	WARRANTED IRONSTONE CHINA
ELSMORE (THOMAS) & SON	PARISIAN GRANITE
ELSMORE, FORESTER & CO.	IMPROVED OPAQUE CHINA
EMBERTON, WILLIAM	TUNSTALL
EMPIRE PORCELAIN CO. (LTD.)	EMPIRE WORKS
EMPIRE PORCELAIN CO. (LTD.)	STOKE ON TRENT
EVANS & GLASSON	BEST GOODS
EVANS & GLASSON	SWANSEA
EVANS & GLASSON	SWANSEA POTTERY
EVANS, D. J. & CO.	SWANSEA
EVANS, D. J. & CO.	SWANSEA POTTERY
FELL, THOMAS (& CO.)(LTD.)	IMPROVED STONEWARE
FELL, THOMAS (& CO.)(LTD.)	IRONSTONE CHINA STOKE WORKS
FELL, THOMAS (& CO.)(LTD.)	LONDON
FELL, THOMAS (& CO.)(LTD.)	NEW CASTLE
FELL, THOMAS (& CO.)(LTD.)	PORCELAIN OPAQUE
FELL, THOMAS (& CO.)(LTD.)	REAL IRONSTONE
FELL, THOMAS (& CO.)(LTD.)	STONE CHINA
FERRYBRIDGE POTTERY	GRANITE CHINA
FERRYBRIDGE POTTERY	KNOTTINGLEY POTTERY
FERRYBRIDGE POTTERY	OPAQUE GRANITE CHINA
FOLCH, STEPHEN (& SONS)	GENUINE STONE CHINA
FOLCH, STEPHEN (& SONS)	IMPROVED IRONSTONE CHINA
FOLCH, STEPHEN (& SONS)	IMPROVED IRONSTONE CHINA STOKE WORKS
FOLCH, STEPHEN (& SONS)	STOKE WORKS
FORD & CHALLINOR & CO.	PATENT
FORD & CHALLINOR & CO.	PEARL IRONSTONE CHINA
FORD & RILEY	TRADE MARK
FORD & SONS (LTD.)	BURSLEM
FORD, JOHN & CO.	EDINBURGH
FORD, SAMUEL & CO.	BURSLEM
FORD, SAMUEL & CO.	LINCOLN POTTERY
FORD, SAMUEL & CO.	SEMI PORCELAIN
FORDY & PATTERSON (& CO.)	SHERIFF HILL POTTERY
FORESTER, THOMAS & SON(S)(LTD.)	PHOENIX CHINA
FORESTER, THOMAS & SON(S)(LTD.)	PHOENIX WARE
FORESTER, THOMAS SON & CO.	FORESTERS
FOWLER THOMPSON & CO.	PRESTOPANS
FOWLER THOMPSON & CO.	SEMI CHINA
FOWLER THOMPSON & CO.	WATSON'S POTTERY (See)
FOWLER, THOMPSON (& CO.)	WATSON, WM. & CO. (See)
FREAKLY & FARRALL	IRONSTONE CHINA
FURNIVAL, J. & CO.	REAL VITRIFIED IRONSTONE CHINA
FURNIVAL, J. & CO.	STAFFORDSHIRE
FURNIVAL, JACOB & CO.	COBRIDGE
FURNIVAL, JACOB & CO.	IRONSTONE
FURNIVAL, JACOB & CO.	IRONSTONE CHINA
FURNIVAL, JACOB & CO.	PEARL VITRIFIED IRONSTONE CHINA
FURNIVAL, JACOB & CO.	REAL IRONSTONE CHINA
FURNIVAL, JACOB & CO.	STAFF
FURNIVAL, JACOB & CO.	WHITE GRANITE
FURNIVAL, JACOB & THOMAS	STONE CHINA
FURNIVAL, THOMAS & CO.	IRONSTONE
FURNIVAL, THOMAS & CO.	REAL IRONSTONE
FURNIVAL, THOMAS & SONS	COBRIDGE
FURNIVAL, THOMAS & SONS	IRONSTONE
FURNIVAL, THOMAS & SONS	STAFFS
FURNIVAL, THOMAS & SONS	TRADE MARK

FURNIVAL, THOMAS (& CO.)	OPAQUE PORCELAINE
FURNIVALS (LTD.)	COBRIDGE
FURNIVALS (LTD.)	ROYAL SEMI PORCELAIN
FURNIVALS (LTD.)	TRADE MARK
GALLOWAY & ATKINSON	ALBION POTTERY
GATER, HALL & CO.	CORONA
GATER, HALL & CO.	CORONA WARE
GATER, HALL & CO.	OVERHOUSE
GEDDES, JOHN (&SON)	GLASGOW
GEDDES, JOHN (&SON)	VERREVILLE GLASGOW
GELSON BROS.	HANLEY
GIBSON & SONS (LTD.)	ALBANY & HARVEY POTTERIES
GIBSON & SONS (LTD.)	BURSLEM
GIBSON & SONS (LTD.)	HARVEY POTTERY
GILDEA, WALKER (& CO.)	LATE MAYERS
GILDEA, WALKER (& CO.)	TRADE MARK
GLASGOW POTTERY	CALEDONIAN POTTERY
GLOBE POTTERY CO. LTD.	COBRIDGE
GLOBE POTTERY CO. LTD.	SEMI PORCELAIN
GLOBE POTTERY CO. LTD.	SHELTON
GLOBE POTTERY CO. LTD.	VITRIFIED
GODWIN, ROWLEY & CO.	STAFFORDSHIRE
GODWIN, ROWLEY & CO.	STAFFORDSHIRE STONE CHINA
GODWIN, ROWLEY & CO.	STONE CHINA
GODWIN, THOMAS	BURSLEM
GODWIN, THOMAS	IRONSTONE
GODWIN, THOMAS	NEW WHARF
GODWIN, THOMAS	OPAQUE CHINA
GODWIN, THOMAS	STONE CHINA
GODWIN, THOMAS	WHARF
GODWIN, THOMAS & BENJAMIN	NEW WHARF(E)
GODWIN, THOMAS & BENJAMIN	SEMI CHINA
GODWIN, THOMAS & BENJAMIN	STONE CHINA
GOODFELLOW, THOMAS	IRONSTONE
GOODFELLOW, THOMAS	IRONSTONE CHINA
GOODFELLOW, THOMAS	PATENT
GOODWIN(S) & HARRIS	OPAQUE CHINA
GOODWIN, JOHN	IRONSTONE
GOODWIN, JOHN	LONGTON
GOODWIN, JOHN	SEACOMBE POTTERY
GOODWIN, JOHN	THE QUEEN'S ROYAL IRONSTONE
GOODWIN, JOHN & CO.	IRONSTONE
GOODWIN, JOHN & CO.	LIVERPOOL
GOODWIN, JOSEPH	IRONSTONE
GOODWIN, JOSEPH	TUNSTALL
GORDON, GEORGE	OPAQUE CHINA
GREEN & CLAY	TRADE MARK
GREEN(S)	DON POTTERY
GREEN, GEO.	KILNHURST OLD POTTERY
GREEN, GEORGE	KILNHURST OLD POTTERY
GREEN, T. G. & CO. (LTD.)	GRESLEY
GREEN, THOMAS	FENTON
GREEN, THOMAS	FENTON POTTERIES
GREENOCK POTTERY	CLYDE POTTERY CO.
GRIFFITHS, BEARDMORE & BIRKS	STAFFORDSHIRE IRONSTONE CHINA
GRIMWADE BROS.	ATLAS BONE CHINA
GRIMWADE BROS.	STOKE UPON TRENT
GRIMWADE BROS.	TRADE MARK
GRIMWADES LTD.	SEMI PORCELAIN
GRIMWADES LTD.	STAFFORDSHIRE
GRIMWADES LTD.	STOKE ON TRENT
GRIMWADES LTD.	STOKE POTTERY
GRIMWADES LTD.	UPPER HANLEY POTTERY
GRIMWADES LTD.	UPPER HANLEY POTTERY CO. (LTD.)
GRINDLEY, W. H. & CO. (LTD.)	ROYAL IRONSTONE CHINA
GRINDLEY, W. H. & CO. (LTD.)	SEMI PORCELAIN
GRINDLEY, W. H. & CO. (LTD.)	TRADE MARK
GRINDLEY, W. H. & CO. (LTD.)	TUNSTALL
GROSE & CO.	STOKE UPON TRENT
GROSE & CO.	STONE CHINA
GROVE & STARK	LONGTON
GUEST & DEWSBERRY	SOUTH WALES POTTERY
HACKWOOD & CO.	IRONSTONE CHINA
HALL, RALPH (& CO.) or (& SON)	STONE CHINA
HAMILTON, ROBERT	CALIS
HAMILTON, ROBERT	STOKE
HAMMERSLEY & ASBURY	LONGTON
HANCOCK, SAMPSON (& SONS)	DUTCHESS CHINA (THE)
HANCOCK, SAMPSON (& SONS)	OPAQUE CHINA
HANCOCK, SAMPSON (& SONS)	ROYAL CORONATION WARE
HANCOCK, SAMPSON (& SONS)	STOKE ON TRENT
HANDLEY, JAMES & WILLIAM	STONE CHINA
HARDING & COCKSON	COBRIDGE
HARLEY, THOMAS	LANE END
HARTLEY GREENS & CO.	LEEDS POTTERY
HARVEY, C. & W. K.	HARVEY
HARVEY, C. & W. K.	IRONSTONE
HARVEY, C. & W. K.	OPAQUE CHINA
HARVEY, C. & W. K.	OPAQUE PORCELAIN

HARVEY, C. & W. K.	REAL IRONSTONE CHINA
HARVEY, J. & CO.	OPAQUE PEARL
HAWLEY, PHILIP & CO.	KILNHURST OLD POTTERY
HAWLEY, PHILIP & COOK	KILNHURST OLD POTTERY
HAWLEY, SIMPSON	KILNHURST OLD POTTERY
HAWLEY, THOMAS	KILNHURST OLD POTTERY
HEALD, WILLIAM	KILNHURST OLD POTTERY
HEATH, J. & CO.	IMPERIAL STONE
HEATH, THOMAS	BURSLEM
HEATHCOTE, CHARLES & CO.	CAMBRIA
HERCULANEUM POTTERY	LIVERPOOL
HERON, ROBERT (& SON)	KIRKCALDY, SCOTLAND
HICKS & MEIGH	FRENCH CHINA
HICKS & MEIGH	IMPROVED STONE CHINA
HICKS & MEIGH	INDIAN STONE CHINA
HICKS & MEIGH	STONE CHINA
HICKS, MEIGH & JOHNSON	REAL STONE CHINA
HICKS, MEIGH & JOHNSON	STONE CHINA
HOLDCROFT, PETER & CO.	PEARL
HOLLAND & GREEN	LATE HARVEY
HOLLAND & GREEN	REAL IRONSTONE CHINA
HOLLAND & GUEST	SOUTH WALES POTTERY
HOLLAND, W. T.	YNYSMEDW POTTERY
HOLLAND, WILLIAM	SOUTH WALES POTTERY
HOLLINSHEAD & KIRKHAM (LTD.)	HOLKIRKWARE
HOLLINSHEAD & KIRKHAM (LTD.)	IMPERIAL IRONSTONE CHINA
HOLLINSHEAD & KIRKHAM (LTD.)	IRONSTONE
HOLLINSHEAD & KIRKHAM (LTD.)	LATE WEDGWOOD
HOLLINSHEAD & KIRKHAM (LTD.)	TRADE MARK
HOLLINSHEAD & KIRKHAM (LTD.)	TUNSTALL
HOLLINSHEAD & KIRKHAM (LTD.)	WOODLAND
HOLLINSHEAD & KIRKHAM (LTD.)	WOODLAND (POTTERY)
HOPE & CARTER	BURSLEM
HOPE & CARTER	STONE CHINA
HOPKIN & VERNON	BURSLEM
HUDDEN, JOHN THOMAS	LONGTON
HUGHES, E. & CO.	FENTON
HUGHES, E. & CO.	ROYAL CHINA
HUGHES, THOMAS	BURSLEM
HUGHES, THOMAS	GRANITE CHINA
HUGHES, THOMAS	IMPERIAL FRENCH PORCELAIN
HUGHES, THOMAS	IRONSTONE CHINA
HUGHES, THOMAS	LONGPORT
HUGHES, THOMAS & SON (LTD.)	IRONSTONE CHINA
HUGHES, THOMAS & SON (LTD.)	IRONSTONE WARE
HUGHES, THOMAS & SON (LTD.)	ROYAL PATENT IRONSTONE
HUGHES, THOMAS & SON (LTD.)	SEMI PORCELAIN
HUGHES, THOMAS & SON (LTD.)	TRADE MARK
HULSEY & ADDERLEY	TRADE MARK
HUMPHREY'S BROS.	TUNSTALL
JACKSON, JOB & JOHN	HERCULANEUM
JACKSON, JOB & JOHN	WARRANTED
JAMIESON, JAMES & CO.	BO'NESS
JAMIESON, JAMES & CO.	PORCELAIN OPAQUE
JOHNSON BROS. (HANLEY) LTD.	ROYAL IRONSTONE CHINA
JOHNSON BROS. (HANLEY) LTD.	ROYAL IRONSTONE WARE
JOHNSON BROS. (HANLEY) LTD.	ROYAL SEMI PORCELAIN
JOHNSON, REUBEN	HANLEY
JOHNSON, REUBEN	STONE CHINA
JOHNSON, SAMUEL LTD.	BRITANNIA POTTERY
JOHNSON, SAMUEL LTD.	BURSLEM
JONES & SON	SUPERIOR STAFFORDSHIRE WARE
JONES, A.B. & SONS (LTD.)	GRAFTON CHINA
JONES & WALLEY	NEW PORCELAIN
JONES, ALBERT E. (LONGTON) LTD.	PALISSY
JONES, FREDERICK (& CO.)	LONGTON
JONES, FREDERICK (& CO.)	PATENT IRONSTONE CHINA
JONES, FREDERICK (& CO.)	PEARL IRONSTONE
JONES, FREDERICK (& CO.)	PEARL IRONSTONE CHINA
JONES, G. F.	IRONSTONE
JONES, G. F.	STOKE ON TRENT
JONES, GEORGE	ROYAL PATENT IRONSTONE
JONES, GEORGE (& SONS)(LTD.)	CRESENT (POTTERY) CHINA
JONES, GEORGE (& SONS)(LTD.)	STOKE ON TRENT
JONES, GEORGE (& SONS)(LTD.)	STONE CHINA
JONES, GEORGE & SONS	IRONSTONE CHINA
KEELING & CO. (LTD.)	BURSLEM
KEELING & CO. (LTD.)	LASOL (WARE)
KEELING & CO. (LTD.)	LATE MAYERS
KEELING, SAMUEL & CO.	HANLEY
KEELING, SAMUEL & CO.	NEW STONE
KEMP & CO.	CALEDONIAN POTTERY
KENT, JAMES (LTD.)	LONGTON
KENT, JAMES (LTD.)	ROYAL SEMI CHINA
KENT, JAMES (LTD.)	YE OLD FOLEY WARE
KILNHURST OLD POTTERY	MALPASS, WILLIAM
KNIGHT, ELKIN & CO.	IRONSTONE CHINA
KNIGHT, ELKIN & CO.	OPAQUE FELSPAR CHINA
KNIGHT, JOHN KING	FOLEY
KNIGHT, JOHN KING	OPAQUE GRANITE CHINA
KNOTTINGLEY POTTERY	FERRYBRIDGE POTTERY
LAWLEY'S LTD. (Retailers)	NORFOLK POTTERY STONE
LIDDLE, ELLIOT & SON	BERLIN IRONSTONE
LIDDLE, ELLIOT & SON	ELLIOT BROS. (See)
LIVESLEY, POWELL & CO.	BEST
LIVESLEY, POWELL & CO.	IRONSTONE
LIVESLEY, POWELL & CO.	IRONSTONE CHINA
LOCKITT, WILLIAM H.	DURA-WARE
LOCKITT, WILLIAM H.	HANLEY
LOCKETT & HULME	OPAQUE CHINA
LONGTON POTTERY CO. LTD.	BLUE BELL WARE
LONGTON POTTERY CO. LTD.	LONGTON
MACHIN & POTTS	PATENT
MACHIN & POTTS	ROYAL VITRESCENT ROCK CHINA
MACINTYRE, JAMES & CO. (LTD.)	BURSLEM
MACINTYRE, JAMES & CO. (LTD.)	IRONSTONE CHINA
MADDOCK & GATER	STAFFORDSHIRE POTTERIES
MADDOCK & GATER	TRADE MARK
MADDOCK & SEDDON	STONE CHINA
MADDOCK, JOHN	IRONSTONE CHINA
MADDOCK, JOHN	STONE CHINA
MADDOCK, JOHN & SONS (LTD.)	BURSLEM
MADDOCK, JOHN & SONS (LTD.)	IRONSTONE CHINA
MADDOCK, JOHN & SONS (LTD.)	ROYAL IVORY
MADDOCK, JOHN & SONS (LTD.)	ROYAL SEMI PORCELAIN
MADDOCK, JOHN & SONS (LTD.)	ROYAL STONE CHINA
MADDOCK, JOHN & SONS (LTD.)	ROYAL VITREOUS
MADDOCK, JOHN & SONS (LTD.)	ROYAL VITRIFIED
MADDOCK, JOHN & SONS (LTD.)	STAFFORDSHIRE POTTERIES
MADDOCK, JOHN & SONS (LTD.)	STONE CHINA
MADDOCK, JOHN & SONS (LTD.)	TRADE MARK
MADDOCK, JOHN & SONS (LTD.)	VITRIFIED
MAILING, C. T. & SONS (LTD.)	CETEM WARE
MAILING, C. T. & SONS (LTD.)	HYLTON POT WORKS
MAILING, C. T. & SONS (LTD.)	NEW CASTLE (ON TYNE)
MAILING, C. T. & SONS (LTD.)	NEWCASTLE-ON-TYNE
MAILING, C. T. & SONS (LTD.)	TRADE MARK
MALKIN, WALKER & HULSE	LONDON
MANN & CO.	HANLEY
MARE, JOHN	BRITISH COBALT BLUE
MARPLE, TURNER & CO.	IRONSTONE CHINA
MARSH, JACOB	OPAQUE CHINA WARRANTED
MARSHALL, JOHN & CO.	BO'NESS (POTTERY)
MARSHALL, JOHN (& CO.)(LTD.)	BEST GOODS
MASON, C. J. (& CO.)	FENTON
MASON, C. J. (& CO.)	FENTON STONE WORKS
MASON, C. J. (& CO.)	GRANITE CHINA
MASON, C. J. (& CO.)	LANE DELPH
MASON, C. J. (& CO.)	NEW STONE CHINA
MASON, C. J. (& CO.)	PATENT IRONSTONE CHINA
MASON, C. J. (& CO.)	SEMI CHINA WARRANTED
MASON, C. J. (& CO.)	STAFFORDSHIRE POTTERIES
MASON, CHARLES JAMES (& CO.)	BANDANA WARE
MASON, CHARLES JAMES (& CO.)	BRITISH NANKIN CHINA (OR POTTERY)
MASON, CHARLES JAMES (& CO.)	CAMBRIAN ARGIL
MASON, CHARLES JAMES (& CO.)	IMPROVED IRONSTONE CHINA
MASON, CHARLES JAMES (& CO.)	MASON'S
MASON, CHARLES JAMES (& CO.)	WARRANTED
MASON, G. M. & C. J.	FENTON STONE WORKS
MASON, G. M. & C. J.	IRONSTONE CHINA
MASON, G. M. & C. J.	MASON'S
MASON, G. M. & C. J.	MASON'S PATENT IRONSTONE CHINA
MASON, G. M. & C. J.	PATENT IRONSTONE CHINA
MASON, G. M. & C. J.	SEMI CHINA WARRANTED
MASON, JAMES	PATENT IRONSTONE CHINA
MASON, MILES	BRITISH NANKIN CHINA
MAUDESLEY, J. & CO.	STONEWARE
MAYER & ELLIOTT (See MAYER BROS. & ELLIOTT)	BERLIN IRONSTONE
MAYER & ELLIOTT (See MAYER BROS. & ELLIOTT)	IRONSTONE
MAYER & NEWBOLD	NEW OPAQUE
MAYER & NEWBOLD	OPAQUE CHINA
MAYER, T. & J.	LONGPORT
MAYER, T. J. & J.	CHINESE PORCELAINE
MAYER, T. J. & J.	DALE HALL POTTERY
MAYER, T. J. & J.	IMPROVED BERLIN IRONSTONE
MAYER, T. J. & J.	IMPROVED IRONSTONE
MAYER, T. J. & J.	IMPROVED IRONSTONE CHINA
MAYER, T. J. & J.	IRONSTONE
MAYER, T. J. & J.	LONGPORT
MAYER, T. J. & J.	PATENT
MAYER, T. J. & J.	STONEWARE
MAYER, THOMAS	IMPROVED STONE CHINA
MAYER, THOMAS	LONGPORT
MAYER, THOMAS	STAFFORDSHIRE
MAYER, THOMAS	STOKE
MAYER, THOMAS	STOKE UPON TRENT
MCLACHLAN, DONALD & BROWN	CLYDE POTTERY CO. (LTD.)

MEAKIN & CO.	COBRIDGE
MEAKIN & CO.	IRONSTONE
MEAKIN & CO.	IRONSTONE CHINA
MEAKIN BROS. & CO.	MEAKIN & CO. (See)
MEAKIN, ALFRED (LTD.)	PARIS WHITE IRONSTONE
MEAKIN, ALFRED (LTD.)	PARISIAN GRANITE
MEAKIN, ALFRED (LTD.)	REAL IRONSTONE CHINA
MEAKIN, ALFRED (LTD.)	ROYAL IRONSTONE CHINA
MEAKIN, ALFRED (LTD.)	ROYAL SEMI PORCELAIN
MEAKIN, ALFRED (LTD.)	TUNSTALL
MEAKIN, CHARLES	HANLEY
MEAKIN, CHARLES	ROYAL IRONSTONE
MEAKIN, CHARLES	ROYAL IRONSTONE CHINA
MEAKIN, HENRY	IRONSTONE CHINA
MEAKIN, J. & G.	PARIS WHITE IRONSTONE
MEAKIN, J. & G. (LTD.)	EASTWOOD WORKS
MEAKIN, J. & G. (LTD.)	HANLEY
MEAKIN, J. & G. (LTD.)	IRONSTONE
MEAKIN, J. & G. (LTD.)	IRONSTONE CHINA
MEAKIN, J. & G. (LTD.)	PEARL CHINA
MEAKIN, J. & G. (LTD.)	REAL CHINA
MEAKIN, J. & G. (LTD.)	SEMI PORCELAIN
MEAKIN, J. & G. (LTD.)	SOL
MEIGH, CHARLES	ENAMEL PORCELAIN
MEIGH, CHARLES	FRENCH CHINA
MEIGH, CHARLES	IMPERIAL STONE CHINA
MEIGH, CHARLES	IMPROVED IRONSTONE
MEIGH, CHARLES	IMPROVED IRONSTONE CHINA
MEIGH, CHARLES	IMPROVED STONE CHINA
MEIGH, CHARLES	IRONSTONE
MEIGH, CHARLES	PORCELAIN OPAQUE
MEIGH, CHARLES	STONE
MEIGH, CHARLES & SON	CHINA
MEIGH, CHARLES & SON	HANLEY
MEIGH, CHARLES & SON	IMPROVED FELSPAR
MEIGH, CHARLES & SON	IRONSTONE CHINA
MEIGH, CHARLES & SON	OPAQUE PORCELAIN
MEIGH, CHARLES & SON	STAFFORDSHIRE
MEIGH, JOB (& SON)	HANLEY
MEIGH, JOB (& SON)	IMPROVED CHINA
MEIGH, JOB (& SON)	IMPROVED STONE CHINA
MEIGH, JOB (& SON)	OLD HALL
MEIKLE BROS. (Canadian Importers)	LIVERPOOL
MEIKLE BROS. (Canadian Importers)	ROYAL OPAQUE CHINA
MEIR, JOHN	STONE CHINA
MEIR, JOHN	WARRANTED STAFFORDSHIRE
MEIR, JOHN & SON	IRONSTONE
MEIR, JOHN & SON	IRONSTONE CHINA
MEIR, JOHN & SON	STAFFORDSHIRE
MEIR, JOHN & SON	STONE CHINA
MEIR, JOHN & SON	TUNSTALL
MEIR, JOHN & SON	WARRANTED
MEIR, JOHN & SON	WARRANTED STAFFORDSHIRE
MELLOR, TAYLOR & CO.	REAL IRONSTONE CHINA
MELLOR, TAYLOR & CO.	ROYAL IRONSTONE CHINA
MELLOR, TAYLOR & CO.	SEMI PORCELAIN
MELLOR, TAYLOR & CO.	WARRANTED STONE CHINA
MELLOR, VENABLE, PINDER & CO. (See)	MELLOR, VENABLES & CO.
MELLOR, VENABLES & CO.	IRONSTONE
MELLOR, VENABLES & CO.	ROYAL PATENT
METHVEN, DAVID & SONS	BULLOCH
METHVEN, DAVID & SONS	IMPERIAL
METHVEN, DAVID & SONS	KIRKCALDY POTTERY
METHVEN, DAVID & SONS	PORCELAIN OPAQUE
METHVEN, DAVID & SONS	SCOTLAND
MIDDLESBROUGH POTTERY	LONDON (See)
MIDWINTER, W. R. (LTD.)	BURSLEM
MIDWINTER, W. R. (LTD.)	PORCELON
MILLER, JAMES & CO. LTD.	GLASGOW
MILLER, JAMES & CO. LTD.	NORTH BRITISH POTTERY
MILLER, JAMES & CO. LTD.	PORT DUNDAS POTTERY CO.
MINTON	FELSPAR CHINA
MINTON	FELSPAR PORCELAIN
MINTON	FLORENTINE CHINA
MINTON	IMPROVED STONE CHINA
MINTON	LAWLEYS LTD. (Retailers)
MINTON	M./STONE
MINTON	OPAQUE CHINA
MINTON	SEMI CHINA
MINTON	SEMI NANKIN CHINA
MINTON	STOKE UPON TRENT
MINTON	STONE
MINTON	STONE CHINA
MINTON & BOYLE	IMPROVED STONE CHINA
MINTON (Mid 19th c.)	B.B. (BEST BODY)
MOORE, (SAMUEL) & CO.	SUNDERLAND
MORLEY & ASHWORTH	HANLEY
MORLEY & ASHWORTH	IMPERIAL IRONSTONE
MORLEY & ASHWORTH	MANUFACTURED BY
MORLEY & ASHWORTH	PATENT IRONSTONE CHINA
MORLEY & ASHWORTH	REAL IRONSTONE CHINA
MORLEY & ASHWORTH	STONE CHINA
MORLEY, FRANCIS (& CO.)	IRONSTONE
MORLEY, FRANCIS (& CO.)	MASON'S IRONSTONE
MORLEY, FRANCIS (& CO.)	OPAQUE CHINA
MORLEY, FRANCIS (& CO.)	PATENT
MORLEY, FRANCIS (& CO.)	PATENT IRONSTONE CHINA
MORLEY, FRANCIS (& CO.)	PATENT OPAQUE CHINA
MORLEY, FRANCIS (& CO.)	REAL IRONSTONE
MORLEY, FRANCIS (& CO.)	REAL IRONSTONE CHINA
MORLEY, FRANCIS (& CO.)	REAL STONE CHINA
MORLEY, FRANCIS (& CO.)	ROYAL STONE
MORLEY, FRANCIS (& CO.)	SHELTON
MORLEY, FRANCIS (& CO.)	STONEWARE
MOUNTFORD, GEORGE THOMAS	STOKE
MUIR, ANDREW & CO.	CLYDE POTTERY CO. (LTD.)
MYOTT, SON & CO. (LTD.)	IMPERIAL SEMI PORCELAIN
MYOTT, SON & CO. (LTD.)	SEMI PORCELAIN
MYOTT, SON & CO. (LTD.)	STAFFORDSHIRE
MYOTT, SON & CO. (LTD.)	STOKE
NAUTILUS PORCELAIN CO.	NAUTILUS PORCELAIN
NEAL (JAMES) & CO.	HANLEY
NEW WHARF POTTERY CO.	BURSLEM
NEW WHARF POTTERY CO.	SEMI PORCELAIN
NEWPORT POTTERY CO., LTD.	BURSLEM
OLD HALL (EARTHENWARE) CO. LTD.	IMPERIAL PARISIAN GRANITE
OLD HALL (EARTHENWARE) CO. LTD.	INDIAN STONE CHINA
OLD HALL (EARTHENWARE) CO. LTD.	OLD HALL
OLD HALL (EARTHENWARE) CO. LTD.	OPAQUE PORCELAIN
OLD HALL PORCELAIN WORKS LTD.	OLD HALL
PALISSY POTTERY LTD.	PALISSY
PALISSY POTTERY LTD.	ROYAL WORCESTER
PALISSY POTTERY LTD.	STAFFORDSHIRE
PANKHURST, J. W. & CO.	HANLEY
PANKHURST, J. W. & CO.	IRONSTONE CHINA
PANKHURST, J. W. & CO.	PANKHURST & DIMMOCK (see)
PATTERSON (GEORGE) & CO.	SHERIFF HILL
PATTERSON (GEORGE) & CO.	TYNE POTTERY
PEARSON & CO.	TRADE MARK
PEARSON & CO.	WHITTINGTON MOOR
PEARSON, EDWARD	IRONSTONE CHINA
PEARSON, EDWARD (& SON)	COBRIDGE
PEARSON, FARRALL & MEAKIN	IRONSTONE CHINA
PEARSON, FARRALL & MEAKIN	JOHN FARRALL (See)
PENMAN, BROWN & CO.	ARMITAGE
PENMAN, ROBERT H. & CO.	ARMITAGE
PENMAN, ROBERT, H. & CO.	PENMAN, BROWN & CO. (See)
PETTY & CO.	LEEDS
PHILLIPS & CO.	GARRISON POTTERY
PHILLIPS & CO.	SUNDERLAND POTTERY
PHILLIPS, EDWARD & GEORGE	LONGPORT
PHILLIPS, EDWARD & GEORGE	OPAQUE CHINA
PHILLIPS, GEORGE	BURSLEM
PHILLIPS, GEORGE	LONGPORT
PHILLIPS, GEORGE	OPAQUE CHINA
PHILLIPS, GEORGE	PEARL IRONSTONE CHINA
PHILLIPS, GEORGE & SON	IRONSTONE
PHILLIPS, J.	GARRISON POTTERY
PHILLIPS, J.	SUNDERLAND POTTERY
PHILLIPS, JOHN	HYLTON POT WORKS
PHILLIPS, JOHN	HYLTON POTTERY
PHILLIPS, JOHN	SUNDERLAND POTTERY
PHILLIPS, THOMAS & SON	BURSLEM
PHILLIPS, THOMAS & SON	LONGPORT
PHOENIX POTTERY CO.	N'CASTLE
PINDER, BOURNE & CO.	BURSLEM, STAFFORDSHIRE
PINDER, BOURNE & CO.	IMPERIAL WHITE GRANITE
PINDER, BOURNE & CO.	NILE ST., BURSLEM
PITCAIRNS LTD.	PORCELAIN ROYALE
PITCAIRNS LTD.	TUNSTALL
PLANT, J. & CO.	STOKE POTTERY
PLANT, R. H. & S. L. (LTD.)	TRADE MARK
PLANT, R. H. & S. L. (LTD.)	TUSCAN CHINA
PLYMOUTH POTTERY CO. LTD.	STONE CHINA
PODMORE, WALKER & (CO.)	IMPERIAL GRANITE
PODMORE, WALKER & (CO.)	IMPERIAL IRONSTONE CHINA
PODMORE, WALKER & (CO.)	IRONSTONE
PODMORE, WALKER & (CO.)	PEARL
PODMORE, WALKER & (CO.)	PEARL STONE CHINA
PODMORE, WALKER & (CO.)	PEARL STONE WARE
PODMORE, WALKER & (CO.)	STONEWARE
PODMORE, WALKER & (CO.)	WEDGWOOD
PODMORE, WALKER & (CO.)	WEDGWOOD & CO.
POSSIL POTTERY CO.	GLASGOW
POSSIL POTTERY CO.	NAUTILUS PORCELAIN
POSSIL POTTERY CO.	TRADE MARK
POTTS, WM. WAINWRIGHT	DERBYSHIRE

POTTS, WM. WAINWRIGHT	PATENT
POULSON BROTHERS	FERRYBRIDGE POTTERY
POUNTNEY & ALLIES	HAMILTON
POUNTNEY & ALLIES	IMPROVED STONE CHINA
POUNTNEY & CO. (LTD.)	BRISTOL
POUNTNEY & CO. (LTD.)	BRISTOL ALKALON CHINA
POUNTNEY & CO. (LTD.)	BRISTOL PORCELAIN
POUNTNEY & CO. (LTD.)	BRISTOL POTTERY
POUNTNEY & CO. (LTD.)	BRISTOL SEMI PORCELAIN
POUNTNEY & CO. (LTD.)	GRANITE CHINA
POUNTNEY & CO. (LTD.)	SEMI PORCELAIN
POUNTNEY & GOLDNEY	BRISTOL POTTERY
POUNTNEY & GOLDNEY	MANDARIN OPAQUE CHINA
POWELL & BISHOP	BEST
POWELL & BISHOP	IRONSTONE
POWELL & BISHOP	IRONSTONE CHINA
POWELL, BISHOP & STONIER	ORIENTAL IVORY
PRATT & SIMPSON	SEMI PORCELAINE
PRATT & SIMPSON	STONE CHINA
PRATT & SIMPSON	WARRANTED
PRATT, F. & R. & CO. (LTD.)	FENTON
PRATT, F. & R. & CO. (LTD.)	KAOLIN (WARE)
PURVES, CHARLES	ELGIN POTTERY
RATCLIFFE, WILLIAM	HACKWOOD
RATHBONE, T. & CO.	TRADE MARK
RATHBONE, T. & CO.	TUNSTALL
READ & CLEMENTSON	STONEWARE
READ & CO.	STONEWARE
REED & TAYLOR (& CO.)	FERRYBRIDGE POTTERY
REED & TAYLOR (& CO.)	OPAQUE CHINA
REED & TAYLOR (& CO.)	STONE CHINA
REED, JAMES	STONE CHINA
REED, JAMES	STONEWARE
REEVES, JAMES	FENTON
REEVES, JAMES	STAFFORDSHIRE
REEVES, JAMES	VICTORIA CHINA
REID, WILLIAM (Scotland)	MUSE
REID, WM. & FORSTER	NEW BIGGINS POTTERY
REID, WM. (& SON(S))	MUSE
REID, WM. (& SON(S))	MUSSELBURGH
REID, WM. (& SON(S))	NEW BIGGINS POTTERY
RIDGWAY & ABINGTON	HANLEY
RIDGWAY & ABINGTON	IMPERIAL STONE
RIDGWAY & MORLEY	GRANITE CHINA
RIDGWAY & MORLEY	GRANITE IRONSTONE CHINA
RIDGWAY & MORLEY	HANLEY
RIDGWAY & MORLEY	IMPERIAL STONE
RIDGWAY & MORLEY	IMPROVED GRANITE CHINA
RIDGWAY & MORLEY	OPAQUE CHINA
RIDGWAY & MORLEY	PATENT
RIDGWAY & MORLEY	PATENT IRONSTONE CHINA
RIDGWAY & MORLEY	REAL IRONSTONE CHINA
RIDGWAY & MORLEY	STONEWARE
RIDGWAY, JOHN & WILLIAM	DRESDEN OPAQUE CHINA
RIDGWAY, JOHN & WILLIAM	IRONSTONE CHINA
RIDGWAY, JOHN & WILLIAM	JAPAN OPAQUE CHINA
RIDGWAY, JOHN & WILLIAM	OPAQUE CHINA
RIDGWAY, JOHN & WILLIAM	OPAQUE CHINA
RIDGWAY, JOHN & WILLIAM	REAL IRONSTONE CHINA
RIDGWAY, JOHN & WILLIAM	STOCKTON
RIDGWAY, JOHN & WILLIAM	STONE CHINA
RIDGWAY, JOHN (& CO.)	IMPERIAL STONE
RIDGWAY, JOHN (& CO.)	IMPERIAL STONE CHINA
RIDGWAY, JOHN (& CO.)	OPAQUE CHINA
RIDGWAY, JOHN (& CO.)	PORCELAINE A LA FRANCAISE
RIDGWAY, JOHN (& CO.)	REAL IRONSTONE CHINA
RIDGWAY, JOHN (& CO.)	REAL STONE CHINA
RIDGWAY, JOHN (& CO.)	STONE CHINA
RIDGWAY, JOHN (& CO.)	STONEWARE
RIDGWAY, JOHN (& CO.)	SUPERIOR STONE CHINA
RIDGWAY, JOHN, BATES & CO.	FLORENTINE CHINA
RIDGWAY, MORLEY, WEAR & CO.	GRANITE
RIDGWAY, MORLEY, WEAR & CO.	GRANITE CHINA
RIDGWAY, MORLEY, WEAR & CO.	IMPROVED GRANITE CHINA
RIDGWAY, MORLEY, WEAR & CO.	OPAQUE CHINA
RIDGWAY, MORLEY, WEAR & CO.	REAL IRONSTONE CHINA
RIDGWAY, WM. (& CO.)	ETRUSCAN FESTOON
RIDGWAY, WM. (& CO.)	GRANITE CHINA
RIDGWAY, WM. (& CO.)	IMPERIAL GRANITE CHINA
RIDGWAY, WM. (& CO.)	IMPROVED CHINA
RIDGWAY, WM. (& CO.)	IMPROVED GRANITE CHINA
RIDGWAY, WM. (& CO.)	IMPROVED STONE
RIDGWAY, WM. (& CO.)	OPAQUE CHINA
RIDGWAY, WM. (& CO.)	OPAQUE GRANITE
RIDGWAY, WM. (& CO.)	OPAQUE GRANITE CHINA
RIDGWAY, WM. (& CO.)	QUARTZ CHINA
RIDGWAY, WM. (& CO.)	REAL IRONSTONE CHINA
RIDGWAY, WM. (& CO.)	SHELTON
RIDGWAY, WM. SON & CO.	HANLEY
RIDGWAY, WM. SON & CO.	IMPERIAL STONE
RIDGWAY, WM. SON & CO.	PUBLISHED BY
RIDGWAYS (BEDFORD WORKS) LTD.	BEDFORD WARE (OR WORKS)
RIDGWAYS (BEDFORD WORKS) LTD.	BEDFORD WORKS (OR WARE)
RIDGWAYS (BEDFORD WORKS) LTD.	IRONSTONE CHINA
RIDGWAYS (BEDFORD WORKS) LTD.	IRONSTONE WARE
RIDGWAYS (BEDFORD WORKS) LTD.	IVORY CHINA
RIDGWAYS (BEDFORD WORKS) LTD.	JANROTH (American Importer)
RIDGWAYS (BEDFORD WORKS) LTD.	SEMI CHINA
RIDGWAYS (BEDFORD WORKS) LTD.	SEMI PORCELAIN
RIDGWAYS (BEDFORD WORKS) LTD.	SHELTON
RIDGWAYS (BEDFORD WORKS) LTD.	VITRIFIED
RIDGWAYS (LTD.)	OPAQUE CHINA
RIDGWAYS (LTD.)	ROYAL SEMI PORCELAIN
RIDGWAYS (LTD.)	ROYAL VITRIFIED
RIDGWAYS (LTD.)	STOKE ON TRENT
RILEY, JOHN & RICHARD	OPAQUE CHINA
RILEY, JOHN & RICHARD	SEMI CHINA
RILEY, JOHN & RICHARD	SEMI CHINA WARRANTED
RILEY, JOHN & RICHARD	WARRANTED
ROBINSON & WOOD	STONE CHINA
ROBINSON, JOSEPH	BURSLEM
ROBINSON, WOOD & BROWNFIELD	OPAQUE STONE
ROBINSON, WOOD & BROWNFIELD	OPAQUE STONE CHINA
ROBINSON, WOOD & BROWNFIELD	STONE CHINA
ROBINSON, WOOD & BROWNFIELD	STONEWARE
ROGERS, JOHN (& SON)	CHINESE PORCELAIN
ROGERS, JOHN (& SON)	SEMI CHINA
ROWLEY & CO.	STONE CHINA
ROWLEY, JOSEPH	CALEDONIAN POTTERY
ROWLEY, JOSIAH	GLASGOW
SCOTT (BROS.)(& CO.)(& SONS)	SOUTHWICK POTTERY
SCOTT BROS.	EDINBURGH SCOTLAND
SEWELL(S) & CO.	ST. ANTHONY'S POTTERY
SEWELL(S) POTTERY	ST. ANTHONY'S POTTERY
SHARPE, THOMAS	SWADLINCOTE
SHARPUS	LONDON RETAILERS
SHAW, ANTHONY (& CO.)(&SON(S))	BURSLEM
SHAW, ANTHONY (& CO.)(&SON(S))	IMPERIAL IRONSTONE CHINA
SHAW, ANTHONY (& CO.)(&SON(S))	IRONSTONE
SHAW, ANTHONY (& CO.)(&SON(S))	IRONSTONE CHINA WARRANTED
SHAW, ANTHONY (& CO.)(&SON(S))	MANUFACTURED
SHAW, ANTHONY (& CO.)(&SON(S))	OPAQUE STONE CHINA
SHAW, ANTHONY (& CO.)(&SON(S))	PORCELAIN OPAQUE
SHAW, ANTHONY (& CO.)(&SON(S))	STONE CHINA
SHAW, ANTHONY (& CO.)(&SON(S))	STONE CHINA WARRANTED
SHAW, ANTHONY (& CO.)(&SON(S))	TRADE MARK
SHAW, ANTHONY (& CO.)(&SON(S))	TUNSTALL
SHAW, ANTHONY (& CO.)(&SON(S))	WARRANTED
SHAW, ANTHONY (& CO.)(&SON(S))	WHITE GRANITE
SHAW, C. & J.	STONE CHINA
SHAW, C. & J.	VINCIT VERITAS
SHERIFF HILL POTTERY	GATESHEAD FELL
SHIRLEY, THOMAS & CO.	CLYDE (OR) LADYBURN POTTERY
SHIRLEY, THOMAS & CO.	LADYBURN POTTERY
SHIRLEY, THOMAS & CO.	SAXON
SHIRLEY, THOMAS & CO.	WARRANTED
SIMPSON-BOWMAN HEALD	KILNHURST OLD POTTERY
SKINNER & WALKER	PEARL WARE
SKINNER & WALKER	QUEENS-WARE/STOCKTON
SKINNER & WALKER	STOCKTON
SMITH & FORD	LINCOLN POTTERY
SMITH & FORD	SEMI PORCELAIN
SMITH, FORD & JONES	LINCOLN POTTERY
SMITH, FORD & JONES	PARISIAN WHITE
SMITH, W. (JR.) & CO.	STOCKTON
SMITH, WILLIAM (& CO.)	QUEENS-WARE/STOCKTON
SMITH, WILLIAM (& CO.)	STAFFORD POTTERY
SMITH, WILLIAM (& CO.)	VEDGWOOD
SMITH, WILLIAM (& CO.)	WEDGWOOD WARE
SMITH, WM. & CO.	STONE GRANITE
SNEYD & HILL	HANLEY
SNEYD & HILL	STAFFORDSHIRE POTTERIES
SNEYD, THOMAS	HANLEY
SOHO POTTERY LTD.	COBRIDGE
SOHO POTTERY LTD.	SEMI PORCELAIN
SOHO POTTERY LTD.	SOLIAN WARE
SOHO POTTERY LTD.	TUNSTALL
SOUTH WALES POTTERY	IRONSTONE
SOUTH WALES POTTERY	IRONSTONE CHINA
SOUTH WALES POTTERY	LLANELLY
SOUTH WALES POTTERY	PEARL WHITE IRONSTONE
SOUTHWICK POTTERY	SOUTHWICK
SPODE, JOSIAH	NEW FAYENCE
SPODE, JOSIAH	NEW STONE
SPODE, JOSIAH	PATENT IRONSTONE CHINA
SPODE, JOSIAH	STONE CHINA
ST. JOHN'S STONE CHINAWARE CO. (Canadian)	IMPERIAL IRONSTONE CHINA

ST. JOHN'S STONE CHINAWARE CO. (Canadian)	IRONSTONE CHINA
ST. JOHN'S STONE CHINAWARE CO. (Canadian)	STONE CHINAWARE CO.
STANLEY POTTERY LTD.	LONGTON
STANLEY POTTERY LTD.	ROYAL STANLEY (WARE)
STANLEY POTTERY LTD.	STOKE ON TRENT
STEVENON, RALPH & WILLIAMS	WARRANTED
STEVENSON, A.	WALL, W. G. (See)
STEVENSON, ANDREW	NEW CANTON
STEVENSON, ANDREW	SEMI NANKIN CHINA
STEVENSON, ANDREW	STAFFORDSHIRE
STEVENSON, ANDREW	STAFFORDSHIRE WARRANTED
STEVENSON, ANDREW	WARRANTED
STEVENSON, JAMES & CO.	CLYDE POTTERY CO. (LTD.)
STEVENSON, RALPH	SEMI CHINA WARRANTED
STEVENSON, RALPH	STAFFORDSHIRE
STEVENSON, RALPH	WARRANTED
STEVENSON, RALPH & SON	IMPERIAL STONE
STEVENSON, RALPH & SON	IMPERIAL STONE CHINA
STEVENSON, RALPH & SON	NEW STONE CHINA
STEVENSON, RALPH & WILLIAMS	COBRIDGE
STEVENSON, RALPH & WILLIAMS	ROYAL STONE CHINA
STEVENSON, RALPH & WILLIAMS	SEMI CHINA
STEVENSON, RALPH & WILLIAMS	STAFFORDSHIRE
STEVENSON, RALPH & WILLIAMS	STONE CHINA
STEVENTON, JOHN & SONS LTD.	ROYAL VENTON WARE
STUBBS & KENT	LONGPORT
STUBBS, JOSEPH	LONGPORT
SUNDERLAND POTTERY CO. (LTD.)	SUNDREX
SWANSEA POTTERY	CAMBRIAN POTTERY
SWANSEA POTTERY	CYMBRO STONE CHINA
SWIFT & ELKIN	OPAQUE CHINA
SWIFT & ELKIN	STAFFORDSHIRE STONE CHINA
SWILLINGTON BRIDGE POTTERY	GRANITE CHINA
SWILLINGTON BRIDGE POTTERY	IRONSTONE CHINA
SWILLINGTON BRIDGE POTTERY	OPAQUE GRANITE CHINA
SWINNERTON (LTD.)	HANLEY
SWINNERTON (LTD.)	SEMI PORCELAIN
TAMS & ANDERSON	TAMS (ET. AL.)
TAMS & CO.	SEMI CHINA
TAMS & CO.	TAMS (ET. AL.)
TAMS (ET. AL.)	SEMI CHINA
TAMS, ANDERSON & TAMS	TAMS (ET. AL.)
TAMS, JOHN (& SON)(LTD.)	CHININE
TAMS, JOHN (& SON)(LTD.)	CROWN POTTERY
TAMS, JOHN (& SON)(LTD.)	ELEPHANT BRAND
TAMS, JOHN (& SON)(LTD.)	LONGTON
TAMS, JOHN (& SON)(LTD.)	NANKIN WARE
TAMS, JOHN (& SON)(LTD.)	ROCK STONE
TAMS, JOHN (& SON)(LTD.)	TAMS REGENT
TAMS, JOHN (& SONS)(LTD.)	CROWN POTTERY
TAMS, S. & CO.	TAMS (ET. AL.)
TAMS, S. & CO.	WARRANTED STAFFORDSHIRE
TAYLOR BROS.	HANLEY
TAYLOR BROS.	IRONSTONE CHINA
TAYLOR, WILLIAM	BROOK STREET, HANLEY
TAYLOR, WILLIAM	HANLEY
TAYLOR, WILLIAM	STONE CHINA
THOMPSON, FOWLER (& CO.)	SEMI CHINA
THOMSON, JOHN (& SONS)	ANNENFIELD
THOMSON, JOHN (& SONS)	GLASGOW
THOMSON, JOHN (& SONS)	GRANITE
THOMSON, JOHN (& SONS)	STONEWARE
TILL, THOMAS & SON(S)(LTD.)	BURSLEM
TILL, THOMAS & SON(S)(LTD.)	IRONSTONE
TILL, THOMAS & SON(S)(LTD.)	STONEWARE
TILL, THOMAS & SON(S)(LTD.)	SYTCH POTTERY
TILL, THOMAS & SON(S)(LTD.)	TRADE MARK
TOMKINSON BROS. & CO.	LONGTON
TOMKINSON BROS. & CO.	PEARL
TOMLINSON & CO.	FERRYBRIDGE POTTERY
TOMLINSON & CO.	KNOTTINGLEY POTTERY
TOWNSEND, GEORGE	STAFFORDSHIRE IRONSTONE CHINA
TROUTBECK, E. T.	TUNSTALL
TUNNICLIFF(E), MICHAEL	TUNSTALL
TURNBULL, G. R.	POTTERY
TURNBULL, G. R.	STEPNEY (POTTERY)
TURNER & CO.	KILNHURST OLD POTTERY
TURNER & PHILLIP HAWLEY	KILNHURST OLD POTTERY
TURNER & THOMAS HAWLEY	KILNHURST OLD POTTERY
TURNER & TOMKINSON	PEARL IRONSTONE CHINA
TURNER, (JOHN) & CO.	PATENT IRONSTONE CHINA
TURNER, (JOHN) & CO.	TURNER'S PATENT
TURNER, G. W. & SONS	TUNSTALL
TURNER, G. W. & SONS	TURNERS
TURNER, GODDARD & CO.	ROYAL PATENT IRONSTONE
TWIGG, BENJAMIN & JOHN	KILNHURST OLD POTTERY
TWIGG, DANIEL	KILNHURST OLD POTTERY
TWIGG, JOHN	KILNHURST OLD POTTERY
TWIGG, JOSEPH (& CO.)	NEW HILL
TWIGG, JOSEPH (& CO.)	STONE CHINA
UPPER HANLEY POTTERY CO. (LTD.)	SEMI PORCELAIN
VENABLES, JOHN & CO.	BURSLEM
VENABLES, JOHN & CO.	VENABLES, MANN & CO. (See)
VENABLES, MANN & CO.	BURSLEM
WALKER, THOMAS	IRONSTONE
WALKER, THOMAS	IRONSTONE CHINA
WALKER, THOMAS	TUNSTALL
WALKER, THOMAS HENRY	WARRANTED STONE CHINA
WALLACE & CO.	CAMBRIAN POTTERY
WALLACE, JAMES & CO.	SEMI CHINA
WALLEY, EDWARD	COBRIDGE
WALLEY, EDWARD	INDIAN STONE
WALLEY, EDWARD	IRONSTONE
WALLEY, EDWARD	IRONSTONE CHINA
WALLEY, EDWARD	PARIS WHITE
WALLEY, EDWARD	PEARL WHITE
WALLEY, EDWARD	STAFFORDSHIRE
WALLEY, EDWARD	STONE CHINA
WALLEY, THOMAS	LANE END
WATSON, WILLIAM (& CO.)	FOWLER THOMSON & CO. (See)
WEATHERBY, J. H. & SONS (LTD.)	DURABILITY
WEATHERBY, J. H. & SONS (LTD.)	FALCON WARE
WEATHERBY, J. H. & SONS (LTD.)	HANLEY
WEATHERBY, J. H. & SONS (LTD.)	ROYAL CROWNFORD IRONSTONE
WEATHERBY, J. H. & SONS (LTD.)	SEMI PORCELAIN
WEATHERBY, J. H. & SONS (LTD.)	TUNSTALL
WEDGWOOD & CO.	FERRYBRIDGE POTTERY
WEDGWOOD & CO.	KNOTTINGLEY POTTERY
WEDGWOOD & CO. (LTD.)	IMPERIAL IRONSTONE CHINA
WEDGWOOD & CO. (LTD.)	IMPERIAL PORCELAIN
WEDGWOOD & CO. (LTD.)	IMPERIAL STONE CHINA
WEDGWOOD & CO. (LTD.)	PATENT PARIS WHITE IRONSTONE
WEDGWOOD & CO. (LTD.)	PEARL STONE WARE
WEDGWOOD & CO. (LTD.)	ROYAL SEMI PORCELAIN
WEDGWOOD & CO. (LTD.)	ROYAL STONE CHINA
WEDGWOOD & CO. (LTD.)	SEMI ROYAL PORCELAIN
WEDGWOOD & CO. (LTD.)	STONE CHINA
WEDGWOOD & CO. (LTD.)	STONE GRANITE
WEDGWOOD & CO. (LTD.)	STONEWARE
WEDGWOOD & CO. (LTD.)	TRADE MARK
WEDGWOOD & CO. (LTD.)	WEDGWOOD & CO.
WEDGWOOD'S (J.) WEDGWOOD & SONS (LTD.)	STONE CHINA
WEDGWOOD, JOSIAH (& SONS, LTD.)	ETRURIA
WEDGWOOD, JOSIAH (& SONS, LTD.)	PEARL
WEDGWOOD, JOSIAH (& SONS, LTD.)	SEMI ROYAL PORCELAIN
WEDGWOOD, JOSIAH (& SONS, LTD.)	STONE CHINA
WEDGWOOD, JOSIAH (& SONS, LTD.)	WEDGWOOD
WEDGWOOD, RALPH & CO.	WEDGWOOD
WEDGWOOD, RALPH & CO.	WEDGWOOD & CO.
WHITEHAVEN POTTERY	STONE CHINA
WHITEHAVEN POTTERY	WARRANTED STONE CHINA
WHITEHAVEN POTTERY	WHITEHAVEN
WHITTAKER & CO.	HANLEY
WILEMAN, JAMES F.	FOLEY POTTERIES
WILEMAN, JAMES F.	IRONSTONE CHINA
WILKINSON & HULME	BURSLEM
WILKINSON & WARDLE	DENABY POTTERY(IES)
WILKINSON (JOHN) POTTERY	WHITEHAVEN POTTERY
WILKINSON, ARTHUR J. (LTD.)	BURLEIGH WARE
WILKINSON, ARTHUR J. (LTD.)	BURSLEM
WILKINSON, ARTHUR J. (LTD.)	IRONSTONE CHINA
WILKINSON, ARTHUR J. (LTD.)	LATE ALCOCK, (R.)
WILKINSON, ARTHUR J. (LTD.)	ROYAL IRONSTONE CHINA
WILKINSON, ARTHUR J. (LTD.)	ROYAL PATENT IRONSTONE
WILKINSON, ARTHUR J. (LTD.)	ROYAL SEMI PORCELAIN
WILKINSON, ARTHUR J. (LTD.)	ROYAL STAFFORDSHIRE POTTERY
WILLIAMS, WILLIAM	IRONSTONE
WILLIAMS, WILLIAM	YNYSMEDW POTTERY
WILSON, ISAAC & CO.	MIDDLESBROUGH (POTTERY)
WILTSHAW & ROBINSON (LTD.)	CARLTON CHINA (OR WARE)
WILTSHAW & ROBINSON (LTD.)	STOKE ON TRENT
WINKLE, F. & CO. (LTD.)	COLONIAL POTTERY
WINKLE, F. & CO. (LTD.)	STOKE
WINKLE, F. & CO. (LTD.)	WIELDON WARE
WOLFE & HAMILTON	STOKE
WOOD & BROWNFIELD	COBRIDGE
WOOD & BROWNFIELD	PEARL WHITE
WOOD & BROWNFIELD	REAL IRONSTONE
WOOD & BROWNFIELD	REAL IRONSTONE CHINA
WOOD & BROWNFIELD	STONE CHINA
WOOD & BROWNFIELD	STONEWARE
WOOD & BROWNFIELD	WARRANTED
WOOD & BROWNFIELD	WARRANTED REAL IRONSTONE CHINA
WOOD & CHALLINOR	IRONSTONE
WOOD & CHALLINOR	OPAQUE CHINA

WOOD & CHALLINOR	STONE CHINA
WOOD & HAWTHORNE	IRONSTONE CHINA
WOOD & SON	ROYAL SEMI PORCELAIN
WOOD & SON(S) (LTD.)	IRONSTONE CHINA
WOOD & SON(S) (LTD.)	ROYAL IRONSTONE CHINA
WOOD & SON(S) (LTD.)	WOODS
WOOD, ARTHUR & SON (LONGPORT) LTD.	LONGPORT
WOOD, EDMUND, T.	STONE GRANITE
WOOD, ENOCH	WHITE ENAMEL CHINA
WOOD, ENOCH	WOOD
WOOD, ENOCH & EDWARD	PEARL CHINA
WOOD, ENOCH & SON(S)	BURSLEM
WOOD, ENOCH & SON(S)	BURSLEM WARRANTED
WOOD, ENOCH & SON(S)	CELTIC CHINA
WOOD, ENOCH & SON(S)	IMPERIAL CHINA
WOOD, ENOCH & SON(S)	PATENT
WOOD, ENOCH & SON(S)	SEMI CHINA
WOOD, ENOCH & SON(S)	STAFFORDSHIRE
WOOD, ENOCH & SON(S)	WARRANTED
WOOD, J. WEDGE	STONE GRANITE
WOOD, JOHN & CO. (LTD.)	NEW CASTLE (ON TYNE)
WOOD, JOHN & CO. (LTD.)	STEPNEY (POTTERY)
WOOD, JOHN WEDGE	IRONSTONE
WOOD, JOHN WEDGE	IRONSTONE CHINA
WOOD, JOHN WEDGE	WEDGEWOOD & CO.
WOOD, JOHN WEDGE	WOOD, EDMUND T. (See)
WOOD, RATHBON & CO.	IRONSTONE CHINA
WOOD, SON & CO.	COBRIDGE
WOOD, SON & CO.	IRONSTONE CHINA
WOODNORTH & CO.	WHITEHAVEN POTTERY
WOOLF, LEWIS (& SONS)	FERRYBRIDGE POTTERY
WOOLF, SYDNEY & CO.	FERRYBRIDGE
WOOLISCROFT, GEORGE (& CO.)	IRONSTONE
WOOLISCROFT, GEORGE (& CO.)	IRONSTONE CHINA
YALE & BARKER	SEMI CHINA
YALE & BARKER	WARRANTED
YATES, JOHN	FENTON
YATES, JOHN	WARRANTED/STONE CHINA/FENTON
YNYSMEDW POTTERY	IRONSTONE

APPENDIX B9: CATEGORY MANUFACTURED BY POTTER

POTTER	GDN NO.	B&W	H	F	M	T	W
ADAMS, BENJAMIN	10	X					
ADAMS, HARVEY & CO.	14	X					
ADAMS, WILLIAM & THOMAS	43	X			X		X
ADAMS, WM. & SON(S)(& CO.) LTD.	17-42A	X	X	X	X	X	X
ADDERLEY, WM. ALSAGER & CO.	47-49	X		X			
ADDERLEYS LTD.	50-53	X		X			
ALCOCK, HENRY & CO. (LTD.)	64-65	X		X		X	X
ALCOCK, HENRY POTTERY	66						
ALCOCK, JOHN	67, 69	X		X	X		X
ALCOCK, JOHN & GEORGE	68-70	X		X	X		
ALCOCK, JOHN (JR.) & SAMUEL	71			X			X
ALCOCK, RICHARD	—						X
ALCOCK, SAMUEL & CO.	73-78	X		X	X		X
ALLASON, JOHN	82	X					
ALLERTON, BROUGH & GREEN	—	X					
ALLERTON, CHARLES & SONS	84-91	X		X			
ALLMAN, BROUGHTON & CO.	94-95	X					
ASHWORTH, G. L. & BROS. (LTD.)	137-148	X	X	X	X		X
BADDELEY, JOHN & EDWARD	196-98	X					
BADDELEY, RALPH & JOHN	199-200	X					
BAGGERLEY & BALL	207	X					
BAGSHAW & MEIR (OR MAIER)	208	X					
BAGSTER, JOHN DENTON (SEE BAXTER)	300-301A	X					
BAILEY & BALL	—	X					
BAILEY, W. & D.	—	X					
BAKER & CHETWYND & CO.	—					X	X
BAKER, (W.) & CO. LTD.	230-33	X		X		X	X
BAKER, BEVANS & IRWIN (GLAMORGAN POTTERY)	226-29	X					
BALFOUR, ALEXANDER & CO.	—	X					
BARKER & SON	256-56A	X		X	X		
BARKER & TILL	—	X		X			
BARKER BROS. (LTD.)	247-49			X			
BARKER, SAMUEL & SON (DON POTTERY)	260-63	X		X			
BARKER, SUTTON & TILL	258-59	X					
BARKERS & KENT (LTD.)	264-66	X		X			
BARLOW, THOMAS	267	X					
BARROW & CO.	—	X					X
BATES & BENNETT	287			X			
BATES, BROWN-WESTHEAD & MOORE	288						
BATES, ELLIOTT & CO.	289-90	X					
BATES, GILDEA & WALKER	292			X			
BATES, WALKER & CO.	293-93A	X					
BATHWELL & GOODFELLOW	294	X					
BATKIN, WALKER & BROADHURST	295	X					
BAXTER, JOHN DENTON (SEE BAGSTER)	300-301A	X					
BEARDMORE & EDWARDS	306	X					
BEARDMORE, FRANK & CO.	307-07A			X			
BECK, BLAIR & CO.	—	X					
BEECH & HANCOCK	312-13	X		X	X		
BEECH & LOWNDES	—	X					
BEECH, HANCOCK & CO.	311	X			X		
BEECH, JAMES	314	X		X			
BELFIELD & CO.	316	X					
BELL, COOK & CO.	—	X					
BELL, ISAAC & THOMAS	—	X					
BELL, J. & M. P. (& CO.)(LTD.)	317-320	X	X	X	X		X
BELLE VUE POTTERY (HULL)	321-23	X					
BENNETT, J. & CO.	336			X			
BESWICK, ROBERT	—						X
BEVINGTON, (T. & J.) & CO.	351 & 3767	X					
BIRKS, BROS. & SEDDON	374			X			
BISHOP & STONIER (LTD.)	384-88	X		X		X	X
BLACKHURST & TUNNICLIFFE	401			X			
BLACKWELL, JOHN & ANDREW	—	X					
BLAKENEY POTTERY LTD.	—			X			X
BODLEY & CO.	419						
BODLEY & HARROLD	431-32	X					
BODLEY, EDWARD F. & CO. (& SON)	420-23	X	X				
BODLEY, EDWARD F. & SON	424-27	X					
BOLTON, JAMES FLETCHER	—	X					
BOOM, JOSEPH	—	X					
BOOTE, T. & R. (& SON) LTD.	436-41	X		X	X		X
BOOTH & MEIGH	—	X					
BOOTH, THOMAS & CO.	447	X		X			
BOOTH, THOMAS & SON	448	X					
BOOTH, THOMAS G.	449	X					
BOOTH, THOMAS, G. & F.	450	X		X			
BOOTHS (LTD.)	451-54	X		X			
BOULTON, MACHIN & TENNANT	469			X			
BOURNE & LEIGH (LTD.)	482-86			X			
BOURNE, BAKER & BOURNE	—	X					
BOURNE, CHARLES	—	X					
BOURNE, EDWARD	472	X					
BOURNE, JOSEPH (& SON)(LTD.)	473	X					X
BOURNE, NIXON & CO.	489-89A		X				
BOURNE, WILLIAM & CO.	—	X					
BOURNE, WILLIAM (FENTON)	—			X	X		
BOURNE, WILLIAM (LONGTON)	—	X					
BOVEY POTTERY CO. LTD.	493-93A			X			
BOVEY TRACEY POTTERY CO.	498	X					
BOWERS, GEORGE FREDERICK (&CO.)	509-14	X					X
BOYLE, SAMUEL (& SONS)	—	X					
BOYLE, ZACHARIA (& CO.) (& SON(S))	522-23	X					
BRADLEY & CO.	530	X					
BRAMELD & CO. (ROCKINGHAM WORKS)	3351-59	X					
BRANNAM, C. H. (LTD.)	NOT ENGLISH			X			
BRIDGETT & BATES	587-88			X			
BRIDGWOOD & CLARKE	589-90A						X
BRIDGWOOD, SAMPSON (& SON) (LTD.)	591-98	X		X	X	X	X
BRINDLEY, JOHN & CO.	—	X					
BRITANNIA POTTERY CO. LTD.	620	X					
BRITISH ANCHOR POTTERY CO. LTD.	622-24	X		X			
BROADHURST & GREEN	—			X			
BROADHURST, JAMES & SONS (LTD.)	639-41	X					
BROUGHAM & MAYER	649	X		X	X		X
BROWN & STEVENTON, LTD.	653-4			X			
BROWN-WESTHEAD, MOORE & CO.	675-81	X		X			
BROWNFIELD POTTERY LTD.	667-70			X			
BROWNFIELD, WM. (& SON(S))	660-66	X		X	X		
BROWNFIELDS GUILD POTTERY SOCIETY LTD.	667-70			X			
BROWNHILLS POTTERY CO.	671-74	X					
BULLOCK, A. & CO.	704, 704A	X					
BURGESS & GODDARD (IMPORTERS)	—						X
BURGESS & LEIGH (LTD.)	712-18	X		X			
BURGESS, HENRY	710-711					X	X
BURN, JOSEPH & CO.	—	X					
BURTON, SAMUEL & JOHN	734	X					
BUTTERFIELD, WILLIAM & JAMES	736	X					

POTTER	GDN NO.	B&W	H	F	M	T	W
CALEDONIAN POTTERY	—	X					
CALLAND, JOHN & CO.	746-49	X					
CAMBRIAN POTTERY	3757-63	X		X			
CAMPBELLFIELD POTTERY CO. (LTD.)	757-61	X		X			
CAREY, JOHN & SONS	—	X					
CAREY, THOMAS & JOHN	772	X					
CARLTON WARE LTD.	774			X			
CARR & PATTON	—	X					
CARR, JOHN (& CO.)(& SON(S))	778-79	X		X			
CARTWRIGHT & EDWARDS (LTD.)	796-98	X		X			
CAULDON LTD.	681& 84,821-23	X		X			
CERAMIC ART CO. LTD.	828			X			
CERAMIC ART CO.(1905) LTD.	829-30			X			
CHALLINOR & MAYER	—					X	
CHALLINOR, E. & C.	837	X				X	X
CHALLINOR, E. & CO.	836	X		X	X		X
CHALLINOR, EDWARD	835 & 35A	X		X	X		X
CHAPPELL, S. & J. (LEEDS POTTERY)	—	X					
CHESWORTH & ROBINSON	874	X					
CHETHAM & ROBINSON (& SON)	879	X					
CHETHAM & WOOLLEY	—	X					
CHETHAM (& SON)	875-76	X					
CHETHAM, JONATHAN LOWE	877	X					
CHILD & CLIVE	883A	X					
CHILD, SMITH	883	X					
CLARKE, EDWARD (& CO.)	893-96			X			X
CLEMENTSON & YOUNG	911	X		X	X		
CLEMENTSON BROS. (LTD.)	905-909	X		X		X	X
CLEMENTSON, JOSEPH	910-910A	X		X	X	X	X
CLEMENTSON, JOSEPH & SONS	—	X					X
CLEMENTSON, YOUNG & JAMESON	912	X					
CLEVELAND POTTERY CO.	—			X			
CLEWS, JAMES & RALPH	918-19	X	X				
CLIVE, JOHN HENRY	920	X					
CLOSE & CO.	928	X					
CLOSE, J. T. (& CO.)	—			X			X
CLOUGH'S ROYAL ART POTTERY	929						
CLYDE POTTERY CO. (LTD.)	932-36	X		X	X		
CO-OPERATIVE WHOLESALE SOCIETY, LTD.	1053-7			X			
COCHRAN & FLEMING (BRITANNIA POTTERY)	968-72	X		X			
COCHRAN, R. & CO. (VERREVILLE POTTERY)	965-67	X	X	X	X	X	X
COCKSON & CHETWYND (& CO.)	975-76	X		X			X
COCKSON & HARDING	977-79	X		X			
COCKSON & SEDDON	980						X
COLCLOUGH & CO.	983-84			X			
COLLEY, ALFRED & CO. LTD.	999			X			
COLLINSON, CHARLES & CO.	1013	X		X			
COPELAND & GARRETT	1088-95	X		X	X		
COPELAND, W. T. (& SONS LTD.)	1068-80	X		X	X		
CORK & EDGE	1097-1100	X					X
CORK, EDGE & MALKIN	1101	X		X	X		
CORMIE, JOHN	—	X					
CORN, EDWARD	—						X
CORN, W. & E.	1109-13			X	X	X	X
CORNFOOT, COLVILLE & CO.	—	X					
COTTON & BARLOW	1116	X		X			
CUMBERLIDGE & HUMPHREYS	1158-58A			X			
DALTON & BURN	—	X					
DANIEL, H. & R.	—	X					
DANIEL, WALTER	—	X					
DAVENPORT & WILLIAM	—	X					
DAVENPORT, (WM.) ET.AL.	1179-95A	X	X	X	X	X	X
DAVENPORT, BANKS & CO.	1196-96A	X					X
DAVENPORT, BECK & CO.	1197	X					
DAVENPORT, HENRY	—	X					
DAVENPORT, JOHN	—	X					
DAVENPORT, WILLIAM	—	X					
DAVIS (RICHARD) & CO.	1201	X					
DAVIS, COCKSON & WILSON	—	X					
DAVIS, J. H. & J.	—	X		X			X
DAVIS, JOHN HEATH	1204 & 04A						X
DAWSON, (JOHN DAWSON & CO.) ETC.	1107-12	X		X			
DAWSON, THOMAS & CO.	—	X		X			
DEAKIN & BAILEY	4420	X					
DEAKIN & SON(S)(& CO.)	1218	X		X			
DEAKIN, EDWIN	—			X			
DEAN, S. W.	1219			X			
DEANS (1910) LTD.	1222						X
DILLON, FRANCIS	1288-88A	X					X
DILLWYN & CO.	3764-70	X		X			
DIMMOCK & SMITH	1302	X		X			
DIMMOCK, J. & CO.	1289-91	X		X			
DIMMOCK, THOMAS (JR.) & CO.	1297-1301	X	X	X	X	X	

POTTER	GDN NO.	B&W	H	F	M	T	W
DON POTTERY	1309-14	X					
DOULTON & CO. (LTD.)	1327-34	X		X			
DUDSON, JAMES (& J.T. DUDSON)	1409-11	X					
DUDSON, WILCOX & TILL LTD.	1412-13			X			
DUNDERDALE, DAVID & CO.	1416-18	X					
DUNN, BENNETT & CO. (LTD.)	1421-22	X		X			
EDGE, BARKER & BARKER	1437	X					
EDGE, BARKER & CO.	1438	X					
EDGE, MALKIN & CO. (LTD.)	1440-45	X		X		X	
EDGE, WILLIAM & SAMUEL	1436	X		?			
EDWARDS, JAMES	—	X		X	X		X
EDWARDS, JAMES & SON	1446-48	X		X			X
EDWARDS, JAMES & THOMAS	1454-56	X	X		X		
EDWARDS, JOHN (& CO.)	1449-52	X		X		X	X
EDWARDS, THOMAS	—	X		X			X
ELGIN POTTERY	—	X					
ELKIN & CO.	1468A	X					
ELKIN & NEWBON	1467	X					
ELKIN, KNIGHT & BRIDGWOOD	1464	X		X			
ELKIN, KNIGHT & CO.	1465-66	X			X		
ELSMORE & FORESTER	1476-77A	X		X	X	X	X
ELSMORE, (THOMAS) & SON	1478					X	X
EMBERTON, WILLIAM (& CO.)	1485	X		X			
EMERY, FRANCIS J.	1485A	X		X			
EMPIRE PORCELAIN CO. (LTD.)	1488-89	X		X			
EVANS & GLASSON	1519-19A	X					
EVANS, D. J. & CO.	1514-18	X					
FARRALL, JOHN	—					X	
FELL, THOMAS (& CO.)(LTD.)	1530-35	X		X	X		
FENTON, ALFRED & SONS	1536-37						
FERRYBRIDGE POTTERY	1536+	X					
FLACKETT & TOFT	—	X					
FLACKETT, TOFT & ROBINSON	1569			X			
FOLCH, STEPHEN (& SONS)	1581	X					
FORD & CHALLINOR (& CO.) or (FORD & CHALLINOR)	1595-95A	X		X			X
FORD & RILEY	1601-03						
FORD & SONS (LTD.)	1582-86			X			
FORD, JOHN & CO.	1596	X					
FORD, SAMUEL & CO.	1604			X			
FORD, THOMAS (& CO.)	1606		X	X			
FORDY & PATTERSON (& CO.)	—	X					
FORDY, J. & CO.	—	X					
FORESTER, THOMAS & SON(S) (LTD.)	1614-17A			X			
FORESTER, THOMAS SON & CO.	1613			X			
FORRESTER, GEORGE	—	X					
FOWLER THOMPSON & CO.	1625	X					
FREAKLEY & FARRALL	—						X
FURNIVAL, JACOB & CO.	1643	X		X	X	X	X
FURNIVAL, JACOB & THOMAS	1644	X		X			
FURNIVAL, THOMAS & CO.	1645	X		X	X		
FURNIVAL, THOMAS & SONS	1646-50	X	X	X		X	X
FURNIVALS (LTD.)	1651-58A	X		X			X
GARNER, ROBERT (III)	1669	X					
GARRISON (or SUNDERLAND) POTTERY	3740-48	X			X		
GATER, HALL & CO.	1673			X			
GEDDES, JOHN (& SON) (VERREVILLE POTTERY)	1674	X	X				
GELSON BROS.	1675&1727	X					X
GIBSON & SONS (LTD.)	1679-83			X			
GILDEA, JAMES	1696			X			
GILDEA, WALKER (& CO.)	1697-99	X			X		
GIMSON, WALLIS & CO.	1701	X					
GINDER, SAMUEL & CO.	1702	X					
GLAMORGAN POTTERY (SEE: BAKER, BEVANS & IRWIN)	226-29	X					
GLOBE POTTERY CO. LTD.	1710-15			X			
GODDARD & BURGESS (IMPORTERS, USA)	—						X
GODWIN, BENJAMIN E.	1722-23	X					
GODWIN, JOHN & ROBERT	1726-27	X		X	X		
GODWIN, ROWLEY & CO.	1728						
GODWIN, THOMAS	1729-30B	X	X	X	X		
GODWIN, THOMAS & BENJAMIN	1732-34	X					
GOODFELLOW, THOMAS	1738	X		X	X		X
GOODWIN, JOHN (LONGTON)	4459A	X		X	X		
GOODWIN, JOHN (SEACOMBE)	—	X		X			
GOODWINS & BULLOCK	1740						
GOODWINS & ELLIS	1740A	X					
GOODWINS & HARRIS	1743	X					
GOODWINS, BRIDGWOOD & CO.	—	X					
GOODWINS, BRIDGWOOD & HARRIS	1739						
GOODWINS, BRIDGWOOD & ORTON	1739A & B	X					
GORDON, GEORGE	1745-46	X					
GREEN & CLAY	1783					X	

POTTER	GDN NO.	B&W	H	F	M	T	W
GREEN, JOHN & WILLIAM (& CO.) (DON POTTERY)	—	X					
GREEN, T. A. & S.	1796						
GREEN, T. G. & CO. (LTD.)	1797-98	X					
GREEN, THOMAS	1794-95		X	X			
GRIFFITHS, BEARDMORE & BIRKS	1821	X					
GRIMWADE BROS.	1823	X		X			
GRIMWADES LTD.	1824-32	X		X			
GRINDLEY, W. H. & CO. (LTD.)	1842-50	X		X		X	X
GROSE & CO.	—						X
GROVE & STARK	1855-56			X			
HACKWOOD & CO.	1863-64	X					
HACKWOOD & KEELING	1865	X					
HACKWOOD, WILLIAM	1860-67 &3199	X		X			
HACKWOOD, WILLIAM & SON	1868	X					
HALES, HANCOCK & CO. LTD. (RETAILERS)	—						
HALES, HANCOCK & GOODWIN LTD. (RETAILERS)	1879						
HALL, JOHN & RALPH	1886	X					
HALL, JOHN (& SONS)	1885-87	X					
HALL, RALPH (&CO.) OR (& SON)	1888-90A	X	X	X	X		
HALLAM & JOHNSON (HALLAM, JOHNSON CO.)	—			X			
HAMILTON, ROBERT	1901	X					
HAMMERSLEY & ASHBURY	1909-10	X					
HAMMERSLEY, RALPH (& SON(S))	1912-15	X	X	X	X		
HAMPSON & BROADHURST	1919	X					
HANCOCK & WHITTINGHAM	1937-38	X			X		
HANCOCK, SAMPSON (& SONS)	1927-35	X		X			
HANCOCK, WITTINGHAM & CO.	1936	X			x		
HANDLEY, JAMES & WILLIAM	—	X					
HANLEY PORCELAIN CO.	1940			X?			
HARDING & COCKSON	1946-47						
HARDING, JOSEPH	1949	X					
HARDING, W. & G.	—	X					
HARDING, W. & J.	1950	X					
HARLEY, THOMAS	1951-52B	X					
HARRIS, JOHN	—	X					
HARRISON, GEO. (& CO.)	1958	X					
HARTLEY, GREENS & CO. (LEEDS POTTERY)	1963						
HARVEY, C. & W. K. (C. HARVEY & SONS)	1967-69	X					X
HAWLEY BROS. (LTD.)	1978-79	X					
HAWLEY, JOHN & CO.	1980-81	X					
HAWTHORN, JOHN	—						X
HEATH, BLACKHURST & CO.	1998	X					
HEATH, J. (JOSHUA)	1991-92	X		X	X		
HEATH, JOHN	1989	X		X (?)			HEATH,
JOSEPH	1993	X		X	X		
HEATH, JOSEPH & CO.	1994 &A & B	X	X				
HEATH, THOMAS	1995-96	X		X	X		
HEATHCOTE, CHARLES & CO.	2002	X					
HENSHALL & CO.	2005	X	X				
HERCULANEUM POTTERY	2007-12	X					
HERON, ROBERT (& SON)	2014-15	X		X			
HICKS & MEIGH	2019-20	X					
HICKS, MEIGH & JOHNSON	2021-25	X		X			
HILDITCH & HOPWOOD	—			X			
HILDITCH & SON(S) (& CO.)	2027-29	X					
HOBSON, CHARLES (& SON)	2039-41	X					
HOLDCROFT, HILL & MELLOR	2049-49A	X					
HOLDCROFT, PETER & CO.	2048	X		X	X		
HOLLAND & GREEN	2064-65	X					X
HOLLAND, JOHN	2060	X					
HOLLINS, T. & J.	2068	X					
HOLLINS, THOMAS, JOHN & RICHARD	2069	X					
HOLLINSHEAD & KIRKHAM (LTD.)	2071-76	X		X			X
HOLMES, STONIER & HOLLINSHEAD	—	X					
HOPE & CARTER	2088	X		X	X		X
HOPKIN & VERNON	—	X					
HUDDEN, JOHN THOMAS	2104-5	X					
HUGHES, E. & CO.	2114-19			X	X		
HUGHES, ELIJAH & CO.	2113			X	X		
HUGHES, STEPHEN & CO. (S. & E. HUGHES)	—						
HUGHES, THOMAS	2121	X		X		X	X
HUGHES, THOMAS & SON (LTD.)	2122-25	X		X		X	X
HULME & BOOTH	—				X		X
HULME, (JOHN) & SONS	2128	X					
HULME, HENRY & SONS	2129			X			
HULME, THOMAS	—						X
HULSE & ADDERLEY	2132	X					
HULSE, NIXON & ADDERLEY	2133	X					
HUMPHREYS BROS.	—			X			
INDEO POTTERY	2138	X					

POTTER	GDN NO.	B&W	H	F	M	T	W
INGLEBY, THOMAS & CO.	2140	X					
JACKSON & PATTERSON	2169	X					
JACKSON, J. & CO.	2153-54	X			X		
JACKSON, JOB & JOHN	2155-56	X	X				
JAMIESON, JAMES & CO.	—	X			X		
JOHN KING KNIGHT (SEE: KNIGHT, JOHN KING)	2306-07	X					
JOHNSON BROS. (HANLEY) (LTD.)	2176-79	X		X	X	X	X
JOHNSON, SAMUEL LTD.	2186-89			X			
JONES & SON	2223A	X					
JONES & WALLEY	2224A			X			
JONES, ALBERT E. (LONGTON) LTD.	2203-05			X			
JONES, ELIJAH	2214	X					
JONES, FREDERICK (& CO.)	2215			X			X
JONES, GEORGE (& SONS LTD.)	2217-19	X		X			X
KEELING & CO. (LTD.)	2241-45			X			
KEELING, CHARLES	2240	X					
KEELING, JAMES	—	X					
KEELING, SAMUEL & CO.	2247-49	X		X			
KENT, JAMES (LTD.)	2263-67			X			
KIDSTON, R. A. & CO. (VERREVILLE POTTERY)	—	X					
KILNHURST OLD POTTERY	—						
KNIGHT, ELKIN & BRIDGWOOD	2304-04A	X					
KNIGHT, ELKIN & CO.	2301-03	X	X				
KNIGHT, ELKIN & KNIGHT (KNIGHT, ELKIN & CO.)	2305	X					
KNIGHT, JOHN KING (SEE: JOHN KING KNIGHT)	2306-07	X					
LADYBURN POTTERY	—						
LAKIN, THOMAS	2311	X					
LAWLEYS LIMITED (RETAILERS)	2340-41						
LEAR, SAMUEL	2360						X
LEEDS POTTERY (HARTLEY GREEN & CO.)	2362-65& 1963	X	X				
LIDDLE, ELLIOT & SON (& CO.) (ELLIOT BROS.)	1472			X	X		X
LIVESLEY & DAVIS	—						X?
LIVESLEY, POWELL & CO.	2385-87	X			X	X	X
LOCKETT & HULME	2396	X					
LOCKETT, JOHN & THOMAS	—	X					
LOCKHART & ARTHUR	2401-02	X					
LOCKHART, DAVID & SONS (LTD.)	2404-05	X			X		
LOCKHART, DAVID (& CO.)	2403	X			X		
LOCKITT, WILLIAM H.	2406-7	X					
LONGTON POTTERY CO. LTD.	2418-19			X			
LOWNDES & BEECH (see BEECH & LOWNDES)	—	X					
MACHIN & POTTS	2456-56A	X					
MACINTYRE, JAMES & CO. (LTD.)	2818-25	X					
MADDOCK & GATER	—						X
MADDOCK & SEDDON	2476	X					X
MADDOCK, JOHN	2460-61	X		X			
MADDOCK, JOHN & SONS (LTD.)	2462-67	X		X		X	X
MALING, C. T.	2486-87	X		X			
MALING, C. T. & SONS (LTD.)	2487-91			X			
MALINGS (ROBERT)	2484-85	X					
MALKIN, RALPH	2493	X					
MALKIN, WALKER & HULSE	2496&4472	X					
MANN & CO.	2498			X			
MARE, JOHN	2504	X					
MARPLE, TURNER & CO.	—	X					
MARSH & WILLETT	—	X					
MARSH, JACOB	—	X					
MARSHALL, JOHN (& CO.) (LTD.)	2509	X		X	X		
MASON, CHARLES JAMES	2526-29	X		X			
MASON, CHARLES JAMES & CO.	2531-36	X					
MASON, G. M. & C. J.	2537-41	X					
MASON, MILES	2543-45	X					
MASON, WILLIAM	2546	X					
MAUDESLEY, J. & CO.	2557						
MAY, ROBERT	—	X					
MAYER & ELLIOTT	2563-63A	X			X		X
MAYER & NEWBOLD	2574-77	X					
MAYER BROS. & ELLIOTT	—	X			X		X
MAYER, THOMAS	2568-69	X	X		X		
MAYER, THOMAS & JOHN	—	X					
MAYER, THOMAS, JOHN & JOSEPH	2570-71	X		X	X		X
MEAKIN & CO. (MEAKIN BROS & CO.)	—						X
MEAKIN, ALFRED (LTD.)	2581-89	X		X		X	X
MEAKIN, CHARLES	2596						X
MEAKIN, HENRY	2597						X
MEAKIN, J. & G. (LTD.)	2598-2612	X		X			X
MEAKIN, LEWIS	—						X
MEIGH, CHARLES	2614A-2618	X	X	X	X		

POTTER	GDN NO.	B&W	H	F	M	T	W
MEIGH, CHARLES & SON	2620-22	X		X	X		X
MEIGH, CHARLES, SON & PANKHURST	2624	X			X		
MEIGH, JOB (& SON)	2625-28	X					
MEIKLE BROS. (CANADIAN IMPORTERS)	—						X
MEIR, JOHN	2631-32	X		X			
MEIR, JOHN & SON	2633-41	X		X	X		X
MELLOR, TAYLOR & CO.	2647-48	X		X		X	X
MELLOR, VENABLES & CO.	2645-46	X	X	X	X		X
METHVEN, DAVID & SONS	2651-53	X		X	X		X
MIDDLESBOROUGH EARTHENWARE CO.	2654				X		
MIDDLESBOROUGH POTTERY CO.	2655-58	X		X	X		
MIDWINTER, W. R. (LTD.)	2664-65	X		X			
MILLER, JAMES & CO. LTD. (NORTH BRITISH POTTERY)	2896-98	X			X		
MINTON (& VARIOUS PARTNERSHIPS)	2688-2717	X		X	X		
MOORE & CO.	2748			X	X		
MOORE, (SAMUEL) & CO.	2743-47	X					
MORLEY & ASHWORTH	2754-58	X					X
MORLEY, FRANCIS (& CO.)	2759-64	X	X	X	X		X
MOSELEY, JOHN (MOSELEY, JOHN & WILLIAM)	2791	X					
MOUNTFORD, GEORGE THOMAS	2796	X		X			
MUIR, ANDREW (& CO.)	—	X					
MYOTT, SON & CO. (LTD.)	2809-11	X		X			
NAUTILUS PORCELAIN CO.	2838-39			X			
NEALE, (JAMES) & CO.	2841-46& 2850	X					
NEW WHARF POTTERY CO.	2883-86	X		X	X		
NEWPORT POTTERY CO. LTD.	2876	X		X			
NICHOLSON, THOMAS & CO.	2887-88	X					
NORTH BRITISH POTTERY (MILLER, JAMES & CO. LTD.)	2896-98	X			X		
OLD HALL (EARTHENWARE) POTTERY CO.LTD.	2917-22	X		X			X
OULSNAM, W. E. (& SONS)	—						X
PALISSY POTTERY LTD.	2943-43A			X			
PANKHURST & DIMMOCK	—						X
PANKHURST, J. W. & CO. OR (PANKHURST & DIMMOCK)	2952-56	X					X
PATTERSON & CO. (GEORGE PATTERSON)	2976-77	X					
PATTON, JOHN	—	X					X
PEARL POTTERY CO. (LTD.)	2982-84	X		X			
PEARSON & CO.	2985-87	X					
PEARSON, EDWARD (& SON)	—						X
PEARSON, FARRALL & MEAKIN	—					X	
PENMAN, BROWN & CO.	—						X
PETTY & CO.	—	X					
PHILLIPS, EDWARD & GEORGE	3008-09	X	X				
PHILLIPS, GEORGE	3010-11	X		X	X		X
PHILLIPS, THOMAS & SON	3016A	X		X			
PHOENIX POTTERY CO.	—	X					
PINDER, BOURNE & CO.	3038-42			X	X		
PINDER, BOURNE & HOPE	3043-45	X		X	X		X
PITCAIRNS LTD.	3052	X		X			
PLANT, ENOCH	3055			X			
PLANT, J. & CO.	3056			X			
PLANT, R. H. & S. L. (LTD.)	3059-61						
PLYMOUTH POTTERY CO. LTD.	3072	X					
PODMORE, WALKER (& CO.)	3075-80	X	X	X	X		X
POSSIL POTTERY	3101&2839			X			
POULSON BROS. (LTD.)	3104-05	X					
POUNTNEY & ALLIES	3120-25	X					
POUNTNEY & CO. (LTD.)	3106-13	X		X			
POUNTNEY & GOLDNEY	3126-27	X					
POWELL & BISHOP	3132-36	X				X	X
POWELL, BISHOP & STONIER	3137-38	X		X			X
PRATT & SIMPSON	3156						X
PRATT, F. & R. & CO. (LTD.)	3143-53	X			X		
PRATT, JOHN & CO. LTD.	3154	X					
PURVES, CHARLES (ELGIN POTTERY)	—	X					
RAINFORTH & CO.	3195-95A	X					
RATCLIFFE, WILLIAM	3199-3200	X					
RATHBONE, T. & CO.	3204-06	X		X			
READ & CLEMENTSON	3212-12A	X					
READ, CLEMENTSON & ANDERSON	3213	X					
REED & TAYLOR	3217	X					
REED, JAMES	3216	X					
REEVES, JAMES	3218-21	X					
REID, WM. (& SON OR SONS)	—	X					
RIDGWAY & ABINGTON	—			X			
RIDGWAY & MORLEY	3276-78A	X		X	X		
RIDGWAY, JOB	3250-51	X					
RIDGWAY, JOB & SONS	3252	X					
RIDGWAY, JOHN & WILLIAM	3260-66	X	X				

POTTER	GDN NO.	B&W	H	F	M	T	W
RIDGWAY, JOHN (& CO.)	3253-59B	X	X	X	X		X
RIDGWAY, JOHN, BATES & CO.	3268-69	X		X			X
RIDGWAY, MORLEY, WEAR & CO.	3271-75	X		X			
RIDGWAY, SPARKS & RIDGWAY	3299-99A	X		X (?)			
RIDGWAY, WILLIAM (& CO.)	3300-03A	X	X	X	X		
RIDGWAY, WILLIAM SON & CO.	3306-09& 4416	X	X	X			
RIDGWAYS (BEDFORD WORKS) LTD.	3318-23	X		X			
RIDGWAYS (LTD.)	3310-16			X			
RILEY, JOHN & RICHARD	3328-30	X					
ROBINSON & WOOD	3344	X					
ROBINSON, JOHN (& SONS)	—	X		X			
ROBINSON, JOSEPH	3337-37A			X			
ROBINSON, WOOD & BROWNFIELD	3345	X					
ROGERS, JOHN & GEORGE	3367-68	X					
ROGERS, JOHN (& SON)	3369-72	X	X				
ROWLAND & MARSELLUS (IMPORTERS)	—						
SCOTT BROTHERS	3473-75	X					
SEWELL(S) & CO. (ST. ANTHONY'S)	3664A-67	X					
SHARPE BROTHERS & CO. (LTD.)	3493						
SHARPE, THOMAS	3490-92						
SHAW, ANTHONY (&SON(S)) (& CO.)	3496-3500	X	X	X	X	X	X
SHAW, C. & J.	—	X					
SHIRLEY, THOMAS & CO.	3521-22	X			X		
SHORE, COGGINS & HOLT	3531	X					
SHORTHOUSE (& HEATH)(OR & CO.)	3536-39	X					
SKINNER & WALKER	3569-70			X			
SKINNER, GEORGE & CO.	3568	X					
SMITH & BINNALL	3577			X			
SMITH & FORD	3578			X			
SMITH, FORD & JONES	—					X	
SMITH, GEORGE F. (& CO.)	3579-80	X					
SMITH, THEOPHILUS	—	X					
SMITH, WILLIAM (& CO.)	3596-3601	X		X	X		
SNEYD & HILL	3610			X			
SNEYD, THOMAS	3609			X			
SOHO POTTERY (LTD.)	3612-14	X		X			
SOUTH WALES POTTERY	3626-28	X		X	X		
SOUTHWICK POTTERY	3629-41	X		X	X		
SPODE, JOSIAH (ET. AL)	3647-3659B	X					
ST. ANTHONY'S POTTERY (SEWELL(S) & CO.)	—	X					
ST. JOHNS STONE CHINAWARE CO. (CANADIAN)	—						X
STANLEY POTTERY CO.	—	X					
STANLEY POTTERY LTD.	983-84& 3675-6			X			
STEVENSON & GODWIN	—	X					
STEVENSON, ANDREW	3699-3702	X	X				
STEVENSON, RALPH	3703-05	X	X				
STEVENSON, RALPH & SON	3706-07	X					
STEVENSON, RALPH & WILLIAMS	3713-14	X	X				
STEVENTON, JOHN & SONS LTD.	3715	X		X			
STUBBS & KENT	3730	X					
STUBBS, JOSEPH	3728-29	X	X		X		
SUNDERLAND (OR GARRISON) POTTERY	3740-48	X			X		
SWIFT & ELKIN	3773	X					
SWILLINGTON BRIDGE POTTERY	—	X					
SWINNERTON (LTD.)	3774-5	X					
TAMS (ET. AL)	—	X	X				
TAMS, JOHN (& SON)(LTD.)	3791-3800	X		X			
TAYLOR BROS.	—						X
TAYLOR, GEORGE	3805-06	X					
TAYLOR, HARRISON & CO.	—	X					
TAYLOR, WILLIAM	—						X
THOMSON, JOHN (& SONS)	3844-48	X		X	X		
TILL, THOMAS & SON(S)(LTD.)	3853-58	X		X			X
TITTENSOR, CHARLES	3861	X					
TOFT & MAY	—	X					
TOMPKINSON BROS. & CO.	—						X
TOWNSEND, GEORGE	3879	X					
TROUTBECK, E. T.	—	X					
TUNNICLIFF(E), MICHAEL	3887						X
TURNBULL, G. R.	—	X					
TURNER & ABBOTT	3888	X					
TURNER & TOMKINSON	3903-05	X			X		X
TURNER, G. W. & SONS	3890-94	X		X			
TURNER, GODDARD & CO.	3889						X
TURNER, JOHN & WILLIAM (II)	3896-90	X					
TURNER, JOHN (TURNER & CO.)	3896-90	X					
TURNER, WILLIAM	—	X					
TURPIN & CO.	—	X					
TWIGG, JOSEPH (& CO.)(&BROS. & CO.)	3908-13	X	X				
UPPER HANLEY POTTERY CO. (LTD.)	3927-30	X		X	X		
VENABLES & BAINES	3930A	X					
VENABLES, JOHN & CO.	3930B						X

POTTER	GDN NO.	B&W	H	F	M	T	W
VENABLES, MANN & CO. (VENABLES, JOHN & CO.)	3930B						X
VERNON, JAMES (& SON)	3934-34B	X					
WALKER & CARTER	3981	X					
WALKER, THOMAS	3982-83	X		X	X		X
WALLACE, JAMES & CO.	3984	X					
WALLEY, EDWARD	3988-90	X		X	X	X	X
WALSH, WILLIAM	—	X					
WARBURTON, JOHN (COBRIDGE)	4004	X					
WARDLE, JAMES (& CO.)(LTD.)	4013-15			X			
WATSON & CO.	4038-39	X					
WEATHERBY, J. H. & SONS (LTD.)	4043-45	X			X		X
WEDGWOOD & CO. (LTD.)	4055-62	X		X	X	X	X
WEDGWOOD & CO. (RALPH WEDGWOOD & CO.)	4104	X					
WEDGWOOD, JOSIAH (& SONS LTD.)	4073-87	X		X	X		
WHITEHAVEN POTTERY	4515	X					
WHITTAKER & CO.	4127	X					
WHITTAKER, HEATH & CO.	4128	X					
WHITTINGHAM, FORD & CO.	4130			X			
WHITTINGHAM, FORD & RILEY	4131	X					
WILDBLOOD, JOHN & CO.	—	X					
WILEMAN, HENRY	—						
WILEMAN, JAMES & CHARLES	4156-59						X
WILEMAN, JAMES F.	4160-62	X		X		X	X
WILKINSON & HULME	—					X	
WILKINSON, ARTHUR J. (LTD.)	4168-71	X		X		X	X
WILLIAMS, WILLIAM	—			X	X		
WILSON, DAVID (& SONS)	4192	X					
WILSON, ISAAC & CO.	4193-94	X			X		
WILTSHAW & ROBINSON (LTD.)	4200-02			X			
WINKLE, F. & CO. (LTD.)	4213-15	X		X			
WOLFE & HAMILTON	4227-30	X					
WOLFE(S), THOMAS	4228-29	X					
WOOD & BAGGALEY	4239			X			
WOOD & BARKER LTD.	4240			X			
WOOD & BRETTEL	4242-43	X					
WOOD & BROWNFIELD	4242	X		X	X		
WOOD & CALDWELL	4256	X	X	X	X		
WOOD & CHALLINOR	4244	X		X	X		
WOOD & CHALLINOR & CO.	4245	X					
WOOD & HAWTHORNE	4272						X
WOOD & HULME	4273			X			
WOOD & PIGOTT	4277	X		X			
WOOD & SON(S)(LTD.)	4285-88	X		X	X		
WOOD, ARTHUR	4233			X			
WOOD, ARTHUR & SON (LONGPORT) LTD.	4234	X		X	X		
WOOD, EDMUND, T.	—						X
WOOD, ENOCH	4247-50	X		X			
WOOD, ENOCH & SONS	4257-64	X	X				
WOOD, H. J. (LTD.)	—			X			
WOOD, JOHN & CO. (LTD.)	—	X					
WOOD, JOHN WEDG	4276-76B	X		X	X		X
WOOD, RATHBONE & CO.	—						X
WOOD, SON & CO.	4298						X
WOOD, THOMAS & CO.	4283	X					
WOOD, THOMAS & SONS	4284	X		X			
WOOD, WILLIAM & CO.	4299-4301			X			
WOODNORTH & CO. (WHITEHAVEN POTTERY)	4515	X					
WOOLF, LEWIS (& SONS)(& CO.)	4468-68A	X			X		X
WOOLISCROFT, GEORGE (& CO.)	4308	X					
WOOLLEY, RICHARD	4309	X					
WORTHINGTON & HARROP	4365	X					
YALE & BARKER	4381-82	X					
YATES & MAY	—	X					
YATES, JOHN	4383	X					
YNYSMEW POTTERY	4395-97			X			

APPENDIX B10: ADDITIONAL POTTERS RECORDED IN WHITE IRONSTONE

POTTER	LOCATION	DATE
Bates, Elliot & Co.	Longport	1870-75
Beswick, Robert	Tunstall	1842-60
Bodley, Edward F. & Co.	Burslem	1865-75
Brownfield, Wm. & Sons	Cobridge	1850-92
Challinor, Edward	Tunstall	1842-61
Collinson, Charles & Co.	Burslem	1851-73
Edge, Malkin & Co.	Burslem	1870-98
Forester & Hulme	Fenton	1887-93
Gater, Thomas & Co.	Burslem	1885-94
Goodwin, John	Seacombe	1852-64
Hancock, Sampson (& Sons)	Tunstall & Stoke	1858-92-(1935+)
Malkin, Ralph	Fenton	1864-81
Mason, Charles James	Fenton	1849-53
Maudesley, J. & Co.	Tunstall	1862-64
Meigh, Charles	Hanley	1832-50
Mellor, Venables & Baines	—	—
Moore (Bros.)	Longton	1872-1905
Morely & Ashworth*	Hanley	1859-62
Old Hall Earthenware Pottery Co. Ltd.	Hanley	1861-86
Pinder, Bourne & Co.	Burslem	1862-82
Pratt & Simpson	Fenton	1878-83
Ridgway & Clarke*	—	—
Ridgway & Morley	Hanley	1842-44(5)
Ridgway, Wm. & Co.	Shelton	1830-54
Ridgway, Wm. Son & Co.	Hanley	1838-45
Rogers Bros.	Hanley	c.1903
South Wales Pottery**	Llanlley	1839-1922
Turner, G.W. & Sons	Tunstall	1873-95
Venables & Baines	Burslem	1851-53
Wilkinson & Hulme	Burslem	1881-85
Wood & Hulme	Burslem	1882-1905

Wetherbee's White Ironstone notes on pp. 18-21 the foregoing potters as manufacturing White Ironstone. No marks or pattern names are given.

*New additions

** Potter at Llanlley not identified

APPENDIX B11: ELSMORE and FORSTER, PATTERNS, SHAPES and DECORATIVE STYLING

by ARENE BURGESS

1.	Alphabet Plates	—
2.	Arched forget-me-not	(plain) (Reg'd. 1864)
3.	Arched forget-me-not	(copper lustre bands)
4.	Arched forget-me-not	(copper lustre and cobalt blue)
5.	Arched forget-me-not	(bright blue bands)
6.	Arched Panel	—
7.	Big and little ribs	—
8.	Bittersweet	(mulberry, polychrome/on Fanfare shape)
9.	Brush Stroke Tulip & Sprig	(in blue)
10.	Ceres	(plain) (Reg'd.1859)
11.	Ceres	(plain-variant shape)
12.	Ceres	(bright blue)
13.	Ceres	(copper lustre)
14.	Ceres	(yellow & green with lustre)
15.	Ceres	(Rockingham glaze)
16.	Ceres	(yellow lustre)
17.	Columbia	(resembles Sydenham) (Reg'd.1855)
18.	Crystal	(plain)
19.	Crystal	(copper lustre)
20.	Circus	—
21.	Cut Sponged Stamped	(blue bands with red florettes)
22.	Cut Sponged Stamped	(purple bands with green florettes)
23.	Fanfare	—
24.	Gaudy Brush Stroke	(in mulberry, cobalt and yellow)
25.	Gothic	—
26.	Grandmother's Flowers	(in blue)
27.	Grandmother's Flowers	(in purple)
28.	Grandmother's Flowers	(in deep purple)

	with Sponged Border	—
29.	Grape	(plain)
30.	Grape	(copper lustre)
31.	Green Banded	(plain grape)
32.	Greek Key (Olympic)	(Reg'd. 1867)
33.	Holly Stick Spatter	(green and purple florettes with blue bands)
34.	Holly Stick Spatter	(green and red florettes with blue bands)
35.	Holly Stick Spatter	(purple florettes with dark blue bands)
36.	Holly Stick Spatter	(red florettes with green and blue bands)
37.	Laurel Wreath	(plain) (Reg'd. 1867)
38.	Laurel Wreath	(copper lustre)
39.	Laurel Wreath	(George Washington Medallion)
40.	Lily & Vase	(mulberry)
41.	Lily & Vase	(blue with color)
42.	Morning Glory (Halleck Shape)	(plain) (Reg'd. 1867)
43.	Morning Glory	(blue and copper lustre)
44.	Morning Glory	(pink and green with lustre)
45.	Pacific Shape	(Reg'd.1871)
46.	Panelled Decagon	(plain)
47.	Panelled Decagon	(copper lustre)
48.	Parian Ware	—
49.	Portland Shape	(plain)
50.	Portland Shape	(morning glory-copper lustre)
51.	Portland Shape	(reverse teaberry-copper lustre and green)
52.	Portland Shape	(reverse teaberry with blue underlay)
53.	President Shape	—
54.	Puzzle Pitchers	(Fanfare shape with polychrome transfers)
55.	Rose Banded	—
56.	Scallop	—
57.	Simla	(bright blue)
58.	Simla	(deep flow blue)
59.	Simla	(lavender)
60.	Simla	(purple/mulberry)
61.	Strawberry Lustre	—
62.	Sydenham	—
63.	Tobacco Leaf	—
64.	Trumpet Flowers	(blue)
65.	Trumpet Flowers	(lavender-purple)
66.	Trumpet Flowers	(purple with polychrome)
67.	Tulip Shape	(plain) (Reg'd. 1866)
68.	Tulip Shape	(bright blue)
69.	Tulip Shape	(cobalt and copper lustre)
70.	Tulip Shape	(bright and dark blue with copper lustre)
71.	Tulip Shape	(copper lustre)
72.	Tulip Shape	(lavender)
73.	Vaquero	(lavender transfer)

N.B.: These patterns have been recorded by Mrs. Burgess. Many are illustrated in *Wetherbee, White Ironstone* (see Section 16 - White Ironstone With Copper Touch).

APPENDIX B12: DATING MARKS

1810	The appearance of printed or partially printed pattern names.
1813	**Patent Ironstone China** Introduced July 1813/Patent No. 3724, by Charles James Mason.
1813	**Stone China** Introduced by Josiah Spode.
1821-1822	**New Stone** Introduced by Josiah Spode.
1830	**Royal Arms** (and marks) May be noted on many post 1830 pieces.
1830/1840	**"Published By"** Introduced and protected by Sculpture Copyright Act of 1879, and amended in 1914. - "Published By" is followed by name, address and date of first issue.
1834	**Patent Mosaic** A mark introduced by Richard Boote who invented various techniques for decorating vessels with surface designs in contrasting colors.
1837	**Victorian Royal Quarter Arms** noted by omission of the center shield.
1839-1842	New designs were registered with the Board of Trade. Original files are to be found at the Public Record Office in Kew, Surrey.
1840	**Garter-Type Mark** Widely used at this time.
1842-1867	**Registration Marks** Diamond Shape Device protected by the Design Copyright Act (renewable every three years). These records are to be found under the reference numbers: BT43 and 44 at: The Public Record Office Ruskin Avenue Kew, Surrey, England TW9 4DW Phone: 011-44 181-876-3444
1845	**Stafford Knot** Bow Knot Shape, appears widely in use from 1870's/1880's to date.
1848	**Semi-Porcelain** The term was first introduced in 1848 by George Grainger & Co. for an opaque earthenware body.
1850	***"Royal"** Found in some manufacturer's prefixes or trade names after this date.
1861	***Limited** or "LTD" or "LD" introduced at this time.
1863	**"Trade Mark"** Introduced with Merchandise Act of 1862: *"A general point with reference to Royal, Ltd., Trade-Mark, etc. These were not used by all manufacturers, i.e., only limited companies used LTD. Only registered 'Trade Marks' had this wording. Therefore, marks without these features do not necessarily pre-date the given dates." (This was noted in correspondence from Geoffrey Godden, dated April 5, 1994.)
1868-1883	**Registration Mark** Design remains the same but classification positions change; e.g. letter for year now appear on right. - Copyright protection for manufactured shapes or added designs (renewable every three years).
1875	**"Trade Mark"** Introduced with the Trade Mark Act of 1862 and in 1875 was applied to American wares.
1884	**Registration Numbers** Indicate a design or process being registered (renewable every five years). Records dating from September 1909 onwards are to be found at: The Design Registry Room 1124A State House High Holborn London, England WC 1 The Design Registration Records from 1910 onwards are housed at: The Design Registry Room 1124A State House High Holborn London, England WC 1 Inquiries should first be made to: The Patent Office Designs Registry 25 Southampton Buildings London, England WC2A 1AY Phone: 011-44 171 405 8721
1887	**"Made In"** Continued to be used.
1891	**"England"** (Indicates a date after 1880) applied to export wares, in part, due to the Amrican Tariff Act of 1891.
1900	**"Patented"** Indicated the granting of a U.S. patent.
1901	**"U.S. Patent"** Denotes a design/method patent in the U.S.
1902	**"Patent Applied For"** Patent application applied for.
1920	**"Made in England"** Would normally date to post 1920.
1927	**"Designed or Made Expressly For"** Made specifically for one client. May be marked with name and/or with the factory name.
1950	**"Copyright"** Indicates a post 1950 dating.

The use of British Royal Coat of Arms' marks was not limited to Great Britain; it was used extensively in the United States and has been noted on European wares.

Royal Arms Mark
Pre-1837
(NB: Center Shield within a Shield)

Victorian Simple
Quarter Arms
1837+

Garter Mark
1840+

Staffordshire Knot
1845+

It is well to remember that there are no hard and fast rules as to the exact start date of a particular mark. Potters were often slow to change their existing mark to a new required marking. As such, the pre-June 1837 Royal Arms mark could often be found on wares of the 1840's; a fact holding true of subsequent mark changes.

APPENDIX B13: DATING AND DECIPHERING THE REGISTRY DIAMOND MARK 1842-1883

In 1797 British Parliament enacted Sculpture Copyright legislation to protect designers against their works being copied for a period of fourteen years. In 1814 this act was amended, giving the original designer an additional period of fourteen years, provided they were still alive and had not sold the design. This act enabled the designer to mark his work "Published By", followed by name, address and date of first issue or publication. From 1839-1842 two further measures were enacted into law. One extended the Design Act of 1794, giving three months copyright to extend the former act, and the second gave protection to numerous other branches of manufacture; three years to designs in metal and twelve months to the remainder. In 1841 the Copyright on Glass and Ceramics was extended to three years. In 1842 the act was once again amended whereby protection was extended to designs not specifically ornamental in character, as for instance, the shape of a teapot. This Design Copyright Act enabled manufacturers, dealers or designers to register their ornamental designs, signified by a Registry Diamond, which was renewable. Under this act thirteen different design classes were recorded of which ceramics, the subject of this Encyclopedia, are listed as Class IV. This enactment broke the various items of manufacture into different categories that covered most areas of Victorian art. The classes were:

Class I	Ornamental designs in metal
Class II	Ornamental designs in wood
Class III	Ornamental designs in glass
Class IV	Ornamental designs in earthenware (and porcelain), ivory bone and other solid substances
Class V	Ornamental designs - Paperhangings
Class VI	Ornamental designs - Carpets, floor or oil cloth
Class VII	Ornamental designs - Shawls - printed patterns
Class VII	Ornamental designs - Shawls - patterns not printed
Class IX	Yarn, thread - printed
Class X	Woven fabrics - not furniture
Class XI	Woven fabrics - furniture, printed patterns
Class XII	Woven fabrics - patterns not printed
Class XIII	Lace and all other articles

Design protection for the first six classes, was initially for a period of three years. This act was further emended in 1850, allowing for one year's provisional registration. The Copyright Registration Design Act continued until 1883 after which time (commencing with January 1, 1884) a simple registry number (i.e., Rd.1234) was shown on the wares so registered. The period of protection was now extended to five years from the previous three, extended again in 1907 to another five years, with a further five year extension at the discretion of the Comptroller.

The purpose of the registration mark was solely to show that the design or shape was registered at the Patent Office. Pieces may have registration diamonds that are impressed, printed, applied or moulded. Pieces may also have printed marks that may refer to the applied pattern. Some pieces have all of these markings or parts thereof. Countless dies and date stamps for years of issue were produced. Therefore, countless variations in markings exist. It is important to remember that without the registration diamond, a printed or impressed date does not imply registration. Furthermore, foreign manufacturers, retailers and agents also availed themselves of the English Registry system.

For a complete listing of potters' registration dates, the collector and reader may with to refer to Cushion's *British Ceramic Marks*. Specific designer pattern information may be found in Lockett & Godden's *Davenport;* Godden's *Ridgways*; Hughes' *Nineteenth Century Jugs*; Henrywood's *Relief Moulded Jugs* and *Illustrated Guide to British Jugs*; Copeland's *Spode and Copeland Marks*; Peake's *William Brownfield;* Wetherbee's *A Second Look At White Ironstone,* as well as other selected books listed in the Bibliography. Further, Godden's *Staffordshire* includes a section titled "Post-1842 Registered Designs Relating to Staffordshire Porcelains", pp. 509-534. For those who do not have access or cannot get to the Registry Office in England these books serve as excellent sources because they illustrate and note shapes and designs.

- All dates are to be taken with the understanding that some patterns and pieces may have been registered but not issued until a later date, or may have been purchased by other companies and reissued at a later date.
- As with registration numbers, one has to understand that in many cases the date of registry should be used as a reference point and not taken as gospel.

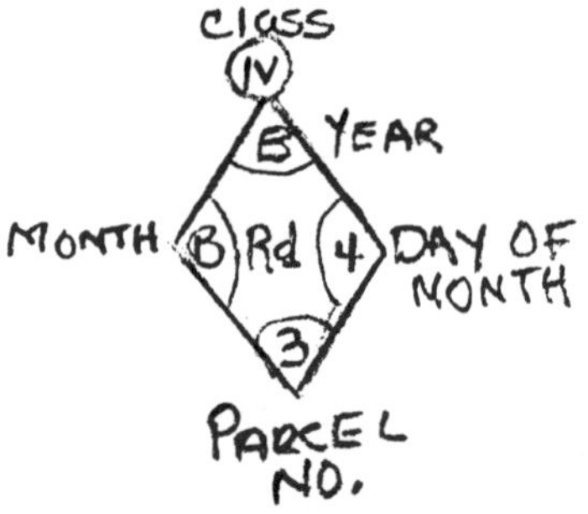

1842-1867
REGISTRY DIAMOND
X
Oct. 4, 1858

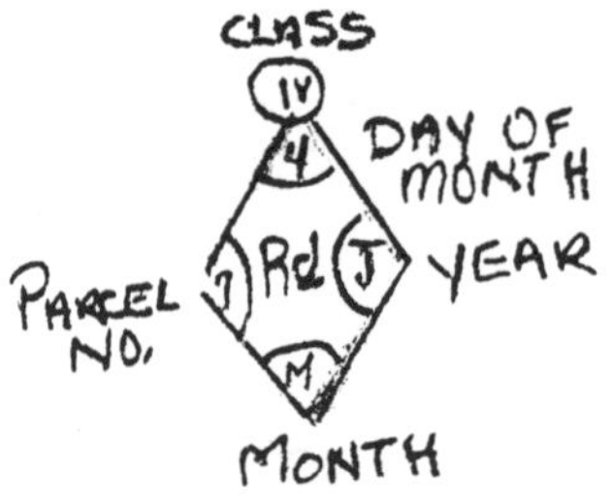

1868-1883*
REGISTRY DIAMOND
X
June 4, 1880

*In 1868 *the positions changed* on the registration diamond; the *top* from year to day of the month, the *right* from day of the month to year, the *bottom* f rom parcel number to month, and the *left* from month to parcel number.
It is important to remember that all dates reflect an opening date of January 1st.

YEAR: 1842-1883

MONTH:	LETTERS	MONTH	LETTERS	MONTH	LETTERS
January	D	May	E	September*	D
February	G	June	M	October	B
March	W	July	I	November	K
April	H	August*	R	December	A

YEAR: 1842-1883

YEAR	LETTER	YEAR	LETTER	YEAR	LETTER	YEAR	LETTER
1842	X	1852	D	1863	G	1874	U
1843	H	1853	Y	1864	N	1875	S
1844	C	1854	J	1865	W	1876	V
1845	A	1855	E	1866	Q	1877	P
1846	I	1856	L	1867	T	1878*	D,W
1847	F	1857*	K	1868	X	1879	Y
1848	U	1858	B	1869	H	1880	J
1849	S	1859	M	1870	C	1881	E
1850	V	1860*	Z	1871	A	1882	L
1851	P	1861	R	1872	I	1883	K
		1862	O			1873	F

*EXCEPTIONS

1857	From September 1-19 the letter "R" is to be noted
1857	From September 20-30 the Letter "D" is to be noted
1860	For December the letter "D" is omitted
1860	For December the letter "K" is substituted
1878	From March 1-6 the letter "W" is to be noted
1878	From March 7-31 the letter "D" is to be noted

APPENDIX B14: REGISTRY DATES, A CHRONOLOGICAL SEQUENCE: 1842-1900

Date	Parcel No.	Reg No.	Potter	Location
September 2, 1841	-	808	EDWARDS, JAMES	BURSLEM
May 30, 1842	-	1266-8	EDWARDS, JAMES	BURSLEM
December 02, 1842	3	2599-00	CLEMENTSON, JOSEPH	SHELTON
December 30, 1842	2	3346	EDWARDS, JAMES	BURSLEM
January 24, 1843	2	4296-7	RIDGWAY, JOHN & CO.	SHELTON
February 21, 1843	1	5266-70	ALCOCK, SAMUEL & CO.	BURSLEM
March 21, 1843	5	5993-4	WEDGWOOD, JOSIAH & SONS	ETRURIA
March 31, 1843	6	6266	ALCOCK, SAMUEL & CO.	BURSLEM
May 02, 1843	4	6978	WEDGWOOD, JOSIAH & SONS	ETRURIA
May 13, 1843	4	7122	JONES & WALLEY	COBRIDGE
June 14, 1843	5	7503-5	ALCOCK, SAMUEL & CO.	BURSLEM
August 30, 1843	8	9678-80	EDWARDS, JAMES	BURSLEM
October 06, 1843	2	10370	EDWARDS, JAMES	BURSLEM
November 10, 1843	3	11292	MINTON & CO.	STOKE
November 28, 1843	5	11690	DIMMOCK, THOS. & CO.	SHELTON
December 14, 1843	10	12331	BOWERS, G. F. & CO.	TUNSTALL
February 15, 1844	9	16264-5	ALCOCK, SAMUEL & CO.	BURSLEM
February 20, 1844	4	16374-5	ALCOCK, SAMUEL & CO.	BURSLEM
March 05, 1844	3	16831	MELLOR, VENABLES & CO.	BURSLEM
March 07, 1844	4	16871	LOCKETT, J. & T.	LANE END
April 03, 1844	3	17566-72	EDWARDS, THOS.	BURSLEM
April 11, 1844	4	17714	HILDITCH & HOPWOOD	LANE END
May 07, 1844	4	18207	DIMMOCK, THOS. & CO.	SHELTON
June 29, 1844	3	19182	DIMMOCK, THOS. & CO.	SHELTON
July 20, 1844	5	19977-9	RIDGWAY, JOHN & CO.	SHELTON
July 30, 1844	2	20322-4	MINTON, HERBERT & CO.	STOKE
August 15, 1844	3	20779	KING, KNIGHT & ELKIN	STOKE
August 21, 1844	7	20169-73	MINTON, HERBERT & CO.	STOKE
September 19, 1844	4	21700-1	RIDGWAY, JN & CO.	SHELTON
September 30, 1844	7	21960	MEIGH, CHARLES	HANLEY
October 14, 1844	4	22158	COPELAND & GARRETT	STOKE
October 17, 1844	3	22192	CLEMENTSON, YOUNG & JAMESON	SHELTON
October 30, 1844	4	22394-6	MINTON, HERBERT & CO.	STOKE
November 06, 1844	4	22424	MINTON, HERBERT & CO.	STOKE
November 11, 1844	5	22490	EDWARDS, JAMES	BURSLEM
November 13, 1844	4	22499-500	RIDGWAY, JOHN & CO.	SHELTON
November 22, 1844	4	22834	DIMMOCK, THOS. & CO.	SHELTON
December 02, 1844	3	22919-20	COPELAND & GARRETT	STOKE
December 07, 1844	4	23207-10	EDWARDS, THOS.	BURSLEM
December 16, 1844	6	23593	RIDGWAY, WILLIAM SON & CO.	HANLEY
December 24, 1844	2	23843	MEIR, JOHN & SON	TUNSTALL
January 11, 1845	6	24846	PHILLIPS, GEORGE	LONGPORT
January 15, 1845	2	24996	CLEMENTSON, YOUNG & JAMESON	SHELTON
January 21, 1845	6	25199	MAYER, T. J. & J.	LONGPORT
February 27, 1845	3	26543	PHILLIPS, GEORGE	LONGPORT
March 05, 1845	1	26608	COPELAND & GARRETT	STOKE
March 06, 1845	5	26617	MINTON, HERBERT & CO.	STOKE
March 17, 1845	10	26939	MINTON, HERBERT & CO.	STOKE
March 20, 1845	1	26949	MINTON, HERBERT & CO.	STOKE
April 25, 1845	2	27350	COPELAND & GARRETT	STOKE
April 26, 1845	3	27354	BOOTE, T. & R., WALLEY & JONES	BURSLEM, COBRIDGE, HANLEY
April 30, 1845	2	27383	FURNIVAL, JACOB & CO.	COBRIDGE
May 08, 1845	2	27451	MINTON, HERBERT & CO.	STOKE
May 10, 1845	3	27482	WALLEY (EDWARD) & T. & R. BOOTE	COBRIDGE & BURSLEM
May 31, 1845	1	27800	MORLEY, FRANCIS	SHELTON
June 19, 1845	1	28150	PHILLIPS, GEORGE	LONGPORT
June 26, 1845	3	28296	MINTON & CO.	STOKE
July 05, 1845	1	28668-71	PHILLIPS, GEORGE	LONGPORT
July 05, 1845	2	28672	WOOD, ENOCH	BURSLEM
July 26, 1845	1	29173	ADAMS, WM. & SONS	STOKE
August 28, 1845	3	29993	CLEMENTSON, JOSEPH	SHELTON
September 04, 1845	3	30161-3	COPELAND & GARRETT	STOKE
September 11, 1845	2	30286	PHILLIPS, THOS. & SON	BURSLEM
September 19, 1845	1	30383	MINTON & CO.	STOKE
October 06, 1845	1	30543-4	MINTON, HERBERT & CO.	STOKE
October 21, 1845	1	30699	COPELAND & GARRETT	STOKE
October 22, 1845	2	30701	CLEMENTSON & YOUNG	SHELTON
November 15, 1845	2	31128	BAYLEY & BALL	LONGTON
November 22, 1845	2	31329	MINTON & CO.	STOKE
December 04, 1845	4	31670-3	RIDGWAY, JOHN	SHELTON
December 27, 1845	2	32553	EDWARDS, JAMES	BURSLEM
December 29, 1845	2	32555	CLEMENTSON, JOSEPH	SHELTON
December 30, 1845	3	32601	FURNIVAL & CLARK	HANLEY
January 07, 1846	2	32698	CLEMENTSON, JOSEPH	SHELTON
January 24, 1846	2	33319	FURNIVAL, JACOB & CO.	COBRIDGE
February 26, 1846	5	34031	MAYER, T. J. & J.	LONGPORT
March 02, 1846	4	34108	MINTON & CO.	STOKE
April 17, 1846	3	34684	COPELAND & GARRETT	STOKE
May 21, 1846	3	35030-1	MINTON, HERBERT & CO.	STOKE
May 26, 1846	2	35116-7	MINTON, HERBERT & CO.	STOKE
June 26, 1846	2	35777	MINTON, HERBERT & CO.	STOKE
June 30, 1846	3	35795	GOODWIN, JOHN	LONGTON
July 11, 1846	1	36047	KNIGHT, J. K.	LONGTON
July 16, 1846	1	36167	RIDGWAY, SON & CO.	HANLEY
July 17, 1846	1	36263	RIDGWAY, JOHN & CO.	SHELTON
July 21, 1846	1	36278	MORLEY, F. & CO.	SHELTON
August 01, 1846	2	36447-8	WEDGWOOD, JOSIAH & SONS	ETRURIA
August 03, 1846	1	36450	WEDGWOOD, JOSIAH & SONS	ETRURIA
August 03, 1846	2	36451-2	MINTON, HERBERT & CO.	STOKE
September 03, 1846	2	37170	PHILLIPS, G.	LONGPORT
September 03, 1846	3	37171-2	MORLEY, F. & CO.	SHELTON
September 14, 1846	4	37254	COPELAND & GARRETT	STOKE
September 26, 1846	2	37419-21	RIDGWAY, JOHN & CO.	SHELTON
September 29, 1846	3	37586	MAYER, T. J. & J.	LONGPORT
October 26, 1846	1	37806	MORLEY, F. & CO.	SHELTON
October 26, 1846	5	37864	EDWARDS, J. (JAMES)	BURSLEM
November 03, 1846	1	37935	RIDGWAY & ABINGTON (WM. & E.)	HANLEY
November 05, 1846	2	37986	PHILLIPS, G.	LONGPORT
November 12, 1846	3	38068	MEIGH, C.	HANLEY
November 16, 1846	2	38113	MINTON, HERBERT & CO.	STOKE
November 21, 1846	2	38291-2	FURNIVAL, THOS. & CO.	HANLEY
December 03, 1846	4	38606	RIDGWAY & ABINGTON (WM. & E.)	HANLEY
December 04, 1846	2	38610	MINTON, HERBERT & CO.	STOKE
December 10, 1846	3	38786	CLEMENTSON, JOSEPH	SHELTON
December 14, 1846	3	39480	EDWARDS, JAMES	BURSLEM
December 14, 1846	4	39481	MINTON & CO.	STOKE
December 16, 1846	1	39519	GOODWIN, JOHN	LONGTON
December 17, 1846	2	39544-5	COPELAND & GARRETT	STOKE
December 29, 1846	2	39703	CHALLINOR, EDWARD	TUNSTALL
December 31, 1846	3	39746	WEDGWOOD, JOSIAH & SONS	ETRURIA
January 09, 1847	4	40104-5	RIDGWAY, JOHN & CO.	SHELTON
January 09, 1847	7	40110	COPELAND & GARRETT	STOKE
February 02, 1847	7	41213	BOOTE, T. & R.	BURSLEM
February 08, 1847	5	41266-7	MAYER, T. J. & J.	LONGTON
February 15, 1847	4	41459-60	COPELAND & GARRETT	STOKE
March 17, 1847	3	42044	WEDGE.WOOD, JOHN	TUNSTALL
March 17, 1847	6	42047-8	RIDGWAY, JOHN & CO.	SHELTON
March 22, 1847	2	42233	BAILEY & BALL	LONGTON
March 23, 1847	7	42279	MINTON, HERBERT & CO.	STOKE
March 30, 1847	1	42363	EDWARDS, JAMES	BURSLEM
April 03, 1847	6	42435	ALCOCK, SAMUEL & CO.	BURSLEM
April 27, 1847	1	42804	ALCOCK, SAMUEL & CO.	BURSLEM
May 12, 1847	4	43154	COPELAND & GARRETT	STOKE
May 14, 1847	1	43170-1	MINTON, HERBERT & CO.	STOKE
June 11, 1847	4	43536	EDWARDS, JAMES	BURSLEM
June 25, 1847	2	43780	EDWARDS, JAMES	BURSLEM
July 05, 1847	5	43916-7	MELLOR, VENABLES & CO.	BURSLEM
July 15, 1847	1	44014-5	MELLOR, VENABLES & CO.	BURSLEM
July 16, 1847	5	44036-9	EDWARDS, JAMES	BURSLEM
July 27, 1847	3	44398	MAYER, T. J. & J.	LONGPORT

Date	Parcel No.	Reg No.	Potter	Location
August 16, 1847	2	45088	EDWARDS, JAMES	BURSLEM
August 17, 1847	2	45091-2	COPELAND, W. T.	STOKE
August 19, 1847	3	45175	MINTON, HERBERT & CO.	STOKE
August 26, 1847	2	45088	EDWARDS, JAMES	BURSLEM
September 09, 1847	3	45730	COPELAND, WILLIAM TAYLOR	STOKE
September 16, 1847	3	45822	COPELAND, WILLIAM TAYLOR	STOKE
September 25, 1847	5	45992	WEDGE.WOOD, JOHN	TUNSTALL
October 02, 1847	5	46192-4	RIDGWAY, JOHN & CO.	SHELTON
October 04, 1847	3	46232	MINTON, HERBERT & CO.	STOKE
October 08, 1847	4	46265	WEDGE.WOOD, JOHN	TUNSTALL
October 13, 1847	1	46299	COPELAND, W. T.	STOKE
October 23, 1847	2	46516-8	MINTON, HERBERT & CO.	STOKE
October 27, 1847	1	46529	RIDGWAY, JOHN & CO.	SHELTON
November 11, 1847	4	46886	MINTON, HERBERT & CO.	STOKE
November 23, 1847	4	47183	WEDGWOOD, J. & CO.	ETRURIA
December 10, 1847	3	47562-3	MINTON & CO. & JOHN BELL	STOKE
December 15, 1847	4	48130	MINTON & CO.	STOKE
January 01, 1848	4	48540-2	BARKER & TILL	BURSLEM
January 18, 1848	2	49040	COPELAND, W. T.	STOKE
February 11, 1848	3	49780-1	MINTON, HERBERT & CO.	STOKE
February 29, 1848	12	50473	MINTON & CO.	STOKE
March 04, 1848	4	50549	MINTON & CO.	STOKE
March 07, 1848	1	50635-6	RIDGWAY & ABINGTON	HANLEY
March 14, 1848	2	50798	COPELAND, W. T.	STOKE
March 15, 1848	2	50803	COPELAND, W. T.	STOKE
March 20, 1848	7	50994	WOOD & BROWNFIELD	COBRIDGE
March 27, 1848	8	51185-91	ALCOCK, J. & S. JNR.	COBRIDGE
April 15, 1848	4	51542	RIDGWAY, JOHN & CO.	SHELTON
April 22, 1848	3	51661	WEDGWOOD, JOSIAH & SONS	ETRURIA
April 27, 1848	4	51763	WEDGWOOD, JOSIAH & SONS	ETRURIA
June 20, 1848	4	52402	BOWERS, G. F. & CO.	TUNSTALL
June 30, 1848	2	52529	COPELAND, W. T.	STOKE
June 30, 1848	3	52530	RIDGWAY & ABINGTON	HANLEY
August 16, 1848	8	53876	PINDER, THOS.	BURSLEM
August 23, 1848	2	54018	WEDGE.WOOD, JOHN	TUNSTALL
August 26, 1848	2	54067	MEIR, JOHN & SON	TUNSTALL
September 15, 1848	3	54438	COPELAND, W. T.	STOKE
September 18, 1848	4	54487	MEIGH, CHARLES	HANLEY
September 30, 1848	7	54662	RIDGWAY, JOHN & CO.	SHELTON
October 17, 1848	3	54901	BOOTE, T. & R.	BURSLEM
November 04, 1848	2	55174	COPELAND, W. T.	STOKE
November 13, 1848	4	55337	COPELAND, W. T.	STOKE
November 21, 1848	5	55456-7	MINTON & CO.	STOKE
November 27, 1848	2	55766	RIDGWAY, JOHN & CO.	SHELTON
December 16, 1848	3	56631-3	EDWARDS, JAMES	BURSLEM
December 28, 1848	2	56845	RIDGWAY, JOHN	SHELTON
January 03, 1849	2	56978	ADAMS, WM. & SONS	STOKE
January 20, 1849	2	57506-8	DAVENPORT, W. & CO.	LONGPORT
February 02, 1849	4	58069	MELLOR, VENABLES & CO.	BURSLEM
February 16, 1849	5	58461	MINTON & CO.	STOKE
February 16, 1849	11	58474	RIDGWAY & ABINGTON	HANLEY
March 13, 1849	2	58874	CLEMENTSON, JOSEPH	SHELTON
March 26, 1849	5	59232	MINTON & CO.	STOKE
March 31, 1849	2	59286	RIDGWAY, JOHN & CO.	SHELTON
April 02, 1849	5	59308	PODMORE, WALKER & CO.	TUNSTALL
April 10, 1849	4	59400	COPELAND, W. T.	STOKE
April 16, 1849	6	59571	MASON, C. J.	LONGTON
May 24, 1849	1	60081	WEDGE.WOOD (MR.)	TUNSTALL
June 07, 1849	3	60265	MAYER, T. J. & J.	LONGPORT
July 16, 1849	2	61347	RIDGWAY & ABINGTON	HANLEY
August 11, 1849	4	61865	COPELAND, W. T.	STOKE
August 15, 1849	2	61986	MINTON, HERBERT & CO.	STOKE
August 17, 1849	2	62003	COPELAND, W. T.	STOKE
August 27, 1849	5	62316	MELLOR, VENABLES & CO.	BURSLEM
September 14, 1849	6	62498	PRATT, F. & R. & CO.	FENTON
September 28, 1849	6	62690-4	RIDGWAY, J. (JOHN)	SHELTON
October 10, 1849	2	62883	RIDGWAY, J. (JOHN)	SHELTON
October 12, 1849	4	62914	MINTON & CO.	STOKE
November 09, 1849	4	63523	COPELAND, W. T.	STOKE
November 17, 1849	2	63718	MINTON & CO.	STOKE
November 22, 1849	2	64319	COPELAND, W. T.	STOKE
December 06, 1849	3	64739	COPELAND, W. T.	STOKE
December 15, 1849	4	64982	MAYER, T. J. & J.	LONGPORT
January 03, 1850	1	65884	DAVENPORT, W. & CO.	LONGPORT
January 14, 1850	4	66266-7	RIDGWAY, J. (JOHN)	SHELTON
February 13, 1850	3	67413	BELL, J. & M. P. & CO. (LTD.)	GLASGOW
March 09, 1850	3	67987	COPELAND, W. T.	STOKE
April 04, 1850	4	68623	MAYER, T. J. & J.	LONGPORT
April 08, 1850	1	68720	CLEMENTSON, J.	SHELTON
April 13, 1850	7	68797	MINTON & CO.	STOKE
April 25, 1850	3	69149	MINTON & CO.	STOKE
June 04, 1850	1	69679	BELL, J. & M. P. & CO. (LTD.)	GLASGOW
June 05, 1850	3	69685	BARKER & SON	BURSLEM
June 21, 1850	4	69884	WALLEY, E.	COBRIDGE
July 02, 1850	2	70088	MAYER, T. J. & J.	LONGPORT
July 16, 1850	5	70364	HARVEY, C. & W. K.	LONGTON
September 09, 1850	5	71843	TILL, THOMAS	BURSLEM
September 16, 1850	8	71952	BELL, J. & M. P. & CO. (LTD.)	GLASGOW
September 16, 1850	9	71953-4	RIDGWAY, J. (JOHN)	SHELTON
September 19, 1850	2	71989	COPELAND, W. T.	STOKE
September 21, 1850	1	72057	MELLOR, VENABLES & CO.	BURSLEM
October 09, 1850	2	72395-6	MINTON & CO.	STOKE
October 17, 1850	6	72544	COPELAND, W. T.	STOKE
November 04, 1850	4	73327	WEDGWOOD, J. & SONS	ETRURIA
November 20, 1850	7	73693	MORLEY, F. & CO.	SHELTON
December 05, 1850	3	74138	MORLEY, F. & CO.	SHELTON
December 19, 1850	6	74786	MAYER, T. J. & J.	LONGPORT
December 20, 1850	6	75148	COPELAND, W. T.	STOKE
February 10, 1851	9	76664	BROWNFIELD, WILLIAM	COBRIDGE
March 17, 1851	13	77481-91	RIDGWAY, J. & CO.	SHELTON
March 31, 1851	4	77986	BELL, J. & M. P. & CO. (LTD.)	GLASGOW
April 09, 1851	2	78268	TILL, THOS. & SON	BURSLEM
April 11, 1851	4	78309-10	BELL, J. & M. P. & CO. (LTD.)	GLASGOW
April 14, 1851	7	78398-401	BELL, J. & M. P. & CO. (LTD.)	GLASGOW
April 26, 1851	3	78634	WALLEY, E.	COBRIDGE
May 30, 1851	4	79085	COPELAND, W. T.	STOKE
June 07, 1851	4	79164	RIDGWAY, J. & CO.	SHELTON
June 11, 1851	2	79183	COPELAND, W. T.	STOKE
June 11, 1851	3	79184	SCRAGG, RALPH	HANLEY
June 19, 1851	5	79300	COPELAND, W. T.	STOKE
July 14, 1851	3	79684	COPELAND, W. T.	STOKE
July 21, 1851	7	79750-3	BOOTE, T. & R.	BURSLEM
July 24, 1851	2	79782	TILL, THOS. & SON	BURSLEM
July 26, 1851	3	79802	COLLINSON, C. & CO.	BURSLEM
August 16, 1851	2	80184	RIDGWAY & ABINGTON	HANLEY
August 26, 1851	3	78634	WALLEY, EDWARD	COBRIDGE
September 02, 1851	4	80365	MAYER, T. J. & J.	LONGPORT
September 19, 1851	3	80629-30	BOOTE, T. & R.	BURSLEM
September 29, 1851	4	80815-16	EDWARDS, JAMES	BURSLEM
September 30, 1851	3	80826	EDWARDS, JAMES	BURSLEM
October 01, 1851	1	80827	COPELAND, W. T.	STOKE
October 10, 1851	4	80910-11	BROWNFIELD, W.	COBRIDGE
October 10, 1851	6	80913	BOOTE, T. & R.	BURSLEM
October 14, 1851	4	80980	TILL, THOS. & SON	BURSLEM
October 16, 1851	4	80989	BROWNFIELD, W.	COBRIDGE
October 21, 1851	3	81057	RIDGWAY, WM.	SHELTON
November 10, 1851	4	81492	SCRAGG, RALPH	HANLEY
November 12, 1851	6	81510-12	MINTON & CO.	STOKE
November 13, 1851	2	81518	MEIGH, CHARLES & SON	HANLEY
November 14, 1851	4	81558	SANDER, GEO. B. (See Hulme & Booth)	LONDON
December 02, 1851	2	81815	MAYER, T. J. & J.	BURSLEM
December 04, 1851	3	81843-4	MINTON & CO.	STOKE
December 05, 1851	5	81864	RIDGWAY, JOHN & CO.	SHELTON
December 08, 1851	8	81960	COPELAND, W. T.	STOKE
January 27, 1852	1	83342	HARDING, W. & G.	BURSLEM
February 17, 1852	1	83826	VENABLES & BAINES	BURSLEM
March 04, 1852	2	84133-4	BROWNFIELD, WM.	COBRIDGE
March 13, 1852	3	84239	RIDGWAY, WM.	SHELTON
March 22, 1852	7	84385	SCRAGG, RALPH	HANLEY
March 24, 1852	3	84406	EDWARDS, JAMES	BURSLEM
March 24, 1852	4	84407	MINTON & CO.	STOKE
March 26, 1852	3	84471	BELL, J. & M. P. & CO. (LTD.)	GLASGOW
April 01, 1852	1	84541	TILL, THOS. & SON	BURSLEM
April 08, 1852	4	84615	TILL, THOS. & SON	BURSLEM
May 14, 1852	5	85081	COPELAND, W. T.	STOKE
May 18, 1852	1	85102	MINTON & CO.	STOKE
June 05, 1852	5	85248	MINTON & CO.	STOKE
June 14, 1852	4	85354	COPELAND, W. T.	STOKE
June 21, 1852	2	85404	LOCKETT, J. & T.	LONGTON
July 05, 1852	3	85619	PANKHURST, J. & CO.	HANLEY
July 23, 1852	3	85803-4	MINTON & CO.	STOKE
August 04, 1852	3	86070-1	COPELAND, W. T.	STOKE
August 13, 1852	5	86126	TILL, THOS. & SON	BURSLEM
August 25, 1852	4	86318	MEIGH, CHARLES & SON	HANLEY
September 03, 1852	7	86473	MINTON & CO.	STOKE
September 15, 1852	5	86649	TILL, THOS. & SON	BURSLEM
September 16, 1852	1	86657	MINTON & CO.	STOKE
September 24, 1852	1	86815	MINTON & CO.	STOKE
October 01, 1852	6	86931	COPELAND, W. T.	STOKE
October 07, 1852	5	87040	SCRAGG, RALPH	HANLEY
October 23, 1852	4	87219	DAVENPORTS, & CO.	LONGPORT
October 25, 1852	2	87228	BROWNFIELD, WM.	COBRIDGE
October 30, 1852	3	87464	MARPLE, TURNER & CO.	HANLEY
November 04, 1852	5	87541	HOLLAND, JOHN	TUNSTALL
November 11, 1852	3	87633	MINTON & CO.	STOKE
November 22, 1852	3	87883	PANKHURST, J. & DIMMOCK, J.	HANLEY
January 03, 1853	3	88808-9	COPELAND, W. T.	STOKE
January 12, 1853	6	88978	GOODFELLOW, THOS.	TUNSTALL
January 14, 1853	3	88987	DAVENPORTS, & CO.	LONGPORT
January 18, 1853	2	89050	DAVENPORTS, & CO.	LONGPORT
February 04, 1853	9	89469	PANKHURST, J. & DIMMOCK, J.	HANLEY
February 10, 1853	2	89626	WOOLISCROFT, GEO.	TUNSTALL
February 12, 1853	3	89661-3	MINTON & CO.	STOKE

Date	Parcel No.	Reg No.	Potter	Location
February 26, 1853	5	89958	COPELAND, W. T.	STOKE
March 10, 1853	2	90253	BELL, J. & M. P. & CO. (LTD.)	GLASGOW
March 17, 1853	5	90360	PANKHURST, J. W. & CO.	HANLEY
March 19, 1853	2	90372	MINTON & CO.	STOKE
April 23, 1853	2	90876	ADAMS, WM. & SONS	STOKE
May 07, 1853	5	91121-4	ALCOCK, JOHN	COBRIDGE
June 14, 1853	2	91405-6	LIVESLEY, POWELL & CO.	HANLEY
June 22, 1853	3	91469	PANKHURST & DIMMOCK	HANLEY
June 24, 1853	3	91487	WOOLISCROFT, GEO.	TUNSTALL
June 24, 1853	11	91512-3	RIDGWAY & CO.	SHELTON
July 18, 1853	4	91737	EDWARDS, JOHN	LONGTON
August 08, 1853	1	92001	SHAW, ANTHONY	TUNSTALL
August 10, 1853	2	92018	HOLLAND & GREEN	LONGTON
September 03, 1853	2	92340	BOOTE, T. & R.	BURSLEM
September 06, 1853	3	92364	MORLEY, F. & CO.	SHELTON
September 21, 1853	2	92631-2	EDWARDS, JAMES	BURSLEM
October 05, 1853	2	92768-70	VENABLES, MANN & CO.	BURSLEM
October 10, 1853	3	92859	BARROW & CO.	FENTON
October 11, 1853	5	92864	SCRAGG, RALPH	HANLEY
October 12, 1853	3	92867	EDWARDS, JAMES	BURSLEM
October 12, 1853	4	92868-9	LIVESLEY, POWELL & CO.	HANLEY
October 19, 1853	4	92952	MINTON & CO.	STOKE
October 22, 1853	1	93008-9	MAYER, T. J. & J.	LONGPORT
November 24, 1853	2	93438-9	TILL, THOS. & SON	BURSLEM
November 26, 1853	2	93452	COPELAND, W. T.	STOKE
November 30, 1853	5	93483	ADAMS, WM. & SONS	STOKE
December 06, 1853	4	93536	ALCOCK, JOHN	COBRIDGE
December 24, 1853	3	93706-7	MOORE, SAMUEL & CO.	SUNDERLAND
December 24, 1853	4	93708	ALCOCK, JOHN	COBRIDGE
January 10, 1854	4	94326	HARDING, W. & G.	BURSLEM
January 14, 1854	3	94632	MOORE, SAMUEL & CO.	SUNDERLAND
January 21, 1854	3	94727	BELL, J. & M. P. & CO. (LTD.)	GLASGOW
January 30, 1854	4	94815	ALCOCK, SAMUEL & CO.	BURSLEM
February 23, 1854	3	95163	COPELAND, W. T.	STOKE
March 11, 1854	4	95275	ALCOCK, SAMUEL & CO.	BURSLEM
March 20, 1854	1	95388	TILL, THOS. & SON	BURSLEM
March 22, 1854	2	95397	EDWARDS, JAMES & SON	LONGPORT
March 24, 1854	3	95420	MINTON & CO.	STOKE
March 31, 1854	1	95469	HOLLAND & GREEN	LONGTON
April 01, 1854	4	95510	BROWNFIELD, WM.	COBRIDGE
April 06, 1854	3	95553	ALCOCK, SAMUEL & CO.	BURSLEM
April 10, 1854	4	95576	ALCOCK, SAMUEL & CO.	BURSLEM
April 11, 1854	5	95587-8	PEARSON, FARRALL & MEAKIN	SHELTON
May 04, 1854	3	95733	RIDGWAY, JOHN & CO.	SHELTON
May 08, 1854	3	95751	BROWNFIELD, WM.	COBRIDGE
June 03, 1854	2	96003	TILL, THOS. & SON	BURSLEM
June 09, 1854	2	96039	MEIGH, CHAS. & SON	HANLEY
June 21, 1854	5	96085-6	BOOTE, T. & R.	BURSLEM
July 18, 1854	2	96296	BOOTE, T. & R.	BURSLEM
July 18, 1854	4	96298	ALCOCK, (SAMUEL) & CO.	BURSLEM
September 05, 1854	3	96773	ALCOCK, SAMUEL & CO.	BURSLEM
September 12, 1854	2	96826	COPELAND, W. T.	STOKE
October 02, 1854	3	96980	BROWNFIELD, WM.	COBRIDGE
October 06, 1854	4	97141	DAVENPORTS, & CO.	LONGPORT
October 09, 1854	4	97160	MAYER, T. J. & J.	LONGPORT
November 10, 1854	5	97659	RIDGWAY, JOHN & CO.	SHELTON
December 27, 1854	3	98640	ALCOCK, SAMUEL & CO.	BURSLEM
December 27, 1854	4	98641	PANKHURST & DIMMOCK	HANLEY
December 29, 1854	1	98648	PRATT, F. & R. & CO.	FENTON
January 06, 1855	4	98786	ALCOCK, SAMUEL & CO.	BURSLEM
January 15, 1855	2	99042	PINDER, BOURNE & HOPE	BURSLEM
January 15, 1855	4	99051	BROUGHAM & MAYER	TUNSTALL
January 19, 1855	3	99086	PANKHURST & DIMMOCK	HANLEY
January 30, 1855	1	99188	EDWARDS, JOHN	LONGTON
February 03, 1855	4	99231	BELL, J. & M. P. & CO. (LTD.)	GLASGOW
February 07, 1855	2	99310	ALCOCK, JOHN	COBRIDGE
February 17, 1855	3	99394	PRATT & CO.	FENTON
February 25, 1855	4	99528	RIDGWAY, J. & CO.	SHELTON
March 01, 1855	5	99538-40	MINTON & CO.	STOKE
March 05, 1855	3	99579	ELSMORE & FORSTER	TUNSTALL
March 17, 1855	1	99679	BAKER, WM.	FENTON
April 07, 1855	7	99814	COPELAND, W. T.	STOKE
April 17, 1855	4	99876	HUGHES, STEPHEN & SON	BURSLEM
April 26, 1855	1	99972-4	BROWNFIELD, WM.	COBRIDGE
April 28, 1855	7	100008	VENABLES, MANN & CO.	BURSLEM
May 10, 1855	5	100094	BEECH, HANCOCK & CO.	BURSLEM
May 14, 1855	3	100116	MINTON & CO.	STOKE
June 07, 1855	4	100246-7	ALCOCK, JOHN	COBRIDGE
June 11, 1855	3	100299	ALCOCK, SAML & CO.	BURSLEM
July 04, 1855	5	100624	THOMPSON, J.	STAFFORDSHIRE
July 24, 1855	1	100816	MEIGH, CHAS. & SON	HANLEY
August 06, 1855	1	101019	DUDSON, JAMES	SHELTON
August 08, 1855	5	101026	EDWARDS, J. & SON	LONGPORT
August 20, 1855	3	101127	FORD, THOS.	SHELTON
August 27, 1855	2	101229-31	BARROW & CO.	FENTON
October 03, 1855	3	101682	MINTON & CO.	STOKE
October 25, 1855	3	102325	CHETWYND, D. (See John Meir & Son)	COBRIDGE
October 29, 1855	6	102355	READE, G. W. (See Meir & Son)	BURSLEM
November 01, 1855	3	102415	WEDGWOOD, JOSIAH & SONS	ETRURIA
November 22, 1855	4	102744	BELL, J. & M. P. & CO. (LTD.)	GLASGOW
November 28, 1855	3	102785	BROWNFIELD, WM.	COBRIDGE
January 05, 1856	3	103103	EDWARDS, J. (JOHN)	LONGTON
January 15, 1856	4	103404	PANKHURST, JAMES & CO.	HANLEY
January 23, 1856	3	103507	MINTON & CO.	STOKE
January 31, 1856	4	103616	WEDGWOOD, JOSIAH & SONS	ETRURIA
March 11, 1856	1	104078	DAVENPORTS, & CO.	LONGPORT
March 12, 1856	3	104090	PRATT & CO.	FENTON
April 07, 1856	2	104313-16	SHAW, A.	TUNSTALL
April 07, 1856	3	104317	BELL, J. & M. P. & CO. (LTD.)	GLASGOW
April 18, 1856	2	104392	BEECH, WILLIAM	BURSLEM
April 18, 1856	3	104393	SCRAGG, RALPH (See George Frederick Bowers)	HANLEY
April 18, 1856	6	104396	WALLEY, E.	COBRIDGE
April 18, 1856	7	104397	RIDGWAY & ABINGTON	HANLEY
April 29, 1856	—	109810	COPELAND, W. T.	STOKE
April 30, 1856	3	104602-3	BROWNFIELD, WM.	COBRIDGE
May 08, 1856	2	104694	MINTON & CO.	STOKE
May 22, 1856	1	104762	MINTON & CO.	STOKE
June 13, 1856	3	105059	MEIGH, CHAS. & SON	HANLEY
June 19, 1856	—	110160	COPELAND, W. T.	STOKE
June 30, 1856	7	105258	CLEMENTSON, J.	SHELTON
July 28, 1856	3	105492	CHALLINOR, E.	TUNSTALL
July 30, 1856	5	105702	EDWARDS, J. & SON	LONGPORT
August 12, 1856	2	105871	PRATT, F. & R. & CO.	FENTON
August 19, 1856	5	105926	PRATT, F. & R. & CO.	FENTON
August 22, 1856	4	105955-9	BOOTE, T. & R.	BURSLEM
September 01, 1856	3	106161	COPELAND, W. T.	STOKE
October 16, 1856	2	106671-2	MINTON & CO.	STOKE
October 22, 1856	3	106770	COPELAND, W. T.	STOKE
November 07, 1856	6	106950	PRATT, F. & R. & CO.	FENTON
November 14, 1856	9	107038	DAVENPORTS, & CO.	LONGPORT
November 27, 1856	3	107708	DAVENPORTS, & CO.	LONGPORT
November 27, 1856	6	107714	BROWNFIELD, WM.	COBRIDGE
November 29, 1856	1	107783-5	WALLEY, E.	COBRIDGE
December 11, 1856	4	107955	COPELAND, W. T.	STOKE
December 18, 1856	2	108052	MAYER & ELLIOT	LONGPORT
December 23, 1856	4	108105	MAYER & ELLIOT	LONGPORT
January 15, 1857	5	108605	PRATT, F. & R. & CO.	FENTON
January 26, 1857	7	108785	EDWARDS, J. (JAMES)	LONGPORT
February 04, 1857	5	108854-5	MEIR, JOHN & SON	TUNSTALL
February 09, 1857	4	108930	MINTON & CO.	STOKE
February 17, 1857	3	109060	MINTON & CO.	STOKE
February 23, 1857	9	109180	PODMORE, WALKER & CO.	HANLEY
March 20, 1857	4	109427	ALCOCK, JOHN	COBRIDGE
April 16, 1857	1	109738	ALCOCK, JOHN	COBRIDGE
April 29, 1857	1	109810	COPELAND, W. T.	STOKE
June 05, 1857	3	110096-7	BROWNFIELD, WM.	COBRIDGE
June 19, 1857	1	110160	COPELAND, W. T.	STOKE
June 25, 1857	1	110247	BELL, J. & M. P. & CO. (LTD.)	GLASGOW
July 30, 1857	2	110780	RIDGWAY, BATES & CO.	SHELTON
September 07, 1857	2	111105	COPELAND, W. T.	STOKE
October 14, 1857	1	111585	RIDGWAY & ABINGTON	HANLEY
October 17, 1857	1	111642	MAYER BROS. & ELLIOT	LONGPORT
October 17, 1857	2	111643-4	BOOTE, T. & R.	BURSLEM
October 22, 1857	1	111677	PRATT & CO.	FENTON
December 04, 1857	4	112350	MINTON & CO.	STOKE
December 09, 1857	2	112354	BROWNFIELD, WM.	COBRIDGE
January 29, 1858	3	112875	COCKSON & HARDING	HANLEY
January 29, 1858	4	112876	WALLEY, E. & W.	COBRIDGE
April 17, 1858	4	113456	RIDGWAY & ABINGTON	HANLEY
April 22, 1858	5	113565	BOOTE, T. & R.	BURSLEM
April 30, 1858	5	113631	MINTON & CO.	STOKE
May 06, 1858	4	113668	EDWARDS, J. (JOHN)	LONGTON
May 25, 1858	4	113864	SHAW, A.	BURSLEM
May 31, 1858	1	113900	HOLLAND & GREEN	LONGTON
May 31, 1858	4	113903	ADAMS, WM.	TUNSTALL
June 02, 1858	1	113905-6	BROWNFIELD, WM.	COBRIDGE
June 23, 1858	6	114048	ALCOCK, SAMUEL & CO.	BURSLEM
July 13, 1858	2	114214	MAYER & ELLIOT	LONGPORT
July 29, 1858	4	114532	ALCOCK, SAMUEL & CO.	BURSLEM
August 24, 1858	2	114763	BROWNFIELD, WM.	COBRIDGE
September 03, 1858	2	115120	SHARPE BROS. & CO.	DERBYSHIRE
September 06, 1858	5	115197	EDWARDS, JAMES	LONGPORT
September 10, 1858	3	115217	EDWARDS, JOHN	LONGTON
September 10, 1858	6	115343	BRIDGWOOD & CLARKE	BURSLEM
October 05, 1858	3	115902	BROWNFIELD, WM.	COBRIDGE
October 05, 1858	3	116176	MINTON & CO.	STOKE
October 07, 1858	1	115953	RIDGWAY & ABINGTON	HANLEY
October 18, 1858	3	116176	MINTON & CO.	STOKE
November 11, 1858	2	116737	WALLEY, E. & W.	COBRIDGE
December 08, 1858	11	117336-8	BOOTE, T. & R.	BURSLEM
December 08, 1858	12	117339	CLEMENTSON, J.	HANLEY

Date	Parcel No.	Reg No.	Potter	Location
December 17, 1858	6	117443	COPELAND, W. T.	STOKE
December 23, 1858	2	117516	CLEMENTSON, J.	HANLEY
December 23, 1858	9	117530	COPELAND, W. T.	STOKE
December 27, 1858	4	117559	CLEMENTSON, J.	HANLEY
January 25, 1859	4	118119	COPELAND, W. T.	STOKE
February 02, 1859	3	118294	BOOTE, T. & R.	BURSLEM
February 03, 1859	2	118303-4	DAVENPORTS, & CO.	LONGPORT
March 21, 1859	7	118891	BOOTE, T. & R.	BURSLEM
March 29, 1859	7	119137	BOOTE, T. & R.	BURSLEM
May 07, 1859	1	119721-2	WALLEY, E. & W.	COBRIDGE
May 10, 1859	2	119760	ALCOCK, SAMUEL & CO.	BURSLEM
May 20, 1859	1	119968	BROWNFIELD, WM.	COBRIDGE
July 02, 1859	2	120560	COPELAND, W. T.	STOKE
August 06, 1859	7	121140	PRATT, F. & R. & CO.	FENTON
August 27, 1859	6	121724	ALCOCK, SAMUEL & CO.	BURSLEM
September 01, 1859	3	121833	EDWARDS, JAMES & SON	LONGPORT
October 12, 1859	4	122959	ADAMS, WM.	TUNSTALL
October 14, 1859	4	123116	COPELAND, W. T.	STOKE
October 25, 1859	1	123389-91	MINTON & CO.	STOKE
October 28, 1859	1	123604	DAVENPORTS, & CO.	LONGPORT
November 02, 1859	3	123738-40	ELSMORE & FORSTER	TUNSTALL
November 05, 1859	4	123816	BROWNFIELD, WM.	COBRIDGE
November 17, 1859	4	124140-3	MINTON & CO.	STOKE
November 23, 1859	4	124274	MINTON & CO.	STOKE
December 10, 1859	5	124653	WEDGWOOD, JOSIAH & SONS	ETRURIA
December 14, 1859	2	124716	WALLEY, E. & W.	COBRIDGE
December 15, 1859	3	124725	MINTON & CO.	STOKE
January 10, 1860	4	125365	COPELAND, W. T.	STOKE
January 23, 1860	7	125863	MAYER & ELLIOT	LONGPORT
February 14, 1860	9	126446-7	COPELAND, W. T.	STOKE
March 01, 1860	2	126950	BATES, BROWN-WESTHEAD & MOORE	HANLEY
March 27, 1860	1	127766	BATES, BROWN-WESTHEAD & MOORE	HANLEY
April 12, 1860	4	127965	MINTON & CO.	STOKE
May 02, 1860	2	128476	MEIR, JOHN & SON	TUNSTALL
May 30, 1860	10	129578	CORN, EDWARD	BURSLEM
June 06, 1860	4	129680-2	BROWNFIELD, WM.	COBRIDGE
June 22, 1860	2	130106	MINTON & CO.	STOKE
June 28, 1860	2	130135	MINTON & CO.	STOKE
August 21, 1860	2	131943	WEDGE.WOOD, JOHN	TUNSTALL
September 24, 1860	3	133411	MINTON & CO.	STOKE
September 29, 1860	7	133788	MINTON & CO.	STOKE
October 18, 1860	4	134591-20	BATES, BROWN-WESTHEAD & MOORE	HANLEY
October 19, 1860	4	134555-7	CLEMENTSON, J.	SHELTON
October 19, 1860	5	134558-9	HOLLAND & GREEN	LONGTON
October 29, 1860	3	134936	MINTON & CO.	STOKE
October 29, 1860	9	134968	BROWNFIELD, WM.	COBRIDGE
November 23, 1860	9	136032	BOOTE, T. & R.	BURSLEM
December 03, 1860	3	136285-6	BATES, BROWN-WESTHEAD & MOORE	HANLEY
December 12, 1860	3	136643	BATES & CO.	HANLEY
January 08, 1861	6	137217	BOOTE, T. & R.	BURSLEM
January 21, 1861	7	137529	WEDGWOOD & CO.	TUNSTALL
February 15, 1861	3	138356	FURNIVAL, J. & CO.	COBRIDGE
February 27, 1861	5	138535	EDWARDS, JAMES & SON	LONGPORT
March 07, 1861	7	138861-2	TURNER & TOMKINSON	TUNSTALL
March 19, 1861	3	139053	COPELAND, W. T.	STOKE
April 05, 1861	3	139360	PINDER, BOURNE & HOPE	BURSLEM
April 06, 1861	1	139369-72	MINTON HOLLINS & CO.	STOKE
April 12, 1861	3	139714-5	DAVENPORTS, & CO.	LONGPORT
April 18, 1861	5	139881	BOOTE, T. & R.	BURSLEM
April 20, 1861	6	139945	PRATT, F. & R.	FENTON
April 25, 1861	2	140200	DUDSON, JAMES	HANLEY
May 03, 1861	8	140367	COPELAND, W. T.	STOKE
May 06, 1861	3	140478	HILL POTTERY COMPANY LTD. (THE)*	BURSLEM
May 06, 1861	5	140480-1	OLD HALL EARTHENWARE CO., THE	HANLEY
May 09, 1861	3	140578-9	BATES, BROWN-WESTHEAD & MOORE	HANLEY
May 13, 1861	7	140679	MINTON & CO.	STOKE
May 31, 1861	3	141114	CORK, EDGE & MALKIN	BURSLEM
June 04, 1861	1	141214	BATES, BROWN-WESTHEAD & MOORE	HANLEY
June 11, 1861	2	141326-7	COPELAND, W. T.	STOKE
June 13, 1861	6	141369	MINTON & CO.	STOKE
July 05, 1861	2	141727	BEECH & HANCOCK	TUNSTALL
July 06, 1861	2	141732	BROWNFIELD, WM.	COBRIDGE
July 18, 1861	4	141869-70	WEDGWOOD, JOSIAH & SONS	ETRURIA
August 19, 1861	7	142755	BOOTE, T. & R.	BURSLEM
August 22, 1861	7	142847	WEDGWOOD & CO.	TUNSTALL
August 23, 1861	2	142850	READE, G. W. (See Charles Meigh & Son)	COBRIDGE
September 06, 1861	6	143313	BROWNFIELD, WM.	COBRIDGE
September 12, 1861	6	143400	PEAKE, J. & J.*	NEWCASTLE
September 17, 1861	2	143702	COPELAND, W. T.	STOKE
October 18, 1861	3	145157	COPELAND, W. T.	STOKE
October 24, 1861	5	145499	HULSEY, NIXON & ADDERLEY	LONGTON
October 28, 1861	7	145686-7	BATES, BROWN-WESTHEAD & MOORE	HANLEY
November 15, 1861	3	146352-4	CLEMENTSON, J.	HANLEY
November 29, 1861	5	146924	WEDGWOOD, JOSIAH & SONS	ETRURIA
December 04, 1861	7	147309-10	BROWNFIELD, WM.	COBRIDGE
December 20, 1861	9	147823	WEDGWOOD & CO.	TUNSTALL
January 11, 1862	5	148517	BROWNFIELD, WM.	COBRIDGE
January 25, 1862	3	148870	BROWNFIELD, WM.	COBRIDGE
February 01, 1862	4	149090	ELLIOT BROS.	LONGPORT
February 10, 1862	8	149292	MINTON & CO.	STOKE
February 27, 1862	4	149673-4	DUDSON, JAMES	HANLEY
March 01, 1862	6	149716	BOOTE, T. & R.	BURSLEM
March 13, 1862	6	149938	COPELAND, W. T.	STOKE
March 13, 1862	7	149939	ADAMS, WM.	TUNSTALL
March 14, 1862	8	149955	KNIGHT, J.	FENTON
March 14, 1862	9	149956	WEDGWOOD & CO.	TUNSTALL
March 14, 1862	10	149957-8	BROWNFIELD, WM.	COBRIDGE
March 22, 1862	9	150152	BOOTE, T. & R.	BURSLEM
March 27, 1862	1	150241	BELL, J. & M. P. & CO. (LTD.)	GLASGOW
March 28, 1862	5	150301-3	BELL, J. & M. P. & CO. (LTD.)	GLASGOW
March 29, 1862	3	150322	MINTON & CO.	STOKE
April 01, 1862	5	150377	WEDGWOOD, JOSIAH & SONS	ETRURIA
April 04, 1862	2	150455	MINTON & CO.	STOKE
April 04, 1862	5	150458	FURNIVAL, J. & T.	COBRIDGE
April 09, 1862	3	150538	OLD HALL EARTHENWARE CO. (LTD.) THE	HANLEY
April 17, 1862	2	151141	TURNER & TOMKINSON	TUNSTALL
May 01, 1862	7	151351	EARDLEY & HAMMERSLEY*	TUNSTALL
May 03, 1862	3	151378	ASHWORTH, G. L. & BROS.	HANLEY
May 09, 1862	9	151568-9	BROWN, T.C.-WESTHEAD, MOORE & CO.	HANLEY
May 14, 1862	3	151672-3	JONES, GEO. & CO.	STOKE
May 16, 1862	—	—	COPELAND, W. T.	STOKE
May 27, 1862	3	151995	CHALLINOR, E.	TUNSTALL
May 29, 1862	5	152013	FURNIVAL, J. & CO.	COBRIDGE
June 24, 1862	5	152709	BROWN, T.C.-WESTHEAD, MOORE & CO.	HANLEY
July 02, 1862	4	152859	MINTON & CO.	STOKE
July 04, 1862	8	152963	CLEMENTSON, J.	HANLEY
July 12, 1862	4	153112	CLEMENTSON, J.	HANLEY
July 14, 1862	2	153127	BEECH & HANCOCK	TUNSTALL
July 19, 1862	6	153366	CLEMENTSON, J.	HANLEY
July 31, 1862	3	153476	JONES & ELLIS*	LONGTON
July 31, 1862	4	153477	MINTON & CO.	STOKE
August 18, 1862	4	153827	HULSEY, NIXON & ADDERLEY	LONGTON
August 19, 1862	4	153844	ASHWORTH, G. L. & BROS.	HANLEY
August 25, 1862	3	154143-4	BODLEY, E. F. & CO.	BURSLEM
August 30, 1862	3	154220	FELL, THOS. & CO.	NEWCASTLE UPON TYNE
August 30, 1862	4	154221	BOOTE, T. & R.	BURSLEM
September 06, 1862	2	154401	MALKIN, WALKER & HULSE	LONGTON
September 11, 1862	3	154678	MINTON & CO.	STOKE
September 17, 1862	6	154812	HOPE & CARTER	BURSLEM
September 22, 1862	7	155103	MINTON & CO.	STOKE
September 26, 1862	1	155220-2	HOPE & CARTER	BURSLEM
October 01, 1862	7	155263-4	FELL, THOS. & CO.	NEWCASTLE UPON TYNE
October 15, 1862	2	156190	TURNER & TOMKINSON	TUNSTALL
October 23, 1862	8	156715-7	BAKER, WM. & CO.	FENTON
November 11, 1862	3	157274	BODLEY, E. F. & CO.	BURSLEM
November 19, 1862	5	157547	WOOLISCROFT, GEO.	TUNSTALL
November 28, 1862	4	157907	MINTON & CO.	STOKE
December 03, 1862	5	158052-3	BROWN, T.C.-WESTHEAD, MOORE & CO.	HANLEY
December 05, 1862	2	158091	BROWNFIELD, WM.	COBRIDGE
December 17, 1862	5	158480	OLD HALL EARTHENWARE CO. (LTD.) THE	HANLEY
December 18, 1862	3	158498	JONES, GEO.	STOKE
January 12, 1863	6	159083	DAVENPORT, BANKS & CO.	ETRURIA
January 16, 1863	2	159123	MINTON & CO.	STOKE
January 16, 1863	8	159153	LIDDLE, ELLIOT & SONS	LONGPORT
January 29, 1863	1	159551	WEDGWOOD, JOSIAH & SONS	ETRURIA
January 30, 1863	3	159573	BOOTE, T. & R.	BURSLEM
February 02, 1863	3	159613	MINTON & CO.	STOKE
February 17, 1863	4	159972	BOOTE, T. & R.	BURSLEM
March 06, 1863	2	160319	ASHWORTH, G. L. & BROS.	HANLEY
March 13, 1863	2	160456	HOPE & CARTER	BURSLEM
March 20, 1863	9	160753-4	PRATT, JOHN & CO.	FENTON
March 21, 1863	2	160759	BEECH & HANCOCK	TUNSTALL
March 21, 1863	4	160761	HULSEY, NIXON & ADDERLEY	LONGTON
March 21, 1863	5	160762	EDWARDS, JAMES & SON	BURSLEM
March 23, 1863	2	160791-2	BODLEY & HARROLD	BURSLEM
April 11, 1863	1	161404	MACINTYRE, J.	BURSLEM

Date	Parcel No.	Reg No.	Potter	Location
April 23, 1863	4	161852	BROWN, T.C.-WESTHEAD, MOORE & CO.	HANLEY
April 25, 1863	1	161861	BEECH & HANCOCK	TUNSTALL
May 11, 1863	3	162261-2	PEARSON, E.	COBRIDGE
May 12, 1863	1	162267	BODLEY & HARROLD	BURSLEM
May 22, 1863	4	162618-9	COPELAND, W. T.	STOKE
May 26, 1863	9	162765	BROWN, T.C.-WESTHEAD, MOORE & CO.	HANLEY
June 04, 1863	4	162976	OLD HALL EARTHENWARE CO. (LTD.) THE	HANLEY
June 08, 1863	15	163188	MINTON & CO.	STOKE
June 08, 1863	16	163189	BROWNFIELD, WM.	COBRIDGE
July 14, 1863	2	164213	TURNER & TOMKINSON	TUNSTALL
July 15, 1863	3	164221	VENABLES, H.	HANLEY
July 20, 1863	3	164353	BROWNFIELD, WM.	COBRIDGE
July 24, 1863	3	164468-9	COPELAND, W. T.	STOKE
July 28, 1863	6	164635	MINTON & CO.	STOKE
August 11, 1863	3	165045-7	TURNER & TOMKINSON	TUNSTALL
August 12, 1863	4	165171	HANCOCK, WHITTINGHAM & CO.	BURSLEM
August 21, 1863	1	165317	CLEMENTSON, J.	HANLEY
August 28, 1863	5	165448	VENABLES, H.	HANLEY
September 07, 1863	6	165720	BOOTE, T. & R.	BURSLEM
September 28, 1863	4	166439	VENABLES, H.	HANLEY
September 28, 1863	6	166441-2	EDWARDS, JAMES & SON	LONGPORT
October 02, 1863	5	166775	VENABLES, H.	HANLEY
October 14, 1863	7	167289	BROWNFIELD, WM.	COBRIDGE
October 17, 1863	1	167374	BOOTE, T. & R.	BURSLEM
October 22, 1863	5	167536	EARDLEY & HAMMERSLEY	TUNSTALL
October 24, 1863	5	167560	WEDGWOOD, JOSIAH & SONS	ETRURIA
October 26, 1863	7	167594-5	OLD HALL EARTHENWARE CO. (LTD.) THE	HANLEY
October 28, 1863	8	167715	JONES, GEO. & CO.	STOKE
October 31, 1863	3	167761-3	WOOD, EDMUND, T.	TUNSTALL
November 03, 1863	5	168132	MEIR, JOHN & SON	TUNSTALL
November 04, 1863	7	168188	BOOTE, T. & R.	BURSLEM
November 06, 1863	1	168234-5	JONES, GEO. & CO.	STOKE
November 26, 1863	12	169553	BROWNFIELD, WM.	COBRIDGE
November 27, 1863	3	169561	BODLEY & HARROLD	BURSLEM
December 02, 1863	5	169774	PANKHURST, J. W.	HANLEY
December 02, 1863	6	169775	BOOTE, T. & R.	BURSLEM
December 18, 1863	4	170294	PRATT, F. & R. & CO.	FENTON
December 23, 1863	2	170418	BROWNFIELD, WM.	COBRIDGE
December 30, 1863	1	170590	BROWN, T.C.-WESTHEAD, MOORE & CO.	HANLEY
January 05, 1864	2	170759	BROWNFIELD, WM.	COBRIDGE
January 11, 1864	5	170883	MALKIN, WALKER & HULSE	LONGTON
February 02, 1864	5	171421	WEDGWOOD, JOSIAH & SONS	ETRURIA
February 05, 1864	5	171520	HOPE & CARTER	BURSLEM
February 13, 1864	6	171673	COPELAND, W. T.	STOKE
February 22, 1864	7	171970	CORK, EDGE & MALKIN	BURSLEM
February 25, 1864	6	172060	LIDDLE, ELLIOT & SON	LONGPORT
March 03, 1864	4	172212	ASHWORTH, G. L. & BROS.	HANLEY
March 12, 1864	5	172559	CORK, EDGE & MALKIN	BURSLEM
March 18, 1864	1	172648	BROWN, T.C.-WESTHEAD, MOORE & CO.	HANLEY
March 22, 1864	3	172815-6	MINTON & CO.	STOKE
March 23, 1864	4	172876	BURGESS & LEIGH	BURSLEM
April 09, 1864	4	173200	WEDGWOOD, JOSIAH & SONS	ETRURIA
April 15, 1864	4	173659	JONES, GEO.	STOKE
April 18, 1864	5	173671	MINTON & CO.	STOKE
April 21, 1864	4	173785	BROWN, T.C.-WESTHEAD, MOORE & CO.	HANLEY
April 21, 1864	8	173799	LIDDLE, ELLIOT & SON	LONGPORT
April 23, 1864	11	173996	ASHWORTH, G. L. & BROS.	HANLEY
April 26, 1864	3	174112	BODLEY & HARROLD	BURSLEM
April 27, 1864	4	174138	HOPE & CARTER	BURSLEM
April 29, 1864	2	174168	BROWNFIELD, WM.	COBRIDGE
May 10, 1864	5	174455-8	JONES, GEO. & CO.	STOKE
June 09, 1864	7	175330	MINTON & CO.	STOKE
June 16, 1864	3	175500	HOPE & CARTER	BURSLEM
June 30, 1864	4	175927	BROWNFIELD, WM.	COBRIDGE
July 09, 1864	5	176164	PINDER, BOURNE & CO.	BURSLEM
July 11, 1864	8	176235-6	PINDER, BOURNE & CO.	BURSLEM
July 18, 1864	6	176597	BODLEY & HARROLD	BURSLEM
July 19, 1864	4	176701	HOPE & CARTER	BURSLEM
July 28, 1864	4	176916	HOLLAND & GREEN	LONGTON
August 20, 1864	10	177912	JONES, GEO. & CO.	STOKE
August 26, 1864	5	178037	BROWN, T.C.-WESTHEAD, MOORE & CO.	HANLEY
September 06, 1864	5	178264	COPELAND, W. T.	STOKE
September 10, 1864	1	178410	MINTON & CO.	STOKE
September 12, 1864	2	178433	MINTON & CO.	STOKE
September 14, 1864	4	178521	BODLEY & HARROLD	BURSLEM
September 16, 1864	6	178597-8	ASHWORTH, G. L. & BROS.	HANLEY
September 19, 1864	1	178680-1	WEDGWOOD, JOSIAH & SONS	ETRURIA
September 21, 1864	1	178693-4	MINTON & CO.	STOKE
September 22, 1864	6	178823-7	WEDGWOOD, JOSIAH & SONS	ETRURIA

Date	Parcel No.	Reg No.	Potter	Location
October 04, 1864	2	179445	JONES, GEO. & CO.	STOKE
October 12, 1864	4	179656	BROWNFIELD, WM.	COBRIDGE
October 28, 1864	4	180453	BODLEY & HARROLD	BURSLEM
October 28, 1864	9	180483	MINTON & CO.	STOKE
October 29, 1864	2	180486	COLLINSON, CHAS. & CO.	BURSLEM
October 31, 1864	3	180569	CORK, EDGE & MALKIN	BURSLEM
November 01, 1864	7	180695	COPELAND, W. T.	STOKE
November 04, 1864	3	180713	LIVESLEY, POWELL & CO.	HANLEY
November 10, 1864	2	181214-5	ELSMORE & FORSTER	TUNSTALL
November 10, 1864	10	181286	JONES, GEO. & CO.	STOKE
November 10, 1864	3	181296	HOPE & CARTER	BURSLEM
November 24, 1864	5	181722	BROWN, T.C.-WESTHEAD, MOORE & CO.	HANLEY
November 29, 1864	1	181843	HOPE & CARTER	BURSLEM
December 10, 1864	8	182249	HOPE & CARTER	BURSLEM
December 31, 1864	6	182699	JONES, GEO. & CO.	STOKE
January 06, 1865	3	182806	HOPE & CARTER	BURSLEM
January 06, 1865	4	182807	MINTON & CO.	STOKE
January 14, 1865	4	183331	JONES, GEO. & CO.	STOKE
February 01, 1865	1	183650-2	MINTON & CO.	STOKE
February 02, 1865	4	183706-7	ASHWORTH, G. L. & BROS.	HANLEY
February 13, 1865	7	183940	PRATT, F. & R. & CO.	FENTON
February 14, 1865	4	183945	LIDDLE, ELLIOT & SON	LONGPORT
February 27, 1865	4	184220	LIVESLEY, POWELL & CO.	HANLEY
March 31, 1865	3	185473	HOPE & CARTER	BURSLEM
April 01, 1865	4	185520	BROWNFIELD, WM.	COBRIDGE
April 03, 1865	4	185613	MINTON & CO.	STOKE
April 22, 1865	5	186266	TILL, THOS. & SONS	BURSLEM
April 22, 1865	7	186273	EDWARDS, JAMES & SON	BURSLEM
April 26, 1865	5	186325	EDWARDS, JAMES & SON	BURSLEM
April 28, 1865	4	186349	HOPE & CARTER	BURSLEM
April 28, 1865	7	186354	ALCOCK, HENRY & CO.	COBRIDGE
May 02, 1865	8	186477	LIVESLEY, POWELL & CO.	HANLEY
May 15, 1865	2	186841	HUDDEN, J. T.	LONGTON
May 17, 1865	2	186901	MINTON & CO.	STOKE
June 06, 1865	6	187358-9	HUDDEN, J. T.	LONGTON
June 14, 1865	6	187574	HILL POTTERY COMPANY LTD. (THE)*	BURSLEM
June 15, 1865	2	187576	HUDDEN, J. T.	LONGTON
June 29, 1865	2	187847-8	BODLEY, ED. F. & CO.	BURSLEM
June 30, 1865	4	187861	HILL POTTERY COMPANY LTD. (THE)*	BURSLEM
July 03, 1865	7	187972	BROWN, T.C.-WESTHEAD, MOORE & CO.	HANLEY
July 12, 1865	3	188167	EDWARDS, JAMES & SON	BURSLEM
August 21, 1865	6	189155	FURNIVAL, J. & CO.	COBRIDGE
August 23, 1865	5	189283	WEDGWOOD, JOSIAH & SONS	ETRURIA
September 14, 1865	2	189718	BROWN, T.C.-WESTHEAD, MOORE & CO.	HANLEY
September 18, 1865	6	189782	LIDDLE, ELLIOT & SON	LONGPORT
September 28, 1865	4	190200	MINTON & CO.	STOKE
September 30, 1865	4	190656	BARKER S. & SON	SWINTON
October 13, 1865	8	190903	BROWN, T.C.-WESTHEAD, MOORE & CO.	HANLEY
October 30, 1865	4	191407-8	BROWNFIELD, WM.	COBRIDGE
November 10, 1865	4	192236	PINDER, BOURNE & CO. & ANTHONY SHAW	BURSLEM
November 23, 1865	10	192793	OLD HALL EARTHENWARE CO. LTD., THE	HANLEY
November 29, 1865	8	192963	EDWARDS, JAMES & SON	BURSLEM
December 23, 1865	3	193844	DUDSON, JAMES	HANLEY
January 02, 1866	4	194063	PRATT & CO.	FENTON
January 03, 1866	6	194194	CLOSE, J. T. & CO.	STOKE
January 13, 1866	2	194450	BODLEY, ED. F. & CO.	BURSLEM
January 17, 1866	4	194537	BURGESS & LEIGH	BURSLEM
January 24, 1866	1	194696	MINTON & CO.	STOKE
January 31, 1866	5	194840	EDWARDS, JAMES & SON	BURSLEM
February 02, 1866	7	194949	COPELAND, W. T.	STOKE
March 02, 1866	2	195644	FORD, CHALLINOR & CO.	TUNSTALL
March 10, 1866	1	195841	OLD HALL EARTHENWARE CO. (LTD.) THE	HANLEY
April 14, 1866	6	196551	WALKER & CARTER	LONGTON
April 14, 1866	7	196552-4	ASHWORTH, G. L. & BROS.	HANLEY
April 16, 1866	8	196619	OLD HALL EARTHENWARE CO. (LTD.) THE	HANLEY
April 18, 1866	4	196651	EDWARDS, JAMES & SON	BURSLEM
April 20, 1866	7	196672-3	BROWNFIELD, WM.	COBRIDGE
May 01, 1866	4	196987-8	FURNIVAL, J. & CO.	COBRIDGE
May 25, 1866	1	197705-6	HOPE & CARTER	BURSLEM
June 12, 1866	1	198135-7	EDWARDS, JOHN	FENTON
June 21, 1866	4	198383-4	PINDER, BOURNE & CO.	BURSLEM
July 19, 1866	5	199186	HUDDEN, J. T.	LONGTON
July 25, 1866	3	199295	JONES, GEO.	STOKE
August 29, 1866	4	200324	BODLEY, ED. F. & CO.	BURSLEM
September 06, 1866	4	200599	PRATT, F. & R. & CO.	FENTON
September 15, 1866	8	201089	ASHWORTH, G. L. & BROS.	HANLEY
October 08, 1866	3	202103-5	MINTON & CO.	STOKE

Date	Parcel No.	Reg No.	Potter	Location
October 13, 1866	3	202493	FURNIVAL, THOS.	COBRIDGE
November 03, 1866	6	203173	MINTON & CO.	STOKE
November 12, 1866	3	203538	COPELAND, W. T.	STOKE
November 14, 1866	8	203817	BROWN, T.C.-WESTHEAD, MOORE & CO.	HANLEY
December 13, 1866	4	204764	LIDDLE, ELLIOT & SON	LONGPORT
December 14, 1866	8	204794	BARKER SAMUEL & SON	SWINTON
December 15, 1866	5	204863	BROWN, T.C.-WESTHEAD, MOORE & CO.	HANLEY
December 19, 1866	5	205088	MEIR, JOHN & SON	TUNSTALL
December 24, 1866	2	205201	HUDDEN, J. T.	LONGTON
January 08, 1867	5	205372	EDWARDS, JAMES & SON	BURSLEM
January 17, 1867	3	205596	BODLEY, ED. F. & CO.	BURSLEM
February 09, 1867	1	206033	BODLEY, ED. F. & CO.	BURSLEM
February 23, 1867	5	206275	WORTHINGTON & HARROP	HANLEY
March 02, 1867	7	206422	WEDGWOOD, JOSIAH & SONS	ETRURIA
March 04, 1867	4	206497	BROWN, T.C.-WESTHEAD, MOORE & CO.	HANLEY
March 05, 1867	6	206517	POWELL & BISHOP	HANLEY
March 06, 1867	4	206522	OLD HALL EARTHENWARE CO. (LTD.) THE	HANLEY
March 09, 1867	3	206564	EDWARDS, JOHN	FENTON
March 11, 1867	2	206662	WEDGWOOD, JOSIAH & SONS	ETRURIA
March 14, 1867	1	206718	DAVENPORT, BANKS & CO.	ETRURIA
March 15, 1867	7	206762-6	BROWNFIELD, WM.	COBRIDGE
March 18, 1867	5	206867-8	COCKSON, CHETWYND & CO.	COBRIDGE
March 19, 1867	5	206881	EDWARDS, JAMES & SON	BURSLEM
March 20, 1867	2	206887	WEDGWOOD, JOSIAH & SONS	ETRURIA
March 21, 1867	10	206961	EDWARDS, JAMES & SON	BURSLEM
March 25, 1867	3	206994	WEDGWOOD, JOSIAH & SONS	ETRURIA
March 26, 1867	4	207024-5	MINTON & CO.	STOKE
April 03, 1867	5	207163	MINTON & CO.	STOKE
April 04, 1867	2	207165	WEDGWOOD, JOSIAH & SONS	ETRURIA
April 04, 1867	9	207201	ELSMORE & FORSTER	TUNSTALL
April 17, 1867	1	207564	HOBSON, CHAS.	BURSLEM
April 24, 1867	2	207636	COPELAND, W. T.	STOKE
May 06, 1867	3	207938	BELL, J. & M. P. & CO. (LTD.)	GLASGOW
May 07, 1867	4	207977	MEIR, JOHN & SON	TUNSTALL
May 08, 1867	6	208002	BROWN, T.C.-WESTHEAD, MOORE & CO.	HANLEY
May 22, 1867	6	208434-5	CLEMENTSON BROS.	HANLEY
June 06, 1867	3	208750	WEDGWOOD, JOSIAH & SONS	ETRURIA
June 11, 1867	6	208819	CLEMENTSON BROS.	HANLEY
June 11, 1867	7	208820	COCKSON, CHETWYND & CO.	COBRIDGE
June 21, 1867	4	209057	BROWNFIELD, WM.	COBRIDGE
June 21, 1867	8	209062	CHETWYND, E. & D.	HANLEY
June 24, 1867	4	209087	CHETWYND, E. & D.	HANLEY
July 04, 1867	5	209362	RIDGWAY, E. J.	HANLEY
July 08, 1867	3	209431	ASHWORTH, G. L. & BROS.	HANLEY
July 12, 1867	5	209530	JONES, GEO.	STOKE
July 15, 1867	2	209556	WEDGWOOD, JOSIAH & SONS	ETRURIA
July 17, 1867	2	209601	CHETWYND, E. & D.	HANLEY
July 25, 1867	3	209726	HOPE & CARTER	BURSLEM
September 17, 1867	3	211290	WEDGWOOD & CO.	TUNSTALL
September 21, 1867	1	211536	ASHWORTH, G. L. & BROS.	HANLEY
September 25, 1867	9	211873-4	POWELL & BISHOP	HANLEY
October 02, 1867	1	211995	MINTON & CO.	STOKE
October 03, 1867	6	212055	MINTON & CO.	STOKE
October 07, 1867	4	212078	MINTON & CO.	STOKE
October 10, 1867	1	212194	BOOTH, THOS.	HANLEY
October 24, 1867	5	212765	FORD, CHALLINOR & CO.	TUNSTALL
October 26, 1867	1	212881	COPELAND, W. T. & SONS	STOKE
October 28, 1867	4	212956	COPELAND, W. T. & SONS	STOKE
October 29, 1867	3	212964	WEDGWOOD, JOSIAH & SONS	ETRURIA
October 30, 1867	3	212974	HUDDEN, J. T.	LONGTON
October 31, 1867	7	213065	POWELL & BISHOP	HANLEY
November 07, 1867	4	213436	EDWARDS, JAMES & SON	BURSLEM
November 18, 1867	9	214000	FORD, CHALLINOR & CO.	TUNSTALL
December 03, 1867	3	214618	COPELAND, W. T. & SONS	STOKE
December 12, 1867	6	214981	PRATT, F. & R. & CO.	FENTON
December 20, 1867	3	215085	WEDGWOOD, JOSIAH & SONS	ETRURIA
January 03, 1868	1	215481	MINTON & CO.	STOKE
January 07, 1868	11	215642	COCKSON, CHETWYND & CO.	COBRIDGE
January 08, 1868	5	215674	BOOTE, T. & R.	BURSLEM
January 10, 1868	2	215705	CORK, EDGE & MALKIN	BURSLEM
January 11, 1868	2	215725	BROWNFIELD, WM.	COBRIDGE
January 13, 1868	2	215735	ASHWORTH, G. L. & BROS.	HANLEY
January 16, 1868	3	215879	OLD HALL EARTHENWARE CO. (LTD.) THE	HANLEY
January 25, 1868	3	216186	HOPE & CARTER	BURSLEM
January 30, 1868	6	216333	FURNIVAL, J. & CO.	COBRIDGE
January 31, 1868	8	216347	WEDGWOOD, JOSIAH & SONS	ETRURIA
January 31, 1868	14	216363	BOOTE, T. & R.	BURSLEM
February 10, 1868	8	216676-8	MINTON & CO.	STOKE
February 12, 1868	1	216699	WEDGWOOD, JOSIAH & SONS	ETRURIA
February 18, 1868	1	216895	WEDGWOOD, JOSIAH & SONS	ETRURIA
February 18, 1868	2	216896-7	BROWN, T.C.-WESTHEAD, MOORE & CO.	HANLEY
February 20, 1868	9	216988	MINTON & CO.	STOKE
February 27, 1868	5	217100	ALCOCK & DIGORY	BURSLEM
March 05, 1868	15	217212	MINTON & CO.	STOKE
March 25, 1868	7	217615	COPELAND, W. T. & SONS	STOKE
March 26, 1868	3	217630	WALKER & CARTER	LONGTON
April 01, 1868	6	217727	MINTON & CO.	STOKE
April 06, 1868	6	217938-9	PINDER, BOURNE & CO.	BURSLEM
April 16, 1868	7	218139	ASHWORTH, G. L. & BROS.	HANLEY
April 21, 1868	6	218285	BEECH & HANCOCK	TUNSTALL
April 23, 1868	8	218387	HAMMERSLEY, R.	TUNSTALL
April 28, 1868	7	218466	GREEN, T. G.	BURTON ON TRENT
May 14, 1868	2	218764	HOPE & CARTER	BURSLEM
May 26, 1868	5	218951	BROWN, T.C.-WESTHEAD, MOORE & CO.	HANLEY
May 26, 1868	6	218952	PINDER, BOURNE & CO.	BURSLEM
May 28, 1868	3	218967	HOLDCROFT & WOOD*	TUNSTALL
May 28, 1868	5	218969-71	MINTON & CO.	STOKE
May 30, 1868	4	219042	BOOTE, T. & R.	BURSLEM
June 08, 1868	4	219174	BURGESS & LEIGH	BURSLEM
June 12, 1868	5	219316-7	BROWNFIELD, WM.	COBRIDGE
June 22, 1868	5	219484	MINTON & CO.	STOKE
July 10, 1868	3	219756	WEDGWOOD, JOSIAH & SONS	ETRURIA
July 20, 1868	2	219942-3	HOPE & CARTER	BURSLEM
July 24, 1868	4	219997	COPELAND, W. T. & SONS	STOKE
August 01, 1868	5	220236-7	BOOTE, T. & R.	BURSLEM
August 13, 1868	1	220772	WEDGWOOD, JOSIAH & SONS	ETRURIA
August 15, 1868	8	220821-4	EDWARDS, JAMES & SON	BURSLEM
August 17, 1868	2	220828	BODLEY, ED. F. & CO.	BURSLEM
August 21, 1868	2	220906	MALKIN, RALPH	FENTON
August 31, 1868	7	221124	BOOTE, T. & R.	BURSLEM
September 01, 1868	1	221125-6	WARDLE, JAMES	HANLEY
September 04, 1868	6	221203-4	GELSON BROS.	HANLEY
September 05, 1868	3	221214	BROWN, T.C.-WESTHEAD, MOORE & CO.	HANLEY
September 09, 1868	4	221311	HOPE & CARTER	BURSLEM
September 09, 1868	5	221312	JONES, F. & CO.	LONGTON
September 09, 1868	6	221313	WEDGWOOD & CO.	TUNSTALL
September 12, 1868	3	221521-2	MINTON & CO.	STOKE
September 14, 1868	4	221548	BOOTH, THOS. & CO.	BURSLEM
September 25, 1868	4	221881-2	MINTON & CO.	STOKE
September 25, 1868	13	222083-4	BROWN, T.C.-WESTHEAD, MOORE & CO.	HANLEY
October 08, 1868	7	222460	MINTON & CO.	STOKE
October 09, 1868	3	222477	HOPE & CARTER	BURSLEM
October 09, 1868	5	222482-4	DAVENPORTS, & CO.	LONGPORT
October 14, 1868	8	222736	JONES, GEO.	STOKE
October 17, 1868	4	223063	MINTON & CO.	STOKE
October 21, 1868	8	223308	BROWNFIELD, WM. (Reg'd by W.P.&G.Phillips)	COBRIDGE
October 22, 1868	5	223314-5	EDWARDS, JAMES & SON	BURSLEM
November 03, 1868	5	223817-8	MINTON & CO.	STOKE
November 03, 1868	6	223819	BROWN, T.C.-WESTHEAD, MOORE & CO.	HANLEY
November 06, 1868	13	224090	POWELL & BISHOP	HANLEY
November 09, 1868	5	224172	WEDGWOOD, JOSIAH & SONS	ETRURIA
November 21, 1868	5	224539	MINTON & CO.	STOKE
November 24, 1868	5	224645	BROWN, T.C.-WESTHEAD, MOORE & CO.	HANLEY
November 25, 1868	4	224724	CORK, EDGE & MALKIN	BURSLEM
December 01, 1868	4	224953	BROWN, T.C.-WESTHEAD, MOORE & CO.	HANLEY
December 11, 1868	5	225410	BODLEY, ED. F. & CO.	BURSLEM
December 12, 1868	4	225425	BROWNFIELD, WM.	COBRIDGE
December 14, 1868	7	225447	COCKSON, CHETWYND & CO.	COBRIDGE
December 23, 1868	5	225734	MINTON & CO.	STOKE
December 31, 1868	6	225993	ASHWORTH, G. L. & BROS.	HANLEY
December 31, 1868	7	225994	HAMMERSLEY, R.	TUNSTALL
January 01, 1869	8	226051	JONES, GEO.	STOKE
January 04, 1869	4	226098	MINTON & CO.	STOKE
January 21, 1869	6	226527-8	MINTON & CO.	STOKE
January 22, 1869	5	226570	GELSON BROS.	HANLEY
January 22, 1869	13	226581	BROWN, T.C.-WESTHEAD, MOORE & CO.	HANLEY
January 28, 1869	5	226738	MINTON & CO.	STOKE
February 01, 1869	7	226910	BROWN, T.C.-WESTHEAD, MOORE & CO.	HANLEY
February 09, 1869	5	227219	MINTON & CO.	STOKE
February 11, 1869	10	227277	JONES, GEO.	STOKE
February 15, 1869	1	227307	BOOTH, THOS. & CO.	BURSLEM
February 19, 1869	2	227345	WEDGWOOD, JOSIAH & SONS	ETRURIA
February 22, 1869	6	227403	WEDGWOOD, JOSIAH & SONS	ETRURIA
February 22, 1869	13	227411	PINDER, BOURNE & CO.	BURSLEM
February 27, 1869	5	227518	WEDGWOOD, JOSIAH & SONS	ETRURIA
March 03, 1869	8	227619	TILL, THOS. & SONS	BURSLEM

Date	Parcel No.	Reg No.	Potter	Location
March 06, 1869	8	227668	PRIMAVESI, F.	CARDIFF
March 08, 1869	6	227696	PRATT, F. & R. & CO.	FENTON
March 09, 1869	1	227743-4	JONES, GEO.	STOKE
March 09, 1869	3	227746	JONES, GEO.	STOKE
March 10, 1869	10	227823	PRIMAVESI, F.	CARDIFF
March 24, 1869	1	228141	WILEMAN, J. F.	FENTON
April 1, 1869	1	228290	WOOD & PIGOTT	TUNSTALL
April 02, 1869	6	228377	BROWNFIELD, WM.	COBRIDGE
April 02, 1869	7	228378	MINTON & CO.	STOKE
April 06, 1869	3	228430	BAKER & CHETWYND	BURSLEM
April 07, 1869	2	228455	MINTON & CO.	STOKE
April 12, 1869	5	228573	LIDDLE, ELLIOT & SON	LONGPORT
April 20, 1869	5	228764	LIDDLE, ELLIOT & SON	LONGPORT
May 13, 1869	16	229405	EDWARDS, JAMES & SON	BURSLEM
May 26, 1869	4	229627	BOOTH, THOS.	HANLEY
May 27, 1869	8	229642-4	DAVENPORT(S) & CO.	LONGPORT
June 19, 1869	5	230183-4	BROWNFIELD, WM.	COBRIDGE
June 25, 1869	4	230429	EDWARDS, JAMES & SON	BURSLEM
June 26, 1869	9	230455	MINTON & CO.	STOKE
July 03, 1869	9	230707-8	WEDGWOOD, JOSIAH & SONS	ETRURIA
July 06, 1869	3	230739	MEIR, JOHN & SON	TUNSTALL
July 19, 1869	8	231101	WARDLE, JAMES	HANLEY
July 20, 1869	2	231124	WEDGWOOD, JOSIAH & SONS	ETRURIA
July 23, 1869	6	231215	MINTON & CO.	STOKE
July 24, 1869	4	231222	COPELAND, W. T. & SONS	STOKE
July 27, 1869	4	231256	HUDDEN, J. T.	LONGTON
August 02, 1869	6	231504	COPELAND, W. T. & SONS	STOKE
August 03, 1869	5	231602	EDWARDS, JOHN	FENTON
August 04, 1869	4	231613	TOMKINSON BROS. & CO.	HANLEY
August 19, 1869	6	232307	COPELAND, W. T. & SONS	STOKE
August 26, 1869	6	232474	COPELAND, W. T. & SONS	STOKE
August 31, 1869	6	232586-7	PRATT, JOHN & CO.	LANE DELPH
August 31, 1869	12	232595	COPELAND, W. T. & SONS	STOKE
September 04, 1869	3	232822	MINTON & CO.	STOKE
September 08, 1869	5	232878	COPELAND, W. T. & SONS	STOKE
September 08, 1869	6	232879	PINDER, BOURNE & CO.	BURSLEM
September 09, 1869	3	232890	PRATT, JOHN & CO.	LANE DELPH
September 10, 1869	4	232903	MINTON & CO.	STOKE
September 21, 1869	7	233411	GELSON BROS.	HANLEY
September 30, 1869	8	233864-6	BROWN, T.C.-WESTHEAD, MOORE & CO.	HANLEY
October 01, 1869	3	233923-4	MINTON & CO.	STOKE
October 04, 1869	6	234016	MINTON & CO.	STOKE
October 15, 1869	6	234486	JONES, GEO.	STOKE
October 23, 1869	4	235012	JONES, GEO.	STOKE
October 29, 1869	3	235399-400	MINTON & CO.	STOKE
October 29, 1869	4	235401-2	POWELL & BISHOP	HANLEY
November 02, 1869	12	235589	CLARKE, ED.	TUNSTALL
November 03, 1869	12	235691	BROWN, T.C.-WESTHEAD, MOORE & CO.	HANLEY
November 08, 1869	2	235830	BROWN, T.C.-WESTHEAD, MOORE & CO.	HANLEY
November 10, 1869	3	235974	BROWNFIELD, WM.	COBRIDGE
November 15, 1869	8	236203-7	LIDDLE, ELLIOT & SON	LONGPORT
November 18, 1869	5	236435	ALCOCK & DIGORY	BURSLEM
November 24, 1869	4	236628	MINTON & CO.	STOKE
November 26, 1869	3	236653	MINTON & CO.	STOKE
December 01, 1869	3	236756	JONES, GEO.	STOKE
December 03, 1869	9	236829	BROWNFIELD, WM.	COBRIDGE
December 17, 1869	7	237224	MINTON & CO.	STOKE
December 18, 1869	2	237229	POWELL & BISHOP	HANLEY
December 22, 1869	7	237500	JONES, GEO.	STOKE
December 24, 1869	1	237552	GELSON BROS.	HANLEY
December 28, 1869	2	237565	PRATT, JOHN & CO.	LANE DELPH
December 31, 1869	2	237644	MINTON & CO.	STOKE
January 01, 1870	5	237691	BROWN, T.C.-WESTHEAD, MOORE & CO.	HANLEY
January 03, 1870	4	237742	JONES, GEO.	STOKE
January 15, 1870	12	238147-8	LIDDLE, ELLIOT & SON	LONGPORT
January 27, 1870	8	238388	HOBSON, CHAS.	BURSLEM
January 29, 1870	3	238436	MINTON & CO.	STOKE
February 01, 1870	6	238527-8	BROWN, T.C.-WESTHEAD, MOORE & CO.	HANLEY
February 03, 1870	13	238595-6	BROWN, T.C.-WESTHEAD, MOORE & CO.	HANLEY
February 04, 1870	7	238603	POWELL & BISHOP	HANLEY
February 09, 1870	2	238663	WEDGWOOD, JOSIAH & SONS	ETRURIA
February 10, 1870	8	238688	MINTON & CO.	STOKE
February 15, 1870	6	238898-9	BROWN, T.C.-WESTHEAD, MOORE & CO.	HANLEY
February 25, 1870	2	239139	MINTON & CO.	STOKE
February 28, 1870	6	239239	MINTON & CO.	STOKE
March 02, 1870	4	239304	MINTON & CO.	STOKE
March 07, 1870	6	239422	HOBSON, CHAS.	BURSLEM
March 08, 1870	1	239424-6	JONES, GEO.	STOKE
March 10, 1870	1	239474	JONES, GEO.	STOKE
March 10, 1870	9	239510	POWELL & BISHOP	HANLEY

Date	Parcel No.	Reg No.	Potter	Location
March 14, 1870	4	239548	BROWN, T.C.-WESTHEAD, MOORE & CO.	HANLEY
March 15, 1870	6	239585	TILL, THOS. & SONS	BURSLEM
March 16, 1870	2	239590-1	MINTON & CO.	STOKE
March 25, 1870	4	239969	HOPE & CARTER	BURSLEM
March 25, 1870	5	239969-70	MINTON & CO.	STOKE
March 26, 1870	1	240000-1	MINTON & CO.	STOKE
March 28, 1870	9	240079	OLD HALL EARTHENWARE CO. LTD., THE	HANLEY
April 07, 1870	9	240383	CORK, EDGE & MALKIN	BURSLEM
April 07, 1870	10	240384-5	BAKER & CO.	FENTON
April 07, 1870	11	240386	ADAMS, HARVEY & CO.	LONGTON
April 09, 1870	1	240458	MINTON & CO.	STOKE
April 14, 1870	7	240570	MINTON & CO.	STOKE
May 13, 1870	8	241474	BROWN, T.C.-WESTHEAD, MOORE & CO.	HANLEY
May 17, 1870	7	241544	BROWN, T.C.-WESTHEAD, MOORE & CO.	HANLEY
May 18, 1870	6	241567-8	BATES, ELLIOTT & CO.	LONGPORT
May 21, 1870	6	241649	OLD HALL EARTHENWARE CO. LTD., THE	HANLEY
May 21, 1870	12	241666	EDWARDS, JAMES & SON	BURSLEM
May 25, 1870	7	241754	EDWARDS, JAMES & SON	BURSLEM
May 26, 1870	5	241960	MINTON & CO.	STOKE
May 30, 1870	15	242077	JONES, GEO.	STOKE
June 03, 1870	8	242154	PRATT, F. & R. & CO.	FENTON
June 07, 1870	16	242234	BOOTH, THOS.	HANLEY
June 09, 1870	3	242391	BROWN, T.C.-WESTHEAD, MOORE & CO.	HANLEY
June 10, 1870	1	242392-4	BROWNFIELD, WM.	COBRIDGE
June 11, 1870	3	242439	EDWARDS, JAMES & SON	BURSLEM
June 17, 1870	7	242503-8	MINTON HOLLINS & CO.	STOKE
June 22, 1870	1	242634-5	ADAMS, HARVEY & CO.	LONGTON
June 22, 1870	3	242637-8	MINTON HOLLINS & CO.	STOKE
June 27, 1870	1	242715	JONES, GEO.	STOKE
July 05, 1870	5	242859	BAKER & CO.	FENTON
July 08, 1870	7	243049-50	WARDLE, JAMES	HANLEY
July 13, 1870	8	243176	EDWARDS, JAMES & SON	BURSLEM
July 14, 1870	9	243197-9	MINTON HOLLINS & CO.	STOKE
July 15, 1870	1	243207	COPELAND, W. T. & SONS	STOKE
July 16, 1870	2	243235	WARDLE, JAMES	HANLEY
July 19, 1870	6	243352	PRATT, F. & R. & CO.	FENTON
July 20, 1870	5	243368	BOOTH, THOS.	HANLEY
July 21, 1870	1	243378	BOOTH, THOS.	HANLEY
July 22, 1870	1	243385	CORK, EDGE & MALKIN	BURSLEM
August 04, 1870	4	243646	WARDLE, JAMES	HANLEY
August 09, 1870	2	243807	BROWNFIELD, WM.	COBRIDGE
August 22, 1870	4	244137-8	BOOTE, T. & R.	BURSLEM
August 23, 1870	6	244173	JONES, GEO.	STOKE
August 25, 1870	5	244223	BOOTE, T. & R.	BURSLEM
September 10, 1870	9	244741	MINTON & CO.	STOKE
September 16, 1870	5	244961	MINTON & CO.	STOKE
September 19, 1870	2	244976	BROWNFIELD, WM.	COBRIDGE
September 27, 1870	4	245227	ELSMORE & FORSTER	TUNSTALL
September 28, 1870	11	245265	GELSON BROS.	HANLEY
October 04, 1870	8	245464	MINTON & CO.	STOKE
October 06, 1870	4	245604	MINTON & CO.	STOKE
October 07, 1870	3	245620	MINTON & CO.	STOKE
October 08, 1870	9	245668	POWELL & BISHOP	HANLEY
October 19, 1870	2	245985-6	JONES, GEO.	STOKE
October 22, 1870	2	246149	BROWNFIELD, WM.	COBRIDGE
October 25, 1870	6	246181	BROWN, T.C.-WESTHEAD, MOORE & CO.	HANLEY
November 04, 1870	9	246927	BROWN, T.C.-WESTHEAD, MOORE & CO.	HANLEY
November 09, 1870	8	247047	MEIR, JOHN & SON	TUNSTALL
November 10, 1870	5	247071-3	MINTON & CO.	STOKE
November 10, 1870	10	247079-80	BROWNFIELD, WM.	COBRIDGE
November 12, 1870	8	247255	MINTON HOLLINS & CO.	STOKE
November 22, 1870	3	247944	JONES, GEO.	STOKE
November 24, 1870	3	248041	MINTON & CO.	STOKE
November 24, 1870	8	248049	BATES, ELLIOTT & CO.	LONGPORT
November 25, 1870	1	248051	MINTON & CO.	STOKE
November 25, 1870	2	248052	TURNER, GODDARD & CO.	TUNSTALL
November 26, 1870	9	248114-6	BOOTE, T. & R.	BURSLEM
December 01, 1870	7	248242	BROWNFIELD, WM.	COBRIDGE
December 02, 1870	11	248294	BROWN, T.C.-WESTHEAD, MOORE & CO.	HANLEY
December 05, 1870	4	248309-15	MINTON HOLLINS & CO.	STOKE
December 16, 1870	5	248869	BATES, ELLIOTT & CO.	LONGPORT
December 17, 1870	11	248899	BATES, ELLIOTT & CO.	LONGPORT
December 19, 1870	9	248953	ADAMS, HARVEY & CO.	LONGTON
December 27, 1870	4	249104	EDWARDS, JAMES & SON	BURSLEM
January 02, 1871	2	249235	GELSON BROS.	HANLEY
January 06, 1871	3	249331	MINTON & CO.	STOKE
January 07, 1871	8	249356	BATES, ELLIOTT & CO.	LONGPORT
January 10, 1871	7	249439	JONES, GEO.	STOKE

Date	Parcel No.	Reg No.	Potter	Location
January 26, 1871	8	249903-6	MINTON HOLLINS & CO.	STOKE
January 30, 1871	2	249972	GELSON BROS.	HANLEY
February 02, 1871	3	250020	EDWARDS, JAMES & SON	BURSLEM
February 08, 1871	9	250231	MACINTYRE, JAMES & CO.	BURSLEM
February 11, 1871	9	250291	BROWN, T.C.-WESTHEAD, MOORE & CO.	HANLEY
February 13, 1871	6	250366	EDGE, MALKIN & CO.	BURSLEM
February 13, 1871	9	250369	POWELL & BISHOP	HANLEY
February 13, 1871	10	250370	BODLEY, ED. F. & CO.	BURSLEM
February 15, 1871	7	250416-8	POWELL & BISHOP	HANLEY
February 20, 1871	2	250478-9	ELSMORE & FORSTER & CO.	TUNSTALL
March 14, 1871	4	250954	PRATT, JOHN & CO.	LANE DELPH
March 15, 1871	10	251013	BATES, ELLIOTT & CO.	LONGPORT
March 27, 1871	1	251246	BROWNFIELD, WM. & SON	COBRIDGE
March 29, 1871	1	251329	FURNIVAL, THOS. & SON	COBRIDGE
April 22, 1871	4	251966	PRATT, JOHN & CO.	STOKE
April 24, 1871	4	251988	WEDGWOOD, JOSIAH & SONS	ETRURIA
April 26, 1871	12	252068	MINTON HOLLINS & CO.	STOKE
April 29, 1871	7	252157	EDWARDS, JAMES & SON	BURSLEM
May 01, 1871	9	252171-3	BROWN, T.C.-WESTHEAD, MOORE & CO.	HANLEY
May 02, 1871	4	252177-80	BROWNFIELD, WM. & SON	COBRIDGE
May 03, 1871	4	252188	JACKSON, JOHN & CO.	ROTHERHAM
May 09, 1871	9	252387	LIDDLE, ELLIOT & CO.	LONGPORT
May 11, 1871	13	252487	POWELL & BISHOP	HANLEY
May 13, 1871	6	252503	ELSMORE & FORSTER	TUNSTALL
May 24, 1871	10	252756	MEIR, JOHN & SON	TUNSTALL
June 02, 1871	4	253017	BROWN, T.C.-WESTHEAD, MOORE & CO.	HANLEY
June 07, 1871	7	253069	GROVE, F. W. & STARK, J.	LONGTON
June 16, 1871	9	253335	TWIGG, JOHN	YORKSHIRE
June 17, 1871	3	253339-40	MINTON & CO.	STOKE
June 19, 1871	9	253378-9	PINDER, BOURNE & CO.	BURSLEM
June 22, 1871	1	253472	TILL, THOS. & SONS	BURSLEM
June 23, 1871	9	253571	BATES, ELLIOTT & CO.	LONGPORT
July 04, 1871	8	253796-8	COPELAND, W. T. & SONS	STOKE
July 15, 1871	2	254030	BOOTH, THOS.	HANLEY
July 25, 1871	12	254239	BATES, ELLIOTT & CO.	LONGPORT
July 29, 1871	6	254344	HOPE & CARTER	BURSLEM
August 09, 1871	7	254757	BATES, ELLIOTT & CO.	LONGPORT
August 18, 1871	10	254899	PRATT & CO.	FENTON
August 28, 1871	5	255267	WARDLE, JAMES	HANLEY
August 29, 1871	2	255274	JONES, GEO.	STOKE
August 30, 1871	4	255320	BARLOW, THOS.	LONGTON
August 31, 1871	9	255333	DAVIS, J. H. & J.	HANLEY
September 15, 1871	10	255825	BARLOW, THOS.	LONGTON
September 19, 1871	2	255849	MINTON & CO.	STOKE
September 25, 1871	8	256079	BROWN, T.C.-WESTHEAD, MOORE & CO.	HANLEY
September 28, 1871	5	256215	BOOTH, THOS. & CO.	TUNSTALL
October 04, 1871	7	256357-60	MINTON & CO.	STOKE
October 04, 1871	9	256362	PINDER, BOURNE & CO.	BURSLEM
October 09, 1871	8	256538	RIDGWAY, E. J. & SONS	HANLEY
October 10, 1871	3	256582	HUDDEN, J. T.	LONGTON
October 10, 1871	6	256586	BROWN, T.C.-WESTHEAD, MOORE & CO.	HANLEY
October 14, 1871	6	256687	BOOTH, THOS. & CO.	TUNSTALL
October 14, 1871	7	256688	WEDGWOOD, JOSIAH & SONS	ETRURIA
October 19, 1871	6	256907	COPELAND, W. T. & SONS	STOKE
October 31, 1871	5	257258	MINTON & CO.	STOKE
November 03, 1871	5	257366	WILEMAN, J. F.	FENTON
November 15, 1871	4	257728	THOMPSON, J. & SONS	GLASGOW
November 23, 1871	6	257944-6	FORD, THOS.	HANLEY
December 01, 1871	6	258095	JONES, GEO.	STOKE
December 22, 1871	6	258949	PRATT, F. & R.	FENTON
December 23, 1871	3	258956-7	JONES, GEO.	STOKE
December 29, 1871	10	259053	BROWN, T.C.-WESTHEAD, MOORE & CO.	HANLEY
January 01, 1872	6	259077	EDGE, MALKIN & CO.	BURSLEM
January 06, 1872	1	259271	MINTON & CO.	STOKE
January 20, 1872	6	259854	JONES, GEO.	STOKE
January 30, 1872	7	260081	COPELAND, W. T. & SONS	STOKE
February 02, 1872	11	260240-1	TURNER & TOMKINSON	TUNSTALL
February 03, 1872	4	260255-6	JONES, GEO.	STOKE
February 15, 1872	3	260463	POWELL & BISHOP	HANLEY
February 16, 1872	7	260504-6	JONES, GEO.	STOKE
February 22, 1872	3	260640	MINTON & CO.	STOKE
March 04, 1872	3	260868	JONES, GEO.	STOKE
March 04, 1872	4	260869-70	MINTON & CO.	STOKE
March 04, 1872	6	260872	MINTON HOLLINS & CO.	STOKE
March 07, 1872	7	260992-3	ADAMS, HARVEY & CO.	LONGTON
March 07, 1872	10	260998	BATES, ELLIOTT & CO.	BURSLEM
March 08, 1872	5	261006-8	MINTON HOLLINS & CO.	STOKE
March 13, 1872	8	261120	MINTON HOLLINS & CO.	STOKE
March 16, 1872	6	261190	MINTON & CO.	STOKE
March 18, 1872	6	261207	MINTON & CO.	STOKE
March 22, 1872	8	261394	BROWN, T.C.-WESTHEAD, MOORE & CO.	HANLEY

Date	Parcel No.	Reg No.	Potter	Location
April 05, 1872	4	261638	WEDGWOOD & CO.	TUNSTALL
April 05, 1872	5	261639	MINTON & CO.	STOKE
April 09, 1872	6	261724	BROWN, T.C.-WESTHEAD, MOORE & CO.	HANLEY
April 10, 1872	11	261749	FURNIVAL, THOS. & SON	COBRIDGE
April 17, 1872	13	261976	RIDGWAY, E. J. & SONS	HANLEY
April 19, 1872	5	262013	MINTON HOLLINS & CO.	STOKE
April 24, 1872	5	262203	PRATT, JOHN & CO. LTD.	LANE DELPH
May 02, 1872	9	262425-6	ADAMS, HARVEY & CO.	LONGTON
May 02, 1872	11	262428-9	FURNIVAL, THOS. & SON	COBRIDGE
May 03, 1872	9	262471-2	MINTON & CO.	STOKE
May 03, 1872	11	262474	BATES, ELLIOTT & CO.	BURSLEM
May 06, 1872	8	262493	BATES, ELLIOTT & CO.	BURSLEM
May 06, 1872	9	262494-5	MINTON HOLLINS & CO.	STOKE
May 11, 1872	4	262672	BOOTH, THOS. & SONS	HANLEY
May 27, 1872	1	262951	JONES, GEO.	STOKE
May 27, 1872	3	262953	MINTON HOLLINS & CO.	STOKE
May 29, 1872	2	262990	JONES, GEO.	STOKE
May 30, 1872	1	262999-3000	MINTON & CO.	STOKE
June 05, 1872	3	263134	HOPE & CARTER	BURSLEM
June 06, 1872	6	263162	BROWNFIELD, WM. & SON	COBRIDGE
June 07, 1872	4	263191	MINTON HOLLINS & CO.	STOKE
June 11, 1872	5	263315	WEDGWOOD, JOSIAH & SONS	ETRURIA
June 11, 1872	12	263348	COPELAND, W. T. & SONS	STOKE
June 18, 1872	3	263496-7	ASHWORTH, G. L. & BROS.	HANLEY
June 18, 1872	4	263498-9	MINTON HOLLINS & CO.	STOKE
June 21, 1872	7	263541	MINTON HOLLINS & CO.	STOKE
June 22, 1872	5	263561	MINTON & CO.	STOKE
June 22, 1872	8	263565	BROWNFIELD, WM. & SON	COBRIDGE
June 22, 1872	1	263771	BROWN, T.C.-WESTHEAD, MOORE & CO.	HANLEY
July 02, 1872	3	263885	WEDGWOOD, JOSIAH & SONS	ETRURIA
July 13, 1872	5	264081	GELSON BROS.	HANLEY
July 16, 1872	5	264206-7	MINTON HOLLINS & CO.	STOKE
July 20, 1872	3	264306-7	JONES, GEO.	STOKE
July 24, 1872	2	264490	ADAMS, W. & T.	TUNSTALL
July 29, 1872	7	264613	DIMMOCK, J. & CO.	HANLEY
July 31, 1872	3	264636-7	MINTON & CO.	STOKE
August 02, 1872	1	264685-6	RIDGWAY, E. J. & SONS	HANLEY
August 14, 1872	4	265105	BOOTH, T. & CO.	TUNSTALL
August 16, 1872	1	265167-8	BROWNFIELD, WM. & SON	COBRIDGE
September 02, 1872	8	265687	BATES, ELLIOTT & CO.	BURSLEM
September 12, 1872	6	265969	MINTON HOLLINS & CO.	STOKE
September 25, 1872	9	266628-31	MINTON HOLLINS & CO.	STOKE
September 26, 1872	2	266633	JONES, F.	LONGTON
October 07, 1872	7	266959	BROWN, T.C.-WESTHEAD, MOORE & CO.	HANLEY
October 11, 1872	5	267060-4	WEDGWOOD, JOSIAH & SONS	ETRURIA
October 12, 1872	10	267103-4	BATES, ELLIOTT & CO.	BURSLEM
October 14, 1872	4	267112	MINTON HOLLINS & CO.	STOKE
October 17, 1872	8	267265	WEDGWOOD, JOSIAH & SONS	ETRURIA
October 18, 1872	5	267317-9	JONES, GEO.	STOKE
October 30, 1872	2	267523	WILEMAN, J. F.	FENTON
October 30, 1872	5	267527	BROWNHILLS POTTERY CO. (THE)	TUNSTALL
November 12, 1872	4	267839	MINTON & CO.	STOKE
November 14, 1872	13	267893-5	BROWNFIELD, WM. & SON	COBRIDGE
November 18, 1872	3	267972	HOLLAND & GREEN	LONGTON
November 30, 1872	8	268309	BELFIELD & CO.	PRESTONPANS
December 02, 1872	5	268322	BROWN, T.C.-WESTHEAD, MOORE & CO.	HANLEY
December 04, 1872	3	268388	PRATT, JOHN & CO. LTD.	LANE DELPH
December 10, 1872	2	268724-5	MINTON & CO.	STOKE
December 11, 1872	8	268748-9	OLD HALL EARTHENWARE CO. LTD., THE	HANLEY
December 14, 1872	5	268806-7	BROWNFIELD, WM. & SON	COBRIDGE
December 24, 1872	1	269197	COCKSON & CHETWYND	COBRIDGE
December 27, 1872	4	269269	ADAMS, JOHN (Executors of)	LONGTON
December 27, 1872	8	269275	MEIR, JOHN & SON	TUNSTALL
January 10, 1873	1	269585	JONES, GEO.	STOKE
January 13, 1873	4	269621	COPELAND, W. T. & SONS	STOKE
January 29, 1873	1	269993-7000	MINTON HOLLINS & CO.	STOKE
February 01, 1873	1	270042-50	MINTON HOLLINS & CO.	STOKE
February 12, 1873	4	270354	BATES, ELLIOTT & CO.	BURSLEM
February 15, 1873	1	270385	MINTON & CO.	STOKE
February 25, 1873	6	270700	JONES, GEO.	STOKE
February 27, 1873	4	270751	TILL, THOS. & SONS	BURSLEM
February 27, 1873	8	270755	MINTON HOLLINS & CO.	STOKE
March 06, 1873	1	270131-2	MINTON & CO.	STOKE
March 06, 1873	9	271057	BROWNHILLS POTTERY CO. (THE)	TUNSTALL
March 26, 1873	6	271561-2	JONES, GEO.	STOKE
April 03, 1873	6	271851	MINTON & CO.	STOKE
April 19, 1873	2	272206	MINTON & CO.	STOKE
April 23, 1873	6	272293	GELSON BROS.	HANLEY
April 28, 1873	5	272364-5	POWELL & BISHOP	HANLEY
April 29, 1873	3	272384-5	JONES, GEO.	STOKE
May 03, 1873	2	272637-8	TILL, THOS. & SONS	BURSLEM

Date	Parcel No.	Reg No.	Potter	Location
May 03, 1873	7	272642-6	BROWNFIELD, WM. & SON	COBRIDGE
May 03, 1873	8	272647-8	MINTON & CO.	STOKE
May 06, 1873	2	272662	MINTON & CO.	STOKE
May 12, 1873	8	272835	BROWN, T.C.-WESTHEAD, MOORE & CO.	HANLEY
May 16, 1873	6	272983	MINTON HOLLINS & CO.	STOKE
May 29, 1873	8	273251	FORD, THOS.	HANLEY
May 30, 1873	15	273376	BROWN, T.C.-WESTHEAD, MOORE & CO.	HANLEY
June 11, 1873	4	273662-3	BATES, ELLIOTT & CO.	BURSLEM
June 19, 1873	3	273804	PINDER & BOURNE & CO.	BURSLEM
June 30, 1873	3	274054-5	MINTON HOLLINS & CO.	STOKE
July 03, 1873	9	274162	MINTON HOLLINS & CO.	STOKE
July 04, 1873	7	274183	BROWN, T.C.-WESTHEAD, MOORE & CO.	HANLEY
July 28, 1873	2	274663	HOBSON, CHAS.	BURSLEM
July 28, 1873	8	274701	MEIR, JOHN & SONS	TUNSTALL
July 31, 1873	1	274725-6	MINTONS	STOKE
August 05, 1873	2	274804	BAKER & CHETWYND	BURSLEM
August 14, 1873	10	275050	BROWN, T.C.-WESTHEAD, MOORE & CO.	HANLEY
August 25, 1873	1	275514-5	JONES, GEO.	STOKE
August 30, 1873	2	275661	BROWN, T.C.-WESTHEAD, MOORE & CO.	HANLEY
September 02, 1873	8	275755	EDGE, MALKIN & CO.	BURSLEM
September 04, 1873	3	275816	MINTONS	STOKE
September 10, 1873	7	275994	POWELL & BISHOP	HANLEY
September 15, 1873	3	276151	BROWN, T.C.-WESTHEAD, MOORE & CO.	HANLEY
September 16, 1873	4	276159	BROWN, T.C.-WESTHEAD, MOORE & CO.	HANLEY
September 19, 1873	4	276338	BROWN, T.C.-WESTHEAD, MOORE & CO.	HANLEY
September 25, 1873	8	276517	ADAMS, HARVEY & CO.	LONGTON
September 29, 1873	2	276566	BROWNFIELD, WM. & SON	COBRIDGE
October 06, 1873	6	276816-7	BROWN, T.C.-WESTHEAD, MOORE & CO.	HANLEY
October 11, 1873	6	277136	MINTONS	STOKE
October 13, 1873	3	277148-9	JONES, GEO.	STOKE
October 22, 1873	6	277385	MINTONS	STOKE
November 03, 1873	3	277844	HOPE & CARTER	BURSLEM
November 03, 1873	4	277845-7	JONES, GEO.	STOKE
November 06, 1873	6	277969	WEDGWOOD & CO.	TUNSTALL
November 10, 1873	7	278169	BROWN, T.C.-WESTHEAD, MOORE & CO.	HANLEY
December 04, 1873	6	278821	OLD HALL EARTHENWARE CO. LTD., THE	HANLEY
December 05, 1873	1	278822	ADAMS, HARVEY & CO.	LONGTON
December 05, 1873	8	278867	BROWNFIELD, WM. & SON	COBRIDGE
December 10, 1873	12	279180	JONES, GEO. & SONS	STOKE
December 27, 1873	7	279437	JONES, GEO. & SONS	STOKE
January 01, 1874	3	279476-7	BATES, ELLIOTT & CO.	BURSLEM
January 10, 1874	15	279655-6	DAVENPORTS, & CO.	LONGPORT
January 20, 1874	3	279938	POWELL & BISHOP	HANLEY
January 21, 1874	7	279964	COPELAND, W. T. & SONS	STOKE
January 23, 1874	5	280010	MEIR, JOHN & SON	TUNSTALL
February 09, 1874	5	280344	BODLEY & CO.	BURSLEM
February 11, 1874	2	280350	BOOTH, THOS. & SONS	HANLEY
February 19, 1874	1	280609	JONES, GEO. & SONS	STOKE
February 25, 1874	7	280786	JONES, GEO. & SONS	STOKE
February 26, 1874	7	280802-4	MINTON HOLLINS & CO.	STOKE
March 03, 1874	4	280907	JONES, GEO. & SONS	STOKE
March 04, 1874	3	280919	MINTONS	STOKE
March 13, 1874	6	281106	DIMMOCK, J. & CO.	HANLEY
March 14, 1874	2	281129	MINTONS	STOKE
March 17, 1874	5	281190	POWELL & BISHOP	HANLEY
March 21, 1874	5	281301	POWELL & BISHOP	HANLEY
March 24, 1874	4	281319	MINTONS	STOKE
March 28, 1874	3	281429-30	JONES, GEO. & SONS	STOKE
April 15, 1874	7	281822	MINTONS	STOKE
April 20, 1874	7	281871-80	MINTON HOLLINS & CO.	STOKE
April 21, 1874	8	281899	JONES, GEO. & SONS	STOKE
April 22, 1874	1	281902	BROWNFIELD, WM. & SON	COBRIDGE
April 23, 1874	8	281954	BROWN, T.C.-WESTHEAD, MOORE & CO.	HANLEY
April 25, 1874	2	281984	JONES, GEO. & SONS	STOKE
April 29, 1874	7	282088	RIDGWAY, SPARKS & RIDGWAY	HANLEY
April 29, 1874	9	282091	FURNIVAL, T. & SON	COBRIDGE
April 30, 1874	2	282098	BOOTH, THOS. & SONS	HANLEY
May 05, 1874	3	282134	BATES, ELLIOTT & CO.	BURSLEM
May 09, 1874	3	282218-9	JONES, GEO. & SONS	STOKE
May 11, 1874	3	282252	THOMPSON, JOHN & SONS	GLASGOW
May 11, 1874	4	282253	HOLLAND & GREEN	LONGTON
May 20, 1874	11	282497	BATES, ELLIOTT & CO.	BURSLEM
May 21, 1874	5	282526	MINTONS	STOKE
May 22, 1874	8	282555	MINTONS	STOKE
May 23, 1874	4	282567-8	JONES, GEO. & SONS	STOKE
June 06, 1874	2	282799-802	BROWNFIELD, WM. & SON	COBRIDGE
June 16, 1874	6	282982	COCKSON & CHETWYND	COBRIDGE
June 17, 1874	7	283041	EDGE, MALKIN & CO.	BURSLEM
June 18, 1874	1	283050	MINTONS	STOKE
June 25, 1874	5	283266-8	FORD, THOS.	HANLEY
June 26, 1874	4	283275	PINDER, BOURNE & CO.	BURSLEM
July 10, 1874	2	283547	MINTONS	STOKE
July 13, 1874	6	283570-1	BROWN, T.C.-WESTHEAD, MOORE & CO.	HANLEY
July 27, 1874	1	283980	HULSEY & ADDERLEY	LONGTON
July 30, 1874	5	284053	MINTON HOLLINS & CO.	STOKE
August 01, 1874	8	284131-5	MINTONS	STOKE
August 01, 1874	9	284136	COCKSON & CHETWYND	COBRIDGE
August 06, 1874	7	284204	BROWN, T.C.-WESTHEAD, MOORE & CO.	HANLEY
August 08, 1874	2	284254-5	BROWNFIELD, WM. & SON	COBRIDGE
August 15, 1874	4	284417	BATES, ELLIOTT & CO.	BURSLEM
August 22, 1874	6	284562	HUDDEN, J. T.	LONGTON
August 28, 1874	4	284699-700	JONES, GEO. & SONS	STOKE
September 01, 1874	3	284791	TILL, THOS. & SONS	BURSLEM
September 03, 1874	12	284884-5	COCKSON & CHETWYND	COBRIDGE
September 04, 1874	3	284897	MINTONS	STOKE
September 05, 1874	7	284920	FURNIVAL & SON	COBRIDGE
September 07, 1874	3	284936-7	BOOTH, THOS. & SONS	HANLEY
September 10, 1874	3	285013	BROWNFIELD, WM. & SON	COBRIDGE
September 12, 1874	1	285181	MINTONS	STOKE
September 15, 1874	2	285282	JONES, GEO. & SONS	STOKE
September 30, 1874	4	285776	BROWNFIELD, WM. & SON	COBRIDGE
October 06, 1874	3	286000	MINTONS	STOKE
October 06, 1874	4	286001	GROVE, F. W. & STARK, J.	LONGTON
October 10, 1874	4	286134	MINTONS	STOKE
October 12, 1874	2	286171	POWELL & BISHOP	HANLEY
October 17, 1874	8	286369-70	BATES, ELLIOTT & CO.	BURSLEM
October 21, 1874	8	286424	JONES, GEO. & SONS	STOKE
October 28, 1874	9	286563	PINDER, BOURNE & CO.	BURSLEM
November 02, 1874	3	286715	EDWARDS, JAMES & SON	BURSLEM
November 03, 1874	4	286720-2	CORN, W. & E.	BURSLEM
November 06, 1874	3	286759	BROWNFIELD, WM. & SON	COBRIDGE
November 07, 1874	4	286774-80	FORD, THOS.	HANLEY
November 10, 1874	3	286794	JONES, GEO. & SONS	STOKE
November 12, 1874	3	286931	MINTONS	STOKE
November 12, 1874	12	286942	BATES, ELLIOTT & CO.	BURSLEM
November 20, 1874	12	287317	PRATT, F. & R. & CO.	FENTON
November 25, 1874	7	287438-9	MINTON HOLLINS & CO.	STOKE
December 01, 1874	5	287598	COPELAND, W. T. & SONS	STOKE
December 04, 1874	6	287638	BARLOW, THOS.	LONGTON
December 07, 1874	8	287694-7	BROWN, T.C.-WESTHEAD, MOORE & CO.	HANLEY
December 08, 1874	2	287699	JONES, GEO. & SONS	STOKE
December 10, 1874	4	287731	PINDER, BOURNE & CO.	BURSLEM
December 12, 1874	3	287776	JONES, GEO. & SONS	STOKE
December 18, 1874	6	287982	JONES, GEO. & SONS	STOKE
December 18, 1874	11	287990-7	MINTON HOLLINS & CO.	STOKE
January 02, 1875	4	288241-2	BROWN, T.C.-WESTHEAD, MOORE & CO.	HANLEY
January 06, 1875	3	288276-8	MINTON HOLLINS & CO.	STOKE
January 16, 1875	9	288502	BROWNHILLS POTTERY CO. (THE)	TUNSTALL
January 18, 1875	8	288521	BROWN, T.C.-WESTHEAD, MOORE & CO.	HANLEY
January 20, 1875	4	288553-6	BROWNFIELD, WM. & SON	COBRIDGE
January 21, 1875	2	288682	JONES, GEO. & SONS	STOKE
January 23, 1875	9	288755-8	BROWN, T.C.-WESTHEAD, MOORE & CO.	HANLEY
January 28, 1875	5	288830	MINTONS	STOKE
February 05, 1875	5	289076	BOOTE, T. & R.	BURSLEM
February 09, 1875	1	289172	PINDER, BOURNE & CO.	BURSLEM
February 09, 1875	2	289173	JONES, GEO. & SONS	STOKE
February 12, 1875	6	289280	MADDOCK, J. & SONS	BURLSEM
February 17, 1875	7	289334	MINTONS	STOKE
February 23, 1875	5	289503	MADDOCK, J. & SONS	BURLSEM
February 23, 1875	6	289504	JONES, GEO. & SONS	STOKE
March 05, 1875	2	289769	BROWNFIELD, WM. & SON	COBRIDGE
March 12, 1875	5	289874-6	JONES, GEO. & SONS	STOKE
March 24, 1875	13	290153	MINTON HOLLINS & CO.	STOKE
March 24, 1875	14	290154-5	BROWN, T.C.-WESTHEAD, MOORE & CO.	HANLEY
March 30, 1875	1	290186	BOOTH, THOS. & SONS	HANLEY
March 31, 1875	5	290209-10	BROWNFIELD, WM. & SON	COBRIDGE
April 03, 1875	7	290259	DIMMOCK, J. & CO.	HANLEY
April 03, 1875	9	290261-2	BODLEY, E. F. & SON	BURSLEM
April 07, 1875	3	290352	MINTONS	STOKE
April 09, 1875	6	290393-4	BROWNFIELD, WM. & SON	COBRIDGE
April 10, 1875	7	290407-8	POWELL & BISHOP	HANLEY
April 15, 1875	5	290500	MALKIN, R.	FENTON
April 17, 1875	1	290738	PINDER, BOURNE & CO.	BURSLEM
April 20, 1875	1	290787	DIMMOCK, J. & CO.	HANLEY
April 20, 1875	2	290788	MINTONS	STOKE
April 22, 1875	4	290843-6	MINTON HOLLINS & CO.	STOKE
May 07, 1875	7	291109	JONES, GEO. & SONS	STOKE

Date	Parcel No.	Reg No.	Potter	Location
May 07, 1875	8	291110	BURGESS & LEIGH	BURSLEM
May 20, 1875	4	291440	BATES, ELLIOTT & CO.	BURSLEM
May 20, 1875	3	291444	DIMMOCK, J. & CO.	HANLEY
May 22, 1875	1	291458	HOLLAND & GREEN	LONGTON
May 26, 1875	6	291518-20	BROWN, T.C.-WESTHEAD, MOORE & CO.	HANLEY
May 28, 1875	10	291556	CAMPBELLFIELD POTTERY CO. (LTD.)	GLASGOW
May 31, 1875	8	291568	JONES, GEO. & SONS	STOKE
May 31, 1875	18	291611	RIDGWAY, SPARKS & RIDGWAY	HANLEY
June 02, 1875	9	291749-51	MINTON HOLLINS & CO.	STOKE
June 07, 1875	3	291882	ADAMS, W. & T.	TUNSTALL
June 10, 1875	6	292005	BROWNFIELD, WM. & SON	COBRIDGE
June 12, 1875	6	292035	MADDOCK & GATER	BURSLEM
June 12, 1875	10	292042	FURNIVAL, THOS. & SON	COBRIDGE
June 15, 1875	5	292080	WEDGWOOD, JOSIAH & SONS	ETRURIA
June 19, 1875	6	292184	TILL, THOS. & SONS	BURSLEM
June 26, 1875	2	292367-70	JONES, GEO. & SONS	STOKE
July 05, 1875	1	292542	BROWNFIELD, WM. & SON	COBRIDGE
July 23, 1875	10	293035	BROWN, T.C.-WESTHEAD, MOORE & CO.	HANLEY
July 27, 1875	5	293114	GROVE, F. W. & STARK, J.	LONGTON
July 28, 1875	7	293129	MINTON HOLLINS & CO.	STOKE
August 19, 1875	7	293748	GROVE, F. W. & STARK, J.	LONGTON
September 02, 1875	3	294147	ELSMORE, T. & SON	TUNSTALL
September 13, 1875	2	294434-5	JONES, GEO. & SONS	STOKE
September 14, 1875	9	294514	MINTON HOLLINS & CO.	STOKE
September 18, 1875	2	294571-2	JONES, GEO. & SONS	STOKE
September 21, 1875	1	294595	COCHRAN, R. & CO.	GLASGOW
September 25, 1875	3	294662	GROVE, F. W. & STARK, J.	LONGTON
September 28, 1875	6	294768-9	BROWN, T.C.-WESTHEAD, MOORE & CO.	HANLEY
September 30, 1875	4	294825-7	EDWARDS, JOHN	FENTON
October 02, 1875	6	294906	WEDGWOOD, JOSIAH & SONS	ETRURIA
October 11, 1875	4	295001	POWELL & BISHOP	HANLEY
October 11, 1875	10	295014-5	BROWNHILLS POTTERY CO. (THE)	TUNSTALL
October 16, 1875	8	295131	BURGESS, LEIGH & CO.	BURSLEM
October 28, 1875	3	295443	MINTON HOLLINS & CO.	STOKE
November 05, 1875	3	295551-3	JONES, GEO. & SONS	STOKE
November 08, 1875	4	295792-8	MINTON HOLLINS & CO.	STOKE
November 08, 1875	8	295803	COPELAND, W. T. & SONS	STOKE
November 12, 1875	1	295908	JONES, GEO. & SONS	STOKE
November 12, 1875	2	295909	BURGESS, LEIGH & CO.	BURSLEM
December 01, 1875	2	296475	BROWNFIELD, WM. & SON	COBRIDGE
December 01, 1875	9	296508	GELSON BROS.	HANLEY
December 03, 1875	4	296513	JONES, GEO. & SONS	STOKE
December 06, 1875	8	296644	MEIR, JOHN & SON	TUNSTALL
December 10, 1875	3	296770	MINTONS	STOKE
December 11, 1875	5	296813	GROVE, F. W. & STARK, J.	LONGTON
December 13, 1875	8	296834-49	MINTON HOLLINS & CO.	STOKE
December 15, 1875	2	296939-40	MINTONS CHINA WORKS	STOKE
December 15, 1875	3	296941-5	MINTONS	STOKE
December 24, 1875	6	297221	BATES, WALKER & CO.	BURSLEM
December 29, 1875	5	297245	EDGE, MALKIN & CO.	BURSLEM
December 29, 1875	6	297246-7	BROWN, T.C.-WESTHEAD, MOORE & CO.	HANLEY
December 30, 1875	2	297250	MINTONS	STOKE
December 30, 1875	8	297276	MINTON HOLLINS & CO.	STOKE
January 04, 1876	4	297342	MINTONS	STOKE
January 22, 1876	6	297809-11	JONES, GEO. & SONS	STOKE
January 24, 1876	1	297817	MINTONS	STOKE
January 24, 1876	6	297863-4	BATES, WALKER & CO.	BURSLEM
January 26, 1876	2	297977	EDE, MALKIN & CO.	BURSLEM
January 26, 1876	3	297978	POWELL & BISHOP	HANLEY
January 28, 1876	8	298018	EDWARDS, JAMES & SON	BURSLEM
January 29, 1876	3	298027-9	BROWNFIELD, WM. & SON	COBRIDGE
February 01, 1876	2	298049	BROWNFIELD, WM. & SON	COBRIDGE
February 02, 1876	7	298063	WEDGWOOD, JOSIAH & SONS	ETRURIA
February 02, 1876	12	298069	RIDGWAY, SPARKS & RIDGWAY	HANLEY
February 03, 1876	5	298077	POWELL & BISHOP	HANLEY
February 04, 1876	6	298103	MINTONS	STOKE
February 08, 1876	9	298235	BATES, WALKER & CO.	BURSLEM
February 19, 1876	5	298458	JONES, GEO. & SONS	STOKE
February 22, 1876	3	298480-3	MINTON HOLLINS & CO.	STOKE
February 29, 1876	9	298693	DIMMOCK, J. & CO.	HANLEY
March 02, 1876	8	298821	GELSON, T. & CO.	HANLEY
March 02, 1876	11	298832	BROWNHILLS POTTERY CO. (THE)	TUNSTALL
March 10, 1876	8	299076-8	MINTON HOLLINS & CO.	STOKE
March 14, 1876	5	299177	BROWN, T.C.-WESTHEAD, MOORE & CO.	HANLEY
March 17, 1876	5	299236	MINTONS	STOKE
March 24, 1876	7	299380	BATES, WALKER & CO.	BURSLEM
March 30, 1876	4	299497-9	JONES, GEO. & SONS	STOKE
April 08, 1876	6	299773	BATES, WALKER & CO.	BURSLEM
April 11, 1876	4	299819	GELSON, THOS. & CO.	HANLEY
April 12, 1876	4	299830	POWELL & BISHOP	HANLEY
April 12, 1876	11	299852	DIMMOCK, J. & CO.	HANLEY
April 21, 1876	7	300020	MINTON HOLLINS & CO.	STOKE
April 21, 1876	10	300037-8	FURNIVAL & SON	COBRIDGE
April 27, 1876	3	300260	MINTONS	STOKE
May 08, 1876	7	300421-3	BROWN, T.C.-WESTHEAD, MOORE & CO.	HANLEY
May 10, 1876	3	300463	JONES, GEO. & SONS	STOKE
May 11, 1876	9	300491	PRATT, F. & R. & CO.	FENTON
May 16, 1876	7	300603-4	MINTONS	STOKE
May 22, 1876	4	300683-5	WEDGWOOD, JOSIAH & SONS	ETRURIA
May 24, 1876	3	300746	MINTONS	STOKE
May 29, 1876	8	300809-10	JONES, GEO. & SONS	STOKE
June 03, 1876	2	301030	MINTONS	STOKE
June 07, 1876	1	301087	GELSON, THOS. & CO.	HANLEY
June 08, 1876	4	301099	MINTONS	STOKE
June 09, 1876	6	301164	COPELAND, W. T. & SONS	STOKE
June 15, 1876	1	301254	MEIR, HENRY & SON	TUNSTALL
June 15, 1876	9	301267-9	MINTON HOLLINS & CO.	STOKE
June 19, 1876	2	301302	WEDGWOOD, JOSIAH & SONS	ETRURIA
June 21, 1876	4	301330	MINTONS	STOKE
June 22, 1876	4	301341	GELSON, THOS. & CO.	HANLEY
June 23, 1876	5	301402	MINTONS	STOKE
June 26, 1876	6	301443-4	MINTON HOLLINS & CO.	STOKE
July 01, 1876	4	301591	TAMS, JOHN	LONGTON
July 01, 1876	3	301598-90	MINTONS	STOKE
July 03, 1876	2	301596	FORD & CHALLINOR	TUNSTALL
July 05, 1876	1	301619	TILL, THOS. & SONS	BURSLEM
July 05, 1876	7	301641	COPELAND, W. T. & SONS	STOKE
July 10, 1876	3	301877	GELSON, THOS. & CO.	HANLEY
July 26, 1876	3	302125	JONES, GEO. & SONS	STOKE
July 28, 1876	10	302178	GELSON, THOS. & CO.	HANLEY
July 28, 1876	11	302179	POWELL & BISHOP	HANLEY
August 25, 1876	8	302901	PRATT, F. & R. & CO.	FENTON
September 05, 1876	5	303289-90	BATES, WALKER & CO.	BURSLEM
September 06, 1876	9	303308	PINDER & BOURNE & CO.	BURSLEM
September 06, 1876	10	303309	BROWNFIELD, WM. & SONS	COBRIDGE
September 09, 1876	9	303456-7	BROWN, T.C.-WESTHEAD, MOORE & CO.	HANLEY
September 12, 1876	6	303522-3	JONES, GEO. & SONS	STOKE
September 18, 1876	10	303677	ASHWORTH, G. L. & BROS.	HANLEY
September 20, 1876	3	303731-2	HOLLINSHEAD & KIRKHAM	BURSLEM
September 22, 1876	3	303757	POWELL & BISHOP	HANLEY
September 26, 1876	5	303853	HOPE & CARTER	BURSLEM
September 26, 1876	10	303918	BROWN, T.C.-WESTHEAD, MOORE & CO.	HANLEY
September 28, 1876	10	303942	HOPE & CARTER	BURSLEM
October 07, 1876	3	304129-31	BROWNFIELD, WM. & SONS	COBRIDGE
October 07, 1876	4	304132-3	WEDGWOOD, JOSIAH & SONS	ETRURIA
October 07, 1876	6	304144-5	ADAMS, WM.	TUNSTALL
October 09, 1876	1	304149-50	JONES, GEO. & SONS	STOKE
October 17, 1876	4	304376	BROWN, T.C.-WESTHEAD, MOORE & CO.	HANLEY
October 17, 1876	9	304383	WARDLE & CO.	HANLEY
October 19, 1876	3	304428	BURGESS, LEIGH & CO.	BURSLEM
October 20, 1876	2	304454-66	MINTONS	STOKE
October 21, 1876	3	304473	EDGE, MALKIN & CO.	BURSLEM
October 23, 1876	2	304489	MINTONS	STOKE
October 31, 1876	2	304910-4	BROWNFIELD, WM. & SONS	COBRIDGE
November 08, 1876	3	305080	JONES, GEO. & SONS	STOKE
November 08, 1876	9	305090	BROWNFIELD, WM. & SONS	COBRIDGE
November 09, 1876	10	305150	BELFIELD & CO.	PRESTONPANS
November 13, 1876	3	305181	MINTONS	STOKE
November 14, 1876	2	305189	WEDGWOOD, JOSIAH & SONS	ETRURIA
November 14, 1876	8	305195	CLEMENTSON BROS.	HANLEY
November 18, 1876	3	305233	MINTON HOLLINS & CO.	STOKE
November 18, 1876	7	305264	MINTON HOLLINS & CO.	STOKE
November 23, 1876	5	305312	ADAMS, WM.	TUNSTALL
November 24, 1876	15	305461-2	FURNIVAL, THOS. & SONS	COBRIDGE
November 29, 1876	11	305568	FURNIVAL, THOS. & SONS	COBRIDGE
December 05, 1876	2	305684	WEDGWOOD & CO.	TUNSTALL
December 11, 1876	2	305829	TAMS, JOHN	LONGTON
December 14, 1876	1	305934	ADAMS, HARVEY & CO.	LONGTON
December 14, 1876	11	305973	DIMMOCK, J. & CO.	HANLEY
December 18, 1876	9	306100	BEECH, JAMES	LONGTON
December 21, 1876	2	306202	GROVE, F. W. & STARK, J.	LONGTON
December 28, 1876	6	306367	ADAMS, HARVEY & CO.	LONGTON
January 20, 1877	2	307028	GROVE, F. W. & STARK, J.	LONGTON
January 24, 1877	10	307213	BROWNFIELD, WM. & SONS	COBRIDGE
January 25, 1877	6	307236	WOOD & CO.	BURSLEM
January 25, 1877	7	307237-9	JONES, GEO. & SONS	STOKE
January 26, 1877	3	307258	MINTONS	STOKE
January 26, 1877	4	307259	POWELL & BISHOP	HANLEY
February 01, 1877	6	307432	EDWARDS, JAMES & SON	BURSLEM
February 03, 1877	4	307506-7	MINTON HOLLINS & CO.	STOKE
February 07, 1877	3	307551	HOLLAND & GREEN	LONGTON
February 07, 1877	7	307570-2	BROWNFIELD, WM. & SONS	COBRIDGE
February 09, 1877	7	307603	ROBINSON & CO.	LONGTON
February 09, 1877	11	307613	BROWN, T.C.-WESTHEAD, MOORE & CO.	HANLEY
February 12, 1877	3	307646	BEECH, JAMES	LONGTON

Date	Parcel No.	Reg No.	Potter	Location
February 15, 1877	10	307794	MINTON HOLLINS & CO.	STOKE
February 19, 1877	2	307877	BROWNFIELD, WM. & SONS	COBRIDGE
February 21, 1877	6	307906	MINTONS	STOKE
February 21, 1877	9	307909	COPELAND, W. T. & SONS	STOKE
February 24, 1877	3	307983	HUGHES, THOS.	BURSLEM
February 27, 1877	2	308010	MINTONS	STOKE
March 01, 1877	4	308116-21	HALLAM, JOHNSON & CO.	LONGTON
March 08, 1877	14	308329	COPELAND, W. T. & SONS	STOKE
March 10, 1877	7	308357	JONES, GEO. & SONS	STOKE
March 20, 1877	3	308650-2	CLEMENTSON BROS.	HANLEY
March 20, 1877	8	308662	DIMMOCK, J. & CO.	HANLEY
March 24, 1877	1	308781-2	POWELL & BISHOP	HANLEY
March 31, 1877	7	308916	BODLEY, E. F. & CO.	BURSLEM
April 03, 1877	1	308918	POWELL & BISHOP	HANLEY
April 05, 1877	2	308934	FORD, CHALLINOR & CO.	TUNSTALL
April 12, 1877	11	309233	DIMMOCK, J. & CO.	HANLEY
April 23, 1877	4	309617	TAMS, JOHN	LONGTON
May 02, 1877	2	309818-21	JONES, GEO. & SONS	STOKE
May 04, 1877	13	309917	OLD HALL EARTHENWARE CO. LTD., THE	HANLEY
May 05, 1877	4	309922	WEDGWOOD, JOSIAH & SONS	ETRURIA
May 12, 1877	7	310034	FURNIVAL, THOS. & SONS	COBRIDGE
May 16, 1877	5	310175	BROWNFIELD, WM. & SONS	COBRIDGE
May 18, 1877	6	310267	WEDGWOOD, JOSIAH & SONS	ETRURIA
May 22, 1877	5	310359-61	BROWNFIELD, WM. & SONS	COBRIDGE
May 24, 1877	8	310448	BROWN, T.C.-WESTHEAD, MOORE & CO.	HANLEY
May 30, 1877	13	310556	FURNIVAL, T. & SONS	COBRIDGE
June 08, 1877	7	310761-4	MINTON HOLLINS & CO.	STOKE
June 09, 1877	3	310775-6	BAKER & CO.	FENTON
June 13, 1877	2	310909	BAKER & CO.	FENTON
June 15, 1877	7	310972	RIDGWAY, SPARKS & RIDGWAY	HANLEY
June 19, 1877	4	311031	FORD & CHALLINOR	TUNSTALL
June 22, 1877	3	311141	WALKER & CARTER	STOKE
June 22, 1877	14	311187	BODLEY, E. F. & CO.	BURSLEM
June 26, 1877	11	311366	FURNIVAL, T. & SONS	COBRIDGE
June 28, 1877	9	311423	FURNIVAL, T. & SONS	COBRIDGE
July 02, 1877	3	311523	COPELAND, W. T. & SONS	STOKE
July 06, 1877	2	311626	MINTONS	STOKE
July 09, 1877	2	311711	MINTON HOLLINS & CO.	STOKE
July 14, 1877	2	311883-4	TAMS, JOHN	LONGTON
July 17, 1877	9	312019-21	EDWARDS, JAMES & SON	BURSLEM
July 23, 1877	2	312125	EDWARDS, JON	FENTON
July 25, 1877	5	312187	FORD, CHALLINOR & CO.	TUNSTALL
July 26, 1877	6	312311-4	MINTON HOLLINS & CO.	STOKE
July 31, 1877	2	312422	MINTON HOLLINS & CO.	STOKE
August 17, 1877	11	313080	RIDGWAY, SPARKS & RIDGWAY	HANLEY
August 18, 1877	6	313099-101	MINTON HOLLINS & CO.	STOKE
August 18, 1877	7	313102	FURNIVAL & SON	COBRIDGE
August 25, 1877	2	313324	WOOD, WM. & CO.	BURSLEM
August 25, 1877	3	313325-9	MINTON HOLLINS & CO.	STOKE
August 28, 1877	9	313381	BROWN, T.C.-WESTHEAD, MOORE & CO.	HANLEY
September 11, 1877	3	314046	TURNER, G. W. & SONS	TUNSTALL
September 19, 1877	5	314292	MINTON HOLLINS & CO.	STOKE
September 20, 1877	3	314385	WEDGWOOD, JOSIAH & SONS	ETRURIA
September 22, 1877	7	314470-1	MINTONS	STOKE
September 22, 1877	13	314480	MINTON HOLLINS & CO.	STOKE
September 25, 1877	5	314548	MINTONS	STOKE
October 02, 1877	7	314890	BATES, WALKER & CO.	BURSLEM
October 10, 1877	3	315102	EDWARDS, JOHN	FENTON
October 10, 1877	5	315104-5	BROWNFIELD, WM. & SONS	COBRIDGE
October 15, 1877	2	315271-2	JONES, GEO. & SONS	STOKE
October 16, 1877	6	315400-1	POWELL & BISHOP	HANLEY
October 19, 1877	8	315473	MINTON HOLLINS & CO.	STOKE
October 19, 1877	13	315479	BROWN, T.C.-WESTHEAD, MOORE & CO.	HANLEY
October 24, 1877	10	315565	GROVE, F. W. & STARK, J.	LONGTON
October 24, 1877	14	315574	PRATT, F. & R. & CO.	FENTON
October 30, 1877	7	315684	WEDGWOOD & CO.	TUNSTALL
October 31, 1877	6	315765	JONES, GEO. & SONS	STOKE
November 05, 1877	4	315918	POWELL & BISHOP	HANLEY
November 06, 1877	11	315954-6	BROWNFIELD, WM. & SONS	COBRIDGE
November 07, 1877	2	316090	MINTONS	STOKE
November 07, 1877	10	316101	PINDER, BOURNE & CO.	BURSLEM
November 15, 1877	12	316309	BROWN, T.C.-WESTHEAD, MOORE & CO.	HANLEY
November 20, 1877	9	316502	EDWARDS, JAMES & SONS	BURSLEM
November 21, 1877	8	316526	DAVENPORTS, & CO.	LONGPORT
November 22, 1877	1	316542-3	OLD HALL EARTHENWARE CO. LTD., THE	HANLEY
November 22, 1877	13	316560	HANCOCK, B. & S.	STOKE
November 24, 1877	7	316605	DIMMOCK, J. & CO.	HANLEY
December 06, 1877	4	316863	MINTONS	STOKE
December 14, 1877	1	317112	DIMMOCK, J. & CO.	HANLEY
December 21, 1877	6	317404	MINTONS	STOKE
December 21, 1877	10	317410	FURNIVAL, T. & SONS	COBRIDGE
December 22, 1877	5	317427-8	BROWNFIELD, WM. & SONS	COBRIDGE
December 29, 1877	6	317494	BROWN, T.C.-WESTHEAD, MOORE & CO.	HANLEY
January 03, 1878	4	317537-9	MINTON HOLLINS & CO.	STOKE
January 09, 1878	4	317692-4	BROWNHILLS POTTERYCO. (THE)	TUNSTALL
January 14, 1878	1	317756	MADDOCK, J. & SONS	BURLSEM
January 14, 1878	3	317758	ADAMS, WM.	TUNSTALL
January 14, 1878	6	317763	MINTON HOLLINS & CO.	STOKE
January 15, 1878	5	317780	WEDGWOOD, JOSIAH & SONS	ETRURIA
January 22, 1878	6	317940	DIMMOCK, J. & CO.	HANLEY
January 24, 1878	6	318041	COPELAND, W. T. & SONS	STOKE
January 25, 1878	9	318107-8	BROWNFIELD, WM. & SONS	COBRIDGE
January 28, 1878	11	318141	BROWN, T.C.-WESTHEAD, MOORE & CO.	HANLEY
January 30, 1878	3	318158-9	JONES, GEO.	STOKE
January 30, 1878	15	318189-90	BROWNHILLS POTTERY CO. (THE)	TUNSTALL
January 31, 1878	1	318210	HANCOCK, B. & S.	STOKE
February 01, 1878	4	318239	JONES, GEO. & SONS	STOKE
February 01, 1878	11	318265-6	MINTON HOLLINS & CO.	STOKE
February 09, 1878	6	318469	DIMMOCK, J. & CO.	HANLEY
February 11, 1878	5	318543-4	BROWN, T.C.-WESTHEAD, MOORE & CO.	HANLEY
February 20, 1878	6	318800	MINTON HOLLINS & CO.	STOKE
February 28, 1878	3	319041	DUNN, BENNETT & CO.	HANLEY
March 05, 1878	2	319190	GROVE, F. W. & STARK, J.	LONGTON
March 06, 1878	5	319201	MINTON HOLLINS & CO.	STOKE
March 07, 1878	4	319219	EDWARDS, JOHN	FENTON
March 09, 1878	1	319278-9	BROWNHILLS POTTERY CO. (THE)	TUNSTALL
March 09, 1878	11	319296	POWELL & BISHOP	HANLEY
March 13, 1878	1	319370	MINTONS	STOKE
March 13, 1878	10	319394	COPELAND, W. T. & SONS	STOKE
March 25, 1878	9	319679	EMERY, F. J.	BURSLEM
March 27, 1878	6	319725-6	TURNER, G. W. & SONS	TUNSTALL
March 27, 1878	15	319867-72	MINTON HOLLINS & CO.	STOKE
April 02, 1878	6	320030	BELFIELD & CO.	PRESTONPANS
April 10, 1878	4	320281	MINTONS	STOKE
April 17, 1878	4	320482	MINTONS	STOKE
April 17, 1878	14	320568-9	RIDGWAY, SPARKS & RIDGWAY	HANLEY
April 20, 1878	2	320606	FURNIVAL, THOS. & SONS	COBRIDGE
April 24, 1878	2	320669	BROWNFIELD, WM. & SONS	COBRIDGE
April 30, 1878	7	320874-5	WEDGWOOD, JOSIAH & SONS	ETRURIA
May 03, 1878	2	321028	WEDGWOOD, JOSIAH & SONS	ETRURIA
May 08, 1878	9	321231-2	BATES & BENNETT	COBRIDGE
May 14, 1878	6	321361	ELSMORE, & SON	TUNSTALL
May 17, 1878	12	321575	DIMMOCK, J. & CO.	HANLEY
May 23, 1878	3	321704	WEDGWOOD, JOSIAH & SONS	ETRURIA
May 24, 1878	2	321726	WEDGWOOD, JOSIAH & SONS	ETRURIA
May 29, 1878	9	322039	MINTON HOLLINS & CO.	STOKE
June 04, 1878	9	322168	FURNIVAL, F. & SONS	COBRIDGE
June 05, 1878	14	322223-4	COPELAND, W. T. & SONS	STOKE
June 07, 1878	1	322309	JONES, GEO. & SONS	STOKE
June 08, 1878	8	322390	WOOD, WM. & CO.	BURSLEM
June 12, 1878	10	322471	ADAMS, HARVEY & CO.	LONGTON
June 13, 1878	2	322476	TAMS, JOHN	LONGTON
June 19, 1878	7	322597-8	BODLEY, E. F. & CO.	BURSLEM
June 27, 1878	7	322931-2	WEDGWOOD, JOSIAH & SONS	ETRURIA
June 29, 1878	1	322948	WOOD, SON & CO.	COBRIDGE
July 01, 1878	1	322971	BURGESS & LEIGH	BURSLEM
July 03, 1878	2	323132	MINTONS	STOKE
July 08, 1878	6	323396	WEDGWOOD, JOSIAH & SONS	ETRURIA
July 09, 1878	8	323434	MINTONS	STOKE
July 09, 1878	9	323435	WEDGWOOD, JOSIAH & SONS	ETRURIA
July 09, 1878	10	323436	DIMMOCK, J. & CO.	HANLEY
July 10, 1878	14	323508	BATES & BENNETT	COBRIDGE
July 12, 1878	4	323604	WEDGWOOD, JOSIAH & SONS	ETRURIA
July 12, 1878	13	323626	LEAR, SAMUEL	HANLEY
July 12, 1878	15	323628	BROWN, T.C.-WESTHEAD, MOORE & CO.	HANLEY
July 15, 1878	1	323650-1	PRATT & SIMPSON	FENTON
July 17, 1878	9	323774-5	ADAMS, WM.	TUNSTALL
July 20, 1878	6	323893	MEIR, JOHN & SON	TUNSTALL
July 26, 1878	3	324177	WEDGWOOD, JOSIAH & SONS	ETRURIA
July 30, 1878	2	324324	WEDGWOOD, JOSIAH & SONS	ETRURIA
July 30, 1878	6	324336	POWELL, BISHOP & STONIER	HANLEY
July 30, 1878	12	324347	CLARKE, E.	LONGPORT
July 31, 1878	8	324383	MINTONS	STOKE
July 31, 1878	13	324388	EDWARDS, JAMES & SON	BURSLEM
August 07, 1878	3	324730	HUGHES, THOS.	BURSLEM
August 23, 1878	7	325319	DIMMOCK, J. & CO.	HANLEY
September 09, 1878	5	325992-4	BROWNFIELD, WM. & SONS	COBRIDGE
September 10, 1878	2	326006	WEDGWOOD, JOSIAH & SONS	ETRURIA
September 13, 1878	5	326155	ASHWORTH, G. L. & BROS.	HANLEY
September 28, 1878	5	326970-1	MINTON HOLLINS & CO.	STOKE
September 30, 1878	1	327000	MINTONS	STOKE
October 02, 1878	2	327035	MINTONS	STOKE
October 03, 1878	8	327110	HUDDEN, J. T.	LONGTON
October 04, 1878	8	327227	PRATT, F. & R. & CO.	FENTON
October 08, 1878	7	327360	BATES, GILDEA & WALKER	BURSLEM
October 09, 1878	9	327392	WEDGWOOD, JOSIAH	ETRURIA

Date	Parcel No.	Reg No.	Potter	Location
October 11, 1878	8	327556	MINTON HOLLINS & CO.	STOKE
October 14, 1878	8	327625-6	COPELAND, W. T. & SONS	STOKE
October 23, 1878	1	328018	BROWNHILLS POTTERY CO. (THE)	TUNSTALL
October 23, 1878	11	328144-5	PINDER & BOURNE & CO.	BURSLEM
October 24, 1878	1	328146	FURNIVAL, T. & SONS	COBRIDGE
October 24, 1878	2	328147	DIMMOCK, J. & CO.	HANLEY
October 26, 1878	4	328320	BROWNFIELD, WM. & SONS	COBRIDGE
October 30, 1878	3	328436-7	MINTON HOLLINS & CO.	STOKE
October 30, 1878	5	328439-40	MINTONS	STOKE
November 04, 1878	1	328699	EDGE, MALKIN & CO.	BURSLEM
November 05, 1878	11	328774	BURGESS, H.	BURSLEM
November 06, 1878	3	328795	LEAR, SAMUEL	HANLEY
November 15, 1878	11	329147	PRATT, F. & R. & CO.	FENTON
November 16, 1878	5	329157	DIMMOCK, J. & CO.	HANLEY
November 23, 1878	2	329456	CHALLINOR, E. & C.	FENTON
November 26, 1878	14	329673	BOOTE, T. & R.	BURSLEM
November 27, 1878	9	329709	MACINTYRE, J. & CO.	BURSLEM
November 29, 1878	14	329782-3	CORN, W. & E.	BURSLEM
December 02, 1878	7	329901	BROWN, T.C.-WESTHEAD, MOORE & CO.	HANLEY
December 03, 1878	9	329922	MACINTYRE, J. & CO.	BURSLEM
December 04, 1878	2	329939	BROWNFIELD, WM. & SONS	COBRIDGE
December 06, 1878	3	330061	MINTONS	STOKE
December 07, 1878	2	330097	SHAW, A.	BURSLEM
December 19, 1878	8	330485	HUGHES, THOS.	BURSLEM
December 27, 1878	13	330677	BOOTE, T. & R.	BURSLEM
January 07, 1879	7	330920	COPELAND, W. T. & SONS	STOKE
January 08, 1879	11	330965-6	MINTON HOLLINS & CO.	STOKE
January 09, 1879	8	330997-8	BROWNFIELD, WM. & SONS	COBRIDGE
January 14, 1879	5	331152	NEW WHARF POTTERY CO., THE	BURSLEM
January 16, 1879	3	331228	HANCOCK, B. & S.	STOKE
January 16, 1879	13	331342	PRATT, F. & R. & CO.	FENTON
January 22, 1879	4	331458	DUNN, BENNETT & CO.	HANLEY
January 28, 1879	11	331597	COPELAND, W. T. & SONS	STOKE
January 29, 1879	2	331600	FURNIVAL, T. & SONS	COBRIDGE
February 01, 1879	13	331775	CLEMENTSON BROS.	HANLEY
February 03, 1879	1	331777	WEDGWOOD, JOSIAH & SONS	ETRURIA
February 05, 1879	7	331892-3	MINTONS	STOKE
February 08, 1879	1	332030	MINTONS	STOKE
February 14, 1879	4	332251	FURNIVAL, T. & SONS	COBRIDGE
February 24, 1879	3	332607-9	ADAMS, W. & T.	TUNSTALL
February 25, 1879	4	332642	MINTONS	STOKE
February 28, 1879	1	332823	CHETWYND, E.	STOKE
February 28, 1879	7	332831	CLEMENTSON BROS.	HANLEY
March 01, 1879	1	332837	FURNIVAL, T. & SONS	COBRIDGE
March 04, 1879	4	332938	GROVE, F. W. & STARK, J.	LONGTON
March 06, 1879	10	333047	POWELL, BISHOP & STONIER	HANLEY
March 12, 1879	4	333210	EDGE, MALKIN & CO.	BURSLEM
March 12, 1879	12	333235-6	COPELAND, W. T. & SONS	STOKE
March 13, 1879	1	333241-4	DAVENPORT, WM. & CO.	LONGPORT
March 13, 1879	14	333301	CLEMENTSON BROS.	HANLEY
March 14, 1879	9	333319	CLARKE, E.	LONGPORT
March 17, 1879	2	333368	POWELL, BISHOP & STONIER	HANLEY
March 18, 1879	1	333431	WEDGWOOD, JOSIAH & SONS	ETRURIA
March 19, 1879	2	333485	HAWTHORNE, J.	COBRIDGE
March 28, 1879	6	333801	CLEMENTSON BROS.	HANLEY
March 29, 1879	4	333813	BECK, BLAIR & CO.	LONGTON
April 03, 1879	9	334030	BROWN, T.C.-WESTHEAD, MOORE & CO.	HANLEY
April 04, 1879	12	334052-3	PINDER, BOURNE & CO.	BURSLEM
April 09, 1879	5	334137	ALCOCK, H. & CO.	COBRIDGE
April 10, 1879	12	334200	BROWN, T.C.-WESTHEAD, MOORE & CO.	HANLEY
April 15, 1879	6	334241-2	BROWN, T.C.-WESTHEAD, MOORE & CO.	HANLEY
April 23, 1879	8	334508	BROWN, T.C.-WESTHEAD, MOORE & CO.	HANLEY
April 24, 1879	3	334531	WEDGWOOD, JOSIAH & SONS	ETRURIA
May 05, 1879	1	334860-1	FURNIVAL, T. & SONS	COBRIDGE
May 05, 1879	6	334897	BATES, GILDEA & WALKER	BURSLEM
May 06, 1879	7	334923-5	BRIDGWOOD, SAMPSON & SON	LONGTON
May 13, 1879	4	335148-51	PINDER & BOURNE & CO.	BURSLEM
May 13, 1879	8	335167-8	CLEMENTSON BROS.	HANLEY
May 14, 1879	9	335182	BROWN, T.C.-WESTHEAD, MOORE & CO.	HANLEY
May 19, 1879	1	335308-9	BROWNFIELD, WM. & SONS	COBRIDGE
May 21, 1879	5	335496	ADAMS, HARVEY & CO.	LONGTON
May 23, 1879	2	335551-2	BRIDGWOOD, SAMPSON & SON	LONGTON
May 23, 1879	14	335608	ADAMS, HARVEY & CO.	LONGTON
May 29, 1879	2	335715	TAMS, JOHN	LONGTON
May 29, 1879	12	335739-40	PINDER, BOURNE & CO.	BURSLEM
May 30, 1879	10	335791	DIMMOCK, J. & CO.	HANLEY
May 31, 1879	4	335805	MINTON HOLLINS & CO.	STOKE
June 10, 1879	4	336030	FURNIVAL, T. & SONS	COBRIDGE
June 11, 1879	8	336075	TILL, THOS. & SONS	BURSLEM
June 13, 1879	13	336132	BROWN, T.C.-WESTHEAD, MOORE & CO.	HANLEY
June 18, 1879	4	336185	GROVE, F. W. & STARK, J.	LONGTON

Date	Parcel No.	Reg No.	Potter	Location
June 24, 1879	11	336415	WEDGWOOD, JOSIAH & SONS	ETRURIA
June 25, 1879	1	336417	CLEMENTSON BROS.	HANLEY
June 30, 1879	12	336586-7	BIRKS BROS. & SEDDON	COBRIDGE
July 02, 1879	2	336676	WEDGWOOD, JOSIAH & SONS	ETRURIA
July 07, 1879	2	336917	WILEMAN, J. F.	FENTON
July 08, 1879	1	336930	MINTONS	STOKE
July 08, 1879	16	336967-8	BROWN, T.C.-WESTHEAD, MOORE & CO.	HANLEY
July 09, 1879	12	337058	BROWN, T.C.-WESTHEAD, MOORE & CO.	HANLEY
July 16, 1879	14	337177	BROWN, T.C.-WESTHEAD, MOORE & CO.	HANLEY
July 25, 1879	4	337497	MINTONS	STOKE
July 26, 1879	6	337536	MINTON HOLLINS & CO.	STOKE
July 31, 1879	2	337660	MINTONS	STOKE
August 06, 1879	6	337958	WARDLE & CO.	HANLEY
August 13, 1879	2	338135	GROVE, F. W. & STARK, J.	LONGTON
August 27, 1879	13	338872	BATES, GILDEA & WALKER	BURSLEM
September 04, 1879	6	339193	BROWN, T.C.-WESTHEAD, MOORE & CO.	HANLEY
September 10, 1879	13	339373	BROWN, T.C.-WESTHEAD, MOORE & CO.	HANLEY
September 17, 1879	4	339685-6	BROWNFIELD, WM. & SONS	COBRIDGE
September 18, 1879	10	339979	BROWN, T.C.-WESTHEAD, MOORE & CO.	HANLEY
September 26, 1879	4	340431	HUDDEN, J. T.	LONGTON
September 29, 1879	3	340569	EDGE, MALKIN & CO.	BURSLEM
October 09, 1879	1	341137	BATES, GILDEA & WALKER	BURSLEM
October 10, 1879	2	341151	BROWN, T.C.-WESTHEAD, MOORE & CO.	HANLEY
October 15, 1879	1	341347	MINTONS	STOKE
October 16, 1879	16	341500	MINTON HOLLINS & CO.	STOKE
October 17, 1879	2	341502	ASHWORTH, G. L. & BROS.	HANLEY
October 18, 1879	3	341629	WEDGWOOD, JOSIAH & SONS	ETRURIA
October 27, 1879	9	341997	BODLEY, E. F. & CO.	BURSLEM
October 29, 1879	5	342098	MINTONS	STOKE
October 29, 1879	7	342100	CLEMENTSON BROS.	HANLEY
October 30, 1879	4	342158	MINTONS	STOKE
November 03, 1879	12	342396	MINTON HOLLINS & CO.	STOKE
November 06, 1879	2	342461	WEDGWOOD, JOSIAH & SONS	ETRURIA
November 15, 1879	16	342925-7	COPELAND, W. T. & SONS	STOKE
November 17, 1879	2	342929	POWELL, BISHOP & STONIER	HANLEY
November 19, 1879	5	343017	POWELL, BISHOP & STONIER	HANLEY
November 20, 1879	4	343070-1	ELSMORE, & SON	TUNSTALL
November 21, 1879	6	343148	MINTONS	STOKE
November 28, 1879	5	343530	BROWNFIELD, WM. & SONS	COBRIDGE
November 29, 1879	3	343585	MINTONS	STOKE
November 29, 1879	4	343586	BROWN, T.C.-WESTHEAD, MOORE & CO.	HANLEY
December 02, 1879	4	343652-3	BROWN, T.C.-WESTHEAD, MOORE & CO.	HANLEY
December 02, 1879	5	343654	ELSMORE, & SON	TUNSTALL
December 06, 1879	2	343815-6	BOOTE, T. & R.	BURSLEM
December 10, 1879	14	344077	CLEMENTSON BROS.	HANLEY
December 17, 1879	11	344387	RIDGWAYS	STOKE
December 19, 1879	1	344452	CLEMENTSON BROS.	HANLEY
December 20, 1879	5	344478	WEDGWOOD, JOSIAH & SONS	ETRURIA
December 22, 1879	2	344503	MINTONS	STOKE
January 07, 1880	4	344963	BOOTE, T. & R.	BURSLEM
January 07, 1880	8	344972	MINTON HOLLINS & CO.	STOKE
January 08, 1880	9	344997	OLD HALL EARTHENWARE CO. LTD., THE	HANLEY
January 13, 1880	1	345131	BROWN, T.C.-WESTHEAD, MOORE & CO.	HANLEY
January 21, 1880	7	345469-71	PINDER, BOURNE & CO.	BURSLEM
January 22, 1880	2	345481	MINTONS	STOKE
January 22, 1880	8	345493-4	MINTON HOLLINS & CO.	STOKE
January 23, 1880	5	345511	MINTONS	STOKE
January 26, 1880	11	345719	BROWNFIELD, WM. & SONS	COBRIDGE
January 27, 1880	13	345798	WARDLE & CO.	HANLEY
January 28, 1880	3	345801	BROWN, T.C.-WESTHEAD, MOORE & CO.	HANLEY
January 28, 1880	12	345833	POWELL, BISHOP & STONIER	HANLEY
February 03, 1880	11	345952	POWELL, BISHOP & STONIER	HANLEY
February 09, 1880	18	346202	WHITTINGHAM, FORD & RILEY	BURSLEM
February 10, 1880	4	346208-10	MINTONS	STOKE
February 12, 1880	4	346360	ADDERLY, W. A.	LONGTON
February 12, 1880	7	346363	BROWNFIELD, WM. & SONS	COBRIDGE
February 14, 1880	14	346467	BATES, GILDEA & WALKER	BURSLEM
February 24, 1880	2	346832	MINTONS	STOKE
February 25, 1880	18	346920	CLEMENTSON BROS.	HANLEY
February 26, 1880	6	346952-3	MINTON HOLLINS & CO.	STOKE
March 08, 1880	4	347344	FURNIVAL, T. & SONS	COBRIDGE
March 12, 1880	4	347476	ADDERLY, W. A.	LONGTON
March 16, 1880	3	347599	WILEMAN, J. F. & CO.	FENTON
March 16, 1880	12	347646-7	MACINTYRE, J. & CO.	BURSLEM
March 17, 1880	6	347660	WEDGWOOD, JOSIAH & SONS	ETRURIA
March 22, 1880	4	347838	POWELL, BISHOP & STONIER	HANLEY

Date	Parcel No.	Reg No.	Potter	Location
March 25, 1880	6	348018	MINTONS	STOKE
April 12, 1880	6	348606-8	BATES, GILDEA & WALKER	BURSLEM
April 15, 1880	11	348761	RIDGWAYS	STOKE
April 22, 1880	5	349027	GRINDLEY, W. H. & CO.	TUNSTALL
April 26, 1880	1	349221	FURNIVAL, T. & SONS	COBRIDGE
April 29, 1880	4	349340-1	MINTONS	STOKE
April 30, 1880	6	349380	FURNIVAL, T. & SONS	COBRIDGE
May 03, 1880	3	349438-43	BROWNFIELD, WM. & SONS	COBRIDGE
May 10, 1880	6	349693	POWELL, BISHOP & STONIER	HANLEY
May 13, 1880	8	349852-3	MINTONS	STOKE
May 13, 1880	15	349869	MINTON HOLLINS & CO.	STOKE
May 14, 1880	26	349939	BATES, GILDEA & WALKER	BURSLEM
May 25, 1880	4	350098	BROWNFIELD, WM. & SONS	COBRIDGE
May 26, 1880	6	350142	MINTONS	STOKE
June 01, 1880	4	350251	MINTONS	STOKE
June 07, 1880	6	350476	DIMMOCK, J. & CO.	HANLEY
June 08, 1880	1	350477	JONES, GEO. & SONS	STOKE
June 10, 1880	12	350613	DIMMOCK, J. & CO.	HANLEY
June 11, 1880	3	350616	WEDGWOOD, JOSIAH & SONS	ETRURIA
June 16, 1880	3	350972	WEDGWOOD & CO.	TUNSTALL
June 17, 1880	4	351025	LEAR, SAMUEL	HANLEY
June 17, 1880	15	351058	RIDGWAYS	STOKE
June 17, 1880	16	351059	MACINTYRE, J. & CO.	BURSLEM
June 17, 1880	21	351064	DIMMOCK, J. & CO.	HANLEY
June 19, 1880	11	351186	WEDGWOOD, JOSIAH & SONS	ETRURIA
June 22, 1880	1	351259	GRINDLEY, W. H. & CO.	TUNSTALL
July 07, 1880	5	351910	MINTONS	STOKE
July 07, 1880	15	351928	EMERY, F. J.	BURSLEM
July 12, 1880	4	352094	MINTONS	STOKE
July 13, 1880	12	352138	BARLOW, THOS.	LONGTON
July 15, 1880	3	352192	DUNN, BENNETT & CO.	HANLEY
July 15, 1880	4	352193	GROVE, F. W. & STARK, J.	LONGTON
July 28, 1880	2	352872	BROWNHILLS POTTERY CO. (THE)	TUNSTALL
July 31, 1880	8	353079	OLD HALL EARTHENWARE CO. LTD., THE	HANLEY
August 04, 1880	3	353108	PINDER, BOURNE & CO.	BURSLEM
August 11, 1880	14	353543	CLEMENTSON BROS.	HANLEY
August 14, 1880	12	353713-4	DAVENPORT, WM. & CO.	LONGPORT
August 18, 1880	3	353818	WEDGWOOD, JOSIAH & SONS	ETRURIA
August 21, 1880	10	354081	ADDERLY, W. A.	LONGTON
August 23, 1880	6	354093-4	BROWN, T.C.-WESTHEAD, MOORE & CO.	HANLEY
September 03, 1880	3	354639	BROWN, T.C.-WESTHEAD, MOORE & CO.	HANLEY
September 11, 1880	3	355091-100	BROWNFIELD, WM. & SONS	COBRIDGE
September 14, 1880	6	355169	MINTONS	STOKE
September 15, 1880	6	355231	ASHWORTH, G. L. & BROS.	HANLEY
September 15, 1880	12	355255-7	MINTON HOLLINS & CO.	STOKE
September 25, 1880	6	355651-4	MINTON HOLLINS & CO.	STOKE
September 27, 1880	5	355745-6	MARSHALL, JOHN & CO.	BO'NESS, SCOTLAND
September 29, 1880	3	355947-8	BROWNHILLS POTTERY CO. (THE)	TUNSTALL
October 06, 1880	4	356163	WEDGWOOD, JOSIAH & SONS	ETRURIA
October 12, 1880	4	356514	MINTONS	STOKE
October 13, 1880	5	356532	WEDGWOOD, JOSIAH & SONS	ETRURIA
October 20, 1880	10	356970	BURGESS & LEIGH	BURSLEM
October 22, 1880	4	357039	BODLEY, E. F. & SON	BURSLEM
October 26, 1880	13	357298-9	MINTON HOLLINS & CO.	STOKE
October 27, 1880	20	357429	TAMS, J.	LONGTON
October 27, 1880	21	357430	WOOLISCROFT, G. & SON	ETRURIA
November 02, 1880	2	357609	GRINDLEY, W. H. & CO.	TUNSTALL
November 04, 1880	4	357656-7	ADAMS, W. & T.	TUNSTALL
November 04, 1880	15	357724-5	MINTON HOLLINS & CO.	STOKE
November 09, 1880	4	357954	WEDGWOOD, JOSIAH & SONS	ETRURIA
November 18, 1880	14	358500	MINTONS	STOKE
November 24, 1880	4	358747	GROVE, F. W. & STARK, J.	LONGTON
November 24, 1880	5	358748	BATES, GILDEA & WALKER	BURSLEM
December 06, 1880	2	359292	POWELL, BISHOP & STONIER	HANLEY
December 07, 1880	10	359321-6	PINDER, BOURNE & CO.	BURSLEM
December 15, 1880	15	359668-71	BROWNFIELD, WM. & SONS	COBRIDGE
December 18, 1880	2	359784	BATES, GILDEA & WALKER	BURSLEM
December 24, 1880	8	359997	BROWN, T.C.-WESTHEAD, MOORE & CO.	HANLEY
December 29, 1880	7	360042-4	DOULTON & CO.	LAMBETH
December 31, 1880	1	360100	OLD HALL EARTHENWARE CO. LTD., THE	HANLEY
January 06, 1881	2	360331	HANCOCK, B. & S.	STOKE
January 20, 1881	3	360900	MINTONS	STOKE
January 21, 1881	11	360954	ADAMS, W. & T.	TUNSTALL
January 26, 1881	4	361116-7	MINTON HOLLINS & CO.	STOKE
February 08, 1881	5	361537	GROVE, F. W. & STARK, J.	LONGTON
February 08, 1881	6	361538-41	BROWNFIELD, WM. & SONS	COBRIDGE
February 11, 1881	10	361668	EMERY, F. J.	BURSLEM
February 15, 1881	6	361748	ADDERLY, W. A.	LONGTON
February 17, 1881	2	361813	MURRAY & CO.	GLASGOW
February 25, 1881	14	362166	MACINTYRE, J. & CO.	BURSLEM
February 28, 1881	3	361170	WOOLISCROFT, G. & SON	HANLEY
March 03, 1881	5	362423	DIMMOCK, J. & CO.	HANLEY
March 08, 1881	3	362548	GROVE, F. W. & STARK, J.	LONGTON
March 19, 1881	4	363026-7	MINTONS	STOKE
March 23, 1881	4	363157	MINTONS	STOKE
March 24, 1881	2	363206-7	PINDER, T. S.	BURSLEM
March 24, 1881	3	363208	ADDERLY, W. A.	LONGTON
March 31, 1881	2	363461	HUDDEN, J. T.	LONGTON
April 07, 1881	9	363732	OLD HALL EARTHENWARE CO. LTD., THE	HANLEY
April 08, 1881	3	363739	WEDGWOOD & CO.	TUNSTALL
April 12, 1881	4	363849-50	MINTONS	STOKE
April 14, 1881	10	363975	MINTONS	STOKE
April 16, 1881	17	364110	MARSHALL, J. & CO.	BO'NESS, SCOTLAND
April 19, 1881	5	364118	BOOTE, T. & R.	BURSLEM
April 23, 1881	7	364238	WILEMAN, J. F.	FENTON
April 28, 1881	12	364488	COPELAND, W. T. & SONS	STOKE
April 30, 1881	4	364529	WEDGWOOD, JOSIAH & SONS	ETRURIA
May 03, 1881	4	364604	WOOD, WM. & CO.	BURSLEM
May 04, 1881	3	364625-7	BROWNFIELD, WM. & SONS	COBRIDGE
May 05, 1881	2	364648	ADAMS, W. & T.	TUNSTALL
May 11, 1881	3	364941	TAMS, J.	LONGTON
May 13, 1881	2	365005	MINTONS	STOKE
May 16, 1881	2	365066	WEDGWOOD, JOSIAH & SONS	ETRURIA
May 20, 1881	11	365206	ADDERLY, W. A.	LONGTON
May 21, 1881	3	365211	POWELL, BISHOP & STONIER	HANLEY
May 24, 1881	5	365391	ASHWORTH, G. L. & BROS.	HANLEY
May 24, 1881	6	365392-3	MINTONS	STOKE
May 24, 1881	7	365394	EMERY, F. J.	BURSLEM
May 25, 1881	3	365424	POWELL, BISHOP & STONIER	HANLEY
May 25, 1881	10	365445-6	WEDGWOOD, JOSIAH & SONS	ETRURIA
May 26, 1881	7	365461	WOOLISCROFT, G. & SON	HANLEY
May 30, 1881	1	365539	FURNIVAL, T. & SONS	COBRIDGE
June 01, 1881	3	365730	MINTONS	STOKE
June 04, 1881	3	365852	FURNIVAL, T. & SONS	COBRIDGE
June 07, 1881	3	365875	BODLEY, E. F. & SON	BURSLEM
June 13, 1881	1	366015	LEAR, S.	HANLEY
June 21, 1881	13	366220-2	BIRKS BROS. & SEDDON	COBRIDGE
June 21, 1881	20	366246	GILDEA & WALKER	BURSLEM
July 02, 1881	5	366643	FURNIVAL, T. & SONS	COBRIDGE
July 06, 1881	7	366809	WEDGWOOD, JOSIAH & SONS	ETRURIA
July 09, 1881	10	366922-3	WARDLE & CO.	HANLEY
July 14, 1881	6	367133-4	BROWN, T.C.-WESTHEAD, MOORE & CO.	HANLEY
July 25, 1881	2	367418	DAVIS, J. H.	HANLEY
July 28, 1881	14	367538	RIDGWAYS	STOKE
July 30, 1881	3	367549	BRIDGWOOD, SAMPSON & SON	LONGTON
July 30, 1881	5	367551	MINTONS	STOKE
July 30, 1881	15	367590	COPELAND, W. T. & SONS	STOKE
August 05, 1881	12	367892-3	PINDER, BOURNE & CO.	BURSLEM
August 10, 1881	13	368044	OLD HALL EARTHENWARE CO. LTD., THE	HANLEY
August 23, 1881	3	368802	GROVE, F. W. & STARK, J.	LONGTON
August 24, 1881	11	368942	BOOTE, J. & R.	BURSLEM
August 27, 1881	3	369202	LEAR, S.	HANELY
August 27, 1881	9	369215-8	GILDEA & WALKER	BURSLEM
August 29, 1881	7	369248	ADAMS, W. & T.	TUNSTALL
September 16, 1881	3	370636	JONES, GEO. & CO.	STOKE
September 23, 1881	21	370470-2	MINTON HOLLINS & CO.	STOKE
September 27, 1881	9	370611	PINDER, BOURNE & CO.	BURSLEM
September 28, 1881	13	370633	GILDEA & WALKER	BURSLEM
September 29, 1881	3	370636	JONES, GEO. & SONS	STOKE
September 30, 1881	3	370702-3	DAVENPORTS LTD.	LONGPORT
September 30, 1881	15	370725-8	MINTONS	STOKE
October 04, 1881	6	370885	BROWNFIELD, WM. & SONS	COBRIDGE
October 07, 1881	27	371098	MINTONS	STOKE
October 12, 1881	14	371330-1	MINTONS	STOKE
October 13, 1881	5	371339	BOOTE, T. & R.	BURSLEM
October 22, 1881	1	371959	MINTONS	STOKE
October 26, 1881	8	372138	MINTONS	STOKE
October 26, 1881	16	372172	BROWN, T.C.-WESTHEAD, MOORE & CO.	HANLEY
October 29, 1881	3	372347	BOOTE, T. & R.	BURSLEM
October 29, 1881	4	372348	BROWNFIELD, WM. & SONS	COBRIDGE
October 29, 1881	11	372376	WARDLE & CO.	HANLEY
October 29, 1881	14	372379	MINTON HOLLINS & CO.	STOKE
November 02, 1881	1	372489-90	BROWN, T.C.-WESTHEAD, MOORE & CO.	HANLEY
November 08, 1881	1	372918	BOOTE, T. & R.	BURSLEM
November 09, 1881	6	372979	GROVE, F. W. & STARK, J.	LONGTON
November 19, 1881	3	373541	BRIDGWOOD, SAMPSON & SON	LONGTON
November 22, 1881	9	373615	TAMS, J.	LONGTON
December 10, 1881	7	374579	BROWN, T.C.-WESTHEAD, MOORE & CO.	HANLEY
December 16, 1881	3	374782	MINTONS	STOKE
December 24, 1881	5	375054	BROADHURST, J.	FENTON
January 04, 1882	2	375426-7	COPELAND, W. T. & SONS	STOKE
January 04, 1882	9	375444	PRATT, F. & R. & CO.	FENTON

Date	Parcel No.	Reg No.	Potter	Location
January 07, 1882	2	375494	GRINDLEY, W. H. & CO.	TUNSTALL
January 07, 1882	11	375580	RIDGWAYS	STOKE
January 10, 1882	5	375599	LEAR, S.	HANLEY
January 18, 1882	10	376032	ROBINSON & SON	LONGTON
January 26, 1882	5	376425	HUDDEN, J. T.	LONGTON
January 30, 1882	2	376528	HOLLINSHEAD & KIRKHAM	TUNSTALL
January 30, 1882	3	376529	GROVE, F. W. & STARK, J.	LONGTON
February 01, 1882	1	376580	EDGE, MALKIN & CO.	BURSLEM
February 03, 1882	4	376672-3	BROWN, T.C.-WESTHEAD, MOORE & CO.	HANLEY
February 04, 1882	10	376754	MINTON HOLLINS & CO.	STOKE
February 08, 1882	7	376839	WARDLE & CO.	HANLEY
February 15, 1882	4	377048	GROVE, F. W. & STARK, J.	LONGTON
February 16, 1882	6	377135-7	MINTONS	STOKE
February 18, 1882	5	377273	WILEMAN, J. F. & CO.	FENTON
February 23, 1882	17	377488-9	MINTON HOLLINS & CO.	STOKE
March 01, 1882	12	377780	MINTON HOLLINS & CO.	STOKE
March 07, 1882	7	378051	MINTON HOLLINS & CO.	STOKE
March 13, 1882	3	378252	HUDDEN, J. T.	LONGTON
March 15, 1882	3	378337	POWELL, BISHOP & STONIER	HANLEY
March 15, 1882	4	378338	MURRAY & CO.	GLASGOW
March 20, 1882	5	378643	ADDERLY, W. A.	LONGTON
March 23, 1882	2	378739	ADAMS, W. & T.	TUNSTALL
April 04, 1882	2	379212-3	BROWNFIELD, WM. & SONS	COBRIDGE
April 11, 1882	6	379434	JONES, GEO. & SONS	STOKE
April 11, 1882	7	379435-6	MINTON HOLLINS & CO.	STOKE
April 21, 1882	7	379767	BRIDGWOOD, SAMPSON & SON	LONGTON
April 27, 1882	14	380072	NEW WHARF POTTERY CO., THE	BURSLEM
May 02, 1882	5	380194	ASHWORTH, G. L. & BROS.	HANLEY
May 06, 1882	5	380418	POWELL, BISHOP & STONIER	HANLEY
May 08, 1882	18	380549-50	DAVENPORTS LTD.	LONGPORT
May 09, 1882	3	380553-4	ALCOCK, H. & CO.	COBRIDGE
May 09, 1882	7	380558	BROWNFIELD, WM. & SONS	COBRIDGE
May 09, 1882	11	380564	MINTON HOLLINS & CO.	STOKE
May 10, 1882	4	380571-2	EDWARDS, JOHN	FENTON
May 13, 1882	6	380789	JONES, GEO. & SONS	STOKE
May 24, 1882	4	381376	MINTON HOLLINS & CO.	STOKE
May 24, 1882	21	381434	DOULTON & CO.	BURSLEM
May 25, 1882	11	381480	ADDERLY, W. A.	LONGTON
May 27, 1882	3	381568	LEAR, SAMUEL	HANLEY
May 30, 1882	5	381611	GRINDLEY, W. H. & CO.	TUNSTALL
June 05, 1882	6	381805	MINTONS	STOKE
June 09, 1882	4	381965-6	ADDERLY, W. A.	LONGTON
June 13, 1882	11	382126	SHAW, A. & SON	BURSLEM
June 13, 1882	14	382130-1	WARDLE & CO.	HANLEY
June 21, 1882	5	382407-8	BRIDGWOOD, SAMPSON & SON	LONGTON
June 21, 1882	11	382472	OLD HALL EARTHENWARE CO. LTD., THE	HANLEY
June 23, 1882	1	382593-4	WEDGWOOD, JOSIAH & SONS	ETRURIA
June 23, 1882	5	382598	BURGESS & LEIGH	BURSLEM
July 03, 1882	2	382842	MINTONS	STOKE
July 06, 1882	4	383020-1	BROWNFIELD, WM. & SONS	COBRIDGE
July 14, 1882	3	383436-7	JONES, GEO. & SONS	STOKE
July 14, 1882	10	383468	WARDLE & CO.	HANLEY
July 17, 1882	8	383549	WOOD & SON	BURSLEM
July 19, 1882	7	383641	WARDLE & CO.	HANLEY
July 20, 1882	1	383694-6	EDWARDS, JOHN	FENTON
July 22, 1882	8	383802	JONES, GEO. & SONS	STOKE
July 25, 1882	9	383869-71	BROWNHILLS POTTERY CO. (THE)	TUNSTALL
July 28, 1882	3	384078	HAWLEY & CO.	LONGTON
July 31, 1882	2	384160-1	BRIDGWOOD, SAMPSON & SON	LONGTON
July 31, 1882	9	384171-2	MINTONS	STOKE
August 05, 1882	4	384353-4	BROWNFIELD, WM. & SONS	COBRIDGE
August 21, 1882	2	385106	TAMS, JOHN	LONGTON
August 25, 1882	2	385129	MINTONS	STOKE
August 26, 1882	4	385490	WOOD, WM. & CO.	BURSLEM
August 28, 1882	2	385527	BELFIELD & CO.	PRESTONPANS
August 28, 1882	9	385544	MINTONS	STOKE
August 29, 1882	12	385623	BROWNFIELD, WM. & SONS	COBRIDGE
September 06, 1882	2	385954	HAWLEY & CO.	LONGTON
September 08, 1882	5	386085-6	MINTONS	STOKE
September 19, 1882	2	386542	GRINDLEY, W. H. & CO.	TUNSTALL
September 28, 1882	4	387147-8	BROWN, T.C.-WESTHEAD, MOORE & CO.	HANLEY
September 28, 1882	22	387229	BRIDGETT & BATES	LONGTON
September 29, 1882	2	387231-2	BROWNHILLS POTTERY CO. (THE)	TUNSTALL
October 06, 1882	2	387598-603	MINTONS	STOKE
October 09, 1882	3	387771	COPELAND, W. T. & SONS	STOKE
October 11, 1882	3	387958-60	BRIDGWOOD, SAMPSON & SON	LONGTON
October 11, 1882	4	387961	WOOD & SON	BURSLEM
October 12, 1882	17	388200	FURNIVAL, T. & SONS	COBRIDGE
October 16, 1882	4	388296	WOOD & SON	BURSLEM
November 08, 1882	2	389554	MINTONS	STOKE
November 10, 1882	10	389793	RIDGWAYS (Made by Dudson)	STOKE
November 10, 1882	12	389795-7	PRATT & SIMPSON	FENTON
November 11, 1882	2	389801	POWELL, BISHOP & STONIER	HANLEY
November 13, 1882	1	389893	EDGE, MALKIN & CO.	BURSLEM
November 13, 1882	2	389894	BRIDGWOOD, SAMPSON & SON	LONGTON
November 21, 1882	8	390264	GILDEA & WALKER	BURSLEM
November 24, 1882	19	390588	MINTON HOLLINS & CO.	STOKE
November 27, 1882	3	390617	ALCOCK, H. & CO.	COBRIDGE
November 27, 1882	5	390619	WILEMAN, J. F. & CO.	FENTON
December 02, 1882	8	390976	MINTON HOLLINS & CO.	STOKE
December 06, 1882	2	391068-9	BROWN, T.C.-WESTHEAD, MOORE & CO.	HANLEY
December 13, 1882	4	391361-2	MINTONS	STOKE
December 13, 1882	5	391363-4	WEDGWOOD, JOSIAH	ETRURIA
December 14, 1882	6	391409	LEAR, S.	HANLEY
December 15, 1882	3	391460	OLD HALL EARTHENWARE CO. LTD., THE	HANLEY
December 22, 1882	2	391818	GROVE, F. W. & STARK, J.	LONGTON
December 23, 1882	4	391855	WILEMAN, J. F.	FENTON
December 23, 1882	12	391917	NEW WHARF POTTERY CO., THE	BURSLEM
December 27, 1882	1	391929	NEW WHARF POTTERY CO., THE	BURSLEM
January 03, 1883	14	392362	FURNIVAL, T. & SONS	COBRIDGE
January 04, 1883	5	392403	BROWN, T.C.-WESTHEAD, MOORE & CO.	HANLEY
January 08, 1883	5	392590	COPELAND, W. T. & SONS	STOKE
January 09, 1883	3	392626	POWELL, BISHOP & STONIER	HANLEY
January 09, 1883	4	392627	BODLEY, E. F. & SON	LONGPORT
January 09, 1883	11	392652	DAVENPORTS LTD.	LONGPORT
January 10, 1883	17	392693	GILDEA & WALKER	BURSLEM
January 13, 1883	17	392809	BOOTE, T. & R.	BURSLEM
January 17, 1883	3	392888	GRINDLEY, W. H. & CO.	TUNSTALL
January 23, 1883	8	393099	BODLEY, E. F. & SON	LONGPORT
January 23, 1883	10	393102-3	COPELAND, W. T. & SONS	STOKE
January 24, 1883	1	393107	BRIDGWOOD, SAMPSON & SON	LONGTON
January 24, 1883	2	393108-9	BROWNFIELD, WM. & SONS	COBRIDGE
January 25, 1883	3	393177	BROWNHILLS POTTERYCO. (THE)	TUNSTALL
January 27, 1883	8	393298	TURNER, G. W. & SONS	TUNSTALL
January 29, 1883	6	393310	BROWNFIELD, WM. & SONS	COBRIDGE
January 29, 1883	7	393311-2	GRINDLEY, W. H. & CO.	TUNSTALL
January 30, 1883	1	393323	BODLEY, E. F. & SON	LONGPORT
January 30, 1883	12	393362	WEDGWOOD & CO.	TUNSTALL
January 31, 1883	14	393413	MINTON HOLLINS & CO.	STOKE
February 01, 1883	3	393418	BRIDGWOOD, SAMPSON & SON	LONGTON
February 02, 1883	4	393495	HANCOCK, S.	STOKE
February 02, 1883	17	393539	WEDGWOOD & CO.	TUNSTALL
February 03, 1883	3	393548	MINTONS	STOKE
February 07, 1883	4	393714	HAWLEY & CO.	LONGTON
February 12, 1883	3	394086	DUNN, BENNETT & CO.	HANLEY
February 14, 1883	3	394185	GRINDLEY, W. H. & CO.	TUNSTALL
February 15, 1883	5	394215	DAVIS, J. H.	HANLEY
February 17, 1883	13	394371	TURNER, G. W. & SONS	TUNSTALL
February 19, 1883	1	394374	ADDERLY, W. A.	LONGTON
February 20, 1883	13	394443	DAVENPORTS LTD.	LONGPORT
February 20, 1883	17	394448	GILDEA & WALKER	BURSLEM
February 21, 1883	3	394452	JONES, GEO. & SONS	STOKE
February 22, 1883	21	394600	OLD HALL EARTHENWARE CO., THE	HANLEY
February 24, 1883	12	394676	WEDGWOOD, JOSIAH & SONS	ETRURIA
February 28, 1883	3	394765	TILL, THOS. & SONS	BURSLEM
March 08, 1883	20	395316-7	BODLEY, E. F. & SON	LONGPORT
March 15, 1883	3	395622	FURNIVAL, T. & SONS	COBRIDGE
March 17, 1883	8	395703	MINTONS	STOKE
March 20, 1883	4	395819	WEDGWOOD, JOSIAH & SONS	ETRURIA
March 24, 1883	3	396056	BRIDGWOOD, SAMPSON & SON	LONGTON
March 30, 1883	1	396200-1	MINTONS	STOKE
March 30, 1883	9	396245	MINTON HOLLINS & CO.	STOKE
April 02, 1883	3	396313	POULSON, T. & E. L.	CASTLEFORD
April 21, 1883	1	397227	WILEMAN, J. F. & CO.	FENTON
April 24, 1883	7	397311	ASHWORTH, G. L. & BROS.	HANLEY
April 25, 1883	14	397376	PRATT & SIMPSON	FENTON
April 27, 1883	18	397513	DAVIS, J. H.	HANLEY
April 27, 1883	19	397514	POWELL, BISHOP & STONIER	HANLEY
May 02, 1883	4	397609-11	BROWN, T.C.-WESTHEAD, MOORE & CO.	HANLEY
May 08, 1883	6	397829-30	BOOTH, T. G. & F.	TUNSTALL
May 11, 1883	5	398059	PLANT, R. H. & CO.	LONGTON
May 22, 1883	11	398425	POWELL, BISHOP & STONIER	HANLEY
May 23, 1883	7	398436	BOOTH, T. G. & F.	TUNSTALL
May 24, 1883	3	398479	BROWNHILLS POTTERY CO. (THE)	TUNSTALL
May 25, 1883	4	398519	ADDERLY, W. A.	LONGTON
May 31, 1883	17	398784	WARDLE & CO.	HANLEY
June 02, 1883	9	398849-55	MINTON HOLLINS & CO.	STOKE
June 04, 1883	8	398877-8	CLEMENTSON BROS.	HANLEY
June 08, 1883	2	399068	ALCOCK, H. & CO.	COBRIDGE
June 09, 1883	2	399135-6	BRIDGWOOD, SAMPSON & SON	LONGTON
June 09, 1883	6	399143	MINTONS	STOKE
June 11, 1883	2	399147	GROVE, F. W. & STARK, J.	LONGTON
June 13, 1883	3	399319	BELFIELD & CO.	PRESTONPANS
June 13, 1883	7	399336	PRATT & SIMPSON	STOKE
June 14, 1883	2	399367-70	GROVE, F. W. & STARK, J.	LONGTON
June 18, 1883	11	399554	TAMS, JOHN	LONGTON
June 18, 1883	12	399555-9	BROWNFIELD, WM. & SONS	COBRIDGE

Date	Parcel No.	Reg No.	Potter	Location
June 20, 1883	3	399640	BOOTE, T. & R.	BURSLEM
June 20, 1883	4	399641	MINTONS	STOKE
June 20, 1883	16	399675	CORN, W. & E.	BURSLEM
June 21, 1883	22	399822	WARDLE & CO.	HANLEY
June 23, 1883	4	399875	WEDGWOOD, JOSIAH & SONS	ETRURIA
June 25, 1883	5	399891	FORD & RILEY	BURSLEM
June 25, 1883	10	399897-8	BROWNFIELD, WM. & SONS	COBRIDGE
July 02, 1883	4	400146	EDGE, MALKIN & CO.	BURSLEM
July 04, 1883	7	400348	BROWNFIELD, WM. & SONS	COBRIDGE
July 05, 1883	6	400367	GROVE, F. W. & STARK, J.	LONGTON
July 05, 1883	19	400462	FURNIVAL, T. & SONS	COBRIDGE
July 10, 1883	11	400583-4	MACINTYRE, J. & CO.	BURSLEM
July 11, 1883	4	400596	WEDGWOOD, JOSIAH & SONS	ETRURIA
July 19, 1883	4	400941	DAVENPORTS LTD.	LONGPORT
July 19, 1883	21	400994	JONES, GEO. & SONS	STOKE
July 20, 1883	11	401035	HOLLINSHEAD & KIRKHAM	TUNSTALL
July 21, 1883	3	401040	BRIDGETT & BATES	LONGTON
July 23, 1883	3	401087	WEDGWOOD, JOSIAH & SONS	ETRURIA
July 26, 1883	1	401296	ADDERLY, W. A.	LONGTON
July 27, 1883	4	401410	BROWN, T.C.-WESTHEAD, MOORE & CO.	HANLEY
July 30, 1883	10	401553	BROWNFIELD, WM. & SONS	COBRIDGE
July 31, 1883	3	401593	BOOTE, T. & R.	BURSLEM
August 01, 1883	4	401624	JONES, GEO. & SONS	STOKE
August 01, 1883	9	401653	BROWN, T.C.-WESTHEAD, MOORE & CO.	HANLEY
August 02, 1883	3	401663-4	DAVENPORTS LTD.	LONGPORT
August 08, 1883	9	401842	RIDGWAY, J. & E.	STOKE
August 22, 1883	1	402560-1	BROWNHILLS POTTERY CO. (THE)	TUNSTALL
August 25, 1883	11	402839	BROWNFIELD, WM. & SONS	COBRIDGE
August 31, 1883	6	403110	CORN, W. & E.	BURSLEM
August 31, 1883	7	403111	WILEMAN, J. F. & CO.	FENTON
September 05, 1883	3	403298-9	BROWNFIELD, WM. & SONS	COBRIDGE
September 07, 1883	19	403501-4	POWELL, BISHOP & STONIER	HANLEY
September 11, 1883	4	403665	WEDGWOOD, JOSIAH & SONS	ETRURIA
September 14, 1883	1	403805-6	ADAMS, W. & T.	TUNSTALL
September 14, 1883	2	403807	MINTONS	STOKE
September 21, 1883	4	404196	BROWN, T.C.-WESTHEAD, MOORE & CO.	HANLEY
September 25, 1883	4	404328	GROVE, F. W. & STARK, J.	LONGTON
September 25, 1883	5	404329-30	BRIDGWOOD, SAMPSON & SON	LONGTON
September 29, 1883	4	404571	BRIDGWOOD, SAMPSON & SON	LONGTON
October 02, 1883	15	404643	MELLOR, TAYLOR & CO.	BURSLEM
October 04, 1883	4	404745	BRIDGWOOD, SAMPSON & SON	LONGTON
October 06, 1883	2	404870	GRINDLEY, W. H. & CO.	TUNSTALL
October 08, 1883	2	404901-2	BOOTH, T. G. & F.	TUNSTALL
October 12, 1883	13	405336	BRIDGETT & BATES	LONGTON
October 13, 1883	3	405341	WOOD & SON	BURSLEM
October 13, 1883	11	405363-4	BROWNFIELD, WM. & SONS	COBRIDGE
October 17, 1883	5	405466	NEW WHARF POTTERY CO., THE	BURSLEM
October 20, 1883	3	405724	ADDERLY, W. A.	LONGTON
October 20, 1883	4	405725-9	BROWNFIELD, WM. & SONS	COBRIDGE
October 23, 1883	6	405855	DIMMOCK, J. & CO.	HANLEY
October 24, 1883	11	405946-8	MINTON HOLLINS & CO.	STOKE
October 27, 1883	1	406046	BROWNHILLS POTTERY CO. (THE)	TUNSTALL
October 30, 1883	2	406140	MARSHALL, J. & CO.	BO'NESS, SCOTLAND
October 30, 1883	3	406141	NEW WHARF POTTERY CO., THE	BURSLEM
October 30, 1883	17	406187	ROBINSON, J.	BURSLEM
November 01, 1883	27	406372	DAVENPORT'S LTD. (1881-87)	LONGPORT
November 05, 1883	13	406511	ALCOCK, H. & CO.	COBRIDGE
November 06, 1883	3	406516	CHALLINOR, E. & C.	FENTON
November 07, 1883	2	406561	CORN, W. & E.	BURSLEM
November 10, 1883	10	406782	BROWNFIELD, WM. & SONS	COBRIDGE
November 13, 1883	10	406875	BOOTH, T. G. & F.	TUNSTALL
November 15, 1883	17	407063	FURNIVAL, T. & SONS	COBRIDGE
November 21, 1883	3	407333	EMERY, F. J.	BURSLEM
November 23, 1883	7	407601	MINTON HOLLINS & CO.	STOKE
November 24, 1883	3	407601	POWELL, BISHOP & STONIER	HANLEY
November 26, 1883	2	407623	ADDERLY, W. A.	LONGTON
November 26, 1883	3	407624	BRIDGWOOD, SAMPSON & SON	LONGTON
December 05, 1883	2	408035	MALKIN, EDGE & CO.	BURSLEM
December 08, 1883	8	408136	WILEMAN, J. F. & CO.	FENTON
December 14, 1883	4	408288	BROWNHILLS POTTERY CO. (THE)	TUNSTALL
December 15, 1883	13	408356	BOOTH, T. G. & F.	TUNSTALL
December 29, 1883	4	408849	POWELL, BISHOP & STONIER	HANLEY
March 29, 1884	-	-	DAVENPORT'S LTD. (1881-87)	LONGPORT — (#4310)
March 29, 1884	-	-	DAVENPORT'S LTD. (1881-87)	LONGPORT — (#4312)
March 29, 1884	-	-	DAVENPORT'S LTD. (1881-87)	LONGPORT — (#4311)
March 23, 1885	-	-	DAVENPORT'S LTD. (1881-87)	LONGPORT — (#24402)
July 25, 1885	-	-	DAVENPORT'S LTD. (1881-87)	LONGPORT — (#30422)
September 22, 1885	-	-	DAVENPORT'S LTD. (1881-87)	LONGPORT — (#34191)
April 09, 1886	-	-	DAVENPORT'S LTD. (1881-87)	LONGPORT — (#46849)
September 15, 1886	-	-	DAVENPORT'S LTD. (1881-87)	LONGPORT — (#56252)
April 01, 1900	-	-	WOOD & BROWNFIELD (AGENTS)	#355747
April 01, 1900	-	-	WOOD & BROWNFIELD (AGENTS)	#358427
May 01, 1900	-	-	WOOD & BROWNFIELD (AGENTS)	CROMER, STUART AND MIMOSA

For information purposes, selected dates for Davenports Ltd and Wood & Brownfield (as agents) have been included.

APPENDIX B15: PART I - REGISTRY NUMBERING SEQUENCE, 1839-1884

NUMBER	DATE	NUMBER	DATE
1	AUG. 1839	198000	JUNE 1866
300	APR. 1840	205850	FEB. 1867
700	JUNE 1841	217400	MAR. 1868
1000	JAN. 1842	227800	MAR. 1869
8500	JULY 1843	240500	APR. 1870
21500	APR. 1844	248450	MAY 1871
30000	AUG. 1845	261800	APR. 1872
43500	JUNE 1847	271200	MAR. 1873
58800	MAR. 1849	280600	FEB. 1874
72300	OCT. 1850	288700	JAN. 1875
878000	NOV. 1852	299000	MAR. 1876
102900	DEC. 1855	308300	MAR. 1877
111600	OCT. 1857	322500	JUNE 1878
119225	APR. 1859	331500	JAN. 1879
133000	SEPT. 1860	350400	JUNE 1880
144400	OCT. 1861	362000	FEB. 1881
154600	SEPT 1862	376100	JAN. 1882
163400	JUNE 1863	383100	JAN. 1883
183000	JAN. 1865	408900	JUNE 1884

APPENDIX B15: PART II - REGISTRY NUMBERING SEQUENCE, 1884-1996

NUMBER	DATE	NUMBER	DATE	NUMBER	DATE	NUMBER	DATE
1	1884	612431	1913	839230	1942	950046	1971
19754	1885	630190	1914	839980	1943	955342	1972
40480	1886	644935	1915	841040	1944	960708	1973
64520	1887	653521	1916	842670	1945	965185	1974
90483	1888	658988	1917	845550	1946	969249	1975
116648	1889	662872	1918	849730	1947	973838	1976
141273	1890	666128	1919	853260	1948	978426	1977
163767	1891	673750	1920	856999	1949	982815	1978
185713	1892	680147	1921	860854	1950	987910	1979
205240	1893	687144	1922	863970	1951	993012	1980
224720	1894	694999	1923	866280	1952	998302	1981
246975	1895	702671	1924	869300	1953	1004456	1982
268392	1896	710165	1925	872531	1954	1010583	1983
291241	1897	718057	1926	876067	1955	1017131	1984
311658	1898	726330	1927	879282	1956	1024174	1985
331707	1899	734370	1928	882949	1957	1031358	1986
351202	1900	742725	1929	887079	1958	1039055	1987
368154	1901	751160	1930	891665	1959	1047478	1988
385180	1902	760583	1931	895000	1960	1056076	1989
403200	1903	769670	1932	899914	1961	1061406	July 1990
424400	1904	779292	1933	904638	1962	2000000	Aug 1 1990
447800	1905	789019	1934	909364	1963	2003720	1990
471860	1906	799097	1935	914536	1964	2012047	1991
493900	1907	808794	1936	919607	1965	2019933	1992
518640	1908	817293	1937	924510	1966	2028110	1993
535170	1909	825231	1938	929335	1967	2036116	1994
552000	1910	832610	1939	934515	1968	2044229	1995
574817	1911	837520	1940	939875	1969	2053112	1996
594195	1912	838500	1941	944932	1970	—	—

From January 1884 registration numbers have the prefix "Rd" or "Rd No." The numbering sequence stopped with 1061406 in July, 1990, and the new sequence for designs filed after August 1, 1990 starts with 2000000. The above

chart (which are the numbers noted by most authors) does not give exact dates, rather it provides a general year span, with an opening date of January 1st. For an exact listing of dates by month and year with corresponding registration numbers for the years 1884 - 1945, refer to John A. Bartlett. *British Ceramic Art, 1870-1940*. Atglen, PA, Schiffer Publishing, Ltd. 1993, p. 233. For example, Mr. Bartlett lists: No. 139,296-165,353 for Nov. 29, 1889 - Jan. 27, 1891, and 165,354-185,824 for Jan. 27, 1891 - Jan. 5, 1892.
Please note that designs were actually registered on these dates as opposed to dates on the piece itself, which were the dates the pattern was issued. Even this is ambiguous and requires further research, as the potter could have commenced manufacture of the pattern before or after the date was actually registered. When only the year of manufacture is noted, without a registration number, the date was taken from various sources.

INTRODUCTION: APPENDICES B16, 17, 18, 19 & 20: ALPHABETICAL and CHRONOLOGICAL LISTINGS OF REGISTRY DATES 1842-1883

Introduction to Appendices B16 and B17:

Design registrations record the name and address, as recorded by the potter, manufactory, retailer or agent who wanted to safeguard, via registration, a certain shape or added design. Class IV is the registry designation used for earthenware. This is noted on the uppermost portion of the Registry Diamond. (See Appendix B13: Dating and Deciphering the Registration Mark, 1842-1883). This category may include porcelain, relief jugs, parian, majolica and other types of earthenware. Potters could and did use a registered shape or design as they saw fit, and it may appear on other earthenware media. A design appearing on an earthenware dinner set did not prohibit the potter from using the same design on a porcelain tea set. Likewise, a shape with embossing registered for a tea set may also have been used on a dinner or desert set and/or selected embossed motifs transposed onto jugs. All may bear the same registry number of the original design page recorded in the Registry Office. This Appendix is an abridged version of Cushion's registry listing of those shapes and/or designs and primarily relates to those potters included in this Encyclopedia.

- Cushion notes the first recorded *ironstone* registry with the new diamond designation as September 22, 1843.

The prior registry system, 1839-1842, was not ignored and there were potters who continued with printed markings which included wording such as "...published by," "...applied for," "...entered at the Registry Office."

In effect, both systems ran parallel; the registry diamond starting in 1842 and the other, with printed text and registry date which started in 1839. An example of the latter type registry is evidenced with James Edwards registry of May 30, 1842, as cited in *White Ironstone Notes*, Vol. 5, No. 1, Summer 1998, p. 11:

"To prevent this shape from
being copied it was entered
at the Registry Office of
Designs, May 30, 1842 by
James Edwards
1267"

Similarly, a jug may read (refer to *Hughes*, Vol. II, p. 22):

"Ridgway & Abington
December 3, 1846
Rd. No. 38606"

At times there may be inconsistencies relative to the location of potteries. A case in point would be Mayer Bros., for whom the location is given as Longport, which was a hamlet in Burslem prior to its incorporation in Burslem. As such, both names may appear in this registry listing. Furthermore, confusion may arise between the names of Mayer & Elliot and Mayer Bros. & Elliot. This was the same company registering under two different trade titles. Likewise, there may have been a change in company title, as is noted by Charles Meigh, who registered as C. Meigh, Charles Meigh and subsequently Chas. Meigh & Son. Other changes such as locale name changes may be noted, e.g., Lane End to Longton or Lane Delph (Fenton), or Foley (Fenton). In 1812 Shelton and Hanley were united and either name may appear prior to and/or after this unification. It all depended upon what the potter or his agent found more convenient. Further muddying the issue is the fact that frugality prevailed. Old letterhead was not thrown away but, rather, used until finished, which, of course, created a conflict regarding locales. The reader is asked to be aware of these discrepancies as well as registry spelling errors, and should refer to the Appendix B12, Dating Marks, as well as to Appendix B13: Dating & Deciphering the Registration Mark, 1842-1883.

An "X" after the number denotes that an exact date of registry shape has not been confirmed. Hugh Wakefield's *Victorian Pottery*. London. Herbert Jenkins, 1962, pp. 183-186, notes in Appendix III "Design Registration for Scenic Patterns" (between 1839 and 1870), five additional potters not covered by this Encyclopedia. I have cited these potters and marked their names within the listing of registries with an asterisk.

A reference category section has been included. For category listing refer to Introduction to Appendix B18.

Introduction to Appendix B18:

Appendix B18 is a chronological listing of all potters as recorded by this author and noted in the English Pattern Section of this Encyclopedia, with the inclusion of a category section. Numbers 1 - 6 below are code numbers for patterns and/or shapes, as recorded under Patterns Listed by Potter. Number 7 is for recorded jugs; see Earthenware, Parian & Porcelain Jugs, Appendix B20. Numbers 8 - 13 are additional references (see Frequently Referenced Works for exact titles). They are:

CATEGORY LISTING CODING

1 - Flow Blue	8 - Godden's Staffordshire
2 - Mulberry	9 - Miscellaneous
3 - Tea Leaf/Copper Lustre	10 - Peake
4 - White Ironstone	11 - Godden's Ridgway
5 - Blue and White	12 - Godden's Davenport
6 - Historic Blue	13 - Copeland, II
7 - Jugs	

Introduction to Appendix B19: Appendix B19 is as above, but formatted alphabetically by potter.

Introduction to Appendix B20: Appendix B20 records Jugs & Parian ware from the following sources:

1 - Peake,
2 - Hughes, Vol. I
3 - Hughes, Vol. II
4 - Peake, Unpublished Notes
5 - Geoffrey Godden's registration files to be illustrated in Geoffrey Godden's *New Revised Handbook of Marks*, Barrie & Jenkins, London, 1998 or 1999.

For those wishing to pursue further research on Parian Ware, see *Godden's Guide to English Porcelain*, Wallace-Homestead Book Co., Radnor, PA, 1992, pp. 173-177 for a check list of Parian Manufacturers; Geoffrey Godden, *English China.* London, Barrie & Jenkins, 1985, Section 13, pp. 291-326, "The Parian Body"; and *The Parian Phenomenon*. Paul Atterbury, editor, Somerset, England, Richard Dennis, 1989. A listing of Teapot designs [named] abstracted from Peake's *Brownfield*, p. 182, Appendix 7 is included below.

POTTER	DATE OF REGISTRY	REGISTRY NO.	PATTERN NAME
Alcock, J.	Dec. 24, 1853	93708	Bluebell
Ashworth, G.L. & Bros.	Mar. 6, 1863	160319	Halifax
Ashworth, Geo. L. & Bros.	June 18, 1872	263497	Alton
Baker & Chetwynd	Apr. 6, 1869	228430	U.S.A.
Bodley, E.F. & Son	Oct. 22, 1880	357039	Storks
Boote, T. & R.	Oct. 6, 1881	370998	Tunis
Brownfield, Wm.	May 20, 1859	119968	Shamrock
Brownfield, Wm.	June 12, 1868	219317	Cone
Brownfield, Wm*	Oct. 21, 1868	223308	Westminster
Brownfield, Wm.	June 19, 1869	230184	Severn
Brownfield, Wm.	June 10, 1870	242394	Nice
Brownfield, Wm. & Son	June 6, 1874	282802	Aston
Brownfield, Wm. & Sons	Oct. 31, 1876	304911	Man & Gourd
Brownfield, Wm. & Sons	Oct. 31, 1876	304913	Fish
Brownfield, Wm. & Sons	Jan. 26, 1880	345719	Basket
Brownfield, Wm. & Sons	Feb. 8, 1881	361540	Mistletoe
Brownfield, Wm. & Sons	Feb. 8, 1881	361541	Mistletoe
Brownfield, Wm. & Sons	Oct. 13, 1883	405363	Clamshell
Edge, Malkin & Co.	Mar. 12, 1879	333210	Cockatoo
Elsmore & Forster	Nov. 10, 1864	181214	Olympic
Jones, Geo.	June 27, 1870	242715	Pineapple
Jones, Geo. & Sons	June 26, 1875	292367	Monkey
Lear, Samuel	May 27, 1882	381568	Sunflower (?)
Mintons	Jan. 24, 1875	297817	Cockerell
Mintons	Apr. 17, 1878	320482	Tortoise
Mintons	Oct. 2, 1878	327035	Porcupine
Moore Bros.	May 11, 1874	282249	Camel
Venables, Mann & Co.	Oct. 5, 1853	92768	Baltic
Wedgwood, Josiah & Sons	May 22, 1876	300683	Boston

*The registry is in the name of W.P. & G. Phillips, a London retailer. It is, however, a Brownfield shape.
Collectors wishing to further research shape and design registries should consult such works as Lockett & Godden's *Davenport*, Godden's *Ridgway*, Peake's *Brownfield*, *Copeland* amongst others.

APPENDIX B16: REGISTRY DATES, A CHRONOLOGICAL SEQUENCE WITH CATEGORY OF MANUFACTURE, 1842-1883 AS RECORDED WITH A REGISTRY DIAMOND*

*Two registry dates are included that are prior to the first recorded Ironstone date recorded by Cushion, using the Diamond Registry System; that date being September 22, 1842/ No. 1694 by James Dixon & Sons of Sheffield.

DATE	POTTER	LOCATION	CATEGORY
Sept. 2, 1841	EDWARDS, JAMES & THOMAS	BURSLEM	2, 5
May 2, 1842	EDWARDS, JAMES	BURSLEM	5
December 02, 1842	CLEMENTSON, JOSEPH	SHELTON	5
December 30, 1842	EDWARDS, JAMES	BURSLEM	10
January 24, 1843	RIDGWAY, JOHN & CO.	SHELTON	
February 21, 1843	ALCOCK, SAMUEL & CO.	BURSLEM	
March 21, 1843	WEDGWOOD, JOSIAH & SONS	ETRURIA	5, 7, 10
March 31, 1843	ALCOCK, SAMUEL & CO.	BURSLEM	
May 02, 1843	WEDGWOOD, JOSIAH & SONS	ETRURIA	
May 13, 1843	JONES & WALLEY	COBRIDGE	7, 10
June 14, 1843	ALCOCK, SAMUEL & CO.	BURSLEM	1
August 30, 1843	EDWARDS, JAMES	BURSLEM	1, 2, 4, 5
October 06, 1843	EDWARDS, JAMES	BURSLEM	
November 10, 1843	MINTON & CO.	STOKE	
November 28, 1843	DIMMOCK, THOS. & CO.	SHELTON	1
December 14, 1843	BOWERS, G. F. & CO.	TUNSTALL	8
February 15, 1844	ALCOCK, SAMUEL & CO.	BURSLEM	
February 20, 1844	ALCOCK, SAMUEL & CO.	BURSLEM	
March 05, 1844	MELLOR, VENABLES & CO.	BURSLEM	
March 07, 1844	LOCKETT, J. & T.	LANE END	7
April 03, 1844	EDWARDS, THOS.	BURSLEM	4
April 11, 1844	HILDITCH & HOPWOOD	LANE END	1, 8
May 07, 1844	DIMMOCK, THOS. & CO.	SHELTON	1
June 29, 1844	DIMMOCK, THOS. & CO.	SHELTON	1, 2, 5
July 20, 1844	RIDGWAY, JOHN & CO.	SHELTON	5
July 30, 1844	MINTON, HERBERT & CO.	STOKE	
August 15, 1844	KING, KNIGHT & ELKIN	STOKE	5, 7
August 21, 1844	MINTON, HERBERT & CO.	STOKE	8
September 19, 1844	RIDGWAY, JN & CO.	SHELTON	4
September 30, 1844	MEIGH, CHARLES	HANLEY	7
October 14, 1844	COPELAND & GARRETT	STOKE	
October 17, 1844	CLEMENTSON, YOUNG & JAMESON	SHELTON	5
October 30, 1844	MINTON, HERBERT & CO.	STOKE	8
November 06, 1844	MINTON, HERBERT & CO.	STOKE	
November 11, 1844	EDWARDS, JAMES	BURSLEM	5
November 13, 1844	RIDGWAY, JOHN & CO.	SHELTON	
November 22, 1844	DIMMOCK, THOS. & CO.	SHELTON	1, 2
December 02, 1844	COPELAND & GARRETT	STOKE	1, 5
December 07, 1844	EDWARDS, THOS.	BURSLEM	
December 16, 1844	RIDGWAY, WILLIAM SON & CO.	HANLEY	6, 7
December 24, 1844	MEIR, JOHN & SON	TUNSTALL	5
January 11, 1845	PHILLIPS, GEORGE	LONGPORT	5
January 15, 1845	CLEMENTSON, YOUNG & JAMESON	SHELTON	
January 21, 1845	MAYER, T. J. & J.	LONGPORT	4, 7
February 27, 1845	PHILLIPS, GEORGE	LONGPORT	
March 05, 1845	COPELAND & GARRETT	STOKE	
March 06, 1845	MINTON, HERBERT & CO.	STOKE	8
March 17, 1845	MINTON, HERBERT & CO.	STOKE	
March 20, 1845	MINTON, HERBERT & CO.	STOKE	7
April 25, 1845	COPELAND & GARRETT	STOKE	5

DATE	POTTER	LOCATION	CATEGORY
April 26, 1845	BOOTE, T. & R., WALLEY & JONES	BURSLEM, COBRIDGE, HANLEY	6
April 30, 1845	FURNIVAL, JACOB & CO.	COBRIDGE	5
May 08, 1845	MINTON, HERBERT & CO.	STOKE	7, 8
May 10, 1845	WALLEY (EDWARD) & T. & R. BOOTE	COBRIDGE & BURSLEM	7
May 31, 1845	MORLEY, FRANCIS	SHELTON	1, 2, 4, 5, 6
June 19, 1845	PHILLIPS, GEORGE	LONGPORT	4
June 26, 1845	MINTON & CO.	STOKE	
July 05, 1845	PHILLIPS, GEORGE	LONGPORT	
July 05, 1845	WOOD, ENOCH	BURSLEM	5
July 26, 1845	ADAMS, WM. & SONS	STOKE	5
August 28, 1845	CLEMENTSON, JOSEPH	SHELTON	
September 04, 1845	COPELAND & GARRETT	STOKE	
September 11, 1845	PHILLIPS, THOS. & SON	BURSLEM	
September 19, 1845	MINTON & CO.	STOKE	8
October 06, 1845	MINTON, HERBERT & CO.	STOKE	8
October 21, 1845	COPELAND & GARRETT	STOKE	2, 5
October 22, 1845	CLEMENTSON & YOUNG	SHELTON	1, 5
November 15, 1845	BAYLEY & BALL	LONGTON	7,
November 22, 1845	MINTON & CO.	STOKE	7, 8
December 04, 1845	RIDGWAY, JOHN	SHELTON	1, 5
December 27, 1845	EDWARDS, JAMES	BURSLEM	
December 29, 1845	CLEMENTSON, JOSEPH	SHELTON	
December 30, 1845	FURNIVAL & CLARK	HANLEY	7, 8
January 07, 1846	CLEMENTSON, JOSEPH	SHELTON	5
January 24, 1846	FURNIVAL, JACOB & CO.	COBRIDGE	
February 26, 1846	MAYER, T. J. & J.	LONGPORT	
March 02, 1846	MINTON & CO.	STOKE	7, 8
April 17, 1846	COPELAND & GARRETT	STOKE	8
May 21, 1846	MINTON, HERBERT & CO.	STOKE	4
May 26, 1846	MINTON, HERBERT & CO.	STOKE	7, 8
June 26, 1846	MINTON, HERBERT & CO.	STOKE	8
June 30, 1846	GOODWIN, JOHN	LONGTON	1, 2, 5
July 11, 1846	KNIGHT, J. K.	LONGTON	
July 16, 1846	RIDGWAY, SON & CO.	HANLEY	1, 4, 7, 11
July 17, 1846	RIDGWAY, JOHN & CO.	SHELTON	5
July 21, 1846	MORLEY, F. & CO.	SHELTON	
August 01, 1846	WEDGWOOD, JOSIAH & SONS	ETRURIA	2x, 10
August 03, 1846	MINTON, HERBERT & CO.	STOKE	
August 03, 1846	WEDGWOOD, JOSIAH & SONS	ETRURIA	1, 2x
September 03, 1846	MORLEY, F. & CO.	SHELTON	7, 10
September 03, 1846	PHILLIPS, G.	LONGPORT	5
September 14, 1846	COPELAND & GARRETT	STOKE	5
September 26, 1846	RIDGWAY, JOHN & CO.	SHELTON	
September 29, 1846	MAYER, T. J. & J.	LONGPORT	7, 10
October 26, 1846	EDWARDS, J. (JAMES)	BURSLEM	1
October 26, 1846	MORLEY, F. & CO.	SHELTON	
November 03, 1846	RIDGWAY & ABINGTON	HANLEY (WM. & E.)	
November 05, 1846	PHILLIPS, G.	LONGPORT	5
November 12, 1846	MEIGH, C.	HANLEY	7
November 16, 1846	MINTON, HERBERT & CO.	STOKE	1
November 21, 1846	FURNIVAL, THOS. & CO.	HANLEY	1, 5
December 03, 1846	RIDGWAY & ABINGTON	HANLEY (WM. & E.)	7, 11
December 04, 1846	MINTON, HERBERT & CO.	STOKE	
December 10, 1846	CLEMENTSON, JOSEPH	SHELTON	
December 14, 1846	EDWARDS, JAMES	BURSLEM	
December 14, 1846	MINTON & CO.	STOKE	8
December 16, 1846	GOODWIN, JOHN	LONGTON	5
December 17, 1846	COPELAND & GARRETT	STOKE	
December 29, 1846	CHALLINOR, EDWARD	TUNSTALL	5
December 31, 1846	WEDGWOOD, JOSIAH & SONS	ETRURIA	2x
January 09, 1847	COPELAND & GARRETT	STOKE	1
January 09, 1847	RIDGWAY, JOHN & CO.	SHELTON	1, 5x
February 02, 1847	BOOTE, T. & R.	BURSLEM	7
February 08, 1847	MAYER, T. J. & J.	LONGTON	7, 10
February 15, 1847	COPELAND & GARRETT	STOKE	
March 17, 1847	RIDGWAY, JOHN & CO.	SHELTON	5x
March 17, 1847	WEDGE.WOOD, JOHN	TUNSTALL	4, 5x
March 22, 1847	BAILEY & BALL	LONGTON	9
March 23, 1847	MINTON, HERBERT & CO.	STOKE	8
March 30, 1847	EDWARDS, JAMES	BURSLEM	2x
April 03, 1847	ALCOCK, SAMUEL & CO.	BURSLEM	4, 7
April 27, 1847	ALCOCK, SAMUEL & CO.	BURSLEM	4, 7
May 12, 1847	COPELAND & GARRETT	STOKE	
May 14, 1847	MINTON, HERBERT & CO.	STOKE	7, 8
June 11, 1847	EDWARDS, JAMES	BURSLEM	2x
June 25, 1847	EDWARDS, JAMES	BURSLEM	1, 2x
July 05, 1847	MELLOR, VENABLES & CO.	BURSLEM	5
July 15, 1847	MELLOR, VENABLES & CO.	BURSLEM	1
July 16, 1847	EDWARDS, JAMES	BURSLEM	1, 2x,
July 27, 1847	MAYER, T. J. & J.	LONGPORT	4
August 16, 1847	EDWARDS, JAMES	BURSLEM	2x
August 17, 1847	COPELAND, W. T.	STOKE	7, 13
August 19, 1847	MINTON, HERBERT & CO.	STOKE	8
August 26, 1847	EDWARDS, JAMES	BURSLEM	1x
September 09, 1847	COPELAND, WILLIAM TAYLOR	STOKE	5

DATE	POTTER	LOCATION	CATEGORY
September 16, 1847	COPELAND, WILLIAM TAYLOR	STOKE	1
September 25, 1847	WEDGE.WOOD, JOHN	TUNSTALL	1, 4, 5x
October 02, 1847	RIDGWAY, JOHN & CO.	SHELTON	1, 5x
October 04, 1847	MINTON, HERBERT & CO.	STOKE	8
October 08, 1847	WEDGE.WOOD, JOHN	TUNSTALL	1, 4, 5x
October 13, 1847	COPELAND, W. T.	STOKE	
October 23, 1847	MINTON, HERBERT & CO.	STOKE	
October 27, 1847	RIDGWAY, JOHN & CO.	SHELTON	
November 11, 1847	MINTON, HERBERT & CO.	STOKE	8
November 23, 1847	WEDGWOOD, J. & CO.	ETRURIA	
December 10, 1847	MINTON & CO. & JOHN BELL	STOKE	
December 15, 1847	MINTON & CO.	STOKE	8
January 01, 1848	BARKER & TILL	BURSLEM	5
January 18, 1848	COPELAND, W. T.	STOKE	
February 11, 1848	MINTON, HERBERT & CO.	STOKE	
February 29, 1848	MINTON & CO.	STOKE	
March 04, 1848	MINTON & CO.	STOKE	8
March 07, 1848	RIDGWAY & ABINGTON	HANLEY	7
March 14, 1848	COPELAND, W. T.	STOKE	
March 15, 1848	COPELAND, W. T.	STOKE	
March 20, 1848	WOOD & BROWNFIELD	COBRIDGE	2
March 27, 1848	ALCOCK, J. & S. JNR.	COBRIDGE	1, 2, 4
April 15, 1848	RIDGWAY, JOHN & CO.	SHELTON	
April 22, 1848	WEDGWOOD, JOSIAH & SONS	ETRURIA	
April 27, 1848	WEDGWOOD, JOSIAH & SONS	ETRURIA	
June 20, 1848	BOWERS, G. F. & CO.	TUNSTALL	8
June 30, 1848	COPELAND, W. T.	STOKE	5
June 30, 1848	RIDGWAY & ABINGTON	HANLEY	
August 16, 1848	PINDER, THOS.	BURSLEM	
August 23, 1848	WEDGE.WOOD, JOHN	TUNSTALL	4, 5
August 26, 1848	MEIR, JOHN & SON	TUNSTALL	5
September 15, 1848	COPELAND, W. T.	STOKE	5
September 18, 1848	MEIGH, CHARLES	HANLEY	7
September 30, 1848	RIDGWAY, JOHN & CO.	SHELTON	4
October 17, 1848	BOOTE, T. & R.	BURSLEM	7
November 04, 1848	COPELAND, W. T.	STOKE	7, 8
November 13, 1848	COPELAND, W. T.	STOKE	8
November 21, 1848	MINTON & CO.	STOKE	7, 8
November 27, 1848	RIDGWAY, JOHN & CO.	SHELTON	
December 16, 1848	EDWARDS, JAMES	BURSLEM	4
December 28, 1848	RIDGWAY, JOHN	SHELTON	
January 03, 1849	ADAMS, WM. & SONS	STOKE	1, 2
January 20, 1849	DAVENPORT, W. & CO.	LONGPORT	
February 02, 1849	MELLOR, VENABLES & CO.	BURSLEM	2x, 5x
February 16, 1849	MINTON & CO.	STOKE	
February 16, 1849	RIDGWAY & ABINGTON	HANLEY	7, 11
March 13, 1849	CLEMENTSON, JOSEPH	SHELTON	2, 5
March 26, 1849	MINTON & CO.	STOKE	8
March 31, 1849	RIDGWAY, JOHN & CO.	SHELTON	
April 02, 1849	PODMORE, WALKER & CO.	TUNSTALL	1, 2, 5
April 10, 1849	COPELAND, W. T.	STOKE	
April 16, 1849	MASON, C. J.	LONGTON	
May 24, 1849	WEDGE.WOOD (MR.)	TUNSTALL	1, 2, 5
June 07, 1849	MAYER, T. J. & J.	LONGPORT	
July 16, 1849	RIDGWAY & ABINGTON	HANLEY	
August 11, 1849	COPELAND, W. T.	STOKE	13
August 15, 1849	MINTON, HERBERT & CO.	STOKE	10
August 17, 1849	COPELAND, W. T.	STOKE	1, 5
August 27, 1849	MELLOR, VENABLES & CO.	BURSLEM	2, 2x, 5
September 14, 1849	PRATT, F. & R. & CO.	FENTON	
September 28, 1849	RIDGWAY, J. (JOHN)	SHELTON	5
October 10, 1849	RIDGWAY, J. (JOHN)	SHELTON	
October 12, 1849	MINTON & CO.	STOKE	8
November 09, 1849	COPELAND, W. T.	STOKE	7, 8
November 17, 1849	MINTON & CO.	STOKE	7, 8
November 22, 1849	COPELAND, W. T.	STOKE	5
December 06, 1849	COPELAND, W. T.	STOKE	10
December 15, 1849	MAYER, T. J. & J.	LONGPORT	
January 03, 1850	DAVENPORT, W. & CO.	LONGPORT	1, 2
January 14, 1850	RIDGWAY, J. (JOHN)	SHELTON	5x
February 13, 1850	BELL, J. & M. P. & CO. (LTD.)	GLASGOW	5
March 09, 1850	COPELAND, W. T.	STOKE	5
April 04, 1850	MAYER, T. J. & J.	LONGPORT	
April 08, 1850	CLEMENTSON, J.	SHELTON	5
April 13, 1850	MINTON & CO.	STOKE	8
April 25, 1850	MINTON & CO.	STOKE	
June 04, 1850	BELL, J. & M. P. & CO. (LTD.)	GLASGOW	5
June 05, 1850	BARKER & SON	BURSLEM	5, 7
June 21, 1850	WALLEY, E.	COBRIDGE	5, 7
July 02, 1850	MAYER, T. J. & J.	LONGPORT	7
July 16, 1850	HARVEY, C. & W. K.	LONGTON	4
September 09, 1850	TILL, THOMAS	BURSLEM	
September 16, 1850	BELL, J. & M. P. & CO. (LTD.)	GLASGOW	5x, 10
September 16, 1850	RIDGWAY, J. (JOHN)	SHELTON	5x
September 19, 1850	COPELAND, W. T.	STOKE	5
September 21, 1850	MELLOR, VENABLES & CO.	BURSLEM	4
October 09, 1850	MINTON & CO.	STOKE	10
October 17, 1850	COPELAND, W. T.	STOKE	
November 04, 1850	WEDGWOOD, J. & SONS	ETRURIA	

DATE	POTTER	LOCATION	CATEGORY
November 20, 1850	MORLEY, F. & CO.	SHELTON	
December 05, 1850	MORLEY, F. & CO.	SHELTON	
December 19, 1850	MAYER, T. J. & J.	LONGPORT	7
December 20, 1850	COPELAND, W. T.	STOKE	5
February 10, 1851	BROWNFIELD, WILLIAM	COBRIDGE	
March 17, 1851	RIDGWAY, J. & CO.	SHELTON	10
March 31, 1851	BELL, J. & M. P. & CO. (LTD.)	GLASGOW	
April 09, 1851	TILL, THOS. & SON	BURSLEM	
April 11, 1851	BELL, J. & M. P. & CO. (LTD.)	GLASGOW	
April 14, 1851	BELL, J. & M. P. & CO. (LTD.)	GLASGOW	
April 26, 1851	WALLEY, E.	COBRIDGE	7
May 30, 1851	COPELAND, W. T.	STOKE	7, 8
June 07, 1851	RIDGWAY, J. & CO.	SHELTON	
June 11, 1851	COPELAND, W. T.	STOKE	5
June 11, 1851	SCRAGG, RALPH	HANLEY	
June 19, 1851	COPELAND, W. T.	STOKE	5
July 14, 1851	COPELAND, W. T.	STOKE	8
July 21, 1851	BOOTE, T. & R.	BURSLEM	4, 10
July 24, 1851	TILL, THOS. & SON	BURSLEM	
July 26, 1851	COLLINSON, C. & CO.	BURSLEM	1
August 16, 1851	RIDGWAY & ABINGTON	HANLEY	7, 11
August 26, 1851	WALLEY, EDWARD	COBRIDGE	8
September 02, 1851	MAYER, T. J. & J.	LONGPORT	4
September 19, 1851	BOOTE, T. & R.	BURSLEM	4
September 29, 1851	EDWARDS, JAMES	BURSLEM	4
September 30, 1851	EDWARDS, JAMES	BURSLEM	4x
October 01, 1851	COPELAND, W. T.	STOKE	
October 10, 1851	BOOTE, T. & R.	BURSLEM	4
October 10, 1851	BROWNFIELD, W.	COBRIDGE	
October 14, 1851	TILL, THOS. & SON	BURSLEM	
October 16, 1851	BROWNFIELD, W.	COBRIDGE	7
October 21, 1851	RIDGWAY, J. & CO.	SHELTON	7,11
November 10, 1851	SCRAGG, RALPH	HANLEY	
November 12, 1851	MINTON & CO.	STOKE	5, 8
November 13, 1851	MEIGH, CHARLES & SON	HANLEY	7
November 14, 1851	SANDER, GEO. B. (See Hulme & Booth)	LONDON	2
December 02, 1851	MAYER, T. J. & J.	BURSLEM	4, 7
December 04, 1851	MINTON & CO.	STOKE	
December 05, 1851	RIDGWAY, JOHN & CO.	SHELTON	
December 08, 1851	COPELAND, W. T.	STOKE	
January 27, 1852	HARDING, W. & G.	BURSLEM	5
February 17, 1852	VENABLES & BAINES	BURSLEM	5
March 04, 1852	BROWNFIELD, WM.	COBRIDGE	
March 13, 1852	RIDGWAY, WM.	SHELTON	5
March 22, 1852	SCRAGG, RALPH	HANLEY	
March 24, 1852	EDWARDS, JAMES	BURSLEM	5
March 24, 1852	MINTON & CO.	STOKE	8
March 26, 1852	BELL, J. & M. P. & CO. (LTD.)	GLASGOW	7
April 01, 1852	TILL, THOS. & SON	BURSLEM	10
April 08, 1852	TILL, THOS. & SON	BURSLEM	
May 14, 1852	COPELAND, W. T.	STOKE	8, 10
May 16, 1852	COPELAND, W. & T.*	STOKE	5
May 18, 1852	MINTON & CO.	STOKE	8
June 05, 1852	MINTON & CO.	STOKE	7, 8
June 14, 1852	COPELAND, W. T.	STOKE	5
June 21, 1852	LOCKETT, J. & T.	LONGTON	7
July 05, 1852	PANKHURST, J. & CO.	HANLEY	
July 23, 1852	MINTON & CO.	STOKE	7, 8
August 04, 1852	COPELAND, W. T.	STOKE	1
August 13, 1852	TILL, THOS. & SON	BURSLEM	7
August 25, 1852	MEIGH, CHARLES & SON	HANLEY	7
September 03, 1852	MINTON & CO.	STOKE	7, 8
September 15, 1852	TILL, THOS. & SON	BURSLEM	
September 16, 1852	MINTON & CO.	STOKE	7, 8
September 24, 1852	MINTON & CO.	STOKE	8
October 01, 1852	COPELAND, W. T.	STOKE	5
October 07, 1852	SCRAGG, RALPH	HANLEY	
October 23, 1852	DAVENPORTS, & CO.	LONGPORT	2, 4, 5
October 25, 1852	BROWNFIELD, WM.	COBRIDGE	10
October 30, 1852	MARPLE, TURNER & CO.	HANLEY	5
November 04, 1852	HOLLAND, JOHN	TUNSTALL	5
November 11, 1852	MINTON & CO.	STOKE	
November 22, 1852	PANKHURST, J. & DIMMOCK, J.	HANLEY	
January 03, 1853	COPELAND, W. T.	STOKE	1
January 12, 1853	GOODFELLOW, THOS.	TUNSTALL	
January 14, 1853	DAVENPORTS, & CO.	LONGPORT	3, 4, 8, 10
January 18, 1853	DAVENPORTS, & CO.	LONGPORT	8
February 04, 1853	PANKHURST, J. & DIMMOCK, J.	HANLEY	4
February 10, 1853	WOOLISCROFT, GEO.	TUNSTALL	4, 5
February 12, 1853	MINTON & CO.	STOKE	
February 26, 1853	COPELAND, W. T.	STOKE	7, 8
March 10, 1853	BELL, J. & M. P. & CO. (LTD.)	GLASGOW	1, 2
March 17, 1853	PANKHURST, J. W. & CO.	HANLEY	
March 19, 1853	MINTON & CO.	STOKE	1
April 23, 1853	ADAMS, WM. & SONS	STOKE	4
May 07, 1853	ALCOCK, JOHN	COBRIDGE	4, 10
June 14, 1853	LIVESLEY, POWELL & CO.	HANLEY	7, 10
June 22, 1853	PANKHURST & DIMMOCK	HANLEY	7
June 24, 1853	RIDGWAY & CO.	SHELTON	

DATE	POTTER	LOCATION	CATEGORY
June 24, 1853	WOOLISCROFT, GEO.	TUNSTALL	5
July 18, 1853	EDWARDS, JOHN	LONGTON	4
August 08, 1853	SHAW, ANTHONY	TUNSTALL	1, 5
August 10, 1853	HOLLAND & GREEN	LONGTON	
September 03, 1853	BOOTE, T. & R.	BURSLEM	4
September 06, 1853	MORLEY, F. & CO.	SHELTON	
September 21, 1853	EDWARDS, JAMES	BURSLEM	4
October 05, 1853	VENABLES, MANN & CO.	BURSLEM	4
October 10, 1853	BARROW & CO.	FENTON	
October 11, 1853	SCRAGG, RALPH	HANLEY	
October 12, 1853	EDWARDS, JAMES	BURSLEM	
October 12, 1853	LIVESLEY, POWELL & CO.	HANLEY	3, 4
October 19, 1853	MINTON & CO.	STOKE	8
October 22, 1853	MAYER, T. J. & J.	LONGPORT	2, 4
November 24, 1853	TILL, THOS. & SON	BURSLEM	
November 26, 1853	COPELAND, W. T.	STOKE	
November 30, 1853	ADAMS, WM. & SONS	STOKE	
December 06, 1853	ALCOCK, JOHN	COBRIDGE	
December 24, 1853	ALCOCK, JOHN	COBRIDGE	
December 24, 1853	MOORE, SAMUEL & CO.	SUNDERLAND	
January 10, 1854	HARDING, W. & G.	BURSLEM	
January 14, 1854	MOORE, SAMUEL & CO.	SUNDERLAND	
January 21, 1854	BELL, J. & M. P. & CO. (LTD.)	GLASGOW	
January 30, 1854	ALCOCK, SAMUEL & CO.	BURSLEM	7
February 23, 1854	COPELAND, W. T.	STOKE	7, 13
March 11, 1854	ALCOCK, SAMUEL & CO.	BURSLEM	8
March 20, 1854	TILL, THOS. & SON	BURSLEM	
March 22, 1854	EDWARDS, JAMES & SON	LONGPORT	4
March 24, 1854	MINTON & CO.	STOKE	
March 31, 1854	HOLLAND & GREEN	LONGTON	4
April 01, 1854	BROWNFIELD, WM.	COBRIDGE	7, 10
April 06, 1854	ALCOCK, SAMUEL & CO.	BURSLEM	8
April 10, 1854	ALCOCK, SAMUEL & CO.	BURSLEM	8
April 11, 1854	PEARSON, FARRALL & MEAKIN	SHELTON	4
May 04, 1854	RIDGWAY, JOHN & CO.	SHELTON	4x
May 08, 1854	BROWNFIELD, WM.	COBRIDGE	
June 03, 1854	TILL, THOS. & SON	BURSLEM	7
June 09, 1854	MEIGH, CHAS. & SON	HANLEY	7
June 21, 1854	BOOTE, T. & R.	BURSLEM	
July 18, 1854	ALCOCK, (SAMUEL) & CO.	BURSLEM	8
July 18, 1854	BOOTE, T. & R.	BURSLEM	4
September 05, 1854	ALCOCK, SAMUEL & CO.	BURSLEM	4, 8
September 12, 1854	COPELAND, W. T.	STOKE	7, 8
October 02, 1854	BROWNFIELD, WM.	COBRIDGE	
October 06, 1854	DAVENPORTS, & CO.	LONGPORT	4, 8
October 09, 1854	MAYER, T. J. & J.	LONGPORT	1
November 10, 1854	RIDGWAY, JOHN & CO.	SHELTON	4x, 5
December 27, 1854	ALCOCK, SAMUEL & CO.	BURSLEM	7, 8
December 27, 1854	PANKHURST & DIMMOCK	HANLEY	7
December 29, 1854	PRATT, F. & R. & CO.	FENTON	
January 06, 1855	ALCOCK, SAMUEL & CO.	BURSLEM	5x, 8
January 15, 1855	BROUGHAM & MAYER	TUNSTALL	4
January 15, 1855	PINDER, BOURNE & HOPE	BURSLEM	
January 19, 1855	PANKHURST & DIMMOCK	HANLEY	4, 7
January 30, 1855	EDWARDS, JOHN	LONGTON	4
February 03, 1855	BELL, J. & M. P. & CO. (LTD.)	GLASGOW	2
February 07, 1855	ALCOCK, JOHN	COBRIDGE	4, 7
February 17, 1855	PRATT & CO.	FENTON	10
February 25, 1855	RIDGWAY, J. & CO.	SHELTON	
March 01, 1855	MINTON & CO.	STOKE	8
March 05, 1855	ELSMORE & FORSTER	TUNSTALL	3, 4
March 17, 1855	BAKER, WM.	FENTON	
April 07, 1855	COPELAND, W. T.	STOKE	5
April 17, 1855	HUGHES, STEPHEN & SON	BURSLEM	4
April 26, 1855	BROWNFIELD, WM.	COBRIDGE	7
April 28, 1855	VENABLES, MANN & CO.	BURSLEM	
May 10, 1855	BEECH, HANCOCK & CO.	BURSLEM	
May 14, 1855	MINTON & CO.	STOKE	8
June 07, 1855	ALCOCK, JOHN	COBRIDGE	4
June 11, 1855	ALCOCK, SAML & CO.	BURSLEM	5x, 8
July 04, 1855	THOMPSON, J.	STAFFORDSHIRE	
July 24, 1855	MEIGH, CHAS. & SON	HANLEY	4, 10
August 06, 1855	DUDSON, JAMES	SHELTON	7
August 08, 1855	EDWARDS, J. & SON	LONGPORT	
August 20, 1855	FORD, THOS.	SHELTON	8
August 27, 1855	BARROW & CO.	FENTON	4
October 03, 1855	MINTON & CO.	STOKE	8
October 25, 1855	CHETWYND, D. (See John Meir & Son)	COBRIDGE	4
October 29, 1855	READE, G. W. (See Meir & Son)	BURSLEM	4
November 01, 1855	WEDGWOOD, JOSIAH & SONS	ETRURIA	
November 22, 1855	BELL, J. & M. P. & CO. (LTD.)	GLASGOW	
November 28, 1855	BROWNFIELD, WM.	COBRIDGE	7
January 05, 1856	EDWARDS, J. (JOHN)	LONGTON	4
January 15, 1856	PANKHURST, JAMES & CO.	HANLEY	4, 7
January 23, 1856	MINTON & CO.	STOKE	7, 8, 10
January 31, 1856	WEDGWOOD, JOSIAH & SONS	ETRURIA	
March 11, 1856	DAVENPORTS, & CO.	LONGPORT	8
March 12, 1856	PRATT & CO.	FENTON	
April 07, 1856	BELL, J. & M. P. & CO. (LTD.)	GLASGOW	

DATE	POTTER	LOCATION	CATEGORY
April 07, 1856	SHAW, A.	TUNSTALL	3, 4
April 18, 1856	BEECH, WILLIAM	BURSLEM	10
April 18, 1856	RIDGWAY & ABINGTON	HANLEY	7
April 18, 1856	SCRAGG, RALPH (See George Frederick Bowers)	HANLEY	4
April 18, 1856	WALLEY, E.	COBRIDGE	2, 7
April 29, 1856	COPELAND, W. & T.*	STOKE	5
April 30, 1856	BROWNFIELD, WM.	COBRIDGE	7
May 08, 1856	MINTON & CO.	STOKE	8
May 22, 1856	MINTON & CO.	STOKE	8
June 13, 1856	MEIGH, CHAS. & SON	HANLEY	7
June 19, 1856	COPELAND, W. & T.*	STOKE	5
June 30, 1856	CLEMENTSON, J.	SHELTON	5
July 28, 1856	CHALLINOR, E.	TUNSTALL	2
July 30, 1856	EDWARDS, J. & SON	LONGPORT	
August 12, 1856	PRATT, F. & R. & CO.	FENTON	
August 19, 1856	PRATT, F. & R. & CO.	FENTON	
August 22, 1856	BOOTE, T. & R.	BURSLEM	4
September 01, 1856	COPELAND, W. T.	STOKE	
October 16, 1856	MINTON & CO.	STOKE	8, 10
October 22, 1856	COPELAND, W. T.	STOKE	7, 8, 13
November 07, 1856	PRATT, F. & R. & CO.	FENTON	
November 14, 1856	DAVENPORTS, & CO.	LONGPORT	1x, 4
November 27, 1856	BROWNFIELD, WM.	COBRIDGE	10
November 27, 1856	DAVENPORTS, & CO.	LONGPORT	1x, 4
November 29, 1856	WALLEY, E.	COBRIDGE	1, 3, 4, 6
December 11, 1856	COPELAND, W. T.	STOKE	
December 18, 1856	MAYER & ELLIOT	LONGPORT	4
December 23, 1856	MAYER & ELLIOT	LONGPORT	
January 15, 1857	PRATT, F. & R. & CO.	FENTON	
January 26, 1857	EDWARDS, J. (JAMES)	LONGPORT	
February 04, 1857	MEIR, JOHN & SON	TUNSTALL	4
February 09, 1857	MINTON & CO.	STOKE	7, 8
February 17, 1857	MINTON & CO.	STOKE	8
February 23, 1857	PODMORE, WALKER & CO.	HANLEY	4
March 20, 1857	ALCOCK, JOHN	COBRIDGE	4
April 16, 1857	ALCOCK, JOHN	COBRIDGE	
April 29, 1857	COPELAND, W. T.	STOKE	13
June 05, 1857	BROWNFIELD, WM.	COBRIDGE	10
June 19, 1857	COPELAND, W. T.	STOKE	7, 13
June 25, 1857	BELL, J. & M. P. & CO. (LTD.)	GLASGOW	
July 30, 1857	RIDGWAY, BATES & CO.	SHELTON	4
September 07, 1857	COPELAND, W. T.	STOKE	
October 14, 1857	RIDGWAY & ABINGTON	HANLEY	7, 11
October 17, 1857	BOOTE, T. & R.	BURSLEM	4
October 17, 1857	MAYER BROS. & ELLIOT	LONGPORT	5
October 22, 1857	PRATT & CO.	FENTON	
December 04, 1857	MINTON & CO.	STOKE	8
December 09, 1857	BROWNFIELD, WM.	COBRIDGE	7
January 29, 1858	COCKSON & HARDING	HANLEY	7
January 29, 1858	WALLEY, E. & W.	COBRIDGE	3, 7
April 17, 1858	RIDGWAY & ABINGTON	HANLEY	
April 22, 1858	BOOTE, T. & R.	BURSLEM	
April 30, 1858	MINTON & CO.	STOKE	8
May 06, 1858	EDWARDS, J. (JOHN)	LONGTON	
May 25, 1858	SHAW, A.	BURSLEM	5
May 31, 1858	ADAMS, WM.	TUNSTALL	3, 4
May 31, 1858	HOLLAND & GREEN	LONGTON	
June 02, 1858	BROWNFIELD, WM.	COBRIDGE	
June 23, 1858	ALCOCK, SAMUEL & CO.	BURSLEM	8
July 13, 1858	MAYER & ELLIOT	LONGPORT	
July 29, 1858	ALCOCK, SAMUEL & CO.	BURSLEM	7, 8
August 24, 1858	BROWNFIELD, WM.	COBRIDGE	10
September 03, 1858	SHARPE BROS. & CO.	DERBYSHIRE	7, 10
September 06, 1858	EDWARDS, JAMES	LONGPORT	4
September 10, 1858	BRIDGWOOD & CLARKE	BURSLEM	
September 10, 1858	EDWARDS, JOHN	LONGTON	
October 05, 1858	BROWNFIELD, WM.	COBRIDGE	7
October 05, 1858	MINTON & CO.	STOKE	7
October 07, 1858	RIDGWAY & ABINGTON	HANLEY	7
October 18, 1858	MINTON & CO.	STOKE	
November 11, 1858	WALLEY, E. & W.	COBRIDGE	2, 3, 7
December 08, 1858	BOOTE, T. & R.	BURSLEM	4
December 08, 1858	CLEMENTSON, J.	HANLEY	3, 4
December 17, 1858	COPELAND, W. T.	STOKE	
December 23, 1858	CLEMENTSON, J.	HANLEY	
December 23, 1858	COPELAND, W. T.	STOKE	
December 27, 1858	CLEMENTSON, J.	HANLEY	
January 25, 1859	COPELAND, W. T.	STOKE	8
February 02, 1859	BOOTE, T. & R.	BURSLEM	
February 03, 1859	DAVENPORTS, & CO.	LONGPORT	8
March 21, 1859	BOOTE, T. & R.	BURSLEM	4, 7
March 29, 1859	BOOTE, T. & R.	BURSLEM	7
May 07, 1859	WALLEY, E. & W.	COBRIDGE	3, 7
May 10, 1859	ALCOCK, SAMUEL & CO.	BURSLEM	8
May 20, 1859	BROWNFIELD, WM.	COBRIDGE	7
July 02, 1859	COPELAND, W. T.	STOKE	8
August 06, 1859	PRATT, F. & R. & CO.	FENTON	
August 27, 1859	ALCOCK, SAMUEL & CO.	BURSLEM	7, 8

DATE	POTTER	LOCATION	CATEGORY
September 01, 1859	EDWARDS, JAMES & SON	LONGPORT	4
October 12, 1859	ADAMS, WM.	TUNSTALL	
October 14, 1859	COPELAND, W. T.	STOKE	5
October 25, 1859	MINTON & CO.	STOKE	10
October 28, 1859	DAVENPORTS, & CO.	LONGPORT	
November 02, 1859	ELSMORE & FORSTER	TUNSTALL	3, 4
November 05, 1859	BROWNFIELD, WM.	COBRIDGE	7
November 17, 1859	MINTON & CO.	STOKE	
November 23, 1859	MINTON & CO.	STOKE	
December 10, 1859	WEDGWOOD, JOSIAH & SONS	ETRURIA	
December 14, 1859	WALLEY, E. & W.	COBRIDGE	2, 7
December 15, 1859	MINTON & CO.	STOKE	8
January 10, 1860	COPELAND, W. T.	STOKE	5
January 23, 1860	MAYER & ELLIOT	LONGPORT	4
February 14, 1860	COPELAND, W. T.	STOKE	8
March 01, 1860	BATES, BROWN-WESTHEAD & MOORE	HANLEY	7, 8
March 27, 1860	BATES, BROWN-WESTHEAD & MOORE	HANLEY	8
April 12, 1860	MINTON & CO.	STOKE	8
May 02, 1860	MEIR, JOHN & SON	TUNSTALL	4
May 30, 1860	CORN, EDWARD	BURSLEM	
June 06, 1860	BROWNFIELD, WM.	COBRIDGE	7
June 22, 1860	MINTON & CO.	STOKE	
June 28, 1860	MINTON & CO.	STOKE	
August 21, 1860	WEDGE.WOOD, JOHN	TUNSTALL	5
September 24, 1860	MINTON & CO.	STOKE	
September 29, 1860	MINTON & CO.	STOKE	
October 18, 1860	BATES, BROWN-WESTHEAD & MOORE	HANLEY	
October 19, 1860	CLEMENTSON, J.	SHELTON	3, 4
October 19, 1860	HOLLAND & GREEN	LONGTON	4
October 29, 1860	BROWNFIELD, WM.	COBRIDGE	7
October 29, 1860	MINTON & CO.	STOKE	7, 8
November 23, 1860	BOOTE, T. & R.	BURSLEM	4
December 03, 1860	BATES, BROWN-WESTHEAD & MOORE	HANLEY	
December 12, 1860	BATES & CO.	HANLEY	7
January 08, 1861	BOOTE, T. & R.	BURSLEM	11
January 21, 1861	WEDGWOOD & CO.	TUNSTALL	7
February 15, 1861	FURNIVAL, J. & CO.	COBRIDGE	
February 27, 1861	EDWARDS, JAMES & SON	LONGPORT	4
March 07, 1861	TURNER & TOMKINSON	TUNSTALL	
March 19, 1861	COPELAND, W. T.	STOKE	5
April 05, 1861	PINDER, BOURNE & HOPE	BURSLEM	7
April 06, 1861	MINTON HOLLINS & CO.	STOKE	
April 12, 1861	DAVENPORTS, & CO.	LONGPORT	4
April 18, 1861	BOOTE, T. & R.	BURSLEM	
April 20, 1861	PRATT, F. & R.	FENTON	7
April 25, 1861	DUDSON, JAMES	HANLEY	7
May 03, 1861	COPELAND, W. T.	STOKE	
May 06, 1861	HILL POTTERY COMPANY LTD. (THE)*	BURSLEM	
May 06, 1861	OLD HALL EARTHENWARE CO., THE	HANLEY	7
May 09, 1861	BATES, BROWN-WESTHEAD & MOORE	HANLEY	7
May 13, 1861	MINTON & CO.	STOKE	
May 31, 1861	CORK, EDGE & MALKIN	BURSLEM	7
June 04, 1861	BATES, BROWN-WESTHEAD & MOORE	HANLEY	7, 8
June 11, 1861	COPELAND, W. T.	STOKE	5, 7
June 13, 1861	MINTON & CO.	STOKE	
July 05, 1861	BEECH & HANCOCK	TUNSTALL	7
July 06, 1861	BROWNFIELD, WM.	COBRIDGE	7
July 18, 1861	WEDGWOOD, JOSIAH & SONS	ETRURIA	
August 19, 1861	BOOTE, T. & R.	BURSLEM	
August 22, 1861	WEDGWOOD & CO.	TUNSTALL	7
August 23, 1861	READE, G. W. (See Charles Meigh & Son)	COBRIDGE	4
September 06, 1861	BROWNFIELD, WM.	COBRIDGE	
September 12, 1861	PEAKE, J. & J.*	NEWCASTLE	
September 17, 1861	COPELAND, W. T.	STOKE	5
October 18, 1861	COPELAND, W. T.	STOKE	5,7
October 24, 1861	HULSEY, NIXON & ADDERLEY	LONGTON	
October 28, 1861	BATES, BROWN-WESTHEAD & MOORE	HANLEY	8
November 15, 1861	CLEMENTSON, J.	HANLEY	3, 4, 7
November 29, 1861	WEDGWOOD, JOSIAH & SONS	ETRURIA	7
December 04, 1861	BROWNFIELD, WM.	COBRIDGE	7, 8
December 20, 1861	WEDGWOOD & CO.	TUNSTALL	
January 11, 1862	BROWNFIELD, WM.	COBRIDGE	
January 25, 1862	BROWNFIELD, WM.	COBRIDGE	7
February 01, 1862	ELLIOT BROS.	LONGPORT	7
February 10, 1862	MINTON & CO.	STOKE	
February 27, 1862	DUDSON, JAMES	HANLEY	7
March 01, 1862	BOOTE, T. & R.	BURSLEM	
March 13, 1862	ADAMS, WM.	TUNSTALL	4
March 13, 1862	COPELAND, W. T.	STOKE	5,7
March 14, 1862	BROWNFIELD, WM.	COBRIDGE	2
March 14, 1862	KNIGHT, J.	FENTON	
March 14, 1862	WEDGWOOD & CO.	TUNSTALL	
March 22, 1862	BOOTE, T. & R.	BURSLEM	4,7
March 27, 1862	BELL, J. & M. P. & CO. (LTD.)	GLASGOW	1x, 2x
March 28, 1862	BELL, J. & M. P. & CO. (LTD.)	GLASGOW	1x, 2x, 7
March 29, 1862	MINTON & CO.	STOKE	7
April 01, 1862	WEDGWOOD, JOSIAH & SONS	ETRURIA	
April 04, 1862	FURNIVAL, J. & T.	COBRIDGE	

DATE	POTTER	LOCATION	CATEGORY
April 04, 1862	MINTON & CO.	STOKE	8
April 09, 1862	OLD HALL EARTHENWARE CO. (LTD.) THE	HANLEY	7
April 17, 1862	TURNER & TOMKINSON	TUNSTALL	
May 01, 1862	EARDLEY & HAMMERSLEY	TUNSTALL	
May 01, 1862	EARDLEY & HAMMERSLEY*	TUNSTALL	
May 03, 1862	ASHWORTH, G. L. & BROS.	HANLEY	
May 09, 1862	BROWN, T.C.-WESTHEAD, MOORE & CO.	HANLEY	8
May 14, 1862	JONES, GEO. & CO.	STOKE	
May 27, 1862	CHALLINOR, E.	TUNSTALL	5
May 29, 1862	FURNIVAL, J. & CO.	COBRIDGE	7
June 24, 1862	BROWN, T.C.-WESTHEAD, MOORE & CO.	HANLEY	
July 02, 1862	MINTON & CO.	STOKE	
July 04, 1862	CLEMENTSON, J.	HANLEY	4x,7
July 12, 1862	CLEMENTSON, J.	HANLEY	4x
July 14, 1862	BEECH & HANCOCK	TUNSTALL	7
July 19, 1862	CLEMENTSON, J.	HANLEY	4x
July 31, 1862	JONES & ELLIS*	LONGTON	
July 31, 1862	MINTON & CO.	STOKE	
August 18, 1862	HULSEY, NIXON & ADDERLEY	LONGTON	7
August 19, 1862	ASHWORTH, G. L. & BROS.	HANLEY	11
August 25, 1862	BODLEY, E. F. & CO.	BURSLEM	8
August 30, 1862	BOOTE, T. & R.	BURSLEM	
August 30, 1862	FELL, THOS. & CO.	NEWCASTLE UPON TYNE	
September 06, 1862	MALKIN, WALKER & HULSE	LONGTON	
September 11, 1862	MINTON & CO.	STOKE	
September 17, 1862	HOPE & CARTER	BURSLEM	4x
September 22, 1862	MINTON & CO.	STOKE	
September 26, 1862	HOPE & CARTER	BURSLEM	4x, 7
October 01, 1862	FELL, THOS. & CO.	NEWCASTLE UPON TYNE	
October 15, 1862	TURNER & TOMKINSON	TUNSTALL	
October 23, 1862	BAKER, WM. & CO.	FENTON	4, 7
November 11, 1862	BODLEY, E. F. & CO.	BURSLEM	8
November 19, 1862	WOOLISCROFT, GEO.	TUNSTALL	
November 28, 1862	MINTON & CO.	STOKE	8
December 03, 1862	BROWN, T.C.-WESTHEAD, MOORE & CO.	HANLEY	8
December 05, 1862	BROWNFIELD, WM.	COBRIDGE	7
December 17, 1862	OLD HALL EARTHENWARE CO. (LTD.) THE	HANLEY	
December 18, 1862	JONES, GEO.	STOKE	
January 12, 1863	DAVENPORT, BANKS & CO.	ETRURIA	4
January 16, 1863	LIDDLE, ELLIOT & SONS	LONGPORT	7
January 16, 1863	MINTON & CO.	STOKE	7, 8
January 29, 1863	WEDGWOOD, JOSIAH & SONS	ETRURIA	
January 30, 1863	BOOTE, T. & R.	BURSLEM	4
February 02, 1863	MINTON & CO.	STOKE	8
February 17, 1863	BOOTE, T. & R.	BURSLEM	
March 06, 1863	ASHWORTH, G. L. & BROS.	HANLEY	
March 13, 1863	HOPE & CARTER	BURSLEM	7
March 20, 1863	PRATT, JOHN & CO.	FENTON	7
March 21, 1863	BEECH & HANCOCK	TUNSTALL	7
March 21, 1863	EDWARDS, JAMES & SON	BURSLEM	
March 21, 1863	HULSEY, NIXON & ADDERLEY	LONGTON	
March 23, 1863	BODLEY & HARROLD	BURSLEM	5, 5x, 7
April 11, 1863	MACINTYRE, J.	BURSLEM	7
April 23, 1863	BROWN, T.C.-WESTHEAD, MOORE & CO.	HANLEY	
April 25, 1863	BEECH & HANCOCK	TUNSTALL	7
May 11, 1863	PEARSON, E.	COBRIDGE	4
May 12, 1863	BODLEY & HARROLD	BURSLEM	
May 22, 1863	COPELAND, W. T.	STOKE	1, 5, 8
May 26, 1863	BROWN, T.C.-WESTHEAD, MOORE & CO.	HANLEY	8
June 04, 1863	OLD HALL EARTHENWARE CO. (LTD.) THE	HANLEY	
June 08, 1863	BROWNFIELD, WM.	COBRIDGE	
June 08, 1863	MINTON & CO.	STOKE	8
July 14, 1863	TURNER & TOMKINSON	TUNSTALL	
July 15, 1863	VENABLES, H.	HANLEY	
July 20, 1863	BROWNFIELD, WM.	COBRIDGE	
July 24, 1863	COPELAND, W. T.	STOKE	5, 7
July 28, 1863	MINTON & CO.	STOKE	
August 11, 1863	TURNER & TOMKINSON	TUNSTALL	
August 12, 1863	HANCOCK, WHITTINGHAM & CO.	BURSLEM	7
August 21, 1863	CLEMENTSON, J.	HANLEY	3, 4
August 28, 1863	VENABLES, H.	HANLEY	
September 07, 1863	BOOTE, T. & R.	BURSLEM	
September 28, 1863	EDWARDS, JAMES & SON	LONGPORT	
September 28, 1863	VENABLES, H.	HANLEY	
October 02, 1863	VENABLES, H.	HANLEY	
October 14, 1863	BROWNFIELD, WM.	COBRIDGE	7
October 17, 1863	BOOTE, T. & R.	BURSLEM	4
October 22, 1863	EARDLEY & HAMMERSLEY	TUNSTALL	
October 24, 1863	WEDGWOOD, JOSIAH & SONS	ETRURIA	
October 26, 1863	OLD HALL EARTHENWARE CO. (LTD.) THE	HANLEY	
October 28, 1863	JONES, GEO. & CO.	STOKE	
October 31, 1863	WOOD, EDMUND, T.	TUNSTALL	4, 7
November 03, 1863	MEIR, JOHN & SON	TUNSTALL	4
November 04, 1863	BOOTE, T. & R.	BURSLEM	
November 06, 1863	JONES, GEO. & CO.	STOKE	
November 26, 1863	BROWNFIELD, WM.	COBRIDGE	
November 27, 1863	BODLEY & HARROLD	BURSLEM	
December 02, 1863	BOOTE, T. & R.	BURSLEM	
December 02, 1863	PANKHURST, J. W.	HANLEY	4
December 18, 1863	PRATT, F. & R. & CO.	FENTON	7
December 23, 1863	BROWNFIELD, WM.	COBRIDGE	10
December 30, 1863	BROWN, T.C.-WESTHEAD, MOORE & CO.	HANLEY	8
January 05, 1864	BROWNFIELD, WM.	COBRIDGE	
January 11, 1864	MALKIN, WALKER & HULSE	LONGTON	
February 02, 1864	WEDGWOOD, JOSIAH & SONS	ETRURIA	
February 05, 1864	HOPE & CARTER	BURSLEM	
February 13, 1864	COPELAND, W. T.	STOKE	7, 8
February 22, 1864	CORK, EDGE & MALKIN	BURSLEM	
February 25, 1864	LIDDLE, ELLIOT & SON	LONGPORT	7
March 03, 1864	ASHWORTH, G. L. & BROS.	HANLEY	
March 12, 1864	CORK, EDGE & MALKIN	BURSLEM	2, 7
March 18, 1864	BROWN, T.C.-WESTHEAD, MOORE & CO.	HANLEY	8
March 22, 1864	MINTON & CO.	STOKE	
March 23, 1864	BURGESS & LEIGH	BURSLEM	7
April 09, 1864	WEDGWOOD, JOSIAH & SONS	ETRURIA	
April 15, 1864	JONES, GEO.	STOKE	
April 18, 1864	MINTON & CO.	STOKE	
April 21, 1864	BROWN, T.C.-WESTHEAD, MOORE & CO.	HANLEY	8
April 21, 1864	LIDDLE, ELLIOT & SON	LONGPORT	7
April 23, 1864	ASHWORTH, G. L. & BROS.	HANLEY	
April 26, 1864	BODLEY & HARROLD	BURSLEM	
April 27, 1864	HOPE & CARTER	BURSLEM	
April 29, 1864	BROWNFIELD, WM.	COBRIDGE	7
May 10, 1864	JONES, GEO. & CO.	STOKE	
June 09, 1864	MINTON & CO.	STOKE	8
June 16, 1864	HOPE & CARTER	BURSLEM	
June 30, 1864	BROWNFIELD, WM.	COBRIDGE	
July 09, 1864	PINDER, BOURNE & CO.	BURSLEM	
July 11, 1864	PINDER, BOURNE & CO.	BURSLEM	
July 18, 1864	BODLEY & HARROLD	BURSLEM	
July 19, 1864	HOPE & CARTER	BURSLEM	
July 28, 1864	HOLLAND & GREEN	LONGTON	
August 20, 1864	JONES, GEO. & CO.	STOKE	
August 26, 1864	BROWN, T.C.-WESTHEAD, MOORE & CO.	HANLEY	
September 06, 1864	COPELAND, W. T.	STOKE	5
September 10, 1864	MINTON & CO.	STOKE	7
September 12, 1864	MINTON & CO.	STOKE	
September 14, 1864	BODLEY & HARROLD	BURSLEM	
September 16, 1864	ASHWORTH, G. L. & BROS.	HANLEY	
September 19, 1864	WEDGWOOD, JOSIAH & SONS	ETRURIA	
September 21, 1864	MINTON & CO.	STOKE	
September 22, 1864	WEDGWOOD, JOSIAH & SONS	ETRURIA	
October 04, 1864	JONES, GEO. & CO.	STOKE	
October 12, 1864	BROWNFIELD, WM.	COBRIDGE	7
October 28, 1864	BODLEY & HARROLD	BURSLEM	7
October 28, 1864	MINTON & CO.	STOKE	8
October 29, 1864	COLLINSON, CHAS. & CO.	BURSLEM	6, 7
October 31, 1864	CORK, EDGE & MALKIN	BURSLEM	7
November 01, 1864	COPELAND, W. T.	STOKE	8
November 04, 1864	LIVESLEY, POWELL & CO.	HANLEY	7
November 10, 1864	ELSMORE & FORSTER	TUNSTALL	3, 4
November 10, 1864	HOPE & CARTER	BURSLEM	
November 10, 1864	JONES, GEO. & CO.	STOKE	
November 24, 1864	BROWN, T.C.-WESTHEAD, MOORE & CO.	HANLEY	8
November 29, 1864	HOPE & CARTER	BURSLEM	7
December 10, 1864	HOPE & CARTER	BURSLEM	
December 31, 1864	JONES, GEO. & CO.	STOKE	
January 06, 1865	HOPE & CARTER	BURSLEM	5x
January 06, 1865	MINTON & CO.	STOKE	8
January 14, 1865	JONES, GEO. & CO.	STOKE	
February 01, 1865	MINTON & CO.	STOKE	8
February 02, 1865	ASHWORTH, G. L. & BROS.	HANLEY	
February 13, 1865	PRATT, F. & R. & CO.	FENTON	
February 14, 1865	LIDDLE, ELLIOT & SON	LONGPORT	
February 27, 1865	LIVESLEY, POWELL & CO.	HANLEY	
March 31, 1865	HOPE & CARTER	BURSLEM	5x
April 01, 1865	BROWNFIELD, WM.	COBRIDGE	7
April 03, 1865	MINTON & CO.	STOKE	
April 22, 1865	EDWARDS, JAMES & SON	BURSLEM	
April 22, 1865	TILL, THOS. & SONS	BURSLEM	5
April 26, 1865	EDWARDS, JAMES & SON	BURSLEM	
April 28, 1865	ALCOCK, HENRY & CO.	COBRIDGE	

DATE	POTTER	LOCATION	CATEGORY
April 28, 1865	HOPE & CARTER	BURSLEM	5x
May 02, 1865	LIVESLEY, POWELL & CO.	HANLEY	7
May 15, 1865	HUDDEN, J. T.	LONGTON	
May 17, 1865	MINTON & CO.	STOKE	8
June 06, 1865	HUDDEN, J. T.	LONGTON	
June 14, 1865	HILL POTTERY COMPANY LTD. (THE)*	BURSLEM	
June 15, 1865	HUDDEN, J. T.	LONGTON	
June 29, 1865	BODLEY, ED. F. & CO.	BURSLEM	7, 8
June 30, 1865	HILL POTTERY COMPANY LTD. (THE)*	BURSLEM	
July 03, 1865	BROWN, T.C.-WESTHEAD, MOORE & CO.	HANLEY	8
July 12, 1865	EDWARDS, JAMES & SON	BURSLEM	7
August 21, 1865	FURNIVAL, J. & CO.	COBRIDGE	
August 23, 1865	WEDGWOOD, JOSIAH & SONS	ETRURIA	
September 14, 1865	BROWN, T.C.-WESTHEAD, MOORE & CO.	HANLEY	8
September 18, 1865	LIDDLE, ELLIOT & SON	LONGPORT	4
September 28, 1865	MINTON & CO.	STOKE	
September 30, 1865	BARKER S. & SON	SWINTON	
October 13, 1865	BROWN, T.C.-WESTHEAD, MOORE & CO.	HANLEY	8
October 30, 1865	BROWNFIELD, WM.	COBRIDGE	7
November 10, 1865	PINDER, BOURNE & CO. & ANTHONY SHAW	BURSLEM	
November 23, 1865	OLD HALL EARTHENWARE CO. LTD., THE	HANLEY	
November 29, 1865	EDWARDS, JAMES & SON	BURSLEM	
December 23, 1865	DUDSON, JAMES	HANLEY	7
January 02, 1866	PRATT & CO.	FENTON	
January 03, 1866	CLOSE, J. T. & CO.	STOKE	4
January 13, 1866	BODLEY, ED. F. & CO.	BURSLEM	8
January 17, 1866	BURGESS & LEIGH	BURSLEM	5
January 24, 1866	MINTON & CO.	STOKE	8
January 31, 1866	EDWARDS, JAMES & SON	BURSLEM	7
February 02, 1866	COPELAND, W. T.	STOKE	8
March 02, 1866	FORD, CHALLINOR & CO.	TUNSTALL	5
March 10, 1866	OLD HALL EARTHENWARE CO. (LTD.) THE	HANLEY	
April 14, 1866	ASHWORTH, G. L. & BROS.	HANLEY	4, 5x
April 14, 1866	WALKER & CARTER	LONGTON	5
April 16, 1866	OLD HALL EARTHENWARE CO. (LTD.) THE	HANLEY	
April 18, 1866	EDWARDS, JAMES & SON	BURSLEM	
April 20, 1866	BROWNFIELD, WM.	COBRIDGE	7
May 01, 1866	FURNIVAL, J. & CO.	COBRIDGE	
May 25, 1866	HOPE & CARTER	BURSLEM	
June 12, 1866	EDWARDS, JOHN	FENTON	4
June 21, 1866	PINDER, BOURNE & CO.	BURSLEM	
July 19, 1866	HUDDEN, J. T.	LONGTON	
July 25, 1866	HOPE & CARTER	STOKE	
July 25, 1866	JONES, GEO.	STOKE	
August 29, 1866	BODLEY, ED. F. & CO.	BURSLEM	
September 06, 1866	PRATT, F. & R. & CO.	FENTON	7
September 15, 1866	ASHWORTH, G. L. & BROS.	HANLEY	5x
October 08, 1866	MINTON & CO.	STOKE	8
October 13, 1866	FURNIVAL, THOS.	COBRIDGE	7
November 03, 1866	MINTON & CO.	STOKE	8
November 12, 1866	COPELAND, W. T.	STOKE	
November 14, 1866	BROWN, T.C.-WESTHEAD, MOORE & CO.	HANLEY	8
December 13, 1866	LIDDLE, ELLIOT & SON	LONGPORT	7
December 14, 1866	BARKER SAMUEL & SON	SWINTON	
December 15, 1866	BROWN, T.C.-WESTHEAD, MOORE & CO.	HANLEY	8
December 19, 1866	MEIR, JOHN & SON	TUNSTALL	7
December 24, 1866	HUDDEN, J. T.	LONGTON	
January 08, 1867	EDWARDS, JAMES & SON	BURSLEM	
January 17, 1867	BODLEY, ED. F. & CO.	BURSLEM	8
February 09, 1867	BODLEY, ED. F. & CO.	BURSLEM	8
February 23, 1867	WORTHINGTON & HARROP	HANLEY	
March 02, 1867	WEDGWOOD, JOSIAH & SONS	ETRURIA	
March 04, 1867	BROWN, T.C.-WESTHEAD, MOORE & CO.	HANLEY	8
March 05, 1867	POWELL & BISHOP	HANLEY	
March 06, 1867	OLD HALL EARTHENWARE CO. (LTD.) THE	HANLEY	
March 09, 1867	EDWARDS, JOHN	FENTON	
March 11, 1867	WEDGWOOD, JOSIAH & SONS	ETRURIA	
March 14, 1867	DAVENPORT, BANKS & CO.	ETRURIA	
March 15, 1867	BROWNFIELD, WM.	COBRIDGE	7, 8
March 18, 1867	COCKSON, CHETWYND & CO.	COBRIDGE	
March 19, 1867	EDWARDS, JAMES & SON	BURSLEM	
March 20, 1867	WEDGWOOD, JOSIAH & SONS	ETRURIA	
March 21, 1867	EDWARDS, JAMES & SON	BURSLEM	
March 25, 1867	WEDGWOOD, JOSIAH & SONS	ETRURIA	
March 26, 1867	MINTON & CO.	STOKE	
April 03, 1867	MINTON & CO.	STOKE	
April 04, 1867	ELSMORE & FORSTER	TUNSTALL	3, 4
April 04, 1867	WEDGWOOD, JOSIAH & SONS	ETRURIA	
April 17, 1867	HOBSON, CHAS.	BURSLEM	
April 24, 1867	COPELAND, W. T.	STOKE	8
May 06, 1867	BELL, J. & M. P. & CO. (LTD.)	GLASGOW	7
May 07, 1867	MEIR, JOHN & SON	TUNSTALL	
May 08, 1867	BROWN, T.C.-WESTHEAD, MOORE & CO.	HANLEY	8
May 22, 1867	CLEMENTSON BROS.	HANLEY	4
June 06, 1867	WEDGWOOD, JOSIAH & SONS	ETRURIA	7
June 11, 1867	CLEMENTSON BROS.	HANLEY	3
June 11, 1867	COCKSON, CHETWYND & CO.	COBRIDGE	
June 21, 1867	BROWNFIELD, WM.	COBRIDGE	10
June 21, 1867	CHETWYND, E. & D.	HANLEY	
June 24, 1867	CHETWYND, E. & D.	HANLEY	
July 04, 1867	RIDGWAY, E. J.	HANLEY	11
July 08, 1867	ASHWORTH, G. L. & BROS.	HANLEY	
July 12, 1867	JONES, GEO.	STOKE	4
July 15, 1867	WEDGWOOD, JOSIAH & SONS	ETRURIA	
July 17, 1867	CHETWYND, E. & D.	HANLEY	
July 25, 1867	HOPE & CARTER	BURSLEM	5
September 17, 1867	WEDGWOOD & CO.	TUNSTALL	5
September 21, 1867	ASHWORTH, G. L. & BROS.	HANLEY	7
September 25, 1867	POWELL & BISHOP	HANLEY	
October 02, 1867	MINTON & CO.	STOKE	
October 03, 1867	MINTON & CO.	STOKE	
October 07, 1867	MINTON & CO.	STOKE	
October 10, 1867	BOOTH, THOS.	HANLEY	7
October 24, 1867	FORD, CHALLINOR & CO.	TUNSTALL	5
October 26, 1867	COPELAND, W. T. & SONS	STOKE	8
October 28, 1867	COPELAND, W. T. & SONS	STOKE	8, 9
October 29, 1867	WEDGWOOD, JOSIAH & SONS	ETRURIA	
October 30, 1867	HUDDEN, J. T.	LONGTON	
October 31, 1867	POWELL & BISHOP	HANLEY	7
November 07, 1867	EDWARDS, JAMES & SON	BURSLEM	
November 18, 1867	FORD, CHALLINOR & CO.	TUNSTALL	5
December 03, 1867	COPELAND, W. T. & SONS	STOKE	13
December 12, 1867	PRATT, F. & R. & CO.	FENTON	
December 20, 1867	WEDGWOOD, JOSIAH & SONS	ETRURIA	7
January 03, 1868	MINTON & CO.	STOKE	
January 07, 1868	COCKSON, CHETWYND & CO.	COBRIDGE	4,7
January 08, 1868	BOOTE, T. & R.	BURSLEM	4
January 10, 1868	CORK, EDGE & MALKIN	BURSLEM	5
January 11, 1868	BROWNFIELD, WM.	COBRIDGE	
January 13, 1868	ASHWORTH, G. L. & BROS.	HANLEY	
January 16, 1868	OLD HALL EARTHENWARE CO. (LTD.) THE	HANLEY	
January 25, 1868	HOPE & CARTER	BURSLEM	5x
January 30, 1868	FURNIVAL, J. & CO.	COBRIDGE	1, 4, 7
January 31, 1868	BOOTE, T. & R.	BURSLEM	
January 31, 1868	WEDGWOOD, JOSIAH & SONS	ETRURIA	
February 10, 1868	MINTON & CO.	STOKE	8
February 12, 1868	WEDGWOOD, JOSIAH & SONS	ETRURIA	
February 18, 1868	BROWN, T.C.-WESTHEAD, MOORE & CO.	HANLEY	1, 7
February 18, 1868	WEDGWOOD, JOSIAH & SONS	ETRURIA	8
February 20, 1868	MINTON & CO.	STOKE	
February 27, 1868	ALCOCK & DIGORY	BURSLEM	8
March 05, 1868	MINTON & CO.	STOKE	8
March 25, 1868	COPELAND, W. T. & SONS	STOKE	
March 26, 1868	WALKER & CARTER	LONGTON	7
April 01, 1868	MINTON & CO.	STOKE	8
April 06, 1868	PINDER, BOURNE & CO.	BURSLEM	
April 16, 1868	ASHWORTH, G. L. & BROS.	HANLEY	
April 21, 1868	BEECH & HANCOCK	TUNSTALL	
April 23, 1868	HAMMERSLEY, R.	TUNSTALL	1, 6
April 28, 1868	GREEN, T. G.	BURTON ON TRENT	
May 14, 1868	HOPE & CARTER	BURSLEM	5x
May 26, 1868	BROWN, T.C.-WESTHEAD, MOORE & CO.	HANLEY	
May 26, 1868	PINDER, BOURNE & CO.	BURSLEM	
May 28, 1868	HOLDCROFT & WOOD*	TUNSTALL	
May 28, 1868	MINTON & CO.	STOKE	
May 30, 1868	BOOTE, T. & R.	BURSLEM	7
June 08, 1868	BURGESS & LEIGH	BURSLEM	
June 12, 1868	BROWNFIELD, WM.	COBRIDGE	7
June 22, 1868	MINTON & CO.	STOKE	
July 10, 1868	WEDGWOOD, JOSIAH & SONS	ETRURIA	
July 20, 1868	HOPE & CARTER	BURSLEM	5x
July 24, 1868	COPELAND, W. T. & SONS	STOKE	7, 8
August 01, 1868	BOOTE, T. & R.	BURSLEM	
August 13, 1868	WEDGWOOD, JOSIAH & SONS	ETRURIA	
August 15, 1868	EDWARDS, JAMES & SON	BURSLEM	
August 17, 1868	BODLEY, ED. F. & CO.	BURSLEM	5
August 21, 1868	MALKIN, RALPH	FENTON	5
August 31, 1868	BOOTE, T. & R.	BURSLEM	
September 01, 1868	WARDLE, JAMES	HANLEY	
September 04, 1868	GELSON BROS.	HANLEY	7
September 05, 1868	BROWN, T.C.-WESTHEAD, MOORE & CO.	HANLEY	1x, 8
September 09, 1868	HOPE & CARTER	BURSLEM	5x, 7

DATE	POTTER	LOCATION	CATEGORY
September 09, 1868	JONES, F. & CO.	LONGTON	4, 7
September 09, 1868	WEDGWOOD & CO.	TUNSTALL	5
September 12, 1868	MINTON & CO.	STOKE	
September 14, 1868	BOOTH, THOS. & CO.	BURSLEM	5
September 25, 1868	BROWN, T.C.-WESTHEAD, MOORE & CO.	HANLEY	1x, 8
September 25, 1868	MINTON & CO.	STOKE	
October 08, 1868	MINTON & CO.	STOKE	
October 09, 1868	DAVENPORTS, & CO.	LONGPORT	8
October 09, 1868	HOPE & CARTER	BURSLEM	5x
October 14, 1868	JONES, GEO.	STOKE	
October 17, 1868	MINTON & CO.	STOKE	8
October 21, 1868	BROWNFIELD, WM. (Reg'd by W.P.&G.Phillips)	COBRIDGE	7
October 22, 1868	EDWARDS, JAMES & SON	BURSLEM	
November 03, 1868	BROWN, T.C.-WESTHEAD, MOORE & CO.	HANLEY	1x, 8
November 03, 1868	MINTON & CO.	STOKE	8
November 06, 1868	POWELL & BISHOP	HANLEY	
November 09, 1868	WEDGWOOD, JOSIAH & SONS	ETRURIA	
November 21, 1868	MINTON & CO.	STOKE	8
November 24, 1868	BROWN, T.C.-WESTHEAD, MOORE & CO.	HANLEY	1x, 8
November 25, 1868	CORK, EDGE & MALKIN	BURSLEM	7
December 01, 1868	BROWN, T.C.-WESTHEAD, MOORE & CO.	HANLEY	1x, 8
December 11, 1868	BODLEY, ED. F. & CO.	BURSLEM	
December 12, 1868	BROWNFIELD, WM.	COBRIDGE	7
December 14, 1868	COCKSON, CHETWYND & CO.	COBRIDGE	7
December 23, 1868	MINTON & CO.	STOKE	7
December 31, 1868	ASHWORTH, G. L. & BROS.	HANLEY	7
December 31, 1868	HAMMERSLEY, R.	TUNSTALL	6x
January 01, 1869	JONES, GEO.	STOKE	
January 04, 1869	MINTON & CO.	STOKE	8
January 21, 1869	MINTON & CO.	STOKE	8
January 22, 1869	BROWN, T.C.-WESTHEAD, MOORE & CO.	HANLEY	1x, 8
January 22, 1869	GELSON BROS.	HANLEY	
January 28, 1869	MINTON & CO.	STOKE	
February 01, 1869	BROWN, T.C.-WESTHEAD, MOORE & CO.	HANLEY	1x, 8
February 09, 1869	MINTON & CO.	STOKE	8
February 11, 1869	JONES, GEO.	STOKE	
February 15, 1869	BOOTH, THOS. & CO.	BURSLEM	
February 19, 1869	WEDGWOOD, JOSIAH & SONS	ETRURIA	1
February 22, 1869	PINDER, BOURNE & CO.	BURSLEM	
February 22, 1869	WEDGWOOD, JOSIAH & SONS	ETRURIA	
February 27, 1869	WEDGWOOD, JOSIAH & SONS	ETRURIA	
March 03, 1869	TILL, THOS. & SONS	BURSLEM	
March 06, 1869	PRIMAVESI, F.	CARDIFF	
March 08, 1869	PRATT, F. & R. & CO.	FENTON	
March 09, 1869	JONES, GEO.	STOKE	
March 09, 1869	JONES, GEO.	STOKE	
March 10, 1869	PRIMAVESI, F.	CARDIFF	
March 24, 1869	WILEMAN, J. F.	FENTON	
April 1, 1869	WOOD & PIGOTT	TUNSTALL	5
April 02, 1869	BROWNFIELD, WM.	COBRIDGE	
April 02, 1869	MINTON & CO.	STOKE	8
April 06, 1869	BAKER & CHETWYND	BURSLEM	
April 07, 1869	MINTON & CO.	STOKE	8
April 12, 1869	LIDDLE, ELLIOT & SON	LONGPORT	
April 20, 1869	LIDDLE, ELLIOT & SON	LONGPORT	
May 13, 1869	EDWARDS, JAMES & SON	BURSLEM	
May 26, 1869	BOOTH, THOS.	HANLEY	7
May 27, 1869	DAVENPORT(S) & CO.	LONGPORT	4
May 27, 1869	DAVENPORT, & CO.	LONGPORT	
June 19, 1869	BROWNFIELD, WM.	COBRIDGE	7
June 25, 1869	EDWARDS, JAMES & SON	BURSLEM	
June 26, 1869	MINTON & CO.	STOKE	8
July 03, 1869	WEDGWOOD, JOSIAH & SONS	ETRURIA	
July 06, 1869	MEIR, JOHN & SON	TUNSTALL	
July 19, 1869	WARDLE, JAMES	HANLEY	
July 20, 1869	WEDGWOOD, JOSIAH & SONS	ETRURIA	
July 23, 1869	MINTON & CO.	STOKE	
July 24, 1869	COPELAND, W. T. & SONS	STOKE	8
July 27, 1869	HUDDEN, J. T.	LONGTON	
August 02, 1869	COPELAND, W. T. & SONS	STOKE	8
August 03, 1869	EDWARDS, JOHN	FENTON	
August 04, 1869	TOMKINSON BROS. & CO.	HANLEY	
August 19, 1869	COPELAND, W. T. & SONS	STOKE	8
August 26, 1869	COPELAND, W. T. & SONS	STOKE	8
August 31, 1869	COPELAND, W. T. & SONS	STOKE	8
August 31, 1869	PRATT, JOHN & CO.	LANE DELPH	
September 04, 1869	MINTON & CO.	STOKE	
September 08, 1869	COPELAND, W. T. & SONS	STOKE	8
September 08, 1869	PINDER, BOURNE & CO.	BURSLEM	
September 09, 1869	PRATT, JOHN & CO.	LANE DELPH	
September 10, 1869	MINTON & CO.	STOKE	
September 21, 1869	GELSON BROS.	HANLEY	4

DATE	POTTER	LOCATION	CATEGORY
September 30, 1869	BROWN, T.C.-WESTHEAD, MOORE & CO.	HANLEY	1x, 8
October 01, 1869	MINTON & CO.	STOKE	
October 04, 1869	MINTON & CO.	STOKE	
October 15, 1869	JONES, GEO.	STOKE	
October 23, 1869	JONES, GEO.	STOKE	
October 29, 1869	MINTON & CO.	STOKE	
October 29, 1869	POWELL & BISHOP	HANLEY	3, 3x, 4, 4x
November 02, 1869	CLARKE, ED.	TUNSTALL	
November 03, 1869	BROWN, T.C.-WESTHEAD, MOORE & CO.	HANLEY	1x, 8
November 08, 1869	BROWN, T.C.-WESTHEAD, MOORE & CO.	HANLEY	1x, 8
November 10, 1869	BROWNFIELD, WM.	COBRIDGE	7
November 15, 1869	LIDDLE, ELLIOT & SON	LONGPORT	2, 7
November 18, 1869	ALCOCK & DIGORY	BURSLEM	8
November 24, 1869	MINTON & CO.	STOKE	8
November 26, 1869	MINTON & CO.	STOKE	
December 01, 1869	JONES, GEO.	STOKE	
December 03, 1869	BROWNFIELD, WM.	COBRIDGE	
December 17, 1869	MINTON & CO.	STOKE	
December 18, 1869	POWELL & BISHOP	HANLEY	3x, 4x, 7
December 22, 1869	JONES, GEO.	STOKE	
December 24, 1869	GELSON BROS.	HANLEY	
December 28, 1869	PRATT, JOHN & CO.	LANE DELPH	5
December 31, 1869	MINTON & CO.	STOKE	
January 01, 1870	BROWN, T.C.-WESTHEAD, MOORE & CO.	HANLEY	1x, 8
January 03, 1870	JONES, GEO.	STOKE	
January 15, 1870	LIDDLE, ELLIOT & SON	LONGPORT	
January 27, 1870	HOBSON, CHAS.	BURSLEM	7
January 29, 1870	MINTON & CO.	STOKE	8
February 01, 1870	BROWN, T.C.-WESTHEAD, MOORE & CO.	HANLEY	1x, 8
February 03, 1870	BROWN, T.C.-WESTHEAD, MOORE & CO.	HANLEY	1x, 8
February 04, 1870	POWELL & BISHOP	HANLEY	7
February 09, 1870	WEDGWOOD, JOSIAH & SONS	ETRURIA	
February 10, 1870	MINTON & CO.	STOKE	8
February 15, 1870	BROWN, T.C.-WESTHEAD, MOORE & CO.	HANLEY	1x, 8
February 25, 1870	MINTON & CO.	STOKE	
February 28, 1870	MINTON & CO.	STOKE	
March 02, 1870	MINTON & CO.	STOKE	8
March 07, 1870	HOBSON, CHAS.	BURSLEM	
March 08, 1870	JONES, GEO.	STOKE	
March 10, 1870	JONES, GEO.	STOKE	
March 10, 1870	POWELL & BISHOP	HANLEY	
March 14, 1870	BROWN, T.C.-WESTHEAD, MOORE & CO.	HANLEY	1x, 8
March 15, 1870	TILL, THOS. & SONS	BURSLEM	
March 16, 1870	MINTON & CO.	STOKE	8
March 25, 1870	HOPE & CARTER	BURSLEM	
March 25, 1870	MINTON & CO.	STOKE	
March 26, 1870	MINTON & CO.	STOKE	8
March 28, 1870	OLD HALL EARTHENWARE CO. LTD., THE	HANLEY	
April 07, 1870	ADAMS, HARVEY & CO.	LONGTON	
April 07, 1870	BAKER & CO.	FENTON	
April 07, 1870	CORK, EDGE & MALKIN	BURSLEM	
April 09, 1870	MINTON & CO.	STOKE	
April 14, 1870	MINTON & CO.	STOKE	8
May 13, 1870	BROWN, T.C.-WESTHEAD, MOORE & CO.	HANLEY	1x, 8
May 17, 1870	BROWN, T.C.-WESTHEAD, MOORE & CO.	HANLEY	1x, 8
May 18, 1870	BATES, ELLIOTT & CO.	LONGPORT	
May 21, 1870	EDWARDS, JAMES & SON	BURSLEM	
May 21, 1870	OLD HALL EARTHENWARE CO. LTD., THE	HANLEY	
May 25, 1870	EDWARDS, JAMES & SON	BURSLEM	
May 26, 1870	MINTON & CO.	STOKE	7
May 30, 1870	JONES, GEO.	STOKE	
June 03, 1870	PRATT, F. & R. & CO.	FENTON	
June 07, 1870	BOOTH, THOS.	HANLEY	
June 09, 1870	BROWN, T.C.-WESTHEAD, MOORE & CO.	HANLEY	8
June 10, 1870	BROWNFIELD, WM.	COBRIDGE	7
June 11, 1870	EDWARDS, JAMES & SON	BURSLEM	
June 17, 1870	MINTON HOLLINS & CO.	STOKE	
June 22, 1870	ADAMS, HARVEY & CO.	LONGTON	
June 22, 1870	MINTON HOLLINS & CO.	STOKE	
June 27, 1870	JONES, GEO.	STOKE	7
July 05, 1870	BAKER & CO.	FENTON	
July 08, 1870	WARDLE, JAMES	HANLEY	
July 13, 1870	EDWARDS, JAMES & SON	BURSLEM	
July 14, 1870	MINTON HOLLINS & CO.	STOKE	
July 15, 1870	COPELAND, W. T. & SONS	STOKE	7, 8
July 16, 1870	WARDLE, JAMES	HANLEY	

DATE	POTTER	LOCATION	CATEGORY
July 19, 1870	PRATT, F. & R. & CO.	FENTON	
July 20, 1870	BOOTH, THOS.	HANLEY	
July 21, 1870	BOOTH, THOS.	HANLEY	
July 22, 1870	CORK, EDGE & MALKIN	BURSLEM	7
August 04, 1870	WARDLE, JAMES	HANLEY	
August 09, 1870	BROWNFIELD, WM.	COBRIDGE	
August 22, 1870	BOOTE, T. & R.	BURSLEM	
August 23, 1870	JONES, GEO.	STOKE	
August 25, 1870	BOOTE, T. & R.	BURSLEM	
September 10, 1870	MINTON & CO.	STOKE	8
September 16, 1870	MINTON & CO.	STOKE	
September 19, 1870	BROWNFIELD, WM.	COBRIDGE	
September 27, 1870	ELSMORE & FORSTER	TUNSTALL	
September 28, 1870	GELSON BROS.	HANLEY	
October 04, 1870	MINTON & CO.	STOKE	7
October 06, 1870	MINTON & CO.	STOKE	
October 07, 1870	MINTON & CO.	STOKE	8
October 08, 1870	POWELL & BISHOP	HANLEY	
October 19, 1870	JONES, GEO.	STOKE	
October 22, 1870	BROWNFIELD, WM.	COBRIDGE	
October 25, 1870	BROWN, T.C.-WESTHEAD, MOORE & CO.	HANLEY	
November 04, 1870	BROWN, T.C.-WESTHEAD, MOORE & CO.	HANLEY	1x
November 09, 1870	MEIR, JOHN & SON	TUNSTALL	
November 10, 1870	BROWNFIELD, WM.	COBRIDGE	
November 10, 1870	MINTON & CO.	STOKE	7, 8
November 12, 1870	MINTON HOLLINS & CO.	STOKE	
November 22, 1870	JONES, GEO.	STOKE	
November 24, 1870	BATES, ELLIOTT & CO.	LONGPORT	
November 24, 1870	MINTON & CO.	STOKE	8
November 25, 1870	MINTON & CO.	STOKE	
November 25, 1870	TURNER, GODDARD & CO.	TUNSTALL	7
November 26, 1870	BOOTE, T. & R.	BURSLEM	4
December 01, 1870	BROWNFIELD, WM.	COBRIDGE	
December 02, 1870	BROWN, T.C.-WESTHEAD, MOORE & CO.	HANLEY	1x
December 05, 1870	MINTON HOLLINS & CO.	STOKE	
December 16, 1870	BATES, ELLIOTT & CO.	LONGPORT	
December 17, 1870	BATES, ELLIOTT & CO.	LONGPORT	
December 19, 1870	ADAMS, HARVEY & CO.	LONGTON	8
December 27, 1870	EDWARDS, JAMES & SON	BURSLEM	
January 02, 1871	GELSON BROS.	HANLEY	
January 06, 1871	MINTON & CO.	STOKE	1x, 5x
January 07, 1871	BATES, ELLIOTT & CO.	LONGPORT	
January 10, 1871	JONES, GEO.	STOKE	
January 26, 1871	MINTON HOLLINS & CO.	STOKE	
January 30, 1871	GELSON BROS.	HANLEY	
February 02, 1871	EDWARDS, JAMES & SON	BURSLEM	
February 08, 1871	MACINTYRE, JAMES & CO.	BURSLEM	
February 11, 1871	BROWN, T.C.-WESTHEAD, MOORE & CO.	HANLEY	8
February 13, 1871	BODLEY, ED. F. & CO.	BURSLEM	8
February 13, 1871	EDGE, MALKIN & CO.	BURSLEM	
February 13, 1871	POWELL & BISHOP	HANLEY	
February 15, 1871	POWELL & BISHOP	HANLEY	
February 20, 1871	ELSMORE & FORSTER & CO.	TUNSTALL	4, 7
March 14, 1871	PRATT, JOHN & CO.	LANE DELPH	
March 15, 1871	BATES, ELLIOTT & CO.	LONGPORT	
March 27, 1871	BROWNFIELD, WM. & SON	COBRIDGE	
March 29, 1871	FURNIVAL, THOS. & SON	COBRIDGE	7
April 22, 1871	PRATT, JOHN & CO.	STOKE	
April 24, 1871	WEDGWOOD, JOSIAH & SONS	ETRURIA	
April 26, 1871	MINTON HOLLINS & CO.	STOKE	
April 29, 1871	EDWARDS, JAMES & SON	BURSLEM	
May 01, 1871	BROWN, T.C.-WESTHEAD, MOORE & CO.	HANLEY	8
May 02, 1871	BROWNFIELD, WM. & SON	COBRIDGE	7
May 03, 1871	JACKSON, JOHN & CO.	ROTHERHAM	
May 09, 1871	LIDDLE, ELLIOT & CO.	LONGPORT	
May 11, 1871	POWELL & BISHOP	HANLEY	
May 13, 1871	ELSMORE & FORSTER	TUNSTALL	
May 24, 1871	MEIR, JOHN & SON	TUNSTALL	
June 02, 1871	BROWN, T.C.-WESTHEAD, MOORE & CO.	HANLEY	8
June 07, 1871	GROVE, F. W. & STARK, J.	LONGTON	
June 16, 1871	TWIGG, JOHN	YORKSHIRE	
June 17, 1871	MINTON & CO.	STOKE	1x, 5x
June 19, 1871	PINDER, BOURNE & CO.	BURSLEM	7
June 22, 1871	TILL, THOS. & SONS	BURSLEM	
June 23, 1871	BATES, ELLIOTT & CO.	LONGPORT	
July 04, 1871	COPELAND, W. T. & SONS	STOKE	8
July 15, 1871	BOOTH, THOS.	HANLEY	7
July 25, 1871	BATES, ELLIOTT & CO.	LONGPORT	
July 29, 1871	HOPE & CARTER	BURSLEM	
August 09, 1871	BATES, ELLIOTT & CO.	LONGPORT	
August 18, 1871	PRATT & CO.	FENTON	
August 28, 1871	WARDLE, JAMES	HANLEY	
August 29, 1871	JONES, GEO.	STOKE	
August 30, 1871	BARLOW, THOS.	LONGTON	7
August 31, 1871	DAVIS, J. H. & J.	HANLEY	
September 15, 1871	BARLOW, THOS.	LONGTON	
September 19, 1871	MINTON & CO.	STOKE	1x, 5x
September 25, 1871	BROWN, T.C.-WESTHEAD, MOORE & CO.	HANLEY	7, 11
September 28, 1871	BOOTH, THOS. & CO.	TUNSTALL	
October 04, 1871	MINTON & CO.	STOKE	1x, 5x
October 04, 1871	PINDER, BOURNE & CO.	BURSLEM	
October 09, 1871	RIDGWAY, E. J. & SONS	HANLEY	
October 10, 1871	BROWN, T.C.-WESTHEAD, MOORE & CO.	HANLEY	
October 10, 1871	HUDDEN, J. T.	LONGTON	
October 14, 1871	BOOTH, THOS. & CO.	TUNSTALL	5
October 14, 1871	WEDGWOOD, JOSIAH & SONS	ETRURIA	
October 19, 1871	COPELAND, W. T. & SONS	STOKE	7, 8
October 31, 1871	MINTON & CO.	STOKE	1x, 5x
November 03, 1871	WILEMAN, J. F.	FENTON	
November 15, 1871	THOMPSON, J. & SONS	GLASGOW	
November 23, 1871	FORD, THOS.	HANLEY	8
December 01, 1871	JONES, GEO.	STOKE	
December 22, 1871	PRATT, F. & R.	FENTON	
December 23, 1871	JONES, GEO.	STOKE	
December 29, 1871	BROWN, T.C.-WESTHEAD, MOORE & CO.	HANLEY	8
January 01, 1872	EDGE, MALKIN & CO.	BURSLEM	7
January 06, 1872	MINTON & CO.	STOKE	8
January 20, 1872	JONES, GEO.	STOKE	
January 30, 1872	COPELAND, W. T. & SONS	STOKE	8
February 02, 1872	TURNER & TOMKINSON	TUNSTALL	
February 03, 1872	JONES, GEO.	STOKE	
February 15, 1872	POWELL & BISHOP	HANLEY	7
February 16, 1872	JONES, GEO.	STOKE	
February 22, 1872	MINTON & CO.	STOKE	8
March 04, 1872	JONES, GEO.	STOKE	
March 04, 1872	MINTON & CO.	STOKE	
March 04, 1872	MINTON HOLLINS & CO.	STOKE	
March 07, 1872	ADAMS, HARVEY & CO.	LONGTON	8
March 07, 1872	BATES, ELLIOTT & CO.	BURSLEM	7
March 08, 1872	MINTON HOLLINS & CO.	STOKE	
March 13, 1872	MINTON HOLLINS & CO.	STOKE	
March 16, 1872	MINTON & CO.	STOKE	
March 18, 1872	MINTON & CO.	STOKE	8
March 22, 1872	BROWN, T.C.-WESTHEAD, MOORE & CO.	HANLEY	
April 05, 1872	MINTON & CO.	STOKE	8
April 05, 1872	WEDGWOOD & CO.	TUNSTALL	
April 09, 1872	BROWN, T.C.-WESTHEAD, MOORE & CO.	HANLEY	
April 10, 1872	FURNIVAL, THOS. & SON	COBRIDGE	7
April 17, 1872	RIDGWAY, E. J. & SONS	HANLEY	
April 19, 1872	MINTON HOLLINS & CO.	STOKE	
April 24, 1872	PRATT, JOHN & CO. LTD.	LANE DELPH	
May 02, 1872	ADAMS, HARVEY & CO.	LONGTON	8
May 02, 1872	FURNIVAL, THOS. & SON	COBRIDGE	7
May 03, 1872	BATES, ELLIOTT & CO.	BURSLEM	
May 03, 1872	MINTON & CO.	STOKE	
May 06, 1872	BATES, ELLIOTT & CO.	BURSLEM	
May 06, 1872	MINTON HOLLINS & CO.	STOKE	
May 11, 1872	BOOTH, THOS. & SONS	HANLEY	7
May 27, 1872	JONES, GEO.	STOKE	7
May 27, 1872	MINTON HOLLINS & CO.	STOKE	
May 29, 1872	JONES, GEO.	STOKE	
May 30, 1872	MINTON & CO.	STOKE	8
June 05, 1872	HOPE & CARTER	BURSLEM	
June 06, 1872	BROWNFIELD, WM. & SON	COBRIDGE	
June 07, 1872	MINTON HOLLINS & CO.	STOKE	
June 11, 1872	COPELAND, W. T. & SONS	STOKE	13
June 11, 1872	WEDGWOOD, JOSIAH & SONS	ETRURIA	2x
June 18, 1872	ASHWORTH, G. L. & BROS.	HANLEY	
June 18, 1872	MINTON HOLLINS & CO.	STOKE	
June 21, 1872	MINTON HOLLINS & CO.	STOKE	
June 22, 1872	BROWN, T.C.-WESTHEAD, MOORE & CO.	HANLEY	8
June 22, 1872	BROWNFIELD, WM. & SON	COBRIDGE	
June 22, 1872	MINTON & CO.	STOKE	
July 02, 1872	WEDGWOOD, JOSIAH & SONS	ETRURIA	2x
July 13, 1872	GELSON BROS.	HANLEY	
July 16, 1872	MINTON HOLLINS & CO.	STOKE	
July 20, 1872	JONES, GEO.	STOKE	
July 24, 1872	ADAMS, W. & T.	TUNSTALL	
July 29, 1872	DIMMOCK, J. & CO.	HANLEY	
July 31, 1872	MINTON & CO.	STOKE	
August 02, 1872	RIDGWAY, E. J. & SONS	HANLEY	
August 14, 1872	BOOTH, T. & CO.	TUNSTALL	
August 16, 1872	BROWNFIELD, WM. & SON	COBRIDGE	
September 02, 1872	BATES, ELLIOTT & CO.	BURSLEM	7
September 12, 1872	MINTON HOLLINS & CO.	STOKE	
September 25, 1872	MINTON HOLLINS & CO.	STOKE	

DATE	POTTER	LOCATION	CATEGORY
September 26, 1872	JONES, F.	LONGTON	7
October 07, 1872	BROWN, T.C.-WESTHEAD, MOORE & CO.	HANLEY	8
October 11, 1872	WEDGWOOD, JOSIAH & SONS	ETRURIA	2x
October 12, 1872	BATES, ELLIOTT & CO.	BURSLEM	
October 14, 1872	MINTON HOLLINS & CO.	STOKE	
October 17, 1872	WEDGWOOD, JOSIAH & SONS	ETRURIA	2x
October 18, 1872	JONES, GEO.	STOKE	7
October 30, 1872	BROWNHILLS POTTERY CO. (THE)	TUNSTALL	t
October 30, 1872	WILEMAN, J. F.	FENTON	8
November 12, 1872	MINTON & CO.	STOKE	
November 14, 1872	BROWNFIELD, WM. & SON	COBRIDGE	8
November 18, 1872	HOLLAND & GREEN	LONGTON	
November 30, 1872	BELFIELD & CO.	PRESTONPANS	
December 02, 1872	BROWN, T.C.-WESTHEAD, MOORE & CO.	HANLEY	8
December 04, 1872	PRATT, JOHN & CO. LTD.	LANE DELPH	
December 10, 1872	MINTON & CO.	STOKE	
December 11, 1872	OLD HALL EARTHENWARE CO. LTD., THE	HANLEY	7
December 14, 1872	BROWNFIELD, WM. & SON	COBRIDGE	7, 8
December 24, 1872	COCKSON & CHETWYND	COBRIDGE	7
December 27, 1872	ADAMS, JOHN (Executors of)	LONGTON	
December 27, 1872	MEIR, JOHN & SON	TUNSTALL	
January 10, 1873	JONES, GEO.	STOKE	
January 13, 1873	COPELAND, W. T. & SONS	STOKE	7
January 29, 1873	MINTON HOLLINS & CO.	STOKE	
February 01, 1873	MINTON HOLLINS & CO.	STOKE	
February 12, 1873	BATES, ELLIOTT & CO.	BURSLEM	
February 15, 1873	MINTON & CO.	STOKE	
February 19, 1873	BEVINGTON, T. & J.	HANLEY	8
February 25, 1873	JONES, GEO.	STOKE	8
February 27, 1873	MINTON HOLLINS & CO.	STOKE	
February 27, 1873	TILL, THOS. & SONS	BURSLEM	
March 06, 1873	BROWNHILLS POTTERY CO. (THE)	TUNSTALL	
March 06, 1873	MINTON & CO.	STOKE	
March 26, 1873	JONES, GEO.	STOKE	8
April 03, 1873	MINTON & CO.	STOKE	8
April 19, 1873	MINTON & CO.	STOKE	
April 23, 1873	GELSON BROS.	HANLEY	7
April 28, 1873	POWELL & BISHOP	HANLEY	
April 29, 1873	JONES, GEO.	STOKE	
May 03, 1873	BROWNFIELD, WM. & SON	COBRIDGE	8
May 03, 1873	MINTON & CO.	STOKE	
May 03, 1873	TILL, THOS. & SONS	BURSLEM	
May 06, 1873	MINTON & CO.	STOKE	8
May 12, 1873	BROWN, T.C.-WESTHEAD, MOORE & CO.	HANLEY	7, 8
May 16, 1873	MINTON HOLLINS & CO.	STOKE	
May 29, 1873	FORD, THOS.	HANLEY	8
May 30, 1873	BROWN, T.C.-WESTHEAD, MOORE & CO.	HANLEY	8
June 11, 1873	BATES, ELLIOTT & CO.	BURSLEM	
June 19, 1873	PINDER & BOURNE & CO.	BURSLEM	7
June 30, 1873	MINTON HOLLINS & CO.	STOKE	
July 03, 1873	MINTON HOLLINS & CO.	STOKE	
July 04, 1873	BROWN, T.C.-WESTHEAD, MOORE & CO.	HANLEY	8
July 28, 1873	HOBSON, CHAS.	BURSLEM	
July 28, 1873	MEIR, JOHN & SONS	TUNSTALL	
July 31, 1873	MINTONS	STOKE	8
August 05, 1873	BAKER & CHETWYND	BURSLEM	
August 14, 1873	BROWN, T.C.-WESTHEAD, MOORE & CO.	HANLEY	8
August 25, 1873	JONES, GEO.	STOKE	
August 30, 1873	BROWN, T.C.-WESTHEAD, MOORE & CO.	HANLEY	8
September 02, 1873	EDGE, MALKIN & CO.	BURSLEM	
September 04, 1873	MINTONS	STOKE	8
September 10, 1873	POWELL & BISHOP	HANLEY	
September 15, 1873	BROWN, T.C.-WESTHEAD, MOORE & CO.	HANLEY	
September 16, 1873	BROWN, T.C.-WESTHEAD, MOORE & CO.	HANLEY	
September 19, 1873	BROWN, T.C.-WESTHEAD, MOORE & CO.	HANLEY	8
September 25, 1873	ADAMS, HARVEY & CO.	LONGTON	8
September 29, 1873	BROWNFIELD, WM. & SON	COBRIDGE	8
October 06, 1873	BROWN, T.C.-WESTHEAD, MOORE & CO.	HANLEY	8
October 11, 1873	MINTONS	STOKE	
October 13, 1873	JONES, GEO.	STOKE	
October 22, 1873	MINTONS	STOKE	
November 03, 1873	HOPE & CARTER	BURSLEM	
November 03, 1873	JONES, GEO.	STOKE	
November 06, 1873	WEDGWOOD & CO.	TUNSTALL	
November 10, 1873	BROWN, T.C.-WESTHEAD, MOORE & CO.	HANLEY	

DATE	POTTER	LOCATION	CATEGORY
December 04, 1873	OLD HALL EARTHENWARE CO. LTD., THE	HANLEY	
December 05, 1873	ADAMS, HARVEY & CO.	LONGTON	8
December 05, 1873	BROWNFIELD, WM. & SON	COBRIDGE	8
December 10, 1873	JONES, GEO. & SONS	STOKE	
December 27, 1873	JONES, GEO. & SONS	STOKE	
January 01, 1874	BATES, ELLIOTT & CO.	BURSLEM	
January 10, 1874	DAVENPORTS, & CO.	LONGPORT	8
January 20, 1874	POWELL & BISHOP	HANLEY	
January 21, 1874	COPELAND, W. T. & SONS	STOKE	7, 8
January 23, 1874	MEIR, JOHN & SON	TUNSTALL	
January 30, 1874	JONES, GEORGE (& SONS)	STOKE	8
February 09, 1874	BODLEY & CO.	BURSLEM	8
February 11, 1874	BOOTH, THOS. & SONS	HANLEY	
February 19, 1874	JONES, GEO. & SONS	STOKE	
February 25, 1874	JONES, GEO. & SONS	STOKE	7
February 26, 1874	MINTON HOLLINS & CO.	STOKE	
March 03, 1874	JONES, GEO. & SONS	STOKE	5
March 04, 1874	MINTONS	STOKE	
March 13, 1874	DIMMOCK, J. & CO.	HANLEY	
March 14, 1874	MINTONS	STOKE	8
March 17, 1874	POWELL & BISHOP	HANLEY	
March 21, 1874	POWELL & BISHOP	HANLEY	
March 24, 1874	MINTONS	STOKE	8
March 28, 1874	JONES, GEO. & SONS	STOKE	
April 15, 1874	MINTONS	STOKE	8
April 20, 1874	MINTON HOLLINS & CO.	STOKE	
April 21, 1874	JONES, GEO. & SONS	STOKE	
April 22, 1874	BROWNFIELD, WM. & SON	COBRIDGE	
April 23, 1874	BROWN, T.C.-WESTHEAD, MOORE & CO.	HANLEY	8
April 25, 1874	JONES, GEO. & SONS	STOKE	7
April 29, 1874	FURNIVAL, T. & SON	COBRIDGE	7
April 29, 1874	RIDGWAY, SPARKS & RIDGWAY	HANLEY	
April 30, 1874	BOOTH, THOS. & SONS	HANLEY	7
May 05, 1874	BATES, ELLIOTT & CO.	BURSLEM	
May 09, 1874	JONES, GEO. & SONS	STOKE	
May 11, 1874	HOLLAND & GREEN	LONGTON	7
May 11, 1874	THOMPSON, JOHN & SONS	GLASGOW	
May 20, 1874	BATES, ELLIOTT & CO.	BURSLEM	
May 21, 1874	MINTONS	STOKE	8
May 22, 1874	MINTONS	STOKE	8
May 23, 1874	JONES, GEO. & SONS	STOKE	8
June 06, 1874	BROWNFIELD, WM. & SON	COBRIDGE	8
June 16, 1874	COCKSON & CHETWYND	COBRIDGE	
June 17, 1874	EDGE, MALKIN & CO.	BURSLEM	7
June 18, 1874	MINTONS	STOKE	8
June 25, 1874	FORD, THOS.	HANLEY	8
June 26, 1874	PINDER, BOURNE & CO.	BURSLEM	7
July 10, 1874	MINTONS	STOKE	8
July 13, 1874	BROWN, T.C.-WESTHEAD, MOORE & CO.	HANLEY	
July 27, 1874	HULSEY & ADDERLEY	LONGTON	8
July 30, 1874	MINTON HOLLINS & CO.	STOKE	
August 01, 1874	COCKSON & CHETWYND	COBRIDGE	7
August 01, 1874	MINTONS	STOKE	
August 06, 1874	BROWN, T.C.-WESTHEAD, MOORE & CO.	HANLEY	
August 08, 1874	BROWNFIELD, WM. & SON	COBRIDGE	8
August 15, 1874	BATES, ELLIOTT & CO.	BURSLEM	
August 22, 1874	HUDDEN, J. T.	LONGTON	
August 28, 1874	JONES, GEO. & SONS	STOKE	8
September 01, 1874	TILL, THOS. & SONS	BURSLEM	7
September 03, 1874	COCKSON & CHETWYND	COBRIDGE	7
September 04, 1874	MINTONS	STOKE	8
September 05, 1874	FURNIVAL & SON	COBRIDGE	
September 07, 1874	BOOTH, THOS. & SONS	HANLEY	
September 10, 1874	BROWNFIELD, WM. & SON	COBRIDGE	10
September 12, 1874	MINTONS	STOKE	
September 15, 1874	JONES, GEO. & SONS	STOKE	
September 30, 1874	BROWNFIELD, WM. & SON	COBRIDGE	8
October 06, 1874	GROVE, F. W. & STARK, J.	LONGTON	
October 06, 1874	MINTONS	STOKE	
October 08, 1874	JONES, GEO. & SONS	STOKE	
October 10, 1874	MINTONS	STOKE	8
October 12, 1874	POWELL & BISHOP	HANLEY	
October 17, 1874	BATES, ELLIOTT & CO.	BURSLEM	
October 21, 1874	JONES, GEO. & SONS	STOKE	8
October 28, 1874	PINDER, BOURNE & CO.	BURSLEM	
November 02, 1874	EDWARDS, JAMES & SON	BURSLEM	
November 03, 1874	CORN, W. & E.	BURSLEM	4, 7
November 06, 1874	BROWNFIELD, WM. & SON	COBRIDGE	8
November 07, 1874	FORD, THOS.	HANLEY	
November 10, 1874	JONES, GEO. & SONS	STOKE	8
November 12, 1874	BATES, ELLIOTT & CO.	BURSLEM	
November 12, 1874	MINTONS	STOKE	
November 20, 1874	PRATT, F. & R. & CO.	FENTON	
November 25, 1874	MINTON HOLLINS & CO.	STOKE	
December 01, 1874	COPELAND, W. T. & SONS	STOKE	8

DATE	POTTER	LOCATION	CATEGORY
December 04, 1874	BARLOW, THOS.	LONGTON	
December 07, 1874	BROWN, T.C.-WESTHEAD, MOORE & CO.	HANLEY	
December 08, 1874	JONES, GEO. & SONS		0
December 10, 1874	PINDER, BOURNE & CO.	BURSLEM	
December 12, 1874	JONES, GEO. & SONS	STOKE	
December 18, 1874	JONES, GEO. & SONS	STOKE	8
December 18, 1874	MINTON HOLLINS & CO.	STOKE	
January 02, 1875	BROWN, T.C.-WESTHEAD, MOORE & CO.	HANLEY	8
January 06, 1875	MINTON HOLLINS & CO.	STOKE	
January 16, 1875	BROWNHILLS POTTERY CO. (THE)	TUNSTALL	
January 18, 1875	BROWN, T.C.-WESTHEAD, MOORE & CO.	HANLEY	8
January 20, 1875	BROWNFIELD, WM. & SON	COBRIDGE	8
January 21, 1875	JONES, GEO. & SONS	STOKE	8
January 23, 1875	BROWN, T.C.-WESTHEAD, MOORE & CO.	HANLEY	8
January 28, 1875	MINTONS	STOKE	8
February 05, 1875	BOOTE, T. & R.	BURSLEM	
February 09, 1875	JONES, GEO. & SONS	STOKE	
February 09, 1875	PINDER, BOURNE & CO.	BURSLEM	
February 12, 1875	MADDOCK, J. & SONS	BURSLEM	
February 17, 1875	MINTONS	STOKE	8
February 23, 1875	JONES, GEO. & SONS	STOKE	8
February 23, 1875	MADDOCK, J. & SONS	BURLSEM	
March 05, 1875	BROWNFIELD, WM. & SON	COBRIDGE	8
March 12, 1875	JONES, GEO. & SONS	STOKE	7
March 24, 1875	BROWN, T.C.-WESTHEAD, MOORE & CO.	HANLEY	8
March 24, 1875	MINTON HOLLINS & CO.	STOKE	
March 30, 1875	BOOTH, THOS. & SONS	HANLEY	7
March 31, 1875	BROWNFIELD, WM. & SON	COBRIDGE	8
April 03, 1875	BODLEY, E. F. & SON	BURSLEM	8
April 03, 1875	DIMMOCK, J. & CO.	HANLEY	
April 07, 1875	MINTONS	STOKE	7, 8
April 09, 1875	BROWNFIELD, WM. & SON	COBRIDGE	8
April 10, 1875	POWELL & BISHOP	HANLEY	
April 15, 1875	MALKIN, R.	FENTON	
April 17, 1875	PINDER, BOURNE & CO.	BURSLEM	
April 20, 1875	DIMMOCK, J. & CO.	HANLEY	
April 20, 1875	MINTONS	STOKE	8
April 22, 1875	MINTON HOLLINS & CO.	STOKE	
May 07, 1875	BURGESS & LEIGH	BURSLEM	7
May 07, 1875	JONES, GEO. & SONS	STOKE	8
May 20, 1875	BATES, ELLIOTT & CO.	BURSLEM	
May 20, 1875	DIMMOCK, J. & CO.	HANLEY	
May 22, 1875	HOLLAND & GREEN	LONGTON	
May 26, 1875	BROWN, T.C.-WESTHEAD, MOORE & CO.	HANLEY	8
May 28, 1875	CAMPBELLFIELD POTTERY CO. (LTD.)	GLASGOW	
May 31, 1875	JONES, GEO. & SONS	STOKE	
May 31, 1875	RIDGWAY, SPARKS & RIDGWAY	HANLEY	
June 02, 1875	MINTON HOLLINS & CO.	STOKE	
June 05, 1875	BROWNFIELD, WM. & SON	COBRIDGE	
June 07, 1875	ADAMS, W. & T.	TUNSTALL	
June 10, 1875	BROWNFIELD, WM. & SON	COBRIDGE	1
June 12, 1875	FURNIVAL, THOS. & SON	COBRIDGE	7
June 12, 1875	MADDOCK & GATER	BURSLEM	
June 15, 1875	WEDGWOOD, JOSIAH & SONS	ETRURIA	
June 19, 1875	TILL, THOS. & SONS	BURSLEM	
June 26, 1875	JONES, GEO. & SONS	STOKE	8
July 05, 1875	BROWNFIELD, WM. & SON	COBRIDGE	8
July 23, 1875	BROWN, T.C.-WESTHEAD, MOORE & CO.	HANLEY	
July 27, 1875	GROVE, F. W. & STARK, J.	LONGTON	
July 28, 1875	MINTON HOLLINS & CO.	STOKE	
August 19, 1875	GROVE, F. W. & STARK, J.	LONGTON	
September 02, 1875	ELSMORE, T. & SON	TUNSTALL	
September 13, 1875	JONES, GEO. & SONS	STOKE	7, 8
September 14, 1875	MINTON HOLLINS & CO.	STOKE	
September 18, 1875	JONES, GEO. & SONS	STOKE	8
September 21, 1875	COCHRAN, R. & CO.	GLASGOW	
September 25, 1875	GROVE, F. W. & STARK, J.	LONGTON	
September 28, 1875	BROWN, T.C.-WESTHEAD, MOORE & CO.	HANLEY	8
September 30, 1875	EDWARDS, JOHN	FENTON	7
October 02, 1875	WEDGWOOD, JOSIAH & SONS	ETRURIA	
October 11, 1875	BROWNHILLS POTTERY CO. (THE)	TUNSTALL	7
October 11, 1875	POWELL & BISHOP	HANLEY	
October 16, 1875	BURGESS, LEIGH & CO.	BURSLEM	
October 28, 1875	MINTON HOLLINS & CO.	STOKE	
November 05, 1875	JONES, GEO. & SONS	STOKE	8
November 08, 1875	COPELAND, W. T. & SONS	STOKE	8
November 08, 1875	MINTON HOLLINS & CO.	STOKE	
November 12, 1875	BURGESS, LEIGH & CO.	BURSLEM	
November 12, 1875	JONES, GEO. & SONS	STOKE	
December 01, 1875	BROWNFIELD, WM. & SON	COBRIDGE	8
December 03, 1875	JONES, GEO. & SONS	STOKE	

DATE	POTTER	LOCATION	CATEGORY
December 06, 1875	MEIR, JOHN & SON	TUNSTALL	
December 10, 1875	MINTONS	STOKE	8
December 11, 1875	GROVE, F. W. & STARK, J.	LONGTON	
December 13, 1875	MINTON HOLLINS & CO.	STOKE	
December 15, 1875	MINTONS	STOKE	8
December 15, 1875	MINTONS CHINA WORKS	STOKE	
December 18, 1875	GELSON BROS.	HANLEY	
December 24, 1875	BATES, WALKER & CO.	BURSLEM	
December 29, 1875	BROWN, T.C.-WESTHEAD, MOORE & CO.	HANLEY	8
December 29, 1875	EDGE, MALKIN & CO.	BURSLEM	
December 30, 1875	MINTON HOLLINS & CO.	STOKE	
December 30, 1875	MINTONS	STOKE	8
January 04, 1876	MINTONS	STOKE	8
January 22, 1876	JONES, GEO. & SONS	STOKE	
January 24, 1876	BATES, WALKER & CO.	BURSLEM	
January 24, 1876	MINTONS	STOKE	8
January 26, 1876	EDE, MALKIN & CO.	BURSLEM	
January 26, 1876	POWELL & BISHOP	HANLEY	4x, 7
January 28, 1876	EDWARDS, JAMES & SON	BURSLEM	7
January 29, 1876	BROWNFIELD, WM. & SON	COBRIDGE	7, 8
February 01, 1876	BROWNFIELD, WM. & SON	COBRIDGE	
February 02, 1876	RIDGWAY, SPARKS & RIDGWAY	HANLEY	
February 02, 1876	WEDGWOOD, JOSIAH & SONS	ETRURIA	
February 03, 1876	POWELL & BISHOP	HANLEY	4x
February 04, 1876	MINTONS	STOKE	8
February 08, 1876	BATES, WALKER & CO.	BURSLEM	
February 19, 1876	JONES, GEO. & SONS	STOKE	
February 22, 1876	MINTON HOLLINS & CO.	STOKE	
February 29, 1876	DIMMOCK, J. & CO.	HANLEY	7
March 02, 1876	BROWNHILLS POTTERY CO. (THE)	TUNSTALL	
March 02, 1876	GELSON, T. & CO.	HANLEY	
March 10, 1876	MINTON HOLLINS & CO.	STOKE	
March 14, 1876	BROWN, T.C.-WESTHEAD, MOORE & CO.	HANLEY	8, 11
March 17, 1876	MINTONS	STOKE	8
March 24, 1876	BATES, WALKER & CO.	BURSLEM	
March 30, 1876	JONES, GEO. & SONS	STOKE	8
April 08, 1876	BATES, WALKER & CO.	BURSLEM	
April 11, 1876	GELSON, THOS. & CO.	HANLEY	
April 12, 1876	DIMMOCK, J. & CO.	HANLEY	
April 12, 1876	POWELL & BISHOP	HANLEY	4x
April 21, 1876	FURNIVAL & SON	COBRIDGE	3, 4
April 21, 1876	MINTON HOLLINS & CO.	STOKE	
April 27, 1876	MINTONS	STOKE	8
May 08, 1876	BROWN, T.C.-WESTHEAD, MOORE & CO.	HANLEY	8
May 10, 1876	JONES, GEO. & SONS	STOKE	8
May 11, 1876	PRATT, F. & R. & CO.	FENTON	
May 16, 1876	MINTONS	STOKE	8
May 22, 1876	WEDGWOOD, JOSIAH & SONS	ETRURIA	
May 24, 1876	MINTONS	STOKE	8
May 29, 1876	JONES, GEO. & SONS	STOKE	8
June 03, 1876	MINTONS	STOKE	8
June 07, 1876	GELSON, THOS. & CO.	HANLEY	
June 08, 1876	MINTONS	STOKE	8
June 09, 1876	COPELAND, W. T. & SONS	STOKE	7
June 15, 1876	MEIR, HENRY & SON	TUNSTALL	
June 15, 1876	MINTON HOLLINS & CO.	STOKE	
June 19, 1876	WEDGWOOD, JOSIAH & SONS	ETRURIA	7
June 21, 1876	MINTONS	STOKE	8
June 22, 1876	GELSON, THOS. & CO.	HANLEY	
June 23, 1876	MINTONS	STOKE	8
June 26, 1876	MINTON HOLLINS & CO.	STOKE	
July 01, 1876	MINTONS	STOKE	8
July 01, 1876	TAMS, JOHN	LONGTON	
July 03, 1876	FORD & CHALLINOR	TUNSTALL	
July 05, 1876	COPELAND, W. T. & SONS	STOKE	8
July 05, 1876	TILL, THOS. & SONS	BURSLEM	7
July 10, 1876	GELSON, THOS. & CO.	HANLEY	
July 26, 1876	JONES, GEO. & SONS	STOKE	8
July 28, 1876	GELSON, THOS. & CO.	HANLEY	
July 28, 1876	POWELL & BISHOP	HANLEY	4x
August 25, 1876	PRATT, F. & R. & CO.	FENTON	
September 05, 1876	BATES, WALKER & CO.	BURSLEM	
September 06, 1876	BROWNFIELD, WM. & SONS	COBRIDGE	8, 10
September 06, 1876	PINDER & BOURNE & CO.	BURSLEM	7, 8
September 09, 1876	BROWN, T.C.-WESTHEAD, MOORE & CO.	HANLEY	8
September 12, 1876	JONES, GEO. & SONS	STOKE	8
September 18, 1876	ASHWORTH, G. L. & BROS.	HANLEY	
September 20, 1876	HOLLINSHEAD & KIRKHAM	BURSLEM	7
September 22, 1876	POWELL & BISHOP	HANLEY	4x
September 26, 1876	BROWN, T.C.-WESTHEAD, MOORE & CO.	HANLEY	
September 26, 1876	HOPE & CARTER	BURSLEM	
September 28, 1876	HOPE & CARTER	BURSLEM	7, 8
October 07, 1876	ADAMS, WM.	TUNSTALL	7
October 07, 1876	BROWNFIELD, WM. & SONS	COBRIDGE	8

DATE	POTTER	LOCATION	CATEGORY
October 07, 1876	WEDGWOOD, JOSIAH & SONS	ETRURIA	
October 09, 1876	JONES, GEO. & SONS	STOKE	
October 17, 1876	BROWN, T.C.-WESTHEAD, MOORE & CO.	HANLEY	
October 17, 1876	WARDLE & CO.	HANLEY	7
October 19, 1876	BURGESS, LEIGH & CO.	BURSLEM	7
October 20, 1876	MINTONS	STOKE	
October 21, 1876	EDGE, MALKIN & CO.	BURSLEM	7
October 23, 1876	MINTONS	STOKE	
October 31, 1876	BROWNFIELD, WM. & SONS	COBRIDGE	8
November 08, 1876	BROWNFIELD, WM. & SONS	COBRIDGE	8
November 08, 1876	JONES, GEO. & SONS	STOKE	1, 8
November 09, 1876	BELFIELD & CO.	PRESTONPANS	
November 13, 1876	MINTONS	STOKE	8
November 14, 1876	CLEMENTSON BROS.	HANLEY	7
November 14, 1876	WEDGWOOD, JOSIAH & SONS	ETRURIA	
November 18, 1876	MINTON HOLLINS & CO.	STOKE	
November 18, 1876	MINTON HOLLINS & CO.	STOKE	
November 23, 1876	ADAMS, WM.	TUNSTALL	
November 24, 1876	FURNIVAL, THOS. & SONS	COBRIDGE	3, 4
November 29, 1876	FURNIVAL, THOS. & SONS	COBRIDGE	7
December 05, 1876	WEDGWOOD & CO.	TUNSTALL	
December 11, 1876	TAMS, JOHN	LONGTON	
December 14, 1876	ADAMS, HARVEY & CO.	LONGTON	8
December 14, 1876	DIMMOCK, J. & CO.	HANLEY	7
December 18, 1876	BEECH, JAMES	LONGTON	
December 21, 1876	GROVE, F. W. & STARK, J.	LONGTON	7
December 28, 1876	ADAMS, HARVEY & CO.	LONGTON	8
January 20, 1877	GROVE, F. W. & STARK, J.	LONGTON	1
January 24, 1877	BROWNFIELD, WM. & SONS	COBRIDGE	
January 25, 1877	JONES, GEO. & SONS	STOKE	8
January 25, 1877	WOOD & CO.	BURSLEM	7
January 25, 1877	WOOD, WM. & CO.	BURSLEM	
January 26, 1877	MINTONS	STOKE	
January 26, 1877	POWELL & BISHOP	HANLEY	8
February 01, 1877	EDWARDS, JAMES & SON	BURSLEM	
February 03, 1877	MINTON HOLLINS & CO.	STOKE	
February 07, 1877	BROWNFIELD, WM. & SONS	COBRIDGE	8, 10
February 07, 1877	HOLLAND & GREEN	LONGTON	
February 09, 1877	BROWN, T.C.-WESTHEAD, MOORE & CO.	HANLEY	8
February 09, 1877	ROBINSON & CO.	LONGTON	
February 12, 1877	BEECH, JAMES	LONGTON	
February 15, 1877	MINTON HOLLINS & CO.	STOKE	
February 19, 1877	BROWNFIELD, WM. & SONS	COBRIDGE	
February 21, 1877	COPELAND, W. T. & SONS	STOKE	8
February 21, 1877	MINTONS	STOKE	8
February 24, 1877	HUGHES, THOS.	BURSLEM	
February 27, 1877	MINTONS	STOKE	8
March 01, 1877	HALLAM, JOHNSON & CO.	LONGTON	
March 08, 1877	COPELAND, W. T. & SONS	STOKE	8
March 10, 1877	JONES, GEO. & SONS	STOKE	
March 20, 1877	CLEMENTSON BROS.	HANLEY	4
March 20, 1877	DIMMOCK, J. & CO.	HANLEY	
March 24, 1877	POWELL & BISHOP	HANLEY	
March 31, 1877	BODLEY, E. F. & CO.	BURSLEM	8
April 03, 1877	POWELL & BISHOP	HANLEY	
April 05, 1877	FORD, CHALLINOR & CO.	TUNSTALL	7
April 12, 1877	DIMMOCK, J. & CO.	HANLEY	
April 23, 1877	TAMS, JOHN	LONGTON	
May 02, 1877	JONES, GEO. & SONS	STOKE	8
May 04, 1877	OLD HALL EARTHENWARE CO. LTD., THE	HANLEY	
May 05, 1877	WEDGWOOD, JOSIAH & SONS	ETRURIA	
May 12, 1877	FURNIVAL, THOS. & SONS	COBRIDGE	7
May 16, 1877	BROWNFIELD, WM. & SONS	COBRIDGE	8
May 18, 1877	WEDGWOOD, JOSIAH & SONS	ETRURIA	
May 22, 1877	BROWNFIELD, WM. & SONS	COBRIDGE	8
May 24, 1877	BROWN, T.C.-WESTHEAD, MOORE & CO.	HANLEY	8
May 30, 1877	FURNIVAL, T. & SONS	COBRIDGE	
June 08, 1877	MINTON HOLLINS & CO.	STOKE	
June 09, 1877	BAKER & CO.	FENTON	
June 13, 1877	BAKER & CO.	FENTON	4
June 15, 1877	RIDGWAY, SPARKS & RIDGWAY	HANLEY	5
June 19, 1877	FORD & CHALLINOR	TUNSTALL	
June 22, 1877	BODLEY, E. F. & CO.	BURSLEM	7, 8
June 22, 1877	WALKER & CARTER	STOKE	
June 26, 1877	FURNIVAL, T. & SONS	COBRIDGE	7
June 28, 1877	FURNIVAL, T. & SONS	COBRIDGE	
July 02, 1877	COPELAND, W. T. & SONS	STOKE	7, 8
July 06, 1877	MINTONS	STOKE	8
July 09, 1877	MINTON HOLLINS & CO.	STOKE	
July 14, 1877	TAMS, JOHN	LONGTON	
July 17, 1877	EDWARDS, JAMES & SON	BURSLEM	7
July 23, 1877	EDWARDS, JON	FENTON	
July 25, 1877	FORD, CHALLINOR & CO.	TUNSTALL	7
July 26, 1877	MINTON HOLLINS & CO.	STOKE	
July 31, 1877	MINTON HOLLINS & CO.	STOKE	

DATE	POTTER	LOCATION	CATEGORY
August 17, 1877	RIDGWAY, SPARKS & RIDGWAY	HANLEY	
August 18, 1877	FURNIVAL & SON	COBRIDGE	
August 18, 1877	MINTON HOLLINS & CO.	STOKE	
August 25, 1877	MINTON HOLLINS & CO.	STOKE	
August 28, 1877	BROWN, T.C.-WESTHEAD, MOORE & CO.	HANLEY	8
September 11, 1877	TURNER, G. W. & SONS	TUNSTALL	
September 19, 1877	MINTON HOLLINS & CO.	STOKE	
September 20, 1877	WEDGWOOD, JOSIAH & SONS	ETRURIA	
September 22, 1877	MINTON HOLLINS & CO.	STOKE	
September 22, 1877	MINTONS	STOKE	
September 25, 1877	MINTONS	STOKE	8
October 02, 1877	BATES, WALKER & CO.	BURSLEM	
October 10, 1877	BROWNFIELD, WM. & SONS	COBRIDGE	
October 10, 1877	EDWARDS, JOHN	FENTON	
October 15, 1877	JONES, GEO. & SONS	STOKE	8
October 16, 1877	POWELL & BISHOP	HANLEY	
October 19, 1877	BROWN, T.C.-WESTHEAD, MOORE & CO.	HANLEY	8
October 19, 1877	MINTON HOLLINS & CO.	STOKE	
October 24, 1877	GROVE, F. W. & STARK, J.	LONGTON	
October 24, 1877	PRATT, F. & R. & CO.	FENTON	7
October 30, 1877	WEDGWOOD & CO.	TUNSTALL	
October 31, 1877	JONES, GEO. & SONS	STOKE	
November 05, 1877	POWELL & BISHOP	HANLEY	
November 06, 1877	BROWNFIELD, WM. & SONS	COBRIDGE	8, 10
November 07, 1877	MINTONS	STOKE	
November 07, 1877	PINDER, BOURNE & CO.	BURSLEM	7
November 15, 1877	BROWN, T.C.-WESTHEAD, MOORE & CO.	HANLEY	8
November 20, 1877	EDWARDS, JAMES & SONS	BURSLEM	
November 21, 1877	DAVENPORTS, & CO.	LONGPORT	12
November 22, 1877	HANCOCK, B. & S.	STOKE	
November 22, 1877	OLD HALL EARTHENWARE CO. LTD., THE	HANLEY	
November 24, 1877	DIMMOCK, J. & CO.	HANLEY	
December 06, 1877	MINTONS	STOKE	8
December 14, 1877	DIMMOCK, J. & CO.	HANLEY	
December 21, 1877	FURNIVAL, T. & SONS	COBRIDGE	
December 21, 1877	MINTONS	STOKE	
December 22, 1877	BROWNFIELD, WM. & SONS	COBRIDGE	7, 8
December 29, 1877	BROWN, T.C.-WESTHEAD, MOORE & CO.	HANLEY	8
January 03, 1878	MINTON HOLLINS & CO.	STOKE	
January 09, 1878	BROWNHILLS POTTERY CO. (THE)	TUNSTALL	
January 14, 1878	ADAMS, WM.	TUNSTALL	
January 14, 1878	MADDOCK, J. & SONS	BURLSEM	
January 14, 1878	MINTON HOLLINS & CO.	STOKE	
January 15, 1878	WEDGWOOD, JOSIAH & SONS	ETRURIA	
January 22, 1878	DIMMOCK, J. & CO.	HANLEY	
January 24, 1878	COPELAND, W. T. & SONS	STOKE	8
January 25, 1878	BROWNFIELD, WM. & SONS	COBRIDGE	8
January 28, 1878	BROWN, T.C.-WESTHEAD, MOORE & CO.	HANLEY	8
January 30, 1878	BROWNHILLS POTTERY CO. THE)	TUNSTALL	
January 30, 1878	JONES, GEO.	STOKE	7, 8
January 31, 1878	HANCOCK, B. & S.	STOKE	
February 01, 1878	JONES, GEO. & SONS	STOKE	
February 01, 1878	MINTON HOLLINS & CO.	STOKE	
February 09, 1878	DIMMOCK, J. & CO.	HANLEY	
February 11, 1878	BROWN, T.C.-WESTHEAD, MOORE & CO.	HANLEY	
February 20, 1878	MINTON HOLLINS & CO.	STOKE	
February 28, 1878	DUNN, BENNETT & CO.	HANLEY	7
March 05, 1878	GROVE, F. W. & STARK, J.	LONGTON	
March 06, 1878	MINTON HOLLINS & CO.	STOKE	
March 07, 1878	EDWARDS, JOHN	FENTON	
March 09, 1878	BROWNHILLS POTTERY CO. (THE)	TUNSTALL	
March 09, 1878	POWELL & BISHOP	HANLEY	8
March 13, 1878	COPELAND, W. T. & SONS	STOKE	7
March 13, 1878	MINTONS	STOKE	
March 25, 1878	EMERY, F. J.	BURSLEM	
March 27, 1878	MINTON HOLLINS & CO.	STOKE	
March 27, 1878	TURNER, G. W. & SONS	TUNSTALL	
April 02, 1878	BELFIELD & CO.	PRESTONPANS	
April 10, 1878	MINTONS	STOKE	
April 17, 1878	MINTONS	STOKE	
April 17, 1878	RIDGWAY, SPARKS & RIDGWAY	HANLEY	
April 20, 1878	FURNIVAL, THOS. & SONS	COBRIDGE	4, 7
April 24, 1878	BROWNFIELD, WM. & SONS	COBRIDGE	
April 30, 1878	WEDGWOOD, JOSIAH & SONS	ETRURIA	
May 03, 1878	WEDGWOOD, JOSIAH & SONS	ETRURIA	8
May 08, 1878	BATES & BENNETT	COBRIDGE	
May 14, 1878	ELSMORE, & SON	TUNSTALL	
May 17, 1878	DIMMOCK, J. & CO.	HANLEY	
May 23, 1878	WEDGWOOD, JOSIAH & SONS	ETRURIA	
May 24, 1878	WEDGWOOD, JOSIAH & SONS	ETRURIA	
May 29, 1878	MINTON HOLLINS & CO.	STOKE	
June 04, 1878	FURNIVAL, F. & SONS	COBRIDGE	7

DATE	POTTER	LOCATION	CATEGORY
June 05, 1878	COPELAND, W. T. & SONS	STOKE	8
June 07, 1878	JONES, GEO. & SONS	STOKE	
June 08, 1878	WOOD, WM. & CO.	BURSLEM	
June 12, 1878	ADAMS, HARVEY & CO.	LONGTON	8
June 13, 1878	TAMS, JOHN	LONGTON	
June 19, 1878	BODLEY, E. F. & CO.	BURSLEM	
June 27, 1878	WEDGWOOD, JOSIAH & SONS	ETRURIA	
June 29, 1878	WOOD, SON & CO.	COBRIDGE	
July 01, 1878	BURGESS & LEIGH	BURSLEM	7
July 03, 1878	MINTONS	STOKE	
July 08, 1878	WEDGWOOD, JOSIAH & SONS	ETRURIA	
July 09, 1878	DIMMOCK, J. & CO.	HANLEY	
July 09, 1878	MINTONS	STOKE	8
July 09, 1878	WEDGWOOD, JOSIAH & SONS	ETRURIA	
July 10, 1878	BATES & BENNETT	COBRIDGE	
July 12, 1878	BROWN, T.C.-WESTHEAD, MOORE & CO.	HANLEY	
July 12, 1878	LEAR, SAMUEL	HANLEY	7
July 12, 1878	WEDGWOOD, JOSIAH & SONS	ETRURIA	
July 15, 1878	PRATT & SIMPSON	FENTON	
July 17, 1878	ADAMS, WM.	TUNSTALL	
July 20, 1878	MEIR, JOHN & SON	TUNSTALL	7
July 26, 1878	WEDGWOOD, JOSIAH & SONS	ETRURIA	
July 30, 1878	CLARKE, E.	LONGPORT	
July 30, 1878	POWELL, BISHOP & STONIER	HANLEY	
July 30, 1878	WEDGWOOD, JOSIAH & SONS	ETRURIA	
July 31, 1878	EDWARDS, JAMES & SON	BURSLEM	
July 31, 1878	MINTONS	STOKE	
August 07, 1878	HUGHES, THOS.	BURSLEM	
August 23, 1878	DIMMOCK, J. & CO.	HANLEY	
September 09, 1878	BROWNFIELD, WM. & SONS	COBRIDGE	8
September 10, 1878	WEDGWOOD, JOSIAH & SONS	ETRURIA	
September 13, 1878	ASHWORTH, G. L. & BROS.	HANLEY	
September 28, 1878	MINTON HOLLINS & CO.	STOKE	
September 30, 1878	MINTONS	STOKE	
October 02, 1878	MINTONS	STOKE	
October 03, 1878	HUDDEN, J. T.	LONGTON	
October 04, 1878	PRATT, F. & R. & CO.	FENTON	
October 08, 1878	BATES, GILDEA & WALKER	BURSLEM	
October 09, 1878	WEDGWOOD, JOSIAH	ETRURIA	
October 11, 1878	MINTON HOLLINS & CO.	STOKE	
October 14, 1878	COPELAND, W. T. & SONS	STOKE	8
October 23, 1878	BROWNHILLS POTTERY CO. (THE)	TUNSTALL	7
October 23, 1878	PINDER & BOURNE & CO.	BURSLEM	
October 24, 1878	DIMMOCK, J. & CO.	HANLEY	
October 24, 1878	FURNIVAL, T. & SONS	COBRIDGE	
October 26, 1878	BROWNFIELD, WM. & SONS	COBRIDGE	8
October 30, 1878	MINTON HOLLINS & CO.	STOKE	
October 30, 1878	MINTONS	STOKE	
November 04, 1878	EDGE, MALKIN & CO.	BURSLEM	7
November 05, 1878	BURGESS, H.	BURSLEM	
November 06, 1878	LEAR, SAMUEL	HANLEY	
November 15, 1878	PRATT, F. & R. & CO.	FENTON	
November 16, 1878	DIMMOCK, J. & CO.	HANLEY	
November 23, 1878	CHALLINOR, E. & C.	FENTON	
November 26, 1878	BOOTE, T. & R.	BURSLEM	
November 27, 1878	MACINTYRE, J. & CO.	BURSLEM	
November 29, 1878	CORN, W. & E.	BURSLEM	
December 02, 1878	BROWN, T.C.-WESTHEAD, MOORE & CO.	HANLEY	8
December 03, 1878	MACINTYRE, J. & CO.	BURSLEM	
December 04, 1878	BROWNFIELD, WM. & SONS	COBRIDGE	8
December 06, 1878	MINTONS	STOKE	
December 07, 1878	SHAW, A.	BURSLEM	4
December 19, 1878	HUGHES, THOS.	BURSLEM	
December 27, 1878	BOOTE, T. & R.	BURSLEM	
January 07, 1879	COPELAND, W. T. & SONS	STOKE	8
January 08, 1879	MINTON HOLLINS & CO.	STOKE	
January 09, 1879	BROWNFIELD, WM. & SONS	COBRIDGE	8, 10
January 14, 1879	NEW WHARF POTTERY CO., THE	BURSLEM	
January 16, 1879	HANCOCK, B. & S.	STOKE	
January 16, 1879	PRATT, F. & R. & CO.	FENTON	7
January 22, 1879	DUNN, BENNETT & CO.	HANLEY	
January 28, 1879	COPELAND, W. T. & SONS	STOKE	5
January 29, 1879	FURNIVAL, T. & SONS	COBRIDGE	7
February 01, 1879	CLEMENTSON BROS.	HANLEY	
February 03, 1879	WEDGWOOD, JOSIAH & SONS	ETRURIA	
February 05, 1879	MINTONS	STOKE	8
February 08, 1879	MINTONS	STOKE	8
February 14, 1879	FURNIVAL, T. & SONS	COBRIDGE	
February 24, 1879	ADAMS, W. & T.	TUNSTALL	
February 25, 1879	MINTONS	STOKE	
February 28, 1879	CHETWYND, E.	STOKE	
February 28, 1879	CLEMENTSON BROS.	HANLEY	
March 01, 1879	FURNIVAL, T. & SONS	COBRIDGE	7
March 04, 1879	GROVE, F. W. & STARK, J.	LONGTON	
March 06, 1879	POWELL, BISHOP & STONIER	HANLEY	
March 12, 1879	COPELAND, W. T. & SONS	STOKE	5
March 12, 1879	EDGE, MALKIN & CO.	BURSLEM	

DATE	POTTER	LOCATION	CATEGORY
March 13, 1879	CLEMENTSON BROS.	HANLEY	7
March 13, 1879	DAVENPORT, WM. & CO.	LONGPORT	1, 8
March 14, 1879	CLARKE, E.	LONGPORT	
March 17, 1879	POWELL, BISHOP & STONIER	HANLEY	
March 18, 1879	WEDGWOOD, JOSIAH & SONS	ETRURIA	
March 19, 1879	HAWTHORNE, J.	COBRIDGE	4
March 28, 1879	CLEMENTSON BROS.	HANLEY	7
March 29, 1879	BECK, BLAIR & CO.	LONGTON	
April 03, 1879	BROWN, T.C.-WESTHEAD, MOORE & CO.	HANLEY	
April 04, 1879	PINDER, BOURNE & CO.	BURSLEM	
April 09, 1879	ALCOCK, H. & CO.	COBRIDGE	
April 10, 1879	BROWN, T.C.-WESTHEAD, MOORE & CO.	HANLEY	
April 15, 1879	BROWN, T.C.-WESTHEAD, MOORE & CO.	HANLEY	10
April 23, 1879	BROWN, T.C.-WESTHEAD, MOORE & CO.	HANLEY	8
April 24, 1879	WEDGWOOD, JOSIAH & SONS	ETRURIA	
May 05, 1879	BATES, GILDEA & WALKER	BURSLEM	
May 05, 1879	FURNIVAL, T. & SONS	COBRIDGE	
May 06, 1879	BRIDGWOOD, SAMPSON & SON	LONGTON	
May 13, 1879	CLEMENTSON BROS.	HANLEY	
May 13, 1879	PINDER & BOURNE & CO.	BURSLEM	7
May 14, 1879	BROWN, T.C.-WESTHEAD, MOORE & CO.	HANLEY	8
May 19, 1879	BROWNFIELD, WM. & SONS	COBRIDGE	8
May 21, 1879	ADAMS, HARVEY & CO.	LONGTON	8
May 23, 1879	ADAMS, HARVEY & CO.	LONGTON	8
May 23, 1879	BRIDGWOOD, SAMPSON & SON	LONGTON	
May 29, 1879	PINDER, BOURNE & CO.	BURSLEM	
May 29, 1879	TAMS, JOHN	LONGTON	
May 30, 1879	DIMMOCK, J. & CO.	HANLEY	
May 31, 1879	MINTON HOLLINS & CO.	STOKE	
June 10, 1879	FURNIVAL, T. & SONS	COBRIDGE	
June 11, 1879	TILL, THOS. & SONS	BURSLEM	
June 13, 1879	BROWN, T.C.-WESTHEAD, MOORE & CO.	HANLEY	8
June 18, 1879	GROVE, F. W. & STARK, J.	LONGTON	
June 24, 1879	WEDGWOOD, JOSIAH & SONS	ETRURIA	
June 25, 1879	CLEMENTSON BROS.	HANLEY	
June 30, 1879	BIRKS BROS. & SEDDON	COBRIDGE	
July 02, 1879	WEDGWOOD, JOSIAH & SONS	ETRURIA	
July 07, 1879	WILEMAN, J. F.	FENTON	8
July 08, 1879	BROWN, T.C.-WESTHEAD, MOORE & CO.	HANLEY	8
July 08, 1879	MINTONS	STOKE	8
July 09, 1879	BROWN, T.C.-WESTHEAD, MOORE & CO.	HANLEY	8
July 16, 1879	BROWN, T.C.-WESTHEAD, MOORE & CO.	HANLEY	8
July 25, 1879	MINTONS	STOKE	8
July 26, 1879	MINTON HOLLINS & CO.	STOKE	
July 31, 1879	MINTONS	STOKE	8
August 06, 1879	WARDLE & CO.	HANLEY	7
August 13, 1879	GROVE, F. W. & STARK, J.	LONGTON	
August 27, 1879	BATES, GILDEA & WALKER	BURSLEM	2
September 04, 1879	BROWN, T.C.-WESTHEAD, MOORE & CO.	HANLEY	8
September 10, 1879	BROWN, T.C.-WESTHEAD, MOORE & CO.	HANLEY	8
September 17, 1879	BROWNFIELD, WM. & SONS	COBRIDGE	8
September 18, 1879	BROWN, T.C.-WESTHEAD, MOORE & CO.	HANLEY	8
September 26, 1879	HUDDEN, J. T.	LONGTON	
September 29, 1879	EDGE, MALKIN & CO.	BURSLEM	
October 09, 1879	BATES, GILDEA & WALKER	BURSLEM	
October 10, 1879	BROWN, T.C.-WESTHEAD, MOORE & CO.	HANLEY	8
October 15, 1879	MINTONS	STOKE	8
October 16, 1879	MINTON HOLLINS & CO.	STOKE	
October 17, 1879	ASHWORTH, G. L. & BROS.	HANLEY	
October 18, 1879	WEDGWOOD, JOSIAH & SONS	ETRURIA	
October 27, 1879	BODLEY, E. F. & CO.	BURSLEM	7, 8
October 29, 1879	CLEMENTSON BROS.	HANLEY	
October 29, 1879	MINTONS	STOKE	
October 30, 1879	MINTONS	STOKE	8
November 03, 1879	MINTON HOLLINS & CO.	STOKE	
November 06, 1879	WEDGWOOD, JOSIAH & SONS	ETRURIA	
November 15, 1879	COPELAND, W. T. & SONS	STOKE	8
November 17, 1879	POWELL, BISHOP & STONIER	HANLEY	
November 19, 1879	POWELL, BISHOP & STONIER	HANLEY	
November 20, 1879	ELSMORE, & SON	TUNSTALL	
November 21, 1879	MINTONS	STOKE	7, 8
November 28, 1879	BROWNFIELD, WM. & SONS	COBRIDGE	8
November 29, 1879	BROWN, T.C.-WESTHEAD, MOORE & CO.	HANLEY	8
November 29, 1879	MINTONS	STOKE	

DATE	POTTER	LOCATION	CATEGORY
December 02, 1879	BROWN, T.C.-WESTHEAD, MOORE & CO.	HANLEY	8
December 02, 1879	ELSMORE, & SON	TUNSTALL	
December 06, 1879	BOOTE, T. & R.	BURSLEM	7
December 10, 1879	CLEMENTSON BROS.	HANLEY	
December 17, 1879	RIDGWAYS	STOKE	
December 19, 1879	CLEMENTSON BROS.	HANLEY	7
December 20, 1879	WEDGWOOD, JOSIAH & SONS	ETRURIA	
December 22, 1879	MINTONS	STOKE	
January 07, 1880	BOOTE, T. & R.	BURSLEM	
January 07, 1880	MINTON HOLLINS & CO.	STOKE	
January 08, 1880	OLD HALL EARTHENWARE CO. LTD., THE	HANLEY	
January 13, 1880	BROWN, T.C.-WESTHEAD, MOORE & CO.	HANLEY	8
January 21, 1880	PINDER, BOURNE & CO.	BURSLEM	
January 22, 1880	MINTON HOLLINS & CO.	STOKE	
January 22, 1880	MINTONS	STOKE	8
January 23, 1880	MINTONS	STOKE	8
January 26, 1880	BROWNFIELD, WM. & SONS	COBRIDGE	8
January 27, 1880	WARDLE & CO.	HANLEY	7
January 28, 1880	BROWN, T.C.-WESTHEAD, MOORE & CO.	HANLEY	8
January 28, 1880	POWELL, BISHOP & STONIER	HANLEY	
February 03, 1880	POWELL, BISHOP & STONIER	HANLEY	
February 09, 1880	WHITTINGHAM, FORD & RILEY	BURSLEM	
February 10, 1880	MINTONS	STOKE	
February 12, 1880	ADDERLY, W. A.	LONGTON	8
February 12, 1880	BROWNFIELD, WM. & SONS	COBRIDGE	
February 14, 1880	BATES, GILDEA & WALKER	BURSLEM	7
February 24, 1880	MINTONS	STOKE	8
February 25, 1880	CLEMENTSON BROS.	HANLEY	
February 26, 1880	MINTON HOLLINS & CO.	STOKE	
March 08, 1880	FURNIVAL, T. & SONS	COBRIDGE	
March 12, 1880	ADDERLY, W. A.	LONGTON	8
March 16, 1880	MACINTYRE, J. & CO.	BURSLEM	
March 16, 1880	WILEMAN, J. F. & CO.	FENTON	8
March 17, 1880	WEDGWOOD, JOSIAH & SONS	ETRURIA	
March 22, 1880	POWELL, BISHOP & STONIER	HANLEY	
March 25, 1880	MINTONS	STOKE	8
April 12, 1880	BATES, GILDEA & WALKER	BURSLEM	
April 15, 1880	RIDGWAYS	STOKE	
April 22, 1880	GRINDLEY, W. H. & CO.	TUNSTALL	7
April 26, 1880	FURNIVAL, T. & SONS	COBRIDGE	
April 29, 1880	MINTONS	STOKE	8
April 30, 1880	FURNIVAL, T. & SONS	COBRIDGE	7
May 03, 1880	BROWNFIELD, WM. & SONS	COBRIDGE	8, 10
May 10, 1880	POWELL, BISHOP & STONIER	HANLEY	7
May 13, 1880	MINTON HOLLINS & CO.	STOKE	
May 13, 1880	MINTONS	STOKE	8
May 14, 1880	BATES, GILDEA & WALKER	BURSLEM	
May 25, 1880	BROWNFIELD, WM. & SONS	COBRIDGE	8, 10
May 26, 1880	MINTONS	STOKE	
June 01, 1880	MINTONS	STOKE	8
June 04, 1880	CLEMENTSON BROS.	HANLEY	
June 07, 1880	DIMMOCK, J. & CO.	HANLEY	
June 08, 1880	JONES, GEO. & SONS	STOKE	8
June 10, 1880	DIMMOCK, J. & CO.	HANLEY	8
June 11, 1880	WEDGWOOD, JOSIAH & SONS	ETRURIA	7
June 16, 1880	WEDGWOOD & CO.	TUNSTALL	
June 17, 1880	DIMMOCK, J. & CO.	HANLEY	
June 17, 1880	LEAR, SAMUEL	HANLEY	7
June 17, 1880	MACINTYRE, J. & CO.	BURSLEM	
June 17, 1880	RIDGWAYS	STOKE	
June 19, 1880	WEDGWOOD, JOSIAH & SONS	ETRURIA	
June 22, 1880	GRINDLEY, W. H. & CO.	TUNSTALL	
July 07, 1880	EMERY, F. J.	BURSLEM	7
July 07, 1880	MINTONS	STOKE	8
July 12, 1880	MINTONS	STOKE	8
July 13, 1880	BARLOW, THOS.	LONGTON	
July 15, 1880	DUNN, BENNETT & CO.	HANLEY	
July 15, 1880	GROVE, F. W. & STARK, J.	LONGTON	7
July 28, 1880	BROWNHILLS POTTERY CO. (THE)	TUNSTALL	
July 31, 1880	OLD HALL EARTHENWARE CO. LTD., THE	HANLEY	
August 04, 1880	PINDER, BOURNE & CO.	BURSLEM	
August 11, 1880	CLEMENTSON BROS.	HANLEY	
August 14, 1880	DAVENPORT, WM. & CO.	LONGPORT	8
August 18, 1880	WEDGWOOD, JOSIAH & SONS	ETRURIA	
August 21, 1880	ADDERLY, W. A.	LONGTON	8
August 23, 1880	BROWN, T.C.-WESTHEAD, MOORE & CO.	HANLEY	8
September 03, 1880	BROWN, T.C.-WESTHEAD, MOORE & CO.	HANLEY	
September 11, 1880	BROWNFIELD, WM. & SONS	COBRIDGE	8
September 14, 1880	MINTONS	STOKE	8
September 15, 1880	ASHWORTH, G. L. & BROS.	HANLEY	
September 15, 1880	MINTON HOLLINS & CO.	STOKE	
September 25, 1880	MINTON HOLLINS & CO.	STOKE	
September 27, 1880	MARSHALL, JOHN & CO.	BO'NESS, SCOTLAND	
September 29, 1880	BROWNHILLS POTTERY CO. (THE)	TUNSTALL	7
October 06, 1880	WEDGWOOD, JOSIAH & SONS	ETRURIA	
October 12, 1880	MINTONS	STOKE	
October 13, 1880	WEDGWOOD, JOSIAH & SONS	ETRURIA	
October 20, 1880	BURGESS & LEIGH	BURSLEM	7
October 22, 1880	BODLEY, E. F. & SON	BURSLEM	8
October 26, 1880	MINTON HOLLINS & CO.	STOKE	
October 27, 1880	TAMS, J.	LONGTON	7
October 27, 1880	WOOLISCROFT, G. & SON	ETRURIA	5
November 02, 1880	GRINDLEY, W. H. & CO.	TUNSTALL	7
November 04, 1880	ADAMS, W. & T.	TUNSTALL	
November 04, 1880	MINTON HOLLINS & CO.	STOKE	
November 09, 1880	WEDGWOOD, JOSIAH & SONS	ETRURIA	
November 18, 1880	MINTONS	STOKE	8
November 24, 1880	BATES, GILDEA & WALKER	BURSLEM	
November 24, 1880	GROVE, F. W. & STARK, J.	LONGTON	
December 06, 1880	POWELL, BISHOP & STONIER	HANLEY	
December 07, 1880	PINDER, BOURNE & CO.	BURSLEM	7
December 15, 1880	BROWNFIELD, WM. & SONS	COBRIDGE	8
December 18, 1880	BATES, GILDEA & WALKER	BURSLEM	
December 24, 1880	BROWN, T.C.-WESTHEAD, MOORE & CO.	HANLEY	8
December 29, 1880	DOULTON & CO.	LAMBETH	7
December 31, 1880	OLD HALL EARTHENWARE CO. LTD., THE	HANLEY	
January 06, 1881	HANCOCK, B. & S.	STOKE	
January 20, 1881	MINTONS	STOKE	
January 21, 1881	ADAMS, W. & T.	TUNSTALL	1
January 26, 1881	MINTON HOLLINS & CO.	STOKE	
February 08, 1881	BROWNFIELD, WM. & SONS	COBRIDGE	8, 10
February 08, 1881	GROVE, F. W. & STARK, J.	LONGTON	
February 11, 1881	EMERY, F. J.	BURSLEM	
February 15, 1881	ADDERLY, W. A.	LONGTON	8
February 25, 1881	MACINTYRE, J. & CO.	BURSLEM	
February 28, 1881	WOOLISCROFT, G. & SON	HANLEY	
March 03, 1881	DIMMOCK, J. & CO.	HANLEY	7
March 08, 1881	GROVE, F. W. & STARK, J.	LONGTON	7
March 09, 1881	MINTONS	STOKE	
March 23, 1881	MINTONS	STOKE	8
March 24, 1881	ADDERLY, W. A.	LONGTON	8
March 24, 1881	PINDER, T. S.	BURSLEM	
March 31, 1881	HUDDEN, J. T.	LONGTON	
April 07, 1881	OLD HALL EARTHENWARE CO. LTD., THE	HANLEY	
April 08, 1881	WEDGWOOD & CO.	TUNSTALL	
April 12, 1881	MINTONS	STOKE	8
April 14, 1881	MINTONS	STOKE	8
April 16, 1881	MARSHALL, J. & CO.	BO'NESS, SCOTLAND	
April 19, 1881	BOOTE, T. & R.	BURSLEM	
April 23, 1881	WILEMAN, J. F.	FENTON	
April 28, 1881	COPELAND, W. T. & SONS	STOKE	5
April 30, 1881	WEDGWOOD, JOSIAH & SONS	ETRURIA	7
May 03, 1881	WOOD, WM. & CO.	BURSLEM	
May 04, 1881	BROWNFIELD, WM. & SONS	COBRIDGE	7, 8
May 05, 1881	ADAMS, W. & T.	TUNSTALL	
May 11, 1881	TAMS, J.	LONGTON	
May 13, 1881	MINTONS	STOKE	8
May 16, 1881	WEDGWOOD, JOSIAH & SONS	ETRURIA	7
May 20, 1881	ADDERLY, W. A.	LONGTON	8
May 21, 1881	POWELL, BISHOP & STONIER	HANLEY	
May 24, 1881	ASHWORTH, G. L. & BROS.	HANLEY	
May 24, 1881	EMERY, F. J.	BURSLEM	
May 24, 1881	MINTONS	STOKE	
May 25, 1881	POWELL, BISHOP & STONIER	HANLEY	
May 25, 1881	WEDGWOOD, JOSIAH & SONS	ETRURIA	
May 26, 1881	WOOLISCROFT, G. & SON	HANLEY	
May 30, 1881	FURNIVAL, T. & SONS	COBRIDGE	
June 01, 1881	MINTONS	STOKE	
June 04, 1881	FURNIVAL, T. & SONS	COBRIDGE	
June 07, 1881	BODLEY, E. F. & SON	BURSLEM	8
June 13, 1881	LEAR, S.	HANLEY	
June 21, 1881	BIRKS BROS. & SEDDON	COBRIDGE	8
June 21, 1881	GILDEA & WALKER	BURSLEM	
July 02, 1881	FURNIVAL, T. & SONS	COBRIDGE	5
July 06, 1881	WEDGWOOD, JOSIAH & SONS	ETRURIA	
July 09, 1881	WARDLE & CO.	HANLEY	7
July 14, 1881	BROWN, T.C.-WESTHEAD, MOORE & CO.	HANLEY	8
July 25, 1881	DAVIS, J. H.	HANLEY	
July 28, 1881	RIDGWAYS	STOKE	
July 30, 1881	BRIDGWOOD, SAMPSON & SON	LONGTON	
July 30, 1881	COPELAND, W. T. & SONS	STOKE	8
July 30, 1881	MINTONS	STOKE	
August 05, 1881	PINDER, BOURNE & CO.	BURSLEM	
August 10, 1881	OLD HALL EARTHENWARE CO. LTD., THE	HANLEY	7

DATE	POTTER	LOCATION	CATEGORY
August 23, 1881	GROVE, F. W. & STARK, J.	LONGTON	
August 24, 1881	BOOTE, J. & R.	BURSLEM	
August 27, 1881	GILDEA & WALKER	BURSLEM	7
August 27, 1881	LEAR, S.	HANELY	7
August 29, 1881	ADAMS, W. & T.	TUNSTALL	
September 16, 1881	JONES, GEO. & CO.	STOKE	8
September 23, 1881	MINTON HOLLINS & CO.	STOKE	
September 27, 1881	PINDER, BOURNE & CO.	BURSLEM	
September 28, 1881	GILDEA & WALKER	BURSLEM	
September 29, 1881	JONES, GEO. & SONS	STOKE	7
September 30, 1881	DAVENPORTS LTD.	LONGPORT	8
September 30, 1881	MINTONS	STOKE	
October 04, 1881	BROWNFIELD, WM. & SONS	COBRIDGE	10
October 07, 1881	MINTONS	STOKE	8
October 12, 1881	MINTONS	STOKE	8
October 13, 1881	BOOTE, T. & R.	BURSLEM	
October 22, 1881	MINTONS	STOKE	8
October 26, 1881	BROWN, T.C.-WESTHEAD, MOORE & CO.	HANLEY	8
October 26, 1881	MINTONS	STOKE	8
October 29, 1881	BOOTE, T. & R.	BURSLEM	
October 29, 1881	BROWNFIELD, WM. & SONS	COBRIDGE	8
October 29, 1881	MINTON HOLLINS & CO.	STOKE	
October 29, 1881	WARDLE & CO.	HANLEY	7
November 02, 1881	BROWN, T.C.-WESTHEAD, MOORE & CO.	HANLEY	8
November 08, 1881	BOOTE, T. & R.	BURSLEM	
November 09, 1881	GROVE, F. W. & STARK, J.	LONGTON	
November 19, 1881	BRIDGWOOD, SAMPSON & SON	LONGTON	
November 22, 1881	TAMS, J.	LONGTON	
December 10, 1881	BROWN, T.C.-WESTHEAD, MOORE & CO.	HANLEY	8
December 16, 1881	MINTONS	STOKE	8
December 24, 1881	BROADHURST, J.	FENTON	
January 04, 1882	COPELAND, W. T. & SONS	STOKE	8, 13
January 04, 1882	PRATT, F. & R. & CO.	FENTON	
January 07, 1882	GRINDLEY, W. H. & CO.	TUNSTALL	
January 07, 1882	RIDGWAYS	STOKE	
January 10, 1882	LEAR, S.	HANLEY	7
January 18, 1882	ROBINSON & SON	LONGTON	
January 26, 1882	HUDDEN, J. T.	LONGTON	
January 30, 1882	GROVE, F. W. & STARK, J.	LONGTON	1, 7
January 30, 1882	HOLLINSHEAD & KIRKHAM	TUNSTALL	7
February 01, 1882	EDGE, MALKIN & CO.	BURSLEM	7
February 03, 1882	BROWN, T.C.-WESTHEAD, MOORE & CO.	HANLEY	8
February 04, 1882	MINTON HOLLINS & CO.	STOKE	
February 08, 1882	WARDLE & CO.	HANLEY	
February 15, 1882	GROVE, F. W. & STARK, J.	LONGTON	
February 16, 1882	MINTONS	STOKE	
February 18, 1882	WILEMAN, J. F. & CO.	FENTON	8
February 23, 1882	MINTON HOLLINS & CO.	STOKE	
March 01, 1882	MINTON HOLLINS & CO.	STOKE	
March 07, 1882	MINTON HOLLINS & CO.	STOKE	
March 13, 1882	HUDDEN, J. T.	LONGTON	
March 15, 1882	POWELL, BISHOP & STONIER	HANLEY	
March 20, 1882	ADDERLY, W. A.	LONGTON	8
March 23, 1882	ADAMS, W. & T.	TUNSTALL	8
April 04, 1882	BROWNFIELD, WM. & SONS	COBRIDGE	8, 10
April 11, 1882	JONES, GEO. & SONS	STOKE	
April 11, 1882	MINTON HOLLINS & CO.	STOKE	
April 21, 1882	BRIDGWOOD, SAMPSON & SON	LONGTON	
April 27, 1882	NEW WHARF POTTERY CO., THE	BURSLEM	
May 02, 1882	ASHWORTH, G. L. & BROS.	HANLEY	7
May 06, 1882	POWELL, BISHOP & STONIER	HANLEY	
May 08, 1882	DAVENPORTS LTD.	LONGPORT	8
May 09, 1882	ALCOCK, H. & CO.	COBRIDGE	
May 09, 1882	BROWNFIELD, WM. & SONS	COBRIDGE	8
May 09, 1882	MINTON HOLLINS & CO.	STOKE	
May 10, 1882	EDWARDS, JOHN	FENTON	7
May 13, 1882	JONES, GEO. & SONS	STOKE	
May 24, 1882	DOULTON & CO.	BURSLEM	
May 24, 1882	MINTON HOLLINS & CO.	STOKE	
May 25, 1882	ADDERLY, W. A.	LONGTON	8
May 27, 1882	LEAR, SAMUEL	HANLEY	
May 30, 1882	GRINDLEY, W. H. & CO.	TUNSTALL	
June 05, 1882	MINTONS	STOKE	
June 09, 1882	ADDERLY, W. A.	LONGTON	7
June 13, 1882	SHAW, A. & SON	BURSLEM	
June 13, 1882	WARDLE & CO.	HANLEY	7
June 21, 1882	BRIDGWOOD, SAMPSON & SON	LONGTON	
June 21, 1882	OLD HALL EARTHENWARE CO. LTD., THE	HANLEY	
June 23, 1882	BURGESS & LEIGH	BURSLEM	
June 23, 1882	WEDGWOOD, JOSIAH & SONS	ETRURIA	7
July 03, 1882	MINTONS	STOKE	
July 06, 1882	BROWNFIELD, WM. & SONS	COBRIDGE	
July 14, 1882	JONES, GEO. & SONS	STOKE	8
July 14, 1882	WARDLE & CO.	HANLEY	7
July 17, 1882	WOOD & SON	BURSLEM	
July 19, 1882	WARDLE & CO.	HANLEY	
July 20, 1882	EDWARDS, JOHN	FENTON	7
July 22, 1882	JONES, GEO. & SONS	STOKE	7
July 25, 1882	BROWNHILLS POTTERY CO. (THE)	TUNSTALL	7
July 28, 1882	HAWLEY & CO.	LONGTON	
July 31, 1882	BRIDGWOOD, SAMPSON & SON	LONGTON	
July 31, 1882	MINTONS	STOKE	
August 05, 1882	BROWNFIELD, WM. & SONS	COBRIDGE	
August 21, 1882	TAMS, JOHN	LONGTON	
August 25, 1882	MINTONS	STOKE	8
August 26, 1882	WOOD, WM. & CO.	BURSLEM	
August 28, 1882	BELFIELD & CO.	PRESTONPANS	
August 28, 1882	MINTONS	STOKE	7
August 29, 1882	BROWNFIELD, WM. & SONS	COBRIDGE	
September 06, 1882	HAWLEY & CO.	LONGTON	7
September 08, 1882	MINTONS	STOKE	
September 19, 1882	GRINDLEY, W. H. & CO.	TUNSTALL	
September 28, 1882	BRIDGETT & BATES	LONGTON	
September 28, 1882	BROWN, T.C.-WESTHEAD, MOORE & CO.	HANLEY	
September 29, 1882	BROWNHILLS POTTERY CO. (THE)	TUNSTALL	
October 06, 1882	MINTONS	STOKE	
October 09, 1882	COPELAND, W. T. & SONS	STOKE	8
October 11, 1882	BRIDGWOOD, SAMPSON & SON	LONGTON	7
October 11, 1882	WOOD & SON	BURSLEM	
October 12, 1882	FURNIVAL, T. & SONS	COBRIDGE	7
October 16, 1882	WOOD & SON	BURSLEM	
October 21, 1882	TAMS, J.	LONGTON	
November 08, 1882	MINTONS	STOKE	8
November 10, 1882	PRATT & SIMPSON	FENTON	7
November 10, 1882	RIDGWAYS (Made by Dudson)	STOKE	
November 11, 1882	MINTON HOLLINS & CO.	STOKE	
November 11, 1882	POWELL, BISHOP & STONIER	HANLEY	
November 13, 1882	BRIDGWOOD, SAMPSON & SON	LONGTON	
November 13, 1882	EDGE, MALKIN & CO.	BURSLEM	
November 21, 1882	GILDEA & WALKER	BURSLEM	
November 24, 1882	MINTON HOLLINS & CO.	STOKE	
November 27, 1882	ALCOCK, H. & CO.	COBRIDGE	
November 27, 1882	WILEMAN, J. F. & CO.	FENTON	8
December 02, 1882	MINTON HOLLINS & CO.	STOKE	
December 06, 1882	BROWN, T.C.-WESTHEAD, MOORE & CO.	HANLEY	8
December 13, 1882	MINTONS	STOKE	
December 13, 1882	WEDGWOOD, JOSIAH	ETRURIA	7
December 14, 1882	LEAR, S.	HANLEY	7
December 15, 1882	OLD HALL EARTHENWARE CO. LTD., THE	HANLEY	
December 22, 1882	GROVE, F. W. & STARK, J.	LONGTON	7
December 23, 1882	NEW WHARF POTTERY CO., THE	BURSLEM	7
December 23, 1882	WILEMAN, J. F.	FENTON	
December 27, 1882	NEW WHARF POTTERY CO., THE	BURSLEM	
January 03, 1883	FURNIVAL, T. & SONS	COBRIDGE	
January 04, 1883	BROWN, T.C.-WESTHEAD, MOORE & CO.	HANLEY	
January 08, 1883	COPELAND, W. T. & SONS	STOKE	8
January 09, 1883	BODLEY, E. F. & SON	LONGPORT	
January 09, 1883	DAVENPORTS LTD.	LONGPORT	8
January 09, 1883	POWELL, BISHOP & STONIER	HANLEY	7
January 10, 1883	GILDEA & WALKER	BURSLEM	
January 13, 1883	BOOTE, T. & R.	BURSLEM	
January 17, 1883	GRINDLEY, W. H. & CO.	TUNSTALL	
January 23, 1883	BODLEY, E. F. & SON	LONGPORT	
January 23, 1883	COPELAND, W. T. & SONS	STOKE	8, 13
January 24, 1883	BRIDGWOOD, SAMPSON & SON	LONGTON	
January 24, 1883	BROWNFIELD, WM. & SONS	COBRIDGE	8
January 25, 1883	BROWNHILLS POTTERY CO. (THE)	TUNSTALL	
January 27, 1883	TURNER, G. W. & SONS	TUNSTALL	
January 29, 1883	BROWNFIELD, WM. & SONS	COBRIDGE	
January 29, 1883	GRINDLEY, W. H. & CO.	TUNSTALL	
January 30, 1883	BODLEY, E. F. & SON	LONGPORT	
January 30, 1883	WEDGWOOD & CO.	TUNSTALL	
January 31, 1883	MINTON HOLLINS & CO.	STOKE	
February 01, 1883	BRIDGWOOD, SAMPSON & SON	LONGTON	
February 02, 1883	HANCOCK, S.	STOKE	
February 02, 1883	WEDGWOOD & CO.	TUNSTALL	
February 03, 1883	MINTONS	STOKE	
February 07, 1883	HAWLEY & CO.	LONGTON	7
February 12, 1883	DUNN, BENNETT & CO.	HANLEY	
February 14, 1883	GRINDLEY, W. H. & CO.	TUNSTALL	
February 15, 1883	DAVIS, J. H.	HANLEY	
February 17, 1883	TURNER, G. W. & SONS	TUNSTALL	7
February 19, 1883	ADDERLY, W. A.	LONGTON	8
February 20, 1883	DAVENPORTS LTD.	LONGPORT	8
February 20, 1883	GILDEA & WALKER	BURSLEM	
February 21, 1883	JONES, GEO. & SONS	STOKE	8
February 22, 1883	OLD HALL EARTHENWARE CO., THE	HANLEY	
February 24, 1883	WEDGWOOD, JOSIAH & SONS	ETRURIA	
February 28, 1883	TILL, THOS. & SONS	BURSLEM	

DATE	POTTER	LOCATION	CATEGORY
March 08, 1883	BODLEY, E. F. & SON	LONGPORT	8
March 15, 1883	FURNIVAL, T. & SONS	COBRIDGE	
March 17, 1883	MINTONS	STOKE	8
March 20, 1883	WEDGWOOD, JOSIAH & SONS	ETRURIA	7
March 24, 1883	BRIDGWOOD, SAMPSON & SON	LONGTON	
March 30, 1883	MINTON HOLLINS & CO.	STOKE	
March 30, 1883	MINTONS	STOKE	
April 02, 1883	POULSON, T. & E. L.	CASTLEFORD	
April 21, 1883	WILEMAN, J. F. & CO.	FENTON	
April 24, 1883	ASHWORTH, G. L. & BROS.	HANLEY	
April 25, 1883	PRATT & SIMPSON	FENTON	
April 27, 1883	DAVIS, J. H.	HANLEY	
April 27, 1883	POWELL, BISHOP & STONIER	HANLEY	8
May 02, 1883	BROWN, T.C.-WESTHEAD, MOORE & CO.	HANLEY	8
May 08, 1883	BOOTH, T. G. & F.	TUNSTALL	
May 22, 1883	POWELL, BISHOP & STONIER	HANLEY	8
May 23, 1883	BOOTH, T. G. & F.	TUNSTALL	
May 24, 1883	BROWNHILLS POTTERY CO. (THE)	TUNSTALL	
May 25, 1883	ADDERLY, W. A.	LONGTON	8
May 31, 1883	WARDLE & CO.	HANLEY	7
June 02, 1883	MINTON HOLLINS & CO.	STOKE	
June 04, 1883	CLEMENTSON BROS.	HANLEY	
June 08, 1883	ALCOCK, H. & CO.	COBRIDGE	
June 09, 1883	BRIDGWOOD, SAMPSON & SON	LONGTON	
June 09, 1883	MINTONS	STOKE	
June 11, 1883	GROVE, F. W. & STARK, J.	LONGTON	
June 13, 1883	BELFIELD & CO.	PRESTONPANS	
June 13, 1883	PRATT & SIMPSON	STOKE	
June 14, 1883	GROVE, F. W. & STARK, J.	LONGTON	
June 18, 1883	BROWNFIELD, WM. & SONS	COBRIDGE	8, 10
June 18, 1883	TAMS, JOHN	LONGTON	7
June 20, 1883	BOOTE, T. & R.	BURSLEM	
June 20, 1883	CORN, W. & E.	BURSLEM	
June 20, 1883	MINTONS	STOKE	
June 21, 1883	WARDLE & CO.	HANLEY	7
June 23, 1883	WEDGWOOD, JOSIAH & SONS	ETRURIA	
June 25, 1883	BROWNFIELD, WM. & SONS	COBRIDGE	8
June 25, 1883	FORD & RILEY	BURSLEM	
July 02, 1883	EDGE, MALKIN & CO.	BURSLEM	
July 04, 1883	BROWNFIELD, WM. & SONS	COBRIDGE	8
July 05, 1883	FURNIVAL, T. & SONS	COBRIDGE	7
July 05, 1883	GROVE, F. W. & STARK, J.	LONGTON	
July 10, 1883	MACINTYRE, J. & CO.	BURSLEM	
July 11, 1883	WEDGWOOD, JOSIAH & SONS	ETRURIA	
July 19, 1883	DAVENPORTS LTD.	LONGPORT	8
July 19, 1883	JONES, GEO. & SONS	STOKE	8
July 20, 1883	HOLLINSHEAD & KIRKHAM	TUNSTALL	8
July 21, 1883	BRIDGETT & BATES	LONGTON	
July 23, 1883	WEDGWOOD, JOSIAH & SONS	ETRURIA	
July 26, 1883	ADDERLY, W. A.	LONGTON	7
July 27, 1883	BROWN, T.C.-WESTHEAD, MOORE & CO.	HANLEY	
July 30, 1883	BROWNFIELD, WM. & SONS	COBRIDGE	8
July 31, 1883	BOOTE, T. & R.	BURSLEM	
August 01, 1883	BROWN, T.C.-WESTHEAD, MOORE & CO.	HANLEY	
August 01, 1883	JONES, GEO. & SONS	STOKE	8
August 02, 1883	DAVENPORTS LTD.	LONGPORT	8
August 08, 1883	RIDGWAY, J. & E.	STOKE	
August 22, 1883	BROWNHILLS POTTERY CO. (THE)	TUNSTALL	
August 25, 1883	BROWNFIELD, WM. & SONS	COBRIDGE	8, 10
August 31, 1883	CORN, W. & E.	BURSLEM	
August 31, 1883	WILEMAN, J. F. & CO.	FENTON	8
September 05, 1883	BROWNFIELD, WM. & SONS	COBRIDGE	8
September 07, 1883	POWELL, BISHOP & STONIER	HANLEY	8
September 11, 1883	WEDGWOOD, JOSIAH & SONS	ETRURIA	7
September 14, 1883	ADAMS, W. & T.	TUNSTALL	
September 14, 1883	MINTONS	STOKE	
September 21, 1883	BROWN, T.C.-WESTHEAD, MOORE & CO.	HANLEY	
September 25, 1883	BRIDGWOOD, SAMPSON & SON	LONGTON	
September 25, 1883	GROVE, F. W. & STARK, J.	LONGTON	1
September 29, 1883	BRIDGWOOD, SAMPSON & SON	LONGTON	
October 02, 1883	MELLOR, TAYLOR & CO.	BURSLEM	
October 04, 1883	BRIDGWOOD, SAMPSON & SON	LONGTON	
October 06, 1883	GRINDLEY, W. H. & CO.	TUNSTALL	
October 08, 1883	BOOTH, T. G. & F.	TUNSTALL	
October 12, 1883	BRIDGETT & BATES	LONGTON	
October 13, 1883	BROWNFIELD, WM. & SONS	COBRIDGE	8
October 13, 1883	WOOD & SON	BURSLEM	
October 17, 1883	NEW WHARF POTTERY CO., THE	BURSLEM	
October 20, 1883	ADDERLY, W. A.	LONGTON	
October 20, 1883	BROWNFIELD, WM. & SONS	COBRIDGE	8
October 23, 1883	DIMMOCK, J. & CO.	HANLEY	7
October 24, 1883	MINTON HOLLINS & CO.	STOKE	
October 27, 1883	BROWNHILLS POTTERY CO. (THE)	TUNSTALL	
October 30, 1883	MARSHALL, J. & CO.	BO'NESS, SCOTLAND	7

DATE	POTTER	LOCATION	CATEGORY
October 30, 1883	NEW WHARF POTTERY CO., THE	BURSLEM	
October 30, 1883	ROBINSON, J.	BURSLEM	
November 01, 1883	DAVENPORT'S LTD. (1881-87)	LONGPORT	
November 01, 1883	DAVENPORTS LTD.	LONGPORT	
November 05, 1883	ALCOCK, H. & CO.	COBRIDGE	
November 06, 1883	CHALLINOR, E. & C.	FENTON	
November 07, 1883	CORN, W. & E.	BURSLEM	
November 10, 1883	BROWNFIELD, WM. & SONS	COBRIDGE	
November 13, 1883	BOOTH, T. G. & F.	TUNSTALL	
November 15, 1883	FURNIVAL, T. & SONS	COBRIDGE	
November 21, 1883	EMERY, F. J.	BURSLEM	
November 23, 1883	MINTON HOLLINS & CO.	STOKE	
November 24, 1883	POWELL, BISHOP & STONIER	HANLEY	8
November 26, 1883	ADDERLY, W. A.	LONGTON	8
November 26, 1883	BRIDGWOOD, SAMPSON & SON	LONGTON	
December 05, 1883	MALKIN, EDGE & CO.	BURSLEM	
December 08, 1883	WILEMAN, J. F. & CO.	FENTON	
December 14, 1883	BROWNHILLS POTTERY CO. (THE)	TUNSTALL	
December 15, 1883	BOOTH, T. G. & F.	TUNSTALL	
December 29, 1883	POWELL, BISHOP & STONIER	HANLEY	8

APPENDIX B17: REGISTRY DATES, ALPHABETICAL BY POTTER: WITH CATEGORY OF MANUFACTURE, 1842-1883

POTTER	DATE	LOCATION	CATEGORY
ADAMS, HARVEY & CO.	April 07, 1870	LONGTON	
ADAMS, HARVEY & CO.	June 22, 1870	LONGTON	
ADAMS, HARVEY & CO.	December 19, 1870	LONGTON	8
ADAMS, HARVEY & CO.	March 07, 1872	LONGTON	8
ADAMS, HARVEY & CO.	May 02, 1872	LONGTON	8
ADAMS, HARVEY & CO.	September 25, 1873	LONGTON	8
ADAMS, HARVEY & CO.	December 05, 1873	LONGTON	8
ADAMS, HARVEY & CO.	December 14, 1876	LONGTON	8
ADAMS, HARVEY & CO.	December 28, 1876	LONGTON	8
ADAMS, HARVEY & CO.	June 12, 1878	LONGTON	8
ADAMS, HARVEY & CO.	May 21, 1879	LONGTON	8
ADAMS, HARVEY & CO.	May 23, 1879	LONGTON	8
ADAMS, JOHN (Executors of)	December 27, 1872	LONGTON	
ADAMS, W. & T.	July 24, 1872	TUNSTALL	
ADAMS, W. & T.	June 07, 1875	TUNSTALL	
ADAMS, W. & T.	February 24, 1879	TUNSTALL	
ADAMS, W. & T.	November 04, 1880	TUNSTALL	
ADAMS, W. & T.	January 21, 1881	TUNSTALL	1
ADAMS, W. & T.	May 05, 1881	TUNSTALL	
ADAMS, W. & T.	August 29, 1881	TUNSTALL	
ADAMS, W. & T.	March 23, 1882	TUNSTALL	8
ADAMS, W. & T.	September 14, 1883	TUNSTALL	
ADAMS, WM.	May 31, 1858	TUNSTALL	3, 4
ADAMS, WM.	October 12, 1859	TUNSTALL	
ADAMS, WM.	March 13, 1862	TUNSTALL	4
ADAMS, WM.	October 07, 1876	TUNSTALL	7
ADAMS, WM.	November 23, 1876	TUNSTALL	
ADAMS, WM.	January 14, 1878	TUNSTALL	
ADAMS, WM.	July 17, 1878	TUNSTALL	
ADAMS, WM. & SONS	July 26, 1845	STOKE	5
ADAMS, WM. & SONS	January 03, 1849	STOKE	1, 2
ADAMS, WM. & SONS	April 23, 1853	STOKE	4
ADAMS, WM. & SONS	November 30, 1853	STOKE	
ADDERLY, W. A.	February 12, 1880	LONGTON	8
ADDERLY, W. A.	March 12, 1880	LONGTON	8
ADDERLY, W. A.	August 21, 1880	LONGTON	8
ADDERLY, W. A.	February 15, 1881	LONGTON	8
ADDERLY, W. A.	March 24, 1881	LONGTON	8
ADDERLY, W. A.	May 20, 1881	LONGTON	8
ADDERLY, W. A.	March 20, 1882	LONGTON	8
ADDERLY, W. A.	May 25, 1882	LONGTON	8
ADDERLY, W. A.	June 09, 1882	LONGTON	7
ADDERLY, W. A.	February 19, 1883	LONGTON	8
ADDERLY, W. A.	May 25, 1883	LONGTON	8
ADDERLY, W. A.	July 26, 1883	LONGTON	7
ADDERLY, W. A.	October 20, 1883	LONGTON	
ADDERLY, W. A.	November 26, 1883	LONGTON	8
ALCOCK & DIGORY	February 27, 1868	BURSLEM	8
ALCOCK & DIGORY	November 18, 1869	BURSLEM	8
ALCOCK, (SAMUEL) & CO.	July 18, 1854	BURSLEM	8
ALCOCK, H. & CO.	April 09, 1879	COBRIDGE	
ALCOCK, H. & CO.	May 09, 1882	COBRIDGE	

POTTER	DATE	LOCATION	CATEGORY
ALCOCK, H. & CO.	November 27, 1882	COBRIDGE	
ALCOCK, H. & CO.	June 08, 1883	COBRIDGE	
ALCOCK, H. & CO.	November 05, 1883	COBRIDGE	
ALCOCK, HENRY & CO.	April 28, 1865	COBRIDGE	
ALCOCK, J. & S. JNR.	March 27, 1848	COBRIDGE	1, 2, 4
ALCOCK, JOHN	May 07, 1853	COBRIDGE	4, 10
ALCOCK, JOHN	December 06, 1853	COBRIDGE	
ALCOCK, JOHN	December 24, 1853	COBRIDGE	
ALCOCK, JOHN	February 07, 1855	COBRIDGE	4, 7
ALCOCK, JOHN	June 07, 1855	COBRIDGE	4
ALCOCK, JOHN	March 20, 1857	COBRIDGE	4
ALCOCK, JOHN	April 16, 1857	COBRIDGE	
ALCOCK, SAML & CO.	June 11, 1855	BURSLEM	5x
ALCOCK, SAMUEL & CO.	February 21, 1843	BURSLEM	
ALCOCK, SAMUEL & CO.	March 31, 1843	BURSLEM	
ALCOCK, SAMUEL & CO.	June 14, 1843	BURSLEM	1
ALCOCK, SAMUEL & CO.	February 15, 1844	BURSLEM	
ALCOCK, SAMUEL & CO.	February 20, 1844	BURSLEM	
ALCOCK, SAMUEL & CO.	April 03, 1847	BURSLEM	4, 7
ALCOCK, SAMUEL & CO.	April 27, 1847	BURSLEM	4, 7
ALCOCK, SAMUEL & CO.	January 30, 1854	BURSLEM	7
ALCOCK, SAMUEL & CO.	March 11, 1854	BURSLEM	8
ALCOCK, SAMUEL & CO.	April 06, 1854	BURSLEM	8
ALCOCK, SAMUEL & CO.	April 10, 1854	BURSLEM	8
ALCOCK, SAMUEL & CO.	September 05, 1854	BURSLEM	4, 8
ALCOCK, SAMUEL & CO.	December 27, 1854	BURSLEM	7, 8
ALCOCK, SAMUEL & CO.	January 06, 1855	BURSLEM	5x, 8
ALCOCK, SAMUEL & CO.	June 23, 1858	BURSLEM	8
ALCOCK, SAMUEL & CO.	July 29, 1858	BURSLEM	7, 8
ALCOCK, SAMUEL & CO.	May 10, 1859	BURSLEM	8
ALCOCK, SAMUEL & CO.	August 27, 1859	BURSLEM	7, 8
ASHWORTH, G. L. & BROS.	May 03, 1862	HANLEY	
ASHWORTH, G. L. & BROS.	August 19, 1862	HANLEY	11
ASHWORTH, G. L. & BROS.	March 06, 1863	HANLEY	
ASHWORTH, G. L. & BROS.	March 03, 1864	HANLEY	
ASHWORTH, G. L. & BROS.	April 23, 1864	HANLEY	
ASHWORTH, G. L. & BROS.	September 16, 1864	HANLEY	
ASHWORTH, G. L. & BROS.	February 02, 1865	HANLEY	
ASHWORTH, G. L. & BROS.	April 14, 1866	HANLEY	4, 5x
ASHWORTH, G. L. & BROS.	September 15, 1866	HANLEY	5x
ASHWORTH, G. L. & BROS.	July 08, 1867	HANLEY	
ASHWORTH, G. L. & BROS.	September 21, 1867	HANLEY	7
ASHWORTH, G. L. & BROS.	January 13, 1868	HANLEY	
ASHWORTH, G. L. & BROS.	April 16, 1868	HANLEY	
ASHWORTH, G. L. & BROS.	December 31, 1868	HANLEY	7
ASHWORTH, G. L. & BROS.	June 18, 1872	HANLEY	
ASHWORTH, G. L. & BROS.	September 18, 1876	HANLEY	
ASHWORTH, G. L. & BROS.	September 13, 1878	HANLEY	
ASHWORTH, G. L. & BROS.	October 17, 1879	HANLEY	
ASHWORTH, G. L. & BROS.	September 15, 1880	HANLEY	
ASHWORTH, G. L. & BROS.	May 24, 1881	HANLEY	
ASHWORTH, G. L. & BROS.	May 02, 1882	HANLEY	7
ASHWORTH, G. L. & BROS.	April 24, 1883	HANLEY	
BAILEY & BALL	March 22, 1847	LONGTON	9
BAKER & CHETWYND	April 06, 1869	BURSLEM	
BAKER & CHETWYND	August 05, 1873	BURSLEM	
BAKER & CO.	April 07, 1870	FENTON	
BAKER & CO.	July 05, 1870	FENTON	
BAKER & CO.	June 09, 1877	FENTON	
BAKER & CO.	June 13, 1877	FENTON	4
BAKER, WM.	March 17, 1855	FENTON	
BAKER, WM. & CO.	October 23, 1862	FENTON	4, 7
BARKER S. & SON	September 30, 1865	SWINTON	
BARKER SAMUEL & SON	December 14, 1866	SWINTON	
BARKER & SON	June 05, 1850	BURSLEM	5, 7
BARKER & TILL	January 01, 1848	BURSLEM	5
BARLOW, THOS.	August 30, 1871	LONGTON	7
BARLOW, THOS.	September 15, 1871	LONGTON	
BARLOW, THOS.	December 04, 1874	LONGTON	
BARLOW, THOS.	July 13, 1880	LONGTON	
BARROW & CO.	October 10, 1853	FENTON	
BARROW & CO.	August 27, 1855	FENTON	4
BATES & BENNETT	May 08, 1878	COBRIDGE	
BATES & BENNETT	July 10, 1878	COBRIDGE	
BATES & CO.	December 12, 1860	HANLEY	7
BATES, BROWN-WESTHEAD & MOORE	March 01, 1860	HANLEY	7, 8
BATES, BROWN-WESTHEAD & MOORE	March 27, 1860	HANLEY	8
BATES, BROWN-WESTHEAD & MOORE	October 18, 1860	HANLEY	
BATES, BROWN-WESTHEAD & MOORE	December 03, 1860	HANLEY	
BATES, BROWN-WESTHEAD & MOORE	May 09, 1861	HANLEY	7
BATES, BROWN-WESTHEAD & MOORE	June 04, 1861	HANLEY	7, 8
BATES, BROWN-WESTHEAD & MOORE	October 28, 1861	HANLEY	8

POTTER	DATE	LOCATION	CATEGORY
BATES, ELLIOTT & CO.	May 18, 1870	LONGPORT	
BATES, ELLIOTT & CO.	November 24, 1870	LONGPORT	
BATES, ELLIOTT & CO.	December 16, 1870	LONGPORT	
BATES, ELLIOTT & CO.	December 17, 1870	LONGPORT	
BATES, ELLIOTT & CO.	January 07, 1871	LONGPORT	
BATES, ELLIOTT & CO.	March 15, 1871	LONGPORT	
BATES, ELLIOTT & CO.	June 23, 1871	LONGPORT	
BATES, ELLIOTT & CO.	July 25, 1871	LONGPORT	
BATES, ELLIOTT & CO.	August 09, 1871	LONGPORT	
BATES, ELLIOTT & CO.	March 07, 1872	BURSLEM	7
BATES, ELLIOTT & CO.	May 03, 1872	BURSLEM	
BATES, ELLIOTT & CO.	May 06, 1872	BURSLEM	
BATES, ELLIOTT & CO.	September 02, 1872	BURSLEM	7
BATES, ELLIOTT & CO.	October 12, 1872	BURSLEM	
BATES, ELLIOTT & CO.	February 12, 1873	BURSLEM	
BATES, ELLIOTT & CO.	June 11, 1873	BURSLEM	
BATES, ELLIOTT & CO.	January 01, 1874	BURSLEM	
BATES, ELLIOTT & CO.	May 05, 1874	BURSLEM	
BATES, ELLIOTT & CO.	May 20, 1874	BURSLEM	
BATES, ELLIOTT & CO.	August 15, 1874	BURSLEM	
BATES, ELLIOTT & CO.	October 17, 1874	BURSLEM	
BATES, ELLIOTT & CO.	November 12, 1874	BURSLEM	
BATES, ELLIOTT & CO.	May 20, 1875	BURSLEM	
BATES, GILDEA & WALKER	October 08, 1878	BURSLEM	
BATES, GILDEA & WALKER	May 05, 1879	BURSLEM	
BATES, GILDEA & WALKER	August 27, 1879	BURSLEM	2
BATES, GILDEA & WALKER	October 09, 1879	BURSLEM	
BATES, GILDEA & WALKER	February 14, 1880	BURSLEM	7
BATES, GILDEA & WALKER	April 12, 1880	BURSLEM	
BATES, GILDEA & WALKER	May 14, 1880	BURSLEM	
BATES, GILDEA & WALKER	November 24, 1880	BURSLEM	
BATES, GILDEA & WALKER	December 18, 1880	BURSLEM	
BATES, WALKER & CO.	December 24, 1875	BURSLEM	
BATES, WALKER & CO.	January 24, 1876	BURSLEM	
BATES, WALKER & CO.	February 08, 1876	BURSLEM	
BATES, WALKER & CO.	March 24, 1876	BURSLEM	
BATES, WALKER & CO.	April 08, 1876	BURSLEM	
BATES, WALKER & CO.	September 05, 1876	BURSLEM	
BATES, WALKER & CO.	October 02, 1877	BURSLEM	
BAYLEY & BALL	November 15, 1845	LONGTON	7,
BECK, BLAIR & CO.	March 29, 1879	LONGTON	
BEECH & HANCOCK	July 05, 1861	TUNSTALL	7
BEECH & HANCOCK	July 14, 1862	TUNSTALL	7
BEECH & HANCOCK	March 21, 1863	TUNSTALL	7
BEECH & HANCOCK	April 25, 1863	TUNSTALL	7
BEECH & HANCOCK	April 21, 1868	TUNSTALL	
BEECH, HANCOCK & CO.	May 10, 1855	BURSLEM	
BEECH, JAMES	December 18, 1876	LONGTON	
BEECH, JAMES	February 12, 1877	LONGTON	
BEECH, WILLIAM	April 18, 1856	BURSLEM	10
BELFIELD & CO.	November 30, 1872	PRESTONPANS	
BELFIELD & CO.	November 09, 1876	PRESTONPANS	
BELFIELD & CO.	April 02, 1878	PRESTONPANS	
BELFIELD & CO.	August 28, 1882	PRESTONPANS	
BELFIELD & CO.	June 13, 1883	PRESTONPANS	
BELL, J. & M. P. & CO. (LTD.)	February 13, 1850	GLASGOW	5
BELL, J. & M. P. & CO. (LTD.)	June 04, 1850	GLASGOW	5
BELL, J. & M. P. & CO. (LTD.)	September 16, 1850	GLASGOW	5x, 10
BELL, J. & M. P. & CO. (LTD.)	March 31, 1851	GLASGOW	
BELL, J. & M. P. & CO. (LTD.)	April 11, 1851	GLASGOW	
BELL, J. & M. P. & CO. (LTD.)	April 14, 1851	GLASGOW	
BELL, J. & M. P. & CO. (LTD.)	March 26, 1852	GLASGOW	7
BELL, J. & M. P. & CO. (LTD.)	March 10, 1853	GLASGOW	1, 2
BELL, J. & M. P. & CO. (LTD.)	January 21, 1854	GLASGOW	
BELL, J. & M. P. & CO. (LTD.)	February 03, 1855	GLASGOW	2
BELL, J. & M. P. & CO. (LTD.)	November 22, 1855	GLASGOW	
BELL, J. & M. P. & CO. (LTD.)	April 07, 1856	GLASGOW	
BELL, J. & M. P. & CO. (LTD.)	June 25, 1857	GLASGOW	
BELL, J. & M. P. & CO. (LTD.)	March 27, 1862	GLASGOW	1x, 2x
BELL, J. & M. P. & CO. (LTD.)	March 28, 1862	GLASGOW	1x, 2x, 7
BELL, J. & M. P. & CO. (LTD.)	May 06, 1867	GLASGOW	7
BEVINGTON, T. & J.	February 19, 1873	HANLEY	8
BIRKS BROS. & SEDDON	June 30, 1879	COBRIDGE	
BIRKS BROS. & SEDDON	June 21, 1881	COBRIDGE	8
BODLEY & CO.	February 09, 1874	BURSLEM	8
BODLEY & HARROLD	March 23, 1863	BURSLEM	5, 5x, 7
BODLEY & HARROLD	May 12, 1863	BURSLEM	
BODLEY & HARROLD	November 27, 1863	BURSLEM	
BODLEY & HARROLD	April 26, 1864	BURSLEM	
BODLEY & HARROLD	July 18, 1864	BURSLEM	
BODLEY & HARROLD	September 14, 1864	BURSLEM	
BODLEY & HARROLD	October 28, 1864	BURSLEM	7
BODLEY, E. F. & CO.	August 25, 1862	BURSLEM	8
BODLEY, E. F. & CO.	November 11, 1862	BURSLEM	8
BODLEY, E. F. & CO.	March 31, 1877	BURSLEM	8
BODLEY, E. F. & CO.	June 22, 1877	BURSLEM	7, 8
BODLEY, E. F. & CO.	June 19, 1878	BURSLEM	
BODLEY, E. F. & CO.	October 27, 1879	BURSLEM	7, 8
BODLEY, E. F. & SON	April 03, 1875	BURSLEM	8

POTTER	DATE	LOCATION	CATEGORY
BODLEY, E. F. & SON	October 22, 1880	BURSLEM	8
BODLEY, E. F. & SON	June 07, 1881	BURSLEM	8
BODLEY, E. F. & SON	January 09, 1883	LONGPORT	
BODLEY, E. F. & SON	January 23, 1883	LONGPORT	
BODLEY, E. F. & SON	January 30, 1883	LONGPORT	
BODLEY, E. F. & SON	March 08, 1883	LONGPORT	8
BODLEY, ED. F. & CO.	June 29, 1865	BURSLEM	7, 8
BODLEY, ED. F. & CO.	January 13, 1866	BURSLEM	8
BODLEY, ED. F. & CO.	August 29, 1866	BURSLEM	
BODLEY, ED. F. & CO.	January 17, 1867	BURSLEM	8
BODLEY, ED. F. & CO.	February 09, 1867	BURSLEM	8
BODLEY, ED. F. & CO.	August 17, 1868	BURSLEM	5
BODLEY, ED. F. & CO.	December 11, 1868	BURSLEM	
BODLEY, ED. F. & CO.	February 13, 1871	BURSLEM	8
BOOTE, J. & R.	August 24, 1881	BURSLEM	
BOOTE, T. & R.	February 02, 1847	BURSLEM	7
BOOTE, T. & R.	October 17, 1848	BURSLEM	7
BOOTE, T. & R.	July 21, 1851	BURSLEM	4, 10
BOOTE, T. & R.	September 19, 1851	BURSLEM	4
BOOTE, T. & R.	October 10, 1851	BURSLEM	4
BOOTE, T. & R.	September 03, 1853	BURSLEM	4
BOOTE, T. & R.	June 21, 1854	BURSLEM	
BOOTE, T. & R.	July 18, 1854	BURSLEM	4
BOOTE, T. & R.	August 22, 1856	BURSLEM	4
BOOTE, T. & R.	October 17, 1857	BURSLEM	4
BOOTE, T. & R.	April 22, 1858	BURSLEM	
BOOTE, T. & R.	December 08, 1858	BURSLEM	4
BOOTE, T. & R.	February 02, 1859	BURSLEM	
BOOTE, T. & R.	March 21, 1859	BURSLEM	4, 7
BOOTE, T. & R.	March 29, 1859	BURSLEM	7
BOOTE, T. & R.	November 23, 1860	BURSLEM	4
BOOTE, T. & R.	January 08, 1861	BURSLEM	11
BOOTE, T. & R.	April 18, 1861	BURSLEM	
BOOTE, T. & R.	August 19, 1861	BURSLEM	
BOOTE, T. & R.	March 01, 1862	BURSLEM	
BOOTE, T. & R.	March 22, 1862	BURSLEM	4,7
BOOTE, T. & R.	August 30, 1862	BURSLEM	
BOOTE, T. & R.	January 30, 1863	BURSLEM	4
BOOTE, T. & R.	February 17, 1863	BURSLEM	
BOOTE, T. & R.	September 07, 1863	BURSLEM	
BOOTE, T. & R.	October 17, 1863	BURSLEM	4
BOOTE, T. & R.	November 04, 1863	BURSLEM	
BOOTE, T. & R.	December 02, 1863	BURSLEM	
BOOTE, T. & R.	January 08, 1868	BURSLEM	4
BOOTE, T. & R.	January 31, 1868	BURSLEM	
BOOTE, T. & R.	May 30, 1868	BURSLEM	7
BOOTE, T. & R.	August 01, 1868	BURSLEM	
BOOTE, T. & R.	August 31, 1868	BURSLEM	
BOOTE, T. & R.	August 22, 1870	BURSLEM	
BOOTE, T. & R.	August 25, 1870	BURSLEM	
BOOTE, T. & R.	November 26, 1870	BURSLEM	4
BOOTE, T. & R.	February 05, 1875	BURSLEM	
BOOTE, T. & R.	November 26, 1878	BURSLEM	
BOOTE, T. & R.	December 27, 1878	BURSLEM	
BOOTE, T. & R.	December 06, 1879	BURSLEM	7
BOOTE, T. & R.	January 07, 1880	BURSLEM	
BOOTE, T. & R.	April 19, 1881	BURSLEM	
BOOTE, T. & R.	October 13, 1881	BURSLEM	
BOOTE, T. & R.	October 29, 1881	BURSLEM	
BOOTE, T. & R.	November 08, 1881	BURSLEM	
BOOTE, T. & R.	January 13, 1883	BURSLEM	
BOOTE, T. & R.	June 20, 1883	BURSLEM	
BOOTE, T. & R.	July 31, 1883	BURSLEM	
BOOTE, T. & R., WALLEY & JONES	April 26, 1845	BURSLEM, COBRIDGE, HANLEY	6
BOOTH, T. & CO.	August 14, 1872	TUNSTALL	
BOOTH, T. G. & F.	May 08, 1883	TUNSTALL	
BOOTH, T. G. & F.	May 23, 1883	TUNSTALL	
BOOTH, T. G. & F.	October 08, 1883	TUNSTALL	
BOOTH, T. G. & F.	November 13, 1883	TUNSTALL	
BOOTH, T. G. & F.	December 15, 1883	TUNSTALL	
BOOTH, THOS.	October 10, 1867	HANLEY	7
BOOTH, THOS.	May 26, 1869	HANLEY	7
BOOTH, THOS.	June 07, 1870	HANLEY	
BOOTH, THOS.	July 20, 1870	HANLEY	
BOOTH, THOS.	July 21, 1870	HANLEY	
BOOTH, THOS.	July 15, 1871	HANLEY	7
BOOTH, THOS. & CO.	September 14, 1868	BURSLEM	5
BOOTH, THOS. & CO.	February 15, 1869	BURSLEM	
BOOTH, THOS. & CO.	September 28, 1871	TUNSTALL	
BOOTH, THOS. & CO.	October 14, 1871	TUNSTALL	5
BOOTH, THOS. & SONS	May 11, 1872	HANLEY	7
BOOTH, THOS. & SONS	February 11, 1874	HANLEY	
BOOTH, THOS. & SONS	April 30, 1874	HANLEY	7
BOOTH, THOS. & SONS	September 07, 1874	HANLEY	
BOOTH, THOS. & SONS	March 30, 1875	HANLEY	7
BOWERS, G. F. & CO.	December 14, 1843	TUNSTALL	8
BOWERS, G. F. & CO.	June 20, 1848	TUNSTALL	8

POTTER	DATE	LOCATION	CATEGORY
BRIDGETT & BATES	September 28, 1882	LONGTON	
BRIDGETT & BATES	July 21, 1883	LONGTON	
BRIDGETT & BATES	October 12, 1883	LONGTON	
BRIDGWOOD & CLARKE	September 10, 1858	BURSLEM	
BRIDGWOOD, SAMPSON & SON	May 06, 1879	LONGTON	
BRIDGWOOD, SAMPSON & SON	May 23, 1879	LONGTON	
BRIDGWOOD, SAMPSON & SON	July 30, 1881	LONGTON	
BRIDGWOOD, SAMPSON & SON	November 19, 1881	LONGTON	
BRIDGWOOD, SAMPSON & SON	April 21, 1882	LONGTON	
BRIDGWOOD, SAMPSON & SON	June 21, 1882	LONGTON	
BRIDGWOOD, SAMPSON & SON	July 31, 1882	LONGTON	
BRIDGWOOD, SAMPSON & SON	October 11, 1882	LONGTON	7
BRIDGWOOD, SAMPSON & SON	November 13, 1882	LONGTON	
BRIDGWOOD, SAMPSON & SON	January 24, 1883	LONGTON	
BRIDGWOOD, SAMPSON & SON	February 01, 1883	LONGTON	
BRIDGWOOD, SAMPSON &SON	March 24, 1883	LONGTON	
BRIDGWOOD, SAMPSON &SON	June 09, 1883	LONGTON	
BRIDGWOOD, SAMPSON &SON	September 25, 1883	LONGTON	
BRIDGWOOD, SAMPSON &SON	September 29, 1883	LONGTON	
BRIDGWOOD, SAMPSON &SON	October 04, 1883	LONGTON	
BRIDGWOOD, SAMPSON &SON	November 26, 1883	LONGTON	
BROADHURST, J.	December 24, 1881	FENTON	
BROUGHAM & MAYER	January 15, 1855	TUNSTALL	4
BROWN, T.C.-WESTHEAD, MOORE & CO.	May 09, 1862	HANLEY	8
BROWN, T.C.-WESTHEAD, , MOORE & CO.	June 24, 1862	HANLEY	
BROWN, T.C.-WESTHEAD, MOORE & CO.	December 03, 1862	HANLEY	8
BROWN, T.C.-WESTHEAD, MOORE & CO.	April 23, 1863	HANLEY	
BROWN, T.C.-WESTHEAD, MOORE & CO.	May 26, 1863	HANLEY	8
BROWN, T.C.-WESTHEAD, MOORE & CO.	December 30, 1863	HANLEY	8
BROWN, T.C.-WESTHEAD, MOORE & CO.	March 18, 1864	HANLEY	8
BROWN, T.C.-WESTHEAD, MOORE & CO.	April 21, 1864	HANLEY	8
BROWN, T.C.-WESTHEAD, MOORE & CO.	August 26, 1864	HANLEY	
BROWN, T.C.-WESTHEAD, MOORE & CO.	November 24, 1864	HANLEY	8
BROWN, T.C.-WESTHEAD, MOORE & CO.	July 03, 1865	HANLEY	8
BROWN, T.C.-WESTHEAD, MOORE & CO.	September 14, 1865	HANLEY	8
BROWN, T.C.-WESTHEAD, MOORE & CO.	October 13, 1865	HANLEY	8
BROWN, T.C.-WESTHEAD, MOORE & CO.	November 14, 1866	HANLEY	8
BROWN, T.C.-WESTHEAD, MOORE & CO.	December 15, 1866	HANLEY	8
BROWN, T.C.-WESTHEAD, MOORE & CO.	March 04, 1867	HANLEY	8
BROWN, T.C.-WESTHEAD, MOORE & CO.	May 08, 1867	HANLEY	8
BROWN, T.C.-WESTHEAD, MOORE & CO.	February 18, 1868	HANLEY	1, 7
BROWN, T.C.-WESTHEAD, MOORE & CO.	May 26, 1868	HANLEY	
BROWN, T.C.-WESTHEAD, MOORE & CO.	September 05, 1868	HANLEY	1x, 8
BROWN, T.C.-WESTHEAD, MOORE & CO.	September 25, 1868	HANLEY	1x, 8
BROWN, T.C.-WESTHEAD, MOORE & CO.	November 03, 1868	HANLEY	1x, 8
BROWN, T.C.-WESTHEAD, MOORE & CO.	November 24, 1868	HANLEY	1x, 8
BROWN, T.C.-WESTHEAD, MOORE & CO.	December 01, 1868	HANLEY	1x, 8
BROWN, T.C.-WESTHEAD, MOORE & CO.	January 22, 1869	HANLEY	1x, 8
BROWN, T.C.-WESTHEAD, MOORE & CO.	February 01, 1869	HANLEY	1x, 8
BROWN, T.C.-WESTHEAD, MOORE & CO.	September 30, 1869	HANLEY	1x, 8
BROWN, T.C.-WESTHEAD, MOORE & CO.	November 03, 1869	HANLEY	1x, 8
BROWN, T.C.-WESTHEAD, MOORE & CO.	November 08, 1869	HANLEY	1x, 8
BROWN, T.C.-WESTHEAD, MOORE & CO.	January 01, 1870	HANLEY	1x, 8
BROWN, T.C.-WESTHEAD, MOORE & CO.	February 01, 1870	HANLEY	1x, 8
BROWN, T.C.-WESTHEAD, MOORE & CO.	February 03, 1870	HANLEY	1x, 8
BROWN, T.C.-WESTHEAD, MOORE & CO.	February 15, 1870	HANLEY	1x, 8

POTTER	DATE	LOCATION	CATEGORY
BROWN, T.C.-WESTHEAD, MOORE & CO.	March 14, 1870	HANLEY	1x, 8
BROWN, T.C.-WESTHEAD, MOORE & CO.	May 13, 1870	HANLEY	1x, 8
BROWN, T.C.-WESTHEAD, MOORE & CO.	May 17, 1870	HANLEY	1x, 8
BROWN, T.C.-WESTHEAD, MOORE & CO.	June 09, 1870	HANLEY	8
BROWN, T.C.-WESTHEAD, MOORE & CO.	October 25, 1870	HANLEY	
BROWN, T.C.-WESTHEAD, MOORE & CO.	November 04, 1870	HANLEY	1x
BROWN, T.C.-WESTHEAD, MOORE & CO.	December 02, 1870	HANLEY	1x
BROWN, T.C.-WESTHEAD, MOORE & CO.	February 11, 1871	HANLEY	8
BROWN, T.C.-WESTHEAD, MOORE & CO.	May 01, 1871	HANLEY	8
BROWN, T.C.-WESTHEAD, MOORE & CO.	June 02, 1871	HANLEY	8
BROWN, T.C.-WESTHEAD, MOORE & CO.	September 25, 1871	HANLEY	7, 11
BROWN, T.C.-WESTHEAD, MOORE & CO.	October 10, 1871	HANLEY	
BROWN, T.C.-WESTHEAD, MOORE & CO.	December 29, 1871	HANLEY	8
BROWN, T.C.-WESTHEAD, MOORE & CO.	March 22, 1872	HANLEY	
BROWN, T.C.-WESTHEAD, MOORE & CO.	April 09, 1872	HANLEY	
BROWN, T.C.-WESTHEAD, MOORE & CO.	June 22, 1872	HANLEY	8
BROWN, T.C.-WESTHEAD, MOORE & CO.	October 07, 1872	HANLEY	8
BROWN, T.C.-WESTHEAD, MOORE & CO.	December 02, 1872	HANLEY	8
BROWN, T.C.-WESTHEAD, MOORE & CO.	May 12, 1873	HANLEY	7, 8
BROWN, T.C.-WESTHEAD, MOORE & CO.	May 30, 1873	HANLEY	8
BROWN, T.C.-WESTHEAD, MOORE & CO.	July 04, 1873	HANLEY	8
BROWN, T.C.-WESTHEAD, MOORE & CO.	August 14, 1873	HANLEY	8
BROWN, T.C.-WESTHEAD, MOORE & CO.	August 30, 1873	HANLEY	8
BROWN, T.C.-WESTHEAD, MOORE & CO.	September 15, 1873	HANLEY	
BROWN, T.C.-WESTHEAD, MOORE & CO.	September 16, 1873	HANLEY	
BROWN, T.C.-WESTHEAD, MOORE & CO.	September 19, 1873	HANLEY	8
BROWN, T.C.-WESTHEAD, MOORE & CO.	October 06, 1873	HANLEY	8
BROWN, T.C.-WESTHEAD, MOORE & CO.	November 10, 1873	HANLEY	
BROWN, T.C.-WESTHEAD, MOORE & CO.	April 23, 1874	HANLEY	8
BROWN, T.C.-WESTHEAD, MOORE & CO.	July 13, 1874	HANLEY	
BROWN, T.C.-WESTHEAD, MOORE & CO.	August 06, 1874	HANLEY	
BROWN, T.C.-WESTHEAD, MOORE & CO.	December 07, 1874	HANLEY	
BROWN, T.C.-WESTHEAD, MOORE & CO.	January 02, 1875	HANLEY	8
BROWN, T.C.-WESTHEAD, MOORE & CO.	January 18, 1875	HANLEY	8
BROWN, T.C.-WESTHEAD, MOORE & CO.	January 23, 1875	HANLEY	8
BROWN, T.C.-WESTHEAD, MOORE & CO.	March 24, 1875	HANLEY	8
BROWN, T.C.-WESTHEAD, MOORE & CO.	May 26, 1875	HANLEY	8
BROWN, T.C.-WESTHEAD, MOORE & CO.	July 23, 1875	HANLEY	
BROWN, T.C.-WESTHEAD, MOORE & CO.	September 28, 1875	HANLEY	8
BROWN, T.C.-WESTHEAD, MOORE & CO.	December 29, 1875	HANLEY	8
BROWN, T.C.-WESTHEAD, MOORE & CO.	March 14, 1876	HANLEY	8, 11
BROWN, T.C.-WESTHEAD, MOORE & CO.	May 08, 1876	HANLEY	8
BROWN, T.C.-WESTHEAD, MOORE & CO.	September 09, 1876	HANLEY	8
BROWN, T.C.-WESTHEAD, MOORE & CO.	September 26, 1876	HANLEY	
BROWN, T.C.-WESTHEAD, MOORE & CO.	October 17, 1876	HANLEY	
BROWN, T.C.-WESTHEAD, MOORE & CO.	February 09, 1877	HANLEY	8
BROWN, T.C.-WESTHEAD, MOORE & CO.	May 24, 1877	HANLEY	8
BROWN, T.C.-WESTHEAD, MOORE & CO.	August 28, 1877	HANLEY	8
BROWN, T.C.-WESTHEAD, MOORE & CO.	October 19, 1877	HANLEY	8
BROWN, T.C.-WESTHEAD, MOORE & CO.	November 15, 1877	HANLEY	8
BROWN, T.C.-WESTHEAD, MOORE & CO.	December 29, 1877	HANLEY	8
BROWN, T.C.-WESTHEAD, MOORE & CO.	January 28, 1878	HANLEY	8
BROWN, T.C.-WESTHEAD, MOORE & CO.	February 11, 1878	HANLEY	
BROWN, T.C.-WESTHEAD, MOORE & CO.	July 12, 1878	HANLEY	
BROWN, T.C.-WESTHEAD, MOORE & CO.	December 02, 1878	HANLEY	8
BROWN, T.C.-WESTHEAD, MOORE & CO.	April 03, 1879	HANLEY	
BROWN, T.C.-WESTHEAD, MOORE & CO.	April 10, 1879	HANLEY	
BROWN, T.C.-WESTHEAD, MOORE & CO.	April 15, 1879	HANLEY	10
BROWN, T.C.-WESTHEAD, MOORE & CO.	April 23, 1879	HANLEY	8
BROWN, T.C.-WESTHEAD, MOORE & CO.	May 14, 1879	HANLEY	8
BROWN, T.C.-WESTHEAD, MOORE & CO.	June 13, 1879	HANLEY	8
BROWN, T.C.-WESTHEAD, MOORE & CO.	July 08, 1879	HANLEY	8
BROWN, T.C.-WESTHEAD, MOORE & CO.	July 09, 1879	HANLEY	8
BROWN, T.C.-WESTHEAD, MOORE & CO.	July 16, 1879	HANLEY	8
BROWN, T.C.-WESTHEAD, MOORE & CO.	September 04, 1879	HANLEY	8
BROWN, T.C.-WESTHEAD, MOORE & CO.	September 10, 1879	HANLEY	8
BROWN, T.C.-WESTHEAD, MOORE & CO.	September 18, 1879	HANLEY	8
BROWN, T.C.-WESTHEAD, MOORE & CO.	October 10, 1879	HANLEY	8
BROWN, T.C.-WESTHEAD, MOORE & CO.	November 29, 1879	HANLEY	8
BROWN, T.C.-WESTHEAD, MOORE & CO.	December 02, 1879	HANLEY	8
BROWN, T.C.-WESTHEAD, MOORE & CO.	January 13, 1880	HANLEY	8
BROWN, T.C.-WESTHEAD, MOORE & CO.	January 28, 1880	HANLEY	8
BROWN, T.C.-WESTHEAD, MOORE & CO.	August 23, 1880	HANLEY	8
BROWN, T.C.-WESTHEAD, MOORE & CO.	September 03, 1880	HANLEY	
BROWN, T.C.-WESTHEAD, MOORE & CO.	December 24, 1880	HANLEY	8
BROWN, T.C.-WESTHEAD, MOORE & CO.	July 14, 1881	HANLEY	8
BROWN, T.C.-WESTHEAD, MOORE & CO.	October 26, 1881	HANLEY	8
BROWN, T.C.-WESTHEAD, MOORE & CO.	November 02, 1881	HANLEY	8
BROWN, T.C.-WESTHEAD, MOORE & CO.	December 10, 1881	HANLEY	8
BROWN, T.C.-WESTHEAD, MOORE & CO.	February 03, 1882	HANLEY	8
BROWN, T.C.-WESTHEAD, MOORE & CO.	September 28, 1882	HANLEY	
BROWN, T.C.-WESTHEAD, MOORE & CO.	December 06, 1882	HANLEY	8
BROWN, T.C.-WESTHEAD, MOORE & CO.	January 04, 1883	HANLEY	
BROWN, T.C.-WESTHEAD, MOORE & CO.	May 02, 1883	HANLEY	8
BROWN, T.C.-WESTHEAD, MOORE & CO.	July 27, 1883	HANLEY	
BROWN, T.C.-WESTHEAD, MOORE & CO.	August 01, 1883	HANLEY	
BROWN, T.C.-WESTHEAD, MOORE & CO.	September 21, 1883	HANLEY	
BROWNFIELD, W.	October 10, 1851	COBRIDGE	
BROWNFIELD, W.	October 16, 1851	COBRIDGE	7
BROWNFIELD, WILLIAM	February 10, 1851	COBRIDGE	

POTTER	DATE	LOCATION	CATEGORY
BROWNFIELD, WM.	March 04, 1852	COBRIDGE	
BROWNFIELD, WM.	October 25, 1852	COBRIDGE	10
BROWNFIELD, WM.	April 01, 1854	COBRIDGE	7, 10
BROWNFIELD, WM.	May 08, 1854	COBRIDGE	
BROWNFIELD, WM.	October 02, 1854	COBRIDGE	
BROWNFIELD, WM.	April 26, 1855	COBRIDGE	7
BROWNFIELD, WM.	November 28, 1855	COBRIDGE	7
BROWNFIELD, WM.	April 30, 1856	COBRIDGE	7
BROWNFIELD, WM.	November 27, 1856	COBRIDGE	10
BROWNFIELD, WM.	June 05, 1857	COBRIDGE	10
BROWNFIELD, WM.	December 09, 1857	COBRIDGE	7
BROWNFIELD, WM.	June 02, 1858	COBRIDGE	
BROWNFIELD, WM.	August 24, 1858	COBRIDGE	10
BROWNFIELD, WM.	October 05, 1858	COBRIDGE	7
BROWNFIELD, WM.	May 20, 1859	COBRIDGE	7
BROWNFIELD, WM.	November 05, 1859	COBRIDGE	7
BROWNFIELD, WM.	June 06, 1860	COBRIDGE	7
BROWNFIELD, WM.	October 29, 1860	COBRIDGE	7
BROWNFIELD, WM.	July 06, 1861	COBRIDGE	7
BROWNFIELD, WM.	September 06, 1861	COBRIDGE	
BROWNFIELD, WM.	December 04, 1861	COBRIDGE	7, 8
BROWNFIELD, WM.	January 11, 1862	COBRIDGE	
BROWNFIELD, WM.	January 25, 1862	COBRIDGE	7
BROWNFIELD, WM.	March 14, 1862	COBRIDGE	2
BROWNFIELD, WM.	December 05, 1862	COBRIDGE	7
BROWNFIELD, WM.	June 08, 1863	COBRIDGE	
BROWNFIELD, WM.	July 20, 1863	COBRIDGE	
BROWNFIELD, WM.	October 14, 1863	COBRIDGE	7
BROWNFIELD, WM.	November 26, 1863	COBRIDGE	
BROWNFIELD, WM.	December 23, 1863	COBRIDGE	10
BROWNFIELD, WM.	January 05, 1864	COBRIDGE	
BROWNFIELD, WM.	April 29, 1864	COBRIDGE	7
BROWNFIELD, WM.	June 30, 1864	COBRIDGE	
BROWNFIELD, WM.	October 12, 1864	COBRIDGE	7
BROWNFIELD, WM.	April 01, 1865	COBRIDGE	7
BROWNFIELD, WM.	October 30, 1865	COBRIDGE	7
BROWNFIELD, WM.	April 20, 1866	COBRIDGE	7
BROWNFIELD, WM.	March 15, 1867	COBRIDGE	7, 8
BROWNFIELD, WM.	June 21, 1867	COBRIDGE	10
BROWNFIELD, WM.	January 11, 1868	COBRIDGE	
BROWNFIELD, WM.	June 12, 1868	COBRIDGE	7
BROWNFIELD, WM.	December 12, 1868	COBRIDGE	7
BROWNFIELD, WM.	April 02, 1869	COBRIDGE	
BROWNFIELD, WM.	June 19, 1869	COBRIDGE	7
BROWNFIELD, WM.	November 10, 1869	COBRIDGE	7
BROWNFIELD, WM.	December 03, 1869	COBRIDGE	
BROWNFIELD, WM.	June 10, 1870	COBRIDGE	7
BROWNFIELD, WM.	August 09, 1870	COBRIDGE	
BROWNFIELD, WM.	September 19, 1870	COBRIDGE	
BROWNFIELD, WM.	October 22, 1870	COBRIDGE	
BROWNFIELD, WM.	November 10, 1870	COBRIDGE	
BROWNFIELD, WM.	December 01, 1870	COBRIDGE	
BROWNFIELD, WM. & SON	March 27, 1871	COBRIDGE	
BROWNFIELD, WM. & SON	May 02, 1871	COBRIDGE	7
BROWNFIELD, WM. & SON	June 06, 1872	COBRIDGE	
BROWNFIELD, WM. & SON	June 22, 1872	COBRIDGE	
BROWNFIELD, WM. & SON	August 16, 1872	COBRIDGE	
BROWNFIELD, WM. & SON	November 14, 1872	COBRIDGE	8
BROWNFIELD, WM. & SON	December 14, 1872	COBRIDGE	7, 8
BROWNFIELD, WM. & SON	May 03, 1873	COBRIDGE	8
BROWNFIELD, WM. & SON	September 29, 1873	COBRIDGE	8
BROWNFIELD, WM. & SON	December 05, 1873	COBRIDGE	8
BROWNFIELD, WM. & SON	April 22, 1874	COBRIDGE	
BROWNFIELD, WM. & SON	June 06, 1874	COBRIDGE	8
BROWNFIELD, WM. & SON	August 08, 1874	COBRIDGE	8
BROWNFIELD, WM. & SON	September 10, 1874	COBRIDGE	10
BROWNFIELD, WM. & SON	September 30, 1874	COBRIDGE	8
BROWNFIELD, WM. & SON	November 06, 1874	COBRIDGE	8
BROWNFIELD, WM. & SON	January 20, 1875	COBRIDGE	8
BROWNFIELD, WM. & SON	March 05, 1875	COBRIDGE	8
BROWNFIELD, WM. & SON	March 31, 1875	COBRIDGE	8
BROWNFIELD, WM. & SON	April 09, 1875	COBRIDGE	8
BROWNFIELD, WM. & SON	June 05, 1875	COBRIDGE	
BROWNFIELD, WM. & SON	June 10, 1875	COBRIDGE	1
BROWNFIELD, WM. & SON	July 05, 1875	COBRIDGE	8
BROWNFIELD, WM. & SON	December 01, 1875	COBRIDGE	8
BROWNFIELD, WM. & SON	January 29, 1876	COBRIDGE	7, 8
BROWNFIELD, WM. & SON	February 01, 1876	COBRIDGE	
BROWNFIELD, WM. & SONS	September 06, 1876	COBRIDGE	8, 10
BROWNFIELD, WM. & SONS	October 07, 1876	COBRIDGE	8
BROWNFIELD, WM. & SONS	October 31, 1876	COBRIDGE	8
BROWNFIELD, WM. & SONS	November 08, 1876	COBRIDGE	8
BROWNFIELD, WM. & SONS	January 24, 1877	COBRIDGE	
BROWNFIELD, WM. & SONS	February 07, 1877	COBRIDGE	8, 10
BROWNFIELD, WM. & SONS	February 19, 1877	COBRIDGE	
BROWNFIELD, WM. & SONS	May 16, 1877	COBRIDGE	8
BROWNFIELD, WM. & SONS	May 22, 1877	COBRIDGE	8
BROWNFIELD, WM. & SONS	October 10, 1877	COBRIDGE	
BROWNFIELD, WM. & SONS	November 06, 1877	COBRIDGE	8, 10

POTTER	DATE	LOCATION	CATEGORY
BROWNFIELD, WM. & SONS	December 22, 1877	COBRIDGE	7, 8
BROWNFIELD, WM. & SONS	January 25, 1878	COBRIDGE	8
BROWNFIELD, WM. & SONS	April 24, 1878	COBRIDGE	
BROWNFIELD, WM. & SONS	September 09, 1878	COBRIDGE	8
BROWNFIELD, WM. & SONS	October 26, 1878	COBRIDGE	8
BROWNFIELD, WM. & SONS	December 04, 1878	COBRIDGE	8
BROWNFIELD, WM. & SONS	January 09, 1879	COBRIDGE	8, 10
BROWNFIELD, WM. & SONS	May 19, 1879	COBRIDGE	8
BROWNFIELD, WM. & SONS	September 17, 1879	COBRIDGE	8
BROWNFIELD, WM. & SONS	November 28, 1879	COBRIDGE	8
BROWNFIELD, WM. & SONS	January 26, 1880	COBRIDGE	8
BROWNFIELD, WM. & SONS	February 12, 1880	COBRIDGE	
BROWNFIELD, WM. & SONS	May 03, 1880	COBRIDGE	8, 10
BROWNFIELD, WM. & SONS	May 25, 1880	COBRIDGE	8, 10
BROWNFIELD, WM. & SONS	September 11, 1880	COBRIDGE	8
BROWNFIELD, WM. & SONS	December 15, 1880	COBRIDGE	8
BROWNFIELD, WM. & SONS	February 08, 1881	COBRIDGE	8, 10
BROWNFIELD, WM. & SONS	May 04, 1881	COBRIDGE	7, 8
BROWNFIELD, WM. & SONS	October 04, 1881	COBRIDGE	10
BROWNFIELD, WM. & SONS	October 29, 1881	COBRIDGE	8
BROWNFIELD, WM. & SONS	April 04, 1882	COBRIDGE	8, 10
BROWNFIELD, WM. & SONS	May 09, 1882	COBRIDGE	8
BROWNFIELD, WM. & SONS	July 06, 1882	COBRIDGE	
BROWNFIELD, WM. & SONS	August 05, 1882	COBRIDGE	
BROWNFIELD, WM. & SONS	August 29, 1882	COBRIDGE	
BROWNFIELD, WM. & SONS	January 24, 1883	COBRIDGE	8
BROWNFIELD, WM. & SONS	January 29, 1883	COBRIDGE	
BROWNFIELD, WM. & SONS	June 18, 1883	COBRIDGE	8, 10
BROWNFIELD, WM. & SONS	June 25, 1883	COBRIDGE	8
BROWNFIELD, WM. & SONS	July 04, 1883	COBRIDGE	8
BROWNFIELD, WM. & SONS	July 30, 1883	COBRIDGE	8
BROWNFIELD, WM. & SONS	August 25, 1883	COBRIDGE	8, 10
BROWNFIELD, WM. & SONS	September 05, 1883	COBRIDGE	8
BROWNFIELD, WM. & SONS	October 13, 1883	COBRIDGE	8
BROWNFIELD, WM. & SONS	October 20, 1883	COBRIDGE	8
BROWNFIELD, WM. & SONS	November 10, 1883	COBRIDGE	
BROWNFIELD, WM. (Reg'd by W.P.&G.Phillips)	October 21, 1868	COBRIDGE	7
BROWNHILLS POTTERY CO. (THE)	October 30, 1872	TUNSTALL	t
BROWNHILLS POTTERY CO. (THE)	March 06, 1873	TUNSTALL	
BROWNHILLS POTTERY CO. (THE)	January 16, 1875	TUNSTALL	
BROWNHILLS POTTERY CO. (THE)	October 11, 1875	TUNSTALL	7
BROWNHILLS POTTERY CO. (THE)	March 02, 1876	TUNSTALL	
BROWNHILLS POTTERY CO. (THE)	January 09, 1878	TUNSTALL	
BROWNHILLS POTTERY CO. (THE)	January 30, 1878	TUNSTALL	
BROWNHILLS POTTERY CO. (THE)	March 09, 1878	TUNSTALL	
BROWNHILLS POTTERY CO. (THE)	October 23, 1878	TUNSTALL	7
BROWNHILLS POTTERY CO. (THE)	July 28, 1880	TUNSTALL	
BROWNHILLS POTTERY CO. (THE)	September 29, 1880	TUNSTALL	7
BROWNHILLS POTTERY CO. (THE)	July 25, 1882	TUNSTALL	7
BROWNHILLS POTTERY CO. (THE)	September 29, 1882	TUNSTALL	
BROWNHILLS POTTERY CO. (THE)	January 25, 1883	TUNSTALL	
BROWNHILLS POTTERY CO. (THE)	May 24, 1883	TUNSTALL	
BROWNHILLS POTTERY CO. (THE)	August 22, 1883	TUNSTALL	
BROWNHILLS POTTERY CO. (THE)	October 27, 1883	TUNSTALL	
BROWNHILLS POTTERY CO. (THE)	December 14, 1883	TUNSTALL	
BURGESS & LEIGH	March 23, 1864	BURSLEM	7
BURGESS & LEIGH	January 17, 1866	BURSLEM	5
BURGESS & LEIGH	June 08, 1868	BURSLEM	
BURGESS & LEIGH	May 07, 1875	BURSLEM	7
BURGESS & LEIGH	July 01, 1878	BURSLEM	7
BURGESS & LEIGH	October 20, 1880	BURSLEM	7
BURGESS & LEIGH	June 23, 1882	BURSLEM	
BURGESS, H.	November 05, 1878	BURSLEM	
BURGESS, LEIGH & CO.	October 16, 1875	BURSLEM	
BURGESS, LEIGH & CO.	November 12, 1875	BURSLEM	
BURGESS, LEIGH & CO.	October 19, 1876	BURSLEM	7
CAMPBELLFIELD POTTERYCO. (LTD.)	May 28, 1875	GLASGOW	
CHALLINOR, E.	July 28, 1856	TUNSTALL	2
CHALLINOR, E.	May 27, 1862	TUNSTALL	5
CHALLINOR, E. & C.	November 23, 1878	FENTON	
CHALLINOR, E. & C.	November 06, 1883	FENTON	
CHALLINOR, EDWARD	December 29, 1846	TUNSTALL	5
CHETWYND, D. (See John Meir & Son)	October 25, 1855	COBRIDGE	4
CHETWYND, E.	February 28, 1879	STOKE	
CHETWYND, E. & D.	June 21, 1867	HANLEY	
CHETWYND, E. & D.	June 24, 1867	HANLEY	
CHETWYND, E. & D.	July 17, 1867	HANLEY	
CLARKE, E.	July 30, 1878	LONGPORT	
CLARKE, E.	March 14, 1879	LONGPORT	
CLARKE, ED.	November 02, 1869	TUNSTALL	
CLEMENTSON & YOUNG	October 22, 1845	SHELTON	1, 5
CLEMENTSON BROS.	May 22, 1867	HANLEY	4
CLEMENTSON BROS.	June 11, 1867	HANLEY	3
CLEMENTSON BROS.	November 14, 1876	HANLEY	7
CLEMENTSON BROS.	March 20, 1877	HANLEY	4
CLEMENTSON BROS.	February 01, 1879	HANLEY	
CLEMENTSON BROS.	February 28, 1879	HANLEY	

POTTER	DATE	LOCATION	CATEGORY
CLEMENTSON BROS.	March 13, 1879	HANLEY	7
CLEMENTSON BROS.	March 28, 1879	HANLEY	7
CLEMENTSON BROS.	May 13, 1879	HANLEY	
CLEMENTSON BROS.	June 25, 1879	HANLEY	
CLEMENTSON BROS.	October 29, 1879	HANLEY	
CLEMENTSON BROS.	December 10, 1879	HANLEY	
CLEMENTSON BROS.	December 19, 1879	HANLEY	7
CLEMENTSON BROS.	February 25, 1880	HANLEY	
CLEMENTSON BROS.	June 04, 1880	HANLEY	
CLEMENTSON BROS.	August 11, 1880	HANLEY	
CLEMENTSON BROS.	June 04, 1883	HANLEY	
CLEMENTSON, J.	April 08, 1850	SHELTON	5
CLEMENTSON, J.	June 30, 1856	SHELTON	5
CLEMENTSON, J.	December 08, 1858	HANLEY	3, 4
CLEMENTSON, J.	December 23, 1858	HANLEY	
CLEMENTSON, J.	December 27, 1858	HANLEY	
CLEMENTSON, J.	October 19, 1860	SHELTON	3, 4
CLEMENTSON, J.	November 15, 1861	HANLEY	3, 4, 7
CLEMENTSON, J.	July 04, 1862	HANLEY	4x,7
CLEMENTSON, J.	July 12, 1862	HANLEY	4x
CLEMENTSON, J.	July 19, 1862	HANLEY	4x
CLEMENTSON, J.	August 21, 1863	HANLEY	3, 4
CLEMENTSON, JOSEPH	December 02, 1842	SHELTON	5
CLEMENTSON, JOSEPH	August 28, 1845	SHELTON	
CLEMENTSON, JOSEPH	December 29, 1845	SHELTON	
CLEMENTSON, JOSEPH	January 07, 1846	SHELTON	5
CLEMENTSON, JOSEPH	December 10, 1846	SHELTON	
CLEMENTSON, JOSEPH	March 13, 1849	SHELTON	2, 5
CLEMENTSON, YOUNG & JAMESON	October 17, 1844	SHELTON	5
CLEMENTSON, YOUNG & JAMESON	January 15, 1845	SHELTON	
CLOSE, J. T. & CO.	January 03, 1866	STOKE	4
COCHRAN, R. & CO.	September 21, 1875	GLASGOW	
COCKSON & CHETWYND	December 24, 1872	COBRIDGE	7
COCKSON & CHETWYND	June 16, 1874	COBRIDGE	
COCKSON & CHETWYND	August 01, 1874	COBRIDGE	7
COCKSON & CHETWYND	September 03, 1874	COBRIDGE	7
COCKSON & HARDING	January 29, 1858	HANLEY	7
COCKSON, CHETWYND & CO.	March 18, 1867	COBRIDGE	
COCKSON, CHETWYND & CO.	June 11, 1867	COBRIDGE	
COCKSON, CHETWYND & CO.	January 07, 1868	COBRIDGE	4,7
COCKSON, CHETWYND & CO.	December 14, 1868	COBRIDGE	7
COLLINSON, C. & CO.	July 26, 1851	BURSLEM	1
COLLINSON, CHAS. & CO.	October 29, 1864	BURSLEM	6, 7
COPELAND & GARRETT	October 14, 1844	STOKE	
COPELAND & GARRETT	December 02, 1844	STOKE	1, 5
COPELAND & GARRETT	March 05, 1845	STOKE	
COPELAND & GARRETT	April 25, 1845	STOKE	5
COPELAND & GARRETT	September 04, 1845	STOKE	
COPELAND & GARRETT	October 21, 1845	STOKE	2, 5
COPELAND & GARRETT	April 17, 1846	STOKE	8
COPELAND & GARRETT	September 14, 1846	STOKE	5
COPELAND & GARRETT	December 17, 1846	STOKE	
COPELAND & GARRETT	January 09, 1847	STOKE	
COPELAND & GARRETT	February 15, 1847	STOKE	
COPELAND & GARRETT	May 12, 1847	STOKE	
COPELAND, W. & T.*	May 16, 1852	STOKE	5
COPELAND, W. & T.*	April 29, 1856	STOKE	5
COPELAND, W. & T.*	June 19, 1856	STOKE	5
COPELAND, W. T.	August 17, 1847	STOKE	7, 13
COPELAND, W. T.	October 13, 1847	STOKE	
COPELAND, W. T.	January 18, 1848	STOKE	
COPELAND, W. T.	March 14, 1848	STOKE	
COPELAND, W. T.	March 15, 1848	STOKE	
COPELAND, W. T.	June 30, 1848	STOKE	5
COPELAND, W. T.	September 15, 1848	STOKE	5
COPELAND, W. T.	November 04, 1848	STOKE	7, 8
COPELAND, W. T.	November 13, 1848	STOKE	8
COPELAND, W. T.	April 10, 1849	STOKE	
COPELAND, W. T.	August 11, 1849	STOKE	13
COPELAND, W. T.	August 17, 1849	STOKE	5
COPELAND, W. T.	November 09, 1849	STOKE	7, 8
COPELAND, W. T.	November 22, 1849	STOKE	5
COPELAND, W. T.	December 06, 1849	STOKE	10
COPELAND, W. T.	March 09, 1850	STOKE	5
COPELAND, W. T.	September 19, 1850	STOKE	5
COPELAND, W. T.	October 17, 1850	STOKE	
COPELAND, W. T.	December 20, 1850	STOKE	5
COPELAND, W. T.	May 30, 1851	STOKE	7, 8
COPELAND, W. T.	June 11, 1851	STOKE	5
COPELAND, W. T.	June 19, 1851	STOKE	5
COPELAND, W. T.	July 14, 1851	STOKE	8
COPELAND, W. T.	October 01, 1851	STOKE	
COPELAND, W. T.	December 08, 1851	STOKE	
COPELAND, W. T.	May 14, 1852	STOKE	8
COPELAND, W. T.	June 14, 1852	STOKE	5
COPELAND, W. T.	August 04, 1852	STOKE	
COPELAND, W. T.	October 01, 1852	STOKE	5
COPELAND, W. T.	January 03, 1853	STOKE	
COPELAND, W. T.	February 26, 1853	STOKE	7, 8
COPELAND, W. T.	November 26, 1853	STOKE	
COPELAND, W. T.	February 23, 1854	STOKE	7, 13
COPELAND, W. T.	September 12, 1854	STOKE	7, 8
COPELAND, W. T.	April 07, 1855	STOKE	5
COPELAND, W. T.	September 01, 1856	STOKE	
COPELAND, W. T.	October 22, 1856	STOKE	7, 8, 13
COPELAND, W. T.	December 11, 1856	STOKE	
COPELAND, W. T.	April 29, 1857	STOKE	13
COPELAND, W. T.	June 19, 1857	STOKE	7, 13
COPELAND, W. T.	September 07, 1857	STOKE	
COPELAND, W. T.	December 17, 1858	STOKE	
COPELAND, W. T.	December 23, 1858	STOKE	
COPELAND, W. T.	January 25, 1859	STOKE	8
COPELAND, W. T.	July 02, 1859	STOKE	8
COPELAND, W. T.	October 14, 1859	STOKE	5
COPELAND, W. T.	January 10, 1860	STOKE	5
COPELAND, W. T.	February 14, 1860	STOKE	8
COPELAND, W. T.	March 19, 1861	STOKE	5
COPELAND, W. T.	May 03, 1861	STOKE	
COPELAND, W. T.	June 11, 1861	STOKE	5, 7
COPELAND, W. T.	September 17, 1861	STOKE	5
COPELAND, W. T.	October 18, 1861	STOKE	5,7
COPELAND, W. T.	March 13, 1862	STOKE	5,7
COPELAND, W. T.	May 22, 1863	STOKE	5, 8
COPELAND, W. T.	July 24, 1863	STOKE	5, 7
COPELAND, W. T.	February 13, 1864	STOKE	7, 8
COPELAND, W. T.	September 06, 1864	STOKE	5
COPELAND, W. T.	November 01, 1864	STOKE	8
COPELAND, W. T.	February 02, 1866	STOKE	8
COPELAND, W. T.	November 12, 1866	STOKE	
COPELAND, W. T.	April 24, 1867	STOKE	8
COPELAND, W. T. & SONS	October 26, 1867	STOKE	8
COPELAND, W. T. & SONS	October 28, 1867	STOKE	8, 9
COPELAND, W. T. & SONS	December 03, 1867	STOKE	13
COPELAND, W. T. & SONS	March 25, 1868	STOKE	
COPELAND, W. T. & SONS	July 24, 1868	STOKE	7, 8
COPELAND, W. T. & SONS	July 24, 1869	STOKE	8
COPELAND, W. T. & SONS	August 02, 1869	STOKE	8
COPELAND, W. T. & SONS	August 19, 1869	STOKE	8
COPELAND, W. T. & SONS	August 26, 1869	STOKE	8
COPELAND, W. T. & SONS	August 31, 1869	STOKE	8
COPELAND, W. T. & SONS	September 08, 1869	STOKE	8
COPELAND, W. T. & SONS	July 15, 1870	STOKE	7, 8
COPELAND, W. T. & SONS	July 04, 1871	STOKE	8
COPELAND, W. T. & SONS	October 19, 1871	STOKE	7, 8
COPELAND, W. T. & SONS	January 30, 1872	STOKE	8
COPELAND, W. T. & SONS	June 11, 1872	STOKE	13
COPELAND, W. T. & SONS	January 13, 1873	STOKE	7
COPELAND, W. T. & SONS	January 21, 1874	STOKE	7, 8
COPELAND, W. T. & SONS	December 01, 1874	STOKE	8
COPELAND, W. T. & SONS	November 08, 1875	STOKE	8
COPELAND, W. T. & SONS	June 09, 1876	STOKE	7
COPELAND, W. T. & SONS	July 05, 1876	STOKE	8
COPELAND, W. T. & SONS	February 21, 1877	STOKE	8
COPELAND, W. T. & SONS	March 08, 1877	STOKE	8
COPELAND, W. T. & SONS	July 02, 1877	STOKE	7, 8
COPELAND, W. T. & SONS	January 24, 1878	STOKE	8
COPELAND, W. T. & SONS	March 13, 1878	STOKE	7
COPELAND, W. T. & SONS	June 05, 1878	STOKE	8
COPELAND, W. T. & SONS	October 14, 1878	STOKE	8
COPELAND, W. T. & SONS	January 07, 1879	STOKE	8
COPELAND, W. T. & SONS	January 28, 1879	STOKE	5
COPELAND, W. T. & SONS	March 12, 1879	STOKE	5
COPELAND, W. T. & SONS	November 15, 1879	STOKE	8
COPELAND, W. T. & SONS	April 28, 1881	STOKE	5
COPELAND, W. T. & SONS	July 30, 1881	STOKE	8
COPELAND, W. T. & SONS	January 04, 1882	STOKE	8, 13
COPELAND, W. T. & SONS	October 09, 1882	STOKE	8
COPELAND, W. T. & SONS	January 08, 1883	STOKE	8
COPELAND, W. T. & SONS	January 23, 1883	STOKE	8, 13
COPELAND, WILLIAM TAYLOR	September 09, 1847	STOKE	5
COPELAND, WILLIAM TAYLOR	September 16, 1847	STOKE	
CORK, EDGE & MALKIN	May 31, 1861	BURSLEM	7
CORK, EDGE & MALKIN	February 22, 1864	BURSLEM	
CORK, EDGE & MALKIN	March 12, 1864	BURSLEM	2, 7
CORK, EDGE & MALKIN	October 31, 1864	BURSLEM	7
CORK, EDGE & MALKIN	January 10, 1868	BURSLEM	5
CORK, EDGE & MALKIN	November 25, 1868	BURSLEM	7
CORK, EDGE & MALKIN	April 07, 1870	BURSLEM	
CORK, EDGE & MALKIN	July 22, 1870	BURSLEM	7
CORN, EDWARD	May 30, 1860	BURSLEM	
CORN, W. & E.	November 03, 1874	BURSLEM	4, 7
CORN, W. & E.	November 29, 1878	BURSLEM	
CORN, W. & E.	June 20, 1883	BURSLEM	
CORN, W. & E.	August 31, 1883	BURSLEM	
CORN, W. & E.	November 07, 1883	BURSLEM	
DAVENPORT'S LTD. (1881-87)	November 01, 1883	LONGPORT	

POTTER	DATE	LOCATION	CATEGORY
DAVENPORT(S) & CO.	May 27, 1869	LONGPORT	4
DAVENPORT, & CO.	May 27, 1869	LONGPORT	
DAVENPORT, BANKS & CO.	January 12, 1863	ETRURIA	4
DAVENPORT, BANKS & CO.	March 14, 1867	ETRURIA	
DAVENPORT, W. & CO.	January 20, 1849	LONGPORT	
DAVENPORT, W. & CO.	January 03, 1850	LONGPORT	1, 2
DAVENPORT, WM. & CO.	March 13, 1879	LONGPORT	1, 8
DAVENPORT, WM. & CO.	August 14, 1880	LONGPORT	8
DAVENPORTS LTD.	September 30, 1881	LONGPORT	8
DAVENPORTS LTD.	May 08, 1882	LONGPORT	8
DAVENPORTS LTD.	January 09, 1883	LONGPORT	8
DAVENPORTS LTD.	February 20, 1883	LONGPORT	8
DAVENPORTS LTD.	July 19, 1883	LONGPORT	8
DAVENPORTS LTD.	August 02, 1883	LONGPORT	8
DAVENPORTS LTD.	November 01, 1883	LONGPORT	
DAVENPORTS, & CO.	October 23, 1852	LONGPORT	2, 4, 5
DAVENPORTS, & CO.	January 14, 1853	LONGPORT	3, 4, 8, 10
DAVENPORTS, & CO.	January 18, 1853	LONGPORT	8
DAVENPORTS, & CO.	October 06, 1854	LONGPORT	4, 8
DAVENPORTS, & CO.	March 11, 1856	LONGPORT	8
DAVENPORTS, & CO.	November 14, 1856	LONGPORT	1x, 4
DAVENPORTS, & CO.	November 27, 1856	LONGPORT	1x, 4
DAVENPORTS, & CO.	February 03, 1859	LONGPORT	8
DAVENPORTS, & CO.	October 28, 1859	LONGPORT	
DAVENPORTS, & CO.	April 12, 1861	LONGPORT	4
DAVENPORTS, & CO.	October 09, 1868	LONGPORT	8
DAVENPORTS, & CO.	January 10, 1874	LONGPORT	8
DAVENPORTS, & CO.	November 21, 1877	LONGPORT	12
DAVIS, J. H.	July 25, 1881	HANLEY	
DAVIS, J. H.	February 15, 1883	HANLEY	
DAVIS, J. H.	April 27, 1883	HANLEY	
DAVIS, J. H. & J.	August 31, 1871	HANLEY	
DIMMOCK, J. & CO.	July 29, 1872	HANLEY	
DIMMOCK, J. & CO.	March 13, 1874	HANLEY	
DIMMOCK, J. & CO.	April 03, 1875	HANLEY	
DIMMOCK, J. & CO.	April 20, 1875	HANLEY	
DIMMOCK, J. & CO.	May 20, 1875	HANLEY	
DIMMOCK, J. & CO.	February 29, 1876	HANLEY	7
DIMMOCK, J. & CO.	April 12, 1876	HANLEY	
DIMMOCK, J. & CO.	December 14, 1876	HANLEY	7
DIMMOCK, J. & CO.	March 20, 1877	HANLEY	
DIMMOCK, J. & CO.	April 12, 1877	HANLEY	
DIMMOCK, J. & CO.	November 24, 1877	HANLEY	
DIMMOCK, J. & CO.	December 14, 1877	HANLEY	
DIMMOCK, J. & CO.	January 22, 1878	HANLEY	
DIMMOCK, J. & CO.	February 09, 1878	HANLEY	
DIMMOCK, J. & CO.	May 17, 1878	HANLEY	
DIMMOCK, J. & CO.	July 09, 1878	HANLEY	
DIMMOCK, J. & CO.	August 23, 1878	HANLEY	
DIMMOCK, J. & CO.	October 24, 1878	HANLEY	
DIMMOCK, J. & CO.	November 16, 1878	HANLEY	
DIMMOCK, J. & CO.	May 30, 1879	HANLEY	
DIMMOCK, J. & CO.	June 07, 1880	HANLEY	
DIMMOCK, J. & CO.	June 10, 1880	HANLEY	8
DIMMOCK, J. & CO.	June 17, 1880	HANLEY	
DIMMOCK, J. & CO.	March 03, 1881	HANLEY	7
DIMMOCK, J. & CO.	October 23, 1883	HANLEY	7
DIMMOCK, THOS. & CO.	November 28, 1843	SHELTON	1
DIMMOCK, THOS. & CO.	May 07, 1844	SHELTON	1
DIMMOCK, THOS. & CO.	June 29, 1844	SHELTON	1, 2, 5
DIMMOCK, THOS. & CO.	November 22, 1844	SHELTON	1, 2
DOULTON & CO.	December 29, 1880	LAMBETH	7
DOULTON & CO.	May 24, 1882	BURSLEM	
DUDSON, JAMES	August 06, 1855	SHELTON	7
DUDSON, JAMES	April 25, 1861	HANLEY	7
DUDSON, JAMES	February 27, 1862	HANLEY	7
DUDSON, JAMES	December 23, 1865	HANLEY	7
DUNN, BENNETT & CO.	February 28, 1878	HANLEY	7
DUNN, BENNETT & CO.	January 22, 1879	HANLEY	
DUNN, BENNETT & CO.	July 15, 1880	HANLEY	
DUNN, BENNETT & CO.	February 12, 1883	HANLEY	
EARDLEY & HAMMERSLEY	May 01, 1862	TUNSTALL	
EARDLEY & HAMMERSLEY	October 22, 1863	TUNSTALL	
EARDLEY & HAMMERSLEY*	May 01, 1862	TUNSTALL	
EDE, MALKIN & CO.	January 26, 1876	BURSLEM	
EDGE, MALKIN & CO.	February 13, 1871	BURSLEM	
EDGE, MALKIN & CO.	January 01, 1872	BURSLEM	7
EDGE, MALKIN & CO.	September 02, 1873	BURSLEM	
EDGE, MALKIN & CO.	June 17, 1874	BURSLEM	7
EDGE, MALKIN & CO.	December 29, 1875	BURSLEM	
EDGE, MALKIN & CO.	October 21, 1876	BURSLEM	7
EDGE, MALKIN & CO.	November 04, 1878	BURSLEM	7
EDGE, MALKIN & CO.	March 12, 1879	BURSLEM	
EDGE, MALKIN & CO.	September 29, 1879	BURSLEM	
EDGE, MALKIN & CO.	February 01, 1882	BURSLEM	7
EDGE, MALKIN & CO.	November 13, 1882	BURSLEM	
EDGE, MALKIN & CO.	July 02, 1883	BURSLEM	
EDWARDS, J. & SON	August 08, 1855	LONGPORT	
EDWARDS, J. & SON	July 30, 1856	LONGPORT	

POTTER	DATE	LOCATION	CATEGORY
EDWARDS, J. (JAMES)	October 26, 1846	BURSLEM	1
EDWARDS, J. (JAMES)	January 26, 1857	LONGPORT	
EDWARDS, J. (JOHN)	January 05, 1856	LONGTON	4
EDWARDS, J. (JOHN)	May 06, 1858	LONGTON	
EDWARDS, JAMES	May 2, 1842	BURSLEM	5
EDWARDS, JAMES	May 30, 1842	BURSLEM	4
EDWARDS, JAMES	December 30, 1842	BURSLEM	10
EDWARDS, JAMES	August 30, 1843	BURSLEM	1, 2, 4, 5
EDWARDS, JAMES	October 06, 1843	BURSLEM	
EDWARDS, JAMES	November 11, 1844	BURSLEM	5
EDWARDS, JAMES	December 27, 1845	BURSLEM	
EDWARDS, JAMES	December 14, 1846	BURSLEM	
EDWARDS, JAMES	March 30, 1847	BURSLEM	2x
EDWARDS, JAMES	June 11, 1847	BURSLEM	2x
EDWARDS, JAMES	June 25, 1847	BURSLEM	1, 2x
EDWARDS, JAMES	July 16, 1847	BURSLEM	1, 2x,
EDWARDS, JAMES	August 16, 1847	BURSLEM	2x
EDWARDS, JAMES	August 26, 1847	BURSLEM	1x
EDWARDS, JAMES	December 16, 1848	BURSLEM	4
EDWARDS, JAMES	September 29, 1851	BURSLEM	4
EDWARDS, JAMES	September 30, 1851	BURSLEM	4x
EDWARDS, JAMES	March 24, 1852	BURSLEM	5
EDWARDS, JAMES	September 21, 1853	BURSLEM	4
EDWARDS, JAMES	October 12, 1853	BURSLEM	
EDWARDS, JAMES	September 06, 1858	LONGPORT	4
EDWARDS, JAMES & SON	March 22, 1854	LONGPORT	4
EDWARDS, JAMES & SON	September 01, 1859	LONGPORT	4
EDWARDS, JAMES & SON	February 27, 1861	LONGPORT	4
EDWARDS, JAMES & SON	March 21, 1863	BURSLEM	
EDWARDS, JAMES & SON	September 28, 1863	LONGPORT	
EDWARDS, JAMES & SON	April 22, 1865	BURSLEM	
EDWARDS, JAMES & SON	April 26, 1865	BURSLEM	
EDWARDS, JAMES & SON	July 12, 1865	BURSLEM	7
EDWARDS, JAMES & SON	November 29, 1865	BURSLEM	
EDWARDS, JAMES & SON	January 31, 1866	BURSLEM	7
EDWARDS, JAMES & SON	April 18, 1866	BURSLEM	
EDWARDS, JAMES & SON	January 08, 1867	BURSLEM	
EDWARDS, JAMES & SON	March 19, 1867	BURSLEM	
EDWARDS, JAMES & SON	March 21, 1867	BURSLEM	
EDWARDS, JAMES & SON	November 07, 1867	BURSLEM	
EDWARDS, JAMES & SON	August 15, 1868	BURSLEM	
EDWARDS, JAMES & SON	October 22, 1868	BURSLEM	
EDWARDS, JAMES & SON	May 13, 1869	BURSLEM	
EDWARDS, JAMES & SON	June 25, 1869	BURSLEM	
EDWARDS, JAMES & SON	May 21, 1870	BURSLEM	
EDWARDS, JAMES & SON	May 25, 1870	BURSLEM	
EDWARDS, JAMES & SON	June 11, 1870	BURSLEM	
EDWARDS, JAMES & SON	July 13, 1870	BURSLEM	
EDWARDS, JAMES & SON	December 27, 1870	BURSLEM	
EDWARDS, JAMES & SON	February 02, 1871	BURSLEM	
EDWARDS, JAMES & SON	April 29, 1871	BURSLEM	
EDWARDS, JAMES & SON	November 02, 1874	BURSLEM	
EDWARDS, JAMES & SON	January 28, 1876	BURSLEM	7
EDWARDS, JAMES & SON	February 01, 1877	BURSLEM	
EDWARDS, JAMES & SON	July 17, 1877	BURSLEM	7
EDWARDS, JAMES & SON	July 31, 1878	BURSLEM	
EDWARDS, JAMES & SONS	November 20, 1877	BURSLEM	
EDWARDS, JAMES & THOMAS	September 2, 1841	BURSLEM	2, 5
EDWARDS, JOHN	July 18, 1853	LONGTON	4
EDWARDS, JOHN	January 30, 1855	LONGTON	4
EDWARDS, JOHN	September 10, 1858	LONGTON	
EDWARDS, JOHN	June 12, 1866	FENTON	4
EDWARDS, JOHN	March 09, 1867	FENTON	
EDWARDS, JOHN	August 03, 1869	FENTON	
EDWARDS, JOHN	September 30, 1875	FENTON	7
EDWARDS, JOHN	October 10, 1877	FENTON	
EDWARDS, JOHN	March 07, 1878	FENTON	
EDWARDS, JOHN	May 10, 1882	FENTON	7
EDWARDS, JOHN	July 20, 1882	FENTON	7
EDWARDS, JON	July 23, 1877	FENTON	
EDWARDS, THOS.	April 03, 1844	BURSLEM	4
EDWARDS, THOS.	December 07, 1844	BURSLEM	
ELLIOT BROS.	February 01, 1862	LONGPORT	7
ELSMORE & FORSTER	March 05, 1855	TUNSTALL	3, 4
ELSMORE & FORSTER	November 02, 1859	TUNSTALL	3, 4
ELSMORE & FORSTER	November 10, 1864	TUNSTALL	3, 4
ELSMORE & FORSTER	April 04, 1867	TUNSTALL	3, 4
ELSMORE & FORSTER	September 27, 1870	TUNSTALL	
ELSMORE & FORSTER	May 13, 1871	TUNSTALL	
ELSMORE & FORSTER & CO.	February 20, 1871	TUNSTALL	4, 7
ELSMORE, & SON	May 14, 1878	TUNSTALL	
ELSMORE, & SON	November 20, 1879	TUNSTALL	
ELSMORE, & SON	December 02, 1879	TUNSTALL	
ELSMORE, T. & SON	September 02, 1875	TUNSTALL	
EMERY, F. J.	March 25, 1878	BURSLEM	
EMERY, F. J.	July 07, 1880	BURSLEM	7
EMERY, F. J.	February 11, 1881	BURSLEM	
EMERY, F. J.	May 24, 1881	BURSLEM	
EMERY, F. J.	November 21, 1883	BURSLEM	

POTTER	DATE	LOCATION	CATEGORY
FELL, THOS. & CO.	August 30, 1862	NEWCASTLE UPON TYNE	
FELL, THOS. & CO.	October 01, 1862	NEWCASTLE UPON TYNE	
FORD & CHALLINOR	July 03, 1876	TUNSTALL	
FORD & CHALLINOR	June 19, 1877	TUNSTALL	
FORD & RILEY	June 25, 1883	BURSLEM	
FORD, CHALLINOR & CO.	March 02, 1866	TUNSTALL	5
FORD, CHALLINOR & CO.	October 24, 1867	TUNSTALL	5
FORD, CHALLINOR & CO.	November 18, 1867	TUNSTALL	5
FORD, CHALLINOR & CO.	April 05, 1877	TUNSTALL	7
FORD, CHALLINOR & CO.	July 25, 1877	TUNSTALL	7
FORD, THOS.	August 20, 1855	SHELTON	8
FORD, THOS.	November 23, 1871	HANLEY	8
FORD, THOS.	May 29, 1873	HANLEY	8
FORD, THOS.	June 25, 1874	HANLEY	8
FORD, THOS.	November 07, 1874	HANLEY	
FURNIVAL & CLARK	December 30, 1845	HANLEY	7, 8
FURNIVAL & SON	September 05, 1874	COBRIDGE	
FURNIVAL & SON	April 21, 1876	COBRIDGE	3, 4
FURNIVAL & SON	August 18, 1877	COBRIDGE	
FURNIVAL, F. & SONS	June 04, 1878	COBRIDGE	7
FURNIVAL, J. & CO.	February 15, 1861	COBRIDGE	
FURNIVAL, J. & CO.	May 29, 1862	COBRIDGE	7
FURNIVAL, J. & CO.	August 21, 1865	COBRIDGE	
FURNIVAL, J. & CO.	May 01, 1866	COBRIDGE	
FURNIVAL, J. & CO.	January 30, 1868	COBRIDGE	1, 4, 7
FURNIVAL, J. & T.	April 04, 1862	COBRIDGE	
FURNIVAL, JACOB & CO.	April 30, 1845	COBRIDGE	5
FURNIVAL, JACOB & CO.	January 24, 1846	COBRIDGE	
FURNIVAL, T. & SON	April 29, 1874	COBRIDGE	7
FURNIVAL, T. & SONS	May 30, 1877	COBRIDGE	
FURNIVAL, T. & SONS	June 26, 1877	COBRIDGE	7
FURNIVAL, T. & SONS	June 28, 1877	COBRIDGE	
FURNIVAL, T. & SONS	December 21, 1877	COBRIDGE	
FURNIVAL, T. & SONS	October 24, 1878	COBRIDGE	
FURNIVAL, T. & SONS	January 29, 1879	COBRIDGE	7
FURNIVAL, T. & SONS	February 14, 1879	COBRIDGE	
FURNIVAL, T. & SONS	March 01, 1879	COBRIDGE	7
FURNIVAL, T. & SONS	May 05, 1879	COBRIDGE	
FURNIVAL, T. & SONS	June 10, 1879	COBRIDGE	
FURNIVAL, T. & SONS	March 08, 1880	COBRIDGE	
FURNIVAL, T. & SONS	April 26, 1880	COBRIDGE	
FURNIVAL, T. & SONS	April 30, 1880	COBRIDGE	7
FURNIVAL, T. & SONS	May 30, 1881	COBRIDGE	
FURNIVAL, T. & SONS	June 04, 1881	COBRIDGE	
FURNIVAL, T. & SONS	July 02, 1881	COBRIDGE	5
FURNIVAL, T. & SONS	October 12, 1882	COBRIDGE	7
FURNIVAL, T. & SONS	January 03, 1883	COBRIDGE	
FURNIVAL, T. & SONS	March 15, 1883	COBRIDGE	
FURNIVAL, T. & SONS	July 05, 1883	COBRIDGE	7
FURNIVAL, T. & SONS	November 15, 1883	COBRIDGE	
FURNIVAL, THOS.	October 13, 1866	COBRIDGE	7
FURNIVAL, THOS. & CO.	November 21, 1846	HANLEY	5
FURNIVAL, THOS. & SON	March 29, 1871	COBRIDGE	7
FURNIVAL, THOS. & SON	April 10, 1872	COBRIDGE	7
FURNIVAL, THOS. & SON	May 02, 1872	COBRIDGE	7
FURNIVAL, THOS. & SON	June 12, 1875	COBRIDGE	7
FURNIVAL, THOS. & SONS	November 24, 1876	COBRIDGE	3, 4
FURNIVAL, THOS. & SONS	November 29, 1876	COBRIDGE	7
FURNIVAL, THOS. & SONS	May 12, 1877	COBRIDGE	7
FURNIVAL, THOS. & SONS	April 20, 1878	COBRIDGE	4, 7
GELSON BROS.	September 04, 1868	HANLEY	7
GELSON BROS.	January 22, 1869	HANLEY	
GELSON BROS.	September 21, 1869	HANLEY	4
GELSON BROS.	December 24, 1869	HANLEY	
GELSON BROS.	September 28, 1870	HANLEY	
GELSON BROS.	January 02, 1871	HANLEY	
GELSON BROS.	January 30, 1871	HANLEY	
GELSON BROS.	July 13, 1872	HANLEY	
GELSON BROS.	April 23, 1873	HANLEY	7
GELSON BROS.	December 18, 1875	HANLEY	
GELSON, T. & CO.	March 02, 1876	HANLEY	
GELSON, THOS. & CO.	April 11, 1876	HANLEY	
GELSON, THOS. & CO.	June 07, 1876	HANLEY	
GELSON, THOS. & CO.	June 22, 1876	HANLEY	
GELSON, THOS. & CO.	July 10, 1876	HANLEY	
GELSON, THOS. & CO.	July 28, 1876	HANLEY	
GILDEA & WALKER	June 21, 1881	BURSLEM	
GILDEA & WALKER	August 27, 1881	BURSLEM	7
GILDEA & WALKER	September 28, 1881	BURSLEM	
GILDEA & WALKER	November 21, 1882	BURSLEM	
GILDEA & WALKER	January 10, 1883	BURSLEM	
GILDEA & WALKER	February 20, 1883	BURSLEM	
GOODFELLOW, THOS.	January 12, 1853	TUNSTALL	
GOODWIN, JOHN	June 30, 1846	LONGTON	1, 2, 5
GOODWIN, JOHN	December 16, 1846	LONGTON	5
GREEN, T. G.	April 28, 1868	BURTON ON TRENT	

POTTER	DATE	LOCATION	CATEGORY
GRINDLEY, W. H. & CO.	April 22, 1880	TUNSTALL	7
GRINDLEY, W. H. & CO.	June 22, 1880	TUNSTALL	
GRINDLEY, W. H. & CO.	November 02, 1880	TUNSTALL	7
GRINDLEY, W. H. & CO.	January 07, 1882	TUNSTALL	
GRINDLEY, W. H. & CO.	May 30, 1882	TUNSTALL	
GRINDLEY, W. H. & CO.	September 19, 1882	TUNSTALL	
GRINDLEY, W. H. & CO.	January 17, 1883	TUNSTALL	
GRINDLEY, W. H. & CO.	January 29, 1883	TUNSTALL	
GRINDLEY, W. H. & CO.	February 14, 1883	TUNSTALL	
GRINDLEY, W. H. & CO.	October 06, 1883	TUNSTALL	
GROVE, F. W. & STARK, J.	June 07, 1871	LONGTON	
GROVE, F. W. & STARK, J.	October 06, 1874	LONGTON	
GROVE, F. W. & STARK, J.	July 27, 1875	LONGTON	
GROVE, F. W. & STARK, J.	August 19, 1875	LONGTON	
GROVE, F. W. & STARK, J.	September 25, 1875	LONGTON	
GROVE, F. W. & STARK, J.	December 11, 1875	LONGTON	
GROVE, F. W. & STARK, J.	December 21, 1876	LONGTON	7
GROVE, F. W. & STARK, J.	January 20, 1877	LONGTON	1
GROVE, F. W. & STARK, J.	October 24, 1877	LONGTON	
GROVE, F. W. & STARK, J.	March 05, 1878	LONGTON	
GROVE, F. W. & STARK, J.	March 04, 1879	LONGTON	
GROVE, F. W. & STARK, J.	June 18, 1879	LONGTON	
GROVE, F. W. & STARK, J.	August 13, 1879	LONGTON	
GROVE, F. W. & STARK, J.	July 15, 1880	LONGTON	7
GROVE, F. W. & STARK, J.	November 24, 1880	LONGTON	
GROVE, F. W. & STARK, J.	February 08, 1881	LONGTON	
GROVE, F. W. & STARK, J.	March 08, 1881	LONGTON	7
GROVE, F. W. & STARK, J.	August 23, 1881	LONGTON	
GROVE, F. W. & STARK, J.	November 09, 1881	LONGTON	
GROVE, F. W. & STARK, J.	January 30, 1882	LONGTON	1, 7
GROVE, F. W. & STARK, J.	February 15, 1882	LONGTON	
GROVE, F. W. & STARK, J.	December 22, 1882	LONGTON	7
GROVE, F. W. & STARK, J.	June 11, 1883	LONGTON	
GROVE, F. W. & STARK, J.	June 14, 1883	LONGTON	
GROVE, F. W. & STARK, J.	July 05, 1883	LONGTON	
GROVE, F. W. & STARK, J.	September 25, 1883	LONGTON	1
HALLAM, JOHNSON & CO.	March 01, 1877	LONGTON	
HAMMERSLEY, R.	April 23, 1868	TUNSTALL	1, 6
HAMMERSLEY, R.	December 31, 1868	TUNSTALL	6x
HANCOCK, B. & S.	November 22, 1877	STOKE	
HANCOCK, B. & S.	January 31, 1878	STOKE	
HANCOCK, B. & S.	January 16, 1879	STOKE	
HANCOCK, B. & S.	January 06, 1881	STOKE	
HANCOCK, S.	February 02, 1883	STOKE	
HANCOCK, WHITTINGHAM & CO.	August 12, 1863	BURSLEM	7
HARDING, W. & G.	January 27, 1852	BURSLEM	5
HARDING, W. & G.	January 10, 1854	BURSLEM	
HARVEY, C. & W. K.	July 16, 1850	LONGTON	4
HAWLEY & CO.	July 28, 1882	LONGTON	
HAWLEY & CO.	September 06, 1882	LONGTON	7
HAWLEY & CO.	February 07, 1883	LONGTON	7
HAWTHORNE, J.	March 19, 1879	COBRIDGE	4
HILDITCH & HOPWOOD	April 11, 1844	LANE END	1, 8
HILL POTTERY COMPANY LTD. (THE)*	May 06, 1861	BURSLEM	
HILL POTTERY COMPANY LTD. (THE)*	June 14, 1865	BURSLEM	
HILL POTTERY COMPANY LTD. (THE)*	June 30, 1865	BURSLEM	
HOBSON, CHAS.	April 17, 1867	BURSLEM	
HOBSON, CHAS.	January 27, 1870	BURSLEM	7
HOBSON, CHAS.	March 07, 1870	BURSLEM	
HOBSON, CHAS.	July 28, 1873	BURSLEM	
HOLDCROFT & WOOD*	May 28, 1868	TUNSTALL	
HOLLAND & GREEN	August 10, 1853	LONGTON	
HOLLAND & GREEN	March 31, 1854	LONGTON	4
HOLLAND & GREEN	May 31, 1858	LONGTON	
HOLLAND & GREEN	October 19, 1860	LONGTON	4
HOLLAND & GREEN	July 28, 1864	LONGTON	
HOLLAND & GREEN	November 18, 1872	LONGTON	
HOLLAND & GREEN	May 11, 1874	LONGTON	7
HOLLAND & GREEN	May 22, 1875	LONGTON	
HOLLAND & GREEN	February 07, 1877	LONGTON	
HOLLAND, JOHN	November 04, 1852	TUNSTALL	5
HOLLINSHEAD & KIRKHAM	September 20, 1876	BURSLEM	7
HOLLINSHEAD & KIRKHAM	January 30, 1882	TUNSTALL	7
HOLLINSHEAD & KIRKHAM	July 20, 1883	TUNSTALL	8
HOPE & CARTER	September 17, 1862	BURSLEM	4x
HOPE & CARTER	September 26, 1862	BURSLEM	4x, 7
HOPE & CARTER	March 13, 1863	BURSLEM	7
HOPE & CARTER	February 05, 1864	BURSLEM	
HOPE & CARTER	April 27, 1864	BURSLEM	
HOPE & CARTER	June 16, 1864	BURSLEM	
HOPE & CARTER	July 19, 1864	BURSLEM	
HOPE & CARTER	November 10, 1864	BURSLEM	
HOPE & CARTER	November 29, 1864	BURSLEM	7
HOPE & CARTER	December 10, 1864	BURSLEM	
HOPE & CARTER	January 06, 1865	BURSLEM	5x
HOPE & CARTER	March 31, 1865	BURSLEM	5x

POTTER	DATE	LOCATION	CATEGORY
HOPE & CARTER	April 28, 1865	BURSLEM	5x
HOPE & CARTER	May 25, 1866	BURSLEM	
HOPE & CARTER	July 25, 1866	STOKE	
HOPE & CARTER	July 25, 1867	BURSLEM	5
HOPE & CARTER	January 25, 1868	BURSLEM	5x
HOPE & CARTER	May 14, 1868	BURSLEM	5x
HOPE & CARTER	July 20, 1868	BURSLEM	5x
HOPE & CARTER	September 09, 1868	BURSLEM	5x, 7
HOPE & CARTER	October 09, 1868	BURSLEM	5x
HOPE & CARTER	March 25, 1870	BURSLEM	
HOPE & CARTER	July 29, 1871	BURSLEM	
HOPE & CARTER	June 05, 1872	BURSLEM	
HOPE & CARTER	November 03, 1873	BURSLEM	
HOPE & CARTER	September 26, 1876	BURSLEM	
HOPE & CARTER	September 28, 1876	BURSLEM	7, 8
HUDDEN, J. T.	May 15, 1865	LONGTON	
HUDDEN, J. T.	June 06, 1865	LONGTON	
HUDDEN, J. T.	June 15, 1865	LONGTON	
HUDDEN, J. T.	July 19, 1866	LONGTON	
HUDDEN, J. T.	December 24, 1866	LONGTON	
HUDDEN, J. T.	October 30, 1867	LONGTON	
HUDDEN, J. T.	July 27, 1869	LONGTON	
HUDDEN, J. T.	October 10, 1871	LONGTON	
HUDDEN, J. T.	August 22, 1874	LONGTON	
HUDDEN, J. T.	October 03, 1878	LONGTON	
HUDDEN, J. T.	September 26, 1879	LONGTON	
HUDDEN, J. T.	March 31, 1881	LONGTON	
HUDDEN, J. T.	January 26, 1882	LONGTON	
HUDDEN, J. T.	March 13, 1882	LONGTON	
HUGHES, STEPHEN & SON	April 17, 1855	BURSLEM	4
HUGHES, THOS.	February 24, 1877	BURSLEM	
HUGHES, THOS.	August 07, 1878	BURSLEM	
HUGHES, THOS.	December 19, 1878	BURSLEM	
HULSEY & ADDERLEY	July 27, 1874	LONGTON	8
HULSEY, NIXON & ADDERLEY	October 24, 1861	LONGTON	
HULSEY, NIXON & ADDERLEY	August 18, 1862	LONGTON	7
HULSEY, NIXON & ADDERLEY	March 21, 1863	LONGTON	
JACKSON, JOHN & CO.	May 03, 1871	ROTHERHAM	
JONES & ELLIS*	July 31, 1862	LONGTON	
JONES & WALLEY	May 13, 1843	COBRIDGE	7, 10
JONES, F.	September 26, 1872	LONGTON	7
JONES, F. & CO.	September 09, 1868	LONGTON	4, 7
JONES, GEO.	December 18, 1862	STOKE	
JONES, GEO.	April 15, 1864	STOKE	
JONES, GEO.	July 25, 1866	STOKE	
JONES, GEO.	July 12, 1867	STOKE	4
JONES, GEO.	October 14, 1868	STOKE	
JONES, GEO.	January 01, 1869	STOKE	
JONES, GEO.	February 11, 1869	STOKE	
JONES, GEO.	March 09, 1869	STOKE	
JONES, GEO.	March 09, 1869	STOKE	
JONES, GEO.	October 15, 1869	STOKE	
JONES, GEO.	October 23, 1869	STOKE	
JONES, GEO.	December 01, 1869	STOKE	
JONES, GEO.	December 22, 1869	STOKE	
JONES, GEO.	January 03, 1870	STOKE	
JONES, GEO.	March 08, 1870	STOKE	
JONES, GEO.	March 10, 1870	STOKE	
JONES, GEO.	May 30, 1870	STOKE	
JONES, GEO.	June 27, 1870	STOKE	7
JONES, GEO.	August 23, 1870	STOKE	
JONES, GEO.	October 19, 1870	STOKE	
JONES, GEO.	November 22, 1870	STOKE	
JONES, GEO.	January 10, 1871	STOKE	
JONES, GEO.	August 29, 1871	STOKE	
JONES, GEO.	December 01, 1871	STOKE	
JONES, GEO.	December 23, 1871	STOKE	
JONES, GEO.	January 20, 1872	STOKE	
JONES, GEO.	February 03, 1872	STOKE	
JONES, GEO.	February 16, 1872	STOKE	
JONES, GEO.	March 04, 1872	STOKE	
JONES, GEO.	May 27, 1872	STOKE	7
JONES, GEO.	May 29, 1872	STOKE	
JONES, GEO.	July 20, 1872	STOKE	
JONES, GEO.	October 18, 1872	STOKE	7
JONES, GEO.	January 10, 1873	STOKE	
JONES, GEO.	February 25, 1873	STOKE	8
JONES, GEO.	March 26, 1873	STOKE	8
JONES, GEO.	April 29, 1873	STOKE	
JONES, GEO.	August 25, 1873	STOKE	
JONES, GEO.	October 13, 1873	STOKE	
JONES, GEO.	November 03, 1873	STOKE	
JONES, GEO.	January 30, 1878	STOKE	7, 8
JONES, GEO. & CO.	May 14, 1862	STOKE	
JONES, GEO. & CO.	October 28, 1863	STOKE	
JONES, GEO. & CO.	November 06, 1863	STOKE	
JONES, GEO. & CO.	May 10, 1864	STOKE	
JONES, GEO. & CO.	August 20, 1864	STOKE	
JONES, GEO. & CO.	October 04, 1864	STOKE	

POTTER	DATE	LOCATION	CATEGORY
JONES, GEO. & CO.	November 10, 1864	STOKE	
JONES, GEO. & CO.	December 31, 1864	STOKE	
JONES, GEO. & CO.	January 14, 1865	STOKE	
JONES, GEO. & CO.	September 16, 1881	STOKE	8
JONES, GEO. & SONS	December 10, 1873	STOKE	
JONES, GEO. & SONS	December 27, 1873	STOKE	
JONES, GEO. & SONS	February 19, 1874	STOKE	
JONES, GEO. & SONS	February 25, 1874	STOKE	7
JONES, GEO. & SONS	March 03, 1874	STOKE	5
JONES, GEO. & SONS	March 28, 1874	STOKE	
JONES, GEO. & SONS	April 21, 1874	STOKE	
JONES, GEO. & SONS	April 25, 1874	STOKE	7
JONES, GEO. & SONS	May 09, 1874	STOKE	
JONES, GEO. & SONS	May 23, 1874	STOKE	8
JONES, GEO. & SONS	August 28, 1874	STOKE	8
JONES, GEO. & SONS	September 15, 1874	STOKE	
JONES, GEO. & SONS	October 08, 1874	STOKE	
JONES, GEO. & SONS	October 21, 1874	STOKE	8
JONES, GEO. & SONS	November 10, 1874	STOKE	8
JONES, GEO. & SONS	December 08, 1874		0
JONES, GEO. & SONS	December 12, 1874	STOKE	
JONES, GEO. & SONS	December 18, 1874	STOKE	8
JONES, GEO. & SONS	January 21, 1875	STOKE	8
JONES, GEO. & SONS	February 09, 1875	STOKE	
JONES, GEO. & SONS	February 23, 1875	STOKE	8
JONES, GEO. & SONS	March 12, 1875	STOKE	7
JONES, GEO. & SONS	May 07, 1875	STOKE	8
JONES, GEO. & SONS	May 31, 1875	STOKE	
JONES, GEO. & SONS	June 26, 1875	STOKE	8
JONES, GEO. & SONS	September 13, 1875	STOKE	7, 8
JONES, GEO. & SONS	September 18, 1875	STOKE	8
JONES, GEO. & SONS	November 05, 1875	STOKE	8
JONES, GEO. & SONS	November 12, 1875	STOKE	
JONES, GEO. & SONS	December 03, 1875	STOKE	
JONES, GEO. & SONS	January 22, 1876	STOKE	
JONES, GEO. & SONS	February 19, 1876	STOKE	
JONES, GEO. & SONS	March 30, 1876	STOKE	8
JONES, GEO. & SONS	May 10, 1876	STOKE	8
JONES, GEO. & SONS	May 29, 1876	STOKE	8
JONES, GEO. & SONS	July 26, 1876	STOKE	8
JONES, GEO. & SONS	September 12, 1876	STOKE	8
JONES, GEO. & SONS	October 09, 1876	STOKE	
JONES, GEO. & SONS	November 08, 1876	STOKE	1, 8
JONES, GEO. & SONS	January 25, 1877	STOKE	8
JONES, GEO. & SONS	March 10, 1877	STOKE	
JONES, GEO. & SONS	May 02, 1877	STOKE	8
JONES, GEO. & SONS	October 15, 1877	STOKE	8
JONES, GEO. & SONS	October 31, 1877	STOKE	
JONES, GEO. & SONS	February 01, 1878	STOKE	
JONES, GEO. & SONS	June 07, 1878	STOKE	
JONES, GEO. & SONS	June 08, 1880	STOKE	8
JONES, GEO. & SONS	September 29, 1881	STOKE	7
JONES, GEO. & SONS	April 11, 1882	STOKE	
JONES, GEO. & SONS	May 13, 1882	STOKE	
JONES, GEO. & SONS	July 14, 1882	STOKE	8
JONES, GEO. & SONS	July 22, 1882	STOKE	7
JONES, GEO. & SONS	February 21, 1883	STOKE	8
JONES, GEO. & SONS	July 19, 1883	STOKE	8
JONES, GEO. & SONS	August 01, 1883	STOKE	8
JONES, GEORGE (& SONS)	January 30, 1874	STOKE	8
KING, KNIGHT & ELKIN	August 15, 1844	STOKE	5, 7
KNIGHT, J.	March 14, 1862	FENTON	
KNIGHT, J. K.	July 11, 1846	LONGTON	
LEAR, S.	June 13, 1881	HANLEY	
LEAR, S.	August 27, 1881	HANELY	7
LEAR, S.	January 10, 1882	HANLEY	7
LEAR, S.	December 14, 1882	HANLEY	7
LEAR, SAMUEL	July 12, 1878	HANLEY	7
LEAR, SAMUEL	November 06, 1878	HANLEY	
LEAR, SAMUEL	June 17, 1880	HANLEY	7
LEAR, SAMUEL	May 27, 1882	HANLEY	
LIDDLE, ELLIOT & CO.	May 09, 1871	LONGPORT	
LIDDLE, ELLIOT & SON	February 25, 1864	LONGPORT	7
LIDDLE, ELLIOT & SON	April 21, 1864	LONGPORT	7
LIDDLE, ELLIOT & SON	February 14, 1865	LONGPORT	
LIDDLE, ELLIOT & SON	September 18, 1865	LONGPORT	4
LIDDLE, ELLIOT & SON	December 13, 1866	LONGPORT	7
LIDDLE, ELLIOT & SON	April 12, 1869	LONGPORT	
LIDDLE, ELLIOT & SON	April 20, 1869	LONGPORT	
LIDDLE, ELLIOT & SON	November 15, 1869	LONGPORT	2, 7
LIDDLE, ELLIOT & SON	January 15, 1870	LONGPORT	
LIDDLE, ELLIOT & SONS	January 16, 1863	LONGPORT	7
LIVESLEY, POWELL & CO.	June 14, 1853	HANLEY	7, 10
LIVESLEY, POWELL & CO.	October 12, 1853	HANLEY	3, 4
LIVESLEY, POWELL & CO.	November 04, 1864	HANLEY	7
LIVESLEY, POWELL & CO.	February 27, 1865	HANLEY	
LIVESLEY, POWELL & CO.	May 02, 1865	HANLEY	7
LOCKETT, J. & T.	March 07, 1844	LANE END	7
LOCKETT, J. & T.	June 21, 1852	LONGTON	7

POTTER	DATE	LOCATION	CATEGORY
MACINTYRE, J.	April 11, 1863	BURSLEM	7
MACINTYRE, J. & CO.	November 27, 1878	BURSLEM	
MACINTYRE, J. & CO.	December 03, 1878	BURSLEM	
MACINTYRE, J. & CO.	March 16, 1880	BURSLEM	
MACINTYRE, J. & CO.	June 17, 1880	BURSLEM	
MACINTYRE, J. & CO.	February 25, 1881	BURSLEM	
MACINTYRE, J. & CO.	July 10, 1883	BURSLEM	
MACINTYRE, JAMES & CO.	February 08, 1871	BURSLEM	
MADDOCK & GATER	June 12, 1875	BURSLEM	
MADDOCK, J. & SONS	February 12, 1875	BURLSEM	
MADDOCK, J. & SONS	February 23, 1875	BURLSEM	
MADDOCK, J. & SONS	January 14, 1878	BURLSEM	
MALKIN, EDGE & CO.	December 05, 1883	BURSLEM	
MALKIN, R.	April 15, 1875	FENTON	
MALKIN, RALPH	August 21, 1868	FENTON	5
MALKIN, WALKER & HULSE	September 06, 1862	LONGTON	
MALKIN, WALKER & HULSE	January 11, 1864	LONGTON	
MARPLE, TURNER & CO.	October 30, 1852	HANLEY	5
MARSHALL, J. & CO.	April 16, 1881	BO'NESS, SCOTLAND	
MARSHALL, J. & CO.	October 30, 1883	BO'NESS, SCOTLAND	7
MARSHALL, JOHN & CO.	September 27, 1880	BO'NESS, SCOTLAND	
MASON, C. J.	April 16, 1849	LONGTON	
MAYER & ELLIOT	December 18, 1856	LONGPORT	4
MAYER & ELLIOT	December 23, 1856	LONGPORT	
MAYER & ELLIOT	July 13, 1858	LONGPORT	
MAYER & ELLIOT	January 23, 1860	LONGPORT	4
MAYER BROS. & ELLIOT	October 17, 1857	LONGPORT	5
MAYER, T. J. & J.	January 21, 1845	LONGPORT	4, 7
MAYER, T. J. & J.	February 26, 1846	LONGPORT	
MAYER, T. J. & J.	September 29, 1846	LONGPORT	7, 10
MAYER, T. J. & J.	February 08, 1847	LONGTON	7, 10
MAYER, T. J. & J.	July 27, 1847	LONGPORT	4
MAYER, T. J. & J.	June 07, 1849	LONGPORT	
MAYER, T. J. & J.	December 15, 1849	LONGPORT	
MAYER, T. J. & J.	April 04, 1850	LONGPORT	
MAYER, T. J. & J.	July 02, 1850	LONGPORT	7
MAYER, T. J. & J.	December 19, 1850	LONGPORT	7
MAYER, T. J. & J.	September 02, 1851	LONGPORT	4
MAYER, T. J. & J.	December 02, 1851	BURSLEM	4, 7
MAYER, T. J. & J.	October 22, 1853	LONGPORT	2, 4
MAYER, T. J. & J.	October 09, 1854	LONGPORT	1
MEIGH, C.	November 12, 1846	HANLEY	7
MEIGH, CHARLES	September 30, 1844	HANLEY	7
MEIGH, CHARLES	September 18, 1848	HANLEY	7
MEIGH, CHARLES & SON	November 13, 1851	HANLEY	7
MEIGH, CHARLES & SON	August 25, 1852	HANLEY	7
MEIGH, CHAS. & SON	June 09, 1854	HANLEY	7
MEIGH, CHAS. & SON	July 24, 1855	HANLEY	4, 10
MEIGH, CHAS. & SON	June 13, 1856	HANLEY	7
MEIR, HENRY & SON	June 15, 1876	TUNSTALL	
MEIR, JOHN & SON	December 24, 1844	TUNSTALL	5
MEIR, JOHN & SON	August 26, 1848	TUNSTALL	5
MEIR, JOHN & SON	February 04, 1857	TUNSTALL	4
MEIR, JOHN & SON	May 02, 1860	TUNSTALL	4
MEIR, JOHN & SON	November 03, 1863	TUNSTALL	4
MEIR, JOHN & SON	December 19, 1866	TUNSTALL	7
MEIR, JOHN & SON	May 07, 1867	TUNSTALL	
MEIR, JOHN & SON	July 06, 1869	TUNSTALL	
MEIR, JOHN & SON	November 09, 1870	TUNSTALL	
MEIR, JOHN & SON	May 24, 1871	TUNSTALL	
MEIR, JOHN & SON	December 27, 1872	TUNSTALL	
MEIR, JOHN & SON	January 23, 1874	TUNSTALL	
MEIR, JOHN & SON	December 06, 1875	TUNSTALL	
MEIR, JOHN & SON	July 20, 1878	TUNSTALL	7
MEIR, JOHN & SONS	July 28, 1873	TUNSTALL	
MELLOR, TAYLOR & CO.	October 02, 1883	BURSLEM	
MELLOR, VENABLES & CO.	March 05, 1844	BURSLEM	
MELLOR, VENABLES & CO.	July 05, 1847	BURSLEM	5
MELLOR, VENABLES & CO.	July 15, 1847	BURSLEM	1
MELLOR, VENABLES & CO.	February 02, 1849	BURSLEM	2x, 5x
MELLOR, VENABLES & CO.	August 27, 1849	BURSLEM	2, 2x, 5
MELLOR, VENABLES & CO.	September 21, 1850	BURSLEM	4
MINTON & CO.	November 10, 1843	STOKE	
MINTON & CO.	June 26, 1845	STOKE	
MINTON & CO.	September 19, 1845	STOKE	8
MINTON & CO.	November 22, 1845	STOKE	7, 8
MINTON & CO.	March 02, 1846	STOKE	7, 8
MINTON & CO.	December 14, 1846	STOKE	8
MINTON & CO.	December 15, 1847	STOKE	8
MINTON & CO.	February 29, 1848	STOKE	
MINTON & CO.	March 04, 1848	STOKE	8
MINTON & CO.	November 21, 1848	STOKE	7, 8
MINTON & CO.	February 16, 1849	STOKE	
MINTON & CO.	March 26, 1849	STOKE	8
MINTON & CO.	October 12, 1849	STOKE	8
MINTON & CO.	November 17, 1849	STOKE	7, 8
MINTON & CO.	April 13, 1850	STOKE	8
MINTON & CO.	April 25, 1850	STOKE	
MINTON & CO.	October 09, 1850	STOKE	10
MINTON & CO.	November 12, 1851	STOKE	5, 8
MINTON & CO.	December 04, 1851	STOKE	
MINTON & CO.	March 24, 1852	STOKE	8
MINTON & CO.	May 18, 1852	STOKE	8
MINTON & CO.	June 05, 1852	STOKE	7, 8
MINTON & CO.	July 23, 1852	STOKE	7, 8
MINTON & CO.	September 03, 1852	STOKE	7, 8
MINTON & CO.	September 16, 1852	STOKE	7, 8
MINTON & CO.	September 24, 1852	STOKE	8
MINTON & CO.	November 11, 1852	STOKE	
MINTON & CO.	February 12, 1853	STOKE	
MINTON & CO.	March 19, 1853	STOKE	1
MINTON & CO.	October 19, 1853	STOKE	8
MINTON & CO.	March 24, 1854	STOKE	
MINTON & CO.	March 01, 1855	STOKE	8
MINTON & CO.	May 14, 1855	STOKE	8
MINTON & CO.	October 03, 1855	STOKE	8
MINTON & CO.	January 23, 1856	STOKE	7, 8, 10
MINTON & CO.	May 08, 1856	STOKE	8
MINTON & CO.	May 22, 1856	STOKE	8
MINTON & CO.	October 16, 1856	STOKE	8, 10
MINTON & CO.	February 09, 1857	STOKE	7, 8
MINTON & CO.	February 17, 1857	STOKE	8
MINTON & CO.	December 04, 1857	STOKE	8
MINTON & CO.	April 30, 1858	STOKE	8
MINTON & CO.	October 05, 1858	STOKE	7
MINTON & CO.	October 18, 1858	STOKE	
MINTON & CO.	October 25, 1859	STOKE	10
MINTON & CO.	November 17, 1859	STOKE	
MINTON & CO.	November 23, 1859	STOKE	
MINTON & CO.	December 15, 1859	STOKE	8
MINTON & CO.	April 12, 1860	STOKE	8
MINTON & CO.	June 22, 1860	STOKE	
MINTON & CO.	June 28, 1860	STOKE	
MINTON & CO.	September 24, 1860	STOKE	
MINTON & CO.	September 29, 1860	STOKE	
MINTON & CO.	October 29, 1860	STOKE	7, 8
MINTON & CO.	May 13, 1861	STOKE	
MINTON & CO.	June 13, 1861	STOKE	
MINTON & CO.	February 10, 1862	STOKE	
MINTON & CO.	March 29, 1862	STOKE	7
MINTON & CO.	April 04, 1862	STOKE	8
MINTON & CO.	July 02, 1862	STOKE	
MINTON & CO.	July 31, 1862	STOKE	
MINTON & CO.	September 11, 1862	STOKE	
MINTON & CO.	September 22, 1862	STOKE	
MINTON & CO.	November 28, 1862	STOKE	8
MINTON & CO.	January 16, 1863	STOKE	7, 8
MINTON & CO.	February 02, 1863	STOKE	8
MINTON & CO.	June 08, 1863	STOKE	8
MINTON & CO.	July 28, 1863	STOKE	
MINTON & CO.	March 22, 1864	STOKE	
MINTON & CO.	April 18, 1864	STOKE	
MINTON & CO.	June 09, 1864	STOKE	8
MINTON & CO.	September 10, 1864	STOKE	7
MINTON & CO.	September 12, 1864	STOKE	
MINTON & CO.	September 21, 1864	STOKE	
MINTON & CO.	October 28, 1864	STOKE	8
MINTON & CO.	January 06, 1865	STOKE	8
MINTON & CO.	February 01, 1865	STOKE	8
MINTON & CO.	April 03, 1865	STOKE	
MINTON & CO.	May 17, 1865	STOKE	8
MINTON & CO.	September 28, 1865	STOKE	
MINTON & CO.	January 24, 1866	STOKE	8
MINTON & CO.	October 08, 1866	STOKE	8
MINTON & CO.	November 03, 1866	STOKE	8
MINTON & CO.	March 26, 1867	STOKE	
MINTON & CO.	April 03, 1867	STOKE	
MINTON & CO.	October 02, 1867	STOKE	
MINTON & CO.	October 03, 1867	STOKE	
MINTON & CO.	October 07, 1867	STOKE	
MINTON & CO.	January 03, 1868	STOKE	
MINTON & CO.	February 10, 1868	STOKE	8
MINTON & CO.	February 20, 1868	STOKE	
MINTON & CO.	March 05, 1868	STOKE	8
MINTON & CO.	April 01, 1868	STOKE	8
MINTON & CO.	May 28, 1868	STOKE	
MINTON & CO.	June 22, 1868	STOKE	
MINTON & CO.	September 12, 1868	STOKE	
MINTON & CO.	September 25, 1868	STOKE	
MINTON & CO.	October 08, 1868	STOKE	
MINTON & CO.	October 17, 1868	STOKE	8
MINTON & CO.	November 03, 1868	STOKE	8
MINTON & CO.	November 21, 1868	STOKE	8
MINTON & CO.	December 23, 1868	STOKE	7
MINTON & CO.	January 04, 1869	STOKE	8

POTTER	DATE	LOCATION	CATEGORY
MINTON & CO.	January 21, 1869	STOKE	8
MINTON & CO.	January 28, 1869	STOKE	
MINTON & CO.	February 09, 1869	STOKE	8
MINTON & CO.	April 02, 1869	STOKE	8
MINTON & CO.	April 07, 1869	STOKE	8
MINTON & CO.	June 26, 1869	STOKE	8
MINTON & CO.	July 23, 1869	STOKE	
MINTON & CO.	September 04, 1869	STOKE	
MINTON & CO.	September 10, 1869	STOKE	
MINTON & CO.	October 01, 1869	STOKE	
MINTON & CO.	October 04, 1869	STOKE	
MINTON & CO.	October 29, 1869	STOKE	
MINTON & CO.	November 24, 1869	STOKE	8
MINTON & CO.	November 26, 1869	STOKE	
MINTON & CO.	December 17, 1869	STOKE	
MINTON & CO.	December 31, 1869	STOKE	
MINTON & CO.	January 29, 1870	STOKE	8
MINTON & CO.	February 10, 1870	STOKE	8
MINTON & CO.	February 25, 1870	STOKE	
MINTON & CO.	February 28, 1870	STOKE	
MINTON & CO.	March 02, 1870	STOKE	8
MINTON & CO.	March 16, 1870	STOKE	8
MINTON & CO.	March 25, 1870	STOKE	
MINTON & CO.	March 26, 1870	STOKE	8
MINTON & CO.	April 09, 1870	STOKE	
MINTON & CO.	April 14, 1870	STOKE	8
MINTON & CO.	May 26, 1870	STOKE	7
MINTON & CO.	September 10, 1870	STOKE	8
MINTON & CO.	September 16, 1870	STOKE	
MINTON & CO.	October 04, 1870	STOKE	7
MINTON & CO.	October 06, 1870	STOKE	
MINTON & CO.	October 07, 1870	STOKE	8
MINTON & CO.	November 10, 1870	STOKE	7, 8
MINTON & CO.	November 24, 1870	STOKE	8
MINTON & CO.	November 25, 1870	STOKE	
MINTON & CO.	January 06, 1871	STOKE	1x, 5x
MINTON & CO.	June 17, 1871	STOKE	1x, 5x
MINTON & CO.	September 19, 1871	STOKE	1x, 5x
MINTON & CO.	October 04, 1871	STOKE	1x, 5x
MINTON & CO.	October 31, 1871	STOKE	1x, 5x
MINTON & CO.	January 06, 1872	STOKE	8
MINTON & CO.	February 22, 1872	STOKE	8
MINTON & CO.	March 04, 1872	STOKE	
MINTON & CO.	March 16, 1872	STOKE	
MINTON & CO.	March 18, 1872	STOKE	8
MINTON & CO.	April 05, 1872	STOKE	8
MINTON & CO.	May 03, 1872	STOKE	
MINTON & CO.	May 30, 1872	STOKE	8
MINTON & CO.	June 22, 1872	STOKE	
MINTON & CO.	July 31, 1872	STOKE	
MINTON & CO.	November 12, 1872	STOKE	
MINTON & CO.	December 10, 1872	STOKE	
MINTON & CO.	February 15, 1873	STOKE	
MINTON & CO.	March 06, 1873	STOKE	
MINTON & CO.	April 03, 1873	STOKE	8
MINTON & CO.	April 19, 1873	STOKE	
MINTON & CO.	May 03, 1873	STOKE	
MINTON & CO.	May 06, 1873	STOKE	8
MINTON & CO. & JOHN BELL	December 10, 1847	STOKE	
MINTON HOLLINS & CO.	April 06, 1861	STOKE	
MINTON HOLLINS & CO.	June 17, 1870	STOKE	
MINTON HOLLINS & CO.	June 22, 1870	STOKE	
MINTON HOLLINS & CO.	July 14, 1870	STOKE	
MINTON HOLLINS & CO.	November 12, 1870	STOKE	
MINTON HOLLINS & CO.	December 05, 1870	STOKE	
MINTON HOLLINS & CO.	January 26, 1871	STOKE	
MINTON HOLLINS & CO.	April 26, 1871	STOKE	
MINTON HOLLINS & CO.	March 04, 1872	STOKE	
MINTON HOLLINS & CO.	March 08, 1872	STOKE	
MINTON HOLLINS & CO.	March 13, 1872	STOKE	
MINTON HOLLINS & CO.	April 19, 1872	STOKE	
MINTON HOLLINS & CO.	May 06, 1872	STOKE	
MINTON HOLLINS & CO.	May 27, 1872	STOKE	
MINTON HOLLINS & CO.	June 07, 1872	STOKE	
MINTON HOLLINS & CO.	June 18, 1872	STOKE	
MINTON HOLLINS & CO.	June 21, 1872	STOKE	
MINTON HOLLINS & CO.	July 16, 1872	STOKE	
MINTON HOLLINS & CO.	September 12, 1872	STOKE	
MINTON HOLLINS & CO.	September 25, 1872	STOKE	
MINTON HOLLINS & CO.	October 14, 1872	STOKE	
MINTON HOLLINS & CO.	January 29, 1873	STOKE	
MINTON HOLLINS & CO.	February 01, 1873	STOKE	
MINTON HOLLINS & CO.	February 27, 1873	STOKE	
MINTON HOLLINS & CO.	May 16, 1873	STOKE	
MINTON HOLLINS & CO.	June 30, 1873	STOKE	
MINTON HOLLINS & CO.	July 03, 1873	STOKE	
MINTON HOLLINS & CO.	February 26, 1874	STOKE	
MINTON HOLLINS & CO.	April 20, 1874	STOKE	
MINTON HOLLINS & CO.	July 30, 1874	STOKE	

POTTER	DATE	LOCATION	CATEGORY
MINTON HOLLINS & CO.	November 25, 1874	STOKE	
MINTON HOLLINS & CO.	December 18, 1874	STOKE	
MINTON HOLLINS & CO.	January 06, 1875	STOKE	
MINTON HOLLINS & CO.	March 24, 1875	STOKE	
MINTON HOLLINS & CO.	April 22, 1875	STOKE	
MINTON HOLLINS & CO.	June 02, 1875	STOKE	
MINTON HOLLINS & CO.	July 28, 1875	STOKE	
MINTON HOLLINS & CO.	September 14, 1875	STOKE	
MINTON HOLLINS & CO.	October 28, 1875	STOKE	
MINTON HOLLINS & CO.	November 08, 1875	STOKE	
MINTON HOLLINS & CO.	December 13, 1875	STOKE	
MINTON HOLLINS & CO.	December 30, 1875	STOKE	
MINTON HOLLINS & CO.	February 22, 1876	STOKE	
MINTON HOLLINS & CO.	March 10, 1876	STOKE	
MINTON HOLLINS & CO.	April 21, 1876	STOKE	
MINTON HOLLINS & CO.	June 15, 1876	STOKE	
MINTON HOLLINS & CO.	June 26, 1876	STOKE	
MINTON HOLLINS & CO.	November 18, 1876	STOKE	
MINTON HOLLINS & CO.	November 18, 1876	STOKE	
MINTON HOLLINS & CO.	February 03, 1877	STOKE	
MINTON HOLLINS & CO.	February 15, 1877	STOKE	
MINTON HOLLINS & CO.	June 08, 1877	STOKE	
MINTON HOLLINS & CO.	July 09, 1877	STOKE	
MINTON HOLLINS & CO.	July 26, 1877	STOKE	
MINTON HOLLINS & CO.	July 31, 1877	STOKE	
MINTON HOLLINS & CO.	August 18, 1877	STOKE	
MINTON HOLLINS & CO.	August 25, 1877	STOKE	
MINTON HOLLINS & CO.	September 19, 1877	STOKE	
MINTON HOLLINS & CO.	September 22, 1877	STOKE	
MINTON HOLLINS & CO.	October 19, 1877	STOKE	
MINTON HOLLINS & CO.	January 03, 1878	STOKE	
MINTON HOLLINS & CO.	January 14, 1878	STOKE	
MINTON HOLLINS & CO.	February 01, 1878	STOKE	
MINTON HOLLINS & CO.	February 20, 1878	STOKE	
MINTON HOLLINS & CO.	March 06, 1878	STOKE	
MINTON HOLLINS & CO.	March 27, 1878	STOKE	
MINTON HOLLINS & CO.	May 29, 1878	STOKE	
MINTON HOLLINS & CO.	September 28, 1878	STOKE	
MINTON HOLLINS & CO.	October 11, 1878	STOKE	
MINTON HOLLINS & CO.	October 30, 1878	STOKE	
MINTON HOLLINS & CO.	January 08, 1879	STOKE	
MINTON HOLLINS & CO.	May 31, 1879	STOKE	
MINTON HOLLINS & CO.	July 26, 1879	STOKE	
MINTON HOLLINS & CO.	October 16, 1879	STOKE	
MINTON HOLLINS & CO.	November 03, 1879	STOKE	
MINTON HOLLINS & CO.	January 07, 1880	STOKE	
MINTON HOLLINS & CO.	January 22, 1880	STOKE	
MINTON HOLLINS & CO.	February 26, 1880	STOKE	
MINTON HOLLINS & CO.	May 13, 1880	STOKE	
MINTON HOLLINS & CO.	September 15, 1880	STOKE	
MINTON HOLLINS & CO.	September 25, 1880	STOKE	
MINTON HOLLINS & CO.	October 26, 1880	STOKE	
MINTON HOLLINS & CO.	November 04, 1880	STOKE	
MINTON HOLLINS & CO.	January 26, 1881	STOKE	
MINTON HOLLINS & CO.	September 23, 1881	STOKE	
MINTON HOLLINS & CO.	October 29, 1881	STOKE	
MINTON HOLLINS & CO.	February 04, 1882	STOKE	
MINTON HOLLINS & CO.	February 23, 1882	STOKE	
MINTON HOLLINS & CO.	March 01, 1882	STOKE	
MINTON HOLLINS & CO.	March 07, 1882	STOKE	
MINTON HOLLINS & CO.	April 11, 1882	STOKE	
MINTON HOLLINS & CO.	May 09, 1882	STOKE	
MINTON HOLLINS & CO.	May 24, 1882	STOKE	
MINTON HOLLINS & CO.	November 11, 1882	STOKE	
MINTON HOLLINS & CO.	November 24, 1882	STOKE	
MINTON HOLLINS & CO.	December 02, 1882	STOKE	
MINTON HOLLINS & CO.	January 31, 1883	STOKE	
MINTON HOLLINS & CO.	March 30, 1883	STOKE	
MINTON HOLLINS & CO.	June 02, 1883	STOKE	
MINTON HOLLINS & CO.	October 24, 1883	STOKE	
MINTON HOLLINS & CO.	November 23, 1883	STOKE	
MINTON, HERBERT & CO.	July 30, 1844	STOKE	
MINTON, HERBERT & CO.	August 21, 1844	STOKE	8
MINTON, HERBERT & CO.	October 30, 1844	STOKE	8
MINTON, HERBERT & CO.	November 06, 1844	STOKE	
MINTON, HERBERT & CO.	March 06, 1845	STOKE	8
MINTON, HERBERT & CO.	March 17, 1845	STOKE	
MINTON, HERBERT & CO.	March 20, 1845	STOKE	7
MINTON, HERBERT & CO.	May 08, 1845	STOKE	7, 8
MINTON, HERBERT & CO.	October 06, 1845	STOKE	8
MINTON, HERBERT & CO.	May 21, 1846	STOKE	4
MINTON, HERBERT & CO.	May 26, 1846	STOKE	7, 8
MINTON, HERBERT & CO.	June 26, 1846	STOKE	8
MINTON, HERBERT & CO.	August 03, 1846	STOKE	
MINTON, HERBERT & CO.	November 16, 1846	STOKE	1
MINTON, HERBERT & CO.	December 04, 1846	STOKE	
MINTON, HERBERT & CO.	March 23, 1847	STOKE	8
MINTON, HERBERT & CO.	May 14, 1847	STOKE	7, 8
MINTON, HERBERT & CO.	August 19, 1847	STOKE	8

POTTER	DATE	LOCATION	CATEGORY
MINTON, HERBERT & CO.	October 04, 1847	STOKE	8
MINTON, HERBERT & CO.	October 23, 1847	STOKE	
MINTON, HERBERT & CO.	November 11, 1847	STOKE	8
MINTON, HERBERT & CO.	February 11, 1848	STOKE	
MINTON, HERBERT & CO.	August 15, 1849	STOKE	10
MINTONS	July 31, 1873	STOKE	8
MINTONS	September 04, 1873	STOKE	8
MINTONS	October 11, 1873	STOKE	
MINTONS	October 22, 1873	STOKE	
MINTONS	March 04, 1874	STOKE	
MINTONS	March 14, 1874	STOKE	8
MINTONS	March 24, 1874	STOKE	8
MINTONS	April 15, 1874	STOKE	8
MINTONS	May 21, 1874	STOKE	8
MINTONS	May 22, 1874	STOKE	8
MINTONS	June 18, 1874	STOKE	8
MINTONS	July 10, 1874	STOKE	8
MINTONS	August 01, 1874	STOKE	
MINTONS	September 04, 1874	STOKE	8
MINTONS	September 12, 1874	STOKE	
MINTONS	October 06, 1874	STOKE	
MINTONS	October 10, 1874	STOKE	8
MINTONS	November 12, 1874	STOKE	
MINTONS	January 28, 1875	STOKE	8
MINTONS	February 17, 1875	STOKE	8
MINTONS	April 07, 1875	STOKE	7, 8
MINTONS	April 20, 1875	STOKE	8
MINTONS	December 10, 1875	STOKE	8
MINTONS	December 15, 1875	STOKE	8
MINTONS	December 30, 1875	STOKE	8
MINTONS	January 04, 1876	STOKE	8
MINTONS	January 24, 1876	STOKE	8
MINTONS	February 04, 1876	STOKE	8
MINTONS	March 17, 1876	STOKE	8
MINTONS	April 27, 1876	STOKE	8
MINTONS	May 16, 1876	STOKE	8
MINTONS	May 24, 1876	STOKE	8
MINTONS	June 03, 1876	STOKE	8
MINTONS	June 08, 1876	STOKE	8
MINTONS	June 21, 1876	STOKE	8
MINTONS	June 23, 1876	STOKE	8
MINTONS	July 01, 1876	STOKE	8
MINTONS	October 20, 1876	STOKE	
MINTONS	October 23, 1876	STOKE	
MINTONS	November 13, 1876	STOKE	8
MINTONS	January 26, 1877	STOKE	
MINTONS	February 21, 1877	STOKE	8
MINTONS	February 27, 1877	STOKE	8
MINTONS	July 06, 1877	STOKE	8
MINTONS	September 22, 1877	STOKE	
MINTONS	September 25, 1877	STOKE	8
MINTONS	November 07, 1877	STOKE	
MINTONS	December 06, 1877	STOKE	8
MINTONS	December 21, 1877	STOKE	
MINTONS	March 13, 1878	STOKE	
MINTONS	April 10, 1878	STOKE	
MINTONS	April 17, 1878	STOKE	
MINTONS	July 03, 1878	STOKE	
MINTONS	July 09, 1878	STOKE	8
MINTONS	July 31, 1878	STOKE	
MINTONS	September 30, 1878	STOKE	
MINTONS	October 02, 1878	STOKE	
MINTONS	October 30, 1878	STOKE	
MINTONS	December 06, 1878	STOKE	
MINTONS	February 05, 1879	STOKE	8
MINTONS	February 08, 1879	STOKE	8
MINTONS	February 25, 1879	STOKE	
MINTONS	July 08, 1879	STOKE	8
MINTONS	July 25, 1879	STOKE	8
MINTONS	July 31, 1879	STOKE	8
MINTONS	October 15, 1879	STOKE	8
MINTONS	October 29, 1879	STOKE	
MINTONS	October 30, 1879	STOKE	8
MINTONS	November 21, 1879	STOKE	7, 8
MINTONS	November 29, 1879	STOKE	
MINTONS	December 22, 1879	STOKE	
MINTONS	January 22, 1880	STOKE	8
MINTONS	January 23, 1880	STOKE	8
MINTONS	February 10, 1880	STOKE	
MINTONS	February 24, 1880	STOKE	8
MINTONS	March 25, 1880	STOKE	8
MINTONS	April 29, 1880	STOKE	8
MINTONS	May 13, 1880	STOKE	8
MINTONS	May 26, 1880	STOKE	
MINTONS	June 01, 1880	STOKE	8
MINTONS	July 07, 1880	STOKE	8
MINTONS	July 12, 1880	STOKE	8
MINTONS	September 14, 1880	STOKE	8
MINTONS	October 12, 1880	STOKE	

POTTER	DATE	LOCATION	CATEGORY
MINTONS	November 18, 1880	STOKE	8
MINTONS	January 20, 1881	STOKE	
MINTONS	March 09, 1881	STOKE	
MINTONS	March 23, 1881	STOKE	8
MINTONS	April 12, 1881	STOKE	8
MINTONS	April 14, 1881	STOKE	8
MINTONS	May 13, 1881	STOKE	8
MINTONS	May 24, 1881	STOKE	
MINTONS	June 01, 1881	STOKE	
MINTONS	July 30, 1881	STOKE	
MINTONS	September 30, 1881	STOKE	
MINTONS	October 07, 1881	STOKE	8
MINTONS	October 12, 1881	STOKE	8
MINTONS	October 22, 1881	STOKE	8
MINTONS	October 26, 1881	STOKE	8
MINTONS	December 16, 1881	STOKE	8
MINTONS	February 16, 1882	STOKE	
MINTONS	June 05, 1882	STOKE	
MINTONS	July 03, 1882	STOKE	
MINTONS	July 31, 1882	STOKE	
MINTONS	August 25, 1882	STOKE	8
MINTONS	August 28, 1882	STOKE	7
MINTONS	September 08, 1882	STOKE	
MINTONS	October 06, 1882	STOKE	
MINTONS	November 08, 1882	STOKE	8
MINTONS	December 13, 1882	STOKE	
MINTONS	February 03, 1883	STOKE	
MINTONS	March 17, 1883	STOKE	8
MINTONS	March 30, 1883	STOKE	
MINTONS	June 09, 1883	STOKE	
MINTONS	June 20, 1883	STOKE	
MINTONS	September 14, 1883	STOKE	
MINTONS CHINA WORKS	December 15, 1875	STOKE	
MOORE, SAMUEL & CO.	December 24, 1853	SUNDERLAND	
MOORE, SAMUEL & CO.	January 14, 1854	SUNDERLAND	
MORLEY, F. & CO.	July 21, 1846	SHELTON	
MORLEY, F. & CO.	September 03, 1846	SHELTON	7, 10
MORLEY, F. & CO.	October 26, 1846	SHELTON	
MORLEY, F. & CO.	November 20, 1850	SHELTON	
MORLEY, F. & CO.	December 05, 1850	SHELTON	
MORLEY, F. & CO.	September 06, 1853	SHELTON	
MORLEY, FRANCIS	May 31, 1845	SHELTON	1, 2, 4, 5, 6
NEW WHARF POTTERY CO., THE	January 14, 1879	BURSLEM	
NEW WHARF POTTERY CO., THE	April 27, 1882	BURSLEM	
NEW WHARF POTTERY CO., THE	December 23, 1882	BURSLEM	7
NEW WHARF POTTERY CO., THE	December 27, 1882	BURSLEM	
NEW WHARF POTTERY CO., THE	October 17, 1883	BURSLEM	
NEW WHARF POTTERY CO., THE	October 30, 1883	BURSLEM	
OLD HALL EARTHENWARE CO. (LTD.) THE	April 09, 1862	HANLEY	7
OLD HALL EARTHENWARE CO. (LTD.) THE	December 17, 1862	HANLEY	
OLD HALL EARTHENWARE CO. (LTD.) THE	June 04, 1863	HANLEY	
OLD HALL EARTHENWARE CO. (LTD.) THE	October 26, 1863	HANLEY	
OLD HALL EARTHENWARE CO. (LTD.) THE	March 10, 1866	HANLEY	
OLD HALL EARTHENWARE CO. (LTD.) THE	April 16, 1866	HANLEY	
OLD HALL EARTHENWARE CO. (LTD.) THE	March 06, 1867	HANLEY	
OLD HALL EARTHENWARE CO. (LTD.) THE	January 16, 1868	HANLEY	
OLD HALL EARTHENWARE CO. LTD., THE	November 23, 1865	HANLEY	
OLD HALL EARTHENWARE CO. LTD., THE	March 28, 1870	HANLEY	
OLD HALL EARTHENWARE CO. LTD., THE	May 21, 1870	HANLEY	
OLD HALL EARTHENWARE CO. LTD., THE	December 11, 1872	HANLEY	7
OLD HALL EARTHENWARE CO. LTD., THE	December 04, 1873	HANLEY	
OLD HALL EARTHENWARE CO. LTD., THE	May 04, 1877	HANLEY	
OLD HALL EARTHENWARE CO. LTD., THE	November 22, 1877	HANLEY	
OLD HALL EARTHENWARE CO. LTD., THE	January 08, 1880	HANLEY	
OLD HALL EARTHENWARE CO. LTD., THE	July 31, 1880	HANLEY	
OLD HALL EARTHENWARE CO. LTD., THE	December 31, 1880	HANLEY	
OLD HALL EARTHENWARE CO. LTD., THE	April 07, 1881	HANLEY	
OLD HALL EARTHENWARE CO. LTD., THE	August 10, 1881	HANLEY	7

POTTER	DATE	LOCATION	CATEGORY
OLD HALL EARTHENWARE CO. LTD., THE	June 21, 1882	HANLEY	
OLD HALL EARTHENWARE CO. LTD., THE	December 15, 1882	HANLEY	
OLD HALL EARTHENWARE CO., THE	May 06, 1861	HANLEY	7
OLD HALL EARTHENWARE CO., THE	February 22, 1883	HANLEY	
PANKHURST & DIMMOCK	June 22, 1853	HANLEY	7
PANKHURST & DIMMOCK	December 27, 1854	HANLEY	7
PANKHURST & DIMMOCK	January 19, 1855	HANLEY	4, 7
PANKHURST, J. & CO.	July 05, 1852	HANLEY	
PANKHURST, J. & DIMMOCK, J.	November 22, 1852	HANLEY	
PANKHURST, J. & DIMMOCK, J.	February 04, 1853	HANLEY	4
PANKHURST, J. W.	December 02, 1863	HANLEY	4
PANKHURST, J. W. & CO.	March 17, 1853	HANLEY	
PANKHURST, JAMES & CO.	January 15, 1856	HANLEY	4, 7
PEAKE, J. & J.*	September 12, 1861	NEWCASTLE	
PEARSON, E.	May 11, 1863	COBRIDGE	4
PEARSON, FARRALL & MEAKIN	April 11, 1854	SHELTON	4
PHILLIPS, G.	September 03, 1846	LONGPORT	5
PHILLIPS, G.	November 05, 1846	LONGPORT	5
PHILLIPS, GEORGE	January 11, 1845	LONGPORT	5
PHILLIPS, GEORGE	February 27, 1845	LONGPORT	
PHILLIPS, GEORGE	June 19, 1845	LONGPORT	4
PHILLIPS, GEORGE	July 05, 1845	LONGPORT	
PHILLIPS, THOS. & SON	September 11, 1845	BURSLEM	
PINDER & BOURNE & CO.	June 19, 1873	BURSLEM	7
PINDER & BOURNE & CO.	September 06, 1876	BURSLEM	7, 8
PINDER & BOURNE & CO.	October 23, 1878	BURSLEM	
PINDER & BOURNE & CO.	May 13, 1879	BURSLEM	7
PINDER, BOURNE & CO.	July 09, 1864	BURSLEM	
PINDER, BOURNE & CO.	July 11, 1864	BURSLEM	
PINDER, BOURNE & CO.	June 21, 1866	BURSLEM	
PINDER, BOURNE & CO.	April 06, 1868	BURSLEM	
PINDER, BOURNE & CO.	May 26, 1868	BURSLEM	
PINDER, BOURNE & CO.	February 22, 1869	BURSLEM	
PINDER, BOURNE & CO.	September 08, 1869	BURSLEM	
PINDER, BOURNE & CO.	June 19, 1871	BURSLEM	7
PINDER, BOURNE & CO.	October 04, 1871	BURSLEM	
PINDER, BOURNE & CO.	June 26, 1874	BURSLEM	7
PINDER, BOURNE & CO.	October 28, 1874	BURSLEM	
PINDER, BOURNE & CO.	December 10, 1874	BURSLEM	
PINDER, BOURNE & CO.	February 09, 1875	BURSLEM	
PINDER, BOURNE & CO.	April 17, 1875	BURSLEM	
PINDER, BOURNE & CO.	November 07, 1877	BURSLEM	7
PINDER, BOURNE & CO.	April 04, 1879	BURSLEM	
PINDER, BOURNE & CO.	May 29, 1879	BURSLEM	
PINDER, BOURNE & CO.	January 21, 1880	BURSLEM	
PINDER, BOURNE & CO.	August 04, 1880	BURSLEM	
PINDER, BOURNE & CO.	December 07, 1880	BURSLEM	7
PINDER, BOURNE & CO.	August 05, 1881	BURSLEM	
PINDER, BOURNE & CO.	September 27, 1881	BURSLEM	
PINDER, BOURNE & CO. & ANTHONY SHAW	November 10, 1865	BURSLEM	
PINDER, BOURNE & HOPE	January 15, 1855	BURSLEM	
PINDER, BOURNE & HOPE	April 05, 1861	BURSLEM	7
PINDER, T. S.	March 24, 1881	BURSLEM	
PINDER, THOS.	August 16, 1848	BURSLEM	
PODMORE, WALKER & CO.	April 02, 1849	TUNSTALL	1, 2, 5
PODMORE, WALKER & CO.	February 23, 1857	HANLEY	4
POULSON, T. & E. L.	April 02, 1883	CASTLEFORD	
POWELL & BISHOP	March 05, 1867	HANLEY	
POWELL & BISHOP	September 25, 1867	HANLEY	
POWELL & BISHOP	October 31, 1867	HANLEY	7
POWELL & BISHOP	November 06, 1868	HANLEY	
POWELL & BISHOP	October 29, 1869	HANLEY	3, 3x, 4, 4x
POWELL & BISHOP	December 18, 1869	HANLEY	3x, 4x, 7
POWELL & BISHOP	February 04, 1870	HANLEY	7
POWELL & BISHOP	March 10, 1870	HANLEY	
POWELL & BISHOP	October 08, 1870	HANLEY	
POWELL & BISHOP	February 13, 1871	HANLEY	
POWELL & BISHOP	February 15, 1871	HANLEY	
POWELL & BISHOP	May 11, 1871	HANLEY	
POWELL & BISHOP	February 15, 1872	HANLEY	7
POWELL & BISHOP	April 28, 1873	HANLEY	
POWELL & BISHOP	September 10, 1873	HANLEY	
POWELL & BISHOP	January 20, 1874	HANLEY	
POWELL & BISHOP	March 17, 1874	HANLEY	
POWELL & BISHOP	March 21, 1874	HANLEY	
POWELL & BISHOP	October 12, 1874	HANLEY	
POWELL & BISHOP	April 10, 1875	HANLEY	
POWELL & BISHOP	October 11, 1875	HANLEY	
POWELL & BISHOP	January 26, 1876	HANLEY	4x, 7
POWELL & BISHOP	February 03, 1876	HANLEY	4x
POWELL & BISHOP	April 12, 1876	HANLEY	4x
POWELL & BISHOP	July 28, 1876	HANLEY	4x
POWELL & BISHOP	September 22, 1876	HANLEY	4x
POWELL & BISHOP	January 26, 1877	HANLEY	8

POTTER	DATE	LOCATION	CATEGORY
POWELL & BISHOP	March 24, 1877	HANLEY	
POWELL & BISHOP	April 03, 1877	HANLEY	
POWELL & BISHOP	October 16, 1877	HANLEY	
POWELL & BISHOP	November 05, 1877	HANLEY	
POWELL & BISHOP	March 09, 1878	HANLEY	8
POWELL, BISHOP & STONIER	July 30, 1878	HANLEY	
POWELL, BISHOP & STONIER	March 06, 1879	HANLEY	
POWELL, BISHOP & STONIER	March 17, 1879	HANLEY	
POWELL, BISHOP & STONIER	November 17, 1879	HANLEY	
POWELL, BISHOP & STONIER	November 19, 1879	HANLEY	
POWELL, BISHOP & STONIER	January 28, 1880	HANLEY	
POWELL, BISHOP & STONIER	February 03, 1880	HANLEY	
POWELL, BISHOP & STONIER	March 22, 1880	HANLEY	
POWELL, BISHOP & STONIER	May 10, 1880	HANLEY	7
POWELL, BISHOP & STONIER	December 06, 1880	HANLEY	
POWELL, BISHOP & STONIER	May 21, 1881	HANLEY	
POWELL, BISHOP & STONIER	May 25, 1881	HANLEY	
POWELL, BISHOP & STONIER	March 15, 1882	HANLEY	
POWELL, BISHOP & STONIER	May 06, 1882	HANLEY	
POWELL, BISHOP & STONIER	November 11, 1882	HANLEY	
POWELL, BISHOP & STONIER	January 09, 1883	HANLEY	7
POWELL, BISHOP & STONIER	April 27, 1883	HANLEY	8
POWELL, BISHOP & STONIER	May 22, 1883	HANLEY	8
POWELL, BISHOP & STONIER	September 07, 1883	HANLEY	8
POWELL, BISHOP & STONIER	November 24, 1883	HANLEY	8
POWELL, BISHOP & STONIER	December 29, 1883	HANLEY	8
PRATT & CO.	February 17, 1855	FENTON	10
PRATT & CO.	March 12, 1856	FENTON	
PRATT & CO.	October 22, 1857	FENTON	
PRATT & CO.	January 02, 1866	FENTON	
PRATT & CO.	August 18, 1871	FENTON	
PRATT & SIMPSON	July 15, 1878	FENTON	
PRATT & SIMPSON	November 10, 1882	FENTON	7
PRATT & SIMPSON	April 25, 1883	FENTON	
PRATT & SIMPSON	June 13, 1883	STOKE	
PRATT, F. & R.	April 20, 1861	FENTON	7
PRATT, F. & R.	December 22, 1871	FENTON	
PRATT, F. & R. & CO.	September 14, 1849	FENTON	
PRATT, F. & R. & CO.	December 29, 1854	FENTON	
PRATT, F. & R. & CO.	August 12, 1856	FENTON	
PRATT, F. & R. & CO.	August 19, 1856	FENTON	
PRATT, F. & R. & CO.	November 07, 1856	FENTON	
PRATT, F. & R. & CO.	January 15, 1857	FENTON	
PRATT, F. & R. & CO.	August 06, 1859	FENTON	
PRATT, F. & R. & CO.	December 18, 1863	FENTON	7
PRATT, F. & R. & CO.	February 13, 1865	FENTON	
PRATT, F. & R. & CO.	September 06, 1866	FENTON	7
PRATT, F. & R. & CO.	December 12, 1867	FENTON	
PRATT, F. & R. & CO.	March 08, 1869	FENTON	
PRATT, F. & R. & CO.	June 03, 1870	FENTON	
PRATT, F. & R. & CO.	July 19, 1870	FENTON	
PRATT, F. & R. & CO.	November 20, 1874	FENTON	
PRATT, F. & R. & CO.	May 11, 1876	FENTON	
PRATT, F. & R. & CO.	August 25, 1876	FENTON	
PRATT, F. & R. & CO.	October 24, 1877	FENTON	7
PRATT, F. & R. & CO.	October 04, 1878	FENTON	
PRATT, F. & R. & CO.	November 15, 1878	FENTON	
PRATT, F. & R. & CO.	January 16, 1879	FENTON	7
PRATT, F. & R. & CO.	January 04, 1882	FENTON	
PRATT, JOHN & CO.	March 20, 1863	FENTON	7
PRATT, JOHN & CO.	August 31, 1869	LANE DELPH	
PRATT, JOHN & CO.	September 09, 1869	LANE DELPH	
PRATT, JOHN & CO.	December 28, 1869	LANE DELPH	5
PRATT, JOHN & CO.	March 14, 1871	LANE DELPH	
PRATT, JOHN & CO.	April 22, 1871	STOKE	
PRATT, JOHN & CO. LTD.	April 24, 1872	LANE DELPH	
PRATT, JOHN & CO. LTD.	December 04, 1872	LANE DELPH	
PRIMAVESI, F.	March 06, 1869	CARDIFF	
PRIMAVESI, F.	March 10, 1869	CARDIFF	
READE, G. W. (See Charles Meigh & Son)	August 23, 1861	COBRIDGE	4
READE, G. W. (See Meir & Son)	October 29, 1855	BURSLEM	4
RIDGWAY & ABINGTON	November 03, 1846	HANLEY (WM. & E.)	
RIDGWAY & ABINGTON	December 03, 1846	HANLEY (WM. & E.)	7, 11
RIDGWAY & ABINGTON	March 07, 1848	HANLEY	7
RIDGWAY & ABINGTON	June 30, 1848	HANLEY	
RIDGWAY & ABINGTON	February 16, 1849	HANLEY	7, 11
RIDGWAY & ABINGTON	July 16, 1849	HANLEY	
RIDGWAY & ABINGTON	August 16, 1851	HANLEY	7, 11
RIDGWAY & ABINGTON	April 18, 1856	HANLEY	7
RIDGWAY & ABINGTON	October 14, 1857	HANLEY	7, 11
RIDGWAY & ABINGTON	April 17, 1858	HANLEY	
RIDGWAY & ABINGTON	October 07, 1858	HANLEY	7
RIDGWAY & CO.	June 24, 1853	SHELTON	
RIDGWAY, SON & CO.	July 16, 1846	HANLEY	1, 4, 7, 11
RIDGWAY, BATES & CO.	July 30, 1857	SHELTON	4
RIDGWAY, E. J.	July 04, 1867	HANLEY	11
RIDGWAY, E. J. & SONS	October 09, 1871	HANLEY	
RIDGWAY, E. J. & SONS	April 17, 1872	HANLEY	

POTTER	DATE	LOCATION	CATEGORY
RIDGWAY, E. J. & SONS	August 02, 1872	HANLEY	
RIDGWAY, J. & CO.	March 17, 1851	SHELTON	10
RIDGWAY, J. & CO.	June 07, 1851	SHELTON	
RIDGWAY, J. & CO.	February 25, 1855	SHELTON	
RIDGWAY, J. & E.	August 08, 1883	STOKE	
RIDGWAY, J. (JOHN)	September 28, 1849	SHELTON	5
RIDGWAY, J. (JOHN)	October 10, 1849	SHELTON	
RIDGWAY, J. (JOHN)	January 14, 1850	SHELTON	5x
RIDGWAY, J. (JOHN)	September 16, 1850	SHELTON	5x
RIDGWAY, JN & CO.	September 19, 1844	SHELTON	4
RIDGWAY, JOHN	December 04, 1845	SHELTON	1, 5
RIDGWAY, JOHN	December 28, 1848	SHELTON	
RIDGWAY, JOHN & CO.	January 24, 1843	SHELTON	
RIDGWAY, JOHN & CO.	July 20, 1844	SHELTON	5
RIDGWAY, JOHN & CO.	November 13, 1844	SHELTON	
RIDGWAY, JOHN & CO.	July 17, 1846	SHELTON	5
RIDGWAY, JOHN & CO.	September 26, 1846	SHELTON	
RIDGWAY, JOHN & CO.	January 09, 1847	SHELTON	1, 5x
RIDGWAY, JOHN & CO.	March 17, 1847	SHELTON	5x
RIDGWAY, JOHN & CO.	October 02, 1847	SHELTON	1, 5x
RIDGWAY, JOHN & CO.	October 27, 1847	SHELTON	
RIDGWAY, JOHN & CO.	April 15, 1848	SHELTON	
RIDGWAY, JOHN & CO.	September 30, 1848	SHELTON	4
RIDGWAY, JOHN & CO.	November 27, 1848	SHELTON	
RIDGWAY, JOHN & CO.	March 31, 1849	SHELTON	
RIDGWAY, JOHN & CO.	December 05, 1851	SHELTON	
RIDGWAY, JOHN & CO.	May 04, 1854	SHELTON	4x
RIDGWAY, JOHN & CO.	November 10, 1854	SHELTON	4x, 5
RIDGWAY, SPARKS & RIDGWAY	April 29, 1874	HANLEY	
RIDGWAY, SPARKS & RIDGWAY	May 31, 1875	HANLEY	
RIDGWAY, SPARKS & RIDGWAY	February 02, 1876	HANLEY	
RIDGWAY, SPARKS & RIDGWAY	June 15, 1877	HANLEY	5
RIDGWAY, SPARKS & RIDGWAY	August 17, 1877	HANLEY	
RIDGWAY, SPARKS & RIDGWAY	April 17, 1878	HANLEY	
RIDGWAY, WILLIAM SON & CO.	December 16, 1844	HANLEY	6, 7
RIDGWAY, WM.	October 21, 1851	SHELTON	7,11
RIDGWAY, WM.	March 13, 1852	SHELTON	5
RIDGWAYS	December 17, 1879	STOKE	
RIDGWAYS	April 15, 1880	STOKE	
RIDGWAYS	June 17, 1880	STOKE	
RIDGWAYS	July 28, 1881	STOKE	
RIDGWAYS	January 07, 1882	STOKE	
RIDGWAYS (Made by Dudson)	November 10, 1882	STOKE	
ROBINSON & CO.	February 09, 1877	LONGTON	
ROBINSON & SON	January 18, 1882	LONGTON	
ROBINSON, J.	October 30, 1883	BURSLEM	
SANDER, GEO. B. (See Hulme & Booth)	November 14, 1851	LONDON	2
SCRAGG, RALPH	June 11, 1851	HANLEY	
SCRAGG, RALPH	November 10, 1851	HANLEY	
SCRAGG, RALPH	March 22, 1852	HANLEY	
SCRAGG, RALPH	October 07, 1852	HANLEY	
SCRAGG, RALPH	October 11, 1853	HANLEY	
SCRAGG, RALPH (See George Frederick Bowers)	April 18, 1856	HANLEY	4
SHARPE BROS. & CO.	September 03, 1858	DERBYSHIRE	7, 10
SHAW, A.	April 07, 1856	TUNSTALL	3, 4
SHAW, A.	May 25, 1858	BURSLEM	5
SHAW, A.	December 07, 1878	BURSLEM	4
SHAW, A. & SON	June 13, 1882	BURSLEM	
SHAW, ANTHONY	August 08, 1853	TUNSTALL	1, 5
TAMS, J.	October 27, 1880	LONGTON	7
TAMS, J.	May 11, 1881	LONGTON	
TAMS, J.	November 22, 1881	LONGTON	
TAMS, J.	October 21, 1882	LONGTON	
TAMS, JOHN	July 01, 1876	LONGTON	
TAMS, JOHN	December 11, 1876	LONGTON	
TAMS, JOHN	April 23, 1877	LONGTON	
TAMS, JOHN	July 14, 1877	LONGTON	
TAMS, JOHN	June 13, 1878	LONGTON	
TAMS, JOHN	May 29, 1879	LONGTON	
TAMS, JOHN	August 21, 1882	LONGTON	
TAMS, JOHN	June 18, 1883	LONGTON	7
THOMPSON, J.	July 04, 1855	STAFFORDSHIRE	
THOMPSON, J. & SONS	November 15, 1871	GLASGOW	
THOMPSON, JOHN & SONS	May 11, 1874	GLASGOW	
TILL, THOMAS	September 09, 1850	BURSLEM	
TILL, THOS. & SON	April 09, 1851	BURSLEM	
TILL, THOS. & SON	July 24, 1851	BURSLEM	
TILL, THOS. & SON	October 14, 1851	BURSLEM	
TILL, THOS. & SON	April 01, 1852	BURSLEM	10
TILL, THOS. & SON	April 08, 1852	BURSLEM	
TILL, THOS. & SON	August 13, 1852	BURSLEM	7
TILL, THOS. & SON	September 15, 1852	BURSLEM	
TILL, THOS. & SON	November 24, 1853	BURSLEM	
TILL, THOS. & SON	March 20, 1854	BURSLEM	
TILL, THOS. & SON	June 03, 1854	BURSLEM	7
TILL, THOS. & SONS	April 22, 1865	BURSLEM	5
TILL, THOS. & SONS	March 03, 1869	BURSLEM	
TILL, THOS. & SONS	March 15, 1870	BURSLEM	
TILL, THOS. & SONS	June 22, 1871	BURSLEM	
TILL, THOS. & SONS	February 27, 1873	BURSLEM	
TILL, THOS. & SONS	May 03, 1873	BURSLEM	
TILL, THOS. & SONS	September 01, 1874	BURSLEM	7
TILL, THOS. & SONS	June 19, 1875	BURSLEM	
TILL, THOS. & SONS	July 05, 1876	BURSLEM	7
TILL, THOS. & SONS	June 11, 1879	BURSLEM	
TILL, THOS. & SONS	February 28, 1883	BURSLEM	
TOMKINSON BROS. & CO.	August 04, 1869	HANLEY	
TURNER & TOMKINSON	March 07, 1861	TUNSTALL	
TURNER & TOMKINSON	April 17, 1862	TUNSTALL	
TURNER & TOMKINSON	October 15, 1862	TUNSTALL	
TURNER & TOMKINSON	July 14, 1863	TUNSTALL	
TURNER & TOMKINSON	August 11, 1863	TUNSTALL	
TURNER & TOMKINSON	February 02, 1872	TUNSTALL	
TURNER, G. W. & SONS	September 11, 1877	TUNSTALL	
TURNER, G. W. & SONS	March 27, 1878	TUNSTALL	
TURNER, G. W. & SONS	January 27, 1883	TUNSTALL	
TURNER, G. W. & SONS	February 17, 1883	TUNSTALL	7
TURNER, GODDARD & CO.	November 25, 1870	TUNSTALL	7
TWIGG, JOHN	June 16, 1871	YORKSHIRE	
VENABLES & BAINES	February 17, 1852	BURSLEM	5
VENABLES, H.	July 15, 1863	HANLEY	
VENABLES, H.	August 28, 1863	HANLEY	
VENABLES, H.	September 28, 1863	HANLEY	
VENABLES, H.	October 02, 1863	HANLEY	
VENABLES, MANN & CO.	October 05, 1853	BURSLEM	4
VENABLES, MANN & CO.	April 28, 1855	BURSLEM	
WALKER & CARTER	April 14, 1866	LONGTON	5
WALKER & CARTER	March 26, 1868	LONGTON	7
WALKER & CARTER	June 22, 1877	STOKE	
WALLEY (EDWARD) & T. & R. BOOTE	May 10, 1845	COBRIDGE & BURSLEM	7
WALLEY, E.	June 21, 1850	COBRIDGE	5, 7
WALLEY, E.	April 26, 1851	COBRIDGE	7
WALLEY, E.	April 18, 1856	COBRIDGE	2, 7
WALLEY, E.	November 29, 1856	COBRIDGE	1, 3, 4, 6
WALLEY, E. & W.	January 29, 1858	COBRIDGE	3, 7
WALLEY, E. & W.	November 11, 1858	COBRIDGE	2, 3, 7
WALLEY, E. & W.	May 07, 1859	COBRIDGE	3, 7
WALLEY, E. & W.	December 14, 1859	COBRIDGE	2, 7
WALLEY, EDWARD	August 26, 1851	COBRIDGE	8
WARDLE & CO.	October 17, 1876	HANLEY	7
WARDLE & CO.	August 06, 1879	HANLEY	7
WARDLE & CO.	January 27, 1880	HANLEY	7
WARDLE & CO.	July 09, 1881	HANLEY	7
WARDLE & CO.	October 29, 1881	HANLEY	7
WARDLE & CO.	February 08, 1882	HANLEY	
WARDLE & CO.	June 13, 1882	HANLEY	7
WARDLE & CO.	July 14, 1882	HANLEY	7
WARDLE & CO.	July 19, 1882	HANLEY	
WARDLE & CO.	May 31, 1883	HANLEY	7
WARDLE & CO.	June 21, 1883	HANLEY	7
WARDLE, JAMES	September 01, 1868	HANLEY	
WARDLE, JAMES	July 19, 1869	HANLEY	
WARDLE, JAMES	July 08, 1870	HANLEY	
WARDLE, JAMES	July 16, 1870	HANLEY	
WARDLE, JAMES	August 04, 1870	HANLEY	
WARDLE, JAMES	August 28, 1871	HANLEY	
WEDGE.WOOD (MR.)	May 24, 1849	TUNSTALL	1, 2, 5
WEDGE.WOOD, JOHN	March 17, 1847	TUNSTALL	4, 5x
WEDGE.WOOD, JOHN	September 25, 1847	TUNSTALL	1, 4, 5x
WEDGE.WOOD, JOHN	October 08, 1847	TUNSTALL	1, 4, 5x
WEDGE.WOOD, JOHN	August 23, 1848	TUNSTALL	4, 5
WEDGE.WOOD, JOHN	August 21, 1860	TUNSTALL	5
WEDGWOOD & CO.	January 21, 1861	TUNSTALL	7
WEDGWOOD & CO.	August 22, 1861	TUNSTALL	7
WEDGWOOD & CO.	December 20, 1861	TUNSTALL	
WEDGWOOD & CO.	March 14, 1862	TUNSTALL	
WEDGWOOD & CO.	September 17, 1867	TUNSTALL	5
WEDGWOOD & CO.	September 09, 1868	TUNSTALL	5
WEDGWOOD & CO.	April 05, 1872	TUNSTALL	
WEDGWOOD & CO.	November 06, 1873	TUNSTALL	
WEDGWOOD & CO.	December 05, 1876	TUNSTALL	
WEDGWOOD & CO.	October 30, 1877	TUNSTALL	
WEDGWOOD & CO.	June 16, 1880	TUNSTALL	
WEDGWOOD & CO.	April 08, 1881	TUNSTALL	
WEDGWOOD & CO.	January 30, 1883	TUNSTALL	
WEDGWOOD & CO.	February 02, 1883	TUNSTALL	
WEDGWOOD, J. & CO.	November 23, 1847	ETRURIA	
WEDGWOOD, J. & SONS	November 04, 1850	ETRURIA	
WEDGWOOD, JOSIAH	October 09, 1878	ETRURIA	
WEDGWOOD, JOSIAH	December 13, 1882	ETRURIA	7
WEDGWOOD, JOSIAH & SONS	March 21, 1843	ETRURIA	5, 7, 10
WEDGWOOD, JOSIAH & SONS	May 02, 1843	ETRURIA	
WEDGWOOD, JOSIAH & SONS	August 01, 1846	ETRURIA	2x, 10
WEDGWOOD, JOSIAH & SONS	August 03, 1846	ETRURIA	2x

POTTER	DATE	LOCATION	CATEGORY
WEDGWOOD, JOSIAH & SONS	December 31, 1846	ETRURIA	2x
WEDGWOOD, JOSIAH & SONS	April 22, 1848	ETRURIA	
WEDGWOOD, JOSIAH & SONS	April 27, 1848	ETRURIA	
WEDGWOOD, JOSIAH & SONS	November 01, 1855	ETRURIA	
WEDGWOOD, JOSIAH & SONS	January 31, 1856	ETRURIA	
WEDGWOOD, JOSIAH & SONS	December 10, 1859	ETRURIA	
WEDGWOOD, JOSIAH & SONS	July 18, 1861	ETRURIA	
WEDGWOOD, JOSIAH & SONS	November 29, 1861	ETRURIA	7
WEDGWOOD, JOSIAH & SONS	April 01, 1862	ETRURIA	
WEDGWOOD, JOSIAH & SONS	January 29, 1863	ETRURIA	
WEDGWOOD, JOSIAH & SONS	October 24, 1863	ETRURIA	
WEDGWOOD, JOSIAH & SONS	February 02, 1864	ETRURIA	
WEDGWOOD, JOSIAH & SONS	April 09, 1864	ETRURIA	
WEDGWOOD, JOSIAH & SONS	September 19, 1864	ETRURIA	
WEDGWOOD, JOSIAH & SONS	September 22, 1864	ETRURIA	
WEDGWOOD, JOSIAH & SONS	August 23, 1865	ETRURIA	
WEDGWOOD, JOSIAH & SONS	March 02, 1867	ETRURIA	
WEDGWOOD, JOSIAH & SONS	March 11, 1867	ETRURIA	
WEDGWOOD, JOSIAH & SONS	March 20, 1867	ETRURIA	
WEDGWOOD, JOSIAH & SONS	March 25, 1867	ETRURIA	
WEDGWOOD, JOSIAH & SONS	April 04, 1867	ETRURIA	
WEDGWOOD, JOSIAH & SONS	June 06, 1867	ETRURIA	7
WEDGWOOD, JOSIAH & SONS	July 15, 1867	ETRURIA	
WEDGWOOD, JOSIAH & SONS	October 29, 1867	ETRURIA	
WEDGWOOD, JOSIAH & SONS	December 20, 1867	ETRURIA	7
WEDGWOOD, JOSIAH & SONS	January 31, 1868	ETRURIA	
WEDGWOOD, JOSIAH & SONS	February 12, 1868	ETRURIA	
WEDGWOOD, JOSIAH & SONS	February 18, 1868	ETRURIA	8
WEDGWOOD, JOSIAH & SONS	July 10, 1868	ETRURIA	
WEDGWOOD, JOSIAH & SONS	August 13, 1868	ETRURIA	
WEDGWOOD, JOSIAH & SONS	November 09, 1868	ETRURIA	
WEDGWOOD, JOSIAH & SONS	February 19, 1869	ETRURIA	
WEDGWOOD, JOSIAH & SONS	February 22, 1869	ETRURIA	
WEDGWOOD, JOSIAH & SONS	February 27, 1869	ETRURIA	
WEDGWOOD, JOSIAH & SONS	July 03, 1869	ETRURIA	
WEDGWOOD, JOSIAH & SONS	July 20, 1869	ETRURIA	
WEDGWOOD, JOSIAH & SONS	February 09, 1870	ETRURIA	
WEDGWOOD, JOSIAH & SONS	April 24, 1871	ETRURIA	
WEDGWOOD, JOSIAH & SONS	October 14, 1871	ETRURIA	
WEDGWOOD, JOSIAH & SONS	June 11, 1872	ETRURIA	2x
WEDGWOOD, JOSIAH & SONS	July 02, 1872	ETRURIA	2x
WEDGWOOD, JOSIAH & SONS	October 11, 1872	ETRURIA	2x
WEDGWOOD, JOSIAH & SONS	October 17, 1872	ETRURIA	2x
WEDGWOOD, JOSIAH & SONS	June 15, 1875	ETRURIA	
WEDGWOOD, JOSIAH & SONS	October 02, 1875	ETRURIA	
WEDGWOOD, JOSIAH & SONS	February 02, 1876	ETRURIA	
WEDGWOOD, JOSIAH & SONS	May 22, 1876	ETRURIA	
WEDGWOOD, JOSIAH & SONS	June 19, 1876	ETRURIA	7
WEDGWOOD, JOSIAH & SONS	October 07, 1876	ETRURIA	
WEDGWOOD, JOSIAH & SONS	November 14, 1876	ETRURIA	
WEDGWOOD, JOSIAH & SONS	May 05, 1877	ETRURIA	
WEDGWOOD, JOSIAH & SONS	May 18, 1877	ETRURIA	
WEDGWOOD, JOSIAH & SONS	September 20, 1877	ETRURIA	
WEDGWOOD, JOSIAH & SONS	January 15, 1878	ETRURIA	
WEDGWOOD, JOSIAH & SONS	April 30, 1878	ETRURIA	
WEDGWOOD, JOSIAH & SONS	May 03, 1878	ETRURIA	8
WEDGWOOD, JOSIAH & SONS	May 23, 1878	ETRURIA	
WEDGWOOD, JOSIAH & SONS	May 24, 1878	ETRURIA	
WEDGWOOD, JOSIAH & SONS	June 27, 1878	ETRURIA	
WEDGWOOD, JOSIAH & SONS	July 08, 1878	ETRURIA	
WEDGWOOD, JOSIAH & SONS	July 09, 1878	ETRURIA	
WEDGWOOD, JOSIAH & SONS	July 12, 1878	ETRURIA	
WEDGWOOD, JOSIAH & SONS	July 26, 1878	ETRURIA	
WEDGWOOD, JOSIAH & SONS	July 30, 1878	ETRURIA	
WEDGWOOD, JOSIAH & SONS	September 10, 1878	ETRURIA	
WEDGWOOD, JOSIAH & SONS	February 03, 1879	ETRURIA	
WEDGWOOD, JOSIAH & SONS	March 18, 1879	ETRURIA	
WEDGWOOD, JOSIAH & SONS	April 24, 1879	ETRURIA	
WEDGWOOD, JOSIAH & SONS	June 24, 1879	ETRURIA	
WEDGWOOD, JOSIAH & SONS	July 02, 1879	ETRURIA	
WEDGWOOD, JOSIAH & SONS	October 18, 1879	ETRURIA	
WEDGWOOD, JOSIAH & SONS	November 06, 1879	ETRURIA	
WEDGWOOD, JOSIAH & SONS	December 20, 1879	ETRURIA	
WEDGWOOD, JOSIAH & SONS	March 17, 1880	ETRURIA	
WEDGWOOD, JOSIAH & SONS	June 11, 1880	ETRURIA	7
WEDGWOOD, JOSIAH & SONS	June 19, 1880	ETRURIA	
WEDGWOOD, JOSIAH & SONS	August 18, 1880	ETRURIA	
WEDGWOOD, JOSIAH & SONS	October 06, 1880	ETRURIA	
WEDGWOOD, JOSIAH & SONS	October 13, 1880	ETRURIA	
WEDGWOOD, JOSIAH & SONS	November 09, 1880	ETRURIA	
WEDGWOOD, JOSIAH & SONS	April 30, 1881	ETRURIA	7
WEDGWOOD, JOSIAH & SONS	May 16, 1881	ETRURIA	7
WEDGWOOD, JOSIAH & SONS	May 25, 1881	ETRURIA	
WEDGWOOD, JOSIAH & SONS	July 06, 1881	ETRURIA	
WEDGWOOD, JOSIAH & SONS	June 23, 1882	ETRURIA	7
WEDGWOOD, JOSIAH & SONS	February 24, 1883	ETRURIA	
WEDGWOOD, JOSIAH & SONS	March 20, 1883	ETRURIA	7
WEDGWOOD, JOSIAH & SONS	June 23, 1883	ETRURIA	
WEDGWOOD, JOSIAH & SONS	July 11, 1883	ETRURIA	

POTTER	DATE	LOCATION	CATEGORY
WEDGWOOD, JOSIAH & SONS	July 23, 1883	ETRURIA	
WEDGWOOD, JOSIAH & SONS	September 11, 1883	ETRURIA	7
WHITTINGHAM, FORD & RILEY	February 09, 1880	BURSLEM	
WILEMAN, J. F.	March 24, 1869	FENTON	
WILEMAN, J. F.	November 03, 1871	FENTON	
WILEMAN, J. F.	October 30, 1872	FENTON	8
WILEMAN, J. F.	July 07, 1879	FENTON	8
WILEMAN, J. F.	April 23, 1881	FENTON	
WILEMAN, J. F.	December 23, 1882	FENTON	
WILEMAN, J. F. & CO.	March 16, 1880	FENTON	8
WILEMAN, J. F. & CO.	February 18, 1882	FENTON	8
WILEMAN, J. F. & CO.	November 27, 1882	FENTON	8
WILEMAN, J. F. & CO.	April 21, 1883	FENTON	
WILEMAN, J. F. & CO.	August 31, 1883	FENTON	8
WILEMAN, J. F. & CO.	December 08, 1883	FENTON	
WOOD & BROWNFIELD	March 20, 1848	COBRIDGE	2
WOOD & CO.	January 25, 1877	BURSLEM	7
WOOD & SON	July 17, 1882	BURSLEM	
WOOD & SON	October 11, 1882	BURSLEM	
WOOD & SON	October 16, 1882	BURSLEM	
WOOD & SON	October 13, 1883	BURSLEM	
WOOD, EDMUND, T.	October 31, 1863	TUNSTALL	4, 7
WOOD, ENOCH	July 05, 1845	BURSLEM	5
WOOD, SON & CO.	June 29, 1878	COBRIDGE	
WOOD, WM. & CO.	January 25, 1877	BURSLEM	
WOOD, WM. & CO.	June 08, 1878	BURSLEM	
WOOD, WM. & CO.	May 03, 1881	BURSLEM	
WOOD, WM. & CO.	August 26, 1882	BURSLEM	
WOOLISCROFT, G. & SON	October 27, 1880	ETRURIA	5
WOOLISCROFT, G. & SON	February 28, 1881	HANLEY	
WOOLISCROFT, G. & SON	May 26, 1881	HANLEY	
WOOLISCROFT, GEO.	February 10, 1853	TUNSTALL	4, 5
WOOLISCROFT, GEO.	June 24, 1853	TUNSTALL	
WOOLISCROFT, GEO.	November 19, 1862	TUNSTALL	
WORTHINGTON & HARROP	February 23, 1867	HANLEY	

APPENDIX B18: EARTHENWARE, JUGS & PARIAN WARE: CHRONOLOGICAL LISTING WITH PATTERNS AND SOURCE

Reg. Date	Parcel	Reg. No.	Potter	Pattern	Reference
December 30, 1842	2	3346	EDWARDS, JAMES	Untitled	5
March 21, 1843	5	5993-4	WEDGWOOD, JOSIAH & SONS	Untitled	2
May 13, 1843	4	7122	JONES & WALLEY	Peacock Jug/Hops	2,4,5
September 30, 1844	7	21960	MEIGH, CHARLES	Bacchanalian Dance	1,3,4
January 21, 1845	6	25199	MAYER, T. J. & J.	Rossi	2
March 20, 1845	1	26949	MINTON, HERBERT & CO.	Dancing Amorini	1,3
May 08, 1845	2	27451	MINTON, HERBERT & CO.	Putti	2
May 10, 1845	3	27482	WALLEY (EDWARD) & T. & R. BOOTE	Ranger	1,3
November 15, 1845	2	31128	BAYLEY & BALL	Untitled	4
December 30, 1845	3	32601	FURNIVAL & CLARK	Falstaff	1
March 02, 1846	4	34108	MINTON & CO.	Untitled	2,6
May 26, 1846	2	35116-7	MINTON, HERBERT & CO.	Fruits & Wheat, Society of Arts, Vintage,	1,3,4,6
July 16, 1846	1	36167	RIDGWAY, SON & CO.	Vines in Framework	3
August 01, 1846	2	36447-8	WEDGWOOD, JOSIAH & SONS	Untitled	5
August 03, 1846	2	36451-2	MINTON, HERBERT & CO.	Untitled	5
September 29, 1846	3	37586	MAYER, T. J. & J.	Gothic Figures	5
November 12, 1846	3	38068	MEIGH, C.	York Minster	1,3
December 03, 1846	4	38606	RIDGWAY & ABINGTON	Oak	2,3
February 02, 1847	7	41213	BOOTE, T. & R.	Samuel & Eli	3
February 08, 1847	5	41266-7	MAYER, T. J. & J.	Rossi	5
April 03, 1847	6	42435	ALCOCK, SAMUEL & CO.	Rustic/Ranger	2
April 27, 1847	1	42804	ALCOCK, SAMUEL & CO.	Naomi/Arabic	1,2,3,6
May 14, 1847	1	43170-1	MINTON, HERBERT & CO.	Hops Jug	1,4,6
August 03, 1847	3	44872	ROSE, JOHN & CO.	Untitled	5
August 17, 1847	2	45091-2	COPELAND, W. T.	Adam & Eve/ Portland	5
August 19, 1847	3	45175	MINTON, HERBERT & CO.	Una & The Lion	6
October 04, 1847	3	46232	MINTON, HERBERT & CO.	Dorothea	6
December 10, 1847	3	47562-3	MINTON & CO. & JOHN BELL	Untitled	6
March 07, 1848	1	50635-6	RIDGWAY & ABINGTON	Bulrush, Hops & Barley/Harvest,	1,3
September 18, 1848	4	54487	MEIGH, CHARLES	Trellis Jug	1,3

Reg. Date	Parcel	Reg. No.	Potter	Pattern	Reference
October 17, 1848	3	54901	BOOTE, T. & R.	Infant Samuel/ Samuel & Eli	3
November 04, 1848	2	55174	COPELAND, W. T.	Grapevine/ Convolvulus	2,4,6
November 13, 1848	4	55337	COPELAND, W. T.	Vine	6
November 21, 1848	5	55456-7	MINTON & CO.	Hops	3
February 16, 1849	11	58474	RIDGWAY & ABINGTON	Sylvan	1,3
February 26, 1849	2	58578	ROSE, JOHN & CO.	Shell & Flowers	2
March 26, 1849	5	59232	MINTON & CO.	Untitled	6
March 27, 1849	2	59245	COPE & EDWARDS	Untitled	6
August 15, 1849	2	61986	MINTON, HERBERT & CO.	Squirrel & Bee	5
November 09, 1849	4	63523	COPELAND, W. T.	Lily Of The Valley	1
November 17, 1849	2	63718	MINTON & CO.	Bird & Ivy	2
December 06, 1849	3	64739	COPELAND, W. T.	Untitled	5
June 21, 1850	4	69884	WALLEY, E.	Diana	2,3
July 02, 1850	2	70088	MAYER, T. J. & J.	Birdnesting	1,3,4
September 16, 1850	8	71952	BELL, J. & M. P. & CO.	Untitled	5
October 09, 1850	2	72395-6	MINTON & CO.	Untitled	5
December 19, 1850	6	74786	MAYER, T. J. & J.	Family Jug/ Convolvulus	1,3,4
March 17, 1851	13	77481-91	RIDGWAY, J. & CO.	Bouquet Jug	5
April 26, 1851	3	78634	WALLEY, E.	Ceres	1,2,3
May 30, 1851	4	79085	COPELAND, W. T.	Nymphea/Lotus	1
July 14, 1851	3	79684	COPELAND, W. T.	Untitled	6
July 21, 1851	7	79750-3	BOOTE, T. & R.	Untitled	5
August 16, 1851	2	80184	RIDGWAY & ABINGTON	Nineveh	1,3
October 21, 1851	3	81057	RIDGWAY, WM.	Willie	1
November 13, 1851	2	81518	MEIGH, CHARLES & SON	Thistle	1,3
December 02, 1851	2	81815	MAYER, T. J. & J.	Paul & Virginia	1
March 26, 1852	3	84471	BELL, J. & M. P. & CO.	Untitled	2
April 01, 1852	1	84541	TILL, THOS. & SON	Floral	2
April 21, 1852	4	84837	RAY, GEO.	Dancers	3
June 05, 1852	5	85248	MINTON & CO.	Greek Key	2
June 21, 1852	2	85404	LOCKETT, J. & T.	Bacchanalin Cherubs	1,3
July 23, 1852	3	85803-4	MINTON & CO.	Medieval Revelry, Plain Jug	2,6
August 13, 1852	5	86126	TILL, THOS. & SON	Untitled	3
August 25, 1852	4	86318	MEIGH, CHARLES & SON	Four Seasons	1,3
September 03, 1852	7	86473	MINTON & CO.	Ivy	2,6
September 16, 1852	1	86657	MINTON & CO.	Mermaid/Merman & Cupid	2,6
October 25, 1852	2	87228	BROWNFIELD, WM.	Mazeppa	5
November 25, 1852	4	88037	KEYS & MOUNTFORD	Untitled	6
January 12, 1853	6	88978	GOODFELLOW, THOS.	Niagra	5
February 11, 1853	6	89646	WORTHINGTON, THOS. & GREEN, J.	Untitled	2
February 26, 1853	5	89958	COPELAND, W. T.	Harvest Barrel	2,3,6
May 07, 1853	5	91121-4	ALCOCK, JOHN	Untitled	5
June 07, 1853	3	91329	WOOD, GEO. & CO.	Untitled	2
June 14, 1853	2	91405-6	LIVESLEY, POWELL & CO.	Lily,Julius Ceaser	2
June 22, 1853	3	91469	PANKHURST & DIMMOCK	Snake & Dog	1
January 30, 1854	4	94815	ALCOCK, SAMUEL & CO.	Ivy	4
February 23, 1854	3	95163	COPELAND, W. T.	Victoria,Wellington	2
March 27, 1854	3	95448	BAGULEY, GEO.	Garland & Cupid	2,5
March 27, 1854	6	95451	DEAVILLE, J.	Untitled	2
April 01, 1854	4	95510	BROWNFIELD, WM.	Kent	2
April 15, 1854	1	95611	BAGULEY, GEO.	Untitled	5
June 03, 1854	2	96003	TILL, THOS. & SON	DaVid & Goliath/ Cain & Abel	2
June 09, 1854	2	96039	MEIGH, CHAS. & SON	Untitled	4
September 12, 1854	2	96826	COPELAND, W. T.	Hop Jug/Tulip Jug	1,3,6
October 31, 1854	2	97508	RAY, GEO.	Bird Feeding	5
December 27, 1854	3	98640	ALCOCK, SAMUEL & CO.	Royal Patent Jug	4,6
December 27, 1854	4	98641	PANKHURST & DIMMOCK	Ivy	3,4
January 04, 1855	2	98696	WORTHINGTON & GREEN	Cup Tosser	5
January 19, 1855	3	99086	PANKHURST & DIMMOCK	Untitled	2
February 07, 1855	2	99310	ALCOCK, JOHN	Untitled	2
February 17, 1855	3	99394	PRATT & CO.	Cupid & Bow	5
March 13, 1855	4	99653	WARBURTON & BRITTON	Untitled	2
April 26, 1855	1	99972-4	BROWNFIELD, WM.	Plain Jug,Linen Fold Jug	4
May 14, 1855	3	100116	MINTON & CO.	Untitled	6
July 04, 1855	5	100624	THOMPSON, J.	Three Graces	5
July 24, 1855	1	100816	MEIGH, CHAS. & SON	Untitled	5
August 06, 1855	1	101019	DUDSON, JAMES	Pinapple Jug	3
September 27, 1855	4	101624	BEVINGTON, SAML. & SON	Sacrifice Of Iphigenia	2
November 28, 1855	3	102785	BROWNFIELD, WM.	Wicker	4
January 15, 1856	4	103404	PANKHURST, JAMES & CO.	Home & Abroad	3
January 23, 1856	3	103506	ROBERTS J.	Untitled	2
January 23, 1856	3	103507	MINTON & CO.	Wheat & Leaf	2,5,6
April 18, 1856	2	104392	BEECH, WILLIAM	May They Ever Be United	5
April 18, 1856	6	104396	WALLEY, E.	George Washington	1,3
April 18, 1856	7	104397	RIDGWAY & ABINGTON	John Barleycorn	1
April 30, 1856	3	104602-3	BROWNFIELD, WM.	Gothic Ivy	1,4
June 13, 1856	3	105059	MEIGH, CHAS. & SON	Amphitrite	1,3,4
June 28, 1856	3	105223	WORTHINGTON & GREEN	Untitled	2,5
October 16, 1856	2	106671-2	MINTON & CO.	Untitled	5
October 22, 1856	3	106770	COPELAND, W. T.	Tulip	6
November 27, 1856	6	107714	BROWNFIELD, WM.	Untitled	5
February 09, 1857	4	108930	MINTON & CO.	Hops & Barley	2,6
April 19, 1857	1	110160	COPELAND, W. T.	Untitled	7
June 05, 1857	3	110096-7	BROWNFIELD, WM.	Trade Scantia	5
June 19, 1857	1	110160	COPELAND, W. T.	Untitled	2, 7
June 19, 1857	2	110161	WILKINSON & RICKHUSS	Aquatic	2
October 14, 1857	1	111585	RIDGWAY & ABINGTON	Fuchsia	1,3
December 09, 1857	2	112354	BROWNFIELD, WM.	Arrowhead	2
January 29, 1858	4	112876	WALLEY, E. & W.	Haverlock	4
July 29, 1858	4	114532	ALCOCK, SAMUEL & CO.	Bulrush/ Draped Linenfold	2,6
August 24, 1858	2	114763	BROWNFIELD, WM.	Floral	5
September 03, 1858	2	115120	SHARPE BROS. & CO.	Corn On The Cob	2,5
October 05, 1858	3	115902	BROWNFIELD, WM.	Jewel Jug	3
October 05, 1858	3	116176	MINTON & CO.	Pinapple Jug	3
October 07, 1858	1	115953	RIDGWAY & ABINGTON	Oporto	2
October 29, 1858	2	116468	GREEN, B.	Untitled	5
November 11, 1858	2	116737	WALLEY, E. & W.	Gleaner	1,3,4
February 08, 1859	6	118415	LEVESON HILL (Excrs. of)	Untitled	2
March 21, 1859	7	118891	BOOTE, T. & R.	Four Panels	2,5
March 29, 1859	7	119137	BOOTE, T. & R.	Enville	4,5
May 07, 1859	1	119721-2	WALLEY, E. & W.	Vintage	2
May 20, 1859	1	119968	BROWNFIELD, WM.	Shamrock	2
May 26, 1859	1	120096	LOCKETT, BAGULEY & COOPER	Untitled	2
August 27, 1859	6	121724	ALCOCK, SAMUEL & CO.	Daniel In The Lion's Den	6
October 25, 1859	1	123389-91	MINTON & CO.	Untitled	5
November 05, 1859	4	123816	BROWNFIELD, WM.	Fern	1,3
December 14, 1859	2	124716	WALLEY, E. & W.	Sportman/ Diamond Checkerboard	1,4
March 01, 1860	2	126950	BATES, BROWN-WESTHEAD & MOORE	Untitled	6
May 19, 1860	9	129129	LOCKETT, BAGULEY & COOPER	Untitled	2
June 06, 1860	4	129680-2	BROWNFIELD, WM.	Eglantine	1
January 08, 1861	6	137217	BOOTE, T. & R.	Untitled	5
January 21, 1861	7	137529	WEDGWOOD & CO.	Untitled	5
April 05, 1861	3	139360	PINDER, BOURNE & HOPE	Acanthus	2,8
April 20, 1861	6	139945	PRATT, F. & R.	Untitled	5
April 25, 1861	2	140200	DUDSON, JAMES	Barley/Wheat Ears	2,3
May 06, 1861	5	140480-1	OLD HALL EARTHEN-WARE CO., THE	Untitled	2,5
May 09, 1861	3	140578	BATES, BROWN-WESTHEAD & MOORE	Untitled	5
May 31, 1861	3	141114	CORK, EDGE & MALKIN	Basketweave	1,4
June 04, 1861	1	141214	BATES, BROWN-WESTHEAD & MOORE	Untitled	2,6
June 11, 1861	2	141326	COPELAND, W. T.	Untitled	5
July 04, 1861	2	141715	LOCKETT & COOPER	Untitled	5
July 05, 1861	2	141727	BEECH & HANCOCK	Coral & Seaweed	5
July 06, 1861	2	141732	BROWNFIELD, WM.	Donatello	4
August 22, 1861	7	142847	WEDGWOOD & CO.	Sylvan / Stylized Bloom	1,8
September 18, 1861	7	143679	BEECH, WM.	Untitled	5
October 11, 1861	3	144767	MOUNTFORD & SCARRATT	Untitled	5
October 15, 1861	3	144896	LEVESON HILL (Excrs. of)	Untitled	5
October 18, 1861	3	145157	COPELAND, W. T.	Untitled	5
November 15, 1861	3	146352-4	CLEMENTSON, J.	Untitled	2
November 29, 1861	5	146924	WEDGWOOD, JOSIAH & SONS	Doric	4
December 04, 1861	7	147309-10	BROWNFIELD, WM.	Union	1,4,6
December 05, 1861	5	147322	TILL, BULLOCK & SMITH	Untitled	5
January 25, 1862	3	148870	BROWNFIELD, WM.	International	1,3
February 01, 1862	4	149090	ELLIOT BROS.	Untitled	2
February 27, 1862	4	149673-4	DUDSON, JAMES	Untitled	2
March 13, 1862	6	149938	COPELAND, W. T.	Untitled	5
March 22, 1862	9	150152	BOOTE, T. & R.	Venetia	5
March 28, 1862	5	150303	BELL, J. & M. P. & CO.	Untitled	5
March 29, 1862	3	150322	MINTON & CO.	Untitled	5
April 09, 1862	3	150538	OLD HALL EARTHEN-WARE CO. LTD., THE	Prince Consort	1,3,4
May 09, 1862	9	151568	BROWN, T. C. WESTHEAD-MOORE & CO.	Untitled	5
May 29, 1862	5	152013	FURNIVAL, J. & CO.	Untitled	5
July 04, 1862	8	152963	CLEMENTSON, J.	Untitled	5
July 14, 1862	2	153127	BEECH & HANCOCK	Gothic Floral	2,3,4
August 18, 1862	4	153827	HULSE, NIXON & ADDERLEY	Untitled	5
August 19, 1862	4	153844	ASHWORTH, G. L. & BROS.	Untitled	5
September 12, 1862	2	154693	COOPER, THOS.	Untitled	5
September 26, 1862	1	155200-2	HOPE & CARTER	Untitled	5
October 23, 1862	8	156166	BAKER, WM. & CO.	Untitled	5

Reg. Date	Parcel	Reg. No.	Potter	Pattern	Reference
December 09, 1862	5	158221	COOPER, THOMAS	Edward & Alexandra	4
January 16, 1863	2	159123	MINTON & CO.	Untitled	2,6
January 16, 1863	8	159153	LIDDLE, ELLIOT & SONS	Circular	1,3
March 13, 1863	2	160456	HOPE & CARTER	Untitled	2,
March 13, 1863	3	160457	WILKINSON & SONS	Untitled	5
March 20, 1863	8	160752	WORTHINGTON & GREEN	Untitled	5
March 20, 1863	9	160753	PRATT, JOHN & CO.	Untitled	5
March 21, 1863	2	160759	BEECH & HANCOCK	Foliage Plants	4
March 21, 1863	4	160761	HULSE, NIXON & ADDERLEY	Untitled	5
April 11, 1863	1	161404	MACINTYRE, J.	Untitled	2
April 25, 1863	1	161861	BEECH & HANCOCK	White Fawn	1
April 30, 1863	3	162021	WILKINSON & SON	Untitled	5
May 15, 1863	10	162304	HARDING & COTTERILL	Untitled	2
May 22, 1863	4	162618-9	COPELAND, W. T.	Untitled	6
August 12, 1863	4	165171	HANCOCK, WHITTINGHAM & CO.	Untitled	5
October 14, 1863	7	167289	BROWNFIELD, WM.	Albion	1,3
October 31, 1863	3	167612	WOOD, EDMUND, T.	Untitled	5
November 19, 1863	10	168765	KIRKHAM, WM.	Untitled	2
December 18, 1863	4	170294	PRATT, F. & R. & CO.	Holly & Mistletoe	4
December 23, 1863	2	170418	BROWNFIELD, WM.	Untitled	5
February 13, 1864	6	171673	COPELAND, W. T.	Pansey	1,3,6
February 25, 1864	6	172060	LIDDLE, ELLIOT & SON	Untitled	5
February 29, 1864	6	172183	HAMSPON, J. & D.	Untitled	5
March 12, 1864	5	172559	CORK, EDGE & MALKIN	Untitled	5
March 23, 1864	4	172876	BURGESS & LEIGH	Giraffe	2
April 21, 1864	4	173785	BROWN, T. C. WESTHEAD-MOORE & CO.	Pineapple	6,8
April 21, 1864	8	173799	LIDDLE, ELLIOT & SON	Corn Cob	1,3
April 29, 1864	2	174168	BROWNFIELD, WM.	Argos	1
May 09, 1864	3	174424	BOUGHTON, R. T.	Untitled	5
June 09, 1864	7	175330	MINTON & CO.	Untitled	6
July 02, 1864	3	175959	WOOD & SALE (Transfered to Dudson 2/65)	Untitled	2,8
September 10, 1864	1	178410	MINTON & CO.	Untitled	5
October 12, 1864	4	179656	BROWNFIELD, WM.	Tyrol	2
October 28, 1864	4	180453	BODLEY & HARROLD	Untitled	4
October 29, 1864	2	180486	COLLINSON, CHAS. & CO.	Untitled	4
October 31, 1864	3	180569	CORK, EDGE & MALKIN	Untitled	5
November 04, 1864	3	180713	LIVESLEY, POWELL & CO.	Untitled	5
November 29, 1864	1	181843	HOPE & CARTER	Stylized Flowers	1
December 09, 1864	1	182203	KIRKHAM, WM.	Untitled	5
January 06, 1865	4	182807	MINTON & CO.	Untitled	6
April 01, 1865	4	185520	BROWNFIELD, WM.	Florence	2,3
May 02, 1865	8	186477	LIVESLEY, POWELL & CO.	Untitled	5
June 29, 1865	2	187847-8	BODLEY, ED. F. & CO.	Wheatshef	2,6
July 12, 1865	3	188167	EDWARDS, JAMES & SON	Strapwork	2
October 30, 1865	4	191407-8	BROWNFIELD, WM.	Tiverton	1
December 23, 1865	3	193844	DUDSON, JAMES	Argyle	2,3
January 31, 1866	5	194840	EDWARDS, JAMES & SON	Untitled	5
September 06, 1866	4	200599	PRATT, F. & R. & CO.	Untitled	4
October 13, 1866	3	202493	FURNIVAL, THOS.	Untitled	5
November 03, 1866	6	203173	MINTON & CO.	Untitled	6
November 15, 1866	4	203912	GRANGER, GEO. & CO.	Classical Figures	3
December 13, 1866	4	204764	LIDDLE, ELLIOTT & SON	Untitled	5
December 19, 1866	5	205088	MEIR, JOHN & SON	Untitled	2
March 15, 1867	7	206762-6	BROWNFIELD, WM.	Cashmere	1,3,6
May 06, 1867	3	207938	BELL, J. & M. P. & CO.	Fishwives	2,3
June 06, 1867	3	208750	WEDGWOOD, JOSIAH & SONS	Caterer	2
June 21, 1867	4	209057	BROWNFIELD, WM.	Napoleon	5
July 04, 1867	5	209362	RIDGWAY, E. J.	Fluted Jug	6
September 21, 1867	1	211536	ASHWORTH, G. L. & BROS.	Arches & Medallions	2,3
October 10, 1867	1	212194	BOOTH, THOS.	Untitled	2
October 28, 1867	4	212956	COPELAND, W. T. & SONS	Oak Motifs	6
October 31, 1867	7	213065	POWELL & BISHOP	Hops Jug	2
December 03, 1867	3	214618	COPELAND, W. T. & SONS	Untitled	7
December 20, 1867	3	215085	WEDGWOOD, JOSIAH & SONS	Untitled	5
December 27, 1867	1	215314	BEBBINGTON, J. & J. B.	Four Ages Of Woman	3
January 07, 1868	8	215636	THOMPSON BROS.	Untitled	5
January 07, 1868	11	215642	COCKSON, CHETWYND & CO.	Untitled	5
January 30, 1868	6	216333	FURNIVAL, J. & CO.	Untitled	5
February 05, 1868	4	216451	ADAMS, SCRIVENER & CO.	Untitled	5
February 05, 1868	8	216470	HODGKINSON, E.	Untitled	5
February 18, 1868	2	216897	BROWN, T. C. WESTHEAD-MOORE & CO.	Untitled	5
February 27, 1868	5	217100	ALCOCK & DIGORY	Untitled	6
March 05, 1868	15	217212	MINTON & CO.	Untitled	5
March 26, 1868	3	217630	WALKER & CARTER	Untitled	5
May 13, 1868	1	218664	ADAMS, SCRIVENER & CO.	Untitled	5
May 30, 1868	4	219042	BOOTE, T. & R.	Untitled	5
June 12, 1868	5	219316-7	BROWNFIELD, WM.	Hampton	2
July 16, 1868	3	219833	HACKNEY & CO.	Untitled	5
July 24, 1868	4	219997	COPELAND, W. T. & SONS	Arches & Scrolls	1,6
July 30, 1868	6	220183	ADAMS, SCRIVENER & CO.	Untitled	5
September 04, 1868	6	221203	GELSON BROS.	Untitled	5
September 09, 1868	5	221312	JONES, F. & CO.	Victor	5
October 09, 1868	3	222477	HOPE & CARTER	Untitled	5
October 17, 1868	4	223063	MINTON & CO.	Untitled	5
October 21, 1868	8	223308	BROWNFIELD, WM. (Reg'd by W.P.&G.Phillips)	Westminster	1
November 21, 1868	5	224539	MINTON & CO.	Untitled	6
November 25, 1868	4	224724	CORK, EDGE & MALKIN	Ruth	1,3
December 14, 1868	7	225441	COCKSON, CHETWYND & CO.	Untitled	5
December 23, 1868	5	225734	MINTON & CO.	Pineapple Jug	1
December 31, 1868	6	225993	ASHWORTH, G. L. & BROS.	Dagmar	4
February 02, 1869	4	226928	YEARSLEY, GEO.	Untitled	6
March 01, 1869	8	227558	WORTHINGTON & SON	Untitled	5
March 24, 1869	1	228141	WILEMAN, J. F.	Untitled	5
May 26, 1869	4	229627	BOOTH, THOS.	Sweep Race	3
June 19, 1869	5	230183-4	BROWNFIELD, WM.	Severn	2,3
September 22, 1869	10	233527	BAILEY, W. & J. A.	Untitled	5
September 30, 1869	8	233864-6	BROWN, T. C. WESTHEAD-MOORE & CO.	Untitled	6
October 26, 1869	2	235158	ELLIS, JAMES & SON	Corn Cob	4,6
October 29, 1869	4	235942	POWELL & BISHOP	Untitled	5
November 15, 1869	8	236203-7	LIDDLE, ELLIOT & SON	Fern	4
December 18, 1869	2	237229	POWELL & BISHOP	Untitled	2
January 27, 1870	8	238388	HOBSON, CHAS.	Untitled	5
February 04, 1870	7	238603	POWELL & BISHOP	Untitled	5
March 23, 1870	9	239793	BLACKSHAW, J. & CO.	Untitled	5
April 07, 1870	11	240386	HARVEY ADAMS & CO.	Untitled	5
May 05, 1870	1	241231	OLDHAM, JAMES & CO.	Untitled	5
May 26, 1870	5	241960	MINTON & CO.	Untitled	5
June 10, 1870	1	242392-4	BROWNFIELD, WM.	Nile, Plain,	2,3,4
June 27, 1870	1	242715	JONES, GEO.	Pineapple	5
July 15, 1870	1	243207	COPELAND, W. T. & SONS	Aesthetic/Marsh Marigold/Leaves in Cartouche	1,2,3,6
July 22, 1870	1	243385	CORK, EDGE & MALKIN	Medallion	1
October 04, 1870	8	245464	MINTON & CO.	Untitled	5
November 10, 1870	5	247071-3	MINTON & CO.	Marne	4
November 25, 1870	2	248052	TURNER, GODDARD & CO.	Untitled	5
February 20, 1871	2	250479	ELSMORE & FORSTER	Untitled	5
March 29, 1871	1	251329	FURNIVAL, THOS. & SON	Untitled	5
May 02, 1871	4	252177-80	BROWNFIELD, WM. & SON	Worcester	3
May 06, 1871	1	252258	PHILLIPS, W. P. & G. & PEARCE	Untitled	5
July 15, 1871	2	254030	BOOTH, THOS.	Untitled	2
August 30, 1871	4	255320	BARLOW, THOS.	Untitled	5
September 25, 1871	8	256079	BROWN, T. C. WESTHEAD-MOORE & CO.	Untitled	2
October 19, 1871	6	256907	COPELAND, W. T. & SONS	Oriental Band	3,6
January 01, 1872	6	259077	EDGE, MALKIN & CO.	Untitled	2
February 15, 1872	3	260463	POWELL & BISHOP	Untitled	5
March 07, 1872	10	260998	BATES, ELLIOTT & CO.	Convolvulus	3
April 10, 1872	11	261749	FURNIVAL, THOS. & SON	Untitled	5
May 02, 1872	11	262429	FURNIVAL, THOS. & SON	Untitled	5
May 11, 1872	4	262672	BOOTH, THOS.	Untitled	5
May 27, 1872	1	262951	JONES, GEO.	Untitled	5
June 03, 1872	6	263106	WATCOMBE TERRA COTTA CLAY CO.	Untitled	5
June 11, 1872	12	263348	COPELAND, W. T. & SONS	Untitled	7
July 02, 1872	2	263883-4	ROBINSON & LEADBEATER	Untitled	6
July 15, 1872	4	264194	ROBINSON & LEADBEATER	Untitled	6
September 02, 1872	8	265687	BATES, ELLIOTT & CO.	Untitled	2
September 26, 1872	2	266633	JONES, F.	Untitled	2
September 26, 1872	5	266636	CARTLIDGE, W. E.	Untitled	5
October 18, 1872	5	267317	JONES, GEO.	Untitled	5
October 30, 1872	5	267527	BROWNHILLS POTTERY, THE	Untitled	5
December 11, 1872	8	268749	OLD HALL EARTHEN-WARE CO., THE	Untitled	5
December 14, 1872	5	268806-7	BROWNFIELD, WM. & SON	Cupid	1,3,6
December 24, 1872	1	269197	COCKSON & CHETWYND	Untitled	5
December 27, 1872	8	269270	SCRIVENER, R. G. & CO.	Untitled	5
January 13, 1873	4	269621	COPELAND, W. T. & SONS	Untitled	5
January 15, 1873	2	269690	WORTHINGTON & SON	Untitled	5
February 19, 1873	14	270600-1	BEVINGTON, J. & T.	Untitled	6
February 25, 1873	6	270700	JONES, GEO.	Untitled	6
April 23, 1873	6	272293	GELSON BROS.	Untitled	5
May 12, 1873	8	272835	BROWN, T. C. WESTHEAD-MOORE & CO.	Untitled	2,6
May 30, 1873	15	273376	BROWN, T. C. WESTHEAD-MOORE & CO.	Untitled	6
June 19, 1873	3	273804	PINDER & BOURNE & CO.	Untitled	2
August 30, 1873	2	275661	BROWN, T. C. WESTHEAD-MOORE & CO.	Untitled	6
September 25, 1873	10	276522	BEECH, JANE	Untitled	5
November 12, 1873	3	278185	WORTHINGTON & SON	Untitled	5
February 09, 1874	5	280344	BODLEY & CO.	Untitled	6
February 14, 1874	9	280492	WORTHINGTON & SON	Untitled	5
February 19, 1874	1	280609	JONES, GEO. & SONS	Untitled	5
March 27, 1874	2	281404	WORTHINGTON & SON	Untitled	5
March 30, 1874	1	281437	WORTHINGTON & SON	Untitled	5

Reg. Date	Parcel	Reg. No.	Potter	Pattern	Reference
April 25, 1874	2	281984	JONES, GEO. & SONS	Untitled	5
April 29, 1874	9	282091	FURNIVAL, T. & SON	Untitled	5
April 30, 1874	2	282098	BOOTH, THOS. & SONS	Untitled	5
May 11, 1874	4	282253	HOLLAND & GREEN	Untitled	5
June 17, 1874	7	283041	EDGE, MALKIN & CO.	Trentham	4
June 26, 1874	4	283275	PINDER, BOURNE & CO.	Untitled	2
August 01, 1874	9	284136	COCKSON & CHETWYND	Untitled	5
September 01, 1874	3	284791	TILL, THOS. & SONS	Untitled	5
September 03, 1874	12	284884-5	COCKSON & CHETWYND	Untitled	5
September 10, 1874	3	285013	BROWNFIELD, WM. & SON	Bangor/Mandarin/ HongKong/Audley	5
October 10, 1874	4	286134	MINTONS	Cat Jug	6
November 03, 1874	4	286721	CORN, W. & E.	Untitled	5
December 08, 1874	2	287699	JONES, GEO. & SONS	Untitled	5
January 23, 1875	9	288756	BROWN, T. C. WESTHEAD-MOORE & CO.	Untitled	5
January 29, 1875	1	288861	WORTHINGTON & SON	Untitled	5
March 05, 1875	2	289769	BROWNFIELD, WM. & SON	Untitled	2
March 12, 1875	5	289874-6	JONES, GEO. & SONS	Untitled	5
March 30, 1875	1	290186	BOOTH, THOS. & SONS	Ribbons & Tassels	3
April 07, 1875	3	290352	MINTONS	Untitled	2,6
May 07, 1875	8	291110	BURGESS & LEIGH	Untitled	5
May 26, 1875	6	291518-20	BROWN, T. C. WESTHEAD-MOORE & CO.	Untitled	6
June 12, 1875	10	292042	FURNIVAL, THOS. & SON	Untitled	5
June 26, 1875	2	292367-70	JONES, GEO. & SONS	Untitled	6
September 13, 1875	2	294434-5	JONES, GEO. & SONS	Untitled	2,6
September 30, 1875	4	294827	EDWARDS, JOHN	Untitled	5
October 11, 1875	10	295014	BROWNHILLS POTTERY CO., THE	Untitled	5
November 08, 1875	8	295803	COPELAND, W. T. & SONS	Untitled	6
December 29, 1875	6	297246-7	BROWN, T. C. WESTHEAD-MOORE & CO.	Untitled	6
January 24, 1876	6	297863	BATES, WALKER & CO.	Untitled	5
January 26, 1876	3	297978	POWELL & BISHOP	Untitled	5
January 28, 1876	8	298018	EDWARDS, JAMES & SON	Untitled	5
January 29, 1876	3	298027-9	BROWNFIELD, WM. & SON	Yeddo	1,3,6
February 29, 1876	9	298693	DIMMOCK, J. & CO.	Untitled	5
March 14, 1876	5	299177	BROWN, T. C. WESTHEAD-MOORE & CO.	Untitled	5
March 17, 1876	5	299236	MINTONS	Untitled	6
March 23, 1876	8	299366	BODLEY, E. J. D.	Untitled	5
March 28, 1876	8	299474	WITHENSHAW, W. E.	Untitled	5
April 27, 1876	3	300260	MINTONS	Untitled	6
May 08, 1876	7	300423	BROWN, T. C. WESTHEAD-MOORE & CO.	Untitled	5
June 03, 1876	2	301030	MINTONS	Untitled	6
June 09, 1876	6	301164	COPELAND, W. T. & SONS	Untitled	5
June 19, 1876	2	301302	WEDGWOOD, JOSIAH & SONS	Untitled	2
July 05, 1876	1	301619	TILL, THOS. & SONS	Untitled	5
July 18, 1876	3	301984	SOANE & SMITH	Untitled	5
September 06, 1876	9	303308	PINDER & BOURNE & CO.	Early Cartouche	2,6
September 06, 1876	10	303309	BROWNFIELD, WM. & SONS	Water Jug	5,6
September 09, 1876	9	303456	BROWN, T. C. WESTHEAD-MOORE & CO.	Untitled	5
September 20, 1876	3	303732	HOLLINGSHEAD & KIRKHAM	Untitled	5
September 28, 1876	10	303942	HOPE & CARTER	Untitled	2
October 07, 1876	2	304128	HARROP, WM.	Untitled	2
October 07, 1876	6	304144-5	ADAMS, WM.	Untitled	5
October 17, 1876	9	304383	WARDLE & CO.	Untitled	5
October 19, 1876	3	304428	BURGESS, LEIGH & CO.	Untitled	5
October 21, 1876	3	304473	EDGE, MALKIN & CO.	Untitled	2
November 08, 1876	3	305080	JONES, GEO. & SONS	Untitled	6
November 14, 1876	8	305195	CLEMENTSON BROS.	Untitled	5
November 17, 1876	3	305222	BANKS & THORLEY	Untitled	5
November 29, 1876	11	305568	FURNIVAL, THOS. & SONS	Untitled	5
December 14, 1876	11	305973	DIMMOCK, J. & CO.	Untitled	5
December 21, 1876	2	306207	GROVE, F. W. & STARK, J.	Untitled	5
January 25, 1877	6	307236	WOOD & CO.	Untitled	5
February 02, 1877	7	307497	WORCESTER ROYAL PORCELAIN CO., LTD.	Untitled	5
February 07, 1877	7	307570-2	BROWNFIELD, WM. & SONS	Medieval Jug	5
April 05, 1877	2	308934	FORD, CHALLINOR & CO.	Untitled	5
May 12, 1877	7	310034	FURNIVAL, THOS. & SONS	Untitled	5
June 01, 1877	2	310599	HAMMERSLEY, J. & R.	Untitled	5
June 07, 1877	2	310710	HOLDCROFT, JOSEPH	Untitled	2
June 26, 1877	11	311366	FURNIVAL, T. & SONS	Untitled	5
July 02, 1877	3	311523	COPELAND, W. T. & SONS	Untitled	2,6
July 17, 1877	9	312019-21	EDWARDS, JAMES & SON	Stylized Floral	2
July 25, 1877	5	312187	FORD, CHALLINOR & CO.	Untitled	2
September 28, 1877	9	314675	HOLDCROFT, JOSEPH	Untitled	2
October 10, 1877	5	315104-5	BROWNFIELD, WM. & SONS	Olympus	5
October 24, 1877	14	315574	PRATT, F. & R. & CO.	Birds In Bamboo	2,3
November 06, 1877	11	315954-6	BROWNFIELD, WM. & SONS	Leek	5,6
November 07, 1877	10	316101	PINDER, BOURNE & CO.	Japanese Sprays	1
December 01, 1877	6	316764	OAKS, CLARE & CHADWICK	Untitled	5
December 22, 1877	5	317427-8	BROWNFIELD, WM. & SONS	Hudson	1,3,6
December 29, 1877	6	317494	BROWN, T. C. WESTHEAD-MOORE & CO.	Untitled	6
February 28, 1878	3	319041	DUNN, BENNETT & CO.	Untitled	2
March 09, 1878	11	319296	POWELL & BISHOP	Untitled	2
March 13, 1878	10	319394	COPELAND, W. T. & SONS	Untitled	5
April 20, 1878	2	320606	FURNIVAL, THOS. & SONS	Untitled	5
May 03, 1878	2	321028	WEDGWOOD, JOSIAH & SONS	Under The British Flag	6
May 21, 1878	11	321693	BANKS & THORLEY	Untitled	5
June 04, 1878	9	322168	FURNIVAL, F. & SONS	Untitled	2
July 01, 1878	1	322791	BURGESS & LEIGH	Turin	5
July 12, 1878	13	323626	LEAR, SAMUEL	Untitled	5
July 20, 1878	6	323893	MEIR, JOHN & SON	Untitled	5
October 23, 1878	1	328018	BROWNHILLS POTTERY CO., THE	Untitled	2
November 04, 1878	1	328699	EDGE, MALKIN & CO.	Tuscan	5
November 05, 1878	17	328790-2	BODLEY, E. J. D.	Untitled	6
December 02, 1878	7	329901	BROWN, T. C. WESTHEAD-MOORE & CO.	Untitled	6
January 09, 1879	8	330997-8	BROWNFIELD, WM. & SONS	Swirling Fish, Yesso Jug	5
January 16, 1879	13	331342	PRATT, F. & R. & CO.	Toucan	2
January 29, 1879	2	331600	FURNIVAL, T. & SONS	Untitled	5
March 01, 1879	1	332837	FURNIVAL, T. & SONS	Untitled	5
March 13, 1879	1	333241-4	DAVENPORT, WM. & CO.	Untitled	6
March 13, 1879	14	333301	CLEMENTSON BROS.	Untitled	5
March 28, 1879	6	333801	CLEMENTSON BROS.	Untitled	2
May 13, 1879	4	335148	PINDER, BOURNE & CO.	Untitled	5
June 13, 1879	13	336132	BROWN, T. C. WESTHEAD-MOORE & CO.	Untitled	6
July 09, 1879	12	337058	BROWN, T. C. WESTHEAD-MOORE & CO.	Untitled	6
July 16, 1879	14	337177	BROWN, T. C. WESTHEAD-MOORE & CO.	Untitled	6
August 06, 1879	6	337958	WARDLE & CO.	Untitled	5
October 15, 1879	1	341347	MINTONS	Untitled	6
October 27, 1879	9	341997	BODLEY, E. F. & CO.	Untitled	6
November 21, 1879	6	343148	MINTONS	Untitled	2,6
December 06, 1879	2	343815	BOOTE, T. & R.	Untitled	5
December 19, 1879	1	344452	CLEMENTSON BROS.	Untitled	5
January 16, 1880	8	345288	FIELDING, S. & CO.	Untitled	5
January 27, 1880	13	345798	WARDLE & CO.	Untitled	5
January 28, 1880	3	345801	BROWN, T. C. WESTHEAD-MOORE & CO.	Untitled	6
February 14, 1880	14	346467	BATES, GILDEA & WALKER	Untitled	6
February 24, 1880	11	346870	HARROP, WM. & CO.	Grecian	5
March 08, 1880	10	347360	HARROP, W. & CO.	Untitled	5
March 12, 1880	4	347476	ADDERLEY, W. A.	Untitled	5
April 19, 1880	11	348913	WORCESTER ROYAL PORCELAIN CO., LTD.	Untitled	5
April 22, 1880	5	349026	GRINDLEY, W. H. & CO.	Untitled	5
April 30, 1880	6	349380	FURNIVAL, T. & SONS	Untitled	5
May 05, 1880	13	349528	FIELDING, S. & CO.	Untitled	5
May 10, 1880	6	349693	POWELL, BISHOP & STONIER	Untitled	5
May 13, 1880	8	349852	MINTONS	Untitled	5
May 25, 1880	4	350098	BROWNFIELD, WM. & SONS	Missouri	5,6
June 08, 1880	1	350477	JONES, GEO. & SONS	Untitled	6
June 10, 1880	4	350555	BODLEY, E. J. D.	Untitled	5
June 10, 1880	12	350613	DIMMOCK, J. & CO.	Untitled	6
June 11, 1880	3	350616	WEDGWOOD, JOSIAH & SONS	Wicker	5
June 15, 1880	4	350848	BUCKLEY, WOOD & CO	Untitled	5
June 17, 1880	4	351024	LEAR, SAMUEL	Untitled	5
June 17, 1880	20	351063	CRYSTAL (PALACE) PORCELAIN CO., THE	Untitled	6
July 07, 1880	15	351928	EMERY, F. J.	Untitled	2
July 12, 1880	4	352094	MINTONS	Untitled	5
July 15, 1880	3	352192	DUNN, BENNETT & CO.	Untitled	5
August 14, 1880	12	353713-4	DAVENPORT, WM. & CO.	Untitled	6
September 29, 1880	3	355947-8	BROWNHILLS POTTERY CO., THE	Untitled	5
September 30, 1880	4	355987	WORCESTER ROYAL PORCELAIN CO., LTD.	Untitled	5
October 20, 1880	10	356970	BURGESS & LEIGH	Roman	5
October 22, 1880	12	357088	AYNSLEY, J. & SONS	Untitled	5
October 27, 1880	20	357429	TAMS, J.	Untitled	5
October 30, 1880	6	357560	JONES & HOPKINSON	Untitled	2
November 02, 1880	2	357609	GRINDLEY, W. H. & CO.	Untitled	5
November 10, 1880	13	358141	BEDNALL & HEATH	Avon	5
December 07, 1880	10	359213	PINDER, BOURNE & CO.	Untitled	5
December 29, 1880	7	360042	DOULTON & CO.	Sportsman	5
February 08, 1881	6	361538-41	BROWNFIELD, WM. & SONS	Water Jug	5
February 11, 1881	10	361668	EMERY, F. J.	Untitled	5
March 03, 1881	5	362423	DIMMOCK, J. & CO.	Untitled	2
March 08, 1881	3	362458	GROVE, F. W. & STARK, J.	Untitled	5
March 17, 1881	9	362992	SHORTER & BOULTON	Untitled	5
March 24, 1881	3	363208	ADDERLEY, W. A.	Untitled	6

Reg. Date	Parcel	Reg. No.	Potter	Pattern	Reference
April 09, 1881	5	363793	PLANT, R. H. & CO.	Untitled	6
April 11, 1881	1	363800	BEVINGTON, A. & CO.	Untitled	6
April 30, 1881	4	364529	WEDGWOOD, JOSIAH & SONS	Carlyle	5
May 04, 1881	3	364625-7	BROWNFIELD, WM. & SONS	Mistletoe,Hudson	3,6
May 06, 1881	4	364736	PLANT, R. H. & CO.	Untitled	6
May 16, 1881	2	365066	WEDGWOOD, JOSIAH & SONS	Beaconsfield	5
June 01, 1881	13	365793	MORTLOCK, J. & CO.	Untitled	5
June 16, 1881	8	366078	FIELDING, S. & CO.	Untitled	5
June 21, 1881	13	366220-2	BIRKS BROS. & SEDDON	Untitled	6
July 09, 1881	10	366923	WARDLE & CO.	Untitled	5
July 14, 1881	6	367134	BROWN, T. C. WESTHEAD-MOORE & CO.	Untitled	5
August 10, 1881	13	368044	OLD HALL EARTHEN-WARE CO., LTD., THE	Untitled	5
August 27, 1881	3	369202	LEAR, S.	Untitled	5
August 27, 1881	9	369216	GILDEA & WALKER	Untitled	5
September 29, 1881	3	370636	JONES, GEO. & SONS	Ivy Bower	4
September 30, 1881	3	370702	DAVENPORTS, LTD.	Untitled	5
October 04, 1881	6	370885	BROWNFIELD, WM. & SONS	Water Jug	5
October 07, 1881	27	371098	MINTONS	Untitled	6
October 08, 1881	3	371102	ADAMS & SLEIGH	Pompadour	5
October 20, 1881	1	371866	BEGLEY, THOS.	Parnell	5
October 29, 1881	11	372376	WARDLE & CO.	Untitled	5
November 02, 1881	1	372489-90	BROWN, T. C. WESTHEAD-MOORE & CO.	Untitled	6
November 09, 1881	7	372980	BODLEY, E. J. D.	Untitled	6
November 21, 1881	1	373575	BEVINGTON, JOHN	Swan	3
November 23, 1881	13	373707	SHORTER & BOULTON	Untitled	5
November 25, 1881	1	373821	ADAMS & SLEIGH	Untitled	5
December 20, 1881	9	374948	BEDNALL & HEATH	Untitled	5
December 21, 1881	3	374955	GROSVENOR, F.	Untitled	5
January 04, 1882	2	375426-7	COPELAND, W. T. & SONS	Untitled	7
January 10, 1882	5	375599	LEAR, S.	Untitled	5
January 30, 1882	2	376528	HOLLINGSHEAD & KIRKHAM	Untitled	5
January 30, 1882	3	376529	GROVE, F. W. & STARK, J.	Untitled	5
February 01, 1882	1	376580	EDGE, MALKIN & CO.	Untitled	5
March 20, 1882	5	378643	ADDERLEY, W. A.	Untitled	6
March 27, 1882	10	378959	SHORTER & BOULTON	Untitled	5
March 30, 1882	17	379080	FIELDING, S. & CO.	Untitled	5
April 04, 1882	2	379212-3	BROWNFIELD, WM. & SONS	Untitled	5,6
May 02, 1882	5	380194	ASHWORTH, G. L. & BROS.	Untitled	5
May 05, 1882	2	380401	WOOD, HINES & WINKLE	Untitled	5
May 06, 1882	6	380419	WHITTAKER, EDGE & CO.	Lily	5
May 10, 1882	4	380572	EDWARDS, JOHN	Untitled	5
May 10, 1882	14	380676	FIELDING, S. & CO.	Untitled	5
June 09, 1882	4	381965	ADDERLEY, W. A.	Untitled	5
June 13, 1882	14	381131-2	WARDLE & CO.	Untitled	5
June 23, 1882	1	382594	WEDGWOOD, JOSIAH & SONS	Untitled	5
July 03, 1882	3	382843	BODLEY, E. J. D.	Untitled	6
July 04, 1882	3	382859	WRIGHT & RIGBY (Gen. Booth)	Untitled	2,8
July 14, 1882	10	383641	WARDLE & CO.	Untitled	5
July 20, 1882	1	383694	EDWARD, JOHN	Untitled	5
July 22, 1882	8	383802	JONES, GEO. & SONS	Untitled	5
July 25, 1882	9	383869-71	BROWNHILLS POTTERY CO., LTD., THE	Untitled	5
August 21, 1882	8	385129	ADAMS & BROMLEY	Untitled	5
August 28, 1882	9	385544	MINTONS	Untitled	5
September 06, 1882	2	385954	HAWLEY & CO.	Untitled	5
September 11, 1882	4	386178	ADAMS & BROMLEY	Untitled	5
October 09, 1882	3	387771	COPELAND, W. T. & SONS	Untitled	6
October 11, 1882	3	387958	BRIDGWOOD, SAMPSON & SON	Untitled	5
October 12, 1882	17	388200	FURNIVAL, T. & SONS	Untitled	5
November 10, 1882	12	389797	PRATT & SIMPSON	Untitled	5
November 14, 1882	3	389911-2	STEEL, EDWARD	Falstaff	6
November 15, 1882	7	390005	FIELDING, S. & CO.	Untitled	5
November 21, 1882	4	390255	HOLDCROFT, J.	Untitled	5
December 13, 1882	5	391364	WEDGWOOD, JOSIAH	Untitled	5
December 14, 1882	6	391409	LEAR, S.	Untitled	5
December 22, 1882	2	391818	GROVE, F. W. & STARK, J.	Untitled	5
December 27, 1882	1	391929	NEW WHARF POTTERY CO.	Untitled	5
January 09, 1883	3	392626	POWELL, BISHOP & STONIER	Untitled	5
January 23, 1883	10	393102-3	COPELAND, W. T. & SONS	Queen Anne Jug	7
February 06, 1883	1	393668	WOOD, HINES & WINKLE	Untitled	5
February 07, 1883	4	393714	HAWLEY & CO.	Untitled	5
February 07, 1883	5	393715	MOUNTFORD & THOMAS	Cockatoo	5
February 17, 1883	13	394371	TURNER, G. W. & SONS	Untitled	5
February 19, 1883	1	394374	ADDERLEY, W. A.	Untitled	5
February 22, 1883	6	394556-61	HALL & READ	Untitled	4
March 04, 1883	3	395818	WOOD, E. A.	Untitled	2
March 08, 1883	5	395284	MASSEY, M.	Untitled	5
March 08, 1883	20	395316-7	BODLEY, E. F. & SON	Untitled	6
March 20, 1883	3	395818	WOOD, E. A.	Untitled	5
March 20, 1883	4	395819	WEDGWOOD, JOSIAH & SONS	Untitled	2
April 03, 1883	3	396316	WARBURTON, E.	Untitled	5

Reg. Date	Parcel	Reg. No.	Potter	Pattern	Reference
April 10, 1883	1	396648	BANKS & THORLEY	Untitled	5
May 02, 1883	4	397609-11	BROWN, T. C. WESTHEAD-MOORE & CO.	Untitled	6
May 07, 1883	8	397819	FIELDING, S. & CO.	Untitled	2
May 23, 1883	7	398436	BOOTH, T. G. & F.	Untitled	5
May 31, 1883	17	398784	WARDLE & CO.	Untitled	5
June 18, 1883	11	399554	TAMS, JOHN	Untitled	5
June 18, 1883	12	399555-9	BROWNFIELD, WM. & SONS	Gentleman Jug	5,6
June 21, 1883	22	399822	WARDLE & CO.	Untitled	5
July 05, 1883	19	400462	FURNIVAL, T. & SONS	Untitled	5
July 19, 1883	4	400941	DAVENPORTS LTD.	Untitled	6
July 19, 1883	21	400994	JONES, GEO. & SONS	Untitled	6
July 26, 1883	1	401296	ADDERLEY, W. A.	Untitled	5
August 01, 1883	4	401624	JONES, GEO. & SONS	Untitled	6
August 02, 1883	3	401663-4	DAVENPORTS LTD.	Untitled	6
August 03, 1883	17	401769	BODLEY, E. J.	Untitled	6
August 17, 1883	5	402346	BODLEY, E. J. D.	Untitled	6
August 24, 1883	12	402736	MOUNTFORD & THOMAS	Untitled	5
August 25, 1883	11	402839	BROWNFIELD, WM. & SONS	Montana	2
September 07, 1883	19	403501-4	POWELL, BISHOP & STONIER	Untitled	6
September 11, 1883	4	403665	WEDGWOOD, JOSIAH & SONS	Untitled	2
September 20, 1883	12	404175	HALL & READ	Untitled	5
September 24, 1883	9	404317	JONES & HOPKINSON	Untitled	5
October 08, 1883	1	404900	HOLLINSON & GOODALL	Untitled	5
October 13, 1883	11	405363-4	BROWNFIELD, WM. & SONS	Untitled	6
October 23, 1883	6	405855	DIMMOCK, J. & CO.	Albany	5
October 26, 1883	7	406043	JONES & HOPKINSON	Untitled	5
October 30, 1883	2	406140	MARSHALL, J. & CO.	Untitled	5
October 30, 1883	17	406187	ROBINSON, J.	Untitled	5
November 01, 1883	1	406223	BEVINGTON, A. & CO.	Untitled	6
November 01, 1883	25	406370	WOOD, HINES & WINKLE	Untitled	5
November 01, 1883	26	406371	FIELDING, S. & CO.	Untitled	2
November 26, 1883	2	407623	ADDERLEY, W. A.	Untitled	6
December 15, 1883	15	408357	HOLLINSON & GOODALL	Untitled	5

APPENDIX B19: EARTHENWARE, JUGS & PARIAN WARE: ALPHABETICAL LISTING WITH PATTERNS AND SOURCE

Potter	Reg. Date	Parcel	Reg. No.	Pattern	Reference
ADAMS & BROMLEY	August 21, 1882	8	385129	Untitled	5
ADAMS & BROMLEY	September 11, 1882	4	386178	Untitled	5
ADAMS & SLEIGH	October 08, 1881	3	371102	Pompadour	5
ADAMS & SLEIGH	November 25, 1881	1	373821	Untitled	5
ADAMS, SCRIVENER & CO.	February 05, 1868	4	216451	Untitled	5
ADAMS, SCRIVENER & CO.	May 13, 1868	1	218664	Untitled	5
ADAMS, SCRIVENER & CO.	July 30, 1868	6	220183	Untitled	5
ADAMS, WM.	October 07, 1876	6	304144-5	Untitled	5
ADDERLEY, W. A.	March 12, 1880	4	347476	Untitled	5
ADDERLEY, W. A.	March 24, 1881	3	363208	Untitled	6
ADDERLEY, W. A.	March 20, 1882	5	378643	Untitled	6
ADDERLEY, W. A.	June 09, 1882	4	381965	Untitled	5
ADDERLEY, W. A.	February 19, 1883	1	394374	Untitled	5
ADDERLEY, W. A.	July 26, 1883	1	401296	Untitled	5
ADDERLEY, W. A.	November 26, 1883	2	407623	Untitled	6
ALCOCK & DIGORY	February 27, 1868	5	217100	Untitled	6
ALCOCK, JOHN	May 07, 1853	5	91121-4	Untitled	5
ALCOCK, JOHN	February 07, 1855	2	99310	Untitled	2
ALCOCK, SAMUEL & CO.	April 03, 1847	6	42435	Rustic/ Ranger	2
ALCOCK, SAMUEL & CO.	April 27, 1847	1	42804	Naomi/ Arabic	1,2,3,6
ALCOCK, SAMUEL & CO.	January 30, 1854	4	94815	Ivy	4
ALCOCK, SAMUEL & CO.	December 27, 1854	3	98640	Royal Patent Jug	4,6
ALCOCK, SAMUEL & CO.	July 29, 1858	4	114532	Bulrush/ Draped Linenfold	2,6
ALCOCK, SAMUEL & CO.	August 27, 1859	6	121724	Daniel In The Lion's Den	6
ASHWORTH, G. L. & BROS.	August 19, 1862	4	153844	Untitled	5
ASHWORTH, G. L. & BROS.	September 21, 1867	1	211536	Arches & Medallions	2,3
ASHWORTH, G. L. & BROS.	December 31, 1868	6	225993	Dagmar	4
ASHWORTH, G. L. & BROS.	May 02, 1882	5	380194	Untitled	5
AYNSLEY, J. & SONS	October 22, 1880	12	357088	Untitled	5
BAGULEY, GEO.	March 27, 1854	3	95448	Garland & Cupid	2,5
BAGULEY, GEO.	April 15, 1854	1	95611	Untitled	5

Potter	Reg. Date	Parcel	Reg. No.	Pattern	Reference
BAILEY, W. & J. A.	September 22, 1869	10	233527	Untitled	5
BAKER, WM. & CO.	October 23, 1862	8	156166	Untitled	5
BANKS & THORLEY	November 17, 1876	3	305222	Untitled	5
BANKS & THORLEY	May 21, 1878	11	321693	Untitled	5
BANKS & THORLEY	April 10, 1883	1	396648	Untitled	5
BARLOW, THOS.	August 30, 1871	4	255320	Untitled	5
BATES, BROWN-WESTHEAD & MOORE	March 01, 1860	2	126950	Untitled	6
BATES, BROWN-WESTHEAD & MOORE	May 09, 1861	3	140578	Untitled	5
BATES, BROWN-WESTHEAD & MOORE	June 04, 1861	1	141214	Untitled	2,6
BATES, ELLIOTT & CO.	March 07, 1872	10	260998	Convolvulus	3
BATES, ELLIOTT & CO.	September 02, 1872	8	265687	Untitled	2
BATES, GILDEA & WALKER	February 14, 1880	14	346467	Untitled	6
BATES, WALKER & CO.	January 24, 1876	6	297863	Untitled	5
BAYLEY & BALL	November 15, 1845	2	31128	Untitled	4
BEBBINGTON, J. & J. B.	December 27, 1867	1	215314	Four Ages Of Woman	3
BEDNALL & HEATH	November 10, 1880	13	358141	Avon	5
BEDNALL & HEATH	December 20, 1881	9	374948	Untitled	5
BEECH & HANCOCK	July 05, 1861	2	141727	Coral & Seaweed	5
BEECH & HANCOCK	July 14, 1862	2	153127	Gothic Floral	2,3,4
BEECH & HANCOCK	March 21, 1863	2	160759	Foliage Plants	4
BEECH & HANCOCK	April 25, 1863	1	161861	White Fawn	1
BEECH, JANE	September 25, 1873	10	276522	Untitled	5
BEECH, WILLIAM	April 18, 1856	2	104392	May They Ever Be United	5
BEECH, WM.	September 18, 1861	7	143679	Untitled	5
BEGLEY, THOS.	October 20, 1881	1	371866	Parnell	5
BELL, J. & M. P. & CO.	September 16, 1850	8	71952	Untitled	5
BELL, J. & M. P. & CO.	March 26, 1852	3	84471	Untitled	2
BELL, J. & M. P. & CO.	March 28, 1862	5	150303	Untitled	5
BELL, J. & M. P. & CO.	May 06, 1867	3	207938	Fishwives	2,3
BEVINGTON, A. & CO.	April 11, 1881	1	363800	Untitled	6
BEVINGTON, A. & CO.	November 01, 1883	1	406223	Untitled	6
BEVINGTON, J. & T.	February 19, 1873	14	270600-1	Untitled	6
BEVINGTON, JOHN	November 21, 1881	1	373575	Swan	3
BEVINGTON, SAML. & SON	September 27, 1855	4	101624	Sacrifice Of Iphigenia	2
BIRKS BROS. & SEDDON	June 21, 1881	13	366220-2	Untitled	6
BLACKSHAW, J. & CO.	March 23, 1870	9	239793	Untitled	5
BODLEY & CO.	February 09, 1874	5	280344	Untitled	6
BODLEY & HARROLD	October 28, 1864	4	180453	Untitled	4
BODLEY, E. F. & CO.	October 27, 1879	9	341997	Untitled	6
BODLEY, E. F. & SON	March 08, 1883	20	395316-7	Untitled	6
BODLEY, E. J.	August 03, 1883	17	401769	Untitled	6
BODLEY, E. J. D.	March 23, 1876	8	299366	Untitled	5
BODLEY, E. J. D.	November 05, 1878	17	328790-2	Untitled	6
BODLEY, E. J. D.	June 10, 1880	4	350555	Untitled	5
BODLEY, E. J. D.	November 09, 1881	7	372980	Untitled	6
BODLEY, E. J. D.	July 03, 1882	3	382843	Untitled	6
BODLEY, E. J. D.	August 17, 1883	5	402346	Untitled	6
BODLEY, ED. F. & CO.	June 29, 1865	2	187847-8	Wheatshef	2,6
BOOTE, T. & R.	February 02, 1847	7	41213	Samuel & Eli	3
BOOTE, T. & R.	October 17, 1848	3	54901	Infant Samuel/ Samuel & Eli	3
BOOTE, T. & R.	July 21, 1851	7	79750-3	Untitled	5
BOOTE, T. & R.	March 21, 1859	7	118891	Four Panels	2,5
BOOTE, T. & R.	March 29, 1859	7	119137	Enville	4,5
BOOTE, T. & R.	January 08, 1861	6	137217	Untitled	5
BOOTE, T. & R.	March 22, 1862	9	150152	Venetia	5
BOOTE, T. & R.	May 30, 1868	4	219042	Untitled	5
BOOTE, T. & R.	December 06, 1879	2	343815	Untitled	5
BOOTH, T. G. & F.	May 23, 1883	7	398436	Untitled	5
BOOTH, THOS.	October 10, 1867	1	212194	Untitled	2
BOOTH, THOS.	May 26, 1869	4	229627	Sweep Race	3
BOOTH, THOS.	July 15, 1871	2	254030	Untitled	2
BOOTH, THOS.	May 11, 1872	4	262672	Untitled	5
BOOTH, THOS. & SONS	April 30, 1874	2	282098	Untitled	5
BOOTH, THOS. & SONS	March 30, 1875	1	290186	Ribbons & Tassels	3
BOUGHTON, R. T.	May 09, 1864	3	174424	Untitled	5
BRIDGWOOD, SAMPSON & SON	October 11, 1882	3	387958	Untitled	5
BROWN, T. C. WESTHEAD-MOORE & CO.	May 09, 1862	9	151568	Untitled	5
BROWN, T. C. WESTHEAD-MOORE & CO.	April 21, 1864	4	173785	Pineapple	6,8
BROWN, T. C. WESTHEAD-MOORE & CO.	February 18, 1868	2	216897	Untitled	5
BROWN, T. C. WESTHEAD-MOORE & CO.	September 30, 1869	8	233864-6	Untitled	6
BROWN, T. C. WESTHEAD-MOORE & CO.	September 25, 1871	8	256079	Untitled	2
BROWN, T. C. WESTHEAD-MOORE & CO.	May 12, 1873	8	272835	Untitled	2,6
BROWN, T. C. WESTHEAD-MOORE & CO.	May 30, 1873	15	273376	Untitled	6
BROWN, T. C. WESTHEAD-MOORE & CO.	August 30, 1873	2	275661	Untitled	6
BROWN, T. C. WESTHEAD-MOORE & CO.	January 23, 1875	9	288756	Untitled	5
BROWN, T. C. WESTHEAD-MOORE & CO.	May 26, 1875	6	291518-20	Untitled	6
BROWN, T. C. WESTHEAD-MOORE & CO.	December 29, 1875	6	297246-7	Untitled	6
BROWN, T. C. WESTHEAD-MOORE & CO.	March 14, 1876	5	299177	Untitled	5
BROWN, T. C. WESTHEAD-MOORE & CO.	May 08, 1876	7	300423	Untitled	5
BROWN, T. C. WESTHEAD-MOORE & CO.	September 09, 1876	9	303456	Untitled	5
BROWN, T. C. WESTHEAD-MOORE & CO.	December 29, 1877	6	317494	Untitled	6
BROWN, T. C. WESTHEAD-MOORE & CO.	December 02, 1878	7	329901	Untitled	6
BROWN, T. C. WESTHEAD-MOORE & CO.	June 13, 1879	13	336132	Untitled	6
BROWN, T. C. WESTHEAD-MOORE & CO.	July 09, 1879	12	337058	Untitled	6
BROWN, T. C. WESTHEAD-MOORE & CO.	July 16, 1879	14	337177	Untitled	6
BROWN, T. C. WESTHEAD-MOORE & CO.	January 28, 1880	3	345801	Untitled	6
BROWN, T. C. WESTHEAD-MOORE & CO.	July 14, 1881	6	367134	Untitled	5
BROWN, T. C. WESTHEAD-MOORE & CO.	November 02, 1881	1	372489-90	Untitled	6
BROWN, T. C. WESTHEAD-MOORE & CO.	May 02, 1883	4	397609-11	Untitled	6
BROWNFIELD, WM.	October 25, 1852	2	87228	Mazeppa	5
BROWNFIELD, WM.	April 01, 1854	4	95510	Kent	2
BROWNFIELD, WM.	April 26, 1855	1	99972-4	Plain Jug, Linen Fold Jug	4
BROWNFIELD, WM.	November 28, 1855	3	102785	Wicker	4
BROWNFIELD, WM.	April 30, 1856	3	104602-3	Gothic Ivy	1,4
BROWNFIELD, WM.	November 27, 1856	6	107714	Untitled	5
BROWNFIELD, WM.	June 05, 1857	3	110096-7	Trade Scantia	5
BROWNFIELD, WM.	December 09, 1857	2	112354	Arrowhead	2
BROWNFIELD, WM.	August 24, 1858	2	114763	Floral	5
BROWNFIELD, WM.	October 05, 1858	3	115902	Jewel Jug	3
BROWNFIELD, WM.	May 20, 1859	1	119968	Shamrock	2
BROWNFIELD, WM.	November 05, 1859	4	123816	Fern	1,3
BROWNFIELD, WM.	June 06, 1860	4	129680-2	Eglantine	1
BROWNFIELD, WM.	July 06, 1861	2	141732	Donatello	4
BROWNFIELD, WM.	December 04, 1861	7	147309-10	Union	1,4,6
BROWNFIELD, WM.	January 25, 1862	3	148870	International	1,3
BROWNFIELD, WM.	October 14, 1863	7	167289	Albion	1,3
BROWNFIELD, WM.	December 23, 1863	2	170418	Untitled	5
BROWNFIELD, WM.	April 29, 1864	2	174168	Argos	1
BROWNFIELD, WM.	October 12, 1864	4	179656	Tyrol	2
BROWNFIELD, WM.	April 01, 1865	4	185520	Florence	2,3
BROWNFIELD, WM.	October 30, 1865	4	191407-8	Tiverton	1
BROWNFIELD, WM.	March 15, 1867	7	206762-6	Cashmere	1,3,6
BROWNFIELD, WM.	June 21, 1867	4	209057	Napoleon	5
BROWNFIELD, WM.	June 12, 1868	5	219316-7	Hampton	2
BROWNFIELD, WM.	June 19, 1869	5	230183-4	Severn	2,3
BROWNFIELD, WM.	June 10, 1870	1	242392-4	Nile, Plain,	2,3,4
BROWNFIELD, WM. & SON	May 02, 1871	4	252177-80	Worcester	3
BROWNFIELD, WM. & SON	December 14, 1872	5	268806-7	Cupid	1,3,6
BROWNFIELD, WM. & SON	September 10, 1874	3	285013	Bangor/ Mandarin/ HongKong/ Audley	5
BROWNFIELD, WM. & SON	March 05, 1875	2	289769	Untitled	2
BROWNFIELD, WM. & SON	January 29, 1876	3	298027-9	Yeddo	1,3,6
BROWNFIELD, WM. & SONS	September 06, 1876	10	303309	Water Jug	5,6
BROWNFIELD, WM. & SONS	February 07, 1877	7	307570-2	Medieval Jug	5
BROWNFIELD, WM. & SONS	October 10, 1877	5	315104-5	Olympus	5
BROWNFIELD, WM. & SONS	November 06, 1877	11	315954-6	Leek	5,6
BROWNFIELD, WM. & SONS	December 22, 1877	5	317427-8	Hudson	1,3,6
BROWNFIELD, WM. & SONS	January 09, 1879	8	330997-8	Swirling Fish, Yesso Jug	5
BROWNFIELD, WM. & SONS	May 25, 1880	4	350098	Missouri	5,6
BROWNFIELD, WM. & SONS	February 08, 1881	6	361538-41	Water Jug	5
BROWNFIELD, WM. & SONS	May 04, 1881	3	364625-7	Mistletoe, Hudson	3,6
BROWNFIELD, WM. & SONS	October 04, 1881	6	370885	Water Jug	5
BROWNFIELD, WM. & SONS	April 04, 1882	2	379212-3	Untitled	5,6
BROWNFIELD, WM. & SONS	June 18, 1883	12	399555-9	Gentleman Jug	5,6

Potter	Reg. Date	Parcel	Reg. No.	Pattern	Reference
BROWNFIELD, WM. & SONS	August 25, 1883	11	402839	Montana	2
BROWNFIELD, WM. & SONS	October 13, 1883	11	405363-4	Untitled	6
BROWNFIELD, WM. (Reg'd by W.P.&G.Phillips)	October 21, 1868	8	223308	Westminster	1
BROWNHILLS POTTERY CO., LTD., THE	July 25, 1882	9	383869-71	Untitled	5
BROWNHILLS POTTERY CO., THE	October 11, 1875	10	295014	Untitled	5
BROWNHILLS POTTERY CO., THE	October 23, 1878	1	328018	Untitled	2
BROWNHILLS POTTERY CO., THE	September 29, 1880	3	355947-8	Untitled	5
BROWNHILLS POTTERY, THE	October 30, 1872	5	267527	Untitled	5
BUCKLEY, WOOD & CO	June 15, 1880	4	350848	Untitled	5
BURGESS & LEIGH	March 23, 1864	4	172876	Giraffe	2
BURGESS & LEIGH	May 07, 1875	8	291110	Untitled	5
BURGESS & LEIGH	July 01, 1878	1	322791	Turin	5
BURGESS & LEIGH	October 20, 1880	10	356970	Roman	5
BURGESS, LEIGH & CO.	October 19, 1876	3	304428	Untitled	5
CARTLIDGE, W. E.	September 26, 1872	5	266636	Untitled	5
CLEMENTSON BROS.	November 14, 1876	8	305195	Untitled	5
CLEMENTSON BROS.	March 13, 1879	14	333301	Untitled	5
CLEMENTSON BROS.	March 28, 1879	6	333801	Untitled	2
CLEMENTSON BROS.	December 19, 1879	1	344452	Untitled	5
CLEMENTSON, J.	November 15, 1861	3	146352-4	Untitled	2
CLEMENTSON, J.	July 04, 1862	8	152963	Untitled	5
COCKSON & CHETWYND	December 24, 1872	1	269197	Untitled	5
COCKSON & CHETWYND	August 01, 1874	9	284136	Untitled	5
COCKSON & CHETWYND	September 03, 1874	12	284884-5	Untitled	5
COCKSON, CHETWYND & CO.	January 07, 1868	11	215642	Untitled	5
COCKSON, CHETWYND & CO.	December 14, 1868	7	225441	Untitled	5
COLLINSON, CHAS. & CO.	October 29, 1864	2	180486	Untitled	4
COOPER, THOMAS	December 09, 1862	5	158221	Edward & Alexandra	4
COOPER, THOS.	September 12, 1862	2	154693	Untitled	5
COPE & EDWARDS	March 27, 1849	2	59245	Untitled	6
COPELAND, W. T.	August 17, 1847	2	45091-2	Adam & Eve/Portland	5
COPELAND, W. T.	November 04, 1848	2	55174	Grapevine/ Convolvulus	2,4,6
COPELAND, W. T.	November 13, 1848	4	55337	Vine	6
COPELAND, W. T.	November 09, 1849	4	63523	Lily Of The Valley	1
COPELAND, W. T.	December 06, 1849	3	64739	Untitled	5
COPELAND, W. T.	May 30, 1851	4	79085	Nymphea/ Lotus	1
COPELAND, W. T.	July 14, 1851	3	79684	Untitled	6
COPELAND, W. T.	February 26, 1853	5	89958	Harvest Barrel	2,3,6
COPELAND, W. T.	February 23, 1854	3	95163	Victoria, Wellington	2
COPELAND, W. T.	September 12, 1854	2	96826	Hop Jug/ Tulip Jug	1,3,6
COPELAND, W. T.	October 22, 1856	3	106770	Tulip	6
COPELAND, W. T.	April 19, 1857	1	110160	Untitled	7
COPELAND, W. T.	June 19, 1857	1	110160	Untitled	2, 7
COPELAND, W. T.	June 11, 1861	2	141326	Untitled	5
COPELAND, W. T.	October 18, 1861	3	145157	Untitled	5
COPELAND, W. T.	March 13, 1862	6	149938	Untitled	5
COPELAND, W. T.	May 22, 1863	4	162618-9	Untitled	6
COPELAND, W. T.	February 13, 1864	6	171673	Pansey	1,3,6
COPELAND, W. T. & SONS	October 28, 1867	4	212956	Oak Motifs	6
COPELAND, W. T. & SONS	December 03, 1867	3	214618	Untitled	7
COPELAND, W. T. & SONS	July 24, 1868	4	219997	Arches & Scrolls	1,6
COPELAND, W. T. & SONS	July 15, 1870	1	243207	Aesthetic/ Marsh Marigold/ Leaves in Cartouche	1,2,3,6
COPELAND, W. T. & SONS	October 19, 1871	6	256907	Oriental Band	3,6
COPELAND, W. T. & SONS	June 11, 1872	12	263348	Untitled	7
COPELAND, W. T. & SONS	January 13, 1873	4	269621	Untitled	5
COPELAND, W. T. & SONS	November 08, 1875	8	295803	Untitled	6
COPELAND, W. T. & SONS	June 09, 1876	6	301164	Untitled	5
COPELAND, W. T. & SONS	July 02, 1877	3	311523	Untitled	2,6
COPELAND, W. T. & SONS	March 13, 1878	10	319394	Untitled	5
COPELAND, W. T. & SONS	January 04, 1882	2	375426-7	Untitled	7
COPELAND, W. T. & SONS	October 09, 1882	3	387771	Untitled	6
COPELAND, W. T. & SONS	January 23, 1883	10	393102-3	Queen Anne Jug	7
CORK, EDGE & MALKIN	May 31, 1861	3	141114	Basketweave	1,4
CORK, EDGE & MALKIN	March 12, 1864	5	172559	Untitled	5
CORK, EDGE & MALKIN	October 31, 1864	3	180569	Untitled	5
CORK, EDGE & MALKIN	November 25, 1868	4	224724	Ruth	1,3
CORK, EDGE & MALKIN	July 22, 1870	1	243385	Medallion	1
CORN, W. & E.	November 03, 1874	4	286721	Untitled	5
CRYSTAL (PALACE) PORCELAIN CO., THE	June 17, 1880	20	351063	Untitled	6

Potter	Reg. Date	Parcel	Reg. No.	Pattern	Reference
DAVENPORT, WM. & CO.	March 13, 1879	1	333241-4	Untitled	6
DAVENPORT, WM. & CO.	August 14, 1880	12	353713-4	Untitled	6
DAVENPORTS LTD.	July 19, 1883	4	400941	Untitled	6
DAVENPORTS LTD.	August 02, 1883	3	401663-4	Untitled	6
DAVENPORTS, LTD.	September 30, 1881	3	370702	Untitled	5
DEAVILLE, J.	March 27, 1854	6	95451	Untitled	2
DIMMOCK, J. & CO.	February 29, 1876	9	298693	Untitled	5
DIMMOCK, J. & CO.	December 14, 1876	11	305973	Untitled	5
DIMMOCK, J. & CO.	June 10, 1880	12	350613	Untitled	6
DIMMOCK, J. & CO.	March 03, 1881	5	362423	Untitled	2
DIMMOCK, J. & CO.	October 23, 1883	6	405855	Albany	5
DOULTON & CO.	December 29, 1880	7	360042	Sportsman	5
DUDSON, JAMES	August 06, 1855	1	101019	Pinapple Jug	3
DUDSON, JAMES	April 25, 1861	2	140200	Barley/Wheat Ears	2,3
DUDSON, JAMES	February 27, 1862	4	149673-4	Untitled	2
DUDSON, JAMES	December 23, 1865	3	193844	Argyle	2,3
DUNN, BENNETT & CO.	February 28, 1878	3	319041	Untitled	2
DUNN, BENNETT & CO.	July 15, 1880	3	352192	Untitled	5
EDGE, MALKIN & CO.	January 01, 1872	6	259077	Untitled	2
EDGE, MALKIN & CO.	June 17, 1874	7	283041	Trentham	4
EDGE, MALKIN & CO.	October 21, 1876	3	304473	Untitled	2
EDGE, MALKIN & CO.	November 04, 1878	1	328699	Tuscan	5
EDGE, MALKIN & CO.	February 01, 1882	1	376580	Untitled	5
EDWARD, JOHN	July 20, 1882	1	383694	Untitled	5
EDWARDS, JAMES	December 30, 1842	2	3346	Untitled	5
EDWARDS, JAMES & SON	July 12, 1865	3	188167	Strapwork	2
EDWARDS, JAMES & SON	January 31, 1866	5	194840	Untitled	5
EDWARDS, JAMES & SON	January 28, 1876	8	298018	Untitled	5
EDWARDS, JAMES & SON	July 17, 1877	9	312019-21	Stylized Floral	2
EDWARDS, JOHN	September 30, 1875	4	294827	Untitled	5
EDWARDS, JOHN	May 10, 1882	4	380572	Untitled	5
ELLIOT BROS.	February 01, 1862	4	149090	Untitled	2
ELLIS, JAMES & SON	October 26, 1869	2	235158	Corn Cob	4,6
ELSMORE & FORSTER	February 20, 1871	2	250479	Untitled	5
EMERY, F. J.	July 07, 1880	15	351928	Untitled	2
EMERY, F. J.	February 11, 1881	10	361668	Untitled	5
FIELDING, S. & CO.	January 16, 1880	8	345288	Untitled	5
FIELDING, S. & CO.	May 05, 1880	13	349528	Untitled	5
FIELDING, S. & CO.	June 16, 1881	8	366078	Untitled	5
FIELDING, S. & CO.	March 30, 1882	17	379080	Untitled	5
FIELDING, S. & CO.	May 10, 1882	14	380676	Untitled	5
FIELDING, S. & CO.	November 15, 1882	7	390005	Untitled	5
FIELDING, S. & CO.	May 07, 1883	8	397819	Untitled	2
FIELDING, S. & CO.	November 01, 1883	26	406371	Untitled	2
FORD, CHALLINOR & CO.	July 25, 1877	5	312187	Untitled	2
FORD, CHALLINOR & CO.	April 05, 1877	2	308934	Untitled	5
FURNIVAL & CLARK	December 30, 1845	3	32601	Falstaff	1
FURNIVAL, F. & SONS	June 04, 1878	9	322168	Untitled	2
FURNIVAL, J. & CO.	May 29, 1862	5	152013	Untitled	5
FURNIVAL, J. & CO.	January 30, 1868	6	216333	Untitled	5
FURNIVAL, T. & SON	April 29, 1874	9	282091	Untitled	5
FURNIVAL, T. & SONS	June 26, 1877	11	311366	Untitled	5
FURNIVAL, T. & SONS	January 29, 1879	2	331600	Untitled	5
FURNIVAL, T. & SONS	March 01, 1879	1	332837	Untitled	5
FURNIVAL, T. & SONS	April 30, 1880	6	349380	Untitled	5
FURNIVAL, T. & SONS	October 12, 1882	17	388200	Untitled	5
FURNIVAL, T. & SONS	July 05, 1883	19	400462	Untitled	5
FURNIVAL, THOS.	October 13, 1866	3	202493	Untitled	5
FURNIVAL, THOS. & SON	March 29, 1871	1	251329	Untitled	5
FURNIVAL, THOS. & SON	April 10, 1872	11	261749	Untitled	5
FURNIVAL, THOS. & SON	May 02, 1872	11	262429	Untitled	5
FURNIVAL, THOS. & SON	June 12, 1875	10	292042	Untitled	5
FURNIVAL, THOS. & SONS	November 29, 1876	11	305568	Untitled	5
FURNIVAL, THOS. & SONS	May 12, 1877	7	310034	Untitled	5
FURNIVAL, THOS. & SONS	April 20, 1878	2	320606	Untitled	5
GELSON BROS.	September 04, 1868	6	221203	Untitled	5
GELSON BROS.	April 23, 1873	6	272293	Untitled	5
GILDEA & WALKER	August 27, 1881	9	369216	Untitled	5
GOODFELLOW, THOS.	January 12, 1853	6	88978	Niagra	5
GRANGER, GEO. & CO.	November 15, 1866	4	203912	Classical Figures	3
GREEN, B.	October 29, 1858	2	116468	Untitled	5
GRINDLEY, W. H. & CO.	April 22, 1880	5	349026	Untitled	5
GRINDLEY, W. H. & CO.	November 02, 1880	2	357609	Untitled	5
GROSVENOR, F.	December 21, 1881	3	374955	Untitled	5
GROVE, F. W. & STARK, J.	December 21, 1876	2	306207	Untitled	5
GROVE, F. W. & STARK, J.	March 08, 1881	3	362458	Untitled	5
GROVE, F. W. & STARK, J.	January 30, 1882	3	376529	Untitled	5
GROVE, F. W. & STARK, J.	December 22, 1882	2	391818	Untitled	5
HACKNEY & CO.	July 16, 1868	3	219833	Untitled	5
HALL & READ	February 22, 1883	6	394556-61	Untitled	4
HALL & READ	September 20, 1883	12	404175	Untitled	5
HAMMERSLEY, J. & R.	June 01, 1877	2	310599	Untitled	5
HAMSPON, J. & D.	February 29, 1864	6	172183	Untitled	5
HANCOCK, WHITTINGHAM & CO.	August 12, 1863	4	165171	Untitled	5
HARDING & COTTERILL	May 15, 1863	10	162304	Untitled	2

Potter	Reg. Date	Parcel	Reg. No.	Pattern	Reference
HARROP, W. & CO.	March 08, 1880	10	347360	Untitled	5
HARROP, WM.	October 07, 1876	2	304128	Untitled	2
HARROP, WM. & CO.	February 24, 1880	11	346870	Grecian	5
HARVEY ADAMS & CO.	April 07, 1870	11	240386	Untitled	5
HAWLEY & CO.	September 06, 1882	2	385954	Untitled	5
HAWLEY & CO.	February 07, 1883	4	393714	Untitled	5
HOBSON, CHAS.	January 27, 1870	8	238388	Untitled	5
HODGKINSON, E.	February 05, 1868	8	216470	Untitled	5
HOLDCROFT, J.	November 21, 1882	4	390255	Untitled	5
HOLDCROFT, JOSEPH	June 07, 1877	2	310710	Untitled	2
HOLDCROFT, JOSEPH	September 28, 1877	9	314675	Untitled	2
HOLLAND & GREEN	May 11, 1874	4	282253	Untitled	5
HOLLINGSHEAD & KIRKHAM	September 20, 1876	3	303732	Untitled	5
HOLLINGSHEAD & KIRKHAM	January 30, 1882	2	376528	Untitled	5
HOLLINSON & GOODALL	October 08, 1883	1	404900	Untitled	5
HOLLINSON & GOODALL	December 15, 1883	15	408357	Untitled	5
HOPE & CARTER	September 26, 1862	1	155200-2	Untitled	5
HOPE & CARTER	March 13, 1863	2	160456	Untitled	2
HOPE & CARTER	November 29, 1864	1	181843	Stylized Flowers	1
HOPE & CARTER	October 09, 1868	3	222477	Untitled	5
HOPE & CARTER	September 28, 1876	10	303942	Untitled	2
HULSE, NIXON & ADDERLEY	August 18, 1862	4	153827	Untitled	5
HULSE, NIXON & ADDERLEY	March 21, 1863	4	160761	Untitled	5
JONES & HOPKINSON	October 30, 1880	6	357560	Untitled	2
JONES & HOPKINSON	September 24, 1883	9	404317	Untitled	5
JONES & HOPKINSON	October 26, 1883	7	406043	Untitled	5
JONES & WALLEY	May 13, 1843	4	7122	Peacock Jug/ Hops	2,4,5
JONES, F.	September 26, 1872	2	266633	Untitled	2
JONES, F. & CO.	September 09, 1868	5	221312	Victor	5
JONES, GEO.	June 27, 1870	1	242715	Pineapple	5
JONES, GEO.	May 27, 1872	1	262951	Untitled	5
JONES, GEO.	October 18, 1872	5	267317	Untitled	5
JONES, GEO.	February 25, 1873	6	270700	Untitled	6
JONES, GEO. & SONS	February 19, 1874	1	280609	Untitled	5
JONES, GEO. & SONS	April 25, 1874	2	281984	Untitled	5
JONES, GEO. & SONS	December 08, 1874	2	287699	Untitled	5
JONES, GEO. & SONS	March 12, 1875	5	289874-6	Untitled	5
JONES, GEO. & SONS	June 26, 1875	2	292367-70	Untitled	6
JONES, GEO. & SONS	September 13, 1875	2	294434-5	Untitled	2,6
JONES, GEO. & SONS	November 08, 1876	3	305080	Untitled	6
JONES, GEO. & SONS	June 08, 1880	1	350477	Untitled	6
JONES, GEO. & SONS	September 29, 1881	3	370636	Ivy Bower	4
JONES, GEO. & SONS	July 22, 1882	8	383802	Untitled	5
JONES, GEO. & SONS	July 19, 1883	21	400994	Untitled	6
JONES, GEO. & SONS	August 01, 1883	4	401624	Untitled	6
KEYS & MOUNTFORD	November 25, 1852	4	88037	Untitled	6
KIRKHAM, WM.	November 19, 1863	10	168765	Untitled	2
KIRKHAM, WM.	December 09, 1864	1	182203	Untitled	5
LEAR, S.	August 27, 1881	3	369202	Untitled	5
LEAR, S.	January 10, 1882	5	375599	Untitled	5
LEAR, S.	December 14, 1882	6	391409	Untitled	5
LEAR, SAMUEL	July 12, 1878	13	323626	Untitled	5
LEAR, SAMUEL	June 17, 1880	4	351024	Untitled	5
LEVESON HILL (Excrs. of)	February 08, 1859	6	118415	Untitled	2
LEVESON HILL (Excrs. of)	October 15, 1861	3	144896	Untitled	5
LIDDLE, ELLIOT & SON	February 25, 1864	6	172060	Untitled	5
LIDDLE, ELLIOT & SON	April 21, 1864	8	173799	Corn Cob	1,3
LIDDLE, ELLIOT & SON	November 15, 1869	8	236203-7	Fern	4
LIDDLE, ELLIOT & SONS	January 16, 1863	8	159153	Circular	1,3
LIDDLE, ELLIOTT & SON	December 13, 1866	4	204764	Untitled	5
LIVESLEY, POWELL & CO.	June 14, 1853	2	91405-6	Lily,Julius Ceaser	2
LIVESLEY, POWELL & CO.	November 04, 1864	3	180713	Untitled	5
LIVESLEY, POWELL & CO.	May 02, 1865	8	186477	Untitled	5
LOCKETT & COOPER	July 04, 1861	2	141715	Untitled	5
LOCKETT, BAGULEY & COOPER	May 26, 1859	1	120096	Untitled	2
LOCKETT, BAGULEY & COOPER	May 19, 1860	9	129129	Untitled	2
LOCKETT, J. & T.	June 21, 1852	2	85404	Bacchanalin Cherubs	1,3
MACINTYRE, J.	April 11, 1863	1	161404	Untitled	2
MARSHALL, J. & CO.	October 30, 1883	2	406140	Untitled	5
MASSEY, M.	March 08, 1883	5	395284	Untitled	5
MAYER, T. J. & J.	January 21, 1845	6	25199	Rossi	2
MAYER, T. J. & J.	September 29, 1846	3	37586	Gothic Figures	5
MAYER, T. J. & J.	February 08, 1847	5	41266-7	Rossi	5
MAYER, T. J. & J.	July 02, 1850	2	70088	Birdnesting	1,3,4
MAYER, T. J. & J.	December 19, 1850	6	74786	Family Jug/ Convolvulus	1,3,4
MAYER, T. J. & J.	December 02, 1851	2	81815	Paul & Virginia	1
MEIGH, C.	November 12, 1846	3	38068	York Minster	1,3
MEIGH, CHARLES	September 30, 1844	7	21960	Bacchanalian Dance	1,3,4
MEIGH, CHARLES	September 18, 1848	4	54487	Trellis Jug	1,3,
MEIGH, CHARLES & SON	November 13, 1851	2	81518	Thistle	1,3
MEIGH, CHARLES & SON	August 25, 1852	4	86318	Four Seasons	1,3
MEIGH, CHAS. & SON	June 09, 1854	2	96039	Untitled	4

Potter	Reg. Date	Parcel	Reg. No.	Pattern	Reference
MEIGH, CHAS. & SON	July 24, 1855	1	100816	Untitled	5
MEIGH, CHAS. & SON	June 13, 1856	3	105059	Amphitrite	1,3,4
MEIR, JOHN & SON	December 19, 1866	5	205088	Untitled	2
MEIR, JOHN & SON	July 20, 1878	6	323893	Untitled	5
MINTON & CO.	March 02, 1846	4	34108	Untitled	2,6
MINTON & CO.	November 21, 1848	5	55456-7	Hops	3
MINTON & CO.	March 26, 1849	5	59232	Untitled	6
MINTON & CO.	November 17, 1849	2	63718	Bird & Ivy	2
MINTON & CO.	October 09, 1850	2	72395-6	Untitled	5
MINTON & CO.	June 05, 1852	5	85248	Greek Key	2
MINTON & CO.	July 23, 1852	3	85803-4	Medieval Revelry,Plain Jug	2,6
MINTON & CO.	September 03, 1852	7	86473	Ivy	2,6
MINTON & CO.	September 16, 1852	1	86657	Mermaid/ Merman & Cupid	2,6
MINTON & CO.	May 14, 1855	3	100116	Untitled	6
MINTON & CO.	January 23, 1856	3	103507	Wheat & Leaf	2,5,6
MINTON & CO.	October 16, 1856	2	106671-2	Untitled	5
MINTON & CO.	February 09, 1857	4	108930	Hops & Barley	2,6
MINTON & CO.	October 05, 1858	3	116176	Pinapple Jug	3
MINTON & CO.	October 25, 1859	1	123389-91	Untitled	5
MINTON & CO.	March 29, 1862	3	150322	Untitled	5
MINTON & CO.	January 16, 1863	2	159123	Untitled	2,6
MINTON & CO.	June 09, 1864	7	175330	Untitled	6
MINTON & CO.	September 10, 1864	1	178410	Untitled	5
MINTON & CO.	January 06, 1865	4	182807	Untitled	6
MINTON & CO.	November 03, 1866	6	203173	Untitled	6
MINTON & CO.	March 05, 1868	15	217212	Untitled	5
MINTON & CO.	October 17, 1868	4	223063	Untitled	5
MINTON & CO.	November 21, 1868	5	224539	Untitled	6
MINTON & CO.	December 23, 1868	5	225734	Pineapple Jug	1
MINTON & CO.	May 26, 1870	5	241960	Untitled	5
MINTON & CO.	October 04, 1870	8	245464	Untitled	5
MINTON & CO.	November 10, 1870	5	247071-3	Marne	4
MINTON & CO. & JOHN BELL	December 10, 1847	3	47562-3	Untitled	6
MINTON, HERBERT & CO.	March 20, 1845	1	26949	Dancing Amorini	1,3
MINTON, HERBERT & CO.	May 08, 1845	2	27451	Putti	2
MINTON, HERBERT & CO.	May 26, 1846	2	35116-7	Fruits & Wheat, Society of Arts,Vintage,	1,3,4,6
MINTON, HERBERT & CO.	August 03, 1846	2	36451-2	Untitled	5
MINTON, HERBERT & CO.	May 14, 1847	1	43170-1	Hops Jug	1,4,6
MINTON, HERBERT & CO.	August 19, 1847	3	45175	Una & The Lion	6
MINTON, HERBERT & CO.	October 04, 1847	3	46232	Dorothea	6
MINTON, HERBERT & CO.	August 15, 1849	2	61986	Squirrel & Bee	5
MINTONS	October 10, 1874	4	286134	Cat Jug	6
MINTONS	April 07, 1875	3	290352	Untitled	2,6
MINTONS	March 17, 1876	5	299236	Untitled	6
MINTONS	April 27, 1876	3	300260	Untitled	6
MINTONS	June 03, 1876	2	301030	Untitled	6
MINTONS	October 15, 1879	1	341347	Untitled	6
MINTONS	November 21, 1879	6	343148	Untitled	2,6
MINTONS	May 13, 1880	8	349852	Untitled	5
MINTONS	July 12, 1880	4	352094	Untitled	5
MINTONS	October 07, 1881	27	371098	Untitled	6
MINTONS	August 28, 1882	9	385544	Untitled	5
MORTLOCK, J. & CO.	June 01, 1881	13	365793	Untitled	5
MOUNTFORD & SCARRATT	October 11, 1861	3	144767	Untitled	5
MOUNTFORD & THOMAS	February 07, 1883	5	393715	Cockatoo	5
MOUNTFORD & THOMAS	August 24, 1883	12	402736	Untitled	5
NEW WHARF POTTERY CO.	December 27, 1882	1	391929	Untitled	5
OAKS, CLARE & CHADWICK	December 01, 1877	6	316764	Untitled	5
OLD HALL EARTHEN- WARE CO. LTD., THE	April 09, 1862	3	150538	Prince Consort	1,3,4
OLD HALL EARTHEN- WARE CO., LTD., THE	August 10, 1881	13	368044	Untitled	5
OLD HALL EARTHEN- WARE CO., THE	May 06, 1861	5	140480-1	Untitled	2,5
OLD HALL EARTHEN- WARE CO., THE	December 11, 1872	8	268749	Untitled	5
OLDHAM, JAMES & CO.	May 05, 1870	1	241231	Untitled	5
PANKHURST & DIMMOCK	June 22, 1853	3	91469	Snake & Dog	1
PANKHURST & DIMMOCK	December 27, 1854	4	98641	Ivy	3,4
PANKHURST & DIMMOCK	January 19, 1855	3	99086	Untitled	2
PANKHURST, JAMES & CO.	January 15, 1856	4	103404	Home & Abroad	3
PHILLIPS, W. P. & G. & PEARCE	May 06, 1871	1	252258	Untitled	5
PINDER & BOURNE & CO.	June 19, 1873	3	273804	Untitled	2
PINDER & BOURNE & CO.	September 06, 1876	9	303308	Early Cartouche	2,6
PINDER, BOURNE & CO.	June 26, 1874	4	283275	Untitled	2

Potter	Reg. Date	Parcel	Reg. No.	Pattern	Reference
PINDER, BOURNE & CO.	November 07, 1877	10	316101	Japanese Sprays	1
PINDER, BOURNE & CO.	May 13, 1879	4	335148	Untitled	5
PINDER, BOURNE & CO.	December 07, 1880	10	359213	Untitled	5
PINDER, BOURNE & HOPE	April 05, 1861	3	139360	Acanthus	2,8
PLANT, R. H. & CO.	April 09, 1881	5	363793	Untitled	6
PLANT, R. H. & CO.	May 06, 1881	4	364736	Untitled	6
POWELL & BISHOP	October 31, 1867	7	213065	Hops Jug	2
POWELL & BISHOP	October 29, 1869	4	235942	Untitled	5
POWELL & BISHOP	December 18, 1869	2	237229	Untitled	2
POWELL & BISHOP	February 04, 1870	7	238603	Untitled	5
POWELL & BISHOP	February 15, 1872	3	260463	Untitled	5
POWELL & BISHOP	January 26, 1876	3	297978	Untitled	5
POWELL & BISHOP	March 09, 1878	11	319296	Untitled	2
POWELL, BISHOP & STONIER	May 10, 1880	6	349693	Untitled	5
POWELL, BISHOP & STONIER	January 09, 1883	3	392626	Untitled	5
POWELL, BISHOP & STONIER	September 07, 1883	19	403501-4	Untitled	6
PRATT & CO.	February 17, 1855	3	99394	Cupid & Bow	5
PRATT & SIMPSON	November 10, 1882	12	389797	Untitled	5
PRATT, F. & R.	April 20, 1861	6	139945	Untitled	5
PRATT, F. & R. & CO.	December 18, 1863	4	170294	Holly & Mistletoe	4
PRATT, F. & R. & CO.	September 06, 1866	4	200599	Untitled	4
PRATT, F. & R. & CO.	October 24, 1877	14	315574	Birds In Bamboo	2,3
PRATT, F. & R. & CO.	January 16, 1879	13	331342	Toucan	2
PRATT, JOHN & CO.	March 20, 1863	9	160753	Untitled	5
RAY, GEO.	April 21, 1852	4	84837	Dancers	3
RAY, GEO.	October 31, 1854	2	97508	Bird Feeding	5
RIDGWAY & ABINGTON	December 03, 1846	4	38606	Oak	2,3
RIDGWAY & ABINGTON	March 07, 1848	1	50635-6	Bulrush, Hops & Barley/ Harvest	1,3
RIDGWAY & ABINGTON	February 16, 1849	11	58474	Sylvan	1,3
RIDGWAY & ABINGTON	August 16, 1851	2	80184	Nineveh	1,3
RIDGWAY & ABINGTON	April 18, 1856	7	104397	John Barleycorn	1
RIDGWAY & ABINGTON	October 14, 1857	1	111585	Fuchsia	1,3
RIDGWAY & ABINGTON	October 07, 1858	1	115953	Oporto	2
RIDGWAY, SON & CO.	July 16, 1846	1	36167	Vines in Framework	3
RIDGWAY, E. J.	July 04, 1867	5	209362	Fluted Jug	6
RIDGWAY, J. & CO.	March 17, 1851	13	77481-91	Bouquet Jug	5
RIDGWAY, WM.	October 21, 1851	3	81057	Willie	1
ROBERTS J.	January 23, 1856	3	103506	Untitled	2
ROBINSON & LEADBEATER	July 02, 1872	2	263883-4	Untitled	6
ROBINSON & LEADBEATER	July 15, 1872	4	264194	Untitled	6
ROBINSON, J.	October 30, 1883	17	406187	Untitled	5
ROSE, JOHN & CO.	August 03, 1847	3	44872	Untitled	5
ROSE, JOHN & CO.	February 26, 1849	2	58578	Shell & Flowers	2
SCRIVENER, R. G. & CO.	December 27, 1872	8	269270	Untitled	5
SHARPE BROS. & CO.	September 03, 1858	2	115120	Corn On The Cob	2,5
SHORTER & BOULTON	March 17, 1881	9	362992	Untitled	5
SHORTER & BOULTON	November 23, 1881	13	373707	Untitled	5
SHORTER & BOULTON	March 27, 1882	10	378959	Untitled	5
SOANE & SMITH	July 18, 1876	3	301984	Untitled	5
STEEL, EDWARD	November 14, 1882	3	389911-2	Falstaff	6
TAMS, J.	October 27, 1880	20	357429	Untitled	5
TAMS, JOHN	June 18, 1883	11	399554	Untitled	5
THOMPSON BROS.	January 07, 1868	8	215636	Untitled	5
THOMPSON, J.	July 04, 1855	5	100624	Three Graces	5
TILL, BULLOCK & SMITH	December 05, 1861	5	147322	Untitled	5
TILL, THOS. & SON	April 01, 1852	1	84541	Floral	2
TILL, THOS. & SON	August 13, 1852	5	86126	Untitled	3
TILL, THOS. & SON	June 03, 1854	2	96003	David & Goliath/ Cain & Abel	2
TILL, THOS. & SONS	September 01, 1874	3	284791	Untitled	5
TILL, THOS. & SONS	July 05, 1876	1	301619	Untitled	5
TURNER, G. W. & SONS	February 17, 1883	13	394371	Untitled	5
TURNER, GODDARD & CO.	November 25, 1870	2	248052	Untitled	5
WALKER & CARTER	March 26, 1868	3	217630	Untitled	5
WALLEY (EDWARD) & T. & R. BOOTE	May 10, 1845	3	27482	Ranger	1,3
WALLEY, E.	June 21, 1850	4	69884	Diana	2,3
WALLEY, E.	April 26, 1851	3	78634	Ceres	1,2,3
WALLEY, E.	April 18, 1856	6	104396	George Washington	1,3
WALLEY, E. & W.	January 29, 1858	4	112876	Haverlock	4
WALLEY, E. & W.	November 11, 1858	2	116737	Gleaner	1,3,4
WALLEY, E. & W.	May 07, 1859	1	119721-2	Vintage	2
WALLEY, E. & W.	December 14, 1859	2	124716	Sportman/ Diamond Checkerboard	1,4
WARBURTON & BRITTON	March 13, 1855	4	99653	Untitled	2
WARBURTON, E.	April 03, 1883	3	396316	Untitled	5
WARDLE & CO.	October 17, 1876	9	304383	Untitled	5
WARDLE & CO.	August 06, 1879	6	337958	Untitled	5
WARDLE & CO.	January 27, 1880	13	345798	Untitled	5
WARDLE & CO.	July 09, 1881	10	366923	Untitled	5
WARDLE & CO.	October 29, 1881	11	372376	Untitled	5
WARDLE & CO.	June 13, 1882	14	381131-2	Untitled	5
WARDLE & CO.	July 14, 1882	10	383641	Untitled	5
WARDLE & CO.	May 31, 1883	17	398784	Untitled	5
WARDLE & CO.	June 21, 1883	22	399822	Untitled	5
WATCOMBE TERRA COTTA CLAY CO.	June 03, 1872	6	263106	Untitled	5
WEDGWOOD & CO.	January 21, 1861	7	137529	Untitled	5
WEDGWOOD & CO.	August 22, 1861	7	142847	Sylvan / Stylized Bloom	1,8
WEDGWOOD, JOSIAH	December 13, 1882	5	391364	Untitled	5
WEDGWOOD, JOSIAH & SONS	March 21, 1843	5	5993-4	Untitled	2
WEDGWOOD, JOSIAH & SONS	August 01, 1846	2	36447-8	Untitled	5
WEDGWOOD, JOSIAH & SONS	November 29, 1861	5	146924	Doric	4
WEDGWOOD, JOSIAH & SONS	June 06, 1867	3	208750	Caterer	2
WEDGWOOD, JOSIAH & SONS	December 20, 1867	3	215085	Untitled	5
WEDGWOOD, JOSIAH & SONS	June 19, 1876	2	301302	Untitled	2
WEDGWOOD, JOSIAH & SONS	May 03, 1878	2	321028	Under The British Flag	6
WEDGWOOD, JOSIAH & SONS	June 11, 1880	3	350616	Wicker	5
WEDGWOOD, JOSIAH & SONS	April 30, 1881	4	364529	Carlyle	5
WEDGWOOD, JOSIAH & SONS	May 16, 1881	2	365066	Beaconsfield	5
WEDGWOOD, JOSIAH & SONS	June 23, 1882	1	382594	Untitled	5
WEDGWOOD, JOSIAH & SONS	March 20, 1883	4	395819	Untitled	2
WEDGWOOD, JOSIAH & SONS	September 11, 1883	4	403665	Untitled	2
WHITTAKER, EDGE & CO.	May 06, 1882	6	380419	Lily	5
WILEMAN, J. F.	March 24, 1869	1	228141	Untitled	5
WILKINSON & RICKHUSS	June 19, 1857	2	110161	Aquatic	2
WILKINSON & SON	April 30, 1863	3	162021	Untitled	5
WILKINSON & SONS	March 13, 1863	3	160457	Untitled	5
WITHENSHAW, W. E.	March 28, 1876	8	299474	Untitled	5
WOOD & CO.	January 25, 1877	6	307236	Untitled	5
WOOD & SALE (Transfered to Dudson 2/65)	July 02, 1864	3	175959	Untitled	2,8
WOOD, E. A.	March 04, 1883	3	395818	Untitled	2
WOOD, E. A.	March 20, 1883	3	395818	Untitled	5
WOOD, EDMUND, T.	October 31, 1863	3	167612	Untitled	5
WOOD, GEO. & CO.	June 07, 1853	3	91329	Untitled	2
WOOD, HINES & WINKLE	May 05, 1882	2	380401	Untitled	5
WOOD, HINES & WINKLE	February 06, 1883	1	393668	Untitled	5
WOOD, HINES & WINKLE	November 01, 1883	25	406370	Untitled	5
WORCESTER ROYAL PORCELAIN CO., LTD.	February 02, 1877	7	307497	Untitled	5
WORCESTER ROYAL PORCELAIN CO., LTD.	April 19, 1880	11	348913	Untitled	5
WORCESTER ROYAL PORCELAIN CO., LTD.	September 30, 1880	4	355987	Untitled	5
WORTHINGTON & GREEN	January 04, 1855	2	98696	Cup Tosser	5
WORTHINGTON & GREEN	June 28, 1856	3	105223	Untitled	2,5
WORTHINGTON & GREEN	March 20, 1863	8	160752	Untitled	5
WORTHINGTON & SON	March 01, 1869	8	227558	Untitled	5
WORTHINGTON & SON	January 15, 1873	2	269690	Untitled	5
WORTHINGTON & SON	November 12, 1873	3	278185	Untitled	5
WORTHINGTON & SON	February 14, 1874	9	280492	Untitled	5
WORTHINGTON & SON	March 27, 1874	2	281404	Untitled	5
WORTHINGTON & SON	March 30, 1874	1	281437	Untitled	5
WORTHINGTON & SON	January 29, 1875	1	288861	Untitled	5
WORTHINGTON, THOS. & GREEN, J.	February 11, 1853	6	89646	Untitled	2
WRIGHT & RIGBY (Gen. Booth)	July 04, 1882	3	382859	Untitled	2,8
YEARSLEY, GEO.	February 02, 1869	4	226928	Untitled	6

APPENDIX B20: EARTHENWARE & JUGS, INCOMPLETE REGISTRY DATA

Potter	Location	Parcel	Reg. No.	Date	Pattern	Source
DUDSON, JAMES (7)	HANLEY	5	247901	November 21, 1870	Muses Jug	4, 5
KEENE, RICHARD, W.	*	*	103872	February 22, 1856	Here We Are Jug	1, 5
MINTONS	STOKE	4	292914	December 13, 1882	Untitled	4, 5
PACKES, J.	LONDON	6	243145	July 12, 1870	Untitled	4, 5
SANFORD ESTATE CLAY POTTERY CO.	DORSETSHIRE	4	130112	June 23, 1860	Untitled	1, 5
SANFORD ESTATE CLAY POTTERY CO.	DORSETSHIRE	5	130541-2	July 6, 1860	Victoria Regina Jug	3, 5
SANFORD ESTATE CLAY POTTERY CO.	DORSETSHIRE	5	131339	August 1, 1860	Prince of Wales Jug	1, 5
SANFORD ESTATE CLAY POTTERY CO.	DORSETSHIRE	9	132167-8	September 28, 1860	Loyal Volunteers Jug	2, 5
UNKNOWN	*	*	388793	October 1882*	Untitled	4

I would like to thank Geoffrey Godden for supplying data and filling in missing information, as was available:
An asterisk (*) within a data field indicates that no further information was available.
The foregoing incomplete information has been compiled from the following sources.

1 Peake, *William Brownfield*, See pp. 173*174, 184*185
2 Hughes, Vol. I, See No. 120, 141
3 Hughes, Vol. II, See No. 120
4 Peake, Unpublished Notes
5 Geoffrey Godden's registration files to be illustrated in Geoffrey Godden's *New Revised Handbook of Marks*,Barrie & Jenkins, London, 1999

(*Who were sources number 6, 7, 8?)

Part III. EUROPEAN POTTERS, PATTERNS & MARKS

This European Section is short in comparison to the English and American, because to my knowledge very little has been written by either English or European researchers on the various categories of Ironstone-type Earthenwares, their marks, patterns and brief histories, as covered in this Encyclopedia. This is the first comprehensive look into the production of European potteries. The listing is short and primarily covers Blue and White Transferware, Flown Blue and Mulberry Wares, because examples in the other categories have not been located by this author. Extensive correspondence with various museums and authors yielded limited information on potteries in eight countries. It is just of late that publications, articles and research have come forth.

The format of this section is in alphabetical order, listing potters by country. The countries included are: Belgium, Czechoslovakia, France, Germany, The Netherlands, Portugal, Russia and Sweden.

As Mr. Godden did not catalog European potters, there is no Godden number referenced in this section. The letter "C" will precede all KAD numbers, e.g.:

KAD NO.	MARK		DATING
C1	G. L.	GUILLAUME LAMBERT	(1859-1863)
C2	G. LAMBERT MAASTRICHT	GUILLAUME LAMBERT	
C3	G. L. & CO.	GUILLAUME LAMBERT	

KEY TO LETTERS PRECEDING "KAD NO."
A = AMERICAN (POTTERS)
B = ENGLISH (POTTERS)
C = EUROPEAN (POTTERS)

Additionally, potters are listed in alphabetical order, so inclusions start with the letter "A" and continue on with "A Bros.", "A B", "A & B", etc.

POTTERY LISTING BY COUNTRY

Belgium
- Boch Fréres
- J.B. Cappellmans Ainé/W. Smith & Sie
- Mouzin Lecat & Co.

Czechoslovakia
- August Nowotny & Co.

France
- David Johnston et Cie
- Keller & Guerin/Luneville
- Jean Pouyat
- Utzschneider/Sarreguemines
- J. Vieillard & Cie

Germany
- Franz Anton Mehlem
- Reinhold Schlegelmilch
- Schmidt & Co.
- Villeroy & Boch

The Netherlands
- Clermont and Chainaye/Maastricht
- Guillaume Lambert (& Co.)
- Petrus Regout (& Co.)
- Société Céramique

Portugal
- Gilman & Co./Sacavem

Russia
- T.J. Kuznetzoff

Sweden
- GEFLE Porcelains AB
- Gustavsberg (Vänge)
- Rörstand
- Upsala/Ekeby

BELGIUM

BOCH

KAD NO. | MARK

Boch Frères
Keramis Pottery
Saint Vaast-La Louvière (Belgium), 1841-1980
Subsequently acquired by de Sphinx, Maastricht, Netherlands
With the partition of Luxembourg and Belgium, the Belgian members of the Boch family moved to Keramis (La Louvière in 1841 and established the Keramis Pottery in 1844/1845).

C1 **BOCH FRERES KERAMIS** — Printed marks of differing design, often accompanied by a laurel branch, c.1844-1870.

C2 

Printed mark, c.1850-1910.

C2A **B. F.**
C2B **B. F. K.** — Printed marks of differing design and pattern name. Mark often includes full name or initials "B.F." or "B.F.K.", c.1850-1910.

KAD NO.	MARK	

C3
C4
C5
C6
C7

Typical Examples Include:

c.1850+ **c.1850-1920** **c.1870+** **c.1900+**

Printed marks noted accompanying undecorated white wares.
- Back mark found in green on ordinary earthenwares.
- Back mark found in black on finer quality earthenwares.

C8
C9
C10
C11

Typical Examples Include:

c.1870-1882 **c.1882-1886** **c.1887-1910**

C12 

Printed mark, c. 1910-1966.

C13 

Printed Pottery trade-mark "KERAMIS" noted c.1925(27)-1935.

- Wetherbee, *White Ironstone A Collector's Guide*, p. 185, fig. 18, notes a glass dryer made by Boch Frères.

For further reading, refer to John P. Cushion. *Manuel de la Céramique Européenne*, Fribourg, Switzerland, Office du Livre. 1987; Dieter Zühlsdorff, *Marken Lexikon, Porzellan und Keramik Report, 1885-1935*. Stuttgart, Germany. Arnoldsche, 1988. P. 543(3), 670.

In materials sent to me by Boch Frères, *Collection Journal No. 39*, March 1994 and *Marketing Directory, 1841-1966*, records and photos indicate patterns in both Blue and White and Flow Blue. See p. 82 for a Flow Blue service and p. 84 for the pattern "Althea". It is evident that this pottery is an area ripe for research of both manufacturing history and patterns.

PATTERNS
BLUE & WHITE TRANSFERWARE

CATEGORY	PATTERN
M	Denttello
G	Napoleon
G	Orphans
G	Visité à la Ferme

BELGIUM

CAPPELLMANS

KAD NO.	MARK	
		J.B. Cappellmans Ainé/W. Smith & Sie* **Jemappes near Mons, Belgium, 1845-1857** **Subsequently, J.B. Cappellmans (Till) (1870)**
C14	**J.B. CAPPELLMANS AINE** **W. SMITH & CO.** **BRUXELLES**	Printed or impressed marks of differing design. Pattern name often included, 1845-1857.
C15	**J.B. CAPPELMANS AINE** **W. SMITH & CIE** **BRUXELLES/BORDURE**	- Additional dated markings noted.

*See English potter, William Smith (& Co.), pp. 336-337

For further reading, refer to *NCS Newsletter* No. 100, Dec. 1995, pp. 39-46 for an article by John Cockerill, titled "English Earthenware Made In Belgium".

Patterns in earthenware have been noted, but not fully described. These were printed in blue, green, violet, decorated in Flown Blue and then highlighted in imitation gold.

PATTERNS

Actine
Bridge
Chasse
Chateau
Chinois
Famille Royale
Fountain
Indian
Indian Sports
Dermesse
Lion
Marble
Mois
Napoleon
Orhans
Palestine
Parturages
Renaissance
Rosace
Sacred History of Joseph and His Brothers
Selected Views
Simplon
Subjets Champêtres
Subjets Militaires
Subjets Réligieux
Vues
Vues Des Indies
Warbler
Willow

BELGIUM

MOUZIN LECAT

Mouzin Lecat & Co.
Nimy, Belgium, 1851-1898
(The seat of the Master School of Ceramics)

Bousies Family	**1781-1849**
Jean-Pierre Mouzin	**1849-1851**
Mouzin Lecat & Co.	**1851-1898**
Société Anonyme	**1898-1920**
Petrus Regout (of Maastricht, Holland)	**1921-1951**

C16 **MOUZIN LECAT & CO. NIMY** — Printed mark, pattern name included, c.1851-1898.
- Société Céramique acquires firm in 1920-(1951), see p. 650.

PATTERNS
FLOW BLUE

CATEGORY	PATTERN
O	Pavillons Chinois

- P. Williams, *Flow Blue*, Vol. 1, p. 138, notes a pattern "FLORA" marked "NIMY-BELGIUM", with the initials "H.J."

CZECHOSLOVAKIA

NOWOTNY

KAD NO. MARK

August Nowotny & Co.
Altrohlau, Bohemia, 1823-1884
(Presently, Stara Role, Czechoslovakia)
Formerly, Benedict Hasslacher (1813-1823)
Subsequently, Moritz Zdekauer (1884-1907)
-From 1823-1839 produced only Faience and Earthenware
-From 1839-1884 produced Household, Table & Decorative Porcelain

C17 **NOWOTNY** Impressed name mark, c.1823-1848.

C18
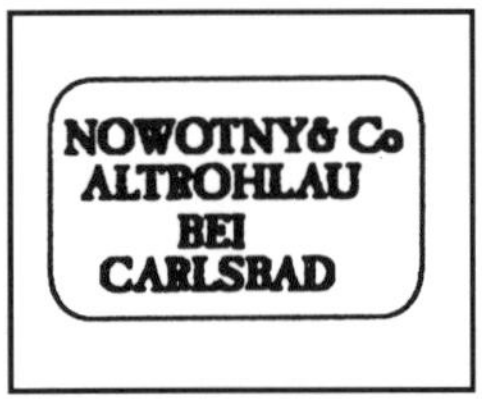

Impressed mark noted by P. Williams, *Flow Blue*, Vol. 2, p. 126 "BOUQUET". Also shown in *Thorn*, p. 26, Mark No. 9. Note spelling "CARLSBAD", 1823-1884.

C19
C20

Printed marks of differing design. Pattern name often included, 1838-1884.

C21

Impressed mark, 1838-1848. Note spelling "KARLSBAD".

C22

Impressed name mark, 1838-1848.

C23
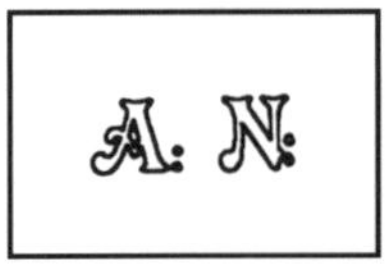

Impressed initial mark, c.1850-1870.

C24

Impressed initial mark "& C", 1870+.

For further reading, refer to *Thorn; Cushion;* and Robert E. Röntgen, *Marks on German, Bohemian and Austrian Porcelain, 1710 to the Present*, Schiffer Publishing Ltd., Atglen, Pennsylvania, 1981

PATTERNS
BLUE & WHITE TRANSFERWARE

CATEGORY	**PATTERN**
C	Grecian Urn

FLOW BLUE

CATEGORY	**PATTERN**
F	Bouquet

FRANCE

JOHNSTON

KAD NO | MARK

David Johnston et Cie
Bordeaux, France, 1834-1845
Subsequently, Jules Vieillard & Cie (1845-1895)

DATES	POTTERY	OWNER/PARTNERSHIP
c.1834-1845	David Johnston et Cie	David Johnston
c.1844	David Johnston et Cie	Jules Vieillard becomes technical and commercial advisor
c.1845-1895	Jules Vieillard et Cie	Jules Vieillard buys company
c.1895	Jules Vieillard et Cie	Company closed

C25 **DAVID JOHNSTON** — Printed or impressed marks of differing design. Pattern name often included, 1834-1845.

C26 **DAVID JOHNSTON & CO.**

C27 **DAVID JOHNSTON & CIE**

C28 

Printed triple crescent mark, 1834-1845.
- The triple crescent mark was continued from David Johnston (1834-1845).
- See J. Vieillard & Cie, p. 641.

For further reading, refer to *Coysh*, Vol. 2, p. 116 for additional comments and marks; *J. Vieillard & Cie, Éclectisme et Japonisme (Catalogue des Céramiques et dessins)*, published by Musée des Arts Decoratifs, Bordeaux Exhibit of October 24-December 10, 1986.

FRANCE

KELLER & GUERIN/LUNEVILLE

Keller & Guerin
Luneville, France, c.1790-1892

Jacques Chambrette founded pottery.	**c.1718-1758**
Gabriel Chambrette (son) takes over pottery.	**c.1758-1772**
Manufactured wares called CYFFLE.	**c.1766-1778**
Charles Loyal (son-in-law) comes into business.	**c.1786**
Business known as Keller & Guerin	**c.1790-1892**
Keller dies.	**c.1830**
Paris warehouse established.	**c.1877**
Business known as Keller, Guerin & St. Clement.	**c.1892**
Business established as a Société Anonyme.	**c.1922**
- Potteries located at Luneville, Badoniller and St. Clement.	
Edouard Fenal is director.	**c.1922-1955**

C29 **K & G LUNEVILLE** — Printed marks of differing design. Pattern name often included, 1892-1922.

Typical Examples Include:

C30
C31
C32

c.1850-1880 **c.1889+** **c.1889-1922**

Printed marks of differing design. Pattern name often included, c.1880s-1922.

KAD NO. | MARK

Petra Williams notes numerous patterns and refers to Thorn's marks. Upon checking these in *Thorn*, p. 7, Mark No's 1-3 (which are reproduced below), the type of patterns would indicate the late Victorian period into the 20th century.

Typical Examples Include:

C33
C34
C35

c.1879+

c.1889+

c.1889+

"GERMANY" added after 1891. Refer to the 1887 Act of Parliament, Merchandise Marks Act of the UK, and the US McKinley Tariff Act of 1891.
- A floral punch bowl with the wording (in red) TOM & JERRY is recorded in *Gaston,* Vol. 2, p. 449.
- It would appear that the factory produced only semi-porcelain from, c.1922-1955.

For earlier marks (1769-1780) refer to Ludwig Danckert, *Dictionary of European Porcelain*; J. Cushion, *Manual de la Céramique Europèene.* Fribourg, Switzerland, Office du Livre, 1987, pp. 357-358; *Karmason*, pp. 180-184; and *Snyder*, Vol. 2, p. 72

BLUE AND WHITE TRANSFERWARE SINGLE PATTERNS

CATEGORY	PATTERN
M	Chase
P/O	Timor

FLOW BLUE

CATEGORY	PATTERN
P/O	"The Arc"
F	Eglantine
M/A	Luneville
M	"Luneville Blue"
M/F	"Luneville Onion"
M	Opaque
F	Parpetta
F	Tom & Jerry
F	Violet

MULBERRY WARES

CATEGORY	PATTERN
F	Eglantine

FRANCE

POUYAT

Jean Pouyat
St. Yrieix (Haute-Vienne), France, 1842-1888
Subsequently, La Céramique (1888-1902)

Francois Pouyat opens factory at St. Yrieix near Limoges.	**c.1780**
Factory expanded	**c.1785-1786**
Pouyat takes over Hause Russinger at Cortile.	**c.1797-1820**
Pouyat is principal stockholder in Russinger.	**c.1800**
Pouyat sells interest in Russinger to son Jean (and two other sons).	**c.1810**
Pouyat Frères buys out old associates of a factory located in Fours Hievre.	**c.1820-1865**
Jean Pouyat opens manufactory at Place des Carmes.	**c.1842**
Jean Pouyat dies and 3 sons, Emile, Leonard & Charles Louis, take over pottery under name of Pouyat Frères and continue marks. Also open a second factory in St. Leonard.	**c.1849**
A. Dubreuil & Baron de la Bastide take over as directors. Company takes on name of La Céramique and continues mark.	**c.1888-1902**
Company purchased by William Guerin who forms Societé Guerin-Pouyat.	**c.1922-1923**
Company now called Société Guerin, Pouyat, Elite, Ltd.	**c.1923-1932**

KAD NO. MARK

C36 **J.P.** **L**

Printed marks of differing design. Pattern name often included, 1842-1888.

- As in England "L" would denote (area) Longton. In France it signifies "Limoges" (region). Initials continued by successors. "FRANCE" added c.1888-1902.

For further reading, refer to *Gaston*, Vol. 1, Plate 398, Mark No. 144; and Danckert's *Dictionary of European Porcelain*, pp. 342-343.

FLOW BLUE CATEGORY	PATTERN
F	Decor

FRANCE

UTZSCHNEIDER/SARREGUEMINES

Utzschneider/Sarreguemines
- and Various locations
Lorraine (France), 1799-1942
Subsequently, Villeroy & Boch (1942-1945)

Sarreguemines established by Fabry and Jacobi.	**c.1790**
Sarreguemines taken over by Utzschneider.	**c.1799-1836**
Sarreguemines taken over by Baron Alexandre de Geiger (son-in-law).	**c.1836**
Expanded into a second factory in Sarreguemines.	**c.1858**
Opened a third factory in Sarreguemines.	**c.1862**
Opened a fourth factory in Sarreguemines.	**c.1869**
Ceased production in 3rd and 4th factories during war.	**c.1870**
Paul de Geiger (son of Baron Alexandre) takes over as Director.	**c.1871-1913**
After Lorraine was annexed by Germany in 1871, part of factory moves into France. Also opened new factory in Digoin on the Saone-et-Loire.	**c.1876**
Name "DIGOIN" was included on marks of Sarreguemines.	**c.1877**
Factories of Sarreguemines, Digoin and Vitry Le François "reunited" and back in operation after W.W. I.	**c.1919-1942**
Business taken over by Villeroy & Boch during W.W. II.	**1942-1945**
Sarreguemines realigns with a group in Luneville.	**1979-1982**
Business renamed Sarreguemines-Bâtiment.	**1982**

C37

Printed marks of differing design. Pattern name often included, c.1840-1850.

C38

Printed marks of differing design. Pattern name often included, c.1850s.

C39

Printed variation of above mark, c.1886-1920.

KAD NO. | MARK

Typical Examples Include:

C40
C41
C42

Printed marks (Crest of Lorraine) of differing design. Pattern name often included, c.1850-1940. "MADE IN GERMANY" c.1888-1918, and "FRANCE" after 1920.

Typical Examples Include:

C43
C44
C45
C46
C47
C48

c.1850-1920

c.1864-1895

c.1888-1918

c.1890s

1920+

c.1940+

Variations of above mark are noted.

For further reading, refer to *Les Marques de Fabrique*. Edition Association des Amis du Musée de Sarreguemines, France 1990; Emile Decker & Christian Thevenin, *Faiences de Sarreguemines*, Nancy, France. Presses Universitaires de Nancy, 1992; *Karmason*, pp. 180-181; and *Snyder,* Vol. 2, pp. 72-73.

BLUE AND WHITE TRANSFERWARE SINGLE PATTERNS

CATEGORY	PATTERN
G	Favor
P/F	"Floral Vase"
G	Galilee
S	Gondorf Rhine #8
M	Royat
P/O	Timor (continued by Villeroy & Boch)
O	Willow

FLOW BLUE

CATEGORY	PATTERN
M/F	Bryonia (continued by Villeroy & Boch)
F	Fleurs
-	Floral Splendid
M/A	Persian Fans
M/A	Persian Medallion
M/A	Persian Moss
M/A	Persian Scroll
S	Pretoria
-	Quebec
-	Rhine Grape

MULBERRY WARES

CATEGORY	PATTERN
F	Anemone
F	Bryonia
S	Canards
F	Carmen
O	Corinthe
F	Erica
F	Flore
-	Fuchsia
-	Glaiful
F	Jardinière
O	Pevard
M	Rewowa

FRANCE

VIEILLARD

KAD NO.	MARK
C49	**J.V.C.**
C50	**J. VIEILLARD & CO.**
C51	**J. VIEILLARD & CO. BORDEAUX**
C52	**A. VIEILLARD PORCELAINE**

J. Vieillard & Cie
Bordeaux, France, 1845-1895
Formerly, David Johnston (c.1834-1845)

Printed or impressed marks of differing design. Pattern name often included, 1845-1895.
- The triple crescent mark was continued by J. Vieillard & Cie, c.1845-1895.
- See David Johnston & Cie, p. 637.

Typical Examples Include:

C28
C53
C54

- Arman, *China & Glass Quarterly,* Vol. 1, Oct./Nov. 1997, No. 4, p. 29 illustrates a back mark on a transfer plate that poses a problem. The back mark reads "MADE BY JOHNSTON/LONGPORT" (see Mark C28). The plate is a transfer plate with a portrait bust titled "MAXIMILLIANO PRIMERO/ EMPERADOS DE MEXICO", who ruled Mexico from 1864-1867. Johnston as potter in Longport has not been identified. It is possible, for marketing purposes that Vieillard used an English marking and exported through England - which may have had cheaper export tariffs to Mexico.

For further reading and marks, refer to *J. Vieillard & Cie, Eclectisme et Japonisme (Catalogue des Céramiques et des dessins)*, published by the Musée des Arts Décoratifs, Bordeaux for an exhibition of the works of Vieillard that was mounted October 24-December 10, 1986. This catalogue is well illustrated with both production examples and marks.

PATTERNS
FLOW BLUE

CATEGORY	PATTERN
F	Bordeaux

GERMANY

MEHLEM

Franz Anton Mehlem
Rhineland, Germany 1836-1920
Formerly, Stoneware Factory, Bonn (1755-1836)
Subsequently, Villeroy & Boch, Mettlach (1921-1931)

C55 

Printed initial mark, c.1887-1920.
- "MADE IN GERMANY" dates from 1887.

C56 

Printed or impressed mark. Pattern name often included, c.1887-1920. (*Gaston,* Vol. 1, Mark No 149, notes an additional unidentified impressed marking "DM/D" with the above circular impressed mark.)

KAD NO. | MARK

C57 

Printed mark "ROYAL/BONN" c.1890-1920.
- Mark without "ROYAL" dates from 1888.

C58 

Printed "Tower" mark, 1896-1920. See *Snyder*, Vol. 1, p. 117 for additional markings.
For further reading, refer to Danckert's *Dictionary of European Porcelain*, p. 43 "Bonn", pp. 85-86 and "Damm"; Robert E. Röntgen *Marks on German, Bohemian and Austrian Porcelain, 1710 to the Present*. Schiffer Publishing, Ltd., Atglen, PA, 1981; and J. Cushion. *Manuel de la Céramique Europénne.* Fribourg, Switzerland, Office du Livre, 1987, p. 437. "Poppelsdorf".

BLUE & WHITE TRANSFERWARE

CATEGORY	PATTERN
S	Rosenguirlande

FLOW BLUE

CATEGORY	PATTERN
S	Libertas
S	Malta
F	Meissen
O	Tokio
F	Wild Rose

GERMANY

SCHLEGELMILCH

Reinhold Schlegelmilch
Suhl & Tillowitz Potteries, Silesia,
Germany, 1869-1938
Subsequently, Lothar Schlegelmilch
Presently, Tulovice, Poland
- Suhl Pottery moved to Tillowitz in 1932

C59 

Printed mark incorporating the name Reinhold Schlegelmilch as "RS", 1869-1938.

C60 

C61 

Printed "House" trademark, 1898-1920. Registered December 10, 1898/No. 34775.
- "GERMANY" after 1891. (See *Snyder*, Vol. 2, p. 23)

C62 

Printed trademark "RST" registered May 23, 1916/No. 210505, c.1916-1938.

C63 

Printed mark, "EPOS", c.1927-1938.

KAD NO. **MARK**

Selected "RS" Printed Marks Include:

C64
C65
C66
C67

1904-1932

1904-1938

1904-1938

1904-1938

For further reading on German, Bohemian marks, etc. refer to *R.E. Röntgen, Gaston,* Vol. 1, pl. 412, and Clifford Schlegelmilch's *My Ancestor's China.*

PATTERNS
FLOW BLUE

CATEGORY	**PATTERN**
F	"Card Holder"
M	"Trinket Box"

- These pieces have not been seen by the author, and after extensive conversations with collectors in the United States, **no ironstone type earthenware has been confirmed for this firm.**

GERMANY

SCHMIDT

Schmidt & Co.
"Victoria" AG Porcelaine Factory,
Altrohlau, Bohemia (currently, Stara Role, Czechia) Germany, 1883-1945

C68 

Printed mark, c.1891-1918.
- Note spelling of "CARLSBAD", an earlier version of "KARLSBAD".

C69 

Printed mark "GEMMA", c.1894-1945.

C70 

Printed Crown mark with various country designations, 1904-1945:

- with "Austria" below 1904-1918

C71 

- with "Czechoslovakia" below 1918-1939

C72 

- with "Germany" 1939-1945

KAD NO. **MARK**

- Blakeney Art Pottery, England, 1968, also uses the marking "Victoria", see p. 113, refer to *Cushion*, p. 157.
- with "Victoria" 1919-1939

For further reading, refer to *Gaston*, Vol. 1, pl. 397; and *Pictorial Souvenirs of Britain* by Ian T. Henderson, London, David & Charles, 1974.

PATTERNS

FLOW BLUE

CATEGORY	**PATTERN**
G	"Two Ladies"

GERMANY

VILLEROY & BOCH

Villeroy & Boch
Mettlach (Saar), Germany and various other European locations, 1836-present
Formerly, Jean François Boch (1809-1836) and
Nicholas Villeroy (1791-1836)

C73 

Printed or impressed mark of the Wallerfangen Pottery, 1861-1876.

C74
C75

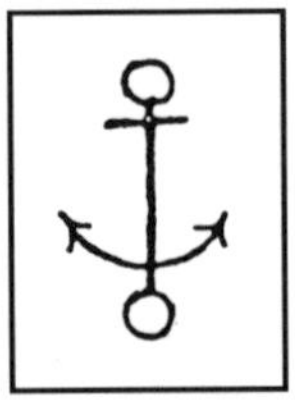

Impressed marks on earthenware. Mark C74 dates from 1824-1836, Mark C75 dates from 1836-1850.

Selected Marks Noted on Stoneware (Mettlach Pottery):

C76
C77
C78

c.1850-1860 **c.1860**

Printed initial mark "V&B". Pattern name often included, c.1860-1880

C79
C80
C81

C82 

Printed "GENERAL MARK", 1874-1918. "GENERAL MARK" continued by individual potteries, each noted by its own name: "Dresden", "Septfontaines/Luxemburg", "Schramberg", and "Wallerfangen" Note that mark "GRANIT" will accompany Granit wares.

KAD NO. **MARK**

Selected marks, 1876-1915, include:

C83
C84
C85

Septfontaines/ Luxemburg (1876-1915)

Schramberg (from 1833-1912)

Wallerfangen (1876-1915)

- An Importer's mark "N.S.&S. NY., SAXONY" has been noted.
- The above marks are found in various colors and were continued on to 1931 with the additional marking "MADE IN SAAR-BASIN".

Selected "Dresden" Marks, 1856-1945, May Include:

Marks found on Tiles & Ceramics

C86
C87
C88
C89

c.1887-1945

Decorative Colored Glazed Wares & Sanitary Wares

(1928)-1945

Additional Marks May Include:

C90
C91
C92

c.1885-present Mettlach (1809-present) Stone Ware only

(1895)-1912 Schramberg (1883-1912) Majolica only

1911-1912 Schramberg (1893-1912)

PATTERNS
BLUE AND WHITE TRANSFERWARE
SINGLE PATTERNS

CATEGORY	PATTERN
F	"Aster"
F	"Blue Rose"
S	Burgenland
A	Dresden
P/O	Timor

FLOW BLUE

CATEGORY	PATTERN
M	Alba
F	Aldine
F	Althea
F	Anemone
M	Bramble
O	"Chinoiserie"
F	Daisy
M	Dresden
F	Elbe
M	Fasan
F	Hellem
O	India ["Cockatoo at Fountain"]
F	Jardiniere
F/M	"Onion-Flora"
F	Rinceaux
M	Rubens
O	"Tonquin II"
S	Turkey

MULBERRY WARES

CATEGORY	PATTERN
F	Bryonia
O	India ["Cockatoo at Fountain"]
F	"Oriental Flowers"

For further reading, refer to Cushion, *Manual de la Céramique Europénne*; *Röntgen*, p. 37; *Gaston*, Vol. 1, Marks 151, 152; *Karmason*, pp. 194-195; and *Snyder*, pp. 73, 88.

THE NETHERLANDS

CLERMONT

Clermont and Chainaye
Maastricht, Holland, c.1850-1859
Subsequently, Guillaume Lambert (1859-1863)

KAD NO.	MARK	
C93	C.C.	Impressed marks of varying design. Pattern name often included, c.1850-1859.
C94	C & C MAASTRICHT	-Initials "C.C." also used by William Ridgway, Son & Co. (1841-1846). See KAD B2055 and *Snyder*, *Historic Staffordshire*, p. 78 for pattern "Catskill Moss".
C95	C & C PEARL MAASTRICHT	
C96		Printed mark. Pattern name often included, c.1850-1859. - Mark may also include a signed marking, impressed as above, c.1850-1859. For further reading, refer to *A. Polling*, pp. 74-78 for additional information on Guillaume Lambert; Marie-Rose Bogaers, *Drukdecors op Maastrichts Aardewerk, 1850-1900*. Lochem, The Netherlands, Uitgeversmaatschappij, Antiek Lochem bv, 1992, pp. 170-171 for a listing of patterns for Clermont and Chainaye, and pp. 201-202 for information on N.A. Bosch, 1853-1854 - 1866/1867.

THE NETHERLANDS

LAMBERT

KAD NO.	MARK	
		Guillaume Lambert (& Co.) **Maastricht, Holland, 1859-1863** **Formerly, Clermont and Chainaye (1850-1859)** **Subsequently, Société Céramique (1863-1958)**
C97	**G.L.**	Impressed initial marks accompanied with five pointed impressed star. Pattern name included, 1859-1863.
C98	**G. LAMBERT MAASTRICHT**	Printed name mark, 1859-1863.
C99		Printed marks of various design. Pattern name often included, 1859-1863.
C100	**G.L. & CO.**	Printed initial/name mark, 1859-1863.

For further reading, refer to *Polling*, pp. 79-82. Also refer to Marie-Rose Bogaers, *Drukdecors op Maastrichts Aardewerk 1850-1900*. Lochem, The Netherlands, Uitgeversmaatschappij, Antiek Lochem bv, 1992, pp. 172-173.

THE NETHERLANDS

PETRUS REGOUT

KAD NO.	MARK	
		Petrus Regout (& Co.) **Maastricht, The Netherlands, 1836-1960** **Petrus Regout c.1836-1880** **P. Regout & Co. c.1880-1899** **P. Regout/De Sphinx c.1899-1960** **Royal Sphinx c.1960-Present**
C101	**PETRUS REGOUT MAASTRICHT**	Impressed mark, 1836-1890. The name Petrus Regout appears in many different forms. - "& CO." added from 1880. - Although company name was changed in 1890, the mark was continued.
C102	**P.R.**	Impressed initial mark, 1850-1890. Various registration marks noted, either impressed or on pad.
C103	**SPHINX**	Impressed mark, 1890-1945. The word "SPHINX" may be replaced by an impressed image of a Sphinx. - It is noteworthy to mention here, that *Coysh*, Vol. 1, p. 299, states that copper plates were provided by Staffordshire engravers in the 1850s, and that patterns are often noted with the makers' initials missing - thus causing confusion as to the country of origin.
C104	**P.R.**	Printed marks, 1850-1880. Markings may be within an oval form.
C105	**P. REGOUT**	- *Polling* shows and interesting marking "WEDGWOOD/P. REGOUT", 1860-1880; evidently cashing in on the famous name Wedgwood.
C106	**P. REGOUT MAASTRICHT**	Printed name marks, 1850-1880.
C107	**PETRUS REGOUT**	

KAD NO.	MARK	
		Typical Marks Include:
C108 C109 C110		  
C111 C112		  c. 1850-1880
		- See *Polling,* pp. 16-20 for a full range of impressed marks
C113	**PETRUS REGOUT & CO. MAASTRICHT**	Printed mark, 1883-1900, which may or may not be marked "MADE IN HOLLAND". "& CO." dates from 1880 and was continued until 1960. "N.V. SPHINX" used from 1928, while older marks remained in use.
C114	**P. REGOUT & CO. MAASTRICHT (PATTERN NAME) MADE IN HOLLAND**	Printed mark noted on export china, 1891+.
		Typical Marks Include:
C115 C116 C117 C118		 **1883-1900 1935-1955**  **1890-1893**  **1891+**  **1935-1960**
C119	**PETRUS REGOUT & CO. MAASTRICHT MADE IN HOLLAND BRITISH REGISTERED DESIGN**	Printed mark, 1935-1950
C120		Printed English Staffordshire Knot, 1855-1880. This mark is based upon prize medals won at the 1851 London Exposition. Refer to *Polling*, pp. 20-22.
C121		Printed mark noted on export wares, 1887-1934. This mark is similar to a Clementson Bros. mark (1865-1916). See p. 148. Refer to *Godden*, Marks No. 906 and 907.

For further reading, refer to Howard Davis. *Chinoiserie Polychrome Decoration on Staffordshire Porcelain 1790-1850*. England, Rubicon Press. 1991. pp. 186-189, Appendix 2 "Staffordshire Engravers Lines With European Potters". Also refer to *FOB* Bulletin No. 89, Autumn 1995, p. 3 for an article by David Furniss titled "Adams 'Lasso' or Amazon Pattern and Petrus Regout 'Indian Traffic' Pattern."

KAD NO.	MARK	
C122	**S-M**	Printed marks for the export market marked "S-M" (Sphinx-Maastricht),Markings "SEMI PORCELANA" and "WHITE STONE" also noted, 1906-1929.
C123		

Typical Examples Include:

C124 

C125 

C126 

C127 

Printed mark evidently for the American market, 1900-1934. Note marking "WHITE GRANITE".

- Many of Regout's Blue and White patterns are also found in polychrome, carmine violet as well as other colors.

For further reading refer to *Polling,* pp. 20-22 and 28-43 for a full range of marks up to 1960; Marie-Rose Bogaers. *Drukdecors op Maastrichts Aardewerk, 1850-1900*. Lochem, The Netherlands. Uitgeversmaatschappij, Antiek Lochem bv, 1992; *FOB* Bulletin No. 56, Summer 1987, p. 12; Bulletin No. 69, Autumn 1990, p. 9, and Bulletin No. 78, Winter 1992-1993, p. 78; Howard Davis *Chinoiserie, Polychrome Decoration on Staffordshire Porcelain, 1790-1850*. London. Rubicon Press, 1991; and *Stoltzfus/ Snyder, p. 139.*

PATTERNS
BLUE AND WHITE TRANSFERWARE
SINGLE PATTERNS

CATEGORY	PATTERN
S	Alpine
-	Amazon
-	Awa
-	Bali
G	Ruth Boaz
P/O	Canton
P/S	Castillo
G	Dancing
P/O	Formosa [Slamat]
P/O	Honc
G	Indian Traffic*
M	Orient
-	Packhorse
P/O	Pajong
P/O	Pekin
-	Pilgrim

CATEGORY	PATTERN
-	Pleasure Party
-	Plough
P/C	Pompeia
P/O	Potiche
P	Red Cross
P/O	Sana (2)
P/O	Slamat
O	Swing
O	Syrian
M	Tancrede
G	Teadrinker
-	Tecla
P/O	Timor
F	Wild Rose
O	Willow

**See *Cluett*, p. 73. See comments, p. 249.

PATTERNS
FLOW BLUE

CATEGORY	PATTERN
S	Abbey (questionable)**
S	Alpine
F	Atlanta
F	Aurorea
O	Chinesch (Chinessch)
M/A	Excelsior
O	Hindostan
O	Honc
S	Lincoln's House (5)
S	Miller
C	Mythology
O	Oriental
O	Pajong
O	Pekin
M/A	Plata (1, & 2)
M	Spinach Leaf (Brush Stroke)
M/A	Superior
O	Timor
O	Vintage

For a full listing of patterns refer to Marie-Rose Bogaers, *Drukdecor op Maastrichts Aardewerk 1850-1900*. Lochem, The Netherlands, Uitgeversmaatschappij, Antiek Lochem bv, 1992. pp. 174-195. It would also be helpful to cross reference patterns with the marks found in *Polling.*

THE NETHERLANDS

SOCIÉTÉ CÉRAMIQUE

KAD NO.	MARK	
		Société Céramique **Maastricht, Holland, 1863-1958** **Formerly, Guillaume Lambert (1859-1863)** - Note that Société Céramique assumed the firm of Mouzin Lecat & Co., Nimy Belgium in 1920, see p. 635.
C128	**S. C.**	Impressed marks with printed pattern name included, 1863-1900.
C129	**SOCIÉTÉ CÉRAMIQUE MAASTRICHT**	Printed marks of differing design, 1863-1958. “HOLLAND” included, 1870-1895. “MADE IN HOLLAND” noted after 1891.
C130	**SOCIÉTÉ CÉRAMIQUE MAESTRICHT HOLLAND**	
C131	**SOCIÉTÉ CÉRAMIQUE MAESTRICHT MADE IN HOLLAND**	

Typical Marks Include:

C132
C133
C134
C135

1870-1880

1870-1895

1891-1900

1900-1957

Note: Ian T. Henderson's *Pictorial Souvenirs of Britain*. David & Charles, London. 1974, pp. 123-126, notes the problems facing all manufacturers relative to the Act of Parliament, Merchandise Marks Act of 1887. This required foreign countries to mark their pieces "*Made In* _______". This act superseded the U.S. McKinley Tariff Act of 1891 which also required the country of origin to be marked on china imports. The British act was aimed at false deception and imposed no custom duties, whereas the American act was protectionist in nature, and imposed custom duties. It is well known that English potters anticipated the Merchandise Marks Act, and they marked their pieces prior to the requisite date of 1891. This practice confuses the issue as to when pieces were truly made. Of course, pieces manufactured for the English Colonies and for home consumption did not have to be marked - thus further confusing exact dating.

PATTERNS
BLUE AND WHITE TRANSFERWARE
SINGLE PATTERNS

CATEGORY	PATTERN
P/S	Alpine
-	Awa
-	Bali
-	Bangor
P/O	Japonais
P/M	Joko
-	Matjan
-	Paddyhalm
-	Paysage
P/O	Potiche
-	Sadi
G	Teadrinker

FLOW BLUE

CATEGORY	PATTERN
O	Amour
M/H	Hannibal
M/A	Regina
-	Splendid

For a further listing of patterns, illustrations and dates refer to Marie-Rose Bogaers, *Drukdecors op Maastrichts Aardewerk 1850-1900*. Lochem, The Netherlands. Uitgeversmaatschappij, Antiek Lochem bv, 1992, pp. 172-173

PORTUGAL

GILMAN/SACAVEM

KAD NO. **MARK**

Gilman & Co.
(A Real Fabrica de Louca de Sacavem), Sacavem (10 miles from Lisbon), Portugal, 1903-1907
Formerly, Baroness Howorth (1896-1903)
Subsequently, Gilman & Comandita (1907-1910)

DATE	NAME	OWNERS/PARTNERS
1850-1880	A Real Fabrica de Louca de Sacavem	Manuel Joaquim Afonso
1880-1896	A Real Fabrica de Louca de Sacavem	Howorths (Guilherme & John Stott) buy out Manuel Joaquim Afonso.
1893-1903	A Real Fabrica de Louca de Sacavem	Baron John Stott Howorth dies, Widow Howorth runs company with James Gilman as manager.
1903-1907	A Real Fabrica de Louca de Sacavem/ "Gilman & Cia"	Baroness Howorth dies. Company now owned and run by James Gilman.
1907-1910	Gilman & Comandita	James Gilman makes son Raul Gilman manager and hires Herbert Gilbert.
1910-1929	Fabrica de Louca de Sacavem	(as above, 1907-1910)
1929-1992	Fabrica de Louca de Sacavem	Herbert Gilbert buys out Raul Gilman. Company now run by Gilbert family.

Printed marks of differing design. Pattern name often included, c.1850-1903.

Selected Marks Include:

C136
C137
C138
C139
C140

1850-1855

1870-1880

1880-1896

1884-1896

1894-1896

C141

Printed marks, 1903-1907. "PORTUGAL" noted after 1891.

- See *Gaston*, Vol. 1, p. 151, pl. 409, Mark No. 156.

For further reading, refer to J. Cushion, *Manuel de la Céramique Europénne,* pp. 328-329.

PATTERNS
FLOW BLUE

CATEGORY	PATTERN
O	"No Pattern Name"
F	Togo

RUSSIA

KUZNETZOFF

T.J. Kuznetzoff
Early 19th century - 1864 Russia
Various locations and family ownerships, 1864-present

C142 **M.C.K.**

P. Williams, *Staffordshire, Vol. 1,* pp. 177-178 notes the pattern "Acropolis" with the printed marking "M.C.K." being of the Bronitzi Pottery (1892-1925).
- Danckert's *Dictionary of European Porcelain*, pp. 198-200 cites some 54 marks for this family of potters.

DATE	POTTERY	OWNER/FAMILY MEMBER
Early 19th -1870	Novocharitonowa Pottery	T.J. Kuznetzoff
1832-?	Duljewo Pottery Established	T.J. Kuznetzoff
?-1864	Duljewo Pottery	S.T. Kuznetzoff
1864-?	Duljewo Pottery	- Kuznetzoff (son of M.S.)
c.1842-end of 19th c.	Riga Porcelain Factory	M.S. Kuznetzoff
1870-	Acquired Kusnezowo Faience Factory	M.S. Kuznetzoff
1878-	Wolchow Factory Built	I.E. Kuznetzoff
1887	Budy Porcelaine Factory Built	M.S. Kuznetzoff near Charkow
1891	Werbiliki (near Twer) acquired Gardner's	M.S. Kuznetzoff Factory
1892-1900	Slawjansk Factory Built	M.S. Kuznetzoff
1892(1900)-1925	Bronitzi took charge of Mercury Factory	I.E. Kuznetzoff
1925-present	Bronitzi, Mercury Factory produced only	I.E. Kuznetzoff utility wares
1900-	Grusinow Works established	I.E. Kuznetzoff

SWEDEN

GEFLE

KAD NO. **MARK**

GEFLE Porcelains AB
Gävle, Sweden, 1910(11)-1936
Formerly, A Pottery & Tile Co. (1850-1910)
Subsequently, Upsala-Ekeby (c.1936-present)

C143 

Printed marks of differing design, 1910(11)-1930.

C144 

Printed marks of differing design, 1930-1936.

For further reading, refer to Tord Gyllenhammer (publisher) *Porslin Modeller Och Dekorer*. Jönkóping, Sweden, 1979

SWEDEN

GUSTAVSBERG (Vänge)

Gustavsberg (Vänge),
Oldenberg Factory nr. Bredsjö, 1786-c.1860 Sweden
(and various other locations from the middle seventeenth century to the present)

C145 **G** — Printed marks, pattern name often included, c. 1810-.

C145A **GUSTAFSBERG**

C146 **GUSTAFSBERG** — Impressed name mark with or without anchor, c.1820-1860.

C147 

KAD NO.	MARK	

Typical Marks Include:

C148
C149
C150

c.1810-

c.1845-

c.1866-

- The spelling Gustafsberg underwent a change in the early twentieth century to Gustavsberg.

For further reading, refer to *Danckert*, pp. 149-150; *Cushion*, pp. 238-239; *Cameron*, p. 150; and Maria Penkala, *European Pottery, A Guidebook for the Collector and Dealer*. Schidam, Netherlands, Interbook International bv, 1980.

PATTERNS

BLUE & WHITE TRANSFERWARE
SINGLE PATTERNS

CATEGORY	PATTERN
F	Asiatic Pheasanats
O	Gonggong
M	Hannibal
M	Lilja
O	London
O	Willow

FLOW BLUE

CATEGORY	PATTERN
M	Agir
Z	"Bluebird"
C	Caesar
F	"Dogwood"
F	Lilium

MULBERRY WARES

CATEGORY	PATTERN
F	Florilla

SWEDEN

RÖRSTAND

Rörstand
Lidköping (near Stockholm) Sweden, 1762-Present
History:

Rörstand founded	**1726**
Rörstand builds the Arabia Porcelain Factory (in Helsinki, Finland)	**1874**
Rörstand acquires the Goteborg Porcelain Factory which was established in 1898 (Sweden)	**1914**
Rörstand sells the Arabia Porcelain Factory	**1916**
Rörstand moves to the Goteborg facilities	**1926**
Rörstand purchases Lidköping Porcelain Factory (established in 1910)	**1929**
Arabia purchases Rörstand	**1929**
Rörstand becomes an independent company	**1931**
Rörstand has a new factory built at Lidköping	**1935**
Rörstand acquired by Upsala/Ekeby	**1964**
Upsala/Ekeby acquired by Arabia Porcelain Factory	**1975**
Arabia acquired by Wärtsîla (a Finnish company)	**1988**
Wärtsîla acquired by Hackman, Rörstand A.B.	**1990**
Company renamed Hackman Houseware & Hackman Tabletop Co.	**1994**

KAD NO.	MARK	
C151	**RÖRSTAND H4**	Printed or impressed marks of differing design. Pattern name often included, c.1830-1850.
C152	**RÖRSTAND 15**	
C153	**4-H RÖRSTAND E LEKSAND**	

KAD NO. | **MARK**

For an earlier history of the pottery and its marks refer to *Cushion*, *Handbook of Pottery & Porcelain Marks*, pp. 240-241, and to his *Manuel de la Céramique Europénne,* pp. 459-461; and *Danckert*, pp. 212-213.

Selected Printed Marks Include:

C154
C155
C156
C157
C158
C159

1850-1860

1852+

1859-1870

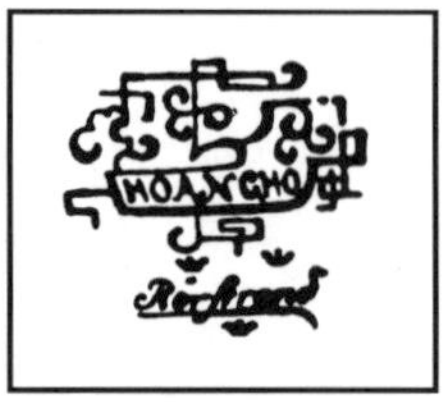

1878

1884

C160 **IRONSTONE CHINA RÖRSTAND** — Impressed marks often accompanying printed pattern name mark, c. 1850-1870 (note two variations).

C161 **IRONSTONE CHINA RÖRSTAND**

For further reading, refer to *FOB,* No. 83, Winter 1993, p. 9; and Bengt Nyström, *Rörstand Porcelains, The Robert Schreiber Collection - Art Nouveau Masterpieces*. New York, London & Stockholm, Abbeville Press, 1996.

PATTERNS

BLUE AND WHITE TRANSFERWARE

SINGLE PATTERNS		**FLOW BLUE**		**MULBERRY WARES**	
CATEGORY	**PATTERN**	**CATEGORY**	**PATTERN**	**CATEGORY**	**PATTERN**
F	Anna	F	"Grasse"	F	"Ivy & Flowers"
S	Arcade	F	"Pense Rörstand"	O	Japan
M	Birgitta	M	Skane	F	"Nosegay"
Z	Elg				
P/O	Japan				
M	Norman				
S	Ruins				

SWEDEN

UPSALA/EKEBY

Upsala/Ekeby
Ekebybruk (outside of Upsala) Sweden, 1886-1975
Subsequently, "Wartila" (a Finnish company) (1975-1990)

Acquisitions:

Gefle Porcelains AB	**1933**
A.B. Karlskrona (Founded in 1918 and until 1968)	**1942**
Acquires Rörstand	**1964**
In turn, acquired by Arabia	**1975**
(Also see Rörstand)	

C162

Printed marks of differing design, pattern name often included, 1886-1984. Trade-mark "UE" from 1920.

KAD NO. **MARK**

C163

Printed marks of Karlskrona continued. Note the addition of "UPSALA-EKEBY", c.1942+.

Typical Marks Include:

C164
C165
C166
C167
C168

1925+

1930+

1936+

1960+

1962-1971

For further reading, refer to *Danckert*, pp. 465-466.

PATTERNS

FLOW BLUE

CATEGORY	PATTERN
M/F	Vinranka (until 1969)

MULBERRY WARES

CATEGORY	PATTERN
F	Mullbär (1943-1964)

FLOWN BLUE - DINNER SERVICES

CATEGORY	PATTERN	DESIGNER	PRODUCTION PERIOD
F	Blå Blom	Paula von Freymann	1964-1967
F	Christina	Arthur Percy	1943
F	Pors	Berit Ternell	1961-1962
-	Scala	Berit Ternell	1958-1961
F	Vinranka	Arthur Percy	1938-1969

FLOWN BLUE - COFFEE & TEA SERVICES

CATEGORY	PATTERN	DESIGNER	PRODUCTION PERIOD
-	Cleo	Arthur Percy	1959
F	Pors	Berit Ternell	1960
F	Vinranka	Arthur Percy	1939-1969

FLOWN BLUE - FANCY GOODS

CATEGORY	PATTERN	DESIGNER	PRODUCTION PERIOD
F	Blå Blad	Arthur Percy	1948-1955
F	Blå Blom	Paula von Freymann	1964
F	Gripsholm	Arthur Percy	1946-1957
-	Mullbär	Ruben Wallström	1943-1964

APPENDIX C1: EUROPEAN POTTERS BY INITIAL

INITIAL	POTTERY
A.N. (& C.)	AUGUST NOWOTNY & CO.
B.F. (K)	BOCH FRERES
B.H.S. & CO.	GILMAN & CO.
C. (&) C.	CLERMONT AND CHAINAYE
E.P.O.S.	REINHOLD SCHLEGELMILCH
F.A.M.	FRANZ ANTON MEHLEM
G.	GUSTAVSBERG
G.L. (& CO.)	GUILLAUME LAMBERT
J.P./L.	JEAN POUYAT
J.V.C. (CO.)	J. VIEILLARD & CIE.
K. & G.	KELLER & GUERIN
K.P.	UPSALA/EKEBY
M.C.K.	T.J. KUZNETZOFF
M.J.A.	GILMAN & CO.
P.R.	PETRUS REGOUT (& CO.)
U. & C.	UTZSCHNEIDER/SARREGUEMINES
UE	UPSALA/EKEBY
V. & B.	VILLEROY & BOCH

APPENDIX C2:CROSS REFERENCE OF BACK MARKS

MARK	POTTERY
(ROYAL) BONN	FRANZ ANTON MEHLEM
BORDEAUX	DAVID JOHNSTON
BORDEAUX	J. VIEILLARD & CIE
CARLSBAD	SCHMIDT & CO.
DIGOIN	UTZSCHNEIDER/SARREGUEMINES
GEMMA	SCHMIDT & CO.
KARLSBAD	AUGUST NOWOTNY & CO.
KARLSKRONA	UPSALA/EKEBY
KERAMIS	BOCH FRERES
LA LOUVIERE	BOCH FRERES
LUNEVILLE	KELLER & GUERIN
MAASTRICHT	CLERMONT AND CHAINAYE
MAASTRICHT	GUILLAUME LAMBERT
MAASTRICHT	PETRUS REGOUT (& CO.)
MAASTRICHT	SOCIETE CERAMIQUE
MEISSEN	FRANZ ANTON MEHLEM
METLACH	VILLEROY & BOCH
NIMY	MOUZIN LECAT & CO.
SACAVEM	GILMAN & CO.
SARREGUEMINES	UTZSCHNEIDER/SARREGUEMINES
SCHRAMSBERG	VILLEROY & BOCH
SPHINX	PETRUS REGOUT (& CO.)
VICTORIA	SCHMIDT & CO.
WALLERFANGEN	VILLEROY & BOCH

Part IV. IMPORTERS, RETAILERS, WHOLESALERS, and AUCTIONEERS Of EARTHENWARE AND SOUVENIR WARES UNITED STATES AND CANADA

From the eighteenth to the twentieth century importers and/or retailers played an important role in distributing table and decorative wares throughout the United States and Canada. As in England, china and earthenware destined for sale and distribution was auctioned on U.S. and Canadian wharves during the late eighteenth and early nineteenth centuries. As towns and cities grew, so did an emerging network of importers, retailers and tradesmen who brought their wares to all areas of the expanding North American continent. Importers and retailers, as well as others, used china and earthenware as an advertising vehicle as is evident by the **printed backstamps** of the American and Canadian Importer listing.

An exception has been noted for the American importer, John Greenfield, importer of china and earthenware (for James & Ralph Clews, 1815-1834), at No. 77 Pearl Street, New York. His marking (the only one recorded to-date) is an **impressed** double circle along with an impressed Clews circular mark (recorded in the *FOB Bulletin* No. 94, Winter '96/'97, p. 8 and *Arman Quarterly*, Vol. 1, July-August 1997, No. 3, p. 8, "Driving a Bear Out of Sugar Canes").

Canada's rich history of china imports paralleled that of the United States. The major waterways of Canada not only helped move wares into the back country, but also served to move goods of the constantly expanding chinaware trade into the United States via the Mississippi, Missouri and Ohio rivers, etc. Later expansion was effected by rail and other avenues of ground transportation. Flow Blue chinaware was the predominant media used and ordered for advertising and special occasion pieces. In addition, military camps, steamship lines, hotels, taverns, etc. placed direct orders for their china/earthenware needs as well as orders for special and/or occasional pieces. Further, pattern and/or maker's marks, backstamps often included advertising marks, as noted, but not limited to:

- SAMPSON BRIDGWOOD & SON (LTD.) "Made for Walker and Pratt Manufacturing Company, Boston, Massachusetts" and "Charles R. Lynde, Importer of China and Glass, 424 Boylston Street, Boston, Massachusetts" marked "Crawford Cooking Ranges." *(Crawford Cooking Ranges has also been noted with a Rowland & Marsellus marking.)*
- BURGESS & LEIGH, Burleigh pattern imprinted with the Harvard University Insignia.
- W.H. GRINDLEY & CO., Melbourne pattern marked "First Baptist Ladies Society, 1904".
- GEORGE JONES & SONS (LTD), Abbey Pattern - a "Shredded Wheat Dish" used as a promotional give-away.
- WOOD & SON(S) (LTD), Trilby Pattern marked "Compliments John A. Hedin & Co., Furniture & Carpets, East Cambridge, Mass."

The late Victorian period ushered in the manufacture of English china "Souvenir" wares, predominantly in blue, another important export commodity to the United States. Many of these "Souvenir" wares are marked and identified by both the potter and importer. With the emergence of department stores, which now brought specialties under one roof, this late Victorian fad found new venues for reaching the market place.

I have attempted to organize this information into a cohesive, but nowhere complete, listing which is separated into four sections:

- **American Importers, Wholesalers, Retailers and Auctioneers, 18th - early 20th century.**(1)
- **American Importers, Wholesalers, Retailers and Auctioneers, 18th - early 20th century.**(2)
- **Canadian Importers, Wholesalers, Retailers and Auctioneers, 18th - early 20th century.**(3)
- **American Importers, Wholesalers, Retailers of "Souvenir" Wares, late 19th - early 20th century.**(4)

American and Canadian Importers, Wholesalers, Retailers and Auctioneers of the 18th-early 20th century which are listed below do not represent the total body of trades people, nor manufacturers. In most cases addresses and dates recorded for retailers, importers and the like may not represent the actual addresses and dates of the company's listed due, in part to conflicting material. This information has been recorded as it was found, and are vignettes gleaned from export records, customs records, bills of lading, correspondence, newspaper ads, etc. Willow Ware imports and retailers have been recorded from ongoing research of backstamp markings.

This is an area that is ripe for further scrutiny. Such research and the resulting data would definitely provide invaluable insight into the dating of imported wares and their respective manufacturers.

For further reading, I would direct the researcher and collector to the following **selected references** (see bibliography for complete titles):

David & Linda Arman
Edwin Atlee Barber
Blue Berry Notes
Arene Burgess
Elizabeth Collard
Neil Ewins
Mary Frank Gaston
Ellen Hill
Sam Laidacker
Ellouise Baker Larsen
Frank Stefano, Jr.
Petra Williams

(1) This section **records information from printed backstamp markings.**
(2) This section **is not recorded from backstamp markings, but abstracted from sources noted above.**
(3) This section records information gleaned from various printed and recorded sources as listed above as well as from bibliography.
(4) This section records information gleaned from various printed and recorded sources as listed above as well as from bibliography.

IMPORTERS, WHOLESALERS, RETAILERS, AUCTIONEERS ENGLISH IMPORTS - 18TH THROUGH EARLY 20TH CENTURY UNITED STATES

IMPORTER	POTTER REPRESENTED
R.J. Allen, Son & Co. 309/311 Market St. Philadelphia, [PA]	F. & R. Pratt & Co.
J.L. Altenbaugh Tiffen, Ohio	Anthony Shaw (& Son(s))
Imported By **Babcock Brothers** Evansville, Indiana	Thomas Goodfellow
Baldwin, Pond & Co. Woonsocket [RI]	Jacob Furnival
L. Barth & Son New York [NYC] (c. 1900)	Wood & Sons, Ltd.
J.D. Bass Boston [MA], America c. 1810	Minton
N.G. Bassett Importer Newburyport [MA] c.1840s	J. & G. Alcock
J.H. Bills & Sons Bolivar Tennessee	Joseph Clementson
Mr. Billsland, Importer (1) 447 Broadway [New York, N.Y.C.] (c. 1840s - 1852)	Chamberlains & Co. Chamberlains/Worcester Manufacturers to the Royal Family STONE CHINA
Clifford Black & Co. Malden, Mass.	Wood & Sons Ltd.
F.J. Blair Importer Corner of Wisconsin & Water Sts., Milwauk*ie*, Wis.	J. Clementson
Manufactured **for** **Bowman & Bowlush** (2) c. 1850+(80)	J. & G. Meakin
Enos Briggs Importers of Earthenware Boston [MA]	Bates, Walker & Co. R. Hall (& Son) (& Co.)
Richard Briggs Boston [MA] c. 1880s	W.T. Copeland & Sons*
John W. Bull No. 70 State Street Hartford [CT] c. 1840s	—
Burley & Co. Chicago [IL] c. 1890s	W.T. Copeland & Sons*

IMPORTER	POTTER REPRESENTED
Burgess & Goddard Importers New York City	S. Bridgwood & Son; John Edwards; Wedgwood & Co.
Imported for **Andrew Castlen** New Albany, Ind. c.1869	Powell & Bishop
P. & I. Chamberlin Importers Louisville [KY]	James & Ralph Clews Enoch Wood & Sons
Clark, Lovering & Co. Importer Baltimore [MD]	Wm. Ridgway (& Son) (& Co.)
Davis Collamore & Co. B'way, Corner 21st S New York [N.Y.C.] c. 1880s	W.T. Copeland & Sons*
Gilman Collamore & Co. Union Square New York [N.Y.C.] c. late 1870s+	W.T. Copeland & Co.* William Davenport & Co. (& possibly Henry, 1881-1887)
Horace Collamore Boston, [MA] (c. 1814-1826)	Bailey & Batkin
Manufactured for **Davenport Bros.** 203 Greenwich St. N.Y. [N.Y.C.] (c. 1842-1890(92))	Joseph Clementson Clementson Bros. (Ltd.)
G. Dummer & Co. China Dealers 112 Broadway N.(New) York [NYC] c. 1810	New Hall (Bone China)
Ebbets & Gale 71 Pearl [St.] New York City [NY] early 1800s	John Davenport
Hugh S. Edmiston 25 West Broadway New York City [NY] 1902-1903	A. Meakin
Evans & Hill Importers Concord, NH	Podmore, Walker (& Co.)
Wm. Everhart Importer * * **J.C. Fairchild** Madison Mich (or marked) WIS c. 1830s	Joseph Clementson
Field & Clark Importers of Earthenware Utica [NY] c. 1822-1829	—
Manufactured for & **Imported by** **Chauncey J. Filley** St. Louis, M.O. (Late 1850s)	Mayer Brothers & Elliott
Manufactured for & **Imported by** **E.A. & S.R. Filley,** St. Louis, M [MO] c. 1854	T.J. & J. Mayer

W.B. Fuller Co. Mansfield [MA]	Wood & Sons Ltd.

IMPORTER	POTTER REPRESENTED
A.S. Gardner & Co. Cleveland - O [OH]	Joseph Clementson
Wm. H. Glenny Importers Buffalo, NY	Wm. Ridgway Son & Co.
J. Greenfield's*** China Store No. 77 Pearl St. New York [N.Y.C.] c. 1824-1832	James & Ralph Clews Job & John Jackson
Townsend Harris (Imported By) Pearl St. New York [N.Y.C.]	T. Mayer
Harris & Chauncey 70 Wall St. New York [N.Y.C.] c. 1826-1829	Enoch Wood & Sons
Henderson & Gaines Importers 45 Canal St. New Orleans [LA] 1836-1866	William Davenport & Co.
Henderson, Walton & Co. Importers 45 Canal St. New Orleans [LA] c. 1834-1836	John Davenport
Henshaw & Jarves Importers of Earthen Ware and Chinaware Boston [MA] c. 1815-1818	Wood & Caldwell
Hill & Henderson Importers New Orleans [LA] c. 1822-1834	James & Ralph Clews[7] John Davenport[7] R. Stevenson & William Enoch Wood & Sons
Geo. T. Horan House Furnishers Charleston [MA]	Wood & Sons Ltd.
Huntington & Brooks 235 Main St. Cincinnati [OH]	Jacob Furnival
J.C. Huntington & Co. 162 Main St. Cincinnati [OH]	Jacob Furnival & Co.
Jenness & Mather Detroit [MI] c. 1850s 80 Pearl Street New York [NYC](3)	T.J. & J. Mayer
Jones, McDuffe & Stratton Importers [Boston, MA] c. 1890s	W.T. Copeland & Sons*
Kent & McMillian Middlebury-O [Ohio]	J. Clementson
T.T. Kissam 145 Maiden Lane New York, [NY] c. 1840s	Charles James Mason (or & Co.)

*For a listing of importer names on backstamps of W.T. Copeland & Sons, 1869-1953, refer to *Copeland*, pp. 94-100.

**See P. Williams, *Flow Blue, Vol. 1*, p. 89 for pattern "Bouquet" marked "F&W".

***See comments for James & Ralph Clews in the introductory part of this section.

IMPORTER	POTTER REPRESENTED
Robert Lawrence [Pearl Street] Cincinnati [OH]	James & Ralph Clews
Chas. Lovering & Co. Importers Baltimore [MD]	Wm. Ridgway (& Co.)
JNO. R. Ludlow & Co. Charleston, So. Ca. [SC] c.1802-1828	Henshall, Williamson & Co. *("Fruit & Flower Border Series")*
H.P. Merrill Sandusky, Ohio c. 1840s - early 50s c. 1845-1853	Joseph Heath
Robert H. Miller Alexandria D.C. c. 1822-1840s	—
Robert Miller (4) Alexandria, Virginia c. 1840	—
Mitchell & Freeman China & Glass Warehouse Chatham St. Boston [MA] c. 1828-1832	Wm. Adams [& Sons] R. Stevenson (& Son)
Samuel E. Moore[10] Importer of China & Earthenware 37 Camp Street New Orleans [LA]	—
John Mortlock (?)	J. Furnival & Co. (c.1845-1870)
Peter Morton [68 Front Street] Hartford [CT] c. 1823-1831	Enoch Wood & Sons
Neff, Warton & Co. Louisville, KY (Kentucky) c. 1832-1839	James & Ralph Clews
Ovington Brothers Brooklyn [NY] c. 1880s	W.T. Copeland & Sons*
Peppard & Callan[8](() Importers Pittsburgh [PA]	Bellevue/Hull Bell [J & M.P.]
Albert Pick & Co. Chicago [IL]	Wood & Son
W.H. Plummer 26 West 22nd or 23rd Street New York [NYC]	Cauldon (Ltd.)
Portland Blue Plate Co. Portland [MAINE]	Burgess & Leigh
A. Reeves & Co. Louisville, [KY] c. 1835-1850	Charles Meigh (& Son)
John Y. Rushton 245 Market Street Philadelphia [PA] 1842-44	Ridgway & Morley
[M. & W.] Sackett & Co. Pittsburgh [PA] 1870s	Edward Clarke (& Co.) (Tunstall)
Hector Sears 226 Greenwich St. New York [N.Y.C.]	J. & G. Alcock

IMPORTER	POTTER REPRESENTED
C.A. Selzer Euclid Ave. Cleveland [OH]	Brown-Westhead Moore & Co.
J.M. Shaw & Co. New York [N.Y.C.] c. 1870s	W.T. Copeland & Sons*
Shawmut Furniture Co. Boston, Mass.	Wood & Sons Pattern noted as "Chain of States"
J.B. Sheriden & Co.[11] Main Street Louisville, K.Y.	—
Sherman & Gillin 138 Pearl St. New York [N.Y.C.]	Job & John Jackson
F.H. Stevens & Co. Hudson , NY	Wm. Adams & Son
T. Sweeney & Son Dealers in Queensware and Manufacturers of Flint Glass 63 Main St. Wheeling [VA]	T. & R. Boote Ltd.
James Tams & Co.[5] Importers/Manufacturers Philadelphia [PA] 1820s-1890s	J. & G. Alcock John Tams, et.al. J. Wedg Wood
Taylor & Wright Importers 62 Pearl Street New York, [N.Y.C.]	Podmore, Walker (& Co.)
H.P. & W.C. Taylor Perfumers Philadelphia [PA] c. 1865	—
I.M. Thompson & Co. Wheeling, VA c. 1826-1845	James & Ralph Clews
Thompson & Parish 10 Pearl Street or 79 Pearl Street New York [N.Y.C.]	J. & G. Alcock
Tilden, Thurber Co. Providence [RI] c.1900	Wm. Adams & Co.
Tyndale and Mitchell No. 219 Chestunt Street Philadel[phia] [PA] c. 1847-1861	Francis Morley & Co.
L. Weafelaer & Co. New York [N.Y.C.] c.1840-1860	Wm. Smith (& Co.), John Wedge-Wood
R.M. Williams 183 Washington St. New York [N.Y.C.]	Ralph Stevenson & William
Peter Wright (& Sons)[6] Importers Philadelphia [PA] U.S.A. 1840+	Thomas Furnival & Co. G. Phillips
Wright & Pike Importers [North 3rd St.] Philadelphia [PA]	J. & G. Alcock
Wright Tyndale and Van Roden [Chestnut Street] Philadelphia [PA] c. 1818-1960s	James & Ralph Clews

(1) Godden notes in *Masons* p 241, Mr. Billsland as an importer of Masons ware.
(2) See *White Ironstone Notes*, Vol. 3, No. 3, Winter 1997, p. 12 for a copy of importer's mark. Also refer to G. Bowman, included in Souvenir Wares Section, as the company may have preceded Bowman & Bowlush.
(3) See *Arman Quarterly*, Vol. 1, 1997, p. 34 where two importer's marks are noted on one piece.
(4) See *Arman, Quarterly*, Vol. 1, 1997, pp. 20-21.
(5) See *Ewins,* pp. 85-86, FN #s 18-21
(6) See *Ewins,* pp. 96, Plate 16
(7) Arman notes in *Historic Staffordshire,* Updated Supplement, "...Errors corrected...Change the attribution of the maker of both the Cities Series and Don Quixote Series from Clews to Davenport."
(8) Sam Laidacker notes in the *American Antique Collector*, Vol. 1, March 1940, No. 9 "...Peppard's were in business and Callan became a lawyer...any time from 1819 to 1848 these men could have had an importing business in addition to their regular work...", p. 189.
(9) See *Arman, First Supplement,* p. 87
(10) See *White Ironstone Notes*, Vol. 4, No. 3, Winter 1998, p. 3
- Both Montgomery Ward and Sears & Roebuck were actively involved in the import of English Earthenware and China to the United States. (1870s+). (Microfilm and catalogs are available at the New York Public Library System, and the Montgomery Ward Catalogs are available on microfim at the University of Wyoming Library.)
(11) See P. Williams, *Staffordshire, Vol. III*, p. 201, where a floral pattern is illustrated, but with no pottery identified.
- Lynne Sussman's *Mocha, Banded, Cat's Eye and Other Factory-Made Slipware, Studies in Northeast Historical Archaeology*, Vol. 1, Parks, Canada. Department of Canadian Heritage, 1997, pp, 82-92, includes an Appendix of Mocha, Banded, Cat's Eye and Other Factory-Made Slipware that provides an extensive listing of English Manufacturers and American Importers of these wares.
N.B.: Refer to Robert Copeland's *Spode & Copeland Marks, pp. 47-50* for special Canadian and American orders & imports, for the 20th century and David & Linda Arman's *Historical Staffordshire, An Illustrated Checklist, First Supplement*. "Importers Marks...1822-1849", pp.97-102.

IMPORTERS, WHOLESALERS, RETAILERS, AUCTIONEERS ENGLISH IMPORTS - 18TH THROUGH EARLY 20TH CENTURY UNITED STATES (Unmarked)

This section represents only a recorded portion (English) of the ceramic import and distribution market in the United States. **Printed backmarks for these retailers/importers have not been recorded to-date.**

As the country expanded, English manufacturers (as well as European) established self directed companies in the United States that oversaw their interests and acted as distributors and/or agents for other English potteries. American retailers and importers acted in like fashion - as distributors and/or agents for English and European manufacturers.

Although not manufacturers, the English company of Goddard & Burgess (see Chronology) developed a niche in the American market as brokers by expediting orders for a vast array of English potters. With payment ensured for goods, Goddard & Burgess were able to dictate to manufacturers those shapes and styles they deemed most marketable. It was not uncommon for such designs to be sent to England by [steam] boat with a turnaround and delivery time back to the United States of approximately five months.

Bill headers, company titles and correspondence often contained spelling and header errors. In the majority, dates and addresses were recorded from these documents as well as from local advertisements and trade directories.

I have noted J. Wedg Wood as Wedgwood, J. (John) in order to differentiate between the names Josiah Wedgwood and Wedge Wood by Smith, and Wedgwood & Co.

They are not, in most cases, the retailers' and/or importers actual years of business, but rather reflect the recorded date from correspondence and/or advertisement.

IMPORTER	POTTER REPRESENTED
John Abbot & James Simpson Philadelphia [PA] c.1795-1800+	Adams, William; Badderley, Ralph; Booth & Sons; Cooper, (Lane End); Hyatt & Harrison; Jackson, Benjamin; Johnson & Bridgwood; Spode, Josiah; Turner, W&J; Weston & Hull; Wood & Caldwell
Adams (3) Philadelphia [PA] c.1838	Adams, W. [William & Sons]
Thomas Adams(3) 248 Pearl Street New York [NYC] early 1820s - 1832	Adams Bros. [Adams, Wm. & Sons];
(W) Adams Bros. (3) New York [NYC] c.1821-1860s	Adams [Wm. & Sons]
John & George Alcock(3) 43 Water [St] New York [NYC] c.1841	Alcock, John & Goerge
R. (Richard) E. Alcock (3) (Son of John Alcock) 42(3) Stone Cor. Coenties Alley New York [NYC] c.1834-1869	Alcock, [Samuel] & Co.
John Alexander 97 Water [St] New York [NYC] c.1841-1846	Wood, Enoch & Sons
Arthenhelt Philadelphia [PA] c.1880	Birks Bros. [& Seddon]
Aspinall New York [NYC] c.1882	Minton
J. Bagshaw(3) Opposite Tunis, Annesley & Co. Office in alley between Walnut & Chestnut Street Wharf. Philadelphia [PA] c.1796-1807 Bagshaw;	Bagshaw & Meir; Bagshaw, Taylor & Co. Taylor & Maier
Bailey, Banks & Biddle Philadelphia [PA] c.1880	Copeland [W.T. & Sons]; Doulton & Co.
J. Baker New York [NYC] c.1855	Wedgwood, J. [John]
T.S. Baldwin & Sons (1) (Jewelers) Painsville, Ohio c.1878	—
G.H. Ball(1) Philadelphia [PA] c.1835	Adams, W. [& Sons]

IMPORTER	POTTER REPRESENTED
Geo. H. Ball(1) 43 Water [St.] New York [NYC] c.1841	Adams Brothers; Alcock, John & George
Flores Bancker New York [NYC] c.1771	Wedgwood, Josiah; Whieldon, Thomas
Bare & West(2) Pearl & Walnut Street Cincinnati [OH] c.1855-1856	Goddard & Burgess/Walley [John]
Barger & Miller Cincinnati, Ohio c.1882	Minton
Thomas J. Barrow (Barrow & Co.) 306 Pearl [St.] New York [NYC] c.1836-1839	Alcock; Mason [C.J. & Co.]; Ridgway
Basset & Co.(1) (Basset & Pierce) 103-105 Broad Street Boston [MA] c.1855-1860	*Boote, T.&R.(1); Meakin, J.&G.
Herbert Beech & Bro. 60 Barclay Street New York [NYC] c.1873	Edwards, John [& Co.]
F.W. Bennett & Co.(4) 28 & 30 Charles Street Baltimore [MD] c.1853-1856 Harvey, Charles [C. & W.K. Harvey]	Adams; Alcock, John; Challinor, E.;
H. Bennett & Co. (3) 12 Murray Street New York [NYC] c.1883-1884	Dunn, Bennett & Co.
Berteau & Dolliver 49 Cedar Street New York [NYC] c.1836	"French Porcelain"
Betts & Gale 71 Pearl [Street] New York [NYC] c. 1807	John Davenport
M.W. Beveridge Georgetown, D.C. Maryland (via Baltimore) c.1882	Minton
T. Birch, Jr. (4) Coffee House Auction Store No. 84 South Second Street Philadelphia [PA] c.1840	—
John Black 139 Front New York [NYC]c.1796 15 Gold Street New York [NYC]c.1801	—
Blair & Pearsons Milwaukee [WI] c.1882	Minton
Edward Boote(3) 20 City Wharf Boston [MA] c.1869	—
Edward Boote(3) 11 East 19 Street New York [NYC]late 1860s 24 College Place New York [NYC] c.1883-1884	—

IMPORTER	POTTER REPRESENTED
Edward Boote(2) Philadelphia [PA] c.1874-1875	Goddard & Burgess/Boote, T.&R.
Boyd & Stroud Philadelphia [PA] c.1857	Wedgwood, J. [John]
George Breed Pitt. [PA] c.1839	Ridgway, Morley, Wear & Co.
Bremar & Neyle Charleston [SC] c.1753	—
Bridgwood & Reeve 281 King Street Charleston [SC] c.1824-1825	Minton
Robert Briggs Boston [MA] c.1855 & 1882	Meakin, J.&G.; Minton
John Bringhurst Philadelphia [PA] c.1793	—
A.J. Brown & Co. Boston [MA] c.1848	Clementson, J. [Joseph]
J.A. Brown & Co. Philadelphia [PA] c.1833	Wood, Enoch & Sons
John W. Bull No. 70 State Street Hartford [CT] c.1847	—
Richard Burlew(1) New York [NYC] c. 1855-1856	—
Burley & Tyrrell Chicago, Ill c.1882	Minton
Edward Butler(1) New York [NYC] c.1869-1876	Davenport, William & Co.; Wedgwood, J. [John]
Cadbury c.1835	Minton, T. [Thomas]
Cahoone & Hail Providence [RI] c.1860s	—
J.E. Caldwell & Co. Philadelphia [PA] c. 1873-1882	Copeland, W.T. & Sons; Harvey, Adams; Minton; Pinder & Co. [Pinder, Bourne & Co.]; Worcester Porcelain Co.
Charles Cartlidge(1) 103 Water Street New York [NYC] c.1834-1846**	Ridgway, W. [& Co.]
Cauffman Philadelphia [PA] c. 1833	Alcock, Sam [& Co.]
E. Caldwell & Co. New York [NYC] c.1848-1849	(Billing to John Whiting, Utica City, New York)
T.G. Chamberlin & Co. (or Chamberlayne) 45 Old Levees Street New Orleans [LA] c.1837-1838	Minton & Boyle

IMPORTER	POTTER REPRESENTED
William Chauncey & Co.(1) New York [NYC] c.1848-1854	Boote, T.&R.
J. Cheesman & Son New York [NYC] c.1841-1842	Wedgwood, J. [John]
Oscar Cheesman New York [NYC] c.1855	Wedgwood, J. [John]
Churchill New York [NYC] c.1834-1835	Bridgwood & Co. (Hanley); Bridgwood, S. (Lane End); Jones, E. (Cobridge); Loundes & Hill; Machin & Co.; Mellor, Venables & Co.; Ray & Tideswell (Lane End); Shaw, Kate
Clark & Andrews Boston [MA] c.1855	Meakin, J.&G.
Clark, Sawyer & Co. Worcester (via Boston) [MA] c.1882	Minton
Clevering (2) Lombard Street Baltimore [MD] c.1855	Goddard & Burgess/Alcock, Samuel & Co.
George, M. Coates (6) Philadelphia [PA] c.1817-1831	—
Callamore, Curtis & Co. Boston [MA] c.1862	Bridgwood & Clarke; Davenport, Banks & Co.; Heath, Blackhurst & Co.; Hughes, Elijah [& Co.]; Liddle, Elliot & Sons; Livesley & Powell [& Co.]; Meakin, J.&G.; Minton & Co.
Davis Collamore 597 Broadway New York [NYC] c.1884-1882	Minton; Wedgwood, [Wm. Smith & Co.]; Wedgwood
Ebenezer Collamore c.1850 E. Collamore & J. Phillips c.1851 John Collamore, Jr. & Co. c.1853 Ebenezer Collamore 293 Broadway, Four doors above Reade Street New York [NYC] c.1847-1859	Wedgwood [Josiah]
Gilman Collamore Boston [MA] c.1813-1818	Bourne, Baker & Bourne; Mayer & James Keeling; Rogers, John [& Son]; Yates, John & William
Gilman Collamore New York [NYC] c.1882	Minton
Horace Collamore 48 Marlboro Street Boston [MA] c.1814-1820	Bailey & Batkin; Bourne, Baker & Bourne; Sarah Brown (Hanley); Hall, John & Ralph; Mayer & Keeling; S. & J. Myatt; Rogers, John & George; Rogers, John & Son; Yates, John
E. P. Conckin New York [NYC] c. 1855	Wedgwood, J. [John]
John A. Conkey & Co. Boston [MA] c.1841-1842	Wedgwood, J. [John]

IMPORTER	POTTER REPRESENTED
Cook & Wright (or Cook, J.W. or Cook, W.W.) 47 North Third Street Philadelphia [PA] c.1833-1836	Boyle, Z [Zachariah]; Henshall, Ridgway, John
David Coope 91 Fulton Street Brooklyn, New York c.1837-1851	Boyle & Minton
Joseph W. Corlies & Co. No. 47 Broadway New York [NY] c.1855	Adams, William & Sons; Boote, T.&R.; Meigh, Chas. & Son; Venables, Mann & Co.; Wedgwood, J. [John]
Cortland & Co. 216 and 216 Baltimore St. Baltimore [MD] c.1866	—
I. Courtney Corner of Drayton St. near ruins of the Episcopal Church A [Atlanta], Georgia c.1802	—
Curtis & Hopper New York [NYC] c.1855	Wedgwood, J. [John]
Cuttler & Amory No. 22 Marlborough St. Boston [MA] c.1796-1797	Wood, Enoch & Caldwell
Davenport Bros. No. 203(7) Greenwich St. New York [NYC] c.1844-1875	Wedgwood, J. [John]
S.W. Davenpport New York [NYC] c.1840s	—
William Davenport & Co. (3) New York [NYC] early 1880s	Davenport & Co.
Davies & Minnett New York [NYC] c.1772	—
Dawson & Hancock New York [NYC] c. 1853-1857	Holland & Green; Livesley & Powell [& Dawson [& Hancock ?] Co.];Walley [John]
Philadelphia [PA] c.1862-1864	Adams, W. [& Son]; Holland [Holland & Green]; Wedgwood & Co.
R.C. Dawson c.1833	Martin, William
S.P. Dewey New York [NYC] c.1841-1842	Wedgwood, J. [John]
S.B. Dibbles c.1842-1843	Wedgwood, J. [John]
Dickson & Lebetter (2) 217 Main Street Cincinnati [OH] c.1855-1856	Goddard & Burgess
E. Dieder No. 45 John Street New York [NYC] c.1847	"French China"
Nathaniel Dougherty (1) New York [NYC] mid-1850s	Edwards, James [& Son] (Dale Hall/Longport)
W. Dudley & Co. Boston [MA] c.1860	Bought from P.H. Whitin & Son
J.B. Dyster c.1856	Wedgwood [Josiah] (Etruria)
A.F. Eberman Philadelphia, [PA] c.1871	Challinior [E.&C.]
Hugh C. Edmiston 25 West Broadway New York [NYC] c.1902-1903	Meakin, Alfred
George Ellis (2) Boston [MA] c.1850-1855	Goddard & Burgess
D. Evans c.1838	Ridgway, W. [William]
Charles Everett Boston [MA] c.1815	Wedwood, Josiah II
F.P. & Co. Boston [MA] ? c.1855	Meakin, J.&G.
M. Farrall Philadelphia [PA] c.1876	Furnival, T. [Thomas & Sons]
H. Ferguson (1) New York [NYC] c.1846***	Ridgway, W. (& Co.)
E.A. & S.R. Filley St. Louis, MS [MO] c.1854	Mayer, T.J.&J.
Dawson Ford Philadelphia [PA] c.1863	Adams, Wm., Jun...
Henry J. Ford (1) 53 Berkmann Street late 1850s 7 S. William Street c.1859 New York [NYC] 97 S. Front Street Philadelphia [PA] c.1853-1856	Clementson, Joseph
J.L. Fox & Co. c.1841-1842	Wedgwood, J. [John]
Fransiloi & Williamson (2) Memphis, Tennessee c.1853	Goddard & Burgess/Walley [John]
Archibald Freeland Manchester, Virginia c.1789	—
French & Co. Boston [MA] c.1882	Minton
Frost & Co. or Herman Frost & Co. New York [NYC] c.1882	Minton
G. Gay Philadelphia [PA] c.1872	Horne & Adams; Pratt, F.&R. (& Co.)
W.H. Glenney 52 & 166 Main Street Baltimore [MD] c.1842-1861	Mason, C.J. (later Morley, F.)
W.H. Glenney (Sons & Co.) Buffalo [NY] Wedgwood, J. [John]	Maddock, John & Sons; Meakin, J.&G.;

IMPORTER	POTTER REPRESENTED
Robert Grace (1) New York [NYC] c.1834	Phillips, George
John Gray (1) 97 Water Street New York [NYC] c.1834-1845	Wood, Enoch & Sons
Will Greenleaf Fronting Cornhill Boston [MA] c.1762	—
(S.B.) Gregory & Co. (2) Albany [NY] c.1845****	Mason [Charles James]; Meigh [Charles]
S.B. Gregory & Co. (2) 88 Warren Street New York [NYC] c.1854-1856	Goddard & Burgess/Meakin, J. & G.
William P. Hacker or W.P. & G.W. Hacker No. 60 North Second Street above Arch Philadelphia [PA] c.1841-1859	Wedgwood, J.[John]
Ritter Hadley New York [NYC] c.1855	Wedgwood, J. [John]
George Hammersley Philadlephia [PA] c.1844-1858	—
W.S. Hammersley & Co. New York [NYC] c.1851	Walley [John]
Charlotte Hammett In the Long Wooden Store Opposite William Prices Esq. Bedon's Alley Charleston [SC] c.1791-1793	—
Hamswell & Co. Buffalo [NY] c.1865	Wedgwood, J. [John]
G. Harker No. 236 Northside Sixth Street between Plum & Western Row Cincinnati [OH] c. 1853	—
Harrison Philadelphia [PA] c.1871	Minton
Hason, Hiss & Co. Baltimore [MD] c.1882	Minton
Joseph Hastings & Sons (1) Boston [MA] c.1851-1861 Walley, John	Bailey, John; *Meigh, Charles & Son;
Samuel Hatch (4) Boston [MA] c.1856	Alcock, John
E.V. Haughwout & Co. Nos. 488, 490 & 492 Broadway New York [NYC] c.1860s	—
Haviland & Co. (3) (of Limoges) 500 Broadway New York [NYC] c.1866	French manufacturers also sold to John Sise [NH]

IMPORTER	POTTER REPRESENTED
Haviland Bros. & Co. (of Limoges) (3) 47 John & 5 Dutch Street New York [NYC]	French manufacturers
Corlies Haydock & Co. (4) 35 William Street New York [NYC] c.1848-1855	Adams, William & Sons; Wedgwood, J. [John]
Henderson & Gains 43 Canal Street New Orleans [LA] c. 1836-1853	Davenport, William & Co.; Mason, C.J. [Charles James](and later Morley, F.)
Henshaw & Jarves Boston [MA] c.1815	Wood & Caldwell
George W. Herring & Co. (2) No. 7 South Charles Street Baltimore [MD] c.1853-1855	Goddard & Burgess/Boote, T.&R.
Hetherington & Kynock Charleston [SC] c.1763	—
William & Thomas Hewitt (3) 16 Chamber Street New York [NYC] c.1806-1823	Sheridan & Hewitt
Hicks, Houston & Co. Nashville [TN] c.1867-1876	Wedgwood, J. [John]
H. Higby (for Monogahela House) Pittsburgh [PA] c.1842-1861	Mason, C.J. [Charles James]; (later Morley, F.)
Thomas Higam No. 30 East Bay Charleston, South Carolina c.1816	—
C.F.A. Hinrichs New York [NYC] c.1864	Cork, Edge & Malkin
Hobson & Boulton New York [NYC] c.1806	Robinson, John & Sons
Hollingsworth (2) 36 South Charles Street Baltimore [MD] c.1853	Goddard & Burgess
Hollingsworth & Hughes Evansville & Indianapolis [IN] c.1842-1861	Mason, C.J. [Charles James] (later Morley, F.)
W.F. Homer & Co. Boston [MA] c.1850-1855	Cork & Edge; Meakin, J.&G.
A. Humphreys Philadelphia [PA] [c.1796]1801	Wedgwood, Josiah
Huntington & Brooks (2) 47 Pearl Street Cincinnati [OH] c.1854-1856	Goddard & Burgess/Walley, John
Cleveland [OH] c.1867	Cork, Edge & Malkin
Hurst & Co. Philadelphia [PA] c.1835	Adams, William

IMPORTER	POTTER REPRESENTED
John C. Jackson (1) 113 Water Street New York [NYC] c.1834-1868	*Davenport, William & Co.; *Jackson, Job & John; *Lockett, John Thomas; *Phillips, George; *Ridgway, John & Co.; Meakin, J.&G.; Sharpe Bros. & Co.; Wedgwood, J. [John]; Wedgwood & Sons
F.&E. Jaeger & Co. Chicago [Il] c.1864-1867	Wedgwood, J. [John]
S. & J. James Philadelphia [PA] c.1836	Stephen Hughes & Co.
Jones & Co. New York [NYC] c.1861	Wedgwood [Josiah]
Jones & Shepard New York [NYC] c.1858	—
Jones, McDuffee & Co. [120] Franklin, Cor. Federal [Street] Boston [MA] [c.1876]-1882(+)	Minton
Chas. Jose & Co. Portland, Maine c.1882	Minton
Kaub, Frymer & Edwards 923 Market Street Philadelphia [PA] c.1876	—
J. Kerr Philadelphia [PA] c.1833-1835	Alcock, Sml (Samuel); Ridgway, J. [John]
Chas. M. Keyer (2) 12 N. Howard Street Baltimore [MD] c.1851-1853	Goddard & Burgess/ Livesley, Powell & Co.
Edward Kistner No. 341 Main Street Between Eighth & Ninth Streets Cincinnati, O [OH] c.1853	—
Kittle & Co. New York [NYC] c.1882	Minton
William Knox Boston [MA] c.1784	Hales & Adams; Wedgwood, Josiah
J.E. Larkin Winsted [CT] c.1880s	Wedgwood & Co.
H. Leonard's & Sons & Co.'s 29 & 31 Monroe Street Grand Rapids, Mich. c.1845-1887+	Boote, T. & R; Doulton; Maddock, John & Sons; Meakin, Alfred; Powell, Bishop & Stonier
Levering (or Lovering) Bros. & Co. (2) 98West Lombard St. Baltimore [MD] c.1853	Goddard & Burgess/Alcock, Samuel & Co
Lewis & Belden c.1855	Wedgwood, J. [John]
H.E. Lewis & Co. Louisville [KY] c.1848-1849	—
Livesley & Davis (3) 5 College Place New York [NYC] c.1870	Trent Pottery (Hanley); Livesley & Davis

IMPORTER	POTTER REPRESENTED
John C. Lloyd New York [NYC] c.1848-1855	Wedgwood, J. [John]
George Lockey Charleston [SC] c.1797	—
Lyon or Thompson & Lyon New York [NYC] c.1855	Meakin, J.&G.; Wedgwood, J. [John]
Maddock (various family members) (3) New York [NYC] c.1854-1880s - Thomas Maddock, c.1854 - John Maddock, Jr., c. 1850s-1869 - W.B. Maddock & Steel, 48 Park Place, New York [NYC], c. 1855-1868 - William Maddock, c. 1869-1880	Importing house(s) for John Maddock [& Sons] Sold to G.F. Melcher [NH]
Maitland, Kennedy & Co. Philadelphia [PA] c.1836	John Wilkinson (Whitehaven Pottery)
J. Marston Bros. (2) 308 West Baltimore Street Baltimore [MD] c.1853-1855	Goddard & Burgess/Walley [John]
Wm. Martin Philadelphia [PA] c.1835	Wood, Enoch & Sons
Masters & Markoe 51 South Street New York [NYC]	—
Mayer (family) (3) New York [NYC] c.1834-1880s - John Mayer, c. 1834-1837 - Thomas Mayer, c.1841-1850s 91 Water [St.], New York [NYC] - Mayer Bros., c.1880s Barclay Street, New York [NYC]	*Boyle, Z. & Son; Mayer, Thomas Mayer [T.J. & J.] *Challinor, E.&C.; * Clementson Bros.; * Mayer, T.J. & J.
W.S. & E.C. McIntosh 415 & 417 South Market Street Albany [NY] c.1836	—
McKetterick & Miller Burlington, Iowa c.1861	Wedgwood, J. [John]
Meakin (family) (3) - George Meakin Boston, [MA], c.1854-1855 9 Barclay Street, New York, [NYC] c.1865-1867 - Meakin & Taylor, 24 College Place, New York [NYC], c1879-1881 - Meakin & Ridgway (Inc.) 129 Fifth Avenue, New York [NYC], c.1892-1967 - Also, Toronto, Canada	Meakin, J.&G.; Pankhurst, [J.W. & Co.] Grindley, W.H. & Co. Meakin, Alfred; Meakin, Charles Adams, William & Son (Ltd.); Beswick (& Sons); Ludlow; Meakin, J.&G.; Ridgway Pottery; Royal Staffordshire [Wilkinson, Arthur, J. Ltd.]
G.F. Melcher Portsmouth [NH] c.1865-1868	Maddock [John & Sons]

IMPORTER	POTTER REPRESENTED
Miller & Coates No. 279 Pearl Street New York [NYC] c.1859-1860	Minton
Jno. L. Monroe (2) 192 Broadway Baltimore [MD] c. 1853	Goddard & Burgess
B.A. Mumford (1) New York [NYC] c.1846	—
Newbold & Cruet (1) 65 Broad Street New York [NYC] c.1839	Barker, Wm. & Co. (late Bourne, Baker & Bourne)
New Holland & Co. Canada (?) c.1855	Meakin, J.&G.
Norcross & Mellon Boston [MA] c.1882	Minton
North & Wheeler (See: Wheeler & Co.)	
Jonathan Ogden (Ogden, Day & Co.) New York [NYC] c.1816-1825	Clews, James & Ralph
C.J. Osbourne New York [NYC] c.1882	Minton
P. Pelatish Page or P.P. Page New York [NYC] c.1855-1859	Wedgwood, J. [John]
N.E. Panney & Co. (For Planters House) No. 80 Main Street St. Louis [MO] c.1842-1861	Mason, C.J. (later Morley, F.)
Parkinson Philadelphia [PA]	Bates (Burslem)
Parr & Banks (2) 159 Baltimore Street Baltimore [MD] c.1853	Goddard & Burgess
Patterson House No. 11 Elm Street Boston [MA] c.1842-1861	Mason, C.J. (later Morley, F.)
J. Philbin New York [NYC] c.1861	Wedgwood [Josiah]
Pierce & Co. Syracuse [NY] c.1865	Wedgwood, J. [John]
Samuel B. Pierce Boston [MA] c.1854-1855	Meakin, L.H. & Co. [Meakin, Lewis Henry & Farrall, John]
Jacob S. Platt New York [NYC] c.1847	Mason, C.J.
Samuel Quincy New York [NYC] c.1870-1875	Furnival, T. [& Sons]; Gelson Bros.; Oulsman, W.
Ramsay & Salt 146 Baltimore Street Baltimore [MD] c.1852	—

IMPORTER	POTTER REPRESENTED
B. Rathbone Bros. c.1855	Meakin, J. & G.
Alexander Read (7) Philadelphia [PA] c.1833-1845	Adams, W. [& Sons]; Boyle, Z. [Zachariah]; Boyle & Minton; Heath, Joseph & Co.; Ridgway, W. [William]; Wedgwood, J. [John]
Rees & Peircey (Rees, Thomas A. & Co.) 78 Maiden Ln New York [NYC] c.1855-1856	"French China"
Frederick Rhinelander New York [NYC] c.1774-1780	Keeling, Anthony
William Ridgway & Co. (and others) (3) 103 Water [St.] New York [NYC] c.1841	Ridgway [and others]; Ridgway & Son; Ridgway, Morley, Wear & Co.
Roberts & Taylor Charleston [SC] c.1772	—
James S. Robertson (1) 94 Church Street New York [NYC] c.1885-1909	Furnivals, Ltd.
Rogers & Co. Boston [MA] c.1875	Sampson (Bridgwood & Son); Davenport (& Co.)
P.&A. Rovoudt or Rovendt 164 North Third Street Philadelphia [PA] c.1839-1848	Challinor, E.; Heath, J. ; Maddock, J.; Morley, F. & Co.; Ridgway, W.
J.D. Rowland Philadelphia [PA] c.1878	Minton; Wedgwood
John Y. Rushton 245 Market Street Philadelphia, [PA] c.1842-1861	Mason, C.J. (later Morley, F.); Ridgway, J. & Co.
M.W. Sackett & Co. Pittsburgh [PA] c.1870s	Clark, Edward (Tunstall)
Caleb Sadler Dubuque, Iowa c.1865	Wedgwood, J. [John]
Sadler & Johnson Dubuque, Iowa c.1865-1866	Wedgwood, J. [John]
Salt, Mear & Schropp Philadelphia [PA] c.1868-1869	Jones [Josiah Ellis]; Jones, F. [Jones, Frederick & Co.]
Sampson & Co. Cincinnati [OH] c.1855	—
Schropp Philadelphia [PA] c.1871	Taylor, W. [William]
Hector Sears & Co. [226 Greenwich Street] New York [NYC] c.1855	Wedgwood, J. [John]
Sergeant & Co. New Orleans [LA] c.1850	—

IMPORTER	POTTER REPRESENTED
J.&S. Seymour New York [NYC] c.1840-1841	Wedgwood, J. [John]
John F. Seymour & Co. (Seymour & Co.) 78 Warren Street New York [NYC] c.1853-1870	Goddard & Burgess/Wedgwood, J. [John]
John Sharkey & Co. Baltimore [MD] c.1855	Wedgwood, J. [John]
Sharples Philadelphia [PA] c.1874-1884	Copeland [W.T. & Co.]; Jervis (Stoke); Minton; Wedgwood, J. [Josiah] Etruria
[J.M.] Shaw & Co. New York [NYC] c.1882	Minton
Sherman & Gillilan (1) 158 Pearl Street New York [NYC] c.1831-1833	Jackson, Job & John; Knight, Elkin & Bridgwood
Sherwood & Hopson (or Hopkins) Utica [NY] c.1855-1865	Wegwood, J. [John]
William Shirley (2) 13 S. Calbart Street Baltimore [MD] c.1853	Goddard & Burgess
John Sise Portsmouth, New Hampshire c.1856-1863	Alcock, J. [John]; Alcock, Sml (& Co.); Haviland & Co. (Limoges)
Skinner & Co. c.1855	Meakin, J.&G.
E.E. Smith Philadelphia [PA] c.1847	Meigh, C. [Charles]
Matthew Smith Baltimore [MD] c.1803-1812	—
E. Snowden Philadelphia [PA] c.1844	Wedgwood, J. [John]
Adam Southern Philadelphia [PA] c.1838-1846	Alcock, Sml [& Co.]; Mellor [Venables] & Co.; Podmore, Walker & Co.; Ridgway, J. & Co.
John Sproston (1) New York [NYC] c.1834-1840s	Davenport, H.&W. & Co.; Henshall & Williamson
D.B. Stedman No. 80 and 82 Broad Street Boston [MA] c.1860-1869	Alcock, Richard; Boote's, T.&R.; Bridgwood, S. & Son; Edwards, John; Liddle, Elliot & Sons'; Pankhurst, J.W. & Co's. - Also sold to W. Dudley & Co.
Steele Bros. Philadelphia [PA] c.1882	Minton
A. Stein Philadelphia [PA] c.1846	Ridgway, J. [& Co.]

IMPORTER	POTTER REPRESENTED
Henry Stevenson (1) (New York [NYC] from 1834-1859) - 161 Chambers Street, c.1834-1837* - 370 Pearl Street, c.1852- - 270 Pearl Street, c.1855- - 271 Pearl Street, c.1859-	Knight, Elkin & Bridgwood; *Stevenson, Ralph & Son
William Stewart Philadelphia [PA] c.1833-1835	Wood, Enoch & Sons
Straus Philadelphia [PA] c.1876	Alcock, H. [Henry & Co.]
Straus & Son New York [NYC] c.1882	Minton
L. Straus & Sons New York [NYC] c.1875	Wedgwood, J. [Josiah] Etruria
Summers & Co. Boston [MA] c.1843	Wedgwood
E. Swan Philadelphia [PA] c.1869	Stanway (Hanley)
Tams (family) (1 & 3) various titles: Tams Bros.; & Co.; James & William; William; S.&J. 298 High [Street] Philadelphia [PA] c.1818-1851	Alcock; Sml [& Co.]; Baggerley & Ball; Bridgwood, S. [Sampson & Co.]; Floyd [Shoebotham]& Co. (Lane End); Godwin, G. and B. C. (Cobridge); Harris & Co. (Lane End); Hughes, S. [Stephen]; Jackson, J.&G.; Pearson, J.[John]; Ratcliffe, R. (Hanley); Reid & Clementson; Rhead & Co. (Burslem); Stevenson, Ralph [& Sons]; Tams, S.; Yates & Meigh
James Taylor (1) New York [NYC] c.1834	Stubbs, Joseph
Taylor, Perkins & Co. New York [NYC] c.1855	Meakin, J.&G.
John Thomas Savannah [GA] c.1819-1824	Minton
Thompson & Lyon 79 Pearl and 46 Stone Street New York [NYC] c.1865-1869	Wedgwood, J. [John]
Tice & Huntington Cincinnati, Ohio c.1882	Minton
Daniel Titus 43 John Street New York [NYC] c.1865-1869	Wedgwood, J. [John]
Tomkinson & Bro. & Co. (1) Philadelphia [PA] c.1862-1868 and **Tomkinson & McElveny** c.1869-1874	Ashworth [G.L. & Bros.]; Bates, Elliot & Co.; Edward, J. [John & Co.]; Tomkinson Bros. & Co. (Hanley)
Trench & Simpson Boston [MA] c.1787	Wedgwood, Josiah

IMPORTER	POTTER REPRESENTED
Tyndale(s) (& Mitchell & Co.) Philadelphia [PA] c.1833-1876 - No. 219 Chestnut Street above 7 th, c.1833-1870 - No. 707 Chestnut Street, c.1871-1885	Alcock, Sml. (& Co.); Clews, R.&J.; Jackson, J.&J.; Machin & Co.; Mason, C.J. (later Morley, F.); Doulton & Co.; Minton & Co.
VanHeusen & Charles Albany [NY] c.1846-1854	Mayer [T.J. & J.]; Meakin, J.&G.; Wedgwood
A. VanWant New York [NYC] c.1882	Minton
Jacob & Thomas Waldon New York [NYC] c.1810	Wedgwood & Byerley
S.W. Waldon & Son Boston [MA] c1855	Meakin, J.&G.
Wanner & Kline & Co. Philadelphia [PA] c.1871	Clementson Bros.
H.N. Ward No. 9 Columbia Street Fort Wayne, Ind. c.1876-1880	Furnival, Thos. & Sons
Webb & Douglas 51 State Street Albany [NY] c.1836	—
Josiah Wedgwood & Sons (1) 162 Fifth Avenue New York [NYC] 1940s	Wedgwood (and others)
Westhead (1) Philadelphia [PA] c.1876 Moore & Co.]	Westhead/Cauldon [Brown, Westhead,
Westmore & Co. Detroit, Michigan c.1865	Wedgwood, J. [John]
Robert C. Westmore New York [NYC] c.1853	—
J.M. (& W.) Westwater & Co. Columbus [OH] c.1864-1867	Wedgwood, J. [John]
W.G. Whedock Janesville, Wisconsin c.1863-1865	Wedgwood, J. [John]
North & Wheeler - 1835 Wheeler & Co. - 1836 Wheeler, Gardiner & Co. 1839-1840 Various Locations in New York State[5]	—
P.H. Whiting & Son Boston [MA] c.1860	Bridgwood, S. & Sons; Mayer & Elliot; Pankhurst, J.W. (& Co.); Wooliscroft, George & Co.
John Whiting Utica City [NY] c.1848-1849	(Billing from E. Cauldwell & Co., New York City)
Wilby & Co. (4) Boston [MA] c.1822-1833	Bailey & Batkin; Booth, J.&T.; Clews, J.&R.; Ridgway, John
Willets [J.&E. or S.&E.] & Co. New York [NYC] c.1840-1863	Wedgwood, J. [John]
Willets & Shepard New York [NYC] c.1869-1874	Brindley, J.
F. B. Williams No. 85 Pearl Street and 52 Stone Street New York [NYC] c.1860	Mayer, T. J. & J.
R.M. Williams (1) 183 Washington Street New York [NYC] c.1830	Stevenson, Ralph & Son
Wilson & Co. New York [NYC] c.1864	Cork, Edge & Malkin
H. Winkley (1) Philadelphia [PA], c.1835-1850s* New York City, c.1841-1848	*Ridgway, John & Co.; Ridgway, Morley, Wear & Co.; Wedgwood, J. [John]
A. Wolf New Orleans [LA] c.1888	—
Woodward & Phelps 37 Barclay St. and 42 Park Place New York [NYC] c.1876	Bridgwood, Sampson & Son; Cockson, Chetwynd & Co.; Edwards; Meakin
Jno Wright, Jr. & Co. 36 Water Street [New York, NYC] 1835-1837	—
Peter Wright & Sons New York [NYC], c.1864	Cork, Edge & Malkin
Peter Wright & Sons No. 37 Walnut Street Philadelphia {PA} c.1840s-1877	Alcock, H. [Henry]; Burgess, H. [Henry]; Bridgwood, S. (& Son); Clementson Bros.; Challinor [E.&C.]; Cork, Edge & Malkin; Corn, W.&E.; Doulton & Watts; Ford (Sandyford)[Ford, Challinor & Co.]; Furnival, T. [& Co.]; Jones, G. & Sons; Pankhurst, J. [J.W. & Co.]; Phillips, George; Powell [Powell & Bishop]; Taylor Bros.; Worthington [& Son]
Wright, Schillin & Co. 1839	—

(1) Company acted as agent for particular potters.
(2) Pottery sold to Goddard & Burgess for the American market.
(3) Family operated sales office in the U.S. and/or sales agent for other English potters.
(4) American auction house in the U.S.
(5) *Arman, Quarterly*, Vol. 1, Oct./Nov. 1997, No. 4, pp. 11-13 "Blue Printed Pottery in the Stock of an Early Nineteenth Century New York General Merchant" by Martin Pulver noting the locations as Albany, Athens, Catskill, Hudson, Oxford, and Walton.
(6) See Lynne Sussman. *Mocha, Banded, Cat's Eye and Other Factory-Made Slipware, Studies in Northeast Historical Archaeology*, Vol. 1, Parks, Canada. Department of Canadian Heritage, 1997, p. 54 where it is noted that Coates was a jobber, buying at auction and reselling to other merchants.
(7) *Godden, Staffordshire* pp. 369-374, in a lengthy and most informative treatise, notes bill of lading as "Shipped by Wm. Adams & Sons" in 1837-1838 for Philadelphia. Alexander Read may be the importer to whom goods were shipped. He further notes that there was an export tax on these goods.
*Denotes exclusive representation for a particular potter; but did not inhibit merchant from selling wares of other potteries.
**See *Ketchum, Jr.*, pp. 71-72.
***See *Ketchum, Jr.*, pp. 72.
****See *Ketchum, Jr.*, pp. 91 & 271-276.

IMPORTERS WHOLESALERS, RETAILERS, AUCTIONEERS, ENGLISH IMPORTS - 18TH THROUGH EARLY 20TH CENTURY CANADA

IMPORTER	POTTER REPRESENTED
S. Alcorn Importer Palace St. Upper Town, Quebec c. 1830s-1840s	—
Robert Anderson St. Paul St. Montreal c. 1840s-1854 (subsequently, Thompson & Wm. Minchin)	—
W.H. Barber Importer Montreal c. 1872-1877	—
Barret & Rae Montreal c. 1870s	J. & G. Meakin
Blackader, Wilkes & Co. Montreal c. 1840s	Clyde Pottery
Boxer Bros. & Co. "Staffordshire Hall" St. Catherine St. Montreal c. 1885 - 1890 (Acquired by John Watson & Co, 1885)	Wm. Brownfield & Sons J. Dimmock & Co.
Robert Britain Dock Street St. John, New Brunswick c. 1847	J. Meir & Son
Burns & Bassett Yellow Store St. Catharines c. 1830s	—
A.B. Buxton "Liverpool House" Water Street St. John, New Brunswick c.1830s	—
Richard Calvert, Jr. St. John's, New Brunswick c.1793	—
John L. Cassidy & Co. (Ltd.) "Nuns Building" Montreal (& Brossaed) 1865-1973+ (?) Ltd. From 1896 Successors to L. Renaud & Cassidy	—
Alexander Christie Queen St. Niagara c. 1850s	—
Thomas Clarkson Auctioneer Toronto c. 1840s	—
Francis Clementson (& Co.) No. 11 Dock St. St. John New Brunswick c. 1853 - c. 1900 (Formerly, Samuel Coopers Old Staffordshire & Yorkshire Warehouse)	Joseph Clementson Clementson Bros.
Francis Clerke St. John New Brunswick c. 1840s	—
Samuel Cooper "Staffordshire & Yorkshire Warehouse" Dock Street St. John, New Brunswick c. 1830s - 1853	Francis Clementson
Cuviller & Co. (Auctioneers) Montreal c. 1817 - ?	Josiah Wedgwood
Adam Darling or **Darling & Jordan** 203 St. James St. Montreal c. 1870s - 1880s	Charles Ford Josiah Wedgwood & Co.
J. P. Davis & Co. Auctioneer Victoria, BC c.1869	—
John Douglas St. Paul St. Montreal c. 1840s - 1860s	—
Douglas & McNiece St. Paul St. Montreal	Thomas Furnival & Sons
Forsyth, Richardson & Co. Montreal c.1824	C.J. Mason
John Glennon No. 65 St. Paul St. Montreal c. 1829 - 1836 (Subsequently, Glennon & Shuter)	Benjamin E. Godwin
John Glennon or "Glennon" Montreal c. 1850 - 1857 (Formerly, John Glennon & Co.)	J.& G. Meakin
John Glennon & Co. Montreal c. 1848 - 1850 (Formerly, Glennon & Bramley)	—
Glennon & Bramley "Old Stand" on Saint Paul St. Montreal c. 1842-1847 (Subsequently, John Glennon & Co.)	John Wood of Brownhills
Glennon & Shuter (or Shuter & Glennon) No. 65 Saint Paul St. Montreal c. 1836-1842 (Subsequently, Glenmore & Bramley)	—
Goodwin & Co. 56 Wellington St. Toronto c. 1856 - 1864	Seacombe Pottery
Goodwin Brothers Lower Town, Quebec c. 1840s - 1860s (Subsequently, McCaghey, Dolbec & Co.)	Seacombe Pottery

IMPORTER	POTTER REPRESENTED
A.M. Greig(Auctioneers) York (Toronto) & Orr's Hotel on Notre Dame St. Montreal c. 1834 - ?	—
Hager & Co.(Retailers) Montreal c. 1855	J. & G. Meakin
Edward Hager & Co. St. Paul St. Montreal c. 1880s (Formerly, Charles Hager)	Thomas Furnival & Sons Belleek (Ireland)
John Hagger No. 293 Corner of St. Paul & St. Peter St. Montreal (?) - c. 1880s	—
William Harris King St. Montreal c. 1810 - (?)	—
Glover Harrison "China Hall" 71-73 King Street East Beleek (Ireland) (1866-1870s) 49 King Street East (c. 1880s-c. 1900) Toronto, Ontario	—
Andrew Hays 7 Saint Sacrament Street (Opposite the Merchant's Exchange) & No. 124 St. Paul St. Montreal c. 1850s - ?	John Ridgway, Bates & Co. Charles Cartledge & Co. Green Point, King's Co., N.Y. (American Pottery)
G. Henderson No. 7 Saulte-au-Matelot St. Quebec c.1820	—
Matthew Hicks & Co. Auctioneer Montreal c.1883	—
Henry Howison Upper Town, Quebec & Corner of St. Paul & Saint Gabriel St. Montreal c. 1870s (Subsequently, Sentenne, Howison & Massue)	—
Irvine, Leslie & Co. Montreal c. 1819	—
J. Jackson No. 3 King St. West Toronto, Ontario c. 1850s - 1860s (68)	Charles James Mason & Co.
J.R. Jennett & Co. Halifax, British Colombia c. 1868	E.F. Bodley & Co.
William Johnson & Son Niagara c.1845	—
Charles H. Jones Market Square York (Toronto) c. 1830s	—
Daniel King St John's, New Brunswick c.1800	—
John Leeming (Auctioneers) Montreal c. 1840s - 1870s	T. & R. Boote; Royal Worcester
Francis Leonard(Auctioneers) St. Paul Street Montreal c. 1823-1850s	—
Alexander Levy Corner of Notre Dame & St. Gabriel Streets Montreal c. 1850s	Royal Worcester
Lovitt & Burrell Milton, Nova Scotia c. 1850s	—
Ludlow & Fraser St. John's, New Brunswick c.1793	—
Thomas McAdam Montreal c. 1835 - ?	—
McCaghey, Dolbec & Co. Lower Town, Quebec c. 1868/69 - 1874 (Subsequently, Francis T. Thomas)	Clementson Bros.
John McDonald & Son Halifax, British Colombia c. 1840 - 1870s	Edge, Malkin & Co. Podmore, Walker & Co.
James McNiece Montreal c. 1860s	—
Adam L. MacNider "Old Distillery Stores" Montreal c. 1832	Derby, Rockingham, Worcester
John A. Monro St. Catherine c.1873	—
Samuel Nelms Charlottetown, Prince Edward Island c.1827	—
N. Norris Toronto, Ontario c. 1840s	—
Thomas Norris Quebec c. 1850s - 1890s	—
Bernard O'Neill (& Co.) 22 Bedford Row Halifax, British Columbia c. 1835 - ?	Fell & Co.
Patton (John) & Co. 49 King Street East Toronto, Ontario c. 1846 - 1860s	Coalport/Coalbrookdale (The advertising term utilized for Coalport was Coalbrookdale.)
John Patton 73 Great St. James St. Montreal Belleek (Ireland) c. 1860s - 1870s	Royal Worcester
Wm. Peddie (& Co.) St. Paul St. Montreal c. 1829 - 1834 (& Co., Walter Peddie) 1834 - 1846	Enoch Wood & Sons

IMPORTER	POTTER REPRESENTED
Thomas J. Potter Auctioneer Montreal c.1880s	—
Rateford & Lugrin St. John's, New Brunswick c.1833	—
Wm. J. Reid & Co. "Crystal Hall" London & Ontario c. 1880s - ?	"Manufactured By Wm. J. Reid & Co."*
Louis Renaud & Cassidy Montreal c. 1860 - 1865 (Formerly, Renaud, Prieur & Co.)	—
Renaud, Prieur & Co. Rue St. Paul Montreal c. 1857-1870 (Formerly, John Glennon)	—
George Rhynas Montreal c.1839	—
F.H. Rous & Co. Belleville, Ontario c. 1850s	—
Thomas Schiefferlin Montreal c.1798	—
William Scott & Son Montreal c.1880s	—
Scott, Montgomerie & Co. Montreal c.1820s	Minton
Sentenne, Howison & Massue Corner of St. Paul & Gabriel St. Montreal c. 1870s (Formerly, Henry Howison & Massue)	—
Henry J. Shaw Auctioneer Montreal c.1870s	—
Shuter & Glennon (see) Glennon & Shuter	
Shuter & Wilkins No. 65 St. Paul St. Montreal c. 1819 - c. 1836 (Formerly, Glennon & Shuter)	—
Shutter & Patterson King St. opposite The Market Place Montreal c. 1834 - 1850s	—
W.W. Smith Missisquoi Bay Eastern Townships of Quebec 1830s	William Davenport
S. & W. Spragg Montreal c. 1820s - ?	Enoch Wood & Sons

IMPORTER	POTTER REPRESENTED
John Sproston St. Paul St. Montreal c. 1850s - ?	—
Street & Ranney Auctioneer St. John's, New Brunswick c.1837	—
A.L. Taylor Missiskoui Lower Canada c.1835	—
Francis T. Thomas (& Co.) Lower Town, Quebec c. 1874 - 1897+ Thomas Co. Ltd. from 1910 (Formerly, McCaghey, Dolbec & Co.)	Britannia Pottery Co.; Robert Cochran; Cochran & Fleming; Fleming/Glasgow
Thomas & Minchin St. Paul Street Montreal 1854 - ? (Formerly, Robert Anderson)	Meakin, J. & G.
Joseph & John Tooker Yarmouth c.1841	—
William Turner Worcester Montreal c. 1832 - 1833+	Josiah Wedgwood (& Sons)

*Wm. J. Reid & Co. were not manufacturers but rather decorators and wholesalers to dealers and private customers. In 1880, under the name of Reid & Co., they contracted agents in Canada to bring in orders. Reid & Co. represented Coalport, Copeland, Derby, Minton, Worcester, and Wedgwood amongst others.

IMPORTER	POTTER REPRESENTED
George Wadsworth No. 92 St. Paul St. Montreal c. 1820s	—
James Wainright Upper End of Copeland's Warf', Halifax c.1791	—
John Watsons & Co. Grey Nun Street Montreal 1860s - 1885 (Subsequently, Boxer Bros.& Co.)	—
Joseph Wedgwood No. 51 St. Paul St. Montreal c. 1816 - 1819	Josiah Wedgwood
A.T. Wiley (Wiley & Co.) 425 Notre Dame St. Montreal c. 1880 - 1890s (Acquired by Cassidy's)	—
S.L. Willett Montreal ? - 1866	—

For further reading on Canadian importers refer to Collard's two books, *A Potter's View* and *Pottery & Porcelain*.

IMPORTERS, WHOLESALERS, RETAILERS OF "SOUVENIR" WARES ENGLISH IMPORTS - LATE 19TH THROUGH EARLY 20TH CENTURY UNITED STATES

IMPORTER	POTTER REPRESENTED
Coleman S. Adler and Sons Inc. Jewelers New Orleans [LA]	A.G. Richard & Co., Ltd.
Almy, Bigelow & Washburn Salem, Mass	Rowland & Marsellus*
Bawo and Dotter Importer N.Y. [N.Y.C.] c. 1864-1910	W.H. Gross; Ridgway(s) Potteries, Ltd.; Rowland & Marsellus*; Spode, Copeland's China**
Heyn Binswanger & Co. Detroit, Mich	Rowland & Marsellus*
Wm. Bluck & Co. (?)	W. Adams & Co.
The Boston Store Erie [PA]	—
A.C. Bosselman & Co. Importers N.Y. [N.Y.C.] c. 1904-1930 1904 - 469 Broadway 1912 - 114 East 16th Street 1915 - 3 East 13th Street 1918 - 248 Lafayette Street 1926 - 164 Fifth Avenue	Ridgway(s) Potteries, Ltd. Rowland & Marsellus (?)*
George H. Bowman Co. Sole Importer Cleveland [OH] 1888-1932 and New York City [N.Y.]	Wm. Adams & Co.; Frank Beardmore & Co., Fenton; Sampson Hancock & Sons; Rowland & Marsellus*; (Royal) Doulton
G.S. Burbank Plymouth [MA] c. 1900 - ?	Rowland & Marsellus*
Burgess & Goddard, Importers New York City [NY] c. 1840s - 1890s	Samson Bridgwood & Son (Ltd.); John Edwards; Goddard & Burgess; Josiah Wedgwood & Sons
Burley & Co. Chicago [IL] c. 1890s - ?	Spode, Copeland's China**
J.G. Doan Middleboro, Mass.	(Foreign)
Nathan-Dohrmann Co. San Francisco [CA] c. 1900	Minton(s)
Wm. Donaldson & Co. Minneapolis, Minn	Rowland & Marsellus*
Drake & Hersey Co. House Furnishers Boston, Mass. c. 1890s	—

IMPORTER	POTTER REPRESENTED
Emerson & Son Milford, New Hampshire	—
Enco National Importers New York [N.Y.C.] 1909 -	Alfred Meakin Ltd.
Ferguson & Day	Wm. Davenport
Fred & Dotties Antiques Birdsboro [PA] 1968+	Blakeney Pottery Ltd.
French, Mitchell, Woodbury Company Importers Boston [MA] 1901-1905	Wm. Adams & Sons
J.R. Gibney New York [NYC]	Thomas Furnival & Sons
Hall Galleries Springfield, Mass. c. 1930s - ?	Spode, Copeland's China**
Hight and Fairfield Co. Butte, Montana	Rowland & Marsellus*
Benj. F. Hunt & Sons, Importer 53 Hanover St. Boston, Mass. c. 1890s - ?	(Foreign)
T.M. James & Sons Kansas City, Missouri c. 1940s	Spode, Copeland's China**
Jones, McDuffee and Stratton Co. Boston, Mass. 1871-1960 Jerome Jones 1853 Louis P. McDuffee 1863 Solomon P. Stratton 1866	Wm. Adams & Co.; Josiah Wedgwood & Sons; Wood & Sons (Ltd.); (and others)
Lazarus & Rosenfeld New York [NY]	(Foreign)
Daniel Low & Co. Salem, Mass.	Josiah Wedgwood & Sons
Marmod, Jacquard, King & Co. (Jewelers) St. Louis [MO]	—
Mellen and Hewes Co. Importers Hartford [CT]	Josiah Wedgwood & Sons
Norcross, Mellen & Co. Boston [MA] c. 1896	Minton(s); Josiah Wedgwood & Sons
Wm. Plummer & Co. New York [NY] c. 1880s+	Josiah Wedgwood & Sons
John H. Roth & Co. "Jonroth" Peoria [IL] c. 1909-1970 Florida, 1970+	Wm. Adams & Son; British Anchor Pottery; Grimwades, Ltd.; Alfred Meakin, Ltd.; Ridgway(s) Potteries, Ltd.; Royal Staffordshire Pottery
Rowland & Marsellus New York [NY] c. 1893-1938	British Anchor Pottery; W.H. Gross; Ridgway(s) Potteries, Ltd.; Royal Fenton; Sampson Hancock & Sons; Wood & Sons (Ltd.); (and others)

IMPORTER	POTTER REPRESENTED
St. Louis Glass & G.Ware Co. St. Louis, MO c. 1904	Wm. Adams & Co.
Shreve, Crump & Low (Co.)*** Boston [MA] c. 1970s	Josiah Wedgwood & Sons
R.D. Sprout Onset, Mass.	—
Steele & Johnson The Fair Fairfield, Iowa	(Foreign)
Stix, Baer & Fuller*** Grand Leader St. Louis, MO. (Subsequently, Dillard's, c. 1985)	Rowland & Marsellus*
Tilden & Thurber Providence [RI] c.1900	—
Van Heusen, Charles & Co. Albany, New York c. 1900-1930s (?)	Josiah Wedgwood & Sons
Van Roden Philadelphia [PA] 1890s+	Minton & Co.
Walker & Pratt Mfg. Co. Boston [MA]	Sampson Bridgwood & Son (Ltd.); Rowland & Marsellus* - "Crawford Range"
C.E. Wheelock & Co. South Bend, Indiana and Peoria, Illinois 1888-1920s (71)	Wm. Adams & Son; Frank Beardmore & Co., Fenton; Minton(s)
Wright, Tyndale & Van Roden Chestnut St. Philadelphia [PA] 1818-1960s	Minton(s)

DEPARTMENT STORES

Abraham & Straus	NY
B. Altman & Co.	NY
Gimbel Brothers	NY
Macy's Dept. Store	NY
Marshall Field & Co.	IL
Rich's Inc.	GA
Charles Schwartz	DC
H. Stern's Co.	NY
L. Strauss & Sons	NY
John Wanamaker' s	PA
Woodward & Lathrop,	DC
F. Woolworth Co. NY	

*Although Rowland & Marsellus were not manufacturers, they were a very important presence in the "Souvenir" Ware market. They had wares manufactured , under their own label, which they then brokered and sold through various distributors in the United States.

**For a listing of importer names on backstamps of W.T. Copeland & Sons, 1869-1953, refer to *Copeland,* pp. 94-100.

***Although not exactly early 20th century, I have included these two importers/ retailers.

N.B.: See Bibliography for additional sources on manufacturers and/or importers of souvenir/commemorative plates. Additionally, Marian Klamkin has a section which includes souvenir plates manufactured by Josiah Wedgwood & Sons and Minton & Co. *See American Patriotic and Political China* by Marian Klamkin, New York, Charles Scribner's Sons, 1973, p. 188-189, 204-205 and 190-191 respectively.

GLOSSARY

Biscuit: Sometimes called "Bisque." Clayware when fired once at about 950c. - 1100c. is transformed into a hard substance without the addition of glaze. Vitrification takes place at higher temperatures.

Body: A ceramic term used to describe the composite material used for the production of a particular type of ceramic such as "Ironstone Body", "Parian Body", etc. The term paste, in the case of porcelain, is often used to mean the same.

Brush Stroke/Gaudy Ironstone: Contrived American terms used interchangeably to define free hand-painted design(s) under and over the glaze (as opposed to transfer designs). It is noted for simple hand-painted (cobalt) floral designs under the glaze, but frequently over glazed in richly decorated colored enamels. Red, yellow, green, gold or copper lustre may be added giving the effect of richly decorated Mason's style Imari Ware.

Ceramic: A general term applied to products that are fired at high temperature. The most common of these clay-based silica compounds are noted as Porcelain, Earthenware, Ironstone, etc.

China Glaze: See Pearlware.

Clobbering: Subsequent over painting with colored enamels on the glaze of previously decorated wares. The term

Clobbered Ware or China refers only to imported decorated wares, usually Chinese in origin, that were further decorated after importation.

Cobalt (Blue): The colorant for all ceramic blue applied under the glaze. Cobalt oxide, originally black, turns to a blue cobalt silicate when heated with the silica in the glaze.

Crazing: The development of fine cracks in the fired glaze of a piece of ceramic caused by shrinkage during the cooling period. Crazing may allow moisture and impurities to discolor the ware. Further shrinkage may be caused by the absorption of moisture in its life in a home, especially if left in contact with moisture for any length of time. This absorption of moisture can cause the biscuit to expand the point where the glaze 'envelope' cannot hold it any more.

Creamware: A refined, light weight cream-colored earthenware body of high quality Ball Clay and Flint, made by applying a pale yellowish lead glaze to the biscuit body and fired at about 900c - 1000c. Renamed "Queensware" by Josiah Wedgwood, c. 1762.

Earthenware: A ceramic body made from clays and silica compounds fired at various temperatures. It is semi-porous and opaque, and is usually glazed to render it impervious to liquids.

Enamel: Usually a lead base opaque or transparent coloring pigment of vitreous nature, colored with metallic oxides and fired to the glaze as decoration at a low kiln temperature of 750c. - 850c. Enamel comes in an almost unlimited range of colors.

Flow Blue: A cobalt blue printing color which diffused into the glaze with the addition of Flow Powder into the saggars during firing. Flow Powder is a mixture of Salt (Sodium Chloride), White Lead and Calcium Carbonate. The process results in blurring of the surrounding printed image. Collectors commonly refer to this distortion as Flown Blue. The term is interchangeable with Flow Blue.

Gaudy Ironstone: See: Brush Stroke

Glaze: A vitreous and often colorless lead powdered oxide solution in which the previously fired Bisque is dipped and fired to coat it with a glass-like coating, resulting in an impervious and permanent surface.

Glost: Also known as Glostware, White Ware or White Glost. Glost is the fixing of the glaze to the biscuit, usually at 1050c. for earthenware, in a "Glost Oven."

Ironstone: A hard, heavy durable earthenware body, patented in 1813 by C.J. Mason. Ironstone describes a ware made to a formula (similar to, if not identical to Stoneware). The name Ironstone, as used today, covers all bodies of this type.
"No potter who aimed at making a pale gray body would dream of putting 20% of iron slag into it! ...Moreover, it is very doubtful if any other 'sane' potter 'experimented' with his formulas... [further] by the middle of the 19th century the term ironstone had been generally applied to poor to medium quality earthenwares; it was no longer vitreous in most cases."(Correspondence from Robert Copeland dated June 1996)

Lead Glaze: A transparent glaze containing Lead Oxide, normally fired at a low temperature of 800c- 1050c.

Lustre (Decoration): A technique of decoration which renders a metallic like appearance. It is produced by metallic colored salts (films) fused to the top of the glaze and results in a shiny surface in imitation of silver, copper, etc. The addition of gold results in red, and gold-chloride in rich purple-red. The addition of silver nitrate yields a yellow-like color. Platinum, silver or copper yield their own color.

Mulberry Ironstone: Transfer printed or hand painted (brush stroke) ironstone with the color coming from manganese carbonate-a blackish, brownish-purplish hue. May be flown (see flow blue).

Outline Printing: A transfer outlined pattern, often in blue, black, biscuit-brown or chestnut-brown, decorated by

Print & Paint: filling in with various underglaze colors and sometimes embellished over the glaze with gold and/or colored enamels.

Pearlware: A white earthenware body similar to Creamware, but with some cobalt stain added to the lead glaze, and refined by Josiah Wedgwood. Pearlware is white or pale gray in appearance and is often confused with Creamware. The period name for this ceramic body was "China Glaze." The modern term is Pearlware.

Polychrome: Any decoration with more than one color under the glaze (as opposed to monochrome). Polychrome may be further embellished with colored enamels and gold over the glaze.
Polychrome printing is transfer printing decorated as above.

Porcelain: A highly refined ceramic body of many varieties (as opposed to earthenware or pottery). When fired at high temperatures porcelain becomes semi-vitreous and translucent. Its translucence depends on the thickness and firing temperature of the piece, and the firing temperature and composition of the paste.

Pottery: A generic term for all ceramic wares made of fired clay. It is often unglazed, coarse and porous (until glazed), as opposed to fine white earthenware.

Queensware: A fine, cream colored, lead glazed earthenware perfected by Josiah Wedgwood in c. 1762 and named after Queen Charlotte (see Creamware).

Relief (Decoration): By molding, casting, stamping and sprigging, a design is formed on a piece of pottery which rises above the plane (surface) of the body and, in effect, protrudes from the surface to a varying degree.

Saggar: A box or container made of fire clay and grog (crushed fired saggars or pitcher fragments) in which pottery ware may be placed for setting in a kiln.

Spatterware: Glazed earthenware crudely decorated by brush or sponge which produces a spatter-type effect, when splashed or spattered in colors such as blue, green and puce.

Sponge Printed (Decorating): Referred to as "dabbing" and/or "sponge-printing" decoration. A process by which the biscuit is "dabbed" with a rough sponge filled with colored slip or "printing" by which portions are cut out of the smooth root of a sponge, thus forming (motif) designs which were further decorated with underglaze colors.

Stilt Marks: Small defects in the glaze caused by the pieces having stood on three or four cone-shaped stilts during firing.

Stone China: Name adopted by Spode, c. 1813-1814. Stone China is a clay body fired at a high temperature of about 1250c. Such firing makes it very dense (thinness of the clay body may give the appearance of translucency) and hard and impervious to liquid without the use of a glaze.

Stoneware: Stoneware is a clay mixed with a proportion of fusible material and fired at high temperatures. It is impervious to liquid even when left unglazed.

Transfer Decorating: A process of decorating by which a printed, decorated pattern is obtained through inking an etched or engraved copper plate with metallic oxide-stained oils. The inked, sized tissue paper is then transferred while still tacky, face down onto the earthenware biscuit (body) surface and secured by brushing with a stiff bristle brush. The tissue paper is washed off in cold water which does not affect the color which is mixed with oil, to leave the image of the design on the article.

Underglaze (Decoration) Decoration applied to the biscuit ware before glazing. All colors used in ceramic decoration are based on metallic oxides and carbonates. Those which will withstand the glost temperatures of 1000c. - 1100c. are more limited than those available for on-glaze decorations which will be fired at below 850c.
Vitreous: Converted to glass. The state of a ceramic body which has been rendered non-porous by firing, without the addition of glaze.

BIBLIOGRAPHY

A library of reference books is essential to every collector, whether beginner or expert. This extended bibliography is the nucleus for which much of the information in this encyclopedia is based. Each book has its own contribution to make. Hardly a month passes by without the publication of a new book or article.

Some offer short anecdotes and histories while some are committed to a given subject. Certain older volumes are often unreliable or dated, leading the reader to search out more current reference works. Older sources, however, should not be ignored, read everything past and present.

Lacking primary sources such as newspapers, periodicals, rate and billing records, general directories and the like, I have had to rely upon secondary sources, as listed in this bibliography, in order to compile my data.

-A-

Andrews, Sandy. *Crested China. The History of Heraldic Souvenir Ware*. Hants, England: Milestone Publications, 1980

Arman, David & Linda. *Anglo-American Ceramics*, Part I. Rhode Island: Oakland Press, 1998

_________. *Historical Staffordshire, An Illustrated Check-List*. Danville, Virginia: Arman Enterprises, 1974.

___________. *Historical Staffordshire, An Illustrated Check-List, First Supplement*. Danville,Virginia: Arman Enterprises, 1977.

Atterbury, Paul. *Cornish Ware, Kitchen and Domestic Pottery by T.G. Green of Church Gresley, Derbyshire*. England: Richard Dennis, Ltd., 1996.

Atterbury, Paul (ed.). *English Pottery & Porcelain*. Clinton, New Jersey: A Main Street Press Book, Universe Books, 1978.

Atterbury,Paul. *The Parian Phenomenon*. Somerset, England: Richard Dennis, Ltd., 1989.

Atterbury, Paul and Batkin, Maureen. *The Dictionary of Minton*. Woodbridge, Suffolk, England: The Antique Collectors Club Ltd., 1990.

Atterbury, Paul & Irvine, Louise. *The Doulton Story, A Souvenir Booklet Produced Originally for the Exhibition Held at the Victoria and Albert Museum, May 12-30, 1979.* Stoke-on-Trent, England: Royal Doulton Tableware Limited, 1979.

-B-

Ball, A. *The Price Guide to Pot Lids and Other Underglaze Multicolour Prints On Ware*. (2nd. edition) Woodbridge, Suffolk, England: Antique Collectors Club, Ltd., 1980.

Baker, John C., B.A., A.M.A. (Revised by), *Sunderland Pottery*. England: Thomas Reed Industrial Press Ltd. and Tyne & Wear County Council Museums, 1984.

Balgade, Susan & Al. *Warman's English and Continental Pottery & Porcelain, an Illustrated Price Guide with Histories and References for Nearly 200 Categories from ABC to Zsolnay*. (2nd ed.) Radnor, Pennsylvania: Wallace-Homestead Book Company, 1991.

Barber, Edwin Atlee, A.M., Ph.D. *Anglo-American Pottery, Old English China With American Views*. (2nd ed), Philadelphia, Pennsylvania: Patterson & White Company, 1901.

_________. *Marks of American Potters*. Ann Arbor, Michigan: Ars Ceramica, Ltd., 1976.

_________. *Marks of American Potters*. Southampton, New York: Cracker Barrel Press, (no date).

_________. *The Pottery and Porcelain of the United States and Marks of American Potters*. New York, New York: Feingold & Lewis, 1976. (Reprint of the 1893 1st ed. with new introduction)

_________. *Tulip Ware of the Pennsylvania-German Potters.* Philadelphia, Pennsylvania: The Pennsylvania Museum and School of Industrial Art, 1903.

Barker, David. *William Greatbatch, A Staffordshire Potter*. London, England: Jonathan Horne Publications, 1990.

Barker, David & Halfpenny, Pat. *Unearthing Staffordshire.* Stoke-on-Trent, England: City Museum and Art Gallery, (Sponsored by Christies), 1990.

Barret, Richard Carter. *Bennington Pottery & Porcelain*. New York, New York: Bonanza Books, 1958.

Bartlett, John A. *British Ceramic Art*. 1870-1940. Atglen, Pennsylvania: Schiffer Publications, 1993.

Batkin Maureen. *Gifts for Good Children, The History of Children's China, Part, II 1890 -1990*. Ilminster, Somerset, England: Richard Dennis Publications, 1996.

_________. *Wedgwood Ceramics, 1846-1959*. London, England: Richard Dennis, 1982

Battie, David and Turner, Michael. *The Price Guide to 19th and 20th Century British Pottery.* (Reproduction), Woodbridge, Suffolk, England: Antique Collectors Club, 1990.

Battie, David. *Guide To Understanding 19th and 20th Century British Porcelain.* Woodbridge, Suffolk, England: Antique Collectors Club, 1994.

Bell, R.C. *Tyneside Pottery*. London, England: Studio Vista, Ltd., 1971.

Bemrose, Geoffrey. *Nineteenth Century English Pottery & Porcelain*. London, England: Faber & Faber, 1952.

Bergesen, Victoria. *Bergesen's British Ceramic Price Guide*. London, England: Barrie & Jenkins, 1992.

Berlard, Charles, H. *Pottery and Porcelain, A Glossary of Terms*. London & Vancouver: David & Charles, 1974.

Berling, Dr. K. (ed.) *Meissen China, An Illustrated History*. New York: Dover Publications, 1972 (1st edition, Berlin 1910).

Berthoud, Michael. *A Compendium of British Cups*. Shropshire, England: Micawber Publications, 1990.(1st edition as "Anthology of British Cups" 1982)

_________. *H & R Daniel, 1822-1846.* Kent, England: Micawber Publications, 1980.

_________. *The Daniel Table Ware Patterns.* Kent, England: Micawber Publications. 1982.

Berthoud, M. & Price, L. *Daniel Patterns on Porcelain*. Kent, England: Micawber Publications, 1997.

Binns, Charles F. *The Story of the Potter*. London, England, New York & Toronto: George Newnes, Limited, and Hodder and Stoughton. 1898.

Blacker, J.F. *A.B.C. of Collecting Old English China*. London, England: Stanley Paul & Co., Ltd., 1912.

_________. *A.B.C. of XIX Century English Ceramic Art*. London, England. Stanley Paul & Co., Ltd., 1911.

Blake, Sylvia. *Flow Blue*. Des Moines, Iowa: Wallace-Homestead Book Company, 1971.

Blum, Mr. & Mrs. Joseph. *Thomas Bentley*. (reprint) New York, New York: The Wedgwood Society of New York, 1975.

Bockol, Leslie. *Willow Ware, Ceramics in the Chinese Tradition*. Atglen, Pennsylvania: Schiffer Publications, 1995.

Bohn, Henry G. *A Guide to the Knowledge of Pottery, Porcelain, and Other Objects of Vertu*. London: Bell & Daldy, 1871.

Bradshaw, Peter. *18th Century English Porcelain Figures, 1745-1795*. Woodbridge, Suffolk, England: Antique Collectors Club, 1981.

Branin, M. Lelyn. *The Early Makers of Handcrafted Earthenware and Stoneware in Central and Southern New Jersey*. Cranbury, New Jersey: Associated University Presses, 1988.

Bunt, Cyril, G.E. *British Potters and Pottery Today.* Leigh-on-Sea, England: F. Lewis Publishers Ltd., 1956.

Burgess, Arene, W. *Souvenir Plates, A Collector's Guide*. Bethalto, Ohio: Privately Published, 1978.

Burgess, Arene, W. *A Collector's Guide to Souvenir Plates.* Atglen, Pennsylvania: Schiffer Publishing, Ltd., 1996.

Burgess, Fred. W. *Old Pottery and Porcelain*. (2nd Impression). New York, New York: G.P. Putnam's Sons, Ltd., 1924.

Burton, William, F.C.S. *A History and Description of English Earthenware and Stoneware.* London, Paris, New York and Melbourne: Cassell & Co., Ltd., 1904.

Burton, W. and Hobson, R.L. *Handbook of Marks on Pottery and Porcelain*. London, England: MacMillan & Co., 1919.

Butler, Joseph T. *Spatterware at Winterthur: An Analysis of Marks, Forms, Shapes, Color and Decoration.* Winterthur, Delaware: Winterthur Museum, 1957.

-C-

Caiger-Smith, Alan. *Lustre Pottery*, New York, New York: New Amsterdam Press, 1985.

Camehl, Ada Walker. *The Blue-China Book, Early American Scenes and History Pictured in the Pottery of the Time*. New York, New York: Dover Publications, Inc., 1971.

Cameron, Elisabeth. *Encyclopedia of Pottery and Porcelain, the Nineteenth and Twentieth Centuries*. London, England: Faber & Faber, Ltd., 1986.

Charleston, Robert J. *World Ceramics, An Illustrated History*. New York, New York: Crescent Books, 1990.

Carter, Tina, M. *Teapots, The Collector's Guide to Selecting, Identifying and*

Displaying New & Vintage Teapots. Philadelphia & London: Courage Books, 1995.

Chaffers, William. *Marks & Monograms on European and Oriental Pottery and Porcelain*, (14th rev. ed.) Los Angeles, California: Borden Publishing Co., (no date—approx. 1968), last edition, 15th, William Reeves, England 1965.

_________. *The New Collector's Hand-Book of Marks and Monograms on Pottery and Porcelain*. (Revised and augmented by Frederick Litchfield) London, England: Reeves and Turner, 1924.

Chalala, Mildred L. & Joseph P. *A Collector's Guide to ABC Plates, Mugs and Things*. Lancaster, Pennsylvania: Pridemark Press, 1980.

_________. *China and Pottery Marks*, New York, New York: Gilman Collamore & Co., Inc.

Charles, Bernard H. *Pottery and Porcelain, A Glossary of Terms*. London, England: David & Charles, 1974.

Christian, Albert. *The Spinning Wheel's Complete Book of Antiques*. (Revised edition) New York, New York: Grosset & Dunlap, 1972/73.

Clark, Garth. *The Potter's Art*. London, England: Phaidon Press, Ltd., 1995.

Clements, Monica Lynn & Patricia Rosser. *Popular Souvenir Plates*. Atglen, Pennsylvania: Schiffer Publishing Ltd, 1998.

Cluett, Robert. *George Jones Ceramics, 1861-1951*. Atglen, Pennsylvania: Schiffer Publishing Ltd, 1998.

Collard, Elizabeth. *Nineteenth-Century Pottery and Porcelain in Canada*. (2nd ed.) Kingston & Montreal, Canada: McGill-Queens University Press, 1994.

_________. *The Potter's View of Canada*. Kingston & Montreal, Canada: McGill-Queens University Press, 1983.

Copeland, Robert. *Blue and White Transfer-Printed Pottery*. Aylesbury, Bucks, England: Shire Publications, Ltd., 1982.

_________. *Copeland's Spode*. Shire Album 309, Aylesbury, Bucks, England: Shire Publications, Ltd., 1993.

_________. *Spode & Copeland Marks* (and Other Relevant Intelligence). London, England: Studio Vista, First Edition 1993, Second Edition 1997.

_________. *Spode's Willow Pattern and Other Designs After the Chinese*. London, England: Artillery House, 1980 and 1990 editions.

Cox, Alwyn & Angela. *Rockingham Pottery & Porcelain, 1745-1842*. London, England: Faber & Faber, 1983.

Cox, George J., ARCA. *Pottery for Artists, Craftsmen & Teachers*. New York, New York: The MacMillan Company, 1914.

Cox, Warren E. *The Book of Pottery and Porcelain, Vol. I*. (8th printing) New York, New York: Crown Publishers, 1953.

_________. *The Book of Pottery and Porcelain, Vol. II*. New York, New York: Crown Publishers, 1945.

Coysh, A.W. *Blue & White Transfer Ware 1780-1840*. London, England: David & Charles, Ltd., 1982.

_________. *Blue Printed Earthenware 1800-1850*. Vermont, U.S.A. & London, England: David & Charles, 1980.

Coysh, A.W. & Henrywood, R.K. *The Dictionary of Blue and White Printed Pottery, Vol. I, 1780-1880*. Woodbridge, Suffolk, England: Antique Collectors Club, Reprinted 1992.

_________. *The Dictionary of Blue and White Printed Pottery, Vol. II 1780-1880*. Woodbridge, Suffolk, England: Antique Collectors Club, Reprinted 1992.

Coysh, A.W. & Stefano, Frank, Jr. *Collecting Ceramic Landscapes*. London, England: Lund Humphries, 1981.

Cruickshank, Graeme. *Scottish Pottery*. Shire Album 191, Aylesbury Bucks, England: Shire Publications, Ltd., 1993.

_________. *Scottish Spongeware*. Edinburgh, Scotland: Scottish Pottery Studies, 1982.

Cushion, John P. *The Connoisseur Illustrated Guides, Pottery & Porcelain*. New York, New York: Hearst Books and London, England: The Connoisseur, 1972.

_________. *Pocket Book of British Ceramic Marks*. Definitive Fourth Edition, Revised and Expanded. London, England: Faber & Faber, 1994.

_________. *Pottery and Porcelain Tablewares*. London, England. Studio Vista, 1976.

Cushion, John P. (in collaboration with W.B. Honey). *Handbook of Pottery and Porcelain Marks*. (fifth edition, revised and expanded), London, England & Boston, Massachusetts: Faber & Faber, 1996.

-D-

Dacre, Norman. *Kilnhurst Old Pottery, 1746-1929*. Kilnhurst, Rotherham, England: Norman Dacre Publisher, 1987.

Dale, Jean. *The Charlton Standard Catalogue of Royal Doulton Jugs*. Canada: Charlton Press, 1993.

Darty, Peter. *The Pocketbook of Porcelain and Pottery Marks*. London, England: Dalton Watson, Ltd., (no date).

Davis, Howard. *Chinoisserie, Polychrome Decoration and Staffordshire*. London, England: Rubicon Press, 1991.

Davis, Peter & Rankine, Robert. *Wemyss Ware, A Decorative Scottish Pottery*. Edinburgh and London: Scottish Academic Press, 1986.

Debolt, C. Gerald. *Debolt's Dictionary of American Pottery Marks*. Paducah, Kentucky: Collectors Books, 1994.

_________. *The Dictionary of American Pottery Marks, Whiteware and Porcelain*. Rutland, Vermont: Charles E. Tuttle Company, 1988.

Decker, Emile & Thevenin, Christian. *Faiences de Sarreguemines*. Nancy, France: Presses Universitaires de Nancy, 1992.

Dietz, Ulsysses Grant. *A New Look at the Spatterware at Winterthur*. Winterthur, Delaware: Winterthur Museum, 1980.

Downman, Rev. Edward A. *English Pottery and Porcelain: A Handbook for the Collector*. London: L. Upcott Gill, 1910.

Drakard, David. (ed.) *Limehouse Ware Revealed*. London, England: The English Ceramic Circle, 1993.

Drakard, David & Holdway, Paul. *Spode Printed Ware*. London, England and New York, New York: Longman Publishing, 1983.

Dudson, Audrey M. *Dudson, A Family of Potters Since 1800*. Stoke-on-Trent, England: Dudson Publications, 1985.

_________. *A Guide to Cheese Dishes from 1750-1940*. Stoke-on-Trent, England: Richard Dennis Publisher, 1993.

Duke, Harvey. *Official Identification and Price Guide to Pottery and Porcelain* (7th ed.), New York, New York: House of Collectibles, 1989.

-E-

Ealestone, Arthur A. & Lockett, Terence A. *The Rockingham Pottery*, New Revised Edition. England: David & Charles, 1973.

Earle, Alice Morse. *China Collecting in America*. New York, New York: Charles Scriber's Sons, 1892.

Eberlein, Harold Donaldson and Ramsdell, Roger Wearne. *The Practical Book of Chinaware*. Garden City, New York: Halcyon House, 1942.

Edwards, Diana. *Black Basalt, Wedgwood and Contemporary Manufacturers*. Woodbridge, Suffolk, England: Antique Collectors Club, 1994.

Edwards, Diana & Hampson, Rodney. *English Dry-Bodied Stoneware, Wedgwood and Contemporary Manufacturers, 1774-1830*. Woodbridge, Suffolk, England: Antique Collectors Club, 1998.

Elliott, G. W. *Some Descriptions of Pottery Making and Working Conditions, 1557-1844*. Hanley, Stoke-on-Trent, England: Albion Galleries.

Emmerson, Robin. *British Teapots and Tea Drinking, 1700-1850*. London, England: H.M.S.O./ Norfolk Museum Service, 1992.

Evans, Lady Maria Millington, M.A. *Lustre Pottery*, New York, New York: E.P. Dutton & Company, (no date).

Eyles, Desmond. *The Doulton Burslem Wares*. London, England: Barrie & Jenkins, Ltd. and Royal Doulton, 1980.

-F-

Fenn, Patricia and Malpa, Alfred P. *Rewards of Merit*. Charlottesville, Virginia: The Ephermera Society of America, (Distributed by Howell Press, Inc.) 1994.

Finegan, Mary. *Johnson Brothers Dinnerware, Pattern Directory & Price Guide*. Boone, North Carolina: Marfine Antiques, 1993.

Finlayson, R.W. *Portneuf Pottery and Other Early Wares*. Don Mills, Canada: Longman, Canada, Ltd., 1972.

Fisher, Stanley W. *British Pottery and Porcelain*. New York, New York: Bell Publishing Company, 1962.

_________. *English Pottery and Porcelain Marks*. DesMoines, Iowa: Wallace-Homestead Book Co., 1970.

Fleming, J. Arnold, O.B.E. *Scottish Pottery*. Glasgow, Scotland: Maclehose, Jackson & Co., 1923.

Flick, Pauline. *Children's China (The Medallion Collector's Series)*. England: Constable Company, Ltd., 1983.

Foil, Richard. *Cumbow China of Abingdon, Virginia*. Abingdon, Virginia: Richard Foil Publisher

Fox, Eleanor J. and Edward G. *Gaudy Dutch*. Pottsville, Pennsylvania: Privately Published, 1968.

Frederick, G., Hays, V., Hill, E., Nelson, L. and Overmeyer, D. *Teapot Body Styles*. Flow Blue International Collectors' Club, 1993 and 1995 Supplement.

Freeman, Larry. *Ironstone China, China Classics, Vol. IV*. Watkins Glen, New York: Century House, 1954.

Frelinghuysen, Alice Cooney. *American Porcelain 1770-1920*. New York, New York: Harry N. Abrams, Inc. 1989.

-G-

Gallo, John. *Nineteenth and Twentieth Century Yellow Ware*. Richfield Springs, New York: Heritage Press, 1985.

Gaston, Mary Frank. *Blue Willow*. Paducah, Kentucky: Collectors Books, 1983 and Rev. 2nd edition 1996.

_________. *A Collector's Encyclopedia of Flow Blue China*. Paducah, Kentucky: Collectors Books, 1983.

_________. *Collector's Encyclopedia of Flow Blue China, Second Series, Identification and Values*. Paducah, Kentucky: Collectors Books, 1994.

Gates, William, C. Jr. *The City of Hills & Kilns*. East Liverpool, Ohio: The East Liverpool Historical Society, 1984.

Gates, William C. and Ormerod, Dana E. *The East Liverpool, Ohio Pottery District, Identification of Manufacturers and Marks*. Ronald L. Michael, Editor. California, Pennsylvania: The Society for Archaeology, 1982.

Glass, Douglas, Fisher, Margaret and Collins, Elizabeth. *Break the Pot - Make the Pot*. London & Glasgow: Adprint Ltd.

Glendinning, Sharon and Kobach, Janice. *Flow Blue Handbook*. Privately Published, Vol. I, 1994, Vol. II, 1995.

Godden, Geoffrey A. *An Illustrated Encyclopaedia of British Pottery and Porcelain, 2nd edition*. Leicester, England: Magna Books, 1992 (1st ed. Barrie & Jenkins 1980).

Godden, Geoffrey A. *Antique Glass and China, A Guide for the Beginning Collector.* New York, New York: Castle Books, 1966.

_________. *British Porcelain, An Illustrated Guide*. New York, New York: Clarkson N. Potter, (1st edition) 1974.

_________. *British Porcelain, An Illustrated Guide*. London, England: Barrie & Jenkins, (Reprinted, & Revised) 1990.

_________. *British Pottery, An Illustrated Guide*. New York, New York: Clarkson N. Potter (1st edition) 1974.

_________. *British Pottery, An Illustrated Guide*. London, England: Barrie & Jenkins, (Reprinted) 1990.

_________. *British Pottery and Porcelain, 1780-1850*. U.S.A: A.S. Barnes & Company, Inc., 1963.

_________. *The Concise Guide to British Pottery and Porcelain*. London, England: Barrie & Jenkins, 1990.

_________. *Encyclopaedia of British Pottery and Porcelain Marks*. New York, New York: Bonanza Books, (1st edition) 1964.

_________. *Encyclopaedia of British Pottery and Porcelain Marks*. London, England: Barrie & Jenkins, (Reprinted & Revised) 1993.

_________. *English China*. London, England: Barrie & Jenkins, 1985.

_________. *Godden's Guide to European Porcelain*. London, England: Barrie & Jenkins, 1993.

_________. *Godden's Guide to Masons China and the Ironstone Wares*. London, England: Antique Collectors Club, (Reprinted & Revised) 1993.

_________. *The Handbook of British Pottery and Porcelain Marks*. London, England: Barrie & Jenkins, (Reprinted) 1993.

_________. *Jewitt's Ceramic Art of Great Britain 1800-1900*. London, England: Barrie & Jenkins, 1985.

_________. *Minton Pottery and Porcelain of the First Period*. London, England: Barrie & Jenkins, 1968.

_________. *Ridgway Porcelains*. London, England: Antique Collectors Club, (2nd Revised ed.) 1985.

Godden, Geoffrey A. (Editor & Contributor) *Staffordshire Porcelain*, London, England: Granada Publishing, 1983.

Godden, Geoffrey A. and Gibson, Michael. *Collecting Lustreware*. London, England: Barrie & Jenkins, 1991.

Godden, Geoffrey A. *Victorian Porcelain*, London, England: Herbert Jenkins, 1961.

Gorely, Jean. *Wedgwood*. New York, New York: Gramercy Publishing Co., 1950.

Grabham, Oxley, M.A., M.B.O.U. *Yorkshire Potteries, Pots & Potters, Annual Report of the Council of the Yorkshire Philosophical Society for 1915.* Presented To The Annual Meeting, February 1915. England: Printed by Coultas & Voulans, Ltd., 1916.

Graham, The Rev. Malcolm. *Cup and Saucer Land*. England: Madgwick, Houlston & Co., Ltd., 1908.

Greaser Arlene & Paul H. *Homespun Ceramics, A Study of Spatterware, 3rd. ed.* Allentown, Pennsylvania: Privately Published, 1964 and 4th ed. 1973.

Green, David. *Pottery Materials & Techniques*. London, England: Faber & Faber, Ltd., 1967.

Guide to English Porcelain. Radnor, Pennsylvania: Wallace-Homestead, (reissue) 1992.

-H-

Haggar, Reginald G. *The Concise Encyclopedia of Continental Pottery & Porcelain*, New York, New York: Hawthorne Books, Inc., 1960.

_________. *Staffordshire Chimney Ornaments*. New York, New York: Pitman Publishing Corp., 1955.

Haggar, Reginald and Adams, Elizabeth. *Mason Porcelain & Ironstone, 1796-1853*. London, England: Faber & Faber, 1977.

Haggar, R.G., Mountford, A. and Thomas, J. *The Staffordshire Pottery Industry, Well Street Pottery*. (An Extract from The Victoria History of the Country of Stafford, Vol. II) Staffordshire, England: Reprinted by Staffordshire County Library, Edited by M.W. Greenslade & J.G. Jenkins, 1981.

Hainbach, Rudolf. *Pottery Decorating*. (Translated by Charles Salter). London, England: Scott, Greenwood & Son, 1907.

Haines, Flora, E. *A Keramic Study, A Chapter in the History of Half a Dozen Dinner Plates*. Bangor, Maine: Published by the Author, 1895.

Halfpenny, Pat. *English Earthenware Figures, 1740-1840*. Woodbridge, Suffolk, England: Antique Collectors Club, (reprint) 1995.

Halfpenny, Pat (Editor). *Penny Plain, Two Pence Coloured. Transfer Printing on English Ceramics, 1750-1850*. Stoke-on-Trent, England: The City Museum & Art Gallery, 1994.

Hallesy, Helen. *The Glamorgan Pottery, Swansea, 1814-1838*. Llandysul, Dyfed, Wales: Gomer Press, 1995.

Halsey, R.T. Haines. *Pictures of Early New York on Dark Blue Staffordshire Pottery*, New York, New York: Dover Publications, 1974.

Hampson, Rodney. *Churchill China, Great British Potters Since 1795*. Keele, England: The Centre for Local History, Department of History, University of Keele, England. (Staffordshire Heritage Series No. 5), 1994.

Hartman, Urban. *Porcelain and Pottery Marks*. New York, New York: Urban Hartman, 1943.

Hawke-Smith, Cameron. *The Making of the Six Towns*. Stoke on Trent, England: City Museum and Art Gallery., 1985.

Hayden, Arthur. *Chats on English China*. New York: Frederick A. Stokes Company, 1920.

_________. *Chats on Old Earthenware*. New York: Frederick A. Stokes Company, 1909.

_________. *Spode and His Successors*. New York, New York: Frederick A. Stokes Company.

Heaivilin, Annise Doring. *Grandma's Tea Leaf Ironstone, A History and Study of English and American Potteries*. Des Moines, Iowa: Wallace-Homestead Book Company, 1981.

Henderson, Ian. *Pictorial Souvenirs of Britain*. London, England: David & Charles, 1974.

Henrywood, R.K. *Bristol Potters 1775-1906*. Bristol, England: Redcliffe Press Ltd., 1992.

_________. *An Illustrated Guide to British Jugs, From Medieval Times to the Twentieth Century.* England: Swanhill Press, 1997.

_________. *Relief Moulded Jugs, 1820-1900*. London, England: Antique Collectors Club, 1985.

Hill, Ellen, R. *Mulberry Ironstone, Flow Blue's Best Kept Little Secret*. Madison, New Jersey: Mulberry Hill Publications, 1993 (1994 and 1996 Supplements).

Hill, Susan. *The Shelley Style*. Stratford-upon-Avon, Warwickshire, England: Jazz Publications, Ltd., 1990.

Hillier, Bevis. *Master Potters of the Industrial Revolution, The Turners of Lane End*. London, England: Cory, Adams & Mackay, 1965.

_________. *Pottery and Porcelain 1700-1914*. New York, New York: Meredith Press, 1968. (A Social history of the Decorative Arts.)

Hoener, Norma Jean. *Flow Blue China: Additional Patterns and New Information*. Flow Blue International Collectors' Club, 1996.

Hollowood, Bernard. *The Story of J. & G. Meakin*. London, England: Bemrose Publicity Co., Ltd., 1957.

Honey, W. B. *English Pottery and Porcelain*. London, England: A & C. Black, Ltd., 1933

_________. *English Pottery and Porcelain*. (3rd ed.), London, England: Adam & Charles Black, 1947.

Hopwood, Irene & Gordon. *Denby Pottery 1809-1997*. London, England: Richard Dennis, 1997.

_________. *The Shorter Connection, A.J. Wilkinson, Clarice Cliff, Crown Devon, A Family Pottery.* London, England: Richard Dennis Publications, 1992.

Howard, David Sanctuary. *New York and the China Trade*. New York: New York Historical Society, 1984

Hudson, Kenneth. *The History of English China Clays*. New York, New York: Augustus M. Kelley Publishers, 1969.

Hughes, G. Bernard. *The Country Life Collector's Pocket Book of China*. London, England: Distributed for Country Life Books by the Hamlyn Publishing Group, Ltd., Reprinted 1978.

_________. *English and Scottish Earthenware, 1660-1860*. London, England: Abbey Fine Arts, 1970.

_________. *Victorian Pottery and Porcelain*. London, England: Spring Books, 1967.

Hughes, G. & Pugh, Robert. *Llanelly Pottery*. Llanelli, Wales: Llanelli Borough Council Public Library, 1990.

Hughes, Kathy. *A Collector's Guide to Nineteenth Century Jugs*. London, England & Boston, Massachusetts: Routledge & Kegan Paul, Plc, 1985.

_________. *A Collector's Guide to Nineteenth Century Jugs, Vol. II*. Dallas, Texas: Taylor Publishing Company, 1991.

Husfloen, Kyle. *Collector's Guide to American Pressed Glass, 1825-1915*. Radnor, Pennsylvania: Wallace-Homestead Book Co., 1992.

Hutchins, Catherine E. (Editor). *Everyday Life in the Early Republic* . Winterthur, Delaware: Henry Francis du Pont Winterthur Museum, 1994. "Changing Consumption Patterns: English Ceramics and the American Market from 1770 to 1840" by George L. Miller, Ann Smart Martin & Nancy S. Dickinson, pp 219-248.

Hyde, J. A. Lloyd. *Oriental Lowestoft, Chinese Export Porcelain*. Newport, Monmouthshire, England: The Ceramic Book Company, 1954.

-I-

Irvine, Louise. *Royal Doulton Series Ware, Volume 1, Subjects from Literature, Popular Illustrators, Historical Characters and Events*. London, England: Richard Dennis, Ltd., 1980.

_________. *Royal Doulton Series Ware, Volume 2, Olde Worlde Imagery*. London, England: Richard Dennis, Ltd., 1984.

_________. *Royal Doulton Series Ware, Volume 3, Doulton in the Nursery*. London, England: 1986.

_________. *Royal Doulton Series Ware, Volume 4, Around the World Flora and Fauna*. London, England: Richard Dennis, Ltd., 1988.

_________. *Royal Doulton Series Ware, Volume 5, Doulton Scenic Wares*. London, England: Richard Dennis, Ltd., 1998.

-J-

Jacobson, Dawn. *Chinoiserie*. London, England: Phaidson Press, Ltd., 1993.

Jenkins, Steven. *Midwinter Pottery, A Revolution in British Tableware* (ed. Paul Atterbury), England: Richard Dennis, 1997.

Jervis, W. Percival. *A Book of Pottery Marks.* Privately Printed, 1897.

Jervis. W.P. *European China, China Classics, Vol. III*. (Introduction by Serry Wood). Watkins Glen, New York: Century House, (reissued) 1953.

Jervis, W.P. and Wood, Serry. *English Staffordshire, China Classics, Vol. VI*. Watkins Glen, New York: Century House, 1953.

Jewitt, Llewellyn. *The History of Ceramic Art in Great Britain,* Vol. 1 & 2, Great Britain and New York: Scribner, Welford & Armstrong, 1878.

_________. *The Ceramic Art of Great Britain*. Dorset, England: New Orchard Editions Ltd., 1985. (Reprint of the 1883 original l2th edition.)

John, W.D. & Baker, Warren. *Old English Lustre Pottery*. Newport, Mon, England: R.H. Johns Ltd., 1951.

Jones, Joan. *Minton, the First Two Hundred Years of Design and Production*. Shrewsbury, England: Swan Hill Press, 1993.

-K-

Karmason, Marilyn G. with Stacke, Joan B. *Majolica, A Complete History and Illustrated Survey*. New York, New York: Harry N. Abrams, Inc., Publishers, 1989.

Kearns, Tim. J. *Knowles Taylor and Knowles, American Bone China.* Atglen, Pennsylvania: Schiffer Publications, Ltd., 1994.

Kelly, Henry E. *Scottish Sponge Printed Pottery, Traditional Patterns, Their Manufacturers and History*. Glasgow, Scotland: The Lomondside Press, 1993.

Kenny, Adele. *Staffordshire Animals, A Collector's Guide to: History, Styles, Values*. Atglen, Pennsylvania: Schiffer Publishing, Ltd., 1998.

Kenny, John B. *The Complete Book of Pottery Making*. New York, New York: Greenberg Publishing, 1952.

Ketchum, William C., Jr. *American Country Pottery, Yellowware & Spongeware.* New York, New York: Alfred A. Knopf, 1987.

_________. *American Pottery and Porcelain, Identification and Price Guide*. New York: Avon Books, 1994.

_________. *American Stoneware*. New York, New York: Henry Holt & Company, 1991.

_________. *Potters and Potteries of New York State, 1650-1900*. (2nd edition). New York: Syracuse University Press, 1987.

Klamkin, Marian. *American Patriotic and Political China.* New York, New York: Charles Scribner's Sons, 1973.

Kovel, Ralph M. and Terry H. *Dictionary of Marks - Pottery and Porcelain*. New York, New York: Crown Publishers, Inc., 1953.

-L-

Laidacker, Sam. *Anglo-American China & Historical American Views & Subjects, Part I.* Bristol, Pennsylvania: Compiled and Published by Sam Laidacker, 1938 (copyright 1954).

_________. *Anglo-American China, Other Than American Views, Part II*. Bristol, Pennsylvania: Compiled and Published by Sam Laidacker, 1951.

_________. *Anglo-American Pottery*. Philadelphia, Pennsylvania: Patterson & White, 1901.

_________. *Standard Catalogue of Anglo-American China, From 1810-1850*. Scranton, Pennsylvania: Published by Sam Laidacker, 1938.

Lambton, Lucina. *Chambers of Delight*. London, England: The Gordon Fraser Gallery Ltd., 1983.

Lang. Gordon. *Miller's Pottery & Porcelain Marks.* London, England: Millers an Imprint of Reed International Books Ltd., 1995.

Larsen, Ellouise Baker. *American Historical Views of Staffordshire China*. New York, New York: Doubleday, Doran & Co., 1939.

_________. *American Historical Views of Staffordshire China, 3rd Edition*. New York, New York: Dover Publications, (Reprinted) 1975.

Lawrence, Heather. *Yorkshire Pots and Potteries*, London, England and Vermont, USA: David Charles, 1974.

Lechler, Doris Anderson. *English Toy China*. Marietta, Ohio: Antique Publications, 1989.

Lehner, Lois. *Lehner's Encyclopedia of U.S. Marks on Pottery, Porcelain & Clay*. Paducah, Kentucky: Collector Books, 1988.

_________. *Ohio Pottery & Glass, Marks and Manufacturers*, Des Moines, Iowa: Wallace Homestead Book Co., 1978.

Lewis, Griselda, A. *A Collectors History of English Pottery.* Woodbridge, Suffolk, England: Antique Collectors Club, 1992.

Lewis, John and Griselda. *Pratt Ware, English & Scottish Relief Decorated and Underglaze Coloured Earthenware, 1780-1840*. New York, New York and Dyfed, United Kingdom: Leo Kaplan, Ltd. and Shire Publications, 1993 (ACC published the English edition).

Lindsey, Bessie, M. *American Historical Glass*. Rutland, Vermont: Charles E. Tuttle Co., 1980.

Litchfield, Frederick. *Pottery and Porcelain, A Guide to Collectors*. London, England: A & C Black, Ltd., 1925.

Little, W.L. *Staffordshire Blue*. London, England: B.T. Batsford, Ltd., (Reprinted) 1987.

Lockett, Terence A. *Collecting Victorian Tiles*. Woodbridge, Suffolk, England: Antique Collectors Club, (Reprinted) 1988.

_________. *Davenport Pottery and Porcelain, 1794 - 1887*. London, England: David & Charles, Newton Abbot, 1972.

Lockett, Terence A. and Godden, Geoffrey A. *Davenport China, Earthenware and Glass, 1794-1887*. London, England: Barrie & Jenkins, 1989.

-M-

Mankowitz, Wolf. *Wedgwood*. London, England: Spring Books, 1953.

Mankowitz, Wolf and Haggar, Reginald G. *The Concise Encyclopedia of English Pottery and Porcelain*. London, England: Andre Deutsch, Ltd., 1968.

May, Harvey. *The Beswick Price Guide* (4th edition). London, England: Francis Joseph, 1997.

May, John and Jennifer. *Commemorative Pottery 1780-1900*. New York, New York: Charles Scribner's Sons, 1972.

McCauley, Robert, H. *Liverpool Transfer Designs on Anglo-American Pottery*. Portland, Maine: The Southworth-Anthoensen Press, 1942.

McClinton, Katharine Morrison. *Antiques in Miniature*. New York, New York: Charles Scribner's Sons, 1970.

McConnell, Kevin. *Spongeware and Spatterware*. Atglen, Pennsylvania: Schiffer Publishing, Ltd., 1990.

McVeigh, Patrick. *Scottish East Coast Potteries, 1750-1840*. Edinburgh, Scotland: John Donald Publishers, Ltd., 1979.

Meteyard, Eliza. *The Life of Josiah Wedgwood from His Private Correspondence and Family Papers*. (Vol. I & II). London, England: Hurst & Blackett,

Publishers, reprinted in 1980.

Milbourn, Maurice and Evelyn. *Understanding Miniature British Pottery and Porcelain, 1730- Present Day*. Woodbridge, Suffolk, England: Antique Collectors Club, Ltd., 1983.

Miller, George, L. *English Ceramics and the American Market: Prices, Marketing and Consumption from 1780-1880*. Williamsburg, Virginia: Colonial Williamsburg Foundation, 1989.

_________. *A Revised Set of Index Values for Classification and Economic Scaling of English Ceramis from 1787 to 1880*. (Vol. 25, No. 1,) Williamsburg, Virginia: Williamsburg Foundation (Historical Archaeology), 1991 London, England. Pottery Publications, 1996.

Miller, George, L., Jones, Oliver R., Ross, Lester A. and Majewski, Teresita (Compilers). *Approaches to Material Culture.* California, Pennsylvania: Research for Historical Archaelogists, The Society for Historical Archaelogy, (California University of Pennsylvania) 1991.

Miller, Judith & Martin. *Victorian Style*. London, England: Reed International Books, Ltd., 1994.

Miller, Philip and Berthoud, Michael. *An Anthology of British Teapots*. Bridgnorth, Shropshire, England: Micawber Publications, 1985.

Moore, N. Hudson. *The Old China Book*. New York, New York: Tudor Publishing Co., (Reprinted) 1948.

Moore, Ralph. *Porcelain & Pottery Tea Tiles*. Marietta, Ohio: Antique Publications, 1994.

Moore, Steven and Ross, Catherine. *Maling, The Trade Mark of Excellence*. Newcastle, England: Tyne & Wear Museums, (Revised Edition) 1992.

Morley-Fletcher, Hugo, Consultant Editor. *Techniques of the World's Great Masters of Pottery and Ceramics*. London, England: Quantum Books, Ltd., 1997.

Morse, Alice Earl. *China Collecting in America*. New York: Scribner, 1892.

-N-

Nance, E. Morton. *The Pottery and Porcelain of Swansea and Nantgarw.* London, England: B.R. Batsford, Ltd., 1942 (Photocopied edition in two volumes).

Niblett, Kathy. *Dynamic Design; The British Pottery Industry, 1940-1990*. Stoke-on-Trent, England: City Museum and Art Gallery, 1990.

Nix, Thomas. *Abbie's Encyclopedia of Children's and Miniature Flow Blue.* Florida: Sentinel Publications, July 1992.

_________. *Abbie's Encyclopedia of Flow Blue, Floral & Art Nouveau.* Florida: Sentinel Publications, July 1992.

_________. *Abbie's Encyclopedia of Oriental and Scenic Flow Blue*. Florida: Sentinel Publications, July 1992.

_________. *Abbie's Enculopedia of Scinde Forms and Shapes*. Florida: Sentinel Publications, July 1992.

The North Staffordshire Pottery Industry and the War. Industrial Study Group supervised by Stephen Coltham, B.A. North Staffordshire, England, 1944.

-O-

Old China. Syracuse, New York: Keramic Studio Publishing Co., 1901-1902.

Ormsbee, Thomas H. *English China and its Marks*. New York, New York: Deerfield Books, Inc., 1967.

Owen, Harold. *The Staffordshire Potter*. London: Grant Richards. 1901.

-P-

Palliser, Mrs. Bury. *The China Collectors Pocket Companion.* London, England: Sampson Low, Marston & Co., Ltd., 1906.

Parkin, W. M. *The Earthenwares of Booths, 1864-1948*. Derbyshire, England: Keeling Collection, 1997.

Paul, E. and Petersen A. (editors) *Collector's Handbook to Marks on Porcelain and Pottery*. Green Farms, Connecticut: Modern Books and Crafts, Inc., 1974.

Peake, Tim. H. *William Brownfield & Son(s), An Illustrated Guide to Brownfield Wares, 1837-1900*. London, England: T.H. Peake Publishers, 1995.

Peel, Derek. *A Pride of Potters, 300 Years of Adams Craftsmanship*. London, England: Arthur Barker, Ltd. and Robert Speller and Sons 1957

Penderill-Church, John. *William Cookworthy 1705-1780*. Truro, Cornwall, England: D. Bradford Barton, Ltd., 1972.

Perrott, E. George, B.A. *Pottery & Porcelain Marks, European, Oriental and USA in Chronological Order.* Bath, England: Gemini Publications, Ltd., 1997.

Pine, Nicholas. *The Concise Encyclopedia and Price Guide to Goss China.* Waterlooville, Hampshire, England: Milestone Publications, 1992.

Pocket Guide to 1880 Table Settings. Watkins Glen, New York: Century House.

Pope, Clive Mason. *A-Z of Staffordshire Dogs.* Kidlington, Oxon, England: Classic Press, 1990.

Potteries Picture Postcards, A Second Portrait of the Six Towns Vol. 2. Shropshire, England: Compiled by The Potteries Postcard Society, 1986 and Vol. 3 1988.

Potteries Picture Postcards, A Second Portrait of the Six Towns Vol. 2. Shropshire, England: Compiled by The Potteries Postcard Society, 1986 and Vol. 3 1988.

Pottery, A History of the Pottery Industry and its Evolution. (Limited Edition) New Jersey: Thomas Maddock's Sons Company, 1910.

Prime, William, C. *Pottery and Porcelain of all Times and Nations*. New York: Harper & Brothers Publishers, 1878.

Pryce, P.D. and Williams, S.H. *Swansea Blue and White Pottery*. Woodbridge, Suffolk, England: Antique Collector's Club, 1973.

Pugh, Gordon. Surgeon Captain P.D., *Naval Ceramics*. Newport, Mon, England: The Ceramic Book Company, 1971.

Pugh, Robert. *Welsh Pottery, A Towy Guide*. Bath, England: Towy Publishing, 1995.

Punchard, Lorraine. *Playtime Pottery & Porcelain From Europe & Asia.* Atglen, Pennsylvania: Schiffer Publishing, Ltd., 1996.

_________. *Playtime Pottery & Porcelain From the U.K. and the U.S.* Atglen, Pennsylvania: Schiffer Publishing, Ltd., 1996.

-Q-

Quail, G. *Nautilus Porcelain, Possil Pottery*. Glasgow, Scotland: Glasgow District Libraries Publications, 1983.

Quinter, David Richard. *Willow!* Burnstown, Ontario, Canada: General Store Publishing House, 1997.

-R-

Rackham, Bernard. *Catalogue of the Herbert Allen Collection of English Porcelain*. (2nd ed.) London, England: Victoria & Albert Museum, 1922.

Ramsay, John. *American Potters and Pottery*, New York, New York: Tudor Publishing Co., 1947.

Ramsey, L.G.G., F.S.A. (Editor) *The Complete Encyclopedia of Antiques*. New York, New York: Hawthorne Books, Inc., 1967.

The Random House Collector's Encyclopedia, Victoriana to Art Deco. New York, New York: Random House, 1974.

Rathbone, Frederick. *Wedgwood By Rathbone (A Reprint in its Entirety of Old Wedgwood)* ed. by Harry M. Buten, England: Buten Museum of Wedgwood, 1968.

Reilly, Robin. *Wedgwood*. (2 Volumes) London, England: MacMillan, Ltd., 1989.

_________. *Wedgwood, The New Illustrated Dictionary*. Woodbridge, Suffolk, England: Antique Collector's Club, 1995.

Reilly, Robin and Savage, George. *The Dictionary of Wedgwood*. Woodbridge, Suffolk, England: Antique Collector's Club, 1980.

Rhead, G. Woolliscroft. *British Pottery Marks*. London, England: Scott, Greenwood & Son, 1910.

_________. *The Earthenware Collector, A Guide to Old English Earthenware*. London, England: Herbert Jenkins Ltd., 1920.

Rhead, G. Woolliscroft and F.A. *Staffordshire Pots and Potters*. London, England: Hutchinson & Co., 1906.

Rice, D.G. *English Porcelain Animals of the 19th Century*. Woodbridge, Suffolk, England: Antique Collector's Club, (Reprinted) 1990.

Riley, Noel. *Gifts For Good Children, The History of Children's China 1790-1890*. London, England: Richard Dennis Publications, 1991.

Robacker, Earl F. *Arts of the Pennsylvania Dutch*. New York, New York: Castle Books, 1965.

_________. *Pennsylvania Dutch Stuff, A Guide to Country Antiques*. Philadelphia, Pennsylvania: University of Pennsylvania Press, (5th edition) 1961.

_________. *Pennsylvania Dutch Stuff, A Guide to Country Antiques*. New York, New York: Bonanza Books, 1964.

_________. *Spatterware and Sponge, Hardy Perennials of Ceramics.* Cranbury, New Jersey: A.S. Barnes & Co, Inc., 1979.

Roberts, Gaye Blake. *Mason's, The First Two Hundred Years.* London, England: Merrell Holberton Publishers Ltd., 1996.

Rogers, Connie. *Willow Ware Made in The U.S.A., An Identification Guide.* Cincinnati, Ohio: Privately Published, 1995.

-S-

Sandon, Henry. *British Pottery and Porcelain for Pleasure and Investment*,. New York, New York: Arco Publishing Co. Inc., 1969.

_________. *Coffee Pots and Teapots for the Collector.* Edinburgh, Scotland: John Bartholomew and Son, Ltd., 1973.

Sandon, John. *The Dictionary of Worcester Porcelain, Vol. 1, 1751-1851*, Woodbridge, Suffolk, England: The Antique Collector's Club, 1996.

Savage, George. *English Ceramics*. New York, New York: Fine Art Books, 1961.
Savage, George & Newman, Harold. *An Illustrated Dictionary of Ceramics*. London, England: Thames & Hudson Ltd., 1992 (Reprint).
Scarratt, William. *Old Times in the Potteries*. Stoke on Trent, England: 1906.
Schiffer, Herbert, Peter & Nancy. *Chinese Export Porcelain, Standard Patterns & Forms 1780-1880.* At Exton, Pennsylvania: Schiffer Publishing, Ltd., 1975.
Sekers, David. *The Potteries*. Shire Album 62, Aylesbury, Bucks, England: Shire Publications, Ltd., 1994.
Shaw, J.T. (ed.) *Sunderland Ware, The Potteries of Wearside*. (4th edition), Sunderland, England: Sunderland Public Libraries, Museum & Art Gallery, (no date).
Shaw, Simeon. *History of the Staffordshire Potteries*. (Originally published in 1829), New York, New York: Praeger Publishers, 1970.
Shuman, John A, III. *The Collector's Encyclopedia of Gaudy Dutch and Welsh.* Paducah, Kentucky: Collector Books, 1991 and updated edition 1998.
Sibson, Florence. *The History of the West Cumberland Potteries*. Hong Kong: Production by Albert Chan Production Ltd., 1991.
Skinner, Deborah S. & Young, Velma. *Miles Mason Porcelain, A Guide to Patterns & Shapes.* Stoke-on-Trent, England: City Museum & Art Gallery, 1992.
Slesin, Suzanne, Rozensztroch, Daniel, Cliff, Stafford. *Everyday Things, Kitchen Ceramics.* New York: Abbeville Press Publishers, 1997.
Smith, Alan. *The Illustrated Guide to Liverpool Herculaneum Pottery 1796-1840.* London, England: Barrie & Jenkins, 1970.
Snyder, Jeffrey B. *Fascinating Flow Blue*. Atglen, Pennsylvania: Schiffer Publishing, Ltd., 1997.
_________. *Flow Blue: A Collector's Guide to Patterns, History and Values*. Atglen, Pennsylvania: Schiffer Publishing Ltd., 1992, revised editions 1996 and 1999.
_________. *Historic Flow Blue, With Price Guide.* Atglen, Pennsylvania: Schiffer Publishing Ltd., 1994.
_________. *Historical Staffordshire, American Patriots & Views*. Atglen, Pennsylvania: Schiffer Publishing Ltd., 1995.
_________. *A Pocket Guide to Flow Blue*. Atglen, Pennsylvania: Schiffer Publications, Ltd., 1995.
_________. *Romantic Staffordshire Ceramics*. Atglen, Pennsylvania: Schiffer Publications, Ltd., 1997.
Solon, L. N. *A Brief History of Old English Porcelain and its Manufactories.* London, England: Bemrose & Sons, Ltd., 1903.
Solon, L. M. *The Art of The Old English Potter.* New York, New York: D. Appelton and Company, 1886.
Spargo, John. *Early American Pottery & China*. Garden City, New York: Garden City Publishing Co., Inc., 1926.
Stefano, Frank Jr. *Check-List of Wedgwood Old Blue Historical Plates and Other Views of the United States.* Brooklyn, New York: Produced by Josiah Wedgwood & Sons Ltd. for the Sole Import of Jones, McDuffee & Stratton Co., Privately Published, 1990.
Starkey, Govin. *'Pottery' The Story of Alfred Meakin (Tunstall) Ltd.*, London, England: Ruthien Publications Press, 1949.
Stefano, Frank Jr. *Pictorial Souvenirs & Commemoratives of North America,* New York, New York: E.P. Dutton & Co., Inc., 1976.
Stoltzfus, Dawn & Snyder, Jeffrey B. *White Ironstone, A Survey of it Many Forms: Undecorated; Flow Blue; Mulberry; Copper Lustre.* Atglen, Pennsylvania: Schiffer Publications, Ltd., 1997.
Stratton, Deborah. *Mugs and Tankards*. London, England: Souvenir Press, 1975.
Stuart, Dennis, editor. *People of the Potteries*. Keele, England: Department of Adult Education, University of Keele, 1985.
Sussman, Lynne. *Canadian Historic Sites (Spode/Copeland Transfer-Printed Patterns)*. Ottawa, Canada: Prepared by the National Historic Parks and Sites Branch, 1979.
_________. *Mocha, Banded, Cat's Eye and Other Factory-Made Slipware, Studies in Northeast Historical Archaeology*, Vol. 1, Parks, Canada: Department of Canadian Heritage, 1997.
_________. *The Wheat Pattern, An Illustrated Survey*. Parks, Canada: National Historic Parks and Sites Branch, 1985.

-T-

Thomas, D & E Lloyd. *The Old Torquay Potteries*. Devon, England, 1978.
Thomas, John. *The Rise of the Staffordshire Potteries*. Bath, England: Adams & Dart, 1971.
Thorn, D. Jurdan. *Handbook of Old Pottery and Porcelain Marks*. New York, New York: Tudor Publishing Co., 1947.
Towner, Donald. *The Leeds Pottery*. London, England: Cory, Adams & Mackay, 1963.
Treadwell, John H. *A Manual of Pottery and Porcelain for American Collectors.* New York: G. P. Putnam & Sons, 1872.
Turner, H.A.B. *A Collector's Guide To Staffordshire Pottery Figures*. New York, New York: Emerson Books, Inc., 1971.
Turner, William, F.S.S. (editior) *William Adams, An Old English Potter*. London, England: Chapman & Hall, Ltd. and Syracuse, New York: The Keramic Studio Publishing Co., 1904.
Twichett, John, F.R.S.A. *In Account With Sampson Hancock, 1860s-1880s*. Burford, Oxon, England: D.J.C. Books, 1996.
Twichett, John, F.R.S.A & Bailey, Betty. *Royal Crown Derby*, New York, New York: Clarkson N. Potter, Inc. 1976.

-U-

Upchurch, Nancy. *Handbook of Tea Leaf Body Styles.* U.S.A.: Published by the Tea Leaf Club International, 1995.

-V-

Verbeek, Susan Jean. *The History and Products of J.H. Weatherby & Sons Ltd., Thomas Lawrence (Longton) Ltd., Falcon China, Ltd.*
The Victorian Pattern Glass & China Book, New York, New York: Arch Cape Press, 1990.
The Victoria History of the Counties of Stafford, Vol. II & Vol. VIII. R. B. Pugh, editor. London, England: University of London Institute of Historical Research, Oxford University Press, 1967 & 1963 respectively.

-W-

Wakefield, Hugh. *Victorian Pottery*. London, England: Herbert Jenkins, Ltd., 1962.
Ward, John. *The Borough of Stoke-Upon-Trent*. London, England: Republished by Webberley, Ltd, (from the original published in 1843), 1984.
Watkins, Chris and Harvey, William and Senft Robert. *Shelley Potteries, The History and Production of a Staffordshire Family of Potters*. London, England: Barrie & Jenkins, (Reprinted) 1994.
Walton, Peter. *Creamware and Other English Pottery at Temple Newsam House, Leeds.* England: Manningham Press, 1976.
Watney, Bernard. *English Blue and White Porcelain of the 18th Century*. London, England: Faber & Faber, Ltd., 1973 (2nd Revised Edition).
Wedgwood, Henry Allen. *People of the Potteries*. New York, New York: Augustus M. Kelley Publishers, 1970.
Wedgwood, Josiah, M.P., C.C. and Ormsbee, Thomas H. *Staffordshire Potter*. New York, New York: McBride & Co., 1947.
_________. *Staffordshire Pottery and its History*. New York, New York: McBride, Nast & Co., 1913.
Weir, Richard. *Six of the Best.* Burton-upon-Trent, England: Trent Valley Publications, 1988.
Westroppp, Hodder M. *Handbook of Pottery and Porcelain*. London: Chatto & Windus, 1880.
Wetherbee, Jean. *A Look At White Ironstone*. DesMoines, Iowa: Wallace-Homestead Book Co., (Photocopy) 1981.
_________. *A Second Look At White Ironstone*. Lombard, Illinois: Wallace-Homestead Book Co., 1993.
_________. *White Ironstone, A Collector's Guide*. Dubuque, Iowa: The Antique Trader, 1996.
Whiter, Leonard. *Spode, A History of the Family, Factory and Wares from 1733-1833.* London, England: Barrie & Jenkins, (Reprinted) 1978.
Whitmyer, Margaret & Ken. *Children's Dishes, (with updated Value Guide)*. Paducah, Kentucky: Collector's Books, 1995.
Wilkinson, V. *Copeland*. Shire Album 306, Aylesbury, Bucks, England: Shire Publications, Ltd., 1993.
Williams, Petra. *Flow Blue China, An Aid To Identification*. Jeffersontown, Kentucky: Fountain House East, (Revised Edition) 1981.
_________. *Flow Blue China, II*. Jeffersontown, Kentucky: Fountain House East, (Revised Edition) 1981.
_________. *Flow Blue China and Mulberry Ware, Similarity and Value Guide*. Jeffersontown, Kentucky: Fountain House East, (Revised Edition) 1978.
Williams, Petra and Weber, Marguerite R. *Staffordshire I, Romantic Transfer Patterns*. Jeffersontown, Kentucky: Fountain House East, 1975.
_________. *Staffordshire II, Romantic Transfer Patterns*. Jeffersontown, Kentucky: Fountain House East, 1978.
_________. *Staffordshire III, Romantic Transfer Patters.* Jeffersontown, Kentucky: Fountain House East, 1998.
Williams, Sydney, B. *Antique Blue and White Spode*. London, England: Omega Books, Ltd., 1987 (Reprint of the Revised 3rd Edition of 1949).

Williams-Wood, Cyril. *English Transfer-Printed Pottery and Porcelain*. London, England: Faber & Faber, 1981.

_________. *Staffordshire Pot Lids and Their Potteries*. London: Faber & Faber, 1972.

Wills, Geoffrey. *English Pottery and Porcelain*. London, England: Guinness Signatures and Garden City, New York: Doubleday & Co., 1969.

Wood, Heather Serry. *English Staffordshire China, Classics No. I*. Watkins Glen, New York: Century House, 1959.

_________. *Hand Painted China, China Classics. No. V*. Watkins Glen, New York: Century House, 1953.

_________. *English Staffordshire China, Classics No. VI*. Watkins Glen, New York: Century House, 1959.

Worth, Veryl Marie. *Willow Pattern China*. Revised 2nd editions. Oakridge, Oregon: H.S. Worth Co., 1979.

FOREIGN PUBLICATIONS

Bogaers, Marie-Rose. *Drukdecors op Maastrichts Aardewerk, 1850-1900*. Antiek, Lochem: b.v., Uitgeversmaatschappij, 1992.

Cushion, John P. *Manual of European Ceramics*. Firbourg, Switzerland: Office du Livre, 1987.

Danckert, Ludwig. *Directory of European Porcelain*. London, England: N.A.G. Press, Ltd., 1992.

_________. *Handbuch des Europaischen Porzellans*. Neuausgabe, Germany: Prestel-Verlag, 1992.

Herlitz-Gezelius, Ann Marie. *Rorstand*. Sweden: Dristianstds Boktryckeri Signum Ab., 1989.

Kumela, C. Marjut, Paatero, Kristina and Rissanen, Kaarina. *Arabia*. Uudenmaan Kirjapaino Oy (Jurkaisija Utgivare), Helsinki, Finland, 1987.

Penkala, Maria, F.R.G.S. *European Pottery, A Guide for the Collector and Dealer.* Schiedam, The Netherlands: Interbook International B.V., 1980.

Polling, A. *Maastrichtse Ceramiek, Merken en Dateringen. P. Regout, (De Sphinx), N.A. Bosch, Clermont en Chainaye, Societe Ceramique, Guillaume Lambert, L. Regout (Mosa), F. Regout, Alfred Regout (Rema)*. Lochem, Netherlands: Utigeversmaatschappij Antiek, 1993.

Rontgen, Robert, E. *Marks on German, Bohemian & Austrian Porcelain, 1710 to the Present*. December 10, 1986, Atglen, Pennsylvania: Schiffer Publishing, Ltd., 1981, Lochem, b.v., 1993.

Schlegelmilch, Clifford, J. *My Ancestors' China, Handbook of Erdmann and Reinhold Schlegelmilch - Prussia - Germany. and Oscar Schlegelmilch - German Porcelain Marks*. Whittemore, Michigan: Privately Published, 1973.

Vieillard, J. et cie, Eclectisme et Japonisme, Catalogue des Ceramiques et des Dessins. Catalogue Realise dan le Cadre de l'Exposition "Vieillar a Bordeaux," October 24 - December 10, 1986.

Zuhlsdorff, Dieter. *Marks/Lexikon, Porcelain and Ceramic Report 1885-1935*. Stuttgart, Germany: Arnoldsche Verlagsanstalt GmbH, 1988.

CATALOGS

A & B Auction Catalog of English Ceramics. February 2, 1998 - February 12, 1998. Marlboro, Massachusetts.

Aberdeen Ceramics. Text by Graeme Cruickshank, Godfrey Evans, editor and Charles Murray. Aberdeen, Scotland: Aberdeen Art Gallery & Museums, 1981.

Bonhams, Chelsea. "Blue Transfer Printed Wares including the F.G. Allen Collection. In Celebration of the 25th Anniversary of the Friends of Blue." Auction, April 21, 1998.

Bo'ness Potteries. Text by Christine Roberts & Beverly Lyon. Scotland. Falkirk Museums with help of The Council for Museums and Galleries in Scotland. 1977

British and Continental Ceramics. Christies, South Kensington. Thursday, September 10, 1998. London, England.

A Catalogue of American Historical China Cup Plates. Richard H. and Virginia A. Wood. Baltimore, Maryland, Privately Published.

A Catalogue of the Boynton Collection of Yorkshire Pottery. A. Hurst. Presented to the Yorkshire Museum 1916 and 1920, Yorkshire, England.

The Campbell Museum Collection (2nd ed. rev.) by Ralph Collier (director). The Campbell Museum, Camden, New Jersey, 1972.

Catalogue of the Herbert Allen Collection of English Porcelain, 2nd edition. Edited by Bernard Rackham, London, England: Victoria & Albert Museum, 1922.

A Celebration of Yorkshire Pots, The Eighth Exhibition from the Northern Ceramic Society, June 29 to September 21, 1997, Clifton Park Museum, Rotherham, England.

Christies, South Kensington, British and Continental Ceramics. July 2, 1998.

The Clyde Pottery, Greenock, 1816-1905. Boa, Denholm, Quail, Scotland: Interclyde District Libraries, 1987.

Collector's Sales and Service, February 1998 Sale of English Ceramics. Middletown, Rhode Island.

Commemorative Catalogue of an Exhibition of English Pottery and Porcelain. The English Ceramic Circle, 1927-1948. London, England: Routledge & Kegan Paul, Ltd., 1948.

Commemoratives, Blue Printed and Other English Pottery. Dreweatt Neate. Donnington Priory, England: September 9-10, 1998.

Creamware & Pearlware (May 18 - Sept. 7, 1986). The Fifth Exhibition from the Northern Ceramics Society, Stoke-on-Trent, England. Edited by Pat Halfpenny and Terence A. Lockett.

Cybis in Retrospect, Catalog of the Exhibition of Boleslaw Cybis, November 21, 1970 to January 3, 1971, New Jersey State Museum, Trenton, New Jersey.

Don Pottery Catalogue, 1801-1893, for the South Yorkshire Exhibition of 1983. Doncaster Museum and Art Gallery, England, 1983.

Doulton Pottery from the Lambeth and Burslem Studios, 1873-1989, Part II. Catalogue of an Exhibition of Pottery at The Fine Art Society, June 24-July 5, 1979. London, England: Richard Dennis Publications, 1975.

Dreweatt-Neate Auction Catalog of The Gibb Collection of Blue Printed and other Pottery, Donnington, Newbury, England, March 26, 1997, as well as other selected catalogs.

The Grand Rapids Price List &Cook Book. H. Leonard's & Sons & Co.'s., Grand Rapids, Michigan, c. 1887.

The Great Exhibition, London, 1851. The Art-Journal Illoustrated Catalogue of the Industries of All Nations, (A Facsimile of the 1851 edition), London, England: Crown Publishers, 1970.

Historical Staffordshire and Collector's Items, William R. & Teresa F. Kurau. Privately Published. Lampeter, Pennsylvania.

Hops & Venom, or Looking Into Frog Mugs. The Marjorie N. Davies Collection Exhibition, March 13 - May 2, 1988, edited by D.S. Skinner, Stoke-on-Trent, England: City Museum and Art Gallery.

International Ceramics Fair and Seminar. "Creamware and Pearlware - Exports to the USA 1750-1830" by Terence A. Lockett. London: Park Lane, June 1994.

James D. Julia Auction Catalog, August 1977 (including the Bagdon collection of Flow Blue), Fairfield, Maine.

Jersey City: Shaping America's Pottery Industry, 1825-1892, An Exhibition at the Jersey City Museum, Jersey City, New Jersey, September 17 - November 22, 1997 (Includes Exhibition Checklist). Compiled by Ellen Denker, Diana Stradling, and the Staff of the Jersey City Museum.

Made in Liverpool, Liverpool Pottery & Porcelain, 1700-1850. The Seventh Exhibition from the Northern Ceramics Society, June 27 - September 19, 1993, Walker Art Gallery, Liverpool and National Museums and Galleries on Merseyside.

Mason's Patent Ironstone Exhibition & Sale, January 17 - February 8, 1987. Samelsbury Hall, Preston, England.

The Montgomery Ward Catalog. Selected Editions.

The Old Vicarage, West Malling, Kent. Christies, South Kensington, Wednesday, September 23, 1998.

People & Pots, An Exhibition from the Northern Ceramic Society. Manchester Museum. Manchester, England. March 3-31, 1976.

The Pottery and Porcelain of New Jersey, 1688-1900. An Exhibition of the New York Museum, Newark, New Jersey. April 8 - May 11, 1947.

The Raven Mason Collection, The Catalogue of the Collection at Keele University. edited by Gay Blake Roberts & John Twitchett. Edinburgh, Scotland: Keele University Press, 1997.

Red-Cliff's Ironstone, Fine China, Retail Price Catalog, January 1962, July 1972, and 1975. Chicago, Illinois: Red-Cliff Company.

The Sears Roebuck Catalog. Selected Editions.

The Sir Leslie Joseph Collection of Welsh Pottery and Porcelain, May 14-16, 1992. London, England: Sotheby's.

Spatterware, September 1 - October 27, 1991. From the Collection of Louis G. & Shirley F. Hecht. Museum of Fine Arts, Hagerstown, Maryland.

Swansea and Nantgarw Potteries, Catalogue of the Collection of Welsh Pottery and Porcelain at the Glynn Vivian Art Gallery. Kildare Meager, S. M.B.E. Swansea, Wales: Swansea Corp., 1949.

True Blue, Transfer Printed Earthenware. The catalogue of an exhibition of British Blue Transfer Printed Earthenware to celebrate the 25th Anniversary of the Friends of Blue. Held at The Wedgwood Museum, Barlaston, Stoke-on-Trent, Staffordshire, March 21 to July 12, 1998. Edited by Gaye Blake Roberts, Oxfordshire, England: Friends of Blue Publishers, 1998.

Vodrey & Bro., Standard American Price List, Manufacturers of Iron-Stone China and Decorated Ware, E. Liverpool, Ohio.

The Victorian Catalogue of Household Goods. (Introduction by Dorothy Bosomworth). London, England: Studio Editions, 1995.

The Victorian Pattern Glass & China Book. New York, New York: Arch Cape Press, 1990.

Victorian Relief-Moulded Jugs, An Exhibition Catalogue From Richard Dennis, December 3-23, 1987. Edited by Jill Rumsey, Printed in Great Britain by Flaydemouse, Yeovil, 1987.

The Wedgwood 1880 Illustrated Catalogue of Shapes. (Introduction by J. K. des Fontaines). London, England: The Wedgwood Society.

The Whitehead Catalogue, 1798, James and Charles Whitehead, Manufacturers, Hanley Staffordshire. (Introduction by Reginald Haggar). Bletchley, England: D. B. Drakard.

JOURNALS, MAGAZINES AND NEWSLETTERS

American Ceramic Circle Bulletin, New York, New York.

Vol. 1, 1970-1971 Ed. by Hedy B. Landman
Vol. 2, 1980 Ed. by Hedy B. Landman
Vol. 3, 1983 Ed. by Hedy B. Landman
Vol. 4, 1985 Ed. by Hedy B. Landman
Vol. 5, 1986 Ed. by Carl C. Danterman
Vol. 6, 1988 Ed. by Meredith Chilton & Olive Koyama
Vol. 7, 1989 Ed. by Meredith Childton & Olive Koyama
Vol. 8, 1992 Ed. by Jacolyn A. Mott
Vol. 9, 1994 Ed. by Jacolyn A. Mott

American Ironstone by Julie Rich, Keynote Address at the White Ironstone China Association, 1996 Convention, published by White Ironstone Collectors Association, Redding Ridge, CT.

The Antique Collector (The American Antiques Collector) edited and published by Sam Laidacker, Scranton, Pennsylvania:

Vol. I, No. 1 - No. 10, February 1939 - May 1940.
Vol. II, No. 1 - No. 10, June 1940 - Summer 1942.
Vol. III, No. 1 - No. 8 (various editions), Winter 1943-No Date.

Antique Journal, Dubuque, Iowa: Babka Publishing Co., (Issues of 1945-1981)

Antique Traders Magazine and Price Guide, Blue and White. Dubuque, Iowa: Everybody's Press, April 1994.

Antique Traders Price Guide to Antiques (Special Focus on Souvenir Plates) Vol. 19, No. 3, Issue 77, Dubuque, Iowa: Everybody's Press.

Antique Trader Weekly (various editions), Dubuque, Iowa: Antique Trader Publications.

Antique Week. (various editions) Knightstown, Indiana: Mayhill Publications,

Antiques and The Arts Weekly. (various editions), Newtown, Connecticut: The Bee Publishing Co., Inc.

Antiques Magazine, October 1976 "The St. Johns Stone Chinaware Company," Elizabeth Collard.

Blueberry Notes. Newsletter of the Flow Blue International Collectors' Club, Selected Issues 1986-Present.

The China & Glass Quarterly, (Vol. 1, No. 1, Jan. - Feb. 1997), David & Linda Arman, Editors. Portsmouth, Rhode Island: The Oakland Press.

The China & Glass Quarterly, (Vol. 1, No. 2, April - May 1997), David & Linda Arman, Editors. Portsmouth, Rhode Island: The Oakland Press.

The China & Glass Quarterly, (Vol. 1, No. 3, July - August 1997), David & Linda Arman, Editors. Portsmouth, Rhode Island: The Oakland Press.

The China & Glass Quarterly, (Vol. 1, No. 4, October - November 1997), David & Linda Arman, Editors. Pottsmouth, Rhode Island: The Oakland Press.

The Commemorative Wares of The Cambrian and Glamorgan Potteries, Swansea and the South Wales Pottery, Llanelli, 1768-1870 (Originally presented at a meeting of the Commemorative Collectors Society) the National Folk Museum of Wales, St.Fagans, Cardiff, Wales. Oct. 7, 1972

The Connoisseur, Vol. IX, No. 34, London, England: Otto, Ltd., June 1904.

Echoes and Reflections. Occasional Paper No. 2 of The Northern Ceramic Society. Wells, England, 1990.

English Ceramic Circle Transactions. Published by the English Ceramic Circle, Grillford, Ltd., Granby, Milton, Keynes, England.

Vol. 8, Part 2, 1972 Vol. 14, Part 1, 1990
Vol. 12, Part 1, 1984 Vol. 14, Part 2, 1991
Vol. 12, Part 2, 1985 Vol. 14, Part 3, 1992
Vol. 12, Part 3, 1986 Vol. 15, Part 1, 1993

"Flow Blue" Susan R. Williams. *The Magazine Antiques*. New York, New York: October 1984.

Friends of Blue. Bulletins of the Friends of Blue, England. Feb. 1971-Present.

"Glasdig No. 2", *Magazine of the Glasgow Urban Archaeology Support Group*, Winter/Spring 1982, Glasgow, *Scotland*.

"William Harry Grindley and His Flow Blue Dishes." William H. Van Buskirk, Big Rock, Illinois, Published by the Flow Blue International Collectors' Club, August 1996.

"William Harry Grindley, Part II". William H. Van Buskirk, Big Rock, Illinois, Published by the Flow Blue International Collectors' Club, June 1997.

Journal of Ceramic History. Vol. No. 7, Stoke, England: George Street Press, 1974.

Journal of Ceramic History. Vol. No. 9, Stoke, England: Stoke on Trent City Museums, 1977.

"Bristol Potters and Potteries, 1600-1800" *Journal of Ceramic History*. Vol. No. 12, by Jackson, Reg. & Philomena and Price Roger, City Museum and Art Gallery, Stoke-upon-Trent, England, 1982.

Journal of Ceramic History, Vol. 13, "John & Richard Riley, China and Earthenware Manufacturers" by Roger Pomfret, City Museum & Art Gallery Stoke-on-Trent, England, 1988.

Journal of Ceramic History, Vol. 14, "Longton Potters, 1700-1865" by Rodney Hampson, City Museum and Art Gallery, Stoke-upon-Trent, England, 1990.

Journal of Ceramic History. Vol. 15, "Supplying The Present Wants Of Our Yankee Cousins... Staffordshire Ceramics and the American Market, 1775-1880" by Neil Ewins, City Museum & Art Gallery, Stoke-on-Trent, 1997.

Journal of the Northern Ceramic Society, Volumes 1 - 14, 1984 - Present.

Little Things Mean A Lot, A Study of White Ironstone Miniatures. by Adele & Dick Armbruster. Presented at the White Ironstone Collectors Convention, May 3, 1997.

A Look at LaBelle (Victorian Flow Blue), Wheeling Potteries. by Richard Southern, An Occasional Paper Presented to the Flow Blue International Collectors' Club Annual Convention, July 1995, Kansas City, Kansas, USA.

The Northern Ceramic Society Newsletter No. 93, March 1994 and September 1994, As well as Selected Newsletters to the Present.

150 Ans De Creation et de Tradition Faiencieres, Boch-Keramis, La Louviere, 1841-1991. Jacues Lefebvre and Dr. Therese Thomas, editors, La Louviere, (Keramik Museum), Belgium, 1991.

Proceedings of the Fourth Annual Convention of the United States Potters Association,Jan. 15 - 16, 1878" (photocopy), Trenton, New Jersey: John L. Murphy State Gazette Printing House.

"John & Richard Riley, China and Earthenware Manufacturers" Roger Pomfret, *Journal of Ceramic History*, Vol. 13, Stoke-on-Trent, England: City Museum & Art Gallery, 1988.

Scottish Industrial History, Vol. 16, Lesley Richmond, ed. Business Archives Council of Scotland, 1993.

Scottish Pottery Historical Review, Huntley House Museum, Edinburgh, Scotland:

1st Historical Review 1975/1976 - "The History & Products of the Scottish Potteries"
5th Historical Reivew, 1979/1980, ed. by Graeme D.R. Cruickshank
6th Historical Review, 1980/1981
9th Historical Review, 1984/1985
10th Historical Review, 1985/1986
11th Historical Review, 1986/1987
12th Historical Review, 1987/1988
13th Historical Review, 1988/1989
14th Historical Review, 1991/1992
15th Historical Review, 1992/1993
18th Historical Review, 1997

Scottish Pottery Society Archive News, No. 3, Spring, 1978. Edinburgh, Scotland.

Scottish Pottery Society Archive News, No. 4, 1979. Edinburgh, Scotland.

The Scottish Pottery Society Bulletin, No. 21. Glasgow, Scotland, September 1995.

Scottish Pottery Studies, No. 1. 1972 . Scottish Pottery Society, "Scottish Spongeware" Graeme Cruickshank.

"Spinning Wheel" National Magazine About Antiques, Hanover, Pennsylvania: Everybody's Press, (Issues of 1947 - 1977).

Tea Leaf Readings. Bulletin of the Tea Leaf Club International, USA, 1980 - Present.

Tiny Times. Newsletter of the Toy Dish Collectors Club. Bethlehem, Connecticut: selected volumes.

The Torquay Collector. Wisconsin, USA: The North American Torquay Society, Jan. 1995.

Tri-State Pottery Festival Plate Turners Handbook, East Liverpool, Ohio, USA, (Issues of 1969-1991).

Victorian Ceramics Group Newsletter, Vol. 3, No. 2, Florence, New Jersey.

The Wheeling Potterys, "The Best Made In America", Catalog No. 31, September 1906.

White Ironstone Body Styles, Copper & Gold Lustre Decorated, 1840-1900, Parts 1 and 2. Published by the Education Committee of the Tea Leaf Club International, U.S.A., 1990.

White Ironstone Notes. Newsletter of the White Ironstone Association, USA, 1994-Present.

INDEX OF AMERICAN POTTERS

INDEX OF ENGLISH POTTERS

Note: An Asterisk (*) after a name indicates that no patterns have been recorded.

For the Index of European Potters, see page 633.